Praise for *The Biographical Encyclopedia of Jazz*

"As with its predecessors, it makes an indelible contribution to the documentation of the lives of the individuals who make the music."

—Stanley Crouch

"An invaluable and distinguished contribution to jazz research and scholarship."

—Dan Morgenstern, Rutgers University

"Recommended . . . for public and academic libraries, especially those supporting strong music collections."

—*Library Journal*

"With more than 3,300 entries, this comprehensive guide puts a century of jazz at readers' fingertips."

—*Miami Herald*

"An indispensable reference source for its comprehensiveness and quality of scholarship."

—*Booklist/Reference Books Bulletin*

"An indispensable research tool for jazz writers, record collectors, musicians, and fans, Leonard Feather's series of biographical dictionaries has served a wide variety of needs for the last 45 years. . . . In this present edition, we find thoroughly updated biographical sketches. . . . All periods and styles of jazz are covered, from early New Orleans jazz to avant-garde and free."

—*JazzTimes*

The Biographical
ENCYCL

OPEDIA

of

Jazz

Leonard Feather & Ira Gitler

with the assistance of *Swing Journal*, Tokyo

OXFORD
UNIVERSITY PRESS

OXFORD
UNIVERSITY PRESS

Oxford University Press, Inc., publishes works that
further Oxford University's objective of excellence
in research, scholarship, and education.

Oxford New York
Auckland   Cape Town   Dar es Salaam   Hong Kong   Karachi
Kuala Lumpur   Madrid   Melbourne   Mexico City   Nairobi
New Delhi   Shanghai   Taipei   Toronto

With offices in
Argentina   Austria   Brazil   Chile   Czech Republic   France   Greece
Guatemala   Hungary   Italy   Japan   Poland   Portugal   Singapore
South Korea   Switzerland   Thailand   Turkey   Ukraine   Vietnam

First published by Oxford University Press, Inc., 1999
198 Madison Avenue, New York, NY 10016
www.oup.com

First issued as an Oxford University Press paperback, 2007
ISBN 978-19-532000-8

Oxford is a registered trademark of Oxford University Press

The Library of Congress has cataloged the hardcover edition as follows:
Feather, Leonard G.
The biographical encyclopedia of jazz / Leonard Feather and Ira Gitler,
with the assistance of Swing journal, Tokyo.
p.   cm.
Rev. and enl. ed. of: The encyclopedia of jazz.
Includes discographies.
ISBN 0-19-507418-1
1. Jazz—Bio-bibliography.   2. Jazz—Discography.
I. Gitler, Ira.   II. Feather, Leonard G. Encyclopedia of jazz.
III. Suingu janaru.   IV. Title
ML102.J3F4   1999
781.65′092′2—dc21   [B]
98-15485

Design: Adam B. Bohannon

9 8 7 6 5 4 3 2 1
Printed in the United States of America
on acid-free paper

TO THE MEMORY OF JANE AND LEONARD
AND TO MARY JO AND FITZ

CONTENTS

Publisher's Note   ix
Preface by Leonard Feather   xi
Preface by Ira Gitler   xiii
Abbreviations   xvii
The Entries, A-Z   3

PUBLISHER'S NOTE

This book is based in part on Leonard Feather's *Encyclopedia of Jazz, The New Encyclo-pedia of Jazz,* and *The Encyclopedia of Jazz in the Sixties* and on a subsequent work by Mr. Feather and Ira Gitler, *The Encyclopedia of Jazz in the Seventies.*

The Biographical Encyclopedia of Jazz is a thorough revision, recasting, and expan-sion of these books.

Leonard Feather and Ira Gitler agreed with Oxford in 1990 to publish this work. Both authors had made significant progress when, in September 1994, Leonard Feather died. Ira Gitler then assumed the responsibility of completing the work. We are aware of the great burden this placed upon him, and we remain greatly impressed with the effort and skill with which he has brought the work to its successful conclusion.

This 2007 edition of *The Biographical Encyclopedia of Jazz* does not update or, for the most part, correct information in the body of each entry. However, in the headings of many biographies there are corrections and updates pertaining to birth places and dates, death places and dates, and nomenclature.

Oxford University Press acknowledges *Swing Journal,* Tokyo, for its contribution toward the editorial preparation costs relating to *The Biographical Encyclopedia of Jazz.*

PREFACE
by Leonard Feather

The Biographical Encyclopedia of Jazz is a new book; as far as has been possible it is a complete volume, neither an update nor a revision of any previous reference work. It includes musicians who were born in the nineteenth century and others who today are still in their twenties.

Because of the vast number of artists entering the field and making a contribution of enough importance to justify their inclusion, the task of producing a work both up to date and all-encompassing was a formidable one. Every attempt has been made to obtain information on any performer whose impact seems likely to prove durable.

The biographical assignments were distributed for the most part along geographical lines: musicians living on or near the East Coast were dealt with by Ira Gitler and his collaborators, while biographies of those primarily associated with the West Coast were contributed by me and/or Don Heckman. Musicians in other areas were divided up simply according to which of us gained access to the data.

Deceased artists were allocated alphabetically: those from A to L were written (or rewritten from earlier versions) by Ira and his team; those from M to Z by Don and/or me. Don's role proved invaluable; as we went along, he with his computer and I with my non-computerized collaboration, it became clear that his role amounted to that of a full-scale associate author/editor.

Others who helped include Gene Lees, former *Down Beat* editor and current editor/publisher of the *Jazzletter,* and Jude Hibler, editor and publisher in the late 1980s of *Jazz Link Magazine*, who provided material on many musicians based in and around San Diego. Frankie Nemko, the British-born, California-based writer, and Celia Wood, a valuable associate in London, supplied many of the British biographies.

The immense job of compiling representative compact disc listings in our portion of the book fell to the encyclopedic Scott Yanow.

As is always the case with reference works, helpful information about the earlier years of the subjects was found in previous print sources. Among them were the *New Grove Dictionary of Jazz*, the Laffont *Dictionnaire du Jazz*, the *Encyclopedia of Jazz*, the *Encyclopedia Yearbooks of Jazz*, the *Encyclopedias of Jazz in the '60s and '70s*, the Italian *Grande Enciclopedia del Jazz*, John Chilton's *Who's Who of Jazz*, the *Guinness Who's Who of Jazz*, and, of course, countless magazines such as *Down Beat, JazzTimes, Jazziz, Coda, Jazz Express, Swing Journal, Musica Jazz, Jazz Magazine, Orkester Journalen*, and others.

For the first six months in the writing and assembling of the book, I had the very helpful secretarial assistance of Sylvia O'Gilvie. From early 1992 I had the invaluable cooperation of Julie Compton and her tireless work in taking dictation, transcribing, and proofreading.

The emergence of so many new players and the proliferation of CDs is a healthy indication of the state of jazz, but it is also a frustration for those of us trying to keep pace with exponentially moving developments. If the present work proves substantially helpful in broadening the awareness of all the major figures and their contributions, Ira and Don and I and our colleagues will feel that it was worth all the effort.

Los Angeles   LEONARD FEATHER
June 1994

PREFACE
by Ira Gitler

I first met Leonard Feather in the spring of 1948, when I was nineteen. He was presenting a show, with recordings and interviews, called "Jazz At Its Best," on WMGM radio in New York City. I had been reading him from 1945 in the pages of *Metronome,* and he was one of my main influences when I began to write about jazz in my high school and college newspapers. I was impressed with the *New 52nd Street Jazz* album he produced for RCA in 1946 and devoured his book, *Inside Bebop,* published in 1949.

In the early '50s, when I was with Prestige Records, Leonard was involved with Duke Ellington's Mercer label, which Prestige distributed. We became better acquainted and, in 1954, when he began work on the first *Encyclopedia of Jazz* for Horizon Press, he asked me to be his chief assistant. I was elated to be involved in a project of this magnitude with one of my journalistic role models.

Working across the table from Leonard every week for an extended period was an invaluable learning experience. I had been writing for Prestige from 1951 and had been published in *Metronome,* but he helped me to start writing for Blue Note and the magazine *Hi-Fi Music at Home*.

I continued to work with him on *The Encyclopedia of Jazz* series through the yearbooks, *The New Encyclopedia of Jazz* (1960) and *The Encyclopedia of Jazz in the Sixties* (1966). In the last I wrote some of the biographies for the first time. When it came time to do *The Encyclopedia of Jazz in the Seventies,* Leonard decided, because of the enormity of the project, that I should be co-author.

In the '80s, Horizon Press, the publisher for the entire series, went out of business. As the decade wore on I tried, via proposals to government endowments and the private sector, to raise funds to begin work on a new encyclopedia, but the '90s arrived with no grant in sight. Then to the rescue came Sheldon Meyer, who has done more for jazz books than any editor in the history of publishing. He had written a letter showing Oxford's interest in the book for me to include in some of the grant proposals, but now he made us a concrete offer. With help from *Swing Journal,* Japan's leading jazz magazine (to which both Leonard and I contributed), we were finally under way.

As there was no edition in the '80s, we opted not to do an encyclopedia of the '90s but rather a completely new book, encompassing full biographies of people from the previous books and the vast number of new musicians who had come up since the 1976 edition. In order to accommodate so many biographies, we decided not to include photographs or special features.

Leonard and I agreed that the main criterion for including fusion players was if they had originally made a reputation in jazz. The yardstick for blues singers was if the main body of their work was done with jazz musicians. In other words, Joe Williams is included, but not Big Joe Williams.

In the early years of this project I had the help of Stephanie Stein and Greg Robinson in the writing of biographies. Ms. Stein wrote for *Jazziz* in 1986 and *Down Beat* from '88 to '92. As a literary editor and annotator for BMG-RCA Victor, she contributed extensively to *The First Label in Jazz, RCA Victor 80th Anniversary, Collector's Edition,* and the *Ellington Centennial Collection.* Her biography of Gil Evans is a work in progress.

Robinson, an accomplished trombonist who tours with the ska group Mephiskapheles, is also a fine jazz journalist, writing for *Windplayer* in the mid 1990s and *JazzTimes* from '96.

My son, Fitz Gitler, was a constant source and force, particularly in educating me in the use of the Apple Powerbook at the outset of the project and in solving problems in the area of computers right through to the finish.

In 1998 I was fortunate to receive the help of Chris Albertson (author of *Bessie,* the definitive biography of Bessie Smith), whose expertise in jazz and computers was a great aid in completing the encyclopedia.

Boston bassist Ben Taylor, referring to *The Penguin Guide to Jazz on CD, Third Edition,* compiled for me an alphabetical list of musicians' recordings, as leaders and side people, which saved invaluable time that I would have spent in further surfing of the index. Additionally I also availed myself of the *All Music Guide to Jazz,* particularly Volume 3, to which Scott Yanow was a major contributor.

It was of inestimable help to have Joellyn Ausanka oversee the copyediting. Her knowledge of jazz, other artistic and cultural milieus, and general information greatly mitigated the task of fine-tuning the book in its final stage.

To dear friend Leila Hadley Luce I cannot give enough thanks for the generous use of her apartment (a veritable library) as a workplace for several years in the middle period of the project.

When Leila's apartment was no longer available, Oxford made office space for me at their New York headquarters, a much appreciated move which helped bring the book closer to fruition.

In the homestretch it was my wife, Mary Jo, who put up with me at home and, alternately prodding and soothing as she had throughout the marathon, helped me to cross the finish line.

I would also like to acknowledge the help of the following people: Jeff Atterton, Dick Bank, Krystian Brodacki, George Buck and *Jazz Beat,* Pino Candini, Rossella Livraga, Gian Mario Maletto, Claudio Sessa and *Musica Jazz*, Michael Chertok, Michael Cuscuna, Len Dobbin, Doug Engel, Kim Ewing, Leonard Gaskin, Jean-Louis Ginibre, Terri Hinte, Brooks Kerr, Kiyoshi Koyama, Adam Lore, Kenny Mathieson, Mark Miller and *The Encyclopedia of Music in Canada*, Dan Morgenstern and The Institute of Jazz Studies, Hank O'Neal, Bob Porter, Brian Priestley and *Jazz: The Rough Guide* (for the amplification of certain British biographies and the addition of some others), Henri Renaud, J. R. Rich, Dick Sudhalter, and Leonard Weinrich.

Discoveries are constantly being made in the area of birth places and dates. In the '80s Gary Giddins uncovered Louis Armstrong's real birth month, day, and year in New Orleans. Ross Kailey of Albuquerque, New Mexico, by writing to city halls and obtaining copies of birth certificates, established new and correct birth years for Charlie Christian, Earl Hines, and Art Tatum. It is not always so easy.

For example, all books agree that Joe Rushton was born in Evanston, Illinois, but for birth dates *Encyclopedia of Jazz* (1960) indicates 4/19/07; *Grove* says 11/1/07; and *Jazz: The Rough Guide,* 11/7/07. When I asked writer John McDonough (based in the Chicago area) to see if he could get the correct date for me in Evanston, the city told him it didn't give out such information.

An even more perplexing case is that of Herb Flemming. *EOJ* lists him as born in Puente, California, 4/5/04; *Grove,* Honolulu, Hawaii, 4/5/1900; and the Laffont *Dictionnaire*, Butte, Montana, 4/5/1898. *EOJ* mentions that Flemming attended the Dobbs Chauncey School in Dobbs Ferry, New York. The school no longer exists, but I thought the Dobbs Ferry Historical Society might have school records in its archives. It didn't. I went with the French, figuring they must know something since he spent so much time there.

One date I changed, using personal experience, was Rudy Williams's birth year. All previous books place it as 1909. I cut my jazz teeth on the recordings of Al Cooper's Savoy Sultans in the late 1930s. My older brother, who bought the 78s and listened and danced to the Sultans at the Savoy, often referred to Rudy, one of his particular favorites, as a teenager. Based on this I have changed the year to 1919.

Many musicians with birth dates early in the century have no death dates. This is because due to their lack of recent activity in the field, nothing is generally known about them. Others have been reported dead, but we have no confirming information. I have chosen to identify this latter group with a d.? in their biography headings.

Each succeeding encyclopedia seeks to rectify past mistakes and uncover new, correct information. We have done this to the best of our abilities.

Here are some keys for understanding the biographies. When the full first name is the one by which a musician is best known, then that and any middle names are used without parenthesis, e.g., BAKER, DAVID NATHANIEL.

When a diminutive or nickname is the main identification, the given and any middle names are in parenthesis, e.g., BAKER, CHET (CHESNEY HENRY). If the middle name is the one in common usage, the first name appears in parenthesis, e.g., BARBARIN, (ADOLPHE) PAUL. A birth name that is not used professionally follows the primary heading, in parenthesis, upper and lower case, and normal order, e.g., BANG, BILLY (William Vincent Walker). A variation of this is BAILEY, MILDRED (Rinker). There is no need to repeat the given name in these instances.

We chose not to include album titles in the CD listings, using the body of a biography for particularly important titles. When someone is part of an anthology, that title is listed. The two basic rules are that the CDs for which someone is the leader are listed first; those recorded as a side person begin with the leader's name, the first prefaced by a w. (for with) and the label in parenthesis. If a musician appears on the same label with a variety of leaders, only the last in a series, separated by semicolons, carries the name of the label, for example w. Dexter Gordon; Grant Green; Lee Morgan; Ike Quebec (BN).

A NOTE ON RECORD LABELS: Many labels are part of larger parent companies. BMG encompasses RCA Victor (which is referred to either as RCA or Victor), Bluebird, and Novus. Vogue usually means the French label as issued in the late '90s on RCA Victor.

32 Jazz, having purchased Muse and Landmark, is now rereleasing material from these labels under its own imprimatur.

Birdology is part of Polygram, Verve's parent, as are Antilles, Emarcy, Mercury, and Metrojazz.

The Duke Ellington recordings listed for Saja have also come out on Atlantic. Rhino has reissued much from the Atlantic catalog. We have listed these as Rhino or Rhino/Atlantic.

Fantasy owns Contemporary, Debut, Galaxy, Good Time Jazz, Jazzland, Milestone, New Jazz, Nocturne, Pablo, Prestige (including Moodsville and Swingville), Riverside, and Specialty. Many sessions have been reissued in the OJC (Original Jazz Classics) series, but we have chosen to identify them by their label of birth, as indeed they are identified in their new configuration and in the Fantasy catalog.

Jazz City is being made available outside of Japan as Evidence.

Of the important independents, Xanadu has been the least reissued on CD and sporadically at that, but most recently by Classic Records of California and Tokuma of Japan. For information concerning all labels, consult the guides mentioned earlier.

New York City   IRA GITLER
April 1999

ABBREVIATIONS

GENERAL

Acad. – Academy
accomp. – accompanist; accompanied; accompanying
app. – appeared; appearance(s); appearing
arr. – arranger; arranged; arrangement(s)
assoc. – associated
asst. – assistant
att. – attended
b. – born
bb – big band
bec. – became; become; becoming
bef. – before
bro. – brother
ca. – circa
coll. – college
collab. – collaboration(s); collaborated
comp. – composer; composed; composition(s)
cond. – conductor; conducted
comp. – composer; composed; composition(s)
cons. – conservatory
cont. – continued
contemp. – contemporary
d. – died
dir. – director; directed
dj – disc jockey
docu. – documentary
dur. – during
educ. – educator; educated
ens. – ensemble

exp. – experience
extens. – extensively; extensive
fath. – father
feat. – featured; featuring
fest. – festival
form. – formed; forming
fr. – from
grad. – graduated
gp. – group
harm. – harmony
hs – high school
improv. – improvisation
incl. – including; included
infl. – influence; influenced
instr. – instrument; instrumental
int'l – international; internationally
jf – jazz festival
join. – joined; joining
jp – jazz party
lab. – laboratory
lead–leader; leading
metro. – metropolitan
mil. – military
mos. – months
moth. – mother
mus. – music; musician(s)
nat'l – national
occ. – occasionally
oct. – octet
orch. – orchestra
orchest. – orchestrated
orig. – original; originally
pc. – piece
perf. – performed; performances; performer

Philharm. – Philharmonic
pl. – player; played; playing
priv. – private; privately
prod. – producer; produced; production
prof. – professional; professionally
profess. – professor
publ. – published; publishing; publication
qnt. – quintet
qt. – quartet
rec. – recording; recorded
remain. – remaining; remained
ret. – return; returned
sch. – school
sess. – session(s)
sist. – sister
spt. – septet
St. – State
start. – started
stud. – studied; studying
sw. – switched
sxt. – sextet
TDWR – Talent Deserving Wider Recognition
tour. – touring; toured
trad. – traditional
trav. – traveled
U. – University
w. – with
wk(s). – week(s)
wkshp. – workshop(s)
yr. – year(s)

COUNTRIES, CITIES, STATES

For birth and death state locations, United States Postal Service abbreviations are used. Otherwise:

Amer. – America
Arg. – Argentina
Austr. – Austria
Austral. – Australia
Balt. – Baltimore
Bklyn. – Brooklyn
Bost. – Boston
B'way – Broadway
BWI – British West Indies
Calif. – California
Can. – Canada
Chi. – Chicago
CIS – Commonwealth of Independent States
Den. – Denmark
Det. – Detroit
Engl. – England
Eur. – Europe; European
Germ. – Germany
KC – Kansas City
LA – Los Angeles
LI – Long Island
LV – Las Vegas
Manh. – Manhattan
Mex. – Mexico
NO – New Orleans
NYC – New York City
NZ – New Zealand
Ont. – Ontario
Phila. – Philadelphia
Pitts. – Pittsburgh
PR – Puerto Rico
Pref. – Prefecture (Japan)
Que. – Quebec
Scand. – Scandinavia
SF – San Francisco
Swed. – Sweden
Wash., D.C. – Washington, District of Columbia

INSTRUMENTS

acdn. – accordion
bgo. – bongo(s)
bjo. – banjo
bs. – bass
bsn. – bassoon
cga. – conga(s)
cl. – clarinet
comp. – composer
crnt. – cornet

dmr. – drummer
dms. – drums
elec. – electric
el-bs. – electric bass
euph. – euphonium
EWI – Electronic Wind Instrument
fl. – flute
flg. – flugelhorn
Fr. hrn. – French horn
gtr. – guitar
hca. – harmonica
kybds. – keyboards
lead. – leader
mand. – mandolin
mello. – mellophone
mrba. – marimba
org. – organ
picc. – piccolo
pno. – piano
pnst. – pianist
rcdr. – recorder
sax(es) – saxophones
    alto; bari.; sop.; tnr. – alto, baritone, soprano, tenor
synth. – synthesizer
tba. – tuba
tbn. – trombone
tmbls. – timbales
tpt. – trumpet
uke. – ukulele
vla. – viola
vln. – violin
vib. – vibraphone
voc. – vocalist; vocal
v-tbn. – valve trombone
wshbd. – washboard
xyl. – xylophone

FESTIVALS

Colo. JP – Colorado Jazz Party
IJF – Idaho (Lionel Hampton) Jazz Festival
MJF – Monterey Jazz Festival
NJF – Newport Jazz Festival
NJF-NY – Newport Jazz Festival–New York
NOJ&HF – New Orleans Jazz and Heritage Festival

LABELS (Audio and Video)

Acc. – Accurate
Aff. – Affinity
AFJS – American Federation of Jazz Societies

Allig. – Alligator
Amer. Mus. – American Music
Amo. – Amosaya
Ant. – Antilles
App. – Appasionato
Arab. – Arabesque
Arb. – Arbors
Arh. – Arhoolie
Ark. – Arkadia
Ast. Pl. – Astor Place
Asyl. – Asylum
Atl. – Atlantic
Aud. – Audiophile
Audq. – Audioquest
Bain. – Bainbridge
Band. – Bandstand
BB – Bluebird
B&B – Black & Blue
Bella. – Bellaphon
Beth. – Bethlehem
BH – Black Hawk
Biog. – Biograph
Bird. – Birdology
BJ – Blue Jackel
BL – Black Lion
Bloom. – Bloomdido
Bluesv. – Bluesville
BM – Blue Moon
BN – Blue Note
Bodes. – Bodeswell
Brown. – Brownstone
Bruns. – Brunswick
BS – Black Saint
Butter. – Butterfly
Cad. – Cadence
Callig. – Calligraph
Cand. – Candid
Cap. – Capitol
CAP – Consolidated Artists Productions
CC – Criss Cross
Cell. – Celluloid
Chall. – Challenge
Chart. – Chartmaker
Chiaro. – Chiaroscuro
Cir. – Circle
Class. – Classics
Col. – Columbia
Comm. – Commodore
Conc. – Concord Jazz
Conn. – Connoisseur
Cont. – Contemporary
Contin. – Continuum
CW – Creative World

Deb. – Debut
Dec. – Decca
Del. – Delmark
Den. – Denon
Disc. – Discovery
Drag. – Dragon
Drey. – Dreyfus
D-T – Double-Time
Elec. Bird – Electric Bird
Elek. – Elektra
Em. – Emarcy
Eve. Star – Evening Star
Ever. – Everest
Evid. – Evidence
EW – East West
Fant. – Fantasy
FF – Flying Fish
Folk. – Folkways
Free. – Freedom
FS – Fresh Sound
Gal. – Galaxy
Gem. – Gemini
GH – Groovin' High
GNP Cres. – Gene Norman
   Presents Crescendo
Gram. – Gramavision
GTJ – Good Time Jazz
High. – Highnote
Hind. – Hindsight
Home. – Homegrown
Hot. – Hothouse
HP – Hip Pocket
H&S – Hot 'n Sweet
IAI – Improvising Artists, Inc.
IC – Inner City
Imp. – Impulse
Ind. Nav. – India Navigation
Insp. – Inspiration
Inter. – Interplay
Intuit. Mus. – Intuition Music
JA – Jazz Alliance
JAR – Jazz Aux Remparts
Jazz. – Jazzology
Jazz Anth. – Jazz Anthology
Jazz Arch. – Jazz Archives
JC – Jazz City
JF – Jazz Focus
JH – Jazz House
JP – Jazz Point
JT – Justin Time
Just. – Justice
Jzld. – Jazzland
Key. Coll. – Keynote Collection
KFW – Knitting Factory
   Works

KJ – King Jazz
Koch Jz. – Koch Jazz
Koko. – Kokopelli
LAJS – Los Angeles Jazz
   Society
Land. – Landmark
Laser. – Laserlight
L. Bleu – Label Bleu
Light. – Lightyear
Lime. – Limetree
Limel. – Limelight
Lip. – Lipstick
Lond. – London
M&A – Music & Arts
Mag. – Magnetic
Main. – Mainstream
Manh. – Manhattan
Maple. – Mapleshade
MB – Metro Blue
MC – Modern Concepts
Merc. – Mercury
Mess. – Messidor
Metro. – Metropolitan
MFP – Music For Pleasure
Mile. – Milestone
Min. Mus. – Minor Music
MM – MusicMasters
Mob. Fid. – Mobile Fidelity
Mon. – Monarch
Mos. – Mosaic
MS – Mythic Sound
Musi. – Musicraft
Nax. – Naxos
N-H – Nagel-Heyer
NJ – New Jazz
NN – New Note
Nob. – Nobility
Noc. – Nocturne
None. – Nonesuch
NW – New World
OK – Okeh
Pab. – Pablo
Palm. – Palmetto
Para. – Paramount
Park. – Parkwood
Penta. – Pentaflowers
Phil. – Philology
Phon. – Phontastic
Pick. – Pickwick
PJ – Pacific Jazz
Polyd. – Polydor
Polyg. – Polygram
Post. – Postcards
Prest. – Prestige
PS – Prime Source

Prog. – Progressive
PW – Paddle Wheel
RCA – includes BMG, Bluebird,
   Novus, Victor
Rear. – Rearward
Red Brn. – Red Baron
Ref. – Reference
Rep. – Reprise
Res. – Reservoir
Rh. – Rhino
Rhap. – Rhapsody
R&T – Razor & Tie
Riv. – Riverside
Roul. – Roulette
Round. – Rounder
SA – Sound Aspects
Sack. – Sackville
Sah. – Sahara
Sav. – Savoy
SB – Sea Breeze
Shan. – Shanachie
Sig. – Signature
Silk. – Silkheart
Smith. – Smithsonian
SN – Soul Note
South. – Southland
Spec. – Specialty
Spl. – Splasc(h)
Spot. – Spotlite
Steep. – SteepleChase
Story. – Storyville
Sunny. – Sunnyside
Sw. Bas. – Sweet Basil
Tel. – Telarc
Ther. – Theresa
32 – 32 Jazz
Timel. – Timeless
Tom. – Tomato
Town. – Town Crier
Tri. – Triloka
Trop. – Tropijazz
UA – United Artists
Up. – Uptown
Vang. – Vanguard
Vart. Jazz – Vartan Jazz
VP – Voice Print
VJ – Vee Jay
WB – Warner Brothers
WC – World Circuit
WH – Windham Hill
WP – World Pacific
WW – West Wind
Vict. – Victor
Voc. – Vocalion
Xan. – Xanadu

GROUPS, PLACES, MAGAZINES, ORGANIZATIONS, and SCHOOLS

AACM – Association for the Advancement of Creative Music

AJO – American Jazz Orchestra

CHJB – Carnegie Hall Jazz Band

DB – Down Beat

Dixie. Hall – Dixieland Hall

Esq. – Esquire

IAJ – International Art of Jazz

IAJE – International Association of Jazz Educators

JATP – Jazz at the Philharmonic

JT – JazzTimes

LCJO – Lincoln Center Jazz Orchestra

L,H&R – Lambert, Hendricks & Ross

LSU – Louisiana State University

Met. – Metronome

MIT – Massachusetts Institute of Technology

MJQ – Modern Jazz Quartet

MM – Melody Maker (England)

MSG – Madison Square Garden

NEA – National Endowment for the Arts

NOCCA – New Orleans Center for the Creative Arts

NORK – New Orleans Rhythm Kings

NPR – National Public Radio

NYJO – National Youth Jazz Orchestra

NYJRC – New York Jazz Repertory Company

NYU – New York University

OBE – Order of the British Empire

ODJB – Original Dixieland Jazz Band

OTB – Out of the Blue

Pres. Hall – Preservation Hall

SJ – Swing Journal (Japan)

TDWR – Talent Deserving Wider Recognition (*Down Beat* poll)

TOBA – Theater Owners' Booking Association

USC – University of Southern California

VA – Veterans Administration

WGJB – World's Greatest Jazz Band

WSQ – World Saxophone Quartet

■ THE BIOGRAPHICAL ENCYCLOPEDIA OF JAZZ ■

a

AACM (ASSOCIATION FOR THE ADVANCE-MENT OF CREATIVE MUSICIANS). A cooperative, nonprofit alliance of musicians strongly oriented toward avant-garde jazz. The AACM was an outgrowth of the Experimental Band, organized by pnst. Muhal Richard Abrams in 1961. Stimulated by NYC's Jazz Composers' Guild and created as a kind of interactive musical networking environment to provide a forum for rehearsals, perfs., and the sympathetic exchange of new musical ideas, the AACM was formalized in May '65, w. Abrams as president. The AACM incl., at various times, Roscoe Mitchell, Anthony Braxton, Joseph Jarman, Lester Bowie, Chico Freeman, Leroy Jenkins, et al. Activities incl. rec. sess., radio shows, and concerts, many of which took place at the U. of Chi.; AACM Festival in NYC, '77; many grants funneled to individuals fr. NEA, Ill. Arts Council, etc. Of the many ensembles that emerged fr. the AACM, among the most prominent were the gp. Air and the gps. of Chico Freeman and George Lewis.

AALTONEN, JUHANI, tnr, alto saxes, fl; b. Kouvola, Finland, 12/12/35. Played w. Heikki Rosendahl in Inkeroinen, 1950s. Moved to Helsinki '61, worked as studio mus. Gained rep. as free jazz and jazz-rock soloist w. Eero Koivistoinen '69–73; Edward Vesala fr. '65; Heikki Sarmanto fr. '69. Studied fl. at Sibelius Acad., also one semester at Berklee Coll. of Mus. '70. Pl. w. Nordic All-Stars '71–2; Helsinki New Music Orch. (UMO) fr. '75; Arild Anderson in Norway late '70s. Led own gps. fr. '74. Tour. w. H. Sarmanto '80s. Gave solo recital on fl. for Tampere Biennale '90. CDs: ECM; w. E. Vesala (ECM).

AARONS, AL (ALBERT W.), tpt, flg; b. Pittsburgh, PA, 3/23/32. Private studies in Pitts. 1947–50; Chi. '51–53; Wayne St. U., Det. '55–57. After pl. w. Yusef Lateef, Barry Harris, and Wild Bill Davis, he joined Count Basie in '61 and remained through '69, then settled in LA. Freelanced w. Henry Mancini, Quincy Jones, Bobby Bryant, Buddy Collette, Gerald Wilson. Worked w. Capp-Pierce Juggernaut; Frank Wess–Harry Edison Orch. '80–90s. Own fav. solo on *Paris Nights* in the Cunninghams' album *Scat Tones M'Bones* (Disc.). CDs: LAJS; w. Basie (Verve; Roul.; Mos.); Capp-Pierce; F. Wess (Conc.); E. Fitzgerald (Pab.).

ABDUL-MALIK, AHMED (Jonathan Timms), bs, oud, cello, vla, vln, tba, pno; b. Brooklyn, NY, 1/30/27; d. Long Branch, NJ, 10/2/93. Father fr. Sudan, pl. vln., N. African tar drm., other instr. Began vln. studies at Vardi's Cons. at age 7. Grad. NYC HS for Perf. Arts. Pl. prof. while in hs, incl. tours w. Fess Williams. Pl. bs. w. Art Blakey 1945, '48; Don Byas '46; Sam (The Man) Taylor '54; Randy Weston '54–7. First rec. w. Weston '56. Pl. and rec. w. Thelonious Monk '57–8. First rec. as leader '58. Studied Middle Eastern mus. w. Jamal Islan and Niam Karakind, Indian mus. w. Dr. Wanamasa Singh. Perf. prog. of non-Western mus. at NYC gallery '57. With Herbie Mann '61; Earl Hines '64. Pl. oud on US State Dept. tour of So. Amer and on rec. w. John Coltrane, both '61. Tour. Nigeria w. Amer. Cultural Society '63. B.S. mus. ed., NYU '69; mus. teacher, NYC pub. schs. '69–85; adjunct prof. of mus., NYU '70–'85; research fellow, Princeton U. '72–3; taught African and Middle Eastern mus. and jazz, Bklyn. Coll. '73. M.A. mus. admin., NYU '77. Pioneer in Jazz Award fr. BMI '84. From '85 studied oud w. Maestro Simon Shaheen. Abdul-Malik pl. a key role in the introduction of elements of non-Western music into jazz. He devoted himself to the study of mus. fr. around the world and its relationship and relevance to the jazz tradition. Favs: Jimmy Blanton; oud, Hamza El Din, Simon Shaheen, Dr. Riad El Soumbati. Polls: *Playboy*. Fests: Tangier '72; Costa del Sol, Oslo, Stockholm, MJF, all '74; Marseilles '78–9; Casablanca '90; Cairo '91. Film: w. Monk *Straight No Chaser*. TV: w. Monk, *Twentieth Century*; *Seven Lively Arts*. CDs: Riv.; w. T. Monk (Riv.; Mile.; Jzld.); R. Weston (Riv.); J. Coltrane (Imp.); H. Mann (Atl.).

ABENE, MIKE (MICHAEL), pno, arr, comp, prod; b. Brooklyn, NY, 7/2/42. Father and grandfath. pl. gtr., mand., vln.; fath. had own band. Aunt on moth.'s side pl. stride pno. Pl. in hs band in Farmingdale, LI, and in Marshall Brown's Int'l Youth Band at NJF 1958. Lessons w. John LaPorta, Wally Cirillo. Att. Manh. Sch. of Mus. as comp. maj. '61–2. Pl. w. Don Ellis '60–1; pl. w. and arr. for Maynard Ferguson '61–5; also pl. at Cork n' Bib on LI w. Clark Terry, Jimmy Nottingham in early '60s, and in LV w. Buddy Rich, Sweets Edison, Georgie Auld '63. Pl. w. Al Cohn–Zoot Sims at Half Note '65–7. Wrote and pl. for jingles and TV fr. '66. Comp. and arr. for 11-pc. band w. Joe Shepley and Burt Collins, late '60s. Duo at Bradley's '72–5, Sweet Basil '78. Arrs. for David Taylor, Jim Pugh, Grover Mitchell bb, Liza Minnelli, Mel Lewis Orch., Dizzy Gillespie United Nation Orch. In recent yrs. has worked as prod. for GRP, winning Grammy in '87 for *Digital Duke* (co-prod. w. Mercer Ellington). He is also prod., arr., and mus. dir. for Group J, jazz vocal gp. Favs: Ellington, Monk; arrs: Ellington, Gil Evans, Mingus. Fests: Stockholm '62; Pori '91; North Sea '91; various Scand. fests. w. Group J. CDs: Stash; w. B. Cobham (GRP); Chris Connor (Cont.); M. Ferguson (Roul., Main.); B. Rich (LRC); as arr: M. Lewis Orch. (MM), D. Gillespie (Enja), G. Mitchell (Ken); as prod.: M. Ellington; Cobham; Eddie Daniels; GRP All-Star bb (GRP).

ABERCROMBIE, JOHN L., gtr, synths, elec 12-string gtr, elec mand; b. Port Chester, NY 12/16/44. Started on gtr. at age 14; some priv. lessons but mostly self-taught until he att. Berklee Coll. of Mus. 1962–6, where he stud. gtr. w. Jack Petersen; theory; harm. Worked w. Johnny "Hammond" Smith '67–8; Dreams '69; Chico Hamilton '70; Jeremy Steig; Gil Evans; Gato Barbieri '71–3; Billy Cobham, Jan. '74–Jan. '75. Dur. that time he also pl. w. Jack DeJohnette, tour. Eur. w. him. He cont. w. DeJohnette in '75 but also began to lead his own trio, incl. Gate-

way w. Dave Holland, DeJohnette, and qt. In the late '70s pl. w. DeJohnette's New Directions. Duos w. Ralph Towner into the '80s. Pl. w. Kenny Wheeler qnt. '88; w. Wheeler's qnt. and bb '90, tour. w. him US '91; Eur. '92. Perf. and rec. Mingus's *Epitaph* w. Gunther Schuller. Gateway revived several times over the yrs., incl. '94. Has also collab. in trio w. Marc Johnson, Peter Erskine. Abercrombie, an imaginative improviser, is at home in a variety of contexts and uses devices such as the volume pedal and phase shifter in the service of the music rather than as gimmicks. Early infls.: Jim Hall, Bill Evans, Rollins, Coltrane. Fests: Montreux w. Hamilton '71; Antibes w. G. Evans; NJF-NY; Montreux w. Barbieri '74; many int'l since. Poll: *DB* Critics TDWR '75. CDs: ECM; Steep.; w. Towner (ECM); Cobham (Atl.); DeJohnette; Wheeler; Colin Walcott; Barre Phillips; J. Garbarek (ECM); J. Lovano; M. Petrucciani (BN); J. Hall (MM); M. Tyner; N. Lan Doky (Mile.); P. Erskine (Den.); G. Evans (BB).

ABNEY, DON (JOHN DONALD), pno; b. Baltimore, MD, 3/10/23; d. Los Angeles, 1/20/00. Studied priv. in Balt., then pl. Fr. hrn. w. army band. Pl. in Balt. w. Buddy Johnson, ca. 1946. Moved to NYC '47. Studied at Manh. Sch. of Mus., pl. w. Eddie Gibbs at Vill. Vanguard '47; Snub Mosely '48; Wilbur De Paris '48–9. Worked as single at Sherry Netherland Hotel, also w. Billy Williams '50–1. Pl. w. Bill Harris–Kai Winding, '51; Chuck Wayne, '52; Sy Oliver, Louis Bellson, Thelma Carpenter '53–4. Accomp. Ella Fitzgerald w. JATP '54–7; Carmen McRae '58–9; Fitzgerald '61. On staff at NBC fr. '60. Moved to LA '62, pl. w. Stanley Wilson, Benny Carter in TV orchs. Pl. w. Stan Kenton's Neophonic Orch. '66; own trio '69–71; cond. for Rosemary Clooney '70; Pearl Bailey-Louis Bellson '71–4; Jack Jones '75. Visited Japan '79. Moved there '80 and married a Japanese woman, settling outside of Tokyo. Most of his work has been in clubs. Ret. after illness in '93 to play at concert staged for him by Japanese mus. Favs: Nat Cole, Art Tatum, Ellis Larkins. Film: *Pete Kelly's Blues* '55. TV: w. Pearl Bailey. Rec. w. Eddie South '47; Carol Sloane '82. CDs: w. E. Fitzgerald (Dec.; Verve); B. Carter (Verve); Lucky Thompson (Imp.).

ABRAMS, LEE (Leon Curtis Abramson), dms; b. Brooklyn, NY, 1/6/25; d. Brooklyn, 4/20/92. Raised in Bklyn. Served in army 1943–6; then worked w. Roy Eldridge to '47; various gps. on 52nd St. incl. Coleman Hawkins, J.J. Johnson, Eddie "Lockjaw" Davis. Pl. w. Andy Kirk orch.; Eddie Heywood trio '48. Tour. w. Hot Lips Page; rejoin. Heywood; briefly w. Illinois Jacquet, winter '51–2; Oscar Pettiford '52; Lester Young to '53; then freelanced w. Al Haig et al.

Led workshops and taught jazz in Bklyn. In '80s pl. in bro. Ray's bb. Film: *Joe Albany . . . a Jazz Life* '80. CDs: w. Eldridge (Dec.); Duke Jordan (RCA); Wynton Kelly (BN); Eddie Davis; Bennie Green in *Prestige First Sessions, Vol. 3* (Prest.).

ABRAMS, MUHAL RICHARD (Abrahams), pno, comp, cl; b. Chicago, IL, 9/19/30. Studied pno. fr. age 17. Four yrs. at Chi. Mus. Coll., then self-taught. Pl. first prof. gig at age 18. Arr. for King Fleming band 1950. Pl. pno. w. Walter Perkins; MJT+3 fr. '55. Freelanced in Chi. w. Miles Davis, Max Roach, Sonny Rollins, Johnny Griffin. Formed own bb, the Experimental Band, in Chi. '61; sidemen incl. Eddie Harris, Victor Sproles. Founded AACM '65; as the first dir. of this organization, he strongly infl. younger members incl. Lester Bowie, Anthony Braxton, Geo. Lewis, Joseph Jarman. Moved to NYC '77. Pl. in duos w. Lewis, Braxton, Leroy Jenkins, Amina Claudine Myers, late '70s; also led gps. and a bb. Comp. for Kronos String Qt., mid '80s. Led qnt. w. Stanton Davis, John Purcell, late '80s. Series of concerts at Ethical Culture Society in '90s. Favs: Nat Cole, Art Tatum, James P. Johnson. Poll: *DB* Critics TDWR '74. CDs: BS; Del.; w. A. Braxton (Del.); Chico Freeman (Ind. Nav.); Marty Ehrlich (NW); Eddie Harris (Rhino/Atl.); Leroy Jenkins; George Lewis (BS).

ABRAMS, RAY (Raymond Joseph Abramson), tnr sax; lead; b. Brooklyn, NY, 1/23/20; d. Brooklyn, 7/6/92. Brother of Lee Abrams. Studied w. fath., who pl. vln. and cl. Pl. locally w. Bklyn. gps. Member of house bands at Monroe's Uptown House and 78th St. Taproom, early 1940s. Pl. in D. Gillespie's first bb '45–6; tour. Eur. w. Don Redman '46; ret. To US and form. own band, pl. at the Savoy. Join. Andy Kirk '47–8; w. Gillespie again in '49. Tour. w. Hot Lips Page '49–50; pl. w. various small gps. incl. R. Eldridge '52; Slim Gaillard; Bill Harris; Paul Gayten's r&b band. Taught jazz in Bklyn. Led own bb in '80s and early '90s. Rec. w. Bill Harris; B. DeFranco; T. Gibbs. CDs: w. K. Clarke in *The Bebop Revolution* (BB); Gillespie (Musi.; Sav.; Band.); C. Hawkins (Del.).

ACEA, JOHNNY (JOHN ADRIANO), pno, tpt, arr; b. Philadelphia, PA, 10/11/17; d. ca. late '80s. Freelanced fr. late 1930s on tpt. w. Jimmy Gorham, Sammy Price; tnr. sax w. Doc Bagby; pno. w. various gps. In army, '44–6; moved to NYC '47. Pl. w. Lockjaw Davis at Minton's '47–8; Dizzy Gillespie bb '49–50; James Moody '51; Illinois Jacquet '51–2; Dinah Washington '52; Cootie Williams '53; Jacquet '53–4. Freelanced w. Joe Newman, Eddie Jefferson, others fr. '55. Favs: Art Tatum, Bud Powell. CDs: w.

Joe Newman–Al Cohn (FS); Jacquet (Verve); Grant Green (BN).

ACHILLES, BOB (ROBERT W.), saxes, fl, cl; b. Evansville, IN, 9/30/37. Graduated fr. U. of Ill. 1960, w. B.S. in mus. ed. Moved to LA, studied w. Lyle "Spud" Murphy, worked w. local commercial gps. In '63, he joined Harry James band and became feat. instrumentalist, mostly on cl. Left James '67; two yrs. w. LV house bands '67–9; copyist, arr., and studio work in LA '69–75. In '75 retired from mus. to enter Christian ministry; occasionally pl. cl. to illustrate his beliefs at religious retreats and gatherings. CDs: w. James (Verve).

ACUNA, ALEX (Alejandro Neciosup-Acuna), dms, perc; b. Pativilca, Peru, 12/12/44. Studied tpt. and pno.; self-taught on perc. Studio mus. at age 16; worked in LV w. Perez Prado 1964. Fr. mid '60s to mid '70s, freelanced in studios and bands in LV, LA, and PR. First prominent in jazz as perc. w. Weather Report '75–6 and dmr. '76–7; app. on album *Heavy Weather*. Formed own gp., Koinonia, '80; also worked or rec. w. Lee Ritenour; Clare Fischer '78–9; Ella Fitzgerald '80; Tania Maria '83; Chick Corea; Paco De Lucia '84; Joni Mitchell '85; active into the '90s as a freelancer and studio player. CDs: Tonga; w. Weather Report; J. Zawinul (Col.); B. Enriquez (GNP).

ADAMS, GEORGE RUFUS, tnr sax; b. Covington, GA, 4/29/40; d. Brooklyn, NY, 11/14/92. Began on pno. at age 11, pl. in church. Took up sax in hs and pl. w. sch. band. Studied under Wayman Carver at Clark Coll. First prof. exp. w. band backing blues singers Jimmy Reed, Howlin' Wolf, Lightnin' Hopkins in Atlanta. Tour. w. Sam Cooke 1961. Moved to Ohio '63; to NYC '68. Pl. w. Roy Haynes '69–73; Charles Mingus '73–6; Gil Evans '75–78; McCoy Tyner '76–9. Fr. '79 co-lead. of gp. w. Don Pullen. Also cont. rec. as lead. Tour. in Eur. w. Pullen, incl. apps. at fests. Also pl. Eur. Fests. w. Evans in '80s. Worked w. James "Blood" Ulmer in Phalanx. Prominent soloist in premiere of Mingus's *Epitaph*; tour. w. Mingus Dynasty into '92. Big-toned, gospel, and blues-oriented style infl. by Coltrane's later period. CDs: BN; Timel.; SN; w. Mingus (Rhino/Atl.); Mingus Dynasty (Col.); M. Tyner (BN); J. Ulmer (In+Out; Moers; DIW); G. Evans (Ant.; Evid.); Craig Harris (SN).

ADAMS, PEPPER (PARK III), bari sax; b. Highland Park, MI, 10/8/30; d. Brooklyn, NY, 9/10/86. Began on tnr. sax and cl. in Rochester, N.Y. At 12 met Harry Carney; three yrs. later in Det., he sw. to bari. sax and by 1947 was a member of Lucky Thompson's band. Divided his time between gigging and working in an auto plant until serving w. the army in Korea '51–3, incl. pl. for Special Services shows. Pl. at Bluebird Club in Det. w. James Richardson, backing visiting star soloists, then w. Kenny Burrell's gp. Moved to NYC Jan. '56, work. w. the Maynard Ferguson and Stan Kenton orchs. bef. joining Chet Baker and spending some time on the West Coast. Ret. to NYC '58; w. Benny Goodman '58–9; Thelonious Monk at Town Hall '59; on road w. Lionel Hampton '62–3. Fr. '58 to '62 he co-led qnt. w. Donald Byrd. A charter member of the Thad Jones–Mel Lewis orch. fr. '65, he remained w. it into '76; also pl. and rec. w. David Amram's gp. In the late '70s and into the '80s, he tour. Engl. and the Continent several times, pl. w. local rhythm sections. Was part of Count Basie tribute at Grande Parade du Jazz, Nice, in mid '80s. Early infls: Coleman Hawkins, Chu Berry, Carney, Barry Harris. Gary Carner, his discographer and biographer, has characterized Adams's style as having "very long, tumbling, double-time melodic lines. And that raw, piercing, bark-like timbre." CDs: Just Jazz; FS; Res.; Muse; Sav.; Riv.; Mile.; w. Mingus (Deb.); C. Baker; Monk; T. Thielemans; J. Griffin; P.J. Jones (Riv.); Thad Jones (Riv.; LRC); G. Ammons; C. Hawkins; J. Coltrane (Prest.); R.R. Kirk (Merc.); L. Morgan; D. Byrd; E. Jones; D. Gillespie (BN); C. Fuller; L. Hampton (Timel.); H. O'Brien (CC); Denny Christianson (JT); J. Henderson; F. Hubbard (BL); P. Leitch (Res.).

ADDERLEY, CANNONBALL (JULIAN EDWIN), alto sax; sop sax; comp; b. Tampa, FL, 9/15/28; d. Gary, IN, 8/8/75. Father was a jazz crntst.; entire family musical. Stud. brass and reed instruments at hs in Tallahassee, Fla., 1944–8, forming first jazz gp. w. band dir. Leander Kirksey as adviser. Fr. '48 to '56, Adderley was band dir. at Dillard HS in Ft. Lauderdale, Fla., and had his own jazz gp. in So. Fla, '48–50. While serving in the army '50–2, he bec. leader of the 36th Army Dance Band. In '52, led own gp. in Wash., D.C., where he studied at the US Naval Sch. of Mus. He led another army band at Ft. Knox, '52–3. The nickname Cannonball evolved from "Cannibal," a name given by hs colleagues in tribute to his vast appetite. Adderley first attracted attention in the NYC jazz community when he sat in w. Oscar Pettiford at the Café Bohemia in the summer of '55, whereupon he rec. for Sav., but soon moved to the Em. label. In spring '56 he and his bro. Nat began tour. w. their own gp. When it disbanded in late '57, he joined Miles Davis until Aug. '59, then tour. as feat. soloist w. George Shearing's bb. In Oct. '59, the Adderley bros. reformed their qnt., playing bop imbued w. an infectious, highly rhythmic gospel spirit that made it one of

the most popular gps. in jazz dur. the early '60s. Such hit records as "Work Song," "Dis' Here," and "Mercy, Mercy, Mercy" produced a rash of "soul-jazz" fusion gps. Fr. '59 to '65, the qnt.'s pnsts. incl. Junior Mance; Bobby Timmons; Barry Harris; Victor Feldman; Joe Zawinul; George Duke; Hal Galper; and Michael Wolff. Drummer Louis Hayes and bs. Sam Jones formed the core of the rhythm section. Yusef Lateef was added in '61 and replaced by Charles Lloyd in '63 until July '65, when the gp. ret. to qnt. size. Through the mid and late '60s, the gp. maintained a stable personnel, w. Roy McCurdy, dms., Victor Gaskin, bs. (later replaced by Walter Booker), and Zawinul. In the late '60s, Adderley began doubling on sop. and occasionally electrified his alto sax. Fr. '62 he was married to actress Olga James. He suffered a massive fatal stroke while on tour in Indiana. Memorabilia from his career is housed in Tallahassee at Fla. A&M's Black Archives Research Center and Museum. Considered an articulate spokesman for jazz, Adderley was also involved in a variety of nonplaying activities. He was a member of the committee for NEA; Black Academy of Arts and Letters; NARAS board of governors; Jazz Advisory Panel for the JFK Center for the Perfoming Arts; and active as clinician for coll. jazz wkshps. The advisory board for Harvard U.'s Artist-in-Residence program, on which he served, was posthumously renamed after him. He also produced albums by Dexter Gordon, Bud Powell, and Wes Montgomery. Earliest infls. were Benny Carter and Charlie Parker; later ones included Miles Davis, John Coltrane, Bill Evans, and the modal harmony that affected them all. Polls: *DB* Critics, New Star '59; *DB* Critics & Readers '60–1; *DB* Readers '68–71; *DB* Hall of Fame '75; *Playboy* '61–6. Int'l apps: Japan, Eur. '63; Engl. '64. Fests: NJF; MJF; Montreux; Cannes; Pori; tour. eastern and western Eur. as part of "NJF in Eur." package '72; Alaska Fest. of Mus. '75. Films: *Play Misty for Me*; *Soul To Soul*; *Save the Children*. TV: hosted *90 Minutes*, a 13-week series, '72; David Frost show; *Tonight Show*; Nancy Wilson show; *Playboy After Dark*; acting role in one sequence of *Kung Fu*. Publ: *Play Saxophone Like Cannonball Adderley*, Robbins Mus. Corp. Comps: "Sack O' Woe"; "Introduction to a Samba"; "Them Dirty Blues"; "Savior" (lyrics by Olga James); *Suite Cannon*, a three-part work: co-comp. w. Nat the mus. for *Big Man*, based on the legend of John Henry. CDs: BN; Em.; Riv; Mile.; Cap.; Sav.; w. John Benson Brooks; Bill Evans; Sam Jones; K. Dorham; P.J. Jones; J. Heath (Riv.); M. Davis (Col.); Gil Evans (PJ); N. Adderley (Jzld.); K. Clarke (Sav.).

ADDERLEY, NAT (NATHANIEL), crnt, comp; b. Tampa, FL, 11/25/31; d. Lakeland, FL, 1/2/01. Brother of Cannonball Adderley. Studied tpt. first,

1945–6, bef. sw. to crnt. when he pl. in army band '51–3. Worked w. L. Hampton '54–5, then w. Cannonball Adderley '56–7. While Cannonball was a sideman w. Miles Davis, Nat pl. w. J. J. Johnson '57–8 and W. Herman '59. Rejoined Cannonball '59 and remained until his bro.'s death '75. In '76, founded a gp. w. Ken McIntyre and John Stubblefield. Dur. '80s and '90s, cont. lead. small gps. w. Sonny Fortune, Larry Willis, Walter Booker, Jimmy Cobb, Vincent Herring, Rob Bargad, et al., frequently tour. Eur. and Japan. Adderley is highly regarded for his comps. "Work Song," "Sermonette," and "Jive Samba"; noted also for his humorous dissertations and introductions, which in a way are parallel to his effervescent solo style, which at first mixed elements of Clark Terry w. Dizzy Gillespie and then added some mid '50s Miles Davis. His son, Nat Adderley Jr., is a kybd. player active in soul and r&b. CDs: Riv.; Sav.; Land.; Evid.; Enja; Steep.; Sw. Bas.; In+Out; w. C. Adderley (Sav.; Em.; Riv.; Cap.; Mile.; Land.); Riverside Reunion Band (Mile.); K. Clarke (Sav.); James Clay (Riv.); Red Garland (Gal.); Paul Gonsalves (Jzld); D. Ellington (Saja).

ADDISON, BERNARD S., gtr; b. Annapolis, MD, 4/15/05; d. Rockville Centre, NY, 12/18/90. Played vln. and mand. as a child. In 1920, he moved to Wash., D.C., where he was a schoolmate of Claude Hopkins. As bjost. he co-led a gp. w. Hopkins in early '20s; then dates in Phila. w. Rex Stewart bef. traveling to NYC w. Sonny Thompson. Fr. mid '20s, he worked for five yrs. as sideman and lead. at Smalls' Paradise, NYC. Sw. to gtr. '28 and worked w. Art Tatum first in Milton Senior Band, then as accomp. to Adelaide Hall '30; also w. Louis Armstrong '30; Luis Russell; Sam Wooding; Fats Waller '31–2; F. Henderson '33–4; Adrian Rollini '35. Tour. US and Eur. '36–8 as accomp. to Mills Bros. Pl. w. Stuff Smith '38–9; Sidney Bechet '40; led own band until army service; in '45, after discharge, he made a USO tour w. Snub Mosley. Tour. w. Ink Spots in US and Can. dur. '50s; pl. w. Eubie Blake '58; also accomp. Juanita Hall. A highly regarded rhythm gtrst. in the '30s, he took up classical gtr. in the late '50s. Cont. freelancing in '60s but devoted most of his energies to teaching. Fests: Great South Bay, w. Henderson Reunion Band, '57; NJF '60 w. Blake. Rec. for BB as a leader '35, and British 77 label '61. CDs: w. Jelly Roll Morton; Bechet; Henderson (BB); Louis Armstrong; D. Ellington; B. Holiday (Col.).

ADILIFU, KAMAU MUATA (Charles Sullivan), tpt, flg, comp; b. NYC, 11/8/44. Two uncles, Herman and Hubie James, pl. tpt. (latter still active in NYC). Stud. w. Hubie James 1954–6, '61, and pl. w. his orch. '62; then stud. w. Cecil Collins at Manh. Sch. of Mus. '62–7 (B. Mus. '67). Pl. w. theater pit bands fr. '65; Donald McKayle Dance Co. '67; Lionel Hampton '68; Roy Haynes Hip Ens. '69; Count Basie '70; Lonnie Liston Smith '71; NYJRC '72; Norman Connors '73; Thad Jones–Mel Lewis '74; Sonny Fortune '75. Led own Black Legacy bb, also qt. and qnt. '75–80. Pl. w. Jazzmobile Dream Band '80; Geo. Gruntz bb '80–2; Mercer Ellington orch. '81; McCoy Tyner bb '85–92; John Clark '95. Also pl. and rec. w. Ricky Ford; Kenny Barron; Abdullah Ibrahim; Walter Davis Jr.; Woody Shaw; others. Taught at Bennington Coll. summer '77. Favs: Miles Davis, Lee Morgan. Fests: Eur. w. Tyner bb '90. TV: PBS *Black Journal* w. Billy Taylor '75. LPs: Strata-East, Inner City. CDs: Arab.; w. Tyner (Mile.; Bird.); M. Ellington (GRP).

ADLER, LARRY (LAWRENCE), hca; pno; comp; b. Baltimore, MD, 2/10/14; d. London, 8/9/01. After app. in Ziegfeld's *Smiles* 1931, he became a national name and was seen in films; in *Many Happy Returns* '34, he was accomp. by Duke Ellington orch. Scored a big hit while app. in London '35; lived in London, tour. extensively on the Continent, bef. ret. to the US '39. Pl. clubs accomp. by Ellis Larkins, a relationship that cont. in the '80s. Teamed w. Dizzy Gillespie for TV app. '59. Although living in London again fr. '49, he cont. to visit US for engagements, incl. a successful NYC run at the Cookery in late '70s; and the Ballroom in '86, where he employed a special player pno. that allowed him to duet w. George Gershwin. Rec. debut as leader in London '34; as sideman w. Stephane Grappelli and Django Reinhardt, Paris '38; John Kirby, NYC '44. Perhaps the world's best-known hca. pl., Adler perf. classical and pop material as well as jazz. Book: autobiography, *It Ain't Necessarily So*, London '84. Columnist for *Boz*, London, in '90s. TV: duets w. D. Gillespie '59; Bill Evans. CDs: Merc.; Newport Classics; w. D. Reinhardt (DRG).

AFFIF, RON (RONALD ANTHONY), gtr, bs, pno; b. Pittsburgh, PA, 12/30/66. Uncle, Ron Anthony, was gtrst. w. Sinatra and George Shearing. Began on dms. at age 12, then sw. to gtr. Studied in Pitts. w. Joe Negri, Jenny Condonato, Eric Suseoff. Pl. in Pitts. w. Dave Budway, Negri, Suseoff. Moved to LA 1984. Pl. w. Dave Pike; Dick Berk; Andy Simpkins; Sherman Ferguson; John Pisano; Ron Anthony '84–8. Moved to NYC '89. Pl. w. Leon Parker; Ralph Lalama; Philip Harper; Sheila Jordan; Harvie Swartz; Sam Newsome; Kevin Mahogany; Cecil Brooks III; Bill Mays; Jerry Weldon; Jay Collins; Tim Armacost; Essiet Essiet '89–95. Led a trio w. Essiet and Jeff "Tain" Watts at Zinc Bar fr. '95. Favs: Pat Martino,

Joe Pass, Wes Montgomery. Fests: Eur. fr. '87; Japan fr. '88; Korea fr. '92. CDs: Pab.; w. J. Pisano (Pab.).

AKAGI, KEI, pno, kybds; b. Sendai, Japan, 3/16/53. Spent childhood yrs. in Cleveland, OH; stud. at local mus. sch. Ret. to Japan in early teens; studied philosophy and music comp. in Tokyo. Ret. to US as phil. student at UC–Santa Barbara while cont. to pl. and comp. Rejecting a future as coll. profess., became full-time mus. at 25 and moved to LA. In 1970s, pl. w. Blue Mitchell; Art Pepper; Eddie Harris; Flora Purim–Airto Moreira; in '80s w. Joe Farrell; Alan Holdsworth; Jean-Luc Ponty; James Newton; Al DiMeola; Miles Davis '89–90; in '90s w. Stanley Turrentine. Fav. own solo on *Playroom*, Mesa/Blue Moon Recs. Taught jazz pno. priv. '78–85. CDs: PW; w. B. Shew (MAMA); Joey Sellars (Nine Winds).

AKIYOSHI, TOSHIKO, comp, pno; b. Dairen, Manchuria, 12/12/29. Studied classical pno. 1936–45. To Japan w. family '46. Took up jazz '47. Pl. w. Yamada in Fukuoka, then in Tokyo w. various gps. '49–51; own gp. fr. Aug. '51. While visiting Japan w. JATP, Nov. '53, Oscar Peterson heard her, and Norman Granz rec. her w. his rhythm section. Broke up her gp. Sept. '54; formed oct. for radio, TV; won local awards as Japan's leading pnst. In Jan. '56 arrived in Bost. Studied at Berklee on scholarship, also priv. w. Margaret Chaloff. As protégée of George Wein, pl. at his Storyville club and at NJF and bec. active as comp. for student and faculty orchs. Married to Charlie Mariano '59–65, dur. which time they led own qt., spending much of her time in Japan but also teaching at summer jazz clinics in Reno and Salt Lake City '64 and '65. Own radio prog. NYC '67–8. Debut as comp.-cond. at Town Hall Oct. '67. Own qt. at Expo '70 in Japan. Married to Lew Tabackin, she became involved in a series of ventures, incl. Japanese tour w. qt. '71. In '72 she and Tabackin moved to LA, where they gigged locally w. a qt. and in '73 formed a 16-piece band that rapidly achieved worldwide popularity. Akiyoshi won *DB* poll as arr. fr. '78 and both as comp. and arr. annually fr. '82, in addition to a series of awards for the orch. as best bb. She was the first woman and Asian to win in any of these categories. Honored for her fifty yrs. in jazz by Japanese Embassy in NYC, '96. Like Duke Ellington, she is an excellent pnst. but regards the orch. as her principal means of expression. In her LA band and the one she formed after ret. to NYC in '82, she has used Japanese dmrs., effectively incorporating Japanese culture into her mus. She is known for her exquisite, flute-oriented writing for the reed section, w. Tabackin as a feat. soloist, and has a talent for writing charts that employ complex voicings while retaining the essence of swing. Cont. to lead a trio, reorganizing the bb only when it is called for. From '98 it was in residence, once a week, at Birdland. As a pnst., she was clearly inspired by Bud Powell, whose infl. is reflected in her music, notably on the album *Remembering Bud*. Unlike most bb leaders, she writes all her band's arrs. and most comps. (she arr. a few tunes by Tabackin). Following an association w. RCA, she rec. for her own label, Ascent, but her '92 Carnegie Hall concert was released by CBS/Sony. Comps. incl. "Kogun," "Sumie," "Long Yellow Road," "Tales of a Courtesan," "March of the Tadpoles," "American Ballad," "Henpecked Old Man," and "Tanuki's Night Out." CDs: RCA; Col.; Ken; Insights; Denon; Evid.; Conc.

AKLAFF, PHEEROAN (Paul Maddox), dms; b. Detroit, MI, 1/27/55. Brother classical pnst. Assoc. w. the free jazz movement fr. 1975, when he pl. w. Jay Hoggard. Worked w. Leo Smith's New Dalta Ahkri in New Haven, Conn.; then in NYC w. Oliver Lake Trio, Anthony Davis–James Newton Qt. '78–9; Davis's Episteme fr. '81; Lake's Jump Up fr. '83; Henry Threadgill's Air '82–3; and Very Very Circus fr. '84. Pl. w. Ray Anderson, Mark Helias '89; Craig Harris's Tailgaters '90s. Rec. as. a lead. for Gram., *Fits Like a Glove* '83. CDs: w. Davis; Anderson (Gram.); Air (BS); Lake (BS; Gram.); Helias (Enja); Newton (BN).

ALBAM, MANNY (EMMANUEL), comp, arr, cond; b. Samana, Dominican Republic, 6/24/22; d. Croton, NY, 10/2/01. To NYC at age of 6 wks. Studied cl. at Stuyvesant HS. Prof. debut w. Don Joseph qnt. on alto sax 1940. Later pl. (usually bari. sax) and wrote for many bands incl. Muggsy Spanier '41; Bob Chester '42; Georgie Auld '42–5; Boyd Raeburn '43–5. After army service '45–6, pl. w. Herbie Fields, Bobby Sherwood, Sam Donahue '47; Charlie Barnet '48–9. Fr. '50 gave up pl. to concentrate on writing and by '55 was one of the busiest arrs. in NYC. Rec. numerous albums for RCA and Coral '55–7. Arrs. for rec. dates by Stan Kenton; Woody Herman; Gerry Mulligan; Buddy Rich; Coleman Hawkins; Carmen McRae; Dizzy Gillespie; others. Cont. stud. w. Tibor Serly '59–60. Taught at Eastman Sch. '67–92; Glassboro St. (now Rowan Coll.) '72–87; Manh. Sch. of Mus. fr. '93. Mus. Dir. of BMI's Jazz Comp. Wkshp. fr. '86. Worked in Engl. '60, '87, '88 incl. Royal Phil.; recs. w. Tubby Hayes; Ronnie Ross; w. UMO orch. in Finland '88; Germ. '89 w. Radio Cologne, Stuttgart, Frankfurt orchs., cond. concerts for Red Rodney, Phil Woods, B. Shank, L. Konitz; Metropole Orch., Netherlands '94; Herb Geller, Stuttgart '95, rec. for Germ. IRS label. Has written symphonic arrs.

of comps. by Roland Hanna; Billy Taylor; and J.J. Johnson (*Lament*); also chamber mus. for trombonists Jim Pugh and Dave Taylor; and tubaist Harvey Phillips; mus. for films, TV (PBS w. Billy Taylor; M. McPartland); commercials. His rec. of *West Side Story* was nominated for a Grammy '58. Favs: Bill Holman, Bob Brookmeyer, Al Cohn, Thad Jones, Johnny Mandel, Strayhorn/Ellington. Fest: Imatra, Finland, '95. John S. Wilson wrote in the *NY Times*: "Albam has the ability to orchestrate in terms that can be translated into a loose, swinging performance as well as the willingness to create strong-lined ensembles and study supporting frameworks for his soloists rather than sketchy outlines which merely serve as springboards for a succession of solo performances." CDs: *Sketches from the Book of Life* (LRC); w. Hank Jones and Meridian String Qt. (LRC); Coleman Hawkins (Imp.); Meredith D'Ambrosio (Sunny.); J. Lovano (BN).

ALBANY, JOE (Joseph Albani), pno; b. Atlantic City, NJ, 1/24/24; d. New York City, 1/12/88. Sisters are classical pnst., operatic sop. Studied acdn. as a child. After taking up pno. in high sch., he moved to Calif. at age 17 and worked w. Leo Watson. Member of Benny Carter orch. 1943 before ret. to the East. Worked in NYC w. Max Kaminsky, Rod Cless at the Pied Piper. Rec. w. Georgie Auld '45. Ret. to Calif. '46; pl. w. Charlie Parker and Howard McGhee, rec. w. Lester Young. A private session w. Warne Marsh was issued on Riverside label in '57, reviving interest in Albany, but he remained in relative obscurity. Worked in small SF club '60; wrote some songs rec. by Anita O'Day. Pl. w. Charles Mingus at Village Gate, NYC '63; Russ Morgan, LV '64. Moved to Eur. '72, ret. permanently the following yr., first in LA bef. settling in NYC in late '70s. Intensive practice strengthened his left hand, and he pl. many solo jobs as well as gp. work at the West End, Sweet Basil. As solo pno. opened Kool JF tribute to Charlie Parker, '80. Infl. at first by Tatum and Basie, later by Bud Powell and Monk, Albany was also strongly shaped by Parker. Drug addiction hampered him through much of his career, but his many perfs. dur. the '80s leavened his legendary status to a certain extent. Beset by illness dur. the latter part of the decade, incl. a brain tumor. Film: *Joe Albany—A Jazz Life*, documentary by Carole Langer '80. CDs: Riv.; Steep.; FS; Story.; w. L. Young (BN).

ALBERT, DON (Albert Dominique), tpt, lead; b. New Orleans, LA, 8/5/08; d. San Antonio, TX, 1/80. Uncle was Natty Dominique; also a relative of Barney Bigard. Pl. in parade bands in NO in early 1920s; then tour. in Southwest w. Alphonso Trent's second band '25; pl. w. Troy Floyd '26–9. In '30s and '40s led his own Texas-based bands whose sidemen incl. Alvin Alcorn, Louis Cottrell Jr., and Herb Hall. Rarely playing, Albert concentrated on managing, leading, and arr. Band app. in Mex., Can., and NYC '37. Pl. at the Palace Theater, NYC '49. He ret. to active pl., worked w. small gps. fr. the '50s, when he moved to San Antonio, Texas, to the mid '70s. Sat in w. Buddy Tate's band, NYC '66; pl. at NOJF '69. Film: *Beale Street Mama* '46. Rec. "Rockin' and Swingin'" (Voc.) '36. LP: *Echoes of New Orleans* (South.). CD: one track on *The Real Kansas City* (Col.).

ALCORN, ALVIN ELMORE, tpt; b. New Orleans, 9/7/12; d. New Orleans, 7/17/03. Son tptr. Sam Alcorn. Stud. mus. w. bro. Oliver, cl. and sax; tpt. w. George McCullum Jr. Pl. w. Clarence Desdune's band 1928; led own band bef. joining A. J. Piron '30–1; Sunny South Syncopators '31. Worked w. Don Albert '32–7; again w. Piron '37. Pl. w. Sidney Desvigne '41–50, also briefly w. Tab Smith in mid '40s. Fr. '47 was active as decorator for real estate co.; also pl. w. Papa Celestin '51; Octave Crosby '51–4; then to Calif., pl. w. Kid Ory '54–6, tour. Eur. w. him '56; also worked w. Bill Mathews in LV '55. Coll. concert tour sponsored by Rev. Alvin Kershaw '56. Ret. to NO, pl. dates w. George Lewis '58; Bill Mathews, Paul Barbarin '59. Apps. in NYC '69. Perf. regularly as lead. and sideman into the '80s. Tour. Eur. w. NO All-Stars '66; as soloist '73, '74, '76; w. Chris Barber '78; tour. Austral. '73. Favs: Armstrong, Red Allen, Benny Carter. Film: *The Benny Goodman Story* w. Ory '55; *Live and Let Die* '73. Rec. w. Eureka Brass band '59 and late '60s. CDs: Story.; w. Ory (GTJ).

ALDEBERT, LOUIS, pno, voc; b. Ismailiya, Egypt, 6/8/31; **ALDEBERT, MONIQUE** (née Dozo), voc; b. Monaco, 5/5/31. Louis sang w. Blue Stars and the Double Six of Paris; Monique sang in clubs w. Don Byas; Django Reinhardt; Bobby Jaspar; and the Double Six. The Aldeberts moved to the US in 1967, sang in LV shows and perf. in LA '69, where they worked in night clubs alone or backed by small gps. Toured Japan '91. Their ingenious arrs. of jazz and pop tunes, and their own originals, some in French, have a unique, unpretentious charm. CD: w. Double Six (CMP Amplitude).

ALDEN, HOWARD VINCENT, gtr, tnr-bjo; b. Newport Beach, CA, 10/17/58. Began on tnr-bjo. at age 10. Studied gtr. in LA w. Jimmy Wyble, Howard Roberts, Joe Diorio 1975–8, then one yr. at Gtr. Inst. of Tech. Gigs on bjo. fr. age 12. Pl. w. Disneyland band '76–7; various Calif. dixie. gps. '78; Page

Cavanaugh '78–9; Red Norvo '79. Made rec. debut w. Wild Bill Davison '81. Moved to NYC '82. Pl. w. Joe Bushkin '82–5; Joe Williams '83–6; Woody Herman '84; Warren Vaché, Ruby Braff since '84; H. Alden–Dan Barrett Qnt. since '85; Newport All-Stars since. '91; Kenny Davern in '90s. Pl. for jazz cruises, parties since '86. Taught at the Gtr. Inst. of Tech. '78–80. As versatile as he is expert within a wide repertoire. Favs: Barney Kessel, Geo. Van Eps, Charlie Christian. Polls: *JT* Best Emerging Gtr. '90. Fests: Eur. since '86. JVC-NY. CDs: Conc., incl. duets w. Van Eps; w. Braff; Scott Hamilton; Susannah McCorkle; Ken Peplowski; Flip Phillips; W. Vaché (Conc.); Benny Carter (MM); Claude Williams (Prog.); K. Davern (Arb.).

ALEMAN, OSCAR MARCELO, gtr; b. Resistencia, Argentina, 2/20/09; d. Buenos Aires, Argentina 10/14/80. Orphaned in Brazil at age 10, he learned cavaquinho. Studied gtr. in teen yrs. Formed gtr. duo Los Lobos w. Gaston Bueno Lobo 1924; pl. w. dancer Harry Fleming in Spain late '20s. Led Baker Boys, acc. Josephine Baker in Paris '31; w. Freddy Taylor's Swing Men from Harlem '33–5; also led band w. Frank "Big Boy" Goudie at Le Chantilly. Pl. jam sessions w. Bill Coleman; Willie Lewis; Arthur Briggs; Django Reinhardt. First jazz recs. in mid '30s, incl. Taylor '35; Coleman '36; Eddie Brunner '38; Danny Polo '39. Rec. as lead. in Eur. '39–40. Ret. to Buenos Aires early '40s, rec. and pl. until his death. Used finger-picking technique like Reinhardt, whom he admired, but was known for personal, full, low-register sound. Infl. by the mus. of Brazil and his native Argentina. CDs: Acoustic Disc; Jazz Time.

ALESS, TONY (Anthony Alessandrini), pno; b. Garfield, NJ, 8/22/21; d. NYC, 9/23/85. Played w. Bunny Berigan at 17; later w. Johnny McGhee, Teddy Powell, Vaughn Monroe 1940–2. Army to '44; then briefly w. Charlie Spivak before replacing Ralph Burns w. Woody Herman '45. Left in '46; taught three yrs. at NY Cons. bef. going into radio work; on staff at WNEW Radio, NYC, for a yr.; replaced Elliot Lawrence on daily Jack Sterling show, CBS, Feb. '54. Own comp. *Long Island Suite* rec. on LP of same title for Roost '55. CDs: w. Stan Getz (Prest.); W. Herman (Col.).

ALEXANDER, ERIC WELLS, tnr sax; b. Galesburg, IL, 8/4/68. Moved to Olympia, Wash., at age 2. Studied pno. fr. age 6 or 7; sax fr. age 13, first priv., then in public sch. system. Cont. mus. educ. at U. of Indiana 1986–7; Wm. Paterson Coll., N.J. '87–90. Moved to Chi. and began working, first w. vocalist Lenny Lynne. Rec. debut w. Charles Earland, the

orgst. w. whom he has pl. since '91. Won 2nd prize in Thelonious Monk Competition '91. Moved to NYC and has pl. w. Cecil Payne; Eddie Henderson; Harold Mabern; Danny Moore; Vanguard Jazz Orch.; Mickey Roker; Shirley Scott fr. '92. Favs: Coltrane, George Coleman, Joe Henderson, Sonny Stitt. CDs: Del.; CC; w. One For All (Sharp Nine); Earland; Randy Johnston (Muse); C. Payne (Del.); Joe Magnarelli; Steve Davis; Tenor Triangle (CC); Michael Weiss (DIW); Rob Mazurek (Hep).

ALEXANDER, MONTY (MONTGOMERY BERNARD), pno; b. Kingston, Jamaica, 6/6/44. Mother sang in church. Pl. calypso and boogie-woogie by ear at early age; priv. studies 1952–8. Moved to Miami, Fla., '61, where he was heard by Frank Sinatra, whose friend Jilly Rizzo hired him for his NYC club, Jilly's, in '67. Played and rec. w. Milt Jackson and Ray Brown in late '60s and early '70s. Early work showed strong Oscar Peterson infl. Formed own trio '74; tour. Eur. '74–80. Cont. to lead own gps. into '90s, sometimes in a Nat Cole tribute; also collab. w. steel dmrs. Othello Molineaux and Boogsie Sharpe; Triple Treat w. Brown, Herb Ellis. Doug Ramsey characterized Alexander's playing as containing "a rhythmic concept charged by the dance music of the Caribbean Islands," and talked of his "piquantly hesitant placement of notes at precisely the correct strategic spots behind the beat." Favs: Nat Cole, Art Tatum. Films: soundtracks for *Bird*; *For Love of Ivy*. Fests: Japan and Eur. fr. '74, incl. Montreux '77; solo pno. at JVC-NY '96. TV: Merv Griffin; *Nightwatch*. CDs: Conc.; MPS; Chesky; Verve; SN; Lime.; w. M. Jackson; D. Gillespie (Pab.); Ernestine Anderson; R. Brown (Conc.).

ALEXANDER, MOUSEY (ELMER), dms; b. Gary, IN, 6/9/22; d. Orlando, FL, 10/9/88. Father pl. vln. Studied dms. at Roy Knapp Sch. in Chi. 1948; in NYC w. Sam Ulano. Pl. w. Jimmy McPartland '48–50; M. McPartland '52–3; Sauter-Finegan '53–5; Johnny Smith '55–6; B. Goodman '56–7. App. w. Bud Freeman at Eddie Condon's '58; then w. Condon's house band '59. Made a Eur. tour w. Georgie Auld '60; So. Amer. tour w. Goodman '61; Goodman sxt. '66–7. Tour. Sweden and Czechoslovakia w. Paul Anka '66. Worked as contractor for jingles '62–5. Fr. '65 formed a long-term assoc. w. Al Cohn–Zoot Sims gp.; also fronted his own gps. at Plaza 9 '68–9, Half Note '74; pl. w. Clark Terry orch. '69–72 and gigged in '72 w. Lee Konitz, Sonny Stitt, James Moody. Tour. Eur. w. Sy Oliver '73; pl. w. Doc Severinsen on *Tonight* '73; w. Sims, Terry, spring '74. Fr. '67 many apps. at Colo. JP; also Odessa (Tex.) JP '71, '75. Lived and pl. in Fla. in the '80s. Suffered heart attack '73; two more in '76. Resumed career through medication and therapy. In Aug. '80, seven weeks after form. and pl. w. his own bb, he suffered a severe stroke. Moved to Orlando, Fla., June '81. Had quadruple by-pass operation Jan. '82. Through intensive therapy, rehabilitated himself, resumed pl., lectured and gave drm. demonstrations to patients at stroke seminars in Fla. hospitals. Freelanced in central Fla. Last NYC app. w. Auld at Blue Note, May '87. Originally infl. by Buddy Rich, he also admired Wash., D.C., dmr. Joe Timer. In later yrs. he incorporated certain facets of Art Blakey's work. Rec. w. L. Konitz for Mile. '71; own LP, *The Mouse Roars* (Famous Door) '79. CDs: w. Z. Sims (Pab.); B. Goodman (MM); B. Clayton (Prest.).

ALEXANDER, ROLAND E., tnr, sop saxes, pno; b. Boston, 9/25/35; d. Brooklyn, NY, 6/14/06. From musical family. Received B. Mus. Bost. Cons. 1958, then moved to NYC. Pl. in early '60s w. John Coltrane; Matthew Gee; Philly Joe Jones; Mal Waldron; Roy Haynes; Max Roach; Blue Mitchell. Worked w. Sonny Rollins '65. Freelancing in NYC area in '90s. Favs: Charlie Parker, Coltrane, Rollins, Ornette Coleman, Joe Henderson, Johnny Griffin. LPs: *Pleasure Bent* (Prest.); w. Charli Persip (Beth.); Blue Mitchell (UA). CDs: w. H. McGhee (Aff.); M. Roach (Atl.); J. Spaulding (Muse); as pnst. w. P. Chambers (BN).

ALEXANDER, VAN (Al Feldman), comp, arr; b. NYC, 5/12/15. Mother a concert pnst. Studied w. Otto Cesana. First prof. arr., "Keepin' Out of Mischief," sold to Chick Webb for $5 in 1936. His arr. of "A-Tisket, A-Tasket" for Ella Fitzgerald in '38 was elected to the Grammy Hall of Fame in '86. Formed own orch. in '38 that lasted into '43 and pl. at B'way movie palaces. Moved to Calif. Fr. mid '50s his career has been devoted to arr. and cond. for TV and movies. He has arr. and cond. for Mildred Bailey; Ella Fitzgerald; Lena Horne; Peggy Lee; Dakota Staton; Kay Starr; Frank Sinatra; Sarah Vaughan; Benny Goodman; Stan Kenton; Jack Teagarden; Bunny Berigan; Lionel Hampton; Teddy Hill; Willie Bryant; Lucky Millinder. Infl.: Victor Young. Favs: Billy May, Pete Rugolo. Own LP, *Home of Happy Feet* (Cap.). CDs: w. Chick Webb–Ella Fitzgerald (Dec.).

ALEXANDRIA, LOREZ (Dolorez Alexandria Nelson, née Turner), voc; b. Chicago, IL, 10/14/29. Sang gospel and choral mus. 1940s and early '50s; later worked Chi. clubs. Rec. four albums '57–9; perf. w. Ramsey Lewis '58. Rec. six albums in early '60s, w. sidemen from C. Basie band; Howard McGhee; and Wynton Kelly Trio. Moved to LA '64; has cont. to perf. at So. Calif. venues and rec. occasionally (incl.

Lorez Alexandria Sings the Songs of Johnny Mercer, Cont.). A talented voc. whose low-keyed style kept her in the shadow of such better-known performers as Sarah Vaughan and Ella Fitzgerald. CDs: Muse; Trend.

ALI, RASHIED (Robert Patterson), dms; b. Philadelphia, PA, 7/1/35. Younger bro., dmr. Muhammad Ali, worked w. Albert Ayler, Archie Shepp, Frank Wright. Studied at Granoff Sch. and priv. Worked w. saxophonist Len Bailey and various local gps., incl. r&r bands. Forced to give up pl. prof., he drove a cab for almost two yrs., then resumed pl. w. Arnold Joyner and others. After moving to NYC in 1963, he began to be known in avant-garde circles, worked w. Pharoah Sanders; Bill Dixon; Paul Bley; Shepp; Marion Brown; Sun Ra; Ayler. Joined John Coltrane Nov. '65, worked at first as part of a two-dms. setup w. Elvin Jones, remain. until Coltrane's death in '67, and cont. w. Alice Coltrane for a time bef. forming his own gp. '68. Pl. w. Sonny Rollins, '68; recs. and gigs w. J. McLean, A. Coltrane, Bud Powell, '69. Concerts, coll. jobs, and clubs, '70–1. Org. NY Jazz Musicians Fest. '72. Form. his own Survival Recs. '73 and opened restaurant-club, Studio 77/Ali's Alley '74, maintaining it until summer '79. With Milford Graves and Andrew Cyrille, participated in a concert series called *Dialogue of the Drums* mid '70s. In '80s worked w. James Ulmer's Phalanx. App. in Berlin w. Evan Parker '91. Tour. Japan w. S. Rollins '63; Coltrane '66. Comp: suite, *New Directions in Jazz.* TV: *The Jazz Set*, PBS '71; *The Story of Jazz*, BMG docu. '91. Fests: NJF '71–2. CDs: w. Coltrane; Shepp (Imp.); David Murray (BS).

ALIAS, (CHARLES) DON, perc, cga, dms; b. NYC, 12/25/39; d. NYC, 3/28/06. Studied pno. and gtr. as a youth, but learned perc. "on the streets" and through one-on-one w. Mongo Santamaria, Armando Peraza, etc. Pl. w. Dizzy Gillespie and Eartha Kitt at NJF 1957. Earned B.S. in biochemistry fr. Carnegie Inst. and worked as biochemist in Bost. '62–8. Made rec. debut w. Johnny Lytle '62. Att. Berklee Sch. '66–7 and pl. around Bost. w. Chick Corea; Alan Dawson; Tony Williams. Ret. to NYC '67. Rec. and Eur. tour w. Miles Davis '69. Pl. and rec. in '70s w. Charles Mingus; M. Santamaria; Elvin Jones; Stan Getz; Herbie Hancock; Jaco Pastorius; Pat Metheny; Blood, Sweat and Tears; Santana; etc., then form. Stone Alliance w. Gene Perla, Kenny Kirkland, Steve Grossman, and Jan Hammer. In early '80s, Alias moved to Montreal, Can., and formed 5-perc. band, Kebekwa. Ret. to NYC '86, pl. w. Carla Bley; David Sanborn; '89–90. Active in studio in recent yrs., rec. w. K. Kirkland; Michael Brecker; Al Jarreau; Charlie

Haden. Favs: A. Peraza, Tata Guines, Patato Valdez. Polls: *DB* TDWR. Fests: NJF '57; many others. TV: *Night Music* w. D. Sanborn. CDs: w. M. Davis (Col.; WB); M. Brecker; K. Kirkland; Kevin Eubanks (GRP); Carla Bley (Watt); Steve Swallow (XtraWatt); Joey Calderazzo; Gil Goldstein (BN); Charlie Haden (Polyd.); Bob Mintzer (DMP); David Sanborn (Rep.; Elek.); Jeremy Steig (LRC); Mike Stern (Atl.); Victor Lewis (Audq.).

ALLAN, JAN BERTIL, tpt, pno; b. Falun, Sweden, 11/7/34. Father was bsst. and vlnst. in 1920s and '30s. Studied pno. fr. age 6, sw. to tpt. at 14, when he became interested in jazz. First prof. gigs '51; moved to Stockholm, worked w. George Riedel. Later pl. w. Lars Gullin–Rolf Billberg '54–5; Carl-Henrik Norin '55–7. Co-led a qnt. w. Billberg '60–3, and led his own orch. '63–8, pl. mus. ranging fr. jazz and pop to jazz-rock. Worked w. Swedish Radio Jazz Gp. '68–75. Won Golden Record from *Orkester Journalen* for best jazz rec., "Ceramics" '70. Pl. w. Riedel's Trio con Tromba '82. Freq. app. at jazz fests. throughout Eur., as well as TV in Germ., Den., Sweden, etc. Often pl. w. visiting Amer. jazzmen, incl. Thad Jones; John Lewis; Warne Marsh; Bob Brookmeyer. Has had concurrent career as elementary particle physicist at Stockholm U. Rec. for Four Leaf Clover (Swedish label) as leader and w. Thad Jones; also w. Trio con Tromba for Phono suecia 1. CD: w. L. Konitz (Drag.).

ALLEN, CARL LEE, dms, perc, comp; b. Milwaukee, WI, 4/25/61. Brother E.J. is trptr. and arr.; moth. sings gospel mus. Studied in Milwaukee publ. sch. 1969–79; U. of Wis.–Green Bay '79–81; w. Steve Bagby at William Paterson Coll. '81–3. Pl. first jazz gig w. Sonny Stitt and Red Holloway '77. Pl. w. James Moody '80; Richard Davis's Wisconsin Connection '80–2; Freddie Hubbard '82–90; Donald Harrison–Terence Blanchard '86–9; Jackie McLean '86–90; Woody Shaw '87–9; Geo. Coleman fr. '87; own qnt. fr. '89; Randy Weston '90–1; D. Harrison, Vincent Herring, Benny Green fr. '90; Donald Byrd, Jazz Futures '91; NY Jazz Giants, Mulgrew Miller fr. '92. Allen has been active as a clinician and lecturer fr. '82. A hard-driving, explosive pl. Favs: Art Blakey, Elvin Jones, Billy Higgins. Fests: Eur., Japan fr. '83. TV: apps. on PBS. CDs: Alfa; Timel.; w. B. Green (BN); D. Harrison (Cand.); J. McLean (Tri.); F. Hubbard (BN; Alfa); Donald Brown (Muse); V. Herring (MM); Steve Wilson (CC).

ALLEN, ED (EDWARD CLIFTON), tpt; b. Nashville, TN, 12/15/1897; d. NYC, 1/28/74. Raised in St. Louis, Mo., where he stud. pno. and crnt. fr.

1907. Prof. debut in local roadhouse at age 16. Pl. in Seattle, Wash. '16 w. pnst. Ralph Stevenson. Following two yrs. w. Charlie Creath on Streckfus Lines Mississippi riverboats, led own band on SS *Capitol* '22. Assocs. incl. Gene Sedric, Walter Thomas, Pops Foster, Johnny St. Cyr. After working in NO w. his own Whispering Gold Band, he moved to Chi. '24, where he pl. w. Earl Hines at an after-hours club. Arrived in NYC '25, as a member of Joe Jordan's Sharps and Flats in Ed Daily's Black & White Show. With Leroy Tibbs at Connie's Inn '27–9. Own qt. at Tony Pastor's in early '40s, but fr. '30s worked mostly in taxi dance halls. At New Gardens on E. 14th St. w. Benton Heath band fr. '45 until illness ended his full-time pl. career. Rec. w. Elmer Snowden '61. Known for use of mutes, particularly the wa-wa, in the manner of King Oliver. Rec. often w. Clarence Williams '27–37; noted solo on Bessie Smith's "Nobody Knows You When You're Down and Out" '29. CDs: w. Williams (Class.); Bessie Smith (Col.); E. Snowden (Prest.).

ALLEN, GENE (Eugene Sufana), bari sax; also bscl.; b. East Chicago, IN, 12/5/28. Studied pno. and cl. fr. age 8. Pl. w. Louis Prima 1944–7; Gene Williams '48; Claude Thornhill '48–50; Tex Beneke '51–3; Sauter-Finegan '53–5; Tommy Dorsey '56–7; Benny Goodman '58, incl. Brussels World's Fair, and again in '62; Gerry Mulligan '57, '60–2; also many gigs w. Nat Pierce band at Birdland, etc. '59–60. Rec. w. Manny Albam, Woody Herman late '50s, early '60s. Feat. w. Sauter-Finegan on "Hey, Lulu"; "Finegan's Wake"; "Alright, Already." CD: w. Sauter-Finegan (BB).

ALLEN, GERI ANTOINETTE, pno, kybds; b. Pontiac, MI, 6/12/57. Father is amateur pnst. Husband is tptr. Wallace Roney. Began on vln.; pno. fr. age 7. Stud. w. Patricia Wilhelm, then w. Marilyn Jones at Cass Tech HS; B.A. Howard U.; M.A. in ethnomusicology, U. of Pitts. Pl. w. James Newton, Oliver Lake's Jump Up 1982. Pl. in late '80s–90s w. Joseph Jarman; Lester Bowie; Jay Hoggard; Ralph Peterson; Wallace Roney; Steve Coleman's Five Elements; Kelvyn Bell's Kelvynator; Roy Brooks' Artistic Truth; Marcus Belgrave; Ralph Armstrong; Donald Walden; Endangered Species; Gary Thomas; Wayne Shorter; Dave Holland bb; Roscoe Mitchell bb; Dewey Redman; Betty Carter; John Stubblefield; Frank Lowe; Chico Freeman; Vernon Reid's Living Colour. Also co-leads duo w. Greg Osby; trio w. Charlie Haden, Paul Motian. Member of Wallace Roney gp. fr. '96. Accomp. Abbey Lincoln on soundtrack to film *Drugstore Cowboy* '89. Allen leads a trio and qt. and has perf. as a solo pnst. Tour. w. Ornette Coleman's qt. '94. Has taught at New Engl.

Cons. and is a faculty member at Howard U. Comp. musical theater piece, *Fur on the Belly*, for Amer. Mus. Theater Fest. Favs: Mary Lou Williams, Thelonious Monk, Cecil Taylor, Andrew Hill, Art Tatum. Awards: Eubie Blake Awd. '89; Distinguished Alumnae fr. Howard U.; JAZZPAR '96. Polls: TDWR, *DB* Critics '93–4. Fests: all major fr. '82. Film: *Kansas City* '96. CDs: BN; DIW; SN; w. Franco Ambrosetti; J. Stubblefield (Enja); Cecil Brooks III (Muse); Osby (BN; JMT); Betty Carter; band fr. *Kansas City* (Verve); Steve Coleman; Paul Motian; Gary Thomas (JMT); Buddy Collette; F. Lowe (SN); C. Freeman; D. Redman (BS); Oliver Lake (BS, Gram.); Ralph Peterson; Woody Shaw (BN); Reggie Workman (Post.); Roney (WB).

ALLEN, HARRY ADAMS, tnr sax; b. Washington, DC, 10/12/66. Father was bb dmr. Family moved to LA 1967, then to Rhode Island '77. Began on acdn. and cl., then pl. in band w. fath. and sist. Joined mus. union at age 11. Studied at Rutgers U. '84–8. Pl. w. Doc Cheatham; Yank Lawson; Bob Haggart; Maxine Sullivan; Jonah Jones; Gus Johnson; George Wein; G. Masso; Dave McKenna; etc. Co-led qt. w. John Colianni, and worked freq. w. John Bunch; Oliver Jackson; Bucky and John Pizzarelli; Dan Barrett; Chuck Riggs. A solid, mainstream swinger, parallel to Scott Hamilton but w. his own personality. Favs: Ben Webster, Stan Getz, Scott Hamilton. Fests: JVC-NY '91; Eur. '90–1. TV: Jerry Lewis Telethon '84; Austr. TV w. James Moody '91. CDs: RCA; Prog.; N-H; John Marks; w. John Pizzarelli (RCA).

ALLEN, MARSHALL, alto sax; also cl, fl, oboe; b. Louisville, KY, 5/25/24. Mother a singer. Start. on cl. at 10. Pl. w. army band. Worked w. Art Simmons in Paris 1949–50, dur. which time he also studied at Cons. of Mus. Met Sun Ra when he moved to Chi. '51 and fr. '56 has been a member of Sun Ra's organization; after Sun Ra's death he became dir. Has also pl. w. Olatunji; rec. w. Paul Bley for ESP. Favs: Hodges, Byas, Hawkins but plays in a more avant-garde style. Films: *Individual*, w. mus. by Bill Dixon; *Cry of Jazz*. CDs: w. Sun Ra (Evid.; BL; DIW; hatArt; BS; A&M; Leo).

ALLEN, MOSE (MOSES), bs, tba, voc; b. Memphis, TN, 1907; d. NYC, 2/2/83. Played in band w. Jimmy Crawford at Le Moyne Coll. First rec. w. Chickasaw Syncopators 1932 on "Chickasaw Stomp," where Allen has a "preaching" voc. in a *sprechstimme* style. Joined Jimmie Lunceford summer '28, sw. fr. tba. to bs. in '32. Left Lunceford to become a store-owner in NYC. Until the end of the '60s also pl. mus. part-time. One of the first bs. pls. to use amplification. Rec: "Rhythm Is Our Business" w. Lunceford '34. CD: w. Lunceford (Dec.).

ALLEN, RED (HENRY JR.), tpt; voc; b. Algiers, LA, 1/7/08; d. NYC, 4/17/67. His fath., who led a brass band in and around NO for over forty yrs., died in 1952. As a child, Henry Jr. marched in his father's band. He pl. w. George Lewis in '23; John Handy '25; and on riverboats w. Fate Marable '26. After working w. Fats Pichon in '27, he joined King Oliver in Chi., later pl. more riverboat dates. Brought to NYC by RCA Victor in '29, he rec. four sides w. members of Luis Russell's band. He then joined Russell, remaining w. him into '32; Charlie Johnson '32–3; Fletcher Henderson '33–4; Mills Blue Rhythm Band '34–7. Fr. '37 to '40 he pl. in Russell's band under the leadership of Louis Armstrong. In late '40, he formed a sxt., which over next ten yrs. pl. long residencies at clubs in NYC, Bost., Mass., and Calif., the longest being at the Garrick Lounge in Chi. from fall '43 to summer '45. In a front line that also incl. alto saxst. Don Stovall, his main sidekick was tbnst. J.C. Higginbotham. In '52–3 Allen was a regular soloist at the Central Plaza, NYC. Fr. April '54 to May '65 he was a member of the trad.-oriented house band at the Metropole Café. Dur. this period he also tour. w. his own band and as a soloist. In the fall of '59, he first tour. Eur. as a sideman w. Kid Ory. Visited Engl. as a soloist in '63, '64, '66. Dur. the '60s, he also fronted his own gps. at various NYC clubs. Toured Engl. again in Feb. '67, but by then was seriously ill w. cancer. Originally infl. by Armstrong, Allen developed a personal style in terms of rhythm and timbre. He rightfully deserves the place between Armstrong and Eldridge in jazz tpt. lineage. Given his forward-looking '33 solo on Henderson's "Queer Notions," in which he uses a whole tone scale, it is not surprising that Don Ellis in a '65 *DB* article called him "the most avant-garde trumpet player in New York City," adding, "What other trumpeter plays such asymetrical rhythms, but makes them swing?" Fests: NJF '57. TV: *The Sound of Jazz*, CBS '57. CDs: BB; Class.; w. F. Henderson (Col.); S. Bechet (BB).

ALLEN, STEVE (STEPHEN VALENTINE PATRICK WILLIAM), songwriter, pno, voc; b. NYC, 12/26/21. First prominent as TV comedian in 1950s; also pl. competent swing pno. As host of NBC's *Tonight Show* and other TV programs he presented many jazz artists. Often assoc. w. Terry Gibbs. Became a prolific songwriter and by '85 was listed in *Guinness Book of World Records* as the most prolific comp. of modern times. Among his more than four thousand works are "This Could Be the Start of Something Big," "Impossible," "Picnic," and the lyrics to "South Rampart Street Parade" and "Gravy Waltz." Allen, who pl. the title role in the '55 film *The Benny Goodman Story*, has written several original scores for stage, films, and TV. Own TV series: *Jazz Scene USA* '61–2. Videos: *Jazz Scene USA* shows (Shanachie); *An Introduction to Jazz Piano* (Homespun). Rec. for Dot; Dec.; Em. CDs: Conc.

ALLEY, VERNON CREEDE, bs; b. Winnemucca, NV, 5/26/15; d. San Francisco, 10/3/04. Grandfather pl. vln. Studied cl. and pno. at Sacramento, SF colls. Start. w. Wes Peoples band 1937; Saunders King '37–9; own band '39–40; Lionel Hampton '40–2; Count Basie '42; navy band '42–6. Then own band off and on mainly in SF; also own TV show and DJ shows in SF. Led bands in '80s, often accomp. visiting star soloists. Cont. to pl. casuals and club dates into '90s. Gigged and rec. w. Jimmy Witherspoon and Ralph Sutton '59. Film: *Reveille with Beverly* w. Basie '43. Recs. w. Hampton, Basie, Jack Sheedy '49; Flip Phillips '52; Charlie Mariano '53. CDs: w. Hampton (Dec.); Phillips (Verve).

ALLISON, MOSE JOHN JR., pno, voc, comp; b. Tippo, MS, 11/11/27. Started on pno. w. priv. teacher at age 6. Studied tpt. in hs and led NO-style gp. Early listening to Armstrong, Nat Cole, Sonny Boy Williamson, Tampa Red, John Lee Hooker, et al. Army service 1946–7. B.A. fr. Louisiana St. U., where he studied English and writing '50. First visited NYC '51. Tour. Texas and Louisiana w. own pno. trio. Moved to NYC '56 and worked w. S. Getz off and on '56–7; G. Mulligan '58. Pl. at Vanguard and Great South Bay JF w. own trio '58; fr. Feb. to April '59, pl. in Paris, Stockholm, Copenhagen w. local rhythm sections. Often w. Al Cohn–Zoot Sims at Half Note, NYC '59. Began rec. as trio lead. for Prest. in '57 incl. two tracks on tpt. but didn't pl. it again after his horn was stolen fr. a Phila. club in which he was appearing. Since the '60s he has worked mainly in clubs w. a trio, singing his own songs, Ellington, and other standards, and pl. pno. in a wry, eclectic, swinging style. His perfs. reveal an unconventional mixture of a traditional vocal style and a relatively modern approach to the pno. Many of the British blues and rock musicians of the '60s were infl. by him. Favs: Williamson, Ellington, Monk, Gillespie. Comps: *Back Country Suite* (incl. "Parchman Farm"); "If You Live"; "Your Mind Is On Vacation"; "Everybody's Cryin' Mercy"; "I Don't Worry About a Thing." CDs: Prest.; Rhino/Atl.; Col. (box); BN; w. Cohn-Sims (Dec.; Evid; BN).

ALLYN, DAVID (Albert DiLello), voc; b. Hartford, CT, 7/19/23. Father pl. Fr. horn w. Hartford Symph.;

moth. was singer. Start. singing prof. in hs, infl. by Bing Crosby. With J. Teagarden 1940–2. Served w. First Army Division '42 and was awarded Purple Heart. After discharge joined Van Alexander Orch.; then w. Henry Jerome. After singing on radio, he joined Boyd Raeburn '44–6, rec. "Forgetful" and "I Only Have Eyes For You" w. arrs. by George Handy. Rec. Rodgers and Hart songs w. Johnny Richards for Disc. in early '50s; Jerome Kern songs w. Johnny Mandel arrs. for WP '58. Worked w. S. Kenton in LA '60; Count Basie at Basin St. East and Lake Tahoe '64. Also worked the Playboy Club circuit '60–64. Drug problems hampered his career, but fr.'68 he did rehab. counseling for drug addicts at Phoenix House and Halfway House, NYC; Addiction Services in Hartford; and, in '70s, for Veterans Admin. in LA. In '75 he rec. an LP, *Don't Look Back*, for Xan. accomp. by Barry Harris. Lived in Minneapolis, Minn., in early '80s, then moved to NYC, worked at Gregory's. In the '80s, fronted a bb at various venues, cont. in '90s at Red Blazer Too and w. qt. at La Place on the Park. A superb ballad singer w. a fine sense of phrasing and a rich sound, his work is informed by the many excellent musicians w. whom he has performed. TV: *The World of Lenny Bruce* '59; *Tonight Show* '63; *Today*; Merv Griffin; Mike Douglas '67. CDs: Aud.; w. Raeburn (Sav.).

ALMARIO, JUSTO PASTOR GOMEZ, saxes, fl, cl; b. Sincelejo, Colombia, 2/18/49. Professional debut at 13 w. Alex Acosta Orch. in Colombia; at 17, tour. US w. "Cumbia Colombia" Band on cultural exchange tour. Studied at Berklee Sch. on full scholarship. To NYC 1971, to pl. w. Mongo Santamaria. While w. Roy Ayers '76–9, settled in LA. In '80s, worked w. Freddie Hubbard and was member of gp. Koinonia for ten yrs.; also w. Clayton-Hamilton band '89; own band off and on fr. '85. CDs: MCA; BM; w. Poncho Sanchez; Tania Maria (Conc.); Diane Reeves (BN); Louis Bonilla (Cand.); B. Shew (MAMA).

ALMEIDA, LAURINDO, gtr, comp, arr; b. São Paulo, Brazil, 9/2/17; d. Van Nuys, CA, 7/26/95. Studied at Escola Nacional de Music, Rio de Janeiro. Primarily a concert gtrst., he led his own orch. and worked as a radio staff mus. bef. leaving Rio 1947. Fr. 1947 to '50 he gained recognition in the US as a feat. soloist w. Stan Kenton Orch. For next twenty-five yrs. did freelance studio and club work in LA and wrote scores for seventeen films. Received five Grammys in the classical, pop, and jazz categories, as well as an Oscar and *DB* movie poll for his film scores. In '54 he rec. precursor of bossa nova movement w. Bud Shank for PJ. Fr. '74 to '75 co-led The LA Four w. Shank, Ray Brown, and Shelly Manne;

tour. NZ, Austral., and Mex. w. the gp. in '75. Rec. many classical and bossa nova albums, incl. duos w. his wife, lyric soprano Deltra Eamon, and w. Ray Brown. His pubs. incl. *Guitar Tutor in Three Courses*; *Contemporary Moods for Guitar*; *Popular Brazilian Music*; and *Laurindo Almeida Guitar Method*. CDs: Conc.; PJ; w. LA Four (Conc.); S. Getz (Verve); MJQ (Atl.); R. Brown (Bell); Kenton (Mos.); B. Shew (MAMA).

ALPERT, TRIGGER (HERMAN), bs; b. Indianapolis, IN, 9/3/16. Studied mus. at Indiana U. 1938–9. Pl. w. Alvino Rey '40; join. Glenn Miller in Oct. of that yr., remaining through the end of the Miller army band '44. After discharge worked briefly w. Tex Beneke, Woody Herman; did radio series w. Benny Goodman, then staff work at CBS, incl. several yrs. on Garry Moore show. Worked w. Frank Sinatra '46–50; W. Herman Qnt. '47. Cited by George Simon in *Met.* as one of the greatest bssts., w. exceptional tone and fine beat, he was extremely active in the rec. studios between '45 and '62, pl. w. Louis Armstrong; Roy Eldridge; Ella Fitzgerald; Tony Mottola; Ray McKinley; Bud Freeman; Muggsy Spanier; Jerry Jerome; Artie Shaw; Coleman Hawkins; Sauter-Finegan; Gene Krupa; Buddy Rich. Left CBS in '65. Active in radio and TV jingles until '70, when he bec. a full-time photographer. Rec. own LP, *Trigger Happy!* (Riv.) '56, w. Al Cohn, Zoot Sims, Urbie Green. CDs: w. Miller; Sauter-Finegan (BB); *East Coast Sounds* (the former *Trigger Happy!*) w. Sims, Cohn (Jzld.).

ALTENA, MAARTEN VAN REGTEREN, bs; comp; b. Amsterdam, Netherlands 1/22/43. Studied at Amsterdam Cons., 1961–7. Assoc. w. mus. of the Dutch Instant Comps.' Pool. Often heard in concert and on recs. w. Han Bennink. Rec. w. Steve Lacy, Kenny Wheeler, own gps. A key figure in the Dutch avant-garde, he tour. US, Can., '84, '88, '90. CDs: hatArt; w. Willem Breuker (Entr'acte).

ALTSCHUL, BARRY, dms, perc, comp, arr; b. Bronx, NY, 1/6/43. Father pl. mand.; sist. studied pno. and voice at Juilliard. Studied w. Charli Persip 1961–2; Sam Ulano '69–70; Lee Konitz '72. Pl. w. Paul Bley Trio '64–70; Jazz Comp. Guild Orch. '64–8; Carmell Jones–Leo Wright in Eur. '68; Sonny Criss, Hampton Hawes in Calif., Tony Scott in NYC '69; Circle w. Chick Corea, Anthony Braxton, Dave Holland '70–2; Braxton; Sam Rivers '73–7; own gps. w. sidemen incl. Anthony Davis; Ray Anderson, Glenn Ferris, Mark Helias, Andy McKee fr. '78. Worked freq. in Eur. fr. the late '60s. Pl. w. D. Holland; Babs Gonzales; Steve Lacy; Jimmy Owens;

Karl Berger; J.R. Monterose; Johnny Griffin; Gato Barbieri; Slide Hampton; Andrew Hill; Dave Liebman; Mike Nock; Paul Winter; Roswell Rudd; Gary Peacock, many others in US and Eur. '60s–70s. Lived mainly in Eur. '82–92, leading a 20-pc. bb in France, subsidized by the French Cultural Affairs Dept. Ret. to NYC in '92 and has since divided his time between US and France. Has taught at clinics at Harvard, Oberlin, NYU, Berklee, etc., and has perf. as guest percst. w. the Indianapolis and Taos Symphs. He has also worked in recent yrs. as a rec. prod. Known mainly for his intuitive, creative work in avant-garde circles, Altschul's musicality enables him to fit in any style. Favs: Philly Joe Jones, Roy Haynes, Art Blakey, Elvin Jones. Fests: Eur., Asia, Africa, So. Amer., Carib. TV: *Tonight Show* w. Paul Bley '66. CDs: SN; IAI; w. Braxton (hatArt); P. Bley (SN); Circle; Dave Holland (ECM); C. Corea (BN); A. Hill (Freedom); Sam Rivers (Red).

ALVAREZ, CHICO (ALFRED), tpt; b. Montreal, Que., Canada, 2/3/20; d. Las Vegas, NV, 8/1/92. Raised in Inglewood, Calif.; studied vln., pno. for ten yrs. bef. starting on tpt. Pl. w. Stan Kenton 1941–51, except for army service '43–6 and a few mos. w. Charlie Barnet, Red Norvo, and Benny Carter in late '40s while Kenton was disbanded. Feat. on early Kenton recs. incl. "Machito," "Harlem Holiday." In '52, opened mus. store in Hermosa Beach; also worked w. Latin bands as songwriter, arr., and tptr. Fr. '58 to '82 worked in LV hotels, accomp. Ella Fitzgerald, Sarah Vaughan, et al. Organized the LV Jazz Band in early '80s and was feat. at Sacramento Dixieland Jubilee '85. Fav: Louis Armstrong. CDs: w. Kenton (Cap., Mos.).

ALVIN, DANNY (Daniele Viniello), dms; b. NYC, 11/29/02; d. Chicago, IL, 12/6/58. Son was Teddy Walters, gtrst.-voclst. who pl. on 52nd St. in mid 1940s. Prof. debut w. Aunt Jemima (Edith Wilson) '18; pl. w. Sophie Tucker at Reisenweber's '19. Moved to Chi. '22 and pl. w. Jules Buffano; Charlie Straight; Elmer Schoebel; Frankie Quartell. After working in various bands, incl. commercial orchs., and leading own gp., he join. Art Hodes '33. Moved back to NYC '36, worked w. Sidney Bechet; George Brunis; Buck Clayton; Wild Bill Davison; Wingy Manone; Joe Marsala. Ret. to Chi. '47 and pl. w. Doc Evans bef. forming the Kings of Dixieland '49, w. which he pl. own club, Basin Street, and rec. in the '50s. Originally inspired by Tony Spargo and, later, Zutty Singleton, Alvin pl. in a loud, flamboyant style. Own LP on Stepheny '58. CDs: w. Pee Wee Russell (Comm.); Hodes and Bechet–Albert Nicholas in *Hot Jazz* (BN).

ALVIS, HAYES JULIAN, bs, tba, arr; b. Chicago, IL, 5/1/07; d. NYC, 12/29/72. Played dms., then tba. in hs ROTC. Member of the dm. corps of Chi. *Defender* Boys' Concert Band along w. Lionel Hampton, Sid Catlett. Pl. dms. w. Jelly Roll Morton 1927–8, but began to learn basics of tba. fr. Lawson Buford and bs. fr. Quinn Wilson. Pl. tba. w. Earl Hines '28–30. Moved to NYC w. Jimmie Noone '31; worked on bs. and tba. w. Mills Blue Rhythm Band '31–4, '36, doubling at times as road manager. Pl. w. Duke Ellington '35–8; own gp. w. Freddy Jenkins in *Blackbirds* revue '38; Benny Carter '38–9; Joe Sullivan trio '40, '42; Bobby Burnett, Louis Armstrong '40–2; army band under Sy Oliver '43–5. After the war, worked w. Dave Martin '46–7; and as house bsst. at Café Society, NYC; freelanced w. Sy Oliver, etc. Ran successful interior decorating business bef. shipping out as merchant seaman on SS *United States*. Ret. to NYC May '58 and join. Wilbur De Paris. Alvis also studied dentistry and held a pilot's license. In his later yrs., worked at Local 802, AFM. Among his last apps. were Eur. tours w. Jay McShann '70 and Tiny Grimes '71. Recs: his arr. of "Blue Nights" w. Hines; early bs. solo on "Rhythm Spasm" w. Mills Blue Rhythm; tba. solo on "Truckin'" w. Ellington. CDs: w. Ellington (Dec.); Mills Blue Rhythm Band (Hep); Jabbo Smith (Class.); Leonard Feather's All-Stars in *52nd Street Swing* (Dec.).

AMBROSE, BERT, lead; b. London, England, 1897; d. Leeds, England, 6/18/71. Family emigrated to the US when he was very young. He worked in NYC as a mus. dir. 1917–22 and rec. for Col. '23. Later in the '20s he was active as mus. dir. in London, and fr. '27 his band incl. Amer. mus. He was popular mainly in the '30s, when he headed what was then the leading British swing band, feat. arrs. by Sid Phillips, cl. solos by Danny Polo. He led bands of various sizes until '56 when he turned to management; fr. '66 he devoted his time to guiding the career of singer Kathy Kirby. He suffered a fatal collapse in a TV studio. Rec. for Dec. in mid '30s. CDs: ASV; Pearl.

AMBROSETTI, FLAVIO, alto sax; b. Lugano, Switzerland, 10/8/19. Father of tptr. Franco Ambrosetti. Stud. w. private teachers and at mus. sch. in Lugano, first on pno. Inspired by hearing Coleman Hawkins in Switz. in late 1930s, he pl. w. many Swiss gps., app. w. Hazy Osterwald band at Paris JF '49. With own qnt. pl. many concerts and fests. in Italy and other Eur. countries. In the mid '60s this gp. incl. his son Franco, George Gruntz, and Daniel Humair. They were the basis for The Band, an orch. that tour. Eur. '72 and rec. twice in the '70s, incorporating such pls. as Dexter Gordon, Phil Woods, Woody Shaw.

Grad. w. engineering degree fr. Politecnicum, Zurich '45, he was the gen. mgr. of family wheel co. until his retirement in '92. Fav: C. Parker. One of the first Europeans to successfully play in the bop style. Fests: Lugano (founder) '62; Prague '66; MJF; Pori '67; Ljubljana '70; Bologna '73. Comps: "Gentilino Serenade"; "Looking Forward"; "Our Suite Dig"; "Age of Prominence"; "El Comendador (Nebulosa)." The Band's MPS rec. *Alpine Power Plant* won as best jazz rec. in Italy '73. CDs: Enja.

AMBROSETTI, FRANCO, tpt, flg, comp; b. Lugano, Switzerland, 12/10/41. Son of Flavio Ambrosetti. Studied pno. 1952–9; self-taught on tpt. fr. '59. Made prof. debut '61. Led own gp. in Zurich, early to mid '60s. Pl. w. fath.'s gp. '63–70. Rec. w. Geo. Gruntz '64; also rec. w. Gato Barbieri under leadership of bs. Giorgio Azzolini. Won first prize for tpt. at Vienna Int'l Jazz Competition '66. Made US debut w. father's qnt. '67. Led own gp. w. Gruntz, Daniel Humair, Ron Mathewson, late '60s early '70s. Formed The Band w. fath., Gruntz, Humair '72; this gp. later became known as the Geo. Gruntz Concert Jazz Band. Freelanced in Eur. fr. '70s w. Phil Woods; Dexter Gordon; Cannonball Adderley; Joe Henderson; Michael Brecker–Mike Stern; Hal Galper; Kenny Clarke; et al. Rec. as lead. w. sidemen incl. M. Brecker; Kenny Kirkland; John Scofield; Ron Carter; Bennie Wallace; Phil Woods; Dave Holland; Kenny Barron; Victor Lewis; Seamus Blake. Also in the '70s, earned a master's degree in economics fr. the U. of Basel. Manages his family's business, which supplies wheels to Eur. vehicle manufacturers. In recent yrs., Ambrosetti has cont. to perf. w. the Geo. Gruntz Concert Jazz Band and lead his own qt., incl. NYC club gigs. A highly articulate, fiery, world-class soloist. Comps: score for Germ. film *Die Reise* by Markus Imhof '86; "Pistrophallopus"; "Gin and Pentatonic"; "Blues for Ursula"; "Close Encounter." Favs: Clifford Brown, Miles Davis, Freddie Hubbard, Kenny Dorham. Polls: Best Rec. for *The Band* in Ital. critics poll '73; Montreux JF Awd.; '80, '82; RAI Best Eur. Mus. '85. Fests: all major in Eur. fr. '62; Monterey JF w. fath.'s gp. '67. TV: Eur. TV. CDs: Enja; BN; w. Gruntz ; Flavio Ambrosetti (Enja).

AMMONS, ALBERT C., pno; b. Chicago, IL, 9/23/07; d. Chicago, 12/2/49. Father of Gene Ammons. Early assoc. of Pinetop Smith and Meade Lux Lewis. He and Lewis were drivers for the Silver Taxicab Co. in 1924, while pl. rent parties, etc. as pnsts. Began pno. at age 10. Worked in clubs w. François Mosely's Louisiana Stompers '29; William Barbee and his Headquarters '30–1; Louis P. Banks Chesterfield orch. '32–4. Led own band '34–8. Rec.

for Dec. as leader '36. To NYC for app. w. Lewis and Pete Johnson (The Boogie-Woogie Trio) at *From Spirituals to Swing* Carnegie Hall concert. App. at Café Society, NYC, and rec. for Col. and BN '39, all of which helped to spark a national boogie-woogie craze. Frequently worked w. Johnson incl. series of recs. '41. In that year accidentally cut off the tip of a finger but resumed pl. w. Johnson. Later suffered partial paralysis in both hands but recovered. Pl. at Pres. Truman's inaugural Jan. '49. In his last days, he often perf. at Mama Yancey's Parlor in Chi. His "Boogie-Woogie Stomp" '36 was modeled after Pinetop's "Boogie Woogie," but Ammons developed an individual style and became one of the finest interpreters of boogie-woogie. Rec. "St. Louis Blues" w. son, Gene, '47; "Benson's Boogie" w. Lionel Hampton '49. CDs: Milan; multiple tracks on *Barrelhouse Boogie* (BB); tracks in *The 1940s Mercury Sessions* (Merc.).

AMMONS, GENE (EUGENE aka JUG), tnr sax; b. Chicago, IL, 4/14/25; d. Chicago, 7/23/74. Son of Albert Ammons; studied music under Capt. Walter Dyett at Du Sable HS. Left Chi. at age 18 to tour. w. King Kolax. First gained prominence as member of Billy Eckstine's band 1944–7; then led own gps. in Chi. Replaced Stan Getz w. Woody Herman '49; form. gp. w. Sonny Stitt in '50, which feat. their tnr. battles; disbanded in '52. Ammons then led several gps., mainly based in Chi. His problems w. narcotics severely disrupted his career in the '50s and '60s, incl. incarceration '58–60 and '62–9. Resumed touring, backed by a rhythm section. Following ill health in the spring of '74, he was hospitalized in Chi. w. cancer in July and died of pneumonia. Infl. by Lester Young and, later, bop phraseology, Ammons was originally considered part of the "cool" school. He later became known in the r&b field for his sweet ballad and honking style, but he ret. to the mainstream of jazz. His big sound and driving beat established him as one of the giants of modern jazz saxophone. TV: *Just Jazz*, PBS '71. CDs: Prest.; Sav.; Em.; w. Eckstine (Sav.); W. Herman (Cap.); A. Ammons in *The 1940s Mercury Sessions* (Merc.).

AMRAM, DAVID WERNER III, Fr hrn, pno, various fls, shenai, dumbek, cga, perc, gtr, comp, arr; b. Philadelphia, PA, 11/17/30. Cousin of cond. Otto Klemperer. Introd. to jazz by fath. and uncles, world mus. by uncle who was merchant seaman. Began on bugle. Stud. tpt., pno. at Curtis Inst. of Mus.; pl. Fr. horn fr. age 14. In Wash., D.C., fr. 1943. Pl. tpt. w. Louis Brown '43; Fr. horn w. Dick Leith '46; Buddy Rowell–Ed Dimond Latin Jazz Band '50–2; Nat'l Symph., own sxt. w. Spencer Sinatra '51–2. In army in Eur. '52–5. Pl. in Germ. w. Jutta Hipp, Albert Man-

gelsdorff '53–5; in Paris w. Henri Renaud, Stephane Grappelli, Sadi, Lionel Hampton '55. Moved to NYC '55. Pl. w. Sahib Shihab–Kenny Burrell '55–6; own qt. w. Geo. Barrow '55–71; Charles Mingus '56; Oscar Pettiford orch. '56–8; Pepper Adams–Jerry Dodgion '57; Kenny Dorham '59. Pl. concerts w. Dizzy Gillespie fr. '57. Began comp. for TV, films, and theater in late '50s. Scored films *The Young Savages, Splendor in the Grass* '60; *The Manchurian Candidate, Seven Days in May* '63. Mus. dir. of Lincoln Ctr. Repertory Theater '63–5; also comp. for NY Shakespeare Fest., B'way shows. First opera, *The Final Ingredient,* premiered on network TV '65. Composer-in-residence w. NY Philharm. '66–7. Pl. w. Freddie Redd '66; Mingus, Jeremy Steig '68; own qt. w. Pepper Adams '70. Beginning in the mid '60s, often app. w. major orchs. as a guest cond., then led a jazz gp. for the second half of the program. Premiered *Triple Concerto* '70; pl. w. Mary Lou Williams in her Mass '71; own qt. w. Paquito D'Rivera '85; Pepper Adams–Jerry Dodgion '88. Has perf. at folk mus. fests and led wkshps. at colls., hs, and parks all over the world fr. the early '70s. Autobiography, *Vibrations* (Viking) '68. Other major works incl. concerti for bassoon, horn, and vln., pieces based on Native Amer. themes, and an operatic treatment of Shakespeare's *Twelfth Night.* A master of many non-Eur. instruments and a pioneer in the field of world mus., he was awarded an honorary doctorate fr. U. of Hartford '88. Favs: Fr. horn: Julius Watkins; pno: T. Monk, T. Flanagan; arr: Gil Evans, B. Strayhorn. Fests: all major. Film: *Pull My Daisy.* TV: *The Final Ingredient*, ABC-TV '65. LPs: RCA; Col., incl. *The Young Savages* soundtrack; Dec. CDs: FF; New Chamber Music; w. Kenny Dorham (Riv.); O. Pettiford (Imp.); *The Manchurian Candidate* soundtrack (Premier).

AMSTELL, BILLY (WILLIAM), tnr sax, cl; b. London, England, 8/20/11. Professional debut in Glasgow. Worked in London early 1930s, w. Jack Harris, Roy Fox, then prominently as feat. soloist w. Ambrose from '32. Rejoin. Harris '39; worked w. Geraldo '43–5; then back w. Ambrose and later w. BBC dance orch. Frequently heard w. George Chisholm and w. own gps.; cont. active into '80s. Amstell played an important role in early British jazz, both on cl. and tnr. sax. CDs: w. Spike Hughes (Largo).

AMY, CURTIS EDWARD, saxes; b. Houston, TX, 10/11/29; d. Los Angeles, 6/12/02. Played cl. in childhood. Pl. tnr. sax in army band. B.S. in mus. ed. fr. Kentucky St. Coll. 1952; taught sch. in Tenn. To LA '55; pl. w. Amos Milburn r&b gp.; led sxt. and rec. w.

Dupree Bolton '62; pl. w. Gerald Wilson band. Originally inspired by Gene Ammons and Sonny Stitt, he was mainly prominent on the West Coast in the '50s and '60s; also tour. w. Ray Charles in latter decade. CDs: PJ; w. G. Wilson (PJ).

ANDERS, JORGE (Etzensberger), tnr sax, cl, arr; b. Buenos Aires, Argentina, 4/18/39. Father was classical vlnst. who perf. in various Eur. orch. bef. moving to Argentina in 1936. Studied classical cl. in Buenos Aires w. prof. Eliseo Rosas; self-taught on sax. Formed own trio and qt. '56. Made rec. debut '64, w. Santiago Giacobbe qnt. Also pl. w. Rodolfo Alchourron; Alfredo Remus; Quinteplus; and own gps. bef. moving to NYC in '79. Arr. for Machito; Mel Lewis Jazz Orch.; Mousey Alexander bb; Mercer Ellington. Pl. and rec. w. Butch Miles '80–5. Cl. soloist w. Ellington orch. '82–7. Has had own bb since '85. Favs: Charlie Parker, Benny Goodman, Zoot Sims; arrs: Ellington, Strayhorn, Thad Jones. LP w. B. Miles (Famous Door). CDs: Jazz Workshop.

ANDERSEN, ARILD, bs; b. Oslo, Norway, 10/27/45. Studied w. George Russell. First prof. gig w. Jan Garbarek qt., later in various gps. w. Garbarek, 1967–73; also w. Don Cherry, '68; accomp. singer Karin Krog fr. '67. App. at fests. w. G. Russell '69; in France w. Stan Getz '70; in Norway w. Sonny Rollins. To US '72; pl. w. P. Bley; Sam Rivers; Steve Kuhn; Sheila Jordan; others; for balance of '70s, he worked throughout Eur. w. Jon Eberson; Knut Riisnaes; Lars Jansson; others. Pl. w. Charlie Mariano '80; Kenny Wheeler, Paul Motian '81; then on and off w. Alphonse Mouzon; also led a qnt., Masqualero, in '80s, touring Eur.; app. at the Village Vanguard '86. CDs: ECM; w. Garbarek (ECM); Karin Krog (Meantime).

ANDERSON, ANDY (EDWARD), tpt; b. Jacksonville, FL, 7/1/10. Studied tpt. at Fla. St. Coll.; St. Emma Coll. of Belmead, Va. Pl. in Fla. w. Luckey Roberts. To NYC w. Roberts in 1926 to work w. George Howe and Luis Russell; perf. and rec. w. Jelly Roll Morton '28–9; w. Benny Carter at the Arcadia Ballroom; occ. rec. w. Clarence Williams through '31. Join. Mills Blue Rhythm Band '30–4, then pl. w. Charlie Turner's Arcadians, staying when band was fronted by Fats Waller '35. In late '30s, pl. w. Hazel Scott and Joe Sullivan; w. Frankie Newton 10-pc. band '41, then ceased full-time mus. activities. CDs: w. L. Armstrong (JSP); Mills Blue Rhythm Band (Hep); J.R. Morton (BB); King Oliver (Aff.); C. Williams (BBC).

ANDERSON, CAT (WILLIAM ALONZO), tpt; b. Greenville, SC, 9/12/16; d. Norwalk, CA, 4/29/81.

Studied at Jenkins Orphanage and pl. in its bands. First inspiration was Louis Armstrong. Tour. w. the Carolina Cotton Pickers 1932–6, then join. Doc Wheeler's Sunset Royals in '41 and pl. w. Lucky Millinder, Erskine Hawkins bef. join. Lionel Hampton in summer of '42. Feat. on "Loose Wig." With Duke Ellington '44–7; after lead. own band for three yrs., rejoin. Ellington '50, leaving again in '59. Fr. '61 to '71, app. often w. Ellington, taking part in Eur. and Asian tours and utilizing his phenomenal, high-register abilities in many of Duke's suites, e.g., "Ad Lib on Nippon" in *The Far East Suite*. Settled in San Fernando Valley, Calif., in Jan. '71 and became involved in Hollywood studio work. Also freelanced w. own gp.; Ellington alumni gps.; Bill Berry orch. In addition to his high-note expertise, he also pl. convincing growl style, sounding on ballads like Harry James, as in "The Eighth Veil" w. Ellington. Fests: NJF-NY, MJF, Concord. TV: shows w. Ellington; Julie Andrews; Merv Griffin. Film: *Lady Sings the Blues*. Book: *The Cat Anderson Trumpet Method: Dealing w. Playing in the Upper Register*. CDs: B&B; w. Ellington (BB; Col.; Atl.).

ANDERSON, CHRIS, pno; b. Chicago, IL, 2/26/26. Self-taught, he grew up captured by the harmony he heard when watching Hollywood films as a pre-teen. While in hs, he pl. in Chi. South Side blues bars. A job in a rec. store introduced him to the mus. of Nat Cole, Tatum, and Ellington, as well as Debussy and Ravel. Pl. w. Sonny Stitt in mid '1940s; then w. Charlie Parker, Howard McGhee at Pershing Ballroom. To '60, pl. w. local mus. Wilber Ware; Von Freeman; et al. In the course of serving as house pno. at several clubs, he backed Sonny Rollins; Clifford Brown; Gene Ammons; Stan Getz. Accomp. Dinah Washington on tour '61. Was fired after six weeks, but decided to stay in NYC, where he rec. for Riv. Although he worked intermittently, Anderson, who is blind and suffers fr. a brittle bone condition, became legendary among mus. Has been a regular solo perf. at Barry Harris's annual concerts. In '90s led trio and co-led qt. w. Roni Ben-Hur; app. at La Belle Epoque and Small's NYC; pl. in concert w. Charlie Haden at Cami Hall, NYC, July '97. Herbie Hancock, who encountered him in '60, said of him in '90: "Chris's music . . . has affected me deeply. After hearing him play once, I begged him to let me study with him. Chris Anderson is a master of harmony and sensitivity. I shall be forever be indebted to him and to his very special gift." "With Chris it's not the line," said Haden. "It's all about improvising with chords, and I love it." CDs: Maple.; Alsut; Haden-Anderson (Naim); Charlie Parker (Sav.); Sun Ra (Round).

ANDERSON, CLIFTON ELLIOT, tbn; b. NYC, 10/5/57. Both parents musicians; uncle is Sonny Rollins. Began on dms.; Rollins gave him his first tbn. at age 7. Studied at HS of Mus. and Art 1970–4; Manh. Sch. of Mus. '74–8. Pl. w. Stevie Wonder '79; Rollins fr. '83; Slide Hampton's World of Trombones '83–5. Founded music prod. co., Change The World Prods., '87. Pl. w. Frank Foster's Loud Minority '88; James Jabbo Ware fr. '88; Abdullah Ibrahim, Muhal Richard Abrams '89–90; McCoy Tyner bb '91–2; Mingus bb '93–4. Favs: J.J. Johnson, Slide Hampton. Fests: all major w. Rollins. Film: *Saxophone Colossus* w. Rollins. TV: Eur. TV w. Rollins. CDs: Mile.; w. Rollins (Mile.); Abrams (BS); Art Ens. of Chi. (DIW); Robin Eubanks (JMT).

ANDERSON, ERNESTINE IRENE, voc; b. Houston, TX, 11/11/28. First prof. job w. Russell Jacquet 1943; w. Johnny Otis '47–9, L. Hampton '52–3. Rec. debut w. Gigi Gryce, Nov. '55. Toured Scand. w. Rolf Ericson '56. Her album, *Hot Cargo*, rec. in Sweden, became a hit and led to US recs. for Merc. By mid '60s, her popularity had declined, and she remained based in Engl. for the next decade. Re-established herself through a series of recs. for Conc. fr. '76, and had a hit w. "Never Make Your Move Too Soon." Toured Japan and Eur. w. Philip Morris Superband '85. Based in Seattle, Wash., she cont. to pl. clubs and fests around the world. An emotionally strong perf. who is particularly effective on blues and ballads. CDs: Conc.; w. Gigi Gryce (Sav.); two tracks on *The Ladies* (Sav.).

ANDERSON, FRED JR., tnr sax; b. Monroe, LA, 3/22/29. Moved to Evanston, Ill., 1939; self-taught on tnr. since age 12. A founding member of AACM '65; he greatly influ. many of his fellow band members, incl. tbn. George Lewis; Chico Freeman; Douglas Ewart. Rec. w. Joseph Jarman '66–7; toured Eur. w. own qnt. '74, '78; rec. w. the gp. Neighbours in Germ. '79, w. Austrian pianist/comp. Dieter Glawichnig. Has owned the Velvet Lounge nightclub in Chi. since '82, where he occasionally perf. on weekends into the '90s. CDs: Okka Disk; Nessa; Messsage; Moers; w. Neighbours (MRC); J. Jarman (Del.).

ANDERSON, IVIE MARIE, voc; b. Gilroy, CA, 7/10/05; d. Los Angeles, CA, 12/28/49. Studied singing near her home town, then at age 6 in Wash., D.C. Prof. debut in a LA club ca. 1921. Sang at the Cotton Club, NYC 1925. On the road w. Sissle and Blake's *Shuffle Along*; then ret. to LA, working w. Paul Howard, Curtis Mosby, and Sonny Clay, w. whom she also tour. Austral. In a mus. revue '28; later

that yr., she tour. US as single. Sang w. Earl Hines at Grand Terrace, Chi. '30. Join. Duke Ellington '31, introducing "It Don't Mean a Thing" '32. Until an asthmatic condition forced her to leave the band in '42, she was a valuable part of the orch., swinging the up-tempo numbers—sometimes w. effective use of scat—and treating the ballads w. warmth and a well-rounded timbre. She was equally at home w. blues. Owned a LA restaurant, Ivie's Chicken Shack. Film: sang "All God's Children Got Rhythm" in '37 Marx Bros. film *A Day at the Races*. CDs: w. Ellington (BB).

ANDERSON, JAY, bs, comp; b. Ontario, CA, 10/24/55. Began on pno. bef. sw. to bs. Grad. w. B. Mus. fr. Calif. St., Long Beach, 1978. Much exp. in classical field. Pl. and rec. w. Woody Herman '78–9; Carmen McRae '79–81. Moved to NYC '81 and has since been busy as freelancer. Pl. w. Red Rodney–Ira Sullivan '81–6 and then w. Rodney until '90. On and off w. Toshiko Akiyoshi–Lew Tabackin '81–'90. Pl. and rec. w. Bennie Wallace '85–7; Warren Bernhardt '88–91; Michael Brecker '89–90. Pl. w. Randy Brecker on U.S. State Dept. tour of East. Eur. '89. Also perf. w. Steve Khan; Michel Legrand; Mel Lewis; Joey Calderazzo; Clark Terry; Bob Brookmeyer; Toots Thielemans; many others. Much jingle and non-jazz studio work. Favs: Paul Chambers, Dave Holland, Albert Stinson, Charlie Haden. CDs: w. R. Rodney (Den.; Steep.); B. Wallace (Den.); M. Brecker (GRP); B. Belden (Sunny.; BN); J. Calderazzo (BN); Joe Albany (Ken; Bella.); Warren Bernhardt; Garry Dial (DMP); Brian Lynch (CC); P. Delano (Verve).

ANDERSON, RAY ROBERT, tbn, voc, tuba, cga; b. Chicago, IL, 10/16/52. Began stud. tbn. in fourth grade at U. of Chi. lab. sch; tbnst. Geo. Lewis began on same day, w. same teacher. Moved to Minneapolis, Minn., 1968 to attend Macalester Coll., pl. in local r&b bands. Pl. w. Keshavan Maslak, Charles Moffett, Stanley Crouch in Calif. bef. moving to NYC in '72. Pl. w. Jimmy Giuffre '73–5; Barry Altschul '76–81. Made rec. debut w. Gerry Hemingway '76. Replaced Geo. Lewis w. Anthony Braxton '77. Form. own gp., Slickaphonics, w. Mark Helias '79. Began singing in '83 after Bell's palsy left one side of his face paralyzed. Has since overcome this obstacle by adopting an asymmetrical embouchure. With Carla Bley '85–6; Geo. Russell '85–6; Charlie Haden since '86; Geo. Gruntz since '87. An expressive, eclectic, expansive soloist who makes use of multiphonics and many of the traditional tbn. effects. Favs: Vic Dickenson, Frank Rosolino, J.C. Higginbotham, Jack Teagarden. Polls: *DB* '86. Fests: Moers '79 w. Roscoe

Mitchell–Leo Smith Orch., many others. TV: *Night Music* w. Charlie Haden. CDs: hatArt; Gram.; Enja; w. Slickaphonics (Teldec); Tim Berne (SN); C. Haden (Polyd.); Mark Helias (Enja); G. Hemingway (SA); John Scofield (Gram.); Bennie Wallace (Enja; BN); Lew Soloff (Sw. Bas.).

ANDERSON, WESS (WESSELL), alto, sop, sopranino saxes; b. Brooklyn, NY, 11/27/64. Studied classical pno. at age 12 for three yrs. bef. fath.—a prof. dmr. who had tour. w. Cecil Payne—introduced him to jazz. Sw. to alto after hearing Charlie Parker at age 14. Studied w. Roland Alexander; then at Jazzmobile wkshps. w. F. Wess; F. Foster; Charles Davis. Sat in w. Sonny Stitt at Blue Coronet. Encouraged by Branford Marsalis to attend Southern U. in Baton Rouge, La., he stud. under Alvin Batiste for five yrs. and then join. Wynton Marsalis's band in 1988, app. int'l w. him fr. that time. His first rec. as a leader, *Warm Daddy in the Garden of Swing* '94, uses his nickname in the title. CDs: Atl.; w. W. Marsalis (Col.).

ANDRE, WAYNE, tbn, comp; b. Manchester, CT, 11/17/31; d. NYC, 8/26/03. Studied w. private teacher in Hartford, Conn., 1946. Att. Hartt Sch. of Mus. '48–9; Schillinger House '49–50. Pl. first prof. gigs in Hartford w. Al Lepak and William Cully. Pl. w. Charlie Spivak '50–1, then w. air force band in Korean War. Upon discharge, pl. w. Sauter-Finegan Orch. '55; Woody Herman '56. Made rec. debut w. Kai Winding Spt. '56. Att. Manh. Sch. of Mus. '58–62. Orig. member of Gerry Mulligan Concert Jazz Band '61. Member of CBS Staff Orch. '61–4. Very active as freelancer. Pl. w. Benny Goodman '61–2; Quincy Jones '62; also many rec. sess. w. such vocs. as Frank Sinatra; Peggy Lee; Dinah Washington; Sarah Vaughan. Tour. USSR w. Goodman '62. Pl. w. Thad Jones–Mel Lewis '67; Clark Terry bb '67–8. Ret. to Goodman Orch. '78–9; also rec. w. rock gp. Steely Dan in '70s. With Jaco Pastorious '84. Form. own spt. '84. Tour. USA and Eur. w. Mingus "Epitaph" Orch. '91. Teach. tbn. at Mannes Sch. of Mus. In recent yrs., Andre has become more involved in comp. and arr. In May '91 he premiered an ext. work for tbn. and symph. orch. in Oslo, Norway. Favs: Urbie Green, J.J. Johnson, Slide Hampton. Polls: NARAS Most Val. Studio Player '82, '86. Fests: many, in UK, Norway, France, Greece, Germ., Italy, Spain, Switz. TV: *Ed Sullivan Show* w. Pearl Bailey '68. CDs: w. Geo. Benson (A&M; CTI); Lockjaw Davis (RCA); Maynard Ferguson (Main.); B. Goodman (Lond.).; Dexter Gordon (Col.).; Freddie Hubbard (CTI); Gerry Mulligan (Verve); Wes Montgomery (Verve).

ANDREWS, ERNIE (ERNEST), voc; b. Philadelphia, PA, 12/25/27. Moved to LA before age of 10; sang in church choir. Amateur contest appearance resulted in first rec. deal w. G&G Recs.; worked w. Harry James late 1950s. Cont. active in LA clubs, w. occasional fest. apps. fr. '60s into '90s. Tour. w. Gene Harris Superband '90. App. at Blue Note, NYC, w. Ray Brown '95. A talented ballad and blues singer whose pop interpretations are tinged w. a jazz flavor. CDs: Muse, High.; w. Gene Harris (Conc.); Harper Bros. (Verve).

ANTOLINI, CHARLY, dms; b. Zurich, Switzerland, ca. 1935. In mid 1950s pl. and rec. w. Bill Coleman and Albert Nicholas in Paris and Zürich. Worked w. Eur. Dixieland gps. '50s to early '60s. Moved to Stuttgart, Germ. '62; pl. w. Suddeutscher Rundfunk bb; rec. w. Wolfgang Dauner '64; Stuff Smith '67; Baden Powell '67. Studio mus. '69–71; also pl. w. Kurt Edelhagen's band, touring Soviet Union; pl. w. L. Hampton '80; B. Goodman '81. CDs: Bell; w. B. Dennerlein (Bebab).

APPLEYARD, PETER, vib, all mallet and perc instr; b. Cleethorpes, Lincolnshire, England, 8/26/28. Studied pno. w. Albert Wells; self-taught percussionist. Began pl. dms. 1941; vib. '45. Pl. for servicemen dur. WWII and w. Felix Mendelsohn's Orch.; RAF band '46–8; many bands in Scotland and Engl. '48–9; to Bermuda w. Jack Wallace '49 for two yrs. Emigrated to Can. '51. Joined Calvin Jackson Qt. '53–6, then formed own qt. tour. Can. and US. Had own TV series in Can. Tour. int'l w. B. Goodman '72–80. Eur. w. Peanuts Hucko in '80s; tours w. Buddy DeFranco, Herbie Mann '89–90. Many app. at jazz parties in US. Won gold rec. for *Swing Fever* '83. Feat. soloist w. Mel Tormé, fall '91. His presentation incl. comic impressions of such vibs. as Norvo; Hampton; Jackson; Gibbs. Named to the Order of Canada '92. CDs: Conc.; w. B. Goodman (Lond.).

ARBELLO, FERNANDO, tbn; b. Ponce, PR, 5/30/07; d. San Juan, PR, 7/26/70. Studied tbn. fr. age 12, pl. w. sch. orch. and symph. gp. of Ponce. In NYC pl. w. the orchs. of Earle Howard 1927; Wilbur De Paris '28; June Clark '29–30. Fr. '31 to '34 worked w. Claude Hopkins, rec. solo on "Chasin' All the Blues Away" '34. With Chick Webb '34–5; Fletcher Henderson '35–6; Lucky Millinder '36–7; Billy Hicks '37; briefly w. Edgar Hayes, Fats Waller, Hopkins again; Benny Carter, Zutty Singleton '40; Henderson '41; Marty Marsala '41–2. Fr. '42 to '46 w. Jimmie Lunceford. Own band in '50s; Rex Stewart in Bost. '53; Machito '60. At end of '60s, he ret. to PR and led his own gp. '69. Valued by leaders as a solid section man. CDs: w. C. Hopkins (Class.).

ARCHEY, JIMMY (JAMES H.), tbn; b. Norfolk VA, 10/12/02; d. Amityville, NY, 11/16/67. Took up tbn. at 12; studied mus. at Hampton Inst. 1915–19. To NYC '23, working w. Ed Howard, Ed Small '24; Edgar Hayes '26–7; Arthur Gibbs, Joe Steele, King Oliver '29, rec. w. him '30. Between '31 and '37, his main affiliation was Luis Russell, who fronted orch. for Louis Armstrong. Solo on "Mahogany Hall Stomp" '36. Pl. w. Willie Bryant '38–9; Benny Carter '39–42; short stays w. Coleman Hawkins, Ella Fitzgerald, Cab Calloway, Duke Ellington; Claude Hopkins '44–5; Noble Sissle '46–9. With Mezz Mezzrow in France '48; Bob Wilber at Savoy Café, Bost. '48–50. Tour. Eur. w. own gp. '52; again w. Mezzrow '54–5; Earl Hines '55–62, most notably at Hangover Club, SF. Also worked w. Muggsy Spanier. In Feb. '66 he tour. Eur. w. NO All-Stars. Strong swing style marked by wide range and vigorous attack. Radio: Rudi Blesh's *This Is Jazz* series '47. Film: *Jazz Dance* '54. CDs: GHB; Story.; w. L. Armstrong (Dec.); S. Bechet (BN; Sav.); Benny Carter (B&B; BB); Wild Bill Davison (Jazz.); Bunk Johnson (Story.; Amer. Mus.); Lil Armstrong (Riv.); King Oliver (Aff.); Red Allen (Class.); Earl Hines (Riv.).

ARMACOST, TIM (TIMOTHY MICHAEL), tnr, sop saxes, cl, fl; b. Los Angeles, CA, 12/8/62. Mother, Roberta Bray Armacost, is classical concert pnst.; many mus. in family. Introduced to jazz by fath., a diplomat and jazz fan. Grew up in US and Japan. Began on fl. at age 7; cl. at 8; sw. to tnr. sax at 15. Pl. in Wash., D.C., w. Bob Israel bb 1979–81. Stud. w. Doc Ross at U. of Maryland; Bobby Bradford at Pomona Coll. Also priv. studies w. Charlie Shoemake. Pl. in Tokyo w. Michiyuki Kozaki '83–4; in LA w. Moment's Notice Qnt. '83, '85. Moved to Amsterdam, Netherlands, after grad. fr. Pomona '85; pl. w. Amer. and Dutch mus. incl. OYEZ '86–8; Klaus Ignatzek, Claudio Roditi '88; Amsterdam Jazz Qnt. '90. In Japan w. Fumio Itabashi '88. Head of sax dept. at Sweelinck Cons., Amsterdam, '87–91. Ret. to US in '91. Pl. in NYC w. David White fr. '91; Maria Schneider Orch. '95; Valery Ponomarev Universal Language fr. '95; David Murray bb, New Legacy bb '96; Larry Gillespie bb fr. '96. Stud. tabla w. Vijay Ateet in New Delhi, India, '92. Tour. Eur. w. Intercontinental Jazz Trio fr. '95; Ugetsu fr. '96. Led own gps. in US, Eur., Japan, India fr. '85 w. sidemen incl. Kenny Barron, Billy Hart, Tom Harrell, Ray Drummond. Armacost stud. Zen Buddhism w. master in Kyoto, Japan, fr. '83 and speaks Dutch and Japanese fluently. Favs: Rollins, Mobley, Coltrane. Fests: North Sea w. Amsterdam Jazz Qnt. '91; Jazz Yatra, Bombay, w. own qt. '96. TV: Japan, Poland, Spain. CDs: Timel.; Conc.; D-T; Via; w. Ugetsu (Mons);

Ignatzek (Timel.); Rick Hollander (YvP; Timel.; Conc.); David White (Cad.; CIMP); H. Meurkens (Conc.).

ARMSTRONG, LIL (Lillian Hardin), pno, comp, voc; b. Memphis, TN, 2/3/1898; d. Chicago, IL, 8/27/71. Studied for a concert career at Fisk U. but moved to Chi. 1917; worked as a song demonstrator bef. join. Freddie Keppard's Original Creole Jazz Band. Led own band at Dreamland ca. '20. With King Oliver to LA '21 and back in Chi. until '24, dur. which time she met Louis Armstrong, who became her second husband in '24. At her urging, he left for NYC in the fall, to join Fletcher Henderson. When he ret. to Chi. in Nov. '25, they teamed up in the band she was already leading. Pl. an important role in her husband's career, writing material, pl. and singing on recs. by Armstrong's Hot Five (sometimes Lil's Hot Shots) and Hot Seven '25–7. Rec. for Col. under name NO Wanderers '26. While tour. w. Keppard ca. '28 and pl. w. Johnny Dodds '28–9, she earned a teacher's degree fr. Chi. Mus. Coll. '28 and a postgrad. degree fr. NY Coll. of Mus. '29. Separated fr. Armstrong '31, divorced '38. Dur. '30s, she rec. and worked as house pnst. for Decca. Led own bands in Chi. and NYC incl. all–female orch. at the Harlem Opera House '31, Regal Theater, Chi. '34. Also pl. w. Ralph Cooper '31; Red Allen and Zutty Singleton '40. In '40s, she studied tailoring, made a tuxedo for Louis, and expected to retire from mus., but the jazz revival movement pulled her back. Worked in Engl. and France w. Peanuts Holland, Michel Attenoux, and Sidney Bechet and as soloist in clubs '52. Ret. to US, she app. at Red Arrow in suburban Chi. '52–60. Rec. for Riv. '61. She was working on an autobiography when she died while pl. a concert dedicated to Armstrong's memory at Chi.'s Civic Center Plaza. Rec. for Dec. in all-star context '37–40. Comp: "Struttin' With Some Barbecue" (with Armstrong); "Jazz Lips"; "Skid-dat-de-dat"; "Hear Me Talkin'"; "Just for a Thrill," which became a '59 hit by Ray Charles. TV: *Chicago and All That Jazz*, NBC '61. CDs: Riv.; w. Armstrong/Oliver (Mile.); Armstrong (Col.).

ARMSTRONG, LOUIS DANIEL (aka SATCHMO, POPS); tpt, voc; b. New Orleans, LA, 8/4/01; d. NYC, 7/6/71. His moth., Mayann, from Boutte, La., was the granddaughter of slaves. She was married at 15 to Willie, a turpentine worker, who abandoned her when Louis was a small child. She and Louis lived in abject poverty at Liberty and Perdido Streets in NO's Third Ward, better known as Storyville; he also spent some of his early childhood w. his paternal grandmoth., Josephine. Armstrong began singing several yrs. bef. he started pl. crnt. When he was about 7, he and some friends sang on the streets for spare change; many yrs. later, singing became an integral part of Armstrong's showmanship. At age 11, while selling coal for a family named Karnofsky, he was able to afford a cornet. A turning point in his childhood came on January 1, 1913, when he celebrated the New Year by firing a gun in the street. Arrested, he was sent to the city's Colored Waifs' Home where he eventually pl. alto horn, bugle, and, finally, crnt. in the Home's band; he stud. there w. Peter Davis and was soon pl. picnics and parades w. the band. When released from the Home after two yrs., he worked a variety of jobs, but was already determined to become a musician.

Still a teenager, he was befriended by King Oliver, who became his mentor and main musical infl. When Oliver left for Chi. in '18, Armstrong replaced him in Kid Ory's band, the most prominent jazz band in NO at that time. That same yr., Armstrong married an ex-prostitute, Daisy, but the union was brief. Armstrong worked w. Ory, and on riverboats w. Fate Marable '18–21, solid experiences that helped him develop into a skilled professional by the summer of '22, when Oliver asked him to join his band as second crntst. at Lincoln Gardens in Chi. At that time, Oliver's Creole Jazz Band had a strong impact on the Chi. jazz scene, highlights being remarkable unison crnt. breaks by Oliver and Armstrong. He made his rec. debut w. Oliver, incl. first recorded solo, on "Chimes Blues" '23. It was in the Creole Jazz Band that Armstrong met Lillian Hardin, the pnst. in the band. On Feb. 25, 1924, she became the second Mrs. Armstrong. In Oct. '24, while working w. Lil in Ollie Powers' Dreamland band, he left for NYC to join Fletcher Henderson at the Roseland Ballroom. He tour. extensively w. Henderson in spring and summer of '25. Dur. this time, Armstrong's playing caused a sensation; he was recognized as an innovator and the foremost "hot" soloist in jazz, much in demand accomp. blues singers like Bessie Smith and Mamie Smith on recs. He left Henderson in Nov. '25 to ret. to the Dreamland in Chi., where Lil was now leading her own band, and began rec. his extraordinary series of Hot Five and Hot Seven sides for Okeh, incl. debut as a scat singer on "Heebie Jeebies." Early in '26, while working w. Erskine Tate's orch. at the Vendome Theatre, he sw. to tpt. for appearance sake. A few mos. later, he was doubling in Carroll Dickerson's orch. at the Sunset Cabaret, billed as "Louis Armstrong, World's Greatest Trumpet Player." The Hot Five/Seven recs. earned Armstrong a world-wide reputation—the emotional intensity and basic simplicity of his solos had no parallel in jazz, and his rapport w. such sidemen as Earl Hines, Kid Ory, Zutty Singleton, and Johnny Dodds remains memorable.

Back in New York in '29, he fronted the Dickerson band at Connie's Inn in Harlem and doubled in a featured role in the revue *Hot Chocolates* at the Hudson Theatre on B'way. This was a pivotal point in Armstrong's career, marking the start of his fronting a bb and focusing more on popular songs than on blues and original instrumentals. For six mos. in '30 he toured, backed by Luis Russell's orch., and, fr. July '30 to spring '31, he was featured w. Les Hite's band at Frank Sebastian's Cotton Club in Calif. Russell teamed w. him again dur. the late '30s. Most of the large orch. Louis fronted fr. this time until 1946 were undistinguished, but his recorded solos, even on material of lesser value, remain impressive. After the Calif. trip, Armstrong ret. to Chi., then took a new band to NO in June '31—his first visit home in nine yrs. Meanwhile the phenomenal reception of his records led to his first Eur. trip, headlining a variety show at the London Palladium, July '32. Dur. this visit, *MM* editor P. Mathison Brooks unwittingly gave him the nickname "Satchmo" by garbling an earlier nickname, "Satchelmouth." In '33, Armstrong ret. to Eur. for a tour that lasted until Jan. '35, fronting various mediocre bands that were assembled for him. Back in the US, he was sidelined by lip trouble but in '36 went to Hollywood to take part in the film *Pennies from Heaven* w. Bing Crosby.

In the next few yrs. he made a transition to the personality-entertainer whose popularity stretched far beyond jazz. Novelty songs such as "Ol' Man Mose," "You Rascal You," and "Brother Bill" became his most requested numbers, and vocals pl. an increasingly dominant role in his act. His Dec. recs., fr. '35 to '42, often teamed him w. such pop artists as Bing Crosby and the Mills Bros., as well as w. Polynesian and Hawaiian gps., but there was also jazz. In Jan. '44 he celebrated his first victory in the *Esq.* poll w. his fellow winners in the first jazz concert ever held at the Metropolitan Opera House, NYC. In '47 he app. w. the Edmond Hall Sxt. at Carnegie Hall, then had major acting role in the film *New Orleans*. Instead of assembling another bb after the assignment was completed, he led a sxt. feat. Jack Teagarden, Barney Bigard, Dick Cary, Arvell Shaw, and Sid Catlett. This became the All Stars, a highly successful touring gp. whose sidemen, collectively, incl. pnsts. Earl Hines, Joe Bushkin, Marty Napoleon, and Billy Kyle; Bob McCracken, Edmond Hall, Peanuts Hucko, Joe Darensbourg, and Joe Muranyi, cl.; Trummy Young, Tyree Glenn, tbn.; Dale Jones, Milt Hinton, Jack Lesberg, Mort Herbert, bs.; and dmrs. Cozy Cole, Kenny John, Barrett Deems, and Danny Barcelona. Mounting interest in Armstrong as a symbol of Amer. jazz led to more frequent trips abroad after WWII: Nice JF '48; Eur. tours '49, '52; Japanese tour '54; UK,

Ghana '56; spring '57; six-month Eur. tour '59, incl. Spoleto, Italy, where he was wrongly diagnosed as having suffered a heart attack. He resumed pl. in NYC a few weeks later. Important recs. in the '50s incl. Col. LPs paying tribute to W.C. Handy and Fats Waller; and Verve collaborations w. Ella Fitzgerald and Oscar Peterson.

In '60 he toured Africa twice, the second time under the auspices of the US St. Dept. Other foreign travels in this decade incl. Europe, Mexico, and an extensive, nineteen-country tour of Africa '61; Europe '62; Australia, New Zealand, Hong Kong, Korea, Japan, Hawaii '63; Australia, New Zealand, Singapore, India, Japan, Formosa, Okinawa '64; Czechoslovakia, East and West Germany, Romania, Yugoslavia, Hungary, England, France, Holland, Sweden, Denmark '65. During this tour he played before an audience of 93,000 in the Budapest Football Stadium. Armstrong's group remained active on a full time basis. In '66 he played a summer season at the Jones Beach Marine Theatre on Long Island. In the spring of '67 he was ill for two months but shortly afterward resumed his schedule, playing concerts in Dublin, Antibes, St. Tropez, and Majorca. Early in '68, after a few American engagements, Armstrong and his All Stars played at the San Remo Festival. In June they appeared at the New Orleans JF, then went immediately to England for a series of successful concerts before ret. to the US. In Sept. he was taken seriously ill and was confined to Beth Israel Hospital in NYC for two months. Released in Jan. '69, he suffered a relapse and was back in again in Feb. His public apps. in the second half of the year were limited to guest shots.

Although under doctors' orders not to play trumpet, in '70 Armstrong made numerous TV appearances as a singer. He talked and sang at a special birthday concert held at the Shrine Auditorium in LA and the following week appeared in a *Salute to Satch* tribute at the NJF. He resumed playing in Sept., co-starring in a LV show with Pearl Bailey and, in October, flew to London to sing and play at a benefit concert. During '71 he continued to perform occasionally, but after playing for two weeks at the Empire Room of the Waldorf-Astoria in NYC, he suffered a heart attack and went into the hospital on March 5. On May 6 he was allowed to go home, but his health was precarious, and early in the morning on July 6 he died in his sleep at his home in Corona, Queens.

Polls: Won many *Esq.* awards as tpt. and voc. in '40s; countless int'l magazine polls; in '60s and '70s, both critics and readers polls as voc. in *DB*. Additional stage performances: as Bottom in *Swingin' the Dream* '39; in *The Real Ambassadors* with Dave Brubeck at Monterey JF '62. Additional films: *Artists and Models*; *Every Day's a Holiday* '37; *Going Places '38; Cabin in the Sky* '42; *Pillar to Post* '45; *The Strip; Glory Alley; A Song Is Born; The Glenn Miller Story; The Five Pennies; High Society; Jazz on a Summer's Day* '58; *La Paloma; The Night Before the Premiere; Auf Wiedersehen* (all Germany) '59; *A Girl, a Guitar and a Trumpet* '59 (Denmark); *Paris Blues* '60; *Where the Boys Are* '65; *A Man Called Adam* '66; *Hello Dolly* '69. Books: autobiographies *Swing That Music* '36 and *Satchmo: My Life in New Orleans* (Prentice-Hall) '54; biographies *Louis: The Louis Armstrong Story*, Max Jones and John Chilton (Little, Brown) '71; *Louis Armstrong: An American Genius*, James Lincoln Collier (Oxford) '83; *Satchmo*, Gary Giddins (Anchor Books) '88; *Louis Armstrong: An Extravagant Life*, Lawrence Bergreen (Broadway) '97. As a popular singer his biggest hits were "Mack the Knife" '56; "Hello Dolly" '64; and "What a Wonderful World" fr. '68, which achieved its success after inclusion in the film *Good Morning Vietnam* '87. CDs: Col., incl. boxed set, *Portrait of the Artist As a Young Man*; RCA, incl. boxed set; BB; Dec.; Verve; Disney; Louis Armstrong and Ella Fitzgerald, *Porgy and Bess*; Louis Armstrong and Oscar Peterson (Verve); Louis Armstrong and King Oliver (Mile.); w. Fletcher Henderson (Col.).

ARNOLD, HARRY (Harry Arnold Persson), lead, comp; also saxes, cl; b. Hälsingborg, Sweden, 8/7/20; d. Stockholm, Sweden, 2/11/71. Father pl. valve tbn. Studied alto sax, cl. 1937–8. Began arr. '38 after learning by "analyzing works by different composers between Basie and Ravel." Own 12-pc. band at Amiralen dance hall, Malmö, Sweden for seven yrs. from April '42. With Thore Ehrling, as tnr. sax, arr. '49–52. Own band again for weekends in Malmö '52–4. Served as comp., cond., arr. for Europa Films, Stockholm. Leader of Swedish Radio bb '56–65 (it became known in US as "Jazztone Mystery Band" on Jazztone label). Later recs. on Atl., Merc. First instrumental infl: Benny Carter; fav. arrs: Sy Oliver, Quincy Jones. Arnold's orch. incl. Arne Domnerus, Bengt Hallberg, Bjarne Nerem, Åke Persson; the orch. made recs. w. Coleman Hawkins, Nat Adderley, and Benny Bailey. Quincy Jones wrote arrs. for the band '58. LPs: Merc.; Atl. CDs: w. T. Ehrling (Drag.).

ARNOLD, HORACEE EMMANUEL, dms, comp, pno, gtr; b.Wayland, KY, 9/25/37. Older bro. got him interested in jazz. Always wanted to pl. dms. but didn't until stationed in Calif. w. coast guard 1957. Studied art, piano at LA City Coll.; encouraged to pursue dms. by Maurice Miller, dmr. w. Harold Land. Ret. to Louisville, Ky., '58. Pl. w. Roland Kirk '58; in Indianapolis, Ind., w. Kirk, David Baker bb '59. Pl. briefly in NYC w. Hasaan, Henry Grimes '59, then in trio in Louisville w. Kirk Lightsey, Cecil McBee. Moved to NYC '60. Pl. w. Chas. Mingus and R. Kirk '60. Tour. Asia w. Alvin Ailey dance co. '62. Pl. w. Barry Harris; Bud Powell '62; Hugh Masekela–Miriam Makeba '63–5; Tal Farlow–Don Friedman '66. Stud. comp. w. Heiner Stadler '66; classical gtr. w. Hy Gubernik, Ralph Towner '66–9. Led gp. The Here And Now Company in concerts and wkshps. in NYC schools '67–70; sidemen incl. Karl Berger, Robin Kenyatta, Sam Rivers, Joe Farrell, Mike Lawrence. Coordinator for Jazzmobile and led own gps. '69–72. Pl. w. Chick Corea's Return To Forever, Stan Getz '72–3. Tour. Japan w. Archie Shepp '78. Formed gp. Colloquium III w. Billy Hart, Freddie Waits late '70s; taught wkshps. at NY Drummers' Collective. Freelanced and pl. w. Dave Friedman, '80s. Arnold taught at Wm. Paterson Coll. in the '80s. Favs: Roy Haynes, Tony Williams, Clifford Jarvis. Infls: Corea, Zawinul, Ellington, Shorter. Own LPs for Col. TV: *The People*, *Round Trip* on CBS, early '70s. CDs: w. C. Corea (Den.; LRC); Billy Harper (SN); Gust Tsilis (Enja).

ARODIN, SIDNEY J. (Arnondrin), cl, saxes; b. Westwego, LA, 3/29/01; d. New Orleans, LA, 2/6/48. Studied cl. fr. age 11. Pl. w. Johnny Stein on Mississippi riverboats. To NYC 1922, pl. w. Original NO Jazz Band for three yrs. With New Orleans Rhythm Masters in San Antonio, Tex., '26; in NO w. NO Harmony Kings, Wingy Manone '27; Halfway House Orch., Monk Hazel, occasionally doubling on tin whistle '28. Worked in KC dur. summer '33; w. Louis Prima NYC '34; also Manone and NORK. Led own band at Puppy House, NO '39–40. Fr. '41 illness curtailed his perf. Noted as co-comp. w. Hoagy Carmichael of "Lazy River." Rec. w. Jones and Collins Astoria Hot Eight; Manone; Hazel; Abbie Brunies; Johnnie Miller; Prima. CDs: w. Sharkey Bonano (Timel.); Manone (Collectors Classics).

ARONOV, BEN (BENJAMIN JAMES), pno, kybd; b. Gary, IN, 10/16/32. Studied at U. of Tulsa, then at. Manh. Sch. of Mus. Pl. w. Jerry Wald early 1950s; Lighthouse All-Stars, June Christy in LA late '50s; Terry Gibbs '58–60; Lena Horne '59–60; Al Cohn–Zoot Sims '67–86; Jim Hall '67–72; Lee Konitz '75–80; Benny Goodman '86–8; Ken Peplowski since '89. Favs: Hank Jones, McCoy Tyner, Keith Jarrett. Fests: Japan '67–81; Germany '78. CDs: Arb.; Prog.; w. B. Goodman (MM); Jim Hall (Mile.); Lee Konitz (Chiaro.; SN); Harvie Swartz (Gram.); W. Vaché; Peplowski (Conc.); Eddie Bert (FS); Z. Sims (32).

ART ENSEMBLE OF CHICAGO. Organized in Paris 1961, first as a qt. w. Roscoe Mitchell, Joseph Jarman, Lester Bowie, and Malachi Favors; later as a qnt. w. Don Moye '70. Strongly infl. by free jazz elements that flowed from Muhal Richard Abrams' Chi.-based Experimental Band and the AACM. Based in France '69–71, perf. throughout Eur. and on TV, recs. and for film scores. In '70s and '80s the gp. made numerous concert, fest., and club apps. in US. Fr. '80s cont. to tour US and France. Perfs. are a mixture of theatricality and mus.: the stage filled w. instruments, incl. bs. sax, bjo, el-bs., log dms., bike horns, gongs, whistles, and more conventional instruments. The players often have painted faces and app. in such costumes as grass skirts, straw boaters, and hard hats. David Spitzer wrote of the gp.: "The members of [the Art Ensemble of Chi.] produce musical sounds which run the gamut from the traditional to the absurd and the surreal. They also include valid, humorous vocal discourses and cries, as well as atypical sounds produced on traditional instruments." CDs: ECM; DIW.

ARVANITAS, GEORGES, pno, org; b. Marseilles, France, 6/13/31. Studied classical pno. fr. ages 5 to 18. Pl. w. local trad. bands. Moved to Paris 1952, worked w. Mezz Mezzrow, Albert Nicholas, Bill Coleman, and many visiting Americans, incl. Dexter Gordon, Sonny Stitt, Donald Byrd. Led own gp. for two yrs. at Blue Note in Paris. Visited NYC twice in mid '60s, working there w. Ted Curson '64; Yusef Lateef for nine mos. '65. Back in Paris, he cont. to perf. w. visiting Americans. Tour. Japan w. Michel Legrand '72, and in Italy w. Sonny Criss and Sonny Stitt; worked w. Pepper Adams; Curson; Dizzy Gillespie; James Moody; and others in '80s. Infls: Bud Powell, Bill Evans. Awarded Prix Django Reinhardt '59. Rec. w. Anita O'Day for MPS at Berlin JF '70. Video: w. Coleman Hawkins (Shan.). CDs: w. Hawkins (Stash); D. Murray (FS); Chet Baker; Stuff Smith (France's Concert); Int'l Pescara Jam Sessions (Phil.).

ASCHER, KEN (KENNETH LEE), pno, kybds, comp, arr; b. Washington, DC, 10/26/44. Began on pno. in Chi. at age 5. Family moved to Atlanta 1950s. Jazz gigs and club dates in Atlanta fr. age 16. Studied elementary arr. fr. age 16 and classical pno. until '67; Ascher's teachers incl. William Beller at Columbia U. Received B.A., M.A., and Ph.D. in comp. fr. Columbia; taught mus. history at Columbia '62–4. Worked as commercial studio mus. in NYC fr. '66. Pl. w. Woody Herman '66–7; Steve Lawrence–Eydie Gormé '69–70; Art Blakey ca. '71; Paul Williams '72–3; Marvin Stamm, Thad Jones–Mel Lewis Orch. and Qt. '70s. Also worked at Half Note club, accomp.

Zoot Sims; Ruby Braff; Anita O'Day; Maxine Sullivan; Jimmy Rushing. As a studio musician, comp., and arranger, Ascher has worked on many bestselling albums by pop artists, incl. Paul Williams; John Lennon; Barbra Streisand; James Taylor; Billy Joel. With Williams, he collab. on the song scores for the films *A Star Is Born* '76 and *The Muppet Movie* '79. Ascher's songs have been rec. by such jazz vocalists as Carmen McRae, Cleo Laine. Favs: O. Peterson, Keith Jarrett, Herbie Hancock, Bill Evans, Chick Corea; arrs: Johnny Mandel, Gil Evans, Bill Holman, Nelson Riddle, Don Costa. Polls: '76 Golden Globe Awd. for song "A Star Is Born"; NARAS MVP, elec. kybd. '84. Fests: Eur. w. W. Herman '67. TV: app. w. Paul Williams on *Tonight Show*; David Frost show. LPs w. Marvin Stamm (Palo Alto); Johnny Hartman (Perception). CDs: w. Warren Bernhardt (DMP); as arr. w. Lennon (Cap.); Streisand (Col.).

ASCIONE, JOE (JOSEPH V.), dms, perc, comp; b. Brooklyn, NY, 3/14/61. Maternal grandfath. pl. all instruments, incl. harp, oboe, vln., pno., mand., gtr.; all male cousins pl. dms. as did paternal grandfath. and uncle. Studied w. Greg Proios 1971–5; Charli Persip '77–81; also at Hofstra U. and the New Sch. Pl. w. The Hot Club '87–9; Joyce DeCamilo '89–90; Billy Mitchell Qt. '91–6. Made rec. debut w. Dick Cary '91. Pl. and rec. w. Sam Pilafian–Frank Vignola's Travelin' Light '92–4; also pl and rec. w. Cab Calloway; Della Reese; Al Hirt. Freelanced w. Milt Hinton; Jay McShann; Roland Hanna; Dick Hyman; Flip Phillips; Scott Hamilton; James Moody; George Coleman; others. Favs: Buddy Rich, Baby Dodds, Jo Jones, Gene Krupa. Fests: Santiago, Chile, w. Arnie Lawrence '92; Sweden w. Travelin' Light 93; Germ. '95; Berne JF '96. TV: *Good Day NY*. CDs: N-H; w. Phillips-Hinton (Chiaro.); Vignola-Mitchell (Conc.); Travelin' Light (Tel.).

ASH, MARVIN (Ashbaugh), pno; b. Lamar, CO, 10/4/14; d. Encino, CA, 8/21/74. Raised in Kansas, where he pl. w. Wallie Stoefer. Worked w. Connie Conrad, Herman Waldman, Jack Crawford in early 1930s. Moved to Tulsa, Okla., pl. on staff of local radio station. Well known in LA area since '42, when he moved there. Pl. at Hangover Club and w. Wingy Manone. Rec. own LPs on Dec.; Cap.

ASH, VIC (VICTOR), tnr sax, cl, fl; b. London, England, 2/9/30. Studied priv. 1945. Pl. w. Kenny Baker '51–3, Vic Lewis '53–5; accomp. Hoagy Carmichael, Cab Calloway on British visits '55. Led own qt. '56–8, and sxt. '58–60; tour. US w. own gp. '57–8; w. Vic Lewis band '59. Led Jazz Five w. Harry Klein '60–3, sometimes backing such visiting Amer.

jazzmen as Miles Davis, D. Brubeck, and D. Gillespie. Won *MM* polls for eight yrs. Pl. w. Ray Charles '61; John Dankworth '63–5; worked in Bermuda '66–9. Fr. '70s worked mostly as studio mus., often backing non-jazz artists such as Frank Sinatra and Shirley MacLaine. Rec. w. own gp. for Nixa '56.

ASHBY, DOROTHY JEANNE, harp, pno; b. Detroit, MI, 8/6/32; d. Santa Monica, CA, 4/13/86. Father Wiley Thompson, a self-taught gtrst., gave her harm. lessons. Further studies at Cass Tech. HS; Wayne St. U. where she was mus. ed. major. Studied vocal techniques; sang folk songs on local radio. Gave pno. recitals; pl. pno. for choir; harp in Wayne St. orch. In '53, a yr. after buying a harp, she pl. first prof. job in Phila. club. Concerts w. Louis Armstrong, Woody Herman '57. Worked in Det. clubs for the most part but also in NYC. Hosted own jazz talk show on WJR radio, Det. '60s. Wrote book on jazz and modern harm. for harp and cello. Moved to Calif. and worked as studio mus. on recs. by Stanley Turrentine, Sonny Criss in mid '70s. Favs: Oscar Peterson, Billy Taylor, George Shearing. Kenny Dorham said of her in *DB*: "Miss Ashby is taking care of business, which is quite a job with this traditionally clumsy instrument." Rec. LPs for Atl.; NJ; Argo; Jzld.; Cadet. CDs: Prest.; Sav.

ASHBY, HAROLD KENNETH, tnr sax; b. Kansas City, MO, 3/27/25; d. NYC, 6/13/03. Brother Herbert pl. alto; bro. Alex, tpt. Began on cl., sw. to tnr. in vocational sch. Self-taught. In navy 1943–5; did not play dur. that time. Pl. in KC w. Tommy Douglas '46–7; Walter Brown–Jay McShann '48–9. Met Ben Webster, who became his mentor, in KC '49. Moved to Chi. '50, pl. and rec. w. blues mus. incl. Willie Dixon; Willie Mabon; Otis Rush; Memphis Slim; Lowell Fulson; Jimmy Witherspoon; Chuck Berry '50s. Moved to NYC '57, freelanced w. Milt Larkin; Mercer Ellington; Count Basie. Introduced to Duke Ellington by Ben Webster '58. Subbed w. Ellington fr. '60, then joined band in '68 and remained until '75, one yr. after Ellington's death. Has worked mainly as a single at jazz parties and in Eur. fr. '75. Favs: Hawkins, Don Byas, Webster. Fests: Eur., Asia, So. Amer., Africa w. Ellington; Eur. as single. App. in *Ellington Reeds* concert at NJF-NY '86. TV: *Reminiscing in Tempo* (PBS Ellington special). CDs: Stash; CC; Gem.; w. Ellington (Fant.; Saja; Sequel Jazz; Pablo); Cat Anderson (B&B); Bennie Wallace (Den.); B. Golson (Ark.).

ASHBY, IRVING C., gtr; b. Soommerville, MA, 12/29/20; d. Perris, CA, 4/22/87. From a mus. family; start. on uke. at age 7; Stud. gtr. fr. 9. Att. New Eng.

Cons. but refused scholarship and worked w. Bost.-area bands. Pl. w. Lionel Hampton 1940–2. In LA worked w. Eddie Beal, etc. Replaced Oscar Moore in King Cole Trio, Oct. '47, tour. Eur. w. him '50. After pl. in trio w. Gerry Wiggins, join. Oscar Peterson for JATP's first Eur. trip '52. Freelancing and teaching in LA '50s. Wrote and pl. background mus. for State Dept. docu. film at USC Sch. of Cinema '63; pub. *Guitar Work Book* '67. Left LA for semi-retirement in Perris '69, concentrating on landscape design, sign painting, teaching orch. and gtr. at hs; also at U. of Calif., Riverside '71. Infl. chiefly by Charlie Christian, he rec. w. Fats Waller; Lester Young; Wardell Gray; Erroll Garner; Louis Jordan; Charles Mingus; and Illinois Jacquet. CDs: w. Nat Cole (Mos.; Cap.); C. Basie (Pab.); B. Holiday; I. Jacquet; Charlie Parker (Verve); A. Previn (BL); F. Waller (BB); Lester Young (BN).

ASHTON, BILL (William Richard Allingham), saxes, comp, lead; b. Blackpool, England, 12/6/36. Studied at Oxford 1957. Prof. debut as mus. in France '62. Taught French in London. In '65, became founder and mus. dir. of the National Youth Jazz Orch., which made extensive use of British repertoire by Tubby Hayes; Stan Tracey; Harry South; John Dankworth. The NYJO has made numerous apps. before royalty and has toured the US, USSR, Portugal, Austral., Turkey. Awarded an MBE '78. Comps: "London," "No Flowers By Request," "Accident Prone," "Blood Orange," "Blenkinsop's Blues." The NYJO has its own magazine and record label.

ASMUSSEN, SVEND (HAROLD CHRISTIAN), vln, voc; also vla, bs, gtr, pno, vib; b. Copenhagen, Denmark, 2/28/16. Studied w. priv. teachers in Copenhagen 1922–32. Prof. debut at 17 in local theater. Fr. '33 to '43 led gp. patterned after style of Joe Venuti's Blue Four. Tour. in Den. w. Mills Bros. '37 and Fats Waller '38. Also tour. w. Josephine Baker '38; Valaida Snow '39. Later worked as actor and comedian. Cruises around the world in '50s. Fr. '58 to '61 he co-led the Swe-Danes, a trio w. gtr. Ulrik Neumann and singer Alice Babs, touring US in '58; w. Babs in Scan. '69–72; Brazil '74. Joint apps. and rec. w. other vlnsts., notably Stuff Smith and Stephane Grappelli '66; Grappelli and Ray Nance w. Ellington, Atl. '63. Many film and TV apps. incl. Ed Sullivan, Dinah Shore. Despite a tendency to work in pop settings, Asmussen has a reputation as an elegant, swinging vlnst. and a spirited singer. Favs: Stuff Smith, Didier Lockwood. Fests: Antibes '65; MJF '75. Rec. w. John Lewis (Atl.) '62; Toots Thielemans, (A&M) '72; Ed Thigpen. CDs: Phon.; Sig.; Asmussen/Grappelli (Story.); w. Oscar Aleman

(Acoustic Sound); J-L. Ponty (MPS); D. Grisman (Zebra).

ATKINSON, LISLE ARTHUR, bs, pno; b. NYC, 9/16/40. Mother pl. pno., fath. pl. bs. Began on vln. and sw. to bs. Att. HS of Mus. and Art, then Manh. Sch. of Mus. Pl. w. Freddy Cole trio 1959–61; many recs. w. Nina Simone '62–6; rejoin. F. Cole '67. Was member of Bill Lee's NY Bass Vln. Choir fr. late '60s to early '70s. In early '70s, pl. w. Stanley Turrentine, Wynton Kelly Trio; later pl. w. Billy Taylor Trio; Kenny Burrell Trio; NY Jazz Quartet; Dakota Staton; Frank Foster's Loud Minority; Grady Tate Trio. Recs. w. Geo. Coleman Oct., Howard McGhee Qt. Also acc. voc. incl. Betty Carter, Johnny Hartman, Joe Williams, and pl. w. own bs. qt. In '80s rec. and perf. w. Charles Sullivan; Nancy Wilson; Eddie Harris. Form. Neo Bass Ens. '85. Pl. w. Benny Carter since '85; Grover Mitchell bb '87–8; Ernie Wilkins–Joe Newman Qnt. '89; Lee Konitz since '88. Also instr. at Jazzmobile Wkshp. in NYC since '71. Favs: Richard Davis, Charles Mingus. Fests: Nice '89 w. Wilkins-Newman, others in UK, Spain, France, Italy, Sweden, Japan. TV: *Today*; *Like It Is*. CDs: w. G. Coleman (Charly); Benny Carter (Limel.); Betty Carter (Roul.); Richard Wyands (DIW); Helen Humes (Muse); Hal Singer (FNAC).

AULD, GEORGIE (John Altwerger), tnr, alto, sop saxes, lead; b. Toronto, Ont., Canada, 5/19/19; d. Palm Springs, CA, 1/8/90. Moved to Bklyn., N.Y., 1929. Began on alto ca. '30; won Rudy Wiedoft scholarship 31. Start. on tnr. in '35 after hearing a Coleman Hawkins rec. Led own band at Nick's ca. '36. Pl. w. Bunny Berigan '37–8; Artie Shaw '38–9. Took over Shaw band '40, then led own new gp. Pl. w. Jan Savitt, early '40; Benny Goodman bb and sxt. '40–1; Shaw '41–2. In army '43, then led own bb '43–6; sidemen incl. Serge Chaloff, Joe Albany, Stan Levey, Al Porcino. Freelanced. w. own small gp. '47–9. Ran own club, Tin Pan Alley, NYC. Led 10-pc. band, also app. as actor in B'way play *The Rat Race* '49. Led qnt. w. Frank Rosolino, Tiny Kahn '50–1, then rec. as lead. for Coral label w. vocal chorus accomp. Moved to Calif., opened Melody Room club in Hollywood '54; led bb w. Lunceford-style arrs. by Billy May, mid '50s. Ret. to NYC '58, worked as studio mus. App. mainly in LV in '60s, incl. w. Benny Goodman '66. Tour. Eur. and So. Amer. as soloist and cond. w. Tony Martin fr. '67. Auld freelanced as a studio mus. in LA fr. the late '60s, but enjoyed his greatest popularity as a jazz soloist in Japan. By '75 he had toured Japan twelve times and released fifteen albums there, many of them hits. Strongly infl. by Ben Webster, he picked up on bebop in the mid '40s; his pl. then showed essences of the Lester Young sch., later often reflecting Gene Ammons. Fests: Colo. JP in late '80s. Film: both as an actor on screen and saxophonist on the soundtrack for *New York, New York* '77. TV: *Art Ford's Jazz Party*. CDs: Musi.; w. B. Berigan (Jass; BB; Hep); Benny Carter (Class.); B. Goodman (Col.; Vintage Jazz); Charlie Christian; Billie Holiday (Col.); Barney Kessel (Cont.); C. Hawkins (Del.); A. Shaw; C. Basie (BB); Met. All-Stars (RCA); Anita O'Day (Verve).

AUSTIN, CUBA, dms; b. Charleston, WV, ca. 1906; d. Bombay, India, after 1960. First prof. experience as tap dancer. Pl. off and on w. William McKinney's Synco Jazz Band, early 1920s–'26, then full-time w. McKinney's Cotton Pickers '26–31. After McKinney's band split into two factions in '26, Austin led the Original Cotton-Pickers '31–4. Lived in Balt., Md., fr. '34, owned business and pl. w. Rivers Chambers and own trio. Rec. w. The Chocolate Dandies '28. CDs: w. McKinney's Cotton Pickers (BB; Class.); Benny Carter (Charly).

AUSTIN, LOVIE (Cora Calhoun), pno, comp; b. Chattanooga, TN, 9/19/1887; d. Chicago, IL, 7/10/72. Piano stud. at Roger Williams U., Nashville; Knoxville Coll. Gained experience on vaudeville circuit, led own band 1923. As mus. dir for Paramount label, she accomp. many singers in Chi. area, incl. Ida Cox, Alberta Hunter, Ma Rainey; also rec. w. her own Blues Serenaders, which often incl. her lover, tptr. Tommy Ladnier. Worked as mus. dir. of Monogram Theater, Chi., for twenty yrs.; cond. pit band at Joyland Theater for nine. Led own trio, adding mus. such as Tommy Ladnier, Johnny Dodds. Worked as war plant inspector for two yrs. dur. WWII; also pl. w. own traveling shows and in theaters. Fr. late '40s pl. at Jimmy Payne's dancing school; worked as asst. trainer for St. Anselm's Kindergarten. Mary Lou Williams cited her as an inspiration. Fav: Duke Ellington; imp. infl: Ladnier. Comp.: "Graveyard Blues," rec. by Bessie Smith. Rec. again w. Alberta Hunter '61. LP w. Blues Serenaders on Fountain. CDs: w. Hunter (Riv.); Johnny Dodds (Aff.); w. Ladnier in *The Jazz Trumpet* (Prest.).

AUTREY, HERMAN, tpt; b. Evergreen, AL, 12/4/04; d. NYC, 6/14/80. Studied alto horn from 1913, making debut w. fath.'s orch. at 14. Sw., to tpt. '18. Moved to Pitts. '23. Worked w. local bands, then tour. in South, lead. own band in Fla. '26. Lived and work. in Bost., Wash., D.C., and Phila. Pl. w. Doc Hyder '33, then, later in the yr., moved to NYC and join. Charlie Johnson at Small's Paradise. Prominent

w. Fats Waller and his Rhythm '34–41; also pl. first tpt. w. Fletcher Henderson '35. With Claude Hopkins '38–9, also w. Charlie Turner, Luis Russell in this period. With Stuff Smith '42, later lead. this gp. on West Coast. Own gp. at Musical Bar, Phila. '45; freelanced w. own band in Can. late '40s. Jam sessions at Jimmy Ryan's, Stuyvesant Casino, NYC early '50; own gp. in Can., Bklyn., late '50s. Gigs w. Lester Lanin, Conrad Janis, and at Eddie Condon's, late '50s, after recovering from serious auto accident '54. Led own qt. at Embers '60. Became part of the Saints and Sinners, organized by Red Richards, tour. Eur. w. them '67, '69. Freelanced in NYC mid '70s, occ. subbing at Jimmy Ryan's. A strong, economical player, orig. infl. by Armstrong, and a singer w. ties to Waller. Rec. w. Saints and Sinners for MPS; Sack. CDs: w. Waller (BB; Stash); C. Hopkins (Class.); Swingville All-Stars (GTJ).

AVERY, TEODROSS, tnr, sop saxes; b. Fairfield, CA, 7/2/73. Began stud. classical gtr. at age 10. Sw. to alto sax at 13 and pl. in junior hs ens. Heard Coltrane and Dexter Gordon's mus. and took up tnr. in hs. In the SF Bay area sat in w. Blakey; Elvin Jones; Freddie Hubbard; Donald Byrd; Cedar Walton; and the Marsalis brothers, who encouraged him. Attended Berkeley HS in senior yr. Stud. w. Joe Henderson. Went to Berklee Coll. on scholarship; in first yr. won Clifford Brown–Stan Getz Fellowship Award and National Found. for Advancement of the Arts Award. In second yr. form. own gp. and work. around Bost. Won Sony Innovation Award '93 and perf. at Alice Tully Hall, NYC. Rec. debut for GRP in same yr. Favs: Rollins, J. Henderson, Coltrane, G. Ammons. CDs: GRP; Imp.; w. Carl Allen (Atl.).

AYERS, ROY E., vib, voc; b. Los Angeles, CA, 9/10/40. Father pl. tbn; stud. w. moth., a pno. teacher, fr. age 5. Lionel Hampton gave him vib. mallets at 6; got first set of vib. at age 12. Studied harm. at Jefferson HS; further mus. stud. at LA City Coll. Pl. w. Gerald Wilson orch., Jack Wilson; co-led qt. w. Hampton Hawes 1963. Gigs w. Chico Hamilton; Phineas Newborn; Teddy Edwards; Curtis Amy early to mid '60s. Led own qt. '65–6; pl. w. Herbie Mann '66–70; own crossover gp., Ubiquity, using electronics in '70s. Perf. soundtrack to '73 film *Coffy*, issued as LP on Polyd. Had own label, Uno Melodic, in '80s. Pl. and rec. as lead. and w. pop gps. involved w. acid jazz, rap in '80s and '90s, incl Guru's Jazzmatazz '93. Favs: Miles Davis, Marvin Gaye, Gil Scott-Heron. Early vib. favs: Milt Jackson, Bobby Hutcherson, Cal Tjader, Victor Feldman. Polls: *DB* '66, '71; *Blues & Soul*. Fests: LV JF '62; Africa, Asia, Eur., etc. Rec. debut w. Vi Redd '62. CDs: JH; GrooveTown; w.

Herbie Mann (Atl.); Leroy Vinnegar (Cont.); Jack Wilson (FS).

AYLER, ALBERT, tnr, sop, alto saxes; bagpipes; comp; b. Cleveland, OH, 7/13/36; d. NYC, sometime in Nov. 1970, on or after 11/5/70. Began stud. alto sax w. fath., a vlnst. and tnr. saxist, at age seven. As a teenager, began pl. prof. w. r&b bands; tour. w. Little Walter in 1952. During army service '59–62, he pl. in army concert bands and switched to tnr.; occ. pl. in Paris clubs while stationed in France '60–1. Stayed in Eur. after discharge; led bop trio in Sweden; w. Cecil Taylor in Copenhagen, winter of '62–3. Moved to NYC in '63, occ. perf. w. Taylor. In summer '64, formed a qt. w. Don Cherry, Gary Peacock, Sunny Murray; tour. Eur. in late '64. His successive sidemen were equally prominent in NYC's avant-garde jazz community and at times included both Peacock and Henry Grimes on bs.; Ayler's bro. Don, tpt.; Murray, Beaver Harris, or Milford Graves, dms.; Call Cobbs, pno. or harpsichord. Though his radical mus., stemming from the "free jazz" developments in the '60s, never found a steady following, Ayler rec. frequently, and his work was often critically acclaimed. He did perf. occ. at NYC clubs and coll. concerts. His gp. pl. at NJF '66 and toured Eur. briefly in Nov. of that yr. In '69 he reverted to a more blues-rooted style, suggesting his early r&b experience. Soon after ret. to NYC from a Eur. tour, he was reported missing; his body was found in NYC's East River on Nov. 25. Critic Joachim Berendt found "the joyous air of the folk musician" in Ayler's work. Michael Cuscuna wrote: "The music of Albert Ayler remains among the most unique and haunting in the history of black American music . . . of all the players of the 1960s avant-garde, including the geniuses, the competent musicians, and the lame hucksters, Ayler's music seemed to evoke the strongest reaction, be it pro or con . . . [he offered] simple, unforgettable melodies, such as *Ghosts*, which many feel to be the anthem of 1960s black music." Polls: *DB* Critics New Star '69. CDs: Free.; Imp.; Sonet; DIW; ESP; Jazz View. *Wings* (SN) contains Giorgio Gaslini's pno. transcriptions of a number of Ayler's comps.

b

BABASIN, HARRY (Babasian), bs, cello; b. Dallas, TX, 3/19/21; d. Los Angeles, CA, 5/21/88. Raised in Vernon, Tex. Began on bs. and cello as teenager, then stud. at No. Texas St. Coll. Fellow students were Jimmy Giuffre, Herb Ellis, Gene Roland. Pl. w. territory bands in Midwest, early 1940s. To NYC '45, pl. w. Gene Krupa, Charlie Barnet, Boyd Raeburn. Moved to Calif., late '45. Pl. w. Raeburn '45–6; Benny Goodman '46–7. Made first jazz pizzicato cello recs. w. Dodo Marmarosa '47. Tour. w. Woody Herman '48, then freelanced as studio mus. in Hollywood. Founded Nocturne rec. co., early '50s. Pl. cello in own gp., The Jazzpickers, '56; pl. briefly w. Harry James '59. Babasin received an M.A. in comp. fr. San Fernando Valley St. Coll. '61. He pl. in a duo w. pianist Phil Moody fr. '63. Film: app. in *A Song Is Born* '48. LPs: PJ; Em.; Disc; VSOP. CDs: Noct.; PJ; Em; Disc.; VSOP; w. B. Goodman (Cap.); Laurindo Almeida (WP); Chet Baker; Sonny Criss; Bob Gordon (FS); Barney Kessel (Cont.); D. Marmarosa (Jz. Class.); B. Raeburn (Sav.).

BABS, ALICE (Alice Nilsson Sjöblom), voc; b. Kalmar, Sweden, 1/26/24. Studied at Royal Academy fr. 1956. Represented Sweden at Paris JF '49. Active in films, TV, and on stage, she join. forces w. vlnst. Svend Asmussen and gtrst. Ulrik Neumann to form the Swe-Danes '59–63. In '63 the purity of her voice, coupled w. a sense of swing, attracted the attention of Duke Ellington, w. whom she made many apps., rec. w. him on Reprise and app. in some of the sacred concerts incl. the second, NYC '68, and the third, London '73. In the latter yr. she also sang at NJF-NY. Though largely inactive in later yrs., she still made occ. apps. at events dedicated to Ellington, incl. hosting Int'l Ellington Conference, Stockholm '94. Honors: appointed as Royal Court singer, the only non-opera singer given that title, by King of Sweden '72; elected to Royal Academy '74. Infls: Ivie Anderson, B. Holiday, Ellington, J. Hodges. CD: *Second Sacred Concert* w. Ellington, incl. "Heaven"; "T.G.T.T" (Prest.).

BADEN POWELL (Roberto Baden Powell de Aquino), gtr; b. Varre-e-Sai, Brazil, 8/6/37; d. Rio de Janeiro, 9/26/00. Father and grandfath. well-known mus.; prof. fr. age 15. Early participant in bossa nova; co-wrote "Samba Triste" w. Billy Blanco in 1959; studio gtr. for many bossa nova albums '59–61. Comp. over fifty Afro-samba style tunes w. lyricist Vinicius de Moraes. Rec. w. Herbie Mann '62; led own gps. fr. '66. In '70s and '80s worked mostly in Eur., releasing numerous albums, sometimes in assoc. w. jazz artists, incl. Stephane Grappelli. Occ. US tours, incl. one w. Stan Getz. CDs: BL; Verve; Tropical; Mile.

BADGLEY, BOB (ROBERT L.), bs; b. Det., MI, 6/23/28. Studied at Cass Tech HS 1944–5. In SF w. Virgil Gonsalves; LA w. Tommy Gumina, Dick Stabile, Bobby Troup, Matty Matlock '67–70. Hotel bands in LV in '70s; on the road w. F. Sinatra '79; Bob Florence Trio '79–86. Best known dur. world tours w. Joe Williams '84–90, also backed Pia Zadora '86. Favs.: J. Patitucci, E. Gomez, S. LaSpina, N-H.Ø. Pedersen. CDs: w. J. Williams (Verve); Sue Raney (Disc.).

BADRENA, MANOLO, perc, dms, gtr, pno; b. San Juan, PR, 3/17/52. Sister is a choreographer. Began on pno., stud. priv. and at Miami-Dade Coll. Freelanced w. Art Blakey bef. join. Weather Report, w. whom he made rec. debut 1977. Pl. and rec. w. George Duke '77; Herb Alpert '78; first rec. as lead. prod. by Alpert '79. Pl. w. Spyro Gyra; Gil Evans Orch. '87-8; Ahmad Jamal '88; Steve Khan since '84; Lew Soloff since '87; Carla Bley. Many recs. w. rock mus. incl. Joni Mitchell; Debbie Harry; Talking Heads; Andy Summers. Also pl. for B'way shows and TV and film soundtracks. Cont. to devote himself to the study of world mus., w. emphasis on int'l perc. styles. Favs: Trichy Sarkaran, Changuito; arr: Gil Evans. Fests: Eur., Hawaii, Brazil; Japan since '81. Polls: *DB, Modern Drummer, Ad Lib.* TV: Arsenio Hall show, Joan Rivers show. CDs: w. Weather Report (Col.); A. Jamal; Mike Stern (Atl.); S. Khan (GRP, Polyd.); Bob Berg (Den.); Carla Bley (Watt); Brecker Bros. (Novus); L. Soloff (Electric Bird); Ronnie Cuber; Harvie Swartz (Gram.).

BAGLEY, DON (DONALD NEFF), bs, comp; b. Salt Lake City, UT, 7/18/27. Started w. Hollywood Teenagers 1944. Three yrs. in navy, also worked w. Shorty Sherock, Wingy Manone, Dick Pierce, '40s. In '50 was recommended to Stan Kenton by Jimmy Rowles; stayed w. Kenton '50-54; w. Les Brown '56. Active fr. '60s as arr. for NBC-TV mus. variety shows; in '70s scored mus. for TV shows, incl. *Barnaby Jones, Quincy,* and *Murder, She Wrote.* Rec. series of Christmas albums incl. Sarah Vaughan, Mormon Tabernacle Choir. Favs. incl. John Clayton, bs. and arr.; Rob Pronk, arr. CDs: w. Kenton; Shorty Rogers (Cap.); Zoot Sims; Lee Konitz (Vogue).

BAILEY, BENNY (ERNEST HAROLD), tpt; b. Cleveland, OH, 8/13/25; d. Amsterdam, 4/14/05. Studied pno., fl. at Central HS. Took up tpt., stud. at Cleveland Cons. and w. George Russell. Prof. debut w. Bull Moose Jackson in Buffalo 1941; then to LA w. Scatman Crothers '44. Pl. w. Jay McShann '47; Teddy Edwards. Tour. Eur. w. D. Gillespie band '47-8; then w. L. Hampton '49-53, incl. Sweden, where he remained, working w. Harry Arnold radio band '57-9. Join. Quincy Jones band in Eur., pl. w. it there and in US '59-60. Moving to Germ. in '60, he worked w. Berlin Radio Band for two yrs; Max Greger in Munich for five yrs.; later w. Radio Suisse Romande, and as member of the Clarke-Boland band early '60s-73; worked w. George Gruntz in mid '70s. Pl. w. Eric Dolphy in Germ. '61, and in '80s w. many visiting Amers., incl. the Paris Reunion Band '86. Living in Amsterdam since '91. Qt. w. co-leader Ferdinand Povel '93. In '95 and '96 he visited US for gigs at Village Vanguard as a single, adding vocs. to his repertoire and evoking Armstrong, Eldridge, and Gillespie within sixteen bars in one number. A supe-

rior bebop tpt. stylist w. a powerful tone and range. First infls: Tommy Enoch, Freddie Webster; favs: Miles Davis, Art Farmer. Fests: Montreux w. L. McCann, E. Harris '69; Middleheim w. Boland gp. '74; Northsea '95. Made film w. O. Pettiford in Germ. '59. LPs: *From Vienna with Jazz* w. Friedrich Gulda on Col.; tracks, "Meet Benny Bailey" w. Arnold on Merc.; "Concerto for Benjamin and Jonathan" w. Jon Eardley on *International Jazz Workshop* (Em.). CDs: Cand.; Enja; TCB; Gem.; Hot.; w. Q. Jones (Merc.; R&T; Qwest); Stan Getz (DIW; Drag.); Dolphy (Cand.; Enja); Basie (Roul.; Verve); Berlin Contemp. Jazz Orch. (ECM); Dexter Gordon (Col.; Steep.); Tony Coe (Hot.); Eddie Harris (Rhino/Atl.); F. Redd (Mos.); S. Shihab (Rear); B. Golson (Prest.).

BAILEY, BUSTER (WILLIAM C.), cl; b. Memphis, TN, 7/19/02; d. NYC, 4/12/67. Started on cl. at age 13; later stud. w. Franz Schoepp of Chi. Symph., who also taught Benny Goodman. Pl. w. W. C. Handy orch. in 1917, remaining w. him until '19, when he moved to Chi. and worked w. Erskine Tate '19-22. He first achieved recognition while w. King Oliver '23-4; both he and Louis Armstrong left Oliver to join Fletcher Henderson in NYC. Bailey pl. w. Henderson fr. '24-7; until '37 he rejoin. Henderson for brief periods and was feat. on many of his recs. Tour. Eur. w. Noble Sissle '29; pl. w. various NYC bands, then w. Sissle again '31-3; Mills Blue Rhythm '34-6. He join. John Kirby in spring of '37 and pl. w. him regularly until '44, then on and off '45-6; Wilbur De Paris '46-9. In early '50s he led own qt. and worked w. Red Allen; w. Big Chief Russell Moore '52-3; pit orch. of *Porgy and Bess* '53-4; then rejoin. Allen at Metropole. He also occ. made app. in symph. orchs. under Leon Barzin, Everette Lee, Dmitri Mitropoulos. Briefly w. Tyree Glenn '59; then w. Wild Bill Davison '61-3; Saints and Sinners '63-4. He join. L. Armstrong's All-Stars in '65. Bailey was the first classically trained clst. to become a major jazz artist. Considered a pioneer on his instrument, his fluid, academic, yet swinging style distinguished him in the swing and pre-swing eras. Fests: NJF '57, '59; Great South Bay '57; Shakespeare Fest., Can. '58. Film: app. in *Splendor in the Grass* '62. LP: Felsted. CDs: w. Kirby (Col.); Henderson (Col.; BB); Red Allen; L. Hampton (BB); Armstrong (Aff.; Verve); Victoria Spivey/Lucille Hegamin (Prest.); Buck Clayton (Riv.); Nat Cole (Cap.); Wild Bill Davison (Jazz.); Roy Eldridge (Col.; Dec.); Bessie Smith; Billie Holiday (Col.); Teddy Grace (Timel.); Swingville All-Stars (GTJ).

BAILEY, COLIN JAMES, dms; b. Swindon, England, 7/9/34. Drums since age 4; pno. and theory

1946–9. Debut as accomp. to vaudeville pnst. Toured US, Austral. w. Austral. Jazz Qt. 1960–1. Moved to SF, worked w. Vince Guaraldi trio to Dec. '62. Dur. '60s, pl. w. Victor Feldman; George Shearing; Chet Baker; Ray Brown; Joe Pass; Joao Gilberto; Jim Hall; Clare Fischer. Japan w. Benny Goodman, Mar. '64, also other jobs w. Goodman qt., band. Subbed for Tony Williams in Miles Davis qt. TV series staff job w. Terry Gibbs combo. Dur. '70s, trav. w. Vic Damone, plus jobs w. Gibbs; R. Kellaway; Pass; Feldman; Joe Williams; Lockjaw Davis; Sweets Edison, Al Hirt. Often subbed in *Tonight Show* band. Eur. tours in '83 and '85 w. Richie Cole, Ernestine Anderson '89; Carol Sloane '90, '91; and Joe Pass '91. Two drum books w. worldwide distribution. Taught clinics, master classes, and at No. Tex. St. U. Favs: Jimmy Cobb, P.J. Jones, Joe Morello. CDs: w. Feldman (Conc.); Goodman (Limel.); Guaraldi (Fant.); Pass (Pab.).

BAILEY, CRAIG, alto, sop saxes, fl, cl; b. Cincinnati, OH, 2/3/60. Began on cl. at age 13. B. Mus., U. of Miami–Coral Gables 1984. Moved to NYC '85, first gigs subbing for Bobby Watson. Lead alto w. Charli Persip Superband II '85–7. Substitute teacher in NYC schs. '85–9. Pl. w. Panama Francis's Savoy Sultans, Nancie Banks bb '86–8; Jimmy Heath–Slide Hampton bb '87. Received NEA award '88. Lead alto sax w. Ray Charles Orch. '87–91; alto sax and cl. w. Bobby Watson Tailor Made bb '93; alto and sop. w. Ray Mantilla Space Station '94. Tour. w. *Black and Blue* revue '95–7. Bailey has been a member of the TanaReid Qnt. fr. '91 and leads his own qnt. and spt. Favs: alto: Cannonball Adderley; fl: Hubert Laws; arr: Oliver Nelson. Fests: all major w. P. Francis, TanaReid, B. Watson, own gps. TV: Greek TV w. own qnt. '97. CDs: Cand.; w. TanaReid (Conc.; Evid.); The Colossal Saxophone Sessions (Evid.); N. Banks (Invitation).

BAILEY, DAVE (SAMUEL DAVID), dms; b. Portsmouth, VA, 2/22/26. Raised in Philadelphia, Officer in AAF 1942–6. Moved to NYC '47, stud. under GI bill at Mus. Center Cons. An early disciple of Max Roach and Art Blakey, he pl. w. Herbie Jones '51–3; gigged w. Al Sears; Johnny Hodges; Lou Donaldson; Charles Mingus; Horace Silver; and Curtis Fuller. Acquired a major reputation while working w. Gerry Mulligan '55–9. Pl. w. Ben Webster '58; Billy Taylor '59; Art Farmer–Benny Golson Jazztet '59. Tour. in Brazil in '59, he stud. the bossa nova rhythms and demonstrated them on such recs. as Fuller's rec. of *South American Cooking* for Epic '61. In '60s, pl. w. Clark Terry–Bob Brookmeyer qnt.; then w. Terry '66–9. By the late '60s he had largely withdrawn fr.

pl., worked as a flight instr. at Westchester County Airport. Fr. '69 to '73 flew a Lear jet for F. Lee Bailey. Replaced B. Taylor as dir. of Jazzmobile '73. Films: soundtrack w. Lars Gullin for Italian movie in Milan '59; w. Mulligan, *The Subterraneans* '59. LPs: as leader, *One Foot in the Gutter*; *Into Something* (Epic); *Bash* (Jazzline). CDs: w. Mulligan (Col.; Verve; PJ); B. Taylor (Riv.); A. Farmer; L. Donaldson (BN); C. Fuller (Sav.); R. Kellaway (FS); C. Rouse (Col.); Grant Green (BL); B. Strayhorn (Red Brn.).

BAILEY, DEREK, gtr; b. Sheffield, England, 1/29/30; d. London, 12/25/05. Grandfather, prof. pno., bjost.; uncle, George Wing, prof. gtrst. Moved to London 1966; pl. free jazz w. John Stevens; Evan Parker; Paul Rutherford; et al. Join. Spontaneous Mus. Ens., which worked w. Tony Oxley's sxt. '68–73. Organized a trio, Iskra 1903, w. Rutherford and Barry Guy '70; form. a rec. co., Incus, w. Oxley and Parker. Fr. '76, led gp. Company, tour. Eur., Japan, Africa, and No. Amer.; also cont. to perf. as a soloist or in duos. In '77, started Company Week, a yearly, five-day, int'l fest of improvisation, held in London. A strong believer in free improv. and creative musical thinking, Bailey has had a powerful infl. on such younger players as Alan Holdsworth and Bill Frisell. Book: *Improvisation: Its Nature and Practice in Music* (Latimer Press, London) '80. TV: *On the Edge*, series based on his book. CDs: Incus; w. Peter Kowald; Cecil Taylor; Globe Unity Orch. (FMP).

BAILEY, DONALD ORLANDO (DUCK), dms, hca; b. Philadelphia, PA, 3/26/33. Self-taught. Also pl. tbn., saxes and pno. First prof. job w. Jimmy Smith for eight yrs. fr. 1955. Freelanced in LA fr. mid '60s w. Jack Wilson; Hampton Hawes; Freddie Hubbard; Joe Pass; Gene Ammons; Bobby Hutcherson; Gerald Wilson; Jimmy Rowles. In '70s app. as hca. soloist; occasionally billed as "Harmonica Man." Also pl. w. Bill Cosby; assisted Sonny Terry in movie sound track for *Buck and the Preacher*. One of the most respected and tasteful dmrs. of his generation. CDs: w. Jimmy Smith (BN); Bebop and Beyond (BM); G. Benson (Verve); P. Christlieb (Capri); H. Hawes (Cont.).

BAILEY, MILDRED (Rinker), voc, pno; b. on Coeur d'Alene reservation in Idaho near Tekoa, WA, 2/27/07; d. Poughkeepsie, NY, 12/12/51. Went to sch. in Spokane. Her bro., Al Rinker, was one of the orig. Rhythm Boys w. Paul Whiteman's band (w. Bing Crosby and Harry Barris). She began her professional career as a teenager, accomp. silent movies and as a song demonstrator; tour. w. revues and perf. on radio in Calif. W. Whiteman, 29–'33 and bec. the first female band voc. That yr. she began her prolific rec. career w. "What Kind O' Man Is You," w. Eddie Lang's orch. In '33, she married Red Norvo, a Whiteman sideman '33–4, and they settled in NYC. In '34–5 she was feat. regularly on the radio shows of George Jessel and Willard Robison. In '36, Norvo expanded the gp. he form. in '35 to a 12-pc. band that he and Bailey co-led to '39. They were billed as "Mr. and Mrs. Swing," and their band, known for its soft, subtle swing, was very popular and rec. regularly for Brunswick. She became known as the "Rockin' Chair Lady" after rec. Hoagy Carmichael's "Rockin' Chair" in '32. In '39 she was a frequent guest on Benny Goodman's radio show. Fr. '40, despite a recurrent illness, she worked as a single at Café Society, the Blue Angel, and other NYC clubs; in the mid '40s she had her own CBS radio show. Although seriously ill w. diabetes and heart trouble, she cont. perf. in '49 and was featured w. Joe Marsala in Chi., summer '50. In '51, after some tour., she was hospitalized in Poughkeepsie, where she died at the end of the yr. Bailey was originally inspired by Bessie Smith, Ethel Waters, and other early female blues singers. Partly of Native Amer. ancestry, she was the first non-black singer accepted in jazz, noted for her unique light soprano voice, jazz-inspired phrasing, flawless articulation, and innate sense of swing. Her many recs. w. Norvo, Teddy Wilson, John Kirby, Goodman, Coleman Hawkins, and others have earned her a lasting place in jazz history. CDs: Col.; Dec.; TOM; Vintage Jazz Classics; w. Norvo; R. Eldridge (Col.); B. Berigan (Pro Arte); Dorsey Bros. (Hep).

BAILEY, PEARL MAE (aka PEARLIE MAE), voc; b. Newport News, VA, 3/29/18; d. Philadelphia, PA, 8/17/90. Raised in Wash., D.C., and Phila. Bro. Bill was an entertainer, sist. Eura, a voc. In 1933, she won an amateur dancing contest at the Pearl Theater, Phila., and started working in touring shows. In the mid '30s she won a singing contest at the Apollo in NYC and soon was perf. w. several bbs, incl. Noble Sissle and Edgar Hayes. She perf. in USO tours fr. '42, then tour. w. Cootie Williams' bb '43–4. Her solo app. at the Village Vanguard '44 was followed by a long engagement at the Blue Angel '44–5 and an assoc. w. Cab Calloway. In '46 she starred in the B'way musical *St. Louis Woman* and scored hits on Col. recs. w. "Legalize My Name," "It's a Woman's Prerogative," and "Tired"—she repeated the latter song in her first film app., *Variety Girl* '47. By the late '40s, she was known nationally as a comedienne, but much of her work as a singer retained jazz qualities. She app. in several other films and on TV. In '52 she married Louis Bellson, w. whom she perf. and rec. regularly through the '60s. Won a Special Tony in

'68 for her starring role in an all-black version of *Hello, Dolly,* which ran on B'way '67–9. In '76 she announced her retirement fr. perf. to serve as a UN delegate, but eventually resumed tour., concert, and broadcast apps., often despite severe health problems. In '78, she was feat. at Pres. Carter's White House jazz party. Fest: Concord JF '74. Films: *Carmen Jones* '54; *That Certain Feeling* '56; *St. Louis Blues* '58; *All the Fine Young Cannibals* '60. Broadway: *House of Flowers* '54–5. TV: own series on ABC '70s. Book: autobiography, *The Raw Pearl* '68. CDs: Col.; Roul.

BAIN, BOB (ROBERT FURNISS), gtr; b. Chicago, IL, 1/26/24. Studied gtr. w. Joe Wolverton and comp. w. Mario Castelnuovo Tedesco. Joined Freddie Slack 1943, T. Dorsey '45–46; Bob Crosby '46–47; Harry James '47–48; André Previn Qt. '48–49; Phil Moore Four '49–50; then freelance studio gtr. in Hollywood until he join. Doc Severinsen's *Tonight Show* band in '72, remaining there for next twenty yrs. Rec. "Unforgettable" w. Nat Cole, "Opus One" w. T. Dorsey, many dates w. Nelson Riddle/Sinatra and H. Mancini. Favs: Django Reinhardt, Charlie Christian, Les Paul. CDs: w. L. Bellson (Pab.); T. Dorsey (BB; Hep); B. Holiday (Dec.).

BAKER, CHET (CHESNEY HENRY), tpt, voc; b. Yale, OK, 12/23/29; d. Amsterdam, Netherlands, 5/13/88. Family moved to Calif. in 1940. Start. mus. training at Glendale Junior HS; pl. tpt. in marching and dance bands. Drafted in '46; pl. in 298th Army Band in Berlin, Germ.; discharged in '48. Studied theory and harm. at El Camino Coll., LA. Re-enlisted to join Presidio Army Band in SF '50–2; dur. this period sat in nightly at Bop City. In '52, Baker pl. several dates on the West Coast w. Charlie Parker bef. join. Gerry Mulligan. Gained major recognition w. Mulligan's pianoless qt. His quiet, clear tone and subdued solos epitomized the "cool" style that Mulligan helped engender, and his sound was widely emulated. In '53 Baker left Mulligan, rejoined Parker briefly, and formed his own gps. In '55–6 he toured Eur., Iceland, and Engl.; in winter '57, tour. US w. Birdland All-Stars, then Scand. and Italy. Fr. '59 to '64, he lived in Eur., where he was often in legal trouble due to drug addiction; he served a prison sentence in Italy '60–1; was arrested in Germ. in '62, and sent to Switzerland instead of serving a sentence. In '64, after spending some time in a Germ. sanatorium, he ret. to the US, living and pl. w. his own qt. in NYC and LA to '68. Then, while in SF, he suffered severe injuries, incl. the loss of his teeth, fr. an assault by hoodlums; he stopped pl. for two yrs., then—w. the aid of methadone—gradually started making a comeback. In '74–5 he pl. in NYC and ret. to prominence through new recs. and a reunion w. Mulligan. In '70s he was again perf. frequently, cont. to do so until his tragic death in Amsterdam '88, after a fall or push fr. the window of his hotel room. Baker had a light pure sound and succinct phrasing that directly descended from Miles Davis, yet had its own distinct lyricism. When he made his comeback in the mid '70s, John Wilson of the *NY Times* said that he had "more range and assertiveness within the wistfully ruminative style with which he has always been associated." His singing voice was small, but his ballad style had an appealing intimacy, and his scatting was superbly musical. Polls: *DB* Critics New Star '53; *DB* Readers '53–4; *Met.* '54–5; *MM* '55; Germ. *Jazz Echo* '56, '58; *Playboy* '58. Film: *Let's Get Lost*, docu., '89. Book: autobiography, *As Though I Had Wings: The Lost Memoir* (St. Martin's Press) '97. CDs: boxed set, PJ; BB; Col.; Up.; Em.; Riv.; Jzld.; Gal.; Cont.; Mile.; Prest.; CC; Steep.; Enja; FS; Phil.; A&M; Timel.; Red; SN; w. Mulligan; Art Pepper (PJ); Miles Davis; Lighthouse All-Stars (Cont.); Stan Getz (FS; Sonet; Story.); Jim Hall (CTI); Lars Gullin (Drag.); Charlie Haden (SN); Charlie Parker (Stash).

BAKER, DAVID NATHANIEL, tbn, comp, cello, educ; b. Indianapolis, IN, 12/21/31. Earned Master of mus. ed. degree from Ind. U.; worked w. local bands and L. Hampton while earning doctorate. In Calif. w. Stan Kenton 1956; Maynard Ferguson '57; led own bb in Indianapolis '58–9. Awarded *DB* Hall of Fame scholarship to Berklee Sch. '59; att. Sch. of Jazz, Lenox, Mass., '59–60. Pl. w. Q. Jones and George Russell, early '60s. Problems w. his jaw forced him to sw. fr. tbn. to cello in '62; by the '70s he was pl. both instruments. Taught at Ind. U. from '66, eventually achieving position of Distinguished Profess. of Mus. and Dir. of Jazz Studies. Many comps. for various combinations of classical and jazz ens. *Levels*, a concerto for solo string bs., jazz band, winds, and strings, was nominated for a Pulitzer Prize '73. Received Int'l Assoc. of Jazz Educs. Hall of Fame Award '81. In '92 was Pres. of the National Jazz Service Organization and a member of the National Council for the Arts. Mus. dir. of Smithsonian Jazz Orch. fr. '91. CDs: Smithsonian; w. G. Russell (Riv.).

BAKER, GINGER, dms; b. London, England, 8/19/40. Began on tpt., also stud. theory. While at sch. sw. to dms., pl. w. jazz bands of various styles. Met bs. Jack Bruce and worked w. him in the gps. of Alexis Korner and Graham Bond, early 1960s. Form. Cream, one of the first jazz-rock gps., w. Bruce and Eric Clapton '66. When it disbanded in '69, he and Clapton became part of the newly formed Blind Faith. Then he led Air Force which feat. tnr. sax Harold McNair and Phil Seamen, dms. In the early '70s, after a sojourn in Nigeria—where he operated his own rec. studio, worked and rec. w. Fela Kuti and the band Salt—he ret. to the UK and resumed lead. own gps. and working as a sideman in other rock units. Moved to Italy in '80s but, after semi-retirement, was back pl. by mid decade. In '94 and '96, he rec. as a trio lead w. Bill Frisell and Charlie Haden. CDs: Atl.

BAKER, KENNY (KENNETH), tpt, crnt, flg; b. Withersnea, Yorks., Eng., 3/1/21; d. Felpham, Eng., 12/7/99. Learned pno. at home; took up crnt. at 12 in local brass band. Made prof. debut in London 1939. Pl. w. Lew Stone '41; Geo. Chisholm '44; also worked w. Maurice Winnick; Jack Hylton; Bert Ambrose; Sid Millward. Pl. lead tpt. and arr. for Ted Heath '44–9. Studio and film work '49–51, incl. *The Red Shoes;* tpt. solos for Kay Kendall in *Genevieve* '54, etc. Led own gp., Baker's Dozen, on BBC radio prog. *Let's Settle For Music* '51–9. Pl. w. MM All-Stars '57–8. Rec. w. Benny Goodman '69; George Chisholm '71, '73; Johnny Patrick, pl. mus. of Harry James, '76. Form. show, *Best Of British Jazz*, w. Betty Smith, Don Lusher, which tour. fr. '76. In the '80s, Baker pl. in revivals of Ted Heath's mus. He pl. solo tpt. on the soundtracks to the TV progs. *The Beiderbecke Affair* and *The Beiderbecke Tapes*. Max Jones observed that Baker "has maintained the highest musical standards, and his enthusiasm for jazz in the mainstream idiom." LPs on Dormouse. Baker's CDs, *The Louis Armstrong Connection* on Magic Music, recreate Armstrong's recs. in a combination of his tpt. and dubbing of Armstrong's orig. vocals. Other CDs: Horatio Nelson; Big Bear.

BAKER, SHORTY (HAROLD J.), tpt; b. St. Louis, MO, 5/26/14; d. NYC, 11/8/66. Studied dms. first but made his debut on tpt. in orch. of his bro., tbnst. Winfield Baker, late 1920s. Pl. w. Fate Marable and, in Chi., w. Erskine Tate, early '30s; in St. Louis w. Eddie Johnson's Cracker Jacks '32–3. Worked w. Don Redman '36–8; Teddy Wilson bb '39–40; Andy Kirk '40–2, where he met Mary Lou Williams, whom he married '42; pl. w. her band. An association begun w. Duke Ellington, Jan.-April '38, was resumed in Nov. '43. He remained w. Ellington until Dec. '51, excepting army service '44–6; feat. on "Trumpet No End," Williams' arr. of "Blue Skies" '46; also "Times A-Wastin'" '44; "Three Cent Stomp" '47. Freelanced in East w. Teddy Wilson, Ben Webster '52; w. Johnny Hodges band '54–5. Rejoin. Ellington, May '57 until Sept. '59. Formed own qt., pl. at Embers; also worked as sideman at Metropole Café, NYC. Rec. w. Bud

Freeman. A lyrical, economic player w. a fine tone and an excellent sense of dynamics. CDs: Shorty Baker/Doc Cheatham (Prest.); Ellington (Col.; BB; Prest.; Saja); J. Hodges (Prest.; Vogue); E. Fitzgerald (Verve); Russell Procope in *Giants of Small Band Swing*, Vol. 1 (Riv.).

BALES, BURT (BURTON FRANK), pno, voc; also mello, bari sax; b. Stevensville, MT, 3/20/16; d. San Francisco, CA, 10/26/89. Private pno. study from age 12; pl. in speakeasies in Santa Cruz, Calif., early 1930s. In '40s worked w. Lu Watters '42; Bunk Johnson '43; Dude Martin '44; own gp. and solo work '45–9. Briefly rejoined Watters '59; then w. Turk Murphy in SF '49–50. Rec. as a leader in '49, '50, and '57. Played w. Bob Scobey '50 and '53; Marty Marsala '54. Living in SF, worked at Pier 23 as solo pnst. '54–66. In '66, went to electronics sch., grad. in '69 as electronic tech. Returned to active perf. '75, pl. mainly solo. Fr. '75 into '80s freelanced in SF clubs incl. Washington Square Bar & Grill. Favs: Jelly Roll Morton, F. Waller, J.P. Johnson, J. Sullivan, Don Ewell, Ralph Sutton. CDs: Burt Bales–Paul Lingle, *They Tore My Playhouse Down* (GTJ); w. Bunk Johnson; T. Murphy; B. Scobey; and *The Good Time Jazz Story*, boxed set (GTJ); Frank Goudie (Story.).

BALL, KENNY (KENNETH DANIEL), tpt, voc; b. Ilford, Essex, England, 5/22/30. Played tpt. as a teen; in 1950s worked w. Dixie gps. of Charlie Galbraith, Sid Phillips, and Eric Delaney. First rec. as lead. '57; organized own band, The Jazzmen, '58. Prod. several hit singles incl. "I Love You Samantha" and "Midnight in Moscow," both '61. Did cabaret work and then suffered lip trouble in mid '60s; ret. to active pl. '68 for Louis Armstrong London concerts. Tour. Engl. and Eur. in '70s w. The Jazzmen. Many TV apps., incl. *Morecambe & Wise* series '64–72, made him a popular figure in Engl. in the '80s. First Engl. jazz gp. to tour Soviet Union '85. Cont. to tour and rec. into the '90s. Favs: Armstrong, Beiderbecke, Kenny Baker, Clifford Brown. A melodic improviser w. a strong, warm sound. LPs: Timel.; Pye. CDs: Kaz; MFP.

BALL, RONNIE (RONALD), pno; b. Birmingham, England, 12/22/27; d. NYC, 1984. At 15 pl. w. local bands. Moved to London 1948, rec. w. Tony Kinsey, Ronnie Scott, Victor Feldman. Worked in bands on Cunard ocean liners bet. Southhampton and NYC bef. emigrating to US '52, cont. his stud. w. Lennie Tristano. Pl. w. Chuck Wayne '52; Lee Konitz '53–5. Rec. own album, and w. J.J. Johnson–Kai Winding for Sav. '56. Moved to Calif., worked w. Warne Marsh qnt. '56–7; own trio w. Red Mitchell, Dennis

Budimir fall '57. Pl. w. Buddy Rich and Winding combos '58, bef. join. Gene Krupa qt. Oct. '58 for clubs and fests. Brief stint w. Roy Eldridge '59. Accomp. Chris Connor '61–3. Recs. w. Konitz, Marsh, Ted Brown, LA '56; Sims-Cohn-Dorham, Rio '61. CDs: w. Konitz (BL); Marsh in *Tristano & Marsh* (Cap.); Marsh (VSOP); Krupa (Verve); K. Clarke; H. Mobley (Sav.); A. Pepper (Cont.).

BALLAMY, IAIN MARK, saxes; b. Guildford, England, 2/20/64. Alto fr. 1978, then tnr. Led qnt. '83; soon after, joined John Graham Collier in band that later became known as Loose Tubes. Rec. w. Gil Evans for film *Absolute Beginners* '85; has also been active as teacher and comp. App. at MJF '93. CDs: w. John Donaldson (Koch Jz.); Michael Gibbs (Ah Um).

BALLANTYNE, JON WILLIAM, pno, comp; b. Prince Albert, Sask., Canada, 10/8/63. Raised in Saskatoon; introduced to jazz by fath., Fred, a pnst. Studied w. Maisie Calverly 1973–81; at No. Tex. St. U. '82–5; Banff Jazz Wkshp. '81, '84–5. Pl. w. Woody Herman Orch. '87; Joe Henderson '89–90. Own trio in Montreal in '90s; some apps. at Sweet Basil, NYC. Polls: Concours de Jazz de Montreal prize '86; Juno Award '89. Fests: Paris '86; US, Japan, Eur. w. Henderson '89–90; all major in Can. CDs: JT; w. John Nugent (Unity).

BALLARD, BUTCH (GEORGE EDWARD), dms; b. Camden, NJ, 12/26/17. Played w. Fats Waller; worked w. Cootie Williams 1942. Served in navy dur. WWII. Pl.w. L. Armstrong '46; Lockjaw Davis at Minton's; I. Jacquet '47. Led own band in Phila., '47–8. Join. Mercer Ellington '48; Count Basie '49; tour. Eur. w. Duke Ellington, along w. Sonny Greer, '50. Work w. Ellington again for a few mos. '53. Dur. the late '50s led own band in Phila., other eastern cities, and Can. Backed Nina Simone, Dinah Washington, Sonny Stitt, etc. at Showboat in Phila. Fr. early '80s teaching in Phila. Tour. Eur. fests. w. Clark Terry's Spacemen '89. CDs: w. Ellington (Cap.); Basie (BB); Terry (Chiaro.); w. Eddie Vinson in *The 1940s Mercury Sessions* (Merc.).

BALTAZAR, GABE (GABRIEL RUIZ JR.), alto sax, fl, cl; b. Hilo, HI, 11/1/29. Musical family; stud. at Interlochen Mus. Camp, Peabody Cons., and LA St. Coll. Moved to Calif. in mid 1950s. Rec. w. dmr. Paul Togawa for Mode '57. Worked w. Lighthouse All-Stars '60; Stan Kenton '60–5; Neophonic Orch. '65–6; in '60s also app. w. Howard Rumsey; Shelly Manne; Oliver Nelson; Gil Fuller; Onzy Matthews; Victor Feldman; Terry Gibbs; Don Ellis. Living in Hawaii '70s and '80s; Deputy Bandmaster of Royal

Hawaiian Band fr. '69. Active pl. and teach. jazz in Hawaii fr. early '70s. Rec. own bb '79. App. at Kenton fiftieth anniversary celebration at Newport Beach, Calif., '91. CDs: VSOP; FS; w. Kenton (Cap.; CW); *Back to Balboa*, Kenton 50th anniversary celebration (MAMA).

BANG, BILLY (William Vincent Walker), vln, comp; b. Mobile, AL, 9/20/47. Began on bongos, sw. to vln. at 12. Studied at Stockbridge Sch. 1961–3; Queens Coll., NYC, and w. Leroy Jenkins '73. Pl. in Music Ens. w. Daniel Carter, Dewey Johnson '72–5; Survival Ens. '75; Frank Lowe Orch.; String Trio of NY w. James Emery, John Lindberg '77; Ronald Shannon Jackson and Decoding Society '79–80; Marilyn Crispell '81–3; Sun Ra Orch. fr. '82; w. Sonny Sharrock in the band Material. Solomonic Sxt. w. Ahmed Abdullah fr. '90; also much freelance. Bang taught at the U. of Nebraska '81. Favs: Coltrane, Jackie McLean, Dolphy. Fests: Eur., Japan, Hong Kong. Films: app. in film w. Sun Ra. TV: PBS. CDs: JT; SN; Celluloid; w. String Trio of NY; Marilyn Crispell (BS); Kip Hanrahan (Amer. Clave); J. Lindberg; Das Pferd (ITM); Kahil El Zabar (SA).

BANK, DANNY (DANIEL BERNARD), bari sax, fl, cl, b-cl; b. Brooklyn, NY, 7/17/22. Played and rec. w. Charlie Barnet 1942–4; Benny Goodman '45–6; Paul Whiteman '46–7; Jimmy Dorsey '47–8. Rejoin. Barnet '48–9. With Artie Shaw '49–50; Tommy Dorsey '50–1. Freelance in NYC fr. '51, mainly as highly valued section man in studio bbs. Rec. in bb w. Charlie Parker '52; Dizzy Gillespie '54–5; Cannonball Adderley '56; Miles Davis–Gil Evans, on b-cl., '57–62; Johnny Hodges '66–7, '70; Louis Armstrong '70; many others. Perf. w. B. Goodman in '86. Tour. Japan in '89 w. Gunther Schuller and bb perf. Duke Ellington comps. In mid '90s w. Jimmy Heath bb. Favs: Harry Carney, Jack Washington. CDs: w. C. Barnet (Dec.); M. Davis (Col.); Clifford Brown (Em.); Eddie "Lockjaw" Davis (BB); Art Farmer (Prest.); D. Gillespie; C. Parker; Gene Krupa; Wes Montgomery; Jimmy Smith (Verve); Billie Holiday (Polyd.); Helen Merrill (Verve; Em.); Oliver Nelson (RCA); Buddy Rich (Sequel); G. Wallington; Stanley Turrentine (BN).

BANKS, BILLY (WILLIAM), voc; b. Alton, IL, ca. 1908; d. Tokyo, Japan, 10/19/67. Best known for a series of 1932 recs. made under his name or as the Rhythmakers w. Fats Waller; Red Allen; Eddie Condon; Tommy Dorsey; Pee Wee Russell; Zutty Singleton. Join. Noble Sissle in '34 and worked at Billy Rose's Diamond Horseshoe '38–48. In '52 tour. Engl. and the Continent as variety artist, then Asia and Aus-tral., settling in Japan after '57. CD: w. S. Bechet (Class.); Mills Blue Rhythm Band (Hep).

BANKS, CLARENCE LEROY, tbn; b. Englewood, NJ, 6/13/52. Cousin is club date org. Wife is comp.-arr. Nancie Banks in whose bb he perfs. Studied w. Chas. Levine at Dwight Morrow HS, 1969–71; Curtis Fuller at Jazzmobile '70–1; Arnold Frome at Fairleigh Dickinson U. '72–4. Pl. w. Slide Hampton's World of Tbns. '79–80; Kid Creole and the Coconuts '80–1; *Ain't Misbehavin'* world tour '81–2; Charli Persip Superband '81–3; Count Basie Orch. fr. '84. Favs: J.J. Johnson, Slide Hampton, Frank Rosolino. Fests: all major w. Basie Orch. Film: *The Cotton Club*. TV: Cosby Show w. Basie Orch. CDs: w. S. Hampton (BL); C. Persip (SN); C. Basie (Den.; Tel.); Diane Schuur–Basie Orch (GRP); Nancie Banks (CAP).

BAQUET, GEORGE F., cl; b. New Orleans, LA, 1883; d. New Orleans, 1/14/49. Father, clst. Theogene V. Baquet (b. & d. NO, 1858–1920), founded Excelsior Brass Band in 1880 and led it until '04. Bro., Achille (Joe) Baquet, cl. (b. NO, 11/15/1885; d. Hollywood, CA, 11/20/56), worked w. Papa Jack Laine's Reliance Brass Band and in NYC fr. '15 w. Jimmy Durante's Original NO Jazz Band, w. whom he rec. '18–20 bef. moving to LA in '20. George pl. E-flat cl. in fath.'s Lyre Club Symph. Orch. at age 14. Pl. w. Onward Brass Band, '00; Manuel Perez's Imperial Orch., '01–2. Other than the period '02–4, when he tour. w. P. T. Wright's Georgia Minstrels, he worked in NO w. a variety of bands, inc. Buddy Bolden, John Robichaux '04; Superior Band '06; Magnolia and Olympia Orchs. '08–14, until he left for LA to pl. w. Bill Johnson's Original Creole Orch., which app. in Chi., NYC. Gigged in NYC '16, incl. Coney Island. Moved to Phila. '17, where he led own gp. NO Nighthawks, known as George Baquet's Swingsters dur. '30s. Rec. w. Jelly Roll Morton '29: "Burnin' the Iceberg," "Tank Town Bump," "Sweet Anita Mine." Infl. on Sidney Bechet, Jimmie Noone. It has been suggested that the famed cl. solo on "High Society," generally attributed to Alphonse Picou, is actually Baquet's creation. CDs: w. Bessie Smith (Col.); Jelly Roll Morton (BB).

BARANCO, WILBERT, pno, voc; b. United States, ca. 1912. Worked w. Curtis Mosby in early 1930s; later pl. in band dur. mil. service. Rec. in LA '45 w. Ernie Andrews as well as his own trio, incl. Charles Mingus; also accomp. Dinah Washington w. Lucky Thompson's All-Stars. Organized Rhythm Bombardiers w. former servicemen; gp. rec. w. Vic Dickenson, Willie Smith, Dizzy Gillespie, et al. Rec. w.

Mingus, '46; led own trio, '47. Fr. late '40s worked as mus. teacher. CDs: w. D. Washington (Del.).

BARBARIN, (ADOLPHE) PAUL, dms; b. New Orleans, LA, 5/5/1899; d. New Orleans, 2/17/1969. Father, Isadore Barbarin (b. NO, 9/24/1872; d. 6/12/60), was grandfath. of Danny Barker, pl. mello. and alto horn w. Onward Brass Band, Excelsior, Tuxedo Brass Bands. Rec. w. Bunk Johnson 1945. Bro. Louis pl. dms., pl. w. Onward Brass Band '18 and w. Kid Rena, Punch Miller, Sidney Desvigne; fr. '37, Louis pl. w. Papa Celestin and Albert French and was active until retirement in '82. Paul began on cl. at 15, dms. at 16. Pl. w. Silver Leaf Orch. and Young Olympia Bd. Went to Chi. '17 to work in stockyards; by '18, had pl. w. King Oliver, Jimmie Noone. Ret. to NO '20, pl. w. Albert Nicholas. Worked w. Oliver in Chi. '24–7. Back to NO '27 for jobs w. Fats Pichon, Armand Piron. To NYC '28, pl. w. Luis Russell. Orch. sometimes under leadership of Louis Armstrong or Jelly Roll Morton '29–35. Fr. '35, band led by Armstrong; Barbarin remained into '39 when he ret. to NO. Pl. in Chi. w. Red Allen '42–3; worked w. Sidney Bechet '44; Art Hodes, Chi. '53; own band NYC, LA '55. However, fr. '39 until his death, most of his pl. was on snare and bass dms. w. brass bands and small gps. in NO. Reformed Onward Brass Band '60. While leading it in the pre–Mardi Gras Proteus Carnival parade, he died of a heart attack. TV: *Today* '56; *Wide, Wide World* '58. Comp.: "Bourbon St. Parade." Recs. as lead. Atl.; Riv.; Nob. CDs: Atl.; Story.; tracks on *Recorded in New Orleans, Vol.1* (GTJ); w. Armstrong (Col.; Dec.); King Oliver; Johnny Dodds (Aff.).

BARBARO, CLIFFORD, dms; b. NYC, 6/7/38. Father pl. tbn. Start. on dms. in band at George Washington HS. Stud. briefly w. Philly Joe Jones in 1960s; Stanley Spector '69–70. Pl. w. Lionel Hampton '69; Ray Bryant; then w. John Hicks '74; Betty Carter '74–8; Charles Tolliver '78–83; Sadik Hakim '80; Barry Harris '83; Jon Hendricks '83–7; Sun Ra '87–9; Walter Bishop Jr. in '80s; New York HardBop Qnt. fr. '95; James Carter '97; Sherman Irby '98. In trio, Bop Juice, w. Ralph Lalama and bs. Joel Forbes at Savoy Lounge fr. '98. Favs: Philly Joes Jones, Louis Hayes, Tony Williams, Jack DeJohnette. Pl. at Pescara JF, Italy, w. Bishop '95. CDs: w. NY Hard-Bop Qnt. (TCB); Sun Ra (BL); Betty Carter (Roul.); Tolliver (Strata-East); Irby (BN).

BARBER, BILL (JOHN WILLIAM), tba; b. Hornell, NY, 5/21/20. Son is prof. club date mus. Received B. Mus. fr. Juilliard 1942; M. Mus. Ed. fr. Manh. Sch. of Mus. Pl. w. 7th Army Band '42–5;

K.C. Philharm. '45–7; Claude Thornhill '47–8; Miles Davis Nonet '49; Sauter-Finegan Orch. '52–4; Pete Rugolo '54; Miles Davis–Gil Evans '57–62; Geo. Shearing '59; Goldman Concert Band fr. mid '60s; also much freelance work incl. B'way shows, TV, City Center Ballet. Taught mus. in public sch. on Long Island, NY, fr. '60. Pl. w. Gerry Mulligan Rebirth of the Cool band '92. Barber is cons. the first mus. to pl. mod. jazz on the tba. Fav. arr: Gil Evans. Fest: Eur. w. Mulligan '92. CDs: w. Mulligan (GRP); M. Davis (Cap.; BN; Col.); Kenny Burrell; Gil Evans (Verve); John Coltrane (Imp.).

BARBER, CHRIS (DONALD CHRISTOPHER), tbn; bandleader; b. Welwyn Garden City, England, 4/17/30. Played vln., sop. sax first; later stud. tbn., bs. at Guildhall Sch. of Mus. Start. first band 1949; helped organize band w. Ken Colyer '53; took it over himself '54. The band, which pl. traditional NO-style mus., enjoyed phenomenal success through '50s, pl. to packed houses all over Eur. Band tour. US, in wake of hit rec. of Sidney Bechet's "Petite Fleur" '59; app. at MJF. Barber's band was one of the first to rediscover Scott Joplin rags and perf. them. He also occ. worked w. such non-traditional mus. as Bertie King and Joe Harriott and helped expand British understanding of r&b by importing such Amer. blues mus. as Sonny Terry, Muddy Waters, Brownie McGhee for apps. in Engl. His American Jazz Band, feat. Sidney DeParis, Hank Duncan, and Edmond Hall, rec. two albums, starting '59. In early '60s, the gp. was reorganized as Chris Barber's Jazz and Blues Band, often employing blues and rock mus.; many tours of Eur., '60s and '70s. In '76 toured Engl. w. "Echoes of Ellington," feat. Russell Procope and Wild Bill Davison. Collaborated w. NO pnst. Dr. John in a show, *Take Me Back to New Orleans*, perf. in US, Engl., and Eur. '81–2. The band remained active into the '90s, occ. changing style and orientation to adapt to new ideas in pop mus. and jazz. CDs: Story., Timel.; BL; Teldec; Zounds; Bell; w. Louis Jordan (BL).

BARBIERI, GATO (LEANDRO J.), tnr sax, comp, arr; b. Rosario, Argentina, 11/28/34. Uncle pl. tnr. sax. Attracted to jazz after hearing Charlie Parker rec. Studied at Infancia Desvalida, Rosario 1944. Family moved to Buenos Aires '47. Studied cl. priv. '47–52; also stud. alto, comp., then tnr. fr. age 20. Pl. w. Lalo Schifrin '53. After coming to prominence in Buenos Aires, Barbieri lived in Brazil for several mos. ca. '61, then moved to Rome '62. Pl. in Eur. w. Ted Curson, Jim Hall, Don Cherry '65–7. Rec. w. Cherry in NYC '67. Comp. mus. for Gianni Amico film *Notes for a Film on Jazz*, ca. '68. After leaving Cherry, Barbieri began to focus on the fusion of jazz and Latin mus. He rec. his first Amer. LP as a lead., *The Third World*, for the Flying Dutchman label in '69, then ret. to Argentina in '70. He won a Grammy award in '72 for his score to the film *Last Tango in Paris*, and in '73 began tour. w. a large gp. of So. Amer. mus. In the mid '70s, he began to perf. in a more commercial style, but by the late '80s ret. to his So. Amer. roots. Polls: *DB* TDWR '72. Fests: all major fr. '71. Film: app. in *Last Tango in Paris*. CDs: ESP; Imp.; RCA; Aff.; w. Carla Bley (ECM); D. Cherry (Mos.; Magnetic); Charlie Haden (Imp.); Jazz Comp. Orch. (JCOA).

BARBOUR, DAVE (DAVID MICHAEL), gtr; b. NYC, 5/28/12; d. Malibu, CA, 12/11/65. Played bjo. in coll., then gtr. w. Wingy Manone 1934; Red Norvo '35-6; Lenny Hayton '36-7; Hal Kemp '38; Artie Shaw '39; also w. Raymond Scott, Glenn Miller. Was active dur. '30s as a studio mus., rec. w. Louis and Lil Armstrong; Mildred Bailey; Teddy Wilson; Bunny Berigan. With Benny Goodman '42-3 where he met Peggy Lee. Married '43-52, he was her mus. dir., co-writing w. her such hits as "Manana" and "It's a Good Day." Dur. this period, he also rec. w. Jack Teagarden; Charlie Barnet; Boyd Raeburn. Pl. in Havana w. Woody Herman band '49. In '50s accomp. Nellie Lutcher, Jeri Southern for recs. App. as actor in film, *Secret Fury*, w. Claudette Colbert '51. In mus. retirement from mid '50s, he rec. w. Benny Carter '62. CDs: w. Goodman; B. Holiday (Col.); Benny Carter (Prest.); Nat Cole (Cap.); Teddy Grace (Timel.); Louis Armstrong; Lil Armstrong; B. Berigan (Class.).

BARCELONA, DANNY (DANIEL), dms; b. Honolulu, HI, 7/23/29. Self-taught. Tour. Far East w. Trummy Young's Hawaii Dixie All-Stars 1948-51. When Young joined Louis Armstrong in '52, Barcelona took over as lead. of the gp. until '53. Pl. w. revues and club date bands at Hawaiian resorts '53-7, then moved to NYC '57. Pl. w. Louis Armstrong fr. '58 until Armstrong's death in '71, then ret. to Honolulu. Pl. w. local gps. '71-9, then moved to Monterey Park, Calif., '79. Favs: Gene Krupa, Buddy Rich, Max Roach. Fests: all major fr. '58; Nice JF w. NYJRC '77. Film & TV: apps. w. Armstrong. CDs: w. Armstrong (Col.; Verve; LRC; Roul.; Story.; EPM Musique).

BAREFIELD, EDDIE (EDWARD EMMAN-UEL), saxes, cl, arr; b. Scandia, IA, 12/12/09; d. NYC, 1/3/91. Studied pno. at 10, alto sax at 13, pl. by ear until 17; cl. at cons. in Chi. 1930. First prof. job w. Edgar Pillows' Night Owls in Des Moines, Iowa, '26; in late '20s and early '30s pl w. such territory units as Isier's Gravy Show; West Va. Ravens; the Ethiopian

Serenaders; Oscar "Bernie" Young, etc. Led and co-led small gps. in Minneapolis bef. join. Bennie Moten '32; pl. w. Zack Whyte '33; briefly led his own band; then w. the Cotton Pickers. Worked w. Cab Calloway '33-6 and off and on to '58. To LA mid '30s; pl. w. Charlie Echols; form. own bb '36; worked w. Les Hite '37. Join. Fletcher Henderson '38; Don Redman '38; Ella Fitzgerald '40. Own band '40; also pl. w. Coleman Hawkins, Benny Carter, et al; staff mus. at ABC and WOR radio, NYC, '42-6; w. Duke Ellington '47. Cond. pit orchs. and orchestrated for B'way musicals '48-70. Mus. dir. for *Streetcar Named Desire* '48-9. With Sy Oliver at Zanzibar, NYC, '50; to Brazil and Uruguay w. Calloway '51; tour. w. Redman '53; briefly pl. w. Dukes of Dixieland '55; also freelanced extensively, incl. as mus. dir. for Calloway's revues in Miami, LV, '57. Tour. Eur. w. Sammy Price '58. Cond. and arr. *Jazz Train* revue in Eur. '60. Pl. w. Paul Lavalle '63, '65; Wilbur De Paris '64, Saints & Sinners '69. Member of orch. for Ringling Bros. and Barnum & Bailey Circus '71-82; cont. freelancing into '90s, w. Stan Rubin; the Harlem Blues and Jazz Band; and Illinois Jacquet's orch. Although primarily an alto sax for most of his career, he ret. to his first love, tnr. sax, in his last yrs. A dependable section player and soloist, Barefield also was a talented orchestrator who wrote charts for Moten—incl. "Toby," which feat. him on cl.; Calloway; Glenn Miller; Paul Whiteman; B. Goodman; J. Dorsey; etc. Fav: Benny Carter. Fav. own solo: "Moonglow" w. Calloway. Film: app. w. Calloway in *The Singing Kid* '36; *Everyday's a Holiday* w. Armstrong '37; *The Night They Raided Minsky's* '68. LP: *The Indestructible Eddie Barefield* (Famous Door). CDs: w. Basie (BB); Benny Carter (BB; Class.); Calloway; Don Redman; Pete Johnson; L. Hampton (Class.); Milt Hinton (Chiaro); F. Henderson; B. Holiday (Col.); B. Moten (BB; Class.); Coleman Hawkins (Prest.).

BARGAD, ROB (ROBERT CARL), pno; b. Boston, MA, 9/7/62. Father is amateur gtrst., pnst., crnst., bsst. Began pno. lessons at age 8. Pl. first gigs while att. New Trier HS, Northfield, Ill. Att. Rutgers U. (N.J.) jazz prog. 1981-4. Recommended to Lionel Hampton by Paul Jeffrey, who was a profess. at Rutgers. Moved to NYC '84, pl. w. Leo Johnson, Little Jimmy Scott, Dakota Staton bef. join. Hampton in '87. Pl. w. own qt. since '88; Nat Adderley qnt. since '91. Bargad has also worked w. the Harper Bros. and Dakota Staton Trio, and led own bb, Jazz Unit 17. Favs: Wynton Kelly, Hampton Hawes, Larry Willis. Fests: Eur. and Japan. TV: two PBS specials w. L. Hampton; Eur. TV w. Hampton and N. Adderley. CDs: CC; w. N. Adderley (ALCR; Land.).

BARGERON, DAVE (DAVID WAYNE), tbn, b-tbn, euph, tba; b. Athol, MA, 9/6/42. Grandfather on fath.'s side had family band, The Musical Bargerons, that pl. dances and concerts in New Engl. 1930s-40s. Began on pno. at age 7; sw. to tbn. at age 11. B. Mus., Bost. U. '64. Pl. tbn. and tba. in dixieland bands in NYC and Bost., and taught inst. mus. in NYC sch. until Jack Jeffers got him a job in Clark Terry bb '68. Made rec. debut w. Ernie Wilkins bb '68. Perf. and rec. w. Doc Severinsen's New Generation Brass '68–9; Blood, Sweat and Tears '70–8; Jaco Pastorius '80–3. Pl. w. Howard Johnson's Gravity since '68; Gil Evans Orch. since '72; Bob Mintzer since '80; Geo. Gruntz since '80; Geo. Russell since '89. In '91, Bargeron app. w. Miles Davis and Quincy Jones pl. Gil Evans arr. at Montreux and rec. w. Gerry Mulligan's Re-birth of the Cool band. Favs: Carl Fontana; arrs: Gil Evans, G. Russell. Polls: NARAS Most Val. Pl., bs-tbn. '89. Fests: Eur., Asia, Austral. and NZ every yr. since '70. CDs: w. B, S and T (Col.); B. Mintzer (DMP); G. Mulligan (GRP); Geo. Gruntz (Enja); Peter Erskine (Den.); G. Evans (Elec. Bird; Jazz Door; New Tone; BH); D. Sanborn (Elek.);Chris Hunter (Sw. Bas.); M. Davis–Q. Jones (WB).

BARKER, BLUE LU (Louise Dupont), voc; b. New Orleans, LA, 11/13/13; d. New Orleans, 5/7/98. Sang and danced locally; married Danny Barker 1930 and rec. series of blues sess. for Dec., Apollo, and Cap. in '30s and '40s. After ret. to NO, she cont. to app. occ. in public and took part in a jazz cruise w. husband on the *Norway* in '87. CDs: w. Willie Pajeaud (504).

BARKER, DANNY (DANIEL MOSES), gtr, bjo, voc, comp; b. New Orleans, LA, 1/13/09; d. New Orleans, 3/13/94. Studied cl. w. Barney Bigard, dms. w. his uncle, Paul Barbarin, later taking up uke. and bjo. Tour. southern states w. Little Bro. Montgomery, Lee Collins, and others in 1920s. Moved to NYC '30, sw. fr. bjo. to gtr. and pl. w. Dave Nelson '31; Fess Williams; Albert Nicholas; James P. Johnson; then a series of bbs incl. Lucky Millinder '37–38; Benny Carter '38; Cab Calloway '39–46. Pl. on trad. revival recs. and radio shows reverting to bjo. in NYC '47, LA '48–49. Back in NYC, worked w. Conrad Janis and Wilbur De Paris, and own band. Also w. Eubie Blake at NJF '60 and Cliff Jackson at Ryan's '63. Fr. '65 to '75 he was curator of the NO Jazz Museum, then became Grand Marshal of the Onward Brass Band for seven yrs. An eloquent spokesman for early NO jazz, he gave lectures and wrote articles while cont. to app. occ. w. various gps. and w. his wife, Blue Lu Barker. App. w. Wynton Marsalis and NO gps. at Lincoln Center '90. Lifetime Achievement Award fr. National Endowment for the Humanities '91. Books:

Bourbon Street Black w. Jack Buerkle '73; *A Life in Jazz* '86. His comps. incl. "Save the Bones for Henry Jones," rec. by Nat Cole; and "Don't You Make Me High," rec. w. Blue Lu Barker. CDs: w. Red Allen; Teddy Wilson (Class.); C. Calloway (Class.; Col.); Sir Charles Thompson (Del.); P. Barbarin (Atl.); W. Marsalis; Dirty Dozen Brass Band (Col.); Mary Osborne (Stash); Wille Pajeaud (504); Bob Wilber (Cir.); Wild Bill Davison (Jazz.).

BARKER, GUY, tpt; b. London, England, 12/26/57. Studied at Royal Coll. of Mus. Received encouragement fr. Clark Terry, Dizzy Gillespie. Pl. w. Mike Westbrook Orch.; John Dankworth Orch.; Stan Tracey sxt., oct., bb; Peter King; Gil Evans Orch. in Engl., US; Ornette Coleman; Carla Bley. Awards from Wavendon All Music; British Jazz Awards. His work encompasses a wide stylistic range. Pl. on many movie soundtracks, TV and radio shows. Rec. w. Joe Henderson; Nat Adderley; Gil Evans. CDs: Spot.; w. Van Morrison (Verve); Tommy Smith (BN; Honest); C. Bley (Watt); Joe Gallivan (Cad.); Mel Tormé (Conc.); Stan Tracey (BN; Steam); M. Westbrook (Enja); Barbara Thompson (Vera Bra); Keith Nichols (Stomp Off); Nat. Youth Jazz Orch. (NYJO).

BARKER, THURMAN, dms, perc; b. Chicago, IL, 1/8/48. Studied at Roosevelt U.; early participant in AACM. In mid and late 1960s pl. w. Anthony Braxton; Joseph Jarman; Muhal Richard Abrams; and Kalaparusha Maurice McIntyre. Rec. and tour. w. Braxton '78–80; Sam Rivers '79–80; trio work w. Jarman and Rivers '85; marimba w. Cecil Taylor qnt. '87. Book: incl. in *As Serious As Your Life*, Valerie Wilmer '80. CDs: w. Art Ensemble of Chi. (Nessa); M.R. Abrams (BS; Del.); Billy Bang (SN); A. Braxton (hatArt); J. Jarman (Del.); John Lindberg (WW); Roscoe Mitchell (Chief); Butch Morris (SA); Amina Myers (BS); Sam Rivers (Tom.); Cecil Taylor (Leo; SN).

BARKSDALE, EVERETT, gtr; b. Detroit, MI, 4/28/10; d. Inglewood, CA, 1/29/86. Started on alto sax, gtr., and bs.; early exp. in dance schs. Pl. w. Erskine Tate, Chi. 1930; Eddie South '32–9; Benny Carter Orch., NYC '40; Herman Chittison trio; Leon Abbey; Buster Browne '42; Cliff Jackson; Lester Boone '44. Led own qt. '42–5; staff mus. for CBS w. Jubilaires on Arthur Godfrey show '42–4. With Art Tatum trio '49–55. Mus. dir. for Billy Kenny and Inkspots; tour. Eur. and Can. Rejoin. Tatum Sept. '56 for last gigs. Took up el-bs. and doubled w. Buddy Tate '58–9. On staff ABC-TV and freelance work '60s. Later, worked in Calif. into the '70s. Stylistically somewhere between Charlie Christian and Al Casey. Pl.

and contracted many rec. sess. for Lena Horne; Sammy Davis; Al Hirt, etc. Also rec. w. Armstrong; Tate; Sarah Vaughan; Dinah Washington. CDs: w. Tatum (Cap.); Red Allen (BB); Sidney Bechet; Benny Carter (BB; Class); B. Holiday (Dec.).

BARNES, EMILE (MILÉ), cl; b. New Orleans, LA, 2/18/1892; d. New Orleans 3/2/70. Brother is Polo Barnes. Stud. w. Lorenzo Tio Jr.; Alphonse Picou; George Baquet; Big Eye Nelson. First job w. Buddy Petit. Fr. 1919 through '20s partnered w. Chris Kelly. In '30s join. Wooden Joe Nicholas's Camellia Band, but also worked at making mattresses. Dur. late '40s, he pl. w. Kid Howard. CD: Amer. Mus.

BARNES, GEORGE, gtr; b. Chicago Heights, IL, 7/17/21; d. Concord, CA, 9/5/77. Studied w. fath., a mus. profess. Own qt. for Midwest tour 1935–7; NBC staff in Chi. '37–42; Bud Freeman at College Inn '42. Army to '46. ABC radio staff, Chi., to Nov. '51, when he moved to NYC for TV and rec. work. Under contract to Dec. as gtrst., comp., and arr. Duo w. Carl Kress for several yrs., until latter's death, June '65. Freelanced until he teamed w. Bucky Pizzarelli '69–72. Formed qt. w. Ruby Braff for NJF-NY '73, app. at fests. in US and Eur. incl. concert tour w. Tony Bennett '73–4. Voted best new grp. of the yr. by *Hi-Fidelity* '75, but disbanded that summer. In this time, he also worked w. Joe Venuti and once again w. Freeman. One of first elec. gtrsts. '31. Self-designed gtrs.; taught at Famous Gtrs. Sch.; wrote four gtr. books, incl. *How to Arrange for the Guitar.* TV: w. Tony Bennett. Comp.: "Something Tender"; *Suite for Octette*; "It's Like the Fourth of July"; "Frolic for Basses." Also collab. w. daughter, Alexandra. Early recs. w. Big Bill Broonzy; Blind John Davis; Washboard Sam; first elec. gtr. rec. '37. Recs. w. Carl Kress, Louis Armstrong; Bud Freeman; B. Pizzarelli; Joe Venuti; T. Bennett. CDs: Barnes–Kress (Jass); w. Braff (Conc.); Krupa and Rich (Verve); Bill Broonzy (Col.).

BARNES, JOHN, woodwinds; b. Manchester, England, 5/15/32. Played and rec. on cl. w. Zenith Six bef. moving to London 1955; later pl. alto sax w. Delta Jazzmen; took up bari. sax w. Alan Elsdon's band '61–4 and made it his principal instrument. Worked w. Alex Welsh, mid '60s to late '70s. Fr. '79, perf. and made numerous recs. w. Humphrey Lyttelton's band. LP: Callig.; CD: w. Welsh (BL).

BARNES, POLO (PAUL D.), cl, sop sax; also alto, tnr, and bari saxes; b. New Orleans, LA, 11/22/01; d. New Orleans, 4/13/81. Brother of Emile Barnes. Att. St. Paul Lutheran Coll. Took up alto sax 1919 and w.

Lawrence Marrero form. Original Diamond Band, later known as the Young Tuxedo Band. Join. Kid Rena '22; Maple Leaf Orch. '23; Papa Celestin's Original Tuxedo Band '23. While w. Papa Celestin made reputation and gained popularity w. rec. of his comp. "My Josephine." Pl. w. Chick Webb '27; King Oliver '27, and again '31, '34–5. Tour. and rec. w. Jelly Roll Morton '28–9. Worked w. own band in NO '32–3; Chester Zardis '35; Kid Howard '37–9, '41; navy bands, Algiers, La. '42–5; Celestin's Tuxedo Band '46–51. Moved to Calif. and left mus. '52–7. Ret. to NO '59; join. Paul Barbarin's band '60. Member of Young Men fr. NO at Disneyland on riverboat '61–4. Back to NO '64, perf. at Preservation and Dixieland Halls. Tour. Eur. '73, '74. Ill health ended his mus. career '77. Own recs. on Icon; Camelia; CSA; as sideman w. Celestin; Morton, sop. sax solo on "Deep Creek Blues"; Peter Bocage; Kid Sheik Colar. CDs: Amer. Mus.; w. Morton (BB); Kid Thomas (Amer. Mus.).

BARNET, CHARLIE (CHARLES DALY), alto, tnr, sop saxes; lead; b. NYC, 10/26/13; d. San Diego, CA, 9/4/91. Started on pno. at an early age, saxophone at 12. Scion of a wealthy family whose urgings that he become a corp. lawyer he stubbornly resisted. Led his own band on a transatlantic liner at 16, making numerous ocean crossings; later went to the South Seas and Latin Amer. First prominent in jazz circles as lead. of band at the Paramount Hotel, NYC, 1932 and on recs. w. Red Norvo for Col. '34. Successful rec. career incl. '39 bb hit, "Cherokee." A volatile tnr. stylist and Hodges-infl. alto man, he also pl. soprano sax, leading the reed section, as on his '44 hit, "Skyliner." His '39–41 band was a fine Ellington-infl. swing outfit, feat. arrs. by Billy May and himself. Barnet pl. at Harlem's Apollo Theater in '33 and was one of the first white bandleaders to feature African-Amer. mus. extensively, beginning w. Frankie Newton in '37 and incl. Lena Horne; Trummy Young; Peanuts Holland; Howard McGhee; Oscar Pettiford; and Clark Terry. Other mus. and singers feat. w. him incl. Chubby Jackson; Neal Hefti; Ralph Burns; Buddy DeFranco; Frances Wayne; Fran Warren; and Kay Starr. His '49 band was bop flavored. A colorful personality, married six times, Barnet often made newspaper headlines and was one of the most talked about figures in jazz in the late '30s and early '40s. In the early '60s, he limited his activities to occ. gigs w. a pickup gp. By '65 he was semiretired, but assembled a band that app. in Hollywood, LV, and NYC, winter of '66–7; NJF '69; Can. Exposition, Toronto; Disneyland '72. Barnet was also involved in mus. publ. and the restaurant business. Book: *Those Swinging Years* w. Stanley Dance (LSU Press) '84. Films: *Syncopation* '42; *The Fabulous*

Dorseys '47; *A Song Is Born* '48. TV: a taped hour-long TV concert remains unreleased. CDs: BB; Dec.; Cir.; w. R. Norvo (Hep).

BARON, JOEY, dms, comp; b. Richmond, VA, 6/26/55. Began on dms. in 1964; pl. in hs marching band and was working local gigs fr. age 14. Att. Berklee Coll. for two yrs. Worked w. Carmen McRae in LA '76. In NYC in the '80s pl. in gps. w. Red Rodney; Jay McShann; Jim Hall; Toots Thielemans; Fred Hersch; Mark Murphy; Tim Berne; Hank Roberts; Bill Frisell. Own trio, Barondown, w. Steve Swell, tbn., and Ellery Eskelin, tnr. sax, reflects his eclecticism and ability to perf. in many genres. CDs: w. Barondown (Avant; NW); w. Berne (JMT); Zorn (Elek.; DIW); Frisell (Elek.; None.); J. Scofield (BN); D. Douglas (Arab.).

BARONE, GARY ANTHONY, tpt, flg, dms, educ; b. Detroit, MI, 12/12/41. Father, Joe Barone, pl. tpt. w. Bob Crosby; bro. Mike pl. tbn. Stud. at Mich. State U. 1964; San Fernando Valley State Coll. '65–7. Late '60s, early '70s, pl. w. Stan Kenton; LA Neophonic Orch.; Gerald Wilson; Bud Shank; Mike Barone; Frank Zappa; Willie Bobo; Frank Strazzeri; and in US, Italy, and Engl. w. Shelly Manne. Also taught brass at univ. clinics. Fr. '71, comp., arr., and feat. soloist in TV and film studios, incl. work w. L. Schifrin; D. Grusin; Tom Scott; John Rubinstein; and *Tonight Show* orch. Dur. '80s, perf. w. Dick Berk; Pete Christlieb; Chuck Israels; Barney McClure; John Stowell; Rob Thomas; and bands of John Clayton and Gary Hobbs. App. at many jazz fests., taught at Dick Grove Sch. of Mus., and led Gary Barone Jazz Qt. Favs: Miles Davis, Freddie Hubbard. CDs: w. Barone Bros. (Palo Alto); S. Manne (Main.).

BARONE, MIKE (MICHAEL), tbn, comp; b. Detroit, MI, 12/27/36. Raised in Cleveland, Ohio; stud. w. fath. and member of Cleve. Symph. Army 1956–9. In LA fr. '59, working w. Sy Zentner, Louis Bellson; Quincy Jones; Dizzy Gillespie; Maynard Ferguson. Led own bb at Donte's '67–70, dur. which time he also co-led combo w. bro. Gary. In late '60's, he made series of albums for Liberty under the name *Trombones Unlimited*. Later very active as comp./arr. for *Tonight Show* orch., Academy Awards show, Grammy Awards, etc. Later settled in Colo., where he cond. clinics. Won Shelly Manne award for extended concert work, *Themes and Variations*, for New Amer. Orch. in LA. CDs: w. Barone Bros. (Palo Alto); Oliver Nelson (Imp.).

BARRETT, DAN (DANIEL PATRICK), tbn, v-tbn, crnt, comp, arr; b. Pasadena, CA, 12/14/55.

Older bro. had surf-rock band in early 1960s. Began on pno., then sw. to tbn. in fifth grade; began pl. crnt. in junior hs, self-taught. Pl. in hs w. many second gen. NO mus. who had settled in So. Calif.: Barney Bigard; Joe Darensbourg; Alton Purnell; Eddie Miller; Ed "Montudie" Garland, Nappy Lamare. Join. Local 47 at 16 w. help of former Kid Ory band tptr. Andy Blakeney. Stud. w. Frank Demond; Bill Campbell; Al Jenkins. Att. Long Beach State U. as mus. ed. maj. '75–7, but left sch. to perf. at Breda Oude Stijl JF, Netherlands, w. Sunset Mus. Co. Pl. w. many Calif. trad. jazz bands incl. Crown City Jazz Band, w. Bigard, Darensbourg, Blakeney, and in dixieland bands at Disneyland and Busch Gardens. Pl. and arr. for Tony Romano '81–3 at Hotel Laguna bef. moving to NYC in '83. Pl. w. Widespread Jazz Orch. '83–5; Eddie Condon's Jazz Band '83–5. Feat. w. Woody Herman at NY Pops conc. '84. Pl. and arr. for Benny Goodman '85–6; Joe Bushkin '86; Buck Clayton's Swing Band '87–9. Has co-led the Howard Alden–Dan Barrett Qnt. since mid '80s. Pl. tbn. on soundtracks for *The Cotton Club* and *Brighton Beach Memoirs*, and comp. and pl. for PBS drama, *Rocket to the Moon*. Also pl. crnt. w. var. trad. jazz bands in NYC and LA. One of the best of the neo-mainstream tbn. pl., he can range back and forward in jazz history w. ease and expertise, delivering a big, smooth sound. Favs: Lawrence Brown, Jack Teagarden, Vic Dickenson, Louis Armstrong. Polls: *DB* TDWR '90. Fests: Breda '77–83, '87, '90; Bern '84; Edinburgh '81, '88–9; Montreux '83; Nice '88–90; Oslo '89. CDs: Arb.; Conc.; w. Alden-Barrett Qnt.; Warren Vaché; Rosemary Clooney; Mel Tormé; Concord All-Stars (Conc.); B. Clayton (Stash); B. Goodman (Limel.); Marty Grosz (Jazz.); Bushkin (DRG).

BARRETT, DARREN WINSTON, tpt, flg; b. Manchester, England, 6/19/67. Father pl. alto sax. Went to grade sch. in Toronto, Can. Became serious about the tpt. in hs. Stud. at Berklee Coll. of Mus., B.A. 1990; Queens Coll.'s Aaron Copland Sch. of Mus., M.A., jazz perf. '93; M.S., mus. ed. '95; and Thelonious Monk Inst. of Jazz at New Engl. Cons., Diploma in Jazz Perf. '97. Also stud. at Columbia U. Teachers at various schs. incl. Donald Byrd; Jimmy Heath; William Fielder; William Vacchiano; Charles Schluter. Was principal tpt. Queen's Coll. Choral Society '92–93; Queen's Coll. Orch. '92–94. Pl. w. Antonio Hart Qnt. '90–5; Slide Hampton's Jazzmasters '93; Roy Hargrove bb '95; Thelonious Monk Inst. Ens. '95–7; Greg Tardy Qnt.; and Jackie McLean Qnt. fr. '98. Taught beginning band, jazz band, and general music, tutored priv. at Louis Armstrong Middle Sch., Queens, N.Y., '94–5; priv. studio at New Engl. Cons. Prep Sch., teach. tpt. methods, improv. techniques, fr. '97. Pl. in France and Spain w. Hart; France w. Hampton; India and Thailand w. Thelonious Monk Inst. Ens., March '96. Barrett, who has a good sense of pace and strong chops, can play with the swagger of Lee Morgan and the edge of Woody Shaw. Favs: Clifford Brown, Miles Davis. Won 1st Place in Thelonious Monk Tpt. Competition '97. CDs: J Curve; w. A. Hart (Novus); Monk Inst. of Jazz.

BARRETT, SWEET EMMA, pno, voc; b. New Orleans, LA, 3/25/1897; d. New Orleans, 1/28/83. Self-taught. Pl. in Original Tuxedo Orch. w. co-leads. Papa Celestin and William Ridgely 1923–5; then under Ridgely to '36; also worked w. Sidney Desvigne; Armand Piron; John Robichaux. After a long period of inactivity, she began a comeback '47. In '50s worked at Happy Landing. Career boosted in '61, when she made her rec. debut on Riv.'s "Living Legends" series. Soon she was successfully leading Preservation Hall band for int'l tours; also worked in Memphis, Minneapolis, and in '65 at Disneyland. App. often at The Quarter, NO; concerts for NO jazz club. Suffered a stroke in '67, but despite a paralyzed left side, cont. to perf. until her death. Her trademark was a red skull cap and matching pair of bright red garters w. attached bells that jingled rhythmically and earned her the sobriquet the "Bell Gal." Rec. for South.; Jazz. CDs: Riv.; GHB.

BARRETTO, RAY (RAYMOND), cga, perc, lead; b. NYC, 4/29/29; d. Hackensack, NJ, 2/17/06. In army 1946–9; first experience in jam sessions while stationed in Germ. Freelanced in NYC w. Lou Donaldson, Donald Byrd, etc. '49–53. Encouraged by Charlie Parker w. whom he jammed at the Apollo Bar. Began pl. professionally w. Eddie Bonnemere '53–4; Pete Terrace '54; Jose Curbelo '54–7; Tito Puente '57–61; Bonnemere's Latin Jazz Combo and Herbie Mann's gp. '61–2. Pl. and rec. W. Cannonball Adderley, Gene Ammons, Red Garland, Dizzy Gillespie '50s. Left Mann in '62 to form own gp. A leader in the salsa field, he perf. at jazz clubs in NYC and int'l into the '90s. In mid '90s pl. several engagements w. his New World Spirit band in Paris. The first cga. pl. to blend well in a straight-ahead jazz setting; also a powerful perf. in Latin jazz. Favs: Chano Pozo, Tata Guines. Fr. '60s through '80s released more than twenty albums on Fania label. CDs: BN; Conc.; Owl; Mess.; w. Gillespie (Verve); Eddie "Lockjaw" Davis; C. Adderley (Riv.); Ammons; Garland; Jimmy Forrest; S. Stitt; O. Nelson (Prest.); L. Donaldson; Kenny Burrell; S. Turrentine (BN); Eddie Harris; Freddie Hubbard (Atl.); Wes Montgomery (Riv., Verve); Joe Zawinul (FS).

BARRITEAU, CARL, cl; b. Trinidad, 2/7/14. Raised in Venezuela. After moving to London, was main soloist w. Ken "Snake Hips" Johnson's West Indian Swing Band, fr. 1937 until Johnson's death in an air raid; '41. Won the *MM* poll on cl. for seven consecutive yrs.; later form. own gp. and pl. for US troops in Eur., Africa, and S.E. Asia. Moved to Austral. and retired '70.

BARRON, BILL (WILLIAM JR.), tnr, sop sax; fl; comp; educ; b. Philadelphia, PA, 3/27/27; d. Middletown, CT, 9/21/89. Piano at 7 for two yrs. Studied tnr. sax at 13 in mus. dept. at Mastbaum HS, where Johnny Coles was a classmate. B.A. in comp., Combs Coll. of Mus., Phila.; Ph.D. in Education, U. of Mass., Amherst, 1975. Tour. w. Carolina Cottonpickers. Pl. in army special band unit w. Randy Weston, Ernie Henry. Discharged in '46, he stud. comp. and theory at Ornstein Sch. of Mus., Phila. Worked w. various gps. in Phila. '48–58, incl. Red Garland, Jimmy Golden, Jimmy Heath. To NYC '58, pl. w. Cecil Taylor; Donald Byrd; C. Mingus; Philly Joe Jones '61; then most often as co-leader w. Ted Curson through first half of '60s, incl. Eur. tours. In '70s led own qt. and also app. w. bro., Kenny, in Barron Bros. gp. fr. '68 to '74; however, his main occupation was dir. of jazz wkshp. at MUSE (Bedford-Lincoln Neighborhood Museum, operated by the Bklyn Children's Museum). Later he became jazz workshop coordinator for NEW MUSE (the Community Museum of Bklyn.). Fr. '74, he devoted himself more to teaching, beginning w. City Coll., CUNY, where he taught improv. using embellishments. Fr. Sept. '75 he was asst. profess. of mus. and dir. of Afro-Amer. mus. at Wesleyan U., where he became chairman of the Mus. Dept. '84. Panelist for Nat'l Conf. of Black Amer. Mus. at Black Expo, Chi. '71; CBA Symposium '72. Received NEA grant for comp. Early infl: Dexter Gordon. Although Barron's work of the early '60s resembled Coltrane's, Curson has said that he "was playing like this in Philadelphia a number of years ago, when John Coltrane was still playing alto." Fests: Kongsberg w. Y. Lateef '66. TV: interview, *Inside Bed-Stuy,* WNEW '70; w. Curson, WNET '72. Comps: "Ode to An Earthgirl"; "Motivation"; "Hold Back Tomorrow." Recs. w. Mingus. CDs: Sav.; Muse; Joken; w. Curson (BL); P.J. Jones (Riv.).

BARRON, KENNY (KENNETH), pno, comp; also bs, tba; b. Philadelphia, PA, 6/9/43. Older bro. tnr. saxophonist Bill Barron; two bros. and two sists. also pl. pno. Studied classical pno. in Phila. 1949–58; bs. in hs 56–9. First job w. Mel Melvin '57; band also incl. Bill Barron. Pl. w. Philly Joe Jones, Jimmy Heath '59; Yusef Lateef in Det. '60. Moved to NYC

'61. Pl. w. Bill Barron–Ted Curson; James Moody at Five Spot '61; Roy Haynes '62; Dizzy Gillespie '62–6; Stanley Turrentine '66; Freddie Hubbard '67–9; Jimmy Owens; Esther Marrow, late '60s; Yusef Lateef '71–4; Stan Getz '74; Buddy Rich '74–5; Lateef '75; Ron Carter '75–8. Also pl. in '70s w. Milt Jackson, Jimmy Heath. Freelanced extens. fr. '79. Led trio w. Buster Williams, Ben Riley '79–81. Co-founded Sphere w. Charlie Rouse, Williams, Riley '82–6; gp. reformed w. Gary Bartz '98. Pl. w. Stan Getz '87–91. Barron toured India w. Chico Freeman in '83 and again w. his own qnt. in '87. In '92, he was part of a world tour sponsored by the Phillip Morris Co. Leading own trio and qnt. in '90s. Taught at Jazzmobile Wkshp. '72–3; Rutgers U. fr. '73. One of the finest and most versatile mainstream pnsts. whose scope has incl. Brazilian mus. in the '90s. Favs: Tommy Flanagan, Hank Jones, Barry Harris. Fests: Eur. fr. '64; Japan fr. '79. TV: NBC *Positively Black* w. Lateef, R. Carter; ABC *Like It Is* w. E. Marrow. Films: pl. on soundtracks of *School Daze*; *Do the Right Thing*. Comps: a number of well-crafted originals of which "Voyage" is the most pl. by other mus. CDs: Verve; Cand.; Conc.; Enja; Limel.; CC; Red; 32; Muse; w. Bill Barron (Sav.); Barry Harris; Gary Bartz; Paquito D'Rivera (Cand.); Ella Fitzgerald; J.J. Johnson–Al Grey (Pab.); S. Getz (Em.; Conc.); D. Gillespie (Verve); Lionel Hampton, Buddy Rich (LRC); Tom Harrell (CC); Joe Henderson (Mile.); Bobby Hutcherson (Land.); Woody Shaw; Sheila Jordan (Muse); Y. Lateef (Atl.); Frank Morgan (Ant.); Valery Ponomarev (Res.); V. Mayhew (Chiaro.).

BARTH, BRUCE DAVID, pno; b. Pasadena, CA, 9/7/58. Grew up in NYC. Moth. pl. classical pno.; bro. is ragtime gtrst. Pno. lessons fr. age 5. Stud. at New Engl. Cons. w. Jaki Byard, George Russell 1982–4; later w. Norman Simmons in NYC. Pl. in Bost. w. G. Russell bb '83; Orange Then Blue Band '84–6; also own trio. Taught at Berklee Coll. of Mus. '85–8. Ret. to NYC '88. Pl. w. Nat Adderley briefly '89; Vincent Herring '90; Stanley Turrentine '90–1; Terence Blanchard fr. '90. Barth curr. teaches at LIU-Bklyn. Favs: H. Hancock, M. Tyner, Red Garland. Fests: Eur. w. Herring, Blanchard; Japan w. Adderley, Blanchard. Film: cameo app. in *Malcolm X* '92. TV: BET, Canadian and Japanese TV w. Blanchard. CDs: Enja; w. Blanchard (Col.); Herring (MM); Steve Wilson (CC); Randy Johnston (Muse); G. Russell (BN).

BARTZ, GARY LEE, alto, sop sax, comp; b. Baltimore, MD, 9/26/40. Father ran local jazz club, North End Lounge. Studied alto fr. age 11. First gigs as teenager in fath.'s club. Studied at Juilliard Sch. of

Mus. 1957–8; jammed w. Freddie Hubbard, Lee Morgan, Pharoah Sanders while in NYC. Ret. to Balt. '58, stud. at Peabody Cons. Made prof. debut w. Max Roach–Abbey Lincoln '64, then pl. w. Art Blakey '65–6. Form. own gp. Ntu Troop '67. Pl. w. Roach; Chas. Tolliver; Blue Mitchell '68–9; McCoy Tyner off and on '68–76; Miles Davis '70–1. Rec. w. Woody Shaw for Cont. '70. In late '70s, did studio work w. Norman Connors and Phyllis Hyman in LA. Signed w. the Cap. label '77 for disco-funk genre recs. Re-emerged in jazz '88, and in the '90s was one of its most potent players, combining his Parker roots w. post-bop infls. Join. reorganized Sphere '98. Scored ABC-TV special *About Time* '72. Polls: *DB*, *MM* '72. Fests: w. Ntu Troop, Kongsberg; Montreux, where he rec. "I've Known Rivers," '73. CDs: Atl.; Cand.; Steep.; w. Donald Brown (Muse); Louis Hayes (Cand.); M. Tyner (BN); M. Davis (Col.); W. Shaw (Mos.); P. Delano; Sphere; R. Hargrove (Verve); M. Cowings–K. Kalesti (Em.); Buster Williams (TCB).

BASCOMB, DUD (WILBUR ODELL), tpt; b. Birmingham, AL, 5/16/16; d. NYC, 12/25/72. An original member of the 'Bama State Collegians while in hs, he came to NYC in 1934. Remained after Erskine Hawkins became leader in '38. Solos on "Tuxedo Junction," "Hot Platter," "Gin Mill Special," often wrongly attributed to Hawkins. Excellent w. mutes. Left to form sxt., then a bb, w. his bro. Paul '45–6, and led own gp. on 52nd St. bef. pl. w. Duke Ellington '47. In early '50s, own qnt. in N.J. Fr. mid to late '50s theater dates and one-nighters w. Jackie Wilson. Led own gp. and bb '61–3 and was a busy freelancer dur. the '60s and early '70s. Pl. in off-B'way prod. *Cindy* '66; pit orch. for *Purlie* '70; app. on soundtracks for *It's a Mad, Mad, Mad World* '63; *Midnight Cowboy* '69; *Legend of Nigger Charlie* '72. Three tours of Japan w. Sam the Man Taylor, fr. '63; Eur. w. Buddy Tate '68–70. Such young bop tptrs. as Miles Davis, Fats Navarro, and Idrees Sulieman all knew his "Tuxedo Junction" solo; Dizzy Gillespie praised him as an infl. on "modern trumpet players . . . like the way Clifford Brown phrased notes—Dud Bascomb was doing some of that. 'Bli-bli'—grace notes." Comp. "Country Boy," rec. by Hawkins '42. Solo on "Women" w. Ellington. Rec. w. Tate for MPS. CDs: w. Erskine Hawkins (BB).

BASCOMB, PAUL, tnr sax; b. Birmingham, AL, 2/12/12; d. Chicago, IL, 12/2/86. Brother of Dud Bascomb. Won scholarship to Alabama St. Coll., where he was a founder of sch.'s first dance orch., 'Bama State Collegians. Dur. summer vacations, also toured w. Jean Calloway, C.S. Belton's Society Syncopators.

With the exception of a period in 1938–9, when he was absent from the Erskine Hawkins's band, his career paralleled his bro.'s to '47, after which he led his own gps., incl. long stays at Smalls' Paradise, NYC; El Sino, Det.; Robert's Show Lounge and the Esquire, Chi., '50s, '60s. Remain. active into mid '80s. Fest: Grande Parade du Jazz, Nice '78. Fluent soloist in the manner of Chu Berry, his most famous solo is "Sweet Georgia Brown" w. Hawkins '40. Other recs. w. Count Basie '40 (but no solos); Dinah Washington '56; Little Esther; the Flamingos; own gp., Merc. CDs: Del.; w. Hawkins (BB).

BASIE, COUNT (WILLIAM), pno, org, lead, comp; b. Red Bank, NJ, 8/21/04; d. Hollywood, FL, 4/26/84. Basie studied mus. w. his moth. and pl. pno. fr. childhood, picking up rudiments of ragtime fr. early Harlem pnsts. He later studied org. informally w. Fats Waller. He made his prof. debut in NYC as an accomp. in vaudeville; replaced Waller in an act called Katie Crippen and Her Kids; and also worked w. June Clark, Sonny Greer, and others. While traveling w. the Gonzelle White show on the Keith Circuit, he found himself stranded in KC when the outfit broke up in 1927. After recovering fr. an illness, he accomp. the Whitman Sisters and pl. for silent movies. He pl. w. Walter Page's Blue Devils, a band that incl. Jimmy Rushing, for a yr. '28–9. After the Blue Devils broke up, Basie and some of the other members join. Bennie Moten. This band stayed together until Moten's death in '35. It cont. under the leadership of Moten's bro., Buster, but Basie, starting a gp. of his own, the Barons of Rhythm, at the Reno Club, soon had hired the best of Moten's men. The band gradually grew to nine pcs. and began broadcasting fr. the club on a local station, W9XBY. It was at this time that Basie acquired his nickname.

When John Hammond heard a broadcast, he headed for KC to hear the band in person—then decided to bring it to NYC. The band augmented its personnel, came to NYC in '36, opened at Roseland, and made its first recs. for Dec. in Jan. '37. By the following yr., when it triumphed at the Famous Door on 52nd St., the band had become internationally famous, due in large measure to Basie's simple, somewhat elliptical pno. style and feather-light rhythm section that fr. March '37 comprised Freddie Green, gtr.; Jo Jones, dms.; and Walter Page, bs.; Rushing's vocals; and the individualism of such soloists as Lester Young, Herschel Evans, Earl Warren, Buck Clayton, Harry Edison, Benny Morton, and Dicky Wells; also the charts—some by Eddie Durham and various band members, others spontaneously developed "head" arrs. Through the '40s,

despite the occ. loss of key personnel, Basie maintained a band whose contagious rhythmic pulsation and superlative team spirit, combined w. a succession of inspired soloists, remained unique in jazz. The band feat. a number of outstanding mus. incl. saxists Buddy Tate, Don Byas, Lucky Thompson, Illinois Jacquet, and Paul Gonsalves; tpts. Al Killian, Joe Newman, and Emmett Berry; tbns. Vic Dickenson and J.J. Johnson. Among the female vocs. were Billie Holiday and Helen Humes. Except for a period in '50–1, when economic conditions compelled him to front a spt. (incl. Clark Terry, Wardell Gray, and Buddy DeFranco), Basie led a bb continuously until his death, gaining a global reputation for his undying allegiance to the beat, his loyalty to the blues as a basic form, and his ability to produce recs. of unflaggingly high caliber.

Basie reorganized the bb in '52, w. much encouragement fr. Billy Eckstine. This orch. has been referred to as the "New Testament" band as opposed to the original "Old Testament" '30s-'40s outfit. The personnel incl. Joe Newman, tpt.; Paul Quinichette, Eddie "Lockjaw" Davis, tnrs.; Marshal Royal, alto; and Gus Johnson, dms. That same yr., the band began a long assoc. w. Birdland in NYC. In '54, when the band made its first tour of Eur., and '55, Basie's twentieth anniversary as a leader, other new stars were feat., among them Thad Jones and Joe Wilder, along w. Newman, tpts.; Bennie Powell and Henry Coker, tbns.; Frank Foster and Frank Wess, tnrs.; Sonny Payne, dms. Singer Joe Williams, who had worked w. the spt. in '50, rejoined Basie in late '54 and helped the band achieve a new, even wider level of popularity, particularly through the hit rec. "Every Day" '55. Dur. this period, most of the arrs. were by Ernie Wilkins and Neal Hefti, w. additional scores by Johnny Mandel, Foster, and others. The band tour. overseas w. tremendous success, tour. Engl. twice in '57. On the second occasion, Basie's became the first US band ever to pl. a Royal Command perf. for the Queen. Basie also set a precedent pl. thirteen weeks in the roof ballroom of the Waldorf-Astoria Hotel, NYC, June-Sept. '57, the first black jazz orch. to pl. there. Although the vocs. who followed the departure of Williams in '60 never matched his stature, Basie's career cont. on an upward trend in terms of popularity. The band's instrumental albums of original material enjoyed limited success, but an LP entitled *Hits of the '50s and '60s*, w. Quincy Jones, arrs. based on pop songs of the day, was an immediate hit. Basie followed up w. a series of similar albums, w. arrs. by Billy Byers. In '65–6 the band rec. mainly for Frank Sinatra's Reprise label, and made several highly acclaimed albums and personal apps. w. him—the union was mutually beneficial. The band also rec. and app. in concert w. Tony Bennett and did an album w. Sammy Davis Jr. Other arrs. who contributed to the band's book in the '60s and thereafter were Sammy Nestico; Chico O'Farrill; Benny Carter; Eric Dixon; and Bill Holman. Fr. '60 to '66, the band lost tpts. Newman and Jones, and saxists Marshall Royal, Wess and Foster. It did four cruises on the QE2 dur. the late '60s and early '70s and in Jan. '71 went to Austria for the first time. In '73–4, Basie made several recs. for Norman Granz, w. small bands feat. other prominent mus., incl. Oscar Peterson; Eddie "Lockjaw" Davis; Zoot Sims. Basie suffered a heart attack in the summer of '76 and rested until Jan. '77. Nat Pierce replaced him at the pno. dur. this time. The band incl. Sonny Cohn, Pete Minger, tpts; Al Grey, Curtis Fuller, Mel Wanzo, Bill Hughes, tbns.; Bobby Plater, Danny Turner, altos; Jimmy Forrest, Eric Dixon, tnrs.; Butch Miles, dms. Struck by severe arthritis in the early '80s, Basie used a small motor scooter to get him on and off stage. Mainstay sidemen at this time, in addition to the enduring Freddie Green, were Kenny Hing, tnr. sax; Dennis Wilson, tbn; Bob Ojeda, tpt; John Williams, bari. sax; Dennis Mackrel, dms.

After Basie's death, Thad Jones ret. to the US from Copenhagen, Den., to lead the band fr. '85 until his death, Feb. '86. Frank Foster assumed leadership '86–95, at which time Grover Mitchell took over. As the '90s draw to a close, the Basie band cont. to be a favorite at int'l fests. Polls: big band: *Esq.* Silver Award '45; *DB* Readers poll '55, '57–61; as bb, dance '62–3; *DB* Critics '54–7; *Met.* '58–60; Basie on pno.: *Met.* '42–3; *DB* Hall of Fame '58. Films: *Stage Door Canteen* '43; *Blazing Saddles* '74; Bruce Ricker's *The Last of the Blue Devils* '91, in video (Rhap.). Books: *The World of Count Basie*, Stanley Dance (Scribner's) '80; *Good Morning Blues*, w. Albert Murray (Random House) '85. CDs: Dec.; Col.; BB; Verve; Roul.; Pab.; Mos.; w. Moten (BB); Basie/Ellington (Col.); *From Spirituals to Swing* (Vang.); under Foster's dir. (Den.); under Mitchell's dir., *Count Plays Duke* (MAMA).

BASILE, JOHN, gtr, comp; b. Boston, MA, 3/5/55. Father pl. gtr. Att. New Engl. Cons., then stud. w. William Leavitt at Berklee; later w. Barry Galbraith in NYC. Pl. w. Red Norvo Trio 1978. In '79 received NEA grant for jazz comp. Freelance since '79 w. Michael Moore; Tom Harrell; Emily Remler; George Mraz; Peggy Lee; Morgana King; Ruby Braff. Made rec. debut in '85 w. own LP incl. Eddie Gomez. Tour. Eur. w. Clark Terry, Sweets Edison, Buddy Tate '88. Favs: Jim Hall, Galbraith, Frank Sinatra. Has subbed for Hall as teacher at New Sch.; given own seminars in Italy. Fests: Germ., Belgium, Switzerland '88; Italy since '89. CDs: Chesky; Phil.; FS; ProJazz, Mus. Heritage.

BASS, MICKEY (LEE ODDIS III), bs, comp, arr, pno, brass, fl; b. Pittsburgh, PA, 5/2/43. Mother was a singer; grandmother was a pno. teacher. Studied bs. w. William Lewis in Pitts. Pl. in All-City HS Orch. Att. Howard U. Coll. of Fine Arts 1961–3, stud. w. Bernard Mason and maj. in mus. ed. First job in NYC w. Hank Mobley at Theresa Hotel '64. Pl. w. Bennie Green; Jackie McLean; Art Blakey; Sonny Rollins. With Bobby Timmons '65; Gloria Lynne '65–8; Carmen McRae '67. Att. NYU '67–8. Pl. w. Billy Eckstine '68–9; Blakey '70; then worked w. Freddie Hubbard, Miriam Makeba bef. ret. to Blakey. Instr. at Jazzmobile Wkshp., NYC, since '75. Taught bs. and improv. at Duke Ellington Sch. of the Arts, Wash., D.C., '75–8. Had weekly radio show in NYC. Pl. w. Duke Jordan at Churchill's, NYC '76. Adjunct profess. of mus., Hartt Coll. '80–4. Received NEA comp. grant '80. Chairman for Nat'l Assoc. of Jazz Educs. '84–6. East Coast rep. for Sarah Vaughan '85–6. Own qt. w. Carter Jefferson, John Hicks, Michael Carvin '87. Led Manhattan Burn Unit w. D. Schnitter, E. Gladden '95. Hosted cable TV arts prog. in NYC '88. Bass's comps. and arrs. have been pl. and rec. by Lee Morgan; Hank Mobley; Art Blakey; Chico Hamilton; Jaki Byard; Gloria Lynne; Bobby Timmons; Al Hibbler; Ramon Morris. Has co-auth. mus. textbook w. Billy Taylor. He has also worked as prod. for Chiaro. label. Infls: C. Parker, M. Davis, Coltrane. Fests: NJF-NY w. F. Hubbard '71, Blakey '73; many others in Eur. and Japan. TV: w. F. Hubbard, Gp. W, Bost.; Canadian Broad. Co.; Billy Eckstine Show, WNBC-NYC; w. A. Blakey WNEW-NYC; NHK-Japan; Frank Foster, *Today*. CDs: Chiaro.; w. PJ Jones (Sonet); Blakey (Prest.).

BASSO, GIANNI (GIOVANNI), tnr sax, cl, sop sax; b. Asti, Italy, 5/24/31. Brother pl. bs. Began on cl.; stud. at Asti Cons. 1937–44. Pl. in Belgium w. bb, own combos '46–50; also w. Amer. mus. in Belgium and Germ. Ret. to Italy '50, pl. w. dance bands of Kramer Gorni; Beppe Mojetta; Angelo Brigada. Pl. w. Gil Cuppini '55, then form Sestetto Italiano w. Oscar Valdambrini '57. Basso and Valdambrini accomp. many visiting mus. incl. Billie Holiday; Lionel Hampton; Gerry Mulligan; Chet Baker; Lee Konitz; Art Farmer; Conte Candoli; Zoot Sims; Phil Woods; Frank Rosolino; and Joe Venuti, '57–74. Worked w. Armando Trovajoli bb '57–8; Maynard Ferguson bb '65; Slide Hampton–Dusko Gojkovic bb '72; B.P. Convention bb '75; Kenny Clarke–Francy Boland bb '70s-'80s; Thad Jones bb, '81; Lalo

Schifrin–Sarah Vaughan '84; Frank Sinatra Jr. '89; Natalie Cole, '92. Tour. US, '91. Basso has taught at the cons. of Turin '78–80; Milan '90–2; Asti fr. '92. Favs: Getz, Webster, Byas, F. Foster, Rollins. Polls: *Musica Jazz*. Fests: all major in Eur. Films: *La Prima Notte di Quiete* w. M. Ferguson; *I Soliti Ignoti* w. Baker; *Crimen* w. Valdambrini. TV: Eur. TV. CDs: Penta.; Fonola; Spl.; w. Baker (Jazzl.); Helen Merrill (Liuto); Goykovic (Enja).

BASSO, GUIDO, tpt, flg, arr, comp; b. Montreal, Que., Canada, 9/27/37. Child prodigy on tpt. Studied at Conservatoire de Musique de Montreal. Played in dance bands in teens; hired at 18 by Vic Damone to go on the road. Worked in Louie Bellson band and trav. w. Pearl Bailey 1957–60. Moved to Toronto '60, became top studio mus., lead., TV mus. dir., rec. artist. Led orch. on two bbs for Toronto apps. of Benny Goodman; Quincy Jones; Duke Ellington; and Dizzy Gillespie. Many recs. w. Rob McConnell's Boss Brass and as leader of own gps. Noted as a top jazz player on tpt. and flg. w. lyrical style, magnificent tone, and long, intricate, fluent lines. CDs: Innov.; w. McConnell (Conc.; SB).

BATES, DJANGO, kybds, E-flat horn, comp; b. Beckenham, England, 10/2/60. Mainly self-taught on pno., tpt., vln. but stud. all of these fr. 1971–7 at Center for Young Mus. in London and at Morley Coll. '77–8. Pl. w. Tim Whitehead's qt., Borderline, for three and a half yrs. fr. '81. Join. Dudu Pukwana's gp., Zila, '83. Founder-member of Loose Tubes '83, for which he did most of the comp. Pl. w. Ken Stubbs's qt., First House, in mid '80s; also founder-member of Bill Bruford's Earthworks; worked w. him up to '94 when he left to lead own gps., incl. Human Chain, which he start. in '79, and Delightful Precipice, form. in '91. Has also collab. w. George Russell; George Gruntz; Michael Gibbs; and in duo w. concert pnst. Joanna MacGregor. His infls. reflect a wide and varied mus. spectrum. Polls: *Wire*, Best comp., '87,'91; Mus. of Year, '87. CDs: JMT; Ah Um; w. Loose Tubes (Editions EG).

BATISTE, ALVIN, cl, comp; b. New Orleans, LA, 11/7/32. While in hs, pl. w. Ed Blackwell. First job w. Guitar Slim and Ukulele Lemon. In army in early 1950s, then jammed w. Ornette Coleman in LA '56. Freelanced in NO, worked as hs mus. educ., late '50s; also tour. w. Ray Charles '58. When he grad. fr. Southern U. in Baton Rouge, La., pl. *Mozart Clarinet Concerto* w. NO Symph. Form. the Jazzstronauts '69. Taught jazz course at Southern U., '69–mid '80s. His students incl. Branford Marsalis; Donald Harrison; Herlin Riley. Began rec. w. Cannonball Adderley in early '70s, but album was never completed. App. on

Adderley's final LP, *Lovers* '75. Pl. w. Billy Cobham '70s; rec. w. John Carter's Clarinet Summit fr. '81. Tour. and rec. w. Freddie Hubbard's Satchmo Legacy Band, late '80s. Batiste absorbed the mus. of his NO heritage and classical mus. bef. becoming infl. by C. Parker. His extended comps. have been perf. by the NO Symph. Orch. Fests: led 60-member coll. ens. at NO JF '69; pl. at Montreux w. Cobham '70s. CDs: Col.; w. Wynton Marsalis (Col.); Clarinet Summit (Ind. Nav.); Satchmo Legacy Band (SN); American Jazz Qnt. (BS); Ernie Wilkins (Bird.); Marlon Jordan (Arab.).

BATTLE, EDGAR W. (PUDDINGHEAD), tpt, comp.-arr; also v-tbn, alto sax; b. Atlanta, GA, 10/3/07; d. NYC, 2/6/77. Took up tpt. at age 8. While stud. at Morris Brown Coll., form. Dixie Serenaders 1922; later led Dixie Ramblers, also pl. w. other leaders incl. Eddie Heywood Sr. Worked w. Gene Coy '28; Andy Kirk '30; Blanche Calloway '31; own band '33; Sam Wooding; Benny Carter; Alex Hill '34; Willie Bryant, tripling v-tbn., alto sax, also arr. '35–6. In latter yr., he also perf. on radio broadcasts of *George White's Scandals*. After lead. own band '37, gave up pl. to concentrate on comp.-arr. for Cab Calloway; Earl Hines; Count Basie; Fats Waller; Paul Whiteman; Jack Teagarden; Louis Prima. Rec. comps. w. Kirk, "Puddin' Head Serenade"; C. Calloway, "Ratamacue," "Crescendo in Drums," "Hard Times"; Hines, "Topsy Turvy (Hard Times)," "Yellow Fire"; Basie, "Topsy" (co-comp. Eddie Durham). Recs. as sideman: w. Kirk; Blanche Calloway; Willie Bryant. CDs: w. Benny Carter (BB).

BAUDUC, RAY (RAYMOND), dms; b. New Orleans, LA, 6/19/06; d. Houston, TX, 1/8/88. Studied w. fath., crntst. Jules Bauduc Sr., and bro., dmr. Jules Jr. (b. ca. 1904). First prof. engagement replacing bro. in theater orch. Worked w. Emmett Hardy; Six Nola Jazzers. Tour. w. Johnny Bayersdorffer 1924; Scranton Sirens led by vlnst. Billy Lustig '25. In NYC, pl. w. Joe Venuti–Eddie Lang '26 and made rec. debut w. Memphis Five. With Freddie Rich, Hotel Astor Orch., and in London, doubl. as tap dancer '26–8. Member of Ben Pollack orch. '28–34; also worked and rec. dur. this time w. Miff Mole; Red Nichols; Jack Teagarden; Benny Goodman; Wingy Manone; Louis Prima; Glenn Miller. Gained great recognition w. Bob Crosby band '35–42. Rec. duet w. Bob Haggart of their comp. "Big Noise from Winnetka," in which he pl. w. his sticks on Haggart's bs. strings. After serving in WWII, led a band w. Gil Rodin; also own ens. Reunited briefly w. Crosby '47; then Jimmy Dorsey '47–50; Jack Teagarden '51–5. Co-led gp. w. Nappy Lamare in southern Calif. and

US tours '56–9. In '60s freelanced on West Coast incl. w. Pud Brown '67 and others. Retired to Tex. in early '70s, perf. occ. w. local mus. near his home in Bellaire. Films: *Holiday Inn* w. Bing Crosby '42; *The Fabulous Dorseys* '47. Book: *Dixieland Drumming*, pub. Chi. '37. Recs. w. Pollack; Gene Gifford; Bunny Berigan; Bing Crosby; Teagarden; Pete Fountain; Lamare. CDs: w. Bob Crosby (Dec.); Teagarden (BB; Arb.; ASV); Johnny Wiggs (Story.); *Swing is Here* (BB); M. Spanier (ASV).

BAUER, BILLY (WILLIAM HENRY), gtr; b. Bronx, NY, 11/14/15; d. Melville, NY, 12/5/02. Father was song-and-dance man who worked briefly on B'way bef. becoming a printer. Began on uke. and bjo. bef. sw. to gtr. in early 1930s. First prof. job pl. bjo. in speakeasy '28. Pl. solo bjo. on radio '29. Pl. w. Jerry Wald '40; made rec. debut w. Carl Hoff '41; worked w. Abe Lyman at Lincoln Hotel '42. Had own sxt., w. Flip Phillips on cl., Ray Turner on tnr., bef. join. Woody Herman's First Herd '42. With Herman until '45, then pl. briefly w. Benny Goodman and Jack Teagarden, but was importantly involved w. Lennie Tristano's gps. '45–9. Taught at NY Cons. of Mod. Mus. '46–9. Rec. w. Met. All-Stars '47–53. Staff gtrst. at NBC '50–8, then tour. Eur. w. Goodman. Own gps. on LI '60–2, then pl. w. Ice Capades '63–7; B'way shows '67–70. Pl. freq. w. Lee Konitz '50s–'60s. Opened gtr. sch. '70. Wrote four books for gtr. stud. After freelancing in the '70s, Bauer worked mainly as an educ. in '80s and '90s. Favs: Wes Montgomery. Polls: *DB* '49–50; *Met.* '49–53. Fests: Sweden, Norway, Germany, Brussels World's Fair w. B. Goodman '58. Films: *The Hustler*. CDs: w. Coleman Hawkins (Imp.); W. Herman (Col.; RCA); L. Tristano (Cap.); L. Konitz (Prest.); Charlie Parker (Verve; Spot.; Jazz Anth.); Buddy Rich (Sequel); Met. All-Stars (RCA); J.J. Johnson (Sav.); Goodman (Hep; Limel.).

BAUZA, MARIO, tpt, alto sax, cl, comp, arr; b. Havana, Cuba, 4/28/11; d. NYC, 7/11/93. Studied cl. at Municipal Cons. of Mus., Havana. Pl. bs-cl. in Havana Symph.; Felipe Valdes' Cuban Typical Orch. 1925. Rec. in NYC w. Antonio Mario Romeu's Charanga Orch. '26. Moved to NYC '30. Perf. w. Cuban comps. Antonio Machin, Don Azpiazu. Worked w. Noble Sissle '32. Tptr. and mus. dir. w. Chick Webb '33–8. Pl. w. Don Redman '38–9; Cab Calloway '39–41. Bauza was responsible for bringing the young Dizzy Gillespie into Calloway's band, where he gave him a grounding in Afro-Cuban mus. Join. Machito's Afro-Cubans '41; later became mus. dir. In his time w. Machito Afro-Cubans '41–76, where he pl. alto sax as well as tpt., he was infl. in helping to bring about a fusion of Afro-Cuban mus. and jazz. Worked mainly

as leader and mus. dir. fr. '76, pl. salsa as well as jazz. Tour. Eur. w. own band '92. Comps: "Tanga"; "Mambo Inn"; "Sambia." Fav. arrs: Chico O'Farrill, Quincy Jones, Gil Fuller. CDs: Mess.; w. C. Calloway (Class.); Ella Fitzgerald (Dec.); Louis Jordan (JSP); Machito (Col.; Pab.; Verve); one track w. Machito in *The Jazz Scene* (Verve); Gillespie-Machito (Pab.); C. Parker (Verve); C. Webb (Dec.; Hep).

BEAL, CHARLIE, pno; b. Los Angeles, CA, 9/14/08; d. San Diego, CA, 8/91. Older bro. of Eddie Beal. Pl. at Sebastian's Cotton Club w. Les Hite 1930. To Chi. '40, where he pl. at Grand Terrace w. Jimmie Noone; Erskine Tate; Frankie Jaxon. Replaced Teddy Wilson in Louis Armstrong band '33. After working w. Carroll Dickerson and Noble Sissle, moved to NYC, pl. at Adrian's Tap Room. Joined Eddie South '36, then served in army, moved to LA, and took part in L. Armstrong film, *New Orleans*. Worked in Eur. fr. late '48, ret. to Calif. for work at Raquet Club. CDs: w. Armstrong (BB).

BEAL, EDDIE, pno, comp; b. Redlands, CA, 6/13/10; d. Los Angeles, CA, 12/15/84. Studied pno. w. moth.; vln. at sch. Percussionist w. sch. symph. Came to LA as dmr. 1931, but sw. to pno. after a yr.; pl. w. Charlie Eccles, Earl Dancer. Pl. in Shanghai w. Teddy Weatherford, Buck Clayton '34–6, then worked in Calif., rec. w. Maxine Sullivan '39. Dur. '40s, served in army; acc. Billie Holiday; Ivie Anderson; rec. w. Jimmy Mundy; Herb Jeffries; Helen Humes; Red Callender; Claude Trenier. Fr. late '40s app. and rec. w. own gps., but later was mainly active as songwriter and publisher. Tours w. L. Rawls '70. Fr. Dec. '74 to Jan. '75 feat. in concerts w. Tommy Dorsey band under dir. of M. McEachern. Film: *Sparkle*. TV: *Sanford & Son*. Best-known comps: "Softly," rec. by Georgia Carr; "All Because of You," rec. by Dinah Washington. Stan Kenton rec. both these numbers and "Skoot," which Beal co-wrote w. Erroll Garner. A competent pnst., Beal was better known in later yrs. for his songs.

BEAL, JEFF, tpt, flg, kybds; b. Hayward, CA, 6/20/63. Studied tpt. fr. age 8 in public schools and priv. Degree fr. Eastman Sch. of Mus. 1985, receiving eleven *DB* student awards for tpt., jazz comp., and arr. Moved to NYC '85, pl. in Latin bands and bought a small electronic studio to rec. his own mus. incl. *Liberation* '87. In addition to his increasingly individual tpt. style, Beal has comp. many classical chamber wks., incl. concerto feat. John Patitucci; bb charts; and originals integrating electronics into improvised settings. Favs: Miles Davis, Kenny Wheeler, Woody Shaw. CDs: Ant.; Tri.

BEAN, FLOYD R., pno, comp; b. Grinnell, IA, 8/30/04; d. Cedar Rapids, IA, 3/9/74. Led own band 1919. Worked at Linwood Inn, Davenport, Iowa, where Bix Beiderbecke sat in '23; w. Bunny Berigan in Cy Mahlberg's band '26; Jack Jenney in Earl Hunt band '30. Studied arr. in Chi. '33 and pl. w. Eddie Neibauer '34–5; Jimmy McPartland '37–9; Bob Crosby '39; Wingy Manone '40. Own trio, then w. Boyd Raeburn '43; Jess Stacy '45 as second pno. and arr. Worked w. Paul Mares, Sidney Bechet '48; Miff Mole '50; Muggsy Spanier '50–5; Georg Brunis '53–7 and '58–9; Bob Scobey '58; Bill Reinhardt '60. Moved to Cedar Rapids '64. Fav. and greatest infl: Earl Hines. Rec: *Chicago Jazz* w. McPartland '39 (Decca); other recs. w. Spanier '50; own 45s, '56. CD: w. Bob Crosby (Halcyon).

BEASLEY, JOHN, kybds, arr; b. Shreveport, LA, 10/10/58. Musical family; grandfath. pl w. territory bands in 1920s, moth. a bandleader and mus. ed., fath. taught in jazz program at No. Tex. St. U. Stud. pno. fr. age 8; also pl. gtr., dms., and sax w. rock bands, and oboe in hs. Moved to LA '77; pl. r&b dates and jazz gigs w. Tony Dumas, Ralph Penland, et al.; w. Sergio Mendes '80. Mostly studio work in '80s; also pl. w. Chick Corea; Stanley Clarke; Michael Franks; Hubert Laws; prod. mus. for TV shows. First rec. as leader, *Cauldron* '91; Brazil tour w. H. Laws, B. Hutcherson, and Joe Henderson '92. CDs: WH; w. Laws (Limel.); B. Neidlinger (K2B2); J. Patitucci (GRP).

BEASON, BILL (WILLIAM), dms; b. Louisville, KY, 1908. Studied at Wilberforce U. Join. Horace Henderson's Collegians 1924, then pl. w. Henderson throughout '20s. Moved to NYC ca. '30. Pl. w. Bingie Madison, Jelly Roll Morton, Clarence Williams, King Oliver '30–1. Tour. Eur. and rec. w. Teddy Hill '35–7. Pl. w. Dicky Wells in Paris '37; Don Redman '38–9; Roy Eldridge '39. Replaced Chick Webb in Chick Webb Orch. when illness forced the leader to retire '39. Remained in band under Ella Fitzgerald's leadership until '41, then pl. w. H. Henderson '41; John Kirby off and on fr. '43; Eddie Heywood '44; Ben Webster '45; Sy Oliver, Earl Bostic '47. By the '50s he was inactive in mus. CDs: w. R. Eldridge (Col.); E. Fitzgerald (Class.); J.R. Morton (BB); K. Oliver (Aff.; Class.).

BECHET, SIDNEY JOSEPH, sop sax, cl; b. New Orleans, LA, 5/14/1897; d. Paris, France, 5/14/59. Four bros. all pl. instr. Began pl. bro. Leonard's cl. at age 6. Stud. w. Geo. Baquet fr. age 8; also stud. w. Lorenzo Tio Jr., Big Eye Nelson, but primarily self-taught. Sat in w. Freddie Keppard ca. 1905. By '14,

Bechet had pl. w. Jack Carey; Buddy Petit; Eagle Band of NO. Tour. Texas and South w. Clarence Williams, Louis Wade '14–16. Pl. w. King Oliver's Olympia Band in NO '16. Moved to Chi. '17; worked w. Oliver, Keppard, Tony Jackson, Lawrence Duhé '17–19. Moved to NYC, late '19. Freelanced, then joined Will Marion Cook's Southern Syncopated Orch. In '19, Bechet tour. the Continent w. Cook, and Engl., where he was described by the Swiss conductor Ernest Ansermet as "an extraordinary clarinet virtuoso" and "an artist of genius." Bought straight sop. sax in London. Pl. w. Bennie Peyton in Paris '19–21. Ret. to NYC '21. Pl. briefly w. Duke Ellington '24. Bechet opened Club Basha in Harlem in the mid '20s; Johnny Hodges acquired Bechet infl. while perf. there. Rec. w. Clarence Williams's Blue Five, also w. blues singers, incl. Mamie Smith, Rosetta Crawford '24–5. Freelanced in US and Eur. in mid '20s, incl. Eur. tour. w. Black Revue '25; Moscow w. Tommy Ladnier '27. Join. Noble Sissle in Paris '28. Pl. w. Sissle in Eur. and US off and on '28–38; also led own gps. incl. NO Feetwarmers w. Ladnier '32. Co-owned tailor shop in NYC w. Ladnier '38–9. Bechet was rediscovered as part of the NO revival that began ca. '39. Led own trio at Nick's, then app. several times w. Eddie Condon at Town Hall. Went to Chi. in early '40s w. own gp. that incl. Vic Dickenson, Sid Catlett. Also pl. and rec. in '40s w. Big Four (Muggsy Spanier, Carmen Mastren, Wellman Braud); Mezz Mezzrow. Bechet made freq. trips to Eur. fr. '49, then settled permanently in Paris '51. In France, Bechet transcended his jazz fame and was treated like a show-business celebrity. He made several hit recs. incl. "Petite Fleur," '52. Generally considered along w. Louis Armstrong as one of the earliest consummate jazz artists, he was the first jazz mus. to master the sop. sax. On that instrument he had a wide, sunny vibrato w. a powerful sound able to compete w. tpts. in carrying a lead. Bechet's infl. is considerable, but largely indirect, coming through other mus. such as Johnny Hodges, Buster Bailey, and Duke Ellington and later through his student Bob Wilber. In '97, his centennial, he was celebrated at many fests. and in programs at Carnegie Hall and Lincoln Center. A collection of material relating to Bechet's life and work is in the library of the Arkansas Arts Center at Little Rock. Polls: *Record Changer* All-Time All-Star '51. Book: autobiography, *Treat It Gentle* '60; *The Wizard of Jazz*, John Chilton, '87. CDs: BB; Class.; BN; BL; Vogue; JSP; Jazz.; KJ; w. Louis Armstrong (Col.; Dec.; Aff.); Jelly Roll Morton (BB); Charlie Parker (Stash); Clarence Williams (EPM).

BECK, GORDON, pno; comp; b. London, England, 9/16/36. Studied classical pno. at ages 12–15.

Worked as a draftsman bef. beginning a career as a mus. 1961. Fr. '62 to '66 pl. w. gps. of Tony Kinsey, Tubby Hayes; acc. Annie Ross; backed Helen Merrill, Joe Henderson, Lee Konitz, Phil Woods et al. w. his own trio at Ronnie Scott Club '66–9. Extensive Eur. and US tours w. P. Woods European Rhythm Machine '69–72; app. at NJF '71. In '73 was a member of George Gruntz's Piano Conclave; fr. '73 to '75 led own gp., Gyroscope. Toured Austral., Japan, and US w. Alan Holdsworth '85; pl. and rec. w. Didier Lockwood, Billy Hart, and Cecil McBee, late '80s. Became involved w. computers, sequencers, and synthesizers in '90s. Pl. solo pno. concerts in Eur., Israel, US. Active as jazz educ. at Barry Jazz Summer Sch. in Wales '74–87. CDs: JMS; w. Ian Carr (Core); Holdsworth; D. Humair (JMS); H. Merrill (Owl); M. Tormé (PW).

BECK, JOE (JOSEPH A.), gtr; b. Philadelphia, PA, 7/29/45. Mother, bro., sist. amateur mus. Stud. pno. w. moth. 1951–4. Pl. w. Paul Winter, Charles Lloyd '64; Don Payne '64–5; Gary McFarland '64–6; Tony Bennett, Astrud Gilberto '65; Mike Mainieri, Chico Hamilton '66; Peggy Lee '66–9; Jeremy Steig '68–9; Joe Farrell '71–3; Larry Coryell '76; own gps. since '74. Also rec. in '70s w. Jack McDuff; Gato Barbieri; Gene Ammons; Woody Herman; Buddy Rich; Maynard Ferguson; Paul Simon. One of the the first jazz-rock gtrs. Beck worked as a dairy farmer '68–71 and '88–90. Duo w. Ali Ryerson fr. '96. Favs: John Scofield, Jim Hall. Polls: NARAS Most Val. Player '84–9. TV: *Hot Licks* instructional video. CDs: DMP; w. Miles Davis; M. Ferguson (Col.); L. Coryell (Novus); Blue Mitchell (Main.); David Sanborn (WB); Gil Evans (Enja); L. Hampton (Limel.); Jane Jarvis (Aud.); J. Leonhart (Sunny.); H. Merrill (Em.); G. Niewood (DMP); B. Rich (LRC); B. Torff (Bassline).

BECK, PIA (PIETERNELLA), pno, voc; b. The Hague, Netherlands, 9/18/25. Ran away fr. home in teens; pl. w. Miller Sxt. 1944–9; did USO shows. Led own trio fr. '49; visited US in '52 and freq. thereafter; operated nightclubs in Netherlands and Spain. Rec. "Pia's Boogie" for Philips '50. Favs: Peterson, Garner, Mary Lou Williams, Fitzgerald, Vaughan. Autobiography, *The Pia Beck Story*, publ. in Amsterdam '78.

BECKETT, FRED (FREDERICK LEE), tbn; b. Nellerton, MS, 1/23/17; d. St. Louis, MO, 1/30/46. Trombone w. hs band. Moved to KC, then join. Johnson's Crackerjacks, St. Louis, 1934. Bet. '37–9 w. bands of Buster Smith; Tommy Douglas; Andy Kirk; Prince Stewart; Nat Towles. Pl. w. Harlan Leonard

'39–40; Lionel Hampton '40–4. Became infected w. fatal TB while in mil. service '45. Rec. solos on Leonard's "My Gal Sal," "Skee," and "A La Bridges," '40, which impressed the young J.J. Johnson, who considered him the first great modern tbn. Also rec. w. Hampton '41–2. CDs: w. Hampton (Dec.; Jazz Magic).

BEDFORD, RONNIE (RONALD HILLIER), dms, tmbls, mrba, tympani; b. Bridgeport, CT, 6/2/31. Mother sang and pl. acc.; sists. pl. pno.; bro. pl. tpt. Stud. priv. in Bridgeport 1941–4; joined Bridgeport Mus. Union at age 16. Studied in NYC w. Fred Albright, Willie Rodriguez '49–52. Pl. w. Louis Prima '50–1; 2nd Army Bagpipe Band '52–4; Billy May–Sam Donahue '54–6, Sam Donahue '56–7; Richard Maltby, Buddy Morrow, Boyd Raeburn, Les and Larry Elgart '57–9; Eddie Condon, Joe Bushkin, Hank Jones, Marian McPartland, Pee Wee Russell, Chuck Wayne, Jimmy Giuffre '58–60. Worked on B'way w. Don Elliot qt. in *A Thurber Carnival* '59–60; w. Peter Matz in *No Strings* '61–2. Pl. w. Johnny Richards '62–8; Al Cohn–Zoot Sims, Wild Bill Davison, Red Norvo, Phil Woods, Jimmy Raney, Toshiko Akiyoshi, Teddy Wilson, Lee Konitz, Ruby Braff '62–70; bbs incl. Benny Goodman, Marshall Brown's Newport Youth Band, Warren Covington's Tommy Dorsey Orch., Vincent Lopez, Skitch Henderson '63–9; Rod Levitt Oct. '63–85; Jack Reilly, Sheila Jordan, Warren Chiasson fr. '60s; Morris Nanton, Harold Lieberman's Jazz Impact '70–86; B. Goodman Sxt. and Oct., '74–5; Red Norvo, Barbara Carroll '77; Benny Carter '77–86; Buddy DeFranco, Arnett Cobb, Herb Ellis–Barney Kessel, Sweets Edison, Jack Sheldon, Dick Sudhalter '78–86. House dmr. at Newport and Kool JFs '80–5. Bedford moved to Wyoming in late '85 to take a teaching position at Northwest Coll. He presented a concert of the mus. of Claude Bolling in Billings, Mont., New Year's Eve '89. Cont. to perf. w. his own trio and qt. at fests. and to book his own tours as Ronnie Bedford and Friends. Favs: M. Roach, B. Rich, S. Manne. Fests: Eur. w. Goodman '75; Mexico City '79 w. DeFranco. TV: Ed Sullivan, Steve Allen, *Today*; Edie Adams, Mickey Rooney specials; Jazz at the Smithsonian video w. Benny Carter. CDs: w. Hank Jones; Dick Meldonian (Prog.); B. Carter (MM; Pab.); DeFranco (Pab.).

BEIDERBECKE, BIX (LEON), crnt, pno, comp; b. Davenport, IA, 3/10/03; d. NYC, 8/6/31. His moth. pl. pno. Beiderbecke began pl. pno. at 3 and crnt. at 13, though he pl. left-handed for the first eight yrs. He attended hs in Davenport 1919–21. Dur. this time, he sat in and pl. prof. w. various bands, incl. those of Wilbur Hatch, Floyd Bean, and Carlisle Evans. To discourage his interest in jazz, his family sent him to Lake Forest Acad., near Chi., in '21, but he was expelled in May '22 for frequent truancy, mostly musically related. While still at the acad., he form. the Cy-Bix Orch. w. dmr. Walter "Cy" Welge, and went to Chi. regularly to pl. w. the Ten Foot Band, among others, and to hear jazz. He ret. to Davenport briefly that summer, then moved to Chi. to join the Cascades Band, working on Lake Mich. excursion boats. Fr. fall '22 to fall '23, he gigged around Chi., at times ret. to Davenport to work for his fath., a merchant. In Oct. '23, he joined the Wolverines in Hamilton, Ohio, and soon became the band's main attraction. Dur. the next yr., they pl. in and around Chi., tour. the Midwest, and rec. for Gennett; they began a long residency at the Cinderella Ballroom, NYC, in Sept. '24 and did some further rec. bef. Beiderbecke left in Nov. Dur. '24 he also began a long musical partnership w. saxist Frankie Trumbauer. After a brief spell w. Jean Goldkette, he ret. to Chi. in '25 where he pl. w. Charlie Straight's commercial band. He was fired after a month. In Feb., he briefly enrolled at Iowa State U., then resumed gigging around Chi. and sitting in w. the city's foremost artists, incl. King Oliver, Louis Armstrong, and Jimmie Noone. In Sept. '25, he join. Trumbauer, who was then leading a band in St. Louis under Goldkette's auspices. After the summer season '26, Beiderbecke and Trumbauer joined Goldkette to Sept. '27. After a month stint w. the short-lived Adrian Rollini Orch. in NYC, Beiderbecke and Trumbauer join. Paul Whiteman in Indianapolis. Beiderbecke officially remained w. Whiteman until spring '30, though he had many extended absences due to his deteriorating health, and spent some time back in Davenport the last year of his life. From the summer of '30, when he did a four-day tryout w. the Casa Loma Band, he worked freelance, mostly in NYC, and cont. rec., though he was severely curtailed by his ill health. In the winter of '31, he briefly had a regular spot on the *Camel Hour* radio show and played occ. dates that spring. In the summer of '31, he moved fr. his Manh. apt. to Sunnyside, Queens. He was treated by a doctor the last few days of his life and died at home of lobar pneumonia.

Dur. his lifetime, Beiderbecke was appreciated by virtually only a handful of mus. and fans. It wasn't until after his death that he acquired legendary status, partly through Dorothy Baker's novel *Young Man With a Horn*, which is very loosely based on his life. Beiderbecke was known chiefly for his exquisite tone and extremely lyrical improvisations. He was probably the first white jazz mus. to be admired and imitated by black mus.: Rex Stewart and others learned his solo on Trumbauer's rec. of "Singin' the Blues" note for note. Himself inspired by Emmett Hardy, a

white tptr., Armstrong, Joe Smith, and others, Beiderbecke's followers were legion, incl. Bobby Hackett and Jimmy McPartland. As a pnst. and comp., he was among the first to incorporate Debussy's harmonic ideas in a jazz idiom. Of his four piano comps., the most famous is "In a Mist" (also known as "Bixology"), the others being "Flashes," "Candlelights," and "In the Dark." All were notated and edited for publication by arranger Bill Challis '30. In his short career, Beiderbecke often perf. highly commercialized arrs. and was, at times, surrounded by mus. of a much lesser stature, yet he left a legacy of performances unmatched for subtlety and finesse. Films: *Bix: "Ain't None of Them Play Like Him Yet,"* Brigitte Berman; *Bix: An Interpretation of a Legend*, Pupi Avati '90. Books: *Bix: Man and Legend*, R.M. Sudhalter, P.R. Evans, W. Dean-Myatt '74; *Remembering Bix: A Memoir of the Jazz Age*, Ralph Berton '74. CDs: Col.; BB; Mile.; w. Hoagy Carmichael (BB).

BEIRACH, RICHIE (RICHARD), pno, kybds, comp; b. NYC, 5/23/47. Studied classical and jazz pno. and comp. at Berklee Coll. of Mus. and Manh. Sch. of Mus. (B.A. 1972). Pl. w. Stan Getz '72; Dave Liebman's Lookout Farm '73–6. Formed own trio Eon '76. Founding member of John Abercrombie Qt. '78. Co-led gp. Quest w. Liebman '81–mid '80s. He has also worked w. Freddie Hubbard, Lee Konitz, Chet Baker. His varied infls. range fr. Tatum, Bud Powell, and Bill Evans to Corea, Hancock, and Tyner; many modern classical comps.; and C. Parker, M. Davis, and Coltrane along w. soul perfs. He has rec. solo pno. in the Maybeck Hall series on Conc.; and in duo on Tri. w. George Coleman. CDs: Conc.; Tri.; Owl; Core; Konnex; w. Liebman (CMP; Story.; Core); Abercrombie (ECM); John Scofield (Enja); Chet Baker (A&M); Ron McClure; Mike Richmond (Steep.).

BELDEN, BOB (JAMES ROBERT), arr, sop, tnr saxes, pno, synth; b. Evanston, IL, 10/31/56. Mother sings, bro. and sis. pl. pno. Family moved to Goose Creek, So. Carolina, in late 1950s. Began on pno., then sw. to alto sax at age 11. Pl. w. bro.'s rock band '69–71, then stud. at No. Tex. St. U. '73–8. Pl. w. Denton Dues Band '77; Woody Herman '79–80; Donald Byrd '82–5. Sub. w. Mel Lewis Orch. '84–5. Pl. w. Michael Legrand '85–7; Joe Chambers since '87; Red Rodney, Ray Mantilla '88; Bob Belden Ens. since '89. Belden has taught comp. at the New Sch. since '90, and prod. two recs. for Red Rodney. Other rec. projects have incl. his own comps. for *Treasure Island*, and adventuresome, personal interpretations of the opera *Turandot*; the mus. of Sting; and the mus. of Prince. Wrote the arrs. for Herbie Hancock's *The*

New Standard and Joe Henderson's *Porgy and Bess*, both Verve; and Bernard Purdie's *Soul to Jazz II*, ACT, which he also produced. Fests: Eur. '79–80, '88, '90; So. Amer. '80, '87. TV: apps. w. Herman and Legrand. CDs: BN; MB; Sunny.; w. Herman (Conc.); Glenn Wilson (Sunny.).

BELGRAVE, MARCUS, tpt, educ, comp, arr; b. Chester, PA, 6/12/36. Cousin is Cecil Payne. Encouraged at an early age by his fath. and bro., both brass pl., and, when he was 17, by Clifford Brown, Belgrave was working prof. by the time he entered hs. Came to national attention in mid 1950s and early '60's pl. w. Ray Charles band while stationed in air force. Moved to Det. in '63, where he co-founded the jazz studies program at Det. Metro Arts Complex; was an orig. faculty member of the Oakland U. Jazz Stud. Program; founded the Jazz Development Wkshp. in Det. His students have incl. Geri Allen; Robert Hurst; Kenny Garrett; and James Carter. App. in Classical Jazz series at Lincoln Center, NYC, in '90s. Rec. w. Bobby Blue Bland; Aretha Franklin; Eric Dolphy; McCoy Tyner; Max Roach; Joe Cocker. CDs: w. G. Allen (BN); R. Hurst (DIW); LCJO (Col.); Charles Mingus; Ray Charles (Rh./Atl.); David Murray (Red Brn.); David Newman (Muse); K. Lightsey (CC); C. Payne (Del.); C. Amy (PJ).

BELL, (SAMUEL) AARON, bs, comp; also pno, tba, tpt, euph; b. Muskogee, OK, 4/24/22; d. Bronx, NY, 7/28/03. B.A. as mus. ed. major at Xavier U., NO, 1942; M.A. fr. NYU '51; Columbia U. '75; Ph.D. fr. Columbia '77. After navy duty '41–6, join. Andy Kirk '47 bef. ret. to Muskogee to teach mus. in hs. Pl. w. Ed Wilcox; Lucky Millinder; Herman Chittison; Teddy Wilson; Lester Young; Eddie Heywood; Johnny Smith; Dorothy Donegan; Mat Mathews. Had own trio at Concord Hotel in upstate N.Y., Dec. '54–May '56. Pl. briefly w. Billy Taylor trio, fall '59. Join. Duke Ellington spring '60, remain. until Oct. '62. Then pl. in pit bands; comp. for off-B'way theater '69–72. Resident comp., La Mama Experimental Theater '70–3; mus. dir. for Elmsford (N.Y.) Dinner Theater '74–5. App. at NJF-NY w. Paul Jeffrey '73; Corky Corcoran '74. In '78 he pl. in Eur. in an Ellington alumni unit under the dir. of Cat Anderson, and did the Eur. fest. circuit as pnst., occ. doubling bs., w. C. Terry Spacemen '89. Dir. of Instrumental and Jazz Program, Essex Coll., Newark, N.J., '70–5, Chairman of Perf. Arts Dept. fr. '77. Retired fr. teach. '94. Cont. to lead voc. gp., S.W.A.T. Team; also gp. and bb for coll. concerts. Comps: *Bicentennial Symphony*; *Watergate Sonata* for pno.; *Rondo Schizo* for cl. and pno.; *Frugal Fugue* for combo. Fav: Pettiford. CDs: w. Ellington (Col.; BB; BL; Imp.; Saja;

Red Brn.; Fant.); J. Hodges (BB; Pab.); J. Coltrane (Imp.); B. Holiday (Verve); J. Rushing (Vang.); L. Young (Story.); C. Anderson (B&B); H. Ashby (Stash).

BELL, GRAEME, pno, comp; b. Melbourne, Australia, 9/7/14. Six years classical studies. Form. band w. bro. Roger in late 1930s. Led first Austral. jazz band to tour Eur. '47. Founded the Swaggie label in '49; helped arr. Rex Stewart's visit to Austral. '49 and rec. w. him. Tour. Japan '54 and '87; led series of all-star gps. in '60s and '70s and became established as Austral.'s foremost trad. jazz mus. In April '90, he took his 6-pc. band to China and southeast Asia. Rec. album w. Japanese band in Sydney '91. Favs. incl. Fats Waller, Teddy Wilson, Earl Hines, Dollar Brand, Ralph Sutton. Awards: Queen's Medal '77; MBE '78. App. at Edinburgh JF w. Humphrey Lyttelton '93. Book: *Graeme Bell, Australian Jazzman*, Child & Assocs. (Austral.) '88. CDs: EMI/Axis (Austral.).

BELLETTO, AL (ALPHONSE JOSEPH), alto, bari saxes; cl; b. New Orleans, LA, 1/3/28. Played cl. in hs. Began pl. prof. after acquiring a sax. Led own gp. while att. Loyola U., where he earned a bachelor's degree in mus. ed. Received M. Mus. fr. La. State U. Worked w. Sharkey Bonano; Leon Prima; Wingy Manone; Dukes of Dixieland. Toured w. own sxt. fr. Dec. 1952. The gp. was incorporated into the Woody Herman Orch. '58–9. Worked in NO fr. '60s. Favs: Charlie Parker, Count Basie, Stan Kenton. Rec. LPs for Cap. CDs: fr. '69 NO JF, one track, *What's New* on *Jazz Festival Masters* (Scotti Bros.); w. Herman (Evid.).

BELLSON, LOUIE or LOUIS (Luigi Paulino Alfredo Francesco Antonio Balassoni), dms, comp, lead; b. Rock Falls, IL, 7/6/24. Won contest run by Gene Krupa for best dmr. under the age of 18, 1940. Pl. w. Ted Fio Rito; Benny Goodman bef. and after army service in '43; Tommy Dorsey '47–9. Worked in small gp. w. Charlie Shavers and Terry Gibbs '50. After working in Calif. w. Harry James, Bellson, Willie Smith, and Juan Tizol, quit James to join Ellington, Mar. '51. Ellington rec. several of Bellson's originals, incl. "The Hawk Talks," "Skin Deep," and "Ortseam." Left Ellington Jan. '53, shortly after his marriage to Pearl Bailey, whom he accomp. off and on until her death in '90. Also worked w. Dorsey '55–6; Basie '62; Dorsey ghost band '64; Ellington '65–6; James '66. Dur. '50s, rec. extensively for Norman Granz w. Art Tatum; Oscar Peterson; Buddy De Franco; Louis Armstrong; Ella Fitzgerald; et al., and tour. w. JATP '55, '67, and, in Eur., '72. For more than twenty yrs., he has led bbs internationally, w. personnel drawn fr. pools of musicians in NYC, LA, and Chi. In the '90s he has often tour. w. a qnt. Among his better-known sidemen have been Don Menza; Pete Christlieb; Ted Nash; Cat Anderson; Ross Tompkins; Bobby Shew; Blue Mitchell; Sam Noto; and Joe Romano. Universally respected as a mus. who combines enthusiasm and a driving beat w. an astonishing technique, incl. the use of two bs. dms., he was described by Ellington as "The world's greatest drummer.... Louis Bellson has all the requirements for perfection in his craft." Received Amer. Jazz Masters Award fr. NEA '94. CDs: MM; Pab.; Conc.; Limel.; w. T. Dorsey (Hep); Ellington (Col.; Pab.; Saja; GRP); Basie (Roul.; Pab.); L. Armstrong; Benny Carter; R. Eldridge (Verve); O. Peterson; E. Fitzgerald; Art Tatum; S. Vaughan; JATP (Pab.); J. Hodges (Prest.; Verve).

BENEKE, TEX (GORDON), tnr sax, voc, lead; b. Fort Worth, TX, 2/12/14; d. Costa Mesa, CA, 5/30/00. Played sop. sax as child. Territory bands in 1930s, incl. Ben Young '35–7. Recommended by Gene Krupa, he join. Glenn Miller band '38; became the band's best known sideman. Tenor solos on classic sides, incl. "String of Pearls" and "In the Mood," singing on such hits as "Chattanooga Choo Choo" and "I've Got a Gal in Kalamazoo." App. w. Miller band in the films *Sun Valley Serenade* '41 and *Orchestra Wives* '42. That yr., when Miller dissolved band to enter mil., Beneke tour. w. the old band's voc. gp., the Modernaires, then led a navy dance band in Okla. After WWII, he led a Miller-styled orch. w. sanction of the Miller estate administrators, '46–50; cont. to dir. his own, similarly styled orch. into '90s, usually incl. singers and instrumentalists fr. the orig. Miller organization. Polls: *DB* '41–2; *Met.* '41–2. CDs: w. Miller; *Met.* All-Stars (BB).

BENFORD, TOMMY (THOMAS P.), dms; b. Charleston, WV, 4/19/05; d. Mt. Vernon, NY, 3/24/94. Mother pl. pno., org.; fath. pl. tba., dms. Bro. Bill pl. tba. Learned mus. w. bro. at Jenkins Orphanage in So. Carolina. Tour. Engl. w. Orphanage band 1914. Stud. dms. w. Steve and Herbert Wright. First prof. job w. Green River Minstrel Show '20. Pl. w. Marie Lucas; Edgar Hayes; Charlie Skeete; Jelly Roll Morton; Bill Benford; Fats Waller; Duke Ellington '20s. Pl. in Eur. w. Eddie South, Sy Devereaux '32; Freddie Taylor '36–7; Willie Lewis '38–41. Rec. in Eur. w. South; Eddie Brunner; Coleman Hawkins; Bill Coleman; Benny Carter; Django Reinhardt. Pl. in US w. Noble Sissle '43; Snub Mosley '46–8; Bob Wilber '48–9; Jimmy Archey '50–2; Rex Stewart '53; Muggsy Spanier in Can. '54; Leroy Parkins, Bob Pilsbury on Cape Cod '56–9; house bands at Central

Plaza, Jimmy Ryan's, late '50s; Freddy Johnson '59. Tour. Eur. w. *Jazz Train* under dir. of Eddie Barefield '60–1. Pl. w. Joe Thomas, Edmond Hall, Danny Barker '63; Saints and Sinners '63–8; Franz Jackson '68. Pl. w. Bob Greene's *World of Jelly Roll Morton* at NJF-NY and Lincoln Center '73–4; Clyde Bernhardt's Harlem Blues and Jazz Band '73–81; B. Greene '82. App. on tribute to C. Hawkins at NJF-NY '83. Favs: Sid Catlett, Buddy Rich. CDs: w. J.R. Morton (BB; JSP; Class.); C. Hawkins (ASV; Timel.); Django Reinhardt (Aff.); Benny Carter (B&B).

BENJAMIN, JOE (JOSEPH RUPERT), bs; b. Atlantic City, NJ, 11/4/19; d. Livingston, NJ, 1/26/74. Raised in NYC; stud. vln. w. Hall Johnson. Protégé of bsst. George Duvivier. Worked as mus. copyist for Jimmie Lunceford, Billy Moore Jr. Pl. w. Mercer Ellington 1946; Billy Taylor (bs.), Artie Shaw, Fletcher Henderson '50. Second bs. w. Duke Ellington at Met. Opera concert, Jan. '51; intermittently assoc. w. Ellington as copyist, sideman, and publ. co. employee. Worked w. Dizzy Gillespie, Paris '52; tour. w. Sarah Vaughan '53–5; Gerry Mulligan '57; Dave Brubeck, Ellis Larkins '58. Club work w. Sweets Edison; Ben Webster; Tyree Glenn. Many recs. as studio mus. In '70s worked again w. D. Ellington. Died of heart attack several weeks after auto accident. Fav: Blanton. Broadway: *The Nervous Set* '59. CDs: w. Vaughan (Em.); Mulligan; Brubeck (Col.); Barry Harris (Riv.); Mulligan-Desmond; K. Burrell; B. Holiday (Verve); Ellington (Col.; Pab., Atl.); J. Hodges (BB); E. Dolphy; RR Kirk; J. Richardson (Prest.).

BENJAMIN, SATHIMA BEA, voc; b. Capetown, South Africa, 10/17/36. Sang hymns in church bef. discovering pop mus. in Capetown. Prof. debut 1959, w. Dollar Brand (Abdullah Ibrahim); after their marriage, the duo moved to Eur. where they met Duke Ellington, w. whom she sang several times. The couple settled in NYC. Benjamin sang at '65 NJF; rec. several albums for Ekapa, the best known of which was *Sathima Sings Ellington* '79. In '92, an album, *Southern Touch*, in which she is backed by Kenny Barron, Buster Williams, and Billy Higgins, was released on an Enja CD.

BENNETT, BETTY, voc; b. Lincoln, NE, 10/23/21. First stud. w. moth., a jazz pnst. Moved to Hamburg, Iowa, at 6; stud. voice, planning to be an opera singer. Sang w. Georgie Auld 1943; had own radio show as member of WAVES '45. After WWII, sang w. Claude Thornhill '46; Alvino Rey '47–9; Stan Kenton All-Stars '49; Charlie Ventura '49–50. Worked as a single in SF '50–1; w. Charlie Barnet '52. Married André

Previn '52 and retired. Resumed singing in '58 w. Benny Goodman, then semiretired until she moved to London '63; worked as resident singer at Ronnie Scott's Club '64–6. Back to LA late '60s, working as a secretary-researcher for a TV producer fr. '67. After marrying gtrst. Mundell Lowe, she resumed singing and perf. regularly w. him in US and Eur. A splendid, jazz-infl. singer noted for her interpretation of sophisticated lyrics. CDs: FS.

BENNETT, LOU (Jean-Louis Benoit), org, comp; b. Philadelphia, PA, 5/18/26. Father was fr. Martinique. Studied pno. w. moth. and aunt. In army where he pl. tba. in band 1943–6; then led own Nat Cole–style trio in Balt. fr. '47. Began pl. org. '56; tour. w. own trio '57–9. Moved to Paris '60, pl. at Blue Note w. Jimmy Gourley, Kenny Clarke. Pl. and rec. w. Clarke, René Thomas, Donald Byrd '60s. Tour. Eastern Eur. '66. In '78 conceived and built an org. called "The Bennett Machine," which enabled him to prod. many other instrumental voices such as pno., vib. Led qnt. w. Gerard Badini '80s. Bennett has not perf. in the US since he app. at '64 NJF. Favs: Wild Bill Davis, Jackie Davis, Jimmy Smith. Fests: all major in Eur. fr. '60. Many film and TV apps. in Eur. CD: w. Clarke in *Americans in Europe* (Imp.).

BENNETT, MAX RAMON, bs, el-bs, comp; b. Des Moines, IA, 5/24/28. Raised in KC and Oskaloosa, Iowa. Pl. tbn. as teenager, then gtr. Stud. at U. of Iowa. Pl. w. Herbie Fields 1949; Georgie Auld, Terry Gibbs, Charlie Ventura '50–1. In army '51–3. Tour. w. Stan Kenton '54–5, then settled in LA. Pl. w. own combo at Lighthouse, also backed Peggy Lee. Accomp. Ella Fitzgerald w. JATP '57–8. Worked as studio mus. in LA '58–60. Pl. w. Terry Gibbs '59. Tour. w. Peggy Lee, cond. orch. '61–3. Ret. to work as studio mus., began pl. el-bs. '63. Pl. w. Jimmy Rowles Trio at Carriage House, LA, fr. '63; freelance w. Shorty Rogers, Pete Jolly, also bbs led by Mike Barone, Bud Brisbois, Jack Daugherty '60s. Pl. w. Quincy Jones off and on '68–80; Tom Scott's LA Express '72–7, backing Joni Mitchell '73–4, '76. Pl. and rec. w. Crusaders '72–3, '75; Aretha Franklin '77; Victor Feldman '84; others. Formed own gp., Freeway, '84. Bennett comp. much of the repertoire of LA Express and Freeway. His songs w. orig. lyrics were rec. by Peggy Lee. CDs: w. Mel Tormé (Charly); LA Express (A&M); Charlie Mariano (FS; Aff.); Bob Cooper; T. Gibbs (Cont.); Ella Fitzgerald (Verve); Coleman Hawkins (Pab.); Kenton (Status); Joni Mitchell (Asylum).

BENNETT, TONY (Anthony Dominick Benedetto), voc.; b. Astoria, Queens, NY, 8/3/26. In 1948, stud. at Amer. Theatre Wing under the GI Bill. Worked as a singing waiter at age 17. Pearl Bailey discovered him; Bob Hope changed his stage name fr. Joe Bari to Tony Bennett. In '51, Bennett rec. "Boulevard of Broken Dreams," his first hit. In '62 he scored w. "I Left My Heart in San Francisco," and it became his signature song. In the '60s he perf. w. the orchs. of Basie, Ellington, and Herman. His assoc. w. jazz was further marked by the use of such mus. as saxists Zoot Sims and Al Cohn; and crntsts. Bobby Hackett and Ruby Braff. The latter tour. w. him in '71–3 and backed him in a qt. w. gtrst. George Barnes '73–4. Fr. '66 to '72 Bennett employed John Bunch as his pnst/mus. dir.; and, in the same capacity, Ralph Sharon '56–68 and fr. '80. Pl. most countries of the world, app. in fests. at Mt. Hood; Ravinia (Chi.); North Sea; NYC; SF. As a painter, he first exhibited in Chi. in '77 and has since shown in Engl., France, and in many US cities. TV: *Tonight Show* many times; *Nat Cole Show;* BBC-TV, 100th Anniv. of Royal Albert Hall w. London Philharm., cond. by R. Farnon. Movies: *King; The Oscar.* Awards: one of six vocalists selected by *Life* magazine as Best Amer. Standard Singers of all time; Honorary Doctorate from Berklee. Video: *Tony Bennett Live: Watch What Happens* (Sony). CDs: Col.; DRG; w. B. Evans (DRG; Fant.); Basie (Col.; BN).

BENNINK, HAN (HENDRIKUS JOHANNES), dms; b. Zaandam, Netherlands, 4/17/42. Studied at art sch. first. Mainly self-taught, but helped by fath., a radio mus. In 1966, w. Willem Breuker and Misha Mengelberg, started the Instant Comps.' Pool, an independent rec. co., for which he rec. solo and w. various small gps. His bro. Peter, a saxist, was a frequent associate. Pl. w. many visiting Amers. incl. Eric Dolphy; Ben Webster; Sonny Rollins; Steve Lacy; Cecil Taylor. Bennink's work was noted for its unorthodox variety of equipment and for drawing on mus. fr. many other cultures, incl. Africa, Japan, Tibet. He has long been considered one of Eur.'s outstanding and most versatile percsts. Favs: Kenny Clarke, Ed Blackwell. Won Bird jazz award at North Sea Fest. '87. CDs: w. Breuker (BVHAAST; Entr'acte); Derek Bailey; Company (Incus); P. Brotzman; Globe Unity Orch.; Cecil Taylor; Peter Kowald (FMP); Don Cherry; Dexter Gordon (Aff.); E. Dolphy (Em.); Major Holley; Joe van Enkhuizen (Timel.); L. Konitz (Phil.); Mengelberg (SN); Andy Sheppard (Ant.); ICP Orch. (BVHAAST).

BENSKIN, SAMMY (SAMUEL), pno, comp, arr; b. NYC, 9/27/22; d. Teaneck, NJ, 8/92. Played w. Bardu Ali 1940; Bobby Burnet at Café Society '41; Stuff Smith '42; Gene Sedric, Don Redman, Al

Cooper '43; Freddie Green, Billie Holiday, Benny Morton '45. Worked as soloist and w. own trio fr. '45. Pl. w. Three Flames '54; then app. in Wm. Saroyan's *The Time of Your Life* at the City Center '55. Accomp. singers fr. mid '50s, incl. Roy Hamilton '55; Al Hibbler '58–9; also Titus Turner; Diahann Carroll; Dinah Washington. Pl. w. Stan Rubin '58; *Time of Your Life* at Brussels World's Fair '59. Benskin worked mainly as a voc. coach, arr., and rec. prod. fr. '60, pl. occ. gigs as a single. He pl. in NYC in the mid '80s w. the Harlem Blues and Jazz Band. Rec. w. Freddie Green; (Duke), ca. '45; Bennie Morton (BN) '45; John Hardee (BN) '46. CDs: w. B. Holiday (Dec.); tracks w. Hardee, Morton in *The Blue Note Swingtets* (BN).

BENSON, GEORGE, gtr, voc; b. Pittsburgh, PA, 3/22/43. Stepfather, a gtrst., taught him uke. and pl. Charlie Christian recs. for him. In 1954, he started on gtr. and rec. four pop sides for RCA's "X" label. Tour. w. Jack McDuff '62–5, rec. w. him as sideman and leader. Benson then formed own qt. '65, rec. for Col. In '70s, rec. for A&M and CTI w. larger gps. In '76, *Breezin'*, his first WB album, won the Record of the Year Grammy and catapulted Benson to world-class stardom; since then, he has been better known as a voc. rather than a gtrst. He has since won other Grammys, mostly in pop and r&b categories. As a crossover artist, he has rec. w. Ivan Lins; Chet Atkins; Freddie Hubbard; Patti Austin; Miles Davis; Herbie Hancock; Tony Bennett; Quincy Jones; Earl Klugh; the Count Basie Orch.; Billy Cobham; and many others. He has app. on countless domestic and int'l TV shows; comp. the title song for *The Greatest*, a film about Muhammad Ali; and made many fest. apps. worldwide. He headlined a week-long *Guitar Legends* event in Seville, Spain, at the '92 Expo site. Makes effective use of a technique of singing wordlessly in unison w. his improv. gtr. solos. In his occ. jazz apps., he has cont. to reveal a strong linkage w. Charlie Christian. CDs: Prest.; CTI/CBS; Col.; WB; Verve; w. McDuff (Prest.; Conc.); Hank Crawford (Mile.); Ronnie Cuber (Elec. Bird); M. Davis (Col.); S. Turrentine; Lou Donaldson (BN); F. Hubbard (CTI); Jean-Luc Ponty (Atl.).

BENTON, WALTER BARNEY, tnr sax; b. Los Angeles, CA, 9/9/30. Father pl. sax; sist. pl. pno. Stud. C-melody sax in jr. hs. First gigs at local USO. Pl. w. army bands at Ft. Lewis, Wash., 1950–2; Yokahama, Japan, '53. In LA, rec. w. Kenny Clarke and in jam session w. Clifford Brown–Max Roach '54. Pl. w. Perez Prado '54–7, incl. tour of Asia '56. Freelanced in LA '57–9, then led own gp. in NYC '59–61. Also pl. and rec. w. Roach, Abbey Lincoln, Julian Priester in NYC bef. ret. to LA '61. Pl. w. Gerald Wil-

son '60s. Rec. w. John Anderson '66. Favs: Lucky Thompson, Milt Jackson , Charlie Parker. CDs: w. K. Clarke; M. Jackson (Sav.); Clifford Brown (Em.); Eric Dolphy; A. Lincoln; Roach (Cand.); Q. Jones (Imp.).

BERG, BOB (ROBERT), tnr, sop saxes; b. NYC, 4/7/51; d. Amangansett, NY, 12/5/02. Raised in Bklyn.; stud. at HS for Perf. Arts, then Juilliard. Tour. w. Jack McDuff 1969; Horace Silver '73–6; Cedar Walton '77–83; rec. *Visitation* w. Sam Jones '78. Join. Miles Davis '84–7; rec. *You're Under Arrest* '85. In '91, was feat. on Gary Burton's *Cool Nights* and Mike Stern's *Odds and Evens*. Toured Caribbean and Central Amer. for US State Dept., early '92. LP: Xan. CDs: Den.; Stretch; Red; w. Davis (Col.); Sam Jones; Kenny Drew (Steep.); Kenny Drew Jr. (JC); Tom Harrell (Cont.); B. Dennerlein; Leni Stern (Enja); Mike Stern (Atl.); Cedar Walton (Muse); Eastern Rebellion (Timel.); Niels Lan Doky (Mile.; Story.); Gary Burton (GRP); B. Higgins (Red); J. Chambers (Cand.).

BERG, THILO, dms; b. Dortmund, Germany, 4/23/59. Parents are mus. teachers; bro. pl. Fr. horn.; sist. a classical singer. Took up tpt., cl., pno. bef. concentrating on dms. Studied in Trossingen 1977–81. Pl. w. SWF Radio Orch. to '81; own bb '86–92; it tour. w. Art Farmer '87; Slide Hampton '88, '90, '91; Bob Mintzer '90, '91. Berg worked w. Louis Stewart–Heiner Franz qt. '88–9; John Gordon's Trombones Unlimited '91–2; Barbara Morrison qt. '92–3. Active as a rec. prod. for Clark Terry and others on the Mons label in Germ. Pl. in NYC '90, '91. Does clinics and wkshps. for Tama Drums. Favs: Carl Allen, Jeff Hamilton, Jeff "Tain" Watts. Fest: Leverkusen w. B. Morrison, '93. Rec. debut in Germ., '81. CDs: Mons; w. B. Morrison; J. Gordon (Mons).

BERGER, DAVID, arr, comp, tpt; b. NYC, 3/30/49. Mother was amateur pnst. Stud. at Berklee Coll. of Mus. 1966; Ithaca Coll. '67–71, B. Mus. '71; Eastman Sch. of Mus. '67–81; Manh. Sch. of Mus. '85–6, M. Mus. Jazz Comp. '86. Also stud. w. Rayburn Wright; Jimmy Maxwell; Ludmila Ulehla; Edward Green. Pl. w. local bands in Ithaca '67–71. Moved to NYC '71, form. own rehearsal band. Pl. w. Jimmy Maxwell '72–80; Lee Castle '73. Pl. and arr. for Mercer Ellington '74; Chuck Israels Nat'l Jazz Ens. '75–80; Gunther Schuller '80. Berger has comp. and arr. for Buddy Rich orch.; Thad Jones–Mel Lewis Orch.; Clark Terry; Bill Watrous; WGJB; Lee Konitz Nonet; Stan Getz; Buddy DeFranco; Stanley Turrentine; Roland Hanna; Wynton Marsalis; Betty Carter; Dr. Michael White; LCJO. Cond. LCJO '88–94. Led specially assembled orchs. for Ellington Society concerts '94–5. In '96 he wrote one and a half hours of extra material to go w. the Ellington/Strayhorn *Nutcracker Suite* and cond. an orch. on a six-city US tour incl. perfs. at the Bklyn. Acad. of Mus. Berger has also arr. for theater, TV, and commercials as well as for the films *The Cotton Club* and *Brighton Beach Memoirs*. He has taught jazz courses at Jersey City State Coll. '79–82; Montclair St. Coll. '85–7; LIU '85–9; Hartt Coll. of Mus. '86; Wm. Paterson Coll. fr. '86; New Sch. '89–91; Manh. Sch. of Mus. '85–6 and fr. '88. Berger has received numerous NEA comp. grants. His transcriptions and arrs. have been published by Classic Editions, Hal Leonard, Columbia Pictures, Jazz Heritage, and Charles Colin. Favs: Duke Ellington, Billy Strayhorn. Fests: Eur. '81. TV: *A Classical Jazz Christmas* w. LCJO. CDs: as cond. w. LCJO (Col.).

BERGER, KARL (KARLHANNS), vib, pno, perc, comp; b. Heidelberg, Germany, 3/30/35. Began on pno. at age 8. Stud. at Heidelberg Cons. 1948–54; U. of Berlin '55–63 (Ph.D. '63). Pl. in house bands at Le Chat-Qui-Peche, Paris, and Cave 54, Heidelberg; also concerts w. Steve Lacy, Eric Dolphy, late '50s-early '60s. Tour. Eur. w. Gato Barbieri–Don Cherry '65–6. Moved to NYC '66. Pl. w. Pharoah Sanders; John McLaughlin; Lee Konitz; D. Cherry; Masahiko Sato; Ingrid Sertso; Carlos Ward; S. Lacy; Roswell Rudd; Clifford Thornton; Marion Brown; also Young Audiences educ. concerts w. Sam Rivers–Reggie Workman '66–72. Led own gps. off and on fr. '66. Artist-in-res. at Wesleyan Univ., Cornish Inst., U.C.-San Diego, Evergreen Coll., Texas Tech.; also taught at New Sch., NYC, late '60s-early '70s. With Ornette Coleman, founded Creative Mus. Studio as an independent jazz stud. prog. in collab. w. SUNY–New Paltz '72. Tour. and rec. w. Woodstock Wkshp. Orch. w. D. Cherry, L. Konitz, Oliver Lake, Leroy Jenkins '70s. Artist-in-res. at Antioch Coll., Naropa Inst., Banff Sch. of Arts '72–82. Pl. w. Lee Konitz, Dave Holland, Ed Blackwell fr. '72. Has received several comp. grants fr. NEA, NY State Council on Arts, etc. fr. '72. Comp.-in-res. for West Germ. radio and TV network WDR, also comp. and dir. orch. for Kool JF '82–5. Tour. Africa w. own qt. w. perc. Babatunde Olatunji. Comp. jazz ballets *The Bird* and *Monk and the Robbers* for WDR radio bb and orch.; commercial comp. and arr. for Bill Laswell's Material Prod. in NYC; also pl. w. Dave Brubeck, Hozan Yamamoto '85–8. Pl. w. Mingus Epitaph; Tom Tedesco; Cameron Brown; Blackwell Project; Rhythm-Changes w. Sonny Sharrock; Structure w. Anthony Cox, Dewey Redman, Geri Allen; D. Cherry; Joe Lovano '89–90. Led wkshp. at World Mus. Inst., NYC and Longy Sch. of Mus., Bost. '89–90. Rec.

duets w. gtrst. Paul Koji Sligihara '91. Rec. own *Moondance Suite* w. voc. Ingrid Sertso '92. Polls: *DB* critics TDWR vib. '68, '71, '74–5; *Jazz Forum* twice in '70s. Fests: all major fr. '66. TV: Eur. TV; video w. D. Brubeck. CDs: BS; Enja; ITM; L+R; Bella.; w. Mingus Epitaph (Col.); D. Cherry (A&M; Mag.; Mos.); J. Lovano (Enja); Carla Bley (ECM); L. Konitz (Mile.); Alan Silva (ESP).

BERGHOFER, CHUCK (CHARLES CURTIS), bs; b. Denver, CO, 6/14/37. Played tba. and tpt. in hs; bs. at 18. Moved to LA 1945; pl. w. Bobby Troup–Herb Ellis '58; opening attraction at Shelly's Manne Hole, Nov. '60. Also worked w. Russ Freeman; Conte Candoli; Richie Kamuca; Howard Roberts; Barney Kessel; Ben Webster; Jimmy Rowles; Zoot Sims; et al., but mainly active fr. the '60s as a studio mus., perf. on the soundtracks of hundreds of theatrical and TV films. CDs: w. S. Manne (Cont.); Zoot Sims (Pab.); Bob Cooper (Disc.); Mel Tormé; Rosemary Clooney; Frankie Capp (Conc.); *The Tenor Trio* (JMI); T. Ranier (Cont.).

BERGONZI, JERRY, saxes; also el-bs, pno, dms; b. Boston, MA, 10/21/47. Took up cl. at 8, alto at 12, tnr. at 14. Stud. priv. w. Joe Viola while in hs. After four yrs. at Lowell U. in Mass., pl. el-bs in local bands. To NYC 1972; after some yrs. gigging w. Tom Harrell, Harvie Swartz, et al., he join. Two Generations of Brubeck '73. Work. w. Dave Brubeck qt. '79–81; then ret. to Bost. '81, regularly teaching and pl. w. his own qt., Con Brio, and trio, Gonz. Toured Eur. w. George Gruntz bb and in combo w. dmr. Daniel Humair. Has also collab. w. Mulgrew Miller; Joachim Kuhn; Tiger Okoshi. Favs: Coltrane, Rollins, Shorter, Joe Henderson. CDs: Red; BN; w. Brubeck (Conc.); J. Calderazzo (BN); Bennie Wallace (Den.); Humair (L. Bleu); Gruntz (Enja; TCB); Alex Riel (Stunt).

BERIGAN, BUNNY (ROWLAND BERNARD), tpt, voc; b. Hilbert, WI, 11/2/08; d. NYC, 6/2/42. Played vln., tpt. in grandfath.'s orch. Worked w. NORK, coll. dance bands at U. of Wisc., 1920s. To NYC w. Frank Cornwell '29, then Hal Kemp '30, incl. Eur. tour; Rudy Vallee, Freddie Rich, Paul Whiteman '32–3; Dorsey Bros. '34; Benny Goodman '35–6; Tommy Dorsey '37. Left to form bb, which he led '37–40. Rejoin. Dorsey for six mos. '40. Hospitalized in NYC '42, he died of pneumonia. Berigan's midwestern background, alcoholism, iconoclasm, musical compromises, and early demise parallel the life of Bix Beiderbecke. Infl. by Beiderbecke and Armstrong, he pl. w. a lyrical beauty, particularly in the lower register. Rec. many

Beiderbecke comps. w. own band; also many other titles for RCA, incl. his biggest hit, which he both sang and pl., "I Can't Get Started" '37. Other well-known solos incl. "Sometimes I'm Happy," "King Porter Stomp," "Blue Skies" w. Goodman; "Marie," "Song of India" w. Dorsey; "Billie's Blues" w. B. Holiday. Polls: *Met.* '37, '39. Film: *Syncopation* '42. Book: *Bunny Berigan: Elusive Legend of Jazz*, Robert Dupuis (LSU) '93. CDs: BB; Hep; Jass; Pro Arte; w. B. Goodman; J. Teagarden; Fats Waller (BB); Holiday (Col.); Red Norvo; A. Rollini (Aff.); Gene Gifford in *Swing is Here* (BB); Dorsey Bros. (Hep); L. Armstrong (Dec.).

BERK, DICK (RICHARD ALAN), dms, Latin perc.; b. San Francisco, CA, 5/22/39. Studied at Berklee Sch. of Mus. 1959–60. Pl. NYC clubs w. Nick Brignola; Ted Curson–Bill Barron; Mingus; Walter Bishop, Monty Alexander, Freddie Hubbard. Moved to LA in '68 and worked w. Gabor Szabo; Cal Tjader; Milt Jackson; Ray Brown; Phineas Newborn; Georgie Auld; the Cunninghams; Richie Cole; Nat Adderley; George Duke; Jean-Luc Ponty; Blue Mitchell. Numerous concerts and fests. in US, Eur. Moved to Portland, Ore., in '90. Pl. w. Leroy Vinnegar; John and Jeff Clayton; Ernestine Anderson; James Williams; Dave Frishberg. Form. gp., Jazz Adoption Agency, in '90s. An intelligent, hard-swinging player in keeping w. the dmr./leaders he names as favs: Max Roach, Elvin Jones, Art Blakey, Philly Joe Jones. Fest: MJF w. Billie Holiday '58. Stage: acting role in *Idiot's Delight* w. Jack Lemmon; *Hoagy, Bix and Wolfgang Beethoven Bunkhouse*. Films: *New York, New York*; *Raging Bull*; *Scarface*. TV: apps. w. Merv Griffin; Mike Douglas; *Hogan's Heroes*; *It Takes a Thief*; *Emergency*. CDs: Res.; Nine Winds; w. Nick Brignola (Res.); Cal Tjader (Fant.); Ted Curson (BL); Jessica Williams (JF).

BERMAN, SONNY (SAUL), tpt; b. New Haven, CT, 4/21/25; d. NYC, 1/16/47. Took up tpt. after bro., also tptr., died in diving accident. Pl. w. Louis Prima, Sonny Dunham, T. Dorsey, Georgie Auld, Harry James, B. Goodman 1940–5. Join. Woody Herman Feb. '45, feat. as soloist w. Woodchoppers gp. and bb. Infl. by Eldridge and Gillespie, he was an adventurous and warm soloist whose great potential was eclipsed by a drug-related heart attack. Rec. solos w. Herman: "Your Father's Mustache"; "Sidewalks of Cuba"; "Pam"; "Let It Snow"; w. Met. All-Stars, "Metronome All Out" '46; Bill Harris on Dial incl. "Woodchopper's Holiday"; "Nocturne" '46. LP on Esoteric, reissued as *Beautiful Jewish Music* on Onyx. CDs: w. Herman (Col.; Laser.); Auld in C. Hawkins' *Rainbow Mist* (Del.); Ralph Burns in *The*

Jazz Scene (Verve); Woodchoppers in *The 1940—The Small Groups: New Directions* (Col.).

BERNE, TIM, alto and bari saxes; b. Syracuse, NY, 10/16/54. Took up sax in hs and became interested in jazz after att. concerts by Sun Ra. After a stay in Calif., he moved to NYC in 1974, stud. briefly w. Anthony Braxton, and then apprenticed w. Julius Hemphill. Form. own label, Empire, '79 and rec. albums in Calif. and NYC, then rec. for Soul Note w. such mus. as Ray Anderson; Herb Robertson; Paul Motian; Hank Roberts; Joey Baron. With last two, form. Miniature, a cooperative trio. While working as a clerk at Tower Records, he signed w. Col. '86. Rec. w. John Zorn on *Spy vs Spy* '89; tour. Eur. in duo with Marilyn Crispell '91. In the '90s, he led gps. Caos Totale and Bloodcount, which rec. for JMT. "The main objective with Bloodcount," says Berne, "is to de-emphasize the usual soloistic approach inherent in small group 'jazz' and create more of a chamber music approach to improvisation. . . . In a sense we are all co-composers in sharing the direction of each piece." CDs: JMT; SN; w. J. Baron; H. Roberts; Peter Herborn (JMT); M. Formanek (Enja; SN); Zorn (None.); G. Gruntz (TCB); M. Helias; Nels Cline (Enja); Lindsey Horner (Op. Mds.).

BERNHARDT, CLYDE (EDRIC BARRON), tbn, voc; b. Gold Hill, NC, 7/11/05; d. Newark, NJ, 5/20/86. Raised in Harrisburg, Pa. Studied tbn. 1922; start. pl. prof. '23. Moved to NYC '28, worked w. Ray Parker and Honey Brown '29–30; King Oliver, who feat. him as singer, '31; Alabamians '31–2; Billy Fowler '32–3; Vernon Andrade '34–7; Edgar Hayes '37–42, incl. Eur. tour. '38. Also worked w. Horace Henderson '41; Fats Waller '42; Jay McShann '42–3; Cecil Scott '43–4; Luis Russell, Claude Hopkins '44; Bascomb bros. '45. Own gp. the Blue Blazers '46–8. Rejoin. Russell '48–51; Joe Garland '52–70. Led Harlem Blues & Jazz Band '72–9; then join. Legends of Jazz to '86. Fine blues singer and supple tbnst. Book: *I Remember Eighty Years of Black Entertainment, Big Bands and the Blues* (U. of Penn. Press) '86. Recs. as lead. on Musi., Derby, Barron; as sideman w. Alex Hill, Edgar Hayes. CD: w. Pete Johnson (Sav.).

BERNHARDT, WARREN, pno, kybds; b. Wausau, WI, 11/38. Classically trained; gave first concert 1948. Pl. jazz while att. coll. in Chi. Toured US and Latin Amer. w. Paul Winter Sxt. '61–4. In late '60s, pl. w. Clark Terry; George Benson; Gerry Mulligan; and many studio gps. and singers. In late '70s, assoc. w. Jack DeJohnette; also worked w. Mike Mainieri '75–80; co-led Steps Ahead w. Mike Brecker '84–5;

also pl. in trio w. Jimmy Cobb and Dave Holland '85–6. Worked as mus. teacher and film comp. The work of pnst. Bill Evans is a recurring theme in Bernhardt's perfs. They were close friends fr. '62 until Evans' death in '80. In '92, he rec. *Reflections* w. Jay Anderson, bs., and Jeff Hirshfield, dms. Bernhardt has been praised for his technical facility, melodic invention, and harmonic sensibility. CDs: DMP; w. W. Marsalis (Col.); George Young (PW).

BERNHART, MILT, tbn; b. Valparaiso, IN, 5/25/26. Took up tba. 1936; tbn. '38, then priv. studies. Join. Boyd Raeburn at age 16 in Chi.; later in LA w. Teddy Powell; army '44–6. Off and on w. Stan Kenton '46–51; also, in that period, briefly rejoin. Raeburn '47, and pl. w. B. Goodman '48–9. Dur. '50s, worked w. Maynard Ferguson '50–5; Lighthouse All-Stars '52–3; Shorty Rogers '52–4; Columbia Pictures staff '55–8; then mainly active in film and TV studios. Later devoted his time to running a travel agency and organizing bb concerts. Pres. of the Big Band Academy of Amer. His round yet edgy sound was vital to the shaping of Kenton's tbn. section. CDs: w. Kenton (Cap.; Mos.); Goodman (Hep); Lighthouse All-Stars (Cont.); S. Rogers (BB); Anita O'Day (Verve); Kenton Reunion boxed set (MAMA).

BERNSTEIN, ARTHUR (ARTIE), bs; b. Brooklyn, NY, 2/4/09; d. Los Angeles, CA, 1/4/64. Childhood stud. on cello, later sw. to bs. as sideline. He became prof. mus while stud. law at NYU 1930. Worked w. Ben Pollack, Red Nichols '31; Dorsey Bros. studio band '32–4; many rec. dates through '30s. Pl. w. Benny Goodman '39–41, moved to Calif. for film studio work. After AAF service in WWII, return. to Hollywood studios. Won *DB* award '43. Recs. w. Red Norvo '33; Mildred Bailey '35; Teddy Wilson and Billie Holiday '36; Claude Thornhill, Larry Clinton '37; Goodman, Hampton '39; Met. All-Stars '41; Serge Chaloff '46. CDs: *From Spirituals to Swing* (Vang.); w. Goodman; R. Eldridge; B. Holiday (Col.); Dorsey Bros.; T. Wilson (Hep); L. Hampton (BB); Norvo; A. Rollini (Aff.); Chaloff (Mos.); some of these Chaloff tracks also w. W. Herman (Laser.).

BERNSTEIN, PETER ANDREW, gtr, pno; b. NYC, 9/3/67. Began on pno. Stud. w. Attila Zoller, Gene Bertoncini, Ted Dunbar; then w. Jim Hall, Donald Byrd, Jimmy Cobb at New Sch. 1988. Pl. w. Arnie Lawrence '84. Lived in Paris '87–8, then pl. w. Jesse Davis '88–91; Jimmy Cobb '89. Also pl. w. Lee Konitz; Junior Cook; Michael Weiss; Lou Donaldson; Larry Goldings; Joshua Redman; own gps. Jim Hall, who mentored Bernstein, called him "the most impressive young guitarist I've heard" and praised

his "swing, logic, feeling and taste. Pete has paid attention to the past as well as the future." Favs: Wes Montgomery, Grant Green, Hall. CDs: CC; w. J. Davis (Conc.); L. Donaldson (Mile.); Mike Hashim (Stash); Mel Rhyne (CC); L. Goldings (Min. Mus); J. Hall (MM); G. Keezer (DIW); Bubba Brooks (TCB).

BERRIOS, STEVE, dms, perc, tpt; b. NYC, 2/24/45. Father, Steve Sr., was dmr. w. Marcellino Guerra, Noro Morales, Miguelito Valdez, Pupi Campo. Began mus. stud. on bugle at age 11, later pl. tpt. w. George Wheeler and the Jazz Disciples, winning the Apollo Amateur Hour five times. Later pl. prof. w. Pucho and the Latin Soul Bros., etc. However he was fascinated by his fath.'s dms. and pl. them along w. recs. in the house. Julito Collazo, his godfath., gave him instruction. At age 19 Steve Sr. gave him his job w. the Latin house band at the Great Northern Hotel on West 57th St., where he worked for several yrs. Dur. close to twenty yrs. on and off w. Mongo Santamaria, he began doubling on timbales. Also tour. and rec. w. Miriam Makeba; Leon Thomas; Kenny Kirkland; Randy Weston and Paquito D'Rivera; Max Roach's M'Boom. Pl. w. Jerry Gonzalez's Fort Apache Band fr. 1981. Rec. w. own band for Mile. Dmr. Billy Hart says: "No other drummer really has anywhere near as total command of these two worlds, Afro-Cuban music and modern bebop, w. an absolutely spiritual *and* cultural understanding of both these realms." CDs: Mile.; with Santamaria (Pab.; Mile.); M. Brecker (GRP); J. Gonzalez (Enja; Sunny.); R. Mantilla (Red); Wallace Roney (Muse); Hilton Ruiz (Cand.; Novus); Bobby Watson (Col.); R. Weston (Free.).

BERROA, IGNACIO, dms; b. Havana, Cuba, 7/8/53. Began on vln. Studied at Cuban Nat'l Sch. of Arts 1964–7; Nat'l Cons. of Mus. '68–70; then pl. in Cuban army band. Pl. in Cuba w. Felipe Dulzaides '72–5; experimental gp. ICAIC '75–9; Cuban Orch. of Mod. Mus. '79–80; Cuban Orch. of Radio and TV '79–80. Moved to NYC '80 and pl. w. Paquito D'Rivera, Dizzy Gillespie Qt. '81–3; McCoy Tyner '81; Machito bb '81, 83–7. Also worked w. Clark Terry; Dave Valentin; Hilton Ruiz; Daniel Ponce; David Amram; Lou Donaldson; James Moody; Jaco Pastorius. Pl. w. D. Gillespie gp. and bb '87–8; United Nation Orch. fr. '89 until Gillespie became ill. Film: soundtrack for *Beat Street*. Fests: many w. Gillespie. CDs: w. P. D'Rivera; M. Tyner (Col.); D. Gillespie (Enja); Mike Longo (CAP).

BERRY, BILL (WILLIAM R.), crnt; b. Benton Harbor, MI, 9/14/30; d. Los Angeles, 11/13/02. Father pl. bs. prof. in 1930s; moth. an orgst. W. territory band, late '40s. Studied at Cincinnati Coll. of Mus. '54; Berklee '55–7, pl. w. Herb Pomeroy. With Woody Herman '57–60; Maynard Ferguson '61; Duke Ellington '62; then w. Ellington's second string orch. for *My People* show in Chi. '63. In later yrs., occ. join. orch. under Mercer Ellington. Active in NYC studios and w. Thad Jones–Mel Lewis '66–8; also led own bb. After moving to LA in '71, freelanced, working occ. w. his own LA Big Band. With Louis Bellson in Engl. '80; Japan, '81, '83,'87–8. Active at MJF, where he led the HS All-Stars annually from '81; mus. dir. '85; also mus. dir. at Otter Crest JF '80–1. Clinics in US, Eur., and Japan. Co-producer, w. wife Betty, of Int'l Jazz Party in LA '91–2, feat. Japanese and US mus. With his own band, Berry drew heavily on the Ellington-Strayhorn repertoire, sometimes using the orig. arrs. w. such Ellington alumni as Buster Cooper and Britt Woodman. CDs: Conc.; w. Scott Hamilton; J. Hanna; R. Clooney; F. Capp (Conc.); Ellington (Atl.; BL; Col.; Saja; Story.; Fant.); J. Rowles (JVC); C. Hawkins (Imp); J. Hodges (BB).

BERRY, CHU (LEON BROWN), tnr sax; b. Wheeling, WV, 9/13/08; d. Conneaut, OH, 10/30/41. From mus. family; was orig. inspired by Coleman Hawkins. Began on alto sax, pl. in hs and West Va. St. Coll. Chose mus. over football and join. Sammy Stewart bb on tnr. sax 1929; moved from Chi. to NYC '30. Pl. w. Cecil Scott, Otto Hardwicke; then w. Benny Carter '32; Charlie Johnson. With Teddy Hill '33–5; Fletcher Henderson '35–6. Join. Cab Calloway '37, where he starred until he was killed in car crash. Fr. his Hawkins infl. he built a personal style marked by hard-swinging fluidity at fast tempos and a lush, mellow ballad approach. Linked by Don Byas, he exerted an infl. on bop era saxophonists. Polls: *DB* '37; *Met.* '37, '39. Recs. w. F. Henderson, own comp. "Christopher Columbus"; Calloway, "Ghost of a Chance," "Bye Bye Blues"; C. Basie, "Cherokee," "Lady Be Good"; also w. Lionel Hampton; Red Norvo; Red Allen; Gene Krupa; Wingy Manone; Teddy Wilson. CDs: Comm.; Jazz Arch.; Zeta; w. Fletcher Henderson (Col.; BB); C. Calloway (Class.; Col.); Basie (Dec.); L. Hampton (BB); Benny Carter (B&B); R. Eldridge (Col.); R. Norvo (Aff.); T. Wilson (Hep).

BERRY, EMMETT, tpt; b. Macon, GA, 7/23/15; d. Cleveland, OH, 6/22/93. Raised in Cleveland. Studied w. symph. mus. Join. Chi. Nightingales in Toledo, Ohio, 1932. Moved to NYC '33, gigged around Albany, N.Y. '34–6. Pl. w. F. Henderson '36–9, then H. Henderson '40. With Earl Hines, Teddy Wilson '41–2; Raymond Scott at CBS '42–3; L. Hampton, D. Redman, B. Carter '43; John Kirby '44; Eddie Hey-

wood '45; Count Basie '45–50. Briefly w. Jimmy Rushing '51, he then worked w. Johnny Hodges '51–4; Hines, Cootie Williams '55. Tour. France and No. Africa w. Sammy Price, Jan.-May '56. Six wks. w. I. Jacquet; w. F. Henderson reunion band at Great South Bay Jazz fest. '57. Started retail mus. business NYC, Dec. '58, but remained active as player; tour. Eur. w. Buck Clayton, fall '59 and in '61. Dur. early '60s, he worked in LA, incl. band backing Nat Cole. Ret. to NYC '65; pl. w. Peanuts Hucko '66; Wilbur De Paris '67; Big Chief Moore '68; Buddy Tate '69. Ret. to Cleveland due to ill health '70. Solid mainstream soloist out of Armstrong, Eldridge, Clayton. Fav. own solo: "Jappa" w. Hodges. TV: *The Sound of Jazz,* CBS. Recs. w. H. Henderson; C. Cole; A. Sears; J. Rushing; Basie; Clayton; Jacquet. CDs: *The Sound of Jazz* (Col.); w. Ed Hall (Comm.); F. Henderson (Col.); Basie (Col.; BB); Benny Carter (BB); Clayton (Steep.); D. Byas; Seventh Avenue Stompers (Sav.); I. Jacquet (Mos.); B. Holiday (Col.; Dec.); Jo Jones; J. Rushing (Vang.); Pee Wee Russell (Cand.); Buddy Tate (BL); Johnny Hodges (Suisa).

BERRY, STEVE (STEPHEN JOHN), bs, cello; b. Gosport, England, 8/24/57. Grandfather, Joseph Berry, is a dixieland dmr. Studied at Guildhall Sch. of Mus. 1983–4. Began working locally; founder-member of 21-pc. jazz orch., Loose Tubes, '84, for which he comp. and arr. much of the repertoire. Fr. '87 to '91, own trio w. Mark Lockheart, Peter Fairclough. In '91 member of Mike Westbrook Big Band. Fr. '83, he visited much of Eur., Can., US, Morocco, Turkey. Frequent BBC national radio apps. Feat. in TV docu. w. Loose Tubes '86–87. His trio album named to Ten Best Jazz Albums by *The Guardian* '88. Teaches bs. and cello, especially in improv. wkshps. Recs. w. Loose Tubes, Django Bates, Ian Carr, Billy Jenkins. LP: *Trio* (Loose Tubes). CD: w. Loose Tubes (Editions EG); Ian Carr (MMC); Billy Jenkins (Allmusic; De Core Music; VSOP; Wood Wharf).

BERT, EDDIE, tbn; b. Yonkers, NY, 5/16/22. Began on alto horn in jr. hs. Studied w. Benny Morton while Count Basie Orch. was at Famous Door on 52nd St. 1938; later stud. w. Miff Mole, Trummy Young; earned B. Mus. and M. Mus. fr. Manh. Sch. of Mus. '57. Pl. w. Sam Donahue '40; Red Norvo '41–3; Woody Herman, Charlie Barnet '43; army band led by Bill Finegan '44–5; Herbie Fields '46; Stan Kenton '47–8; Benny Goodman '48–9; Herman '50; Kenton, Bill Harris's three-tbn. gp. '51; Herbie Fields, Ray McKinley '52; own gps. fr. '52; Les Elgart '54; Kenton '55; Charles Mingus off and on '55–74; Tony Aless–Seldon Powell '56. Guest cond.

and soloist at Caracas JF '57, '64. Pl. w. Elliot Lawrence '58–68; Goodman off and on '58–86; Urbie Green, Thelonious Monk '59; Gil Melle '62; Chubby Jackson '62–3; Monk '64; Thad Jones–Mel Lewis Orch. '67–72; Bobby Rosengarden Orch. on Dick Cavett TV show '68–72; N.Y. Jazz Repertory Co. '73–8; L. Hampton '76–80; Monk '81; Illinois Jacquet bb; Galt MacDermott's New Pulse Band '84–6; John Lewis–led Amer. Jazz Orch.; Walt Levinsky Great Amer. Swing Orch., Loren Schoenberg Orch. fr. '86; Gene Harris's Philip Morris Superband '89; Mingus Epitaph fr. '89. Worked extens. in B'way pit bands incl. *Bye Bye Birdie, Pippin, Ain't Misbehavin'* '60–86. Led qnt. w. J.R. Monterose in live session for Fresh Sound label at Birdland, NYC '91. Guest of honor at the N.Y. Brass Conference '90. Taught at Essex Coll. '81–2; U. of Bridgeport '84–6; and is the author of the *Eddie Bert Trombone Method* (Chas. Colin Publ.). Bert is an accomplished photographer whose photos have been publ. in the books *Jazz Giants* and *To Bird With Love,* and on the cover of the Spotlite album *The Band That Never Was.* Polls: *Met.* Musician of Year '55. Fests: all major. Film: *Jam Session* w. Charlie Barnet '43. TV: *Swing into Spring* '64; *Let's Dance* w. B. Goodman '86. CDs: FS; Sav.; w. Benny Carter; L. Schoenberg; Norvo (MM); Barnet (Dec.); Hampton (Timel.); Gene Harris (Conc.); T. Jones–M. Lewis (Royal; LRC); C. Mingus (Deb.; Rhino); T. Monk (Riv.); Coleman Hawkins; Phil Woods (FS;); Duke Jordan; E. Wilkins (Sav.); Teddy Charles (Atl.); M. Ferguson (BB); Goodman (BN; Hep; MM); J. Heath (Verve); C. Terry (Vang.); Tommy Talbert (Modern Concepts; Chart.).

BERTON, VIC (Victor Cohen), dms; b. Chicago, IL, 5/7/1896; d. Hollywood, CA, 12/26/51. Father pl. and taught vln., bro. Ralph was jazz critic. Began pl. prof. w. fath.'s dance orch.; regular pit dmr. at Alhambra Theater in Milwaukee, Wisc., at age 7. Stud. w. Josef Zettleman of Chi. Symph. Pl. w. Sousa's Navy Band in WWI. In 1920s, pl. w. Paul Whiteman, Vincent Lopez, and other dance bands. Worked and rec. w. Red Nichols '26–9, using a pair of machine kettle dms. as "hot tympani" to pl. bs. parts for novelty effects. Possibly the first dmr. to transfer the cymbal fr. the bass dr. to an early model of the high-hat, which he patented in '26. Led own bands; pl. w. Miff Mole, and w. Bix Beiderbecke in the Wolverines, bringing them to NYC '24. In late '30s sw. fr. dance band work to Hollywood studios. Pl. w. N.Y. Philharm. and was feat. soloist w. LA Philharm. Chosen by Igor Stravinsky as perc. for West Coast perfs. of *L' Histoire du Soldat.* Co-comp., w. Art Kassel, of "Sobbin' Blues" '22. CDs: w. Nichols (ASV); Beiderbecke (Col.; JSP); J. Teagarden (BB); J.Venuti (CDS; Yazoo).

BERTONCINI, GENE, gtr; b. NYC, 4/6/37. Learned tunes fr. bro. who pl. jazz acdn. Stud. architecture at Notre Dame U.; gtr. w. Johnny Smith, Chuck Wayne. Pl. w. Richie Levister, Joe Puma, Danny Pucillo, Julie Roggiero late 1950s; own gps. fr. '59; Buddy Rich Qnt. '61; Marine Corps. Band '61–2. Freelance in early '60s, then pl. w. Skitch Henderson's *Tonight Show* band for two yrs. in mid '60s. Pl. and rec. w. Lena Horne, Carol Sloane, Morgana King '68–70. Toured US and Can. w. own trio '71–8. Formed duo w. Michael Moore, late '70s. Also pl. and rec. w. Hubert Laws; Clark Terry; Wayne Shorter; Lalo Schifrin; Michel Legrand; Paul Desmond; Ron Carter. Has taught at Eastman Sch. of Mus.; New Engl. Cons.; NYU; and New Sch. Whitney Balliett called him "an affecting, highly original guitarist who moves easily back and forth between classical and jazz guitar." Favs: Jim Hall, Wes Montgomery, Ed Bickert, Lenny Breau. Fests: Italy '87; Norway '89. Book: *Approaching the Guitar,* KJOS Music. CDs: Stash; w. W. Shorter (BN); Chas. McPherson (Main.); R. Kellaway (Chiaro.); M. Moore (Stash; Chiaro.); H. Laws (CTI).

BERTRAND, JIMMY (JAMES), dms, xyl, wshbd; b. Biloxi, MS, 2/24/1900; d. Chicago, IL, 8/60. Cousin, dmr. Andrew Hilaire. To Chi., where he worked w. Erskine Tate at the Vendome Theater 1918–28. Pl. sessions w. Tiny Parham '26; Jimmy Blythe '27; Blind Blake '28. Pl. w. Dave Peyton '28, then w. Parham, Lee Collins, Junie Cobb '32; Eddie South '31–3; Reuben Reeves '34. Although he cont. to lead his own band until '45, fr. the end of '20s devoted much time to teaching. His pupils incl. Lionel Hampton and Sid Catlett. One of the best of the wshbd. players, he rec. as lead. of Washboard Wizards in late '20s w. sidemen Louis Armstrong, Johnny Dodds. Also recs. w. E. Tate, E. South. CDs: w. J. Dodds (Dec.; Aff.; Timel.; BB); F. Keppard (KJ); South (DRG).

BEST, DENZIL DECOSTA, dms, comp; b. NYC, 4/27/17; d. NYC, 5/24/65. Father pl. tba. Stud. pno. at age 6, then tpt. Pl. w. Chris Columbus 1940 and in early sess. at Minton's. After recovering fr. protracted lung disease '40–1, he gigged on pno. and bs., then took up dms. '43. After working w. local bands, he pl. w. Ben Webster for nine mos. '43–4; Coleman Hawkins '44–5; Illinois Jacquet '46; tour. Sweden w. Chubby Jackson '47–8. Join. George Shearing '49, where his strong but subtle brushwork helped establish the qnt.'s highly identifiable sound. Remain. w.

Shearing until auto accident temporarily curtailed his career '52. Resumed work w. Artie Shaw '54. Tour. w. Erroll Garner '56–7. Remaining in NYC, he pl. w. Lee Evans, Cecil Young '58–9; gigged w. Nina Simone, Tyree Glenn '59. Calcium deposits in his wrists hampered him in later yrs. He fractured his skull in a fall down a flight of subway steps and died the following day. Celebrated for his comps, many of which remain standards: "Move"; "Dee Dee's Dance"; "Wee" (aka "Allen's Alley"); "Nothing But D. Best"; and w. T. Monk, "Bemsha Swing." Recs. w. Jacquet, Shaw, Jackson, Stuff Smith, Jack Teagarden. CDs: w. Hawkins (Cap.); Garner (Col.); Lee Konitz (Prest.); Shearing (Sav.; Verve); F. Navarro (Sav.); B. Webster (Prog.).

BEST, JOHNNY (JOHN McCLANIAN JR.), tpt; b. Shelby, NC, 10/20/13. Studied pno. briefly, then tpt fr. 1926. Att. Duke U. and U. of No. Caro., '30–6. With Les Brown '36–7; C. Barnet '37; Artie Shaw '37–9; Glenn Miller '39–42. Navy service '42–5, then radio shows w. Bob Crosby and Jerry Gray '47–53; w. Billy May '53. Tour. int'l. w. Ray Coniff '70s and '80s. Subbed for Billy Butterfield in WGJB '70s. To Japan w. Zeke Zarchy '90. Owned and operated an avocado orchard in Pauma Valley, Calif., '50–82. Although partially paralyzed in '82 accident, he cont. pl., mainly in San Diego, Calif., area. CDs: w. Miller (BB); Shaw (BB; Aff.; ASV); Hep).

BEST, SKEETER (CLIFTON), gtr; b. Kinston, NC, 11/20/14; d. NYC, 5/27/85. Studied w. moth., a pno. teacher. Prof. debut w. Abe Dunn's local band, early 1930s. Worked w. Slim Marshall, Phila. '35–40; Earl Hines '41–2; Erskine Hawkins '42. Navy '42–45. Pl. w. Bill Johnson gp. '45–9; USO tour of Far East w. Oscar Pettiford '51–2. Freelanced in NYC w. own trio and w. Paul Quinichette; Jesse Powell; Kenny Clarke; Sir Charles Thompson in mid and late '50s. Rejoin. Thompson in '60s. Taught gtr. in later yrs. Rec. w. Hines '42, '77; Mercer Ellington '58. CDs: w. Milt Jackson and Ray Charles (Atl.); D. Gillespie (Verve); Howard McGhee (Sav.); Etta Jones (Prest.); I. Quebec (Mos.); Hines (BB); Lucky Thompson (Imp.).

BETTI VAN DER NOOT, DINO A., comp, arr, pno; b. Rapallo, Italy, 9/18/36. Mother and cousin classical pnsts. Stud. at Scuola Musicale, Pavia, 1946–51; privately in Milan '59; Berklee Coll. of Mus. '70s. In Italy, led combos '57–60. Not active in mus. in '60s. Led amateur bb '69–78; prof. bb '82. His bb sidemen incl. Franco Ambrosetti; Paul Bley; Bob Cunningham; Bill Evans; David Friedman;

Danny Gottlieb; Donald Harrison; Paul Motian; Steve Swallow; others '85. Betti van der Noot is chairman of B Communications, a prominent Milan ad agency, and has comp. many jingles. He led a bb in NYC, Sept. '87. His comps. are narratives rife w. color, ranging fr. the boldest hues to the most subtle and revealing a sensitive, inventive melodist and lapidarian master of orchestral skills. Fav. arrs: Ellington, Strayhorn, Woody Herman, Ralph Burns, Stan Kenton. Fests: Ital. fests fr. '58. Polls: Rec. of Year in *Musica Jazz* critics poll '87, '89. TV: Ital. TV. CDs: Innowo; SN.

BETTS, KEETER (WILLIAM THOMAS), bs; also dms; b. Port Chester, NY, 7/22/28; d. Silver Spring, MD, 8/6/05. Stud. dms. in grade sch. and hs. Sw. to bs. on grad. 1946. After one yr. w. priv. teach. began pl. local jobs. With Earl Bostic, Apr. '49–Sept. '51; Dinah Washington, Nov. '51–'56; brief stay w. Adderley bros. bef. settling in Wash., D.C., '57. Pl. there w. C. Byrd at Showboat '57–64. Tour. Engl. and Saudi Arabia w. Woody Herman '59. Worked w. B. Timmons '64. Fr. '65 to '78 assoc. w. T. Flanagan, incl. accomp. Ella Fitzgerald, which he cont. into the '80s. In '90s many jazz cruises on SS *Norway*. Active as educ. consultant to WBET-TV jazz. Favs: R. Brown, Blanton, Pettiford. CDs: w. N. Adderley; C. Byrd; Sam Jones (Riv.); Lockjaw Davis; E. Fitzgerald (Pab.); Clifford Brown; D. Washington (Em.); T. Flanagan (Pablo; Gal.); Stan Getz (Verve); B. De Franco (Conc.); J. Mance; Soft Winds (Chiaro.).

BEY, ANDY (ANDREW W. JR.), voc, pno, comp; b. Newark, NJ, 10/28/39. Began pl. pno. by ear at age 3; att. Arts HS of Mus. & Art in Newark. Studied pno. w. Sanford Gold in 1965. Voice coaching fr. Nat Jones and Romney Fell but basically self-taught singer. In early '50s app. on TV as a "Startime Kid" w. Connie Francis, etc. With Louis Jordan at Apollo Theater '53. For more than ten yrs. perf. in gp. Andy & the Bey Sisters w. his siblings, vocs. Salome and Geraldine; tour. extensively in Eur. '58–9. As a single worked w. Thad Jones–Mel Lewis Orch. in early '70s; also w. Umajo Ens. led by Mtume. Tour. w. Horace Silver '87, incl. Eur. JF circuit. Infl. by a wide variety of singers, fr. Ella Fitzgerald and Sarah Vaughan to Aretha Franklin and Ray Charles, and instrumentalists. Bey's deep, resonant, gospel and blues-derived style did not always adapt well to some of his forays w. Silver. Comp: *Celestial Blues*. Rec. w. M. Roach '68; Duke Pearson '69; H. Silver '70; G. Bartz '70; S. Clarke '72. Own LP: Atl., '73. CDs: Evid.; w. C. Harris (JMT); David Murray (DIW); Pharoah Sanders (Evid.).

BHUMIBOL ADULYADEJ (Ramma IX Bhumibol); cl, saxes; b. Cambridge, MA, 12/5/27. Raised in US and Switzerland. Learn. cl. in latter, lead. 7-pc. band while in sch.; then stud. other reeds. Favors sop. sax. Infl. by Benny Goodman and by Thai music. Became King of Thailand, ninth ruler of the Chakri dynasty, but cont. to perf. frequently w. such visiting Amer. mus. as Goodman, who was in Thailand, Dec. '56; J. Teagarden; L. Hampton. In '96, he jammed w. Warren Vaché, Benny Carter, etc. Has comp. some jazz originals.

BIAGI, GIAMPAOLO, dms; b. Florence, Italy, 8/5/45. Parents were amateur mus. Began on pno. Pl. w. Jimmy Harris at Red Garter-Florence, mid 1960s. Came to NYC in late '60s, pl. at Red Garter-NYC '67–8, then w. Jimmy Harris in Atlanta, Ga., '69–70. Freelance in Eur. and US '71–2, then pl. w. Chet Baker in NYC '73; Hazel Scott '78–9; house band at Latin Quarter '80. Settled in NYC permanently in early '80s; freelance since '81 w. Scott Hamilton; Nat Pierce; Doc Cheatham; John Bunch; Bob Wilber; Milt Hinton; Richard Wyands; Warren Vaché; Kenny Davern; etc. Favs: K. Clarke, S. Manne, Osie Johnson. Fests: Eur.; also Bermuda '89, Brazil '90. TV: apps. w. John and Bucky Pizzarelli, Mary Martin, Sylvia Syms, Margaret Whiting. CDs: w. K. Davern (MM); Vaché (Conc.).

BICKERT, ED (EDWARD ISAAC), gtr; b. Hochfield, Man., Canada, 11/29/32. Studied in Vernon, British Col., 1943; pl. dance dates w. fath., a fiddler, and moth., a pnst. Moved to Toronto, worked w. local gps. incl. Norman Symonds; Ron Collier; Phil Nimmons; Moe Koffman. Visited US Nov. '56, gigged at Birdland. A longtime member of Rob McConnell's Boss Brass, he is also an active studio mus. and accomp. to visiting artists fr. US, who regard him as Can.'s leading gtrst. CDs: Conc.; JA; w. Rob McConnell (Conc.; SB); Paul Desmond (CTI; Tel.); Ernestine Anderson; Benny Carter; R. Clooney; Concord All-Stars; K. Peplowski; M. Tormé (Conc.); Oscar Peterson (Pab.); B. Tate (Sack.).

BICKFORD, BILL (WILLIAM CAMPBELL), gtr; b. Norwalk, CT, 7/7/56. Father pl. concertina and pno.; older bro. pl. classical gtr. Began pl. gtr. at age 14, imitating Lightnin' Hopkins. Stud. w. Linc Chamberland 1970–3; Berklee Coll. of Mus. '74–5; City Coll. of NY '77–9. Also stud. comp. and arr. w. Ed Summerlin and Mario Davidofsky. Led own jazz qt. as teenager. Subbed for Linc Chamberland in jam session band at Rapson's, Stamford, Conn., early '70s; pl. w. Dave Liebman; Pee Wee Ellis; Lynn Christie. Pl. w. r&b band '75–7; Larry Elgart Orch.

'77–86. Made rec. debut w. John McNeil '79. Pl. w. Defunkt '82–92; Jim Pepper '84–91; Donald Byrd, Dr. Lonnie Smith, mid '80s; Jack McDuff '86; Liquid Hips w. ex-Defunkt members John Mulkerin, Kenny Martin. Pl. w. Ed Schuller's Eleventh Hour fr. '91; Billy Cobham–Wolfgang Schmid; Jack Walrath's Masters of Suspense fr. '96. Bickford has led his own trio, Bigfood, fr. '88. He has taught at the Gitarrentage and Jazz Days wkshps. in Germ. fr. '92. Favs: Robert Johnson, Villa-Lobos, Prince. Fests: all major. TV: Germ. w. Defunkt '92. LP w. McNeil (Steep.). CDs: Tutu; w. Defunkt (Ant.; DIW; Enemy); E. Schuller (Tutu).

BIG MAYBELLE (Maybel Louise Smith), voc; b. Jackson, TN, 1924; d. Cleveland, OH, 1/23/72. As a child, she sang blues and was a member of the Church of God in Christ choir. At age 9, she won a voc. contest at Memphis Cotton Carnival. Sang w. Dave Clark in Memphis and w. Tiny Bradshaw 1947–50. For the rest of her career, she app. mainly as a single, her flamboyant, shouting style often accomp. by such tnr. saxophonists as Budd Johnson and Sam "the Man" Taylor. Film: *Jazz On a Summer's Day*, prod. at NJF '58; video of same (New Yorker). CDs: Sav.; Okeh.

BIGARD, BARNEY (ALBANY LEON), cl, tnr sax, comp; b. New Orleans, LA, 3/3/06; d. Culver City, CA, 6/27/80. Uncle, vlnst. Emile Bigard, taught him mus. basics; bro. Alex was dmr.; cousins were Natty Dominique and A.J. Piron. Became prof. mus. only after essaying other jobs, incl. photoengraving. Studied cl. w. Lorenzo Tio Jr., doubling on tnr. sax when he join. Albert Nicholas 1922. After brief stints w. Octave Gaspard, Amos White, and Luis Russell, he rejoin. Nicholas and went w. him to Chi. '24. With King Oliver at Plantation Café '25–7; Charlie Elgar in Milwaukee, summer '27; to NYC w. Russell, fall '27, bef. join. Duke Ellington, Jan. '28. Except for a short period dur. summer '35, pl. w. Ellington through June '42. Settled in Calif. '42, led own combo, join. Freddie Slack '43–4; pl. w. Kid Ory bef. join. Louis Armstrong '46–55, w. the exception of a few mos. in Calif. at end of '52. Led own gps. in LA and LV w. Cozy Cole Nov. '58–Mar. '59; rejoin. Armstrong '60–1. Concerts and gigs w. Earl Hines, Muggsy Spanier, Ben Pollack in early '60s; Rex Stewart '66–7. Tour. colls., hs w. Art Hodes, Wild Bill Davison, Eddie Condon '71. Colo. JP '71–3; numerous fests in US and abroad incl. NJF, Nice, Pescara, San Sebastian, Bordeaux '74–5. Tour. Switzerland w. New Ragtime Jazzband '75 App. at Nice JF '79. Dur. his Ellington yrs., he established himself as a major voice on his instrument and as one of the orch.'s distinctive, integral sounds. His pl. in the *chalumeau* register on an Albert system cl. was the very embodiment of the NO reed tradition. Yet he brought to it his personal style, further defined by glissandos and intricate runs. Bigard collab. w. Ellington on several comps., beginning w. "Mood Indigo" '30, and incl. "Ducky Wucky," "Saturday Night Function," "Clarinet Lament" ("Barney's Concerto"), and "C-Jam Blues." Polls: *Esq.* Silver Award '44, '46–7. Films: *New Orleans* '47; *St. Louis Blues* '57; *Musical Biography of Barney Bigard*, docu. for French TV. Autobiography: *With Louis and the Duke*, ed. by Barry Martyn (Oxford) '86. CDs: Jazz.; tracks in *Greenwich Village Jazz*, Pick.; w. Ellington (BB; Col.; Dec.); Armstrong (Col.; BB; Dec.; Roul.); Morton (BB; Col.); Cootie Williams (B&B); Rex Stewart (B&B; Aff.; Riv.); D. Reinhardt; King Oliver (Aff.); J. Dodds (Dec.; Aff.).

BIJMA, GREETJE, voc; b. Stiens, Netherlands, 4/22/56. Self-taught. Gave priv. concerts of improvised songs, then worked as singer w. saxist Alan Laurillard's gp. Led own qnt. fr. 1985; worked w. Direct Sound voc. gp. '88; Willem Breuker Kollektief fr. '90. An experimental singer who uses jazz and other disciplines to create fresh sounds, she became in '90 the first woman to receive the Netherlands' highest jazz honor, the Boy Edgar Award. CDs: Enja; w. Breuker (BVHAAST).

BILK, ACKER (BERNARD STANLEY), cl; b. Pensford, England, 1/28/29. Played pno., org. first; sw. to cl. when in Royal Engineers. Formed first band in Bristol, then migrated to London, app. w. Ken Colyer's band. Started Paramount Jazz Band,which still exists, in 1951. Had int'l pop hit in '61 w. "Stranger on the Shore." Tour. int'l incl. US, Middle East, Far East. Own radio show *Acker's Half Hour*; owns two publ. firms. Some half dozen recs. on Pickwick and Kaz labels. CDs: Philips; Timel.; Apricotmusic; w. Humphrey Lyttelton (Callig.).

BILLBERG, ROLF GUNNAR, alto, tnr saxes, cl; b. Lund, Sweden, 8/22/30; d. Uddevalla, Sweden 8/17/66. Played cl. in mil. band, Uddevalla, 1948. In '50s, on hearing Charlie Parker and Lennie Tristano, he sw. fr. concert cl. to jazz; worked on tnr. sax w. local gps. and w. Sven Sjöholm's orch. in Göteborg. Moved to Stockholm and pl. alto and tnr. w. Simon Brehm '54; Lars Gullin '54–5. CDs: w. Gullin (Drag.).

BILLINGS, JOSH (FRANK R.), dms; b. Chicago, IL, 1904; d. NYC, 3/13/57. Parents both doctors. Promising artist and enthusiastic fan of the Austin High Gang, whose members inspired him to pl. jazz.

In 1929, he and Mezz Mezzrow went to NYC—where the Austin High Gang had gone a yr. earlier—and became part of a reorganized Mound City Blue Blowers. He pl. w. whisk brooms on a suitcase covered in wrinkled wrapping paper and kicked the case w. his heel for bs-drm. effects. Rec. "Tailspin Blues" w. the Blue Blowers, incl. Jack Teagarden, Eddie Condon, Red McKenzie '29. Remained friendly w. the Chi. musicians but was employed as a band boy w. Ray Noble in the mid '30s. Worked as a lithographer in Chi., but moved back to NYC when Condon opened his own club in Greenwich Village '46. CDs: w. Teagarden (BB; ASV); M. Spanier (ASV).

BIONDI, RAY (REMO), gtr, vln, mand; also tpt; b. Cicero, IL, 7/5/05; d. Chicago, IL, 1/28/81. First stud. vln. in childhood; took up mand. fr. age 12. Worked mainly in Chi. as vlnst. 1927–35, rec. w. Wingy Manone, Danny Altier. Doubled tpt. and vln. in Chi. and after moving to NYC '36 w. Joe Marsala, sometimes replacing Eddie Condon on gtr. Gtrst. w. Gene Krupa '38–45 (vln. in '44); moved back to Chi. '45. Pl. w. Krupa again '50–1 bef. settling down in Chi. Freelanced on gtr. and mand.; taught fr. '61; worked w. Art Hodes, etc., fr. '66. Rec. w. Marsala; Krupa; M. Spanier; L. Armstrong '53; W. Herman '56; on el-vln. w. Johnny Wicks and the Swinging Ozarks '52. CDs: w. Krupa (Col.); C. Terry (Chess).

BISCOE, CHRIS (CHRISTOPHER DENNIS), alto, sop, tnr, bari saxes; alto cl, fl, picc; b. East Barnet, England, 2/5/47. Self-taught, first on alto sax. Stud. English and education at Sussex U. 1965–8. Moved to London. Pl. w. NYJO 1970–73; Mike Westbrook fr. '79; also form. own qt. '79; another qt., Full Monte, was form. in '88 and has cont. into '90s. Fr. '83–93 tour. w. Brotherhood of Breath; worked w. Didier Levallet in France fr. '85; George Russell's Living Time '86–95; tour. w. Hermeto Pascoal's bb in UK '94. Has also worked and rec. w. Andy Sheppard. Many BBC-TV apps. Leader of jazz wkshps.; presented concerts at Bath Fest. CDs: Walking Wig; Slam; w. Brotherhood of Breath; M. Westbrook (Venture); G. Russell (Label Bleu).

BISHOP, JOE (JOSEPH), flg, arr; b. Monticello, AR, 11/27/07; d. Houston, TX, 5/12/76. Professional debut on tba. Later began pl. flg., worked w. Isham Jones 1930–5; Woody Herman '36–40. When he rejoin. Herman '42, he was also a staff arr. contributing charts for "Woodchopper's Ball" '39; own comps., "Blue Prelude" and "Blue Flame," Herman's theme song '41. Active as freelance arr. fr. '42, but health problems limited his activities fr. '51. Rec. w. Cow Cow Davenport '38. CDs: w. Herman (Dec.).

BISHOP, WALLACE HENRY, dms; b. Chicago, IL, 2/17/06; d. Hilversum, Netherlands, 5/2/86. After stud. dms. w. Jimmy Bertrand, pl. w. blues pnst. Thomas Dorsey fr. 1923 and Richard M. Jones '27. Worked w. Jelly Roll Morton; also w. Les Hite, Erskine Tate '28–30. Received recognition while w. Earl Hines '31–7. Pl. and rec. w. Jimmie Noone '41; Coleman Hawkins '43; Phil Moore '44–5; Sammy Price, John Kirby '46; Sy Oliver, Billy Kyle '47. Tour. Eur. w. Buck Clayton '49–50, remain. to work in Switzerland '50. Tour. w. George Johnson '51. Took up residence in Netherlands '51, gigging w. pnsts. Rob Pronk, Pia Beck, Franz Elsen dur. '51–6; also on continent w. Don Byas, Ben Webster, Kid Ory, Hines. By end of '70s, he had reduced his pl. activities. Rec. w. L. Armstrong, Billie Holiday '49; Buddy Tate, Milt Buckner, J. Letman, Tiny Grimes '67–8. Book: *The Wallace Bishop Story*, Netherlands '81. CDs: w. Buckner (B&B); Clayton; Willie "The Lion" Smith (Vogue); Hines (Class.; Red. Bar.; Vogue); B. Holiday (Dec.); Sonny Stitt in *Opus De Bop* (Sav.).

BISHOP, WALTER F. JR., pno, comp; b. NYC, 10/4/27; d. NYC, 1/24/98. Father was an ASCAP songwriter who worked w. Art Tatum; Fats Waller, Eubie Blake; James P. Johnson; Ram Ramirez. Pl. w. Alan Jackson, Louis Metcalf 1945. In air corps '45–7, then pl. w. Art Blakey '47–9; Miles Davis '49; Andy Kirk bb '50; Charlie Parker '51–4. Inactive in mus. in mid to late '50s. Pl. w. Allen Eager, Philly Joe Jones '59. Stud. w. Hall Overton at Juilliard '61–9. Led own trio w. Jimmy Garrison, G.T. Hogan '61; pl. briefly w. Cannonball Adderley '62; Les Spann, Sam Jones '63; Charlie Parker Memorial All-Stars '64; own qt. w. Frank Haynes, then Harold Vick, mid '60s. Moved to LA in '69. Pl. and rec. w. Blue Mitchell; Supersax; Terry Gibbs; Harold Land; Bobby Hutcherson; Stanley Turrentine; Art Farmer; and own gp., 4th Cycle, '69–75; also lectured at LA area universities and stud. w. Spud Murphy. Ret. to NYC '76. Pl. w. Clark Terry bb '76; own gps. in NYC clubs fr. '76. Acted in play about Billie Holiday, *They Were All Gardenias*, '79. Pl. w. Bill Hardman–Junior Cook '80. Perf. solo concert at Carnegie Recital Hall '83. Pl. w. all-star gps. and own gps. in NYC and Eur. '80s-'90s; Charlie Parker Memorial Band w. Tom Kirkpatrick, Harold Jefta fr. '92. Bishop was a guest lecturer at Hartt Coll. of Mus. '79–82. Author of two instructional books, *A Study in 4ths* and *A Further Study in 4ths* (Caldon Publ.). Comps: "Coral Keys"; "Sweet Rosa." Bishop was a poet who often incorporated his poetry on jazz subjects into his musical performances; was a member of Poets Four, a poetry society that also incl. Gavin Moses, Ron Cephus Brown, and Will Sales. Infls: Bud Powell, Charlie Parker. Favs: Barry Harris, Tommy Flanagan, Benny Green. Fests: Eur. fr. '63; Jap. fr. '80s. TV: Joe Franklin '80. Video: *Walter Bishop Master Class* (Jazz Video Int'l). CDs: BL; DIW; FS; Red; w. Charlie Parker Memorial Band (Timel.); Ch. Parker (Verve); Miles Davis; S. Getz (Prest.); Jackie McLean (BN); K. Dorham (Deb; BN; BL); Blue Mitchell (Main.); Art Blakey (BN; DIW; FS; Drag.); R.R. Kirk (Merc.); Archie Shepp (Den.); Sonny Stitt (BL); Ken McIntyre (NJ); Charlie Rouse (Jzld.); Milt Jackson (Sav.).

BIVONA, GUS, cl; b. New London, CT, 11/25/15; d. Woodland Hills, CA, 1/5/96. Studied alto in Stamford, Conn., 1934; worked locally bef. moving to NYC '37. Pl. w. Hudson-Delange '37, Bunny Berigan '38, Teddy Powell '39, feat. as cl. soloist. Led own band in Larchmont, N.Y., then worked w. B. Goodman '40; Jan Savitt and Les Brown, early '41; mil. service '42, leading own naval air force band. Pl. w. T. Dorsey '45, Bob Crosby '46; MGM staff mus. fr. '47. Often assoc. w. Steve Allen on TV, recs., and in clubs fr. '58. Later freelanced in LV bef. lead. own bb and gps. in southern Calif. clubs. Fav: B. Goodman. CDs: w. Bunny Berigan (Hep); T. Dorsey (BB; Jass).

BLACK, DAVE (DAVID JOHN), dms; b. Philadelphia, PA, 1/23/28; d. Alameda, CA, 12/4/06. House dmr. at Blue Note in Phila.; backed Charlie Parker, Georgie Auld, Buddy De Franco, et al., fr. 1948. Joined D. Ellington, Oct. '53; toured w. band until '55; later worked w. trad. gps., incl. Bob Scobey, '57–60. CDs: w. Ellington (Cap.).

BLACKBURN, LOU, tbn; b. Rankin, PA, 11/12/22; d. Berlin, Germany, 6/7/90. Studied at Roosevelt U., Chi.; eight yrs. in US Army, incl. two yrs. in Eur. w. 7th Army Symph. Pl. w. Charlie Ventura 1956; house band at Club Harlem, Atlantic City, N. J., '57; then join. L. Hampton '57–8; eight mos. w. D. Ellington '61. Settled in LA, worked in film studios. Lived in Eur. fr. '70, mainly in Switz. and Berlin; led Mombasa, which incl. African mus. pl. mixture of African and Western mus. built on polyrhythms, comp. and arr. by Blackburn. CDs: w. Ellington (Col.); Mingus (Rhino).

BLACKMAN, CINDY (CYNTHIA REGINA), dms; b. Yellow Springs, OH, 11/18/59. Grandmother was prof. pnst; moth. prof. vlnst; uncle pl. vib., gtr. First lessons on pno. and gtr. Stud. dms. w. private teachers 1972–8; at Berklee Coll. of Mus. '78–9; informally in NYC w. Art Blakey. Pl. w. locals bands, then w. Sam Rivers '82; Geo. Braith–Tommy Turrentine '82–4; Wallace Roney on and off '82–92; Jackie McLean '85–6; Joe Henderson '87; Larry Coryell '88–9; Don Pullen '89–93; Angela Bofill '92–3. Favs: Blakey, T. Williams, Roach, E. Jones, PJ Jones. TV: TBS Black History Month special w. Blakey. CDs: Muse; Free Lance; w. W. Roney (Muse); Santi Debriano (Free Lance); Jacky Terrasson (OMD); SaxEmble (Qwest).

BLACKWELL, ED (EDWARD B.), dms; b. New Orleans, LA, 10/10/29; d. Hartford, CT, 10/8/92. Originally infl. by pl. of Paul Barbarin, Baby Dodds, Zutty Singleton. Pl. in r&b band led by Plas Johnson, Raymond Johnson, late 1940s. Met Ornette Coleman in NO '49. Moved to LA '51, pl. w. Coleman. Worked in Texas '53–6, then ret. to NO '56, rec. w. Orig. Amer. Jazz Qnt., incl. Alvin Batiste, Ellis Marsalis. Moved to NYC '60. Pl. w. Coleman '60–1; Eric Dolphy–Booker Little at Five Spot '61; Randy Weston '65–7 incl. African tour; Mose Allison '67; Coleman fr. '67. Also pl. and rec. in '60s w. Don Cherry, Archie Shepp. Artist-in-residence at Wesleyan U. '75 and taught there on and off fr. that time. Tour. w. Old And New Dreams '76. Pl. in '70s-'80s w. Cherry; Coleman; A. Braxton; D. Redman; David Murray. Stricken w. kidney disease in '72, he was sustained by a dialysis machine for the rest of his life. A master of polyrhythmics, he was the perfect accomp. for both Coleman and Cherry, blending elements from NO, bebop, Africa, and the Caribbean into a style that was often referred to as "songlike" or "speechlike." CDs: Enja; BS; w. Coleman (Atl.; Rhino; Novus); Cherry (ECM; Mos.; Aff.; A&M); Coltrane (Atl.); E. Dolphy (Prest.); Donald Harrison (PW); J. Lovano (Enja; BN); D. Murray (BS; DIW); D. Redman; Old and New Dreams (BS; ECM); M. Waldron (SN); Jane Ira Bloom (Enja); R. Anderson (Gram.); Amer. Jazz Qnt.; K. Berger (BS).

BLADE, BRIAN, dms, comp; b. Shreveport, LA, 7/25/70. Father a Baptist minister. Start. on vln; dms. at ages 13–17 in church; also snare drum in hs symph. band. Lessons w. teach., stud. Morris Goldenberg book. Showed promise as tournament tennis pl. but became involved in jazz through listening to recs. Moved to NO 1988, pl. in coffee shops w. Nicholas Payton, Chris Thomas. Pl. duets w. John Vidacovich; sat in w. Ellis Marsalis, later tour. w. him and Courtney Pine in Engl. Pl. in street parades and w. Mardi Gras Indians. Learned fr. Herlin Riley. Kenny Garrett heard him pl w. Harry Connick in NYC and hired him for his *Black Hope* album '92. Pl. w. Garrett; Delfeayo Marsalis; Joshua Redman qt. Collab. w. Joni Mitchell '97. Own band fr. '98 draws on jazz, r&b, etc. Favs: Elvin Jones, Tony Williams, Billy

Higgins. Fests: Eur., Japan w. Redman. CDs: BN; w. Garrett; Redman; Mehldau; Bob James (WB); Kevin Hays; Steven Masakowski (BN); New Orleans Collective (Evid.); *Warner Jams, Vol. 1* (WB).

BLAIR, LEE L., bjo, gtr; b. Savannah, GA, 10/10/03; d. NYC, 10/15/66. Left-handed and self-taught on bjo., gtr.; brief stud. w. Mike Pingatore. Began pl. in dancing sch. w. Charlie Skeete 1926; Bill Benford '27; Jelly Roll Morton '28. Tour. w. Morton '28–9; also worked w. Billy Kato '28, '30–1. Pl. w. Luis Russell at Connie's Inn '34, stay. w. same orch. under L. Armstrong '35–40. Freelanced dur. '40s and bef. join. Wilbur De Paris '55. With De Paris '55–6, '58, also tour. Africa '57. In late '50s, ran chicken farm in upstate N.Y., also gigging in NYC in '60s. Brief reunion w. De Paris '64; also pl. that summer in bjo. trio w. Danny Barker at N.Y. World's Fair. Recs. w. Morton, Armstrong, De Paris; also w. Dick Cary, Pee Wee Erwin '59; Leonard Gaskin '62. Feat. w. De Paris on "Banjoker," Atl. CDs: w. Morton (BB); Armstrong (Dec.); Swingville All-Stars (GTJ).

BLAKE, EUBIE (JAMES HUBERT), comp, pno, lead; b. Baltimore, MD, 2/7/1883; d. NYC, 2/12/83. Blake began stud. org. at age 6 when his parents, both former slaves, bought an instrument for their home. Later stud. theory w. Llewellyn Wilson, cond. of the Balt. Colored Symph. As a teenager, Blake started pl. pno. in bordellos and for rent parties, and comp. songs. In 1901, he tour. w. a medicine show, then worked as an accomp. for Madison Reed. Fr. '07 to '15, he pl. solo pno. at the Goldfield Hotel, Balt. In '15, he and Noble Sissle became a perf. and songwriting team, beginning a working friendship that lasted until Sissle's death in '75; they co-led several orchs., wrote musicals, revues, and numerous songs, incl. "I'm Just Wild About Harry," and had a hit w. "It's All Your Fault," as perf. by Sophie Tucker. Sissle and Blake moved to NYC ca. '17, to join James Reese Europe's Society Orch., which soon became Europe's 369th Infantry Band. After WWI, Sissle and Blake toured the US w. Europe's orchestra and formed the Dixie Duo, a vaudeville act. In '21 they wrote and produced the first successful black musical, *Shuffle Along*, which had more than a yr.'s run on B'way and toured the US. In '25–6, they toured Eur. as a duo. In the late '20s and '30s, Blake contributed to many shows, including *Blackbirds* and *Atrocities of 1932*. In the late '30s, he resumed working w. Sissle; they toured w. their own USO show dur. WWII. Blake retired officially in '46, stud. comp. at NYU, and completed a series of courses in the Schillinger System. He and Sissle occ. reunited for special concerts and broadcasts.

In the '50s, renewed public interest in ragtime created a demand for Blake as a perf. and lecturer, establishing him as one of ragtime's foremost living experts. His comeback got a boost in '69 w. the release of *The 86 Years of Eubie Blake* (a two-record Col. set), and a highly successful app. at the first NO Jazz Fest. In '72, Blake started his own rec. and publ. co., Eubie Blake Music. Fr. '73, the yr. of his 90th birthday, he made countless apps. w. and without Sissle, incl. perfs. w. the Boston Pops Orch.; fests in Switz., Den., and Norway; and a Carnegie Hall Concert w. Benny Goodman. In '74 he rec. five pno. rolls for the QRS co. In '78 he pl. at President Carter's White House Jazz Party, and his life was made the subject of a successful B'way musical, *Eubie*. Blake received numerous awards and honorary degrees: ASCAP '72; Bklyn. Coll. '73; Dartmouth; Rutgers; New Engl. Cons. '74; U. of Maryland '79; Presidential Medal of Freedom '81. His mus. and research materials are housed at the Eubie Blake Cultural Center, Balt. As both a comp. and pnst., Blake—along w. James P. Johnson and Fats Waller—was a major contributor to the "Harlem-stride" style that evolved in the '20s. A prolific songwriter, he is credited w. over three hundred comps., many of which had the syncopated ragtime feel that characterized much of Amer. popular song fr. 1900 through the '20s. Favs: "One Leg Willie" Joseph; Johnny Guarnieri. Fests: NJF '71; Scott Joplin Fest, Sedalia, Mo.; MJF; Montreux, Nice '74; Nice '78. Film: docu., *Reminiscing with Sissle and Blake* '74. Book: *Reminiscing with Sissle and Blake*, Robert Kimball/William Bolcolm (Viking) '72. Comps: "The Charleston Rag" 1899; "Chevy Chase"; "Fizz Water Rag"; "I'm Just Wild About Harry"; "Memories of You"; "You're Lucky to Me"; "Love Will Find a Way"; "Lovin' You the Way I Do." LPs: Col.; 20th Century Fox; Eubie Blake Music. CDs: Quicksilver; Biograph.

BLAKE, RAN, pno, comp; b. Springfield, MA, 4/20/35. Studied w. Ray Cassarino as teenager; then att. Bard Coll., N.Y., 1956–60 (B.A. '60); also att. School of Jazz, Lenox, Mass. Stud. w. Oscar Peterson, John Lewis, Gunther Schuller. Pl. in duo w. Jeanne Lee fr. '57, incl. Eur. tour '63; mainly solo pno. fr. mid '60s. Music columnist for *Morningsider* '60–2. Taught at New Engl. Cons. fr. '67; Chairman of Third Stream Dept. fr. '73. Also taught at Hartford Cons. '72–5. Collab. w. Ricky Ford on and off in '70s. Rejoin. Lee for duo rec. '89. Has also worked w. singers Dominique Eade, Eleni Odoni. Blake is one of the foremost theorists and perfs. of the Third Stream movement. He says that his "sources are Alfred Hitchcock, Thelonious Monk and Charles Ives . . . I do everything I can to broaden myself, and I use

the techniques of a jazz musician but sound somewhat European." Favs: Monk, Geo. Russell, Mildred Falls, Ray Charles, Max Roach. Awards: Guggenheim Fellowship for comp. '82; MacArthur Grant '88. Fests: all major '62–83. TV: Eur. TV. Book: *The Primacy of the Ear*, in preparation. CDs: hatArt; GM; M&A; Maple.; SN; w. J. Lee (BB; Owl); Franz Koglmann (hatArt).

BLAKE, RON (RONALD EVANS), tnr, sop saxes; b. St. Thomas, VI, 9/7/65. Began on gtr. at age 8. Sw. to sax after hearing parents' Coltrane and Cannonball Adderley recs. Studied classical sax at Charlotte Amalie HS, St. Thomas, 1979–80; Interlochen Arts Acad. '81–2; Northwestern U. '82–6. Dur. this period, Blake's teachers incl. Lynn Klock, James Forger, Frederick Hemke; he also won numerous classical competitions. Formed own jazz gp. '86. Decided to sw. focus to jazz after meeting Gary Bartz '87. Pl. w. Roland Hanna, Bobby Hutcherson, Milwaukee Symph. Orch. '87; Bobby Broom '88–91; Clark Terry–Louie Bellson bb, Nancy Wilson, Bethany Pickens '89. Att. Northeastern Ill. U., Chi., '89. Pl. w. Chi. Jazz All-Stars '89–90; Akio Sasajima '90. Moved to Tampa, Fla., '90; was Asst. Profess. of Jazz Studies at U. of So. Fla. '90–2. Gigs w. Bartz '91; Chi. Civic Orch. '92. Moved to NYC '92. Pl. w. Benny Golson, Eddie Henderson, Marc Cary fr. '92; Roy Hargrove, Art Farmer fr. '93; Slide Hampton bb '94; Johnny Griffin '95; form. 4–Sight w. Peter Martin, Rodney Whitaker, Greg Hutchinson '98. Favs: Von Freeman, Golson, Shorter. Fests: Virgin Islands JF fr. '87; Red Sea JF fr. '90; Eur., Japan w. Hargrove fr. '93. TV: PBS *Live From Lincoln Center*, WBET, w. Hargrove. CDs: w. 4–Sight (N2K); Hargrove (Verve; Novus); A. Farmer (Arab.); M. Cary (Enja; Arab.); Jimmy Smith; Stephen Scott (Verve); Golson (Mile.).

BLAKE, SEAMUS, tnr, sop saxes; b. London, England, 12/8/70. Family moved to Vancouver, Br. Col., Canada, 1973. Began on vln. Stud. at Berklee Coll. of Mus. '88–92. Pl. w. Victor Lewis fr. '92; Kevin Hays, Franco Ambrosetti fr. '93. Also freelanced w. Billy Drummond '93; Mingus bb '94. Led late night sessions at Blue Note, NYC, '95. Tour. w. G. Gruntz '96. Blake solos w. a lucid, fiery presence that immediately makes him one of the bright young reedmen of the '90s. Favs: Coltrane, Rollins, Joe Henderson, Shorter. Fests: Cork, '95. CDs: CC; w. V. Lewis (Red); K. Hays (BN); Ambrosetti (Enja); B. Drummond (CC); Mingus bb (Drey.); Gruntz (TCB).

BLAKENEY, ANDY (ANDREW), tpt; b. Quitman, MS, 6/10/1898; d. Baldwin Park, CA, 2/12/92. After pl. in Chi. w. King Oliver, Doc Cook, et al., he moved to LA in 1926 and join. Johnny Mitchell, whose band incl. L. Hampton, Les Hite. Worked in silent films and early radio; bbs, small gps., brass bands and symphonic orchs. Pl. w. Paul Howard's Quality Serenaders; "Tin Can" Henry; Leon Herriford. Join. L. Hampton '35; led own band in Hawaii '36–41; Ceele Burke orch. '42–6; Horace Henderson '46; Kid Ory '47; then led own gps. Tour. Eur. w. Legends of Jazz '74. Recs. w. Sonny Clay; Reb Spikes '26; C. Burke '40s; Ory '47; Eagle Brass Band '84. After Blakeney's death, Floyd Levin wrote: "Andy's career, spanning most of the history of jazz, was a vital element in establishing the music and sustaining its popularity." CDs: w. Legends of Jazz (GHB); Eagle Brass Band; Ory (Amer. Mus.).

BLAKEY, ART (aka Abdullah Ibn Buhaina), dms, lead; b. Pittsburgh, PA, 10/11/19; d. NYC, 10/16/90. Took pno. lessons in sch. and by the age of 14 was leading a prof. dance band. Self-taught on dms. Pl. w. Mary Lou Williams at Kelly's Stable, NYC, 1942; Fletcher Henderson Orch. '43–4; led own bb briefly in Bost. '44. Join. Billy Eckstine Orch. in St. Louis, Mo., '44; pl. w. Eckstine '44–7. Organized rehearsal band, the Seventeen Messengers, '47; also rec. w. oct. under name Jazz Messengers. Trav. in Africa, stud. mus. and Islamic culture '48–9. Pl. w. Lucky Millinder '49; Buddy De Franco '51–3. Perf. as leader and sideman w. Clifford Brown, Miles Davis, etc., at Birdland Monday sessions '54. Form. Jazz Messengers w. Horace Silver, Kenny Dorham, Hank Mobley, Doug Watkins '55. When Silver left the gp. in '56, Blakey assumed sole leadership. The Jazz Messengers were the archetypal hard-bop gp. of the late '50s, playing a forceful brand of bop w. an emphasis on the music's blues roots. Sidemen fr. this time incl. tptrs. Donald Byrd, Bill Hardman, and Lee Morgan; altoist Jackie McLean; tenorists Johnny Griffin, Benny Golson, and Wayne Shorter; and pnsts. Sam Dockery, Junior Mance, Walter Davis, and Bobby Timmons. Dur. this period he also led rec. sessions w. drm. ens. that mixed jazz drmrs. w. African percussionists. Fr. '62 to '65, the Jazz Messengers incl. Freddie Hubbard, Wayne Shorter, and Curtis Fuller. After the breakup of this sxt. in early '65, Blakey ret. to qnt. format. In the mid '60s, the gp. feat. Chuck Mangione and Keith Jarrett. Jazz Messengers fr. the late '60s and early '70s incl. tptrs. Woody Shaw, Olu Dara, and Bill Hardman; tenorists Billy Harper, Carter Jefferson, David Schnitter; and pnsts. Cedar Walton, Joanne Brackeen. In '71–2 Blakey took occasional breaks fr. leading the Messengers to tour w. Dizzy Gillespie, Sonny Stitt, Kai Winding, Thelonious Monk, and Al McKibbon as

the Giants of Jazz. He took part in a memorable drm. battle w. Max Roach, Buddy Rich, Elvin Jones at Radio City as part of NJF-NY '74. Blakey's sidemen fr. the late '70s and early '80s incl. tptrs. Valery Ponomarev, Wynton Marsalis, and Terence Blanchard; saxists Schnitter, Bobby Watson, Branford Marsalis, Donald Harrison, Jean Toussaint; and pnsts. James Williams, Donald Brown, and Mulgrew Miller. His last band incl. tptr. Brian Lynch, tnr. sax Javon Jackson, pnsts. Benny Green and Geoff Keezer. Blakey was a key figure in the evolution of modern jazz and an infl. stylist on his instrument. His innovations incl. introducing African drumming techniques into jazz, and the trademark closing of the hi-hat on beats two and four that underscored his driving sense of rhythm. His ability to spot and nurture young talent is unsurpassed in the music's history. The large number of leading musicians who went on to stardom after pl. in Blakey's gp. have led some to refer to the Messengers as the "finishing school" of modern jazz. Favs: Max Roach, Sid Catlett, Cozy Cole. Polls: *DB* New Star '53. Film: soundtrack for *Les Femmes Disparaissent*, France '58. Video: *The Jazz Messenger* (Rhapsody Films) '87. Fests: all major int'l incl. lead. bb at Mt. Fuji, Japan. CDs: BN; Col.; Atl.; Riv.; Prest.; Imp.; Timel.; Conc.; PW; SN; A&M; w. Eckstine (Sav.); Clifford Brown; Kenny Burrell; Lou Donaldson; Kenny Dorham; Johnny Griffin; Hank Mobley; Horace Silver; Jimmy Smith (BN); Miles Davis; Sonny Rollins (BN; Prest.); T. Monk (BN; Riv.; BL); James Williams (Em.); B. DeFranco (Mos.).

BLANCHARD, TERENCE OLIVER, tpt, comp; b. New Orleans, LA, 3/13/62. Father stud. opera, was member of Harlem Harmony Kings; aunt pl. pno. and teaches mus. Began on pno. at age 4. Stud. classical tpt. w. Geo. Jenson, pno. w. Ellis Marsalis at NOCCA 1978–80. Stud. w. Kenny Barron, Paul Jeffrey, Bill Fiedler at Rutgers Univ. '80. Pl. w. Lionel Hampton '80–1; Art Blakey '82–6. Co-led gp. w. Donald Harrison '84–9. Blanchard has led own gp. fr. '91. App. at Lincoln Center pl. commissioned works, incl. *Romantic Defiance* '93. He has participated on the soundtracks of Spike Lee's films fr. '87, either as perf. or comp., incl. *School Daze, Do the Right Thing, Mo' Better Blues, Jungle Fever, Malcolm X, Crooklyn,* and *Clockers.* His work w. Branford Marsalis on the soundtrack to *Mo' Better Blues* earned a Grammy nomination. Scored *The Promised Land* for TV. Infl. by Miles Davis, Clifford Brown, F. Hubbard, W. Shaw, he cites other infls. as Coltrane, Ellington, Monk, Shorter. Polls: *DB* TDWR; *JT* Emerging Artist. Fests: all major fr. '82. Film: app. in *Malcolm X.* TV: *Tonight Show* '92. CDs: Col.; w. Harrison

(PW); Blakey (Conc.; Timel.; PW); Benny Green (CC); Ralph Peterson (BN); Billy Pierce (Sunny.).

BLAND, JACK, gtr, bjo; b. Sedalia, MO, 5/8/1899; d.? Started Mound City Blue Blowers w. Dick Slevin on kazoo and singer Red McKenzie. They rec. "Arkansas Blues" and "Blue Blues" in Chi. 2/23/24; it was a sensation and reputedly sold a million copies. Later that year, w. guitarist Eddie Lang added, the gp. visited Engl. In '30s in NYC, Bland rec. w. Billy Banks, his own Rhythm Makers, and other gps.; in '40s rec. w. George Wettling; Marty Marsala; Art Hodes; Muggsy Spanier; then moved to LA and retired, ca. '44. CDs: w. J. Teagarden (BB; ASV); Spanier (ASV); Red Allen (Hep); Fats Waller (CDS); Hodes (Dormouse).

BLANDING, WALTER JR., tnr sax; b. Cleveland, OH, 8/14/71. Father was prof. jazz bsst.; moth., Audrey Shakir, is jazz pnst. and voc.; grandmoth., Ruby Patton, prof. gospel and classical pnst. and orgst. Started on C-melody and alto sax. Stud. w. Barry Harris off and on fr. 1980; at LaGuardia HS, NYC, '85–9; New Sch. fr. '89. Pl. w. parents at Village Gate '87–9; Reggie Workman '89; Cab Calloway, Count Basie Orch., Roy Hargrove '90; Milt Hinton–Honi Coles '91; Harper Bros. fr. '91. Blanding won a Yamaha Young Talent Award in '89 and was a finalist in the Thelonious Monk Int'l Sax. Competition in '91. He then worked w. Wynton Marsalis. Moved to Israel '97, pl. and teach., also bringing in mus. fr. US for perfs. Member of LCJO beginning w. Dizzy Gillespie tribute '97. Favs: Coltrane, Rollins, C. Parker. Fests: Eur. fr. '90. TV: *Cosby Show*; *Tonight Show* '91. CDs: w. Tough Young Tenors (Ant.); Harper Bros (Verve).

BLANTON, JIMMY (JAMES), bs; b. Chattanooga, TN, 10/5/18; d. Los Angeles, CA, 7/30/42. Studied vln.; mus. theory w. uncle; and bs. at Tenn. St. Coll. Pl. w. pnst.-moth.'s band. Moved to St. Louis, Mo., at end of 1937, working w. Fate Marable on the riverboats and w. the Jeter-Pillars orch. Hearing him in late '39, Duke Ellington immediately hired Blanton, who became a vital part of the Ellington orch. until late '41, when TB forced him into an LA sanitarium. Establishing himself as a distinctive voice and rhythmic force within the Ellington organization, Blanton ushered the bs. into the modern era. His impeccable intonation was most clearly evident in his horn-like pizzicato solos, which took the instrument far beyond its heretofore standard walking, quarter-note style. As a soloist and ensemble player, he demonstrated a high degree of harmonic acuity. His style profoundly infl. an entire generation of bssts., most significantly

Oscar Pettiford, Red Callender, Ray Brown, Charles Mingus. Blanton took part in some of the seminal '41 Harlem jam sessions, and—but for his untimely death—seemed destined to become a member of the Gillespie-Parker inner circle. Recs. w. Ellington: duo, "Plucked Again," "Pitter Panther Patter," "Mr. J.B. Blues," "Body and Soul"; w. orch., "Across the Track Blues," "Jack the Bear," "Conga Brava," "Ko-Ko," "Harlem Air Shaft." CDs: w. Ellington (BB).

BLEY, CARLA (Borg), comp, arr, pno, org, lead; b. Oakland, CA, 5/11/38. Father was pno. teach. and church orgst., moth. pl. pno. Daughter, Karen Mantler, pl. kybds., hca. Bley stud. pno. w. parents, then pl. in church for weddings and funerals. Moved to NYC 1955; worked as pnst. and cigarette girl in jazz clubs. Married Paul Bley '57 and began writing mus. for him, Geo. Russell, Jimmy Giuffre, Art Farmer. Worked w. Charles Moffett and Pharoah Sanders '64. Founded Jazz Composer's Orch. w. second husband, Mike Mantler '64, and two yrs. later founded Jazz Comp. Orch. Assoc., which commissions and prod. new jazz comps. Comps. rec. by P. Bley '65; Jazz Comp. Orch. '66, Gary Burton '68; Charlie Haden's Liberation Mus. Orch. '69–70. In '71, she completed an extended piece, *Escalator Over the Hill*, which led to awards and grants incl. Guggenheim Fellowship '72; Oscar du Disque de Jazz '73; NEA and Creative Artists Prog. grants, mid '70s. Start. WATT label w. M. Mantler '70s. Pl. and rec. in '70s and '80s w. M. Mantler; Gato Barbieri; Dave Holland; Roswell Rudd; Steve Swallow. In '90s pl. in duo w. Swallow and in trio w. him and Andy Sheppard. Received many other awards for comps. incl. NY Jazz Award '79; Deutcher Shallplattenpreis '85; Prix Jazz Moderne '91. Comp. soundtrack for film, *Mortelle Randonnee*, '85. Visiting Prof. of Mus. at Coll. of Wm. and Mary '90. Fav: Billy Strayhorn. Polls: *DB* '80s, '91; *JT* '90; Hi Fi Vision '90. Fests: NJF '65; Eur. fr. '75; Japan. Rec. own comp., *Churches,* for ECM at Umbria Jazz, Italy, '96. Film: pl. on soundtrack of *Holy Mountain* '73. TV: *Night Music* '90. Wrote opera, based on Malcolm Lowry's *Under the Volcano*, '85. Comps: "A Genuine Tong Funeral"; "Sing Me Softly of the Blues"; "Ida Lupino"; "Ad Infinitum"; "Wrong Key Donkey." CDs: ECM; WATT; w. C. Haden (BN; Imp.; ECM; Polydor); M. Mantler (WATT); S. Swallow (XtraWatt).

BLEY, (H.) PAUL, pno, kybds, comp; b. Montreal, Que., Canada, 11/10/32. Cousin Jonathan is classical concert pnst. Began on vln. at age 5; pno. at 8. Received junior diploma fr. McGill Cons. at age 11; also stud. at Quebec Cons. Led hs band; own qt. at

Chalet Hotel, Montreal, 1945–8. Form. trio w. ex-members of the Oscar Peterson Trio, Ozzie Roberts and Clarence Jones, when Peterson left for US '49, and pl. at Alberta Lounge; then moved to NYC '50. Studied pno., comp., cond. at Juilliard '50–4. Hosted weekly TV show for Jazz Wkshp. of Montreal '52. Freelanced in NYC w. Jackie McLean–Donald Byrd, Pete Brown, Charlie Parker, Ben Webster, Lester Young, early '50s; led own gps. fr. '54. Tour. midwestern colls. '55. Moved to LA in '56; tour. West Coast colls. '57–9. Married Carla Bley '57 (divorced ca. '66). Pl. w. Ornette Coleman–Don Cherry '58; own gp. w. Scott La Faro, Bobby Hutcherson '59. Ret. to NYC '59. Pl. w. Charles Mingus '60; Jimmy Giuffre, Don Ellis, Sonny Rollins, Gary Peacock early '60s; own gp. w. Steve Swallow, Pete LaRoca, Giuseppi Logan '64. Member of Jazz Comp. Guild '64–5. Pl. w. Annette Peacock, late '60s-73. Bley began experimenting w. electronic instruments in the early '70s. For his Paul Bley Synthesizer Show, he would stack four kybds., an acoustic pno., elec. pno., clavinet, and synth. Tour. Eur. as a solo pnst. '73–5. Founded Improvising Artists Inc., a prod. co., w. artist Carol Goss '74; prod. recs. by self, also Sam Rivers–Dave Holland, Ran Blake, others. Has cont. to perf. and rec. as a leader and solo pnst. into the '90s; also in a trio w. Giuffre and Swallow. He says his ambition is to "deconstruct" free jazz. Has taught improv. at New Engl. Cons. fr. '92. Favs: Giuffre, Beiderbecke. Fests: all major fr. '61. Film: *Imagine the Sound* w. Cecil Taylor, Archie Shepp, Bill Dixon; also Can. jazz history short w. Stan Kenton '52. CDs: Deb.; ECM; DIW; SN; Owl; MM; Evid.; Sav.; ESP Disk; Steep.; hatArt; JT; IAI; BL; Post.; Splasc(h); w. Chet Baker (Steep.); C. Parker (Up.); Jimmy Giuffre (ECM; hatArt; IAI; Owl); Franz Koglmann (hatArt); Lee Konitz (Evid.; IAI); B. Altschul (IAI); Jaco Pastorius (DIW; IAI); Sonny Rollins (BB); Charlie Haden (Verve); B. Ditmas (Post.); J. Surman (ECM); Mingus; Don Ellis (Cand.).

BLOOM, JANE IRA, sop, alto saxes; b. Newton, MA, 1/12/55. Studied w. Joseph Viola in Bost. 1968–77, also at Yale U. '72–7, M. A., grad. magna cum laude; and w. Geo. Coleman in NYC '77–8. Pl. w. Jay Clayton Qnt. '78–83; George Coleman Oct. '79; David Friedman Qnt. '80–1; David Lahm All-Stars '84–5; Outskirts '89–91; Cleo Laine '91. Bloom has taught clinics and master classes at Harvard, Yale, Wellesley, New Engl. Cons., UCLA, U. of Mich., etc.; in '89, she became the first mus. commissioned by NASA; the resulting comp., *Most Distant Galaxy,* is incl. in her CD *Art & Aviation.* Kevin Whitehead called her tone "one of the most gorgeous of any soprano saxophonist," and praised her "haunt-ingly lyrical ballad conceptions." Favs: Joe Viola. Polls: *DB* TDWR '83–91. Fests: various in Eur., US fr. early '80s. TV: CBS *Sunday Morning*; score for *Shadow of a Doubt*, NBC. Video: app. in *Reed Royalty* (Jazz Images). Comps: *Einstein's Red/Blue Universe*, prem. at Carnegie Hall '94; jazz score for Pilobolus Dance Co. CDs: Arab.; Enja; Col.; w. D. Lahm (Generation); Cleo Laine (RCA).

BLOWERS, JOHNNY (JOHN G. JR.), dms; b. Spartanburg, SC, 4/21/11; d. Westbury, NY, 7/17/06. Played w. Eddie Condon, Bunny Berigan, Bobby Hackett, Pee Wee Russell in NYC 1930s and '40s. Extens. studio work in '50s and '60s. Tours w. Sy Oliver; WGJB; Harlem Blues and Jazz Band. Rec. w. Louis Armstrong; Billie Holiday; Sidney Bechet; Ella Fitzgerald; et al. Visited Eur., Engl. '81. In '91, pl. on SS *Norway* jazz cruise. Cont. to work w. Harlem Blues and Jazz Band and own gp. Book: *Johnny Blowers: Back Beats and Rim Shots* (Scarecrow). CDs: w. Berigan (BB; Jass); E. Condon; E. Fitzgerald; B. Holiday (Dec.); Teddy Wilson (Hep).

BLUIETT, HAMIET A. JR., bari sax, contralto cl, bs-fl; b. St. Louis, MO, 9/16/40. Raised in Lovejoy and Brooklyn, Ill. Began on pno., tpt., then sw. to cl. at age 8; fl. at age 18; bari. sax at age 20. Stud. w. aunt Mattie Chambers, a choir dir., 1943–4; Geo. Hudson '48–55; then at So. Ill. U. '57–60. After navy service, moved to St. Louis in mid '60s. Assoc. w. Black Artists Gp.; pl. w. Lester Bowie; Bobo Shaw; Julius Hemphill; Oliver Lake. Moved to NYC '69; free-lanced and pl. w. Sam Rivers bb; Olatunji. Pl. w. Charles Mingus Qnt. w. Don Pullen '72–5. Formed World Sax. Qt. w. Hemphill, Lake, David Murray '76. Pl. w. Don Braden Oct. '97. Has five-octave range on the bari. and an expansive tone to match. Favs: Carney, Leo Parker, P. Adams. Awards: SESAC '91. CDs: BS; SN; Tutu; Maple.; w. World Sax. Qt. (BS; Moers; Elek. Mus.; Elek. None.; Mingus (Atl.); J. Stubblefield; Abdullah Ibrahim; Arthur Blythe (Enja); R. Weston (Verve); L. Bowie (ECM); Ebony Brass Qnt.; Andy McKee (Maple.).

BLYTHE, ARTHUR MURRAY, alto, sop saxes; comp, arr; b. Los Angeles, CA, 7/5/40. Grew up in San Diego, pl. in sch. bands fr. age 9. Stud. w. former Jimmie Lunceford saxist Kirtland Bradford, mid 1950s; also w. David Jackson. Ret. to LA '60. Pl. w. Horace Tapscott '63–73; Owen Marshall '67; Stanley Crouch's Black Music Infinity '67–73. In this period he was known as Black Arthur. Moved to NYC '74. Pl. w. Chico Hamilton '74–7; Gil Evans '76–80; Lester Bowie, Jack DeJohnette '78–80; also w. Leon Thomas; Ted Daniel; Julius Hemphill. Led own gps.

in '70s incl. avant-garde qnt. w. Abdul Wadud, Bob Stewart, Bobby Battle, James Blood Ulmer, or Kelvyn Bell; In The Tradition w. Fred Hopkins, Steve McCall, Stanley Cowell, or John Hicks. Blythe experimented w. pop mus. briefly in the early '80s, then form. the all-star, free jazz sxt., The Leaders, in '84. Worked mainly as a lead. fr. '80 but also replaced J. Hemphill in World Saxophone Quartet '90. An emotional pl., he reflects strong gospel and blues roots w. abstract qualities that seem to derive fr. Eric Dolphy. Pl. on soundtracks for films: *Sweet Jesus Preacher; As Above, Also Below; Coonskin.* Favs: Coltrane, C. Parker, Harold Land, Daniel Jackson, Dolphy; comps.: Ellington, Monk. CDs: Ind. Nav., Enja; w. The Leaders; L. Bowie (BS); J. DeJohnette (ECM); G. Evans (Ant.; Zeta); H. Tapscott (Novus); M. Tyner (Mile.; Red. Bar.); Mose Allison (BN); World Sax. Qt. (Elek. None.).

BLYTHE, JIMMY (JAMES LOUIS), pno; b. Louisville, KY, 1/1901; d. Chicago, IL, 6/21/31. Moved to Chi. in his teens, stud. w. Clarence Jones. Rec. first pno. solos, "Chicago Stomp," "Armour Ave. Struggle," for Paramount in 1924. During the '20s, he rec. many sess. accomp. singers for Para., incl. Ma Rainey. Rec. w. Jimmy Bertrand's Washboard Wizards '27; State Street Ramblers '28–9, '31; J.C. Cobb and his Grains of Corn '28–9. Led many sess. for Para. w. sidemen incl. Johnny Dodds, Freddie Keppard, Roy Palmer. One of the first boogie- woogie pnsts., he was a versatile soloist well versed in the blues idiom. CDs: w. Johnny Dodds (BB; Dec.; Aff.; Timel.); one track each w. Barrelhouse Five and State Street Ramblers in *History of Classic Jazz* (Riv.).

BOBO, WILLIE (William Correa), tmbls, perc, voc; b. NYC, 2/28/34; d. Los Angeles, CA, 9/15/83. Father a folk-gtrst. from Puerto Rico. Raised in Spanish Harlem; self-taught on bongos from age 14. Began as bandboy w. Machito, then pl. w. Latin bands in NYC; later w. Perez Prado. Given the nickname "Bobo" by Mary Lou Williams on 1951 rec. date. Worked w. Tito Puente '54–8; Cal Tjader '58–61; Herbie Mann '61–3. After extensive work as sideman for Latin and jazz gps., formed own band in LA '66, for work at clubs, concerts, fests. Moved to Calif., '69. In the '70s, he added voc. to his perfs. Fav: Jimmy La Vaca, tmbls., who pl. w. Luis Del Campo in NYC '50s. Bobo's bands blended jazz, Latin, and r&b in an exciting, entertaining way. Fests: Int'l Song Fest., Venezuela; Latin Jazz Fest, MSG; MJF w. Tjader '59; NJF w. Mann '63. Film: *Soul to Soul* w. Santana in Ghana. TV: actor-mus. for Bill Cosby comedy series, late '70s. Recs. as lead. on Verve, Roulette. Recs. as sideman w. Miles Davis; Chico

Hamilton; Cannonball Adderley; Terry Gibbs. CDs: w. Tjader (Fant.; Verve); H. Hancock; Ike Quebec (BN); Les McCann (Rhino); Oliver Nelson (RCA); Wes Montgomery (Verve).

BOHANNON, STEVE, dms, org; b. 1947; d. Victorville, CA, 10/21/68. Father, Hoyt Bohannon, pl. tbn. w. Harry James. Worked w. Stan Kenton and pl. org. w. Howard Roberts qt., but was best known as dmr. w. Don Ellis orch. He was killed instantly when a car in which he was riding collided w. a truck. Rec. w. Ellis for PJ. CDs: w. Ellis (GNP Cres.).

BOHANON, GEORGE ROLAND JR., tbn, bs.-tbn, euph; b. Detroit, MI, 8/7/37. Studied at Det. Institute of Mus. Arts. Led vocal-instrumental gp., The Premieres, 1956–60. First prominent w. Barry Harris, Yusef Lateef, Ernie Wilkins '59–60; then join. Chico Hamilton qnt. '62–3. Later freelanced w. many gps. in Calif., incl. Quincy Jones, Marty Paich, Johnny Mandel, Jack Elliott; tour. Japan w. Benny Carter '84; world tour w. Gene Harris Philip Morris Superband '90–1. CDs: w. Clayton-Hamilton Band (Capri); Gene Harris; F. Capp (Conc.); Jimmy Smith; Sonny Rollins (Mile.); Milt Jackson (Qwest); GRP All-Star bb (GRP).

BOLAND, FRANCY (FRANÇOIS), comp, lead, pno; b. Namur, Belgium, 11/6/29; d. Geneva, Switz., 8/12/05. Studied fr. age 8. Pl. w. Bob Shots at Paris JF 1949; w. Al Goyens in Germ. '50. Arr. for Bobby Jaspar, Bernard Peiffer, Henri Renaud, Fats Sadi '51–4. Pnst.-arr. w. Aime Barelli band '54–5. Tour. Germ., France, Italy w. Chet Baker '55–6. Lived in US '57–8, arr. for Count Basie, Benny Goodman. Ret. to Eur. '58, arr. for Werner Müller, Kurt Edelhagen bb in Frankfurt. Form. Clarke-Boland bb w. Kenny Clarke '59. The band, which incl. many Amer. expatriates as well as Eur. mus., rec. w. such feat. soloists as Lockjaw Davis; Stan Getz; Johnny Griffin; Benny Bailey. After the band broke up in '73, Boland moved to Geneva, Switzerland, where he cont. to comp. and arr. for Eur. jazz orchs. Occ. perf. and rec. as the leader of small gps.; sidemen incl. son Chris on gtr. and B. Bailey. Rec. bb album as lead. '76; comp. and arr. for Sarah Vaughan's rec. of poems by Pope John Paul II '84. Like Duke Ellington, he tailored his charts to the musical personalities of his sidemen. His comps. for the Clarke-Boland bb incl. "Sabbath Message"; "Sax No End"; "Griff's Groove," for Johnny Griffin. Extended works incl. *All Blues*, a three-part suite; *Fellini 712; Off-Limits; Change of Scene*, for Stan Getz. Fests: all major in Eur. fr. '59. CDs: w. Clarke-Boland (MPS; RTE); Chet Baker (Em.).

BOLDEN, BUDDY (CHARLES JOSEPH), crnt; b. New Orleans, LA, 9/6/1877; d. Jackson, LA, 11/4/31. Acknowledged to be the first of the NO "trumpet kings," the details of his life have been greatly colored by exaggerations and fanciful accounts. City records listed him as a plasterer, but he was known to own a barber shop and edit a scandal sheet called *The Cricket*. After finishing sch. in 1894, he took up the crnt. Pl. w. Charley Galloway in '95 bef. form. his own semi-prof. gp. w. cl. Frank Lewis and valve tbn. Willie Cornish. Bunk Johnson was a band member '95–9. In the first five yrs. of the twentieth century, his band enjoyed great popularity in black dance halls and honky tonks and pl. for picnics and parades. Samuel Charters, in his book *Jazz: New Orleans*, says: "[Bolden] was so popular he sometimes had six or seven bands going in one night, and he'd go from one to another playing his specialties, 'Make Me a Pallet on the Floor,' 'Bucket's Got a Hole In It' and 'Funky Butt, Funky Butt, Take It Away.' " In '06, Bolden began to suffer periods of mental derangement, and tbnst. Frankie Dusen took over as leader. His last known job was a funeral w. the Allen Brass Band in '07. His mental problems, compounded by alcoholism, caused his internment at the East Louisiana State Hospital, 6/5/07, where he spent the rest of his life. It was said that when Bolden played, the sound of his horn could be heard all over the city. His was a powerful style w. a hard rhythmic drive and particularly poignant expression on slow blues. He supposedly rec. on an Edison cylinder in the late '90s, but no evidence has ever surfaced. Nevertheless, as a transitional figure between ragtime and what was to be called jazz, he was a link to this later mus. through his infl. on Freddie Keppard, Bunk Johnson, etc. His 6-pc. band set standards for the small NO ensembles that followed. Books: *In Search of Buddy Bolden, First Man of Jazz*, Donald M. Marquis '78; novel, based on Bolden's life, *Coming Through Slaughter*, Michael Ondaatje '76.

BOLDEN, WALTER LEE, dms, comp, arr; b. Hartford, CT, 12/17/25. Studied at Julius Hartt Sch. of Mus., Hartford 1945–7. Pl. w. Gigi Gryce '45–8; Horace Silver '48–50; Stan Getz; Gerry Mulligan '50–1; Howard McGhee '51–3; George Wallington, Teddy Charles '53; Matt Matthews '54–5; Carmen McRae, Sonny Rollins, Tony Scott, Miriam Makeba-Ray Bryant '58; L,H&R, Al Cohn–Zoot Sims, Bennie Green, Abbey Lincoln, G. Shearing '59; Bobby Short '65; own gps. since '73. Coord. of Arts for N.Y. Project Create '74–6. Pl. in '80s w. Ray Bryant; Johnny Hartman; Junior Mance; Art Farmer; Heath Bros; w. Walter Bishop Jr.; Annie Ross in '90s. Contributed comps. to the book of A. Taylor's Wailers: "Mr.

A.T."; "Stressed Out"; "Harlem Mardi Gras." Favs: Roach, PJ Jones, Blakey, Kenny Clarke; arrs: Gigi Gryce, Horace Silver, Tadd Dameron. Fests: Austral. '59; Switzerland '82; Japan '82, '88–9. TV: *Positively Black* w. J. Hartman. CDs: w. Mulligan (Prest.); J.J. Johnson (FS); Getz (Roul.); J. Mance (JSP); C. Hawkins (Prest.; Dec.); McGhee (Aff.).

BOLLENBACK, PAUL NORRIS, gtr; b. Hinsdale, IL, 6/6/59. Father pl. tpt. Raised in Westchester County, N.Y., fr. age 5. Became interested in mus. at 7. After two and a half yrs. in New Dehli, India, he ret. to NYC area, pl. in Westchester rock bands. Moved to Wash., D.C., in 1976. Stud. at U. of Miami as perf. major 1979–81; priv. stud. in ear training and comp. w. Dr. Asher Zlotnik in D.C. area '82–90; also help fr. pnst. Lawrence Wheatley. Pl. w. Buck Hill; Keter Betts; Marc Copland; Charlie Byrd. Has also worked w. Stanley Turrentine; Ron Holloway; Paul Bley; Arturo Sandoval; Joe Kennedy; Jimmy Bruno; Balt. Symph.; Navy Commodores. Began pl. w. Gary Thomas early '80s. Best known for his work w. Joey DeFrancesco, whom he met at Kennedy Center in summer of '90 when both were part of a concert feat. Dizzy Gillespie, James Moody, etc. Tour. in Eur. w. Thomas in '80s and cont. w. DeFrancesco in '90s incl. Poland, Russia, Bulgaria, Greece, Spain. App. w. local pl. in Netherlands, France. Co-feat. w. Jimmy Ponder in *The Jazz Guitarists* at Kennedy Center '92. A hot player w. strong blues feeling. Favs: George Benson, Pat Martino, John Scofield. Pl. Vail JP w. DeFrancesco '96. Awards: SESAC Outstanding Comp. '91; grant from Va. Commission on the Arts and NEA to comp. and perf. *New Music for Three Jazz Guitars* at Blues Alley, Wash., D.C., '91. TV: *Tonight Show*, *Today*, *Good Morning America*, *Entertainment Tonight*, w. DeFrancesco; acoustic gtr. on *America's Most Wanted* '91. Rec. debut w. Thomas '87. CDs: Chall.; w. DeFrancesco (Col.; Muse; Big Mo); Thomas (Enja; JMT); R. Holloway (Mile.).

BOLLING, CLAUDE, lead, pno, comp; b. Cannes, France, 4/10/30. Studied in Nice and Paris. Won amateur jazz contest 1944. Form. own combo '45; made prof. debut pl. for US Army in Nice '45. Pl. w. Chippie Hill at Paris JF '48; Club St. Germain '49–52. Pl. w. Amer. mus. incl. L. Hampton, R. Eldridge, Rex Stewart, Cat Anderson, P. Gonsalves, M. Mezzrow, etc., late '40s-early '50s. Led own bb, Show Biz Band, fr. '55; sidemen incl. Roger Guerin, Gerard Badini. Bolling cont. to perf. and rec. w. Amer. mus. incl. Sidney Bechet, Don Byas, Kenny Clarke, Buck Clayton '50s-'60s. Comp., arr., led studio band for French singers incl. Sacha Distel; Mireille Mathieu; Mouloudji; Juliette Greco. Bolling wrote mus. for the films *Borsalino* '70 and *Catch Me a Spy*; TV prog. *To Bix Or Not to Bix*; musical comedy *Monsieur Pompadour*. Also led vocal gp. Les Parisiennes. He is noted for his semiclassical comps., which he has rec. w. Jean-Pierre Rampal, Maurice André; and his interpretations of Ellington material. Favs: Tatum, Hines, Ellington. Polls: Grand Prix du Disque (six times). CDs: Col.; Milan; w. Hampton (Vogue); Eldridge (Vogue).

BOLTON, (BEWIS) DUPREE, tpt; b. Oklahoma City, OK, 3/16/29; d. Alameda, CA, 6/5/93. Left home at 14. In 1944 pl. w. Buddy Johnson in NYC; join. Benny Carter's bb '45, but left the mus. scene in '46, his career disrupted by drug abuse. Re-emerged in '59 w. Harold Land and rec. "The Fox," which established his reputation. Arrested for narcotics and did not work until '62 w. Curtis Amy. After another prison sentence, he pl. briefly w. Bobby Hutcherson '67, bef. his incarceration. Cont. to pl. while at the Joseph Harp Correctional Center in Tulsa, Okla., recording there in '80. After his release, he pl. a gig w. Dexter Gordon in Oklahoma City '82, then ret. to the West Coast, but remained in obscurity. CDs: w. H. Land (Cont.); C. Amy (PJ).

BOLTRO, FLAVIO, tpt, flg; also pno, gtr; b. Torino Italy, 5/5/61. Father, Dante, a prof. tptr., gave him first lessons at age 9. Grad. fr. G. Verdi Cons. of Torino, 1982. Began prof. career alternating between jazz and classical. Pl. w. symph. orch. of RAI and orch. of Regio Theater, Torino. Was part of the gp. Lingomania, led by Maurizio Gianmarco '84–6; pl. jazz fests. in Umbria, Paris, and Montpellier. Also worked w. Mario Rusca '85–6, incl. Montreal JF '86. Led own trio w. Furio Di Castri, Manhu Roche '87. Join. Giovanni Tommaso '88–'92 and tour. US w. him in '89. Has also worked w. Mario Rai bb; Ricardo Fassi qt.; Enrico Intra sxt. In '91 pl. w. national orch. of AMY (Assoc. of Jazz Mus.), dir. by G. Gaslini. Apps. at jazz fests. w. Bob Berg, Dave Liebman, Don Cherry, Billy Hart, Richie Beirach '84–9; Jimmy Cobb, F. Hubbard '90; Clifford Jordan, Red Holloway '91. Favs: Clifford Brown, Miles Davis, Chet Baker. CDs: Red; Penta.; w. Tommaso; Piero Bassini (Red); Phil Woods (Phil.); S. Grossman (Phrases); Fassi; Giuseppe Costa; Massimo Farao; Giovanni Mazzarino; Stefano Sabatini (Spl.); Roberto Gatto (Gala); M. Petrucciani (Drey.).

BONAFEDE, SALVATORE, pno; b. Palermo, Italy, 8/4/62. Studied classical pno. at Palermo Cons. 1973–9. Moved to Bost. '86; stud. at Berklee Coll. of Mus. '86–9. Pl. w. Jerry Bergonzi, Ricky Ford '87–9. Freelance w. Kenny Burrell; Archie Shepp; Sam Rivers; Lew Tabackin; Bob Berg; Reggie Workman; Gary Bartz. Moved to NYC '90, pl. w. Mel Lewis Orch., own gps. With Groove Collective fr. '93. Poll: *Musica Jazz* '91. Fests: Eur. fr. '85. CDs: Ken; Penta.; w. Bergonzi (Red); Enzo Randisi (Spl.); Pierre Vaiana (CELP).

BONANO, SHARKEY (JOSEPH GUSTAF), tpt, voc; b. Milneburg, LA, 4/9/02; d. New Orleans, LA, 3/27/72. Played w. local NO bands such as Chink Martin, 1921, and Freddy Newman. To NYC for tryout w. the Wolverines, but instead join. Jimmy Durante '24. Ret. to the South and led his own band on riverboats '25. Worked w. Jean Goldkette '27 and led the Melody Masters w. Leon Prima '28–30. With Larry Shields in Calif. bef. ret. to NO, where he worked fr. '30 to '36. Made rec. debut as leader on Dec. '36, then sw. to Vocalion. After pl. w. Ben Pollack '36, he led his own band, the Sharks of Rhythm, in NYC. Popular for his Armstrong-derived tpt. and voc., modeled along the lines of Wingy Manone and Louis Prima. Also pl. occ. w. the revived ODJB. Following mil. service '49, he settled in NO and form. a band that made numerous successful recs. and accomp. Lizzie Miles for Cap. Gigged in NYC Feb. '55, Sept. '59. In mid '50s also tour. US for Hilton Hotels' shows. Worked into the '60s, though illness reduced his pl. activities. Pl. NOJF '69. Recs. w. Norman Brownlee, Johnnie Miller, Monk Hazel '20s. CDs: Timel.; Story.; tracks in *Recorded in New Orleans, Vol. 1* (GTJ).

BOND, JIMMY (JAMES EDWARD JR.), bs, tba; b. Philadelphia, PA, 1/27/33. Played bs. in jr. hs.; bs. and tba. in hs. Grad. fr. Juilliard 1955. While in sch., pl. w. Gene Ammons, Louie Bellson, Charlie Parker, et al. With Chet Baker '55–6; Ella Fitzgerald '56–7; Buddy DeFranco '57. Tour. w. George Shearing, then settled in LA '59; worked w. Paul Horn Qnt. '59–61; after that, primarily active in Hollywood studios into '80s, although occ. pl. or rec. w. Jazz Crusaders, Gerald Wilson, Curtis Amy, Gil Fuller '65. Active in real estate since early '70s; perfs. w. Buddy Collette, et al. CDs: w. Art Pepper; Elmo Hope (Cont.); C. Baker (PJ; Em.; FS); Dizzy Gillespie (BN); Lars Gullin (Drag.).

BONNER, JOE (JOSEPH LEONARD), pno, comp; b. Rocky Mount, NC, 4/20/48. Grandfather was in minstrel shows; moth. sang; fath. pl. vln. Stud. mus. fr. elementary sch. through Booker T. Washington HS and pl. w. local jazz gps. while att. Va. St. Pl. w. Roy Haynes 1970–1; F. Hubbard '71–2; Pharoah Sanders '72–4; also w. Thad Jones–Mel Lewis; Harold Vick; Max Roach; Leone Thomas; Billy

Harper. While living in Copenhagen, Den., he tour. Eur. w. Harper '78–9. Ret. to US '80, later pl. in NYC and Denver. Infl. by tptrs. and saxists as well as pnsts., he employs a palette of impressionist colors. Favs: Tyner, Hancock, Mingus. Rec. w. Johnny Dyani '79, '83. CDs: Evid.; Steep.; w. Harper (BS); Sanders (Evid.); Sonny Simmons (WW).

BONNIER, BESS, pno, voc, comp; b. Detroit, MI, 5/26/28. Studied classical pno. in Det. public sch. for five yrs.; then two yrs. w. Bendetsen Netzorg. Stud. Art Tatum solos w. H. DeRemer, three yrs. Pnst. w. dance band at Jefferson Jr. HS, Det. 1941. Pl. w. Mike Norsesian while in sch. '44–6, then freelanced w. Kenny Burrell, Leo Osebald, Billy Mitchell, Doug Watkins, Paul Chambers, Bill Spencer, Art Mardigan, Johnny and Marion DeVita, Major Holley, Pepper Adams, Al Aarons '46–54. Pl. w. Dave Heard–Tate Houston '54–5; own trio '55–60; Jack Brokensha '60–1; own trio '61–5; Brokensha '65–70. Led own gps. fr. '70. Artist-in-res. in Det. public schs. '73–6. Perf. at Det. Piano Summit, NYC, '82; solo pno. at Kool JF, SUNY-Purchase '83. She taught mus. at Grosse Pointe North HS '80, '90–4. Established Grosse Pointe Acad. of Mus. '94. Completed a songbook of orig. comps. in '90. Comp: *Suite William*, jazz accomp. to Shakespearean texts. Named Woman of the Year by Wayne St. U. and Artist of the Year by the Mich. Foundation for the Arts '86; Rec. Governor's Award fr. state of Mich. '90. Favs: Tommy Flanagan, Barry Harris, Hank Jones, Bill Evans. Fests: Montreux-Detroit fest annually. TV: local TV in Det. LPs: Argo; Noteworks (own label). CDs: Noteworks; w. Brokensha (AEM).

BOOKER, BERYL, pno, voc; b. Philadelphia, PA, 6/7/22; d. Berkeley, CA, 9/30/78. Self-taught. Worked in clubs w. local combos and own gps. in early 1940s. To NYC w. Slam Stewart '46, remaining w. trio off and on to '51. Join. Dinah Washington as accomp. '51–3. Then form. own all-female trio w. Bonnie Wetzel, bs., and Elaine Leighton, dms.; tour. Eur. w. *Jazz Club U.S.A.* Jan. '54 and rec. w. Don Byas for Vogue in Paris. After trio broke up, dur. summer '54, worked at the Embers and other NYC clubs w. combos incl. a new trio. With Stewart again '55–7; and Washington '59 for several mos. incl. July gig in Stockholm, Sweden. Cont. to pl. and rec. into the '70s. Booker gained recognition in the '40s w. Stewart, and throughout her career showed herself to be an authoritative and swinging Garner-infl. pianist, who perhaps never received all the attention she deserved. Rec. debut as leader for RCA '46, w. Mary Osborne; later rec. for Em. w. such sidemen as Budd Johnson, S. Stewart, John Collins, and Oscar

Pettiford. CDs: tracks w. own trio in *The Women* (BB); w. B. Holiday (BN).

BOOKER, WALTER M. JR. bs; b. Prairie View, TX, 12/17/33; d. NYC, 11/24/06. Family moved to Wash., D.C., in 1942. Fath. pl. pno., cl.; stud. cl. w. fath. fr. '42. Received degree in psych. fr. Morehouse Coll. '56; pl. alto sax and cl. in coll. band. Began pl. bs. while in army '56–8. After discharge, stud. w. Joseph Willens in Wash. Pl. w. JFK Qnt. '60–3; Shirley Horn '64. Moved to NYC Oct. '64 to pl. w. Donald Byrd. Pl. w. Sonny Rollins, Ray Bryant '65; Art Farmer '66–7; Thelonious Monk, Stan Getz mid '60s; Cannonball Adderley '68–75. Rec. w. Betty Carter '76; Nick Brignola, Billy Higgins '79; Richie Cole–Phil Woods '80; John Hicks '81–3; Pharoah Sanders, Nat Adderley '82; Clifford Jordan '84. Cont. to pl. w. N. Adderley in '90s. Favs: Percy Heath, Israel Crosby. Film: app. w. C. Adderley in *Play Misty For Me* '71. CDs: w. C. Adderley (Fant.; Cap.); N. Adderley (Evid.; In + Out; Land.; Sw.Bas.); Rollins (Imp.); K. Barron (Cand.); S. Grossman; John Hicks (DIW); Clifford Jordan (SN); Junior Cook; S. Cowell (Steep.); W. Shorter (BN); B. Higgins (Timel.); Claude Williams (Prog.).

BOONE, RICHARD, tbn, voc; b. Little Rock, AR, 2/24/30; d. Copenhagen, Denmark 2/10/99. At 5, sang solo in Baptist church; at 12 pl. tbn. in sch. band. Joined army at 18, five yrs. in Germ. and France in Special Service Orch.; then back to Little Rock to study at Philander Smith Coll. Moved to LA 1960, rec. as sideman on *The Resurgence of Dexter Gordon* for Jzld. Pl. w. Della Reese off and on to '66. Tour. w. Count Basie '66–9, earning popularity for his pl. and unique, comedic singing, which incl. his own brand of blues scat and yodeling. After freelancing in Eur., settled in Copenhagen '71, working w. Thad Jones, Danish Radio bb to '85; Ernie Wilkins fr. '86; also substitute teacher at cons. In '87, organized the Sophisticated Ladies (female pno., bs., and dms.), tour. w. them throughout Eur. Perf. for three weeks at club in Nairobi, Kenya, '90. Favs: Tony Bennett, Carmen McRae, Sarah Vaughan, B. Eckstine. Rec. in Vienna w. Leo Wright '90. Own LP for Nocturne '69. CDs: Story.; w. Basie (Sequel; Jazz Arch.); Benny Carter; Thad Jones (Story.); D. Gordon (Jzld.; Steep.).

BOOTH, JUINI aka JOONY (ARTHUR EDWARD), bs, cello, pno, bs; b. Buffalo, NY, 2/12/48. Piano lessons at 8; bs. at 12. Stud. at Buff. Community Mus. Sch. 1962–3. Pl. w. Chuck Mangione '64–5; Art Blakey '66–7. Freelance '68–70 w. Donald Byrd; Dollar Brand; K. Dorham; Tal Farlow;

Shelly Manne; Thelonious Monk; Albert Ayler, etc. Pl. w. Freddie Hubbard '68–71; Tony Williams Lifetime '71–3; McCoy Tyner '74–6; Elvin Jones, Charles Tolliver '77–8. Freelance w. Beaver Harris, Steve Grossman, Sonny Stitt, Chet Baker '79–88. Pl. w. Sun Ra fr. '89. Favs: Scott LaFaro, Paul Chambers, F. Rabbiatt; arrs: Gil Evans, Abdullah Ibrahim, Ellington. Fests: Eur., So. Amer., Africa, Japan fr. '71. Awards: CAPS; NEA '78. Films: *Round Trip* w. Larry Rivers. TV: *Night Music* w. Sun Ra '89. CDs: w. Tyner (Mile.); Grossman (Red); Sonny Simmons (ESP); Chico Freeman (Cont.).

BOSE, STERLING BELMONT (aka BOZO), tpt; b. Florence, AL, 2/23/06; d. St. Petersburg, FL, 6/58. Worked w. NO bands in early 1920s bef. moving to St. Louis, where he pl. w. Crescent City Jazzers; Arcadian Serenaders at Arcadia Ballroom '24–6. Was infl. by Bix Beiderbecke, whom he heard in Frankie Trumbauer orch. dur. this period. Pl. w. Jean Goldkette in KC '27–8; Chi. radio orch. '29; Ben Pollack '30–3, moving w. him to NYC. Dur. remainder of '30s, he freelanced, perf., and rec. w. the bands of Joe Haymes '34; Tommy Dorsey '35; Ray Noble, Benny Goodman '36; Glenn Miller '37; Bob Crosby '38–9; Bobby Hackett '39. After pl. four mos. at Nick's, early '40s, pl. briefly w. Bob Zurke's bb and Jack Teagarden. Freelanced in Chi. bef. ret. to NYC '43, working at Nick's again w. Miff Mole, Art Hodes; Town Hall concerts w. Eddie Condon. After another short period in Chi., he settled in Fla., app. w. own bands. Gravely ill, he took his own life w. a gun. Recs. w. Goldkette, Teagarden, Pollack, T. Dorsey, Goodman, Crosby, Zurke, Johnny Mercer. CDs: w. Condon (Jazz.); Bob Crosby (Dec.; CDS; Swaggie; Jazz Arch.); Dorsey Bros. (Hep); T. Dorsey; Goodman (BB); Teagarden; F. Waller (ASV).

BOSTIC, EARL EUGENE, alto sax, comp; b. Tulsa, OK, 4/25/13; d. Rochester, NY, 10/28/65. Clarinet and alto in hs and Boy Scout bands. Stud. harmony, theory, and several inst. at Xavier U., NO. Pl. locally w. Joe Robichaux, 1934; then w. Ernie Fields, Clarence Olden bef. tour. w. Charlie Creath–Fate Marable '35–6. To NYC '38, where he was feat. in bands of Don Redman, Edgar Hayes, Cab Calloway, and arr. for Paul Whiteman, Louis Prima, Ina Ray Hutton; later Artie Shaw, Lionel Hampton. Worked w. Hot Lips Page and also led own band at Mimo Club; pl. tpt., gtr., alto '41. With Hampton '43–4, then formed own bands '45, rec. w. bb for Majestic, small gp. for Gotham. Combining his technical facility w. a clarion-toned, extroverted style, he became a phenomenally successful r&b recording star for King, beginning w. "Flamingo" '51 and con-

tinuing w. "Temptation," "Moonglow," "Cherokee," "You Go to My Head." On the strength of these hits, his gp. was a strong tour. attraction; sidemen incl. John Coltrane; Blue Mitchell; Stanley Turrentine; Benny Golson; Jaki Byard. A heart attack drastically curtailed his career in '56, but he resumed pl. on a part-time basis in '59, mostly taking jobs close to his LA home. Moved to Det. '65, and went on the road again, but suffered a second, fatal heart attack. Polls: voted to *Playboy* all-star band, '59, app. at Playboy JF same yr. Comps: "Let Me Off Uptown," "The Major and the Minor," "Brooklyn Boogie." Recs. w. L. Hampton, Hot Lips Page. Own last sess. incl. such sidemen as Groove Holmes, Joe Pass, Shelly Manne w. arrs. by Buddy Collette. CDs: King; w. Hampton (BB); Page (Comm.); Rex Stewart (Prest.).

BOSWELL, CONNEE (CONNIE), voc; b. New Orleans, LA, 12/3/07; d. NYC, 10/11/76. Suffered a polio attack as an infant, which confined her to a wheelchair throughout her career. Stud. cello at 4, later pno., sax, tbn. Occasionally pl. latter three instruments w. Boswell Sisters, the voc. trio she form. w. her sists. Martha and Helvetia (Vet) in 1931. The tightly knit trio—a precursor to the Andrews Sisters—gained int'l popularity through its recs. w. the Dorsey Bros., Benny Goodman, Red Nichols, and Don Redman, and via frequent radio apps. In '35, when her sists. married and ret. fr. music, she launched her career as a soloist. Her relaxed sense of swing, apt timing, and warm feeling, contrasted w. the stiffer, on-the-beat vocs. of earlier jazz and infl. many singers, most notably Ella Fitzgerald. Films: *Big Broadcast of 1932*, w. Boswell Sisters; *Artists and Models* '37; *Kiss the Boys Goodbye* '41; *Syncopation* '42. Recs: w. Boswell Sisters, Bing Crosby, and others. LP w. updated version of Original Memphis Five '56. CDs: w. Bob Crosby (Halcyon; Swaggie).

BOTHWELL, JOHNNY, alto sax; b. Gary, IN, 5/23/19; d.? After hearing Johnny Hodges, he bought an alto sax. In 1940 gigged in Chi. on tnr., then alto. Moved to NYC, pl. w. Woody Herman '43; Sonny Dunham '44–6. Prominent in Boyd Raeburn's progressive bb '44–5. Pl. w. Gene Krupa '45. Led own sxt. '46; own bb '46–7; residency at Tin Pan Alley Club, Chi. '48. Own big and small bands through '50, when he retired fr. full-time mus. and moved to Miami, Fla. Excellent lead pl. and Hodges-inspired ballad stylist. Rec. for Sig. '45–7. CDs: Hep; w. Raeburn (Sav.).

BOTSCHINSKY, ALLAN, tpt, flg, comp; b. Copenhagen, Denmark, 3/29/40. Father pl. classical bassoon, pno. Tpt. lessons at 11; at 14 began stud. at Royal Danish Cons. Pl. w. Ib Glindemann bb 1956–9;

Jazz Qnt. '60, w. Bent Axen, Niels-Henning Ørsted Pedersen '59–63. Gained exp. pl. w. Oscar Pettiford; Stan Getz; Dexter Gordon; Ben Webster; Sahib Shihab; Lee Konitz; and Kenny Dorham. In '63, after being voted Musician of the Year by Danish jazz critics, he was awarded a scholarship to Manhattan Sch. of Mus., NYC, where he stud. w. Cecil Collins. Pl. w. Danish Radio Jazz Gp. '63–5; Danish Radio bb '64–82. Fr. '66, worked as a leader and w. Peter Herbolzheimer's Rhythm Combination and Brass. Form. rec. co., M.A. Music, w. Marion Kaempfert '87. Infl. tonally by Jack Sheldon, Botschinsky is a fluent, melodic pl. who reflects a grounding in swing, bebop, and the Tristano-Konitz sch. Awards: Ben Webster Prize '83; Prize of Honor fr. Danish Comps. Org. '84. Comps: "The Night"; "The Bench"; "The End of a Tune." CDs: M.A. Mus.; w. Kenny Dorham; Dexter Gordon (Steep.); Thad Jones; Ben Webster (Story.); O. Pettiford (BL); P. Herbolzheimer (Rare Bid); Eur. Jazz Ens. (Ear-Rational; M.A. Mus.).

BOUTTE, LILLIAN THERESA, voc; b. New Orleans, LA, 8/6/49. Studied mus.; sang in church choir. First prof. gig w. Allen Toussaint r&b gp. Starred in stage show, *One Mo' Time*. Tour. Eur., 1981–2; formed gp., Music Friends, w. Germ. saxophonist Thomas L'Etienne '83; after their marriage, it became the Boutte-L'Etienne Jazz Ensemble. She cont. frequent tours of US and Eur. into early '90s, incl. Festa New Orleans Music in Ascona, Italy '85–8, and w. Humphrey Lyttelton at the '87 Edinburgh JF and Barbican Arts Centre, London. An impressive perf. w. a traditional, blues and gospel-infl. jazz style. CDs: Callig.

BOWEN, RALPH MICHAEL, tnr, alto, sop saxes; fl, cl; b. Guelph, Ont., Canada, 12/23/61. Grandfather led dance band; bro. Wayne is prof. saxist; wife Geraldine is prof. vlnst. Began on cl. at age 11. Stud. sax at Phil Nimmons clinic, then w. Pat LaBarbera at Banff Sch. of the Arts summer program 1978. Stud. w. LaBarbera '78–83. Pl. in Toronto w. Keith Blackley, Lance Anderson, Rick Tait, own gps. '79–84; Manteca '80–4. Stud. w. David Baker at Indiana U. '82–4. Moved to NYC '85; pl. w. Out of the Blue '85–90; Michael Camilo fr. '86; Horace Silver fr. '88; Jim Beard '91; John Serry, Kenny Drew Jr. fr. '92. Received B. Mus. fr. Rutgers U. '89; M. Mus. '92. Bowen is on the faculty at Rutgers and working toward a doctorate in classical fl. He has led his own gp. fr. '91. Favs: Coltrane, Rollins, J. Henderson, C. Adderley, E. Bostic. Fests: Japan fr. '85; Eur. fr. '86; Brazil '90; Carib. fr. '91. TV: Eur. TV w. OTB; Camilo. CDs: CC; w. Camilo (Epic); OTB; Renee Rosnes: (BN); Benny Carter (MM).

BOWIE, JOSEPH, tbn; b. St. Louis, MO, 1953. Brother of Lester Bowie. Bec. member of Black Artists Guild at 17; pl. w. Oliver Lake, Julius Hemphill; rec. w. Lake 1971, '76. Tour. w. Human Arts Ensemble '72–8; pl. w. St. Louis Creative Ensemble '77–9. Organized a gp., Defunkt, in '80 w. another bro., Byron, pl. a mixture of funk, avant-garde jazz, rock, etc.; rec. an album, *Defunkt*, '81; pl. w. the Ethnic Heritage Ens. '86. CDs: w. Kahil El'z-abar (Chameleon; OpenMinds; Silk.); Vienna Art Orch. and Choir (Amadeo).

BOWIE, LESTER (WILLIAM LESTER), tpt, flg, comp, lead; b. Frederick, MD, 10/11/41; d. Brooklyn, NY, 11/8/99. Father was tpt. pl. and hs band dir.; bro. Byron pl. sax, bro. Joe pl. tbn. Raised in Little Rock, Ark. and St. Louis Studied crnt. w. fath. fr. 1946. Formed first gp., Continentals, 1954; first gigs backing doo-wop gps. Pl. at after-hours clubs while in air force in Tex. '58–60. Pl. w. wife Fontella Bass and Oliver Sain '61. Pl. w. r&b bands in South and Midwest incl. Little Milton, Albert King, early '60s; also tour. w. circus bands. App. on r&b recs. on Chess label. Ret. to St. Louis; led hard-bop gp. there w. dmr. Philip Wilson, ca. '64. Moved to Chi. '65. Founding member and second president of AACM. Formed Art Ens. of Chi. w. Roscoe Mitchell, Joseph Jarman, Malachi Favors '68; pl. w. Art Ens. of Chi. fr. '68. Bowie also helped form the Black Artists Group and the Great Black Music Orch. in St. Louis. Premiered extended comp. *Gettin' to Know Y'All* w. 50-pc. Baden Baden Free Jazz Orch. '69. Led own gps. under name Serious Fun fr. '70s. Rec. in '70s w. Archie Shepp; Sunny Murray; Jimmy Lyons; Cecil Taylor. Tour. Senegal '74, perf. w. local dmrs. Pl. w. NY Hot Tpt. Repertory Co. w. Wynton Marsalis, Ray Copeland '83. Bowie has pl. w. the all-star avant garde gp. The Leaders fr. '86 and has led the all-brass gp. Brass Fantasy fr. '89. Premiered orchestral work at Town Hall, also rec. theme music for *Cosby Show* '90. Worked on film soundtracks w. comp. Philippe Sarde, early '90s. Bowie taught at clinics and was artist-in-res. at Yale, Dartmouth, and Harvard. Joachim Berendt described him as "a Cootie Williams of the avant garde." Favs: Miles Davis, Kenny Dorham, Freddie Hubbard. CDs: BS; DIW; ECM; In+Out; PW; w. Art Ens. of Chi. (Atl.; DIW; ECM; Aff.; Del.; EMI Jazztime; Nessa); Leaders (BS; BH); J. DeJohnette (ECM; Pan); D. Murray (Ind. Nav.); A. Shepp (Aff.; Charly); Kip Hanrahan (American Clave); Khail El'zabar (SA).

BOWLER, PHIL (PHILLIP CHARLES), bs, el-bs; b. NYC, 3/2/48. Began on vln., cello, tbn. Received B. Mus. fr. Hartt Coll. of Mus. 1971. Pl. w. Rahsaan

Roland Kirk '76–7; Hugh Masekela '80; Joe Lee Wilson '81; W. Marsalis '82–3; Slide Hampton's World of Tbns. '83; Terence Blanchard–Donald Harrison '85–6; Jon Faddis, H. Silver, S. Salvador fr. '85; also freelance w. T. Farlow; Jackie McLean; Jaki Byard; Freddie Hubbard; Art Blakey; Phil Woods; Pharoah Sanders; Branford Marsalis; Herman Foster; Lester Bowie, etc. Bowler has led his own gp., Pocket Jungle, w. Bill Dowling, Peter Smith, Beaver Bausch fr. '85; join. McLean in mid '90s. Hosted a jazz radio program on WPKN, Bridgeport, Conn., fr. '86. Favs: Ron Carter, Ray Brown, Percy Heath. Fests: East. Eur. w. Faddis '89; India w. Abdullah Ibrahim '90. TV: NBC *Live at Five*; CBS *Sunday Morning*. CDs: w. Ralph Peterson (BN); Carla White (Mile.); S. Salvador (Stash); W. Marsalis; B. Marsalis (Col.); D. Harrison (Cand.); McLean (BN).

BOWMAN, DAVE (DAVID WALTER), pno; b. Buffalo, NY, 9/8/14; d. Miami, FL, 12/28/64. His parents, Canadians, raised him in Hamilton, Ont. Pl. pno. fr. childhood, stud. mus. at Hamilton Cons. and, later, at Pitts. Mus. Inst. Began prof. w. Ken Steele in Hamilton. Worked w. Jack Hylton in London 1936–7, moving to NYC, where he worked w. Bobby Hackett, Bud Freeman's Summa Cum Laude Orch. at Nick's '37–40. Then pl. w. Jack Teagarden '40; Joe Marsala '41; Muggsy Spanier '41–2. Radio work fr. '43; staff pnst. ABC, NBC, where he accomp. Perry Como. Join. Bud Freeman trio '54–5. Moved to Fla., where he freelanced in late '50s w. hotel bands and Phil Napoleon's trad. combo '64. Drowned in an auto accident. Recs: w. Hackett, Bechet, Lee Wiley, and Eddie Condon; solo pno., "Cow Cow Boogie"; "Stars Fell on Alabama" Sig. '46. CDs: w. Billie Holiday; Roy Eldridge (Dec.); Freeman (Aff., CDS); Teddy Grace (Timel.); Wingy Manone (Prest.); Spanier (ASV; Archives of Jazz).

BOWN, PATTI (PATRICIA ANNE), pno; elkybds, org, voc; b. Seattle, WA, 7/26/31. Mother and three sists. all pl. pno. Sist. Edith Mary was sponsored by Paul Robeson and Orson Welles and presented at Town Hall by Sol Hurok in a concert sponsored by Claire Boothe Luce. Began pl. pno. by ear at age 2, perf. for governor of Wash. Stud. w. priv. teacher, nuns, and at U. of Wash.; graduated fr. U. of Seattle 1955. Led own bands and pl. w. other local Seattle bands while a teenager. To NYC '56; toured Eur. w. Quincy Jones '59–60; pl. w. him again '62. Mus. dir. for Dinah Washington '62–4; Sarah Vaughan '64. In the '60s, she worked and/or rec. w. Gene Ammons; James Moody; Oliver Nelson; Illinois Jacquet; Joe Newman. Also pl. w. Charles Mingus, George Russell, NYJRC. Cont. to freelance,

leading own gps., singing and writing orig. material, into '80s, often app. at Village Gate. Taught at U. of Wash, NYU, Bennington Coll., Rutgers U. A versatile perf., who makes full, two-handed use of the pno., she has rec. w. a wide variety of mus. and voc. fr. jazz to r&b to gospel. Favs: Ellington, Horace Silver, Erroll Garner. Fests: NJF, NJF-NY; '90 Lionel Hampton JF, Moscow, Idaho. Solo concert w. U. of Mexico Symph., Mexico City '79; w. Marian McPartland, Joanne Brackeen at Cornell U. '87. Pl. for B'way show *Purlie* '72–4; as actress, app. Off-B'way in *Christchild* '92. LP: *Patti Bown Plays Big Piano*, Col. '59. CDs: w. Q. Jones (Merc.; R&T); Gene Ammons; Etta Jones (Prest.); B. Eckstine (Em.).

BOYD, CURTIS, dms, comp; b. Brooklyn, NY, 6/9/40. Father sang and pl. pno. Stud. at Chi. Cons.; Bklyn. Acad. of Mus. Stud. arr. w. Adolph Sandole. Pl. w. Cedar Walton, Julian Priester, Wynton Kelly, Frank Strozier, Kenny Dorham, Chick Corea, late '50s; Gloria Lynne '62; Ronnell Bright '63; Carmen McRae '64; Joe Williams '65; Oscar Brown Jr. '66–8; Freddy Cole '68–72. Pl. in '70s w. Chris Woods; Al Cohn; Helen Merrill; Heath Bros.; Harold Ashby; Bob Cranshaw; Sweets Edison, etc. Pl. w. Billy Taylor, Frank Foster, Cecil Payne, Harold Vick, Little Jimmy Scott '78; freelanced '79–84; Billy Taylor '85–7; Bill Doggett, Ernestine Anderson, Joe Williams '88–91. Co-led Art of Jazz wkshp. at Stony Brook Coll. '80–5. Perf. as a guest artist w. the symphs. of San Antonio, Sacramento, Atlanta, Denver, Portland, others '85–7. Boyd has also been involved w. Jazzmobile; the Third St. Mus. Settlement; the Jackie Robinson Foundation; and teaching at Five Towns Coll. on LI. Favs: Roach, Philly Joe Jones, Art Blakey, Roy Haynes. Fests: Japan '64; Singapore w. Taylor '85; Senegal '85; Hungary w. Taylor '86. TV: PBS Trib. to Thelonious Monk w. Taylor and Gerry Mulligan; *Today* w. Oscar Brown Jr. CDs: w. Taylor (Taylor-Made).

BOYD, NELSON, bs; b. Camden, NJ, 2/6/28; d.? Began prof. career in Phila., early 1940s, moving to NYC '47 and pl. w. Coleman Hawkins, Tadd Dameron, Dexter Gordon on 52nd St. Worked w. bands of Charlie Barnet and, briefly, Dizzy Gillespie '48. Tour. Middle East w. Gillespie orch. '56. CDs: w. Charles McPherson; S. Stitt (Prest.); Thelonious Monk (BN); Fats Navarro (BN, Sav.); Miles Davis (Sav., Cap.); Milt Jackson; D. Gordon (Sav.); D. Gillespie (GNP; CAP; Verve).

BRACKEEN, JOANNE (Grogan), pno, comp; b. Ventura, CA, 7/26/38. Grandfather pl. cello, cl. in LA Phil. Orch. Stud. pno. fr. age 9. Att. LA Cons. of Mus.

Pl. w. Teddy Edwards, Dexter Gordon, Harold Land, Charles Lloyd in Calif., late 1950s. Moved to NYC '65. Worked w. Freddie McCoy late '60s; Woody Shaw '69; Dave Liebman '69. Pl. and rec. w. A. Blakey '70–2; Joe Henderson '72–5; Joe Farrell, Sonny Red '73; Sonny Stitt, Horacee Arnold, S. Getz '75–7. Own duo and trio since '72 have incl. Eddie Gomez, Cecil McBee; Sam Jones; Clint Houston; Billy Hart; J. DeJohnette; Freddie Waits. Also worked w. F. Hubbard; Jon Faddis; Toots Thielemans; Pharoah Sanders; Lee Konitz; Eddie Harris; Charlie Shavers, etc. A profess. at the New Sch., Brackeen received NEA comp./perf. grants in '79 and '82, and in the future would like to expand her comp. to symphonic works. Favs: Ornette Coleman, Joe Henderson, Tony Williams. Fests: Eur. every yr. since '72. TV: apps. w. Getz, Henderson, Sanders. CDs: Conc.; Ken; Ant.; Timel.; w. Getz (Steep.).

BRADEN, DON (DONALD KIRK), tnr, sop saxes, fl, pno; b. Cincinnati, OH, 11/20/63. Family moved to Louisville, Ky., in 1967. Began on alto at age 12; tnr. at 13. Mainly self-taught; some lessons w. Mike Tracy, Jamey Aebersold. First gigs w. local funk band at age 15. Att. Harvard U. '81–3, stud. briefly w. Bill Pierce, Jerry Bergonzi. Moved to NYC '84. Pl. w. Harper Bros. '85–6; Wynton Marsalis '86–7; Betty Carter '86–8; Roy Haynes '88–9; Freddie Hubbard '89–91; Larry Ridley's Jazz Legacy Ens., Jeanie Bryson fr. '91; own gps. fr. '80s. Also subbed for Bill Pierce w. Tony Williams '87–91 and Ralph Bowen w. OTB '88. Freelanced extensively w. Kenny Barron; Herbie Hancock; Dianne Reeves; Art Blakey bb; Lonnie Smith; Illinois Jacquet bb; Jack McDuff; others. Braden has worked as a computer consultant fr. '83; he co-owns a software co. in Mass. and wrote the program that tracks ticket sales for the JVC JF-NY. Favs: Coltrane, Rollins, Shorter. Fests: Eur., Japan w. T. Williams, Hubbard. Pl. at Lincoln Center "Battle Royale" for tnrs. w. G. Coleman, J. Redman, D. Murray of which Peter Watrous wrote: "Braden's narratives flowed, always self-analyzing and never careless, even in the most heated contexts." TV: David Brenner, Joan Rivers, *Saturday Night Live* w. Marsalis '87–8; Mt. Fuji JF; '89; Hubbard *Live at the Blue Note* (Jap. TV) '90; mus. dir. of new *Cosby* show '97. CDs: RCA; CC; D-T; Epicure; Land.; w. Melvin Rhyne (CC); Betty Carter; Stephen Scott (Verve); Joris Teepe (Mons).

BRADFORD, BOBBY LEE, crnt, tpt, pno; b. Cleveland, MS, 7/19/34. Played pno. at age 8, crnt at 15. Stud. at Sam Houston Coll. 1952–3 and U. of Tex. '59–61. Pl. w. Ornette Coleman and Eric Dolphy in LA in the early '50s. After four yrs. in air force bands, he moved to NYC where he pl. w. Coleman '61–3

and Quincy Jones '62. Moved to LA in '64; co-led combo w. John Carter on and off '69–91. Taught elementary sch. '66–71, lived in Engl. '71, then briefly to NYC to rejoin Coleman. Fr. mid '70s through '91 taught jazz courses at Pasadena City Coll. and Pomona Coll. Participated in Little Big Horn wkshp. w. Carter, Arthur Blythe, James Newton, et al. '76–8. In '80s, app. w. David Murray Octet; Charlie Haden's Liberation Music Orch.; John Stevens' Freebop; and his own gp., Mo'tet. His son, Dennis Bradford, is a dmr. and one of the founding members of the Jeff Lorber Fusion. LP: *Science Fiction* w. Coleman. CDs: SN; hatArt; w. J. Carter (Gram.; BS; hatArt; Novus); David Murray (BS; DIW).

BRADFORD, CARMEN, voc; b. Austin, TX, 7/19/60. Grandfather was singer Melvin Moore. Fath. is tptr. Bobby Bradford; moth. is singer Melba Joyce. Raised in Pasadena, Calif., she established herself as a popular singer, rec. jingles for TV, also singing country mus. In 1982 she was opening act for the Count Basie Orch. The following yr., Basie hired her to join the band. She remained until '91, establishing herself as a versatile artist w. a strong sound, equally at ease w. ballads, up-tempos, and blues. In '90 she also rec. and perf. w. George Benson. After leaving Basie, worked as a single and rec. on her own. CDs: Amazing; w. Basie (Den.); Benson (WB).

BRADFORD, PERRY (JOHN HENRY; "MULE"), lead, voc, pno., comp; b. Montgomery, AL, 2/14/1893; d. NYC, 4/20/70. Raised in Atlanta, Ga. Traveling w. minstrel shows, he arrived in Chi. in 1909, where he pl. solo pno. and started own band in '10. To NYC '12, lead. own band off and on until '28. First to arr. rec. sess. for a black singer, Mamie Smith. Her '21 rec. of his "Crazy Blues" sold over a million copies and started the blues craze of the '20s. Made several tours w. Smith in early '20s and fr. '23 led rec. gps., incl. Perry Bradford's Jazz Phools, for many sess., backing his own vocs. and those of Alberta Hunter and others. Sidemen incl. L. Armstrong; Buster Bailey; James P. Johnson; Fats Waller; Don Redman. Form. own publ. co. Served prison sentence for violating copyright laws '23. Comps: "Evil Blues"; "You Can't Keep a Good Man Down"; "That Thing Called Love." His '65 autobiography, *Born With the Blues*, is a bitter, rambling narrative that attacks those whom he felt had not given him his due, but also contains useful insights. CDs: w. Louis Armstrong (Aff.); James P. Johnson (Hot 'n' Sweet).

BRADLEY, BILL aka JUNIOR and/or WILL JR. (WILLIAM ACKERSON), dms; b. NYC, 2/15/38; d.? Son of Will Bradley. Began on dms. 1952, turned prof. spring '54, pl. at NYC clubs such as Birdland, Basin St., w. Johnny Smith; Tony Scott; Kai Winding; George Wallington. Played w. Woody Herman Jan.-Apr., '56. Favs: Art Blakey, Philly Joe Jones. LPs: *House of Bradley* (Epic); w. Tony Fruscella (Atl.).

BRADLEY, WILL (Wilbur Schwichtenberg), lead, arr, tbn; b. Newton, NJ, 7/12/12; d. Flemington, NJ, 7/15/89. Raised in Washington, N.J., moving to NYC in 1928, where he worked w. Milt Shaw. Pl. and rec. w. Red Nichols '31–2; CBS studio mus. '31–4; Ray Noble '35–6; CBS again to late '39, when he join. Ray McKinley to form a band whose Col. recs. were highly successful, mainly due to novelty boogie-woogie numbers feat. pnst. Freddie Slack: "Beat Me Daddy, Eight to the Bar"; "Scrub Me Mama With a Boogie Beat"; "Down the Road a Piece"; and the band's theme, "Strange Cargo." After band broke up in '42, he was mainly active as studio player. Pl. briefly w. Sauter-Finegan '53. His favorite solo, "April in Paris," is typical of his smooth ballad style. Class. comps. include a tbn. sonata for the American Comp. League; several large string works; and a brass suite; other works perf. by Dean Dixon, Radiodiffusion, Paris. Fav. class. comp.: Alban Berg. Hobbies incl. silversmithing, gem cutting, wood sculpture, and painting. CDs: Col.; w. B. Goodman (Cap.); T. Dorsey (BB); Bud Freeman (CDS); Woody Herman (Disc.); Red Nichols (ASV); Roy Eldridge (Dec.); C. Parker (Stash).

BRADSHAW, TINY (MYRON), lead, voc, dms; b. Youngstown, OH, 9/23/05; d. Cincinnati, OH, 11/26/58. Studied psychology, later perc. at Wilberforce U.; sang w. Collegians under Horace Henderson. Moved to NYC, pl. dms. w. Marion Hardy's Alabamians, the Savoy Bearcats, Mills Blue Rhythm Band; and sang w. Luis Russell 1932. Form. own band at Renaissance Ballroom '34, rec. "Darktown Strutter's Ball," "Sheik of Araby" for Dec. Sidemen incl. Shad Collins, Happy Caldwell, Russell Procope; later, Sonny Stitt, Big Nick Nicholas. Tour. Japan '45. Rec. several r&b hits in late '40s–early '50s incl. "Soft" w. Red Prysock, tnr. sax. CDs: King.

BRAFF, RUBY (REUBEN), crnt, tpt; b. Boston, MA, 3/16/27. Self-taught. Worked in Boston area w. Pee Wee Russell; Bud Freeman; Urbie Green; Edmond Hall; Sam Margolis; Joe Sullivan; Geo. Wettling; Gene Ramey. Moved to NYC 1953; app. at first NJF '54. Had acting and pl. role in musical *Pipe Dream* '55–6. Although he was widely acclaimed by critics, Braff had trouble finding steady work in the '50s and early '60s when his style was out of fashion. Rec. w. Vic Dickenson '53; Buck Clayton, Urbie Green '54; Bud Freeman, Benny Goodman, own gp. '55. App. in *The Magic Horn*, a televised play about a jazz gp., '55. Tour. w. Newport All-Stars '60s. App. as single in Engl. '65, incl. work w. Alex Welsh. Feat. soloist w. Tony Bennett '71–3. Led qt. w. Geo. Barnes '73–5. Freelanced in NYC fr. '75, incl. subbing for Roy Eldridge at Jimmy Ryan's. Tour. w. NY Jazz Repertory Co. tribute to Louis Armstrong '75. His important collab. since have involved mus. such as Dick Hyman; Gene Di Novi; Scott Hamilton; Ed Bickert; Howard Alden; Roger Kellaway; Gray Sargent, Ellis Larkins. Living on Cape Cod fr. '91. Survived a serious illness in '93 to come back strongly in '94 w. his mellow, burnished sound, particularly so effective in the lower register, and buoyant sense of swing. Fav: Louis Armstrong. Fests: JVC-NY; Nice. Polls: *DB* New Star '55. Film: *This Funny World* w. Bennett. TV: Mike Douglas; *Today*; Eur. TV. CDs: Conc.; Chiar.; Arb.; w. Hyman (Conc.); V. Dickenson; M. Powell (Vang.); Goodman (Cap.; MM).

BRANNON, TEDDY (HUMPHREY J.), pno, arr, comp; b. Moultrie, GA, 9/27/16; d. Newark, NJ, 2/24/89. Cousin of Babs Gonzales. Family moved to Linden, N.J., in early 1920s. Stud. pno. fr. age 9. Pl. w. local dance bands dur. hs, then w. night club band in Newark, N.J., '37–42; led this gp. for a while. Pl. w. Benny Carter '42–4; various combos on 52nd St. '45–6; own trio '47–50; Roy Eldridge, Buddy Rich, Bennie Green '50–2; Johnny Hodges '52–4; Illinois Jacquet '54–7; Jonah Jones '58–60. Also accomp. singers incl. Dinah Washington; Ruth Brown; The Ravens. Fav: Oscar Peterson. CDs: w. Bennie Green (Prest.); D. Byas (Sav.); Carter (Forlane); Eldridge (Dec.); Tab Smith (Del.).

BRASHEAR, OSCAR, tpt, flg; b. Chicago, IL, 8/18/44. Mother a church pnst. Private lessons and studies at DuSable HS. After tour. w. Woody Herman, '67, Basie '68–9, freelanced in Chi. w. Sonny Stitt, Gene Ammons, Dexter Gordon, and James Moody. Active fr. '71 in LA w. Gerald Wilson; Harold Land; Oliver Nelson; Shelly Manne; Quincy Jones; Horace Silver; Duke Pearson. In '70s and '80s, visited Japan many times w. Q. Jones, H. Land, Benny Carter; also North Sea JF w. Wilson '90; Umbria w. Billy Higgins '98. A spirited, fluent soloist, critics have called him a latter-day Clifford Brown. CDs: w. Wilson (Disc.); Teddy Edwards (Verve); Silver (Col.); Land (Muse); Milt Jackson (Qwest); Joe Henderson; Jimmy Smith; S. Rollins (Mile.); Basie (Sequel); Clayton-Hamilton (Capri); Nelson (RCA); B. Golson (Timel.); B. Hutcherson (Ther.).

BRAUD, WELLMAN (Breaux), bs; b. St. James Parish, LA, 1/25/1891; d. Los Angeles, CA, 10/29/66. Began on vln. at 12; started perf. in NO ca. 1910–1, incl. dms. in brass band; gtr. w. A.J. Piron. Worked in string trio at Tom Anderson's. Tour. brought him to Chi. '17. Pl. bs. w. Sugar Johnny '20; Charlie Elgar '20–22. Trav. to Eur. w. Will Vodery's *Plantation Days* '23. In NYC w. Wilbur Sweatman '23; tour. w. burlesque show bef. join. Ellington '27. Stayed w. Ellington into '35 dur. which time he gained a wide reputation through his forceful, though sometimes overstated, beat. Claimed to have advanced the walking bass style. Assumed lead. of Spirits of Rhythm '35–6; own trio in Sheepshead Bay (NYC) restaurant '37–41. Operated a pool hall in Harlem fr. '40; also pl. and/or rec. w. Jelly Roll Morton, Sidney Bechet in early '40s; Bunk Johnson '47. Tour. Eur. w. Kid Ory '56. Moved to Calif. '60, pl. occ. w. Joe Darensbourg, Barbara Dane. Heart ailment restricted his pl. activities. Rec. w. Ellington incl. his own "Double Check Stomp" '30. CDs: w. Ellington (Dec.; BB; Col.); Ory (GTJ); Morton; Bechet (BB); Mezzrow (Story.); Jack Teagarden–Pee Wee Russell; Rex Stewart (Riv.).

BRAUGHAM, CHARLES E., dms, perc; b. Dallas, TX, 10/1/42. Moved to Chi. 1956, pl. in local polka and rock 'n' roll bands. Att. U. of Ill.-Urbana '63–71. Pl. w. U. of Ill. Jazz Band '66–71, incl. Eur. tour '68–9. Pl. w. Ron Dewar–James Knapp '69–70; Jim McNeely–Jon Burr '74–5. In Wash., D.C., '76–8; pl. w. Ron Elliston. Moved to NYC '79; pl. w. Bill Kirchner '79–85; Marian McPartland since '79; Clark Terry since '80; Widespread Jazz Orch. '83–5; Loren Schoenberg '86–9. Ret. to Chi. '86. Apps. for Joe Segal's Jazz Showcase w. Georgie Auld, Al Cohn, M. Allison, Joe Pass. Working w. Bill Porter since '86; Jim Cooper–Bob Dogan since '90. Favs: Mel Lewis, Elvin Jones, Sonny Payne. Fests: Eur. w. Terry, Widespread Orch., Schoenberg Orch. Taught mus. at U. of Ill. '69–71; NYU '82–3. TV: PBS w. Rosemary Clooney and Michael Feinstein '91. Rec. Berlioz *Symphonie Fantastique* w. Sir George Solti, London Records. CDs: w. Jim Cooper; Chuck Hedges (Del.); Kirchner (SB); Dave Gordon (Southport).

BRAXTON, ANTHONY, alto, sopranino, bs, contrabs saxes cl, bs cl, fl, comp; b. Chicago, IL, 6/4/45. Studied w. Jack Gell at Chi. Sch. of Mus., then at Chi. Mus. Coll. and Roosevelt U. Became interested in jazz after meeting Roscoe Mitchell at age 17. Joined AACM in 1966; pl. "free jazz" w. this gp. at Lincoln Center in Chi. Organized Creative Construction Company w. Leroy Jenkins and Leo Smith '67. Made first rec. as a leader w. Jenkins, Smith, Muhal Richard Abrams '67. Earned living as chess hustler, late '60s. To Paris w. Creative Construction Co. '69. Pl. w. Italian gp. Musica Elettronica Viva in NYC '70; Circle w. Chick Corea, Dave Holland, Barry Altschul in NYC and Eur. '70–1. Following the success of his rec. *For Alto* '71, the first unaccomp. sax LP ever made, he pl. solo at Carnegie Hall '72. Led own gps. in US and Eur. '71–6; sidemen incl. Holland; Altschul; Phillip Wilson; Jerome Cooper; Kenny Wheeler; Geo. Lewis. Rec. w. Derek Bailey and Co. in London '74–7; Globe Unity Orch. in Germ. '75. Tour. Engl. w. qt. consisting of Marilyn Crispell, Mark Dresser, and Gerry Hemingway '85, and has led this unit intermittently in the '90s. He taught at Mills Coll. '85–8; Wesleyan U. in early '90s. Orig. infl. by Paul Desmond and Warne Marsh, and later by John Coltrane, Eric Dolphy, Lee Konitz, Ornette Coleman, and Cecil Taylor, Braxton is generally considered one of the foremost free jazz saxophonists. His occasional forays into mainstream jazz improv., on recs. such as *In the Tradition*, have generated mixed reactions from the critical community. As a comp., he has cited Stockhausen and John Cage as major infls. He has frequently used geometric designs and mathematical formulas to title his comps. His larger works incl. pieces for orch. and marching band, and the score to the film *Paris Streets*, commissioned by M.I.T. Other film: *Un Coup de Franc*, France. TV: Italy, Germ., France. Book: *Forces in Motion: Anthony Braxton and the Meta-Reality of Creative Music* (Quartet) '88. CDs: Del.; Leo; hatArt; Hat Hut; M&A; BS; Steep.; w. Circle; Dave Holland (ECM); Max Roach (BS); R. Teitelbaum (hatArt).

BREAKSTONE, JOSHUA, gtr; b. Elizabeth, NJ, 7/22/55. Studied w. Sal Salvador; degree fr. Berklee 1975; M. A. in creative arts fr. NYU '87. Rec. debut '79, w. Joanne Brackeen, Cecil McBee, and Billy Hart. Gigged in NYC '79–81 w. Warne Marsh, Emily Remler, et al., while teaching gtr. and jazz studies at the Rhode Island Cons. of Mus. First solo album, *Wonderful!*, for Sonora '83, feat. Barry Harris. Has since collaborated w. Kenny Barron, Tommy Flanagan, Jimmy Knepper. An even-keeled, subtle pl. who emphasizes single-note lines, Breakstone says, "For me the most thrilling thing about playing is inventing melodies." CDs: Cont.; Evid.; Capri; Mob. Fid.

BREAU, LENNY (LEONARD), gtr; b. Auburn, ME, 8/5/41, d. Los Angeles, CA, 8/12/84. Parents, Hal "Lone Pine" Breau and Betty Cody, were country singers/mus. Began on gtr. at age 8; perf. as Lone Pine Jr. w. parents at age 12. Worked as country gtrst. in Can., stud. jazz w. pnst. Bob Erlendson in Winnipeg. Moved to Toronto 1964, pl. w. own trio, singer Don Franks, others. Also pl. w. TV and studio bands in Toronto and Winnipeg. Briefly in LA, lead. trio and rec. album at Shelly's Manne Hole, mid '60s. Led own gps. and worked w. singers in Toronto '70–2; semiretired to Winnipeg '73–5. Moved back to Ontario '75 and was sporadically active. Pl. w. Chet Atkins, Geo. Benson '77; rec. w. Don Thompson, Claude Ranger '79. Known for his expert use of octave harmonics, he could play impressively at length, weaving an amalgam of jazz, rock, classical, and ethnic musics. Fr. early '80s, he utilized 7–string gtr. w. addition of high A string. Wrote monthly column "Fingerstyle Jazz" for *Guitar Player* '81–4. His death by asphyxiation was ruled a homicide. Favs: Chet Atkins, Tal Farlow, Bill Evans. Films: *Toronto Jazz* '62; *Talmadge Farlow* '81. TV: many apps. on CBC, incl. profile *One More Take* '68. CDs: Guitarchives; MHS; Genes; One Way; Lenny Breau & Chet Atkins, One Way.

BRECKER, MICHAEL LEONARD, tnr, sop saxes, EWI; b. Philadelphia, PA, 3/29/49; d. NYC, 1/13/07. Brother is Randy Brecker; fath. and sist. Emily pl. pno. Stud. w. Vince Trombetta 1965–9; also Joe Allard, Joe Viola, Edgar Grana. Studied comp. '82–6. Pl. w. local gps. in Phila. fr. '66. Moved to NYC '69; pl. w. Edwin Birdsong '70; Dreams w. bro. Randy '70–2; Horace Silver '73; Billy Cobham '74; Brecker Bros. '75–81. Dur. this last period he and Randy opened and operated club, Seventh Avenue South. Pl. w. Steps Ahead '79–86; Pat Metheny '80–1; Michael Brecker Band fr. '87; Herbie Hancock '88; Return of Brecker Bros. '92. He also perf. w. non-jazz artists incl. James Taylor, John Lennon, Joni Mitchell, Paul Simon; worked extensively as a clinician. Brecker's tnr. sax pl. successfully translated John Coltrane's pl. into a broadly popular style that was highly influential upon the younger saxophonists of the '80s and '90s. He was also a pioneer in the use of the EWI. Polls: *DB* '87–8; *Jazziz*; Grammy for Best Jazz Perf. '88. Fests: all major fr. '70s. CDs: GRP; Imp.; w. Brecker Bros. (GRP; RCA); Dreams (Col.); C. Corea (WB); P. Delano (Verve); Claus Ogerman; GRP All-Star BB (GRP).

BRECKER, RANDY (RANDAL E.), tpt, flg; b. Philadelphia, PA, 11/27/45. Father and sist. pl. pno.; bro. Michael pl. reeds. Stud. w. Tony Marchione in Phila., then w. Jerry Coker and David Baker at Indiana U. 1963–6. Left sch. while on tour in Eur. w. Indiana U. Jazz Band. Moved to NYC '67. Pl. w. Blood, Sweat and Tears '67; Horace Silver '68–9; Janis Joplin '68; then w. bbs of Clark Terry, Duke Pearson, Thad Jones–Mel Lewis, Joe Henderson, Frank Foster.

Form. jazz-rock band Dreams w. bro. Michael and Billy Cobham '69. Pl. w. Art Blakey '70; Dreams '69–72; Johnny and Edgar Winter '73; Larry Coryell '73–4; Cobham '74; Mike Longo and Idris Muhammad '74. Pl. w. bro. Michael in Brecker Bros. band '75–81; Jaco Pastorius Word of Mouth Band '82–3; w. Elaine Elias '84–6; own qnt. since '87; also various All-Star bands. In great demand as studio mus. since '70. Favs: Kenny Dorham, Freddie Hubbard, Lee Morgan, Miles Davis. Polls: *DB* TDWR '69; NARAS Most Val. Pl. (five times). Fests: Eur. every yr. since '70s; Japan; Middle East. CDs: BN; Den.; Sonet; GNP Cresc.; w. Blood, Sweat and Tears; Dreams (Col.); Brecker Bros. (GRP; RCA); Lew Tabackin (Conc.); GRP All-Star BB (GRP).

BREHM, SIMON, bs; b. Stockholm, Sweden, 12/31/21; d. Stockholm, 2/11/67. After participating in an amateur contest in 1941, he made prof. debut w. Arne Hülphers. Form. qnt. in '46; rec. w. Royal Swingers, own qnt. incl. Stan Hasselgard '47; and own sxt. w. Hasselgard, Arne Domnerus '46–7. Extremely active in Swedish bop circles dur. '40s and '50s, he pl. and rec. w. many Amer. and Eur. visitors, incl. Hot Lips Page, Teddy Wilson, Tyree Glenn, Zoot Sims, Toots Thielemans, George Wallington, Quincy Jones; also noted Swedish mus. Lars. Gullin, Rolf Ericson. Led own band in Stockholm '51–58. Founded Karusell Records '52; also active as critic, radio prod. Pl. Paris JF '49. Recs: w. Gullin (Drag.).

BREUKER, WILLEM, saxes, cl, comp; b. Amsterdam, Netherlands, 11/4/44. Formed first band, 23 pcs., in 1966. He was assoc. w. Alex von Schlippenbach and the Globe Unity Orch. '65–8; Günter Hampel '66–73; Peter Brotzman '68, '70. In '67 he co-founded, w. Misha Mengelberg and Han Bennink, the Instant Composers' Poll, remaining w. it into '73. Has cont. to collab. w. Bennink on and off over the yrs. as in the New Acoustic Swing Duo. Form. the Willem Breuker Kollektief in '74. Fr. mid '70s this 10-pc. ens. tour. extensively through East. and West. Eur., Mexico, Can., India, and the CIS (formerly USSR); many apps. at North Sea, Bergen, Montreal, Prague, Glasgow fests, etc. In '91, the ens. made its fifth tour of the US. The Kollektief is one of the most orginal and unusual jazz gps. to emerge outside the US, playing everything fr. Weill and Prokofiev to Ellington and Charlie Parker in a style that involves sudden starts and stops, shifts of rhythm, and extensive individual and collective improvisation. CDs: BVHAAST (his own label); Entr'acte; w. Berlin Contemp. Orch. (ECM); Brotzmann (FMP); Leo Cuypers; Hannes Zerbe (BVHAAST); Hampel (Birth; ESP Disk).

BRICE, PERCY, dms, perc, cga; b. NYC, 3/25/23. Mother pl. pno.; aunt was stage actress. Studied vln. and pno. under WPA in 1930s. Pl. w. Luis Russell '44; Benny Carter '45–6; Mercer Ellington '47; Eddie Vinson '48–51; Tiny Grimes '51–3; Oscar Pettiford. Perf. simultaneously w. Lucky Thompson at Savoy Ballroom, Chocolate Williams after-hours at Minton's '53–4. Pl. w. Billy Taylor '54–6; George Shearing '56–8; Kenny Burrell at Minton's '58; Sarah Vaughan '59–61; Harry Belafonte '61–9. Off and on w. Carmen McRae and Ahmad Jamal in '60s. Led own r&b gp. mid '70s. Began working in B'way shows '78; cond. orch. for *Bubblin' Brown Sugar* '81–6. Also worked w. Illinois Jacquet in '80s. Favs: Max Roach, Buddy Rich, Kenny Clarke, Art Blakey. Films: *Sepia Cinderella* w. Mercer Ellington '47; *The Big Beat* w. G. Shearing '57. TV: apps. w. Vaughan, Shearing; Ed Sullivan w. Belafonte; *Tonight Show* w. Taylor. CDs: w. Shearing (Mos.); Billy Taylor (Prest.); Benny Carter (Hep).

BRIDGEWATER, CECIL VERNON, tpt, arr; b. Urbana, IL, 10/10/42. Father, grandfath., and great-grandfath. pl. tpt. Moth., bro., sist., and uncles all mus. Began pl. alto sax and tpt. First prof. gig in uncle's band. Studied w. Haskel Sexton at U. of Ill. 1960–4, '68–70. Tour. Eur. w. U. of Ill. bb '68; Russia, '69. Form. Bridgewater Bros. Band w. bro. Ron, tnr. sax, pl. and rec. off and on '69–89. Join. Horace Silver '70, then pl. and arr. for Thad Jones–Mel Lewis Orch. '70–6. Pl. w. Max Roach since '71. With Art Blakey '72; Jimmy Heath '74–6; Joe Henderson '75; Lena Horne '82–3; Mercer Ellington '85–6; Grover Mitchell bb from '86; Richard Davis since '87; Count Basie Orch. w. Frank Foster '89; own gp. since '89. Bridgewater has had extensive exp. teaching tpt., improv., arr., and bb at Jazzmobile Wkshp., New Sch., LIU, Manh. Sch. of Mus., Five Towns Coll. Favs: Armstrong, Gillespie, Terry; arrs: Gerald Wilson, Quincy Jones, Thad Jones, Duke Ellington. Fests: Eur. yearly since '71; Japan; Brazil '89; Senegal '88; Morocco '72. CDs: Brown.; Mesa; w. Bridgewater Bros. (Den.); M. Tyner (Mile.); M. Roach (SN; Enja); T. Jones–M. Lewis (A&M); Groove Holmes; J. McDuff; Houston Person; M. Carvin (Muse); A. Hart (Novus); J. Stubblefield (SN); A. Ibrahim (Enja); Richard Davis (Hep; Sw. Bas.); Billy Harper (Story.); Dee Dee Bridgewater (Verve).

BRIDGEWATER, DEE DEE (Denise Garrett), voc.; b. Memphis, TN, 5/27/50. Father, Matthew, was prof. tpt. Raised in Flint, Mich.; own trio in jr. hs., then sang w. fath.'s grp. at local dances. Attend. Mich. St. U. 1968; toured Russia w. U. of Ill. band

'69. Married tptr. Cecil Bridgewater '70 and moved to NYC w. him; divorced in mid '70s. Feat. voc. w. Thad Jones–Mel Lewis orch. '72–4; sang Abbey Lincoln's role in the *Freedom Now Suite* at St. Peter's Church. Won Tony award for perf. in B'way musical *The Wiz* '74. Stud. w. Roland Hanna and worked at Hoppers in NYC bef. moving to LA for a pop mus. career '76. Tour. in Eur. w. *Sophisticated Ladies* '84. Settled in France in '86, working as songwriter, actress, and radio/TV personality. Starred in Paris and London productions of *Lady Day* '86–7; hosted French radio show, *Le Jazz Club,* '88. Tour. Far East w. Clark Terry, James Moody, Jimmy McGriff, and others in late '80s. Perf. w. Don Cherry, Sheila Jordan, and Mark Murphy in Robert Wilson's "jazz opera," *Cosmopolitan Greetings,* in Germ.; also in *Black Ballad,* a Paris-based play w. Archie Shepp '92. Bridgewater's lovely, dark-toned voice is her greatest asset, and she is particularly effective as a ballad singer. She has perf. programs of Horace Silver and Ellington material at fests., clubs. Rec. album at Montreux JF '92; tribute to E. Fitzgerald at JVC-NY, '97. CDs: Imp; Verve; Philips.

BRIGHT, RONNELL LOVELACE, pno, comp; b. Chicago, IL, 7/3/30. Studied at U. of Ill., Juilliard, and Roosevelt U. Pl. in navy band 1953; accomp. Carmen McRae '54–5; pl. and rec. w. Rolf Kuhn '56; Dizzy Gillespie bb '57–8. In '65, after tour. as accomp. and cond. for Sarah Vaughan, Lena Horne, Gloria Lynne, and Nancy Wilson, he settled in LA. Member of Supersax '72–4; taught hs '74–5, and became active as comp. By early '90s, had settled in Denver, Colo., as Doctor of Divinity; he and his wife, Rev. Dianne Bright, produce jazz programs at their Harmony Church, often presenting local mus. as guests w. the Harmony Orch. CDs: w. C. Hawkins (Prest.); F. Wess (Sav.); Vaughan (Em.; Merc.).

BRIGNOLA, NICK (NICHOLAS THOMAS), bari, sop, alto saxes; cl, fl; b. Troy, NY, 7/17/36. Grandfather pl. tba. and bari. horn in concert and marching bands incl. John Philip Sousa's; fath. pl. gtr. and uke.; uncle, cl. Began on alto sax, then encouraged by Harry Carney to pl. bari. sax. Pl. w. Reese Markewich 1957; Herb Pomeroy, Cal Tjader, Mastersounds '58; Sal Salvador bb, Woody Herman early '60s; Ted Curson late '60s-70s; Pat Metheny early '80s; Phil Woods Oct., Mingus Superband late '80s; also commercial work. Led own gps. w. Glen Moore, Dave Holland, Phil Markowitz, etc., fr. '59, incl. electric jazz-rock gp. in early '70s. Brignola taught jazz history and improv. at SUNY-Albany '74–86. His inventive bari. lines are delivered w. a dexterity that never detracts fr. the requisite fullness of tone.

Favs: Carney, Pepper Adams. Polls: *JT* '90; NAJE '87; *DB* '97. Fests: Eur. since '70s. TV: PBS: *Portrait of a Jazz Musician*. CDs: Res.; Nightlife; w. P. Woods (Conc.; Chesky); W. Herman (Conc.; Status); Mingus Dynasty (SN); *Three Baritones* (Drey).

BRIL, IGOR (Mikhaylovich), pno, comp; b. Moscow, Russia, 6/9/44. Played w. Yuri Saulsky 1966–9; German Lukyanov '69–70; led own gps. through '70s and '80s, also led dept. of jazz at the Gnessins State Musical and Pedagogical Institute in Moscow. Described by S. Frederick Starr in his book *Red and Hot* as "one of Russia's best musicians of the sixties." CDs: Mob. Fid.

BRILLINGER, JEFF (JEFFREY PAUL), dms; b. Kingston, NY, 7/12/47. Began pl. dms. in grade sch. in Hartford, Conn. Studied w. Alan Dawson and Fred Buda at Berklee 1965–9, then w. Joe Morello in NYC. Pl. in Bost. w. Clark Terry; Zoot Sims; Bob Brookmeyer; Mose Allison; Mel Tormé; Irene Reid; Bobby Short; Morgana King. Moved to NYC '72, and pl. w. Jack McDuff '72; house band at Playboy Club '72–4; Woody Herman '74–5; Horace Silver '75; Chet Baker, Stan Getz '78; Jackie Cain–Roy Kral '81. Freelance in NYC in '80s w. Tom Harrell; John Abercrombie; Bob Berg; Michael Weiss; Jim McNeely; Sal Nistico; Marian McPartland; Dave Liebman; Hubert Laws; Junior Cook, etc. Own qnt. since '89. Favs: Elvin Jones, Jack DeJohnette, Philly Joe Jones. Fests: MJF w. W. Herman '74; Pori JF. CDs: w. Herman (Fant.); C. Baker (Band.; CC; Drey.); Jackie & Roy (Conc.).

BRISKER, GORDON, tnr sax, fl; b. Cincinnati, OH, 11/6/37. Mother taught pno. at Cincinnati Cons. of Mus., where he stud. 1954–6; also stud. at Berklee Sch. '57–8. Pl. w. Woody Herman '60–2; Louie Bellson '64; Bobby Shew '79–81; Joe Farrell bb '84. Mus. dir. for Anita O'Day fr. '87. Arrs. for Bellson, James Brown, Herman, Herb Pomeroy, Rosemary Clooney, *Tonight Show* Orch., etc. In early '90s, he began to write pieces for jazz qt. w. expanded harmonic and rhythmic approaches. CDs: Naxos; w. O'Day (DRG; Swing); Sarah Vaughan (Jazz Band).

BRITTO, CAROL WHITNEY, pno, org, arr; b. Cleveland, OH, 5/20/35. Also pl. cello and tbn. Stud. at Cleveland Inst. of Mus., then at Oscar Peterson's Advanced Sch. of Contemp. Mus. Pl. first gigs in Cleveland at age 16. Moved to Toronto, Ont., 1957; pl. in Can. w. Chet Baker; Benny Carter; Roy Eldridge; Tal Farlow; Al Hibbler; Helen Humes; Milt Jackson; Zoot Sims; Buddy Tate; Clark Terry; Joe

Williams; Phil Woods, etc. Org. for Toronto Blue Jays baseball team '77–9. Perf. at Carnegie Tavern in NYC '78. Moved to NYC '84; pl. w. Al Grey and Buddy Tate; Major Holley; Bobby Rosengarden; Lionel Hampton; taught at New Sch. Favs: Oscar Peterson, Basie, Bill Evans; arrs: Clare Fischer, Ellington, Claus Ogerman. Fests: Kool JF w. Al Grey '84; Bern '90. TV: *Ladies Night Out* w. Anne Murray; *Take 30*, Can. biog. docu. CDs: Town Crier.

BROADBENT, ALAN LEONARD, pno, arr, comp; b. Auckland, New Zealand, 4/23/47. Studied at Royal Trinity Coll. of Mus., Auckland, 1954–60; Berklee Coll., on *DB* scholarship, '66–9; priv. w. Lennie Tristano '66–9. Tour. w. Woody Herman '69–72; wrote extended works for the Herman band, incl. *Blues In The Night Suite* and *Variations on a Scene*, later perf. by Herman w. the Houston Symph. Pl. w. John Klemmer gp. '75. Rec. three albums w. Irene Kral '74–7. Became member of Charlie Haden's Qt. West '88. Won first prize for *Sonata for Violincello and Piano*, Bost. Public Library Mus. Assoc. '69. Other orch. works incl. *Song of Home* '81; *Conversation Piece* '85; *Concerto for Trio and Orchestra* '91; *Jazz Balladen* for Walter Norris and Cologne Radio Symph., cond. by Broadbent '95. Favs: Bud Powell, Bill Evans, Tristano. Poll: *DB* Critics, TDWR as arr. '72. CDs: Conc.; Disc.; Trend; w. Haden; Shirley Horn (Verve); Herman (Fant.); Scott Hamilton; B. Brookmeyer; Mel Tormé (Conc.); Bud Shank (Cont.); Bill Perkins (Interplay); Natalie Cole (Elek.).

BROKENSHA, JACK (JOHN JOSEPH), vib, dms, arr-comp; b. Adelaide, Australia, 1/5/26. Father, a perc., gave him early tuition. Was child xyl. pl. in radio and vaudeville. Member of Austral. Symph. Orch. 1942–4; while in air force '44–6, pl. entertainment unit; tour. w. own gp. for concerts, broadcasts, lounges. Active in Melbourne '47–8; Sydney '49–50; Brisbane '50; Adelaide '51. Moved to Can. '53; w. pnst. Bryce Rohde, form. in '54 the Austral. Jazz Qt. w. reedmen Errol Buddle and Dick Healey. Gp., which at times was a qnt. or sxt., broke up after an Austral. tour in '58, and Brokensha moved to Det. He tour. in Austral., NZ w. Sammy Davis Jr. and Stan Freberg in '59. Form. mus. prod. co. and became active in TV and as a dj. In '90s still lead. own gp. and working w. pnst. Bess Bonnier. Favs: Milt Jackson, Norvo. Rec. w. Rex Stewart in Austral. AJQ rec. LPs for Beth. label. CDs: AEM.

BROMBERG, BRIAN, bs, el-bs, voc; b. Tucson, AZ, 12/5/60. Father and bro. pl. dms. Bromberg started on dms. at age 13 bef. taking up bs. a yr. later, and began classical stud. As teenager he pl. regularly

w. adults; stud. mus. at local university; perf. w. area bands and symphs. Tour. w. Stan Getz at 19, sw. fr. acoustic to el-bs. Worked w. H. Silver; Monty Alexander; Dave Grusin; D. Gillespie; Joe Farrell; Richie Cole; Lee Ritenour; Phil Upchurch; and Freddie Hubbard. Made first album, *A New Day*, for BH 1986. A technically impressive artist, Bromberg has worked w. a variety of instruments, incl. fretted, acoustic, picc., upright, and synth bs. Designed own bs., the B-Quad 4. Bromberg's "performance is one step short of incredible," wrote Leonard Feather. "At times he seems to be producing two melodies simultaneously, using three or four fingers of each hand." Favs: Stanley Clarke, Jaco Pastorius. Fests: a regular at the Lionel Hampton JF, Moscow, Ida., in the '90s. Films: pl. w. Grusin on soundtracks for *The Fabulous Baker Boys*; *Havana*. CDs: Zebra; Nova.

BROOKMEYER, BOB (ROBERT EDWARD), v-tbn, pno, comp, arr; b. Kansas City, MO, 12/19/29. Father was amateur gtrst. Began on cl. Studied at KC Cons. 1947–50. In army '50–1, then pl. pno. w. Tex Beneke '51. Freelance on pno., v-tbn. w. Ray McKinley, Louis Prima, Claude Thornhill, Jerry Wald, Terry Gibbs; then pl. v-tbn. w. Woody Herman '52; Stan Getz '53; Gerry Mulligan off and on '53–7; own gp. '57; Jimmy Giuffre '57–8; G. Mulligan bb '60–5. Led qnt. w. Clark Terry off and on '61–6. Pl. and arr. w. Thad Jones–Mel Lewis Orch.; *Merv Griffin Show* band '65–8. Among his outstanding arrs. for Jones-Lewis were "Willow Tree"; "St. Louis Blues"; and own comp. "ABC Blues." Moved to Calif. '68; pl. w. *Della Reese Show* band '69–70 and worked as studio mus. He was occ. reunited w. Jones-Lewis and Mulligan in the '70s. Pl. in duo w. Jim Hall '78–9, then was mus. dir. for the Mel Lewis Jazz Orch. '80–2. Studied w. Earle Brown, Joel Thome in NYC '83–4. Brookmeyer has worked mainly in Eur. as a freelance comp. and cond. fr. '79. Tour. Engl. w. Tony Coe. Pl. w. Mulligan Tribute band, incl. L. Konitz, R. Brecker '97. Taught adv. jazz comp. at Manh. Sch. of Mus. '85–8 and was mus. dir. of the BMI Jazz Comps. Wkshp. '88–91. Many of his scores are housed in Georges P. Vanier Library of Concordia U., Montreal. In '91 he was awarded an honorary doctorate by the U. of Missouri-KC. As a v-tbnst. he combines a sense of swing, mordant wit, the ability to abstract harmony, and an aptitude for contrapuntal interaction w. an understanding of the entire jazz tradition. Fav: Bill Harris; arrs: Gil Evans, Thad Jones, Geo. Russell. Polls: *DB* New Star '53. Fests: extensive work in Eur. fr. '79. Films: *Jazz On a Summer's Day*. TV: ABC Arts, *Making of a Song* '81; Norwegian TV docu., '81. LPs: Finesse; Verve; UA. CDs: ACT; Prest.; Drag.; Conc.; w. Tony Coe–Bob Brookmeyer

(Story.); G. Mulligan (PJ; RCA; Verve; RTE); C. Terry (Main.); Jones-Lewis; J. Giuffre (Mos.); M. Petrucciani (Drey.); dual pnos. w. B. Evans, *The Ivory Hunters* (BN).

BROOKS, BUBBA (DAVID JR.), tnr sax; b. Fayetteville, NC, 5/29/22; d. NYC, 4/11/02. Father sang in voc. gp., pl. pno.; uncle, J.C. McAllister, pl. alto sax; cousin, Bill McAllister, tnr. Younger bro. was Tina Brooks. Bought tnr. at age 18 and began sitting in w. local band, learning on the job. Took some lessons fr. a local tnr. pl., Archie Simmons, and taught himself by listening to Basie, Ellington, Hampton recs. Moved to Balt., pl. w. the Four Dukes at Club Harlem. Entered army in 1943 where he met James Moody, Dave Burns. Ret. to Fayetteville '44; made rec. debut w. George Barkley. At end of '40s, join. Sonny Thompson band, tour. and rec. w. Wynonie Harris. Left Thompson, '57 and ret. to NYC. Worked w. Clyde McPhatter '60. After pl w. Jimmy McCracklin, join. Bill Doggett for twenty yrs., incl. Eur. tours, remain. until Doggett's death. Was a member of Harlem Blues and Jazzband. First rec. as leader '96. Infls: Hawkins, Byas, Webster, A. Cobb, Jacquet. CDs: Claves; TCB.

BROOKS, HARVEY OLIVER, pno, comp; b. Philadelphia, PA, 2/17/1899; d. Los Angeles, CA, 6/17/68. After tour. and rec. in the early 1920s w. Mamie Smith, moved to Calif., where he co-led the Quality Four w. Paul Howard fr. '23–5; pl. w. Howard's Quality Serenaders '25–30. Pnst. and mus. dir. for Les Hite '31–5, often worked as comp. in Hollywood studios. Wrote "That Dallas Man" and "They Call Me Sister Honky Tonk" for Mae West film *I'm No Angel* '33. In '50s, pl. w. Kid Ory; Teddy Buckner '55–6; Joe Darensbourg '57–60. Fr. '61, he was a member of the Young Men of NO, which he led in '68. CD: w. L. Hampton (CDS).

BROOKS, JOHN BENSON, comp, pno; b. Houlton, ME, 2/23/17; d. NYC, 11/13/99. Mother had scholarship to Peabody Cons. Received instruction on several inst. fr. friends, neighbors, and at sch., then att. New Eng. Cons., Juilliard. Led own band in Bost. 1939, then worked w. Eddie DeLange '40. Also pl. w. Boyd Raeburn, T. and J. Dorsey, Les Brown, et al., in '30s-40s. His "A Night at the Deuces" (fr. *Tales of 52nd Street*) was rec. by Randy Brooks, Dec. '46. Introduced folk jazz combo at Town Hall concert by the Weavers '50. In his folk jazz gps., Brooks attempted to unify folk mus., NO, KC, mainstream, and avant-garde jazz into a single style. Rec. in this style for Vik label. In '59, he arrived at a 12–tone system of comp. and improv. His *Alabama Concerto*, feat. Cannonball Adderley and Art Farmer, was reissued on an Adderley Riverside CD.

BROOKS, ROY, dms, perc; b. Detroit, MI, 9/3/38; d. Detroit, 11/15/05. Inspired to pl. dms. after hearing Elvin Jones at Bluebird. Pl. w. Yusef Lateef, Barry Harris, etc. at El Sino; New Music Society sess. at World Stage. Worked w. Beans Bowles at Lavert's Lounge, then pl. in LV w. Four Tops. Pl. w. Horace Silver Qnt. 1959–64; Lateef '67–70; Pharaoh Sanders '70; James Moody '70–2; Charles Mingus '72–3. Also pl. in early '70s w. Wes Montgomery; Sonny Stitt; Jackie McLean; Dexter Gordon; Dollar Brand; Four Tops. Founding member of M'Boom Re:Percussion '70. Formed own gp., Artistic Truth '73. In '76, Brooks ret. to Det., where he founded a jazz teaching center, Musicians United to Save Indigenous Culture (MUSIC). Led own gp. Aboriginal Perc. Choir, at Det. JF '80. Brooks has cont. to perf. w. Artistic Truth into the '90s. Favs: Roach, E. Jones, Blakey, K. Clarke. Fests: all major '59–70s. TV: *Today, Tonight Show, Like It Is, Positively Black, Dial M For Music.* CDs: Enja; w. H. Silver; Woody Shaw (BN); Stitt (Muse); R. Rodney; M. Roach (Col.; Enja); Lateef (Rhino); A. Ibrahim (Enja); Blue Mitchell (Riv.).

BROOKS, STELLA, voc; b. Seattle, WA, 10/24/15. Started singing in SF, early 1930s. Moved to NYC, '37. Concerts at Town Hall, also rec. for Disc label, accomp. by Frankie Newton, Sidney Bechet, George Brunis, Joe Sullivan; '46. Occ. NYC café apps. in '50s. In early '60s ceased perf. due to throat problems. CDS: Greta Keller/Stella Brooks, Smith./Folk; w. Bechet (Class).

BROOKS, TINA (HAROLD FLOYD), tnr sax, comp; b. Fayetteville, NC, 6/7/32; d. NYC, 8/13/74. Father, David Sr., pl. pno., sang. Moved w. family to NYC 1944. While in hs, stud. C-melody sax. Twin bro., Harry, began pl. sax at same time but gave it up soon after. Took lessons fr. his older bro., David Jr. (Bubba). Sw. to alto, then tnr sax. Pl. dances, etc., w. classmates. In '50, replaced Bubba in Sonny Thompson's band for a few mos. Made rec. debut w. Thompson for King '51. Worked w. local Latin bands, Charles Brown, Joe Morris in early '50s; on the road w. Amos Milburn '53 or '54. Studied harm. w. Herbert Bourne for a yr. Join. L. Hampton's orch. for spring and summer '55. Met tptr. Benny Harris at Blue Morocco club in Bronx, N.Y., '56, and became assoc. w. him, Elmo Hope, et al. in gigs and jamming at Bronx and Harlem clubs. Through Harris began rec. for BN as sideman '58, and lead. '60. In '59–60 was understudy to Jackie McLean in off-B'way prod. *The Connection.* In the '60s pl. Latin and r&b gigs,

tour. briefly w. Ray Charles but app. mostly in Bronx clubs such as Freddie's Bar, the 845 Club and the Blue Morocco w. Hope, Oliver Beener, Don Pullen, etc. Drug addiction impaired his health, and he died of kidney failure. Originally inspired by Lester Young, he also listened closely to Charlie Parker; Dexter Gordon; Wardell Gray; Sonny Rollins; and Hank Mobley. Robert Palmer saw a connection between Brooks's sound and style and the vocalists he heard in his youth. "Like a singer," he wrote, "Brooks gives every phrase its own weight and inner dynamic." CDs: BN; w. Jimmy Smith; F. Hubbard; K. Burrell (BN); Freddie Redd (Mos.).

BROOM, BOBBY (ROBERT JR.), gtr; b. NYC, 1/18/61. Great-grandfather pl. fiddle. Stud. in NYC w. Jimmy Carter 1974–6; Pat Martino '76; at HS. of Mus. and Art '74–8; Berklee Coll. of Mus. '78–9. Pl. w. Al Haig, Walter Bishop in NYC clubs '77. Auditioned for Sonny Rollins at the urging of Haig. Pl w. Rollins–Donald Byrd at Carnegie Hall '77; off-B'way pit band '77–8; Dave Grusin '80; Tom Browne '80–1; Sadao Watanabe fr. '81; Hugh Masekela '81–82; own gp. fr. '82; Art Blakey '82; Sonny Rollins fr. '82; Rodney Franklin, all-star gp. w. Stanley Turrentine, Roy Ayers '83. Moved to Chi. '84. Studied at Columbia Coll., Chi., '84–7, B.A. Mus. Pl. w. Kenny Burrell fr. '85; Miles Davis '87; Max Roach '88; Charles Earland '88–90; Stanley Turrentine fr. '89. Co-lead. ESP w. Darryl Jones, Robert Irving III, Toby Williams. Taught at Hartt Coll. of Mus. '83–4; Assoc. for Adv. of Creative Mus. '85; Amer. Cons., Chi., fr. '85; in Italy w. Thelonious Monk Institute exchange prog. '89; Yamaha clinics fr. '90. Favs: Al Casey, Wes Montgomery, Grant Green, Pat Martino. Fests: all major fr. '80. CDs: GRP; w. ESP (Pioneer-LDC); Rollins; C. Earland (Mile.); Burrell (BN); Turrentine; Watanabe (Elek.); Ronnie Cuber (FS).

BROTZMANN, PETER, tnr sax; b. Remscheid, Germany, 3/6/41. Prominent free jazz figure in the 1960s. Tour. Eur. w. Mike Mantler and Carla Bley '66; worked w. Globe Unity Orch. until '81, also led trio w. Han Bennink and Fred van Hove; in '86 pl. w. Cecil Taylor in Berlin and form. qt., Last Exit, w. Sonny Sharrock, Bill Laswell, and Ronald Shannon Jackson. In '90, he worked w. B-Shops for the Poor in Britain. A pl. of extraordinary intensity, he has been compared to Albert Ayler and Pharoah Sanders. CDs: DIW; FMP; Pathological; w. Last Exit (Enemy); Ginger Baker (ITM); C. Taylor (FMP; SN); Company (Incus); Globe Unity; P. Kowald (FMP).

BROWN, BEN (BENJAMIN FRANKLIN), bs, elbs, gtr; b. Opa-Locka, FL, 8/25/52. Father, a gospel singer; bro., dmr.; sist., vln. Stud. pno. first, then sw. to gtr. at No. Miami Mus. Center. Enrolled at Miami Dade Jr. Coll. 1970, and was offered scholarship to stud. bs. After two yrs. sw. to U. of Miami, grad. w. B.A. '74. Prof. debut on gtr. w. gp. called The Shevrons. In '73 was house bs. at club in Miami, backing B. Kessel, Mose Allison, S. Stitt; pl. w. Miami Symph. for José Iturbi. After pl. concert w. F. Hubbard and S. Turrentine, pl. clubs w. I. Sullivan. Worked w. Lou Rawls '74; B. Rich '75; D. Gillespie '76–9, tour. worldwide; Al Haig in NYC '80. In '81–2 freelanced w. B'way shows: *Sophisticated Ladies, Singing in the Rain, Blues in the Night, But Never Jam Today.* Tour. w. T. Bennett '81; Lena Horne '82–4. Pl. w. Jimmy Heath fr. '85. Tour. w. Gregory Hines fr. '87. Pl. w. Walter Bishop Jr. in Japan '89. Pl. w. Al Grey '94–7; also Sweets Edison. Tour. w. Ruth Brown fr. '96. Adjunct profess. of bass, Queens Coll. '95–7. Fr. '95 has been "Macintosh consultant for fellow musicians who have difficult time understanding how the machines and programs function." Favs: Blanton, Hinton, Pettiford, R. Brown, P. Chambers. B'way: *Jelly's Last Jam* '91–2; *Bring in 'Da Noise, Bring in 'Da Funk* '97–8. TV: subbed for many yrs. on *Sesame Street,* bec. regular '95. CDs: J. Heath (Steep.); A. Grey (Tel.); Mike Longo (CAP); Carol Sloane (Conc.); Horne (BN); Gillespie (Pab.); Rodney Jones (Timel.).

BROWN, BOYCE, alto sax; b. Chicago, IL, 4/16/10; d. Hillsdale, IL, 1/30/59. Began prof. w. band of dmr. Don Carter at age 17. After working briefly in NYC w. Benny Meroff in early 1930s, he ret. to Chi., where he had previously pl. w. Beiderbecke, Spanier, Teschemacher, Condon. Join. Wingy Manone, '33; pl. w. Paul Mares' Friars Society orch. '34–5. Own combo at Liberty Inn '36 to mid '40s. With Chet Roble trio '47–8, Danny Alvin '49. Ret. w. own gp. to Liberty Inn, but in '53 began monastic life as Brother Matthew, a member of the Servite Order. Took his vows in Feb. '56 and w. Father Hugh Calkins, the pnst. in his monastery sessions, gained more publicity than he had received dur. his yrs. in the clubs. In the spring of '56, Brother Matthew participated in a NYC TV jam sess. and rec. a fundraising LP on ABC-Paramount w. Eddie Condon. Royalties fr. both projects went to the missions of the Servite Order in So. Africa. Recs. w. Mares, Charlie LaVere '35; J. McPartland '39; Wild Bill Davison '40.

BROWN, CAMERON LANGDON, bs; b. Detroit, MI, 12/21/45. Studied pno. for six yrs., then sw. to bs. in hs band. While att. Columbia U., he perf. w. a qt. that won awds. at intercollegiate competitions. Rec. in Eur. w. George Russell 1965; then moved to Stock-

holm, Swed.; pl. w. Don Cherry, Bill Barron, Donald Byrd '65–6. Taught elem. sch. in NYC '69–72, then pl. w. Beaver Harris, Hod O'Brien in house band at St. James Infirmary, accomp. Al Cohn–Zoot Sims, Charlie Rouse, Chet Baker, et al. Pl. w. Sheila Jordan, Art Blakey, Archie Shepp, mid '70s. Founding member of Geo. Adams–Don Pullen Qt. '79. Pl. w. Dannie Richmond qt. fr. '80; D. Cherry '86–7; A. Shepp '87. CDs: w. G. Adams–D. Pullen (SN; BN); Beaver Harris; G. Russell (SN); Dewey Redman; Archie Shepp (BS; Enja); Massimo Urbani (Red); Mal Waldron (Enja); E. Blackwell (BS).

BROWN, CLARENCE "GATEMOUTH," gtr, b. Vinton, LA, 4/18/24. Raised in Orange, Tex. Learned gtr. and Texas fiddle mus. fr. fath.. Prof. debut at age 21 as dmr. in San Antonio, Tex. Sw. to gtr. in 1947 after subbing for T-Bone Walker. Rec. series of r&b hits for Peacock label in '50s. In '60s, moved to Nashville, Tenn.; took part in syndicated r&b TV show and rec. series of country singles. Starting in '71, he traveled frequently overseas and rec. many Eur. albums, some released in US by Alligator Recs. In mid '70s, he tour. Africa for US State Dept. App. regularly at Montreux Fest in '70s; pl. in USSR in '79. In '80s he was based in NO, cont. to produce award-winning albums, mostly for Rounder Recs. The *Washington Post* called Brown "as rich and varied as the American music tradition itself." He has a special knack for finding meaningful connections among a wide range of Amer. mus. forms, fr. jazz, blues, bluegrass, and country to swing, funk, and zydeco. CDs: Allig.; Verve; w. Jeannie and Jimmy Cheatham (Conc.); Arnett Cobb; Al Grey; Helen Humes; Jay McShann (B&B).

BROWN, CLEO (CLEOPATRA), pno, voc; b. Meridian, MS, 12/8/09; d. Denver, CO, 4/15/95. Moved w. her family to Chi. 1919. Turned prof. at age 14 w. traveling show. Worked in Chi. and environs in late '20s. Led own gp. at Three Deuces there on and off fr. '30s through '50s; also worked in NYC, Hollywood, SF, LV. Had own radio series on WABC. Career halted by illness '40–2. Said to have learned her boogie-woogie style from her bro., Everett Brown, an associate of Pine Top Smith. Rec. for Dec. w. own qt., incl. Gene Krupa '35–6; and w. Decca All-Stars; also rec. for Hot Shot label. Living in LA when she rec. for Cap. '49. Moved to Denver, Colo., '73 and became involved w. the Seventh Day Adventist Church where she pl. weekly as C. Patra Brown. In '87, Marian McPartland found her and invited her to app. on her radio series *Piano Jazz,* where she sang hymns and gospel songs, incl. some of her own. Early infl. on Dave Brubeck. CD: Audio.

BROWN, CLIFFORD (aka BROWNIE), tpt, comp; b. Wilmington, DE, 10/30/30; d. Bedford, PA, 6/27/56. Began on tpt. 1943. While in hs, he stud. w. band director Harry Andrews; jazz harmony, theory, tpt., pno., vib., bs. w. Robert Lowery; also stud. mus. w. Sam Wooding. Gigs in Phila. w. Miles Davis, Fats Navarro, Charlie Parker '48. Brown was infl. by Navarro's style, and the two were close friends. Studied math at Delaware St. Coll., music at Maryland St. Coll., where he also arr. for coll. band. Hospitalized after car accident June '50–May '51. Pl. and rec. w. Chris Powell's Blue Flames on tpt. and pno. '52–3; Tadd Dameron '53. Toured Eur. w. Lionel Hampton, late '53; rec. while in Eur. w. Gigi Gryce, Art Farmer, Henri Renaud, et al. Freelanced in NYC w. Art Blakey and others '53–4, then formed Brown-Roach Qnt. in '54 w. Max Roach, Geo. Morrow, Richie Powell, Harold Land (replaced by Sonny Rollins '55). Brown was killed in an auto accident while traveling from Phila. to Chi. Although his professional career lasted less than five yrs., he is among the most influential modern trptrs: admired for his broad tone and strong attack; flawless execution in all registers and at all tempos; flowing, logical improvisations; and lyrical ballad playing. His direct infl. is evident in the playing of Lee Morgan and Freddie Hubbard, but he had some effect on practically every jazz trumpeter who came after him. Comps: "Daahoud"; "Joy Spring"; "Tiny Capers." Polls: *DB* New Star '54. TV: Soupy Sales show. CDs: Col.; BN; Prest.; Em.; RCA; w. Roach (Em.; GNP; Mos.); Rollins; Dameron (Prest.); A. Blakey; J.J. Johnson (BN); Sarah Vaughan; Dinah Washington (Em.); Helen Merrill (Verve).

BROWN, DONALD RAY, pno, comp, arr, bs, tpt, dms; b. Desoto, MS, 3/28/54. Raised in Memphis, Tenn. Sist. Waddia is prof. gospel mus.; bro. Graylon is prof. bs. and singer. Fath. pl. gtr. and pno. Moth. and eight other bros. and sists. all amateur mus. Wife Dorothy is classical flst. and pnst. Began on dms., tpt. in jr. hs. First prof. gig in top 40 band pl. bs. parts on tba. 1968. Att. Memphis St. U. on baritone horn scholarship '72–5. Began pl. pno. in coll.; early infls. were cousin, Lloyd Anderson, and James Williams. Pl. w. top 40 bands '68–83. Fr. early '70s, rec. on Stax label w. r&b mus. incl. Ann Peebles; Ollie Nightingale; Ted Taylor; William Bell; Z.Z. Hill; The Soul Children. Pl. el-bs. w. Al Green fr. '75; B.B. King, late '70s. Taught public sch. students in Memphis O.I.C. prog. '77–8. Staff mus. in Memphis studios The Dailey Planet '78–9; Hi Records '79–81. Join. Art Blakey in Oct. '81, then hospitalized for rheumatoid arthritis, April '82. Pl. w. Toots Thielemans, Eddie "Lockjaw" Davis–Johnny Griffin '84;

Freddie Hubbard '85–6. Rejoined Jazz Messengers '86. Tour. Eur. w. Jon Faddis '87; Donald Byrd '88; Jack Walrath '89; Japan w. Kenny Garrett '90. Led own gp. at Clermont, France, JF annually fr. '89. Also freelanced in '80s w. Wynton Marsalis; Eddie Henderson; Louis Hayes; Bobby Hutcherson; Alan Dawson; Bob Moses; Louis Smith; Slide Hampton; Billy Hart; Woody Shaw; Buddy DeFranco–Terry Gibbs; Chris Calloway; Diane Reeves; Clifford Jordan; Kevin Eubanks; Bill Hardman–Junior Cook; Charles McPherson; James Moody; Milt Jackson. Brown's comp. "The Insane Asylum" was rec. by Wynton Marsalis. Other comps. incl. "The Early Bird Gets the Short End of the Stick"; "Capetown Ambush"; "A Bad Case of the Bu's"; "New York"; and "The Smile of the Snake" rec. by Art Farmer, Ralph Peterson, Billy Pierce, James Williams, and others. Arrs. of some of Brown's comps. are avail. fr. Second Floor Music, NYC. Brown has taught at Jamey Aebersold Clinics '80–6; Berklee Coll. of Mus. '83–8; U. of Tenn. at Knoxville fr. '88. His students have incl. Cyrus Chestnut; Danilo Perez; Julian Joseph; Javon Jackson; Sam Newsome. Favs: Ray Charles, Tatum, Waller, Nat Cole, Monk, Bud Powell; comps: Waller, Gershwin, Ellington, Jimmie Lunceford, Fletcher Henderson. Fests: Eur., Japan fr. '81. TV: PBS special w. Blakey; Eur. TV w. Faddis; also Sony and LaserVision videos w. Blakey. CDs: Muse; JC; Sunny.; w. Blakey (Conc.); D. Byrd (Land.); Wallace Roney (Muse); Steve Nelson (Red); Memphis Piano Convention (DIW); Russell Malone (Col.); Billy Pierce (PW).

BROWN, GARNETT, tbn, comp; b. Memphis, TN, 1/31/36. Studied at U. of Arkansas 1954–8; US Naval Sch. of Mus. '59. Pl. w. Luther Steinberg '57–8; Chico Hamilton '62; Sal Savador; George Russell, incl. Swedish tour, '64. Worked w. L. Hampton, Johnny Richards in mid '60s. Fr. '65 through '72 w. Thad Jones–Mel Lewis '66–8; Duke Pearson '67–8; H. Hancock '70–2. Moved to LA July '75, worked w. Capp–Pierce Juggernaut '78; Gerald Wilson, Buddy Collette; also in TV, film, commercial recs.; pit band for *Purlie* in '80s w. Henry Franklin, Hampton, Benny Carter, Clayton/Hamilton. Toured Japan w. Toshiko Akiyoshi bb and Lionel Hampton. Orchestrated mus. for feature film *Harlem Nights*. Poll: *DB* Critics TDWR and *DB* Readers '74; awards fr. BMI, U. of Ark. Active as arr. fr. his NYC days, he wrote extended comps. for NYJRC in '70s; CHJB in '90s. CDs: w. George Russell (Riv); Booker Ervin (Prest.); McCoy Tyner (Mile.); Joe Henderson; D. Gillespie (BN); Woody Shaw (Muse); Roland Kirk (Merc.); Freddie Hubbard (CTI); H. Hancock (Col.); Frank Capp (Conc.); Gil Evans (Enja).

BROWN, LAWRENCE, tbn; b. Lawrence, KS, 8/3/07; d. Los Angeles, CA, 9/5/88. Brought up in Pasadena, Calif.; stud. pno., vln., tba. bef. focusing on tbn. Worked w. Charlie Echols 1926; Curtis Mosby; first recs. w. Paul Howard '29–30. In early '30s, pl. w. Les Hite's band, fronted by Louis Armstrong, bef. join. Duke Ellington '32. Left in '51 w. Johnny Hodges to pl. in latter's small band. Freelance and CBS studio work, NYC, '55–60. Rejoin. Ellington for ten yrs., leaving mus. '70. Settled in Wash., D.C., '70; appointed by Pres. Nixon to Advisory Committee for Kennedy Center. Ret. to Calif. in '72 and became rec. agent for Local 47 of AFM. Brown could lead a section and, w. equal effectiveness, lend his sophisticated, mellow-toned, legato style to blues ("Across the Track Blues") and ballads ("On a Turquoise Cloud"). Although he was best known for his smooth, laid-back perf., his up-tempo solos on such numbers as "Slippery Horn" and "Rose of the Rio Grande" are not easily dismissed. Dur. his last period w. Ellington, he assumed the role of plunger soloist and acquitted himself admirably. Polls: *Esq.* Silver Award, '44–5. LPs: *Inspired Abandon* (Imp.); w. Jackie Gleason (Cap.). CDs: w. Ellington (BB; Col.); Armstrong (Col.); Hodges (BB; Verve; Mos.); Met. All-Stars; Hampton (BB).

BROWN, LES (LESTER RAYMOND), saxes, bandleader; b. Reinerton, PA, 3/14/12; d. Los Angeles, 1/4/01. Studied at Cons. of Mus. in Ithaca, N.Y., 1926–9. Form. Duke Blue Devils while at Duke U. and made first rec. for BB, but band broke up Sept. '37. In '38, after arr. for Larry Clinton and Isham Jones, started a new band that achieved great success as a pop-oriented, swing ensemble, the "Band of Renown." The band became a regular feature on radio (later, TV) shows and on USO tours w. Bob Hope into '80s. Many arrs. by Ben Homer, who wrote score for band's biggest hit, "Sentimental Journey," sung by Doris Day, Brown's vocalist in '40 and '43–6. Soloists w. band incl. Ted Nash; Dave Pell; Butch Stone; Warren Covington; and Abe Most. Brown himself pl. alto and cl. but was never feat. as soloist. Still active w. band into '90s. CDs: Col.; Hind.; Cir.; Fant.

BROWN, MARION JR. alto sax, comp; b. Atlanta, GA, 9/8/35. Played reeds in hs and Army bands. Studied at Clark Coll. until 1965, then moved to NYC, where he rec. w. Archie Shepp, John Coltrane. Prominent as a leader of avant-garde gps. fr. '67. Tour. Eur. w. own gp., incl. Steve McCall, Ambrose Jackson, Gunter Hampel '68–70. Taught African and African-Amer. mus. at Bowdoin Coll., also tour. w. Leo Smith, early '70s. Rec. as lead fr. '73. Studied ethnomusicology at Wesleyan U. mid '70s. Also stud.

So. Indian fl. w. P. Vishwanathan. Rec. w. Günther Hampel in Eur. '83. Comps. incl. "Similar Limits"; "Sound Structure"; "QBIC"; "Porto Novo"; "Geechee Reflections." Rec. *Ascension* w. Coltrane. CDs: ESP; Birth; Freelance; ITM; w. Coltrane; Shepp (Imp.); Hampel (Birth); M. Waldron (Freelance).

BROWN, MARSHALL RICHARD, lead, comp, arr, educ, v-tbn; b. Framingham, MA, 12/21/20; d. NYC, 12/13/83. Father a vaudeville magician; moth. pl. pno. for silent movies. Self-taught on gtr. at age 9, v-tbn. at 16. B.S. cum laude NYU, 1949; M.A. Columbia U., '53. Own band while in hs '37. Pl. and arr. w. Bernie Leighton while in army '42–5. Staff arr. at summer hotel in Adirondacks '49. Band dir., East Rockaway HS, '49–51. While teach. at Farmingdale HS, LI, '51–7, org. and dir. dance band, the Dalers, which scored a success at NJF '57. He was appointed to fest. board and traveled to Eur. w. George Wein to choose members for an Int'l Youth Band, which pl. at Brussels World's Fair and NJF '58. The following yr. he assembled the Newport Youth Band, which pl. at that fest. and others '59–60. Band members who went on to achieve fame incl. Eddie Gomez; Jimmy Owens; Ronnie Cuber; Dusko Goykovich; George Gruntz; Gabor Szabo. Tour. and rec. w. Ruby Braff '60–1; Pee Wee Russell '61–2, '65; Bobby Hackett '64; Eddie Condon '66–7; Roy Eldridge '68–70; Lee Konitz '71–4. Enjoyed success as pop songwriter in '50s w. "Seven Lonely Days"; "The Banjo's Back in Town"; and, in France, "Tout au Bout de la Semaine." Score for *U.S. Steel Hour*, mus. drama '56. Award: Oustanding Educ. of the Yr., Westlake Coll. of Mus., '57. Pl. NJF w. Konitz, '72. Infl: Charlie Parker (jazz); John Dewey (educ.). CDs: w. Konitz (Mile.).

BROWN, OSCAR JR. voc, songwriter; b. Chicago, IL, 10/10/26; d. Chicago, 5/29/05. Acted on network radio soap opera while in hs. Att. nine different colls., then held a variety of jobs incl. advertising copywriter. Ran for Ill. state legislature on Progressive ticket, 1948; also worked for musicians' union and in fath.'s law and real estate offices. Became prof. songwriter after army service '54–6, sometimes working w. Lil Armstrong in Chi. First rec. comp., "Brown Baby," was sung by Mahalia Jackson. Collab. w. Max Roach on *Freedom Now Suite* '60. First rec. as vocalist for Col. '60, then presented orig. mus. play, *Kicks and Company*, in Chi. '61. Host of TV prog. *Jazz Scene USA* '62. App. w. Annie Ross in London revue *Wham! Bam! Thank You Ma'am* '63. Perf. in clubs w. Jonah Jones, Dizzy Gillespie, others '60s. Made club apps. again in '96. Best known for setting lyrics to a number of instr. jazz works incl. Nat Adderley's

"Work Song"; Bobby Timmons's "Dat Dere"; and Miles Davis's "All Blues." CDs: Col.

BROWN, PETE (JAMES OSTEND), alto, tnr sax; b. Baltimore, MD, 11/9/06; d. NYC, 9/20/63. First stud. pno., vln.; sax at 18. Worked around Balt., then to NYC w. Banjo Burney 1927. Pl. w. Charlie Skeete, and w. Freddie Moore's trio '28–34; own combo at Brittwood in Harlem. Original member of John Kirby sxt. '37, leaving a yr. later to form his own band, often perf. w. Frankie Newton at such 52nd St. clubs as Kelly's Stable and the Onyx. His style of jump alto was humorous and wheezy-toned w. a clipped sense of swing. Pl. tnr. in Bklyn. in '40s; also later w. Slim Gaillard at Birdland, but most of his work was on alto. App. w. C. Hawkins at NJF '57. Kidney problems limited his perfs. in later yrs. Last app. w. D. Gillespie at Village Gate late '62. Taught in Bklyn. fr. '30s; students incl. Flip Phillips, Cecil Payne. Paul Desmond cited him as an infl. Rec. own sess. on Dec., Savoy; as sideman w. Kirby; F. Newton; Joe Marsala; Jimmie Noone; Buster Bailey; Willie "The Lion" Smith; Sammy Price; Bernard Addison; Champion Jack Dupree. LP: Beth.; 77. CDs: tracks in *Complete Keynote Collection* (Em).; w. F. Newton; Maxine Sullivan (Aff.); Willie "The Lion" Smith (Timel.); Joe Turner (Atl.); four tracks w. Leonard Feather in *52nd Street Swing* (Dec.).

BROWN, PUD (ALBERT), tnr, cl, tpt; b. Wilmington, DE, 1/22/17; d. New Orleans, LA, 5/27/96. Began pl. sax at age 5; tour. state fairs w. family band 1927 bef. join. vaudeville circuit, pl. in theater orchs. in early '30s. In Chi. '38, he pl. w. Phil Lavant's orch. and w. such mus. as Bud Freeman, Jimmy Dorsey, Bud Jacobson, and Pete Daily. Worked in Shreveport, La., '45–9 bef. moving to LA. In the '50s, he was assoc. w. Nappy Lamare, Jack Teagarden, Kid Ory, Teddy Buckner. Began doubling tpt., crnt. in the '60s. Remained in Calif. to '73, then ret. to Shreveport, often working in NO w. gtrst. Les Muscutt at the Blue Angel. In the '80s he was the cl. in Clive Wilson's Original Camellia Jazz Band in NO and had his own gp. at the Palm Court Café in the '90s. For six mos. '84–85, he worked in Singapore w. dmr. Trevor Richards. Also pl. Lawrence Welk. Rec. w. Armstrong; Les Brown in '40s; his own comp. "Johnson Rag" '50s. CDs: Jazz.

BROWN, RAY (RAYMOND MATTHEWS), bs, comp; b. Pittsburgh, 10/13/26; d. Indianapolis, IN, 7/2/02. Studied pno. at 8; took up bs. and pl. first prof. gig at local club in 1943. Six mos. w. Jimmy Hinsley '44, then toured w. Snookum Russell; moved to NYC '45, joined D. Gillespie combo and, in '46, bb. In '48,

formed trio w. Hank Jones and Charlie Smith. Married to Ella Fitzgerald '48–52, acc. her in clubs and concerts, also on JATP tours. With Oscar Peterson '51 to '66, when he settled in LA. Active in studios; helped form LA Four '74. In late '70s and '80s he became active in management, publ., comp., etc. His comp. "Gravy Waltz," w. Steve Allen lyrics, won a Grammy. Frequently worked in qnt. format w. Milt Jackson. Rec. w. gp., Triple Treat, in late '80s. His trios incl. pnsts. Gene Harris and Monty Alexander in '80s; Benny Green and Geoff Keezer in '90s. Global tours w. Gene Harris bb. Active as educ. w. O. Peterson in Toronto for two and a half yrs., and at UCLA. Won many polls, incl. *Esq.* New Star '47, *Met.* '55–60, *DB* '53–9, *DB* critics '54, *Playboy* '58–60, *Playboy* All-Stars '59–60. A firm, versatile rhythm player w. a rich tone and precise articulation, Brown cont. in the '90s to be in demand for jazz and commercial work while maintaining a parallel career as a businessman and publisher. Books: *Ray Brown Bass Book I.* CDs: Conc.; Tel.; Capri; Cont.; Evid.; w. Gillespie (RCA; Sav.; Pab.); C. Parker; B. Powell; Peterson; Herb Ellis (Verve); Fitzgerald (Verve; Pab.); Ellington (Pab.); LA Four; Monty Alexander; Gene Harris; Triple Treat (Conc.); Milt Jackson (Pab.; Verve; Imp.).

BROWN, RUTH, voc; b. Portsmouth, VA, 1/12/28; d. Henderson, NV, 11/17/06. Began singing in church where her fath. was choir dir. On the road in 1945 w. singer/tptr. Jimmy Brown, whom she married. Worked briefly w. Lucky Millinder band '48, then Blanche Calloway heard her in Wash., D.C., and brought her to NYC, where she began rec. for Atlantic. Rose to int'l fame as r&b star through such '50s hits as "Teardrops from My Eyes"; "5–10–15 Hours"; and "Mama, He Treats Your Daughter Mean." Taught pre-school while living in Deer Park, N.Y. Rec. for Skye label in '69, but suffered poor distribution and changing public taste. During next 20 yrs., her career was often in limbo, though she worked in various stage shows in LA, LV, and off-B'way. After an 8-month Paris run in the musical *Black and Blue* ('85), she triumphed w. a Tony-winning perf. in the B'way production '89. Resumed rec. career on Fant. label, winning a Grammy for her album *Blues on Broadway*. Though best known as an r&b artist, Brown was a superb blues singer who can satisfy jazz fans w. her delivery of ballads and pop songs. In the late '90s, her band incl. gtrst. Rodney Jones, bsst. Ben Brown, and dmr. Akira Tana. Films: *Hairspray; Under the Rainbow.* TV: *Hello, Larry; Checkin' In.* CDs: Atl.; Fant.; BN (accomp. by Thad Jones–Mel Lewis).

BROWN, SAM (SAMUEL T.), gtr, also bs; b. Baltimore, MD, 1/19/39; d. Bloomington, IN, 12/28/77.

Father pl. vln., pno., fl., crnt., and was operatic tnr. Pno. at 4, mand. at 6. At 12, he began pl. gtr. w. hs dance band on weekly TV show. Three yrs. w. paratroopers fr. age 17, incl. last two w. band, where he learned to read mus. Class. gtr. lessons w. Joe Fava, Det. 1958–60; Mannes Coll. of Mus., NYC '60–1; Leonid Bolotine '60–3; harm. and theory w. Fred Wurle; master classes w. Julian Bream, Gustavo Lopez. Pl. w. Miriam Makeba '61–4; Astrud Gilberto, incl. Japanese tour, '65; Ella Fitzgerald '65–6; Ars Nova '66–8; Gary Burton, Keith Jarrett '69–71; Ron Carter '71; Herbie Mann '74; David Matthews fr. '74; Sundays at Gregory's w. Al Haig '75. Concerts and/or gigs w. Stan Getz; Hubert Laws; Jimmy Owens; Charlie Haden; Joe Farrell. Infls: Django Reinhardt, Segovia, Tal Farlow, Johnny Smith, Ravi Shankar. TV: Ed Sullivan w. Makeba, H. Belafonte; *Tonight Show* w. Fitzgerald; *Jazz Special* w. Burton. Arr. rec. sess. for Makeba, Carly Simon. Comps: "My Hoss Knows the Way"; "Sunrise Highs"; "Dance of the Windchimes." Fests: NJF-NY w. G. Burton, S. Getz, G. Mulligan. Rec. w. Burton; H. Mann; Ars Nova; Jeremy Steig; C. Haden; Bill Evans; Makeba; Matthews. CDs: w. Carla Bley (JCOA); Jarrett (Col.; Imp.); C. Haden (Imp.); Thad Jones–Mel Lewis (LRC).

BROWN, SANDY (ALEXANDER), cl; b. Izatnagar, India, 2/25/29; d. London, England, 3/15/75. Self-taught. Led own trad. and swing band in Scotland fr. 1946, w. two yrs. out for mil. service. Moved to London '54, gigging w. Humphrey Lyttelton, Ken Colyer, Chris Barber. Rec. as leader '49–73. Form. w. tptr. Al Fairweather the Fairweather-Brown All-Stars, rec. and working intermittently '55–62. Also pl. and rec. w. Sammy Price, Brian Lemon, Phil Seamen, and, in '74, Earle Warren in US. Infl. by jazz-rock in late '60s. Fav. early solo: "The Last Western." Favs: Johnny Dodds, Eddie Miller, J. Giuffre, Pee Wee Russell. Book: *The McJazz Manuscripts*, pub. posthumously, London '79. Was qualified architect, acoustic physicist. CDs: EMI; Col.; Hep; w. Sammy Price (BL).

BROWN, SCOVILLE TOBY, cl; b. Chicago, IL, 10/13/15; d. NYC, '95. Studied at Chi. Mus. Coll. 1938–9; also w. Simeon Bellison '43–4; Leon Russianoff '54. Pl. w. Louis Armstrong '32–4; Don Redman '39–40; Fats Waller '40–2. In army '43–5, then pl. alto w. Claude Hopkins at Zanzibar '45. Pl. in NYC on Teddy Wilson's CBS radio show, also w. Lucky Millinder late '40s. Led own combo '48–52. Pl. dixie. sessions at Stuyvesant Casino and Central Plaza '52–5. Tour. US, Eur., Middle East w. Lionel Hampton '56–7. Perf. at Lake Champlain Valley fest.

'59, then join. Muggsy Spanier. Favs: Reginald Kell, Goodman, DeFranco, Shaw. CDs: w. L. Armstrong (BB); L. Hampton (RCA); Buck Clayton (Riv.).

BROWN, SONNY (GERALD), dms; b. Cincinnati, OH, 4/20/36; d.? Began pl. on set of dms. belonging to Geo. Russell, whose moth. gave them to Brown. Studied at Woodward HS and Cincinnati Cons. of Mus. In army 1953–6. Pl. in Midwest w. Eddie Vinson, Amos Milburn, Dinah Washington, various gospel gps. '56–60. Known mainly for his assoc. w. Rahsaan Roland Kirk, w. whom he pl. off and on fr. '57. Moved to NYC '61. Worked w. Frank Foster, Randy Weston, Ray Bryant early '60s; Jon Hendricks '63–4; Kenny Burrell for one yr. in mid '60s. House dmr. at Montreux JF '63–4. Freelanced in NYC w. Clifford Jordan; Sonny Rollins; Curtis Fuller; Coleman Hawkins; Zoot Sims; Lee Konitz; Archie Shepp; Sam Rivers, etc. With Bill Lee's NY Bass Choir fr. '68; also co-comp. an opera w. Lee. Rec. w. Attila Zoller–Herbie Hancock '69; tour. Scand. w. Joe Henderson, Ron Carter '70. Taught at Harlem YDA program, '68–73; public schs., Bronx, '69–70; Jazzmobile Wkshp. '72; Jazz Interactions Wkshp., I.S. 44, '73. Favs: Donald Linder, Jo Jones, Sonny Greer, Chris Columbus, Blakey, Roach. TV: *Tonight Show*, *Today* (NBC); *Soul* (NET). CDs: w. R.R. Kirk (Atl.; Merc.); C. Mingus (Col.).

BROWN, STEVE THEODORE, bs; b. New Orleans, LA, 1/13/1890; d. Detroit, MI, 9/15/65. Brother was tbnst. Tom Brown. Began on tba., then sw. to bs. Pl. in bro.'s band, trav. w. it to Chi., May 1915. Joined NORK. With Original Memphis Melody Boys and Midway Dance Orch. '23; Jean Goldkette '24–7; Paul Whiteman '27–8. After a yr. of pl. in KC, worked in Det. dur. '30s and '40s as lead. and freelance. Speaking of Brown in the Goldkette band, saxophonist Doc Ryker said: "At that time, all bands were using tubas, but when they heard him they all switched to string bass. None of them could equal Steve slapping the bass. He had a really distinctive style and an uncanny sense of rhythm." Recs. w. NORK '22; Goldkette; Whiteman; Frank Gillis Dixie Five '50. CDs: w. Beiderbecke (Col.); Whiteman (RCA; Jazz Arch.).

BROWN, TED (THEODORE G.), tnr sax; b. Rochester, NY, 12/1/27. Father led band, pl. bjo., vln., sax. Uncle and grandfather pl. sax in fath.'s band. Stud. bjo. w. fath. fr. 1933, vln. fr. '38, cl. and tnr. fr. '41. Moved to So. Calif. '42, stud. tnr. w. Joe Catalyne '44; classical cl. w. Kalman Bloch '47. Pl. w. Hal Brooks, Lew Gray '45; Brooks–Sully Mason '45–6; army bands '46–7. Moved to NYC '48, stud.

and pl. w. Lennie Tristano '48–55. Pl. w. Jerry Wald '52; Lee Konitz '55; Ronnie Ball–Willie Dennis, Warne Marsh '56. Moved to Lawrence, Mass., '62, pl. infrequently. Did not pl. fr. '67 to '72. After working w. Tony Zano in New Engl. '76, ret. to NYC. Pl. w. Konitz. '76; own qt. '77; Zano '79–80. Made first rec. as lead. for Criss Cross '85. Pl. w. Hod O'Brien '87; Konitz–Rein De Graaff '88; Jack van Poll '92. Brown has worked outside of mus. in the computer field since '64. Favs: Lester Young, Charlie Parker, Zoot Sims. Fests: Holland '87–8; Belg., France, So. Africa '92. TV: *Stars of Jazz* w. W. Marsh '57. CDs: CC; w. Marsh in *Tristano & Marsh* (Cap.).

BROWN, VERNELL JR., pno; b. Los Angeles, CA, 8/13/71. Primarily self-taught on pno. fr. age 4 but first pl. dms. and vln.; changed to pno. when he heard a band teacher pl. boogie woogie, then began stud. jazz and classical pno. Att. LA County HS for the Arts, then transferred to Hamilton HS and took special classes at Cal. St., LA. Signed to A&M Records after Chairman Jerry Moss heard him pl. at a Recording Academy "Jazz in the Schools" program. Also attended Berklee School; won Leonard Feather pno. scholarship, a Yamaha Music Corp. award, and a Best Instrumentalist citation in *DB*'s student mus. awards; finalist in Thelonious Monk Int'l Jazz Pno. Competitions '88 and '89. First album, *A Total Eclipse*, was nominated for NAACP Image Award. CDs: A&M.

BROWN, VERNON, tbn; b. Venice, IL, 1/6/07; d. Los Angeles, CA, 5/18/79. Raised in St. Louis and pl. there w. Frankie Trumbauer at the Arcadia Ballroom 1925-6. With Jean Goldkette in Chi. '28; Joe Gill in Tex. '31; Benny Meroff, Chi. '35. Moved to NYC and pl. w. Mezz Mezzrow '37; Benny Goodman '38–40. With Artie Shaw '40; Jan Savitt '41; Muggsy Spanier '41–2; Casa Loma Orch. '43. Fr. that time he was mainly occupied w. radio and TV studio staff work at ABC in NYC. Led band in Seattle '50, but went back to studio work, occ. tour. w. Goodman incl. Eur. in spring '58. Fests: w. Goodman, Brussels, NJF '58. Worked w. Tony Parenti '63; other gigs, recs., concerts in NYC area w. Cozy Cole, Bud Freeman, Billy Butterfield. Infl. Jack Teagarden. Recs. w. Harry James, Spanier, Mel Powell. CDs: w. Goodman (BB; Col.; Cap.; Hep); Pee Wee Russell (Comm.); L. Hampton (CDS); Shaw (BB); Spanier (ASV Archives of Jazz); bsst. Billy Taylor; B. Freeman (Key. Coll.).

BRUBECK, CHRIS (CHRISTOPHER WILLIAM), el-bs, tbn, pno, gtr, comp, arr, voc; b. Los Angeles, CA, 3/19/52. Father is Dave Brubeck; grandmoth., uncles, three bros. are prof. mus. Began on pno. Stud-

ied tbn. w. Dave Sporney at Interlochen Arts Acad. 1965-9; U. of Michigan, '70-2. Pl. w. bro. Darius fr. '63; own rock gps. '66-76; Addiss and Crofut '69-70; New Heavenly Blue '68-73; Two Generations of Brubeck '70-4; Sky King mid '70s; New Dave Brubeck Qt. '78-88; Larry Coryell '79-80; Brubeck-LaVerne Trio '86; Crofut and Brubeck fr. '90. Brubeck has written two off-B'way musicals, *David: Champion of Israel* and *Happy Hanukkah Reklaw Texas*. In '87 he arr. a Christmas concert for the Houston Symph. and Chorus. His comp. *Wisdom* was premiered in '91 at the Manh. Choral Fest. Fav. el-bs: Flim Johnson; fav. tbn: Trummy Young. Fests: Eur. w. Dave Brubeck, own gps. TV: *Tonight Show* w. Dave Brubeck; *Today* w. Bill Crofut; A&E Cable. CDs: Albany; BH; w. Dave Brubeck (MM; Conc.).

BRUBECK, DANNY (DANIEL PETER), dms; b. Oakland, CA, 5/4/55. Son of Dave Brubeck. Studied at Interlochen Arts Acad. 1970; N.C. Sch. of the Arts '71-3; Berklee '72. Pl. w. fath. and bros. in Two Generations of Brubeck '73; w. New Brubeck Qt. '78; Larry Coryell and Brubeck Bros. '80; Brubeck-LaVerne Trio '84; the Dolphins '88. TV app. on PBS, BBC, NBC *Today* and *Tonight Show*, etc. Favs: Jack DeJohnette, Joe Morello, Alan Dawson. CDs: w. the Dolphins (DMP); Dave Brubeck (MM); Darius Brubeck (B&W).

BRUBECK, (DAVID) DARIUS, pno, comp; b. San Francisco, CA, 6/14/47. Oldest son of Dave Brubeck; named after comp. Darius Milhaud. Pno. lessons to 1961; stud. w. Milhaud '62; stud. comp. w. Donald Martino '63-4; harmony at Mills Coll. '65-7. World tours w. Two Generations of Brubeck '72-5; New Brubeck Qt. '76-8. Appointed lecturer in jazz studies, U. of Natal, Durban, So. Africa; in '92 was assoc. profess. In '87, pl. w. So. African gtrst. Sandile Shange at Montreux JF; celebrated his fath.'s 70th birthday by pl. four of his own arrs. w. London Symph. Orch. '90; app. at Jazz Educators' Convention in Miami, Fla., w. Natal student gp., Jan. '92; also tour. Eur. w. bro., cellist Matthew Brubeck '92. "Living in South Africa," says Brubeck, "has provided many great experiences in cross-cultural music-making, with African and Indian musicians, but also reinforced my respect for jazz as a unique musical tradition." Favs: Monk, Dave Brubeck, Ellington. LPs: *Gathering Forces: Earthrise*; *Larry Coryell & the Brubeck Bros.: Better Than Live*. CDs: B&W; w. Dave Brubeck (LRC; as arr., MM).

BRUBECK, DAVE (DAVID WARREN), pno, comp; b. Concord, CA, 12/6/20. Mother was classical pnst. and teacher; two bros. are mus. teachers; four sons are prof. jazz mus. Studied pno. w. moth. until age 11; pl. w. local bands fr. age 14. Received B. A. in mus. fr. Coll. of the Pacific. Stud. w. Darius Milhaud at Mills Coll., Oakland, Calif. Pl. w. The Band That Jumps 1940–2, then join. army, pl. w. Wolf Pack Band in Eur. '44–5. After discharge, he stud. comp. w. Milhaud, again at Mills Coll. '46–9. Pl. w. own gps. The Three Ds '46–9; experimental oct. w. Paul Desmond, Cal Tjader, Bill Smith '46–9; trio w. Tjader, Norman Bates, or Ron Crotty '49–51. Rose to national prominence in qt. w. Desmond, Gene Wright, Joe Morello '51–68. Brubeck's qt. w. Desmond was one of the most popular jazz gps. of all time, selling millions of recs., incl. the first million-selling jazz LP, *Time Out*, in '60. A recipient of numerous awards, Brubeck was cover subject of *Time* magazine in '54. App. w. Leonard Bernstein and the NY Philharm. in '59. His was the first jazz gp. to make extensive use of odd time signatures, such as "Blue Rondo a la Turk," in 9/8, and "Take Five," in 5/4. Toured Engl. '59; Austral. '60. In '59, he premiered a work by his bro., Howard Brubeck, *Dialogue for Jazz Combo and Symphony*. In the early '60s, he himself began to comp. extended works, incl. *Points on Jazz* for the American Ballet Theatre; *Mr. Broadway* for a CBS-TV show; and a musical theater piece, *The Real Ambassadors*. The latter, written w. his lyricist wife Iola, was introduced at MJF '61 and rec. for Col., but never presented on B'way. After the orig. qt. broke up in '67, Brubeck form. a new qt. w. Gerry Mulligan, Alan Dawson, Jack Six; pl. w. it '72–4. Pl. w. Two Generations of Brubeck w. sons Darius, Dan, and Chris '72–4, then retired to write extended works, incl. an oratorio, *The Light in the Wilderness*, four cantatas, a Mass, and various smaller pieces and tone poems. Pl. w. New Brubeck Qt. '77–9; qt. w. Bill Smith, cl. or Bob Militello, reeds, Six, and Randy Jones fr. '79. In '87, he comp. and perf. mus. commemorating the papal visit. Brubeck received numerous awds. in the '80s incl. Conn. Arts Awd., Nat'l Music Council Awd., Officier de L'Ordre des Arts et Lettres, and BMI Jazz Pioneer Award. He has perf. for every Amer. president since Kennedy. In celebration of his 75th birthday, he pl. two concerts at the National Cathedral in Wash., D.C.: a premiere of a choral work, *This Is the Day*; and an hour-long Mass, *To Hope! (A Celebration)*, comp. in '81. He perf. the Mass in Russia '98. Over the yrs., Brubeck has collaborated w. such artists as Louis Armstrong, Jimmy Rushing, Carmen McRae, et al. Brubeck's early pno. style, which was often heavy in touch and thick w. complex harmonies, evolved in later yrs. into a richer, more melodic, but no less provocative, form of expression. As a jazz comp., he is best known for "In Your Own Sweet Way"; "The Duke"; "Blue Rondo a la Turk." Favs: Tatum, Waller, Ellington. Polls: *DB* '53–5, '59, '62–3, '65; *Billboard* '62, '65–6; *MM* '63; *Playboy* '66–7. Fests: Eur. annually fr. '58, also Asia, Austral., So. Amer. many times. TV: many apps. incl. *Moscow Night Concert* on A&E. CDs: Col., incl. retrospective boxed set; Conc.; Tel.; MM; Fant.; Atl.; A&M; Angel.

BRUBECK, HOWARD R., pno, comp, arr; b. Concord, CA, 7/11/16; d. San Diego, CA, 2/16/93. In 1959, his *Dialogues for Jazz Combo and Symphony Orch.* was perf. at Carnegie Hall by his bro. Dave's qt. and the NY Philharm., cond. by Leonard Bernstein. Taught mus. theory, comp., orchestration, cond. at Mills Coll.; San Diego St. U.; and at Palomar Coll. where the mus. auditorium was named for him, Aug. '92. Favs: Ellington, Strayhorn, Dave Brubeck.

BRUBECK, MATTHEW, cello, pno; b. Norwalk, CT, 5/9/61. Father is Dave Brubeck; three bros., grandmoth., two uncles also prof. mus. Began on pno. at age 7. Studied cello w. Aldo Parisot while att. Choate Sch. and Yale U. 1978–84. Receive M. Mus. fr. Yale '84. Pl. w. various community symph. orchs. bef. joining Bay Area Jazz Comps. Orch. in '88. Pl. w. Jazz Comp. Orch., own duo w. David Widelock fr. '88; Dave Brubeck, Brubeck and Sons fr. '89; E.W. Wainright–African Roots of Jazz, Wally Schnalie '90; Tom Waits fr. '90; own qnt. w. Widelock and Peck Allmond '91; Dutch voc. La Pat '91; duo w. Darius Brubeck, duo w. Melanie Jones, own string trio fr. '92. Brubeck has perf. w. major orchs., incl. London Symph., SF Symph., Cincinnati Symph., and currently is a member of three Bay Area orchs. He taught at San Jose St. '89–90. Favs: Hank Roberts, Mark Summer, Ernst Reijseger. Fests: Eur. '91–2. Film: soundtrack for Jim Jarmusch's *Night on Earth* w. Waits. CDs: Jazzpoint; w. Dave Brubeck (MM); T. Waits (Island); Yale Cellos (Delos).

BRUCE, JACK (JOHN SYMON ASHER), bs; voc, songwriter, kybds, synth, hca; b. Glasgow, Scotland, 5/14/43. Studied Royal Scottish Acad., Glasgow. To London, pl. w. Alexis Korner, Graham Bond and John Mayall, early 1960s. Came to prominence w. English rock gp. Cream '66–8, then rec. own album, *Things We Like*, w. sidemen incl. John McLaughlin. In late '60s, worked w. Larry Coryell, Carla Bley on *Escalator Over the Hill*, Michael Gibbs, et al.; in '70s w. Tony Williams's Lifetime and in Eur. w. Charlie Mariano; rec. w. Soft Machine '80 and app. w. Joachim Kuhn '86. Doubled as a photographer in the '90s. CDs: w. McLaughlin (Col.); Tony Williams (Polyd.); Ginger Baker (ITM); C. Bley (ECM); M. Mantler (Watt); Charly Antolini (Bell).

BRUNIS, GEORG (George Clarence Brunies), tbn; b. New Orleans, LA, 2/6/02; d. Chicago, IL, 11/19/74. Father, a baker who pl. vln.; moth. pl. pno. Sist. pl. gtr.; oldest bro., Rudy, pl. bs. but worked as a brewer. Other siblings became pros, incl. crntst. Richie, who pl. w. Fischer's Brass Band, Papa Jack Laine's Reliance Brass Band; tbnst. Henny, whom Georg held in highest esteem, pl. in No. Calif. and Chi. w. bro. Merritt Brunies. Crntst./tbnst. Merritt led own bands in No. Chi. and Biloxi, Miss. Crntst. Abbie led the Halfway House Orch. in NO and pl. w. Brunies Bros. Dixieland Jazz Band in Biloxi. Cousin Little Abbie was a dmr. in NO but also worked w. Sharkey Bonano in NYC. At age 8, Georg pl. alto horn in family trio and w. Papa Jack Laine, sw. to tbn. at age 10. To Chi. 1920, pl. w. Paul Mares. Following a stint on a Mississippi riverboat, he rejoined Mares in the Friars Society Orch., which became the NORK. Fr. '24–35 worked w. Ted Lewis bef. settling in NYC and becoming a fixture on the local scene, particularly at Nick's. With Muggsy Spanier '39; also pl. often w. Art Hodes, Eddie Condon, and Lewis. Ret. to Chi. late '49 where, fr. '51 to '59, he led own band at Club 1111. He later led combos in Madison, Wisc., and Cincinnati, Ohio, remaining active as a perf. into early '70s. Self-taught, he pl. completely by ear. Had a reputation for not practicing, but was also known to pick up a cold horn and instantly get into high gear. One of the pioneer tailgate stylists, he incorporated a broad sense of humor, which manifested itself in the manipulation of the slide w. his foot, and through his singing such specialties as "Ugly Chile." His fat tone, extensive range, and lyricism can be heard w. NORK on "Tin Roof Blues" '23. Brunis dropped the second "e" from Georg and the "e" from Brunies on the advice of a numerologist. Fests: Playboy JF, Aug. '59. Recs. w. Wolverines, Spanier, Lewis, Bechet, Wingy Manone, and Condon, whose *Windy City Seven* sides for Commodore are said to be Brunis's fav. session. CDs: NORK (Mile., Village); w. Beiderbecke; Sharkey Bonano (Timel.); Wild Bill Davison; Pee Wee Russell, incl. Windy City Seven (Comm.); Hodes (Del.); Bechet (Laser.); Spanier (ASV; BB; CDS; RCA); Waller (CDS); T. Lewis (JSP).

BRUNO, JIMMY (JAMES MICHAEL), gtr; b. Philadelphia, PA, 7/22/53. Took up gtr. at age 7, tutored by his fath. Jimmy Bruno Sr., who once pl. gtr. w. Nat Cole and rec. "Guitar Boogie Shuffle" w. Frank Virtue and the Virtues in 1959. Began prof. career tour. w. Buddy Rich '72–3, incl. Ronnie Scott's, London '73. Worked in LV show rooms '75–85. Fr. '85 to '89, based in LA, where he worked mainly as a studio mus. At the time became a protégé

of Tommy Tedesco, who called him "simply one of the best young talents I've heard in 30 years." Fr. '90, back in Phila. where he teaches at the U. of the Arts and gigs w. own gp. App. at Birdland, NYC '97, rec. there for Concord. Has worked w. Joe Pass; George Van Eps; Doc Severinsen; Lena Horne; Elvis Presley; B.B. King; Sinatra; T. Bennett. Pl. 7-string gtr. made by Bob Benedetto. Favs: Wes Montgomery, Pass, Hank Garland. Book: *Anatomy of a Guitar Player*, co-authored w. Tedesco. CDs: Conc.; w. The Concord Guitar Collective–H. Alden & F. Vignola (Conc.).

BRYAN, MIKE (MICHAEL NEELY), gtr; b. Byhalia, MI, 1916; d. Los Angeles, CA, 8/20/72. Self-taught. Pl. in and around Memphis 1934. With Red Nichols in Chi. '35. Led own band in Greenwood, Miss., '38–9. Established his reputation w. Benny Goodman '40–1; then brief stints w. Bob Chester, Artie Shaw, Jan Savitt. Following army service '42–5, he pl. on 52nd St. w. various gps., rec. w. Slam Stewart, and Clyde Hart's oct., which incl. Charlie Parker, Dizzy Gillespie. With Goodman band again '45–6. Later worked in Hollywood studios and operated an LA music store. In '60s, he prod. jazz films feat. Armstrong, Ellington, Condon, etc., sponsored by Goodyear Rubber for foreign TV. Tour. Vietnam w. Martha Raye bef. his death of leukemia. Bryan soloed on Hart's '45 rec. of "4–F Blues," but he was mainly a rhythm gtrst. CDs: w. Goodman (Col.); Shaw (BB); Slam Stewart; E. Garner (Sav.); R. Eldridge (Dec.).

BRYANT, BOBBY (ROBERT O. SR.), tpt; b. Hattiesburg, MS, 5/19/34. B. Mus. Ed. fr. Cosmopolitan Sch. of Mus., Chi., where he pl. w. Red Saunders and other local bands. Mus. dir. for Billy Williams, then six yrs. w. Vic Damone, incl. int'l tours. Settled in LA, working w. Oliver Nelson and Gerald Wilson, and as feat. soloist w. countless rec. gps. in pop and r&b areas. Freelanced in LA since the 1980s, incl. w. the Capp-Pierce Juggernaut. Bryant can be heard in such films as *Lady Sings the Blues*, *Assault on a Queen*, and *Harlem Nights*; also on TV film *Roots II, Part I*. Developed course in jazz theory and improv. which he taught priv. at Bost. Cons. and Englewood HS in Chi., and at many coll. clinics. A powerful perf. and talented comp., he is well known for his stalwart upper tpt. range. His son, Bobby Bryant Jr., is a tnr. saxist. CDs: w. Clayton-Hamilton Jazz Orch. (Capri); Gene Harris (Conc.); Nelson (Imp.); Monk (Col.); Mingus (Rhino); Lockjaw Davis (Prest.); J. Griffin (Riv.).

BRYANT, CLORA, tpt; also pno, dms; b. Denison, TX, 5/30/29. Father was a whistler and bird caller;

moth. a singer. Bro. Fred pl. tpt., bro. Mel sang and danced. Grew up listening to all the bbs. Started on pno., then added tpt. because she wanted "to go to the football games as a member of high school marching band." Stud. w. Profess. Conrad O. Johnson while in hs 1942; priv. in LA w. Lloyd Reese '45. Pl. w. hs swing band at road house outside Denison, and in Okla., '42–3. Offered scholarship to Oberlin but opted for Prairie View U. in Tex. because of its all-girl orch. Pl. w. it '43–5, incl. military bases and Apollo Theater, NYC. Transferred to UCLA '45. (Ret. in '78 to get degree.) Pl. one wk. w. Sweethearts of Rhythm at Million Dollar Theater '46; also Darlings of Rhythm '46; Four Vees '47; Queens of Swing '48–9; Jack McVea all-girl orch. '50; Sepia Tones '51. Pl. at the Lighthouse '51; w. Eric Dolphy '56; LV w. Damita Jo '60; tour. w. Billy Williams Revue '60–2; act w. bro., Mel & Clora '63–5; Bill Berry bb '68; Barry White all-girl orch. '75; own gp., Swi-bop, '76–93. Tour w. Johnny Otis '80–2. Pl. w. Jimmy and Jeannie Cheatham '86–9, incl. Eur. tours. As a result of writing a letter to Mikhail Gorbachev, she pl. ten days in the Soviet Union '89. Has taught music at Taft HS, Woodland Hills, Calif.; jazz history at UCLA, USC, Santa Monica Coll., El Camino Coll. Favs: Dizzy Gillespie, Louis Armstrong, Roy Eldridge, Charlie Shavers. LPs: *Gal With A Horn*, Mode '57; w. Linda Hopkins, *How Blue Can You Get,* Quicksilver. CD: w. J. & J. Cheatham (Conc.).

BRYANT, RAY (RAPHAEL HOMER), pno, comp; b. Philadelphia, PA, 12/24/31. Mother pl. pno.; sis. is music teacher in Phila.; bro. Tommy Bryant, nephews are Kevin and Robin Eubanks. Began pl. pno. at age 6; pl. bs. in jr. hs. First prof. gigs at age 12; joined mus. union at 14. Pl. w. bro. Tommy and local gps. Stud. and pl. w. Elmer Snowden. Learned bebop style by listening to Red Garland, who moved to Phila. in the mid 1940s. Tour. w. Tiny Grimes '48–9, then freelanced in Phila. and Syracuse, N.Y., '49–50. Pl. at Billy Krechmer's club in Phila., backing Krechmer, Jack Teagarden, Johnny Smith '51–3. House pnst. at Blue Note in Phila., pl. for Charlie Parker, Miles Davis, Lester Young, J.J. Johnson–Kai Winding, Sonny Stitt, others '53–6. Accomp. Carmen McRae w. Specs Wright, Ike Isaacs '56–7; also made first rec. as lead. w. this trio for Prest. '57. Pl. w. Coleman Hawkins at NJF, rec. w. Dizzy Gillespie '57. Moved to NYC '58. Pl. w. Jo Jones Trio w. Tommy Bryant '58; Sonny Rollins, Charlie Shavers, Curtis Fuller, own trio '59. In '60, Bryant had a hit w. his comp. "Little Susie"; another comp., "Changes," was rec. by Miles Davis; "Cubano Chant" by Art Blakey and others. A powerful blues pl. noted for his versatility, Bryant has worked mainly in a trio or as a single fr.

'60, but rec. w. Elmer Snowden Sxt. '61, and w. Zoot Sims, Benny Carter, and others for the Pablo label in the '70s. He has tour. Eur. regularly fr. '73, when he app. as a solo pnst. at MJF. Favs: Tatum, Teddy Wilson, Bud Powell. Polls: *DB* New Star '60. Fests: Eur. fr. '73; Japan fr. '70s. CDs: Col.; Em.; Prest.; NJ; Pab.; Em.; B&B; w. M. Davis; C. Hawkins; T. Grimes; Art Taylor (Prest.); D. Gillespie (Verve); S. Rollins (Prest.; Imp); Jo Jones (Vang.); Lee Morgan (BN); B. Golson; O. Nelson (NJ); Benny Carter; Z. Sims (Pab.); M. Roach (Merc.); Al Grey (B&B).

BRYANT, RUSTY (ROYAL G.), tnr , alto sax; b. Huntington, WV, 11/25/29; d. Columbus, OH, 3/25/91. Raised in Columbus fr. 1935. Fath., a mortician and amateur mus., bought him a tpt., later alto sax. At age 13, pl. w. Archie (Stomp) Gordon band. In navy '48–9, stationed in Bost., where he heard Sam Rivers, Jaki Byard, Nat Pierce, others. Ret. to Columbus, where he pl. briefly w. Tiny Grimes, then led own gp. at Carolyn Club for five yrs. Rec. for Dot label in '50s; had several hit singles in honking r&b style, notably "Night Train." Fr. '56 to '58 his band voc. was Nancy Wilson. In the '60s the band toured extensively in the East and Midwest, often under the leadership of org. Hank Marr. Bryant resumed rec. as a leader for Prest. in '69. CDs: Prest.; w. Charles Kynard (BGP).

BRYANT, TOMMY (THOMAS), bs; b. Philadelphia, PA, 5/21/30; d. Philadelphia, 1/3/82. From mus. family: moth. led church choir; sist. pl. pno. and sang; bro. is Ray Bryant. Took up bs. at age 12; later stud. at Mastbaum HS. Began prof. pl. w. Phila. small gps., notably Billy Krechmer; also backed visiting soloists. Pl. w. Elmer Snowden 1949–52; in army '54–6, incl. band. Own trio '57; w. Jo Jones '58–9; Charlie Shavers '59–63. Through the '60s, pl. off and on w. Ray Bryant trio. Fr. early '70s up to his death, he app. w. Ink Spots as bs. and voc. Favs: O. Pettiford, Slam Stewart. CDs: w. Dizzy Gillespie (Verve); Elmer Snowden (Riv.); Jo Jones (Van.); Barney Wilen (FS); Coleman Hawkins (Band.).

BRYANT, WILLIE (WILLIAM STEVEN), lead, voc; b. New Orleans, LA, 8/30/08; d. Los Angeles, CA, 2/9/64. Moved to Chi. 1912. Stud. tpt. but made prof. debut as soft shoe dancer '26, worked in vaudeville as dancer and singer into '33. Fr. '34 until Feb. '39, and again '46–8, he led own bb that rec. for Victor '35–6; Dec. '38; sidemen incl. Benny Carter, Teddy Wilson, Ben Webster. Later known as the unoffical mayor of Harlem, he app. as a comic emcee in nightclubs and at the Apollo Theater, incl. TV show, and worked as a jazz disc jockey on WHOM.

Fr. '46 to '48 he led another bb. Worked in LA as stage and screen actor in his last yrs. Comp. his band's theme, "It's Over Because We're Through." CDs: BB; Class.; Jazz Arch.

BRYSON, JEANIE, voc; b. NYC, 3/10/58. Grandmother stud. at Juilliard and pl. pno.; moth. is songwriter-pnst. Connie Bryson; fath. was Dizzy Gillespie. Raised in East Brunswick, N.J. Pl. pno. in first grade; fl. in fifth grade. Majored in anthropology and minored in ethnomusicology at Livingston Coll., Rutgers U., where she sang Native Amer. and Javanese songs; Indian ragas; stud. harm. w. Kenny Barron. After grad. in 1981, she worked in Post Office but sang jazz in clubs at night. Left her day job in '87 and start. perf. full time. App. at Trumpets, N.J. '90, '93; Sign of the Dove, NYC '93. Eur. tours '92–3. Reviewing her perf. at the Village Vanguard, Peter Watrous wrote: "Bryson has created a performance language rare in its ability to portray desire and humor as part of everyday life. . . . She edits herself, turning nuance and suggestion into statements of power." CDs: Tel.; w. Terence Blanchard; Grover Washington (Col.).

BUCKNER, MILT (MILTON BRENT), pno, org; b. St. Louis, MO, 7/10/15; d. Chicago, IL, 7/27/77. Brother of Ted Buckner. Raised in Det. While stud. at Det. Art Inst. for two yrs., began pl. w. local bands incl. Harlem Aristocrats, Dixie Whangdoodles. Wrote arr. for Earl Walton, 1930. While w. dmr. Don Cox's band '32–4, "to give the 5–piece orch. more depth," he developed a technique of parallel chord patterns, later dubbed the "locked hands" style when he employed it in Lionel Hampton's orch. Pnst. and arr. w. McKinney's Cotton Pickers '34; then w. Cox and Jimmy Raschel in mid-late '30s. Join. Hampton as pno.-arr. Nov. '41, remaining into '48. Briefly led own bb, which rec. for MGM '48. Rejoin. Hampton '50–2, doubling on Hammond org., which became his main inst. in '52, when he formed his own trio. Also worked, often in Eur., w. Illinois Jacquet '66, again in mid '70s; Buddy Tate '66; duo w. Jo Jones '69; Hampton '71. Fests: NJF '68, '70–5; Nice '74–5; MJF '70. Comps: "Hamp's Boogie Woogie"; "Overtime"; "The Lamplighter." CDs: Prog.; B&B; w. Hampton (BB; GRP; B&B); Al Casey; Arnett Cobb; Helen Humes; J. McShann; Slam Stewart; Tate (B&B); Jacquet (BB; B&B; BL; Prest.).

BUCKNER, TED (THEODORE GUY), alto sax; also sop and bari sax; b. St. Louis, MO, 12/14/13; d. Detroit, MI, 4/12/76. Brother of Milt Buckner, w. whom he pl. in J. Raschel's orch. 1935. Also worked w. McKinney's Cotton Pickers and other Det. bands.

Became prominent w. Jimmie Lunceford '38–43, soloing on such tunes as "Margie," "Down by the Old Mill Stream," "Ain't She Sweet," and "Well, All Right Then." Own gps. in Det. '40s; tour. w. Todd Rhodes in early '50s., then again active as lead. Pl. on Johnny Ray's first recs; later app. on many rec. Motown sess. Pl. w. revived edition of McKinney's Cotton Pickers in '70s. Eur. tour. w. Sammy Price, '75. CDs: w. Lunceford (Dec.).

BUCKNER, TEDDY (JOHN EDWARD), tpt, voc; b. Sherman, TX, 7/16/09; d. Los Angeles, CA, 9/22/94. Raised in Calif. First pl. prof. at age 15. Pl. in Shanghai w. Buck Clayton 1934; back in LA, join. L. Hampton band, becoming leader when Hampton left to go w. Benny Goodman '36. Pl. in '40s w. Benny Carter; Hampton again; and Kid Ory '49–53. In Feb. '54 began a long run lead. own band at Beverly Cavern, LA, and rec. w. sidemen incl. Trummy Young, J. C. Heard, Albert Nicholas, Edmond Hall; rec. in Eur. w. Sidney Bechet '58. His comp. "Parisian Encounter" led to his popularity in France. Own gps. in LA at 400 Club '59–61; The Huddle '62–6; then became permanent musical fixture at Disneyland, leading NO-style gp. until retirement in '85. Strongly infl. by Louis Armstrong, for whom he was a stand-in dur. the making of *Pennies From Heaven* '36. Portrayed Armstrong on TV in *Hello Louis* '70, and ABC's *Louis Armstrong: Chicago Style* '75. Other films incl. *Pete Kelly's Blues*; *Hush, Hush, Sweet Charlotte*. CDs: Vogue; w. Hampton (Dec.); Ory (GTJ; Col.); Doc Cheatham; Sammy Price (B&B); B. Holiday (Col.; Aff.).

BUDIMIR, DENNIS MATTHEW, gtr; b. Los Angeles, CA, 6/20/38. Studied pno. 1947; gtr. '48. Worked prof. in LA fr. '52, pl. w. Ken Hanna '55; Keith Williams '57–8; Harry James '58; Chico Hamilton '59; Bud Shank '60 and Peggy Lee '60–1. In army '61–3, then freelanced in LA as studio mus. w. Julie London; Quincy Jones; Lalo Schifrin; Marty Paich; Dave Grusin; Don Ellis; Gil Mellé. Has worked w. such rock stars as George Harrison and Ringo Starr; w. pop singers Doris Day, Johnny Mathis; and such jazz pl. as Johnny Mandel, Milt Jackson, Ray Brown. A highly respected, versatile studio sess. pl., Budimir won the NARAS Most Valuable Player award '75–80, then the Emeritus award. Tour. Japan w. Bobby Troup '63. Early infls: Jimmy Raney; Tal Farlow. CDs: w. Dizzy Gillespie (BN; Moon); Chico Hamilton (FS); Milt Jackson (Pab.); Carmen McRae (BN); Oliver Nelson (RCA).

BUDWIG, MONTY (MONTGOMERY), bs; b. Pender, NE, 12/26/29; d. Los Angeles, CA, 3/9/92.

Studied bs. in hs. Early exp. w. Anson Weeks 1950; Vido Musso '51; and various gigs around SF. After three yrs. in air force band, moved to LA '54. Worked w. Zoot Sims; Barney Kessel. Join. Red Norvo trio for fourteen mos. '54–5. Pl. w. Woody Herman combo in LV '55; Herman bb '56–7; Shelly Manne '58–60; '66 and off and on into late '70s. With Benny Goodman for NYC concerts and tour. of Japan '64; Austral. tour '73. Tour. So. Amer. w. Carmen McRae '74. Fr. the '60s he also enjoyed an extensive studio career, incl. movies and TV shows w. Steve Allen, Johnny Carson, Judy Garland, Merv Griffin; w. T. Gibbs on Regis Philbin show '65. He worked and/or rec. w. Rosemary Clooney; Conti Candoli; Peggy Lee; Mundell Lowe; Oscar Peterson; Frank Sinatra; Sarah Vaughan; and Joe Williams. Pl. w. Lighthouse All-Stars in Japan, Belgium, and at North Sea JF, MJF '91. Fr. '75, rec. regularly for Conc. label. Favs: Blanton, Pettiford, Ray Brown, Red Mitchell. CDs: w. Norvo (BB); Manne; Lennie Niehaus (Cont.); Richie Kamuca–B. Holman (HiFi); Mike Wofford (Disc.); Vince Guaraldi (Fant.); Lighthouse All-Stars (Cont.; Cand.); Toshiko Akiyoshi; Al Cohn; Herb Ellis; Stan Getz; Scott Hamilton; Dave McKenna; Kessel (Conc.); Bill Evans (Verve); C. Candoli (BR).

BULLOCK, HIRAM, gtr, b. Osaka, Japan, 9/11/55. Started on pno. at age 3 in Balt., Md.; pl. bs. in hs while living in Panama. Hearing John McLaughlin in 1972 inspired him to pl. gtr., which he stud. w. Pat Metheny at U. of Miami. To NYC in '75 w. singer Phyllis Hyman; rec. w. Michael Brecker, Billy Joel, Kenny Loggins, Barbra Streisand within first yr.; then many studio dates w. Steely Dan, James Taylor, Paul Simon, Roberta Flack, the Brecker Bros., et al. Rec. three albums w. the 24th St. Band, feat. Will Lee, Steve Jordan, and Cliff Carter. After two yrs. w. Paul Schaeffer band on David Letterman show, he form. own band, making debut on Atl. album, *From All Sides* '86. Pl. solo on Sting's rec. of "Little Wing." For three yrs. he was a regular on David Sanborn's *Night Music* TV series. Cont. to tour w. own gps. and perf. regularly w. Sanborn and Al Jarreau, Gil Evans, Miles Davis, Carla Bley. CDs: Atl.; w. Gil Evans (Gram.; Elec. Bird; New Tone); Sanborn (WB); Carla Bley; Steve Swallow (Watt); Brecker Bros (Novus); Jaco Pastorius (Big World Music; DIW); John Scofield (Gram.).

BUNCH, JOHN L. JR. pno; b. Tipton, IN, 12/1/21. Studied pno. and harm. at age 11; first gigs w. band at age 12. Pl. w. Dixieland band bef. entering army. Didn't play for three yrs. while in service dur. WWII, which incl. time spent as POW in Germ. Studied speech at U. of Ind. 1946–50. Pl. w. Tinker Reason Trio, Anderson, Ind., '51. Join. Woody Herman '56,

remain. into '57. Pl. w. Benny Goodman '57–8; Maynard Ferguson '58; Urbie Green '59; Buddy Rich '60. Led own gps. fr. late '50s. Pl. w. Goodman early '60s, incl. tour of USSR '62; Al Cohn–Zoot Sims at Half Note, NYC, '61–2; Gene Krupa Qt. '61–4; Wild Bill Davison '65; own duo at Luigi's, NYC, '65–6; Buddy Rich bb '66. Accomp. and mus. dir. for Tony Bennett '66–72. Pl. w. Goodman '73; Rich '74; own trio in NYC and British West Indies '73–5; Goodman, Pearl Bailey, Louie Bellson '80s; Scott Hamilton fr. '82; WGJB, '91. As a young pnst., he made a smooth transition fr. swing to bop, maintaining the best elements of both in his own subtly elegant manner. Favs: Bud Powell, Teddy Wilson. Fests: all major w. Goodman, Scott Hamilton. TV: *This Is Music*; Tony Bennett specials; also apps. w. Goodman, Pearl Bailey, Tom Jones, Dean Martin, et al. LPs: w. own trio, qt., qnt. on Famous Door '75–80. CDs: Arb.; Conc.; Chiaro.; LRC; w. Goodman (RCA; Col.; Lond.; Limel.); Herman; S. Hamilton; Chris Flory; Maxine Sullivan; K. Peplowski; R. Braff; W. Vaché (Conc.); J. Venuti (Chiaro.); Flip Phillips (Chiaro., Conc.); M. Ferguson (Roul.); Yank Lawson (Jazz.); L. Bellson (MM; Limel.); Rich (PJ; BGO; Sequel).

BUNKER, LARRY (LAWRENCE BENJAMIN), dms, vib; b. Long Beach, CA, 11/4/28; d. Los Angeles, 3/8/05. Accordion, pno., dms. in hs. Army 1946–8, then first prof. job w. bop spt. on Miss. riverboat. Dur. two yrs. gigging in Calif. on pno., picked up vib.; join. Howard Rumsey at Lighthouse, Jan. '51. Pl. w. Art Pepper, Georgie Auld '52, back to Rumsey in fall. With Gerry Mulligan, Jan.-Sept. '53; six mos. on daily Bob Crosby TV show to Mar. '54; also brief. w. Barney Kessel, Stan Getz. Often worked w. Peggy Lee unit '55–60. In early '60s, pl. at Shelly's Manne Hole w. Clare Fischer; worked w. Bud Shank '62, incl. concert in Mexico City. Led own qt. '63; worked w. Fischer, Ralph Pena. Tour., incl. Eur., w. Bill Evans '64–5. To Austral. w. Judy Garland, '64. MJF w. Dizzy Gillespie. Tour. Japan w. Getz, '65. Equally adept on dms. and vib., Bunker was greatly in demand for symph. assignments as well as pop and jazz dates, perf. w. Zubin Mehta; Pierre Boulez; and Michael Tilson Thomas; film and TV jobs w. Quincy Jones; Oliver Nelson; Johnny Mandel; Lalo Schifrin; Dave Grusin; Mulligan; and gigs w. Jim Hall; Zoot Sims; Gary Burton. Collected and restored antiques and made custom instruments and equipment for the perf. of contemporary mus. CDs: w. Mulligan; Chet Baker (PJ); B. Evans (Verve; Riv.); Pepper (Sav.); Hampton Hawes (Prest.); Shorty Rogers; Red Norvo (BB); Bud Shank (Conc.); B. Holiday (Verve); Buddy Collette (Cont.); Bill Perkins (Riv.); Q. Jones (Mob. Fid.); Harry Babasin (Noct.).

BUNN, TEDDY (THEODORE LEROY), gtr; b. Freeport, NY, 1909; d. Lancaster, CA, 7/20/78. From mus. family; self-taught. Prof. debut w. calypso singer. Met Leo Watson and worked w. him in the Washboard Serenaders in late 1920s. Subbed for Fred Guy w. Duke Ellington '29. At Watson's urging, join. Sepia Nephews in Wash., D.C., '32; gp. became the Spirits of Rhythm and enjoyed great success at the Onyx Club and Nick's in NYC. In '37–8, led own small gps.; also w. John Kirby in trio and duo '37. Rejoin. Spirits of Rhythm '39, moving w. them to Calif. '40. Worked w. Edgar Hayes '40s, '50s; Jack McVea, Hawaii '54; Louis Jordan '59. Less frequent perfs. dur. the next decades, incl. tour. w. r&r show late '50s. Recs. w. Spirits of Rhythm; "Sweet Lorraine" w. Jimmie Noone '37; Johnny Dodds; "If You See Me Comin'" w. Mezz Mezzrow–Tommy Ladnier '38; "Summertime" w. Bechet '39; solo sess. for BN '39. CDs: w. Bechet (BN; BB); L. Hampton (BB); Spirits of Rhythm (JSP); Dodds (B&B); James P. Johnson (Hot 'n' Sweet).

BUNNETT, (MARY) JANE, sop, tnr, alto saxes; fl, pic, pno; b. Toronto, Ont., Canada, 10/22/56. Clarinet in school band. Stud. classical pno. and took fl. lessons w. saxist Jane Fair. Pl. traditional Greek mus. bef. form. own qnt. w. husband, tptr. Larry Cramer, 1987. Pl. w. Latin Banda Brava '88; Jane Fair (*Music in Monk Time*); Kenny Wheeler bb '90. Perf. at Havana JF '90, '98; NZ, Austral., Eur.; and collab. w. many mus., incl. Don Pullen; Dewey Redman; Charlie Haden; Carla Bley; G. Rubalcaba; A. Cyrille; Claude Ranger. Since her rec. debut in '88, she has been considered one of the most promising sop. saxists in jazz. Her involvement w. Cuban mus. and musicians has earned her the nickname "Havana Jane." Favs: Lacy, Shorter, Coltrane. CDs: BN; Evid.; Den.; M&A; Paul Bley/Bunnett (JT).

BURBANK, ALBERT, cl; b. New Orleans, LA, 3/25/02; d. New Orleans, 8/15/76. Took up cl. at 17. In 1920s was a member of dmr. Arnold DePass's band; also pl. w. Buddy Petit; Chris Kelly; Punch Miller. Dur. '30s worked in taxi dance halls bef. form. own qt. In navy dur. WWII. With Wooden Joe Nicholas '45, '49; Albert Jiles '46; De De Pierce '47; Herb Morand '49–50; Paul Barbarin '50–2; Kid Clayton '52–3. Join. Kid Ory in LA '54, but ret. to NO in same yr., working at the Paddock Lounge until '66, then w. Albert French at Dixieland Hall. Worked w. Kid Thomas at Preservation Hall '69–73, incl. int'l tour '71. Pl. w. Percy Humphrey '73, but ill health eventually reduced him to a singing role at Preservation Hall. Recs. w. Thomas and Kid Howard. CDs: Story.; w. J. Archey (GHB); Ory;

Barbarin (Story.); Morand; Nicholas (Amer. Mus.); Humphrey (Riv.).

BURKE, RAY (Raymond N. Barrois), cl; sop, tnr saxes; b. New Orleans, LA, 6/6/04; d. New Orleans, 3/21/86. From a mus. family. Self-taught, first on homemade kazoo and cl. Began pl. conventional cl. at 16. Early prof. exp. w. Blind Gilbert; Henry Walde's Melon Pickers, mid 1920s–'30s. Worked briefly in KC in late '30s. Pl. in NO w. Sharkey Bonano, George Hartman, Wooden Joe Nicholas '40s; Johnny Wiggs '52 and again fr. '54; Johnny St. Cyr '54. App. at Preservation Hall w. Punch Miller '60, and often w. Kid Thomas dur. the next twenty yrs. while also owning secondhand store on Bourbon Street. Pl. the NO JF '69. Tour. Eur. '73. Favs: Harry Shields, Leon Roppolo. Recs. w. own bands; Wendell Eugene. CDs: Amer. Mus.; w. Alvin Alcorn; George Girard; Percy Humphrey; Johnny Wiggs (Story.); Ken Colyer; Willie Pajeaud (504); Art Hodes (Del.).

BURKE, SONNY (JOSEPH FRANCIS), arr, lead; b. Scranton, PA, 3/22/14; d. Santa Monica, CA, 5/31/80. Violin and pno. fr. age 5. All-state fullback in hs. Stud. mus. at Duke U. to 1937, where he, Les Brown, and Johnny Long all led student bands. Led 15-pc. coll. band on transatlantic ocean liner one summer. After working in Det. dept. store, he became a freelance arr. for Buddy Rogers, Joe Venuti, Xavier Cugat. To NYC '38, where he took over Sam Donahue's band, touring w. it '39–40. He cross-bred the styles of Jimmie Lunceford and Count Basie, an example of which, "Jimmie Meets the Count," was rec. for OKeh in '40. Through Glenn Miller, he became an arr. for Charlie Spivak '40–2. Arr. for J. Dorsey fr. '42–5. In the '50s, he was rec. dir. and leader for Dec., working w. Ella Fitzgerald, Louis Armstrong, and others; his '51 rec of "Mambo Jambo" was a hit. At Reprise, he prod. all of Frank Sinatra's sess. bef. moving on to WB as head of mus. operations. Later headed own Daybreak label. Favs: Pete Rugolo, Nelson Riddle, John Graas, Shorty Rogers. Arr: "King Porter Stomp," J. Dorsey; "Everything I Have Is Yours," B. Eckstine.

BURKE, VINNIE (Vincenzo Bucci), bs; b. Newark, NJ, 3/15/21. Began on vln. at age 5, then pl. gtr. Worked in war plant, 1942–5, where he lost the use of a finger in an accident. Sw. to bs. In mid to late '40s, pl. w. Joe Mooney; Tony Scott; then three yrs. w. Cy Coleman trio. Pl. briefly w. Sauter-Finegan Orch. in early '50s; Marian McPartland '53. Pl. and rec. w. Gil Mellé mid '50s. House bassist on WNTA-TV show, Art Ford's *Jazz Party* '58. Pl. w. Vic Dickenson '59. Also rec. in '50s w. John Mehegan; Chris Connor;

Eddie Costa; Tal Farlow; and Don Elliot. Worked in early '60s w. Bucky Pizzarelli; Mat Mathews; Bobby Hackett. Gigging in Newark in '90s. LPs: w. Farlow (Xan.). CDs: w. Mellé (Prest.).

BURNET, BOBBY (ROBERT W.), tpt; b. Chicago, IL, 1912; d. Guadalajara, Mexico, 8/3/84. Played dms., pno., bjo. bef. moving to tpt. To NYC where he worked w. Charlie Barnet 1938–40. After leading own sxt. at Café Society and Nick's in NYC, he rejoin. Barnet '41, leaving him in '42 for semiretirement. Rec. w. Freddy Wacker's Windy City Seven '57. Moved to Mex. '58. CDs: w. Barnet (BB Cir.).

BURNO, DWAYNE, bs, comp; b. Philadelphia, PA, 6/10/70. Self-taught. Began pl. at age 16. First major job w. Donald Harrison 1989. Pl. w. Jesse Davis '90 and moved to NYC to join Betty Carter, w. whom he work fr. mid '90 to late '91. Pl. w. Three Baritones Band, Italy '98. Also has led own gp. Favs: Oscar Pettiford, Sam Jones, Ron Carter, Buster Williams; comps: Bud Powell, Thelonious Monk, Kenny Dorham, Wayne Shorter, Bobby Hutcherson. CDs: w. Harrison (Sw. Bas.); V. Herring (Land.); J. Davis (Conc.); S. Wendholt (CC); E. J. Allen (Enja); B. Golson (Ark.); David Schumacher (Amo.).

BURNS, DAVE (DAVID), tpt, flg, arr; b. Perth Amboy, NJ, 3/5/24. Studied priv. w. Antony Aquaviva 1933–7; Nicholas Morrisey '37–41; Carmine Caruso '59–61. Pl. w. Savoy Sultans '42–3, then led an army air force band '43–5. Pl. w. Dizzy Gillespie bb '45–9; Duke Ellington '50–2; James Moody '52–7. Freelance '57–60, then pl. w. Billy Mitchell–Al Grey '61–3; Willie Bobo '63–5. Pl. on Leon Bibb NBC-TV show '65–6. Co-led gp. w. Bill English at Minton's '66–8. Moved to LI, pl. w. Billy Mitchell in *Project Read* '69. Lectured and pl. in schs. w. Int'l Art of Jazz fr. '68; has also taught at SUNY Stony Brook and priv. Burns received an achievement awd. fr. the NAACP. in '57. He was the first to get close to Gillespie's style, and it is hard, at times, to distinguish between the two on the Bebop Boys recs., e.g., "Smokey Hollow Jump," Sav. '46. He later combined this w. his own voice, further flavored by Clifford Brown. Favs: Gillespie, Brown; arrs: Gil Fuller, Tadd Dameron, Quincy Jones. Poll: *Esq.* Fests: Eur. w. Gillespie. TV: Milton Berle w. Ellington '50; Sammy Davis w. Johnny Brown sxt. '65; Leon Bibb '65–6. Films: *Jivin' in Bebop* w. Gillespie '47; *Night Club Scene* w. Ellington '51; *Sweet Love Bitter* '67. LPs: Vang. CDs: w. Gillespie (Sav.; RCA; Roost; GNP Cres.; Vogue); Ellington (Col.; Saja); J. Moody (BN; Prest.); Eddie Jefferson

(Prest.); Milt Jackson (Riv.); J. Griffin (Riv.); G. Wallington; Art Taylor; Dexter Gordon, boxed set (BN).

BURNS, RALPH, comp, arr, pno; b. Newton, MA, 6/29/22; d. Los Angeles, 11/21/01. Studied at New Engl. Cons. 1938–9. First rec. comp., "The Moose," written dur. his yr. as Charlie Barnet's pnst. After six mos. w. Red Norvo, Burns join. Woody Herman in Jan. '44 as pnst. and arr.; in mid '45 he left the road to concentrate on writing. His originals for Herman played a central role in the band's early successes; they incl. "Apple Honey, Bijou" and longer pieces such as *Lady McGowan's Dream* and *Summer Sequence*. The last movement of the latter became known as "Early Autumn," w. lyrics added later by Johnny Mercer. By the '50s, Burns was concentrating on writing for radio, TV, and movies, though he cont. to contribute occ. to Herman's library. In later yrs. his jazz associations were infrequent, but incl. comp. the score for Martin Scorsese's film *New York, New York* in '77. Won the *Esq.* New Star award in '46 and the *DB* award in '52–3. He led jazz gps. on a series of Dec. LPs in the late '50s. CDs: one track, "Introspection," in *The Jazz Scene* (Verve); w. Herman (Col.; Cap.; BB; Laser.); Konitz–Giuffre; Anita O'Day (Verve); Serge Chaloff (Mos.).

BURR, JON (JONATHAN H.), bs, pno, comp; b. Huntington, NY, 5/22/53. Father, bros., and sists. are amateur mus. Began on cl. and bassoon. Was introduced to Marian McPartland, Linc Milliman, and Michael Moore by hs band dir. Sat in w. Chas. Mingus 1969. Att. Berklee summer program '69, then U. of Ill. '70–5. Moved to NYC '75, rooming w. Jim McNeely. Worked w. Buddy Rich bb '76–7; Art Farmer, Chet Baker, Lee Konitz '77; Horace Silver '78; Stan Getz '78. Pl. w. Tony Bennett '80–5; Stephane Grappelli '86; rec. w. Chet Baker '86; then B'way shows and various classical orchs. '87–90. In '90, Burr pl. w. Roland Hanna; Dorothy Donegan; Barbara Cook; Lou Donaldson; Hank Jones. Has led own qt. since '91 and cont. to work w. Donegan in '90s. Burr's comps. have been perf. and rec. by Chet Baker, Mel Lewis bb, Barry Miles. Favs: Ron Carter, Eddie Gomez, Richard Davis, Paul Chambers. Fests: many, w. S. Grappelli, C. Baker, T. Bennett. TV: PBS *Salute to France*; w. T. Bennett, *Tonight Show*; *SCTV*; *Evening at the Pops*. CDs: w. S. Grappelli (Col.); J. McNeely (Muse); C. Baker (Timel.); Hanna (LRC); Donegan (Chiaro.).

BURRAGE, RONNIE (JAMES RENALDO), dms, perc, kybds, voc; b. St. Louis, MO, 10/19/59. Mother pl. pno.; five uncles were mus. Studied pno.

at St. Louis Sch. of Mus., then pl. in drum and bugle corps. Pl. w. bands at Washington U. while in hs. One of Burrage's uncles got him his first prof. gig w. Luther Thomas's Rainbow Glass 1971. Att. No. Tex. St. U. '78. Pl. w. McCoy Tyner '80–3; Dave Valentin–Jerry Gonzales, Sonny Rollins–Pat Metheny, Chico Freeman '83; Jaco Pastorius, Woody Shaw '84; Cedar Walton, Pepper Adams, Woody Shaw–Joe Farrell '85; Third Kind of Blue, Jackie McLean '85–7; Michael Urbaniak '86; Jack Walrath, Ray Anderson '87; Abdullah Ibrahim, Michael Brecker, Freddie Hubbard '88; Robin Eubanks '89; Wayne Shorter, Sonny Fortune, J. Walrath, Richard Davis–Clifford Jordan '90; JoAnne Brackeen '90–1; Blue Brass Connection '90–2; Courtney Pine, Monty Waters '91; Eddie Gomez, S. Fortune, Smithsonian Jazz Orch., Sir Roland Hanna '92. Burrage has led his own trio fr. '90, and his own large gp., Band Burrage, fr. '92. He taught at the Berlin Cons. '85–6 and has taught at the U. of the Arts in Phila. fr. '91. Favs: Elvin Jones, Jack DeJohnette, Roy Haynes; arrs: Oliver Nelson, Julius Hemphill, Quincy Jones. Fests: all major fr. '80 incl. Antibes w. K. Lightsey, '95. CDs: Amadeo; Sound Hills; w. World Sax. Qt. (None.); Eric Person (SN); J. Walrath (Muse, BN); Ray Anderson; B. Dennerlein (Enja); Clifford Jordan; Stanley Cowell; James Williams (DIW); Joe Locke; D. Stryker (Steep.).

BURRELL, DAVE (HERMAN DAVIS II), pno, comp, arr; b. Middletown, OH, 9/10/40. Mother was voc., org., pnst., choir dir. Studied w. Barbara Smith at U. of Hawaii 1958–60. Grad fr. Berklee Coll. of Mus. '65. Pl. w. Tony Williams, Sam Rivers in Bost., then moved to NYC '65. Pl. w. Grachan Moncur III, Marion Brown, then form. Untrad. Jazz Improv. Team w. Byard Lancaster, Bobby Kapp, Sirone '65; 360 Degree Music Experience w. Moncur, Beaver Harris '68. Pl. w. Archie Shepp fr. '69, incl. Pan African Fest. in Algiers '69. Taught mus. at Community Thing Organization wkshp. in Harlem '69. Also pl. and rec. '60s–'70s w. Pharoah Sanders; Beaver Harris; Alan Silva; Sunny Murray. Fr. late '80s assoc. w. David Murray; also w. H. Bluiett; C. McBee. Burrell has travelled extens. and perf. w. indigenous musicians in Jamaica, Haiti, Algeria, Hawaii, Japan, etc. Received NEA grant to comp. jazz suite based on Haitian folk mus., early '70s; also scored French film while in No. Africa. Wrote jazz opera, *Windward Passages*, late '70s. Burrell has comp. and arr. for Shepp, P. Sanders, M. Brown, 360 Degree Exper., and for his own duo, trio, and qt. Comps. incl. "A.M Rag (Margie Pargie)"; "Blue Notes on the Black and White Keys"; "Polynesian Suite"; "Echo"; "La Vie De Boheme," based on Puccini's *La Boheme*. He

scored the play *Witherspoon* for CBS-TV and taught at Queens Coll. '71–3. Favs: JR Morton, Ellington, Monk, B. Powell, Coltrane, Shepp, Grachan Moncur III, Roach, Prokofiev, Puccini, Rimsky-Korsakoff. Fests: all major w. Shepp. TV: *Like It Is* w. Shepp; Italian docu. *Jazz in New York Today*. CDs: Den.; Gazell; hatArt; w. Shepp (Aff.; BS; Charly; Free.; Timel.); Noah Howard; Alan Silva (ESP Disk); D. Murray (BS; DIW; Tutu); P. Sanders (Imp.).

BURRELL, KENNY (KENNETH EARL), gtr, comp; b. Detroit, MI, 7/31/31. Mother was church singer; fath. pl bjo.; bros., Billy and Donald, gtr. Took up gtr. at age 12. Mainly self-taught but stud. classical gtr. in 1952–3. B.A. in mus. comp. and theory fr. Wayne St. U. '55. Pl. w. Candy Johnson '49; Count Belcher '49; Tommy Barnett '50. Led own combo and worked briefly w. Dizzy Gillespie '51, also making rec. debut w. Gillespie on DeeGee. Own gps. until '55, when Oscar Peterson hired him to sub for Herb Ellis in his trio. Moved to NYC freelancing w. own gp. and other combos '55–6. Worked w. Benny Goodman '57. Led own trios, qts. fr. that yr. and cont. to rec. prolifically. In '65 rec. LP, *Guitar Forms*, w. 13-piece band and Gil Evans arrs. for Verve. Tour. Calif. '67; Eur. '69. Own club, The Guitar, in NYC '69. Tour. Japan '70, '71. Began a series of col. seminars '71; since '78 he has taught an annual class on Ellington at UCLA and fr. fall '96 has served as Director of UCLA's Jazz Studies Program. Tour. int'l w. Philip Morris Superband '85–6. His formidable technique is never thrust upon the listener in an obvious way, but in the service of his flexible, melodious lines and inherent intimacy w. the blues. Favs: Christian, Reinhardt, Oscar Moore. Fests: numerous int'l, beginning w. own trio at NJF '59. Polls: winner many times in *DB*; *MM*; *SJ*; *Ebony*. Video: *Club Date*, KPBS-San Diego. B'way: pit bands for *Bye Birdie; How to Succeed in Business Without Really Trying* '60s. Books: *Jazz Guitar; Jazz Guitar Solos*. Comps: "Ode to 52nd Street"; *Asphalt Canyon Suite*; "Midnight Blue"; "Be Yourself"; "Love is the Answer." Rec. on bjo w. Mercer Ellington '84. CDs: Prest. and NJ, incl. dates w. Coltrane; Jimmy Raney; Fant. incl. two double-CD Ellington sets; BN; Verve; Col.; Cont.; Conc.; w. Jimmy Smith (BN; Verve; Mile.); K. Dorham; D. Byrd; M. Allison; I. Quebec; S. Turrentine (BN); Gillespie; K. Clarke; F. Foster; F. Wess; J. Newman (Sav.); Bill Evans (Fant.); Thad Jones; G. Ammons (Prest.); Jerome Richardson (NJ); J. Heath; C. Baker (Riv.); A. Farmer (Cont.); T. Flanagan (Timel.).

BURROUGHS, ALVIN ("MOUSE"), dms; b. Mobile, AL, 11/21/11; d. Chicago, IL, 8/1/50. Played and rec. w. Walter Page's Blue Devils 1928–9; Alphonso Trent '30. Moved to Chi., where he was a member of bands of Horace Henderson '37–8; Earl Hines '38–40; Milt Larkin '41; Benny Carter '42. Led own band bef. join. Red Allen '44–6. Following another stint as leader, he join. George Dixon qt., remaining until his death. Solos w. Hines: "G.T. Stomp"; "XYZ"; "Tantalizing a Cuban." CDs: w. Hines; Hampton (BB); Albert Ammons in *The 1940s Mercury Sessions* (Merc.); Bill Harris in *Key. Coll.* (Em.).

BURROWS, DON (DONALD VERNON); cl, saxes, fl, comp; b. Sydney, Australia, 8/8/28. Studied at Sydney Cons. 1946–48. First rec. date at 16 w. Dixieland gp. App. in concerts, at fests., and on TV (as sideman, leader, soloist, and lecturer) for many yrs., leading gps. of every kind and size. Inspired by Benny Goodman and Buddy DeFranco, he has been called Austral.'s premier jazz clst. Many awards from Austral. mus. magazines; in '72, Queen Elizabeth awarded him the MBE for services to jazz; in '73, the Austral. Prime Minister appointed him to Council for the Arts; helped establish Austral.'s first jazz studies program at Sydney Cons., where he became a teacher. Also app. w. symph orchs.; comp. mus. for many film docus. and TV programs. Took part in Montreal Expo, incl. world's first satellite telecast, '67; Expo 70 in Osaka, Japan. Pl. at NJF-NY '72. Film: *2000 Weeks*. Rec. w. S. Grappelli '77. LPs: Main.; Col. Austral; albums on Cherry Pie label.

BURTIS, SAM, tbn, bs-tbn, tba, euph, pno, synth, comp, arr; b. Far Rockaway, NY, 10/2/48. Began on tba. in third grade, then start. pl. tbn. While in hs on LI met Carmell Jones at Cork 'n' Bib, then Chubby Jackson and John LaPorta, all of whom encouraged him. Pl. w. Chubby Jackson's LI Sound 1963. Att. Ithaca Coll. and Berklee briefly bef. moving to NYC '67. Stud. w. Carmine Caruso, Jimmy Knepper, Jimmy Maxwell, Jack Nowins. Pl. w. Buddy Rich '67; Archie Whitewater '68; own gp. w. Travis Jenkins '68; Larry Harlow '68–72. Pl. and rec. in '70s w. Thad Jones–Mel Lewis Orch.; Lee Konitz Nonet; Dave Mathews; Deodato; John Tropea; Chuck Israels; Jazz Composer's Orch.; Tito Puente; Machito; Eddie Palmieri; many recs. w. Latin bands for Fania label. Freelanced in early '80s, then w. Tito Puente '87–91; Mingus Dynasty '89; Mingus *Epitaph* Orch. '90; mus. dir. for Mingus bb at Time Café in NYC in early '90s. Favs: Teagarden, Nanton, J.J. Johnson, C. Fuller. Fests: many in Asia and Eur. w. B. Rich, Deodato, Jones-Lewis, etc. TV: *Saturday Night Live*. CDs: w. Lee Konitz (Chiaro.; SN); Tito Puente (Conc.); Mingus (Col.).

BURTON, ABRAHAM AUGUSTUS JR., alto, tnr saxes; b. NYC, 3/17/71. Studied w. Bill Saxton; then at LaGuardia HS 1986–9. Became seriously involved w. mus. when his hs teacher, Justin DiCioccio, encouraged him to stud. w. Jackie McLean at Hartt Coll. '89–93. Pl. w. All-City HS Orch., NYC, '89; Collective Expression band in Conn. '89–91; Art Taylor '90–4; Nat Reeves '92. Own qt. fr. '94; Louis Hayes Qt. fr. '98. Favs: McLean, Coltrane, Rollins. Polls: McDonald's best student combo '88; *DB* best combo and soloist '89. Pl. in Spain w. Taylor; Germ. w. Reeves '92. Made film in Eur. w. Taylor. CDs: Enja; w. Taylor (Enja; Verve); Louis Hayes (TCB).

BURTON, GARY, vib, educ. b. Anderson, IN, 1/23/43. Played mrba. in variety shows fr. early age; was helped by country musicians Hank Garland, Boots Randolph, and Chet Atkins; later by jazz players Marian McPartland, Jim Hall, and Herb Pomeroy. Studied at Berklee Sch. 1960–1, dur. which time he rec. own album for RCA '61. Tour. w. George Shearing Qnt. '63, Stan Getz '64–5, while cont. to rec. for RCA. Form. qt. w. Larry Coryell, Bob Moses, Steve Swallow '67. Rec. Carla Bley's *A Genuine Tong Funeral* '68; *Hotel Hello*, a highly artistic duo album w. Swallow, ECM '74. For next two yrs., he incl. Eberhard Weber, bs., in his gp. Became profess. at Berklee '71, teaching improv. and mus. business courses; appointed dean of curriculum '85. Gave many lectures and seminars throughout US, perf. on SS *Norway* jazz cruise w. gp. of his Berklee students, incl. Makoto Ozone, pno., '93. Burton won first place in *DB* readers' poll '68–74; critics' poll '72, 74–5; *DB* Jazzman of the Yr. '68. Honorary doctorate at Berklee '89. He has tour. Eur., Japan, and So. Amer., sometimes under State Dept. auspices. Pl. solo concerts for Russian mus. and critics at US Embassy in Moscow. Among his most notable and successful albums are *Alone At Last*, a solo set on Atl., for which he won a Grammy '70; *Crystal Silence*, ECM '72; *New Tango*, Atl. '88; *Reunion*, GRP '90. In '92, Burton teamed w. Eddie Daniels for a CD and series of concert tributes to Lionel Hampton and Benny Goodman. Though he names Red Norvo, Milt Jackson, and Dave Samuels as his favorite vibists, Burton developed a unique style that shows the infl. of Bill Evans. He has long specialized in the use of four mallets, w. results that are harmonically rich, yet retain the essence of swing. He has also comp. a number of works that suit well his idiosyncratic talent. Teamed up on recs. w. Stephane Grappelli, Keith Jarrett, and Carla Bley. CDs: BB; ECM; GRP; Atl.; w. C. Corea; Ralph Towner; E. Weber (ECM); E. Daniels (GRP); S. Getz (BB); Fred Hersch (JC); Marc Johnson (Em.); Quincy Jones; RR Kirk (Merc.); Steve Swallow (Xtra Watt).

BURTON, RAHN (WILLIAM RON) (aka JABU-LANI), pno, org, comp; b. Louisville, KY, 2/10/34. Piano lessons age 13–17. First prof. job w. local gps. of Tommy Walker, Edgar "Eggeye" Brooks. Tour. Midwest w. Roland Kirk 1953–9, then freelanced for eight mos. in NYC '60. Pl. w. Chris Powell in Syracuse, N.Y. '60–1. Freelanced in Louisville '61–4, then pl. organ w. Geo. Adams trio '64–5. Formed gp. w. Norris Jones (Sirone), Ron Hampton, Lloyd McNeil in Atlanta '65–6. Freelanced in NYC '66, then rejoined R.R. Kirk '67–72. Pl. w. Piano Choir fr. '72; Michael Carvin fr. '74. Burton has led his own gp., African American Connection, fr. '72. Also worked w. Stanley Turrentine, Leon Thomas, Carlos Garnett '70s; Hannibal Peterson, Charlie Rouse '80s. Favs: Peterson, Garner, B. Powell, Silver, Muhal Richard Abrams, Andrew Hill. TV: w. Kirk, *March to Freedom* (Martin Luther King docu.), *Soul* (PBS). CDs: DIW; w. R. R. Kirk (Atl.; Rhino); Beaver Harris (SN); Massimo Urbani (Red).

BUSH, LENNIE (LEONARD WALTER), bs; b. London, England, 6/6/27. Made prof. debut 1944. Pl. and rec. w. Ronnie Scott '49–64; Victor Feldman '52–7; Jimmy Deuchar '54–6; Dizzy Reece '55–7; Tony Crombie '55–8; Alan Clare '56–8; George Chisholm '56–73; Tony Kinsey '57–74. Worked w. Jack Parnell's studio band for ATV '56–60. Also accomp. many visiting mus. at Ronnie Scott's, incl. Stephane Grappelli; Clark Terry; Zoot Sims; Joe Pass; Ben Webster; Carmen McRae; Anita O'Day. Worked w. Benny Goodman's Eur. band '69–72. Rec. w. Eddie Vinson '80. Favs: Ray Brown, Tommy Potter. CDs: w. Feldman (Cont.); Grappelli (Accord; Verve).

BUSHELL, GARVIN PAYNE, cl, sax, oboe, bassoon, fl; b. Springfield, OH, 9/25/02; d. Las Vegas, NV, 10/31/91. Mother taught voice; fath., a comp.; uncles were circus mus. Pno. at age 6, cl. at 13. Moved to NYC 1919, working in vaudeville bef. join. Mamie Smith's Jazz Hounds '21. With Ethel Waters '21–2. Tour. in US, Eur., So. Amer. w. Sam Wooding '25–7. Worked w. Johnny Dunn, Otto Hardwicke '31; Fess Williams '33; Bessie Smith, Fletcher Henderson '34–6; Cab Calloway '36–7; Chick Webb '37–9; Ella Fitzgerald '39–40. Led own gps. in '40s and '50s. Took Omer Simeon's spot w. Wilbur De Paris, Sept. '59, tour. int'l and remain. w. band until '64. To Africa w. Paul Taubman's orch. '64. Pl. w. Cab Calloway '66. Moved to PR '67, then LV, worked as mus. teach. Interviewed extensively in Jan. and Feb. '59 issues of *Jazz Review*. Fav: Benny Goodman. Fests: Great So. Bay '58. Recs. w. M. Smith; Wooding; J. Dunn; B. Smith; Waters. Pl. bassoon. w. Chi.

Civic Orch. '50; also pl. bassoon on rec. w. Louisiana Sugar Babes '28; J. Coltrane '61. CDs: w. Wild Bill Davison (Jazz.); E. Fitzgerald (Dec.); Waller (BB); Gil Evans (Verve); E. Dolphy (WW); Coltrane (Imp.).

BUSHKIN, JOE (JOSEPH), pno, tpt, voc, comp; b. NYC, 11/7/16; d. Santa Barbara, CA, 11/3/04. Private stud. on pno., tpt. Began prof. w. Frank LaMarr at Bklyn. Roseland, 1932. Fr. '35, pl. jobs mainly on pno., incl. gigs w. Joe Marsala and Bunny Berigan, at Famous Door on 52nd St., NYC, '35–6; Eddie Condon–Red McKenzie '36–7. With Berigan again '38; Fats Waller orch. in Chi.; Muggsy Spanier '39; Tommy Dorsey '40–2. Tpt. in army band '42–3; then assistant to David Rose and mus. dir. for orch. w. *Winged Victory* air force show '44–6. Join. Benny Goodman in spring of '46; to Rio De Janeiro w. Bud Freeman at Copacabana Beach Hotel, winter '47. Acted and pl. piano in B'way play *The Rat Race* '49–50. Own qt. opp. Art Tatum at Embers '51; acquired society following; rec. w. Tallulah Bankhead. Pl. w. Louis Armstrong All-Stars on Armstrong–B. Goodman tour '53; led own gps. at Roundtable and Basin Street East, NYC, '60s; El Matador in SF '65. Didn't perf. for five yrs.; lived in Hawaii and, later, Santa Barbara, emerging for occasional jobs incl. tour w. Bing Crosby '76–7. In '80s, he resumed app. in NYC clubs, incl. Café Carlyle '84; St. Regis Hotel's King Cole Room '86; Tavern on the Green '95–6. A superior pnst. of the Teddy Wilson sch. w. a light but firm touch and uplifting swing, and a tasty Armstrong-inspired tpt. Best known comp.: "Oh Look At Me Now"; also "Hot Time in the Town of Berlin"; "How Do You Do Without Me"; "Something Wonderful Happens in Summer." Favs: Tatum, Peterson, Wilson. Fests: Nice; Northsea '86; JVC-NY '96. Film: *The Rat Race* '60. TV: wrote and rec. soundtrack for *Johnny Midnight* w. Edmond O'Brien '60; app. on *Perry Como Show*, *Bell Telephone Hour* in late '50s; Bing Crosby Christmas Special '75. Rec. w. Billie Holiday, Col. '36. For Comm. label '40s: piano solos; duet w. Willie "The Lion" Smith; own gp. feat. Zoot Sims; sideman sess. w. Condon; Lester Young. CDs: DRG; w. Young; Pee Wee Russell (Comm.); Spanier; T. Dorsey (BB); Condon (Dec.); Berigan (Hep; Jass).

BUSHLER, HERB, bs, el-bs; b. NYC, 3/7/39. Piano lessons 1947–9, then sw. to tba. Began pl. bs., doubling on el-bs. fr. '65. Pl. w. Ted Curson '64–5; Gil Evans off and on '67–81; Fifth Dimension '69; David Amram off and on fr. '70; Paul Winter, Blossom Dearie, Tony Williams '71–3; Enrico Rava '73; Joe Farrell '73–4; Harold Vick '75; Ryo Kawasaki in Japan '75–6; David Sanborn '79–81. Collab. w.

comp. Coleridge-Taylor Perkinson on ballet and film scores and concerts '66–80. Conducted Negro Ensemble Co. in productions of *Song of the Lusitanian Bogey* '68; *Man Better Man* '74. Also freelanced in '70s w. Billy Harper, Joe Chambers, Howard Johnson's Substructure. Bushler has perf. as a feat. soloist w. the Toronto, Phila., Cincinnati, Amer., Bklyn., and Rochester symphs. Fav: Coleridge Perkinson. Fests: all major w. Curson, Evans, Tony Williams. CDs: w. Curson (BL); G. Evans (Enja).

BUTLER, BILLY, gtr; b. Philadelphia, PA, 12/15/24; d. Teaneck, NJ, 3/20/91. Toured w. vocal gp., Harlemaires, 1947–9, then led own gp. '49–52. Pl. w. orgs. Doc Bagby '53; Bill Doggett '54–61. While w. Doggett, he co-wrote the org.'s biggest hit, "Honky Tonk." Rec. as studio mus. w. King Curtis '61–2; Dinah Washington, Panama Francis '63; Johnny Hodges '65, '67; Jimmy Smith '66; David "Fathead" Newman '68. Rec. soul-jazz albums as lead. for Prest. '68–70. Pl. w. B'way show bands fr. '68; also worked w. Houston Person '69–71; Norris Turney '75. Rec. album *Guitar Odyssey* w. Al Casey, Jackie Williams '74. Tour. Eur. regularly fr. '76. CDs: w. G. Ammons (Prest.); Lockjaw Davis (B&B); J. Hodges (BB; Verve); R.R. Kirk (Rhino/Atl.).

BUTLER, FRANK, dms; b. Kansas City, MO, 2/18/28; d. Ventura, CA, 7/24/84. Began on dms. in Omaha, Neb., hs. Pl. for USO shows, then w. gps. in KC, and studied w. Jo Jones. To SF, where he accomp. Billie Holiday 1949 and pl. w. Dave Brubeck '50; Edgar Hayes '51–3. Own gp. '53; briefly w. Duke Ellington '54. Moved to LA and worked w. Perez Prado, Curtis Counce '56. Sporadically active, gigging w. Ben Webster, Harold Land, Jimmy Witherspoon, Helen Humes. Co-led band w. Curtis Amy '61; own qnt. '62; stint w. Miles Davis '63; second dmr. w. Elvin Jones in Coltrane's combo late '65. Also worked w. Jimmy Rowles, Terry Gibbs, Teddy Edwards, Conte Candoli, Gerald Wilson, but drug problems kept him from perf. on a consistent basis. Worked for a short time as drug abuse counselor in Youth Outreach Program for LA County Health Dept. In late '70s, his career revived as leader and sideman for Xanadu Recs. Pl. w. Xanadu all-star gp. in Dakar, Senegal, '80, where he also sat in w. the drm. ens. of Doudou Ndiaye Rose. An all-purpose dmr. w. an impeccable sense of time, he combined the airiness of Jo Jones w. the best of the bop dmrs. Favs: Jo Jones, Blakey, Roach, PJ Jones. Fests: MJF; Black Fest. of Arts; Montreux; Dakar. TV: *Stars of Jazz*; also series w. P. Prado. Recs: own albums on Xan.; also w. T. Edwards; Xanadu All-Stars at Montreux. CDs: w. Davis (Col.); Coltrane (Imp.); Art Pepper;

Curtis Counce; Phineas Newborn; Harold Land; H. Humes; Ben Webster (Cont.); D. Coker; Kenny Drew; Sam Noto (Xan.); Sonny Criss (DIW); Red Garland (Gal.); Elmo Hope (BN; Cont.).

BUTLER, HENRY, pno; voc; b. New Orleans, LA, 9/21/49. Began singing at age 7, in choir at Louisiana State Sch. for the Blind; studied classical pno.and voice, and w. Alvin Batiste at Southern U. in Baton Rouge, La.; further studies at Michigan St., earning M. A. in voice 1974. Also priv. lessons w. Professor Longhair, Harold Mabern, and Roland Hanna. Moved to LA '80; rec. debut album '86, w. Freddie Hubbard, Charlie Haden, et al. Moved to NYC '87. In '90, moved to Charleston, Ill., where he became Assoc. Profess. of Mus. at Eastern Ill. U. Gigs at Green Mill, Chi. '95–6. An extremely eclectic musician, Butler's work ranges from r&b, standards and impressionistic music to vocal ballads, spirituals, and orchestral works. An active photographer, *American Photographer* magazine has called him "the first completely blind practitioner of the hobby." Infls: Prof. Longhair, James Booker, Roland Hanna, C. Haden, Harold Mabern, George Duke. CDs: Imp.; WH; Atl.

BUTMAN, IGOR, tnr, sop, alto saxes; b. Leningrad (St. Petersburg), Russia, 10/27/61. Father was an engineer and amateur dmr. Studied cl. and sax at Mussorgsky Mus. Sch. 1975–80. His teacher, Gennady Golstain, encouraged him to listen to the jazz radio shows on Voice of America. Orig. interested in rock, but took up jazz after meeting Golstain. Pl. w. David Goloshchokin, '79–82; Oleg Lundstrem '82–3; Allegro, fall '84–7. To US, stud. under scholarship at Berklee Coll. in Bost. '87–9. While there, gigs w. Gary Burton '87; own gps., one w. Rachel Z, another w. Wolfgang Muthspiel '87–90; worked w. Rebecca Parris '87–9. Own trio at Ryles; Pat Metheny was frequent sitter-in. Sat in w. Grover Washington, then gigged and rec. w. him '88. Pl. w. Valery Ponomarev '89–91. Feat. guest w. Billy Taylor trio at Met. Museum of Art, NYC, '90. Moved to NYC '91. Pl. w. Michael Moriarty qnt. at Fat Tuesday's '92. Led gp. on Wed. at Russian Samovar, NYC, when not traveling, '92–6. Fr. '92, he has ret. to Russia for tours, fest. apps. Form. band w. Eddie Gomez for work in Moscow '92, '94. Pl. w. Joe Locke at Visiones, NYC, '93, '94. Tour. Eur. w. Lionel Hampton '94. Re-formed Allegro w. Nick Levinovsky '95. An accomplished amateur ice hockey pl., he has taught sax to National Hockey League pl. Alexei Kovalev. Butman is a world-class player of hard swing and deep passion. Favs: Cannonball Adderley, Sonny Rollins, Stan Getz. Fests: JVC-NY '88, Boston Globe '89, both w. G. Washington; Salt Lake City '92, '95; L. Hampton Idaho JF '94, '96; Sochi, Russia '95; w. Allegro, JVC-NY '95. Pl. for Presidents Clinton and Yeltsin at *Fifty Years of Victory* celebration, 5/10/95, in Moscow. Rec. debut was w. own gp. for Melodiya label '83. CDs: Impromptu; Soyuz; w. Partners in Time (Evid.); Walter Davis (Maple.); M. Moriarty (DRG).

BUTMAN, OLEG, dms; b. Leningrad (St. Petersburg), Russia, 7/9/66. Brother of Igor Butman, w. whom he has pl. prof. on and off since 1984. Began on balalaika. Sw. to dms. '76. Studied at M.P. Moussorgsky Music Coll. '83–7. Pl. w. David Goloshchokin in Leningrad '86–8; worked at Blue Bird jazz club in Moscow '88–90. To US '90. Pl. w. Richie Cole '88; w. Jon Faddis at Blue Bird, Moscow '89; gigs in Cambridge, Mass., at Ryles w. Pat Metheny '90; NYC w. Monty Alexander '91; Harvie Swartz '92; Goloshchokin at Wetlands, NYC, '97. Favs: Tony Williams, PJ Jones, Elvin Jones. CDs: w. I. Butman (Soyuz).

BUTTERFIELD, BILLY (CHARLES WILLIAM), tpt; b. Middletown, OH, 1/14/17; d. No. Palm Beach, FL, 3/18/88. Tried vln., bs., tbn. bef. pl. tpt. in sch. bands. Worked w. orchs. of Andy Anderson, Austin Wylie 1935. Pl. w. Bob Crosby '37–40; Artie Shaw '40–1; Benny Goodman '41–2; Les Brown '42. CBS and ABC studio mus. '42–5; army '45–6. Own bb '45–7; then led house band at Nick's, NYC '47 bef. ret. to studios. Tour. w. own small gps., concentrating on coll. venues. Moved to Rescue, Va., gigging and teaching locally '59–60. Relocated to Fla. in mid '60s. Fronted own gps. until formation of WGJB '68, tour. w. it in US, Engl., Eur., So. Amer., Austral. Ret. to Fla. '72, freelancing w. own gps., Flip Phillips. An excellent lead player w. a gorgeous tone shown to advantage on "What's New? (I'm Free)" w. Crosby; "Star Dust" w. Shaw; "Blueberry Hill" w. Armstrong. Fests: NJF w. Goodman '58; w. WGJB at NJF '71; NOJF; Berlin. Regular apps. at Colo. JP '60s–'80s. Film: *Second Chorus* w. Shaw. Own recs. on Cap., RCA Vict. CDs: w. WGJB (Rh./Atl.); Bob Crosby; Louis Armstrong; B. Holiday (Dec.); A. Shaw; T. Dorsey; J. Teagarden (BB); B. Goodman (Col.; Limel.); E. Condon (Col.; Jass; Dec.; Jazz.); Buck Clayton (Mos.); P. Hucko (Timel.); Mel Powell (Comm.); Lester Young (Sav.).

BUTTERFIELD, DON, tba; b. Centralia, WA, 4/1/23; d. Cedar Gove, NJ, 11/27/06. In army 1942–6, then stud. at Juilliard. Prof. debut w. Goldman Band. Freelanced in studios, symph. orchs.; also rec. w. Jackie Gleason and worked briefly w. Claude Thornhill Orch. 1950s. Pl. w. Radio City Music Hall Orch. fr. early '50s; Jazz Composers Workshop w. Teddy

Charles, Teo Macero, Chas. Mingus '55–6. Rec. w. own sxt. for Col. '55, then presented the gp. at NJF '58. Contrib. articles to *DB* '62. Pl. w. Dizzy Gillespie Orch. at Antibes JF '62. Concerts w. Mingus '62–3; Dakota Staton, Oliver Nelson '63. Numerous film soundtracks, '50s-60s. Rec. w. Thad Jones–Mel Lewis Orch. '76. One of the first tba. players to be assoc. w. modern jazz. CDs: w. Mingus (Imp.; Rh./Atl.); Cannonball Adderley (Riv.; Cap.); G. Melle; O. Nelson (Prest.); MJQ; T. Charles (Atl.); D. Gillespie; Wes Montgomery; Oscar Peterson; Jimmy Smith; Cal Tjader (Verve); also many classical CDs.

BUTTS, JIMMY (JAMES H.), bs, voc; b. NYC, 9/24/17; d. NYC, 1/8/98. Began on pno. in hs. Pl. bs. w. Dr. Sausage and the Five Pork Chops 1937; Chris Columbus '39–41; Art Hodes '40; Les Hite, briefly, '41; Chris Columbus '41–3; Doc Wheeler's Sunset Royals, Don Redman, early '40s. Perf. in comedy duo w. Wilbert Kirk, early '40s. Rec. w. Tiny Grimes–Charlie Parker '44. Led own trio and freelanced w. Lem Johnson, Sir Chas. Thompson, Trummy Young, Buddy Tate, Josh White, Helen Humes, mid '40s. Join. Dud Bascomb '48. Teamed w. bs.-pnst. Doles Dickens '52–7, then pl. hotel, lounge gigs in duo w. Juanita Smith '57–68. In '68, form. gp. w. wife, voc. Edye Byrde, perf. in NYC area hotels and restaurants. CDs: w. C. Parker (Sav.); Sir Chas. Thompson (Del.).

BYARD, JAKI (JOHN A. JR.), pno, comp, saxes, tpt, bs, tbn, gtr, dms; b. Worcester, MA, 6/15/22; d. Queens, NY, 2/10/99. Mother pl. pno.; fath. pl. bari. horn in marching band. Studied pno. priv., 1930–2. First gigs through Worcester Boys Club. Pl. w. local bands '38–41; army bands '41–6. Pl. in Bost., w. local bands '46–9, then w. Earl Bostic '49–50; Jimmy Tyler in Larry Steele's Smart Affairs '50–2. Pl. tnr. sax w. Herb Pomeroy '52–5; solo pno. at Stable, Bost. '53–5. Freelanced in Bost. in late '50s, then pl. w. Maynard Ferguson '59–62. Came to prominence w. Charles Mingus '62–5, '70. Also pl. and rec. in '60s w. Eric Dolphy; Booker Ervin; Don Ellis; Charlie Mariano; Roland Kirk; own gps. Pl. solo pno. at Village Gate, NYC, late '60s. Led duo at Bradley's, NYC, mid '70s; Apollo Stompers bb fr. late '70s. Byard taught at New Engl. Cons. fr. '69; S.E. Mass. U. fr. '71; Elmo Lewis Sch. of Fine Arts, Bost.; Hartt Coll. of Mus. fr. '75; New Sch.; Manh. Sch. of Mus. He cond. seminars and clinics at U. of Pitts., Smithsonian Inst., Howard U. Byard was noted for his extensive knowledge of the jazz pno. trad. and his ability to apply various trad. styles in a modern context. Byard was shot to death in his home. Favs: Fats Waller, Rube Bloom. Polls: *DB* critics TDWR '66, '71. CDs: Cand.; Conc.; Muse; Prest.; SN; w. Mingus

(Rh./Atl.; Imp.; DIW; Enja); R.R. Kirk (Em.; Merc.); Dolphy; Booker Ervin (Prest.); Ran Blake (SN); Al Cohn–Zoot Sims (32); Ricky Ford (Cand.); A. Shepp (Den.); D. Ellis (NJ; Cand.).

BYAS, DON CARLOS WESLEY, tnr sax; b. Muskogee, OK, 10/21/12; d. Amsterdam, Netherlands, 8/24/72. Mother pl. pno., fath. cl. Start. on vln. and alto sax, pl. latter on first prof. jobs w. Bennie Moten, Terrence Holder, Walter Page's Blue Devils in late 1920s. Own gp., Don Carlos and His Collegian Ramblers, early '30s. Sw. to tnr. and moved to Calif., '33. Worked w. Lionel Hampton '35; Eddie Barefield, Buck Clayton '36, all in LA. To NYC w. Eddie Mallory '37. Short stays w. Don Redman, Lucky Millinder bef. pl. w. Andy Kirk '39–40. Worked w. Edgar Hayes, Benny Carter, then replaced Lester Young in Basie band '41–3. Prominent in 52nd St. clubs w. Coleman Hawkins, Dizzy Gillespie, and own combos '43–6. In fall of '46, he tour. Eur. w. Redman and remained there, living first in France, then, after several yrs., the Netherlands. He achieved great popularity in continental jazz circles, rec. and pl. w. local mus. as well as visiting Amers.: Duke Ellington '50; Quincy Jones; JATP '61. Ret. to US and app. at NJF '70; worked in NYC clubs such as the Vanguard and Club Baron. Tour. Japan w. A. Blakey '71, bef. ret. to the Netherlands, where he died of lung cancer. Stylistically, Byas was a member of the Hawkins sch., but had developed a personal style before he participated in and was infl. by the bebop movement. Won *Esq.* Silver Award '46. Fests: Berlin '65; NJF '70. TV: *Just Jazz*, PBS '71. Comps.: "Byas-a-Drink (Jamboree Jump)"; "Orgasm." First rec. w. Timme Rosenkrantz, "A Wee Bit of Swing," RCA '38. Feat. solo on "Harvard Blues" w. Basie '41. Also recs. w. Hot Lips Page and numerous dates as combo lead. for variety of small labels '44–5. CDs: Col.; Sav.; Class.; BL; two tracks in *American in Europe* (Imp.); duo w. Slam Stewart in *The Commodore Story* (Comm.); w. Basie; B. Holiday (Col.); C. Christian (Jazz Anth.); B. Clayton; R. Eldridge; J. Hodges; Mary Lou Williams (Vogue); A. Kirk (B&B); Louis Armstrong (RCA); C. Hawkins (Pab.); Key. Coll. (Em.); Gillespie (BB).

BYERS, BILLY (WILLIAM MITCHELL III), tbn, comp, arr; b. Los Angeles, CA, 5/1/27; d. Malibu, CA, 5/1/96. A prodigy who began on pno. at 6 and first pl. prof. at age 8 but was forced to give up pno. at 14 due to arthritis. As a tbnst. he pl w. the Hollywood Canteen Kids 1942–3; then freelanced w. movie studios. Spent a yr. at Harvard U. Army service '44–5. Wrote film mus. for three yrs. and then pl. w. Buddy Rich, Georgie Auld '49. To NYC w. Benny Goodman; then worked w. the bands of Charlie Ventura,

Teddy Powell '50. Replaced Johnny Mandel on staff at WMGM, NYC, as arr., cond., tbnst., pnst.; also wrote for Max Liebman's *Show of Shows* on TV. In Feb. '56, went to Paris to work w. producer Ray Ventura on recs., films. Ret. to NYC Nov. '57. Pl. tbn. w. Yves Montand one-man show; Johnny Richards orch. '59. To Eur. as assistant to Quincy Jones w. *Free and Easy* '59–60. Tbn. coach for Paul Newman on *Paris Blues* '61, bef. ret. to NYC, where he assisted Jones at Merc. Recs. into the mid '60s. Moved back to So. Calif.; wrote for Jones until '70. Other writing affiliations were w. Count Basie; Frank Sinatra, w. whom he tour. Japan and Eur. as a sideman '74; Duke Ellington; Sweets Edison; Tommy Dorsey; Sammy Davis; Billy Eckstine; Peggy Lee, etc. Extremely active as comp./arr. for films, TV, records, night club acts, and B'way musicals. Lived in Paris again '83–8. As comp./arr., won eight Emmys and orchestrated three Tony-awarded shows: *A Chorus Line*; *City of Angels*; and *Will Rogers' Follies*. Scored films: *The Pawnbroker* w. Jones; *The Sting* and *The Way We Were* w. Marvin Hamlisch. Favs: Earl Swope, Jack Jenney; arrs: Maurice Ravel, Robert Farnon, Thad Jones, Al Cohn, Johnny Mandel. Own LP, *Impressions of Duke Ellington*, Merc. '60s. CDs: w. Hal McKusick (Prest.); Joe Newman (BL).

BYRD, CHARLIE (CHARLES L.), gtr; b. Suffolk, VA, 9/16/25; d. Annapolis, MD, 12/1/99. Brother Joe is prof. bs.; bro. Jack is amateur jazz gtr. Began stud. at age 10 w. fath.. Pl. for hs dances, then stud. at Virginia Tech and pl. in army band. Met and pl. w. Django Reinhardt in Paris dur. WWII. Stud. theory, comp. at Hartnett Mus. Sch. in NYC. Pl. w. Sol Yaged 1947; Joe Marsala, Barbara Carroll '48; Freddie Slack, '49. Began pl. classical gtr. '50; recitals in DC area. Studied w. Sophocles Papas '50; Andres Segovia '54. Comp. mus. for Tennessee Williams play *The Purification*; also for Agriculture Dept. films, late '50s. Led gp. at own club, Showboat, in DC, '57–66. Pl. w. Woody Herman '59. Perf. on a State Dept. spons. tour of So. Amer. '61, then rec. the hit album *Jazz Samba* w. Stan Getz '62, which spawned the bossa nova craze of the mid '60s. Tour. Eur. w. Les McCann, Zoot Sims '60s. Formed Great Guitars w. Barney Kessel, Herb Ellis '73. Was partner in DC club, Charlie's Georgetown, '80–5. Rec. w. Washington Guitar Qt. in '90s. A master of many idioms, he app. w. Nat'l, Balt., Minn. symphs. and in more than 1,000 coll. concerts. Favs: Charlie Christian, Segovia. Fests: Eur. fr. '50s; So. Amer. fr. '61; numerous apps. in US, incl. NJF, MJF, Conc. Polls: *DB* New Star '59; *DB* Readers '63. TV: Steve Allen, etc. Book: *Charlie Byrd's Melodic Method for Guitar* '73. CDs: Conc.; Riv.; Mile.; w. Getz (Verve).

BYRD, DONALD (DONALDSON TOUSSAINT L'OUVERTURE II), tpt, flg, comp, educ; b. Detroit, MI, 12/9/32. Father a Methodist minister and mus. Stud. Cass Tech HS; Wayne St. U., B. Mus. 1954; Manh. Sch. of Mus., M.A., mus. ed.; w. Nadia Boulanger, Paris, '63; Ph.D. fr. Col. U. Sch. of Educ. '71; Col. U. Teach. Coll. '82 Pl. w. air force bands '51–3. While stationed in Newburgh, N.Y., pl. w. Thelonious Monk in NYC. Ret. to Det., working locally there until moving to NYC, pl. w. George Wallington at Café Bohemia, Aug. to Oct. '55. Join. A. Blakey's Jazz Messengers, Dec. '55. Worked w. Max Roach, summer '56; in '57 he was part of a gp. that gigged around NYC and rec. w. various members as lead.: Red Garland, John Coltrane, Arthur Taylor, or Lou Donaldson; Jazz Lab Qnt. w. Gigi Gryce. In early '58 at Five Spot, qnt. w. Pepper Adams, an assoc. which cont. into '61; also pl. w. Sonny Rollins, Coleman Hawkins, Lionel Hampton, Thelonious Monk, and own qnt. Pl. fests in Juan-Les-Pins; Recklinghausen; Stockholm; Molde; and in '65–6 was arr. for Norwegian Radio Orch. As an educ. he was instructor at Music & Art HS, NYC, and jazz clinics cond. by Nat'l Stage Band Camps. He cont. priv. stud. of the classics, Spanish mus., and many other forms. He taught at Rutgers, Hampton Inst., Howard U., leaving in '75, and, after earning a law degree, No. Caro. Central U. Also taught at Delaware St. in '90s. While Chairman of the Black Mus. Dept. at Howard U. in '73, he utilized some of his students in *Black Byrd*, a BN rec. that became a hit and established him as a pop-soul artist. Prod., but did not play on their Fant. LP, *The Blackbyrds*. Cont. to lecture on mus. and law, as it applies to the mus. business. Favs: Gillespie, Miles Davis, Clifford Brown. Films: in Germ.; France. CDs: BN; Del.; Land.; Sav.; Prest.; w. P. Adams; Kenny Drew; J. Griffin; J. Heath; Monk; Gigi Gryce (Riv.); G. Ammons; K. Burrell; J. Coltrane; A. Farmer; Garland; A. Taylor; Phil Woods (Prest.); Dexter Gordon; J. Henderson; H. Silver (BN); Kenny Clarke; Hank Jones (Sav.); Blakey (Col.); S. Rollins (BN; Mile.); J. McLean (BN; Prest.); Elmo Hope (Mile.); H. Mobley; George Wallington (Sav.; Prest.); Ahmad Jamal (Verve).

BYRD, JOE (GENE), bs; also gtr, fl; b. Chuckatuck, VA, 5/21/33. Brother is Charlie Byrd. Stud. at Peabody Cons., Balt., Md., then freelanced around Balt. Join. Charlie Byrd '64. Favs: Scott La Faro, Keter Betts. CDs: w. C. Byrd (Mile.; Conc.).

BYRNE, BILL (WILLIAM E. JR.), saxes, cl, fl; b. Stamford, CT, 4/26/42. Not to be confused w. Bill Byrne who pl. tpt. w., and was road manager for, Woody Herman fr. 1965 to mid '80s. Educ. at Oak-land HS and SF St. Coll. w. degree in mus. '65. Prof. jobs in Oakland-SF area until join. army '66, where he pl. w. in NORAD Commanders. After discharge, worked w. Harry James in US and Eur. Fr. late '70s freelanced in LA film, TV, and rec. studios. Pl. w. Buddy Rich band '75; Ray Charles '76–7, incl. tour in Africa. Also pl. w. orchs. of B. Berry; Louie Bellson; Terry Gibbs; Neal Hefti; Bob Florence; Bill Holman; Don Menza; Nelson Riddle; and w. Tony Bennett; Lena Horne; Mel Tormé; Sammy Davis Jr. Fr. '73–82 primarily assoc. w. Akiyoshi–Tabackin bb, tour. in Japan, Eur., US. App. in Akiyoshi docu. film, *Jazz Is My Native Language*. Fav: C. Parker. Fests: Belvedere, Can., w. Bellson and Supersax; Conc. w. Berry '74; Chuck Mangione '75. LP: w. Akiyoshi, *Roadgame* (RCA). CDs: w. Bellson (Pab.).

BYRNE, BOBBY (ROBERT), tbn; b. Columbus, OH, 10/10/18. Father was noted mus. teacher at Cass Tech. HS, Det. Studied harp, pno., picc., fl., tbn., cello, perc. Joined Dorsey Bros. at age 16; after the band split in 1935, he remained as tbn. soloist w. Jimmy Dorsey until late '39. Led own band '39–42; Don Redman was arr. in '41. In army '42–5. Led own band '46, then freelanced in NYC late '40s. Led Dixieland combo on Steve Allen TV show '53–4. Rec. as leader for Grand Award '53–4; as studio mus. w. Pearl Bailey, Cannonball Adderley, Cootie Williams, Charlie Barnet, Urbie Green, Lionel Hampton '52–60. Byrne ceased perf. in the late '60s and became an executive for the Command label. CDs: w. Dorsey Bros. (TOM); J. Dorsey (Dec.; ASV); Louis Armstrong (Dec.); C. Barnet (Evid.).

BYRON, DON, cl; b. NYC, 11/8/58. Father pl. bs. in a calypso band; moth. a pnst. Studied classical cl. in hs; att. New Engl. Cons.; pl. w. Greg Osby and was a member of the New Engl. Ragtime Ens. Fr. 1980, pl. in and led klezmer bands; since '85 pl. and rec. in NYC w. Hamiet Bluiett, Ralph Peterson, Reggie Workman, et al.; leads Semaphore, an ens. devoted to new classical mus. First rec. *Tuskegee Experiments*, released '91, which incl. Bill Frisell, Reggie Workman, et al. In '96, released *Bug Music*, w. re-creations of Ellington, John Kirby, and Raymond Scott small gp. recs. Gave children's concerts at Bklyn. Academy of Mus. '98. *DB* said of Byron, "He has the unerring ability to shift mindsets, to work deliberately and imaginatively within the dictates of any chosen idiom." CDs: None.; KFW; w. Bluiett; A. Braxton (BS); Steve Coleman (Novus); Frisell (None.); Craig Harris (JMT); M. Crispell (Leo); Gerry Hemingway (hatArt); David Murray (DIW); Peterson; Cassandra Wilson (BN); B. Previte (Enja); Workman (Leo; M&A).

C

CABLES, GEORGE ANDREW, pno, kybds, comp; b. Brooklyn, NY, 11/14/44. Studied w. moth., a teacher and amateur pnst.; also att. HS. of Perf. Arts 1958–62; Mannes Coll. of Mus. '63–5. At age 18, formed Jazz Samaritans w. Steve Grossman, Clint Houston, Billy Cobham. Arr. for East Harlem Protestant church choir '60s. Worked w. Art Blakey, Max Roach, late '60s; Sonny Rollins '69; Joe Henderson '69–71; Freddie Hubbard '71–6. Pl. pno. and el-pno. in own trio, Cable Car, in LA mid '70s. Pl. w. Gabor Szabo, Bobby Hutcherson mid to late '70s; also w. Woody Shaw; Billy Harper. Worked w. Dexter Gordon at Keystone Korner in SF, Dec. '76, remain. w. Gordon until '78. Rejoin. Blakey in '77 and began an assoc. w. Art Pepper that lasted until the saxist's death in '82. Fr. '80s w. own trio; also w. Bebop and Beyond '84; in NYC mid '90s, w. Pete La Roca Sims' Swingtime; Joe Chambers; others. Cables' comps. have been rec. by Woody Shaw, Woody Herman, Freddie Hubbard, Bobby Hutcherson. Among the best are "Morning Song" and "Helen's Song." Favs: Wynton Kelly, Buddy Montgomery, Hancock, Tyner. Fests: all major. CDs: Cont.; DIW; Steep.; Conc.; w. Bebop and Beyond (BM); D. Gordon (Col.; Steep.); Hubbard (CTI); S. Rollins; J. Henderson (Mile.); Hutcherson (Timel.; Land.); F. Morgan (Cont.; Ant.); Pepper (Gal.; Cont.); Joe Farrell (Cont.); W. Shaw; H. Land (Muse); S. Rogers; B. Forman (Conc.); M. Roach; J. Stubblefield (Enja); C. Rouse (Land.); P. Sims (BN).

CACERES, ERNIE (ERNESTO), cl, bari sax; b. Rockport, TX, 11/22/11; d. San Antonio, TX, 1/10/71. Brothers Emilio and Pinero pl. vln. and tpt.-pno. respectively. Stud. w. Profess. Bolanos; cl. first, then gtr., which he also pl. in last yrs., saxes. Local bands fr. 1928; trio w. bros. early '30s; Emilio's band in Det. and NYC. With Emilio's trio on Benny Goodman's *Camel Caravan* radio show '37. Worked w. Bobby Hackett '38–9, '44–5; J. Teagarden '39–40; Bob Zurke '40; Glenn Miller '40–2; Johnny Long '42; T. Dorsey '43; B. Goodman '43–4; W. Herman '44; Billy Butterfield '44–5; band in army '45. Fr. '42 to '48, app. w. many trad. gps., incl. E. Condon, at Nick's and other NYC clubs. Own qt. '49; daily TV series w. Garry Moore '50–6; w. Hackett sxt. at Henry Hudson Hotel and fests. '56–7; Butterfield in Va. '60–2, bef. settling in San Antonio. Occ. app. w. Jim Cullum; frequent apps. in '60s at Colo. JP. Film apps. w. Miller. Recs. w. Emilio Caceres; Muggsy Spanier; Jimmy McPartland. CDs: w. Miller; Met. All-Stars; Armstrong; Teagarden (BB); Bechet (Laser.); Condon (Dec.; Stash; Jazz.); R. Eldridge (Dec.); B. Hackett (Dormouse Int'l); Goodman (Col.).

CAIN, JACKIE (JACQUELINE RUTH), voc; b. Milwaukee, WI, 5/22/28. Studied w. Don Maya in Chi. 1947–8. Sang w. hs. gps., mid '40s. First prof. job in Jay Burkhart Orch. w. Lou Levy, Jimmy Gourley, Lee Konitz '47–8. Met Roy Kral '47. Began working on voice-horn concept w. Kral in George Davis gp. after hearing Buddy Stewart and Dave Lambert. Perf. w. Kral for Dave Garroway '48. Feat. prominently w. Charlie Ventura '48–9. Married Kral '49. Led sxt. w. Kral incl. cello and gtr. '49, then trios, qts. Cain and Kral had own TV show in Chi. ca. '51–2. The duo sang w. Ventura again in '53, then worked as Jackie & Roy in nightclubs, concerts, and fests fr. '53. Cain has written lyrics to many of her husband's comps. The duo has received six Grammy nominations. In addition to her fine blending in the vocal duo, Cain is a fine solo voc., especially effective on ballads. Favs: Carmen McRae, Shirley Horn, Sarah Vaughan. Polls: *DB*, *Play*. Fests: Eur., Japan, Australia. TV: *Tonight Show*, Merv Griffin, Mike Douglas, *Kraft Music Hall*, Smothers Bros., Dinah Shore, Ernie Ford. CDs: Jackie & Roy: Sav.; Aud.; Fant.; Disc.; DRG; BL; Red Brn.; w. Ventura (Dec.; GNP Cres.).

CAIN, MICHAEL, pno, comp; b. Los Angeles, CA, 4/2/66. Grew up in Las Vegas. Began on pno. at age 4. Stud. classical but showed early interest in improvisation. By age 10 was into a style that encompassed both musics, centered in jazz. Heard recs. of Herbie Hancock, Keith Jarrett. At 14 began working prof. in LV area. At 17 stud. jazz and classical at No. Tex. St. U.; classical research at USC 1985; grad. stud., incl. mus. of Ghana, Bali, India, at Calif. Inst. of the Arts '87–90; received M.F.A. Perf. w. Marlena Shaw; Gerald Wilson; Billy Higgins; New American Orch. Rec. and tour. w. James Newton qt., incl. Eur., '89. Also pl. in separate duos w. Ralph Alessi; Peter Epstein. Moved to NYC '90, pl. w. members of M-Base incl. Greg Osby; Robin Eubanks; Lonnie Plaxico. Rec. as leader for Candid. join. Jack DeJohnette's Special Edition. Worked extens. w. Anthony Cox qt. '90–2 Also tour. and/or rec. w. Dave Holland; Steve Swallow; John Scofield; Steps Ahead; Ray Anderson; Bobby Previte. Fr. '95 to '97 taught at Eastman Sch., Rochester, N.Y., directing small ens. and holding classes in improv., contemp. comp. techniques, history, analysis, and pno. Taught at New Engl. Cons. fr. fall '97. Improv. inspired by everything fr. Beethoven string qts. to pop musician and songwriters. Grant fr. NARAS '88; commission fr. Howard Hanson Inst. for comp. premiered at Presidential Inaugural Gala '97. Fests: MJF, Chi., North Sea w. G. Wilson '90; w. DeJohnette, Mt. Fuji '91; North Sea and other Eur. fests. Favs: Hancock, Jarrett, Art Lande. CDs: Cand.; ECM; MA (Japan); w. DeJohnette (BN; ECM); Ryan Kisor (Col.); Marty Ehrlich (Enja); Steps Ahead (NYC); Robin Eubanks (JMT); Ravi Coltrane (BMG).

CAINE, URI, pno, comp; b. Philadelphia, PA, 6/8/56. Cousin, Alan Marks, was classical pnst. and infl. on him. Began on pno. at age 7. At 13 met Bernard Peiffer and took lessons fr. him. At 16 stud. comp. w. George Rochberg; George Crumb. While in hs pl. w. Bootsie Barnes; also Philly Joe Jones; Hank Mobley; Johnny Coles; Mickey Roker; Bobby Durham; Jymie Merritt; Odean Pope. Stud. at U. of Pa. From 1981 gigged in Phila. and NYC, working w.

Freddie Hubbard; Clark Terry; Benny Golson; Eddie Vinson; Bobby Watson; Gary Thomas; Wallace Roney; Rashied Ali; Steve Grossman; Phil Woods; Max Roach. Rec. debut w. Cornell Rochester–Gerald Veasley, Gramavision '85. Moved to NYC '87, pl. w. Anthony Cox; Smitty Smith; Ralph Peterson; Bob Moses; Tom Harrell; Buddy DeFranco–Terry Gibbs. In early '90s pl. w. Sam Rivers–Barry Altschul; w. Don Byron fr. '90; Dave Douglas fr. '95. Recs. w. own trio. Favs: Miles Davis, Herbie Hancock, Coltrane; arrs: Stravinsky, Frank Zappa, Ellington, Gil Evans. Awards: Pennsylvania Council on the Arts Grant for Musical Comps. '83; runner-up in Great American Jazz Piano Competition '92; grants to write music for the Uptown String Qt.; his homage to Gustav Mahler for the Winter & Winter label won the Composer's Hut Award, Dobbiaco, Italy (formerly Toblach), as Best Mahler rec. of '97. CDs: W&W; JMT; w. Enja Band, *Live at Sweet Basil* (Enja); Byron (KFW; None.; BN); Douglas (NW; Arab.); John Zorn (Tzadik).

CALABRESE, BUCKY (FREDERICK PHILIP), bs; b. Hicksville, NY, 8/6/27; d. Bronx, NY, 6/5/95. Began on pno. at age 10; sw. to bs. at age 24. Stud. at Hartnett Sch. of Mus. under G.I. Bill 1951, then w. Charles Mingus and Clyde Lombardi. Pl. first prof. gigs as sub. for Lombardi. Pl. w. Ray Eberle, Dizzy Gillespie '57; Sal Salvador '58; Kai Winding '59; Stan Kenton '62. Worked w. traditional jazz gps., incl. Edmond Hall '63; E. Condon '64; Max Kaminsky '65. With Teddy Wilson Duo '68; Dave McKenna Duo and Trio '73–4; also pl. for singers, incl. Tony Bennett, Sammy Davis, Diahann Carroll, Matt Dennis. Pl. in '70s and '80s w. Roy Eldridge, Max Kaminsky at Jimmy Ryan's and Metropole; Al Cohn–Zoot Sims at Half Note. With Doc Cheatham at Sweet Basil fr. '87. Favs: O. Pettiford, Ray Brown. Fests: Nice '91 w. Cheatham. TV: *Today* w. M. Dennis '68, Helen O'Connell '69. CDs: w. Kenton (Cap.).

CALDERAZZO, JOEY, pno; b. New Rochelle, NY, 2/27/65. Started pno. at age 8; stud. w. a teacher fr. Juilliard; later w. Richie Beirach. By mid '80s, he replaced Kenny Kirkland in Michael Brecker gp. First solo rec., *In the Door*, for BN '91. CDs: BN; w. Bob Belden; Jerry Bergonzi; Rick Margitza (BN); Michael Brecker (Imp.); Bob Mintzer (Novus); Dave Stryker (Steep.).

CALDWELL, GEORGE O., pno, kybds; b. Clarksdale, MS, 10/19/50. Father pl. tpt.; two bros., sax; sist., pno. Studied classical pno. fr. age 7, first w. priv. teacher, then at Memphis St. U. and Oberlin Cons. Pl.

in theater pit bands at Memphis St., while stud. jazz w. Robert Garner. First prof. jazz gig w. Bill Easley 1975. Pl. w. Sam Green in Oberlin, Ohio, '76–7; Herman Green's Green Machine in Memphis, Tenn., '77–80. Founding member of Midtown Jazzmobile in Memphis '78. Pl. in Memphis w. Louis Smith '81; Geo. Coleman '83; Phineas Newborn '84. Pl. w. Clifford Jordan and Bunky Green in Jackson, Miss. '84. Moved to NYC '85. Pl. w. Panama Francis's Savoy Sultans '85–6; Duke Ellington Orch. '86–7; Count Basie Orch. fr. '89. Caldwell taught at Oberlin '76–77 and priv. in Memphis '79–84. While in Memphis, he developed a course on jazz and blues for public sch. children and was given the W.C. Handy Award. Favs: Phineas Newborn, Donald Brown, Mulgrew Miller. Fests: all major fr. '86. CDs: w. Basie Orch. (Tel.); Carmen Bradford (Amazing).

CALDWELL, HAPPY (ALBERT W.), tnr sax, cl, fl; b. Chicago, IL, 7/25/03; d. NYC, 12/29/78. Started pl. cl. in 1919, studied w. cousin, Buster Bailey. Worked w. Bernie Young's Creole Jazz Band '22–3. After tour. w. Mamie Smith's Jazz Hounds '23, he moved to NYC, and pl. tnr. w. many bands, incl. Elmer Snowden '25; Willie Gant '26; w. Cliff Jackson in revue *Keep Shufflin'* '27; Arthur Gibbs '27–8; Fletcher Henderson, Vernon Andrade '29–33; Tiny Bradshaw, Louis Metcalf '35; also Fats Waller, Hot Lips Page in '30s. Led own gp., the Happy Pals, in Phila. '41–4, and in NYC '41, '45. Led band at Smalls' Paradise '50–3. With Metcalf at Metropole Café, NYC '56 and other gigs through '60; also apps. w. Jimmy Rushing. A Mason, he led a dance band at many of their affairs and was a master of one of their Eastern Star chapter lodges. In '70s, he worked in maintenance at City Coll., NYC, but cont. to gig as a member of The New Amsterdam Mus. Assoc., NYC's oldest African-American mus. org. App. w. own gp. as honoree at Overseas Jazz Club concert '75. Pl. and participated in seminars in Sweden and Den. '75. Active in entertaining senior citizens. Infl. by early Coleman Hawkins style. Rec. "Knocking a Jug" w. Louis Armstrong, Eddie Condon '29; Bubber Miley '30; Billy Banks '32; Red Allen '36; Mezz Mezzrow '37; Jelly Roll Morton '39; Clyde Bernhardt '72–3. CDs: w. Armstrong (Col.); Bechet; Morton; Muggsy Spanier; J. Teagarden (BB); w. Gene Gifford in *Swing Is Here* (BB).

CALHOUN, EDDIE, bs; b. Clarksdale, MS, 11/13/21; d. Paradise Lake, MI, 1/28/94. Grew up in Chi.; self-taught, he made prof. debut w. Prince Cooper in mid 1940s, after army service. Pl. w. Dick Davis '47–9; Ahmad Jamal '49–52; Horace Henderson '52–4; Johnny Griffin '54. Freelanced w. Roy

Eldridge, Billie Holiday, Miles Davis '54–5. Calhoun is best known for his assoc. w. Erroll Garner '55–66. Ret. to Chi. '67. Pl. w. pnst.-singer Norvel Reed '67–8. Operated nightclub, Cal's Place, '72–4. Led own sxt. at Fantasy Club, Chi. '75–80, then pl. w. pnst. Lennie Capp '80–6. Tour. Eur. w. Erwin Helfer's Chi. All-Stars, '86. Cont. to tour in '90s. Favs: Wilbur Ware, Red Callender. Fests: all major w. Garner. TV: many apps. w. Garner. Recs. w. A. Jamal; *Concert By the Sea* w. Garner. CDs: w. Garner (Col.).

CALIMAN, HADLEY, tnr sax; also fl, bs-cl, sop sax; b. Idabel, OK, 1/12/32. Began on cl. at age 14, then sw. to alto and tnr. sax in hs. Tour. w. prof. bands at age 16. Pl. w. Roy Porter bb 1949–51. Stud. at Pomona St. Coll. and SF Cons., early '50s. Remaining in Calif., he led his own gp. and pl. w. Gerald Wilson '67; Don Ellis, Johnny Almond '69; Luis Gasca '71; Hampton Hawes '73; Azar Lawrence '74; Eddie Henderson, Jon Hendricks '75; Bobby Hutcherson '76–7; Freddie Hubbard '79. Also freelanced w. Bobby Bryant, Mongo Santamaria, Willie Bobo, Big Black '60s-'70s. In the '80s, Caliman pl. in a qnt. w. tpt. Nathan Breedlove. Favs: Lester Young, Dexter Gordon, John Coltrane, Joe Henderson. Poll: *DB* TDWR. Fests: Conc., Berkeley. Recs. w. Wilson, Lawrence, Almond, Hawes. LPs: Main., Catalyst. CDs: w. Jessica Williams (JF).

CALLENDER, RED (GEORGE), bs, tba, comp; b. Haynesville, VA, 3/6/16; d. Saugus, CA, 3/8/92. Raised in Atlantic City, N.J.; stud. alto horn, then tba., bs. To NYC 1932; bs. w. bands in Cleveland and Columbus, Ohio, '34–5; to LA '36. Pl. w. Buck Clayton band; first two comp. rec. by Lionel Hampton '37; first rec. date w. Louis Armstrong '37; gave bs. lessons to Charles Mingus '37. Sidelined in movies and rec. w. Nat Cole '38–9; member of Lee and Lester Young band in LA and NYC '40–43; tour., rec. w. own gps. '44–6; seen w. Armstrong in '46 film, *New Orleans*; joined Erroll Garner Trio, rec. w. Charlie Parker, Dexter Gordon, Benny Goodman; toured Hawaii, pl. w. Honolulu Symph. and led own trio in Honolulu '47–50. Dur. '50s and '60s, he was increasingly active in Hollywood studios—the first African-Amer. on staff at NBC in Calif. '64. Pl. w. Stan Kenton's LA Neophonic Orch. '65. His '58 album, *Callender Speaks Low*, was the first to feature tba. as a solo jazz vehicle. Perf. w. Mingus at MJF '64; rec. many film scores w. D. Gillespie, Lalo Schifrin. Att. first World Tba. Symposium '73; tour. Eur. w. Legends of Jazz (Louis Armstrong Memorial Tour) '78, '79. Founded the Wind College w. John Carter, Charles Owens, and James Newton in LA '80s. Remained active, teaching, comp. and perf. until

New Yr.'s Eve, '91, w. Jeannie & Jimmy Cheatham. A highly respected artist on both bs. and tba. Comps: "Pastel"; "Red Light"; "Primrose Lane." Book: autobiography, *Unfinished Dream*, w. Elaine Cohen (Quartet) '85. LPs: Metrojazz; Crown. CDs: w. Armstrong (RCA; Dec.); C. Parker; D. Gordon (Stash); L. Young; Garner; Jacquet; Tormé; Holiday (Verve); Tatum (Pab.); Benny Carter; Red Norvo (BB); Wardell Gray; A. Previn (BL); Newton (Gram.); A. Pepper (PJ); Buddy Collette (Spec.); Dick Hyman (Mile.); John Carter (BS); Cheathams (Conc.); Mingus (Rhino/Atl.); Satchmo Legacy Band (SN).

CALLOWAY, BLANCHE, voc, lead; b. Baltimore, MD, 1902; d. Baltimore, 12/16/78. Sister of Cab Calloway. Began singing in Balt. clubs early 1920s, then to NYC, working as single at Ciro Club, mid 20s. Tour. w. revues bef. moving to Chi. where she rec. w. Louis Armstrong '25; Reuben Reeves '29. App. w. Andy Kirk's orch. at the Pearl Theater in Phila. '31. Hiring some of Kirk's sidemen, she form. an orch. w. which she tour. until '38, when it went bankrupt. Sidemen incl. Vic Dickenson, Ben Webster, Clyde Hart, and Edgar Battle, the latter also serving as arr. Briefly led band again in '40; then worked as single for a few yrs. Dir. a Fla. radio station in early '60s. LPs: w. Reeves (Retrieval); Cab Calloway (French RCA). CD: w. Louis Armstrong (Aff.).

CALLOWAY, CAB (CABELL), voc, lead; b. Rochester, NY, 12/25/07; d. Hockessin, DE, 11/18/94. Brother of Blanche; fath. of Chris. Raised in Balt., Md., where he occasionally sang with the Balt. Melody Boys. Moved with family to Chi. and back to Balt.; then in mid 1920s he returned to Chi. to att. Crane Coll. and app. in *Plantation Days,* at the Loop Theater, w. Blanche, who helped him get the job. In '28, after tour. Midwest with the show, he start. working as a substitute dmr. and emcee at the Sunset Café. in Chi. In '29, he took over leadership of the Alabamians and brought them to NYC, pl. at the Savoy. While in NYC, he was featured in the revue *Hot Chocolates*; simultaneously working regularly w. the Missourians, which soon became Cab Calloway and His Orch. Fr. Feb. '31 to Jan. '32, it was the house band at the Cotton Club, replacing Duke Ellington. In '31, Calloway rec. "Minnie the Moocher," a hit that brought him national attention as the "Hi-De-Ho Man." Though sometimes discounted by critics as a jazz perf., Calloway became one of the most successful leaders of the '30s and '40s and helped further the careers of the outstanding jazz musicians who made up his band, incl. Ben Webster, Chu Berry, Eddie Barefield, Cozy Cole, Milt Hinton, Jonah Jones, and Dizzy Gillespie. Berry was featured

in the Cab Jivers, a small gp. within the band. The orch. tour. Eur. in '34, and, fr. the late '30s to early '40s, the US and Can. Dur. this period, the band rec. frequently and app. in several films, incl. the classic *Stormy Weather* '43. A flamboyant dresser w. flashy movements, Calloway's vocals were a comedic blend of cantorial Hebrew style, jive expressions, and pliant scat. As dynamic as he was on rhythm numbers, he could also deliver a ballad with convincing drama. He disbanded his orch. in '48, forming a sxt., The Cabaliers, perf. w. it and other small gps. until '51, when he re-formed the bb for a Eur. tour and maintained it for most of that yr. Fr. '52 on, he worked mostly in musical theater and night clubs, rather than in jazz venues. George Gershwin originally modeled the *Porgy and Bess* character Sportin' Life after Calloway, and he finally assumed the role in a NYC revival that ran fr. June '52 to Aug. '54, then tour. Eur. and the US. Resumed night club work in mid '50s, mostly as a single, though in the late '50s he occasionally led bbs formed for him by Eddie Barefield for special events and short residencies in NYC, LV, and other cities. In the mid '60s he was featured in the Harlem Globetrotters touring show. In '67, he starred w. Pearl Bailey in a B'way revival of *Hello Dolly*. At the height of the disco fad, he rec. a disco version of "Minnie the Moocher" for RCA Victor. In the '70s and '80s, he resumed perf. and tour. int'l as a single, often backed by a bb. In the '80s he app. on TV and in the film *The Blues Brothers*; in '87, he tour. w. *His Royal Highness of Hi-de-ho*, a show that celebrated his 80th birthday and featured his vocalist daughter, Chris. In June '94, a severe stroke left him incapacitated. He died in a Delaware nursing home five mos. later. Fests: NJF-NY; Umbria Jazz '87; Birmingham, Engl. '89. Films: *The Singing Kid* w. Al Jolson '36; *Big Broadcast of '32*; *Sensations of 1945*; *St. Louis Blues*. Stage: *Pajama Game* w. Barbara McNair; national companies of *Eubie*; *Bubblin' Brown Sugar*. Books: *Hepster's Dictionary* '38; *Of Minnie the Moocher and Me* '76. His private record collection was donated to Bost. U. '76. CDs: Col.; Class.; JSP; ASV; w. Don Redman (Class.).

CAMERON, CLAYTON, dms; b. Los Angeles, CA 2/27/59. At 16, he pl. w. schoolmate Billy Childs, then began rehearsing w. Grant's Music Center Band, which accomp. Ernie Andrews, Jimmy Witherspoon, and others. Living in LV 1982–83, he worked w. Kirk Stuart Trio; pl. w. Joe Williams; rec. w. Gerald Wilson Orch., then joined Sammy Davis Jr. fr. July '83 until his death in '90. In '90–91, tour. w. George Shearing, Joe Williams, and Joe Pass. Prod. instructional video, *The Living Art of Brushes*, widely accepted among mus. educs. "He takes brushes into the 21st century," said Ed Thigpen. Favs: Tony Williams, Jo Jones, Elvin Jones, Roach, Bellson. CDs: w. B. Childs (WH); James Leary; Todd Cochran (Vital); John Quintero (Nova).

CAMERON, JAY, bari. sax, saxes, cl, bs-cl, fl; b. NYC, 9/14/28; d. San Diego, CA, 3/20/01. Began on alto sax. Studied in Hollywood w. Mickey Gillette 1944–7. Freelanced in LA in '40s; pl. w. Bobby Sherwood, Ike Carpenter. Rec. w. Bill Coleman in Paris '49. Worked w. Rex Stewart in France and Italy '49–50. Ret. to US '51; rehearsed on alto w. Gerry Mulligan in Central Park. To Eur. in late '51; pl. w. gp. co-led by Kenny Clarke, James Moody, and Hubert Fol. Tour. Scand. w. Boyd Bachman '53, then pl. in Antwerp and Brussels w. Bobby Jaspar, Rene Thomas '54–5. With Fats Sadi Orch. at Rose Rouge, Paris, spring '55; w. Henri Renaud, Jul.-Nov. '55. Ret. to US; w. Woody Herman Jan.-Jul. '56, then briefly w. Chet Baker, Dizzy Gillespie. Pl. w. Maynard Ferguson, Nov. '57–Nov. '58. Freelanced in NYC '59, then pl. w. Slide Hampton '60–2; Paul Winter '63. Led own gp. w. Jimmy Owens, Dusko Gojkovic. Moved to Poconos '65; pl. w. Bob Dorough and owned mus. store '65–72, then operated various nightclubs. Moved to LV late '74; pl. w. show bands, some jazz gigs '74–96. Tour. Belgium and France '92. Taught jazz to hs students in LV '95–6. Reunited w. Dorough at Poconos JF, Sept. '96. Moved to San Diego '97. Favs: Cecil Payne, Lars Gullin, Pepper Adams. Poll: *DB* TDWR bari. sax '63. LPs: w. S. Hampton (Atl.; Epic); Winter (Col.); Herman (Cap.); A. Hodeir (Sav.). CDs: w. Ferguson (Roul.).

CAMILO, MICHAEL, pno, comp, arr; b. Santo Domingo, Dominican Republic, 4/4/54. Uncles, aunt, sist. are comp. or mus. Began on acdn. at age 4. Stud. pno. at Nat'l Cons. of D.R. from age 9. Camilo decided to bec. a jazz mus. at 15, after hearing an Art Tatum rec. of "Tea for Two." Moved to NYC in the late 1970s; stud. cond., comp., and arr. at Juilliard and Mannes Coll. of Mus. Pl. w. French Toast '80–4; Paquito D'Rivera '82–6; own gps. since '85. Feat. w. Danish Radio bb '89–91. In '91, Camilo participated in tour w. French classical pnsts. Katia and Marielle Labeque, perf. a program of jazz and classical pieces. He has comp. extensively for films and TV, and comp. and cond. many classical works. Camilo's comps. have earned him an Emmy and a Grammy, and he was named one of the "Top Three Jazz Artists of the Year" by *Billboard* in '89 and '90. Favs: Tatum, Peterson, Tyner, Hancock, Bill Evans. Fests: Eur. every yr. since '86; also in Caribbean and Japan '90–1; Cuba '98. TV: PBS, *An Evening with Michel Camilo*; *JVC-Newport JF '91*. CDs: Trop.; Col.; Pro-

Jazz; w. P. D'Rivera (Col.); French Toast (King); B. Lagrene (BN); G. Niewood (DMP).

CAMPBELL, JIMMY (JAMES L.), dms; b. Wilkes-Barre, PA, 12/24/28. Self-taught; began pl. in army in 1947. In '50s, he worked w. Ralph Flanagan, Don Elliott, Claude Thornhill, Maynard Ferguson; Woody Herman '57–9, incl. State Dept. tours of So. Amer. '58, and Eur.-Saudi Arabia '59. Join. Stan Kenton, '59. With Herman again '60–2. In '60s, he pl. in B'way shows. Moved to LV '67, pl. there w. Joe Williams, Julie London, others. Pl. w. George Rock Dixieland Band in San Diego, Calif., '73. Illness curtailed his career that yr. but he ret. to freelancing in LV '83. Favs: Tough, Blakey, Lamond, Roach. Fav. own solo: "Big Chase" on *Roadshow* album w. Kenton. CDs: w. Ferguson (BB); Kenton (Cap.); Phil Woods (FS).

CAMPBELL, JOHN ELWOOD II, pno, vib, org, dms, bs; b. Bloomington, IL, 7/7/55. Many amateur mus. in family. Stud. pno. fr. age 7, then studied perc. and pl. bs. in jazz band at Ill. St. U. Pl. w. hs. band dir., Bill Jacoby, at Bloomington Holiday Inn, early 1970s. Moved to Chi. '76, pl. w. Joe Daley; Bunky Green; Art Hoyle; Jazz Members bb; Ross Traut; own qt. '79–84; also backed visiting soloists, incl. Eddie Harris; Eddie Jefferson; Dave Liebman; Red Rodney. Moved to NYC '84. Pl. w. Stan Getz '84; Clark Terry since '84; Mel Tormé '86–90; also worked w. Ruby Braff; Buddy DeFranco; Terry Gibbs; Scott Hamilton; Milt Jackson; Red Mitchell. Campbell taught pno. at DePaul U. in Chi. '83–4. Favs: Garner, Peterson, Bill Evans. Fests: Japan '79–80, '90; Eur. '81, '90. TV: PBS *Newport '84* w. Getz; *In Performance at the White House* w. Tormé '87. CDs: Cont.; Conc.; w. C. Terry (Chiar.; Delos); Gibbs–DeFranco (Cont.).

CAMPBELL, TOMMY (THOMAS W.), dms; b. Norristown, PA, 2/14/57. Organist Jimmy Smith is a distant uncle and godfath. Raised in Willow Grove, a suburb of Phila. Inspired to pl. dms. after seeing Buddy Rich on TV. Studied at Berklee Coll. of Mus., late 1970s. Early gigs w. Jimmy Smith, Dizzy Gillespie, Curtis Warner. With Gillespie for over two yrs. in '80s, then tour. and rec. w. John McLaughlin, and tour. w. Manhattan Transfer. In '90s, he worked w. Sonny Rollins; Igor Butman. Fests: all major w. Gillespie, McLaughlin, Rollins. TV: *Tonight Show*; *Good Morning America*. CDs: w. Kevin Eubanks (Col.; GRP); Robin Eubanks (JMT); McLaughlin (WB); Rollins (Mile.); C. Freeman; Roots (In+Out).

CAMPISE, TONY (ANTHONY S.), tnr, alto saxes, fl, bs fl, picc, oboe; b. Houston, TX, 1/22/43. Studied alto sax, cl. w. Hal Tennyson 1956–62; improv. w. Jerry Coker in Houston and Calif. '61–3, and briefly w. Lee Konitz; fl. w. Byron Hester '63–71; oboe w. Barbara Hester '67–9. Att. mus. sch. at Sam Houston U.; U. of Houston; Houston Baptist Coll.; and Monterey Peninsula Coll. Pl. in Houston w. Don Cannon '62–5; Paul Schmitt '67–71; Young Audience Jazz Ens. '69–75; Gulf Coast Giants of Jazz '70–3. Three seasons of musicals at Houston Music Theatre '72–4. Lead alto and fl. w. S. Kenton '74. Favs: C. Parker, J. Coltrane, Konitz, Tristano, Dolphy. CDs: Heart; w. Kenton (CW).

CANDIDO (Candido Camero De Guerra), bgo, cga, perc.; b. Regal, Havana, Cuba, 4/22/21. Self-taught. Began on bs., gtr., then sw. to bongos at age 14. Pl. in Havana w. Machito, CMQ radio orch. 1940s; Armando Romeu at Tropicana Club '47–52. Came to US '52. Pl. in *Night In Havana* show at Clover Club, Miami, for six mos; then moved to NYC. Met Dizzy Gillespie, who introduced him to Billy Taylor. Pl. w. Taylor at Le Downbeat club '53–4; Stan Kenton Orch. '54. Busy as freelancer in NYC '56–7, then pl. w. Gillespie gp. '58; JATP w. Gillespie, Stan Getz '60; Tony Bennett at Carnegie Hall '62. Rec. in '50s-'60s w. Kenton; Gillespie; Erroll Garner; G. Shearing; Bennie Green; Art Blakey; Gene Ammons; Duke Ellington; Kenny Burrell; Sonny Rollins; Wynton Kelly; Wes Montgomery; Elvin Jones; Illinois Jacquet; Dinah Washington; Tito Puente; Machito, many others. Tour. w. own Latin jazz combo fr. '50s; sidemen incl. Al Cohn, Phil Woods. Candido has worked mainly as a studio mus. fr. the mid '80s, but has surfaced on jazz scene in the '90s w. C. O'Farrill, Randy Weston, others. Fests: all major fr. '54. TV: Mike Wallace '62; also apps. w. T. Bennett, Lionel Hampton. LPs: ABC-Paramount. CDs: w. W. Montgomery; S. Getz; Gillespie (Verve); S. Rollins (BB); B. Rich (RCA); B. Green; G. Ammons; B. Taylor (Prest.); w. Garner (Merc.); Ellington (Col.); C. Parker (Stash).

CANDOLI, CONTE (SECONDO), tpt, flg; b. Mishawaka, IN, 7/12/27; d. Palm Desert, CA, 12/14/01. Studied tpt. w. bro., Pete Candoli, in 1940. Pl w. gps. in South Bend, Ind. Join. Woody Herman at age 16, dur. hs vacation. Then pl. w. Herman, Jan.-Sept. '45, rec. solo on "Put That Ring on My Finger." Army service '45–6. Tour. in Scand. w. Chubby Jackson sxt., winter '47–8. Pl. w. S. Kenton '48, '52–3; C. Ventura '49; Herman '50; C. Barnet '51. Led own gp. in Chi. '54, then moved to LA and join. Howard Rumsey's Lighthouse All-Stars to '60. Took part in '92 reunion. Freelanced extensively w. Terry Gibbs '60–2; Gerry Mulligan '60–1, incl. Eur. tour; Shelly

Manne '61–72; Kenton's Neophonic Orch. '65–9. Fr. '68 pl. w. Doc Severinsen's *Tonight Show* orch. dur. its West Coast visits and became a permanent member when the show moved to LA in '72. Also pl. for Flip Wilson TV show '70–4. App. w. Supersax on and off fr. '72; acted as clinician at midwest colls.; pl. w. Bill Berry band; and co-led Candoli Bros. w. Pete. Tour. in Eur. w. Frank Rosolino '75. Won LA Jazz Society award '90. A highly respected teacher and perf., he based his style on Gillespie in the mid '40s, adding Miles Davis and Clifford Brown infls. in the '50s. Fests: MJF w. Herman, '60; Candoli Bros. '73; Concord w. Berry '74; IJF w. P. Candoli '94, '96. Film: *Bell, Book and Candle* '58. Other TV orchs: Donn Trenner on Steve Allen show '63–4; Elliot Lawrence on Les Crane show '65. CDs: FS, BR; w. Kenton (Mos.; Cap.); T. Gibbs; Lighthouse All-Stars; S. Manne; Bob Cooper; Art Pepper (Cont.); Sonny Criss (Prest.); S. Getz (Verve); S. Rogers (BB; Cand.); L. Bellson (Conc.; Pab.; Limel.); F. Capp; Gene Harris (Conc.); C. Ventura (Dec.); G. Mulligan (Verve; RTE); R. Kamuca (HiFi); L. Gullin (Drag.); W. Herman; Monk (Col.).

CANDOLI, PETE (WALTER JOSEPH PRIMO), tpt, flg, arr; b. Mishawaka, IN, 6/28/23. Brother of Conte Candoli. Took up bs. first, then Fr. horn at 12. As tptr. pl. w. Sonny Dunham 1940–1; Will Bradley '41–2; Ray McKinley '42; T. Dorsey '43–4; Teddy Powell '44. Earned nickname, "Superman," as powerhouse, high-note perf. w. Woody Herman '44–6. Worked w. Boyd Raeburn '47; Tex Beneke '47–9. Moved to LA, pl. w. Jerry Gray '50–1; Les Brown; S. Kenton. Rec. w. M. Legrand; Quincy Jones; Henry Mancini; Igor Stravinsky. Also active w. coll. mus. seminars. Soundtracks for many films, incl. *Private Hell 36* '54; *Man With the Golden Arm* 55; *Prisoner of Second Avenue* '75; *Save the Tiger* '73. Co-led gps w. bro. Conte '57–62. In '72 sang, danced, pl., and cond. orch. w. his (then) wife, singer Edie Adams. Pl. w. and arr. for L. Hampton's Golden Men of Jazz '95, '96. Though he has more of a studio image than his bro., he is a gifted leadman and soloist. Orig. infl. by tptrs. of the Swing Era, he incorporated elements of Gillespie into his style in the mid '40s. Fests: w. Conte Candoli, MJF '73; IJF, '94, '96; w. L. Hampton, Aurex (Japan) '81; Woody Herman tribute, JVC-NY '96. Film: *Bell, Book and Candle* '58 (also issued on Dot LP). TV: member of bands on Merv Griffin show; *Tonight Show* band. CDs: w. Herman (Col.; BB); T. Dorsey (Hep; Jass); B. Cooper; A. Pepper (Cont.); Benny Carter (BB); M. Paich (Cand.).

CANNON, GERALD LEON, bs; b. Racine, WI, 3/15/58. Father, gtrst., has gp., Gospel Expressions.

Took up el-bs. at age 9. Stud. and pl. w. fath. Further stud. w. Bill Pulice at latter's music store. While at U. Wisconsin-La Crosse met Milt Hinton at a clinic 1978, and sw. to acoustic bs., stud. w. Linda Brewer. Fr. '78 to '82 stud. at Wisc. Cons. of Mus., Milwaukee; also lessons w. Skip Crumby-Bey. Worked locally w. singer Penny Goodwin. In NYC '83–6, worked briefly w. Art Blakey; w. Philip Harper at Blue Note, late night jam sessions; James Williams. Ret. to Milwaukee '86–8, backing visiting mus. such as Dexter Gordon; Cedar Walton; Mose Allison. Brought to NYC by Buddy Montgomery to pl. in duo at Parker Meridien Hotel '89–90. Own sxt., Jazz Elements, in Milwaukee '90–3; also taught at Wisc. Cons. Back to NYC '93, accomp. Andy Bey. Pl. w. Roy Hargrove fr. '94; Frank Foster fr. '97. Has stud. w. Buster Williams fr. '97; also lessons w. Ray Brown, Cachaito. First overseas tour, on Eur. festival circuit, w. Adam Makowicz in '80s. Comps: "Song for Audrey"; "The Dookie Duke"; "Jeanne's Dream." Favs: Sam Jones, Doug Watkins, Ray Brown, Wilbur Ware. CDs: w. Hargrove (Verve); Sherman Irby (BN); Tim Armacost (Conc.).

CAPP, FRANKIE (Frank Cappucio), dms; b. Worcester, MA, 8/20/31. Studied at Bost. U. Replaced Shelly Manne w. Stan Kenton 1951; pl. w. Neal Hefti '52; Billy May '53; Peggy Lee '53–4; Dorothy Dandridge, Betty Hutton, Ella Fitzgerald '56–7; off and on w. André Previn trio '57–64. After many yrs. of studio work, he formed a bb w. pnst. Nat Pierce '75. Billed as Capp-Pierce Juggernaut, it pl. mainly around LA and cont. under Capp's name after Pierce's death in '92. Capp has pl. in every kind of gp., fr. bbs and bebop qts. to Dixieland bands, and he has been a consistently reliable perf. regardless of idiom. CDs: Conc.; w. B. Berry; R. Woodard (Conc.); M. Paich (GNP Cres.); A. Previn (Cont.); *The Tenor Trio* (JMI).

CAREY, MUTT (THOMAS), tpt; b. Hahnville, LA, 1891; d. Elsinore, CA, 9/3/48. Started on dms. but sw. to crnt. in 1912, studied w. bro., Jack, and pl. w. his band until join. Kid Ory '14. Tour. in vaudeville w. the Dodds bros., then to Chi. '17, pl. w. cl. Lawrence Duhe at Dreamland. In '18, ret. to NO, working w. Wade Whaley bef. rejoin. Ory in Calif. '19. Upon Ory's departure in '25, he assumed lead. of gp., later naming it the Jeffersonians. Spent several yrs. pl. intermittently while holding jobs as pullman porter and mail carrier. In '44, he was reunited w. Ory for a Orson Welles network radio broadcast. The traditional jazz revival brought him to NYC in '47, working w. Edmond Hall and other NO mus. In describing Carey's app. w. Ory during an SF perf. Samuel Char-

ters wrote: "He was such a sensation with muted effects he had learned from Oliver, that Oliver was passed over as a Mutt Carey imitator when he played San Francisco a year later." Rec. in the mid '40s w. Hociel Thomas, Ory, and own gp. the New Yorkers. CDs: w. Bunk Johnson (Amer. Mus.); Ory (GTJ; Amer. Mus.; Col.).

CARISI, JOHNNY (JOHN E.), tpt, comp, arr; b. Hasbrouck Heights, NJ, 2/23/22; d. NYC, 10/3/92. First studied tpt. and theory in hs, then comp. w. Stefan Wolpe 1948–50, and tpt. w. Carmine Caruso '53–4. Worked w. several bands fr. '38–43, incl. Babe Russin, George Handy, Herbie Fields; also sat in at Minton's and Monroe's in early '40s. Stationed in New Haven, Conn., dur. WWII, pl. w. Glenn Miller's air force band; also w. Ray McKinley and Lou Stein contingents '43–6. In late '40s, pl. w. Skitch Henderson, Claude Thornhill, Charlie Barnet; became prominent as comp. of "Israel," rec. by Miles Davis Nonet '49. Dur. '50s, his works for chamber gps. were perf. at various concerts, incl. Yale U. symposium; arr. for Barry Galbraith's Guitar Choir '59. Went on St. Dept. tour of southeast Asia and Mideast w. dance troupe '60. Some comp.-arr. for TV and theater in '60s; orchestrator for Anita Loos–Ralph Blane musical *Something About Anne*, choreographed by his wife, dancer Gemze de Lappe; chamber piece for NY Sax Qt. Commissions incl: National Jazz Ensemble, perf. at Wolf Trap, Lincoln Center; Gerry Mulligan's Wilder Winds, perf. at Town Hall, Kennedy Center; works for tba. virtuoso Harvey Phillips. In '70s, he taught at Manhattan Sch. of Mus.; Queens Coll., CUNY '71–3. Pl. w. Brew Moore '69–70. In the '80s, pl. regularly at Jimmy Ryan's; gigs w. Jim Chapin, Loren Schoenberg; arrs. for Max Roach's double qt. Perf. in dixieland band that pl. between innings at Yankee Stadium. Hospitalized for a stroke, he resumed working, but had to reenter the hospital for open heart surgery; he died of complications resulting from that operation. Comps: "Springsville"; "Moon Taj"; "Angkor Wat"; "Lestorian Mode"; arr. for *Urbie Green's Big Beautiful Band* (Project 3); comp.-arr. for Marvin Stamm rec. *Machinations* (Verve). CDs: two tracks on *The Arrangers* (BB); w. Gil Evans (Prest.; Imp.); M. Davis (Cap.; Col.).

CARLISLE, UNA MAE, voc, comp, pno; b. Xenia, OH, 12/26/15; d. NYC, 11/7/56. Discovered by Fats Waller in 1932, while working in Cincinnati, Ohio, as radio mus.; later she worked w. him. Pl. and rec. in Eur. '37–39; made series of Waller-infl. gp. recs. while in Engl. '38. Ret. to US '39, rec. "I Can't Give You Anything But Love" w. Waller. Led own all-star gps. for BB '40–1, incl. Lester Young, Benny Carter,

John Kirby. Dur. this time, she comp. and rec. her biggest hits: "Walkin' by the River" '40; "I See a Million People" '41. Throughout the '40s, she tour., pl. night clubs; own TV and radio series late '40s, '51–3. Retired to Ohio '54 due to ill health. Her pno. style was heavily infl. by Waller. Recs. for Col. w. Don Redman, Bob Chester '50. CD: track on *The Women: Classic Female Jazz Artists* (BB).

CARLSON, FRANKIE (FRANK L.), dms, perc; b. NYC, 5/5/14. Drummer w. orig. Woody Herman band 1937–42. Rec. w. Glenn Miller '39. Settled in LA; pl. w. Benny Goodman '42; rec. w. Red Nichols '44; Georgie Auld '52; June Christy '53. Rec. w. Stan Kenton as percst. '63–5; later pl. in Kenton's Neophonic Orch. '65–6; pl. and rec. w. LA Philharm. Orch. Active at MGM studios, pl. for cartoons, films, TV. Regular on *Dr. Kildare* TV show. Was also commercial radio engineer. Retired to Hawaii. App. on album *Kenton Plays Wagner*, Cap., '64. CDs: w. Herman (Dec.).

CARLTON, LARRY EUGENE, gtr; b. Torrance, CA, 3/2/48. Studied mus. at LA Harbor Coll. 1966–8; Cal St. U., Long Beach, Calif., '68–70. Pl. Disneyland w. Bill Elliot '68; tour. w. 5th Dimension. In '69, he was mus. dir. of NBC children's show, perf. live on camera as "Larry Guitar." Fr. '70, pl. on thousands of rec. sess., TV shows, movies, commercials, etc. Join. Crusaders '73; pl. w. Tom Scott's LA Express, mid '70s. First solo rec. as leader '78; fr. '85 rec. for MCA. Cont. to tour into '90s pl. a mixture of jazz, blues, pop, and rock. In '88, Carlton was shot in the throat by an unknown assailant, bringing his career to a temporary halt. He recovered and resumed pl. in '90. Won NARAS Most Valuable Player Award '73–4. CDs: MCA; GRP; w. Crusaders; J. Klemmer (MCA).

CARMICHAEL, HOAGY (HOAGLAND HOWARD), comp, voc, pno; b. Bloomington, IN, 11/22/1899; d. Rancho Mirage, CA, 12/27/81. Studied pno. w. moth., a prof. pnst.; jazz pno. basics w. Reginald DuValle in Indianapolis, Ind. Pl. for hs dances, then form. own band at Indiana U. Became friendly w. and was infl. by Bix Beiderbecke, who rec. his "Riverboat Shuffle" w. the Wolverines 1924. Pl. pno. w. Jean Goldkette '27; also rec. his "Washboard Blues" w. Paul Whiteman in same yr. To NYC '29, where he was assoc. w. such artists as Louis Armstrong, the Dorsey bros., Benny Goodman, Eddie Lang, Jack Teagarden, Bubber Miley, Clarence Williams, Red Norvo, and Mildred Bailey. A prolific songwriter; many of his comps. became jazz standards: "Star Dust," "Rockin' Chair," "Lazy River,"

"Georgia," "The Nearness of You," "Skylark." Moved to Hollywood, Calif., in mid '30s, app. as pnst. and actor in numerous films '37–54, incl. *To Have and Have Not, The Best Years of Our Lives, Young Man With a Horn.* Active in radio and TV in '40s and '50s; in '60s wrote for and hosted *Bell Telephone Hour*; host for *Project 20* ragtime documentary. Books: two autobiographies, *The Stardust Road* '46 and *Sometimes I Wonder* '65. Visited Japan in '61, '64. His vocal style, idiosyncratic w. a nasal twang, was effective nevertheless. His collection of recs. and scores are housed by the Indiana Archives of Trad. Mus. in Bloomington. LP: PJ, '56. CDs: BB; w. Armstrong (Col.); Lang (ASV).

CARMICHAEL, JUDY (Judith Lea Hohenstein), pno; b. Lynwood, CA, 11/27/52. Mother pl. pno., fath. sang; both amateur. Studied pno. w. moth. fr. age 4; self-taught fr. age 10. Worked as actress, then pl. first prof. gig w. Jo Stafford at age 16. Encouraged by Count Basie, Sarah Vaughan, Benny Carter, she rec. her first album w. Basie sidemen. Moved to NYC 1984, pl. w. Al Hirt, Benny Carter, but mainly as solo stride pnst. She has written a book on stride pno., and received NEA grants to lecture and perf. in schs. across the US in '90–1. Favs: Nat Cole, Fats Waller. Fests: Eur. '83–91; Brazil, '89; China, '92. CDs: C&D; Jazz.

CARNEGIE HALL JAZZ BAND. Formed in December 1991 by Carnegie Hall and George Wein's Festival Productions to present an annual concert series produced by the latter with Jon Faddis as music director. Debut concert was October 22, 1992. In addition to re-creations of past classics from jazz's past, there have been new perspectives on older repertory as well as newly commissioned compositions and arrangements. Composer-arrangers who have contributed include Mike Abene, Manny Albam, Toshiko Akiyoshi, John Clayton, Frank Foster, Slide Hampton, Jimmy Heath, Randy Sandke, and Maria Schneider. Guest soloists have been Michael Brecker, Doc Cheatham, Chick Corea, Wynton Marsalis, T.S. Monk, James Moody, and Clark Terry. Personnel (1999): Faddis, Randy Brecker, Earl Gardener, Lew Soloff, Terell Stafford, Byron Stripling, Tommy Williams, tpt.; Jerry Dodgion, Ralph Lalama, Dick Oatts, Gary Smulyan, Frank Wess, reeds; Robin Eubanks, John Fedchock, Slide Hampton, Doug Perviance, Steve Turre, Dennis Wilson, tbn.; Renee Rosnes, pno.; Todd Coolman, Peter Washington, bs.; John Riley, Lewis Nash, dms. Tours: Japan '94; Argentina, Chile, Uruguay '95; Eur., summer '96; US, fall '96; Italy '97. Pl. Berlin JF '93; Hollywood Bowl; Tanglewood '94; joint concerts w. Lincoln Center Jazz Orchestra at JVC-NY JF '94–5. Radio: regular apps. on *Jazz Set with Branford Marsalis*. CD: BN.

CARNEY, HARRY HOWELL, bari sax, cl, bs cl; b. Boston, MA, 4/1/10; d. NYC, 10/8/74. Studied priv., first pno., then cl., alto sax. Started prof. in 1925 w. Bobby Sawyer, Walter Johnson, Joseph Steel. In '26, his parents allowed Duke Ellington to take him on a road tour w. his band. He moved permanently to NYC in '27, working w. Fess Williams bef. rejoin. Ellington in June. First feat. on alto, doubling cls., he eventually settled on bari. sax, becoming the instrument's most prominent jazz exponent. With his deeply sonorous and vigorous tone, enhanced by his mastery of circular breathing, he became a cornerstone of the Ellington orch. He was the first to seriously explore the bs-cl.as a solo jazz instrument, and his approach to the bari. sax parallels Coleman Hawkins' pioneering on the tnr. From the summer of '74 until his death, Carney cont. to pl. w. the orch. under Mercer Ellington's dir. Co-comp. "Rockin' in Rhythm" w. Ellington '30. Polls: *Esq.* Silver Award '45, '47; *DB* Readers '44–8, '52; *Met.* '44–8; *DB* Critics '53–4, '56, tied w. Mulligan '59, '65–73; EOJ Mus., '56. CDs: two tracks in *The Jazz Scene* (Verve); w. Ellington (Dec.; BB; Col.; Pab.; Atl.; Rep.; Fant.); Hodges (Verve; BB; Imp.); B. Goodman (Col.); Sandy Williams in *Giants of Small Band Swing, Vol. 2* (Riv.); J. Bothwell (Hep).

CARPENTER, DAVE (DAVID EDWARD), bs; b. Dayton, OH, 11/4/59. Studied at Ohio St. U. Pl. w. Buddy Rich 1983–5; moved to NYC '85. Tour. w. Maynard Ferguson '85–6; Woody Herman '86–7; and worked w. small gps. in NYC. Pl. briefly in Ringling Bros.' circus band '88; moved to LA '89. Freelance studio work on acoustic and electric instruments. Also pl. or rec. w. Sal Marquez; Rob Mullins; Ernie Watts; Supersax; the Capp–Pierce Juggernaut; and Billy Cobham. CDs: w. Sal Marquez (GRP); Rob Mullins (Nova); W. Herman (Conc.); Bill Holman (JVC); Lanny Morgan (Cont.); David Arney (Band Together); Bill Perkins; Claude Williamson (FS).

CARR, BRUNO, dms; b. Bronx, NY, 2/9/28; d. Denver, CO, 10/25/93. Cousin of Connie Kay. Self-taught on dms. Sid Catlett helped him get started. Was prof. for seven yrs. After army, 1951–3, he worked as bouncer in a NYC club until '55. Pl. w. Ray Charles, incl. Eur. tour, '60–2; Sarah Vaughan, Betty Carter '63; Lou Donaldson, Shirley Scott '64; also w. Herman Foster; Abbey Lincoln; Wild Bill Davis. Tour. w. Herbie Mann spt. for several yrs. in

mid '60s. Dur. '60s and '70s also worked w. Bobby Timmons; Norman Simmons; Jack Wilson; Monty Alexander; Wynton Kelly. Moved to Denver in early '80s, app. at Colo. JP several times in that decade. Many albums w. Donaldson; Aretha Franklin; Joe Turner; Hank Crawford; Sonny Stitt; Cleanhead Vinson. Favs: Catlett, Chick Webb, Sonny Greer. Film: *Swinging Along* w. Charles '61. TV: *Tonight Show*; Merv Griffin; Perry Como; *Dial M for Music*. CDs: w. Mann (Rh.); Charles (DCC).

CARR, IAN HENRY RANDELL, tpt, flg, kybds, comp; b. Dumfries, Scotland, 4/21/33. Grew up in northeast Engl. Self-taught on tpt. Degree in Engl. lit. at Durham U. Held many unusual jobs bef. deciding on a jazz career in 1960. Served in army '56–8. Pl. and rec. w. Emcee Five, incl. bro. Mike, '60–2. Moved to London and pl. briefly w. Harold McNair; then co-led qnt. w. Don Rendell '62–9. Founder-member of New Jazz Orch., '63; leader-arr. of Animals Big Band '65; also worked w. Joe Harriott, Don Byas, John McLaughlin. Pl. w. Michael Garrick '65–7. In '69 form. own jazz-rock band, Nucleus, which cont. through '88, tour. int'l inc. fests. such as Montreux; Newport '70. Fr. '75 has been assoc. w. the Jazz and Rock Ens., which he helped establish. Pl. w. Mike Gibbs '87; also feat. soloist w. Hamburg Radio Orch. Led own qnt. fr. '89. Worked w. G. Russell's Anglo-American Living Time Orch. Assoc. Prof. at Guildhall Sch. of Mus. and Drama fr. '82; also teaches regularly at Interchange Wkshps., London. Comps: prizewinning score for Paris Biennale '63; *Will's Birthday* for Globe Theatre '74; *Old Heartland* '88; mus. for play *Going Home*, perf. onstage w. own qnt. '90; suite, *Northeastern Song Lives* '91. An int'l recognized tptr. infl. by M. Davis, D. Gillespie, C. Brown, et al., he is also well-known for his writings on jazz, incl. *Music Outside: Contemporary Jazz in Britain* '73; *Miles Davis: a Critical Biography* '82; *Keith Jarrett: The Man and his Music* '91; and collabs. w. Brian Priestley and Digby Fairweather, *Jazz: The Essential Companion* '87; and *Jazz: The Rough Guide* '95. Radio: hour docu. on M. Davis for BBC '90–1; eight 30–minute programs on Davis's mus. as a follow-up. CDs: MMC/EMI; Core; w. Neil Ardley (AMP); M. Gibbs (Venture); United Jazz + Rock Ensemble (VeraBra).

CARR, LODI (Lois Ann Cox-Kasher), voc; b. Marquette, MI, 9/13/33. Parents and older bro. were amateur singers. Self-taught. First sang w. Milt Jackson at age 13. Early exp. perf. in Det. at the World Stage w. Jackson, Roland Hanna, Pepper Adams, Elvin Jones, Thad Jones, Billy Mitchell, Paul Chambers, K. Burrell, ca. '49. First nightclub app. w. Hanna '49. Sang

w. Adams '46–86; W. Gray '47; Tommy Flanagan fr. '49; T. Jones, late '40s-'50s; Curtis Fuller fr. '50. Moved to NYC '53. Sang w. Larry Elgart, Les Elgart, Don Elliott '55; Bobby Timmons '55–8; Claude Thornhill '56–7; Sonny Clark, Kenny Dorham '56–8; Herman Foster, Melba Liston fr. '56; George Duvivier '58. Ret. to Det. '58, then back to NYC '59. In the '50s, she also worked w. Barry Harris; Major Holley; E. Jones; Duke Jordan; Yusef Lateef; Al Klink; Mundell Lowe; Mingus; Hank Mobley; James Moody; Jamil Nasser; Horace Parlan; Bud Powell; Jerry Segal; E. Shaughnessy; Rex Stewart; Sonny Stitt; Doug Watkins; H. Lawson, K. Lightsey, B. Mitchell, fr. '50s. Inactive in '60s-'70s, then worked w. Chris Anderson '82–3; Ron Carter fr. '86; Clifford Jordan, J. Morello, Sahib Shihab '80s; Billy Higgins, M. Holley, Geoff Keezer, Chris McBride, Carmen McRae, Mulgrew Miller, Mickey Roker '80s-90s; Bob Hurst '89–90; Geo. Cables '90–1; Art Blakey's Jazz Messengers, Roy Hargrove '91; Barry Harris '90s. Carr had a weekly gig at the Village Gate '86–92. Favs: Fitzgerald, Vaughan, McRae. Fests: North Sea '86–8; U.S. and Can. fests fr. '80s. CD: Laurie.

CARR, MANCY PECK (aka CARA), bjo, gtr; b. Charleston, WV, ca. 1900. Played w. Carroll Dickerson Orch. in Chi. '24, and again in late 1920s. In '28–9 he rec. w. Louis Armstrong's Hot Five and orch., incl. such classic sides as "Fireworks," "A Monday Date," and "Skip the Gutter." In '29, he came w. Dickerson to NYC, where he cont. to rec. w. Armstrong. After ret. to Chi., he moved to W. Va., where he worked w. his bro. For many yrs., his name was incorrectly spelled as "Cara." CDs: w. Armstrong (Col.).

CARR, MIKE (MICHAEL ANTHONY), org, pno, vib; b. South Shields, England, 12/7/37. Brother of Ian Carr. Pl. pno. and vib. in Emcee Five 1960–2. Worked in Africa '63–5, then pl. org. in Herbie Goins's Nighttimers. Perf. freq. at Ronnie Scott's London, '66–7. Led own trio w. John McLaughlin, late '60s. Tour. w. Ronnie Scott '71–5, incl. perf. at Carnegie Hall, NYC, '74. Tour. Eur. w. own qt. '75–7. Formed jazz-rock gp., Cargo, '80, and cont. to lead it and a trio into the '90s. CDs: Cargogold.

CARRINGTON, TERRI LYNE, dms, comp, voc; b. Medford, MA, 8/4/65. Grandfather, Matt Carrington, pl. w. Waller, Ellington, and Chu Berry; fath., saxist Sonny Carrington, was president of the Bost. Jazz Society. Jammed w. Clark Terry, Dizzy Gillespie, and Rahsaan Roland Kirk bef. she was a teenager. Became youngest mus. to receive scholar-

ship to Berklee Sch. of Mus. after she sat in w. Oscar Peterson at age 11; after grad. hs att. Berklee full time. Since 1985, worked w. Wayne Shorter; Pharoah Sanders; Al Jarreau; David Sanborn; Clark Terry; and others. House dmr. for a few mos. w. Arsenio Hall TV show fr. '89. Tour. Eur. fest. circuit w. Stan Getz '90. CDs: Verve; w. Niels Lan Doky (Story.); Robin Eubanks; Greg Osby; Gary Thomas; Cassandra Wilson (JMT); Mulgrew Miller (Land.); John Scofield (Gram.); Mitchell Forman (Novus).

CARROL, SHELLEY, tnr sax; b. Houston, TX, 10/26/64. Studied and/or pl. w. Arnett Cobb, Don Wilkerson, James Clay, and other "Texas Tenors." Attended Texas Southern U.; B. Mus., w. emphasis in jazz stud., fr. No. Texas St. 1992. In '89, he was also a member of the Duke Ellington Orch. Described by Mercer Ellington as "another of those young men with traditional roots like the Marsalises. He has a personality of his own and is also a good blues singer." CD: w. Sebastian Whitaker (Justice).

CARROLL, BARBARA (Barbara Carole Coppersmith), pno, voc; b. Worcester, MA, 1/25/25. Began pl. pno. at 5, w. priv. tuition fr. age 8. After one yr. at New Engl. Cons., she pl. USO tour w. a trio. To NYC in late '40s; led trio w. Chuck Wayne and Clyde Lombardi at Downbeat Club; rec. debut on Discovery labe, '49. Worked at The Embers in '50s w. trio that incl. bs. Joe Shulman, to whom she was married fr. '54 until his death in '57. Rec. several RCA albums '53–6, later also on Kapp, Verve, and WB labels. App. as actress in the '53 B'way prod. Rodgers and Hammerstein's *Me and Juliet*; perf. w. Benny Goodman at Carnegie Hall; acc. Billie Holiday on *Today* show. Took hiatus fr. perf. to remarry and raise a family, then resumed career in '76; pl. at Bemelmans Bar in NYC's Carlyle Hotel fr. '78. App. at Town Hall tribute to Mary Lou Williams '81; NJF '79; Women's Jazz Fest. in KC; JVC-NY JF '91. TV: *Tonight Show*; Merv Griffin; ABC soap opera *All My Children*. Favs: Bill Evans, Bud Powell. CDs: DRG; After 9; tracks on *The Women* (BB); w. S. Hasselgard (Drag.); Serge Chaloff (Mos.).

CARROLL, JOE "BEBOP" (Joseph Paul Taylor), voc; b. Philadelphia, PA, 11/25/19; d. Brooklyn, NY, 2/1/81. Appeared in the film *Stormy Weather* '43, and w. Paul Bascomb's orch., but is best known for his work w. Dizzy Gillespie 1949–53. Made several recs. w. Gillespie incl.: "Jump-Did-Le-Ba"; "Hey Pete! Let's Eat Mo' Meat"; "In the Land of Oo-Bla-Dee," Victor '49; "Honeysuckle Rose," Cap. '50; and a series for the Dee Gee label, '51–2, incl. "Oo-Shoo-Be-Do-Be," co-comp. w. Gillespie, '52. Rec. debut as leader on Prest. '52; also rec. for Vogue, Epic, and other labels. Tour. Eur. w. Gillespie in '53; then worked and rec. as a single. Tour. w. Woody Herman '64–5, rec. "Wa Wa Blues" '64, then resumed solo career. A virtuoso scat artist, he modeled his comedic vocal style after Leo Watson. CDs: w. Gillespie (BB; RCA; Sav.; Vogue); tracks in *The Bebop Singers* (Prest.).

CARRUTHERS, JOCK (EARL MALCOM), bari sax; b. West Point, MO, 5/27/10; d. Kansas City, MO, 5/5/71. Raised in KC, he stud. mus. at Fisk U. Join. Benny Moten in 1928, then moved to St. Louis, where he worked w. Dewey Jackson '29–30; Fate Marable '31. Best known as member of Jimmie Lunceford's orch. fr. '32 until after Lunceford's death in '47, when the band was co-led by Joe Thomas and Eddie Wilcox. Eventually ret. to KC, playing locally into the late '60s. Recs. w. Lunceford: "Rose Room"; "Harlem Shout"; "I Love You"; "Organ Grinder's Swing." CDs: w. Lunceford (Dec.).

CARRY, SCOOPS (GEORGE DORMAN), alto sax, cl; b. Little Rock, AR, 1/23/15; d. Chicago, IL, 8/4/70. His bro., Ed, led band in Chi. Studied w. moth., who had mus. degree; later harmony, theory, cl. at Chi. Mus. Coll. 1923–32. First orch. at U. of Iowa; then worked in Chi. and tour. w. Boyd Atkins '30. Pl. w. Lucky Millinder early '30s; Ed Carry '34; Zutty Singleton; Fletcher Henderson '36; Roy Eldridge; Mildred Bailey '37; Art Tatum '38; Horace Henderson '39. Best known for his tenure w. Earl Hines '40–7, where he pl. lead alto and served as asst. lead. On leaving Hines, he studied law, eventually taking up practice in Chi., where one of his clients was Local 208 AFM. His mellow, liquid sound is in evidence on his often uncredited solos w. Roy Eldridge on '37 Vocalion sides, and on his own fav. solo, "Jelly Jelly," w. Hines bb '40. CDs: w. Eldridge (Col.); Hines (BB).

CARTER, BENNY (BENNETT LESTER), alto sax, tpt, comp, arr; b. NYC, 8/8/07; d. Los Angeles, 7/12/03. Raised in midtown Manh. until age 16, when his family moved to Harlem. Pno. lessons w. moth., 1917. Bought a crnt. '21, but soon exchanged it for C-melody sax, taking lessons fr. local teachers. Early infls. were tptrs. Bubber Miley and Cuban Bennett, a cousin. First prof. jobs summer '23; pl. w. Willie "The Lion" Smith, switching to alto sax '24, and becoming one of that instrument's most important stylists. Pl. bari. sax w. Earl Hines '25. Went to Wilberforce U., but instead of studying there went on tour w. Horace Henderson's Wilberforce Collegians. Publ. first song, "Nobody Knows," co-written w. Fats Waller, in '27. Fr. '27 to '29 he was mainly w. Charlie Johnson band, but also briefly w. Fletcher Henderson, Duke Ellington. Led reorganized Wilberforce Collegians, '28–9, when he began regularly doubling on tpt. Rejoined F. Henderson '30–31, then briefly w. Chick Webb, but left to join McKinney's Cotton Pickers '31–2. Led own band off and on fr. summer '32 to Jan. '35. Sidemen incl. Teddy Wilson, Chu Berry, Sid Catlett. In spring '33, he organized an all-star band for recs. of comps. by British composer Spike Hughes; on one session he pl. sop. sax. After pl. tpt. w. Willie Bryant band for three mos., Carter sailed for France, joining the Willie Lewis band in Paris on tpt. and alto sax. At instigation of Leonard Feather, he went to Engl. Mar. '36 to arr. for BBC Dance Orch, rec. sess. w. British gps. Dur. a three-year expatriation, he worked in Holland and Scand.; in summer '37, while pl. at a Dutch resort, he rec. w. interracial, int'l band, the first of its kind in jazz history. Back in US, May '38, he formed new band. pl. Savoy Ballroom, Mar. '39, and tour. until fall '42, when he led several small gps. whose sidemen incl. Dizzy Gillespie, Jimmy Hamilton. In '43, he formed a West Coast bb whose sidemen at one time or another incl. Max Roach; Miles Davis; J.J. Johnson; Buddy Rich; Gerald Wilson. His film career started w. *Stormy Weather,* for which he wrote arrs. and pl. on soundtrack. Based in Calif. fr. '44, he worked on movie soundtracks as comp., arr., and perf.; he also app. on screen in *As Thousands Cheer; The View from Pompey's Head; The Snows of Kilimanjaro; An American in Paris.* Fr. '58, when he wrote regularly for *M Squad,* he was mainly active in TV, writing for such series as *Chrysler Theatre, Ironside, Name of the Game.* He cont. to work off and on in films, the last being *Buck and the Preacher* in '72.

By '60, Carter was devoting more time to arr. than to perf.; he became mus. dir. for numerous singers, incl. Peggy Lee; Pearl Bailey; Lou Rawls; and Ray Charles. In the '70s, he was active in jazz educ., mainly at Princeton, where he was a visiting profess. and perf. In '74 he received an honorary Doctor of Humanities degree. Pl. at all leading jazz fests. in US and abroad, also toured Middle East under auspices of State Dept. and USIA, Dec. '75–Jan.'76. From '73, he toured Japan almost annually w. 10- to 17-pc. gps. Throughout the '80s he organized combos and bands for clubs, concerts and fests. By the early '90s, he was the most versatile, continuously active artist in jazz history, and arguably the most honored and talented. He pl. jazz cruises such as the one honoring him on the *Song of America* '94. In March of '96 he was presented in concert at Lincoln Center and received the Kennedy Center Award. Though alto sax remained his primary instrument, Carter's occasional forays on tpt. display a warm tone and highly personal legato style. Until he gave it up in the early '40s, he was also a distinctive clst. (heard on the title track of the RCA CD *All of Me*); he even played tbn. briefly, but only rec. one solo on that instrument. As an arr., Carter's writing for reeds is particularly effective; he has written countless bb charts for such leaders as Benny Goodman; Count Basie (incl. *Kansas City Suite*); Glenn Miller; and Cab Calloway. Carter is the subject of one of the most thorough biographies ever devoted to a jazz musician, *Benny Carter: A Life In American Music,* by Morroe Berger, w. Ed Berger and James Patrick, publ. '82. A one-hour TV docu., *Symphony in Riffs,* was released in US in '92. Carter comps. incl. "Blues In My Heart"; "When Lights are Low"; "Key Largo"; "A Kiss from You"; "Symphony in Riffs"; "Cow Cow Boogie." In '92, Carter completed two extended works, *Harlem Renaissance* and *Japan Suite,* for presentation at a N.J. concert sponsored in part by the NEA. CDs: BB; Imp.; Cont.; MM; Pablo; w. D. Reinhardt (Ark.); C. Neville (Eve. Star).

CARTER, BETTY (Lillie Mae Jones), voc; b. Flint, MI, 5/16/30; d. Brooklyn, NY 9/26/98. Studied pno. at Det. Cons. As teenager, sang w. Charlie Parker and other visiting bebop mus. Made prof. debut after winning amateur contest 1946. Tour. as Lorraine Carter w. Lionel Hampton '48–51. Hampton called her "Betty Bebop," which was later amended to Betty Carter. App. as single in nightclubs and theaters fr. '51; worked w. Miles Davis '58–9; Ray Charles revue '60–3; Sonny Rollins in Japan '64. One of the most thoroughly jazz-oriented singers, orig. showing a strong Sarah Vaughan infl., she led her own trio fr. '69. It was a finishing sch. for countless young mus. such as Benny Green, Mulgrew Miller, Stephen Scott, Cyrus Chestnut, and Jacky Terrasson, just to name the pnsts. In '71, she founded her own rec. co., Bet-Car, whose prods. were later reissued on Verve. She was feat. in the musical *Don't Call Me Man* '75, and perf. w. symph. orchs. under David Amram in NYC and Bost. '82–3. One of the few singers to scat authentically and effectively, Carter continuously stretched her interpretation of standards, drawing praise for her daring and creativity and criticism for taking the material to the point where its essence was no longer relevant. Fav: Billie Holiday. Polls: *DB* Critics, Readers, '89–93; Critics '94. Fests: all major fr. '50s. Perf. at White House '94. CDs: Verve; Roul.; Atl.; Imp.; w. Ray Charles (DCC); King Pleasure (Prest.).

CARTER, BOB (Robert Kahakalau), bs; b. New Haven, CT, 2/11/22. Parents were vaudeville perfs. on Keith circuit. Learned gtr. and bs. fr. fath., who

later became a teacher of Hawaiian mus. Made prof. debut w. fath.'s orch. 1937. Pl. w. local bands in Bost. '37–40, then tour. w. territory bands '40–2. Led own trio in Bost. '44. In army '44–5, then pl. on 52nd St. in NYC w. Dizzy Gillespie; Charlie Parker; Tony Scott; Dexter Gordon; Hank Jones; Ben Webster; Max Roach; Stuff Smith; Charlie Shavers, etc. Tour. and rec. w. Charlie Ventura '47–8; Benny Goodman '49–50; Ventura '53–4. Also rec. w. Buddy DeFranco '49; Joe Mooney '51; Marian McPartland '51, '53; Johnny Smith '52; Lou Stein '55. First comps. rec. by Bob Alexander '53. Stud. comp. and arr. w. Wesley LaViolette in Calif. '56. Pl. and arr. for Red Norvo, Bob Harrington, Shelly Manne '56–7. Moved to Honolulu '57; pl. w. Hawaiian, Japanese, Korean, Filipino mus. Ret. to NYC '58. Pl. w. Bobby Hackett '59; Bill Smith in Eur. '63; Henri Chaix, Oscar Klein in Eur. '69. CDs: w. Red Norvo (BB); Johnny Smith (FS); S. Getz (Roul.); B. Goodman (Col.).

CARTER, JAMES, tnr, alto, bari, sop saxes, bs cl, bs fl, picc; b. Detroit, MI, 1/3/69. Began pl. sax at age 11. Stud. w. Donald Washington and was member of his Bird-Trane-Sco-Now youth band in early 1980s. Dur. summers of teenage yrs, he pl. jazz at Blue Lake Arts Camp in Muskegon County, Mich. Won scholarship to Interlochen classical mus. camp and att. both camps concurrently. Tour. Scand. w. Blue Lake Jazz Ens. '85; ret. to Eur. later in the yr. as member of camp's faculty band, Blue Lake Monster Ens. In '85 he also pl. w. Wynton Marsalis at Blues Alley, Wash., D.C., and tour. w. him dur. the next eighteen mos. After grad. fr. hs., worked and tour. w. Lester Bowie and his NY Organ Ens. Has been member of LCJO; Mingus Dynasty bb. In '93, tour. w. Art Ens. of Chi. and own qt., making his rec. debut as a lead. w. *J.C. on the Set* '93. App. in Julius Hemphill's opera *Long Tongues,* Wash., D.C., '89. Film: Robert Altman's *Kansas City.* CDs: Atl.; DIW; w. Bowie (DIW); Hemphill (BS); Tough Young Tenors (Ant.); Frank Lowe (ITM Pacific); *Kansas City* (Verve); *SaxEmble* (Qwest).

CARTER, JOHN WALLACE, cl, saxes, fl, comp, educ; b. Ft. Worth, TX, 9/24/29; d. Inglewood, CA, 3/31/91. Studied cl. and alto sax; B.A. from Lincoln U., Jefferson City, Mo., 1949; M.A. of mus. ed., U. of Colorado, NTSU '56; Cal. St. U. '61. Teacher in public schs., Ft. Worth '49–61; LA '61–82. Orig. inspired by Parker, Young, Coltrane, he jammed w. Ornette Coleman, Charles Moffett in late '40s; tour. Southwest late '40s, early '50s w. jazz and blues gps. Moved to LA in early '60s, pl. w. Hampton Hawes; Carmell Jones; Harold Land; Phineas Newborn; also taught full-time in LA public sch. system. Form. New

Art Jazz Ens. w. Bobby Bradford '65. Bef. gp. disbanded in '73, it was involved in many lecture-demonstration concerts. Formed own ens. pl. in Eur. '73. Fr. '74, concentrated solely on cl. and comp. Participated in Little Big Horn wkshps. w. Bradford, James Newton, Arthur Blythe '76–8; formed the Wind Coll., a sch. for improv., w. Newton, Red Callender, Charles Owens '83. Led Clarinet Summit, an unaccompanied qt. (three sop. cl. and a bs-cl.) in concert at the Public Theatre, NYC, '81. From the mid '80s on, Carter perf. more actively, in the US and Eur., while also developing and rec. his epic five-part suite, *Roots and Folklore: Episodes in the Development of American Folk Music.* Commissioned by the Public Theater, the suite expresses black history, fr. slave crossings to the great post–Civil War urban migration to New York in the '40s. It skillfully interweaves folk motifs, unusual scoring, and emotionally charged improvisational passages. The rec. of its second movement, *Castles of Ghana,* was hailed as one of the top recs. of '86, bringing Carter belated attention as a cl. virtuoso and powerful contemporary comp. CDs: BS; Gram.; Clarinet Summit (Ind. Nav.); w. Bradford; H. Tapscott (hatArt); J. Newton (Gram.).

CARTER, RON (RONALD LEVIN), bs, piccolo bs, cello, comp, arr; b. Ferndale, MI, 5/4/37. Seven siblings all stud. mus. Began on cello in sch. at age 10; sw. to bs. at Cass Tech. HS., Det. Pl. w. local gp. 1955. Led own gps. in Rochester, N.Y., while earning B.A. in mus. at Eastman Sch. of Mus. '56–9. Pl. w. Chico Hamilton '59. M. Mus. fr. Manh. Sch. of Mus., '61. Freelanced in NYC w. Eric Dolphy, Cannonball Adderley, Jaki Byard, Randy Weston, Bobby Timmons, Monk '59–63. With Art Farmer briefly bef. join. Miles Davis '63. Member of Miles Davis Qnt. w. Shorter, Hancock, Tony Williams '63–8. Pl. w. Friedrich Gulda in Eur. '65; NY Jazz Sxt. fr. '67; NY Bass Choir fr. '69; Lena Horne '70–4; Michel Legrand fr. '71; NY Jazz Qt. '71–6. Rec. as lead. fr. '72. Tour. w. all-star gps., incl. CTI All-Stars, '70–5; V.S.O.P. '76–7, early '80s; Milestone Jazzstars w. Rollins, McCoy Tyner, Al Foster '78. Also freelanced in '70s w. S. Turrentine, Hubert Laws, L. Hampton, Joe Henderson, and worked extens. as studio mus. Carter has pl. piccolo bs., a solo instr. about half the size of a double bs., in his own qt. fr. '75. Freelanced in '80s w. T. Flanagan; Bette Midler; B.B. King; Kronos Qt.; Dexter Gordon; Helen Merrill; Black Composers Orch.; New World Symph.; Bklyn. Philharm., et al. Pl. on soundtrack to *'Round Midnight* '86, winning a Grammy for his comp. "Call Sheet Blues." Carter has also scored films, incl. *Beatrice, Haraka,* and the TV films *Exit Ten* and *A Gathering of Old*

Men. His bs. recs. of the Bach Cello Suites was certified gold '88; in all, he has app. on more than 1000 albums. Rec. w. rap gp. A Tribe Called Quest '91. He is the author of four books: *Building a Jazz Bass Line; Ron Carter Comprehensive Bass Method; Ron Carter Bass Lines;* and *The Music of Ron Carter.* A popular lecturer on the business of mus., Carter is on the faculty of City Coll., N.Y. Favs: Ray Brown, Percy Heath, Paul Chambers. Polls: *DB* New Star '65; *DB* Readers '73–5. TV: NBC Leon Bibb '70–3; *Positively Black;* Howard Cosell '75. CDs: BN; CTI; Evid.; Timel.; Conc.; FNAC; Em.; Mile., NJ; w. M. Davis (Col.); Jim Hall (Mile.); Branford/Wynton Marsalis (Col.); Dolphy (Prest.; Cand.); Hancock (BN; Col.); Tyner (Mile.; BN); Turrentine; Hubbard; Desmond (CTI); Shorter; T. Williams; R. Rosnes; J. Henderson; S. Turrentine (BN); J.J. Johnson (BB); Rollins (BB; Mile.); Getz; Burrell; Stephen Scott (Verve); J. Spaulding; W. Shaw; Wallace Roney; Donald Brown (Muse); Tadd Dameron; Sam Jones; Milt Jackson; B. Timmons; W. Montgomery (Riv.); C. Baker; R. Garland (Gal.); D. Ellis; B. Little (Cand.); A. Farmer; B. Golson (Den.); S. Kuhn (Owl); S. Khan (Polyd.).

CARVER, WAYMAN ALEXANDER, fl; also saxes, cl; b. Portsmouth, VA, 12/25/05; d. Atlanta, GA, 5/6/67. Uncle, D.D. Copeland, dir. municipal band and pl. fl., pno., tpt.; fath., Wayman Sr., pl. cl.; daughter pl. fl., pno. Took up fl. at 14; pl. w. coll. dance band. In NYC, he pl. w. Elmer Snowden 1931–2; Benny Carter '33–4. Carver's solos on a '33 Spike Hughes sess. w. Carter's band are the earliest examples of rec. jazz fl. From '34, he pl. fl. and sax w. Chick Webb and His Little Chicks, remaining w. the band after Ella Fitzgerald assumed leadership '39–40. After WWII, he moved to Atlanta, where he was a profess. of mus., dir. the band program at Clark Coll., and pl. occ. gigs on cl. w. local gp. Favs: D.D. Copeland, fl.; Benny Carter, sax, cl. Fav. own solo: "Sweet Sue" w. Webb '37. CDs: w. Webb (Dec.).

CARVIN, MICHAEL WAYNE, dms; b. Houston, TX, 12/12/44. Father Henry (Hank) Carvin was one of Houston's top dmrs. Stud. w. fath. fr. age 6. First prof. gig w. pnst. Carl Campbell at age 13. Moved to LA 1952; stud. at LA Community Coll. Pl. w. Earl Grant bb '64–5, then w. 266th Army band in Vietnam '65–7. Led own gp. on tour w. Bill Cosby '67. Staff dmr. at Motown Recs. '68–70. Pl. w. B.B. King, George Duke '70; Barbara McNair TV show band, Hugh Masekela '70–1; Dexter Gordon '71; Hampton Hawes '71–2; Bobby Hutcherson '72–3; Larry Young '73; Freddie Hubbard '73–4; Jackie McLean '73–80; McCoy Tyner '74; Pharoah Sanders '74–6;

Alice Coltrane '76–7; own qnt. '76–9; Dizzy Gilles-
pie '79–81; Bridgewater Bros. '80–5; Cecil Taylor
'81; Slide Hampton '81–3; James Moody '81–4;
Hank Jones '85; Illinois Jacquet '85–6; Jon Hen-
dricks '86; Dakota Staton '86–8; own qnt. fr. '89; T.
Hino fr. '90; Abbey Lincoln '91–2; Claudio Roditi fr.
'91. Also freelanced extensively w. Woody Shaw;
Monk Montgomery; Jimmy Smith; Walter Bishop;
Gerry Mulligan; Lonnie Liston Smith, etc. Carvin has
taught at Grant Arts Ctr., LA '70–1; Community
Learning Ctr., Oakland, Calif. '72; Creative Arts
Develop. Ctr., NYC, '73; U. of Hartford, Hartford
Artists Collective, Jazzmobile Wkshp. '73–5; Vallek-
ilde Music Clinics, Denmark, '74–5; NYC Public
Schs. '80–1; Rutgers U., Prof. Perc. Ctr. '80–4;
Drummers Collective '84–5. Founded the Michael
Carvin Sch. of Drumming '85. He is the author of the
instr. book *Something for All Drummers* (Arual).
Favs: Henry Carvin. Fests: Eur. fr. '64; Japan fr. '80.
TV: Barbara McNair '70–1; *Like It Is*; also videos w.
Betty Carter, Dakota Staton, Slide Hampton. CDs:
Muse; Steep.; w. Hino (BN); Hawes (FS); McLean
(Steep.).

CARY, DICK (RICHARD DURANT), pno, tpt,
mello, alto horn, tbn, comp, arr; b. Hartford, CT,
7/10/16; d. Glendale, CA, 4/6/94. Studied vln.
1920–30; comp. w. Stefan Wolpe '47–52. Pl. vln. w.
Hartford Symph. while in hs. Rec. on pno. w. Joe
Marsala '42. House pnst. at Nick's, NYC, '42–3. Pl.
and arr. w. Benny Goodman '43; pl. w. Glen Gray,
Brad Gowans '43. While in army '44–6, rec. w. Muggsy Spanier, Wild Bill Davison. Pl. w. Billy Butterfield
'46; Jean Goldkette '47; Louis Armstrong All-Stars
'47–8; Jimmy Dorsey '49–50. On staff at WPIX
'49–50; also mello. and arr. for Eddie Condon TV
shows. Pl. tpt. at Eddie Condon's '54. Arr. and pl. w.
Bobby Hackett at Henry Hudson Hotel, NYC, '56–7.
Rec. in '50s w. Pee Wee Russell, Bud Freeman, Jimmy
McPartland; also arr. for Dorsey Bros. Arr. and pl. alto
horn and tbn. w. Max Kaminsky '58–9. Premiered
comp. *Georgia Sketches* at Great So. Bay JF '58.
Formed experimental gp. out of nucleus of Hackett
band '59. Moved to LA late '59; freelanced w. Red
Nichols; Bob Crosby; Ben Pollack; Matty Matlock.
Toured Austral., NZ, Japan w. Condon '64. Very active
as comp. and arr. in '60s, organizing rehearsal bands
incl. a brass qnt., reed oct., woodwind qnt. Also led
dance band feat. Abe Most in swing era re-creations.
Led 9-pc. band for jazz concerts in parks and sch. fr.
'70. Arrs. feat. on soundtrack of film *The Great Gatsby*
'74. Rec. in Eur. w. Barrelhouse Jazzband '75. Cary
cont. to tour, pl. tpt., alto horn, and pno., throughout
the '70s and '80s. His Tuesday Night Band, a gp. of
studio mus. who met weekly in his home for twenty

yrs., was feat. at the LA Classic JF '92. Favs: tpt.,
Eldridge; pno., Tatum; arr., Eddie Sauter. TV: *The Jazz
Show*; Dick Van Dyke special. CDs: w. Armstrong;
Teagarden (BB); B. Freeman (RCA); Condon
(Chiaro.; Jazz.); Hackett (Dormouse).

CARY, MARC ANTHONY, pno, comp; b. NYC,
1/29/67. Great-grandmother was opera singer and
pnst.; grandfath., a cousin of Cootie Williams, pl. tpt.
in the latter's band in the South; moth. pl. cello and vln.
Began on tpt., dms., cello. Raised in Wash., D.C. Early
studies w. Elnora Oxendine, then at Duke Ellington
Sch. of Mus. Won several pno. competitions while in
hs, incl. Leonard Feather Awd. Stud. w. John Malachi
early 1980s; Walter Davis Jr. '85–9; Mulgrew Miller
'87; Calvin Jones at U. of D.C., late '80s. Pl. in D.C. w.
Frontline Jazz Ens. '84–6; U. of D.C. Jazz Band
'87–9; also taught at Oxendine Mus. Acad. Moved to
NYC '89. Pl. w. Betty Carter '89–91; Arthur Taylor's
Wailers fr. '89; Roy Hargrove Qnt. fr. '91. Own gp. in
late '90s. Cary has also freelanced w. Harper Bros.;
Marlon Jordan; Wallace Roney; Terence Blanchard;
Freddie Hubbard. Favs: Monk, Ellington, Walter
Davis, Bud Powell. Fests: all major fr. '89. Film: *Mr.
A.T.* w. Taylor. CDs: Enja; Arab.; w. Taylor (Enja);
Hargrove (Novus); Betty Carter (Verve).

CASEY, ALBERT ALOYSIUS, gtr; b. Louisville,
KY, 9/15/15; d. NYC, 9/11/05. Father pl. dms.; uncle
pl. sax and acdn. Began on uke. Studied gtr. at Martin
Smith Mus. Sch., NYC. Came to prominence w. Fats
Waller's Rhythm and orch., 1934–43. Made more
than 230 recs. w. Waller, incl. "Buck Jumpin'," his
best-known solo '41. Pl. w. Teddy Wilson orch.
'39–40; Buster Harding '40; Chu Berry '41. Also rec.
in late '30s-40s w. Frankie Newton; Mezz Mezzrow;
Teddy Wilson; Billie Holiday; James P. Johnson; Earl
Hines; Sid Catlett. After Waller's death in '43, perf.
w. other former members of Waller's band under dir.
of Pat Flowers. Pl. w. Clarence Profit Trio '44; led
own trio fr. '44. Waller helped sw. him fr. acoustic to
electric gtr. in early '40s. Feat. w. King Curtis '57–61.
Rec. in Paris w. Helen Humes, Jay McShann, and as
leader '73. Pl. w. Harlem Blues and Jazz Band fr. '80;
also w. Harlem All-Stars at Louisiana Club, NYC, in
'90s. In '90s, Casey toured Eur. annually as a single.
Poll: *Esq.* Gold Awd. '44–5. Fests: Eur.; JVC-NY '98.
Rec. as leader for Cap. '45. CDs: Swingville; B&B;
tracks as lead. in *Classic Capitol Jazz Sessions*
(Mos.); w. Waller (BB, Stash); Newton (Aff.);
Satchmo Legacy Band (SN); Slam Stewart; J.
McShann (B&B); Louis Armstrong; J. Teagarden; L.
Hampton (BB); Esquire All-Stars; Chu Berry
(Comm.); M. Hinton (Chiaro.); B. Holiday (Col.);
King Curtis (Tru-Sound).

CASEY, BOB (ROBERT HANLEY), bs.; gtr; b. Johnson County, IL, 2/11/09; d. Marion, IL, 4/9/86. Started on tnr-bjo. at 14, then gtr.; picked up bs. at age 20; self-taught. In 1926–7 pl. dances in southern Ill. and St. Louis, Mo. Fr. '29, pl. bs. and doubled on gtr. Moved to Chi. and worked w. Wingy Manone; Muggsy Spanier, '33; staff mus. at NBC. Tour. and rec. w. Spanier '39; ret. to Chi. when gp. disbanded, and worked w. Charlie Spivak, et al. Moved to NYC, join. Brad Gowans at Nick's '43; pl. regularly there and at Condon's for yrs. In '50s, he worked w. Art Hodes; Bobby Hackett. Moved to Fla. '57; w. Dukes of Dixieland '62. Pl. sporadically fr. late '60s, incl. engagements in NYC '71. Recs. w. Wild Bill Davison '43, '45; Hackett '43, '44; Ralph Sutton; Joe Sullivan '50s. CDs: w. Spanier (BB); Davison (Comm.).

CASEY, FLOYD, dms, washboard; b. Poplar Bluff, MO, 1900; d. NYC, 9/7/67. Worked on riverboats in the early 1920s. Pl. in St. Louis w. Dewey Jackson, Ed Allen's Whispering Gold Band '22, and others. Moved to NYC in mid '20s and was feat. on many Clarence Williams recs. fr. '27, incl. "Cushion Foot Stomp," Okeh '27; w. tbn. George Wilson at Capitol Palace '27. In '30s, he pl. many taxi dance halls; w. Jimmy Reynolds '41. Rejoin. Allen's band; then they both join. pnst. Benton Heath at the New Gardens on 14th St., NYC, into the '60s. Rec. w. Elmer Snowden on a sess. that also incl. Allen '61. CDs: w. Snowden (Prest.); Williams (CDS).

CASTLE, LEE (Aniello Castaldo), tpt, lead; b. NYC, 2/28/15; d. Hollywood, FL, 11/16/90. Started on tpt. at age 15. As Lee Castaldo, pl. first prominent prof. job w. Joe Haymes 1935; Artie Shaw '36, '41; on and off w. Tommy Dorsey '37–41, who sent him to study w. Dorsey's fath. on family farm in Lansford, Pa. Also pl. w. Jack Teagarden, Glenn Miller '39; Will Bradley '41; Benny Goodman '43. Led own band sporadically in '38 and throughout '40s. Start. using name of Castle in '42. Join. Dorsey Bros. Orch. in '53, as feat. soloist, and, at times, lead. On Jimmy Dorsey's death in '57, Castle assumed leadership of his orch., remaining w. it through mid '80s. Fervent Louis Armstrong disciple. Films: *Stage Door Canteen* '43; *The Girls They Left Behind* w. Goodman. TV w. Dorseys: *Stage Show*; Patti Page; George Jessel; *NBC Bandstand*. Recs. w. org. Glenn Hardman (incl. Lester Young), Col. '39. CDs: w. T. Dorsey (BB; Tax); Shaw (BB; Hep).

CASTLEMAN, JEFF (JEFFRY ALAN), bs, el-bs; b. Los Angeles, CA, 1/27/46. Studied w. Ralph Pena at U. of Calif., Riverside. Made prof. debut w. Si Zentner in LV 1964. Pl. w. Louis Bellson off and on

'65–7; Joe Castro '66. Rec. w. Johnny Hodges–Earl Hines '67. Pl. w. Duke Ellington Orch. '67–9; first bs. to pl. el-bs. w. Ellington band. Married Ellington's vocalist, Trish Turner, and settled in LA '69. Tour. w. Sarah Vaughan; Tony Bennett '70. Pl. w. Shelly Manne '71–3. Worked mainly as studio mus., pl. el-bs., fr. mid '70s. CDs: w. Ellington (Fant.; Prest.; BB; Saja); Sinatra-Ellington (Rep.); S. Manne (Main.).

CASTRO, JOE (JOSEPH A.), pno, comp; b. Miami, AZ, 8/15/27. Raised in Pittsburg, Calif., pl. prof. fr. age 15. Att. San Jose St. Coll. Served in army, where he pl. in band, 1946–7. Form. own trio, working on West Coast and Hawaii for several yrs. Became protégé of Doris Duke. Accomp. June Christy and Anita O'Day '59 into '60s. Join. Teddy Edwards '59, rec. w. him and under own name, '60. Mus. dir. for Tony Martin '61–3. Acc. Christy in Austral. '63. Later, accomp. singers and worked in show bands in LV. Made occasional trips to Hawaii; app. w. Honolulu Symph. '66. Pl. at Beverly Hills Hotel '67–8; trio around LA '69. Fr. '70, arr. and cond. for pop acts in LV; arr. for Joe Williams, C. Basie, Al Hibbler '73. Fr. '70–4, wrote and cond. film projects for Sutherland Associates, employing Buddy Collette, Jack Sheldon, Frank Rosolino. Fav: Tatum; infls: Ravel, C. Parker. LPs: Atl.; bb on own label, Clover. CDs: w. Edwards (Cont.).

CASTRO-NEVES, (CARLOS) OSCAR (DE) (Oscar Neves), gtr, comp; b. Rio de Janeiro, Brazil, 5/15/40. Born a triplet in a highly musical family. Started on cavaquinho (similar to uke.); as teenager, pl. in gp. w. his bros., app. in nightclubs and on radio and TV. As teenager, he was active w. early bossa nova movement in Rio; comp. standards "Patinho Feio" (Ugly Duckling) and "Onde Esta Voce?" (Where Are You?). Perf. at first bossa nova concert at Carnegie Hall in Nov. 1962; in mid '60s, tour. w. Stan Getz; Lalo Schifrin; Dizzy Gillespie; Laurindo Almeida; et al. Settled in LA '67; pl. w. Paul Winter Consort '69–70; mus. dir. and feat. gtr. w. Sergio Mendes for ten yrs.; fr. '70s, pl. and/or rec. w. Getz; Flora Purim; Ella Fitzgerald; Milt Jackson; Quincy Jones; Joao Gilberto; Lee Ritenour; et al. Comp. and arr. mus. for films: *Blame It On Rio, Gabriela*; and orch. mus. for *Short Circuit II, Dirty Rotten Scoundrels*, etc. In '92, prod. two albums for Toots Thielemans. Prod. and comp. mus. for TV docu., *Reflections Through a Brazilian Eye*. Versatile and talented, Castro-Neves is a fine comp., arr., and gtrst. whose sound Leonard Feather described as one of pure "crystalline beauty." CDs: JVC; w. Fitzgerald (Pab.); J. Klemmer (MCA).

CATHCART, DICK (CHARLES RICHARD), tpt, voc; b. Michigan City, IN, 11/6/24; d. Los Angeles, CA, 11/8/93. Father pl. crnt.; three bros. have all been prof. mus. Began on cl. at age 4, sw. to tpt. at 13; later stud. w. Geo. Wendt, Louis Maggio. First job w. Rob Barnes at Indiana U. Pl. w. Ray McKinley, Alvino Rey 1942; AAF Radio Orch. '43–6; Bob Crosby '46. Worked as MGM studio mus. '46–9, then pl. w. Ben Pollack '49–50; Ray Noble '50–1; Frank DeVol, '51–3. Led own combo, Pete Kelly's Big Seven, fr. '51. The band was feat. in *Pete Kelly's Blues*—the radio series, the '55 film, and the '59 TV series. Dubbed solos for Billy May in film *Nightmare* '55. Also perf. on soundtracks to films *Dragnet* '54; *Battle Stations* '55. Did short stint on the road as singer w. the Modernaires in '50s; also worked as voc. in '60s. App. w. Dick Cary's band at Sacramento JF '85. Re-form. Big Seven and app. as soloist at fests. often w. pnst. Ray Sherman. The smooth clarity of his sound drew comparisons w. Beiderbecke but he named as his favs: Armstrong, Hackett, Butterfield. LPs connected w. Pete Kelly: RCA, Col., WB; *Bix MCMLIX,* WB. CDs: w. Harry James (Verve); Pollack (Jazz.).

CATHERINE, PHILIP, gtr; b. London, England, 10/27/42. English moth., Belgian fath. Family moved to Brussels after WWII. Became prof. at age 17. Tour. w. Lou Bennett 1959. In the '60s pl. w. Jack Sels; Fats Sadi; and on Belgian radio. Began pl. rock-jazz, work. w. Jean-Luc Ponty Dec. '70–June '72. Stud. for a yr. at Berklee Coll. of Mus. At the end of '73 he started a gp. called Pork Pie w. C. Mariano and Jasper van't Hof. He also pl. w. the Mike Gibbs band and Klaus Doldinger's Jubilee and Niels-Henning Ørsted Pedersen. In '76 he scored in a duet w. Larry Coryell at the Berlin JF; they then tour. together in Eur. and app. at various major fests. in Eur. and the US '77–8. In later yrs. Bireli Lagene join. them for perfs., often in tribute to Django Reinhardt. In between, in the '80s he worked in a trio w. Didier Lockwood and Christian Escoude; also Chet Baker. Favs: Reinhardt, Rene Thomas, J. McLaughlin, Coryell. CDs: Drey.; CMP; Elek.; Inak; Sept; CC; w. Baker (Phil.; Timel.; Enja; CC; Drey.); Coryell (ACT); Kenny Drew (Steep.; SN); Eur. Jazz Ens. (M.A. in mus.); Dexter Gordon; NHØ-Pedersen (Steep.); Grappelli (Musidisc; Bird.); Roff Kuhn (Blue Flame); Barney Wilen (IDA).

CATINGUB, MATT (MATTHEW MOODY), alto, other saxes, pno, dms, comp; b. No. Hollywood, CA, 3/25/61. Son of singer Mavis Rivers. Mainly self-taught. Start. w. moth. in clubs and concerts at age 16. Pl. w. Louie Bellson band at 17, off and on since then; Akiyoshi–Tabackin Band 1981–83. Dir. of jazz ensembles at Grove Sch. of Mus. '83–84. Accomp. Toni Tennille fr. '88; Jack Jones fr. '90. Favs: Cannonball Adderley, Phil Woods, David Sanborn; arrs: Nelson Riddle, Billy May. CDs: SB, incl. perfs. by M. Rivers; w. Bellson (Pab.); Tom Kubis (SB).

CATLETT, BUDDY (GEORGE JAMES), bs, sax, cl; b. Long Beach, CA, 5/13/33. Studied sax and cl. in Seattle, Wash., then bs. Played sax w. Bumps Blackwell band, which at times incl. Quincy Jones, Ernestine Anderson, and Ray Charles 1947–51. Then bs. became his main instrument, and he pl. w. Horace Henderson '56–7; Johnny Smith '58–59; Cal Tjader '59. Toured Eur. w. Q. Jones '59–60; pl. w. Junior Mance, Chico Hamilton, Johnny Griffin–Eddie "Lockjaw" Davis '60; Count Basie '61–4; Maynard Ferguson '64–5; Louis Armstrong '65–9; Roy Eldridge, Roland Hanna, Tyree Glenn '69–70. In '78, after freelancing in NYC, he ret. to Seattle, where he has been active on bs. and saxes in local gps. Favs: Ray Brown, Milt Hinton. CDs: w. Louis Armstrong; Basie; Ella Fitzgerald (Verve); Benny Bailey; Phil Woods (Cand.); Griffin-Davis (Jazzl.); C. Hawkins (Imp.); Mel Tormé (Stash).

CATLETT, SID (SIDNEY, "BIG SID"), dms; b. Evansville, IN, 1/17/10; d. Chicago, IL, 3/25/51. Studied pno. first, then dms., pl. latter w. sch. drum and bugle corps. Prof. debut w. Darnell Howard 1928; then w. Sammy Stewart, w. whom he went to NYC '30. Pl. w. Elmer Snowden '31; Benny Carter '33; Rex Stewart, Eddie Condon, McKinney's Cotton Pickers '34; Jeter-Pillars '34–5; Fletcher Henderson '36; Don Redman '36–8. Feat. in Louis Armstrong orch. '38–42, also pl. w. Benny Goodman '41. Worked w. Teddy Wilson '42–4. Led own gps. in Hollywood, Calif., '44–5; NYC, '46. Join. Louis Armstrong's All-Stars '47, remain. w. him for two yrs. Freelanced, primarily in Chi., until his death. An infl. stylist and melodic soloist w. a tremendous sense of swing, who was able to pl. w. both traditionalists and modernists dur. the bebop transition. Mel Powell told Whitney Balliett: "[t]his giant of a man had no peer as a percussionist. After all, he was playing on nothing but a set of traps. . . . Yet he invariably sounded like he was playing delicately tuned drums. . . . His sensitivity and delicacy of ear were extraordinary. So was his time." Films: *Smash Your Baggage* w. Snowden '33; *Jammin' the Blues* '44. Polls: *Esq.* Gold Award '44–5. Fest.: Nice '48. CDs: four tracks w. own gp. in *Classic Capitol Jazz Sessions* (Mos.); w. Billie Holiday, Albert Ammons, Chu Berry, Esquire All-Stars, Chocolate Dandies, and own qt. in *The Commodore Story* (Comm.); Louis Armstrong (BB; Dec.); Bechet (BB;

BN); Eldridge (Col.; Dec.); Goodman (Col.); Gillespie (Sav.); Ellington; Hampton (BB); Carter (B&B); Holiday (Dec.; Story.); Mezzrow (Story.); Buddy Rich; T. Wilson (Hep); Tatum (BL); Lester Young (Key.).

CAVASENO, JOEY (JOSEPH HARRY), alto sax, cl; b. Mineola, NY, 6/2/67. Father was amateur saxist, uncle pl. vln. Stud. w. Chasy Dean, Arnie Lawrence, then at Rutgers U. and the New Sch. Was discovered by Lionel Hampton while pl. in all-star hs jazz band. Feat. on cl. w. Hampton 1985, then pl. w. Arvell Shaw '85–6. Made rec. debut w. Doc Cheatham–Geo. Kelly '87. Pl. w. Illinois Jacquet '86–90; Panama Francis since '87; Bobby Forrester since '91. Has also worked w. Clark Terry, the Duke's Men, Wild Bill Davis, Henry Butler; led own qnt. Favs: Johnny Hodges, Charlie Parker, Lou Donaldson. TV: Regis Philbin. CDs: w. Cheatham (Stash); Jacquet (Atl.).

CELESTIN, PAPA (OSCAR PHILLIP), crnt, lead; Napoleonville, LA, 1/1/1884; d. New Orleans, LA, 12/15/54. Early interest in gtr. and mand., then took up tpt. and tbn. To NO in 1906, pl. w. Indiana Brass Band; in '08 w. Henry Allen Sr.'s Excelsior Brass Band; led own Tuxedo Band '10–13. Co-led Original Tuxedo Orch. w. William Ridgley '17–25. When the partnership w. Ridgley ended, Celestin led his own Tuxedo Jazz Orch., which enjoyed popularity in the NO area. Forced out of mus. dur. the Depression, he worked in a shipyard through WWII. Reorganized Tuxedo Jazz Orch. in '46; app. on radio and TV in early '50s. Perf. for Pres. Eisenhower '53. In '54, a bust of Celestin was presented to the Delgado Museum of NO. Although not noted as a great soloist, his use of mutes was effective, and he was a compelling vocalist and all-around perf. Recs. w. own band for Okeh, Col. CDs: GHB; Folk Lyric.

CEROLI, NICK, dms; b. Warren, OH, 12/22/39; d. Los Angeles, CA, 8/11/85. Played in Youngstown and Cincinnati while in sch. bef. join. Ralph Marterie, 1958. Between '59–65 work. in Chi., LV, and LA w. Marterie; Ray Anthony; Lionel Hampton; Gerald Wilson; Les Brown; Terry Gibbs. Rec. w. Jack Teagarden; Stan Kenton's LA Neophonic Orch. '66; Herb Alpert's Tijuana Brass '65–9. In '70s, he did studio work in LA, also pl. w. Pete Jolly; Zoot Sims; Richie Kamuca; Bill Berry; Bob Florence; Clark Terry; Pete Christlieb. Favs: PJ Jones, Elvin Jones, Buddy Rich. Fest: MJF w. Wilson, '63. TV: *Tonight Show*; Merv Griffin show. Book: *Modern Approach to Independence, Vols. I & II* (Try Publ., Hollywood, Calif.). LPs: w. Berry (Conc.); Florence (Trend);

Christlieb (Bosco); Christlieb–Warne Marsh (WB). CDs: w. Bobby Jaspar (FS); Z. Sims (Pab.).

CERRI, FRANCO, gtr, bs; b. Milan, Italy, 1/29/26. Son Stefano is prof. bs. and mus. teach. Self-taught fr. age 18. First prof. gig w. Kramer Gorni 1945. Pl. w. Gorni off and on '45–62; Flavio Ambrosetti off and on '48–70; Django Reinhardt '49; Stephane Grappelli off and on '49–72; Joe Turner '56; Daniel Humair off and on '56–90; Billie Holiday, Mal Waldron, Lee Konitz '59; Chet Baker '59–61; Kenny Clarke off and on '59–70; Enrico Intra fr. '60; Franco Ambrosetti off and on '60–80; Martial Solal, Buddy Collette '61; L. Konitz '62; Bud Shank '63; Lou Bennett '69–71; M. Solal, Phil Woods '70; Johnny Griffin '70–2; P. Woods '72; Tony Scott off and on '72–8; L. Konitz '74; Dado Moroni off and on '76–92; James Moody, Reggie Johnson '85; Barney Kessel '87–9; Tal Farlow '91; Ray Brown, L. Konitz '92. Cerri leads a qt. w. Enrico Intra, as well as a gtr. qt. In '86, he and Intra co-founded Musica Oggi, an organization for the promotion of jazz in Italy, and Civici Corsi Di Jazz, a jazz sch. in Milan. Author of two gtr. methods (Edizioni Fabbri, Edizioni Ricordi), he teaches advanced courses at the Civici Corsi Di Jazz. Favs: Jim Hall, B. Kessel; later infl: Rene Thomas. Polls: Diapason, Al Numero Uno awards; Ital. Critics Poll every yr. since '48. Fests: all major in Eur.; US '66; w. Italian all-stars at Town Hall '93. TV: More than six hundred apps. as host and guest on Eur. TV. LPS: RCA; Voce del Padrone; Col. CDs: DIRE; w. C. Baker (Jzld.).

CHALLIS, BILL (WILLIAM H.), arr; b. Wilkes-Barre, PA, 7/8/04; d. Wilkes-Barre, 10/4/94. Began on pno., then pl. sax; later led student band at Bucknell U. Join. Jean Goldkette as staff arr. 1926; formed close assoc. w. Bix Beiderbecke. Join. Paul Whiteman Orch. w. Beiderbecke '27. One of the pioneers in bb arr., he wrote jazz-oriented arrs. for Frankie Trumbauer rec. sess. and for Whiteman, some of which feat. Beiderbecke's crnt. improvs. scored for the tpt. section, incl. "Lonely Melody"; "Changes"; "Dardanella"; "San." He notated and edited Beiderbecke's pno. comps. for publ. '30. After leaving Whiteman in '30, Challis freelanced as an arr. for Trumbauer; Fletcher Henderson; Dorsey Bros.; Casa Loma Orch.; Lennie Hayton; several radio orchs.; and Artie Shaw, for whom he arr. "Blues in the Night." Later wrote for Bobby Hackett; Manhattan Transfer. Arr. Beiderbecke's pno. comps. for gtr. qnt. led by Bucky Pizzarelli for Monmouth-Evergreen '74. In '86, working fr. memory and by scaling down the Whiteman charts which had been preserved at Williams Coll., he rewrote the original Goldkette charts, which had been lost. They were rec. by Vince Giordano's Nighthawks. CDs: own '36 orch., Circle; *The Goldkette Project* (Circle); as arr.: w. Whiteman, Goldkette, F. Henderson (BB), A. Shaw (RCA).

CHALOFF, SERGE, bari sax; b. Boston, MA, 11/24/23; d. Boston, 7/16/57. Father, Julius, pl. pno. w. Bost. Symph; moth., Margaret, renowned pno. teacher at New Engl. Cons. and priv. Stud. pno. and cl., but self-taught on bari. after listening to Harry Carney, Jack Washington. Worked w. Tommy Reynolds 1939; Dick "Stinky" Rogers '41–2; Shep Fields '43; Ina Ray Hutton '44; Boyd Raeburn, Georgie Auld, Jimmy Dorsey '45. The emergence of Charlie Parker infl. him dur. this period, and by the time he pl. w. Auld's combo on 52nd St. he was already translating a fluent bop line to the bari. sax, previously regarded as cumbersome. With Herman '47–9, becoming a member of the celebrated "Four Brothers" sax section, which enhanced his reputation. Ret. to Bost., where he led a gp. and taught in the early '50s. On his own recs. and as a sideman on mid to late '40s small gp. recs., his virtuosity was impressive, but his finest work may be found on his own '55 Cap. LP *Boston Blow Up,* incl. an extraordinary rendition of "Body and Soul." Drug problems hampered his career and cancer partially paralyzed him. Polls: *DB* '49–51; *Met.* '49–53. CDs: *The Complete Serge Chaloff Sessions,* 4–CD box on Mos.; Up.; Cool 'N Blue; BL; w. Herman (Cap.; Col.; Laser.).

CHAMBERS, HENDERSON CHARLES, tbn; b. Alexandria, LA, 5/1/08; d. NYC, 10/19/67. Early exp. w. Morehouse Coll. band, Atlanta, Ga. Pl. w. various territory bands, incl. Neil Montgomery 1931; Doc Banks '32; Zack Whyte '34; Al Sears '35–6; Tiny Bradshaw '37–8. Moved to NYC '39, worked at the Savoy w. Chris Columbus '39–40; Louis Armstrong '41–43. Freelanced w. Don Redman '43; various gps. at Café Society, incl. Ed Hall '46–8; Tour. w. Lucky Millinder '50–2; Jerry Fielding '54. Also in '50s pl. and rec. w. Sy Oliver, Mel Powell; to Miami, Fla., w. Cab Calloway; subbed w. Duke Ellington '57; Mercer Ellington '59. Tour. w. Ray Charles '61–3; Count Basie '64–6. Org. rehearsal band w. Edgar Battle '67. Favs: Bobby Byrne, Benny Morton. CDs: w. Buck Clayton (Mos.); Jimmy Rushing (Vang.); Basie (Aff.).

CHAMBERS, JOE (JOSEPH ARTHUR), dms, pno, vib, comp; b. Stoneacre, VA, 6/25/42. Brother is Stephen Chambers, aka Talib Rasul Hakim, classical comp. Pl. pno. then dms. in family band. Att. Chester HS, Chester, Pa., then Phila. Cons. 1960–1, and American U. '61–3. Pl. w. Eric Dolphy '63; Freddie Hubbard '64–6; Lou Donaldson '65; Sam Rivers '65; Wayne Shorter '65–7; Chick Corea '66;

Miroslav Vitous '69. Also worked in '60s w. Jimmy Giuffre; Andrew Hill; Donald Byrd; Duke Pearson; Archie Shepp; Joe Henderson; Stan Getz; Herbie Hancock; McCoy Tyner. Chambers was an orig. member of Max Roach's perc. ens., M'Boom Re:Percussion, founded in '70. It was at this time that he began studying mallet instruments. Pl. w. Charles Mingus '71–3; own gps. since '74. Also pl. in '70s w. S. Rollins; Tommy Flanagan–Art Farmer; Joe Zawinul. Chambers received an NEA comp.'s grant '75. Rec. album of pno. music '80. Pl. w. Chet Baker '82; Ray Mantilla's Space Station, mid '80s; also pl. on soundtracks of three Spike Lee films. Mark Griffith wrote in *Modern Drummer*: "When you consider some of the special aspects of playing the vibes (such as dampening and muting) you gain important insight into his drumming." Favs. and infls: Roach, Elvin Jones, Kenny Clarke, Roy Haynes. Polls: *DB* New Star, '69. Fests: Eur. every yr. since '67; Mt. Fuji '85–7. Pl. own suite *The Almoravid,* at Carnegie Hall, '74. CDs: 32; BN; Den.; Cand.; Muse; w. W. Shorter; J. Henderson; B. Hutcherson; F. Hubbard; Andrew Hill (BN); C. Mingus (Col.; Atl.); Corea; Zawinul; Vitous (Atl.); M'Boom (Col.; SN; BM); D. Murray (BS); K. Hays (Steep.); S. Grossman (Red); A. Shepp (Imp.; Den.); R. Woodard (Cand.); C. Baker (Enja); Woody Shaw (32); Stanley Cowell (Conc.; BL).

CHAMBERS, PAUL LAURENCE DUNBAR JR., bs; b. Pittsburgh, PA, 4/22/35; d. NYC, 1/4/69. Started on bari. horn and tba. In Det. fr. age 13, took up bs. in 1949 and soon began working w. local mus., incl. Kenny Burrell. In Apr. '54, he went on the road w. Paul Quinichette for eight mos. bef. settling in NYC, where he pl. w. Bennie Green; Sonny Stitt; Joe Roland; J.J. Johnson and Kai Winding; and George Wallington. Fr. '55 to '63, he was an integral part of the various highly acclaimed Miles Davis rhythm sections, along w. Red Garland, Philly Joe Jones, Bill Evans, Wynton Kelly, and Jimmy Cobb. During this period, he also app. on numerous Prest. sess. w. Garland and Arthur Taylor. Form. trio w. Kelly and Cobb in '63, working as a unit for two and a half yrs., incl. backing Wes Montgomery for a yr. '65–6. Freelanced in NYC w. Tony Scott, Barry Harris, and others. Fell ill w. TB in latter part of '68. He displayed a large, resonant tone and broad-bottomed pulse and contributed dexterous arco and pizzicato solos. Polls: New Star Awards, *DB* Critics and Mus.' Mus. in Encyclopedia Yearbook '56. Favs: Blanton, Pettiford. Book: *The Music of Paul Chambers,* transcriptions of twenty of his solos, '84. Much in demand, he rec. w. a wide variety of musicians. CDs: BN; w. Davis (Prest.; Col.); Coltrane (Prest.; BN; Atl.); J.J. Johnson

(Prest.; Col.); Wes Montgomery (Riv.; Mile.; Verve); D. Gordon; J. Griffin; S. Clark; H. Mobley; I. Quebec (BN); S. Criss; R. Garland; G. Evans; S. Rollins; A. Taylor; G. Wallington (Prest.); K. Dorham; J. Heath; Kenny Drew; W. Kelly; Blue Mitchell; C. Terry (Riv.); A. Pepper; P. Newborn (Cont.); C. Adderley (Sav.; Em.); Milt Jackson (Atl.; BN; Imp.).

CHAMBLEE, EDDIE (EDWIN LEON), tnr sax, cl; b. Atlanta, GA, 2/24/20. Father pl. tpt.; moth. pl. pno. Received sax from fath. on 12th birthday. Grew up in Chi., where he att. Wendell Phillips HS. Worked as mus. while studying law for one yr. at U. of Chi. In army band 1941–6, then led own combo w. Osie Johnson '46. Led own gps. in Chi. '47–54; pl. w. Lionel Hampton '54–7. Married to Dinah Washington (whom he met through Wendell Phillips) '57–8; perf. and rec. w. Washington dur. this time. Pl. w. Cozy Cole '59–60; Milt Buckner '76; L. Hampton '77–8; Count Basie Orch. '82. Led own gp. every Sat. at Sweet Basil in NYC, '82–92, until ill health forced him to retire. Fests: Eur., Japan. LPs: B&B; Merc. CDs: w. Washington (Em.); M. Buckner; A. Cobb (B&B); Hampton (B&B; BB; Timel.).

CHAPIN, THOMAS, alto, mezzo-sop saxes, fl; b. Manchester, CT, 3/9/57; d. Providence, RI, 2/13/98. Studied at Hartt Coll. of Mus., Hartford, w. J. McLean, Paul Jeffrey 1976–8; B.A. fr. Livingston Coll. of Rutgers U., stud. w. Jeffrey, Ted Dunbar, K. Barron '78–80. Lead alto and fl. as mus. dir. w. L. Hampton '81–6; tour. Japan, So. Amer., Eur., and US incl. major fests., TV, and radio apps. Pl. w. Chico Hamilton qt. '89, incl. tour of Eur. From '88 he led his own trio and Spirits Rebellious gp. Pl. and rec. w. Machine Gun, where he was known as "Rage"; Motation; Ned Rothenberg Double Band; also pl. w. Gatemouth Brown; Walter Thompson bb; Alborada Latina; Flamenco Latina; Amenacer. He became ill while tour. in Africa, Jan. '97, developing leukemia that kept him inactive most of the following mos. His last perf. was 2/1/98 at a benefit for him in his birth-place of Manchester, where he made an unscheduled playing app. on stage. Chapin was a spontaneous, inventive improviser who pl. w. much heart, humor, and soul. Mike Zwerin described his "post-Ornette Coleman alto saxophone" as "'out' while in. In bounds out of bounds, if that makes sense. When in mainstream mode, he resembles his teacher Jackie McLean." Favs: Rahsaan Roland Kirk, Hermeto Pascoal, C. Parker, J. McLean, Debussy. Fests: w. Hampton, NJF-NY; Nice; North Sea; w. Hamilton, Leverkeusen; Maastricht '89; w. own gps., NJF-Saratoga '87; JVC-Saratoga '90; Knitting Factory '90, '96, '97; Vitoria '94; Umbria '96; JVC-NY,

Litchfield, Conn. '97. Film: *Music Man/Thomas Chapin*, as mus. and collage artist '90 (also in video). TV: Venezuela, Panama '87; Madrid Public TV '90; NJF '95 on PBS '96. Book: *10 Compositions* (Peace Park Pub., BMI '85). CDs: KFW; Arab.; Mu; Enemy; w. Hampton (Timel.); Rothenberg (Moers); Tom Varner (NW); Michael Musillami (Stash; Evid.); Axel Zwingenberger (Vagabond); Mario Pavone (KFW); D. Lahm (Generation).

CHARLAP, BILL (WILLIAM MORRISON), pno; b. NYC, 10/15/66. Mother is voc. Sandy Stewart; fath., comp. Moose Charlap; bro. Tom, bs. Dick Hyman is distant cousin. Began pl. pno. at age 3. Grad. of HS of the Perf. Arts, he stud. jazz and classical pno. w. Jack Reilly; Kenny Barron; Richie Beirach; Eleanor Hancock. Pl. w. Gerry Mulligan 1988–90; Helen Merrill '90; pno. duos w. Dick Hyman; Roger Kellaway; Derek Smith; Roland Hanna; Marian McPartland. Also pl. w. Marvin Stamm; Jay Leonhart; Joe Roccisano bb; and own duo, trio. Has accomp. Sheila Jordan; Barbara Lea; Carol Sloane; Sandy Stewart. Join. Phil Woods qnt. '95. A standout even in the field of bright young pianists to emerge in the '90s. Favs: Glenn Gould, Svatoslav Richter, Vladimir Horowitz. Fests: Eur. '88–90 w. G. Mulligan; Japan '90 w. H. Merrill; Mt. Hood, Ore., w. Red Mitchell; Jazz in July series at 92nd St. YMHA, NYC. TV: w. Mulligan. CDs: Conc.; Prog.; Chiaro.; Cinema City; w. Mulligan (GRP; A&M); Woods (Conc.); Jon Gordon (Chiaro.); J. Leonhart (DRG); S. Stewart (Cabaret); Stamm (MM).

CHARLES, DENIS (aka DENNIS), dms, perc; b. St. Croix, VI, 12/4/33; d. NYC, 3/26/98. Family pl. perc. instruments. At age 9, he pl. bongos w. Rhythm Makers. Moved to NYC w. two bros. 1945. Pl. congas, bongos in calypso, mambo bands, w. bro. Frank in late '40s. In '54 began teaching himself to pl. drum kit by listening to Art Blakey, Roy Haynes. Pl. w. Cecil Taylor '55–61, incl. app. w. Taylor and Archie Shepp in Jack Gelber's play *The Connection* '61. Pl. and rec. w. Steve Lacy '57, '63–4, '79, '82; Gil Evans '59; Sonny Rollins '62; A. Shepp '67. Largely inactive in '70s, then emerged in early '80s as member of Jazz Doctors w. Billy Bang, Frank Lowe; also pl. w. Wilbur Morris; Jemeel Moondoc; Joel Forrester. Tour. in Eur. w. Outlaws in Jazz, incl. Jac Berrocal, Daunik Lazro, Didier Levallet '93. Rec. duet album *Bangception* w. Bang, '82. Rec. in '80s w. Bang, Rob Brown. Made rec. debut as lead. '89. CDs: Silk.; Eremite; Wobbly Rail; w. C. Taylor (Cont.; BN); Bang (SN); Lacy (Prest.; hatArt; SN); Wilbur Morris (DIW); Rob Brown (Silk.).

CHARLES, RAY (Ray Charles Robinson), pno, alto sax, voc, comp-arr; b. Albany, GA, 9/23/30; d. Beverly Hills, CA, 6/10/04. Grew up in Greenville, Fla. Blind fr. age 6. Studied at St. Augustine's Sch. for the Blind; left at 15. Pl. w. local bands in Fla. fr. 1947. Moved to Seattle, where, fr. '50, he led a Nat Cole/Charles Brown–styled trio. Also tour. as pnst.-mus. dir., arr. for Lowell Fulson '50–2. Formed own band '54 and, using a blend of gospel and blues, rec. a succession of r&b hits for Atl., incl. "I Got a Woman," "Drown in My Own Tears," and "Hallelujah I Love Her So" '55–6. By the end of the '50s he was a world figure, having perf. at NJF, Carnegie Hall, and in Eur., pl. a mixture of jazz standards, pop, and gospel melodies. Singing blues in an authentic fashion with great energy and emotion, he also showed modern jazz infl. in his pl. (named Louis Jordan, Tatum, Bud Powell, Nat Cole and Oscar Peterson among his favorites). Early sidemen incl. David "Fathead" Newman; Don Wilkerson; Hank Crawford; Leroy Cooper. In the '60s, he had a string of pop hits, incl. "Georgia on My Mind"; "Ruby"; "Hit the Road Jack"; "I Can't Stop Loving You"; "Born To Love." His soulful treatment of country and western songs started a trend, but he did not abandon jazz. Instrumental recs. incl. sess. w. Milt Jackson on which he pl. alto sax. Own labels, Tangerine in the '60s and Crossover, briefly, in the '70s. Won *DB* critics poll New Star award as singer '58; Lifetime Achievement Award fr. NARAS '88. Films: acting role in Irish prod., *Ballad in Blue*; sang the soundtrack theme for *The Cincinnati Kid*. Book: *Brother Ray* w. David Ritz (Dial Press). CDs: Atl.; WB; Pab.; Rhino; Col.; DCC Compact Classics.

CHARLES, TEDDY (Theodore Charles Cohen), vib, comp, pno, perc; b. Chicopee Falls, MA, 4/13/28. Mother pl. pno. for silent movies; bro. was self-taught pnst. in Fats Waller style; sist. pl. harp. Studied dms. in hs. Moved to NYC 1946. Pl. on 52nd St., where he was helped by Max Roach, Red Norvo; began pl. pno. w. help fr. Hank Jones. Stud. dms., perc., vib., pno. at Juilliard Sch. of Mus. '47. Pl. vib. and dms. w. Bob Astor, '47; pno., vib. w. Randy Brooks '48; Benny Goodman Orch., Nov. '48. Made rec. debut w. Chubby Jackson bb '49. Pl. w. Buddy DeFranco '49; Artie Shaw Orch. '50; then formed qnt. w. Jackie Paris. Freelanced w. Anita O'Day; Oscar Pettiford; DeFranco bb; Roy Eldridge; Slim Gaillard. Led own gps. fr. early '50s. Stud. comp., arr. w. Hall Overton '50s; began rec. own comps. in series titled New Directions for Prest. Participated in Chas. Mingus's Jazz Composers Wkshp. '54–5. Led own Tentet at NJF '56. Mus. dir. for Prest. '56–7; Jubilee '58; Bethlehem '58–9; Warwick, Motown '60s. Also

worked as salvage diver; owned sailboat charter co. fr. '50s. Rec. w. Tentet for Atl. label '57–88; sidemen incl. Art Farmer; Gigi Gryce; J.R. Monterose; Joe Harris; Jimmy Raney; comps. by Geo. Russell, Jimmy Giuffre, Gil Evans and himself. Led New Directions qnt. on coll. concert tours fr. '64. Fr. '61 divided his time bet. mus. and captaining his charter sailboats, w. emphasis on the latter. Perf. in Italy w. Max Roach at Verona JF '88. Duo w. Harold Danko in '90s. Gigged in Key West, Fla., winters '95, '96; gp. incl. Johnny O'Neal. As a priv. teacher, Charles taught four-mallet technique to Terry Gibbs, Don Elliott, Tito Puente, Warren Chiasson. His comps. and recs. of the '50s, using modality and polytonality, presaged jazz of the following decades. Favs: Hampton, M. Jackson, Bobby Hutcherson, Chiasson; arrs: George Russell, Bob Brookmeyer, John Carisi, Gil Evans, Ellington, Strayhorn. Polls: *DB* New Star '54; *Met*. Mus. of Yr. '56; Jazz Composers Journal citation '89. Fests: NJF '56–64; Kool JF '84–5 w. Tentet. Film: app. w. Dizzy Gillespie, Stan Getz, Geo. Handy, Chubby Jackson in never released film by Gjon Mili. TV: own show on WPIX-TV, NYC, '54. Rec. w. Aretha Franklin; Earl Bostic. CDs: Atl.; Prest.; NJ; SN; w. Wardell Gray; Brookmeyer; T. Macero (Prest.) Miles Davis; Mingus (Debut).

CHASE, BILL (William Chiaiese), tpt, comp; b. Boston, MA, 1935; d. nr. Jackson, MN, 8/9/74. Studied at Berklee Coll. of Mus. w. Herb Pomeroy, rec. w. his bb 1957. Join. Maynard Ferguson as lead tpt. '58. Rec. w. Stan Kenton, NYC, and app. w. Woody Herman at MJF '59. Worked w. Herman on and off for ten yrs.; tour. in Eur. w. him '69. Formed Chase, a 9-pc. jazz-rock gp. comprising four tpts., org., rhythm section, and voc. *Chase*, its '71 debut LP on Epic, was voted number one pop album of the yr. in *DB* Reader's Poll. His suite *Ennea* on the band's second album was not as well received, and the gp. disbanded. Dur. a '74 comeback tour, Chase and three members of his band died in a plane crash. A powerful lead pl. and versatile all-around tpt. CDs: w. Herman (Col.; Moon); Ferguson (Roul.; Mos.).

CHEATHAM, DOC (ADOLPHUS ANTHONY), tpt, voc; b. Nashville, TN, 6/13/05; d. Washington, DC, 6/2/97. Cousin, Mason Johnson, pl. tpt. Began on dms., crnt., and sop. sax. Self-taught; later stud. theory w. Tom Timothy, "a tune detective in New York." Pl. in band at B.F.S. Boys Club 1910 at Phillips Chapel. In early '20s, he worked in pit band at Bijou Theater, backing Bessie, Mamie, and Clara Smith; Ethel Waters. Moved to Chi. and join. Midwest territory band, the Synco Jazzers, led by John Williams, husband of Mary Lou Williams, '26. Pl. in Chi. w. Albert

Wynn at Dreamland Café; Lil Armstrong; Louis Armstrong at Vendome Theater '26; in Phila. w. Wilbur DeParis '26; Bobby Lee's Cotton Pickers '27; in NYC w. Chick Webb '28. Tour. Eur. w. Sam Wooding '28–30. Pl. w. Marion Hardy, McKinney's Cotton Pickers '30; Cab Calloway '31–9; Benny Carter at Arcadia Ballroom '32; Teddy Wilson '39–40; also pl. in '30s w. Fletcher Henderson, Don Redman. A mysterious illness put him in the hospital for nine weeks in '39. After going to Paris to recuperate, he app. there w. Buck Clayton–Coleman Hawkins at the Hot Club '40. Ret. to the US, he pl. w. Carter again '40–1; Teddy Hill '41. Still troubled by ill health, he worked for a time in the post office and ran his own teaching studio. Pl. w. Eddie Heywood Sxt. '43–5; Hot Lips Page '46; Marcelino Guerra, incl. French tour, '50; Perez Prado, incl. Buenos Aires, '52; also app. w. Billie Holiday. Worked at Storyville in Bost., w. Vic Dickenson '53–4. Pl. at Jimmy Ryan's and w. Latin bands in NYC, incl. Machito, fr. mid '50s. Tour. Eur. w. Sammy Price '58; Africa w. Herbie Mann '60. Led own gp. at International Hotel, NYC, '60–5. Pl. w. Benny Goodman Sxt. '67; Ricardo Rey '67–70; Lionel Hampton; Barrelhouse Jazz band in Eur. '70; B'way show *Two Gentlemen of Verona* '71; Red Balaban and Cats '72–4; Countsmen; Sy Oliver '74; NYJRC at Carnegie Hall, Geo. Wein–Dick Hyman '70s. Cheatham led a gp. at Sweet Basil Sunday brunch fr. '80. Tribute concert by Highlights in Jazz '82. App. w. Dizzy Gillespie at Blue Note '92. Orig. known as a lead trumpeter, Cheatham blossomed into a soloist in later adulthood. His unhurried lyricism informed his thoughtful improvs., often topped off by the clarity of his upper register. As a singer, he displayed a warm, gentle, understated style. In his late 80s and early 90s, he was considered by many to be in his musical prime. He attributed his longevity and resilience to a healthy diet, and lifelong abstention fr. cigarettes, drugs, and alcohol. Fests: Eur., Africa fr. '50s; tribute at JVC-NY '91. TV: *Sound of Jazz* '57; ABC *Nightline* '96. Book: *Ad Lib Chord Reading* (B. Feldman & Co., London). First rec. w. Ma Rainey '26. CDs: Col; Park.; B&B; Sack.; Jazz.; Natasha; *Doc Cheatham and Nicholas Payton* (Verve); w. Gillespie (Tel.); B. Holiday; E. Heywood (Comm.); B. Clayton; M. Hinton (Chiaro.); Benny Carter (BB); L. Hampton (Timel.); B. Goodman (MM); Sammy Price (B&B); Pee Wee Russell (BL); B. Tate (Story.); Shorty Baker (Prest.); Swingville All-Stars (GTJ).

CHEATHAM, JEANNIE (Jean E. Evans), kybds, voc, comp, arr; b. Akron, OH, 8/14/37. From a mus. family, she began singing in Baptist church at age 5. Began studying classical pno. at age 6, but sw. to jazz at 13 after hearing an Erskine Hawkins rec. In 1950s,

she began pl. in house bands, backing such singers as Dakota Staton; Joe Williams; Al Hibbler; T-Bone Walker; Jimmy Rushing. Married Jimmy Cheatham in '61, lived in NYC and Wisc.; moved to San Diego, Calif., in '78. Form. Sweet Baby Blues Band w. husband '84, and began singing such crowd-pleasing, humorous songs as "Meet Me with Your Black Drawers On." Favs: Bud Powell, Mike Wofford, Wynton Kelly, Basie, B. Evans. Fests: Conc., Chi., MJF, Mt. Hood, KC, North Sea, Nice, New Zealand. Polls: *JT* Critics '90; *DB* '91; ASCAP Popular Mus. Award '84–91. TV: *Three Generations of the Blues*, PBS, '83. Radio: M. McPartland's *Piano Jazz*. CDs: Conc.

CHEATHAM, JIMMY (JAMES R.), tbn, bs tbn, comp, arr; b. Birmingham, AL, 6/18/24; d. San Diego, CA, 1/12/07. Musical roots in the Baptist church. Moved to Buffalo, N.Y., in late 1930s; pl. w. Rev. Walker's Community Concert Band, which incl. top sidemen fr. such NYC-based bands as Fletcher Henderson; Don Redman; McKinney Cotton Pickers; Cab Calloway; Jimmie Lunceford; Count Basie. To the West Coast in '51, worked w. Wardell Gray; Buddy Collette; Benny Carter; and Gerald Wilson. Ret. to Buffalo in '54; met and married Jeannie Evans in '61. Tour. w. Maynard Ferguson in '61. Fr. '62 to '72, he freelanced in NYC, arr. for films, commercials; mus. dir. for Chico Hamilton Productions. In '72, he tour. w. Ellington. Form. Sweet Baby Blues Band w. his wife in '84 and began rec. a series of successful albums for Conc. Jimmy and Jeannie taught at U. of Wisc. in late '70's bef. moving to San Diego in '78. Profess. of mus. at UCSD since '78, teach. improv. and black music history, and, since '86, Dir. UCSD Jazz Program. Fests: Conc., Chi., MJF, Mt. Hood, KC, North Sea, Nice, New Zealand. Polls: *JT* Critics '90; *DB* '91. TV: *Three Generations of the Blues*, PBS '83. CDs: Conc.

CHEKASIN, VLADIMIR, saxes, kybds, comp; b. Sverdlovsk, Russia, 2/24/47. Greatly esteemed in former Soviet Union, he took up vln., then cl. and sax, leading bands from 1967. Living in Vilnius fr. '71, worked off and on w. pnst. V. Ganelin and percst. Vladimir Tarasov. Won first prize in jazz competition in Prague '71 and began rec. that yr. Led student band while teaching at Lithuanian State Cons. '82; later led various gps. and bands. He names both jazz and classical artists among his infls. and has been compared to Rahsaan Roland Kirk and Ben Webster. App. in film *Taxi Blues* '89, pl. w. Hal Singer. CDs: w. Ganelin Trio (Leo; hatArt).

CHERICO, GENE (EUGENE), bs; b. Buffalo, NY, 4/15/35; d. Santa Monica, CA, 8/12/94. Began on drms. but studied bs. as physical therapy after injuring arm in train accident while a member of army band, early 1950s. Cont. studies in Bost., at Berklee, where he met Toshiko Akiyoshi, w. whom he worked off and on for many yrs. Pl. w. Herb Pomeroy '57–9, and in '60s w. Maynard Ferguson; Red Norvo; Benny Goodman; George Shearing; Stan Getz; Dick Grove; Peggy Lee; and others. In '70s, tour. w. Frank Sinatra; Nancy Wilson. Work in LA studios; wrote and pl. bs. theme on segments of Rod Serling's *Night Gallery*. Fest: Concord w. T. Gibbs '73. In the mid '80s, he was diagnosed w. a serious illness that severely curtailed his pl. career. CDs: w. Akiyoshi (Cand.; RCA; FS); Paul Desmond (BB); Getz (Verve); Bill Perkins (Inter.).

CHERRY, DON (DONALD EUGENE), pocket tpt, crnt, tpt, perc, doussn'gouni, tambura, sitar, fl, comp; b. Oklahoma City, OK, 11/18/36; d. nr. Malaga, Spain, 10/19/95. Daughter Jan pl. vln. and sings; stepdaughter Neneh is pop singer; son David pl. synth. in LA; son Eagle Eye is dmr. in Bklyn. Fath. owned Cherry Blossom club in Okla. City; Charlie Christian, Fletcher Henderson pl. there. Family moved to LA 1940. Began pl. tpt. in jr. hs; form. first band, Jazz Messiahs, w. Billy Higgins and altoist Geo. Newman ca. '49. Cherry att. Sam Adams HS but was expelled for cutting classes to pl. w. Jefferson HS bb. Studied harm. w. Newman, Jefferson's arr. Heard Charlie Parker–Chet Baker at Tiffany club. Gigged in LA w. Red Mitchell, Dexter Gordon, Wardell Gray, etc. fr. '51. Met James Clay, Ornette Coleman '53. Rec. w. Coleman for Contemporary label '58. Began pl. pocket tpt. '59. When Coleman was signed by Atlantic '59, he and Cherry were sponsored to att. the Sch. of Jazz in Lenox, Mass., Aug. '59. Came to NYC w. Coleman to pl. at Five Spot, fall '59. Rec. w. John Coltrane '60. Left Coleman ca. '62; pl. briefly w. Steve Lacy, Sonny Rollins '63. Founding member of NY Contemporary Five w. Archie Shepp, John Tchicai '63. Pl. in Eur. w. Contemp. Five '63–4; Albert Ayler '64; own gp. w. Gato Barbieri in Paris and NYC '64–6. Also pl. w. indigenous mus. in No. Africa, mid '60s. Pl. w. Geo. Russell in Stuttgart, Germ., '65; Giorgio Gaslini in Milan, Italy, '66. Freelanced in NYC and Eur., late '60s. Artist-in-res. at Dartmouth Coll. '70, then moved to Sweden '71; pl. w. wife Moki at Museum of Mod. Art in Stockholm. Pl. at NJF-NY in Central Park w. Organic Music Theater. Artist-in-res. at Creative Music Studio, Woodstock, N.Y., '74, then stud. voice and tabla in India w. Ustad Zia Mahuddin Daggar '74; stud. Turkish mus., late '70s. Pl. and rec. w. Collin Walcott '77, and w. him and Nana Vasconcelos in gp., Codona, late '70s–'84. Fr. '76 he, Dewey Redman, Charlie Haden, and

Ed Blackwell pl. as New and Old Dreams, rec. in '80. Worked w. rock mus. Lou Reed. Visiting artist at Harvard U. '80. Tour. West Africa, Austral. '81. Stud. Flamenco mus. in Spain '83. Formed own gp., Nu, w. Carlos Ward, Vasconcelos '84. Pl. w. all-star gp., The Leaders, '84–6; w. Indian mus. at Jazz Yatra, Bombay, '84; Jabbo Smith at Berlin JF '86. Reunion tour and rec. w. Coleman, Charlie Haden, Ed Blackwell '87. Rec. for A&M as lead. w. Haden, James Clay, Billy Higgins '89. Cherry settled in SF in the '80s and pl. w. Peter Apfelbaum's Heiroglyphics Ens. and his own gps. Nu and Multikulti. Made another reunion tour w. Coleman, '93. Films: soundtracks for *New York Eye and Ear Control*; *Holy Mountain*. CDs: A&M; BN; ECM; Mag.; Aff; w. Coleman (Cont.; Atl.); Coltrane (Atl.); Rollins (RCA); Codona; C. Haden; Collin Walcott (ECM); Old and New Dreams (ECM; BS); Jazz Composers Orch.; Carla Bley (JCOA); Johnny Dyani (Steep.); A. Ayler (Free.; ESP); S. Lacy (NJ); C. Rouse (Land.); Sun Ra (A&M); H. Ruiz (Novus); F. Lowe (SN); P. Bley (Musidisc).

CHERRY, EDWARD E. JR., gtr, bs, pno; b. New Haven, CT, 10/12/54. Mother was amateur pnst. Began on cl. in elem. sch., then sw. to gtr. in jr. hs. Stud. gtr. priv. for two yrs., then at Berklee Coll. of Mus. 1973. Pl. w. Tim Hardin '73; Jimmy McGriff '74–5; Dizzy Gillespie '78–92; Sam Rivers '83–4; Brownie McGhee '85; Kenny Burrell Jazz Gtr. Band '86; Paquito D'Rivera '91; Pheeroan Aklaff fr. '91; Roy Hargrove '97. Favs: Grant Green, Jimi Hendrix, Wes Montgomery. Fests: Eur. fr. '80; China w. Bobby Battle, '85. TV: *A Night in Tunisia* w. Gillespie '80–1; PBS, *A Dream Deferred* '84. CDs: GH; w. P. D'Rivera (Chesky); Jon Faddis (Epic); Aklaff (Gram.); Gillespie (Pab.; Enja); H. Threadgill (BS); Andy McKee (Maple.).

CHESKY, DAVID, pno, comp, arr; b. Miami Beach, FL, 10/29/56. Began pl. pno. at age 5. Studied pno. w. Sanford Gold, John Lewis; comp. w. David Del Tredici. Own bb debuted at Storyville, NYC, 1977, pl. at NJF-NY the same yr. Founded Chesky Recs., a label praised for its sound quality, '89. Has prod. numerous sess. w. such leaders as McCoy Tyner; Tom Harrell; Phil Woods; Clark Terry; Paquito D'Rivera; Luizi Bonfa; Bucky Pizzarelli; and Fred Hersch. Rec. LP, *Rush Hour*, for Col. '79. CDs: Chesky, incl. albums of chorinhos and tangos, acc. by Romero Lubambo.

CHESTNUT, CYRUS, pno, comp; b. Baltimore, MD, 1/17/63. Grandfather a minister and church pnst.; fath. a pnst. who began teaching him at age 7.

As a boy, he pl. at the Mt. Calvary Star Baptist Church; his mus. is still infl. by his gospel roots. Att. Peabody Prep. Inst. and Berklee Coll. of Mus., where he received several scholarships: Eubie Blake 1982; Oscar Peterson '83; Quincy Jones '84. Grad. w. deg. in jazz comp. and arr. '85. Worked w. Jon Hendricks, incl. Eur. fests., '89; Terence Blanchard–Donald Harrison; Wynton Marsalis; Betty Carter. Member of LCJO '95–6, incl. Eur. tour, summer '95. "Mr. Chestnut draws deeply on the black musical tradition, and outside of the standard debts owed to the jazz pianists Bud Powell, Thelonious Monk, McCoy Tyner, Ahmad Jamal and others," wrote Peter Watrous in a club review for the NY Times, "his playing was filled with references to church music and the blues. It came out in his touch and his rhythms and the way he valued the use of music as a direct translation for expression. And it came in the feeling of joy that permeated his playing." App. in Robert Altman's film and video, Kansas City. LP w. Blanchard–Harrison (Col.). CDs: Atl.; Evid.; w. Carl Allen (Atl.); Carter; C. McBride; R. Hargrove; Kansas City soundtrack (Verve); M. Carvin (Muse); Dave Young (JT); Kathleen Battle (Sony Classical); Harrison (Cand.; Sw. Bas.); R. Burrage (Sound Hills); Bud Shank (Mile.).

CHIASSON, WARREN, vib, pno, perc, comp; b. Cheticamp, N.S., Canada, 4/17/34. Many mus. on moth.'s side; fath. pl. vln. Raised in Sydney, N.S. Classical vln. lessons for six yrs; then pl. gtr., pno., tbn. Mainly self-taught; stud. briefly w. Lennie Tristano, Geo. Russell in late 1950s. Pl. w. army band in Halifax '51–5. Pl. xyl. in coll., vib. fr. '57. Studio work for CBC in Halifax, N.S., '57–9. Came to NYC to sell a song '59, met George Shearing's manager. Pl. w. Shearing, '59–61, incl. Austral. tour '60. Pl. w. B'way show Foxy tour. co. in Dawson City, Yukon, '62. App. w. Gunther Schuller, Milton Babbitt, Eric Dolphy, Richard Davis in Perspectives of New Music concert at Carnegie Recital Hall '62. Pl. in NYC w. own gps. and orchs., incl. Buddy Morrow, Vaughn Monroe, Warren Covington, Sammy Kaye, Tex Beneke, Rusty Dedrick; Lee Castle, early '60s; house band at NYC World's Fair '64–5; Bill Dixon, Grachan Moncur III '67. Led gp. w. Jimmy Garrison, Sonny Brown, Arnie Lawrence '67–72. B'way show Hair '68–72; Brainchild in Phila. '73. Hosted weekly sess. at Signs of the Zodiac, NYC, '68–70. Pl. w. Shearing off and on '72–4; Chet Baker '74; solo vibes at Gregory's, NYC '75; Roberta Flack '75. Much freelance work w. Frank Strozier; Lee Konitz; Al Dailey; Joe Farrell; also gtrs., incl. Jim Hall; Jimmy Raney; Chuck Wayne; Tal Farlow; Joe Puma; Dick Garcia; Gene Bertoncini. Subbed for Lionel Hampton at the '88 re-creation of the '38 Carnegie Hall concert. In '80s and '90s also worked as solo pnst. Taught at St. Mary's U., Halifax, '77–8, and is the author of a vib. method, The Contemporary Vibraphonist (Col. Pict. Publ.). Comps: "Bossa Nova Scotia"; "Ultramarine"; "Bravel." Favs: Milt Jackson, Teddy Charles, Cal Tjader. Fests: Austral. '60; Carib. '86. TV: Roberta Flack in Concert; Sat. Night Live; many apps. on CBC. CDs: Empathy; Audio.; w. Shearing (Mos.); Dolphy (Enja).

CHILDERS, BUDDY (MARION), tpt; b. St. Louis, MO, 2/12/26. Self-taught; sch. band in Bellville, Ill. Auditioned for Stan Kenton, Dec. 1942, and pl. w. the band seven times '43–54. Also pl. w. Benny Carter '44; Les Brown '47; Woody Herman '49; Frank Devol '50–1; Tommy Dorsey; '51–2; Georgie Auld and Charlie Barnet '54. Freelanced in LA and LV fr. mid '50s; worked regularly w. Frank Sinatra fr. '80s. Worked and rec. w. Akiyoshi-Tabackin bb '81. Also led own band in Chi., in late '80s. Known principally as a fine lead tptr., Childers is also a capable jazz soloist. Own LP on Liberty. CDs: Cand.; w. Kenton (Cap.); J. Leitham (USA); Carmen McRae (BN); Anita O'Day (Moon); Marty Paich (Cand.); André Previn (BL); Shorty Rogers (BB).

CHILDS, BILLY (WILLIAM EDWARD), pno, kybds, comp; b. Los Angeles, CA, 3/8/57. B. Mus. in comp., USC. Studied jazz harm. w. Herb Mickman, classical pno. w. Leon Simmons. First prof. jazz gig was a two-wk. tour of Japan w. J.J. Johnson and Nat Adderley 1977. Worked mainly w. Freddie Hubbard '78–84, incl. several Eur. tours. In late '70s, he tour. Japan w. Hubbard, Marlon Jordan, and Dianne Reeves, whose accomp. he was intermittently fr. '79. Based in LA in '80s, he pl. many local dates w. own qt. (usually w. Bob Sheppard, Tony Dumas, Mike Baker). Also pl. w. Eddie Daniels; Alan Holdsworth; Bobby Hutcherson; and Branford Marsalis. A versatile comp. and soloist who absorbs musical knowledge fr. all cultures, Childs aspires to achieve what he describes as the depth and profundity of John Coltrane's music. Premiered his Concerto for Piano and Jazz Chamber Orchestra at MJF '94. Favs: Hancock, Tyner, Jarrett, Corea; comps: Ellington, Hindemith, Hancock, Honneger, Wm. Walton. CDs: WH; w. Hubbard (Pab.); Daniels (GRP); Bruce Forman (Conc.); Bunky Green (Delos); Holdsworth (Cream); Grover Washington (Elek.).

CHILTON, JOHN JAMES, tpt, flg, comp; b. London, England, 7/16/32. Led own band 1954–7, then pl. and arr. w. Bruce Turner's Jump Band '58–63; Alex Welsh '63; Mike Daniels bb '63–5. Led own gp., Swing Kings, '66–8. Co-led Feetwarmers w.

Wally Fawkes '69–73, then became sole leader in '74. The Feetwarmers have tour. extensively as a backup gp. for singer George Melly. Chilton has authored several important jazz books, incl. *Who's Who of Jazz: Storyville to Swing Street* (London, 1970); books about McKinney's Cotton Pickers, the Jenkins Orphanage bands, and Bob Crosby's Bob Cats; and biographies of Louis Armstrong (w. Max Jones), Billie Holiday, Coleman Hawkins, and Sidney Bechet. CDs: w. G. Melly (Legacy).

CHIRILLO, JAMES LOUIS, gtr, bjo, comp, arr; b. Waltham, MA, 5/2/53. Grandfather pl. first tpt. in NYC Sanitation Dept. band 1924–46. First prof. gig w. rock band Heart '71. Stud. gtr. w. Al Galante in Bellevue, Wash., '73; Bellevue Comm. Coll. '73–4; Al Turay in Seattle, Wash., '74; Jack Peterson at No. Tex. State U. '75–8; Tiny Grimes '82–4; Remo Palmier fr. '92. Stud. comp., arr. at No. Tex. State and in NYC w. John Carisi '88–92; Bill Finegan fr. '92. Pl. w. mil. band at West Point '79–82; Tiny Grimes '83; Haywood Henry, Eddie Durham, Eddie Barefield, Al Casey, Earle Warren, Joe Newman, Percy France at West End, NYC, '83–91; Benny Goodman Orch. '85–6; Sal Mathews at Hyatt Hotel, NYC, '83–8; Buck Clayton bb '87–91; Ken Peplowski fr. '87; Ruby Braff '88; Dick Sudhalter, Kenny Davern fr. '88; Claude Williams, Loren Schoenberg fr. '89; Jack Wilson fr. '90; Smithsonian Jazz Orch. fr. '91. Toured UK w. Peanuts Hucko, '91. Chirillo's arrs. have been rec. by the Schoenberg Orch. Favs: Grant Green, Freddie Green, Dick McDonough; arrs: Ellington, Strayhorn, Eddie Sauter, Bill Finegan. Fests: all major w. Goodman, Clayton. TV: *Let's Dance* w. Goodman '85. CDs: w. Schoenberg; Goodman (MM); Joe Wilder (Eve. Star); C. Williams (Arh.); Peplowski (Conc.).

CHISHOLM, GEORGE, tbn; b. Glasgow, Scotland, 3/29/15; d. Milton Keynes, Bedfordshire, England, 12/6/97. Inspired by Jack Teagarden, he gigged around Glasgow as teenager. To London 1936; worked w. Teddy Joyce. Member of Benny Carter's int'l band in Holland, summer of '37; also rec. w. Ambrose, Coleman Hawkins, Fats Waller and own gps. in late '30s. Pl. w. and arr. for the RAF Squadronaires fr. '41. After WWII, freelanced in radio, TV, and led own gps. Pl. w. Louis Armstrong at Hungarian Relief Fund benefit '56. In '82, having recuperated fr. heart surgery, he tour. w. Keith Smith. From mid '80, he made several apps. at Colo. JP. Considered by many to be one of Engl.'s most original jazz instrumentalists, he was a superlative musician with an ageless style. Retired fr. active pl. '95. Awarded the OBE '84. Radio: BBC Show Band fr. '52, incl. *Goon Show*. TV: *Black and White Minstrel Show* '50s. CDs: w. Carter (Class.; Pearl); Hawkins (ASV); John Petters (CMJ); Waller (EMI Pathe/Jazztime); Mike Westbrook (Transatlantic/Line).

CHITTISON, HERMAN ("IVORY"), pno; b. Flemingsburg, KY, 10/15/08; d. Cleveland, Ohio, 3/8/67. Studied in Nashville, Tenn., and at Kentucky St. Coll. Began prof. w. Zack Whyte, Cincinnati, Ohio, 1928–31; tour. as pnst. for Stepin Fetchit. Moved to NYC early '30s, acc. Adelaide Hall, Ethel Waters, rec. w. Clarence Williams '30, '33. Join. Willie Lewis w. whom he went to Paris and pl. w. on and off '35–8; also tour. w. Louis Armstrong '34. Form. Harlem Rhythm Makers w. other members of Lewis's band, and tour. Egypt w. it '38–40. Ret. to NYC, acc. Fetchit again '40; Mildred Bailey '41; perf. on CBS radio show *Casey, Crime Photographer* '42–51. Form. trio and became a fav. through long engagements at the Blue Angel and other supper clubs in NYC and Bost., through '50s and early '60s. Perf. dur. his last yrs. in Akron and Cleveland, Ohio. A tasteful, Tatum-inspired pl. w. fluent technique. CDs: IAJRC; w. George Wettling in *Key. Coll.* (Em.); Louis Armstrong (Dec.); C. Williams (CDS).

CHRISTIAN, BUDDY (NARCISSE J.), bjo; also gtr, pno; b. New Orleans, LA, ca. 1895; d. New Orleans, ca. 1958. Played w. many bands in NO fr. 1910; pno. w. King Oliver '15–16 bef. moving to NYC '19, where he pl. bjo. and pno. Worked w. Willie "The Lion" Smith '19; Lucille Hegamin '21, '26; June Clark '23. Bjo. duo. w. Fred Jennings '29, after which his career becomes obscure. Rec. many sess. w. Clarence Williams, incl. the Blue Five w. Louis Armstrong and Sidney Bechet; w. Red Onion Jazz Babies '24; own band for OKeh '26. CDs: w. Armstrong (Aff.); Bechet (Media; EPM Musique); Williams (EPM/Hot 'n Sweet).

CHRISTIAN, CHARLIE (CHARLES), gtr; b. Dallas, TX, 7/29/16; d. NYC, 3/2/42. Raised in Oklahoma City, Okla. Stud. w. fath., a blind gtrst.; his bros., Edward and Clarence, were also mus. Playing locally, Christian quickly established he was a mus. who was admired fr. early on. An innovator on gtr., musically and technically, he pl. an amplified acoustic gtr. as early as 1937. His influences included Eddie Durham and Lester Young. He pl. bs. for Alphonso Trent and gtr. w. other bands, incl. Anna Mae Winburn, Nat Towles, and Lloyd Hunter; also worked with Jeter-Pillars band in St. Louis, and Lesley Sheffield in Oklahoma City. John Hammond heard him and recommended him to Benny Goodman. Hammond arranged that Christian audition for Goodman in Aug. '39 in LA at the Victor Hugo Hotel;

Goodman hired him on the spot. Christian was soon featured on Goodman's radio broadcasts and with his newly formed sxt. In the early '40s, he participated in the seminal sessions in Harlem at Minton's and Monroe's Uptown House, where his harmonic sophistication, ingenious phrasing, and hornlike solos contributed much to the early language of bop. Tragically, Christian's role here and his work with Goodman abruptly ended: he contracted tuberculosis in mid '41 and spent his last few months in an NYC hospital. Through the wide exposure Christian gained during his stay with Goodman, he quickly achieved fame as an outstanding soloist. As the first modern jazz gtrst. to play single-line improvisations on the elec. gtr., he influenced a small army of gtrsts. who followed in his wake: Barney Kessel, Herb Ellis, Kenny Burrell, Tal Farlow, et al. His work alongside other bop pioneers is strikingly shown in some sess. rec. by Jerry Newman at Minton's and Monroe's. First issued in an album of 78s and later on LP, these tracks have been reissued on CD. Polls: *DB* '39–41; *Met.* '41–2. Rec. on acoustic gtr. w. Edmond Hall for BN '41. CDs: Jazz Anth.; Col. (incl. Goodman sxt. & bb); w. Jerry Jerome (Arb.); L. Hampton (BB; CDS); E. Hall (BN); *Spirituals to Swing* (Vang.).

CHRISTIAN, EMILE JOSEPH, tbn; bs; b. New Orleans, LA, 4/20/1895; d. New Orleans, 12/3/73. From mus. family. Bro. Frank Joseph (b. NO, 9/3/1897; d. 11/27/73) pl. brass instrs., mostly known on crnt. Pl. w. bros. in local bands, incl. Papa Jack Laine, Alfred "Baby" Laine. Led own gp., Frank Christian's Ragtime Band, 1910–18; to Chi. then NYC '18. Recs. w. Jimmy Durante '18–20. Ret. to Chi. as lead. Bro. Charles (b. NO, 7/25/1885; d. 6/11/64) did not become a full-time mus., but pl. tbn. in Frank's band and other NO orchs. Emile pl. tbn. w. bros. in local bands and slide crnt., bs., cl. w. Frank's orch. Worked w. Merritt Brunies in NO and Chi. ca. '16. Join. Bert Kelly in Chi. '17; then w. Orig. NO Jazz Band, led by Brunies, in Chi. Replaced Eddie Edwards in ODJB in NYC '18; tour. and rec. w. ODJB in Engl. '19–20. Ret. to NYC, pl. w. Phil Napoleon's Memphis Five '21, bef. ret. to Eur. where he remained for twenty yrs., working all over the Continent and in India: w. Eric Borchard Orch., Berlin, '24; Leslie Sterling, Paris, and Lud Gluskin, Germ., '27–30. Pl. in Belgium, Norway, Den. in mid '30; pl. in Bombay and tour. intercontinentally as only white member of Leon Abbey's orch. After WWII, ret. to NO, pl. there through late '60s w. such mus. as Leon Prima, Sharkey Bonano, George Girard. Tour. w. Louis Prima '57. Fav: T. Dorsey. Fests: Disneyland '67; NO, '68–9. Pl. bs. on George Girard Story. LP. CD: ODJB (BB).

CHRISTIAN, JODIE MORRIS, pno; b. Chicago, IL, 2/2/32. Both parents pl. pno. Stud. at Chi. Sch. of Mus. 1943. Pl. in church and sch., danced in talent shows, and sang w. Sharps and Flats and Thorne Gospel Crusaders 1945. Form. own voc. gp., The Ensemble of Rhythm, '51. First gigs on pno. w. Ron Hall, Von Freeman. Pl. at officers club while in air force in Japan '54. Pl. w. Ira Sullivan, Johnny Griffin at Cotton Club, Chi., '58–9; Lester Young '59; Coleman Hawkins early '60s. Founding member of AACM. Freelanced extens. w. Gene Ammons; Sonny Stitt; Eddie Harris; S. Rollins; Don Byas; Milt Jackson; Benny Carter; Frank Foster; S. Getz; Buddy Montgomery; Roscoe Mitchell. Christian is mus. dir. for The Lyon and Healy Mus. Sch. and the Better Boys Republic, and a member of Jazz Express, which presents concerts in Chi. public schs. Favs: Nate Coleman, Tatum, Buddy Wheaton. Fests: Int'l tours w. E. Harris '69, '91; Roscoe Mitchell '90; Art Porter '92. TV: Mike Douglas w. E. Harris; Ch. 11 Jazz (Chi. PBS) w. Byas. CDs: Del.; w. R. Mitchell (BS); Von Freeman; Louis Smith (Steep.); I. Sullivan; Lin Halliday; Mike Smith (Del.); E. Harris (Rh.); Ammons–Dexter Gordon (Prest.).

CHRISTIANSON, DENNY (DENNIS RICHARD), tpt, arr, comp, lead; b. Rockford, IL, 9/12/42. Studied at Navy Sch. of Mus., Wash., D.C. Pl. at Harrah's Casino in Lake Tahoe, Nev. 1971–5, then worked as studio mus. and arr. in LA '75–80. Moved to Montreal, Can. '80. Pl. w. studio orchs., also taught at U. of Montreal '83–4; Concordia U. '86–7; McGill U. '88–90. Christianson has led his own bb since '81 at fests in Can. and Eur.; rec. w. Pepper Adams as feat. soloist '86. He became a naturalized Can. citizen in '91. Fests: all major in Can. and Eur. CDs: JT.

CHRISTIE, (RONALD) KEITH, tbn; b. Blackpool, England, 1/6/31; d. London, England, 12/16/80. Began at age 14, then stud. at Guildhall Sch. of Mus., London. Pl. w. Humphrey Lyttelton 1949–51; Christie Brothers' Stompers w. bro. Ian, cl., Ken Colyer '51–3; John Dankworth '53–5; Tommy Whittle '55–6; Ted Heath '56–8; Bobby Lamb–Ray Premru '60. Freelanced in '60s-70s incl. Tubby Hayes bb; Kenny Wheeler bb; trad. jazz work w. Lyttelton, Max Harris; tour. Eur. w. B. Goodman '70–2. Worked w. London company of *Bubbling Brown Sugar* in late '70s, but was injured when he fell from the raised theater set. Pl. w. Best of British Jazz after recuperating. Favs: Louis Armstrong, Jack Teagarden, C. Parker, Al Cohn. Fests: US w. Heath. LPs: w. Lyttelton (Dormouse); Hayes (Fontana). CDs: *Christie Brothers' Stompers* (Cadillac); w. Dankworth (Sepia); Goodman (Verve); B. Rich (Sequel).

CHRISTIE, LYN (LYNDON VAN), bs, el-bs, comp; also tpt, kybds; b. Sydney, Australia, 8/3/28. Raised in New Zealand. Fath. pl. sax and was pres. of mus. union in Christchurch, NZ. Moth. pl. pno.; bros. pl. dms. and bassoon. Self-taught. First gigs w. parents' dance band, then w. Martin Winiata, Julian Lee on weekly radio broadcasts. Grad. fr. Otago Medical Sch., worked as doctor, pl. infreq. dur. this time. Ret. to Sydney in 1961 to practice medicine, but soon bec. involved w. mus. Led own qt.; also rec. w. Errol Buddle '63; Judy Bailey '64. Moved to NYC '65. Was chief resident at Yonkers (N.Y.) Gen. Hosp. '66–8, then stud. w. Homer Mensch at Juilliard Sch. of Mus. '68–9. Freelanced in duos w. Eddie Thompson; J. Byard; David Lahm; Patti Bown; Lance Hayward; R. Hanna; Freddie Redd; Pat Rebillot; Mike Abene; Dick Katz; gps. w. Jeremy Steig; Tal Farlow; Don Heckman; Paul Winter; Al Cohn–Zoot Sims; Chet Baker; Daphne Hellman; Ahmad Jamal; Ted Curson; Clark Terry; Chico Hamilton; bbs incl. Thad Jones–Mel Lewis; Buddy Rich; Dick Cone; Bobby Rosengarden. Also pl. w. Westchester, Northeast. Penna., and Ridgefield symph. orchs. Tour. and rec. w. Toshiko Akiyoshi '71; Attila Zoller '71, '74. Pl. at Colo. JP '71–3. Led own gps. fr. '73 w. sidemen incl. Randy Brecker; John Scofield; Walter Bishop Jr.; Vic Juris. Join. faculty at Westchester Cons. '73, where he start. annual June JF '80. Also taught in Scranton, Penna., pub. schs. and at U. of Scranton; Mercy Coll. '78–90; West. Conn. St. U. '79–90; Lehman Coll. '89–95; and Manhattanville Coll., fr. '88. Rec. w. Mike Mainieri '68; Tal Farlow '76, '81; D. Hellman '85. Comp. several film scores. Favs: Blanton, Ray Brown, Pettiford, P. Chambers. TV: Austral. Broad. Comm. '61–5; *Something New* w. Leon Bibb '69; *Our Amer. Mus. Heritage* '72; *Positively Black* w. Marlena Shaw '75, all NBC. CDs: ABC; w. T. Purrone (Steep.); Farlow (Col.; Guitarchives); L. Hayward (Island, Town.).

CHRISTLIEB, PETE (PETER), tnr sax, fl, many woodwinds.; b. Los Angeles, CA, 2/16/45. Father, Don, pl. bassoon w. Igor Stravinsky. First prof. job w. his teacher, Bob Cooper. Pl. w. Jerry Gray 1963–4; Chet Baker '64; Si Zentner '65; Woody Herman '66; Louie Bellson '67. Member of Doc Severinsen's *Tonight Show* orch. '72–92 but cont. to work frequently w. Bellson and others, incl. Basie; Goodman; Shelly Manne; Gene Ammons; Frank Rosolino; Carl Fontana. Led own qt. fr. '80s; also pl. w. Capp-Pierce Juggernaut. Form. rec. co., Bosco, '81, rec. own gp.; Bellson; Bob Florence. He has a vigorous, full-bodied style that reflects the modern Lester Young disciples and Sonny Rollins. Named Most Valuable Player Emeritus by NARAS. LPs: Bosco; *Apogee* w. Warne

Marsh (WB). CDS: JMI; Pete Christlieb–Bob Cooper (Capri); w. Bellson (Pab.; Conc.); Capp (Conc.); Conte Candoli (BR); Bill Holman (JVC); Severinsen (Amherst); Anthony Wilson (MAMA).

CHRISTY, JUNE (Shirley Luster aka Sharon Leslie), voc; b. Springfield, IL, 11/20/25; d. Sherman Oaks, CA, 6/21/90. Began w. local bands in 1938, bef. singing w. a variety of bands in Chi., incl. Boyd Raeburn. Replaced Anita O'Day, one of her models, w. Stan Kenton in '45, remaining into '49. In '46, she married tnr. saxist Bob Cooper, w. whom she app. in Calif. clubs '49–50. Toured w. Kenton in the '50s; Ted Heath '57–8; Cooper, Eur. '56, Eur. and So. Africa '58. Visited Austral. and gave concerts in Japan '64; club gig in Engl. '65. Semiretired from mid '60s, she occ. took nightclub jobs in No. Hollywood and SF. Guest app. w. Kenton at NJF-NY '72; Eur. fests. w. Shorty Rogers '85. Polls: *DB* top female voc. w. a band '46–8, '50; *Met.* poll, '47. Fav: Sarah Vaughan. Scored hit w. "Tampico," her first rec. w. Kenton '45. Began rec. as single '49. "Something Cool" typified her cool, throaty delivery. CDs: Cap.; w. Kenton (Cap.; Mos.).

CINELU, MINO (DOMINIQUE), perc; b. St. Cloud, France, 3/10/57. Family orig. fr. Martinique. Raised in Paris. First gigs accomp. singers, then worked w. Jef Gilson. Pl. w. bros. Patrice and Jean-Jacques in trio Chute Libre 1972–7. Moved to NYC ca. '78. Pl. and rec. w. Dizzy Gillespie and Gato Barbieri, then led Mino Cinelu Ens. w. Bob Cunningham, Arnie Lawrence, Andy Bey, Ricky Ford '80–3. Rec. and tour. w. Miles Davis in early '80s, then join. Weather Report '84. Member of trio, Drummers' Music, w. Fabiano, Victor Jones '84–5, then led trio w. John Scofield, Darryl Jones '85. Led qnt., Who's Who, w. Kevin Eubanks, Onaje Allen Gumbs, Victor Bailey '87. Cont. to perf. intermittently w. Miles Davis in '80s. CDs: w. M. Davis (Col.; WB); K. Barron (Em.; Verve); Robin Eubanks (JMT); D. Sanborn (WB); G. Evans (Elec. Bird); Gil Goldstein (WP); J. Stubblefield (Enja); Harvie Swartz (Gram.); Ernie Watts (CTI).

CIRILLO, WALLY (WALLACE JOSEPH), pno, comp; b. Huntington, NY 2/4/27; d. Boca Raton, FL, 5/5/77. Navy 1944–6. Studied at NY Cons. of Modern Mus. '48–50. Received two master's degrees in comp. under Vittorio Giannini '58; in mus. ed. from Man. Sch. of Mus. '60; stud. experimental comp. w. John Cage at New Sch. Local jazz concerts early '52. Pl. in Chi. in early '50s, w. Chubby Jackson–Bill Harris gp. '53. Perf. own comps. at Carnegie Hall and Museum of Modern Art, NYC, w. Jazz Composers

Workshop in '50s. In '54, he led and perf. w. Teo Macero and Charles Mingus on Sav. rec. of his comp. "Trans-Season," said to be first 12–tone jazz work. Pl. w. John La Porta '56. Also comp. three symph., chamber works, experimental electronic jazz pcs. Taught pno. and comp. '59–60. Moved to Boca Raton, Fla. '61, pl. w. Phil Napoleon '64; Flip Phillips, Ira Sullivan '60s; also taught at U. of Miami, Miami-Dade Jr. Coll., Fla. Int'l U. '75. Pl. in Miami w. Terry Gibbs '72; Anita O'Day '73. Duo recs. and perfs. w. gtrst. Joe Diorio '72–5. Infls.: "everyone from Pinetop Smith to Karlheinz Stockhausen." Favs: Tatum, Tristano. CDs: w. Mingus (Deb.); J.J. Johnson–Kai Winding (Sav.).

CLARE, KENNY (KENNETH), dms; b. London, England, 6/8/29; d. London, 1/11/85. While in mil. service dur. WWII, he pl. in student band. Then worked w. Oscar Rabin's dance band 1949–54. Pl. w. Jack Parnell bef. join. Johnny Dankworth Orch. '55–60. In the '60s, he was a sess. mus. for various bands, incl. Ted Heath, Johnny Spence; second dmr. for Clarke-Boland Big Band '67–72; int'l tours w. Dankworth and Cleo Laine. Recs. as co-lead. w. Ronnie Stephenson; as sideman w. Milt Buckner; Joe Pass; Stephane Grappelli; Michel Legrand; Shorty Rogers. CDs: w. Clarke-Boland (MPS); Dankworth (Sepia); Grappelli; J.L. Ponty (MPS).

CLARK, BILL (WILLIAM E.), dms; b. Jonesboro, AR, 7/31/25; d. Atlanta, GA, 7/30/86. Worked w. Lester Young 1950; briefly w. Duke Ellington '51; also pl. w. Mary Lou Williams in early '50s; w. Lena Horne, Paris '52; Hazel Scott. Rec. w. Dizzy Gillespie's bb and small gps. '52; pl. and rec. w. George Shearing '53–5; w. Toots Thielemans '55; Ronnell Bright w. Jackie Paris; Rolf Kuhn '56–7; again w. M.L. Williams '57–60. Recs. w. Lester Young '50; M. L. Williams '51; D. Gillespie '52; George Shearing '55; Kuhn '56. CDs: w. Young (Verve); Gillespie (Vogue).

CLARK, BUDDY (WALTER JR.), bs, arr; b. Kenosha, WI, 7/10/29; d. Mission Hills, CA, 6/8/99. Studied at Chi. Mus. Coll. 1948–9. Worked in Chi. w. Bud Freeman, Bill Russo gps.; tour. w. Tex Beneke '51–4. Moved to LA '54; tour. w. Les Brown '55–6; pl. in '50s w. Red Norvo, Dave Pell; MJF w. Med Flory '58; to Eur. w. Jimmy Guiffre '59. Active as studio mus. fr. '60s. Often accomp. Peggy Lee fr. '56. Co-founder of Supersax, w. Flory, '72; his arr. for Supersax incl. "Parker's Mood"; "Lover Man"; "Ko-Ko"; "A Night In Tunisia." Broke w. Flory and left Supersax in late '75. Relatively inactive since then. CDs: w. Supersax (Cap.); Terry Gibbs; Barney Kessel

(Cont.); Gerry Mulligan (LRC; Verve); Anita O'Day (Verve).

CLARK, CHARLES E., bs, cello; b. Chicago, IL, 3/11/45; d. Chicago, 4/15/69. Studied classical bs. w. Davis Bethe and Joseph Guastefeste, first bs. of Chi. Symph; jazz bs. w. Wilbur Ware. Start. pl. prof. in 1963; join. Muhal Richard Abrams' Experimental bb; one of founding members of AACM '65, and perf. in affiliated gps. led by Abrams, Joseph Jarman, Leroy Jenkins. Also member of Chi. Civic Orch., the official training orch. of the Chi. Symph. Suffered a cerebral hemorrhage after an orch. rehearsal and died almost instantly. The Civic Orch. established an annual scholarship in his name. *DB* noted "the power and youthful exuberance of his playing." CDs: w. M. R. Abrams; J. Jarman (Del.).

CLARK, JOHN TREVOR, Fr-hrn, pno; b. Brooklyn, NY, 9/21/44. Grandfather was church orgst. and choir dir. Pl. gtr., tpt. w. local gps. in jr. hs. Stud. w. Gunther Schuller, Jaki Byard, Ran Blake, George Russell at New Engl. Cons. 1970–3. Pl. w. Paul Jeffrey Oct. '74–8; Gil Evans Orch. '74–88; Carla Bley '77–9; Jaco Pastorius '81; G. Russell '82; McCoy Tyner bb fr. '86. Clark has led his own gp. fr. '73. Favs: Vincent Chancey, Willie Ruff, Julius Watkins. Polls: *DB*; NARAS Most Val. Player. Fests: Eur. fr. '76; Japan '76, '84; Brazil '86. TV: *Saturday Night Live* w. Quincy Jones, Aaron Neville. CDs: Post.; HMM; ECM; w. G. Evans (ProJazz); Jimmy Knepper (SN); G. Gruntz (TCB).

CLARK, JUNE (ALGERIA JUNIUS), tpt; b. Long Branch, NJ, 3/24/1900; d. NYC, 2/23/63. Moved w. family to Phila. in 1908; studied pno. w. moth. as child; learned bugle w. a boy's gp., then studied tpt. priv. and pl. in brass band. Listened to a lot of jazz when his job as Pullman porter took him to NO. Pl. w. James P. Johnson on his first prof. gig, a touring revue, *Black Sensations*; they both left the show in Toledo, Ohio, and form. gp. w. tbn. Jimmy Harrison. In '20, Clark ret. to Phila.; tour. w. Willie "The Lion" Smith '21–2, and w. shows on the TOBA theatre circuit. Worked in Buick factory in Det. bef. rejoin. Harrison; together they join. Fess Williams and went to NYC ca. '23. Clark settled in NYC; led own gps. at several clubs, Ed Small's, Palace Gardens, Tango Gardens '24–30; also worked w. other gps. In '30s, led own bands and pl. w. various bands in NYC and Phila., incl. George Baquet, Charlie Skeete. In '37, he ret. fr. full-time pl. due to health problems, but worked for a while as Louis Armstrong's road manager. Fr. '39 to '41, he was in a sanitorium for TB. Once recovered, he worked as mus.

adviser to several bands; mus. asst. to Earl Hines '44. His last job, in the '50s, was as road manager for boxer Sugar Ray Robinson, but severe illness forced his retirement shortly bef. his death. Rec. w. W. Smith (Col.) '25; Duke Ellington (Bruns.) '27. CDs: w. Smith; Ellington (Class.).

CLARK, MIKE (MICHAEL JEFFREY), dms; b. Sacramento, CA, 10/3/46. Father is part-time dmr. Began on dms. at at age 5; fath. took him to clubs to sit in w. jazz mus. fr. age 7. Self-taught. As a child, pl. w. Mike Lala, Murphy Campo, and Clarence "Frogman" Henry in NO. Freelanced in SF Bay Area mid 1950s-early '60s. Pl. w. Vince Guaraldi Trio '67–71; Woody Shaw '71; Mike Nock, Eddie Henderson, Joe Henderson '72–3. Led own gps. w. Paul Jackson, Jack Walrath '71–3. Pl. briefly w. Mose Allison, then join. Herbie Hancock late '73. Pl. w. Hancock '73–6; off and on '76–7. Came to prominence w. success of Hancock's hit album *Thrust* '74. Tour. US and Eur. w. Brand X '77–8, then pl. w. E. Henderson–Julian Priester in Bay Area '78–9. Moved to NYC '80; co-led gp. w. Jack Walrath '80–2. Tour. Japan w. Hancock–Wayne Shorter '82. Pl. w. Jack Wilkins Trio and freelanced in NYC fr. '83; rejoined Walrath mid '80s. Tour. Eur. w. Chet Baker late '80s. Clark has taught at the Drummers Collective in NYC. Favs: Tony Williams, Elvin Jones, PJ Jones. Fests: all major fr. '73. Film: *Death Wish* w. Hancock. TV: several Charlie Brown soundtracks w. Guaraldi. CDs: Stash; Enja; w. Hancock (Col.); Jack Wilkins (MM).

CLARK, SONNY (CONRAD YEATIS), pno; b. Herminie, PA, 7/21/31; d. NYC, 1/13/63. Began mus. studies on pno. at age 4, then bs. and vib. Moved to Calif. in 1951 w. bro., who also pl. pno. Worked w. Wardell Gray, then, briefly, in SF w. Vido Musso, Oscar Pettiford. Settled in LA, rec. w. Teddy Charles-Wardell Gray '53; worked w. Buddy DeFranco qt., '53–6, tour. Eur. '54. Also pl. and rec. in mid '50s w. Sonny Criss; Frank Rosolino; Howard Rumsey's Lighthouse All-Stars. Moved to NYC in '57, acc. Dinah Washington; fr. '57 to '62, freelanced w. Sonny Rollins, Johnny Griffin, Charles Mingus; also led trio w. Sam Jones, Arthur Taylor. Hospitalized in late '62 for a leg infection, was released in early Jan. and died of heart attack a few days later. One of the top stylists of the Bud Powell school. *Voodoo*, an album devoted to his comps., was rec. by John Zorn and the Sonny Clark Memorial Qt. '85. CDs: BN; Up.; Bain.; w. Dexter Gordon; Grant Green; Lee Morgan; Ike Quebec (BN); B. Holiday (Verve); W. Gray (Prest.); Philly Joe Jones; S. Rollins (Riv.); Lighthouse All-Stars (Cont.); S. Turrentine (Time); Jimmy Raney (RCA).

CLARKE–BOLAND BIG BAND. Cologne-based bb, organized by Kenny Clarke and comp.-pnst. Francy Boland w. promoter Gigi Campi. First rec., *Jazz Is Universal*, was released 1961. Frequent apps. and recs. bef. disbanding in '73. Among the personnel were Sahib Shihab; Benny Bailey; Idrees Sulieman; Åke Persson; Johnny Griffin; Ronnie Scott, et al. The band was universally praised for its hard swinging perfs. and well-crafted arrs. CDs: MPS; RTE; Verve; (sxt.) Rear.

CLARKE, GEORGE F., tnr sax; b. Memphis, TN, 8/28/11. Studied under Jimmie Lunceford at Manassas HS, Memphis. Joined Lunceford's band until 1933. Pl. w. Guy Jackson in Buffalo, N.Y. '33–4; Stuff Smith, Lil Armstrong '35; S. Smith '39. Led own gp. at Anchor Bar in Buffalo '42–54. Joined Cootie Williams in NYC '54. Tour. Eur. w. Williams '59; Africa w. Cozy Cole '62. Favs: Coleman Hawkins, Ben Webster, Don Byas, Eddie "Lockjaw" Davis.

CLARKE, KENNY (KLOOK; Kenneth Clarke Spearman aka Liaqat Ali Salaam), dms; b. Pittsburgh, PA, 1/2/14; d. Montreuil-sous-Bois, France, 1/26/85. From a mus. family; fath. pl. tbn., bros. dms. and bsst. Studied pno., tbn., dms., vib., and theory in hs. While still a teenager, started working prof. in Pitts. w. Leroy Bradley, remaining w. the band for five yrs. Played w. major jazz gps., incl. Roy Eldridge, 1935; Jeter-Pillars band in St. Louis. Moved to NYC toward the end of '35. His half-bro. Frank Clarke, a bsst., join. him fr. Calif. in '36. They worked w. Lonnie Simmons at the Black Cat in Greenwich Village. Freddie Green was on gtr., and Clarke developed parts of his modern style to come. Join. Edgar Hayes in '37; pl. w. Claude Hopkins for several mos. bef. working w. Teddy Hill '39–40 alongside Dizzy Gillespie. In early '40–1, Clarke, Thelonious Monk, and Nick Fenton made up the nucleus of the house band at Minton's. The now legendary Minton's after-hours sess. is where Clarke, Monk, Gillespie, Charlie Christian and other musicians fleshed out the ideas that developed into bebop. It was also here that Clarke acquired his nickname, "Klook" (fr. "Klookmop"), referring to his unexpected bass drm. and snare drm. accents. In '41–2, Clarke toured with Louis Armstrong for a few mos.; worked w. Ella Fitzgerald's band, then Benny Carter's. He pl. w. Red Allen in Chi. for a yr. and a half bef. ret. to NYC, where he led own band at Kelly's Stables, sometimes fronted by Coleman Hawkins. Served in army '43–6, pl. tbn. with army stage band in Paris. After discharge, he ret. to NYC and worked w. Gillespie '46; Tadd Dameron '47; rejoin. Gillespie for Eur. tour in

'48, remaining in Paris for a few mos., recording and teaching. Back in NYC, he worked at the Royal Roost with Dameron and many other gps. In '51, he was a member of the gp. backing Billy Eckstine on a concert tour, and later in yr. became a founding member of Milt Jackson Qt., which in April '52 became the Modern Jazz Qt. Clarke remained with the gp. to '55, then freelanced, often at the Café Bohemia, and rec. extensively w. a variety of musicians. In summer of '56, Clarke join. Jacques Helian's band in Paris, subsequently working there w. visiting US artists, incl. Miles Davis; Bud Powell '59–62; and the Three Bosses w. Powell, Pierre Michelot. In France, he also pl. on soundtrack of *Ascenseur Pour L'Echafaud* '57; app. in *Liaisons Dangereuses* '60; and comp. the film scores for *On N'enterre Pas Dimanche* '59; *La Rivière du Hibou* '61. From '60 to '73, he co-led an oct. and the Clarke-Boland Big Band w. Francy Boland; over the yrs., sidemen incl. fellow US expatriates Johnny Griffin, Idrees Sulieman, Sahib Shihab; Zoot Sims; Eur. personnel incl. Ronnie Scott; Derek Humble; Dusko Goykovich. The band app. at numerous Eur. jfs. In '72, he made a rare US visit to participate in the Duke Ellington Fellowship program at Yale U. After Clarke-Boland disbanded in '73, he perf. and taught in Paris and often toured w. a small gp.; he was the "house drummer" at Montreux JF '73, pl. and rec. w. Dexter Gordon, Gene Ammons, etc. He cont. to be quite active until his death, visiting the US again, briefly, in '79 and, for the Kool JF '84.

A pioneering, highly infl. drummer himself, Clarke once cited Max Roach and Big Sid Catlett as his favorites on that instrument. With Gillespie and Parker, he was a key figure in the early days of bebop and, as such, made fundamental contributions to the stylistic evolution of modern jazz drumming. He was the first drummer to depart fr. the old sock-cymbal style and develop a more subtle approach; instead he used the ride cymbal to carry the rhythm and the bass and snare for punctuation, enhancing the polyrhythmic quality that early on became an element of bop phrasing. Book: *Klook: The Story of Kenny Clarke*, Mike Hennessey (Quartet) '90. Comps.: "Salt Peanuts" w. Gillespie; "Epistrophy" w. Monk; "Rue Chaptal" (possibly w. Kenny Dorham), aka "Royal Roost"; and "Tenor Madness." CDs: JazzTime; Sav.; w. Clarke-Boland, MPS; RTE; Rear; two tracks in *Americans in Europe* (Imp.); w. E. Hayes (Class.); Sidney Bechet (BB; Vogue); Charlie Christian (Jazz Anth.); Gillespie (BB; Sav.; Vogue; Philips); Miles Davis (Cap.; Prest.; BN); MJQ; Gene Ammons; Art Farmer; S. Rollins (Prest.); Monk (Riv.); C. Parker (Verve; BN); Bud Powell (BL; Drey.; MS; RCA); Milt Jackson (Gal.; Sav.; BN); J. J. Johnson (Sav.; BN); Fats Navarro (Sav.; BN; Mile.); Thad Jones; K. Dorham (Deb.); Hank Jones; C. Adderley (Sav.); D. Gordon (BN); Zoot Sims; Martial Solal (Vogue).

CLARKE, PETE (FRANK), alto sax, bari sax, cl; b. Birmingham, AL, 3/10/11; d. NYC, 3/27/75. Brothers Dick Clarke and Arthur "Babe" Clarke, tpt. and sax respectively. Pl. w. J. Neal Montgomery's Collegiate Ramblers 1927; Wayman Carver's Ramblers '29; Chick Webb '30–6. Rec. w. Duke Ellington '36. Pl. w. Louis Armstrong '37–8; Teddy Wilson Orch. '39–40. Rec. w. Rex Stewart '46, then tour. Eur. w. Don Redman. Pl. w. John Kirby briefly '47; w. Happy Caldwell at Smalls' Paradise, NYC early '50s. Freelanced extensively in '60–70s incl. gigs w. Danny Barker in early '60s and occasional apps. at Jimmy Ryan's in the early '70s. CDs: w. C. Webb (Hep; Dec.); Louis Armstrong (BB); Ellington (Col.; Red Brn.); T. Wilson (Class.); Henry Red Allen (Tax).

CLARKE, STANLEY M., el-bs, comp; b. Philadelphia, PA, 6/30/51. Studied mus. as a child; later at Phila. Mus. Acad. w. Ed Adrian, Neil Courtney. Started on acdn., sw. to vln., cello, and bs.; took up el-bs. in hs, pl. w. r&b and rock bands locally. Worked w. Horace Silver for six mos. 1970; then w. Joe Henderson for a yr.; elec. and acoustic bs. w. Pharoah Sanders '71; tour. w. Stan Getz '72. Dur. this period, he also worked for brief periods w. Gil Evans, Mel Lewis, and, again, w. Silver. He join. Chick Corea '72–7 and was one of the founding members of Corea's new gp., Return to Forever, in which he pl. only el-bs. After leaving Corea, he was active and successful w. jazz, fusion, and rock bands, and w. his own gps. for concerts and recs. In the early '80s, he frequently worked w. George Duke; together they scored a hit with Clarke's single "Sweet Baby" '81. In '83 he rejoin. Return to Forever for a US tour. Tour. w. concerts of unaccomp. el-bs. playing '86; rec. *If This Bass Could Only Talk* '88. Revived partnership w. Duke '89; the join. avant-pop gp. Animal Logic. Began writing for film soundtracks. His credits incl.: *The Five Heartbeats*; *Passenger 57*; *Boyz in the Hood*; *Remember the Time*; *Higher Learning*; *Poetic Justice*. Infls: Blanton, Oscar Pettiford, Paul Chambers, Scott La Faro, Coltrane, Miles Davis. Clarke is a master of both acoustic and el-bs. Fests: many apps. at NJF-NY and Eur. events in '70s and '80s. Polls: *DB* Critics New Star, acoustic bs. '73–4; el-bs. '74; *DB* Readers, '74–5. Comps: "Children of Forever"; "Bass Folk Song"; "Light As a Feather." CDs: Epic; Epic Soundtrax; Col.; w. Corea (Polyd.; Verve; Stretch); Stan Getz; John McLaughlin (Col.); E. Elias (Den.).

CLARKE, TERRY (TERENCE MICHAEL), dms, perc; b. Vancouver, B.C., Canada, 8/20/44. Studied w. Jim Blackley in Vancouver 1960–5. Worked w. visiting US mus., incl. Barney Kessel, Vince Guaraldi, and local mus. Moved to SF '65, pl. w. John Handy '65–7; Fifth Dimension '67–70; tour. US, Can., Eur. Moved to Toronto '70, freelance w. Don Thompson; Ed Bickert; Moe Koffman; Oscar Peterson; Rob McConnell (reg. member of Boss Brass); Frank Rosolino; Blue Mitchell; James Moody; Chet Baker; Art Pepper; Herb Ellis; Al Cohn–Zoot Sims; George Coleman; etc. Moved to NYC '85, pl. w. Jim Hall; Toshiko Akiyoshi bb; Jay Leonhart; Roger Kellaway; Joe Roccisano; ret. at times to pl. w. McConnell. Favs: Elvin Jones, Tony Williams, Shelly Manne. Fests.: MJF '65 w. Handy; Eur.; Japan since '72. TV: *Tonight Show*, Ed Sullivan, Dick Cavett. CDs: w. McConnell (Conc.; SB); O. Peterson (Pab.); J. Hall (Conc.; MM; Tel.); Akiyoshi (Col.); Bickert; K. Peplowski; E. Remler (Conc.); D. Cheatham; J. McShann; B. Tate (Sack.); Oliver Jones (JT).

CLATWORTHY, BENN, tnr sax; b. London, England, 5/17/55. Grandmother was actress Gertrude Lawrence. Picked up sax as teenager, pl. in rock and funk bands; moved to LA mid 1980s; stud. w. Phil Sobel; Charlie Shoemake; pl. w. Cedar Walton, Jimmy Cleveland, Lionel Hampton; own bands, feat. Cecilia Coleman, pno., fr. '85. Dedicated artist who makes living solely as jazz mus. Favs: D. Gordon, Coltrane, Rollins. CDs: Disc.

CLAXTON, ROZELLE, pno, arr; b. Memphis, TN, 2/5/13. Mother, fath., four sists., three bros. all pl. pno. Took org. and pno. lessons fr. age 11; oldest sist. taught him to read mus. Pl. house parties fr. age 12; made daily broadcasts on Memphis radio at age 15. Stud. w. Jimmie Lunceford, then pl. w. Clarence Davis's Rhythm Aces fr. late '20s; W.C. Handy took over the band in '31. Freelanced in KC w. Bennie Moten, Harlan Leonard, Ernie Fields '33–40. Stud. arr. w. Leonard. Moved to Chi. '40; pl. w. Eddie South, Walter Fuller, Roy Eldridge. Pl. briefly w. Lucky Millinder in NYC early '40s. In army '43–5, then worked w. Geo. Dixon '46–9. Arr. for Earl Hines, J. Lunceford, Red Norvo, Count Basie, Andy Kirk '40s-50s. Studied at Chi. Conserv., received B. Mus. '52, M. Mus. '54; also active as a teacher. Accomp. Pearl Bailey at Chez Paree, Chi. '58. Pl. and rec. w. Franz Jackson's Original Jass All-Stars fr. '59. Tour. as Pearl Bailey's accomp. '78–83. Freelanced in Chi. fr. '83. Favs: Tatum, Hines, Waller, Wilson, JP Johnson. Rec. w. Fields on Vocalion; Jackson on Philips; Pinnacle. CDs: w. Jackson (Riv.).

CLAY, JAMES EARL, tnr sax, fl; b. Dallas, TX, 9/8/35; d. Dallas, 1/12/95. Studied alto sax in hs. Start. pl. prof. w. sch. dir. who took on gigs. First rec. sess. w. Larance Marable for Jazz West, LA 1957. Ret. to Dallas '58; went into mil. service '59. Lived and pl. mostly in Tex. for the rest of his life, but made one NYC app. w. Red Garland at Lush Life in late '70s. Fav: Sonny Rollins. CDs: Riv.; Ant.; w. Wes Montgomery (Riv.; Mile.); Don Cherry (A&M); Red Mitchell (Cont.).

CLAYTON, BUCK (WILBUR DORSEY), tpt, comp, arr; b. Parsons, KS, 11/12/11; d. NYC, 12/8/91. Father pl. sousaphone in church band and sang in choir. Studied pno. w. fath. fr. age 6; tpt. age 17–19. Pl. in church orch. 1930–2, then moved to Calif. '32. Pl. w. Duke Ellighew band at Red Mill taxi dance hall '32–4, then led own 14-pc. band. Teddy Weatherford took Clayton's band to Shanghai, where they worked at the Canidrome '34–6. Ret. to Calif., then join. Count Basie in KC '36. Came to prominence as soloist ("Fiesta in Blue," etc.) and arr. w. Basie '37–43; his arrs. incl. "It's Sand Man"; "Taps Miller"; "Red Bank Boogie." In army '43–6; freelanced in NYC '46–9. Made first of many trips to France '49. Tour. w. JATP '49–51, then pl. in NYC w. Joe Bushkin '51–3; also worked w. Tony Parenti, Jimmy Rushing, own combos. Made many "jam sess." recs. for Columbia as leader and arr. '50s; also arr. for Duke Ellington, Harry James. Pl. w. Benny Goodman Orch., Teddy Wilson '57; NJF tour of Eur. '59; Eddie Condon '59–64. Tour. Eur. frequently fr. late '50s, incl. perfs. w. Sidney Bechet at Brussels World's Fair '58; w. own gp. at Hot Club de France 30th Anniversary celebration, Paris '62; w. Humphrey Lyttleton in UK '63. Embouchure problems forced Clayton to stop pl. tpt. in '72. He worked briefly in the insurance dept. at local 802 in NYC, then left to concentrate on comp. and arr. Arr. jam sess. dates for Chiaro. label '70s. Clayton resumed pl. tpt. in the late '70s, making a St. Dept. tour of Africa '77. Taught at Hunter Coll. '75–80. Tour. Eur. as leader of Basie alumni band, The Countsmen, '83, then ceased pl. again to focus on arr. Clayton debuted a new bb at the Bklyn. Museum in Nov. '86. Fr. that date until his death, he led this orch. on several int'l tours and contributed over 100 charts to the band's book. His biography, *Buck Clayton's Jazz World*, by Nancy Miller Elliott, was publ. in '86. Favs: Sweets Edison, Joe Newman, Ruby Braff, Warren Vaché; arrs: Quincy Jones, Nat Pierce. Polls: *Esq.* Gold Awd., Best Mus. in Armed Forces '45; NEA Jazz Master Award '90. Films: app. in *Benny Goodman Story* '56; *Jazz On a Summer's Day* '60. CDs: Chiaro.; Col.; Riv.; Prest.; Mos.; NH; BL; Stash;

Steep.; Story.; Verve; w. Basie (Dec.; Col.); Billie Holiday (Col.; Verve); E. Condon (Chiaro.); B. Goodman (Col.; MM); E. Hines (Vogue); Lyttelton (Phil.); Lester Young (Comm.; Key.); JATP (Verve).

CLAYTON, JAY (Judith Colantone), voc; b. Youngstown, OH, 10/28/41. Studied at Miami U., Ohio 1959–63, then moved to NYC. Active in jazz and new mus. Perf. w. Steve Reich; Muhal Richard Abrams; John Cage; Jane Ira Bloom; et al. Member of improv. voc. qt., Vocal Summit, w. Urszula Dudziak, Norma Winstone, and Michelle Hendricks. Recs. w. Abrams; Cage; Jerry Granelli; Don Lanphere; Paul McCandless. Taught voc. jazz at CCNY, Bud Shank Workshop, and mus. schs. in Cologne, Berlin, Munich, Germ. In '92, she was on jazz faculty at Cornish Coll. of the Arts in Seattle, Wash. "As far as vocal innovation goes," wrote Fred Bouchard in *Jazz Times*, "Jay Clayton is precariously on the cutting edge." CDs: Hep; ITM; Anima; Jay Clayton and Fred Hersch (Sunny.); w. M.R. Abrams (BS); Lanphere (Hep); String Trio of N.Y. (West Wind; ITM).

CLAYTON, JOHN (JOHNNIE LEE JR.), bs, arr, lead; b. Los Angeles, CA, 8/20/52. Mother pl. pno. and org. in Baptist church. Bro. is reedman Jeff Clayton (b. Los Angeles, 2/4/54). After pno. lessons for a few yrs. as child, he took up bs. in junior hs at age 13. Classical lessons at 16 until he discovered Ray Brown's "Workshop in Jazz Bass" evening courses at UCLA 1969. At Brown's urging, he also took a yr. of classical lessons; also stud. el-bs. w. Carol Kaye. Began coll. stud. at LA Valley Coll. '70–1. Transferred to attend Indiana U., grad. '75. Brown start. him prof., helping him to get a bs. and introducing him to name musicians. Worked w. Murray McEachern Qt. '71; Henry Mancini TV show, *The Mancini Generation*, '72; Monty Alexander Trio w. Jeff Hamilton. '75–7; C. Basie Orch. '77–9; Amsterdam Phil. Orch., Netherlands '80–4. Fr. '85, he co-led the Clayton-Hamilton Jazz Orch., the Clayton Bros., and join. Brown in Superbass. Worked annually as lead. and sideman in Eur. fr. '76. Many trips to Asia and Austral. fr. '78. From '74, taught priv. and annually at mus. schs., summer jazz camps, grade schs., universities. Bass profess.: Mus. Cons. in The Hague, Netherlands '81–4; Long Beach St. U. '85–7; USC fr. '87. Appointed to head Hollywood Bowl jazz program '99. Has written for the Northwest Chamber Orch.; Amer. Jazz Phil.; Iceland Symph.; Amsterdam Philharm. and Metropole Orch., Netherlands; Hollywood Bowl Orch. (*Maestro!: The Benny Carter Suite*, '97); and Richmond Symph. Arr. "Star Spangled Banner" for Whitney Houston to sing at Super Bowl XXV, in Tampa, Fla. Favs: Brown, Israel Crosby, Christian

McBride, Milt Hinton; arrs: Ellington, Johnny Mandel, Robert Farnon. Won LA Jazz Society's Comp./Arr. award. Film: wrote arrs. for Dr. John in *101 Dalmatians*; *Bogus*. CDs: Clayton-Hamilton (Capri); Superbass (Capri; Tel.); Clayton Bros. (Qwest; Capri; Conc.); w. Jeff Hamilton; Ernestine Anderson; Benny Carter; C. McRae; R. Woodard; M. McPartland (Conc.); Monty Alexander (Conc.; Polyd.; MPS); Milt Jackson (Pab.; Atl.; Qwest); Basie (Pab.); B. Kessel (Cont.).

CLESS, ROD (GEORGE RODERICK), cl; b. Lenox, IA, 5/20/07; d. NYC, 12/8/44. From mus. family; began. cl. in hs. First prof. job in Des Moines, Iowa, 1925, where he met Frank Teschemacher; to Chi. '27, pl. w. Teschemacher, Bud Freeman; join. Charlie Pierce's orch. '28; Louis Panico '29. Pl. cl. and alto sax w. small gps. and dance bands, incl. Jess Stacy's qt., in Chi. late '20s-mid '30s. Moved to NYC, join. Muggsy Spanier '39; Art Hodes '40–1; Marty Marsala '41; Georg Brunis, Bobby Hackett '42; Wild Bill Davison, Hodes '43. Enroute home fr. a job w. Max Kaminsky at the Pied Piper '44, Cless fell, and died four days later. Infls: Johnny Dodds, Jimmie Noone, Teschemacher, Freeman. Recs. as lead for B&W '44; as sideman w. Teschemacher '28; Spanier '39; Hodes '40; Kaminsky '44. CDs: w. Spanier (BB); Hodes (Dormouse); J. Teagarden (Conifer).

CLEVELAND, JIMMY (JAMES MILTON), tbn; b. Wartrace, TN, 5/3/26. Army service, 1944–6; stud. at Tenn. State A&I U.; pl. at Carnegie Hall w. coll. band. Worked w. Lionel Hampton '49–53, incl. Eur. tour. Freelanced in NYC, winning *DB* Critics Poll New Star Award '55. Off and on w. Johnny Richards '57–60; pl. and rec. w. Dizzy Gillespie; member of house band on TV series *The Subject Is Jazz*. Pl. w. Gerry Mulligan '59; toured Eur. w. Quincy Jones in show *Free and Easy* '59–60. Commercial TV and studio work in NYC mid and late '60s, and fr. early '70s in LA. In '80s, pl. w. Hampton, Gerald Wilson and led his own 9-pc. band; pl. on the soundtrack of '91 film, *Dingo*. A articulate, highly virtuosic player, Cleveland's rapid-style playing has met w. some criticism for his excessive use of technique, but he always keeps his distinctive tone intact. Own LP for Em. '55. CDs: w. Frank Wess; Gigi Gryce (Sav.); Art Farmer; Lockjaw Davis; Eddie Jefferson (Prest.); Lucky Thompson (Imp.); Gil Evans (Prest.; Verve; Enja); Benny Golson (Cont.); L. Hampton (BB); Clifford Brown (RCA); J. Richardson (NJ).

CLINTON, LARRY, comp, arr, lead, tpt; b. Brooklyn, NY, 8/17/09; d. Tucson, AZ, 5/2/85. Mother was concert soprano. Self-taught. Pl. briefly w. Ferde Grofé 1932. Arr. for Isham Jones; Claude Hopkins '33; Dorsey Bros. '35–6; Glen Gray '36–7; Louis Armstrong; Tommy Dorsey; Bunny Berigan '37. Led own successful swing band '37–41. In air force '42–6, then resumed leading band '48–50. Worked in publ. and rec. business fr. '50s. A&R dir. for Kapp Recs. '58–9. Clinton bec. famous in the late '30s for his swing arrs. of Eur. classical works, incl. "My Reverie," after Debussy '38; "Our Love," after Tchaikovsky '39. Well-known arrs. for others incl. "Dusk in Upper Sandusky" for Jimmy Dorsey; "The Dipsy Doodle"; "Satan Takes a Holiday" for T. Dorsey. A collection of Clinton's scores and other materials is in the Amer. Heritage Center of the U. of Wyoming at Laramie. Favs: Fletcher Henderson, Igor Stravinsky. CDs: Cir.; as arr. w. J. Dorsey (Dec.); w. T. Dorsey (RCA).

CLOONEY, ROSEMARY, voc; b. Maysville, KY, 5/23/28; d. Beverly Hills, CA, 6/29/02. Worked as a duo w. her sist., Betty, in Tony Pastor's band late 1940s. In '50s, she rec. a string of pop hits and app. in films, incl. *White Christmas*. Her '56 jazz-based album w. Duke Ellington, *Blue Rose*, caught many by surprise. She cont. her foray into jazz in '77, w. a number of swing-oriented Conc. albums and NYC club apps., backed by mainstream gps. that incl. Warren Vaché and Scott Hamilton. Though not basically a jazz singer, she attracted a following among jazz audiences in the '80s and '90s. TV: PBS specials, and commercials. Film: *White Christmas* '54. CDs: Conc.; w. Ellington (Col.).

COATES, JOHN FRANCIS JR., pno; also vib; b. Trenton, NJ, 2/17/38. Father was a jazz pnst. and mus. teacher. Stud. at Mannes and Dalcroze schls. in NYC; priv. w. Urana Clark 1945–56. While still in hs, he rec. as leader of a trio w. Wendell Marshall and Kenny Clarke. After grad. in '56, he join. Charlie Ventura for two yrs., then enrolled at Rutgers U. After receiving his degree, he settled in the small town of Delaware Water Gap, Pa., where he was editor, comp. and arr. for Shawnee Press. He pl. frequently at the Deer Head Inn, where such mus. as Al Cohn, Zoot Sims, and Phil Woods sat in w. him. Keith Jarrett, who as a teenager was often brought to the Deer Head by his moth., is said to have been infl. by Coates. In '77, he left Shawnee Press to devote himself more fully to pl. and comp. in several genres, incl. one hundred choral arr.; two mus. comedies; fifty songs, "which are important to me in my jazz playing." Favs: John Coates Sr., Art Tatum. TV: apps. w. Ventura; Barry Miles; Bernard Peiffer. Rec. on vib. w. Peiffer for Polyd. CDs: Sav.

COBB, ARNETT (Arnette Cleophus Cobbs), tnr sax; b. Houston, TX, 8/10/18; d. Houston, 3/24/89. Studied pno. w. grandmoth.; also vln., C-melody sax, tpt. Prof. debut w. Frank Davis 1933; Chester Boone '33–6; Milton Larkin '36–42. Replaced Illinois Jacquet in Lionel Hampton's band '42–7, then, having established a reputation, left to form his own band, but a spinal operation in '48 prevented him from pl. for a couple of yrs. Reorganized the band in '51; was active touring until seriously injured in a car accident in '56. Resumed tour. w. the band in '57–8, then ret. to Houston, where he managed the Ebony Club and intermittently led own bb through the '60s, though recurrent illness often prevented him fr. perf. Feat. at Club Magnavox, Houston, summer '70. A '73 concert w. Jacquet at Town Hall, NYC, reactivated his career; he made his first, and very successful, Eur. tour. that year. Tour. Eur. again w. Hampton '78. Through the mid '80s, he toured the US and Eur. extensively, often w. the Texas Tenors, which incl. Jacquet and Buddy Tate. Cobb was an emotionally charged, soulful musician whose robust sound perfectly characterizes the term "Texas Tenor." CDs: Prest., incl. *Very Saxy* w. C. Hawkins, Lockjaw Davis, Tate; Del.; B&B; Fant.; SN; Timel.; Prog.; w. Milt Buckner; Al Casey; Al Grey; J. McShann; Helen Humes (B&B); Hampton (Dec.; Timel.).

COBB, JIMMY (JAMES WILBUR), dms; b. Washington, DC, 1/20/29. Primarily self-taught, but studied briefly w. Jack Dennett of the Nat'l Symph. Pl. in marching band at Armstrong HS 1946. Worked in Wash., D.C., w. Charlie Rouse, Leo Parker, Frank Wess, Rick Henderson, Billie Holiday, Pearl Bailey late '40s. Tour. and pl. w. Earl Bostic '50–1; Dinah Washington on and off '52–6; Cannonball Adderley '57–8; Stan Getz–Dizzy Gillespie '58; Miles Davis '58–63. Form. trio w. Wynton Kelly, Paul Chambers '63–9; trio acc. J.J. Johnson, Wes Montgomery, and others. When Chambers died in '69, Kelly and Cobb stayed together until '71, at which time Cobb joined Sarah Vaughan. Accomp. Vaughan throughout '70s, then pl. w. Richie Cole, Sonny Stitt, Nat Adderley, Ricky Ford, Buddy DeFranco–Terry Gibbs, Hank Jones, Nancy Wilson, Joe Albany in '80s. Pl. w. Kenny Drew in Japan '81; Art Farmer '83; Tommy Flanagan '86. Cont. his assoc. w. N. Adderley into '90s. Teaches in the New Sch. Jazz Program and leads own gp., Cobb's Mob. Favs: Roach, Kenny Clarke, Blakey, PJ Jones, Buddy Rich. Poll: *Playboy*. Fests: all major fr. '50s. Film: w. David Amram on soundtrack of *Seven Days to May* '63. TV: Robert Herridge series w. Miles Davis, Gil Evans '59; *Sarah Vaughan Live From Wolf Trap*; PBS, *So Nobody Else Can Hear* '83–6. CDs: Fable; w. Davis (Col.);

Coltrane (Atl.; Prest.); Montgomery (Riv.; Mile.; Verve); Howard McGhee (BL); Stitt; R. Ford; D. Newman (Muse); K. Drew (Steep.); P. Gonsalves (Jazz.); K. Dorham; W. Kelly; B. Timmons (Riv.); N. Adderley (Riv.; Evid.; In+Out; SB; Land.); C. Adderley (Em.; Land.); A. Pepper (Cont.); D. Washington (Em.); B. DeFranco (Conc.); K. Barron (Cand.); P. Bernstein (CC).

COBB, JUNIE (JUNIUS C.), cl, alto, tnr saxes, bjo, pno; b. Hot Springs, AR, ca. 1896; d. ca. '70. As teenager pl. pno. in combo w. Johnny Dunn. Moved to Chi. ca.1920, became known as a multi-instrumentalist. Led own band at Club Alvadere '20–1. Pl. bjo. w. King Oliver '24–7; Jimmie Noone '28–9. Rec. as lead. for Vocalion '26–9. Worked in Eur. for six mos., then led bands in Chi. clubs, early '30s. Accomp. singer Annabelle Calhoun until ca. '46, then worked as solo pnst. Ceased full-time perf. in '55, but rec. own album for Riv.'s *Chicago: The Living Legends* series, w. A. Calhoun '61. Cont. to pl. frequently until his death. Recs. w. Johnny Dodds; Noone; Tiny Parham. CDs: Riv.; w. Dodds; Noone (Aff.).

COBHAM, BILLY (WILLIAM C.), dms, perc, comp; b. Panama, 5/16/44. Family to NYC 1947. Began "fooling around" w. timbales at age 2. By age 8, he was sitting in w. his fath., a pnst., in public perfs. Pl. in drum and bugle corps; stud. at HS of Mus. and Art '59. Pl. w. Jazz Samaritans, incl. George Cables, Clint Houston, and other schoolmates. Army bands '65–8, also worked w. Billy Taylor trio at the Hickory house, NYC, dur. last half of '67. Rec. debut w. George Benson on *Giblet Gravy*, '68. Tour. w. Horace Silver, Feb.-Oct. '68. In the '70s he was quite active w. studio work, pl. on soundtracks of films (*Shaft*), TV series (*Mission Impossible*), and jingles. Pl. w. Stanley Turrentine and Kenny Burrell bef. join. Brecker bros. to form. early jazz-rock gp, Dreams, '69–70. Dur. this time, he also rec. *Bitches Brew; Live-Evil;* and *Jack Johnson* w. Miles Davis. Rec. and worked w. John McLaughlin's Mahavishnu Orch. '71–2; own band fr. '73, incl. frequent work in Eur. In Sept. '75, form. new qt., Spectrum, which incl. George Duke, John Scofield. Member of Paul Shaffer's *Saturday Night Live* TV band '78. Moved to Zurich in '80 and for next twenty yrs. maintained residence there, ret. to US often. He became a major figure in the jazz-rock fusion movement. Won *DB* Readers Poll, '73–5. Own albums for Atl. '73–6; Col. '77–80; Elek./Musician '82–3; GRP fr. '85; also prod. albums for Airto Moreira, David Sancious, Richard Davis, Pete and Sheila Escovedo. Early infls: Garner, Eckstine, Tito Puente, Stan Levey, Sonny Payne, Jo Jones, Gus Johnson. CDs: GRP; Atl.; Inak;

w. M. Davis; McLaughlin/Mahavishnu (Col.); Benson (Col.; Verve); Ron Carter; L. Coryell; F. Hubbard; Milt Jackson (CTI); S. Rollins; M. Tyner (Mile.).

COCHRAN, TODD (aka BAYETE), pno, synth, comp; b. San Francisco, CA, 9/3/51. Parents both mus. Priv. stud. fr. age 6; B. Mus. in 1970 fr. Trinity Coll., London, after several yrs. of stud. correspondence course; also stud. at San Jose U. First prominent dur. two yrs. w. Bobby Hutcherson–Harold Land gp. Style involved contemporary harmonic and basic ethnic rhythms calling for, he said, "an understanding for the African-American experience." Cochran worked in many other areas, w. Santana; Jeff Beck; Quincy Jones; George Benson; Maynard Ferguson; and Freddie Hubbard. CDs: Vital Music; w. Hubbard (BN).

COCUZZO, JOE (JOSEPH G.), dms, comp, arr; b. Boston, MA, 9/17/37. Both parents were amateur mus.: fath. pl. mand., gtr., vln.; moth. sang. Older bro., Danny, pl. dms. Began on dms. in Boston pub. schs. at age 8; later stud. w. Geo. L. Stone, Carl E. Gardner. Pl. in Chi. w. Ralph Marterie, 1957–9, then join. Woody Herman, '59–60. In army, stationed at Ft. Dix, N.J. '60. Pl. w. M. McPartland off and on fr. '60; Don Ellis, also Les and Larry Elgart Orch. '61–5. Tour. w. Gary McFarland '66; Tony Bennett '69–71. Pl. w. Tommy Furtado in NYC '71–3, then tour. w. Bennett '75–80; Harry James '80–1; Rosemary Clooney off and on '83–93. Also tour. w. Diahann Carroll; Vic Damone; Julius La Rosa; Sylvia Syms. Cocuzzo has worked as a songwriter and lyricist fr. '85; his song "Christmas Time of Year" is publ. by Warner Bros. In recent yrs., he has worked as lyricist w. Brazilian comp. Ivan Lins. Favs: Krupa, Jo Jones, Roy Haynes, Rich, Bellson, Al Foster; arrs: Johnny Mandel, Torrie Zito, Nelson Riddle, Gil Evans. Fests: all major w. Bennett, others. TV: special w. Leonard Bernstein and N.Y. Philharm. '65; Ed Sullivan, *Tonight Show*, Mike Douglas w. Bennett; *Today* w. R. Clooney. LPs: w. Garner (Merc.); McFarland (Imp.). CDs: w. J. Bunch (LRC); Clooney (Conc.); John Pizzarelli (Novus).

COE, TONY (ANTHONY GEORGE), tnr, sop saxes, cl; b. Canterbury, England, 11/29/34. Studied cl., but self-taught on saxes; later studied comp. Pl. in army band 1953–6, w. Joe Daniels, Nat Gonella. With Humphrey Lyttelton '57–62. Moved his focus fr. alto to tnr. Turned down job w. Basie '65, then rejoined Lyttelton; pl. w. John Dankworth '66–9; Clarke-Boland '69–73. In '70s, worked w. Derek Bailey's Company; Stan Tracey; and own gps., incl. one w.

Kenny Wheeler; another w. T. Oxley. Fr. '71, pl. w. classical and contemp. mus. ens. Matrix. Tour. Eur. w. United Jazz and Rock Ensemble '78; UK w. Mike Gibbs band '83. Movies and recs. w. Henry Mancini, incl. feat. tnr. sax soloist in *Pink Panther* series. In '87, mus. dir. for London prod. of the play *Lady Day*. Best known comp.: "Zeitgeist." An outstanding soloist, especially on cl., his tnr. style is derived, in part, fr. Paul Gonsalves. CDs: Story.; hatArt; Hot.; w. Clarke-Boland (MPS); Bob Moses (Gram.); Lyttelton (Phil.); Tracey (Steam); Norma Winstone (ECM).

COGGINS, GIL (GILBERT LLOYD), pno; b. NYC, 8/23/28; d. NYC, 2/15/04. Began pl. pno. as child, but did not take it seriously until after his army discharge. Pl. w. Miles Davis; Lester Young early 1950s. Worked as real estate salesman '54. Perf. in NYC at Minton's Playhouse, West End in early '70s. Pl. w. Ed Lewis '74–5. Semiretired fr. early '80s, but app. w. Sonny Rollins in reunion concert at Beacon Theater, NYC '96. Favs: Tatum, Bud Powell, Nat Cole, Hank Jones, Shearing. CDs: w. Miles Davis (BN); Jackie McLean (NJ); John Coltrane (Prest.).

COHEN, AVISHAI, bs, comp; b. Naharia, Israel, 4/20/70. Around age 9 or 10 start. fooling around on piano. Began formal pno. stud. at 11. Family moved to St. Louis when he was 14. Became interested in jazz. Pl. pno. w. hs jazz band. Sw. to el-bs. after bs. teacher told him about Jaco Pastorius. At 16 family ret. to Israel. Att. Music & Arts HS in Jerusalem for a yr. before concentrating on music full time. Gigged at local clubs and made two apps. at Red Sea JF. Was mustered into Israeli army 1988. Pl. rock bs. gtr. in army band. Resumed his career, adopting acoustic bs. Moved to NYC, Jan. '92. For a yr. worked at moving and construction jobs and practiced bs. Then became part of NY scene, pl. w. Paquito D'Rivera; Leon Parker; Wynton Marsalis. Join. Danilo Perez trio '95; also app. often at Small's in band w. Ravi Coltrane, Steve Wilson, Jason Lindner, Jeff Ballard. Rec. w. Perez on *Panamonk* '96. A meeting w. Chick Corea led to first rec. as a leader for the Stretch label. In '98 he join. Corea's new gp., Origin. Favs: Pastorius, Mingus, Jymie Merritt, Bach, Stevie Wonder. CDs: Stretch; w. Corea (Stretch); Perez; Nnenna Freelon (Conc.).

COHEN, GREG (GREGORY PETER), bs, comp, arr; b. Los Angeles, CA, 7/13/53. Mother was amateur classical gtr. Bro. Danny is singer/songwriter. Began on gtr., then bs-gtr.; early exp. pl. in r&b bands w. bro. Stud. at Cal. State-Sonoma 1971–3; in Valencia at Cal. Inst. of the Arts '76–7. Pl. w. Tom Waits fr. '78; Teddy Edwards, Frankie Randell '80–2; Jack

Sheldon '81; Mimmo Locasciulli fr. '86; Ken Peplowski, Peter Ecklund fr. '88; Marty Grosz fr. '89; Ed Polcer, Bobby Gordon fr. '90; David Sanborn, Danny Barker, Jackie & Roy '91; Kenny Davern fr. '91; Rick Fay '92; Annie Ross '92–3; Lou Reed, Bill Frisell, '92–4; John Zorn, Woody Allen fr. '92; Laurie Anderson fr. '93; Randy Sandke fr. '94; Gerald Wiggins '95–6. Cohen has comp. works for St. Ann's in Bklyn. and the Lincoln Center Theater. Has worked on and off as a vln. bow maker. Favs: Jimmy Blanton, Walter Page; arr: Gil Evans. Fests: Eur., Asia, Austral. fr. '77. Film: apps. in *Maxie; Short Cuts; One From the Heart*. CDs: DIW; w. K. Peplowski (Conc.); D. Sanborn; Tom Waits (Elek); Marty Grosz (Jazz.; Stomp Off); Zorn (DIW); *Weird Nightmare*, mus. of C. Mingus (Col.).

COHN, AL (ALVIN GILBERT), tnr sax, bari sax, cl, bs-cl; b. NYC, 11/24/25; d. East Stroudsburg, PA, 2/15/88. Wives were Marilyn Moore and Flo Handy, both voc.; son, Joe, pl. gtr. Began pno. study at age 6 and cl. at 12; self-taught on tnr., which he took up as a teenager. Pl. w. Joe Marsala's bb 1943; pl. and arr. w. George Auld to end of '46. He pl. a succession of jobs with various progressive bbs, incl. Boyd Raeburn '46; Alvino Rey. First gained attention in jazz circles while working w. Buddy Rich in NYC, summer of '47, but it was as a member of Woody Herman's band fr. Jan. '48 to Apr. '49 that his reputation was truly established. Replaced Herbie Steward in the "Four Brothers" sax section, pl. alongside Serge Chaloff, Stan Getz, and Zoot Sims. Cohn and Sims thus began one of the most productive musical relationships in jazz. They both left Herman in '49 and briefly worked w. Artie Shaw in NYC. Cohn then retired fr. full-time mus. until the spring of '52, when he began working intermittently w. Elliot Lawrence until '58, and started freelancing, mainly as an arr. He wrote for Jack Sterling's CBS radio show and *Your Hit Parade*; TV shows incl. Andy Williams, Pat Boone, Steve Allen. In '55–6, he was a staff mus. for RCA Victor, working as tnr. player and/or arr. on countless albums, some under his own leadership. In '57, Cohn and Sims formed a qnt., which they maintained into the early '80s. The gp. didn't really stabilize until '59, when it app. at the Randall's Island JF and, subsequently, several long annual runs at the Half Note, NYC. The qnt. app. in clubs and concerts in NYC, Toronto, Can., Wash., D.C.; tour. Scand. '78; Japan '78. Cohn also led his own qt. in the '70s, app. at NY Jazz Museum '75; and made guest apps. at Condon's. In the '70s-80s, he was also active on B'way, as well as in NYC clubs and at Eur. fests. In '80s, he tour. and rec. w. Concord All-Stars; tnr. trio w. Buddy Tate, Scott Hamilton. Cohn was a swinging, modern Basie-oriented arr. and tnr. of the Lester

Young sch. His tone darkened later in his career, and he pl. more on the beat w. some Sonny Rollins added to the mix. Underrated by the public, his playing was always admired by his contemporaries for its structure, sound, and swing. Favs: Sims, Sonny Stitt, Charlie Parker; arrs: Johnny Mandel, Neal Hefti. Fests: NJF w. Sims '66; NJF-NY w. Herman alumni '72; Molde '75; Colo. JP '68–72, '74–5 into '80s. Film: tnr. solos on soundtrack of *Lenny* '74. TV: arr. award winning specials *Anne Bancroft Show*; *S'Wonderful, S'Marvelous, S'Gershwin* '69–70; Tony Award show in '70s. On B'way: principal arr. for *Raisin* '73; *Music, Music, Music* '74; *Sophisticated Ladies* '81; tnr. sax soundtrack for stage version of *I'm Not Rappaport*. Comps: "The Goof and I"; "Tasty Pudding"; "The Underdog" (aka "Ah-Moore"); "Lady Chatterley's Mother." LPS: many on Xan. CDs: Sav.; Prest.; Conc.; Evid.; Red. Brn.; JazzHouse; Timel.; w. Sims (BB; Muse; 32; Evid.; Sonet; Dec.); O. Pettiford (RCA); Getz; M. Davis; Coltrane (Prest.); B. Holiday (Verve); J. Knepper (Steep.); Concord All-Stars (Conc.); Totti Bergh (Gem.).

COHN, JOE (JOSEPH MARK), gtr, tpt, bs; b. Flushing, NY, 12/28/56. Son of Al Cohn and voc. Marilyn Moore. Studied at Berklee 1975–8 as gtr. major, and in '90 as tpt. major. Worked w. Freddy Cole '79; Buddy DeFranco '79–80; Bob Mover '80–1; two tours of Engl. w. fath. Pl. w. Nick Brignola '80–2; Zoot Sims '83; Artie Shaw bb '84–90; Al Grey '88–91. In '90s, he worked w. Duffy Jackson; Doug Raney. Rec. w. Raney for Double-Time label '97. Recs. w. DeFranco, Shaw, Grey, and Cohn. Perf. at Colo. JP '84–5 and '88; *Norway* Jazz Cruise '88–90; JVC JF, Eur. '90; North Sea JF; Pescara JF. Taught priv. for five yrs. in Bost. area; clinician w. Al Grey, L. Hampton Music Sch. at U. of Idaho '91. CDs: D-T; w. Grey (Chiaro; Capri; Arb.); DeFranco (Conc; Pab.).

COHN, SONNY (GEORGE THOMAS), tpt; b. Chicago, IL, 3/14/25; d. Chicago, 11/7/06. Began pl. as a child, inspired by Roy Eldridge, Charlie Shavers. Pl. in Chi. w. Richard Fox 1942; Walter Dyett '43–5; Red Saunders off and on '45–60, dur. which time the band was in residence at Club DeLisa. Worked at Regal Theater w. bands passing through Chi. Pl. w. Louis Bellson, Erskine Hawkins '50s. Join. Count Basie Orch. '60 and stayed until Basie's death in '84, doubling as road manager fr. '74. CDs: w. Basie (Pab.; Rep.; Roul.; Verve; Den.); Milt Jackson w. Basie (Pab.); Jodie Christian; Tab Smith (Del.).

COKER, DOLO (CHARLES MITCHELL), pno; alto sax; b. Hartford, CT, 11/16/27; d. Los Angeles,

CA, 4/13/83. Studied mus. in Florence, So. Caro., where he was raised, and Mather Acad. in Camden, So. Caro. First prof. jobs in Phila. w. Ben Webster 1946; Kenny Dorham '55; Sonny Stitt; Gene Ammons, Lou Donaldson '58; Philly Joe Jones '59; Dexter Gordon '60–1, incl. stage prod. of *The Connection*. Moved to LA in '60, lead. own trio at various clubs through '72. In '70s, worked in LA w. Herb Ellis; Blue Mitchell; Red Rodney; Supersax; Lee Konitz; again w. Stitt; Red Foxx Show in concert; also sch. concerts w. Sonny Criss '73, '74; Jack Sheldon, Richard Boone, Dexter Gordon '74; Teddy Edwards '75; Sweets Edison '75, '77. In March '80, he app. at a Club Med JF in Dakar, Senegal w. Xanadu Rec.'s all star band, incl. Al Cohn, Billy Mitchell, Leroy Vinnegar and Frank Butler. This incl. the first Africa-wide broadcast of a jazz concert, and the first rec. of an Amer. jazz gp. in Africa. Coker was also a pno. teacher and voc. coach. Favs. and infls.: Tatum, Hank Jones, Red Garland. TV: *Rosey Grier Show* '68; *In Name Only*, Screen Gems '69; *Della Reese Show* '69; *Festival in Black*, KCET '71; *Black Omnibus* '73; *Lucy Show*; *Sanford & Son*. Fests: Watts Summer JF, '70–2. Comps: "Lovely Lisa"; "Field Day"; "Affair in Havana." Recs. as lead. for Xan.: *Dolo!* '76; *All Alone* '78. Own fav. rec.: A. Pepper's *Intensity* '60. CDs: w. Pepper (Cont.); Gordon (Jzld.); S. Criss (Muse); H. Edison (Pab.); PJ Jones (Riv.).

COKER, HENRY L., tbn; Dallas, TX, 12/24/19; d. Los Angeles, CA, 11/23/79. Studied mus. at Wiley Coll. Prof. debut w. John White in 1935. Worked w. Nat Towles '37–9; then moved to Hawaii, pl. w. local gps. Ret. to mainland, working w. Benny Carter '44–6; Eddie Heywood 46–7; Illinois Jacquet '45. Due to illness, he worked intermittently '49–51. Best known as feat. tbn. soloist w. Count Basie '52–63, making numerous recs., apps., and tours w. the band. Studio work in NYC, then tour. w. Ray Charles '66–71. For most of '70s, he freelanced in LA; rejoin. Basie briefly in '73; Charles in '76. Film: soundtrack, *Lady Sings the Blues* '72. Rec. solos on "Paper Moon" w. Heywood; "Flyin' Home," "Hot Rod" w. Jacquet; "Straight Life," "Peace Pipe" w. Basie. CDs: w. T. Dameron (Prest.); Jacquet (BB; Verve; Mos.); Basie (Verve; Roul.); F. Wess; K. Clarke; F. Foster; Milt Jackson (Sav.).

COKER, JERRY, educ, arr, tnr sax; b. South Bend, IN, 11/28/32. Both parents were jazz mus. Stud. pno., cl., fl., bassoon, tnr. sax, comp. Pl. w. Fred Dale's Indiana U. band. Join. Woody Herman 1953; left in mid '54 to move to West Coast; pl. concert tour w. Stan Kenton. Attended Yale U. on scholarship for comp. '58. Dur. '60s, he became prominent jazz educ. and lead. of coll. bands. Directed jazz program at Sam Houston St. Coll. '60–2; Monterey Peninsula Coll. '63–4; Indiana U. '65; Miami U. '66. His Indiana U. ens. took first place in Intercollegiate Fest. at Notre Dame '65; made St. Dept. tour of Near East '66. Profess. of mus., U. of Tenn., in mid '80s. Favs: Getz, Sims, Cohn. Book: *Improvising Jazz* (Prentice Hall) '64. Own LP; also *The Herdsmen Play Paris* (Fant.). Other recs. w. Herman (Verve; Col.); Mel Lewis; Clare Fischer (PJ). CDs: w. Herman (Disc.).

COLAR, KID "SHEIK" (George Cola), tpt; lead; b. New Orleans, LA, 9/15/08; d. Detroit, MI, 11/7/96. Studied informally w. Wooden Joe Nicholas. Form. first band when he was 17. Pl. around NO through 1943. Attended USAF Mus. Sch. '43–5. After his mil. discharge, he pl. w. own band bef. join. George Lewis '49; w. Eureka Brass Band fr. '52; also w. Harold Dejan's Olympia Brass Band in '50s. In the early '60s, he led own gps. whose sidemen incl. Capt. John Handy and Cié Frazier. Tour. Engl. w. Barry Martyn '63; several tours w. Handy in late '60s, incl. Eur. '66. In the '70s, he app. often at Preservation Hall. Tour. Engl. as soloist '76; cont. tour. actively in the '80s, mainly w. the Preservation Hall Band. CDs: Amer. Mus.

COLE, COZY (WILLIAM RANDOLPH), dms; b. East Orange, NJ, 10/17/06; d. Columbus, OH, 1/29/81. Private stud. in childhood; made own sticks in manual training class at sch. First inspiration was Sonny Greer. Prof. debut w. Wilbur Sweatman, NYC 1928. Led own band in late '20s. Rec. w. Jelly Roll Morton '30; pl. w. bands of Blanche Calloway and Benny Carter in early '30s; Willie Bryant '35–6; Stuff Smith, Jonah Jones at Onyx Club '36–8. Rose to prominence as member of Cab Calloway band Feb. '39–42. Important rec. solos incl. "Crescendo in Drums"; "Paradiddle"; "Ratamacue." Pl. w. Raymond Scott Orch. on CBS radio staff '42–5, while also stud. perc. at Juilliard and w. Saul Goodman of the NY Phil. Rec. w. Dizzy Gillespie '45. Feat. in B'way prod. *Carmen Jones* and, w. Benny Goodman, in *Seven Lively Arts* '45–6. Freelanced in NYC as sideman and leader bef. join. Louis Armstrong '49–53, incl. Eur. tours '49, '52. Operated drum sch. w. Gene Krupa fr. Mar. '54 until Krupa's death in '73. App. regularly at Metropole Café, NYC '55–8. Tour. Engl. and Continent w. Jack Teagarden, Earl Hines fall '57. His rec. of "Topsy" was an int'l hit in '58, enabling him to lead his own gp. through the '60s. Tour. West Africa w. qnt. for St. Dept. cultural exchange program '62–3. Pl. w. Jonah Jones at the Embers '69. Worked mainly as a freelancer in the

'70s; tour. Eur. w. Benny Carter qt. in revue *A Night in New Orleans* '76. Favs: Krupa, Jo Jones, Buddy Rich, Louie Bellson. Fests: NJF '73 w. Calloway reunion band; Nice '74. Poll: *Esq.* Silver Award '44. Films: *Make Mine Music*; *The Glenn Miller Story*; soundtrack for *The Strip*. TV: app. on Arthur Godfrey, Garry Moore, Steve Allen shows. Books: *Modern Drum Technique*; *Gene Krupa & Cozy Cole Drum Book* (Mills Music); *Cozy Cole, William V. Kessler— Modern Studies for Drums* (BMI). CDs: w. own gp., Roy Eldridge in *Key. Coll.* (Em); Eldridge; C. Hawkins (Dec.); L. Hampton; J. Teagarden; Jelly Roll Morton; Red Allen (BB); Gillespie; Shearing (Sav.); Calloway (Col.); Armstrong (BB; Dec.); E. Condon (Jazz.); Benny Carter (B&B); B. Holiday (Col.; Dec.); Frankie Newton; Stuff Smith (Aff.); Rex Stewart; Buck Clayton (Riv.); Teddy Wilson (Hep).

COLE, FREDDY (LIONEL FREDERICK), pno; voc; b. Chicago, IL, 10/15/31. Youngest of five children; moth. and three bros. (Eddie, Ike, and Nat "King" Cole) all pl. pno. Began on pno. ca 1938 and sang in fath.'s church choir. First prof. job at 15. Local jobs at Capitol Lounge; after brief road tour, he ret. home to cont. his educ. at Roosevelt Coll. Stud. at Juilliard '51; then at New Engl. Cons., grad. in '56 w. master's degree. Pl. Café Society, NYC, early '50s; his rec. of "Whispering Grass," was a mild hit; regular US and int'l tours w. small gps. fr. '60s. His career took an upturn in the late '90s. Although his pno. style is quite different, Cole's vocal timbre and approach resembles that of his famous bro. While his repertoire incl. songs assoc. w. Nat, he asserts his autonomy w. songs like "I'm Not My Brother, I'm Me." Favs: Eckstine, Johnny Hartman, Oscar Peterson, Ahmad Jamal, John Lewis. LPs: Dinky. CDs: Fant.; Sunny.

COLE, JUNE (LAWRENCE), bs, tba; also voc; b. Springfield, OH, 1903; d. NYC, 10/10/60. Began pl. tba. prof. in 1923 w. Synco Jazz Band, which became McKinney's Cotton Pickers. Left the band in '26 to join Fletcher Henderson. In '28, he sailed to Eur. to tour w. Bennie Peyton, then Sam Wooding. In '31, after Wooding disbanded, Cole stayed in Eur., working intermittently w. Willie Lewis through the '30s; due to severe illness and prolonged stays at the American Hospital in Paris, he stopped perf. '36–9. Resumed working w. Lewis. '39–41, when band ret. to US. Through the '40s, he led small gps. in NYC; also worked w. Willie "The Lion" Smith '47. Dur. the early '50s, he led a band at Club 845, NYC, and ran own record store in Harlem. Cont. pl. into late '50s. CDs: w. Henderson (Col.; BB); Bessie Smith (Col.).

COLE, NAT "KING" (Nathaniel Adams Coles), pno, voc; b. Montgomery, AL, 3/17/17; d. Santa Monica, CA, 2/15/65. Cole was raised in Chi. in a musical family; bros. Isaac, Eddie, and Freddy were prof. mus. Fr. age 12, he sang and pl. org. in church where his fath. was pastor; by 17, he was leading his own gp., the Royal Dukes. Made rec. debut in 1936 w. Eddie Cole's band, the Solid Swingers. That same year, he form. a band to tour vaudeville circuit w. a revival of Eubie Blake's revue *Shuffle Along*. In '37, when the show broke up in LA, he settled there and started working in night clubs as a solo pnst. In '39, he formed the orig. King Cole Trio, w. Oscar Moore, gtr., and Wesley Prince, bs. The gp. rec. for Dec. in '40 and '41 and worked in Hollywood and NYC clubs. In '42, he rec. w. Lester Young for the Philo label; their perfs. on "I Can't Get Started"; "Indiana"; "Body and Soul"; and "Tea for Two" became benchmarks in their individual careers. In '43, the trio sw. to the Cap. label and rec. its first national hit, "Straighten Up and Fly Right." From the mid to late '40s, Cole maintained the trio, occasionally working and rec. in other contexts, incl. a celebrated '44 app. w. JATP. Starting w. "The Christmas Song" '46, Cole began making voc. recs., accomp. by studio orchs. and strings. A succession of vocal hits, incl. "Mona Lisa" and "Nature Boy," established him as one of the country's leading popular singers and led to his own sponsored radio series (Wildroot Cream Oil '48–9). In '56, he became the first major African-American perf. to host his own network TV series, a 15-minute NBC musical variety show that was expanded to a star-studded half hour, but left the air a year later due to viewer and sponsor apathy. From '50 until his death, Cole was an internationally acclaimed entertainer, whose considerable talent as a jazz pnst. and singer was almost totally obscured by his commercial success. He perf. in supper clubs, toured extensively as a solo artist, and, dur. the early '60s, staged his own revues: *The Merry World of Nat King Cole*, LA '61, and *Sights and Sounds*, which toured in '63. He appeared in several movies, most notably *St. Louis Blues*, in which he portrayed W.C. Handy, and *The Nat King Cole Story*, a feature based on his life; in '64, he made his final film appearance in *Cat Ballou*. In Dec. '64, he was operated on for a malignant tumor and died in a Santa Monica hospital two mos. later. After his death, his widow, Maria Cole, formed the Nat King Cole Cancer Foundation. As a popular singer, Cole's unique tonal quality, a mixture of velvet and smoke, enriched even the most mundane Tin Pan Alley songs and lent a jazz tinge to his more up-tempo recs. Since Louis Armstrong, his was the first male voice rooted in the jazz tradition to win such widespread popular acceptance. Though in his later yrs. Cole rarely perf. as a jazz pnst., his earlier work in that genre has infl. such musicians as Oscar Peterson, Red Garland, and Tommy Flanagan, and cont. to received newfound admiration. Cole evolved fr. the Earl Hines sch., mastering fluid, melodic right-hand lines, and a spare, yet harmonically advanced left-hand comping style. Polls: *Esq.* Gold, pno. '46; *Esq.* Silver '47; *Met.* '47–9; *Esq.* Silver, voc. '46–7; *DB*, small combo '44–7; *Met.* '45–8. CDs: boxed set of Cap. recs., Mos.; Dec.; Cap.; BL; w. Lester Young (BN; Verve); JATP (Verve); L. Hampton (BB).

COLE, NATALIE, voc; b. Los Angeles, CA, 2/6/50. Daughter of Nat and Maria Cole. Stage debut at age 11 in fath.'s revue at Greek Theatre, LA. Her own career from mid '70s to late '80s was devoted mainly to r&b and pop material, which earned her Grammy awards and multimillion rec. sales. Among her better known LPs are *Inseparable* '75; *Unpredictable* '77; then, after a long rec. hiatus, *Everlasting* '87. In '91, she changed her style and made an album of songs rec. by her fath. On the title track, "Unforgettable," state-of-the-art technology enabled her to sing a seamless duet w. him, resulting in a surprise hit and the establishment of her identity as a jazz-based perf. Since '92, she has cont. to tour internationally w. partial jazz accomps..; in '94, she won a Grammy for *Take a Look*. CDs: Elek.

COLE, RICHIE (RICHARD), alto sax; b. Trenton, NJ, 2/29/48. Father owned a jazz club; heard jazz from a very early age. Start. on gtr. at age 5; picked up alto sax at 10. Studied w. Phil Woods as a teenager; after hs graduation, att. Berklee Coll. of Mus. on scholarship. Left after two yrs. to join Buddy Rich 1969. Dur. early '70s, he worked w. Doc Severinsen; L. Hampton; Manhattan Tranfer; also form. own gp. Closely assoc. w. Eddie Jefferson, w. whom he pl. fr. '75 until Jefferson's death in '79. Since then has led own gps, incl. Alto Madness. A hard-driving, Woods-influenced pl., he sometimes detracts from his performances w. overdone comedy. CDs: Heads Up; Muse; Conc.; Mile.; w. Jefferson (Muse); Rich (BGO); S. Stitt (32).

COLE, RUPERT, alto sax; cl; b. Trinidad, BWI, 8/8/09. Father of Ronnie Cole, dms., vib. Stud. cl. in Barbados. Moved to NYC in 1924. Sw. to alto, on which he start. pl. prof.; recs. w. Bill Brown '29; tour. w. Horace Henderson to '31; Don Redman '31–8; Louis Armstrong's orch. '38–44. Briefly w. Redman again bef. join. Cootie Williams' bb '45–6. In '50s worked w. Lucky Millinder; occ. w. Wilbur De Paris. Ret. from full-time mus, but still freelanced dur. '60s; pl. regularly w. George Wettling's trio '64. CDs: w. Armstrong (Dec.).

COLEMAN, BILL (WILLIAM JOHNSON), tpt, voc; b. Centreville, KY, 8/4/04; d. Toulouse, France, 8/24/81. Began tpt. studies in 1916. Debut w. children's orch. in Cincinnati, Ohio, w. Ernest Moore '18. Pl. w. J.C. Higginbotham and Edgar Hayes. Taught himself to read mus. To NYC where he worked w. Cecil and Lloyd Scott '26–7; Luis Russell '29, '31–2; Cecil Scott '29–30; Charlie Johnson '30. To France w. Lucky Millinder '33. Worked w. Teddy Hill '34–5. Ret. to Paris, worked w. Freddy "Snake Hips" Taylor '35–6; briefly w. Qnt. of the Hot Club of France '36; then w. Willie Lewis '36; Leon Abbey in Bombay, India '36–7. After pl. w. Lewis again in Paris '37–8, form. Harlem Rhythm Makers w. Herman Chittison and other Lewis sidemen, pl. in Egypt '38–40, incl. Shah of Iran's wedding reception, Alexandria '39. Back in NYC, he worked w. Benny Carter, Fats Waller '40; Teddy Wilson '40–1; Andy Kirk '41–2; Waller orch.; tour. South w. Noble Sissle, Ellis Larkins '42; Mary Lou Williams '44; to Calif. w. John Kirby '45; USO tour of Japan and Philippines '45–6; Sy Oliver '46–7; Billy Kyle '47–8. In Dec. '48, he moved back to Paris, where he enjoyed great popularity among French jazz fans through his residency at Trois Mailletz fr. '54. Tour. extensively on the Continent through '60, w. band that incl. Dicky Wells, Guy Lafitte, Zutty Singleton. Tour. Engl. '66 '67; Africa '71–2. Orig. infl. by Louis Armstrong, he evolved a personal, legato, swinging style, marked by a mellow, lambent tone. Fests: Juan-les-Pins w. Basie '61; Nice '74. Awarded French Order of Merit '75. French films: *Respectful Prostitute*; *Printemps a Paris*. CDs: Topaz; Class; BL; w. Bechet; Buck Clayton (Vogue); Benny Carter (B&B); Ben Webster (BL); B. Holiday (Col.); D. Reinhardt (Ark.).

COLEMAN, CECILIA, pno; b. Long Beach, CA, 9/8/62. Studied jazz w. Charlie Shoemake, classical w. Dr. Allan Giles; B. Mus. in pno. fr. Cal. St.-Long Beach. From 1984, she freelanced w. many groups in LA area, incl. Cece Worrell; Bob Keane; Benn Clatworthy; Jimmy Cleveland; Chuck Flores; Jack Sheldon; Phil Upchurch. Won Shelly Manne New Talent Award fr. LA Jazz Society '84. CDs: Resurgent; w. Benn Clatworthy (Disc.).

COLEMAN, DENARDO, dms; b. Los Angeles, CA, 4/19/56. The son of Ornette Coleman and the poet Jayne Cortez. Started on dms. at age six; at 10 rec. *The Empty Foxhole* w. his father. Soon after, worked w. him in clubs and on tour. Inspired by Billy Higgins, Ed Blackwell, and Charles Moffett. Often pl. in tandem w. Jack DeJohnette. Has cont. to work regularly w. Ornette Coleman and act as his business mgr. CDs: w. O. Coleman (BN; Col.; Repertoire); w. P. Metheny (Geffen).

COLEMAN, EARL, voc; b. Port Huron, MI, 8/12/25; d. NYC, 7/12/95. Family moved to Leland, Miss., 1927. Childhood friend of Jimmy Grissom, who later sang w. Duke Ellington. Moved to Indianapolis, Ind. '39; sang w. Ernie Fields, Bardu Ali. With Jay McShann '43; Earl Hines, King Kolax '44. To Calif. w. McShann '45. Rec. "This Is Always," "Dark Shadows" w. Charlie Parker '47; "Yardbird Suite," "Stranger in Town" w. Fats Navarro, Max Roach '48. Inactive for several yrs., then worked w. Gene Ammons '54. Rec. w. Art Farmer, Gigi Gryce; Sonny Rollins '56. Resumed tour. and rec. as a leader in '60. App. w. Gerald Wilson in LA '60; Don Byas in Paris '62. Steady gigs in NYC at Birdland and Village Gate '62 to mid '60s. Worked w. Billy Taylor, Frank Foster bb, mid '60s; also one-nighters at Playboy club. Moved to LA '68; app. at Redd Foxx's club; freelanced, also w. Bill Berry, Gerald Wilson orchs. Worked in Cincinnati, St. Louis, '75. Fav: Billy Eckstine. Fests: NJF-NY; North Sea '89. TV: Billy Taylor show, '66. CDs: Prest.; w. C. Parker (Mos.; Stash); Sonny Rollins; G. Ammons (Prest); Miles Davis (BL); Etta Jones (Muse).

COLEMAN, GEORGE EDWARD, tnr, alto, sop saxes; b. Memphis, TN, 3/8/35. Brother pl. alto; son, George Jr., pl. dms. Began on alto, self-taught. Pl. alto w. B.B. King 1952–5. Moved to Chi. '56, pl. tnr. w. Walter Perkins's MJT+3, John Gilmore, Ira Sullivan '56–8. Moved to NYC '58, pl. w. Max Roach '58–9; Slide Hampton '60–2; Wild Bill Davis '62; Miles Davis '63–4; Ossie Davis–Ruby Dee '64; Lionel Hampton '65; Lee Morgan '66; also pl. w. Charles McPherson, Elvin Jones, Shirley Scott fr. '65. Led own oct., qt. fr. '74; also pl. w. Cedar Walton. Coleman pl. alto on the soundtrack to Dick Gregory's film *Sweet Love Bitter*, based on the life of Charlie Parker. He has taught at LIU, New Sch., NYU, Lenox Sch. of Mus. Pnst. Harold Mabern has been a constant in his '90s qts. App. at Lincoln Center "Jazz Tenor Battle Royale" in mid '90s. A tnr. sax master who, in relation to his high level of accomplishment, is undervalued by the public. Favs: Frank Foster, Sonny Rollins, Joe Henderson. Fests: all major fr. early '60s. Films: app. in *Sweet Love Bitter; Freejack*. CDs: Verve; Timel.; Evid.; JH; Charly; w. M. Davis (Col.); H. Hancock; Jimmy Smith; Booker Little (BN); Cedar Walton (Timel.); R. Beirach (Tri.); James Williams (DIW); Elvin Jones (Enja); Mabern; Chet Baker (Prest.); Mingus (Atl.); M. Roach (Riv.); Louis Smith (Steep.); H. McGhee (BL); H. Ruiz (Novus).

COLEMAN, IRA NOEL, bs; b. Stockholm, Sweden, 4/29/56. Lived in France 1956–68; Germ. '68–82. Parents, both artists, had many mus. friends incl. Art Taylor, Max Roach, Charles Mingus, Johnny Griffin. Studied electronics and engineering '75–7; in French mil. '78–9; att. Cologne Cons. of Mus. '80. Moved to Bost. to study at Berklee Coll. of Mus. '82–4. Moved to NYC '84. Pl. w. Archie Shepp '84; Freddie Hubbard '85; Mercer Ellington orch. '86; Betty Carter '87–9; Tony Williams, Monty Alexander fr. '89. Favs: Ron Carter, Dave Holland, Miroslav Vitous. Polls: *SJ* Trio of Yr. w. Mulgrew Miller, Smitty Smith '85. Fests: Eur. fr. '85; Japan fr. '89. TV: Cosby Show w. Betty Carter; Bravo cable w. Herbie Hancock; T. Williams; own trio. CDs: w. T. Williams; J. Henderson; R. Rosnes (BN); Franco Ambrosetti (Enja); M. Alexander (Chesky); Betty Carter; P. Delano (Verve); Branford Marsalis; T. Shook; Marlon Jordan (Col.); Carl Allen (Alfa); Billy Pierce (Sunny.); Vincent Herring (Land.; MM); Mulgrew Miller (Land.).

COLEMAN, ORNETTE, alto sax, comp, tnr sax, tpt, vln; b. Ft. Worth, TX, 3/19/30. Influenced by his cousin, a mus. teacher, he was self-taught on alto fr. age 14, then sw. to tnr. two yrs. later. Pl. w. local bands 1946–8; carnival band '49. Tour. w. Clarence Samuels' r&b gp., then settled in NO, working mostly at day jobs. Ret. to Ft. Worth '50, then went to LA w. Pee Wee Crayton's r&b gp. After a couple of yrs. back in Ft. Worth, he ret. to LA. While working as an elevator operator, he studied harmony and theory textbooks and developed a new style divorced fr. the conventional concept of improv. based on chord patterns. While working in obscure clubs in LA, he came to the attention of Red Mitchell, Percy Heath. Made rec. debut on Cont. label '58. Signed w. Atlantic, att. Lenox Sch. of Jazz '59. Opened at Five Spot, NYC, w. Don Cherry, Charlie Haden, Billy Higgins autumn '59. Coleman's new style of jazz was the source of much controversy among jazz mus. and listeners fr. that time. Rec. seven albums for Atl. (six w. Cherry) '60–2; also perf. at NJF and MJF, and at Town Hall '62. The album *Free Jazz*, rec. w. a double qt. w. Cherry, Freddie Hubbard, Eric Dolphy in '60, contained thirty-seven minutes of collective, improv. babel which strongly infl. the avant-garde of the '60s and '70s. Stud. tpt. and vln., did not perf. '63–4. Appeared at Village Vanguard, tour. Eur. in trio w. David Izenzon, Charles Moffett '65. Coleman's perfs. on tpt. and vln. brought him even more controversy, and strong criticisms fr. mus. such as Miles Davis and Chas. Mingus. Pl. w. qt. and Phila. Woodwind Qnt. at Village Theater '67; w. Don Cherry at NYU '69. Led qt. w. Dewey Redman, Charlie Haden,

Ed Blackwell, or son Denardo Coleman late '60s. Focused on comp., perf. occasionally at own Artists House in Soho, NYC early '70s; extended comps. incl. *Forms and Sounds for Wind Quintet*; *Skies of America*. The latter was perf. w. symph. orch. at NJF '72. Led gp. w. James Blood Ulmer, Haden, Denardo Coleman, Barbara Huey, mid '70s. Led gp. Prime Time fr. '75. Rec. and tour. w. Pat Metheny '85–6. Coleman received Guggenheim Fellowships for comp. in '67 and '74; MacArthur Grant '94. A film about his life, *Ornette: Made in America*, was dir. by Shirley Clarke and released in '84. Two concerts entitled *Ornette Coleman Celebration* were given at Weill Recital Hall '87. In '97, several nights were devoted to his music at Lincoln Center, incl. *Skies of America* and gp. perfs. Scored and perf. on soundtrack of films *Naked Lunch* '92; *Philadelphia*. Polls: *DB* Jazzman of Yr. '66, '71; *DB* Hall of Fame '69; *DB* Rec. of Yr. for *At the Golden Circle*, Vol. 1, '66; won *DB* Critics Poll '67, '72–4; *DB* Readers '72–4. Form. own label, Harmolodic, released through Verve. CDs: Harmo./Verve; Col.; Atl.; Cont.; BN; w. Metheny (Geffen); Rolf Kuhn (Intuit.).

COLEMAN, STEVE, alto sax, fl, comp; b. Chicago, IL, 9/20/56. Started on vln., then alto sax. After early exposure to the mus. of Von Freeman and Bunky Green, his fath. introduced him to mus. of Charlie Parker. In NYC in mid 1970s, he worked w. Thad Jones–Mel Lewis Orch.; Bob Brookmeyer; David Murray; Sam Rivers; Slide Hampton; Abbey Lincoln. Later founded the Bklyn.-based progressive jazz collective, M-Base, and began rec. w. his gp., the Five Elements, whose early recs. stressed iconoclastic combinations of avant-garde techniques and funky rhythms. In '92, he released *Rhythm In Mind*, a more straight-ahead venture feat. Von Freeman, Kenny Wheeler, Kevin Eubanks, Tommy Flanagan, et al. "My language comes directly from the language of older cats like my musical idols Charlie Parker, J. Coltrane, Lester Young, Miles Davis, and Louis Armstrong, to name a few," says Coleman. "Without their language, my language wouldn't be possible." In '95, he rec. extensively w. Five Elements at the Hot Brass Club. Fest: NJF-NY '92; San Sebastian '97. CDs: Novus; JMT; DIW; w. Franco Ambrosetti; Abbey Lincoln (Enja); Robin Eubanks; Cassandra Wilson (JMT); Dave Holland (ECM); T. Jones–M. Lewis (WW); Lewis (Tel.); David Murray; Sam Rivers (BS); Greg Osby (BN).

COLES, JOHNNY (JOHN), tpt, flg; b. Trenton, NJ, 7/3/26; d. Philadelphia, PA, 12/21/97. Began pl. in 1939; mainly self-taught. Pl. w. mil. band '41; Slappy And His Swingsters '45–8; Eddie Vinson '48–51.

Co-led gp. w. Philly Joe Jones '51, then pl. w. Bull Moose Jackson '52; James Moody '56–8; Gil Evans Orch. '58–64; Charles Mingus off and on mid '60s incl. Eur. tour '64. Rec. w. Duke Pearson and as leader '60s, also co-led gp. w. Geo. Coleman. Pl. w. Herbie Hancock Sxt. '68–9. Rec. soundtrack to Bill Cosby's *Fat Albert* TV series '69. Pl. w. Ray Charles Orch. '69–70; Duke Ellington Orch. '70–4. Rejoin. Charles after Ellington's death in '74. Worked w. A. Blakey '76; PJ Jones's Dameronia, Mingus Dynasty early '80s; Count Basie Orch. '85–6. Moved to SF '85 but was back in Phila. in '90s. Fav: Miles Davis. Poll: *DB* Critics New Star '65. CDs: BN; CC; w. Gil Evans (Verve; Enja); C. Mingus (Jazz Workshop; Musidisc); H. Hancock; Joe Henderson (BN); K. Burrell (Verve); C. Earland; Buck Hill; Etta Jones (Muse); Gene Harris (Conc.); Frank Morgan (Cont.); D. Byrd (BL); Ray Crawford (Cand.).

COLIANNI, JOHN, pno; b. Paterson, NJ, 1/7/63. Father, an ex-pnst., stimulated his interest. Priv. studies 1976–9; began on tpt. and pno., but dropped tpt. lessons in '79. Prof. debut '78 w. Keter Betts at Blues Alley, Wash., D.C. Tour. w. Lionel Hampton Feb. '82–Dec. '84. Has played NYC clubs intermittently since '83. Won third place in Thelonious Monk pno. competition '87. Many dates w. Oliver Jackson qt. fr. '88. Full time accomp. for Mel Tormé in early '90s but cont. to freelance w. Woody Allen and others. Favs: Teddy Wilson, Monty Alexander, Mel Powell, Dave McKenna. CDs: Conc.; w. Tormé (Conc.; Tel.); Harry Allen (Mastermix); Hampton (Timel.).

COLLETTE, BUDDY (WILLIAM MARCELL), saxes, cl, fl, comp; b. Los Angeles, CA, 8/6/21. Studied fl., sax, cl., and pno. w. various teachers in LA and SF; also comp. and arr. via Schillinger System w. George Tremblay 1938–87. In '40s, he worked w. Cee Pee Johnson; Les Hite; Gerald Wilson; Benny Carter. One of the first black musicians to break into commercial radio and TV, he pl. for the Groucho Marx show, taking leave of absence '56 to tour w. Chico Hamilton Qnt. From '60s, he concentrated on studio jobs, w. occasional jazz dates, incl. LA Neophonic. Taught at various colls. in LA area fr. '74. Has written everything from TV jingles and industrial film mus. to a three-part fugue for nine instruments and a 12–tone suite for harp and fl. Helped start Legend Rec. co. '73–5. One of the most adaptable and respected mus. in the LA area. Fests: put together bbs at MJF for Mingus; Monk '64; Gillespie '65; Gil Evans '66. Pl. w. reunited Hamilton qnt. at Verona JF, Italy, '89. CDs: Cont.; SN; w. Hamilton; J. Newton (SN); Gillespie (BN); B. Kessel; Lyle Murphy; H. Rumsey–Lighthouse All-Stars (Cont.); R. Norvo

(BB); Mingus (Rh.); Jimmy Smith (Mile.); H. Bluiett (BS); Q. Jones (Imp.).

COLLEY, SCOTT, bs; b. Los Angeles, CA, 11/24/63. Older bro. pl. dms. Won scholarship to Calif. Inst. of Arts, 1984, also studied w. Charlie Haden, Fred Tinsley. Pl. w. Carmen McRae fr. '86 into early '90s; also w. Clifford Jordan; Art Farmer; John Scofield; James Newton; Joe Lovano; Billy Hart; Lew Tabackin; Al Foster; Fred Hersch, etc. Pl. w. T.S. Monk '91–3; Jim Hall fr. '91; gp., Lan Xang, 'fr. 97. Favs: Mingus, Haden, Holland, Pastorius. CDs: CC; Freelance; Steep.; w. Hall (Tel.); R. Hargrove; C. Hollyday (Novus); Hersch (Chesky); Rebecca Franks (Just.); McRae (Den.); Rich Perry; S. Slagle; H. Danko; D. Stryker (Steep.); Ted Rosenthal (JA); B. Charlap (CC); Chris Potter (Conc.); P. Martino (BN); Lan Xang (Mythology).

COLLIE, MAX (JOHN MAXWELL), tbn; b. Melbourne, Australia, 2/21/31. Formed own jazz band in home town, having been assoc. w. the orig. Graeme Bell band. In 1962, he moved to Engl., joined London City Stompers, and soon took over as lead., changing the band's name to Max Collie's Rhythm Aces. Rec. first LP in '71. In '75, the band won the World Jazz Championship against the top fourteen US and Can. traditional bands. The band continues to tour internationally. In '85–6, Collie presented the "New Orleans Mardi Gras" in over one hundred perfs. w. some twenty-five of them in UK concert halls. His discography is vast, incl. many recs. for BL, Reality, and French labels. CDs: Timel.; Reality.

COLLIER, (JAMES) GRAHAM, comp, arr, bs, kybds; b. Tynemouth, England, 2/21/37. Father was dmr. for silent movies. Pl. tpt. in army band 1954–61. Won *DB* scholarship to Berklee Coll. of Mus., where he stud. w. Herb Pomeroy, William Curtis '61–3. Tour. US w. Lee Castle's Jimmy Dorsey Orch., then ret. to Engl. '63. Formed own gp., Graham Collier Music, '64; sidemen have incl. Harry Beckett, John Surman, Kenny Wheeler. This band was the first in Engl. to extensively tour schs. presenting a concert and lecture program. Formed bb, Hoarded Dreams, to perf. comp. of same name at Bracknell JF '83. Formed rehearsal orch. that later became Loose Tubes '84. Collier is curr. Dir. of Jazz Studies at the Royal Acad. of Mus., London. He has comp. for plays, films, and TV, and is the author of several books, incl. *Inside Jazz* (Quartet) and *Jazz: A Student's and Teacher's Guide* (Cambridge). He has owned and managed the British rec. label Mosaic (not to be confused with the Amer. reissue label) fr. '74. Awarded the OBE medal in '87. Favs: Gil Evans,

Duke Ellington, Charles Mingus. CDs: RAM; Boathouse.

COLLINS, BURT (BURTON I.), tpt; b. Bronx, NY, 3/27/31. Moved to Phila. at age 9; stud. tpt. at 14. Worked w. Neal Hefti 1955; feat. sideman w. Woody Herman '56; same yr. also worked w. Dizzy Gillespie; Claude Thornhill. Pl. w. Johnny Richards bb, when it was active, fr. '57–9; again in '64; Elliot Lawrence '58; Urbie Green '59. Active studio mus. in '60s and '70s, pl. for B'way shows, incl: *Bye Bye Birdie* '60; *How to Succeed in Business . . .* '61–2. Many club dates in mid '60s. Pl. w. Duke Pearson's bb '67–70; David Matthews bb '75; Lee Konitz Nonet '75–7. Early infl: Harry James. Fav: Clifford Brown. Fest: Randall's Island, w. C. Adderley bb, early '60s. TV: jazz soloist w. band on Les Crane Show '65; specials w. Victor Borge; Jonathan Winters. Feat. solo on "New Girl" w. Pearson '67. Off B'way: taped solos for *Side Man* '98. CDs: w. Herman (Evid.); Duke Pearson (BN); G. Benson (A&M); Konitz (Chiaro.).

COLLINS, CAL (CALVIN), gtr; b. Medora, IN, 5/5/33; d. Dillsboro, IN, 8/26/01. Played mand. w. local bluegrass gps.; mainly self-taught on gtr., which he took up at age 13. As a teenager, pl. w. Andy Simpkins, Harold Jones. Worked w. George Mehas qt. in Hamilton, Ohio, 1950s. After two yrs. in army, moved to Cincinnati, working in clubs, radio, and TV. Gained wider recognition w. Benny Goodman fr. '76 to '80. In this period and '80s tour. w. Scott Hamilton and Warren Vaché in LA, Portland, and Seattle, w. trips to Japan, Austral. Led gps. in Cincinnati in the '90s, incl. a qt. w. flg. Jerry Van Blair; and traveled as a single to Japan, Eur., UK, So. Africa. First inspired by Art Tatum and Fats Waller, rather than gtrs., he acknowledged the infl. of Nat Cole's cohorts, Oscar Moore, Irving Ashby, John Collins; also named Django Reinhardt and George Van Eps among his favs. Taught master classes and cond. clinics. CDs: Conc.; w. Hamilton; Vaché; Al Cohn; Woody Herman; Rosemary Clooney; Conc. All-Stars (Conc.); Goodman (Lond.).

COLLINS, DICK (RICHARD HARRISON), tpt, crnt, flg; b. Seattle, WA, 7/19/24. Grandfather pl. picc. w. Queen Victoria's Royal Band. Fath., Fred, had own band, and Collins was mascot 1929–31. Bro., Bob, pl. tbn. w. Dave Brubeck Oct. Stud. w. Red Nichols' fath., San Jose, Calif. '29–30; Grace Adams East, Oakland, Calif., '34–5; Darius Milhaud, Alexander Tansman, Paris '48. B.A., SF St. U.; M.S., USC. Own radio show on KGO, SF, '30, where he sang, accomp. by sist. on gtr. Pl. w. Earl Gladman

Orch. '38–40, "a mixed band with a black leader. Played small towns always 'across the tracks.' " Pl. w. Brubeck Qnt. and Oct. '46–7, '49–50; Hubert Fol's Be-Bop Minstrels in France, Netherlands '48; Charlie Barnet '51; Charles Mingus Orch. early '50s; Alvino Rey '52; Charlie Mariano Sxt. '53; Woody Herman '54–6, incl. Eur. tour. '54; Les Brown on and off '58–66, incl. tours of Eur., Asia, Africa; Nat Pierce Qnt. '78; Capp-Pierce Juggernaut '90s. Collins has served as mus. librarian for the Calif. Institute for the Arts '68–9; librarian, Nat'l Information Center for Earthquake Engineering, Cal. Tech '70; LA Public Library, Art and Mus. Dept. '72–86. Favs: Armstrong, Berigan, Eldridge. Awarded Prix de Disques for *H2O* by *Jazz Hot* magazine, Paris '48. Films: docu. on D. Milhaud '50s; W. Herman band, Germ. '54. TV: several seasons w. Bob Hope, Steve Allen, Dean Martin shows. Comp. mus. for Tennessee Williams' *At Liberty*, Idlewild (Calif.) Art Fest. '58. His *Diptych* pl. at Long Beach (Calif.) Music Fest. '61. Rec. w. Mingus for Fentone ca. '50. LPs: *The Herdsmen Play Paris* (Fant.); two under his own name for RCA Victor, one of which was reissued on CD by RCA in Spain. CDs: w. Brubeck (Col.; Fant.); P. Desmond; Tjader (Fant.); Herman (Disc.); N. Pierce (Hep); Kenny Clarke (Jazz Time).

COLLINS, JAY HOWARD, tnr sax; b. NYC, 7/22/68. Father pl. fl.; stepfath. pl. blues gtr. and hca. Studied at Wilson HS in Portland, Ore., later w. Steve Coleman at Dave Holland Jazz Wkshp. 1989; Andrew Hill '92. Pl. in Portland w. Ron Steen off and on fr. '87; Jerry Hahn '89; Akbar Depriest '89–90; Dick Berk '90. In NYC '90, pl. w. Joe Beck, Tex Allen. Ret. to Portland '91, pl. w. Crazy 8's, Leroy Vinnegar, Mel Brown, Berk. Favs: Rollins, Hawkins, Lockjaw Davis. TV: PBS, PDX Jazz Summit '91. CDs: Res.; w. Berk (Res.); R. Steen (House).

COLLINS, JOHN ELBERT, gtr; b. Montgomery, AL, 9/20/13; d. Los Angeles, 10/4/01. Early study w. his moth., Georgia Gorham, a pnst. and bandleader, who rec. for Black Swan. Worked in Chi. w. Art Tatum 1935; Roy Eldridge '36–9; in NYC fr. '40, pl. w. Lester Young; Billie Holiday; Benny Carter; Dizzy Gillespie; Fletcher Henderson; then in the army '42–6. To Eur. '48 in trio w. Slam Stewart and Erroll Garner. Pl. and rec. w. Tadd Dameron, NYC '49. Join. Nat Cole Sept. '51, remaining until Cole's death '65; then on and off for the next six yrs. w. Bobby Troup. Tour. France and Spain w. own trio '83; feat. soloist w. Carmen McRae '88. Cont. to gig occ. in LA into '90s, but worked mainly as priv. teacher. Won *Esq.* New Star Award, '47; awarded LA Jazz Society Award; also Smithsonian and Rutgers U. Award for outstanding contribution to jazz. One of the most underrated of Christian-inspired gtrsts., he was kept in obscurity in the '50s as the result of his constant touring w. Cole. CDs: w. Fats Navarro–Dameron (Cap.); Cole (Mos.; Cap.; Laser.); McRae (Conc.; Den.); Joe Williams (Delos); Ray Brown (Conc.); Tatum (Dec.); Milt Jackson (Pab.); I. Jacquet (BB; Verve); R. Eldridge (Col.; Dec.).

COLLINS, JOYCE, pno, educ, voc, arr, comp; b. Battle Mountain, NV, 5/5/30. Studied pno. fr. age 4. Encouraged by Dave Brubeck and Reno jazz mus., she moved to Calif. to stud. priv., grad. in 1949 w. a B.A. in mus. fr. SF St. U. To LA, where she began jazz career in local clubs, then worked in NYC, LV, Paris, and Mexico City in '50s and '60s. Tour. w. Frankie Carle '54; sat in regularly w. Bob Cooper at The Lighthouse '58; made rec. debut as lead. for Jazzland '61. Pl. ten yrs. in rec. bands and w. major TV sitcoms. Rec. w. Frank Butler, Paul Horn and Gene Estes bb; albums as pnst., voc., and arr. w. Bill Henderson '75, '82. Tour. w. Bill Cosby, Horn, and app. at KC Women's JF and Int'l Art of Jazz, LI, N.Y. First woman to cond. a show band in LV. First female member of AFM board of dir. '60–4. Named NAJE Outstanding Jazz Educ. in '80, '86. Radio apps. w. Marian McPartland and on own program feat. women jazz comps. and lyricists. Fr. '74 taught jazz pno., harm., and hist. at Dick Grove Sch. of Mus. Perf. in Brazil '91. CDs: Dodo; Disc.; Aud.

COLLINS, LEE (LEEDS), tpt; b. New Orleans, LA, 10/17/01; d. Chicago, IL, 7/3/60. Studied mus. w. tptr. fath. and tbnst. uncle. Fr. 1913 pl. w. Young Eagles, Columbia Band, and Young Tuxedo Orch., among other NO bands; in '15 pl. w. Louis Armstrong, Kid Shots Madison for Zulu Club parade; also sideman w. Papa Celestin, Zutty Singleton. In '24, he replaced Louis Armstrong in King Oliver band at Lincoln Gardens in Chi. Tour. extens. as lead. and sideman dur. late '20s and early '30s. Celebrated for his '29 Vict. recs. w. saxist Davey Jones in Jones and Collins Astoria Hot Eight. Worked in early '30s w. Luis Russell in NYC; Dave Peyton in Chi.; w. Chicago Ramblers in '32; Dodds bros; Z. Singleton; Mezz Mezzrow. In '30s, pl. w. Lovey Austin's Blues Serenaders; Jimmy Bertrand '40. Fr. mid '45, led own trio at Victory Club on Clark St., but also gigged w. Chippie Hill '46; Kid Ory '48; Art Hodes '50–1; Joe Sullivan, Calif. '53. Eur. tours w. Mezzrow '51, '54. Illness dur. second tour ended his pl. career. A wide-toned, rhythmically exciting player, he was considered to be one of the leading descendants of such pioneers as Buddy Bolden and Bunk Johnson,

but also showed the infl. of Armstrong and Red Allen. Book: *Oh, Didn't He Ramble*: *The Life Story of Lee Collins*, F.J. Gillis and J.W. Miner '74. CDs: w. Morton (Riv.); Mezzrow (Vogue); Jones and Collins Astoria Hot Eight in 3–CD set, *New Orleans-Chicago-New York* (BBC).

COLLINS, RUDY (RUDOLPH ALEXANDER), dms; b. NYC, 7/24/34. Studied tbn. at Seward Park HS; dms. at Wurlitzer Sch. of Mus.; later stud. w. Sam Ulano 1953–7; Charlie Tappin. Start. pl. prof. for club dates and dances '52; w. Hot Lips Page; Cootie Williams '53; Eddie Bonnemere '53–6. Apps. in '56 w. Johnny Smith at Birdland, NYC; Roy Eldridge at the Bohemia; at Town Hill in Brooklyn w. Austin Powell '57–8; also freelanced in late '50s w. Cab Calloway; Carmen McRae; Cecil Taylor. Join. Herbie Mann '59, tour. Africa '60; w. Dizzy Gillespie '62–6. In '67–8, he tour. w. Ray Bryant; Kenny Burrell; Woody Herman; apps. w. Junior Mance; Lloyd Price; Harry Belafonte '69. Also pl. in pit bands for *Purlie*; *Hair*. In '70s, cont. as active freelance mus.; worked w. Earl Hines trio '72; NYC clubs w. Duke Pearson, Lee Konitz '73; Randy Weston, Count Basie '74; tour. US and Can. w. Cleo Laine–John Dankworth '74. Taught dms. at Bklyn. Children's Museum fr. '69. Favs: Roach, Jo Jones, PJ Jones, Persip. Fests: NJF, w. J.J. Johnson and Kai Winding '56; Toronto, w. C. Basie '74. TV: apps. w. Gillespie '71; Weston '74; special w. Laine-Dankworth '75. CDs: w. Mann (Atl.); Gillespie (Philips); Q. Jones; RR Kirk (Merc.).

COLLINS, SHAD (LESTER RALLINGSTON), tpt; b. Elizabeth, NJ, 6/27/10; d. NYC, 6/78. Father was a minister. Raised in Lockport, N.Y. To NYC, pl. in band org. by Charlie Dixon, fronted by Cora LaRedd 1928. Worked w. Eddie White '29–30; Chick Webb '31; Benny Carter '33; Tiny Bradshaw '34. Join. Teddy Hill '36, tour. Engl. and France w. him '37. Remained in Paris, where he pl. and rec. w. Dicky Wells; ret. to US, join. Count Basie band '39. With Carter, Freddie Moore '40; Lester Young sxt., Kelly's Stable '41; then w. Cab Calloway on and off '41–6. Pl. w. Buster Harding '48; w. Al Sears, and tours. w. Jimmy Rushing in early '50s. R&B dates w. Sam "The Man" Taylor '55. Fr. '60s, did occ. club dates. CDs: w. Basie (Dec.); Basie in *From Spirituals to Swing*; Vic Dickenson (Vang.); Paul Quinichette (Prest.); Benny Carter (B&B).

COLTRANE (née McLeod), **ALICE** (Turiya Sagittinanda), pno, harp, org; b. Detroit, MI, 8/27/37; d. West Hills, CA, 1/12/07. Early classical stud. fr. 1944. After working locally w. Terry Pollard, Kenny

Burrell, Yusef Lateef, she tour. and rec. w. Terry Gibbs '62–3. Dur. this time, she met John Coltrane, whom she married in '65. Replacing McCoy Tyner in '66, she was a regular member of Coltrane's gps. until his death in '67. Fr. late '60s, she led a number of gps., incl. Joe Henderson, Pharoah Sanders, Carlos Ward, Jimmy Garrison, Ron Carter, Charlie Haden, Rashied Ali. Relocated to LA '72; created an Indian-style ashram, the Vedantic Center, for the study of Eastern religions '75; had own TV series in LA in mid '80s. Cont. to perf. occ. and, in '87, tour. Eur. w. a qnt. that incl. her sons, Oran and Ravi Coltrane, on saxophones. (A third son, John Jr., died a few yrs. earlier.) From late '80s, she sponsored an annual John Coltrane Fest. w. awards for young mus. and a concert that usually featured her own perf. mainly on org. and harp. Orig. a bebop-oriented pl., Coltrane, in later yrs. leaned toward impressionistic arpeggios. CDs: Imp.; w. J. Coltrane (Imp.); McCoy Tyner (BN).

COLTRANE, JOHN WILLIAM, tnr, sop sax, comp, lead; b. Hamlet, NC, 9/23/26; d. NYC, 7/17/67. Father, a tailor, pl. several instruments. Studied E-flat alto horn, cl., then alto sax in hs. After moving to Phila., he stud. at the Ornstein Sch. of Mus. and Granoff Studios. Made prof. debut w. lounge band in Phila. 1945. Pl. alto w. Navy band in Hawaii '45–6, and w. Joe Webb, King Kolax '46–7; tnr. w. Eddie Vinson '47–8; both instr. w. Dizzy Gillespie '49–51; Earl Bostic '52–3. Also pl. in early '50s w. Jimmy Heath, Howard McGhee, various r&b bands. Pl. tnr. exclusively fr. '53, working w. Johnny Hodges '53–4, bef. coming to prominence w. Miles Davis Qnt., w. Red Garland, Paul Chambers, Philly Joe Jones '55–7. Pl. w. Thelonious Monk at Five Spot, NYC '57. Rejoined Davis '58; also freelanced w. R. Garland, P. Chambers, Donald Byrd, Cannonball Adderley, Bill Evans, others '58–60. Began pl. sop. sax in '60. Debuted own qt. at Jazz Gallery, NYC, May '60. After trying various mus., incl. Steve Kuhn, Pete La Roca, and Billy Higgins, Coltrane hired McCoy Tyner, Elvin Jones '60, and Jimmy Garrison '61. Art Davis was occ. added on second bs., and Eric Dolphy pl. off and on w. the gp. '61–3. Reggie Workman and Roy Haynes subbed for Garrison and Jones, when needed. Although his qt. was extremely popular and had an int'l following, Coltrane's ever-evolving style made him a controversial figure on the jazz scene. Around '61, he became involved in the Indian improv. concept, in which improvs. are based on pre-determined modes, or scale arrs., rather than chords. Just as he had been criticized in the late '50s for his verbose, so-called "sheets of sound" approach, he was now attacked for his long solos and use of harsh, highly vocal sounds. Coltrane's innovations led to greater freedom for soloists in the '60s and beyond, taking the mus. away from songs and song patterns; at the same time, however, he cont. to interpret the standard repertoire, rec. several blues numbers and two albums of ballads in the early '60s. By 1965, Coltrane's mus. had reached a stage of religious fervor, emotional force, and hypnotic tension, and Coltrane himself was at the peak of his popularity. It was in this yr. that he rec. "Ascension," a multi-horn, extended exercise in febrile dissonance, a spiritual descendant of Coleman's "Free Jazz." Fr. '65 to '67, the personnel in Coltrane's gp. changed freq. Tyner left in '65; Jones quit in '66 after pl. briefly alongside a second dmr., Rashied Ali. Dissatisfied w. the direction the music was taking, Garrison quit following a two-week tour of Japan '66. New members incl. his wife Alice Coltrane, Pharoah Sanders, and a number of other dmrs. and percs. Coltrane himself began studying the conga around this time. By the time of his death fr. a liver ailment at age 40, he was revered by many for his obsessive pursuit of the musical ideal; his selfless, peaceful demeanor; and his strong religious convictions.

Coltrane is generally considered second only to Charlie Parker in terms of the impact he had on the musical tradition established by Louis Armstrong. He affected the mus. in every major way: harmonically and melodically, rhythmically, tonally, and formally. The Coltrane infl. is apparent in most of the leading saxists of the '60s and '70s, incl. Wayne Shorter; Joe Farrell; Chas. Lloyd; Pharoah Sanders; Archie Shepp; Albert Ayler; John Gilmore. He also spawned countless imitators, though few could approach his technical mastery or emotional depth. Not the least of his accomplishments was to establish the sop. sax as a modern jazz instrument; by the '70s a large number of alto and tnr. saxists doubled on sop. Coltrane's comps. incl. "Naima"; "Cousin Mary"; "Spiral"; "Countdown"; "Giant Steps"; "Mr. P.C."; "Syeeda's Song Flute"; "Moment's Notice"; "Blue Train"; *A Love Supreme*; "Trane's Blues"; "Crescent"; "Impressions." Favs: Dexter Gordon, Sonny Stitt, Sonny Rollins, Stan Getz. Polls: *DB* Critics tnr., sop., New Star combo '61; Hall of Fame, Rec. of Yr. for *A Love Supreme*, Jazzman of Yr., tnr., '65; Coltrane won the *DB* poll annually in at least one category '61–6. Video: *The Coltrane Legacy* '87. Books: transcriptions of Coltrane solos, Andrew White '73; *Chasin' the Trane: The Music and Mystique of John Coltrane*, J.C. Thomas '75; *Coltrane*, C.O. Simpkins '75; *John Coltrane*, Brian Priestley '87. CDs: Prest.; BN; Atl.; Imp.; Sav.; Pab.; Rhino; Roul.; w. M. Davis (Prest.; Col.); T. Monk (Jzld.; Riv.; BN); Tadd Dameron; Sonny Rollins; R. Garland (Prest.); w. C. Adderley (Mec.); Duke Ellington (Imp.).

COLTRANE, RAVI, tnr, sop saxes; b. Huntington, NY, 8/6/65. Son of John and Alice Coltrane; named after Indian sitarist Ravi Shankar. Raised in Woodland Hills, Calif. Stud. sop. sax briefly while in hs; abandoned it when older bro., John Jr., died in auto accident. Began serious study of saxophone at 20; enrolled in Cal Arts; gigged w. Alice Coltrane's bands; fr. 1991 to '93 w. Elvin Jones. Then pl. w. Geri Allen; Kenny Barron; Steve Coleman; Wallace Roney. Co-leader of Grand Central w. Antoine Roney. Describing Coltrane in the Int'l *Herald Tribune*, Mike Zwerin wrote, "The word is out. This is a burgeoning monster." CDs: RCA Vict.; Alfa; w. Cecil Brooks (Muse); Cindy Blackman (High.).

COLUMBUS, CHRIS (Joseph Christopher Columbus Morris aka Joe Morris), dms, lead; b. Greenville, NC, 6/17/02. Father of Sonny Payne. Active as leader 1930s-50s; in residence at Savoy Ballroom for some of this time. Pl. w. Louis Jordan '46-52; Wild Bill Davis late '50s-early '60s.; Damita Jo mid '60s; Duke Ellington '67. Led own gp. in '70s. Tour. Eur. w. Davis, '72. Rec. w. Davis, Al Grey, Floyd Smith '72; Milt Buckner '73. CDs: w. Ellington (Saja); L. Jordan (Band.).

COLYER, KEN (KENNETH; THE GUV'NOR), tpt, also gtr; b. Great Yarmouth, England, 4/18/28; d. South of France, 3/8/88. Brother, Bill, pl. wshbd. and worked as jazz journalist. Self-taught on hca. 1939; while at sea, tpt. '45. Founder and lead. of Crane River Jazz Band '49-53; also worked w. Christie Bros. Stompers, '51. While in merchant marine, he jumped ship in Mobile, Ala., and went to NO where he pl. w. George Lewis and rec. w. Emile Barnes until jailed and deported. Ret. to Engl. and took over Chris Barber band, renaming it Ken Colyer's Jazzmen. Band made debut and recs. in Den. '53, and became a leading British revivalist band of the decade. Pl. in Germ. '54, '59; Gibraltar '56; NYC and New Engl. towns '57. He also sang and pl. gtr. in his own skiffle gp. In the '60s and '70s, Colyer cont. as a lead., app. at his own club, Studio 51, in London. Own label, KC Records, in '60s. Tour. US and Can. '75; pl. w. Can. band at NO Jazz & Heritage Fest. In early '80s, pl. w. his own All-Star Jazzmen. Tour. w. Max Collie's *New Orleans Mardi Gras* show. By '87, illness had curtailed his career. He moved to southern France, where he lived in a trailer until his death. Colyer's bands were inspired by those of George Lewis and Bunk Johnson, but he honed a personalized style. Film: soundtrack for *West 11*, '63, filmed partly at Studio 51. Book: *When Dreams Are in the Dust* '87. CDs: Story.; 504; GHB; Lake; Joy; CMJ; Ken Colyer Trust; Music Mecca; BL; w. Christie Bros. (Cadillac).

COMBELLE, ALIX, cl, tnr sax; b. Paris, France, 6/15/12; d. Mantes, France, 2/27/78. Father was classical saxist; son is dmr. Philippe Combelle. Start. prof. as dmr. 1928-31; sw. to tnr. and cl., pl. w. bs. Bruno '31; Gregor '32-3; Arthur Briggs '34; Guy Pacquinet '34-5; Michel Warlop '34-7; Coleman Hawkins '35, '37. Made many hist. recs. w. Django Reinhardt and Bill Coleman as a member of the Qnt. du Hot Club de France. Pl. w. Benny Carter '38; Tommy Benford, Reinhardt, Phillipe Brun '37-8; Coleman, Ray Ventura '38; Freddy Johnson '39. Led gp., Jazz de Paris '40-5; several bbs through mid '50s. Pl. again w. Coleman '49; Buck Clayton '49-65; L. Hampton '53; Jonah Jones '54. Owned a nightclub in '60s. CDs: w. Benny Carter (B&B); Clayton; Hampton (Vogue); Hawkins (Timel.); QHCF (EMI); Reinhardt (Aff.; Ark.; Prest.); Freddy Johnson (Class.).

COMFORT, JOE (JOSEPH GEORGE), bs; b. Alcorn, MS, 7/18/17; d. Los Angeles, CA, 10/29/88. From a mus. family, he studied tbn. w. fath.; self-taught on bs. Pl. w. L. Hampton, 1946-7; Phil Moore '47; Nat Cole '48-51, incl. Eur. tour. '50. Pl. w. Oscar Moore '52-4; Perez Prado '53; Harry James '54; Billy May '55; Nelson Riddle '56-60; pl.on all Riddle's recs. w. Frank Sinatra. Rec. w. Hampton, Cole, Moore; also Harry "Sweets" Edison; Buddy Rich; Red Norvo; Benny Carter; Stan Kenton; Earl Hines, et al. Though most active in the pop area, Comfort achieved recognition as an excellent jazz player. Orig. infl: Blanton. Favs: Ray Brown, Pettiford, Paul Chambers. TV: Sinatra series, ABC '57; *M Squad* w. Benny Carter '59-60. CDs: w. Cole; H. James; Sinatra (Cap.); Buddy Collette; Gerry Wiggins (Cont.); Hampton (Dec.); Sarah Vaughan (Roul.).

COMPO, PETE (PETER GEORGE), vln, bs; b. Queens, NY, 8/9/32; d. NYC, 4/28/03. Uncle Charles Cacioppo pl. vln., ran mus. sch.; son Charles pl. tnr. sax, fl., gtr. Stud. vln. w. uncle 1938-48, then sw. to bs. in hs '49. Stud. bs. w. Phil Sklar of NBC Symph. '49-52; Slam Stewart '51-2; Homer Mensch of NY Philharm. off and on '56-70; also at Manh. Sch. of Mus. '50-1 '54-5; Nat'l Orch. Assoc. '57-8. Stud. theory w. Bill Rubenstein '62-3; Tony Aless '68-9; comp. w. Edgar D. Grane fr. '91. Pl. bs. w. Conrad Janis '50-1; Stuff Smith '51; Claude Thornhill '51-2; army band '53-4; Herbie Fields '54; C. Thornhill '54-5; Fred Waring '55-6; Charlie Barnet '56; Sol Yaged at Metropole Café; NYC late '50s. Theater work and freelance w. Buster Bailey; Red Allen; Willie "The Lion" Smith; Kenny Davern; Cozy Cole; Boyd Raeburn; Dick Hyman; Buddy Rich; Al Cohn; Paul Motian; Duke Jordan; Zoot Sims; Lionel Hampton; Billy Taylor; Ray Nance; Dick Meldonian; Eddie Barefield; Joe Temperley, etc., fr. '60s. Pl. w. Ken Peplowski, Howard Alden, Jo Jones, Buddy Tate, Al Grey, etc., early '80s. Compo began pl. the vln. again in '84 and gigged on both instr. until a hip injury forced him to give up bs. in '88. A strong swinger on vln. Pl. on soundtracks to films *Raging Bull, A Doctor's Story, Flamingo Kid, Tootsie* '8os. Tour. Eur. as lead. '89–91. Compo founded a private mus. sch. in Ossining, N.Y., in '64, and taught vln. and bs. there '64–74. Fav. vln: Stuff Smith, Svend Asmussen; bs: Ray Brown, Slam Stewart. Polls: *DB* TDWR vln. '89. Fests: Japan '84; Eur. fr. '86. TV: NYC TV w. army band '53–4; Germ. TV '89. CDs: Kaleidoscope; TakeTwelve; w. Cozy Cole (Aff.).

CONDON, EDDIE (ALBERT EDWIN), lead, gtr; b. Goodland, IN, 11/16/05; d. NYC, 8/4/73. Raised in Momence and Chi. Heights, Ill. Self-taught on uke., bjo.; start. working semi-prof. fr. age of 15 w. local bands, incl. Hollis Peavey's Jazz Bandits. Living in Chi. in 1920s, he was closely assoc. w. Austin High Gang, incl. Gene Krupa; Frank Teschemacher; Bud Freeman; Jimmy McPartland; Joe Sullivan. In '27, form. Condon-McKenzie Chicagoans w. Red McKenzie; their initial '27 recs. are acknowledged as classics that laid the foundation for "Chicago Style" jazz. To NYC in '28, worked and rec. w. Mound City Blue Blowers, incl. McKenzie, Josh Billings on suitcase-dms., and Jack Bland, gtr.; tour. w. Red Nichols '29; again w. Blue Blowers '30–1, '33; co-led gp. w. Joe Marsala '36–7. Fr. '37–44, he perf. frequently at Nick's in NYC; w. big bands of Bobby Hackett and, briefly, Artie Shaw. He also opened a Greenwich Village nightclub bearing his name in '46, relocating to East 56th St. in '58, and operating it until '67. Through the '50s, he app. at the club intermittently; in the early '60s not at all. Tour. UK '57; Austral., NZ, Japan '64. He was taken seriously ill after his ret. to US, but recovered. A *Tribute to Condon* concert took place at Carnegie Hall, and he made a brief app. at a '65 TV tribute to him. In '65–6 he was back at Condon's; in '67, he perf. a concert at Disneyland. Co-led all-star band w. Kai Winding at Roosevelt Grill, NYC '69. High school and coll. tour w. Art Hodes, Wild Bill Davison, Barney Bigard '71. His prominence in jazz was not so much as a player, but rather due to his talent for assembling memorable rec. gps., and, fr. '39, promoting jam sess. and concerts. Condon was among the first to organize racially integrated bands, bringing together such musicians as Fats Waller; Jack Teagarden; Big Sid Catlett; Max Kaminsky; Louis Armstrong; Pee Wee Russell; and Wild Bill Davison. In the early '40s, he prod. a series of con-

certs at Town Hall and began to attract prominent people from literary, art, and entertainment circles, garnering much publicity for himself and, more importantly, the brand of jazz he fervently espoused. His abilities as a raconteur made him a stimulating emcee; his dry wit was also manifested in his articles and rec. reviews for various publications, incl. the *New York Journal-American*. After his death, a club bearing his name opened on West 54th Street; it feat. some of the mus. with whom he had been assoc., and flourished as a bastion of Condon-type jazz fr. March '75 to July '85. Poll: *DB* '42–3. Fests: NJF '54, '56; NJF-NY, app. briefly at own tribute '72. Books: *We Called it Music* w. Thomas Sugrue (Henry Holt) '47; *Eddie Condon's Treasury of Jazz* w. Richard Gehman (Dial) '56; *Eddie Condon's Scrapbook of Jazz* w. Hank O'Neal (St. Martin's Press) '73. TV: own series, *Eddie Condon Floorshow*, '48. CDs: Comm.; Dec.; Chiaro.; Col.; Sav.; Mos.; *Town Hall Concerts, Vols. 1–10*; Jazz.; w. Armstrong (Col.); Waller; M. Spanier; Teagarden (BB); Russell (Comm.); Bechet (Laser.); Red Allen (Hep); B. Freeman (Aff.).

CONNICK, HARRY JR., pno, voc, comp; b. New Orleans, LA, 9/11/67. His parents, both lawyers, co-owned a record store and encouraged him in mus. He began fooling around on the pno. at age 3; at 6 pl. at his fath.'s swearing-in ceremony as NO District Attorney; and made rec. debut at 10 w. local dixieland band. Work in Bourbon Street clubs and stud. w. Ellis Marsalis, James Booker. Stud. at NOCCA and took part in several classical pno. competitions. Pl. in funk band w. Delfeayo Marsalis, NYC 1985. At 18, he studied mus. at Hunter Col. and Manh. Sch. of Mus. '85. Worked in clubs and as org./choir dir. at Bronx church. Signed a contract w. Col. and app. to acclaim as singer/pnst. at the Hotel Algonquin's Oak Room, NYC. Furthered his success w. soundtrack vocals for film *When Harry Met Sally* '89. Tour. nationally and in Eur. Pl. to SRO crowds w. own bb at Lunt-Fontanne Theatre on B'way in Nov. '90 and proved to be a charming, charismatic front man. The critical reception was less positive for his week at the Village Vanguard in Feb. '91, w. a qt., that reflected Connick's Thelonious Monk infl. In July '91 he pl. a command perf. at Windsor Castle for Prince Philip's 70th birthday. Cont. to tour int'l w. band. Tour. w. his sxt., Funky Dunky, in the summer of '94, mixing NO funk, rock, and r&b. Films: soundtrack, *Sleepless in Seattle;* as actor, *Memphis Belle* '90; *Little Man Tate* '91; *Copycat* '95. TV: episode of *Cheers*; PBS special for *Great Performances*; Frank Sinatra tribute '90; Oscar telecast '91. Video: *Swingin' Out Live*, tape of PBS show. CDs: Col.

CONNIFF, RAY, comp; tbn; b. Attleboro, MA, 11/6/16; d. San Diego, CA, 10/12/02. Studied w. fath.; pl. w. Dan Murphy 1934; Hank Biagini '36; Bunny Berigan '37–8; Bob Crosby '39–40; Artie Shaw '40–1; also worked in trad. jazz bands led by Bobby Hackett '43; Art Hodes '44. While in army, worked w. Harry James Orch. '42, arr. many pop tunes and riff-based instrumentals. Staff tbnst. at NBC in NYC '54; became arr.-cond. for Col. recs. '55. More or less retired his tbn. and worked on rec. projects for Johnnie Ray; Guy Mitchell; Johnny Mathis. Form. own gp. of singers and mus., the Ray Conniff Singers, who perf. his arrs. in concert and on many pop albums; tour. extensively, incl. Eur., Japan, Mex. In '74, he was the first US artist to rec. in USSR, using Soviet mus. and singers. Though Conniff was a major pop mus. personality, he occ. pl. jazz tbn. as part of his gp.'s concerts and on recs. Teamed w. Billy Butterfield for Col. LP, '58. CDs: w. Berigan; Shaw (BB); Bob Crosby (Dec.); Hodes in *Hot Jazz On Blue Note* (BN).

CONNOR, CHRIS, voc; b. Kansas City, MO, 11/8/27. Studied vln., cl. Sang w. Eddie Sigoloff band at U. of Mo, then w. jazz gp. led by Bob Brookmeyer in KC. To NYC 1949, join. Claude Thornhill, then Jerry Wald; June Christy heard her singing w. Wald and recommended her to Stan Kenton; worked w. Kenton Jan. to July '53 scoring w. *All About Ronnie*. Fr. then on, she worked as a single, rec. several successful albums for Beth. in the '50s, which were well received by the public, but garnered mixed reviews from a jazz press that inevitably compared her to June Christy and Anita O'Day, her predecessors in the Kenton band. In '91, she app. at a Kenton reunion in Newport Beach, Calif. CDs: 32; Atl.; Enja; Cont.; Aud.; w. Kenton (Natasha).

CONNORS, NORMAN (Norman Connor Jr.), dms, perc, comp, prod; b. Philadelphia, PA, 3/1/47. Percussion studies at Juilliard, 1967–8. Active in NYC in mid '60s w. Archie Shepp; Sun Ra; Sam Rivers; Jackie McLean; Pharoah Sanders; others. Tour w. own gp. in '70s. Began rec. for Buddah as leader '72; won gold album for *You Are My Starship* '76; rec. several hit r&b recs. in mid '70s. Rec. for Arista '78–82. Inactive on recs. '82–88, but prod. recs. by Lonnie Liston Smith, Phyllis Hyman, Angela Bofill, Pharoah Sanders, Melba Moore, etc. Fr. '90, he was a contract perf./prod. at Motown recs. CDs: MoJazz.

COOK, DOC (Charles L. Cooke), pno, arr, lead; b. Louisville, KY, 9/3/1881; d. Wurtsboro, NY, 12/25/58. Became Doctor of Mus., Chi. Coll. of Mus., 1926. As early as '09, he was active as comp.-arr. in Det. Moved to Chi. where he led own bands;

best known as leader of house band at Dreamland Ballroom '22–8, which incl. several prominent early jazz men: Freddie Keppard; Jimmie Noone; Jerome Pasquall; Johnny St. Cyr; Andrew Hilaire; Billy Butler. The orch. rec. frequently for Gennett '23; then Col. '26–7; also rec. w. Cookie's Gingersnaps, a sxt. fr. the orch., for Okeh '26. Fr. '28–30, Cook led the orch. at theaters and ballrooms, but long engagements were getting more difficult to obtain; band pl. residency at White City Amusement Park '29 until park closed in '30. Cook moved to NYC '30 and fairly quickly established himself as arr.; staff arr. for Palace Theater '30; then worked until early '40s as staff arr. at RKO and Radio City Music Hall. Retired to N.J.

COOK, JUNIOR (HERMAN), tnr sax; b. Pensacola, FL, 7/22/34; d. NYC, 2/4/92. Father and older bro. pl. tpt. Start. on alto sax in hs, then sw. to tnr. Encouraged by Gigi Gryce. Worked w. Gloria Bell last half of 1957; two mos. w. Dizzy Gillespie bef. join. Horace Silver May '58, remaining until March '64. Pl. w. Blue Mitchell qnt. '64–9. Taught at Berklee Coll. of Mus. in early '70s, then worked w. Freddie Hubbard '73–5. Pl. w. Elvin Jones, and freelanced in NYC w. Keno Duke, George Coleman oct. bef. teaming up w. Louis Hayes '75–6. Form. the Bill Hardman–Junior Cook qnt., working w. Hardman until the latter moved to Paris '88. In the '90s, led own gp. in clubs, app. w. Freddie Redd at Birdland, and was a member of Clifford Jordan's bb. A rhythmically vigorous player who synthesized several bop tnr. styles. Favs: Sonny Stitt, Dexter Gordon, Wardell Gray, S. Rollins. CDs: Steep.; w. Silver (BN); Barry Harris (Prest.); Hayes (Timel.); Mitchell (BN; Riv.); Louis Smith; Hardman (Steep.); Cedar Walton (Prest.; Steep.); Jordan (CC); F. Hubbard (CTI); G. Coleman (Charly); Larry Gales (Cand.); McCoy Tyner (Mile.; Bird.).

COOK, WILL MARION, comp, cond; b. Washington, DC, 1/27/1869; d. NYC, 7/19/44. Studied at Oberlin Cons. at age 13; went to Berlin at age of 16, att. hs and stud. vln. w. Joseph Joachim. Worked as concert vlnst. and cond. After ret. to US, collaborated w. poet Paul Lawrence Dunbar on *Clorindy, the Origin of the Cakewalk* in 1898. This pioneering black musical was a success on B'way, also perf. in London. Between '02 and '07, Cook dir. and comp. mus. for several other shows, incl. *In Dahomey* and *In Bandana Land*. Was mus. dir. of Clef Club w. Tim Brymn. In late '18, org. 15-pc. NY Syncopated Orch., renamed the Southern Syncopated Orch. Band, which tour. US and Eur. in '19, incl. Sidney Bechet, Arthur Briggs, Benny Peyton. In '20, Cook ret. to NYC, cont. his career as cond., mus. promoter, teach. through the '30s; also org. "all-Negro-music" concerts, feat. such mus. as Bechet, James P. Johnson. He was also one of Duke Ellington's mentors. Comps: "I'm Coming Virginia"; "Mandy Lou"; "Mammy."

COOK, WILLIE (JOHN), tpt; b. Tangipahoa, LA, 11/11/23; d. Stockholm, 9/22/00. Raised in East Chicago, Ind. Studied as a teenager. Prof. debut 1940 w. King Perry. Pl. w. Claude Trenier '41; own combo '42; Jay McShann '43; w. Earl Hines off and on '43–8; Lunceford band under Ed Wilcox '48; Dizzy Gillespie '48–50; Gerald Wilson's band in LA '50–1; mus. dir. for Billie Holiday. Went to study in St. Louis, bef. join. Duke Ellington '51–7; Eur. tour '59; '60–1. Freelanced dur. the '60s, mainly in NYC w. Mercer Ellington, Jimmy Jones, et al. until rejoin. D. Ellington '68, pl. w. him intermittently until '73. Moved to Houston, Tex., retired from mus. until '77, when he worked w. Clark Terry; Count Basie. Resettled in Sweden late '70s; dur. early '80s, he pl. w. various Scand. bands; also w. Ernie Wilkins; app. at annual Ellington conferences in Engl. '85; Den. '92. Fav: Clark Terry. Ellington considered him one of his outstanding lead tpts.; he is also an exciting soloist. Opening solo on "Jam with Sam" '52; also feat. on "Upper Manhattan Medical Group" '56. CDs: w. Ellington (Col.; Saja; Red Brn.; M&A; Charly); Basie (Pab.); Gillespie (GNP Cres.).

COOLMAN, TODD FRANCIS, bs, cello; b. Gary, IN, 7/14/54. Began pl. bs. in hs. Att. Ind. U. 1972–5, after which he pl. w. Nat'l Symphony of Mexico for one yr. Freelance in Chi. '76–8, then pl. w. Gerry Mulligan '79; Horace Silver '79–80; Stan Getz '81; Al Haig '81–3; Lionel Hampton bb '81–2; Mel Lewis Orch. '84; Bob Wilber '84–5. Pl. w. James Moody since '85. Received M. Mus. fr. Manh. Sch. of Mus. '86. Pl. w. Benny Golson–Art Farmer '86–9; Terry Gibbs–Buddy DeFranco '88–9; Hal Galper '90–1; Barney Kessel '91. Coolman has been the recipient of two NEA comp.'s grants. Favs: Pettiford, Red Mitchell. Fests: Eur. every yr. since '79; Japan w. L. Hampton. CDs: BRC Int.; w. J. Moody (RCA); T. Gibbs–B. DeFranco; John Campbell (Cont.); Hal Galper (Conc.); Hampton (Timel.); A. Jamal (Bird.); D. Newman (Cand.); R. Schneiderman (Res.).

COON, JACKIE (JACK MERLE), tpt, flg, crnt; b. Beatrice, NE, 6/21/29. Pl. dur. 1950s w. Jack Teagarden; Earl Hines; Charlie Barnet; Louis Prima; in '60s w. Bob Crosby and own Silver Cornet Orch. After a decade at Disneyland '68–78, settled in Big Sur, Calif., freelancing w. Pete Fountain. Eur. tour w. Yank Lawson '87; annual apps. at Classic JF in LA fr. '83.

A respected trad.-oriented soloist. Favs: Armstrong, Eldridge, Gillespie. CDs: Arb.; w. Teagarden (Arb.).

COOPER, AL (LOFTON ALFONSO), alto sax, cl, lead; b. 1911; d. Florida, 10/5/81. Grachan Moncur Jr. is half-bro. Early gigs at 101 Club, NYC; Harlem-on-the Hudson, N.J.; White Towers, Pleasantville, NY. Best known as leader of the Savoy Sultans, house band at Harlem's Savoy Ballroom 1937–46. Rec. for Dec. '38–41. The Sultans, an oct., sometimes a nonet, were known for a infectiously swinging style, dubbed "jump." Main soloists were Rudy Williams, alto sax; Sam Massenberg, tpt. LPs: Dec., '82. CD: Class.

COOPER, BOB (ROBERT WILLIAM), tnr sax, oboe; b. Pittsburgh, PA, 12/6/25; d. Los Angeles, CA, 8/6/93. Studied cl. fr. 1940; tnr. sax fr. '41. Pl. w. Tommy Reynolds '44; join. Stan Kenton at 19; married band's voc., June Christy, '47; left Kenton '51. Freelanced in LA w. Shorty Rogers; Pete Rugolo; Lighthouse All-Stars. Took up oboe, pl. it on rec. w. Bud Shank. Tour. Eur. '58, and Japan '61, w. June Christy. Many yrs. w. Lighthouse All-Stars in '50s and '60s, and w. reorganized gp. fr. '90. Active in '60s as studio mus. and comp. for TV and films. Member of LA Neophonic, which premiered his *Solo For Orchestra*, 66. In '70s and '80s, app. w. Shorty Rogers; Bill Holman; Capp-Pierce Juggernaut; Bob Florence and other bbs in LA area. Awarded LA Jazz Society tribute '89. Concentrating solely on tnr. fr. '91. When Cooper join. Kenton, his infl. was Lucky Thompson; over the yrs. he veered, successively, toward Getz, Sims, and, finally, Cohn. Apps. at Colo. JP in late '80s-early '90s. CDs: Cont.; FS; Trend; Disc.; Pete Christlieb–Bob Cooper (Capri); w. Capp; R. Clooney; Gene Harris (Conc.); Kenton (Cap.); Christy (Disc.; Cap.); Chet Baker; M. Davis; B. Kessel; S. Manne; Lighthouse All-Stars (Cont.); S. Rogers (BB; Cand.); Marty Paich; Vic Lewis–West Coast All-Stars (Cand.).

COOPER, BUSTER (GEORGE), tbn; b. St. Petersburg, FL, 4/4/29. Studied tbn. in hs. Pl. w. 16-pc. band in Fla. Worked w. Nat Towles in Tex.; to NYC, 1950; studied harm. and counterpoint at the Hartnett Sch. Joined L. Hampton '53; toured Eur. w. him dur. a three-year tenure; worked in Apollo Theatre house band, NYC; also pl. w. Lucky Millinder and Benny Goodman; organized Cooper Bros. band w. bro. Steve on bs. In late '50s, Cooper Bros. band backed Josephine Baker at Olympia Theatre in Paris; also worked in Paris w. Curly Hamner '59. Joined Duke Ellington June '60; dur. seven yrs. w. band, he established a decidedly distinct personality w. his explosive, multi-noted playing and colorful use of the plunger mute. Moved back to St. Petersburg, form. qt.

w. bro.; taught a jazz course for a yr. at New Coll. in Sarasota, then moved to LA, July '73. Worked extensively in LA w. Capp-Pierce Juggernaut and the Bill Berry Band; also tour. w. various Ellington alumni and reunion gps. Tour. w. Monk Montgomery in So. Africa '74. Pl. at Duke Ellington conference in Copenhagen '92. Fav: J.J. Johnson. CDs: Blue Lady; w. Ellington (Atl.; Pab.; BB; Prest.; Saja; MM; Fant.); Capp (Conc.); J. Hodges (BB; Imp.); Harry Edison (Pab.); B. Goodman (MM); L. Hampton (Natasha); B. Strayhorn (Red Brn.); Prestige Blues Swingers; Arnett Cobb (Prest.).

COOPER, JEROME, dms, perc, comp; b. Chicago, IL, 12/14/46. Studied w. Oliver Coleman 1958–63; Capt. Walter Dyett at DuSable HS '63–5; Loop Jr. Coll. '67–8. Worked w. Oscar Brown Jr. in Chi. '68; Kalaparusha Maurice McIntyre in Chi. and Nashville '68–9; Rahsaan Roland Kirk '70–1, incl. Eur. tour. Pl. w. Lou Bennett in West Africa '70. Freelanced in US and Eur. w. Dizzy Reece, Noah Howard, Clifford Jordan '70; Steve Lacy in Eur. '70–1; Art Ens. of Chi. '71; Robin Kenyatta, Alan Silva '71–2; Geo. Adams, Sam Rivers, Karl Berger '73; Andrew Hill, Anthony Braxton '74; McIntyre fr. '74 into the '80s. Member of Revolutionary Ens. w. Sirone, Leroy Jenkins '71–7; w. this gp. he sometimes played pno., fl., and bugle. Perf. as unaccomp. soloist '76–80, then pl. w. Cecil Taylor '80. Favs: Art Blakey, Max Roach, Tony Williams. TV: French TV w. R.R. Kirk; *Today* w. Chad Mitchell. CDs: w. Revolutionary Ens. (ESP Disk); Taylor (hatArt).

COPELAND, KEITH LAMONT, dms, tmbls, cga; b. NYC, 4/18/46. Father Ray Copeland. Stud. w. Gene Murvay 1956–60. Pl. club dates '60–3; in air force '63–8. After discharge, stud. w. Walter Perkins Jr. '68, then at Berklee Coll. of Mus. w. Fred Buda '68–70 and Alan Dawson '73–8. Pl. in Bost., and NYC w. Sammy Benskin, Barry Harris, Marvin Gaye '68; Trini Lopez '68–70; Rollins Griffith '68–73; Bill Evans, Jaki Byard '69; Stevie Wonder '71–3; Maggi Scott '75–8. Ret. to NYC '78. Pl. w. Milt Jackson, Johnny Griffin '78; Sam Jones–Tom Harrell bb, Heath Bros. '78–9; Billy Taylor '80–4; Geo. Russell '80–88; Hank Jones since '86. Copeland taught at Berklee '75–8; LIU-Bklyn. '82; Rutgers U. '85; and the New Sch. '87. Favs: Art Blakey, Elvin Jones, Alan Dawson. Fests: Eur. since '79; Jap. since '86. CDs: w. H. Jones; H. Alden (Conc.); Heath Bros. (Col.); Stanley Cowell; P. Bley; Mike Richmond; Larry Schneider; Louis Smith (Steep.); Chris White (Muse); Billy Pierce; M. D'Ambrosio (Sunny.); G. Russell (SN); J. Breakstone (Cont.; PW); Joe Locke (Chief); Chris Connor (Enja).

COPELAND, RAY M., tpt, flg, comp; b. Norfolk, VA, 7/17/26; d. NYC, 5/18/84. Son is dmr. Keith Copeland. Studied classical tpt. priv. and for four yrs. at Wurlitzer Sch. of Mus. Start. pl. w. bands in Bklyn. Join. Cecil Scott in 1945, working at the Savoy; w. Chris Columbus at Small's Paradise '46; tour. w. Mercer Ellington '47–8; w. Al Cooper's Savoy Sultans '48–9. Took day job '50–5 at paper co., but pl. occ. w. Andy Kirk; Lucky Millinder; Lucky Thompson; Sy Oliver. Resumed more active mus. career in mid '50s: w. L. Hampton, Randy Weston '57–8; Tito Puente, Oscar Pettiford '58; Johnny Richards, Gigi Gryce '58–9; Roxy Theatre Orch. late '58–61; also led own 14-pc. band for club dates. Pl. w. Louie Bellson, Pearl Bailey '62–4; Ella Fitzgerald '65. Rejoin. Weston in '66, concerts at U. of Calif.; State Dept. tour. of Africa '67. Tour. Eur. w. Thelonious Monk '68; perf. w. Marian McPartland at LI, N.Y., public schs. '68–9; to Morocco w. Weston '70; participated in Eur. tour of revue, *The Musical Life of Charlie Parker*, fall '74, incl. Romania and Yugoslavia. Perf. in pit band and on rec. for B'way shows: *No, No, Nanette* '70; *Two Gentlemen of Verona* '72. Also led own gps. and concentrated on comp: premiered his *Classical Jazz Suite in Six Movements* at Lincoln Center '70. Active as jazz adjudicator and clinician: taught at Pratt Inst., NYC '68; pl. History of Jazz concerts w. Orch. da Camera in LI, N.Y., public schs. '71–3; also perf. w. Int'l Art of Jazz, same schs. '72–4; clinics at Villanova U. '72, and Del. hs '73–4; taught at Wilmington Sch. of Mus., Del. and N. J. sch. system '73; Jazzmobile Workshop, Fordham U. '74; Hampshire Coll. fr. '79. Infl. by Dizzy Gillespie. Favs: Ernie Royal, Clifford Brown, Joe Wilder; Jimmy Nottingham. Fests: MJF w. Gil Fuller '65; Weston '66; NJF w. Weston '73. Film: soundtrack for *Kiss Her Goodbye* w. J. Richards; *Straight No Chaser* w. T. Monk. Book: *The Ray Copeland Method and Approach to the Creative Art of Jazz Improvisation* (Kaercea Mus. Enterprises) '74. Recs. w. J. Richards; Pettiford. CDs: w. Monk (Prest.; Riv.); Weston (Verve); Pettiford; Betty Carter (Imp.).

COPLAND, MARC (Cohen), pno, comp; b. Philadelphia, PA, 5/27/48. Moved to NYC to pursue career as saxist, then sw. to pno. Self-taught on pno. Rec. on sax as lead. 1973. Led own pno. trio, often w. Gary Peacock, fr. '83. Pl. w. John Scofield '85–6; Bob Belden, Bill Kirchner fr. '85; Dave Samuels fr. '87; Cindy Blackman–Wallace Roney, Astrud Gilberto '88; Herbie Mann's Jasil Brazz '88–9; James Moody; Jim Snidero, Dave Stryker fr.'88; Peter Erskine '89. Fests: Eur., Japan fr. '86. TV: VH-I w. Samuels '87; Moody '88; Eur. TV w. Scofield; Moody. Own gps. incl. trio w. Peacock, Billy Hart;

co-op band w. Dieter Ilg, Jeff Hirshfield; duo w. Ralph Towner; and qnt. w. Randy Brecker, Bob Berg, James Genus, Dennis Chambers. Gary Giddins said, "[Copland] combines the harmonic leverage of Bill Evans and the plainspoken bluesiness of Hampton Hawes," and Bob Belden commented: "One of the most sophisticated and well developed concepts of harmonic movement. He comps by implication rather than stating the obvious." Early infls.: Evans , K. Jarrett. CDs: Sav.; JazzCity; L&R; Future Music; w. B. Belden (Sunny.; BN); J. Moody (Novus); J. Snidero (Red); D. Stryker (Steep.; Someday); S. LaSpina (Steep.).

CORB, MORTY, bs; b. San Antonio, TX, 4/10/17; d. Las Vegas, NV, 1/13/96. Learned to pl. uke. at age 6 and, later, self-taught on gtr. and bs. Began prof. w. dance band in home town at 17; then w. bands in Ark. and Mo. After pl. w. army air force band, moved to LA in 1946 and worked w. Louis Armstrong '47. In '50s, w. Jack Teagarden; Bob Crosby; Jerry Gray; Jess Stacy; Kid Ory; Benny Goodman; then mainly worked on film and TV, incl. *Pete Kelly's Blues* series. Rec. albums w. Matty Matlock; Billy May; Claude Thornhill; Bob Crosby; Alvino Rey; Wild Bill Davison. In early '90s, he gigged mainly w. Dick Cathcart, Abe Most, Pete Fountain. LP w. own gp., *Strictly from Dixie*, for Tops '57. CD: w. Fountain (MCA).

CORCORAN, CORKY (GENE PATRICK), tnr sax, cl, Engl. horn; b. Tacoma, WA, 7/28/24; d. Tacoma, 10/3/79. Discovered by Jimmie Lunceford, start. pl. prof. w. Sonny Dunham at age 16, 1940–1. Join. Harry James Oct. '41, and was feat. soloist until he left the band in '47, having gained prominence through numerous movie and radio apps. w. him. Pl. w. L. Hampton and others at *Just Jazz* concert in Calif. '47. Pl. w. Tommy Dorsey briefly in '48; own gp. '49; rejoin. James that same yr., app. w. him intermittently through the '50s, '60s. Following an illness, he rejoin. James in '74, perf. only as soloist. Also cont. to lead own gps. in LV and on West Coast. Worked as clinician for Leblanc Instr. Co. Concert w. own gp. at NY Jazz Museum '74. Considered a prodigy dur. his early yrs. w. James, he placed second in *DB* polls '43–4. A big-toned soloist of the Hawkins sch., his other favs. incl. Ben Webster, Stan Getz. Fest: NJF-NY w. James '74. LPs: Epic '60; RCS. CDs: w. Hampton, *Just Jazz* (Dec.); James (Cap.; Verve; Jazzline).

COREA, CHICK (ARMANDO ANTHONY), pno, kybds, comp; b. Chelsea, MA, 6/12/41. Started on pno. at 4; studied w. fath., a prof. mus., who exposed him to extensive classical and jazz listening. First significant prof. job was w. Mongo Santamaria in 1962; then Willie Bobo '63; Blue Mitchell '64–6, w. whom he first rec. his own comps. He worked w. Herbie Mann off and on in '65 bef. form. his own gps. for recs. and perfs. In '68, after working w. Sarah Vaughan for a yr., he joined Miles Davis, at a time when Davis was exploring the use of electronic instruments and rock rhythms, initiating jazz "fusion." Through his use of a variety of kybds. and acoustic pno., Corea contributed to the textural complexity that was characteristic of Davis's work in this period, and evident on such albums as *In a Silent Way*; *Bitches' Brew*; *Live/Evil*. Corea and bs. Dave Holland left Davis in '70, intent on incorporating some of Davis's use of extended improv. into a more acoustic context. They formed a trio, Circle, w. dmr. Barry Altschul, and later added Anthony Braxton on woodwinds; this gp. exerted a major infl. on other "free-jazz" oriented gps. dur. this period. By late '71, however, Corea left the band to work alongside Airto and Stanley Clarke w. Stan Getz. In '72, they left Getz to form. Return to Forever, w. Flora Purim and Joe Farrell. In '73, Bill Connors, Lenny White and perc. Mingo Lewis, along with Clarke and Corea, comprised the gp.; the band was now more electronic and rock-oriented and had a large audience; it finally disbanded in '75 (although they did an extensive reunion tour in '83). Corea then formed several ens., exploring different genres and instrumentation; some incorporated classical elements, used small string and brass sections, and de-emphasized electronics; others were wholly electronic; Spanish and Latin infls. also colored a significant portion of Corea's work. In '86, Corea premiered his *Concerto for Piano and Orchestra in Three Movements* in the US and Japan. In '85, he formed the fusion gp. the Elektric Band, w. John Patitucci on bs. and Dave Weckl on dms.; the gp. remained active in the late '90s, often serving as a nucleus for larger ens., in concert and on recs.

Throughout Corea's career, he has cont. to play in acoustic contexts: as a soloist; in duos w. Herbie Hancock and Gary Burton; in qt. w. Mike Brecker, Eddie Gomez, and Steve Gadd; Trio Music w. Roy Haynes and Miroslav Vitous (the latter two gps. were formed in '81). In the summer of '92, he toured with the qt. again, w. Bob Berg replacing Brecker. That same yr., Corea formed his own label, Stretch Records. In '96, he rec. a tribute to Bud Powell and led a gp., incl. Joshua Redman, Wallace Roney, Christian McBride and Roy Haynes, pl. this mus. on a worldwide tour. Formed new gp., Origin, '98 w. Steve Wilson, Steve Davis et al. Earlier in his career, Corea had cited Tatum, Hancock, Tyner, Monk as his favorite pnsts.; and Powell, Tyner, and Bill Evans as major infls. By the mid '70s, he himself was regarded, along with Hancock, as an infl. link in the lineage of modern acoustic jazz pnsts. He had an extraordinary way of lending lyricism to the use of angular whole-tone figures, and, at times, polytonal harmonies, as amply demonstrated by his work on an early album like *Now He Sings, Now He Sobs* '68. Such recs. as *My Spanish Heart* and *Piano Improvisations* uphold Joachim Berendt's view of Corea as "the romanticist of the modern jazz piano." Several of his comps. have become standards: "Spain"; "Windows"; "Crystal Silence"; "La Fiesta"; "Tones for Jones' Bones"; "Captain Marvel"; "500 Miles High." From the early '70s, Corea has been involved in the study of Scientology, which he feels has helped increase awareness in all aspects of life, incl. mus. Polls: *DB* Readers, comp. '73–4; pno. '73; elec. pno. '75; *DB* Critics, New Star, comp. CDs: GRP; BN; Stretch; Atl.; ECM; Polyd.; Verve; w. Davis (Col.); Burton (ECM); GRP All-Star bb (GRP); Getz (Verve; Col.); Hancock; J. McLaughlin (Col.); Gillespie; Wayne Shorter; Blue Mitchell; B. Hutcherson (BN); J. Henderson (Cont.; MPS); Gomez (Den.).

CORNELIUS, CORKY (EDWARD), tpt; b. Indiana, 12/3/14; d. NYC, 8/3/43. Taught mus. by his father. Pl. and rec. w. Les Brown 1937; Benny Goodman '39; Gene Krupa '39–40; Glen Gray's Casa Loma Orch. '41–3. Solo w. Krupa on "Hamtramck" (Okeh '40). CD: w. Goodman (Col.).

CORREA, MAYUTO (MAILTO), perc; b. São Goncalo, Rio de Janeiro, Brazil, 3/9/43. From age 12, he pl. in local bands; form. samba show that won first pl. at local fests. After working in Mex. w. Tamba Four '70, he moved to US; pl. and/or rec. w. Joao Donato, Charles Lloyd, Gabor Szabo, Hugh Masekela, Freddie Hubbard early '70s; later w. Kenny Burrell, Donald Byrd, Gator Barbieri; fr. mid 70s, freelanced as studio mus., songwriter, and comp. music for two plays. CDs: w. C. Tjader (Fant.).

CORYELL, LARRY, gtr, comp, lead; b. Galveston, TX, 4/2/43. Some priv. stud., but mostly self-taught on gtr. Family moved to Wash. when he was 7. At 15, start. pl. w. rock 'n' roll band led by pnst. Mike Mandel. While studying journalism at U. of Wash., he gigged around Seattle. Moved to NYC 1965; worked w. Chico Hamilton. Pl. w. Free Spirits, an early jazz-rock fusion gp. incl. Jim Pepper, Bob Moses; then join. Gary Burton, tour. w. him '67–8. Briefly w. Herbie Mann '69, bef. form. own gp., Foreplay, w. Steve Marcus, Mandel. Form. new gp., Eleventh House, which incl. Randy Brecker, Alphonse Mouzon, Mandel '73, traveling widely, incl. four Eur. tours; Japan

'74. Worked occ. w. John McLaughlin, incl. own album, *Spaces*. In late '70s, pl. hollow-body gtr., app. in small gps. w. John Scofield; Michal Urbaniak; Steve Khan; Philip Catherine; McLaughlin and Paco De Lucia. In late '70s, rec. w. Mingus; Rollins; Grappelli. In the '80s he form. a trio w. Bunny Brunel, Mouzon. In '90s, cont. to tour. w. own gps.; rec. *Live from Bahia* w. Brazilian mus.; and also app. w. The Great Guitars. Steve Lake, writing in *Melody Maker*, said: "To describe Coryell the guitarist as merely agile or inventive would be to do him a serious disservice. He is amazing. Truly everyman's guitarist, able to suggest shades of Montgomery, Hendrix, Reinhardt and Shankar in less time than it takes to say it, and always sounding like himself anyway." Fests: NJF-NY '73–4; Guitar Legends, Seville Spain, '92; Cork JF '94; many others incl. Live Under the Sky, Tokyo '92. Books: *Improvisations from Rock to Jazz*, a collection of his own transcriptions; *Larry Coryell: Jazz Guitar Solos*, transcribed by D. Pritchard '80. Comps: "Rene's Theme"; *Concerto for Guitar and Orchestra*, premiered in Calais, France '92. CDs: Koch; Start; ACT; Novus; String; CTI; Muse; Steep.; Conc.; w. C. Baker (Inak); R. Brecker (BN); Grappelli (Verve); D. Lanphere (Hep); Mann; Mingus (Atl.); E. Remler; Great Guitars (Conc.); J. Walrath (Muse).

COSTA, EDDIE (EDWIN JAMES), pno, vib; b. Atlas, PA, 8/14/30; d. NYC, 7/28/62. Studied pno. w. bro. and priv. teacher; self-taught on vib. Moved to NYC after hs. join. Joe Venuti in 1948. While in army for two yrs., perf. in Japan and Korea. Ret. to NYC, pl. w. Sal Salvador; Tal Farlow; Don Elliott; Kai Winding. Fr. '56 to '62, much in demand as a studio mus. and rec. sideman, due to his excellent reading skills and precise pl. on pno. and vib. Pl. and rec. w. own trio '57; w. Woody Herman on and off '58–9; often w. Coleman Hawkins '59–60. Died in auto accident on West Side Highway, NYC. A hard-driving, percussive player, noted for the rumbling swing of his left hand, he was well versed in bop and post-bop idioms, and, at times, employed an unusual octave-unison keyboard style. Polls: *DB* Critics "New Star" award on pno. and vib. '57. Fest: NJF '57. Recs. w. own trio; as sideman w. Farlow; Herman; Salvador; André Hodeir. CDs: VSOP; w. Gil Evans (Imp.); John Mehegan; O. Pettiford; B. VerPlanck; H. Mann (Sav.); H. McKusick (Prest.).

COSTA, JOHN, pno, comp; b. Arnold, PA, 1/18/22; d. Pittsburgh, PA, 10/11/96. Studied w. Oscar Levant's teacher, and at Carnegie Tech. 1945–51. Received B.A. in comp. Pl. w. Tommy Reynolds '40–2. Freelanced in Pitts. area, later app. on KDKA-

TV and made twice-yearly apps. at the Embers, NYC '50s. Comp. several classical pieces. A regular on children's TV show *Mister Rogers*. CDs: Chiaro.

COSTANZO, JACK (JAMES), bgo, cga; b. Chicago, IL, 9/24/22. Began as dancer in contest-winning team w. wife, Marda Saxon, tour. in early 1940s. After navy service '45, taught dancing at Beverly Hills (Calif.) Hotel. Pl. w. Bobby Ramos orch. 1946; several Latin bands, incl. Lecuona Cuban Boys; Chuy Reyes; Desi Arnaz; Rene Touzet. Tour. and rec. w. Stan Kenton '47–8. With Nat "King" Cole Trio '49–53. Mainly w. pop gps. and singers since then. Gave bongo lessons to Jack Lemmon, Gary Cooper, and Carolyn Jones for movie roles. Films: *Thrill in Brazil*; *Bernadine*; *Visit to a Small Planet* '59. In '90s, he lived in San Diego, Calif., working w. own qnt. CDs: w. Kenton; Cole (Cap.; Mos.); M. Paich (GNP Cres.).

COTTRELL, LOUIS ALBERT JR., cl, tnr sax; b. New Orleans, LA, 3/7/11; d. New Orleans, 3/21/78. Son of Louis Cottrell Sr. Studied cl. w. Lorenzo Tio and Barney Bigard. Played w. the reorganized Golden Rule Orch. in 1925, bef. join. Polo Barnes. In late '20s, pl. for brief periods w. Chris Kelly; Kid Rena; Young Tuxedo Orch; Sidney Desvigne on the SS *Island Queen*. Join. Don Albert's orch. in '29, remaining to '39; tour. US, Can., Mex. in '30s. Ret. to NO, pl. w. Paul Barbarin '40; A.J. Piron on riverboats '41. Rejoin. Desvigne '42–7; Barbarin in '50s. In '60s, worked w. Peter Bocage and led own band. Rec. w. orchs. of Jim Robinson and Bocage, and own trio for Riv. '61. Fr. late '20s, he was prominent in organizing the black mus. branch of NO AFM, Local 496; was its president fr. '40s into '60s. CDs: Riv.

COTTRELL, LOUIS SR., dms; b. New Orleans, LA, 12/25/1878; d. New Orleans, 10/17/27. Son was Louis Cottrell Jr. Played w. John Robichaux's orch. to 1909; also Olympia Orch 1900–14. Went to Chi. w. Manuel Perez '15. Ret. to NO, worked w. A.J. Piron until his death. A pioneering early jazz dmr., Cottrell incorporated the "press roll" into his playing. He was a significant infl. on successive NO dmrs., incl. Baby Dodds, Cié Frazier. CD: w. Piron (Azure).

COUNCE, CURTIS LEE, bs; b. Kansas City, MO, 1/23/26; d. Los Angeles, CA, 7/31/63. As a teenager, he studied vln., bs., tba. Join. Nat Towles 1941–4. Moved to LA, where he worked w. Johnny Otis '45; Edgar Hayes '45–8; then w. Benny Carter; Wardell Gray; Billy Eckstine; Bud Powell; Hampton Hawes; also stud. comp. and arr. w. Spud Murphy dur. this period. Join. Shorty Rogers '54, pl. in clubs and on

concert tour. After working w. Buddy De Franco '56, join. Stan Kenton, tour. Eur. w. him Mar.-May. Form. own gp. Aug. '56 and cont. as a lead. and teacher until his death; sidemen incl. Carl Perkins; Jack Sheldon; Gerald Wilson; Harold Land; Frank Butler. Tour. Austral. w. Benny Carter '60. Fav: Blanton. Fests: MJF w. Coleman Hawkins '59. Films: *Carmen Jones*, *Sweet Smell of Success*, *St. Louis Blues*, *The Five Pennies*. CDs: Cont.; w. W. Gray; Teddy Charles (Prest.); Art Pepper–Chet Baker (PJ); Clifford Brown (Em.); I. Jacquet (Verve); Kenton (Cap.); S. Rogers (BB; Mos.); Lyle Murphy (Cont.).

COWELL, STANLEY A., pno, comp; b. Toledo, OH, 5/5/41. Studied pno. w. Mary Belle Shealy, Elmer Gertz fr. age 4. Perf. as feat. soloist w. Toledo Youth Symph. and Amer. Youth Symph. 1954. Stud. pno. w. Emil Danenberg, comp. w. Richard Hoffman at Oberlin Coll. '58–62, B. Mus.; Mozarteum Acad., Austria '60–1; U. of Wichita '62–3; comp. w. Ingolf Dahl at U. of So. Calif. '63–4; U. of Mich. '65–6, M. Mus. Moved to NYC '66; pl. w. Roland Kirk, Gene McDaniels '66; Marion Brown '66–7. Premiered *New Detroit*, comp. for double sxt. and fl. at U. of Mich. Arts Fest '67. Pl. w. Max Roach '67–70; Miles Davis, Herbie Mann '68; Bobby Hutcherson–Harold Land '68–71; Stan Getz '69; Music Inc. w. Chas. Tolliver '69–73; Gloria Lynne '70. Advisor to Afro-Amer. Mus. Dept. at Oberlin Coll. '71–2. Co-founded Strata-East rec. label '72. Organized and led Piano Choir fr. '72. Formed Collective Black Artists, Inc. w. Reggie Workman, Jimmy Owens '73; mus. dir. of CBA Ens. '73–4. mus. dir. of *Lady Day: A Musical Tragedy* at Bklyn. Acad. of Mus. '73. Pl. w. Donald Byrd '73. Co-mus. dir. of NY Jazz Repertory Co. '74. Pl. w. Clifford Jordan fr. '74; Sonny Rollins '74–5; Heath Bros. fr. '75. Mus. dir. of theater prod. in OH and NYC '76–80. Perf. mainly w. own gps. fr. late '70s; also pl. w. Larry Coryell fr. early '80s; J.J. Johnson '88. Cowell was featured in the Smithsonian Inst.'s Evening of Solo Pno. in '78 and '81. Taught at Amherst Coll. '74–5; CUNY–Lehman Coll. fr. '81; New Engl. Cons. fr. '87. Received a fellowship fr. Meet the Composer in '90 to comp. a work for the Toledo Symph. His *Piano Concerto No. 1,* which is dedicated to Art Tatum, was prem. in '92. Working on three choral-orchestral works, a computer-music project, and a book of orig. etudes for student pnsts. Fests: Eur. fr. '67; Africa '69 '72; Asia '73 '83; West Indies '71; Caribbean '83. TV: Dick Cavett w. Heath Bros. '79–80. CDs: Conc.; Steeple.; DIW; BL; w. J. DeJohnette; Rollins (Mile.); A. Pepper (Gal.); Piano Choir; Tolliver (Strata-East); L. Coryell (Muse; Jazz-point); J.J. Johnson (Ant.); G. Russell (SN); Marion Brown (ESP Disk); Jay Clayton (ITM Pacific).

COWINGS, MARION LINCOLN, voc, gtr, perc; b. NYC, 1/24/46. Mother sang; uncle and sist., Dr. Patricia Cowings, pl. pno. Began on pno. Stud. at HS of Mus. and Art; Manh. Sch. of Mus. At invitation of Jon Hendricks, perf. w. L, H&R at age 15. Soloist in NY Philharm. perf. of Aaron Copland's *Second Hurricane* 1959. Sang w. Pony Poindexter–Ike Isaacs at Randall's Island JF '60; L, H&R, early '60s; own rock and r&b gps. '70–9. Co-led a gp. w. (then) wife Kim Kalesti fr. '80–96. Sidemen incl. Frank Foster; Walter Davis Jr.; Bobby Watson; Kenny Barron; Al Foster; Eddie Gomez; Gary Bartz; Al Grey; Ralph Lalama; Frank Wess; Arnie Lawrence; Slide Hampton; Major Holley; Winard Harper; etc. Resumed solo career '96. Several apps. at Blue Note, acc. by Barron. Assistant profess. of vocal jazz at NYU fr. '87; he has also taught at City Coll., LIU, Jazzmobile Wkshp., and the New Sch. A versatile jazz singer, at ease with a ballad and adept at vocalese. Favs: Tony Bennett, Jon Hendricks, Junior Wells, Ella Fitzgerald. Fests: Eur. fr. '84; Japan fr. '91. CDs: w. Cowings-Kalesti (Em.).

COX, ANTHONY W., bs; b. Ardmore, OK, 10/24/54. Cousin is prof. org. who taught theory to Nat and Cannonball Adderley at Fla. A & M. Studied classical bs. at U. of Wis., Eau Claire, then freelanced in Minneapolis, Minn. Pl. w. Herb Ellis 1980; Chet Baker '81; Charli Persip bb '82–7; Sam Rivers '83; Jack Walrath '83–90; Craig Harris '84–90; Third Kind of Blue '84–7; Michelle Rosewoman '86–9; David Murray bb '87; Arthur Blythe '87–9; Dewey Redman–Ed Blackwell '87–8; Henry Threadgill '88; Kenny Burrell '88–9; Stan Getz '88–90; John Scofield '88–90. With Marty Ehrlich since '82; Geri Allen since '84; Gary Thomas since '87; Joe Lovano since '89; Fred Wesley since '90; also own gps. incl. Rios w. vib. David Friedman. Favs: Mingus, Peacock, Holland. Fests: Eur. since '82; Japan since '90. TV: German TV w. own qt. CDs: Ant.; w. G. Thomas (Enja; JMT); A. Blythe (Col.); Lovano (BN; Enja); Walrath (Muse); Persip (SN); G. Allen (BN; Minor Mus.); Scofield (Gram.); Friedman; B. Previte; Rosewoman; Gust Tsilis; Mitch Watkins; M. Ehrlich (Enja); Wesley (Minor Mus.); A. Donelian (Sunny.).

COX, IDA (Prather), voc, comp; b. Cedartown, GA, 2/25/1896; d. Knoxville, TN, 11/10/67. As child sang in church; left home to join White & Clark's Minstrels; then sang in theaters 1910. To Chi. '22, where she began rec. for the Para. label the following yr. accomp. by Lovie Austin's Blues Serenaders and Fletcher Henderson. In the '30s, she tour. successfully in the South w. her own tent show, accomp. by her husband, pnst.-orgst. Jesse Crump, and the North-

east theatre circuits, incl. Harlem's Apollo, where she was billed as "the Sepia Mae West." John Hammond brought her to NYC in '39 for Carnegie Hall concert, *From Spirituals to Swing*, and Voc.-Okeh rec sess. backed by James P. Johnson, Charlie Christian. A heart attack in '45 curtailed her career, and she retired to live w. her daughter in Knoxville, Tenn., in '49. She did not rec. again until '61, when Chris Albertson brought her to NYC for a Riv. date backed by Coleman Hawkins, Roy Eldridge, Sammy Price, in which she redid some of her own comps. of the '20s, incl. "Wild Women Don't Have the Blues" and "I've Got the Blues for Rampart Street." A leading interpreter of classic blues, she was, w. Ma Rainey, one of Bessie Smith's greatest competitors. CDs: Riv.; also one track each in *History of Classic Jazz* (Riv.), *Spirituals to Swing* (Vang.).

COXHILL, LOL (LOWEN), sop, other saxes, voc; b. Portsmouth, England, 9/19/32. Son, Simon, pl. dms.; daughter, Claire, voc. Priv. stud. 1952–9; gp. stud. w. Aubrey Frank '60–1. First prof. engagement w. Rufus Thomas, tour. and on BBC-TV. Since '58 has predominantly pl. sop. sax w. Otis Spann; Lowell Fulsom; Champion Jack Dupree; Alexis Korner '67–70; Brotherhood of Breath '74–5; Derek Bailey's Company, incl. Anthony Braxton, Steve Lacy, Evan Parker '87–8; Melody Four w. Tony Coe, Steve Beresford. Pl. w. Steve Miller's Delivery at Berlin Free Mus. Fest. '69; cont. tour. int'l w. gps. and in solo. Favs: Bechet, Lucky Thompson, Evan Parker, S. Lacy. Films: *Coxhill*, TCB '72; *Frog Dance*, British Arts Council film & video '80–4; *One Man's Week*, BBC-TV; also as actor in TV series; soundtrack comp. and perf. Book: subject of *The Bald Soprano* by Jeff Nuttall (TakTakTak, Engl.) Recs. w. E. Parker; S. Lacy; D. Bailey, etc. CDs: FMP; w. Company (Incus); The Dedication Orch. (Ogun); George Ricci (Slam).

CRANSHAW, BOB (MELBOURNE ROBERT), bs, el-bs; also tba; b. Evanston, IL, 12/10/32. Father was dmr. in KC; bro. a pnst. in Chi. and NYC. Son, bsst. Tom Barney. Pno. lessons at age 5. Stud. dms. fr. age 9; bs. in hs and coll. Stud. mus. therapy at Bradley, Roosevelt, and Northwestern U. Pl. tba. while w. army in Korea. Founding member of Walter Perkins' MJT+3 in 1950, and came to NYC w. the gp. in '60. Also pl. w. Eddie Harris in Chi. '50s. Pl. w. Junior Mance, Carmen McRae, Joe Williams early '60s; Duke Pearson '62–73; Sonny Rollins fr. '62. Active as studio mus. fr. mid '60s; also pl. w. Bobby Scott; Quincy Jones; Chas. Aznavour; Mary Lou Williams; Billy Taylor. Tour. Eur. and Japan w. Ella Fitzgerald–Oscar Peterson late '60s. House bs. for

Prest. artists at Montreux JF '73. Led own trio at Hopper's, Greenwich Village '75. Pl. w. B'way shows *Jesus Christ Superstar* and *Sergeant Pepper*. One of the few to effectively use the el-bs. in jazz, he has pl. and rec. on it w. Rollins; Horace Silver; Milt Jackson. Favs: Ray Brown, Percy Heath, Israel Crosby, Ron Carter, Scott LaFaro, Bill Lee. Fests: all major fr. '60s. TV: David Frost w. Billy Taylor Orch.; educ. TV incl. *Sesame Street, Electric Company*; *Saturday Night Live* house band. CDs: w. Rollins (Mile.; BB); w. Joe Henderson; Lee Morgan; Donald Byrd; Grachan Moncur III; D. Gordon; G. Green; B. Hutcherson; H. Mobley; H. Silver (BN); W. Montgomery; J. Hodges; K. Barron (Muse); M. Jackson (Pab.; MM; Riv.); P. Bley; Louis Smith; L. Willis (Steep.); C. Walton (Prest.); RR Kirk (Merc.); B. Webster (Enja).

CRAWFORD, HANK (BENNIE ROSS JR.), alto, other saxes, pno, comp.; b. Memphis, TN, 12/24/34. Started on alto sax; pl. w. Phineas Newborn, Booker Little, George Coleman, and others in hs. First prominent w. Ray Charles, 1958; mus. dir. of small gp. and bb; form. own band '63. Fr. '60–70, he rec. twelve albums for Atl.; in the '70s, rec. eight albums w. bbs. for Kudu, returning to a classic soul jazz format on his '83 Mile. album, *Midnight Ramble*. In '81, he toured w. Dr. John and David "Fathead" Newman in Swamp Jam; pl. and rec. w. Jimmy McGriff fr. '86. Fr. late '80s, he worked w. own qt., and occ. w. Newman as part of re-formed Ray Charles small band. Crawford's work as soloist and writer reveals an intense blues essence. He has had a significant infl. on David Sanborn and, through him, on a generation of young, funk-styled alto saxists. CDs: Mile.; Atl.; Rh.; w. Fathead Newman (Atl.; Muse; 32); R. Charles (Atl.; Rh.); Richie Cole (Mile.); J. McGriff (Tel.).

CRAWFORD, JIMMY (JAMES STRICKLAND), dms; b. Memphis, TN, 1/14/10; d. NYC, 1/28/80. First stud. alto sax, then self-taught on dms. While a student at Manassas HS, he was heard by his physical ed. instructor, Jimmie Lunceford, and rec. w. Lunceford's Chickasaw Syncopators 1927. Tour. w. Lunceford '29–42, then worked in a defense plant. Gigged w. Ben Webster on 52nd St. until Oct. '43, when he entered mil. service and pl. in army bands under lead. of Walter Gross, Sy Oliver. After his discharge, worked w. Edmond Hall and others at Café Society '45–9; pl. for Fletcher Henderson's show, *Jazz Train*, at Bop City '50. In '52, he began pl. in B'way pit bands for such musicals as *Alive and Kicking, Pal Joey, Mr. Wonderful, Jamaica, Gypsy*. Tour. w. Lena Horne '58. His precise, spirited drumming was one of the cornerstones of the Lunceford orch. As a sideman, Crawford rec. prolifically in a number of contexts,

incl. sess. w. Benny Goodman; Count Basie; Dizzy Gillespie; Bing Crosby; Ella Fitzgerald; Elmer Snowden; Mary Martin; and all of Jackie Gleason's Cap. albums. Fests: Great South Bay w. Rex Stewart's Henderson Reunion Band '57. Film: *The Adventure of Jazz*, Louis & Claudine Panassié '70. CDs: w. Lunceford (Dec.); Snowden (Riv.); C. Hawkins; B. Holiday (Dec.); I. Jacquet (Verve); Q. Jones (Merc.); Dicky Wells in *Giants of Small Band Swing, Vol.1*; B. Clayton (Riv.).

CRAWFORD, RAY (HOLLAND RAYMOND), gtr; b. Pittsburgh, PA, 2/7/24; d. Pittsburgh, 12/30/97. Started on cl. and tnr. sax; stud. pno. and tnr. in hs. Pl. tnr. w. Fletcher Henderson '42–3. When TB forced him to stop pl. reeds, he took up gtr. Pl. w. Ahmad Jamal's first trio in Pitts. '49–50; Chi. '51–6. Resettled in NYC, pl. there w. Jamal '56; Jimmy Smith '58; Gil Evans '59–60; also w. Tony Scott. Moved to LA; freelanced in films, concerts; form. own sxt., incl. Johnny Coles, Cecil Payne '61; worked w. Sonny Stitt '63. Rejoin. Smith in mid '60s; pl. w. him often fr. '71 into '80s; worked w. Sonny Criss '75. Moved to La Jolla, Calif. '83, began pl. tnr. again, cont. w. gtr. Pl. occ. w. Jimmy and Jeannie Cheatham. Taught gtr. at U. Calif.–San Diego Mus. Sch. '87–8. Moved to Pasadena, Calif. '90, teach. and comp. Probably the first gtrst. to create a "bongo" effect w. his fingers on strings. Fav: Gil Evans. Recs. w. Jamal; S. Stitt. Fav. own solos on "La Nevada" in Evans' *Out of the Cool*. CDs: Cand.; Criss (Muse); Evans (Imp.; BN).

CREATH, CHARLIE (CHARLES CYRIL), tpt, lead, sax, acdn; b. Ironton, MO, 12/30/1890; d. Chicago, IL, 10/23/51. Sister was married to Zutty Singleton. From mus. family; began on alto sax. At 16, started pl. tpt. prof. in St. Louis w. circus bands and theater orchs. Led his own gps. in St. Louis and for Streckfus Lines on Miss. riverboats fr. 1916 to '40; had several bands working under his name. Co-led riverboat band w. Fate Marable '27. After long illness in late '20s, he mostly pl. alto sax and acdn., becoming assoc. again w. Marable '35–8. In early '40s, he had own nightclub in Chi. Worked as inspector in airplane factory dur. WWII, but after '45 retired due to poor health. Recs. for Okeh '24–27.

CRISPELL, MARILYN, pno; b. Philadelphia, PA, 3/30/47. Grew up in Balt. Stud. classical mus. at New Engl. Cons. 1964–68, but discovered jazz in '75 after hearing Coltrane's *A Love Supreme*. Worked on and off w. Anthony Braxton in many gps. after being hired in '78 for his Creative Music Orch. In addition to her own trios, pl. in Anthony Davis's opera *X* and

w. Reggie Workman's Ens. '86–92. Tour. Eur. and Can. fr. '78, rec. frequently and teaching at many improv. wkshps. A brilliant virtuoso infl. by, but not imitative of, Cecil Taylor. An explosive style and individual lyricism makes her a lead. voice in free jazz. Favs: Taylor, Paul Bley, Monk. CDs: Cad.; Leo; M&A; BS; FMP; KFW; w. Braxton (M&A; SA; BS; hatArt); Workman (Leo; M&A).

CRISS, SONNY (WILLIAM), alto sax; b. Memphis, TN, 10/23/27; d. Los Angeles, CA, 11/19/77. Moved w. family to LA in 1942; pl. w. Shifty Henry after sch. hours. After hs grad. '46, worked w. Sammy Yates, Johnny Otis, Howard McGhee, Al Killian, Billy Eckstine combo at Billy Berg's; pl. in Gene Norman's "Just Jazz" concerts; Gerald Wilson's orch. Join. JATP '48; made several concert tours, incl. one w. B. Eckstine in early '50s. Freelanced in LA; West Coast tour w. Stan Kenton's *Jazz Showcase '55*; led own gps. '56–7. In the late '50s, he pl. w. Howard Rumsey's Lighthouse All-Stars; tour. w. Buddy Rich '58, and led his own gp. in Chi. '59. Lived in Paris '62–5; pl. w. own gps. at the Blue Note and other clubs; perf. in concert and on TV and radio; and tour. in Germ. and Belg. Ret. to LA in '65 and freelanced. His fine mid '60s recs. for Prest. helped revive his career. Fr. '70 to '74 devoted considerable time to community service, especially teaching; gave a series of concerts for young people dur. Hollywood Bowl summer program '71–2. He was awarded for his contributions to and infl. on So. LA youth. Made Eur. tours in '73, '74, teaching and perf. in US in between. Took his own life with a gun. Strongly infl. by Charlie Parker, particularly Parker's Calif. yrs., but pl. w. a more florid tone that reflected Benny Carter, an earlier infl. TV: Bobby Troup's *Stars of Jazz.* Fests: NJF '68; MJF '77 w. D. Gillespie. CDs: Prest.; Muse; 32; Pab.; w. Wardell Gray (Prest.).

CROMBIE, TONY (ANTHONY JOHN), dms, comp, arr, pno; b. London, England, 8/27/25. Mother was silent movie pnst. Self-taught. Pl. in London clubs fr. 1941, incl. perfs. w. Glenn Miller and Sam Donahue bands. Pl. on ocean liners w. Ronnie Scott late '40s. Tour. Eur. w. Duke Ellington '48, then pl. at Club Eleven and on weekly radio show w. Tito Burns's Acdn. Club Sxt. '48–50. Tour. w. Lena Horne, Carmen McRae, Annie Ross '50–4. House drummer for Engl. Dec. in '50s. Pl. w. R. Scott '51–4 '56; Victor Feldman '54–5. Led own gps. '54–6. Rec. on pno. w. Dizzy Reece '55. Formed Big Band Jazz Inc. '59. House dmr. at Ronnie Scott's '59–61, backing Coleman Hawkins, Ben Webster, Jimmy Witherspoon, J.J. Johnson, others. Comp. extens. for TV dur. this time, incl. scores to thirty-nine TV films in the *Man From Interpol* series. Rec. this mus. for Top Rank LP. Led own gp. in Israel '63, then formed duo w. orgst. Alan Haven '64. Pl. w. Haven in LV '65–6; w. Mike Carr in trio, Pendulum, '70–2; R. Scott '72–5; Georgie Fame's Blue Flames '70s; Peter King, Stan Tracey in '80s. Crombie's comps. have been rec. by Miles Davis; Joe Henderson (each did "So Near, So Far"); Blossom Dearie; Paul Gonsalves; Stephane Grappelli; Ray Nance. CDs: w. V. Feldman (Cont.); I. Jacquet (BL); B. Webster (Philips).

CROOK, HAL (HAROLD E. III), tbn, pno; b. Providence, RI, 7/28/50. Grandfather pl. for silent movies; fath. led swing band in 1940s. Classical pno. lessons fr. age 5. Fath. took him to jam sessions fr. age 13. Met Clark Terry and other established mus., who encouraged him. Pl. w. Terry '66; Duke Bellaire '66–8; Herb Pomeroy since '67; Louis Bellson '68; Woody Herman '68; Lionel Hampton '69. Grad. Berklee Sch. of Mus., B.A. arr. and comp. '71, then pl. w. Doc Severinsen's *Tonight Show* band '71. Out of music, working as truck driver, knife maker, pno. tuner '75–7. Pl. w. Chuck Israels '79,'81; Lew Tabackin–Toshiko Akiyoshi '81; for TV in LA '81–2. Founded Jazz Sch. of San Diego, Calif. '81; teacher '81–6; Prof. at Berklee Sch. since '86. Pl. w. Sal Nistico '88; Clark Terry's Spacemen '88; "XO" w. Jerry Bergonzi '88–9; Phil Woods '89–92. Crook has written a best-selling educ. book, *How to Improvise,* and has led his own gps. off and on since '68. Favs: Jack Teagarden, Bill Harris, Vic Dickenson, Curtis Fuller. Fests: Eur. since 78; Japan since '90. CDs: Ram; Outland; w. P. Woods (Conc.; Chesky; Phil.).

CROSBY, BING (HARRY LILLIS), voc; b. Tacoma, WA, 5/3/03; d. Madrid, Spain, 10/14/77. Older bro. of Bob Crosby. While studying law at Gonzaga U., Spokane, Wash., he form. duo w. singer Al Rinker, pl. dms. and singing. They tour. vaudeville circuit; in 1927, joined Paul Whiteman in LA and were teamed w. Harry Barris. The Rhythm Boys, as the voc. trio was called, achieved national popularity w. Whiteman until his app. in the '30 film, *The King of Jazz.* After that, Crosby left to work as a single. Fr. '31, he enjoyed a highly successful career in radio and such films as the "Road" series w. Bob Hope; *The Birth of the Blues* '41; *Holiday Inn* '42; *High Society* w. Louis Armstrong and Frank Sinatra '56. In '70s, he made int'l tours accomp. by qt. that incl. Joe Bushkin, Johnny Smith, Milt Hinton. One of the first crooners, Crosby was basically a pop music figure, but he was infl. by Armstrong, and he frequently rec. w. jazz mus., incl. Bix Beiderbecke, Frankie Trumbauer, Okeh '28; Duke Ellington, "Three Little Words," Vict. '30; "St. Louis Blues," Col. '32; Don Redman,

Bruns. '32; and on Dec. w. Louis Armstrong '36; Jack Teagarden '41, Bob Crosby '42, Louis Jordan '44, Eddie Heywood '45. CDs: Dec.; Verve; w. Armstrong (Dec.; Verve); Whiteman (BB).

CROSBY, BOB (GEORGE ROBERT), lead, voc; b. Spokane, WA, 8/23/13; d. La Jolla, CA, 3/9/93. Younger bro. of Bing Crosby. Attended Gonzaga U. Prof. debut as singer w. Anson Weeks orch. in 1932. Join. Dorsey Bros. in '34, then fronted a band that incl. former Ben Pollack sidemen '35. The Bob Crosby Orch. achieved great popularity specializing in orchestrated Dixieland. Reedman Gil Rodin was its mus. dir., and the Bobcats, a gp. fr. within the band, achieved its own success, continuing to rec. after '42, when the orch. officially broke up. Prominent members incl. Yank Lawson, tpt.; Eddie Miller, tnr. sax; Bob Haggart, bs; Ray Bauduc, dms. Crosby and his orch. app. in such films as *Presenting Lily Mars* '42; *Reveille with Beverly* '43; and on the soundtrack for *Holiday Inn* '42. Crosby served in the Marines '44-5, and led a service band in the Pacific. As a vocalist, he resembled his bro., especially in the low register. After WWII, he gained renewed popularity as a radio and TV personality through the '50s; his daily CBS show, *Club 15*, and weekly NBC variety show were highly popular. He frequently revived the Bobcats, assembling the original personnel, for recs. and special events. Fr. '60, he cont. to form reunion bands, although mainly occupied w. other business interests. Apps. in LV; tour. Japan and Far East '64; Disneyland '60s and '70s; US concert tours as part of *Big Band Cavalcade* '72-4; cont. to app. w. Bobcats and orch. in '80s and into the '90s. A collection of Crosby's scores and other research materials are housed at the American Heritage Center, U. of Wyoming, Laramie. Fest.: NJF-NY w. Bobcats '75. Additional films: *Sis Hopkins* '41; *As Thousands Cheer* '43; *The Singing Sheriff* 44. Book: *Stomp Off, Let's Go*, publ. in London '83. Comp.: "Silver and Gold"; "Until"; "The Wonderful World of You." CDs: Dec.; Swaggie; Cir.

CROSBY, ISRAEL (CLEM), bs; b. Chicago, IL, 1/19/19; d. Chicago, 8/11/62. Played various brass instrument as a child, incl. tpt., tbn., tba., but sw. to bs. at age 15. In mid 1930s, pl. in Chi. clubs, incl. w. Albert Ammons '35-6. Worked w. Fletcher Henderson '36-9; Horace Henderson '40-1; Teddy Wilson '42. For next few yrs., he freelanced and worked as studio mus., incl. Raymond Scott's CBS orch. '44, and recs. w. Roy Eldridge, Coleman Hawkins, Georgie Auld. Join. Ahmad Jamal '51; pl. w. Benny Goodman band and sxt. '53-4; except for Far East tour w. Goodman '56-7, he rejoin. Jamal '56-62,

when trio broke up. Pl. w. George Shearing qnt. in '62 for a few mos., until slowed by heart disease. An early bs. virtuoso, he first gained visibility through solos on recs. w. Jess Stacy '35; Gene Krupa, incl. "Blues of Israel" '35; Wilson '36; Edmond Hall '41; Auld, Eldridge, Hawkins '44. "[Crosby] played bass parts that were so beautiful you could never write anything that good," said Shearing. "He was one of the most inspiring musicians I played with." CDs: w. Krupa (Verve; tracks in *Swing is Here*, BB); Wilson (Hep); Albert Ammons (Merc.); Eldridge (Col.); Art Hodes in *Hot Jazz on Blue Note*; Edmond Hall (BN); Sam Jones (Riv.).

CROTTY, RON, bs; b. San Francisco, CA, 1929. Was member of early Dave Brubeck gps., incl. the Oct. 1948-50; the trio w. Cal Tjader '50-1; and the original qt. '52-3. Also worked in SF w. Wally Rose; Virgil Gonsalves; Brew Moore; and Earl Hines. Rec. w. his own trio, Vince Guaraldi and Eddie Duran '55. Dur. army service in Engl., he pl. w. many British jazzmen. CDs: w. Brubeck (Fant.; Col).

CROW, BILL (WILLIAM ORVAL), bs, tba, v-tbn, dms; b. Othello, WA, 12/27/27. Mother was radio singer in Seattle, Wash., in 1930s. Began on tpt., then pl. dms. and v-tbn. in army dance bands in '40s. After discharge, Crow worked as dmr. and tbnst. in Seattle bef. taking up bs. in '50. Moved to NYC '50. Pl. dms. w. Mike Riley '51; Pl. bs. and tbn. w. Glen Moore '52, then bs. w. Teddy Charles, Stan Getz '52; Claude Thornhill '53; Terry Gibbs '53-4; Jerry Wald, Marian McPartland '54; Gerry Mulligan Qt. and Concert Jazz Band '56-65. Rejoined McPartland '57-8; Mulligan '58-61. Pl. w. Gene DiNovi, G. Wein, Al Cohn-Zoot Sims '60; Al Cohn, Quincy Jones, Mose Allison, Lee Konitz '61; Benny Goodman '62, incl. World's Fair and USSR tour. With Clark Terry-Bob Brookmeyer '63-6; Eddie Condon's house band '65; Walter Norris gp. at Playboy Club, NYC '66-71; Peter Duchin '71-3; Ted Brown, Al Cohn '76-7; Local 802 All-Stars since '83; also pl. for B'way shows since '74. Crow is an officer in the NYC mus. union and an accomplished writer w. many articles and rec. reviews to his credit, incl. monthly column in union's paper, *Allegro*. His book *Jazz Anecdotes* was publ. in '90; a second book of anecdotes, *From Birdland to Broadway*, in '92, both w. Oxford. Favs: Pettiford, Ray Brown, Percy Heath, Wilbur Ware. Fests: Eur. w. Mulligan '56, '59, '62; Japan '64. Films: *Jazz on a Summer's Day*. Rec. as a leader for Japanese label, Venus, '95. CDs: w. Mulligan (Verve; Merc.; Col.; PJ); Terry-Brookmeyer (Main.); Sims-Brookmeyer (BL); Cohn (Evid.); Sims (Evid.; BL); Getz (Roul.; Verve); Goodman (MM).

CRUMP, JESSE (TINY), pno, org; b. Paris, TX, 1906; d. USA, 4/21/74. Left Dallas, Tex., in 1919; spent thirteen yrs. on TOBA vaudeville circuit. In '20s, he led the first all-black band for Pickwick Hotel's radio station in KC. Accomp. and wrote songs. for blues singer Ida Cox, whom he later married. Tour. w. Cox late '20s-early '30s and accomp. her '23-8, on such memorable Para. sides as "Bearmash Blues" '23; "Coffin Blues," "Rambling Blues" '28. Also rec. w. Billy MacKenzie for Para. '29-30. Fr. '37 to '52, he worked mostly around Muncie, Ind. Moved to SF early '50s, rec. several dixieland albums for Verve w. Bob Scobey '56; pl. w. Marty Marsala '60; also worked as soloist in trad. jazz clubs. CDs: w. Cox in *Great Blues Singers* (Riv.); Scobey (GTJ).

CRUZ, ADAM RAYMOND, dms, perc; b. NYC, 2/13/70. Grandfather was studio tptr. in NYC; fath., Ray Cruz, pl. perc. w. Latin bands, now leads own gp., Cruz Control. Stud. w. fath., then at Rutgers U. and New Sch. Pl. w. Charlie Sepulveda 1990–4; Hilton Ruiz '92–4; Paquito D'Rivera, Steve Turre '93–4; David Sanchez, Leon Parker, Mingus bb, '94–5. Cruz studied pno. in late '90s. Eminently capable of swinging ens., large and small, straight ahead or Latin, and pl. inventive solos. Favs: Roy Haynes, Steve Gadd, Steve Berrios. Fests: Eur. w. Mingus bb; Sanchez. So. Amer. w. Sepulveda. TV: *Bill Cosby Show* '92. CDs: w. Sepulveda (Ant.); Sanchez; Parker (Col.); Mingus bb (Drey.); D'Rivera (Mess.); V. Mayhew (Chiaro.).

CUBER, RONNIE (RONALD EDWARD). bari, tnr saxes, comp, arr; b. Brooklyn, NY, 12/25/41. Father pl. acdn., moth. pno. Pl. cl. w. fath. fr. age 9. Stud. tnr. at Bklyn. Cons. of Mus. Pl. bari. w. Marshall Brown's Newport Youth Band 1958–60; Sal Salvador '61; Slide Hampton '62; Maynard Ferguson '63–5; Geo. Benson '66–7; King Curtis–Aretha Franklin '65–8; Woody Herman '68–70; White Elephant '70–1; Eddie Palmieri '70–6; Lee Konitz '78–9; Rein de Graaf '79–82, then off and on since '85; *Saturday Night Live* band '79–85; Steve Gadd Gang '87–90; in '90s, Little Big Band '91–2; Mingus Dynasty; Dr. John; own gps. since '70s; Three Baritones in late '90s. Cuber also has extensive exp. as a studio mus., doubling on fl. and bs-cl. A robust, thinking jazz pl., at home in Latin jazz and blues/funk as well. Feat. on soundtrack of National Lampoon's *Animal House*, among other films. Favs: Pepper Adams, Harry Carney; arr: Bobby Paunetto. Polls: *DB* '66; NARAS Most Val. Player '79–86. Fests: Eur., Asia, Israel since '76. Films: *The Borgia Stick* w. Geo. Benson; *New York Nights* w. Little Big Band. TV: Grammy Awards '91–2, *Saturday Night Live*, Night Music, David Letterman, etc. LPs: as lead. and sideman (Xan.). CDs: Mile.; Steep.; FS; Pro-Jazz; Elec. Bird; *Three Baritones*, Drey.; w. G. Benson (Col.); C. Herwig (Ast. Pl.); Konitz (Steep.; SN; Chiaro.); M. Tyner; E. Wilkins (Bird.); H. Silver; Dr. John (GRP; WB).

CUESTA, HENRY FALCON, cl; b. McAllen, TX, 12/23/33. Cousin of Ernie Caceres. Raised in Corpus Christi, Tex., where he stud. vln. w. fath., 1940; start. pl. in small gps. at 14. Att. Del Mar Coll. of Mus. for three yrs.; pl. in Corpus Christi Symph. '50–3. After army service, pl. in Midwest hotel bands; then worked w. Shep Fields, Ted Lewis bef. join. Jack Teagarden, June '59. Freelanced in Toronto '63–72; join. Lawrence Welk TV show as feat. soloist '72–84. Later w. Bob Crosby '84–6; tour w. Mel Tormé '90; tribute to Jimmy Dorsey tour '91. Rec. w. Teagarden for Roul.

CUFFEE, ED (EDWARD EMERSON), tbn; b. Norfolk, VA, 6/7/02; d. NYC, 1/3/59. Moved to NYC in mid 1920s; participated in many rec. sess. for Clarence Williams '27–8, '29. Pl. w. Leroy Tibbs at Connie's Inn; Bingie Madison '29; McKinney's Cotton Pickers '30–34; Fletcher Henderson '35–8; Leon Abbey '40; Count Basie '41; Chris Columbus '44. Pl. w. various bands for short periods, incl. Bunk Johnson '47, then left mus. to work as an electrician. His pl. w. C. Williams exemplified the tailgate style of NO tbns. Recs. w. C. Williams, F. Henderson. CDs: w. Benny Carter (Charly); R. Eldridge (Col.); McKinney's Cotton Pickers (BB); King Oliver (Aff.).

CULLAZ, ALBY (ALBERT), bs; b. Paris, France, 6/25/41; d. Paris, 2/8/98. Father, Maurice Cullaz, critic-producer and former president of the French Jazz Academy. Bro. Pierre, gtrst. Took up bs. at 17; turn. prof. in 1963. Pl. w. Johnny Griffin qt. for two yrs.; Jef Gilson '65; tour. in Eur. w. Jean-Luc Ponty; Michel Graillier, Aldo Romano. Worked w. H. Mobley Sxt. '69; also w. René Thomas; D. Gillespie; S. Grappelli; Eddy Louis; Art Taylor; D. Gordon; K. Clarke; Guy Lafitte; Raymond Fol, et al. Won Django Reinhardt Academy prize '72. Recs. w. Gilson; Graillier. LP w. Mobley (BN). CDs: w. J. Albany (FS); S. Grossman (Musidisc).

CULLAZ, PIERRE, gtr; cello; b. Paris, France, 7/21/35. Brother of Alby Cullaz. After stud. pno. and cello, took up gtr. in 1949. Prof. debut w. Michel Hausser '56–7. Work w. Art Simmons '58–9. Following mil. service, pl. w. Martial Solal '62; Eddy Louis '64–5. Fr. '65–70 part of Guitars Unlimited, a 5-gtr. section that worked w. the bands of Claude Bolling;

André Hodeir; Ivan Julien; also accomp. singers such as Claude Nougaro. Active as a teacher at CIM, Paris. Favs: Reinhardt, Wes Montgomery, René Thomas, Milt Jackson. Book: *Methode de Guitare* (A. Leduc editions). Comp. mus. for films w. M. Legrand. Rec. *Anna Livia Plurabelle* w. Hodeir (Epic '66); also sess. w. G. Lafitte (Musidisc); Buck Clayton; Sir Charles Thompson (Vogue). CDs: w. Sarah Vaughan (Em.; Merc.).

CULLEY, WENDELL PHILIPS, tpt; b. Worcester, MA, 1/8/06. Started pl. w. Bost. bands. Moved to NYC, 1929 and pl. w. the Bill Brown Brownies. With Horace Henderson '30; Cab Calloway '30–31. Pl. w. Noble Sissle 1931–7; also in early '40s; L. Hampton '44–9. Pl. w. Sissle again bef. join. Count Basie '52–9. After leaving Basie, ret. from mus., moved to the West Coast and worked in the insurance business. Rec. w. Sidney Bechet in '20s and '30s. Primarily a lead pl., but pl. feat. solos w. Hampton: "Airmail Special"; "Midnight Sun"; Basie: "Li'l Darlin'." CDs: w. Hampton (Dec.); Basie (Verve); Sarah Vaughan (Merc.); Bechet (Class.).

CULLUM, JIM JR., crnt, lead; b. San Antonio, TX, 9/20/41. Father, a cl. pl. in coll. band and w. J. Teagarden in the 1930s, but later went into the grocery business. Form. a family band, Happy Jazz, w. crntst. Jim Jr. who assumed lead. after his fath.'s death in '70s. Sidemen incl. Allan Vaché, cl.; Mike Pittsley, tbn.; John Sheridan, pno. The band has pl., six nights a week, for well over thirty yrs. at the Landing, a club located on San Antonio's Riverwalk in the Hyatt Regency Hotel, broadcasting nationally via the Vintage Jazz Network on approximately two hundred stations. Own rec. cos., Audiophile; Happy Jazz. Over the yrs., the band's guests have incl. Earl Hines; B. Goodman; Bobby Hackett; Joe Venuti. Mus. such as Clark Terry, Dick Hyman, Doc Cheatham have rec. with Cullum. CDs: Pacific Vista; Stomp Off; Aud.; Col.

CULVER, RIC (ERIC C.), tbn, euph; b. Detroit, MI, 4/30/43. Father pl. w. Jean Goldkette bands in 1930s. Studied at Juilliard '61–6 and Mich. State U. '73–5. Prof. career almost totally devoted to large ens. pl. With Glenn Miller Orch. cond. by Buddy DeFranco '60s; Buddy Rich, Louis Bellson, Akiyoshi-Tabackin '70s; Gordon Goodwin, Gordon Brisker, Dave Pell, Bill Holman, Bob Florence '80s. CDs: w. Akiyoshi–Tabackin; Rich (BB); Holman (JVC); Brisker (Disc.); Florence (Capri); Mark Masters (Capri).

CULVER, ROLLIE (ROLLAND PIERCE), dms; b. Fond du Lac, WI, 10/29/08; d. Culver City, CA,

12/8/84. Musical family: two bros. were amateur dmrs.; sist., pnst.; wife pl. pno., vln., tbn. Took up dms. in 1920; pl. in hs band and orch.; app. in theaters as tap dancer. Pl. w. Wally and Heinie Beau in Wis. '30–40. Join. Red Nichols in '41; then w. Joe Sanders, Jimmy Joy '42–4. Rejoin. Nichols '45, staying w. him until his death in '65. Also pl. for and app. in many films, incl. *Say One for Me* w. Bing Crosby '59. With Nichols, USIA tour of Eur. and all of Asia '60; World JF in Japan '64. Major infl: Krupa. Fav: Buddy Rich. Recs. w. Nichols; Jack Delaney and Raymond Burke; Kay Starr; Phil Harris. CDs: w. Nichols (Cap.).

CUNLIFFE, BILL (WILLIAM HENRY JR.), pno; b. Lawrence, MA, 6/26/56. Began pno. and cl. studies at age 9. Studied classical pno. at Phillips Acad. w. Albion Metcalf 1971–75 and at Duke U. fr. '76–79. While at Duke, was introduced to jazz by Mary Lou Williams, who taught him about Tatum, Waller, Garner, others. Furthered his knowledge of swing and bebop at Eastman in '78. In '81, he won *DB* Best Jazz Comp., Outstanding Jazz Arr. Pl. w. Buddy Rich '84–5; tour. periodically w. Frank Sinatra; pl. w. Freddie Hubbard; James Moody; Woody Shaw; Pharoah Sanders; Joe Henderson; George Coleman; Bobby Watson; Art Blakey; Kenny Burrell; Art Farmer. Soloist w. Cincinnati Pops Orch. NEA grant to stud. jazz improv. '88; won Thelonious Monk Jazz Piano Award '89. Moved to LA '89. Pl. w. Clayton–Hamilton Jazz Orch., John and Jeff Clayton Qt. w. Jeff Hamilton; led own gps. Pl. Eur. and US. App. at Otter Crest, Santa Fe, Vail jps. Favs: Tatum, T. Flanagan, H. Hancock. CDs: Disc.; w. Clayton–Hamilton (Capri); Clay Jenkins (Sonic Atmospheres).

CUNNINGHAM, BOB, bs, comp; b. Cleveland, OH, 12/28/34. Played w. local bands in Cleveland, then moved to NYC 1960. Tour. and rec. w. Dizzy Gillespie '61 incl. MJF. Rec. w. Bill Hardman, Eric Dolphy '61; Ken McIntyre '63; Walt Dickerson '65; Frank Foster '65–6; Junior Mance, Freddie Hubbard '66; Jazz Composers Orch. '68; Gary Bartz '69; Leon Thomas '70; also worked w. Art Blakey; Betty Carter; Kenny Dorham; Sun Ra; Art Farmer; Max Roach; Joe Henderson; Pharoah Sanders; Rashied Ali. Pl. w. Yusef Lateef '70–6, incl. tours of US, Eur., and Africa. Led own gp. fr. late '70s. Pl. w. Bross Townsend. Rec. w. World Bass Violin Ens. '82–3. As a comp., Cunningham has worked on several occasions w. choreographers and writers. His scores incl. the dance-drama *Musical Safari in Living Color,* as well as other theater pieces. CDs: w. Lateef (Atl.; Rh.); Hubbard (Atl.); Jazz Composers Orch. (JCOA); A. Shepp (WW).

CUPPINI, GIL (GILBERTO), dms, arr, lead; b. Milan, Italy, 6/6/24; d. Fosdinovo, Italy, 6/15/96. Father was dmr., acdnst. Stud. pno. first in 1935, harm. fr. '39; medicine, surgery at U. of Milan. Inspired by B. Goodman Qt.to become a mus. Took up dms. '46; prof. debut in Switz. '47. Pl. w. Hazy Osterwald in Eur. '49; Kramer Gorni '50; Nunzio Rotondo '52–4, '58–60; also w. Basso-Valdambrini gp. Led own gp. at Taverna Mexico, Milan '55; on radio-TV Italiana '56; pl. w. Armando Trovajoli bb '57; Teddy Wilson in Brussels; Lee Konitz '58. Broadcast concerts on RAI (Italy) dur. the '60s. In the '70s, rec. w. Joe Venuti; late '70s was part of rhythm section (Franco D'Andrea, pno.; Giorgio Azzolino, bs.) that accomp. many Amer. and Eur. mus. Favs: orig. Krupa; then Roach, PJ Jones. Fests: accomp. Trovajoli and Gorni at Paris JF '49; app. often at San Remo fr. '56; w. Int'l Youth Band at NJF '58, rec. w. it for Col. CDs: Red; Jump; Right Tempo Classics; w. J. Venuti (Omega); Lino Patruno (Carosello); Flavio Ambrosetti (Enja).

CURNOW, BOB (ROBERT H.), comp, arr, tbn, bs, pno; b. Easton, PA, 11/1/41. Extensive stud. at Mich. St. U. 1964–7; arr. and comp. w. Russ Garcia and Johnny Richards '61–3; tbn. w. Buddy Baker. Tour. w. Stan Kenton for nine mos. '63. Later gigged w. L. Hampton; Warren Covington; B. Goodman; Sammy Davis; et al. Cond. many coll. bands, incl. Notre Dame jazz ens. '64–70. Rejoin. Kenton in '73 and spent four yrs. as a&r dir., arr., comp., prod., and gen. mgr. of Kenton's Creative World Recs. Wrote such projects as thirty-eight national anthems '72; *Kenton Plays Chicago* '74; and *7.5 On the Richter Scale*. He later served as pres. of IAJE; spent eleven yrs. as Dir. of Bands and Jazz Stud. at Cal. St. U., LA. He also has taught at Mich. St.; Case Western Reserve; guest cond. the Bost. Pops, Cleveland Philharm., and all-state jazz ens. nationwide, incl. the McDonald's All-American HS Jazz Band. Leads the New Jazz Repertory Ens. of Spokane, Wash. and heads Sierra Mus. Publications. Wrote bb arrs. of Pat Metheny and Lyle Mays mus. for the MAMA Foundation '94. Favs: J.J. Johnson; Frank Rosolino; Bill Harris; Bill Holman. CDs: MAMA; w. Kenton (CW).

CURSON, TED (THEODORE), tpt, picc-tpt, flg; b. Philadelphia, PA, 6/3/35. Jimmy, Percy, and Tootie Heath were childhood friends. First band w. Tootie Heath, Sam Reed, Bobby Timmons, Jimmy Garrison. Att. Mastbaum HS in Phila., then studied at Granoff Cons. in 1950s. Pl. w. Charlie Ventura '53. Encouraged by Miles Davis to move to NYC '56, pl. w. Red Garland; Mal Waldron; Philly Joe Jones. Pl. and rec. w. Cecil Taylor '59; Charles Mingus w. Eric Dolphy

'59–62; Archie Shepp early '60s. Co-led gp. w. Bill Barron '62–6, then moved to Den. and pl. reg. at Pori JF. Received grant from Finnish govt. '73. Ret. to NYC '76, led own gp. w. Nick Brignola, Chris Woods; also pl. w. Andrew Hill; Kenny Barron; Lee Konitz; Ernie Wilkins; Steve McCall; Howard Johnson. Led late night jam sess. at Blue Note, NYC '80–3, '90–1. Also worked in '80s as clinician at various universities. Formed '90s gp., Ted Curson & Company. His mus. was used for the soundtrack of Pier Paolo Pasolini's '69 film *Teorema*. Would like to rec. an album w. strings, feat. orig. ballads. Favs: C. Brown, K. Dorham, M. Davis, Gillespie. Poll: *DB* New Star '66. Fests: all major fests in Eur. since '60; also India, Mid. East, No. Africa, Venezuela. Films: *Notes for a Film on Jazz*, w. Gato Barbieri; Eric Dolphy's *Last Date*. TV: *Jazz Set* (PBS), US; *Live from Club Severine*, France; Pori Jazz Fest., Finl.; Jam Session at the Blue Note w. Sadao Watanabe, Japan. CDs: Evid.; Prest.; BL; EPM Musique; Trend; w. Mingus (Cand.; Atl.); Dizzy Reece (Trend); B. Barron (Sav.); Dolphy (Cand.); Gil Evans (Imp.); A. Hill (Free.); Mingus Dynasty (WW); Shepp (Imp.); A. Trzaskowski (Polskie Nagrania).

CURTIS, KING (Curtis Ousley), tnr sax, lead; b. Ft. Worth, TX, 2/7/34 ; d. NYC, 8/13/71. Started on alto sax as a pre-teen; while still in hs, pl. jazz and r&b w. local bands. Sw. to tnr.; opted to tour w. L. Hampton '52, instead of accepting coll. scholarship. With Hampton, developed comp. and arr.; also took up gtr. Left band in NYC, where he quickly became very active as studio mus. in r&b field, often accomp. singers, through the '60s. Own gp., the King Pins, rec. extensively for Prest., Cap., Atco. Appointed mus. dir. for Aretha Franklin '71, app. w. her at Montreux JF. Died of stab wounds after he was involved in a fight in front of a NYC building he owned. TV: mus. dir. for series, *Soul*. CDs: NJ; Prest.; Tru-Sound; w. Oliver Nelson (Prest.).

CUTSHALL, CUTTY (ROBERT DEWEES), tbn; b. Huntington County, PA, 12/29/11; d. Toronto, Ont., Canada, 8/16/68. Began as symph. tbnst. in Pitts. Entered dance band ranks w. Charlie Dornberger 1934; then pl. w. Jan Savitt '39; Benny Goodman '40–2. After army duty '42–6, he rejoin. Goodman until Dec. '46; freelanced in NYC '47; w. Billy Butterfield at Nick's '48. Join. Eddie Condon's house band '49. In '50s, he cont. to work w. Condon incl. tour of Engl., Scotland, early '57. Dur. these yrs., he also worked w. Yank Lawson; Peanuts Hucko; Max Kaminsky; Bob Crosby. Fr. '63 to '66, app. at Colo. JP and was an orig. member of the gp. org. in Denver as the Nine Greats of Jazz. This became the WGJB, but bef. that gp.'s first rec., Cutshall died of a heart attack while working in Toronto w. Condon. Favs: Teagarden, Will Bradley. His exuberant Teagarden-inspired work enlivened sess. w. Condon, Wild Bill Davison, Lawson. CDs: w. Condon (Sav.; Col.); Wild Bill Davison (Story.); Goodman (Col.); Swingville All-Stars (GTJ).

CYRILLE, ANDREW CHARLES, dms, perc; b. Brooklyn, NY, 11/10/39. Played in drum and bugle corps at age 11, then pl. in trio w. Eric Gale. Att. Juilliard and Hartnett Sch. 1960–4; studied briefly w. Philly Joe Jones. Pl. in early '60s w. Mary Lou Williams; Roland Hanna; Coleman Hawkins; Illinois Jacquet; Bill Barron; RR Kirk; Walt Dickerson; Ahmed Abdul Malik; Howard McGhee; Kenny Dorham; Nellie Lutcher; Freddie Hubbard; Babatunde Olatunji. Pl. w. Cecil Tayor '64–75, establ. reputation as leading free jazz dmr. Also pl. w. Jimmy Giuffre, Cedar Walton '64–6; Stanley Turrentine, Gary Bartz, Junior Mance, Benny Powell, Grachan Moncur III '68–9; Joe Mensah, Voices Inc. '70. Rec. album as unaccomp. perc. soloist '69. Artist-in-residence at Antioch Coll. '71–3. Cyrille led a variety of perc. ensembles in the '70s and early '80s, often perf. w. Milford Graves and Rashied Ali. Fr. '75 to early '80s, led MAONO, w. David Ware, Ted Daniel, Sonelius Smith, Lisle Atkinson, Nick DiGeronimo; then The Group, w. Marion Brown, Billy Bang, Fred Hopkins, Ahmed Abdullah; Pieces of Time, w. Kenny Clarke, Don Moye, Graves. Pl. w. Oliver Lake; John Carter; David Murray; Reggie Workman; Muhal Richard Abrams in '80s and '90s. Cyrille teaches at the New Sch. and the Graham Windham Home for Children, and has received three NEA grants for perf. and comp. In '90, he received a Meet the Comp. grant toward a collaboration w. choreographer Cleo Parker Robinson. Favs: Roach, Blakey, Haynes. Fests: Eur. and Japan w. C. Taylor. '74; also w. own gps. since '70s. Films: *On the Other Side of the Tracks*, France. TV: *Positively Black*. CDs: BS; SN; M&A; DIW; w. C. Taylor (BN; Charly; Konnex); Pieces of Time; K. Clarke; B. Bang (SN); Muhal Abrams (BS); C. Bley (Watt); Bobby Bradford; A. Braxton; H. Tapscott (hatArt); D. Murray (hatArt; DIW; Red Brn.); Dickerson (NJ); Hawkins (Prest.); O. Lake; John Carter (Gram); M. Ehrlich (Enja); C. Haden (Imp.).

d

DA COSTA, PAULHINO, perc, comp; b. Rio de Janeiro, Brazil, 5/31/48. Started on perc. 1955, working w. samba gps. and tour. w. Brazilian bands. Moved to US in '73, pl. w. Sergio Mendes for four yrs. He has played on hundreds of pop, jazz, and soul rec. dates incl. sess. for Dizzy Gillespie; Milt Jackson; Freddie Hubbard; Joe Pass; Anita O'Day; and Ella Fitzgerald. A three-time winner of the NARAS Most Valuable Player award '80–82, *DB* called him "one of the most talented percussionists of our time." CDs: Pab.; A&M; w. Terence Blanchard; Fitzgerald (Pab.); H. Hancock (Col.); Gillespie; Pass; M. Davis (WB).

DA FONSECA, DUDUKA (EDUARDO MOREIRA), dms, perc; b. Rio de Janeiro, Brazil, 3/31/51. Wife, Maucha Adnet, sang w. Antonio Carlos Jobim fr. 1984. Stud. in Rio at Villa Lobos Inst., Pro Arte and Guerra Peixe Sch. of Mus., late '60s-early '70s. Came to prominence w. own trio perf. in bossa nova style in concerts and on Brazilian TV '66–8. Pl. w. Mandengo '68, then in various gps. w. Tenorio Jr., Ion Muniz. Moved to NYC '76. Pl. w. Brazilian Express '80; NY Samba Band '82–9; Brazilian All-Stars w. Randy Brecker, Bob Mintzer, Eliane Elias '86–7. Led Trio De Paz w. Nilson Matta, Romero Lubambo fr. '89. Also worked w. Claudio Roditi; Slide Hampton; Astrud Gilberto; Herbie Mann; Antonio Carlos Jobim; Jorge Dalto. Da Fonseca has taught at the Drummers Collective in NYC fr. '85. He is the author of an instructional book, *Brazilian Rhythms for Drumset*. Favs: Edson Machado, Elvin Jones, Jack DeJohnette. Fests: Eur., Japan, So. Amer., Carib. fr. '81. TV: PBS w. Brazilian Express '81; Eur. TV w. H. Mann, A. Gilberto; Portuguese TV w. A. C. Jobim,

'92. CDs: Conc.; w. H. Mann (RBIC); A. Gilberto (Verve); C. Roditi (Cand.); Joanne Brackeen; S. McCorkle (Conc.); Emily Remler (Just.); N.Y. Voices (GRP); John Zorn (None.).

DAHLANDER, BERT (NILS-BERTIL), dms; b. Gothenburg, Sweden, 5/13/28. Father pl. acdn., moth. pno. Originally self-taught on vln. and pno.; later stud. at Juilliard. Pl. w. Thore Ehrling's radio band and own qt. Many visits to US starting in 1954, pl. in Bee Hive house band, Chi., and worked w. Terry Gibbs for a yr. Was briefly known as Bert Dale. Tour. Eur. w. Chet Baker '55–6; then pl. w. Lars Gullin bef. ret. to US '57; rejoin. Gibbs, then worked in Teddy Wilson Trio '57–60. Dur. '60s, he worked mainly in Sweden, incl. gig w. Earl Hines; own TV show '65. Back to US '66, pl. in Aspen, Colo. w. Ralph Sutton. Remained in Aspen, pl. w. many combos, incl. Peanuts Hucko. Ret. to Scand., working w. Alice Babs and in Swedish TV house band. Many int'l tours fr. '70s, also apps. at Colo. JP and other events in Colo. Visited Africa to study perc. '91. In mid '90s, he commuted between Colo. and Sweden, playing in both locales. Has own label, Everyday, in Battlement Mesa, Colo. A spirited swinger, adept w. brushes. Max Roach was an early infl. LPs: Verve; w. Gibbs (Em.); Wilson (Col.). Hines (Chiaro). CDs: Everyday; w. Wilson (Mos.).

DAILEY, ALBERT PRESTON, pno, comp; b. Baltimore, MD, 6/16/38; d. Denver, CO, 6/26/84. Studied pno. at age 6; pno. and comp. at Morgan St. Coll. 1955–6; Peabody Cons., Balt., '56–9. Pl. in house band at Royal Theater, '53–6. Tour. w. Damita Jo '60–3; own trio at Bohemian Caverns, Wash., D.C.,

'63–4. To NYC Mar. '64, pl. w. Bill English at Minton's; gigs w. Dexter Gordon, Roy Haynes, Hank Mobley '65; Sarah Vaughan, Dave Pike, Art Farmer '66; Woody Herman, Art Blakey '68–9; Charles Mingus, Joe Williams, Betty Carter, Thad Jones–Mel Lewis early '70s; Sonny Rollins off and on '70–3; Milt Jackson '72–3; Stan Getz '73–5; Blakey '75; Archie Shepp '77; Gordon '79; duo tour of West Coast w. Getz '84. Dailey also often app. as a solo pnst., his work reflecting noteworthy compositional abilities. Comps: "The Day After the Dawn"; "Bittersweet Waltz"; "Encounter"; "A Lady's Mistake"; *Africa Suite*. Favs: Tatum, Powell; later, Barry Harris, Tommy Flanagan. Fests: MJF w. Herman '67; NJF-NY '73–4; Eur. fests w. Getz '74. NEA Grant '75. LPs: Col. CDs: Steep.; w. L. Coryell (Muse); Walt Dickerson (Steep.); Getz (Col.); Slide Hampton (BL); F. Hubbard (Atl.); Shepp (Den.); B. DeFranco (Pab.).

DAILY, PETE (THAMAN PIERCE), crnt, v-tbn; b. Portland, IN, 5/5/11; d. Los Angeles, CA, 8/23/86. Played bari. horn as a child; then tba. and bs. sax; sw. to crnt. after borrowing one fr. a girl in hs band. Worked in Chi. fr. 1930–40 w. Art Van Damme; Boyce Brown; Bud Freeman; and others. Frank Melrose was a close friend and musical infl. Worked his way to Calif. w. Mike Riley '42; join. Ozzie Nelson; served in merchant marine for a yr. Rejoin. Nelson '45, and began rec. w. own gp., Pete Daily's Chicagoans. Until '54, he rec. for several labels, most notably Cap. Sidemen incl. Joe Darensbourg and Nappy Lamare. In the early '60s, he sw. to v-tbn, moved home to Indiana, and pl. w. Smokey Stover's band. App. at Sacramento JF mid '70s. A stroke in '79 ended his career. CDs: tracks in *Jazz Band Ball; The Good Time Jazz Story* box (GTJ).

DALEY, JOE (JOSEPH ALBERT), tnr sax, cl, fl, comp; b. Salem, OH, 7/30/18; d. Thousand Oaks, CA, 3/5/94. Studied sax w. Larry Teal in Det.; arr. w. Ray McConnell. B. Mus. in comp. fr. Chi. Mus. Coll. 1953. Sideman w. numerous bands in '40s and '50s, incl. Woody Herman '50–1. Also worked for singers, incl. Judy Garland, Tony Bennett. Formed free jazz trio '63. Pl. coll. and hs concerts in Midwest '60s; NJF '63; *DB* JF, Chi., '65. Gigged in Chi. and environs until late '80s when he moved to Calif., where he pl. sporadically. Favs: Charlie Parker, Sonny Rollins. LP fr. NJF '63, RCA.

DALLAS, SONNY (FRANCIS DOMINIC JOSEPH), bs, voc; b. Pittsburgh, PA, 10/27/31; d.? Father pnst, voc.; bro. pl. tbn. Started singing prof. at age 8. Stud. bs. w. Herman Clements in Pitts. 1949.

Pl. w. Charlie Spivak, Ray Eberle, Claude Thornhill, Les Elgart '53–4. Moved to NYC '56. Pl. w. Bobby Scott, Zoot Sims, Sal Salvador, Phil Woods–Gene Quill '57–8; George Wallington '58–9; Mary Lou Williams, Lennie Tristano '59. NJF tour w. Tristano '59. Favs: Red Mitchell, Pettiford, Paul Chambers. LPs w. Phil Woods (Epic); Sal Salvador (Beth.); ML Williams (Roul.). CDs: w. Woods (FS); Tristano (Jazz); L. Konitz (Verve); Nat Pierce (Hep).

D'AMBROSIO, MEREDITH, pno, voc, comp, lyricist; b. Boston, MA, 3/20/41. Husband is pnst. Eddie Higgins. Moth., Sherry Linden, was pnst.-singer; fath., Barry Worth, was semi-classical singer. Stud. at Julia Lubit Sch. of Pno. 1946–7; Rutland Sch. of Mus. and Art '47–9; Schillinger House '52; Berklee Coll. of Mus. '53. Sang on TV at age 17, then w. local bands. Hired as pnst.-singer by local club '53. Stud. art at Bost. Museum Sch. '58–9. D'Ambrosio has worked mainly as a single fr. the '50s. Sidemen in '80s-90s incl. Higgins; Michael Moore; Joel Segal; Tom Harrell; Steve Novosel; Keter Betts; Leroy Vinnegar; Major Holley; Randy Sandke; Yank Lawson; Bob Haggart; Ken Peplowski; Jake Hanna; Jack Sheldon; G. Masso; Bob Dorough; Alan Dawson. A watercolorist, calligrapher, and scrollmaker fr. the mid '50s, D'Ambrosio has taught manuscript writing fr. '70. Taught pno. and voc. at Emerson Coll. '80; U. of Oregon '85; Wesleyan Coll. '89; Frank Demeiro's Jazz Camp '92. Doug Ramsey wrote: "Meredith is an artist. Intelligence. Taste. Restraint. Subtlety. Insinuation. Harmonic sensibility and voice production that seems effortless." Favs: Tatum, Bill Evans, Monty Alexander; arrs: Mingus, Gil Evans, Claus Ogerman. Fests: Italy '85–6; France fr. '85. TV: *Odyssey: Meredith vs. The Arts*, WBZ, Bost. '66; *Forever Gershwin*, WCVB, Bost. '74. CDs: Sunny.

DAMERON, TADD (Tadley Ewing Peake), pno, comp, arr, lead; b. Cleveland, OH, 2/21/17; d. NYC, 3/8/65. Brother, Caesar, who pl. alto sax., tutored him in jazz basics; self-taught on pno. First significant prof. jobs were w. Freddie Webster; Zach Whyte; Blanche Calloway. By 1940, he was established as an arr. in Chi.; then came to NYC w. Vido Musso. He later joined Harlan Leonard in KC and wrote many arrs. for the band's recs. on BB. After war-plant work dur. WWII, he was very active as an arr. in NYC for Jimmie Lunceford; Billy Eckstine; Georgie Auld; Sarah Vaughan. Dur. the late '40s, he also wrote for Dizzy Gillespie, whose orch. premiered his large-scale work, *Soulphony*, at Carnegie Hall in '48. In '47, Coleman Hawkins rec. his "Half Step Down, Please." Dameron also cont. to play pno. dur. this period, w. Babs Gonzales' Three Bips and a Bop '47;

and w. his own gp. on 52nd St. '47. His qnt. and, sometimes, sxt., which feat. Fats Navarro and Allen Eager, was in residence at the Royal Roost for most of '48. In '49, he went to France to app. w. Miles Davis at the Paris Jazz Fest. Remaining in Eur., he worked briefly in London w. Ted Heath as staff arr. After ret. to the US, he worked w. "Bull Moose" Jackson '51–2. In '53, he form. his own band, incl. Clifford Brown and Benny Golson, and pl. the summer season in Atlantic City. Narcotics use severely curtailed his activities in the '50s and led to his incarceration in Lexington, Ky. '58. While there, in '60, he wrote and arr. material for an album by Blue Mitchell. After his release in '61, he resumed his career, rec. as leader and as arr., w. Milt Jackson and Sonny Stitt. He also wrote two charts used by Benny Goodman on his '62 USSR tour. In the early '60s, Dameron's health was failing, and by '63 a series of heart attacks saw him hospitalized several times. His last public app. was at a benefit held for him at the Five Spot, NYC, Nov. '64. He died of cancer a few mos. later. As one of the first important comps. and arrs. of the bebop era, Dameron, who combined swing and beauty, made an indelible contribution to the development of modern jazz. With Gil Fuller, Gil Evans, Gillespie and a handful of others, he was among the first writers to incorporate the harmonic and rhythmic devices of bop in a bb setting. His wide voicings, as much as four octaves apart, gave his small band work a particular richness. Polls: *Esq.* New Star, arr. '47. Comps: "Hot House"; "If You Could See Me Now"; "Good Bait"; "Cool Breeze"; "Lady Bird"; "Our Delight"; "Casbah"; "Fontainebleau"; "On a Misty Night"; "Smooth As the Wind." CDs: Prest.; Riv.; as arr.: w. Gillespie (BB; BN); B. Eckstine (Sav.); Blue Mitchell (Riv.); as pnst., w. C. Brown (Prest); Navarro (BN; Sav.; Mile.); Babs Gonzales (BN); D. Gordon (Sav.).

D'AMICO, HANK (HENRY), cl; b. Rochester, NY, 3/21/15; d. NYC, 12/3/65. Started on vln., then cl. in hs band in Buffalo, N.Y. First prof. gigs on Great Lakes boats between Buffalo and Chi. Worked w. Paul Specht 1936; then Red Norvo '36–9; also led own oct. on radio '38. Pl. w. Bob Crosby, '40–1; own bb 41; briefly w. Les Brown, Norvo, Benny Goodman '42; NBC staff w. Raymond Scott; gigs w. Miff Mole, Tommy Dorsey '43; fr. '44–55, staff mus. at ABC network. Apps. w. Jack Teagarden '54; in late '50s and '60s, worked mainly w. small gps., sometimes lead. his own band. With Morey Feld trio at N.Y. World's Fair '64. A clear-toned, fluid soloist after Goodman. TV: w. Steve Allen. Recs. w. Allen; Wingy Manone; Charlie Shavers; Bob Crosby. CDs: w. T. Dorsey (Hep; Jass); Norvo in *The Keynote Col-*

lection (Em.); Carl Kress in *Classic Capitol Jazz Sessions* (Mos.); Lester Young (Sav.); Eddie Condon (Jazz.).

D'ANDREA, FRANCO (FRANCESCO), pno, kybds; b. Merano, Italy, 3/8/41. Mother is amateur pnst. Started on tpt., cl., sop. sax. Began pl. pno. at age 17. Self-taught. Pl. w. Nunzio Rotondo 1963; Gato Barbieri '64–5. Freelanced w. Johnny Griffin, Dexter Gordon, Steve Lacy, Art Farmer, Don Byas, Hank Mobley, Lucky Thompson, Charles Tolliver, Slide Hampton, Geo. Coleman, others '63–73. Pl. w. Modern Art Trio '68–72; Perigeo Qnt. '72–7; Pepper Adams, Enrico Rava, Joe Farrell '73–83; Kenny Wheeler, Aldo Romano, Africa Djole fr. '83; Giovanni Tommaso qnt. fr. early '80s. D'Andrea has also led his own gps., ranging fr. duo to sept., fr. '78. He has taught at the Siena Jazz Seminars '78–92; Milan C.P.M. fr. '86. Favs: Bill Evans, Monk, Herbie Hancock. Polls: *Musica Jazz* '82, '84–7. Fests: all major in Eur. fr. '63; US '84–5 '91; Can. '83–4; Africa '87; Japan, Israel '92. TV: Eur. TV. CDs: Owl; Penta.; Red; L. Bleu; w. Dave Liebman (Red); L. Konitz (Phil.); Rava (Gala); Romano (Enja; Owl).

DANIELS, DEE, voc; b. Berkeley, CA, 1/11/47. Played vln. through junior hs; pno. through coll.; sang in church. After earning a B.A. in art educ., she taught art in a Seattle, Wash., hs, then quit to take up singing. Dur. a long residency in Eur., in the 1980s, she was befriended by John Clayton Jr., who later prod. her Capri album. Sang w. Wild Bill Davis in France '84; often w. Toots Thielemans in Belgium '84–6; Hank Jones, Tommy Flanagan in Holland '87. Rec. for Timel. in Holland '91. Scored major success in '92 at Lionel Hampton JF in Idaho, where she became a regular. An artist of exceptional promise, who sometimes acc. herself at the pno., Daniels has been highly praised by Clayton, Monty Alexander, and many others who have worked w. her. CDs: Mons; Capri.

DANIELS, EDDIE (EDWARD KENNETH), cl, tnr sax; b. Brooklyn, NY, 10/19/41. Alto sax at 9, cl. at 12; pl. in Newport Youth Band at 16. B.A. fr. Bklyn. Coll. 1963; M.A. from Julliard '66. Prominent w. Thad Jones–Mel Lewis Orch. '66–73, mainly on tnr., occ. on cl. Won *DB* New Star cl. award '68. Then w. New Amer. Orch, premiered a work commissioned for him, Jorge Calandrelli's *Concerto for Jazz Clarinet and Orchestra* '84; it was featured in his first GRP album, *Breakthrough*. Fr. that time, he has concentrated on cl. Rec. a series of albums for GRP, incl. *Memos From Paris* w. Roger Kellaway. Collab. w. Gary Burton on an album, *Benny Rides Again*, dedicated to Benny Goodman and Lionel Hampton. Many apps. w. symph. orchs. and on TV w. Bost. Pops; also pl. w. the Vermeer, Suk, and Composers String Qts. Consistent winner in jazz polls, Daniels has been praised as the most gifted and creative post-bop cl. to emerge in the '80s. CDs: GRP; Prest.; Muse; Ref.; w. Jones-Lewis (LRC); Dave Samuels (GRP); *Digital Duke*, Mercer Ellington (GRP); Rolf Kuhn (Intuit.).

DANIELSSON, PALLE, bs; b. Stockholm, Sweden, 10/15/46. Started on vln. at age 8. Doubled on bs. and hca. at 15. Stud. at Stockholm Royal Acad. of Mus. 1962–6. Pl. in 1960s w. Staffan Abeleen; Eje Thelin; Geo. Russell; Bill Evans; Ben Webster; Charlie Shavers. Co-led gp. Rena Rama w. Bobo Stenson '71–85. Worked in Eur. w. Jan Garbarek '70s.; Keith Jarrett '74–9. Tour. Japan, rec. in NYC w. Garbarek-Jarrett '79. Pl. w. Charles Lloyd early '80s; Michel Petrucciani fr. mid '80s, incl. US tour '84; Kenny Wheeler. Own band, Contra Post. CDs: w. Jarrett; Garbarek-Jarrett; P. Erskine; Colin Walcott; C. Lloyd (ECM); Urs Leimgruber (Enja); A. Manglesdoeff (MPS); Petrucciani (Conc.; BN); Z. Sims (Sonet); Barney Wilen (IDA).

DANKO, HAROLD, pno, comp; b. Sharon, PA, 6/13/47. Father pl. acdn.; two bros. are prof. mus. in Ohio. Family moved to Masury, Ohio, in late 1940s. First gigs accomp. bro.'s woodwind students early '60s, then stud. mus. ed. at Youngstown U. and pl. w. local mus. '65–9. Pl. w. army band on Staten Island, N.Y. '69; Teddy Charles '81–91; Edison Machado '82–8; Butch Miles '85, '87; Dee Dee Bridgewater, '90; also worked w. Chet Baker; Gerry Mulligan; Thad Jones–Mel Lewis; Lee Konitz; Woody Herman; Mel Tormé; Maureen McGovern; Chris Connor; Anita O'Day; own gps. Danko has taught at Jersey City St. Coll. '80–5; Concordia Coll. '81–3; Manh. Sch. of Mus. since '84; New Sch. since '89. In Sept. '98 became member jazz faculty at Eastman Sch. of Mus. His comps. have been rec. by Chet Baker and Lee Konitz. Awarded an NEA Fellowship '95 to perf. his comps. in a series of concerts. Favs: Earl Hines, Bud Powell, Arthur Rubinstein. Polls: Nat'l Assoc. of Concert and Cabaret Arts '80. Fests: Holland w. C. Baker '75; France and Italy w. own gp., '90–1. TV: PBS Jazz in Amer. w. Mulligan; Eur. TV w. Konitz, C. Baker, Mulligan, Jones-Lewis, D. Bridgewater. CDs: Sunny.; JC; Steep.; w. C. Baker (Polyd.; Gal.; Timel.; PW); Konitz (SN; Musi., Steep.); Charles (SN); K. Lightsey; M. D'Ambrosio (Sunny.); Rich Perry (Steep.).

DANKWORTH, ALEC (ALEXANDER WILLIAM TAMBA), bs; b. London, England, 5/14/60.

Father John Dankworth, moth. Cleo Laine, sist. voc. Jacqui Dankworth. Stud. at Guildhall Sch. 1978; Berklee Sch. '78–80. First w. Laine-Dankworth '80–90; rec. and tour. w. Nigel Kennedy '86; join. Clark Tracey Qnt. '86; tour. w. Stephane Grappelli '87; Tommy Smith '88–90; pl. w. Eddie Daniels '89; Abdullah Ibrahim, Julian Joseph Qt., Jean Toussaint in '90s. Form. own qt. '91; also w. Martin Taylor; Buddy DeFranco; Johnny Griffin; Anita O'Day; Mose Allison. Worked in US, Austral. '80–83; Far East '88; Eur. '89. Teaches bs. every yr. on the Wavendon Allmusic Plan; Guildhall Sch. summer course. Has rec. w. all the above. Fest: w. Dave Brubeck at JVC-NY '99. CDs: JH; w. J. Dankworth (Sepia); Clark Tracey (33); Guy Barker (Verve; Spot.); Dave O'Higgins (EFZ); J. Joseph (East West); David Newton (Linn); Toussaint (What Goes Around).

DANKWORTH, JOHN PHILIP WILLIAM, alto, sop saxes, cl, comp; b. London, England, 9/20/27. Wife, Cleo Laine; son, Alec, daughter Jacqui. Pl. cl. in trad. bands in mid 1940s. Stud. at Royal Acad. of Mus. '44–6. Worked in ships' bands on transatlantic crossings '47–8, and was able to visit 52nd Street clubs and reinforce his interest in modern jazz and Charlie Parker's strong infl. Pl. w. Tito Burns sxt.; then help found Club 11 in '48. Led John Dankworth Seven '50–53, when he form. bb that cont. on a regular basis into '64, incl. an app. at NJF '59, and reorg. on an annual basis until '71, when he became mus. dir. for Laine and scaled the band's size down to ten. Tour. w. own qnt. in early '80s. Dur. '60s, Dankworth—who had written arrs. for Ted Heath in the '40s and extensively for his own gps. and bb— became increasingly involved w. film scoring and writing for TV. Comp. and perf. many classical works and cont. to tour w. Laine. In '69, he founded w. Laine the Wavendon Allmusic Plan, a mus. coll. in the Engl. countryside, attended by many aspiring jazz players. He has participated regularly as an instructor and taught master classes at Berklee Coll. of Mus., Bost. In '85, he founded the London Symph. Orch's Summer Pops. As cond., he has worked w. major symph. orchs. in US, Can., Austral., NZ. Formed a new bb in '90 and fr. '93 co-led the Dankworth Generation Band w. his son. Though best known in the US for his role in Laine's career, he remains a top notch comp. and alto player. Comp. for the British mus. theatre; commissions fr. London Philharm. Society; National Theatre; Royal Shakespeare Co.; Houston Ballet; Silver Jubilee of Coventry Cathedral. Awards: won many *Melody Maker* polls in the '50s; CBE '74; "Show Business Personality of the Year" fr. Variety Club '77; Hon. M.A., Open U. '75; Hon. D.

Mus., Berklee Coll. '82. Film writing: *Morgan*; *The Magus*; *Return from the Ashes*; *Modesty Blaise*. CDs: Roul.; Sepia; MCA Classics; JH; w. Laine (RCA; Polyd.); M. Tormé (Conc.).

DAPOGNY, JIM (JAMES), pno, editor, writer; b. Berwyn, IL, 9/3/40. Studied comp. at U. of Ill: B. Mus. 1962; M. Mus. '63; Ph.D. mus. app. '71. Taught jazz theory and history at U. of Mich fr. '66. Rec. as lead. of Chicago Jazz Band '84; also pl. w. State Street Aces; Mysterious Babies; Sippie Wallace. Book: *Ferdinand "Jelly Roll" Morton: The Collected Piano Music* '82. Also contributed transcriptions of works by Morton, Fats Waller, Louis Armstrong, and Earl Hines, Meade "Lux" Lewis, and Thelonious Monk to the book *Smithsonian Classic Jazz Scores*, ed. by Gunther Schuller. CDs: Disc.; w. Clancy Hayes (Del.).

DARA, OLU (Charles Jones III), tpt, crnt, African tpt, hca; b. Louisville, MS, 1/12/41. Raised in Natchez, Miss. Served in navy, then moved to NYC 1963. Adopted Yoruba name '69. In his gp., the Natchezsippi Band and Okra Orchestra, he combines dance rhythms w. West African mus., blues, r&b, and marches. Has also worked as a sideman w. Art Blakey; Oliver Lake; David Murray; Henry Threadgill; Bill Laswell; James Newton; Don Pullen; others. App. in film *Kansas City* '96. Video: *Kansas City*. CDs: Atl.; *Kansas City* (Verve); Charles Brackeen (Silk.); Kip Hanrahan (Amer. Clave); J. Hemphill; Murray; Pullen (BS); Cassandra Wilson (BN).

DARDANELLE (Breckenridge), pno, vib, voc; b. Avalon, MS, 12/27/17; d. Memphis, TN, 8/8/97. Began working prof. in 1930s. Led own trio, incl. Tal Farlow, at Copa Lounge, NYC '45. Trio pl. opposite Nat Cole; Art Tatum. Raising a family took her off the road, and she concentrated on radio and TV as mus. and actress. In early '60s, had her own show out of Chi., w. sons Skip and Brian on dms. and bs. respectively. Lived in Glen Rock, N.J. '66–84 and revived her jazz career. Moved to Oxford, Miss., '85, and became an Artist-in-Residence at U. of Miss. '86. Pl. jazz cruise on QE2 '94. In late '80s, she began to write her memoirs. Never publ., but she rec. two 13–wk. series of excerpts for NPR. CDs: Audio.; Stash.

DARENSBOURG, JOE (JOSEPH WILMER), cl, sop sax; b. Baton Rouge, LA, 7/9/06; d. Van Nuys, CA, 5/24/85. Father was crntst.-lead. of brass band. Stud. cl. w. Alphonse Picou; also vln. and pno. Between 1923 and '26, he pl. w. NO bands, incl. Buddy Petit; then to St. Louis, Mo, working in river-

boat bands w. Fate Marable, Charlie Creath; trav. w. medicine show and circus band. To LA in late '20s, working on alto sax w. Mutt Carey. Moved to Seattle, Wash. '29, remaining until '44 and working all manner of jobs, incl. cruise ships, clubs, and as accomp. for visiting entertainers. Ret. to full-time jazz w. pnst. Johnny Wittwer '44. Moved back to LA, join. Kid Ory '44–54; also Wingy Manone; Gene Mayl; Pete Daily; Teddy Buckner. Led own gp., the Dixie Flyers, in late '50s. World tours w. Louis Armstrong '61–4; numerous gigs at Disneyland '65–9; own band '72–3; join. Legends of Jazz for concerts and tours '73–5. Pl. w. Chris Barber and other trad. bands, Engl. '74. Fests: NJF, MJF, NO; Hollywood Bowl Dixie Jubilee '59. TV: *Stars of Jazz*. Film: biography shot in London '74. Fav. own solos: "Sweet Georgia Brown"; "Yellow Dog Blues," a hit for him in '57. CDs: w. Armstrong (Col.; Story.); Ory (Col.); *Legends of Jazz and Barney Bigard* (GHB).

DASH, (ST.) JULIAN BENNETT, tnr sax; Charleston, SC, 4/9/16; d. NYC, 2/25/74. Started on alto sax, 1932. Made prof. debut in '35 w. Charleston Nighthawks, a band led by Lonnie Simmons, who was his first inspiration. Pl. tnr. sax w. Revellers, then w. 'Bama State Collegians at Alabama St. Teachers Coll. '35–6. Moved to NYC, orig. to stud. embalming, but ended up leading a band at Monroe's Uptown House '36–8. Rejoin. Collegians band, now known as Erskine Hawkins' orch., and remained w. it until mid '50s. Fr. that time, he worked at various day jobs, pl. on weekends; worked w. Marlowe Morris trio at Shalimar, mid '60s; own qnt. '70–1. Fav: Chu Berry. Co-comp. "Tuxedo Junction." Rec. solos w. Hawkins, incl. "No Soap"; "Bicycle Bounce." Rec. w. own gp. and as sideman w. Jimmy Rushing for Master Jazz, early '70s. CDs: w. Hawkins (BB); Buck Clayton (Mos.).

DAVENPORT, COW COW (CHARLES), pno, voc; b. Anniston, AL, 4/23/1894; d. Cleveland, OH, 12/2/55. Father was a pastor; moth. pl. org. Expelled fr. Ala. Theological Seminary for pl. ragtime pno. Fr. 1912, start. pl. in cabarets and bordellos; fr. '14 to 30 tour. w. carnivals and in vaudeville as pnst., singer, dancer. Worked in Storyville, NO, until '17, when he left to tour w. Bessie Smith. Later enjoyed great success in duo w. singer Dora Carr. Settled in Chi. in '20s, trav. w. his Cow Cow Chicago Steppers and accomp. singer Ivy Smith in Chi. '27–9. Talent scout for Vocalion '28–9. After a short time as a rec. store proprietor in Cleveland, he ret. to vaudeville circuit, but was jailed in Montgomery, Ala. In '35, when stranded in Fla., he decided to leave show business. Resettled in Cleveland '37, operating café and working for WPA.

To NYC in '40s, where experienced hard times until '46, when Art Hodes rescued him fr. a men's room job at the Onyx Club and got him radio work and an entrée to ASCAP. Ret. to Cleveland in '48. His claimed authorship of "You Rascal, You" and "Mama Don't Allow It" remains unproven; name does not appear on "Cow Cow Boogie," which he sold outright in '42. Made pno. roll of "Cow Cow Blues" '25; recs. w. D. Carr '24–5; Ivy Smith '27–9; also own sess. Considered to be one of the first exponents of boogie-woogie. CD: *History of Classic Jazz* (Riv.).

DAVENPORT, WALLACE FOSTER, tpt; b. New Orleans, LA, 6/30/25; d. New Orleans, 3/18/04. Played w. Young Tuxedo Brass Band 1938; Papa Celestin '40–1, and again dur. navy service. In late '40s, pl. w. various NO bop and swing mus. Worked intermittently w. Lionel Hampton '53–69, incl. US and Eur. tours; Count Basie '64–6; dur. same period, he also worked occ. w. Ray Charles and Lloyd Price. Ret. to NO in '69, pl. mainly trad. jazz; rec. on own label, My Jazz, '71–6. Resumed tour. in mid '70s, incl. Eur. w. George Wein '74. Led own gps. '76–9. Fr. '76 occ. reunited w. Hampton; frequently perf. in NO. In later yrs., he often worked w. gospel singers, incl. Zion Harmonizers; Aline White. CDs: w. Hampton (Col.; BB; Timel.); Basie (Verve); Arnett Cobb (B&B); Bob Wilber (Cir.).

DAVERN, KENNY (JOHN KENNETH), cl; b. Huntington, NY, 1/7/35. Studied briefly w. David Weber, Joe Napoleon, but primarily self-taught. Join. mus. union at 16. Pl. w. Jack Teagarden 1954; Phil Napoleon '55, '59, '65; Pee Wee Erwin '56, '60; own gp., Salty Dogs, '58; Billy Butterfield fr. '58; Herman Autrey '59; Ruby Braff '60; own gp. at Nick's '61; Eddie Condon's All-Stars, Ted Lewis '62; Dukes of Dixieland '63; Wild Bill Davison, Bud Freeman, Shorty Baker '64; Dick Wellstood, Geo. Wettling '65–8; Wellstood '72; Soprano Summit w. Bob Wilber '73–9. Then gave up sop. to concentrate exclusively on cl., incl. occ. "Summit" reunions. Member of WGJB '78; Lawson-Haggart Band fr. '79. Pl. in off-off B'way show *One Mo' Time* '80. Form. Blue Three w. Wellstood, Bobby Rosengarden '81. Rec. soundtrack to film *The Gig* w. Wellstood, Warren Vaché '84. Davern has toured w. all-star gps. and as single fr. '82. own gps. in '90s. An intense, lyrical player who uses all registers effectively. Favs: Pee Wee Russell, Jimmy Noone, Irving Fazola. Polls: *DB*, *JJ*. Fests: all major fr. '50s. Films: *The Hustler*. TV: PBS. CDs: MM; Arb.; Jazz.; w. Soprano Summit (Conc.; Chiaro.); Wellstood (Chiaro.; Chazz Jazz); Swingville All-Stars (GTJ); Davison; Lawson (Jazz.); Shearing (Conc.).

DAVIS, ART (ARTHUR), bs, educ; b. Harrisburg, PA, 12/5/34. Piano at age 5, then tba.; bs. at 15. Stud. at Juilliard and Manh. Sch. of Mus. B.A., Hunter Coll. 1972; M.A. in mus., psych., CUNY and NYU '76; Ph.D. in psych. '81. Early work w. Harrisburg Symph. Well known in '50s and '60s for assoc. w. John Coltrane, Max Roach '58–9; Dizzy Gillespie '59–60; Gigi Gryce '60; Lena Horne '61–2; NBC-TV staff orch. '62–3; Westinghouse TV '64–9; CBS '69–70. In '60s, rec. and/or perf. w. Quincy Jones; Phil Woods; Art Blakey; McCoy Tyner; Freddie Hubbard; many others. In '70s and '80s bec. active as teacher of jazz, classical mus., and psychology. Theory courses at Orange Coast Coll. fr. '87. Pl. w. Hilton Ruiz '86–7. Author of *The Arthur Davis System for Double Bass* '75. CDs: SN; w. Coltrane (Atl.; Imp.); J. Albany (Story.); Blakey; Gil Evans; Hubbard; Tyner (Imp.); E. Dolphy (Cand.; Enja); Booker Little (BN; Cand.); Gillespie (Verve); Elvin Jones (Riv.); Roach (Imp.; Atl.; Riv.); Oliver Nelson (Prest.).

DAVIS, CHARLES, bari, tnr, alto, sop saxes, comp; b. Goodman, MS, 5/20/33. Studied at Chi. Sch. of Mus. 1948–50; DuSable HS '49–52; then w. John Hauser '51–4. Pl. w. Jack McDuff '54; Sun Ra fr. '54; Billie Holiday, Ben Webster '55–6; Dinah Washington '57–9; Kenny Dorham '59–62; Illinois Jacquet, Lionel Hampton, John Coltrane '60s; Jazz Composers' Orch. '66–76; Donald Byrd '69; Artistry in Music w. Cedar Walton, Hank Mobley, Curtis Fuller '72; Louis Hayes '72–4; Clark Terry bb '73–9. Form. Baritone Saxophone Retinue, six bari. plus rhythm '74. Pl. w. Duke Ellington Orch., Thad Jones–Mel Lewis Orch. '78; Dizzy Reece '79–83; Barry Harris '80–2; Dameronia, Philly Joe Jones '81–4; Abdullah Ibrahim '83–8; Johnny Coles '89; Clifford Jordan bb fr. '90; Three Baritones '98. Davis has held many admin. jobs in mus. incl. mus. dir. for Lloyd Price's Turntable club '68; Monday Night Boat Ride up the Hudson '70; Home of the Id club '71–2; mus. librarian for Spike Lee's *Mo Better Blues* '90. He has received several NEA comp.'s grants and has taught at Bklyn. P.S. 179 '68; Jazzmobile Wkshp., fr. '73; Jazz Cultural Theatre '83–5; New Amsterdam Mus. Assoc. '85–8. Polls: *DB* '64; BMI Jazz Pioneer '84. Fests: all major fr. '59. Film: *The Man With Perfect Timing* w. Ibrahim '86. TV: apps. w. Archie Shepp, Randy Weston, Lucky Thompson, Ibrahim, etc. CDs: Red; w. Dorham (Time); C. Jordan (Mile.); Ibrahim (Tiptoe); C. Walton (Delos); Shirley Scott; Ricky Ford (Muse); J. Griffin; Sam Jones (Riv.); S. Lacy; Cecil Taylor (Cand.); Sun Ra (Evid.; Leo).

DAVIS, EDDIE "LOCKJAW" (EDWARD), tnr sax; b. NYC, 3/2/21; d. Culver City, CA, 11/3/86. In late 1930s, eight mos. after buying a tnr., which he taught himself to play, Davis began working at Clark Monroe's Uptown House. Pl. w. Cootie Williams '42–4; Lucky Millinder '44; Andy Kirk '45–6; Louis Armstrong '46. Own combo, mainly at Minton's '45–52. Join. Basie '52–3; own gp. to '55; then form. trio w. orgst. Shirley Scott, pl. together through '60, except for Eur. tour w. Basie, fall '57; long runs w. trio at Basie's club in NYC '58–9. Co-led qnt. w. Johnny Griffin '60–2; then withdrew fr. active pl. to work as a booking agent for Shaw Artists Corp. Rejoin. Basie, also functioning as road manager, '64, remain. w. him until '73, when he moved to LV. Tour. Eur. w. own gp. '68; w. Norman Granz tour, incl. Ella Fitzgerald, '73; w. revue *The Musical Life of Charlie Parker* '74. Fr. '74, cont. tour. and rec. activity. His unorthodox, jagged, extroverted style combined elements of the Ben Webster wing of swing tnr. w. rhythmic bop figures. Favs: Coleman Hawkins, Herschel. Evans, Ben Webster. Fests: NJF w. Basie, Fitzgerald; Nice; Colo. JP. CDs: Prest., incl. four tracks as leader and two as sideman w. Bennie Green in *Prestige First Sessions, Vol. 3*; Riv.; Pab.; BB; Story.; B&B; Enja; Steep.; Divox; w. Basie (Mos.; Roul.; Pab.; Verve); w. Benny Carter; Fitzgerald; D. Gillespie; Milt Jackson; O. Peterson (Pab.); H. Edison (Riv.; Pab.; B&B); Hawkins; R. Garland (Prest.); F. Navarro (Sav.); Eddie Vinson (B&B).

DAVIS, JESSE, alto sax; comp; b. New Orleans, LA, 9/11/65. Brother, Roger, pl. tba. Began on dms., tpt.; alto sax at 11. Stud. at NOCCA 1982–3; Northeastern Ill. U., Chi., '83–6; William Paterson Coll. (N.J.) '86–7; New Sch. Began lead. own gps. in NYC '86. Pl. w. Illinois Jacquet '87–90. Tour. Japan w. all-star band, incl. Donald Byrd, Jimmy Heath, '91. In '90s, he app. w. LCJO; Battle Royale, altos, at Lincoln Center; Philip Morris All-Stars; George Wein's Newport All-Stars; Nicholas Payton qnt.; Hank Jones qnt. Moved back to NO at end of '95. A fluid player w. a singing sound, infused w. strong blues feeling. Favs: C. Parker, Benny Carter, Sonny Stitt. Fests: all major, incl. all-star gp. w. M. Tormé, JVC-NY, '96; Payton, JVC-NY, San Sebastian, '97. Film and Video: *Kansas City*. CDs: Conc.; w. Cedar Walton (Muse); Tana-Reid; Robert Trowers (Conc.); *Kansas City* band; Stephen Scott (Verve); Sebastian Whittaker (Just.); Fabio Morgera (Ken).

DAVIS, KAY (Kathryn Elizabeth Wimp), voc; b. Evanston, IL, 12/5/20. Voice major, pno. stud. at Northwestern U., 1938–43. Recital work in Chi., bef. join. Duke Ellington, autumn '44. Feat. mainly in wordless vocals in the style Ellington had introduced w. Adelaide Hall in '27. Made film shorts w. the band,

toured Engl. and Continent '48, w. Ellington and Ray Nance; in '50 visited France w. entire band. Left Ellington June '50, married Edward Wimp, retired fr. mus. and settled in Chi. The almost ethereal sound of her precise soprano can be heard to great effect on "Mood Indigo"; "Minnehaha"; "On a Turquoise Cloud"; "Creole Love Call"; and "Transblucency." Film: soundies for Universal w. Ellington. CDs: w. Ellington (RCA; Musi.; Col.; Prest.).

DAVIS, LEM (LEMUEL ARTHUR), alto sax; b. Tampa, FL, 6/22/14; d. NYC, 1/16/70. Played in Tampa w. Charlie Brantley's Collegians 1937–8. Moved to NYC ca. '40; rec. w. Harold Boyce's Harlem Indians '41. Came to prominence in early '40s, pl. on 52nd St. w. Nat Jaffe; Coleman Hawkins; Eddie Heywood; Rex Stewart. Rec. comp. "'Taint Me" w. Heywood '44. Made several recs. as leader '45–6 for Savoy. Pl. w. John Kirby '46, then rejoin. Heywood. Led own gp. and pl. w. pnst. Teacho Wiltshire; Buck Clayton in NYC '50s-60s. LP: own gp. in *Changing Face of Harlem, Vol. 2* (Sav.). CDs: w. Clayton (Mos.); Joe Thomas's Big Six in *Giants of Small Band Swing, Vol. 2* (Riv.).

DAVIS, (THOMAS) MAXWELL, tnr sax, comp, arr; b. Independence, KS, 1/14/16; d. Los Angeles, CA, 9/18/70. Studied vln. and alto sax in Wichita, Kansas, where he led his own band for four yrs. Moved to West Coast in 1936, pl. w. Woodman bros. '36–7; sw. to tnr. while w. Gene Coy in Seattle, Wash. Moved to LA in '37, worked w. Fletcher Henderson; three yrs. in burlesque shows; then to San Diego, Calif., w. Happy Johnson. Dur. '40s, he wrote arr. for Jimmie Lunceford; perf. in early JATP concerts. As a&r dir. for Aladdin Recs. '46–54 , he prod., arr., and pl. (as sideman and leader) on the label's sess. Also worked for other labels, incl. Cap. and B&W. Moved to the Modern label in '54. Fr. '58 to 60, Davis wrote bb arrs. for a series of Crown albums dedicated to Ellington; Basie; Woody Herman; Tommy Dorsey; and Lionel Hampton. Favs: Coleman Hawkins; arr: Sy Oliver. Recs. incl. *Idaho* w. Ray Anthony; also w. Jesse Price; Geechie Smith; Helen Humes; June Christy; Ella Mae Morse; Pete Johnson; Red Callender; Jay McShann; Joe Turner. CDs: w. King Pleasure (BN).

DAVIS, MILES DEWEY JR., tpt, flg, comp, lead; b. Alton, IL, 5/25/26; d. Santa Monica, CA, 9/28/91. Grew up in East St. Louis, Ill. Father, a dentist, gave him a tpt. for his 13th birthday. Studied w. Elwood Buchanan; Joseph Gustat of St. Louis Symph. Pl. in hs band; w. Eddie Randall in St. Louis 1941–3. Clark Terry, whom he heard and met locally, was an early infl. He also met Charlie Parker and Dizzy Gillespie when the Billy Eckstine band pl. an engagement in St. Louis. Came to NYC in the fall of '44 to attend Juilliard, but bef. long was working on 52nd St. Pl. w. Charlie Parker '45–8; also w. Coleman Hawkins on 52nd St.; and the orchs. of Eckstine, Benny Carter in Calif. He led a gp. w. Parker, Kai Winding, Allen Eager at Royal Roost, NYC '48. The same yr., Davis organized a nonet that rec. for Cap. and became known as the "Birth of the Cool" band. The gp. used an instrumentation never bef. heard in jazz, w. French horn and tba. in addition to tpt., tbn., alto and bari saxes, pno., bs., and dms. Arrs. incl. Gil Evans and Gerry Mulligan, who along w. altoist Lee Konitz had been members of the Claude Thornhill Orch. Although the nonet was not a commercial success, it is of historical importance since it initiated the less aggressive and hard-edged style of bebop known as cool jazz, later associated w. the Calif. jazz scene of the 1950s. Pl. w. Sonny Rollins, Art Blakey, Tadd Dameron '49, co-leading combo with Dameron at Paris JF. Own gps. NYC '50–1. Tour. w. gp. Jazz Inc. that incl. Milt Jackson, Zoot Sims, under Symphony Sid's aegis, '52. Also rec. in early '50s w. Parker; Rollins; Blakey; J.J. Johnson; Horace Silver; et al. Led first Miles Davis Qnt. w. John Coltrane, Red Garland, Paul Chambers, Philly Joe Jones '55–7. He was featured on flg. on the album *Miles Ahead* w. Gil Evans and 19-pc. orch. '57. Further celebrated orchestral collab. w. Evans were *Porgy and Bess* '58 and *Sketches of Spain* '60. Led qnt. w. Cannonball Adderley briefly in '58. Scored French film *Ascenseur Pour L'echafaud* by improvising to the film on a screen in studio. Re-formed 1955 qnt., adding Cannonball Adderley as sixth member, '58. Led qnts. and sxts. w. sidemen incl. Red Garland, Bill Evans, Wynton Kelly, P.J. Jones, Jimmy Cobb, Paul Chambers, Sonny Stitt, Jimmy Heath, Hank Mobley '58–63. Recorded the seminal, modal album *Kind of Blue* '59.

Formed qnt. w. Herbie Hancock, Ron Carter, Tony Williams, Geo. Coleman '63; Wayne Shorter repl. Coleman, '64. Davis led this gp., which pl. jazz origs. rather than standards or show tunes, '64–8. Chick Corea and Dave Holland repl. Hancock, Carter '68. Rec. jazz-rock album *In a Silent Way* w. Hancock, Corea, Joe Zawinul, elec. kybds.; John McLaughlin, gtr. '69. Later the same yr., he rec. a harder-edged jazz-rock LP, *Bitches' Brew*, and cont. in this direction w. *A Tribute to Jack Johnson* '70; *Live-Evil* '71; and the more dance-oriented *On the Corner* '72. In the early '70s, Davis occ. used a wah-wah pedal w. his tpt. Illness and injuries sustained in a '72 car accident forced Davis into retirement in the mid '70s. He returned to the scene in '80 and in '81 released the album *We Want Miles*. He began touring w. a new qnt. and sxt. in '81. A few mos. after suffering a stroke in Feb. '82, he resumed activity. Sidemen incl. Robert Irving III ('80–7); Al Foster ('80–5); saxist Bill Evans ('80–4); John Scofield ('82–5); Branford Marsalis ('84–5); Bob Berg ('84–7); J. DeFrancesco, Adam Holtzman ('88); Kei Akagi ('89–90); and Kenny Garrett. Played the classic Gil Evans charts (abetted by Wallace Roney) w. an orch. under the dir. of Quincy Jones at Montreaux JF '91.

Davis, whose early style in Parker's quintet owed much to Freddie Webster, developed his own persona out of Webster and Dizzy Gillespie's styles during his time with Parker. His reflective solos with his own nonet, occupying the horn's middle register for the most part, prompted Barry Ulanov to describe his playing as "a man walking on eggshells." However, Davis's upper-register flights with his and Tadd Dameron's group at the Paris JF and on a Metronome All-Star recording with Gillespie and Fats Navarro (both '49) revealed another side of him. Although he did not concentrate on this aspect, he did employ a harder-edged swing in the '50s and '60s while also winning accolades for his moody, often-muted ballads and judicious use of space. Perhaps because of his very sophistication, he was never accorded proper recognition for his mastery in the blues that ran through his entire career and its many stylistic settings; e.g., "Now's the Time" and "Billie's Bounce" (w. Parker), to "Bluing"; "Walkin'"; "Blues for Pablo"; "Miles Runs the Voodoo Down"; and "Star People."

Favs: Armstrong, Eldridge, Gillespie, Bobby Hackett, Harry James, Clark Terry, Freddie Webster. Polls: *Esq.* New Star '47; *Met.* '51–3, '58–60; *DB* Readers '55, '57–9; *DB* Critics '55 (tie w. Gillespie), '59; *Play.* '60. CDs: WB; Col.; Prest.; BN; Cap.; BL; Sav.; Deb.; Cont.; w. C. Parker (Sav.; Stash; Verve); C. Hawkins (Cap.).

DAVIS, NATHAN TATE, saxes, fl; bs cl, educ; b. Kansas City, KS, 2/15/37. Played w. Jay McShann in KC. Dur. long stay in Eur., tour. w. Art Blakey, worked w. Eric Dolphy, Donald Byrd, and the Kenny Clarke–Francy Boland bb. Ret. to US to head jazz dept. at U. of Pitts. 1969, where he established annual seminars w. concert and a jazz hall of fame. Dur. the next two decades, while remaining active as a tnr. saxist and cont. at U. of Pitts., he lectured extensively and taught saxophone at Oberlin Cons. Tour. w. Paris Reunion Band, Eur. '85. Books: *Writings in Jazz* '85; autobiography, *Paris-Pittsburgh: A Story in Jazz–The Life of Nathan Davis*, co-written w. Gisela Albus, was publ. in Germ. but printed almost entirely in English '91. In the '80s, Davis was the recipient of many academic honors and awards. CDs: DIW; w. Dolphy

(WW); Paris Reunion Band (Gazell); D. Goykovich (Enja); Roots (In&Out).

DAVIS, RICHARD, bs; b. Chicago, IL, 4/15/30. Attended DuSable HS. Stud. priv. w. Rudolph Fahsbender 1945–54; at Vandercook Coll. of Mus., '48–52, B. Mus. Ed.; also at DePaul U., Roosevelt U., City Coll. of Chi. Pl. w. Youth Orch. of Chi. '46–8; Chi. Civic Orch., DePaul and Roosevelt U. orchs. '48–54; local dance bands led by Eddie King, Walter Dyett '52–3; Ahmad Jamal '53–4; Don Shirley '54–5; Benny Goodman, Sauter-Finegan Orch., Charlie Ventura mid '50s. Managed family restaurant bus. mid '50s. Tour. and rec. w. Sarah Vaughan '57–60; pl. w. Kenny Burrell '59; Gunther Schuller's Orch. USA '61–4. Classical jobs w. Igor Stravinsky, Leonard Bernstein early '60s. Following his work w. Eric Dolphy–Booker Little at the Five Spot in '61, Davis became one of the most sought-after modern bssts. Pl. w. Dolphy '61–4; extensive freelancing w. Ben Sidran, Ben Webster, Charles Lloyd, Booker Ervin, Chick Corea, Dave Brubeck, Earl Hines, Stan Getz, Bobby Hackett, Al Cohn–Zoot Sims, Andrew Hill, James Moody, J.J. Johnson, Frank Sinatra, etc. '65–75; also rec. own LPs for Muse and worked w. rock mus., incl. John Lennon; Bruce Springsteen; Van Morrison. Pl. w. Thad Jones–Mel Lewis Orch. '66–72, incl. Russian tour; NYC Bass Choir fr. '69. Perf. w. NY Philharm. '73, '75. Also pl. on film soundtracks, incl. *Holy Mountain*, and jingles. Davis moved to Madison, Wisc., in '77 to take a teaching post at U. of Wisc. and pursue his other passion, raising horses. Pl. in '80s w. J.J. Johnson; McCoy Tyner–Elvin Jones; David Murray–Joe Chambers; Ben Sidran; Barbara London–Phil Wilson; Van Morrison. Davis has led his own qnt., modeled after the Dolphy-Little Qnt., off and on fr. the early '80s. Davis is the author of an instr. book, *Writing on Chords*, and hosts a jazz radio prog. on WMAD. Favs: Eddie Gomez, Ron Carter, Cecil McBee, Gary Karr. Polls: *Jazz* mag., *DB* Critics '66; *DB* TDWR '67–74; *DB* Readers '68–72; ASCAP Awd. (12 times). Fests: all major fr. '65. TV: ABC *Like It Is* w. Bass Choir; *Black Journal*; *Soul Train*; Jerry Lewis Telethon; Barbra Streisand, Bob Hope specials, etc. CDs: DiscUnion; DIW; Hep; SB; w. Dolphy-Little; Booker Ervin; Eddie Daniels; P. Martino; Lucky Thompson (Prest.); Dolphy (Prest.; BN; WW; Enja); A. Hill; Gillespie; B. Hutcherson (BN); G. Evans; Getz; J. Hodges; W. Montgomery (Verve); James Williams; C. Jordan; R. Hanna (DIW); Ben Webster (Riv.); Joe Henderson (Cont.; BN); Jones-Lewis (LRC); Jazz Comp. Orch. (JCOA); NY Unit; L. Soloff; Donald Harrison (PW); Milt Jackson; Elvin Jones (Imp.); C. Walton (Prest.; Steep.); RR Kirk (Em., Merc.).

DAVIS, SAMMY JR., voc; dancer, also dms; b. NYC, 12/8/25; d. Beverly Hills, CA, 5/16/90. From age 4, he tour. w. his fath. and uncle, Will Mastin, as a vaudeville act, the Will Mastin Trio. In 1931, he app. w. Ethel Waters in a film, *Rufus Jones for President*. Except for army service '43–5, he cont. to work w. Mastin Trio until the late '50s, when his fath. and uncle retired. Made rec. debut on Cap. '49, by which time he had established himself as a vocal impressionist. But by '53, when he sw. to Decca., he decidedly had his own voc. style. By mid '50s he had become a major entertainer. Made B'way debut in *Mr. Wonderful* '56, and scored great success in *Golden Boy* '64, repeating his role in London prod. '68. A capable dmr., he occ. subbed w. Lionel Hampton and Woody Herman; also pl. other instruments, incl. tpt., vib. Films: *Porgy and Bess*, '59; *A Man Called Adam* '66. Book: autobiography, *Yes I Can*. CDs: WB; Dec.; *Sammy Davis Jr. Sings and Laurindo Almeida Plays* (Sandstone); w. Basie (Verve).

DAVIS, SPANKY (RONALD J.), tpt, flg, pno; b. Indianapolis, IN, 3/6/43. Mother pl. pno. and taught mus.; bro., Jan, pl. alto sax. Raised in Ft. Wayne, Ind. Began on pno. at age 6; tpt. at age 7. Stud. w. priv. teachers, later w. Geo. Bean in Chi. '71–2; Jimmy Maxwell in NYC '78–9. Pl. w. Thunderbirds '58–9, Silhouettes '59–61 in Ft. Wayne; Jess Gayer Orch. in Grand Island, Nebraska '61–2; Don Glasser in Chi. '63–5; Howard McGhee bb, Sammy Kaye in NYC '66; Tiny Hill in Chi. '66–8. Led own dixieland band in Ft. Wayne '68–9, then pl. in Chi. w. Ralph Marterie '70–4; Bill Reinhardt '77; Jim Beebe's Chi. Jazz '77–8. Moved to NYC '78, began subbing for Roy Eldridge at Jimmy Ryan's. Pl. w. Charlie Palmieri '79; Machito '79–80; Sam Jones bb '79–81. Replaced Eldridge as leader at Ryan's '80 and remained until club closed in Dec. '83. Pl. w. Gerry Mulligan Orch. '80–1; Benny Goodman Sxt. '81–2; Panama Francis's Savoy Sultans '83–6; Butch Miles's Jazz Express, '85–6; Buck Clayton bb '88–91; Annie Ross; Frank Sinatra '91–2. Freelance in '80s-90s w. Buddy Tate; Billy Mitchell; Al Cohn; Scott Hamilton; Jay McShann; Jim Galloway; Bob Haggart; Carl Fontana; Al Grey; Frank Wess; others. Favs: Eldridge, Sweets Edison, Clifford Brown. Fests: Eur. fr. '80; Japan fr. '88. Film: app. in *Machito: A Latin Jazz Legacy*. Rec. w. Butch Miles. CDs: w. Buck Clayton; Panama Francis (Stash); J. DeFrancesco (Col.); Ruth Brown (Fant.).

DAVIS, STANTON JR., tpt, comp; b. New Orleans, LA, 11/10/45. Attended Berklee 1967–9, New Engl. Cons. '69–73. Was program dir. for MIT radio station '68–74. M. Mus. in ethnomusicology fr. Wesleyan U.

'83. Pl. in clubs around Bost., then w. George Russell; Mercer Ellington; Lester Bowie; Charlie Haden; G. Gruntz; Jim Pepper; Bob Stewart; Muhal Richard Abrams; Sam Rivers; Gil Evans; Webster Lewis; Jaki Byard; Max Roach; James Moody. Deep involvement as educ. w. Southeast. Mass. U '76–8; Jazzmobile '80–8; Wellesley Coll. '81–4; Bennington Coll. '80–2; New Engl. Cons. '80–2. Davis has also pl. for TV and B'way shows, incl. *Black and Blue; Ain't Misbehavin'; Sophisticated Ladies*. He has received comp.'s grants fr. the MA Foundation for the Arts and the NEA. Favs: M. Davis, Dorham, Hubbard. CDs: w. Russell (SN); Art Ens. of Chi.; Bowie; Abrams (BS); J. Pepper; Ray Anderson (Enja).

DAVIS, STEVE (STEPHEN; aka Luquman Abdul Syeed), bs; b. Philadelphia, PA, 1929; d. Philadelphia, 8/21/87. Worked locally in Phila., then in NYC w. Lester Young; Jimmy Heath; Sonny Stitt. Pl. w. John Coltrane 1960–1; also worked w. James Moody '61–2. Rec. w. Moody, Dave Burns, Freddie McCoy in '60s. CDs: w. Coltrane (Atl.); Chuck Mangione (Riv.); Eddie Jefferson (Prest.); McCoy Tyner (Imp.).

DAVIS, STEVE (STEPHEN K.), tbn; b. Worcester, MA, 4/14/67. Grandparents, fath. are mus. Began on tpt., then sw. to bari. horn and tba. bef. settling on tbn. Gigs dur. hs at Music Box, Binghamton, N.Y., pl. tbn. and bs. Stud. under Jackie McLean at Hartt Coll. of Mus. 1985–8. Pl. w. Eddie Henderson–Ron Bridgewater '88; own qnt. since '88; Hotep Galeta '88–9; Charli Persip '88–91; Art Blakey '89–90; Geoff Keezer '90; Jackie McLean since '90; Elvin Jones '90–1; Lionel Hampton, Woody Herman '91; Michael Weiss fr. '95; Mingus bb, R. Hargrove bb, fr. '97; C. Corea fr. '97. Faculty: Artist's Collective since '87; Hartt since '91. Favs: J.J. Johnson, Curtis Fuller, Grachan Moncur III, Slide Hampton. Fests: Eur. and Japan w. Blakey '90. TV: WTBS w. Blakey, '89; Eur. TV w. Blakey, '90. CDs: CC; Brown; w. Blakey (Timel.; A&M); J. McLean (Bird.; Toshiba/EMI); Leon Parker (Col.); Corea (Stretch).

DAVIS, TROY JEROME, dms; b. Baton Rouge, LA, 11/29/65. Father, Earl, is pnst; sist. Jodie Davis Whitfield is singer, married to gtrst. Mark Whitfield. Began on dms. at age 3. Stud. at Southern U. 1983–6. Pl. w. Alvin Batiste '83–6; Henry Butler '87; Betty Carter '87–9; Wynton Marsalis '89; Roy Hargrove '90; Marlon Jordan, Mark Whitfield, Terence Blanchard fr. '90. Favs: Elvin Jones, Tony Williams, Jack DeJohnette, Ben Riley. Fests: Eur., Japan fr. '87. TV: Cosby Show w. Betty Carter; *Sunday Night* w. Carter, Branford Marsalis, David Sanborn. CDs: w. Whitfield (WB); Jordan (Col.; Arab.); Blanchard (Col.).

DAVIS, WALTER JR., pno, comp; b. Richmond, VA, 9/2/32; d. NYC, 6/2/90. Raised in East Orange, N.J. Moth. pl. gospel mus.; uncles pnsts. As a teenager, he pl. around Newark; left sch. to go to Montreal, Can., w. Babs Gonzales's gp. Moved to NYC in early '50s, pl. w. Charlie Parker and Max Roach '52, remaining in Roach's gp. through '53; join. Dizzy Gillespie '56, incl. Eur. and Mid-East State Dept. tour; Eur. tour w. Donald Byrd, Art Taylor '58; join. Art Blakey '59. In early '60s, led own trio, duo; worked w. Philly Joe Jones, Jackie McLean. Left mus. mid late '60s, worked as a tailor, designer; stud. and pl. in India '69. Resumed mus. career in NYC: pl. w. Doctor John, Rolling Stones '69; Sonny Rollins '73–4; Blakey '75; NYC apps. w. own trio; apps. w. Blakey all-star gp. '83, '85. Favs: Tatum, Bud Powell. Film: soundtrack of *Bird* '87. TV: *Focus* w. Betty Carter, Wash., D.C. Fests: NJF-NY w. Rollins '74; Blakey '75; Antwerp; Naarden; Toulon; Bologna, '90. Comp: "Greasy"; "Uranus"; "On the Real Side." CDs: BN; JC; Den.; Red; Maple.; Steep.; w. Art Taylor; S. Criss (Prest.); Gillespie (CAP; Verve); Rollins (Mile.); McLean (BN); Archie Shepp (Imp.; Den.).

DAVIS, WILD BILL (WILLIAM STRETHEN), org, pno, arr; b. Glasgow, MO, 11/24/18; d. Moorestown, NJ, 8/17/95. Raised in Parsons, Kansas. Stud. mus. w. fath., a prof. singer; later at Tuskegee Inst. on scholarship; Wiley Coll. While in sch., he pl. pno. and gtr. Moved to Chi., worked w. Milt Larkin as gtr. and arr. 1939–42; arr. for Earl Hines '43; pno. and arr. for Louis Jordan '45–8. Focused on Hammond org. '49 and by '50 had started a trend that had many jazz pnsts. doubling on org. Fr. '51, tour. w. own trio, incl. gtr. and dms. Also cont. as an arr. and scored an enormous success in '55 w. chart of "April in Paris" for Basie. Fr. '50 through mid '60s, pl. summers annually at Grace's Little Belmont Club in Atlantic City, N.J. Tour. w. Duke Ellington '69–71, pl. second pno. when Ellington had a hand ailment '69; also pl. org. and contributed some arr. Dur. '70s, he tour. extens. as soloist, frequently in France, where he made numerous recs. for B&B. Worked w. Lionel Hampton '78–80; cont. activity, '80s and '90s. Though now considered a pioneering jazz orgst., Davis's forceful style earned him more popularity in r&b circles than in jazz in the '50s and '60s. Early favs: Tatum, Hines; org., Waller, Basie. Fests: NJF-NY '73–4; many in Eur.; pno. w. Duke's Men, JVC-NY JF. Own LPs on Epic; Everest; RCA. CDs: B&B; w. Arnett Cobb (Prest.); J. Hodges (BB; Verve); E. Fitzgerald (Verve); F. Morgan (Cont.; FS); Illinois Jacquet (B&B; Verve); Slam Stewart; Buddy Tate; Eddie Vinson; Lockjaw Davis (B&B); Ellington (Fant.; Atl.); L. Hampton; Chris Barber (Timel.).

DAVIS, WILL (WILLIAM E.), pno; b. Chicago, IL, 2/17/26; d. Detroit, MI, 3/24/84. Father pl. cl. Stud. priv. in Roanoke, Va., later at Det. Cons. Pl. w. Snookum Russell, Paul Bascomb, early 1940s; Howard McGhee in Chi. '46; Milt Jackson, Sonny Stitt, Wardell Gray in Det. House pnst. at Crystal Bar, backing Coleman Hawkins, Lester Young, Charlie Parker–Miles Davis '53. Freelanced in NYC in '50s, incl. Kenny Burrell Qt. Favs: Billy Kyle, Sir Charles Thompson, Bud Powell, Tatum, John Lewis. LP: Sue. CDs: w. Jackson-Stitt (Gal.); Burrell (Prest.).

DAVISON, WILD BILL (WILLIAM EDWARD), crnt, lead; b. Defiance, OH, 1/5/06; d. Santa Barbara, CA, 11/14/89. First instruments. were bjo., mand., gtr; then sw. to mello., crnt.; pl. bjo. and mello. in hs band. Worked w. local bands., incl. Chubb-Steinberg orch. w. which he made rec. debut 1924; band pl. in NYC as Omer-Hicks orch. '26. Went to Chi.; pl. w. Seattle Harmony Kings '27; various Chi. bands, incl. Benny Meroff, to '32. He form. a bb w. Frank Teschemacher '31, but bef. it could open, in March '32, Teschemacher was killed in an accident as he and Davison drove back fr. a rehearsal. Davison moved to Milwaukee, Wisc., and worked as leader and sideman there, also frequently in Chi. '33–41; dur. this period, he doubled on v-tbn. Moved to NYC in spring '41; led own band at Nick's to '42. In '43, he led a gp. in Bost.; recreated ODJB for dancer Katherine Dunham's revue; pl. at Jimmy Ryan's, NYC. Served in army fr. late '43 to '45. After discharge, he pl. w. Art Hodes at Village Vanguard, then led own band in St. Louis, bef. becoming a regular at Eddie Condon's '45–57. Tour. Engl. w. Condon '57, initiating an annual int'l tour routine that he maintained for the rest of his career. Tour w. own band in '64; solo tours throughout '60s. Moved to LA '60, but was mostly on the road; extensive US tours '60–6, but also ret. to Nick's for a yr. '62–3; Metropole Café '64. Between '65 and '75, Davison pl. and/or rec. w. over 100 different bands, incl. Can., Engl., Dan., and Swiss. Led Jazz Giants '68; US tour w. Bigard, Condon, Hodes '71. Fr. '73 to '75, he was based in Wash., D.C., working only occ.; cont. to pl. in Eur. '70s, '80s. Celebrated 80th birthday w. concert at Town Hall, NYC. Early infl: Beiderbecke. Favs: Armstrong, Hackett. One of the most colorful figures fr. the late '20s Chi. scene, his playing was described by John Wilson of the *NY Times* as "the cockiest, sassiest, even blowsiest trumpet style in jazz." His big, vibrant sound never lost the vigor and ebullience that helped establish his mus. individuality in a much earlier era. Fests: Colo. and Odessa, Tex., JPs '65–6; Big Horn JF '72; Det. JF '73–4; Nice '74; NJF '78. TV: Tribute to Condon '64. Book: *The Wildest One* by Hal Willard (Avondale Press) '96. CDs: Comm.; Sack.; Jazz.; w. Pee Wee Russell (Comm.); Bechet (Mos.); Condon (Col.; Sav.; Jazz.); w. Bechet; Hodes in *Hot Jazz on Blue Note* (BN).

DAWSON, (GEORGE) ALAN, dms, vib; b. Marietta, PA, 7/14/29; d. Lexington, MA, 2/23/96. Father pl. pno., gtr., sang; moth. pl. pno., sang. Stud. w. Chas. Alden in Bost. 1947–51. Pl. w. Tasker Crosson '43–4; Hopeton Johnson '45; Jimmy Martin '47; Buster Daniels, Wilbur Pinckney, Phil Barboza, Art Royall, Ike Roberts '48; Ray Perry, Frankie Newton '49; Sabby Lewis '50–1; Serge Chaloff '51. Mil. service '51–3, pl. in army band bef. join. Lionel Hampton for three mos., incl. Eur./Africa tour. Pl. w. Sabby Lewis '53–6, then join. faculty of Berklee Coll. of Mus. While there, he pl. w. John and Paul Neves '58–61; Al Vega '59; Herb Pomeroy '61–2; house band at Lennie's on the Turnpike '62–70; Dave Brubeck '68–75; qt. w. Bill Pierce, James Williams in '80s. Also extensive freelance w. Roy Eldridge; Charlie Shavers; Buck Clayton; Red Allen; Phil Woods; Coleman Hawkins; Zoot Sims; Al Cohn; Booker Ervin; Sonny Stitt; Budd Johnson; Jaki Byard; Junior Mance. With Byard and Richard Davis he helped form an extraordinary rhythm section which made some exceptional recs. w. Ervin for Prest. '63–4. Dawson is the author of *A Manual for the Modern Drummer* w. Don De Micheal '64; and *Blues and Odd Time Signatures* '72. His students at Berklee incl. Tony Williams; Clifford Jarvis; Harvey Mason; Joe LaBarbera. He was a resourceful, musical drummer w. unerring time built into his drive. Favs: Jo Jones, S. Catlett, M. Roach, R. Haynes. Polls: *DB* New Star '65; *Mod. Drummer* Best Small Gp. '85; Bost. Jazz Society '85. Fests: Eur. fr. '65; Japan fr. '78; Cascais JF, Portugal, '91. TV: PBS specials w. Brubeck, Oscar Peterson. CDs: w. Ervin; Byard; S. Criss; T. Farlow; D. Gordon; I. Jacquet (Prest.); C. Brown (RCA; Prest.); Woods; S. Stitt (Muse; 32); Brubeck (Col.; Atl.); H. Alden; K. Peplowski; R. Braff (Conc.); C. Neville (Eve. Star); Hampton (BB); R. Hanna; Hank Jones (B&B); Donald Brown (JC); Satchmo Legacy Band (SN).

DE ARANGO, BILL (WILLIAM), gtr; b. Cleveland, OH, 9/20/21; d. East Cleveland, 12/26/05. Studied at Ohio State U.; pl. w. local gps. 1939–42; army '42–4. Pl. w. Ben Webster on 52nd St., NYC. In '45–6, he rec. w. Charlie Parker; Dizzy Gillespie; Lockjaw Davis; Ike Quebec. Pl. w. Ray Nance, then led own gp. feat. Terry Gibbs in NYC and Chi. Moved back to Cleveland '48. Except for a sess. for Em. in '54, he was relatively inactive as a player for quite a while, devoting his time instead to running a mus. store and coaching gtr. students. Later, he occ. pl. w. pnst. Bill Dinasco and, in the late '60s, briefly managed Henry Tree, a rock gp. w. which he also rec. anonymously '70. Pl. at Comeback Inn in Venice, Calif., late '80s. He had a fluid, modern style that in the '40s placed him in the vanguard of bop gtrsts. He used a sensitive, Germ.-made pedal to improvise "beginning with little figures and then extending them fr. a softer vein to really wild." In '90s, pl. at the Barking Spider in Cleveland. LP: w. Red Norvo (Xan,). CDs: GM; w. Gillespie (BB).

DE BREST, SPANKY (JAMES), bs; b. Philadelphia, PA, 4/24/37; d. Philadelphia, 3/2/73. Began pl. locally w. Marian Anderson's nephew, Jimmy DePreist, and Lee Morgan. To NYC, working w. Art Blakey fr. Jul. 1956 to Apr. '58; ret. to Phila. and join. J.J. Johnson sxt. Nov. '58 for two yrs., then pl. w. Phila. pnst. Harold Corbin. A long illness disrupted his career fr. late '50s. Favs: Percy Heath, Pettiford, R. Brown, W. Ware. Recs. w. J.J. Johnson. CDs: w. Blakey (Col.; BB; Atl.; BN; Sav.); C. Jordan (Riv.); L. Morgan (FS); J. Coltrane (Prest. boxed set); Ray Draper (NJ).

DE FAUT, VOLLY (VOLTAIRE), cl, saxes; b. Little Rock, AR, 3/14/04; d. So. Chicago Hts., IL, 5/29/73. Raised in Chi.; stud. vln. at age 6; cl. and sax at 14. Worked w. Sig Meyers 1922; NORK '23; perf. and rec. w. Merritt Brunies '24–6. In '26, he went to Det. w. Ray Miller; also pl. w. Isham Jones, Jean Goldkette's orch. '28–9. Through '30s, did radio work; staff mus. at WGN, Chi.; then in army. Also active as a dog-breeder, he only gigged intermittently fr. mid '40s: w. Bud Jacobson '45; Doc Evans '50; Art Hodes '53. He remained relatively unknown although he was among the best Chi. cls. who had mastered the NO style. Towards the end of his career, he used a electronic amplification device on his cl. Recs: w. Brunies; M. Spanier '24; Jelly Roll Morton '25; Goldkette '28; Hodes '53 and '68. CDs: w. The Bucktown Five in *Bix Beiderbecke and the Chicago Cornets* (Mile.); Stomp Six in *Riverside History of Classic Jazz* (Riv.); Hodes (Del.); Spanier (ASV).

DE GRAAFF, REIN, pno; b. Groningen, Netherlands, 10/24/42. Studied priv. 1952–6. Pl. w. Jenna Meinema '57. Formed own trio and qt. '60. Pl. in Germ. w. Jazzopators '62–3. Pl. w. local gps. while stationed w. Dutch army at NATO base in Germ. '63. Pl. w. Erwin Somer '63–4. Led qt. w. Dick Vennik fr. '64. Pl. w. Gijs Hendriks '64–5. Visited US in late '67, sat in w. Lee Morgan; Hank Mobley; Elvin Jones. Pl. w. René Thomas '73–4. De Graaf has accomp. many Amer. mus. in Eur. incl. Mobley; Mor-

gan; Johnny Griffin; Art Taylor; Clifford Jordan; Cecil Payne; Dexter Gordon; Clark Terry; Sonny Stitt; Kenny Dorham; Milt Jackson; Philly Joe Jones; Arnett Cobb; Charlie Rouse; Billy Mitchell; Pepper Adams; Lee Konitz; Bud Shank; Art Farmer; others. He perf. in the US in '70s w. Ronnie Cuber; Valery Ponomarev; Evelyn Blakey; Paul Jeffrey; Curtis Fuller. Favs: Bud Powell, L. Tristano, Hampton Hawes, Barry Harris. Polls: Boy Edgar Awd. '80; Bird Awd. '86. Fests: all major Eur. TV: Eur. TV w. Terry, Benny Bailey, own gps. CDs: Timel.; w. Al Cohn; Griffin; Cobb; T. Edwards; M. Holley; Fathead Newman; D. Pike (Timel.).

DE HAAS, EDDIE (EDGAR O.), bs, gtr; b. Bandoeng, Java (now Indonesia), 2/21/30. Father pl. fl. Pl. gtr. in Bandoeng, then moved to Netherlands in 1946. In Eur., pl. bs. w. Pia Beck '50; Wally Bishop, Don Byas '51; Bill Coleman '52–3; Martial Solal '52–6; Henri Renaud '55; Chet Baker '55–6. Moved to NYC, pl. w. Larry Sohn, Terry Gibbs, Miles Davis '57; Blossom Dearie, Kai Winding, Benny Goodman, Charlie Mariano–Toshiko Akiyoshi '58; Roy Haynes, Kenny Burrell, Chris Connor '59–61; Johnny Mathis '62; Gene Krupa '64–5. Freelance in Chi. since '68. Favs: Pettiford, Ray Brown. Fests: Eur.; Japan, Mex. w. Gene Krupa; Chi. JF since '75. Films: *Let's Get Lost* w. Chet Baker. TV: Steve Allen '63; WTTW-Chi. w. Joe Williams. CDs: w. Roy Haynes (NJ); C. Baker (Em.; Jazz Anthol.; Accord); Sonny Stitt (Verve); Von Freeman; Louis Smith (Steep.); M. Mezzrow (Jazz Time).

DE LA ROSA, FRANK (FRANCISCO ESTABAN JR.), bs; b. El Paso, TX, 12/26/33. Father and bro. both mus. Stud. at LA Cons. of Mus. 1956–8. Worked w. Latin gps. until '59, then moved to LV to work in casino bands. Ret. to LA '65; pl. w. Don Ellis '66–8; Sweets Edison '68–9; Ella Fitzgerald '69–72; Don Menza '72–5; Sarah Vaughan '74–5. CDs: w. Fitzgerald (Pab.).

DE MERLE, LES (LESTER WILLIAM), dms, comp; also perc, pno; b. Brooklyn, NY, 11/4/46. Studied dms. and perc. w. Bob Livingston, NYC, 1960–5; attended Berklee Coll. of Mus., stud. theory and harm. w. Alf Clausen. Worked w. Lionel Hampton at 16; w. Billy Williams Revue, Connie Haines '65; Lee Castle–Jimmy Dorsey band '66. Form. his first gp. in '67 w. Randy Brecker, Arnie Lawrence; in late '60s gigged around NYC w. Joe Farrell; Lee Konitz; others. Moved to LA in '71; form. own gp., Transfusion. In '72, he opened the Cellar Theater, which was the gp.'s home base and a showcase for young artists. App. at NJF '74 w. Harry James. Publ:

Jazz-Rock Fusion, Vols I & II (Try Pubs., Hollywood, Calif.). CD: w. Richie Cole (Muse).

De NICOLA, TONY (ANTONIO EMEDIO), dms, educ; b. Pennington, NJ, 9/2/27; d. Philadelphia, 9/2/06. Brother Robert prof. tpt. and master brass instrument and mouthpiece maker. Stud. pno., theory; dms. at age 12 in grade sch. Pl. in hs, American Legion, firehouse marching bands; polka bands; and dance bands in night clubs. Army air force 1946–7, pl. in AF and Special Services bands. Pnst. Donn Trenner got him start. w. Chick Foster band in Midwest '48. Left Foster w. Trenner and went to SF '49, pl. there that yr. Helped at grandparents' tavern in Trenton '50, then pl w. Freddy Martin orch. '50–1. Pl. w. Charlie Ventura on and off '51–8. Join. Harry James '58–62. Pl. w. Billy Butterfield, Charlie Shavers, Atlantic City, N.J., and NYC '63. Taught in Trenton public schls. Went to Trenton St. Coll., B.S. '72; M.S. '74. Fr. '72 taught dms., perc., form. jazz bands at Trenton St. Ret. in '92 but taught three more yrs. as adjunct. Own gp. in Phila. and a fixture at Forrestal Conference Center, Princeton, fr. '90. A regular with the Kenny Davern quartet, De Nicola was praised by the leader for his swing and taste. Favs: Jo Jones, Krupa, Rich, Tough, Dodds, Catlett. Video: *Flip Phillips' 80th Birthday Party* (Arb.). CDs: w. Davern (Arb.); Greg Cohen (DIW); H. James (Verve).

DE PARIS, SIDNEY, tpt; b. Crawfordsville, IN, 5/30/05; d. NYC, 9/13/67. Studied w. fath., profess. of mus.; bro., Wilbur De Paris. Debut w. Sam Taylor, Wash., D.C., 1924. Pl. w. Charlie Johnson in NYC '26–31; McKinney's Cotton Pickers '31; Don Redman '32–6; Willie Bryant, C. Johnson, M. Mezzrow '37–8; Zutty Singleton '39–41; Benny Carter '40–1; Art Hodes, Charlie Barnet '41. Worked w. Wilbur De Paris's band '43–5; Claude Hopkins '46. Teamed up again w. Wilbur '47, app. w. him off and on until his death. Strong, punching style in the NO tradition, marked by growl work and use of cup mute. CDs: De Paris Bros. *The Complete Commodore Recordings*; *The Complete Edmond Hall/ James P. Johnson/ Sidney De Paris/ Vic Dickenson Blue Note Sessions* (Mos.); w. Jelly Roll Morton; McKinney's Cotton Pickers (BB); S. Bechet (Mos.; BB); Benny Carter (BB; B&B); Lucille Hegamin; Victoria Spivey (Prest.); J.C. Higginbotham in *Giants of Small Band Swing, Vol. 2* (Riv.); Swingville All-Stars (GTJ); w. own gps. and gps. of Bechet, James P. Johnson, Edmond Hall in *Hot Jazz on Blue Note* (BN).

DE PARIS, WILBUR, tbn; b. Crawfordsville, IN, 1/11/1900; d. NYC, 1/3/73. Studied w. fath. Began on alto horn, pl. in fath.'s circus band, then worked on TOBA circuit. Went to NO in 1922 w. Mack's Merrymakers. Fr. '25, he led own gp. in Phila. Worked in NYC w. Leroy Smith '28; Orig. Blue Rhythm Band '30; Dave Nelson '31. To Eur. w. Noble Sissle '31, and again w. Teddy Hill '37. Pl. w. Louis Armstrong '38–41; Ella Fitzgerald's orch. '41; Roy Eldridge bb '43; led own band, incl. bro. Sidney '43–5; w. Duke Ellington '45–7. In '47, he rejoin. Sidney to form De Paris Bros. Orch. at Jimmy Ryan's, then remained in residence there into '62, under his own name. When he led band on St. Dept. tour of Africa '57, Sidney took over gp. at Ryan's. Jobs at Broken Drum; Room at the Bottom, NYC '64; worked w. Guy Lombardo Show at Jones Beach '65; gigs and one-nighters in Midwest and Toronto, Can., '66. After Sidney's death, Wilbur's activity diminished, but pl. a few dates w. new gp. '72. De Paris's gps. played an infectious blend of NO and swing styles. The tight arrs. and skillful mixture of harmonic and rhythmic elements derived fr. swing bands was not unlike Jelly Roll Morton's gps. of the '20s, and the repertoire ranged fr. NO standards to current material. TV: *The Subject Is Jazz*, NBC, '58. Films: *The Small Hours; The Pirate; Windjammer*. Fests: Cannes, Antibes '60. Between '52 and '60, De Paris rec. six LPs as leader for Atl. CDs: De Paris brothers, *The Complete Commodore Recordings* (Mos.); w. Ellington; Jelly Roll Morton (BB); Louis Armstrong; R. Eldridge (Dec.); J. Hodges (Prest.).

DE ROSA, CLEM (CLEMENT RICHARD), dms, arr, comp, educ; b. Brooklyn, NY, 5/20/25. Son is dmr., Richard; daughter, Dianne, pl. woodwinds w. Clark Terry. Began on sax. Att. Juilliard Sch. of Mus.; M. Mus. fr. Manh. Sch. of Mus. Early experience pl. in clubs on Long Island, N.Y., w. Billy Watt, Harry Altman; and w. John LaPorta in NYC. Fr. 1945–55, he worked w. Jimmy Dorsey; Vaughn Monroe; Georgie Auld; Boyd Raeburn; Mingus; Bobby Hackett; Thad Jones; Coleman Hawkins; Ben Webster; Teo Macero; Kenyon Hopkins; Sonny Stitt; Teddy Wilson; Bill Harris; Chubby Jackson. Fr. '55 to '85, De Rosa was active mainly as an educ. He formed the first elem. sch. jazz ens. in '55 and was named N.Y. State Teacher of the Yr. in '61. Past president of the Int'l Assoc. of Jazz Educators; founded and cond. McDonald's Tri-State HS Jazz Ens.; exec. dir. of Int'l Foundation for Jazz. Led and cond. Glenn Miller Orch. '81–2; Bert Kaempfert Memorial Orch. '87. De Rosa has co-authored books on jazz educ. w. Mel Lewis, Dick Hyman, Michael Moore; also own book, *Teaching Rhythm Through Words*. He was inducted into the IAJE Hall of Fame in '90. Favs: Jo Jones, Mel Lewis, Shelly Manne; arrs: Gil Evans, Thad Jones, Bill Holman. Films: *Radio Days* w. Woody

Allen. TV: Johnny Carson; Merv Griffin; Arlene Francis; Joe Franklin. CDs: w. C. Mingus (Debut boxed set); G. Miller Orch. (GRP).

DE ROSA, RICHARD JEROME, dms, comp, arr, educ; b. Huntington, NY, 11/25/55. Father is Clem De Rosa; bro., sist., uncles all prof. mus. Began on dms., then learned tpt., Fr. hrn., pno. Received B. Mus. in mus. educ., Jersey City (N.J.) St. Coll. 1977; M. Mus. in comp., Manh. Sch. of Mus. '85. Pl. w. Marian McPartland '74–9; Roland Haynes '75; Paul Lavalle '78; Peter Nero '78–9. Pl. and rec. w. Gerry Mulligan Qt., Concert Jazz Band, and bb fr. '79. Also pl. w. Harry Sheppard '81–3; Sal Salvador '82; Chris Connor '82; Bob Haggart '84; Laura Taylor '85–6; Jay Leonhart, Ray Alexander '90. De Rosa has much exp. as an educ., teach. at Ramapo Coll. '78–80; Jersey City St. Coll. '78–82; Hartt Coll. of Mus. '82–4; Man. Sch. of Mus. since '82; Lehman Coll. '85; Princeton U. '85–7; Central Conn. St. Coll. '85–9; Vandercook Coll. of Mus. '90–1; Duquesne U., Pa., Biola U., LA '91. Asst. dir. of McDonald's HS Jazz Ens. '82–8. De Rosa's arrs. have been rec. by Gerry Mulligan; Mel Lewis bb; Glenn Miller Orch. Fav: Jack DeJohnette; arrs: Claus Ogerman, Michael Gibbs. Fests: Eur. since '79; So. Amer., '85; Austral., '89. TV: w. M. McPartland, *Good Morning America* '74, *Today* '75: Joe Franklin w. Sheppard '80. Book: *Concepts for Improvisation* (Hal Leonard). CDs: w. G. Mulligan (GRP; A&M; Swing); Jackie & Roy (Aud.); Nancy Harrow and B. Brookmeyer (Gazell); as arr.: w. G. Dial–D. Oatts (DMP); Mel Lewis (Atl.).

DE WILDE, LAURENT, pno, comp; b. Washington, DC, 12/19/60. Born of French parents, he spent his first four yrs. in the US, incl. NYC, bef. moving to France. After philosophy study at the École Normale Superieure, he took up residence in NYC 1982–3. Att. the jazz program at LIU '84–6; also stud. w. Jim McNeely and Mulgrew Miller. Pl. at Sweet Basil and the Angry Squire. App. w. Eddie Henderson qt.; also accomp. Greg Osby; Donald Harrison; Ernie Watts; Vincent Herring; Bud Shank; Antonio Hart; Joshua Redman. Ret. to Paris in '90, pl. there and tour. in Eur.; concert in Damascus, Syria. Signed w. Sony/Columbia. Howard Mandel calls him "a sparkling melodist and a harmonically playful, dynamics-sensitive pianist, reveling in strong rhythms." Book: *Monk,* which won "Best Book of the Yr." fr. the Academie du Jazz. De Wilde won a Victoire prize as "best new jazz talent." CD: Col.; IDA; w. E. Henderson (IDA).

DEAN, DONALD WESLEY, dms; Kansas City, MO, 6/21/37. Raised in KC; active in LA fr. 1961, w.

Kenny Dorham. Also pl. w. Harold Land; Gerald Wilson; George Shearing; Dexter Gordon; Jack Wilson; Phineas Newborn; Hampton Hawes; others. Rec. w. Carmell Jones for PJ '62. Member of Les McCann's gp. '68–72, rec. the popular album *Swiss Movement*. In mid '70s, pl. w. Jimmy Smith, feat. on Verve album *Bluesmith*. Later worked in Horace Tapscott gp. CDs: w. McCann (Rh.; Night).

DEAN, VINNIE (Vincent Divittorio), alto sax, fl, cl; b. Mt. Vernon, NY, 8/8/29. Played w. Shorty Sherock, Johnny Bothwell 1946; Charlie Spivak '47–50; Charlie Barnet '48–9; Elliott Lawrence '51–2; Stan Kenton '52–3. Rec. w. Ralph Burns Orch. '52–4; Eddie Bert combo for Disc. '53; Jazztone '55. Pl. w. Carl Erca at Log Cabin in Armonk, N.Y., mid '50s, also managed rec. store in Mt. Vernon. Led own qt. in Yonkers, also freelanced w. C. Barnet '58; Benny Goodman, Geo. Williams, E. Lawrence, Urbie Green, Hal McKusick '59; Sal Salvador '60. Fr. the '50s, Dean operated a rec. studio, licensed booking agency, and publ. co. Fav: Charlie Parker. CDs: w. Kenton (Cap.); Tony Bennett (Col.).

DEARIE, BLOSSOM, voc, pno, comp; b. East Durham, NY, 4/28/26. Sang w. vocal gps. in mid 1940s, incl. Blue Flames w. Woody Herman; Blue Reys w. Alvino Rey. Also pl. pno. in cocktail lounges. Rec. "Moody's Mood For Love" w. King Pleasure '52, then worked in Paris w. Annie Ross. While in Paris, she form. a vocal gp., the Blue Stars, for which she wrote some of the arrs.; sidemen incl. Fats Sadi, Roger Guerin. The gp.'s rec. of "Lullaby of Birdland," sung in French, was a hit both in France and the US. Two other gps., the Double Six of Paris and the Swingle Singers, evolved out of the Blue Stars. Married Bobby Jaspar in Paris ca. '55. Ret. to NYC '56; rec. as lead. w. Herb Ellis; Ray Brown; Jo Jones. Came to prominence singing and pl. w. her own trio in NYC and LA clubs fr. '56. By the '70s, she was also app. regularly at Ronnie Scott's in London. In NYC dur. '80–90s she perf. at the Ballroom, Russian Tea Room, and Danny's Skylight Room. Rec. for own label, Daffodil, fr. '74. Dearie's repertory incl. many of her own songs, incl. "I'm Shadowing You," w. lyrics by Johnny Mercer; "Sweet Georgie Fame"; "Hey John." She was the recipient of the first Mabel Mercer Found. Award in '85. A highly original perf. combining a sweet, insouciant, soprano voice w. buoyant, harmonically interesting pno. CDs: Verve; Mastermix; w. King Pleasure; Stan Getz (Prest.).

D'EARTH, JOHN (John Edward Dearth II), tpt, flg, dms, pno, pennywhistle, clay fls and ocarinas, perc, comp, arr; b. Framingham, MA, 3/30/50. Grew up in

Holliston, Mass. Father, Philip, is an amateur dmr.; great-uncle a vaudeville tbnst. Fath. taught him dms. w. brushes and brass tray at age 2; bought him first tpt. at 8. Taught self scales and "took things off records." At 10, he became inspired by Shorty Baker's work on Ellington's "Willow Weep For Me." Learned to read mus. in elementary sch.; further studies w. band dir. Alvin Ezer at Holliston HS. Stud. tpt. priv. w. Ziggy Minichiello; then jazz theory and bb arr. w. Boots Mussulli 1963–7, worked in his Milford Area Youth Orch. Stud. w. John Coffey of Bost. Symph. In '69–70, he commuted fr. Mass. to N.J. every Monday to stud. arr. w. Thad Jones. Att. Harvard '68–71, stud. theory w. Louise Vosgerchian. Moved to NYC '71. Stud. w. Carmine Caruso and Vince Penzarella; theory w. Richie Beirach; also informally w. Kirk Nurock. Considers Bob Moses, whom he met in '70, as "one of my important 'teachers.' " Worked w. Ken Sawyer's Big Nine '64–9; duo w. Doug Davis, trio adding Bennie Wallace '68–71; Fire & Ice, w. Don Grolnick '68–70. Took part in early '70s NYC "loft scene" w. dmr. Robert Jospe; Randy Brecker; B. Wallace; John Abercrombie; Dave Liebman; Free Life Communication; Sam Rivers' Studio Rivbea; Mark Morganelli's Jazzmania. Pl. w. Larry Elgart '72–6; own qt. '73; David Berger's rehearsal band '73–4; Gunter Hampel '74; National Jazz Ens. '75–8; David Lahm gps. '75–84; B. Moses gps. '73–84; Cosmology, co-led w. singer/songwriter Dawn Thompson and Jospe '73–84; Tito Puente '79–80; Deodato '74–6; Al Porcino Orch., Ed Palermo bb '74–6; Dave Matthews mid '70s; Lee Konitz Nonet '76–7; Buddy Rich '77; L. Hampton '77–8; Thad Jones–Mel Lewis bb '76; Lewis bb '78–80; Nurock '82; Harvie Swartz '79–80; fr. '82 own qnt., sxt., spt., w. Dawn Thompson (his wife fr. '86); Jane Ira Bloom '83; Emily Remler '83–5; Charlottesville Swing Orch. fr. '85; Doug Richards' Great Amer. Mus. Ens. fr. '86; Secrets '87–9; Visions '84–9; George Gruntz '91–5, incl. tour. China '92; Bruce Hornsby fr. '93; Klaus Konig '95. Has worked. in Can., Eur., So. America. Has taught fr. '69 incl. Johnny Colon East Harlem Mus. Sch. mid '70s; songwriting w. wife, summers at U. of Virginia, '84–90. Jazz Ens., which he taught fr. mid '80 at UVA, was incorporated into university's curriculum in '90; for its concerts he has imported guests such as Liebman; Michael Brecker; Clark Terry; Joe Henderson et al. Fr. '88 has also taught at Virginia Commonwealth U. jazz program. Favs: "Besides Armstrong and Miles Davis, who are beyond category," Harry Edison, Lee Morgan, Clifford Brown; arrs: Ellington, Gil Evans, Thad Jones, Brookmeyer. Awards: NEA grants '74, '89. Film: score for docu. *West Main Street*. Video: *Miles Davis at Montreux* '91. TV: w. Great Amer.

Mus. Ens., *Music of Armstrong and Ellington,* PBS '90; John D'earth Spt., PBS '94. CDs: Conc.; Enja; w. David Lahm (Generation); E. Remler (Conc.); Gruntz (Enja; TCB); D. Liebman (Cand.); Jae Stinnet (Heart); Konig (Enja).

DEBRIANO, SANTI (Alonso Santi Wilson Debriano Santorino), bs, gtr, berimbau, gimbre; b. Panama Republic, 6/27/55. Father, Alonso, is well-known comp. of Panamanian songs. Maternal grandfath., Walter Woods, was dmr. and lead.; paternal grandfath. was church org. Grew up in NYC, began on bs. in public sch. Stud. comp. and political sci. at Union Coll. 1972–6 w. B.A.; bs. at New Engl. Cons. '76–7; ethnomusicology at Wesleyan U. '89–91 w. M.A. Pl. w. Archie Shepp '78–82; Sam Rivers '83–5; John Carter, Geri Allen '85; Oliver Lake fr. '86; Jim Pepper '87–9; Kirk Lightsey '87–90; '95; Sonny Fortune fr. '88; George Adams '89–91; Don Pullen '89–92; Billy Hart fr. '89; Panamaniacs '91–2; Lightsey fr. '95. Debriano has taught at Wesleyan and the New Sch. Favs: Ray Brown, Dave Holland, M. Vitous. Fests: Eur. fr. '80; Japan fr. '88; Panama '92. Film: *Imagine the Sound* w. Shepp; feat. in Marc Huraux's *Check the Changes*. CDs: Free Lance; w. Lightsey (Sunny.; Timel.); G. Adams; S. Fortune (BN); Stanley Cowell (Conc.); Billy Hart (Arab.); O. Lake (Gram.); Karl Berger (SN); Jay Collins (Res.); G. Cables; L. Willis (Steep.); J. Chambers (Cand.); Shepp; Jim Pepper (Enja); David Murray (Red Brn.).

DEDRICK, RUSTY (LYLE F.), tpt, comp; b. Delevan, NY, 7/12/18. Brother, Arthur, pl. tbn. w. Red Norvo. Att. Fredonia State Teachers Coll.; stud. comp. priv. w. Paul Creston, Stephan Wolpe. Pl. w. Dick Stabile, 1938–9; Red Norvo '39–41; Claude Thornhill '41–2. Served in army '42–5, then pl. three mos. w. Ray McKinley '46. Rejoin. Thornhill '46–7. Worked in NYC as freelance studio mus. and arr. late '40s-60s. Dur. this time, he comp. and arr. for Don Elliott; Maxine Sullivan; Lee Wiley; others. Pl. w. Urbie Green '67. Mus. dir. of the Free Design '69–70, then pl. w. Lionel Hampton '70–1. Join. jazz dept. of Manh. Sch. of Mus. '71. Comp. and arr. mainly for educ. field fr. '70s. Comps. incl. *The Modern Art Suite; Suite for Alto Sax and Trumpet.* Favs: Armstrong, Berigan, M. Davis, Don Elliott. Fests: Colo. JP, '74. LPs: Esoteric; Counterpoint; Four Corners; Monmouth-Evergreen; w. Elliott (Riv.). CD: w. M. Sullivan (Aud.).

DEEMS, BARRETT B., dms, lead; b. Springfield, IL, 3/1/13; d. Chicago, IL, 9/15/98. Joined Paul Ash at 15; led own gps. on and off through 1930s; Joe Venuti orch. '38–44; Red Norvo '48; Charlie Barnet '51;

Muggsy Spanier '52; Louis Armstrong '54–8. Own gp. at Brass Rail, Chi., '59–60. Pl. and rec. w. Jack Teagarden '60–4; off and on w. Dukes of Dixieland fr. '64. Then in Chi. w. Bill Reinhardt at Jazz Ltd. '66–70. Subbed in WGJB '71–5; tour. Eur. w. Benny Goodman '76. To So. Amer. in early '80s w. Wild Bill Davison and Eur. w. Keith Smith. While based in Chi., cont. to freelance into mid '90s, incl. own bb. Dur. his yrs. w. Armstrong, Deems was greatly respected for his speed, propulsive style, and well-rounded technique. Film: *Rhythm Inn* '51; *High Society* '56. TV: *Timex Jazz* '72. Book: *Drummer's Practice Routine* (Martin Dixon, publ., Miami). CDs: Del.; w. Armstrong (Col.; Dec.); *Chicago Jazz Summit* (Atl.).

DeFRANCESCO, JOEY, org, comp, tpt; b. Springfield, PA, 4/10/71. Father, John, an electrician, was kybd. pl. and has pl. org. duets on Col. CD w. his son. Won student competition in hs. In 1987, took third place in Thelonious Monk Piano Competition. This led to his being signed by Col. Recs. Tour. Eur. w. Miles Davis. Lived in Scottsdale, Ariz., bef. moving to Delaware in mid '90s. Has tour. w. his own org. gp. within which he also developed into a confident tptr. DeFrancesco has done much to bring the Hammond org. back to popularity; though his style has been compared to that of Jimmy Smith, he has clearly moved out on his own. Pl. w. J. McLaughlin Trio on Eur. summer fest. circuit '96. Other fests: Vitoria; Vail JP. CDs: Col.; Muse; Big Mo; High; w. M. Davis (WB); Didier Lockwood (Drey.); McLaughlin (Verve); H. Person (Muse).

DeFRANCO, BUDDY (BONIFACE FERDINAND LEONARD), cl; b. Camden, NJ, 2/17/23. Brother, Leonard, pl. bs. Stud. mand. first, then cl. at age 9. Attended Mastbaum Sch. in Phila.; at age 14, won Tommy Dorsey National Swing Contest. Began bb career in 1939 w. Johnny "Scat" Davis. Join. Gene Krupa '41; Ted Fio Rito and Charlie Barnet '42–3; Tommy Dorsey '44–5. Settled in Calif., pl. w. Boyd Raeburn '46; T. Dorsey again '47–8. In '50, he joined the Count Basie Sept., remaining for a yr., then led his own bb, for which he wrote many of the arrs. Despite its excellence, the band did not enjoy commercial success and for the next several yrs., DeFranco led a qt. feat. Kenny Drew or Sonny Clark on pno., Milt Hinton or Gene Wright on bs., Art Blakey or Bobby White on dms. Led a qt. on Jazz Club USA Eur. tour Jan. '54. DeFranco's career suffered due to the cl.'s decline in popularity as a jazz instrument; in the early '60s, he co-led a gp. w. acdnst. Tommy Gumina for a while, but made a living as nominal leader of the Glenn Miller Orch. '66–74. By the '80s, his reputation had begun to rise again; he app. intermittently as

co-leader of a qnt. w. Terry Gibbs, making frequent jf and jazz cruise apps. and giving clinics at universities. He toured the Far East, Austral., NZ, So. Africa, and Arg. DeFranco's extraordinary technique, broad scope, tone, fire, and imagination established him as the top clst. of modern jazz, a near counterpart to Dizzy Gillespie and Charlie Parker. He won the *DB* Readers Poll as early as '45, and cont. to win dozens of int'l polls. His peerless virtuosity and creativity is superbly displayed on his own recs. and sess. w. Art Tatum and Oscar Peterson. Favs: Goodman, Shaw, Eddie Daniels. CDs: boxed set of *Complete Verve Buddy DeFranco/Sonny Clark*, Mos.; Pab.; Cont.; Conc.; w. Gibbs (Cont.); Tatum; Peterson (Pab.); R. Kuhn (Intuit.).

DeJOHNETTE, JACK, dms, comp, pno; b. Chicago, IL, 8/9/42. Studied classical pno. for ten yrs.; grad. Amer. Cons. of Mus., Chi.; active w. T-Bone Walker and other blues bands, as well as w. such avant-gardists as Muhal Richard Abrams; Roscoe Mitchell. To NYC 1966; joined John Patton; worked for over two yrs. w. Charles Lloyd; w. Stan Getz '68; also pl. w. Betty Carter; Jackie McLean; John Coltrane; Thelonious Monk; Freddie Hubbard; Bill Evans; Keith Jarrett; Chick Corea. Joined Miles Davis in spring of '70; feat. on the albums *Bitches' Brew* and *Live-Evil*; dur. next two yrs., he rec. own albums, frequently doubling on melodica, pno., clavinet, and org. w. occ. vocs. In '71, he organized the gp. Compost; later led other gps., incl. New Directions and Special Edition. He has worked w. Pat Metheny; is part of Jarrett's Standards Trio, and the Gateway Trio w. John Abercrombie, Dave Holland. In the early '90s, he rec. w. Joey Calderazzo; Gonzalo Rubalcaba; Mark Whitfield; and Ryan Kisor. Comp. five-movement suite for the Rova Saxophone Qt. Since late '80s, his Special Edition gp. has incl. Greg Osby and Gary Thomas, saxes; Lonnie Plaxico, bs.; and, more recently, Michael Cain, kybds.; Steve Gorn, reeds. DeJohnette originally came to prominence as a dmr., but his work fr. the late '70s often showcased his considerable skills as a comp. and pnst. He collaborated w. Bobby McFerrin for *Extra Special Edition*, BN '94. Awards: *Modern Drummer* polls; honorary doctorate fr. Berklee '90. CDs: ECM; BN; Imp.; Land.; Prest.; Mile.; MCA; Manh.; w. M. Davis; J. McLaughlin; Kisor (Col.); Metheny; Holland; Jarrett; J. Garbarek; Abercrombie; G. Peacock; T. Rypdal; J. Surman; M. Goodrick; K. Wheeler (ECM); Bill Evans (Verve); J. Lovano; J. Scofield; W. Shorter (BN).

DEL FRA, RICCARDO, bs, comp, arr; b. Rome, Italy, 2/20/56. Three uncles are amateur mus. Began on gtr. at age 14. Stud. bs. at Frosinone Cons. Pl. in Italy w. Sestetto Piana-Valdambrini; Gerardo Iacoucci; Claudio Fasoli; Gianni Basso; Sax Machine; Enrico Pieranunzi; also backed Kai Winding, Art Farmer as freelancer. Tour. w. Chet Baker off and on 1979–88; also pl. w. Herve Sellin; Barney Wilen; Charles Loos; Jacques Pellen; Johnny Griffin; Toots Thielemans. Freelanced in Eur. w. Sonny Stitt; James Moody; Dizzy Gillespie; Lee Konitz; Benny Carter; Joe Newman; Horace Parlan; Vernel Fournier; Clifford Jordan, etc. Del Fra has taught at the Arpes sch. in Paris, where he lives, fr. '92. His piece *Silent Call*, for jazz qt. and fifteen strings, was premiered at the Paris JF '92. Favs: Paul Chambers, Scott LaFaro; arrs: Gil Evans, Claus Ogerman, Thad Jones. Polls: Grand Prix FNAC '89. Fests: USA '90 w. Toots Thielemans; Japan '86 w. Chet Baker; '91–2 w. Thielemans. Films: w. C. Baker: *Live at Ronnie Scott's*; *Chet's Romance*; *An Evening with Chet Baker*. TV: Eur. TV. CDs: IDA; w. Baker (Timel.; Red; WW); Wilen (IDA); Joe Diorio (RAM).

DELAMONT, GORDON ARTHUR, comp, tpt; b. Moose Jaw, Sask., Canada, 10/27/18; d. Toronto, Ont., Canada, 1/16/81. Raised in Vancouver, Can. Stud. tpt. w. father. Moved to Toronto, 1939; pl. lead tpt. in dance bands and CBC radio orchs. Led own band in Toronto and southern Ont. '45–9. Stud. briefly w. Maury Deutsch in NYC '49, then opened own teaching studio in Toronto. Pupils incl. Peter Appleyard; Moe Koffman; Rob McConnell; many other well-known Can. jazz mus. Led rehearsal band '53–62; jazz oct. '60s. Delamont was recognized as a leader of the Can. third stream movement. His *Ontario Suite* for soprano voice and orch. was perf. daily at Expo '67; the same year his *Collage No. 3* and *Song and Dance* were rec. by the Ron Collier Orch. w. Duke Ellington as soloist. His best-known work, *Three Entertainments For Saxophone Quartet*, was rec. by the NY Sax. Qt. He is the author of several popular textbooks, incl. *Modern Arranging Techniques; Modern Harmonic Techniques; Modern Contrapuntal Techniques* (Delevan Publ.).

DELANEY, JACK MICHAEL, tbn; b. New Orleans, LA, 8/27/30; d. New Orleans, 9/22/75. Studied at Southeastern La. Coll. Pl. w. Johnny Reininger 1949–51; Sharkey Bonano '51–3, '55–6; Tony Almerico '53–4, '56–8. Also worked as staff member of WDSU-TV. Fr. '58, he pl. w. Leon Kellner at Roosevelt Hotel, NO. Fav: J. Teagarden. Recs. as a lead. '53, '55; as sideman w. Ken Colyer '52; Lizzie Miles mid '50s; Pete Fountain '56–7. CDs: w. Bonano (Story.; GHB); Johnny Wiggs (Story.).

DELANO, PETER FRANKLIN, pno, comp; b. NYC, 9/28/76. Father is amateur jazz saxophonist; bro., Oliver, pl. gtr. and leads blues band. Began pno. at age 6; pl. blues progressions at 9. Stud. w. Garry Dial 1988–90. Stud. theory in the New School's Jazz Program and took ens. classes there w. Reggie Workman, Andrew Cyrille '90–1. Join. All City HS Ens. '91. Att. Columbia U. fr. '94, taking yr. off '96–7. Gigs as lead. in NYC fr. '88, incl. solo pno. at the Blue Note; trio at Iridium '95. Pl. w. Mark Whitfield fr. '98. A wunderkind ready to expand on his unlimited promise. Fests: JVC-NY, North Sea; Montreux; Aarhus (Den.) '94; Saratoga, Istanbul, Vitoria, North Sea, Pori '95. Favs: Hancock, Jarrett, Tyner. CDs: Verve.

DEMICHEAL, DON (DONALD ANTHONY), dms, vib, perc, journalist; b. Louisville, KY, 5/12/28; d. Skokie, IL, 2/4/82. Taught perc. and led own band locally 1951–60. Moved to Chi. in '60 to become managing editor of *Down Beat*; editor-in-chief '61–7. Fr. '61 to '64, he also compiled and edited the *Jazz Record Review* for *DB*. Subsequently he edited periodicals that were not devoted to jazz. Form. the Swingtet in '75, pl. vib.; sidemen incl. cl. Jerry Fuller; Chuck Hedges. Pl. dms. w. Kenny Davern and Art Hodes in the Hot Three, app. at Bechet's, NYC, in '70s. Pres. of Jazz Institute of Chi. '74–8. As the Institute's program dir., he helped develop the first Chi. JF '79. Rec. w. the Hot Three, under Davern's name, for Monmouth-Evergreen '79.

DENNARD, KENWOOD MARSHALL, dms, pno, vcl; b. Brooklyn, NY, 3/1/56. Parents both prof. singers; cousin is mus. dir. and pno. for Harry Belafonte, Hugh Masekela. Began pl. pno. at age 3, dms. at age 8, then sang in gospel choir w. Luther Vandross, Nat Adderley Jr. at Apollo Theater and on TV. Att. Mannes Sch. of Mus. and Manh. Sch. of Mus. while in hs. Stud. w. Gary Chaffee and Alan Dawson at Berklee 1973–6, also w. Nadia Boulanger at Fontainebleau Sch. of Fine Arts '75. Pl. and rec. w. Pat Martino '76; Brand X '77; then freelanced w. Dizzy Gillespie; Phyllis Hyman; Pharaoh Sanders; Manh. Transfer. Metarhythmic Orch., one-man-band w. Dennard singing, pl. kybds. and dms. simultaneously, since '84. Led own gps. Quintessence and Turn of the Century '84–7; Jaco Pastorius '85–7; then freelanced w. Wayne Shorter; Belafonte; Bobby McFerrin; Sting; Stanley Jordan; Gil Evans Orch; Lew Soloff; others. In '91, Dennard perf. w. Miles Davis and the Gil Evans Orch. at Montreux. Dennard is also active as an educ. and has written many educ. articles. Favs: Elvin Jones, Zigaboo Modeliste, Billy Cobham. Fests: Eur. TV: Johnny Carson; David Frost; Merv

Griffin; *Sesame Street*. CDs: w. Pastorius (Big World); Stanley Jordan (BN); Lew Soloff (ALCR).

DENNERLEIN, BARBARA, org, synth; b. Munich, Germany, 9/25/64. Took up org. at age 11. By 15 was pl. in local clubs. Rec. four albums for her own label, Bebap Records; tour. extensively throughout Eur. Rec. *Straight Ahead*, 1988, feat. Ray Anderson. Dennerlein cites Jimmy Smith and Larry Young as principal infls. App. at Sweet Basil in NYC '91 and jammed w. George Benson at his home. In album, *Hot Stuff*, which explored Latin, jazz, rock, and funk, she employed a digital interface that enabled her Hammond org. and synthesizers to virtually collaborate through the use of MIDI. Int'l regarded as one of the most promising and individual of a new generation of orgsts. CDs: Verve; Enja.

DENNIS, KENNY (KENNETH CARL), dms; b. Philadelphia, PA, 5/27/30. Worked locally, then in 1950s w. Earl Bostic; Jackie Davis; Erroll Garner; Sonny Stitt; Billy Taylor. Freelanced in NYC w. Monk; Mingus; Miles Davis. In '60, after working w. Phineas Newborn, he moved to CA to pl. w. Lena Horne. Worked '60–3 as house dmr. at Rubaiyat Room in LA. Fr. '63 to '64, he toured w. Nancy Wilson, to whom he was married at the time. Later devoted most of his time to administrative work as manager/publisher, etc., pl. only occ. CDs: w. Mal Waldron (Prest.); S. Rollins (FS).

DENNIS, MATT (MATTHEW LOVELAND), pno, songwriter, voc; b. Seattle, WA, 2/11/14. Sang and pl. w. Horace Heidt 1933; staff arr./comp. for Tommy Dorsey in early '40s. First rec., his comp. "Relax," was arr. by Gil Evans and rec. by the voc. gp. Six Hits and A Miss '40. Settling in LA in late '40s, he worked as a single in supper clubs; then for many yrs. teamed w. his wife, voc. Ginny Maxey. Best-known songs, "Everything Happens To Me"; "Angel Eyes"; "Let's Get Away From It All"; "Will You Still Be Mine?"; "Violets for Your Furs." CDs: some of his LPs for RCA have been reissued in Japan; new CD *Angel Eyes* w. Ginny Maxey '91 (BMG, Japan).

DENNIS, WILLIE (William DeBerardinis), tbn; b. Philadelphia, PA, 1/10/26; d. NYC, 7/8/65. Mainly self-taught, but also stud. w. Lennie Tristano. Worked w. Elliot Lawrence 1946; then Claude Thornhill; Sam Donahue. Pl. w. Benny Goodman at Brussels World's Fair; Woody Herman on St. Dept. tour of Latin America '58. App. w. many gps. in '50s, incl. Howard McGhee; Charlie Ventura; Coleman Hawkins; Tristano; Kai Winding. Member of Mingus's bands in

Calif. and NYC '56–9; Buddy Rich qnt. '59. Pl. w. Gerry Mulligan's Concert Jazz Band in '60s; tour. USSR w. Goodman '62. Also very active in rec. and TV studios. Married to singer Morgana King. Died in a Central Park auto accident. His tumbling, convoluted style, showing the Tristano infl., was carried by a burry tone. CDs: w. Mingus in *The Complete Debut Recordings*, incl. tbn. quart. w. Winding, J.J. Johnson, B. Green (Deb.); Mingus (Col.; Atl.); Mulligan (Verve; RTE); Goodman (MM); Herman (Evid.); Phil Woods (Cand.).

DESMARAIS, LORRAINE, pno; b. Montreal, Que., Canada, 8/15/56. Received M. Mus. in classical pno. fr. McGill U., Montreal, 1979; stud. w. Kenny Barron in NYC '84. Pl. w. own trio '85–6; Tiger Okoshi at Montreal JF, Paquito D'Rivera '88; own gp. Vision, w. Jean-Pierre Zanella, Michel Donato '91; own qt. in NYC and Bost. '92. Pl. duo concerts w. Joanne Brackeen, Marian McPartland '92. Desmarais has won First Prize at the Montreal JF '84; Jacksonville Jazz Pno. Competition '86. She has taught at College St.-Laurent, Montreal fr. '79; U. of Montreal fr. '85. Favs: Bill Evans, Russell Ferrante, Lyle Mays, Herbie Hancock. "Desmarais evokes the piano stylings of McCoy Tyner and Chick Corea."—*Keyboard Magazine*. Fests: Switzerland, '85; France, '87, '89; Calgary, Singapore, Indonesia, Philippines '88; Moscow '91. CDs: Scherzo; Jazzimage.

DESMOND, PAUL (Paul Emil Breitenfeld), alto sax; b. San Francisco, CA, 11/25/24; d. NYC, 5/30/77. Father was arr. and org. for silent movies. Stud. cl. at SF Polytechnic HS; SF State. Join. Jack Fina 1950; Alvino Rey '51. Most of his active career was as a member of the Dave Brubeck qt., fr. its inception in '51 until Dec. '67, when it disbanded. Among his major contributions to Brubeck's success in the early '60s was his comp. "Take Five," the gp.'s biggest hit and the first major jazz work in 5/4 time. Tour. extensively w. Brubeck, incl. Eur. and the Middle East, '58; Engl. w. the NJF show '59. In '72, he reunited w. Brubeck for The Two Generations of Brubeck tour of US fests and Eur. Rarely a club perf., he led a gp. at the Half Note '74; several times at Bourbon St. in Toronto, Can., '74–5. In '75, he also pl. jazz cruise w. Brubeck on SS *Rotterdam*, resulting in an album of Desmond-Brubeck duets. In '70s, he rec. as a lead. w. various gps., incl. Jim Hall. He died of lung cancer. A bright, witty man whose unfinished memoirs, *How Many of You Are There in the Quartet?*, never reached beyond the first chapter, which was published in *Punch* in '73. Desmond, who once stated a desire to make his alto "sound like a dry martini," was a pure-toned, lyrical player of original melodic invention. Favs: Parker, Konitz, Pete Brown. Fests: NO '69; MJF '75; w. Brubeck, NJF fr. '58; MJF '62; NJF-NY '72, '73,'75. Polls: *DB*, new star on alto '53; *DB* '55–9; *Met.* '55–60; *Play.* '57–60. TV: Timex jazz show '72. CDs: RCA, boxed set; BB; Fant.; CTI; Telarchive; Desmond–G. Mulligan (BB); w. Brubeck (Col.; A&M; Fant.; Mob. Fid.); Chet Baker (A&M); MJQ (Atl.); Mulligan (Verve); J. Hall (CTI).

DESVIGNE, SIDNEY, crnt; b. New Orleans, LA, 9/11/1893; d. Pacoima, CA, 12/2/59. During the 1910s he pl. at 101 Ranch Café in Storyville, NO red light district; also worked w. Excelsior Brass Band, Maple Leaf orch. Pl. second crnt. to Louis Armstrong w. Fate Marable on riverboats, moving up to lead tpt. when Armstrong join. King Oliver. Led bands on other riverboats in the late '20s and '30s; also had a bb in NO. In '45, he moved to So. Calif., where he operated a nightclub. Rec. w. Marable for Okeh '24.

DEUCHAR, JIMMY (JAMES), tpt, flg, mello, comp; b. Dundee, Scotland, 6/26/30; d. Dundee, 9/8/93. From mus. family. Both his sons are mus. Stud. tpt.; start. pl.in local jazz band. Pl. at Club Eleven in London while serving in RAF; join. Johnny Dankworth there 1950–1; Jack Parnell '52; Ronnie Scott '53–4; Tony Crombie '55; tour. w. Lionel Hampton '56; rejoin. Scott, incl. US tour '57. Moved to Germ. and became soloist w. Kurt Edelhagen '57–9. Again w. Scott '60–2; Tubby Hayes '62–4. Fr. '66, rejoin. Edelhagen as staff arr. and soloist; also worked w. Clarke-Boland bb '65–71. Ret. to Engl. '71, arr. for BBC; mostly active as arr. through '70s. Moved back to Scotland in early '70s. Wrote for BBC jazz orchs. and Charlie Watts bb. Fav. own pl. on TV w. Benny Golson '60s. One of UK's best modern tpts. A Dameron-infl. comp.-arr., he made major contributions to the band libraries of Scott and others. Comps: "Portrait of Elvin"; "Drum In" (for Edelhagen); *U.K. Suite* (for Clarke-Boland); *Concerto for Joe*, dedicated to J. Temperley. Recs. as lead. on Tempo, Cont.; sideman w. Zoot Sims. CDs: w. Victor Feldman (Cont.); Jack Sharpe (JH); Clarke-Boland (MPS); Hayes (Redial).

DI CASTRI, FURIO, bs; b. Milan, Italy, 9/12/55. Brother pl. gtr. and sax. Began on tpt. Stud. priv. fr. 1966. Awarded a rec. contract after his jazz-rock band won first prize in a talent contest '73. Pl. in Eur. w. Chet Baker '79; Massimo Urbani '79–81; Maurizio Giammarco, incl. perfs. w. Lingomania '79–86; C. Baker, Michael Petrucciani '81–3; Enrico Rava '81–8, again in '90s; Philip Catherine '83; John Tay-

lor '85; C. Baker '85–6; Dino Saluzzi, M. Urbani '86; J. Taylor '87–8; Joe Henderson, Pharoah Sanders, Paul Bley '88; Aldo Romano fr. '88; P. Bley '90. Pl. w. M. Petrucciani–Chas. Lloyd in Calif. '81. Di Castri led a trio w. Flavio Boltro and Manhu Roche '87–9; backed Joe Lovano in Italy '88. He has led a qt. w. Stefano Cantini, Danilo Rea, and M. Roche fr. '88, and a duo w. Paolo Fresu fr. '89. Taught at the Siena summer jazz clinic fr. '89. Favs: Paul Chambers, Scott La Faro. Polls: *Musica Jazz*, '82, '84. Fests: all major in Eur.; US '81; Can. '89; Turkey '87; Israel '90. TV: Sudwestfunk on Germ. TV '89. CDs: Owl; Spl.; A Tempo; w. Baker (Phil.); Romano (Owl; Enja); Rava (Gala; SN; ECM; Inak); Petrucciani (IRD); Fresu (Owl); Saluzzi (ECM); Urbani (Red); Stefano Sabatini (Spl.).

DI MEOLA, AL, gtr; b. Jersey City, NJ, 7/22/54. First instrument was acdn. Stud. priv. fr. age 8; also at Berklee Coll. 1971. Pl. w. Barry Miles in jazz-rock gp. Returned to Berklee to study arr., but join. Chick Corea's Return To Forever '74. Led his own gps. pl. high-energy fusion on a series of Col. albums; also rec. two flamenco albums w. fellow gtrsts. John McLaughlin and Paco DeLucia '82 and '83; in late '80s, he worked w. acoustic gtr. and synths, incl. a trio w. Bireli Lagrene and Larry Coryell. Led the Al Di Meola Project in mid '80s. After a four-yr. absence fr. recs., he ret. in '91 w. two albums, *World Sinfonia*, and *Kiss My Axe*, infl. by the legendary "New Tango" master Astor Piazzolla and feat. the Argentine bandoneon player Dino Saluzzi. Tour. w. J-L Ponty and Stanley Clarke in a trio, Rite of Strings, '95. CDs: Col.; Mesa; BM; Manh.; BN; Tom.; w. Corea (Polyd.).

DI NOVI, GENE (EUGENE), pno; b. NYC, 5/26/28. Studied pno. w. Lucille Green, NYC 1950–1. In LA dur. '60s, he stud. pno. w. Jacob Gimpel; counterpoint w. Mario Castelnuovo-Tedesco. Prof. debut '42; pl. w. Henry Jerome '43; Joe Marsala '44; Boyd Raeburn,'45–6; Buddy Rich '47; solo at Three Deuces, NYC, and w. Chuck Wayne, Stan Hasselgard '47–8; Anita O'Day, Chubby Jackson bb '49. Backed singers in '50s, incl. Peggy Lee, Tony Bennett, and, fr. '55 to '59, Lena Horne. With Benny Goodman at Basin St. East '59. In '60s, wrote mus. for films on West Coast; moved to Toronto, Can., early '70s; rec. w. Ruby Braff in '80s. Accomplished pnst., orig. inspired by Bud Powell. Rec. debut on *Slightly Dizzy* w. Marsala, Nov.'45. Pl. *Expo 90* in Osaka, Japan, '90 and rec. own trio sess. CDs: Cand.; w. Lester Young (BN); Marsala (Class.); Goodman (Cap.).

DI PIPPO, ANGELO, acdn, arr, pno; b. Providence, RI, 9/6/35. Father and five bros. all amateur mus. Fath. owned mus. store in Providence. Took lessons in Prov. fr. 1938, then stud. arr. and comp. at Holy Cross Coll. and C.W. Post U. Moved to NYC after coll. '52, pl. w. society bands at Plaza Hotel. Worked in NYC in late 50s, early 60s w. Tony Scott; Max Kaminsky; Bobby Hackett; Tony Parenti; Edmond Hall; Eddie Condon; also own qt. w. Sam Most; Joe Benjamin; Ted Sommer. Made rec. debut '60 w. own Apollo LP, *The Jazz Accordion*; since then he has rec. more than twenty acdn. albums. He has also worked extensively on B'way, and on film and TV soundtracks. As an arr. and cond. in recent yrs., he has worked w. Robert Merrill since '75; Lynn Roberts '84; Billy Eckstine '85; Connie Haines '86; Roberta Peters since '86. Has also written classical arrs. for oboist Bert Lucarelli and comp. Michel Michelet. Favs: Art Van Damme, Ernie Felice; arrs: Don Sebesky, Bob Florence. Fests: NJF twice w. own qt. Films: apps. pl. acdn. in *The Godfather*; *Lovers and Other Strangers*; *The Deadly Hero*. TV: Johnny Carson, w. own gps.; MTV w. rock gp., the Ramones. CDs: Stash; as arr. w. Eckstine (Kimbo).

DIAL, GARRY, pno, comp; b. Montclair, NJ, 7/2/54. Mother pl. classical pno. Studied w. Elston Husk, Mary Lou Williams 1969–73; Charlie Banacos fr. '72; and at Berklee Coll. of Mus. '71–3; Manh. Sch. of Mus. '88–90, B.A. and M.A. Pl. w. own trio fr. '76; Dial and Oatts w. Dick Oatts fr. '85; Red Rodney–Ira Sullivan 77–94; Charli Persip–Gerry LaFurn Superband '80–3; Joe Morello '82–5; Mel Lewis qt. & bb '86–90; Gerry Mulligan '88–9; also worked w. Dizzy Gillespie, Nat Adderley '80; James Moody '81. Has taught at the New Sch. fr. '89; Manh. Sch. of Mus. fr. '90. Ruth Ellington enlisted Dial to record the entire Duke Ellington catalog, incl. many prev. unrec. and unperf. comps. for the Ellington family's private library '79. Comps: "How Do You Know?"; "Turn and Let Me Hold You"; "A Fine Line." Favs: Bill Evans, W. Kelly, Hancock, Jarrett, Tyner. Fests: all major fr. '79. CDs: Contin.; DMP; w. Dial and Oatts (DMP); Rodney-Sullivan (Den.; Contin.); James Morrison (WB); Joel Spencer–Kelly Sill (JA); C. Fambrough (K-Jazz).

DiCIOCCIO, JUSTIN, dms, perc; b. Buffalo, NY, 3/31/41. Received B. Mus. fr. Eastman Sch. of Mus. 1963; M. Mus. fr. Manh. Sch. of Mus. '71; Certif. fr. Eastman Sch. of Mus. Pl. w. dance bands in Buffalo, then w. Chuck Mangione '62–3; Sammy Nestico '63–9. Freelanced fr. '69 w. Don Menza; Sam Noto; Sal Nistico; Phil Woods; Red Rodney; Clark Terry; Arnie Lawrence; Jay Leonhart; also much commercial work. DiCioccio is the founder and dir. of the

Jazz Studies prog. at NYC's LaGuardia HS. Out of this came an All-City Jazz Band whose alumni incl. Jimmy Owens, Kenny Washington, and Michael Leonhart. He was prog. dir./cond. of the McDonald's HS Jazz Ens. '79–91 and dir. of jazz bands at Princeton U. '80–5. Dir. of the Grammy All-Amer. HS Jazz Band prog., he became prog. dir. of Carnegie Hall's Jazzed educ. prog. '95. As member of the faculty at Manh. Sch. of Mus., in addition to his professorial duties, he is involved in a program called Music in Action, which sends students to teach at inner-city schs. Became head of jazz dept. spring '99. Publ. many articles in mus. ed. magazines, such as *Modern Drummer*; *Music Educators Journal*. His method books are publ. by Music and Art Publications. Favs: Blakey, Roach, PJ Jones. Fests: Italy '92. Film: app. in *Fame*. TV: *Today*, Merv Griffin.

DICKENSON, VIC (VICTOR), tbn; b. Xenia, OH, 8/6/06; d. NYC, 11/16/84. Studied org.; fr. 1922, worked on tbn. w. local bands around Cleveland, Ohio. Join. Speed Webb '27; Zack Whyte '32; Blanche Calloway '33–6; Claude Hopkins '36–9; Benny Carter '39, '41; Count Basie '40–1; then w. Hot Lips Page, Sidney Bechet, Frankie Newton '41, '42–3; Eddie Heywood '43–5 in NYC and Calif. Freelanced and led own gps. on West Coast '47–8. Moved to Bost., freelanced and led gps. there and in NYC through mid 50s, then resettled in NYC, pl. mostly w. dixieland gps. Pl. w. Red Allen at the Metropole Café '58; Wild Bill Davison '61–3; also tour. Germ. w. George Wein '61. Fr. '63 to '68, he pl. and arr. for Saints and Sinners, a band he co-led w. Red Richards. In '60s, he also was a regular at Condon's; tour. Asia and Austral. w. Condon '64; Eur. '65. Fr. '68 to '70 w. Bobby Hackett; WGJB '70–2; again w. Hackett '73 in NYC, Toronto, Can., New Engl. Fr. '75, w. Balaban & Cats at Condon's. Cont. high activity until his death. One of the greatest swing era trombonists, Dickenson was wrongly pigeonholed as a dixieland player. His highly distinctive tone and style was warm, witty, and fluent. Comps: "Alone"; "Constantly"; "I'll Try." Polls: *Esq.* Silver Award '46–7; *DB* Critics '71–4. Fests: Cannes '59; MJF '64; Columbus JF '65; Pescara, San Sebastian '74; Nice '74–5; also NJF-NY '70s incl. Newport Hall of Fame; Colo. JP annually. TV: *The Magic Horn*; *The Sound of Jazz* '57; Tribute to Condon '64; *Just Jazz*, PBS '71 w. Hackett. CDs: Vang.; Story.; w. Lester Young (BN; Verve); Hackett (Chiaro.); Condon (Col.; Chiaro.); R. Braff; Pee Wee Russell (BL); Benny Carter (BB; B&B); Basie (Col.; Pab.); Bechet (BN; BB; BL); C. Hawkins (Cap.); Swingville All-Stars (GTJ); Davison (Jazz.); B. Tate (Story); Wardell Gray (Crown); J. Rushing (Vang.).

DICKERSON, CARROLL, vln, lead; b. 1895; d. Chicago, IL, 10/57. An active leader in Chi. dur. the 1920s, form. first band in '20; residency at Sunset Café '22–4, sidemen incl. Buster Bailey, Andrew Hilaire. In late '24, form. band for 48–wk. tour on the Pantages Circuit. Ret. to Chi. '26, re-form. band for Sunset, feat. Louis Armstrong on tpt. and voc; became house band at Savoy Dance Hall '27–9. In spring of '29, band went to NYC, gigging w. Armstrong as leader, Dickerson as cond. Again under Dickerson's name, the band had residency at Connie's Inn fr. late spring '29 until it broke up the following spring. Dickerson worked briefly w. Mills Blue Rhythm Band and tour. w. King Oliver bef. ret. to Chi. In early '30s, he form. a new band; sidemen in '34–5 incl. Zutty Singleton, Zinky Cohn; led house band at Swingland '37. Left mus. for two yrs; resumed role as a lead. in '39, cont. through '40s, incl. long engagement at the Rhumboogie. Though not a prominent jazz mus. himself, Dickerson was a capable lead. w. distinctive sidemen. Armstrong used several band members for some Hot Five recs. Dickerson's band also acc. Armstrong on OKeh dates in late '20s. Recs. as lead: "Symphonic Raps," w. Armstrong and Hines '28; as sideman w. Armstrong: "Ain't Misbehavin'," "That Rhythm Man," OKeh '29. CDs: w. Armstrong (Col.).

DICKERSON, (LOWELL) DWIGHT, pno; b. Los Angeles, CA, 12/26/44. Studied at Berklee Coll., 1965; also priv. in Bost., w. Ray Santisi, Margaret Chaloff; B.A. fr. Calif. State-LA '73. Pl. w. numerous gps in '70s, incl. Sergio Mendes; Bola Sete; James Moody; Larry Gales; Bobby Bryant; Charles Lloyd; Red Holloway; Bobby Hutcherson; Sahib Shihab. Organized his own trio '77, w. Carl Burnett and Louis Spears; rec. *Sooner or Later*, Disc. '78; form. qt. '80; tour. in Japan, Korea, New Zealand, sometimes singing. Pl. w. Holloway on *Song of America* jazz cruise '94. CDs: Night Life; w. N. Brignola (Night Life); Ricky Woodard (Cand.).

DICKERSON, WALT, vib, comp, arr; b. Philadelphia, PA, 1931. Brothers are classical vlnst., voc.; moth. pl. pno. and sang in church choir. Pl. several instruments bef. sw. to vib. Grad. fr. Morgan St. Coll., Balt., Md., 1953. In army '53–5, then worked as real estate agent in Calif. while leading a gp. that incl. Andrew Hill and Andrew Cyrille. Came to NYC '60, worked at Birdland; Vanguard; Five Spot; Minton's; Wells'; Versailles. Pl. w. Sun Ra '65–late '60s. Rec. *Impressions of a Patch of Blue*, an orig. arr. of Jerry Goldsmith's mus. for the film *A Patch of Blue* w. Sun Ra, MGM '65. Did not perf. late '60s-75, then moved to northern Eur. Worked in Eur. w. Sun Ra, Pierre

Dorge, Richard Davis '70s. An innovative vib. player, Dickerson's melodic and harmonic approach to the instrument is thought to prefigure that of Bobby Hutcherson and Karl Berger. Polls: *DB* New Star '62. CDs: NJ; Steep.; SN; w. Pierre Dorge (Steep.).

D'IMPERIO, DANNY (DANIEL LOUIS), dms; b. Sidney, NY, 3/14/45. Father was pnst. Robert D'Imperio. Grandfath. and two sons also prof. mus. Began on pno., then took up tpt. Sw. to dms. after hearing Louis Bellson w. Dorsey Bros. Orch. First prof. gig w. fath.'s band at age 12; fath. also introduced him to mus. incl. Spiegle Wilcox, Pee Wee Hunt. Pl. w. local bands in Syracuse 1957–62, then w. Salt City Six '62; Jimmy Cavallo '63; pl. bass w. Pee Wee Hunt '63; Vince Falcone–Tony Leonardi '64; Salt City Six '64–5. In army '65–8, pl. w. army bands. After discharge, spent six mos. as house dmr. at Three Rivers Inn, Syracuse, N.Y., then pl. w. Dana Valery '69–70; Glenn Miller Orch. '70–2; Gap Mangione '73; Maynard Ferguson '74–5; Woody Herman '76–7, incl. 40th Anniversary Carnegie Hall Concert; Tony Bennett '78; Barry Kiener, Andy Mackintosh '79; Eddie Jefferson–Richie Cole '80; Gap Mangione '81; Louis Armstrong Alumni Band '82. House dmr. at Eddie Condon's, NYC '83–5. Replaced Buddy Rich in Rich bb after leader suffered heart attack in '83, then organized and led Metropolitan Bopera House '83–6. House dmr. at club in Marco Island, Fla., '86–7, then tour. w. Rich band following leader's death. Own gps. and freelance in NYC since '88, incl. Gene Krupa Legend w. Anita O'Day '89; Les Elgart Band '89–90; Anita O'Day '91; Village Vanguard Orch. '96. Favs: P.J. Jones, Blakey, Sonny Payne. Fests: NJF-NY '74; Belvedere JF '74; Kool JF-Honolulu '77; Sacramento JF '84; JVC JF '88; Toronto de Maurier JF '93 and '95. TV: Mike Douglas w. Woody Herman, M. Ferguson, Liza Minnelli, T. Bennett; David Letterman w. John Pizzarelli '97; PBS w. Ferguson, Herman, Della Reese. CDs: Sack.; VSOP; w. Met. Bopera House (VSOP); Ferguson (Col.); J. Pizzarelli–D. Sebesky Orch. (RCA); Glenn Miller Reunion Band (Laser.); A. O'Day (Disques Swing).

DIORIO, JOE (JOSEPH LOUIS), gtr, comp; b. Waterbury, CT, 8/6/36. Influenced by his uncle, who pl. gtr. and other stringed instruments, stud. at Berdice Sch. of Mus. 1949–54, then self-taught. After exp. w. local bands, established himself in early and mid '60s by pl. and rec. w. Eddie Harris; Sonny Stitt; Bennie Green; Bunky Green; Ira Sullivan; Nicky Hill and other Chi. jazzmen; Stan Getz; Pete and Conte Candoli; and Monty Budwig. In Fla., he comp. and pl. for TV docu. and worked on local TV shows. Pl. at the JFK Center for Perf. Arts in Wash., D.C., in '71. Perf. in the Netherlands '77–'78; France '80; Brazil '85; Italy '87–'90; and Austr. '89. Capable classical as well as jazz gtrst., Diorio has written several publications and, since '75, taught at U. of Miami, USC, and at the Musicians Institute. Diorio is also a painter and sculptor. Favs: Tony Mottola, Django Reinhardt, Jim Hall. Book: *21st Century Intervallic Designs* '78. CDs: RAM.

DIRTY DOZEN BRASS BAND, THE. Organized in NO in 1970s as a musical adjunct to the Dirty Dozen Social and Pleasure Club. Orig. form. to pl. for funerals and parades, the 8-pc. ens. turned to a much more eclectic repertoire in the '80s. Pl. on bills w. Wynton Marsalis and the Grateful Dead and rec. w. Manhattan Transfer; the Neville Bros.; Buckwheat Zydeco; et al. Since '82, tours to more than thirty countries, incl. Montreux, Umbria '84, and North Sea JFs. Personnel, which has remained stable since late '70s, incl.: Gregory Davis and Efrem Towns, tpts.; Charles Joseph, tbn.; Kirk Joseph, sousaphone; Roger Lewis, bari. sax; Kevin Harris, tnr. sax; Lionel Batiste, bs. dm.; Jenell Marshall, snare dm. CDs: Col.

DISLEY, DIZ (WILLIAM CHARLES), gtr; b. Winnipeg, Man., Canada, 5/27/31. Raised in Wales and Yorkshire, Engl. Began on bjo., then sw. to gtr. at age 14 after hearing Django Reinhardt. Rec. w. Yorkshire Jazz Band 1949. In mil., then att. art coll. Moved to London '53. Worked as newspaper cartoonist and pl. w. Mick Mulligan '53; Ken Colyer '54; Cy Laurie, Sandy Brown '56–7. Led own swing gp., Soho String Qt., and pl. w. skiffle gps. late '50s. Pl. w. Kenny Ball, Alex Welsh '60s; also perf. at folk clubs and on radio, TV. Pl. w. Stephane Grappelli '73–83, then re-form. Soho String Qt. '83. App. w. Bireli Lagrene in Reinhardt tribute concert at Kool JF, NYC '84. CDs: w. Grappelli (BL; MPS); Lagrene (Inak); J.-L. Ponty (MPS).

DISTEL, SACHA (ALEXANDRE), gtr, voc; b. Paris, 1/29/33. Nephew of well-known bandleader Ray Ventura. Stud. pno. at age 5, gtr. fr. 1948. Worked w. Bernard Peiffer '52; Henri Renaud, Sandy Mosse, Bobby Jaspar '53; also w. Martial Solal; Barney Wilen; Rene Urtreger; Kenny Clarke; others. Rec. *Afternoon In Paris* w. John Lewis '57. Later became best-known as a pop singer, but cont. to work occ. as a jazz artist. Wrote ballad, "The Good Life." Favs: Charlie Parker, Jim Raney, Kenny Burrell, Tal Farlow, Charlie Christian. CDs: w. Jaspar (Em.).

DITMAS, BRUCE, dms, drum machine, kybds, perc, comp; b. Atlantic City, NJ, 12/12/46. Grew up in Miami, Fla. Father pl. tbn. w. bbs in 1940s, then w. show bands in Miami. Began on pno. Stud. w. Tony Crisetello, then att. Stan Kenton clinics at Indiana U., Michigan St. U. '62–3. Pl. w. Ira Sullivan in Fla. '62–4; tour. w. Judy Garland '64–5. Moved to NYC '66, accomp. singers, incl. Barbra Streisand, Della Reese, Leslie Uggams, Sheila Jordan '66–70. Pl. w. Joe Newman, Jazz Interactions Orch. '71; Gil Evans Orch. '71–7; Enrico Rava fr. '71; Stardrive, Atmospheres w. Clive Stevens, Steve Kuhn, Albert Dailey, Future Shock w. Brecker bros. '72; New Wilderness Preservation Band '72–3; Paul Bley, Lee Konitz, Chet Baker '74–5; Stan Getz '75. Solo concerts and recs. on electronic dms. fr. '76. Feat. w. Gil Evans '79–85; Italian fusion gp. New Perigeo '83. Lived in Italy '86–7, pl. w. Dino Saluzzi–Enrico Rava, Rita Marcotulli–Pietro Tonolo. Ret. to NYC '88 to cont. work w. kybds. and synth. dms. Pl. w. Bigfood, own trio, D3, since '88. Resident comp. for Independent Theater Co. '88–90. Pl. w. Pat Hall, Oil-Can '91; Karl Berger since '91. Ditmas received an NEA grant in '90 to orchestrate *The Dream of Four Directions*, an opera by Patricia Burgess. He comp. the score for the film *Deathscape* and has comp. and perf. extensively for jingles and TV since '90. Favs: Jack DeJohnette, Elvin Jones, Billy Hart; arrs: G. Evans, Geo. Russell. Fests: Eur. since '70s. CDs: Post.; w. Ralph Simon (Post.); D3; Bigfood (Tutu); G. Evans (RCA); Rava (SN); J. Pastorius (DIW); Saluzzi (ECM).

DIVA. An excellent all-female bb formed in 1993 by former Buddy Rich dmr. and manager Stanley Kay, dmr. Sherrie Maricle, and arr. John LaBarbera. Sidewomen have included Ingrid Jensen, tpt.; Virginia Mayhew, saxes. CD on the Diva label.

DIXON, BILL (WILLIAM ROBERT), tpt, flg, comp; b. Nantucket, MA, 10/5/25. Mother was writer and blues singer. Family moved to NYC in 1933. Stud. painting at Bost. U., then tpt. at Hartnett Cons., NYC '46–51. Led own gps. fr. '50s. Pl. w. Cecil Taylor fr. '59; Archie Shepp '62–3. In '64, Dixon organized and prod. the "October Revolution" concerts at the Cellar Café in NYC, which helped introduce avant-garde mus. such as Sun Ra; Roswell Rudd; Paul Bley; Milford Graves; David Izenzon; and Dixon himself to a wider audience. Also in '64, Dixon helped establish the Jazz Composers' Guild, whose charter members incl. Taylor; Paul and Carla Bley; Mike Mantler; Sun Ra; Shepp; and Rudd. He worked w. dancer Judith Dunn fr. '65–75, prod. many concerts that combined free jazz and dance. In '67, he helped found the Free Cons. of the U. of the Streets in NYC. Dixon has had extensive experience as an educ., teach. or lecturing at Ohio St. U. '66; George

Washington U. '67; Columbia U. '67–70; Bennington Coll. since '68; U. of Wisc. '71–2; Middlebury Coll. '86; Yale U. '90; Wesleyan U. '90; Northeastern U. '90. Dixon has also lectured on African-Amer. mus. and culture in Italy, Austria, Israel, and at the Smithsonian Institution's Ellington Symposium. He is a member of the Jazz Advisory Committee of the New Engl. Foundation for the Arts and has served on committees of the NEA. In '86 he publ. *L'Opera: A Collection of Letters, Writings, Musical Scores, Drawings and Photographs*. Favs: M. Davis, Gillespie, Navarro, Clark Terry, Thad Jones. Polls: *Jazz Mag*. Mus. of the Yr. '76; BMI Jazz Pioneer Award '84. Fests: NJF '66; many in Eur. since '76. Films: feat. in *Imagine the Sound* '81. CDs: SN; w. Taylor (BN).

DIXON, CHARLIE (CHARLES EDWARD), bjo, arr; b. Jersey City, NJ, ca. 1898; d. NYC, 12/6/40. Worked w. various bands in NYC and Bost.; join. Sam Wooding at the Nest Club, NYC, 1922. Rec. w. Fletcher Henderson '23; pl. w. his orch. and wrote arrs. fr. '24–8; contributed charts to Henderson after leaving band. Led band accomp. dancer Cora LaRedd. Throughout the '30s, he was active as arr.-comp., writing for Chick Webb and Plantation Club shows. Arr: "Harlem Congo" for Webb '37. CDs: w. Henderson (Col.; BB); as arr. w. Webb (Dec.).

DIXON, ERIC ("BIG DADDY"), tnr sax, fl, comp; b. Staten Island, NY, 3/28/30; d. NYC, 10/19/89. Played bugle as a child, then took up tnr. sax at age 12; as teenager stud. priv. w. Peter Luisetti. Prof. debut in 1950; pl. mus. in army, 1951–3. Freelanced in NYC, incl. working w. Cootie Williams '54; Johnny Hodges '55; Benny Green '56; started doubling fl. In late '50s, he pl. w. Bill English qt.; house band at the Apollo; dmr. Curly Hamner, w. whom he tour. Eur. in '59. Join. Quincy Jones '60, tour. Eur. and rec. w. him in '61. Fr. early '62, he was feat. soloist on tnr. and fl. w. Count Basie; also contributed to band's book. In '72, he left to run The Meeting Place, a Staten Island restaurant, w. his wife, but rejoin. Basie '75–84. A strong-toned, vibrant tnr. soloist and first-rate flst. w. a modern, bluesy style. Favs: Paul Gonsalves, Lockjaw Davis. Comps: "Eric's Edge," "The Meeting Place." Arrs. for Basie: "It's Only a Paper Moon" '65; "Frankie and Johnny" '67. Recs. as leader; also w. Roy Eldridge, Mast. Jazz. CDs: w. Basie (Verve; Roul.; Den.; Pab.; Mos.); Bennie Green; Oliver Nelson (Prest.); Mal Waldron (NJ).

DODDS, BABY (WARREN), dms; b. New Orleans, LA, 12/24/1898; d. Chicago, IL, 2/14/59.

Brother of cl. Johnny Dodds and early associate of Louis Armstrong, Papa Celestin, King Oliver. Pl. in NO and w. Fate Marable's riverboat bands 1918–21. Worked w. Oliver '21–2, first in SF, then Chi '22–3; Honore Dutrey, Freddie Keppard and Johnny Dodds '24. Fr. '25 to '30, he pl. under leadership of Willie Hightower; Lil Armstrong; Charlie Elgar; others. Pl. w. bro. Johnny at Kelly's Stables '27–9 and many other locations throughout the '30s; also ran taxi business w. bro. Bill. Fr. '36 to '39, he worked intermittently as house dmr. at Three Deuces. Pl. w. Jimmie Noone '40–1; Bunk Johnson '45, incl. app. in NYC. After brief return to Chi., he was active in NYC w. Art Hodes '46, '47, and as regular member of band on Rudi Blesh's *This Is Jazz* radio series '47. Pl. w. Art Hodes '48, bef. ret. to Chi. where he worked w. Miff Mole '48–9. A series of strokes, beginning w. one suffered in NYC in spring '49, slowed his activities, but he soon cont. working: w. Conrad Janis '49; Natty Dominique '51, '52; an app. at Jimmy Ryan's Dec. '52; and w. Don Frye late '54. Despite partial paralysis, he pl. sporadically in Chi. to '57. In his final yrs. he also rec. a series of drm. solos w. commentary for Amer. Mus., an extraordinary document of the early NO-style of drumming. He has been praised by colleagues fr. Louis Armstrong to Max Roach. Germ. jazz critic Joachim-Ernst Berendt called him "one of the greatest figures in NO jazz," and Nat Hentoff wrote (in *Jazz Makers*): "Increasingly overlooked have been the intrinsic values of Baby's style; his developed insights into the basic nature of jazz drumming; elements in his work that. . .helped to form certain aspects of modern jazz percussion." Others felt that he messed up the beat when he played to the crowd, and Grossman and Farrell in *The Heart of Jazz* allowed that he had "an occasional tendency to overexuberance that is sometimes damaging in ensembles." Poll: *Record Changer* All-Time, All-Star '51. Fests: Nice w. Mezz Mezzrow '48. Book: *The Baby Dodds Story*, as told to Larry Gara, LA '59. Made many historic recs. w. Jelly Roll Morton; J. Dodds; S. Bechet; own gp. CDs: Amer. Mus.; w. Morton (BB); Bechet (BB; Laser.); Louis Armstrong (Col.; Dec.; BBC); J. Dodds (Dec.; BB); Bunk Johnson (Amer. Mus.); Earl Hines (BB); George Lewis (Amer. Mus.); Wooden Joe Nicholas; Noone (Milan); Mezzrow (Story.); Wild Bill Davison (Jazz.).

DODDS, JOHNNY, cl; b. New Orleans, LA, 4/12/1892; d. Chicago, IL, 8/8/40. Older bro. of Baby Dodds. Took up cl. at 17; mainly self-taught, though he had some lessons w. Lorenzo Tio Jr. First full-time mus. engagement was w. Kid Ory 1911; stayed w. Ory until '18; also tour. w. Fate Marable's riverboat band '17. In '18, he tour. w. Billy Mack, worked w. Mutt Carey, and made his first trip to Chi. Back in NO, he rejoin. Ory '19. Ret. to Chi. in '20, to pl. w. King Oliver, w. whom he remained into '23, incl. stay at Lincoln Gardens and booking in Calif. '21. In '24, Dodds took over as lead. of Freddie Keppard's house band at Kelly's Stables, remaining there to '30. In '30s, he led own gp. at several Chi. clubs, incl. Three Deuces '38. He and his bros. also drove taxis for a living. He was struck by a heart attack in the spring of '39 and did not pl. again until Jan. '40, when he app. w. his own qt. Disbanded gp. due to dental problems, but soon resumed playing on weekends w. a qt. led by his bro. Baby Dodds. Dur. his last few mos., he rarely pl., focusing instead on overseeing apartment houses that he owned. Although he was not the technical equal of such NO cls. as Sidney Bechet and Jimmie Noone, Dodds's warm vibrato, strong blues feeling, and imaginative ensemble playing made him one of the greats of the NO sch. His first recs. were the famous Oliver sess. in Richmond, Ind., and Chi. '23. Fr. '25, he also participated in many historic recs. w. Louis and Lil Armstrong and Jelly Roll Morton. Fr. '27, he rec. as leader. His only trip to NYC was for a '38 rec. w. Charlie Shavers. His last rec. was w. Natty Dominique '40. CDs: Dec.; BB; w. Armstrong-Oliver (Mile.); Oliver (Dec.); Armstrong (Col.); BBC); J.R. Morton (BB); Keppard (King Jazz); Junie C. Cobb (Collector's Classics); in *History of Classic Jazz* (Riv.).

DODGE, JOE (JOSEPH GEORGE), dms; b. Monroe, WI, 2/9/22. Raised in SF; stud. w. SF Symph. dmr. In mil. 1942–6, pl. in army bands, where he met Paul Desmond. Form. gp. w. Desmond '47; tour. w. Nick Esposito '48–9. Held a day job at a bank '50–3, occ. pl. w. Jack Sheedy; dixieland gp. Tour. w. Dave Brubeck '53–6, then made his living outside mus., pl. weekend gigs in Oakland, Calif., area. Favs: Roach, Blakey. CDs: w. Brubeck (Fant.; Col.); Desmond (Fant.).

DODGION, DOTTIE (Dorothy Giaimo), dms, voc; b. Brea, CA, 9/23/29. Father a prof. dmr. in SF. Married Jerry Dodgion. Started as singer; mainly self-taught. Was rescued by Mary Kay in Springfield, Ill., when stranded by comedian she worked for as voc.-straight "man"; form. trio as dmr. w. Mary Kay's bro. and wife, worked her way back to SF. Started subbing and sitting in, became serious about dms. in mid 1950s. Pl. w. Nick Esposito, C. Mingus in SF. Moved to NYC, worked w. Benny Goodman '61; Marian McPartland '64; Billy Mitchell–Al Grey Qnt. Pl. in Toronto, Can., w. Wild Bill Davison; LV w. Carl Fontana, Gus Mancuso; coll. tours w. Eugene Wright; w. Cohn-Sims at Half Note, NYC, then join. Ruby

Braff Qt. Separated fr. husband and moved back to Calif. in mid '70s; worked in Lake Tahoe, Nev, as dmr. and voc.; pl. in LA w. Mancuso, Wright '75. Served as mus. dir. for Wash., D.C., club bef. ret. to NYC '79; w. Melba Liston '80. Infl: Sid Catlett, Jo Jones; Kenny Clarke. A sensitive dmr. who fits into every modern jazz context. Fests: Concord w. Braff '72. Recs. w. Braff; Davison (Chiaro.); M. McPartland (Halcyon). CDs: Arb, as voc.

DODGION, JERRY DAWSON, alto sax, cl, fl, arr; b. Richmond, CA, 8/29/32. Began pl. alto sax in elem. sch. While in hs, he pl. in local bbs w. Rudy Salvini, John Coppola, Chuck Travis. Briefly att. UC-Berkeley, then pl. w. Paul Desmond in Alvino Rey bb; also pl. fl. in National Guard Band. Pl. w. Gerald Wilson 1953–4; Benny Carter '55; Charlie Mariano '57; Red Norvo '58–61. Left Norvo to freelance in NYC '61. Pl. and rec. w. Benny Goodman '61–2, incl. tours of So. Amer. and USSR; Oliver Nelson '61–7; Quincy Jones '60s; Count Basie '66; Duke Pearson '67–9. Also pl. w. own gp. w. wife, Dottie, and subbed for Al Cohn–Zoot Sims at Half Note mid '60s. Dodgion was an orig. member of the Thad Jones–Mel Lewis Orch. in '66, and stayed w. the band as lead alto (fr. '71) and arr. until '79. Busy as freelancer in NYC throughout '70s; pl. and rec. w. Richard Davis; B. Goodman; Herbie Hancock; Blue Mitchell; David Amram. Rec. w. Red Mitchell and Tommy Flanagan, PW '79; w. Marian McPartland '79, '86. Pl. w. Dizzy Gillespie bb '87–8; Grover Mitchell bb '88–91; Gene Harris and Philip Morris Superband '89–91; Buck Clayton bb '91. Favs: Hodges, Benny Carter, Parker; arrs: Ellington, Strayhorn, Thad Jones. Fests: Eur. and Asia w. Jones-Lewis; also Eur. w. Gillespie '87–8, Clayton '91. CDs: w. Jones-Lewis (A&M; BN); H. Hancock; R. Brecker; J. Henderson (BN); Flanagan-Mitchell (PW); S. McCorkle; M. McPartland; G. Harris (Conc.); J. Sheldon (Up.); Goodman (MM); J. J. Johnson (BB); Ron Carter (Mile.).

DOGGETT, BILL (WILLIAM BALLARD), org, pno, comp; b. Philadelphia, PA, 2/6/16; d. NYC, 11/13/96. Played pno. w. Jimmy Gorman, then led own band accomp. Lucky Millinder, 1938. Pl. w. Jimmy Mundy '39; Millinder '40–2. Pnst. and arr. w. Ink Spots '42–4. Freelanced w. Jimmy Rushing, Lucky Thompson, Illinois Jacquet, Willie Bryant, mid '40s. Wrote arr. of Monk's "'Round Midnight" for Cootie Williams orch. '44. Replaced Wild Bill Davis w. Louis Jordan '49–51. Took up org. '51, infl. by Davis. Rec. w. Ella Fitzgerald '51. Very successful as r&b artist in late '50s; his biggest hit was "Honky Tonk" '56. Arr. and cond. album for Fitzgerald '63.

Cont. to tour w. combo throughout '60s, incl. perf. at numerous benefits for the civil rights movement. Rec. w. Della Reese '66. Tour. Eur. regularly w. own gp. fr. '70s; also pl. reunion gigs w. Ink Spots. Polls: *Cashbox* top r&b perf. '57–9. Fests: Eur. w. own combo. CDs: King; After Hours; w. E. Fitzgerald (Verve; Dec.); Willis Jackson (Del.); B. Tate (BL; B&B); Jordan (Band.); Eddie Vinson (B&B).

DOKY, NIELS LAN, pno, comp; b. Copenhagen, Denmark, 10/3/63. Father, a doctor, pl. gtr.; moth., a singer; bro., Christian Minh Doky (b. Copenhagen, 2/7/69), bs. Took up classical gtr. at age 7; pno., after discovering ragtime, 1974. At 13, pl. w. various orchs. Met Thad Jones '78, who advised him to go to US. In '84, after three yrs. of study at Berklee Coll., Bost., he moved to NYC and pl. w. David Sanborn; Ray Barretto; Thad Jones. Rec. for Danish Story. label and Milestone, w. Randy Brecker; Bob Berg; John Abercrombie; John Scofield; N.H.Ø. Pedersen; Christian Minh Doky; others. *The Penguin Guide to Jazz* cited his "dazzling fluency...biting, percussive touch...decisive, linear manner." CDs: Story.; Mile.; w. J. Abercrombie (Maracatu); Lars Danielsson; U. Wakenius (L+R); C.M. Doky; Hans Ulrik (Story.); T. Harrell (Cont.); Tommy Smith (BN).

DOLDINGER, KLAUS, tnr, sop saxes, cl, kybds, comp; b. Berlin, Germany, 5/12/36. Studied pno. fr. 1947, cl. fr. '52, at Robert Schumann Cons., Dusseldorf. Led amateur dixieland band fr. '52. Won several awards on alto sax at jazz competitions '55–6. Perf. in NO, Chi., NYC w. a trad. jazz gp., Feetwarmers, and a hard bop gp., Oskar's Trio '60. Back in Germ., pl. in jazz wkshp. w. visiting US mus., incl. Kenny Clarke, Johnny Griffin, Max Roach, Donald Byrd, Don Ellis, Sahib Shihab, Idrees Sulieman '63–4. Formed own hard bop qnt. w. Ingfried Hoffman as sideman. Tour. No. Africa, Middle East, Scand. '64; So. Amer., spons. by West Germ. govt. '65; Asia '69. Formed Motherhood '70; the gp. changed its name to Passport in '71. Tour. US w. own combo '75. Comps. incl. *Jazz Concertino* for jazz qt. and symph. orch. Fr. '70s, he has mainly been occupied w. writing for films and TV, incl. the scores to the films *Das Boot* and *The Eternal Story*. A collection of Doldinger's comps. for Passport was publ. in Germ. in the '70s. Favs: Bechet, C. Parker, Coltrane, Ornette Coleman, Gil Evans, M. Davis. Polls: won several Germ. jazz and rock polls in '70s. Fests: all major in Eur. w. Passport early '70s. TV: Eur.; Asia; So. Amer. TV. CDs: Atl.; BM.

DOLPHY, ERIC ALLAN, alto sax, cl, bs-cl, fl, comp; b. Los Angeles, CA, 6/20/28; d. Berlin, Germany, 6/29/64. Began on cl. while in jr. hs; later stud. w. Lloyd Reese. Pl. alto sax for dances while a teenager. Stud. mus. at LA City Coll. Pl. lead alto sax and made first recs. w. Roy Porter 1948–50; then US Army to '52, when he transferred to US Navy Sch. of Mus. In '53, he ret. to LA, working w. George Brown, Gerald Wilson, Buddy Collette, Eddie Beal '53–8. Gained wide recognition w. Chico Hamilton '58–9. Moved to NYC in '60, join. Charles Mingus, app. regularly at the Showplace. Rec. *Free Jazz* w. Ornette Coleman '60. A qnt., formed w. Booker Little, app. often at the Five Spot '61. He tour. Eur. dur. the summer of '61, incl. Stockholm, Copenhagen. That yr., he also started an assoc. w. John Coltrane, incl. late fall Eur. tour. Left Coltrane in Mar. '62 and formed gp. w. Freddie Hubbard; later that yr. he became part of Orchestra USA. Until '64, he was also very active as a freelancer, rec. for several labels as a lead. and sideman. In early '64, he rejoin. Mingus for Eur. tour and decided to stay and live in Paris. Rec. w. Dutch and Scand. rhythm sections. While in Berlin for a club date, Dolphy died suddenly of a heart attack precipitated by diabetes. Originating fr. the tradition of Charlie Parker, Dolphy played lines whose contours stemmed fr. Parker but used dissonant harmonies and a raw intonation that was even more pronounced on bs-cl. "He had such a big sound," said Mingus, "as big as Charlie Parker's...inside that sound was a great capacity to talk in his music about the most basic feelings...he knew that level of the language that very few musicians get down to." Don Heckman wrote: "In Dolphy's hands the bass clarinet was never an awkward instrument; it possessed, instead, a serpentine aliveness that coiled with vitality." Dur. his brief career, Dolphy displayed remarkable versatility that allowed him to perf. romantic ballads, blues, and twentieth-century art music in an equally compelling manner. In addition to Parker, his infls. ranged fr. NO marching bands to the sounds of birds, the latter applying to his flute. Coltrane said of him: "My life was made much better by knowing him. He was one of the greatest people I've ever known, as a man, a friend and a musician." Favs: Buddy Collette, C. Parker. Fests: NJF w. Hamilton '59; "rebel" fest. at Newport, Antibes, both w. Mingus '60. Polls: *DB* New Star on alto sax, fl., misc. instrument '61; *DB* Hall of Fame '65. Videos: *Last Date*, Rhap.; w. Mingus (Shan.; Vidjazz). Books: *Dolphy Series Limited*, transcriptions of Dolphy solos by Andrew White; *Eric Dolphy: A Musical Biography and Discography*, V. Simosko and B. Tepperman, '74. CDs: Prest., incl. 9–disc box; NJ; BN; Enja; Em.; Cand.; w. Hamilton (FS); Mingus (Rh./Atl.; Cand.); O. Coleman; John Lewis (Atl.); J. Coltrane; Roach (Imp.); Oliver Nelson (NJ; Imp.); G. Evans (Verve); Sxt. of Orch. USA

(BB); Booker Little; Abbey Lincoln (Cand.); Ron Carter; K. McIntyre; M. Waldron (NJ); Lockjaw Davis (Prest.); G. Russell (Riv.); Andrew Hill (BN).

DOMANICO, CHUCK (CHARLES LOUIS), bs; b. Chicago, IL, 1/20/44. Started on tpt.; sw. to bs. in hs. Moved to LA in mid 1960s; pl. and rec. w. Don Ellis at MJF '66. Later in gps. led by Tom Scott, Roger Kellaway, and Victor Feldman; also pl. in Kellaway's Cello Qt.; rec. w. Shelly Manne '77–80. In '80s, he worked mainly in studios, but pl. gigs w. Jack Sheldon band in '92, rec. w. Shirley Horn, and join. reorganized Kellaway Cello Qt. CDs: w. Shirley Horn (Verve); Victor Feldman; Barney Kessel; Gerry Mulligan (A&M); Oliver Nelson (RCA); Anthony Ortega (hatArt).

DOMINIQUE, NATTY (ANATIE), tpt; b. New Orleans, LA, 8/2/1896; d. Chicago, IL, 8/30/82. Cousin of Barney Bigard, uncle of Don Albert. Tried perc. bef. sw. to tpt.; stud. w. Emanuel Perez and pl. in his brass band in 1913. Went to Chi., then Det., pl. in various brass bands. After WWI, he became prominent on Chi. jazz scene, pl. intermittently w. Carroll Dickerson's orch. to '24, incl. apps. w. Louis Armstrong; w. Jimmie Noone for two yrs; Jelly Roll Morton '23; worked regularly w. Johnny Dodds '25–40. Fr. early '40s, a heart condition curtailed Dominique's pl.; he became a skycap at Chi. airport, emerging occ. to pl. w. Baby Dodds and others; led his own gps. dur. the '50s. Recs. w. J.R. Morton, J. Dodds in '20s; Noone, Dodds '40. CDs: Amer. Mus.; w. J. Dodds (Dec.; BB).

DOMNERUS, ARNE, alto sax, cl; b. Stockholm, Sweden, 12/20/24. Started w. Thore Ehrling and Simon Brehm bands. Pl. at Paris JF 1949. Fr. '51 to '68, he led own combo, which incl. other leading Swedish jazz mus., Lars Gullin, Gunnar Svensson. Also part of Swedish Radio Big Band '56–65; led its successor, the Radiojazzgruppen, '67–78. Cont. active career in the '80s. Pl. w. Bengt Hallberg at Swed. Embassy, NYC. Tour. US and Can. in '91, incl. app. at Sweet Basil, NYC. Sweden's foremost alto player; also a very capable cl. soloist. CDs: Drag.; three tracks in *North American Tour 1991*, Caprice; w. Clifford Brown; J. Moody (Prest.); George Russell (SN); L. Gullin; D. Gillespie (Drag.); B. Hallberg (Phon.).

DONAHUE, SAM KOONTZ, tnr sax, tpt, arr, lead; b. Detroit, MI, 3/8/18; d. Reno, NV, 3/22/74. Played first prof. job at newly legalized beer garden in River Rouge while still in sch. Led own band 1933–8; pl. w. Gene Krupa '38–40; w. Harry James, Benny Good-man '40. Own band in NYC '40–2; entered navy, where he took over lead. of Artie Shaw's Navy Band, which he molded into one of the best service bands '44–5. Pl. battle of the bands against Glenn Miller's AAF orch. in London; Donahue became wartime fav. through UK broadcasts. Ret. to NYC after discharge; led own band and taught at Hartnett Studios to '51, when he spent six mos. back in navy. Then w. T. Dorsey '52; fronted Billy May's orch. on tour '54–6. Fr. '57 to '59, he led own band. Pl. w. Stan Kenton '60–1. Fr. '61 to '65, he fronted T. Dorsey orch., which became part of a popular show feat. alumni Charlie Shavers and the Pied Pipers. The show tour. Japan as part of World JF '64; So. Amer., the Orient '65. In '66, the band, without Dorsey's name, was reduced to an oct. and Donahue soon retired. Capable, big-toned tnr. man of the Hawkins sch., but his greatest talent was as a bb organizer and leader. His bb rec. for Cap. CDs: w. Kenton (Cap.; Status).

DONALD, PETER ALEXANDER, dms; b. San Francisco, CA, 5/15/45. Raised in Woodside, Calif., until he moved to Bost., at age 14. Stud. priv. w. Alan Dawson 1964–9; comp. at Berklee Coll. '68–70. Pl. w. John La Porta's Bost. Youth Band '66–8. First major job w. Red Norvo '65. Living in LA, he pl. w. Carmen McRae '72–74; Akiyoshi-Tabackin bb '74–79; John Abercrombie Qt. '78–82; Denny Zeitlin Trio '85; Bob Florence '87. Tour. and rec. extensively in US, Eur., and Japan. Also active as contractor and prod. for commercial advertising dates. Teacher and perc. program dir. at Grove Sch. of Mus. fr. '85. Author of several publications on drum technique. Favs: Roy Haynes, Bernard Purdie, Peter Erskine. CDs: Abercrombie (ECM); Akiyoshi-Tabackin (RCA); Z. Sims (Pab.); B. Florence (USA); Zeitlin (WH).

DONALDSON, BOBBY (ROBERT STANLEY), dms; b. Boston, MA, 11/29/22; d. NYC, 7/2/71. From mus. family, incl. eldest bro. Don, who was mus. dir. for Fats Waller in late 1930s. Pl. w. Tasker Crosson and other local bands '39–41. Mil. service '41–5, incl. army band w. Russell Procope in NYC. Tour. w. Cat Anderson '46; stud. at Schillinger House '47; worked w. Paul Bascomb, Willis Jackson; Edmond Hall at Café Society '50–2; also gigs w. Sy Oliver, Lucky Millinder, Andy Kirk; Buck Clayton at Basin St. '53–4; Benny Goodman; Red Norvo at the Metropole Café; Dorothy Donegan, Eddie Condon and many other gps. in NYC. In '57, he pl. w. Seventh Ave. Stompers, incl. Vic Dickenson, Buster Bailey, Emmett Berry; in '58, w. Max Kaminsky, Teddy Wilson, then join. Eddie Heywood. Very active as studio mus. fr. mid '50s. Died of a heart attack. Favs: Jo

Jones, Shadow Wilson, Buddy Rich. Recs. as lead. '58, '60; as sideman w. Clayton; Helen Merrill; Mel Powell; Ruby Braff; Goodman; Basie; Hodges; Jackson. Comp: "Don-Que-Dee." CDs: *Seventh Avenue Stompers* (Sav.); w. R. Braff (BL; Aff.); M. Powell (Vang.); B. Goodman (Cap.; MM); H. Mann (Prest.; Sav.); C. Fuller; C. Byrd (Sav.).

DONALDSON, LOU (LOUIS A.), alto sax, cl, dms; b. Badin, NC, 11/1/26. Mother taught pno.; bro. is school band dir. in Louisville, Ky.; two sists. are amateur mus. Began on cl. at age 15. Stud. w. moth., then at Greensboro A&T Coll. and Great Lakes Naval Station. In navy band w. Willie Smith, Clark Terry, Ernie Wilkins mid 1940s. After discharge, moved to NYC, stud. at Darrow Inst. of Mus.; also sat in w. Sonny Stitt; Charlie Parker; others. Pl. w. Hot Lips Page '48–9; Dud Bascomb '50–4; Milt Jackson, Thelonious Monk '52. Rec. w. Art Blakey, Clifford Brown, Horace Silver, Curly Russell '54 for Blue Note; then led own sess. for the label. He became known as an r&b player in the '60s, after app. on recs. such as Jimmy Smith's hit, *The Sermon*, and making a series of funk-directed LPs for Blue Note, but has since ret. to a more bebop-oriented, yet bluesy style. Donaldson has made over seventy-five recs. as a leader since the '50s, and is still in high demand as a leader and soloist. In '90s qt. incl. Dr. Lonnie Smith, Peter Bernstein. Awarded an honorary doctorate fr. Greensboro A&T '82. Favs: Parker, Hodges, Earl Bostic; arr: Oliver Nelson. Polls: *DB*. Fests: Eur.; Japan, incl. multiple tours yearly since late '60s. CDs: Col.; BN; Timel.; Mile.; w. Blakey; Clifford Brown; J. Smith; Milt Jackson; Monk (BN); G. Ammons (Prest.); Cedar Walton (Evid.).

DONATO, MICHEL ANDRÉ, bs, pno; b. Montreal, Que., Canada, 8/25/42. Father, Roland, pl. tnr. sax, led band; uncle Maurice pl. pno. Stud. w. Roger Charbonneau at Montreal Cons. 1960–3; also w. Thomas Martin. Pl. w. Montreal Symph. '64; Aquarius Rising w. Claude Ranger, Brian Barley '68–9; Carmen McRae, Michel Legrand, Pierre Leduc, Lee Gagnon, others '60s. Moved to Toronto '69; pl. w. Lenny Breau; Moe Koffman; Bernie Senensky; Don Thompson; Sonny Greenwich; Alvin Pall; C. Ranger. Also accomp. Benny Carter, Art Farmer, Milt Jackson, Dave McKenna in Toronto clubs, and worked as studio mus. World tour w. Oscar Peterson '72–3. Pl. w. Bill Evans in Can. in '70s, but declined an offer to join the pianist's trio. Rec. w. Gerry Niewood '76; Buddy DeFranco '77. Ret. to Montreal '77. Began teaching at McGill U., U. of Montreal '80. Pl. w. own qnt. '82; Karen Young '83–90, occas. singing and pl. pno.; Oscar Peterson w. Montreal Symph. '84; Lor-

raine Desmarais fr. '84; Montreal All-Stars '85; duo w. Alain Caron fr. '90. Donato established a TV and film mus. prod. co. w. James Gelfand, Jean Dury '91. Favs: Scott LaFaro, Pettiford, Percy Heath, Mingus. Polls: Concours de Jazz de Montreal prize '82. Fests: all major w. Peterson '72–3; Pompeii JF w. own qnt. '82. TV: *Everything Goes* w. M. Koffman; *Jazz En Liberté* '65–70. LPs: w. Peterson (Japan. Col.); Senensky; D. Thompson. CDs: w. Oliver Jones (JT); Desmarais (Scherzo).

DONEGAN, DOROTHY, pno, b. Chicago, IL, 4/6/24; d. Los Angeles, CA, 5/19/98. Early encouragement fr. Art Tatum. Stud. at Chi. Cons., Chi. Mus. Coll., and USC in LA. Worked in cocktail lounges, app. in film, *Sensations of 1945*, then to NYC for play, *Star Time*, w. which she later toured. Donegan's career was mainly limited to night clubs, such as the Embers in NYC, where her flamboyant personality and visual antics tended to distract fr. the fact that she was an exceptional pnst. w. a formidable technique, compelling swing, rich harmonic sense, and broad repertoire. In the late '80s, she received belated recognition in clubs, concerts, int'l fests., and on jazz cruises. Her perfs. incl. verbal humor and impressions of other pnsts. and voc., the latter most often parodic. Her trio in the '90s most often consisted of Jon Burr, bs.; and Ray Mosca, dms. In '92, she won a $20,000 NEA award as an "American Jazz Master," which she accepted at a Miami convention of NAJE. She lectured at Northeastern U., Harvard, and the Manh. Sch. of Mus. In the late '90s she was diagnosed w. cancer, and she was forced to retire in the fall of '97. In '98, while seeking treatment in Mexico, she fell into a coma fr. which she never recovered. Favs: Tatum; V. Horowitz. CDs: Chiaro.; Timel.; Aud.; CMA; B&B; Story.

DONELIAN, ARMEN HRANT, pno, comp; b. Queens, NY, 12/1/50. Father pl. vln.; two uncles, bros., sis. all amateur mus. Stud. at Westchester Cons. 1957–69; Columbia U. '68–72 w. B.A.; priv. w. Richie Beirach '72–4. Pl. w. Ryerson Swing Band '64–8; Columbia U. bb '68–72. Freelance '72–5, then pl. w. Mongo Santamaria '75–6; Lionel Hampton, Chet Baker, Horacee Arnold, Ray Barretto '76–7; Sonny Rollins '77–8; Ted Curson '78–9; Billy Harper '79–83; Anne Marie Moss fr. '79; Paquito D'Rivera '84–5. Own gps. fr. '72. Donelian has taught at Westchester Cons. '72–5 '83–6; New Sch. fr. '86; Wm. Paterson Coll., N.J. Author of *Training the Ear: For the Improvising Musician* (Advance). Received grants fr. NEA and Meet the Composer, and was Artist-in-Residence at the Center for Electronic Music '89, and at the N.J. State Council on the Arts

'89–91. Arts Jazz Perf. Fellowship fr. NEA '94. Favs: V. Horowitz, Jimmy Yancey, Bill Evans, Bud Powell. Comp: "Stargazer." Fests: Carib. '75–6; Eur. fr. '79. TV: NYC, Can., Eur. TV. CDs: Sunny.; Odin; Atlas; w. Roy Ayers (Polyd.).

DORGE, PIERRE, gtr, comp, lead; b. Copenhagen, Denmark, 2/28/46. Led own gps. fr. 1960. His Copenhagen Jazz Qnt. won first prize in Radio Denmark jazz competitions '61–3. Pl. w. John Tchicai bb, Cadentia Nova Danica '69–71, then perf. w. various free-jazz and jazz-rock gps. '71–7. Own qt., Thermaenius, which pl. in a style infl. by Balkan folk mus., fr. '78. Led New Jungle Orch. fr. '80. It app. at Jazz Yatra, Bombay '84; was chosen Danish State Ens. for '93–6; and pl. at Sweet Basil, NYC '97. Dorge has continued to collab. w. Tchicai and lead his own gps. CDs: Dacapo; Steep.; Olufsen; w. Walt Dickerson; Tchicai; Khan Jamal (Steep.).

DORHAM, KENNY (McKINLEY HOWARD), tpt, comp; also tnr sax; b. Fairfield, TX, 8/30/24; d. NYC, 12/5/72. Father pl. gtr.; moth. and sis. pl. pno.; first stud. pno. w. sis. at age 7; tpt. in hs. Debut w. dance band at Wiley Coll., where he att. pharmacy sch. Army '42; member of boxing team. In 1943, after visiting Oakland, Calif., he pl. in Houston, Tex., w. Russell Jacquet. To NYC, pl. w. several pioneering bands in mid '40s through '50s: Dizzy Gillespie '45, doubling as blues singer; Billy Eckstine '46; Lionel Hampton '47; Mercer Ellington '48. Join. Charlie Parker '48–50. Freelanced early '50s; founding member of Art Blakey's Jazz Messengers '54; form. Jazz Prophets, a similar gp., in '55. Replaced Clifford Brown in Max Roach–C. Brown qnt. '56–8. In the summers of '58 and '59, he taught at Lenox Sch. of Jazz, Mass. Own gps. '58–9, apps. at Five Spot. In '60s, freelanced, tour. Eur. often, also taught and comp. Co-led qnt. w. Joe Henderson '62–3; tour. Scan. w. own gp. winter of '63–4; also pl. w. Hank Mobley. Other activities: fr. '64 he was a consultant for HARYOU-ACT, an NYC anti-poverty program; DB rec. reviewer fr. '65. Attended NYU graduate sch. of mus. late '60s. He also taught at the sch. Ill in his last yrs., he pl. only occ. bef. he died of kidney failure. One of the pioneers of bop tpt., he was a sure-fingered, assertive player whose harmonic prowess and characteristic style continues to infl. new generations of musicians. Favs: M. Davis, D. Gillespie. Fests: Paris JF '49; Longhorn JF, Austin, Tex., '66. Films: soundtrack work for A Song Is Born, MGM '48; comp. score, pl. and app. in French films, Witness in the City; Dangerous Liaisons '59. His "Fragments of an Autobiography" was pub. in Music '70, DB's annual for '69. Comps: "Dead End"; "Prince Albert";

"Una Mas"; "Blue Spring"; "Lotus Blossom"; "Epitaph"; "Blue Bossa"; "Whistle Stop"; "Trompeta Toccata." Some have credited him w. authorship of the oft-played and rec. "The Theme." CDs: BN; Riv.; BL; Steep.; Time; Deb.; NJ; w. Thelonious Monk; Blakey; H. Silver; J. Henderson; A. Hill (BN); Parker (Verve; Sav.); Rollins; Dameron; H. Mobley; P. Woods (Prest.); Roach (Em.); C. Walton (Prest.; Steep.); Gillespie; F. Navarro; C. Payne (Sav.); E. Dolphy (Cand.); M. Jackson (Sav.; Riv.); B. Golson (Riv.); H. Land (Jzld.); O. Nelson (NJ).

DOROUGH, BOB (ROBERT LROD), pno, voc, comp; b. Cherry Hill, AR, 12/12/23. Wrote for and pl. w. jr. hs band in Tex. army band 1943–5, pl. sax, cl., pno. Stud. at No. Tex. St. U. '46–9; Columbia U. '49–52. Began career as night club perf. In early '50s, he spent two yrs. as mus. dir. for Sugar Ray Robinson dur. the boxer's career as entertainer, then lived in Paris '54–5. First album as leader, Devil May Care, for Beth. '56. In LA '58–61, jammed w. Ornette Coleman and others; also had small film roles. Sang "Blue Xmas" and "Nothing Like You" on Col. date w. Miles Davis '62. Fr. '60s, he had success w. songs like "Comin' Home Baby" and "Just About Everything." Wrote a number of songs and was mus. dir. for much praised children's TV series of animated two-minute educational spots, Schoolhouse Rock '73–85, then resumed career as night club artist in US and Eur., most often accomp. by bs. Bill Takas. Schoolhouse Rock ran again fr. '91. A witty writer and creative melodist, Dorough sings in a casual, down-home, bluesy style which serves him well as a jazz entertainer. Fests: Kool NY '80; JVC-NY '97. CDs: BN; Bloom.; Red; Evid.; Beth.; Phil.; Scharf-Dorough; Orange Blue; w. M. Davis (Col.); Harold Danko (Sunny.).

DORSEY, JIMMY (JAMES), alto sax, cl, lead; b. Shenandoah, PA, 2/29/04; d. NYC, 6/12/57. Father, a coal miner turned mus. teacher and band dir., taught Jimmy crnt. and tbn. at very early age; bro. was tbnst. Tommy Dorsey. At age 8, he pl. in fath.'s brass band; took up tnr. and alto sax in 1915. Worked briefly in a coal mine ca. '17, but left to devote himself to mus. Form. Dorsey's Novelty Six (later called Dorsey's Wild Canaries) w. Tommy around '19. The gp. pl. long engagement in Balt., Md., and was one of first jazz bands to broadcast on radio. When it disbanded in '21, the bros. join. Billy Lustig's Scranton Sirens. In Sept. '24, Jimmy join. California Ramblers in NYC and tour. w. them; w. Jean Goldkette '25. Fr. '25 to '30, he freelanced w. prominent rec. and radio bands in NYC; tour. w. Paul Whiteman, Red Nichols; and rec. w. Nichols; Bix Beiderbecke; Eddie Lang;

and Joe Venuti. Pl. and made first Eur. tour w. Ted Lewis in spring of '30. On his return to US, he resumed his studio activity, incl. work w. Fred Rich; André Kostelanetz; Rudy Vallee; Lennie Hayton. Dur. the late '20s and early '30s, he also co-led a band w. Tommy for studio work and specific gigs, occ. doubling on tpt., crnt. In the spring of '34, the band became a full-time outfit, making its official debut in July at Sands Point Beach Club on Long Island, N.Y., where it remained for the summer. The band—whose sidemen incl. Bunny Berigan, Charlie Spivak, Glenn Miller, Ray McKinley, Bob Crosby—pl. at the Glen Island Casino, N.Y., in spring of '35. That June, mounting tension and sibling rivalry erupted into a heated on-stage disagreement, which ended w. Tommy walking off the stand and leaving the band. Jimmy cont. as lead. and the orch. became one of the most popular dance bands of the late '30s and early '40s. With vocalists Bob Eberly and Helen O'Connell, the band toured, made regular radio and films apps., and had several hit recs. In the spring of '53, the bros. reunited to co-lead the Dorsey Bros. Orch. Jimmy took over after his bro.'s death in '56, but a battle w. cancer eventually forced him to turn the leadership over to Lee Castle. Dorsey's commercial success as a band leader sometimes obscured his importance as a reed player whose impressive technique and highly polished improv. style infl. many, incl. Charlie Parker. The orch. scored several commercial hits, incl. "So Rare," which was rec. some mos. bef. his death and became a posthumous hit. Polls: alto sax, *DB* '37–9; *Met.* '39–41. Films: band apps. in *That Girl From Paris* '36; *Shall We Dance* '37; *Lady Be Good* '41; *The Fleet's In* '42; *I Dood It!* '43. *The Fabulous Dorseys*, a biopic w. Tommy '47. TV: *Stage Show* weekly CBS series w. Tommy, '55–6. CDs: Dec.; Hep; w. Dorsey Bros. Orch. (Hep); tracks w. Dorsey Bros., Calif. Ramblers in *The Music of Prohibition* (Col.); Louis Armstrong (Dec.); Beiderbecke (Col.; BB).

DORSEY, LEON LEE, bs, el-bs; b. Pittsburgh, PA, 3/12/58. Bachelor's degree fr. Oberlin Coll.; master's fr. U. of Wisc., Manh. Sch. of Mus. Doctoral study under Ron Carter at City Coll., N.Y., fr. '92. Pl. w. Lionel Hampton '86–8; Benny Carter '87; Don Pullen; Art Blakey '89; Dizzy Gillespie '90. Also pl. w. Freddie Hubbard; John Lewis; Kenny Clarke; Jon Hendricks; Sweets Edison; Paquito D'Rivera; Dorothy Donegan; Stanley Turrentine; Art Farmer; Ellis Marsalis. Favs: Ron Carter, Paul Chambers, Ray Brown. In '92, he pl. and rec. w. The Daou, a progressive alternative dance/rock gp. Worked w. Cassandra Wilson '93–6; Kevin Mahogany '96–7; own gps. fr. '95. Fests: Eur., So. Amer, Japan fr. '80s. Film: role in

Japanese remake of *Breakfast at Tiffany's*. CDs: Land.; w. Hampton (Glad-Hamp); Art Blakey (BS; Timel.); Oliver Lake (Gram.); A. Prysock (Mile.).

DORSEY, TOMMY (THOMAS), tbn, lead; b. Shenandoah, PA, 11/19/05; d. Greenwich, CT, 11/26/56. Studied tpt. w. fath., later concentrated on tbn. In early yrs. he was equally well known on both instruments, recording several hot tpt. solos in 1927, but became celebrated for his tbn. pl., which was characterized by an exceptional tone and legato ballad style. His career closely paralleled that of his bro., Jimmy. By '30, he had become one of the most successful freelance radio and rec. trombonists. In '35 he split w. Jimmy and formed his own band, using members of Joe Haymes's orch. "I'm Getting Sentimental Over You," which he first rec. w. a Dorsey Bros. pick-up gp. in '32, became the band's theme song. This band was highly successful dur. the swing era, due, in part, to an extraordinary supporting cast, incl. tptrs. Bunny Berigan, Pee Wee Erwin, Charlie Spivak, Yank Lawson, Charlie Shavers, Ziggy Elman; reed players Johnny Mince, Buddy De Franco, and Bud Freeman; pnst. Joe Bushkin; dmrs. Dave Tough, Buddy Rich, Louie Bellson; vocs. Jack Leonard, Frank Sinatra, Jo Stafford, Connie Haines, and The Pied Pipers; and such arrs. as Sy Oliver, Paul Weston, Axel Stordahl. Among the band's most popular numbers were "Marie"; "Song of India"; and "Boogie Woogie." A small band within the band, the Clambake Seven, pl. in a traditional, post-NO style. Fr. '54 to '56, the Dorsey Bros. hosted *Stage Show,* a weekly CBS-TV musical variety show, whose guests incl. Elvis Presley making his TV debut. Dur. this period, the band often worked at the Statler Hotel, NYC. Dorsey died fr. choking on food. In '58, and into the '70s, a Tommy Dorsey "ghost" band tour. the US under the dir. of tbn. Warren Covington—it was later taken over by Buddy Morrow. Polls: *DB* '36–9; *Met.* '37, '39–46. Films: *Las Vegas Nights* '41; *Ship Ahoy!* '42; *DuBarry Was a Lady, Girl Crazy, Presenting Lily Mars* '43; *Broadway Rhythm* '44; *Thrill of a Romance* '45; *The Fabulous Dorseys* '47. CDs: BB; Hep; Dorsey Bros., Calif. Ramblers in *The Music of Prohibition* (Col.); w. Bix Beiderbecke (Timel.; BB; Mile.); J. Teagarden; Fats Waller; Ellington (BB).

DOUBLE SIX OF PARIS. French voc. sxt. form. in 1959 by Mimi Perrin. Its repertory consisted of jazz themes to which Perrin added lyrics. Members at various times incl. Monique Aldebert-Guerin; Christiane Legrand; Louis Aldebert; Ward Swingle; Roger Guerin; Eddy Louiss. The gp. rec. mus. by Quincy Jones '59–60; also rec. w. Dizzy Gillespie '63; Jerome Richardson '64. The name Double Six referred to the gp.'s practice of overdubbing recs. to give the impression of a 12–voice gp. The original Double Six disbanded in '65, after which Perrin led another gp. by the same name. Jef Gilson led the Double Six briefly in '66 while Perrin was ill, but this gp. was also disbanded in the autumn of '66. CD: w. Gillespie (Philips).

DOUGHERTY, EDDIE (EDWARD), dms; b. NYC, 7/17/15; d. NYC, 12/14/94. Began on dms. at age 13. Rec. in 1930s w. Taft Jordan; Frank Froeba; Mildred Bailey; Harry James; Billie Holiday; Frankie Newton; Pete Johnson; Meade "Lux" Lewis. Also pl. w. band at Dicky Wells' club in Harlem. Subbed for Dave Tough w. Bud Freeman '40, then pl. w. F. Newton, Joe Sullivan, Benny Carter '41; Benny Morton '44–5; others. Rec. w. Cliff Jackson, Mary Lou Williams '44; Clyde Bernhardt '46. Also worked in '40s w. Wilbur De Paris; Teddy Wilson; Albert Nicholas; others. Ceased full-time activity but cont. to pl. into the '80s. CDs: w. James P. Johnson; Tatum (Dec.); B. Holiday (Col.; Comm.); F. Newton; Albert Ammons; M. Bailey (Topaz); Harry James; Bechet (Class.).

DOUGLAS, DAVE (DAVID DEUEL), tpt, comp, lead; b. East Orange, NJ, 3/24/63. Grew up in Montclair, N.J., Westchester County and Woodstock, N.Y. Fath. amateur pnst. Start. on pno. at age 5; tbn. at 7; tpt. at 9. At 11 began improv. w. Music Minus One recs. When 15, dur. a hs yr. abroad, pl. jazz w. mus. in Barcelona, Spain. Stud. comp. and tpt. at Berklee Coll. of Mus. 1981–2 and New Engl. Cons. '82–3. At the latter, John McNeil introduced him to the Carmine Caruso method. Moved to NYC '84, completing his stud. at NYU w., among others, Caruso, Jim McNeely, Joe Lovano. Pl. in the streets, perf. w. other young mus.; also pl. w. art rock, experimental, and straight ahead bands. Tour int'l w. Horace Silver for three mos. '87. Back to NYC, form. first band '87; Mosaic Sxt. '88–91; qnt., New and Used, fr. '89; string gp. '92. Worked w. Don Byron's klezmer band '90–4. In '93, became involved w. Balkan folk mus., form. Tiny Bell Trio; in same yr. began pl. w. John Zorn, incl. Eur. tour; also tour. Eur. w. Myra Melford '94. Has rec. homages to Booker Little, Wayne Shorter. His *Sanctuary* feat. a double qt. updating of *Free Jazz* and *Ascension* for the Avant label. *DB* said of him: "An outstanding player, gifted with a wonderfully fluid style and a deep bag of timbral effects, he's also a terrific writer and arranger, with a rare sensitivity for unfolding, mid-length works." Favs: Miles Davis, Wayne Shorter, Stravinsky. Fests: Berlin; Vienna; MJF. CDs: Arab.; Avant; SN; NW; hatArt; KFW; Konnex; Songlines; w. Zorn (DIW; evva;

Tzadik); Byron (Elek.); Uri Caine (JMT; Winter and Winter); Melford (hatHut; Gram.); Mark Dresser (KFW; SN); Greg Cohen (DIW); V. Herring (MM); F. Hersch; M. Formanek (Enja); A. Braxton–Mario Pavone (KFW).

DOUGLAS, TOMMY (THOMAS), cl, saxes; b. Eskridge, KS, 11/9/06; d. Sioux Falls, SD, 3/9/65. Self-taught dur. hs in Topeka, Kans.; while stud. at Bost. Cons. 1924–8, he was assoc. w. Johnny Hodges; Harry Carney; Otto Hardwicke. First prof. jobs in KC, mainly on alto sax and cl. Between '27 and '31, he worked w. Benny Moten, Jap Allen; also w. George E. Lee '30–1; J.R. Morton in Chi. '31; Clarence Love '32–3; Benny Moten, again '34. Wrote arrs. for Love and Casa Loma orch. Led own bbs. in South and Midwest '30–42, one of which was the nucleus of Harlan Leonard's Rockets in '36. His sidemen incl. Paul Webster; Jo Jones; Charlie Parker; Fred Beckett; Ted Donnelly. In later yrs., he led small gps around KC; pl. briefly w. Duke Ellington '51. Favs: Hodges, Carney, Buster Smith, Buster Bailey. Recs. w. J. McShann for Cap., '44; Julia Lee, Merc., '45. CDs w. McShann (Class.); tracks w. Lee in *The 1940s Mercury Sessions* (Merc.).

DOUGLASS, BILL (WILLIAM V.), dms; b. Sherman, TX, 2/28/23. From a musical family. Worked in LA w. Benny Carter in mid 1950s; Red Callender '54–8; Cal Tjader, Art Tatum '56; Gerry Wiggins, Red Norvo '56–7; Harry Babasin '57. Dur. '60s, he freelanced w. June Christy, Lena Horne, and Kay Starr, and taught at Drum City. Fr. '85 to '90 he was treasurer of Local 47, Musicians' Union. Pl. w. Wild Bill Davis and Judy Carmichael at a fest. in Colorado '83. CDs: w. Tatum (Pab.); Norvo (BB); Wiggins; B. Collette (Spec.); Charlie Byrd; Marian McPartland (Conc.).

DOWDY, BILL, dms; b. Benton Harbor, MI, 8/15/33. Began pl. dms. in hs; worked in trio on weekend gigs and radio progs. After grad., he joined Rupert Harris's band. In army until 1954, then moved to Chi. Stud. dms. at Roosevelt U. Pl. in Chi. w. Johnny Griffin, J.J. Johnson, and local blues bands. Formed gp., the Four Sounds, in South Bend, Ind. The gp. became the Three Sounds in '57, and worked in Wash., D.C., bef. coming to NYC in Sept. '58. Other members were Gene Harris, Andy Simpkins. Dowdy left the gp. in '66. CDs: w. Three Sounds; Lou Donaldson (BN).

DRAPER, RAY (RAYMOND ALLEN), tba; b. NYC, 8/3/40; d. NYC, 11/1/82. Father, Barclay, pl. tpt. w. name bands, rec. w. Jelly Roll Morton; moth., a concert pnst. Entered HS of Perf. Arts after audition on tba; further stud. at Manh. Sch. of Mus. Pl. sess. w. own gp. for Jazz Unlimited at the Pad, Birdland, winter 1956-7. Worked w. Jackie McLean, Donald Byrd '56; Max Roach qnt. '58-9. Problems w. addiction kept him inactive in mus. '59-64. Form. gp. w. Philly Joe Jones in LA, summer '64; co-led qnt. w. Hadley Caliman '65; Big Black '56-7; also pl. w. Horace Tapscott, rec. soundtracks w. Quincy Jones. Own 9-pc. rock gp., Red Beans & Rice, '68-9. In '69, he moved to London where he served as mus. dir. for Ronnie Scott Directions; comp.-arr. for 10-pc. band, Sweetwater Canal. Tour. Eur. as lead. w. Arthur Conley show; also worked w. Kenneth Terroade; Archie Shepp; Don Cherry; Doctor John. Ret. to US '71 w. Doctor John, cont. w. him until '72. Worked w. Cathy Chamberlain's Rag & Roll Revue '74-5; w. Doctor John in LA '75; Howard Johnson's Gravity '77. Taught theory and harm., rec. stud. techniques, etc. at U. of the Streets, NYC, and Wesleyan U., Conn.; received NEA grant for comp. '73-4. Draper, an innocent bystander, was fatally shot outside a check-cashing facility dur. the course of a hold-up. Favs: Bill Barber; former teacher, Henry Edwards. Infl: Miles Davis, Sonny Rollins. Fests: NJF w. Roach '58. Films: *Amougee*, Belgium. TV: *Jazz Set*, PBS '71. Comp: *Fugue for Brass Ensemble*, pl. at NYU; "Fil-ide." Recs. w. Jack McDuff, Doctor John. CDs: NJ.; w. John Coltrane; Sonny Criss; J. McLean (Prest.).

DREARES, AL (ALBERT ALFRED), dms; b. Key West, FL, 1/4/29. Father pl. tpt. Childhood friend of Fats Navarro. Stud. at Hartnett Cons., NYC 1949. Tour. w. Paul Williams band '53-4. Pl. w. Teddy Charles '55; Charles Mingus; Randy Weston '56; Freddie Redd; Kenny Burrell '57; Gigi Gryce '58; Jerome Richardson; Phineas Newborn '59. Also led own combos in NYC '50s. Rec. w. Bennie Green '59-60; Mal Waldron '60-7; Frank Strozier '62; Freddie McCoy '68; Harold Ousley '72; Paul Quinichette '76; Slide Hampton '78. Led own gp. at club in Bklyn, N.Y. '79-83. Moved to Miami, Fla., '85. Favs: Art Blakey, Philly Joe Jones. CDs: w. Redd; R. Weston (Riv.).

DRESSER, MARK, bs; b. Los Angeles, CA, 9/26/52. Mother pl. pno. Began pl. pno. at age 5, then sw. to bs. at age 12. Took gp. classes w. Red Mitchell, Ray Brown 1968. Stud. w. Marray Grodner and David Baker at Indiana U. '70-1, then w. Bertram Turetzky at UC-San Diego fr. '71. Pl. w. Black Music Infinity, w. Stanley Crouch, Bobby Bradford, Arthur Blythe, James Newton, David Murray, Walter Lowe '71; San Diego Symphony '75. Moved to NYC '75, pl. w. David Murray–Butch Morris, also duo perf. w.

Ray Anderson. Then moved to New Haven, Conn., pl. w. Leo Smith; Anthony Davis; Gerry Hemingway; Pheeroan akLaff; Mark Helias. Ret. to San Diego '77 to work w. CETA prog. Pl. w. Diamanda Galas–Jim French; Charles McPherson; also Klezmer bands. Rec. and tour. Eur. w. Ray Anderson '80. Moved to Rome, Italy in '83 to study and perf. w. own gps. Dresser ret. to US '86 to join Anthony Braxton. Since then he has worked w. Tim Berne; John Zorn; Anthony Davis; Marty Ehrlich; Don Byron; Bobby Previte; Fred Frith; Anthony Coleman. Form. string trio, Arcado, w. Hank Roberts, Mark Feldman '88. Pl. w. Tambastics w. Gerry Hemingway, Robert Dick, Denman Maroney since '90; own qnt., Force Green, since '92. Fests: Rivbea Loft JF w. Murray '75; Eur. since '80; Japan. TV: *Night Music* w. T. Berne '90. CDs: A&M; w. Arcado; Berne; Roberts (JMT); R. Anderson (Enja; Gram.); Braxton (BS; Leo; hatArt); B. Bradford (SN); Zorn (Elek. Mus.); M. Crispell (Leo); Hemingway (hatArt).

DREW, JOHN DEREK, bs; b. Sheffield, Yorkshire, England, 12/23/27. Studied pno. as a child, then bs. priv. in Liverpool fr. age 16. Moved to London 1945; freelanced w. show and pop bands incl. two yrs. w. Billy Ternent on BBC. Immigrated to US '54; working w. Les Elgart. Moved to West Coast; pl. w. Gene Krupa '55-6; Stan Getz '56; Neal Hefti, Nat Pierce '56-7; Miami Symph., Barbara Carroll '57. Freelanced in NYC, incl. gigs w. Peggy Lee '58; Marian McPartland, Sauter-Finegan, others '59. Rec. in late '50s w. Toshiko Akiyoshi; Dick Garcia; Dave McKenna; Joe Saye; Benny Carter; Bobby Scott. Favs: Blanton, Ray Brown, Red Mitchell, Hinton. CDs: w. Krupa (Verve); McKenna (Col.).

DREW, KENNY (KENNETH SIDNEY), b. NYC, 8/28/28; d. Copenhagen, Denmark, 8/4/93. Son is pnst. Kenny Drew Jr. Stud. priv. fr. age 5; first recital at 8; att. HS of Mus. and Art; prof. debut as accomp. for Pearl Primus dance sch. First rec. w. Howard McGhee for BN 1950. Worked w. Coleman Hawkins, Lester Young, Charlie Parker '50-1; Buddy De Franco '52-3. Moved briefly to Calif., working w. own trio in LA and SF. Ret. to NYC '56; accomp. Dinah Washington; tour. w. Art Blakey; then free-lanced w. J. Coltrane; Donald Byrd; Johnny Griffin; others; pl. w. Buddy Rich '58-9. Settled in Eur. '61, first in Paris, later in Copenhagen '64; pl. at Jazzhus Montmartre w. Dexter Gordon and visiting soloists, incl. Kenny Dorham; Hank Mobley; Joe Henderson; Sonny Rollins. Formed duo w. bs. Niels-Henning Ørsted Pedersen mid '60s; later a highly acclaimed trio w. dmr. Alvin Queen. Drew also app. w. Paris Reunion Band. Form. a music publ. firm, Shirew

Publishing, and rec. label, Matrix. Fr. his earliest recs., he pl. w. a precise touch, balancing boppish melodic improv. w. block chording that incl. refreshingly subtle harmonizations. Fests: Juan-Les-Pins w. Paris Reunion Band '85; Bologna '90. CDs: BN; Riv.; Steep.; Mile.; SN; Timel.; w. John Coltrane (BN); Chet Baker; Toots Thielemans (Riv.); S. Rollins; Sonny Stitt (Prest.); A. Blakey (Col.); Dexter Gordon (BN; BL; Steep.); J. Griffin (Riv. BL; Steep.); A. Farmer (NJ; SN); J. McLean (BN; Steep.); Benny Carter; C. Hawkins; Stuff Smith (Story.); Nathan Davis; Dusko Goykovich (DIW); Clifford Brown (Em.); Ben Webster (BL; Story.).

DREW, KENNY JR., pno, comp; b. NYC, 6/14/58. At 5, he began pno. study w. his grandmoth., who had also taught his fath. Stud. classical repertoire through his early teens w. his aunt, Marjorie. Discovered jazz at 17, also listening to pop and funk. Pl. in several funk bands in NYC area. First jazz gigs subbing for John Hicks 1985. Then, in Key West, Fla., pl. solo and duo six nights a wk. at a local club, Captain Hornblower's, learning a wide repertoire of standards. Met Charnett Moffett and rec. w. him '86. Went on road w. Stanley Jordan '88; pl. w. OTB; then form. own trio w. Charnett and Cody Moffett, pl. in Japan. Won Great Amer. Jazz Piano Competition at Jacksonville JF (Fla.) '90. Pl. w. Stanley Turrentine; Mingus bb; Faddis/Slide Hampton/Jimmy Heath sxt. in '90s; also w. CHJB; Steve Turre; Jack Walrath; David Sanchez; Jack Wilkins; Michael Mossman; Ronnie Cuber; Steve Slagle. He has also begun to gain a reputation as a classical pnst. Pl. both jazz and classical at Barossa Fest. in Austral. in '96. At same fest. in '97 app. w. classical/chamber-jazz trio led by sax/fl. Daniel Schnyder; the gp. has pl. concerts in Switzerland, NYC. He has also rec. w. Schnyder and bs-tbn. David Taylor in separate dates by each comp. An accomplished, two-handed pnst. whose style is both romantic and hard-swinging, from boogie-woogie and barrelhouse to bop, Bach, and Brazil. Favs: Kenny Drew, Hancock, Bill Evans, O. Peterson, C. Corea, Jarrett. Has incl. selections by Thelonious Monk in many of his albums. Fests: Kyoto; Eur. w. Mingus bb; solo pno., JVC-NY '96. Comps: "Coral Sea"; "Third Phase"; "Las Palmas"; "The Flame Within." CDs: Conc.; Claves; JC; Ant.; TCB; Ark.; Meldac; w. Mingus bb (Drey.); Bubba Brooks (TCB); R. Cuber; Ron McClure (Steep.); Charnett Moffett (BN); Cody Moffett (Tel.); Pete Yellin (Alfa); D. Schnyder (Enja).

DREW, MARTIN, dms; b. Northampton, England, 2/11/44. Began pl. at age 6; stud. for three yrs. w. George Fierstone, who helped him get started prof. In 1974, he pl. w. Oscar Peterson at Ronnie Scott's Club and was Peterson's regular dmr. fr. '80, incl. int'l tours. In '75, he joined Ronnie Scott's band at the latter's club, accomp. many renowned visitors such as Zoot Sims, Scott Hamilton, Phil Woods, Dexter Gordon, and has worked w. Gil Evans; Bill Holman; Manny Albam; Stan Getz; Yehudi Menuhin; Bud Shank; countless others. Rec. debut in '75 w. Red Rodney, Bill LeSage & the Bebop Preservation Society. Also leads own gp. Apps. on many TV shows w. Peterson and Scott, at home and abroad. Won "British Jazz Awards 1990" as "Drummer of the Year." Teaches priv. and in clinics. Own album, *Martin Drew Band* (Lee Lambert). CDs: w. Peterson (Pab; Tel.); Monty Alexander; Benny Carter; B. DeFranco; F. Hubbard (Pab.); R. Scott; A. Sandoval (JH); Spike Robinson; J. Temperley (Hep).

DREWES, GLENN WILLIAM, tpt, flg, crnt, picc-tpt, pno; b. NYC, 4/24/49. Father, Barry, was tptr. pl. in NYC, 1930s-40s, later choirmaster at West Point Acad. Bro. Billy is saxophonist w. Vanguard Jazz Orch. Began on pno. at age 8; pl. tpt. fr. age 12. Received B.S. in mus. ed. fr. Crane Sch. of Mus., Potsdam U. First gig in strip club on Long Island, N.Y. '66–8. Pl. w. Lionel Hampton '71–2, '75–6; Woody Herman '77–9; Buddy Rich '81; Gerry Mulligan '81–5; Frank Sinatra '82; Liza Minnelli '82–5; Toshiko Akiyoshi–Lew Tabackin '83–4; Mel Lewis Orch. (now Vanguard Jazz Orch.) fr. '84; Dizzy Gillespie bb '87; Gene Harris bb '88. Also pl. w. Don Sebesky; Doc Severinsen NY Band; Louis Bellson bb; *Sat. Night Live* Band. Drewes has worked on B'way fr. '84 and was jazz soloist w. the show *City of Angels*. He has taught at the U. of Bridgeport (Conn.), and app. on billboards and in print ads for Kool cigarettes. Favs: Lee Morgan, Blue Mitchell, Sweets Edison. Fests: all major w. bbs fr. early '70s. CDs: w. Mel Lewis Orch.; Bellson (MM); Gene Harris (Conc.); Harry Connick Jr. (Col.); T. Talbert (Chart).

D'RIVERA, PAQUITO, sop, alto, tnr saxes, cl, EWI; b. Havana, Cuba, 6/4/48. Father, Tito Rivera, pl. classical sax; son, Franco D'Rivera, pl. cl. Stud. w. fath.; perf. in public fr. age 6. Pl. Weber *Clarinet Concerto No. 2* at Nat'l Theater, Havana, at age 10. Stud. at Havana Cons. fr. age 12. In army band fr. 1965, then app. as soloist w. Cuban Nat'l Symphony '67. Cond. and pl. w. Orchestra Cubana de Musica Moderna in early '70s, then founded gp., Irakere, w. Chucho Valdes, ca. '73. Irakere won a Grammy in '79 and toured, incl. apps. at NJF and MJF '78. D'Rivera remained until '80, when he relocated to Spain. Moved to NYC in early '80s, pl. w. David Amram; Dizzy Gillespie; McCoy Tyner; Carmen McRae;

Sarah Vaughan; Phil Woods; Stanley Turrentine; Lionel Hampton; Tito Puente; Freddie Hubbard; others. D'Rivera has since led his own qnt., sxt., and bb, and worked as co-mus. dir. of Gillespie's United Nation Orch. On Dizzy's death, he assumed full leadership. He has perf. classical sax. works w. the Nat'l Symph., the Bklyn. Philharmonia, and the Ohio Symph. In '91, he received a lifetime achievement awd. fr. Latin Jazz USA for his contributions to Latin mus.; the same yr., he was the guest of honor at the Heineken JF in PR. Cont. to fuse Cuban and jazz music and combine technique w. fervor on alto sax and cl. With Andy Narell and Dave Samuels form. Caribbean Jazz Project '93. Favs: Charlie Parker, Benny Goodman. Polls: ACE, Hispanic Critics of NY '87; Bravo '90. Fests: all major since early '70s. TV: PBS special, David Letterman, CBS *Sunday Morning*. CDs: Col.; Chesky; Trop.; Cand.; w. Ed Cherry (GH); Gillespie (Enja); Claudio Roditi (Cand.); Clark Terry (Chesky); Irakere (Col.); Caribbean Jazz Project (Heads Up).

DROOTIN, BUZZY (BENJAMIN), dms; b. near Kiev, Russia, 4/22/20; d. Englewood, NJ, 5/21/00. Came to US at age 5; family settled in Bost. Fath. and bros. Al and Lewis are musicians. First prof. gigs w. local gps. 1936. Tour. w. Ina Ray Hutton '40; Al Donahue '41–2. Pl. in Chi. w. Jess Stacy, Wingy Manone mid '40s. Moved to NYC '47. Pl. w. Eddie Condon '47–51, then w. Bobby Hackett; Billy Butterfield; Jimmy McPartland. Worked for George Wein at Mahogany Hall, Bost., '53–5. Ret. to NYC '55, pl. w. Ralph Sutton, Wild Bill Davison, Pee Wee Erwin, Condon, Ruby Braff fr. '55; Hackett '57–60; Dukes of Dixieland '62–mid '60s; Hackett, Jack Teagarden, Condon, Roy Eldridge, Newport All-Stars mid '60s. Bandleader at El Morocco, NYC '66. Tour. w. Jazz Giants w. Wild Bill Davison '67–9, then led own gp., B.D.'s Jazz Family, w. Herman Autrey, Benny Morton '69–70. Freelanced in NYC '71–2, then ret. to Bost. where he joined bro. Al and nephew Sonny in the Drootin Bros. Band at Scotch & Sirloin, other local venues. Dur. the '70s and '80s, he freq. app. w. all-star gps. at jfs incl. LA Classic '84. TV: PBS special *Buzzy's Family*; *Today*; *Tonight* show w. Dukes of Dixieland. LPs: w. Hackett-Teagarden (Cap.); Ruby Braff (Epic); G. Wein (Smash); Jazz Giants (Sack.). CDs: w. Bechet; S. Chaloff; Pee Wee Russell (BL); Condon (Sav.); L. Konitz (Phil.).

DRUMMOND, BILLY (WILLIS ROBERT JR.), dms, perc; b. Newport News, VA, 6/19/59. Father was dmr. and jazz fan. Wife is pnst. Renee Rosnes. Pl. in r&b dance bands fr. age 8, then stud. at Shenandoah Cons. of Mus. Pl. w. Out of The Blue 1988–9;

Joe Henderson '88–9; Horace Silver '89; Ralph Moore since '89; Rosnes since '89; John Faddis '89–91; Bobby Hutcherson '90–1; Buster Williams since '90; Charles Tolliver '91; Lew Tabackin–Toshiko Akiyoshi since '91; Hank Jones '91; Nat Adderley '91. Favs: Philly Joe Jones, Tony Williams, Joe Chambers, Jack DeJohnette. Fests: Eur. and Japan, incl. first Int'l Moscow JF, w. B. Williams. TV: Mt. Fuji JF w. OTB '88; VH-1 Ben Sidran Show w. Bud Shank. CDs: CC; w. OTB; Rosnes; J. Henderson (BN); Hutcherson (Land.); V. Herring (MM; Land.); Adderley; F. Ambrosetti (Enja); S. Wendholt; S. Newsome (CC); Billy Pierce (PW); Steve Kuhn (Res.).

DRUMMOND, RAY ("BULLDOG"), bs, comp; b. Brookline, MA, 11/23/46. Father was in army, family lived in US and Eur. Pl. brass instruments fr. 1954; began pl. bs. in '61. Received B.A. in political science fr. Claremont Coll. '68; M.B.A. fr. Stanford Business Sch. '71. Own qt. in SF '77. Moved to NYC '77. Pl. w. Michael White; Bobby Hutcherson; Woody Shaw; David Murray; Thad Jones–Mel Lewis Orch.; Johnny Griffin; Wynton Marsalis; Hank Jones. Own gps. fr. mid '80s, incl. qnt., sxt., qt.; w. Kenny Barron fr. early '80s. In the '80s and '90s, he was the bs. of choice for many gps., incl. Milt Jackson, Kenny Werner, Toots Thielemans. Infls. and favs: Paul Chambers, Mingus, Hinton, George Duvivier, Scott LaFaro. CDs: Nilva; CC; DMP; Arab.; w. George Coleman (Evid.; JH; Verve); Stan Getz; Hal Galper (Conc.); Gary Smulyan; Michael Weiss (CC); T. Akiyoshi (Evid.); John Hicks (Evid.; Timel.); D. Murray; Chris Anderson; R. Mathews (DIW); G. Bartz; H. Edison; C. Roditi (Cand.); Benny Green (BN); K. Barron (Res.); W. Marsalis; B. Marsalis; Mingus Dynasty (Col.); Art Farmer; L. Konitz (SN); Carl Fontana (Up.); S. Hampton (BL); T. Harrell (CC; Cont.); T. Chapin (Arab.).

DUDZIAK, URSZULA, voc; also perc, synth, comp; b. Straconka, Poland, 10/22/43. Studied pno. at mus. sch. in Zielona-Gora; later stud. voice in Warsaw. Inspired by Ella Fitzgerald, she took up singing in the late 1950s. Join. Krzystof Komeda's gp. in '62, where she met vlnst. Michal Urbaniak, whom she married in '67. Worked w. Urbaniak's gp. in Scand. '65–9. First received attention in the US through her unique '72 rec. w. Adam Makowicz, "Newborn Light." Came to US in '74, settled in NYC, cont. to work w. Urbaniak. Comp. mus. for ballet, N.Y. Dance Collective '74. Worked w. Archie Shepp, Lester Bowie '84. Member of Vocal Summit w. Bobby McFerrin, Jay Clayton, Lauren Newton, Jeanne Lee. Tour. w. Norma Winstone in late '80s. Apps. in *Jazz Nativity*, NYC, in '90s.

Infl: Miles Davis, K. Komeda, Wayne Shorter, Billie Holiday. Dudziak is an immensely skilled vocalist whose range spans nearly five octaves. Although she was not the first singer to achieve startling effects through the use of such electronic devices as tape-echo and ring modulators, she was the first to achieve prominence w. them within a vocalese context. On the negative side is an emphasis on quirkiness rather than music. Fests: Warsaw '69–72; Molde '71; Pescara '72; Int'l Jazz Jamboree, Warsaw '85; Umbria Jazz w. Gil Evans '87. Comps., which are largely improv., incl.: "Dear Christopher Komeda"; "Darkness and Newborn Light"; "Bandi and Bamse" (latter two in collab. w. Makowicz). Recs. as lead: Ari. '75; IC '79. CDs: w. Urbaniak (Col.; Polskie Nagrania); The Monday Night Orch. (SN).

DUKE, DOUG (DOUGLAS) (Ovidio Fernandez), org, pno, bsn, acdn, tpt; b. Buenos Aires, Argentina, 1920; d. Rochester, NY, 11/30/73. Studied classical pno. at age 6; start. pl. pipe org. at 10. Began trav. at 15. "I was always running away w. a band. They [his parents] could never find me." Pl. w. Jan Savitt, Lionel Hampton, Dick Stabile, Mal Hallett in 1940s. Led own gps. at Frank Dailey's Meadowbrook in N.J.; Hickory House in NYC '50s. In '60s operated a small space called The Music Room in Rochester. Many mus. pl. gigs and sat in there. A two-CD issue on the Valley Vue label, Palm Springs, Calif., called *Doug Duke & Company, The Music Room*, feats. him w. Charlie Byrd; Vic Dickenson; Roy Eldridge; Bobby Hackett; Hampton; Coleman Hawkins; Mat Mathews; Ray Nance; Charlie Shavers; Clark Terry; Toots Thielemans; Teddy Wilson; and others in recs made at The Music Room '65–8.

DUKE, GEORGE, pno, kybds, comp, prod; b. San Rafael, CA, 1/12/46. Extensive classical training in SF; grad. fr. SF State U. w. M.A. in comp 1969. While in coll., he pl. in house rhythm section for the Both/And Club; also worked in LA w. Don Ellis, Jean-Luc Ponty, Frank Zappa late '60s and early '70s. Joined Cannonball Adderley '71, touring Eur. w. him, then rejoin. Zappa until '75. Fr. mid '70s, he was mostly active in pop, soul, and funk fields, leading gp. w. Billy Cobham, teaming up w. Stanley Clarke for the Clarke-Duke project, and rec. w. John Scofield '88. Arr. "Backyard Ritual" for Miles Davis's *Tutu* '86. Though he still occ. reveals his considerable jazz talents, Duke was, in the '90s, working primarily in commercial areas of mus. CDs: Col.; WB; Verve; w. Brecker Bros. (RCA); Cobham (Atl.); M. Davis; D. Sanborn (WB); Herb Ellis (Conc.); JL Ponty (BN; Atl.); S. Rollins (Mile.); J. Scofield (Gram.); Sadao Watanabe (Elek.).

DUKES OF DIXIELAND. This NO-based gp. is best known for a long run in the 1950s at the Famous Door on Bourbon St. The leaders were tptr. Frank Assunto (b. NO, 1/29/32; d. NO, 2/25/74) and tbast. Fred Assunto (b. Jennings, LA, 12/3/29; d. Las Vegas, NV, 4/21/66); fr. '55, their father, Papa Jac Assunto (b. Lake Charles, LA, 11/1/05; d. NO, 1/5/85), pl. w. them on tbn. and bjo., but he ret. to teaching when Fred died. The band's recs. on Roulette, RCA, and Audio Fidelity were highly successful, particularly dur. the late '50s when they rec. w. Louis Armstrong. They toured Japan in '64. After the deaths of Fred and Frank, the band cont. w. replacements; in the late '70s and early '80s it app. at its own Duke's Place club in the Monteleone Hotel, NO. Re-form. as an interracial gp. in '85. CDs: Col.; ProJazz; Laser.; *Sound of Bix*, (Leisure Jazz).

DUMAS, TONY, bs; b. Los Angeles, CA, 10/1/55. In the early 1970s, he worked w. Johnny Hammond Smith; Kenny Burrell; Freddie Hubbard; rec. w. Patrice Rushen. Active as studio mus. fr. mid '70s; rec. w. Nat Adderley and J.J. Johnson in Japan '77. Numerous other recs., incl. dates w. Art Pepper; Joe Farrell; Billy Higgins; Joe Henderson. In early '90s, he was in great demand in the LA area, perf. w. such artists as Ernie Watts; Rushen; Billy Childs; and Joe Henderson. Dumas makes the Blitz double bs., designed by John Dawson. CDs: w. Pepper (Cont.; Gal.); Childs (WH); Johnson (Pab.); Henderson; Farrell; G. Cables (Cont.); Higgins (Red; Evid.); R. Woodard (Cand.); E. Daniels (GRP).

DUNBAR, TED (EARL THEODORE DUNBAR JR.), gtr, comp, tpt, v-tbn; b. Port Arthur, TX, 1/17/37; d. New Brunswick, NJ, 5/29/98. Brother pl. pno., sax, tba. Self-taught. Led dance band at Lincoln HS, also pl. parades and club dates. Stud. pharmacology and pl. in bands at Tex Southern U. 1955–9. Worked in Houston w. Arnett Cobb '56–8; Don Wilkerson '57–9; Joe Turner '58; own qnt. '60. Moved to Indiana '61, pl. w. David Baker '61–3; subbed for Wes Montgomery in trio '62–3. Moved to Dallas '63, pl. w. Fathead Newman '63; Red Garland '64; Billy Harper, James Clay '64–5. Moved to NYC '65, pl. in B'way pit bands; w. Frank Foster bb '66–82; Billy Mitchell, Seldon Powell, Jazzmobile w. Billy Taylor, Jimmy Heath, McCoy Tyner late '60s-70s; Harold Ousley '69; Ron Jefferson Choir '69–70; Larry Ridley '70; Tony Williams Lifetime '71–2; Sonny Rollins, Geo. Wein, Ben Riley–Ron Carter '73; Joe Newman, Grady Tate, Joe Chambers, Roy Haynes, Chuck Israels' Nat'l Jazz Ens., Charles Rouse-Bill Lee, Richard Davis '74–5; Gil Evans Orch. '74–6; Jimmy Heath, Billy Harper, Billy Taylor, Oliver Nelson, Frank Wess '76; Charles Mingus bb '77; Jazz Professors of Rutgers U., Harold Vick, Sam Rivers '78; Rufus Reid '79; Jimmy Smith, Dizzy Gillespie, Mickey Tucker '80; Donald Byrd–Alan Dawson, David Baker '81; Philly Joe Jones, Grover Washington, Monty Alexander '82; Richard Davis '86; Kenny Burrell '87; Dave Brubeck '88; Roger Kellaway '89; Buddy Montgomery, Donald Byrd, Rufus Reid, Geo. Coleman '89–90; Frank Wess bb '90; Joe Williams, Billy Taylor, Smithsonian Orch. '92. Dunbar taught at Jazzmobile fr. the late '60s and at Rutgers U. fr. '71. He wrote several instructional books, incl. *A System of Tonal Convergence for Improvisors, Composers and Arrangers.* His students incl. Kevin Eubanks; Vernon Reid; Nile Rodgers; Rodney Jones; Ed Cherry; William Ash. Favs: Segovia, Oscar Moore, Wes Montgomery; arrs: Ellington, Gil Evans, Gerald Wilson. Fests: Eur. fr. '71; Japan fr. '85. LP: Xan. CDs: Steep.; F. Wess; J.J. Johnson (Conc.); Mickey Tucker (Steep.); L. Donaldson (BN); Frank Foster (Den.); Buddy Montgomery (Land.); Fathead Newman (Cand.); B. Taylor (Taylor-Made); Randy Weston (Verve); H. Bluiett (SN).

DUNCAN, HANK (HENRY JAMES), pno; b. Bowling Green, KY, 10/26/1896; d. Long Island, NY, 6/7/68. Studied pno. at Central HS in Louisville and at Fisk U., Nashville, Tenn. Led own gp. in Louisville in 1919, incl. tbn. Jimmy Harrison. Moved to NYC in early '20s, pl. w. Fess Williams '25–30, incl. Savoy ballroom to '28; King Oliver '31; Sidney Bechet's NO Footwarmers '32–3; Charles "Fat Man" Turner at the Arcadia '34–5. Join. F. Waller's bb as second pno '35, tour. US, and perf. cutting contests w. Waller as regular part of show. Apps. in Bost. w. Bechet, Bunk Johnson '45. Opened at Nick's in Greenwich Village, NYC, as solo pno. in Mar. '47, remaining there until May '55; then trio w. Zutty Singleton, Louis Metcalf at Metropole Café, NYC, to '56; ret. to Nick's until '63, when it closed. Illness curtailed his pl. in later yrs. Pioneer of stride pno. Recs. as lead. (B&W) '44. As sideman w. Waller (HMV) '35; Tony Parenti (Jazztone) '55; Wild Bill Davison (Jazz). CDs: w. Bechet; Oliver (BB).

DUNHAM, SONNY (ELMER LEWIS), tpt, tbn, lead; b. Brockton, MA, 11/16/14; d. Florida, 6/18/90. Sister Louise (1906–40) was a prof. saxist. Start. on v-tbn. at age 7, slide at 11. Start. working w. local bands at 13. Moved to NYC in late 1920s, pl. w. Ben Bernie for a few mos.; dur. two yrs. w. Paul Tremaine, he sw. to tpt., occ. doubling on tbn. Briefly led own orch., then join. Glen Gray's Casa Loma Orch. as feat. tpt., '32. Remained to '36 and led own band again to early '37; disbanded and went to Eur.; back

in US, he rejoin. Casa Loma Orch. until '40. Led own bands in '40s; sidemen incl. Corky Corcoran, Pete Candoli, Zoot Sims. His theme song was "Memories of You." Briefly w. Bernie Mann, Tommy Dorsey '51. In the '60s, he cont. to lead own gps. mostly in Fla. Poll: *Met.* '37, tpt. Recs. w. Casa Loma on Dec. CDs: Cir.; w. Metronome All-Stars; J. Teagarden (BB); Casa Loma (Col.).

DUNLOP, FRANKIE (FRANCIS), dms; b. Buffalo, NY, 12/6/28. Brother pl. pno.; fath., gtr. Began pno. studies at age 9, at Buffalo Youth Ctr.; sw. to dms. at 10, stud. w. member of Buffalo Symph. First prof. job on dms. at 16; pl. w. small gps. around western N.Y. 1948–50; briefly w. Big Jay McNeely, ca. '50. Rec. debut w. Moe Koffman '50. After ret. fr. army service '53, he led own combo for a yr. Pl. w. Skippy Williams '54; then moved to NYC, pl. three wks. w. Monk-Coltrane at Five Spot '55; Sonny Stitt, Charles Mingus mid '50s; Sonny Rollins '58. Tour. w. Maynard Ferguson '58–60; Lena Horne; and briefly w. Duke Ellington '60. With Monk again '61–3, tour. Eur. '61; Japan '63. In mid '60s, he worked as a songwriter; also app. on concert tours perf. a comedy, jazz, and pantomime act. Pl. w. Rollins '66–7; then freelanced in NYC, incl. subbing in B'way pit bands for *The Me Nobody Knows*; *Promises, Promises*; *Purlie* '67–70; also led own gps. dur. this time. In early '70s, he again perf. w. own jazz pantomime act in NYC, LA, Santa Monica, Calif. Tour. w. Earl Hines '73–4. In mid '70s, worked w. various bands in Catskills and Pocono mountain resorts. Pl. w. L. Hampton on and off '75–81. Illness ended his career. Dunlop incorporated urgent rhythmic effects w. melodic tonalities. Favs: Max Roach, Philly Joe Jones, Lex Humphries. B'way: *Inner City* '71–3. CDs: w. Wilbur Ware (Riv.); Monk (Riv.; Col.); Ferguson (Mos.); Rollins (Imp.); Ray Crawford (Cand.); Mingus (BB); L. Hampton (B&B; Timel.); Bill Barron (Sav.).

DUNN, JOHNNY, tpt; b. Memphis, TN, 2/19/1897; d. Paris, France, 8/20/37. Attended Fisk U. Perf. as soloist in local theaters 1915–16. Served in France '17–18. After army, he ret. to US and worked in NYC and elsewhere w. W.C. Handy '18–20; Mamie Smith's Jazz Hounds '20–1. Form. own Jazz Hounds, acc. voc. Edith Wilson '21–2. Join. Will Vodery's Plantation Orch. '22, Eur. tour '23. To Engl. w. *Blackbirds* revue '26. Ret. to US, led own orch. in NYC '27, '28; in Chi. '28; back to Eur. '28, '29 w. Lew Leslie, Noble Sissle. In early '30s, he led own band in Eur., app. in France, Belgium, Netherlands; also pl. in Paris orch. accomp. Josephine Baker. Pl. in Den. '35. Lived last few yrs. of his life in Holland. He was, bef.

Armstrong, one of the first infl. tpts., and among the first to make extensive use of the "wa-wa" mute style. Recs: for Col. '22, '24, '28; w. E. Wilson '22, Col.; w. Jelly Roll Morton, Fats Waller, J.P. Johnson '28. CDs: w. Clarence Williams (EPM/Hot 'N Sweet); tracks w. The Plantation Orch. in *Black Jazz in Europe, 1926–30* (EMI Pathé/Jazztime).

DUPREE, CHAMPION JACK (William Thomas), pno, voc; b. New Orleans, LA, 7/4/10; d. Hanover, Germany, 1/21/92. Orphaned by a fire, he lived in Colored Waifs' Home for Boys until age 14, when a foster family took him in. Stud. pno. w. a pnst. in a barrelhouse club and began pl. prof. in 1930. Received the nickname "Champion" when he boxed for a living dur. the Depression. After his last match in Indianapolis '40, he settled there for several yrs., singing and pl. pno. in clubs. Moved to NYC ca. '44. The folk/blues revival of the '60s boosted his career and eventually brought him to Eur., where he rec. and pl. clubs, fests. He referred to himself as one of the last of the barrelhouse pno. players, whose blues reflect the life of urban and Southern rural blacks. "My songs," he said, "tell about my experiences in life or what I saw in the lives of other people." Made rec. debut on Okeh '40. Later sess. for Joe Davis, Apollo, Continental, King. LP: Atl. CDs: Col.; Story.; w. Axel Zwingenberger (Vagabond).

DURAN, EDDIE (EDWARD LOZANO), gtr; b. San Francisco, CA, 9/6/25. Brothers Carlos and Manuel pl. bs. and pno. w. Cal Tjader in 1950s. As a child, he sang in amateur contests w. bro. Manuel. Stud. pno. fr. '32, then took up gtr. '37. Stud. for seven mos. but mainly self-taught; pl. first prof. gig at age 15. In navy two yrs., then worked in SF w. Freddie Slack; Flip Phillips; Charlie Parker; Stan Getz; George Shearing; Vince Guaraldi; Red Norvo; Earl Hines. Rec. in '50s w. Tjader; Getz; Ron Crotty; Jerry Coker; own gp. Led own trio '60–7, then rec. w. Tjader early '70s. Pl. w. Benny Goodman '76–81; Tania Maria early '80s. Duran spent some time in NYC in the late '80s but has led a qt. in SF in the '90s. LPs: Fant., Conc. CDs: w. Tjader; Guaraldi; Getz (Fant.); Tania Maria (Conc.).

DURAN, MANNY (MANUEL SANCHEZ), tpt, flg, claves; b. Alamogordo, NM, 6/11/26; d. NYC, 10/30/06. Grandfather pl. cl. Stud. at U. of New Mexico 1946–50, later w. Carmine Caruso, Adolf Sandole in NYC '75–80. Pl. w. Lacho Acuna's mariachi band in Alamogordo '37–44; Don Sando while in air force at Chanute Field, Ill. '44–5; Frank Packard, Glen Burns in Albuquerque, '46–50. Pl. in LA and SF w. Billy Higgins, Don Cherry, Speed Parsons, Lin Halli-

day, Lawrence Marable, others '54–5. Moved to NYC '56. Worked as a waiter at Café Bohemia for a yr., sitting in w. bands app. there and doing a week of subbing for Roy Eldridge. Then pl. w. Noro Morales; Billy Butterfield; Phil Woods; Kai Winding; Charlie Rouse; Machito; Mongo Santamaria; Eddie Palmieri; Ricardo Rey; Kako; Arsenio Rodriguez; Warne Marsh. Led own small gps. fr. '70 incl. co-lead. gp. w. Carla White '80–5. Also cont. to freeelance, pl. and rec. w. Ray Barretto, Mario Bauza, Vladimir & Conjunto 66. Favs: Kenny Dorham, Dizzy Gillespie. Fests: Finland w. Machito '79. Film: *Heroina* (Mex.) w. Kako. TV: PBS w. Cal Massey. CDs: Stash; w. Gillespie-Machito (Pablo); Bauza (Mess.).

DURHAM, BOBBY (ROBERT JOSEPH), dms; b. Philadelphia, PA, 2/3/37. Father, a prof. tap dancer known at Nat Leroy, danced w. Fish Bros.; uncle, Leon, danced in duo known as Mock & Pock; moth., Theresa, taught him tap and voc. Began dancing at age 2. Start. on dms. in O.V. Catto Drum Corps, Junior HS band; Quaker City Band & Orch.; Bok Vocational HS; Queen Cons.; Marine Corps Band & Drum Corps. Stud. w. Charles Simmons, pl. congas and traps set. Pl. w. Stan Hunter; Lloyd Price; Wild Bill Davis; Al Grey fr. 1962; Lionel Hampton '62; Slide Hampton '64; Duke Ellington '66; Oscar Peterson '66–71; Ella Fitzgerald '73–80; also w. Shirley Scott; Billy Mitchell; Grant Green; Clara Ward; James Brown; Tommy Flanagan. Has taught priv. and served as clinician. Favs: Roach; Blakey; Haynes. Fests: "Everywhere but Russia, Alaska, Arabia." Idaho JF w. L. Hampton; Vail '96; Trapani, Italy '95. CDs: B&B; w. Peterson (MPS; Phil.; Pab.; Tel.); T. Flanagan; Fitzgerald; J. Pass; Lockjaw Davis; R. Eldridge; Gillespie (Pab.); S. Stitt (B&B); P. Minger (JA); J. McShann (Chiaro.); Al Grey (B&B; Stash, Chiaro.; Capri; Arb.); Sweets Edison (Cand.); J. McDuff (Red).

DURHAM, EDDIE, gtr, tbn, comp, arr; b. San Marcos, TX, 8/19/06; d. NYC, 3/6/87. From a mus. family: fath. pl. vln; six bros. pl. instruments; stud. mus. w. older bro. First pl. bjo., then took up tbn. and perf. on both tbn. and gtr. throughout his career. In 1921, he tour. in minstrel shows w. Durham Bros. Band, which he co-dir. w. bro. Allen. Pl. in Southwest territory bands, incl. those of Walter Page, Edgar Battle '26–8. Worked w. Bennie Moten '29–33; wrote several important arrs. for band, incl. "Moten Swing"; also experimented w. gtr. amplification. Moved to NYC in '34 to arr. for Willie Bryant. Pl. and arr. for Jimmie Lunceford: "Avalon"; "Pigeon Walk"; "Lunceford Special"; "Blues in the Groove" '35–7; Count Basie: "Time Out"; "Topsy"; "Swingin' the

Blues"; "Jumpin' at the Woodside" '37–8; early recs. on elec. gtr. w. Basie and Lester Young's Kansas City Five and Six. In late '30s, he was very active as arr. incl: "Slip Horn Jive"; "Glen Island Special"; and "Wham" for Glenn Miller '39; also wrote for Artie Shaw, Ina Ray Hutton, Jan Savitt. Co-comp. "Topsy" w. Edgar Battle; also co-comp. "I Don't Want to Set the World on Fire." In '40, he form. a bb; mus. dir. for Int'l Sweethearts of Rhythm '41–3; briefly dir. his own all-female band '45. Fr. late '40s to mid '60s, freelanced as perf., arr.; led own small gps. Became a real estate agent in '64; then ret. to mus. w. Buddy Tate '69. Co-led gp. w. Franc Williams at West End Café, NYC, mid '70s. In his last yrs., apps. w. the Countsmen; Harlem Blues and Jazz Band, incl. Eur. tours. Among the first el-gtrsts., he was a key infl. on Charlie Christian. His classic arrs. epitomize the swinging riff style of the KC bands of the '30s. CDs: w. Basie (Dec.; Hep); Lunceford, as arr. (Dec.; Class.); Young (Comm.); Moten; Benny Carter; Miller, as arr. (BB).

DUTCH SWING COLLEGE BAND. Popular Dutch gp. founded in 1945 by cl. Peter Schilperoot and pnst. Frans Vink as an offshoot of a jazz sch., the Dutch Swing College, established by the two in '44. Fr. '48 the gp. app. at virtually every major Eur. jazz fest. Tour. Engl. '49. Tour. w. feat. Amer. mus., incl. Sidney Bechet '49–50, '53–4; Hot Lips Page '51; Albert Nicholas '54. Schilperoot left the band in '55. He was replaced by Jan Morks, and pnst. Joop Schrier became the leader. Schilperoot ret. as leader in '59. Personnel over the yrs. incl. tpts. Joost van Os, Kees van Dorsser, Wybe Buma, Oscar Klein, Ray Kaart and Bert de Kort; tbns. Wim Kolstee and Dick Kaart; cls. Dim Kesber, Jan Morks, Bob Kaper; Arie Ligthart, bjo.; Bob van Oven and Henk Bosch van Drakesteyn, bs.; Arie Merkt, Andre Westendorp, Louis de Lussanet, and Huub Janssen, dms. The band tour. and rec. prolifically starting in '45. In the '60s and throughout the '70s feat. artists incl. Jimmy Witherspoon; Bud Freeman; Joe Venuti; Nelson Williams; Teddy Wilson; Billy Butterfield. In the '70s, Schilperoot established his own rec. label, DSC Productions, and was knighted by Queen Juliana of the Netherlands. He died in '90 but the band cont. to perf. in Eur. In '85 an anniversary album, *40 Years*, was released on the Philips label. CDs: Timel.; Philips; PMF.

DUTREY, HONORE, tbn; b. New Orleans, LA, 1894; d. Chicago, IL, 7/21/35. Brothers Pete and Sam pl. vln. and cl. respectively. Pl. w. King Oliver, 1907; various NO brass bands, incl. Melrose, Excelsior, to '17; also w. Buddy Petit; J. Robichaux; Jimmie Noone. Join. navy in '17; then settled in Chi., where he rejoin. Oliver '19–24, participating in many rec. sess. Led own band briefly in '24; later worked w. Carroll Dickerson bb, Johnny Dodds, Louis Armstrong '27. Left mus. in '30 due to poor health. Highly esteemed by early jazz scholars as one of the foremost tbnsts. of his time. Recs. w. Oliver '23. CDs: w. Armstrong (Col.); Oliver (Mile.); Dodds (Dec.; BB; B&B).

DUVIVIER, GEORGE B., bs, arr, comp; b. NYC, 8/17/20; d. NYC, 7/11/85. Studied vln. at Cons. of Mus. and Art. Asst. concertmaster of Central Manh. Symph. Orch. at age 16. Then took up bs., stud. comp., arr. at NYU. Pl. w. Coleman Hawkins 1940–1; Eddie Barefield, Lucky Millinder '42–3. Army service '43–5. Fr. '43 to '47, he was staff arr. for Lunceford, who had bought his first arr. in '42. Perf., comp. and arr. originals for Sy Oliver's MGM recs. '47. Two Eur. tours w. Nellie Lutcher '50. Strongly assoc. w. Lena Horne, incl. Eur. trips; also app. w. Pearl Bailey, Billy Eckstine, Terry Gibbs, Don Redman in the '50s; Bud Powell trio '53–7. Admitted to ASCAP '57. A superb accomp. and supple soloist, he pl. and rec. w. a wide variety of singers and instrumentalists fr. Kate Smith to Sinatra, Benny Goodman to Eric Dolphy. Through '70s and '80s, he was a regular at the Colo. JP. Worked often w. Benny Carter, Hank Jones. Favs: Blanton, Ray Brown; arr: Rugolo, Shorty Rogers, Neal Hefti. A sought-after studio mus., Duvivier pl. on soundtracks for such films as *Requiem for a Heavyweight*, *Serpico*, *The Godfather*; countless jingles, incl. wearing requisite black eye in the Tareyton cigarettes "I'd Rather Fight Than Switch" campaign. TV: three yrs. w. Bobby Rosengarden orch. for Dick Cavett, ABC, in '70s. Comps: "Autumn Landscape"; "Porch Light." Book: *Bassically Speaking: An Oral History of George Duvivier*, Edward Berger and David Chevan (Scarecrow) '94. CDs: w. Bud Powell (Verve; BN; RCA); A. Cohn–Z. Sims; S. Stitt; H. Jones (Muse); J. Venuti–Sims; Soprano Summit; G. Mulligan (Chiaro.); Benny Carter (Verve; Pab.); C. Hawkins; G. Ammons; A. Cobb; E. Davis; Dolphy (Prest.); Ron Carter (NJ); Basie (Roul.); Goodman (Cap.; MM); Sonny Clark; S. Turrentine (Time); B. Webster (Col.); Jimmy Smith; S. Getz; Wes Montgomery (Verve); I. Jacquet; E. Larkins; Slam Stewart; Sir Roland Hanna; Sir Charles Thompson; S. Grappelli (B&B).

e

EADE, DOMINIQUE FRANCES, voc, pno, arr; b. Ruislip, England, 6/16/58. Sister Anne is prof. voc. and pnst.; bro. Geo. pl. el-bs and gtr.; husband is sax-ist Allan Chase. Stud. at Vassar Coll. 1976–8; Berklee Coll. of Mus.,'78–9; New Engl. Cons. '79–82 and '87–9. First gigs as solo act in Stuttgart, Germ., cof-feehouses while in hs. Perf. w. Joe McPhee in Pough-keepsie, N.Y. '76–8; duo w. Ran Blake in Bost. '79; own qt. in Bost. '79–82. Co-led qnt. Genso '83–5. Perf. w. Ran Blake Qnt. w. Ricky Ford '85–6; Taylor McLean '85–9; trio w. Donald Brown, John Lock-wood '85–8; Orange Then Blue w. Geo. Schuller, various new music gps. '85–90; Dave Holland '87; Butch Morris '88; duo and qt. w. Mick Goodrick '88–9; Stanley Cowell, John Damian–Bill Frisell '89; Damian '89–90. Moved to NYC '90. Perf. w. John Medeski at Vill. Gate; trio w. Bruce Barth–Ira Cole-man '91; duo w. Ben Sher fr. '92. Eade has taught and arr. for the a capella choir at New Engl. Cons. fr. '84. Favs: Billie Holiday, Sarah Vaughan, Ella Fitzgerald; comps: Monk, Ellington, Strayhorn, Shorter. Fests: Norway '80; Sweden '83; France '92. TV: PBS *La Plaza* w. Victor Mendoza '85. CDs: RCA; Acc.

EAGER, ALLEN, tnr, alto sax; b. NYC, 1/10/27; d. Daytona Beach, FL, 4/13/03. Studied cl. at 13 w. Dave Weber of NY Philharm. Parents bought him tnr. and he auditioned for Woody Herman at 15; later stud. w. Ben Webster. Tour. w. Bobby Sherwood at 16; later w. Sonny Dunham, Shorty Sherock, Hal McIntyre 1943; Herman '43–4; Tommy Dorsey; and Johnny Bothwell gp. '45. Pl. on 52nd St., NYC, w. various gps., incl. own qt. '45–7. Rec. w. Coleman Hawkins–led 52nd St. all-star gp. for RCA '46. Spent most of '48 pl. w. Tadd Dameron at Royal Roost, NYC; in late '40s and early '50s, he pl. several times w. Buddy Rich bb. Gave up mus. briefly to teach ski-ing and horseback riding, then form. a qt. in '53; pl. at The Open Door in Greenwich Village '54–5; worked sporadically w. Howard McGhee and Oscar Pettiford. After pl. in Paris '56–7, he was largely inactive in mus. but made an app. pl. alto sax at the Charles Min-gus–Max Roach Newport rebel fest. '60. In '61, he took up sports car racing, winning first prize in the GT division at Sebring, Fla. Resumed pl. in early '80s; toured Eur., sometimes w. Chet Baker. Kept a low profile after that, but pl. occ. in Fla., gigged at West End Café, NYC '82, and, in '86, Jazz Show-case, Chi. Inspired by Lester Young and later infl. by Charlie Parker, Eager was one of the most gifted young tnr. men of his generation, an instinctive pl. w. an innate sense of time. Made rec. debut as leader for Sav. '46. and rec. as a sideman w. Dameron, Dave Lambert, others incl. Tony Fruscella, Atl., '55; own LP for Up. '82. Favs: Sonny Rollins, Zoot Sims, Al Cohn. Fests: Lester Young Tribute at NJF-NY '82; Umbria Jazz w. D. Gillespie '83. CDs: four tracks w. K. Winding on *In the Beginning...Bop* (Sav.); w. Fats Navarro (Mile.; BN); C. Hawkins (Vict.); Esq. All-Amer. Poll Winners (BB); G. Mulligan (Prest.; PJ); Bothwell (Hep); Serge Chaloff (Cool 'N Blue).

EARDLEY, JON (JONATHAN), tpt; b. Altoona, PA, 9/30/28; d. Cologne, Germany, 4/2/91. Father pl. tpt. w. Paul Whiteman, Isham Jones, and introduced him to Armstrong and Beiderbecke recs. Took up tpt. at 11; pl. w. circuses and fairs every summer ages 15 to 22. Began pl. jazz in AAF band while stationed in Wash., D.C. 1946–9. Pl. w. Buddy Rich '49; then, after discharge, pl. w. Gene Williams orch. in NYC

'49–50. Ret. to Altoona and form. his own gp. reflecting new infls., Parker and Gillespie. To NYC '53, taking part in sess. at Open Door, where he became assoc. w. Phil Woods, w. whose qnt. he pl. and rec. '54. With G. Mulligan qt. fall '54–5. Worked w. Hal McIntyre bef. rejoin. Mulligan for Eur. tour w. sxt. '56, remain. into '57. Back to Altoona in '57 and remained largely inactive in mus. until '63, when he moved to Brussels to pl. w. Belgian radio and TV orch. Join. WDR Radio Big Band, Cologne, Germ. '69. Apps. at Eur. concerts and fests: Comblain-la-Tour '64; rec. "Concerto for Benjamin and Jonathan" w. Benny Bailey in Germ. '64; pl. in Netherlands '69–70; w. Chet Baker in Cologne '81. App. w. WDR Band at Jazz Yatra, Bombay '84. Rec. in NYC '89. Eardley applied the hot swing and bright lyricism of his early infls. to his harmonically informed modernism. CDs: Prest.; NJ; w. Woods (NJ); Mulligan (PJ); Z. Sims (EMI/Pathe Jazztime); Joachim Kuhn (CMP); Carmen McRae (Qwest).

EARLAND, CHARLES, org, sop sax, synth, el-pno, comp; b. Philadelphia, PA, 5/24/41; d. Kansas City, MO, 12/11/99. Began on alto sax in hs; schoolmates incl. Pat Martino, Lew Tabackin, Bobby Timmons. Pl. tnr. sax. w. Temple U. band, Jimmy McGriff 1958. Led own gp. fr. early '60s; began pl. org. in '63. Pl. w. Lou Donaldson '68–9, then formed own trio. First album *Soul Crib*. 1969's *Black Talk* was a hit and resulted in a contract w. Prest. Tour. w. own gp. fr. '70; double on sop. sax fr. '73. Pl. on soundtrack to film *The Dynamite Brothers* '74. Comps. incl. "Black Talk," incl. in soundtrack of *Fritz the Cat*; "Auburn Delight"; "Never Ending Melody"; "Morgan"; "Tyner." Fests: NJF-NY '73–4; Montreux JF '70s. CDs: Muse; Prest.; Mile.; w. Donaldson (BN).

EASLEY, BILL, saxes, cl; b. Olean, NY, 1/13/46. Father, Robert pl. dms.; moth., Lois, pno. Took up cl. at age 10, after seeing *The Benny Goodman Story*; by age 13 he was pl. w. his parents' band. To NYC 1964, to study at Juilliard; drafted in '65. Tour. US w. George Benson Qt. '68–70. After a yr. in Pitts., he moved to Memphis '71; spent next nine yrs. as a member of Isaac Hayes Movement; tour. w. Mercer Ellington's band. In the '70s and '80s, Easley, who plays almost all woodwind instruments, was primarily a theatre and studio mus., ret. occ. to jazz, incl. apps. w. Jimmy McGriff; Roland Hanna; James Williams. Worked in B'way pit bands for *Sophisticated Ladies*; *Black and Blue*. In '90s, he pl. in NYC w. AJO, Illinois Jacquet bb, and LCJO. A talented saxist, well-versed in traditional styles, he is also an accomplished cl. soloist. Favs: Cannonball Adderley, Barney Bigard. Has taught at William Paterson Coll.

CDs: Mile; Sunny.; w. J. Williams (Sunny.); Claude Williams (Prog.); LCJO; J. DeFrancesco (Col.); Charles Earland (Mile., Muse); Geoff Keezer; Harold Mabern (DIW); Ed Thigpen (Timel.).

EASTMAN, MADELINE LOUISE, voc; b. San Francisco, CA, 6/27/54. Married to dmr. Vince Lateano. Stud. theory, harm., voice at Coll. of San Mateo and priv. Inspired by Billie Holiday. Rec. w. Full Faith & Credit band on Palo Alto Records 1983. Taught jazz singing at jazz camp, co-developed voc. program at Stanford U.; workshop, clinics at Sonoma State Coll. To Japan '89, w. Monterey All-Stars, incl. Bill Berry. Her recs. reveal an exceptionally strong jazz sensitivity and phrasing. CDs: MadKat.

EATON, JOHN LIVINGSTON, pno; b. Washington, DC, 5/29/34. Great-grandfather, William Carleton, was well-known operatic baritone and actor in Amer. and Engl. theater, and dir. of first US D'Oyly Carte Co. Self-taught on pno. Yale U. 1952–6, grad. as an Engl. lit. major. Intended to pursue career as teacher but "succumbed to my first love, jazz, and became a professional musician." Stud. w. Alexander Lipsky '60–85. First gig at age 22 w. Wild Bill Whelan at Bayou, Wash., D.C. Encouraged by Ralph Sutton, Willie "The Lion" Smith; Teddy Wilson; George Shearing. Army service '58. Worked w. Whelan '59–60; led own band, which incl. Buck Hill; Stuff Smith; Jay Leonhart; Billy Taylor Jr. (bs.); George "Dude" Brown. Pl. w. Tommy Gwaltney Trio '64–5. Fr. '68 to '72, he led house trio at Blues Alley, Wash., D.C., backing Roy Eldridge; Buck Clayton; Ray Nance; Don Byas; Clark Terry; Thad Jones; Zoot Sims; Wild Bill Davison; Bobby Hackett; Tony Parenti; Vic Dickenson; Maxine Sullivan; Kenny Davern; Stuff Smith; Billy Butterfield; others. Pl. at Piano Spectacular, Kool JF at Waterloo Village, N.J. '82–4; in NYC at Hanratty's '82–4, Fortune Garden '88; solo concert for Pres. and Mrs. Reagan at White House '88; solo perfs. at Wolf Trap Perf. Arts Center, Va. '90–7. App. as solo perf./lecturer in over two hundred programs for Smithsonian Inst. in Wash., incl. "American Popular Song" series, and on road '78–97. Pl. jazz cruises, incl. SS *Norway* Floating JF '88–91; SS *Viking Sky* '95; feat. soloist at Esther Honan Int'l Pno. Competition, Calgary, Can. '93. Feat. lecturer and perf. for Chautauqua Inst., televised by WNED, Buffalo, N.Y. '90, '93. Taught classical and jazz pno. '65, priv. fr. '65. Nat Hentoff wrote in *The Nation*: "Eaton is the complete pianist. A bemused master of just about the whole spectrum of jazz language." Favs: Tatum, Tommy Flanagan, Bill Evans. TV: American Popular Song series, PBS; *Larry King Live*. Radio: M. McPartland's *Piano Jazz*;

All Things Considered (NPR); Radio Smithsonian; Voice of America. Rec. debut w. Stuff Smith, Verve '60. CDs: Chiaro.; w. Cliff Leeman; Davison (Jazz.).

ECKERT, JOHN W., tpt; b. NYC, 3/13/39. Studied at Eastman Sch. of Mus. 1957–61; No. Tex. St. U. '61–3. First prof. gig pl. at Poconos resort '59. Pl. w. own sxt. in Rochester, N.Y. '60–1; Stan Kenton '63; Maynard Ferguson '65–7. Also pl. w. Gerry Mulligan; Benny Goodman; Buck Clayton; Lee Konitz Nonet; Woody Herman; Sam Rivers; Sam Jones; Joe Henderson; Toshiko Akiyoshi bb; Grover Mitchell bb; Muhal Richard Abrams; AJO; Frank Wess Orch.; Louis Bellson bb; Loren Schoenberg bb. Taught tpt. at Bridgeport U. '79–81; Jersey City St. Coll. '81–3. Favs: Kenny Dorham, M. Davis, Louis Armstrong. Fests: Eur. and Asia '68. CDs: w. Konitz (Chiaro.; SN); Akiyoshi; Mitchell (Ken); K. Peplowski (Conc.); B. Goodman; Schoenberg (MM).

ECKERT, RANDY DARRELL, tpt, flg; b. Monticello, NY, 8/16/48. Father was amateur tbnst. Began on bugle, tbn. Hired by Barry Saperstein while in hs. Stud. at U. of Miami 1966–72. Pl. in Miami w. touring r&b gps., incl. Temptations, Marvin Gaye, Miracles, Gladys Knight '66–70; Sammy Davis Jr. Orch. '68–75; also pl. w. Ira Sullivan, Jaco Pastorius. Tour. Japan w. Michel Legrand Orch. '75. Pl. w. Mel Tormé bb in Fla. '75–8. Moved to NYC '78, pl. w. Sam Jones–Tom Harrell '78–9; Machito '78–80; Tito Puente '80–2; Jaki Byard's Apollo Stompers '80–6; Charli Persip Superband '80–9; Illinois Jacquet bb '88–92; Panama Francis's Savoy Sultans '89; Lionel Hampton Orch. '90; Clifford Jordan bb fr. '91. Eckert taught at U. of Miami '72. Favs: Armstrong, Clifford Brown, K. Dorham. Fests: Jap. w. Legrand '75; Eur. w. Jacquet '88–92. TV: *Today* w. Jacquet; Jap. TV w. Legrand; BBC w. Hampton, Jacquet.

ECKINGER, ISLA, bs, tbn, comp; b. Dornach, Switzerland, 5/6/39. Father pl. oboe, Engl. horn. After cello lessons 1947–52, studied tbn. '56–9 and worked locally in Basel. Took up bs. at age 21. Self-taught. Fr. '65, he worked as freelance bs., pl. throughout Eur., Japan, and US. House bs. at the Domicile, in Munich, Germ. '70s. In '80s, form. gp., Hot Mallets, pl. vib. and tbn. Moved to Hollywood '87, but cont. to travel extensively. World tour, incl. Far East, w. George Robert Qt. in late '91. Some of his comps. have been rec. by Horace Parlan; Clifford Jordan; Benny Bailey; and others. Rec. w. Hot Mallets; also w. Frank Rosolino; Lee Konitz; George Robert. CDs: w. Eddie Davis (Divox); Wild Bill Davison; Cees Slinger (Timel.); S. Grappelli (Verve); Lillian Terry; G. Manusardi (SN); Buck Clayton

(Sack.); George Robert (TCB); Mal Waldron (ECM); Clark Terry–Geo. Robert (Mons.).

ECKSTINE, BILLY ("MR. B" OR "B") (William Clarence Eckstein), voc; b. Pittsburgh, PA, 7/8/14; d. Pittsburgh, 3/8/93. Sang in clubs in Buffalo, N.Y.; Det.; two yrs. at Club De Lisa in Chi. With Earl Hines's band 1939–43, singing and occ. pl. tpt. After rec. such hits as "Jelly Jelly" and "Skylark" w. Hines, he form. his own bb, whose collective personnel incl. Dizzy Gillespie; Fats Navarro; Miles Davis; Kenny Dorham; Gene Ammons; Dexter Gordon; Budd Johnson; Lucky Thompson; Frank Wess; Charlie Parker; Leo Parker; Tommy Potter; and Art Blakey.; arrs. by Johnson; Tadd Dameron; and Jerry Valentine; and voc. Sarah Vaughan. Eckstine was a competent mus. who sometimes pl. v-tbn. w. his band, but his vocals and striking good looks brought him enormous popularity. Dur. its three yr. life, fr. June '44, the Eckstine band was a virtual cradle of bebop, but its commercial recs. suffer fr. poor sound quality and do not truly represent the vitality of the live perfs. Among the first black singers whose appeal transcended race, Eckstine cont. to work and rec. as a single into the early '90s, by which time his voice had a quavery vibrato in the upper register, but he maintained the warmth of his middle register, and his style. In his nightclub act he also pl. tpt., gtr. and danced. Won the *Esq.* New Star Award '46; *DB* poll '48–52. CDs: Sav.; Verve; Merc.; Em.; Roul; Stax; w. Hines (Class.; BB); C. Parker (Stash); S. Vaughan (Em.); S. Hasselgard (Drag.).

EDELHAGEN, KURT, lead, pno, cl, sax; b. Herne, Westphalia, Germany, 6/5/20; d. Cologne, Germany, 2/8/82. Father, an amateur vlnst., start. him w. lessons at age 8; stud. pno. for five yrs.; cl. at 14. Grad. fr. "Folkwang-Schule" in 1941; was in advanced class for classical cond. when called into army same yr. After WWII, led own gp. at British army club in Herne '45; own bb fr. '46, pl. at US clubs in Bad Kissingen '46; Heidelberg, Munich '47; Frankfurt '48; regular broadcasts on Armed Forces Network. His orch. was feat. on Germ. radio in Nuremberg '49–52; Baden-Baden '52–7; won the *Jazz-Echo* poll fr. '53 as best Germ. jazz orch.; Westdeutscher Rundfunk, Cologne fr. '57. Founded first sch. of jazz on university level at Cologne Staatliche Hochschule Für Musik '58; band pl. premiere of Liebermann's *Concerto for Jazz Band & Symph. Orch.* '55. His radio orch., incl. such prominent Eur. mus. as Derek Humble, Dusko Gojkovic, Rob Pronk, perf. throughout Eur.; tour. USSR and East Germ. '64; Middle East '68. Westdeutscher Rundkunk disbanded the orch. in '73, but Edelhagen cont. to pl. and arr. light dance mus. for the station. Favs: Basie,

Kenton; pno: Tatum, Peterson. Dur. the late '50s and '60s, his band, which combined execution and punch, was considered one of Eur.'s finest. Recs. for Bruns, Polydor in Germ; w. Caterina Valente, Dec. CD: w. Stan Getz (Laser.).

EDISON, HARRY "SWEETS," tpt; b. Columbus, OH, 10/10/15; d. Columbus, 7/27/99. An uncle showed him scales, but he was essentially self-taught. While in hs, pl. w. bs. Earl Hood's band and Morrison's Grenadiers. Pl. w. Jeter-Pillars Orch. in Cleveland 1933–5, then St. Louis. To NYC '37; six mos. w. Lucky Millinder. Joined Count Basie in Dec. '37 and remained until the band broke up, Feb. '50. App. in Gjon Mili's celebrated film short *Jammin' the Blues* '44. Tour. w. Buddy Rich band, in Eur. w. Josephine Baker; pl. w. JATP; worked w. Benny Carter on sound tracks and freelanced in Hollywood. Fr. '54, he was in Nelson Riddle Orch. as feat. soloist on many Sinatra sess. Tour. often w. Pearl Bailey and Louie Bellson. Joe Williams' mus. dir. '61. Rejoined Basie briefly on many occs.; in '60s, worked regularly at Memory Lane club in LA. Teamed frequently w. Eddie "Lockjaw" Davis. Through '70s and into '90s he worked often in Eur. Mus. dir. for comedian Redd Foxx in '70s. In '90s was still active, tour. int'l w. Lionel Hampton's Golden Men of Jazz and heading own qnt. In '97 was a stand-out in an all-star tribute to Nat Cole at Carnegie Hall. Edison's distinctive sound and approach was well established dur. his Basie yrs. A great example of his use of dynamics is on Basie's Col. rec., "Miss Thing." He often made subtle use of simple riffs, swinging an entire passage merely by repeating one note or phrase; some of these phrases became clichés but remain an attractive aspect of his persona. Film soundtrack: *Lady Sings the Blues*. TV: *Hollywood Palace; Leslie Uggams Show*. Between '36 and '92, he took part in countless rec. dates w. Illinois Jacquet; Ray Brown; Woody Herman; Shorty Rogers; and others. CDs: Riv.; Pab.; B&B; Cand.; Orange Blue; w. Basie (Dec.; Col.; BB; Pab.); L. Young (Verve) incl. *Lester Young Trio*, which contains Edison-led tracks w. Dexter Gordon; G. Mulligan (A&M); Benny Carter; Z. Sims; Tatum; Joe Turner; O. Peterson (Pab.); H. Ellis; G. Harris; F. Wess (Conc.); B. Holiday (Col.; Verve); E. Fitzgerald (Cap.; Verve); Sinatra (Cap.); B. Webster (Verve; Col.); Joe Williams (Roul.); Red Norvo (BB); B. Kessel (Cont.); Hampton (Tel.); Ellington; Harper Bros. (Verve).

EDWARDS, EDDIE (EDWIN BRANFORD), tbn; b. New Orleans, LA, 5/22/1891; d. NYC, 4/9/63. Played vln. at 10, tbn. at 15. Freelanced w. brass bands; after brief time w. Johnny Stein's Dixie Jass Band, he became a charter member of ODJB 1916.

Apart fr. a short army stint and work w. Jimmy Durante's band, Edwards stayed w. ODJB to '25. Led own gp. at Silver Slipper, NYC '25–7; pl. w. society bands in '30s and '40s. Took part in revival of ODJB '36. Tour. w. reorganized ODJB for Katherine Dunham show '43–4. Club dates w. own jazz sxt. in early '60s. Powerful ensemble pl. Favs: Mole, Higginbotham, Teagarden. Comps: co-comp. of "Tiger Rag"; "Fidgety Feet"; "Original Dixieland One-Step." CDs: w. ODJB (BB; Comm.).

EDWARDS, TEDDY (THEODORE MARCUS), tnr sax, cl; b. Jackson, MS, 4/26/24; d. Los Angeles, 4/20/03. Started on alto sax; worked w. local gps. in 1930s. Worked briefly in Det. and Tampa, Fla., tour. w. Ernie Fields '44, then settled in LA '45. Pl. w. Roy Milton '45, then sw. to tnr. w. Howard McGhee '45. With Benny Carter '48; original Lighthouse All-Stars '49–52; Max Roach–Clifford Brown '54; Gerald Wilson '54–64; Leroy Vinnegar '58; Terry Gibbs '59. In '60s, pl. w. Benny Goodman, McGhee; Basie, Gillespie bbs; and Milt Jackson–Ray Brown Qnt. Worked w. Bill Berry Band, Capp-Pierce Juggernaut in '70s; toured Japan '76 w. Jackson-Brown Qnt. Debuted his Brasstring ensemble in *Blue Saxophone* '77, and cont. to use it intermittently into the '90s; comp. and perf. own comps. w. Belgian Radio Orch. '82–5; tour. int'l w. Tom Waits and wrote soundtrack for his movie, *One From the Heart*. Began rec. for Polygram Jazz, France '91. Edwards has been a consistent perf. whose work has kept pace w. the times, while retaining a strong connection w. tradition. He has grown in acceptance as a comp., as well. CDs: Cont.; Prest.; Ant.; Steep.; Timel.; Verve; w. H. McGhee (Jz. Class.); Leroy Vinnegar; Helen Humes (Cont.); Groove Holmes (Prest.); S. Vaughan (Roul.); B. Goodman (MM); R. Weston (Verve); King Pleasure (HiFiJazz); F. Redd (Mile.).

EFFORD, BOB (ROBERT T.), bari sax, all woodwinds; b. London, England, 4/6/28. Mainly self-taught; prof. debut 1943. Pl. in Engl. w. Teddy Foster; Vic Lewis; Geraldo; Ted Heath; Tony Kinsey; Johnny Keating; John Dankworth. Toured Eur. twice w. Benny Goodman; also on Heath's final US tour. Moved to US '76; active on LA jazz and pop scene w. Ray Anthony; Bob Crosby; Bill Berry; Capp-Pierce; Bill Holman; Les Brown; Dave Pell. A solid section player and a capable sax soloist. Favs: Coleman Hawkins, Lester Young, Johnny Hodges. CDs: w. B. Florence (Trend; Disc.); Bill Holman (JVC); Dave Pell (Headfirst); F. Capp (Conc.).

EGAN, MARK McDANEL, el-bs, bs, comp; b. Brockton, MA, 1/14/51. Mother pl. pno., org.; fath.

pl. tpt. Stud. w. Jerry Coker at U. of Miami 1969–75. Pl. w. own gp. '72; Ira Sullivan '73–4; Phyllis Hyman '75–6; Eumir Deodato '77. Moved to NYC '77, pl. and rec. w. David Sanborn. Stud. priv. in NYC w. Jaco Pastorius, Dave Holland. Pl. w. Walter Bishop Jr. '77–8; Pat Metheny–Danny Gottlieb '77–80; Flora Purim–Airto Moreira '80–4; Stan Getz '81; Bill Evans '82; Lew Soloff, Randy Brecker since '83; Gil Evans Orch. since '83; Michael Franks since '84; Joe Beck since '86; Dave Liebman '86; Sophie Hawkins, David Wilcox '91; also own gp. Elements w. Danny Gottlieb since '82. Egan has worked extensively as a prod., incl. nine of his own recs. and sess. for Bill Evans and Steve Khan–Danny Gottlieb. He has also comp. and pl. for TV and film soundtracks. Favs: Dave Holland, Miles Davis; comp: Gil Evans. Fests: Eur. and Japan since '77. CDs: BM; w. Elements (Ant.; RCA); G. Evans (Elec. Bird; Jazz Door); Metheny (ECM); Soloff (PW; Sw. Bas.); Liebman (Owl); Jim Hall; Ernie Watts (CTI); Getz (Em.); A. LaVerne (Jazzline).

EHRLICH, MARTY (MARTIN LEWIS), saxes, cl, fl, comp; b. St. Paul, MN, 5/31/55. Studied at U. City (Mo.) HS 1968–72; New Engl. Cons. '73–7. Pl. w. Human Arts Ens. while in hs, then w. Jerome Harris, Jaki Byard, Geo. Russell '73; Anthony Braxton, John Lindberg, Leo Smith '79; Leroy Jenkins '81; Anthony Davis, Muhal Richard Abrams, Julius Hemphill '82; John Carter '85; Wayne Horvitz, Bobby Previte '86; John Zorn '88; also pl. w. Barry Altschul; Jack DeJohnette; Don Grolnick; Friedrich Gulda; Chico Hamilton; Mark Helias; Robin Holcomb; Oliver Lake; Butch Morris; Rod Williams. Ehrlich has led his own qt., pl. orig. comps., fr. '88; own Dark Woods Ens.; his bb comps. have been perf. by NY Comp.'s Orch. Received comp. grants from NEA; NY Council on the Arts; Meet the Comp.; etc. Fests: Eur. fr. '79. CDs: Enja; NW; Muse; SA; w. Anthony Cox (Muse); J. Carter (Gram.); Abrams; Braxton (BS); Mario Pavone (KFW); Grolnick (BN); Helias (Enja); Hemphill (Elex. Mus.; BS); Previte (Gram.; Enja); Russell (SN); Zorn (None.).

EINARSSON, TÓMAS RAGNAR, bs, comp; b. Blönduás, Iceland, 3/25/53. Studied w. classical bs. in Reykjavík and Copenhagen; prod. radio programs and wrote jazz columns for daily Icelandic newspaper. Acc. many visiting musicians, incl. Chet Baker; Kenny Drew; Frank Lacy. In 1991, his gp. represented Iceland in a Nordic jazz fest. in Oslo. Einarsson has rec. several albums as leader or co-leader, feat. some thirty of his comps., all well received by Scand. critics. CDs: Skifan; PS:Músík.

EITHER/ORCHESTRA. A 10-pc. (four brass, three saxes, three rhythm), Bost.-based ens. founded in 1985 by saxist and comp. Russ Gershon (b. Manhasset, NY, 8/11/59), it developed fr. a rehearsal band to a prof. outfit in a relatively short time. Numerous tours of US. Perf. and rec. collaborations have incl. mus. such as Lee Konitz; Illinois Jacquet; Charlie Rouse; Julius Hemphill; Cab Calloway; George Russell. Its eclectic mix of repertoire incl. Ellington; Mingus; Monk; Silver; Bennie Moten; Bing Crosby; King Crimson; Gershon originals. CDs: Acc.

EKYAN, ANDRÉ (Echkyan), cl, alto sax; b. Meudon, France, 10/24/07; d. near Alicante, Spain, 8/9/72. Self-taught. Led band at Le Perroquet in Paris 1920s. Pl. w. Jack Hylton in London '30–1; Gregor '32–3; Tommy Dorsey '36. Rec. as leader '35–46; accomp. by Django Reinhardt '37–41. Pl. and rec. w. Tommy Benford, Benny Carter, Coleman Hawkins '37; also pl. w. Ray Ventura '38; Joe Turner, Jack Butler, Frank Goudie '39; Ventura '41; Bobby Nichols '45; Mezz Mezzrow '40s. Rec. w. Reinhardt's Quintette du Hot Club de France '50. Was an infl. on Michel De Villers. CDs: w. Benny Carter (B&B); Reinhardt (Aff.; Class.).

ELDRIDGE, JOE (JOSEPH), alto sax; b. Pittsburgh, PA, 1908; d. Pittsburgh, 3/5/52. Professional debut in NYC, 1927. In late '20s, he led Elite Serenaders in NYC and Pitts. Worked w. Speed Webb and Cecil Scott in early '30s. Co-led band w. bro., Roy Eldridge, '33. Pl. w. McKinney's Cotton Pickers '34; Blanche Calloway '35–6; Roy Eldridge oct. and bb, '36–40; Buddy Johnson '41; Zutty Singleton qt. '41–3. After leading own gp. at Jimmy Ryan's, he rejoin. Singleton in LA '43. Tnr. sax w. R. Eldridge '44; Hot Lips Page '45. Gigged in Canada in late '40s. Ret. to NYC '50; taught priv. '51. Rec. "Mahogany Hall Stomp" w. R. Eldridge bb '39. CDs: w. R. Eldridge (Col.; Dec.).

ELDRIDGE, ROY; "LITTLE JAZZ" (DAVID), tpt, fl, voc, dms; b. Pittsburgh, PA, 1/30/11; d. Valley Stream, NY, 2/26/89. Studied w. older bro., Joe. Started on dms. at age 6. Pl. first gig New Yr.'s Eve, 1917, w. bro. Early prof. experience w. carnivals, pl. tpt., tba., dms.; after getting stranded in Little Rock, Arkansas, he worked w. Oliver Muldoon '27. Ret. to Pitts., where, for a few mos., he led his own band, Roy Elliott and his Palais Royal Orch. Then worked in St. Louis bcf. join. Horace Henderson for eight mos. in '28; ret. to Pitts. and resumed studies w. his bro. Worked briefly w. Zach Whyte, then w. Speed Webb's band '29–30, taking over as leader in Flint, Mich. Moved to NYC in '30 and pl. w. several dance bands: Cecil Scott (where Otto Hardwicke dubbed him "Little Jazz"); Elmer Snowden; Charlie Johnson at Small's. Pl. w. Teddy Hill's orch., then tour. w. Connie's *Hot Chocolates* revue. In '33, he once again ret. to Pitts., co-led a band w. his bro., then join. McKinney's Cotton Pickers in Balt., Md. '34. Ret. to NYC in '35, rejoining Hill at the Savoy; Eldridge and Chu Berry were now the band's principal soloists. Though he once cited Louis Armstrong, Rex Stewart, and Red Nichols as his formative infls., Eldridge drew significantly fr. such saxophonists as Benny Carter and Coleman Hawkins; by the mid '30s, he had developed an original style and become a vital figure in the evolution of jazz trumpet style. His first rec. solo was w. Hill on a '35 date; later that yr., he led his own band at the Famous Door and join. Fletcher Henderson as featured soloist, once again sharing honors w. Berry. On leaving Henderson in '36, he form. an oct. to pl. at the Chi. club Three Deuces, where he remained through '37, except for brief absences. The gp., which incl. Joe Eldridge as sax.-arr., became widely popular through nightly broadcasts; a '38 tour incl. the gp.'s debut at the Savoy, NYC. His work w. Hill and Henderson and recs. by the Three Deuces gp. ("Heckler's Hop," "After You've Gone," etc.) deeply infl. Dizzy Gillespie's early style. Eldridge quit the mus. business for a few mos. in '38 to study radio engineering. In Oct., he resumed pl. as a guest w. Mal Hallett's orch. in NYC; the next mo. he was back at the Famous Door w. his own band, which became the house band at the Arcadia Ballroom '39–40, pl. dates at the Apollo, and in residence at Kelly's Stable fr. Apr. to Oct. '40.

By the late '30s, Eldridge was recognized as one of the Swing Era's greatest improvisers. Courted by white swing bands, he joined Gene Krupa's as feat. soloist and singer fr. '41 to '43, when the band broke up. Eldridge gained national prominence w. Krupa, leaving a legacy that incl. his superb solo on "Rockin' Chair" and '41 hit voc. duet w. Anita O'Day, "Let Me Off Uptown." In '43-4, Eldridge led small gps. in NYC and Chi. and worked as staff mus. w. Paul Baron's orch. at CBS in NYC and on Mildred Bailey's radio series. Tour. w. Artie Shaw '44–5, then had various bands of his own. Ret. to Krupa for a few mos. in '49, but left to join the first national JATP tour. Tour. Eur. w. Benny Goodman in '50, remained in Paris, working there and tour. to great acclaim in Eur. as a single, also app. w. Sidney Bechet, Charlie Parker, and others. A week after his ret. to NYC in April '51, he was leading a small band at Birdland, where he app. regularly through the '50s. He was feat. annually in Norman Granz events in the '50s and '60s, which incl. US and Eur. tours w. either JATP or smaller shows w. Ella Fitzgerald and Oscar Peterson.

During these yrs., he primarily pl. in small gps., devoting his playing time almost equally to flg. and tpt. In the '50s and early '60s, he frequently app. w. a qnt., co-led w. Coleman Hawkins; also pl. many dates w. cl. Sol Yaged and led his own small gps. at the Village Vanguard, The Embers, etc. He accomp. Ella Fitzgerald '63–5; pl. w. Count Basie summer of '66; led own qnt. w. Richie Kamuca on and off '65–'70, incl. a long run at the Half Note, NYC, in late '69 and early '70. Tour. Eur. w. "Jazz from a Swingin' Era" '67; cont. extensive tour. throughout the '70s w. JATP and other Granz shows, and as a single. Took over as house leader at Jimmy Ryan's fr. '70 to '80, when he suffered a severe stroke. From then on, he perf. only as singer, dmr., and pnst., gradually cutting down on his activities as the decade wore on. Eldridge's style combined power, speed, wed to agility and range, harmonic awareness, a brilliant tone w. a tearing edge, overall ebullience, and a highly competitive nature. The core of the great spirit he displayed on trumpet never left him. Polls: *DB*, '42, '46; Hall of Fame '71; *Met.*, '44–6; *Esq.* Silver Award '45. Fests: Great South Bay '57; Berlin '65, '67; Montreux w. Gillespie, Clark Terry '65; NO '69; MJF '71, '74; w. own gp. at dedication of NYC's Louis Armstrong stadium, NJF-NY '73; Pres. Carter's White House JP '78. In '81, Eldridge was given a tribute concert in which he took part by Kool JF-NY. Film: *Ball of Fire* w. Krupa '41. TV & video: *The Sound of Jazz* '57; *Just Jazz*, PBS '71; WNET; episode on *Route 66* w. Ethel Waters, Jo Jones, C. Hawkins. CDs: Col.; Dec.; Pab.; Verve; Vogue; w. F. Henderson; Krupa (Col.); Shaw (BB); Basie (Pab.; Verve); JATP; Parker; Gillespie; Ellington; Fitzgerald; Jacquet; Lester Young (Verve); E. Snowden (BL); Ida Cox (Riv.); Hawkins (Pab.; Verve); Joe Turner; Tatum; Peterson (Pab.); B. Holiday (Col.; Verve); Mingus; Dolphy (Cand.).

ELF, MARK STEPHEN, gtr; b. Queens, NY, 12/13/49. Studied w. Ralph Patt, Chuck Wayne 1967; Barry Galbraith '68–71; at Berklee Coll. of Mus. '69–71; classical gtr. w. William Matthews '72–3. Pl. w. Billy Mitchell '69–71; Gloria Coleman '72–3; Ruth Brisbane '73. Pl. educ. concerts w. Billy Mitchell, Ruth Brown '74–5. Led own gps. in NYC and Eur. fr. '74. Pl. at Apollo Theater w. Freddie Hubbard, Joe Williams, Nat and Cannonball Adderley, Les McCann '75. Gigs w. Junior Cook, Lou Donaldson, Percy Brice–Vicky Barnes '76. Feat. soloist w. Mel Lewis, Jim McNeely, and Gtr. Wkshp. at Kool JF '81. Jazz cruises w. Joe Newman, Benny Powell, Billy Mitchell, Groove Holmes '86-7. Pl. w. Dizzy Gillespie '88; Clark Terry '89; Chile w. Arnie Lawrence '90; St. Lucia w. Marion Cowings–Kim Kalesti '92; Clark Terry, Al Grey, Milt Hinton at tribute to Jane Jarvis '93. Elf has taught at SUNY–Stony Brook '81; Five Towns Coll. fr. '91. He has also pl. w. B'way shows incl. *The Wiz* '76; *Bubblin' Brown Sugar* '78. Favs: Tal Farlow, Joe Pass, Wes Montgomery. TV: Germ. TV w. Gillespie '88; own show on local NYC cable, mid '90s. CDs: Jen Bay; Alerce; HalfNote; w. Ray Drummond (HalfNote); C. Earland (Prest.); Heiner Stadler (JA).

ELIAS, ELIANE, pno, comp; b. São Paulo, Brazil, 3/19/60. Studied w. moth., who was a classical pnst. and had a large collection of Amer. jazz rec. A prodigy, Elias had transcribed solos by Art Tatum, Bud Powell, Erroll Garner, and others by the time she was 12. After pl. straight-ahead jazz in São Paulo restaurants, she vacationed in Paris, where she met Eddie Gomez, who heard her tape and suggested she move to NYC. First US gig w. Steps Ahead, then form. own trio and began rec. for BN. Married tpt. Randy Brecker '83; separated in early '90s. In '91, she rec. a Brazilian-oriented album using synths. and wordless vocals, revealing a gift for combining Brazilian mus. and jazz. Fests: Umbria '84. CDs: Den.; BN, incl. *Solos & Duets* w. guest H. Hancock.

ELIZALDE, FRED (FEDERICO), pno, comp, lead; b. Manila, Philippines, 12/12/07; d. Manila, 1/16/79. Studied at Cambridge U., Engl., where he form. a band, the Quinquaginta Ramblers, w. bro. Manuel 1926. Opened at Savoy Hotel, London '28 w. gp. of Amer. and Brit. mus., incl. Adrian Rollini; Chelsea Quealey; Harry Gold. Band broke up in '29. Stud. classical mus. in Spain, and under Maurice Ravel in France '30–2. Ret. to UK for series of jazz recs. '32. Operated radio station in Manila fr. '32, occas. ret. to UK for classical concerts. Comps. incl. suite *The Heart of a Nigger,* premiered June '27 by Bert Ambrose Orch. at London Palladium; also many pieces for solo pno. which he rec. for Dec. and Bruns. in '20s and '30s. CD: Fred Elizalde and His Cambridge Undergraduates are incl. in *Hot British Dance Bands* (Timel.).

ELLINGTON, DUKE (EDWARD KENNEDY ELLINGTON), comp, pno, lead; b. Washington, DC, 4/29/1899; d. NYC, 5/24/74. Father of Mercer Ellington; grandfath. of gtrst. Edward Ellington and dancer Mercedes Ellington. His fath., a butler, wanted his son to be an artist. Ellington studied pno. fr. age 7; first comp. was "Soda Fountain Rag." He stud. art at Armstrong HS, winning a poster contest sponsored by NAACP, and music at sch. and w. Henry Grant. Strongly infl. by local ragtime pnsts., he turned down a scholarship to Bklyn.'s Pratt Institute,

remaining in D.C., where he pl. gigs and painted signs. By June 1918, when he married Edna Thompson, he was doing very well supplying bands for parties and dances. In '23, he came to NYC w. Sonny Greer and Otto Hardwicke to join Wilbur Sweatman's band, but soon had to ret. to D.C. Later that yr., Elmer Snowden sent for him to join his band, the Washingtonians, in NYC. Other members were Otto Hardwicke, bs. and saxes; Arthur Whetsol, tpt.; Greer, dms; Snowden pl. banjo and saxes. Ellington soon assumed leadership and added Bubber Miley; Tricky Sam Nanton; Harry Carney; Rudy Jackson; Wellman Braud. When Snowden left, he was replaced by Fred Guy. Such early recs. as "East St. Louis Toodle-oo" and "Black and Tan Fantasy" reveal the emerging sound of Ellington's ensemble writing and unique soloists. He wrote his first revue score, *Chocolate Kiddies,* in '24; although the show never made it to B'way, it ran for two yrs. in Germ. After four yrs. at the Kentucky Club, w. summer gigs in New Engl. and short stints at other clubs, the Ellington Orch. moved to the Cotton Club on 12/4/27, remaining there until '32; also app. in film *Check and Double Check* w. Amos and Andy in '30. At the Cotton Club, the band was join. by Barney Bigard; Johnny Hodges; Freddie Jenkins; and Cootie Williams, who replaced Miley. Ellington's first pop hit music was "Mood Indigo," originally rec. in '30 as "Dreamy Blues." Characteristic of the Cotton Club band were the plunger mute styles of Miley (later Williams) and tbnst. Joe "Tricky Sam" Nanton, sometimes emulated vocally by Baby Cox—it became known as "jungle" music. Ellington rec. "Creole Love Call," the first wordless jazz vocal, w. Adelaide Hall in '27; and began writing extended comps. w. *Creole Rhapsody* '31, followed by *Reminiscing in Tempo* '35, and *Diminuendo in Blue/Crescendo in Blue* '37. He was the first jazz comp. to circumvent the limitations of the three-minute, 78 RPM disc by rec. his longer comps. on two or four sides. He was also the first to use a miniature concerto form to build a comp. around a jazz soloist; early examples are "Clarinet Lament" for Bigard, "Echoes of Harlem" for Williams, both '35. In '38 Rex Stewart was featured in "Boy Meets Horn."

In '33, Ellington made a highly successful tour of Eur. w. an enlarged band that incl. two new tbns., v-tbn Juan Tizol and soloist Lawrence Brown, for a total of six brass and four reeds. Returning to the US, he had popular hits w. "Solitude" and "Sophisticated Lady" '33; "In a Sentimental Mood" '35. Musicians welcomed his approach, in which the orchestration was as important as the melody: "Daybreak Express"; "Rude Interlude"; "Stompy Jones"; "Harlem

Speaks," etc. Bef. tour. Eur. again in '39, he made three key additions to the band: Ben Webster, tnr.; Jimmy Blanton, bs.; and Billy Strayhorn, arr., comp., second pnst. Among the outstanding recs. made '39–42, when a AF of M rec. ban went into effect, are "Concerto for Cootie"; "Ko-Ko"; "Jack the Bear"; "Cottontail"; "Warm Valley"; "Harlem Air Shaft"; and Strayhorn's comps.: "Chelsea Bridge"; "Johnny Come Lately"; and "Take the A Train," which became the band's theme. Dur. this period, the band also app. in the '41 revue *Jump For Joy*, in Hollywood, Calif., pl. an Ellington score that incl. Ivie Anderson singing "I Got It Bad and That Ain't Good." In '46 he wrote the score for the B'way musical *Beggar's Holiday*. While Europeans recognized Ellington as a comp. and artist of concert stature, the orch. had been confined to pl. in nightclubs, theaters, and dance halls in the US; that began to change in January '43, when the orch initiated a series of annual concerts at NYC's Carnegie Hall w. the premiere of *Black, Brown and Beige*. Subsequent works written especially for the concert hall incl. *Deep South Suite*; *Blutopia*; *Blue Belles of Harlem*; *Liberian Suite*; *New World A-Comin'*; and *The Tattooed Bride*. *Harlem (A Tone Parallel to Harlem)* was premiered at the Metropolitan Opera House in '51. Four yrs. later, at Carnegie Hall, the orch. was combined w. the Symphony of the Air for the premiere of *Night Creature*.

Although the band's personnel had remained remarkably consistent throughout the '30s, it changed frequently in the '40s. In '40, Cootie Williams left to join Benny Goodman and was replaced by Ray Nance. Bigard left in '42, Tizol in '44; Nanton died in '46. The orch. was enlarged again, and by '46 had 18 members. Added in the '40s were Taft Jordan; Harold "Shorty" Baker; Jimmy Hamilton; Oscar Pettiford; and vocs. Kay Davis; Herb Jeffries; and Al Hibbler. In '48, Ellington tour. Engl. and France w. Nance and Kay Davis, pl. w. local musicians. In '50 the entire band again tour. Eur.; sidemen incl. Ernie Royal; Al Killian; Paul Gonsalves; and Quentin Jackson. After twenty-three yrs. as lead alto, Johnny Hodges left the band in '51, taking Sonny Greer and Lawrence Brown w. him. They were replaced by three members of the Harry James Orch.: Willie Smith, Louie Bellson, and Tizol. Bellson's drive briefly rejuvenated the band, but by '53 he and Smith had left and morale was low. Hodges rejoined the band in '55, and in '56 the band made its now-legendary app. at the NJF, highlighted by Gonsalves' electrifying 27-chorus solo on *Diminuendo and Crescendo in Blue*. This led to a new contract w. Col. and a '57 CBS-TV special, *A Drum Is a Woman*. An Ellington-Strayhorn suite, *Such Sweet Thunder*, was premiered at Town Hall that same yr. In '58, the band rec. w. Ella Fitzgerald

and app. w. her at Carnegie Hall. There were Eur. tours in '58–9 and frequent apps. at US fests fr. '56. Ellington wrote and rec. the score to the film *Anatomy of a Murder* in '59, winning three Grammys. *Suite Thursday*, inspired by works of John Steinbeck, premiered at the MJF '60. He scored the pilot and comp. theme for the TV series *Asphalt Jungle* and the score for film *Paris Blues* '61. Annual Eur. tours '62–6. In '61 the Ellington and Basie bands combined for a Col. album, *First Time*. The following yr., he made a qt. rec. w. John Coltrane; a gp. rec. w. Coleman Hawkins; and a trio sess. w. Charles Mingus and Max Roach. In '63, he comp. the mus. for the Stratford Shakespeare Festival production of *Timon of Athens*, and helped organize a "second Ellington Orch.," supervised by Strayhorn, which pl. for the stage production *My People* in Chi., commissioned by the Century of Progress Exposition. A '63 St. Dept. tour of the Near and Middle East was cut short by the assassination of President Kennedy but inspired the extended work *Impressions of the Far East,* better known as *The Far East Suite*. Trips to Japan in '64 and the Virgin Islands '65 inspired *Ad Lib On Nippon* (incorporated in the rec. of *The Far East Suite*) and *The Virgin Islands Suite*. His *The Golden Broom and the Green Apple* was commissioned by the NY Philharm. '65. The following yr., he perf. at the World Festival of Negro Arts, Dakar, Senegal; then toured Japan; and wrote the score for the film *Assault on a Queen*. Major soloists in Ellington's band dur. the '60s incl. Nance; Cat Anderson; Cootie Williams (who rejoined in '62); Buster Cooper; Lawrence Brown (rejoined in '60); Hodges; Gonsalves; and Jimmy Hamilton. Harold Ashby came aboard as a a regular in '68; Norris Turney in '69. He led his orch. and a large choir in a concert of original sacred mus. at Grace Episcopal Cathedral, SF, Sept. '65. Other Sacred Concerts followed at Coventry Cathedral in Engl. '66, and the Cathedral of St. John the Divine in NYC '68. When Strayhorn died in '67, the band memorialized him w. an album of his comps. entitled *And His Mother Called Him Bill*.

On Ellington's 70th birthday, in '69, he was honored w. a banquet, dance, and all-star jam session at the White House and presented w. the Presidential Medal of Freedom by Pres. Nixon. On New Yr.'s Day '70, the band embarked on a tour of Southeast Asia, Japan, and Austral. That yr., he also premiered the *Togo Brava Suite* at the NJF and toured the Soviet Union. Following a '72 tour of the Far East, he taped a TV special, *Duke Ellington—We Love You Madly,* in LA w. Quincy Jones and former sidemen, and a TV special in Paris. He perf. his Third Sacred Concert at Westminster Abbey, Oct. '73. Illness prevented him from traveling w. the band in Jan. '74, but he joined the band intermittently in Feb. and Mar., dur. which time a docu. film, *On the Road with Duke Ellington*, was made. He was hospitalized in NYC for the last two mos. of his life. A memorial service was held at the Cathedral of St. John the Divine on May 27. The next day, under the leadership of Mercer Ellington, the band flew to Bermuda to honor a commitment Duke had made while on his deathbed. Mercer continued to lead the Duke Ellington Orch. until his death in '96 when tptr. Barrie Lee Hall assumed the leadership. In 1998 Mercer's son, Paul Mercer Ellington, took up reins as the orch. began a weekly series at Birdland, NYC.

The first Ellington biography, *Duke Ellington* by Barry Ulanov, was published by Creative Age in 1946 and later taken over by Farrar, Straus and Young. He has since been the subject of many books, including *The World of Duke Ellington*, Stanley Dance (Da Capo) '70; *Jazz Masters of the Thirties*, Rex Stewart (Da Capo) '72; *Celebrating the Duke*, Ralph J. Gleason (Da Capo) '75; *Duke*, Derek Jewell (W.W. Norton) '77; *Duke Ellington in Person*, Mercer Ellington and Stanley Dance '78; *Duke Ellington*, James L. Collier (Oxford) '87; *Ellington: The Early Years*, Mark Tucker (U. of Illinois) '91; *The Duke Ellington Reader*, Mark Tucker (Oxford) '93; *Duke Ellington: Beyond Category*, John Edward Hasse (Simon & Schuster) '93. An autobiographical memoir, *Music Is My Mistress*, published in 1973 by Doubleday, contains a virtually complete list of Ellington's compositions. An Ellington commemorative stamp was issued by the U.S. Postal Service on 4/29/86. Favs: Willie "The Lion" Smith, Fats Waller, Luckey Roberts, James P. Johnson. Polls: *Met.* band '45; *Esq.* Gold Awd. arr. and band '45–7; *DB* Readers band '42, '44, '46, '48; *DB* Readers fav. soloist '48; *DB* Readers comp. '57–8; *DB* Critics '53, '58–9; *DB* Hall of Fame '56; NAACP Spingarn Medal for achievement '59; elected to National Institute of Art and Letters '70; inducted into Royal Swedish Academy of Music '71; many more honors. Fests: all major fr. '56. Additional films: *Black and Tan* '29; w. Mae West, *Belle of the Nineties* '34; *Hit Parade of 1937*; *Cabin in the Sky* '43; puppetoon, *Date With Duke* '47; *Duke Ellington at the White House* '69. Additional TV: *The Duke*, special on Can. CBS '64; *Duke Ellington Swings Through Japan*, CBS '64; NET '66; PBS, Some of this film and TV material is available on video. CDs: RCA; Col.; BB; Dec.; BN; Imp.; Pab.; Prest.; Atl.; Saja; Roul.; MM; Fant.; BN; w. Sinatra (Rep.); Fitzgerald (Pab.; Verve); Coltrane (Imp.); *Money Jungle* w. Mingus, Roach (BN).

ELLINGTON, MERCER KENNEDY, comp, tpt; b. Washington DC, 3/11/19; d. Copenhagen, Den-

mark, 2/8/96. Son of Duke Ellington; fath. of Paul Mercer Ellington. Stud. alto sax., tpt., mainly in NYC at Columbia U., Juilliard. Formed his first band in 1939; members briefly incl. Dizzy Gillespie; Clark Terry; Calvin Jackson; and arrs. by Billy Strayhorn, prior to his join. Duke. Army '43–5, mainly in band under Sy Oliver. Again led own band, off and on, and for a few mos. in '50; pl. E-flat horn in Duke Ellington Orch. After running Mercer Recs. label '50–52, w. L. Feather, he left mus., worked as a salesman, tour. w. Cootie Williams as road mgr. and tpt. '54. For several yrs. he was a successful DJ in NYC, but gave it up in '65 to join his fath. as tpt. and mgr. On Duke's death in May '74, he took over leadership of the band, gave up tpt., and did very little comp., but was successful in retaining most of the original spirit of the orch. In later yrs., he lived mainly in Copenhagen, but cont. to spend enough time in the US, and on occ. tours of Eur. and Japan, to keep the band organized. Mus. dir. and cond. for *Sophisticated Ladies*, revue based on his fath.'s music '81–3. Cond. *Queenie Pie*, Ellington's only opera, in Phila., and at Kennedy Center in Wash., D.C. Though Mercer was a talented comp., his work always remained in the shadows of his father and Billy Strayhorn. His comps. incl. "Pigeons and Peppers"; "Things Ain't What They Used To Be"; "Blue Serge"; "Moon Mist"; "The Girl In My Dreams"; "John Hardy's Wife"; and "Jumpin' Punkins." In his later yrs., he took some of his father's unfinished work, completed it and rec. it, most notably *The Three Black Kings*. He also co-comp. (w. his father) "Music Is My Mistress," named for Duke's autobiography. Book: *Duke Ellington in Person* w. Stanley Dance '78. Recs. w. own band: "Ditty a La Dizzy," Aladdin '46; "Metronome All Out," Musicraft '46; "You Name It," Sunrise '47. LPs: Coral; Fant. CDs: GRP; MM; w. D. Ellington (RCA; Fant.; Pab.; Prest.).

ELLINGTON, RAY, dms, lead; b. London, England, 1915; d. London, 2/28/85. Son, Lance, is tbn. First prof. job w. Harry Roy 1937–42. Sang w. Tito Burns's BBC Accordion Club Sxt. '47, then form. own gp. w. Lauderic Caton, Dick Katz, Coleridge Goode. Gigs at Downbeat Club, London '48. Rec. w. Ray Nance for Parlophone Super Rhythm Style series, using pseudonym Reggie Pitts. Came to prominence through weekly BBC radio apps. on *The Goon Show* '51–60. He cont. to lead a qt. in London clubs fr. the '60s until the time of his death. Rec. for Pye label.

ELLIOTT, DON (Don Elliott Helfman), vib, mello, tpt, bongos, voc; b. Somerville, NJ, 10/21/26; d. Weston, CT, 7/5/84. Studied pno. at age 6; acdn. at 8.

Pl. bari. horn and mello. in hs band; tpt. in local dance bands. Assoc. w. pnst. Bill Evans in teenage yrs. Stud. harm. at Juilliard 1944–5. Pl. tpt. in army band; also gunner on B-29; discharged late '46. Stud. arr. and took up vib. at U. of Miami '47. Worked w. Jan Raye trio '48; then, as voc., w. Hi, Lo, Jack & the Dame '48–9; tpt., vib. on staff of radio station WMCA, NYC, bef. join. George Shearing '50–1; Teddy Wilson at Embers; briefly w. Benny Goodman '52; mello. and vib. w. Terry Gibbs '52–3; Buddy Rich '53. Led own qt. '54–60, also freelanced in NYC. Hit rec., "Uh-Oh," w. Sascha Burland as The Nutty Squirrels. He also showed his humorous side in a routine where he parodied various prominent vibists. In the '60s, he functioned successfully as comp. and prod. for national radio and TV commercials, game shows, and specials. Also operated two 16–track rec. studios, where he did multi-voice overdubs for the Don Elliott "Voices," used by Quincy Jones for the soundtracks of films: *The Pawnbroker*; *$*; *Heat of the Night*; *Hot Rock*; *The Getaway*. Comp., arr., and prod. soundtrack for film, *The Happy Hooker*; backed Roberta Flack's rec. of "Smiling" w. twenty reproductions of his own voice. B'way: wrote mus. and led qt. on-stage for *Thurber Carnival* '60; scores for *Tobacco Road*; *The Opposite Sex*. Resumed pl. career w. NY Jazz Ens. at Carnegie Hall and w. Gerry Mulligan at Westport Country Playhouse '74; guest soloist w. NYJRC's tribute to Q. Jones; own gp. at coll. concerts; Stryker's Pub, NYC '75. Polls: *DB* on misc. inst. '53–7. Fests: NJF in '50s; Nice in '80s. CDs: w. Paul Desmond (Fant.); Shearing (Verve); M. Davis (FS); Eckstine (Em.).

ELLIS, DON (DONALD JOHNSON), tpt, comp, lead; b. Los Angeles, CA, 7/25/34; d. Los Angeles, 12/17/78. Mother was a church org. Led own dance bands in jr. hs. Stud. tpt., B. Mus. in comp. at Bost. U. 1956. Worked w. Ray McKinley '56; army jazz bands in Germ. '57–8; Charlie Barnet '58; Maynard Ferguson '59; George Russell sxt. '61–2. Fr. '61 in NYC, he also led own trio at Village Vanguard; qt. at Wells' '62. Form. Improv. Wkshp. Orch. for apps., incl. TV. Involved in "third stream" and jazz "happenings." Tour. Poland '62, Scand. '63. Soloist w. NY Philharm. in Larry Austin's *Improvisations* '63; perf. in Gunther Schuller's *Journey Into Jazz* '64. To LA where he began grad. stud. at UCLA and form Hindustani Jazz Sxt. w. Hari Har Rao and a new 23-pc. band '64. Asst. to comp. Lukas Foss at SUNY-Buffalo under Rockefeller grant '64–5. Ret. to LA where he re-form. own orchs. '65. His innovative orch. used Latin perc.; saxes tripling cl. and fl.; made wide use of odd time signatures; also el. string qt.; voc. qt. as instrumental section; Echoplex for rec. of extended solos; quarter tones for solos and for passages by entire tpt. section.; fusion of jazz and Indian mus.; Fender-Rhodes pno., clavinet, ring modulator, and phaser. Gave priv. lessons in theory, comp., tpt. on both coasts; taught arr. at UCLA; *Introduction to Jazz*, San Fernando Valley St. Coll. Ellis was enjoying a reputation as a restless experimenter without allegiance to any one wing of the avant-garde, when he was struck by a serious heart attack in '75. Following his recuperation, dur. which time he undertook writing projects for various studios, he resumed pl. activity by yr.'s end on the "superbone," a valve-slide tbn. orig. made for Maynard Ferguson. Favs: Dizzy Gillespie, Fats Navarro, Clark Terry. Polls: *DB*, new star tpt. '62. In the '60s and early '70s, the band tour. regularly on the West Coast and app. at such fests as NJF '61; First Int'l JF, Wash., D.C. '62; MJF '66, '77; NJF, Antibes, '69; Jazz Yatra, Bombay '78. His leading an all-star orch. at Berlin JF '68 became the focus of a TV special, *Birth of a Band*. Other TV apps.: Conc., Calif., spec. '69; Soupy Sales spec.; more in Hollywood, Hamburg, Paris, Montreal, Antibes. Film: his score for *The French Connection* was awarded Grammy '71. Publ: *New Rhythm Book* '72; *Quarter Tones* '75. Wrote several articles for *DB* '65–9. Comps: "Tragedy"; "Indian Lady"; "Turkish Bath"; "Variations for Trumpet." Commissions: *Synthesis* for Stan Kenton's Neophonic Orch.; *Contrasts for Two Orchestras and Trumpet* for Zubin Mehta and LA Philharm.; *Reach*, a cantata for chorus and orch., for Berlin JF. CDs: Col.; GNP Cres.; Cand.; NJ; w. Dolphy (Enja); Eddie Harris (Rh.); George Russell (Riv.).

ELLIS, HERB (MITCHELL HERBERT), gtr; b. Farmersville, TX, 8/4/21. Played hca., bjo., then gtr. Stud. at No. Tex. St. Coll. 1941–3. Join. Glen Gray's Casa Loma Orch. '44. Tour. w. Jimmy Dorsey '45–8, then spent five yrs. as member of Soft Winds, instrumental-vocal trio w. John Frigo, bs.; Lou Carter, pno. Replaced Barney Kessel in Oscar Peterson's trio '53, tour. w. JATP, visiting Eur. often. Left Peterson in Nov. '58; accomp. Ella Fitzgerald '58–62. Also backed Julie London. Member of house band on Steve Allen TV show '61–4; Regis Philbin '64–5. Based in LA in '60s and '70s, he was mainly active in studio work, pl. for the Joey Bishop, Della Reese, and Merv Griffin shows, but fr. '72 he pl. many concerts, clubs, seminars in gtr. duo w. Joe Pass. Later tour. w. the Great Guitars, which incl. Charlie Byrd and Kessel. Fr. '90, he and Ray Brown were occasionally reunited w. Peterson, incl. Japanese, Eur. tours. Living in Fairfield Bay, Ark., in the '90s, but remained active in the forefront of the jazz scene, as an outstanding soloist in the Charlie Christian tradition, playing clean, fluent lines, especially effective in the blues idiom. Comp: "Detour Ahead." Fests: all major int.; Conc. Mus.; Colo. JP. CDs: Verve; Conc.; Just.; *The Soft Winds, Then and Now* (Chiaro.); w. J. Dorsey (Hep); Three Guitars; Monty Alexander; Al Cohn; Jake Hanna; Gene Harris (Conc.); Terry Gibbs (Cont.); Sonny Stitt; Ben Webster; Lester Young; I. Jacquet; Tatum; Roy Eldridge; Benny Carter; Louis Armstrong; S. Getz; Gillespie; J.J. Johnson; B. Holiday (Verve); C. Hawkins (Verve; Pab.); Pass (Pab.); O. Peterson (Verve; MPS; Pab.; Tel.).

ELMAN, ZIGGY (Harry Finkelman), tpt, tbn, cl, saxes, lead; b. Philadelphia, PA, 5/26/14; d. Los Angeles, CA, 6/26/68. Raised in Atlantic City, N.J., fr. age 4, he pl. w. Alex Bartha at the Steel Pier, mainly on tbn., 1930-6. Join. Benny Goodman on tpt. '36, and was a key section man and soloist into '40, feat. on such numbers as "Bei Mir Bist du Schoen" and "And the Angels Sing," where his use of the Yiddish "freilich" style gave his solos a distinctive excitement. His strong, hot and brassy style is best exemplified on "Gin for Christmas," rec. w. Lionel Hampton '39. Worked w. Joe Venuti '40; Tommy Dorsey '40-7, w. time out for army service '43-6. Moved to LA, where he led own bands '47-9, app. at the Palladium and rec. for MGM; also back w. T. Dorsey '47-8. Film, radio, TV, rec. work from '49 w. Dinah Shore; Bing Crosby; Paul Weston orch. In '55, he was seen in *The Benny Goodman Story*, but, due to ill health, his soundtrack was dubbed by Manny Klein. Continued poor health forced semiretirement in '56, and he worked only on a limited basis until his death. Fav: Harry James. Polls: *DB* '40-1, '43-5, '47; *Met.* '41-3. Comps: "And the Angels Sing"; "Zaggin' With Zig." CDs: Cir.; w. Goodman (BB; Col.; Hep); Hampton; Met. All-Stars (BB); T. Dorsey (BB; Hep); Sarah Vaughan (Col.).

ELMER, STEVE, pno, dms; b. Brooklyn, NY, 10/6/41. Cousin Bobbi Lynn Elmer pl. bs. w. Latin bands in 1950s-60s. Began on dms. in Bklyn. public sch. '54. First gig w. qt. in Catskills at age 13, then pl. w. tpt. Shelly Gordon at 16. Freelanced as dmr. in NYC fr. '55, then stud. perc. w. Moe Goldenberg at Manh. Sch. of Mus. '59-60. Dms. w. Pepe Morreale '61-3; Bobby Hackett '62-4; All-Amer. Brass Band on tour of Africa '64. Stud. pno. w. Lennie Tristano '65-71. Received B.S. in mus. educ. fr. Hofstra U. '67; M.A. in comp. fr. Queens Coll. '71. Later stud. classical pno. w. Arminda Canteros '85-7; Jon Verbalis '89-91. House pno. at Jazzmania Society '76-7. Pl. pno. in duo w. Ralph Hamperian fr. '87; w. Jazz Mentality fr. '90. President of Bklyn. Heights Orch. '90-3. Elmer taught mus. in NJ and NYC public schs.

'67-9. He was dir. of jazz studies at Queens Coll. '72-6, and has also taught jazz history and perf. at Hunter Coll. and York Coll. He contributed chapters on jazz and rock to the textbook *Music: An Appreciation* (McGraw-Hill). Favs: Bill Evans, Bud Powell, Teddy Wilson; dms: Zutty Singleton, Gene Krupa, Max Roach. CDs: w. Jazz Mentality (VAI).

ENEVOLDSEN, BOB (ROBERT MARTIN), v-tbn, tbn, bs, bari horn, tnr sax, etc.; b. Billings, MT, 9/11/20; d. Los Angeles, 11/19/05. Grew up in musical family; grad. U. of Montana 1942; grad. degree in mus. theory, U. of Utah. First prof. job w. fath. in a pit band. for mus. show '33. Army '42-6. In LA in '50s; very active in jazz, rec. and/or pl. w. Shelly Manne; Shorty Rogers; Marty Paich; Leonard Feather; Bill Holman; Bob Florence; Terry Gibbs; Gerry Mulligan; Dave Pell; arr./orchestrator for Bobby Troup, Steve Allen. In '60s, pl. for many TV shows, incl. Ray Anthony; Steve Allen; Woody Woodbury; Peter Marshall; and w. LA Neophonic Orch. With Bob Crosby, Jack Lesberg '70s; Tex Beneke, Bill Holman, Mel Tormé, Lighthouse All-Stars '80s. A versatile, talented multi-instrument perf., he was best-known for his v-tbn. work. Still freelanced actively in LA in '90s. CDs: VSOP; w. Holman (JVC); G. Mulligan (Cap.); M. Tormé (Conc.; Stash); T. Gibbs; S. Manne; L. Niehaus; Art Pepper; Lighthouse All-Stars (Cont.); Rogers (BB); Paich (GNP Cres.; Cand.); Tommy Newsome (Laser.).

ENGELS, JOHN, dms; b. Groningen, Netherlands, 5/13/35. Many dmrs. in family; fath. pl. w. Coleman Hawkins, Nat Gonella; bro. is prof. bs. Self-taught. Pl. w. Pia Beck, Mary Lou Williams 1953; Kid Dynamite-Sammy Walker '54-5. In Dutch army '55-7, pl. w. Piet Noordijk, Rob Madne. Pl. w. Cees Slinger Trio backing Getz, Byas, Phil Woods, Zoot Sims, Frank Rosolino, Benny Bailey, Julius Watkins '57-61. Co-founded Diamond Five at Club Scheherazade, Amsterdam '59. Pl. w. Boy Edgar bb, Theo Loevendie Trio, Louis van Dijk Trio '61-75, which backed Woody Shaw and D. Gillespie. Received gov. grant to study w. Mel Lewis in NYC '83. Tour w. Chet Baker '86-7; Monty Alexander, Charlie Rouse, Jimmy Knepper, Mingus Dynasty '89. Pl. w. many Dutch mus. and backed singers incl. Betty Carter; Helen Merrill; Abbey Lincoln; Rita Reys; Nina Simone; Jon Hendricks. Taught at the Rotterdam, Amsterdam, Zwolle, and Utrecht Cons. fr. '86. As house dmr. at the North Sea JF fr. '75, pl. w. Hank Jones; Benny Carter; Lew Tabackin; Al Cohn; Lee Konitz; Freddie Hubbard; Tommy Flanagan. Favs: Mel Lewis, M. Roach, Elvin Jones, Shelly Manne, Jeff Hamilton, Billy Higgins. Polls: Ferdinand Povel Awd. '80; Bird Awd. '85; Boy Edgar Prize '88; *Drum Mag.* (Holland) '89–91. Fests: No. Amer.; Indonesia; Dubai. TV: Eur. TV. CDs: w. Chet Baker (Timel.; PW); A. Cobb; T. Edwards (Timel.); Klaus Ignatzek (yvp).

ENGLISH, BILL, dms; b. NYC, 8/27/25. Played and rec. w. r&b musicians incl. Sonny Thompson, Chi. 1951–2; Amos Milburn, LA '54. Pl. in NYC w. Erskine Hawkins, Bennie Green '56. Led own qt. and pl. in house band at Apollo Theater, late '50s. Pl. and rec. w. Earl Hines '60. Rec. w. Prestige Blues Swingers, Joe Newman, Quincy Jones, Gene Ammons '61; Stanley Turrentine '63; Kenny Burrell '63–4; Eddie Jefferson '68–9; Eric Dixon '74. CDs: w. Burrell (BN); Green; Jefferson; Newman; C. Hawkins (Prest.).

ENRIQUEZ, BOBBY "WILDMAN" (ROBERTO T.), pno, vib, perc, arr; b. Bacolod City, Philippines, 5/20/43; d. Stayton, OR, 8/6/96. Self-taught, did not read mus. Began on pno. Sang and pl. w. Coca-Cola Tops, sponsored by Coca-Cola 1956–8. Moved to Manila '60, pl. w. Vestre Roxas-Tony Scott '60. App. w. Bayside 10-pc. Latin band w. Tito Puente in Hong Kong '61. Moved to Taiwan, pl. w. house band at Tainan Officers' Mess, US Air Force base '61–3. Led own trio w. Lonnie Baylon, Feliz Velasquez at Ft. Buckner Officers' Club in Okinawa '64–7. Arr. and cond. for Filipino revue, *Moses and the Hi-Brows,* perf. at LV hotels '67. Music dir. for Don Ho in Hawaii '68–70. Moved to LV; perf. w. Danny Moore, the Jades, the Adorables '71–2. Tour. US and Can. w. Bet E. Martin Show '72. Moved to SF, led own trio at Miyako Hotel '73. Ret. to Hawaii, led. qt. and pl. solo pno. at Moana Hotel, Waikiki '75–80. Tour. US and Eur. w. Richie Cole's Alto Madness '81; Dizzy Gillespie '82–3. Command perf. for Ferdinand and Imelda Marcos at Malacanang Palace '82; also led trio w. Rufus Reid, Billy Higgins at Pitt Inn, Tokyo, and perf. w. Bingo Miki and Tokyo Symph. Moved to NYC '84. Detained in Philippines for political reasons '84–5. Ret. to NYC, led own trio fr. '86. Pl. w. Richie Cole at Toronto JF '90. Enriquez, whose fath. was a martial arts instructor, held a black belt in Shorin-ryu (Okinawan style) karate. He was named an Ambassador of Goodwill by Philippine president Corazon Aquino. Highly skilled and able to swing w. abandon, he often crossed the line into pyrotechnical excess but could also harness his flamboyance for tender moments. Favs: Gillespie, J.J. Johnson, Puente. Polls: *SJ* Artist of Yr. '82; Entertainer of Yr., Philippines '90. Fests: all major fr. '81; Vail JP '96. TV: Johnny Carson, Mike Douglas w. Don Ho '68; Joe Franklin '82; Merv Griffin and Eur. TV w. Gilles-

pie '83. LP: w. R. Cole (Muse). CDs: Evid.; GNP Cres.

ERICSON, ROLF, tpt, flg; b. Stockholm, Sweden, 8/29/22; d. Stockholm, 6/16/97. Studied at Katarina Mus. Sch. and w. priv. teachers. Worked w. Swedish bands 1938–47. He may well have pl. w. more famous bbs and gps. than any other jazz mus. Moved to NYC '47. Pl. w. Charlie Barnet '49; Woody Herman '50; Benny Carter, Wardell Gray, Elliot Lawrence '49–50; in Sweden w. Arne Domnerus '50–1, also tour. there w. Charlie Parker. Back to US, pl. w. Charlie Spivak '52–3; Harry James; Jimmy and Tommy Dorsey; TV w. Les Brown. Worked w. Lighthouse All-Stars '53. Tour. w. Cecil Payne, Duke Jordan, Ernestine Anderson, and others in Sweden '56. Ret. to US, he worked w. Dexter Gordon; Harold Land, Stan Kenton; Herman; Maynard Ferguson; Far East tour w. Buddy Rich, all bet. '56 and '60. Tour. in Scand. w. Bud Powell, Lars Gullin, Brew Moore, Kenny Dorham, and in US w. Benny Goodman, Gerry Mulligan '61–5. Pl. w. Charles Mingus '62–3; Rod Levitt '63–5. Member of Duke Ellington orch. '63–4. Led own bb in Sweden, late '60s. Living in Germ. '71–80, worked in radio studios and tour. extens. in Eur., app. at different times w. D. Ellington and Mercer Ellington dur. this period. Later, in the US, he worked w. the WGJB and the bbs of Basie, Bill Berry, Capp-Pierce Juggernaut, Clayton-Hamilton, Louie Bellson. In his seventies, he remained a fluent soloist and all around tptr. who absorbed the infls. of all the masters. He was awarded a lifetime achievement grant from the Swedish government and a golden record by the magazine *Orkester Journalen* '84. CDs: Drag.; w. Land; C. Baker; M. Davis; Lighthouse All-Stars (Cont.); D. Gordon (Steep.); C. Parker (Story.); G. Russell (SN); Ellington (MM; Pab.; Atl.); J. Hodges (Imp.); Strayhorn (Red Brn.).

ERSKINE, PETER CLARK, dms, perc, synth; b. Somers Point, NJ, 5/6/54. From age 6, he att. Stan Kenton's National Stage Band camps for several yrs. Stud. priv. w. Alan Dawson and others. Further studies at Interlochen Arts Acad. and Indiana U. First prof. job w. Kenton 1972–76; then w. Maynard Ferguson. Join. Weather Report '78–82, rec. five albums w. the gp., incl. *8:30.* In '79, he also pl. and rec. w. Steps, aka Steps Ahead, remaining w. that gp. until '86. Later settled in Calif. and rejoin. Joe Zawinul in Weather Update, the follow-up band to Weather Report; also w. John Abercrombie's qt. '87; Bob Mintzer's bb; Warren Bernhardt's trio. Many recs., incl. dates w. Don Grolnick; Eliane Elias; Gary Burton–Pat Metheny; Rickie Lee Jones; Jan Garbarek. A powerful perf., whose rhythm pl. alongside Jaco Pastorius was one of the most attractive aspects of Weather Report's music. Favs: Elvin Jones, Billy Cobham, Mel Lewis, Grady Tate, Jack DeJohnette, Paul Motian. CDs: Den.; Ah Um; ECM; Novus; Cont.; w. Weather Report (Col.); J. Abercrombie; J. Garbarek; G. Peacock; R. Towner; K. Wheeler; Marc Johnson (ECM); Bernhardt; A. LaVerne (DMP); Mintzer (DMP; Novus); Kenton (CW); M. Brecker (Imp.); Burton; E. Daniels; J. Patitucci (GRP); Elias; Grolnick; J. Calderazzo (BN); George Cables; J. Farrell; J. Henderson (Cont.); Mike Mainieri (NYC).

ERVIN, BOOKER TELLEFERRO II, tnr sax; b. Denison, TX, 10/31/30; d. NYC, 8/31/70. Father, a tbnst., worked w. Buddy Tate. Pl. fath.'s horn in hs band 1939–40. Air force '50–3; self-taught on tnr. sax while stationed on Okinawa w. air force; then stud. at Berklee Sch. for two yrs. Worked w. Ernie Fields '54–5. Pl. in Dallas and Denver '56–7. After a short time in Pitts., he moved to NYC, May '58; join. Charles Mingus in Nov. and remain. w. him to '62; also worked w. the Playhouse Four at Minton's Playhouse w. Horace Parlan, Al Harewood, George Tucker. Pl. w. Randy Weston '60, incl. Negro Arts Fest. in Lagos, Nigeria. Tour. Greenland w. USO unit '62. With Weston again for rec. '63, Little Theater concert '64. Freelanced in Eur. '64–6; Scand. clubs, late '64, then Blue Note in Paris, club in Barcelona '65; Berlin, Munich '66; also pl. concerts in Italy, Norway, TV show in Amsterdam. Eur. again in '68, then own gps. in US. Died of kidney disease. With a sound as big as the great outdoors and a tidal, rhythmic drive, he was in the lineage of the Texas tenors. The series of "Book" recs. for Prest. between '63–5 are particularly evocative. Infls: Lester Young, Dexter Gordon, Sonny Stitt. Although he named Coltrane as his favorite, he was less indebted to him than were the majority of his contemporaries. Fests: Randall's Island w. J. Bunch '58, Roland Hanna '59; NJF, Antibes w. Mingus '60. Comps: "Mojo"; "A Lunar Tune"; "A Day to Mourn"; "No Booze Blooze"; "Eerie Dearie"; "Number Two." CDs: Prest.; Cand.; Sav.; w. Mingus (Col.; Atl.; BN; Cand.); E. Dolphy (Prest.); R. Weston (Verve).

ERWIN, "PEE WEE" (GEORGE), tpt; b. Falls City, NE, 5/30/13; d. Teaneck, NJ, 6/20/81. Raised in KC, Mo. Father, who gave him first horn and lessons, was a tptr. w. territory bands. Pl. w. Eddie Kuhn 1927; Joe Haymes '31–3; Isham Jones '33–4; Freddie Martin '34. To NYC where he did radio work w. Benny Goodman '34–5, and worked w. Ray Noble '35. With Goodman '36; Tommy Dorsey off and on '37–9; Raymond Scott '39; own bb '41–2. Active as a studio mus. to '49, app. often at Nick's through '50s. In the

'60s, he was a CBS staff mus.; weekly jazz radio show w. Ed Joyce in mid '60s. Pl. many jazz concerts, incl. two tours of Scand., Germ., UK w. Kings of Jazz '74. "Pee Wee's timeless," said Joe Newman. "What he played doesn't fit into any categories—it's not Dixieland or bop, just a great musician playing what he feels." Recs. w. Dick Hyman; NYJRC; Jackie Gleason in *Music for Lovers* series on Cap. Prod. *Jazz: The Personal Dimension* for Rutgers U. at Carnegie Hall. App. often at Colo., Odessa JPs. KCJF; NYJRC; Jazztage, Hanover, Germ. '74; Nice JF '75. In '60s, he ran a tpt. sch. w. Chris Griffin. Publs: *Pee Wee Erwin Teaches Trumpet* (Charles Colin); *A Wee Bit of Dixie*—duets (Award Music Co.). Own LPs: Qualtro. CDs: w. T. Dorsey; B. Goodman (BB); Sandy Williams in *Giants of Small Band Swing*, Vols. 1&2 (Riv.); Swingville All-Stars (GTJ).

ESCHETE, RON (RONALD PATRICK), gtr; b. Houma, LA, 8/19/48. Father, who pl. gtr. and sang, showed him his first chords. Stud. classical gtr. at Loyola U. Pl. in jazz, country, and r&b bands in home town and in NO. Tour. w. Buddy Greco 1969. Moved to So. Calif. '70. Worked in TV and taught at several colls., incl. Guitar Inst., fr. '76. Pl. and/or rec. w. Dave Pike, Clayton Bros. in '70s; Milt Jackson, Ray Brown, Gene Harris, Herman Riley, Dewey Erney, and own grps. in '80s, incl. tours in Eur. and Japan w. Brown, Tommy Gumina. Also pl. w. Charlie Shoemake; Lionel Hampton; D. Gillespie. Join. Gene Harris qt. '91. Of Eschete's Conc. solo album, Jim Ferguson wrote: "[H]e more than meets the considerable challenge that seven-string guitar poses, demonstrating a singular command of sophisticated chordal concepts supported by infectious grooves—a delicate balance that very few guitarists achieve with such perfection and grace." Fests: MJF Gtr. Ens. '83; Lionel Hampton JF, Idaho, w. Harris in '90s. Books: *Key Correlation; Melodic Chord Phrases; The Jazz Guitar Soloist.* CDs: Conc.; w. Ray Brown; Gene Harris; E. Anderson; J. McDuff (Conc.); Andy Simpkins (Disc.); Warne Marsh (Story.).

ESCOUDÉ, CHRISTIAN, gtr; b. Angouleme, France, 9/23/47. Father and uncle Gousti Malha, gtsts. fr. whom he began learning at age 10. Five yrs. later he was working locally as a prof., often at Amer. bases. Fr. 1968 to '71 he pl. w. Aime Barelli in Monte Carlo. At the end of '71 he went to Paris, pl. in a "bal musette." In '72 he became part of Eddy Louiss's trio. Pl. w. Steve Potts in gp. Recent History '73; own trio '73–4; Confluence w. Didier Levallet '75–6. Form. Swing String System and worked w. it, sporadically, to '87. In mid '70s also form. duo w. cellist

Jean-Charles Capon. Freelanced w. Michel Portal; Slide Hampton; Martial Solal; Jean-Claude Fohrenbach. Duo tour of US, Brazil, Japan w. John McLaughlin. Pl. w. Solal bb '81; led new qt. 82; duo w. Didier Lockwood '83; trio w. Philip Catherine; Trio Gitan w. Babik Reinhardt, Boulou Ferre '87; duo w. Michel Graillier '87; qt. w. Jean-Michel Pilc '88; oct. w. four gtrs., incl. J. Gourley, '89; Village Vanguard w. Hank Jones '90; Gipsy Trio, w. B. Reinhardt, Birele Lagrene added '92; rec. in LA w. Lou Levy, Bob Magnusson, Billy Higgins '93. Fests: Samois, dedicated to Django Reinhardt, often fr. '78; Nice '78, rec. w. J. Lewis; pl. w. Getz, Bill Evans, F. Hubbard, L. Konitz; Dakar w. René Utreger, '79; Patrimonio, Corsica, w. B. Reinhardt, B. Lagrene '93. Award: Django Reinhardt prize '76. CDs: Em., Verve; Charlie Haden–Christian Escoude (Drey.); w. John Lewis (Em.).

ESCUDERO, RALPH (RAFAEL), bs, tba; b. Manati, PR, 7/16/1898; d. Puerto Rico, 4/10/70. Took up bs. w. sch. band at age 12. To NYC, where he pl. w. the New Amsterdam Musical Association 1920–1. He was pl. w. Wilbur Sweatman at the Howard Theater in Wash., D.C., when Fletcher Henderson heard him and hired him '23. Stayed w. Henderson until '26, then join. McKinney's Cotton Pickers until '31. Subsequently worked w. Kaiser Marshall's Bostonians; the Savoy Bearcats; and W.C. Handy. Ret. to Puerto Rico, where he worked through the '60s. CDs: w. Henderson (Col.); McKinney's Cotton Pickers (BB).

ESKELIN, ELLERY LANE, tnr sax; b. Wichita, KS, 8/16/59. Raised in Balt., Md.; both parents mus. First lessons w. moth., who pl. org. w. her own gps. Stud. at Towson State U. and priv. w. George Coleman and Dave Liebman. Moved to NYC 1983; worked w. Jack McDuff; Liebman; others. Since late '80s, he has been a member of Joint Venture, a gp. w. Paul Smoker, Drew Gress, and Phil Haynes. Described by Peter Watrous in the *NY Times* as "an appealing soloist who mixes an understanding of bebop with the freedom of free improvisation." CDs: SN; Cad.; PS; SGL; Eremite; hatology; w. Joint Venture (Enja).

ESSIET, ESSIET OKON, bs; b. Omaha, NE, 9/1/56. Both parents from Nigeria. Two bros., two sist. all pl. instruments. Began on vln. at age 10; sw. to bs. in hs in Portland, Ore. 1970. Pl. w. Don Moye, Abdullah Ibrahim fr. '82; Art Blakey and the Jazz Messengers '88–91; Bobby Watson and Horizon fr. '91; Freddie Hubbard fr. '94. Also freelanced w. Benny Golson, Jackie McLean, Curtis Fuller, Cedar Walton, Louis Hayes '82–8. Made rec. debut w.

Ibrahim '83. Freelanced w. Bobby Hutcherson, Geri Allen, Geo. Adams, Kenny Barron '91–4. Essiet taught bs. at the Hague Cons., Netherlands '85. Favs: Paul Chambers, Ron Carter, Israel Crosby, Ray Brown. Fests: all major fr. '81. CDs: w. A. Ibrahim (Enja); Blakey (A&M; Timel.); Watson (Col.); Dr. John (WH); D. Kikoski (Epic); Ralph Peterson–Geri Allen (BN); V. Ponomarev (Res.); I. Butman (Soyuz).

EUBANKS, KEVIN, gtr; b. Philadelphia, PA, 11/15/57. Nephew of Tommy and Ray Bryant; bro. is tbn. Robin Eubanks. Stud. vln. 1965, tpt. '68, then gtr.; basically self-taught. Local gigs w. funk-rock bands at age 13; stud. at Berklee Sch. '76. Joined Art Blakey '80; to NYC '81. Tour. or rec. w. Roy Haynes; Sam Rivers; Slide Hampton. Rec. several albums for GRP fr. '84, incl. *Sundance*, on which he pl. electric and acoustic instruments in a variety of styles. Began working w. Dave Holland '91, rec. for ECM. Join. Branford Marsalis in *Tonight Show* band '92, assuming leadership in '95. Took own gp. on St. Dept. tour to Pakistan, Jordan. In '80s, he was a clinician at Umbria Jazz in Perugia, Italy, for four summers; also taught at Rutgers U. and Banff Sch. of Fine Arts in Can. One of the most adaptable gtrsts. of his generation. CDs: BN; GRP; w. Blakey (Timel.); Robin Eubanks; Greg Osby; Gary Thomas (JMT); Gary Burton (GRP); James Williams; E. Higgins; M. D'Ambrosio (Sunny.); Steve Coleman (Novus); D. Holland (ECM); K. Lightsey (CC); H. Mabern (DIW); Ralph Moore (Res.); J.-L. Ponty (FNAC).

EUBANKS, ROBIN DERRICK, tbn; b. Philadelphia, PA, 10/25/55. Entire family is musical; Kevin Eubanks is bro.; Ray and Tommy Bryant are uncles; two other bros. also mus. Stud. at Phila. Settlement Mus. Sch. 1964–72; Temple U. '72–5; Phila. Coll. of Perf. Arts '75–8; then w. Slide Hampton '79–80. Pl. prof. in funk gps. fr. childhood. Pl. w. Sun Ra '78; Slide Hampton's World of Tbns. '78–81; Art Blakey '80; Jimmy McGriff '80; Kevin Eubanks '83–4; Dave Holland '86–7; Blakey '87–8; Steve Coleman '87–8; Abdullah Ibrahim '88–9; McCoy Tyner bb; Ronald Shannon Jackson late '80s; Bobby Previte since '90; E.T.Q. w. Steve Turre since '90; also own gp. since '89. Received NEA perf. grant '91. Eubanks is one of the founders of the M-BASE Collective and is interested in applying electronic effects to the tbn. He has lectured at Berklee Coll. of Mus.; New Engl. Cons.; Jackson St. U.; and bef. the Int. Tbn. Assoc. Favs: J.J. Johnson, Slide Hampton, Curtis Fuller, Al Grey. Polls: *DB* TDWR '89–91; *SJ* '91. Fests: Eur., Japan, Austral. since '86. Film: app. in *The Cotton Club*. TV: *Saturday Night Live*; *Motown at the Apollo*; '92 Grammy Awds. CDs: JMT; w. Blakey

(Timel.; SN; PW); D. Holland (ECM); G. Osby (BN); Steve Coleman (JMT; Novus); B. Hardman (Steep.); G. Harris; Marvin Smith (Conc.); Mark Helias; Ibrahim (Enja); R. S. Jackson (Virgin); B. Marsalis; Bobby Watson (Col.); McCoy Tyner (Mile.); Hank Roberts; Cassandra Wilson (JMT).

EUELL, JULIAN THOMAS, bs; b. NYC 5/23/29. Took up bs. in 1944. In army '45–7. Stud. at 3rd St. Settlement House; pl. w. Sonny Rollins, Jackie McLean, Art Taylor '47. Gave up pl. to work in post office '49–52. Began formal studies w. Charles Mingus 1952, then at Juilliard w. Stuart Sankey, Fred Zimmerman '53–6; also w. Hall Overton, John Mehegan dur. this period. Spent yr. in Columbia U. mus. dept. '54–5. Worked w. Elmo Hope '52; Benny Harris '52–3; Charlie Rouse '53–4; Joe Roland '55; Freddie Redd '56; Gigi Gryce qnt. '56–7; Phineas Newborn '57. Stud. at NYU '51–4, att. Columbia U. to receive B.S. in sociology; active in youth work in Newark, N.J., from Jan. '58 to fall '59. At this time he was semi-active in mus., pl. w. Mal Waldron on and off '58–60; Randy Weston '59; Abbey Lincoln '59–60. Also perf. w. Mingus "on many occasions when he used two basses—he doubled on piano." Pl. w. Kenny Dorham gp. From '62 to '66 Dir. of Arts and Cultural Prog. at HARYOU-ACT in Harlem. Hired Dorham, Jackie McLean for concerts in the community. Pl. until '68. Then went back to school. Ph.D. in Amer. studies, George Washington U. '73. Assistant Secretary for Public Service at the Smithsonian Institution '70–82, where—as part of his responsibility for the Division of Performing Arts—he aided the expansion of the Institution's commitment to jazz. Director of Oakland Museum, History-Art-Science '83–88; Director of Louis Armstrong House '91–5. Had start. pl. again '86. In '90s gigging in Wash., Balt. w. Larry Willis; various gps. at Bertha's; concert w. Ellis Larkins. Taught in jazz wkshps. w. Hall Overton; did jazz hist. wkshps. for Portland schs. Film: pl. on soundtrack of *The Cool World*. Favs: Pettiford, Mingus, Paul Chambers, Ron Carter, Rufus Reid. CDs: w. Waldron; Coltrane-Quinichette; Gryce (Prest.).

EUROPE, JIM (JAMES REESE), lead, comp; b. Mobile, AL, 2/22/1881; d. Boston, MA, 5/10/19. Moved to Wash., D.C., bef. the age of 10, studying vln. and pno. there w. asst. dir. of US Marine Band. To NYC 1904, where he first worked as pnst., then as dir. of mus. comedies. Took part in avant concert of syncopated mus. w. singer Ernest Hogan '05. Org. the Clef Club, a mus. assoc. and clearing house for black mus. His band was the first black gp. to rec. '13, and, in '14, he presented a Carnegie Hall concert feat. 125

mus. and singers. Tour. w. Vernon and Irene Castle '14. Worked in NYC clubs. As a lieutenant dur. WWI, he org. the 369th Infantry Regiment Band, an excellent mil. unit that also became known for its jazz concerts in a successful tour of France '18. Ret. to US in '19, and tour. triumphantly bef. being fatally knifed by Herbert Wright, one of his dmrs., in a nightclub confrontation. Europe's music is more accurately characterized as ragtime, but he was on the cutting edge of jazz, and he employed jazz mus. Book: *A Life in Ragtime*, Reid Badger (Oxford) '95. Rec. *Memphis Blues* for Pathé '19. CD: IAJRC; Memphis Archives.

EVANS, BILL (WILLIAM DAVID), tnr, sop saxes, pno; b. Clarendon Hills, IL, 2/9/58. Father pl. pno. w. Ill. Symph. Stud. pno. fr. age 6; sax and cl. fr. age 12. Gave classical pno. concerts at 16. Stud. at No. Tex. St. U.; William Paterson Coll., N.J.; priv. w. Dave Liebman in Chi., then moved to NYC 1978. Join. Miles Davis on Liebman's recommendation '80. Pl. w. Davis '80–4; Elements w. Mark Egan, Danny Gottlieb on and off fr. '82; John McLaughlin–Mahavishnu Orch. '84–6; Michael Franks '87; Herbie Hancock '89; Lee Ritenour '90; Andy Summers '91. Evans has led his own gp. fr. '83, full-time fr. '91. Favs: Sonny Stitt, Joe Henderson, Sonny Rollins. Fests: Eur. since '81. CDs: BN; Col.; Lip.; PW; JC; w. M. Davis (Col.); Elements (Ant.); Dave Grusin (N2K).

EVANS, BILL (WILLIAM JOHN), pno, comp; b. Plainfield, NJ, 8/16/29; d. NYC, 9/15/80. Studied pno., vln., fl. Led gp. w. bro., Harry, and Don Elliott 1945. B.F.A. fr. Southeastern Louisiana Coll. Pl. in trio w. Mundell Lowe, Red Mitchell ca. '49. Worked w. Herbie Fields for six mos. '50; then in army '51–4, pl. fl. in band. Pl. w. Jerry Wald, Tony Scott, Geo. Russell '54–5. Freelanced in NYC and studied at Mannes Coll. of Mus., NYC '55–6. Made LP debut, *New Jazz Conceptions,* w. own trio for Riv. label '56. Rec. w. Chas. Mingus '56, then pl. w. Miles Davis, Feb.-Nov. '58; rec. *Kind of Blue* w. Davis '59. On faculty of Sch. of Jazz, Lenox, Mass., summer '59; feat. in John Lewis score for film *Odds Against Tomorrow* '59. Led trio w. dmr. Paul Motian, bs. Scott LaFaro (later repl. by Chuck Israels) on dates for Riv. '59–61; also rec. in duo w. Jim Hall '59. Won Grammy awd. '63 for album *Conversations With Myself,* on which he pl. two and three pno. tracks by overdubbing. Led trio w. bs. Gary Peacock, Eddie Gomez; dmrs. incl. Marty Morell, Joe Hunt, Philly Joe Jones, Eliot Zigmund, Shelly Manne fr. '60s. In the latter part of the '70s and until his death, his trio incl. Marc Johnson, bs., and Joe LaBarbera, dms. Evans, who had been addicted to heroin, broke his habit in '70, but became involved w. cocaine in '79, which proved fatal. Evans acknowledged Bud Powell, Lennie Tristano, and Horace Silver as infls., but also incorporated essences of Ravel, Debussy, and Scriabin. His style had a lasting effect on subsequent pnsts. Chick Corea; Herbie Hancock; Keith Jarrett; Steve Kuhn; Hampton Hawes; Paul Bley; Michel Petrucciani, and many others. Gene Lees called him "the most influential pianist of his generation, altering the approach to tone and harmony. He rapidly found his own personality and built a style on subtle rhythmic displacement, fresh and sometimes ambiguous chord voicings, thoughtful voice leadings, and an exquisite golden tone that has been much imitated but never reproduced." Polls: numerous *DB* Critics and Readers polls; *Play*. All-Stars' All-Stars. Awards: Grammys in '68, '70, '71. Fests: all major. TV: *Camera Three; Jazz Adventures; Jazz Set* (PBS, '71); many apps. on Eur. TV. Publ.: *Bill Evans*, a volume of transcriptions, Ft. Lauderdale, Fla. '65. A collection of materials relating to his life and work is housed at Southeastern La. U. Comps: "Peri's Scope"; "Very Early"; "34 Skidoo"; "Waltz for Debby"; "Comrade Conrad"; "NYC's No Lark"; "Turn Out the Stars"; "Blue in Green." CDs: boxed sets: *The Complete Fantasy Recordings*; *The Complete Riverside Recordings*; *The Secret Sessions*, Mile.; Verve box; also individual CDs on these labels (incl. *The Tony Bennett/Bill Evans Album*, Fant.) and Col.; his collaboration w. Jim Hall and two-pno. date w. Bob Brookmeyer, respectively, may be found under his name on BN; w. G. Russell (BB; Dec.); M. Davis (Col.); C. Adderley (Riv.); C. Mingus (Beth.); Konitz-Giuffre; S. Getz (Verve;); Tony Scott (FS; Sunny.); A. Farmer (BN).

EVANS, DOC (PAUL WESLEY), crnt; b. Spring Valley, MN, 6/20/07; d. Minneapolis, MN, 1/10/77. Played vln., pno., dms., sax, but was crntst. w. band at Carleton Coll., class of 1929. Gave up sax to concentrate solely on crnt. '31. Led amateur bands in Minneapolis–St. Paul area dur. '30s; also taught sch. for a yr. and raised champion cocker spaniels. Ret. to mus. full-time w. Red Dougherty '39. In mid '40s, he worked in both Chi. and NYC, leading combo incl. Joe Sullivan '40–1; also worked w. Eddie Condon. Ret. to Minneapolis, pl. and rec. w. Bunk Johnson '47. Pl. w. Miff Mole '49. Worked on West Coast, but most of his pl. was done in Minneapolis, where his gp. enjoyed high popularity. Cond. the Mendota Symph. Rec. at the Manassas JF '75. Own recs. on Audio label; and as sideman w. Turk Murphy on Col. CDs: Jazz.

EVANS, GIL (Ian Ernest Gilmore Green), arr, comp, pno, lead; b. Toronto, Ont., Canada, 5/13/12; d. Cuernavaca, Mexico, 3/20/88. Self-taught. His family

lived in various places in the Northwest bef. settling in Berkeley, Calif., when Evans was 8. Here he first attended sch. formally, and a family friend gave him some pno. lessons. The family moved to Stockton, Calif., in 1928. While in hs, he pl. solo pno. at the Stockton Hotel and other local jobs. He formed his first band while in junior coll., and merged w. another young bandleader, bs. Ned Briggs. This 10-pc. band modeled itself on the then-popular Casa Loma Band. Evans, who later cited Louis Armstrong as a profound early infl., also emulated the mus. of Fletcher Henderson, Don Redman, and Duke Ellington in his writing for this band, which became house band at the Rendevous Ballroom, Balboa Beach, Calif., for two yrs. fr. Sept. '35; personnel incl. Jimmy Maxwell, tpt.; Buddy Cole, pno.; Vido Musso, cl.; Stan Kenton sometimes subbed on pno. The band tour. the Pacific Northwest in February-March '37. That fall, voc. Skinnay Ennis took over as leader, retaining Evans as arr. and pnst. The band settled in Hollywood, working there intermittently through '39, and was regularly feat. on Bob Hope's Pepsodent radio show fr. '38. In '39, when Claude Thornhill was hired for the show, he quickly became a major infl. on Evans. Thornhill ret. to NYC in '40 to start his own orch. and hired Evans as an additional arr. in '41. Evans stayed w. him until '48, except for army service from '43 to '46. Some of Thornhill's techniques—incl. voicings for mixed brass and woodwinds, and horns without vibrato—were adapted by Evans, who gave them a finishing touch. His arrs. incl. the use of Fr. horns, fl., tba., and other instruments that were not normally used in jazz dur. those yrs. He culled ideas fr. classical and twentieth-century music, producing orchestral textures that bore his individual stamp.

Evans settled in NYC in '47 and began writing some stunning bebop arrs. for Thornhill, attracting the attention of such musicians as Miles Davis, Gerry Mulligan, John Lewis, and John Carisi, who often congregated at Evans' apartment. Their exchange of ideas resulted in the Miles Davis Nonet—a scaled-down version of the Thornhill band—and a unique series of Cap. recs. (the so-called "Birth of the Cool" sessions) incl. Evans' arrs. of "Boplicity" and "Moondreams," which exemplified his masterful, eloquent interweave of soloist and score, amid subtly shifting textures. Although these recs. caused quite a stir among musicians, Evans' career languished for a few yrs. Through the mid '50s, he freelanced and did some arrs. for singers, incl. Tony Bennett; Johnny Mathis; and Helen Merrill; charts for Billy Butterfield's bb; and *La Plus Que Lente* for Mulligan's sxt. He finally reconnected w. Davis in '57, expanding on the ideas they had begun to flesh out in the late '40s. Their collaborative friendship bore three successive masterpieces between '57–60, *Miles Ahead, Porgy and Bess,* and *Sketches of Spain,* all of which gave Evans belated, widespread critical acclaim. Through the mid '60s, Evans also rec. several albums as a leader: *Big Stuff; New Bottle, Old Wine;* and *Out of the Cool.* Through inventive, evocative arrs., he had an uncanny ability to make the works of such disparate comps. as Irving Berlin, Kurt Weill, Jelly Roll Morton, and Thelonious Monk seem uniquely his own. Besides Davis, Evans' charts became enhancing frames for such players as Cannonball Adderley; Steve Lacy; Phil Woods; Budd Johnson; Eric Dolphy; Kenny Burrell; Paul Chambers; and Elvin Jones. In those yrs., Evans was more in demand in the studio than on the bandstand, but he formed gps. for specific NYC dates, incl. stints at the Apollo and Birdland in '59, and six weeks at the Jazz Gallery in '64. Fr. the late '60s through the '70s, he maintained a rehearsal band that perf. and rec. sporadically, but his activity increased in his final yrs. The band had an increasingly experimental nature, on which Evans thrived; fr. the late '60s on, his scores incorporated synthesizers and rock rhythms and were structurally flexible, allowing for gp. and individual improvisation. As always, the personnel consisted of some of NY's finest musicians, incl. Lew Soloff; David Sanborn; George Adams; Billy Harper; John Scofield; Howard Johnson; Pete Levin; and John Clark, some of whom pl. w. him on and off for over fifteen yrs. The band perf. at the MJF in '66; weekly at the Village Vanguard in '70; toured Eur. in '71; debuted in Japan '72; pl. at Westbeth, the artists's community where Evans lived, summer '72. Fr. '73 to '75, it app. somewhat regularly at the Village Vanguard. As one of the initial mus. dir. of NYJRC, Evans perf. three concerts w. his orch. under its auspices: *Jazz in the Rock Age; Gil Evans Retrospective;* and *The Music of Jimi Hendrix.* In the early '80s, the band perf. in the prestigious *Jazz at the Public* concert series at the Public Theater, NYC. In April 1983, the orch. began regular Monday night apps. at Sweet Basil in NYC.

His increased visibility revivified his career on several fronts: he collaborated on film scores w. pop stars David Bowie and Robbie Robertson; was in demand on the int'l fest. circuit; and was involved w. several diverse rec. projects. His app. w. Sting at Umbria Jazz '87 was a Eur. media event, though his band's highly charged nightly sets in the ruins of a church caused a far more profound musical sensation. Since his death, the Monday Night orch. has cont. under the leadership of his son, Miles Evans. Several rarely perf. Evans arrs. have been presented, most notably the AJO concert of Evans' Thornhill arrs., spring '91; and a Montreux '91 concert feat. Miles Davis in a re-creation of *Sketches of Spain* and *Miles*

Ahead, organized by Quincy Jones. One of the most innovative jazz arr./comps., Evans conts. to be very infl., second, perhaps, only to Ellington, in the striking individuality of his work. Upon his death, Miles Davis commented: "He never wasted a melody, he never wasted a phrase...Students will discover him, they'll have to take his music apart layer by layer. That's how they'll know what kind of genius he was." Awards: Guggenheim Fellowship for comp. '68; founding artist of the John F. Kennedy Center '72; National Music Award '76; perf. at the White House for Jimmy Carter '78; BMI Jazz Pioneer Award '82; honorary doctorate from New Engl. Cons. '86; Amer. Jazz Masters Fellowship from NEA '86. Fests: MJF '66; NJF tour '73; Umbria Jazz '74; Kool Fest. '82–3; North Sea, Umbria Jazz, Free Jazz, Rio de Janeiro '87. Books: *Gil Evans,* Raymond Horricks (Hippocrene Books) '84; *Las Vegas Tango,* Laurent Cugny. Video: *Gil Evans* (View Video). Film scores: O. Lee's *The Sea is Your Future; Absolute Beginners; The Color of Money.* Arrs. for Thornhill: "Buster's Last Stand"; "Donna Lee"; "Anthropology"; "Yardbird Suite"; "Robbins' Nest"; "Early Autumn"; "There's a Small Hotel." Comps: "La Nevada"; "Las Vegas Tango"; "Hotel Me"; "Eleven"; "Anita's Dance"; "Bud and Bird." CDs: BN; Prest.; Imp.; Verve; BB; Atl.; Ant.; Evid.; Em.; w. M. Davis (Cap.; Col.); H. Merrill; S. Lacy; L. Konitz; K. Burrell (Verve).

EVANS, HERSCHEL, tnr sax; cl; b. Denton, TX, 1909; d. NYC, 2/9/39. Turned prof. in 1926, pl. w. Southwestern territory bands beginning w. Edgar Battle, T. Holder, and then going on to Troy Floyd '29–31; Bennie Moten '33–5; Hot Lips Page, Dave Peyton '34. To LA w. Lionel Hampton '35, also worked there w. Buck Clayton. Ret. to KC and join. Count Basie in late '36, rising to prominence w. an approach that translated the warm, big-toned Coleman Hawkins style into what became the cornerstone of Texas tnr. and exerted a seminal infl. on Buddy Tate; Arnett Cobb; Illinois Jacquet. Until his death, he and Lester Young, w. their contrasting styles, were chief ingredients in the success of the Basie sound. Solos w. Basie: "Blue and Sentimental"; "One O'Clock Jump"; "John's Idea"; also on own comps., "Doggin' Around" and "Texas Shuffle." Recs. w. Mildred Bailey, Harry James. CDs: w. Basie (Dec.); *Spirituals to Swing* (Vang.); L. Hampton (BB); B. Holiday (Col.).

EVANS, MILES IAN GILMORE, tpt, lead; b. NYC, 7/5/65. Son of Gil and Anita Evans; bro. Noah is rock bs. and prod. Began on dms. Stud. at Mus. and Art HS, NYC. First sat in w. Gil Evans Orch. at MJF

7/5/1974. Stud. w. members of orch., incl. Lew Soloff, Jon Faddis. Pl. w. all-British Gil Evans Orch. '82; Gil Evans Monday Night Orch. at Sweet Basil, NYC fr. '83. Tour. Japan w. Evans–Miles Davis '83; Evans–Jaco Pastorius '84. When his fath. died in '88, he took over as leader. He was a member of the orch. assembled by Quincy Jones that perf. Gil Evans charts w. Miles Davis at Montreux JF '91. Favs: Miles Davis. Fests: all major in Eur. fr. '82; Brazil Free Jazz Fest. '87. TV: *Ghost of Faffner Hall*, HBO. CDs: w. Gil Evans Orch. (SN); w. M. Davis–Q. Jones (Qwest).

EVANS, "STUMP" (PAUL ANDERSON), alto, bari sax; b. Lawrence, KS, 10/18/04; d. Douglas Co., KS, 8/29/28. Studied mus. w. fath. Began on alto horn, sw. to tbn. bef. taking up alto sax. In the early 1920s, he concentrated on bari. sax. Moved to Chi. where he worked w. Bernie Young, King Oliver '23; Dixie Syncopators '26. Rec. on alto sax w. Jelly Roll Morton '27, and later pl. w. the bands of Jimmy Wade and Erskine Tate until TB ended his career. Recs: w. Oliver, "Alligator Hop" '23; Tate, "Static Strut" '26; Morton, "Wild Man Blues"; "Hyena Stomp." CDs: w. Oliver (Dec.); Armstrong-Oliver (Mile.); Morton (BB).

EWELL, DON (DONALD TYSON), pno; b. Baltimore, MD, 11/14/16; d. Pompano Beach, FL, 8/9/83. Brother, Ed Lynch, pl. tbn. w. Casa Loma orch. Stud. classical pno. at Maryland Inst. of Fine Arts; in mid 1930s, majored in comp. at Peabody Cons., Balt. Pl. w. local gps.and led own trio bef. join. a swing band, the Townsmen '36–40; learned bb arr. here; led own trio again '41. Pl. fl., picc. w. mil. bands dur. WWII; after discharge, he moved to NYC. Worked w. Bunk Johnson '46–7; Doc Evans '47; Sidney Bechet '48. Moved to Chi. '49, pl. w. Muggsy Spanier '49; Miff Mole '49–50; George Brunis. Learned blues pl. fr. Jimmy Yancey in late '40s; own band in St. Louis '51. Worked in Chi. w. Eddie Wiggins '52; Lee Collins '53; also own gps. Moved to Calif. to pl. w. Kid Ory '53–5; as soloist at Hangover, SF; then mainly w. Jack Teagarden fr. summer of '56–64, incl. tour of Asia. Settled in NO for a few yrs,. mid to late '60s, lead. own gps. and as sideman. Duo w. Willie "The Lion" Smith at Village Gate, and for rec., NYC '67. Join. Dukes of Dixieland in Fla. '69, perf. w. band in NO, France '71; Engl. '80. Also made solo apps. in Eur. '71; was house pnst. at Royal Orleans Hotel, NO '78. Disciple of Jelly Roll Morton, who, w. James P. Johnson and Fats Waller, was a major infl. CDs: Solo Art; GTJ; George Lewis–Don Ewell (Del.); w. Kid Ory (GTJ); Teagarden (Jazz.); Albert Burbank (Story.).

EWING, "STREAMLINE" (JOHN R.), tbn; b. Topeka, KS, 1/19/17. Studied at Jefferson HS in LA. Prof. debut through Gene Coy. Extensive name band experience incl. Horace Henderson 1938; Earl Hines '38–9, '41–2; short stints w. bbs of Louis Armstrong; Lionel Hampton; then Jimmie Lunceford '43–5; Cab Calloway '46; Jay McShann '48; Cootie Williams '50. Moved to Calif., pl. w. George Jenkins, Gerald Wilson off and on fr. '53; Teddy Buckner fr. '56. Tour. Eur. '85 and Japan '90, w. Johnny Otis. Freelancing in LA in recent yrs., Ewing is best known through his recs. w. Hines, incl. "Grand Terrace Shuffle"; "Yellow Fire"; "XYZ"; "Windy City Jive"; "Swingin' On C." Favs: Tommy Dorsey, J.J. Johnson. CDs: w. Hines (Class.; BB).

FADDIS, JON, tpt, flg, pno, comp, lead; b. Oakland, CA, 7/24/53. One sister sings, other pl. pno. Began on tpt. at age 8. Stud. w. Bill Catalano, who introduced him to Dizzy Gillespie's music 1964. Later stud. improv. w. Bill Atwood; tpt. w. Carmine Caruso; Mel Broiles; Vince Penzarella. Stud. comp. w. Edgar Grana '85–90. Pl. w. r&b bands in Oakland fr. age 13, then w. rehearsal bands in SF incl. Rudy Salvini; Cus Cousineau; Don Piestrup. Joined Lionel Hampton immediately after grad. hs '71. Moved to NYC '72, pl. w. Thad Jones–Mel Lewis Orch. '72–5; Charles Mingus '72–3; Gil Evans, Chuck Mangione '72; Gillespie fr. '74. Worked as studio mus. mid '70s–early '80s. App. w. Gillespie at White House "In Performance" '82. Pl. w. own qnt. fr. '82; Philip Morris Superband, late '80s. Faddis has also perf. and rec. w. Duke Ellington Orch.; Count Basie Orch.; Art Blakey; McCoy Tyner; Dexter Gordon; Cab Calloway; Joe Williams; Ella Fitzgerald; Sarah Vaughan; James Moody; Milt Jackson; etc. He served as mus. dir. of the Gillespie bb and the United Nation Orch. fr. '87 to '92; the Carnegie Hall 100th Anniv. bb '91. Faddis has travelled extens. as a lecturer and clinician; in '92 was appointed mus. dir. of the Carnegie Hall Jazz Band and in '99 to the faculty of Purchase Coll. St. U., N.Y. Known for his mastery of the Gillespie style, often playing an octave higher than Dizzy, Faddis has brought other elements to his work from some of the Swing Era giants and personalized his playing. Tour. US, on own and w. LCJO '94. Favs: Gillespie, Armstrong, Eldridge, M. Davis, C. Brown, Snooky Young. Polls: *DB* TDWR '74–5. Fests: all major fr. '77. Films: soundtracks for *The Gauntlet; Bird; The Wiz; The Burning Spear; A Winter in Lisbon.* TV: Johnny Carson, Arsenio Hall w. Gillespie; David Letterman; *Saurday Night Live.* LP: w. Oscar Peterson (Pab.). CDs: Epic; Conc.; w. CHJB (BN); Gillespie (Pab.; Tel.); Monty Alexander (Chesky); Ed Cherry (GH); K. Burrell (Fant.); M. Jackson (East-West); Mingus (Rh.); Mingus Big Band (SN); M. Tyner (Mile.).

FAGERQUIST, DON (DONALD A.), tpt; b. Worcester, MA, 2/6/27; d. Los Angeles, CA, 1/24/74. Began prof. w. Mal Hallett 1943. Pl. w. G. Krupa '44–5, again in '48. Led own gp. backing Anita O'Day '49; then w. A. Shaw '49–50; W. Herman '51–2; Les Brown, Dave Pell Octet '53–9. On staff at Paramount Studios from Jan. '56, but also worked w. P. Rugolo '56–61; M. Tormé '56–7; L. Bellson '59; L. Almeida '62. Died of kidney disease. Originally inspired by Roy Eldridge, later infl. by Gillespie, he was a leading soloist in the West Coast movement of the '50s. Rec. w. Krupa; Shaw; Brown; S. Manne; John Graas; Tormé; Pell; A. Pepper. CDs: VSOP; w. Bob Cooper (Cont.); Herman (Disc.); Pepper (Pac. Jazz); S. Rogers (BB); Tormé (Stash); Krupa (Hep).

FAHN, MIKE (MICHAEL JEFF), v-tbn, tbn; also dms, bari horn, scat voc.; b. Queens, NY, 12/16/60. Father was jazz drummer in 1950s, pl. w. Billy May; Tex Beneke; Lionel Hampton. Began on dms, then tpt., bari. horn, tbn. Moved with parents to LA '77. Pl. w. Frank Strazzeri, Don Menza '78–82; Dick Berk '84; own gps. w. Bob Sheppard, Tad Weed, John Patitucci, Peter Donald '85–8. Also worked in '80s w. Bob Cooper; Conte Candoli; Pete Christlieb; Shorty Rogers. Pl. w. Maynard Ferguson '89–91; Terry Gibbs, Woody Herman Orch., Bill Holman bb, Kim Richmond, Andy Simpkins, D. Berk '90; Jack Sheldon, Louis Bellson '92. Moved back to NYC '93; pl. w. Toshiko Akiyoshi bb, Loren Schoenberg bb, Roland Vasquez '94, then freelanced. Leonard Feather called him "one of the few genuine virtuoso performers on the valve trombone." Favs: Bob Brookmeyer, J.J. Johnson. Polls: New Talent Awd., LA Jazz Society '87. CDs: Cexton; w. Berk (Res.; Nine Winds); Catingub (SB); B. Cooper (Disc.); Andy Simpkins (MAMA).

FAIRWEATHER, DIGBY (RICHARD JOHN CHARLES), long-model crnt, tpt; b. Rochford, Essex, England, 4/25/46. Both parents musical, fath. prof. First stud. dms., euph., vln., cl., tpt. Fr. 1970 worked in local Essex bands and his own Dig's Half Dozen. Rec. debut w. Alex Welsh '75. Turned prof. '77. Was founder-member of Keith Nichols' Midnite Follies Orch.; join. the co-op qt. Velvet; rec. solo albums. Voted BBC Jazz Society's Mus. of the Yr. '79. Fr. that time became co-dir., w. pnst. Stan Barker, of non-profit educ. trust, Jazz College. App. w. A. Welsh Reunion Band '83–7; Pizza Express All-Stars '80–3; Brian Priestley's Special Sept. '81; led own qt.; re-form. Kettners Five w. Tiny Winters. Led Jazz Superkings fr. '87; worked w. Great British Jazz Band fr. 94. Founded the Assoc. of Brit. Jazz Mus. and the Nat'l Jazz Foundation Archive '87. Helped to estab. jazz section of Brit. Mus. Union '90. Presenter of jazz radio shows on London FM; BBC Radio 2 in '90s. Fests: Northsea; Nice; Cork. TV: Nat Gonella tribute. Books: *How to Play Trumpet* '85; *Jazz: The Essential Companion* '87; *Jazz: The Rough Guide* '95. CDs: BL; Big Bear; FMR; w. Great Brit. Jazz Band (Cand.); Val Wiseman (Big Bear); S. McCorkle (Conc.).

FAMBROUGH, CHARLES, bs, comp; b. Philadelphia, PA, 8/25/50. Father was bass singer in church choir. In seventh grade began ten yrs. of classical bs. study w. Neil Courtney of Phila. Orch. Fellow student was Stanley Clarke, whom he interested in modern jazz. Prof. work fr. 1968 as member of house band for Mike Douglas TV show; worked at the Concord Hotel in Catskill Mts. backing name acts; r&b club dates in NYC. Worked w. Andy Aaron's Mean Machine, pop gp. in Phila., '69. Grover Washington was feat. sax. When Washington form. his own gp. in '70, Fambrough join. him for three and a half yrs.; then pl. w. Airto Moreira '75–8; McCoy Tyner '78–80; Art Blakey '80–4; Wynton Marsalis '81–2; also gigs w. F. Hubbard; R.R. Kirk; Shirley Scott; R. Hargrove; K. Barron; H. Silver; R. Haynes; Courtney Pine. Rec. as lead. for CTI label '91–3 w. all-star casts. Recs. on Mile. w. Tyner. CDs: CTI; w. Blakey (Timel.; Conc.); Marsalis (Col.).

FAME, GEORGIE (Clive Powell), voc, org; b. Leigh, Lancashire, England, 6/26/43. Played w. Rory and the Blackjacks in London at age 16. Form. Blues Flames to back pop singer Billy Fury, winning recognition at the Flamingo Club in Soho, early '60s. Won British polls as top male jazz voc. Many concerts and fests.; feat. soloist w. big band of pnst. Harry South, which incl. Ronnie Scott, Tubby Hayes. In 1966–8 own West End theatre production and a season at London's Mayfair Theatre. Tour. Continent w. C. Basie band '67–8; sang w. J. Hendricks, Annie Ross at Berlin JF '68. First US app. '70, w. own group, Shorty. In '70s co-starred in Brit. TV series, *The Price of Fame*, tour. w. re-vamped Blue Flames gp. Blossom Dearie wrote song for him, "Sweet Georgie Fame." In '80s, rec. tributes to such personal idols as Hoagy Carmichael; in '90s mus. dir. for Van Morrison. CDs: Go Jazz/VeraBra; Conn.; w. Morrison (Verve).

FARLEY, ED, tpt; b. Newark, NJ, 7/16/04. Played w. Red McKenzie at Onyx club, 1935; then co-led gp. w. trombonist Mike Riley and briefly had the most popular comedy-jazz gp. on 52nd St. w. hit song, "The Music Goes Round and Round," before fading into obscurity.

FARLOW, TAL (TALMADGE HOLT), gtr; b. Greensboro, NC, 6/7/21; d. Sea Bright, NJ, 7/25/98. Worked as sign painter, then began pl. gtr. 1943. Self-taught; orig. inspired by Charlie Christian. Gigged in Phila. First major job w. trio led by pnst. Dardanelle at Copa Lounge, NYC '47. Pl. w. Marjorie Hyams '48; Buddy DeFranco '49; Red Norvo '50–3; Artie Shaw's Gramercy 5 '53–4; Norvo '54–5. Semi-retired '55–60, then almost completely inactive fr. '60 except for occas. apps. at clubs near his home in Sea Bright. Pl. weekends w. Don Friedman, Vinnie Burke for a short time at club in Asbury Park '65. Came out of retirement '67 for two-mo. stint at NYC club, The Frammis; also rec. w. Sonny Criss. Pl. w. Geo. Wein's Newport All-Stars '68–70. Participated in making of documentary film *Talmage Farlow* '81. In the early '80s, Farlow began to app. more regularly in public, while cont. to teach priv. Replaced B. Kessel in the Great Guitars early '90s. As a young guitarist, Farlow was interested in jazz through hearing Art Tatum. Charlie Christian's recordings with Benny Goodman gave him a strong focus, enhanced later by Lester Young and shaped further by the collaborations of Parker and Gillespie. Farlow was a master technician (using his thumb for speed), with a great ear and a down home feeling. He had his own method for playing harmonized solos. Furthermore, he built an octave-divider, which he operated with his foot, for playing doubled lines. Favs: Christian, J. Raney, Kessel, Jim Hall. Fests: NJF '68–9, '73. Polls: *DB* Critics New Star '54. Video: *Talmage Farlow* (Rhap.). Book: *Tal Farlow Guitar Method* (Guitar Player Prod.). CDs: Verve; Prest.; Conc.; w. Norvo (Sav.; BB); Shaw (MM); Pettiford (RCA); DeFranco (Prog.).

FARMER, ADDISON GERALD, bs; b. Council Bluffs, IA, 8/21/28; d. NYC, 2/20/63. Raised in Phoenix, Ariz., moving to LA in 1945 where he pl. w. C. Parker, Miles Davis '46; Teddy Edwards '47; Howard McGhee, Benny Carter, Jay McShann '48; Gerald Wilson '53. Moved to NYC '54, stud. bs. w. Fred Zimmerman; pno., theory at Juilliard and Manhattan Sch. of Mus. Worked w. twin bro., Art Farmer, in Farmer–Gigi Gryce qnt. '54–5; then w. T. Charles; S. Getz. Charter member of Art Farmer–Benny Golson gp. Oct. '59; w. M. Allison '60–2. Died from reaction to the synergy of two medications. Favs: Pettiford, R. Brown, P. Heath. CDs: w. Art Farmer (Prest.; Cont.; BN); G. Ammons; Bennie Green; T. Macero (Prest.); M. Allison (Prest.; Rh./Atl.); M. Waldron (NJ).

FARMER, ART (ARTHUR STEWART), tpt, flg, flumpet; b. Council Bluffs, IA, 8/21/28; d. NYC, 10/4/99. Twin bro. of Addison Farmer. Raised in Phoenix, Ariz. Stud. pno. at age 6, later vln. and tba.; took up tpt. at 14. To LA in 1945 where he worked w. Horace Henderson; Floyd Ray. Trav. east w. Johnny Otis; freelanced in NYC '47–8 and stud. w. Maurice Grupp. Ret. to West Coast '48 and worked w. Benny Carter; Gerald Wilson; Jay McShann; Roy Porter. Pl. w. Wardell Gray '51–2. After tour. for a yr. w. L. Hampton in Eur. and US '52–3, he settled in NYC, co-leading a gp. w. Gigi Gryce off and on '54–6. Pl. w. Horace Silver '56–8; Gerry Mulligan '58–9, incl. apps. in films, *I Want to Live; The Subterraneans*. In '59 he and Benny Golson form. The Jazztet, which stayed together until '62. Around this time Farmer sw. fr. tpt. to flg., worked often w. Jim Hall '62–4; then form. new qt. feat. Steve Kuhn. After working in Eur. '65–6, ret. to US and led combo w. Jimmy Heath. In '68 moved to Vienna and join. Austrian Radio Orch.; also worked w. Clarke-Boland and Peter Herbolzheimer bbs. Tour. Eur. and Orient w. Jimmy Smith gp. '72. In the '70s, he rarely ret. to US, but increased his perf. visits after '80. Re-form. the Jazztet w. Golson for a brief time '82. In the '80s and '90s led gps. annually in NYC, first at Sweet Basil w. Clifford Jordan; later at Village Vanguard w. Jerome Richardson, Ron Blake. In '91 he began pl. the flumpet, a new horn w. a sound between a tpt. and flg., designed for him by David Monette. His playing was always marked by a consistent lyricism, sensitivity, and personal tone quality; these attributes broadened and deepened in the '90s. Fests: pl. w. both Charles Mingus Jazz Wkshp. and Lester Young qnt. at NJF '55; many int'l fests w. own gps. since then, incl. Cork JF '94. Special guest soloist at Lincoln Center for *Jeru: The Music of Gerry Mulligan* w. LCJO '96. Video: *Art Farmer: Jazz at the Smithsonian* (Sony). Publ: transcriptions of nine flg. solos, *Art Farmer Solos* (D. Erjavec, Rottenburg, Baden-Wurttemberg, Germ.) '84. CDs: Arab.; Atl.; L+R; Main.; BN; Conc.; Chess; Cont.; Den.; Prest.; NJ; CTI; Mon.; SN; Enja; w. Hall (Tel.); Gigi Gryce (Sav.); G. Ammons; C. Brown; W. Gray; S. Rollins; G. Melle; D. Byrd (Prest.); M. Waldron (NJ); Golson (Cont.); Mulligan (Col.); G. Russell; J.J. Johnson (BB); Q. Jones (Imp.); D. Jordan (Steep.); T. Charles (Atl.).

FARNHAM, ALLEN, pno, kybds, comp; b. Boston, MA, 5/19/61. Mother is pnst. and orgnst. Began on tpt. at age 10; pno. lessons at age 12, then pl. jazz in hs. Stud. classical and jazz pno. at Oberlin Cons. 1979–83. Moved to Cleveland '83; stud. pno. w. Andrius Kuprevicius and classical Indian music w. Ramnad V. Ragavan. Pl. in Cleveland w. Kenny Davis–Ernie Krivda and worked as studio mus. '82–4. Moved to NYC '85. Pl. w. Roland Vasquez '85–6; Special EFX '86; Mel Tormé–Marty Paich '87; Ernestine Anderson '90; Susannah McCorkle fr. '91; also own gps. Farnham has worked as a producer and promoter for the Concord rec. label fr. '86. He received an NEA grant to fund a series of concerts in '89. Favs: Art Tatum, Keith Jarrett, Oscar Peterson. Fests: Japan fr. '87. CDs: Conc.; w. S. McCorkle; M. Tormé (Conc.); G. Tsilis (Enja).

FARNSWORTH, JOSEPH ALLEN, dms; b. Holyoke, MA, 2/21/68. Musical family; fath. is a mus. teacher, one bro. pl. tbn., another saxist w. Ray Charles. Stud. w. Art Taylor, Alan Dawson; B. Mus., William Paterson Coll., N.J., 1986–90. Pl. w. Junior Cook '91; worked w. George Coleman; Cecil Payne; Annie Ross. Tour. Far East w. Jon Hendricks '91; Jon Faddis '92; Benny Green '95; six-week Eur. tour w. Benny Golson, *Celebrating 40 Years of Benny Golson's Music* in '96. Favs: Roach, Blakey, Art Taylor, Billy Higgins. Rec. soundtrack for *Ed's Next Move* w. Golson. CDs: w. Cook (Steep.); Eric Alexander (CC; Del.); Cecil Payne (Del.); Golson (Ark.; Mile.); Steve Davis (CC); Michael Weiss (DIW); One For All (Sharp Nine).

FARRELL, JOE (Joseph Carl Firrantello), tnr, sop saxes; flutes; all reeds, except bsn; b. Chicago Heights, IL, 12/16/37; d. Los Angeles, CA, 1/10/86.

Father pl. gtr., bro., mand.; bro.-in-law—local Chi. mus. in late 1930s-early '40s—start. him on cl. in '48. Stud. tnr. sax w. Joe Sirolla at Roy Knapp Mus. Sch., Chi. '53; majored in fl. at U. of Ill. w. Charles DeLaney. B.S. in mus. ed. '59. Pl. w. Ralph Marterie '57, also jamming w. many Chi. mus. incl. Ira Sullivan, Nicky Hill. To NYC '60, pl. w. Maynard Ferguson '61; Slide Hampton '62; Tito Rodriguez '62–4; George Russell Sxt., incl. Eur. tour Oct. '64; Jaki Byard '65; three yrs. w. Thad Jones–Mel Lewis orch. from '66; also w. Elvin Jones trio '67–70. Briefly w. W. Herman '65; Horace Silver late '60s; Herbie Hancock. With Chick Corea in '70s, incl. Eur. and Jap. tours w. Return to Forever. Led own qt. '74–5. Extremely active in NYC studios in late '60s and early '70s, rec. w. Santana; Billy Cobham; the Rascals; the Band; Aretha Franklin; James Brown. In '78, he moved to LA, where he led his own qt. and 18-piece band. He was active in both jazz and rock during the '70s, but in '79 join. Mingus Dynasty, touring US and Eur., as he also did w. Louis Hayes '83, and Joanne Brackeen '84; pl. w. Woody Shaw '85. A tnr. saxist of great energy and invention, he was also a strong sop. saxist and a particularly full-bodied alto flautist. Insp. and infl: Parker, Rollins, Coltrane, B. Powell, I. Sullivan, J. Griffin, Byard, E. Jones. Polls: *DB* Critics, New Star, tnr. '68, fl. '69; *DB* Readers, sop. sax '69; MM '68. Fests: NJF w. Ferguson '60; E. Jones '68 '72; as soloist '73–4; Molde, Pori '71–2; own gp. at Berlin JF '73. CDs: Cont.; CTI; Timel.; w. E. Jones (BN); Pat Martino; Byard (Prest.); Corea (ECM; Verve); Mingus (Rh./Atl.); G. Benson (CTI); Jones-Lewis (LRC).

FARROW, ERNIE (ERNEST), bs; also dms, pno; b. Huntington, WV, 11/13/28; d. Detroit, MI, 7/14/69. Half-sister is Alice Coltrane. Stud. pno. in NYC w. uncle, Charles Lewis. Raised in Detroit. Pl. bs. w. own combo in hs. Worked w. Terry Gibbs 1954; Stan Getz '55; Barry Harris, in Det. '50s, NYC '60s. Pl. w. Y. Lateef on and off, from '56 to mid '60s; also own trio at the Bluebird, Det. '58; Red Garland trio '60. Ret. to Det. '64, form. a qnt. and a 10-pc. band, the Big Sound; also app. as sideman w. Jack Brokensha; Harold McKinney; et al. Reinstituted jazz policy at the Bluebird '69, and was lead. his qnt. there when he lost his life in a swimming pool accident. Favs: Blanton, Ray Brown, Pettiford, Junior Raglin. Recs. w. Harris; Gibbs; Johnny Williams. CDs: w. Lateef (NJ; Prest.; Sav.; Imp.).

FASOLI, CLAUDIO, tnr, sop saxes, pno; b. Venice-Lido, Italy, 11/29/39. Grandmother was singer; bro. is pnst. Stud. priv. in Venice 1955–7, then self-

taught. Pl. w. Open Jazz Group '61–4; Giorgio Buratti '66–7; Guido Manusardi '69–71; Perigeo Qnt. '72–7; Giorgio Azzolini, Tullio De Piscopo '77–8; Lydian Sound Orch. fr. '88; Giorgio Gaslini fr. '89; Grande Orch. Nazionale '91–2. Led own gps. fr. '79 w. sidemen incl. Kenny Wheeler; Niels H.Ø. Pedersen; Barry Altschul; Mick Goodrick; Tony Oxley; John Surman; Lee Konitz. Fasoli has taught and lectured on improv. at cons. in Siena '78–97; Caserta '82; Terni '83; Vicenza '84–90; Milano '84–92; Padova '88–92. Favs: Konitz, Wayne Shorter. Polls: Ital. Critics Poll '78; Siena Jazz Assoc. '92. Fests: all major in Eur.; Can. '77; USA '77, '89; Mex. '91. TV: Perigeo special '73; *C. Fasoli Qt. Live!* '84. CDs: Ram; SN; Spl.; Nueva; w. Gaslini; Wheeler (SN).

FATOOL, NICK (NICHOLAS), dms; b. Milbury, MA, 1/2/15; d. Los Angeles, 9/26/00. Played w. gps. around Providence, R.I. Worked w. Joe Haymes in NYC 1937; George Hall '38; Benny Goodman '39–40; Artie Shaw '40–1; briefly w. Claude Thornhill and Jan Savitt '42 bef. join. Alvino Rey '42–3. Settled on West Coast '43, pl. w. Harry James; also studio mus., incl. rec. sess. w. Billy Butterfield; L. Armstrong; Erroll Garner; Jess Stacy; Glen Gray; others; Bing Crosby Show '56–8; concerts w. Bob Crosby orch. '57–9. Participated annually in Frank Bull–Gene Norman Dixieland Jubilees through '40s and '50s. Worked w. Pete Fountain intermittently '62–5; tour. Far East w. Bob Crosby '64; app. w. L. Armstrong at Hollywood Palace, mid '60s; gigs w. Fountain again, at his NO club '67–9; Bob Crosby, Phil Harris in LV '69–73; also apps. w. Matty Matlock, Dick Cary, Peanuts Hucko in '70s. Since '72, has also been a prof. golf teacher. Cont. to work around LA into '80s; tour. Eur. w. Crosby '81. Fests: Sacramento; Aspen; Concord; San Diego. Film: pl. on soundtracks for *Pete Kelly's Blues*; *The Five Pennies.* CDs: w. Goodman (Col.; Vang.); Shaw; L. Hampton (BB); Nat Cole (Cap.); Yank Lawson (Audio.); S. Hasselgard (Phon.); B. Holiday (Dec.).

FAULK, DAN (DANIEL M.), tnr, sop saxes, cl; b. Philadelphia, PA, 11/22/69. Six bros. are musicians. Stud. w. Heath Krieger in Prescott, Ariz. 1984–7; Bill Pierce at Berklee Coll. of Mus. '87–8; Joe Lovano at Wm. Paterson Coll. '88–91; priv. stud. w. Barry Harris, Benny Golson in early '90s. First gigs w. salsa band in Ariz. '83; then pl. w. fusion band there '83–6. Worked w. TanaReid fr. '91; Ed Cherry, Valery Ponomarev '92; Craig Bailey's Unit 6 fr. '92; J. J. Johnson '96. Favs: Rollins, Coltrane, C. Parker, W. Shorter, D. Gordon, J. Henderson. Polls: *DB* student awd. '91. TV: N.J. Network w. college band. CDs: CC; w.

TanaReid (Conc.); Eijiro Nakagawa and Funk 55; Tatsi Nakamura (King).

FAVORS, MALACHI (Brother Malachi Favors Magoustous), bs, comp; b. Chicago, IL, 8/22/37. From a religious family. Initially insp. by Charlie Parker; Oscar Pettiford; Wilbur Ware. Began pl. bass after high sch. Pl. and rec. w. Andrew Hill 1958–60; also pl. w. Dizzy Gillespie; Freddie Hubbard; lounge gigs w. pnsts and orgnsts. Met Roscoe Mitchell, Muhal Richard Abrams '61. Pl. w. Abrams' Experimental Band fr. that time. With Roscoe Mitchell Art Ens. fr. '65; w. the addition of Joseph Jarman the gp. bec. the Art Ens. of Chi. In France w. Art Ens. of Chi. '69–71. Settled in Chi. '71; led gps. through '80s. In addition to bs., Favors has also perf. and rec. on zither, melodica, hca., bjo., and perc. with the Art Ens. of Chi. Rec. w. Jimmy Lyons; A. Shepp; Mitchell. CDs: w. Art Ens. of Chi. (Nessa; Aff.; Del.; ECM; DIW); L. Bowie (BS); Mitchell (Chief; BS; Ahmed Abdullah; Charles Brackeen; Dennis Gonzalez (Silk.); Shepp (Aff.; Charly); Kahil El'zabar (SA).

FAVRE, PIERRE, dms; b. Le Locle, Neuchatel, Switzerland, 6/2/37. Self-taught. Prof. debut 1954. Worked in bop, Dixieland, and free jazz gps; heard w. Manfred Schoof on *European Echoes*. After employment by Paiste Cymbals, led a trio w. Irene Schweizer on pno. and George Mraz on bs., later augmented by saxist Evan Parker. Long association w. French saxist Michel Portal in '70s. From '80, worked w. singer Tamia, touring US w. her '85. Led perc. gp., feat. Paul Motian and Nana Vasconcelos, using a variety of bells, gongs, cymbals and other adventurous percussion instruments. Rec. w. Santana '68, Mal Waldron 71; Albert Mangelsdorff '76; Barre Phillips '81. CDs: ECM; w. Joe McPhee; Portal (hatArt); D. Saluzzi; J. Surman (ECM); Schweizer (Intakt).

FAZOLA (Irving Henry Prestopnik), cl; b. New Orleans, LA, 12/10/12; d. New Orleans, 3/20/49. Studied C-melody sax and cl. from age 13. Pl. w. Candy Candido; Louis Prima; S. Bonano; Armand Hug. Join. Ben Pollack 1935, and went to Chi. w. him the following yr. Worked w. Gus Arnheim '36; Glenn Miller '37–8; Bob Crosby, also feat. w. Bob Cats, Mar. '38–Aug. '40; Jimmy McPartland '40; Tony Almerico '40–1; Claude Thornhill '41; Muggsy Spanier '41–2; Teddy Powell '42–3; Horace Heidt '43. During these yrs., he visited NO periodically, and eventually, due to ill health, resettled there permanently, working intermittently until his death w. Almerico, Louis and Leon Prima, and his own small gps. Louis Prima gave him the name Fazola, and he

eventually legalized it, dropping Irving as well as his surname. His style was a comfortable blend of the NO clarinet tradition and elements of swing, and he was known for his ease of execution and pure, lyrical sound that helped shape the Miller and Thornhill reed sections. Recs: "My Inspiration" w. Crosby. Polls: *DB* '40, '41. CDs: Key. Coll. (Em.); w. B. Holiday (Col.); Crosby (Dec.); Bonano (Timel.).

FEATHER, LEONARD GEOFFREY, comp, piano, journalist; b. London, England, 9/13/14; d. Sherman Oaks, CA, 9/22/94. Studied at St. Paul's School and University Coll., London 1920–32; pno. and cl. lessons, but self-taught as arr. and comp. Prod. and comp. for rec. sessions by Benny Carter and George Chisholm in London early '30s; was instrumental in hiring of Carter for BBC Dance Orch. Moved to NYC mid '30s; in next decade prod. and comp. for sess. by L. Armstrong; D. Ellington; D. Gillespie; et al. In '40s, organized jazz concerts at Carnegie Hall; produced debut recs. of Sarah Vaughan; George Shearing; Dinah Washington. His "Evil Gal Blues," "Salty Papa Blues," and "Blowtop Blues" launched Washington's career. Continued to comp., produce, and arr. (incl. charts for C. Basie) from '40s. After publication of *Inside Bebop* '49 and the release of the initial *Encyclopedia of Jazz* '55, was best known as an important jazz journalist, commentator, and critic. Relocated to LA '60; became main jazz critic for *LA Times*; taught jazz courses and seminars at Loyola Marymount U. '72–4; UC Riverside '73; Cal State Northridge, and UCLA '87–90. Reviews and articles appeared in periodicals and magazines around the world, incl. *Esquire, Playboy, Show, Down Beat, Metronome, JazzTimes, Swing Journal* (Japan), *Musica Jazz* (Italy); his *LA Times* columns were syndicated world wide. Although most visible as the best-known writer on jazz in the world, Feather was a gifted musician, comp., and producer whose musically creative work also had an impact upon jazz. Among his more than 200 published compositions are "How Blue Can You Get" (a hit for B. B. King); "Blues for Yesterday" (rec. by Armstrong); "Old Man Rebop" (rec. by Gillespie); "I Remember Bird" (rec. by Cannonball Adderley; Phil Woods; Oliver Nelson); "Signing Off" (rec. by Sarah Vaughan; Ella Fitzgerald; André Previn); "Born on a Friday" (rec. by Cleo Laine); and "Twelve Tone Blues" (rec. by Yusef Lateef). Among his numerous awards and commendations are the first journalism Grammy ever given by NARAS '64; an Emmy nomination as producer of KNBC's *The Jazz Show* '71; a CPB award for excellence in local programming on KUSC's *The Leonard Feather Show*; *Down Beat*'s Lifetime Achievement Award '83; an honorary Doctorate of Music from Berklee College of Music '84; a Greater Los Angeles Press Club Journalism Award '85; the Deems Taylor/ASCAP Distinguished Journalism Award '87. CDs: Class.; *Night Blooming Jazzmen* (Main.); w. Joe Marsala (Class.).

FEATHER, (BILLIE JANE LEE) LORRAINE, voc, lyricist; b. NYC, 9/10/48. Daughter of Leonard Feather. Named for her moth., who sang prof. as Jane Leslie; her mother's ex-roommate, Peggy Lee; her godmother, Billie Holiday; and the song "Sweet Lorraine." As pre-teen took pno. lessons fr. John Lewis in NYC. Raised in LA fr. 1960. Two yrs. as theater arts major at LA Community Coll., moved back to NYC late '60s to pursue career as singer; app. in concert and Broadway versions of *Jesus Christ Superstar*. Worked w. bands; sang backup for Petula Clark, Grand Funk Railroad; then own act, perf. in cabarets. Ret. to LA in '70s, work. at Parisian Room, The Little Club, Donte's. Jake Hanna recommended her to Carl Jefferson, and she rec. for Concord. Join. Ricard Perry's vocal gp., Full Swing, app. and rec. several albums w. it in the '80s. Became active as lyricist and occ. solo perf. Lyrics for "Creole Love Call" rec. by Cleo Laine as "Love Call"; lyrics for "Chelsea Bridge"; "Rockin' in Rhythm"; and Charlie Barnet's "The Right Idea," rec. by Full Swing. Favs: Holiday, Nat Cole, Sinatra. Fests: Monterey; Playboy; Kool w. Full Swing. Film: sang on soundtrack for *Dick Tracy; For the Boys*. TV: has written for *Beverly Hills 90210; Family Matters; The Days of Our Lives; Santa Barbara*. Also co-wrote songs for Disney's *Dinosaurs*. In '96 wrote lyrics for the finale of the Summer Olympics opening ceremony, "Faster, Higher, Stronger," sung by Jessye Norman. LP: Conc.; w. Full Swing (Planet; Cypress/A&M). CDs: *The Body Remembers*, released on Bean Bag, reissued on Award, w. most of the material co-written by her husband, Tony Morales, ex-dmr. w. the Rippingtons.

FEATHERSTONHAUGH, BUDDY (RUPERT EDWARD LEE), bari sax; also tnr sax, cl; b. Paris, France, 10/4/09; d. London, England, 7/12/76. Studied at sch. in Sussex, Engl. Debut w. Pat O'Malley in Hendon 1927. As a tnr. sax, he rec. w. Spike Hughes '30–1; tour. w. L. Armstrong band '32. Led own gp. when in RAF during WWII; it evolved into Radio Rhythm Club Sextet for the BBC '43–5; also pl. in Iceland '46. In late '40s, semiretired from jazz, worked as auto salesman. Then as bari. sax, led own piano-less qnt. in jazz clubs '56–8; tour. Middle East for Brit. War Office '57. One of the few Brit. jazz men of his generation to make the transition to modern jazz. Fav: Mulligan. Recs: w. Valaida Snow '35;

Benny Carter '37; own qnt. '56–8. CDs: w. Carter (Class.; Conifer); L. Feather (Class.); Spike Hughes (Kings Cross Music).

FEDCHOCK, JOHN WILLIAM, tbn, arr, comp; b. Cleveland, OH, 9/18/57. Studied at Ohio St. U. 1975–9 (B. Mus., B. Mus. Ed. '79); arr. w. Rayburn Wright at Eastman Sch. of Mus. '79–80, '85 (M. Mus. '85). Pl. and arr. w. Woody Herman Orch. '80–7; Gerry Mulligan Concert Jazz Band, Louis Bellson bb '88; Bob Belden Ens. fr. '89; Bellson bb '90. Fedchock co-led a bb w. Maria Schneider fr. '89–92. In that yr. he started his own bb. Taught at Eastman Summer Wkshp. '85, and has worked extens. as a clinician w. hs and coll. bands fr. '88. Chuck Berg called him "a melodist of note, with an absolutely gorgeous sound and a fleet, supple technique." Favs: Fontana, Slide Hampton, Rosolino, J.J. Johnson, Urbie Green; arrs: Thad Jones, Bill Holman. Fests: Japan '82; Eur. fr. '83. TV: Montreux JF '83 (Swiss TV); Woody Herman's BB Celebration '84, West Va. Jazz Fest '87 (PBS); Big Bands at Disneyland (Disney Channel); Woody Herman and the Ultimate Herd '86 (video). Fav. own solo: "Caravan" on Res. CDs: Res.; w. Herman; R. Clooney (Conc.); Belden (Sunny.; BN); Schneider (Enja).

FELD, MOREY, dms; b. Cleveland, OH, 8/15/15; d. Bow Mar, CO, 3/28/71. Self-taught on dms. from 1933. Pl. w. Ben Pollack '36; Joe Haymes '38; briefly w. Bud Freeman '40; B. Goodman '43–5, and occ. into '60s; Buddy Morrow spring '46. In that same yr., began an assoc. w. Eddie Condon that incl. work. at Condon's club '65. Worked w. B. Butterfield '52; B. Hackett '53; P. Hucko '54; ABC staff '55–60; form. own sxt. '55. Led own trio at NY World's Fair '64. Opened dms. sch. '66. In '68, moved to Calif. before join. Hucko in Denver and, in the same yr., becoming orig. dmr. in World's Greatest Jazz Band. He died in a fire at his home. Favs: Rich, Lamond. Fests: NJF '65; Colo. JP in '60s. Film: *Sweet and Lowdown* w. Goodman. Recs: w. Jess Stacy '40; T. Wilson, Slam Stewart, Norvo mid '40s. LP: Kapp '56. CDs: w. Goodman (Col.; MM); S. Getz (Roost); Wild Bill Davison (Jazz.); Freeman (Aff.).

FELDER, WILTON LEWIS, tnr sax, bs, comp; b. Houston, TX, 8/31/40. Orig. came to prominence as founding member of gp. known in 1950s as Modern Jazz Sextet, later as Nite Hawks; fr. '60 as Jazz Crusaders and fr. '72 as the Crusaders. In late '60s began to double on el-bs. and was in constant demand for rock, pop, and r & b sessions, rec. w. A. Shepp; Bobby Bryant; Blue Mitchell; Groove Holmes; Grant Green; Stanley Turrentine; Carmen McRae; Dizzy

Gillespie; et al. From the mid '80s, after the other founding members departed, Felder and Joe Sample were co-leaders of the Crusaders. The group continued to record into the early '90s incl. a reunion w. Wayne Henderson. Felder's best playing—as a hard-edged, bop-tinged, blues tenor saxophonist—took place on the Jazz Crusaders albums from the early '60s. CDs: Par; w. Crusaders (PJ; GRP).

FELDMAN, VICTOR STANLEY, pno, vib, perc, comp; b. London, England, 4/7/34; d. Los Angeles, CA, 5/12/87. Mainly self-taught through listening to bros.; was hailed as a genius when he pl. a job on dms. at age 7. Rec. debut at 8; took up pno. at 9. Stud. at London Coll. of Mus. Pl. vib. w. Carlo Krahmer at 14. Led trio w. two bros. 1941–7; guest star w. Glenn Miller AEF band '44; also w. Vic Lewis; Ted Heath; Ronnie Scott. Went to Switzerland w. Ralph Sharon '49; to India w. Eddie Carroll '53–4. Moved to US Oct. '55; tour. w. Woody Herman, Jan. '56–June '57; briefly w. Buddy DeFranco. Settled in LA, worked w. Lighthouse All-Stars, Oct. '57–Aug. '59. Stud. arr. w. Marty Paich '59. Tour. w. Cannonball Adderley '60–1. Ret. to LA; stud. film scoring w. Leith Stevens. Worked mainly in Hollywood studios, but also app. w. own trio. Accomp. Peggy Lee, incl. trips to London, Monte Carlo '61. As vib., tour. w. Benny Goodman to USSR '62. Worked w. Miles Davis '63. Turning down Davis's offer to remain w. the gp., he opted to stay in LA, where he was an active studio perf., mainly as a perc. Accomp. June Christy in London '65. In '70s, he worked often w. John Guerin, Chuck Domanico, Tom Scott, in jazz and jazz-rock contexts. His affiliations in the '80s incl. Steely Dan, Joni Mitchell, and the Generation Band w. his sons. An extremely versatile performer, particularly fluent on pno. and vib., Feldman was highly regarded by his contemporaries. Favs: Jackson, Norvo, Tatum, John Lewis, Catlett, Tiny Kahn, Roach, Rich, Kenny Clarke, Art Taylor; arrs: Ellington, Mulligan, Lewis. Polls: five magazine awards as Britain's number one vibes man; *DB* Critics new star vib. '58. Fests: Paris JF '52; Colo. JP '71; Canadian JF '74. Film: pl. on soundtrack for *Sandpiper; Harlow*; comp. two science and art films for UCLA. TV: pl. for *Peter Gunn*. Publs: *All Alone by the Vibraphone* (Gwyn Publ., Sherman Oaks, Calif.); *Musician's Guide to Chord Progression* (Try Publ., Hollywood, Calif.). Comps: "Seven Steps to Heaven," first rec. by M. Davis '63; collab. w. George Russell in writing score for ballet, *Encounter Near Venus*, perf. by Ballet Pacifica '75. CDs: Cont.; Riv.; TBA; w. C. Adderley (Land.; Pab.); Davis (Col.); S. Manne; Bob Cooper; B. Kessel; S. Rollins; L. Vinnegar (Cont.); James Clay; Sam Jones; Bill Perkins (Riv.); J.J. Johnson; Z. Sims (Pab.); Wes Montgomery (Riv.; Mile.); F. Rosolino (Spec.).

FELIX, LENNIE (LEONARD JACOBUS), pno; b. London, England, 8/16/20; d. London, 12/29/81. Started stud. pno. at age 10; infl. by Waller, Tatum, Hines. Evolved quickly as a soloist, also worked in trios and combos. Pl. w. Freddy Randall 1950. To NYC, pl. w. Red Allen; Buster Bailey; John Kirby. Refused Kirby's offer of a regular spot and ret. to London, where he join. Harry Gold '53, leaving him to tour Far East '54; Eur. '55. Pl. at Le Boeuf sur le Toit, Paris, where he replaced Garland Wilson '56. Feat. soloist w. Wally Fawkes '57–8. Work. in Vienna '59; then trav. between Engl. and the Continent in '60s and '70s. Pl. w. Nat Gonella '60. From '61 app. on numerous radio and TV shows and rec. as both soloist and trio lead. Injuries fr. being hit by a reckless driver on a London street led to his death. Recs. on Brit. Col., Nixa, Upright. LP w. Randall on Dormouse. CD: w. Bruce Turner (Lake).

FERGUSON, MAYNARD (WALTER), tpt, v-tbn, lead; b. Montreal, Que., Canada, 5/4/28; d. Ventura, CA, 8/23/06. Studied at French Cons. of Mus. in Montreal. First US app. w. Boyd Raeburn 1948; solo act at Café Society in which he pl. saxes and several brass instruments; later w. J. Dorsey. Left Canada '49; pl. w. Charlie Barnet; joined Stan Kenton Jan '50 and remained until '53, building an int'l following w. his upper register work, fantastic technique, and screaming solos. Freelanced in LA for three yrs.; led all-star bands in NYC and LA '56–7. Own 13-piece band intermittently until '67; toured Engl. w. Anglo-Amer. band, then led all-English band. Visited India '68; became disciple of J. Krishnamurti and worked at fusing jazz w. classical Indian music. Has since made annual spiritual pilgrimages to India and is Visiting Profess. of Western Music at the Rishi Valley School near Madras. In '70s, living in Ojai, Calif., enjoyed several pop rec. successes, incl. "MacArthur Park" '70, and "Gonna Fly Now," the theme from *Rocky,* '78. Disbanded his 12-piece ensemble in '84; in '86 formed a funk-jazz group, High Voltage, which he led until '88, w. minimal critical success. In '89, he organized Big Bop Nouveau, which enjoyed far better critical and commercial acceptance. Perf. at "Back To Balboa," Kenton reunion fest. in Newport Beach, Calif. '91. Ferguson came to the US jazz scene as an anomaly. Although his forays into the stratosphere helped win the *DB* poll '50–2, he later revealed a more balanced style, playing solos in the normal trumpet register and doubling effectively on v-tbn. He brought to prominence such arr. as Willie Maiden; Bill Holman; Slide Hampton; and such sidemen as Don Ellis; Lanny Morgan; Mike Fahn; and others. Was active as an educ. in clinics and wkshps. Film: soundtrack for *The Ten Commandments*. CDs: Mos.;

Conc.; Roul.; Main.; BB; Hot Shot; Intima; w. Clifford Brown, D. Washington (Em.); Kenton (Cap.); S. Rogers (BB).

FERGUSON, SHERMAN EUGENE, dms, comp; b. Philadelphia, 10/31/44; d. Los Angeles, 1/22/06. Began prof. w. Charles Earland in late 1960s. Worked w. Pat Martino; Kenny Burrell; Benny Carter; Freddie Hubbard; Eddie Harris; Shorty Rogers; Teddy Edwards; Buddy Collette; Bobby Shew; Johnny Hartman. Fests: Eur., Japan, Brazil; w. S. Rogers, Chi. JF. Rec. debut w. Pat Martino '69. TV: acted in *Days and Nights of Molly Dodd* '87. Favs: R. Haynes, Roach, DeJohnette. CDs: w. Carter (MM); Joe Wilder (Eve. Star); Shew (Pausa; Delos); Burrell (Muse); M. Wofford (Disc.); Bud Shank (Cand.; Cont.); Holly Hofmann (Capri); Bobby Bradford (SN); Harris (Timel.); Warne Marsh (Story.); Martino (Prest.; Muse).

FERRIS, GLENN ARTHUR, tbn, comp; b. Los Angeles, CA, 6/27/50. Studied classical tbn. w. several teachers 1959–68; jazz theory and improv. w. Don Ellis '64–6; John Klemmer '69. Pl. w. Ellis '66–70; Revival '69–71; Beach Boys, Tim Buckley '71; Frank Zappa's Mothers of Invention '72; Harry James '73–4; Billy Cobham '74–6; Bobby Bradford '70s. Also freelanced in various classical, pop, rock, and soul ens. Form. 10-pc. band, Celebration, which incl. Bobby Bradford; John Carter; James Newton; also duo w. Milcho Leviev '77. Moved to France '80. Rec. w. Planete Carree of saxman Jean-Pierre Debarbat. Rec. w. Tony Scott '81, then tour. Eur. w. Jack Walrath '82–3; pl. w. Orchestre National Du Jazz of Antoine Hervé '87–8; app. w. gps. of Peter Scharli; Generations, led by Didier Levallet; and Henri Texier's qt., Azur. A risk-taking improviser capable of pl. in many genres. Fests: Eur. fests w. Ellis, Cobham, Walrath. LPs w. Ellis (Col.). CDs: w. B. Altschul; Tony Scott (SN); Cobham (Atl.); F. D'Andrea (Penta.); S. Lacy (Novus; hatArt); Orchestre National Du Jazz (L. Bleu); M. Solal (Drey.); D. Frishberg (Bloom.); Walrath (Steep.).

FEZA, MONGEZI, tpt; also fl; b. Queenstown, So. Africa, 1945; d. London, England, 12/14/75. Began on tpt. at age 8. Pl. w. Ronnie Beer's Swinging City Six. Join Chris McGregor's Blue Notes in 1962, later moving to London w. the gp., after perf. at Antibes JF '64. He became involved w. the founding of McGregor's larger ens., Brotherhood of Breath, pl. important solo and ensemble roles. In '72, moved to Denmark, pl. w. Johnny Dyani and perc. Okay Temiz and rec. w. them for the Swedish Sonet label. In '73, he rec. w. his former McGregor bandmate, Dudu Pukwana, for Caroline recs. Hot, rhythmic pl., who utilized choked effects, sometimes on pocket tpt. CD: w. Blue Notes; Brotherhood of Breath (Ogun).

FIELD, GREGG, dms, comp; b. Oakland, CA, 2/21/56. Extensive freelance work in LA on *Merv Griffin* show, *Saturday Night Live*; also pl. w. Donald Byrd; Quincy Jones; Herbie Hancock; Wayne Shorter; Mel Tormé. Start. in 1981, worked several stints w. the Count Basie band before and after Basie's death. To Japan for Fujitsu-Concord JFs '89–90, w. Frank Wess–Harry Edison band. Prod. album for Ray Anthony all-star band in '90. Heard w. Bill Berry and LA bb at Hollywood concerts '91; also led his own ens., feat. several Basie alumni, in LA in the early '90s. A reliable, dynamic, big band drummer, he has taught at the U. of So. Calif. CDs: w. Basie (Pab.); Wess-Edison (Conc.).

FIELDER, ALVIN, dms; b. Meridian, MS, 11/23/35. Musical family; bro. William is Dir. of Jazz Studies at Rutgers U. Began pl. in 1948; after hs pl. w. local band of Duke Oatis; stud. perc. w. Ed Blackwell while working on pharmacy degree at Xavier U. and Tex. Southern U. In mid and late '50s worked in Houston w. r & b acts such as Lowell Fulsom, Amos Milburn, and Eddie Vinson; studio work for Duke Recs. From '59 to '68 active in Chicago w. Sun Ra Arkestra '60–1, and was charter member of the AACM, perf. w. Muhal Abrams; Roscoe Mitchell; Fred Anderson; et al. Ret. to Miss. '68, to run family pharmacy. Active in obtaining grants to bring contemporary musicians to Miss.; in '70s worked in Atlanta and Dallas w. local gps., incl. recs. w. Improvisational Arts Qnt., one of the most important new music gps. Fest: apps. in '80s in NO, Holland, France, Germany, Netherlands; also pl. at Festival Int'l de Louisiane, '91. CDs: w. Roscoe Mitchell (Del.); Charles Brackeen; Dennis Gonzales (Silk.).

FIELDS, HERBIE (HERBERT), tnr, alto, sop saxes, cl; b. Elizabeth, NJ, 5/24/19; d. Miami, FL, 9/17/58. Studied at Juilliard 1936–8. Worked w. Raymond Scott; Leonard Ware trio; Hot Lips Page. During army service led band at Ft. Dix '41–3. Upon discharge led own band, but broke it up in '44 and join. Lionel Hampton for a yr., feat. on cl. Led sess. for Savoy which marked Miles Davis's rec. debut '45. Had own band again from early '46 which rec. for RCA. Depressed over his relative inactivity in the late '50s, he committed suicide. Polls: *Esq.* New Star on alto '45. Took part in sess. at Minton's in '41 w. Page, Joe Guy, et al., some of which has been issued on Onyx and Xanadu LPs. CDs: Met. All-Stars (BB); M. Davis (Sav.); O. Pettiford (Topaz); Helen Humes (Class.); Hampton (Class.; Dec.).

FIELDS, KANSAS (CARL DONNELL), dms; b. Chapman, KS, 12/5/15; d. Chicago, IL, 5/95. Moved w. family to Chi. when he was 14; start. stud. dms. at age 15. Began pl. prof. in 1933 w. tpt. Eddie Mullens; club dates. In late '30s pl. w. Johnny Long, Jimmie Noone, Walter Fuller; w. King Kolax '40; Roy Eldridge '41; also led own band before moving to NYC. In '41–2 worked w. E. Fitzgerald; Benny Carter; Edgar Hayes; Charlie Barnet; also w. Parker, Gillespie at Minton's '42. Served in marines '42–5; after discharge join. Cab Calloway '45; then gigged w. Eddie Condon; Willie "The Lion" Smith; again w. Eldridge. Pl. w. Sidney Bechet at Jimmy Ryan's '47; Gillespie '49; own gp. at Café Society Downtown '51. Tour. Eur. w. Babs Gonzales and M. Mezzrow '53. Settled in France in '54; worked w. other US mus., incl. such expatriates and visitors as Albert Nicholas; Bill Coleman; Peanuts Holland; and at the Brussels World's Fair w. Bechet '58; apps. at many other Eur. fests. Ret. to Chi. '64, active as studio mus. and perf. w. local gps. through late '70s. Infl. by Sid Catlett. Recs: w. L. Hampton; Mezzrow; Buck Clayton. CDs: w. Gillespie; Joe Williams (Sav.); Bud Powell (Disc.; MS); Mel Powell (Comm.); E. Condon (Jass); C. Hawkins (Stash).

FINCH, CANDY (OTIS, JR.), dms; b. ca. 1934; d. Seattle, WA, 7/13/82. Father, tnr. sax Otis Finch. Pl. in Det. clubs in 1950s. Pl. and rec. w. Shirley Scott '61, '64; Stanley Turrentine '62, '64; Milt Jackson '65; D. Gillespie '66–9. Other recs. w. Billy Mitchell '62; Al Grey '62–3; G. Ammons '71. Worked as a studio mus. in LA, before moving to Seattle '78, where he led combo. CDs: w. Turrentine (BN; Imp.); Gillespie (Imp.); Scott (Prest.).

FINCK, DAVID E., bs, el-bs; b. Rochester, NY, 8/26/58. Parents both amateur mus. Stud. w. Sam Goradetzer and Michael Shahan of Phila. Symph.; grad. fr. Eastman Sch. of Mus. 1980. Pl. w. Woody Herman '80–1, then moved to NYC. Freelance '81–9, incl. work w. Joe Williams; Annie Ross; Mel Lewis Orch.; Al Cohn; Ernestine Anderson; Rosemary Clooney; Tom Harrell; Jerry Dodgion; Phil Woods; Clark Terry; Al Grey; etc. Pl. w. Paquito D'Rivera Ens.; Steve Kuhn Trio since '89; also pl. w. Freddie Hubbard; Makoto Ozone; Eddie Daniels. Favs: P. Chambers, S. LaFaro, R. Brown, R. Carter, M. Moore. Fests: Eur. since '81; Japan since '91; also Panama '90; Israel '91; Argentina '92. Film: cameo app. in *Big* w. Tom Hanks. TV: *Today* w. R. Clooney. CDs: w. Kuhn (Conc.; Res.); P. D'Rivera (Mess.; Chesky); J. Basile (Chesky); C. Roditi (Mile.).

FINDERS, MATT (MATTHEW KEN), tbn, bs tbn, tba; b. Livermore, CA, 2/12/60. B.A. in mus., San Jose State U. Pl. w. Clark Terry band 1981; Chuck Israels '81; Mel Lewis Orch. '83–8; T. Akiyoshi '84–92; Benny Goodman '84–5; Slide Hampton World of Trombones '86; Cologne Radio Big Band '89; Buck Clayton bb '90–l; AJO '90–1; Smithsonian Repertory Band '91–2; off and on w. Loren Schoenberg bb '83–92. Moved to LA to become member of Branford Marsalis house band on *Tonight Show* May '92. Favs: Frank Rosolino, Jack Teagarden, J.J. Johnson. CDs: w. Schoenberg; Goodman (MM); Grover Mitchell (Ken); Akiyoshi (Col.; Ken); B. Mintzer (dmp); P. Erskine (Den.).

FINEGAN, BILL (WILLIAM J.), lead, arr, pno; also comp; b. Newark, NJ, 4/3/17. Parents, sist. and bro. all pl. pno. Stud. priv.; also at hs and coll.; later at Paris Cons. While in coll., form. student band; first prof. work w. own pno. trio in a restaurant. His first real break in the arr. field came through Tommy Dorsey who, after buying Finegan's score for "Lonesome Road," played it for Glenn Miller, who offered Finegan a job in 1938; stayed w. Miller as staff arr. until '42, arr. some of the band's biggest hits, incl. "Little Brown Jug"; "Sunrise Serenade"; "Song of the Volga Boatman"; also wrote music for films feat. the band, *Sun Valley Serenade* '41; *Orchestra Wives* '42. Work. for T. Dorsey as arr. on and off to '52, incl. music for film *The Fabulous Dorseys* '47; arrs. for Dorsey incl. "Bingo, Bango, Boffo" '46, "Pussy Willow" '49. Stud. w. Stefan Wolpe '47–8. Lived in France and Engl. '48–50, further stud. at Paris Cons. and in Engl. In '52, join. forces w. Eddie Sauter to form Sauter-Finegan bb, which remained together until '57 and was notable for its varied instrumentation—extra percussion, English horn, piccolo, bs. cl.—and generally adventuresome spirit. Collab. w. Sauter again in '59, writing jingles for TV and radio. Cont. to write commercials through the '60s. In '70s, wrote arrs. for the Glenn Miller orch. and the Mel Lewis orch. Sauter-Finegan reunion concert at Town Hall '86. Taught jazz stud. at Univ. of Bridgeport, Conn., through late '80s. Fav. arrs: Sauter, Sy Oliver, Gerry Mulligan. Never really active as a soloist, Finegan's fav. own work on record is a chest solo on Sauter-Finegan's "Midnight Sleigh Ride." "I beat on my chest to simulate the sound of a sleigh horse running on hard-packed snow; this is probably my finest effort on wax—or snow." Comps: for Sauter-Finegan, "Doodletown Fifers." CDs: w. Sauter-Finegan; arrs. for Miller; Dorsey (BB).

FISCHER, CLARE D., pno, org, kybds, cello, cl and sax; b. Durand, MI, 10/22/28. Musical family, bro. an arr. and bass tptr. Raised in Mich.; started on tba. and vln.; pno. at age 9; began comp. at 12. Took up cello, cl., sax at hs in Grand Rapids. Began arr. in teens, writing book for own band 1944. Completed studies at Mich. St. U. w. B. Mus. '52; M. Mus. '55. Moved to LA '57. Pnst. and mus. dir. for Hi-Los '57–62, incl. Eur. tour '58. Cond./arr. for D. Gillespie's album *A Portrait of Duke Ellington* '60. His first trio LP, *First Time Out*, revealed a unit heavily influenced by Bill Evans and Scott La Faro. From early '60s, active in Latin music w. Cal Tjader; feat. on some of the first American bossa nova recordings, innovating use of organ and other electric kybds. Led several gps., incl. Salsa Picante '78; 2+2, which incl. voc. qt., early '80s. In late '80s an accident restricted his mus. activities but he became very active again in the '90s, writing for a wide variety of perfs. fr. Natalie Cole and Prince to Richard Stoltzman and Paul McCartney. Feat. at NAJE convention, Miami '92. Best known compositions are "Pensativa" and "Elizete." Fav. arrs: Strayhorn, Mulligan. Fest: North Sea '94. CDs: JMI; Disc.; Conc.; w. Tjader (Fant.); Gillespie (Verve).

FISHKIN, ARNOLD (Fishkind), bs; b. Bayonne, NJ, 7/20/19. Raised in Freeport, Long Island; was a childhood neighbor and friend of Chubby Jackson. Start. on vln. at age 8; bs. at 14. Pl. w. Bunny Berigan's orch. 1937; J. Teagarden '40–1; w. Les Brown before serving in army '42–6. After discharge pl. w. Dick Stabile, Jerry Wald '45–6. Join. Lennie Tristano trio in Freeport '46. Went to West Coast w. Charlie Barnet, pl. w. him '46–7; settled in Calif. Pl. w. the Butch Stone Band in Hollywood, sidemen incl. Stan Getz, Shorty Rogers. Ret. to NYC, rejoin. Tristano '48–9; Lee Konitz '49–51. Freelance radio work '50; through '50s and '60s; staff mus. at ABC and CBS; also many rec. sess., incl. Don Elliott; Billy Bauer; Mel Powell; Howard McGhee; Hank Jones. Ret. to LA '66, active as studio mus. Favs: Blanton, R. Brown. CDs: w. Teagarden (Jass); Konitz (Prest.); Tristano (Prest.; Cap.; Key. Coll., Em.) ; C. Jackson (Em.); M. Ferguson; C. Hawkins (BB); C. Parker (Stash); S. Hasselgard (Drag.).

FITZGERALD, ELLA, voc; b. Newport News, VA, 4/25/17; d. Beverly Hills, CA, 6/15/96. Raised in Yonkers, N.Y., where she sang with a school glee club but was more interested in dancing. She planned to dance at an amateur show but changed her mind, due to nerves, at the last minute and sang. Appearing in several amateur hours, she won first prize, a week's work at the Harlem Opera House. Soon after, in 1932, her mother died and she went to an orphanage but then lived with an aunt in Harlem. Singing at

another amateur show in '34 at the Apollo Theater, she was heard by Benny Carter and Bardu Ali, conductor of the Chick Webb orchestra. They recommended her to Webb, with whom she soon earned great popularity, mainly at the Savoy Ballroom. She made her record debut w. Webb on "Love and Kisses" in June '35 and had her first major hit in '38 w. "A-Tisket, A-Tasket," on which she collaborated w. arr. Van Alexander in adapting the old nursery rhyme. After Webb's death in '39 she became nominal leader of the band for two years. She then appeared as a soloist in clubs and theaters. Fr. '46 she worked often w. Norman Granz, app. on his annual tours and visiting Eur. and Japan w. his Jazz at the Philharmonic troupe. Her accompanying trio was led by bassist Ray Brown, her husband from '47 to '53. Her recs. for Decca incl. hit-making collaborations w. the Ink Spots and Louis Jordan, and ranged from inferior pop material to a sublime Gershwin duet album w. Ellis Larkins. Late in '55 she ended her twenty-year affiliation w. Decca, took on Granz as her personal manager, and soon after began recording for his new Verve label. Under his guidance she appeared in person and on records w. Duke Ellington; Count Basie; Oscar Peterson; Joe Pass; Louis Armstrong; et al. Granz recorded her singing Cole Porter; Jerome Kern; Irving Berlin; Rodgers & Hart; the Gershwins; Duke Ellington; Harold Arlen; and Johnny Mercer. These "Song Book" albums helped immeasurably in establishing her w. a broader audience. She was presented in concert w. the Boston Pops in '72 and by '75 had app. w. more than forty symphony orchs throughout the US.

Ella Fitzgerald's talent established her as the ultimate jazz singer, and the favorite female singer of virtually all her contemporaries, who admired her bell-like tonal clarity, great flexibility and range, and brilliant rhythmic style. She was the first singer to make completely effective use of bebop-oriented scat variations; her versions of "Lady Be Good," "Flying Home," "How High the Moon" and others were widely influential. Her main piano accomps. were Paul Smith, beginning in '56 and continuing off and on until the end of her career; and Tommy Flanagan '63–5; '68–78. From the early '70s Fitzgerald was plagued by poor health, starting with a series of eye problems in '71. In the '80s she suffered from other illnesses, including a major heart condition and diabetes. By '89 she had pared down her schedule to very occasional concerts. Despite a widening vibrato, much of the brilliance of her earlier work could still be heard, and her explorations in the upper register were undiminished. By the mid '90s, confined to a wheel chair, she had ceased to perform. Orig. infl: Connee Boswell. Fests: NJF-NY; Nice; Juan-Les-

Pins; Montreux; Baalbek, Lebanon; some of these perfs. were nights devoted solely to her. Films: *Pete Kelly's Blues* '55; *St. Louis Blues* '58; *Let No Man Write My Epitaph* '60. TV: two Frank Sinatra specials; Timex special; own shows for BBC; Carol Burnett show, etc. Video: *Ella and Duke at Antibes*. Polls and Awards: *DB* Readers poll starting in '37 and often through the decades; the *DB* Critics poll often fr. its inception in the '60s and '70s; the *Esq.* Gold award in '46 and Silver award in '47; US National Medal of the Arts '87; French Commandeur Des Arts et Lettres '90. Book: *Ella Fitzgerald*, Stuart Nicholson (Victor Gollancz) '93. CDs: Dec.; Verve; Pab.; Cap.; w. B. Goodman (BB); C. Webb (Dec.); B. Rich (Hep); Basie; Ellington; C. Parker; Peterson (Verve); J. Pass; JATP (Pab.).

FLANAGAN, TOMMY LEE, pno; b. Detroit, 3/16/30; d. NYC, 11/16/01. Began on cl. at age 6, sw. to pno. at 11. Made prof. debut w. 1945, then pl. w. Lucky Thompson, Milt Jackson, Rudy Rutherford '46–8; Billy Mitchell, Thad Jones, Elvin Jones late '40s. In army '51–3. Pl. w. Mitchell, Kenny Burrell '54–5. Moved to NYC '56; pl. w. Oscar Pettiford, Ella Fitzgerald '56; J.J. Johnson '56–7; Miles Davis '57; own gps. fr. '57; Johnson '58; Tyree Glenn, Sweets Edison '59–60; Coleman Hawkins '61; Jim Hall '61–2; Fitzgerald '63–5; Tony Bennett '66; Fitzgerald '68–78. Flanagan, who made a reputation as an outstanding accomp. through his assoc. w. Fitzgerald worked almost exclusively in a trio format fr. '78. His trios, perf. internationally, incl. such rhythm teams as Geo. Mraz and Kenny Washington; Peter Washington–K. Washington; and P. Washington w. Lewis Nash. He had a wide-ranging repertoire, steeped in Ellington, Monk, the bebop canon, and the American Songbook, and was a particularly acute interpreter of Strayhorn, Dameron, and Thad Jones. His combination of harmonic sophistication and lyric swing, transported by a silken touch, placed him in the upper echelon of jazz pnsts. Favs: Tatum, Bud Powell, Nat King Cole, Teddy Wilson. Polls: *DB* Critics & Readers; *JT*. Awards: Danish Jazzpar '92; NEA Jazz Master '96. Fests: all major fr. late '50s. CDs: BN; Verve; Timel.; Enja; Gal.; Prest.; Pab.; Den.; DIW; Sav.; Evid.; Flanagan–Hank Jones (Gal.); Flanagan–K. Barron (Den.); w. Fitzgerald; Benny Carter; Gillespie (Pab.); Burrell; M. Davis; G. Ammons; D. Gordon; B. Ervin (Prest.); S. Rollins (Prest.; Mile.); J. Coltrane (Atl.); C. Hawkins (Prest.; Verve; Imp.); Steve Coleman (Novus); P. Woods (Prest.; Cand.; Chesky); C. Terry; Mingus; Benny Bailey; Dolphy (Cand.); J.J. Johnson; G. Mulligan (Col.); Red Rodney; K. Clarke; C. Fuller; Wilbur Harden (Sav.); Wes Montgomery; M. Jackson; J. Heath; P.J. Jones (Riv.).

FLANIGAN, PHIL (PHILIP H.), bs; b. Geneva, NY, 6/28/56. Father is amateur saxist and clst. Began on pno., then tbn. and gtr. before sw. to bs. Stud. at Eastman Sch. of Mus. w. Oscar Zimmerman 1972–4; New Engl. Cons. '74–5. Pl. w. Chris Flory '75; Widespread Jazz Orch. '76; Scott Hamilton since '76; Bob Wilber '77–81; Benny Goodman '77–83; Smithsonian Repertory Ens. '80–1; Warren Vaché '81–3; John Bunch '83–9; Red Norvo '84; Louis Bellson '88–9; Ira Sullivan '90–2. Wilber describes his work as "the most melodic bass solos in jazz." Favs: Pettiford, LaFaro, Ray Brown. Fests: Eur., Japan; JVC-NY '98. Film: app. in *The Bell Jar* '79. TV: *Today* w. S. Hamilton '79, '81; *Moon Over Miami*, ABC '93. CDs: *New York Toast* on own label, Philophile; w. Hamilton; Vaché; F. Phillips; Flory; R. Clooney (Conc.); Bunch (Arb.; Conc.); Eddie Higgins (Sunny.); K. Davern (MM); Wilber (Arb.; Chiaro.; Bodes.); Widespread Depression (Stash).

FLAX, MARTY (Martin Flachsenhaar), bari sax; b. NYC, 10/7/24; d. Las Vegas, NV, 5/3/72. Pl. w. Chubby Jackson, 1949; W. Herman '50; Louis Jordan '51; P. Rugolo '54; L. Millinder, Perez Prado, Les Elgart '56. Tour. Middle East and So. Amer. w. D. Gillespie orch. for State Dept. '56; Woody Herman St. Dept. tour of So. Amer. '58. Own gp. at Café Society '57; tnr. sax w. C. Thornhill '59; Buddy Rich '66–7. From the late '60s, pl. in LV hotel and lounge bands. Recs: w. C. Jackson, "Father Knickerbocker"; Sam Most. CDs: w. Gillespie (Verve; CAP); w. Jackson in *The Jazz Arrangers, vol. 2* (Col.).

FLEMMING, HERB (Niccolaiih El-Michelle), tbn, voc; b. Butte, MT, 4/5/1898; d. NYC, 10/3/76. Of North African descent. Stud. mus., pl. mello. and euph. at Dobbs Chauncey Sch., Dobbs Ferry, N.Y. 1910–13; tbn., cello, theory at Frank Damrosch's Cons., NYC '19; later stud. at St. Cecilia Acad., Florence; Univ. di Roma, Italy. Join. Jim Europe's 15th NY Nat. Guard band '17; trav. to France in Europe's 369th US Infantry band. Discharged fr. service in NYC '19. Worked w. Fred Tunstall '21; Lafayette Theater orch. '22. Join. Sam Wooding pit band for *Chocolate Kiddies* revue, Berlin '25, and subsequently tour. Eur. w. him '25; also S. Amer. '27. With Lew Leslie's *Blackbirds* revue, NYC, London, Paris '29. Led International Rhythm Aces in Eur. '29; rejoin. Wooding in Berlin '30; then led gp. for Josephine Baker's *Joie de Paris* revue; tour. w. own revue to Buenos Aires. Between '33–5, pl. Paris; Calcutta; San Remo, Italy. App. as voc. in Berlin '35–7; also served as interpreter for US Olympic Team. Join. Fats Waller in Chi. late '40s, worked w. him on and off to '42. After pl. w. Noble Sissle, went to Calif., worked as an IRS agent '43–9. Mus. engagements during this period incl. apps. in films, *Pillow to Post*; *No Time for Romance*. Ret. to full-time pl. and singing NYC '49, first as freelance, then w. Red Allen '53–8. To Spain '64, perf. throughout country; also in Italy and Germ. Ret. to NYC '76. Stylistically a transitional figure between the tbn. pioneers, such as Kid Ory, and later, more sophisticated players such as Jimmy Harrison. Recs: w. J. Europe '19; Johnny Dunn '21; Perry Bradford '24; Wooding '25; Freddie Johnson '33; Waller '42; Red Allen '55 '60. CD: Waller (BB).

FLORENCE, BOB (ROBERT CHASE), pno, comp, arr, lead; b. Los Angeles, CA, 5/20/32. Mother a pnst. for silent movies. Began stud. pno. bef. he was 4. Gave first recital at age 7 and cont. classical stud. until 18. First arrs. were written while a student at LA City Coll., where he stud. w. Bob MacDonald in early 1950s. Stud. comp. w. Dr. Wesley LaViolette. Wrote two arrs. for Harry James rec. date. Comp., arr. for Alvino Rey '56–7; Les Brown '56. First prominent when his arrangement of "Lazy River" was a hit for Si Zentner 1961. Arr. for many jazz and blues artists, incl. Stan Kenton; Louis Bellson; Buddy Rich; Jimmy Witherspoon; Sergio Mendes; et al. Wrote for TV shows, incl. Red Skelton, Dean Martin, Andy Williams. Mus. dir. for Vicki Carr '73–7. Own bands in '60s. From '78 has led big band, the Bob Florence Limited Edition, in LA and is a favored accomp. for many singers. Florence's craftsman-like charts never fail to swing and provide excellent showcases for his soloists. Serves as clinician, adjudicator, or guest instructor for coll. mus. programs. Favs: Ellington, Holman, Brookmeyer. CDs: Disc.; USA; MAMA; FS.

FLORES, CHUCK (CHARLES WALTER), dms, perc; b. Orange, CA, 1/5/35. Raised in Santa Ana, Calif. Fath. prof. gtr. Stud. w. Shelly Manne 1952–58 and two yrs. w. Murray Spivack. Rec. debut w. Shorty Rogers band. Pl. w. Woody Herman '54–55, incl. Eur. tour; Bud Shank Qt. '56–57, then w. Art Pepper; Claude Williamson. Australian w. Stan Kenton '58; Mexico w. LA Four '75. Pl. w. Akiyoshi–Tabackin Orch.; Laurindo Almeida; Bill Perkins; Med Flory; Tony Rizzi; George Van Eps; Joe Diorio. Has presented "History of Jazz" concerts at schools since '60s w. qt. incl. Bob Summers, Gordon Brisker, Bob Magnusson, and others. Favs: Elvin Jones, Steve Gadd. Rec. w. Cy Touff (PJ); Al Cohn (RCA) '55; own qnt. for Conc. '77. CDs: w. Almeida; Touff (PJ); Pepper (BN).

FLORY, CHRIS (CHRISTOPHER GLEN), gtr; b. NYC, 11/13/53. Primarily self-taught, w. eight mos.

of lessons in NYC 1971. Pl. rock and blues fr. age 13, then jazz gigs w. Scott Hamilton in Providence, R.I., and upstate N.Y. Pl. w. Hamilton since '75; Flip Phillips, Illinois Jacquet, Hank Jones–Milt Hinton '76; Jo Jones '76–81; Bob Wilber '77–80; Buddy Tate '78–80; Benny Goodman '78–83; Ruby Braff '82–5; Maxine Sullivan '83–6; Widespread Jazz Orch. since '83; Goodman '86; Judy Carmichael since '86; Buck Clayton bb '88–92; Loren Schoenberg bb since '89; Oliver Jackson '90; Panama Francis '91; also own gps. since '74. Flory has taught gtr. priv. since '75. Favs: C. Christian, W. Montgomery, Bill Jennings. Fests: Eur. since '79; Japan '83, '85, '86 w. Hamilton. TV: PBS w. Bob Wilber '85–9; also various w. Goodman. CDs: Conc.; D-T; w. Hamilton; R. Clooney; Maxine Sullivan (Conc.); Braff (Phon.; Conc.); Phillips (Conc.; Chiaro.); Wilber (Chiaro.).

FLORY, MED (MEREDITH IRWIN), alto sax, comp, voc; b. Logansport, IN, 8/27/26. Studied cl. priv. After Air Corps, B.A. in Philosophy at U. of Indiana 1950; then joined Claude Thornhill, feat. on cl. Later pl. w. Art Mooney; lead tnr. sax w. Woody Herman '53; led own band, NYC '54. Relocated to LA '56; app. as singer on Ray Anthony TV series '56–7 led own rehearsal band at first Monterey Fest '58. Became active as film and TV actor incl. roles in *Mannix; Lassie; Bonanza; Policewoman*; also wrote and doctored motion picture scripts. Early in '72, w. Buddy Clark, he developed the concept of Supersax. Group made its debut at Donte's in No. Hollywood, Nov. '72. Tour. Canada '74; Japan, Jan. '75. Fests: Newport West, Concord, Monterey '73; Orange Coast '74. LPs: w. own bb, Jazz Wave (Jubilee); w. Thornhill (Trend); Supersax (MPS; Col.). CDs: w. Supersax (Cap.).

FOLDS, CHUCK (CHARLES WESTON), pno; b. Cambridge, MA, 5/4/38. Grew up in Evanston, Ill., stud. w. Northwestern U. faculty. Att. Yale U. 1957–60, then stud. classical pno. w. Richard McClanahan in NYC '60s. Pl. in concerts w. Yale Jazz Band feat. Chet Baker, Kenny Clarke, Stan Getz '56–60. Worked w. Danny Alvin at Basin St., Chi. '57. Moved to NYC '60; pl. w. Joe Thomas, Ruby Braff, Pee Wee Russell, Max Kaminsky at Eddie Condon's and Metropole early '60s; Village Stompers '63–4; Peanuts Hucko, Geo. Wettling '64; Shorty Baker, Conrad Janis, Red Allen '65. Editor for Amer. Heritage Pub. Co. '65–9. Pl. w. Bob Crosby, Tony Parenti '60s; Roy Eldridge at Jimmy Ryan's '71–3; Bobby Hackett '73–4; Wild Bill Davison, Jimmy McPartland, Buck Clayton–Maxine Sullivan, Countsmen, Joe Venuti, Buddy Tate, etc. '70s. Solo pno. at the Cookery '74–80. Pl. w. Maxine Sullivan

'74–5; World's Greatest Jazz Band '75–80; Doc Cheatham fr. '75; Buck Clayton, Cheatham, Vic Dickenson, Johnny Mince at Crawdaddy '77–9. Gigs at West End w. Cheatham; Earle Warren; Percy France; Russell Procope; Franc Williams; also solo pno. at Ryan's and Condon's late '70s. Trio and solo at Hors D'Oeuvrerie at World Trade Center '80–90; freelanced fr. '90 w. Bucky Pizzarelli; Warren Vaché; Joel Helleny; Harlem Blues and Jazz Band; at Cajun restaurant w. Jon Seiger. Folds app. w. Cheatham at Sweet Basil Sunday brunch fr. '80; also other gigs w. Cheatham. Has led Sweet Basil brunch since Cheatham's death in '97. He is a freq. perf. in the NYU Highlights in Jazz series, and was a feat. soloist in '88 concert, *Satch 'N Fats*. Effective stride player, whose primary infl. was Donald Lambert, and valued accomp. to singers. Fests: NJF-NY w. Eldridge '73; Bob Crosby, WGJB '75; JVC-NY w. Cheatham and solo pno. '91; Nice '91; Sarasota; Toronto '92. CDs: Arb.; w. Cheatham (Col.); Rick Fay (Arb.).

FONTANA, CARL CHARLES, tbn; b. Monroe, LA, 7/18/28; d. Las Vegas, 10/10/03. Studied w. fath., a saxist; pl. in his band 1941–5. First prominent w. Woody Herman '50–2; later w. Al Belletto '52–3 and '57–8; Lionel Hampton '54; Hal McIntyre '54–5; Stan Kenton '55–6; Kai Winding '56–7. Worked in show bands in Las Vegas from '57; tour. w. Herman in '50s and '60s. With Benny Goodman in LV '66; many jazz parties in Colorado, Texas, etc. In LA, pl. with Supersax and Louis Bellson; gigs and recs. w. World's Greatest Jazz Band; co-led gp. w. Jake Hanna '75; tour. Japan w. Georgie Auld late '70s. Despite the limited quantity of his jazz work, due to his LV residency, Fontana was regarded as the most fluid, innovative trombonist after J.J. Johnson and Kai Winding. CDs: TNC-Jazz; Up.; Hanna/Fontana (Conc.); w. Herman (Disc.); Don Sickler (Up.); Kenton (Cap.); M. Solal (Vogue); B. Shew (MAMA).

FORD, JIMMY (JAMES MARTIN), alto sax; also voc, cl; b. Houston, TX, 6/16/27; d. Houston, 3/6/94. Began on cl., then alto sax in Houston. Pl. w. Johnny "Scat" Davis orch. 1946–7; Milt Larkin '47–8. Toured Midwest w. K. Winding, Jan. '48. Pl. tnr. sax w. Tadd Dameron Sxt. at Royal Roost, NYC, April-Aug. '48. Ret. to Houston but came to NYC again fall '49, as alto saxist. Pl. w. Red Rodney March-Nov. '51 and rec. w. him. App. w. Bud Powell Sxt. on various Monday nights at Birdland, May '51–Aug. '52. After several yrs. in Houston join. Maynard Ferguson as lead alto and featured soloist, doubling as "boy singer," '57–60. Ret. to Houston once more where he pl. w. Arnett Cobb, Eddie Vinson, et al., and led own gp. w. tpt. Stephen Fulton. During the earlier part of his career he also perf. w. Boyd Raeburn; Shorty Sherock; Shelly Manne; D. Gillespie; G. Mulligan; L. Hampton. Tour. Eur. w. Cobb, Calvin Owens '86. Favs: Charlie Parker, Sonny Stitt. CDs: Champion; w. Red Rodney in *Prestige First Sessions, Vol. 3* (Prest.); Ferguson (Mos.).

FORD, JOE (JAMES ALLEN), alto, sop saxes, comp, arr, pno; b. Buffalo, NY, 5/7/47. Aunt pl. alto sax; many other mus. in family. Stud. in Buffalo publ. sch.; then at Central St. U., B.S. in mus. ed. 1968. Also stud. sax w. John Sedola; Robert Enoch; Ken McIntyre; Jackie McLean; Frank Foster; pno. w. Robert Roseboro; Zenobia Powell Perry; perc. w. Joe Chambers. Pl. and rec. w. Sam Jones; Lester Bowie; McCoy Tyner; Jimmy Owens; Idris Muhammed; Rey Scott; Charles Fambrough; John Blake; Jerry Gonzalez's Fort Apache Band; Larry Willis; Avery Sharpe; collective gp. Birthright. Also app. w. symph. orchs. incl. Buffalo, Rochester, Milwaukee. Ford has taught at Central St. U. '66; Buffalo publ. schs. '68–72; Buffalo publ. library '74–5; Williamsburg Mus. Center, Bklyn. fr. '80; Orange, N.J. Board. of Educ. '83–8; Mind Builders Creative Arts Sch., Bronx '83–8. Clinician w. Buffalo Jazz Ens. fr. '74. Currently leads the Black Art Sax. Qt. and The Thing bb. Pl. w. Chico O'Farrill bb '96. Rec. *Meet the Composer* grants in '90, '91. Favs: Bechet, J. McLean, Coltrane; arr: Quincy Jones. Fests: all major w. M. Tyner; J. Gonzalez. CDs: w. M. Tyner (Mile.; Birdology); J. Blake; J. Gonzalez (Sunny.); Malachi Thompson (Del.); L. Willis (Steep.); R. Burrage (Sound Hills).

FORD, RICKY (RICHARD ALLEN), tnr sax; b. Boston, 3/4/54. Started on dms.; took up tenor sax 1969, inspired by Rahsaan Roland Kirk. Stud. at New Engl. Cons. w. Bill Saxton; rec. w. Ran Blake. Tour. w. Duke Ellington Orch. under Mercer Ellington '74–6. Replaced George Adams in Charles Mingus band '76 and began gigging as leader '77. In '79 join. Mingus alumni gp. led by Dannie Richmond, but from '80s worked mainly as a leader; also as sideman w. L. Hampton '81; Mingus Dynasty, incl. Eur. tours '82; Abdullah Ibrahim '86; Beaver Harris and, in '90s, w. Pete LaRoca Sims. Has taught at Brandeis U. A powerful and fluent soloist showing links to Hawkins; D. Gordon; Rollins. Debut album for New World '77. CDs: Cand.; Muse; w. R. Blake; S. Lacy; Mingus Dynasty; G. Russell; M. Waldron (SN); Richard Davis (Hep; Sw. Bas.); Hampton; D. Richmond (Timel.); Mingus (Rhino; Atl.); M. Tyner (Mile.); Ibrahim (Enja); P. Sims (BN).

FORD, ROBBEN LEE, gtr; b. Woodlake, CA, 12/16/51. Father pl. country music on gtr., hca. in

Wyoming. Stud. sax at age 11 in hs; self-taught on gtr. fr. 13. Moved to SF 1970; form. Charles Ford band (named for his father) w. bro. Pat; also worked w. Charlie Musselwhite's Blues Band '70. Bro. Mark join. Charles Ford band; rec. for Arhoolie. Pl. w. Jimmy Witherspoon '72–3; tour. w. Tom Scott's LA Express backing Joni Mitchell, and w. George Harrison *Dark Horse* tour '74. Recs. w. Barbra Streisand and Kenny Loggins '74. Form. Yellowjackets w. Russell Ferrante, Jimmy Haslip and Ricky Lawson '78; studio session work '79–82; pl. and rec. as soloist w. Michael McDonald '84–5. Tour. Japan w. Sadao Watanabe '85 and '87; pl. w. Miles Davis '86. From late '80s perf. and rec. w. own groups. A strong blues-based gtr. stylist, Ford began to concentrate on pop-oriented vocal music in the '90s. Fests: major fests w. Witherspoon. TV: PBS, *One of a Kind* '70s. CDs: WB; GRP; Avenue; Stretch.

FORESYTHE, REGINALD, comp, arr, pno; b. London, England, 5/28/07; d. London, 12/23/58. Began on pno. at age 8; later pl. for dances and accomp. singers. Worked w. various film companies in Calif. 1920s. In '30 went to Chi. where he wrote Earl Hines's theme song, "Deep Forest." Ret. to London, app. at the Café de la Paix w. 10-piece band '33. Ret. to NYC '34 and was guest artist w. Paul Whiteman. During this trip, he made many recs. for Col. w. B. Goodman; Toots Mondello; Hymie Shertzer; John Kirby; et al. Ret. to London '35, app. at the 400 Club w. own orch., as well as in a Brit. film. After serving as an intelligence officer in RAF during WWII, he pl. in various clubs in London and environs. One of the most original arrs. of his time, he was among the first to make use of woodwinds in jazz. Comps: "Dodging a Divorcee"; "Serenade to a Wealthy Widow"; "Southern Holiday: a Phantasy of Negro Moods."

FORMAN, BRUCE LLOYD, gtr; b. Springfield, MA, 5/14/56. Studied pno. for six yrs. but sw. to gtr. in 1970. Became interested in jazz through listening to saxists and tptrs. In SF area in the '70s, stud. w. Jackie King at Poly Tech HS. Pl. w. bs. Ratzo Harris; pno. Smith Dobson; then other local gps. Gigged in NYC w. Roland Hanna and Sam Jones '72. Pl. w. Richie Cole '78–82, then form. own gps. incl. one w. Bobby Hutcherson, George Cables '85. Pl. and/or rec. w. Eddie Jefferson; Freddie Hubbard; Ray Brown; Joe Farrell; Tom Harrell; Mark Murphy; Grover Washington. Pl. in Eur., Japan. Has cond. seminars in universities and hs., incl. Stanford; U. of North Carolina; UC Berkeley; No. Texas U. Favs: W. Montgomery, G. Benson, Grant Green, Joe Pass. Fest: Monterey '83, w. Mundell Lowe, John Collins,

Ron Eschete. CDs: Conc.; w. Dave Eshelman (SB); Hutcherson (Land.).

FORMAN, MITCHEL, pno, kybds.; b. Brooklyn, NY, 1/24/56. Lessons at age 7; late stud. at coll. and Manh. Sch. of Mus. 1974–78. After pl. w. rock bands in hs, join. Clem De Rosa bb at 16. First prominent w. Gerry Mulligan Qt. and bb '78–80; Stan Getz '81–83; John McLaughlin Mahavishnu Orch. '84–86; regularly w. Wayne Shorter from '87. Also gigs during '80s and early '90s w. Phil Woods; John Scofield; Mike Stern; Astrud Gilberto; Mel Tormé; Gary Burton; Pat Metheny; Carla Bley. Own trio in '90s; also w. jazz-rock band Metro. Favs: H. Hancock, Kenny Werner, Keith Jarrett. Fests: solo pno. at NJF '80. Rec. *Now & Then: A Tribute to Bill Evans* w. sidemen Eddie Gomez and Jack DeJohnette for Novus '92. CDs: Lip.; SN; Novus; AMM-Jazzline; w. G. Burton (GRP); Bill Evans-ts. (JC; Lip.); Getz (Em.); McLaughlin (Verve); Scofield (Gram.); Tony Smith (BN); Giulio Visibelli (Spl.).

FORMANEK, MICHAEL GEORGE, bs, comp; b. San Francisco, CA, 5/7/58. Began on gtr. and el-bs. but stopped pl. el-bs. in 1983. Stud. bs. priv. '73–83, then stud. comp. w. Robert Aldridge '89–90. Began prof. career w. Bishop Norman Williams after Williams pl. a concert w. Formanek's hs stage band '74. Was introduced to Eddie Henderson, Woody Shaw, Dave Liebman, etc. by Williams at SF jam sessions. Pl. w. Williams '74–6; Henderson '76; Joe Henderson '76–7; Mark Isham '76–8; Dave Liebman '77–9. Moved to NYC '78, pl. w. Herbie Mann '79–80; Media Band at West Germ. Radio, Cologne, Feb. '80–Jan. '81; Michael Franks '81; own gp., Gallery '82–3; Dave Friedman since '82; Dave Samuels '82–3; Stan Getz '83–4; Toshiko Akiyoshi–Lew Tabackin '83–4; Gerry Mulligan '85–6; Freddie Hubbard '86–90; Fred Hersch '88–91; Terumasa Hino since '89; Mingus Dynasty bb fr. '91. Also own gps. w. Tim Berne, Greg Osby since '90. Taught bs. and gp. improv. at LIU '88–9. Favs: Mingus, Dave Holland, Charlie Haden. Fests: Eur. since '79; Asia since '81; So. Amer. '85. TV: Eur. TV w. D. Friedman, F. Hubbard. CDs: Enja; SN; w. James Emery (KFW); Fred Hersch (Sunny.; JC); A. Pepper (Cont.); Franco Ambrosetti; Daniel Schnyder; A. Zoller (Enja); Jane Ira Bloom (Arab.); Eddie Daniels (GRP); M. D'Ambrosio (Sunny.); B. Mintzer (dmp); Mark Murphy (Muse); Ronnie Cuber (FS); Leni Steren (Lip.).

FORREST, JIMMY (JAMES ROBERT JR.), tnr sax; b. St. Louis, MO, 1/24/20; d. Grand Rapids, MI, 8/26/80. Played in hs and w. band of moth., Eva

Dowd, later org. at St. James AME Church. Worked around St. Louis w. Dewey Jackson, Fate Marable, Jeter-Pillars in 1930s. Pl. w. Don Albert '38; J. McShann '40–2; Andy Kirk '42–7; then own combo in St. Louis '47–8, before replacing Ben Webster in Duke Ellington orch. for nine mos. '49–50. Most often feat. w. own gps. in '50s, but also pl. w. Harry Edison '58–60. Lived and pl. in St. Louis or LA for different periods bef. join. Count Basie '73; left in '77 to form qnt. w. Al Grey. Pl. in an earthy, big-toned, hard driving style. Favs: W. Gray, G. Ammons, D. Gordon. Comp: "Night Train," derived from Ellington's "Happy Go Lucky Local," was an r&b hit in '51. CDs: Del.; Prest.; NJ; w. Basie (Pab.); Grey (B&B); O. Nelson; Betty Roché; Prestige Blues-Swingers (Prest.); Joe Williams (Roul.); Ellington (Col.).

FORRESTER, JOEL, pno; b. New Kensington, PA, 5/2/46. Brother and two sists. are prof. mus. Stud. in SF in early 1970s, then received criticism and encouragement fr. Thelonious Monk '76–7. Pl. w. own gps. and Microscopic Septet, which he co-founded. Also accomp. silent films at Thalia Theater, NYC. Written more than 750 comps. Favs: Monk, James P. Johnson, Erroll Garner. Fests: Eur. w. Micro. Spt. since '85. Film: app. in German film *Only the Dead Know Brooklyn*. CDs: w. Micro. Spt. (Osmosis; Stash).

FORTUNE, SONNY (CORNELIUS), alto, sop saxes, fl; b. Philadelphia, PA, 5/19/39. Began on sax at age 18. Stud. at Wurlitzer Sch. of Mus., Granoff Sch. of Mus., also priv. w. Roland Wiggins. Pl. w. local r&b bands; Chris Columbus; Betty Burgess; Carolyn Harris before coming to NYC 1967. Pl. briefly w. Elvin Jones '67, then w. Mongo Santamaria '68–70; lived in LA for seven mos. bef. moving back to NYC and working w. Leon Thomas '70; McCoy Tyner '71–3; Roy Brooks '73. Briefly led own gp. then pl. w. Buddy Rich '74; Miles Davis '74–5. Led own gps. fr. June '75. Also pl. for two yrs. w. Nat Adderley Qnt.; seven yrs., on and off, w. E. Jones Jazz Machine. In '87–8 was part of Coltrane Legacy Band which incl. Tyner, R. Workman, E. Jones. Film: *The Crossing Guard*. TV: *48 Hours*, CBS. CDs: BN; w. M. Davis (Col.); N. Adderley (Evid.; Sw. Bas.); E. Jones; A. Ibrahim (Enja); Tyner (Mile.); M. Carvin (Muse); Mingus (Atl.); M. Waldron (SN).

FOSTER, AL (ALOYSIUS), dms; b. Richmond, VA, 1/18/44. Raised in NYC. Given set of dms. at age 10; encouraged by fath. who pl. bs. Learned about jazz dms. fr. listening to Max Roach recs.; as a teenager was also very infl. by Sonny Rollins. Pl. w.

Hugh Masekela 1960; Ted Curson, Illinois Jacquet '62–4; Blue Mitchell '64; Lou Donaldson, K. Winding '66. Pl. w. M. Davis from '72 to '75, incl. extens. tour.; tour. w. S. Rollins, McCoy Tyner, Ron Carter in Milestone Jazzstars, fall '78. Rejoin. Davis '80, incl. tours '81. Since early '80s also led own gps.; very active freelance mus., incl. work w. Steve Kuhn; Joanne Brackeen; Joe Henderson; frequent apps. w. Quest w. Richie Beirach, Dave Liebman in mid '80s; Tyner; J. McLean; Rollins; F. Hubbard; Henderson; M. Petrucciani. A versatile player, he is particularly notable for the way his rapport greatly enhanced the performances of both Davis and Rollins. Favs: Roach, Arthur Taylor. CDs: w. Davis; B. Marsalis (Col.); Steve Kuhn (Owl; Post.; JC); R. Workman (Post.); Rollins (Mile.); Duke Jordan; Sam Jones; D. Gordon (Steep.); T. Flanagan; F. Hubbard (Enja); D. Byrd; J. Heath; B. Hutcherson (Land.); P. D'Rivera; G. Bartz (Cand.); J. Henderson (BN; Red; Verve); Tyner (Mile.; Chesky); J. Brackeen; A. LaVerne; V. Shafranov; Chris Potter (Conc.).

FOSTER, ALEX (PAUL ALEXANDER), cl, fl, picc, alto sax, other saxes; b. Oakland, CA, 5/10/56. Grandfather perf. in B'way musicals; bro. Frank is vln. in LA; sist. Dawn is cellist w. San Jose Symph. Stud. at SF Cons.; Curtis Inst. of Mus.; Inst. of Advanced Mus. Study, Valais, Switz. Pl. w. Oakland Symph., SF Light Opera, Red Garter Ragtime Band, Mike Wolff–Alex Foster Qnt. 1970–2; Duke Pearson bb, Clark Terry bb, Chuck Israels Orch., New World Symph., Chico Hamilton, Thad Jones–Mel Lewis '72–5; Jack DeJohnette's Directions, Nancy Wilson, Nat Adderley, Freddie Hubbard '75–7; Answering Service w. Mike Wolff, *Ain't Misbehavin'* '77–9; Royal Phil. Orch., Don Sebesky '79–81; Jaco Pastorius '82–4; Lenny Pickett and the Borneo Horns, *Saturday Night Live* Band '85–90; Paul McCartney, Michael Franks '89; Gil Evans Orch. fr. '89; Mingus Epitaph–Dynasty bb fr. '90. Feat. on the soundtrack to the '91 film *Awakenings*. Favs: Charlie Parker, Cannonball Adderley, Coltrane, Wayne Shorter. Fests: Eur., Japan fr. '73. Film: *Rico* w. Dean Martin. TV: *Saturday Night Live*. CDs: Big World; TruSpace; w. M. Tyner (Mile.); J. DeJohnette (ECM); Andy McKee (Maple.); M. Davis (WB); Chris Hunter (PW; Sw. Bas.); Mingus Dynasty (Col.); Mingus BB (Drey.).

FOSTER, FRANK BENJAMIN III, tnr, sop, alto, cl, comp, arr; b. Cincinnati, OH, 9/23/28. Mother was amateur pnst. Stud. pno. at Cosmopolitan Sch. of Mus., Cincinnati; harmony at Walnut Hills HS 1942–6; sax at Central State U. Ohio. Pl. w. dance bands in Cincinnati fr. '42; Andrew Johnson Orch.

'43; Jack Jackson's Jumping Jacks '43–5; Earle Warren '44; own bb '45–6; Wilberforce Collegians '46–9. Moved to Det. in '49, pl. w. Snooky Young '49; Phil Hill '50–1. In army '51–3, then join. Count Basie Orch. Pl. and arr. w. Basie '53–64; arrs. incl. "Shiny Stockings"; "Down for the Count"; "Blues Backstage," etc. Pl. and arr. w. Woody Herman '64. Pl. w. Lloyd Price Orch., dir. by Slide Hampton, '64. Led own bb and small gps. '64–71; Duke Pearson bb, late '60s; Thad Jones–Mel Lewis Orch. off and on, late '60s–'76; Elvin Jones Jazz Machine '70–8. Led Frank Foster's Non-Electric Co., Loud Minority bb, Living Color Band '72–86. Pl. w. Buddy Rich '76; Clark Terry bb '70s; led Jazzmobile bb at Winter Olympics '80 for which he comp. *Lake Placid Suite*; qnt. w. Frank Wess '83–6. Led the Count Basie Orch. fr. June '86 to July '95. Early models incl. Wardell Gray, Sonny Stitt. A later Coltrane infl. took away some of his individuality for a time, and he failed to feature himself enough as leader of the Basie band; began a resurgence w. small gp. work after mid '95. Served as a music consultant in the NYC public schools '71–2 and has taught at SUNY-Buffalo and Queens Coll. Awarded an honorary doctorate fr. Central St. U. in '83. Favs: Joe Henderson, W. Shorter, Coltrane; arrs: Oliver Nelson, T. Dameron, Thad Jones, Gil Evans, Slide Hampton, Jimmy Heath, Ernie Wilkins. Fests: all major fr. '53. CDs: Prest.; Pab.; Den.; Arab.; Steep.; Conc.; w. C. Basie Orch. (Den.; Verve; BL; Roul.; Tel.); Elmo Hope (BN; Prest.); Joe Newman (Prest.; BL); M. Alexander (Chesky); Monk; K. Burrell; I. Jacquet (Prest.); D. Byrd; F. Wess (Sav.); E. Jones (Riv.; Imp.).

FOSTER, (NORMAN) GARY, alto sax, fl, cl, educ; b. Leavenworth, KS, 5/25/36. Graduated from U. of Kansas w. B. Mus. in woodwinds and mus. educ. Moved to LA 1961; became assoc. w. Clare Fischer '62. Active in the studio scene as well as with bbs incl. L. Bellson fr. '68; Mike Barone '69–70; Fischer '69–75. He also pl. w. Dennis Budimir '63–4; J. Rowles '68; Warne Marsh '68–73. With the Akiyoshi–Tabackin West Coast band throughout its duration '73–82; dur. that time, he also worked w. Ed Shaughnessy 74–6, and L. Almeida '74–7; founded Nova Music Studios, a gp. of teacher-performers in Pasadena. An eclectic and virtuosic musician inspired by the Lennie Tristano sch. of improv., he was infl. by Lee Konitz and Marsh. CDs: Conc.; w. Akiyoshi–Tabackin (RCA); Clare Fischer (Disc.); Marsh (hatArt); A. Broadbent; Jim Self; R. Clooney; C. Tjader; M. Tormé (Conc.); Milt Jackson (Qwest).

FOSTER, HERMAN, pno; b. Philadelphia, PA, 4/26/32; d. NYC, 4/3/99. Blind from birth. Began on cl., C-mel. sax, and bs. Stud. at Overbrook Sch. for the Blind. Pl. w. King Curtis early 1950s; Eric Dixon '53; Lou Donaldson fr. '53; Bill English, Seldon Powell '56–7; King Curtis '58–61; Al Casey '60. Led own trio w. Earl May, sometimes backing Gloria Lynne '60–3. Pl. in '80s-90s w. Donaldson; Gail Winters; Frank Vignola qt.; own trio w. Jay Leonhart or Jon Burr at Village Gate. Used a locked-hands chordal style as a contrast to his single-note attack. Favs: Milt Buckner, E. Garner, J. Mance, Mike Renzi; comp: Max Steiner. CDs: Timel.; Casey (Prest.; Swingville); Donaldson (BN; Muse).

FOSTER, POPS (GEORGE MURPHY), bs; b. McCall, LA, 5/18/1892; d. San Francisco, CA, 10/30/69. Older bro., Willard, pl. bjo. and gtr. Family moved to NO 1902. Stud. cello for three yrs., then bs. Debut w. Rosseals orch. '06; then w. Magnolia orch., Kid Ory '08; also w. Tuxedo and Eagle bands; A. J. Piron and King Oliver. Worked w. Fate Marable on St. Louis riverboats '17–21, doubling tba.; also in St. Louis w. Charlie Creath and Dewey Jackson. To LA in '23, where he pl. w. Ory, Mutt Carey, and at various taxi dance halls to '25. After brief time back in St. Louis, pl. w. Oliver at the Savoy, NYC '28; then w. similar personnel under Luis Russell '29–35; and L. Armstrong '35–40. Hospitalized from spring to Sept. '40; briefly w. Teddy Wilson before pl. w. Happy Caldwell '40–1; form. duo w. gtr. Isidore Langlois '41. From '42 to '45 work. in the NYC subways, but continued to gig. Worked w. S. Bechet '45; Art Hodes '45–6; on Rudi Blesh's *This Is Jazz* radio series. Pl. at Nice JF and tour. in France w. Mezz Mezzrow '48. Worked in Boston w. Bob Wilber, Jimmy Archey '49–51. Eur. w. Archey '52, and at Jimmy Ryan's '53. Regular at Central Plaza, app. in *Jazz Dance*, filmed there in '54. Pl. in NO w. Papa Celestin '54; tour. Eur. and No. Africa w. Sammy Price Dec. '55–May '56; in June moved to SF to work w. Earl Hines at Club Hangover '56, remaining w. him into early '60s. With Elmer Snowden trio '63–4. Tour. Eur. w. NO All-Stars '66. One of the first to popularize the string bs. in jazz, he utilized both the slapping and walking techniques. Polls: *DB* '36; *Record Changer* All-Time, All-Star '51. Book: *The Autobiography of Pops Foster, New Orleans Jazzman* (U. of Cal. Press) '71. Fav. own rec. "Mahogany Hall Stomp" w. Armstrong '29. CDs: w. Armstrong (Col.; Dec.); Lil Armstrong (Riv.); Bechet (Mos.; BN; Jazz.); J.R. Morton (BB; B&B); Mezzrow (Story.); Waller (BB); Bunk Johnson (Amer. Mus.); Wild Bill Davison (Jazz.).

FOUNTAIN, PETE (PETER DEWEY JR.), cl; b. New Orleans, LA, 7/3/30. Clarinet at age 12; at 18, pl. w. Junior Dixieland Band. A yr. later he join. Phil

Zito's International Dixieland Band. In 1950, founded Basin Street Six. Led own gps., also pl. w. Dukes of Dixieland in '55 in Chi.; Tony Almerico and Al Hirt in NO. Acquired national name through apps. on Lawrence Welk TV show '57–9, after which he bought a club in NO and perf. there frequently; also pl. regularly for several years in LV. Best known in later years through occ. apps. on the *Tonight Show*. Infls: Goodman, Fazola. Book: *A Closer Walk: The Pete Fountain Story* w. B. Neely (Henry Regnery) '72. CDs: MCA; Ranwood; BB; RCA-Camden; GHB; Jazz.; w. Hirt (Monument).

FOURNIER, VERNEL ANTHONY, dms; b. New Orleans, 7/30/28; d. Jackson, MS, 10/28/00. Began on parade drum at age 10. Stud. w. Sidney Montague in grammar sch. and at Xavier Prep HS. Pl. w. Young Swingsters 1938–45; Dooky Chase '42; on Bourbon St. w. Adam Cato, Harold Dejan '43. Stud. at Alabama St. Coll., pl. w. Collegians '45–6. Moved to Chi. '46. Pl. w. King Kolax '46–8; Paul Bascomb, Tom Archia, Teddy Wilson '49–53. Backed soloists incl. Gene Ammons; Sonny Stitt; Lester Young; Wardell Gray; J.J. Johnson–Kai Winding; Ben Webster; Howard McGhee; Stan Getz; Bud Freeman as member of Norman Simmons' house band at Bee Hive club '53–5. Pl. and tour. w. Ahmad Jamal '57–62; Geo. Shearing '62–4. Pl. w. Larry Novak's house band at Mister Kelly's, Chi. '65; Ahmad Jamal '66; Nancy Wilson '67; own trio at Salaam, Chi. '67–79. Moved to NYC '80. Pl. in '80s–90s w. Joe Williams; Billy Eckstine; John Lewis; Barry Harris; Clifford Jordan. Taught at the New Sch. Jazz Program. In May '94 he suffered a stroke that severely curtailed his pl. activity. A master of the loosely swinging, subtly accented NO drumming tradition, which he demonstrated, along w. other NO dmrs. Earl Palmer and Ed Blackwell in concert at CCNY '91. Favs: Paul Barbarin, Ike Day, Art Blakey. Fests: Eur., Asia, So. Amer. w. Jamal, Shearing, Jordan; Umbria w. Jamal '87. TV: Jap. TV w. B. Eckstine. CDs: TCB; w. C. Jordan (Mile.; SN; CC); A. Jamal (Chess); Sam Jones (Riv.); Shearing (Mos.).

FOWLER, BRUCE, tbn, comp; b. Salt Lake City, UT, 7/10/47. Son of educator William Fowler. Stud. at U. of Utah, No. Tex. St. Pl. w. Woody Herman 1968–9; Frank Zappa '72–5 and '88–9; Buddy Rich '76; Don Van Vliet '75–7; T. Akiyoshi '79–82; Bingo Miki '82–5, also often w. Fowler Bros. family band fr. '80. App. in Robert Altman film *Short Cuts* late '93; comp. and arr. for many films incl. *Batman Returns*; *A League of Their Own*. Favs: J.J. Johnson, Urbie Green, Carl Fontana, Frank Rosolino. CDs: Fossil; Terra Nova; w. Fowler Bros. (Fossil).

FOWLER, ED (EDWARD GRANT), el-bs, kybds; b. Salt Lake City, UT, 7/30/57. Brother of Bruce, Steve, Tom, Walt. Stud. at U. of Colorado, 1975–7. Gigs around Salt Lake City, then joined band, Blind Melon Chitlin '73–5. Pl. w. Fowler Bros. band, Air Pocket '78–93; Jon Crosse Quartet '80; Bruce Fowler band '91. Ambition: to compose in idiom ranging from contemporary jazz to atonal classical vein, often merging elements of both. Favs: J. Pastorius, M. Vitous. Fav. own solo: pno. on title track of *Ants Can Count* (Terra Nova). CDs: w. Fowler Bros. (Fossil); Steve Fowler (Fossil; Eclipse).

FOWLER, STEVE (STEVEN COTTAM), fl, alto sax; b. Chicago, IL, 3/8/49. Father, Dr. William Fowler, is noted jazz educ./comp. Bros. Bruce, Tom, Walt, Ed all well-known musicians. Stud. under father's program at U. of Utah. Tour. w. Fowler Bros. band fr. 1974; also Ladd Mackintosh '75 to present; Phil Wright Qt. '87–91; many Latin, jazz, rock bands in '80s and '90s. Tour. Japan '91 w. Eikichi Tazawa. Favs: Ornette Coleman, J. Coltrane. CDs: Fossil; w. Fowler Bros. (Fossil).

FOWLER, TOM (THOMAS WILLIAM), bs, vln, comp; b. Salt Lake City, UT, 6/10/51. Son of educ. William Fowler. Pvt. vln. and bs. as youngster; one year at U. of Utah. Pl. w. Fowler Bros. family band from 1971; also Frank Zappa '73–5; George Duke, Jean-Luc Ponty fr. '75; Hildegarde Neff fr. '81; Ray Charles in '90s. Favs: J. Pastorius, N.H.Ø. Pedersen. CDs: Fowler Bros.; Bruce Fowler (Fossil).

FOWLER, WALT (WALTER ERNEST), tpt, flg, kybds; b. Salt Lake City, UT, 3/2/55. Father profess. of music at U.'s of Utah, Colorado. Four bros. all musicians. In addition to traveling w. Fowler Bros. band from 1974, he tour. w. Frank Zappa; Billy Cobham; Johnny "Guitar" Watson; Buddy Rich; Ray Charles in the '70s; Brandon Fields fr. '80; George Benson '85–7; Diana Ross '89–92; Billy Childs '90–3. Many Eur. tours fr. '75 w. Zappa, Ross et al.; Japan, Austral. '89 and '91. CDs: Fowler Bros (Fossil); w. Zappa (Barking Pumpkin); Brandon Fields (Nova).

FOWLER, WILLIAM L., educ, comp, gtr; b. Salt Lake City, UT, 7/4/17. Mother taught pno.; fath. a bs. pl. Sons, Bruce, Tom, Steve, Walt, and Ed, all professional musicians. Army band director in France and Germ. 1942–6. Stud. at U. of Utah '46–54, then became prof. of music there until '73, and from '73 to '88 at the U. of Colorado. Long active as outstanding teacher, writing columns for *DB* and *Keyboard*; publishing 23 gtr., bs., and kybds. instruction books; dir. clinics at Mobile JF. Favs: Johnny Smith, Joe Pass,

Segovia; comp: Ellington. CDs: Fossil Records, of which he is president.

FOWLKES, CHARLIE (CHARLES BAKER), bari sax; b. Brooklyn, NY, 2/16/16; d. Dallas, TX, 2/9/80. Studied alto, tnr. saxes, cl., vln. Pl. bari. sax w. Tiny Bradshaw 1938–44; L. Hampton '44–8; then worked w. Arnett Cobb '48–51. Dur. this period he also doubled as the manager of singer Wini Brown, his wife. Pl. w. C. Basie '51–69. After a knee injury, left band and remained in NYC, pl. at Westbury Music Fair, etc. Rejoin. Basie, June '75. Basically a section man, he was feat. on "Misty" w. Basie. Fav: Carney. CDs: w. Basie (Verve; Pab.; Roul.); B. Clayton (Mos.); Hampton (Dec.).

FRANCIS, PANAMA (DAVID ALBERT), dms, lead; b. Miami, FL, 12/21/18; d. Orlando, FL, 11/11/01. Grandfather was choirmaster; tptr. Harold Newchurch and gtrst. Preston (The Ghost) Marshall are cousins. Started pl. at age 4. Pl. in Fla. w. Brolla Roberts 1927; Booker T. Washington Sch. band '30; Geo. McCaskill Orch. '31; George Kelly Cavaliers '34; Fla. Collegians, Charlie Brantley Orch. '38. Moved to NYC '38. Pl. w. Tab Smith '38; Billy Hicks '38–9; Roy Eldridge Orch. at Arcadia Ballroom '39–40; Lucky Millinder Orch. at Savoy Ballroom '40–6; own gp. at Savoy '46; Willie Bryant '46–7; Cab Calloway '47–52; Duke Ellington Orch., Charlie Shavers, Slim Gaillard '52; Conrad Janis Dixieland Five '53. Took own gp. to Monte-video, Uruguay, Mar. '54. Worked as studio mus. for the Platters; Brook Benton, Frankie Avalon, Jackie Wilson, Little Willie John, etc., and freelanced w. Illinois Jacquet, Sy Oliver, Tony Bennett, Ray Charles, Buddy Holly, Carmen McRae, Jimmy Witherspoon et al. '52–63. Owned grocery store '59. House dmr. for Cadillac Industrial Show '63–6. Accomp. Dinah Shore '66–9. Moved to LA '69. Pl. w. Ray Coniff Orch. '69–72. Worked as studio mus. and freelanced w. Joe Williams, Teddy Wilson, Calloway '69–73, then ret. to NYC '73. Pl. w. Sy Oliver Orch. '73–9; NY Jazz Repertory Co. '73–9; Coniff '75, '80–2; gp. at Contemporary Hotel, Walt Disney World '76–8. Led own gp., the Savoy Sultans, in NYC and Eur. fr. '79. Pl. w. Sultans, over a five-yr. period, at Rainbow Room in '80s; worked w. Benny Goodman qt. '82. In '90s living between NYC and Orlando. His career has been slowed by illness in '95 and again, after gigging in Fla. in '96–7, at the end of the latter yr. He has received citations fr. the Hot Club of France, the NY Jazz Society, and the Smithsonian. Favs: Chick Webb, Jo Jones, Buddy Rich. Fests: Latin Amer. w. Calloway '47; all major fr. '79 w. Sultans; also pl. Meridien Hotel in Paris '86, '87; Hilton Hotel, Hong

Kong '88. Films: *Hi-De-Ho Man* w. Calloway; *Rock Around the Clock* w. Allan Freed; *The Learning Tree* w. Gordon Parks; *Lady Sings the Blues* w. Diana Ross; *Angel Heart.* Broadway: *Marathon '33; Never Live Above a Pretzel Factory; Fantasticks; West Side Story.* TV: apps. w. Dinah Shore; Jackie Gleason; Ed Sullivan. CDs: B&B; Stash; w. Calloway (WW); Millinder (Class.); Ray Bryant; M. Buckner; A. Cobb; E. Hines; Joe Turner (B&B); L. Hampton (Timel.); Willis Jackson (Del.); Statesmen of Jazz (Arb.).

FRANKLIN, HENRY "SKIPPER," bs; b. 10/1/40. Studied w. Al McKibbon and George Morrow. Worked w. Curtis Amy, Roy Ayers, Hugh Masekela 1960s. Toured US and Europe w. Hampton Hawes '71; pl. w. Esther Phillips '73–4; Bobby Hutcherson, Gerald Wilson '74; Freddie Hubbard '75. Frequent app. w. Pharoah Sanders through '84; C. Basie '86; Teddy Edwards '90–1. Book: *Bassically Yours.* CDs: Hawes (FS); Woody Shaw (Cont.); Dennis Gonzales (Silk.).

FRANKS, MICHAEL, voc, comp; b. La Jolla, CA, 1944. Studied Engl. lit. at U. of Calif.; M.A. from U. of Oregon. First rec. in mid 1970s w. such sidemen as Joe Sample, Kenny Barron, Ron Carter, etc. Tour. and rec. as a solo act into '90s. His comps. have been rec. by David Sanborn; Carmen McRae; Mark Murphy; Manhattan Transfer; et al. Not specifically a jazz singer, Franks sings with a soft, breathy quality remininscent of the early pop/jazz efforts of Mel Tormé and Page Cavanaugh; his recs. almost always employ first-rate jazz rhythm sections. CDs: WB.

FRANKS, REBECCA COUPE, tpt, flg, comp; b. Aptos, CA, 1/27/61. Musical family; raised in Santa Cruz, Calif. Played prof. at age 15. In addition to her jazz work, pl. w. salsa gps., classical orchs., circus bands. To NYC 1988; B.F.A. degree from New School. Her fiery, hard bop–based tpt. style was heard at the '90 Monterey Jazz Festival. Bill Cosby hired her for his album *Appreciation* on Polygram, and for the *Playboy* Jazz Festival in '91. Stud. w. Art Farmer; Wallace Roney; Laurie Frink; and Walter Davis Jr. CDs: Just.; Phil.

FRANZELLA, SAL JR., cl, comp; b. New Orleans, LA, 4/25/15; d. New Orleans, 11/8/68. Father, clst. in old French Opera Co. Began on pno. at age 9; took up alto sax, cl. at age 12. Stud. w. Jean Paquay, who also taught Fazola; T. Parenti. Join. mus. union at 12; pl. in Saenger Theatre at 15. Tour. w. Louis Prima, then ret. to NO. In 1936 tour. w. Benny Meroff, after extensive local perf. and radio jobs. Left band in NYC and began some studio work for CBS; join. Isham Jones '37; P. Whiteman '38; NBC staff '41–7. Resettled in

Calif., studio work through '50s and '60s. From '55 made regular apps. w. symphs., incl. Buffalo; concert work on cl., bs. cl., alto sax. Moved back to NO in later yrs., pl. jazz gigs and perf. w. NO Pops. Favs: Goodman, J. Mince, Shaw, Abe Most. CDs: Mildred Bailey (Dec.); Jess Stacy (ASV).

FRAZIER, CIE (JOSIAH), dms; b. New Orleans, LA, 2/23/04; d. New Orleans, 1/10/85. Studied w. Louis Cottrell Sr. Cousin of bjo. Lawrence Marrero, w. whom he pl. in Golden Rule Band 1922; Young Tuxedo Orch. mid '20s. Worked w. Papa Celestin's Tuxedo Jazz Orch. and Tuxedo Brass Band '27; A. J. Piron '28; Sidney Desvigne '32. Pl. in WPA bands dur. the Depression; US Navy dance band dur. service '42–5. During '50s worked w. Celestin; Percy Humphrey; George Williams' brass band; Eureka Brass Band. He was a regular at Preservation Hall from '61 to '83. Eur. tours w. Pres. Hall band. Considered to be an exemplar of the NO dms. style. Films: *The Cincinnati Kid* '65; *American Music from Folk to Jazz and Pop* '69. Recs. w. Celestin '27; Wooden Joe Nicholas '45; Kid Howard '61. CDs: w. George Lewis (Del.); Percy Humphrey (Story.); Jim Robinson (GHB).

FREELON, (CHINYERE) NNENNA, voc; b. Cambridge, MA, 7/28/ca. 54. Early infls. were voc. gps. such as The Stylistics and The Spinners. Later listened to Odetta, Miriam Makeba, Nina Simone, Abbey Lincoln, Billy Eckstine, Ella Fitzgerald, and Sarah Vaughan. Grad. fr. Simmons Coll. in Bost., then moved to Durham, N.C.; worked in hospital administration but cont. to devote time to woodshedding her vocal craft. Perf. w. Dr. Billy Tayor; Yusef Lateef; and Toshiko Akiyoshi. In 1990, at the Southern Arts Federation Jazz Forum in Atlanta, met Ellis Marsalis who introduced her to George Butler. This led to her first CD for Columbia '92. As a single she opened for Ray Charles and Al Jarreau in concert perfs. Made Philip Morris Eur. tour '92. Began rec. for Concord in '96. From '97 tour. int'l and rec. w. T.S. Monk Tentet. Jack Massarik has written: "The Ns have it. Natural, nascent. A nerveless nightingale." Favs: Vaughan, Fitzgerald, Simone. Awards: Billie Holiday Award fr. French Academie du Jazz for *Heritage* album '93; Eubie Blake Award '93. CDs: Col.; Conc.; w. T.S. Monk (N2K).

FREEMAN, BUD (LAWRENCE), tnr sax; b. Chicago, IL, 4/13/06; d. Chicago, 3/15/91. Some studies as a youth; debuted in 1923 on C-mel. sax, sw. to tnr. in '25. In the early '20s, he was one of the Austin High Gang, incl. Frank Teschemacher, Dick and Jimmy McPartland, Dave Tough. In '27, he went to NYC to work w. Ben Pollack, leaving him to visit Paris w. Tough in '28. He returned to the US in '29 and, in the next few yrs., divided his time between the popular and jazz fields, pl. and rec. frequently w. Red Nichols; Joe Haymes; Roger Wolfe Kahn; Pollack. He was feat. w. Ray Noble '35, then join. T. Dorsey '36–8; B. Goodman '38. In '39, he recorded w. his own group, Summa Cum Laude, and from this point on he was mostly assoc. w. small bands. He served in the army '43–5, and went to the Aleutians w. an army band. After being discharged, he returned to NYC and pl. w. Eddie Condon late '46–7. In '47, he led a trio, incl. Joe Bushkin, at the Copacabana Hotel in Rio de Janeiro; also spent a yr. in Chile and Peru '52–3. Through the rest of the '50s and '60s, he led his own gps., incl. a trio engagement at Condon's in '58; NJF in late '50s. During the '50s, he also became interested in modern jazz forms, and stud. w. L. Tristano. During the '60s, he app. at many jazz fests., incl NJF, MJF, DB, Pitts.; also tour. Austral., New Zeal., Japan '63; Eur. Int'l JF '64. He was a charter member of WGJB, pl. w. it '68–74. Honored by an NYJRC program, in which he also perf. '74. He moved to London in late '74, lecturing and pl. at universities throughout Brit.; also lived in Dublin before ret. to Chi. in the late '70s.

By the late '20s, Freeman had evolved a completely original voice on tnr. As the first white innovator on the instrument, his highly personal sound, with miminal use of vibrato, stood in sharp contrast to the more ornate style prevalent in that era. He once said that he was originally infl. more by dmrs. and tap dancers than by other saxophonists, which accounts for the rhythmic vigor of his playing. Later on, his tone was compared to Lester Young's. He was also the first tenor man to be accepted in the traditional circles promoted by Eddie Condon. As his many excellent recorded solos show, he cont. to refine his style and maintain his integrity of personality throughout his lengthy career. Polls: *Met.* '37; *DB* '38. Fests: NJF-NY '72, w. Friends of E. Condon. TV: comps. for NBC spectacular *Making of a Pro* '63; *Tonight Show*. Books: *You Don't Look Like a Musician* (Det.) '74; *If You Know of a Better Life, Please Tell Me* (Dublin) '76. Comps: "The Eel"; "That D Minor Thing"; "Song of the Dove"; "Uncle Haggart's Blues." CDs: Prest.; BL; Class.; w. E. Condon (Dec.; Col.); B. Goodman; B. Holiday (Col.); Benny Carter; T. Dorsey; M. Spanier; J. Teagarden (BB); Elmer Snowden (BL); *The Commodore Story*; Pee Wee Russell (Comm.); Swingville All-Stars (GTJ); Teddy Grace (Timel.).

FREEMAN, CHICO (EARL LAVON JR.), tnr sax, lead; b. Chicago, IL, 7/17/49. Son of Von Freeman.

Start. on pno. at age 7; inspired by Miles Davis, start. pl. tpt. as a teenager; switched to tnr. while attending Northwestern U., 1967–72, where he majored in math, then mus. ed. Pl. w. r&b and blues gps., incl. Memphis Slim, Junior Wells; also stud. w. Muhal Richard Abrams and pl. in Abrams' bb; became member of AACM. Worked and stud. w. other AACM mus. such as Fred Anderson, Adegoke Steve Colson, J. Jarman, R. Mitchell, A. Braxton; also worked w. uncle, gtrst. George Freeman. In '74 began grad. stud. in comp. at Governors State U.; feat. soloist w. the school's bb, tour. Brazil '76. Moved to NYC in '76, worked w. H. Threadgill; Sun Ra; Sam Rivers' orch.; H. Bluiett; D. Pullen, incl. Eur. tour '76; Elvin Jones '77. Start. lead. own qt. in late '70s; his gps. have incl. such mus. as Abrams; John Hicks; C. McBee; R. Workman; Jay Hoggard; Don Moye; Steve McCall. Tour. Eur. w. AACM bb. '79. Worked w. Jack DeJohnette's Special Edition early '80s. Occ. pl. in a qnt. w. his fath. With Moye, Pullen, Arthur Blythe, Don Cherry form. the Leaders in '84; tour. Japan w. additional personnel; worked w. new edition of Leaders to '87, incl. Blythe; Moye; McBee; Kirk Lightsey; Lester Bowie. In late '80s, also tour. w. own quart.; Branford Marsalis; John Hicks; Ray Drummond. In '88 pl. in Solomonic Qt. w. Ahmed Abdullah, Charles Moffett, Wilbur Morris. Freeman, who in the past had pl. w. Machito, Ray Barretto, Eddie Palmieri, and El Gran Combo, also tour. in Cuba. In the late '90s, with his gp. Guataca, he became more directly involved in Latin jazz or, as he calls it, Jazz Latin. CDs: Ind. Nav.; Cont.; BS; In+Out; DRG; JH; w. DeJohnette (ECM); The Leaders; Don Pullen (BS); Kirk Lightsey (Sunny.); Roots (In+Out).

FREEMAN, RUSS (RUSSELL DONALD), pno; b. Chicago, 5/28/26; d. Las Vegas, 6/27/02. Cousin of comp. Ray Gilbert, singer Joanne Gilbert. Stud. classical pno. in LA 1934–8. Prominent w. many jazz gps. on West Coast from late '40s, incl. Howard McGhee–Charlie Parker '47; Dexter Gordon '47; Charlie Barnet '51, Chet Baker off and on '53–7; B. Goodman '55–9, off and on; Shelly Manne '56–7. Fr. '70s, mainly active in commercial work, except for four albums made for Japan: *Among Friends* w. Art Pepper '78; *Funk 'n Fun* w. Bill Watrous and Pepper '79; *Blow & Ballad* w. Sonny Stitt and Pepper '80; and *One On One* w. Shelly Manne '82. Mariah Carey recorded his orig. composition, "The Wind," w. her own lyrics on *Emotions* (Col.). Annie Ross wrote lyrics to and rec. his melody "Music Is Forever" (DRG). A major West Coast jazz figure in the '50s whose work was much valued for its strong rhythmic inflections. Favs: Tatum, Bud Powell, J. Albany, H. Silver. CDs: PJ; w. Baker (Mos.; PJ; Cont.); Manne;

Miles Davis; Lighthouse All-Stars (Cont.); Clifford Brown (PJ; also BN/PJ boxed set); Goodman (MM); L. Konitz (Phil.); C. Parker (Stash; Spot.); Pepper (PJ; BN; Sav.; Cont.); S. Rogers (BB); S. Chaloff (BL).

FREEMAN, VON (EARL LAVON), tnr sax, comp; b. Chicago, IL, 10/3/22. Father of Chico Freeman; bros. are George, gtr., and Eldridge "Bruz," dms. Start. on cl. and C-mel. sax at age 7; stud. w. Capt. Walter Dyett at Du Sable HS; Gene Ammons and Bennie Green were classmates. Pl. w. Horace Henderson 1940–1; US Navy Hellcats '41–5; briefly w. Sun Ra '48–9. Most of his work has been in small clubs in and around Chi. He and his bros. were the house band at the Pershing Hotel '46–50, accomp. such mus. as C. Parker; Roy Eldridge; Lester Young. Form. qt. w. bros. and Ahmad Jamal, replaced by Andrew Hill '51. In early '60s worked w. blues mus. Jimmy Reed; Gene Chandler; Otis Rush; w. Milt Trenier '66–9. From '69 concentrated on jazz again; pl. w. D. Gordon for Joe Segal's "Charlie Parker Month" concerts, Aug. '70; own qt. often incl. Dave Shipp, bs.; John Young, pno. Occ. pl. in qnt. w. son, Chico. First NYC club gig as leader, Vill. Vanguard '94. Terry Martin, writing of him, said: "The harmonic and rhythmic innovations of the boppers, particularly Parker, and the latter modal players, have been absorbed into a style that, while it builds on the foundation of Hawkins' power and arpeggiated convolutions, and Lester's melodrhythms, emerges as something quite unique." Recs. as lead: *Have No Fear* (Nessa); *Doin' It Right Now* (Atl.). CDs: Col.; Chief; DIW; Steep.; w. C. Parker (Sav.); C. Freeman (BS; Ind. Nav.); Louis Smith (Steep.); Steve Coleman (Novus; DIW); Strata Institute (DIW).

FRESU, PAOLO, tpt, flg; b. 2/10/61, Berchidda, Sardinia, Italy. Self-taught; pl. tpt. at age 11 in village band; early exp. in traditional Sardinian bands. Taken w. jazz ca. 1980, and moved to the mainland to pursue his interest. Earned degree at Cagliari Cons.; also stud. at Bologna Cons. w. Enrico Rava. Comp. for orchs. and theater gps., wrote for magazines, and taught at various music schs. early '80s. Has taught at Siena Jazz Seminars fr. late '80s; also in Atlanta, Boston, Melbourne. After att. Siena Jazz Seminar '82, he formed a qnt. w. saxophonist Tino Tracanna '84. Work w. Roberto Ottaviano qt. '84–5; Tiziana Ghiglioni '86. Own Fresu Project '86–88; ongoing assoc. with Furio di Castri fr. '88; Aldo Romano fr. '88; Gianluigi Trovesi fr. '91. Fresu has also worked w. Bruno Tommaso '86–88 and w. Tommaso's "Buster Keaton" nonet fr. '88; Mimmo Cafiero '86–89; Barga Jazz Orch. '86–90; Giovanni Tommaso qnt. '87–90 inc. visit to US; Paolo Damiani gps. '84–91; Big

Bang Orch. '89–92. Also pl. w. Albert Mangelsdorff, Franco D'Andrea, Kenny Wheeler, Tony Oxley, John Taylor, Muhal Richard Abrams, Gerry Mulligan, Dave Liebman, Enico Rava, Paul Rutherford, Dave Holland, Lee Konitz, Evan Parker, Michael Nyman, Richard Galliano, John Zorn, John Abercrombie, Ralph Towner, Jerry Bergonzi in '80s and '90s. Infl. by Miles Davis, Fresu displays an extremely expressive tone and sensitive, emotional style. Fests: Eur.; Japan; U.S.; Can.; India; Israel; Senegal. Polls: many Ital. polls and awds. CDs: Spl.; Owl; w. G. Tommaso (Red); Big Bang; Phil Woods (Phil.); Tracanna; Damiani; Paolo Carrus; Guido DiLeone; Giuseppe Emmanuele (Spl.); Romano (Owl; Enja); Cosmo Intini (Timel.).

FRIEDMAN, DAVID, vib, dms, perc, pno; b. NYC, 3/10/44. Father is amateur vlnst. Stud. dms. w. Stanley Krell 1955; marimba, xylophone fr. '60. Perc. major at Juilliard; also stud. w. Saul Goodman; Moe Goldenberg. Later stud. w. Teddy Charles; Hall Overton. Subbed w. NY Phil., Met. Opera Orch. early '60s. Pl. contemp. classical music w. Luciano Berio in Eur. and US. Worked w. Tim Buckley; Horace Silver; Hubert Laws; Horacee Arnold; Wayne Shorter; Joe Chambers; Don Sebesky. Toured US and Eur. as clinician for Ludwig Drum Co. '70s. Rec. and tour. w. Dave Samuels in the Mallet Duo vibes-marimba combo '75; co-led qt. Double Image w. Samuels '77–80. Rec. w. Daniel Humair '79; Chet Baker '82. Friedman has taught at Manh. Sch. of Mus. and the Inst. for Advanced Musical Studies, Montreux, Switz. He is the author of a vib. method: *Vibraphone Technique: Dampening and Pedaling* (Berklee Press). Favs: Luciano Berio, Bill Evans, Milt Jackson. Polls: *DB* TDWR vib. '74, '75 (tie w. Karl Berger). Fests: NJF w. H. Laws, H. Arnold '73. CDs: Enja; w. Double Image; Baker (Enja); H. Laws (CTI); Humair (Blue Flame; Owl); Jim Pugh (dmp); Larry Schneider (Label Bleu).

FRIEDMAN, DON (DONALD ERNEST), pno, comp; b. San Francisco, CA, 5/4/35. Studied classical pno. priv. 1940–50; at Los Angeles City Coll. '54–5. Pl. at LA jam sessions, then worked w. Dexter Gordon, Shorty Rogers, Buddy Collette, Buddy DeFranco '56. Pl. w. Chet Baker, Ornette Coleman '57. Moved to NYC '58, pl. w. own trio, and w. Donald Byrd–Pepper Adams Qnt. Solo pno. at Five Spot; and worked w. Herbie Mann late '50s; Booker Little '61; Jimmy Giuffre '64; Chuck Wayne '66–7; also own gp. w. Attila Zoller since '60s. Pl. w. Clark Terry off and on since late '60s. Taught pno. and comp. at NYU fr. '70 and rec. a grant from the National Council of the Arts '73. In the '80s, Friedman worked w.

Bob Bodley; John Shaw; Urs Leimgruber in the coop gp. Reflexionen; Eiji Nakayama; own trios. Pl. w. Terry fr. '95 incl. Eur. tours '96–7. Tour. in Switz., Germ. w. Lee Konitz '96. Pl. in Italy, US w. hca. pl. Bruno DeFilippi. Favs: Tatum, B. Powell, B. Evans, Corea, Jarrett. Polls: *DB* TDWR '62. Fests: Eur. since '63; Japan since '80. CDs: Steep.; Alfa; Conc.; Prog.; Apollon; Riv.; SN; w. Mann (Atl.); L. Tabackin (Conc.); Little; Dolphy (Cand.); Terry (Chesky); Zoller (Act); Collette (Cont.); Leimgruber (Enja; Timel.); Joe Henderson (Mile.); D. Lanphere (Hep); Konitz (hatArt); DeFilippi (Giants of Jazz).

FRIEDMAN, IZZY (IRVING), cl, saxes; b. Linton, IN, 12/25/03. Studied w. local teacher, then pl. in theater orch.; moved to Chi. 1923; stud. w. principal cl. of Chi. Symph. To NYC '24; stud. comp. and cond.; join. Vincent Lopez '25–6. Free-lanced in NYC until joining Paul Whiteman '28–30; also rec. w. Bix Beiderbecke; Eddie Lang; Frankie Trumbauer; et al. App. w. Whiteman in film, *King of Jazz*, then settled in Hollywood. Active in film studios until '49; formed own music and sound effects company, providing service for hundreds of films and TV shows fr. '50 to '63, when he retired. CDs: w. Beiderbecke (Col.); Lang (ASV); Venuti–Lang (BBC).

FRIESEN, DAVID, bs, comp; b. Tacoma, WA, 5/6/42. Studied pno and gtr. first. Did not pl. bs. until he was in the army at age 19; stud. with a member of the Seattle Symph. Sis. is actress Dyan Cannon. In 1960s, Friesen pl. w. John Handy in Vancouver and w. Marian McPartland, then for two yrs. w. Joe Henderson in SF. Tour. Eur. w. Billy Harper, met Ted Curson in Denmark and pl. w. him at MJF '77. Later worked w. Ricky Ford; Duke Jordan. In '85, pl. duos w. Paul Horn and w. Mal Waldron at Montreal JF. In later years, his instrument was the lighter weight Oregon bass, which he designed himself. From '87, worked and rec. w. gtrst. Uwe Kropinski and pnst. Denny Zeitlin. Occ. does solo bass programs. His technique, enabling him to bow and pluck w. both hands, earned him widespread acceptance from his peers. CDs: ITM; Global Pacific; w. K. Drew; Jordan (Steep.); M. Nock (Tomato); Harper (BS); Waldron (SN); Handy (Boulevard); Zeitlin (WH; Conc.).

FRIGO, JOHNNY, vln, bs; b. Chicago, IL, 12/27/16. Started on vln. at age 7. Tba. in jr. hs band; tba., vln., and tpt. in hs. Join. Chico Marx band 1942, singing in qt. w. Mel Tormé. After coast guard service '43–5, join. Jimmy Dorsey band, then formed Soft Winds w. Dorsey's rhythm section: Herb Ellis, gtr.; Lou Carter, pno.; Frigo, bs. Dur. this time, he composed "Detour Ahead." Fr. '51 was a busy studio mus. in Chi., mainly pl. bs., working often in duo w. pianist Dick Marx. In '81, resumed pl. vln. Ray Brown, Herb Ellis, and Monty Alexander invited him to join them at the Loa club in Santa Monica. This led to recs. as lead. and sideman; apps. at the Colo. JP. Although Frigo had rec. on vln. in the mid '50s, it was not until '88 that he became internationally known as one of the foremost jazz soloists on the instrument. CDs: Chesky; *The Soft Winds: Then and Now* (Chiaro.); w. M. Alexander (Conc.); Ellis (Just.); M. D'Ambrosio (Sunny.); Holly Cole (BN); Helen Merrill (Verve).

FRISELL, BILL (WILLIAM RICHARD), gtr; b. Baltimore, MD, 3/18/51. Father pl. tba., bs. in hs; grandfath. pl. vln., crnt. Began on cl., tnr. sax.; sw. to gtr. at age 11, inspired by blues gtrs. incl. Otis Rush, B.B. King. First gigs pl. for school dances, fraternity parties as teenager. Stud. at U. of No. Colorado; w. Michael Gibbs, Herb Pomeroy at Berklee Coll. of Mus. Also stud. w. Dale Bruning; Johnny Smith; Jim Hall. Lived in Belgium '78, studied comp. and pl. in Eur. w. M. Gibbs; Eberhard Weber. Moved to NYC '79. House gtrst. for ECM label in '80s. Rec. as lead. fr. '82. Pl. and rec. w. P. Motian; John Zorn; Tim Berne; Robin Holcomb; Wayne Horvitz; Marc Johnson; Paul Bley; Lyle Mays; Billy Hart; Bob Moses. Also rec. w. John Scofield; Julius Hemphill; Bobby Previte. Moved to Seattle '89. He mixes elements fr. just about every musical genre and uses synths. and a volume pedal to achieve effects akin to wind instrs. and elec. kybds. Favs: Jim Hall, Jimi Hendrix, Wes Montgomery, Robert Johnson. Polls: *DB* elec. gtr. twice. Fests: Eur., Japan, Brazil fr. '78. CDs: Elek.; ECM; None.; Min. Mus.; w. P. Motian (JMT; ECM; SN); J. Zorn (DIW; Elek.; hatArt); W. Horvitz; D. Byron; J. Hemphill (Elek. None.); Gary Peacock (Post.); P. Bley; K. Wheeler; J. Garbarek; E. Weber; Marc Johnson (ECM); Scofield (BN); B. Previte; B. Moses (Gram.); J. Lovano (SN).

FRISHBERG, DAVE (DAVID L.), pno, voc, songwriter, comp; b. St. Paul, MN, 3/23/33. Mostly self-taught on pno.; mus. theory stud. at U. of Minn. Air Force service, 1955–7. Worked in NYC w. Kai Winding '59–60; Carmen McRae '60–1; at Eddie Condon's '61–4, Gene Krupa Qt. and Ben Webster '62–3; Al Cohn–Zoot Sims '63–71. In LA from '68–76, often worked w. Bill Berry; Jack Sheldon; and Herb Alpert. Fr. '78, app. chiefly as soloist, pl. and singing his own witty songs, for most of which he wrote both lyrics and music. They include "I'm Hip" (co-written w. B. Dorough); "My Attorney"; "Bernie"; "Van Lingle Mungo"; "Peel Me a Grape"; "The Wheelers and Dealers"; "El Cajon"; "Dear Bix"; "You Are There";

"Dodger Blue." In addition to his songwriting, he is also a gifted and whimsical jazz pianist, whose albums usually display his broad knowledge of jazz history w. tunes from the '20s and '30s and medleys devoted to such instrumentalists as Johnny Hodges. CDs: Fant.; Conc.; Arb.; Bloom.; Sterling; w. Berry; S. McCorkle; K. Peplowski (Conc.); Bud Freeman (BL); J. Rushing (BB).

FRUSCELLA, TONY, tpt; b. Orangeburg, NJ, 2/14/27; d. NYC, 8/14/69. Lived in an orphanage until age of 14. Start. pl. at 15; began teaching himself, then stud. w. Jerome Canudie. Entered army in 1945, pl. in 2nd Div. band. Worked w. Chick Maures '48; Lester Young briefly in '50, again in '54; sess. w. Don Joseph, Brew Moore '53; G. Mulligan '54, incl. NJF; pl. w. Stan Getz for eight mos. in '55, also rec. for Verve; also rec. as lead. for Atl. '55. From the late '50s, mostly inactive due to drug-related problems. Died of cirrhosis and heart failure a few weeks after his release from a three-month hospital stay. Dan Morgenstern's obituary in *DB* described him as "a poet of the trumpet with a veiled, haunting sound." Favs: Joe Thomas, Phil Sunkel, Gillespie. Comps: "Moatz"; "Baite." Red Mitchell wrote and rec. lyrics to Fruscella's solo on "I'll Be Seeing You." CDs: Cool 'N Blue; w. Getz (Verve).

FRYE, DON (DONALD O.), pno; b. Springfield, OH, 1903; d. NYC, 2/9/81. Started pno. at 13; stud. priv. While still in hs pl. locally w. Lloyd and Cecil Scott, then went to NYC w. them 1924, perf. through early '30s, incl. dates at the Savoy. Worked w. Freddie Moore '33–7; orig. member of J. Kirby '37 sxt.; Lucky Millinder, ca. '38–9; then pl. and rec. w. Frankie Newton '39. Worked w. Zutty Singleton '40; apps. on West Coast '43. Ret. to NYC, pl. long engagement at Village Vanguard; then house pnst. at Jimmy Ryan's fr. '44 to mid '50s. Infl: Waller, Tatum. Recs. w. the Scotts '27, '29; King Oliver '29, '30; Clarence Williams '34; Edmond Hall '44; as soloist '45; Danny Barker '58; Cecil Scott '59. CDs: w. Newton (Aff.); Red Allen (BB).

FULBRIGHT, DICK (RICHARD W.), bs, tba; b. Paris, TX, 1901; d. NYC, 11/17/62. Played w. Alonzo Ross orch. 1926–8; then w. Lucky Roberts in Fla. Moved to NYC in late '20s, pl. w. Bingie Madison, Elmer Snowden '31–2. Join. Teddy Hill mid '30s, Eur. tour '37. After ret. to US, worked in NYC w. Billy Hicks at St. Regis Hotel; w. Dave Martin at St. George Hotel, Bklyn; Zutty Singleton late. '39–40; again w. Martin '41; Alberto Socarras '43–7. Freelanced in '50s, incl. Cootie Williams '50; Noble Sissle. Retired in '58. Recs. w. Teddy Hill, Dicky

Wells (in Paris) '37. CDs: w. Bechet (JSP); Benny Carter (Charly); R. Eldridge (Col.); Frankie Newton; King Oliver; Django Reinhardt (Aff.; Ark.).

FULFORD, TOMMY, pno; b. 1912; d. NYC, 12/16/56. Played w. Blanche Calloway in Indianapolis, Ind. 1936, then moved to NYC. Pl. w. Snub Mosley '36; Chick Webb '36–9. After Webb's death in '39, Fulford cont. to work w. the band under Ella Fitzgerald '40–2. Perf. as solo pnst. '40s-early '50s. Pl. w. Tony Parenti '55–6. CDs: w. Webb; Fitzgerald (Dec.); Ellington small gps. in *The Duke's Men* (Col.).

FULLER, CURTIS DUBOIS, tbn, comp; b. Detroit, MI, 12/15/34. Orphaned at age 6; older sist. was classical pnst. Inspired to pl. tbn. after a social worker took him to hear Illinois Jacquet feat. J.J. Johnson. Pl. tbn. and bari. horn in band at Cass Tech HS, where Donald Byrd, Paul Chambers were classmates 1949–52. Worked in aircraft factory '53, then pl. w. Cannonball Adderley's army dance band at Ft. Knox, Ky. '53–5. Pl. w. Yusef Lateef at Bluebird Inn, Det. '55–6. Also stud. intermittently w. J.J. Johnson; Frank Rosolino; Barry Harris dur. this time. Entered Wayne St. U. '56, where his roommate was Joe Henderson. Pl. in gp. Bone And Bari w. Pepper Adams, Kenny Burrell while at Wayne St. Rec. w. Adams, John Coltrane for Transition label in Boston '56. Joined Miles Davis Qnt. as sixth member in Det. '57; pl. a few dates at Café Bohemia, NYC, but the gp. broke up a few days later. App. on nineteen albums in '57, incl. perfs. w. Lateef; Coltrane; Clifford Jordan; Paul Quinichette; Lou Donaldson; Jackie McLean; Lee Morgan; Sonny Clark; Bud Powell; and six dates as leader. Two wks. as bs-tbnst. w. Dizzy Gillespie Orch. '57. Pl. six mos. w. Lester Young '58; Gil Evans Orch., Benny Golson '59; Art Farmer–Benny Golson Jazztet '59–60; Quincy Jones Orch. '60–1. Join. Art Blakey's Jazz Messengers '61. Tour. So. Amer. w. Coleman Hawkins, spons. by US State Dept., summer '61. Pl. w. Blakey '61–5, incl. Japan tour '63; also rec. as lead. w. bb dir. by Manny Albam '62. Freelanced w. Q. Jones, Lee Morgan, Hank Mobley, McCoy Tyner, Wayne Shorter, Joe Henderson, others late '60s. Tour Eur. w. D. Gillespie Reunion bb '68. Worked sporadically in early '70s w. Stanley Turrentine; Jimmy Heath; Chas. Tolliver; Bill Hardman; then join. Count Basie Orch. '75. Pl. w. Basie '75–8; Blakey,'77–8; Giant Bones w. Kai Winding '79–80; Golson '80–1. Pl. in '80s w. reunion gps. incl. Jazz Messengers, Jazztet. Formed Timeless All-Stars w. Cedar Walton, Billy Higgins, Bobby Hutcherson early '80s. Taught under Jackie McLean at Hartt Coll. of Mus. fr. '90. Arrs. of some of Fuller's comps. have been publ. by Second Floor Music. Favs: J.J. Johnson, Jimmy Cleveland, Bob Brookmeyer, Urbie Green. Polls: *DB* New Star '57. CDs: Prest.; NJ; Timel.; Sav.; w. Blakey (BN; Imp.; Riv.; Timel.); Lateef (Sav.; Riv.); Basie (Pab.); Coltrane; Bud Powell; J. Henderson; Mobley; L. Morgan; Shorter; Jimmy Smith; S. Turrentine (BN); Jazztet (Chess; Timel.); A. Farmer; Satchmo Legacy Band (SN); Flanagan; W. Harden; F. Wess (Sav.); Golson (NJ; Timel.; Drey.); J. Heath; P. J. Jones; Blue Mitchell (Riv.); J. McLean (NJ); P. Woods (Cand.); F. Hubbard (Imp.); J. Griffin (Ant.); Q. Jones; R.R. Kirk (Merc.); L. Hampton (Timel.); S. Hampton (BL).

FULLER, GIL (WALTER GILBERT), comp., arr; b. Los Angeles, CA, 4/14/20; d. NYC, 5/26/94. Raised in Calif. and Newark, N.J. As a teenager, wrote for Floyd Ray; Tiny Bradshaw. Stud. engineering at NYU, then ret. to West Coast; wrote for Les Hite 1940–2. Ret. to NYC after army service '42–5. Wrote arrs. for J. Lunceford; Woody Herman; Charlie Barnet; Count Basie; Artie Shaw; Benny Carter; Machito; Tito Puente. Best known as one of the first comp.-arr. to work in the bop idiom; he wrote pioneering scores for Billy Eckstine and Dizzy Gillespie, whose bb he helped assemble and direct in '46. Comp.-arr. for Gillespie's Carnegie Hall concert '48; also wrote for James Moody gp.; own bb rec. for Disc. In the '50s, his musical career was somewhat erratic; owned several mus. publ. firms; worked in real estate and engineering; worked briefly for Stan Kenton; freelanced. Ret. to Calif. in '57, did some film scoring; briefly had own rec. label, Orovox, '60–1; arr. Ray Charles first C&W rec. '62. Career was uplifted in '65 when he wrote mus. for Gilles-pie's app. w. Kenton's Neophonic Orch; mus. dir. for MJF house orch. Org. Gillespie Reunion BB for Berlin JF '68, rec. by MPS. When jazz was shaken up by the innovations of Parker and Gillespie, Fuller provided the effective orchestral counterpart for their improvisational contributions. His outstanding early arrs. for Gillespie, incl. "Ray's Idea," "Manteca," "Oop-Bop-Sh-Bam," "Swedish Suite," "One Bass Hit," and "Things to Come" (based on Gillespie's *Bebop*), rank as modern jazz classics. Fuller also anticipated the fusion of jazz and Afro-Cuban elements early on, writing for Machito and Tito Puente in the '40s. He wrote many backgrounds for singers, as well as stock arrs. for music publ. Despite his unquestionable versatility, he once said: "Everywhere I went they tagged me as a bebop writer. The fact that I was a trained, experienced all-around musician meant nothing to them. Being a pioneer has its disadvantages." Publ: *The Dizzy Gillespie Series for Jazz Orchestra* (Argus Publs. Inc., Maywood, N.J.). Recs. as lead.: Disc; WP. Co-comp: "One Bass Hit";

"Ray's Idea"; "Manteca"; "Swedish Suite." CDs: as arr. for Gillespie (Sav.; BB; PJ; GNP Cres.).

FULLER, JESSE, voc., gtr; b. Georgia, 3/1897; d. Oakland, CA, 1/28/76. Worked as a tap dancer, singer, and blues gtrst., but was not a full-time mus. Worked in construction and—dur. silent picture days, in Hollywood—pl. a bit part in *The Thief of Baghdad* w. Douglas Fairbanks in 1924. Renowned in the SF Bay area for his perfs. on the fotella, a home-made, one-man-band inst. App. at folk and jazz fests in Calif., pl. in Engl. early '60. Owned a shoeshine parlor in Oakland. Began rec. in late '50s. He admitted to no mus. infl., saying: "I have been my own favorite on my own instrument." CDs: GTJ; Prest.

FULLER, WALTER "ROSETTA," tpt, voc; b. Dyersburg, TN, 2/15/10; d. San Diego, CA, 4/20/03. Father pl. mello. in brass band. Prof. debut w. medicine show 1924, then moved to Chi. '25. Pl. w. Sammy Stewart '27–30; Irene Edie '30; Earl Hines '31–7; Horace Henderson '37–8; Hines '38–41. Fuller's singing on Hines's '34 hit "Rosetta" earned him his nickname. Led own gps fr. '41 in Chi., LA, and, fr. '46, in San Diego where he served on the Board of Dirs. of the SD Mus. Union and perf. into the '80s. Fuller was orig. inspired by Louis Armstrong and later, Red Allen, Sweets Edison, and Roy Eldridge. Fav: Armstrong. Film: app. in *Submarine Command* w. William Holden. CDs: w. Hines; L. Hampton (BB).

g

GADD, STEVE (Stephen K. Gadda), dms; b. Rochester, NY, 4/9/45. Uncle, who pl. bs. dm. in mil. band, showed him rudiments at age 7. Began serious stud. in 1957, having sat in w. Dizzy Gillespie at a local club a yr. earlier. Later stud. at Manh. Sch. of Mus. for two yrs. bef. sw. to the Eastman Sch. While there, pl. w. Chick Corea; Chuck Mangione; Gap Mangione; Joe Romano; Frank Pullara. After three yrs. w. an army band, he worked w. a bb in Rochester; in qt. w. Warren Bernhardt, Eddie Gomez, and George Young. To NYC '72 in trio w. Tony Levin, Mike Holmes. Rec. w. Chet Baker '74. Worked w. Stuff '74–5; Corea '75–81; Ben Sidran '78. A founding member—w. the Brecker bros.—of Steps Ahead, he left it in '81, then worked w. Masahiko Sato; Manhattan Jazz Qnt.; Joe Farrell; Herbie Hancock; Bob James; Steve Khan; Ron Carter; Roland Hanna; also w. Al Di Meola; Paul Simon; Stevie Wonder; Barbra Streisand; Paul McCartney; Aretha Franklin; Al Jarreau. Form. the Gadd Gang w. Ronnie Cuber, Gomez '88. Pl. w. Corea qt. for Eur. fests. '92; M. Petrucciani trio, in Eur., US '97. Favs: Elvin Jones, Tony Williams, Jack DeJohnette, Buddy Rich, Louie Bellson. CDs: w. Baker (CTI); G. Benson; Weather Report (Col.); C. Bley (Watt); Brecker Bros. (Novus); Corea (Polyd.; Verve; Stretch); R. Cuber (Elec. Bird); E. Elias; E. Gomez (Den.); R.R. Kirk (Atl.); Manhattan Jazz Qnt. (PW; SB); D. Sanborn (WB); G. Washington (Elek.).

GAFA, AL (ALEXANDER), gtr; b. Brooklyn, NY, 4/9/41. Self-taught. Fr. 1946 to '49 he worked as an NYC studio mus.; also w. gps. of K. Winding; Sam Donahue; Duke Pearson; concerts w. M. Legrand. Pl. w. orch. accomp. Sammy Davis '69–70; mus. dir. and accomp. for Carmen McRae '70–1. Pl. w. D. Gillespie '71; again '74–6, incl. Eur. tour w. *The Musical Life of Charlie Parker*, fall '74. Pl. w. Al Haig '78–80; own trio '78–81, both at Gregory's. Accomp. Johnny Hartman from late '70s to '82 at Marty's, Fat Tuesday's, etc. Own trio at World Trade Center in early '80s and again '87–91. Worked in B'way pit orchs. in musicals such as *Annie, Cats, La Cage aux Folles* '82–6. Concentrating on writing originals '92. Comps: "Dirty Dog"; "Behind a Moonbeam"; "Barcelona." Recs: own LP *Leblon Beach*, Pablo; others w. C. McRae (Atl.); J. Hartman (Bee Hive); Mike Longo; J. Albany; D. Pearson. CDs: w. Gillespie (Pab.); S. McCorkle (Conc.).

GAILLARD, SLIM (BULEE), gtr, pno, vib, perc, voc; b. Santa Clara, Cuba, 1/1/16; d. London, England, 2/26/91. Previous reference books have cited Det. as his birthplace, but in his 1986 autobiography, *I Was There*, he wrote that he was born in Cuba and that his father, a chief steward on an ocean liner, accidentally left him behind on the island of Crete when he was 12 yrs. old. According to his narrative, he eventually worked his way to the US, settling in Det. He app. in vaudeville as a solo variety act, pl. gtr., tnr. sax, and vib., as well as singing and dancing. Moved to NYC in '37, where he form. duo w. bassist Slam Stewart. Their '38 recording of "Flat Foot Floogie" on Voc. was a huge success and brought them national recognition; radio series on WNEW. Gaillard moved to LA '41, still occ. perf. w. Stewart to '43, but became best-known as a comedian-lead. of small gps. App. in several films in '40s; occ. in later yrs. army service '43–4; then ret. to LA, pl. clubs such as the Regency and Billy Berg's w. bs.

Tiny "Bam" Brown; Leo Watson. In '46 rec. *Opera in Vout* (co-comp.) w. Brown, a tour de force of the nonsense syllable–styled songs, incorporating "o-rooney," "o-reeney, "vout," and "voutie," that made Gaillard such a popular entertainer. Often pl. pno. with his outsize hands palms upward. In mid '40s made series of recs. for various small labels w. Parker, Gillespie, others. Radio broadcasts late '40s. From mid '50s to '70s, career went into decline; was motel manager in San Diego '63; in '70s owner of an orange farm in Seattle. Reunion w. Stewart at MJF '70. Moved to London early '80s, app. regularly in clubs; Nice JF '82; Village West club, NYC, Nov. '83. Eur. apps. w. the Slapcats, a French gp.; recs. w. Buddy Tate in London; single w. Brit. jazz-rap gp., the Dream Warriors, "Easy to Put Together, But Hard to Take Apart." Films: *Hellzapoppin'; Star Spangled Rhythm; Almost Married; Sweetheart of Sigma Chi; Go, Man, Go; Absolute Beginners.* TV: *Roots 2* '78; BBC series '89. Comps.: "Tutti Frutti"; "Poppity Pop." Recs: as lead., Verve, Hep. CDs: Verve; Hep; Class.; Slim & Slam, *The Groove Juice Special*, Col.; w. Parker (Sav.).

GALBRAITH, BARRY JOSEPH, gtr; b. Pittsburgh, PA, 12/18/19; d. Burlington, VT, 1/13/83. Self-taught; started on bjo.; sw. to gtr. after hearing Eddie Lang. First pl. in local clubs; early work w. Red Norvo; Teddy Powell, Babe Russin. Member of Claude Thornhill orch. 1941–2, then again '46–7; also w. Hal McIntyre '42; NBC and CBS staff mus. from '47–70. Tour w. S. Kenton '53. By '55, was regarded as one of the most prominent gtrsts. on the NYC rec. scene, participating in hundreds of sess. for popular and jazz LPs. USO tour to Iceland '57. An immaculate pl., he was also one of several mus., incl. Milt Hinton, Osie Johnson, who gathered informally to play the arrs. of George Russell, Gil Evans in the '50s. On faculty of jazz dept. at City Coll., CUNY '70–5. Favs: Christian, Raney, Farlow. Rec. w. Tal Farlow '54; Gil Evans, feat. on "Barry's Tune" '61. Film: *After Hours* '61. Book: *Barry Galbraith Guitar Study Series.* CDs: w. C. Hawkins (Riv.; Imp.; BB); G. Evans (Imp.; Verve); G. Russell (BB); C. Adderley (Riv.); E. Dolphy (Enja); C. Thornhill (Col.); Sheila Jordan (BN); Clifford Brown; H. Merrill; D. Washington (Em.); Thad Jones–Mel Lewis (LRC).

GALE, ERIC, gtr; b. NYC, 9/20/38; d. Baja California, Mexico, 5/25/94. Worked briefly as a chemist before beginning musical career in early 1960s. Self-taught; early exper. w. r&b bands. Rec. as sess. mus. w. King Curtis '63–70; Johnny Hodges–Clark Terry '66; Jimmy Smith '67; David "Fathead" Newman, Sonny Stitt '68; D. Newman, Mongo Santamaria,

Aretha Franklin '70. House guitarist for CTI label fr. '70; rec. w. Grover Washington Jr.; Stanley Turrentine; Bob James; others '71–7. Rec. first album as lead. for Kudu label '73. Lived in Jamaica briefly, then joined r&b gp. Stuff '75. Formed own gp. '82. CDs: Pinnacle; Disc.; Col.; w. S. Turrentine; G. Washington (CTI).

GALES, LARRY (LAWRENCE BERNARD), bs, comp, cello; b. NYC, 3/25/36; d. Sylmar, CA, 9/12/95. Began lessons w. third cousin, Geo. Duvivier, at age 11. Pl. bs. and cello in hs gps., then att. Manh. Sch. of Mus. 1956. Pl. w. Steve Pulliam '59; J.C. Heard; Buddy Tate '60; Eddie Davis–Johnny Griffin; Bennie Green '61; Herbie Mann; Charlie Rouse '62; Sonny Stitt, Junior Mance '63–4; Joe Williams w. Junior Mance Trio '64; Mary Lou Williams off and on '64 to late '60s; Thelonious Monk '65–9. Moved to Calif. '69; pl. w. Erroll Garner; Willie Bobo; Joe Williams; Red Rodney; Harold Land; Sweets Edison early '70s. Pl. in Calif. w. Bill Berry bb '73–4; Benny Carter '73–5; tour. Japan & US. Rec. in '70s w. Blue Mitchell; Jimmy Smith; Sonny Criss; Clark Terry; Dave Frishberg; Joe Turner; Kenny Burrell. Active as an educator and clinician and received many citations for his work in public schools. Favs: Paul Chambers, Wilbur Ware, Ron Carter. Fests: all major w. T. Monk; pl. at Candid label's Parker & Monk concert, JVC-NY '93. TV: app. in TV movie *The Morning After.* CDs: Cand.; w. Monk (Col.); Griffin-Davis (Jzld.); B. Tate (Prest.); Eddie Harris (Timel.); Burrell (32).

GALLIANO, RICHARD, acdn, bandoneon, comp; b. Cannes, France, 12/12/50. Began acdn. stud. at age 4 w. fath. At 12 won a competition among "young prodigies." Cont. to stud. acdn. and also took courses in harm., counterpoint, and tbn. at Nice Cons. Moved to Paris 1973, where he accomp. many singers. For seven yrs. was lead., arr., and comp. for Claude Nougaro, incl. rec. sessions and mus. for films. In the '80s worked w. C. Baker; J. Gourley; E. Louiss; M. Portal; Steve Potts trio; Daniel Goyonne trio; duo w. Ron Carter; and cellist Jean-Charles Capon w. Louis Sclavis, Mark Ducret. From the early '90s has carried forth Astor Piazzolla's "new tango," combining it w. his grounding in the French musette genre. Won Django Reinhardt Prize for rec. *The New Musette* '91. Collaborated w. gtrsts. Philip Catherine; and Bireli Lagrene w. whom he app. at Vienna JF '94. His virtuosity and versatility has brought new possibilities for the acdn. and enabled him to pl. convincingly in a variety of styles fr. Jimmy Gourley to Michel Portal. CDs: Drey.; Gourley-Galliano, *Flyin' the Coop*, 52e Rue Est.

GALLON, RAY (RAYMOND LEWIS), pno; b. NYC, 5/20/58. Father is amateur pianist. Stud. w. Jaki Byard 1976; John Lewis '78–81. Att. City Coll., received B.F.A. '82, M.A. in comp. '89. Pl. w. Ron Carter fr. '86; Sheila Jordan '86–7; Lionel Hampton '88–90; Geo. Adams fr. '89; Harper Bros. '91; also Dakota Staton; Charli Persip. Gigs w. B. Golson; Mingus Dynasty BB '92. Taught harmony and improv. at City Coll. from '87. App. w. Herb Harris qt. in concert at City Coll. '95. Gigged w. A. Farmer; L. Tabackin; B. Golson; TS Monk fr. '97. Join. Monk, late '98. Favs: Tatum, Monk, B. Powell. Fests: Eur. w. Hampton, Harper Bros.; Japan w. G. Adams. TV: *Tonight Show* w. Harper Bros.; Jap. TV w. Harper Bros., G. Adams; also videos w. Hampton. CDs: w. Harper Bros (Verve); G. Adams (BN); TS Monk (N-coded).

GALLOWAY, JIM (JAMES BRAIDIE), sop, tnr, bari saxes, cl, comp; b. Kilwinning, Ayrshire, Scotland, 7/28/36. Wife, Rosemary, pl. bs. Began on cl. Stud. at Glasgow Sch. of Fine Arts 1954–8. Pl. w. Alex Dulgleish's Scottish All-Stars; own gp. Jazz Makers '61–4. Moved to Toronto, Canada '64. Galloway joined Metro Stompers in '66 and led the gp. fr. '68; Stompers toured '68–70 and have been active intermittently in Tor. fr. '70. Accomp. Buck Clayton; Wild Bill Davison; Vic Dickenson; Jay McShann; Buddy Tate in Toronto clubs '70s. Pl. fests., jazz parties, etc. as single and w. all-star gps. fr. '76. Led Wee Big Band, a jazz repertory orch., in Tor. fr. '79. Hosted live jazz radio show in Tor. '81–7. Premiered extended work *Hot and Suite* w. Scottish Nat'l Orch. '85. Worked as booking agent for several Toronto jazz clubs and has been artistic dir. of the city's Du Maurier Downtown JF fr. '87. Infl: Bechet. CDs: M&A; Sack.; w. Art Hodes (M&A); Doc Cheatham (Sack.).

GALPER, HAL (HAROLD), pno, comp, arr; b. Salem, MA, 4/18/38. Studied classical pno. 1944–9. Galper became int. in jazz after hearing Herb Pomeroy, Serge Chaloff at Boston club The Stables, across the street fr. his hs. Stud. at Berklee '56–9, also w. Ray Santisi; Jaki Byard; Herb Pomeroy; Margaret Chaloff. Pl. in Boston w. Pomeroy Qnt. and bb; Sam Rivers '59–60. In Paris '60. Ret. to US, pl. w. Rivers '61–3; Chet Baker '63–5; Phil Woods '65; Randy Brecker '66; P. Woods '67; Donald Byrd '68; Joe Henderson '69; Bobby Hutcherson–Harold Land '70; Stan Getz '71; Cannonball Adderley '73–5; Lee Konitz '75; C. Baker '76; own qnt. w. Randy and Michael Brecker '77–8; John Scofield '78–9; Slide Hampton, Cannonball Adderley Brotherhood '80. Pl. and arr. for Phil Woods '80–90. Galper has led his own trio w. Todd Coolman, Steve Ellington fr. '90. He has app. as a lecturer and clinician at many univs. in the US and Eur. and currently teaches at the New Sch. He is head of a nonprofit org., The Arts and Educ. Team, which addresses financial and other concerns of mid-career musicians. In '90, Berklee awarded Galper an Artist's Diploma. Favs: Miles Davis, Ahmad Jamal. Fests: all major fr. '60. CDs: Red; Jazz; Steep; Enja; Conc.; w. P. Woods (Conc.; Red; Den.); C. Baker (FS; Phil.); S. Rivers (BN); C. Adderley (Fant.); T. Harrell; L. Konitz (Steep.); R. Brecker (BN); D. Gillespie (Timel.); J. Scofield (Enja).

GANELIN, VYACHESLAV SHEVELEVICH, pno, comp; also kybds, fl, perc, gtr; b. Kraskov, Russia, USSR, 12/17/44. Played in dance bands fr. 1961, then form. jazz trio '64. Grad. fr. Lithuanian State Cons., Vilnius, '68. Form. free jazz duo w. Vladimir Tarasov '69. With the addition of Vladimir Chekasin in '71 this gp. became the Ganelin Trio, later known as the G-T-Ch Trio. Perf. mainly in USSR, Eastern Eur., Cuba '70s; Western Eur. fr. '80s. Rec. for Soviet state-owned label Melodiya fr. '76; later, tapes smuggled out of Russia were released on the British Leo label, accomp. by strong disclaimers that the musicians were not responsible for the release of the tapes. The gp. perf. in '86 at the Jazz Yatra fest. in India and the JVC fest. in NYC before disbanding in '87. Ganelin's comps. incl. a ballet, an opera, and a rock opera. Since immigrating to Israel in '87, Ganelin has formed a new trio w. bassist Victor Fonarev and drummer Mika Markovich. Rec. w. Andrew Cyrille '91. Fests: w. Ganelin Trio, West Berlin '80; Italy '81; UK '84; Bombay; NYC '86. CDs: hatArt; Leo; Melodiya; w. Andrew Cyrille (M&A); Petrs Vysniauskas (Leo).

GANLEY, ALLAN, dms, comp, arr; b. Tolworth, Surrey, England, 3/11/31. Became interested in jazz at age 10; began practicing dms. at 16. In Royal Air Force 1949–51, then pl. w. Jack Parnell '53; Johnny Dankworth '53–5; Bert Ambrose '54; Derek Smith '55; New Jazz Gp. w. Smith; Dizzy Reece '56. Also rec. in '50s w. Mary Lou Williams; Vic Ash; Cleo Laine; Ronnie Scott. Tour. US w. Ronnie Scott '57. Co-led Jazzmakers w. Ronnie Ross '58–60. Tour. US w. Jazzmakers '59, incl. perf. at NJF. Rec. w. Dave Brubeck '61. Pl. w. Tubby Hayes '62–4; Stan Tracey '65. House drummer at Ronnie Scott's club accomp. visiting Amer. artists incl. Dizzy Gillespie; Art Farmer; Freddie Hubbard; Roland Kirk; Clark Terry–Bob Brookmeyer; Benny Golson; Maynard Ferguson; Stan Getz; Jim Hall '64–7. Also rec. in '60s w. C. Laine–J. Dankworth; Blossom Dearie.

Stud. arr. at Berklee Coll. of Mus. '70. Ret. to Engl., led bb w. sidemen incl. Vic Ash; Kenny Wheeler; Chris Pyne '76–86. Freelanced in Engl. throughout '70s-80s; rec. in '70s w. Jim Hall; Al Haig. Arr. for Ronnie Ross; Peter King; BBC Radio BB; others fr. '80s. Maintains a busy schedule, pl. club and festival dates in the UK and abroad. Pl. & rec. w. pnst. Dave Newton in early '90s. Favs: Roach, Rich, Haynes. Polls: *MM* several times. TV: British TV w. C. Terry–B. Brookmeyer; B. Golson; M. Ferguson. LPs: w. Haig (Spot.). CDs: w. Scott Hamilton (Conc.); S. Gaillard; Spike Robinson (Hep); J. Dankworth (Sepia); Martin Taylor (Linn).

GARBAREK, JAN, tnr, sop saxes, fl; b. Mysen, Norway, 3/4/47. Self-taught. Worked w. own gps. in Norway. Gained notice in Eur. jazz circles in mid 1960s through Krysztof Komeda and George Russell; pl. fests. in Warsaw. In late '60s worked and stud. w. Russell; form. qt. w. Terje Rypdal that frequently app. w. Russell's band. He also app. w. Chick Corea; Don Cherry; Keith Jarrett; other Scand. all-star gps. From '73 led own trio. Join. Jarrett's qt. '77, tour. Eur. and US. In late '70s form. own gp. w. kybd. Eberhard Weber, gtr. David Torn, dmr. Michael Di Pasqua.; tour. Eur., US, Japan, Norway '82. Comp. most of the work he rec. Infl: Coltrane, Russell, M. Davis, Jarrett; Norwegian folk music. Many recs. as lead. for ECM.; also w. Ralph Towner; Charlie Haden. In '93 he rec. *Officium* w. the Hilliard Ensemble, a British voc. qt. specializing in 12th- to 16th-century liturgical works. CDs: ECM; w. Haden; Jarrett; G. Peacock; Rypdal; Weber; Towner; K. Wheeler (ECM); Russell (SN).

GARCIA, DICK (RICHARD JOSEPH), gtr; b. NYC, 5/11/31. Great-grandfather pl. command perf. for King of Spain; grandfath. and fath. both gtrsts. Self-taught from age 9; stud. for a yr. in 1944–5. Terry Gibbs heard him at a Greenwich Village jam sess. and recommended him to Tony Scott, w. whom Garcia first pl. in '50; again in '55–6. Worked w. George Shearing '52, incl. tour of continental US, Honolulu. Freelanced in NYC, incl. Joe Roland '55. Rejoin. Shearing '59. Fav. own rec.: *Jazzville, USA, Vol. II*, Dawn, w. own qt. Favs: Farlow, Kessel, Raney. Garcia is an extraordinarily gifted guitarist, unusually fluent in phrasing and style. Recs. w. Shearing (MGM); Milt Buckner (Cap.); Lenny Hambro (Col.); Scott (Vict.). CD: w. Shearing (Verve).

GARCIA, RUSS (RUSSELL), comp, arr, tpt; b. Oakland, CA, 4/12/16. Attended San Francisco St. Coll.; priv. stud. w. Mario Castelnuovo-Tedesco and others. Worked locally, then w. Horace Heidt; Al Donahue; NBC staff work in Hollywood. Own recs.

'55–7 (incl. *Rocky Road*, Beth.) which identified him as a prominent voice in West Coast–style jazz. Arrs. for Buddy DeFranco '53–4; Charlie Barnet '56; Roy Eldridge '57; Johnny Hodges '58; Ray Brown '60; and others. Motion picture scores for Universal, Warner Bros., Disney, etc.; comp. for Stan Kenton's Neophonic Orchestra '65. *Variations for Fluegel-horn, String Quartet, Bass and Drums*, a mixed jazz-classical composition, rec. in '79. Author of an influential guide to arranging. CDs: Trend.

GARDNER, DERRICK EARL, tpt; b. Chicago, IL, 6/3/65. Father, tptr. Burgess Lamar Gardner, has pl. w. Count Basie; Ray Charles; Cannonball Adderley; Eddie Harris; etc.; has chaired the jazz stud. depts. at Norfolk St. U.; Governor St. U.; Cal. St.-Fullerton. Moth., Effie Tyler Gardner, pno., org., taught at Hampton U. for nineteen yrs., chaired the mus. dept. Lectures and teaches clinics in mus. educ. and is minister of mus. at several Hampton, Va., area churches. Bro., Vincent Ramal Gardner, has pl. tbn. w. Basie; LCJO; Marcus Roberts; Frank Foster; Illinois Jacquet. Cousin, Brian Gardner, tnr. sax, tours. in US w. r&b bands. Stud. pno. and tpt. at Hampton U. 1983–7; Indiana U. '88–91. First prof. job was eleven dates w. Ringling Bros & Barnum & Bailey Circus; recommended by tpt. instructor Robert Ransome. Has led own Jazz Prophets in NYC fr. '88. Pl. w. Basie '91–6; Craig Bailey qnt. fr. '93; CHJB '95–6; F. Foster qnt. fr. '96; bb fr. '97; Roy Hargrove bb fr. 97; also in '97 w. Charles Mingus bb; Vanguard Jazz Orch.; Rufus Reid sxt.; Cecil Brooks qt. Worked worldwide w. Basie; Eur. w. Bailey; Foster; also eight-mo. tour w. *Black and Blue*. Dir. of Indiana U. "Soul Revue" '90–1. Teaches priv. in NYC. Favs: F. Hubbard, C. Brown, Woody Shaw. CDs: w. Basie (Tel.; Jazz); Bailey (Cand.); Foster (Arab.); Lena Horne (BN); T. Puente (RMM).

GARDNER, EARL WESLEY JR., tpt, flg; b. NYC, 4/19/50. Wife, Cecelia, pl. vln. w. Max Roach Double Qt.; B'way shows. Stud. at Mus. and Art HS, then at Temple U. Pl. w. Thad Jones–Mel Lewis Orch. fr. 1976, cont. w. Mel Lewis Orch.; Vanguard Orch.; Geo. Gruntz '78; McCoy Tyner bb; *Sat. Night Live* band fr. '85; Dizzy Gillespie bb fr. '87; Gene Harris bb '89; Mingus Epitaph '90–1; Charlie Haden Liberation Orch. '90–2; Lester Bowie Brass Fantasy '91–2. Also pl. w. Amer. Jazz Orch.; Clifford Jordan bb; Clark Terry bb; repertory gps. at Lincoln Ctr. and Carnegie Hall fr. '89. Gardner has pl. on several movie soundtracks incl. *Stardust Memories; School Daze*. Favs: Jon Faddis, Woody Shaw, Wynton Marsalis, Freddie Hubbard, Snooky Young. Fests: Eur. fr. '76. TV: *Sat. Night Live* fr. '85; Emmy Awds.

'87. CDs: w. Tyner (Mile.; Bird.); Lewis (Tel.; MM); B. Marsalis (Col.); G. Dial (dmp); C. Haden (Verve); R. Eubanks (JMT); G. Benson (WB); CHJB (BN).

GARLAND, ED "MONTUDIE" (EDWARD BERTRAM), bs; b. New Orleans, LA, 1/9/1885; d. Los Angeles, CA, 1/22/80. First pl. washtub bs. w. Kid Ory; bs. and snare dm., tba. in NO marching bands fr. 1908, incl. Excelsior '10; Imperial, Security '11. Worked w. Buddy Bolden '04; Freddie Keppard '08. Pl. w. Ory's Brownskin Babes '10. Moved to Chi. '14, worked at Deluxe Café; later w. Emmanuel Perez; Freddie Keppard. Join. King Oliver in '16 and pl. w. his band in LA '21, remaining there when Oliver ret. to Chi. Pl. taxi dance halls in LA; led own One Eleven band '29–33. Fr. '44–55, after yrs. in obscurity, was heard again w. Ory, then w. Earl Hines at Hangover Club in SF '55–6; Turk Murphy '57; to France w. Ory '57; freelanced on West Coast; worked at Disneyland '69. App. in revue, *A Night in New Orleans*, LA '73 '74; honored as "oldest living jazz sideman" by Pres. Ford and LA Mayor Bradley dur. Sept. '74 perf. Join. Barry Martyn's Legends of Jazz '74, tour. US, Eur. An early employer of slapping and pizzicato in jazz context; his expressive arco pl. heard to advantage on '44 rec. w. Ory, "Blues for Jimmy." Favs: Arvell Shaw, Pops Foster. Fests: NO J&H, w. Ory '71. Film: *Imitation of Life* '59. TV: w. Legends on *Dinah Shore* show '75. Fav. own rec: "Muskrat Ramble" w. Ory; many recs. w. Ory '22, '44. CDs: w. Ory (GTJ; Story.); Bunk Johnson; Albert Burbank (Story.); Barney Bigard and Legends of Jazz (GHB).

GARLAND, JOE (JOSEPH COPELAND), comp-arr, tnr sax; also sop, bari saxes, cl; b. Norfolk, VA, 8/15/03; d. Teaneck, NJ, 4/21/77. Studied at Aeolian Cons. in Baltimore; Shaw U. Pl. in coll. bands and orchs; join. Seminole Syncopators 1924; w. Elmer Snowden in NYC '25; Leon Abbey '27, incl. S. Amer. tour. Worked w. Mills Blue Rhythm band '32–6, also as arr; short stints w. Edgar Hayes '37; Don Redman '38; also Lucky Millinder. Join. L. Armstrong's bb '39, taking over as dir. fr. Luis Russell '40; stayed w. Armstrong until '47, except for some freelance work '43–4. In late '40s, worked w. Herbie Fields; Claude Hopkins; Earl Hines. Semi-retired from mus. in '50s, working as a housing inspector. Fr. '59, he and bro., tptr. Moses Garland, occ. led bb comprised of former swing era mus. in NYC-NJ area for club dates. Was also active as photographer and received degrees from three photography schs. Best known as the comp. of "Leap Frog," Les Brown's theme; G. Miller's theme, "In the Mood," which he adapted from the riff "Tar Paper

Stomp," popularized by Wingy Manone. Other comps: "Congo Caravan"; "There's Rhythm in Harlem"; "Serenade to a Savage." Recs. as sideman w. Seminole Syncopators (Okeh) '24; Mills Blue Rhythm (Voc.) '33, (Col.) '33, '35; Ellington (Bruns.) '33. CDs: w. J. R. Morton (BB); Mills Blue Rhythm (Hep); Armstrong (Dec.).

GARLAND, RED (WILLIAM M.), pno; b. Dallas, TX, 5/13/23; d. Dallas, 4/23/84. First pl. cl., stud. w. Prof. A.S. Jackson and Buster Smith; sw. to pno. at age 18. Discovered by Hot Lips Page in Dallas. Fr. 1945 to '55, he worked in NYC and Phila. w. an impressive array of mus., incl. Page; Charlie Parker; Coleman Hawkins; Roy Eldridge; and Ben Webster. Fr. '55 to '57, he received major recognition as a member of the Miles Davis qnt., which also incl. Paul Chambers and Philly Joe Jones. In '57, he freelanced, pl. in NYC w. Donald Byrd; John Coltrane; and Art Taylor; rejoin. Davis in '58. Form. own trio in '59, tour. US; made series of recs. for Prest. w. his trio and qnt. that incl. Coltrane, Byrd, and Taylor. Dur. his work w. Davis and Coltrane, he was a sideman on such seminal recs. as *Cookin'*, *Relaxin'*, *Milestones* w. Davis; *Soultrane, Tranein' In* w. Coltrane. To Phila. in mid '60s, pl. weekends. Ret. to Dallas in '65 when his moth. died, working at Club Arandas and Woodmen Auditorium fr. '66; also pl. in LA '66. To NYC for a month, spring '71, pl. weekends at east side club Pegleg's and rec. two LPs for MPS; ret. to Dallas in June. After yrs. of relative obscurity, made a successful but brief comeback in the late '70s, incl. gigs at Lush Life, NYC, and on recs. In the yrs. following his time w. Davis, Garland became an infl. in his own right, infusing post-bop pno. w. a bluesy, swinging solidity underscoring his subtle, melodic solos. Favs: Tatum, Bud Powell, Hank Jones. CDs: Prest.; Gal.; Timel.; w. Davis (Prest.; Col.); Coltrane; C. Hawkins; J. McLean; Rollins; A. Cobb; A. Taylor; Lockjaw Davis (Prest.); C. Parker (BN); A. Pepper (Cont.).

GARNER, ERROLL LOUIS, pno, comp; b. Pittsburgh, PA, 6/15/21; d. Los Angeles, CA, 1/2/77. Father pl. tpt.; bro. Linton, sist. Martha, pno. Began playing at age 3, a totally self-taught musician who never learned to read music. A classmate of Dodo Marmarosa and an early associate of Billy Strayhorn at Westinghouse HS. By age 7, heard on radio station KDKA with a gp. called the Kan-D-Kids. Also subbed for pnsts., incl. Fate Marable, on the Allegheny riverboats. In 1937, started to pl. prof. w. local gps. and w. Leroy Brown's orch. from '38–41. Played solo pno. at local bars incl. Mercurs; for silent films at local cinema; and org. at sanctified churches on Sundays. Moved to NYC in '44 and pl. solo at several clubs on 52nd St., incl. the Three Deuces and Tondelayo's. After subbing for Art Tatum in Tatum's trio with Slam Stewart and Tiny Grimes, he remained when Stewart became leader in '45. Garner then formed his own trio, w. bs. and dms., a setting he favored throughout his career. In '47, while leading a trio in Calif. with Red Callender and Doc West, he recorded with Charlie Parker. In May '48 his trio pl. in Paris during a week of jazz at the Marigny Theatre. His solo concert debut was in '50 at Cleveland's Music Hall. In '52, with Tatum, Meade Lux Lewis, and Pete Johnson, he was part of "Piano Parade" that toured the US. From '45–9, Garner made many recs. for various labels on a freelance basis bef. signing exclusively with Col.; in '54 he joined Merc., but rejoin. Col. in '56. His celebrated '55 *Concert By the Sea*, rec. in Carmel, Calif., was released in '56. He formed his own label, Octave Records, in '54 and rec. for it periodically, '59–73.

From the late '50s until his death, Garner enjoyed tremendous popular success. He toured Eur. for the first time in the winter of '57–8 and made frequent tours of Engl. and the Continent in the '60s. In '57, he debuted w. the Cleveland Symphony, the first of several apps. he subsequently made with symph. orchs. In '58 he was the first and only jazz artist booked by the impresario Sol Hurok, remaining under his aegis to '62. The following yr., he scored a hit with his recording of "Misty," his own comp., which became one of the most rec. songs of the '60s and has since won many awards.

Throughout the '50s and '60s he was one of a handful of jazz musicians who enjoyed frequent TV exposure; he app. on the shows of Ed Sullivan; Garry Moore; Steve Allen; Ernie Ford; Jackie Gleason; Merv Griffin; Perry Como; the *Bell Telephone Hour*; *Today* and *Tonight* shows. In the late '60s he starred at the International Television Festival in Montreux and was also commissioned to comp. the festival's theme. In the same period, he was the only US artist to app. at the ROTF Eurovision Gala.

By the early '70s Garner was still a fantastically popular concert artist and fest. attraction; he gave his first South Amer. tour and app. at Antibes '70; first tour of Far East '72; and perf. at several galas on the French Riviera '73–4. In '74–5 he performed w. the National Symph. in Wash., D.C., and symphonies in Honolulu, Louisville, Indianapolis, and Det. In early '75, he contracted a severe case of pneumonia fr. which he never recovered.

Garner achieved wide-spread recognition through his highly individualistic and oft-emulated style. By the late '40s, his orchestral style of piano playing had become signature: his left hand played a steady swinging pulse of spread block chords, akin to a rhythm guitar, to accompany his brilliant, right-hand melodic lines and variations, often utilizing striking, octave-encompassing, dramatic, right-hand chordal passages. Over the yrs. his bs. and dm. accomps. incl. Oscar Pettiford and J.C. Heard; John Simmons and Shadow Wilson; Wyatt Ruther and Fats Heard; Eddie Calhoun and Kelly Martin. On Latin percussion he utilized Jose Mangual and, on recs., Candido. Polls: *Esq.* New Star '46; *DB* Readers Poll '49, '56–8; *DB* Critics '57; *Met.* '58–60; many ASCAP awards for "Misty." Films: re-recorded "Misty" for *Play Misty for Me* '71; comp. theme for *A New Kind of Love* '63; his recs. are also heard on the soundtracks of Woody Allen's *Another Woman*; *Alice*; *Deconstructing Harry*. TV: subject for *Just Jazz* '71; many apps. on Eur. TV. Comps: "Gaslight"; "Up In Erroll's Room"; "Solitaire"; "Feeling Is Believing"; "Dreamy"; "That's My Kick"; "Nightwind"; "Other Voices"; "Passing Through," published by Octave Music, a company he formed in '54. Books: *Erroll Garner Songbooks* (Cherry Lane Music); stage band arrs. of Garner songs (Kendor Music). Ballet: music for *Fast Company* perf. by Dayton Ballet Company and the Princeton Ballet Company. Book: *Erroll Garner: The Most Happy Piano*, a bio-discography by James Doran (Scarecrow Press) '85. Through the efforts of his longtime manager, Martha Glaser, in addition to reissues there have also been productions of heretofore unreleased material. CDs: Tel.; Col.; Em.; Verve; Merc.; Sav.; w. C. Parker (Stash); S. Stewart (Sav.); W. Gray (Crown).

GARNER, LINTON S., pno, comp; also tpt, alto horn, bass horn; b. Greensboro, NC, 3/25/15; d. Vancouver, B.C., Can., 2/6/03. Brother of Erroll Garner. Sists. Martha, Ruth, Berniece, also pl. pno. Stud. pno. in Pitts. 1923; tpt. '24. Pl. tpt. in hs and in local bands that incl. Art Blakey, Billy Eckstine. Gave up tpt. '35, ret. to pl. pno. Pl. w. Larry Steele revue; Burns Campbell mid '30s. Worked in Rochester, N.Y., for two yrs., then at McVann's Club in Buffalo, N.Y., until '40, when he joined a band from Pitts. that was fronted by Fletcher Henderson '41–3. In army '43–5, then pl. w. and arr. for Billy Eckstine Orch. '46–7. Accomp. for comedian Timmie Rogers '47–50. Rec. in 'late '40s w. Fats Navarro; Allen Eager; Babs Gonzales; B. Eckstine. Also freelanced as accomp. w. dancer Teddy Hale; as arr. w. Earl Coleman; D. Gllespie, who rec. his "Minor Walk" '47, and "Duff Capers" '48. Rec. as leader of trio w. Al Hall, Jimmie Crawford for Enrica '59. Hotel lounge pianist in Vancouver, Can., fr. mid '74. An accomplished pnst. whose style in no way resembled his bro.'s. CDs: w. Eckstine (Sav.); B. Gonzales (BN).

GARNETT, ALVESTER CAROLL, dms; b. Richmond, VA, 7/17/70. Mother and uncles were active in church choir. Stud. pno., voice, and dms. as a child; started stud. formally at age 5 at Community Mus. Sch. at Va. Commonwealth U. Also stud. tap dance and African dance; stud. African perc.; and later accomp. African dance troup. Cont. formal stud. through hs; mus. major at Va. Commonwealth, concert and orch. perc.; private classes w. Max Roach; Victor Lewis; Ed Blackwell. Awarded Third Place (tie) in Thelonious Monk Competition, NYC 1992. First worked prof. w. Betty Carter '93, Abbey Lincoln '93–6. Also cites Clark Terry as a great help in his early career. Pl. w. Cyrus Chestnut Trio fr. '95; Roy Hargrove Qnt. and bb '96; tour. Eur. w. Phil Woods, spring '96. Favs: Roach, E. Jones, P.J. Jones. TV: BET; w. Abbey Lincoln. CDs: w. Chesnut (Atl.); Lincoln; Teddy Edwards; C. Escoudé (Verve).

GARNETT, CARLOS, tnr sax, comp; also sop, bari saxes, fl; b. Red Tank, Canal Zone, 12/1/38. Self-taught on tnr. sax from age 16. Pl. Latin music as a teenager; pl. tnr. w. US mus., servicemen stationed in Canal Zone. Moved to NYC 1962, worked w. various rock gps. Serious self-study of "science of music" from '65. Join. F. Hubbard '68, rec. first album w. him; A. Blakey '69–70; briefly w. C. Mingus '70. Form. own gp. Universal Black Force, worked from '70–2; during same period pl. w. Mtume; also pl. w. Andrew Hill; Brother Jack McDuff. Pl. w. M. Davis '72; Norman Connors '72–5. Re-formed own gp. '75. Worked in NYC '94; own qt. at Blue Note '98. Infl: Coltrane, H. Mobley, H. Land, W. Shorter. Fests: NJF w. Blakey '69; NJF-NY w. Connors '74. Comp: "Mother of the Future"; "Holy Waters"; "Carlos Two." LP w. Connors, Buddah–Cobble. CDs: High.; 32; Muse; w. Davis (Col.); Hill (BN).

GARRETT, DON (DONALD RAPHAEL), bs; cls, saxes, fls, shakuhachi; b. El Dorado, AR, 2/28/32; d. Champaign, IL, 8/14/89. Studied mus. under Capt. Walter Dyett at DuSable HS, Chi. Worked in Chi. w. Ira Sullivan 1960–2; a charter member of Muhal Richard Abrams' Experimental Band '61. In mid-'60s rec. w. Coltrane; pl. w. Archie Shepp '66, again in '73; gigs in Paris w. Frank Wright and Jean-Luc Ponty '71. From late '70s, tours in Eur., No. Africa w. his wife, Zusaan Kali Fasteau, in their gp. the Sea Ensemble; perf. on many non-Western instr., incl. bamboo flutes of his own make and design. Recs. w. Sullivan; Eddie Harris; Dewey Redman; Joseph Jarman. CDs: w. Coltrane (Imp.); R.R. Kirk (Chess).

GARRETT, KENNY, alto sax; b. Detroit, MI, 10/9/60. Influenced by his stepfath., who pl. sax,

developed early interest in jazz. Stud. cl. and fl. w. Bill Wiggins; then took part in wkshp. cond. by Marcus Belgrave in mid 1970s. After hs grad., join. the Duke Ellington orch. in '78 for three and a half yrs. where he was mentored by Harold Minerve. Moved to NYC '82; pl. in pit orchestra for Ellington musical, *Sophisticated Ladies*. Pl. at Tin Palace w. George Coleman; worked in the orchs. of Mel Lewis; Frank Foster; Dannie Richmond's qnt. Rec. deb. as lead. for Criss Cross '84. Worked w. Freddie Hubbard '84; Out of the Blue '85; join. Art Blakey '85; from late '80s to early '90s, pl. w. Miles Davis; also w. Sting, Peter Gabriel, et al. on Amnesty International tour to Middle East and Africa. After Davis's death form. own gp. and began to tour internationally. He emerged from the Davis band as a strong leader, a new maturity enhancing his already obvious talent as saxophonist and composer. Won *DB* Readers Poll '96. Videos: *Miles and Quincy, Live at Montreux; Miles in Paris*, WB. CDs: WB; Atl.; CC; PW; w. M. Davis (WB); Blakey (PW; Delos; Pro Jazz); Stephen Scott (Verve); OTB; Geri Allen (BN); T. Harrell (CC); Mulgrew Miller (Land.; Novus); W. Roney; W. Shaw; C. Blackman (Muse); Hubbard (Enja); Mercer Ellington (MM).

GARRICK, MICHAEL, pno, pipe org, kybds, comp; b. Enfield, England, 5/30/33. Parents musical. B.A.. in Engl. lit. at London U. Self-taught as mus. but did take some classes at Ivor Mairants' Central Sch. of Dance Mus. 1953–56. Att. Berklee Coll. of Mus. '75–6. Form. own qt. '58, becoming quite involved w. Poetry and Jazz concerts; own qnt., w. Joe Harriott, Shake Keane; trio '63–92; sxt. fr. '66. Pl. w. Don Rendell–Ian Carr qnt. '65–9; Neil Ardley's New Jazz Orch. '64–6; Threesome fr. '77; Chris Hunter '82–4; Dave Green fr. '83; own sxt. Flybinite fr. '83; Kenny Wheeler orch.; Duncan Lamont orch. '88–91; own bb '85–92. Teacher at Royal Acad. of Mus., London. Wrote for Rendell–Carr; in '67 comp. *Jazz Praises*, a cycle of religious pieces for own sext. and choir, rec. in St. Paul's Cathedral '68. Comps: "Black Marigolds"; "Dusk Fire"; "Cold Mountain"; "The Royal Box"; "Bovingdon Poppies." Stud. Indian mus., reflected in some of his comps. Favs: Bill Evans, John Taylor, Ellington, Herbie Hancock. Other infls: John Lewis, K. Wheeler. Pl. in Germ. '58; Antibes '68; Singapore '82. Rec. for Argo & Hep labels fr. '64. CDs: Jazz Academy.

GARRISON, ARV (ARVIN CHARLES), gtr; also bs; b. Toledo, OH, 8/17/22; d. Toledo, 7/30/60. Grandmother was prof. pnst. Self-taught; start. on uke. at age 9; gtr. for church socials; pl. lodge dances at 12; hs dances. Form. own combo, which pl. at Kenmore Hotel, Albany, N.Y. Pl. w. Don Seat in Pitts. Form. own trio 1941, which worked on both coasts to '48; from '46 known as Vivien Garry Trio, after his wife, the trio's bs. In '50s perf. in Toledo where he resettled. A fine-toned, Reinhardt-inspired gtrst., whose mid '40s recs. w. Parker; Gillespie; H. McGhee demonstrate his early affinity with bop. He drowned while having an epileptic seizure. Fav. own rec: his comp., "Five Guitars in Flight," incl. B. Kessel, Tony Rizzi, I. Ashby, Gene Sargent, w. Earl Spencer orch. B&W '47. CDs: w. Parker (Dial); Howard McGhee (Jz. Class.).

GARRISON, JIMMY (JAMES EMORY), bs; b. Miami, FL, 3/3/34; d. NYC, 4/7/76. Moved to Phila. at age 10. Start. on cl. in hs, sw. to bs. as a senior. After grad., began worked w. local bands incl. Bobby Timmons; Al Heath. Moved to NYC in 1958, pl. w. Philly Joe Jones; Lennie Tristano; Benny Golson; Curtis Fuller; Kenny Dorham; Bill Evans. Back w. Jones '60. Worked w. Ornette Coleman at the Five Spot; US tour '61. From '61 to '66, he was a fundamental force in John Coltrane's gps., on records and in concert; tour. int'l. After leaving Coltrane, he co-led gp. w. Hampton Hawes '66; pl. w. Archie Shepp '67–8, incl. Eur. tour; Elvin Jones trio '68–9. In '70–1, he taught at Bennington Coll., Verm., and Wesleyan U., Conn. Pl. w. Alice Coltrane '72; rejoin. Elvin Jones '73–4. His pl. was curtailed by a hand impairment in latter part of '74; lung operation in '75. By the end of '75, he was a substance abuse counselor as house supervisor for Project Create and planned to resume playing. He died of lung cancer. A formidable bassist, he was the perfect accompanist for Coltrane, providing driving walking lines, ostinato effects, and emotionally charged improvisations, often employing a flamenco-like, strumming technique. He was also a master of double and multiple stops, lending a melodic, gtr.-like quality to his playing. Favs. and infl: Percy Heath, Ray Brown. Fests: NJF w. Jones; NJF-NY w. Shepp '73. Comp: "Tapestry in Sound"; "Ascendant"; "Sweet Little Maia." Recs. w. E. Jones; J. McLean (BN). CDs: w. Coltrane (Imp.; Pablo); Rollins; M. Tyner; Ellington (Imp.); P.J. Jones (Riv.); O. Coleman (Atl.; BN); K. Dorham (Bain.); W. Bishop (BL); C. Fuller; Bill Barron (Sav.); Cal Massey (Cand.); E. Jones (Imp.).

GARRISON, MATT (MATTHEW JUSTIN), el-bs, pno; b. NYC, 6/2/70. Father bassist Jimmy Garrison; moth. Roberta pl. pno., gtr., and sings; sist. Joy is a voc. Family moved to Rome when Matt was age 8. Began on el-bs. at 15. Ret. to US to live w. Jack DeJohnette 1987. Stud. at Berklee Coll. of Mus. '89–92; informally w. Dave Holland '89–90;

DeJohnette '89–95. First prof. gig touring w. Gary Burton '92–5; other early gigs w. Betty Carter; Mick Goodrick; Mike Gibbs; Lyle Mays. Pl. and rec. w. Bob Moses '92–5. Tour. w. Tiger Okoshi; Bela Fleck '94–5. Pl. and rec. w. Andy Milne '94–5; Steve Coleman '94–6. Member of Gil Evans Orch. at Sweet Basil '94–6. Also freelance. w. Joe Zawinul; Mino Cinelu; Peter Erskine; Roy Hargrove; Josh Redman; Gil Goldstein; many others. Favs: Jimmy Garrison, Jaco Pastorius, Art Tatum. Fests: all major '92–6. CDs: w. B. Moses (Gram.); Pat Metheny (Rep.); S. Coleman (Novus); w. Joe Zawinul (Escapade).

GARZONE, GEORGE S., tnr sax, fl, cl, sop sax; b. Cambridge, MA, 9/23/50. Grew up in family of musicians. Began on cl.; pl. club dates w. uncles fr. age 12. Stud. at Berklee Coll. of Mus. Tour. w. Tom Jones, Engelbert Humperdinck, Buddy Rich 1972–3. Has led own gp., The Fringe, in Boston fr. '72. Made rec. debut w. The Fringe '80. Garzone has taught at Berklee, New Engl. Cons., and the New Sch. In the '90s has been work. on an improv. technique which he calls The Cross Intervallic Triadic Approach. "This allows the improvisor to create dissonant melodies over chord changes in a melodic and triadic way. I have an example over the standard tune 'Have You Met Miss Jones' where I play a written solo of mine behind the melody of the tune." Favs: Coltrane, Shorter, D. Liebman, J. Lovano, M. Brecker. Polls: Boston Music Awards w. The Fringe. CDs: Arab.; NYC; Garzone-Lovano, NYC; w. Bob Moses (Gram.).

GASKIN, LEONARD, bs; b. Brooklyn, NY, 8/25/20. Studied pno., then bs. in hs and privately. Part of house band at Monroe's in Harlem w. D. Jordan and M. Roach in 1943; worked w. Dizzy Gillespie at the Downbeat '44; then freelanced w. such mus. as E. South; C. Shavers; C. Parker; Don Byas; E. Garner. Join. E. Condon '56, incl. Brit. tour '57. Left Condon to pursue studio work '60. In '70s and '80s apps. w. Sy Oliver; Panama Francis, International Art of Jazz; Oliver Jackson Trio '78–87, incl. several Eur. tours. In '90s pl. w. Big Nick Nicholas at Red Blazer; own trio at Deanna's in lower Manh. Favs: Pettiford, Duvivier. Pl. Edinburgh JF '90; made speaking tour of Senegal for Dizzy Gillespie Society of Dakar '94. CDs: w. M. Davis; K. Pleasure (Prest.); Swingville All-Stars (GTJ); Condon (Col.); Garner (Verve); Getz (Roul.); J.J. Johnson (Sav.); J. Teagarden (BB).

GASKIN, (RODERICK) VICTOR, bs, gtr; b. Bronx, NY, 11/23/34. Father fr. Virgin Islands, pl. calypso flute; uncles also mus. Started on mand. and gtr. Stud. gtr. w. uncles and fath., then w. Charlie Richards fr. 1944. Taught self to pl. bs. while in Marines '52–4. Stud. bs. w. Al McKibbon '60–2; Stuart Sankey; Al Brehm; Ralph Pena '60s; Richard Davis; Billy Taylor '70s. First gigs w. Eli Fountaine II '54. Pl. on West Coast w. Kirt Bradford–Betty Roche '57; Mike Wofford '58; Paul Horn at Shelly's Manne Hole '60–2. Freelance in LA w. Harold Land; Curtis Amy; Roy Ayers; Oscar Brown, Jr.; etc. fr. '61. Pl. w. Les McCann '63–6; Cannonball Adderley '66–9. Moved to NYC '69, freelance w. T. Monk; Thad Jones–Mel Lewis Orch.; B'way shows. Pl. w. Duke Ellington Orch. '69; Harlem Phil., West End Symph. fr. '69; Chico Hamilton '70; John Mayall Blues Band '71; Hugh Masekela, NY Jazz Qt., Harold Vick, Archie Shepp, Roland Hanna, Leon Thomas, Dee Dee Bridgewater, Hal Galper '70s; Geo. Shearing '76. Pl. in '80s w. Doc Cheatham; Hank Jones; Frank Foster; Clark Terry; Jimmy Heath; Lena Horne. Gaskin was a member of the Billy Taylor Trio, early '70s–'93. Taught bs. and improv. at U. of Mass.-Amherst, Queens Coll., and the Jazzmobile Wkshp. Fr. '74 has also worked as prof. photog. Favs: Ray Brown, Israel Crosby, Blanton, Ron Carter. Fests: Japan '67; Eur. '67–73; Africa, India w. Taylor '84. CDs: w. B. Taylor (Taylor-Made; GRP); C. Terry (Chesky); B. Easley (Sunny.); C. Adderley (Cap.); Ellington (Fant.).

GASLINI, GIORGIO, pno, comp; b. Milan, Italy, 10/22/29. Began on pno. at age 6; fath. helped him study. Gave first public perf. at age 13, then led own orch., duo w. Achille Scotti. Pl. w. bb in Galbiate-Lecco 1942; I Diavoli Del Ritmo Trio in Galbiate '43. Led own qt. in Milan '46; made rec. debut w. trio w. Gil Cuppini, Gino Stefani '47. Pl. w. Ochestra Del Momento '47–8; w. duo on radio and in concerts '48. Premiered comp. *Temo E Relazione* at San Remo JF w. oct. '57. Stud. pno., comp., cond. at Giuseppe Verdi Conserv., Milan, late '50s-early '60s. Cond. symph. orch. in concerts '58–60. Comp. and pl. on soundtrack of Antonioni's film *La Notte* '60. Led own qt. w. Gianni Bedori, Bruno Crovetto, Franco Tonani fr. '63. Scored Vermuccio film *Un Amore* '65. Wrote first Ital. jazz opera, *Colloquio Con Malcolm X*, prem. at Teatro Margherita, Genoa '70. Other large works incl. the operas *Quartett Of Life* and *Thel*, as well as symphonies and ballets incl. *Contagio* and *Drakon*. In the '70s, Gaslini began perf. in hospitals, factories, and cinemas as well as at univs. and in concert halls. In '76 he became the first Ital. mus. to be invited to a major Amer. JF (New Orleans). He has perf. in Eur. w. Duke Ellington; Miles Davis; Cecil Taylor; Max Roach; Gato Barbieri; Don Cherry; Steve Lacy; Bill Evans; and many others. Perf. in US

as unaccomp. soloist '80, '86; w. qt. '81. In '85, Gaslini was the first jazz musician to be officially invited to perf. in China. His recs. include personal interpretations of Monk, Ayler, and Schumann. Lee Jeske wrote of a live perf. in NYC: "Gaslini manages to play across styles with very little pretension...he handily encompasses the blues, classical romanticism, stride piano, avant-garde explosions and numerous other jazz and non-jazz flavorings." Gaslini taught jazz courses at St. Cecilia Cons., Rome '72–3; Verdi Cons., Milan '79–80. His instruc. books, *Musica Totale* and *Tecnica E Arte Del Jazz*, are considered the basic Ital. jazz texts. He has scored more than forty films and twenty TV progs. and has continued to perf., rec., and tour actively into the '90s. A biography by Adriano Bassi was publ. in '86 by Ed. Muzzio. Favs: Tatum, B. Powell, Tristano, C. Taylor. Polls: Ital. Critics Prize, six times. Fests: all major in Eur.; No. Amer.; Mid-East; India; Africa fr. late '70s. CDs: SN; Dischi della Quercia.

GATES, GIACOMO (Agostini), voc; b. Bridgeport, CT, 9/14/50. Father pl. class. and "gypsy" vln., listened to Basie; Ellington; Calloway; and symphs. At age 6 chose to sing instead of dancing at tap dance recital. Stud. gtr. w. Mickey LeDonne (fath. of Mike LeDonne) 1958–64; pno. w. Gerry Aiello '88; theory w. Bill Finegan at U. of Bridgeport '89. Pl. gtr. as teenager in bands w. older mus. Learned standards but pl. "for fun." Stud. civil eng. for two yrs. in coll.; worked at construction jobs all over US; also has been tractor-trailer driver, carpenter, life guard, painter, twenty-one dealer, limo driver, landscaper, bouncer, and gandy dancer. After att. summer music fest. and singing wkshp. in Fairbanks, Alaska '87 became active musically. Encour. by Grover Sales, moved back to East Coast and pursued prof. career. Worked around Conn. w. accomp. trios; also w. Richie Cole NYC '91, Bost. '93; Walter Bishop; Lou Donaldson '93. App. at Billy Eckstine Tribute, Blue Note '93. Cond. wkshps. and seminars in Conn., Mass., and N.J. Wrote lyrics to Monk's "Five Spot Blues (Five Cooper Square)"; and "Take Five" incl. P. Desmond solo, the latter praised by D. Brubeck. Gates has been described by Owen McNally as "a bebop and blues singer who is keeping the tradition of Eddie Jefferson alive and well." Favs: Jefferson, Joe Williams, Joe Carroll, M. Allison, Jon Hendricks. Fests: New Haven '89, '94; Phila. '89; Clearwater '91; Detroit/Montreux '92. CDs: dmp; Sharp Nine.

GATTO, ROBERTO, dms, comp, arr; b. Rome, Italy, 10/6/58. Mother was classical singer; uncle was pop drummer. Stud. at Conservatorio di St. Cecilia in Rome; later w. Vincenzo Restuccia of RAI Orch. Pl.

w. Roma Jazz Trio w. Enzo Pietropaolo, Danilo Rea 1975; Enrico Rava, Maurizio Giammarco '76; Enrico Pieranunzi '77; Giovanni Tommaso fr. '80; Piana-Valdambrini Sextet '82; Lingomania '84–9; own gps. Freelanced in Eur. w. Chet Baker; Freddie Hubbard; Lester Bowie; Art Farmer; Kenny Wheeler; Lee Konitz; Gato Barbieri; Bob Berg; Steve Lacy; Johnny Griffin; Geo. Coleman; Dave Liebman; Phil Woods; Michael Brecker; Curtis Fuller; Kai Winding; Tommy Flanagan; Cedar Walton; Kenny Kirkland; many others. Comp. for films and TV. Taught at the Siena jazz seminar. Favs: E. Jones, P. Motian, J. DeJohnette; arrs: Gil Evans, Claus Ogerman. Polls: *Musica Jazz* w. Lingomania '85–7; Drum Club '89–92. Fests: all major in Eur. fr. '80; USA '85–9; Dakar '88; Jerusalem '89. TV: RAI special, other Eur. TV. CDs: Inak; Gala; w. B. Berg; Franco D'Andrea; G. Tommaso; M. Urbani (Red); C. Fuller–Roma Jazz Trio (Timel.); Pieranunzi (yvp); P. Woods (Phil.); Stefano Battaglia; Stefano Sabatini (Spl.).

GAUDRY, MICHEL, bs; b. Normandie, France, 9/23/28. Began on pno., cl. Stud. bass at Geneva Cons. Pl. at Mars Club, Paris fr. 1957, accomp. Billie Holiday; Carmen McRae. Rec. w. Quentin Jackson; Art Simmons '59; Double Six '60–2. Pl. w. Simmons at Nancy Holloway Club '61. Pl. at Blue Note, Paris, w. Bud Powell; Kenny Clarke; Sonny Criss; Stuff Smith–Stephane Grappelli; many others '62–late '60s. Worked mainly as commercial studio mus. fr. late '60s, also accomp. pop singers. Pl. in duo w. Jimmy Gourley at Bilboquet '74. Pl. w. Quincy Jones, André Previn, Phil Woods, Wes Montgomery, Barney Kessel '60s; Sam Woodyard, Lionel Hampton, Raymond Fol, Cat Anderson '70s; Jimmy Owens, Irvin Stokes mid '80s. Gaudry has written articles on the bs. for *Jazz Hot* and *Jazz Magazine*, and has also worked as a cartoonist. Favs: Red Mitchell, Ray Brown, Scott LaFaro, Paul Chambers. Fests: all major in Eur. TV: BBC w. All-Eur. bb '67; French TV w. Grappelli; Clarke; Herb Geller; Johnny Griffin; German TV w. Montgomery. CDs: w. Cat Anderson (B&B); K. Clarke (Jazz Time); Grappelli (BL); B. Powell (BL; MS); J. Lewis (Em.).

GAYLE, CHARLES, tnr sax, bs cl, pno; b. Buffalo, NY, 2/28/39. Worked for Western Electric and Bethlehem Steel but devoted time to pno. study before takng up tnr. sax. Dur. the 1960s took part in the avant-garde scene in NYC. Moved back to Buffalo '69. Two yrs. later ret. to NYC, pl. in street and subways; also lofts and underground clubs. In '84 Peter Kowald heard him in a concert w. Sunny Murray and invited him to Eur. Founded own trio in NYC for Lower East Side Fest. '87. Pl. in France '93. Rec.

three LPs for Silkheart label. A presence on NYC's "downtown" scene, Gayle's honks, screams, and use of overtones link him to the energy, noise element players of the '60s. CDs: KFW; BS; Silk.; Victo; Gayle-William Parker-Rashied Ali, *Touchin' On Trane*, FMP.

GEBLER, JEAN-PIERRE PAUL, bari, tnr saxes; b. Brussels, Belgium, 10/5/38. Many opera singers on moth.'s side of family. Began on tnr.; stud. w. priv. teachers and for one year at Lille Cons., France. Pl. w. Belgians Jacques Pelzer, Bobby Jaspar, Benoit Quersin, and French gps. at Rose Noire club, Brussels 1957–8; also pl. w. Chet Baker; Barney Wilen; Kenny Clarke in Paris. To Portugal '59; led own gp. Hot Club of Portugal at fests. Moved to Madrid late '59, pl. w. Chuck Israels; Perry Robinson; Arnie Wise; Jon Mayer. Ret. to Portugal '63, re-formed Hot Club. Pl. w. Gerry Mulligan in Portugal '65, then tour. Spain and Portugal w. Dexter Gordon '67. After working in advertising in '70s, Gebler formed a qnt. w. Belgian musicians in the early '80s. He has cont. to work w. this gp. into the '90s, making freq. tours of Eur. Favs: Gerry Mulligan, Pepper Adams, Lars Gullin. Film: app. in Portuguese film *Nouvelle Vogue*. LP: LDH '81. CD: Igloo.

GEE, MATTHEW JR., tbn; b. Houston, TX, 11/25/25; d. NYC, 7/18/79. Father pl. bs; bro., Herman, tbn. As a child pl. tpt., then bari. horn; infl. by hearing Trummy Young, start. tbn. at age 11. Stud. at Alabama St. Coll., later at Hartnett Studios in NYC. Pl. w. C. Hawkins; after army service, w. D. Gillespie in 1946, doubling on bari. horn. In late '40s worked w. tpt. Joe Morris; G. Ammons–S. Stitt '50; Join. Count Basie '51; Illinois Jacquet '52–4, incl. Eur. tour. In mid '50s worked at various Brooklyn clubs; w. Sarah Vaughan Show to Eur. '56; briefly w. Gillespie '57. Monday nights at Birdland; w. house band at the Apollo '59. Pl. w. Duke Ellington off and on from '59–63; contributed some comps. In later yrs., perf. occasionally w. small gps., incl. P. Quinichette; Brooks Kerr. A fluent bop tbn., infl. by J.J. Johnson, Bennie Green. Comps: "Wow"; "Gee!" Recs: Riv. '56; w. Gillespie '49, '55. CDs: Riv.; w. Ellington (Col.), incl. his own comp. "The Swingers Get the Blues Too"; G. Ammons; King Pleasure; S. Stitt (Prest.); L. Donaldson (BN); Basie; Jacquet (Verve); J. Griffin (Riv.).

GEISSMAN, GRANT, gtr, comp; b. Berkeley, CA, 4/13/53. Raised in San Jose, Calif., fr. age 2. Early infls. were his grandfath., who pl. bjo., and the Beatles, who have cont. to fascinate him; one of the foremost collectors of Beatles memorabilia. Also listened to recs. by records by Kenny Burrell; Wes Montgomery; and B.B. King. At Calif. St. Northridge learned more about jazz fr. Gerald Wilson and Louis Bellson. Quit school to join Chuck Mangione in 1976; solo on "Feels So Good," earned him great popularity. After leaving Mangione, he rec. a series of albums and became busy in the studios as a perf. and comp. A respected artist with excellent jazz and pop credentials. CDs: BM; Conc.

GELLER, HERB (HERBERT ARNOLD), alto sax; other saxes, cl, fl; b. Los Angeles, CA, 11/2/28. Mother pl. pno. for silent movies. Worked w. Joe Venuti 1946, before moving to NYC '49, to perform and rec. w. Claude Thornhill. Married Lorraine Walsh '51and returned to LA where he was active in '50s West Coast jazz scene w. Billy May '52; Maynard Ferguson '54–6; Shorty Rogers and Bill Holman; and his own qt. Also off and on late '50s w. B. Goodman and Louie Bellson. Moved to Germ. '62; pl. w. Benny Bailey; Kenny Clarke in West Berlin Radio Orch.; in Cologne w. Friedrich Gulda; and then to Hamburg where he settled permanently '65. Pl. and arr. for Norddeutscher Rundfunk. Professor at Hamburg and Bremen Cons. Dur. a return visit to US rec. w. Benny Carter '91. Favs: C. Parker, Benny Carter, Johnny Hodges. Poll: *DB* New Star '55. CDs: VSOP; Enja; FS; Hep; w. Chet Baker (PJ; Enja); C. Brown; Dinah Washington (Em.); Ferguson; Rogers (BB); Carter; Goodman (MM); B. Kessel; Shelly Manne (Cont); M. Paich (Cand.); T. Talbert (Modern Concepts).

GELLER, LORRAINE (Lorraine Winifred Walsh), pno; b. Portland, OR, 9/11/28; d. Los Angeles, CA, 10/13/58. Toured w. Anna Mae Winburn's International Sweethearts of Rhythm 1949–52; freelanced in NYC w. Bonnie Wetzel. In '51, married alto sax Herb Geller and moved to LA. Worked w. S. Rogers, M. Ferguson, Z. Sims '53–4; also apps. w. Parker; Gillespie; Getz. Pl. w. Herb Geller qt. '54–5, and sporadically until her death. Also accomp. Kay Starr '57; Lenny Bruce. Excellent soloist showing infl. of her favs: Tatum, B. Powell, H. Silver. Fav. own solo: "Alone Together," w. H. Geller (Em.) '56. Fests: MJF w. Bill Holman; Mel Lewis '58. Rec. as. lead. on Dot '56; w. Red Mitchell (Cont.) '57. CDs: w. M. Davis; R. Mitchell (Cont.).

GENUS, JAMES HORACE JR., bs; b. Hampton, VA, 1/20/66. Began on gtr. at age 6. Stud. briefly w. Ellis Marsalis 1986, pl. w. him '86–7; Hamiet Bluiett '88–9; Horace Silver, Cedar Walton, Harper Bros. '89; Stanley Turrentine '89–90; Roy Haynes, Don Pullen '89–91; Jon Faddis, Renee Rosnes fr. '89; Kenny Garrett '90; Vincent Herring, Greg Osby, New

York Voices '90–1; Dianne Reeves, Benny Golson, Nat Adderley '91; Ralph Moore, Geoff Keezer fr. '91; Bob Berg, Brecker Bros. fr. '92. Favs: Ray Brown, Ron Carter, Paul Chambers. Fests: Eur., Japan fr. '89. CDs: w. Pullen; Osby; T.S. Monk (BN); Adderley (Enja; Alfa); Faddis (Epic); Herring (MM); Berg (Stretch); Kevin Hays (Steep.); Keezer; James Williams (DIW); Sam Newsome; Steve Wilson (CC); Didier Lockwood; Golson (Drey.); D. Douglas (Arab.).

GEORGE, KARL CURTIS, tpt; b. St. Louis, MO, 4/26/13. Played w. McKinney's Cotton Pickers, 1933; Cecil Lee. Worked w. Jeter-Pillars orch. before pl. w. Teddy Wilson orch. '39–40; L. Hampton orch. '41–2. Served in army '42–3, then settled in Calif., worked w. S. Kenton '43; Benny Carter '44; short spell w. C. Basie '45; Happy Johnson '46. Led own rec. gps. '45–6, sidemen incl. Buddy Tate; J.J. Johnson; Lucky Thompson. Also rec. w. several other gps. at this time incl. C. Mingus; L. Thompson. From late '40s on suffered from very poor health, retired to St. Louis. Recs. w. Teddy Wilson; Slim Gaillard; Oscar Pettiford. CDs: w. D. Washington (Del.).

GERSH, SQUIRE (William Girsback), bs; b. San Francisco, CA 5/13/13. Played w. local commercial gps.; was part of the SF "revivalist" movement, worked w. Lu Watters; Bob Scobey; Turk Murphy; Mutt Carey; Bunk Johnson. Pl. w. Louis Armstrong 1956–8, incl. South American tour Oct. '57. Tour. Europe w. Kid Ory Aug.-Nov. '59. Favs: Several NO bs. and Jimmy Blanton. CDs: w. Scobey; Murphy (GTJ).

GERSON, ROY, pno; b. Malverne, NY, 6/7/62. Father Alvin, led Moonlighters dance band on Long Island 1966–76; sist. Robin is actress-vocalist. Stud. classical pno. w. Miriam Freundlich '67–79, then w. Ernest Ulmer at Manh. Sch. of Mus. '79–81. Pl. w. Moonlighters '70–6; Erskine Hawkins '79; Sol Yaged '81; Widespread Jazz Orch. '82. Has led his own gp., the Swingtet, fr. '90. Favs: Peterson, Tatum, Waller, Garner. Films: app. in *The Cotton Club; Crimes and Misdemeanors; Stella; The Palermo Connection; Sessions*. TV: Joe Franklin. CDs: JA.

GETZ, STAN (STANLEY), tnr sax; b. Philadelphia, PA, 2/2/27; d. Malibu, CA, 6/6/91. Started on bs. in NYC, then bassoon; attended James Monroe HS in Bronx, N.Y.; pl. in All-City Orch. Stud. saxophone w. Bill Sheiner. Began pl. prof. in 1942 w. Dick "Stinky" Rogers; the next year worked w. Jack Teagarden; Dale Jones; Bob Chester; w. Stan Kenton '44–5; then briefly w. Benny Goodman and Tommy Dorsey. In

'47, after pl. with several other bands, moved to Calif., working there w. Butch Stone and his own trio in Hollywood. In Sept. of that yr., join. Woody Herman's newly formed Second Herd, remaining w. Herman to '49. Getz, Zoot Sims, Serge Chaloff, and Herb Steward (replaced by Al Cohn) comprised the celebrated "Four Brothers" in the tune of that name which gave the band its signature sound. Getz began to attain recognition with Herman, particularly with his featured solo on the band's '48 recording of "Early Autumn."

After leaving Herman, Getz formed his own quartet, which included Al Haig on pno. From this time on, his lyrical approach, decidedly modern style, and cool sound earned him wide popularity. In '51, he toured Scand. for the first time. The following year he did studio work for NBC in NYC and rec. "Moonlight in Vermont" w. gtrst. Johnny Smith. He then started leading his own gps. again, usually a quintet; the classic five being the unit which rec. at Storyville in Bost.: Haig, Jimmy Raney, Teddy Kotick, and Tiny Kahn.

During the mid to late '50s, Getz's career was disrupted both by drug abuse and his inclination to work in Eur. While visiting Stockholm in '55, he was taken seriously ill and recuperated for several mos. in Scand. and Africa. When he returned to the US, he resumed touring night clubs w. a qt; made JATP tours in '57 and '58; and was very active on the coll. circuit. In '58, he settled in Copenhagen and worked throughout Eur. until he ret. to US in '61.

Though Getz's reputation as a style-setter in the post-bop "cool" era and one of the top tnr. players of the '50s still held, the reception upon his return was somewhat disappointing. Dur. his absence, the more aggressive sounds of John Coltrane had grabbed the jazz audience's interest. However, his '62 album *Focus*, featuring unusual arrs. by Eddie Sauter, received critical acclaim and was considered a major artistic achievement.

Getz's real career breakthrough in the early '60s was a result of his collaboration with gtrst. Charlie Byrd on the album *Jazz Samba*, which feat. the music of Antonio Carlos Jobim. The record became one of the biggest-selling albums in jazz history and established Getz as the first US artist to successfully integrate the sound and rhythm of bossa nova with jazz. Though the genre became a '60s craze, Getz's related albums, incl. *Jazz Samba Encore* w. Luiz Bonfa and *The Girl From Ipanema* sung by Astrud Gilberto, have become classics, and elements of Brazilian music have left an indelible imprint on jazz. The Getz–Gilberto album was voted best jazz perf. in '64, and went on to become one of the biggest cross-selling albums ever.

Dur. these yrs. of phenomenal success, Getz cont.

to mature as a peerless melodist, whose lyricism was often deliberately contrasted with moments of flawless, solid swinging—his effort to combat the image of being solely a "sensitive" player. From '69 to '72, Getz maintained residences in NYC and near Marbella, Spain, working frequently throughout Eur. w. his own qt.; he also rec. w. the Clarke-Boland orch. for MPS in '71. During this time, Getz commissioned Chick Corea, who had first worked with him in '67, to write pieces for a new gp. he was planning that incl. Corea, Stanley Clarke, Tony Williams, and Airto Moreira. They debuted in NYC in '72 and soon rec. *Captain Marvel* (released in '75). The gp. worked through the mid '70s; later personnel incl. Hank Jones and Kenny Barron. Getz also performed at NJF annually and in late '74 tour. Eur. w. "NJF in Europe" show.

In addition to aiding the careers of Corea, Moreira, and Barron, fr. the late '60s on, Getz helped launch several other promising artists, incl. Gary Burton, Steve Swallow, and Joanne Brackeen. In '75, he broadened his base by producing a "Stan Getz Presents" series for Col., incl. recs. w. Jimmy Rowles and Joao Gilberto and concerts. In the mid '80s, Getz had resettled in the Bay Area, where he perf. regularly and taught at Stanford U. fr. 86. Despite his bouts of illness, he tour. successfully on the Eur. summer fest. circuit in the second half of the decade and in '90. Kenny Barron was a constant in his last quartets, and they rec. a dramatic duo CD, *People Time*.

In the late '50s, Getz cited Lester Young, Herbie Steward (a strong infl. on him in the '40s), Zoot Sims, Al Cohn, and Charlie Parker as his favorite musicians. Throughout his career, their infls. filtered through but Getz's style remained basically unaltered since it was honed in the late '40s and early '50s. His tone did deepen somewhat, as did his soul, through his continuing maturation. In the view of most critics and fellow musicians, he was one of the most melodically creative stylists in the history of the tenor sax.

Polls: *Met.* '50–60; *DB* Readers '50–9; *DB* Critics '53–8. Fests: all major. Films: *The Benny Goodman Story* '56; *Get Yourself a College Girl*; *The Hanged Man*; soundtrack for *Mickey One*. CDs: Prest.; Fant.; Verve; Em.; BN; RCA; Roul.; Col.; Conc.; Mos.; Steep.; Music Club; four tracks in *Opus De Bop* (Sav.); w. Herman (Col.; Cap.; BB); Bill Evans (Mile.); Johnny Smith (Roul.); D. Gillespie; L. Hampton; E. Fitzgerald; Abbey Lincoln; collaborations w. Gillespie; J.J. Johnson; Mulligan (Verve); O. Peterson (Pab.).

GHIGLIONI, TIZIANA, voc; b. Savona, Italy, 10/25/56. Studied improv. at clinics w. Giorgio Gaslini; voc. technique w. soprano G. Ravazzi 1979–80. Led own gps. w. sidemen incl. Pietro

Tonolo, Paolo Fresu, Roberto Ottaviano, Stefano Battaglia fr. '81. Sang w. Paolo Damiani '83; Giovanni Tommaso '87; in duos w. Giancarlo Schiaffini '84; Mal Waldron; Paul Bley '90. Co-led trios w. Enrico Rava–M. Waldron '89; Steve Lacy–M. Waldron '90; Lee Konitz–S. Battaglia '92. Led a qt. that feat. S. Lacy '91. Has written original lyrics in English to many comps. by musicians w. whom she has worked. Favs: B. Holiday, Cathy Berberian, Jay Clayton. Fests: Poland '85; France '89, '91; Germ. '92. TV: Ital. CDs: Spl.; Phil.; SN; Musidisc; NewSoundPlanet; w. Bley; Roberto Ottaviano (Spl.); Chico Freeman (BS); Konitz (Phil.).

GIAMMARCO, MAURIZIO, tnr, sop, alto saxes, comp, arr; b. Pavia, Italy, 10/17/52. Studied harm. w. Gino Marinuzzi at Karl Berger's Creative Music Studio 1975; sax lessons w. Joe Allard. Pl. w. jazz-rock gp. Blue Morning '68–72; Giancarlo Schiaffini; Giorgio Gaslini; Mario Schiano '73–4; Suonosfera duo w. Andrea Centazzo; own qt. fr. '76; Italian folk music gp. Canzoniere Del Lazio '76–7; Enrico Pieranunzi '78–9; trio w. Furio Di Castri, Roberto Gatto '79–80; New Perigeo '80–1; Aldo Romano '83. Led gps. Lingomania '84–9; M.G.Day After Band '90–1. Worked w. Dave Liebman; Billy Cobham '90–1. Also freelanced w. Chet Baker; Lester Bowie; Peter Erskine; Kenny Wheeler; others; comp. and arr. for films, theater, dance. Giammarco leads a qt. and a duo w. Amedeo Tommasi. He teaches sax and improv. at St. Louis Music Sch. in Rome and the Jazz U. in Terni. Polls: Ital. Critics Poll '81; RAI 1 Jazz '84; Musica Jazz '84–5 '87. Fests: all major in Eur.; also USA; Africa. TV: two concerts w. Lingomania on Ital. TV. CDs: Gala; Spl.; Fonit; W. Massimo Moriconi (Penta.); Stefano Sabatini (Spl.).

GIBBS, EDDIE (EDWARD LEROY), gtr, bjo, bs; b. New Haven, CT, 12/25/08. Raised in NYC fr. age 10. Began on bjo., which he stud. in mus. schs. Pl. w. Eubie Blake, Charlie Johnson, Billy Fowler, Wilbur Sweatman late 1920s. Stud. gtr. w. Elmer Snowden '32. Tour. and rec. w. Edgar Hayes '37–8; while in Eur. w. Hayes he rec. w. Kenny Clarke '38. Pl. w. Teddy Wilson '40; Eddie South, Chick Bullock '40–1; Dave Martin fr. '41. Freelanced w. Luis Russell, Claude Hopkins, Cedric Wallace '40s. Rec. w. Eddie Barefield '46. Pl. bjo. w. Wilbur De Paris '52–5. Began pl. bs. '59, stud. w. Bass Hill. Pl. bs. w. Henry Goodwin, Cecil Scott, Claude Hopkins, others fr. '60. CDs: w. Edgar Hayes; Eddie South; Teddy Wilson (Class.).

GIBBS, GERRY (GERALD SCOTT), dms, perc; comp; b. NYC, 1/15/64. Son of Terry Gibbs. Stud. for

one semester at Berklee Coll. of Mus. Pl. w. Doug Carn 1986; Terry Gibbs–Buddy DeFranco, also Buddy DeFranco Qt. fr. '87; Alice Coltrane fr. '89; Philip Harper fr. '90; Joe Lovano fr. '92. Also freelance w. Don Pullen; McCoy Tyner; Reggie Workman; Richie Beirach; Gary Burton; Cedar Walton; Phil Woods. Gigs w. Frank Morgan, Steve Allen, Eddie Henderson fr. '90. Own gp. w. Ravi Coltrane mid '90s. Favs: DeJohnette, E. Jones, Mel Lewis, B. Rich, Blakey, Tony Williams, Don Moye. TV: Steve Allen Show '70. CDs: Qwest; w. T. Gibbs–B. DeFranco; John Campbell (Cont.).

GIBBS, MIKE (MICHAEL), tbn, comp; also pno; b. Salisbury, South Rhodesia (now Harare, Zimbabwe), 9/25/37. Studied pno. priv. 1944–54; tbn. '54–61. Stud. arr. and comp. at Berklee Coll. of Mus. '59–62 (B. Mus. '62); Boston Cons. (diploma '63). Stud. w. Geo. Russell; Gunther Schuller; J.J. Johnson at Sch. of Jazz, Lenox, Mass. '61. Stud. priv. w. Schuller '62; w. Xenakis, Lukas Foss, Aaron Copland, Schuller at Tanglewood Summer School '63; priv. w. Schuller '62. Pl. tbn. w. Herb Pomeroy bb, early '60s. Comp. and arr. for Gary Burton off and on fr. '61. Living in England fr. '65; pl. w. Graham Collier '65–7; also John Dankworth–Cleo Laine, Tubby Hayes. Led own gps. '68–74; also arr. for radio, TV, films, and worked as studio mus. Perf. w. radio orchs. in Den., Swed., Germ., early '70s. Ret. to US as comp.-in-residence at Berklee '74–83. Toured UK '75–8; perf. own comps. w. Eur. radio orchs. '78–81. Left Berklee to concentrate on work as freelance comp., arr., and rec. prod. '83. Worked w. J. Dankworth, Michael Mantler, Pat Metheny, John McLaughlin fr. '83; also pop acts incl. Joni Mitchell; Whitney Houston; Peter Gabriel; Sister Sledge. Ret. to London '85. Tour. w. John Scofield '91. Gibbs's comps. incl. "Sweet Rain"; "And On The Third Day"; "Family Joy." Favs: Gil Evans, Charles Ives, Olivier Messiaen. Polls: *MM* comp., arr., BB '73–4; *MM* Rec. of Yr. '74. CDs: Act; Ah Um; Venture; Virgin; w. Bob Moses (Gram.).

GIBBS, TERRY (Julius Gubenko), vib, perc, comp, lead; b. Brooklyn, NY, 10/13/24. Father and bro. both prof. musicians; started on xylophone, dms., and tympani. In 1936, won Major Bowes Amateur Hour contest. In army three years. Then club dates w. Bill De Arango; first record date w. Aaron Sachs for Manor, June '46. With Tommy Dorsey; Chubby Jackson '47 incl. Swed. tour; Buddy Rich '48; then Woody Herman for a year. Left to form own band, gave it up in '50 to form sextet w. Louie Bellson and Charlie Shavers. Form. own band again and did Mel Tormé TV show. With Benny Goodman Sxt. '51; fr.

late '50s active mainly in LA where he formed a bb staffed with such West Coast jazz names as Bob Cooper, Med Flory, Conte Candoli, Lou Levy, et al. early in '59. Worked frequently for Steve Allen as musical director through '60s, '70s, and '80s, sometimes using two-finger technique while engaging him in pno. duets. Led house band on Regis Philbin TV series, writing all original music '64; spent much of his time playing for TV in '70s. From '80, co-led a group intermittently w. Buddy DeFranco, recalling the context, if not the style of the Benny Goodman small gps. Won *DB* New Star bb award in '62 and various other awards as vibsts. (incl. six times *DB* and *Met.*). One of the first great bop vib., Gibbs was a contemporary of Milt Jackson in the mid '40s. His tremendous vitality and powerful natural beat have made him a bop equivalent of Lionel Hampton, although his inspiration comes from Parker and Gillespie. LPs: Xan.; Em.; Merc. CDs: Cont.; Gibbs-DeFranco, Cont.; w. Herman (Cap.); Goodman (Col.); Rich (Hep); Getz (Prest.).

GIBSON, ANDY (ALBERT ANDREW), comp, arr; also tpt; b. Zanesville, OH, 11/6/13; d. Cincinnati, OH, 2/10/61. Studied some vln.; then self-taught on tpt. Pl. in band fr. Cumberland, Md., led by Lou Redman, bro. of Don. Worked w. Zack Whyte 1932–3, incl. comp.-arr; McKinney's Cotton Pickers '34–5; Blanche Calloway '36. Settled in NYC; on and off w. Lucky Millinder '36–7, then gave up pl. to concentrate on writing. In '37, on D. Ellington's recommendation, he start. writing for Charlie Barnet and worked for him intermittently for ten yrs.; also for Count Basie '38–42; Cab Calloway; Harry James. In mil. service '42–5, pl. tpt. and lead. army band in Eur.; after discharge, moved to Calif. and rejoin. Barnet. Resettled in NYC in '48 to freelance. In '55, he was staff arr. at King Recs., later became A&R exec. In late '50s wrote some arrs. for Camden LP. Retired in Ohio. One of the better, yet less-publicized, writers from the late swing era. Favs: Ellington, Hefti, Sy Oliver. Comps: "The Hucklebuck"; "The Great Lie"; "I Left My Baby." Arrs. for Basie incl. "Tickle Toe"; "Louisiana"; "The World Is Mad"; "Shorty George"; for Barnet, "Shady Lady"; "Charleston Alley"; "Blue Juice"; for Calloway, "A Ghost of a Chance."

GIBSON, BANU, voc; b. Dayton, OH, 10/24/47. Grew up in Hollywood, Fla. Trained as a dancer and took singing lessons w. an opera teacher at age 9. Sang in sch. musicals; sang and danced in a Miami Beach nightclub production, and tour. w. it 1969–72; perf. in a Roaring '20s revue at Disneyland '72–77. After teaching herself bjo. and gtr., she form. New Orleans Hot Jazz Orch., a classic jazz spt., on April 1,

'81. Founded own rec. label, New Orleans Hot Jazz; starred at many traditional jazz fests., app. on a few PBS-TV specials, incl. *The Great Chefs of New Orleans*; app. w. her band at symph. pops concerts; tour. Europe in '86 w. Wild Bill Davison and in '88. Became known as one of the most exciting singers in the classic jazz idiom. CDs: NO Hot Jazz.

GIBSON, DAVE (DAVID F.), dms, perc; b. Philadelphia, PA, 3/7/53. Mother was amateur singer. Began on pno.; dms. at age 12. Stud. at Temple U. 1974–9 (B. Mus.) First gigs w. r&b bands in Phila., then pl. w. house band at Valley Forge Music Fair '79–80; Jimmy McGriff '80–1; house band at Sheraton Valley Forge hotel '81–5; Joe Sudler Swing Machine backing Clark Terry, Freddie Hubbard, Stanley Turrentine, Frank Foster, and others '85–91; Woody Herman '89–91; Count Basie Orch. fr. '91; Diane Schuur fr. '95. Gibson taught mus. in the Phila. public sch. system '70s and is currently a consultant for cultural organizations in Phila. Favs: Roach, Blakey, Sonny Payne, Mickey Roker, Butch Ballard. Fests: Eur. fr. '88; Japan '91. TV: app. on *Sesame Street*. CDs: w. Basie; Sweets Edison (Tel.); Odean Pope (SN); Schuur (Atl.).

GIBSON, FRANK JR., dms; b. Auckland, New Zealand, 2/19/46. Made debut at age 8, pl. duets w. his drummer fath. Extensive freelance work w. jazz and pop artists in New Zealand. Lived in London 1977–80, pl. w. Alan Holdsworth; Tony Coe; George Chisholm; Peter Ind; and many others in jazz and rock. Back in NZ, made several award-winning albums w. Brian Smith; Jacqui Fitzgerald; and Phil Broadhurst. Rec. w. Alan Broadbent in LA '87–9. Favs: P.J. Jones, E. Jones, Tony Williams. CDs: w. Broadbent (Disc.; Trend).

GIFFORD, GENE (HAROLD EUGENE), comp, arr, gtr; also bjo; b. Americus, GA, 5/31/08; d. Memphis, TN, 11/12/70. Attended hs in Memphis, where he start. arr. Tour. w. own bands 1925–6; Blue Steele '28–9. Join. Jean Goldkette's Orange Blossoms in '29, which evolved into the Casa Loma orch., a cooperative band with Glen Gray as lead. Fr. '30–9 Gifford is best known as the chief arr. for the orch., which was very popular on coll. campuses. His riff-based writing style was an infl. on swing band arrs. Will Hudson; Nat Leslie; Archie Bleyer; the young Gil Evans; many of his charts were perf. by F. Henderson (most notably "Casa Loma Stomp") and other bands in the pre-swing and swing yrs. Led his own band on sess. for Victor in '35, incl. Bunny Berigan. After leaving Casa Loma, freelanced for dance and radio bands. Also worked as draftsman-engineer, stevedore. Wrote for Bob Strong '43–4; Tommy Reynolds '44–5; CBS staff in NO '45; USO tours '45–6; w. Glen Gray again '48–9; then freelance. During the '50s, he worked as radio engineer and audio consultant. In '69 settled in Memphis, teaching theory and counterpoint. His arrs. for Casa Loma are in the Robert Dodge Library at Northeastern U., Boston. Comps: "Smoke Rings" (Casa Loma's theme); "Black Jazz"; "White Jazz"; "Maniac's Ball." CD: own gp. in *Swing Is Here* (BB); *see also* **GRAY, GLEN.**

GILBERTO, ASTRUD, voc; b. Bahia, Brazil, 1940. Family moved to Rio when she was 2. Fath. was painter, teacher. Came to prominence after she rec. the song "The Girl From Ipanema" w. her then husband Joao Gilberto, Antonio Carlos Jobim, and Stan Getz on the Verve LP Getz/Gilberto '63. A shortened version of the song was released in '64 and bec. a hit, with Gilberto's gentle, breathy voice setting the style for bossa nova singing in the US. Tour. w. Getz and rec. own bossa nova albums, singing in English and Portuguese '60s. In '80s she added Michael Franks songs and some American standards to her repertoire. Perf. in NYC as lead. of a gp. that incl. Jerry Dodgion '83. Cont. to perf. and rec. in the bossa nova idiom into the '90s. Although the first female Brazilian singer to define the jazz-related bossa nova style for US audiences, Gilberto was later eclipsed by perfs. such as Flora Purim; Elis Regina; Gal Costa; et al. CDs: Verve; CTI; Den.; w. Getz (Verve).

GILBERTO, JOAO, voc, gtr, comp; b. Juaseiro, Bahia, Brazil, 6/31. From musical family. Bec. interested in mus. in boarding sch. and listened to Amer. jazz, esp. Gerry Mulligan, as teenager. Pl. dms. in local band in Juaseiro. Self-taught on gtr., he worked as a solo perf. Join. vocal gp. Garotos da Lua and remain. until gp. broke up in early 1950s. Moved to Rio de Janeiro; w. Antonio Carlos Jobim developed a style of singing and gtr. pl. based on the samba that bec. known as bossa nova. The success of his rec. of Jobim's "Desafinado" '57, signalled the ascent of the bossa nova in Brazil. Rec. "Chega de Saudade" and own comp. "Bim-bam" w. Jobim '58. In '59, the duo rec. an LP that served as the inspiration for the '62 Stan Getz/Charlie Byrd album *Jazz Samba*. Sang and pl. gtr. on album *Getz/Giberto* w. Getz, Jobim, and then-wife Astrud Gilberto '63. A single fr. the LP, "The Girl From Ipanema," became a hit in '64. App. At Umbria Jazz '96, '98. CDs: WB; Tropical; World Pacific; Elek. Mus.; w. Getz (Verve).

GILLESPIE, DIZZY (JOHN BIRKS), tpt, comp, voc, pno, lead; b. Cheraw, SC, 10/21/17; d. Engle-wood, NJ, 1/6/93. Father, who died in 1927, was an amateur bandleader and gave Dizzy a working knowledge of several instruments. Started on tbn. at age 14, then switched to tpt. a year later. Studied harmony and theory at Laurinburg Inst., No. Carolina '32–5; cont. to practice tpt. and pno. on his own. Moved to Phila. '35 to be with family. First prof. gig w. Frankie Fairfax; Charlie Shavers was also in the band and helped Dizzy learn Roy Eldridge solos. Dizzy earned his nickname for his zany behavior while w. Fairfax's gp. Moved to NYC '37, replacing Eldridge in the Teddy Hill band. Toured Europe w. Hill, then played w. Al Cooper's Savoy Sultans, Alberto Socarras, bef. rejoin. Hill in '38. Played w. Mercer Ellington '39, then joined Cab Calloway where he developed an interest in Afro-Cuban music through friendship w. section mate Mario Bauza. Met Charlie Parker in KC while on road w. Calloway '40. With Calloway, Gillespie had already begun to evidence some elements of the bebop style, of which he and Parker are generally considered to be the prime architects. He participated in after-hours jam sessions in NYC w. Parker, Thelonious Monk, Kenny Clarke, et al. from '41.

After leaving Calloway in '41, Gillespie freelanced w. Ella Fitzgerald; Coleman Hawkins; Benny Carter; and others. He toured w. Charlie Barnet and Les Hite in early '42, recording a prophetic solo on the latter's *Jersey Bounce*. Pl. w. Calvin Jackson; Lucky Millinder '42. Pl. w. Charlie Parker in Earl Hines Orch. '43. Co-led a combo on 52nd St. w. Oscar Pettiford '43–4; on a Coleman Hawkins date in Feb. '44, he recorded his comp., "Woody'n You," which is considered to be the first formal statement of the music to become known as bebop. He then joined Billy Eckstine's forward-looking bb as tptr. and mus. dir., but was back in NYC by '45, beginning to rec. prolifically for an assortment of labels. In the spring he and Parker pl. w. a qnt. at the Three Deuces on 52nd St.; at this time they made the seminal bebop combo recs., "Hot House"; "Shaw 'Nuff"; and "Salt Peanuts." He briefly led own bb, then, in December, he and Parker took a group to Hollywood to play at Billy Berg's, where they were appreciated mainly by other musicians. Gillespie returned to NYC in early '46 and opened on 52nd St. w. his own sxt., which soon became a reorganized bb. This time, a '47 RCA rec. contract enabled him to sustain the band until '50. In this orch. he experimented w. Afro-Cuban jazz, hiring perc. Chano Pozo, who is heard on recs. of Geo. Russell's "Cubana Be–Cubana Bop" and his own "Manteca," written w. Pozo. By the end of '47, Gillespie's rhythm section consisted of John Lewis, Ray Brown, and Kenny Clarke, who later formed the MJQ. w. Milt Jackson, a Gillespie regular from '46.

Other Gillespie sidemen incl. J.J. Johnson; Dave Burns; Ernie Henry; John Brown; Sonny Stitt; James Moody; Jimmy Heath; Paul Gonsalves; John Coltrane; Yusef Lateef; Cecil Payne.

Dizzy's harmonic acumen made him "the theoretician" (as Budd Johnson called him) of the then new movement. He was also one of its vanguard soloists, with thought-provoking ideas and rhythmic stimulation in the way he played off the beat w. death-defying leaps or coming-from-behind multi-noted explosions. Also notable was his ebullient personality: verbal (incl. his superb scat singing) and visual humor; and signature beret, heavy horn-rimmed glasses, goatee, and (occasional) leopard-skin jacket.

Following the breakup of his bb, Gillespie toured briefly w. Stan Kenton as featured soloist, then formed a sxt. Co-founded Dee Gee Records w. Dave Usher '51. Despite a hit w. "Oo-Sho-Be-Do-Be," the label was not a financial success, and the masters were leased by Savoy. In '53, he began playing a tpt. with an upswept bell, which became his trademark. He toured w. JATP '53–late '50s. In spring '56 a new bb, organized for Gillespie by Quincy Jones, toured the Near and Middle East, subsidized by the US St. Dept. This was the first time the US government had ever accorded official recognition and economic aid to jazz. In the summer of '56, he went on another St. Dept. tour, this time to So. Amer. Gillespie kept the band together until '58, then led a qnt. In '60 Gillespie's gp. incl. Leo Wright and Junior Mance. Lalo Schifrin replaced Mance '61.

He toured Argentina w. a combo, also led a bb at MJF '61, where he premiered Schifrin's *The New Continent* in '62, w. a large orch. dir. by Benny Carter. In '63 he recorded an improvised, unaccompanied soundtrack to docu. film about Dutch painter Karel Appell. Placed on ballot by admirers as independent candidate for President in '63 Calif. primary. Re-formed qnt. w. James Moody, Kenny Barron '64. Reunited w. Gil Fuller at MJF '65. Mike Longo replaced Barron '66; when Moody left in the late '60s, he was replaced by gtrst. George Davis, whom Al Gafa replaced in '71. Other sidemen in '60s-70s incl. el-bs. Frank Schifano; Russell George; Phil Upchurch; Chuck Rainey; Alex Blake; Earl May; dmrs. Candy Finch; David Lee; Mickey Roker.

A Eur. tour w. the Reunion Big Band '68 incl. former Gillespie sidemen Sahib Shihab; Cecil Payne; Curtis Fuller; Ted Kelly. Gillespie made a world tour with the Giants of Jazz; Thelonious Monk; Sonny Stitt; Kai Winding; Al McKibbon; Art Blakey '71-2. With his own combo, he toured the Virgin Islands '73; Eur. '74; Eur. and Mediterranean '75. Perf. at "Tribute To Dizzy Gillespie" concert, Avery Fisher Hall '75.

In the '80s he cont. to tour, appearing at fests. worldwide. His protegé, Jon Faddis, became his alter ego and in a touring bb, toward the end of the decade, the musical dir. It was also in '88 that he founded the United Nation Orch. which toured in Africa '89; Can. and So. Amer. '91. In '92, at the beginning of his 75th yr., Gillespie spent the first two mos. in residence at the Blue Note club, NYC, in special celebratory programs w. various trumpeters and, then, saxophonists who app. w. him in an all-star rotation. Recs. of these perfs., *To Diz With Love* and *To Bird With Love,* were issued on Telarc.

Gillespie received many awards in the last years of his life, incl. Bashere of Iperu from Nigeria '89; Commandant D'Ordre Des Arts Et Lettres from France '89; Grammy Lifetime Achievement Awd. '89; Nat'l Medal Of Arts '89; ASCAP Duke Awd. '90; Kennedy Center Honor '90. He held twenty honorary degrees fr. universities incl. Columbia, Rutgers, New Engl. Cons., Queens Coll. His comps., many of which are jazz standards, incl. "Woody'n You"; "A Night in Tunisia"; "Salt Peanuts"; "Groovin' High"; "Blue 'N Boogie"; "Bebop"; "Dizzy Atmosphere"; "That's Earl Brother"; "Con Alma"; "Tour De Force"; "Kush"; "Bro. King"; "Olinga." With Parker he co-wrote "Anthropology" and "Shaw 'Nuff. " Polls: *Esq.* New Star '45, Silver Awd. '47; *Met.* '47–50; *DB* Readers '56; *DB* Critics '54 '55 (tie w. Miles Davis) '56–7, '71–5; Handel Medallion fr. NYC '72; Inst. of High Fidelity Mus. of Yr. '75. Films: *Jivin' in Bebop* '47; ad libbed dialogue for soundtrack of animated short, *The Hole* '60s; soundtrack music for *The Cool World* '63; another animated short, *Voyage to Next,* used his voice early '70s; documentary, *A Night in Havana* '85; acted and played in feature film, *Winter in Lisbon* '90. TV: many apps. on PBS; tpt. special w. Al Hirt early '70s; many apps. on *Tonight Show,* etc. Books: *To Be Or Not to Bop* w. Al Fraser (Doubleday) '79; *Groovin' High* by Alyn Shipton (Oxford) '99. CDs: RCA; Sav.; GNP Cres.; Vogue; Imp.; A&M; Tel.; BN; Timel.; ProJazz; Enja; Milan; Verve; Pab.; four tracks in *Prestige First Sessions, Vol. 3* (Prest.); United Nation Orch. (Enja); JT; w. Charlie Christian (Jazz Anth.); L. Hampton (BB); Parker (Stash; Deb.; Verve; Sav.; French Col.); Norvo (Jz. Class.); Calloway; J. Marsala (Class.); Ellington (Col.); Bebop & Beyond (BM); O. Peterson (Pab.); R. Eldridge (Verve); Moody (Novus); JATP (Verve; Pab.).

GILMORE, JOHN E., tnr sax, cl, bs-cl, sop sax; b. Summit, MS, 10/29/31; d. Philadelphia, PA, 8/20/95. Studied cl. fr. age 14 under Capt. Walter Dyett at DuSable HS in Chicago. Pl. w. air force band 1948–52; Jack Scott in San Antonio, Tex. '51; Geo.

Eskridge, Earl Hines bb '52. Pl. in Chi. w. Sun Ra '53–61; Willie Jones (pno.) '56; King Kolax '57; Willie Mabon, Wilbur Campbell '58; Andrew Hill, Johnny Griffin, Miles Davis, Dinah Washington '59; Red Saunders '60; Al Smith '61. Pl. in NYC w. Gloria Coleman–Grant Green '62; Lloyd Price bb, dmr. Buster Smith–Bu Pleasant '63; B.B. King, Paul Bley '64; Art Blakey, Frank Foster '65; Charles Mingus '66; McCoy Tyner, Philly Joe Jones, Walter Bishop '67; Geo. Russell, Arthur Taylor, Al Grey '68; Olatunji Drums of Passion, Melba Liston bb '69; Lex Humphries '72. Worked w. Sun Ra fr. '62, alternating as leader w. Marshall Allen after Sun Ra's death in '93. Favs: C. Hawkins, Rollins, Coltrane; comp./arr.: Sun Ra, Monk, G. Russell. Fests: Eur.; Asia; Africa w. Ra. Polls: *DB* TDWR. Video: *Charlie Mingus 1968*; *Sun Ra: A Joyful Noise* '80 (Rhap.). CDs: *Blowing in from Chicago*, Clifford Jordan–John Gilmore, BN; w. Sun Ra (Evid.; ESP Disk; BL; hatArt; Aff.; BS; DIW; A&M; Leo); M. Tyner (Imp.); A. Hill (BN); Pete (La Roca) Sims (32).

GILMORE, STEVE (STEVEN DIRK), bs, el-bs; b. Trenton, NJ, 1/21/43. Primarily self-taught but stud. briefly w. Ray Brown. First prof. gigs w. hs mus. teacher at age 14. Pl. w. Ira Sullivan 1967–9; Baker's Dozen bb '67–70; Flip Phillips, late '60s; Mose Allison '72; Thad Jones–Mel Lewis '74–5; Al Cohn–Zoot Sims '74–88; Richie Cole in '70s; also John Coates; Dave Frishberg; Toshiko Akiyoshi. A member of Phil Woods gps. fr. '74. In the mid '80s two books of transcriptions of Gilmore's bass lines were publ. by F. Boaden, New Albany, Ind. Favs: Red Mitchell, Michael Moore. Fests: many in Eur.; Asia; No. and So. Amer. CDs: w. P. Woods (Conc.; Ant.; Chesky); Dave Liebman (Cand.; Red); Frishberg (Conc.); Cole (Muse); T. Harrell (Steep.); Gillespie (Timel.); C. Baker (Phil.).

GIOIA, TED, pno, voc; b. Los Angeles, CA, 10/21/57. Piano stud. at age 7; at 20, began teaching at Stanford U. and became key figure in developing its jazz stud. program. In 1988 his book, *The Imperfect Art*, was publ. by Oxford and won the ASCAP/Deems Taylor Award. His first CD, *The End of the Open Road*, was issued in '88 on Quartet Records. Gioia also prod. rec. sess. w. Bobby Hutcherson; John Handy; others. Other books: *West Coast Jazz; History of Jazz* (both Oxford).

GIORDANO, VINCE (VINCENT JAMES), lead, tba, bs sax, bs, gtr, bjo, dms, pno; b. Brooklyn, NY, 3/11/52. Began on vln., sw. to tba. in seventh grade. First gigs w. dixieland combos on Long Island mid 1960s. Stud. arr. w. Bill Challis '67–70. Pl. w. Smith

St. Society Jazz Band '60s-70s; US Navy Show Band '70–2; Clyde McCoy '73–4; New Paul Whiteman Orch. '74; Bob Greene '75–6; NY Jazz Repertory Co. '78; Bix Beiderbecke Mem. Jazz Band '79–80; tours w. Leon Redbone '70s; State St. Aces, Chicago Rhythm '80s. Pl. on the soundtracks of Woody Allen's *Zelig* and *The Purple Rose of Cairo* and has led his own jazz repertory ens., the Nighthawks, fr. the '70s. Favs: Adrian Rollini, Beiderbecke, Armstrong, C. Hawkins. Fests: Breda, Holland '79. Films: app. in *The Cotton Club; Bloodhounds on Broadway*; *Bix* (Italy). CDs: w. Challis, *The Goldkette Project* (Cir.); w. *Chicago Jazz Summit* (Atl.); Nighthawks (GHB).

GIRARD, ADELE, harp; also pno, voc; b. 1913; d. Denver, CO, 9/7/93. Although she had worked w. the Harry Sosnick orch., it was not until she join. the gp. of Joe Marsala that her talents as a jazz harpist were revealed. Worked at the Hickory House on 52nd St., NYC, fr. 1937 w. Marsala, whom she married in the same yr. CDs: w. Marsala (Class.) and in *Greenwich Village Sound* (Pick.); Barbara Lea (Prest.); Bobby Gordon (Arb.).

GIRARD, GEORGE, tpt, voc; b. New Orleans, LA, 10/7/30; d. New Orleans, 1/18/57. Became prof. tptr. after grad. fr. Jefferson HS 1946. Toured nat'l w. Johnny Archer's Orch. Pl. in NO w. Phil Zito; Joe Mares. Helped organize Basin Street Six '50, app. w. it until he form. own gp. to pl. at Famous Door in French Quarter '54. Pl. at annual Dixieland Jubilee in LA, fall '54. His career was interrupted by cancer and he underwent surgery, Jan. '56. In the spring he recovered enough to pl. for four mos. before he was again forced into inactivity. Noted for his clear-toned, driving style. Last rec. date was produced by Dr. Edmond Souchon for Good Time Jazz, Apr. '56. Rec. two LPs for Vik; one w. Basin St. Six (GHB). CDs: Story.; one track in *The Good Time Jazz Story* (GTJ); w. Armand Hug in *Classic Capitol Jazz Sessions* (Mos.).

GISBERT, GREG (GREGORY LYLE), tpt, flg, crnt; b. Mobile, AL, 2/2/66. Father pl. pno. and sax; moth., tpt. First gigs on dms. w. fath. at age 10, then pl. tpt. in dance bands while in hs. Stud. at Jamey Aebersold Clinic 1981; Clark Terry Clinic '82–4; Berklee Coll. of Mus. '84–5. Pl. w. Buddy Rich '85–6; Woody Herman '87–9; Gary Burton '89; John Fedchock–Maria Schneider, Toshiko Akiyoshi–Lew Tabackin fr. '89; Mingus Epitaph '90–2; Frank Wess; Clark Terry fr. '90; Mickey Tucker, Buck Clayton bb '91; Danny D'Imperio fr. '91; Norman Simmons '92; also freelance w. singers incl. Sarah Vaughan; Joe

Williams; Ella Fitzgerald; Sammy Davis Jr.; Mel Tormé; Tony Bennett. Has co-led qnt. w. John Gunther fr. '93. Favs: Terry, T. Harrell, Tim Hagans. Polls: *DB* HS Soloist '84. Fests: Eur. since '86. TV: Eur. TV, Jerry Lewis Telethon w. Rich. CDs: CC; w. Gunther (Capri); M. Tucker (Steep.); D. D'Imperio (VSOP; Sack.); S. McCorkle (Conc.); J. Fedchock (Res.).

GISMONTI, EGBERTO, gtr, pno, comp; b. Carmo, Brazil, 12/5/47. Piano fr. 1954, later stud. comp. in Paris w. Nadia Boulanger. Back in Brazil '66; self-taught on gtr., infl. by Baden Powell. Variously pl. 6–, 8–, and 10–string gtr. From '66–9, tour. US, first w. Airto Moriera and Flora Purim, later w. Nana Vasconcelos. Rec. w. Paul Horn '76; Charlie Haden '80. In late '70s, began stud. music of Xingu Indians, and incorporating it into his comps. Worked w. gps. and as soloist into '90s, perf. at UCLA '90 and at the Blue Note, NYC, on a bill w. Hermeto Pascoal. CDs: ECM; w. Haden (ECM).

GIUFFRE, JIMMY (JAMES PETER), cl, saxes, fl, bs-fl, comp, arr; b. Dallas, TX, 4/26/21. Studied cl. fr. 1930. Received B. Mus. fr. No. Texas St. Univ. '42. Later stud. comp. at USC for one semester in early '40s and w. Wesley LaViolette '46–60; cl. w. Art Bloom '61–4; reedmaking w. Kal Opperman '63; fl. w. Jimmy Politis '68–73. Pl. w. Army Air Force Orch. '44; tnr. sax w. Dallas Symph. on *Porgy and Bess* '46. Pl. and arr. w. Boyd Raeburn '46; Jimmy Dorsey '48; Buddy Rich '50. In '48, Giuffre was recommended to Woody Herman by Stan Getz and Shorty Rogers; the success of Giuffre's comp. "Four Brothers" brought him wide recog. as a comp./arr. Pl. and arr. w. Herman '50; Rogers '51; Lighthouse All-Stars '52; MJQ '57; JATP '50s. Comp. concert pcs. for larger gps., string orch., etc. fr. late '50s. Has led trios, beginning w. Bob Brookmeyer and Jim Hall and was renowned for his Lester Young infl., chalumeau cl. Later he had rhythm sections such as Paul Bley–Steve Swallow, Don Friedman–Barre Phillips, Richard Davis–Joe Chambers, Kiyoshi Tokunaga–Randy Kaye fr. '56. Reunited w. Bley–Swallow '93. Giuffre's trio was prominent in the free jazz movement of the early '60s. He has also led a qt. fr. '60. Worked mainly as a comp. and educ. in the late '60s and early '70s, but resumed perf. '75. Taught at New Engl. Cons. for fourteen yrs.; NYU for ten yrs.; New Sch. for three yrs. His comps. incl. ballets (*The Castle; Manikins*); choral works (*Life's Music*); string qts.; several film scores. Publ. instructional book, *Jazz Phrasing and Interpretation*, late '60s. Favs: Barney Bigard, C. Parker, Rollins, Coltrane, Lester Young. Polls: *DB* New Star tnr. '55;

DB New Star bari. '56; *DB* cl. '57 '63; *Met.* cl. '58–9; Jazz Podium '60s. Fests: Eur. fr. '59; Japan w. S. Rogers '85. Film: *Jazz on a Summer's Day*. TV: *The Sound of Jazz*. CDs: Col.; Mos.; SN; ECM; FS; Atl.; Choice; IAI; Owl; Konitz-Giuffre (Verve); w. W. Herman (Col.; BB; Cap.); R. Norvo (BB); B. Rich (Hep); Rogers (Cap.; BB); T. Charles (Prest.); C. Baker; S. Manne; L. Niehaus; Lighthouse All-Stars; John Lewis (Cont.); MJQ (Atl.).

GLADDEN, EDDIE (EDWARD), dms; b. Newark, NJ, 12/6/37; d. Newark, 9/30/03. Began pl. dms. in sch. band; infl. by Max Roach, Art Blakey, and two local drummers, Bobby Thomas and Buddy Mack. First prof. gig in Newark 1962. Worked in Newark w. Freddie Roach, Larry Young, Johnny Coles, Woody Shaw, Buddy Terry, Mickey Tucker '60s. Pl. w. Kenny Dorham, Grant Green, Jimmy McGriff late '60s; James Moody '72; Shirley Scott '74–5; Richie Cole, Eddie Jefferson, Cecil Payne, Horace Silver, mid '70s; Dexter Gordon '77–82; Mickey Bass '95. CDs: w. Larry Young (BN; Mosaic); D. Gordon (BN; Col.; Steep.); C. Jordan; K. Lightsey; J. Raney (CC); R. Cole; E. Jefferson (Muse); J. Stubblefield (SN); C. Baker (Timel.; CC).

GLASEL, JOHN SAMUEL, tpt, flg, sop tba; b. NYC, 6/11/30. Mother taught pno.; sist. pl. pno. and sang prof. Began on crnt. Stud. priv. w. William Vacchiano; Murray Karpilovsky; Carmine Caruso; Maurice Grupp; also at Yale U. (grad. 1951 w. B.A.); and Yale Sch. of Mus. (grad. in '52 w. B. Mus.). Prof. debut w. Bob Wilber '45; pl. w. New Haven Symph. fr. '53–5, also worked w. chamber gps., subbing in Radio City Mus. Hall orch. Member of co-op gp. The Six w. Wilber and others '54–6. Worked w. Glenn Miller orch. under Ray McKinley May-June '56; B'way pit orchs.: *Bells Are Ringing* '57–9; *Once Upon a Mattress* '59. Pl. w. Bill Russo orch. July-Aug. '59. Weekends w. Woody Herman in '60s. More B'way work for *Camelot; Sweet Charity*; etc. In '70s pl. w. Dick Cone bb, incl. Sundays at the Half Note. Worked in Frank Sinatra's "New York" band on East Coast and foreign tours '80–2. Was adjunct instructor of tpt. at Columbia Teach. Coll. '69–82. Elected President of Local 802, AFM '82, serving fr. '83–92; member of AFM Executive Board '85–9; trustee AFM Employers' Pension Fund '87–92. Favs: Armstrong, Gillespie. TV: many specials w. Elliot Lawrence '70–82; thirteen weeks w. *Saturday Night* band. Rec. own LP for Golden Crest incl. his *Music For Brass Quintet* '63; w. The Six for Beth.; other LPs w. Barry Miles; Gus Vali; Jimmy McPartland; Sinatra. CD: w. Johnny Carisi in Gil Evans' *Into the Hot* (Imp.).

GLASSER, DAVID, alto sax, fl, cl; b. NYC, 6/3/62. Studied at HS of Mus. & Art and w. Barry Harris; then received B. Mus. and M. Mus. fr. Eastman Sch. of Mus. Pl. w. Harris, Bill Dobbins, Count Basie Orch. 1989–91; Frank Foster '91; Illinois Jacquet fr. '91; Clark Terry gp. fr. mid-'90s. Glasser was a semifinalist in the Thelonious Monk Int'l Sax. Competition '91. Favs: Hodges, C. Parker. Fests: Eur.; Japan; Brazil w. Basie Orch. Film: app. in *Fame* '79. CDs: w. Basie (Den.); G. Benson (WB); Jon Hendricks (Atl.); Terry (Chiaro.).

GLENN, (EVANS) TYREE, tbn, vib; b. Corsicana, TX, 11/23/12; d. Englewood, NJ, 5/18/74. Sons are mus.: Tyree Jr., vibes, tnr. sax; Roger, fl., vib. Pl. w. local bands as a youth; then w. Tommy Mills in Wash., D.C., and Va., 1934–6. Pl. w. Charlie Echols in LA '36; Eddie Barefield on West Coast '36–7; then join. Eddie Mallory accomp. Ethel Waters to '39; briefly w. Benny Carter '39; Cab Calloway '40–6. Tour. Eur. w. Don Redman '46, and remained for solo gigs until '47. After ret. to US, join. Duke Ellington '47–51. Tour. Scand. as soloist '51. Replaced Tiny Kahn on vibes on Jack Sterling's daily CBS radio show '53–63. Through '50s and '60s was also staff mus. and occ. actor at WPIX-TV; other studio work; led own gps. in clubs. Pl. w. L. Armstrong All-Stars '65–71, except during Armstrong's illness in '68; own gp. at the Roundtable '69; also pl. occ. w. Ellington in these yrs. Originally infl. by J.C. Higginbotham, he developed into an all-purpose swing stylist who utilized plunger techniques, particularly in his Ellington yrs. Feat. on vib. in "Bye Bye Blues" w. Calloway '40. Fest: NJF-NY '72. Comp: "Sultry Serenade," later known as "How Can You Do a Thing Like That to Me?" Own recs: Roost; Roul. CDs: w. Ellington (Col.; Prest.); Armstrong (Col.; Verve); Clark Terry (Riv.); C. Calloway (Class.; Col.); B. Holiday (Col.); Carter (B&B; BB); Rex Stewart (Prest.); C. Terry (Riv.); S. Hasselgard (Phon.); Buck Clayton (Mos.).

GLOW, BERNIE, tpt; b. NYC, 2/6/26; d. Manhasset, NY, 5/8/82. Studied priv. fr. age 9; HS of Mus. and Art. While a teenager, worked w. Louis Prima for a two-week theater date. Tour. w. Richard Himber 1943; Raymond Scott CBS house band '44–5; Artie Shaw '45–6; Boyd Raeburn '47; Woody Herman '47–9. Staff mus. at WMGM '50–5. From '50s to '60s, very prolific studio mus., acknowledged more as an excellent lead player than a soloist. He took part in numerous sess. w. mus. such as Herman; B. Goodman; Miles Davis and Gil Evans; M. Albam; D. Gillespie; J.J. Johnson; Gunther Schuller. In '70s, cont. to do occ. sess., incl. recs. w. G. Benson; G. Bar-

bieri. CDs: w. Herman (Cap.; Col.); Davis–Evans (Col.); tracks in *The Birth of the Third Stream* (Col.).

GOINES, LINCOLN, bs, el-bs; b. Oakland, CA, 10/2/53. Many amateur mus. in family. Began on tpt. then sw. to cello and bs. Stud. w. members of Vancouver, B.C., symph. First prof. gig at topless bar in Vancouver 1971. Made rec. debut w. Julian Priester '72. Pl. w. Idris Muhammed '78–9; Ryo Kawasaki '78–82; Barry Miles–Terry Silverlight fr. '78; Nancy Wilson '79; John Scofield '79–80; Bob Mintzer, Dave Valentin fr. '79; Bill Connors '80–3; Tania Maria '81–2; Sonny Rollins '82–3; Eliane Elias–Randy Brecker fr. '82; Paquito D'Rivera fr. '84; Herbie Mann '87–8; Leni Stern fr. '87; Ronnie Cuber fr. '88; Mike Stern–Bob Berg fr. '89. Goines is the author of an instruc. book, *Afro-Cuban Grooves for Bass and Drums* (Manh. Music/DCI). Favs: Paul Chambers, Jimmy Garrison, Ron Carter, Jaco Pastorius, Alfonso Johnson. Fests: all major fr. '80s. TV: PBS w. T. Maria; D. Valentin. CDs: w. Valentin (GRP); B. Mintzer (DMP); Bob Berg (Den.); Mike Stern (Atl.); E. Elias (BN).

GOINES, VICTOR, tnr, sop saxes, cl, bs-cl; b. New Orleans, LA, 8/6/61. Began on cl. at age 6. Stud. w. Carl Blouin, who start. him on sax in hs band. Cont. on cl. and sax at Loyola U., where he received a degree in mus. ed. 1984. Fr. '83, he stud. w. Ellis Marsalis and tour. int'l in his qt. '84. Fr. '87, he stud. for his Master's at Virginia U.-Richmond; degree in '90. Dur. these yrs., he app. in NYC w. Lionel Hampton; Bobby Watson; Jack McDuff; Ruth Brown; pit band for B'way musical, *Black and Blue*. In '93, he join. Wynton Marsalis spt., remaining into '94, when he became a member of the LCJO. On the faculty of U. of NO. CDs: two on own NO-based Rosemary Joseph label: *Genesis* '91; *Joe's Blues* '98; w. W. Marsalis; LCJO (Col.).

GOLD, MILT (MILTON), tbn, pno; b. Scranton, PA, 3/22/29. Father pl. classical cl. After elementary instr., self-taught on tbn. by pl. along w. bb recs. and behind recs. by Frank Sinatra; Dick Haymes; Helen Forrest; others. "To make the slide trombone sound like a B-flat tenor sax was also the way it began and remained, naturally, in the subconscious mind with the instrument and away from it." Learned dms., pno. later. Worked in Pocono Mts. in Pa. w. Sal Zumo orch. 1945. Began tour. w. Shorty Sherock '46–8; Herbie Fields '48; Anita O'Day sxt.; Bill Harris–Shelly Manne sxt. '49; Joe Holiday qnt.; w. Nat Pierce orch. in Bost. '50; then tour. w. Claude Thornhill, doubling as relief dmr. '51. Pl. w. Med Flory band, NYC '52. Tour. w. New Concepts in Jazz;

pl. tbn. w. Kenton; pno. w. Getz. Pl. w. Pete Rugolo orch.; tour. w. B. Eckstine–Peggy Lee '54. Worked as sideman and lead. in Catskill Mts. resort hotels '54–5; w. Jimmy Palmer orch., incl. as arr. '56. Worked in radio broadcast orch. in "occupied Berlin" '63. In '90s perf. as club date mus. on pno., dms. Comps. rec. by Al Cohn (Em.) '53; Nick Travis (RCA); Seldon Powell (Prest.) '54. Favs: "The royal family of jazz excluding trombone players." CDs: w. Jon Eardley (Prest.); Kenton (Vogue/Sigla); S. Chaloff (Up.).

GOLDBERG, STU (STUART WAYNE), pno, org, synth, comp; b. Malden, MA, 7/10/54. Raised in Seattle. Grad. magna cum laude in pno. and comp. from U. of Utah at age 19. Best known through US and Eur. tours w. John McLaughlin 1974–6 and '79–80. Tour. w. Miroslav Vitous; Al Di Meola '76; Freddie Hubbard '76–7; to Eur. w. Alphonse Mouzon '76–7; and Charlie Mariano '78–9. Countless radio, TV apps. in Eur. From early '80s, pno. tours, jazz fests. in US, Eur.; film and rec. sessions in LA. LPs: several as lead. '78–82 (MPS); w. Mariano (CMP). CDs: w. McLaughlin; Wayne Shorter (Col.).

GOLDIE, DON (Donald Elliott Goldfield), tpt; b. Newark, NJ, 2/5/30; d. Miami, FL, 11/19/95. Mother, Claire St. Claire, was concert pnst.; fath., Harry "Goldie" Goldfield, tptr., asst. cond. w. Paul Whiteman for more than fifteen yrs. Stud. vln., pno., then tpt. at age 10. Won scholarship at 11; stud. w. private teachers. Pl. first job at 14 w. father's orch. Army 1951–4. Pl. w. Joe Mooney '56–8; Neal Hefti '59. Also worked w. Lester Lanin; Buddy Rich. Join. J. Teagarden June '59, pl. w. him into early '60s. Member of Jackie Gleason's orch. on Gleason's '60s TV show. Became prominent in Miami music circles in '70s and cont. to pl. hotels, clubs, and Dixieland fests. such as Sacramento JF. Own gps. incl. Lords of Dixieland and Jazz Express. Noted for his musical and physical resemblance to Billy Butterfield, he was also renowned for his accurate vocal impressions of Louis Armstrong, pl. an energetic, melodic brand of traditional jazz, sometimes using a muffler mute of his own design to achieve a singular sound. Favs: Butterfield, Armstrong, Berigan. Rec. w. Rich; Hefti (Coral); and Teagarden (Roul.). CDs: Jazz.; w. Teagarden (Jazz Band).

GOLDINGS, LARRY, pno, org; b. Boston, MA, 8/28/68. Raised in Newton, Mass. Both parents stud. and appreciated pno. Classical lessons at age 9; heard an O. Peterson rec. at 12. Stud. jazz in Eastman Sch. Summer Jazz camp. Lived in NYC from 1986 when

he came to stud. at New Sch. Jazz Program as member of first graduating class. During New Sch. yrs. pl. regularly in jams at Augie's on upper B'way w. Peter Bernstein; Bill Stewart; et al. Accomp. Jon Hendricks '87–9. In '87 began to double org. In '90s join. Maceo Parker's gp. on org., tour. in US and Eur.; also pl. pno. w. Christopher Hollyday; Jim Hall. Tour. w. John Scofield qt. Own trio, pl. pno. and org., sometimes alternating on same gig, as on QE2 Jazz Cruise '96 and displaying a standard of excellence on each instr. Favs: Peterson, Dave McKenna. CDs: Verve; Novus; WB; Min. Mus.; w. G. Burton (GRP); Hall (MM); J. Scofield (BN); Hollyday (Novus); M. Parker (Verve; Min. Mus.); D. Stryker (Steep.); B. Previte (Enja).

GOLDKETTE, JEAN, lead, pno; b. Valenciennes, France, 3/18/1899; d. Santa Barbara, CA, 3/24/62. Lived in Greece and Russia until family moved to the US in 1911, settling in Chi. Trained as a concert pnst. as a child. Moved to Detroit in '21, form. own band. Though not a jazz mus. himself, he became an important organizer and agent for many bands during the '20s, incl. McKinney's Cotton Pickers and the Orange Blossoms, which became the Casa Loma Orch. His agency, the National Amusement Corp., handled as many as twenty bands throughout the Midwest during the late '20s. His main orch., which was based at the Graystone Ballroom, Det., incl. such sidemen as J. Venuti; E. Lang; B. Beiderbecke; F. Trumbauer; the Dorsey brothers. App. as soloist w. Det. Symph. '30. From '30s, for the most part, gave up lead. and organizing orchs., though he re-form. a couple of bands in '45, '47. App. as concert pnst. in '50s; also became president of the Nat'l Actors Foundation, a nonprofit org. dedicated to developing new talent. Moved to Calif. in '61, where he died of a heart attack the following yr. In '59 he did a reunion LP for Camden. CDs: Bix Beiderbecke, Vol. 2, incl. Goldkette's '27 recs. (Masters of Jazz); Bill Challis's *The Goldkette Project* (Cir).

GOLDSBY, JOHN MARK, bs; b. Louisville, KY, 12/10/58. Began on pno., gtr., then pl. el-bs. in rock bands. Stud. w. Daniel Spurlock, Louisville Symph. 1976–7. Pl. w. Jamey Aebersold and Jimmy Raney in Louisville '76–80; also pl. w. Buddy DeFranco; Johnny Hartman; Barney Kessel; Dave Liebman; Jay McShann; Buddy Tate; Helen Humes; David Leonhart. Moved to NYC '80, pl. w. Albert Dailey; Benny Bailey; Sal Nistico; Jaki Byard. Pl. w. Bob Wilber; Smithsonian Repertory Ens. '82; Claude Bolling, Hubert Laws, Larry Coryell, Jack Wilkins, Jean-Pierre Rampal '84; Roger Kellaway '86; Helen Merrill since '86; Loren Schoenberg since '87; Ken

Peplowski since '88; AJO since '89. With Ted Rosenthal, Bob Kindred at NYC Grand Hyatt fr. '86. Currently w. Smithsonian Jazz Orch.; Bill Mays trio. Goldsby perf. on soundtrack to *The Cotton Club* '84. He has taught at Jamey Aebersold summer jazz clinics '81–92; LIU '86–8; and Nassau Community Coll. '91–2, and is currently on the faculty of William Paterson Coll. Received NEA perf. grants in '88, '90, '93. The "John Goldsby Plays Oscar Pettiford" concert, NYC, was funded by the '90 grant. Guest speaker at the Int'l Society of Bassists convention in '91. Favs: Pettiford, P. Chambers. Fests: Eur.; Japan w. Helen Merrill; Eur. w. Louis Bellson. TV: *Tonight Show* w. C. Bolling–H. Laws '85. Books: *Bowing Techniques for the Improvising Bassist; Bass Notes.* CDs: Conc.; w. AJO; Schoenberg (MM); R. Sandke; Peplowski (Conc.).

GOLDSTEIN, GIL, pno, synth, acdn, comp, arr; b. Washington, DC, 11/6/50. First instr. was acdn. "That's how I learned to improvise. I grew up with it." Freelance in D.C. area fr. 1966. Received B. Mus. fr. U. of Maryland '73; M. Mus. fr. U. of Miami '74; Ph.D. Union Grad. Sch. '78. Pl. w. Pat Martino '75–8; Lee Konitz '76–8; Ray Barretto '82–4; Astrud Gilberto '82–8; Stan Getz, Chet Baker '83; Gil Evans Orch. fr. '83; Michael Franks '87–9; Jim Hall '88–90. Own Zebra Coast orch. fr. early '90s; pl. w. James Moody in mid '90s. Comp. and arr. extens. for film and TV and taught at the New Sch., NYC '85–91. Prod. P. Metheny's *Question and Answer* album. Ret. to doubling acdn. '83. Favs: Bill Evans; arr: Gil Evans. TV: Montreux JF w. M. Davis '91; Sting w. Gil Evans '87. Book: *The Jazz Composer's Companion* (Consolidated Mus.). CDs: WP; BN; solo acdn. (Big World); w. Gil Evans (King; Elec. Bird; Jazz Door); Eddie Harris; Bernard Purdie (Act); M. Davis; Moody (WB); C. Baker (Phil.); B. Cobham (Inak); Hall (Conc.; MM); P. Martino (Muse); Mike Stern (Atl.); D. Liebman (Owl); Petrucciani (BN); Metheny (Geffen).

GOLIA, VINNY, saxes, cl, fl, comp; b. Bronx, NY, 3/1/46. First app. on recs. as an artist, painting album covers for Chick Corea and others. Stud. sax w. Dave Liebman; Anthony Braxton. Moved to LA 1973, pl. w. John Carter; Bobby Bradford. Start. own label, 9 Winds Recs. '77, rec. various small gps. and bbs. A student of chamber music, the versatile Golia plays some twenty instruments, incl. the entire reed family. He has tour. and/or rec. w. George Gruntz; Tim Berne; Braxton; and others, and rec. duets w. bassist Bertram Turetzky. Golia is regarded as an important figure on the avant-garde West Coast jazz scene. CDs: 9 Winds; w. Figure 8 (BS).

GOLSON, BENNY, comp, tnr sax; b. Philadelphia, PA, 1/25/29. Pno. at age 9, sax at 14; stud. at Howard U. 1947–50. Join. Bull Moose Jackson '51; Tadd Dameron, a member of the band, encouraged him to arrange. In '53–4, pl. w. Dameron; L. Hampton; Johnny Hodges; w. Earl Bostic '54–6, then toured S. America w. D. Gillespie '56, and remained w. the band until it broke up, Jan. '58. In and around his stint w. Art Blakey ('58–9), he became well known as the comp. of such tunes as "Whisper Not"; "I Remember Clifford"; "Stablemates"; "Along Came Betty"; "Blues March"; "Killer Joe", and "Are You Real?" Left Blakey Feb. '59; co-led Jazztet w. Art Farmer fall '59–62. In '63, became mainly active as comp.; in '64, stopped pl. and visited Eur. several times for comp./arr. assignments. Wrote soundtracks for films and TV in Eur. and US. Resumed pl. occ. in '70, but claims he did not feel comfortable pl. a horn until '82, when he revived the Jazztet. Dur. the next decade, he cont. to compose regularly on studio assignments but also led small gps. in Eur. and US. Went on a St. Dept.–sponsored cultural tour of southeast Asia '87, after which Philip Morris assigned him to Bangkok to write mus. for Bangkok Symph. In his first recs. w. Dameron his style was strongly infl. by Don Byas and Lucky Thompson; later showed a Coltrane infl., but fr. the '80s had absorbed it into his personal blend. As an educ. he has lectured, perf., and/or given clinics at NYU; Stanford; U. of Pitts.; Rutgers; William Paterson Coll. (two yrs. as scholar-in-residence); and Berklee. As a comp. has an exceptional gift for creating memorable melodies, sometimes with unusual harmonic structures. *Two Faces* for symph. orch. premiered at Alice Tully Hall, NYC, Oct. '92. Awards: Guggenheim Fellowship for comp. '94; NEA Jazz Masters '97. Early infls: Hawkins, Webster. TV: scores for *M*A*S*H*; *Mission Impossible*; *Mannix*; *Mod Squad*; etc.; BBC, London; feature films in Paris; Munich. CDs: Mile.; Cont.; Riv.; NJ; Prest.; Den.; SN; Ark.; Timel.; Den.; Drey.; w. C. Brown (Prest.); Jazztet (Chess; Cont.); Farmer (Cont.; SN; BN); Gillespie (Verve; Tel.); Blakey (BN); Dick Katz (Res.); P.J. Jones; W. Kelly; A. Lincoln; Blue Mitchell (Riv.); Lem Winchester (NJ); Dolphy (Enja); C. Fuller; S. Shihab (Sav.); Milt Jackson (BN); S. Turre (Ant.); R. R. Kirk (Merc.).

GOLSTAIN, GENNADY L'VOVICH (Gol'-shteyn), saxes, woodwinds, comp; b. Moscow, USSR, 1/25/38. Studied cl. at mus. sch. in Leningrad, grad. 1956; self-taught on saxes and fl. Best known as lead alto and arr. for Yusef Vainstein orch., as well as for a qnt. out of the ens. In '70s pl w. Vladimir Ludvikovsky and Oleg Lundstrem. Form. own early ens., Pro Anima '78, and taught sax at Mussorgsky Music

Sch. in Leningrad. A talented soloist, Golstain was discussed in Frederick Starr's *Red and Hot: The Fate of Jazz in the Soviet Union* (Oxford) '83. A rec. titled *Leningrad Jazz Festival*, which feat. him both w. Vainstain's orch. and in a qnt. w. tpt. Constantin Nosov, was released on a Vee-Jay LP '65.

GOMEZ, EDDIE (EDGAR), bs, comp; b. Santurce, PR, 10/4/44. Family moved to NYC in early 1950s. Moth. pl. pno. Began on bs. at age 12. Stud. w. Fred Zimmerman '58, then at HS of Mus. and Art; Juilliard Sch. of Mus. '62–5. Pl. w. Marshall Brown's Newport Youth Band '59–61; Les Elgart, Larry Elgart, Warren Covington, Sal Salvador '61; house band at Playboy Club backing Monty Alexander, Kai Winding, etc. '62; Rufus Jones '63; Marian McPartland '64; Joe Henderson, Tommy Turrentine, Jaki Byard '63–4, also Bobby Hackett, Johnny Richards, Edmond Hall, Buck Clayton, Pee Wee Russell; Paul Bley '64–5; Gerry Mulligan, Gary McFarland '65; Jim Hall '66; Bill Evans Trio '66–77. Subbed for Ron Carter w. Miles Davis '67–8. Pl. w. Jeremy Steig fr. '67; Jack DeJohnette's New Directions w. Lester Bowie, John Abercrombie '77–9; Chick Corea fr. '77; Steps Ahead '79–82; Hank Jones '79–84; DeJohnette '85; Joanne Brackeen. Gomez has led his own gp. fr. '88, incl. perf. in Moscow '92. He has app. as a guest soloist w. the Tashi Ens. and the Kronos Qt. Favs: Paul Chambers, Scott LaFaro, Ray Brown. Polls: *DB* TDWR '68; MJF Awd. '91. Fests: all major fr. '66. TV: Joan Lunden show w. own gp. '90. CDs: Col.; Den.; Stretch; B&W Mus.; w. Evans (Verve; Fant.; Mile.; Col.); M. Mainieri (NYC); Konitz; Tyner (Mile.); Brackeen (Ant.; Conc.); Steig (Enja); K. Werner (Sunny.); DeJohnette (ECM; Mile.; Land.); Corea (Verve; Polyd.; Stretch); Bley; Giuseppi Logan (ESP Disk); W. Bernhardt; A. LaVerne (dmp); Petrucciani; R. Brecker; E. Elias (BN).

GOMEZ, EDSEL ROBERT (Rentas), pno; b. Bayamon, PR, 8/9/62. Sister pl. pno., org. Began pno. lessons at age 5 after trying to copy sist.; various teachers until 1980. Stud. at Berklee '80–5, where he won a Count Basie award and grad. w. B. of Mus. Had band w. friends '72–3, pl. his transcriptions of Eddie Palmieri mus. Prof. salsa singer Mario Feliciano came to a rehearsal and hired Gomez for his band '74–5. Between '75–80 pl. w. many local bands, incl. Ismael Rivera; Pete "El Conde" Rodriguez. While at Berklee pl. w. Orch. Tropica; Adalberto Santiago; Celia Cruz; Don Byron; Claudio Roditi; Bill Pierce; Chick Corea. Pl. and rec. w. Luis "Perico" Ortiz in NYC before moving to Brazil '86. Pl. all over that country as well as in Uruguay, Chile. Stud. different Brazilian styles and rhythms. Worked in

B'way-type shows and ran a rec. studio doing TV commercials for major products and political campaigns; wrote mus. for the theater. Began trav. to NYC and Eur. '90. Perf. in NYC w. "Eddie Palmieri Latin Pianos in Concert"; also worked at Iridium, Knitting Factory, concerts, and Canadian tour w. Byron '96. Moved to NYC Feb. '97 and join. David Sanchez qnt.; also worked w. Patato Valdes at Bistro Latino in Manh.; gigged w. Conrad Herwig; Roditi; Machito Orch. Has taught priv. and at Souza Lima Cons., São Paulo, Brazil. Favs: Ellington, Hancock, Kenny Kirkland. CDs: own trio w. Eddie Gomez, I. Berroa at the '93 Heineken JF (Heineken); w. Byron (None.); Sanchez (Col.); Raul de Souza (RGE, Braz. label).

GONELLA, NAT (NATHANIEL CHARLES), tpt, voc, lead; b. London, England, 3/7/08; d. Gosport, Hampshire, England, 8/6/98. Pl. and rec. w. dance bands incl. Billy Cotton 1929–33; Roy Fox '31–2; Ray Noble '31, '33–4; Lew Stone '32–5. Had hit rec. w. "Georgia On My Mind," w. Stone '32. Led own gps. fr. '32, most prominently the Georgians w. bro. Bruts Gonella, also a tptr., as sideman '34–9. Visited NYC, rec. for Parlophone w. Benny Carter; Buster Bailey; John Kirby and perf. at Hickory House '39. Ret. to London, led gp. the New Georgians '40–2; after the war, New Georgians bb. Worked less freq. in late '40s, early '50s. Form. New Georgia Jazz Band '58. Cont. to perf. and rec. throughout the '60s and '70s. He ceased playing in the early '80s but cont. to sing. An important infl. in Brit. trad. jazz. Book: *Georgia On My Mind: The Nat Gonella Story*, R. and C. Brown (Horndean) '85. CDs: Parade; Philips; Cedar.

GONSALVES, PAUL ("MEX"), tnr sax; b. Boston, MA, 7/12/20; d. London, England, 5/15/74. Raised in Pawtucket, R.I. Start. on gtr. at age 16; then took up tnr. In early 1940s, was feat. w. Sabby Lewis in Bost. Army service '42–5. Pl. w. Count Basie '46–9; Dizzy Gillespie bb '49–50. Join. D. Ellington '50, remain. w. him for the rest of his career, except for brief periods. Dur. the '56 NJF, he stunned the audience with his now-legendary 27–chorus solo on "Diminuendo and Crescendo in Blue." At first identified by his similarities to Ben Webster, Gonsalves emerged over the yrs. as a unique soloist in his own right with a breathy warm sound, heard to great effect on ballads, and virtuosic, urgent, serpentine lines of harmonic complexity. In poor health in later yrs., he died just ten days bef. Ellington himself passed away. Recs. as a lead. (Jzld.) '60; w. J. Hodges, Lawrence Brown (Imp.); Ray Nance (Black Lion) '70. CDs: Jzld.; BL; Sonny Stitt–Paul Gonsalves (Imp.); w. R. Eldridge (Fant.);

Ellington (Col.; BB; Atl.; Pab.; Em.; MM; BL; Prest.); C. Terry (Riv.); John Lewis (Atl.); Hodges (Imp.; Prest.; BB); Basie (Col.; BB); Strayhorn (Red Brn.).

GONZALES, BABS (Lee Brown), voc; b. Newark, NJ, 10/27/19; d. Newark, 1/23/80. Studied pno., dms. App. briefly w. Charlie Barnet; Benny Carter 1943. In '46 form. voc. trio, Babs' Three Bips and a Bop, w. Tadd Dameron and gtrst. Pee Wee Tinney; pl. the Onyx Club on 52nd St. augmented by cl. Tony Scott. First rec. for BN '47 was his comp. "Oop-Pop-a-Da," popularized later by Dizzy Gillespie. Perf. as soloist in late '40s; series of recs. w. prominent bop mus. for Cap. '49. Active as disc jockey, jazz promoter.; perf. w. James Moody '51–4, also was his manager. Eur. apps. as soloist '51, '53. Active as a single through '60s; also in '70s incl. annual Eur. perfs. Created Expubidence, own rec. and publ. company. In '75, pl. in Eur. clubs; u. tour in Netherlands; dates w. L. Hampton. A colorful character and innovative dresser, whose scat singing was typified by the use of vowel sounds. Fests: NJF-NY '74; Montreux; Laren; Cologne; Gothenberg '75. Books: *I Paid My Dues*; *Movin' On Down De Line* (Expubidence Publ., Newark). Comps: "Weird Lullaby," aka "Lullaby of the Doomed"; and "When Lovers They Lose." Rec. w. Moody (EmArcy) '51. CDs: BN; tracks in *East Coast Jive* (Del.); w. C. Parker (Mos.).

GONZALEZ, JERRY, tpt, cga; b. Bronx, NY, 6/5/49. Father sang w. conjuntos; introduced him to the music of Armstrong and Parker as well as Puente and Machito and bought and taught him tpt. Some yrs. later took up cga., inspired by Mongo Santamaria. With bro., bs. Andy Gonzalez (b. NYC, 1/1/51) he perf. in various gps., pl. Latin and jazz incl. Monguito Santamaria. Both bros. att. NY Coll. of Mus. Jerry pl. gig in Washington, D.C., w. D. Gillespie at age 19. Worked w. Eddie Palmieri 1971; Manny Oquendo's Conjunto Libre. Pl. and rec. w. Clifford Thornton's Grupo Experimental '72. Also app. w. Kip Hanrahan; M. Tyner; T. Williams; K. Dorham; A. Shepp; Joe Chambers; Woody Shaw; K. Lightsey. Founded the Fort Apache Band '80, which has incl. A. Gonzales; K. Kirkland; S. Turre; Jorge Dalto; Sonny Fortune; S. Berrios; Carter Jefferson; J. Stubblefield; Joe Ford; and Larry Willis. Band had breakthrough w. *Rumba Para Monk*, an album of T. Monk's comps. arr. by Gonzales. Worked as conguero w. Chico O'Farrill bb '97. Fav: Miles Davis. Fests: many int'l w. Ft. Apache; as single, Bologna '90. CDs: Mile.; Sunny.; Enja; w. Franco Ambrosetti (Enja); B. Belden (BN); C. Blackman (FreeLance); Don Byron (Elek. None.); C. Fam-

brough (CTI); Lightsey (CC); J. Williams (Sunny.); Willis (Steep.); Pastorius (Big World).

GOODMAN, BENNY (BENJAMIN DAVID), cl, lead; b. Chicago, IL, 5/30/09; d. NYC, 6/13/86. First studies at Kehelah Jacob Synagogue fr. 1919; then played in band and studied with James Sylvester at Jane Addams' Hull House '20. Further studies with Franz Schoepp for two years ca. '20. Made professional debut at Central Park Theater, Chi., w. Benny Meroff, doing an imitation of Ted Lewis '21. Entered Harrison HS '22, pl. occasionally w. Austin HS Gang including Bud Freeman; Jimmy McPartland; Frank Teschemacher; Dave Tough; others. Joined musicians union '23, playing with Murph Podolsky, Jules Herbevaux. Met Bix Beiderbecke on lake excursion boat summer '23. Joined Ben Pollack in LA '25; recording first solo on "He's the Last Word" with Pollack in Chi. '26. Came to NYC with Pollack '28; also freelanced with Sam Lanin; Nat Shilkret; Meyer Davis. Goodman left Pollack in Sept. '29 to become a studio musician. Rec. with Red Nichols, Ben Selvin, Ted Lewis, Johnny Green, Paul Whiteman, others '29–34. Also played on B'way in Gershwin's *Strike Up the Band* and *Girl Crazy* '30, and Richard Whiting's *Free For All* '31. He began an assoc. w. Teddy Wilson and John Hammond ca. '31. Organized a 12–pc.band spring '34. Played at Billy Rose's Music Hall and rec. for Columbia. Arrs. for the band at this time were Deane Kincaide, Will Hudson, Benny Carter; Goodman pl. tenor sax on Carter's charts, which feat. sax soli calling for four saxes. The band was featured on the *Let's Dance* program on NBC radio Nov. '34–May '35. The show's budget allowed Goodman to buy new arrangements, and he was encouraged by John Hammond to hire Fletcher Henderson. Henderson's arrs., Goodman's exacting leadership, and distinctive soloists Bunny Berigan, Jess Stacy, and Gene Krupa, who joined in late '34, established the character of the band. After playing a brief engagement at the Roosevelt Hotel in NYC, Goodman embarked on his first tour, sponsored by Willard Alexander and the Music Corp. of America spring '35. The band's performance on Aug. 21 at the Palomar Ballroom in LA was broadcast nationwide and is often cited as the beginning of the Swing Era.

Goodman made his first combo studio session as a leader '35, a trio rec. with Teddy Wilson and Gene Krupa. He took Wilson on the road in early '36 and became the first major white bandleader to break the "color barrier," adding Lionel Hampton to form a qt. Aug. '36. The Goodman Orch. was phenomenally popular '36–9, perf. on the CBS radio program *Camel Caravan* and appearing in films, *Big Broadcast of 1937* and *Hollywood Hotel*. On Jan. 16, '38,

Goodman gave an historic concert at Carnegie Hall w. his band, gps., and soloists fr. the bands of Count Basie and Duke Ellington. Now popularly known as the "King of Swing," his feat. sidemen incl. Harry James; Ziggy Elman; Vernon Brown; Vido Musso. Arrs. incl. Jimmy Mundy; Edgar Sampson; Mary Lou Williams; and Horace Henderson. Goodman was also the first jazz musician to achieve wide success as a classical perf. when he rec. Mozart's *Clarinet Quintet* w. Budapest String Qt. and gave a classical recital at Town Hall '38. He also commissioned the comp. *Contrasts* from Béla Bartók and premiered it at Carnegie Hall Jan. '39. He led a sxt. in the B'way production *Swingin' the Dream*, fall '39.

Due to illness Goodman disbanded July '40, but re-formed the band a few months later w. several musicians who had come aboard in late '39, including Charlie Christian and Johnny Guarnieri; they form. the sxt. w. addition of Cootie Williams and Georgie Auld; and arr. Eddie Sauter. Dur. the rec. ban he cut V-Discs for the armed forces '42–4; and app. on stage in the revue *The Seven Lively Arts* w. his sxt., incl. Red Norvo and Slam Stewart '44. From 1945–50 he led a bb and sxt, off and on, incl. his flirtation w. bebop '47–9 that incl. such sidemen as Wardell Gray; Doug Mettome; and, in the sxt., clst. Stan Hasselgard. He also commissioned clarinet concertos fr. Copland and Hindemith in '47 and performed with all major US symphony orchestras fr. '40s. He mainly led small gps. fr. '50, beginning with the sxt. that feat. Roy Eldridge and Zoot Sims, and toured Europe in that year. The original trio was reunited for a benefit perf. '51. He rec. the soundtrack to the film *The Benny Goodman Story*, in which Steve Allen portrayed him '55. A tour of the Far East was sponsored by the US State Dept. '56–7. The Goodman band was fronted by Urbie Green in '57, but in '58 Goodman app. with the band and singer Jimmy Rushing in the Amer. Pavilion at the Brussels World's Fair.

Goodman led all-star orchestras on St. Dept.–sponsored trips to So. America '61; USSR '62; Japan '64. He toured with and perf. as feat. soloist w. symphony orchs. '60s-70s. In '78 he led an orchestra at a concert commemorating the fortieth anniversary of the first Carnegie Hall concert. Received Kennedy Center Honor award '82. That yr., he was also awarded the Sanford Medal fr. Yale U.'s Sch. of Music, where he gave master classes. His scores, recs., and other materials are in Yale's collection. A selection was published in the book *Goodman Papers* '93, and MusicMasters has issued the recs.

The possessor of a flawless technique and warm liquid sound, Goodman—who in his youth had listened to Leon Ropollo, Johnny Dodds, and Jimmie Noone—was in his peak a hot, swinging player, even if he did not use a "dirty" tone, as he had in the late '20s.

Polls: *Playboy* '57–61; *Esq.* Gold Awd. '44–7; *DB* fav. soloist '43–7 '49; *DB* Critics '54 (tie) '56; *DB* Readers '73; *Met.* '40–9. Films: *Powers Girl* '42; *Stage Door Canteen* '43; *Sweet and Lowdown* '44; soundtrack for Disney's *Make Mine Music* '45; *A Song Is Born* '48. TV: *Swing Into Spring* '58–9; *The World of Benny Goodman* '62; '66; *Tonight Show* '66; *Merv Griffin* '68; Timex special '72; Swedish TV '72; BBC-TV '73; NBC special '74; PBS *Tribute to John Hammond* '75; PBS special '80s. Books: *The Kingdom of Swing*, B. Goodman and I. Kolodin '39; bio-discography, *Benny Goodman: Listen to His Legacy*, D.R. Connor (Scarecrow) '88; *Benny Goodman and the Swing Era*, James L. Collier (Oxford) '89; *Swing, Swing, Swing: The Life and Times of Benny Goodman*, Ross Firestone (Norton) '93. CDs: Col., Cap.; RCA; Decca; MM; w. Hasselgard (Drag.); B. Holiday (Col.); Adrian Rollini (Aff.); J. Teagarden (BB); T. Wilson (Class.).

GOODMAN, WAYNE MATHEW, tbn, bs-tbn, euph, v-tbn; b. Brooklyn, NY, 11/26/68. Began tbn. stud. at age 11. Grad. fr. HS of Perf. Arts, NYC 1986. Att. Bklyn Coll. '86–8; William Paterson Coll. (N.J.) '88–91, bachelor's degree in jazz stud. and perf.; Manh. Sch. of Mus., master's in jazz stud. '95. First prof. gig at 15. Began to make a living w. local Latin jazz bands while in coll. Justin DiCioccio introduced him to David Berger. Stud. w. Berger; Rufus Reid; Steve Turre; Harold Mabern at Wm. Paterson. Later stud. for a yr. w. Barry Harris '93. Took part in educ. video, *The Barry Harris Workshop Video* '94. Pl. w. Jon Hendricks' band, Explosion '93–5. Has been a member of the LCJO since '94 and has led own NO band in and around NYC, focusing on the music of Jelly Roll Morton and King Oliver; also active as a teacher and clinician. Adept w. the plunger mute and at ease in a variety of jazz styles. Favs: J.J. Johnson, Lawrence Brown, Curtis Fuller, Tricky Sam Nanton; arrs: Ellington, Basie, Gil Evans, Thad Jones. Tour. and pl. at fests. in US; So. Amer.; Eur.; Asia. Pl. at White House w. W. Marsalis, Marian McPartland, Al Grey, Dr. Michael White, and others, as part of "The Millennium Council" for Pres. and Mrs. Clinton, Sep. '98. TV: *Live from Lincoln Center* '94, '98. Radio: *Making the Music*, PBS, perf. of Ellington's *Harlem*. Rec. debut w. Chico Mendoza '93. CDs: w. W. Marsalis and LCJO (Col.); Mendoza (Rogsan Swing).

GOODRICK, MICK, gtr; b. Sharon, PA, 6/9/45. Began on gtr. at age 12; att. Stan Kenton summer music camps. Stud. at Berklee Sch. of Mus. in mid 1960s, then taught at Berklee for four yrs. Rec. w. Woody Herman '70. Led trio w. Alan Broadbent, Rick Laird; duo w. Pat Metheny in Bost. early '70s. Tour. and rec. w. Gary Burton '73–5; also pl. in '70s w. Jack DeJohnette; Joe Williams; Astrud Gilberto. Pl. w. Charlie Haden '82, tour. w. his Liberation Orch. '85; w. DeJohnette's Special Edition fr. '87. Pl. at JVC-NY Fest. tribute to Jim Hall '90. Book: *The Advancing Guitarist* (Hal Leonard) '87. CDs: ECM; Ram; CMP; w. Burton (ECM); DeJohnette (Imp.; BN); C. Fasoli (Ram); C. Haden (ECM; Verve); Hall (MM).

GOODWIN, BILL (WILLIAM RICHARD), dms, perc; b. Los Angeles, CA, 1/8/42. Father, Bill, was well-known film actor, radio announcer; moth. was prof. dancer. Pno. lessons 1947–54, then stud. sax w. Frank Chase. Self-taught on dms., w. encouragement fr. Stan Levey; Shelly Manne; Mel Lewis; Freddy Gruber; Dexter Gordon. First prof. gig w. Charles Lloyd '59. Pl. w. Lloyd '59–61; Bud Shank '61–3; Mike Melvoin off and on '61–5; Frank Rosolino '62; Harold Rumsey, Art Pepper '64; Paul Horn '65–6; Roger Williams, Gabor Szabo '67; Geo. Shearing '68. Also pl. in LA w. Shorty Rogers; Joe Pass; Joe Williams; Tony Bennett. Join. Gary Burton '69, then moved to NYC. Pl. w. Burton–Keith Jarrett '69–71; Toshiko Akiyoshi '71; Stan Getz '72; Nat'l Jazz Ens., Gerry Mulligan '73–4; Al Cohn–Zoot Sims, Children of All Ages '74; Phil Woods fr. '74; Tom Waits '75. Also pl. w. Stephane Grappelli; Bill Evans; Bob Dorough; Mose Allison; Manh. Transfer; Michel Legrand; Geo. Robert; Tom Harrell; own gps. Goodwin has taught master classes at Eastman, Harvard, No. Texas St. U., and has worked extens. as a rec. prod. for Woods, Harrell, etc. fr. '79. Favs: Roy Haynes, Billy Higgins, Pete LaRoca, Billy Hart. Fests: all major fr. '69. TV: *Tonight Show* w. Paul Horn '65, Geo. Shearing '68. CDs: TCB; FS; w. Woods (Mile.; Conc.; Red; Den.); Harrell (Chesky; Cont.; Steep.); Dave Liebman (Red); L. Tabackin (Vart.); D. Frishberg (Conc.); H. Galper (Enja); Gillespie (Timel.); C. Baker (Phil.).

GOODWIN, HENRY CLAY, tpt; b. Columbia, SC, 1/2/10; d. NYC, 7/2/79. Mother, Blossom Harrison, was a honky-tonk pnst. Stud. priv. and at Armstrong HS, Wash., D. C.; dms., tba., then tpt. Went to Eur. w. Claude Hopkins band, incl. Sidney Bechet, to acc. Josephine Baker 1925. To Buenos Aires w. Paul Wyer '26. Ret. to NYC, worked w. Elmer Snowden, Cliff Jackson late '20s. To Eur. w. L. Millinder '33; back in NYC w. Willie Bryant '33; Charlie Johnson '34–6; Cab Calloway '36; Edgar Hayes '37–40, incl. Eur.

tour. '40; w. S. Bechet '41; Cecil Scott '42–4. Freelanced, then w. Art Hodes '46; Eur. tour w. Mezz Mezzrow '48, incl Nice JF; w. Bob Wilber in Boston late '48–9; Jimmy Archey '50–1, Eur. tour '52; in SF w. Earl Hines '56. Ret. to NYC, pl. w. George Stevenson '59; freelanced through '60s w. dixieland gps. at Metropole, other clubs. Plunger and growl specialist. CDs: w. Bechet (BB).

GORDON, BOB (ROBERT RESNICK), bari sax; born St. Louis, MO, 6/11/28; d. San Diego, CA, 8/28/55. Stud. at Westlake Coll. Start. pl. w. dance bands at age 18, incl. Shorty Sherock; Lee Williams; Jimmy Palmer. Worked w. Alvino Rey 1948–51; Billy May '52; Horace Heidt '52–3. In '52–5, many rec. sess. w. such prominent mus. as Shelly Manne; Maynard Ferguson; Chet Baker; Stan Kenton; Clifford Brown. This promising young pl., infl. by Gerry Mulligan, was killed in an auto accident while on the way to play a concert w. Pete Rugolo. Polls: *DB* Critics New Star '55. LP: PJ, '54. CDs: V.S.O.P./Tampa; FS; w. Brown; Baker (PJ); Lennie Niehaus (Cont.).

GORDON, BOBBY (ROBERT CAMERON), cl, ts; b. Hartford, CT, 6/29/41. After stud. at Berklee Sch. of Mus. 1959–60, he stud. cl. priv. w. Joe Marsala, whose infl. he reflects. Based in Chi. in the '60s, was able to pl. w. Bobby Hackett; Max Kaminsky; Wild Bill Davison; and Muggsy Spanier. Later, pl. w. Jim Cullum; Leon Redbone. Worked in Engl. in '78 and France in '82. Pl. and rec. w. Marty Grosz's Orphan Newsboys. Living in San Diego since the '70s, app. regularly on the trad. jazz circuit. Fests: JVC-NY; Elkhart JP; LA Classic Jazz; LA JP; Toronto Jazz. TV: *Tonight Show;* Steve Allen. CDs: Arb.; w. Grosz (Stomp Off); Redbone (Private Music).

GORDON, DEXTER KEITH, tnr, sop sax, comp; b. Los Angeles, CA, 2/27/23; d. Philadelphia, PA, 4/25/90. Father was doctor whose patients incl. Duke Ellington, Lionel Hampton. Began on cl. at age 13; sw. to alto sax at age 15. Stud. harmony, theory w. Lloyd Reese and pl. in Reese's rehearsal band w. Chas. Mingus; Buddy Collette. Quit school 1940; began pl. tnr. sax and join. local band, Harlem Collegians. Pl. w. Lionel Hampton '40–3; made rec. debut w. Hampton '42. Ret. to LA '43, pl. w. Lee Young; Jesse Price; also rec. as lead. w. Nat Cole as sideman. Pl. briefly w. Fletcher Henderson orch., Louis Armstrong bb '44. Moved to NYC late '44, pl. w. Billy Eckstine Orch. Gordon's recs. w. Eckstine and his own for Savoy established him as a leading figure in the bop movement. On 52nd St. he pl. w. Charlie Parker at the Spotlite and led own gp. at Three

Deuces; recorded with both Parker and Gillespie. He traveled to Calif. summer '46. Pl. two mos. w. Cee Pee Johnson in Honolulu, then returned to NYC late '47. Pl. w. Tadd Dameron '49 and gigged on 52nd St. Rec. a series of saxophone duels w. Wardell Gray '47–52. Led combos in Calif. in '50s. Acted, comp., and led qt. in West Coast prod. of Jack Gelber's play, *The Connection*. Cont. to lead own gps., then moved to NYC '62. After tour. Eng. and the Continent in fall '62, Gordon settled in Copenhagen. Worked extens. in Eur., also took part in Danish prod. of *The Connection* and was feat. in Danish film '60s. Perf. in US clubs during first half of '65 and made occas. visits thereafter, but pl. mainly at Eur., fests and at Copenhagen's leading jazz club, Montmartre. Began pl. sop. sax in '70s. Tour. Japan '75. Visited NYC '76, where people lined up around the block to hear him at the Village Vanguard; he returned permanently to US '77, fronting his own gp., which featured Woody Shaw, and rec. for Col. Gordon starred in the '86 film, *Round Midnight*, about an expatriate American jazz musician living in Eur., and was nominated for an Oscar. He made several Eur. festival tours in the '80s. Strongly infl. by Lester Young, Gordon combined the Young and Hawkins schs. with the infl. of Charlie Parker to become the first to translate Parker's language to the tnr.; was a strong early infl. on Sonny Rollins and John Coltrane, among others. A volume of Gordon solo transcriptions was publ. by Lennie Niehaus in '79. Polls: *DB* Critics '71; *DB* Mus. of Yr. '78, '80; Jazz Hall of Fame '80. Fests: all major fr. '60s. Films: *Unchained*; *Awakenings*. TV: PBS *Just Jazz* '71; actor, *Crime Story* '88. Videos: Rhap.; Shan.; D. Gordon–B. Webster, Vid Jazz. CDs: BN, incl. boxed set; Prest.; Sav.; Col.; Steep.; Stash; Polyd.; BL; w. Eckstine; Gillespie; Fats Navarro (Sav.); Wardell Gray (Prest.); Sir Charles Thompson (Del.); H. Hancock (BN); Stan Levey (Aff.); J. McLean (Steep.).

GORDON, FRANK ALFRED, tpt, flg; b. Milwaukee, WI, 9/27/38. Attended Wisconsin U.-Milwaukee; Roosevelt U., Chi.; Governors St. U., Park Forest, Ill. Stud. w. Bunky Green; Donald Byrd. Pl. w. local gps. in Milwaukee and Chi. 1960s. Join. AACM in Chi. '68; pl. w. Anthony Braxton; Kalaparusha Maurice McIntyre; AACM bb. Pl. w. Eldee Young–Red Holt '70; own sxt., The Awakening w. Ken Chaney '71; Thad Jones–Mel Lewis Orch. '76; Art Blakey, Sam Rivers '77; w. Lena Horne on B'way '81. Pl. in '80s and '90s w. David Murray bb; Charlie Haden; Illinois Jacquet bb; John Stubblefield; John Hicks; Clifford Jordan bb; own gps. Favs: Clifford Brown, Lee Morgan, Freddie Hubbard. Fests: Eur. '76–8 w. Jones-Lewis; '77 w. Rivers; '90 w. Jacquet;

Hamburg '91 as soloist. Film: app. in *The Cotton Club*. TV: Lena Horne, *The Lady and Her Music*. CDs: SN; w. Ebony Brass Qnt. (Maple.); C. Persip (SN); M.R. Abrams (BS).

GORDON, JOE (JOSEPH HENRY), tpt; b. Boston, MA, 5/15/28; d. Santa Monica, CA, 11/4/63. Studied at New Engl. Cons. w. Fred Berman. Worked selling sandwiches on Boston-Albany train line 1947; sold newspapers around local clubs to gain entry to mus. community. Led own combo at the Savoy in Bost. '47. Then worked w. Georgie Auld, Lionel Hampton, Charlie Parker on and off '52–5; Art Blakey '54; Don Redman '55. Tour. Mid-East w. Dizzy Gillespie bb spring '56; pl. w. Horace Silver '56. Ret. to Bost., form. own gp., then worked w. Herb Pomeroy orch. '56–8. Moved to LA, pl. w. Harold Land; Dexter Gordon; Benny Carter; Barney Kessel; w. Shelly Manne '58–60. Freelanced in last yrs. Died in fire in his room. Favs: Gillespie, Eldridge. Film: w. Manne, *The Proper Time*. Recs. as lead. for Merc. '55; Cont. '61; w. Gillespie; Blakey (Em.). CDs: w. Monk (Riv.); Gillespie (Verve); Manne; Kessel; Helen Humes (Cont.); Charlie Mariano (Prest.); C. Parker (Up.); Land (Jzld.).

GORDON, JON BARRY, alto, sop saxes; b. Staten Island, NY, 12/23/66. Mother was singer whose first husband was Calif. bari. saxist Bob Gordon. Stud. at HS. of Perf. Arts 1980–4; Manh. Sch. of Mus. '84–8; also w. Phil Woods, who inspired him to pl. jazz. Pl. w. Eddie Chamblee in jam sessions at Sweet Basil. Worked w. Red Rodney '88; Loren Schoenberg since '88; Bill Mays '90; Ron McClure since '90; own qt. Won Thelonious Monk competition '96. Gordon's playing and writing are solidly grounded but adventuresome in extending harmonies and form. He says, "I try to write modern but not lose the melodic sense." Favs: C. Parker, Coltrane, C.Adderley, Benny Carter, Woods, C. McPherson. Fests: Oslo '87–91; jazz cruises. Theater: *Jazz Nativity*. CDs: Chiaro.; Gem.; CC; w. Bill Mays (Conc.); J. Fedchock (Res.).

GORDON, WYCLIFFE A. ("PINECONE"), tbn, tba, cl, bsn, pno, bs, dms; b. Waynesboro, GA, 5/29/67. Many mus. in family. Began on pno. but mainly self-taught on tbn., start. at age 12. In hs in Augusta, Ga., was selected for All-State Concert & Jazz Band and McDonald's All-American Marching Band & Jazz Band. During his soph. yr. at Fla. A&M U., Wynton Marsalis first heard him pl. and was impressed. Pl. w. various all-county and all-state bands, then w. Herb Harris III 1988; Marcus Roberts '88–9; Scotty Barnhart, Wynton Marsalis fr. '89; Lincoln Center Jazz Orch. fr. '90; Word Of Mouth, Playback '92. An ebullient player with a robust style rooted in the NO tradition and swing. Favs: Tricky Sam Nanton, J.J. Johnson, Slide Hampton, Vic Dickenson, Dicky Wells. Fests: all major w. Marsalis. Film: cameo app. in *Tune in Tomorrow*. CDs: Wycliffe Gordon–Ronald Westray (Atl.); w. Marsalis; LCJO (Col.); Marcus Roberts (Col.; Novus).

GOTTLIEB, DANNY (DANIEL RICHARD), dms, perc; b. NYC, 4/18/53. Mother pl. vln. in amateur orchs. Began on cello. Received B. Mus. fr. U. of Miami 1975, then stud. w. Joe Morello and Mel Lewis in NYC. Pl. w. pop singer Bobby Rydell '75, then Pat Martino '75; Gary Burton, Joe Farrell, Clark Terry '76; Pat Metheny '77–82; Stan Getz, Flora Purim early '80s; Michael Franks '83. Formed own gp. w. Mark Egan '81, which became Elements '83. Pl. w. John McLaughlin–Mahavishnu Orch. '84–7; Al Di Meola '86; Randy Brecker, Eliane Elias '87; Gil Evans Orch. '87–8; Blues Bros. Band '89–91; Manh. Jazz Qnt. '90; Eddie Gomez since '91; also gigs w. Chip Jackson; Jeremy Steig; Warren Bernhardt; Lew Soloff; Richard Stoltzman. Has also done extens. sess. and film work. Film: co-comp., w. Egan, music for *Blown Away* '85. Favs: Joe Morello, Jack DeJohnette, Mel Lewis. Polls: *Modern Drummer* '85. Fests: Eur.; Japan since '75. TV: VH-1 *New Visions* w. Egan. CDs: Big World; w. G. Burton; P. Metheny (ECM); Elements (Ant.; RCA); B. Brookmeyer (Act); McLaughlin (Verve); Soloff (PW); H. Laws (MM); Bernhardt (DMP); G. Evans (Elec. Bird; Jazz Door); A. LaVerne (Steep.; JC).

GOURLEY, JIMMY (JAMES PASCO JR.), gtr, voc, comp; b. St. Louis, MO, 6/9/26. Father founded Monarch Cons. of Mus. in Hammond, Ind.; son Sean is gtrst. Began on gtr. at 10. Pl. in student bb w. Lee Konitz on tnr. sax 1941. Tour. w. commercial bands in La. '43–4; in navy '44–6. Repl. Jimmy Raney w. Jay Burkhart band in Chi. '46–8. Freelanced in Chi. w. Vido Musso, Anita O'Day, Gene Ammons, Sonny Stitt, Jackie Cain–Roy Kral '48–50. Lived in Paris '51–4; worked w. Henri Renaud, also led own gps. at Tabou, Ringside. Rec. in Paris w. Zoot Sims; L. Konitz; Gigi Gryce; Clifford Brown; Bob Brookmeyer; Roy Haynes; et al. Pl. w. Chubby Jackson in Chi. '56, then ret. to Paris in Dec. '57. Pl. six mos. w. Art Simmons at Mars Club '58. With Kenny Clarke, co-led house band at Paris Blue Note backing visiting soloists '59–63. Rec. w. Lester Young '59. Tour. Switz., Italy w. own qt. '64. Back at Blue Note '64–5, then led own qt. at Chat Qui Peche '65–6. Rejoin. Clarke in trio w. Lou Bennett Feb. '66; Bennett was later repl. by Eddy Louiss. Perf. on soundtracks to

films *Paris Blues* (w. Ellington); *Ballade Pour Un Voyou*. Lived in Canary Islands, perf. there at Half Note club which he helped found '70–2. Ret. to Paris, led own qt. at Club St. Germain; duo at Bilboquet '74; sang and pl. solo gtr. at Caveau de la Montagne '75. Perf. solo at Sweet Basil, NYC, summer '75. Led trio in Eur. '70s-80s. Currently leads a duo w. his son Sean in Paris. Gourley is credited with introducing a smooth, Lester Young–influenced style of guitar playing to Eur., which had previously been dominated by Django Reinhardt. Favs: Charlie Christian, Jimmy Raney. Fests: many in Eur. Film: app. w. K. Clarke in *The Only Game in Town*, w. Elizabeth Taylor, Warren Beatty. LPs as lead. on Uptown; Bingow. CDs: Bloom.; Up.; Gourley–Richard Galliano (52 rue Est); w. Christian Escoude (Em.); C. Brown; Sims; Brookmeyer; Konitz (Vogue); Stan Getz (LRC); Lester Young; Grappelli (Verve); w. Clarke; Bill Smith in *Americans in Europe* (Imp.).

GOWANS, BRAD (ARTHUR BRADFORD), tbn, cl, arr; b. Billerica, MA, 12/3/03; d. Los Angeles, CA, 9/8/54. Learned to pl. several inst. at his moth.'s school. First prof. job w. Rhapsody Makers Band, on cl., some slide tbn. Then w. Tommy De Rosa's NO Jazz Band, replacing Sidney Arodin. In 1926, switched to crnt., pl. w. Joe Venuti; Jimmy Durante; also recs. w. Red Nichols, Mal Hallett '26–8. After brief inactive period in early '30s, concentrated more on tbn., pl. w. Bobby Hackett '36; Wingy Manone on v-tbn; Hackett again, doubling on sax '38; Joe Marsala; Bud Freeman; w. Eddie Condon at Nick's '40. In '39–40 also wrote arr. for Freeman and Lee Wiley; invented a combination slide and valve tbn. he called a "valide." Pl. w. Ray McKinley '42; Art Hodes '42–3; Max Kaminsky '45; Condon '46; join. Jimmy Dorsey '48; Nappy Lamare '49. Moved to West Coast '51, freelanced. Spent his last yr. in LV w. Ed Skrivanek's sxt. On cl. and tbn. considered, respectively, a disciple of Larry Shields and Eddie Edwards of ODJB. Wrote many successful arr. for trad.-style bands, incl. Freeman's Summa Cum Laude orch. Rec. as lead., Vict. '46; w. Freeman (Vict.). CDs: w. Kaminsky (Jazz.); Pee Wee Russell (Comm.); M. Spanier (BB).

GOYKOVICH, DUSKO (Dusan Gojkovic), tpt, comp; b. Jajce, Yugoslavia, 10/14/31. Studied at Acad. of Mus. in Belgrade 1948–53, then pl. w. Belgrade radio dance orch. Moved to Germ. '55; pl. w. Frankfurt All-Stars, Max Greger Orch. '55–6; Kurt Edelhagen's radio orch. '57–60; Marshall Brown's Int'l Youth Band at NJF '58. Moved to USA '61. Stud. comp. and arr. at Berklee Coll. of Mus. '61–3, then pl. w. Maynard Ferguson '63–4; Woody Herman

'64–6. Ret. to Germ. '66. Pl. w. Int'l Jazz Quintet w. Sal Nistico '66–mid '70s; Mal Waldron, Jimmy Woode, Philly Joe Jones late '60s; Kenny Clarke–Francy Boland bb '68–73; Peter Herbolzheimer bb early '70s. Led own qnt. in Munich fr. '67; own 12–pc. band Summit w. Slide Hampton '74–5. Pl. w. Alvin Queen in '80s. Goykovich has arr. for Eur. radio orchs. and has taught at the Swiss Jazz Sch. in Berne and the Munich Jazz Sch. His comps. reflect the infl. of Yugoslavian folk music. He is the author of a jazz tpt. method in German, *Anleitung zur Improvisation fur Trompete* (Soehne-Mainz) '68. Favs: Eldridge, Gillespie, K. Dorham, C.Brown, M. Davis. CDs: Enja; DIW; Sound Hills; w. Clarke–Boland (MPS); Nathan Davis (DIW); W. Herman (France's Concert).

GOZZO, CONRAD JOSEPH, tpt; b. New Britain, CT, 2/6/22; d. Burbank, CA, 10/8/64. Studied w. fath., a tpt. teacher. Replaced one of his fath.'s students in Isham Jones's band 1938. Between '39–41, worked w. Tommy Reynolds; R. Norvo; Johnny Scat Davis; Bob Chester; w. C. Thornhill '41–2; three months w. B. Goodman. From '42–5, in navy w. Artie Shaw band, pl. lead. Rejoin. Goodman '45. In '45–6 member of W. Herman's first Herd; then w. Boyd Raeburn; Tex Beneke. Settled in LA '47, pl. on Bob Crosby's radio broadcasts '47–'51. From the mid '50s on, he was a very prominent LA sess. mus., highly regarded as a powerful lead tpt. Participated in numerous recs. w. Herman '51–7; Ray Anthony '51–8; Billy May '51–64; Shorty Rogers '53–7; also Stan Kenton; Goodman. He died of a heart attack. Recs: as lead., Vict. '55. Feat. on "Stars Fell On Alabama" w. Herman (Col.). CDs: w. H. James (Cap.); B. Rich (Verve); S. Rogers (BB).

GRAAS, JOHN, Fr. horn, comp; b. Dubuque, IA, 10/14/24; d. Van Nuys, CA, 4/13/62. Trained as a classical Fr. horn pl.; while in hs, won a national solo contest and scholarship to Tanglewood, where he pl. under Koussevitsky. First horn w. Indianapolis Symph. 1941–2; left to pl. w. C. Thornhill; own band in army '42–5. After discharge, was member of Cleveland Symph. '45–6; Tex Beneke '46–8; concert tours w. S. Kenton '49–50; also stud. comp. w. L. Tristano late '40s. Settled in Hollywood early '50s; continued stud. comp. w. S. Rogers and his teacher, Wesley La Violette. Worked as freelance; first horn w. Universal Studios; pl. on many TV shows; also wrote film and TV scores for RKO, Warner's, etc.; tour. w. Liberace. Dur. '50s, also work w. Jazz Lab, a gp. incl. Jimmy Giuffre, Marty Paich; led own gps., which at times incl. Giuffre; Paich; Shorty Rogers; Bud Shank; Gerry Mulligan; Shelly Manne; others. Con-

sidered a jazz pioneer on Fr. horn, he was equally devoted to stretching modern jazz developments, as both a perf. and comp. Comps. incl. two commissions for the Cincinnati Symph.: *Jazz Symphony No. 1*; *Jazz Chaconne No. 1*. His comps. vary fr. unpretentious, swinging jazz to a technically brilliant, though sometimes over-heavy incorporation of Eur. classical infl. Active as a soloist and teach. until his sudden death, caused by a heart attack. Ball State U. has a collection of his scores. Polls: *Met.*, misc. inst. '55. Recs. as lead. on Merc., Dec., Kapp; w. Kenton; Mulligan; Rogers; Bob Cooper (Cap.); Rugolo (Col.). CDs: w. Rogers (BB).

GRAETTINGER, BOB (ROBERT), comp, arr; b. Ontario, CA, 10/31/23; d. Los Angeles, CA, 3/12/57. Studied sax at age 9; comp. at Westlake Coll. of Mus., LA. Prof. debut at 16 w. Bobby Sherwood, pl. and writing. For the next several yrs., worked as both pl. and comp.-arr. w. Benny Carter; Johnny Richards; Alvino Rey; Jan Savitt; then turned his full attention to comp. Decided to devote himself to writing. Join. S. Kenton 1947; first orig. comp for Kenton, "Thermopylae," rec. '47; a symphonic piece, *City of Glass*, was perf. by Kenton '48, rev. and rec. in '51. Other comps. rec. by Kenton, for Cap.: "This Modern World"; "House of Strings"; "Incident in Jazz." During his last yrs., illness curtailed his work. Graettinger was an extraordinarily gifted modern comp. Gunther Schuller has written: "If Graettinger sounds like anybody it is Ives—in the music's multi-layered complexity, textural density and non-tonal language (especially *City of Glass*)—anticipating (not following) many of the European and American avant-garde experiments of the '50s and '60s. Much of the same can be said of his jazz-oriented works and arrangements. Pieces like 'Laura,' 'Autumn in New York' or 'Incident in Jazz' are radically new in relation to the canon of those post-war years, neither bowing to the influence of Ellington nor the beboppers." CD: *Stan Kenton Plays Bob Graettinger* (Cap.).

GRAMERCY FIVE. Group name used by Artie Shaw. The first, in 1940, feat. Billy Butterfield on tpt. and Johnny Guarnieri on harpsichord; the second, in '45, incl. Roy Eldridge, Barney Kessel, and Dodo Marmarosa. The last, which was Shaw's final unit before he retired, feat. Hank Jones, pno.; Joe Roland, vib.; and Tal Farlow or Joe Puma, gtr. All three ensembles were effective vehicles for displaying the individual skills of Shaw and his sidemen. CDs: BB; MM.

GRANELLI, JERRY (GERALD JOHN), dms; also vib, pno; b. San Francisco, CA, 12/30/40. Father and uncle drmrs. Stud. vln. for a yr., later dms. w. Joe Morello, his first main infl. After club dates in SF area join. Vince Guaraldi 1962. Form. own gp., the Jazz Ensemble '64. Worked w. Jon Hendricks; John Handy; Martial Solal; Jack Sheldon; Jimmy Witherspoon; and, over his career, a wide variety of mus. fr. Maynard Ferguson to Ornette Coleman. Recs. and clubs w. Denny Zeitlin fr. summer '64 to '67. Tour. w. Mose Allison fr. '70s through the '90s. Moved to Boulder, Col. '76 to co-dir. the mus. dept. of the Naropa Institute. Form. own band, Visions. In '80 took teaching position at Cornish Coll. of the Arts in Seattle. Perf. w. Ralph Towner, Gary Peacock in US, Eur. '80–3. Moved to Halifax, Nova Scotia, to bec. the dir. of the dept. of jazz and popular mus. at the Canadian Cons. of Mus. In '90s has led qnt. w. Jane Ira Bloom, Julian Priester, David Friedman, Anthony Cox; incl. Eur. tour '93. In mid '90s professor at Hochschule der Kunst in Berlin and lead. new band, UFB, w. gtrs. Kai Bruckner, Christian Kogel; Andreas Walter, bs., which also app. in Can. Favs: P.J. Jones, R. Haynes, Rich, Roach, Morello. Film: score, pl. by his gp., for *Jim the Man*, based on a Herbert Gold story, shown at SF Film Festival '65. CDs: Intuit. Mus.; Evid.; w. Guaraldi (Fant.); Allison (Atl.); Jay Clayton (ITM Pacific); R. Towner (ECM).

GRANT, DARRELL LEMONT, pno; b. Pittsburgh, PA, 5/30/62. Raised in Lakewood, Colo., a suburb of Denver. Moth. is gospel singer. Younger sist. and bro. pl. pno. and gtr., respectively, in family gospel band, which perf. in churches and nursing homes. Fath. read poetry and scripture; the band was also feat. on a weekly radio broadcast. Stud. priv. w. William Sible at Denver Piano Cons. 1969–80. At age 15 joined first prof. gp., Pearl Street Jazz Band, which perf. at Denver clubs and rec. two albums. Moved to Rochester, N.Y., to attend Eastman Sch. of Mus. '80–4; (B. Mus. in applied mus. '84). Grad. studies in jazz at U. of Miami '84–6; M. Mus. in jazz perf. '86. While in Miami worked w. Duffy Jackson; Pete Minger. Moved to NYC '86. Pl. w. Woody Shaw '86; Junior Cook–Bill Hardman '86–7; Charli Persip Superband '86–8. Tour. w. Betty Carter '88–9. Led own gp., Current Events, '88–91. Pl. w. Kevin Eubanks, James Newton, Terence Blanchard '89; Greg Osby's Sound Theatre '89–91; Frank Morgan '90–1. Mus. Dir. of American Tap Dance Orch. '90–3. Pl. w. Craig Harris's Tailgater's Tales; Roy Haynes fr. '90; Bill Lee '91–2; Phyllis Hyman '91–4; Chico Freeman '92; Tony Williams '92–3; Robin Eubanks fr. '92; Sonny Fortune '94; Santi Debriano's Panamaniacs, Jane Bunnett fr. '95. Cont. to lead own gp. Peter Watrous wrote: "He has figured out how to bring together all the various ploys that a modern rhythm section can use and meld them so that a performance is rarely stationary. It is a type of rhythm section virtuosity that is becoming more and more common, and Mr. Grant and his band have mastered it." Favs: Jarrett, Hancock, Stanley Cowell, James Williams. Fests: Japan; Eur. fr. '88. CDs: CC; w. Current Events (Verve/Forecast); G. Osby (BN); C. Harris; C. Persip (SN); Don Braden (CC).

GRAPPELLI, STEPHANE (orig. Grappelly), vln, pno, comp; b. Paris, France, 1/26/08; d. Paris, 12/1/97. Received first vln. from fath., with whom he studied. He also attended the Paris Cons. but was mainly self-taught. At age 15 pl. pno. at a local cinema accomp. silent films and also perf. in clubs and restaurants. His listening incl. the recs. of Armstrong; Beiderbecke; and Venuti. Pl. in band at Ambassadeurs club when he was 19. For several years alternated between pno. and vln. w. Gregor and his Gregorians; then worked as vln. and alto saxist w. Alan Romans band in Montparnasse district. Met Django Reinhardt, and they co-founded the Quintet of the Hot Club of France 1934. The group achieved international prominence on records as the first significant non-American jazz group. In England when WWII broke out, Reinhardt returned to France while Grappelli, remaining in London, worked extensively w. George Shearing. Worked w. Reinhardt again after the war in Engl. and France until '48. Became more visible in '66, rec. w. Violin Summit (Svend Asmussen, Jean-Luc Ponty, and Stuff Smith). First US app. at NJF '69. Rec. w. classical vlnst. Yehudi Menuhin '73, '75, and '79. He cont. to tour. int'l, leading a trio or qt., app. at most of the major jazz fests., incl. *Tribute to Django* at Kool JF, NYC '84. His gtr. associates incl. Denny Wright, Diz Disley in '70s; Martin Taylor in '80s; Bucky Pizzarelli in '90s. His 80th birthday was celebrated w. a Carnegie Hall concert. Rec. prolifically w. Duke Ellington; Oscar Peterson; John Lewis; Earl Hines; Martial Solal; Joe Venuti; Barney Kessel; Gary Burton; Michel Petrucciani; David Grisman; et al. Grappelli was the third important violinist to emerge in jazz after Joe Venuti and Eddie South. As a pnst., he leaned toward a florid, romantic style in direct contrast w. the swinging rhythms of his violin playing, but could also generate a gentle stride. CDs: Tel.; Verve; BL; Conc.; Pab.; Drey.; Angel; Vang.; Linn.; Atl.; GRP; Den.; B&B; Mile.; Owl; WB; w. Kessel (BL); South (DRG); Peterson (Pab.); C. Haden (Verve); C. Hawkins (Timel.); *see also* **REINHARDT, DJANGO.**

GRAVES, MILFORD, dms; b. Queens, NY, 8/20/41. Began on cga., sw. to dms. at age 17. Self-taught, later stud. tabla w. Wasantha Singh 1965.

Came to prominence through app. w. Giuseppi Logan and NY Arts Qt. in the "October Revolution" concert series '64. Pl. w. Jazz Composers Orch. '64–5; Paul Bley '65; Hugh Glover fr. '65; Don Pullen '66; Albert Ayler '67. Taught music at Black Arts Repertory Theater, Harlem '60s. Participated in "Dialogue of the Drums" concert series w. Andrew Cyrille, Rashied Ali mid '70s. Rec. w. A. Cyrille, Kenny Clarke, Don Moye '83. On faculty of Bennington Coll. fr. '73. Polls: *DB* Critics TDWR '67. Fests: NJF w. Jazz Composers Orch. '65, A. Ayler '67, various '73–4; Eur. fests. '70s. Film: *Lord Shango* '74. TV: *Positively Black*, *Inside Bed-Stuy*, Martin Luther King special on Metromedia '70s. CDs: ESP Disk; w. Ayler (Imp.); Logan; Bley; NY Art Qt. (ESP Disk); Kenny Clarke (SN); David Murray (DIW).

GRAVINE, ANITA, voc; b. Carbondale, PA, 4/11/46. Father sang; moth. pl. pno. and hca. Bro. Mickey was jazz and studio tbn. in NYC and LA. Moved to NYC mid 1960s. Stud. voice w. Julio Berracol mid '60s; Helen Hobbs Jordan late '60s; Michael Warren '90s. Also stud. pno., theory w. Tony Aless. First job w. Larry Elgart Orch. Also sang w. Warren Covington, Urbie Green, Buddy Morrow bands mid '60s. Freelanced in NYC area w. Vinnie Burke, Roy Eldridge, Milt Hinton, Hank Jones, Chick Corea, Eddie Gomez late '60s-early '70s. Lived in Germany late '70s-early '80s, perf. infreq. Ret. to NYC mid '80s. Worked w. Mike Abene fr. mid '80s. Also freelanced w. Tom Harrell; Geo. Mraz; Billy Hart; Gary Burton. Taught jazz voc. at Mannes Coll. of Mus. mid '80s. In the early '90s, Gravine formed a film and video prod. co., Sargasso Productions. In '93 she was named director of video programming for the Cultural Heritage Museum of N.J. Favs: Frank Sinatra, Peggy Lee, Chet Baker. Fests: Italy fr. '86. LPs: Prog.; Stash. CD: JA; SN.

GRAY, GLEN ("SPIKE"; Glen Gray Knoblaugh), alto sax, lead; b. Roanoke, IL, 6/7/06; d. Plymouth, MA, 8/23/63. Studied at Illinois Wesleyan Coll.; left to work as cashier on Santa Fe Railroad. Pl. alto sax w. amateur bands 1926–7; in '27 join. Orange Blossoms, one of J. Goldkette's dance orchs. Band pl. long engagement at the Casa Loma Hotel in Toronto in '28; in NYC '29, the band incorporated as the Casa Loma orch; app. at Roseland, began rec. for Okeh same yr. Became an immensely popular band in the '30s, especially on the coll. circuit. Some of its best-known personnel were Pee Wee Hunt; Clarence Hutchenrider; Gene Gifford. In '33–4, the band perf. on the first radio show to broadcast swing. It was one of the first white big bands to have a deliberate jazz policy, drawing on the sound of black bands. From

'37, the band was billed under Gray's name; rec. regularly for Dec. to '42, Merc. in '46. Ill health disrupted Gray's activities in early '50s; he occ. led studio orchs. from '56–62, perf. Casa Loma and swing repertory. Northeastern U., Boston, houses material assoc. w. Gray and Casa Loma. Recs: Okeh '29; Bruns., Vict. Dec. '30–5. CD: Col.; Cir.; "Casa Loma Stomp" in *Anthology of Big Band Swing* (Dec.).

GRAY, JERRY (Generoso Graziano), comp, arr, lead; b. Boston, MA, 7/3/15; d. Dallas, TX, 8/10/76. Started stud. vln. w. fath. at age 7; also acdn., solfeggio. Led own band 1931; arr. for Sonny Kendis. Tour. w. A. Shaw '36–9, first as vln., then as arr.; scored Shaw's hit version of "Begin the Beguine," rec. '38 for Bluebird. Join. G. Miller as head arr. '39; wrote such popular charts as "Pennsylvania 6–5000"; "String of Pearls"; "Sun Valley Jump"; "I Dreamt I Dwelt in Harlem"; "The Spirit Is Willing." With Miller's AAF band during WWII; awarded bronze medal in '46 for keeping band together after Miller's death. Later settled in Hollywood; led orch. for own radio show '46–52; freelanced; mus. dir. for *Bob Crosby Show*; staff arr. for Warner Bros. '62. In '70s led bands for clubs, sess. in Texas. Film scores: *The Glenn Miller Story* '54; *What Did You Do in the War, Daddy?* '66. Recs: Decca; Lib.; Tops; Voc. CDs: w. Miller; Shaw (BB).

GRAY, WARDELL, tnr sax; b. Oklahoma City, OK, 2/13/1921; d. Las Vegas, NV, 5/25/55. Raised in Det.; first stud. cl., then alto sax. Worked w. local bands while still a teenager, incl. Jimmy Rachel; Benny Carew. Pl. w. Earl Hines 1943–5 before moving to West Coast and worked w. Benny Carter '46; Billy Eckstine '47; Vernon Alley. Dur. this period, he bec. prominent through recs. and concert apps. for promoter Gene Norman and jam sess. w. Dexter Gordon; made "The Chase," first version of famous rec. w. Gordon '47; also recs. w. C. Parker, incl. "Relaxin' at Camarillo." In '48, went to NYC w. Goodman sxt.; at the Royal Roost w. Count Basie orch., Tadd Dameron sxt.; w. Goodman's bb late '48–9; Basie again in small gp. and bb '50–1. Spent his last few yrs. freelancing on West Coast and in Midwest, incl. work w. Sonny Criss; Hampton Hawes; Frank Morgan; frequent rec. sess., incl. Louis Bellson '52–3. A descendant of the Lester Young sch., he later came under the infl. of C. Parker, showing a vigorous, fuller tone and harder attack. While pl. a hotel engagement w. Benny Carter in LV, he died mysteriously, his body found along the road in the desert. Film: *Forgotten Tenor*, Abraham Ravett '96. Comps: "Twisted"; "Stoned" aka "Bedlam." CDs: Prest.; BL; Crown; FS; w.

Parker; Gordon (Stash); F. Navarro, in Dameron sxt. (BN; Mile.); B. Goodman (Cap.; Mos.; Hep); S. Hasselgard (Drag.; Phon.); Basie (Col.); C. Baker (FS); Frank Morgan (GNP Cres.); S. Criss (FS; DIW); *Jazz West Coast Live*, Vols. 1–3 (Sav.); w. Bellson in *Classic Capitol Jazz Sessions* (Mos.).

GRECO, BUDDY (ARMANDO), pno, voc, arr; b. Philadelphia, PA, 8/14/26. Studied w. fath., a music critic, who had radio show in Phila. Led trio 1944–49; joined Benny Goodman as pnst., singer, and arr. '49–52; tour. Engl. and France in '50. In later yrs. he opted for a more commercial style, pl. synths., singing pop songs and working the supper club and casino circuit in LV, Atlantic City, Monte Carlo, etc. Co-hosted a CBS-TV show w. Buddy Rich '67. In return to his jazz roots, rec. an album backed by Grover Washington Jr., Buddy DeFranco, Ernie Watts et al. '91. Tour. in a concert tribute to B. Goodman feat. a swing band led by Peanuts Hucko '92. Remained a capable, bop-inspired pianist and a singer in the classic pop tradition. CDs: Bay Cities; Total; w. Goodman (Cap.; Mos.).

GREEN, BENNIE, tbn; also bari horn; b. Chicago, IL, 4/16/23; d. San Diego, CA, 3/23/77. From mus. family; bro. Elbert pl. tnr. sax w. Roy Eldridge. Stud. tbn. at DuSable HS. Start. pl. prof. w. local gps. Join. Earl Hines in 1942, where he came under Dizzy Gillespie's infl.; remain. w. Hines to winter '48, except '43–5, w. 343rd Army Band in Ill. Worked briefly w. Gene Ammons; bec. more widely known pl. clubs and concerts w. Charlie Ventura '48–50. Tour. w. Hines's gp. '51–3; then led own gps. through '60s, often feat. prominent tnr. saxes, such as Charlie Rouse; Lockjaw Davis; Jimmy Forrest; Johnny Griffin. Several apps. w. Duke Ellington in '68, '69; then resettled in LV; pl. in hotel show bands; also occ. recs. as sideman in '70s; made last rec. at NJF-NY '72. One of the most dexterous and velvet-toned modern tbnsts. Favs: Lawrence Brown, Tommy Dorsey, Bobby Byrne, J.J. Johnson, M. Gee. Fest: NJF '69. TV: *Duke Ellington Sacred Concert*. Publ: *Be Bop Trombone Solos* (Belwin Mills, NYC). Comp: "I Wanna Blow Now." CDs: Prest.; Jzld.; four-tbn. sess. in *Charles Mingus: The Complete Debut Recordings* (Debut); w. Miles Davis (Prest.); S. Vaughan (Col.); B. Gonzales; I. Quebec (BN); S. Gaillard (Verve); Ventura (Dec.; GNP Cres.); Joe Williams (Sav.); Jo Jones (FS); Buck Clayton (Mos.).

GREEN, BENNY (BENJAMIN MORRIS WAGNER), pno, comp; b. NYC, 4/4/63. Grew up in Berkeley, Calif. His fath., a tnr. sax pl., interested him in jazz. Stud. classical pno. at 7; fr. 9 stud. priv. w.

Carl Andrews; Dick Whittington; Bill Bell; Ed Kelly; Smith Dobson. Pl. in Berkeley HS band. Worked w. Joe Henderson, Woody Shaw, Eddie Henderson, Hadley Caliman, Peter Apfelbaum in SF early 1980s. To NYC '82, stud. w. Walter Bishop Jr.; Walter Davis Jr.; and Larry Willis. Pl. w. Bobby Watson before join. Betty Carter '83. Became part of Art Blakey's Jazz Messengers '87–9. Worked w. Freddie Hubbard '89–92. Has led own trio and pl. w. Ray Brown's trio fr. '92. When Oscar Peterson received the Glenn Gould Prize in Canada '93 he made Green his choice as the first winner of the Gould Protégé Prize. Adept w. a single line, Green also pl. w. two-handed chordal power and can go deep into the blues. By the mid '90s his own personality was emerging more clearly. Early infl: Monk, M. Tyner. Favs: Tatum, Nat Cole, B. Powell, Peterson, Wynton Kelly, B. Evans, Hancock. CDs: BN; CC; w. Blakey (SN; PW; Evid.); Hubbard (Alfa; MM; Timel.); Betty Carter (Verve); Ralph Moore (Res.; Land.); R. Brown (Tel.); Jazz Futures (Novus); Don Braden; Jim Snidero; J. Swana (CC); Lew Tabackin (Conc.); Mingus Dynasty (Col.); S. Turre (Ant.).

GREEN, BILL (WILLIAM EARNEST), all woodwinds; b. Kansas City, KS, 2/25/28; d. Los Angeles, 7/29/96. Studied cl. Pl. w. WPA band in KC. Grad. fr. LA Cons. w. B.A., M.A. 1947–52. Bec. busy freelancer. Worked w. Gerald Wilson, Benny Carter in '50s; Nelson Riddle fr. '60; Louis Bellson off and on for 30 years; also Q. Jones; Buddy Rich; O. Nelson. For eight yrs. during late '50s and early '60s he led an all-star gp. at Marty's in LA. Pl. cl. w. Highland Park Symph. During '80s, accomp. Sarah Vaughan; Ella Fitzgerald; and many other singers; also pl. w. Capp–Pierce Juggernaut; L. Hampton; W. Herman; and Clayton-Hamilton Band. Taught at UCLA, USC, Cal. St., many hs. Though best known as a reliable section musician, Green was an excellent soloist on bari. and sop. saxes. Favs: Benny Carter, Lucky Thompson, C. Parker, D. Byas. Fests: MJF w. Gil Fuller Orch. '65. Award: Educ. of the Yr. fr. LA Jazz Society '91. Film: *Young Man with a Horn*. TV: *M Squad*; *Benson*; *Shogun*; *Flip Wilson*; etc. LP: Everest. CDs: w. Clayton-Hamilton Band (Capri); Capp; Gene Harris (Conc.); Gillespie; C. McRae (BN); O. Nelson (Imp.; RCA); B. Collette (Cont.).

GREEN, BUNKY (VERNICE JR.), alto, other saxes, fl, cl; b. Milwaukee, WI, 4/23/35. Mainly self-taught, infl. by Charlie Parker. Pl. local jobs in Milwaukee until 1960. On recommendation of Lou Donaldson, worked w. Chas. Mingus in NYC and LA briefly '57. Moved to Chi. '60; pl. w. Nicky Hill; Ira Sullivan; Andrew Hill; Red Saunders; Louis Bellson.

Stud. at Roosevelt U. '63. At Notre Dame Intercoll. JF, won trip to Algiers under US govt. sponsorship '64. Led pit band at Gai Paris club, Chi. '65. Tour. Eur. w. Renegades, incl. Steve Coleman, Craig Handy, Joe Lovano summer '96. Holder of a master's degree fr. Northwestern U., he taught at Chi. State U. '72–9; dir. the jazz studies program at U. of No. Florida fr. early '90s. CD: Delos; w. Travis Shook (Col.); C. Terry (Delos).

GREEN, CHARLIE ("BIG GREEN"), tbn; b. Omaha, NE, ca. 1900; d. NYC, 2/36. Played w. brass bands in Omaha and Tulsa; w. Omaha Night Owls ca. 1920; Frank "Red" Perkins '20–3; tour. w. carnival shows. Settled in NYC, worked w. F. Henderson '24–7, and intermittently through '30. Well known as sideman on many Bessie Smith recs. for Col. '24–5, '27–30, where his expressive, often gruff style was appropriate accomp. Briefly w. June Clark; then join. Fats Waller, James P. Johnson for *Keep Shufflin'* revue '28; Zutty Singleton, Benny Carter '29. Pl. occ. w. Elmer Snowden, Chick Webb '30; Jimmie Noone, McKinney's Cotton Pickers '31; Sam Wooding, Don Redman '32. Pl. regularly w. Webb '32–3; again w. Carter '33; Webb '34; Louis Metcalf '35; Kaiser Marshall. He froze to death outside his home in Harlem. CDs: w. B. Smith (Col.); Henderson (BB; Col.).

GREEN, DAVE (DAVID JOHN), bs; b. London, England, 3/5/42. Self-taught. First pl. prof. w. Don Rendell–Ian Carr qnt. 1963–9; Humphrey Lyttelton '65–83; Stan Tracey '67–78, where he accomp. many visiting Amers. such as Coleman Hawkins; Sonny Rollins; Benny Carter; Zoot Sims. Form. own gp., Fingers '79. Pl. w. Michael Garrick fr. '64; Peter King fr. '82; Didier Lockwood '85–6; Charlie Watts's Charlie Parker–based qnt. fr. '91. Favs: Blanton, Ron Carter, Charlie Haden, Wilbur Ware. Tour. Yugoslavia w. Fingers '84. Fests: Nice JF '84; Berne JF w. Jim Galloway–Carl Fontana gp. '85. Won Brit. Jazz Awards '87, '89, '92. LP w. Fingers, *Fingers Remember Mingus*, Spot., '79. CDs: Linn; w. C. Watts (Contin.); S. Tracey (BN); Scott Hamilton (Conc.).

GREEN, FREDDIE (Frederick William Greene), gtr; b. Charleston, SC, 3/31/11; d. Las Vegas, NV, 3/1/87. Moved to NYC 1930 to finish sch. Musically self-taught; start. pl. guitar at the age of 12. While pl. at the Black Cat Café in Greenwich Village w. Kenny Clarke '36, was heard by John Hammond, who recommended him to Count Basie. Debuted w. Basie in Phila., March '37, remaining w. him almost continuously until Basie's death in '84. He was also constantly in demand for rec. dates, incl. sess. w. Benny Goodman; Mildred Bailey; Billie Holiday; Teddy Wilson; Benny Carter; Lester Young; Lionel Hampton; Buck Clayton; Joe Sullivan; Illinois Jacquet. Long considered the definitive rhythm guitarist, his light, steady strumming on unamplified gtr. was an invaluable component of Basie's sound for almost fifty years. His very rare solo passages may be heard to good effect w. Bro. John Sellers on Vang. '54; "Memories Ad Lib" w. Basie and Joe Williams (Roul.). Polls: *DB* Critics '58. Comps: "Down for Double"; "Corner Pocket," aka, w. lyric, "Until I Met You." CDs: Freddie Green–Al Cohn (BB); Herb Ellis and Freddie Green (Conc.); *Spirituals to Swing* (Welk-Vang.); w. Basie (Col.; Dec.; Verve; Roul.; Pab.; Mos.); L. Young (Comm.; Key.; Sav.); B. Clayton (Col.); Manhattan Transfer (Atl.).

GREEN, GRANT, gtr; b. St. Louis, MO, 6/6/35; d. NYC, 1/31/79. Son Greg is jazz gtrst. who goes by name Grant Green Jr. Began stud. gtr. while in grade sch. Start. pl. w. local gps. in 1944. Worked w. both r&b and jazz combos in '50s, incl. Jimmy Forrest; Sam Lazar; Jack McDuff. His work w. McDuff, and later Larry Young, Big John Patton, helped set standard in '50s and '60s for trios w. org., gtr., dms. Moved to NYC '60 and began to rec. LPs for BN which were very well received. In '60s, made frequent recs. in a wide variety of contexts; also led own gps. around NYC. Inactive due to personal problems '67–9, then resumed rec. for BN. Lived in Detroit '74. Perf. mus. for film *The Final Comedown*. A Christian-inspired gtrst., his blues-based, linear approach to the instr. was also infl. by J. Raney; C. Parker; and other horn players. Polls: *DB* Critics New Star '62. Book: *Grant Green: Rediscovering the Forgotten Genius of Jazz Guitar*, Sharony Andrews Green (Miller Freeman) '99. CDs: BN; BL; Mos.; w. L. Morgan; H. Mobley; Joe Henderson; I. Quebec; S. Turrentine; Larry Young (BN); J. Hodges (Verve).

GREEN, JESSE, pno, comp, arr; b. Stroudsburg, PA, 6/7/71. Father is tbnst. Urbie Green; moth., Kathy Preston, is jazz singer; other relatives musical. Began on pno. at age 2; stud. w. Rachel Carr; John Scully. Began pl. tbn. in school band but gave it up after fifteen yrs. to concentrate on pno. Stud. classical pno. fr. age 14 w. Dr. Robert Miller at East Stroudsburg Univ. Self-taught in jazz; occ. lessons w. David Liebman; Phil Woods. First gigs accomp. moth. at Poconos resorts. Pl. w. Frank Russo 1989; Urbie Green fr. '89. Led own gp. at resorts and at Deer Head Inn, Delaware Water Gap, fr. '89. Made rec. debut for Chiaro. label '92. Favs: Peterson, B. Evans, Hancock; arrs: Nelson Riddle, Woods, Donald Fagan. Jazz cruises '94, '95. Polls: *DB* student comp. awd. '88. CDs: Chiaro.; w. U. Green (Chiaro.).

GREEN, LIL (LILLIAN), voc; b. Chicago, IL, 12/22/19; d. Chicago, 4/14/54. Started perf. in Chi. clubs in 1930s. From '40–45, rec. regularly for BB, accomp. by Big Bill Broonzy; scored big hits w. "Romance in the Dark" and "Why Don't You Do Right," which was later popularized by Peggy Lee. In '40s, worked in Det.; tour. the South w. Broonzy; also tour. w. Tiny Bradshaw, incl. apps. in NYC at Café Society; Apollo; Savoy; worked w. Luis Russell '44. Then worked mostly around Chi. until her death. Recs. for Alad. '49; Atl. '51. LP: Vict.

GREEN, THURMAN ALEXANDER, tbn; b. Longview, TX, 8/12/40; d. Los Angeles, CA, 6/19/97. Began pl. tbn. in jr. hs. Moved to LA to attend Compton Coll. in 1958. Pl. in US Navy band '61–5; then ret. to LA, pl. many rec. dates, TV and movie soundtracks. Eur. tour w. Mercer Ellington '87; Japan tours w. Benny Carter '88–9, '91. Concerts and jazz clubs w. Gerald Wilson; Louie Bellson; Clayton–Hamilton Band; Bill Berry LA bb; H. Tapscott. Co-lead. w. Buster Cooper of qnt. '88–92, incl. Monterey JF '87, '90–1. Own trio album, *Cross Current,* released on B.J. '89. CDs: Maple; Buster Cooper–Thurman Green (Blue Lady); w. Miles Davis–Michel Legrand (WB); Clayton–Hamilton (Capri); G. Wilson (Disc.); Gene Harris; F. Capp (Conc.); Al Aarons (LAJS).

GREEN, URBIE (URBAN CLIFFORD), tbn; b. Mobile, AL, 8/8/26. Two older bros. both tbnsts. Wife, Kathy Preston, is voc.; son, Jesse, pnst. Stud. pno. w. moth., then began on tbn. at age 12. Pl. w. Tommy Reynolds, Bob Strong bands at 16. At 17, while at prof. sch. in Hollywood, worked w. Jan Savitt. Pl. w. Frankie Carle 1945–7; G. Krupa '47–50. Came to prominence w. Woody Herman '50–3. Worked as studio mus. in NYC fr. '53. Participant in recorded jam sessions w. Buck Clayton '53–4. Pl. w. B. Goodman Orch. at Waldorf-Astoria '56; also app. in *Benny Goodman Story* '56. Fronted Goodman band on three-month tour '57. Form. own band, pl. coll. concerts, dances '58; at Birdland, NYC '59. Pl. w. Count Basie Orch. '63; Elliot Lawrence band on Les Crane's *Nightlife* TV show '65. Led Tommy Dorsey Orch. at Riverboat, NYC '66–7. Also led own band at Riverboat '66–9; in '69 the band was an electric jazz-rock gp. Was among the all-stars who perf. at White House for Duke Ellington's 70th birthday party '69. Led combos at clubs, incl. London House, Blues Alley, Royal Box '70s. Occ. tours w. Goodman in '70s. Pl. at many Colo. JPs. Active as clinician fr. '70s. Has raised cattle on a farm in Penn. fr. '60s. Green's sound is characterized by a full, mellow tone and exceptional control and ease of delivery. Polls: *DB* Critics New Star '54. TV: *Dial M for Music*; Mike

Douglas; *The Main Event* w. Frank Sinatra '70s. CDs: Chiaro.; w. B. Clayton (Mos.; Chiaro.); Basie; E. Fitzgerald; Gillespie; W. Montgomery; Jimmy Smith (Verve); G. Evans (Imp.); C. Hawkins (Imp.; BB); Gene Harris (Conc.); Goodman (MM); Herman (Verve; Disc.); Q. Jones (Imp.; Merc.).

GREENFIELD, HAYES aka HAZE (HAROLD), alto sax, saxes, comp, arr; b. Poughkeepsie, NY, 7/7/57. Studied at Berklee Coll. of Mus. 1974–8, then priv. w. Hal Galper, Jaki Byard, Geo. Coleman '80–5. Pl. w. Jaki Byard; Rashied Ali; Tom Harrell; Norman Simmons; Mike Stern; Jeff Williams; Leroy Williams; Bill Frisell; Ray Drummond; Ron McClure; Don Friedman; Hiram Bullock; Jerome Harris; Joe Lee Wilson. Led own gp. fr. '86. Has scored several short films and TV progs. incl. PBS docus. He was feat. on the soundtrack of the film *Reunion,* starring Jason Robards. Favs: J. McLean, C. Parker, C. Adderley, Dolphy, Konitz. Fests: Eur. w. own gp. fr. '88. CDs: Owl; BlackHawk; SpecialMusic.

GREENLEE, CHARLES (Greenlea), tbn; b. Detroit, MI, 5/24/27; d. Springfield, MA, 1/22/93. First stud. w. American Legion drum and bugle corps. Pl. bari. horn, dms., mello. in grammar sch. Pl. w. local band while att. Cass Tech. HS. Pl. w. Floyd Ray 1944; Lucky Millinder, Buddy Johnson, Benny Carter '45; Dizzy Gillespie '46. Led own band w. Tommy Flanagan, Billy Mitchell, Frank Foster '47. Pl. w. Lucky Thompson '48; Gillespie '49–50; Gene Ammons '50. In the late '40s he was known by his, then, Muslim name, Harneefan Mageed. Retired from music '51, then ret. w. Yusef Lateef '57. Resumed pl. full-time w. Maynard Ferguson '59. Pl. in '60s w. John Coltrane; Archie Shepp; Sam Rivers; Collective Black Artists Orch. Taught at U. Mass.-Amherst. Rec. as lead. for Baystate label '75. Fav: J.J. Johnson. CDs: w. Roland Kirk (Mer.); Slide Hampton (Atl.); Coltrane (Imp.); Shepp (BS; Free.).

GREENWICH, SONNY (Herbert Lawrence Greenidge), gtr; b. Hamilton, Ont., Canada, 1/1/36. While in late teens, received a gtr. from his fath. Self-taught. In his early 20s worked in r&b bands, Toronto bars, and jazz clubs. A meeting w. John Coltrane in Buffalo, according to Gene Lees, reinforced his spiritual leanings, which strongly infl. his style. Tour. w. John Handy 1966–7; briefly w. Hank Mobley, then in '68 led a gp. in NYC incl. Jimmy Garrison, Jack DeJohnette. After working for a short while w. Miles Davis in Toronto in '69, he rec. w. a gp. co-led w. Don Thompson. Living in the Montreal area since late '60s, retired from music for several yrs. Highly regarded by Elvin Jones and Gary Burton, both of whom offered him jobs at one time. CDs: Kleo; w. Meantime, a gp. incl. his son, gtrst. Sonny Greenwich Jr. (JT).

GREER, SONNY (WILLIAM ALEXANDER), dms; b. Long Branch, NJ, 12/13/1895; d. NYC, 3/23/82. Professional debut w. Harry Yerek in N.J. dur. WWI. Met Duke Ellington in Wash., D.C., in 1919, and their careers ran parallel almost immediately, fr. Ellington's early days as a leader. Greer debuted with Ellington in March '20 and rem. w. him until March '51 when he join. Johnny Hodges' small gp. until Sept. '51. Through '50s, he freelanced in NYC w. Louis Metcalf, Red Allen '52–3, incl. Bermuda; w. various gps. at the Embers '56–8; Tyree Glenn '59; Eddie Barefield, J.C. Higginbotham '60s; own band at the Garden Café '67, '71. Pl. fairly regularly w. Brooks Kerr trio fr. '72; apps. w. him at NYJRC, Churchill's, Gregory's '74. Active until shortly before his death. Greer was noted for the colorful personality he lent to the Ellington orch., as well as his vital role in the rhythm section. During the band's residency at the Cotton Club in the '20s, his exotic and elaborate percussion effects contributed greatly to the jungle numbers Ellington devised for the club's shows, and later to such tunes as "Ring Dem Bells." Without ever taking extensive solos, he was showy or subtle, as the particulars of a score or mood of a performance dictated, and his artistry especially came forth in the early '40s, when he and Jimmy Blanton were a team. Film: *The Night They Raided Minsky's* '67; *Sonny*, a short docu. '68. TV: many apps. on Art Ford Show '50s, *Today* '74. In the '30s and early '40s, he rec. w. Rex Stewart, Hodges, Bigard, and Cootie Williams in small Ellington contingents; also w. L. Hampton; Esq. All-Stars. CDs: six tracks as lead. in *Classic Capitol Jazz Sessions* (Mos.); w. Ellington (BB; Dec.; Col; Prest.; MM; Saja); Hampton; Esq. All-Stars (BB); Hodges (B&B; Prest.; Vogue); R. Stewart; C. Williams (B&B).

GRENADIER, LARRY (LAWRENCE ALBERT), bs, el-bs; b. San Francisco, CA, 2/6/66. Father, Albert, pl. tpt.; bros. Phil and Steve pl. tpt. and gtr. respectively. Began on tpt. at age 10; began pl. elec. bs. at 11, bs. at 13. Received B. A. fr. Stanford U. 1989. Pl. w. Larry Vuckovich '82–6; Chas. McPherson '82; Joe Henderson '84–8; Steve Smith's Vital Information '87–8; Stan Getz '88–9; Gary Burton '90; J. Henderson, Danilo Perez '93–4. Pl. in '94 w. Tom Harrell; Joshua Redman; Betty Carter; also Native Colors w. Ralph Moore, Renee Rosnes, Billy Drummond; then w. Brad Mehldau into late '90s. Grenadier was on the faculty of Mannes Sch. of Mus.

'90–3. Favs: Paul Chambers, Ron Carter, Jimmy Garrison. Fests: Eur. fr. '90. CDs: w. Chris Potter; Walter Norris (Conc.); Seamus Blake (CC); Kevin Hays (Steep.); D. Perez (Novus); Mike Stern (Atl.); Mehldau (WB).

GREY, AL (ALBERT THORNTON), tbn, marching-tbn; b. Aldie, VA, 6/6/25; d. Scottsdale, AZ, 3/24/00. Raised in Pottstown, Pa. Fath. pl. tpt., sax, tbnst.; son is tbn. Mike Grey. Began pl. bari. horn at age 4 in Goodwill Boys' Band, which his fath. led. Stud. tbn. w. fath.; pl. tba. in hs band. Bugle and drum master in navy at Great Lakes Training Center 1942; began pl. tbn. again in order to join navy dance band. Pl. w. navy bands in Hingham, Mass. '43; Grosse Isle, Mich. '44–5. Joined Benny Carter on day of his discharge fr. navy '45. Rec. w. Chocolate Dandies w. Carter, Buck Clayton, Ben Webster, Sid Catlett for Swing; Carter bb w. Dexter Gordon, Don Byas, Freddie Green, et al. for Deluxe '46. Pl. w. Jimmie Lunceford '46–7; Lucky Millinder '47–8. Began using plunger mute while w. Lionel Hampton '48–52. Worked as studio mus. for Decca in NYC '52–3. Led own gp. on tour w. Gatemouth Brown in southern US '53. Pl. w. Arnett Cobb '54–7; Dizzy Gillespie bb, Oscar Pettiford Birdland Band '57; Count Basie Orch. '57–61. Co-led sxt. w. Billy Mitchell '61. Freelanced and rec. several albums as lead. '61–4. Pl. w. Quincy Jones briefly '64, then rejoined Count Basie as feat. soloist. Pl. w. Basie '64–77; freelanced, tour. w. Jazz at the Philharmonic '70s-early '80s. Rec. two-tbn. album w. J.J. Johnson for Pablo label '84. Co-led qnt. w. various tnr. sax pl. incl. Billy Mitchell, Buddy Tate, Jimmy Forrest, Al Cohn '80s. Formed qnt. w. son Mike Grey, Joe Cohn, J.J. Wiggins, Bobby Durham '88. Expanded the gp. to a sxt. w. the addition of tnr. saxophonist Rob Scheps '91. Pl. w. L. Hampton's Golden Men of Jazz in '90s; in mid decade ret. to lead own gp. Grey was generally considered one of the masters of the plunger style but his expressive, ebullient playing was present on open horn as well. In later years he was also heard pl. marching tbn., a compact valve instrument. He pl. on numerous film soundtracks incl. *The Color Purple*; *As Thousands Cheer*. Author of instructional book, *Plunger Techniques* (Second Floor Music) '87. Favs: J.J. Johnson, Trummy Young. Polls: *DB* '61; *DB* Best New Gp. '61. Fests: all major w. Basie; own gps. TV: Timex; Eur. TV. CDs: Arb.; Capri; Chiaro.; B&B; Gem.; Story.; w. J.J. Johnson; E. Fitzgerald (Pab.); Basie (Verve; Roul.; Pab.); L. Morgan–W. Kelly (Spec.); Ray Brown; F. Wess (Conc.); Carter (Hep); Gillespie; Joe Williams (Verve); J. McShann; C. Terry (Chiaro.); Hampton (BB; Tel.); Tate (Res.); Eddie Vinson (B&B); Mercer Ellington (GRP).

GRIFFIN, CHRIS (GORDON), tpt; b. Binghamton, NY, 10/31/15; d. Danbury, CT, 6/18/05. Played
w. local bands fr. age 12; prof. gig in NYC taxi-dance
hall at 15. Pl. w. Charlie Barnet 1933–5; Rudy Vallee,
Joe Haymes, Benny Goodman '36–9. Also rec. w.
Miff Mole, Mildred Bailey, Teddy Wilson '30s. On
staff at CBS fr.'39. Pl. w. Jimmy Dorsey '40; Goodman off and on '40s-50s. Ran tpt. school w. Pee Wee
Erwin '60s. Tour. Eur. w. W. Covington '74. CDs: w.
Goodman (BB; Col.); B. Holiday (Col.; Dec.); Wilson (Class.); Carl Kress in *Classic Capitol Jazz Sessions* (Mos.).

GRIFFIN, JOHNNY (JOHN ARNOLD III), tnr
sax; b. Chicago, 4/24/28. Mother sang; fath. pl. crnt.
Began on cl.; stud. w. Walter Dyett at DuSable HS. Pl.
w. Lionel Hampton 1945–7; Joe Morris '47–50; Jo
Jones '50; Arnett Cobb '51; Philly Joe Jones, Percy
Heath, Gene Ramey, ca. '50. During this time he also
practiced regularly w. Thelonious Monk and Bud
Powell. In army band in Hawaii '51–3, then worked in
Chi. bef. ret. to NYC in '57. Pl. w. Art Blakey '57;
Monk '58. Worked in Chi '58–60, occ. ret. to NYC for
rec. dates. Co-led qnt. w. Eddie "Lockjaw" Davis
'60–2. Trav. to Eur. '62, then moved to Paris '63,
where he pl. at Blue Note club w. Bud Powell; Kenny
Clarke; Kenny Drew; Art Taylor. Tour. Eur. w. Monk
'67. Feat. soloist in Clarke–Boland bb '67–9. Moved
to Bergambacht, Netherlands '73, lived there until he
ret. to France '80. Feat. at Montreux JF '75 w. Count
Basie, Dizzy Gillespie. Tour. extens. in '70s, sometimes w. Eddie Davis and/or Arnett Cobb. Apps. w.
Paris Reunion Band in '80s. From late '70s has tour.
annually in US. His '90s rhythm section was Michael
Weiss, Peter and Kenny Washington. Griffin, known
as "The Little Giant," has long had a reputation as "the
fastest gun alive." Although he still burns like a comet
that takes one on an orbital ride, he not only adrenal-
izes the listener but makes one feel and think with his
combination of soul and intellect at medium and bal-
lad tempos as well. Fav: Charlie Parker. Comps:
"You've Never Been There"; "Take My Hand"; "The
Way It Is"; "Dance of Passion." Fests: all major. Film:
The Jazz Life Featuring Johnny Griffin, shot at Village
Vanguard '85. CDs: Ant.; BN; Riv.; Gal.; Steep.; BL;
Timel.; Davis–Griffin (Prest.); Griffin–Davis (Jzld.);
w. Blakey (Atl.; BB); Hampton (GRP); D. Gordon
(Col.); Monk; C. Baker; T. Dameron; E. Jefferson; P.J.
Jones; Blue Mitchell; W. Montgomery; C. Terry;
Wilbur Ware (Riv.); Basie; Gillespie (Pab.);
Clarke–Boland (MPS); I. Sullivan (Del.); Powell (BL;
MS); R. Hargrove (Verve); Phil Woods (BN).

GRIFFITH, MILES LLOYD, voc, African drum,
pno, cl; b. Brooklyn, NY, 5/13/69. Family fr.
Trinidad. Moth., voc.; fath., voc., steel drum. Aunt,
Calypso Rose, "is, and has been, the queen of calypso
for at least 30 years." Griffith and his six siblings all
sing; bro. Mervyn Jr. pl. pno., org. Stud. mus. at P.S.
256 w. Isaiah Ruffin, incl. ear training through spirituals and classical mus. 1977–81. Singing/acting
understudy for Paul Simon film, *One Trick Pony,* '79.
Further exposure to various kinds of mus. at Satellite
Jr. HS. Sang w. Boys Choir of Harlem '82–3, '85.
Made thirty-state tour. w. Boys Choir '83; entered La
Guardia HS of Music & Arts fall '83. Met Charnett
Moffett, Stephen Scott, Justin Robinson. Stud. w. Ms.
Ext and Judy Gray. Heard and was infl. by Jay Clayton. Led own gp. w. Scott, Ari Roland, Greg Hutchinson. Met Barry Harris and participated in his sessions
at the Jazz Cultural Theater '86–8. Stud. in Pete
Yellin's jazz program at LIU on full scholarship
'88–91, grad. w. a B.F.A. Clyde Criner was an important infl. there. Stud. comp., arr., comping at Queens
Coll. w. Donald Byrd, Roland Hanna, Jimmy Heath
'93; also sang w. bb. In '94 Heath presented him w.
the Louis Armstrong Scholarship and he grad. w. a
master's in voc. perf. '95. Voc. instructors have incl.
Marion Cowings '87–90; Rahim-Ausar Sahu '90–1;
Richard Harper '94. From '89 to '95 had various
combos, often involving tbnst. Jamal Haynes. Singer
Evelyn Blakey took him to sing w. her all over the
city, tutoring him informally. Worked w. James
Williams' Progress Report '92; Bill Lee's Family
Tree Singers; percst. David Pleasant '93. Sang a lead
role in premiere of Wynton Marsalis's *Blood on the
Fields* Apr. '94, tour. w. it in '97. Own qt. perf. in
Who Dat Killed Better Days Jones by poet Carl Han-
cock Rux; gigged at Iridium '94. Join. Jon Hendricks
Explosion; sang w. J. Heath bb spring '95. Fr. '96 w.
Jack Walrath Masters of Suspense. Walrath says:
"Miles Griffith is a Renaissance man among contem-
porary singers. He can scat, shout, croon, preach and
deliver a ballad like no one you have ever heard. This
is the future of jazz and blues vocal." Has taught voc.
at LIU; New Sch. in '90s. Favs: B. Holiday, L. Arm-
strong, Calypso Rose. Fests: Bern (Switz.), France,
SF w. Hendricks; Panasonic Village JF, NYC, w. R.
Hargrove bb '95; JVC-NY w. J. Williams '97. Tours:
Senegal w. Bill Saxton '94; Germ. w. Walrath '96;
own tour in Israel '97. Film: as actor in *Ragtime.*
CDs: w. Marsalis, *Blood on the Fields* (Col.); J.
Williams (Evid..); Walrath w. WDR bb (ACT); Mark
Elf (Jen-Bay); Bill Mobley (Space Time); one track
in *A Cool Yule* (BN).

GRIMES, HENRY ALONZO, bs; b. Philadelphia,
PA, 11/3/35. Studied vln. in jr. hs; later tba. at Mastbaum HS. Moved to NYC early 1950s. Stud. at Juilliard, then tour. w. Arnett Cobb; Willis Jackson. Pl. in

Phila. w. Bobby Timmons, Lee Morgan, Tootie Heath mid '50s. Worked w. Anita O'Day, Sonny Rollins '57; Gerry Mulligan '57–8. At Newport JF '58 he perf. w. the gps. of Benny Goodman; Lee Konitz; S. Rollins; Tony Scott; Thelonious Monk. Pl. w. Lennie Tristano '58, then tour. Eur. w. Rollins '59. Came to prominence pl. free jazz w. Cecil Taylor '61–6; Perry Robinson '62; S. Rollins '62–3; Albert Ayler '64–6; Don Cherry '65–6. Retired from music '67. Favs: Ray Brown, Pettiford, Mingus, Wilbur Ware. Film: *Jazz On A Summer's Day* w. Monk '58. TV: apps. w. Mulligan '57–8. LP: own trio (ESP). CDs: w. Don Cherry (Mos.); Rollins (RCA; DIW); A. Ayler (Imp.; Freedom; ESP Disk); G. Evans; Pharoah Sanders (Imp.); Goodman (MM); Konitz (Phil.); S. Lacy (hatArt); Mingus (Deb.); Mulligan (PJ); Scott (FS); Taylor (BN); Charles Tyler; Frank Wright (ESP Disk).

GRIMES, TINY (LLOYD), gtr; b. Newport News, VA, 7/7/16; d. NYC, 3/4/89. Began on dms. Self-taught on pno., began pl. in amateur shows around Wash., D.C., 1935. Pl. pno. and danced at Rhythm Club, NYC '38. Taught self to pl. 4–string elec. gtr., pl. w. Cats and a Fiddle '40–1; Art Tatum–Slam Stewart '43–4. Pl. w. own gp., Rocking Highlanders, on 52nd St. '44–7; also rec. as lead. w. Charlie Parker '44. Moved to Cleveland '47. Tour. midwest w. own gp. '51–5, then settled in Phila. Ret. to NYC, pl. in clubs in Harlem and Greenwich Village, NYC '60. Tour. France w. Milt Buckner '68; Jay McShann '70. Took part in all-star gtr. concert at Town Hall '71. Led own gps. at Cookery and West End, NYC '70s. Also pl. w. Countsmen, Earl Hines '72. Grimes cont. to perf. and rec. in NYC until his death. Favs: Charlie Christian, Snags Allen, Johnny Smith. Rec. for BN w. own gp., Ike Quebec, John Hardee in '44–6 period. CDs: Prest.; B&B; as lead. and sideman in *The Blue Note Swingtets* (BN); w. Charlie Parker (Sav.); Tatum (Dec.); J. Hodges (BB); Buck Clayton (Riv.); B. Holiday (Dec.; BN); I. Jacquet (Prest.); A. Cobb (France's Concert).

GRISMAN, DAVID, mand; b. Passaic, NJ, 3/23/45. Started on pno.; switched to mand. at 15. Early recs. with the Even Dozen Jug Band; Earth Opera; and Jerry Garcia; active sideman in 1970s w. Judy Collins; James Taylor; Bonnie Raitt; et al. By late '70s, more jazz elements surfaced in Grisman's work; rec. two duos w. Stephane Grappelli. In early '80s rec. several albums feat. a hybrid blend of jazz and bluegrass Grisman described as "Dawg music"; rec. w. Danish vlnst. Sven Asmussen '87. CDs: Grisman–Martin Taylor (Acoustic Disc); *Svingin With Svend* (Zebra); w. F. Vignola (Conc.).

GROLNICK, DON (DONALD), pno, org, comp, arr; b. Brooklyn, NY, 9/23/47; d. NYC, 6/1/96. Father pl. gtr. Began on acdn. Stud. pno. w. Ray Thompson; Jerry Citron; sax w. John LaPorta. Att. Tufts U. Pl. w. Dreams 1969–71; Brecker Bros. '72–4; Steps Ahead early '80s; Joe Lovano–Josh Redman '93. Grolnick worked extens. w. pop mus. incl. James Taylor fr. '74; Linda Ronstadt '77–mid '80s, incl. recs. w. Nelson Riddle; Bonnie Raitt; Steely Dan. He prod. recs. for Michael Brecker; Bob Berg; Peter Erskine; John Scofield; and toured Eur. w. Joe Henderson, Randy Brecker, Eddie Gomez, Victor Lewis '91. App. w. own Latin Jazz gp. at Blue Note, NYC '94. Mus. dir. for Rainforest Foundation Carnegie Hall concert '95. In his own recs. of the '90s, Grolnick used a front line of tpt., tnr. sax, tbn., and bs. cl. to give his writing a personal sound. Favs: Basie, Garner, B. Evans, W. Kelly, Hancock, K. Kirkland. Fests: Eur.; Japan fr. early '70s. TV: *Tonight Show*, *Sat. Night Live*, David Letterman, etc., w. Brecker Bros.; Taylor; Ronstadt; Bette Midler. CDs: BN; WB; w. Dreams (Col.); Bob Mintzer (DMP); M. Brecker (Imp.); Brecker Bros. (Novus); P. Erskine (Cont.; Den.; AhUm); Scofield (Gram.); Mike Stern (Atl.).

GROSS, MARK IVAN, alto, sop saxes; b. Baltimore, MD, 2/20/66. Brother Vincent is tptr. in Maryland. Began on alto sax at age 6. Stud. at Berklee Coll. of Mus. Pl. w. Jack McDuff 1989; Lionel Hampton Orch. '89–92; Harper Bros. '92; Delfeayo Marsalis fr. '93. Gross has taught music in the Brooklyn public schs. Favs: C. Adderley, C. Parker, C. McPherson. Fests: Eur. '88–92; Japan '92. Film: app. w. L. Hampton Orch. in *Malcolm X*. CDs: w. D. Marsalis (Novus); Yoichi Kobayashi (King); *Five Guys Named Moe* soundtrack (Col.).

GROSSMAN, STEVE (STEVEN), tnr, sop saxes; b. Brooklyn, NY, 1/18/51. Older bro. Hal pl. tpt. and teaches at Berklee Coll. of Mus. Grew up in Pitts. Began on alto sax at age 8, then sop. at 16, tnr. at 17. Pl. w. The Uniques w. Hal Grossman, Jimmy Sutherland 1964–5. Stud. at Juilliard Sch. of Mus. '67–9. Pl. in Jazz Samaritans w. Geo. Cables, Lenny White '68–9; Miles Davis '69–71; Lonnie Liston Smith '71; Elvin Jones off and on '71–6; Stone Alliance, w. Gene Perla, Don Alias '75–7; Gil Evans Orch. '80; own gps. w. Tyler Mitchell, Reggie Johnson, Art Taylor, Joe Chambers, Cedar Walton, Tom Harrell, etc. fr. '81. Worked w. Eddie Gomez's Next Futures, Michael Petrucciani, Miles Davis–Jackie McLean '91; Joe Henderson–McCoy Tyner '92. Based in Bologna, Italy, dur. the '90s lead. own qt. Ret. to NYC several times to rec. for Dreyfus label, once live at Sweet Basil. A player of unrelenting swing and tough tenderness whose earlier infls. were Coltrane, Shorter, he turned, in the '80s, more toward the middle period Rollins for inspiration and funneled that through his own sound and psyche. Favs: C. Parker, Rollins, J. Coltrane, Sal Nistico, Jackie McLean. Fests: all major fr. '70. TV: Eur. CDs: Drey.; Musidisc; Timel.; Red; DIW; Phrases; w. Davis (Col.); E. Jones (BN).

GROSZ, MARTY (MARTIN OLIVER), gtr, bjo, voc; b. Berlin, Germany, 2/28/30. Father was artist George Grosz. Family moved to NYC 1933. Self-taught fr. age 12. Freelance in Chic. '48, in NYC '48–51. Worked w. John Dengler; also co-led dixie. band w. Dick Wellstood, Tommy Benford '51. In army '51–4, then moved to Chi. Tour. Midwest and Canada w. own gps. '54–6. Led trio at Gaslight Club, Chi. '57–64, then toured '65–70. Led house band at Blackstone Hotel, Chi. '71; own oct., Sounds of Swing, early '70s. Ret. to NYC '75; pl. w. NY Jazz Repertory Orch. '75; Soprano Summit '75–8; Dick Meldonian at Hoboken House early '80; D. Wellstood's Friends of Fats; Classic Jazz Qt; The Orphan Newsboys; also freelance extens. A fine rhythm gtr. w. an eclectic repertoire; also a witty raconteur. Favs: Carl Kress, Julian Bream, Teddy Bunn. Polls: *Jazzology* '85. Fests: Eur. fr. '75; Japan fr. '88. Film: app. briefly in *Tootsie*. TV: PBS Bix Beiderbecke prog. '75; *Today*. CDs: Jazz.; Stomp Off; J and M; N-H; w. Orphan Newsboys; Classic Jazz Quartet; Meldonian; Randy Sandke (Jazz.); Maxine Sullivan (Stash).

GROVE, DICK (RICHARD DEAN), comp, arr, pno, educ; b. Lakeville, IN, 12/18/27; d. Las Vegas, NV, 12/26/98. Studied at Denver U.; worked in LA w. John Graas; led own band fr. 1962; rec. *Little Bird Suite* for PJ '63. Arr. for Paul Horn; Nancy Wilson; Buddy Rich; etc. Founded Dick Grove Music Workshops in San Fernando Valley '73. The sch. grew to include hundreds of students but in '92 ran into financial difficulties, shut down, and was replaced by a smaller sch. in the same Van Nuys location.

GRUBER, FREDDIE, dms, educ; b. Bronx, NY, 5/27/27. Father a ballroom dancer. Through pnst. Joe Springer, stud. w. Henry Adler 1941–2; also w. Freddie Albright; Moe Goldenberg. Billy Gladstone showed him his approach to the snare drum. Hung out w. Morey Feld; Mickey Scrima. Practiced w. Cozy Cole. Form. lifelong friendship w. Buddy Rich. Began pl. prof. '43. Worked w. Ram Ramirez trio at Riviera in Greenwich Village in '40s; also w. Benny Ventura. Barry Ulanov wrote a rave column in *Metronome* '47 extolling his polyrhythmic conception. Pl. w. Tony Scott, Jackie Paris '47–8; Rudy

Vallee '48; Davey Schildkraut, Tony Fruscella, Buddy DeFranco '49; in '50 was part of Gene Roland's rehearsal band that incl. Charlie Parker; Zoot Sims; Al Cohn; Red Rodney. Roomed w. Philly Joe Jones early '50s. Pl. w. Oscar Pettiford at Snookie's '52. Moved to Calif., May '55, then six mos. in LV bef. settling in LA '56. Shelly Manne helped him get union card but he stayed in the underground, pl. and running the sessions at the Caprice '58–61 w. such participants as bs. LaFaro; Peacock; Haden; George Morrow; Ben Tucker; Herbie Lewis; and Elmo Hope; Hamp Hawes; Dexter Gordon; Joe Gordon; Bobby Hutcherson; Joe Albany; Walter Norris; Dave Pike. Later gigged at the Digger. Pl. w. Art Pepper mid '60s. Taught informally in club kitchens bet. sets, at poolside while he swam laps, bef. setting up shop in the back of Terry Gibbs's music store '65–7; then beg. teaching at home. John Guerin was an early pupil. Taught Don Ellis, "who wanted to learn to pl. his own charts," '70s. In '80s bec. a guru for countless jazz and rock dmrs. incl. Dave Weckl; Peter Erskine; Steve Smith; Adam Nussbaum; Neal Peart; Anton Fig; Ian Wallace; Jim Keltner; et al. Clinician for Zildjian; Vic Firth; and DW Drums of which he is co-founder. Clinics in Holland, Germ, Belg. Favs: Jo Jones, Rich, Haynes, P.J. Jones, Clarke, Roach, Blakey. CD: w. *The Band That Never Was* (Spot.).

GRUNTZ, GEORGE, pno, comp/arr, lead; b. Basel, Switzerland, 6/24/32. Studied at cons. in Zurich at age 14; won several prizes at Swiss amateur jazz fests.; worked regularly at Café Atlantis in Basel 1950s. App. at NJF w. Int'l Youth Band '58; in early '60s worked w. Eur. trio that accomp. tour. US jazz players. Tour. Far East w. Helen Merrill '63; member of Phil Woods's orig. European Rhythm Machine '68–9. Fr. '70 to '84, mus. dir. of Zurich Playhouse; served as dir. of Berlin JF '72–94. In '72, w. Flavio and Franco Ambrosetti and Daniel Humair, form. an all-star bb called The Band which tour. in Eur. with an all-star int'l cast '72, '76. He assumed leadership in '78, and it became known as the George Gruntz Concert Jazz Band; sidemen at various times have incl. Jon Faddis; Tom Harrell; Jimmy Knepper; Charlie Mariano; Benny Bailey; et al. In '73, created Piano Conclave, a European cooperative of pnsts. Tour. So. Amer. '84; US '87, w. GG-CJB, incl. Lee Konitz; Sheila Jordan; Joe Henderson; etc.; in '89 worked in trio w. Adam Nussbaum and Mike Richmond; w. GG-CJB tour. Eur. and Israel '90; China '92. Sidemen in '90s incl. Lew Soloff; Mike Mossman; Howard Johnson; Chris Hunter; Seamus Blake; Ray Anderson. He has cont. his assoc. w. Franco Ambrosetti down through the yrs., gigging w. him in Switzerland; tour.

in Germ. '93; and app. at Cork JF '94. Among his comps. are a jazz opera, *Money*, based on a text by Amiri Baraka and premiered in NYC '82; an oratorio, *The Holy Grail of Jazz and Joy* '82; and *Cosmopolitan Greetings*, a second opera, based on Allen Ginsberg writings '88. GG-CJB won *DB* critics poll, TDWR, '92. CDs: hatArt; Enja; TCB; MGB; w. Franco Ambrosetti (Enja).

GRUSIN, DAVE, pno, kybds, comp; b. Denver, CO, 6/26/34. Studied mainly at U. of Colorado; after serving in marines, he became mus. dir. for Andy Williams 1959–66. Rec. w. Benny Goodman '62; qnt. date for CBS '64, feat. Thad Jones, Frank Foster. Dur. the '70s, he became active as arr. in LA for Sarah Vaughan; Peggy Lee; Mel Tormé; and Carmen McRae; and worked w. Tom Scott; Gerry Mulligan; and Lee Ritenour; also collab. closely w. Quincy Jones. Accomp. his then-wife, Ruth Price, at Shelly's Manne Hole '66. Grusin moved away fr. mainstream jazz to experience great success as an Oscar-winning comp. for motion pictures. With his partner, the former dmr. Larry Rosen, he became dir. of GRP Records, which prod. many pop, fusion, and jazz albums in the '80s and '90s. CDs: GRP; w. Don Grusin; GRP All-Star bb (GRP); Mulligan (Tel.).

GRUSIN, DON (HENRI), pno, synth, comp; b. Denver, CO, 4/22/41. Brother of Dave Grusin. Stud. and taught economics. In late 1960s, pl. w. Gary Burton; Zoot Sims; et al. in Denver. Moved to No. Calif. '72, pl. w. Latin jazz gp., Azteca. After trip to Japan w. Quincy Jones in '75, he left the academic world permanently for music. To LA '76, worked and rec. with gp., Friendship (incl. Lee Ritenour, Ernie Watts, Abraham Laboriel) '78. First solo album '81. Prod. Ernie Watts album, *Musician* '85. Rec. duo album w. bro. Dave '88. Interested in mus. fr. other cultures. Would like to "integrate other music into my own tradition of jazz, folk, square dance and classical." His career, like that of his bro., has been mainly in the areas of pop-jazz, fusion, etc. CDs: GRP; w. Joe Pass (Pab.).

GRYCE, GIGI (GEORGE GENERAL; aka BASHEER QUSIM), alto sax, fl, comp; b. Pensacola, FL, 11/28/25; d. Pensacola, 3/17/83. Attended mus. sch. in Hartford, Conn., where he was raised; start. on cl., later took up fl., alto sax, pno. Worked w. local bands fr. 1946; led own 23–piece orch., incl. Horace Silver, at auditorium in Hartford. Stud. at Boston Cons. '48–51, majoring in classical comp., incl. stud. w. Alan Hovhaness. Went to Paris on Fulbright in '52, stud. w. Nadia Boulanger and Arthur Honegger. After ret. to US in '53, went to NYC, perf.

and rec. w. Max Roach; Clifford Brown; Howard McGhee; w. Tadd Dameron in Atlantic City; same yr., six-mos.' tour. w. L. Hampton, incl. Eur. Pl. w. Art Farmer '54–6; fr. '56 to '58 pl. w. own gp., the Jazz Lab Qnt., incl. Donald Byrd; app. at NJF '57; also comp. and arr. for many rec. dates. In '59, led own gp. at the Five Spot; Cork 'N Bib; other clubs. In '60s, stopped perf. and spent much of his time teaching, incl. some time spent in Ghana. Taught in NYC sch. system dur. '60s-'70s. P.S. 53 in the Bronx was renamed Basheer Qusim Sch. A gifted modern soloist, whose first-rate skills as a player, as well as a comp. and arr. can be heard on recs. w. Dizzy Gillespie; Oscar Pettiford; Art Farmer. Favs: Parker, Carter, Konitz. Book: *Blue Concept: The Music and Life of Gigi Gryce*, Noal Cohen and David Griffith (Ascon Prods, Inc.). Comps: "Minority"; "Hymn to the Orient"; "Nica's Tempo"; three symphs. and various chamber works. CDs: NJ; Riv.; Sav.; w. Farmer (Prest.); T. Monk (Riv.); B. Golson (Cont.); Teddy Charles (Atl.); C. Brown (Prest.; BN; Sav.; Vogue); Duke Jordan (Sav.); M. Roach (Deb.); Gillespie (Verve).

GUARALDI, VINCE (VINCENT ANTHONY), pno, comp; b. San Francisco, CA, 7/17/28; d. Menlo Park, CA, 2/6/76. Musical family; uncle, Muzzy Marcellino, a TV mus. dir.; another uncle, Joe Marcellino, was an SF bandleader who helped him get start. prof. While apprenticing at *SF Daily News* in 1949, he almost lost a finger in an accident, causing him to switch to mus. full-time. Pl. w. Cal Tjader trio in SF '50; Bill Harris, Chubby Jackson orch. '53; G. Auld '53; S. Criss '55; tour. w. W. Herman '56–7; again w. Tjader '57–9; w. Herman tour. Brit., Saudi Arabia '59; join. Lighthouse All-Stars '59. In '60s, pl. mainly w. own trio around SF; in '63, frequent apps. w. gtrst. Bola Sete. In '60s, achieved recognition as a comp., incl. "Cast Your Fate to the Wind," which became a hit. From '63 prod. soundtracks for the *Peanuts* TV series and specials, which he comp. and perf., incl. *Charlie Brown's Christmas* '65; Oscar nomination for mus. for film, *A Boy Named Charlie Brown*. In '65, also wrote an orig. jazz mass, perf. at Grace Cathedral, SF. Cont. to pl. concerts and occ. club apps. in Bay Area; died of a heart attack. John S. Wilson once wrote: "He has an exceptional knack for catching and projecting the spirit of a tune." Recs. w. Bola Sete. CDs: Fant.; w. C. Tjader (Fant.).

GUARNIERI, JOHNNY (JOHN A.), pno, comp; b. NYC, 3/23/17; d. Livingston, NJ, 1/7/85. Descendant of Guarnerius family of vln. makers. Stud. classical pno. fr. 1927. Became interested in jazz after meeting Art Tatum and Willie "The Lion" Smith early '30s. Pl. w. George Hall dance band '37; Benny Goodman '39–40; Artie Shaw '40–1; rec. on harpsichord w. Shaw's Gramercy Five '40; Goodman again '41; Jimmy Dorsey '42–3; Raymond Scott's CBS radio orch., doubling w. his own trio at the Onyx Club on 52nd St.; also pl. w. Cozy Cole early '40s. Fr. '43 to '47, Guarnieri was one of the most recorded artists in jazz, working w. Cole; Lester Young; Slam Stewart; Roy Eldridge; Ben Webster; Coleman Hawkins; Rex Stewart; Don Byas; Louis Armstrong; etc. Join. staff at NBC in NYC late '40s. Moved to Calif. '62; pl. solo pno. at Hollywood Plaza Hotel '63–5. In the late '60s, specialized in playing in 5/4 time and rec. an entire album in this meter. Perf. orig. pno. concerto in 5/4 at Wilshire Ebell Theater, LA '70. Spent most of early '70s pl. solo pno. at Tail O' The Cock restaurant in No. Hollywood but did tour. Eur. w. Slam Stewart '74; all-star pno. gp. '75. Fests: Concord '70; NJF-NY '74; Nice '75. TV: Art Ford's *Jazz Party*; pilot, *After Hours*, w. Hawkins; Eldridge. Able to emulate the pno. styles of Waller (he also imitated his singing), Wilson, Basie, he liked to explore what he called "multiple sounds—a modern take-off on Bach, but with a French Impressionist approach." A master of stride piano, he comp. more than 3,500 pieces in his lifetime incl. a musical show, *What a Perfect Business*. Book: *From Ragtime to Tatum* (Schirmer). CDs: w. B. Goodman (Col.); Shaw; Teagarden (BB); L. Young (Sav.; Key.); Armstrong (BB); V. Dickenson; Buddy Tate (Story); J. Dorsey (Dec.); Grappelli; S. Stewart (B&B); Ruby Braff (Aff.).

GUERIN, JOHN PAYNE, dms; b. Hawaii, 10/31/39; d. West Hills, CA, 1/5/04. Raised in San Diego; self-taught on dms. His teen-age jazz gp. won coll. jazz fest. at Lighthouse 1957. Pl. w. Buddy DeFranco '59–60; moved to LA '63; pl. w. George Shearing '65–6. Perf. and rec. in late '60s w. Thelonious Monk; Donald Byrd; Roger Kellaway; Victor Feldman; Ray Brown; and others; from '68 active in TV, film, and rec. studios. In '73, he founded LA Express w. Tom Scott; toured and rec. w. Joni Mitchell; in late '70s, early '80s rec. w. Joe Farrell; Bobby McFerrin; Milt Jackson; et al. Active as prod. and arr. throughout '80s but ret. to active jazz perf. '89, w. new version of LA Express. Film: pl. on soundtrack of *Bird* '88. CDs: w. Ray Brown (Conc.); Monk (Col.); G. Mulligan (A&M); J-L. Ponty (BN); H. Rumsey Lighthouse All-Stars (Cont.).

GULDA, FRIEDRICH, pno, comp, fl, bari sax, voc; b. Vienna, Austria, 5/16/30. Studied pno. fr. age 7 w. Professors F. Pazofsky and B. Seidlhofer at State Acad. of Music 1942–7. Won int'l competition at Geneva '46. Pl. at classical music fests. in Prague

'47, Vienna '48; many concerts throughout Eur. and So. Amer. Made Carnegie Hall debut in Fall '50 and was hailed by critics as one of the greatest classical pno. talents of his generation. Became interested in jazz after attending NYC jazz clubs. Perf. on Aust. radio w. Aust. All-Stars incl. Karl Drewo, Joe Zawinul '56. In NYC, sat in w. MJQ, then led gp. at Birdland and at NJF '56; sidemen incl. Idrees Sulieman, Phil Woods, Jimmy Cleveland. Perf. in Aust. jazz circles while cont. to tour as a classical pnst. Began pl. wooden fl. late '50s; bari sax ca. '60. Perf. at jazz wkshp. in Hamburg '61. Formed large orch. w. sidemen incl. Benny Bailey; Nat Peck; rec. comps. *Music for Three Soloists and Band* and *Music for Piano and Band, No. 1* '63. Made combined classical and jazz tour of So. Amer. w. Jimmy Rowser, Albert Heath '64. Premiered Euro-jazz Orch. on TV in Germ. and Austr. '64; sidemen incl. Joe Zawinul; Art Farmer; J.J. Johnson; Herb Geller; Freddie Hubbard; Kenny Wheeler; Sahib Shihab; Ron Carter; Jimmy Woode; Mel Lewis. Perf. comp. *Music for Piano and Band, No. 2* w. Los Angeles Neophonic Orch. '65. Led own orch. until '66. Founded jazz competition in Vienna '66; founded Int'l Musikforum in Ossiach, Aust. '68. In the late '60s and early '70s Gulda rec. as a jazz singer under the pseudonym Albert Golowin. Member of free jazz trio Anima w. Jorg Fuchs, Limpe Fuchs '72. Pl. at Eur. fests. w. Cecil Taylor '76; Don Cherry and the Revolutionary Ens. '77. Also helped organize several fests. incl. the Friedrich Gulda Fest. in Gmunden, Aust. '78. Hosted two music progs. on Aust. TV '81. Perf. a Mozart pno. concerto w. Chick Corea in Eur. '83–4. Worked w. drummer and singer Ursula Anders '80s. Gulda's comps. incl. two pno. concertos, a concerto for cello and brass band, as well as many vocal, orchestral, and solo pno. pieces. Orig. infl. by Bud Powell, Gulda's briskly articulate jazz playing is not comparable to the level of his classical performances, but he has consistently attempted to introduce his audiences to unusual musical experiences. His published writings incl. *Worte zur Muzik, Munich* '71. Fests: all major in Eur. LP: at Birdland (RCA) '56. CDs: as classical pianist (Lond.).

GULLIN, LARS GUNNAR VICTOR, bari sax, comp; also pno; b. Visby, Sweden, 5/4/28; d. Vissefjärda, Sweden, 5/17/76. Started pl. bugle in military band at 13, then cl.; later stud. pno. Turned to jazz in late 1940s. Moved to Stockholm '48, pl. pno. w. Charles Redland; alto sax w. Arthur Osterwall. From '49 to '51, pl. w. Seymour Osterwall; start. arr. for the band and sw. to bari sax after hearing Gerry Mulligan in late '49. Worked w. Arne Domnerus '51–3; tour. Eur. w. own gp. '54. In '50s, also rec. w. numerous US mus. visiting Sweden, incl. Zoots Sims; Stan

Getz; James Moody; Lee Konitz. Active in Italy late '50s, incl. tour w. Chet Baker '59. From early '60s, mostly concentrated on solo work and comp. Died of a heart attack. Pl. many fests. throughout Scand., Engl., Italy. Polls: *DB* New Star '54, first Eur. mus. to win US jazz poll. In '68, was honored as Sweden's leading jazz mus. as part of annual artists' awards; bari sax. award fr. Swedish newspaper *Expressen* '73. TV film: *Danny's Dream*, about his life as a mus. '68–9. Comps: *Concerto for Piano and Orch.*; *Danny's Dream*; *Aesthetic Lady*; *Jazzamour-Affair Suite. Areos Aromatic Atomica Suite*, his last work, was rec. by Swedish Radio Jazz Gp. '76. Recs. as a lead. for Atl.; East-West; Em.; and Eur. labels. As sideman w. S. Getz (Roost; Verve); Sims; Moody (Prest.); CDs: Drag.; w. C. Brown (Prest.); Getz (DIW); Brew Moore (BL); A. Shepp (Steep.).

GUMBS, ONAJE ALLAN BENTLEY, pno, comp, arr; b. NYC, 9/3/49. Cousins are prof. mus. Stud. w. May Tolland 1956–67; at Mus. and Art HS '63–7; w. T. Richard Patterson at SUNY-Fredonia '67–71; later w. David Baker at Indiana U. Pl. w. Andrew Langston '65–6; Dwight Gassaway '67–71; Errol Rolle '68; Fredonia bb '68–70; Kenny Burrell, Paul Gresham '71; Zimbabwe Nat'l Rhythm Troupe, Buffalo, N.Y. '71–2; Norman Connors '72; Natural Essence '72–4; Jimmy Owens, Collective Black Artists Ens., Frank Foster's Loud Minority '75; Buster Williams '75–77; Betty Carter '76; Nat Adderley, Phillis Hyman (mus. dir.) '76–7; Woody Shaw (mus. dir.), Noel Pointer '77–9; Angela Bofill (mus. dir.) '80; Sadao Watanabe '81; Sathima Bea Benjamin, Jeffrey Osborne–Deniece Williams (mus. dir.) '82; Watanabe '83–4; Jay Hoggard on and off fr. '83; S.B. Benjamin '84; Shunzo Ohno '84–5; Stanley Jordan '85; Watanabe '86; Gwen Guthrie (mus. dir.) '87; Michael Carvin '90; Terumasa Hino '90–1; Jeff Majors '92. Led own gp. Snowflight fr. '82. Gumbs has prod. recs. for Will Downing; Vanessa Rubin; Marlena Shaw; as well as his own recs. He has comp. for woodwind qt. and chamber orch. In '92, his comp. "Dare to Dream" was chosen as the theme song for NYC's City Volunteer Corps. Favs: Barron, Hancock, Flanagan, Llew Matthews, Hank Jones. Fests: Eur.; Japan; Africa; etc. fr. '77. TV: *NBC: Live from Studio 88, Sunday Night* w. David Sanborn. CDs: MCA; N. Adderley (Steep.); W. Shaw (32); J. Moody (Novus); w. Kevin Eubanks; Billy Cobham (GRP); T. Hino (BN); John Blake (Gram.); Watanabe (Elek.); Ronald Shannon Jackson (Virgin); as arr: w. W. Downing (Island); V. Rubin (RCA).

GUMINA, TOMMY (THOMAS J.), acdn, polychord; b. Milwaukee, WI, 5/20/31. Studied in Mil-

waukee, Chi., and at Loyola U. Pl. w. Harry James Band 1953–6; Buddy DeFranco–Tommy Gumina Qt. '59–63. On staff at ABC '64–7, then pl. w. Nelson Riddle '65–8. In '65, began to concentrate on design and marketing of musical instruments as pres. of Polytone Musical Instruments. From '73 to '75, pl. w. Art Pepper–Tommy Gumina Qt., and fr. '87 to '92 w. Joe Pass–Tommy Gumina Trio. *DB* poll winner early '60s. Recs. w. DeFranco; Pepper; and Pass. CDs: w. Pepper (Story.).

GUNN, RUSSELL, tpt; b. Chicago, IL, 10/20/71. Family moved to East St. Louis, Ill., in 1979. At age 9 began on tpt. Decided at 15 that he wanted a jazz career. At *DB* MusicFest U.S.A. in '89 he was selected as "best high school trumpet player in the United States." In same competition the East St. Louis Lincoln HS Jazz Band won first prize as well. Tour. w. band that summer to Montreux and North Sea JFs. Stud. at Jackson St. U. in Mississippi for one yr. Came to NYC '94 to pl. w. Wynton Marsalis in premiere of *Blood on the Fields*. Worked w. LCJO; Jimmy Heath bb. With Branford Marsalis's Buckshot LeFonque gp. '95. Has also perf. w. Marcus Roberts; James Moody; John Hicks; Oliver Lake; tour. w. bluesman Johnny Taylor. Pl. lead tpt. w. Miss. Symph. on Gunther Schuller's *Journey into Jazz* '90. Rec. on soundtrack for TV show *Moon Over Miami*. Favs: C. Brown, M. Davis, B. Little. CDs: Muse; High.; w. B. Marsalis (Col.); Lou Reed (WB).

GUNTHER, JOHN, tnr, sop saxes, comp, arr.; b. Denver, CO, 8/30/66. Grew up in suburban Aurora. Began on alto sax at age 9 in school band. Pl. w. Joy Caylor band 1979–84. Began jamming w. tptr. Greg Gisbert at El Chapultepec in Denver '83. Stud. at Berklee Coll. of Mus. '86–9. Moved to Chi. '89. Pl. w. Woody Herman '90–1. Did two-yr. teach. apprenticeship at U. of Miami '92–3; post-grad. degree '93. Backed Dizzy Gillespie; Michael Brecker; Joe Henderson as member of Miami U. orch.; also tour. Brazil w. it '92. Trav. to NYC to stud. w. J. Lovano on NEA grant '92. Moved to NYC '93 and form. qnt. w. Gisbert. Pl. w. W. Herman orch. at JVC-NY '96. A solid post-bop pl. beginning to stretch boundaries. Own trio in late '90s. Favs: Coltrane, Shorter, Lovano. CDs: CIMP; Capri; Convergence; Synergy Music.

GURTU, TRILOK, perc; b. Bombay, India, 10/30/51. Grandfather a music scholar and sitar pl.; moth. a star singer of *thumri*, a light classical vocal style. Stud. classical tabla from age 5; interest in jazz, soul, rock, and world mus. inspired by a bro., also a percst. Worked in Eur. in mid 1970s; moved to NYC '76. Pl. and rec. w. Don Cherry; Charlie Mariano;

Barre Phillips; Karl Berger late '70s. Toured Europe w. Jan Garbarek early '80s; worked w. John Abercrombie; Archie Shepp; et al.; pl. w. Oregon fr. '86; John McLaughlin trio fr. '88. A remarkable percst. who has effectively combined the complexity of Indian rhythmic *talas* with an ability to play a hard-swinging jazz groove. CDs: CMP; w. McLaughlin (Verve); Oregon (ECM; VeraBra); Shankar (ECM); D. Gottlieb (Atl.).

GUSTAFSSON, RUNE URBAN, gtr; b. Göteborg, Sweden, 8/25/33. Uncle pl. gtr. Began on gtr. at age 14; participated in amateur contests, orig. planning to become ballad singer. Pl. w. Bert Dahlander 1952–4; Putte Wickman '54–6, '57–9; Hacke Bjorksten '56. Pl. and rec. w. Arne Domnerus Orch. fr. '59. Rec. w. Jan Johansson '60s. Worked as studio mus. in pop and jazz fields. Tour. US and Can. w. Domnerus Trio '91. Rec. as lead. for Sonet label '77; w. Zoot Sims for Pablo '78, '84. Favs: Raney, Farlow, J. Hall, Kessel. CDs: w. A. Domnerus, *North American Tour 1991* (Caprice); Hallberg (Phon.); G. Russell (SN).

GUY, FRED, gtr, bjo; b. Burkeville, GA, 5/23/1899; d. Chicago, IL, 11/22/71. Grew up in NYC, pl. bjo. w. local bands. Join. Duke Ellington 1925. Sw. to gtr. '34; stud. w. Eddie Lang. When Guy retired fr. music in '49, Ellington did not replace him. Although Guy had been an important member of the rhythm section in the early Ellington band, his role had become greatly diminished w. the arrival of Jimmy Blanton in '40. Guy managed the Parkway Ballroom in Chi. fr. '49. CDs: w. Ellington (RCA; Col.); J. Hodges (Suisa).

GUY, JOE (JOSEPH LUKE), tpt; b. Birmingham, AL, 9/20/20; d. Birmingham or NYC, ca. 1962. Raised in NYC. Early experience in late 1930s pl. w. Fats Waller; Teddy Hill; feat. tpt. in Coleman Hawkins' bb '39–40; Charlie Barnet '41. Frequently pl. at Minton's w. Thelonious Monk, Kenny Clarke in '41–2, dur. the incubation period of bop. Worked w. Cootie Williams' bb '42; introduced several Monk comps. to the band's book, incl. " 'Round Midnight" and "Epistrophy," soloing on the latter. In '45, tour. w. JATP and pl. on the first JATP rec. to be released. From '45 to '47, closely assoc. w. Billie Holiday, socially and musically. Later moved to Phila. and was inactive from '50 on. Originally inspired by Roy Eldridge, he came under Gillespie's infl. in the Minton's period, incorporating some of the latter's devices in his style. LP: *Trumpet Battle at Minton's* (Xan.). Recs. w. Hot Lips Page; Christian '41. CDs: w. Hawkins (BB); Holiday (Dec.; Verve); Christian (Jazz Anth.); *The Complete Jazz at the Philharmonic on Verve, 1944–1949* (Verve).

GWALTNEY, TOMMY (THOMAS O.), cl, alto sax, vib, xyl; b. Norfolk, VA, 2/28/21. Studied w. Ernie Caceres, Peanuts Hucko. Pl. w. coll. bands, then in army band early 1940s. Sw. to vib. temporarily after sustaining lung damage in war. Pl. in NYC w. Charlie Byrd, Sol Yaged '46–7; Bobby Hackett '56–7; Billy Butterfield '58–9. Led own gps. in Norfolk and Wash., D.C., '59–61. Pl. w. C. Byrd '62–3, then ret. to Norfolk '65. Prod. and promoted Va. Beach JF '59–61, '65. Opened club, Blues Alley, in Wash. '65, worked there regularly w. gp. incl. Steve Jordan. Perf. and rec. at Manassas, Va., JF '66–73. Favs: Hucko, Goodman, Fazola. LP: *Goin' to Kansas City* feat. Buck Clayton (Riv.) '60. CDs: w. Hackett (Dormouse).

h

HACKETT, BOBBY (ROBERT LEO), tpt, crnt, gtr; b. Providence, RI, 1/31/15; d. Chatham, MA, 6/7/76. Son of a blacksmith, sixth of nine children. Son, Ernie Hackett, active as jazz dmr. in '70s. Start. on uke., he left school at 14 and began pl. gtr., bjo., vln., w. local bands and in Syracuse. In 1933, pl. mainly crnt., was part of trio w. Pee Wee Russell and Teddy Roy, perf. in various Boston and Providence clubs. In '36 took over lead. of Ted Marsh's band at the Theatrical Club, Boston, w. Brad Gowans writing arrs. Though he was mainly infl. by Armstrong dur. this period, he eventually became more closely identified w. the lyrical style of Bix Beiderbecke. Went to NYC in '37, pl. gtr. w. Joe Marsala, doubling on crnt; own band at Nick's '38–9; own bb at the Famous Door and on tour '39; disbanded and join. Horace Heidt '39–40; w. Glenn Miller on gtr., occ. crnt. '41–2. In '43, NBC staff; also tour. w. Katherine Dunham dancers '43; w. Glen Gray '44–6. ABC staff for several yrs. from '46; frequent apps. at Nick's; tour. East Coast w. own band early '50s. In '53–5 he earned wide recognition through a series of mood albums on Capitol led by Jackie Gleason, w. whom he also app. in person. TV shows w. Martha Wright; other broadcasts. Fr. '56 to '58, led a sxt. at the Henry Hudson Hotel and for brief tours and jazz fests., then led qt. in NYC clubs and on tours. Pl. w. B. Goodman '62–3, incl. Mex.; worked frequently w. Tony Bennett in mid '60s. Moved to Cape Cod '69, where he was often feat. at Dunfey's. Pl. w. Vic Dickenson in NYC and US tour '70; in '70s also feat. guest w. WGJB; tour. Eng. '74; apps. at Michael's Pub '75. Hospitalized for two weeks in May '76, he perf. on June 4 after his release, then died of a heart attack three days later. From his first days in NYC, Hackett was an important force in jazz. While he made his name as a crntst. and tptr., he remained a proficient gtrst. His melodic style has been praised by musicians of every description, and his beautifully burnished sound easily complemented a variety of jazz idioms. Fests: NJF w. Dickenson '70; many apps. at NJF-NY; Colo. JP. TV: *Just Jazz* w. Dickenson; PBS '71. Recs. as lead: Epic; Cap. CDs: Project 3; Jazz.; Hackett-Dickenson (Chiaro.); as lead. and sideman in *The Commodore Story* (Comm.); w. Armstrong; Miller; Teagarden (BB); Goodman; B. Holiday (Col.); Condon (Dec.; Stash; Sav; Jazz.; Comm.); Pee Wee Russell (Comm.); T. Wilson (Hep); Teddy Grace (Timel.); Gleason (Cap.).

HADEN, CHARLIE (CHARLES EDWARD), bs, comp; b. Shenandoah, IA, 8/6/37. Began perf. career as "little two-year-old Charles Edward...the youngest cowboy singer and yodeler on the air" on the Haden family's Midwest radio show. Took up bs. when his singing career was jeopardized by an occurrence of bulbar polio in his throat; bs. w. Haden Family band to age 15; also perf. w. small band in Springfield, Mo., and on TV show *Ozark Jubilee*. Moved to LA in mid 1950s to study at Westlake Coll. of Modern Music. Pl. w. Art Pepper '57; w. Ornette Coleman in Paul Bley qt. '57–9; and Hampton Hawes '58–9. Moved to NYC '59; app. w. Coleman at historic Five Spot date late '59. In early '60s pl. w. Denny Zeitlin trio, Archie Shepp, et al; rejoin. Coleman '66; also worked on and off w. Keith Jarrett and w. the Jazz Composers Orchestra; Tony Scott; Roswell Rudd; Red Norvo; Mose Allison; etc. In '69 he formed the Liberation Music Orchestra; in '76 he organized Old and New Dreams w. former Coleman sidemen Don

Cherry, Dewey Redman, and Ed Blackwell. Rec. w. variety of small ens. '70s through '90s, incl. two recs. of duets w. various musicians. In late '70s spent two years in a SF rehab program to deal w. a chemical dependency problem. Perf. and rec. w. new versions of Liberation Music Orch. '80s and '90s; form. Quartet West w. Ernie Watts, Alan Broadbent '86; also co-led trio w. Paul Motian and Geri Allen; rec. w. among others, Abbey Lincoln; Tom Harrell; David Sanborn; Gonzalo Rubalcaba; Stan Getz; Hank Jones; Kenny Barron. Artistic Director of Jazz Program at CalArts, LA. *DB* critic poll winner for bs. '82–90. Haden's warm, resonant sound, more classical than jazz in its timbre, is the perfect foundation for a playing style that reaches for primal musical essence rather than convoluted technical virtuosity. The best evidence of his skill is the ability to play with artists whose styles range fr. Coleman's open-ended improvising to Stan Getz's complex chordal variations. "The beauty of the art form of jazz," Haden told *NY Newsday*, "[is that] it gets people's attention with living in the moment." CDs: Verve; ECM; Drey.; SN; Old and New Dreams (ECM; BS); Konitz-Mehldau-Haden (BN); Haden-Chris Anderson (Naim); w. O. Coleman; Coltrane (Atl.); J. Redman (WB); Barron (Verve); J. Lovano; J. Scofield; Rubalcaba (BN); P. Bley (Musi.; SN); C. Bley (JCOA; Watt); A. Pepper (Cont.); K. Jarrett (Atl.; Imp.; ECM; Col.); Zeitlin; Motian (ECM); G. Allen (SN; DIW; JMT).

HADI, SHAFI (Curtis Porter), tnr sax, alto sax, comp; b. Philadelphia, PA, 9/21/29. Piano lessons fr. grandmoth. at age 6. Pl. w. r&b bands incl. Paul Williams; Griffin Bros.; Ruth Brown. Stud. comp. at Howard U., U. of Det. Pl. w. Chas. Mingus 1956–8. Collab. on soundtrack of John Cassavetes' film *Shadows* '58. Rejoined Mingus '59. Also active as a painter in '50s. CDs: w. Mingus (Col.; Atl.; Beth.; in *The Complete Debut Recordings*, Deb.).

HAGANS, TIM, tpt; b. Dayton, OH, 8/19/54. Lessons in grade sch. fr. Kermit Simmons. Majored in mus. ed. at Bowling Green St. U. 1972–4. Att. Stan Kenton jazz camp dur. summers; join. Kenton orch. '74–7; then pl. w. Woody Herman for six weeks fr. Jan. '77 bef. moving to Sweden and pl. w. Thad Jones Eclipse; Ernie Wilkins; Sahib Shihab; Danish and Swedish Radio Bands; also taught at U. of Lund and Jazz Inst. of Malmö. Moved to Cincinnati '82, pl. w. Blue Wisp bb, while teaching tpt., improv., jazz history at U. of Cincinnati. To Bost. '84, pl. w. Jimmy Mosher; Bert Seager; Orange Then Blue; taught at Berklee Coll. of Mus. Relocated in NYC '87, pl. w. Mel Lewis; Joe Lovano; Fred Hersch; Geo. Russell; John Hart; Marc Copland; Bob Belden; Andy La-

Verne; Bob Mintzer; Gil Evans; Maria Schneider; also own gp. w. Vic Juris, Scott Lee, Jeff Williams. In '87 Hagans received an NEA grant to comp. a suite for bb. Fests: Sweden since '77. CDs: BN incl. Freddie Hubbard tribute co-led w. Marcus Printup; MoPro; w. Kenton (CW); Belden (Sunny.; BN); A. LaVerne (Steep.); P. Delano (Verve); Lovano; John Hart; Rick Margitza (BN); Maria Schneider (Enja); Copland (JC); Thad Jones (Story.); R. McClure; S. Slagle (Steep.); Orange Then Blue (GM); J. Fedchock (Res.).

HAGGART, BOB (ROBERT SHERWOOD), bs, arr; b. NYC, 3/13/14; d. Venice, FL, 12/3/98. Many amateur mus. in family. Stud. gtr. w. Geo. Van Eps 1930. Pl. bs., uke., bjo., tba., tpt. in Douglaston HS on Long Island '31; later stud. harm., comp. w. Ruppert Graves, Tom Timothy, Stefan Wolpe, and bs. w. Fred Zimmerman in NYC '45–8. Pl. bs. w. local gps. '31–3; Bob Sperling at eastern resorts '33–5. Came to prominence as bs. and arr. w. Bob Crosby '35–42. Freelanced as jazz and commercial studio mus. in NYC '44–68; made many dixieland recs. w. Yank Lawson in '50s. Scored musical *Mad Avenue*, also started own jingle company '50s. On staff at NBC '60s. Formed WGJB w. Lawson '68. Tour. w. WGJB '68–88. In recent years, Haggart perf. w. all-star gps. and reunions of the WGJB. He was the author of the *Bob Haggart Bass Method* (Robbins) '40. Comps: "What's New"; "South Rampart Street Parade"; "My Inspiration"; "Big Noise From Winnetka"; "Dogtown Blues." Favs: Geo. Mraz, Michael Moore, Milt Hinton; arrs: Eddie Sauter, Bill Finegan, Bill Holman, Marty Paich, Benny Carter. Polls: *Met.* '37, '39–44; *DB* '37–42, '44. Fests: all major w. WGJB. TV: *Tonight Show*, *Today*, etc. on NBC; apps. w. Bob Crosby '85; Benny Goodman '86; Dick Hyman trio incl. White House gig '90. Lived and pl. in Fla. in '90s. CDs: Jazz.; w. WGJB (Rh./Atl.; World Jazz; Project 3); w. Lawson (Audio.; Jazz.); Bob Crosby; B. Holiday; E. Fitzgerald (Dec.); E. Condon (Dec.; Stash; Jazz.); Armstrong; Ellington; Teagarden (BB); K. Davern (MM); B. Freeman (BL); w. Manone (Prest.); F. Phillips (Chiaro.); S. Vaughan (Col.).

HAGOOD, KENNY "PANCHO" (KENNETH), voc; b. Detroit, MI, 1926; d. Farmington, MI, 11/9/89. Debut at age 17 w. Benny Carter. Sang w. Dizzy Gillespie orch., ballads and scat duets w. Dizzy 1946–8; Tadd Dameron at the Roost '48. Lived in Chi. and Paris before ret. to Det. in mid '80s, worked there and environs. Infl. by B. Eckstine, Sarah Vaughan. Rec. w. Monk '48; Miles Davis '50; Guy Lafitte '60. CDs: w. Gillespie (Sav.; BB; GNP Cres.); Monk (BN); C. Parker (Mos.); Davis (Cap.).

HAHN, JERRY DONALD, gtr, b. Alma, NE, 9/21/40. Studied at Wichita St. U. and did first prof. pl. in Kansas. Moved to SF 1962, pl. in hotel and studio bands. In '64 join. John Handy, app. w. him at the MJF '65–6. Tour. w. Fifth Dimension '68; pl. w. Gary Burton '68–9. Form. Jerry Brotherhood '70. Lecturer at Wichita St. '72; contributor to *Guitar Player* '74–8. Led own qt. Active in Portland, Ore., in late '80s w. Dave Friesen, etc. Moved to Denver '93. A fluent pl., comfortable in a wide variety of musical settings. Early infl: Barney Kessel. Favs: Wes Montgomery, Kenny Burrell, Howard Roberts. Fests: w. Burton, Berlin '68, NJF '69; w. own qt., Wichita '74–5. LP: Arh. CDs: Enja; w. Handy (Koch Jz.); Bennie Wallace (Enja).

HAIG, AL (ALAN WARREN), pno; b. Newark, NJ, 7/22/24; d. NYC, 11/16/82. Raised in Nutley, N.J. Stud. pno. and theory as a child and in coll., where he also stud. harp, cl., and sax. Pl. w. coast guard bands 1942–4; club dates around Bost.; briefly w. Jerry Wald orch. In '45, he was very active pl. w. most of the early, significant bop bands on 52nd St., incl. D. Gillespie–C. Parker. Pl. on countless rec. sess., incl. such classic Parker–Gillespie Guild sides as "Hot House," "Salt Peanuts," "Shaw 'Nuff," '45. In late '45 was in Calif. w. Charlie Barnet; also at Billy Berg's w. Parker–Gillespie into early '46. In late '40s w. J. Dorsey orch.; also pl. w. B. Webster; Coleman Hawkins, Fats Navarro; Lockjaw Davis. Pl. w. Parker qnt. for Paris JF '49. From '49 to '51, worked mainly w. S. Getz, then became virtually inactive until '54 when he join. C. Baker. Pl. briefly w. Gillespie's bb fr. late '56 into early '57; worked in Bermuda '59; w. Perry Lopez '60. In the '60s lapsed into obscurity, pl. in cocktail lounges and clubs around NYC and N.J. In the '70s he successfully resumed his jazz activities. Pl. w. own duo at Bradley's '73; to Eur. same yr., apps. at clubs in Paris, Copenhagen, radio broadcasts; solo and trio at Gregory's, NYC '74–5; in Nov. '74 reunited w. Jimmy Raney for Carnegie Recital Hall concert; trio at Sweet Basil '75. In the late '70s made several trips to Eur., pl. in Engl., Paris, Sweden, Belgium, Den. Dur. these yrs., he made several recs., solo and trio, for Spotlite, Interplay, Choice, Inner City. Along w. Bud Powell, Haig was among the first and best of the bop pnsts., who quickly adapted Parker and Gillespie's melodic and harmonic ingenuity to the pno. His technical expertise made him seem relaxed, even at whirlwind tempos, and his numerous late '40s recs. as sideman for an incredible array of musicans display the sensitivity and prowess that made him so much in demand. Comp.: *Piano & String Quartet* '75. CDs: FS; Prog.; w. Gillespie (BB; Sav.); Parker (Verve; Sav.; Phil.); Leo Parker in *Prestige First Sessions, Vol. 1*; Wardell Gray; P. Woods–D. Byrd (Prest.); Getz (Prest.; Roul.; Mos.; Verve; BN); R. Rodney in *Key. Coll.* (Em.); Baker (FS; Riv.); Barnet (Dec.).

HAKIM, SADIK (Argonne Thornton), pno; b. Duluth, MN, 7/15/22; d. NYC, 6/20/83. Nickname "Dents." Some called him "Dense," which he did not appreciate. Adopted Muslim name after converting to Islam in 1947. Fr. mus. family: grandfath. was mus. professor; moth. and others pl. chamber mus. Stud. theory w. grandfath.; self-taught on pno. Left home in '40, worked in Peoria, Ill., w. Fats Dudley; in Chi. w. Jesse Miller '42; was heard by B. Webster, whom he join. in NYC late '44 for fifteen months. In '45 pl. on historic C. Parker sess. for Savoy, incl. "Thrivin' on a Riff"; also "Dexter's Deck" w. D. Gordon. Pl. w. L. Young '46–8; Slam Stewart, Louis Metcalf in Can. late '40s. Tour. w. James Moody orch. '51–4. In mid 50's freelanced around NYC; own qt. in Mt. Vernon, N.Y.; w. Buddy Tate orch. '56–9. In '59 pl. and comp. for co-op Brooklyn gp., incl. summer dances for the Mayor's Committee for Live Music. Form. own gp. in early '60s; also freelanced; pl. w. S. Rollins '64. Moved to Montreal ca. '66, pl. in nightclubs; led own trio and qt. at Expo '67, '68; made many radio broadcasts. Tour. Eur. for six months '72; long Eur. tour again in '75 before app. at fest. in Duluth '76; then ret. to NYC. Tour. Japan '79–80. An important early bop pnst. with a quirky, singular style. Favs: Tatum, B. Powell. Comps: *The London Suite*; "Liliane"; "A Prayer for Liliane." Fav. own solos: "Jumpin' With Symphony Sid"; "No Eyes Blues" w. L. Young, Aladdin '47. LPs: *East and West of Jazz*, split w. D. Jordan, Charlie Parker label '62; *Duke Ellington Memorial*; *The London Suite*, CBC; Prog. '78. CDs: Steep.; w. Parker; D. Gordon (Sav.); L. Young (BN); Moody (Prest.)

HALE, CORKY (Merrilyn Cecilia Hecht), harp, pno, voc, fl; b. Freeport, IL, 7/3/31. Studied priv. and at Chicago Music Cons. and Interlochen, Mich. Worked w. bands in 1950s, incl. Freddy Martin; David Rose; Liberace; Harry James; and Ray Anthony. In '60s harp w. Tony Bennett, pno. w. Clark Terry and Doc Severinsen. Rec. w. Kitty White, also on MGM album, *Cats Versus Chicks*. Less active in '70s and '80s; married to songwriter Mike Stoller. New career in '90s as TV/movie prod. but occ. app.in clubs. Hale showed an exceptionally modern approach to the harp and great harmonic sensitivity as a pnst. LP: GNP Cres. CD: w. Chet Baker (PJ).

HALL, ADELAIDE LOUISE, voc; b. Brooklyn, NY, 10/20/01; d. London, England, 11/7/93. Professional debut on B'way in chorus line of Noble Sissle & Eubie Blake's *Shuffle Along* 1921; tour. Eur. w. *The Chocolate Kiddies* revue '25. Achieved her most lasting fame 10/26/27 when she recorded two wordless vocals, "Creole Love Call" and "The Blues I Love To Sing," w. the Duke Ellington Orch. Feat. in *Blackbirds of '28* on Broadway; visited Engl. first time '31. Tour. US '32 w. Art Tatum as her accompanist. Became British citizen '38; rec. w. Fats Waller '38. Many apps. on British TV, films, and stage. Returned to US '57, app. in B'way musical *Jamaica* w. Lena Horne. Return visits to US in '79, '80, and 83. Perf. in *Blacks on Broadway* at Lincoln Center for NJF-NY '80 and at Carnegie Recital Hall '88. A celebration of her 90th birthday was held at the Queen Elizabeth Hall. She rec. regularly for British Decca between '39–45 and for Col. (UK) in the '70s. CDs: *Hall of Memories, 1927–39* (Conifer); w. Ellington (BB); Waller (EMI-Pathe); Tatum (Collectors Items).

HALL, AL (ALFRED WESLEY), bs; b. Jacksonville, FL 3/18/15; d. NYC, 1/18/88. Raised in Phila. Start. on cello, tba.; sw to bs. 1932. Began work. w. local bands '33–5; then w. Billy Hicks in NYC '36–7; Skeets Tolbert '37–8. Pl. w. Teddy Wilson orch. '39; sxt. '40–1; pl. in trios w. Ellis Larkins, Mary Lou Williams '42–4; w. Kenny Clarke '43; CBS staff work on Mildred Bailey show '43–4; also B'way, studio mus. from mid '40s on. In '45 he began an assoc. w. Erroll Garner, which cont. on and off to '63. Pl. briefly at Condon's '47. From '47 to '50, had own label, Wax Recs., whose catalogue was later bought by Atl. Tour. w. Garner, also briefly w. Basie '52. Freelanced for most of '50s; active as B'way mus. through '50s and 60s; worked w. Yves Montand, Harry Belafonte late '50s. Cont. extensive freelance and rec. work through '60s and '70s; pl. w. Phil Moore '65; B. Goodman '66, incl. tour of Belgium; Hazel Scott '69; Tiny Grimes '71; Alberta Hunter '77–8. In '80s, pl. regularly w. Doc Cheatham at Sweet Basil, NYC. Had also stud. TV production, and at times was active as a video editor in '60s. Orig. infl: John Kirby, Billy Taylor. Favs: Blanton, Hinton, R. Brown, Pettiford, Duvivier. Fest.: NJF w. Eubie Blake '60. Broadway: *Jamaica*, subbing for Duvivier '58; J. Robbins' *Ballet USA* '58. Recs. w. T. Wilson (Col.) '41; K. Clarke '46; Garner (Col.); Ellington-Hodges (Verve). CDs: w. Clarke in *The Bebop Revolution* (BB); w. B. Holiday (Col.); Ellington; J. Hodges; H. Merrill (Verve); Armstrong; Teagarden (BB); S. Stitt in *Opus De Bop*; F. Navarro (Sav.); P. Gonsalves (BL); Goodman (MM); Wilson (Hep).

HALL, EDMOND, cl, saxes; b. New Orleans, LA, 5/15/01; d. Boston, MA, 2/11/67. Musical family;

fath., Edward, pl. cl; all five sons were musicians, the most prominent being Edmond and Herb. Edmond start. on gtr. but taught himself cl. and, at 17, began pl. in local bands, incl. Bud Russell 1919; Jack Carey. Tour. w. Buddy Petit fr. '21 to '23, then w. Mat Thomas. Moved to Jacksonville, Fla., worked w. Eagle Eye Shields '24–5; joined Alonzo Ross's Miami-based De Luxe Syncopators, rec. w. this band in Savannah '27 and went to NYC w. it in '28. After it disbanded two weeks later, he worked w. several NY bands, incl. Billy Fowler's. Join. Charlie Skeete in the fall of '29 and cont. w. the band when Claude Hopkins took over '30, remaining to '35 (doubling on bari. sax). Worked w. Lucky Millinder '36; Billy Hicks '37–8; Zutty Singleton, Joe Sullivan, Lionel Hampton '39; Red Allen '40–1; Teddy Wilson '42–4. Led own band in Bost. '48–8 and Calif. '50. Join. house band at Condon's, NYC '50; left in '55 to replace Barney Bigard w. Louis Armstrong for tours of US, Austral., Eur. Semi-retired after leaving Armstrong in '58. Pl. and taught in Ghana for several mos. in late '59. Dur. the '60s he tour. Eur. several times; apps. w. Condon, Jimmy McPartland; feat. soloist w. Dukes of Dixieland on Japan tour '64. His last perfs. were at a Carnegie Hall concert and at the *Bost. Globe* Fest. He died of a heart attack. Hall, who pl. Albert system cl. w. a sharp, reedy tone and warm style, was perhaps the most technically proficient of the NO clarinetists. He rec. prolifically in the '30s and '40s and was equally at home in the swing and NO styles. Polls: *Esq.* Silver Award '45 in NYC. Fests: Colo. JP fr. '62. TV: apps. w. Yves Montand; *Today*. Book: *Profoundly Blue*, Manfred Selchow '88. Own recs. on BN '41, Comm. '43. CDs: BN; Story.; tracks as lead. and sideman in *The Blue Note Jazzmen* (BN); *The Commodore Story* (Comm.); w. Armstrong (Col.; Verve; BL; Pab.); Ruby Braff (BL); Condon (Dec.; Stash; Sav.; Jazz.); Wild Bill Davison (Jazz.); L. Hampton (BB); V. Dickenson (Vang.); B. Holiday (Col.); Bunk Johnson (Amer. Mus.); Swingville All-Stars (GTJ).

HALL, HERB (HERBERT), cl, reeds; b. Reserve, LA, 3/28/07; d. San Antonio, TX, 3/6/96. Younger bro. of Edmond Hall. Started on gtr., then borrowed bro. Robert's cl. Left home to join band in Baton Rouge 1927; later pl. in NO w. Sidney Desvigne. Pl. in Texas, Southwest, and South w. Don Albert '29–40; worked w. bands on air force base in San Antonio before moving to NYC '45. Tour. Eur., No. Africa w. Sammy Price '55–6. Pl. at Eddie Condon's late '50s. Pl. w. Wild Bill Davison '67–9; Don Ewell in Can. '70; Saints & Sinners '72; Bob Greene '73; Balaban & Cats fr. '74; Bob Greene '75. Ret. to San Antonio '77 and went into semi-retirement. A warm-toned, lyrical player. Favs:

Edmond Hall, Jimmie Noone, Omer Simeon. Fests: Manassas, Va.; Windsor, Ont.; NJF-NY w. Greene '73. CDs: Jazz.; w. Maxine Sullivan (Audio.); Swingville All-Stars (GTJ).

HALL, JIM (JAMES STANLEY), gtr, comp.; b. Buffalo, NY, 12/4/30. First learned pno., sw. to gtr. at age 10. By 13, pl. prof. in Cleveland. Att. Cleveland Inst. of Mus. Left Ohio for LA in 1955, where he join. the Chico Hamilton Qnt. Member of Jimmy Giuffre Trio w. Bob Brookmeyer '57. In early '60s pl. w. Lee Konitz; Sonny Rollins; Art Farmer. Traded the tour. life for studio work, incl. the Merv Griffin TV orch. in mid '60s. Led duos w. Ron Carter or Jack Six and other small gps. fr. '66. An innovator in duo experimental combinations, Hall pl. clubs w. Brookmeyer in early '70s; in '84 perf. a symph. piece, comp. by Brookmeyer, w. Stockholm Radio Symph. Rec. two LPs w. classical vlnst. Itzhak Perlman w. André Previn as pnst./cond.; Red Mitchell, bs.; and Shelly Manne, dms. In '90s led own qt. w. Gil Goldstein, Steve LaSpina, Terry Clarke. Recs. in a duo setting w. Bill Evans, George Shearing, Mitchell, and Carter remain peerless. Special concerts incl. The White House for Duke Ellington's 70th Birthday Party; the J. Hall Invitational, JVC-NY '90; Carnegie Hall w. Rollins '91; Smithsonian Inst.; others. Pl. fests. worldwide. Polls: *DB* Critics; *DB* Readers; *JT*. In '98 awarded Danish Jazzpar prize. Berklee instituted J. Hall Scholarship Fund. Hall is known for creative chord extensions, voicings, and space in his solos, "I loved Art Tatum's fearlessness about chords," he says, "but Bartok influenced my linear writing; he was my hero." Teaches jazz ens. at the New Sch. and cond. seminars worldwide. Film: *Jim Hall: A Life in Progress* '99. Book: *Exploring Jazz Guitar* (Hal Leonard) '91. CDs: MM; Tel.; CTI; Verve; Conc.; Den.; Mile.; BN; w. Chico Hamilton (Mos.); B. Evans (Mile.; BN; Verve); Rollins (RCA); Desmond (RCA; WB); Petrucciani (BN); Shearing-Hall (Conc.); H. Hawes; B. Webster (Cont.); Konitz (Mile.); Farmer; Giuffre; John Lewis; O. Coleman (Atl.); Dolphy (Enja); Getz (Verve; BB).

HALL, MINOR ("RAM"), dms; b. Sellers, LA, 3/2/1897; d. Sawtelle, CA, 10/16/59. Raised in NO. Began prof. in 1914, subbing for his older bro. Tubby; w. Kid Ory '16. Moved w. family to Chi. '17; replaced Tubby in Lawrence Duhe's band. Served in army '18–19, then ret. to Chi. Pl. w. K. Oliver in Calif. '21–2; in Chi. w. Jimmy Noone '26. Moved to Calif., pl. w. Mutt Carey '27–32; also pl. regularly w. Winslow Allum in '30s. Army again for six months in '42, w. honorable discharge. Pl. an important role in NO revival w. Ory in '40s, rejoin. him in '42, remain-

ing w. him until taken ill w. cancer during Eur. tour in '56. Pl. occ. w. NO Creole Jazz Band in '59 before being hospitalized. Film: w. Ory, *Tailgate Man From New Orleans* '56. Recs: w. Ory (Dec.) CDs: w. Armstrong (RCA; BB); Ory; D. Ewell (GTJ).

HALL, SKIP (ARCHIE), org, pno, arr; b. Portsmouth, VA, 9/27/09; d. Ottawa, Ont., Canada, 11/80. Brother-in-law of Sy Oliver. Start. stud. at age 8 w. fath.; later at Martin-Smith Sch., NYC. Began pl. in sch. bands, rent parties, and gigs in Harlem. Fr. 1931 to '38, led own band in Cleveland. Fr. late '30s to mid '40s, worked as freelance arr. Pl. pno. occ. w. J. McShann '40–4, writing arrs. of "Cherokee" and "Sepian Bounce." While in army during WWII, led 132nd band in Engl. Worked as freelance sess. mus. after discharge. Began long assoc. w. Buddy Tate in late '40s, mostly on org.; pl. w. Tate's orch. from '50 to 55; led own trio '55–6; perf. as soloist '58; pl. w. George James '63; tour. Eur. w. Tate '68. Fav: Tatum. Recs. as lead. '49; w. Hot Lips Page '49. LPs: w. Wells; Tate (Felsted).

HALL, TUBBY (ALFRED), dms; b. Sellers, LA, 10/12/1895; d. Chicago, IL, 5/13/46. Brother of Minor Hall. Raised in NO, start. pl. dms. as a teenager. From 1913 to '16, pl. w. Frank Dusen's Eagle Band; the Crescent Band; Silverleaf Band. Moved to Chi., pl. w. Lawrence Duhe's band '18. Rejoin. band under K. Oliver's lead. '20 after two yrs. army service in WWI. Became prominent pl. w. Jimmy Noone, Carroll Dickerson, Louis Armstrong in '20s; in '30s w. Armstrong, Noone in Chi.; also w. Frankie "Half Pint" Jaxon. Led own gps. in '35, '45–6. Rec. w. Noone (Dec.) '36, '40. CDs: w. Armstrong (BBC; JSP).

HALLBERG, BENGT, pno, comp; b. Gothenburg, Sweden, 9/13/32. Studied pno. w. Sixten Eckerberg in Gothenburg 1944–6; comp. w. Lars-Erik Larsson, counterpoint w. Ake Udden at Royal Acad. of Mus. in Stockholm '54–7. Pl. w. Thore Jederby '48; Kenneth Fagerlund '49. Came to prominence when he tour. and rec. in Sweden w. Stan Getz '50. Rec. w. all-star Swedish gp. '51; w. Clifford Brown, Art Farmer '53. Led own trio, closely assoc. w. Lars Gullin and other top Swedish jazz mus. Pl. w. Swedish Radio bb '56–63, also worked as commercial studio arr. and mus. Pl. w. Radiojazzgruppen; Arne Domnerus Sxt. fr. '69. Increasingly active as comp. fr. late '50s, beginning w. a string qt. '57. Other works incl. *Collaboration* for string qt. and rhythm section '63; *Kain*, a ballet for symph. orch. and rhythm, premiered by Royal Swedish Opera '64; *Lyrisk Ballad* for two jazz pnst. and orch. '68; *Music for Jazz Combo and Symph. Orch.* '69; *Beat Rondo* '71. Writing for radio and TV. Soloist in Geo. Russell's comp. *Living Time*; also pl. w. Ove Lind '70s. Formed Trio Con Tromba w. Jan Allan, Georg Riedel early '80s. Pl. w. Domnerus at Swed. Embassy, NYC '80s. Favs: Teddy Wilson, Bud Powell, Lennie Tristano, Keith Jarrett. Poll: *Estrad* Mus. of Yr. '54. Books: *Modern Jazz Piano* (Westin & Co.) and *Beginner's Course* (Reuter & Reuter). Rec. "Farewell Blues" on acdn. '81. CDs: Phon.; w. C. Brown (Prest.); Getz (DIW); Domnerus (FXCD); Ove Lind; Roy Williams (Phon.).

HALLIDAY, LIN, tnr sax; b. De Queen, AR, 6/16/36; d. Chicago, 1/25/00. Raised in Little Rock, Ark. Start. on cl. and sax. After grad. fr. hs he went to LA where he met Joe Maini and pl. gigs and at jam sessions. Spent 6 mos. in Wisconsin, woodshedding w. Sonny Rollins recs., then moved to NYC 1958. Briefly in Calif. again before ret. to NYC '59; replaced Wayne Shorter in Maynard Ferguson's Birdland band. After pl. w. the gps. of Louie Bellson and Philly Joe Jones he lost his cabaret card and wended his way back to Hollywood via Little Rock before ending up in Chi. Settled in Nashville to raise a family ca. '66. Did studio and club dates, Jerry Lee Lewis Telethons, etc. In '78 severely injured his knees and was bed-ridden for an extended period of recuperation. Moved to Chi. '80 and pl. at the Green Mill, Get Me High Lounge, the Bop Shop, and Joe Segal's Jazz Showcase. Favs: Rollins, C. Parker. CDs: Del.; w. Brad Goode; Eric Alexander (Del.).

HAMBRO, LENNY (LEONARD WILLIAM), alto sax, cl, fl, arr; b. Bronx, NY, 10/16/23; d. McKee City, NJ, 9/26/95. Mother was ragtime pianist; son, Lee, a mus. Started on sop. sax before sw. to alto sax and cl. in 1938–9. Stud. w. Bill Sheiner along w. Stan Getz, who was a schoolmate at James Monroe HS. Pl. w. Gene Krupa '42–3, then w. 379th A.S.F. Band in Newport News, Va. '43–6. Pl. w. Billy Butterfield '46; Bobby Byrne '47; Vincent Lopez; Pupi Campo. Rejoin. Krupa '47–51. First rec. as lead. for Savoy '51. Stud. cl. w. Leon Russianoff and fl. w. Henry Zlotnick in NYC '51–6. Pl. w. and managed Ray McKinley orch. '51–2; pl. jazz and lead alto w. Machito off and on '52–6; also freelance in NYC '52–6, worked w. Chico O'Farrill, Joe Loco, own qt.; accomp. singers at Paramount Theater; did studio work and teaching. Organized and pl. w. new Glenn Miller Band led by McKinley '56–64. His qnt. was feat. within band when it tour. Eur., Africa '57, '58. Hambro worked as a booking agent in '64 and was involved in writing and prod. jingles and film music fr. '67, winning several advertising industry awards. In '80 moved to Atlantic City area, serving as entertainment dir. for Claridge Hotel; then as mus. dir. for Bally's '83 bef. pl. in band at Trump Castle. Eur. gigs

w. Peter Duchin. Also pl. conventions, Phila. jazz clubs w. own bands and gps; cont. mus. relationship w. O'Farrill. Moved to Fla. in '91, acting as booking agent, pl. in jazz clubs, and teach. privately. His best known comp. is "The Lonely One," which was rec. by Nat Cole in '55. Feat. on "Pure Emotion" in O'Farrill's CD of same name. Favs: C. Parker, J. Hodges, B. Goodman; arrs: N. Hefti, J. Mandel, O'Farrill. Film: cameo app. in *Serpico*. CDs: w. O'Farrill (Mile.; Verve); G. Miller Band (RCA).

HAMEL, HERSH (Herschel Himmelstein), bs; b. Los Angeles, CA, 11/13/28. First prof. job w. Charlie Barnet 1950; also led his own bb at LA's Oasis club in the same year. In '57 he worked in trio w. Elmo Hope; to Denver w. Art Pepper Qt. '59. Pl. w. Curtis Amy '62; Pepper qt. '64, incl. rec. debut. To NYC '65; worked w. Toshiko Akyoshi, Jim Hall. Ret. to LA '66; stud. sitar w. Ravi Shankar; pl. w. Pepper again '70s. In '80s worked w. Alvino Rey and led various gps. of his own, incl. such players as Bill Perkins, Frank Strazzeri, et al. In '91–2 pl. w. a trio locally in LA. CDs: w. Pepper (FS).

HAMILTON, BUGS (JOHN), tpt; b. St. Louis, MO, 3/8/11; d. St. Louis, 8/15/47. Played in NYC w. Billy Kato 1930–1; briefly w. Chick Webb early '30s; Kaiser Marshall at Ubangi Club; Bobby Neal '35. Hamilton is best known for his work w. Fats Waller '38–42. Pl. w. Eddie South '43. Died of tuberculosis at age 36. CDs: w. Waller (BB).

HAMILTON, CHICO (FORESTSTORN), dms; b. Los Angeles, CA, 9/21/21. Began on cl. Formed band in hs w. Ernie Royal; Charles Mingus; Illinois Jacquet; Buddy Collette; Jack Kelso. Pl. w. Floyd Ray, Lionel Hampton 1940; Slim Gaillard–Slam Stewart, Lorenzo Flennoy, Lester Young, T-Bone Walker, Duke Ellington '41. In army '42–6; stud. dms. w. Jo Jones. Pl. w. Jimmy Mundy, Count Basie, and at Billy Berg's as house dmr. late '40s. Worked w. Lena Horne '48–55; also other singers, incl. Billy Eckstine; Ella Fitzgerald; Sarah Vaughan; Nat Cole; Sammy Davis Jr.; Billie Holiday. Member of orig. Gerry Mulligan Qt. '52. Beginning in '55 Hamilton led his own qnt. w. cello, guitar, fl. and bs. Orig. personnel incl. B. Collette; Jim Hall; Fred Katz; Carson Smith; later Paul Horn; John Pisano; Nate Gershman; Eric Dolphy. Hamilton briefly replaced the cello w. a tpt.; personnel in early '60s incl. Charles Lloyd; Gabor Szabo; Albert Stinson. In '65 Hamilton form. his own jingle, TV, and film music prod. co. but cont. to be active in jazz. Led own gps. w. Arnie Lawrence, Richard Davis, Larry Coryell '66; Arthur Blythe, Barry Finnerty, Steve Turre '75; also many recs. as lead. in late '70s. Hamilton has been a teacher at the New Sch. since '87, and in '89 reunited his '55 qnt. for a Eur. tour and rec. session. He is currently lead. own gp., pl. w. Andrew Hill, and working on his autobiography. Favs: Jo Jones, Sid Catlett, Sonny Greer. Polls: *DB* '57. Fests: Eur. since '57 incl. MJF and North Sea JF '72–3. Films: *Sweet Smell of Success* '57; *Jazz On a Summer's Day* '60. CDs: Mos. (boxed set); SN; Imp.; PJ; Disc.; FS; w. Horne (BB); Holiday (Verve); L. Young; John Lewis (BN); Mulligan (PJ; Cap.); R. Norvo (BB); Buddy Tate (BL); Slim & Slam (Col.).

HAMILTON, JEFF (JEFFREY RAY), dms; b. Richmond, IN, 8/4/53. Studied at Indiana U, where he met John Clayton, who recommended him to Murray McEachern, then the leader of the Tommy Dorsey band 1974. After a stint w. L. Hampton in '75, rejoin. Dorsey; later w. Monty Alexander Trio '77; Woody Herman '77–8. In Jan. '78 he replaced Shelly Manne in the LA 4; also freelanced w. Ella Fitzgerald; Rosemary Clooney; Peter Nero; and Count Basie. In Jan. '88 he and John Clayton formed their own bb, which enjoyed considerable success in the LA area. Also pl. frequently w. Ray Brown Trio from '88; world tour with Philip Morris Superband '89; pl. w. Oscar Peterson off and on from '90. Many yrs. as staff member of Bud Shank Workshop in Port Townsend, Wash. A regular at Colo. JP in '80s-90s. CDs: Conc.; Mons; Clayton-Hamilton Orch. (Capri); w. Alexander (Conc.; Verve); R. Brown (Conc.; PW); Scott Hamilton; Dave Frishberg; Gene Harris; Herman; LA 4; Shearing; Tormé (Conc.); Milt Jackson (Pab.); Shank (JVC); Magnolia Jazz Band and Art Hodes (GHB); T. Talbert (SB); Jiggs Whigham (Capri).

HAMILTON, JIMMY (JAMES), cl, tnr sax, comp; b. Dillon, SC, 5/25/17; d. St. Croix, VI, 9/20/94. Raised in Phila. At age 7 start. stud. tbn., pno., tpt., saxes. Pl. tpt. w. Frank Fairfax, where his section mates incl. D. Gillespie, C. Shavers 1935; also pl. w. Lonnie Slappy. Then tnr. sax, cl. w. Lucky Millinder, Jimmy Mundy '39; Teddy Wilson orch. '39–41; Benny Carter sxt. '41–2; Eddie Heywood, Yank Porter '42. In May '43 replaced Chauncey Haughton in Duke Ellington orch. Became the principal cl. soloist and fr. late '40s was also feat. on tnr. sax. Remained w. Ellington until June '68. Moved to St. Croix where he pl. and taught cl. In '80s pl. w. Mercer Ellington in US; also w. the Spacemen, a gp. of Ellington alumni. Tour. as single in Eur. App. in concert w. John Carter's "Clarinet Summit" at the Public Theater, NYC '81, and rec. w. it for Ind. Nav. Pl. in concert for the Ellington Society, NYC May '81. A technically accomplished clarinetist with a cool, clear, liquid tone, he exhibited a throatier sound and more combustible approach on tnr. Solos w. Ellington: "Air Conditioned Jungle"; "Tattooed Bride"; "Flippant Flurry"; "Island Virgin"; "Ad Lib On Nippon"; on tnr., "Hy'a Sue"; "Bensonality"; "One O' Clock Jump." Polls: *Esq.* New Star award '46; *DB* Critics New Star '62. CDs: as lead in *The Blue Note Swingtets* (BN); w. Ellington (Col.; Atl.; Prest., Pab.); Hodges (Verve; Imp.; BB); B. Holiday (Col.); Lucky Thompson (FS); *Clarinet Summit* (Ind. Nav.).

HAMILTON, SCOTT, tnr sax; b. Providence, RI, 9/12/54. Mother's cousin is Ralph Burns. Began on pno. and cl. Pl. blues hca. in local gps. 1968–70. Began focusing on tnr. sax at age 16. Gained experience w. tnr.-org. gigs in Providence. Tour. NY–New Eng. '71–6 w. Hamilton-Bates Blue Flames. Moved to NYC '76, pl. w. Hank Jones; Tiny Grimes; Anita O'Day; house band at Eddie Condon's; and w. John Bunch, who recommended him to Benny Goodman; w. Goodman '76–8. Maintained a mus. partnership w. Warren Vaché fr. '76. Worked w. Concord All-Stars '78–82; Cleanhead Vinson–Buddy Tate '79–80; Goodman '82; Ruby Braff '82–8; Geo. Wein fr. '82, incl. Newport JF All-Stars. Also pl. in '80s w. Woody Herman; Rosemary Clooney. Hamilton has led his own qnt. off and on fr. '77, at one time feat. Maxine Sullivan, but has also tour. as a single since the early '80s. Hamilton came along at a time when his mainstream melodicism and swing, derived fr. Hawkins, Webster, and Young, swam against the prevailing tide. His excellence enabled him to transcend trends and succeed as an individual. In recent yrs. his stylistic inclinations have factored in some Zoot Sims. Favs: Jacquet, Getz. Polls: *JJ* '78. Fests: Eur.; Japan; Austral. fr. '78. First LP on Famous Door w. John Bunch '77. CDs: Prog.; more than thirty Conc. albums as lead. incl. collab. w. G. Mulligan; F. Phillips; D. McKenna; K. Peplowski; and Spike Robinson; *Tour De Force* w. Al Cohn and Buddy Tate; w. Braff (Conc.; Phon.); Benny Carter; C. Byrd; Clooney; Herman; Cohn; Gene Harris; Concord All-Stars; Maxine Sullivan; S. McCorkle; Cal Tjader (Conc.); Phillips; B. Wilber (Chiaro.).

HAMMER, BOB (HOWARD ROBERT), comp, arr, pno; b. Indianapolis, IN, 3/3/30. Played w. local gps. in Mich. fr. age 15. Stud. at Mich. St. U.; Manh. Sch. of Mus. Pl. w. Gene Krupa, Sauter-Finegan Orch., Lionel Hampton, Chas. Mingus, Jimmy Knepper, Jimmy Dorsey, Red Allen, Woody Herman 1950s-early 60s. As staff arr. for Impulse label in '60 he arr. for Mingus, Johnny Hartman; comp. and arr. for W. Herman, Clark Terry. Favs: Bud Powell, Nat Cole, Tatum, Horace Silver; arrs: Ellington, Mingus, Bill Holman, Johnny Carisi, Eddie Sauter. CDs: w. Mingus (FS; BN).

HAMMER, TARDO (RICHARD ALAN), pno; b. Queens, NY, 2/26/58. Mother pl. pno. Stud. w. Sal Mosca 1965–8 but primarily self-taught. Pl. w. Warne Marsh '80; Richard Vitale fr. '81; Charlie Rouse '83; Bill Hardman–Junior Cook '85–90; Johnny Griffin '86; Bopera House fr. '86; Lionel Hampton '87; Lou Donaldson '88–9; own qnt. w. J. Cook '89; Art Farmer–Clifford Jordan '89–90; Vernel Fournier '90. Also pl. in '80s w. Geo. Coleman; Gary Bartz; Al Cohn; C Sharpe; Mel Lewis; Harold Ashby; etc. Accomp. Annie Ross in late '90s. Favs: Tatum, B. Powell, Monk. Fests: Japan w. Vitale, Fournier '90. CDs: Sharp Nine; w. Bopera House (VSOP); Doug Lawrence (Fable); Vitale (Timel.).

HAMPEL, GUNTER, vib, woodwinds, pno, comp; b. Goettingen, Germany, 8/31/37. Studied architecture and mus. 1948; led own gp. from '58; tour. Eur. w. frequent radio and TV apps. Comp. mus. for films. Has perf. occasionally in US but is best known for his work in Eur., Africa, Asia, So. America. Numerous recs. of own gps.; also rec. w. Marion Brown and Jeanne Lee; rec. w. composer Krzysztof Penderecki, Don Cherry and the New Eternal Rhythm Orchestra '71. Formed Galaxie Dream Band '72, cont. to work with it into '90s. Dozens of recs. on his label, Birth Records, incl. sessions w. Cecil Taylor; Archie Shepp; Enrico Rava; Jimmy Lyons; et al. CDs: Birth; w. Taylor (SN; FMP).

HAMPTON, LIONEL LEO, vib, dms, pno, voc, lead; b. Louisville, KY, 4/20/08; d. NYC, 8/31/02. Raised in Kenosha, Wis., and Chi. Stud. at Holy Rosary Acad., Kenosha. Later pl. dms. in *Chicago Defender* Newsboys' Band. Moved to Calif. 1928, pl. dms. w. Paul Howard Orch., Eddie Barefield, Les Hite. Began pl. vib. dur. period when Louis Armstrong was fronting Hite band. Made rec. debut on vib. on "Memories of You" w. Armstrong Oct. '30. Organized own band to pl. at Sebastian's Cotton Club, LA '34. Heard by Benny Goodman, who used him on a rec. date w. Teddy Wilson, Gene Krupa Aug. '36. Pl. vib. w. Goodman Qt., also subbed on dms. in bb '36–40. While w. Goodman, Hampton also made a series of popular all-star recs. for Victor feat. sidemen fr. top jazz bands. Led own bb fr. Sept. '40. Had huge hit w. "Flying Home," rec. May '42. Hampton led one of the most popular bands of the '40s, emphasizing excitement and showmanship. Sidemen incl. Illinois Jacquet; Dexter Gordon; Arnett Cobb; Johnny Griffin; Fats Navarro; Clifford Brown; Joe Newman; Ernie Royal; Clark Terry; Art Farmer; Quincy Jones; Cat Anderson; Al Grey; Charles Mingus; Wes Montgomery; band vocalists incl. Joe Williams; Dinah Washington; Betty Carter; Aretha Franklin. By the

'50s Hampton's band had assimilated many elements of the popular rhythm & blues style. Made frequent tours of Eur., No. Africa, Israel w. bb fr. mid '50s. Tour. Japan, Philippines, Taiwan '63. Formed Jazz Inner Circle sxt. '65; instrumentation was vibes, organ, tpt., two saxes, dms. Started own rec. label Glad-Hamp w. wife Gladys early '60s. Worked mainly w. small bands in '60s and '70s except for occasional bb reunions. Pl. w. reunited Goodman Qt. at NJF-NY '73. Active in Republican politics fr. '72 when he campaigned for Nixon and N.Y. Gov. Nelson Rockefeller; later campaigned for Reagan and Bush. Founded Lionel Hampton Development Corp., which developed low income housing in the inner city early '70s. Appointed Goodwill Ambassador to Far East by NYC Mayor John Lindsay '74. Pl. at White House for Pres. Carter '78, also formed rec. label Who's Who In Jazz. Began leading bb again full-time in '80s and cont. into '90s. Appointed by Pres. Bush to Board of the Kennedy Center '91. Awarded Kennedy Center Honor '92; National Medal of Arts '96. Leader of all-star gp. Golden Men of Jazz which has incl. Sweets Edison, Clark Terry, Pete Candoli, Al Grey, James Moody, Buddy Tate, Benny Golson, Hank Jones, Junior Mance, Milt Hinton, Grady Tate fr. '91.

Chiefly responsible for popularizing the vib. as a jazz instrument, Hampton was known for his onstage charm, strong leadership, and unfailing sense of swing. Illness curtailed his playing time in the late '90s. He held more than fifteen hononary doctorates fr. universities in the US and abroad; was honorary chairman of the Jazz Foundation's Musicians Emergency Fund. In '84 he began playing at the U. of Idaho's jazz festival; in '85 the fest. was named for him; and in '87 the university's music sch. was renamed the Lionel Hampton Sch. of Music. Fav: Milt Jackson; arr: Frank Foster. Polls: *Met.* '44–6; *Esq.* New Star '45; *DB* Critics '54; *Play.* '57–60. Fests: all major. Films: *A Song Is Born* '48; *Benny Goodman Story* '55. Book: *Hamp* w. James Haskins (Warner Books) '89. CDs: Tel.; RCA; Dec.; Imp.; Verve; Timel.; Vogue; B&B; w. Goodman (RCA; Col.; Lond.); Armstrong (Dec.); Tatum (Pab.); T. Wilson (Hep); M. McPartland (JA).

HAMPTON, SLIDE (LOCKSLEY WELLINGTON), tbn, comp, arr; b. Jeannette, PA, 4/4/32. Mother, fath., four bros., four sists. all musicians. Raised in Indianapolis. Began on tpt. then sw. to tbn. after a yr. Self-taught, plays left-handed. Pl. w. family band 1945–52; Buddy Johnson blues band '53–4; Lionel Hampton '55–7. Pl. and arr. w. Maynard Ferguson bb '58–9. Form. own oct. w. Freddie Hubbard, Booker Little, Julian Priester, Geo. Coleman '59. Briefly w. Dizzy Gillespie bb '60. Mus. dir. for Lloyd

Price early '6os, then pl. w. Art Blakey; Thad Jones–Mel Lewis Orch. To Eur. w. Woody Herman Orch. '68. Settled in Berlin; arr. for European radio orchs. and own gps. Ret. to US '77. Led World of Trombones, which consisted of nine tbns. w. rhythm section. Also led Collective Black Artists Orch.; Manhattan Plaza Composers Orch. Pl. w. Jimmy Heath, Kenny Barron, Ron Carter, and Art Taylor in Continuum, a gp. dedicated to the mus. of Tadd Dameron. Has led a 12-pc. gp., the Jazz Masters, which made its debut at the Village Vanguard in Feb. 1993, performing Hampton's arrs. of Gillespie comps. Sidemen incl. J. Heath; Jon Faddis; Roy Hargrove; Claudio Roditi; Antonio Hart; David Sanchez; Danilo Perez. Very active as a teacher in the New York area. A superior arr. and soloist who is able to combine speed and tone on the tbn. Favs: Armstrong, L. Young, C. Parker, J.J. Johnson, Gillespie, Coltrane. Fests: all major in Eur. fr. '68; JVC-NY; Colo. JP. Film: *Winter in Lisbon* w. Gillespie. TV: many apps. on Eur. TV. CDs: BL; CC; LRC; w. Jazz Masters (Tel.); A. Farmer; Gillespie (Enja); J. Hall (Tel.); M. Alexander (Chesky); Robin Eubanks (JMT); Ferguson (Roul.); D. Gordon (Col.); Herman (Conc.); P.J. Jones (Gal.); Mingus (Rh./Atl.); R. Schneiderman (Res.); M. Tyner (Bird.).

HANCOCK, HERBIE (HERBERT JEFFREY), pno, kybds, comp, lead; b. Chicago, IL, 4/12/40. First pno. lessons at age 7; perf. Mozart pno. concerto w. Chi. Symph. at age 11. Formed own jazz band at Hyde Park HS; att. Grinnell Coll. in Des Moines, Iowa; perf. w. Lee Morgan, Hank Mobley, and Coleman Hawkins while still att. coll. To NYC w. Donald Byrd's band; rec. w. Byrd 1961. First session as a leader, *Takin' Off*, '62 incl. his hit comp, "Watermelon Man." Briefly w. Eric Dolphy '62–3 bef. join. Miles Davis '63–8 as a member of a rhythm section that also incl. Tony Williams and Ron Carter. While w. Davis, Hancock rec. as leader and sideman w. various other gps. Among notable works were "Cantaloupe Island"; "Maiden Voyage"; "Dolphin Dance"; "Speak Like A Child"; and "Riot." As "Speak Like A Child" was released, Hancock left Davis to form his own sxt. Moved to LA '72. By '73 w. release of *Headhunters* and the single "Chameleon," the gp. had become essentially an electric funk unit. From mid '70s, Hancock alternated between the commercial work w. various editions of the Headhunters and his Rockit Band, and more traditional work w. VSOP, the latter usually w. Ron Carter or Buster Williams, bs.; Tony Williams or Al Foster, dms.; Wayne Shorter or Branford Marsalis, saxes; and Freddie Hubbard or Wynton Marsalis, tpt. Several duo-pno. tours w. Chick Corea '76–89; pno.

tours w. Oscar Peterson '80s. In the '90s he tour. w. own trio and a qt. w. Pat Metheny, Dave Holland, Jack DeJohnette; also New Standard All-Stars, w. some of the same personnel plus Jon Scofield and Michael Brecker, playing jazz versions of music by Prince; Stevie Wonder; the Beatles; etc. His film scores incl. *Blow-Up, The Spook Who Sat by the Door* '73; *Death Wish* '75; *A Soldier's Story* '84; *Round Midnight*, in which he acted and the score of which won him an Oscar '87; *Action Jackson* '88; and *Colors*. Polls and Awards: *DB* Readers Poll as Jazzman of the Year '74; Honorary Doctorate from the Berklee School of Music; Grammy awards; American Music Award; MTV Video Award; and Cleo Award. From '88 to 90, hosted the cable-TV music variety program *Showtime Coast to Coast*. CDs: BN; Col.; Verve; WB; Qwest; Merc.; *Blow-Up* soundtrack (Rhino); w. Miles Davis (Col.); Byrd; Joe Henderson; Grant Green; Bobby Hutcherson; Lee Morgan; Stanley Turrentine; Tony Williams; Renee Rosnes (BN); Corea (Verve; Polyd.); B. Goodman (MM); Hubbard (BN; CTI); Shorter (BN; Col.; Verve); B. Marsalis; W. Marsalis (Col.); S. Rollins; Joe Williams (BB); R. Carter (Mile.).

HANDY, CAPT. JOHN, alto sax, cl; b. Pass Christian, MS, 6/24/1900; d. Pass Christian, 1/12/71. Father, John Sr., headed family band, incl. Capt. John's younger bros., Julius and Sylvester. First took up gtr., mand., and dms., and was perf. in family band by age 15. At 16 self-taught on cl. and pl. w. Punch Miller, Kid Rena, etc. To NO in 1918, pl. there and in Baton Rouge through the '20s. In '28 took up alto sax; tour. southern states w. bro. Sylvester in Louisiana Shakers '32. Worked w. Kid Howard; Jim Robinson, Lee Collins in '30s; Charlie Creath in St. Louis '38. In NO pl. w. the Young Tuxedo Brass Band '40s; Kid Clayton '50s; Kid Sheik Colar '61; Preservation Hall Jazz Band, tour. Engl., the Cont., Can., Japan '67. Fest: NJF, '70. Rec. own album for RCA '67. CDs: GHB; Amer. Mus.

HANDY, CRAIG MITCHELL, tnr sax, sop sax, alto sax, fl, cl; b. Oakland, CA, 9/25/62. Mother pl. pno. Began on gtr. at age 9; sw. to pno. at 10, tbn. at 11, alto sax at 12. Won Charlie Parker Scholarship to No. Texas St. U. but decided to major in psychology. Pl. w. Galen Jeter's Dallas Jazz Orch. 1983–6; Abdullah Ibrahim '87–90; Roy Haynes, Mingus Dynasty fr. '87; Art Blakey, Wynton Marsalis, John Hicks '88–9; own qt. '88–90. Tour. Eur. as single '90–2. Soloist in Thelonious Monk tribute concert at Lincoln Center, NYC '92. Mus. dir. of Chartbusters, an all-star rec. gp. which pays homage to labels such as Blue Note, Prestige. Handy has taught at the Henry St. Settlement in NYC. Favs: D. Gordon, C. Jordan, Coltrane, Rollins,

J. Henderson. Film: seen and heard in *Kansas City* '96. TV: rec. theme music for Bill Cosby show '89–90; scored and perf. mus. for *The Cosby Mysteries* '94. CDs: Arab; w. Haynes (Evid.); Chartbusters (NYC; Prest.); Mingus Dynasty (SN; Col.); Mingus Big Band (Drey.); P. Delano; Stephen Scott; band fr. *Kansas City* (Verve); Charles Sullivan; Ray Drummond (Arab.); Bob Belden (Sunny.); A. Ibrahim (Enja).

HANDY, GEORGE JOSEPH (Hendleman), comp, arr, pno; b. Brooklyn, NY, 1/17/20; d. Harris, NY, 1/8/97. Mother pl. pno. Stud. w. her fr. age 5, then at Juilliard Sch. of Mus., NYU, and priv. w. Aaron Copland. Pl. w. Michael Loring 1938–9. In army '40, then pl. w. Raymond Scott and began writing mus. '41. Pl. and arr. w. Boyd Raeburn '44–5, then worked as songwriter at Paramount studios in LA '45. Pl. and arr. w. Raeburn '46; his notable arrs. for Raeburn incl. "There's No You"; "Tonsillectomy"; "Dalvatore Sally." Also arr., for Alvino Rey, "Stocking Horse"; Ina Ray Hutton; Herbie Fields; Armed Forces Radio Service. After rec. his extended comp. *The Bloos* in '46, Handy lapsed into obscurity until the mid '50s, when he rec. two albums as a lead. for RCA's Label X. Comp., arr. and pl. pno. for Zoot Sims recs. on ABC-Paramount and Riv. '56–7; wrote for NY Sax. Qt. '60s, incl. *New York Suite* '64. Handy was a rec. reviewer for *DB* in the late '60s. Living in upstate Sackett Lake, N.Y., in his later yrs. Fav: Johnny Mandel. Polls: *Esq.* Silver Awd. '47. Rec. w. Vivien Garry Trio for Sarco, '45; comp. *Diggin' For Diz* and rec. it w. Charlie Parker and D. Gillespie for Dial '46. CDs: *The Bloos* in *The Jazz Scene* (Verve); w. Raeburn (Sav.); C. Parker (Stash); Sims (Riv.).

HANDY, JOHN RICHARD III, alto sax, comp; b. Dallas, TX, 2/3/33. Not related to Capt. John Handy. Moved to LA 1943–4; back to Dallas '44–8, where he became interested in boxing and won amateur featherweight championship '47. Self-taught on cl. from '46, he began on alto in '49 when family ret. to Calif. Stud. theory. Army service '53–5, then back to coll. Moved to NYC and worked w. Charles Mingus '58–9; Randy Weston '59. Form. own gp. '59, pl. at Birdland, Five Spot, concert at UN. Tour. Swed., Den. for US gov't. as soloist '61. Moved to Calif. and was feat. soloist w. Santa Clara Symph., SF St. Coll. Symph. Band '63. Rejoin. Mingus '64 and app. w. him at MJF. A yr. later at same fest. scored major hit w. own band feat. Michael White on vln. Tour. w. Monterey All-Stars '66. Pl. in Gunther Schuller's opera, *The Visitation*, SF '67. Fr. '68 to '70 he taught jazz at Stanford; Cal. St.; UC-Berkeley. New band w. Mike Nock, White '68. Concerts in '71 w. sarod player Ali Akbar Khan in gp. called Rainbow, blending Indian music and jazz. Pl.

his *Concerto for Jazz Soloist and Orchestra* w. SF Symph. '70; Stockton Symph. '71; NO Symph. '72. Other comp: "Spanish Lady"; "Tears For Ole Miss"; "If We Only Knew." Later Handy gps. experimented w. jazz-rock, but he later returned to jazz, working w. Mingus Dynasty and the gp. Bebop And Beyond. A good example of his later work is the '88 *Excursion in Blue*. Handy was inspired by Parker but also came under Dolphy's infl. and reflects both in style and sound. Film: soundtrack for *Boo's Up and Down*, Swed. '61. CDs: Quart.; reissue of '65 Monterey JF perf. orig. on Col. (Koch); w. Mingus (Col.; Rhino; BN; Fant.; SN); S. Stitt (32).

HANDY, W.C. (WILLIAM CHRISTOPHER), comp, crnt, lead; b. Florence, AL, 11/16/1873; d. NYC, 3/28/58. Studied at Kentucky Mus. Coll. Tour. w. various bands; pl. crnt., later soloist and bandmaster of Mahara's Minstrels 1896–1903; during this period also stud. mus. and taught at Huntsville Agricultural and Mechanical Coll. Then tour. w. own bands, mostly in the South. To NYC '17 w. his own Memphis Orch.; moved there the next yr. and set up mus. publ. company; also made numerous recs. w. own bands '17–23. Tour. w. Jelly Roll Morton '26; Clarence Davis '32; pl. at the Apollo w. vlnst. Billy Butler's orch. '36. His autobiography, *Father of the Blues*, was first published in '41. Though he led bands periodically through the '40s, he was mainly recognized for his own songs, as a collector and documentor of trad. blues themes, and as an important music publisher. His first well-known song was "Memphis Blues," publ. in '12; it was orig. entitled "Mr. Crump" and was written in '09 as a campaign tune for Memphis politician E. H. "Boss" Crump. "St. Louis Blues" '14 was his most famous song: others were "Yellow Dog Blues" '14; "Joe Turner Blues" '15; "Beale Street Blues" '16; "Loveless (Careless) Love" '21; "Aunt Hagar's Blues" '22. He gradually lost his vision through the '30s and was totally blind by the '40s; he was also partially disabled fr. a severe fall in the subway in '43. He remained active, conducting business at his B'way office until a few mos. bef. his death. The '57 film *St. Louis Blues* starred Nat King Cole as Handy and was loosely based on his life. His songs have been rec. countless times by a wide variety of jazz mus. Several whole albums have been devoted to his music. CD: *Louis Armstrong Plays W.C. Handy* (Col.).

HANNA, JAKE (JOHN), dms; b. Roxbury, MA, 4/4/31. Studied w. Stanley Spector. Local gigs before air force service. House dmr. at Storyville in Bos. mid 1950s. On and off w. W. Herman '57 and '62–4; also w. Toshiko Akiyoshi '57 in Boston; Maynard Ferguson

'58; Marian McPartland Trio in NYC '59–61. Briefly w. Duke Ellington; Bobby Hackett; Harry James; and Herb Pomeroy. Pl. on Merv Griffin TV show '64–75, moving to LA w. the show in '70. On West Coast worked regularly w. Supersax, rec. innumerable albums for Concord Jazz, and led small gp. w. Carl Fontana. Adept in many idioms and effective in small gps. or bbs, he has been a welcome presence at events such as the Colo. JP and the LA Classic JF in the '90s. CDs: Arb.; Conc.; w. Supersax (Cap.); Basie; Benny Carter (Pab.); Scott Hamilton; Akiyoshi; H. Alden; A. Cohn; D. McKenna; M. McPartland; B. Kessel (Conc.); Herman (Verve; BB; Conc.); Yank Lawson (Jazz.); Herb Ellis (Conc.; Just.); Dan Barrett (Arb.).

HANNA, SIR ROLAND PEMBROKE, pno, comp, arr, cello; b. Detroit, MI, 2/10/32; d. Hackensack, NJ, 11/13/02. Father was preacher, pl. sax; bro. pl. tpt., vln. Began on pno. at age 11. First interest was classical music; later given jazz infl. by friend Tommy Flanagan. Stud. at Cass Tech. High Sch., Det.; Eastman Sch. of Mus.; Juilliard Sch. of Mus. Pl. in Det. w. Emmet Slay 1948; Tommy Dee Dot '49. In army '50–2, pl. w. Billy Towles. Led own gps. fr. '53. Pl. w. Benny Goodman Orch. '58, incl. NJF, Brussels World's Fair; Chas. Mingus '59; Sarah Vaughan '60; Carmen McRae '65; Thad Jones–Mel Lewis Orch. '66–74, incl. tour of Soviet Union '72; Coleman Hawkins '67. Perf. solo concerts at Olympia Theatre, Paris '68. Pl. w. Bobby Rosengarden's Dick Cavett Show Orch. '73; solo pno. at Montreux JF '74; NY Jazz Qt. '75; Zoot Sims off and on '70s; LCJO '86–92; Broadway show *Black and Blue* '87; Smithsonian Jazz Orch. '92. In his later years, Hanna was involved in comp. chamber music and orchestral works, incl. a 3-movement work for pno., winds, and strings premiered by the NY Philomusica Chamber Ens., and a jazz ballet, *Desert Knights*, premiered by the BalletMet of Columbus, Ohio. In '93 he was guest soloist w. the Det. Symph. in a perf. of his comp. *Oasis*. Hanna taught at Manh. Sch. of Mus.; Eastman Sch.; New Sch.; and was assoc. prof. at the Aaron Copland Sch. of Mus., Queens Coll. Knighted by the late William Tubman, Pres. of Liberia, during a benefit tour of Africa in '70. Favs: Tatum, Arthur Rubinstein, T. Flanagan. Fests: all major fr. '58. TV: *An Evening With Carmen McRae and the Roland Hanna Trio* (NET). CDs: Town Crier; MM; Conc.; B&B; Story.; DIW; LRC; Free.; w. NY Jazz Qt. (Enja); Mingus (Merc.; Col.; Rhino); Mingus Dynasty (SN); Jim Hall; Ron Carter (CTI); Carl Fontana (Up.); Terence Blanchard; LCJO (Col.); Kenny Burrell; J. Henderson (BN); Benny Carter; Ellington; Goodman (MM); Richard Davis (DIW; Hep; SB); B. Easley

(Mile.); Grappelli (BL; B&B); J. Knepper (Steep.; SN); Jones/Lewis (LRC); J. Heath (Verve).

HARA, NOBUO, lead, comp, tnr, sop, alto saxes, cl; b. Toyama Pref., Japan, 11/19/26. Began on tpt. at age 14. Pl. sax and stud. classical mus. while in navy band 1943–5. After WWII, pl. jazz in officers' club in Tokyo. Formed Sharps And Flats bb '52. The band often accomp. visiting American singers and was very popular through the '70s, making innumerable apps. in movies and on TV. Received standing ovation at NJF '67. Perf. at fests. in '80s. Pl. thirtieth anniv. concert at Budokan, Tokyo '81; also won Fumio Nanri award for contributions to Japanese jazz the same yr. Won Grand Prix Awd. for fortieth anniversary concert which feat. guests incl. Sadao Watanabe '91. Hara's bb has rec. over 100 albums. Polls: *SJ* '56–70, '72, '90–2. CDs: King; WB; Atl.

HARA, TOMONAO, tpt; b. Kanagawa Pref., Japan, 10/21/66. Began on tpt. at age 11; pl. w. brass band in public sch. Self-taught. Became interested in jazz while at coll. in Nagoya. Pl. in Nagoya w. Sunao Wada, Kenji Mori, Kunio Ota. Pl. at Now's The Time Wkshp. at Pit Inn, Tokyo, 1989–91. Encouraged by Wynton Marsalis '90. Pl. w. Koichi Hiroki, Atsushi Ikeda, Yoichi Murata, Kosuke Mine, Fumio Karashima '90–2; Junko Onishi, Motohiko Hino, Makoto Kuriya's X-Bar Unit, Yutaka Shiina, Shigeo Maruyama's Suikyoja Orch., Yoshio Katari bb fr. '92. Co-leads a qnt. w. Masahiko Osaka. Considered by some Japanese critics to be the most important Japanese trumpeter since Terumasa Hino. Favs: C. Brown, Marsalis. Polls: *SJ* Critics New Star '90–2. CDs: PW; w. K. Hiroki (Lui).

HARDAWAY, BOB (ROBERT BENSON), saxes, cl; b. Milwaukee, WI, 3/1/28. Father, J.B. "Bugs" Hardaway, creator of film cartoon characters Bugs Bunny and Woody Woodpecker. Darrell Caulker, film comp., helped him get start. in mus. Pl. first cl. in air force band 1946; wrote and cond. *Air Force Frolics* '47, which tour. Caribbean. Stud. at LA City Coll. '49–50. Pl. w. Ray Anthony '52, '55; Hal McIntyre '53; Billy May, Woody Herman '50s; Bob Florence '50s through '80; Stan Kenton, Mel Tormé, Jimmy Rowles, Bud Shank, Buddy DeFranco '60s; Benny Goodman, Chuck Flores '70s. From '80 to '91, worked w. Roger Neumann and, in '91, w. Yank Lawson and Bob Haggart. Tour. Japan in '70s and '80s; from '60 to 80 was extremely active as a studio musician. Rec. solos w. May; Jerry Gray; Herman. LP: Beth. CDs: w. Goodman (MM); Neumann (SB).

HARDEE, JOHN, tnr sax; b. Corsicana, TX, 12/20/18; d. Dallas, TX, 5/18/84. From mus. family;

start. on pno., then mello., C-melody sax, crnt.; concentrated on sax as teenager; made prof. debut on alto at 13. Attended Bishop Coll., led a band there; left sch. to tour w. Don Albert 1937–8; ret. to coll., grad. '41. Pl. cl. in army bands while doing military service '41–4. After discharge, moved to NYC; pl. in jam sess. at Minton's and active on 52nd St, worked w. Tiny Grimes '46–7, at times accomp. Billie Holiday. Fr. '46 to '48, rec. frequently as lead. and sideman. In late '40s moved to Wichita Falls, Tex.; led gp. for five yrs. In '55, settled in Dallas, where he taught at Oliver Wendell Holmes Jr. HS, led sch. bands to '76; also pl. in clubs as lead. to early '60s. In '75 app. at Nice JF w. "Lockjaw" Davis, I. Jacquet. Inspired by Chu Berry, Hardee played in the tradition of the big-toned, hard-swinging Texas tenors; his heated, strongly swinging solos were completely without artifice. Recs. as lead., BN '46; Sittin' In With '48; Black & Blue; as sideman w. R. Procope; E. Bostic; T. Grimes '46; H. Humes '47; Billy Taylor '49. LP: box, shared w. I. Quebec (Mos.). CDs: as lead and sideman in *The Blue Note Swingtets* (BN); w. Procope in *Giants of Small Band Swing, Volume 1* (Riv.).

HARDEN, WILBUR, flg, tpt; b. Birmingham, AL, 1925. Played w. blues bands of Roy Brown; Ivory Joe Hunter; also navy band 1950s. Moved to Detroit late '50s; replaced Curtis Fuller in Yusef Lateef gp. '57. Rec. as lead. w. John Coltrane '58. Harden ceased full-time playing in '59 after he became ill. He was one of the first jazz trumpeters to rec. on flg. Favs: Miles Davis, Navarro, Gillespie, Thad Jones, Clifford Brown. CDs: Sav.; w. Coltrane (Prest.); Fuller; T. Flanagan (Sav.).

HARDING, BUSTER (LAVERE), arr, pno; b. Ontario, Canada, 3/19/17; d. NYC, 11/14/65. Grew up in Cleveland, Ohio. Self-taught at first; then stud. w. Schillinger in NYC. Own band in Cleveland, then join. Marion Sears as pnst. Lived in Can. for a yr., then moved to NYC in 1938. Arr. and second pno. for Teddy Wilson's bb '39–40; also led qt. at Nick's '40. Staff arr. for C. Calloway '41–2; then was prolific freelance arr., whose more notable charts incl. "Little Jazz" for A. Shaw; "A Smooth One," "Jonah Joins the Cab" for C. Calloway; also wrote arrs. for B. Goodman; E. Hines; C. Hawkins; L. Millinder. In early '40s he wrote many arrs. for C. Basie, incl. "9:20 Special"; "Rockin' the Blues"; later, "Mad Boogie"; "Hobnail Boogie"; "Rusty Dusty Blues"; "Paradise Squat"; "Nails." In late '40s led own gp., occ. accomp. B. Holiday; pl. w. R. Eldridge's big band. Cont. writing in '50s, incl. sess. arrs. for Holiday; "Confusion" and other orig. comps. for D. Gillespie. A first-class swing arr., he did his last writing for

Jonah Jones, w. whom he also pl. briefly in early '60s. CDs: w. Eldridge (Dec.); Holiday (Royal).

HARDMAN, BILL (WILLIAM FRANKLIN JR.), tpt; b. Cleveland, OH, 4/6/33; d. Paris, France, 12/6/90. Uncle, John Lathan, pl. bs. w. James Moody. Stud. tbn. as well as tpt. Pl. w. T. Dameron while in hs; w. Tiny Bradshaw from 1953 to 55; Jackie McLean '55; Mingus '56; Blakey '56–8; Horace Silver briefly '58; Lou Donaldson on and off '59–66; Lloyd Price '63; Blakey again '66–9, rejoin. in '70, the same yr. in which he form own gp., the Brass Company; active w. both gps. in early '70s; also gigs w. Mingus; Collective Black Artists' Ensemble. Form. qnt. w. Junior Cook in late '70s, cont. the collaboration until he moved to Paris '88. Favs: Clifford Brown, Miles Davis, Donald Byrd, Gillespie. Speaking of his infl. Hardman said: "Miles started me in one way, and then I heard Clifford, who took his thing from Dizzy and Fats (Navarro)...and that straightened me out in a manner of speaking." Polls: *DB* Critics, New Star '73. Fests: NJF w. Mingus, '56; RIJF w. Blakey, '56; Baltimore w. C. Rouse, B. Golson '59; NJF-NY w. Mingus '73; Blakey '75; JazBo '90, Bologna. CDs: Steep.; w. Eddie Jefferson; McLean; M. Waldron (Prest.); Blakey (BB; PJ; Col.; BN; Sav.); Stitt (Muse).

HARDWICKE, OTTO ("TOBY"), alto, sop saxes; also bs sax; b. Washington, DC, 5/31/04; d. Washington, 8/5/70. A friend of Duke Ellington from childhood; start. on string bs. and C-melody sax before concentrating on alto. Worked w. Ellington in Elmer Snowden's band and other local bands from 1918. Went w. Ellington to NYC '23; left the band in '28, tour. Eur. w. Noble Sissle; also worked w. Fats Waller. Rejoin. Ellington '32, remaining w. him to '45, then soon retired fr. mus. to a farm in Maryland. Died after a long illness. His unique singing tone on alto was a key element on the orig. '20s recs. of "Black and Tan Fantasy"; "Birmingham Breakdown"; etc. Feat. soloist on orig. version of "Sophisticated Lady" '33, which he co-comp. Rec. as sideman w. Sonny Greer (Cap.) '45. CDs: w. Ellington (Col.; BB; Dec.); w. Greer in *Classic Capitol Sessions* (Mos.); J. Teagarden (BB); Jimmy Hamilton in *The Blue Note Swingtets* (BN).

HARDY, HAGOOD, comp, arr, vib, pno, perc; b. Angola, IN, 2/26/37; d. Hamilton, Ont., Canada, 1/1/97. Raised in Oakville, Ont. Began on pno. at age 9, stud. w. Edna Lawrence, Ellen Scott. Began pl. vib. in clubs while earning B.A. in political science at U. of Toronto mid 1950s. Led own gp. in Toronto '57–61. Pl. in US w. Gigi Gryce '61; Herbie Mann

'61–2; Martin Denny in Hawaii and LV '62–4; Geo. Shearing '64–7. Led trio in Toronto '67; pop gp. Montage '69–74. Worked as studio mus. fr. early '70s. A Salada Tea jingle he wrote in '72 became a hit rec., "The Homecoming," in '75. Films: scored *Second Wind* '75; *Rituals* '76; *Klondike Fever* '79; also many TV progs. incl. CBC's *Anne of Green Gables* '85; many CBS-TV films. Perf. own music as soloist w. symph. orch. or small gp. in concerts fr. '76. Led jazz gp. in Toronto '80s. Infls: Milt Jackson, Cal Tjader. Rec. w. Morocco, hard bop sxt. '90. Polls: Juno Awd. '75; *Billboard* '76; BMI Canada '77; Gemini Awd. '85. CDs: Duke Street; w. Morocco (Sack.); Mann (Rh./Atl.); Shearing (Mos.).

HAREWOOD, AL (ALPHONSE), dms; b. Brooklyn, NY, 6/3/23. Brother Eustace pl. dms.; learned to pl. by watching him. Pl. w. local gps., then w. J.J. Johnson–Kai Winding 1954–6; Gigi Gryce, Art Farmer, David Amram, Geo. Barrow mid '50s; Curtis Fuller–Benny Golson '58–9; Lou Donaldson '59–61; Horace Parlan '60–1; Grant Green '61–3; Mary Lou Williams '62; Stan Getz '62–4; D. Amram '67–8. Pl. in '70s w. Chuck Wayne; C. Fuller; H. Parlan; Lisle Atkinson; Newport All-Stars; in '80s w. Lee Konitz; Norman Simmons; and the Bklyn. Philharm. Accomp. many voc. incl. Joe Williams; Blossom Dearie; Carmen McRae; Betty Carter; Dakota Staton. Taught at Livingston Coll. of Rutgers U. '73–5. A dmr. of taste who never overplays but always swings. Favs: Webb, Roach, Blakey, K. Clarke, P.J. Jones. Fests: NJF, MJF, etc. fr. '50s. TV: *Today* w. Benny Carter, Marian McPartland '91. CDs: w. D. Gordon; G. Green; J. Henderson; I. Quebec; S. Turrentine (BN); Benny Carter (MM); Betty Carter (Roul.; Verve); G. Benson (Accord); Simmons (Milljac); T. Akiyoshi (Evid.); J. Breakstone (PW); B. Ervin (Cand.); C. Fuller (Sav.); Konitz (SN); B. Tate (Res.).

HARGROVE, ROY (ANTHONY JR.), tpt, flg, comp, lead, b. Waco, TX, 10/16/69. Lived in Mart, Tex., until 1977 when his family moved to Dallas. Stud. tpt. at Arts Magnet HS, where he was invited by Wynton Marsalis to sit in w. his band. He also sat in w. Dizzy Gillespie; Bobby Hutcherson; Herbie Hancock; Freddie Hubbard; and Marsalis at the Caravan of Dreams nightclub in Ft. Worth. Pl. in Eur. w. Frank Morgan summer '87. Marsalis arr. for him to travel and study further after his grad. in June '88. Pl. w. Jack McDuff qnt., Clifford Jordan sxt. in Eur. '88. Guest app. w. Art Blakey bb, Renee Rosnes at Mt. Fuji Fest., Japan '88; also w. J. Griffin qt. '88. Stud. at Berklee on a *DB* scholarship '88–9; at New School '90. From '90 toured int'l w. own qnt.; also w. Jazz Futures Octet and other gps., all feat. Antonio Hart.

Made rec. debut w. *Diamond In The Rough* (RCA/Novus) '91. In same yr. app. in Sonny Rollins concert at Carnegie Hall and rec. w. him. On commission fr. Jazz at Lincoln Center wrote *The Love Suite: In Mahogany*, a comp. in five movements for tpt., perf. '93 at Alice Tully Hall. Cont. to lead own gps. and fr. '95 off and on own bb. As a result of pl. in Havana JF '96 w. his qnt., form. band called Crisol, mixing pnst. Chucho Valdes and Cuban percs. w. American horn players such as Gary Bartz, David Sanchez, and Frank Lacy. Band rec. at Umbria Winter Jazz, Orvieto Jan. '97. Tour. w. Crisol in US and Eur. at major fests. '97. Then led sxt., qnt. Whether playing in the hard bop or Afro-Cuban groove, Hargrove's fire is unquenchable and his spirit energizing but he is no less effective as a sensitive balladeer. Early infls: C. Brown, Lee Morgan. Fav: F. Hubbard. CDs: Novus; Verve; w. Jazz Futures (Novus); Rollins (Mile.); James Clay; Frank Morgan; J. McLean (Ant.); Steve Coleman; Antonio Hart (Novus); Charles Fambrough (CTI); Helen Merrill; Stephen Scott (Verve); Ralph Moore (Land.); Ricky Ford (Muse); Superblue (BN).

HARLEM BLUES AND JAZZ BAND. Founded by Dr. Albert Vollmer in 1973; brought together veteran pl. fr. the 1920s and '30s. First lead. was tbnst.-vocst. Clyde Bernhardt and incl. Franc Williams and George James. In the '80s it was led by tptr. Bobby Williams and feat. Eddie Durham, George Kelly, and Al Casey. Personnel has incl. Johnny Letman, Haywood Henry, Candy Ross, Dill Jones, Ram Ramirez, Sammy Benskin, Johnny Williams (bs.), Tommy Benford, Johnny Blowers; voc. Laurel Watson. Tour. int'l fr. '76. Pl. for one yr. at Ginger Man restaurant, NYC, then Sullivan's '97–8.

HARPER, BILLY R., tnr sax, fl, comp, arr; b. Houston, TX, 1/17/43. Entire family sings. Stud. at Evan E. Worthing HS; No. Texas St. U. 1961–5. Pl. w. local r&b bands, own qnt. fr. age 16; own sxt. at No. Texas St.; James Clay mid '60s. Moved to NYC '66, pl. w. Gil Evans '67–76; Art Blakey '67–'70; Lee Morgan '69–71; Thad Jones–Mel Lewis Orch. fr. '69 to 77; Elvin Jones '70; Donald Byrd '70–2; Max Roach '70–8. Worked mainly with his own qnt. fr. '75. He taught improv. in N.J. publ. sch. '73 and at Livingston Coll. '75. His album *Black Saint* was named Record of the Yr. by the Modern Jazz League of Tokyo '76. Comp.: "Thoroughbred"; "Trying to Make Heaven My Home." Foreign tours for USIS '90s. Concert at Miller Theatre, NYC '95. Harper's qnt. incl. Eddie Henderson, Francesca Tanksley, and Newman T. Baker. Favs: James Clay, Don Wilkerson, Kenny Dorham. Infs. incl. Coltrane, Rollins, Richard "Dicky

Boy" Lillie. Polls: *DB* TDWR '74–5; Houston Jazz Mus. of Yr. '92. Fests: Eur., Japan fr. late '60s; Africa w. Max Roach '70s; Latin Amer. w. own gp. '83. TV: NBC Big Apple '66; Eur. TV. CDs: BS; SN; Steep.; Evid.; Story.; w. G. Evans (Enja; BB); Jones–Lewis (LRC); Lee Morgan (FS); M. Tyner (Bird.); R. Weston (Free.; Verve).

HARPER, HERBIE (HERBERT), tbn; b. Salina, KS, 7/2/20. Raised in Amarillo, Tex., and in Colo. Gave up an engineering scholarship to go on the road w. a Tex. band. In 1940s working w. Johnny "Scat" Davis, G. Krupa, Charlie Spivak before settling in Hollywood '47. With B. Goodman '47; C. Barnet '48; S. Kenton '50; Jerry Gray '50–2. Also pl. w. Teddy Edwards gp. '49. Concert w. Billie Holiday '49. Active as lead. and sideman in West Coast movement of the '50s, rec. w. June Christy; Maynard Ferguson; Ray Brown before join. NBC studio orch. '55. Served on Board of Dir. Local 47, AFM '56–8. Worked w. Bob Florence periodically from '50s into '80s. Favs: Urbie Green, J.J. Johnson, Carl Fontana. Own rec. dates in '50s for Nocturne; Bethlehem; Mode; Liberty; Tampa. In '80s rec. for Sea Breeze. Co-led pianoless qnt. w. Bill Perkins in '80s which rec. for VSOP. CDs: Noct.; VSOP; w. Steve White (Noct.); Holiday (Story.); Florence (C5); Roger Neumann (SB); M. Paich (Cand.).

HARPER, PHILIP, tpt; b. Baltimore, MD, 5/10/65. Played in bro. Danny's rock band bef. pl. w. Jimmy McGriff; Little Jimmy Scott. Along w. bro. Winard, pl. w. Jackie McLean 1983. Formed Harper Bros. gp. w. Winard '85. In '87 join. Art Blakey. Stud. at Wm. Paterson Coll. Member of Mingus BB in '90s. CDs: Harper Bros., Verve; w. Blakey (PW; SN); Mingus BB (Drey.); Joe Chambers (Cand.); Cecil Brooks III; Houston Person; Etta Jones (Muse); Errol Parker (Sah.); Cedar Walton (Evid.).

HARPER, (HIRAM) WINARD, dms; b. Baltimore, MD, 6/4/62. Younger bro. Philip pl. tpt.; older bro. Danny pl. tpt., pno. Began pl. dms. at age 5; three yrs. later pl. w. bro. Danny's rock gp. Hearing Brown-Roach rec. of "Jordu" got him interested in jazz. Pl. w. Dexter Gordon, Johnny Griffin 1983; Betty Carter '84–8; Harper Bros. w. Philip '85–92; Stan Getz '87; Ray Bryant, Houston Person fr. '90; Tommy Flanagan trio, mid '90s. Favs: Billy Higgins, Roy Haynes, Billy Hart, Max Roach. Polls: *DB* Best Emerging Band (Harper Bros.). Fests: Eur. fr. '84; Japan fr. '87. TV: *Johnny Carson*. CDs: Savant; Epicure; Harper Bros.; Verve; w. Houston Person; Jimmy Ponder (Muse); Ray Bryant (Em.); James Clay (Ant.).

HARRELL, TOM (THOMAS STRONG), tpt, flg, comp; b. Urbana, IL, 6/16/46. Family moved to Los Altos, Calif. 1952. Start. on tpt. at age 8, beginning to pl. jazz almost immediately. Began pl. w. gps. and jamming in Bay Area at 13. Stud. arr. w. Tony Baker at Stanford U., grad. w. degree in music comp. '69; tour. w. Stan Kenton '69; Woody Herman '70–1; Azteca '72. Pl. w. Horace Silver Quint. '73–7; Bob Berg '74; Chuck Israels' National Jazz Ens. '76; Mel Lewis orch. '81, '82; rec. and pl. w. Lee Konitz; Bill Evans; Bob Brookmeyer; Lionel Hampton. Pl. first gig w. Phil Woods '79; became regular member of gp. '84. Left to form own gp. '89. Pl. and rec. w. George Robert '87. Member of Charlie Haden's Liberation Orch. fr. '88. Pl. w. N.Y. Jazz Giants '92. Diagnosed w. schizophrenia while still in coll.; must take powerful medication to maintain chemical balance and shut out outside distractions. A powerful post-bop trumpeter whose strong tone and precise articulation are complemented by an acute harmonic sense and a warm lyric quality. Woods has said: "I've played with some great musicians and I've never played with anyone better than Tom Harrell." Favs: Gillespie, Clifford Brown, Miles Davis, Hubbard. Comps. incl. "Journey to the Center"; "Rado"; "Sail Away"; "Bouquet." CDs: RCA; Cont.; Chesky; CC; Steep.; Musi.; w. Phil Woods (Conc.; Chesky; Red; Den.); W. Herman (Chess); H. Silver (BN); S. Grossman (Drey.); Leon Parker (Col.); Steve Kuhn (Post.); B. Shew (MAMA); Don Braden; P. Catherine; R. Lalama; M. LeDonne; Hod O'Brien; John Swana (CC); C. Baker (Phil.); Donald Brown (Muse); Michael Cochrane; J. Lovano; G. Russell (SN); Gillespie-Woods (Timel.); C. Haden; H. Merrill (Verve); Jim Hall (Den.); Konitz (Steep.).

HARRIOTT, JOE (ARTHURLIN), alto, bari, tnr saxes; b. Kingston, Jamaica, 7/15/28; d. London, England, 1/2/73. Studied cl. at a boys' sch. as a youngster; join. dance band after leaving sch. and pl. in local gps. w. Bogey Gaynair and Dizzy Reece. Emigrated to Engl. in 1951; freelanced until join. Pete Pitterson. Achieved recognition pl. w. Tony Kinsey '54, incl. Paris JF; Ronnie Scott's big band '55; pl. w. various small combos. Form. own qnt. in '58. Tour. Engl. w. MJQ in late '59. After illness in '60 resumed pl., start. independently experimenting w. "free jazz" ideas, emphasizing ensemble textures, and breaking away from conventional harmonic and melodic ideas. He was also involved w. fusion of jazz and Indian mus.; join. poet Michael Garrick's gp. in '65, combining poetry and jazz. In '60s also tour. as freelance soloist. *Abstract*, his '60s LP for Cap., was enthusiastically received both in the US and Engl. His playing and his free-form comps. were considered among the best of the '60s Brit. jazz avant-garde. Favs: C. Parker, C. Ventura. Recs. as lead. on Jazzland; Brit. Col.; Melodisc; w. Garrick (Argo); Sonny Boy Williamson (Marmalade); *Indo-Jazz Fusions* w. vlnst./comp. John Mayer (EMI); A. Bilk; Stan Tracy; Laurie Johnson (Brit. Col.). CD: w. Chris Barber (Chris Barber Collection).

HARRIS, BARRY DOYLE, pno, comp, educ; b. Detroit, MI, 12/15/29. Mother, a church pianist, gave him lessons fr. age 4. Pl. w. jazz band at amateur show 1946. Strongly infl. by Charlie Parker, Bud Powell, and Thelonious Monk of whose music he is a foremost interpreter. Pl. w. house band at Blue Bird club, Det., backing Miles Davis; Sonny Stitt; Max Roach; Thad Jones; Wardell Gray; et al. Also pl. at Rouge Lounge w. Lee Konitz; Lester Young; et al. Active as educ., utilizing own theory of bebop instruction, fr. '56. Pl. w. Max Roach briefly '56. Left Det. w. Cannonball Adderley '60, settling in NYC. Led own trio, qnt. fr. early '60s. Pl. w. Yusef Lateef, early '60s; Coleman Hawkins off and on '65–9; Chas. McPherson, '60s; Lateef '70. Led duos at various NYC bars and restaurants late '60s-'70s. Wrote six arrs. for strings for C. McPherson concert, Det. '74. Pl. solo piano at NJF-NY '75. Perf. often w. tap dancer Jimmy Slyde. Inaugurated Lincoln Center's Penthouse piano series Jan. '97. In '82 Harris founded the Jazz Cultural Center, a school/perf. space where he taught until it closed in '87. He cont. teaching his workshops, extremely popular among young musicians, at other NYC sites; and present. annual concert extravaganzas at Symphony Space w. profs. and students, incl. a large voc. ens. drawn fr. the latter gp. His comps. incl. "Luminescence"; "Like This!"; "Nicaragua"; "Even Steven"; "Just As Though You Were There"; "Nascimento." Favs: C. Parker, B. Powell, Monk. Fests: all major. Awards: NEA Jazz Masters '89; Bird Award, North Sea JF '91. TV: PBS w. Hawkins '69; Dutch TV w. Lateef '70. Video: *The Barry Harris Workshop Video* (Bop City Prods.); documentary in progress by Checkerboard Film Foundation, video by Albert Maysles. CDs: Prest.; Riv.; Conc.; w. Cannonball Adderley (Riv.); McPherson; J. Moody; I. Jacquet; A. Farmer; E. Jefferson (Prest.); F. Rosolino (Sav.); L. Morgan; H. Mobley (BN); Dexter Gordon (Prest.; BN); C. Hawkins (Imp.); Dave Young (JT); J. Sheldon (Up.); Stitt (32); Lateef (Riv.; Rh./Atl.); S. Grossman (Drey.); C. Jordan (SN).

HARRIS, BEAVER (WILLIAM GODVIN), dms; b. Pittsburgh, PA, 4/20/36; d. NYC, 12/22/91. Mother a dancer who also pl. pno. Stud. w. Stanley Leonard at Carnegie Tech; pno. and comp. w. Charles Bell; w. Kenny Clarke and Dante Agostini at Premier Drum Sch. and Clinic, Paris; perc. w. Richard Fitz, Marshall

Brown, NYC. Nickname derived from early days as a baseball player. Pl. ball as member of Special Services while in army; also began gigging while at Ft. Knox; then local gps. around Pitts. after discharge. To NYC 1963, worked w. S. Rollins; T. Monk; J. Henderson; F. Hubbard; from '66 w. Roswell Rudd. Join. Archie Shepp '67, tour. Eur. w. him and also pl. there w. Albert Ayler. In '68 form. the 360 Degree Music Experience w. Grachan Moncur and Dave Burrell. Personnel changes dur. the late '70s and '80s incl. Ken McIntyre; H. Bluiett; Ricky Ford; and Don Pullen, who served as co-lead. He also pl. w. Cecil Taylor; and in Haiti w. L. Konitz; E. Gomez; and Jim Hall. Made NJF tour of Japan w. Shepp, Konitz, G. Barbieri '73. Worked w. a variety of gps. led by C. Baker, C. Rouse, A. Cohn at St. James Infirmary, a Greenwich Village club owned by Rudd and Hod O'Brien. Mus. dir. for Black and Puerto Rican Culture Program. Pl. for stage prod. *Slave Ship* '71, *Lady Day* at Brooklyn Acad. of Mus. Infl: Clarke, Roach, Haynes, Musa Kaleem, Rollins. Comps: "African Drums"; lyrics for "Money Blues"; "Attica Blues"; "Ballad for a Child," all for Shepp albums. CDs: SN; yvp; w. Shepp (Imp.; Free.; BS); Albert Ayler (hatArt; Phil.; Imp.); L. Coryell (Muse); V. Herring (MM); Jazz Comp. Orch. (JCOA); S. Lacy (BS); M. Urbani (Red).

HARRIS, BENNY (BENJAMIN; "LITTLE BENNY"), tpt, comp; b. NYC, 4/23/19; d. San Francisco, CA, 2/11/75. Self-taught; pl. French horn in children's band at age 12; took up tpt. 1937. Part of Harlem jazz scene in late '30s w. Monk, Gillespie, et al.; worked w. Tiny Bradshaw '39; Earl Hines '41, '43; also in '40s w. Benny Carter; Pete Brown; John Kirby; Herbie Fields; Don Redman; Don Byas; C. Hawkins; Monk; gigs w. Gillespie orch. late '40s; Parker combo early '50s. Moved to Calif. '52, but was not active in mus. An early Gillespie disciple whose lasting contributions are his comps. "Ornithology," based on the opening phrase of Parker's "Jumpin' Blues" solo; "Little Benny" (aka "Ideology"; "Crazeology"; "Bud's Bubble"); "Wahoo" (based on "Perdido" and aka "Lion's Den"); "Reets and I." Rec. w. Clyde Hart (Sav.) '44. CDs: w. Parker (Verve); D. Byas (Sav.); B. Powell (MS).

HARRIS, BILL (WILLARD PALMER), tbn; b. Philadelphia, PA, 10/28/16; d. Hallandale, FL, 8/21/73. Played tpt., tnr. sax, other instr.; start. pl. tbn. prof. when he was 22. First major job was w. Buddy Williams 1942; tour. w. G. Krupa, Ray McKinley; to NYC w. Bob Chester; became prominent through work. w. B. Goodman '43–4. Led own gp. at Café Society Uptown '44; best known as tbn. w. W. Herman's orch. '44–6; feat. incl. "Bijou"; "Everywhere."

Cont. work. w. Herman on and off through '59. Pl. w. C. Ventura '47; from '50 tour. annually w. JATP. Through '50s also led small gps. Settled in Fla. in late '50s, semi-retiring; also worked as DJ in Miami. Tour. Eur. w. B. Goodman, fall '59. In '60s lived for a while in LV; worked in lounges there, doubling on gtr. w. Charlie Teagarden; Red Norvo. One of the definitive tbn. stylists of the '40s, his ballads were warm and burry; at up-tempo, he preached and shouted, reflecting in part one of his original models, J.C. Higginbotham. Harris was widely influential and imitated in modern jazz until the advent of J.J. Johnson. Polls: *DB* '45–54; *DB* Critics '53–4; *Esq.* New Star Award '45; *Esq.* Gold Award '46–7; *Met.* '46–55. Film: soundtrack of *Sweet and Lowdown* w. Goodman. Rec. as a lead. on Em.; w. C. Ventura (Verve); Chubby Jackson (Argo). CDs: Fant.; w. Herman (Cap.; Col.); C. Parker; A. O'Day; F. Phillips; *The Jazz Scene* (Verve); JATP (Verve; Pab.); w. Goodman (MM); E. Condon (Jazz.); Nat Cole (Cap.).

HARRIS, BILL (WILLIE), gtr, comp; b. Nashville, NC, 4/14/25; d. Washington, DC, 12/17/88. Son is bsst. and gtrst. Joe Harris. Stud. pno. w. moth., then pl. org. in fath.'s church. Stud. gtr. briefly at age 12. Bugler in army in Eur. 1943–5. Stud. jazz gtr. priv. in Wash., D.C. '45; classical gtr. w. Sophocles Papas at Columbia Sch. of Mus., Wash., late '40s. Pl. w. local gps. '45–50, then w. r&b gp., The Clovers, '50–8. Encouraged by Mickey Baker, Harris made his first jazz rec. '56. Pl. solo and w. own gps. in Wash. fr. '58; own qnt. at Village Vanguard '60; JFK Qnt. '62; Soc. of Classical Gtr., NYC fr. '62. Received NEA composer's grant '72; comps. incl. "Blue Medley"; "Watergate Blues"; "Wes Montgomery Suite." Tour. France '72–3. Started own rec. co. '77. A well-known and respected gtr. teacher and author of instructional books, Harris prod. the annual Kenny Burrell Gtr. Seminar fr. '71. He specialized in pl. solo, unamplified, acoustic gtr. Favs: Oscar Moore, B. Kessel, Les Paul, Reinhardt, Christian, John Collins. LPs: Em.; B&B.

HARRIS, CHARLIE (CHARLES PURVIS), bs; b. Alexandria, VA, 1/9/16. Studied vln. and bs. in Baltimore. Tour. w. Mac Crockette 1939–43, Lionel Hampton '44–9; rec. w. Wynonie Harris '45; Herbie Fields; Milt Buckner; and Arnett Cobb. Joined Nat Cole '51, making tours of Europe and Australia w. him. Recorded w. Cole '52, '56; Stuff Smith '56; and, in '60, in ensemble conducted by Stan Kenton. CDs: w. Hampton (Dec.); Cole (Cap.).

HARRIS, CRAIG S., tbn, didjeridu, comp; b. Hempstead, NY, 9/10/53. Played in r&b bands as teenager. Stud. theory, arr., comp. w. Ken McIntyre at

SUNY, Old Westbury, N.Y. (B.A. 1976). Recommended by Pat Patrick, he join. Sun Ra and worked w. him '76–8; toured w. Abdullah Ibrahim '79–81. In the '80s he pl. w. Jaki Byard; Olu Dara; David Murray; Henry Threadgill, incl. Jazz Yatra, India, '84; Lester Bowie; Charlie Haden; Muhal Richard Abrams; Cecil Taylor; and Sam Rivers. From '79 he worked as lead. of several gps. incl. Tailgater's Tales, Aqaustra, and Cold Sweat. Pl. in the pit orch. of Lena Horne's *The Lady and Her Music* '82; collab. w. dance company, Urban Bushwomen, on *Points* '85, again in '88 on his comp. *Heat* at The Kitchen, NYC '88. Comps.: "Harlem Night Song"; "Nigerian Sunset"; "Shelter"; "Blackout in the Square Root of Soul." Awarded Guggenheim Fellowship for music comp. '91. CDs: SN; JMT; w. Abrams (BS); Bowie (ECM); Ibrahim (Enja); Murray (BS; DIW).

HARRIS, EDDIE, tnr sax, elec sax, tpt, pno; b. Chicago, IL, 10/20/34; d. Los Angeles, CA, 11/5/96. Professional debut as pno. w. Gene Ammons' band in Chicago. After army service, late 1950s, had a major hit w. rec. of "Exodus." Comp. "Freedom Jazz Dance," popularized by Miles Davis and established as a jazz standard. Most of his work in the late '60s was done with the electric sax, an acoustic instrument pl. through an electronic attachment called a Varitone, principally w. r & b and rock recs. Held the US patent for the reed tpt., which he pl.on several recs. Join. Les McCann's soul-jazz gp. '69; rec. hit song, "Compared to What," at Montreux JF '68; also rec. w. rock musicians Steve Winwood and Jeff Beck. In the '70s ret. to a more trad. bop style but cont. to experiment w. such odd combinations as tpt. and tbns. fitted w. reed mouthpieces, as well as saxes fitted w. brass mouthpieces. Tour. Eur. '86–91; Hong Kong '90, Israel '91. LP: Eddie Harris–Ellis Marsalis (Spindletop). CDs: Act; VJ; Rh./Atl.; Enja; MM; Timel.; Steep.; Virgin; w. McCann (Atl.; MM); Buddy Montgomery (Land.); H. Parlan (Steep.); H. Silver (Col.); B. Purdie (Act).

HARRIS, GENE (EUGENE HAIRE), pno, kybds; b. Benton Harbor, MI, 9/1/33; d. Boise, ID, 1/16/00. Played prof. fr. age 7 in a trick piano act; by 12 had own radio show. Join. army in 1951; pl. in 82nd Airborne Band, where he learned to read music. Tour. w. various bands '54–6, before form. The Four Sounds, which in '57 became The Three Sounds, w. Andy Simpkins and Bill Dowdy. The trio remained together for nearly a decade, rec. more than 2 dozen albums, incl. many blues-oriented interpretations of show tunes and standards. In '66 Dowdy departed, and Simpkins followed in '68; Harris led various permutations of The Three Sounds in late '60s and early '70s, rec. music that leaned heavily toward jazz-rock. Retired from touring in '77 and settled in Boise, Ida., as director of music for the Idanha Hotel. Ret. to more conventional jazz activity w. a qt. in LV '80 and w. Ernestine Anderson in Seattle; app. w. Benny Carter in '85 at the Concord JF and w. Ray Brown's trio at the Half Note in NYC. In '89 assembled the Philip Morris Super Band which tour. internationally to great acclaim through '91. Form. new qt. '91 w. Ron Eschete, Luther Hughes, Paul Humphrey. *The Gene Harris Trio Plus One* was awarded the French *Grand Prix du Disque* '85. Film: solo pno. on soundtrack of *Malice*. CDs: Conc; Harris–Scott Hamilton (Conc.); w. Three Sounds; S. Turrentine (BN); R. Brown (Conc.; PW); Benny Carter; E. Anderson (Conc.); A. O'Day (Verve); James Clay (Riv.); Milt Jackson (Pab.).

HARRIS, HERB (HERBERT III), tnr sax, sop sax; b. Washington, DC, 7/8/68. Brother Robert is r&b gtr., pno., and songwriter. Began on cl. in jr. hs, then sw. to alto sax in hs, tnr. sax in coll. Stud. political science at Fla. A&M. Pl. w. Marcus Roberts off and on 1989–91; Wynton Marsalis '91–2. Tour. w. Jazz Futures II summer '92. Pl. w. Phillip Harper '92. Own gp. at Aaron Davis Hall, NYC '94. Was member of LCJO and in '95 a featured guest at CHJB concert. Favs: C. Parker, Rollins, Coltrane. Fests: Eur., Japan, So. Amer. CDs: *Tough Young Tenors* (Ant.); w. M. Roberts (RCA); W. Marsalis (Col.).

HARRIS, JEROME ESTESE, gtr, el-bs; b. Flushing, NY, 4/5/53. Began on acdn., then pl. vln. in sch. orch. Self-taught on gtr. 1966–73. Stud. psychology at Harvard '69–73 (B.A.); Afro-Amer. mus. and gtr. at New Engl. Cons. '73–7 (B. Mus.). Pl. in local soul and gospel gps. as teenager, then in pop, funk, gospel, and jazz gps. while in college and cons. Pl. w. Ran Blake, Billy Thompson, Jezra Kaye, Bo Winiker '78; Clarice Taylor '78–9; Sonny Rollins '78–81, again fr. '84; Stanton Davis '78–83; Marty Ehrlich off and on '78–90; Michael Gregory Jackson '78–82; Ricky Ford '79; Dwight Andrews '79–80; Amina Claudine Myers fr. '79; Oliver Lake '80–6; Bob Moses '81–7; Geo. Russell bb '82; Julius Hemphill '83, '87; Gunter Hampel '84; Juli Kohl '84–5; Jay Hoggard '84–6; Living Colour '85; Ricky Ford; Black Rock Coalition Orch. '86–7; Sherry Winston '87–8; Henry Threadgill '88; Bobby Previte '88–91; Renee Manning fr. '88; Hank Roberts '89–90; Ned Rothenberg, Bob Stewart fr. '89; Samm Bennett & Chunk '91; Ray Anderson '93. Led his own gps. fr. '87. Fests: Eur., Japan fr. '79. TV: Japanese, Italian TV w. Rollins. CDs: NW; MinorMusic; Muse; w. Rollins (Mile.); O. Lake (Gram.; BS); B. Previte (Gram.; Enja); B. Moses (Gram.); A.C. Myers (Novus; MinorMusic);

N. Rothenberg (Moers); S. Bennett (KFW); Mark Helias (Enja); B. Frisell (ECM); Hemphill (Elek. Mus.); Russell (SN).

HARRIS, JOE, tbn, voc; b. Sedalia, MO, 1908; d. Fresno, CA, summer 1952. Started on tbn. at age 16. Pl. w. territory bands in Okla., Tex., Can. Pl. w. Joe Haymes in Springfield, Mo., ca. 1930; Frankie Trumbauer in Chi. '32. Replaced Jack Teagarden w. Ben Pollack '33. Freelanced in NYC '34, then pl. w. Bob Crosby '35; Benny Goodman '35–6. Moved to Hollywood '36. Work. as studio mus. and pl. w. Spud Murphy '38; Pollack '40; Pee Wee Erwin '42; others. Rejoin. Goodman '43. Pl. w. Eddie Miller, mid '40s. Worked as studio mus. and pl. w. local gps. late '40s–'52. CDs: w. Goodman; Teagarden (RCA).

HARRIS, JOE (JOSEPH ALLISON), dms, perc; b. Pittsburgh, PA, 12/23/26. Studied priv. at age 15. Introd. to bop style by Ray Brown and Art Blakey. Pl. w. Dizzy Gillespie off and on 1946–8, incl. Gillespie–Charlie Parker at Carnegie Hall '47; Arnett Cobb '48; Billy Eckstine '50; Erroll Garner '52; James Moody '54; house band at Apollo and extensive freelance early '50s. Stud. tympani, xylophone w. Alfred Freise; pl. w. Young Men's Symph. at City Center, early '55. Harris settled in Stockholm after tour. Sweden w. Rolf Erickson '56. Moved to Germany '61. Pl. on Radio Free Berlin and w. Kenny Clarke–Francy Boland bb '61–6. Moved to LA '67. Worked w. Benny Carter; w. house band at Playboy Club; and taught dms. at Eubanks Sch. of Mus. '67. Tour. w. Ella Fitzgerald '68. Ret. to Germany '70. Pl. in Munich w. Max Greger Orch., also w. Jimmy Woode, Fritz Pauer, Peter Herbolzheimer at Club Domicile '71. Pl. at Jazz Wkshp. in Hamburg. Ret. to Pitts. '72; pl. w. house band at Walt Harper's fr. '72. Harris taught at U. of Pitts. '72–86. In '83, Harris received a grant to stud. trad. music in Japan. Favs: Roach, Blakey, Rich, Saul Goodman. Fests: Eur. fr. '56; Japan fr. '83. CDs: w. Gillespie (RCA; Roost; Prest.; Sav.); Milt Jackson; H. McGhee (Sav.) ; Teddy Charles (Atl.); J. Moody; K. Pleasure (Prest.); G. Russell (BB); Clarke-Boland; Sahib Shihab (Rear.).

HARRIS, JOHN "IRONMAN" (Harrison Jr.), dms; b. Bridgeport, CT, 1/15/35. Introduced to mus. by his fath., a dancer w. bbs. Began stud. dms. at age 8. Horace Silver and Phineas Newborn were first major infl. in his career; pl. w. Newborn in 1959, bef. join the army. While in the service in Eur., pl. gigs w. Bud Powell; René Thomas; Elmo Hope; Dexter Gordon; etc. After army, ret. to Bridgeport '61. Pl. w. Silver, tour. Japan and rec. *Tokyo Blues* on Blue Note. Worked w. Mitchell–Ruff Trio, Johnny "Hammond"

Smith. Moved to LA '70, worked w. Carmen McRae; Harold Land; Curtis Peagler; Oscar Brashear; Jimmy Cleveland; Charles McPherson. Jeannie and Jimmy Cheatham invited him to join their jam sessions in San Diego in '80. Moved there '83 and in '84 join. Cheathams' Sweet Baby Blues Band. Also pl. w. Seahawk Trio. Fav: Jo Jones. Fests: w. Cheathams, Chi.; Concord; Playboy; MJF; New Zealand; North Sea. TV: *Tonight Show*; *Today*; Emmy-winning TV film, *Three Generations of the Blues*. LPs: w. Johnny Hammond Smith. CDs: w. Cheathams (Conc.).

HARRIS, STEFON DELEON, vib, mrba, perc; b. Albany, NY, 3/23/73. Began on pno.; classical lessons w. Richard Albagli. Stud. at Eastman and Manh. Sch. of Mus. 1991–7. Pl. w. Max Roach's gp. and M'Boom '94; Tim Warfield, Bobby Watson's Horizon, own sxt., Ashanti '95; Buster Williams, Wess Anderson, Eric Reed, LCJO '96. Taught priv. at Manh. Sch. of Mus. and the Jazzmobile Wkshp. fr. '95. Favs: B. Hutcherson, Milt Jackson, Steve Nelson. Fests: Eur. '89, '95, '97; Russia '94. CDs: BN; w. Williams (TCB; Claves); Terell Stafford (Cand.); Russell Gunn (Muse); Warfield (CC); S. Turre; J. Henderson (Verve); LCJO (Col.).

HARRIS, WYNONIE "MR. BLUES," voc; b. Omaha, NE, 8/24/15; d. Los Angeles, CA, 6/14/69. Started as a comedian and dancer, doubling on dms.; also led small gps. in Omaha. Settled in LA in early 1940s. Join. Lucky Millinder in '44 as voc., app. in LA, Bost., NYC. Also sang w. I. Jacquet, rec. "Wynonie's Blues" (Apollo) '45; w. Ernie Fields '46; L. Hampton '48; Dud Bascomb '49. Then led own r&b band. Own recs. on Aladdin, Apollo, in his typical, frantic, blues-shouting style. CDs: Del.; w. Jacquet (Mos.).

HARRISON, DONALD, sop, alto, tnr saxes; b. New Orleans, LA, 6/23/60. Father sang w. Mardi Gras Indians; moth., sists., cousin are amateur mus. Began on alto sax. Stud. in NO w. Kidd Jordan; Ellis Marsalis; Henry Butler. Pl. w. local r&b gps., Doc Paulin Brass Band 1974–9; NO Pops '79; also pl. w. Terence Blanchard. Stud. w. Alvin Batiste at Southern U. '79, then w. Joe Viola at Berklee Coll. of Mus. '80–1. Led own org. trio in Bost. '80, then began pl. w. Roy Haynes in NYC on weekends '80–1. Through Haynes he met Jack McDuff and Art Blakey. Pl. w. McDuff '81; Blakey, along w. Blanchard '82–6; Tony Williams, Don Pullen '85; Harrison-Blanchard Qnt. '87–8; Miles Davis '87; Blakey '89; Bill Lee's Mo Betta Qt. '89–90; Guardians of the Flame Mardi Gras band fr. '89; Nat Adderley '91. Harrison has led his own qt. fr. '90. He taught at the New Sch. '89–90 and

pl. on the soundtrack to Spike Lee's *Do the Right Thing*. His recent recs. have focused on the fusion of modern jazz w. elements of trad. NO music. Favs: Bechet, Parker, Coltrane; arr.: Ellington. Polls: *DB* TDWR alto sax '85; Sony Innovators awd. Fests: Eur., Asia fr. '82; So. Amer. TV: PBS Blakey documentary. CDs: Cand,; SB; PW; w. Harrison-Blanchard (Col.); Blanchard–Harrison (Evid.; Conc.); Blakey (Timel.; Conc.; PW); Donald Brown (Sunny.); L. Coryell; Jim Hall; T. Rosenthal (CTI); Tony Williams; G. Keezer (BN); Errol Parker (Sah.); Don Pullen (BS); Mickey Tucker (Steep.).

HARRISON, JIMMY (JAMES HENRY), tbn; b. Louisville, KY, 10/17/1900; d. NYC, 7/23/31. Raised in Det. from age 6. Pl. w. combos there and in the Midwest after having taught himself tbn. at 15. Moved w. family to Toledo, Ohio, where he worked in family restaurant and pl. semi-pro baseball. After pl. and singing in a tour. minstrel show, he located in Atlantic City 1919; led own trio and pl. w. Charlie Johnson, Sam Wooding. Pl. w. Hank Duncan in Det.; then in Toledo w. June Clark and James P. Johnson. Tour. w. various shows '21–3; to NYC w. Fess Williams '23; Charlie Smith, June Clark '24; Billy Fowler, D. Ellington, Elmer Snowden '25–6. From early '27 to '31, on and off w. F. Henderson; dur. this period he pl. frequently w. C. Johnson at Small's Paradise. A stomach ailment hospitalized him in '30, and although he resumed pl. w. Henderson and worked w. Chick Webb spring-summer '31, the illness proved to be fatal. According to Benny Carter, who was his closest friend and associate in several bands, and other contemporaries who heard him extensively, Harrison, often called "the father of swing trombone," was the first truly great jazz trombonist and remains unsurpassed for warm feeling, tone, and style. Some of his most effective records were made with Carter's Chocolate Dandies group in '30. As a singer, he liked to imitate the late Bert Williams, one example being his vocal on Henderson's "Somebody Loves Me" '30. His playing infl. J. Teagarden, D. Wells, T. Dorsey and many others. CDs: w. Henderson (BB; Col.); Carter (B&B; Charly); C. Johnson (Hot 'n' Sweet); Webb (Hep; Dec.); Clarence Williams (EPM).

HARROW, NANCY, voc; b. NYC, 10/3/30. B.A. from Bennington Coll. Worked w. Tommy Dorsey band 1958, then clubs in NYC and Paris '61–4. Debut album on Cand. '60, feat. Buck Clayton, Dicky Wells, Kenny Burrell, Buddy Tate, Milt Hinton, and others. Rec. for Atl. '62, accomp. incl. Phil Woods, John Lewis, and Willie Dennis. Out of music '64–75; worked as ed. of literary magazine, *The American Journal*. Ret. to singing '75 at The Cookery, NYC.

Has since recorded frequently for the US and Japanese market and appeared at Michael's Pub and other NYC venues. European radio and TV from '86. A sensitive artist notable for her tasteful choice of material and unpretentiously appealing style. CDs: Gazell; Audio.; SN; Cand.

HART, ANTONIO, alto sax; b. Baltimore, MD, 9/30/68. Took up sax at age 7. Stud. classical sax for four yrs. at Baltimore Sch. for the Arts; att. Berklee Coll. of Mus. where he stud. w. Joe Viola, Andy McGhee, Billy Pierce. Pl. w. James Williams; Out of the Blue; sat in w. Art Blakey. Tour. in Eur. w. Roy Hargrove 1987; again w. Jazz Futures '91. Form. own gp., rec. for Novus '91. Stud. at Queens Coll. w. Jimmy Heath. Tour. w. Phil Woods, Vincent Herring in Alto Summit '97. Infl. by Sonny Stitt, Cannonball Adderley; later by C. Parker, Johnny Hodges, Earl Bostic, Kenny Garrett. CDs: Imp.; Novus; *Alto Summit* (Mile); w. Roy Hargrove (Novus); Cecil Brooks (Muse); Benny Green (BN).

HART, BILLY (WILLIAM WALTER), dms; b. Washington, DC, 11/29/40. Grandmother was concert pnst. Self-taught. Became interested in jazz after hearing Charlie Parker recs. given to him by Buck Hill. Turned prof. w. Hill, Shirley Horn, John Malachi. Rec. debut w. Buck Clarke 1960. Pl. w. Horn '61–4; Jimmy Smith '64; Wes Montgomery '64–8; Eddie Harris, Pharoah Sanders '68–9; Marian McPartland '69; Herbie Hancock '70–3; McCoy Tyner '73–4; Stan Getz off and on '74–80s. Also rec. w. Miles Davis, Jimmy Rowles, Niels H.Ø. Pedersen, Clark Terry, Lee Konitz, S. Horn '70s; Chico Freeman, James Newton '80s. Pl. w. Mingus Dynasty '80; The Great Friends w. S. Fortune, Billy Harper, Eddie Henderson, Stanley Cowell, Reggie Workman '82 incl. tour of Japan; Quest w. Dave Liebman, R. Beirach, Ron McClure fr. '82; Great Jazz Trio w. Hank Jones, Mads Vinding '88; Dizzy Gillespie Diamond Jubilee All-Star '92. Has tour. w. own gp. incl. J. Stubblefield, D. Kikoski, D. Fiuczynski fr. '88. Formed percussion gp. Coloquium III w. Freddie Waits, Horacee Arnold '92; they led perc. wkshps. at Drummers' Collective, NYC. Has given clinics from '83 incl. West. Mich. U. '92. A very precise player who extracts delicate colors from his cymbals but is equally adept in firing up ensembles from the straight ahead to more avant expressions. Favs: "Besides Max Roach, too many to name." Polls: *DB* Critics TDWR '74. Rec. LPs *Enhance* (A&M) '77; *Oshumare* '85 and *Rah* '88 (Gram.). CDs: Arab.; w. S. Getz (Col.; Conc.); M. Davis (Col.); Charles Lloyd (ECM); Chico Freeman (Ind. Nav.); G. Bartz; P. Bley; N.H.Ø. Pedersen; D. Gordon; D. Jordan; S. Horn; B. Hill

(Steep.); H. Galper (Steep.; Conc.); L. Coryell; P. Martino (Muse); N. Brignola; P. Leitch (Res.); D. Liebman (Story.); Mingus Big Band; L. Konitz; J. Knepper (SN); R. Moore; J. Coles (CC); T. Harrell (Cont.); Jimmy Smith (Verve).

HART, CLYDE, pno, arr; b. Baltimore, MD, 1910; d. NYC, 3/19/45. Professional debut w. Gene Coy in 1929; then pnst.-arr. w. Jap Allen '30–1; Blanche Calloway to '35; McKinney's Cotton Pickers '35. To NYC '36, led own quart. at the Brittwood in Harlem; arr. for Andy Kirk; pl. solo pno. in clubs. Join. Stuff Smith late '36–38; worked w. Lucky Millinder, Roy Eldridge, Lester Young, Frankie Newton before join. John Kirby late '42. Also worked w. Oscar Pettiford. Gigs w. Wilbur DeParis, Walter "Foots" Thomas, Tiny Grimes '44; own gp. on 52nd St. in autumn. Pl. w. Don Byas combo into early '45, before tuberculosis limited his performing apps. Wrote arrs. for Paul Baron's CBS orch. Although he did not live to translate the new bebop style to his right hand, Hart was an important transitional pnst. of whom Pettiford said: "He was the first to play the modern-style left hand. He told me as long as I was playing that much bass, he didn't need to play rhythm in the left hand, and he could just use it to establish chord changes." Comps: "Puddin' Head Serenade" for A. Kirk; "In the Bag" for L. Hampton; "Bu-Dee-Daht" w. Budd Johnson for C. Hawkins. CDs: w. L. Hampton (BB); Chu Berry (Comm.); C. Hawkins (Del.); B. Webster (Prog.); Byas; Young; C. Parker; Gillespie (Sav.).

HART, JOHN STEPHEN, gtr, el-bs; b. Ft. Belvoir, VA, 6/15/61. Mother pl. pno. Picked up gtr. at age 12. Stud. w. Dave Gould in Sarasota, Fla., 1975–7, then w. Randall Dollahan at U. of Miami '79–83, where he made transition fr. fusion to jazz. Freelanced in Sarasota fr. '76, pl. w. Ira Sullivan; Lou Donaldson; then pl. w. Duffy Jackson in Miami '80–1; Bernard Purdie '83; Jose Luis Rodriguez '83–4. Moved to NYC '84. Pl. w. Jack McDuff '86; own trio fr. '86; Lou Donaldson, Jim Pepper, Rick Margitza '88; Margitza, Mike Mainieri, Jimmy Smith '90; Terumasa Hino fr. '90; own qt. w. Chris Potter, Bill Moring, Andy Watson fr. '92. Favs: Wes Montgomery, Jim Hall, Grant Green. Fests: Eur., Japan fr. '90; w. Larry Goldings on QE2 '96. CDs: BN; w. T. Hino; Bob Belden (BN); J. McDuff (Muse).

HARTE, ROY, dms; b. NYC, 5/27/24. Cousin of Dave Pell. Began on dms. at age 10; stud. w. Dave Tough fr. age 13. While in hs, worked simultaneously w. Muggsy Spanier and Dizzy Gillespie. Later pl. w. Bobby Sherwood; Boyd Raeburn; Lucky Millinder; Vido Musso. Gigged in Cuba w. Billie Holiday, Clyde Hart. Worked as studio mus. in Calif., incl. rec. Disney soundtracks and pop recs. for Cap. '50s. President of Hollywood Drum City fr. 1950. With Harry Babasin '53–5; Dick Bock's PJ label shared office space w. them at Drum City. Perf. in LA w. Babasin '50s. Author of several drum instruction books. Favs: D. Tough, Buddy Rich. CDs: w. Babasin; B. Shank; Herbie Harper (Noct.).

HARTMAN, JOHNNY (JOHN MAURICE), voc; also pno; b. Chicago, IL, 7/31/23; d. NYC, 9/15/83. Began pl. pno. and singing at age 8; stud. at DuSable HS; scholarship to Chi. Musical Coll., concentrating on voice, 1939. Worked locally bef. entering mil. service, WWII. In '47 he won first prize in an amateur contest, a week's engagement w. Earl Hines's orch.; remained w. band until it broke up a few mos. later. Sang w. Dizzy Gillespie's orch. '47–9; Erroll Garner '49. Then developed a successful career as a soloist, perf. in clubs, on TV, tour. internationally. Dur. '60s he perf. and rec. w. John Coltrane. Tour. Japan w. Roland Hanna, George Mraz '81; also rec. w. them. Rich, smooth baritone in what was originally an Eckstine-derived style. His recs. of country and popular songs, "By the Time I Get To Phoenix," "Raindrops Keep Falling on My Head," also had wide appeal. Infl: Eckstine, Sinatra. Fests: London '59; Japan '63; Austral. '68; NJF-NY '75. TV: Sammy Davis; *Tonight Show*; *Today*; specials in Austral.; Eur. Recs.: w. E. Garner '49; as lead. for Beth. '55; Imp. '63; *Once in Every Life* (BH) '81. CDs: FS; Imp.; w. Coltrane (Imp.); Gillespie (BB).

HARTOG, JIM (JAMES P.), bari, sop saxes, comp, arr; b. San Mateo, CA, 3/10/50. Grandmother, uncles were prof. mus. Stud. pno. 1956–67, sax fr. '72. Received B.A. in history fr. Grinnell Coll. '71, B. Mus. fr. New Engl. Cons. '80. Pl. w. Baird Hersey '76; Jaki Byard '71–81; Tom Varner '79–83; Karl Berger '82; Wayne Horvitz–Bobby Previte '87; 29th Street Sax. Qt. fr. '83; also freelance w. Tito Puente; Bob Belden; Tom Pierson; Candido, etc. Profess. of Jazz Saxophone at Sweelinck Cons., Amsterdam '90–2. Favs: Pepper Adams, Harry Carney, Serge Chaloff. Fests: Eur. fr. '83 w. Sax Qt. TV: Eur. TV w. Sax Qt. CDs: Planet X; NewNote; w. 29th St. Sax Qt. (Ant.); w. Bobby Watson (NewNote).

HASHIM, MICHAEL J., alto, sop saxes, comp; b. Geneva, NY, 4/9/56. Started band w. Chris Flory, Phil Flanigan 1972; own trio at Hobart Coll. '73–4. Att. Creative Mus. Wkshp. w. Dave Holland, Milford Graves, Leroy Jenkins, Lee Konitz, summer '74; lessons w. Jimmy Lyons, Andy McGhee, Phil Woods, Albert Regni in NYC '74–83; also infl. by Jimmy Rowles, a close friend. Pl. w. C. Flory '75–6; Wide-

spread Jazz Orch. '76–92; Muddy Waters '76; Jo Jones '77; Brooks Kerr–Sonny Greer '78; August Darnell '78; own qt. fr. '79; Gatemouth Brown '86; Judy Carmichael fr. '87 incl. gigs at the Kickerbocker, NYC, fr. '90; Ink Spots '88–91; annual trips as soloist to Engl. fr. '89; Hashim–Mike LeDonne gp. fr. '89; Sammy Price–Eddie Barefield '90. In '92, as part of a Carmichael tour, sponsored by the USIS, he was a member of the first official jazz gp. to play in China since '49. Co-composed the score for PBS drama *Rocket to the Moon* '87; comp. and perf. a full-length score for choreographer Ann Cooper Albright, Oberlin Coll. '91. Favs: B. Carter, C. Parker, J. Hodges. Fests: Eur. incl. Cork w. Benny Bailey '93; Caribbean w. Widespread Orch. Film: soundtrack for *I'm Not Rappaport* '97. CDs: Stash; 33; Hep; w. Widespread Orch. (Stash); Carmichael (C&D).

HASLANGER, (JAMES) ELIAS, tnr, alto, sop, bari saxes, cl, fl, pno; b. Austin, TX, 7/9/69. First stud. on alto sax w. La Falco "Corky" Robinson at Austin HS; then w. Harvey Pittel at U. of Texas, where he was a member of the Jazz Orch., Jazz Combos, Wind Ens., Symph. Orch., Sax Choir, and Sax Qt. 1987–92. Pl. w. U. Tex. Wind Ens., Engl. '91; Jazz Orch., Scot. '92. Gigged prof. in Austin fr. '91 w. violist Will Taylor; James Polk, former mus. dir. for Ray Charles; and tpt. Martin Banks. Moved to NYC in fall '92 to attend Manh. Sch. of Mus., stud. w. Dick Oatts. In spring '93 ret. to Austin and began freelancing w. many gps. and start. own qt. Fr. '95 worked and rec. w. swing band, the Lucky Strikes. Began stud. for master's degree at Southwest Texas St. U., San Marcos, Tex., fall '95. Pl. in Jazz Ens., backing visiting players such as Clark Terry, Frank Foster, and Al Grey; trav. to North Sea, Montreux fests, '95, '98. Received M. Mus. in composition '98. Won two *DB* student awards: jazz combo '96; soloist '97. Has taught priv. and as theory teach. asst. at Southwest Tex. Favs: Getz, Coltrane, C. Parker. CDs: Heart; w. Taylor (Amazing).

HASSELGARD, STAN (AKE), cl; b. Bollnas, Sweden, 10/4/22; d. near Decatur, IL, 11/23/48. Raised in Uppsala, pl. w. local amateur gp., Royal Swingers, early 1940s. Worked prof. w. Arthur Osterwall '44–5; Simon Brehm '46–7; rec. in Sweden w. Brehm and Bob Laine; also w. Tyree Glenn. Master's degree fr. Uppsala U. '47. Came to NYC in summer '47 to study art history at Columbia U. Apps. in LA w. Johnny White; C. Basie's rhythm section at Just Jazz concert; International All-Stars w. Wardell Gray, Dodo Marmarosa. During that yr., he rec. as lead. for Cap., w. B. Kessel, R. Norvo. Late '47 join. B. Goodman sxt. until it disbanded summer '48, being the only clst. that Goodman ever allowed to be featured w. him. Originally infl. by Goodman, he gravitated toward bebop after his arrival in the US and would have undoubtedly been one of the important clst. had he survived his 20s. In Oct. '48 led qnt. at Three Deuces in NYC, incl. Max Roach, Chuck Wayne, Barbara Carroll. Died in a car accident, a few hours after a V-Disc rec. session as lead. Recs. on Swed. labels; Cap. '47; w. Gray, Spot. '47–8. CDs: Drag.; Phon.; six tracks in *Classic Capitol Jazz Sessions* (Mos.).

HAUGHTON, CHAUNCEY, cl, sax, pno; b. Chestertown, MD, 2/26/09; d. Tarrytown, NY, 7/1/89. Began on pno. at age 8, then took up cl. and sax in coll. band. Pl. w. local gps., incl. Elmer Calloway, bro. of Cab, late 1920s-early '30s. Moved to NYC w. Gene Kennedy Orch. '32. Pl. w. Blanche Calloway '32–5; Claude Hopkins, Noble Sissle, Fletcher Henderson, Chick Webb mid '30s; Cab Calloway '37–40; Benny Carter '40; Ella Fitzgerald '40–2; Duke Ellington '42–3. In army '43–5. Tour. Eur. w. Don Redman '46, then pl. briefly in Scand. '47. Back w. Calloway in late '40s, '58. CDs: w. Calloway (Class.); Ellington (BB; Prest.); Carter (BB); Fitzgerald (Dec.).

HAVENS, BOB (ROBERT LEROY), tbn, vib; b. Quincy, IL, 5/03/30. Studied vln. at age 6, then tbn. and pno. at 7. First prof. job w. Ralph Flanagan 1955; w. George Girard, Al Hirt in late '50s. Feat. soloist on Lawrence Welk TV show '60–82; frequent apps. at trad. jazz clubs. Pl. and tour. w. bbs of Harry James '83 and '88; Benny Goodman Tribute Band, led by Peanuts Hucko '87–90; Bob Crosby '80–9; and Tex Beneke '91. Small gp. perf. in the '80s w. Ray Linn's Chicago Stompers '82–3; Heinie Beau Sxt. '82–4; Keith Smith, in Engl. '84; Great Pacific Jazz Band '84–91; World's Greatest Jazz Band '85. Made symph. debut as soloist w. the Florida Symphonic Pops in Boca Raton '90. Served as a sheriff of LA County and perf. w. a gp. called the Los Angeles County Sheriff's Rhythm Posse Band. Recs. w. Pee Wee Irwin; Ray Linn; Dick Cary; Heinie Beau; WGJB; and Jackie Coon. CDs: GHB; Honey; w. Great Pacific Jazz Band (Sacramento Stomp); New Orleans Classic Jazz Orch. (Stomp Off); Ed Polcer; Pete Fountain (Jazz.).

HAVILAND, MATT (MATTHEW RYDER), tbn, comp, arr; b. Des Moines, IA, 6/17/61. Family moved to N.J. soon after birth. Stud. w. Tony Salvatori at summer jazz wkshp. in Ramapo 1978–80; then w. Phil Wilson, Herb Pomeroy, Ken Pullig at Berklee Coll. of Mus. '79–83; also w. Slide Hampton and Barry Harris in NYC '83–4. Pl. w. Charli Persip since '84; Slide Hampton's World of Tbns. '86–7; Illinois Jacquet bb '87–90; own qnt. w. Vincent Herring, feat.

orig. comps. since '88. In '89 Haviland was accepted into the BMI Jazz Comp. Wkshp. and received an NEA grant to comp. an extended work for bb. His arrs. have been rec. by the Harper Bros. and the Charli Persip Superband. Favs: Teagarden, J.J. Johnson, Rosolino; arrs: Ellington, G. Evans, Mingus. Fests: Eur. and Caribbean since '87. TV: CBS *Sunday Morning* w. Jacquet. CDs: w. Persip (SN); Bill Warfield (Inter.).

HAWES, HAMPTON, pno; b. Los Angeles, CA, 11/13/28; d. Los Angeles, 5/22/77. Father a clergyman; grew up listening to spirituals; self-taught. Prof. debut while at LA Polytechnic HS. Worked w. Big Jay McNeely 1944; pl. w. Dexter Gordon, Wardell Gray, Sonny Criss in '40s; Howard McGhee, incl. perfs. w. Charlie Parker '50–1; Shorty Rogers and Howard Rumsey combos '51–2. In army '52–4; then led own trio feat. Red Mitchell, tour. clubs throughout US. In '58 he was arrested for possessing narcotics and went to prison; he was pardoned by Pres. John F. Kennedy in '63 and resumed mus. career w. an app. on Steve Allen's TV show. Pl. in Jon Hendricks' concert, *Evolution of the Blues,* '64; in LA clubs w. Harold Land, Jackie McLean. In '65 reunited w. Mitchell for long club engagement at Donte's in LA; co-led gp. w. Jimmy Garrison '66. Fr. Sept. '67 to June '69 tour. the world. Ret. to LA, pl. in duo w. Leroy Vinnegar. Led trio in London, Paris, Copenhagen '71. To '74 active in LA clubs; also Eur. fests. incl. Montreux, Nice. In '74 duo w. bs. Carol Kaye; Mario Suraci '75. Dur. mid '70s he also pl. concerts and rec. w. Joan Baez '74. Rec. duo album w. Charlie Haden '76. Originally inspired by C. Parker and Bud Powell, he was admired for his crisp, well-thought-out lines and rhythmic emphasis. In '70s, his style underwent a radical change as he experimented w. and perf. mainly on electronic keyboards, utilizing modal concepts and the extended use of vamps, but ret. to acoustic pno. near the end of his career. Polls: *DB* Critics, *Met.* New Star '56. Book: autobiography *Raise Up Off Me: A Portrait of Hampton Hawes* w. D. Asher (Coward, McCann & Geoghegan) '74, won Deems Taylor Award. LP: *The Challenge,* solo pno. rec. for Japanese Vict. '68. CDs: Cont.; FS; BL; Hampton Hawes–Freddie Redd (Prest.); w. Gray (Prest.); Rogers (BB; Cap.); Criss (Prest.; FS; DIW); Gordon (Sav.); A. Farmer; B. Kessel; S. Rollins; Lighthouse All-Stars (Cont.); C. Haden (Verve); A. Pepper (Sav.; Cont.); C. Parker (Mos.).

HAWKINS, COLEMAN RANDOLPH ("HAWK"; "BEAN"), tnr sax, lead; b. St. Joseph, MO, 11/21/04; d. NYC, 5/19/69. First studies were on piano with his moth. from age 5. He then switched to cello at 7; tenor sax at age 9. His first prof. gigs were school dances ca. 1916. Attended hs in Chi., then studied harmony, comp. at Washburn Coll., Topeka, Kansas. Pl. w. orch. at 12th St. Theater, KC '21, then tour. w. Mamie Smith's Jazz Hounds '22–3. Freelanced w. Wilbur Sweatman, others in NYC, then joined Fletcher Henderson '23. While with Henderson, Hawkins also pl. w. Ginger Jones–Charlie Gaines at Garden Of Joy and Cecil Smith–Lou Hooper at Renaissance Casino. He rose to stardom w. Henderson and in '34 left the band to tour Engl. as a single. Pl. w. Jack Hylton in Engl. '34; pl. and rec. w. Dutch gp., The Ramblers, in Laren, Netherlands, '35, '37; also rec. w. Eur. gp. in Zurich '36; and w. own gps., incl. Benny Carter, Stephane Grappelli, Django Reinhardt in Paris '37. Toured Engl., sponsored by Selmer Instrument Co. '39 bef. making an eagerly anticipated ret. to NYC in July '39. He opened at Kelly's Stable w. a 9-piece gp. on Oct. 5, and six days later rec. his famous solo on "Body and Soul," which became a hit and forever established him as a major jazz name. In '40 he formed an orch., rec. and pl. at Golden Gate Ballroom, Savoy Ballroom, Apollo Theater. Led small gps. mainly in Chi. and Midwest '41–3. Early in '44 he led what is considered to be the first bop rec. date for the Apollo label w. a gp. that incl. Dizzy Gillespie. Thelonious Monk became his pnst. later that yr., and he cont. to employ younger mus. in his gps., incl. Miles Davis, Fats Navarro, J.J. Johnson, Milt Jackson, late '40s-50s. The sxts. he took to Chi. and Calif. in '44–5 incl. Howard McGhee; Sir Charles Thompson; Denzil Best; and Oscar Pettiford. Back in NYC, late '45, he led a qt., often feat. Hank Jones, on 52nd Street. He joined JATP, which took him to Calif. again in April '46. Pl. off and on w. own gps. and JATP '46–51. He rec. an unaccomp. improv., "Picasso," for Norman Granz's *Jazz Scene* project in '48. Toured Eur. w. own gps. '48–50, '54. App. in *Seven Ages of Jazz* concerts '58–9. Pl. w. Roy Eldridge at fests. from late '50s. Rec. w. Duke Ellington '62. In the '60s his gp. comprised Tommy Flanagan and/or Barry Harris, Major Holley, Eddie Locke. He played a set w. Sonny Rollins at the NJF in '63 and did a studio rec. w. him later that year. Hawkins' health began to fail in the mid '60s, and in '67 he collapsed onstage in Toronto. Following his last JATP tour in '67, he then toured Eur. w. Oscar Peterson. A tour of Den. scheduled for early '68 was cancelled due to ill health. Hawkins' last performance took place on April 20, 1968, at the North Park Hotel in Chi.

Hawkins was the first important jazz tenor saxophone soloist and the most infl. figure in the evolution of the instrument. He was the first jazz soloist to apply his creativity, with artistic and commercial success, to the refashioning of a ballad. His huge sound was an inspiration for swing and bop players alike incl. Illinois Jacquet; Arnett Cobb; Lucky Thompson; Dexter Gordon; and Sonny Rollins. An early admirer of Charlie Parker and Dizzy Gillespie, he showed a remarkable ability to stay abreast of new developments in jazz over the course of his career. Fr. '45 he surrounded himself w. innovative younger musicians. As a result, his playing continued to evolve until the final years of his life.

Polls: *DB* '39; *DB* critics '59; *Esq.* Gold Awd. '44–7; *Met.* '45–7. Film: *The Crimson Canary* '45. Video: *After Hours*, Hawkins–Roy Eldridge (Rhap.); *Tenor Legends*, Hawkins; Dexter Gordon (Shan.). TV: *Tonight Show* '55; *Sound of Jazz* '57; acted in episode of *Route 66*; many other apps. CDs: RCA, incl. *Sonny Meets Hawk*; BB; Cap.; Prest.; Riv.; Verve, incl. *The Jazz Scene*; Imp.; Pab.; Sav.; Charly (ASV); w. D. Ellington (Imp.); F. Henderson (BB; Col.); McKinney's Cotton Pickers; Red Allen; L. Hampton (BB); Benny Carter (B&B); Pee Wee Russell; Roach; Dolphy; A. Lincoln (Cand.); JATP; C. Parker (Verve); B. Powell (BL); Monk (Riv.); Reinhardt (Aff.; Ark.); Holiday; Fitzgerald (Verve).

HAWKINS, ERSKINE RAMSAY, tpt, lead; b. Birmingham, AL, 7/26/14; d. Willingboro, NJ, 11/11/93. Began on dms. at age 7, then pl. tbn. bef. sw. to tpt. at age 13. Led 'Bama State Collegians at Alabama State Teachers Coll. 1934. Brought band to NYC '34. Fr. '38 the gp. was known as the Erskine Hawkins Orch. Came to prominence '39–41 w. apps. at Savoy ballroom and hit recs. for BB incl. "Tuxedo Junction" '39; "After Hours" '40; "Tippin' In" '45. Orig. infl. by L. Armstrong, he took care of his band's high-note work and was billed as "The 20th Century Gabriel." Sidemen incl. Paul and Dud Bascomb; Julian Dash; Haywood Henry; Avery Parrish. Around '53 Hawkins reduced the size of his working gp., pl. occ. reunion gigs w. the big band. Led qt. at the Embers, NYC, in early '60s and at Catskill Mts. resorts '60s-70s. Perf. at NY Jazz Repertory Co. concert paying tribute to Savoy ballroom '74; app. at Nice JF '79. He cont. to perf. until the mid '80s. CDs: BB; Class.

HAWKINS, MARSHALL, bs, pno, dms, org; b. Washington, DC, 7/14/39. A self-taught mus., he began his prof. career in 1965, becoming the youngest bs. pl. to work w. Shirley Horn. He credits her w. being his major infl. in mus. at that point. Pl w. Miles Davis; Roberta Flack; Richie Cole; and has led the Marshall Hawkins Qnt. from '71. Worked in Ghana, Japan, Finland, Den., Swed., France, Spain, Engl., Can., and Mexico. In '74, he app. on the Emmy award-winning TV show *Catch a Rising Star*. Teaching in the jazz stud. dept. at the Idyllwild Sch. of Mus.

and the Arts, Calif. fr. '85. Favs: Monk, Horn, Coltrane, M. Davis, A. Jamal. CDs: w. Horn (Imp.); Lloyd McNeil (Asha); R. Cole (Muse).

HAYES, CLANCY (CLARENCE LEONARD), bjo, voc; b. Caney, KS, 11/14/08; d. San Francisco, CA, 3/13/72. Musical family; seventh son of a seventh son. Start. on dms. as a child; then picked up gtr., later sw. to bjo. Led own band, The Harmony Aces, as a teenager. Pl. w. brother's band in Oakland, Calif. in 1923; then tour. Midwest w. a vaudeville show. Settled in SF in '26; join. NBC staff '28. Built large following in SF and LA, pl. and singing w. Sid Lippman; Raymond Paige; many others. In '38 join. Lu Watters and was a key figure in old-time jazz revival which Watters' Yerba Buena band helped inspire; remained w. Watters through '40s; also pl. w. Bunk Johnson in SF '44. Through '50s worked w. Bob Scobey. In '60s worked as soloist; w. Fire House Five Plus Two; Turk Murphy. Orig. member of World's Greatest Jazz Band, form. in '68, and took part in its first rec. By then, his health was failing due to cancer. Sang in a lively, vaudeville-derived style. Polls: *DB* Critics, New Star singer '54. Comp: *Huggin' and a Chalkin'*, a popular hit '53. Recs. as lead. Audio Fidelity; ABC-Paramount; w. Watters (Verve). CDs: Del.; GTJ; w. Scobey (BB; GTJ); Johnson; Watters (GTJ).

HAYES, EDGAR JUNIUS, pno, arr; b. Lexington, KY, 5/23/04; d. Riverside, CA, 6/28/79. Studied at Fisk U. and Wilberforce U. (B.A. 1922). Prof. debut w. Fess Williams '19; tour. South w. him '22. Led own gps. in Ohio, upstate N.Y. '24–6; pl. long engagement w. his Symphonic Harmonists at the Alhambra, NYC '27–30. Pnst. and principal arr. w. Mills Blue Rhythm Band '31–6, under Baron Lee, L. Millinder. Led own excellent orch. '37–41, tour. Eur., Scand. '38; sidemen incl. Joe Garland, Kenny Clarke. Band became very prominent due to its hit rec. of Hayes's arr. of "Star Dust," rec. Dec. '38. Hayes moved to Riverside, Calif., in '42; pl. solo at Somerset House for twelve yrs. From '54 to 60 pl. solo at Jimmie Diamond's Lounge, San Bernardino; in '60s pl. in Tustin and Newport Beach. Member of LA Pianist Club, which had monthly jam sess., bi-annual concerts. Cont. to pl. clubs into '70s. Rec. w. own orch. (Dec.); as soloist (Dec.), ca. '60. CDs: Class.; w. Mills Blue Rhythm Band (Hep); Red Allen (Class.).

HAYES, LOUIS SEDELL, dms; b. Detroit, MI, 5/31/37. Father was amateur dm. and pno.; cousin Clarence Stamps, dmr.; bro. Gerald is prof. saxist. Another cousin is Prince. Stud. w. fath., then w. Stamps 1948–51; at Wurlitzer Sch. of Mus. '51–2. Led own gp. in local club '52. Pl. w. Yusef Lateef '56,

then moved to NYC. Pl. w. Horace Silver '56–9; Cannonball Adderley '59–65; Oscar Peterson '65–7. Led own gps. w. sidemen incl. Freddie Hubbard, Joe Henderson, James Spaulding, Kenny Barron '67–70. Pl. w. Hubbard '70–1; Peterson '72. Led own sxt.'72–5, then co-led gps. w. Junior Cook '75–6, Woody Shaw '76–7. The Hayes-Shaw gp. backed Dexter Gordon on his ret. to NYC in '76. Cont. to lead his hard-bop qnt. since '77; sidemen have incl. Gary Bartz; Charles Tolliver; Charles McPherson; Curtis Fuller; in '90s, Riley Mullins, Abraham Burton, David Hazeltine, Santi Debriano. Pl. w. McCoy Tyner fr. '80s. Hayes has rec. extens. as a freelance w. C. Jordan; H. Land; Frank Morgan; F. Strozier; Lucky Thompson; S. Stitt; C. Walton; T. Gibbs; many others. Favs: Jo Jones, P.J. Jones, Roach, Tony Williams, Blakey, Rich, K. Clarke. Polls: *DB* New Star '61. Fests: all major fr. '56. TV: PBS w. Adderley. CDs: TCB: Steep.; Timel.; Cand.; Sharp Nine; Louis Hayes–Woody Shaw, TCB; w. C. Adderley (Riv.; Cap.; Mile.); N. Adderley; Sam Jones; Barry Harris; V. Feldman (Riv.); M. Tyner (Mile.; Den.; Timel.); Coltrane; Fuller; P. Woods (Prest.); Peterson (Pab.; MPS); Hubbard (Imp.); D. Gordon (Col.); Silver; S. Clark; G. Green (BN); J. McLean; K. Burrell (NJ); P. Newborn (Cont.); Lateef (Sav.); J.J. Johnson (Col.); W. Montgomery (PJ; Mile.; Riv.); J. Henderson (BN; Mile.); D. Hazeltine (Sharp Nine).

HAYES, TUBBY (EDWARD BRIAN), tnr sax, vib, fl, alto, bari saxes, comp/arr, lead; b. London, England, 1/30/35; d. London, 6/8/73. Father pl. vln. on BBC. Start. stud. vln. at age 8; sw. to tnr. sax at 12; began pl. prof. at 15. Join. Kenny Baker 1951; then pl. w. Bert Ambrose; Vic Lewis; Jack Parnell. Led own octet '55–6. Took up vib. '56, after encouragement from Victor Feldman. In April '57 form. Jazz Couriers w. Ronnie Scott, remaining together to summer '59. Tour. Germ. w. Kurt Edelhagen '59. Led various gps. from '59; form. bb, app. on own TV series '61–2, '63. Pl. w. Ellington Orch. at London's Royal Fest. Hall '64. Made first of many US apps. at the Half Note, NYC '61; others in '62, '64, incl. Jazz Workshop, Boston; Shelly's Manne Hole '65. Many int'l tours w. own gp. incl. Brussels '62; Oslo '63; Vienna '64, '65; Berlin '65. Also app. frequently w. symph. orchs. Fr. '69 to '71, was almost inactive due to illness. Died while undergoing heart operation. A superior, virtuosic soloist, inspired by Parker, Rollins, Getz, Sims, Coltrane. He pl. w. a great vitality and fluency, capable of tender balladry and hard, flat-out swing. Fests: Wash., D.C., Antibes '62; Lugano '63. Films: *All Night Long* '61; *The Beauty Jungle* '64; *Dr. Terror's House of Horrors* '65. Recs. as lead. on Engl. labels incl. Carlton, Fontana, Imp.;

w. Dizzy Reece (BN; Sav); Jimmy Deuchar (Cont.). CDs: Col.; Mastermix; Harlequin; w. V. Feldman (Cont.); R.R. Kirk (Merc.).

HAYMER, HERBIE (HERBERT), tnr sax; b. Jersey City, NJ, 7/24/15; d. Santa Monica, CA, 4/11/49. Started on alto sax at 15. Pl. w. local gps. in early 1930s. Moved to NYC, switched to tnr. sax while work. w Carl Sears–Johnny Watson orch.; briefly w. Rudy Vallee, C. Barnet. Best known as feat. soloist w. Red Norvo '35–7. Then pl. w. J. Dorsey '37–41; W. Herman '41–2; Kay Kyser '42; B. Goodman, Dave Hudkins '43. Army service for a short period '44. Worked w. Red Nichols; then settled in Calif., did studio work, freelanced; w. Goodman again '47. Died in an automobile accident driving home from a Frank Sinatra recording session. Made best recs. w. own qnt. for Sunset '45, incl. C. Shavers; Nat Cole; B. Rich; John Simmons. Reissued under Cole's name. Recs. w. Norvo (Dec.; Bruns.); w. Dorsey (Dec.) CDs: w. Cole (BL; Cap.); J. Dorsey; Herman (Dec.).

HAYMES, JOE, pno, arr, lead; b. Marshfield, MO, 1908. Self-taught. Worked as circus trapeze artist as teenager. Staff arr. for Ted Weems, then form. own band and moved to NYC ca. 1930. In residence at Roseland and Empire ballrooms; sidemen incl. Pee Wee Erwin, Bud Freeman. Buddy Rogers took over Haymes's band in '34; Haymes organized a new band which became the nucleus of the first Tommy Dorsey Orch. '35. Cont. to lead his own gps. in the late '30s, then worked as a studio mus. in LA in the '40s. He later ret. to NYC and became a staff mus. for CBS.

HAYNES, CYRIL N., pno; b. Panama, Canal Zone, 5/8/18. Played w. Savoy Sultans 1937–43. Long stint at Apollo Theatre w. Reuben Phillips Band, followed by extensive tour w. Harlem Globetrotters. In '80s worked mainly as solo pianist at NYC clubs. Rec. w. own gps. for Comet; B&W; w. Billy Hicks (Variety) '37; Savoy Sultans (Dec.) '37; Bigard (B&W) '44. CD: w. Bigard in *Greenwich Village Jazz* (Pick.); Al Cooper's Savoy Sultans; Edmond Hall (Class.); Slim Gaillard (Verve).

HAYNES, FRANK, tnr sax; b. San Francisco, CA, 1931; d. NYC, 11/30/65. Moved to NYC 1960. Pl. w. Randy Weston, Walter Bishop, and others at NYC clubs. Haynes, who never attained prominence, was a driving tenor player whose career was cut short by cancer. LPs: w. Dave Bailey (Epic; Jazzline). CDs: w. K. Dorham; Grant Green (BL); Les McCann (PJ).

HAYNES, GRAHAM BRENTLEY, crnt, flg; b. Brooklyn, NY, 9/16/60. Father is Roy Haynes.

Learned tpt. in junior hs, then stud. priv. w. Dave Burns 1977–80. Theory, harm., classical mus. hist., Queens Coll. '79–81; pl. gospel mus. in local Pentacostal church. Went to his fath.'s gigs, jazz concerts w. parents. First prof. jazz job w. Jaki Byard '78. Pl. w. local funk bands in Queens. Worked w. Byard's Apollo Stompers '78–83; Michael Carvin '81–2; Steve Coleman '79–88, incl. Five Elements and M-Base Collective. Rec. debut w. Coleman on *Motherland Pulse* (JMT) '85. Form. own band No Image '87; also worked sporadically w. many bands incl. David Murray; Hamiet Bluiett; Cassandra Wilson; Abbey Lincoln; Ralph Peterson; Butch Morris; George Russell in NYC, Eur., Japan. Moved to Paris '91, becoming interested in music of Salif Keita; Toure Kunda; Baaba Maal; Cheb Khaled; in '92 rec. "Nocturne Parisian" for Muse, reflecting Afro-Arabian underground. Pl. regularly w. Doudou Ndiaye Rose Jr. Ret. to US '93. Rec. w. own gp. for Verve. App. w. Roy Haynes gp. at Carnegie Hall '96. Favs: M. Davis, Woody Shaw, Fats Navarro. CDs: Verve; Muse; w. Ed Blackwell (Enja); Cassandra Wilson (JMT); Rodney Kendrick (Verve).

HAYNES, (AKILI) JAMAL MSHAURI, tbn, dms, pno, tpt, bari horn, tba, voc; b. Brooklyn, NY, 7/12/72. Mother is gospel singer and pnst.; fath. pl. cga., fl., tpt. Began on pno., dms. Stud. at Music and Art HS; then at the New Sch. Sang and pl. w. Jon Hendricks and New Music Singers 1990; Bill Cosby's Beacons in Jazz Orch. '90–1; Wynton Marsalis, Honi Coles–Milt Hinton at Lincoln Center '91; Art Ens. of Chi.–Soweto, Lester Bowie's Brass Fantasy '91; Charli Persip Superband, Illinois Jacquet bb fr. '91; own qt. fr. '92. Haynes taught basic music under Donald Byrd at the Newark Boys and Girls Club '91. Favs: J.J. Johnson, M. Davis, Coltrane, Ellington. Fests: Eur. w. L. Bowie; I. Jacquet fr. '91. CDs: w. Antonio Hart (Novus); Stephen Scott (Verve).

HAYNES, PHIL (PHILLIP ALAN), dms, perc, comp; b. Hillsboro, OR, 6/15/61. Grandfather pl. sax w. Ted Weems, Paul Whiteman 1915–25. Stud. w. symph. Percussionist '75–79; B. Mus. cum laude Coe Coll., Iowa. To NYC '83; rec. debut w. his qt., Continuum, on Owl Records. Later efforts, "4 Horn Lore" and "4 Horns & What?," feat. his unique qnt. of two brass, two saxes and dms. His comps. have been rec. by Paul Smoker; Joint Venture; et al. Sideman w. Anthony Braxton; Frank Lacy; Dave Liebman; Ron McClure; etc. CDs: Open Minds; w. Ellery Eskelin (Open Minds); Smoker (SA; Enja); Tom Varner (NW).

HAYNES, ROY OWEN, dms, lead; b. Roxbury, MA, 3/13/25. Father pl. org. in church in West Indies. Pl. in Boston w. Sabby Lewis, Frankie Newton, Pete Brown ca. 1944; Luis Russell '45–7; Lester Young '47–9; Kai Winding, Miles Davis, Bud Powell '49; Charlie Parker '49–52; Stan Getz off and on fr. '50; Sarah Vaughan '53–8. Freelanced w. Phineas Newborn; M. Davis; Lee Konitz; then pl. at Five Spot w. Thelonious Monk, own gp. '58. Pl. w. L,H&R, G. Shearing, Lennie Tristano, Kenny Burrell '59. Led own qt. '60–5. Subbed for Elvin Jones w. John Coltrane '61–5. Pl. w. Getz, Gary Burton late '60s. Led own jazz-rock gp. Hip Ensemble fr. '69; sidemen incl. Geo. Adams, Hannibal Peterson. Perf. in Joe Segal's Charlie Parker Month concerts in Chi. '70s, app. w. Billy Taylor at Town Hall, NYC '75. Rec. in late '70s w. Nick Brignola; G. Burton; Hank Jones; Art Pepper; Ted Curson; Joe Albany; Horace Tapscott. Pl. w. Dizzy Gillespie at jazz fests '79, then join. Chick Corea's gp. Trio Music '81. Led own qt. fr. mid '80s. Tour. and rec. w. Corea's Bud Powell tribute '96. Recognized not only for his taste and swing, but the ability to play stimulating, exhortatory fills behind soloists and the invention of his breaks from "fours" to "sixteens." Favs: Blakey, Roach, K. Clarke, P.J. Jones. Polls: *DB* New Star '62. Awards: honorary doctorate fr. Berklee '92; Danish Jazzpar prize '94. TV: Merv Griffin, *Soul*, NET, *Positively Black*. Fests: all major. CDs: NJ; Evid.; Drey.; Freelance; Story.; w. L. Young; M. Jackson (Sav.); C. Parker (Verve; BN; Up.); T. Monk (Riv.); Wardell Gray; M. Davis (Prest.); Stan Getz (Prest.; Roul.; BB; Mos.); B. Powell; F. Navarro; J. McLean; J. Henderson; M. Petrucciani (BN); Eric Dolphy (NJ); Oliver Nelson (NJ; Imp.); Coltrane (Imp.); Rollins (Riv.); Corea (BN; Verve); Vaughan (Em.); Brubeck (Atl.).

HAYS, KEVIN, pno, comp; b. NYC, 5/1/68. Raised in Greenwich, Conn. Fath. pl. pno. Began stud. pno. at age 8 after "picking things up by ear." Summer course at Interlochen, Mich., in 1982; the same yr. bec. interested in jazz through fath.'s rec. collection. Began gigging in Conn. dur. hs. In mid '80s pl. his first NYC job at West Boondock. Around '86 stud. harm. and learned tunes w. Jack Reilly. Stud. classical repertoire and technique w. Eleanor Hancock. While still in hs worked at Mikell's w. dmr. Justin Page; pl. a few solo gigs at the Knickerbocker; and sat in at late hour sess. Pl. w. Nick Brignola in Lake George, N.Y., and at a fest. in Fla. 86. Att. Manh. Sch. of Mus. briefly, then pl. w. Benny Golson, James Moody. Pl. in Spain for three mos. '87–8. Worked w. Harper Bros., incl. Japanese tour '90; then pl. w. Joe Henderson; Joshua Redman; Donald Harrison; Roy Haynes; George Coleman; Joe Chambers; Bob Belden; Eddie

Henderson. Cont. w. Golson but join. Sonny Rollins spring '95. Early infls: O. Peterson, Bill Evans, W. Kelly, P. Newborn, B. Powell. Favs: mus. of M. Davis, Hancock, Shorter, Joe Henderson, Andrew Hill. Comps: "El Matador"; "Emperor Leon"; "Seventh Sense"; "Go Round." CDs: BN; Steep.; JC; w. Belden (BN); Redman (WB); Harper Bros. (Verve); V. Herring (Land.); Golson (Drey.); Rollins (Mile.).

HAYTON, LENNIE (LEONARD GEORGE), pno, arr, comp, lead; b. NYC, 2/13/08; d. Palm Springs, CA, 4/24/71. Studied pno. priv. in NYC. Pl. w. Little Ramblers 1926; Cass Hagen '27; bands; second pno. w. P. Whiteman '28–30. Became prominent in jazz circles through many rec. sess., as pl. and arr., w. F. Trumbauer; B. Beiderbecke; R. Nichols; Joe Venuti. In early '30s was lead. and arr. for Bing Crosby radio show; used such sidemen as Benny Goodman; Artie Shaw; Dorsey bros. Tour. w. own dance band '37–40. Worked as arr., then mus. dir. at MGM Studios in Hollywood '40–53. Married singer Lena Horne in '47; often acted as her mus. dir. in '50s, '60s. Recs. on Roul. CDs: w. Beiderbecke (Col.); J. Teagarden (ASV); Venuti (JSP); Lena Horne; Red Nichols–Miff Mole in *The Jazz Age: New York in the Twenties* (BB).

HAYWOOD, CEDRIC, pno; b. Houston, TX, ca. 1914; d. Houston, 9/9/69. Went to Phyliss Wheatley HS w. Arnett Cobb. He and Cobb join. Chester Boone's band in 1934; pl. w. Milton Larkin '35–40; L. Hampton '41; briefly w. S. Bechet in '42. Moved to SF in '43, pl. w. local gps. After WWII army service, worked w. various combos under R&B singer Saunders King; pl. w. I. Jacquet '48–51. Ret. to SF; w. Cal Tjader qnt. '52; Gerald Wilson '53; active as freelancer before join. Kid Ory's band at the Tin Angel '55–9; tour. Eur. twice w. Ory in '50s. Worked w. Brew Moore in SF in early '60s. Moved back to Houston in '63. From '64 led own bb at Club Ebony until he died following a stroke. CDs: w. Jacquet (BB; Mos.); Ory (GTJ).

HAZEL, MONK (ARTHUR), dms, crnt, mello; b. Harvey, LA, 8/15/03; d. New Orleans, LA, 3/5/68. Father was a dmr. Raised in Gretna and NO. First pl. dms., then given a crnt. by Emmett Hardy, w. whom he pl. in 1920; worked mainly as dmr. but doubled on both instruments throughout career. Early assoc. of Abbie Brunies, pl. w. his Halfway House Dance Orch. '24–5; rec. w. Tony Parenti '25. Fr. late '20s to early '30s, led own Bienville Roof Orch.; rec. sess. for Bruns. '28. Went to NYC, pl. w. Johnny Hyman, Jack Pettis, own band '29–31. Later to Hollywood, worked w. Gene Austin; rec. w. him on crnt. Army service

'42–3; then resumed as dmr. in NO w. Sharkey Bonano. Became inactive for some time due to illness. In '59 worked in NO w. Roy Liberto; w. Bonano in NO, Atlanta, NYC. Recs. on Voc. '34. LPs: South.; w. Bonano (Cap.); Jack Delaney (South). CDs: w. Bonano (GHB; Story.); Bob Havens (GHB).

HAZELTINE, DAVID, pno, org; b. Milwaukee, WI, 10/27/58. Mother prof. voclst., gtrst., perf. on Milwaukee radio and TV through 1950s. Began priv. lessons at age 9; also start. entertaining as a magician at same time. Perf. at children's parties until age 15. Stud. at Wisconsin Cons. of Mus. 1976–9. First instr. was org. He says: "My first and only 'jazz' teacher, Will Green, introduced me to several local organ bars." At 20 became house pnst. at the Jazz Gallery, Milw., where he pl. w. Sonny Stitt; Chet Baker; Pepper Adams; Charles McPherson; Eddie Harris. Also pl. solo pno. and w. trios in local bars. Worked w. Jon Hendricks '81; Junior Cook '82–3; Lainie Kazan '81–3; Brian Lynch fr. '81; Slide Hampton Jazz Masters, Marlena Shaw (as mus. dir.), Louis Hayes qnt. fr. '95. Chairman of Jazz Dept., Wisc. Cons. of Mus. '84–92, teach. jazz theory, improv., ear training, pno. A confident, lyrical player in the bebop tradition with a lilting, uplifting sense of swing. Favs: Buddy Montgomery, Cedar Walton, Barry Harris. Pl. in Denmark '94; Japan '95. Rec. debut w. Hendricks on Muse '82. CDs: Sharp Nine; w. B. Lynch (CC; Sharp Nine); Jim Snidero (CC); M. Shaw (Conc.); L. Hayes (TCB; Sharp Nine); J. Richardson (TCB).

HEARD, FATS (EUGENE M.), dms; b. Cleveland, OH, 10/10/23; d. Cleveland, 12/5/87. Received his first set of dms. at age 8. Began lessons at Outhwaite Jr. HS. Pl. in marching band and orch. at Central HS. Dur. this time pl. a local gig w. Coleman Hawkins. Stud. pno. at Cleveland Inst. of Mus. After navy service in WWII pl. w. Lionel Hampton late 1940s. Freelanced in NYC; then join. Erroll Garner late '52, tour. w. him to June '55. Ret. to Cleveland., tour. occ. w. Teddy Wilson; Sarah Vaughan; and Carmen McRae. Owned Modern Jazz Room in Cleveland fr. '59; then worked as a real estate salesman; had his own realty co. fr. 74. CDs: w. Garner (Col.; Merc.; Verve).

HEARD, J.C. (JAMES CHARLES), dms, lead; b. Dayton, OH, 10/8/17; d. Southfield, MI, 9/30/88. Younger bro., David, a dmr., rec. w. Sonny Stitt 1948. First perf. as dancer in vaudeville shows; began pl. dms. as teenager. Pl. w. local gps. in Det. in mid 1930s, then moved to NYC. Pl. w. Teddy Wilson Orch. '39–40; Benny Carter '42; Cab Calloway '42–5; own sxt. at Cafe Society '46–7; Erroll Garner '48. Freelanced fr. '48 incl. JATP tours in Eur. and

Japan. Moved to Japan '53, led gp. w. Toshiko Akiyoshi, Miyoshi Umeki and worked as single in China, Philippines, and Australia. Ret. to NYC, Nov. '57. Pl. w. JATP '58; T. Wilson, Coleman Hawkins–Roy Eldridge at Metropole, Lester Lanin, own gp. late '50s; also tour. Eur. w. Sammy Price. Led qt. in LA and LV ca. '60. Pl. in NYC w. Dorothy Donegan fr. '62. Ret. to Det. '66, led own trio, sextet, bb. Tour. US and Eur. as single and w. all-star gps. '70s. Heard had an elegant, swinging style, coming out of Jo Jones, which enabled him to make the transition from the big band era into bebop. He was a favorite of D. Gillespie. Favs: Rich, Jo Jones, Roach. Fests: Eur., Asia fr. '48. TV: Mike Douglas '64. CDs: w. Bechet; Benny Carter (BB); C. Hawkins (Class.; Prest.); T. Wilson (Class.; Musi.); Cab Calloway (Mag.; WW); Sir Chas. Thompson (Del.); Gillespie (RCA); Red Norvo (Stash); C. Basie; C. Parker; Ben Webster; Lester Young (Verve); Doc Cheatham; Al Grey; Ellis Larkins; Sammy Price; Eddie Vinson (B&B); Gene Ammons; A. Cobb; Rex Stewart (Prest); B. Holiday (Col.; Verve); S. Vaughan (Col.); Jacquet (B&B; Verve); Pete Johnson (Sav.; Del.); H. McGhee (Sav.); O. Peterson (Pab.).

HEARD, JOHN, bs; b. Pittsburgh, PA, 7/3/38. Played saxes as a teenager; self-taught on bs. After service in air force pl. w. Tommy Turrentine, J. C. Moses, and Booker Ervin in Pittsburgh; later w. Al Jarreau in SF 1966–8. Moved to LA '69; from early '70s worked w. Ahmad Jamal, C. Basie; also w. Akiyoshi–Tabackin '78–9 and w. Louis Bellson and Oscar Peterson in late '70s and early '80s. After extensive freelance work in LA in '80s, gave up music to concentrate on his considerable talent as a painter and sculptor. Two years later, in '91, resumed his playing career. App. often at Colo. JP. CDs: w. Basie; Zoot Sims; Eddie Vinson (Pab.); Bellson (Conc.); George Cables; Frank Morgan; Bud Shank (Cont.); Pharoah Sanders (Evid.); Tete Montoliu (Steep.); Jamal (Tel.); H. Land (Muse); B. Hutcherson; Buddy Montgomery (Land.).

HEATH, JIMMY (JAMES EDWARD), tnr, sop saxes, fl, comp, arr; b. Philadelphia, PA, 10/25/26. Father pl. cl; bros. are Percy and Tootie Heath; son is percst. Mtume. Began on alto sax at age 14. Stud. at Wilmington HS, Wilmington, N.C. 1941–3; summers w. Paul Amoti at Theodore Presser Sch., Phila., same yrs. Pl. w. Calvin Todd–Mel Melvin in Phila. '44; Nat Towles in Omaha, Neb. '45–6; own band in Omaha '46–7. Moved w. bro. Percy to NYC to pl. w. Howard McGhee '47–8; Gil Fuller '49; Dizzy Gillespie bb and sxt. '49–50; Symphony Sid All-Stars, Kenny Dorham '53; Miles Davis '53–5, '59; Gil Evans orch. '59; Donald Byrd '62; Art Farmer '65–7; own qt. '72–4; Heath Bros. w. Percy and Tootie '76–82; own qt. fr. '82. Tour. w. Faddis-Hampton-Heath sxt. in mid '90s. Upon his arrival in NYC in '47, Heath's Parker-derived alto style earned him the nickname "Little Bird." Sw. to tnr. sax soon after arr. in NYC, and also pl. bari. on some sessions. He became increasingly active as a comp./arr. fr. '60s and wrote for Blue Mitchell; Chet Baker; Milt Jackson; Yusef Lateef; Clark Terry; Billy Taylor; and for Eur. radio bbs. Taught at Jazzmobile '66–85; City Coll. NY '73; Housatonic Community Coll., Bridgeport, Conn. '76–8; City Coll., New Sch. '85; was a full professor at Queens Coll. fr. '87, heading the Jazz Master program fr. the mid '90s until his retirement in Jan. '98. Two of Heath's best known comps. are "CTA" and "Gingerbread Boy." His larger works incl. *Afro-American Suite of Evolution* '74; *Three Ears* '88; *Upper Neighbors Suite* '90; *Sweet Jazzmobile* '92. Heath has received numerous awards incl. North Norway Fest. Awd. '70; Honorary Doctorate fr. Sojourner-Douglass Coll. '85; Lionel Hampton Hall of Fame '88; BMI Awd. '90; a chair is endowed in his name at Queens Coll., where he was given the President's Award '98. Heath's music was the subj. of an Amer. Jazz Orch. tribute concert '91. He has also led his own bb in '90s. A CD feat. Heath's new music for bb was prod. by Bill Cosby '92. Favs: C. Parker, L. Young, Ben Webster; arr: Ellington. Fests: all major fr. '47. TV: *The Jazz Set* (PBS) '71; *Cosby Show* '85. CDs: Verve; Steeple.; Land.; Riv.; w. Heath Bros. (Ant.; Conc.); Gillespie, four tracks in *Prestige First Sessions, Vol. 3* (Prest.); Miles Davis; J.J. Johnson (BN); Milt Jackson (Riv.; Imp.; Pab.; MM); N. Adderley; Sam Jones; Blue Mitchell; Elmo Hope (Riv.); C. Terry (Vang.; Chesky); McGhee (Sav.); A. Cobb (SN).

HEATH, PERCY LEROY, bs, baby bs, cello; b. Wilmington, NC, 4/30/23; d. Southampton, NY, 4/28/05. Brothers are Jimmy and Tootie Heath. Fath. pl. cl. in Elks Marching Band, moth. and grandmoth. sang in choir. Began on vln. at age 8, also sang on radio show. Stud. bs. at Granoff Sch. of Mus. in Phila. 1946. First gig w. Red Garland '46, then pl. w. Hollis Hoppers before bec. house bs. at Down Beat Club in Phila. Moved to NYC '47, pl. w. Howard McGhee; Miles Davis; Fats Navarro; J.J. Johnson. With Dizzy Gillespie '50–2, also freelance w. Charlie Parker; Thelonious Monk; Horace Silver; Clifford Brown; etc. In '51 Heath joined the Milt Jackson Qt., w. John Lewis and Kenny Clarke, which was renamed the Modern Jazz Qt. in '52. He was an integral part in the gp.'s success given that his role went far beyond the usual requisites and he excelled in all departments. When the MJQ disbanded temporarily in '75, he form. the Heath Bros. w. his two bros., Tony

Purrone, Stanley Cowell, Akira Tana. One of the most respected and sought-after bassists in jazz, Heath continued to work w. the MJQ and the Heath Bros. dur. the '80s and into the '90s. He held an honorary doctorate from the Berklee Coll. of Mus., and in '88 was named an Officer of Arts and Letters by the French Govt. Won Founders Award from Thelonious Monk Inst. '95. Favs: Jimmy Blanton, Oscar Pettiford, Ray Brown. Polls: *DB* New Star '54. Fests: all major. TV: numerous app. w. MJQ. Comp.: "Watergate Blues." CDs: w. Heath Bros (Ant.; Conc.); MJQ (Prest.; Atl.; Pab.); C. Parker (Verve); Miles Davis (Prest.; BN); Getz; Monk (Prest.); C. Brown (Prest.; BN); C. Adderley; N. Adderley; J. Heath; Bill Evans; E. Hope; W. Montgomery (Riv.); K. Clarke; Gillespie; Gigi Gryce; Duke Jordan; H. McGhee (Sav.); S. Rollins (Prest.; Riv.; BN); H. Silver; J.J. Johnson; John Lewis (BN); K. Dorham (Deb.); Milt Jackson (Prest.; Sav.; BN); Coltrane (Atl.); O. Coleman (Cont.); P. Desmond (BN); Konitz (BL).

HEATH, TED (GEORGE EDWARD), lead, comp, tbn; b. Wandsworth, London, England, 3/30/1900; d. Virginia Water, Surrey, England., 11/18/69. Father was lead. of Wandsworth Borough Band. At age 10, won prize in brass band contest for tnr. horn; start. tbn. at 14. In 1922 while working as a street mus. was discovered by Jack Hylton, who helped him get his first job at Queens Hall Roof, where Hylton was relief pnst. Pl. w. Bert Firman '24–5; Hylton '25–7; Ambrose '27–35; then w. Sid Lipton and Geraldo. Left latter in '44, when BBC hired him to form band for a radio series. In '45 his band also start. pl. concerts at the London Palladium; in later yrs. these became a regular Sunday event. The orch., a well-trained, popular dance band w. first-rate jazz soloists, developed a huge following in Engl. and on the Continent through its broadcasts, tours, and hit recs. His sidemen incl. Ronnie Scott; Jack Parnell; Kenny Baker; Tommy Whittle; Danny Moss; Don Rendell; voc. Lita Roza, Dickie Valentine. Heath's recs. also became popular in the US, and the band made the first of its many US concert tours in '56. Heath often commisssioned charts from such Amer. arrs. as Tadd Dameron and Bill Russo; Brit. writers John Dankworth and Kenny Graham. One of the band's more successful, jazz-oriented albums was Fats Waller's *London Suite* (Lond.). Died after five-yr. illness dur. which the orch. remained active. Recs. on Brit. labels. CDs: w. Benny Carter (Class.; Conifer).

HEATH, TOOTIE (ALBERT aka KUUMBA), dms, comp; b. Philadelphia, PA, 5/31/35. Brother of Percy and Jimmy Heath. Rec. debut w. John Coltrane

1957. Moved to NYC late '50s; pl. w. J.J. Johnson '58–60. Also worked w. Jazztet '60–1 and rec. w. Nat Adderley; Johnny Griffin; Mal Waldron; Kenny Dorham; et al. In '65 after having pl. in Stockholm w. George Russell, he moved there, worked w. Friedrich Gulda; then as house dmr. at the Montmartre, Copenhagen, pl.w. Kenny Drew and Niels-Henning Ørsted Pedersen backing Dexter Gordon; Stuff Smith; Ben Webster; et al. Back in US '68 w. Herbie Hancock sxt. to '69; Yusef Lateef '70–74; Heath Bros. gp. '75–8, also freelancing in Eur. dur. this period. Settled in LA '76 where he was active as an educ. at many local colleges and universities (UCLA, CalArts, Stanford, Santa Monica Coll.), as well as with music appreciation programs for African-American hs children. TV: *The Jazz Set* (PBS) '71; also acted and comp. music for TV episodes of *Easy Street* and *Frank's Place*. A well-rounded musician, Heath has stud. w. well-known musicians in Jamaica, Nigeria, and Ghana. Cont. to app. w. Heath Bros. intermittently in '80s, '90s. Join. MJQ '95. CDs: w. Heath Bros. (Ant.; Conc.); J. Heath (Riv.; Steep.); Coltrane; C. McPherson (Prest.); Milt Jackson; Wes Montgomery; Bobby Timmons; Billy Taylor (Riv.); H. Edison; J. Pass (Pab.); D. Gordon (Prest.; Steep.; BL); J. Griffin (Riv.; BL); Art Farmer (SN; Cont.); C. Hawkins; B. Webster (Story.); J.J. Johnson (Col.); R. R. Kirk (Merc.); Y. Lateef (Rh./Atl.); H. Land (Conc.); A. Braxton; T. Montoliu; Drew (Steep.); W. Marsh (CC); M. Tyner (Imp.).

HECKMAN, DON (DONALD J.), alto sax, comp, journalist; b. Reading, PA, 12/18/35. Clarinet stud. from age 12; B.A. degree in mus. theory, Florida State U. 1961. Perf. at 1st Int'l JF in Washington, D.C. '63, w. John Benson Brooks's 12–tone jazz gp. Cond. jazz radio show on WBAI-FM, NYC '63–4. Pl. and rec. w. Don Ellis '63–4. Concerts and recs. w. Don Heckman–Ed Summerlin Improvisational Jazz Workshop '64–72; perf. at avant-garde October Revolution festival in NYC '64. Comp. music for numerous TV, theatre, and documentary films '64–'84; adjunct profess. of music, City Coll., NYC '68–72. Active as journalist from early '60s, writing for *Met.*, *DB*, *Stereo Review*, *Saturday Review*, *Jazz Review*, *Village Voice*, etc. Pop/rock/jazz critic and Sunday Recordings Editor, *New York Times* '70–3. Produced gold album for Blood, Sweat & Tears, *B, S & T: IV*, '71. Vice-President, East Coast A&R, RCA Records '73–4. Moved to LA '76; wrote dramatic scripts (*Dynasty*; *Big Shamus, Little Shamus*; etc.) and scored music for TV '77–89. Fr. '86 covered jazz, pop and related music for *LA Times*; became the paper's jazz critic '95. M.A. degree from Antioch U. in clinical psychology '94; practicing psychotherapist fr. '95. Articles and essays anthologized in *Jazz Panorama* (Crowell-Collier); *The Urban*

Adventurers (McGraw-Hill); *Black Americans* (Voice of America Forum Lectures). Named BMI Jazz Pioneer '84. LPs include *Heckman-Summerlin Improvisational Jazz Workshop* (Ictus); *Avant-Slant* w. J. B. Brooks (Decca); *Ring Out Joy* (Avant-Garde); *Saturday in the Park* (RCA Camden); etc.

HEFTI, NEAL, tpt, comp; b. Hastings, NE, 10/29/22. Studied tpt. at age 11; wrote first arrs. while in hs for Nat Towles' band. Pl. w. Bob Astor 1941; to Cuba w. Les Lieber; pl. and wrote for Charlie Barnet, Bobby Byrne; arr. for Earl Hines. To LA w. Charlie Spivak '43; worked briefly w. Horace Heidt, then join. W. Herman, Feb. '44. His arrangements—incl. "The Good Earth" and "Wildroot"—played an important part in the success of the Herman band dur. this period. Married Herman's vocalist Frances Wayne, Oct. '45; worked w. Ch. Ventura's bb '46; Harry James '48–9. Composed and rec. "Repetition" for Norman Granz's *Jazz Scene* album featuring Charlie Parker '47. From '50, wrote for C. Basie, originally for the spt., then for the bb, incl. such celebrated numbers as "Li'l Darlin'," "Whirly Bird," "Little Pony," "Kid From Red Bank," "Cute," and dozens of others, playing a major role in establishing the sound of the Basie ensemble dur. those years. He also led his own bb intermittently for a few yrs. fr. '52. From '60s, wrote many TV and film scores, incl. *Batman*, but was inactive as a trumpeter and bandleader. His best-known compositions include "Girl Talk" (lyrics by Bobby Troup); "Fred" (for a Fred Astaire special); themes from *Barefoot In the Park*; *The Odd Couple*; etc. By the early '90s Hefti's tremendous success as a composer had enabled him virtually to retire, though he busied himself editing published collections of his music. From his earliest days with Woody Herman, where he introduced Gillespian passages into the tpt. section, i.e. "Caldonia," Hefti in his writing showed a strong sense of melody and the ability to bring out the most swinging characteristics in every group for which he wrote. CDs: w. Herman (Col.); Basie (Col.; Verve; Pab.); as tpt.: tracks in *Early Bebop* (Merc.); w. Lucky Thompson in *The Bebop Revolution* (BB).

HELIAS, MARK, bs, el-bs, comp; b. New Brunswick, NJ, 10/1/50. Played dms., gtr., el-bs. in rock bands until age 19. Stud. cl., then bs. w. John Smith. Stud. w. Homer Mensch at Livingston Coll. 1971–4; Yale Sch. of Mus. '74–6. Pl. w. Chet Baker '73; own gp. in N.J. w. Herb Robertson '73; Anthony Davis '74; Ed Blackwell fr. '75; Chamber Orch. of New Engl. '75–7; Anthony Braxton '77; David Schnitter '78; Dewey Redman '78–86; Oliver Lake '78; Barry Altschul '79–83; BassDrumBone w. Ray

Anderson, Gerry Hemingway '78–87; Slickaphonics '79–87. Freelance in '80s w. Muhal Richard Abrams; Mike Nock; Bill Barron; Jane Ira Bloom; Marsalis bros.; Mal Waldron; Bennie Wallace; Jerome Harris; David Lopato; Jim Pepper; Julius Hemphill; C. Baker; JB Horns; etc. Pl. w. own gp. since '84; Simon Nabatov since '90; Tim Berne since '91; Ray Anderson Qt. since '91; Corporate Art w. Gary Thomas, Bobby Previte, Christy Doran. Helias has also prod. recs. for Anderson and Lindsey Horner, and received numerous comp. grants and commissions. Favs: Pettiford, Wilbur Ware, Henry Grimes, Gary Peacock, Mingus. Fests: Eur. since '77; Asia. TV: Eur. TV w. various gps. CDs: Enja; w. Slickaphonics (Enja; Teldec); R. Anderson (Gram.); Corporate Art (JMT); D. Redman (Gal.).

HELLENY, JOEL EDWARD, tbn; b. Paris, TX, 10/23/56. Mother is pnst. and teacher. Began on pno., sw. to tbn. at age 7. Stud. one yr. at U. of Ill., but primarily self-taught. Pl. at jam sessions in Ill., then w. Mel Lewis bb 1979; Roy Eldridge at Jimmy Ryan's fr. '79; house band at Eddie Condon's; Benny Goodman '80–2; Mel Lewis '83; Buck Clayton '89–90; Jimmy McGriff '90; Geo. Wein's Newport All-Stars fr. '90; Frank Wess '91. Helleny was a feat. soloist on the soundtrack to *The Cotton Club*. "Helleny," says Peter Straub, "reflects the influence of the older trombonists but it seems based on a vision of music itself rather than one specifically related to his instrument." Favs: Vic Dickenson, Lawrence Brown, Tricky Sam Nanton. Fests: Eur. and Asia since '79. CDs: Arb.; w. Randy Sandke (Stash); Scott Hamilton (Conc.).

HELLMAN, DAPHNE (Van Beuren Bayne Shih), harp; b. NYC, 12/2/15; d. NYC, 8/4/02. Father was amateur vlnst. Stud. harp at age 12 w. Mildred Dilling, learning classical repertoire. Grad. Miss Porter's Academy of Dramatic Art, Farmington, Conn. 1935. Pl. in church, then w. Special Services, US Army in Wash., D.C., and Germ. Pl. w. Ving Merlin All-Girl Band; Billy Rose's Diamond Horseshoe; Ruban Bleu; Versailles, Julius Monk's Upstairs at the Downstairs. Made rec. debut w. Mitch Miller '58; recs. in '60s w. own trio, Hellman's Angels. Pl. every Tuesday night at Village Gate for twenty-eight yrs. until club closed. In '90s app. at Figaro coffee house in Greenwich Village; Wales Hotel on Madison Ave.; Firebird; and Grand Central subway stop on the Lexington Ave. line. Tour. India, Sri Lanka, and Australia regularly since '68; also tour. in Russia. In '70–1 she worked as a photographer's assist. in Vietnam and Cambodia. Fr. '84 pl. in streets of Paris. Pl. w. Phoebe Legere at Fringe Club, Hong Kong, also in Sri Lanka and India '88–92. Hellman conducted jazz harp wkshps. at the U. of Arizona '89–90. Favs: Deborah

Henson-Conant. TV: *Mel Tormé Show*; *Mike Wallace*. LPs: w. Hellman's Angels (Plug); Mitch Miller (Col.). CD: Overdressed Late Guy Productions.

HEMPHILL, JULIUS ARTHUR, alto, sop, tnr saxes, fl, comp; b. Ft. Worth, TX, 1/24/38; d. NYC, 4/2/95. Mother pl. pno. Stud. cl. w. John Carter in Ft. Worth early 1950s; then att. U. of Calif. at Berkeley; North Texas St. U.; Lincoln U. (B.A.) '66. Pl. w. Richard Keil's Boogie Chillun Blues Band early '60s; army band '64; Ike and Tina Turner mid '60s. Hemphill moved to St. Louis in '68 and bec. a founding member of the Black Artists Group, w. Oliver Lake, Lester Bowie, and Hamiet Bluiett. Pl. w. John Hicks and tour. US coll. '71; rec. two albums, *Dogon A.D.* and *Coon Bid'ness* in early '70s, both of which were later released on Arista/Freedom. Pl. w. Anthony Braxton in Chi. '73. Perf. in Paris, Sweden '73; moved to NYC that yr. Pl. w. Paul Jeffrey in NYC '74. Started his own rec. co., Mbari, in '72. In '76 he became a founding member of the World Saxophone Qt., w. Lake, Bluiett, and David Murray. In the '80s worked w. Murray's oct. and the Jah Band, in addition to lead. his own sxt. and trio. Sxt. tour. US and Eur. '90–1. Wrote many extended comps. incl. *Kawaida*; *Obituary*; *Cosmos for Three Parts*; *Last Supper at Uncle Tom's Cabin* for choreographer Bill T. Jones; *Mingus Gold*; *One Atmosphere*; *Long Tongues: A Saxophone Opera*. Favs: C. Parker, C. Adderley, Konitz, Stitt. Fests: Eur. since '73. Film: *The Orientation of Sweet Willie Rollbar* '72. TV: PBS: *Skyline*; *Last Supper at Uncle Tom's Cabin*; *Night Music*; also German TV. CDs: BS; None.; M&A; Sack.; w. Jah Band (Min. Mus.); WSQ (BS; Elek. Mus.); Bill Frisell (Elek. Mus.); Jamaaladeen Tacuma (Gram.).

HEMPHILL, SHELTON "SCAD," tpt; b. Birmingham, AL, 3/16/06; d. NYC, 12/59. Studied at Wilberforce Coll., pl. w. Horace Henderson's Collegians 1924–8. Pl. w. Fred Longshaw, accomp. Bessie Smith '24–5; Benny Carter '28–9; Chick Webb '30–1; Mills Blue Rhythm Band '31–7; Louis Armstrong '37–44; Duke Ellington '44–9. Freelanced in NYC fr. '49. CDs: w. B. Smith (Col.); Webb; Armstrong (Class.); Ellington (BB; Col.); Mills Blue Rhythm Band (Hep).

HENDERSON, BILL (WILLIAM RANDALL), voc; b. Chicago, IL, 3/19/30. Professional debut at age 5, singing and dancing. Army service, then sang in opening show at Blue Note in Chi. Soon after arriving in NYC sang jazz hit "Señor Blues" w. Horace Silver 1958. Perf. w. O. Peterson '63–4; C. Basie '65–6. Settled in LA, worked mainly as actor, but cont. to sing occasionally. Among screen credits were *Trouble Man* '72, TV roles in *Ironside, Happy Days, Sanford & Son.* Sang w. Jon Hendricks in movie, *White Men Can't Jump,* '92. A strongly jazz-oriented singer with an original and piquant timbre. CDs: Suite Beat; Disc.; *Bill Henderson with the Oscar Peterson Trio* (Verve).

HENDERSON, BOBBY (Robert Bolden Henderson; Jody Bolden), pno, tpt; b. NYC, 4/16/10; d. Albany, NY, 12/9/69. Started on pno. at age 9; stud. from 1923. While also stud. bookkeeping, pl. local gigs; some stud. w. F. Waller. Worked as Billie Holiday's regular accomp. in '33, incl. residency at the Onyx. Then lived in upstate N.Y., pl. solo in various cities. Pl. tpt. in army band during WWII; after discharge he again worked as a single in upstate N.Y.; in Albany for most of the '50s. John Hammond rec. him for Vang. in '56; app. at NJF '57; work. in PR '60–1. Moved to Albany late '60s. Very strongly infl. by Harlem stride pianists. Favs: Tatum, Ellington, Waller, T. Wilson, Basie, Clarence Profit. Rec. at Newport JF '57 (Verve); at Count Basie's (Vang.); Chiaro. CDs: Vang.

HENDERSON, EDDIE (EDWARD JACKSON), tpt, flg; b. NYC, 10/26/40. Father sang w. Charioteers; moth. danced as one of the Brown Twins at Cotton Club. Tpt. at age 9; Louis Armstrong gave him first few lessons. Private instruct. 1949–54. Moved to SF w. family at age 14; stud. tpt. at SF Cons. of Mus. '54–6; also some tutelage fr. Miles Davis during this time. Air Force service '58–61. Competed in Nat'l Figure Skating Championships '56–61, the first black to do so. Won Pacific and Midwestern titles. From '61 pursued dual careers, stud. at U. of Calif Berkeley, grad. w. B.S. in zoology '64; M.D. '68, Howard U. During summers from '64, pl. w. John Handy. Gigs w. Handy, Big Black, Philly Joe Jones '68; also pl. w. Tyrone Washington; Joe Henderson; and led own qnt. Interned at French Hosp., SF '68–9. Residency in psychiatry at U. of Calif. Hospital '69–71. Worked w. H. Hancock '69–73; G. Bartz '69–82; Pharoah Sanders '73–82. Tour. w. Art Blakey '73, also '76, '77, '82. Pl. w. Azteca; worked w. Norman Connors '70–78; had a pop hit, "Comin' Through," for Capitol '77. Pl. w. Elvin Jones '78–80; George Coleman '82; J. Griffin '83, '88; Slide Hampton '88; McCoy Tyner '88–93; B. Golson '92. Rec. w. Richard Davis, Stanley Cowell and P. Sanders late '70s-early '80s. Continued to practice medicine both in general practice and psychiatry, full-time '75–85; part-time '85–91. Henderson has been praised by critics for his full round tone, exceptional technique, and attention-riveting ideas. Favs: M. Davis, C. Brown, L. Morgan. Won awards as best horn player

in SF '77, '79, '83, '84. CDs: Mile.; IDA; w. Billy Harper; Kevin Hays; Bartz; Ron McClure; Bertha Hope (Steep.); Mulgrew Miller (Novus); K. Barron (Enja); Victor Lewis (Red); Sanders (Evid.); Tyner (Bird.); Donald Brown (Muse).

HENDERSON, (JAMES) FLETCHER HAMILTON JR., lead, comp, arr, pno; b. Cuthbert, GA, 12/18/1898; d. NYC, 12/29/52. Studied classical mus. w. moth., a pianist. Earned degree in chemistry and math fr. Atlanta U. Moved to NYC 1920 to become a chemist but found work instead as a song plugger w. the Harry Pace–W.C. Handy music publ. co. When Pace founded Black Swan, Henderson joined him as a music director, putting together gps. to back the company's singers, who incl. Ethel Waters. Led band at Club Alabam Jan. '24, then achieved national recognition during ten yrs. at Roseland Ballroom '24–34. Also rec. pno. accomp. for Bessie Smith and many other singers '20s. Although Henderson's band began as a regular dance band, it soon acquired a reputation as the first large grp. to play in the emerging jazz style. Louis Armstrong was feat. jazz soloist w. the band '24–late '25, app. on recs. incl. "Copenhagen"; "Go 'Long Mule"; "Shanghai Shuffle"; and "Sugar Foot Stomp." At the same time, Henderson's music dir. Don Redman developed the basic formula for jazz bb arrs., based on interplay between the brass and reed sections. Redman left Henderson to join McKinney's Cotton Pickers in '27, and Henderson took over comp. and arr. duties. Henderson's classic arrs. fr. this period incl. "King Porter Stomp" and "Down South Camp Meeting"; sidemen incl. tpts. Joe Smith and Rex Stewart; tbns. Charlie Green and Jimmy Harrison; saxes Redman, Benny Carter, who also arr., and Coleman Hawkins; and cl. Buster Bailey.

In '34, financial difficulties forced Henderson to sell some of his best charts to Benny Goodman, who was then forming his own bb. The success of Goodman's recs. of "King Porter Stomp," "Sometimes I'm Happy," "Blue Skies," and others led directly to the immense popularity of the swing style in the years '35–45. Henderson also sold charts to other bandleaders incl. Isham Jones and the Dorsey Bros. He cont. to tour and rec. as a leader until the late '30s. Sidemen fr. this period incl. tpts. Red Allen, Roy Eldridge, Joe Thomas, Emmett Berry; tbns Claude Jones, Keg Johnson, J.C. Higginbotham, Dicky Wells, and Benny Morton; saxes Edgar Sampson, Russell Procope, Hilton Jefferson, Ben Webster, and Chu Berry; bs. John Kirby and Israel Crosby; and dmrs. Walter Johnson and Big Sid Catlett. Henderson joined Goodman as a pnst. for a few months in '39, then resumed leading his band intermittently. He app.

at the Club De Lisa in Chi. '44–5, then wrote arrs. for Goodman in Calif. '46–7. He toured as Ethel Waters' accomp. '48–9. After being inactive due to illness in the first half of '50, he wrote the score w. J.C. Johnson for the show *The Jazz Train*, prod. at Bop City, NYC. He was leading a sxt. at Café Society when he suffered a stroke in Dec. '50, and was bedridden for most of the last two yrs. of his life. In '57–8, Rex Stewart organized and dir. a band of former Henderson sidemen that was heard at the Great South Bay JF and on recs.

Although he led what was often a great band, Henderson's main legacy to jazz is his work as an arranger. The style he popularized was virtually synonymous with swing, and his band served as the model for the popular swing bands of the late '30s and '40s. By the late '40s–50s, many of the characteristics of his arrs. had been assimilated into the mainstream pop music of commercial and TV bands. Walter C. Allen's *Hendersonia*, a comprehensive book of Henderson data, was published by Jazz Monographs '73. Henderson's papers are in the collection of the Amistad Research Center at Tulane U. Polls: *DB* arr. '38–40. CDs: RCA; Dec.; Col.; Class.; Sav.; w. Bessie Smith; Goodman (Col.).

HENDERSON, HORACE W., arr, pno, lead; b. Cuthbert, GA, 11/22/04; d. Denver, CO, 8/29/88. Brother of Fletcher Henderson. Stud. at Atlanta U. and Wilberforce U. Tour. as lead. of Wilberforce Collegians, which later incl. Rex Stewart and Benny Carter mid 1920s. Led own bands until '31, when he joined Don Redman as pianist-arr. Pl. and arr. w. Fletcher Henderson Orch. '33–6, incl. "Hot and Anxious," "Christopher Columbus"; Vernon Andrade '35; also wrote arrs. for Benny Goodman incl. "Japanese Sandman"; "Dear Old Southland"; "Big John Special"; "I Found a New Baby." Led own band w. Ray Nance, Emmett Berry, Israel Crosby in Chi. late '30s. Arr. for Charlie Barnet '41, then tour. as pianist and mus. dir. for Lena Horne. Rec. w. small gps. in Los Angeles '44–5; arr. for bands of Jimmie Lunceford, Earl Hines, Tommy Dorsey, Glen Gray '40s. In the late '40s and early '50s, he led a small r&b band in the Chi. area. Led combo in Minneapolis '58. Henderson cont. to work as a bandleader, perf. in the Denver area fr. the '60s and heading a combo at the Broadmoor Hotel in Colorado Springs into the '80s. He also was involved as a horse breeder. CDs: Class.; as arr. w. F. Henderson (RCA; Dec.; Col.; Class.); Goodman (RCA); B. Carter (B&B); R. Eldridge (Col.); B. Holiday (Dec.).

HENDERSON, JOE (JOSEPH A.), tnr, sop saxes, fl, comp; b. Lima, OH, 4/24/37; d. San Francisco,

6/30/01. Brother pl. sax. Began on dms.; took up tnr. sax at age 13. First prof. gigs w. show bands. Stud. at Kentucky St. Coll. and Wayne St. U., Detroit 1956–60. Pl. w. Sonny Stitt '59, then led own band in Det. '60. Toured world w. army band '60–2. Three mos. in Baltimore, then moved to NYC, pl. w. Jack McDuff '62. Co-led gp. w. Kenny Dorham '62–3; then pl. w. Horace Silver '64–6; Andrew Hill '65; Jazz Communicators w. Freddie Hubbard, Louis Hayes late '60s; Herbie Hancock Sextet '69–70; Blood, Sweat & Tears briefly '71. Worked mainly as a leader fr. '70. Moved to SF mid '70s. Coll. clinics '70s; w. Freddie Hubbard in Calif. '80s. A highly influential saxist who evidenced a wide range of inspirations in his playing, he experienced a resurgence in popularity following the success of his 1992 CD of Billy Strayhorn comps., *Lush Life*. His comps. incl. "Recordame"; "Black Narcissus"; "Inner Urge"; "Isotope"; "The Bad Game"; "Caribbean Fire Dance." Favs: C. Parker, Stitt; comps: Bartók, Hindemith, Stravinsky. Polls: *DB* TDWR '67. CDs: Verve; BN; Mile.; Red; Enja; MPS; w. Dorham; Silver; Hancock; Hill; L. Morgan; Larry Young; Grant Green; R. Rosnes (BN); Konitz (Mile.); Hubbard (CTI); Mulgrew Miller (Novus; Land.); A. Cobb (SN); R. Hargrove; B. Mseleku; S. Scott (Verve); W. Marsalis (Col.); Tyner (BN; Chesky); W. Norris (Conc.); G. Gruntz (hatArt).

HENDERSON, LUTHER, arr, comp, pno; b. Kansas City, MO, 3/14/19. Mother was amateur pianist; fath. semi-prof. singer and actor. Both parents were schoolteachers. Won Harlem amateur contest 1934. Stud. math at City Coll. NY '34–6; mus. at Juilliard Sch. of Mus. '38–42; later at Navy Sch. of Mus. '44–6; New York U. '46–7. Pl. w. Leonard Ware '39–44. Pl. and arr. for Navy Band at Great Lakes Naval Station '44–6; Mercer Ellington '46–7. Pianist and mus. dir. for Lena Horne '47–50. Henderson arr. dance sets, vocal arrs., symphonic adaptations for Duke Ellington fr. '44. He has been mus. dir. for more than forty B'way and off-B'way shows fr. '50 incl. *Ain't Misbehavin'; Funny Girl; Purlie; That's Entertainment; Doctor Jazz; Jelly's Last Jam*. His orig. musicals incl. *Ethel Waters; Crystal Tree; Siren Song; Riviera on the Rocks; Rose Colored Glasses*. He has worked extens. in TV and film, and as a coach, mus. dir., and accomp. w. vocalists incl. Polly Bergen; Nancy Wilson; Dinah Shore; Diahann Carroll; Eartha Kitt; Florence Henderson; Leslie Gore; Robert Goulet–Carol Lawrence; Liza Minnelli. Arr. for Canadian Brass '80s. Twice nominated for a Tony Awd. *Recess*, a film for which he comp. the score, won the Golden Phoenix Awd. Favs: Fletcher Henderson, Sy Oliver, Pete Rugolo, Thad Jones, Ralph Burns. TV: Victor Borge specials; Carol Burnett;

Miss Teen USA Pageant; Polly Bergen; Ed Sullivan; Dean Martin; many other apps. CDs: RCA; as arr.: w. Ellington (Col.); Canadian Brass (RCA); Dee Dee Bridgewater (Philips).

HENDERSON, WAYNE MAURICE, tbn, comp; b. Houston, TX, 9/24/39. Started stud. tbn in sixth grade; fr. early teens was part of the gp. that became known in the 1960s as the Jazz Crusaders and in the '70s as the Crusaders. Pl. coll. campuses, radio and TV shows, clubs throughout the Southwest. After leaving the group in '75, worked as soloist and led own unit '77. Also prod. sess. for many other artists, incl. Ronnie Laws; Bobby Lyle; and Hiroshima; and rec. with George Benson; Roy Ayers; Esther Phillips; Billy Cobham. In '92 launched a new group, The Next Crusade, feat. another former Crusader, Wilton Felder, w. Rob Mullins on kybds., Ndugu Chancler on dms., et al. His comp. include "Young Rabbits"; "Congolese Sermon"; "In A Dream"; "Scratch"; and more recently, "Down Home Transitions" and "Rosa Café." A competent trombonist who has enjoyed great commercial success. CDs: Par; w. Jazz Crusaders (PJ; MoJazz); Crusaders (GRP; MCA; MoJazz).

HENDRICKS, JON (JOHN CARL), voc, songwriter, dms; b. Newark, OH, 9/16/21. Only musician of seventeen children. Sang hymns and spirituals w. moth. in church. As a child, sang at parties and banquets fr. 1929. After family moved to Toledo in '32, he began perf. on the radio, sometimes accomp. by Art Tatum. Moved to Detroit ca. '40, sang w. band of brother-in-law Jessie Jones. In army in Eur. '42–6. After discharge, stud. at U. of Toledo and taught self to pl. dms. Worked as dmr. in Rochester, N.Y., for two years in late '40s. Sang and pl. dms. w. own qt. in Toledo ca. '51. Moved to NYC '52, began working as songwriter. Rec. vocal version of "Four Bros." w. Teacho Wiltshire '52. Worked mainly as office clerk '52–7, while writing songs for Louis Jordan, King Pleasure, others. Rec. new version of "Four Bros." w. Dave Lambert for Decca '57. Hendricks and Lambert joined Annie Ross to rec. "Sing A Song of Basie," (ABC-Paramount) which feat. multitracked vocal settings of Basie charts '58. L,H&R rec. and tour. w. Count Basie Orch. fr. late '58. In high demand as lyricist fr. '59. Hendricks presented a jazz revue, *Evolution of the Blues*, at the Monterey JF '60 to much critical acclaim. Yolande Bavan repl. Ross in the trio in '62, and by '64 the gp. had broken up. Worked as single fr. '64. Moved to London '68, perf. mainly in Eur. and Africa; also began making trio apps. w. wife Judith and daughter Michelle. Ret. to US ca. '72, settled in Mill Valley, Calif. Worked as jazz critic for *SF Chronicle* '73–4, then staged new version of *Evolu-*

tion of the Blues, which ran for five yrs. at the Broadway Theater in SF. Also taught at Cal. State, Sonoma, Stanford, and UC Berkeley around this time. In recent years, Hendricks has perf. most often w. wife Judith, his children Michelle and Aria, Kevin Burke, and Bobby McFerrin. Writing for and app. w. Manhattan Transfer. Feat. perf. and emcee in his 75th birthday celebration at Lincoln Center '96. Major role in W. Marsalis's *Blood on the Fields*. Reunited w. Ross '98. Delivers his storytelling lyrics w. elan and is a master scatter who can sing a convincing pizzicato "bass" solo. His lyrics incl., among many others, "Along Came Betty"; "Desafinado"; "Down for Double"; "Four, Hi-Fly"; "Little Niles"; "Moanin'"; "Now's the Time." He is a member of the Artists Committee of the Kennedy Center. Favs: Tatum, King Pleasure, Max Roach, Art Blakey, Sid Catlett; comps: Quincy Jones, Gigi Gryce, Gil Evans. Polls: *DB* New Star, Readers '59; *Playboy*; *MM* '68. Film: *White Men Can't Jump* '92. TV: many apps. on British TV; French TV film *Hommage à Cole Porter.* CDs: Tel.; w. L,H&R (Col.; Roul.; Imp.); Blakey (Prest.); W. Marsalis; J. Rowles (Col.); Al Grey (Capri); Michelle Hendricks (Muse); King Pleasure (Prest.); Manhattan Transfer (Atl.).

HENDRICKSON, AL (ALTON REYNOLDS), gtr, voc; b. Eastland, TX, 5/10/20. Lived in Calif. fr. 1925. Stud. w. Luis Eliorriage. Join. Artie Shaw '40, pl. w. Gramercy Five. Coast Guard service '42–5. Worked w. Ray Linn; sang and pl. w. Freddie Slack ca. '46, and Benny Goodman '47; also tour. and/or rec. w. Boyd Raeburn, Ray Noble, Woody Herman '47–59; Johnny Mandel '58; Neal Hefti; Bill Holman late '50s. Active in studio work for movies and TV; recs. and films w. Mandel; Hefti, Holman; Nelson Riddle. Pl. on many bossa nova recs. '62–5. Extensive studio work '60s accomp. pop singers w. orchs. of Riddle; Quincy Jones; Lalo Schifrin. Numerous film and TV soundtracks. Member of Guitars Inc. and Guitars Unlimited, rec. gps.; also rec. w. Capp-Pierce Juggernaut '77. Principally active in studios throughout late '70s and '80s. In early '90s, reactivated jazz career, preparing albums in his own home studio on elec. and acoustic guitars. Favs: Segovia, C. Christian. Fest: MJF w. Gillespie, Bellson '62. CDs: w. Goodman (Cap.; Mos.); Shaw (BB); Capp–Pierce (Conc.); B. Kessel (Cont.); A. O'Day; M. Tormé (Verve); Herbie Harper (Noct.).

HENRY, ERNIE (ERNEST ALBERT), alto sax; b. Brooklyn, NY, 9/3/26; d. NYC, 12/29/57. Played vln. at 8; start. alto at 12. Discovered by Tadd Dameron; join. his band at the Famous Door on 52nd St. in 1947. Then worked w. Fats Navarro; also apps. w.

various gps. led by C. Ventura, G. Auld, M. Roach, K. Dorham '47. Pl. w. D. Gillespie's orch. '48–9; I. Jacquet '50–1. Worked only occ. between '52–6; jam sess. in Bklyn.; pl. w. T. Monk '56–7; then w. Gillespie's re-formed orch. '57. He died in his sleep on a morning after app. w. Gillespie at Birdland. Orig. infl. by Parker in a more general way than most young alto saxists of his generation, he already showed an individuality in his recs. w. Dameron. His work as a leader and sideman on Riv. advanced an even more personal expression while retaining his deep feeling for blues-based material. CDs: Riv.; w. Navarro (BN; Sav.); Gillespie (BB; GNP Cres.; Verve); Monk; Dorham; M. Gee (Riv.).

HENRY, HAYWOOD, bari sax, cl, saxes, fl; b. Birmingham, AL, 1/10/13; d. Bronx, NY, 9/15/94. Sister was pianist/organist in Birmingham. Pl. cl. in hs band; Dud Bascomb was also a member. Sist. bought him a tnr. sax. Att. Alabama State Teachers Coll. on football scholarship; pl. in 'Bama State Collegians w. Bascomb, Erskine Hawkins 1931–2. Moved to NYC '34, then rejoin. Collegians on tour '35. Henry remained w. the gp., renamed the Erskine Hawkins Orch., until the mid '50s. Subbed for Harry Carney w. Duke Ellington '40–2. Freelanced in NYC on saxes, cl., fl., fr. mid '50s. Pl. w. Rex Stewart's Fletcher Henderson All-Stars '57–8; r&b gps. fr. '60, many for Alan Freed; Reuben Phillips band at Apollo Theater late '50s-early '60s; also w. Wilbur DeParis, Snub Mosley early '60s; Earl Hines '69–71; NY Jazz Repertory Co. '75. Also rec. in '70s-early '80s w. E. Hawkins; Ella Fitzgerald; Sy Oliver; and as a lead. In '80s and '90s also was part of The Duke's Men and the Harlem Jazz and Blues Band. Perf. in Denmark in '90s. Pl. on soundtracks to Spike Lee's *School Daze* and *Mo' Better Blues*, late '80s. Worked in B'way pit bands fr. late '40s, incl. *Ain't Misbehavin'*, *Black and Blue*. In the '90s rec. w. Charles Brown; Clark Terry; and Bill Doggett; and led a qt. in NYC. Fav: Harry Carney. Fests: all major w. Hines; USSR w. NYJRC, '75. LP: *The Gentle Monster* (Uptown). CDs: w. Bill Doggett (After Hours); Clark Terry (Chiaro.); E. Hawkins (BB); F. Henderson All-Stars (FS); B. Holiday (BN); Eddie Harris (Rh./Atl.); Willis Jackson (Del.) Jacquet (Roul.); S. Turre (Stash).

HENSON-CONANT, DEBORAH, harp; b. Stockton, CA, 11/11/53. Raised in mus. family; first comp. at age 12. Stud. classical harp at UCLA and UC-Berkeley. After several yrs. pl. w. symph. and chamber gps., sat in with jazz gp. in Boston and began concentrating on jazz; added amplification in 1984 and led a popular trio in the Boston area. Seen on a TV show in '88, she was spotted by GRP pres. Larry

Rosen, who signed her to the label. Like the few jazz harpists who preceded her, she has developed a sensitive feeling for improv. in the jazz idiom on this difficult instrument. CDs: GRP.

HERBERT, ARTHUR, dms; b. NYC, 5/28/07. Nephew is Herbie Lovelle. First gigs on Long Island 1930. Pl. in Bklyn. and at Dickie Wells's club in Harlem '31; w. Eddie Williams at Savoy Ballroom '35; own gp., Rhythm Masters, mid '30s; Edgar Hayes '38; Pete Brown '39; Coleman Hawkins '39–40; Eddie Durham '40; Hot Lips Page, Sidney Bechet '41; Geo. James '42–3; Mezz Mezzrow '43; Pete Brown '46; others. Pl. w. Lem Johnson in '60s. CDs: w. Hawkins (BB; Class.); Bechet (BB).

HERBERT, GREGORY DELANO, alto, tnr saxes; also cls., fls; b. Philadelphia, PA, 5/19/47; d. Amsterdam, Netherlands, 1/31/78. Private lessons 1961; Granoff Sch. of Mus. '62. Worked briefly w. D. Ellington '64. Entered Temple U., Sept. '64, remaining there as mus. and sax major '68. Took up tnr. upon join. Woody Herman Oct. '71; tour. w. him int'l until '75. Pl. w. Thad Jones-Mel Lewis Orch. from '75 to '77; also pl. w. Chuck Israels' Nat'l Jazz Ens.; Blood, Sweat & Tears. Favs: J. McLean, C. Adderley, Coltrane, Rollins. Recs. w. Johnny Coles (Main.); Israels (Chiaro.); Jones–Lewis (A&M). CDs: w. Herman, *The Raven Speaks* (Fant.), which incl. his feat. on "Summer of '42"; Chet Baker (Gal.); P. Martino (Prest.).

HERBERT, MORT (Morton Herbert Pelovitz), bs, arr; b. Somerville, NJ, 6/30/25; d. Los Angeles, CA, 6/5/83. Took two lessons on tpt. but taught himself bs. in hs and began pl. local gigs. Worked w. various swing bands dur. 1940s and '50s. In charge of mus. for the navy in Pearl Harbor area '43–6. Went to Rutgers U. '49–52. From Sept. '55 to Jan. '58 was feat. at the Metropole, NYC, w. Sol Yaged and also gigged w. Sauter-Finegan; M. McPartland; D. Elliott. Join. L. Armstrong Jan. '58 and tour. w. him in US and overseas into '61. Passed bar exam and became a Deputy District Attorney, LA County, '62; practicing lawyer '64. Remained active in freelance pl. and writing, especially w. Herb Ellis. Favs: Red Mitchell, Percy Heath, Clyde Lombardi; arrs: Sauter, Hefti, E. Wilkins. Films: w. Armstrong, *The Beat Generation*; *Die Nacht vor der Premiere* '59. Fav. own solo and arr: "I've Got You Under My Skin" in own LP, *Night People* (Sav.). Rec. w. Elliott (Sav.). CDs: w. Armstrong (Roul.; Tax).

HERFURT, SKEETS (ARTHUR), alto, tnr saxes, cl, voc; b. Cincinnati, OH, 5/28/11. Grew up in Denver. Stud. and pl. in bands at U. of Colo. Pl. w. Smith

Ballew 1934; Dorsey Bros. '34–5; Jimmy Dorsey '35–6; Ray Noble; Tommy Dorsey '37–9. Moved to Calif. '40, pl. w. Alvino Rey. In army '44–5. Pl. and rec. w. Benny Goodman '46–7. Worked as studio mus. and led own band fr. mid '40s. Rec. in '50s w. Billy May; Louis Armstrong; Geo. Auld; Jack Teagarden, Stan Kenton. Rec. w. Benny Goodman '61, '64. CDs: w. Armstrong (Class.); T. Dorsey (BB); Mel Tormé (Stash).

HERMAN, WOODY (WOODROW CHARLES), cl, alto, sop saxes, voc., lead; b. Milwaukee, WI, 5/16/13; d. Los Angeles, CA, 10/29/87. Sang and danced in vaudeville as child; started on sax at 9. Left home at 17 w. Tom Gerun band 1929–33; worked w. Harry Sosnik, Gus Arnheim '33; Isham Jones '34–6. Pl. alto, tnr., and sang w. Isham Jones Juniors on Decca records. When Jones disbanded, key sidemen formed co-op band w. Herman as leader '36. Recording for Decca it became known as "The Band That Plays the Blues." "Woodchopper's Ball" '39 was a major hit. Sidemen incl. Saxie Mansfield, tnr sax; Joe Bishop, flg., arr.; Tommy Linehan, pno; Walt Yoder, bs.; Frankie Carlson, dms. In '43 and '44 Herman used Johnny Hodges, Ben Webster, Juan Tizol, Budd Johnson on his rec. sessions. He also commissioned comps. from Dizzy Gillespie, whose "Down Under" '42 pointed the Herman band's direction and that of jazz generally.

As band members were drafted during WWII, Herman bought up their shares until he owned the band. He now began hiring younger, more daring players and modernized the band's sound. By '44 the band incl. Chubby Jackson; Neal Hefti; Ralph Burns; Bill Harris; Flip Phillips; Sonny Berman; Pete Candoli; Billy Bauer; and Dave Tough. Known as Herman's Herd, it included The Woodchoppers, a small contingent fr. within the band. In '46, the band rec. and premiered at Carnegie Hall *Ebony Concerto,* comp. for Herman by Igor Stravinsky. By the end of '46, when it disbanded, the Woody Herman orchestra had won numerous polls, had its own network radio show, and gained worldwide popularity. Herman was now established among the major band leaders. In the fall of '47 Herman reorganized The Second Herd or "Four Brothers" band. The latter name derived from a Jimmy Giuffre comp. that featured three tenors: Stan Getz, Zoot Sims, and Herbie Steward (later replaced by Al Cohn) and bari. saxist Serge Chaloff. It was an all-star aggregation with Shorty Rogers; Red Rodney; Ernie Royal; Earl Swope; Bill Harris; Lou Levy; Chubby Jackson; Don Lamond; and Terry Gibbs but, due to its strong bop orientation, never achieved the popularity of the first Herd. By '49 its nucleus had changed although the formidable book

remained and was now played by such men as Gene Ammons; Milt Jackson; Conte Candoli; and Shelly Manne. By the end of the year, however, Herman had disbanded again. He took a small gp. to Cuba in Dec. '49 and perf. w. it in the US for four mos. into '50. In '52 he formed what was dubbed the Third Herd; its members incl. tbns. Urbie Green and Carl Fontana, and pnst. Nat Pierce, who also served as chief arr. The new band rec. for Herman's own Mars label. This orchestra cont. through most of the decade but was supplanted by a sxt. w. Nat Adderley and Zoot Sims and an all-star alumni big band at the MJF '59. What could be dubbed "The Fourth Herd" coalesced in '62 w. Pierce; Jake Hanna; Sal Nistico; Carmen Leggio; Phil Wilson; Henry Southall; and Bill Chase.

Herman continued to lead a bb more or less regularly for the rest of his life, hiring young players and embracing new ideas and writing, w. works by Herbie Hancock, John Coltrane, and Chick Corea in the repertoire. Following Herman's death the band cont. under tnr. saxist Frank Tiberi, a saxophone section member fr. '69. Herman was a good though not great jazz player. His solos, however, were always appropriate to the composition. He played alto in a lyrical, Johnny Hodges–derived style; clarinet in a more bluesy vein; showed a distinct personality on the soprano; and sang well in a manner reflecting his love for earlier blues models. His real significance was his genius as an organizer and his generosity in showcasing other players. He once told Benny Goodman, "Well, Benny, you always knew how to play the clarinet and I always knew how to organize a band."

His last years were tragic. Unbeknownst to Herman, his manager gambled away the band's payroll taxes. The IRS persecuted Herman without mercy and confiscated his earnings. When illness prevented him from working and thereby making payments, the IRS seized his home. Films: *What's Cookin'?* '42; *Wintertime* '43; *Sensations of 1945* '44; *Earl Carroll's Vanities* '45; *Hit Parade of 1947*; *New Orleans* '47; *Rhapsody in Wood* (soundtrack for George Pal Puppetoon) '47; *Monterey Jazz* '73. Books: *Woody Herman,* Steve Voce '86; *Woodchopper's Ball,* Stuart Troup (Dutton) '90; *Leader of the Band,* Gene Lees (Oxford) '95; *Chronicles of the Herds,* William D. Clancy w. Audree Coke (Schirmer) '95. CDs: Dec.; Col.; Cap.; Verve; Disc.; Fant.; Conc.; BB; Chess; Mob. Fid.; w. Buck Clayton (Mos.); Ruby Braff (Chiaro.).

HERRING, VINCENT DWYNE, alto, sop, tnr saxes, fl, pno; b. Hopkinsville, KY, 11/19/64. Studied at Dean Friedrich's Acad. of Mus., Vallejo, Calif. 1975–81; Cal. St. U. at Chico '81–2; Long Island U.-NYC '89–91. Pl. solo in NYC streets. Worked w.

Lionel Hampton '85–8; David Murray bb '85–7; Horace Silver '87; Larry Coryell, Art Blakey '89; Roy Haynes, Abdullah Ibrahim's Ekaya '89–90; Jack DeJohnette '90; Art Taylor's Wailers '90–1. Has pl. w. Nat Adderley fr. '89; Cedar Walton fr. '90; and also leads his own qnt. Tour. w. Phil Woods, Antonio Hart in Alto Summit '97. Favs: C. Adderley, C. Parker, Coltrane, W. Shorter. Fests: Eur., Japan fr. '86. TV: Eur. and Jap. TV. CDs: MM; Land.; w. N. Adderley (Land.; SB; In+Out); Freddie Hubbard (MM); Donald Brown (Muse); Kevin Hays; Ron McClure; Louis Smith (Steep.); Scott Wendholdt (CC); *Alto Summit* (Mile.).

HERSCH, FRED (FREDERICK S.), pno, comp, arr; b. Cincinnati, OH, 10/21/55. Grandfather pl. vln., founded Charleston, W. Va., Symph.; grandmoth. pl. org. in synagogue. Stud. at Grinnell Coll. 1973; U. of Cinci. Cons. '74; w. Irma Volpe at New Engl. Cons. '75–7 (B. Mus. '77); w. Sophia Rosoff in NYC '80s. Pl. w. local gps. in Cinci. '73–4; Woody Herman Orch. '77; Sam Jones qt. and bb '78–82; Art Farmer '78–84; Billy Harper '79; Joe Henderson off and on '79–89; Jane Ira Bloom fr. '84; Stan Getz '86; Eddie Daniels '86–90; Toots Thielemans fr. '86; Charlie Haden–Liberation Music Orch. '87; James Moody '90; also much exp. in classical field incl. Vienna Art Orch. '92, own gps., and solo perfs. Led a trio w. Michael Formanek, Jeff Hirshfield '88 into '90s; later trio mates are Drew Gress, Tom Rainey. Taught at New Engl. Cons. '80–6; New Sch., Manh. Sch. of Mus. '91. Fr. '84 to '89 he owned a jazz rec. studio in NYC. Received an NEA perf. grant for a trio concert at Town Hall '89. Prod. recs. for GRP and Sony, and was a freelance reviewer for *Entertainment Weekly*. Favs: Earl Hines, Jamal, Paul Bley, Monk. Fests: Eur. fr. '79; Asia fr. '88. TV: *Today* '89; VH-1 New Visions '90. CDs: Chesky; Sunny.; Red; Angel/EMI; Jazz City; None.; Conc.; Varese Sarabande; w. Jane Ira Bloom (Arab.; Enja); A. Farmer (Conc.; SN); B. Harper (SN); M. D'Ambrosio (Sunny); Thielemans (Conc.).

HERWIG, (LEE) CONRAD III, tbn; b. Ft. Sill, OK, 11/1/59. Mother, grandmoth., aunts all mus. Stud. w. Les Benedict and Ira Nepus in Hawaii 1972–7, then at North Texas St. U. '77–80. Pl. w. Red Garland while at No. Texas, then w. Clark Terry '81; Buddy Rich bb '82; Cab Calloway, Slide Hampton, Jack McDuff, Paquito D'Rivera '83; Toshiko Akiyoshi, Mario Bauza fr. '84; Eddie Palmieri since '85; Dave Liebman '89; Max Roach '90. Herwig has toured extens. as a clinician and soloist, and has led his own qnt. since '87. Pl. w. Joe Henderson '98. He received an NEA perf. grant in '88, and in '91 app. w.

Miles Davis at Montreux JF. Favs: Frank Rosolino, Slide Hampton, Carl Fontana. Polls: *Texas Jazz Mag.* '80. Fests: Eur. since '82; also Jap., So. Amer., Carib. TV: BBC w. B. Rich, Tony Bennett '82; Montreux video '91. CDs: Astor Place; Ken; w. Dave Liebman (Owl); S. McCorkle (Conc.); Chris Hunter (PW; SB); Akiyoshi (Ken/Bellaphon); E. Koivistoinen (Timel.); Ron McClure (Steep.); W. Weiskopf (CC).

HEYWOOD, EDDIE JR., pno, comp, lead; b. Atlanta, GA, 12/4/15; d. Miami Beach, FL, 1/2/89. Studied w. fath., a well-known pnst. and lead. fr. 1923. Prof. debut w. theater band '30. Pl. w. Wayman Carver '32; Clarence Love '34–7. Moved to NYC '38, freelanced and pl. in Harlem clubs. Pl. w. Benny Carter '39–40; Zutty Singleton, Don Redman early '40s. Form. own oct. which rec. w. Billie Holiday '41; led own sxt. w. Vic Dickenson, Doc Cheatham at Village Vanguard '43. Had hit w. "Begin the Beguine" '44, which led to steady work in NYC on 52nd St. and in Calif. Unable to perf. '47–50 due to partial paralysis of hands, he resumed pl. in '51, worked mainly w. a trio. His work became increasingly pop-oriented in the '50s, and he had a hit w. his comp. "Canadian Sunset" '56. He was afflicted by paralysis again '66–9 and devoted his attention to comp. and arr. while recovering in Vineyard Haven, Mass. Ret. to active pl. at the Cookery, NYC '72; perf. freq. on Martha's Vineyard and at sch. and coll. concerts in the '70s. He had another long engagement at the Cookery in '84. Polls: *Esq.* New Star '45; BMI Cert. of Achievement '69. Fests: NJF-NY '74. Film: app. w. own sxt. in *The Dark Corner; Junior Prom* '46. CDs: one track, "Begin the Beguine," in *The Commodore Story* (Comm.); w. B. Holiday (Comm.; Col.); B. Carter; Rex Stewart; Sid Catlett; Coleman Hawkins; Edmond Hall; B. Carter (Class.).

HIBBLER, AL (ALBERT), voc; b. Little Rock, AR, 8/16/15; d. Chicago, 4/24/01. Blind from birth; stud. at cons. and sang w. local bands. After winning amateur contests in Memphis, joined Dub Jenkins' band; led own band in San Antonio, Tex., then tour. w. Jay McShann 1942. Toured w. Duke Ellington '43–51, singing in a controversial style, with grotesque tonal distortions, described by Ellington as "tonal pantomime," and an odd, pseudo-cockney accent some critics found inappropriate. Later rec. w. Mercer Ellington, Billy Taylor, Jimmy Mundy, Gerald Wilson, Count Basie '52; and R.R. Kirk '72. Perf. at Louis Armstrong's funeral. Had big commercial hit w. "Unchained Melody." Won *Esq.* New Star Award as Male Singer '47; *DB* Awards for Band Vocalist '48–9. CDs: Atl.; Varese Sarabande; w. Ellington (BB; Col.; Prest.); McShann (Dec.); Kirk (Rh/Atl.).

HICKS, JOHN JOSEPHUS HICKS JR., pno; b. Atlanta, GA, 12/21/41; d. NYC, 5/10/06. First pno. lessons fr. moth., then stud. at Lincoln U., Mo., and at Berklee Coll. of Mus. Pl. w. Little Milton, Albert King 1959, then worked in early '60s w. Oliver Nelson; Grant Green; Sonny Red; Johnny Griffin; Lockjaw Davis; Pharoah Sanders; Kenny Dorham; Lucky Thompson; Lou Donaldson; Joe Henderson. Join. Art Blakey '64. Pl. w. Betty Carter '65–6; Woody Herman '68–9; also w. Freddie Hubbard; Frank Foster; Anita O'Day; Clea Bradford; Etta Jones; Slide Hampton. Pl. in early '70s w. Blakey; Charles Tolliver; Mickey Bass; Woody Shaw; Music Incorporated; Oliver Lake; Lester Bowie; Julius Hemphill; Geo. Coleman; Sonny Stitt; James Moody; Jon Hendricks; also taught improv. and jazz hist. at So. Illinois U. '72–3. Own trio acc. Betty Carter '75–80. Pl. in early '80s w. Arthur Blythe; Chico Freeman; David Murray; Pharoah Sanders. With Bobby Watson '82–3; arr. and pl. for own bb since '84; various ens. w. Elise Wood fr. '85; Mingus Dynasty and bb in '90s. Comp. score for '91 PBS prog. *A People United.* Favs: Bud Powell, Monk, T. Flanagan, Hank Jones. Polls: BMI Awd. '84; MBA Jazz Master Awd. '85. Fests: all major. CDs: DIW; Evid.; DSM; Timel.; Novus; Conc.; Red Brn.; Res.; Maple.; Land.; w. Keystone Trio (Mile.); A. Blythe (Col.); B. Mover (DSM); D. Murray (BS; DIW; Red Brn.); S. Fortune (BN); K. Barron; G. Bartz (Cand.); D. Berk; J. McShann (Res.); H. Bluiett; Art Davis (SN); P. Sanders (Evid.; Timel.); Mingus Dynasty (Col.); V. Herring (MM); R. Hargrove (Novus); Betty Carter (Verve); P. Leitch (Res.; Conc.); B. Watson (Red); O. Lake (Gram.).

HIGGINBOTHAM, J.C. (JACK; JAY C.), tbn; b. Social Circle, GA, 5/11/06; d. NYC, 5/26/73. Raised in Cincinnati, Ohio, where he joined Wes Helvey's band 1924–5. Pl. in Buffalo, N.Y., w. Eugene Primos, Jimmy Harrison '26–7. Moved to NYC '28. Pl. w. Luis Russell '28–31; Chick Webb '31; Fletcher Henderson '31–3; Mills' Blue Rhythm Band (later called Lucky Millinder's Orch.) '34–6. Achieved great recognition as feat. tbn. w. Russell's band under the dir. of Louis Armstrong '37–40. Then w. Red Allen's sxt. through most of the '40s especially in Chicago; later they worked in NYC and Boston, jointly and apart. Led own gp. in Cleveland '55, then pl. clubs in Boston. Pl. w. dixie. gp. at Metropole, NYC '56–early '60s; tour. Eur. w. Sammy Price '58. Pl. in Scand. '63. Rejoin. Louis Armstrong briefly '64; ret. to Copenhagen '65. Perf. occ. w. all-star gps. at fests and in NYC until his death. Higginbotham is considered to be one of the most important swing trombonists, known for a gutsy extrovert style, robust tone, and forceful attack. Polls: *DB* '41–4; *Met.* '43–5; *Esq.*

Gold Awd. '45. Fests: Randall's Island w. Henderson reunion gp late '50s; NJF '63; NJF-NY w. E. Condon all-star gp. '72. CDs: two tracks w. own gp. in *Giants of Small Band Swing, Vol. 2* (Riv.); w. Red Allen; J. Teagarden; F. Waller; B. Carter (BB); F. Henderson (Col.; Class.); Mills Blue Rhythm (Class.); Armstrong (Dec.; Col.); J.R. Morton (BB; B&B); C. Hawkins (BB; Prest.; Jass); Bechet (BB; BN); Lucille Hegamin–Victoria Spivey (Prest.); Pete Johnson (Sav.); Tiny Grimes (Prest.); Buck Clayton (Mos.).

HIGGINS, BILLY, dms; b. Los Angeles, CA, 10/11/36; d. Inglewood, CA, 5/3/01. Began dms. at age 12. Pl. in r&b combos at age 19, worked w. Amos Milburn, Bo Diddley; also w. Jimmy Witherspoon; Brook Benton; Sister Rosetta Tharpe. Gigged w. Don Cherry; James Clay; Walter Benton; Dexter Gordon et al. Join. Red Mitchell qt. 1957. Charter member of original Ornette Coleman Quartet in LA '58 and NYC '59. Pl. w. T. Monk qt., John Coltrane qt. '60; S. Rollins '62–3. Active freelancer w. H. Mobley; L. Morgan; H. Hancock et al. Cont. to work w. Coleman off and on in '60s and '70s. From '70 worked often w. Cedar Walton, incl. Eastern Rebellion; Clifford Jordan; and a variety of other gps. incl. Jackie McLean; Mal Waldron; Milt Jackson; Art Pepper; J.J. Johnson; Joe Henderson; Pat Metheny; Slide Hampton; coleader of Bill Lee's Brass Company '72–3; Chris Anderson '73–4. Involved w. first edition of Charlie Haden's Quartet West mid '80s; Cedar Walton's trio in '90s until kidney disease halted his career. By middecade, with a new kidney, he resumed active playing. A highly sensitive, musical drummer, he was always at home in every setting and was one of the most recorded drummers in jazz. Taught at his Los Angeles studio in '90s. Fests: NJF-NY w. C. Jordan, '73; Verona w. J. Heath '74; many since in US, Eur., Japan. Own gp. at Umbria Jazz '98. Polls: won new star award from *DB* Critics, '60. Film: *Round Midnight* '86; pl. w. Abdullah Ibrahim for *Chocolat* '87. Award: NEA Jazz Masters Fellowship '97. CDs: Red; Timel.; Evid.; w. O. Coleman (Cont.; Rhino/Atl.); Walton (Prest.; CC; Red; SB; Evid.; Muse); Eastern Rebellion (Timel.; MM); Monk (Riv.); D. Gordon (BN; Steep.); Rollins (RCA); D. Cherry; Sun Ra (A&M); Haden (Verve; SN); Stitt (32); L. Morgan; Mobley; D. Byrd; G. Green; H. Hancock; Quebec; S. Clark; J. Henderson (BN); J. McLean (BN; Steep.); J. Redman (WB); Cecil Taylor (Cand.); B. Hutcherson (Cont.); S. Lacy (NJ); R. Hargrove (Novus); S. Hampton (CC); J. Clay (Ant.).

HIGGINS, EDDIE (HAYDN), pno; b. Cambridge, MA, 2/21/32. Studied w. moth., a pianist. Prof. gigs in Chicago nightclubs while attending Northwestern U.

Sch. of Music. Pl. w. George Brunis 1954–6; led own trio for few yrs., perf. at Playboy JF '59. House trio lead. at London House, Chi. '57–69; fr. '63 also active w. studio work. In '70 moved to Ft. Lauderdale, Fla.; led house gp. '78–82 w. Ira Sullivan. Many jazz fests. at home and abroad and annual cruises on the SS *Norway* from mid '80s. Married singer Meredith D'Ambrosio '88; works frequently as her accomp. Many albums from '60 w. Al Grey, Coleman Hawkins, and own gps. Fests: many in Eur.; Japan; Colo. JP '91. TV: *Today* show, '68; apps. on local shows in Chi., Bost., Miami. Radio: M. McPartland's *Piano Jazz* '94. CDs: Sunny.; Solo Art; Venus; w. Lee Morgan; Wayne Shorter (Vee-Jay); D'Ambrosio (Sunny.); George Masso (N-H); Chuck Hedges (Arb.).

HILL, ALEX (ALEXANDER WILLIAM), pno, arr, comp; b. North Little Rock, AR, 4/19/06; d. North Little Rock, 2/1/37. Studied w. his moth. Worked w. Alphonso Trent, then led own gp. 1924 and began touring. Became mus. dir. of traveling show, which he left in LA ca. '27; some studio work on silent film sets in Hollywood; pl. w. local bands, incl. Mutt Carey. Moved to Chicago, worked as pno. and arr. for Jimmie Noone, L. Armstrong, and others in late '20s. To NYC in '30 w. Sammy Stewart; worked briefly w. Andy Kirk, then became staff arr. for Irving Mills org. Fr. '30 to '35 Hill developed a reputation as an arr., wrote charts for Claude Hopkins; D. Ellington; P. Whiteman; Benny Carter; E. Condon; Mills Blue Rhythm Band; F. Waller; Willie Bryant. Left Mills in '35, start. own bb which pl. at the Savoy. A few months later, advanced tuberculosis forced him to retire to his bro.'s home back in Arkansas. Recs. w. Noone (Voc.) '29; Condon (Col.) '33; own band (Voc.) '34. CDs: own orch. w. Jabbo Smith (EPM); w. Noone (Aff.); as arr: w. Mills Blue Rhythm (Class.).

HILL, ANDREW, pno, comp; b. Chicago, IL, 6/30/37. As a boy, sang, pl. acdn., and tap-danced. Appeared in local talent shows 1943–7; learned to pl. blues on pno. '50; pl. w. Paul Williams r&b gp. at age 15, later coming into contact w. name jazzmen at Joe Segal's jam sessions. He came to know Barry Harris, who became an influence, along w. Bud Powell, Tatum, and Monk. To NYC '61 as Dinah Washington's accomp. Came to prominence via his Blue Note albums as leader. and sideman. Lived in LA '62, worked at The Lighthouse and w. Roland Kirk qt. Ret. to NYC '63. Coordinated Black Arts Repertory Theatre '65 and pl. coll. and clubs. Tour. w. Smithsonian Heritage Program '73–4 and received Smithsonian Fellowship '75. From late '70s taught, tour. worldwide, rec. for several different labels. Moved to

Portland, Ore., where he was an associate professor at Portland State U. Studied the musical history of the Japanese community and composed *The American Nikkei Symphony*, which he described as "a symphonic interpretation of a century of immigrant Japanese experience in America." Ret. to the New York area '96; pl. at Knitting Factory; Town Hall; Queen Elizabeth Hall, London; in '97 at Alice Tully Hall for World Music Inst. Has been Guest Artist-in-Residence at Harvard U. and Bennington Coll. Hill was considered to be in the second wave of avant-garde players who followed in the wake of Ornette Coleman and Cecil Taylor but presented a totally personal vision, eschewing the "noise element" players. Reinvented himself in the late '80s-early '90s, collaborating w. Greg Osby, Robin Eubanks. "Pianist-composer Hill made some of the thorniest, most fiendishly constructed, uncategorizable jazz of an era. Though Hill has mellowed...there is still plenty of knottiness."—*The New Yorker*. CDs: BN; Mos.; Free.; SN; w. Joe Henderson; B. Hutcherson; H. Mobley (BN); R.R. Kirk (Merc.); R. Workman (Post.).

HILL, BASS (ERNEST), bs; b. Pittsburgh, PA, 3/14/00; d. NYC, 9/16/64. Worked w. Claude Hopkins 1924–8, incl. Eur. '25, accomp. Josephine Baker. Pl. w. LeRoy Smith, Bill Brown, Charlie Skeete late '20s. In early '30s briefly w. Chick Webb; Benny Carter '31, '33–4; Willie Bryant '35. To Eur. w. Bobby Martin '37; band, renamed The Cotton Club Serenaders, stayed in Eur. to '40. Rejoin. Hopkins, pl. w. him on and off '41–4; w. Zutty Singleton, L. Armstrong '43; Cliff Jackson '44; USO tour w. Herbie Cowens '45–6; w. pno. Minto Kato. Ret. to Eur. '49, worked w. Bill Coleman, Big Boy Goudie. Ret. to US '52, worked regularly w. Happy Caldwell. From '54 also worked as delegate for AFM, NYC. Rec. w. Red Allen on tba. '30; bs. w. Benny Carter, Spike Hughes '35; Hot Lips Page '40. CDs: w. Allen; Carter (Class.).

HILL, BUCK (ROGER), tnr sax; comp; b. Washington, DC, 2/13/27. Began on sop. sax at age 13 but then moved to the alto and tnr. Att. Armstrong HS, where he had the same music teacher who taught Duke Ellington. Pl. first prof. gig at Republic Gardens 1943. With 173rd Ground Force band in Alabama late '40s. After discharge, worked w. Billy White bb; John Malachi at Club Caverns; house band at Howard Theater. Pl. at clubs incl. Showboat Lounge, but fr. '50 to '55 worked as a mail carrier. Then he left the post office and drove a cab while also pl. w. Sonny Stitt; Gene Ammons; Stan Getz; and Max Roach when they came to Wash. Rec. w. Charlie Byrd, with whom he had pl. at the Showboat '58–9.

Ret. to the post office full-time '60 and was intermittently active in jazz. In the early '70s he began to become prominent once more as a mus. in Wash., backing Milt Jackson locally; and worked w. gtr. Bill Harris at the latter's Pigfoot club; Shirley Horn; and Andrew White. Rec. w. local tpt. Allan Houser '73, then as lead. for Steeplechase label '78–81; Muse in '80s. A world-class tnr. saxist who has chosen to stay at home. Favs: Coltrane, Rollins, Ben Webster, C. Hawkins, L. Young. Fests: North Sea '81. CDs: Muse; Steep.; w. Horn (Verve).

HILL, CHIPPIE (BERTHA), voc; b. Charleston, SC, 3/15/05; d. NYC, 5/7/50. Worked as a dancer in an Ethel Waters show, NYC, after leaving home when very young. In early 1920s tour. w. Ma Rainey as singer and dancer; worked on TOBA circuit. Settled in Chi., where she began working w. many prominent mus., incl. King Oliver. In '25–6 made a series of blues recs., accomp. by L. Armstrong, Richard M. Jones; tour. w. Lovie Austin '29; also worked w. Thomas A. Dorsey, Tampa Red. Worked sporadically fr. '30, w. Jimmie Noone at Cabin Inn '37; as single at Club DeLisa '39–40. Out of music '40–6, doing mostly menial work. Resumed active career w. the help of Rudi Blesh, who made a successful series of recs. w. her, accomp. by Lovie Austin; Lee Collins; Baby Dodds; and other important '20s jazz figures, for his Circle label '46. Moved to NYC in '47, pl. residencies at the Village Vanguard and Jimmy Ryan's '47–8; Paris JF; Bessie Smith Memorial concert at Town Hall '48; Riviera Club '49–50; w. Art Hodes' gp. at the Blue Note, Chi. Ret. to NYC, pl. at Ryan's and other clubs. At the height of her reactivated career, she died in an automobile accident. Recs. on Voc. CDs: w. Armstrong (Col.; Aff.); *History of Classic Jazz* (Riv.).

HILL, FREDDY (FREDERICK ROOSEVELT), tpt; b. Jacksonville, FL, 4/18/32. Studied at Florida A & M, where he pl. w. Nat Adderley. Army service, 1953; taught in public sch., '55–7. To LA in late '50s; worked w. Gerald Wilson bb; Earl Bostic. In '60s rec. w. Leroy Vinnegar; Buddy DeFranco; L. Bellson; D. Gillespie; Oliver Nelson; and Wilson. CDs: w. Vinnegar (Cont.); Wilson (PJ).

HILL, TEDDY (THEODORE), lead, saxes; b. Birmingham, AL, 12/7/09; d. Cleveland, OH, 5/19/78. Played dms. in sch. band; sw. to tpt.; then saxes and cl. Tour. w. a show band 1926–7; join. George Howe's band in NYC at the Nest Club '27. Worked w. Luis Russell '28–9, also serving as asst. manager; w. James P. Johnson '32. From '32 start. regularly lead. own bands at Lafayette Theatre;

Ubangi Club; the Savoy; etc.; at times sidemen incl. R. Eldridge; Dicky Wells; Chu Berry; D. Gillespie; Frankie Newton. Tour. Engl. and France in '37. Pl. at NY World's Fair '39. After '40 was no longer active as a lead. but was prominent figure as manager of Minton's Playhouse dur. bop's emergence in the early '40s; remained as manager there into the late '60s; ran Club Baron in Harlem fr. '69 into '70s. Recs. on Voc. '36; BB '37. CDs: Hep; Class.; w. Gillespie (BB); Eldridge (Col.); King Oliver (Aff.); Luis Rusell (JSP); L. Armstrong (Col.); Red Allen (JSP).

HILLYER, LONNIE, tpt; b. Monroe, GA, 3/25/40; d. NYC, 7/1/85. Raised in Detroit. Start. pl. older bro.'s tpt. when bro. went into army in 1951; stud. while in hs; then priv. w. Barry Harris fr.'54; at Larry Teal's music studio while in hs; w. tptr. Bill Horner for a yr. in '58. Pl. at World Stage jam sess. '55–7. Worked w. Yusef Lateef at Minor Key, Det., and Half Note, NYC '59; w. Joe Henderson at the Bluebird, Det. '60. Taught tpt. in Det. before moving to NYC late summer '60 and worked w. Slide Hampton. Best known for his assoc. w. Harris, Charles Mingus; Charles McPherson; all of whom he worked w. regularly into '70s. Pl. w. Mingus '60–1, '64–7. He and McPherson join. Mingus at the same time; they also worked together w. Harris '61–3; co-led a gp. in '66; also pl. w. Charles Davis '66. Pl. w. Mingus again '71–3; apps. w. Harris, McPherson into the '70s. Taught tpt. in NYC. First infl. by his bro.'s Armstrong and Harry James recs., Hillyer named Gillespie, M. Davis, F. Navarro, Freddie Webster as favs. Although not gifted with strong "chops," he was one of the few tptrs. of his generation to understand and utilize the nuances of Gillespie's style. Fests: w. Mingus MJF '64–5; NJF '71; NJF-NY '72. CDs: w. Harris (Riv.); Lateef (NJ); Mingus (Col.; Cand.; VDJ; Mos.); Dolphy (Cand.); McPherson (Prest.; Main.).

HINES, EARL KENNETH (FATHA), pno, comp, lead; b. Duquesne, PA, 12/28/03; d. Oakland, CA, 4/22/83. Father pl. tpt. in Eureka Brass Band; moth. was organist. Raised in Pittsburgh. Stud. tpt. briefly w. fath., pno. w. moth.; stud. classical pno. w. priv. teachers. Led trio in clubs while att. Schenley HS. First full-time job w. singer Lois Deppe in Chicago 1922. Pl. in Chi. w. Sammy Stewart at Sunset Cafe, Erskine Tate at Vendome Theater; tour. w. Carroll Dickerson '25–6. Hines became mus. dir. when Louis Armstrong assumed leadership of Dickerson's band in '27. Briefly managed nightclub w. Armstrong, then pl. w. Jimmie Noone at Apex Club '27–8. Rec. w. Armstrong incl. duet on "Weatherbird" '28. Opened w. own bb at Grand Terrace Dec. '28. Led own bb '28–48. Sidemen in the '30s band incl. Jimmy

Mundy; Budd Johnson; Walter Fuller; Omer Simeon; Darnell Howard; Herb Jeffries; Arthur Lee Simpkins; Ida James; this band had hits incl. "Deep Forest," the band's theme, and "Rosetta," Hines's, best-known comp. In the '40s, the band incl. many bebop mus. incl. Charlie Parker; Dizzy Gillespie; Bennie Green; Benny Harris; Wardell Gray; Shadow Wilson; Billy Eckstine; Sarah Vaughan; hits incl. "Jelly Jelly"; "Boogie Woogie on the St. Louis Blues"; "Stormy Monday Blues." He disbanded '47 and join. Louis Armstrong's All Stars, remaining into '51. Then, after lead. new gp. w. Jonah Jones, Bennie Green, Aaron Sachs, and vocalists Helen Merrill and Etta Jones '52-3, he moved to San Francisco and led his own sxt., incl. Muggsy Spanier, Darnell Howard, and Jimmy Archey, at the Hangover Club into the late '50s; the gp. also broadcast fr. Hangover coast-to-coast on CBS Radio network. Then he tour., incl. Eur. '57; ran Music Crossroads, a short-lived nightclub in Oakland; and generally languished in obscurity. His apps. in three critically acclaimed concerts at the Little Theatre in NYC '64 rekindled his career. Led trio, qt. w. Budd Johnson fr. '64. There were frequent Eur. tours and fest. apps. fr. '65; USSR '66; Latin Amer. w. Oscar Peterson '69; w. Teddy Wilson, Marian McPartland, Ellis Larkins '74. SS *Rotterdam* jazz cruise '75; state dinner at White House '76. Hines was a consummate ensemble pianist and one of the first to play mainly with a linear rather than chordal approach in the right hand, dubbed "trumpet style" piano. Don Schlitten described a Hines 1965 performance as the embodiment of his old orchestra: "He uses his left hand sometimes for accents and figures that would only come from a full trumpet section. Sometimes he will play chords that would have been written and played by five saxophones in harmony. But he is always the virtuoso pianist with his arpeggios, his percussive attack, and his fantastic ability to modulate from one song to another as if they were all one song and he just created all those melodies during his own improvisation."

Polls: *Esq.* Silver Awd. '44; *DB* Hall Of Fame '65; *DB* critics '66-7, '69-73. *Stereo Review* Annual Award '78. Fests: all major fr. '64. Radio: series of five half-hour shows for French Nat'l Broadcasting System, mid '60s. TV: Dick Cavett, Johnny Carson, Merv Griffin, Mike Douglas; Ralph Gleason's *Jazz Casual*. CDs: BB; Col.; B&B; Chiaro.; Riv.; BL; Red Brn.; Class.; GNP Cres.; Del.; NW; Prest.; w. Armstrong (Col.; Dec.); Bechet (BB); Benny Carter (Cont.); Buck Clayton (Chiaro.); J. Dodds; Noone (Dec.); P. Gonsalves; S. Grappelli (BL).

HING, KENNY (KENNETH ALLEN), saxes, cl, fl; b. Portland, OR, 10/25/35. Father pl. bjo.; younger bro. John, gtr. Began on cl. 1944, then stud. w. Eddie Flenner fr. '46. Pl. w. "mickey mouse" and society bands under Johnny Reitz, Wally Heider. Feat. on tnr. sax w. Count Basie Orch. fr. '77, showing a light-footed ability to swing. Favs: Don Byas, Lucky Thompson, Paul Gonsalves, Zoot Sims. Fests: all major w. Basie Orch. CDs: w. Basie (MAMA; Den., Tel.; Pab.); Sarah Vaughan w. Basie, solo on "All the Things You Are" (Pab.).

HINO, MOTOHIKO (TOKO), dms, lead; b. Tokyo, Japan, 1/3/46; d. Tokyo, 5/13/99. Father, Bin, was tap dancer and tpt.; bro. is Terumasa Hino. Worked w. fath. as tap dancer at age 8. Stud. dms. w. Kanji Harada; pl. prof. fr. age 11. First jazz gig w. Konosuke Saijo 1963. Pl. w. Shungo Sawada; Hiroshi Watanabe's Stardusters; then join. Terumasa Hino Qnt. '67. Made rec. debut as lead. '70. When bro. disbanded qnt. and moved to NYC in '75, form. own trio. Rec. w. Kazumi Watanabe '76. In NYC '78-80, pl. w. Joanne Brackeen Trio and freelanced w. Dave Liebman; Joe Henderson; Sonny Rollins; Gary Bartz; T. Hino. In Japan, formed own gp. Zoom '81. Worked in '80s w. T. Hino; Masahiko Sato; Humio Karashima; own trio and qnt. Tour. China '86. Pl. w. Dizzy Gillespie in Osaka '87. Form. ambitious bb, Urbanightroops, '90. Started after-hours jam session at Pit Inn, Tokyo, to help promote young musicians '92. Extens. tour of Japan commemorating 35th year in music business. Hino was generally considered the top jazz drummer in Japan. Died of pancreatic cancer. Favs: Elvin Jones, Tony Williams. Polls: *SJ* Readers '71-9, '82-93; *SJ* Critics '90-2. Fests: all major in Japan; NJF-NY w. T. Hino '73. TV: app. w. Gillespie '87. CDs: Gram.; King; ThreeBlindMice; Meldac; w. D. Liebman–Steve Swallow (FunHouse).

HINO, TERUMASA, tpt, flg, comp, lead; b. Tokyo, Japan, 10/25/42. Father was tap dancer and tpt.; bro., Motohiko Hino. Fath. started him tap-dancing at age 4, pl. tpt. at age 9. Primarily self-taught. Made prof. debut as second tpt. in dance band at US Army camp 1955; pl. w. Hiroshi Watanabe's Stardusters and others at several base camps '57-60. Tour. Indonesia w. Jiro Inagaki '61. Came to prominence w. Hideo Shiraki Qnt., then the top jazz gp. in Japan '64-5. Led own gp. fr. '65. Won first of many *Swing Journal* polls '67. Co-led qnt. w. Masabumi Kikuchi '68. Had hit w. rec. "Hinology" '69-70; pl. at Berlin Jazzstage '71, NJF-NY '72, other Eur. fests '73. Edited Japanese book of Miles Davis transcriptions '75. Moved to NYC, pl. w. Jackie McLean at Five Spot '75. Freelanced w. Larry Coryell, Gil Evans, Hal Galper, Carlos Garnett, Sam Jones, Dave Liebman, Elvin Jones late '70s-early '80s. Many tours of Japan, Eur. fr. '80s. Hino has worked extens. in fusion and pop music as well as jazz. Won *SJ* poll in three categories '90. Helped organize annual All Japan Jazz Aid concert at Budokan '87–92. Received Fumio Nanri awd. for contrib. to Japanese jazz '88. Pl. reunion concert w. M. Kikuchi at Yamaha JF, Hamamatsu; concert w. own gp. for Japan Society, NYC '93. Hino is generally recognized as the top jazz trumpeter to emerge fr. Japan. Kiyoshi Koyama wrote: "In the '90s Hino is back to more straight-ahead jazz, showing great maturity in his ballad playing." Favs: M. Davis, Clifford Brown, Lee Morgan, F. Hubbard, W. Shaw. Polls: *SJ* Readers '67–93; *SJ* Critics '90–2; *SJ* Jazzman of Year '70, '75, '83, '90; *SJ* Rec. of Year '90; *SJ* Jazz Disc Awd. '72, '74. Fests: Mt. Fuji annually fr. '87; Warsaw JF w. own US gp. '91; all major in US and Eur. CDs: Victor, Enja, JVC, Sony, BN; w. Gil Evans (DIW); Hal Galper; M. Waldron (Enja); Motohiko Hino (Gram.); S. Watanabe (Den.); Sam Jones (Steep.); D. Liebman (Timel.); Bob Moses (Open Minds); R. Beirach (Konnex); G. Russell (SN).

HINTON, MILT "JUDGE" (MILTON JOHN), bs; b. Vicksburg, MS, 6/23/10; d. NYC, 12/18/00. Mother pl. pno., org., dir. church choir. Raised in Chicago. For his 13th birthday, his moth. bought him a vln., which he stud. w. Prof. James Johnson 1923–7. Pl. sarousaphone, bs.-horn, tba. '25–30. Stud. music theory, harmony w. Major N. Clark Smith at Wendell Phillips HS '24–9. Switched to string bs. '28. Att. Crane Jr. Coll. '29–30. Stud. bs. w. Paul Steinke in Milwaukee '33–6; Dmitri Shmuklosky in Chi. '36–45. Pl. w. Eddie South off and on '31–6; Zutty Singleton at Three Deuces, Chi. '36; also freelanced in Chi. w. Johnny Long; Tiny Parham; Erskine Tate; Art Tatum; Cassino Simpson; Jabbo Smith. Pl. w. Cab Calloway '36–51. Freelanced in NYC clubs w. Joe Bushkin, Jackie Gleason, Phil Moore '51, then join. Count Basie for two mos. Pl. w. Louis Armstrong '52–3, then on staff at CBS '54. Pl. w. Jimmy McPartland at Metropole Café, Benny Goodman at Basin St. '55. In high demand as studio mus. fr. '56. Pl. concerts w. Ben Webster, Sammy Davis Jr., Judy Garland, Harry Belafonte '60s. Active as lecturer and in youth groups fr. '60s. On staff at ABC, pl. w. Bobby Rosengarden on *Dick Cavett Show,* late '60s-70s. Tour. extens. w. Pearl Bailey fr. early '70s, incl. several perfs. at White House; also tour. Eur. w. Paul Anka, Bing Crosby. House bassist at Michael's Pub, NYC fr. '74 backing Red Norvo; Teddy Wilson; Flip Phillips; Terry Gibbs; Joe Venuti; Bobby Hackett; Dick Wellstood; et al. Taught jazz workshops at Hunter Coll. '80–5; Baruch Coll. fr. '85; Skidmore Coll. summer prog. fr. '88; Interlochen Music Camp '90. He has served as Bass Chairman of the Nat'l Assoc. of Jazz Educs., panel member of NEA, and board member of the Int'l Society of

Bassists. He was a member of the NJF Hall of Fame and held honorary doctorates fr. several US universities. Was an accomplished photographer whose work has been exhibited in the Denver Mus. of Art and the museums of the Rhode Island Sch. of Design, Parsons Sch. of Design, and Rochester Inst. of Technology; and Flushing Town Hall Sept. '98. His photos were publ. in magazines incl. *Popular Photography; Down Beat;* and *Life*; the Classic Jazz Calendar every year fr. '89; and in two books: *Bass Line: The Stories and Photographs of Milt Hinton* (Temple Univ. Press) '88, and *OverTime: The Jazz Photographs of Milt Hinton* (Pomegranate ArtBooks) '91. Hinton was one of the most popular and sought-after bassists on the NYC scene but illness limited his playing engagements toward the end of the '90s.

TV: App on numerous shows; a 90–min. film docu., *The Story of Jazz* '91; the film *A Great Day in Harlem,* which incl. historic footage by his wife, Mona Hinton '94. Favs: Blanton, Ray Brown, Ron Carter, John Clayton, Pettiford, Rufus Reid. Polls: *Esq.* Silver Awd. '44, NARAS Eubie Awd. Films: w. Calloway, *Stormy Weather* '43. CDs: Chiaro.; Prog.; w. Calloway (Class.; Col.); L. Hampton (Tel.; BB; Dec.); Venuti-Sims; Ralph Sutton; B. Wilber; J. McShann; B. Clayton (Chiaro.); Eddie South (DRG); Benny Carter; C. Hawkins; J. Hodges; J. Rushing; Geo. Russell; Joe Williams; M. Ferguson; Freddie Green–Al Cohn (BB); B. Holiday (Col.; Verve); B. Goodman (MM); B. Marsalis; Russell Malone; J. DeFrancesco (Col.); Pee Wee Russell (Cand.); C. Fuller (Sav.); Gil Evans; Helen Merrill (Verve); I. Quebec (BN); Q. Jones; S. Horn; R.R. Kirk (Merc.); W. Montgomery (Riv.); R. Braff; Joe Newman (BL); T. Wilson (Hep; B&B); T. Gibbs (Cont.).

HIPP, JUTTA, pno; b. Leipzig, Germany, 2/4/25; d. Queens, NY, 4/7/03. Began pno. at age 9. Stud. painting at Acad. of Arts, joined local Hot Club for jam sessions dur. WWII. When Russians occupied Leipzig, she fled w. family to Munich. Pl. w. Charles Tabor, then rec. w. Hans Koller 1950–3. Led own qnt. in Frankfurt '53–5. Moved to NYC Nov. '55. Led trio w. Peter Ind, Ed Thigpen at Hickory House '56. Rec. w. Zoot Sims '56. By '58 Hipp had stopped pl. prof. Active as an artist, she supported herself by tailoring. CD: BN.

HIRSHFIELD, JEFF (JEFFREY LEE), dms; b. NYC, 8/22/55. Primarily self-taught. Pl. gigs on Long Island bef. moving to NYC in 1978. Pl. w. Mose Allison '78–9; Woody Herman '79–80; Lonnie Smith '81; Red Rodney–Ira Sullivan '81–5; Toshiko Akiyoshi–Lew Tabackin '85–8; Bennie Wallace '87–8. Hirshfield has also worked w. Jim Hall; Randy Brecker; Toots Thielemans; Eddie Daniels; Eliane

Elias; Geo. Gruntz; John Zorn; Ray Anderson; B. Brookmeyer; Bob Belden; Tim Berne; Tom Harrell; Joey Calderazzo; Michael Formanek; etc. Favs: Pete LaRoca, Paul Motian, Elvin Jones, Tony Williams. Fests: Eur., Japan, Austral. CDs: w. Belden (Sunny.; BN); M. Formanek (Enja); R. Rodney–I.Sullivan (Elektra); J. Abercrombie; S. LaSpina; R. McClure; Rich Perry; S. Slagle; D. Stryker (Steep.); G. Dial (dmp); F. Hersch (Red; Sunny.; JC; Angel); Bill Mays (JA); Bennie Wallace (Den.); Akiyoshi; Jim Snidero (Ken); R. Schneiderman (Res.).

HIRT, AL (ALOIS MAXWELL), tpt; b. New Orleans, LA, 11/7/22; d. New Orleans, 4/27/99. Brother Gerald tbnst. w. NO Symph., Louis Prima, Hirt. Tpt. at age 6. Stud. at Cincinnati Cons. 1940–43 After army service '43–6, tour. w. Jimmy and Tommy Dorsey, Ray McKinley, and Horace Heidt. Staff musician at NO radio station for eight years. Left studio work, form. combo w. Pete Fountain at Pier 600 Club, began rec. dixieland albums for Audio Fidelity label '58. Around '60 Hirt's startling bravura style and impressive physical stature (almost 6 1/2 ft. tall and nearly three hundred lbs.) attracted increasing attention. Dur. the next several yrs. he became a national name and a best-selling RCA artist, running his own eponymous club on Bourbon Street and appearing on many TV shows. Pl. w. symph. orchs. and in '65 app. at Carnegie Hall lead. a bb w. arrs. by Gerald Wilson. Mostly active in NO fr. late '60s, lead. own bands, whose personnel at one time included pianist Ellis Marsalis. CDs: RCA; Novus; ProJazz; Intersound; Monument.

HISEMAN, JON (PHILIP JOHN), dms, elec perc; b. London, England, 6/21/44. Family, music hall entertainers. Received basic mus. training at sch.; mostly self-taught, start. w. pno. and vln. First prof. engagement replacing Ginger Baker in Graham Bond band 1966. P. w. Georgie Fame '67–8; John Mayall '68. Also assoc. w. Mike Taylor; New Jazz Orch. Form. own band, Colosseum '68; Jon Hiseman's Tempest '73. Pl. w. United Jazz and Rock Ens. '76; join. wife Barbara Thompson's Paraphernalia '76. Re-form. Colosseum '94. Tours Eur. annually. Own rec. label, TM; also owns and operates 24–track studio, a mus. publ. co. specializing in jazz (UK pub. for such as B. Golson; O. Coleman; R. Weston, D. Gordon, etc.). Early infls: Joe Morello, R. Haynes, Elvin Jones. Has made more than thirty-five recs. w. Andrew Lloyd Webber (MCA); Howard Riley Trio (CBS); United Jazz & Rock Ens. (Mood); Paraphernalia (MCA); B. Thompson (TM); Colosseum. CDs: Sequel; Pinnacle; w. Thompson (VeraBra).

HITE, LES, lead, alto sax; b. DuQuoin, IL, 2/13/03; d. Santa Monica, CA, 2/6/62. Lived in LA dur. the 1920s, pl. w. many bands incl. Mutt Carey, Curtis Mosby. In '30 took over lead. of Paul Howard's Quality Serenaders. L. Armstrong fronted this band, renamed the New Sebastian Cotton Club Orch., for long periods from '30 to '32; sidemen incl. L. Hampton on dms.; Marshal Royal; Lawrence Brown; etc. Hite remained as lead. of band until the mid '40s; later personnel incl. Britt Woodman; T-Bone Walker; Al Morgan. The band pl. long engagements on the East Coast '37, '40–42; in '42 D. Gillespie was a member. Never really active as a pl., Hite retired when orch. disbanded in '45. He became partner of a successful booking agency in '57. Recs. w. Armstrong (OK)'30, '31; w. own band, "Jersey Bounce" (Hit) '42. CDs: w. Armstrong (Col.).

HO, FRED WEI-HAN (Houn), bari, sop saxes; fl, comp, arr; b. Palo Alto, CA, 8/10/57. Self-taught on fl. fr. age 9, bari. sax fr. age 14. Grad. Harvard U., then worked in construction in Boston area until 1981, when he moved to NYC. Pl. w. Charli Persip Superband '82–7; Change of the Century Orch., Gil Evans Orch. '87. Led the Afro-Asian Music Ens. fr. '82; Asian Amer. Art Ens. '83–88; Journey Beyond the West Orch. fr. '90. In addition to shorter pieces, has written an opera, *A Chinaman's Chance*; a musical theater piece, *A Song for Manong*, and a ballet, *Monkey Meets the Spider Spirits*. Received many awds. and fellowships incl. Duke Ellington Awd. of the Black Mus. Conference '88; NY Foundation for the Arts '89; Chinese for Affirmative Action Awd. '91; several Meet the Comp. grants. Taught and lectured at many US univs. incl. Harvard, Stanford, Cornell, U. of Calif., etc. Favs: Leo Parker, Harry Carney, Pepper Adams. Polls: *Coda* '87–8. Fests: Eur. '87 w. own gps. CDs: SN; Atl.; Asian-Improv; w. Afro-Asian Mus. Ens.; Charli Persip (SN).

HODEIR, ANDRÉ, comp, critic; b. Paris, France, 1/22/21. Studied at Paris Cons. 1942–7; pl. vln. w. Django Reinhardt '47–50. Editor of *Jazz Hot*. Arr. and cond. for James Moody w. strings date, Paris '51. Led Jazz Groupe de Paris w. Bobby Jaspar '54–69, perf. only his own comps. In '70s taught in Paris and at Harvard U. Became best known as a provocative and controversial jazz critic. Books: *Jazz: Its Evolution and Essence*; *Toward Jazz*; *Since Debussy*; *Worlds of Jazz* (Grove). Has written scores for more than thirty films. TV: subject of *A Jazz Portrait*, France '71. Rec. w. Reinhardt, K. Clarke for Swing label '48; a Clarke-led sxt. rec. Hodeir's works for Philips '56; the MJQ rec. his "Around the Blues" '60. Hodeir rec. his "Anna Livia Plurabelle," based on a passage fr. Joyce's *Finnegan's Wake*, for Philips '66.

HODES, ART (ARTHUR W.), pno; b. Nikoliev, Russia, 11/14/04; d. Harvey, IL, 3/4/93. Father and uncle were amateur singers; wife Jan is pianist. Family emigrated to Chi. 1905. Stud. at Hull House, Chi. '14–16. Became interested in jazz through bs. Earl Murphy; later hung out w. Louis Armstrong at Chi. blues bars. First gig at Rainbow Gardens '25. Pl. w. Wolverines, post-Beiderbecke '26; Wingy Manone '29–31; Gene Krupa, Frank Teschemacher, Bud Freeman, Muggsy Spanier, Floyd O'Brien, etc. '30s. Moved to NYC '38, pl. w. Joe Marsala, Mezz Mezzrow '40. Led own gps. fr. '40. Had weekly jazz radio prog. on WNYC '40s. Also founded Jazz Record label and edited *Jazz Record* magazine '43–8. Selected magazine articles have since been published as a book, *Selections from the Gutter*. Pl. w. Sidney Bechet '45–9. Ret. to Chi. '50. Taught at Park Forest Cons. '57–67. In the '60s, Hodes toured coll. with the *Sound of Jazz* lecture-concert program and wrote a monthly column for *Down Beat*. Pl. w. various all-star gps. in US and Eur. '70s. Worked mainly as a soloist fr. '70s, utilizing stride and concentrating on his forte, the blues. His autobiog., *Hot Man*, was publ. in '92. Favs: James P. Johnson, Waller, Ellington, Ray Bryant. Polls: Steinway Mus. of Yr. '57. Fests: Eur. fr. '70; Newport-NY '73; Austral. '85; New Zealand '85–6. TV: hosted *Jazz Alley* series late '60s, won Emmy for program *Plain 'Ol Blues*. CDs: Sack., Park., Jazz., Del.; Albert Nicholas–Art Hodes (Del.); w. Bechet (BN); Magnolia Jazz Band (GHB); own gps. in *Hot Jazz on Blue Note* (BN).

HODGES, JOHNNY (JOHN CORNELIUS; "JEEP"; "RABBIT"), alto, sop saxes; comp; b. Cambridge, MA, 7/25/06; d. NYC, 5/11/70. Started on dms. and pno. before taking up sop. sax at age 14. At first he was self-taught, then took lessons from Sidney Bechet, introduced to him by his sist. Boston was his base through the mid 1920s, but he started working in NYC regularly from '24, when he took Bechet's place in Willie "The Lion" Smith's qt. at the Rhythm Club ca. '24; pl. w. Bechet at Club Basha, Bobby Sawyer '25; Lloyd Scott '26; Chick Webb '27. He worked briefly w. Lucky Roberts before join. Duke Ellington in May '28. In the late '30s, he led a small Ellington contingent for a series of records; they featured tunes that he co-authored w. Ellington and were quite successful. During this period, he also took part in other classic jazz sessions for Lionel Hampton; Teddy Wilson; Earl Hines; and performed at Benny Goodman's Carnegie Hall concert in '38. Hodges stayed w. Ellington until Mar. '51, when he formed his own band w. Lawrence Brown and Sonny Greer. The band scored an r&b hit w. "Castle Rock" and enjoyed modest success. Hodges dissolved the

gp. in spring of '55; he worked that summer on Ted Steele's NBC-TV show, then rejoined Ellington, resuming his role as a true mainstay of the band, except for brief periods: in '58, he worked in Florida w. Billy Strayhorn; in '61 he toured Europe w. several fellow sidemen as the Ellington Giants. In '61, he also teamed w. Wild Bill Davis for a series of very well-received albums. In the early '60s he also recorded w. Strayhorn; Oliver Nelson; and Lawrence Welk. He remained with the Ellington band until he suffered a fatal heart attack at the office of his dentist.

Hodges shared with Benny Carter and Willie Smith the distinction of being one of the definitive alto sax innovators in the great formative years of jazz, primarily in the '30s and '40s. Early in his career, he occasionally doubled on soprano sax, his style inspired by his idol, Sidney Bechet. He brought to jazz a sound that was virtually unprecedented. His warm, sensuous tone became a quintessential part of Ellington's palette and was widely emulated by generations of musicians. His solos were characterized by his profound melodic sense, expressed with a surging, perfect fluency, whether on up-tempo numbers or ballads and blues. As Ellington once said: "Johnny Hodges has complete independence of expression. He says what he wants to say on the horn, and that is *it*. He says it in *his* language, from *his* perspective, which is specific, and you could say that his is pure artistry."

Polls: *Esq.* Silver Award '44, '46; Gold Award '45; *DB* readers '40–9; *DB* Critics '59; *Met.* '45–7. Comps/co-comps. w. Ellington: "Jeep's Blues"; "I'm Beginning to See the Light"; "Hodge Podge"; "Squatty Roo"; "The Jeep Is Jumpin' "; "Good Queen Bess." CDs: Prest.; Verve; BB; Pab.; B&B; Imp.; Vogue, w. Ellington (Dec.; Col.; BB; Prest.; MM; BL; Atl.; Pab.; Story.); Armstrong (RCA); Hampton; Esquire All-Stars (BB); Wild Bill Davis; C. Hawkins; G. Mulligan; C. Parker; E. Fitzgerald (Verve); Goodman; B. Holiday (Col.); Rex Stewart; Cootie Williams (B&B); Strayhorn (Red Brn.); T. Wilson (Hep); O. Nelson (RCA); C. Terry (Riv.).

HOFMANN, HOLLY (VIRGINIA), fl, alto fl; b. Painesville, OH, 4/20/56. Playing in both classical and jazz traditions, stud. at Interlochen Arts Academy; received B. Mus. from Cleveland Inst. of Mus., M. Mus. fr. U. of No. Colorado in 1983, and stud. priv. w. Frank Wess. Slide Hampton heard her in mid '70s and told her that she should pursue a life in jazz. Moved to San Diego in '84. Worked w. Mike Wofford; Spike Robinson; Hampton; Jeannie and Jimmy Cheatham; Cleveland Orch.; Cedar Walton; Mundell Lowe; Sheila Jordan; "Sweets" Edison, Bobby Shew. Pl. at Birdland, NYC '98. Favs: James Moody, Lew

Tabackin. TV/Video: *Club Date*, own qt. w. guest Bobby Shew. CDs: Capri; JA; Azica; w. Joe Bonner (Evid.).

HOFSTRA, DAVID C., bs, el-bs, tba; b. Leavenworth, KS, 5/21/53. Studied at U. of Kansas 1971–3. Pl. w. rock, blues bands in Kansas '71–6, then moved to NYC '76. Stud. at Marshall Brown Wkshp. '79–83, later w. Homer Mensch '89–90. Hofstra became a founding member of the Microscopic Septet in '80 and pl. through late '70s and '80s w. Bobby Previte; John Zorn; Wayne Horvitz; Robin Holcomb; Joel Forrester; Lou Grassi; William Parker; Jemeel Moondoc; Phillip Johnston; Denis Charles. Also pl. w. blues mus. Bobby Radcliff; Earl King; James "Thunderbird" Davis; Grady Gaines; Otis Rush. Favs: Paul Chambers, Oscar Pettiford, Leroy Vinnegar. Fests: Eur. since early '80s. TV: VH-1, *Ben Sidran Show* w. Micro. Spt. CDs: w. Micro. Spt. (Stash; Osmosis); Zorn (Elek. None.); w. Bobby Radcliff (BlackTop); B. Frisell (Elek. Mus.); Previte (SA).

HOGAN, G.T. (GRANVILLE THEODORE JR.), dms; b. Galveston, TX, 1/16/29. Played tnr. sax in hs, then sw. to dms. Pl. w. r&b bands incl. Earl Bostic 1953–5. Moved to NYC '55. Pl. w. Randy Weston, also rec. w. Kenny Drew, Kenny Dorham late '50s. Pl. briefly w. Chas. Mingus ca. '58. Pl. in Paris w. Bud Powell '60; in NYC w. Walter Bishop Jr., Elmo Hope early '60s. Hogan later ret. to Tex. where he was less active as a musician. CDs: w. Dorham; Ernie Henry (Riv.); Bishop (Prest.); Jimmy Ford (Champion).

HOGGARD, JAY, vib, comp; b. Washington, DC, 9/28/54. Raised in Mt. Vernon, N.Y. Began on pno., alto sax. Met Duke Ellington, who inspired him to become a mus., at Sacred Concert 1967. Stud. in World Mus. prog. at Wesleyan U. Pl. and tour. w. Jimmy Garrison, Clifford Thornton, who were on the faculty at Wesleyan '74. Stud. xyl. in East Africa dur. junior yr. After graduating, taught hs in New Haven and pl. at Yale U. w. Anthony Davis, Leo Smith, Pheeroan Ak Laff '76. Moved to NYC '77. Pl. fr. late '70s w. Kenny Burrell; James Newton; A. Davis; Henry Threadgill; Jorge Dalto; Oliver Lake; M. Tyner; Muhal Abrams; Chico Freeman; Ahmed Abdullah; Sam Rivers; Michael Gregory; Cecil Taylor; also in vib. gps. w. Lionel Hampton; Milt Jackson; Bobby Hutcherson. Led own gps. fr.'80s. An artist-in-residence at Wesleyan U. Son-in-law of former NYC Mayor David Dinkins. Fests: Eur. fr. '74; No. Africa, India w. own gp. '85. TV: Spike Lee's *Do It A Capella; Days and Nights of Molly Dodd*; BET Cable w. L. Hampton; *Live at Five*-NYC; *Focus on Jazz*-NYC. CDs: Muse; Cont.; Ind. Nav.; w. Burrell

(Cont.); Jerome Harris (Muse); Freeman (Ind. Nav.); Newton (Gram.; BN).

HOLDER, TERRENCE ("T"), tpt, lead; b. Texas, ca. 1898; d. southern US, near the end of the '60s. First came to prominence as a feat. soloist w. Alphonso Trent 1922–5. Form. territory band, Dark Clouds of Joy, which incl. Andy Kirk, Don Byas '26. When Holder left the band in '29, Kirk assumed leadership. Holder formed a new band, also called the Dark Clouds of Joy, which became well known in the early '30s. Sidemen incl. Keg and Budd Johnson, Jesse Stone, Herschel Evans '29; Earl Bostic '30–2; Carl Smith '31; Lloyd Glenn '31–2; Buddy Tate '30–3. The gp. disbanded ca. '33, and Holder began leading a small gp. He later freelanced in Montana '40s and pl. w. Nat Towles early '50s. A Kansas City legend who infl. many young tpts. incl. Hot Lips Page.

HOLDSWORTH, ALLAN, gtr; b. Bradford, England, 8/6/48. After working in rock gps., first prominent in jazz w. Tony Williams' Lifetime mid 1970s. Also pl. and rec. w. Spontaneous Music Ensemble '77 and Jean-Luc Ponty. From early '80s led own group, IOU, often using the SynthAxe gtr. synth. In '90s living in southern Calif., tour. frequently w. own gps. Much admired by young gtrsts., Holdsworth's corruscating single-note lines have often been compared to the late improvising of John Coltrane. CDs: JMS; w. Ian Carr (Core 9); Jean-Luc Ponty (Atl.); John Stevens (Konnex).

HOLIDAY, BILLIE; LADY DAY (Eleanora Fagan), voc; b. Baltimore, MD, 4/7/15; d. NYC, 7/17/59. Father, Clarence Holiday, pl. bjo. and gtr. in Fletcher Henderson Orch. in early 1930s. Holiday moved to NYC '28 to live w. her moth. Began singing in a small Bklyn. club ca. '30, then at Harlem clubs incl. Pods' And Jerry's; Jerry Preston's Log Cabin; Yeah Man. Discovered by Columbia Recs. talent scout John Hammond while singing at Monette's '33. Made rec. debut w. Benny Goodman Nov. '33. Sang in NYC clubs '33–5, then rec. w. Teddy Wilson Orch. '35–9; as leader of her own all-star combos fr. '36 to 42. The Wilson sides incl. her first work w. Lester Young. Vocalist w. orchs. of Count Basie '37; Artie Shaw '38. Perf. at Café Society Downtown '39. Tour. as single fr. '40. Holiday rose to stardom in the '40s and in '46 app. w. Louis Armstrong and Kid Ory in the film *New Orleans*. Jailed on drug charge after highly publicized trial '47. Tour. Eur. w. Jazz Club USA '54; as single '58. Made final app. at Phoenix Theater, NYC June '59. Herself inspired by Bessie Smith and Louis Armstrong, she is considered by many to be the most important and influential female singer in jazz history. Her phrasing and overall musicianship were held in high regard by many musicians, in particular Lester Young (who named her "Lady Day") and the other members of the Basie band with whom she perf. and rec. in the '30s and '40s. Despite its gradual deepening through the yrs., the timbre of her voice remained compelling, even when her battle against chronic drug and alcohol addiction took its toll on her intonation. Her most commercially successful recs. were "Strange Fruit"; "Fine and Mellow" (Commodore) '39; and *Lover Man,* Decca '44; her own favorite was *Lady in Satin* '58. Polls: *Esq.* Gold Awd. '44, '47; *Esq.* Silver Awd. '45–6; *Met.* '45–6. TV: *The Sound Of Jazz.* CDs: Col.; Dec.; Verve; Comm.; BL; BN; w. JATP (Verve).

HOLIDAY, CLARENCE E., gtr; b. Baltimore, MD, ca. 1900; d. Dallas, TX, 3/1/37. Father of Billie Holiday. Pl. w. Fletcher Henderson Orch. 1928–33, then rec. w. Benny Carter '34; Bob Howard '35. Worked w. Charlie Turner '35; Louis Metcalf '35–6; Don Redman '36–7. CDs: w. Henderson (Col.; Class.); Carter (Charly; JSP).

HOLLAND, DAVE (DAVID), bs, el-bs, cello, comp; b. Wolverhampton, England, 10/1/46. Began on bs. at age 17. Stud. w. James E. Merrit at Guildhall Sch., London, also pl. w. classical orchs. 1964–8. First jazz exp. w. dixie. gps., then pl. w. Ronnie Scott; John Surman; Humphrey Lyttelton; Evan Parker; Kenny Wheeler; Tubby Hayes; Spontaneous Music Ens. Miles Davis heard him in London in '68 and asked him to join his gp. Pl. w. Davis '68–70; Circle w. Chick Corea, Barry Altschul, Anthony Braxton '70–1; Braxton, Karl Berger '70–6; Joe Henderson '72; Paul Bley '72–3; Stan Getz '73–5; Lee Konitz '74; Gateway w. John Abercrombie, Jack DeJohnette '75–7; Sam Rivers '76–80. Led own gp. fr. '82; sidemen have incl. Wheeler; Steve Coleman; Marvin Smith; Julian Priester; Robin Eubanks. Also pl. in '80 w. Kenny Barron. Holland has perf. and rec. as an unaccomp. soloist on bass and cello. He taught in the summer prog. at Banff Sch. of Fine Arts in '82 and joined the faculty of the New Engl. Cons. in '87. Tour. int'l w. P. Metheny, H. Hancock, DeJohnette in '90s. Pl. w. Davis in Paris '91. Tour. int'l w. Davis tribute band '92. Favs: Ray Brown, Mingus, Scott LaFaro, Gary Peacock, Paul Chambers. Polls: *MM* '69; *DB* critics TDWR '73. CDs: ECM incl. *Emerald Tears,* solo album; w. Gateway; Circle; Wheeler; Abercrombie; T. Stanko; C. Walcott (ECM); M. Davis (Col.); S. Coleman (Novus; DIW); Henderson (Verve; Mile.); Corea (BN; ECM); Braxton (hatArt); Muhal Abrams; Karl Berger (BS); Franco Ambrosetti; Barron (Enja); Hank Jones (Em.; Conc.);

Joe Lovano; K. Eubanks (BN); N. Brignola (Res.); L. Tabackin (Conc.); Spontaneous Mus. Ens. (Chronoscope); R. Eubanks; Gary Thomas (JMT); Petrucciani (Drey.); Liebman (Owl); Rivers (Tom.; IAI).

HOLLAND, PEANUTS (HERBERT LEE), tpt, voc; b. Norfolk, VA, 2/9/10; d. Stockholm, Sweden, 2/7/79. Raised in Jenkins' Orphanage in S.C., where he learned to pl. tpt. Pl. w. Alphonso Trent in the Southwest 1929–33; Al Sears '32; led own band '33–8; also pl. brief stints w. Willie Bryant; Jimmie Lunceford; Lil Armstrong '30s. Moved to NYC '39, pl. w. C. Hawkins '41; F. Henderson '41–2; C. Barnet '42–6; own gp. '46. Went to Eur. w. Don Redman '46 and remained there; tour. as a single and worked w. various combos. in Scand. and on the Continent until ill health curtailed his activities in the early '70s. Recs. w. Trent, Champion '33; Barnet, Dec. '42; M. Mezzrow '59; in Paris rec. w. Don Byas; Billy Taylor; et al. CDs: w. Barnet (Dec.); Mezzrow (Jazz Time); Redman (Steep.).

HOLLEY, MAJOR QUINCY JR. (MULE), bs, tba, cello; b. Detroit, MI, 7/10/24; d. Maplewood, NJ, 10/25/90. From musical family. Began on vln., tba. Began pl. bs. while in navy band. After discharge studied at Groth Sch. of Mus. Pl. w. Dexter Gordon–Wardell Gray in Calif., then w. Charlie Parker and Ella Fitzgerald in Det. Made rec. debut w. Oscar Peterson 1950. On staff at BBC-TV, London '54–6. Pl. w. Woody Herman '58, incl. St. Dept. tour of So. Amer.; Al Cohn–Zoot Sims '59–60; Kenny Burrell, Coleman Hawkins, Roy Eldridge, Quincy Jones early '60s; Duke Ellington '64. Freelanced in NYC '64–7, then taught at Berklee Coll. of Mus. '67–70. Pl. w. Pepper Adams–Donald Byrd at Half Note, Jaki Byard at Bradley's, and house band at Jimmy Ryans early '70s. Tour. Eur. w. Helen Humes, Kings of Jazz '70s. Freelanced in NYC and Eur. fr. '70s. Holley worked extens. in TV, radio, and Broadway pit bands, and was involved in community service in NYC. Holley often sang along in unison with his bowed solos, in a style reminiscent of Slam Stewart's. Fests: So. Amer. '58; Eur. fr. '70s; many Colo. JP. TV: PBS w. Eldridge at NJF-NY '73. CDs: B&B; Timel.; w. Stewart (Delos; B&B); Ray Bryant; Harry Edison; Roland Hanna; Humes; G. Wiggins (B&B); Hawkins (Verve; Imp.); Z. Sims (32); Ellington (Pab.); Q. Jones; R.R. Kirk (Merc.); J. McShann; Flip Phillips (Chiaro.); W. Herman (Evid.); Burrell; S. Turrentine (BN); J. Venuti (Sonet); C. Terry (Delos); Buddy Tate (Res.; NW); Harry Allen (Prog.); Konitz (LRC); P. Appleyard (Conc.).

HOLLOWAY, RED (JAMES WESLEY), alto, tnr saxes, voc; b. Helena, AR, 5/31/27. Mother pl. pno., fath. vln. To Chicago at age 5; stud. cl., sax in hs; Chi. Cons. 1948–50. Pl. w. Eugene Wright's band '43–6. Join. army at 19; band master for US 5th Army Band. Back to Chi. in '46. Pl. w. Y. Lateef, Dexter Gordon. From '48 pl. sax for Roosevelt Sykes and many other bluesmen, becoming typecast as mainly a blues pl.; however, he worked in the area w. B. Holiday; S. Rollins; L. Hampton; and many other jazz artists. Toured w. Brother Jack McDuff '63–6. To LA '67; fr. '69 to '84 was talent coordinator and member of house band at the Parisian Room, taking leaves for overseas tours. Worked often on tnr. w. Sonny Stitt until Stitt's death in '82. From early '80s enjoyed growing success, generating excitement with his big sound and hard-driving mainstream-modern style on tnr. and a more ballad-oriented approach on alto. Often teamed w. Clark Terry in '90s; gigged and rec. w. Horace Silver '93. Favs: B.Webster, C. Parker, L. Young; arr: B. Golson. Fests: Marciac, '89; Colo. JP; *Norway* Jazz Cruises. CDs: Chiaro.; Prest.; Conc.; Steep.; High.; w. McDuff; G. Benson (Prest.); Terry (Chiaro.; Delos); Silver (Col.); Ernestine Anderson; Ray Brown; Frank Capp; Concord All-Stars; Carmen McRae (Conc.); Knut Riisnaes (Gem.).

HOLLOWAY, RON (RONALD EDWARD), tnr sax; b. Washington, DC, 8/24/53. Began on alto sax at age 16; sw. to tnr. sax three mos. later. Mainly self-taught. Sat in w. Freddie Hubbard, Sonny Rollins, and Dizzy Gillespie mid '70s. Pl. w. Osiris '77–80; Rootboy Slim '77–87; Gil Scott-Heron '82–9; Gillespie Qnt. '89–92. Led own gp. In '90s. First rec. as leader for Mile '92. A bear-down-hard-bopper who can blow authentic r&b and croon a ballad with warm, blue feeling. Uses the tnr.'s upper register effectively. Favs: Sonny Rollins, John Coltrane. Polls: Wash. Area Music Awards '85–88, '92–3. Fests: Eur. w. Scott-Heron; Eur., So. Africa, Japan, Russia w. Gillespie. Film: *Clara's Heart* w. Whoopi Goldberg '90. Video: *Black Wax* w. Scott-Heron, '82; *Wolf Trap Celebrates Dizzy Gillespie* '87. TV: *Arsenio Hall* '91, *Tonight Show,* '90 w. Gillespie. CDs: Mile.; w. Gillespie (BluesAlley; ProJazz); Scott-Heron (Essential; Arista).

HOLLYDAY, CHRISTOPHER, alto sax; b. Norwood, MA, 1/3/70. First pl. sax at age 9, learned C. Parker solos by age 14. Debut album as leader, *Treaty* 1985, on his own label, Jazzbeat, followed by *Reverence* w. Cedar Walton, Ron Carter, Billy Higgins '88. In '89 was feat. soloist on M. Ferguson's "60th Birthday Tour"; headlined at Village Vanguard; and taped *Christopher Hollyday* for Novus, the first of four recs. for that label. Tour. Eur.; app. w. own band opposite Harry Connick. Pl. the Blue Note, NYC, w.

own qt. '90. His photo appeared in *Time* magazine; made first nat'l tour w. own qt., portions documented in a CBS-TV *Sunday Morning* '91. First inspiration was Charlie Parker but then he became strongly infl. by Jackie McLean. His last two albums feat. many of his own comps. While these pointed toward new growth, RCA dropped his contract in '92 and he exited the jazz scene. Little has been heard of him since. CDs: Novus.

HOLLYDAY, RICHARD T., tpt; b. New Haven, CT, 6/20/65. Brother of Christopher Hollyday. Began playing in Hamden, Conn. 1974 and in Norwood, Mass. '76 stud. w. Leon Merian. The Norwood HS Jazz Ens., in which he was feat. soloist, arr. and lead., became state champion '80–83. After tour. New Engl., leading a quintet with such sidemen as Donald Brown, Terri Lyne Carrington, and Delfeayo Marsalis, he teamed with his bro. as mus. dir. of Hollyday Bros. Qnt. '85–7. From '89 to 92, led own qt. or qnt. in Boston area. Winner of several "Most Valuable Player" awards while in his teens, also worked in Boston as a real estate manager from '85 to '90. CDs: Jazzbeat.

HOLMAN, BILL (WILLIS LEONARD), comp, tnr sax, lead; b. Olive, CA, 5/21/27. Raised in Santa Ana, Calif; Navy service 1944–6; stud. engineering at UCLA '48; counterpoint w. Russ Garcia and music at Westlake College '48–51. Pl. w. C. Barnet '51; joined S. Kenton '52. First comp. for Kenton "Invention for Guitar and Trumpet"; wrote for Kenton off and on into late '70s. Worked w. Shorty Rogers '56–7, arr. for Maynard Ferguson, and co-led a qnt. w. Mel Lewis '58. Contributed to the library of Gerry Mulligan's Concert Jazz Band '60; also arr. for Terry Gibbs; Woody Herman; et al. In '66 discontinued playing as the result of illness but has resumed occ. in recent years. In '70s wrote albums for C. Basie and Zoot Sims; arr. for Buddy Rich; Doc Severinsen; Louis Bellson; and made almost annual trips to Germany to write for West German radio band. Also visited Scandinavia and Engl. for writing assignments. Started own band in LA '75, and gigged w. it locally into '90s. Arrs. for Mel Lewis; Peggy Lee; Sarah Vaughan; Natalie Cole; Della Reese; the Fifth Dimension; The Association; et al. Has also worked w. school bands and clinics, and received various commissions. Hundreds of recordings of Holman's work attest to the skillful, swinging nature of his writing. His contrapuntal-oriented charts for Stan Kenton—notably "Stompin' At The Savoy"—were among the most swinging pieces in the entire Kenton repertoire. André Previn once observed that Holman was "a first rate saxophonist, but his true instrument is the orchestra, and he plays it with musicianship, honesty and brilliance." A more recent example of this is his arr. of "Just Friends" on his JVC CD where the only "solo" is his chart. CDs: JVC; VSOP; w. Kenton (Mos; Cap.); Gibbs; L. Niehaus (Cont.); Rogers (BB); E. Fitzgerald; A. O'Day (Verve); A. Pepper (PJ); R. Kamuca (FS).

HOLMES, CHARLIE (CHARLES WILLIAM), alto sax; b. Boston, MA, 1/27/10; d. Boston, 9/12/85. Childhood friend of Johnny Hodges and Harry Carney. Stud. oboe; pl. w. Boston Civic Symph. in 1926. Moved to NYC w. Carney '27; pl. briefly w. Chick Webb; Henri Saparo; others before join. George Howe, remaining when Luis Russell became lead. Left in '28, rejoin. Saparo, then w. Russell again. Pl. w. Mills Blue Rhythm Band '32; then w. Russell until '40, incl. L. Armstrong as lead. '35–40. Pl. w. Bobby Burnet '41; Cootie Williams' big band '42–5; tour. Far East w. USO show '45–6 w. Jesse Stone. After ret. to US, pl. briefly w. John Kirby, Billy Kyle '47; freelanced. In '50s retired from full-time mus. and worked for an insurance co.; pl. w. Joe Garland's band on weekends; cont. to pl. some dates and rec. in '60s and '70s. Considered one of the better Hodges-style altos in the '30s. Recs. w. Russell '28–9; Armstrong '35–40; Red Allen '29–30; J.C. Higginbotham '30; Al Sears '52; Clyde Bernhardt '72–5; Kustbandet in Sweden '75. CDs: Red Allen (Class.); Armstrong (Col.; Class,); Mills Blue Rhythm (Hep); Luis Russell (JSP); F. Waller; J. Teagarden (BB).

HOLMES, GROOVE (RICHARD ARNOLD), org; b. Camden, NJ, 5/2/31; d. St. Louis, MO, 6/29/91. No formal mus. training. Worked in small clubs for several yrs. before he was discovered in Pittsburgh 1960 by Les McCann, who recommended him to Dick Bock of Pacific Jazz. Beginning in '61 he rec. a series of albums for that label and worked mainly in So. Calif. clubs. Tour. w. own trio from '62. His hit single, "Misty," from the Prestige album *Soul Message*, sold more than 300,000 copies '65. After rec. ten more LPs for Prest., he shifted to Groove Merchant, where he also teamed w. Jimmy McGriff for studio and concert recs. In '76 his gp. incl. kybd. pl. Khalid Moss and Mel Roach, dms. Though he named Jimmy Smith as his fav. blues organ artist, Holmes stated that he was infl. by no other organist: "I listen to none of them—nothing they do interests me; I play completely differently. I listen to bass men." Holmes himself also played bs. Naturally left-handed, he was infl. by Paul Chambers and Ron Carter, and his strong bass pedal line more closely resembles that of a string bass than the bass lines of most organists. CDs: PJ; Prest.; Muse; 32; w. McCann (Rh./Atl.).

HOLOBER, MICHAEL, pno, comp, arr; b. Brooklyn, NY, 4/21/57. Studied at SUNY-Oneonta 1975–9; SUNY-Binghamton '81–2. Pl. w. Slam Stewart '85–6; Nick Brignola fr. '89; Jazz Caucus w. Dave Calarco, Tom Harrell, Jerry Bergonzi fr. '90. Led own Gotham Jazz Orch. at Small's, NYC '96. Holober has taught pno., comp., and ens. at SUNY-Binghamton '82–6; New York U. fr. '87; City Coll. NY fr. '89. Favs: Bill Evans, Chick Corea, Keith Jarrett; arrs: Gil Evans, Bob Brookmeyer. CD: w. Brignola (Res.).

HOLT, RED (ISAAC), dms; b. Rosedale, MS, 5/1/32. Best known for long association w. Ramsey Lewis from 1956–66; co-led, w. bs. Eldee Young, soul jazz group, Young-Holt Unlimited '66–74; later led similar group, Red Holt Unlimited. From '70s worked with educational and community organizations in the Chicago area. CDs: w. Lewis (Chess).

HONDA, TAKEHIRO (TAKASHI), pno, comp, lead; b. Iwate Pref., Japan, 8/21/45. Brothers-in-law are Sadao and Fumio Watanabe; son Tamaya is drummer. Music lessons fr. childhood. Stud. w. Kazuko Nagamine while in hs and at Kunitachi U. of Mus. Left college after two yrs. to pursue jazz career. Pl. in 1960s w. Kazunori Takeda; Fumio Watanabe; then w. Masahiko Togashi. Form. own trio late '60s. Signed rec. deal w. Trio label '69; made six albums in two yrs. Accomp. singer Mieko Hirota '71. Pl. w. Sadao Watanabe '73–8. Rec. two albums w. Ron Carter, Tony Williams '77. Co-led gp. Native Sun w. Kosuke Mine '78–85. Pl. in mid to late '80s w. Toshiyuki Honda; Motohiko Hino; own gp. w. son Tamaya Honda. Formed Earthian All-Star Ens. (EASE) w. K. Mine, Shigeharu Mukai, Takeo Uematsu '92. Pl. educational jazz concerts w. Paul Jackson '93. Polls: *SJ* Readers '74–9. Fests: all major w. Watanabe. CDs: JVC; FunHouse.

HONDA, TOSHIYUKI, sop, alto saxes, fl, comp; b. Tokyo, Japan, 4/9/57. Father was well-known jazz critic, pl. bs. Primarily self-taught. Pl. at Pit Inn in Tokyo while in hs. Decided to become prof. mus. while studying at Seikei U. Pl. w. Geo. Ohtsuka, Ryojiro Furusawa 1976. Stud. comp. and arr. w. Toshio Ogawa. Formed gp. Burning Waves, which rec. its debut album in LA '77. Rec. w. Chick Corea, Miroslav Vitous, Roy Haynes '83. Scored Juzo Itami films *Marusa No Onna* '87; *Marusa No Onna 2* '88; also comp. extensively for TV. Formed gps. Radio Club '87, Re-Lax '92. Fav: Joe Farrell. Polls: *SJ* Readers soprano '84–93; *SJ* Rec. of Year '87. CDs: King-ElectricBird; Toshiba-East World.

HOOD, BILL (WILLIAM HARRISON), bari sax, comp; b. Portland, OR, 12/13/24; d. Portland, 12/1/92. Brother of gtr./zither player Ernie Hood (b. Charlotte, NC, 6/2/23; d. '91). Stud. pno.; self-taught on saxes, woodwinds, and as comp. Cond. for GI show in Pacific after WWII; pl w. Freddie Slack 1946–7. To Calif. in '50s; pl. or rec. w. Bill Holman; Shorty Rogers; Chet Baker; etc.; Monterey JF '58, '62, '65; w. B. Goodman '61, '65; Terry Gibbs '65. Occ. w. Benny Carter '50s–'70s. Toured Japan w. Q. Jones '75; led qnt. w. Jack Nimitz in mid '60s; formed the Love Bros. '74. Worked as studio musician into early '80s. From late '80s, unable to play due to illness. CDs: w. Helen Humes (Cont.); Z. Sims (Pab.); Tormé (Verve; Stash).

HOOGENDIJK, JARMO, tpt; b. Den Helder, Netherlands, 3/28/65. Studied at Royal Cons, The Hague, w. Ack Van Rooyen; also priv. lessons w. Woody Shaw, who introduced Hoogendijk to many American mus. Worked in Europe w. own qnt. since 1984. Taught tpt. at the Cons. of Rotterdam and The Hague since '90. Favs: Armstrong, Shaw, K. Dorham. Polls: Pall Mall Export Award '86. Fests: Eur. since '84; US '88; Can. '92. TV: many app. on Eur. TV w. own qnt. CDs: Timel.; w. Nueva Manteca–Nicky Marrero (Timel.).

HOOPER, LES (LESTER JOSEPH III), comp, arr, pno; b. Jackson, MS, 2/27/40. Early work w. J. Klemmer; Richard Evans; Singers Unlimited in Chicago mid 1960s. Recs. w. Klemmer; Don Ellis; Ben Sidran; etc., but primarily active for many years as a TV and film comp. and as an educ. Comp. *Jazz Rock Symphony* under a grant from National Endowment; other commissions from New Amer. Orch. In early '90s was operating own synth. studio in Sherman Oaks, Calif. Favs: Bill Evans, C. Corea, Clare Fischer. LP: CW.

HOOPER, LOU (LOUIS STANLEY), pno, comp; also org, vln, vla; b. North Buxton, Ont., Canada, 5/18/1894; d. Charlottetown, PEI, Canada, 9/17/77. Father, vlnst. in Can., late 1800s; bros. Fred, tpt.; Arnold, vln. Start. as choir boy, later became soloist at St. Luke's Episcopal Church in Ypsilanti, Mich. Pno. lessons at 10. Grad. from Detroit Cons. 1916; postgrad. studies; B. Mus. '20; also stud. at Columbia U. Teachers Coll. '23–4. Pl. w. Hooper Brothers Orch., Ypsilanti '06; worked w. dance bands in Detroit. Led small concert-party in France dur. WWI '18. Moved to NYC '21, pl. in pit orch. w. Mildred Franklin. Worked w. Elmer Snowden, Bob Fuller '24–8, often accomp. female singers incl. Ethel Waters, Monette Moore. Recs. w. Bubber Miley;

Louis Metcalf; Ma Rainey; pl. shows w. Bessie Smith; Lew Leslie's *Blackbirds of 1928–9*. Accomp. Paul Robeson for six mos. Taught classical pno. at Martin-Smith Mus. Sch., which later became Juilliard. Ret. to Can. '32, began long assoc. w. Myron Sutton's Canadian Ambassadors, w. whom he pl. on and off for next forty yrs.; orch. backed Billie Holiday, Connie's Inn, Montreal '39. Enlisted in Can. Artillery '39, served in Eur. to '45, in charge of Can. Concert Parties.

Rediscovered living in Montreal in '62. Member of Montreal Vintage Mus. Society; feted by Int'l Assoc. of Rec. Collectors '73; prod. an evening of his own works from '18–70. Moved to Prince Edward Island '75, taught at local U. In last yrs., several apps. on CBC. Infl: B. Goodman, C. Christian, B. Beiderbecke, J.P. Johnson, Ralph Sutton, Ellington, Armstrong. Comps: *Ruth*, an oratorio; music to *The Congo*, by Vachel Lindsay; "Wanderlust"; "Cakewalk"; "South Sea Strut"; "Undecided Rag"; "Rainy Day Rag"; "Sunny Day Rag," last three written in '75. Recs: solo piano (CBC); *The Jolly Miners* w. Snowden, Fuller (Historical).

HOPE, BERTHA (Rosemond), pno, comp; b. Los Angeles, CA, 11/8/36. Began stud. classical pno. w. her parents at age 3 and cont. pno. studies until 12 or 13; again at 16. Also pl. cl., vln., cello in sch. orch.; perc. She became interested in jazz through hearing Shelly Manne and Shorty Rogers, but it was listening to Bud Powell on recs. and, finally, in person at the Haig in LA, early '50s, that convinced her to play jazz. Encouraged by Vi Redd; Teddy Edwards; Les McCann. Took lessons w. Richie Powell for six mos. Pl. w. Johnny Otis band. Pl. in local trios. In '58 met Elmo Hope when he came to LA as part of Sonny Rollins gp. He expressed an interest in her music. They married in '60 and moved to NYC the following yr., rec. some duets for Riverside. After his death she resumed her studies and pl. career. Rec. as lead. for Steep. w. Walter Booker, Billy Higgins '90. Active in NYC as solo, duo, trio pno; also member of all-female gp., Jazzberry Jam. CDs: Steep.; Min. Mus.; w. E. Hope (Riv.).

HOPE, ELMO (ST. ELMO SYLVESTER), pno, comp; b. NYC, 6/27/23; d. NYC, 5/19/67. Parents were from West Indies. As a child stud. classical pno. and listened to a lot of classical recs. w. his friend Bud Powell. Won awards for solo recitals from 1938. From '48 to 51 tour. w. Joe Morris's R&B band; then freelanced w. Clifford Brown; S. Rollins; et al. His cabaret card was revoked, preventing him from NYC apps ca. '56; tour. w. Chet Baker '57; settled in LA where he pl. w. Harold Land; w. Lionel Hampton at the Moulin Rouge, Hollywood fall '59. Ret. to NYC '61; pl. only occasionally in his last yrs. due to poor health. With a style that parallels Powell, Hope was a pianist and composer of rare harmonic acuity and very personal interpretation. His wife, pnst. Bertha Hope, said: "He's got a 'stretched out' way of delivery—elastic. He's the epitome of elasticity." CDs: BN; Prest.; Cont.; Riv.; Mile.; w. C. Brown; Lou Donaldson (BN); S. Rollins; J. McLean (Prest.); Land (Cont.).

HOPE, STAN (William Stanley Hope Winfield), pno, gtr; b. Atlantic City, NJ, 7/10/33. Mother was soloist in church choir. Pl. w. family band, the Hope Four, then freelanced fr. age 15. Worked in Atlantic City 1951–3; pl. w. Milt Jackson; Sonny Stitt; James Moody; Dizzy Gillespie; Roy Haynes. Pl. w. Billy Ford '53, then lived w. Charli Persip in Newark, pl. w. Hank Mobley, Joe Holiday. Worked w. Kitty Noble '55–6; Coleman Hawkins, Eric Dixon, Charlie Rouse, Paul Gonsalves '56–8; Ink Spots '58–65. Hope decided to come off the road in '66 and worked for a year w. Slam Stewart and Peck Morrison at the Village Door in Queens, NYC. Since '85 he has worked mainly w. Houston Person and Etta Jones. Fav. arrs: Ernie Wilkins, Marty Paich. Fests: Tokyo '64; Madrid '88; also Caribbean jazz cruises. CDs: w. H. Person–E. Jones (Muse).

HOPKINS, CLAUDE DRISKETT, pno, lead; b. Alexandria, VA, 8/24/03; d. NYC, 2/19/84. Raised in Wash., D.C. Start. on pno. at age 6; stud. mus. and medicine, earning a B.A. in mus. at Howard U., where both parents were faculty. Early inspirations were Chopin; pno. rolls of James P. Johnson, Fats Waller. Pl. in coll. orchs.; led own band in Atlantic City; went to NYC in 1924, pl. briefly w. Wilbur Sweatman. In Sept. '25 to Eur. as mus. dir. of *Revue Negre*, feat. Josephine Baker; band incl. S. Bechet; as Baker's fame took off, the show tour. Eur. and was wildly successful; also tour. Italy and Spain w. own band early '26. Hopkins ret. to US spring '26; led own orch. at Asbury Park, N.J.; Crystal Cavern in Wash., D.C.; Roseland and other NYC clubs. In '30 took over lead. of Charlie Skeete's band at Cocoanut Grove in Harlem, moved to Savoy; Roseland '31–5; Cotton Club '35–6; tour. extensively '37–40. From '30 Hopkins' orch. was one of the most popular black bands in the country, helped by regular radio broadcasts; sidemen at times incl. Edmond Hall; Vic Dickenson; Jabbo Smith. Disbanded '40 but re-form. '41, tour. again to '42. During WWII worked as aircraft inspector at General Motors plant, Linden, N.J.; led company's band; also tour. Can., Ohio w. own band fall '43. In '44, form. new orch. for Club Broadway

residency; also worked as arr. for Phil Spitalny; Tommy Tucker; others. From '44 to '47, led various combos at the Zanzibar; tour. w. novelty qnt. '48–9; own gp. at Cafe Society '50–1. Pl. in a gp. w. Doc Cheatham, Vic Dickenson, the Drootin bros., and Jimmy Woode at George Wein's Mahogany Hall, Boston '52–4; w. Red Allen at the Metropole, NYC '54–5; Herman Autrey late '50s; Sol Yaged '60. From '60 to '66, led own gps. in NYC, also upstate N.Y., Toronto Pl. w. Roy Eldridge at Jimmy Ryan's for several yrs.; nightclubs in N.J. From '67 to '69 w. Wild Bill Davison's Jazz Giants. Active in '70s, incl. several jazz fests. Tour. Eur. w. Dicky Wells, Earle Warren '82. A master of stride with a lyrical bent and a consistent sense of swing. Fests: Concord '73; Andernos, Spain '74; Nice, Manassas '74. Films: *Dance Team*; *Wayward*; *Barbershop Blues*. TV: Nice, '74; WGBH, Boston '75. Comps: "I Would Do Anything For You"; "Crying My Heart Out For You"; "Safari Stomp"; "Late Evening Blues"; "Crazy Fingers"; "Blame It On a Dream." LPs: Prest.; Chiaro. CDs: Class; w. Teddy Wilson; Eubie Blake; Dill Jones, *Jazz Piano Masters: Live at the New School* (Chiaro.).

HOPKINS, FRED (FREDERICK), bs; b. Chicago, IL, 10/11/47; d. Chicago, 1/7/99. Studied w. Capt. Walter Dyett of DuSable HS; trained w. Civic Orch.; later stud. w. Joseph Guastafeste of Chi. Symph. Member of AACM late 1960s; pl w. Kalaparusha Maurice McIntyre '70; Henry Threadgill and Steve McCall in trio, Reflection, '71–2. Relocated to NYC '75; rejoin. Threadgill and McCall in trio, Air. Rec. in late '70s w. Anthony Braxton; Marion Brown; Oliver Lake; David Murray; Hamiet Bluiett; Don Pullen; in '80s w. Bobby McFerrin, World Bass Violin Ensemble. Moved back to Chi. '97; own gp. '98. Favs: Koussevitsky, Wilbur Ware, Richard Davis, Ray Brown. CDs: w. Ahmed Abdullah; Charle Brackeen (Silk); Muhal Abrams; Air; Pullen (BS); Bluiett (BS; Tutu); John Carter (Gram.); Craig Harris; Tom Varner (SN); Oliver Lake (BS; Gram.); D. Murray (WW; BS; DIW); Threadgill (RCA).

HORN, PAUL JOSEPH, fl, saxes; b. NYC, 3/17/30. Graduated from Oberlin Cons. 1952; Manh. Sch. of Music '53. Pl. w. Sauter-Finegan Orch '56; Chico Hamilton '56–8. Led own qnt. early '60s at Shelly's Manne Hole, etc.; in '65 rec. Lalo Schifrin's *Jazz Suite on the Mass Texts*. An early experimenter in modal devices and unusual meters. Moved to Victoria, B.C. '70. During the next twenty yrs., he stud. and later taught Transcendental Meditation; perf. and rec. as a soloist at the Taj Mahal, the Great Pyramid and other exotic locations. In the '80s and early '90s he often was more closely identified w. New Age music than jazz. Autobiography: *Inside Paul Horn* (Harper-Collins) '90. CDs: Black Sun; BMG; Celestial Harmonies; Kuckuck; w. S. Rogers (BB); Tormé (Stash); C. Tjader (Fant.).

HORN, SHIRLEY, pno, voc; b. Washington, DC, 5/1/34; d. Cheverly, MD, 10/21/05. Studied pno. and comp. at Howard U. fr. ages 12 to 18; later majored in music at Howard. Inspired by Oscar Peterson; Ahmad Jamal; Debussy; and Rachmaninoff. An early marriage at 21 slowed her music career; for the most part, worked clubs in the Washington and Baltimore area and rec. only occasionally. Her album, *Embers and Ashes*, caught the attention of Miles Davis, enabling her to open opposite him at the Village Vanguard. In 1963 rec. three LPs for Mercury, but the company insisted that she give up pno. in favor of vocals. An upswing in her career began w. a series of albums for Verve, from '87, the first of which was *I Thought About You. Close Enough For Love* '89 and *You Won't Forget Me* '90 followed. The latter featured guest appearances by Davis and Wynton Marsalis, reaching top of jazz charts. Her longtime accompanists were Charles Ables, bs; Steve Williams, dms. Horn's trio accomp. Carmen McRae on a '91 album. In '98 she rec. a Miles Davis tribute album. Her distinctive timbre and unhurried pace, complemented by subtle piano accompaniment, made for a most singularly effective style. CDs: Verve; Steep.; Merc.; w. Marsalis (Col.); McRae (Novus).

HORNE, LENA, voc; b. Brooklyn, NY, 6/30/17. Started as dancer at Cotton Club 1934. Tour. and rec. w. Noble Sissle Orch. '35–6. After four mos. w. Charlie Barnet's band '40–1, she earned great popularity as a singer at Café Society. Starred in movies in '40s incl. *Cabin in the Sky*; *Stormy Weather*. Although considered by many as a popular singer, has been closely assoc. w. many jazz artists and her work is strongly informed by jazz. Her pnsts. and mus. directors have incl. Horace Henderson, Phil Moore, and Lennie Hayton, whom she married in Paris in '47. Autobiography, *In Person, Lena Horne*, was publ. in '50. She app. in the Broadway musical *Jamaica* '57–9. In early '80s her one-woman show, *The Lady and Her Music*, ran on Broadway for a yr. Fests: JVC-NY: tribute to Billy Strayhorn program '93; evening celebrating her 80th birthday w. presentation of Ella Award for Lifetime Achievement in Vocal Artistry, '97. Rec. w. Artie Shaw (RCA) '41. CDs: BN; BB; DRG; RCA; Three Cherries; DCC Jazz; w. Barnet (Cir.); Sidney Bechet (Class.).

HORNER, TIM (TIMOTHY LEWIS), dms, perc, arr; b. Roanoke, VA, 7/24/56. Father is dmr. and

church choir dir.; moth. is church org.; bro. is jazz pnst. in Boston. Start. listening to jazz recs. at age 8. Began on dms.; later pl. vln. in local symph. orchs. Stud. dms., perc., comp. at Berklee Coll. of Mus. Pl. w. Tommy Dorsey Orch. 1977–8; Herb Pomeroy '78–9. Tour. Germany w. Reiner Schnell bb '79; Japan w. Helen Merrill, Chris Connor, Ernestine Anderson '81–3. Pl. w. Warne Marsh '82–3; Clifford Jordan '83–4; Joe Locke fr. '83; Pepper Adams in Singapore '84; Bobby Enriquez '86–90; Ted Nash fr. '90; Red Rodney briefly '91; Jazz Nativity, Tom Lellis fr. '91; Mark Murphy fr. '92; Maria Schneider bb, Jon Gordon fr. '93; Hendrik Meurkens mid '90s. Favs: Billy Hart, Al Foster, Mel Lewis, Elvin Jones; arrs: Gil Evans, Claus Ogerman, Thad Jones. TV: ABC Morning Show in LA '85. CDs: w. T. Nash (Maple.); Lynn Seaton (Timel.); Bill Mays; Meurkens (Conc.); Jon Gordon (Chiaro.).

HORTON, JOANNE BARBARA ("PUG"), voc; b. Sheffield, England, 5/30/32. Uncle, bs. Hank Hobson, was London freelancer who pl. w. Shearing; Grappelli; Pearl Bailey; Eartha Kitt. Husband is Bob Wilber. Start. singing at age 9 w. local dance bands. Inspired to become singer after hearing Bessie Smith recs. at age 11. Sang w. uncle Colin Whitehead's band 1945–6. Fr. '47 to '60 worked as prof. dancer, actress, and TV artist in UK, Can., and US. Tour. So. Amer. as goodwill ambassador for US goverment '57; resumed singing career in Albany, N.Y. w. Skip Parson's Jazzband '60. Co-led cooperative band, The Jazz Cellar Six, in N.Y., Mass., and Vermont '61–74. Sang Ivie Anderson–related songs at Carnegie Hall w. NYJRC '76. Tour. w. Bob Wilber and Dave McKenna in US, Engl., Sweden '77–9. Form. Bechet Legacy w. Wilber '81–4; tour. w. Smithsonian Jazz Repertory Orch. led by Wilber '81–3. App. w. Wilber in Benny Goodman tribute '88 and in Ellington program at Royal Festival Hall '89. Taught jazz history in Albany sch. system; Wilkes Coll., Pa. Hosted radio talk shows in Albany; Gloucester, Engl. Favs: Bessie Smith, B. Holiday, Ethel Waters, Eva Taylor, Fests: Manassas w. Wild Bill Davison, J. McPartland '74; fr. '78 w. Wilber in Nice; Edinburgh; Northsea; Jazz Yatra, India; Poland; Germ.; Ireland; Spain; Australia. LPs: Fat Cat; w. Wilber (Phon.). CDs: w. Wilber (Arb.; Cir.; Jazz.; Chall.).

HOUSTON, CLINT (CLINTON JOSEPH), bs, gtr, pno; b. New Orleans, LA, 6/24/46; d. NYC, 6/6/00. Father pl. classical pno.; sist. pl. gtr. Family moved to Wash., D.C., in late 1940s, then to NYC in '53. Stud. bs w. Ron Carter '64–6; kybd., harmony at Queens Coll. '66. Also stud. graphic art at Cooper Union and Pratt Inst. Pl. in house band at Slugs w.

boyhood friends Geo. Cables, Lenny White late '60s; Nina Simone '69; Roy Haynes '69–70. Ret. briefly to art sch. '70, then form. Free Life Communications w. Dave Liebman '70. Pl. w. Roy Ayers '71–3, incl. Montreux JF '71. Lived in Germ. '72; pl. w. Kurt Edelhagen in Cologne. Ret. to NYC '73. Pl. w. Charles Tolliver '73–5. In Calif., pl. w. Kai Winding '75; Stan Getz '75–7. Ret. to NYC '77; pl. w. Woody Shaw '77–9; Joanne Brackeen '78–86; Slide Hampton's World of Tbns. '81; Pepper Adams '83; Frank Foster '84–6; Roland Hanna '86. Also pl. in '80s-90s w. Benny Golson; Art Farmer; Curtis Fuller; Freddie Hubbard; Clark Terry; Junior Mance; John Stubblefield; McCoy Tyner; Bobby Watson; Gary Bartz. Bs. and mus. dir. w. Louis Hayes fr. '89. Taught at the New Sch. '89. Favs: Pettiford, Israel Crosby, Scott LaFaro. Fests: Eur. fr. '69; also Japan; China; Africa. TV: CBC w. Sonny Greenwich '69. CDs: Timel.; Story.; w. Hayes (Steep.; Cand.); W. Shaw (Mos.); Tolliver; John Hicks (Strata East); P. Adams (Res.); Bartz (Steep.); H. Bluiett (SN); J. Brackeen (Timel.); Getz (Col.); Stubblefield (Enja).

HOWARD, BOB (Howard Joyner), voc, pno; b. Newton, MA, 6/20/06; d. Mount Kisco, NY, 12/3/86. Moved to NYC in 1926. Worked as soloist in several clubs, incl. long residencies at Famous Door, Hickory House in the '30s; also feat. at the Apollo, Lafayette theaters. Start. rec. in '31; from mid 30s made series of all-star recs. w. Benny Carter; T. Wilson; B. Webster; others. Own radio series from '35; Eur. tour '36; long residency at Mamie's Chicken Shack late '30s. Many apps. on radio; own TV show in '50s. Pl. long engagements in LA, Las Vegas, Montreal. Recs. on Dec., Bruns.

HOWARD, DARNELL, cl; b. Chicago, IL, 7/25/1895; d. San Francisco, CA, 9/2/66. From mus. family; start. on vln. at age 7; lessons w. Charlie Elgar. Pl. w. various bands in Midwest; then to NYC, rec. w. W.C. Handy's orch. in 1917. Ret. to Chi., led own bands; tour. w. Elgar '21; to London w. J.P. Johnson spring '23; Eur. again in '24 w. Singing Syncopators. Back in Chi., pl. w. Carroll Dickerson and Dave Peyton before join. King Oliver '25. Tour. Far East w. New York Singing Syncopators, incl. Shanghai, Philippines, Japan. Ret. to US and rejoin. Oliver '26 in Chi; also pl. w. Erskine Tate, Dickerson, Elgar, and led own band in late '20s. Pl. w. Earl Hines orch. '31–7; in late '30s led own gp. again. Briefly w. F. Henderson, C. Hawkins '41; led own band in Chi. clubs '43–5; w. Kid Ory in Calif. '45. Ret. to Chi., pl. w. various combos. Moved to San Francisco in '48, worked there w. Muggsy Spanier on and off to '53; w. Bob Scobey '53; Jimmy Archey '54. From '55 to 62

w. Hines's small band. Illness curtailed activities in '62; then resumed lead. own gps., also w. Elmer Snowden, Burt Bales. Tour. Eur. w. NO All-Stars early '66. Seriously ill upon return to US, he suffered a stroke and died a few months later of a brain tumor. A prominent figure in the Chicago jazz scene of the '20s, Howard was a warm-toned cl. of the Noone school. He was also heard as a jazz vlnst. dur. his early yrs. w. Hines. Recs. w. Handy (Col.); Hines (Bruns., Dec.; Riv.). CDs: w. Lil Armstrong; Alberta Hunter (Riv.); J. Dodds (Aff.); Hines; J.R. Morton (BB); D. Ewell (GTJ); Oliver (CDS); K. Ory (GTJ; GHB); Naty Dominique (Amer. Mus.).

HOWARD, ED (EDWARD CHARLES), bs, el-bs; b. Washington, DC, 4/9/60. Began on el-bs. Bro. pl. tpt. in hs and encouraged him to keep playing. Took coll. music courses while att. School Without Walls in D.C. 1976–9. Also stud. w. Marshall Hawkins, Buster Williams. Moved out of parents' house and began working prof. at age 16. Pl. in D.C. w. Lawrence Wheatley, then moved to NYC '80. Met many musicians while in house band at Star Café '82–6. Pl. w. Chas. Davis '82–6; Roy Haynes fr. '82; Albert Dailey '83–5; Tex Allen '83–6; Junior Cook '83–91; Clifford Jordan '83–92; Brian Lynch '84–8; Richie Cole, Vernel Fournier, '84–90; Joe Locke fr. '84; Ralph Moore '85–9; Stanley Cowell '86–93; Craig Handy fr. '89; Gary Thomas, Eddie Henderson fr. '90. Also worked w. Stanley Turrentine; Freddie Hubbard; Dizzy Gillespie; John Lewis; Curtis Fuller; Pat Metheny; Barry Harris; Eddie "Cleanhead" Vinson; Billy Higgins; Art Farmer; Roland Hanna; John Hicks; Gary Bartz; Warne Marsh; Joe Lovano; Billy Hart; Benny Green; Buck Hill; Red Holloway; Red Rodney; Jon Faddis; Lee Konitz; Pepper Adams; Anita O'Day; many others. Favs: Paul Chambers, Dave Holland, Mingus, Charlie Haden. Fests: Eur., Japan fr. '84. TV: Jap., Germ. TV. CDs: w. C. Jordan (CC; JazzHeritage); R. Haynes (Freelance; Drey.); G. Thomas (Polyd.); R. Cole (Conc.; Mile.); Dave Kikoski (Tri.).

HOWARD, KID (AVERY), tpt; b. New Orleans, LA, 4/22/08; d. New Orleans, 3/28/66. Started on dms., then took up crnt. under infl. of Chris Kelly. Pl. in several brass bands, incl. Eureka, Allen's, Tuxedo. Led own band from late 1920s in NO and on tour to Chi.; reached his peak as a soloist in early '30s; also pl. in theater orchs. His brass band pl. for Buddy Petit's funeral '31. In mid '40s rec. w. George Lewis for Climax; to '52, lapsed into obscurity, pl. only occasionally. Then pl. regularly w. Lewis, incl. Eur. tour '59. Fell seriously ill '61; after recuperating pl. frequently at Preservation Hall, Dixieland Hall in last years. Died of cerebral hemorrhage. CDs: Amer. Mus.; w. G. Lewis (Amer. Mus.; BN; Story.).

HOWARD, PAUL LEROY, tnr sax, cl, lead; b. Steubenville, OH, 9/20/1895; d. Los Angeles, CA, 2/18/80. From mus. family; start. on crnt., also stud. woodwinds, pno. Moved to LA in 1913 and lived w. uncle, a mus. teacher. First prof. job w. Wood Wilson's Syncopators '16; then w. various bands. In early '20s pl. w. K. Oliver, Jelly Roll Morton on West Coast. Form. own gp. in '23, which varied in size; became best known as the Quality Serenaders in '24, which incl. L. Hampton, Lawrence Brown as sidemen; pl. at Sebastian's Cotton Club '27–9; Kentucky Club. Disbanded in early '30s. Then pl. w. Ed Garland and led own trio before join. L. Hampton '35–6; Eddie Barefield '37. Worked w. Charlie Echols until reform. own band in '39, pl. long residency near LA to '53. Cont. to pl. through the '50s. Recs. for Victor. CD: w. Lionel Hampton 1929 to 1940 (BBC).

HUBBARD, FREDDIE (FREDERICK DE-WAYNE), tpt, flg, comp; b. Indianapolis, IN, 4/7/38. Sist. sang and pl. classical music, spirituals; bro. pl. pno. Stud. mello. at John Hope JHS; tpt. at Arsenal Tech. HS; stud. at Jordan Cons. and w. Max Woodbury of Indianapolis Symph.; local gigs w. Montgomery Bros. Moved to NYC 1958. Pl. at Turbo Village in Brooklyn w. Jay Cameron; own gp. Gigged w. Philly Joe Jones. After stints w. Sonny Rollins, Slide Hampton, J.J. Johnson, Quincy Jones '59–61, join. Art Blakey's Jazz Messengers and achieved int'l prominence. Rec. experimental, avant-garde sess. as sideman w. O. Coleman '60; John Coltrane '65. Had own gp. '64–5; work. w. Max Roach; pl. in Austr. w. Friedrich Gulda. From '66 into the '90s often led own gps., occ. switching fr. jazz to experiments in rock, fusion, and r&b but always reverting to a jazz-oriented style. From '76 to '79 participated w. Herbie Hancock, Wayne Shorter, Ron Carter, Tony Williams in VSOP. Pl. on several film soundtracks incl. *Shaft's Big Score;* H. Hancock's score for *Blow Up.* Continued to lead own gps. Living in LA he has cont. to show a strong adherence to hard bop. Coming out of Clifford Brown his sound, technique, and fire made him an exemplar of the style and a personal voice from within it, infl. many young tptrs. who followed in his jet stream. In the late '80s he developed lip problems and they cont. to plague him in the late '90s, diminishing his powerful attack to a great degree. Comps: "Up Jumped Spring"; "Byrdlike." Won *DB* Critics Poll New Star '61; Readers Poll '73–4. CDs: BN incl. *The Freddie Hubbard/Woody Shaw Sessions;* CTI; BL; Enja; Pab.; MM; Atl.; Imp.; Timel.; w. Blakey (BN; Riv.; Timel.); B. Golson (Den.; Timel.); O. Coleman; Roach; MJQ (Atl.); Coltrane (Prest.; Atl.; Imp.); Dolphy (BN; NJ); Basie; D. Gillespie (Pab.); Bill Evans; J. Heath (Riv.); G. Cables; J. Farrell (Cont.); Tina Brooks; D. Gordon; Hancock; Joe Henderson; B. Hutcherson; J. McLean; W. Shorter (BN); Milt Jackson (CTI); Q. Jones (A&M); R.R. Kirk (Merc.); O. Nelson; S. Rollins (Imp.); K. Lightsey (Timel.); S. Vaughan (Em.); Betty Carter (Verve); S. Turrentine (BN; Fant.); M. Tyner (Mile.); Satchmo Legacy Band (SN).

HUBBLE, ED (JOHN EDGAR), tbn; b. Santa Barbara, CA, 4/6/28. Father was LA radio tbnst. Pl. w. Hollywood Canteen band, LA County Band 1941; Ken Murray's Blackouts '43. Family moved to NYC '44. Att. hs in Scarsdale; co-led gp. w. Bob Wilber '44. Pl. w. Alvino Rey, Buddy Rich, Shorty Sherock, Jess Stacy '45–6; Red McKenzie's Candy Kids '47; also pl. w. Eddie Condon, Geo. Wettling mid '40s. Co-led gp. w. Johnny Windhurst off and on fr. '48. Pl. w. The Six '53–4, then lived in Columbus, Ohio, and Conn. in late '50s. Pl. w. Muggsy Spanier '59–60; Billy Maxted '59–6; Phil Napoleon '62–4; Don Ewell '63; own qt. '64; Jackie Gleason Orch. '64–5; Dukes of Dixieland '66; Dick Wellstood–Kenny Davern '67; Geo. Mauro '67–8; Max Kaminsky at Jimmy Ryan's '68. Taught priv. in NYC '60s; one of his students was Jack Teagarden's son. Pl. w. World's Greatest Jazz Band '69–73; Flip Phillips in Fla. '73–4; Kings of Jazz in Eur. '74; NY Jazz Repertory Orch., Windhurst '75. Hubble was seriously injured in an auto accident in '79 but ret. to work in the early '80s. Moved to Texas ca.'86; pl. w. Jim Cullum Jr. '86–7 and freelanced. Fav: Teagarden. Fests: Nice; NJF-NY; Colo. JP. Recs. w. Doc Evans; Davison; WGJB. CDs: w. R. Braff (Aff.); Cullum (Col.; Stomp Off).

HUCKO, PEANUTS (MICHAEL ANDREW), cl, tnr sax; b. Syracuse, NY, 4/7/18; d. Ft. Worth, TX, 6/19/03. Began pl. at age 11. Prof. debut at 16. Worked as tnr. sax, infl. by Bud Freeman and Eddie Miller, w. the orchs. of Jack Jenney; Will Bradley; Joe Marsala; and Bob Chester; join. Glenn Miller's Army Air Force Band as feat. cl. soloist. After the war pl. w. Benny Goodman and Ray McKinley orchs. before replacing Pee Wee Russell w. Eddie Condon 1947–50. In '50s pl. w. Bobby Hackett; Jack Teagarden; studio work at CBS, ABC; and from '58 to 60 w. Louis Armstrong. Led own band at Condon's Club '64–6. Cl. soloist on L. Welk TV series '70–72; led Glenn Miller Orch. '74; then settled in Denver, lead. qt. feat. his wife, singer Louise Tobin, at his own nightclub. A regular at Dick Gibson's Colo. JPs where his rendition of "Stealin' Apples" was an annual fav. Start. tour. in '87 w. "Salute to Benny Goodman" show, pl. arrs. fr. the old Goodman band. In the '90s remained one of the finest clsts. in the Goodman tradition. CDs: Timel.; Starline; w. Armstrong (BB; Vict.); Bechet (Laser.); Buck Clayton (Jaz Up); B. Rich (Hep); Teagarden (BB); Will Bradley (Tax); Chri Connor (Atl.); Bobby Hackett (Dormouse).

HUDSON, WILL, comp, arr, lead; b. Barstow, CA, 3/8/08; d. South Carolina, 1981. Raised in Detroit. In late 1920s wrote many arrs. for McKinney's Cotton Pickers; Erskine Tate, C. Calloway '32. As a staff arr. for Irving Mills in the '30s, his scores were pl. by Calloway; J. Venuti; F. Henderson; J. Lunceford; Mills Blue Rhythm; also Ina Ray Hutton; D. Redman; E. Hines; other prominent lead. Co-led own bb w. singer Eddie DeLange '36–8; then on his own '39–40. While in service dur. WWII '43–5, arr. for Glenn Miller. Then freelanced for mus. publishers. From '48 stud. at Juilliard, start. comp. symph. mus. and in other genres. By the '50s became obscure and largely inactive in jazz. Arr: "Hocus Pocus," Henderson (BB) '34. Comps: "Moonglow" w. DeLange '34; an entire album of their songs was rec. by J. Guarnieri (Coral).

HUFFSTETER, STEVE (STEVEN C.), tpt, flg; b. Monroe, MI, 2/7/36. Self-taught. Grew up in Phoenix, Ariz.; moved to LA late 1950s; active member of jazz scene '59 to present; pl. w. S. Kenton; Willie Bobo; Poncho Sanchez; Bob Florence; T. Akiyoshi–L. Tabackin; L. Bellson; others; own combos, some in Latin jazz mode '70s, '80s; form. qnt. w. Benn Clatworthy '91. Tour. Argentina w. Bobo '72; w. Akiyoshi several times to Japan and Eur. '70s, '80s. Own band w. wife Dee, a percussionist, to Tahiti '91. At ease in a number of idioms, from Latin to fusion, though excels at bebop. Favs: Hubbard, M. Davis, Gillespie. CDs: w. Akiyoshi–Tabackin (RCA); Florence (MAMA; USA); Natalie Cole (Elek.); D. Schuur (GRP).

HUG, ARMAND, pno, comp; b. New Orleans, LA, 12/6/10; d. New Orleans, 3/19/77. Studied w. moth. Prof. debut at age 13; at 14 start. pl. for silent movies; at 15 in French Quarter taxi dance hall. Pl. w. Harry Shields at the Fern Dance Hall 1926; pl. w. various dance bands. Early assoc. of Irving Fazola; Monk Hazel. In '20s and '30s, pl. w. various NO mus. incl. Louis Prima; Sharkey Bonano. Maritime service '42–5. Then primarily worked as soloist in NO's better hotels and clubs; frequent radio broadcasts; own TV series on local station. Became ASCAP member '59. In '67 given a lifetime contract to pl. at Royal

Orleans Hotel. Fest: NOJF '69. Made over 250 recs., incl. sideman w. Bonano, Johnny Wiggs. As lead. for Para. '53; Golden Crest; Ace. CDs: trio & band in *Classic Capitol Band Sessions* (Mos.); tracks as lead. & sideman in *The Good Time Jazz Story* (GTJ); w. Wiggs (Story.).

HUGHART, JIM (JAMES DAVID), bs; b. Minneapolis, MN, 7/28/36. Both parents, bro., and moth.'s family all musical. Fath. was bs. w. Minneapolis, San Diego Symphs. Bachelor's degree in music theory from U. of Minnesota 1959. After two years in 7th US Army Symph. Orch. '60–1 join. Ella Fitzgerald, tour. w. her for three yrs. and settled in So. Calif., working w. scores of leading singers and bands including five yrs. w. Sinatra; plus Q. Jones; J. Pass; Z. Sims; C. Adderley; J. Griffin; Joe Williams; O. Peterson. Tour. w. Natalie Cole 1991–2. Won NARAS MVP Emeritus Award '87. CDs: w. Chet Baker (Repertoire); Fitzgerald-Ellington (Verve); P. Christlieb (CC); Rosemary Clooney; D. Frishberg (Conc.); Warne Marsh (Story.); Pass (Pab.; Tel.).

HUGHES, BILL (WILLIAM HENRY), tbn, bs-tbn; b. Dallas, TX, 3/28/30. Father pl. tbn. for Elk's Lodge in Wash., D.C. Stud. vln. at Armstrong HS, Wash. 1946. Stud. pharmacy at Howard U. '48–52. Pl. tbn. w. Andy Kirk '49; Frank Wess '50–2; Count Basie '53–7. Rec. w. Osie Johnson combo w. Wess, Thad Jones '55. Not active '57–63, then rejoin. Basie '63. Sw. to bs-tbn. '66. Favs: J.J. Johnson, Urbie Green, Geo. Roberts, Dick Hixson. CDs: w. Basie (Verve; Roul.; Pab.); F. Wess (Sav.).

HUGHES, LUTHER, bs, elec-bs; b. Covington, KY, 12/31/46. From mus. family: uncle pl. gtr.; moth., grandparents church singers. Stud. bs. priv. in Cincinnati 1964; U. of Cinci. Mus. Cons. '65; grad. Cal. State U., Long Beach, '79; US army band, '66–9; house band at Playboy Club w. Roy Meriwether. To LA '71; active sideman w. L. Bellson, Crusaders, C. McRae, Joe Farrell, H. Hawes, Dave Pike '70s; Gene Harris '71–92; H. Silver '85; form. funk/fusion band, Cahoots '85; C. Shoemake '88–92. Mus. dir. El Matador club in Huntington Beach, '91–2. At home in both mainstream and contemporary modes. Favs: LaFaro, R. Brown. CDs: w. Cahoots (ITI); w. G. Harris (Conc.); Shoemake (Chase Mus. Gp.); Ron Eschete (Bain.; Conc.).

HUGHES, SPIKE (PATRICK CAIRNS), comp, bs; b. London, England, 10/18/08; d. London, 2/2/87. Played bs. w. Cambridge U. band; then rec. w. Brit. jazz bands for Dec. in late 1920s and '30s. Pl. w. and wrote for C.B. Cochrane '31; tour. w. Jack Hylton

'31–2. His career peaked in spring '33 when he went to NYC and, w. Benny Carter's help, form. an all-star band, incl. C. Hawkins, Red Allen, to rec. a series of his comps. He then retired from perf., but from '31 to '44 was a critic for *Melody Maker* under pseudonym "Mike"; also was significant in establishing venues for Amer. bands and recs. in Engl. The writing on his Amer. recs. reveals a talent for jazz scoring that was adventurously ahead of its time. Comps: "A Harlem Symphony"; "Six Bells Stampede"; "Nocturne"; "Pastorale"; "Arabesque"; "Donegal Cradle Song"; and jazz ballet, *High Yellow*. LP: Dec. CDs: King's Cross; Largo.

HUMAIR, DANIEL, dms; b. Geneva, Switzerland, 5/23/38. Studied cl., dms., theory fr. age 7. At 15 he pl. dms. in dance bands. Won several prizes at Zurich JF 1958. Tour. Eur. w. own gp. '55–8, then moved to Paris '58. Pl. in Paris w. Barney Wilen; Michel Hausser; Lucky Thompson; Oscar Pettiford; Kenny Dorham; Chet Baker. Pl. w. Martial Solal fr. '59; trio, The Connection, w. Rene Urtreger, Pierre Michelot '60; Swingle Singers '65–7; trio w. Jean-Luc Ponty, Eddy Louiss '68; Phil Woods' European Rhythm Machine '68–73. Freelanced w. Stephane Grappelli, Geo. Gruntz, Jim Hall, Herbie Mann, Lee Konitz, Anthony Braxton, Bill Coleman, Joe Henderson, etc. '71–7. Form. trio w. Henri Texier, François Jeanneau '77. Own trio w. Joachim Kuhn, J.F. Jenny-Clark. Also an accomplished abstract painter with artworks on display at the Museum of Modern Art, Paris. Has app. on the soundtracks of many films incl. *Last Tango in Paris* '72, and publ. a nontraditional drum method entitled *Drum Book*. In '86 named Chevalier des Arts et Lettres by the French govt. Favs: Elvin Jones, DeJohnette. Polls: *DB* New Talent '68, TDWR '70; Prix Charlie Parker, Prix in Honorem '88. Fests: all major fr. late '50s. CDs: Blue Flame; Drey.; Owl; L. Bleu; w. P. Woods (EMI); Franco Ambrosetti; K. Barron; A. Mangelsdorff (Enja); C. Baker (BB); France's Concert); Franco D'Andrea; Larry Schneider (L. Bleu); Grappelli (Verve; BL; Musidisc); B. Jaspar (Mole); Konitz (Steep.); Joachim Kuhn (Owl); H. Merrill (Em.); L. Thompson (Vogue); K. Wheeler (SN); A. Zoller (Act).

HUMBLE, DEREK, alto sax; b. Livingston, England, 1931; d. Easington, England 2/22/71. Played prof. while in teens; tour. and rec. w. Vic Lewis and Kathy Stobart 1951. Pl. w. Ronnie Scott's band '52–6. Active in rec. w. Victor Feldman; Jimmy Deuchar; Tony Crombie in '50s. Pl. w. Kurt Edelhagen's orch. in Cologne '57–67; fr. '61 lead alto w. Kenny Clarke–Francy Boland bb. Victimized by a mugging, he recovered sufficiently to freelance and

pl. w. Phil Seamen's qt. '70–1, but residual effects of his injuries eventually caued his demise. Highly valued as a lead man, he was also a more than capable improviser. Solos w. Clarke-Boland: "New Box"; "November Girl." CDs: w. Clarke-Boland (MPS); Victor Feldman (Cont.).

HUMES, HELEN, voc; b. Louisville, KY, 6/23/13; d. Santa Monica, CA, 9/9/81. Made her first recs. at age 15 w. James P. Johnson. Best known for assoc. w. Count Basie 1938–42; also rec. w. Harry James '38; Pete Brown '42. Settled in Calif. From '45, concentrated mostly on R&B, after scoring a big hit w. "Bebaba-leba," a jump blues, for Aladdin. Also had a hit w. "Million Dollar Secret" '50. Ret. to more of a jazz context in the late '50s, tour. Australia w. Red Norvo; also pl. w. him in Hollywood clubs. App. in West Coast version of the play *Simply Heavenly*. Only occ. active in '60s; spent a yr. in Aust. '64–5. Returned home to Louisville '67, remained there until summer '73, when her participation in tributes to Basie and Armstrong at NJF-NY helped reactivate career; tour. France, Switz., Spain. Toured France again in '74; rec. for Black and Blue; apps. at the Half Note, NYC. In Jan. '75 she began a successful four-mos.' engagement at the Cookery, NYC; rec. her first US album in many yrs. In Mar. '75, she was honored by the city of Louisville and given keys to the city. Body of work w. Basie showed her to be a superior ballad singer who was also effective on rhythm numbers. During her jazz comeback in the mid '70s, Whitney Balliett, in *The New Yorker*, called her "one of the best and most durable of American popular singers who...bears easy comparison with Mildred Bailey and Billie Holiday...[She] is singing better than ever...sharing with us a style of singing and performing that is almost gone." Fests: NJF; French Lick, Indiana '59; NJF-NY '73; NJF; Montreux '74. CDs: Cont.; B&B; Le Chant Du Monde; Muse; tracks in *The 1940s Mercury Sessions* (Merc.); w. Basie (Dec.; Col.); in *Spirituals to Swing* (Vang.); Lester Young (BN).

HUMPHREY, PAUL NELSON, dms, comp; b. Detroit, MI, 10/12/35. Studied pno. to age 8, then began lessons on dms. After hs cont. mus. educ. at Naval Academy, tour. w. unit bands, and pl. w. prominent jazz artists in off hours. After service, tour. and rec. w. Wes Montgomery 1961–62. Also pl. w. Les McCann; Kai Winding; John Coltrane; Joe Williams; Cannonball Adderley; and Harry James Orch. Moved to LA in late '60s to work w. Harry Edison; tour. and rec. w. Sammy Davis Jr.; Diahann Carroll; Burt Bacharach; Nelson Riddle. A versatile drummer, Humphrey has pl. w. R&B and rock groups such as Little Richard; Tina Turner; Smokey Robinson; Jerry

Garcia; The Supremes; has done extensive film, rec., and TV work, and acc. Ella Fitzgerald; Sarah Vaughan; Peggy Lee; Carmen McRae; Mel Tormé; Frank Sinatra; Lou Rawls; Joe Williams. A regular w. Gene Harris in the '90s. Cond. dms. clinics in schools and universities throughout US and has written several instruction books. First solo album, *Cool Aid*, a hit in '71. CDs: Disc.; w. Harris; Ron Eschete; Red Holloway; McRae (Conc.); L. Feather (Main.); Spike Robinson (Capri); Gerald Wilson (Disc.).

HUMPHREY, PERCY GASTON, tpt, voc; b. New Orleans, LA, 1/13/05; d. New Orleans, 8/22/95. Drums at 13, tpt. lessons w. grandfath.; led own band 1925. Pl. w. Eureka Brass band; to Chicago w. Kid Howard '29; odd jobs in '30s; retired '39; ret. to mus. '46. Led Eureka band, w. which he rec. '51. Worked w. George Lewis '51–3; then mostly w. dance bands until '61. Led Crescent City Joymakers in '60s and early '70s, incl. rec. for Riv. '61. Pl mainly at Preservation Hall fr. '61; cont. to perform in NO and tour w. Preservation Hall ensembles into early '90s. CDs: Riv.; GHB; Story.; w. G. Lewis (Amer. Mus.).

HUMPHREY, RALPH S., dms; b. Berkeley, CA, 5/11/44. Studied at San Jose State U. 1964–7; UCLA '68; Cal. State, Northridge '68–9; master's degree in perc. perf. Worked w. Don Ellis orch. '69–73; toured US and abroad; pl. on soundtrack for *The French Connection*; wrote chapter for Ellis's book, *The New Rhythm Book*, '72. Tour. w. Frank Zappa '73–4; later freelanced w. Tony Bennett; Joe Williams; Carmen McRae; Clare Fischer; John Klemme; et al.; rec. w. Ray Pizzi and L. Subramaniam '79; joined Free Flight '82. CDs: w. Free Flight (Silver City/Laurie).

HUMPHREY, WILLIE (WILLIAM JAMES JR.), cl; b. New Orleans, LA, 12/29/00; d. New Orleans, 6/7/94. Lessons w. grandfath., a crntst. and teacher. Worked on riverboats, then to Chi. 1919; pl. w. Freddie Keppard and King Oliver. Ret. to NO '20; pl. w. Kid Rena; to St. Louis '25; pl. w. Fate Marable; back to NO again '32. Worked as teacher; pl. w. Lucky Millinder '35–6; after navy service in WWII, pl. w. Eureka Brass Band; Paul Barbarin, incl. NYC, '55; and own gps. Rec. w. various bands for Riv. '60. Toured Eur. '67, w. Billie and De De Pierce; from '69 pl. regularly w. Percy Humphrey and Preservation Hall gps. into '90s. CDs: GHB; Barbarin (Atl.).

HUMPHRIES, LEX P. III, dms; b. Rockaway, NJ, 8/22/36. Mother pl. vln.; bro. pl. cga. Self-taught. Played w. Chet Baker, Lester Young in Eur. 1956; Dizzy Gillespie, Lee Morgan, Bud Powell '58; Chris Connor '59; Benny Golson–Art Farmer Jazztet

'59–60; Yusef Lateef '60–3; C. Connor '62. Also rec. w. John Coltrane, Junior Mance '59; Donald Byrd, Duke Pearson '59–60; Paul Chambers, Doug Watkins '60; Wes Montgomery '61; McCoy Tyner '63. Pl. African drums and perc. w. Sun Ra '65–81. Freelanced in Philadelphia area fr. '81. Fav: Philly Joe Jones. CDs: w. Jazztet (Chess); Gillespie (Verve); Pearson; Byrd (BN); F. Hubbard (BL); Sun Ra (Evid.); Tyner (Imp.); Montgomery; Lateef (Riv.).

HUMPHRIES, ROGER, dms; b. Pittsburgh, PA, 1/30/44. Nephew of trumpeter Frank Humphries. Began on dms. at age 3. First important job leading own gp. at Carnegie Music Hall, Pitts. 1960. Tour. and rec. w. Horace Silver '64–6. Rec. w. Carmell Jones '65. Pl. w. Ray Charles at Newport JF '68. Rec. w. Nathan Davis '71. Favs: Max Roach, Art Blakey. CDs: w. Silver (BN).

HUNT, GEORGE, tbn; b. Kansas City, MO, ca. 1906; d. Chicago, IL, ca. 1946. Pl. w. Bennie Moten fr. 1932; join. Count Basie at the Reno Club '36; to NYC w. the band same yr.; F. Henderson '37–8. Moved to Chi., worked w. Artie Starck '39; Erskine Tate '40; tour. w. Earl Hines '41. Committed suicide. Feat. solo: "One O'Clock Jump" w. Basie '37. CDs: w. Basie (Dec.); Henderson (Class.); Hines (BB).

HUNT, JOE (JOSEPH GAYLE), dms; b. Richmond, IN, 7/31/38. Studied at Indiana U. 1956–9; Mannes Coll. of Mus., NYC '60. Pl. w. David Baker bb and sxt. '56–9; Geo. Russell '59–62; John Handy '60; Steve Kuhn '64; Stan Getz '64–5; Jim Hall, Gary Burton '66; Bill Evans '66–7; Lee Konitz, Mose Allison '67; Gary McFarland '67–8; Astrud Gilberto '68; Chuck Israels' Nat'l Jazz Ens. '72. In Boston, co-led gps. w. John Scofield, Mike Stern '72–80. Pl. w. Hal McKusick '78–90; Red Rodney '86. Toured Spain w. Barry Harris–Chuck Israels '87. Pl. w. Smithsonian Jazz Masters Orch. '91. Hunt has taught drums, ens., and jazz history at Berklee Coll. of Mus. fr. '71. Favs: Kenny Clarke, Tiny Kahn, Elvin Jones. Fests: So. Amer., Eur., Japan. Film: app. w. S. Getz in *Get Yourself a College Girl* '64. CDs: w. Russell (Riv.); Getz (Verve).

HUNT, PEE WEE (WALTER), tbn, voc, lead; Mt. Healthy, OH, 5/10/07; d. Plymouth, MA, 6/22/79. Mother pl. bjo. and gtr.; fath., vln. Began on bjo. 1924; stud. at Ohio St. U., grad. from Cincinnati Cons. Pl. w. local bands '27, bjo. and tbn; then w. Jean Goldkette '28–9. One of the orig. members of the Casa Loma orch., form. '29; was feat. voc. w. the band, as well as tbn.; remained to '42. Was briefly a disc jockey in Hollywood; also freelance mus. before join. merchant marine '43–5. From '46 to 55, led own combo; scored big hit w. corny satires on Dixieland music, notably his "Twelfth Street Rag" '48; "Oh!" '53. Own recs. on Cap. CDs: w. Casa Loma (Cir.; EPM); Armstrong (Class.).

HUNTER, ALBERTA, voc; b. Memphis, TN, 4/1/1895; d. NYC, 10/18/84. Left home and went to Chi. at 12; prof. debut at 15 in a club called Dago Frank's, staying for two yrs. Later feat. at Hugh Hoskins', the Panama, the Dreamland; during stay at the latter, wrote "Downhearted Blues," which Bessie Smith sang for phenomenally successful rec. debut rec. 1923. To NYC; replaced B. Smith in the B'way show *How Come*, which starred Sidney Bechet in the title role, as a Chinese; ret to Chi., perf. at Pekin Inn and Dreamland, and rec for Paramount. Also rec. (under half-sister's name, Josephine Beatty) w. Clarence Williams Blue Five, which incl. Louis Armstrong, Sidney Bechet. Also rec. under the names Helen Roberts and May Alix, the latter an actual singer. To France in '25, perf. in Paris. Oscar Hammerstein and Jerome Kern heard her perf. at London Flood victim benefit '27 and cast her opposite Paul Robeson in London prod. of *Show Boat*. Remained in Eur. for the most of '30s, perf. and rec. w. Jack Jackson's society orch in London; also in Copenhagen and Paris. Ret. to US in '39 and had own network radio show; also app. on RCA's experimental TV transmissions for World's Fair. Dur. WWII, she headed the first black USO show, eventually making twenty-five USO tours to various Eur. and South Pacific sites; entertained Generals MacArthur and Eisenhower. Understudied three major roles in B'way show *Mrs. Patterson* '54–55. In '56, she retired fr. full-time mus., and entered YWCA Sch. for Practical Nurses. After graduation in '57, she worked at Goldwater Memorial Hospital, Welfare Island, NYC. Except for app. on two '61 albums (Prest. and Riv.), she remained a nurse until the hospital retired her. In '77, she ret. to mus. full-time w. reg app. at The Cookery, NYC, several albums for Col., and tours to So. Amer. and Eur. Films: feat. in *Radio Parade of 1935*, first British feature film w. color; seen briefly in Robert Altman film, *Remember My Name*, for which she also wrote and perf music '78. TV: Many app. On ABC *Good Morning America*; NBC *Today* show; PBS special w. Eubie Blake; Danish and Germ. TV; also commercials. CDs: Prest.; Rov.; Col.; Swing; Stash; Jass; w. Armstrong (Mile.).

HUNTER, CHRIS, alto, tnr, sop saxes, fl, picc; b. London, England, 2/21/57. Studied in Engl. w. Leslie Evans; John Williams; Stan Robinson; Don Rendell.

Tour. and rec. w. Nat'l Youth Jazz Orch. 1976–8. Pl. w. Williams '78; Mike Westbrook '78–9; then made rec. debut as lead. for Original label. Pl. w. own qnt. '81–3; Gil Evans's British Orch. '83. Moved to NYC '84, pl. w. Evans Orch. at Sweet Basil. Also pl. in '80s w. Michael Camilo; Hiram Bullock; Robben Ford; Airto Moreira; Flora Purim; Tania Maria; Michael Franks; Manhattan Transfer; Geo. Gruntz; Manh. Jazz Orch. Favs: Charlie Parker, David Sanborn. Polls: *SJ* Gold Disc '85. Fests: Eur., Japan since '78. CDs: PW; w. Evans (Evid.); Mike Westbrook (Enja); Gruntz (Enja; TCB).

HURLEY, CLYDE L. JR., tpt; b. Ft. Worth, TX, 9/3/16; d. Texas, 9/63. Mother, Esther B. Temple, was pioneer radio singer and pno. in Tex. Stud. pno. briefly, then picked up tpt. by listening to Armstrong recs. Solo tpt. w. TCU jazz band 1932–6. Join. Ben Pollack in Dallas '37; went to Hollywood w. him and did radio work. Left to pl. w. Glenn Miller '39–40; T. Dorsey '40–1; Artie Shaw '41. Then freelanced in film studios '42–3; MGM staff '44–9; NBC Hollywood staff '50–5; then freelanced for Columbia recs., radio, TV, etc. In '50s also perf. w. Dixieland gps., incl. Matty Matlock's Rampart Street Paraders. Also operated cigarette machine vending business. Favs: B. Berigan, Armstrong. Films: *The Five Pennies*; *The Gene Krupa Story*. Rec: feat. on Miller's "In the Mood" '39. CDs: four tks. in the *Keynote Coll.* (Em.); w. Miller; Dorsey (BB).

HURST, BOB (ROBERT LESLIE III), bs, comp; b. Detroit, MI, 10/4/64. Studied gtr. w. Earl Klugh at age 6. A year later, met Percy Heath and decided to take up bs. Received coll. credit while in 8th grade; National Honor Society Presidential Scholar Awardee 1982 in Wash., D.C.; cont. studies at Indiana U. '82–5. Toured w. Marcus Belgrave '82–5; OTB '84–5; W. Marsalis '85–8; Donald Harrison–Terence Blanchard '88; Tony Williams '88–9; B. Marsalis fr. '89. Moved to LA May '92 as regular member of the B. Marsalis band on *Tonight Show*. Also freelanced in LA area. Infl. by Belgrave, and by bs. C. Mingus; P. Chambers; R. Carter. Comps: "Roused About"; "Down for the Cause"; "Detroit Red"; "Incessant Lullaby." Videos: *Blues & Swing* w. W. Marsalis; *The Music Tells You* w. B. Marsalis. Film: soundtrack work on Spike Lee's *Mo' Better Blues* and *Do The Right Thing*. CDs: Col.; DIW; w. W. Marsalis; B. Marsalis (Col.); D. Marsalis (Novus); E. Marsalis (BN; Col.); OTB; R. Margitza; Geri Allen; Woody Shaw; Tony Williams (BN); Donald Brown (Sunny.; Muse); H. Connick; Russell Malone (Col.); Marvin Smith (Conc.); Ricky Ford (Muse); Mulgrew Miller (Land.).

HUTCHENRIDER, CLARENCE BEHRENS, cl; also saxes; b. Waco, TX, 6/13/08; d. NYC, 8/18/91. Took up cl. and sax in early teens; led own gp. in hs. Prof. debut w. Ross Gorman 1928; pl. w. Tommy Tucker '29; Austin Wiley '31. Feat. cl. w. Glen Gray's Casa Loma orch. '31–43. Three yrs. w. Jimmy Lytell on ABC radio, NYC. Freelanced in radio until forced into retirement due to lung ailment '51–2. Worked w. Walter Davidson combo on Long Island in mid '50s; own trio at Gaslight Club '58–68; Bill's Gay Nineties '68 to May '73; Vince Giordano's New California Ramblers and New Orleans Nighthawks in late '70s. Recs: w. Casa Loma, incl. "Black Jazz"; "Maniac's Ball"; "Smoke Rings"; "Casa Loma Stomp"; "No Name Jive." CDs: w. Gray (Cir.; EPM); Armstrong (Class.).

HUTCHERSON, BOBBY (ROBERT) vib, mrba; b. Los Angeles, CA, 1/27/41. Raised in Pasadena, Calif. First inspired by a Milt Jackson record in 1956, bought a set of vib. and was soon pl. local dances and concerts. Stud. w. Terry Trotter and Dave Pike. Worked in LA w. Curtis Amy, Charles Lloyd; then w. Al Grey–Billy Mitchell combo in SF, NYC '61. While freelancing in NYC w. Jackie McLean et al., rec. w. Eric Dolphy for Blue Note. Pl. w. Archie Shepp; Hank Mobley; Charles Tolliver; Grachan Moncur III; then ret. to freelancing in Calif. Pl. Monterey JF w. Gil Fuller '65. Co-led quintet w. Harold Land '68–71. Settling in SF, he perf. mainly in Calif. and overseas w. own gps. and as member of the Timeless All-Stars. In both his vib. and marimba work, has always shown exceptional imagination and fluency, particularly in his use of four mallets. Won *DB* Critics Poll New Star '64. Film: *Round Midnight* '86. CDs: BN; Land.; 32; Evid.; Cont.; Timel.; w. Land (Main.; Muse); Timeless All-Stars; Eddie Marshall (Timel.); S. Stitt (32); D. Gordon (BN; Col.); K. Barron (Verve); Dolphy; Gillespie; G. Green; Joe Henderson; Moncur; Tony Williams; J. McLean (BN); John Hicks; C. Walton; P. Sanders (Evid.); G. Cables; Chico Freeman; Prince Lasha; F. Morgan (Cont.); Ted Rosenthal (CTI); Tyner (Mile.); A. Shepp (Imp.); Bruce Forman (Conc.); D. Byrd (Land.).

HUTCHINSON, GREGORY, dms; b. NYC, 6/16/70. Father is a perc. who lives between Miami and NYC. Stud dms. and pno. at Bklyn. Cons. of Mus.; Manh. Sch. of Mus. Recommended by Garry Dial to Red Rodney, w. whose qnt. he pl. 1989–90. Pl. w. Betty Carter '90–2; Roy Hargrove '92–5; Ray Brown fr. '95; 4–Sight '98. Taught at Stanford U. Jazz Wkshp. '96, '97. Favs: Blakey, P.J. Jones, Tony Williams, Specs Wright. Pl. major fests, worldwide fr. '89. TV: *Tonight Show* w. Hargrove. CDs: w.

4–Sight (N2K); Carter; Joe Henderson (Verve); Joshua Redman (WB); Brown (Tel.); Hargrove (Novus; Verve); Antonio Hart (Novus); A. LaVerne (Tri.); Eric Reed (Cand.; MoJazz).

HUTCHINSON, JIVER (LESLIE GEORGE), tpt, lead; b. Kingston, Jamaica, BWI, 3/16/1906; d. Weeting, Engl., 11/22/59. Worked w. Bertie King's band 1934 before moving to Engl. where he worked w. dmr. Happy Blake's Cuba Club Band; Leslie Thompson's Emperors of Jazz '36. Main jazz soloist w. Geraldo's dance orch in late '30s and early '40s. Form. own band early '44, which incl. many former members of Emperors of Jazz; tour. Great Brit., India, and Eur. When the band broke up in '50, he ret. to Geraldo; also worked as a lead. Perf. w. Mary Lou Williams '52. While on the road w. his band, an auto accident ended his life. Recs. w. Snake Hips Johnson '38; "I Can't Get Started" for Czech. label, Supraphon '47.

HUTTON, INA RAY (Odessa Cowan), lead, voc; b. Chicago, Il, 3/13/16; d. Ventura, CA, 2/19/84. Mother was prof. pnst. In early 1930s she sang and danced in various Broadway shows; w. Gus Edwards at Palace, NYC 1930; Ziegfeld Follies '34. Irving Mills hired her to lead an all-female swing band; the band, the Melodears, became extremely popular under Hutton's direction '35–9. Led male band in '40s; then fronted new all-female orch. for TV. Org. other bands sporadically dur. the '50s, but never regained her earlier stature. At one time married to tptr. Randy Brooks. Film: short, *Accent on Girls* '36.

HUXLEY, CRAIG (Hundley), pno, synths; b. Los Angeles, CA, 11/22/53. A child prodigy, then known as Craig Hundley, whose jazz trio was popular in the late 1960s. Disbanded the gp. to spend time on various studies, including electronics. Invented own instruments such as the Blaster Beam, became a top sess. pl., scored and/or prod. many TV shows and feature films under his newly adopted name. Founded own business, Sonic Atmospheres, which incorporated own recording studios and several rec. labels, mainly Sonic Atmospheres. By then he was involved primarily in New Age mus. Won an Emmy Award in '90 for scoring mini-series *Family of Spies*. CDs: w. Bud Shank (Sonic.).

HYAMS, MARGIE (MARJORIE), vib; b. NYC, 1923. After working w. Woody Herman 1944–5, lead. her own trio '45–8, and rec. w. Mary Lou Williams, she join. the George Shearing Qnt. in January '49 but the following year she married and retired from the business. CDs: *The Women* w. Mary Lou Williams (BB); Herman (Col.; Jass); Shearing (Mos.).

HYDE, DICK "SLYDE" (RICHARD JOHN), tbns, bs, tpt, euph, tba; b. Lansing, MI, 7/4/36. Began tbn. stud. in 4th grade in Hawaii; also stud. at LA City Coll. and Navy Sch. of Mus., Washington, D.C. Pl. and tour. w. US Navy Band where he met Jay Migliori who help. launch his career. Made rec. debut w. S. Kenton Orch. 1960. Rec. and tour. in US and Eur. w. rock, pop, jazz artists, incl. big bands of Ralph Marterie; C. Basie; W. Herman; H. James '60–61; Roger Wagner Orch. and Chorale '66; Carole King '73; Jaco Pastorius '82–83; Frank Sinatra '87–89; also rec. w. Henry Mancini; Bill Conti; Allyn Ferguson; Johnny Mandel; Tom Scott. Recipient of four NARAS MVP awards for tbn. and tba., earning him the title of MVP Emeritus in the NARAS Hall of Fame. Favs: J.J. Johnson, Carl Fontana. CDs: James (Verve); Kenton (Cap.); Diane Schuur (GRP).

HYLTON, JACK, lead; b. Great Lever, Lancashire, England, 7/2/1892; d. London, England, 1/29/65. Directed tour. pantomime company 1909. Pl. org. in theater ca. '13; freelance mus. in clubs. In army dur. WWI. After war, was second pno. w. roof garden band. Became lead. of gp. bearing his name '21. In mid '20s he expanded band to orch. size, pl. long successful engagement at Alhambra Theater. Late '20s to mid '30s, this orch. was tremendously popular in Eur.; tour. continent as vaudeville show unit, doing stage, radio work; also revues, movies; was first Brit. band to broadcast direct to US. Came to US in '35 alone, form. a band in Chi. for some engagements. Ret. to Eng., disbanded his orch. '40. (Mrs. Jack Hylton also led a band in the UK and Eur. '33–7.) In later yrs. Hylton was theatrical prod., incl. *Camelot* '64. His assoc. w. jazz was almost accidental; he was, however, responsible for Ellington's first trip to Engl. '33 and C. Hawkins's '34. Recs. for HMV from '21, incl. two w. Hawkins '39. CDs: Pearl; tracks in *The British Dance Bands* (Timel.); w. C. Hawkins (Charly).

HYMAN, DICK (RICHARD ROVEN), pno, kybds, comp, arr; b. NYC, 3/8/27. Studied w. Teddy Wilson, others. Grad. Columbia Coll. 1948. Solo pno. at Wells' Music Bar; Café Society w. Tony Scott; Bop City w. Red Norvo. Opened Birdland '49 w. Max Kaminsky, Lester Young. Tour. Eur. w. Benny Goodman '50. TV app. w. Charlie Parker, Dizzy Gillespie

'52 on Earl Wilson show. From '50s through '70s active in studio and jazz work, rec. w. Zoot Sims, Toots Thielemans; also arr. for Count Basie; Bobby Hackett; Doc Severinsen. Own Moog synth. rec. '68–9, incl. "The Minotaur," a popular hit. Fr. '70s frequent duos w. Ruby Braff; Roger Kellaway; Dick Wellstood; Derek Smith. Music dir./pnst./orgst. for TV shows: Arthur Godfrey, David Frost, *Eubie Blake's One Hundred Years*. Concerts incl. Bud Freeman's 75th birthday '81; several NYC jazz festival events; George Wein's twenty-fifth anniversary celebration at the White House '78; Australia concert tours in '90s. Fr. '85 artistic dir. for widely acclaimed *Jazz in July* series held at the 92nd St. Y in NYC. Hyman also has appeared at most of the leading jazz parties, incl. Dick Gibson's from '67; NYC clubs incl. Michael's Pub. His film score credits incl. many Woody Allen movies: *Zelig*; *Purple Rose of Cairo*; *Stardust Memories*; *Broadway Danny Rose*; *Radio Days*. Also scored *Scott Joplin/ King of Ragtime*; *Moonstruck*; *Billy Bathgate*. Ballet scores as pnst. and/or comp.: *Piano Man* (Cleveland Ballet); *Eight Jelly Rolls*, *Bix Pieces*, *Bum's Rush* (Twyla Tharp). Comps. incl. *Piano Concerto*; *Ragtime Fantasy*; *Sextet for Clarinets, Piano & Strings*; *Songs from The Plays of Shakespeare*; *Duets for Six Valves*; *Duets in Odd Meter*. Hyman's multi-faceted work as instr., comp., and arr., and his amazing eclecticism as a pnst., enabled him to recreate the styles of every year fr. ragtime to contemporary with a perfect blend of technical, intellectual, and emotional requirements. Typically, in '75, as mus. dir. of the New York Jazz Repertory Co., he tour. the Soviet Union in a Louis Armstrong tribute concert that incl. his recreations of Armstrong's solos arranged for the tpt. section. It has been said that just as Art Tatum was the greatest creative artist in jazz, Hyman is the outstanding recreative pianist and composer. CDs: MM; Ref.; M&A; Omega; Conc.; *Stride Piano Summit* w. Jay McShann et al. (Mile.); Hyman–Kellaway (JazzMania); Hyman–Derek Smith (Jass; Arb.); w. Maxine Sullivan (Audio.; DCC); R. Braff (Conc.); R. Eldridge (Vogue); C. Hawkins (FS); Flip Phillips (Conc.; Chiaro.); J. Venuti (Chiaro.; Sonet); B. Wilber (Chiaro.); Joe Williams (BB); C. Parker (RARE); Mundell Lowe; Mark Murphy; Wes Montgomery (Riv.).

i

IBRAHIM, ABDULLAH (Adolphe Johannes Brand aka Dollar Brand), pno, comp, sop sax, fl, cello; b. Capetown, South Africa, 10/9/34. Studied priv. fr. age 7, pl. in church; then self-taught. Listened to Louis Jordan in his teens. First prof. job w. vocal gp. Streamline Bros.; also subbed w. Tuxedo Slickers. As Dollar Brand, pl. w. Willy Max in Capetown 1959; led own gp., Jazz Epistles, w. Hugh Masekela, Makaya Ntshoko, Kippie Moeketsi '60–1. Moved w. wife, singer Sathima Bea Benjamin, to Zurich '62. Led trio in Eur. '62–5. Duke Ellington, who heard him at a club in Zurich, rec. him for Reprise '63. Pl. at festivals in Juan-les-Pins, Palermo '63; Montmartre club, Copenhagen '64–5. Came to the US and app. at NJF '65. Pl. w. Elvin Jones, also subbed for Ellington on tour '66, then tour. Eur. w. Don Cherry, Gato Barbieri, M. Ntshoko, Johnny Gertze '66–8. Stud. w. Hall Overton. Converted to Islam '68; known by Muslim name fr. mid '70s. Ret. to Africa '68, living in Swaziland, Capetown, and Johannesburg '68–76. Tour. Eur. frequently in mid '70s, mainly as solo pno.; also w. 10–pc. band '74. Moved to NYC '76. Pl. in duo w. Carlos Ward fr. '76; led own spt. Ekaya fr. '83. Led perf. of mixed-media opera, *Kalahari Liberation*, in Eur. '82. Much of Ibrahim's work reflects the influences of South African popular and folk musics, Ellington, and Thelonious Monk. Some of his orchestral work has an impressive African rhythmic sensitivity. Polls: *DB* critics TDWR '75. Fests: prod. fests in Swaziland; all major in Eur. fr. '60s. TV: Eur. TV, incl. apps. w. Danish Radio bb in '60s and '70s. Film: mus. for *Chocolat* '87; *No Fear No Die*. CDs: Enja; BL; Japo; Tiptoe; Kaz; Rep. (as Dollar Brand); w. Barbieri (Aff.).

ILCKEN, WES (WESSEL), dms; b. Hilversum, Netherlands, 12/1/23; d. Loosdrecht, Netherlands, 7/13/57. Learned to pl. dms. in Paris. From 1942 pl. w. Piet van Dijk's orch. Married Rita Reys '45. Form. qnt. '50; tour. Germ. Moved to Sweden '53; ret. to Netherlands, where he really became prominent. Pl. w. Lars Gullin; D. Gillespie; Joe Carroll; H. Mann; Stan Kenton. In '63 a Dutch National Jazz Prize (at first named for him) was established in his honor. Recs: feat. on the three-album series, *Jazz Behind the Dikes* (Philips) '55–6, first important Dutch jazz recs. CD: w. Bob Cooper (FS).

IND, PETER VINCENT, bs; b. Oxbridge, Middlesex, England, 7/20/28. Studied pno., harm. at Trinity Coll. Pl. pno. w. local bands, then began pl. bs. 1947. Worked w. Freddie Barrat, Tommy Sampson '47–8. Pl. on SS *Queen Mary* '49–51; stud. w. Lennie Tristano while in NYC. Immigrated to US '51. Stud. and occ. gigs w. Tristano '51–4. Pl. w. Lee Konitz '54–7; Buddy Rich '57. Owned rec. studio fr. '57. Pl. w. Coleman Hawkins–Roy Eldridge '60–1; also w. Red Allen, Paul Bley. Founded rec. label Wave '61. In '63 moved to Big Sur, Calif., where he bec. the first jazz bs. to give unaccomp. solo concerts. Pl. w. Lee Konitz–Warne Marsh '65, then ret. to Engl. '66 where he cont. to perf., teach, and manage Wave. Tour. w. Konitz-Marsh '75–6. Operated the Bass Clef club in London '84–94. A painter and the author of books, incl. *Cosmic Metabolism* and *Vortical Accretion* (Ziegenhaus). Fav: Jimmy Blanton. CDs: w. Konitz (BL); Tristano (Atl.; Jazz); Marsh-Konitz (Mob. Fid.); Rich (Sequel); Tubby Hayes (Prog.); S. Gaillard (Hep); Bob Wilber (J&M).

INEKE, ERIC, dms; b. Haarlem, Netherlands, 4/1/47. Brother pl. dms. and acdn. in travelling show. Stud. w. John Engels in 1960s but primarily self-taught. Pl. w. Ferdinand Povel '66–71; Rob Agerbeek '69–79; Rein de Graaf since '71; Irv Rochlin '70s; Jimmy Raney '77, '81–3; Free-Fair '77–85; Charles Loos '81–6; Piet Noordijk since '83; Dutch Jazz Orch. since '84; Frans Elsen '88–9; Ben van den Dungen–Jarmo Hoogendijk since '89. As a member of the Rein de Graaf Trio, Ineke has backed many Amer. soloists in Eur., incl. Dexter Gordon; Johnny Griffin; Ben Webster; Frank Foster; Frank Wess; Charles McPherson; Dave Pike; Lew Tabackin; Bud Shank; Bill Perkins; Al Cohn; Harold Land; Pepper Adams; Freddie Hubbard; Curtis Fuller; Geo. Coleman; etc. Ineke teaches in the jazz dept. of the Royal Cons. of The Hague. Favs: Tiny Kahn, Philly Joe Jones, Elvin Jones. Fests: Eur.; US '77, '91 w. de Graaf. TV: many apps. on Eur. TV. CDs: w. Al Cohn; McPherson-Pike; Pike; van den Dungen-Hoogendijk; David Newman (Timel.); Rene Thomas (RTBF).

INGE, EDWARD FREDERICK, cl, saxes, comp, arr; b. Kansas City, MO, 5/7/06; d. Buffalo, NY, 10/8/88. Began on cl. at age 12. Stud. at cons. in St. Louis and Madison, Wis., fr. 1919. Pl. w. Geo. Reynolds '24; Dewey Jackson, Willie Austin '25; Art Sims, Bernie Young '26. Pl. and arr. w. McKinney's Cotton Pickers '29–31; Don Redman '31–9; Andy Kirk '40–3; Jimmie Lunceford, Louis Armstrong '43–5. Led own gps. in Cleveland and Buffalo fr. '45. Inge's most famous arr. is "You're Driving Me Crazy," rec. by McKinney's Cotton Pickers '30. CDs: w. McKinney's Cotton Pickers (Class.); D. Redman (Class.; Hep); "Chant of the Weed" in *An Anthology of Big Band Jazz* (Dec.); Red Allen (Tax); Kirk (B&B); M. L. Williams (Class.; Suisa).

INGHAM, KEITH CHRISTOPHER, pno, celeste, arr; b. London, England, 2/5/42. Attended Oxford U., degree in classical Chinese; stud. pno. priv. in London 1952–6. Pl. w. Sandy Brown, Bruce Turner, Wally Fawkes, Humphrey Lyttelton '64–74. Fr. '66 Ingham pl. w. Amer. mus. touring UK incl. Red Allen; Pee Wee Russell; Benny Carter; Bud Freeman; Bill Coleman; Bobby Hackett; Charlie Shavers; Peanuts Hucko; Ben Webster. Moved to NYC '79; pl. w. World's Greatest Jazz Band '82–3; Benny Goodman '86; Marty Grosz '89–91. Excellent contributions as arr. and accomp. w. Susannah McCorkle and Maxine Sullivan. Favs: Hines, T. Wilson, T. Flanagan, Al Haig, Ellington. Polls: *Jazz* '75. Fests: UK '83–4; Germ. '91. TV: w. various gps. on BBC. CDs: Prog.; Sack.; Stomp Off; w. M. Sullivan (Atl.; Mob. Fid.); Harry Allen (Prog.); Grosz (Jazz.; Stomp Off; J&M).

INOUE, SATOSHI, gtr; b. Kobe, Japan, 11/12/56. Father is amateur gtrst; cousin is rock gtrst. Began on pno. and org. Stud. at Fuji Jazz Sch., Kyoto 1979–81. Led own gps. in Japan '79–89. Tour. Japan w. own gp. feat. Steve Slagle '88. One week in Chi. w. Jack McDuff '90. In NYC fr. '90. On arrival, assisted by Arnie Lawrence, w. whom he pl. and co-led a gp. '91–6. Stud. at New Sch. '91–4; City College '96. Pl. w. Sam Yahel '94. Tour. Japan w. Junior Mance '95; Frank Foster '96; Jimmy Heath '97. Led own trio w. Larry Goldings, Andy Watson fr. '96. Teaches at the New Sch. and Mannes Coll. of Mus. Favs: Jim Hall, Wes Montgomery. Fests: Japan fr. '94. TV: Japanese TV w. J. Heath, J. Mance. Video: mus. dir. and pl. for *Jim Hall Master Class, Vols. 1 & 2* (Rittor Music). CDs: PW; w. Chie Ayado w. Junior Mance (Japanese Independent); Inside Out (PW); Deanna Kirk (Birth); *Jazz Restoration in Japan, Vol. 3* (PW).

INTERNATIONAL SWEETHEARTS OF RHYTHM. The all-female, originally all-black orch. was formed in 1939 at Piney Woods Country Life Sch. in Mississippi. Dur. the most successful yrs., which involved tours of the black theaters and of Amer. bases in Eur., the band was conducted by singer Anna Mae Winburn. It was directed for a while by arr. Eddie Durham and later by Jesse Stone. The orch. disbanded in '49 but Winburn tour. w. other ens. under the Sweethearts name. Personnel of the band incl. Carline Ray, bs.; Tiny Davis, tpt.; Pauline Braddy, dms.; and a white alto saxophonist, Roz Cron. A key figure also was the tenor saxophonist Vi Burnside. The Sweethearts were the subject of a documentary film, *The International Sweethearts of Rhythm: America's Hottest All-Girl Band* '85. Despite severe financial problems, the band maintained its reputation as one of the most underrated large ensembles of the swing era. LP: Rosetta. CDs: two tracks in *The Women* (BB).

INTRA, ENRICO, pno, comp, arr, cond; b. Milan, Italy, 7/3/35. Brother Gianfranco is pnst. and cond. Stud. priv. First prof. gig at age 17. Led own gps. fr. early 1950s incl. trios, combos, bbs, large orchs. Known mainly as a comp., cond., and lead. Rec. w. Milt Jackson '67; Gerry Mulligan '76; Lee Konitz '92. Co-led qt. w. Franco Cerri fr. '81. In '86 they organized a music assoc., Musica Oggi, and a jazz school, Civici Corsi Di Jazz, of which Intra is dir. Current projects incl. large works for symph. orch., incl. an oratorio setting of the biblical *Song of Songs*. Favs: Bill Evans, Keith Jarrett; arrs: Gil Evans, Thad Jones. Fests: France, Belg., Netherlands early '60s; Germ. '85–90; NYC '93. TV: many apps. on Eur. TV as perf. and cond. LPs: Col.; DIRE; Rifi. CDs: DIRE; Ed. Paoline; w. Jazz Class Orch., Intra & L. Konitz, guests.

IRAKERE. Cuban gp. founded in Havana ca. 1973. Its musicians, who had formerly pl. in the Orquesta Cubana de Musica Moderna and other gps., incl. pno. Chucho Valdes; tpts. Arturo Sandoval, Jorge Varona; saxes Carlos Averhoff, Paquito D'Rivera; gtr. Carlos Emilio; and voc. and perc. Oscar Valdes. Irakere's successful US tour in '78–9 was documented on two albums for the Col. label. Rec. w. American musicians in Havana '79, Japan '80. D'Rivera and Sandoval left the gp. in '80 and '81 respectively, but Irakere has cont. to tour extensively. App. at NJF-NY '78; JVC-NY '97. CDs: Col.; JH; Mess.; WP.

IRBY, SHERMAN, alto, sop saxes, cl, fl; b. Tuscaloosa, AL, 3/24/68. Began on vla. in grade sch. but later sw. to alto sax. B.A. in mus. ed. fr. Clark Coll., Atlanta where he perf. w. D. Gillespie; L. Hampton; C. Rouse; and K. Burrell; and at Montreux-Atlanta Mus. Fest. Moved to NYC after pl. on cruise ship Aug. 1994. Worked w. The Temptations, Boys Choir of Harlem, Mingus Dynasty bb, Betty Carter, Wynton Marsalis '95. Join. LCJO for Eur. tour, summer '95, also tour. w. it in US that fall. Tour. w. Marcus Roberts '97. With Roy Hargrove's Crisol in summer '97 for US, Eur. fest. apps.; then w. Hargrove qnrt. incl. Havana JF '98; Umbria Winter Jazz '99. Favs: Stitt, Adderley, Gigi Gryce. CDs: BN; w. Russell Gunn (High.); Marcus Roberts (Col.); Hargrove (Verve); Ann Hampton Calloway; Billy Strich (Touchwind).

IRVIS, CHARLIE (CHARLES), tbn; b. NYC, 1899; d. NYC, ca. 1939. Brother, Gibbie, was pnst. As a child pl. in boys' band w. Bubber Miley. Worked w. Lucille Hegamin's Blue Flame Syncopators 1920–1; then w. Willie "The Lion" Smith. Join. the Washingtonians while still led by Elmer Snowden '24, remaining after Duke Ellington took over to '26; w. Charlie Johnson '27–8. From '23–7 he rec. frequently w. Clarence Williams; also rec. w. Fats Waller late '20s. Tour. w. Jelly Roll Morton '29–30; w. B. Miley '31. During most of the '30s worked mainly w. Snowden and Johnson. Established the plunger-mute and growl style in Ellington's tbn. chair. CDs: w. Ellington (Dec.); Armstrong (Mile.); Bechet (EPM); F. Waller; Morton (BB); C. Williams

(Hot 'N Sweet); King Oliver in *Hist. of Classic Jazz* (Riv.).

IRWIN, CECIL, saxes, cl, arr; b. Evanston, IL, 12/7/02; d. Des Moines, IA, 5/3/35. Worked w. Carroll Dickerson 1924–5; Erskine Tate '27. Pl. w. Junie Cobb; then join. Earl Hines Dec. '28, as tnr. sax and arr. Killed instantly in a bus crash while tour. w. Hines's orch. Recs. w. Richard M. Jones (Gennett) '27; Dixie Rhythm Kings (Brunswick) '29; Harry Dial (Vocalion) '30. CDs: w. Hines (Class.); J. C. Cobb and his Grains of Corn in *New Orleans, Chicago, New York* (BBC).

IRWIN, DENNIS WAYNE, bs, cl; b. Birmingham, AL, 11/28/51. Older brother David is prof. clst.; many other mus. in family. Stud. cl. fr. age 8; also pl. sax in r&b bands. Stud. cl. w. Lee Gibson at No. Texas State 1969–74; began stud. bs. '70. Pl. bs. w. Jim Moore–Barry Ries in Dallas '71–2; Red Garland '73–4. Moved to NYC '75, pl. w. Ted Curson '75; Jackie Paris '75–6; Albert Dailey '75–7; Dom Salvador da Silva fr. '75; Betty Carter '76–7; Mose Allison '76–88; Art Blakey '77–80; Al Haig '77–82; Chet Baker, early '80s; Horace Silver '81; Mel Lewis Orch. '81–90; Toshiko Akiyoshi–Lew Tabackin fr. '86; Johnny Griffin, Scott Hamilton fr. '87; John Scofield fr. '91. Favs: Ali Jackson, Pettiford, Wilbur Ware, Sam Jones. Fests: Eur. fr. '77; Japan fr. '79. CDs: w. Griffin (Ant.); M. Lewis Orch. (MM); Blakey (Em.; Timel.; Conc.); Allison; John Scofield (BN); Joe Cohn (D-T); C. Byrd; S. Hamilton; S. McCorkle; K. Peplowski; Akiyoshi (Conc.); C. Fuller (Timel.); R. Lalama; M. LeDonne; Tad Shull (CC); J. Lovano (SN); V. Ponomarev (Res.); Bennie Wallace (Enja).

ISAACS, IKE (CHARLES EDWARD), bs., tpt, sousaphone; b. Akron, OH, 3/28/23; d. Atlanta, GA, 2/27/81. First cousin is Maxine Sullivan; son, Richard Lett, pl. tpt. Start. on tpt. and tba.; stud. tpt. at Central Mus. Sch., Akron. While in army 1941, Wendell Marshall gave him bs. lessons in exchange for tba. instruction. Pl. w. Tiny Grimes '49; briefly w. air force band; then w. Earl Bostic '51–3; Mat Mathews, Paul Quinichette '53; Bennie Green '54. Ret. to Ohio, form. own gp., the Four Maestros. Married Carmen McRae in '56; tour. for two yrs. as lead. of her trio, incl. Brit. West Indies. Led trio accomp. L,H&R '58–9. Tour. Sweden w. Basie '62. With Gloria Lynne '62–4 as bs. and manager. Settled in LA '64, headed trio at the Pied Piper, before join. Erroll Garner '66–70. Settled in Atlanta; pl. regularly at E.J.'s, where he worked w. Sweets Edison; Chubby Jackson's bb; Zoot Sims; Clark Terry; others. Most important infl: Wendell Marshall. Fav: Ray Brown. Fests: MJF '59, '61, w. L.H.&R.; NJF '62–3, w. Lynne. Film: app. in *They Shoot Horses, Don't They?* Recs. w. Bostic; Bennie Green. CDs: w. L,H&R (Col.); McRae (Dec.); Sweets Edison–Lockjaw Davis (Riv.); Ray Bryant (Prest.); Basie; Joe Williams (Roul.); Digby Fairweather (BL); Garner (Merc.); Grappelli (Verve).

ISRAEL, YORON DAEL, dms, vib, perc; b. Chicago, IL, 11/24/63. Father was amateur gtr. and hca. pl. Stud. pno. and org. fr. age 9 at Bedford Music Sch.; dms. fr. age 11. Pl. tpt. in sch. band. Pl. gospel music in church, then first prof. gig at age 12 in uncle Jerry Williams' band, Inner City. Also stud. w. Edward Poremba; Gary Matts; Marshall Thompson; Thurman Barker; Joel Spencer; Alan Dawson. B. Mus. fr. Roosevelt U.; M. Mus. fr. Rutgers U. Pl. w. Otis Clay 1980–1; Shirley Caesar '81; Hank Crawford '84; Von Freeman '84–7; Jimmy McGriff '88; Kenny Burrell, Jay Hoggard fr. '88; Ahmad Jamal fr. '89; Gloria Lynne '90; Roy Hargrove '90–2; Art Farmer; Vanessa Rubin fr. '90; Geo. Adams '91; Mingus bb '91–3; Abbey Lincoln '91–4; Horace Silver, Bunky Green '92; Sonny Rollins '92–3; Clifford Jordan, Buster Williams '92–4; Lou Donaldson '93; Frank Wess '93–4; Houston Person, Etta Jones '94; Cyrus Chestnut '94–5; James Williams fr. '94; Tony Bennett, Jimmy Witherspoon, Ernestine Anderson, Steve Coleman, Mulgrew Miller, Freddie Cole '95; Chico Freeman '95–6; Joe Lovano fr. '95; Jim Hall '96; Tom Harrell fr. '96. Taught at Rutgers U. and William Paterson Coll.; also priv. fr. '86. Favs: Roach, DeJohnette P.J. Jones. Fests: all major. TV: ABC *Good Morning America* w. Abbey Lincoln; BET on Jazz w. Chas. Fambrough. CDs: BN; Freelance; w. A. Jamal (Tel.); A. Lincoln (Verve); A. Farmer–C. Jordan (Evid.); Fambrough (CTI); Burrell (Cont.); R. Malone (Col.).

ISRAELS, CHUCK, bs, comp; b. NYC, 8/10/36. Began on cello and gtr. while att. jr. hs in Cleveland. Ret. to NYC, stud. at HS of Perf. Arts. Self-taught on bs. fr. 1955. While att. MIT he stud. w. Herb Pomeroy in Boston. Later stud. mus. at Brandeis U. Pl. w. Billie Holiday, Max Roach, Don Elliott, Tony Scott late '50s. Made rec. debut w. Cecil Taylor '58. Pl. w. Bud Powell in Paris '59. Pl. and rec. w. Geo. Russell '59–61; Eric Dolphy '61. Tour. Eur. w. Ballet USA '61. Join. Bill Evans trio after death of Scott La Faro '61. Pl. w. Evans '61–6; J.J. Johnson, Herbie Hancock, Gary Burton '63; Stan Getz '64; Hampton Hawes '65. Did A&R work for Vanguard rec. label '65. Taught during summers at Indian Hill Mus. Wkshp., Stockbridge, Mass., '60s. Stud. comp.

w. Hall Overton '66–71. Led own bb at Village Vanguard, Half Note '66–8. Assoc. cond. for Broadway show *Promises, Promises* '68–71. Travelled to Eur. to perf. own comps. w. Nord Deutscher Rundfunk Orch.; Danish Radio bb '69–70; Swiss radio gp. '70. Received Croft fellowship to stud. w. Gunther Schuller, Bruno Maderna at Tanglewood '71. Assist. profess. in charge of jazz stud. at Bklyn. Coll. fr. '73. Formed National Jazz Ens., the first major jazz repertory orch. '73; sidemen incl. Jimmy Maxwell; Tom Harrell; Sal Nistico; Jimmy Knepper; Rod Levitt; Bill Goodwin. Guest soloists in the first few seasons incl. Lee Konitz; B. Evans; Roy Eldridge; H. Hancock; Phil Woods. Concert at Smithsonian Inst. '75. The ens. disbanded in '78, after which Israels was less active as a perf. Moved to SF '81; Bellingham, Wash. '86. Pl. w. Barry Harris trio at Village Vanguard and Spain in late '90s. Favs: Pettiford, Red Mitchell, John Neves. Fests: all major w. Evans; Getz; Gerry Mulligan; Nat'l Jazz Ens.; etc. CDs: Anima; Audio Ideas; w. Evans (Riv.; Verve); Getz (Verve); Dolphy (Enja; Prest.); H. Hawes (Cont.); Russell (Riv.); R. Clooney (Conc.) Metropole Orch. (Azica.).

ITURRALDE, PEDRO, saxes, cl, comp, arr; b. Falces, Spain, 7/13/29. Began on cl. and sax at age 9; pl. first prof. gig at age 11. Stud. sax at Madrid Cons. and pl. w. local gps. late 1940s. Tour. Middle East and Germ., then led gp. of Germ. musicians in Madrid. Experimented with fusion of flamenco and jazz late '60s; rec. album *Flamenco Jazz* w. sideman Paco de Lucia. Att. Berklee Coll. of Mus. '72. Received prize for comp. "Like Coltrane" at Monaco composers' competition '72. Taught sax at the Madrid Cons. fr. '73 and has continued to perf. and rec. CDs: Spanish BN; w. Juan Carlos Calderone (Span. BN).

IZENZON, DAVID, bs; b. Pittsburgh, PA, 5/17/32; d. NYC, 10/8/79. Started stud. bs. in 1956; received M.A. '63. Worked w. local gps., incl. Dodo Marmarosa '58. Moved to NYC '61, pl. w. Paul Bley; Archie Shepp; Sonny Rollins; Bill Dixon; also w. more mainstream mus. such as Mose Allison. Additionally, worked as classical mus. and taught bs.; Gary Peacock was one of his students. Pl. w. Ornette Coleman on and off in '62, '65–8, incl. Eur. tour. '65–6. In late '60s pl. w. Perry Robinson; Paul Motian; Jaki Byard; form. own qnt., incl. Gato Barbieri; also form. bs. orch. w. Steve Swallow; Buster Williams; Eddie Gomez; Dave Holland; Jimmy Garrison. In '67 start. stud. psychotherapy, earned Ph.D. '73 and began private practice. Wrote book on human emotions and their relationships. From '72, limited his musical activities because his young son, who suffered from brain injury, required intensive care. In '75, his opera, *How Music Can Save the World*, was performed, proceeds going to his son's medical expenses. Izenzon died of a heart attack chasing a thief on the street. He was an exceptionally fine arco improviser. As a player who was swept up by the new wave of jazz in NYC in the early '60s, he was a firm believer in expanding the role of the bass. "So many musicians," he once said, "are so afraid of disorder that they forget to be afraid of slavery. The bassists can no longer be tied down; we must have freedom to establish communication." Fests: NJF-NY '73; NY Mus. Fest. Polls: *DB* New Star '67. Film: unreleased, *Solo Bass and Stripper*. Video: w. Coleman (Rhap.) '66. Comps: "Hymn to Endlessness"; "A Tribute to Bass Players." Recs. w. Byard; Motian. CDs: w. Coleman (BN; ESP); S. Rollins (RCA); A. Shepp (Imp.); P. Motian (ECM).

JACKSON, CALVIN, comp, pno; b. Philadelphia, PA, 5/26/19; d. Encinitas, CA, 12/9/85. Mother was a concert singer. Extensive mus. studies; thirteen yrs. w. private teachers in Phila., at Juilliard, and at NYU. First prof. job w. Frankie Fairfax. Asst. mus. dir. to George Stoll at MGM, Hollywood 1943–7; also wrote arrs. for Harry James '43. Moved to NYC '48, pl. at Café Society w. Mildred Bailey. Settled in Toronto '50, where he had own radio and TV shows. Ret. to West Coast '57, app. as soloist in classical and jazz concerts '61–2; own radio show '65. Film: soundtrack for *Blood and Steel*; Oscar nomination for score to *The Unsinkable Molly Brown*; app. in *Three on a Couch*. TV: soundtrack for series, *The Asphalt Jungle*; apps. on Steve Allen, *The Detectives*; NBC special, *Rehearsing With Calvin*. Comp: *Profile of an American*, dedicated to J. F. Kennedy, perf. by Hollywood Symph. '66. Recs. on Col., Rep.; w. Phil Moore (Verve). CD: w. Buddy Collette (Cont.).

JACKSON, CHIP (CHARLES MELVIN), bs, el-bs; b. Rockville Center, NY, 5/15/50. Brother is dmr. Bob Jackson. Stud. at Berklee Sch. of Mus. 1970–3. Pl. w. Herb Pomeroy, John LaPorta '72; Gary Burton '72–3; Woody Herman '73–4; Chuck Mangione '74–5; Horace Silver, Betty Carter '77; Thad Jones-Mel Lewis bb '78; Hubert Laws '79; G. Burton '80; Stan Getz '82; Elvin Jones '83–5; Al Di Meola '85. Freelanced '85–7, then worked w. Elvin Jones '88–90; Red Rodney '89–90; Roy Haynes '90; Billy Taylor fr. '94. Taught bs. and improv. in Spain in '86 and w. Jamey Aebersold in Chi. in the late '80s. Favs: Wilbur Ware, Richard Davis, Jimmy Garrison. Fests: Eur. and Japan since '85. TV: Newport JF '90 w. Elvin Jones. CDs: JazzKey; w. Red Rodney (Con-

tin.); Joe Beck (DMP); B. Taylor (Ark.); E. Jones (Enja); J. Walrath (Muse); George Young (PW); R. Cuber (Steep.).

JACKSON, CHUBBY (GREIG STEWART), bs, lead, b. NYC, 10/25/18; d. Paway, CA, 10/1/03. Raised in Freeport, LI; stud. cl. 1934, then bs. '35. Worked w. Mike Riley, Johnny Messner, Raymond Scott, Jan Savitt, Terry Shand, Henry Busse '37–41; feat. w. Charlie Barnet '41–3 where for a time he and Oscar Pettiford were a two-bs. team. An important member of Woody Herman band '43–6 as a driving rhythmic force, cheerleader and comic presence. Began pl. 5–string bs. in late '40s. Tour. in Swed. w. own qnt. '47. Pl. w. C. Ventura '47, '51. Rejoin. Herman '48; led own bb, NYC '49; own club, Happy Monster Room, Valley Stream, LI, '49. With Herman again '50 and off and on through '50s; pl. w. C. Ventura '47, '51. Lived in Chi. '53–8, work. in radio and hosting children's daily TV show. Ret. to NYC '58, did more kids' TV; led own trio. Dur. '60s led various sized gps. in Miami, Fla., incl. his son Duffy. In early '70s alternated between LA and LV; fr. mid '70s mostly active in Fla. but resettled in Calif. in late '90s. Pl. w. L. Hampton '78–9. Taught at Stan Kenton Summer Jazz Clinic '64; was jazz dj in Miami Beach '70s; own jazz club in No. Hollywood briefly '73. Won *Esq.* New Star Award '45; Gold Awd. '46–7; *DB* '45. CDs: Gerry Mulligan–Chubby Jackson (Fant); track in *The Jazz Arranger, Vol. 2* (Col); w. Herman (Col.; Cap.; Disc.; Evid.; BB); Barnet (Evid.); Hampton (Timel.); C. Parker (Stash); C. Hawkins (Jass); S. Chaloff (Cool N' Blue); Herman's Woodchoppers in *1940s: The Small Groups: New Directions* (Col.); Neal Hefti; Red Rodney in *Early Bebop* (Merc.).

JACKSON, CLIFF (CLIFTON LUTHER), pno; b. Culpepper, VA, 7/19/02; d. NYC, 5/24/70. Studied priv.; first prof. job was at a dance sch. in Wash., D.C. Married to singer Maxine Sullivan. Pl. in Atlantic City bef. moving to NYC 1923. Join. Lionel Howard's Musical Aces; w. Elmer Snowden '26; form. Krazy Kats '27, rec. for a variety of labels. In '30s worked mostly as a soloist and accomp. to several blues singers, incl. Viola McCoy; Lena Wilson, Sarah Martin, Clara Smith. Pl. w. Sidney Bechet at Nick's '40. Earned great popularity as house pnst. at Café Society '43–51; also tour. w. Eddie Condon '46. In '50s pl. at several NYC clubs; also worked w. Garvin Bushell '59; J. C. Higginbotham '60; Joe Thomas '62. Fr. '63 to '67, he worked at Jimmy Ryan's w. Tony Parenti. Concerts w. his wife '65, helping in her comeback. In residence at the RX Room fr. '68 until he died of heart failure. One of the early Harlem stride and boogie-woogie pnsts., Jackson's own style later expanded upon and modernized his favs., James P. Johnson, Fats Waller. Cut pno. rolls in '24, recs. '30; rec. solo and band sides for B&W '44; Disc solo sess. '45; w. Snowden '27, '61; B. Berigan '35; J. Marsala (incl. Dizzy Gillespie) (B&W) '45. CDs: BL; one track in *History of Classic Jazz* (Riv.); w. Marsala (Class.); Condon (Jass); Bechet (BB; BN); Snowden (Riv.).

JACKSON, DEWEY, tpt; b. St. Louis, MO, 6/21/1900; d.? Started pl. w. Odd Fellows band at age 12. Worked on riverboats w. Charlie Creath fr. 1919; own gps. fr. '20; Fate Marable fr. '24. Pl. w. Andrew Preer at Cotton Club '26. Riverboats w. own gps. '26–41; sidemen incl. John Lindsay; Pops Foster; Willie Humphrey; Don Stovall, Jock Carruthers; Singleton Palmer; Clark Terry. Led bands in St. Louis '40s Pl. often w. S. Palmer in '30s-40, rec. w. him '50. Worked w. Don Ewell's trio '51, led own gps. in '50s. Perf. infrequently in '60s. Rec. for Voc. '26.

JACKSON, DUFFY (DUFF CLARK), dms; also pno, vib, bs, voc; b. Freeport, NY, 7/3/53. Son of Chubby Jackson. Stud. dms. at age 4 w. Don Lamond, later w. Roy Burnes. Also stud. w. father and tap dancer Steve Condos. Pl. w. father's gp. while in sch.; w. Flip Phillips in Fla. 1967. Dur. senior yr. of hs was dmr. for prod. of musical *Hair* in Coconut Grove, Fla. After grad. fr. Miami Beach HS, opened w. Milt Jackson–Ray Brown at Shelly's Manne Hole in LA '71. Pl. w. Kai Winding, Terry Gibbs, Woody Herman, Monty Alexander, Urbie Green '71–2; Lena Horne '72; Benny Carter in Japan '73; Sammy Davis Jr. '74–6. Pl. w. Ella Fitzgerald at Kennedy Ctr. '79. Tour. w. L. Hampton '83. Rec. w. Count Basie '80; Illinois Jacquet bb '88. Led own gp. '95. Favs: Buddy

Rich, Louie Bellson, Gene Krupa, Mel Lewis. Fests: Eur., Japan fr. '70s. TV: apps. w. Sammy Davis Jr. '74–6; PBS w. E. Fitzgerald at Kennedy Ctr. '79. CDs: Mile.; w. Count Basie Orch. (Den.; Pab.); George Benson (WB); Hampton (Timel.); I. Jacquet (Atl.); T. Mauro (Mile.).

JACKSON, FRANZ R., tnr sax, cl, lead, arr; b. Rock Island, IL, 11/1/12. Began on cl. and tnr. sax in hs. Stud. comp. and arr. at Chi. Mus. Coll. Worked w. various bands fr. 1926. Pl. w. Albert Ammons ca. '30; Cassino Simpson '31; Carroll Dickerson at Grand Terrace '32, '34–6; Jimmie Noone '34; Roy Eldridge '37; Fletcher Henderson '37–8. To NYC w. Eldridge '38. Worked in Calif. w. Earl Hines '40–1, then in NYC w. Fats Waller '41; Cootie Williams '42. Pl. in Bost. w. Frankie Newton '42–3. Tour. w. Eldridge '44, then pl. w. Wilbur De Paris '44–5. USO tours w. Jesse Stone and others fr. '46. Two yrs. in Eur. as band manager. Ret. to Chi. ca. '50; pl. bsn. in DePaul U. Community Symph. fr. '51. Form. Original Jass All-Stars w. Bob Shoffner, Al Wynn '57. The gp. pl. a long engagement at Red Arrow Jazz Club in Stickney, Ill., followed by a weekly gig in Chi. at Jazz Ltd. '60–3 and rec. for Riv. '61. Founded Pinnacle rec. label '60. After pl. in NYC in '68, the Orig. Jass All-Stars made several USO tours to Vietnam and the Far East. Rec. w. Art Hodes '74. Formed gp. Jazz Entertainers in Chi. '80. Tour. Eur. as soloist '81. App. in *Chicago Jazz Summit* JVC-NY JF '86. CDs: Riv., Del., Park.; Franz Jackson–Marcus Belgrave, *Live at the Windsor Jazz Festival III* (Park.); tnr. sax; voc. (erroneously credited to Wild Bill Davison) in *Chicago Jazz Summit* (Atl.); w. Hines (BB); Eldridge (Dec.); Lil Armstrong (Riv.).

JACKSON, JAVON ANTHONY, tnr, alto, sop saxes, fl; b. Carthage, MO, 6/16/65. Mother pl. classical pno. Began on alto sax, sw. to tnr. at age 16. Received help fr. pnst. Billy Wallace as teenager. Stud. at Berklee Coll. of Mus. 1985–6, then left to join Art Blakey's Jazz Messengers. Pl. w. Blakey '87–90; Harper Bros. '90–1; Elvin Jones '91; Freddie Hubbard, Charlie Haden Liberation Orch. fr. '91; Bobby Hutcherson '92; Cedar Walton, Louis Hayes fr. '92. Has conducted jazz clinics at schs. and colls. nationwide. Favs: C. Parker, Rollins. Fests: all major fr. '87. Film: app. in *Malcolm X* '92. CDs: CC; BN; w. Blakey (PW; SN; A&M; Timel.; BN); Hubbard (Timel.; MM); E. Jones (Enja); Rebecca Franks (Just.); Benny Green; Brian Lynch (CC); Mickey Tucker (Steep.); Cedar Walton (Evid.).

JACKSON, MILT (MILTON aka BAGS), vib, pno, voc, gtr, comp; b. Detroit, MI, 1/1/23; d. NYC,

10/9/99. At age 7, he sang gospel duets w. bro. Alvin, later a bs. Also took up gtr. Sw. to pno. at age 11; xyl., vib. in teens. Stud. mus. at Mich. State U. Tour. prof. as tenor in gospel vocal qt. early 1940s. Dizzy Gillespie heard him w. a Det. gp. and brought him to NYC '45. Pl. w. Gillespie sxt. '45, bb '46; Howard McGhee, Tadd Dameron, Thelonious Monk, Charlie Parker '48–9. Replaced Terry Gibbs w. Woody Herman Orch. '49–50. Pl. pno. and vib. w. Gillespie '50–2. Rec. as lead. of Milt Jackson Qt. w. John Lewis, Ray Brown, Kenny Clarke '51–2. In late '52 Percy Heath replaced Brown and the gp. was renamed the MJQ. Appointed to faculty of Sch. of Jazz in Lenox, Mass. '57. Feat. in John Lewis's score for film *Odds Against Tomorrow* '59. Rec. vocal album in Italy '64. Dur. summer mos., Jackson led gps. w. Jimmy Heath '60s; Ray Brown early '70s. Jackson left the MJQ in '74, and the gp. disbanded in July of that yr. It was reunited for a concert in the fall, but Jackson worked mainly as a single in '75. App. w. own all-star gp. at MJF '75. Jackson rejoined the MJQ for Japanese concert '81 and annual concert tours beginning in '82. The gp. celebrated its 40th anniv. in 1992. Own qt. fr. '92 w. Mike LeDonne, Bob Cranshaw, Mickey Roker. Jackson was the first bop musician to play vibes and is widely considered among the best jazz vibsts. He was noted for his relaxed, confident sense of time; his sound, which featured subtle dynamics, was crucial to the unique character of the MJQ. His vibrato was much slower than that used by his predecessors, notably Lionel Hampton. The ingrained blues feeling that permeated Jackson's work caused Gillespie to say, "He's sanctified." Polls: *Esq.* New Star '47; *Met.* '56–60; *DB* Readers '55–64, '66–7; *DB* Critics '55–63, '66–8, '70, '73; *Play.* All-Stars '59–60. Awards: National Music; French Bicentennial; Percussion Hall of Fame; *DB* Hall of Fame. Comps: "Bags' Groove": "Bluesology." CDs: Qwest; Prest.; Riv.; Pab.; Atl.; Sav.; BN; Imp.; CTI; MM; Milt Jackson–Sonny Stitt (Gal); Cannonball Adderley–Milt Jackson (Riv); w. MJQ (Prest.; Atl.; Sav.; Verve; Pab.); M. Davis; S. Rollins (Prest.); F. Navarro (BN; Mile.); H. Mobley; Monk (BN); Gillespie (Sav.; Pab.; Prest.); Basie; Benny Carter (Pab.); O. Peterson (Verve; MPS; Pab.); K. Clarke; C. Parker; H. McGhee (Sav.); Dinah Washington (Del.); T. Dameron; W. Montgomery (Mile.).

JACKSON, OLIVER JR. (BOPS), dms, perc, arr; b. Detroit, MI, 4/28/33; d. NYC, 5/29/94. Brother Ali pl. bs., nephews also mus. Stud. w. Merle Auley and at Wayne State Coll. in Det. Pl. in Det. w. Thad Jones; Paul Chambers; Tommy Flanagan; variety act, incl. tap dancing, Bop and Locke w. Eddie Locke 1948–53; Yusef Lateef '54–6; also Wardell Gray;

Rudy Rutherford; Billy Mitchell; Kenny Burrell; Barry Harris. Moved to NYC '54, pl. w. Tony Parenti, then Red Allen at Metropole; Teddy Wilson '57–8; Charlie Shavers '59–61; Buck Clayton '61; Benny Goodman '62; Lionel Hampton '62–4; Earl Hines qt. '66–9, incl. Soviet Union tour; also Erroll Garner; Coleman Hawkin, Roy Eldridge; Illinois Jacquet; etc. Form. JPJ Qt. w. Budd Johnson, Bill Pemberton, Dill Jones '69. Created New Communications in Jazz program for Johns-Manville Corp., which brought JPJ to various cities in US and Can. for hs concerts '71. Pl. w. Sy Oliver '75–80; own gps. fr. '79; also freelanced w. Oscar Peterson; Lionel Hampton; Newport All-Stars; etc. Fests: all major int'l. Perf. and arr. for TV. Acted and pl. in the off-B'way musical, *Song of Singapore*. Polls: *DB* Critics, TDWR '73. CDs: B&B; w. Lateef (Prest.; NJ; Sav.); Hines (Verve; B&B.); G. Ammons (Prest.); Harry Allen (Prog.; Mastermix); Lockjaw Davis (B&B; Divox); V. Dickenson; B. Tate (Story.); P. Gonsalves (BL); D. Gordon; J. Newman (Prest.); Jacquet (Prest.; Roul.; B&B); Newport All-Stars (Conc.); J. Hodges (BB); R. Sandke (N-H).

JACKSON, PRESTON (James Preston McDonald), tbn; b. New Orleans, LA, 1/3/04; d. Blytheville, AR, 11/12/83. Went to Chi. in 1917; start. on tbn in '20; later stud. w. Honore Dutrey, Roy Palmer. First prof. jobs around Chi.; w. Art Simms, Bernie Young (Milwaukee) '25–30; Dave Peyton, Erskine Tate (Chi.) '30, bef. join. L. Armstrong Jan. '31. Tour. w. Armstrong to '32. to Chi., pl. w. Frankie Jaxon '33; Carroll Dickerson, Jimmie Noone, Zilner Randolph fr. '36. Led own band in '40s and occ. dur. the '50s; also gigs w. Natty Dominique. With Lil Armstrong '59; Franz Jackson All-Stars fr. '66; concerts w. Clyde Bernhardt; Little Brother Montgomery; Art Hodes; et al. Moved to NO; pl. at Preservation Hall w. Percy Humphrey '74 and cont. to pl. locally. Eur. tours w. Kid Thomas Valentine '73; NO Joy Makers '74; as lead. of Preservation Hall Band '79. Served on board of dir. of local Chi. AF of M '34–57. In '30s wrote column for *Jazz Hot* and *Hot News*. Autobiography: *Recapturing Yesterday* '74. Made films in Paris, London. Rec. in Sweden w. own band; as lead. for Para. '26; w. Armstrong '31 (solo on "You Rascal You"); J. Noone; B. Dodds; NO Joy Makers; F. Jackson; Barry Martyn. CDs: w. Armstrong (Col.); Lil Armstrong (Riv.); Baby Dodds (Amer. Mus.).

JACKSON, QUENTIN (BUTTER), tbn; b. Springfield, OH, 1/13/09; d. NYC, 10/2/76. Studied pno., vln., org. w. priv. teachers; tbn. w. bro.-in-law, Claude Jones. Worked w. Gerald Hobson 1927–8; Wes Helvey '29–30; McKinney's Cotton Pickers '30–2; Don Redman '32–40; Cab Calloway '40–5. Tour.

Eur. w. Redman '46, then rejoin. Calloway. Member of Duke Ellington band fr. '48 to Nov. '59, specializing in plunger-mute solos à la Tricky Sam Nanton. Join. Quincy Jones Nov. '59, tour. Eur. w. him in *Free and Easy* '59–60. Then w. Count Basie until fall '62. Worked w. Charles Mingus. Rejoin. Ellington briefly spring '63. NYC studio work; house band at Copacabana '64. Gigs w. NYC bands assembled for Louie Bellson '64; Gerald Wilson '66. Member of NYJRC. With Thad Jones–Mel Lewis fr. inception '65 until illness curtailed his activities in '75. Fr. '60s active w. B'way pit orchs. He was pl. for *Guys and Dolls* when stricken w. a fatal heart attack. Rec. solos w. Ellington: "Fancy Dan"; "Jam with Sam"; "Black and Tan Fantasy" '55. Recs. w. McKinney's Cotton Pickers; Q. Jones; Mingus; Basie; Jones-Lewis. CDs: w. Ellington (Col.; Em.; Pab.); Benny Carter (Charly); Basie (Roul.); Clark Terry (Riv.); Mingus (Imp.); J. Hodges (Vogue); Q. Jones; R. R. Kirk (Merc.); O. Nelson (RCA).

JACKSON, RONALD SHANNON, dms; b. Fort Worth, TX, 1/12/40. Piano at age 5; began pl. cl. and dms. in sch. First prof. gig w. James Clay at age 15; also pl. in Dallas w. Leroy Cooper. Stud. history and sociology bef. moving to NYC 1966. Pl. w. Mingus '66; Betty Carter, Stanley Turrentine, Jackie McLean, McCoy Tyner, Kenny Dorham, Joe Henderson bb late '60s. Worked w. Albert Ayler '66–7. Did not perform but cont. to practice '70–5. Pl. w. Ornette Coleman's Prime Time '75–9; Cecil Taylor '78–9; James "Blood" Ulmer '79–80. Form. own gp. Decoding Society '79; sidemen have incl. Vernon Reid; Zane Massey; Henry Scott; Akbar Ali; Billy Bang; Byard Lancaster. Pl. w. Albert Mangelsdorff '80; Garrett List's A-1 Band '82; Craig Harris '86; Last Exit w. Peter Brotzmann, Sonny Sharrock, Bill Laswell fr. '86. Form. gp. Power Tools w. Bill Frisell, Melvin Gibbs '87. Tour. and rec. w. Ulmer late '80s-early '90s. CDs: Ant.; DIW; Virgin; Axiom; Caroline; Plainsphare; w. O. Coleman (A&M); Last Exit (Cell.).

JACKSON, RUDY (RUDOLPH), cl; saxes; b. Fort Wayne, IN, 1901; d. Chicago, IL, ca. 1968. From a mus. family; stud. cl. in hs. Began pl. w. Chi. bands in 1918; Carroll Dickerson early '20s; King Oliver '23–4, briefly in '27, bef. join. Duke Ellington, June-Dec. '27; Noble Sissle '29–33, incl. tours of Eur. When Sissle ret. to US, Jackson went to Bombay, India, where he pl. w. Leon Abbey, Teddy Weatherford mid '30s. He remained in India until the end of WWII, when he ret. to Chi., later worked for Western Union. Recs. w. Sippie Wallace; Ellington; Sissle. CDs: w. Ellington (BB; Dec.); Bechet (Class.).

JACKSON, TONY (ANTHONY), pno, voc, comp; b. New Orleans, LA, 6/5/1876; d. Chicago, IL, 4/20/21. Played at Mahogany Hall and other famed NO bordellos; also w. Bunk Johnson and Adam Olivier ca. 1894. Worked w. Glover Compton in Louisville, Ky. '04. After '05 he traveled extensively and was heard often in Chi. and NYC. Ret. to NO '10–12, then moved to Chi., worked at the De Luxe Cafe, Pekin Cafe. Fr. '17 to his death, led own band, whose occ. members incl. Freddie Keppard; Lorenzo Tio; Wellman Braud; S. Bechet. One of the first important ragtime pnsts., Jackson was admired for his technique, accomp. abilities, and wide, varied repertoire; he was a skillful entertainer and effective vocalist on ballads and blues. In '16 he wrote his most enduring comp., "Pretty Baby." Jackson never recorded, but Jelly Roll Morton, a great admirer, recorded "Pretty Baby," as well as Jackson's "The Naked Dance" and "Michigan Water Blues" for the Library of Congress.

JACKSON, WILLIS (GATOR), tnr sax; also sop sax, Gator horn; b. Miami, FL, 4/25/28; d. NYC, 10/25/87. Began stud. at 10; pno., then cl. Prof. debut at 14 on tnr. sax w. local bands; schoolmates and bandmates incl. C. Adderley, Blue Mitchell. Stud. theory and harmony at Fla. A&M. Worked w. Cootie Williams 1948–55. Rec. own comp. "Gator Tail" w. Williams and acquired nickname Gator. Tour US fr. '55 w. own gp., very often in r&b package w. Dinah Washington; the Ravens; Jackie Wilson, etc. For eight yrs. was married to Ruth Brown, who sang w. him dur. this time. Pl. summer gig annually at Club Harlem, Atlantic City, N.J. fr. '63. His R&B associations have led some people to underestimate his abilities as a jazz player, but he was a very effective communicator in the Illinois Jacquet vein w. touches of Gene Ammons. Infls: Hawkins, Young, H. Evans, B. Webster, C. Parker. TV: Ed Sullivan in '50s; Mike Douglas in '60s; *Dial "M" for Music* w. Father O'Connor. Comps: "Cookin' Sherry," which won French Grand Prix du Disque '59; "This'll Get to Ya"; "Miss Ann"; "Brother Elijah"; "On My Own"; "West Africa"; "The Head Tune." Jackson's Gator horn, a saxophone of his own design, was used for ballads. It hangs almost to the floor, has a round ball w. a small opening for the bell and sounds, as he explained it, "between soprano and alto, and French horn and clarinet." CDs: Prest.; 32; w. Cootie Williams in *The 1940s Mercury Sessions* (Merc.).

JACQUET, (JEAN BAPTISTE) ILLINOIS, tnr, alto saxes, bsn, lead; b. Broussard, LA, 10/31/19; d. Queens, NY, 7/22/04. Family moved to Houston,

Tex. 1923. Danced w. Jacquet Bros., w. orch. led by fath., Gilbert, who pl. bs. and sousaphone. Bros. Julius, Linton, Russell pl. sax, dms., tpt. respectively; sist. Isabella pl. vln., pno., dms.; moth., May, sang. Stud. dms. in hs, then sw. to sop. and alto saxes. Pl. w. Milt Larkin territory band 1938; jammed w. Charlie Parker while on tour in Kansas City. Pl. w. Lionel Proctor, Bob Cooper late '30s. Grad. fr. hs, moved to Los Angeles '39. After jamming w. Nat Cole at a union Labor Day party, Cole introduced him to Lionel Hampton. Sw. to tnr. sax and join. Hampton '41. Rec. famous solo on "Flying Home," considered a major infl. on the r&b school of tenor playing 5/26/42. Left Hampton '43; pl. w. Cab Calloway '43–4, then form. own gp. in Calif. w. Russell Jacquet, Chas. Mingus '44–5. App. w. Lester Young, Jo Jones, et al. in short film *Jammin' the Blues* '44. Rec. own combo dates for Aladdin and Apollo labels '44. Pl. w. Jazz at the Philharmonic '44, scoring jukebox hit w. JATP *Blues Part II* which feat. high register harmonics; Count Basie Orch. '45–6; annual JATP tours '46–57, and was a large part of the troupe's success. Debuted own gp. w. R. Jacquet, Joe Newman, J. J. Johnson, Leo Parker, Sir Chas. Thompson, Al Lucas, Shadow Wilson to sell-out crowd in Wash., D.C. '47. Co-headlined on tours w. Ella Fitzgerald, Sarah Vaughan '48; had jukebox hits incl. "Robbins' Nest"; "Black Velvet." Occ. led full bb for recs., theater dates fr. late '40s, but perf. mainly w. qt. in '50s. Tour. Eur. w. own gps. fr. '54. Began pl. bsn. '59 and received rave reviews when he debuted the instr. in NYC in the mid '60s. Led trio w. Milt Buckner, Jo Jones '66–76; pl. w. Buddy Rich in NYC '74. Led qnt. w. Slam Stewart at fests., on St. Dept. tours, and for Presidents Carter and Reagan '76–early '80s. Tour. Eur. in Texas Tenors w. Buddy Tate, Arnett Cobb '80s. Jacquet was considered to be the archetypical "Texas tenor," w. a sound as big as the great outdoors and a volatile attack, coming out of Herschel Evans but also touched by Lester Young. On alto sax he showed the influence of Charlie Parker. Exciting at faster tempi, he was tender and romantic on ballads. Artist-in-residence at Harvard '83–4; the experience inspired him to form his own bb in '83. The Illinois Jacquet bb cont. to perf. at fests.; jazz cruises, and clubs in Eur., Japan, and the US; rec. *Jacquet's Got It!* on the Atl. label in '86. Polls: Pittsburgh *Courier* '48. Fests: all major in Eur., Japan, US. Films: *Stormy Weather: Sensations of 1944* w. Calloway; *Jammin' the Blues* '44; documentary, *Texas Tenor* '91. TV: Ed Sullivan. CDs: Atl.; BB; Epic; Roul.; Verve; Prest.; BL; B&B; boxed set (Mos.); w. JATP (Verve); L. Hampton (Dec.); C. Basie (Col.; Hep; Verve); Joey DeFrancesco (Col.).

JACQUET, (ROBERT) RUSSELL, tpt, voc; b. Broussard, LA, 12/4/17; d. Los Angeles, CA, 3/4/90. Played w. Floyd Ray 1939; stud. at Wiley Coll., Tex. '40–2, and Texas Southern U. '42–4, where he led bb. Went to Calif. w. bro. Illinois' band. Then led own band at Cotton Club in Hollywood. Rejoin. his bro. '46 and worked w. him intermittently, incl. Eur. tour fall '54. Took up residence in Oakland, Calif. '59, worked w. bro. Linton Jacquet '60; Gerald Wilson in LA '61; concerts w. Benny Carter '62; stud. at USC, pl. w. Hide-Away All-Stars, LA, and w. I. Jacquet '64. Led own band at It Club, LA '65–6. Pl. w. Cedric Haywood in Houston mid '60s. Pl. w. Illinois again in NYC '85. Later worked w. Ike & Tina Turner; form. JRC Records; taught in LA sch. system. Infl. by early Miles Davis. CDs: w. I. Jacquet (BB; Prest.; Mos.); w. Milt Jackson–Sonny Stitt (Gal.).

JAFFE, NAT (NATHANIEL), pno; b. NYC, 1918; d. NYC, 8/5/45. Studied classical pno. while living w. family in Berlin fr. 1921–32. Back in NYC became interested in jazz, but early jobs were pl. cabaret and dance music. Solo pno. at Mammy's Chicken Coop bef. join. Charlie Barnet '38; pl. w. Jack Teagarden '39–40. Became prominent along 52nd St., working as soloist at Kelly's Stable and also lead. trio and sxt., which incl. Charlie Shavers and Don Byas, shortly bef. he died of uremia. One of the most advanced pnsts. of his day, combining Earl Hines and modern infls. Own recs. on B&W '44; Sig.; w. J. Teagarden (Varsity) '40. CDs: w. L. Armstrong (Class.); C. Barnet (BB).

JAMAL, AHMAD (Fritz Jones), pno, el-pno, comp; b. Pittsburgh, PA, 7/2/30. Began on pno. at age 3. Stud. w. Mary Caldwell Dawson, James Miller. Made prof. debut at age 11. After grad. fr. Westinghouse HS, pl. w. Geo. Hudson 1947–8; Four Strings w. Joe Kennedy, Ray Crawford '49–50. Briefly accomp. song and dance act, then pl. w. own trio Three Strings w. at Blue Note, Chi. '51–2. After he converted to Islam in the early '50s, the gp. bec. known as the Ahmad Jamal Trio. The gp. w. Israel Crosby and Vernel Fournier was in high demand following the success of his '58 album *Live at the Pershing*, which stayed in the top 10 for 108 consecutive weeks. Jamil Nasser repl. Crosby in the early '60s; and Frank Gant repl. Fournier in '66. His trio of the '90s has incl. el-bs. pl. by James Cammack. App. w. Cleveland Summer Symph. in concert conducted by Joe Kennedy '65. In the autobiography *Miles*, Miles Davis cites Jamal as a major stylistic influence, both on his use of space in his improvisations and on his selection of tunes; many of the tunes now assoc. w. Davis's '50s qnt.

were rec. by Jamal a few mos. earlier. Also notable are Jamal's employment of tempi changes and dynamics. Jamal occ. rec. and perf. w. symph. orchs. fr. the mid '60s and has maintained a busy touring sched. fr. '58. Comps. incl. "One For Miles"; "Minor Moods"; "Extensions"; "The Awakening"; "Eclipse." Fests: all major fr. '50s. CDs: Chess; Imp.; Tel.; Atl.; Col.

JAMAL, KHAN (Warren Robert Cheeseboro), vbn, mrba, comp, perc; b. Jacksonville, FL, 7/23/46. Grew up in Philadelphia. Moth., Willa Mae McGee, was stride pnst. Began pl. vibes 1964. Stud. at Granoff Sch. of Mus.; Combs Coll. of Mus.; priv. w. Bill Lewis, Abraham Howard Jr. Pl. in '60s-early '70s w. Frank Lowe; Noah Howard; Grachan Moncur III; Dave Burrell; Archie Shepp; Norman Connors; Byard Lancaster; Sam Rivers; Stanley Clarke; Gary Bartz; Sun Ra; Larry Young; Calvin Hill; Ted Daniel; Jerome Cooper; et al. Pl. w. other Sun Ra sidemen in gp. Cosmic Forces late '60s. Formed Sounds of Liberation w. Byard Lancaster early '70s. Music dir. of Phila. Jazz Foundation '70s. Rec. w. Sunny Murray's Untouchable Factor late '70s. Pl. fr. '80 w. Ronald Shannon Jackson's Decoding Society; Joe Bonner; Billy Bang. Toured Eur. as lead. fr. '75. Favs: M. Jackson, Lem Winchester, B. Hutcherson, Walt Dickerson, Bill Lewis, Roy Ayers. CDs: Steep.; Stash; Story.; Gazell; w. Joe Bonner (Steep.).

JAMES, BOB (ROBERT), pno, kybds, comp, arr, prod; b. Marshall, MO, 12/25/39. Began pl. 1944; received master's in comp. fr. U. of Mich. '62. Bop trio won prize at intercollegiate jf at Notre Dame '61. Moved to NYC '63. Pl. briefly w. Maynard Ferguson, then led free jazz gp. '65. Accomp. and mus. dir. w. Sarah Vaughan '65-8. Worked as session mus. in NYC, rec. w. Quincy Jones, Morgana King, Roberta Flack, Dionne Warwick '68-72. Worked as an arr. for the CTI label '73-5; dur. this time arr. albums for Grover Washington Jr.; Stanley Turrentine; Freddie Hubbard; Hank Crawford; Johnny Hammond; Idris Muhammad; Gabor Szabo; Hubert Laws; Ron Carter; Eric Gale; Milt Jackson. Rec. as lead. for CTI '74-5. Joined CBS '75; worked w. pop acts incl. Neil Diamond, Paul Simon. Formed own rec. co. Tappan Zee '77 to promote mus. such as Richard Tee, Mongo Santamaria. James's comps. incl. scores for the B'way musical *The Selling of the President*; the film *Serpico*; and the theme of the popular TV series *Taxi*. He has cont. to rec. as a lead. in the fusion genre. CDs: WB; Col.; ESP; Tappan Zee; collabs. w. David Sanborn; Earl Klugh (WB); w. G. Burton (GRP); Vaughan (Merc.; Em.); tapes w. John Zorn (Elek. None.).

JAMES, ELMER TAYLOR, bs, tba; b. Yonkers, NY, 1910; d. NYC, 7/25/54. Started on tba. w. Gene Rodgers 1928; June Clark '29; Chick Webb '29-32. Sw. to bs., pl. briefly w. Benny Carter, Webb, bef. join. F. Henderson '34; Mills Blue Rhythm under L. Millinder '34-6; w. Edgar Hayes on and off '37-9; Mezz Mezzrow '37-8; Claude Hopkins '40. Retired fr. music and became a bread salesman but app. w. Zutty Singleton trio '42. A strong bs. in the tradition of Pops Foster. Recs. w. Armstrong '32; Henderson; Red Allen '35; Ladnier-Mezzrow '38. CDs: w. Allen; Benny Carter; Jabbo Smith; Henderson; Chick Webb (Class.); Armstrong; Bechet (BB).

JAMES, HARRY HAAG, tpt, lead; b. Albany, GA, 3/15/16; d. Las Vegas, NV, 7/5/83. Parents w. circus; father, w. whom he stud. tpt., was bandleader. Attended hs in Beaumont, Tex., winning a state tpt. championship w. a solo at age 14. Soon after, he pl. w. the Old Phillips Friars; then w. Logan Hancock; Herman Waldman; and in 1935-6 w. Ben Pollack. Join. Benny Goodman in Dec. '36 and gained such popularity that he left to form his own band in Jan. '39. As a bandleader James scored his biggest hits w. non-jazz solos such as "You Made Me Love You" or the more spectacular "Carnival of Venice." Much of his work in the ensuing yrs. was in this vein though he occ. cont. to play jazz in a style reflecting the infl. of his favorites, Muggsy Spanier and Louis Armstrong. In the early '50s, he was semi-retired, living in LA and occ. touring w. the band. After being feat. in *The Benny Goodman Story* '55, he reorganized his band on a more permanent basis. Toured Eur. in Oct. '57 and placed more emphasis on jazz in his perfs., feat. arrs. by Ernie Wilkins, Neal Hefti, and Thad Jones. As a result, the band, which had a strong Basie flavor, became one of the best bbs. Despite the decline of the bb scene, the James orch. remained active and successful in the '60s. In Aug. '60 he undertook a concert and dance tour in Mex.; shortly afterward tour. So. Amer. for the first time; Japan for the first time in April '64; and the following Sept. made his first app. at the MJF; very well received, he ret. '65. In this period his soloists incl. long-time associate Corky Corcoran, tnr. sax; Ray Sims, tbn.; and notably, Buddy Rich. In the late '60s and early '70s the band was still based in LV but cont. to tour int'l: Eur '70, '71; Argentina '81. Married to film star Betty Grable for more than twenty yrs.—divorced in '65. His tpt. style, which in the '40s was inclined toward sentimentality and bravura, later achieved a more jazz-routed groove, inspired by such players as Roy Eldridge and Harry Edison. However, even in his early yrs., his small gp. playing could be, in turn, soulful or reflective, as in "Boo Woo" and "Just a

Mood." Fests: NJF-NY '74–5. Polls: *DB* '37–9; *Met.* '39–46. Films: *Syncopation* '42; *Best Foot Forward* '43; *Bathing Beauty* '44; *Carnegie Hall* '47. Publ: *Harry James Trumpet Method; Harry James Studies and Improvisations* (Robbins Mus.); *Trumpet Blues*, Peter Levinson (Oxford) '99. Scores and other materials are contained in the American Heritage Center, U. of Wyoming. Recs. w. B. Pollack; Teddy Wilson. CDs: Col.; Cap.; Verve; w. Goodman (BB; Col.); Wilson (Class.); B. Holiday (Col.); L. Hampton; J. Teagarden; *The Metronome All-Star Bands* (BB).

JAMES, STAFFORD LOUIS, bs, comp; b. Evanston, IL, 4/24/46. Grandfather pl. tba.; bro. Don pl. tnr. sax; wife Claudine pl. classical gtr. Began on vln. at age 7; pno. at age 14; bs. at age 18. Stud. at Evanston Cons. 1964; w. Richard Payne, Chuck Beatty while in air force '66; Rudolf Fahsbender at Chi. Cons. '67–8; Julius Levine at Mannes Coll. of Mus. NYC '69–70. First gig in NO w. Trevor Koehler '66; also pl. w. Blue Mitchell, Larry Young at afterhours sess. Moved to NYC '68. First gig in NYC w. Monty Alexander at Minton's '68. Pl. w. Sun Ra '68; Pharaoh Sanders, Rashied Ali, Joe Lee Wilson, Lonnie Liston Smith, Archie Shepp, Alice Coltrane '69–70; Danny Mixon fr. '70; Melba Moore '71; Charles Sullivan '71–2; B. Timmons '72; Roy Ayers '72–3; John Hicks, Gary Bartz, Betty Carter fr. '73; Art Blakey '73–4; Cecil, Ron, Dee Dee Bridgewater '74; Al Haig, Barry Harris '74–5; Andrew Hill, Robin Kenyatta, Andrew Cyrille, Chico Hamilton '75; Dexter Gordon, Woody Shaw '76, '80–3; Oliver Lake '77; John Scofield '78. Pl. in '80s w. Dameronia; Bill Hardman; Slide Hampton; Cecil Payne; Jimmy Heath; Ronnie Mathews; Barney Wilen; P. Sanders. James's own '80s gps. incl. a trio w. Marc Cohen, Mike Smith; string and perc. ens. w. Buster Williams, Victor Lewis, Guilherme Franco. Received grants fr. NY State Council on the Arts for comp. *Ethiopia Suite* '85; Viola D'Amore Society for comp. *Sonatina* '86. Moved to Paris in the late '80s. In '89 he formed the Stafford James Project, a trio in which the bs. is the lead melodic instr. The gp. has perf. w. the Nat'l Orch. of France. Taught at the United Nations Int'l Sch. '74–6; Rutgers U. '79; Sydney Cons., Austral. '80; Umbria Jazz Clinics '85–6; New Sch. '86–8. Fav: Ludwig Streicher (Vienna Philharmonic). Fests: Eur., Asia, So. Amer. TV: *Free Time* w. Shepp '71; *A.M. America* w. Betty Carter '75; *Days and Nights of Molly Dodd* '88. LPs: Red; Horo. CDs: w. P. Sanders; B. Wilen; Ronnie Mathews (Timel.); W. Shaw (Col.; Enja); D. Gordon (Col.).

JANIS, CONRAD, tbn; b. NYC, 2/11/28. Father, Sidney, ran art gallery; moth., Harriet, co-wrote *They*

All Played Ragtime w. Rudi Blesh. Many early credits as stage actor. First prof. mus. experience 1949, when he won a jazz band contest for *Record Changer* magazine. Fr. '50 had multiple interests, w. acting apps. in many B'way shows, films, and over 300 TV shows. In '78 formed The Beverly Hills Unlisted Jazz Band, which for several yrs. feat. actor George Segal on bjo., and app. frequently on TV and at traditional jfs. TV: PBS special, *That's a Plenty* '81. Favs: Bill Watrous, Dan Barrett, Bob Havens. Rec. w. Beverly Hills Band. CD: GHB.

JARMAN, JOSEPH, saxes, bsn, oboe, fl, cl, picc, comp, perc, voc; b. Pine Bluff, AR, 9/14/37. Family moved to Chi. early 1940s. Stud. dms. w. Capt. Walter Dyett at DuSable HS '52–5. Pl. sax, cl. in army bands. Further educ. at Wilson Jr. Coll.; Chi. City Coll.; Chi. Cons. Ret. to Chi. '58. Pl. w. Muhal Richard Abrams' Experimental Band fr. '61; Roscoe Mitchell '65. Founding member of AACM '65. Pl. own comp. *Imperfections in a Given Space* w. John Cage '65. Led own gps. fr. '66; perf. solo fr. '67. Premiered theater pieces *Tribute to the Hard Core* '66; *Indifferent Piece For Six* '67. Lectured at Contemp. Music Soc. of the U. of Chi. '67. Dir. of music and theater wkshp. at Circle Pine Center., Delton, Mich., summer '68. Joined Art Ens. of Chi. '69. Also worked w. Anthony Braxton, Oliver Lake, Don Moye, Don Pullen fr. early '70s. In addition to playing a large array of conventional and homemade wind and perc. instruments, Jarman has danced, sung, and recited poetry w. the Art Ens. of Chi. His pl. reveals some infl. fr. Eric Dolphy, and his presentations, marked w. dramatic visual effects, often successfully integrate colorful theatrical elements w. his free-flowing improv. style. CDs: Del.; BS; *The Magic Triangle* w. Pullen, Moye (BS); Art Ens. of Chi. (ECM; Del.; DIW).

JARREAU, AL (ALVIN), voc; b. Milwaukee, WI, 3/12/40. Musical family; first sang in church recital 1944; later w. local jazz gps. in Milwaukee bars. Stud. at Ripon Coll. and U. of Iowa, earning an M.A. in psych. After army service worked as a counselor for the California Division of Rehabilitation '64–8. Pl. small clubs w. George Duke trio; in late '60s decided to abandon psych. for mus. Moved to LA, where he worked at the Troubador, Improv, etc. First album released '75; toured Eur. the following yr. World tour '77; album *Look to the Rainbow* won his first Grammy for Best Jazz Vocal Perf. the same yr; second Grammy for *All Fly Home* '78. Rec. at Wembley Arena, London '85; sang theme song for hit TV series, *Moonlighting*; cont. int'l and US tour. into early '90s. In '92 released his twelfth album on Reprise, *Heaven and Earth*, feat. an interpretation, w.

lyrics, of Miles Davis's "Blue in Green." Jarreau is comfortable in pop, jazz, and r&b. As a jazz singer, he expands on the bop lines of Jon Hendricks by adding a remarkable array of percussive vocal sounds—grunts, groans, pops, etc.—that place him close to Bobby McFerrin. App. w. McFerrin, Hendricks in latter's Lincoln Center concert '96. CDs: WB; Rep.; Zeta.

JARRETT, KEITH, pno, comp; b. Allentown, PA, 5/8/45. Studied pno fr. age 3; first recital at age 7. Prof. musician fr. his teens; early infl. was John Coates Jr. App. as soloist w. Fred Waring's Pennsylvanians. Moved to Bost. 1962; scholarship student at Berklee; worked in Bost. w. own trio and visiting musicians Tony Scott and Roland Kirk. To NYC '65; pl. w. Art Blakey '65–6. First significant visibility w. Charles Lloyd's gp. '66–7; tour of Russia. Also pl. and rec. w. own trio dur. this period. Member of Miles Davis gp. '69–71, pl. electric kybds; also rec. and tour. w. own gp., which incl. Charlie Haden, Paul Motian, and Dewey Redman, early to mid '70s. Began to perf. as pno. soloist '72, in programs which generally incl. two lengthy, spontaneous improvisations reaching across a broad area of stylistic bases. One of the few jazz players of the '70s to resist both electronic enhancement and pop/rock synthesis. Also worked in a much-praised gp. w. Jan Garbarek and a trio w. Gary Peacock and Jack DeJohnette. Rec. improvisations on pipe organ and perf. works fr. the classical pno. repertory. Fr. the late '80s often heard in a classical context. Headed straight-ahead trio in '90s. Hampered by illness at close of century. One of the most gifted musicians of his generation, Jarrett has been an outspoken opponent of commerciality and the dilution of the creative impulse. CDs: ECM; Atl.; Imp.; Col.; w. Blakey (Em.); M. Davis (Col.); F. Hubbard (CTI); P. Motian; K. Wheeler; G. Peacock (ECM); Lloyd (Atl.).

JARVIS, CLIFFORD OSBOURNE, dms, perc; b. Boston, MA, 8/26/41. Began on dms. at age 10; encouraged by fath., a musician. Stud. w. Alan Dawson at Berklee Coll. of Mus. 1953–8. Moved to NYC ca. '59. Rec. w. Randy Weston, Chet Baker '59; Yusef Lateef '60; Freddie Hubbard '60–5; Barry Harris '61–2; Jackie McLean '65; Elmo Hope '66. Also pl. in '60s w. Grant Green, Roland Kirk. Worked w. Sun Ra off and on '62–76. Pl. w. Pharaoh Sanders, Sirone, Clifford Thornton, Sonny Simmons, Alice Coltrane early '70s; Kenny Drew, Walter Davis late '70s. Rec. w. Archie Shepp '85. Jarvis taught at U. of Mass. and other New Engl. colls. He moved to Engl. in the '80s. Pl. w. French tpt. Michel Marre, Harry Beckett, Chris McGregor, Courney Pine in '80s; Jean Toussaint '91.

Favs: Roach, R. Haynes, P. J. Jones, Ed Blackwell. CDs: w. P. Sanders (Imp.); Sun Ra (Evid.; BL); Freddie Hubbard (BN); B. Harris (Riv.); J. Toussaint (World Circuit); A. Shepp (L+R; WW); C. Baker (Riv.); C. Fuller (Sav.); Beckett (WW); K. Drew (Steep.).

JARVIS, JANE NOSSETTE, pno, pipe-org, kybds; b. Vincennes, IN, 10/31/15. Mother was amateur painter; fath. amateur poet. Stud. at Vincennes U. fr. age 9, then in Chi. at Bush Cons., DePaul U., Chi. Cons. Auditioned for children's radio prog., became staff pnst. for WIND at age 12; eventually fired for being underage. First jazz gp. w. Johnny Bothwell 1937. Staff pnst. at radio stations incl. WOC, WJKS, WTMJ, WMAW; own jazz progs. incl. *The Three Jays, Jivin' w. Jarvis*. Pl. org. for Milwaukee Braves. Pl. first date in NYC w. Milt Hinton, Osie Johnson. Pl. w. Eddie Getz '46; Eddie South '54; Dick Clark's rock band early '60s. Organist for NY Mets games at Shea Stadium mid '60 to '79. Vice pres. of Muzak, Inc. '73–9; prod. jazz albums for Muzak w. Bucky Pizzarelli, Clark Terry, Lionel Hampton. Pl. w. Clark Terry bb '80; special dates w. Lionel Hampton incl. Reagan inaugural ball '84. Pl. w. Ed Polcer's band at Eddie Condon's; own gp. at Universal Coalition's Women's JF, NYC; perf. a Cole Porter program w. Tampa Symph. '80. Many duo engagements at Zinno, NYC in '90s. Member of Statesmen of Jazz, tour. in Japan '97. Taught at the Adamant Mus. Sch. (Vermont); Ethel Walker Sch. in Simsbury, Conn. Holds honorary degrees fr. Vincennes U. and Harvard Sch. of Business, and is an honorary Saginaw Indian Chief. "She shows a reverence for the melody but then makes it her own with an infinite variety of voicings."—George H. Buck Jr. Favs: Jess Stacy, Erroll Garner, Dick Hyman. Polls: BMI Music in Sports Awd. Fests: Argentina '73, '76; Scotland '85; Switz. '85, '89. Film: *Radio Days*. TV: CBS *Tribute to Benny Goodman*. CDs: Prog.; w. Hinton (Prog.); Statesmen of Jazz (Arb.).

JASPAR, BOBBY (ROBERT B.), tnr sax, fl; also cl; b. Liege, Belgium, 2/20/26; d. NYC 3/4/63. Grandfather and fath. were mus. Stud. pno. 1937–9; cl. at 16. Worked for Amer. Army Special Service in Germ. Pl. w. Henri Renaud in Paris '50, later w. Bernard Peiffer, Aime Barelli. Led own qnt. '54–6, pl. at Club St. Germain in Paris; also pl. w. visiting Americans incl. Jimmy Raney '54; Chet Baker '55; Blossom Dearie, whom he married, '56. Came to US April '56 and made Amer. debut w. Gil Fuller's band at a concert in NYC. Pl. w. J. J. Johnson '56; Miles Davis '57; Donald Byrd for six mos. '58, incl. Cannes and Knokke Fests. and five mos. at Chat Qui Peche,

Paris. In NYC '59, app. as guest soloist w. Bill Evans trio at Showplace. Worked in accomp. gp. for Chris Connor '60. Ret. to Eur. '61–2, app. in cabarets, fests.: rec. w. Rene Thomas, Chet Baker. When he first arrived in the US, his style and sound were compared w. Stan Getz, but he was further infl. by Zoot Sims and members of the Parker school, such as Sonny Rollins. Rec. w. J. J. Johnson (Col.). CDs: Mole; Riv.; Herbie Mann–Bobby Jaspar; w. Coltrane (Prest.); Hank Jones; John Rae; B. VerPlanck (Sav.); Baker (Em.; BB); Wynton Kelly (Riv.).

JAUME, ANDRÉ, tnr sax, fl, cl, bs-cl woodwinds; b. Marseilles, France, 10/7/40. Studied cl., comp.; pl. w. Phil Woods 1967. Worked w. Steve McCall, et al. '70–1; w. Edmond Toberet '72. Pl. in bb w. Barre Philips '72–3. First solo rec.; tour. Eur. and US in '80s w. Joe McPhee. Stud. comp. in Bost. w. J. Giuffre '86. Various summer fests. w. Buddy Collette. Collab. w. C. Mariano, C. Haden in '90s. French critics have called him a fascinatingly inventive artist on several instruments. CDs: hatArt; CELP; w. Giuffre (CELP); Joe McPhee (hatArt).

JAZZ AT THE PHILHARMONIC. Generic name for concerts started in 1944 by impresario Norman Granz, originally at the Philharmonic Auditorium in LA and later on tour throughout the US and frequently overseas, several mos. a yr. until '57. By rec. many of his concerts and spreading the results over several sides of 12-inch 78 rpm records, Granz was able to anticipate the long-playing record era. Though the concerts were sometimes criticized for flamboyant performances by some of the soloists, many memorable events took place feat. Roy Eldridge, Dizzy Gillespie, Buck Clayton, Charlie Shavers, Howard McGhee on tpts.; J. J. Johnson and Bill Harris on tbns.; Buddy DeFranco on cl.; and many saxists such as Charlie Parker, Flip Phillips, Benny Carter, Lester Young, Willie Smith, Charlie Ventura, Coleman Hawkins, Illinois Jacquet, Stan Getz, Ben Webster, Don Byas; also pnsts. Nat King Cole, Hank Jones, Kenny Kersey, and Oscar Peterson; gtrsts. Barney Kessel and Herb Ellis; drmrs. Gene Krupa, Buddy Rich, Jo Jones, and Louie Bellson; Lionel Hampton on vibes; vocals by Billie Holiday and Ella Fitzgerald; and sometimes the entire Basie and Ellington orchs. After '67, when he presented a farewell tour of the US, Granz gave up the JATP concept but cont. to tour various artists in Eur. His concerts were released on the Clef, Norgran, Verve, and Pablo labels. CDs: Verve, incl. 10–CD box; Pab.

JAZZ CRUSADERS. Also known as the Modern Jazz Sextet, the Nite Hawks, the Crusaders. Orga-

nized in Houston, Texas early 1950s by dmr. Stix Hooper, tnr. saxist Wilton Felder, and pnst. Joe Sample. Later members were tbnst. Wayne Henderson, flst. Hubert Laws, and bsst. Henry Wilson. By the '70s the members had largely dispersed to pursue separate solo careers, although they cont. to record as a gp. CDs: PJ; MCA.

JAZZ MESSENGERS. *See* **BLAKEY, ART.**

JEFFERS, JACK, bs-tbn, tba, comp; b. Montserrat, British West Indies, 12/10/28. Mother pl. pno. and org. in church. Stud. tenor tbn. in Bost. ca. 1950, then pl. in house band at Howard Theatre, Wash., D.C. '52. Pl. w. Buddy Johnson '56–8; Warren Smith since '58; Lionel Hampton '60; Ray Charles '65; Jazz Composers' Orch. '66–8; Clark Terry '66–72; Maynard Ferguson '68; Jaki Byard '78–81; Charlie Haden '80; Carla Bley '81; Amer. Jazz Orch. fr. '87; Mercer Ellington '88; Muhal Richard Abrams since '89; Count Basie Orch. '90. Jeffers has worked extensively as a studio and B'way mus., and holds a law degree fr. NYU. Leads and arr. for his own band, the New York Classics; also pl. w. C. O'Farrill orch. '98. Favs: Slide Hampton, Howard Johnson; arr.: Benny Carter, Jimmy Heath. Fests: Eur. since '66. CDs: w. J. Heath (Verve); Muhal Abrams (BS); C. Bley; C. Haden (ECM); Jazz Composers Orch. (JCOA); C. Tolliver (Strata East).

JEFFERSON, CARTER R., tnr, sop saxes; b. Washington, DC, 11/30/45; d. Cracow, Poland, 12/10/93. Grandfather, both parents amateur mus. Began on cl. at Stepping Stone Sch. of Mus., Wash., at age 12; later stud. w. Louis Von Jones at Howard U. Tour. w. Little Richard; Jimi Hendrix; Temptations; Supremes; Dionne Warwick; etc. fr. age 17. Pl. w. army band in Korea mid 1960s. Moved to NYC '68, stud. mus. ed. at NYU '68–71. Stud. w. Jimmy Heath; Lee Morgan; Joe Henderson; Budd Johnson; Paul West at Jazzmobile Wkshp. Pl. and rec. w. Mongo Santamaria, Art Blakey '70s; Woody Shaw '70s-80s; Jack Walrath '80s. Lived, perf., and taught privately in Paris '87–9. Jefferson taught at Cornish Inst. of the Arts, Seattle '80–2; Passaic HS, N.J. off and on fr. '81; Wayne, N.J. Vocational Sch. '83; Queensboro Commun. Coll., where he was jazz dir. '83–4; Manh. Valley Children's Ctr. '85–7; Lorton Correctional Facility '89. Victim of a brutal mugging in September '91 that left him w. both jaws broken, he then worked w. members of Congress on a plan to provide freelance musicians w. affordable health insurance. He returned to play, in late '92 w. Jerry Gonzalez Fort Apache Band; Malachi Thompson Free Bop Band; and own gps., Blue Fire and Carter Jefferson Qt.

Favs: Bechet, Hawkins, C. Parker, Gonsalves, Coltrane. Fests: Eur., Japan, So. Amer. fr. '70s. CDs: Timel.; w. Blakey (Prest.); M. Thompson (Del.; Jazz-Life); J. Gonzalez (Sunny.; Alfa); W. Shaw (Col.); J. Walrath (BN).

JEFFERSON, EDDIE (EDGAR), voc, lyricist; b. Pittsburgh, PA, 8/3/18; d. Detroit, MI, 5/9/79. Studied tba. in school; also pl. gtr., dms. His father, an entertainer, guided him into show business. Active for many years as a dancer as well as singer. App. at the 1933 Chi. World's Fair w. the original Zephyrs; w. C. Hawkins' band in Chi. '39; as dancer w. the Lanny Ross show '46; member of the team "Billie and Eddie" w. Sarah Vaughan show '50. In the early '40s he began setting lyrics to improvised jazz solos, thus pioneering a technique adopted later by King Pleasure, and popularized nationally by Lambert, Hendricks, and Ross in the late '50s. Jefferson rec. a series of songs in this style, later known as "vocalese," for Hi-Lo '51. Fr. '53 w. James Moody on and off as voc. and manager. Dur. '67 and '68 app. again as tap dancer. Rejoin. Moody '68, remaining w. him until late '73; tour. w. Roy Brooks' gp. Artistic Truth '74–5; Richie Cole '75–9. Favs: C. Calloway, L. Young, Moody. Among his most celebrated interpretations are "Body and Soul," based on the famous Hawkins solo, and "Moody's Mood for Love." Jefferson was fatally shot in front of the Det. club where he was perf. Poll: *DB* Critics TDWR '75. Fest: NJF '69. Film and video: *Eddie Jefferson: Live at the Showcase* (Rhap.), was made days before his death. CDs: Prest.; Riv.; Muse; Evid.: 32; w. Moody (Prest; Chess); Cole (Muse); King Pleasure; tracks in *The Bebop Singers* (Prest.).

JEFFERSON, HILTON W., alto sax; b. Danbury, CT, 7/30/03; d. NYC, 11/14/68. First prof. job on bjo. w. Julian Arthur in Phila. summer 1925; stud. alto sax that same yr.; rejoin, the band, on sax, going to NYC. Pl. w. Claude Hopkins '26–8; Chick Webb '29–30; tour. w. King Oliver '30; briefly w. McKinney's Cotton Pickers '31; F. Henderson '32–4. In late '20s and early '30s also worked w. other bands for brief periods, incl. B. Carter; Elmer Snowden; Charlie Skeete. From '34 on and off w. Webb, Hopkins; freelanced w. others through '30s. Fr. '40 to '51 worked mainly w. C. Calloway; w. D. Ellington for a yr to '53; tour. w. Pearl Bailey fall '53. Retired fr. full-time music in '54, worked as a bank guard. Still pl. regular stints w. Harry Dial, Noble Sissle mid '50s. Fr. late '50s on, pl. w. own. gp. on weekends; Wally Edwards; Fats Greene; Mercer Ellington. One of the outstanding lead alto players, he was also an excellent soloist. Fests: NJF '58 w. ex-Ellingtonians; Great South Bay

JF '57–8; w. Henderson reunion band. Recs. w. Red Allen; Calloway, "Willow Weep for Me" '40; Rex Stewart; Jimmy Rushing; Buster Bailey. CDs: w. Henderson; Buck Clayton; Calloway; Ellington (Col.); C. Hawkins (Prest.); Red Allen (Tax); Oliver (BB); Webb (Dec.; Hep; Tax); T. Wilson (Hep); E. Fitzgerald (Dec.).

JEFFERSON, RON (ROLAND PARRIS), dms; b. NYC, 2/13/26. Studied at NY Sch. of Mus. Pl. w. Roy Eldridge 1950; Coleman Hawkins '51; Joe Roland '55–6; O. Pettiford '56; Lester Young '56–7. In late '50s worked w. Randy Weston; Gil Melle; Horace Silver; Lou Donaldson; Charles Mingus; Freddie Redd; join. Les Jazz Modes '57; left in '58 to move to Calif. In late '50s and early '60s pl. and rec. w. Teddy Edwards; Groove Holmes; Leroy Vinnegar; Carmell Jones; Victor Feldman; et al; also toured and rec. w. Les McCann. Associated w. Roland Kirk's Jazz and People's Movement in early '70s. Notorious for his catch phrase, "Vous êtes swing!" Cable TV show w. dmr. John Lewis, NYC '80s. LP: *Love Lifted Me* (PJ) '61. CDs: w. McCann (PJ); Redd (Prest.); Vinnegar (Cont.).

JEFFERSON, THOMAS (aka LITTLE TOM), tpt; b. Chicago, IL, 6/20/20. Began on dms., then sw. to Fr. horn and tpt. First pl. in Jones's Home (later Municipal Boys' Home) Band, NO, w. Peter Davis, who had taught Louis Armstrong, Kid Rena, Red Allen. Worked w. Celestin Tuxedo Orch. 1936; later w. Sidney Desvigne; Jimmy Davis; Jump Jackson; John Casimir; also TV work in NO. Fav: Armstrong. Film: app. in *Pete Kelly's Blues.* LP: w. George Lewis. CDs: w. Johnny St. Cyr (Amer. Mus.).

JEFFREY, PAUL H., tnr sax, comp, arr, cl, fl; educ; b. NYC, 4/8/33. Studied at Kingston HS; Ithaca Coll. Led own gp. in Atlantic City, NJ 1957. Pl. w. Wynonie Harris, Big Maybelle in Det., St. Louis '57; Illinois Jacquet in No. Carolina '58; B. B. King in South '60. Moved to NYC '61. Pl. w. Sadik Hakim '61; Johnny Brown '64; Howard McGhee qt. and bb '66. Tour. Eur. w. Dizzy Gillespie Reunion bb '68. Pl. w. Billy Gardner, Charles Moffett '69; Count Basie briefly '70; Thelonious Monk off and on '70–5; own oct. fr. '72. Pl., cond., and arr. for Chas. Mingus '77–8; rec. w. Lionel Hampton '79, '82. Taught at Columbia U., Jersey State Coll., U. of Hartford, Rutgers U. as a clinician for Yamaha, but his main assoc. has been at Duke U. as head of jazz dept. Pl. and also ran summer clinics at Umbria Jazz, Italy in mid '80s. Hosted a jazz radio show on WFUV in NYC '70s. Favs: Monk, Ellington, Dameron. Fests: all major w. Monk. TV: Sammy Davis special w. Johnny Brown

'66; Sonny Rollins documentary NET '68; Eur. TV w. Gillespie '68. CDs: w. Hampton (Timel.); Mingus (Atl.).

JEFFRIES, HERB (Umberto Alexander Valentino), voc; b. Detroit, 9/24/11. Worked w. Howard Bunt, Erskine Tate early 1930s; Earl Hines '31–4; Blanche Calloway. Acting in Black Western films in '30s, became known as "The Bronze Buckaroo." Ballad singer w. Duke Ellington Orch. '40–2, scoring a hit w. "Flamingo." After leaving Ellington rec. as soloist, ran nightclubs in LA and Paris, then worked as single in Hollywood nightclubs. In '90s was still actively singing on jazz cruises and in clubs. Rec. w. Sidney Bechet '40; as lead. w. L. Hampton's sidemen, Eddie Beal, Lucky Thompson, Bobby Hackett, Russ Garcia '45–56. Rec. album, *Magenta Moods*, for Exclusive mid '40s. Briefly form. own rec. co., United National Records '78. CDs: WB; Beth.; w. Ellington; Bechet (BB); Hines (Class.).

JENKINS, FREDDY (FREDERIC DOUGLASS; "POSEY"), tpt; b. NYC, 10/10/06; d. Texas, 1978. Played left-handed; start. in boys' military band. While at Wilberforce U. in early 1920s, pl. briefly w. Edgar Hayes; then w. Horace Henderson's Collegians '24–8. Best known as soloist w. D. Ellington '28–34; also in '35 after recovering fr. serious illness. Led Luis Russell's band at Connie's Inn for a brief period '36; w. Ellington again '37. Form. own band w. Hayes Alvis '38 but was forced to give up pl. dur. that yr. due to chronic, severe lung ailment. Active as a songwriter, press agent, mus. adviser in the '40s in NYC, Wash., D.C., Calif. In '60s worked as a disc jockey and press agent in Texas. Rec. w. his Harlem Seven (BB) '35. CDs: tracks w. Harlem Seven in *New Orleans Chicago New York* (BBC); w. Ellington (BB; Dec.); J. R. Morton (Class.).

JENKINS, JOHN JR., alto sax; b. Chicago, IL, 1/3/31; d. NYC, 7/12/93. Began on cl. at DuSable HS under Capt. Walter Dyett; sw. to alto sax after six mos. Took part in Roosevelt Coll. jam sessions organized by Joe Segal 1949–56. Worked w. Art Farmer in Chi. and Cleveland '55; led own qt. at Bee Hive club, Chi., Dec. '55. Moved to NYC '57. Worked briefly w. Chas. Mingus, then rec. as lead. and sideman for Blue Note and other labels. Fr. '62 to '83 was essentially out of music except for a few gigs w. organist Gloria Coleman in '60s. Worked as a messenger in Rockefeller Center area and also became interested in jewelry. Sold his brass work at street fairs and craft shows in '70s. Began to practice his sax seriously again in '80s. In '83 became street mus.; also pl. as back-up on demo recs.; taught priv. Became reassoc.

w. Clifford Jordan in '90 and was a founding member of Jordan's bb. Favs.: C. Parker, J. McLean, S. Stitt, S. Rollins. CDs: BN; Sav.; *Jenkins, Jordan, Timmons* (NJ); *Alto Madness*, J. McLean–John Jenkins (Prest.); *Bird Feathers* (NJ); w. P. Quinichette (Prest.); Hank Mobley (BN); W. Ware (Riv.).

JENKINS, LEROY L., vln, vla, comp, educ; b. Chicago, IL, 3/11/32. Studied w. O. W. Frederick, Bruce Hayden, and at Du Sable High Sch. Received B.S. in mus. ed. fr. Fla. A&M 1961. Taught string instr. in Mobile, Ala., schools '61–5; Chi. schools '65–9; Chi. Urban Poverty Corps '69. Member of AACM '65–9; founded Creative Construction Company w. A. Braxton, Leo Smith '67. Pl. w. Ornette Coleman in Paris '69; Anthony Braxton '69–72; Archie Shepp '69–74; Cecil Taylor '70; Cal Massey '70–3; Albert Ayler '71; Alice Coltrane, Muhal Richard Abrams '71–2; Mtume '72–4; Dewey Redman '74. Formed Revolutionary Ens. w. Sirone, Jerome Cooper '71. Perf. as soloist and w. own gps. fr. '70s; also pl. w. Carla Bley; Don Cherry; Oliver Lake; David Murray; Rashied Ali; Henry Threadgill; etc.; led trio w. Anthony Davis, A. Cyrille '78–9; and qnt. '82–3; pl. w. C. Taylor qnt. '87. Jenkins' comps. incl. *Concerto for Improvised Violin and Orch.; Theme and Improvisation on the B*, string qt.; *Fresh Faust*, a rap opera; and numerous suites and solo and chamber pieces. In '91 the New York City Opera presented the US prem. of Jenkins' opera, *The Mother of Three Sons*. Serves on the board of dirs. of Meet the Composer, Composers' Forum, New Music Alliance, and Amer. Music Center. Artist-in-residence at Carnegie-Mellon Inst. '87–8. Lectured and taught at Antioch Coll., Bard Coll., the Creative Mus. Found. Wkshp., Columbia U., Oberlin Coll., Michigan State U., Williams Coll., etc. Favs: Billy Bang, Terry Jenouve, Mark Feldman. Polls: *DB* '72, '75–83, TDWR '74; NYC Jazz Mag. '79. NEA grant '73. Fests: jazz and classical fests. in Eur. fr. '70s. Film: acted in *Borsalino*. TV: *Improvisation: Four Personal Views: Leroy Jenkins Solo* videos. CDs: Tom.; BS; Revolutionary Ensemble (ESP); w. C. Taylor (Leo); Abrams (Del.; BS); C. Bley; P. Motian (ECM); Braxton (Del.); George Lewis (BS).

JENKINS, MARVIN LEE, pno, org, fl, cl, tnr sax; b. Aultman, OH, 12/8/32. Mother a pnst.; bro. Obie, a bandlead. Stud. mus. fr. age 10; pl. cl. and tnr. sax w. bro.'s band in hs and coll.; grad. Mt. Union Coll. 1954; pl. cl. and sax in army band '54–6. With Barney Kessel on pno. and fl. '59–61. Accomp. Gloria Lynne '62–4. Tour. and rec. w. Della Reese '65–90. Best-known comp., "Big City," rec. by Shirley Horn; Les McCann; Della Reese; et al. Own LPs on Orovox, Reprise.

JENNEY, JACK (TRUMAN ELLIOT), tbn, lead; b. Mason City, IA, 5/12/10; d. Los Angeles, CA, 12/16/45. Started on tpt.; then sw. to tbn., pl. in father's band at age 11. Pl. w. Austin Wylie 1928; Isham Jones early '30s; Mal Hallett '33. Fr. '34 to '38 studio mus. in NYC; form. own studio band '38, then bb, which was a financial disaster, '39–40; w. Artie Shaw '40–2. Married to singer Kay Thompson, w. whom he also rec. Served in navy late '43–4. Active in Hollywood studios until his death. Best known for the quiet beauty of his tone and style, "Star Dust" w. Shaw being the most extraordinary example. Film: *Syncopation* '42. Recs. w. Red Norvo; Glenn Miller; Coleman Hawkins bb. CDs: w. Artie Shaw (BB).

JENNY-CLARK, JEAN-FRANÇOIS, bs; b. Toulouse, France, 7/12/44; d. Paris, France, 10/6/98. Self-taught on bs. Pl. w. Jackie McLean in Paris 1961. Cons. study early '60s, while pl. w. Johnny Griffin, Kenny Drew, and Bud Powell. Worked w. Don Cherry in Eur. and NYC '67; also pl. w. Gato Barbieri; Slide Hampton; Charles Tolliver; worked in trio w. Joachim Kuhn and Daniel Humair; Pork Pie w. C. Mariano, P. Catherine, Aldo Romano '75. Pl. w. Michel Portal, Chet Baker, Michel Petrucciani in '81–4 period. In mid '80s led German-French Jazz Ensemble w. Albert Mangelsdorff; trio, Easy To Read, w. J. Kuhn, D. Humair '85; co-led German-French Jazz Ens. w. A. Mangelsdorff '87. Contemp. concert music perf. w. John Cage; Luciano Berio; Karlheinz Stockhausen; and Pierre Boulez. Won the Prix Django Reinhardt fr. the Academie du Jazz '74. Fests: Montreux '80 w. Mangelsdorff; JVC-NY w. French musicians '89. CDs: CMP; w. C. Baker (WW); Humair (Blue Flame; L. Bleu); J. Kuhn (Owl; CMP); Mangelsdorff (MPS); Helen Merrill (Em.); P. Motian (ECM); Petrucciani; Romano (Owl); G. Russell; C. Fasoli–K. Wheeler (SN).

JEROME, JERRY, tnr sax, cl, fl, cond; b. Brooklyn, NY, 6/19/12; d. Sarasota, FL, 11/17/01. Played in coll. band while stud. medicine. Join. Harry Reser's Clicquot Club Eskimoes in 1935 to earn tuition money but never ret. to sch. Pl. w. Glenn Miller '36–7; Red Norvo '37; WNEW Staff '38; Benny Goodman '38–40; Artie Shaw '40–1. Also rec. w. Lionel Hampton '39–40. Staff conductor at NBC '42–6. A&R head of Apollo Recs. '46–8; ABC-TV '49. Mus. dir. at WPIX-TV '50–4. Comp., arr., and prod. jingles for radio, TV fr. '50s. Ret. to Fla., cont. to pl. club dates and jazz concerts there and in eastern US, incl. jazz series at C.W. Post Coll. '70s; JVC-NY '97. A collection of his scores and other materials is in the American Heritage Center at the U. of Wyoming-Laramie. Film: *Second Chorus* w. A. Shaw '40. Fav: Lester

Young. LPs as leader on ABC-Para., Stinson, MGM. CDs: double disc w. selections fr. '30–'60s and '96 session, Arb; w. Goodman; Shaw; Hampton (RCA).

JETER-PILLARS ORCHESTRA. Formed in 1934 by alto saxist James Jeter and tnr. saxist Hayes Pillars (b. North Little Rock, AR, 4/30/06), both of whom had worked in Alphonso Trent's orch. before it disbanded in 1933. The Jeter-Pillars Orch. was house band at Club Plantation in St. Louis for approx. ten yrs. beginning in '34. Sidemen dur. this time incl. Jimmy Blanton; Harry "Sweets" Edison; Walter Page; Sid Catlett, Floyd Smith; Jo Jones; Kenny Clarke; later Carl Pruitt; Jimmy Forrest. The band made four recs. for Vocalion in '37. After a tour of the Far East and gigs in Chi. and NYC, it disbanded in the early '50s. The Jeter-Pillars Orch. was primarily a dance band that could pl. for shows rather than a jazz unit.

JOBIM, ANTONIO CARLOS ("TOM," pronounced Tone), comp, gtr, pno; b. Rio de Janeiro, Brazil, 1/25/27; d. NYC, 12/8/94. As music dir. for Odeon Records in 1958, he persuaded the company to rec. Joao Gilberto perf. one of his comps., "Chega de Saudade." The record was a surprise hit, enabling Gilberto to rec. an album of Jobim's songs, thus launching the bossa nova craze. Bossa nova gained popularity in the US in '62 w. the release of Stan Getz and Charlie Byrd's album *Jazz Samba*, which feat. Jobim's comp. "Desafinado." The same yr., Jobim app. w. Getz, Gilberto, and Dizzy Gillespie in a concert at Carnegie Hall. Subsequently, he has been best known as the comp. of bossa novas widely perf. by jazz musicians. Other well-known comps. incl. "One Note Samba"; "Girl from Ipanema"; "Quiet Nights (Corcovado)"; "Meditation"; "Jazz Samba"; "Wave"; "Triste." His mus. was heard, along w. the mus. of Luiz Bonfa, on the soundtrack of the Brazilian film *Black Orpheus* '59. Fr. '65 worked in LA, comp. for TV and films. Scored film, *The Adventurers* '69. TV: app. in special w. Frank Sinatra, Ella Fitzgerald. Video: *Antonio Carlos Jobim: All-Star Tribute* (View). CDs: Verve; Polyd.; CTI; RCA; WB; Disc.; A&M; w. Stan Getz–Joao and Astrud Gilberto (Verve); F. Sinatra (Rep.).

JOHANSEN, EGIL "BOP," dms, comp; b. Oslo, Norway, 1/11/34; d. Kykoping, Sweden, 12/4/98. Self-taught. Pl. pno. at age 6; dms. in 1950. Moved to Stockholm '54. Had a thirty-yr. assoc. w. Arne Domnerus. Pl. and/or rec. w. Harry Arnold, Alice Babs in '50s; Bengt Hallberg '50s, '70; Jan Johansson, Svend Asmussen '60s; Palle Mikkelborg. Pl. w. visiting Americans: Dizzy Gillespie; Stan Getz; Eric Dolphy;

Lucky Thompson; Teddy Wilson. Rec. w. own qnt. '57, '76; Herbie Mann, Ernestine Anderson, Tony Scott in '50s; Jimmy Witherspoon '64; Thad Jones '75, '77; Lee Konitz '83. Died two days after collapsing on stage during a performance. Infls: Parker, Gillespie, Roach, Ellington, Tatum. Pl. w. Swedish Radiojazzgruppen fr. '66; comp. and rec. for films and TV. CDs: w. Domnerus (Phon.; in *Jazz at the Pawnshop*, Proprius).

JOHNS, STEVE (STEPHEN SAMUEL), dms; b. Boston, MA, 11/25/60. Uncle, Jimmy Tyler, was saxist w. Sabby Lewis; Basie. Stud. w. Alan Dawson; then at New Engl. Cons. w. Vic Firth, Fred Buda. Pl. w. Jim Pepper 1985; Gary Bartz, Count Basie Orch. 1986–7; Jimmy Owens '87; Nat Adderley '88; Thomas Chapin '88–91; G. Russell Living Time Orch. '88–92; Stanley Turrentine '89; Larry Coryell fr. '90; Diane Schuur, Mingus Epitaph Orch. '91; Billy Taylor Trio fr. '93. Also pl. w. John Hicks; Gil Evans Orch. Favs: Blakey, DeJohnette, Steve Gadd. Fests: all major fr. late '80s. CDs: w. Taylor (GRP; Ark.); Chapin (Arab.); Ed Jackson (New World); Mario Pavone (KFW); John McNeil–Kenny Berger (Synergy).

JOHNSON, BILL (WILLIAM), alto sax, cl, arr; b. Jacksonville, FL, 9/30/12; d. NYC, 7/5/60. Started on pno., then took up sax at 16. Worked w. various bands; then studied at Wisc. Cons., Ill. Cons.; attended Marquette U. in Milwaukee. While there pl. w. Jabbo Smith, et al.; later worked w. Baron Lee and Tiny Bradshaw. Join. E. Hawkins in 1936, remaining w. him to '43. Wrote many arr. for the band and wrote "Tuxedo Junction" w. Hawkins. Inactive in later yrs. CDs: w. E. Hawkins (BB).

JOHNSON, BRUCE ANTHONY, gtr, el-bs; b. Brooklyn, NY, 2/4/47. Father, Austin Johnson, pl. gtr. w. Ink Spots and swing bands in late 1940s. Stud. w. father. Pl. w. Sil Austin–Big Maybelle Soul Review '65; Ray Nance '67; Gil Evans Orch. '70–2; Enrico Rava, John Abercrombie '73–5; Chico Hamilton '76–8; Charles Tolliver '77; Rodney Jones '78; Arthur Blythe '79; Gil Evans '82. Worked mainly as a teacher at City Coll. and Manh. Sch. of Mus. fr. '77. His students have incl. Rodney Jones; Ed Cherry; Ron Miller; Steve Logan; Vernon Reid. Favs: Mingus, O. Peterson, P. Metheny, G. Evans. Polls: TDWR '72–3. Fests: Eur. w. Evans '71; Italy w. Rava '73. CDs: Dire, may be only on LP; w. Ronald Shannon Jackson (Virgin).

JOHNSON, BUDD (ALBERT J.), tnr, sop saxes, comp, arr; also cl, alto & bari saxes; b. Dallas, TX,

12/14/10; d. Kansas City, MO, 10/20/84. Brother of Keg Johnson. Stud. music w. Booker T. Washington's daughter. Start. working as a dmr. 1924, took up tnr sax. in '26; tour. Texas w. William Holloway; then join. Gene Coy '27; T. Holder in Dallas; to KC w. Jesse Stone, w. whom he join. George E. Lee '29. Led combo in Chi. w. Teddy Wilson until they both became part of L. Armstrong orch. '33. Achieved prominence while working w. Earl Hines fr. '34 to '42 as both ten. sax and arr. Arr. for Gus Arnheim '37; pl. w. Fletcher and Horace Henderson bands '38. Johnson's associations w. the most progressive '40s big bands reveal his catalytic role in the transition fr. swing to bop; he injected modern ideas through his playing and/or writing for Hines, Boyd Raeburn, Billy Eckstine, Woody Herman, and Dizzy Gillespie, as well as helping install forward-thinking players in their bands. He was also responsible for organizing the first bop record date: a Coleman Hawkins session featuring Gillespie in '44; was a member, w. Gillespie and Oscar Pettiford, of the first organized bop combo, which pl. at the Onyx on 52nd St. His contributions to bringing about the full emergence of bop have been sorely neglected. His tnr. style drew fr. the Texas tradition, Lester Young, and innovations of Charlie Parker. Pl. w. Don Redman '43; J. C. Heard '46; Sy Oliver '47; Gillespie in mid '40s; and took part in numerous r&b rec. sessions. He tour. Engl. w. Snub Mosley '52; pl. and wrote for Benny Goodman Feb. '56 to June '57, incl. Asian tour. Tour. Eur. in *Free and Easy* w. Quincy Jones '60; worked w. Count Basie in '61, incl. fests. in France and Newport. Between '62 and '65 very active in NYC pl. club dates, writing, and rec. Rejoin. Hines for combo work '65, doubling sop. sax; tour. w. the gp. in the US, USSR, So. America '66–9. In '69 after leaving Hines, Johnson form. and was mus. dir. for JPJ Qt. w. Oliver Jackson, Bill Pemberton, Dill Jones. The gp. app. in clubs and presented concert "rap sessions" and seminars for over 300,000 hs students under the auspices of Johns-Manville, mainly in US, but also in Eur. dur. summer tour '71. Also tour. Eur. w. Charlie Shavers '70; worked intermittently w. Sy Oliver to mid '70s. In '74 was mus. dir. for NYJRC's *Musical Life of Charlie Parker*, which premiered at NJF-NY '74 and tour. in Eur. that fall; guest mus. dir. for NYJRC's second season '74–5, tour. USSR w. L. Armstrong tribute summer '75. Active as clinician at U. of Conn., Rutgers; pl. in Smithsonian concert series '75; also worked w. co-editor David Baker transcribing music fr. recs. for Smithsonian "classic jazz" project. Dur. late '70s until his death, he cont. to be very active, app. at many festivals and teaching at universities. Fests.: w. JPJ, Montreux; Lubljana '71; NJF-NY '72, jam sess. '73; mus. dir. for C. Hawkins Tribute '83;

Nice '74–5; Colo. JP '71–84. TV: w. JPJ, Montreux JF '71, NET; film of hs perf. in Green Cove Springs, Fla., shown on many local stations. Film: *Last of the Blue Devils* '79. Comps: "Tag Along"; "You Dirty Old Man"; "Mr. Bechet"; "Blues for Sale"; "Tribulations." Recs. as lead. on Cadet, Riv., Argo, Master Jazz. CDs: Prest.; Story.; w. Armstrong; Hampton; C. Hawkins; M. Ferguson; J. J. Johnson; J. Rushing (BB); Hines (BB; Col.; B&B); Benny Carter (Pab.); Ben Webster (Verve); Gil Evans (BN; Imp.); Ellington-Basie (Col.); Goodman (MM); R. Eldridge (Pab.); Gillespie; Pete Johnson (Sav.); Basie (Roul.; Pab.); Q. Jones (Merc.; R&T); I. Jacquet (Roul); C. Shavers (B&B); C. Terry (Cand.); B. Clayton (Chiaro.); S. Vaughan (Col.).

JOHNSON, BUDDY (WOODROW WILSON), pno, lead, arr; b. Darlington, SC, 1/10/15; d. NYC, 2/9/77. Sister was voc. Ella Johnson (b. Darlington, 6/22/23). Went to NYC 1938; pl. in small clubs and tour. Eur. in Tramp Band w. Cotton Club Revue until outbreak of war. Ret. to NYC '39; discovered singing his comp. "Stop Pretending" by a Decca executive in Greenwich Village club; rec. the song, which scored a hit. Fr. then to '54, when he sw. to Merc., he was continuously feat. on Dec., first w. a small gp.; later w. a 14-piece band which app. frequently at the Savoy and was a big r&b attraction in the South. His recs. w. this orch., especially those feat. his sist., incl. "Since I Fell For You," are outstanding for their unique beat and the melodic variety attained by Johnson's arrs. within the framework of the blues. Sidemen incl. Don Stovall; Shad Collins; Dan Minor; Geezil Minerve; Slide Hampton. In '60s led small band and active in church welfare work. Comps: "Please Mr. Johnson"; "One of Them Good Ones"; "Doctor Jive Jives"; "Shufflin' and Rollin.'" Recs. for Decca. CD: one track in *The Legendary Big Band Singers* (Dec.).

JOHNSON, BUNK (WILLIAM GEARY), crnt, tpt; b. New Orleans, LA, 12/27/1879; d. New Iberia, LA, 7/7/49. Studied w. Prof. Wallace Cutchey fr. 1887. Pl. w. Adam Olivier Orch. ca. '96; second crnt. w. Buddy Bolden for a few yrs., then tour. w. Georgia's Smart Set minstrel show and pl. on ocean liners. Ret. to New Orleans '10. Pl. w. Billy Marrero's Superior Orch. '10; Frankie Dusen's Eagle Band '11. Left NO '14; taught and pl. in Mandeville, Lake Charles, Baton Rouge. Pl. w. Gus Fortinet in New Iberia and w. Evan Thomas's Black Eagle Band in Crowley, La. '20s. By '34 dental problems forced his retirement fr. music, and he went to work as a field laborer in New Iberia. Rediscovered in '37 by Bill Russell and Fred Ramsey, who had been directed to him by Louis Armstrong and Clarence Williams as a possible source for research. Inclusion in the book *Jazzmen* '39 stimu-

lated interest in his music, and he resumed playing. Moved to SF '43; worked in drugstore and pl. and rec. w. Yerba Buena Jazz Band. Pl. w. Sidney Bechet in Bost. '45; own gp. at Stuyvesant Casino, NYC '45–6. As a focal point of the trad. jazz revival of the '40s, he perf. and rec. freq. until ret. home to New Iberia in '48. D. M. Marquis, in his book *In Search of Buddy Bolden*, and others have argued convincingly that Johnson, who claimed to have been Louis Armstrong's teacher, made up many of the details of his career prior to 1910. Marquis contends that Johnson was actually born in 1889. CDs: GTJ; Amer. Mus.; GHB; Del.; Col.; w. George Lewis (Amer. Mus.).

JOHNSON, "CANDY" (FLOYD), tnr, bari saxes; b. Madison Co., IL, 5/1/22; d. 6/81. Started on dms. ca. 1935, then sw. to alto and tnr. sax. Att. Wilberforce Coll., pl. in sch. band. Join. Ernie Fields and Tiny Bradshaw; then worked as ballad soloist w. Andy Kirk '42–7; pl. w. C. Basie '51–3, then led own band in Det. Fr. '58 to '64 pl. w. Bill Doggett. Retired fr. full-time mus. in '71 but perf. and rec. occ. Tour. France w. Milt Buckner '71; Eur. '73; led gp. at Bowling Green St. U.; briefly replaced Paul Gonsalves w. D. Ellington '74. Recs. w. Doggett (King); Buckner, A. Cobb (B&B). CDs: w. Al Casey; J. McShann (B&B).

JOHNSON, CHARLIE (CHARLES WRIGHT), lead, pno, tbn; b. Philadelphia, PA, 11/21/1891; d. NYC, 12/13/59. Raised in Lowell, Mass. Went to NYC in 1914, first worked as a sideman on tbn. Rose to prominence as a pnst.-lead. of a band that debuted in Atlantic City, N.J., and opened in '25 at Small's Paradise in Harlem. His original personnel incl.: Sidney De Paris, Jabbo Smith, tpt; Charlie Irvis, tbn; Ben Whitted, Benny Waters, sax; Bobby Johnson, bjo.; Cy St. Clair, tba.; Geo. Stafford, dms. Johnson enjoyed an almost uninterrupted reign at Small's for fifteen yrs. His later sidemen incl. such prominent mus. as Benny Carter; Roy Eldridge; Frankie Newton; Dicky Wells; Jimmy Harrison. After the band broke up in '38, Johnson ceased being a full-time lead.; pl. occ. in NYC in the '40s. Ill health curtailed his activities in the '50s. The band rec. several sess. for Victor in its early yrs. Recs. as lead., Vict. CDs: Jazz Arch.; H&S; *Rainy Nights* w. Ellington's Washingtonians in *History of Classic Jazz* (Riv.).

JOHNSON, CHARLTON COX, gtr; b. Memphis, TN, 12/20/56. Father pl. tbn, moth. pno. Start. on gtr in seventh grade; att. Berklee Coll. 1978. Pl. blues and jazz at Club Handy on Beale St. in Memphis '82–5; taught at Memphis State U. and pl. in faculty jazz ensemble '87–89. Joined C. Basie '89 and tour.

int'l. In '92 co-produced and pl. on solo debut album, *Finally Yours*, by Basie's former vocalist, Carmen Bradford. CDs: w. Bradford (Amazing); Basie (Tel.); Basie & G. Benson (WB).

JOHNSON, DEAN D., bss; b. Renton, WA, 9/12/56. Brother Jeff is gtr. Began on pno. Stud. bs. w. Gary Peacock. Stud. pno. and comp. w. James Knapp at Cornish Inst., Seattle 1973–4; Berklee Coll. of Mus. '74–6. Freelanced in Seattle w. visiting soloists incl. Sonny Stitt; Milt Jackson; Lockjaw Davis; Sweets Edison; Clifford Jordan, Barry Harris; Ted Curson; Richie Cole; Clark Terry; Buddy Tate; many others. Pl. w. Jackie Cain–Roy Kral off and on fr. '79. Moved to NYC '80. Led own qt. '85–7. Pl. w. Gerry Mulligan fr. '85; Haze Greenfield fr. '88. Tour. Italy w. Italian-American qt., Passage, '92. Pl. w. Lee Konitz, Nguyen Le fr. '92. Also extens. freelance work w. Dave Liebman; Paul McCandless; Art Lande; Walter Norris; Joe Lovano; Lew Tabackin; Vic Juris; Billy Harper, etc. Favs.: Eddie Gomez, Gary Peacock, Scott LaFaro. Fests: all major w. Mulligan fr. '85. TV: Many apps. w. Mulligan, also w. Jackie & Roy. CDs: w. Mulligan (GRP; A&M; ProArte); H. Greenfield (Owl); N. Le (Musidisc); Passage (Beat); Cain–Kral (Aud.); John McNeil–Kenny Berger (Synergy).

JOHNSON, DICK (RICHARD BROWN), cl, alto, sop saxes, fl; b. Brockton, MA, 12/1/25. Mother a pno. teacher, grad. fr. New Engl. Cons.; uncle, Mickey Lake, arr. for Edwin Franko Goldman band; cousin is prof. singer. Began on cl. at age 16; alto sax at age 19. Pl. in navy band dur. WWII, then stud. cl. w. Norman Carrell at New Engl. Cons. 1947–8. Pl. w. Neal Hefti '52; Charlie Spivak '52–5; Buddy Morrow '55–8; Dave McKenna, own qt. fr. mid '50s; Benny Goodman off and on '59–60; Xavier Cugat '61; Buddy Rich '71; Woody Herman '80. In '83 Artie Shaw selected Johnson to lead the new Artie Shaw Orch. and he has been w. it since. Pl. w. Mel Lewis Orch. in Japan '89. Taught at Berklee Coll. of Mus. '61–2. Johnson plays a clear-toned, boppish clarinet but on alto sax he is capable of blowing the blues in a dirty-toned, jump style. Fav. cl.: Shaw, Goodman, DeFranco, E. Daniels, B. Wilber; alto: C. Parker, Phil Woods. Fests: NJF w. Eddie Costa '57; Eur., Japan fr. '80s; Colo. JP. TV: PBS, *Big Band Ballroom Bash*. LPs: Riv.; Em.; w. Costa (Verve). CDs: Conc.; w. Woody Herman (Conc.); G. Masso (Arb.).

JOHNSON, DINK (OLIVER), pno, dms, cl; b. Biloxi, MS, 10/28/1892; d. Portland, OR, 11/29/54. Started on dms. while living in Biloxi as a child; later pl. pno. in sporting houses there and in NO. Worked

in LV 1913–14 before join. Freddie Keppard on dms. in LA '14. Form. own band, the Louisiana Six; for a while pl. dms. w. Jelly Roll Morton, his brother-in-law; join. Kid Ory '20 on cl., pno. It was this gp. that made the first jazz record by black musicians in '21 for the Sunshine label. Led own gp., the Five Hounds of Jazz, in LA; renamed the Los Angeles Six for Chi. residency '24. Ret. to Calif., pl. pno. in clubs; also at sister's bar in LV. By '40s retired fr. full-time pl. and ran small restaurant in LA. Still played occasionally and made some recs. as pnst. '46–7. CD: Dink Johnson & Charlie Thompson, *The Piano Players* (Amer. Mus).

JOHNSON, FREDDY, pno; b. NYC, 3/12/04; d. NYC, 3/24/61. Accompanied Florence Mills 1922, then form. own gp. in NYC '24. Worked w. Elmer Snowden '25; Billy Fowler '26. Briefly w. Henri Saporo; Noble Sissle; then join. Sam Wooding, tour. Eur. '28. In '29 worked at Bricktop's in Paris, long residency as soloist; also co-led own bb there w. Arthur Briggs. Left France in '34; pl. long engagements at the Negro Palace in Amsterdam w. C. Hawkins, others; join. Willie Lewis in Belg. in '39. Ret. to Amsterdam '41 and opened own club, La Cubana, there. Arrested by the Nazis in '41 and imprisoned in Germ.; repatriated in '44. After returning to US, worked w. George James, Garvin Bushell. In late '40s and '50s was mostly active as teach. and vocal coach but cont. pl. residencies as soloist. Although he was very ill w. cancer, tour. Eur. in '59 w. show, *Free and Easy*; then pl. in Netherlands as solo for a few weeks. He was hospitalized in Copenhagen in fall '60, ret. to NYC and entered St. Barnabas Hospital, where he died a few mos. later. Recs. in Paris for Bruns.; w. Hawkins and Benny Carter in Netherlands. CD: Class.

JOHNSON, GEORGE, alto sax, cl; b. Grand Rapids, MI, 4/25/13. Not to be confused w. tnr. sax who played w. Wolverines. Worked w. Benny Carter early 1930s; to Eur. '35. Pl. w. Willie Lewis's band; rec. w. Garnet Clark. Form. own band '37; pl. in Paris. To US '39; worked w. Frankie Newton '40–1; Raymond Scott '42; John Kirby '43–5; and Rex Stewart '46. Fr. late '40s led gps. in Eur.; settled in Netherlands. CD: w. Buck Clayton (Riv.).

JOHNSON, GUS JR., dms; b. Tyler, TX, 11/15/13; d. Westminster, CO, 2/6/00. Studied pno., bs., and dms. in sch.; first job as child prodigy at age 9 in Houston. Grad. fr. hs in KC; form. voc. gp., the Four Rhythm Aces. Pl. w. Lloyd Hunter in Omaha 1935; Ernest Redd in Iowa '37. With Jay McShann '38–43, incl. NYC trip '41. After army, ret. to McShann, then pl. in Chi. w. Jesse Miller; Eddie Vinson; then w. Earl Hines last bb; Cootie Williams orch. in NYC. Pl. w. Basie briefly '48; Basie spt. '50 into bb until '54. Freelanced in NYC, incl. w. Lena Horne, Buck Clayton '55–7; tour. w. Ella Fitzgerald '57 into '60s; also w. Woody Herman '59–60; at times w. Gerry Mulligan. Join. World's Greatest Jazz band '69, remaining until fall of '74, when he settled in Denver; worked there, often w. Ralph Sutton and Peanuts Hucko's Pied Piper Qnt. Perf. regularly at Dick Gibson's Colorado jazz parties. Sidelined by Alzheimer's disease '91. Favs.: Rich, Jo Jones, Bellson. Poll: *DB* Critics TDWR '71. Comp.: "Under the Moonlight Starlight Blue." CDs: w. McShann (Dec.; B&B); Basie (BB; Col.; BL; Pab.; Verve); Clayton; M. Hinton; Sutton (Chiaro.); Al Cohn (Evid.); Fitzgerald; Holiday (Verve); C. Hawkins (Prest.; Pab.); J. Hodges (BB; Story.); World's Greatest Jazzband (Rh./Atl.); Hucko (Timel.); Z. Sims (Evid.; BL; Biog.); F. Wess (Sav.); Lem Winchester (NJ).

JOHNSON, HOWARD LEWIS, tba, bari, bass saxes; cl, tpt, flg, el-bs, pennywhistle, arr; b. Montgomery, AL, 8/7/41. From age 2 raised in Massillon, Ohio, grad. fr. hs in 1958. Self-taught; began pl. bari. sax. in '54, tba. in '55. In navy '58–62, then to Bost. where he lived w. Tony Williams' family; then to Chi., where he met Eric Dolphy. Moved to NYC '63; pl. w. Charles Mingus '64–6; Hank Crawford '65; King Curtis '65–6; Archie Shepp '66, '68; Buddy Rich '66; Gil Evans fr. '66. Moved to LA '67, pl. w. Oliver Nelson, Gerald Wilson; w. Gil Evans and Miles Davis at Berkeley JF '68. Fr. '71 to '80 Johnson pl. and arr. for many blues and rock mus. incl. Taj Mahal, The Band, Paul Butterfield, John Lennon. In '72 he subbed for Harry Carney w. Duke Ellington and in '74–5 pl. el-bs. w. Gato Barbieri. Pl. w. *Saturday Night Live* band '75–80, leading it '79–80; Reggie Workman '79–84; Jack DeJohnette '83–6; McCoy Tyner bb fr. '84; Dizzy Gillespie bb '87. In '88 Johnson played a principal role in the Geo. Gruntz–Allen Ginsburg jazz opera, *Cosmopolitan Greetings*, at Hamburg State Opera and has cont. w. Gruntz's Concert Jazz Band fr. that time. He has also done extensive freelance and studio work w. Dexter Gordon; Chaka Khan; Carla Bley; Hank Mobley; Frank Strozier; Quincy Jones; etc. Johnson's own gps. have included the 5-tba. ens. Substructure '68–71; 6-tba. ens. Gravity fr. '71; Tuba Libre w. Dave Bargeron fr. '80s, ens. of so-called "miscellaneous" instr., Book of Miscellanies, fr. '82. App. w. Gil Evans and Miles Davis at Montreux in '91. Fr. late '90 he lived in Hamburg, working w. the Norddeutscher Rundfunk bb for four yrs. Ret. to NYC '95. Although he plays many instruments well, Johnson is

best known as the most important and influential tuba soloist in modern jazz. Favs: tba.: Dave Bargeron, Bob Stewart, Red Callender; bari. sax: Nick Brignola, Pepper Adams, John Surman, Hamiett Bluiett, Cecil Payne; arr: Gil Evans. Polls: *DB, MM,* Jazz Forum; NARAS Most Valuable Player (five times); MVP Virtuoso Award. Fests: all major. Film: *The Last Waltz* w. The Band; *Angel Heart; Eddie and the Cruisers*; soundtracks of *School Daze; Mo' Better Blues; Malcolm X; Clockers*. CDs: Verve; w. John Scofield (BN); Muhal Abrams (BS); Franco Ambrosetti: A. Ibrahim (Enja); G. Barbieri (Imp.); T. Blanchard; D. Gordon (Col.); G. Evans (Enja; BB; Ant.; New Tone; Elec. Bird); Gruntz (TCB; MGB); C. Bley; DeJohnette (ECM); M. Davis (WB); T. Jones–M. Lewis (LRC); Tyner (Mile.); Orange Then Blue (GM).

JOHNSON, HOWARD WILLIAM (aka SWAN), alto sax; b. Boston, MA, 1/1/08; d. NYC, 12/28/91. From mus. family; older bro. was gtr.-bjo. Bobby Johnson; nephew is Bunny Cambell. Pl. w. local bands, then moved to NYC ca. 1925, pl. at Bamboo Inn; w. various gps. Worked w. Fess Williams, Billy Kato, James P. Johnson '30–1; w. Elmer Snowden before join. Benny Carter '32; then w. Teddy Hill to late '30s, incl. Eur. tour in '37; recs. in Paris w. Dicky Wells. In early '40s w. Claude Hopkins; tour. South w. Carter; also wrote some arrs. Fr. '42 to '45 in navy, asst. band dir. for navy band. Ret. to NYC after discharge; lead alto w. D. Gillespie bb '46–8. Active as freelance in '50s and '60s; worked w. Lem Johnson. In '70s and '80s cont. to freelance; app. w. Benny Carter reunion band, NJF-NY '72; worked regularly w. Harlem Blues & Jazz Band until his death. CDs: w. Gillespie (BB; Sav.; Vogue); Panama Francis; Benny Carter (B&B); R. Eldridge (Col.).

JOHNSON, JAMES P(RICE), pno, comp, arr; b. New Brunswick, NJ, 2/1/1891; d. NYC, 11/17/55. First studies w. moth. Pl. prof. dur. summer vacations fr. 1904. Family moved to NYC '08. Stud. in NYC w. Bruto Giannini; also learned fr. ragtime pnsts. Abba Labba (Richard McLean), Eubie Blake, Luckey Roberts. Worked in clubs in Hell's Kitchen district of NYC fr. '13. Publ. first comps., "Mama's Blues" and "Stop It Joe" '17. Also pl. at Clef Club and Barron Wilkins' cabaret, toured w. vaudeville acts, and made piano rolls for Aeolian Co. Mus. dir. of road show, *Dudley's Smart Set*; tour. Eur. w. *Plantation Days* revue. Made solo recs. in NYC '21–30, incl. own comps. "Harlem Strut"; "Carolina Shout"; "Keep Off the Grass"; "Jingles"; "You've Got to Be Modernistic"; also rec. w. Bessie Smith, Ethel Waters. Wrote first Broadway musical *Runnin' Wild* '23, incl.

songs "Old Fashioned Love"; "Charleston." Cont. to write for B'way throughout his career. Fr. the mid 20s he began comp. large-scale orchestral works. The first was *Yamekraw*, a piano rhapsody that premiered at Carnegie Hall w. his pupil Fats Waller as soloist '27. Wrote and perf. revue *Keep Shufflin'* w. Waller '28. Other large works incl. *Harlem Symphony* '32; *Jasmine*, a piano concerto '34; *Symphony in Brown* '35; symphonic jazz arr. of *St. Louis Blues* '37; *De Organizer*, a one-act "blues opera" w. libretto by Langston Hughes '40. Unfortunately, most of the scores for Johnson's orchestral works are lost. Pl. and rec. freq. in NYC dur. trad. jazz revival of late '30–40s incl. Eddie Condon's Town Hall concerts. Johnson was partially paralyzed by a stroke in '40 but by '45 had returned to perf. in NYC clubs such as Eddie Condon's and the Pied Piper. App. on radio show *This Is Jazz* '47; worked on show, *Sugar Hill*, in Calif. '49. Suffered a major stroke in '51 that left him incapacitated until his death. Johnson is widely held to be the first great stride piano player, having distilled his style fr. the ragtime, blues, and early jazz influences of his youth. He was a major influence on subsequent generations of pnsts., incl. Fats Waller; Art Tatum; Duke Ellington; Count Basie; Teddy Wilson; Erroll Garner; Jaki Byard; Thelonious Monk; etc. Johnson's papers are in the collection of Fisk Univ. Film: *St. Louis Blues* w. Bessie Smith. CDs: Biog.; Dec.; Class.; Mos.; Smith.; H&S; w. Armstrong; F. Newton (Aff.); Bechet (Laser.); Condon; Wild Bill Davison (Jazz.); Bunk Johnson (Amer. Mus.); K. Oliver (BB); Jack Teagarden–Pee Wee Russell (Riv.); Waller (Biog.; BB); Clarence Williams (CDS); Edmond Hall (BN); as lead. & sideman in *Hot Jazz on Blue Note*, a 4–CD box (BN); *Spirituals to Swing* (Vang.).

JOHNSON, J. J. (JAMES LOUIS), tbn; comp/arr, lead; b. Indianapolis, IN, 1/22/24; d. Indianapolis, 2/4/01. After playing in hs band, join. the territory gp. of Snookum Russell 1942; then three yrs. w. Benny Carter. Worked w. Count Basie '45–6, then gigged w. various small bop combos on 52nd St. Occasional dates w. Woody Herman and Dizzy Gillespie, then joined Oscar Pettiford '51 for USO tour of Far East. Briefly retired fr. music '52–4, worked as blueprint inspector for Sperry Gyroscope; teamed w. Kai Winding '54–6 in "Jay and Kai Quintet." Formed his own gp. for Eur. tour, then reunited w. Winding in '58. First recognition as a comp. in '59, when his *El Camino Real* and *Sketch for Trombone and Orchestra* were perf. by Monterey JF Workshop Orch. In '60–1 created a six-part work, *Perceptions*, commissioned by Dizzy Gillespie, recorded by Verve feat. Gillespie w. a large orch. cond. by Gunther Schuller '61. Later

alternated between comp. and working w. Miles Davis; his own gp.; and Clark Terry and Sonny Stitt for a tour of Japan. Moved to Calif. in '70 to concentrate on a career as composer, arranger, and conductor. For the rest of the '70s and most of the '80s, active in film and TV comp. Film scores incl. *Cleopatra Jones; Top of the Heap; Willie Dynamite*. TV music credits incl. *Barefoot in the Park; Mayberry RFD; The Danny Thomas Show; That Girl; Mod Squad; Six Million Dollar Man; Starsky and Hutch*. In '87 he returned to Indianapolis and reactivated his playing career. Awarded honorary Doctor of Music degree by Indiana U. and received the Indiana Governor's Arts Award '89. Lead. his own qnt., he cont. to be one of the most important voices on his instrument into the '90s.

Johnson was the progenitor of modern jazz trombone playing, the first musician capable of adapting the complex demands of bop to his instrument. His early work was perf. w. such remarkable technical proficiency that many listeners thought he was playing a valve, rather than a slide, trombone. As much imitated and idolized as Gillespie and Parker, he was one of the major voices in the changing development of jazz in the '40s and '50s. A perennial poll-winner. CDs: Sav.; BN; Prest.; Verve; Ant.; Col.; BB; Em.; Pab.; Conc.; w. Benny Carter in *Classic Capitol Jazz Sessions* (Mos.); Basie (Pab.; Cir.); JATP (Verve; Pab.); M. Davis (Cap.; BN); K. Dorham; Rollins; H. Silver (BN); Getz; Fitzgerald; A. Lincoln (Verve); C. Parker (Stash); Gillespie (Sav.); B. Golson (Riv.); M. Jackson (Pab.; Gal.); King Pleasure; S. Stitt (Prest.); Jacquet; Joe Williams (BB); C. Hawkins (BB; Prest.).

JOHNSON, KEG (FREDERIC H.), tbn; b. Dallas, TX, 11/19/08; d. Chicago, IL, 11/8/67. Father was crntst. and choirmaster; younger bro. was Budd Johnson. Stud. music w. Booker T. Washington's daughter and other priv. teachers. Day job w. fath. at Studebaker while gigging on various instr; start. specializing on tbn. 1927. Left job to become full-time mus., pl. w. local gps. In '29 worked w. T. Holder; Jesse Stone; George E. Lee. Worked w. Grant Moore before settling in Chi. early '30s, pl. w. Eli Rice, Eddie Mallory '30–1; Ralph Cooper at the Regal Theater '31–2. Tour. w. L. Armstrong '32–3, rec. his first solo w. him on "Basin St. Blues." Moved to NYC '33, worked w. Benny Carter, F. Henderson '33–4. Join. C. Calloway at the Cotton Club in Jan. '35, remaining w. him except for brief absences to '48. Pl. w. L. Millinder '48–50; briefly w. Gene Ammons '49. Worked w. Eddie Wilcox before moving to Calif. '51, pl. w. Benny Carter '52; briefly w. D. Ellington '53. Retired fr. full-time music for a few yrs., worked as a house decorator. Cont. to pl. regularly, incl. gigs w. Sammy

Franklin, Wardell Gray. Ret. to NYC in late '50s, pl. w. Eddie Barefield '59; Gil Evans '60. Join. Ray Charles's orch. as bs. tbnst. '61, remaining w. band until he died suddenly dur. a tour. Favs; J. Jenney, J. Teagarden. Recs. w. Calloway. CDs: w. Armstrong (BB); Red Allen; Benny Carter; F. Henderson (Class.); Calloway (Class.; Col.); G. Evans (Imp.); Budd Johnson (Prest.); R. Charles (DCC).

JOHNSON, KEN "SNAKE HIPS" (Kendrick Reginald Huymans), lead, dancer; b. Georgetown, Guyana, 6/22/17; d. London, England, 3/8/41. No formal mus. training. Went to London 1929. Inspired to become involved w. dance fr. assoc. w. the black Amer. choreographer Clarence "Buddy" Bradley. Visited US in '35; is said to have danced for F. Henderson. Ret. to London, danced w. the Emperors of Jazz under Leslie Thompson's lead.; in '37 Johnson assumed leadership. Hired Dave Wilkins, other mus. fr. Trinidad; the band, which tour., was sometimes known as the West Indian Orch.; its BBC broadcasts '38–41 at first startled the public because of Johnson's uncompromising attitude in presenting undiluted swing; fr. '39 was resident orch. at the Café de Paris in London. Johnson was killed when the club was hit by a bomb dur. an air raid. Rec. w. West Indian Orch. for Decca '38.

JOHNSON, LEM (LEMUEL CHARLES aka DEACON), tnr sax, cl, voc; b. Oklahoma City, OK, 8/6/09. Played cl. w. local bands, mid 1920s. Began pl. sax '28 and stud. w. Walter Page while a member of Page's Blue Devils. Pl. on radio show w. Sammy Price '29. Pl. w. various bands in Milwaukee early '30s; three yrs. w. Eli Rice, mainly in Minneapolis mid '30s. Tour. w. Earl Hines ca. '36 then moved to NYC '37. Pl. w. Fess Williams, Luis Russell, Louis Jordan '38–9; Buster Harding, Eddie Durham '40; Edgar Hayes, Sidney Bechet '41; Claude Hopkins '42–3. Led own gps. fr. early '40s. Although he ceased working full-time as a musician in the late '40s, he cont. to lead bands into the '60s. CDs: w. Bechet (BB); L. Jordan (Jukebox Lil).

JOHNSON, LONNIE (ALONZO), voc, gtr, vln; b. New Orleans, LA. 2/8/1889; d. Toronto, Ont., Canada, 6/16/70. From mus. family; bro. was pnst., James "Steady Roll" Johnson. As a child, he stud. gtr., vln.; start. pl. prof. in cafes and theaters while a teenager. Sailed to London ca. 1917; pl. in revue there to '19. Ret. to NO and found that most of his family had died dur. flu epidemic. Worked on riverboats w. Charlie Creath; Fate Marable; others '20–2. Settled in St. Louis, Mo. '25; won a blues contest sponsored by OKeh Recs. and made debut on that label pl. gtr.,

pno., vln., kazoo. Enjoyed great success as a blues artist, frequently rec. for OKeh in Chi. and NYC. Rec. gtr. duets w. Eddie Lang (the latter listed as Blind Willie Dunn to conceal interracial teaming); accomp. Victoria Spivey; Spencer Williams; and other vocs; also guest soloist on recs. by Louis Armstrong; Duke Ellington; and the Chocolate Dandies. Moved to Cleveland, Ohio; in '32, pl. on and off w. Putney Dandridge's orch.; occ. radio work; at times took work in a tire factory and steel mill dur. Depression. Settled in Chi. in '37, resumed rec. (for Dec.; BB); pl. at Three Deuces w. Johnny Dodds to '40. Fr. '40 to '42 he led small gps. at other clubs; in mid '40s app. as soloist, using amplified gtr., emphasizing ballads rather than authentic blues. Scored a hit w. his comp., "Tomorrow Night" '48; rec. many singles for King label dur. late '40s and early '50s. Concert app. in London '52; after ret. to US, he moved to Cincinnati for a few yrs. Moved to Phila. in '58, working as a janitor at the Benjamin Franklin Hotel to '59, when local dj Chris Albertson started him on comeback trail w. Prest. album and a reunion w. Duke Ellington at Town Hall, NYC '60. Gained new, young audience dur. '60s folk/blues revival. Tour. Eur. w. the Amer. Folk Blues Fest. '63. In mid '60s, he settled in Toronto, where he perf. regularly and became popular w. local blues fans. Inactive after suffering injuries in an accident in '69, he died of a stroke the following yr. Johnson was one of the first great single-string jazz gtrsts., as demonstrated by his '20s recs. w. Lang; Armstrong; and Ellington. As a blues artist, his vocal and instrumental style was urban rather than rural, but—as early rec. show—he had deep roots in this field. CDs: Prest.; Col.; BB; co-lead, w. V. Spivey, Elmer Snowden (Prest.); w. Armstrong (Col.); Ellington (Col.); Lang (Col.; Yazoo); King Oliver (BBC).

JOHNSON, MANZIE ISHAM, dms; b. Putnam, CT, 8/19/06; d. NYC, 4/9/71. Raised in NYC. Stud. pno. and vln. as a child; later stud. dms. w. a pit musician at the Lincoln Theater. In early 1920s pl. parlor socials w. Fats Waller; James P. Johnson; et al. Worked w. Willie Gant, June Clark, Elmer Snowden '26; Henri Saparo, Joe Steele '27; Horace Henderson '30. Gained recognition for his work w. Don Redman '31–40. Also pl. w. F. Henderson; L. Armstrong; Willie Bryant. Subbed w. D. Ellington; J. Lunceford; led own band at the Palace '38. In early '40s briefly worked w. Redman again '40, '44; also reunited w. J. P. Johnson '40; Frankie Newton '41; regular stints w. Ovie Alston on and off to '44. Military service '44; after discharge rejoin. Alston; led own gps., incl. house band at Camp Unity, Pa. summer '49. Retired fr. full-time mus. in '50 but worked regularly through

'50s and '60s w. Garvin Bushell; Happy Caldwell; and others. Originally inspired by George Stafford and Kaiser Marshall, Johnson was one of the most respected early swing drummers. Recs. in '30s w. Red Allen; Lil Armstrong; M. Mezzrow. CDs: w. Bechet (Mos.; *Hot Jazz* box, BN); Red Allen (Tax); J. R. Morton (BB; B&B).

JOHNSON, MARC, bs; b. Omaha, NE, 10/21/53. Born into a mus. family. Pno. lessons w. fath., then stud. cello; sw. to bs. at age 16. Family moved to Denton, Tex., and he bec. principal bs. in All-State Youth Orch. of Texas. Cont. his stud. at No. Tex. State U. At age 19 began perf. w. Fort Worth Symph. Join. Woody Herman 1977. Achieved prominence as bs. w. Bill Evans Trio '78–80, where the subtlety and precision of his bass lines made him a fortuitous replacement for Eddie Gomez. Then form. a trio w. Joe and Pat LaBarbera. Worked w. Mel Lewis orch. '80; Stan Getz '81–2; John Abercrombie '83. Form. gp., Bass Desires, w. John Scofield, Bill Frisell and rec. w. it for ECM. A series of duets w. Toots Thielemans, Gary Burton was rec. for Em. on *2X4*. Led gp., Right Brain Patrol, w. Ben Monder, Arto Tuncboyaciyan '93. Has also worked w. Bob Brookmeyer, Jim Hall. Early infls: M. Davis, Bill Evans. CDs: Verve; ECM; Em.; Right Brain Patrol (JMT); w. Ralph Towner; Abercrombie (ECM); P. Bley (Steep.); G. Burton; E. Daniels (GRP); Getz; Thielemans (Conc.); Bill Evans (Drey.; Timel.); F. Hersch; Bill Evans, sax (JC); Konitz (SN); E. Pieranunzi (Timel.; SN); Scofield (BN); John Lewis (DRG); Jim McNeely (Owl; Lip.); P. Motian (JMT); A. LaVerne (Steep.; JC); P. J. Jones (Gal.).

JOHNSON, MONEY (HAROLD), tpt, flg, voc; b. Tyler, TX, 2/23/18; d. NYC, 3/28/78. A friend gave him an old crnt. when he was 15; stud. w. Leonard Parker. Soon start. pl. w. Eddie & Sugar Lou; w. his cousin, Red Calhoun, in Dallas 1934. In '36 went w. Skunny Thompson to Tip Top Club in Okla. City, where he jammed w. Charlie Christian. Pl. w. Nat Towles '37–44, worked out of Omaha. Given nickname by Lee Pope, who used to borrow fr. him. Join. Horace Henderson w. many Towles sidemen '42–4; then two yrs. in Rochester w. Bob Dorsey. Briefly w. C. Basie late '44; then alternated pl. w. Cootie Williams '46, '47 and L. Millinder dur. '47. In '50s worked w. Lucky Thompson, Herbie Fields. To So. Amer. w. Panama Francis '53. Pl. in Reuben Phillips house band at the Apollo for several yrs; then active as studio mus. in '60s; also w. Buddy Johnson; Mercer Ellington; show bands at Basin St. East, Copacabana. St. Dept. tour. of Russia w. E. Hines '66, Eur. '68. Pl. w. D. Ellington in '68; replaced Cat Anderson

'69, pl. w. orch. through '71. Cont. as an active mus. through '70s. Infls: Armstrong, Towles. Fests.: NJF, LV w. Ellington '68. Recs. w. Clarence Williams, R. Phillips. CDs: w. Ellington (Fant.; Prest.; Atl.); H. Henderson (Tax); B. Clayton (Chiaro.).

JOHNSON, (JAMES) OSIE, dms, arr, voc; b. Washington, DC, 1/11/23; d. NYC, 2/10/66. Studied harm., theory w. John Malachi and at Armstrong HS; schoolmates incl. Leo Parker, Frank Wess. Pl. w. Harlem Dictators 1941; Sabby Lewis in Bost. '42–3; navy band in Great Lakes, Chi.; w. Willie Smith, Clark Terry, et al. '44–5. Pl. various clubs in Chi.; also freelance arr., incl. Dinah Washington rec. sess., "Fool That I Am"; "It's Too Soon to Know" '47. Tour. w. Earl Hines '52–3; Tony Scott, I. Jacquet, Dorothy Donegan '54; then settled in NYC permanently. Fr. mid '50s became one of the most active freelance jazz mus., as well as a sought-after studio mus.; app. on countless rec. dates; jingles, even as singer; staff mus. at NBC, CBS for extended periods. App. w. Erroll Garner, Cleveland Symph. '57. Died of a kidney ailment after a long illness. Fest: NJF '57. Poll: *DB* Critics New Star '54. TV: *Sound of Jazz*, CBS '57; on video, Vintage Jazz Classics; *Subject Is Jazz*, NBC '58. Recs. as lead., Period, Beth., Vict.; w. Ben Webster. Feat. on Manny Albam's *The Drum Suite*. CDs: w. Al Cohn; M. Ferguson; G. Russell; Joe Williams (BB); Coleman Hawkins (Prest.; BB); S. Stitt–P. Gonsalves (Imp.); Mose Allison (Rh./Atl.); C. Brown (Em.); G. Evans; J. Hodges; Jacquet; Holiday; H. Merrill (Verve); Q. Jones; R. R. Kirk; S. Horn (Merc.); Lucky Thompson (Imp.); Joe Newman (BL); W. Montgomery; Z. Sims (Riv.); Pettiford (Sav.); P. Woods (Cand.); T. Talbert (MC).

JOHNSON, PETE, pno; b. Kansas City, MO, 3/25/04; d. Buffalo, NY, 3/23/67. Started as a dmr. in hs band; pno. fr. 1922. Fr. '26 began gigging on pno. and was heard in many KC clubs through '38, incl. the Hawaiian Gardens, Peacock Inn, Piney Brown's Sunset Cafe; at the latter he teamed up w. singer Joe Turner, a bartender there, and began working w. him regularly. In '38 went to NYC w. Turner to be feat. on B. Goodman's radio show; also app. at the Apollo. Ret. to NYC w. Turner in Dec. '38 for the historic *From Spirituals to Swing* concert at Carnegie Hall, which also feat. fellow boogie–woogie pnsts. Albert Ammons and Meade Lux Lewis; together they helped bring this pno. style to national attention in the late '30s. Dur. this period, Johnson made several recs., some w. Harry James, w. Turner, and solo. In '39 enjoyed great success at Café Society w. Ammons, Lewis in Boogie-Woogie Trio. For the next few yrs. cont. to work there as duo w. Ammons, and at times, Lewis; pl. residencies in Calif. w. Ammons '47–8; also tour. w. Lewis dur. the '40s; pl. long solo engagements. Moved to Buffalo, N.Y. in '50, pl. local gigs. In '52 tour. US w. Piano Parade, incl. Lewis, A. Tatum, E. Garner; also duo tour w. Lewis. Briefly reunited w. Turner '55; apps. w. Jimmy Rushing. Eur. tour w. JATP show; NJF '58. After suffering a heart attack in Dec. '58 was partially paralyzed and playing was sharply curtailed. Went to NYC summer '60 for some rec. sess. and pl. occ. in Buffalo. A benefit was held for him at Palm Garden, NYC '66. The same yr. a concert honoring his 62nd birthday was held at Kleinhans Music Hall, Buffalo; the Buffalo Philharm. pl. arrs. of his comps, "Roll 'Em Pete" and "Wee Baby Blues." Made his final app. w. Turner again at a *Spirituals to Swing* concert at Carnegie Hall in Jan. '67. Johnson, a pioneer boogie-woogie pnst., had an authoritative and vigorous style, which earned him a reputation as one of the few truly outstanding perfs. in this genre. Fest: NJF '58. Book: *The Pete Johnson Story*, compiled and edited by Germ. discographer Hans Mauerer, was publ. by the US and Eur. Fund-Raising Project for Pete Johnson '65; proceeds were to help defray Johnson's medical expenses. Recs. as soloist, Solo Art; as lead., BN '39; w. Joe Turner (Voc.; Arhoolie). CDs: Del.; Milan; Sav.; Class.; tracks in *Spirituals to Swing* (Vang.) and *History of Classic Jazz* (Riv.); w. Turner (Rh./Atl.).

JOHNSON, PLAS (JOHN JR.), tnr sax; b. Donaldsonville, LA, 7/21/31. From mus. family; stud. sop sax w. fath. Pl. tnr. sax w. Johnson Brothers band, incl. bro. Ray, pno. Worked w. Johnny Otis, Charles Brown and bec. very active w. rock & roll dates on West Coast dur. 1950s. Came to prominence as feat. soloist on Henry Mancini's sound track score for the film *The Pink Panther* '63; also as soloist on soundtrack of *Lady Sings the Blues* '72. Join. staff of Merv Griffin TV show '70; fr. '70s to '90s many local gigs and recordings w. Herb Ellis; Bill Berry; the Capp-Pierce Juggernaut; and at Dick Gibson jazz parties in Denver, Colo. A full-toned soloist in the Hawkins-Ben Webster-Don Byas tradition. CDs: Conc.; w. Capp; Herb Ellis; Jake Hanna; Gene Harris (Conc.); Gerald Wilson (MAMA); Joe Pass; Milt Jackson (Pab.); Oliver Nelson (Imp.).

JOHNSON, REGGIE (REGINALD VOLNEY), bs; b. Owensburg, KY, 12/13/40. Played tbn. as youngster and in army bands. Emerged as bsst. '61. Active in 1960s in avant-garde circles w. Bill Dixon '64; Archie Shepp, Bill Barron '64–5; Sun Ra, Roland Kirk '65; Blakey '65–6. Rec. w. Jazz Composers Orch. '68. Worked w. Bobby Hutcherson–Harold Land '70; Kenny Burrell '73–8; Mingus

Dynasty '82; Johnny Coles and Frank Wess '83. In early '80s w. Horace Parlan. Since the mid '80s, as a European expatriate living in Switz., has rec. w. George Robert and others. CDs: w. Robert (JF); Benny Bailey (TCB); Walter Bishop (Red); Blakey (Em.); Marion Brown (ESP Disk); Coles (CC); H. Parlan; Lockjaw Davis (Enja); T. Harrell (Cont.); S. Grossman (Drey.); B. Hutcherson (BN); Shepp (Imp.); Mingus Dynasty; Mingus bb (SN); Land (Conc.).

JOHNSON, SY (SIVERT BERTIL JR.), pno, comp, arr; b. New Haven, CT, 4/15/30. Began on pno., then stud. acdn. In air force 1951–5, he wanted to fly but was put in band, where he met and was inspired by John Towner Williams. Johnson sold his first arrs. to Count Basie while in law school in LA late '50s. Moved to NYC '59 to work w. Ornette Coleman; pl. w. Charles Mingus at Showplace '60; Rod Levitt Oct. '60s. Stud. in NYC w. Lucy Greene; Hall Overton; Rayburn Wright; also stud. at Juilliard and Eastman Sch. of Mus. arrangers wkshp. In the '60s wrote arrs. for Ruby Braff; Marshall Brown; Gerry Mulligan; then for TV and films. Pl. and arr. for Yolande Bavan '66. Arr. for Charles Mingus; Thad Jones–Mel Lewis; Quincy Jones; Lee Konitz '70s; also pl. pno. on occ. w. Konitz Nonet. In the '80s app. as pnst. w. Joe Williams and Frank Sinatra. Arr. for many films, incl. *The Wiz, The Cotton Club, The Color Purple*, as well as for the B'way show *Black and Blue*. Lectured on Charles Mingus at Harvard U., New Engl. Cons., Berklee Sch. of Mus., and worked as a freelance photographer, jazz critic, and voc. coach. Arr. for Mingus bb in '90s. Comp: one-woman show, *A Cast of Thousands* w. lyricist Ellen Schwartz, done in wkshp. perfs.; opera, based on Tolkien's *The Hobbit*, was premiered in Rome at Jazz&Image Fest. '98. Favs: Keith Jarrett, Jimmy Rowles; arrs.: Ellington, Johnny Mandel. TV: *Let's Dance*; PBS w. Eubie Blake. CDs: as pnst.: w. Sinatra (Rep.); as arr.: w. Lavern Baker (DRG); Mingus (Col.; Atl.); Herbie Mann (Koko.; Lightyear).

JOHNSON, WALTER, dms; b. NYC, 2/18/04; d. NYC, 4/26/77. Went to sch. w. Bubber Miley, Benny Carter. Pl. w. Freddie Johnson 1924. Join. Elmer Snowden '25; Billy Fowler '26, before rejoin. Snowden's gp. which succeeded Ellington at the Kentucky Club '27. Fr. '28 worked on and off w. F. Henderson for ten yrs.; also worked w. Leroy Smith, Sam Wooding; w. L. Millinder '38–9; Claude Hopkins '39; C. Hawkins bb; Edgar Hayes '40; rejoin. Henderson '41–2; Millinder again; also house band at Elk's Rendezvous mid '40s. Pl. mostly w. Tab Smith '44–54. Left full-time mus. mid '50s, worked as bank guard, but cont. to freelance through late '50s, '60s. A steady, dependable drummer, Johnson has been credited w. extending the use of the hi-hat. Recs. w. Henderson (Col.; OK; Voc.); C. Hopkins; Willie Bryant; L. Feather. CDs: Red Allen (Tax); Benny Carter (B&B); Charly); F. Henderson (Col.); Tab Smith (Del.).

JOHNSTON, PHILLIP JOHN, sop, alto saxes, comp, arr; b. Chicago, IL, 1/22/55. Studied pno. w. Don Friedman, sax w. Lennie Popkin in NYC and Gordon Fels in SF, but mostly self-taught. Pl. w. rock band in New Jersey 1972–3, then w. John Zorn '74; swing and dixie. bands in SF mid '70s. Pl. w. Joel Forrester since '77; ROVA Sax Qt. fr. '79; Public Servants '80–2; Microscopic Spt. fr. '81; Mikel Rouse '83–5; Bobby Radcliff '84–6; NY Composer's Orch. '86; Joe Gallant '88; Twilight Time fr. '89; Walter Thompson fr. '90. Also pl. in '70s and '80s w. Wayne Horvitz; Bob Montalto; Eliot Sharp; Pat Irwin; Eugene Chadbourne; Lenny Pickett; Robin Holcomb, Zorn; Bobby Previte; Butch Morris; also w. various rock bands. Favs: Steve Lacy, Bechet, C. Parker, C. Adderley, P. Desmond, Mike Hashim; arrs.: Ellington, Strayhorn, Carla Bley. Fests: Eur. w. Micro. Spt. fr. '83. CDs: Avant; BS; w. Micro. Spt. (Stash; Osmosis).

JOLLY, PETE (Peter A. Ceragioli), pno, acdn; b. New Haven, CT, 6/5/32. Studied at age 3 w. fath., an acdn. teacher; started pno. at 8. Moved to LA, worked w. G. Auld 1952; Shorty Rogers '54; Buddy DeFranco '56; Terry Gibbs; Art Pepper '60; and own gps. Fr. '60s mainly active in TV and movie studios, working w. N. Hefti; J. J. Johnson; B. Byers; Don Costa; Artie Butler; etc. In '65 was one of orig. pnsts. to open the famous No. Hollywood jazz room, Donte's. In '92 was working w. own trio and the revived Lighthouse All-Stars. Best known comp. "Little Bird." A facile pnst., Jolly was—in the '60s and '70s—one of the only acdnsts. to develop a contemporary, single-note, bebop-based improvisational style. CDs: Holt; VSOP; w. Pepper; L. Niehaus (Cont.); C. Baker (PJ); Jon Eardley (NJ); B. Goodman (MM); R. Norvo (BB); S. Rogers (BB; Cand.); J. J. Johnson (Pab.).

JONES, BOBBY, tnr, sop saxes, cl, comp, educ; b. Louisville, KY, 10/30/28; d. Munich, Germany, 3/6/80. Started on dms., his father's instr.; sw. to cl. at age 8. First prof. job at 10; fath., who had him listen to recs. of jazz greats, had arr. for him to sit in w. local black combo for important early jazz experience. Later stud. w. Simeon Bellison; Joe Allard; C. Parker; G. Russell. While pl. in local sxt. was hired by Ray McKinley 1949, remain. w. him until mid '50s. Pl.

briefly w. Hal McIntrye, then rejoin. McKinley before entering army, where he met Adderley bros., Junior Mance; led own combo at officer's club. After discharge, worked w. and arr. for Boyd Bennett for two and a half yrs., pl. hillbilly, then r&r. Briefly w. Boots Randolph to Cleveland, remain. there to pl. clubs, TV, radio, teach. Rejoin. McKinley again '59 to Feb '63, when he join W. Herman for a few mos.; left to work in NYC. To NO w. Jack Teagarden. When Teagarden died Jan. '64, Jones ret. to Louisville; start. Louisville Jazz Council; taught woodwinds at Kentucky State Coll. Went to NYC '69; sat in w. C. Mingus fall '70 and eventually became band member, tour. Eur. and Japan '70; Eur. '72. Left Mingus, settled in Belgium, then Holland; Munich in '73, where he form., qnt., Summit, w. Dusko Goykovich, Horace Parlan. Form. own trio '74. When the climate in Munich aggravated his emphysema, concentrated more on comp. and arr. A thoroughly schooled musician, combining bop facility w. a blues spirit, reflecting his southern background, he followed what C. Parker had told him: "First, you master your instrument, then you master the music, and then you forget about all that shit and just play." Poll: *DB* TDWR on cl. '73. Comps.: "Thanks to Trane"; "Ballad for Two Sons"; "Hill Country Suite." LPs: Cobblestone, Enja; w. J. Raney (Muse). CDs: w. Mingus (Col.; DIW); Herman (Verve).

JONES, BUDDY (BURGHER WILLIAM), bs, tba; b. Hope, AR, 2/17/24; d. Carmel Valley, CA, 6/9/00. Met Charlie Parker in KC at age 17. Began pl. bs. in navy. Worked w. Charlie Ventura 1947, then moved to LA. Freelanced w. Joe Venuti, Ina Ray Hutton '49. Moved to NYC '50. Rec. w. Buddy DeFranco '51. Pl. w. Gene Williams, Lennie Tristano, Stan Getz early '50s. Joined Elliot Lawrence Qt. on Jack Sterling CBS radio show '52. Cont. to perf. on the Sterling show until '64. Rec. w. Elliot Lawrence bb '52–7; Al Cohn '54–5; Sam Most, Gene Quill '55; Joe Newman, Manny Albam, Andy Kirk, Phil Woods, Bob Brookmeyer '56. Pl. w. E. Lawrence, Johnny Richards in mid '60s, then studio mus. in Hollywood. Ret. to NYC late '60s; pl. w. Bobby Hackett; Al Cohn; Bill Watrous. Lived in Mt. Bethel, Pa. In '90s lived and gigged in Carmel Valley, CA. Favs: Walter Page, Hinton, Blanton. Recs. w. Cohn; Lawrence; Woods-Quill. CDs: w. Charlie Parker (Phil.).

JONES, (WILLIAM) CARMELL, tpt, comp; also flg, v-tbn; b. Kansas City, KS, 7/19/36; d. Kansas City, 11/7/96. Began on tpt. at age 11. In military 1956–8, then stud., at Kansas U. '58–60. Led own combo in KC, Mo. '60, then moved to Calif. Rec. as lead. for PJ; and w. Harold Land, Bud Shank '61;

Gerald Wilson '61–3; Curtis Amy. Tour. w. Horace Silver '64–5. Moved to Eur. Aug. '65, joined SFB-TV and radio orch. in Berlin as tpt. and staff arr. Gigs all over Eur. in '70s w. own combo, also w. Paul Kuhn, lead. of SFB Orch. Ret. to Kansas City '80. Became artist-in-residence for KC sch. district. Rec. as lead. for Revelation '82. Honored as an Elder Statesman of KC Jazz '91. Inspired by Clifford Brown, he was an excellent exponent of that style. Poll: *DB* TDWR '64. Fests: all major in Eur. CDs: w. H. Silver; J. Henderson (BN); S. Vaughan (Roul.); B. Ervin; C. McPherson (Prest.).

JONES, CLAUDE B., tbn; b. Boley, OK, 2/11/01; d. aboard SS *United States*, 1/17/62. Studied tpt. and dms. priv.; start. on tbn. at 13; pl. tbn. in town band and at Langston HS, where he doubled on tpt., dms. Att. Wilberforce U. In Ohio, 1922, join. Synco Jazz Band, which later became McKinney's Cotton Pickers w. which he pl. '23–29. Worked intermittently w. F. Henderson and Chick Webb '30–4; Don Redman '31–3; Alex Hill '34. Join. Cab Calloway late '34–40; on and off w. C. Hawkins bb '40; also w. Zutty Singleton, Joe Sullivan. Briefly rejoin. Henderson '41, then retired fr. full-time mus. to manage own sausage company; meanwhile cont. to pl. gigs, incl. Benny Carter; Calloway; Redman. Resumed pl. full-time w. D. Ellington on v-tbn. '44–9. Brief spells w. Machito '49; F. Henderson '50; Ellington again '51. In '52 left music permanently, working as officer's steward on SS *United States*. Adept in the trombone's upper register. CDs: w. Henderson (Col.; BB); McKinney's Cotton Pickers; Jelly Roll Morton; Bechet (BB); Calloway (Class.; Col.); Ellington (BB; Col.; Prest.; MM); Don Redman (Class.; Hep); Red Allen–C. Hawkins (Hep); Benny Carter (B&B); C. Webb (Dec.).

JONES, DILL (DILLWYN OWEN), pno; b. Newcastle Emlyn, Wales, 8/19/23; d. NYC, 6/22/84. Became interested in jazz by hearing Fats Waller records on radio in 1930s. Served in Royal Navy '42–6; stud. at Trinity Coll. of Mus., London '46–8; later w. Luckey Roberts in NYC '65. Prof. debut w. Carlo Krahmer and Humphrey Lyttelton '47–8, incl. first Nice JF '48. Became a leading figure in post-WWII British jazz circles; established himself w. own trio; pl. w. Ronnie Scott; Stephane Grappelli; George Chisolm. Dur. '50s hosted BBC Jazz Club on radio; first introduced jazz on BBC-TV. Accomp. L. Armstrong in Hungarian Relief Fund concert '57. While ship's pnst. on *Queen Mary* through '50s, visited NYC many times, made many assoc. w. US jazz mus. Moved to NYC '61, worked w. Yank Lawson '62; Peanuts Hucko, Roy Eldridge, Bob Wilber,

Jimmy McPartland mid '60s; Gene Krupa '67–8; Dukes of Dixieland '68. Charter member of JPJ Qt. w. Budd Johnson, Oliver Jackson, Bill Pemberton '69. In next four yrs. tour. US for John-Mansville in hs concert-seminars; long engagements at Jimmy Weston's; Eur. apps. Left gp. in '74 to freelance; worked as single; also w. WGJB, Earle Warren, Eldridge, McPartland mid '70s. Fr. '73 pl. intermittently w. Countsmen; some apps. w. Harlem Blues & Jazz Band. Infl: L. Roberts, Joe Sullivan, Ellington, Beiderbecke, J. P. Johnson, F. Waller, Willie "The Lion" Smith. Versatile, accomplished performer in Harlem stride, Bixian impressionism, and modern mainstream. Fests: NJF-NY; Monterey; Montreux in '70s. Comps: "West of the Wind"; "Something for Luckey"; "Celtic Twilight." Recs: as soloist, Chiaro; w. JPJ; Lou McGarity; Tony Parenti; Earle Warren. CDs: w. Budd Johnson and JPJ Qt. (Story.); Lyttelton; Bruce Turner (Lake); Parenti (Jazz.); McGarity (Master Jazz); Herb Hall–Joe Muranyi (Fat Cat Jazz); set in *Jazz Piano Masters: Live at the New School* (Chiaro).

JONES, EDDIE (EDWARD), bs; b. NYC, 3/1/29; d. West Hartford, CT, 5/31/97. Raised in Red Bank, N.J., where he was a neighbor and friend of Count Basie's family. Stud. vln. for five yrs., later other strings, tbn., euph., and tba. In hs qualified for N.J. All-State Choir; Orch., on bs.; and first chair tba. in Concert Band. While stud. music educ. at Howard U. fr. 1946 he pl. bs. w. Howard U. Swing Masters and several bands in the Wash., D.C., area w. such mus. as John Malachi; Frank Wess; Benny Golson; and Bill Hughes. Tour. w. Sarah Vaughan '50; Lester Young ca. '51. Degree in mus. ed. '51. Taught mus. for a yr. at Robert Smalls HS, Beaufort, S.C. Ret. to Wash. to prepare for graduate work at Howard but in August '52 join. Count Basie. Rec. in '50s w. Joe Newman; Milt Jackson; Ernie Wilkins; Frank Foster; Frank Wess; Thad Jones; Putte Wickman. Tour. Sweden w. Joe Newman '58. Dur. yrs. w. Basie schooled himself in computer science. Left Basie in '62 and in '63 join. IBM as a systems engineer. Found time to sub for Richard Davis in the Thad Jones–Mel Lewis Orch. and for Art Davis in the B'way show *Sugar* '60s. In the late '80s while working as vice-pres. of an insurance co., began taking two mos. off each yr. to perf. w. G. Wein's Newport All-Stars and in Basie reunion bands. In '90s cont. to work w. Newport All-Stars, incl. QE2 jazz cruise '96; tour. Japan w. F. Wess bb. Gigs w. Danny Doriz at Caveau de L'Huchette, Paris fr. '93; Eur. tour. and Mediterranean jazz cruises fr. '94. Also perf. w. the Manchester Symph., Conn.; the Village Light Opera, NYC; and was on the board of the Hartford Symph. His big sound and steady beat marked him as an extension of Walter Page in Basie's "New Testament" orch. and he retained those qualities throughout his career. Favs: M. Hinton, Ray Brown, Al McKibbon, Nelson Boyd. CDs: w. Basie (Verve; Roul.; BL; Mos.); J. Newman (Prest.; Swingville; BL; FS); Newport All-Stars (Conc.); F. Wess (Say.; Conc.); M. Jackson; C. Hawkins; Hank Jones; K. Clarke, F. Foster (Sav.); Lambert, Hendricks & Ross (Imp.); Lem Winchester (NJ).

JONES, ELVIN RAY, dms, comp, lead; b. Pontiac, MI, 9/9/27; d. Englewood, NJ, 5/18/04. Younger bro. of Hank and Thad Jones. Self-taught; pl. in sch. band. Pl. in army band 1946–9. Pl. w. Thad Jones, Billy Mitchell in house band at Bluebird Inn, Det. '49–52; Teddy Charles, Chas. Mingus at NJF '55. Moved to NYC '56. Pl. w. Bud Powell '56; Pepper Adams–Donald Byrd '58; Tyree Glenn '58–9; Sweets Edison '59–60; also J. J. Johnson; Stan Getz; Sonny Rollins late '50s. Came to prominence w. John Coltrane Qt. '60–6. Building upon the cross-rhythmic developments of Art Blakey, Jones arrived at an innovative approach to the drums in which no beat of the bar was necessarily indicated by a specific accent. This freed the drummer fr. the role of accompanist and allowed him to participate more fully in collective improvisation and the overall sound of the ensemble while still supporting individual soloists. Shortly after Coltrane hired a second drummer, Rashied Ali, Jones left the gp. He pl. briefly w. Duke Ellington in Eur. and Tony Scott in NYC, then form. own gps. fr. '66. Led qt., later a trio, w. Joe Farrell late '60s. In '70s sidemen incl. Frank Foster; Geo. Coleman; Steve Grossman; Dave Liebman; Azar Lawrence; Roland Prince; Gene Perla; David Williams. Toured Eur., Asia, and So. Amer., and perf. many free concerts in schools and prisons fr. '70s. Performed and rec. actively in the '90s w. his Jazz Machine incl. sidemen such as Ravi Coltrane; Nicholas Payton; Delfeayo Marsalis; Sonny Fortune; David Sanchez; Willie Pickens; etc. Favs: Roach, Blakey, K. Clarke, P. J. Jones, R. Haynes. Polls: *DB* Critics '66–75; *DB* Readers '66, '68–9; Hall of Fame. Fests: Eur., Japan fr. '70s. Films: act and pl. in *Zachariah* '70; docu. *Different Drummer* '79. CDs: BN; Enja; Riv.; Evid.; Land.; w. Coltrane (Atl.; Imp.; Pab.); Pepper Adams (Riv.; Sav.; Prest.); S. Rollins (BN; Imp.); J. J. Johnson; W. Marsalis (Col.); M. Tyner (BN; Imp.; Mile.); Grossman (Drey.); M. Davis (Deb.; Col.); Ellington (Imp.); G. Evans (Imp.; Verve; Enja); T. Flanagan (Enja; DIW); Getz; Hank Jones; Stephen Scott (Verve); Gillespie; O. Coleman; G. Green; Joe Henderson; W. Shorter (BN); A. Pepper; P. Newborn (Cont.); Konitz (Mile.; Verve); S. Lacy; A. Farmer; M. Waldron (NJ); James Williams; R. R. Kirk (Em.).

JONES, ETTA, voc; b, Aiken, SC, 11/25/28; d. Mt. Vernon, NY, 10/16/01. Met and perf. w. Buddy Johnson at Apollo Theatre Amateur Hour NYC 1944. Tour. w. Johnson '44–5, then worked w. Stuff Smith at Onyx Club '45; Harlemaires '46; J. C. Heard '48; Earl Hines gp. w. Jonah Jones, Bennie Green, Art Blakey '52–3. Many recs. as a lead. for Prestige label in '60s following gold record success of "Don't Go to Strangers." Join. saxophonist Houston Person in '68, forging a strong friendship and musical partnership. In addition to Person, has perf. in recent yrs. w. Harper Bros.; Benny Green; Christian McBridge. Combines a Billie Holiday infl. w. a strong feeling for the blues. Poll: *DB*. Fests: Japan w. Art Blakey '70; Eur. and Japan many times since. CDs: 32; Muse; Prest.; High.; w. Person (Muse).

JONES, HANK (HENRY), pno; b. Vicksburg, MS, 7/31/18. Older bro. of Thad and Elvin Jones. Raised in Pontiac, Mich. Stud. w. Carlotta Franzell. Orig. infl. by Earl Hines, Fats Waller, Teddy Wilson, Art Tatum. Pl. w. local bands in Mich. and Ohio fr. age 13, then w. Geo. Clark in Buffalo, N.Y. Moved to NYC at invitation of Lucky Thompson 1944; joined Hot Lips Page at Onyx Club on 52nd Street. Was infl. by hearing Al Haig, Bud Powell. Worked w. Andy Kirk, B. Eckstine, John Kirby, C. Hawkins, H. McGhee mid '40s. Toured w. Jazz at the Philharmonic '47. Accomp. Ella Fitzgerald '48–53; also rec. w. Charlie Parker dur, this time. Freelanced extens. in NYC studios fr. '53. Worked w. Benny Goodman off and on '56–8. On staff at CBS '59–75; worked mainly w. bbs incl. Ray Bloch Orch. on Ed Sullivan show but cont. to tour and rec. w. jazz artists. Orig. pnst. in Thad Jones–Mel Lewis Orch. '66. Tour. w. B. Goodman late '60s; Stan Getz early '70s. After the CBS staff was dissolved in '75, led the Great Jazz Trio w. Ron Carter and Tony Williams or Ben Riley in NYC clubs. Buster Williams repl. Carter in '76. Pnst.-cond. of B'dway show *Ain't Misbehavin'* late '70s. By '80 was lead. a trio w. Eddie Gomez and Al Foster; Jimmy Cobb repl. Foster in '82. Rec. projects in the '70s and '80s incl. solo piano recs. and duos w. other pnsts., incl. Tommy Flanagan, Geo. Shearing, and John Lewis. Rec. in Japan w. Sonny Stitt, Geo. Duvivier early '80s. Jones's taste, touch, harmonic wisdom, overall professionalism, and versatility as a soloist, accompanist, and ensemble musician have kept him in high demand for the last forty yrs. He may be heard on literally thousands of albums. Fests: all major as lead., solo pno., sideman. Film: app. w. Sammy Davis Jr. in *A Man Called Adam* '66. TV: *Strolling '20s* w. Harry Belafonte; *Telephone Hour* w. Benny Goodman; Barbra Streisand, Carol Burnett, Al Hirt, Jackie Gleason shows in '60s; ABC *Like It Is* w.

Jackie McLean, Tommy Potter, Max Roach; app. w. trio in CBS soap opera *Love of Life* early '70s. CDs: Verve; Gal.; 32; Muse; Sav.; Conc.; Timel.; Prog.; Story.; Em.; B&B; T. Flanagan–H. Jones, Gal; w. C. Parker; Lester Young; Stan Getz; JATP (Verve); Artie Shaw; B. Goodman (MM); G. Shearing; K. Peplowski; L. Tabackin; T. Farlow (Conc.); Pepper Adams (Sav.; Res.); C. Adderley (Sav.; BN); Joe Wilder; N. Adderley; E. Bert; D. Byrd; K. Clarke; H. Mobley; Lee Morgan; S. Shihab; F. Wess (Sav.); G. Ammons; O. Nelson; D. Gordon (Prest.); Al Cohn (BB); Milt Jackson (Sav.; Riv.; Imp.); J. J. Johnson (Sav.; BB; Col.); C. Hawkins (BB; Imp.; Riv.; Prest.); Elvin Jones; K. Dorham; Wes Montgomery (Riv.); Nat Cole (Cap.); Thad Jones (Deb.); Z. Sims; P. Gonsalves (BL); Lucky Thompson (Prest.; Imp.); J. Hodges (Verve; BB); B. Holiday (Verve); B. Webster (Col.).

JONES, HAROLD J., dms; b. Richmond, IN, 2/27/40. Lived in Chi. fr. 1958, stud. at American Cons. of Mus. '58–63. In early '60s pl. w. Eddie Harris, D. Byrd, Bunky Green; toured int'l w. Paul Winter '61–2. Join. Count Basie, Dec. '67 for five yrs. Moved to LA '72; freelanced in studios and night clubs; worked w. E. Fitzgerald; T. Bennett; S. Davis Jr. Rejoin. Basie briefly in '74; then Japan tour w. Carmen McRae '75. Perf. w. Benny Carter '77 and '79 in Japan, and in '81 in LA. Accomp. S. Vaughan fr. '80 until her death; join. Natalie Cole, June '91, remain. through '92. A superlative bb dmr., Jones was one of the foremost rhythm section players to work w. C. Basie. CDs: w. Basie; Vaughan; Carter (Pab.); Gene Harris; Ernestine Anderson; M. McPartland; Walter Norris; F. Wess (Conc.); D. Hyman (Mile.); Eddie Harris (Rh./Atl.); T. Talbert (SB).

JONES, ISHAM, lead, saxes, comp; also pno; b. Coalton, OH, 1/31/1894; d. Hollywood, FL, 10/19/56. Raised in Saginaw, Mich. Led own band at 18; moved to Chi. in 1915, concentrated on tnr. sax; pl. w. various bands in Chi. and Mich. Led own trio, then orch., which pl. long residency at Hotel Sherman in Chi. fr. early '20s. Band became immensely popular; went to NYC, London '24; tour. US '24–5. Fr. '26 to '36 the orch. enjoyed tremendous recognition. Known more as a "sweet" band than a jazz band, its members incl. jazz mus. such as Jack Jenney; Sonny Lee; Pee Wee Erwin; Howard Smith. Woody Herman pl. and sang for Jones's last orch. and sxt., Isham Jones's Juniors, whose members were the nucleus of Herman's First Herd. After the Juniors disbanded in '36, Jones concentrated more on comp.; also occ. led orchs. In '40s resettled in Colo., ran a general store; moved to Fla. in '55. Died of cancer. Comps: "It Had

To Be You"; "The One I Love Belongs to Somebody Else"; "On the Alamo"; "There Is No Greater Love"; "I'll See You in My Dreams." CD: Parklane.

JONES, JIMMY (JAMES HENRY); pno, arr, cond; b. Memphis, TN, 12/30/18; d. Burbank, CA, 4/29/82. Family moved to Chi. when he was 3. Start. on gtr., then pl. pno w. combos in Chi. Began gaining recognition when pl. w. Stuff Smith 1943; came to NYC w. him '44. Worked w. J. C. Heard '46–7. Recs. for Al Hall's Wax label '47. Tour. w. Sarah Vaughan '47–52, when forced to stop pl. for two yrs. due to illness. Start. working again as freelance in NYC; then rejoin. Vaughan, incl. Eur. tour fall '54; West Indies, South Amer., Cuba '56. Left her to freelance '58, worked w. Ben Webster; Sweets Edison; Ruby Braff; accomp. Anita O'Day, NJF '58; also Morgana King, Dakota Staton. Fr. late '50s, mostly active as arr. and conductor: wrote arr. for *Subject Is Jazz*, NBC-TV series '59; also for M. Ellington, Joe Williams, Milt Jackson and strings '59; H. Belafonte TV shows, incl. *The Strolling '20s* '65; D. Ellington's TV apps. '62–6; led band for Ellington's *My People* show '63. Cond. for Lena Horne, Nancy Wilson. App. w. own trio on *Today* show. Tour. Eur. as mus. dir. for E. Fitzgerald w. Ellington band '66. Fr. '69 resident mus. and arr. in LA, arrs. for rec. dates, TV shows, occ. for Joe Williams. Wrote arr. for Ellington specials, . . . *We Love You Madly* '73; *Cotton Club* '75. Pnst. for K. Burrell '75; gigs w. gtrst. John Collins. Though primarily active as a writer of rare skill, Jones was greatly underrated as a pnst. His style was uniquely attractive, composed mostly of gently played, discreetly distributed, harmonically ingenious chords, though occasionally he played interesting single-line, right hand solos. CDs: tracks w. own gp. in *Giants of Small Band Swing, Vols. 1&2* (Riv.); w. Don Byas (Sav.); Stuff Smith (Prog.); C. Hawkins (BB); S. Vaughan (Col.; Em.); C. Brown (Em.); Burrell (Fant.); Ellington (Col.; Red Brn.); J. Hodges (Imp.; BB); Jacquet (Verve; Roul.); H. Merrill (Em.; Verve); B. Clayton (Riv.; Mos.); C. Terry (Riv.); Thad Jones (JA; FS); as arr: Wes. Montgomery (Riv.); Shirley Horn (Merc.); Fitzgerald (Verve).

JONES, JO (JONATHAN aka PAPA JO), dms; b. Chicago, IL, 7/10/11; d. NYC, 9/3/85. Grew up in Alabama. Stud. mus. for twelve yrs. and bec. proficient on saxes, tpt., and pno. After leaving sch., he joined a carnival and toured the Chautauqua circuit, often working as a tap-dancer and singer. Join. Walter Page's Blue Devils in Oklahoma City late 1920s. Moved to Omaha, Neb. '30; pl. w. Lloyd Hunter. Moved to Kansas City '33. Join. Count Basie Orch. '34. Pl. w. Basie '34–6, then left to pl. w. Page in the

Jeter-Pillars Orch. in St. Louis. By the end of '36 both men were back in Basie's band. Pl. w. Basie '36–44. In army '44–6, then rejoin. Basie '46–8. Pl. w. JATP '47; Illinois Jacquet '48–9; Lester Young '50–1; Joe Bushkin '52–3. Freelanced extensively in '50s, then pl. w. Ella Fitzgerald–Oscar Peterson JATP '57; own trio w. Ray Bryant '57–60; Teddy Wilson; Claude Hopkins, Bryant '60s; Milt Buckner '69–70s; Benny Carter, Joe Bushkin, etc. '70s. Freelanced throughout his career. Even while a star in Basie's band, he did much freelancing, perf. on recs. w. Harry James; Billie Holiday; Lionel Hampton; Teddy Wilson; Benny Goodman; etc. in the '30s and '40s. Jones is generally considered to be the first jazz drummer to transfer the basic rhythmic pulse fr. the bass drum to the high hat. His use of the snare and bass drum to provide irregular accents instead of a steady pulse freed the rhythm section to respond to individual soloists in a way that had previously been impossible. The rhythm section of Basie, Page, Jones, and Freddie Green, dating fr. '37, was the most influential of its time and is considered by many to have set the standard for modern, four-to-the-bar swing. Jones, who was also a clever, tasteful soloist and a master w. the brushes, is the direct stylistic ancestor of more modern drummers such as Kenny Clarke. Fests: all major fr. JATP 47. Polls: *DB* '56. Film: *Jammin' the Blues*, '44. TV: acted in *Route 66* episode w. Ethel Waters, Coleman Hawkins, Roy Eldridge; PBS John Hammond tribute '75. CDs: Pab.; FS; Vang.; w. Basie (Dec.; Col.; BB; Verve); Lester Young (Comm.; Verve; Story.); Coleman Hawkins (Pab.; Story.; Riv.); JATP; Benny Carter; Ellington (Verve); Ellington-Strayhorn (Rev.); G. Ammons; S. Stitt; Gil Evans (Prest.); Tatum (Pab.); Z. Sims; P. Gonsalves; R. Braff (BL); Mingus; Dolphy; Pee Wee Russell (Cand.); Slam Stewart; B. Tate; Joe Turner, pno. (B&B); Goodman (Col.; Cap.); L. Hampton (BB); Jacquet (BB; Verve; B&B); Teddy Wilson (Hep).

JONES, JONAH (ROBERT ELLIOTT), tpt, voc; b. Louisville, KY, 12/31/09; d. NYC, 4/30/00. Played alto horn in local band, then sw. to tpt. Pl. w. Wallace Bryant on Mississippi riverboats ca. 1927; Horace Henderson '28–9; Wesley Helvey '30; Jimmie Lunceford '31; Stuff Smith '32–4; McKinney's Cotton Pickers '35; Stuff Smith at Onyx Club '36–40. Also rec. in '30s w. Teddy Wilson; Billie Holiday; Lionel Hampton; Lil Armstrong; others. Pl. w. Fletcher Henderson '40; Benny Carter '40–1; Cab Calloway Orch. incl. Cab Jivers '41–52; Joe Bushkin '52; Earl Hines '52–3; *Porgy and Bess* pit band '53. Reunited w. Stuff Smith, w. whom he had perf. comedy vocal numbers '53. Led own qt. at Embers, NYC late '50s. Many of the albums of easy-listening jazz that Jones rec. w. this gp., typi-

fied by the shuffle treatment of "On the Street Where You Live," were commercially successful, leading to Jones's apps. on the Fred Astaire TV show in '58 and '59. Toured Eur., Australia, Far East, Mexico '60s; also bec. first jazz musician to lead a gp. at the Rainbow Grill in NYC. Toured Eur. '70. In res. at Rainbow Room '75. Jones perf. into the '80s but in the '90s app. much less regularly. Favs: Armstrong, Gillespie, Berigan. LPs: Cap. CDs: Jonah Jones–Earl Hines, Chiaro; tracks in *The Keynote Collection* (Merc.); w. S. Smith; Adrian Rollini (Aff.); Calloway (Class.; Col.); Benny Carter (BB); Teddy Wilson (Hep); Eddie Condon (Jazz.); Holiday (Col.).

JONES, LEROY JOSEPH JR., tpt, flg; b. New Orleans, LA, 2/20/58. Cousin Isaac Banks pl. tbn.; cousin Sinclair Banks, cl. Stud. in mus. programs of local sch. system 1968. Began on gtr., then to crnt., tpt., bari. horn. Became involved in mus. prof. "growing up in a neighborhood surrounded by veteran musicians. Danny Barker helped me get started." At 13 join. Barker's Fairview Baptist Church Christian Marching Band, perf. as "Little Louis Armstrong" at Super Bowl VI and pl. at the NO J&HF '71, '73. Form. the Hurricane Brass Band '74 and pl. w. it to '76. Worked w. Leroy Bates and Hot Corp. Inc. '76–7; Hollis Carmouche '78–80; also app. in *One Mo' Time* in this period. Founded qnt., New Orleans' Finest, '80–3, incl. gig in Netherlands Nov. '82; also worked w. Louisiana Repertory Jazz Ensemble and Young Tuxedo Brass Band in these yrs. Later tour. Can. w. Eddie Vinson; opened NO's Intercontinental Hotel w. Della Reese. This led to concert tours in Eur., Asia. He remained in Singapore '85–6 w. Camellia Jazz band at Holiday Inn Parkview Hotel. After lead. New Orleans' Finest again '89–90, old friend Harry Connick Jr. asked him to join his new bb and he worked w. him '90–4. In '95 he form. his own qnt. and rec. for Connick's Noptee label. Favs: Armstrong, C. Brown, M. Davis. TV: *Tonight Show; Late Night*; Arsenio Hall. Film: soundtrack for *Sleepless in Seattle* on "A Wink and a Smile." CDs: Noptee/Sony; w. Connick (Col.); Lillian Boutte (Blues Beacon).

JONES, OLIVER THEOPHILUS, pno; b. Montreal, Que., Canada, 9/11/34. Studied w. Daisy Peterson Sweeny, Oscar Peterson's sister, for 12 yrs; was hired for gigs as novelty pnst. in local clubs at age 9 by Peterson's bro. Chuck. His career as jazz pnst. was seriously delayed by a nineteen-year stint as singer Kenny Hamilton's accomp. In 1983 rec. the first of many albums on the Canadian Justin Time label and established himself int'l as a swinging pnst. in the tradition of Peterson and Tatum. Perf. in pops concert w. Montreal Symph. at Montreal JF

'88; duo concert w. Hank Jones at Monterey JF '89; pl. at '90 Montreal JF w. Clark Terry, Herb Ellis, Red Mitchell, and Ed Thigpen; perf. two concerts for Nelson Mandela in Namibia, Africa, and Montreal '90. Several apps. at Lionel Hampton JF in Idaho in '90s. CDs: JT.

JONES, PHILLY JOE (JOSEPH RUDOLPH), dms, lead; b. Philadelphia, PA, 7/15/23; d. Philadelphia, 8/30/85. Played dms. fr. age 4; stud. w. moth., a pno. teacher; dms. w. Cozy Cole. Pl. for several yrs. in local gps., backing D. Gordon, F. Navarro, and other name jazz mus. when they pl. in Phila. Served in army fr. '41; moved to NYC in '47, pl. at various clubs. In '49 worked w. B. Webster in Wash., D.C.; also pl. w. Joe Morris, Tiny Grimes, L. Hampton late '40s. Ret. to NYC '52, pl. at the Downbeat club w. Miles Davis; L. Konitz; Z. Sims. Worked w. Tony Scott '53; T. Dameron '54. Achieved major recognition through his work w. Davis '55–58 and thereafter on and off to '62. Also led own gps. in late '50s and early '60s. Pl. w. Gil Evans '59. Spent much of '64–6 freelancing in LA and SF; visited Japan in '65 w. show feat. four dmrs. After pl. the Berlin JF in '67 w. S. Vaughan and Erroll Garner, decided to remain in Eur. While living in London '67–9, Brit. mus. union prevented him fr. perf., but was active teaching in sch. he organized in Hampstead. Resettled in Paris '69–72; taught w. Kenny Clarke; pl. w. own gp. at Chat Qui Peche; did freelance recs. Dur. this period pl. throughout Eur. w. Slide Hampton; Della Reese; et al.; tour. w. trio opposite Clarke-Boland orch. in Eng.; on own in Italy; Netherlands, Yugoslavia w. D. Goykovich. Led clinics in Stuttgart; own qnt. in Munich. Ret. to Phila. '72, led own gp; form. jazz-rock band, Le Gran Prix '75. Worked w. Bill Evans late '70s; tour. w. Red Garland. In '81 helped form the band Dameronia, which he led, dedicated to the music of T. Dameron. In '84 app. w. Archie Shepp and Amiri Baraka in a jazz and poetry program. A key figure in modern drumming, Jones was cited by Ralph Gleason in the '60s as "the greatest drummer in jazz today." He was as effective playing brushes w. a pnst. as when he played cross-rhythms on cymbals, snare and bass drum w. a larger gp. Along w. Elvin Jones was one of the most electrifying dmrs. to influence jazz in late '50s to mid '60s. Talented dialectician and mimic. Favs: Cozy Cole, Sid Catlett. Fests.: Austria w. D. Gordon, B. Webster. CDs: Riv.; BL; Gal.; Sonet; w. M. Davis (Prest., Col.); Bill Evans (Riv.; Fant.); Dameron (Prest.; Riv.); Elmo Hope (BN; Riv.; Mile); D. Gordon (BN); C. Adderley; C. Baker, B. Golson (Riv.); C. Brown; Coltrane (Prest.; BN); Dorham; K. Drew; A. Farmer; Bennie Green (Prest.); Garland (Gal.; Prest.); Sonny Clark; H.

Mobley; Quebec (BN); R. Rodney (Sav.); Rollins (Prest.; BN).

JONES, QUINCY DELIGHT JR., comp, tpt, pno, lead; b. Chicago, IL, 3/14/33. To Seattle at age 10; tpt. fr. 1947, w. first lessons fr. Clark Terry '50. To Bost. '51, won scholarship to Schillinger House (later known as Berklee Sch. of Mus.), where he stud. before pl. w. L. Hampton for two yrs. Fr. Nov. '53 freelanced in NYC as arr. for O. Pettiford; Art Farmer; Ray Anthony; Count Basie; James Moody; et al. Mus. dir., arr., and member of brass section for Dizzy Gillespie band that traveled under St. Dept. auspices in Near East and So. America '56–7. Left for Paris, May '57; stud. w. Nadia Boulanger; arr. and cond. for Barclay Recs. In '59 organized all-star band to tour w. Harold Arlen blues opera *Free and Easy*. After show closed in Paris in '60, the band was kept together for tours of Eur. and US. In '61 appointed to an a&r job w. Mercury Recs; became vice president '64; fr. '64 to '66 rec. as lead.; also mus. dir. and arr. for Peggy Lee; Sinatra; Eckstine; et al.; numerous apps. as cond. of Count Basie Orch. dur. gigs w. Sinatra. Began career as film writer in '60s, starting w. Swedish picture, *The Boy in the Tree*, followed by American movies *The Pawnbroker; Mirage; The New Centurions; The Hot Rock; The Anderson Tapes; Cactus Flower; In Cold Blood* (for which he won an Oscar in '67); *In the Heat of the Night; The Color Purple*. His TV themes include *Sanford and Son*, themes and other music for various Bill Cosby shows. Also arr. and cond. 43rd Annual Academy Awards presentation '71; many Grammy award shows and other presentations. Dur. the '70s cont. to rec. w. a bb, but his albums became increasingly pop-oriented. In the fall of '74 suffered two brain aneurisms. Two serious operations kept him on the sidelines until March '75, when he reassembled an orch. and toured Japan. In '80 founded his own label, Qwest, and moved primarily into the pop field, producing for many companies, including Columbia, working w. such pop acts as Aretha Franklin; Michael Jackson (*Thriller*), etc. His own album, *Back on the Block*, made brief use of jazz artists (Sarah Vaughan, Joe Zawinul, etc.) in a hybrid setting mixing elements of rap, hip-hop, jazz, etc. In '92 made a co-production deal w. Time-Warner to produce film, TV, records, and publish magazines incl. *Vibe*. A gifted and original jazz arranger-composer, Jones regrettably abandoned his association w. jazz in favor of commercial ventures, although his Qwest label has feat. releases by Milt Jackson, etc. Comps: "Work of Art"; "Stockholm Sweetnin'"; "For Lena and Lennie"; "Jessica's Day." CDs: WB; Imp.; Merc.; R&T; A&M; TCB; w. C. Brown; A. Farmer (Prest.); Gillepie (Verve; CAP); Sinatra-Basie (Rep.).

JONES, RANDY (RANDALL), dms; b. Slough, England, 1/23/44. Self-taught fr. age 11. Pl. in rock and r&b bands in German clubs fr. teenage yrs. Worked in London studios 1965–7; in Engl. w. Maynard Ferguson '67–72. Moved to NYC '73; pl. w. Chet Baker; Bill Watrous bb; Harry James; Buddy DeFranco; Jackie Paris–Anne Marie Moss. Taught at Bridgeport U. '76–8. Pl. w. Dave Brubeck Qt. fr. '79. Favs: Elvin Jones, P.J. Jones, Bellson. Fests: all major. Film: soundtrack of *Ordeal by Innocence* w. Brubeck. TV: *Tonight Show* w. Brubeck. CDs: w. Brubeck (Conc.; Tel.); Ferguson (Col.).

JONES, REUNALD SR., tpt; b. Indianapolis, IN, 12/22/10. Cousin of Roy Eldridge. After debut in Midwest, worked w. Speed Webb, Chick Webb, Willie Bryant, Don Redman in 1930s; Erskine Hawkins, J. Lunceford, D. Ellington '40s; C. Basie '52–7; W. Herman '59; G. Shearing bb '59; then tour. w. Nat Cole's acc. orch., after which he was largely inactive. CDs: w. Lil Armstrong; D. Redman; C. Webb (Class.); Basie (Verve); Benny Carter (JSP).

JONES, RICHARD M(ARINEY; aka MYKNEE), pno, comp; b. Donaldson, LA, 6/13/1892; d. Chicago, IL, 12/8/45. Studied pno. as a child, later w. Richard "Fishing Bread" Barret; also stud. alto horn, crnt., pipe organ. Pl. alto horn and crnt. w. Eureka Brass Band 1902. Fr. '08 to '17 was one of the most prominent pnsts. in NO bordellos, incl. Lulu White's, Josie Arlington's. Also led own bands in clubs; pl. w. various NO bands such as John Robichaux, A. J. Piron. Start. comp. '15; one of his first songs, "Lonesome Nobody Cares," was perf. by Sophie Tucker. Pl. w. Papa Celestin '18; then moved to Chi. '19, worked for Clarence Williams' publ. company. Pl. w. Bernie Young, Willie Hightower, but mainly org. many rec. sess. for OK '25–8. Accomp. Chippie Hill '25–6; led own gp., Jazz Wizards, for many sess. on OK, Vict., Gennett, Para. Ret. to NO '31–2 but went back to Chi. '34, rec. for Dec. '35 w. Herschel Evans; Louis Metcalf; others. Throughout '30 was active as songwriter; acted as talent scout for several rec. companies; occ. tour. w. own bands. Dur. WWII worked at Foote Bros., a defense plant in Chi. His final rec. date was for Session in '44. He cont. to perform until he died. He was the comp. of many songs whose authorship was subsequently much disputed, incl.: "Jazzin' Babies Blues"; "Trouble in Mind"; "Riverside Blues"; "29th and Dearborn"; "Red Wagon." CDs: w. Louis Armstrong (Aff.).

JONES, RODNEY BRUCE, gtr, comp, arr, bs; b. New Haven, CT, 8/30/56. Uncle Eugene Wayman Jones is pnst., cond., choir dir., taught at Fisk U. and founded Heritage House in Phila. Grew up in Nashville and NYC; also lived in Phila. Began on pno. and cello; gtr. at age 6. Stud. gtr. w. Bruce Johnson, also Alex Pascual, Al Gafa; pno. w. John Lewis at City Coll., NY. Pl. w. Jaki Byard's Music Complex Orch. 1975; Chico Hamilton '76; Dizzy Gillespie '76–8. Tour. Eur. w. own gp. w. Kenny Kirkland, Ben Brown, Ronnie Burrage. Gtrst. and arr. w. Lena Horne fr. '83. Rec. w. Maceo Parker; Bill Cosby; Fred Wesley; Kenny Burrell; Stan Getz; Vincent Herring; Tommy Flanagan; Lorez Alexandria; Hilton Ruiz; Ruth Brown; Candy Dulfer; Grover Washington; many others. Worked extens. as a studio mus. and has taught at Manh. Sch. of Mus. fr. '88. His comps. have been rec. by Gillespie; Horne; R. Brown; K. Burrell; Jimmy McGriff; V. Herring. Favs: Wes Montgomery, Grant Green, Bruce Johnson, Pat Metheny. Fests: all major. TV: Merv Griffin '83; *Cosby Show; A Different World; Showtime at the Apollo.* CDs: MM; w. M. Parker (Verve); J. McGriff (Tel.); Horne (BN); Ruiz (Novus).

JONES, RUFUS (aka SPEEDY), dms; b. Charleston, SC, 5/27/36; d. Las Vegas, NV, 4/25/90. Played tpt. in elem. sch. band, then sw. to dms. at age 13. Pl. first prof. gig w. 15-pc. band led by Brant Bassell. Att. Florida A&M on scholarship. Moved to NYC ca. '54. Rec. w. Lionel Hampton in Amsterdam '54. Pl. in NYC w. Hampton '58; Red Allen, Sol Yaged at Metropole '59; Maynard Ferguson '59–63; own qnt. '63–4; Count Basie Orch. '64–6; own gp., house band at Apollo Theater '66; Duke Ellington '66–73. Examples of his dynamic playing can be heard in Ellington's *Far East Suite*. Favs: Roach, Rich, Bellson, P. J. Jones, Blakey. CDs: w. M. Ferguson (Roul.); Basie (Verve); Ellington (BB; Fant.; Atl.); J. Hodges (BB).

JONES, RUSTY (ISHAM RUSSELL II), dms; b. Cedar Rapids, IA, 4/13/32. Great-nephew and godson of bandleader Isham Jones; both parents were prof. musicians. Stud. at U. of Iowa 1960–5; while in sch. pl. w. J. R. Monterose. Pl. w. Judy Roberts in Chi. '68–72; G. Shearing '72–5. Also freelanced in '70s w. Lee Konitz; Mose Allison; Monty Alexander; Ike Cole; Eddie Higgins; Warren Chiasson. Taught at workshops '80s. CDs: w. Grappelli (MPS; Verve); J-L. Ponty; Shearing (MPS).

JONES, SAM (SAMUEL), bs, cello, comp; b. Jacksonville, FL, 11/12/24; d. NYC, 12/15/81. Father pl. pno.; second cousin was Al Hall. Stud. dms. and gtr. while in sch.; pl. dms. in sch. marching band. Pl. w. Tiny Bradshaw in Cincinnati 1953–5; then moved to NYC, still w. Bradshaw, but also worked w. Les Jazz

Modes, K. Dorham '56; I. Jacquet, C. Adderley '57; D. Gillespie '58–9; T. Monk '59. Rejoin. Adderley '59, remaining w. him to '65; contributed several comps. to band's book. Pl. w. O. Peterson '66–9, incl. world tours, JATP. Resettled in NYC '69, worked w. B. Timmon, W. Kelly early '70s; Thad Jones–Mel Lewis qnt, Bass Choir fr. '69; Cedar Walton '71. In late '70s co-led a big band w. Tom Harrell. Orig. inspired by the Lunceford, Basie, and Eckstine bands and early Parker and Gillespie records. Favs: Blanton, R. Brown, Pettiford, Al Hall. Excellent accompanist w. strong walking lines, full of apt, powerfully resilient notes; adept soloist on both bs. and cello. Fests: NJF-NY; major Eur. events. Mus. of the Year, Copenhagen '69. TV: apps. w. Peterson; Bass Choir; C. Terry. Comps: "In Walked Ray"; "Blues for Amos"; "Del Sasser"; "Unit 7." CDs: Riv.; w. Monk; N. Adderley; C. Baker; Blue Mitchell; Bill Evans; W. Montgomery; M. Jackson; Barry Harris; B. Timmons (Riv.); O. Peterson (MPS; Pab.); G. Ammons (Prest.); C. Adderley (Riv.; BN; Mile.; Cap.); Red Garland (Prest.); D. Gordon; N-H. Ø. Pedersen; D. Jordan (Steep.); Stitt (32); Ellington; J. Hodges (Verve); R. Rodney (Muse); J. J. Johnson (Col).

JONES, SLICK (WILMORE), dms; b. Roanoke, VA, 4/13/07; d. NYC, 11/2/69. Studied w. fath. Prof. debut in 1925 w. John Lockslayer. To NYC on scholarship at Damrosch Cons. Pl. w. F. Henderson '35–6; F. Waller on and off to '42; Stuff Smith '42; Una Mae Carlisle, Eddie South '43; Louis Jordan '44; also. w. Claude Hopkins, Hazel Scott, Don Redman mid-'40s. Join. Gene Sedric '46–54; Wilbur De Paris '54; also worked w. De Paris, Doc Cheatham, et al. in Bost. '55. Active again in NYC fr. '59 w. Scoville Brown; Eddie Durham fr. early '60s. After recovering fr. a serious illness in '64 remained fairly active until he died. CDs: w. L. Hampton; F. Waller (BB); Bechet (Mos.; BN).

JONES, SNAGS (CLIFFORD), dms; b. New Orleans, LA, 1900; d. Chicago, IL, 1/31/47. Played w. Buddy Petit, Jack Carey, Papa Celestin, A. J. Piron early 1920s; King Oliver '24; Richard M. Jones, Chippie Hill, Sara Martin '26; State St. Ramblers, Junie Cobb, Jimmy Wade '28. Moved to Milwaukee, then to Chi. in the early '30s. Led own band in Chi. '34. Rec. w. Arthur Sims (OK) '26; Richard M. Jones (Vict.) '29; Punch Miller (Session) '45; pl. w. Bunk Johnson, Darnell Howard '46. Jones acq. his nickname on account of the gaps between his teeth. CDs: w. Junie Cobb (Collector's Classics); Kid Howard; Punch Miller (Amer. Mus.).

JONES, THAD (THADDEUS JOSEPH), tpt, flg, lead, comp, arr; b. Pontiac, MI, 3/28/23; d. Copen-

hagen, Denmark, 8/20/86. Brother of Hank and Elvin Jones. Together they had their own combo in late 1930s. Worked in Saginaw w. S. Stitt; local bands. Pl. in army bands. tour. overseas '43–6. After discharge led own band in Okla. City; w. Billy Mitchell in Det. '50–3. Active w. C. Mingus's Jazz Composers' Workshop '54–5. Became prominent w. C. Basie '54–63. In early '60s wrote for Harry James, Basie. Pl. Lincoln Center w. T. Monk; worked w. G. Mulligan; NJF and Eur. tour w. George Russell '64. Staff mus. at CBS-TV fall '64; form. qnt. w. Pepper Adams '65. In December of that yr. assembled an 18-piece orch. w. Mel Lewis made up of some of the best of NYC jazzmen, who were mainly employed as studio mus. The band debuted at the Village Vanguard in Feb. '66 and quickly acquired a loyal following. Recs. expanded its audience and the Thad Jones–Mel Lewis Orch. became active on the coll. and festival circuit and tour. int'l. Although Jones left the band in the late '70s, the orchestra (subsequently called the Mel Lewis Jazz Orch., then the Vanguard Jazz Orch.) has played at the Vanguard on Monday nights ever since its debut. Early personnel incl: Adams, Jerome Richardson, Jerry Dodgion reeds; Snooky Young, Marvin Stamm tpt.; Bob Brookmeyer, Garnett Brown tbn; Hank Jones pno; Richard Davis bs. Later members incl. Roland Hanna; Jon Faddis; Jimmy Knepper; Billy Harper; George Mraz; Cecil Bridgewater. In the early yrs., writers such as Brookmeyer, Garnett Brown, and Tom McIntosh helped build the band's book, but the majority of the charts were comp. and arr. by Jones. He was an extremely personal writer and a master of phrasing and subtle voicings, who used flutes, reeds, and muted brass ingeniously. "I tried to write for each individual and think of the musicians personally," said Jones. "You have to gear your writing to two different people and still retain your overall technical sound." He led the band, interspersing his piquant, harmonically rich flugelhorn solos to advantage among the arranged segments. Miles Davis once said: "I'd rather hear Thad Jones miss a note than hear Freddie Hubbard make twelve." In between the orch.'s engagements, Jones and Lewis sometimes led a small gp. for gigs in the NYC area. In '79 Jones left his partnership w. Lewis and moved to Denmark, where he had already worked as lead. of Radioens Big Band '77–8. Form. new big band, the Thad Jones Eclipse, which rec. in '79–80. Ret. to US '85 to lead Count Basie Orch., remaining w. band until Feb. '86. Polls: *DB* Critics New Star tpt. '56; as arr. '67; w. Jones-Lewis Orch.: New Star '66; best big band '74–5; *DB* Readers 72–5; *Playboy* All-Stars' All-Stars '75. Comps: "Mean What You Say"; "Consummation;" "Big Dipper"; "Central Park North"; "A Child Is Born"; "Little Pixie"; *Suite for Pops.* Two volumes of Jones's music, pl. by the Mel Lewis Jazz Orch., were released by MusicMasters. CDs: Deb.; JA; BN; Steep; Jones-Lewis, MM, LRC, WW; Thad Jones–Kenny Burrell–Frank Wess, *After Hours,* Prest.; Jones–Pepper Adams, Mile.; w. Basie (Verve; Roul.); Monk (Riv.); Mingus (Deb.); P. Adams (FS); Brookmeyer (Sonet); Burrell (Fant.); K. Drew; H. Parlan (Steep.); Hancock; Joe Henderson (BN); C. Fuller; F. Wess (Sav.); J. J. Johnson; S. Rollins; Joe Williams (BB); M. Jackson; Elvin Jones; Ben Webster (Riv.); Tyner (Imp.); Jimmy Smith (Verve).

JONES, VICTOR F., dms, tpt; b. Newark, NJ, 9/25/54. Brother is percussionist in SF area. Began on tpt. at age 11; dms. at 12. Pl. in rock bands fr. age 15. Stud. classical tpt. for ten yrs. w. Robert Blumenthal, Chas. Hansen. Also stud. at Jazzmobile Wkshp.; Berklee Coll. of Mus. 1973; drum lessons w. Elvin Jones; Freddie Waits; Ed Blackwell. First prof. gig w. Lou Donaldson '73. Made jazz rec. debut w. Jimmy Ponder '76. Tour. w. Johnny Mathis '77; Stan Getz '77–8; Geo. Adams–Don Pullen '81; James Moody '82; Woody Shaw '83; Lanie Kazan '84; Freddie Hubbard, Ramsey Lewis, Gato Barbieri, Stanley Clarke, Phyllis Hyman, Angela Bofill '86; Richie Cole '87; Stanley Turrentine '89; Mino Cinelu '90; Gonzalo Rubalcaba–Charlie Haden '91; Chaka Khan, Mal Waldron, Michel Petrucciani '92. Pl. dms. and tpt. in own gp., Victor Jones R&B-Bop Band fr. '91. Taught at Newark Community Center of the Arts '75–80; New School '89–91. Active in downtown NYC small club scene in '90s. Favs: Blakey, E. Jones, Mitch Mitchell; tpt.: M. Davis, Bill Bruford. Fests: all major fr. '77. Film: app. w. Stan Getz in *The Exterminator: Forest Eyes.* TV: Dick Cavett, Mike Douglas w. Getz; PBS w. Leo Johnson; also Eur., Jap. TV. CDs: Satellites; w. Getz (Col.; RCA); Petrucciani (BN); V. Ponomarev (Res.); Richie Cole (Conc.; Mile.); Donaldson (Timel.); Chico Freeman (BS; JH); Ed Schuller (Tutu); Woody Shaw (Muse).

JONES, VIRGIL, tpt, flg; b. Indianapolis, IN, 8/26/39. First stud. tpt. at Crispus Attucks HS w. Russell Brown. David Baker helped him to join Lionel Hampton 1960. Tour. w. Hampton into '63, incl. trips to Eur., Arg., Nigeria, Japan. Worked around NYC w. Johnny "Hammond" Smith for a yr.; then pl. Latin gigs in Bklyn. and the Bronx. Ret. to the road w. Ray Charles '67–8, incl. Austral. tour. '67. Back in NYC bec. involved w. studio scene. Did B'way show starring Muhammad Ali but "it didn't get off the ground." Pl. in Bobby Rosengarden band on Dick Cavett TV show; Mondays nights at the Vanguard w. Thad Jones–Mel Lewis Orch. and many other jobs for about two yrs. Rec. often as sideman w. various

artists on Prest. label. App. w. I. Jacquet bb; American Jazz Orch.; Smithsonian Masterworks Orch.; Jimmy Heath; Frank Foster; Barry Harris; Charles Davis; Larry Ridley's Jazz Legacy Ens.; McCoy Tyner bb. Member of Dizzy Gillespie bb on tour to Eur., Japan '87, '88. Pl. w. Dameronia '83–9. A valued, versatile section man and accomplished soloist. Favs: Gillespie, C. Brown, F. Hubbard, et al. Film: *She's Gotta Have It.* B'way: *Ain't Misbehavin'; Black and Blue; Jelly's Last Jam.* CDs: w. Milt Jackson (Riv.); Benny Carter (MM); Tyner (Mile.; Bird.); Dameronia (SN); F. Foster (Denon); RR Kirk (Merc.); S. Stitt; H. Mabern; I. Muhammad; Don Patterson (Prest.); J. De Francesco (Col.); C. Earland (Mile.); Billy Harper (BS); Jimmy Heath; Joe Henderson (Verve); Teddy Edwards (High.); TS Monk (N2K); C. Terry (Chiaro.).

JONES, WILLIE (WILLIAM), dms; b. Brooklyn, NY, 10/20/29; d. Brooklyn, 4/9/93. Mainly self-taught. Pl. and rec. w. Thelonious Monk 1953; also pl. in mid '50s w. Cecil Payne; Joe Holiday; Charlie Parker; Kenny Dorham; J. J. Johnson; Lester Young. Rec. w. Elmo Hope '55; Randy Weston '56. Member of C. Mingus's first Jazz Workshop '55–6. In his later yrs. he did much community work incl. getting jazz programs into the public sch. system. Favs: Roach, K. Clarke, Blakey. CDs: w. Monk; Hope (Prest.); Mingus (Deb.; Atl.); L. Young (Jass).

JOPLIN, SCOTT, pno, comp; b. Texarkana, TX, 11/24/1868; d. NYC, 4/11/17. Self-taught until stud. w. German pno. teacher at age 11. Prominent as soloist in St. Louis and Chi. 1890s. Perf. at Chi. World's Fair 1893. Then relocated to Sedalia, Mo., where he became very popular. After another residency in St. Louis moved to NYC '07, but his career went into decline due to illness. Best known as composer of ragtime piano pieces such as "Maple Leaf Rag" 1899 and "The Entertainer" '02, which infl. such early jazz pnsts. as Jelly Roll Morton. Other comps. incl. "Easy Winners"; "Original Rag"; "Sugar Cane Rag"; "Wall Street Rag." Wrote an opera, *Treemonisha* '11, which he produced at his own expense for a single performance in Harlem in '15. Film: the use of his music, particularly "The Entertainer," in *The Sting* '73, sparked a ragtime revival. Book: *King of Ragtime,* Edward A. Berlin (Oxford) '94. CD: *King of Ragtime Writers,* recs. of his piano rolls (Biog.).

JORDAN, CLIFFORD LACONIA, tnr sax, comp; b. Chicago, IL, 9/2/31; d. NYC, 3/27/93. Started on pno.; tnr. sax at age 14. Att. Du Sable HS w. Johnny Griffin; John Gilmore; John Jenkins; et al. To NYC, tour. w. Max Roach, Horace Silver 1957–8; J. J. Johnson '59–60. Formed qnt. w. Kenny Dorham '61–2; in '62 led own gp. w. Andrew Hill, J. C. Moses. Rejoin. Roach '63; Eur. tour w. C. Mingus '64; w. Roach again '65. Worked in Eur. and Africa '69–70. In '70s tour. w. own gps. and taught in NYC public sch. and for Jazzmobile; also pl. in the Magic Triangle, a qt. w. Cedar Walton. Active in various forms of jazz educ. and cont. world travels incl. West Africa/Middle East w. Randy Weston '67 and Senegal w. Dizzy Gillespie '80. Worked often w. Barry Harris qt.; Art Farmer qnt. '80s and '90s. In early '90s fronted bb weekly at Condon's in NYC; Dizzy Gillespie birthday tribute cruise Oct. '92. A blues-tinged, bop-styled musician w. his own interpretation of Lester Young, Jordan's inventiveness w. personal touches earned him respect among the avant-garde of the '60s as well as the fusion players of the '70s. Favs: Young, Rollins, Coltrane, Byas, Mobley. CDs: Mile.; Riv.; Jzld.; Muse; Steep.; SN; CC; DIW; Maple.; w. Dameronia (SN); Dolphy (WW); Farmer (SN; Cont.); Gillespie (Tel.); S. Hampton (CC); John Hicks (Evid.); C. McRae (Den.; Novus); Mingus (Enja; Deb.); Andrew Hill; Mingus bb (SN); Lee Morgan (Jzld.); Fathead Newman (Cand.); Roach (Fant.; Imp.); Cees Slinger (Timel.); C. Walton (Prest.; Steep.; 32).

JORDAN, DUKE (IRVING SIDNEY), pno, comp; b. NYC 4/1/22; d. Valby, Denmark, 8/8/06. Private classical stud. 1930–8; pl. in band at Brooklyn Automotive HS. After grad. join. Steve Pulliam combo, which won prize at NY World's Fair, '39. In '41 pl. w. Clarke Monroe Sxt., which later worked under Coleman Hawkins' leadership at Kelly's Stable. Pl. w. Al Cooper's Savoy Sultans, Roy Eldridge bb at Spotlite on 52nd St. '46. Heard by Charlie Parker while working w. Teddy Walters trio at the Three Deuces. Pl. off and on beginning in '47 for three yrs. w. Parker; became an integral part of the bebop scene. Pl. w. Sonny Stitt and Gene Ammons '50–1; Stan Getz '52–3; 4 mos. w. Eldridge; then Oscar Pettiford and many gps. in and around NYC incl. his own trio. Dur. '50s often pl. w. Cecil Payne; rec. w. Rolf Ericson in Sweden '56. In '59 went to Paris where he co-wrote, w. Jacques Marray, soundtrack mus., incl. "No Problem," for Vadim's *Les Liaisons Dangereuses*. Pl at Open End club, NYC, in '60s. After a hiatus, returned to mus. in early '70s, pl. many NYC duo gigs at Bradley's; Churchill's; etc. Tour. Scandinavia, Netherlands, '73–4 and '77–8, settling in Denmark '78. At a time when many were overwhelmed by Bud Powell, Jordan stood out w. his own touch and rhythmic attack while working in a similar harmonic area. His time w. Parker marked him as a master of introductions. Comps.: "Jordu," which

became a jazz standard; "Flight to Jordan"; "Two Loves"; "Subway Inn." Dur. '50s he was married to singer Sheila Jordan. CDs: Sav.; Steep.; w. Parker (Sav.; Dial); Getz (Verve; Roul.); G. Ammons; w. Don Lanphere in *Prestige First Sessions, Vol. 1* (Prest.); C. Baker; Doug Raney (Steep.); K. Burrell (BN); Stitt (Prest.; Muse); C. Payne; P. Woods; G. Gryce (Sav.); C. Hawkins; Eldridge (Dec); E. Bert (FS).

JORDAN, LOUIS, voc, alto sax, lead; b. Brinkley, AR, 7/8/08; d. Los Angeles, CA, 2/4/75. Studied cl. and sax w. fath. fr. 1915. Pl. w. Ruby Williams in Hot Springs, Ark.; then moved to Phila. where he join. Charlie Gaines in '30. To NYC w. Gaines '34, and occ. ret. to gig w. him in Phila. even after he established a residence in NYC. Short stint w. Kaiser Marshall's band, before join. Leroy Smith's orch. In summer '35 worked w. him in NYC, Cleveland, and Atlantic City into '36. That summer he join. Chick Webb, w. whom he was heard on alto sax and occ. vocals '36–8. Form. his own gp. in '38 and pl. at the Elks' Rendezvous in Harlem. In the next few yrs. Jordan's combo, which became known as the Tympany Five, enjoyed a slow and steady rise to national fame as Jordan feat. himself in voc. blues and novelties. His major hits were "Knock Me a Kiss" and "I'm Gonna Move to the Outskirts of Town," both rec. '41; "Five Guys Named Moe" '42 "Caldonia" '45; and "Choo Choo Ch' Boogie" '46, the last named ultimately selling over a million records. Rec. duets w. Bing Crosby '44; Ella Fitzgerald '45, '49; L. Armstrong '50. Orig. limited to r&b circles, he broke into the front lines of show business through a unique combination of visual showmanship, good musicianship, a strong accent on humor, and a delightfully original and rhythmic vocal style. His hot, liquid, jump-alto style contributed to the overall excitement of his performances. Jordan is generally considered to be the progenitor of the small-gp. r&b idiom that led, dur. the '50s, to the rise of rock 'n' roll. Departing fr. his usual format, he org. a bb for a tour in the fall of '51 and occ. expanded for theater dates. In the early '50s he was intermittently inactive, owing to illness, and confined himself to his Ariz. home but came back strong in the mid '50s. For three yrs., '60–2, he worked as a single. Tour. Engl. in Dec. '62, pl. concerts w. Chris Barber. The following yr. he reorganized w. a new instrumentation feat. an org. The gp. pl. leading nightclubs, Nevada lounges, and service clubs throughout the US. Tour. Asia '67, '68. Thereafter cont. working intermittently, living in LA and lead. a new version of his Tympany Five until Oct. '74, when he was sidelined by a heart attack while working in Sparks, Nev. A second attack proved fatal. His mus. inspired the British production (later on

B'way) *Five Guys Named Moe*. Fests: NJF-NY '74. Films: *Follow the Boys; Meet Miss Bobby Sox* '44; *Swing Parade of '46*; numerous shorts. Comps.: *Five Guys Named Moe*; "Is You Is..."; "Choo Choo Ch' Boogie"; "Saturday Night Fish Fry." CDs: Dec.; Evid.; Rh.; Merc.; Verve; BN; Class.; B&B; Jordan–Chris Barber, BL; w. Armstrong (BB); C. Webb; Fitzgerald (Dec.)

JORDAN, MARLON, tpt, comp; b. New Orleans, LA, 8/21/70. Youngest of seven children of tnr. saxist, mus.-educ. Edward "Kidd" Jordan. Start. on sax, vln., and dms., then moved to tpt. in fourth grade. Stud. priv. and at NOCCA. Became friendly w. Wynton Marsalis. Pl. in local clubs, summer camp sessions at Tanglewood. As a hs freshman auditioned for the NO Symph. and became a feat. soloist 1986–7. First rec. w. his bro., flst. Kent Jordan. After the release of his own album, *For You Only* '90, tour. w. his gp. and also tour. int'l as a member of the Jazz Futures. Ret. to NO, resurfacing in '97 w. a new rec. for Arabesque. CDs: Col.; Arab.; w. Jazz Futures (Novus); Dennis Gonzalez (Silk.); Donald Harrison (Cand.).

JORDAN, SHEILA JEANETTE (née Dawson), voc; b. Detroit, MI, 11/18/29. Raised in Summerhill, Pa., then ret. to Det. while in hs. Stud. pno. 1940–1; harmony, theory w. Lennie Tristano '51–2. Sang dur. sch. yrs.; later, strongly infl. by Charlie Parker, she was part of a trio that wrote words for many of Parker's tunes. Moved to NYC '51. Married to Duke Jordan '52–62. Perf. reg. at Page Three club in Greenwich Vill. early '60s. Discovered by Geo. Russell, who recommended her to Blue Note label '62 Toured US and Eur. '60s-70s. Fr. '65 she perf. jazz liturgies at churches and coll. chapels incl. Cornell, Princeton, NYU. Pl. w. Don Heckman '67–8; Lee Konitz '72; Roswell Rudd '72–5; also jingles, TV work. Artist-in-res. at City College '74. Formed band w. Steve Kuhn '79. Worked in duo w. Harvie Swartz '80s. Jordan is also an accomplished songwriter, whose repertory incl. free jazz, bebop scat choruses, and settings of contemporary American poetry. CDs: BN; Steep.; Muse; w. G. Russell (Riv.); G. Gruntz (TCB); Carla Bley (ECM).

JORDAN, STANLEY, gtr; b. Chicago, IL, 7/31/59. Began on pno. at age 6, then sw. to gtr. at 11. Pl. in rock and soul bands while in sch. Won awd. at Reno, Nev. JF 1976. Stud. electronic mus., theory, comp. at Princeton U. (B. Mus. '81 Pl. w. Dizzy Gillespie, Benny Carter while in coll. Rec. self-prod. debut album as unaccomp. soloist '82. Perf. at Kool, Conc., and Montreux JFs '84–5. Came to prominence w.

commercial success of second album, *Magic Touch*, prod. by Al Di Meola, w. sidemen Onaje Allen Gumbs, Charnett Moffett, Omar Hakim '85. Also pl. in '80s w. Quincy Jones; Michal Urbaniak; Richie Cole. Jordan is noted for his unusual technique. He taps the strings w. both hands, which allows him to pl. contrapuntal lines and comp against his own solos. CDs: BN.

JORDAN, STEVE (STEPHEN PHILIP), gtr; b. NYC 1/15/19; d. Alexandria, VA, 9/13/93. Studied w. Allan Reuss. Prof. debut w. Will Bradley 1939–41; Artie Shaw '41–2; navy band w. Saxie Dowell '42–5; then w. Bob Chester, Freddie Slack. Pl. and rec. w. Glen Gray '45. Rec. w. Johnny Bothwell '45; Boyd Raeburn '44–5, '47. Pl. w. Stan Kenton, J. Dorsey '47, then left mus. to work in prod. dept. at NBC '50–2. Pl. w. Benny Goodman off and on '53–6; Ruby Braff '56–8. Fr. that time almost inactive in mus.; worked in tailor shop '59. Pl. w. Tommy Gwaltney band at Blues Alley, Wash., D.C., fr. '65. Was a regular at Manassas (Va.) JF '66–73. Later worked w. Brooks Tegler's Hot Jazz Band, pl. in Japan. '92. A skilled, strong rhythm gtr. Book: *Rhythm Man: 50 Years in Jazz* co-authored w. Tom Scanlan (U. of Michigan Press) '91. Rec. w. Vic Dickenson; Jimmy Rushing (Vang). CDs: Aud.; w. Bradley (Tax); Goodman (MM); Gene Krupa (Verve); Raeburn (Sav.); Pee Wee Russell (FS); Buck Clayton (Mos.).

JORDAN, (JAMES) TAFT, tpt, voc; b. Florence, SC, 2/15/15; d. NYC, 12/1/81. Played bari. horn in sch. in Norfolk, Va.: finished sch. in Phila.; start. on tpt. in 1929. Pl. w. Doc Hyder in Phila.; join. Chick Webb '33, remaining through E. Fitzgerald's lead. until orch. disbanded in '42. Led own gp. '42; w. D. Ellington '43–7; various bands incl. Lucille Dixon Orch. at the Savannah Club '49–53; tour. w. Don Redman '53; also active as studio mus. Worked w. B. Goodman, incl. Eur. tours '58, '59. In '60s led own qnt.; cont. studio work; pl. for several yrs. on Broadway w. *Hello, Dolly*. App. at E. Fitzgerald tribute NJF-NY '73; NYJRC L. Armstrong tribute '74; w. Earle Warren at West End Cafe '75. Infl. by Armstrong as both player and singer. TV: apps. on *Steve Allen Show*; Jackie Gleason '58. CDs: w. Ellington (BB; Prest.); Goodman (MM); J. Hodges (Prest.; Suisa); Sarah Vaughan; M. Davis (Col.); Webb (Dec.; Hep); Fitzgerald (Dec.); S. Gaillard (Verve).

JOSEPH, JULIAN RAPHAEL NATHANIEL, kybds; b. London, England, 5/11/66. Father, Howard Joseph (Blue Rivers), voc. Stud. pno., cl., perc., Berklee Coll. 1985. Form. own gp. which incl. Courtney Pine among others. Fr. '83 to mid '90s pl. w. C.

Watkiss; J. Toussaint, B. Marsalis; D. Marsalis; Chico Freeman; Von Freeman; Gary Bartz; Bobby McFerrin; Joe Williams. Tour. Eur., US, Can., Australia, Japan. Wrote and rec. score for film, *A Tale of a Vampire* '92. TV: pl. on soundtrack of BBC movies, *Tell Me You Love Me: First Exposure*, plus apps. on *The Late Show, Birdland*, and others. Pl. Gershwin *Concerto in F* and own comp. w. BBC Scottish Symph. '93. Teaches master class and wkshps. at Royal Acad. of Mus. Has won awards fr. DB, NAJE as soloist or member of Berklee Jazz ens. Favs: Ellington, Waller, Monk, Jarrett. Recs. w. Pine, Watkiss, Toussaint, etc. CDs: East West; w. Pine (Island); J. Toussaint (WC); Steve Williamson (Verve).

JURIS, VIC (Victor E. Jurusz Jr.), gtr; b. Jersey City, NJ, 9/26/53. Began sitting in at jam sessions at age 12. Stud. w. Ed Berg, Pat Martino. Pl. w. Eric Kloss 1975–7; Barry Miles '76–80; Don Patterson '76–80; Richie Cole '76–91; Mike Nock '80–3; Sonny Stitt '81; Larry Coryell '84; Michel Legrand '85–6; David Amram '87–91; Phil Woods '90–1. Since '91, Juris has worked w. David Liebman and Gary Peacock, in addition to leading his own qt. w. Tim Hagans, Jay Anderson, and Jeff Hirshfield. Active in educ.; taught at Manh. Sch. of Mus. summer clinics, Castelfranco Veneto, Italy '90s. Favs: Bireli Lagrene, Jim Hall, Chuck Loeb. Fests: Eur., Japan, So. Amer. CDs: Steep.; Muse; Jazzpoint; w. Liebman (Cand.); Lagrene (Inak); R. Cole (Muse; Conc.).

KAHN, TINY (NORMAN), dms, comp, vib; b. NYC, 5/24; d. Martha's Vineyard, MA, 8/19/53. As child won prize pl. hca. Took up dms. at 15 and pl. timp. in hs orch. Worked w. Georgie Auld 1947; Boyd Raeburn '48; Chubby Jackson, Charlie Barnet '49; Stan Getz qnt. '51; Elliot Lawrence on Jack Sterling's daily CBS radio show, mostly on vib. Described by his boyhood friend, Terry Gibbs, as a natural timekeeper and arr., Kahn came out of the Jo Jones tradition and was known for his delicate touch. Self-taught as a writer, he was an infl. on such contemporaries as Johnny Mandel and Al Cohn. He died of a heart attack while on vacation. Rec. comps arrs: "Tiny's Blues" (out chorus by A. Cohn); "Father Knickerbopper," "Flyin' the Coop" for Jackson; "Leo the Lion" for W. Herman. Arrs: "Godchild" for Jackson (on which he scats the theme); "Over the Rainbow" for Barnet. CDs: w. Getz (BN; Mos., Roul.); Red Rodney in *Early Bebop* (Merc.); Jackson in *The Jazz Arranger*, Vol. 2 (Col.); Lester Young (BN).

KALESTI, KIM, voc, pno; b. Pueblo, CO, 6/29/57. Mother pl. vln.; grandfath. pl. acdn. Was known professionally as Kim Shaw prior to early '90s. Stud. w. Roberta Arwood, Delores Vacaro in Colo.; Ray Sullenger in Houston, Tex.; Hal Schaefer in NYC. Sang w. local musical theater fr. 1962; w. two sists. at talent shows, community centers, etc. '62–6. Guest soloist w. Colo. Symph. '66; Houston Pops Orch. '75. Sang w. Arnett Cobb–Kirk Whalum at Houston JF '76. Tour. US and Eur. w. own gp. '77–9. Moved to NYC '80. Perf. at Greene St. Café '80–91. Kalesti perf. w. her then husband Marion Cowings and a 9-pc. band fr. '80 to mid '90s Sidemen incl. Frank Foster; Walter Davis Jr.; Kenny Barron; Bobby Watson; Al Foster; Frank Wess; Larry Willis; Billy Higgins; Ray Anderson; Jimmy Owens; Clark Terry. Perf. as a single in late '90s. Kalesti has taught at NYU fr. '88; New Sch. Jazzmobile Wkshp. '89 Favs: Marion Cowings, Ella Fitzgerald, Tony Bennett, Sarah Vaughan, L,H&R. Fests: Eur. fr. '79; Japan fr. '91. CDs: w. Cowings-Kalesti (Em.)

KAMINSKY, MAX, crnt, tpt; b. Brockton, MA, 9/7/08; d. Castle Point, NY, 9/6/94. Studied w. Henry Pollock in Bost., later w. M. Schlossberg in NYC. Led own band in Bost. fr. 1924. Moved to Chi. '27. Pl. w. Charlie Pearce '28; bands incl. Bud Freeman; Rod Cless; Geo. Wettling; Frank Teschemacher; Jess Stacy; Wingy Manone; Benny Goodman. Tour. New Engl. w. Red Nichols '29. Pl. w. Leo Reisman in Bost. '31–3; Joe Venuti at Delmonico's, NYC '34; Teddy Roy at Cocoanut Grove, Bost. '35; Tommy Dorsey '35–6; Jack Jenney at Onyx Club '36; Artie Shaw; house band at Little Club, Benny Goodman at Pennsylvania Hotel, NYC '37; Summa Cum Laude Band at Nick's, Lee Wiley in Chi. '38; own gp. at NY World's Fair '39; Artie Shaw '40–3; own gps. at Pied Piper, Village Vanguard, Condon's Ryan's, Metropole, etc. fr. '45; society bands, college tours '50s; Jackie Gleason Orch. '60s. App. reg. at Jimmy Ryan's '60s-70s. Kaminsky publ. his autobiog., *Jazz Band; My Life in Jazz*, in '63. Favs: Bix Beiderbecke, Louis Armstrong, Bobby Hackett, Pee Wee Russell. Fests: Eur. w. Jack Teagarden–Earl Hines '57. CDs: Jazz.; w. Art Hodes in *Hot Jazz* box (BN); Pee Wee Russell (Comm.); Jack Teagarden–Pee Wee Russell (Riv.); Teagarden (BB); Shaw (Hep); S. Bechet (BN); Benny Carter (BB; B&B); Freeman; Joe Marsala; Mezz Mezzrow (Class.); E. Condon (Class; Jazz).

KAMUCA, RICHIE (RICHARD), tnr and alto saxes; b. Philadelphia, PA, 7/23/30; d. Los Angeles, CA, 7/22/77. Studied at Mastbaum HS; pl. locally as a teenager w. Ray Bryant; Red Garland; Specs Wright. Worked w. Stan Kenton 1952–3; Woody Herman '54–5; Chet Baker, Maynard Ferguson '57; Lighthouse All-Stars '57–8; Shorty Rogers '59; Shelly Manne '59–61. To NYC, where he freelanced bef. join. Roy Eldridge '66–71; also worked w. Gary McFarland; Gerry Mulligan; Zoot Sims–Al Cohn; Jimmy Rushing; member of Merv Griffin TV show orch., w. which he ret. to LA in '72. Pl. w. Bill Berry bb; co-led qnt. w. Blue Mitchell '75. Visited NYC in spring of that yr. for gig w. Lee Konitz. On tnr., his light-footed, swinging style was derived fr. Lester Young but on one of his three Concord LPs, *Charlie*, he pl. alto w. a Parker infl. CDs: VSOP; HiFi; w. Chet Baker (PJ); B. Berry; R. Brown; Frank Capp (Conc.); Kenny Burrell; Anita O'Day (Verve); Terry Gibbs; Shelly Manne; Art Pepper; Lighthouse All-Stars (Cont.); Lee Konitz (Mile.); S. Kenton (Cap.) Shorty Rogers (BB); Thad Jones–Mel Lewis (LRC).

KANSAS CITY SIX AND SEVEN. A name used for several rec. gps. fr. 1938 into '80s, usually comprising Count Basie sidemen, sometimes incl. Basie himself. The Kansas City Five was an earlier gp. led by Elmer Snowden in '24 and '25; and also a rec. gp. w. Buck Clayton and Eddie Durham that led directly into the Kansas City Six. CDs: Lester Young (Comm.; Verve); Basie (Imp.; Pab.).

KARLSSON, (NILS) STEFAN, pno; b. Vastervik, Sweden, 8/23/65. Father a jazz pnst. To US in '84; stud. for six yrs. at U. of North Texas; toured Mexico, US, and Austral. w. the UNT One O'Clock Band. Worked or rec. w. Herb Ellis; Red Mitchell; Dick Oatts; Marc Johnston; et al. In 1990 signed w. Justice Recs. of Houston, Tex., and freelanced in the Denver, Colo. area. First album, *Room 292*. CDs: Just.; w. Sebastian Whittaker (Just.).

KAROLAK, WOJCIECH, org, pno; b. Warsaw, Poland, 5/2/38. Professional debut w. Jazz Believers 1958; later pl. pno w. J. Matuszkiewicz. Led own trio fr. '62; lived in Sweden fr. '66 to '72. As orgst., pl. w. Red Mitchell, Putte Wickman. Joined Michal Urbaniak '72; pl. clubs, fests., etc. in Germ., Scand., and Benelux countries. In '74 went to US to work w. Urbaniak's gp., Fusion Black. Ret. to Poland to lead gp. called Mainstream. From '84 leader of Karolak Szukalski Bartkowski; active as comp. of jazz-styled works for film and TV. CDs: Jazz Forum; w. Jarek Smietana (Gow; Starling); Urbaniak (Power Bros.).

KATZ, DICK (RICHARD AARON), pno, comp, arr; b. Baltimore, MD, 3/13/24. Studied at Peabody Inst. of Mus. and U. of No. Carolina. In navy 1943–6, then att. Manh. Sch. of Mus. '46–50; stud. w. Teddy Wilson at Juilliard '50. Pl. w. Al Casey on 52nd St. '50; solo pno. at Chez Inez and Ringside in Paris '51; Tony Scott '52–4; Kai Winding–J. J. Johnson '54–5; solo pno. at Music Inn, Lenox, Mass. '56–9; Carmen McRae '59; also extensive freelance in '50s w. Oscar Pettiford; Kenny Dorham; Ben Webster; Chuck Wayne; etc. Pl. w. Philly Joe Jones '60; Jim Hall, Nancy Harrow '61; Orchestra USA '64–5; Bobby Hackett '66; Helen Merrill, Roy Eldridge fr. mid '60s. Worked as prod. for Mile. Recs. '67–71, prod. sessions for Merrill, Lee Konitz. Pl. w. Konitz fr. '72; Ruby Braff, Helen Humes, Maxine Sullivan, Scott Hamilton, duo w. Sam Jones at Bradley's '76–9; Teddy Charles, Jimmy Knepper, Earle Warren–Dicky Wells and own gps. at West End early '80s; Doc Cheatham, Ellington Reeds mid '80s; Benny Goodman '85; AJO fr. '86; Benny Carter, Loren Schoenberg bb late '80s; Buck Clayton bb, solo pno at New Sch. concert series '89–91; Buddy Tate and own gp. at West End Gate '90. Katz wrote a detailed analysis of the pno. style of Nat Cole for the '92 Mos. reissue of Cole's trio recs. He received a Grammy nomination for a similar booklet accomp. the Smithsonian Jazz Piano Coll. Katz served on the bd. of governors for NARAS '77–90. Favs: Hank Jones, Tommy Flanagan, Cedar Walton, Monk, Bill Evans, Wynton Kelly, Kenny Barron, Mulgrew Miller. Fests: all major fr. '50s. TV: *Today* w. Scott Hamilton '78. CDs: Res.; w. L. Schoenberg (MM); Carmen McRae (Dec.); J. J. Johnson (Beth.); Konitz (Mile.); Pettiford; Benny Carter (Imp.); Dorham (Chess); N. Harrow (SN); J. Knepper (CC); Buck Clayton (N-H); AJO (East-West).

KATZ, FRED (FREDERICK), cello; b. NYC, 2/25/19. Studied w. a pupil of Pablo Casals. Mainly active in classical mus. and as studio player. Best known jazz assoc. w. Chico Hamilton qnt. 1955–6; first mus. to pl. both pizzicato and arco jazz solos on cello; wrote much of the mus. for the Hamilton gp. and app. w. it in film *Jazz on a Summer's Day*; also pl. w. Paul Horn '57–8; Carmen McRae '58. Took part in two poetry and jazz recs. w. Ken Nordine '57. Worked as pno. accomp. for Vic Damone; Lena Horne; Tony Bennett; etc. His comp. incl. *Cello Concerto* '61 and *Toccata* '63. In '64 wrote a Jewish liturgical service for cantor, choir, and jazz gp. perf. on CBS. Later taught anthropology at Valley State Coll. In '90s he was away fr. jazz after making an Italian reunion tour w. Hamilton '89. CD: w. Hamilton (SN).

KAY, CONNIE (Conrad Henry Kirnon), dms; b. Tuckahoe, NY, 4/27/27; d. NYC, 11/30/94. Studied pno. w. moth. fr. age 6. Self-taught on dms. fr. age 10; lessons at age 15. Pl. w. Fats Noel 1939; Sir Charles Thompson, Miles Davis at Minton's '44–5; Cat Anderson '45; Lester Young '49–50. Freelanced w. Charlie Parker, Coleman Hawkins, Beryl Booker, Stan Getz '50–2. Rejoined L. Young '52–5. Replaced Kenny Clarke in Modern Jazz Qt. '55. Dur. the MJQ's annual summer vacation, Kay occas. worked w. other gps. incl. Clark Terry, Bud Powell. After the MJQ disbanded in '74, Kay freelanced in NYC w. Tommy Flanagan; John Lewis; Benny Goodman; Soprano Summit; others. House dmr. at Eddie Condon's fr. '75. Pl. concert in Japan w. MJQ '81 and rejoin. re-formed MJQ '82. Suffered stroke in Jan. '92 but ret. to prof. activity in spring of '93. Kay was known for his unobtrusive, precise, painterly drumming. With the MJQ in the '50s, he was one of the first drummers to play triangle, chimes, timpani, finger cymbals, etc. in a modern jazz context. Favs: Sid Catlett, Art Blakey, Max Roach, Kenny Clarke, Shelly Manne. Fests: all major w. MJQ. CDs: w. MJQ (Prest.; Atl.; Col.); w. C. Hawkins; Roy Eldridge; J. J. Johnson; S. Getz (Verve); Bill Evans; Jimmy Heath; Bobby Timmons; Cannonball Adderley (Riv.); Paul Desmond (RCA); Milt Jackson (Prest.)

KAZEBIER, NATE (NATHAN FORREST), tpt; b. Lawrence, KS, 8/13/12; d. Reno, NV, 10/22/69. Raised in Cedar Rapids, Iowa; bro. a tnr. saxist. Stud. tpt. at age 9. Gained experience in dance bands bef. pl. w. Benny Goodman 1935–6. Then to Calif. where he worked w. Ray Noble, Spud Murphy mid '30s; G. Krupa '39–40; Jimmy Dorsey '40–3. Ret. to Calif. after serving in mil. dur. WWII, pl. w. Goodman '46–7; Hollywood studios, Jess Stacy late '40s. Stayed active into the '60s; also taught golf in Reno. Recs. w. Ray Bauduc, Goodman, and Krupa '35. CDs: w. Krupa (Class; BB); Goodman (BB; Hep; Cap.); Stacy (ASV); Bunny Berigan (Topaz); J. Dorsey (Dec.).

KEEZER, GEOFF, pno; b. Eau Claire, WI, 11/20/70. Father pl. dms., taught university mus. classes; moth. pl. Fr. horn, taught and pl. pno. First pno. lessons at age 5. Pl. first gigs w. fath.'s band at age 14. Stud. at U. of Wisc.–Eau Claire 1986–8; Berklee Coll. of Mus. '88–9. Won hs competition and perf. at jazz convention in Atlanta, where he was encouraged by James Williams, who prod. his first album for the Sunny. label Pl. w. Roy Hargrove '89; Art Blakey '89–90; fr. '90 w. Art Farmer; Benny Golson; Jon Faddis; CHJB; George Coleman; Gerry Mulligan; Mingus Dynasty; Cont. Pno. Ens; own gps

A virtuosic, orchestrally oriented player who has continued to grow. Favs: Phineas Newborn Jr., Art Tatum, Ahmad Jamal. Fests: Eur., Japan, etc. fr. '89. CDs: BN; Sunny; DIW; w. Blakey (A&M; Timel.); Hargrove (RCA); Farmer (Enja); J. Hall (Tel.); R. Cuber (Steep.); Cont. Pno. Ens. (Evid.; DIW).

KELLAWAY, ROGER, pno, comp; b. Waban, MA, 11/1/39. Studied classical pno. and bs.; pl. bs. on early gigs w. Jimmy McPartland and Ralph Marterie. After pno. gigs w. Al Cohn–Zoot Sims and Clark Terry–Bob Brookmeyer, he moved to LA in 1966. Pl. nine mos. w. Don Ellis band; mus. dir. for Bobby Darin '67–9. First feature film score, *The Paper Lion* '68; pl. w. Neophonic Orch. the same yr. Began writing for cello qt. feat. Edgar Lustgarten '69; also assoc. w. Tom Scott, Howard Roberts, Chuck Domanico, and John Guerin in small gps. Orchestrated *Beaux J. Poo Boo* for Les McCann and Cincinnati Symph. '70. Wrote mus. for ballet, PAMTGG, commissioned by George Balanchine '71. Comp. "Remembering You," closing theme for *All in the Family*, TV series '71. In '73 rec. first classical comp., *Esque*; tour. w. Joni Mitchell and Tom Scott's LA Express '74; arr. for Supersax and Carmen McRae '75. A skilled pnst., comp., cond., prod., arr., Kellaway has well over one hundred albums to his credit w. such artists as Eddie Daniels; Quincy Jones; Sarah Vaughan; Sonny Rollins; Zoot Sims; Stan Getz, Carmen McRae; Paquito D'Rivera; mimimalist comp. Steve Reich; and classical cellist Yo-Yo Ma. Kellaway's cello recs. on A&M were regarded by some critics as high points in crossover jazz. He has comp. over twenty movie scores, incl. *A Star Is Born*, which won an Academy Award nomination. *Memos From Paradise*, w. pno and orig. mus. by Kellaway, won a Grammy Award. Mus. dir., arr., and cond. of video, *Echoes of Ellington*. Many commissions to comp. orchestral and chamber mus. His concerto, *Songs of Ascent*, for tuba and orch. was commissioned by Zubin Mehta for the NY Philharm. and perf. at Avery Fisher Hall '89. In the early '90s he was commissioned by West Germ. Radio in Cologne to comp. for live concerts, TV, and recs. As pnst., he tour. Eur. and Japan, often w. Red Mitchell, perf. at leading restaurants and clubs. Wrote and perf. in *Fantasy Absolut* for jazz pno. trio and orch., premiered at Carnegie Hall in May '92. CDs: Conc.; Dragon; GRP. Also *Cello Quartet* on A&M; w. K. Burrell; W. Montgomery (Verve); Eddie Daniels (GRP); J. Leonhart (Sunny.); G. Mulligan (A&M); C. Roditi (Mile.); Z. Sims (Pab.); P. Wickman (Drag.).

KELLER, (ARTHUR) GARY, tnr sax, cl, fl; b. Suffern, NY, 6/25/47. Uncle pl. classical cl.; bro. is rock gtrst. Pl. w. rock and dance bands, then w. Lionel Hampton 1972–3; Woody Herman '78; Danny Stiles '77–8; Gerry Mulligan '78–87; in '90s w. Roy Gerson; Don Sebesky bb. Favs: Rollins, Coltrane. Fests: Eur., Japan w. Mulligan. Film: app. in *New York Stories; Crimes and Misdemeanors.* CDs: w. Mulligan (DRG).

KELLEY, PECK (JOHN DICKSON), pno; b. Houston, TX, 10/22/1898; d. Houston, 12/26/80. Led bands in Houston fr. early 1920s w. such sideman as Jack Teagarden, Pee Wee Russell, Leon Roppolo. Although he pl. briefly in St. Louis in '25, Shreveport, La. '27, and NO '34, the majority of his perfs. were in Houston and environs. Beginning in '48, he turned his attention to solo pno., but his first recs.— made in '57, right after he retired as a full-time player —were in a small band context. Kelley held a legendary reputation due to praise over the yrs. fr. Teagarden, reinforced by John Hammond in '39. The '57 sess. was released on the Comm. label in '83. CD: Comm. Coll. (Mos.)

KELLY, CHRIS, crnt; b. Deer Range Plantation, Plaquemine Parish, LA, 10/18/1885 or 1890; d. New Orleans, LA, 8/19/29. Studied w. Prof. Jim Humphrey. Moved to NO in 1915. Around the early '20s, after assuming leadership of Johnny Brown band, the gp. w. which he began his career, he became one of the most colorful and popular figures in NO, frequently participating in cutting contests. Alcoholism hampered his reliability, but he was considered a NO cornet "King" and renowned as a blues player, celebrated for his rendition of "Careless Love." Some believe he was the first to employ the plunger mute. Kid Howard's mentor, he was cited as an infl. on Louis Armstrong.

KELLY, GEORGE, tnr sax, voc, arr; b. Miami, FL, 7/31/15; d. NYC 5/28/98. Studied pno. fr. age 9 to 13, then sw. to alto sax. Formed band at age 15 w. sidemen incl. Panama Francis. Pl. w. Zack White ca. 1938; Al Cooper's Savoy Sultans '41–4; Rex Stewart '46; Lucille Dixon '48–50; Babs Gonzales, Tiny Grimes early '50s. Also led own gp. and worked as studio mus. '50s. Pl. w. Cozy Cole '59–60s. Tour. and rec. in Eur. w. Jay McShann, Tiny Grimes '70. Pl. w. Ink Spots '70–6, then tour. Eur. w. Ram Ramirez '76. Joined Panama Francis's Savoy Sultans '79; Harlem Blues and Jazz Band '80. Led own band on tours of Eur. fr. '80s. Favs: Coleman Hawkins, Lester Young. CDs: w. Doc Cheatham (Natasha); Panama Francis (B&B); Carrie Smith (Evid.); Al Cooper (Class.); Axel Zwingenberger (Vagabond).

KELLY, GUY (EDGAR), tpt, voc; b. Scotlandville, LA, 11/22/06; d. Chicago, IL, 2/24/40. Played w. Toots Johnson in Baton Rouge, La.; Papa Celestin, NO 1927–8; tour. w. Kid Howard '29; Boyd Atkins '30. Moved to Chi. where he worked w. Cassino Simpson '31; Ed Carry '32; Erskine Tate early '30s, '38; Dave Peyton, Tiny Parham, Carroll Dickerson '34, '37–8; Jimmy Noone '34; Albert Ammons '35–6, '39. Recs. w. Celestin, Frankie Jaxon; "Blues Jumped a Rabbit" w. Noone '36. CDs: w. Celestin (Azure); Noone (Class.); Art Tatum (Dec.); tracks in *New Orleans Jazz Giants: 1936–40* (JSP).

KELLY, JULIE (Dimaggio), voc; b. Oakland, CA, 10/28/47. At 15, she sang folk mus. and pl. gtr. w. twin sist. in duets at coffee houses. Lived in Brazil for a yr. 1970; att. Juilliard Sch. of Mus., NYC; ret. to SF in '73. Sang in gp. w. John Handy '74; based in LA area since '80 as singer and clinician. Her '84 debut album, *We're On Our Way,* introduced her best-known rec., "All My Tomorrows," while her later CD for CMG displays maturity and distinctive phrasing. Favs: Ella Fitzgerald, Joe Williams, Marian Anderson. CDs: Pausa; CMG.

KELLY, RED (THOMAS RAYMOND), bs; b. Shelby, MT, 8/29/27; d. Tacoma, WA, 6/9/04. Raised in Seattle, Wash. Picked up bs., w. no previous training, simply because of wartime shortage of musicians. Start. w. pnst. Johnny Wittwer in 1944. On the road w. Tiny Hill '44; Ted Fiorito '45. To NYC, worked w. Randy Brooks '47; Sam Donahue '48. Pl. w. Chubby Jackson's orch. '49. Tour. w. Charlie Barnet; Herbie Fields; and perf. in Honolulu w. Red Norvo Trio '51. After a yr. w. Claude Thornhill, join. Woody Herman Jan. '53. Pl. w. Maynard Ferguson. Rec. and gigged w. Med Flory '56–9; Stan Kenton '57–9. In '60 rec. for PJ w. Red Mitchell and Jim Hall as The Modest Jazz Trio. Tour. on and off w. Harry James fr. '61 to '74, later freelancing in the LV and Seattle areas. With wife Donna, operated a restaurant-bar in Tumwater, a suburb of Olympia, Wash. '74–8. In Nov. '86 they opened Kelly's in Tacoma, where he was the resident bsst., perf. w. such guest pnsts. as Jack Perciful and Joe Castro; Carl Fontana, Pete Christlieb, Jiggs Whigham, and the Basie band are among perfs. who sat in. Favs: Jimmy Blanton, Red Mitchell. Rec. w. Nat Pierce, Dick Collins '54; Lennie Niehaus '57. CDs: w. Herman (Disc.); Kenton (Status); Anita O'Day (Verve).

KELLY, WYNTON, pno; b. Jamaica, British West Indies, 12/2/31; d. Toronto, Ont., Canada, 4/12/71. Moved w. family to Bklyn., N.Y., at age 4. Prof. debut pl. r&b early 1943. Tour. Caribbean w. Ray Abrams gp. at 15. Pl. w. Hal Singer, Lockjaw Davis in late '40s. Accomp. Dinah Washington in late '40s, then w. Dizzy Gillespie early to mid '50s, w. mil. service dur. that time. Made rec. debut as leader on BN '51. Pl. w. Miles Davis '59–63, then led trio w. Paul Chambers and Jimmy Cobb. "He plays with that direct, strongly rhythmic, communicative quality that is one of the great merits of Erroll Garner," wrote John S. Wilson. CDs: Verve; w. Miles Davis (Col.); B. Holiday; Joe Henderson; Wes Montgomery (Verve); A. Blakey (BB); Abbey Lincoln (Riv.); Dizzy Gillespie (Sav.; Verve); J. Coltrane (Atl.); S. Rollins (Riv.; BN); Lorez Alexandria (Imp.); D. Washington (Em.; Merc.); Roland Kirk (Merc.); Curtis Fuller (Sav.); Betty Carter (Imp.); Sonny Red (BN); Babs Gonzales; H. Mobley; J. J. Johnson (BN); I. Jacquet; S. Lacy (Prest.); Mingus (Deb.); Booker Little (Time).

KELSON, JOHN JOSEPH JR. (aka JACKIE KELSO), saxes, fl, cl; b. Los Angeles, CA, 2/27/22. Known dur. most of his career as Jackie Kelso, upon the death of his father in 1998 decided to carry on the family name. In 1930s, he stud. privately and at Gray Cons. in LA. Prof. debut w. Jerome Myart at 15. In '40s, pl. w. C. L. Burke; Barney Bigard; US Navy band w. Marshal Royal; Lucky Thompson; Kid Ory; Benny Carter; Benny Goodman; Lionel Hampton; Roy Milton. From '50s, had long intermittent assocs. w. Johnny Otis; Billy Vaughn; Nelson Riddle; Bill Berry; Capp–Pierce Juggernaut; Ray Anthony; Bob Crosby; Duke Ellington. Also full-time studio work '64–84; rec. w. Mercer Ellington; many overseas tours w. L. Hampton; M. Ellington; B. Vaughn. Stopped all steady work in '84 and traveled the world as a tourist. Subbed occ. w. Basie band fr. '95, then bec. regular, March '98. CDs: w. Basie (MAMA); G. Harris; F. Capp (Conc.).

KENDRICK, RODNEY, pno, comp; b. Philadelphia, PA, 4/30/60. Parents moved to Miami, Fla. soon after. Fath. pl. pno., as did others in family, and all sang gospel. Pl. dms. before taking up pno. Worked w. James Brown; George Clinton; Harold Melvin and the Blue Notes. At 21, he came to NYC to stud. w. Barry Harris. Pl. w. George Benson; Freddie Hubbard; Frank Morgan; and J. J. Johnson. Became part of Abbey Lincoln's accomp. trio 1993. Began rec. w. his own trio '94. Kendrick, who cites Randy Weston and Sun Ra as "heavy influences," says: "My own feeling for groove, rhythm and the joy of the music came from my mother, who used to shout, dance, talk in tongues and play piano in the church, where I first performed on the organ. Even though I played with heavyweights, I got it from my mother first." CDs: Verve.

KENNEDY, CHARLIE (CHARLES SUMMER), alto sax; also tnr sax, cl, fl.; b. Staten Island, NY, 7/2/27. Mother pl. vln.; sist. pno., acdn., org. in church. Stud. cl. at age 12 in Weehawken, N.J. Pl. w. Louis Prima 1943, tnr. solo on "White Cliffs of Dover"; rec. on tnr. for Savoy w. own qt. '45. Alto sax w. Gene Krupa '45–8, feat. on "How High the Moon"; "Disc Jockey Jump"; "I Should Have Kept On Dreaming"; rec. w. Charlie Ventura '46; Chubby Jackson '50; Chico O'Farrill '51–2; Flip Phillips and Herbie Fields '52. Settled in LA; rec. w. Bill Holman '57–60; Art Pepper '59. Pl. MJF w. Med Flory '58. Regularly w. Terry Gibbs band '59–62. In '60s, rec. w. D. Gillespie, pl. at Shelly's Manne Hole, but had retired fr. mus. by early '70s. Fav: C. Parker. Film: *Beat the Band* w. Krupa '47. CDs: w. Gibbs (Cont.); O'Farrill (Verve); C. Jackson in G. Mulligan–Jackson (Fant./Prest.); Krupa (Hep.).

KENNEDY, JOE (JOSEPH J. JR.), vln, comp, arr; b. Pittsburgh, PA, 11/17/23; d. Richmond, VA, 4/17/04. Benny Carter is cousin; uncle was tptr. Theodore "Cuban" Bennett. Son Joseph III pl. Fr. horn, pno., arrs., sings. Introduced to vln. by grandfather, Saunders Bennett 1933. Encouraged by family and Jimmie Lunceford. Pl. w. George Duke Spaulding Sxt. '46; then led Four Strings w. Ray Crawford, Sam Johnson, Edgar Willis '46–49; Ahmad Jamal repl. Johnson '48. Pl. and arr. w. Fred Brown in Pitts. '50; Jay Peters at Virginia St. U. '52; own qnt. in Richmond, Va. '55–63. Also perf. as soloist at colleges and univs. in Virginia '50–8. Arr. for Ahmad Jamal fr. '59, also occ. perf. and rec. w. him. Received M. Mus. fr. Duquesne U. '60 and began teaching in Richmond school system. Headed mus. dept. at Maggie L. Walker HS '60s. Pl. w. Richmond Symph. '63–81. Cond. Cleveland Summer Symph. in premiere of orig. *Suite For Trio and Orch.* feat. Jamal '65. Pl. w. Continentals bb in Richmond '70. Arr. for *DB* Music Wkshp. Publs. Supervisor of music for Richmond public schs., also taught at Va. Commonwealth U. '73. *Dialogue For Flute, Cello and Piano* prem. at Fisk U. Arts Fest. '73. In '94 he completed a commission for the Roanoke Symph., *Sketches for Solo Violin, Jazz Trio and Symphony Orch.*, perf. by several symph. orchs. in US. Dir. of Jazz Studies at Va. Tech. U. in Blacksburg fr. '84 until he retired fr. teaching in June '95. Led his own qt. fr. '81. Pl. concerts w. Billy Taylor in Oct. '91; w. Jon Faddis and Great Amer. Mus. Ens. at Kennedy Center, Wash., D.C., Dec. '91; Taylor at Kennedy Cntr. 95. Taylor feels that Kennedy "combines the best aspects of Eddie South and Stuff Smith." Favs: Jascha Heifetz, Art Tatum, Duke Ellington, Benny Carter. Fests: Eur. and Japan w. B. Carter '79–81; Engl. as soloist '88; Nancy JF &

Paris concert w. Jamal '96. Film: feat. in Brit. docu. *Fiddlers Three* '88. TV: w. Faddis & Great Amer. Mus. Ens., PBS. Rec. debut w. Four Strings, supervised by Mary Lou Williams, for Disc, a subsidiary of Asch Recs. '47. LPs: B&B; Red Anchor; w. Jamal (Argo). CDs: CAP; w. John Lewis (DRG); B. Carter (PW); Billy Taylor (Conc.); Jamal (Verve).

KENNEDY, RAY (RAY HUSTON JR.), pno, kybd, comp; b. St. Louis, MO, 1/6/57. Brother is bsst. Tom Kennedy. Fath. was prof. tptr. but retired in 1950s. Sist. has master's degree in pno. perf. Moth. pl. pno. and sings. Began on bs. and gtr., then sw. to tpt. Stud. in St. Louis w. Profess. Frank Ryll, Tom Wilson, Herb Drury; comp. w. Joe Charles Thompson. Also one yr. at No. Tex. State. Sat in w. Dizzy Gillespie at age 14; pl. first prof. gig at 15. Co-led trio w. bro. '72–6; then pl. w. Joe Charles '75–6; Woody Shaw '76. Pl. kybd. on jingles '75–81; on soundtrack to film *A Pleasure Doing Business* '77. He and bro. pl. w. Nat Adderley '78; Freddie Hubbard '79; Eddie Harris '80; David Sanborn '82. Pl. w. Sonny Stitt '80; James Moody off and on '80–5; Herb Ellis '84. Co-led trio w. bro. and Dave Weckl '89–93. Pl. w. John Pizzarelli fr. '93. Also worked w. vocal gps. incl. NY Voices, Group Five, and in a trio w. Brian Torff, Warren Odze. Active as a clinician in Eur. and the US, and author of an instructional book, *Elements of Jazz*, publ. in Sweden. Favs: Art Tatum, Nat Cole, Keith Jarrett. Fests: Eur., Japan w. Pizzarelli. TV: Can. TV w. Pizzarelli; many apps. w. own trio in St. Louis '72–5. CDs: w. Pizzarelli (RCA); D. Weckl (GRP); Randy Sandke (Conc.; Jazz.); Lew Anderson bb (Sovereign).

KENTON, STAN (STANLEY NEWCOMB), lead, comp, pno; b. Wichita, KS, 12/15/11; d. Los Angeles, CA, 8/25/79. Raised in LA, where he studied pno. w. his moth. and various priv. teachers. Wrote his first arr. in 1928. After pl. w. several local bands, he join. Everett Hoagland as pnst. and arr. in '34, later spending a yr. w. Gus Arnheim and pl. in the bands of Vido Musso and Johnny Davis. In '36–7, he subbed w. Gil Evans orch. at the Rendezvous Ballroom in Balboa Beach, Calif., where on May 30, '41 he debuted his 14–pc. Artistry in Rhythm Orch, whose orig. members incl. Chico Alvarez, tpt; Red Dorris, tnr. sax, voc.; Bob Gioga, bari. sax; and Howard Rumsey, bs., with arr. by Ralph Yaw and Kenton. The band rec. for Dec. '41–2, but did not acquire a national reputation until the '43 Cap. release of "Artistry in Rhythm," the band's theme. With strong inspiration from Jimmie Lunceford's Orch., Kenton's orchestral trademark in these early yrs. was a staccato reed section style; fr. '44 to '45 the band feat. voc. by Anita O'Day, Gene

Howard, and June Christy. Fr. late '45, when Pete Rugolo joined as arr., Kenton did less writing. Dur. the next two yrs., powered by Rugolo's arrs. and such sidemen as Vido Musso, Kai Winding, Eddie Safranski, Art Pepper, Bob Cooper, and Shelly Manne, the orch. gained int'l popularity w. its bold, brassy "Progressive Jazz," which also encompassed Afro-Cuban numbers. In '47, a decline in bb popularity made Kenton briefly dissolve the orch.; worked w. a small gp. of his sidemen at the Sherman Hotel, Chi. In '49 he pl. Carnegie Hall w. a 20-pc. orch. but was ill during part of that year. In Jan. '50 he tour. under the banner "Innovations in Modern Music" w. a 40-pc. orch. that incl. strings. For several yrs. he routinely made a concert tour in the fall and disbanded the orch. each summer. Dur. this period he presented several ambitious concert pieces, incl. Bob Graettinger's *City of Glass*, which the jazz press found to be pretentious and did not embrace. However, in the first half of the '50s, he won them back w. arrs. by Shorty Rogers; Gerry Mulligan; Bill Holman; and Bill Russo; and such sidemen as Pepper; Rogers; Conte Candoli; Lee Konitz; Holman; Zoot Sims; Maynard Ferguson; Frank Rosolino; Charlie Mariano; Lennie Niehaus; and Mel Lewis, which changed the atmosphere to a more swinging bent. Following in the O'Day, Christy tradition, Chris Connor sang w. the band fr. '53 to '54, scoring a hit w. "All About Ronnie." In the summer of '55 Kenton fronted a band of NYC musicians for a weekly TV series, *Music '55*. His vocalist then was Ann Richards, to whom he was married '55–61. In March '56 he took a new band to Engl. for a highly successful concert tour; it marked the end of union restrictions that had kept US bands out of Engl. for civilian audiences since '37. Dur. the next few yrs. he sometimes rec. lush LPs w. strings, aimed at a broader commercial market. From '58 to '60 he toured extensively w. a new band. In the '60s, Kenton employed arrs. Johnny Richards and Gene Roland, both of whom had written for him on and off since the '40s. A 27-piece ensemble with a section of four mellophoniums feat. Roland's arrs.

Kenton took a hiatus from the road in '64 to concentrate on writing. He launched a new project in '65, forming the LA Neophonic Orch.—which incl. many Kenton alumni—for a series of concerts at the LA Mus. Center. A second series was given in '66. Though technically Kenton was not the leader of this orch., he was its guiding force, and much of the music played was of the ambitious, symphonic-jazz nature assoc. w. him through the yrs. Through this ensemble, he introduced works by many comps. writing in the so-called third-stream idiom and brought in such guest soloists as Friedrich Gulda; Dizzy Gillespie; Buddy DeFranco; Gerry Mulligan; and Cal Tjader. In

'66 Kenton was guest cond. of the Danish Radio Orch. In '67 he appeared bef. the Senate Sub-Committee hearings in an attempt to secure revision of mus. copyright laws. The band toured dur. the summer and he lectured at major universities, judged at many music fests. In '68 he pl. a third Neophonic season. The band cont. to tour, and in '71 and '72, when he was sidelined by a serious illness, it cont. under the dir. of others, such as Ken Hanna at the MJF. Fr. '72 to '75 the band tour. Eur. and Japan. Though he experimented with various instrumentations, the band's basic sound remained substantially the same, with arrs. by Hanna, Hank Levy, and Bob Curnow. Usually featuring a 10-man brass section, in which five trombones keynoted the band's style with a somber sonority, Kenton maintained an effective balance between his repertoire of the '40s and '50s and original material, some of it using 5/4 and other meters, some employing Afro-Cuban variations of old numbers, such as "Artistry in Rhythm," all played with a high spirited bravura.

Fifty yrs. after Kenton's debut as a bandleader on Balboa Island, jazz cognoscenti fr. around the world gathered in nearby Newport Beach to celebrate Stan "The Man" and his music. Over 500 people paid $225 each to take part in four days of panel discussions, films, a cruise, a dinner dance, sales of Kenton memorabilia, and many concerts. Participating musicians incl. Buddy Childers' bb; Lee Konitz's Qt.; Bob Florence's Limited Edition; M. Ferguson's Big Bop Nouveau; and the Stan Kenton Alumni Band, with such soloists as Bob Cooper; Bill Perkins; Gabe Baltazar; Bud Shank; Eddie Bert; Jiggs Whigham; C. Candoli; L. Almeida; S. Rogers; A. O'Day; and C. Connor. Guest conds. were Holman; Rugolo; Russo; Levy; Niehaus; and Marty Paich.

Kenton was an outspoken, often controversial, advocate for jazz who also pl. an important part in jazz education. From '59 to '63 he headed the Stan Kenton Clinics, annual events whose faculty incl. many leading jazz and popular musicians. In '66 he formed Creative World Mus. Publications to make the Kenton library available to schs. In '71 he set up a Jazz Orch. in Residence program, taking his band to schs. for one-day to one-week presentations. By '75, he was cond. at least 100 clinics annually, and four week-long summer clinics on coll. campuses. His sch. band arrs. are housed at No. Texas State U., Denton, Tex. Honors: Doctorate of Mus., Redlands U.; Villanova U. '67; Doctorate of Humane Letters, Drury Coll., '74. Like Duke Ellington, Kenton gave his pno. a minimal role in the orch. In the '50s, he produced a series of recs., *Kenton Presents*, for the Capitol label to showcase various sidemen. In '70 he established Creative World Recs. as a direct mail outlet for his and other artists' recs. Fests: NJF-NY '72, '74–5. Polls: band won *DB* '47, '50–4; *Met.* '47–9, '54, '56; *Playboy* '57–60; Kenton was elected to *DB* readers' poll *Hall of Fame* '54. Grammys: *West Side Story* '62; *Adventures in Jazz* '63. TV: *The Crusade for Jazz*, an hour-long special prod. by Kenton '68; he also made numerous appearances as a talk show guest. Film: *The Substance of Jazz* '69. Publ: *Kenton Straight Ahead*, Carol Easton (Wm. Morrow) '73; *Artistry in Rhythm*, Wm. F. Lee (Creative Press) '80. CDs: Mos.; Cap.; *50th Anniversary Celebration: Back to Balboa* (MAMA).

KEPPARD, FREDDIE, crnt; b. New Orleans, LA, 2/27/1890; d. Chicago, IL, 7/15/33. Brother Louis pl. gtr. and tba. Stud. mand., vln., acdn. Pl. crnt. w. Olympia Orch. fr. 1905, later taking over as dir. Left for LA to join Orig. Creole Band in '14, later app. in Chi. '14 and NYC '15–16. Band broke up in '18 and he settled in Chi., first lead. own band, then working w. Bill Johnson; Doc Cook; Ollie Powers; John Wycliffe; Charlie Elgar; Erskine Tate. It has been said that he covered his hand w. a handkerchief so other tpts. could not observe the way he fingered the valves; and that in his NYC period he turned down a chance to be the first to record jazz because he didn't want to be copied. Most of his recs. were done in '26 and after, when he had already passed his peak. According to those who heard him in his early days, he was a performer of extraordinary power and conviction who combined rags and blues in the emerging jazz style. CDs: King, Swiss label; track in *Hist. of Classic Jazz* (Riv.).

KERR, (CHESTER) BROOKS JR., pno; b. New Haven, CT, 12/26/51. Began on pno. at age 7. Made debut at Playback club, New Haven, at 9. Stud. w. Russell Repa in New Haven 1961–3; Sanford Gold in NYC '64–72; Phil Woods, Chris Swansen, Norm Grossman summer '67 at Ramblerny; Valerie Capers summer '68; Willie "The Lion" Smith '69–73; at Manh. Sch. of Mus. and Juilliard '70–2. Led own gp. while att. Dalton Sch., NYC '66–70. Solo pno. gigs in NYC bars and restaurants '70–3. An acknowledged Duke Ellington expert, he pl. w. and assisted Ellington at one-week seminar at U. of Wisconsin '72. Pl. duets w. Willie "The Lion" Smith at Village Gate '73; solo pno. at NJF-NY '73. Led own combo at Churchill's '73–4; sidemen incl. Ray Nance, Matthew Gee; Francis Williams; Paul Quinichette; Paul Gonsalves; Bob Mover; Sam Woodyard; also vocalists Annie Hurewitz, Betty Roche. Subbed for Ellington at Third Sacred Concert at Central Presbyterian Church Apr. '74. Led own trio at West End Café in '74; trio w. Russell Procope, Sonny Greer at Gregory's '74–5. Tour. Engl., Italy, Israel '79; Russia,

'89. Has taught priv. fr. '78. Worked at Hotel Cecil; St. Nick's, intermittently fr. '96. Led band at dedication of Duke Ellington statue at 110th St. & 5th Ave., NYC '97. Favs: Ellington, C. Hawkins, Tatum, R. Eldridge, C. Parker. LPs: own Blue Wail Label; Famous Door feat. Quinichette, Chiaro.

KERSEY, KENNY (KENNETH LYONS), pno; b. Harrow, Ont., Canada, 4/3/16; d. NYC, 4/1/83. Studied pno. w. moth., a mus. teacher, and fath., a cellist. Studied pno. and tpt. at Detroit Inst. of Mus. Arts. Moved to NYC 1936, doubling on tpt. and pno. Pnst. w. Lucky Millinder '39; Frankie Newton and Roy Eldridge, '39–40; Henry Red Allen '41; Cootie Williams and Andy Kirk '42. Pl. tpt. in army bands to Feb. '46. Tour. w. JATP fr. '46 to early '49; gigged w. Eldridge, Buck Clayton Sxt., and as soloist at Lou Terrasi's Hickory Log '48. With Ed Hall in Bost., '49–50; back in NYC w. Allen '51–2; Sol Yaged Trio '52–4, '56–7; Charlie Shavers '55. A bone disease caused him to give up pl. in the late '50s. Although he first gained fame w. Kirk as a boogie-woogie exponent, he later showed himself to be one of the more harmonically adventurous swing pnsts. Comps: "Boogie Woogie Cocktail," rec. first w. Kirk, then w. Allen, who also feat. him in his "K. K. Boogie." CDs: w. Benny Goodman; Billie Holiday (Col.); JATP (Verve); Kirk; Allen (Class.); R. Braff (BL).

KESSEL, BARNEY, gtr; b. Muskogee, OK, 10/17/23; d. San Diego, CA, 5/6/04. Only gtr. study was at age 12 for three mos. w. the Federal Mus. Project of the WPA. Pl. w. local bands in Okla. at 13, then w. territory bands 1938–9, two Okla. coll. bands '40–1. Moved to LA '42; w. Chico Marx band (dir. by Ben Pollack) '42–3; Artie Shaw band and Gramercy Five '44. App. in film short, *Jammin' the Blues*, w. Lester Young et al. '44. Worked w. Charlie Parker '47; Benny Goodman '47, '58; Oscar Peterson Trio '52; w. JATP '52–3, touring 14 countries. In late '50s and through '60s and '70s he worked mainly as freelance studio mus. and arr. for TV, recs., and films. Also tour. w. Newport All-Stars '69. Tour. Austral. and New Zealand w. Charlie Byrd and Herb Ellis '73, and form. gp., Great Guitars. Moved to San Diego, Calif. late '80s but cont. to pl. clubs such as the Vanguard, NYC, and fests. Suffered major stroke spring '92 and was unable to perf. after that. Attended a tribute to him which feat. numerous peers, incl. Ellis, Byrd, Tal Farlow, Kenny Burrell at JVC JF-NY '97. Wrote *The Guitar*, an instruction book; prod. three videos explaining improv. A stylistic disciple of Charlie Christian, Kessel was perhaps the most distinguished exponent of the style since Christian's death. Nat Hentoff described him as "one of the most extraordinarily consistent and emotionally huge improvisers of our era". CDs: Cont.; Conc.; BL; Sonet; Story.; w. C. Parker (Stash; Verve); C. Barnet (Dec.); C. Byrd (Conc.); Benny Carter (BB; Cont.); B. Collette; H. Hawes; H. Humes; S. Rollins; Lighthouse All-Stars (Cont.); B. Webster; L. Young; E. Fitzgerald; B. Holiday; A. O'Day (Verve); O. Peterson (Verve; Pab.); Kid Ory (GTJ); D. Gordon (Sav.); S. Grappell (BL); S. Rogers; A. Shaw (BB); Tatum (Pab.); P. Desmond (Fant).

KESTERSON, BOB (ROBERT, "DINGBOD"), bs; b. Princeton, MO, 9/13/16. Worked w. Sidney Arodin (comp. of "Up A Lazy River") 1937; Anna Mae Winburn '38. Pl. w. Gus Arnheim '42; Harlan Leonard '43–4; and Stan Kenton '44–5. Rec. w. Wynonie Harris and on the historic 1946 Dial sess. w. Charlie Parker and Howard McGhee that produced "Lover Man"; "Be-Bop"; "The Gypsy"; and "Max is Makin' Wax." Later w. Joe Maini, Herb Geller; Kenny Drew; pl. w. Benny Carter in San Diego '52. Moved to LV where he pl. occ. gigs in early '90s. A relatively unknown player (his name is frequently misspelled as Kesterton), he was a participant in some celebrated early bebop sess. CDs: w. C. Parker (Stash); H. McGhee (Jz. Class.).

KHAN, STEVE (Steven Harris Cahn), gtr; b. Los Angeles, CA, 4/28/47. Father is lyricist Sammy Cahn. Began on pno. at age 5. Pl. dms. in surf-rock gp. The Chantays 1965–8, had hit single "Pipeline." Began pl. gtr. at age 19. Received B.A. in comp. and theory fr. UCLA '69. Jammed w. Ron Finney; Clarence MacDonald; Michael Carvin; then worked w. Friends of Distinction; Phil Moore; Wilton Felder. Moved to NYC '70. Worked as studio mus. and pl. w. George Benson; Hubert Laws; Maynard Ferguson; Buddy Rich; also pop acts Steely Dan and Billy Joel early '70s. Pl. in duo w. Larry Coryell '74–5; w. Brecker Bros '74–7; own gp. Eyewitness, w. Anthony Jackson, Steve Jordan, Manolo Badrena '81–90; Weather Update w. Joe Zawinul '86; also freelanced w. Billy Cobham; Freddie Hubbard; Stan Getz; Lonnie Smith; Tom Scott; Bob James; Geo. Duke; Mike Mainieri; etc. Khan is active as a clinician and has publ. three gtr. books: *The Wes Montgomery Gtr. Folio* (Gopam/Plymouth); *Pat Martino Jazz Gtr. Solos—The Early Yrs.* (CPP/Belwin); *Gtr. Wkshp. Series—Steve Khan*) (Warner). Favs: Wes Montgomery, Kenny Burrell, Jim Hall, Grant Green. Fests: all major fr. early '70s. CDs: BM; GRP; Den.; Verve; Evid; w. Miles Davis (WB); Brecker Bros. (BB).

KIBWE, TALIB aka T. K. BLUE (Eugene Ludovic Rhynie), alto, sop, saxes, fl, alto fl, kalimba, comp, arr; b. Bronx, NY, 2/7/53. Father Jamaican; moth. Trinidadian. Godfather pl. tnr. sax in Jamaican band. Began on tpt. at age 8; soon after moved to reeds and fl. B.A. in mus. and psych. fr. NYU.; M.A. in mus. ed. fr. Columbia Teachers Coll. Dur. this time also stud. at Jazzmobile, Jazz Interactions, and Henry St. Settlement programs w. Jimmy Heath; Frank Foster, Ernie Wilkins; Billy Taylor; Clifford Jordan; et al. Pl. w. Jaki Byard's Apollo Stompers 1975; Abdullah Ibrahim, fr. qt. to bb '77–80 incl. tours in Eur., Africa. Moved to Paris '80 where he began a pl. assoc. w. Randy Weston that has cont. into late '90s. Perf. w. Weston in formats fr. duo to orch. w. strings and is presently his mus. dir. Lived in Paris to late '80s and form. own T. K. Odyssey Band, rec. first album as leader, *Egyptian Oasis* (Anais) '86. Tour. East Africa w. band for USIA '89; for St. Dept. West Africa Feb.-March '90; Morocco Oct. '90. Pl. w. Sam Rivers' saxophone orch. "Winds of Manhattan" '82 incl. Bobby Watson, Steve Coleman. Member of Xalam (Senegalese gp.) '84–5; Chico Hamilton qt. '88; Brotherhood of Breath w. Chris McGregor, Archie Shepp '89. Formed TaJa w. James Weidman '92; from that yr. mus. dir. for Spirit of Life Ensemble. Worked as sub. mus. teach. in public sch. system '89–95. Kibwe can pl. sweetly and with an edge, go deep into the blues and connect strongly with his family's African heritage, complementing Weston's music with passion. Favs: Parker, Adderley, Stitt; sop: Coltrane, Shorter; fl: Moody, Laws. Rec. debut w. Ibrahim on *The Journey* (Chiaro.) '77. Fests: many int'l incl. Pan-Jazz in Trinidad w. TaJa '92. CDs: Evid.; Ark.; w. Weston (Verve); Rivers (BS); Benny Powell (Insp.); Shepp–McGregor (52e Rue Est); Spirit of Life Ens. (Rise Up).

KIKOSKI, DAVE (DAVID JAMES), pno, kybds; b. Milltown, NJ, 9/29/61. Father is part-time mus. and teacher. Stud. w. father, then w. Herbie Buccanen and at Berklee Coll. of Mus. (B. Mus. 1983). Pl. w. Roy Haynes fr. '86; Randy Brecker fr. '86; Ralph Moore '87; Bob Berg fr. '88; Billy Hart '89; Red Rodney '90–1; also w. own trio w. Essiet Essiet and Al Foster; David Sanchez; Mingus bb in '90s. Favs: Herbie Hancock, Keith Jarrett, Gil Evans. Fests: Eur. and Japan fr. '86. CDs: Tril.; Free.; Epicure; w. R. Brecker (Den.); R. Rodney (Contin.); R. Haynes (Drey.; Free.); Craig Handy; Billy Hart (Arab.); R. Moore (CC); B. Berg (Stretch); Joe Locke (Steep.); Eero Koivistoinen (Timel.); Chip Jackson (JazzKey).

KIKUCHI, MASABUMI, pno, kybds, comp; b. Tokyo, Japan, 10/19/39. Grew up in Aizuwakamatsu, Fukushima Pref., dur. and after WWII. Began stud. pno. and theory at age 5; grad. fr. comp. dept. of hs of the Tokyo Nat'l U. of Fine Arts and Music 1958. Pl. w. Eddie Iwata, Takatashi Oya's Highway Sons, Shungo Sawada '58–60, then join. Masahiko Togashi's Jazz Academy '61. Tour. Japan and made rec. debut w. Lionel Hampton Orch. '63. Pl. w. Nobuo Hara's Sharps & Flats '64. Gave first recital in Tokyo '65. Pl. w. Sadao Watanabe '66–7; co-led gp w. Terumasa Hino '68. Pl. concert w. Sonny Rollins Jan. '68. Att. Berklee Sch. of Mus. on *DB* scholarship '68–9; stud. comp. w. Wm. Maroof, arr. w. Herb Pomeroy. Ret. to Japan, form. sxt. w. two pnsts. and two dmrs. '70. The sxt.'s rec. of Kikuchi's comp. "Dancing Mist" was a hit in Japan early '70s. Pl. and rec. in Japan w. Gary Peacock, Woody Herman, Mal Waldron, Joe Henderson, Gil Evans '70–2. Moved to NYC to join Elvin Jones Qnt. '73; tour. US w. Jones '74. Has lived in NYC since. Orig. member of N.Y. Jazz Repertory Co. Built rec. studio in Bklyn., experimented w. synth. and computer mus. late '70s-80s. Rehearsed w. Miles Davis '78; also worked occ. w. Gil Evans dur. this period. Active again as perf. fr. late '80s. Form. gps. AAOBB (All Night, All Right, Off White Boogie Band) '89; Tethered Moon trio w. G. Peacock, Paul Motian '91; trio w. James Genus, Victor Jones '92. Reunited w. T. Hino, M. Togashi at Yamaha JF in Hamamatsu, Japan '93. Polls: *SJ* Readers, pno. '68–9, '72–3; Best Combo '71–2; Jazzman of Year '71–3; Rec. of Year '72; kybd. '84. CDs: Em.; Philips; Sony; NEC-Avenue; Tokuma; Glass House; Nippon Crown; w. Tethered Moon (King; W&W); G. Evans (Story.); T. Hino (BN); Helen Merrill (Verve).

KILLIAN, AL (ALBERT), tpt; b. Birmingham, AL, 10/15/16; d. Los Angeles, CA, 9/5/50. Professional debut at 18 in NYC w. Charlie Turner's Arcadians. Pl. w. Baron Lee 1937; Teddy Hill in late '30s; Don Redman, Claude Hopkins '40; C. Basie '40–4; also Charlie Barnet '43, '45–6; L. Hampton spring '45. On the West Coast he pl. w. the orchs. of Earle Spencer and Boyd Raeburn. App. in JATP concerts '46; led own gp. in Calif. and was feat. in "Just Jazz" concert series. Join. D. Ellington Dec. '47, remaining w. him until shortly bef. his death, incl. Eur. tour '50. He was murdered at his home by a psychopathic landlord. Killian excelled in the altissimo register—one of many examples being his own comp., "Y'Oughta," rec. w. Ellington—but he was also a strong, all-purpose mainstream jazz soloist. CDs: w. Charlie Parker; JATP (Verve); T-Bone Walker (Mos.); Lester Young (Sav.); C. Barnet; L. Hampton (Dec.); Basie (Hep); Ellington (Prest.; Col.); Slim Gaillard (Tax); S. Criss (FS; DIW).

KIMBROUGH, FRANK MARSHALL JR., pno; b. Roxboro, NC, 11/2/56. Musical family; began pl. pno at age 4, started formal lessons age 7. Started pl. prof. in churches and w. local gps. Moved to NYC in 1981, led own gps. Winner, Great American Jazz Piano Competition '85. Co-founded Jazz Composers Collective in '92 w. Ben Allison. Leader of Herbie Nichols Project fr. '92—it received NEA Fellowship in 1996. Worked w. Ted Nash fr. '90; Maria Schneider Orch. fr. '94, tour. Eur. fall '96, summer '97. Teaches pno. and improv. at NYU. Favs: Andrew Hill, Paul Bley. Radio: Marian McPartland's *Piano Jazz* '97; Branford Marsalis's *Jazzset* w. Maria Schneider. CD: Maple.; w. Rich Perry (Steep.).

KINCAIDE, (ROBERT) DEANE, comp, bari, tnr saxes; b. Houston, TX, 3/18/11; d. St. Cloud, FL, 8/14/92. During 1930s pl. w. Wingy Manone in Shreveport, La., '32; Ben Pollack in Chi. '33–5, arr. for Benny Goodman and was member of Bob Crosby band '35–6; also w. Woody Herman '37; Manone '38. Pl. and arr. (wrote the chart on *Boogie Woogie*) w. Tommy Dorsey '39–40. In '40s worked w. Joe Marsala; Ray Noble; Muggsy Spanier. Wrote for and pl. w. Ray McKinley bb '46–50. Later wrote for McKinley-led Glenn Miller Orch. Cont. to freelance, pl., writing for TV, etc.; retired in Calif. '82. Kincaide's arrs. for the Crosby orch. were among the first and most successful efforts to translate Dixieland jazz into bb terms. LP: Ever. CDs: four tracks as lead. in *Classic Capital Jazz Sessions* (Mos.); w. Lee Wiley; T. Dorsey (BB); Crosby (Dec.).

KINDRED, BOB (ROBERT HAMILTON), tnr; also sop, alto, bari saxes; clar, fl; b. Lansing, MI, 5/11/40. Brother pl. cl. Moved to Germantown, Pa. at age 4; then Bala Cynwyd, Pa. Stud. cl. fr. 4th to 9th grades w. Homer Smith; tnr. w. Buddy Savitt, Larry McKenna in 10th grade; Dave Shrier 11–12th grades. Inspired by hearing Stan Kenton orch. in 1954. At 16 he pl. cl. w. Pennsylvania Six Pence, a Chicago-style Dixieland gp. from U. of Pa.; app. w. it at Carnegie Hall, in Europe, and on rec. for Kapp. Degree in clinical psychology at Muhlenberg and post-grad. at Lehigh '60–4. During this period, he was also active as mus. therapist for children. Studied briefly w. Phil Woods in '71. Worked w. Charles Earland '71; other tnr.-org. gigs w. Shirley Scott; Groove Holmes; Glenn Miller band Aug. '71–Nov. '72; Woody Herman '72–3; Dick Cone band '80–3; Smithsonian Jazz Rep. Ens. '83–7; Mike Peters' Django's Music '85–7; Ted Rosenthal trio '85–93; own gps. fr. '91. A romanticist with a strong sense of swing and well-developed sound reflecting his classic tnr. infls. Led gp. incl. Don Friedman, Joe Carroll for jazz clinics in hs, colls. '77–81; also educ. for IAJ. Pl. at Ronnie Scott's fr. '96; Zinno fr. '97. Awarded NEA grant for concert tribute

to Ben Webster and Johnny Hodges, which he perf. at Symphony Space '92. Comp. title song, served as co-prod., mus. dir. and perf. for Ann Phillips' *Bending Towards the Light: A Jazz Nativity*, presented annually at St. Bartholomew's Church and/or Lincoln Center, NYC since '86. Favs: Webster, Coltrane, Young, Rollins, Getz. CDs: Cona.; Jazzmania; w. DMP bb (DMP); Ray Alexander (Nerus).

KING, B. B. (RILEY), gtr, voc; b. Itta Bena, MS, 9/16/25. Cousin of Bukka White. First major job in 1949 as disc jockey and singer on Memphis radio, where he also pl. gtr and sang requests. First billed as "The Beale Street Blues Boy," later as "Blues Boy King," which became B. B. King. Rec. debut on Bullet label '49, then sw. to RPM; his "Three O'Clock Blues" reached the number one position on the r&b charts in early '52, staying there for three weeks. This led to tours of major black theaters in Wash., D.C., Balt., and NYC. Firmly established during the '50s, King sw. to Kent Recs. in '58 w. many singles high on the r&b charts. In '62 he moved to the ABC Bluesway label, scoring his biggest hit w. "The Thrill Is Gone" '70. By the mid '70s, he had become a major pop fest. attraction in US and Can. Also had a long series of best-selling albums. Dur. the '70s and '80s King achieved int'l star status, making countless TV apps., incl. acting guest shots on sitcoms. He has infl. a generation of young rock and pop stars, incl. Mike Bloomfield, Eric Clapton, and Elvin Bishop. Numerous awards incl. Humanitarian Award fr. Fed. Bur. of Prisons '72; B'nai B'rith Mus. and Perf. Lodge, NYC '73; *Rec. World* mag. '74. Grammy award '70; NARAS Lifetime Achievement award '87. Maintained demanding tour schedule in late '90s. Book: *The Arrival of B. B. King*, Charles Sawyer (Doubleday) '80. CDs: JCI; MCA; GRP; w. GRP All-Star bb; Larry Carlton (GRP).

KING JONNY (JONATHAN Z.), pno, comp; b. NYC, 2/2/65. Graduate of Princeton U.; Harvard Law Sch. Stud. w. Tony Aless 1979–83; Mulgrew Miller '86. Began leading own gps. in NYC restaurants and clubs at age 17. Pl. w. OTB '88; Joshua Redman '92, '94; Eddie Harris '95. Led own gp. fr. '94. King's comps. have been rec. by Tony Reedus; Billy Drummond; Billy Pierce. He is a practicing copyright and entertainment lawyer at Cowan, Lubowitz, and Lutman in NYC. Favs: Tyner, Hancock, Wynton Kelly. Book: *What Jazz Is: An Insider's Guide to Understanding and Listening to Jazz* (Walker & Co.) '97. CDs: Enja; CC; w. Eric Felton (SN).

KING, MORGANA (Messina), voc; b. Pleasantville, NY, 6/4/30. Father pl. gtr. and sang. Stud. at

Metropolitan Sch. of Mus. Began prof. career as singer in local NYC, N.J. area clubs at 15, then started perf. nationally. Reached high popularity in 1960s through a series of successful albums and singles, notably "A Taste of Honey." Portrayed Mama Corleone in *The Godfather* '72 and *The Godfather II* '74; also seen as Mrs. Sabatino in *Nunzio* '78. She ret. to a more jazz-oriented style in the '70s, rec. a series of albums for Muse in the late '70s and early '80s. CDs: Em.; Main.; Verve.

KING, PETE (PETER JOHN), alto, tnr saxes; b. Kingston-upon-Thames, Surrey, England, 8/11/40. Self-taught, initially on cl. Started in local pubs. Pl. w. J. Dankworth 1961–2; Tubby Hayes bb '67–75; Ray Charles '76. Feat. w. Zoot Sims–Al Cohn; Maynard Ferguson; Red Rodney; Count Basie Band at Royal Albert Hall '90; Tete Montoliu; and others. Fr. '80s he has had own gp.; also app. regularly w. Stan Tracey. To US w. Charlie Watts's Charlie Parker tribute '87, '91; many Eur. tours; Brazil; Japan; Austral.; Hong Kong. Soloist w. Colin Towns's Mask Orch. in '90s. Strongly infl. by C. Parker, his other favs. incl. L. Young, Getz, Coltrane. Film: *Blue Ice* w. Michael Caine; many TV apps. Radio: feat. as soloist, comp.-arr. w. Brussels Radio bb '85. First award '59 *MM* New Star; Brit. Jazz Awards, best alto, fr. '89. Well known for his work w. pop gp., Everything But the Girl, incl. recs. Other recs. w. Philly Joe Jones, Montoliu. Own recs. on Spot.; Miles Music; Blue Silver. CDs: w. Watts (Contin.); Tracey (BN).

KING, TEDDI, voc; b. Boston, MA, 9/18/29; d. NYC, 11/25/77. After grad. fr. hs, she joined the Tributary Theatre. Won singing contest sponsored by Dinah Shore in Bost.; spent a yr. singing for USO and Amer. Theatre Wing. Stud. classical voice, jazz pno. briefly in late '40s. Sang w. George Graham, Jack Edwards bands, then made rec. debut w. Nat Pierce. Tour w. George Shearing Qnt. '52–3. Worked mainly as a single fr. '53. "The particulars of her style were less important than the harmonious wholes she made of her songs. Traces of Lee Wiley and Mildred Bailey showed up but her work was her own."—Whitney Balliett. Film: *Cool Canaries* w. Shearing. LPs: Victor; Coral. CD: Audio; w. Nat Pierce (Hep).

KINSEY, TONY (CYRIL ANTHONY), dms, comp, arr; b. Sutton, Coldfield, England, 10/11/27. Father pl. vln., moth. pl. pno. Pno. lessons at age 7. Stud. dms. w. Bill West in NYC while working on transatlantic liners; later stud. w. Cozy Cole, arr. w. Bill Russo. Founding member of Johnny Dankworth Seven 1950–1. Led own gps. fr. early '50s, sometimes backing visiting artists incl. Oscar Peterson;

Ella Fitzgerald; Lena Horne; Sarah Vaughan. In residence at Flamingo Club, London '53–late '50s. Sidemen in Kinsey's gps. have incl. Bill Le Sage; Joe Harriott, Don Rendell; Ronnie Ross; Peter King; Alan Branscombe. Led own bb fr. '74; co-led bb w. Dankworth fr. '80. Kinsey has written several extended works for jazz orch. and classical ens. and has also comp. extens. for TV and films. He continues to lead a combo in London clubs. Fests: all major in Eur. Fav: Kenny Clarke. LP: *Thames Suite* (Spot.) '76.

KIRBY, JOHN, bs, tba, lead; b. Baltimore, MD, 12/31/08; d. Hollywood, CA, 6/14/52. Started on tbn., then sw. to tba. and bs. Pl. tba. w. Fletcher Henderson 1930–3; bs. w. Chick Webb late '33–5; Henderson '35–6; Mills Blue Rhythm Band '36. In '37 form. own gp. at the Onyx Club, NYC, w. Frankie Newton and Pete Brown, but the personnel changed and the band rose to high popularity w. Charlie Shavers, whose muted tpt. and arrs. were a prime factor in its success; Russell Procope, alto; Buster Bailey, cl.; Billy Kyle, pno.; O'Neill Spencer, dms. The light, breezy sound and unique style of this gp. brought a new element of ingeniously orchestrated finesse to small band jazz. The Kirby sxt. set several precedents for black orchestras, incl. an engagement at the Waldorf-Astoria in NYC and a network radio series, *Flow Gently, Sweet Rhythm*, in '40, which co-starred Kirby's wife, Maxine Sullivan. After '42, the Kirby vogue slowly declined and the band lost much of its character through personnel changes, Billy Kyle's long army stint and Shavers' defection to Tommy Dorsey being major factors. There was a brief revival in '46 w. Kyle's return and Sarah Vaughan as voc., but by the following yr., bookings had sagged and the sxt. was disbanded. The orig. personnel was reassembled for a '50 Carnegie Hall concert (w. Sid Catlett replacing the deceased Spencer), but attendance was poor. Kirby moved to Calif. and spent the last yr. of his life in obscurity while Benny Carter, an old friend, tried to rehabilitate him. He died of diabetes. On bs., Kirby had a light, gentle sound that contrasted w. the heavy-handed plucking of earlier jazz bassists. As a leader, he was perhaps the most important small band leader of the '30s. Among the sxt.'s greatest successes were "Pastel Blue" and "Undecided," written by Shavers, and a large number of swing adaptations of classical works, incl. "Anitra's Dance"; "Humoresque"; "Sextet from Lucia"; and "Bounce of the Sugar Plum Fairy." CDs: Class.; Cir.; w. Billie Holiday (Col.); B. Goodman; L. Hampton (BB); Benny Carter (B&B; BB); Roy Eldridge (Col.; Dec.); Nat Cole (Cap.); Fletcher Henderson (Sav.); Chick Webb (Dec.; Hep); Capitol Jazzmen

(Jazz Unlimited); Red Allen (Hep; Tax); Willie "The Lion" Smith (Timel.); Teddy Wilson (Hep).

KIRBY, STEVE, bs; b. Maumee Valley, OH, 5/23/56. Family moved to St. Louis when he was two months old. Took up elec. gtr., bs. gtr. at age 22 while w. paratroopers at Ft. Bragg, N.C. Stud. at Webster U., St. Louis fr. age 24; B. Mus. 1985. Taught at Webster '84–6 and worked around St. Louis w. blues bands, then r&b, classical, jazz jobs. Received classical scholarship for master's degree at Manhattan Sch. of Mus. '87. Lester Bowie called him for gigs. Ret. to St. Louis and taught at Webster '88–93; also at Washington U., St. Louis; Fontbonne. Won Grand Prize in Hennessy Jazz Search '92. Moved to NYC '93, worked w. Oliver Lake; Claudio Roditi; John Hicks; Slide Hampton; Antonio Hart. Member of Cyrus Chestnut Trio '94–8. Pl. w. Joanne Brackeen; Duke Ellington Orch.; Wallace Roney; Wycliffe Gordon; Steve Turre; James Carter; Wess Anderson. Took part in clinic at Princeton U. '98. Writing book on jazz bass teaching method. Orig. infl., Paul Chambers. Favs: Pettiford, Ray Brown, Wilbur Ware, Ron Carter, George Mraz. TV: *Good Morning America* w. Chestnut, CBS. Has worked as mechanic, factory worker; preacher in North Carolina; and was heavyweight champion of 82nd Airborne Division, US Army '77–8. CDs: w. Chestnut; James Carter (Atl.); Wess Anderson (Leaning House); Denise Jannah (BN).

KIRCHNER, BILL (WILLIAM JOSEPH JR.), saxes, fl, cl, comp, arr; b. Youngstown, OH, 8/31/53. Studied in Ohio w. Albert Caldrone, Sam D'Angelo. Att. Manh. Coll. '71–5 (B.A. English), also stud. mus. w. Lee Konitz '71–3; Harold Danko '73–5. Kirchner moved to Wash., D.C., in '75, where he contributed articles and reviews to the *Wash. Post, DB, JazzTimes*, and *Jazz Magazine*, and was asst. curator for the Smithsonian Jazz Oral History prog. '79. Pl. in D.C. w. Mike Crotty bb, Bernard Sweetney. In '79 he received an NEA grant to study arr. w. Rayburn Wright in Rochester, N.Y. He ret. to NYC in '80 and formed his own nonet, which he has led ever since. Stud. w. John Purcell '85–7; John McNeil '88–91; Bob Brookmeyer and Manny Albam at BMI Comp. Wkshp. '89–91. Also freelanced in '80s w. AJO; Dizzy Gillespie bb; Anita O'Day; Mel Lewis; Mousey Alexander; Bobby Rosengarden; Vince Giordano; Stan Rubin; etc. Co-produced boxed set, and wrote booklet notes for *Big Band Renaissance* (Smith.). Favs: Miles Davis, Wayne Shorter, Bill Evans (pno.); arrs: Ellington, Strayhorn, Gil Evans, Gary McFarland. Polls: *JT* Best Emerging Talent-Arr. '90. Fests: Taiwan '89 w. Mike Abene. Publ: edited *A*

Miles Davis Reader (Smithsonian Press) '98; *Jazz: A Reader's Companion* (Oxford) 2000. CDs: SB; Smith.; w. Chris Connor (Cont.); Dizzy Gillespie (Enja); Lee Konitz (Steep.).

KIRK, ANDY (DEWEY ANDREW), lead; b. Newport, KY, 5/28/1898; d. NYC, 12/11/92. Raised in Denver, Colo. Stud. pno., singing, alto and tnr. sax, and mus. theory w. Wilberforce Whiteman (Paul Whiteman's father) and others. Pl. tba. and bs. sax w. violinist Geo. Morrison's orch. in Denver 1918–early '20s. Moved to Dallas, Tex. '25, then join. Terrence Holder's Dark Clouds of Joy, assuming leadership of the band in '29 and changing the name to Clouds of Joy, or Twelve Clouds of Joy, etc. In '29 he took band to KC, where its popularity rivalled Bennie Moten's. The Kirk band toured almost constantly '30–48 and had a hit in '36 with "Until the Real Thing Comes Along." The band's main arr. was Mary Lou Williams, who was a member of the gp. fr. '29 to '42. Other sidemen incl. Kenny Kersey; Dick Wilson; Don Byas; Shorty Baker; Howard McGhee; Fats Navarro; and, briefly, Charlie Parker. Kirk himself was never a soloist and rarely played in the ens. after the early '30s. He led another gp. in Calif. in the early '50s, then went into the real estate business and later managed the Theresa Hotel in NYC. He cont. into the '70s to occ. lead pickup gps. but devoted much of his later yrs. to work as a Jehovah's Witness. CDs: Dec.; Class.

KIRK, RAHSAAN ROLAND (ROLAND T.), fl, tnr sax, manzello, stritch, cl, tpt, comp; b. Columbus, OH, 8/7/36; d. Bloomington, IN, 12/5/77. Blind fr. the age of 2, he stud. at the Ohio St. Sch. for the Blind. Began on bugle, tpt. at age 9, then sw. to C-melody sax and cl. Pl. w. sch. band fr. 1948. Pl. first prof. gigs w. local gps.; led own gps. in Ohio fr. '51. While on tour w. the Boyd Moore band, he began experimenting w. pl. two instr. simultaneously. Acquiring a manzello and stritch ca. '59, he worked out a way to play three instr. at once, producing three-pt. harmony through the use of trick fingerings. Made his rec. debut in '56, sparking a controversy over his alleged use of gimmickry, but was soon accepted by critics and public alike. Worked in Louisville, then moved to Chi. '60, rec. for Argo. Pl. w. Chas. Mingus for four mos. in '61, then led own gps. in US and Eur. Pl. in Eur. w. Dexter Gordon, Johnny Griffin '63. By '63 Kirk was using the technique of circular breathing to produce uninterrupted sound. Led gp. Vibration Society mid '60s-75. In the early '70s he was the leader of the Jazz and People's Movement, an organization for the promotion of black music. In August '70 the JAPM, led by Kirk and Lee Morgan, interrupted the taping of the *Merv Griffin Show* to protest the dearth of black music and musicians in TV studios. Paralyzed on one side by a stroke in '75, he was able to resume perf. the following yr. A few mos. bef. his death, he founded the Vibration Sch. of Mus. for saxophonists. His knowledge and performing abilities spanned the entire history of jazz. Polls: *DB* Critics '62, '72–3; *DB* Readers '68, '71, '74; *Play.* '71, '73; *Play.* All-Stars '74. Fests: all major fr. '61. Video: *The One Man Twin* (Rh.); Kirk–John Cage (Rhap.). TV: BBC *Tempo* '67; Soul '72. CDs: Em.; Chess; Prest.; Night; PJ; Verve; Atl.; 32; w. C. Mingus (Atl.); Jaki Byard (Prest.).

KIRKLAND, KENNY (KENNETH DAVID), pno, el kybds; b. Brooklyn, NY, 9/28/55; d. Queens, NY, 11/12/98. Educated at Catholic sch.; began pl. pno. at age 6. Stud. at Manh. Sch. of Mus., where he perf. Bach, Beethoven, Liszt, and Brahms. Majored in theory, comp. After graduation, join. vlnst. Michal Urbaniak for two yrs. Pl. w. Billy Harper; Chico Hamilton; Miroslav Vitous. In 1981 he began a long collaboration with Wynton Marsalis, and fr. '85 to '90 toured and rec. with Sting. He toured the world extensively, especially enjoying his visits w. Sting to the Ivory Coast and Zimbabwe. Fr. '92 to '95 he was a member of the *Tonight Show* band under Branford Marsalis. Rec. w. Urbaniak; Vitous; Elvin Jones; Marsalis; Sting. Found dead in his home, apparently of a drug overdose. CDs: GRP; w. Branford Marsalis (Col.); J. Scofield (Novus); Billy Hart; James Newton (Gram.); Courtney Pine (Ant.); Stanley Jordan (BN); D. Gillespie; A. Sandoval; GRP All-Star bb (GRP); Rodney Jones; Michael Brecker (Imp.); Charnett Moffett (Manh.); Robert Hurst (DIW; Col.); Miroslav Vitous (ECM; Evid.); Kenny Garrett (WB); Jeff Watts (Sunny.); Franco Ambrosetti (Enja); Carla Bley (Watt); C. Fambrough; Ernie Watts (CTI); L. Soloff (PW); Sting (A&M).

KISOR, RYAN, tpt; b. Sioux City, IA, 4/12/73. Father pl. tpt. At 10, Ryan pl. w. Eddie Skeets' local dance band. Two yrs. later start. classical stud. at Morningside Coll. but was soon infl. by Clifford Brown. At 15 met Clark Terry and attended his summer jazz camp. Pl. in all-star hs band at 1988 and '89 conventions of IAJE. In Nov. '90 won first place at the Thelonious Monk Institute's tpt. contest and was signed in '91 to rec. for CBS. He enrolled at the Manh. Sch. of Mus., stud. w. Lew Soloff '91. An astonishingly mature talent who made a tremendous impression on the Monk contest's judges: Clark Terry, Nat Adderley, Red Rodney, and Snooky Young. He has since pl. w. Mingus Dynasty; Gil Evans Orch.; Charlie Haden's Liberation Orch.;

Bobby Watson's bb; LCJO; Philip Morris Jazz All-Stars; Pat Metheny; and the Mingus bb. CDs: Col.; Fable; CC; w. G. Mulligan (Tel.); Ray Anderson (Gram.); Dick Katz (Res.); Andy McKee (Maple.); Mingus bb (Drey.); DMP bb (DMP).

KITAMURA, EIJI, cl, alto, tnr saxes; b. Tokyo, Japan, 4/8/29. Self-taught. Started pl. cl. w. Keio U. coll. band. Pl. first prof. gig w. Tetsuro Takahama's Esquire Cats 1950, then pl. w. Saburo Nanbu '51–3; own gp. Cats Herd '54–7; Mitsuru Ono & his 6 Bros '57–60. Jammed w. Benny Goodman in Tokyo '57. Led own qnt. fr. '60. Pl. w. house band on NET-TV's *Morning Show* late '60s-early '70s. Rec. as lead. w. Teddy Wilson '71, '73; as sideman w. Woody Herman; John Lewis; Hank Jones. Received Fumio Nanri awd. for contrib. to Japanese jazz '77. Rec. bop album w. Harold Land '80. Co-organizer w. Bill Berry of Int'l Jazz Party in LA fr. '91. Kitamura has been one of Japan's most popular jazz mus. since the early '70s. Favs: Goodman, Teddy Wilson, Earl Hines. Polls: *SJ* Readers '60–2, '64–92. Fests: MJF annually fr. '78; Conc. JF '80; Jazz Yatra, India '82. TV: many apps. on Japanese TV. CDs: Audio Lab; GML; Teichiku-Union; Song; Apollon; Century.

KLEIN, MANNY (EMANUEL), tpt; b. NYC, 2/4/08; d. North Hollywood, CA, 5/31/94. Professional debut in late 1920s w. Louis Katzman. Pl. in B'way show, *Follow Through*, w. Al Goodman band '28. Fr. then until '37 he pl. on hundreds of commercial and jazz recs. incl. dates w. Joe Venuti; Red Nichols; Dorsey Bros.; Benny Goodman. To LA '37; co-led band w. Frankie Trumbauer '37–8. After stints w. Matty Malneck, Ray Noble, and Artie Shaw, he was mainly active in the studios. App. on numerous film sound tracks, incl. *Rio Bravo, The Benny Goodman Story*, and *From Here To Eternity*. Cont. an active career until '73, when he was incapacitated by a stroke. Klein was an eclectic and skillful perf., both in lead and solo roles, well-known for solos on "By Heck" (w. Dorsey Bros.) and "Somebody Loves Me" (w. Adrian Rollini). CDs: w. Dorsey Bros. (Col.); Louis Armstrong (BB; Vict.); Judy Garland (Dec.); Hoagy Carmichael; B. Goodman (BB); Ella Fitzgerald (Verve); Ethel Waters (Milan); Lena Horne (BB).

KLEIN, MIRIAM, voc; b. Basel, Switzerland, 3/27/37. While married to Austr. tptr. Oscar Klein, she sang w. his Dixieland band but was better known for *Lady Like*, a remarkable '73 album w. Roy Eldridge, Dexter Gordon, and Slide Hampton on which she showed a strong resemblance to Billie Holiday. Also rec. w. Wild Bill Davison. Visited US briefly, but has mainly worked concerts or fests around Eur. Rec. for Dirox, accomp. only by Kirk Lightsey. CDs: App.; Divox.

KLEIN, OSCAR, tpt, gtr; b. Graz, Austria, 1/5/30; d. Plünderhausen, Germ., 12/12/06. Self-taught. Insp. by Cootie Williams, Wild Bill Davison, Roy Eldridge, and guitarists Eddie Condon, Blind Blake, Lightnin' Hopkins. In '60s pl. w. Dutch Swing Coll. Band; was married to and worked w. singer Miriam Klein; also pl. w. visiting Americans, incl. Davison, Joe Venuti. Hosted Pickin' the Blues, a Swiss TV series '75; app. w. Romano Mussolini in Eur. Fest: L. Hampton Idaho JF w. Mussolini '95. CDs: N-H; w. Peter Meyer (N-H).

KLEMMER, JOHN, tnr sax; b. Chicago, IL, 7/3/46. Started on alto sax; also att. Stan Kenton clinics 1960–5. At 21 moved to LA to join Don Ellis, w. whom he tour. US and Eur. Dur. that time he also tour. West Africa w. Oliver Nelson. Best known for jazz-rock style innovations using echo-plex, ring modulator, and other electronic effects. Rec. duos w. Eddie Harris in the '80s. CDs: BB; Imp.; JVC.

KLINK, AL (ALBERT), tnr sax, fl; b. Danbury, CT, 12/28/15; d. Bradenton, FL, 3/17/91. First important job w. Glenn Miller 1939–42; then w. Benny Goodman '42–4; Tommy Dorsey '43, '44–5; WNEW staff early '47. Freelanced in NYC until summer '54, incl. w. Sauter-Finegan orch. '52–3. Join. NBC staff '54. Began assoc. w. WGJB from late '74, incl. Eur. tours to '82. Fav: Lester Young. Recs: chases w. Tex Beneke on Miller's "In the Mood"; bs. sax solo on "Goodnight, Sweetheart" w. the McGuire Sisters. CDs: w. Miller; Lee Wiley; Sauter-Finegan (BB); B. Goodman (Cap.); T. Dorsey (BB; Hep); Yank Lawson (Jazz.); R. Braff (Aff.).

KLOSS, ERIC, saxes, comp, pno, dms; b. Greenville, PA, 4/3/49. Studied sax at Western Pa. Sch. for Blind Children 1959–67; w. Robert Korshan; Henry Marconi; Tom McKinley in Pitts. Began on alto, later added tnr. and sop. Received degree in philosophy fr. Duquesne U. '72. Made prof. debut in Pitts. w. Bob Negri at age 12. Pl. w. Charles Bell at Pitts. Carnegie Mus. Hall '62–3; Walt Harper '65–7; Pat Martino fr. '65. Made rec. debut in '65. Was subject of a docu. film on Pitts. public TV '66. Stud. in NYC w. Lee Konitz; Sonny Stitt; James Moody. Kloss has led his own gps. fr. '65, w. sidemen incl. Jimmy Owens; Booker Ervin; Cedar Walton; Kenny Barron; Chick Corea; Leroy Vinnegar; Bob Cranshaw; Dave Holland; Billy Higgins; Alan Dawson; Jack DeJohnette. Favs: Charlie Parker, Ornette Coleman, Eric Dolphy, John Coltrane. Fests: NJF-NY '73;

Pitts. JF. LPs for Prest.; Muse; Omnisound. CDs: Prest.; w. Pat Martino (Prest.).

KLUGER, IRV (IRVING), dms, vib; b. Brooklyn, NY, 7/9/21; d. Las Vegas, NV, 2/28/06. Studied vln. 1930–34; dms. w. Henry Adler; comp. at NYU. Pl. w. Bob Astor, Georgie Auld '42–3; Bob Chester, Freddie Slack '43–4; Boyd Raeburn '45–7; Herbie Fields, Bobby Byrne '47; Stan Kenton '47–8; Artie Shaw '49 and again '53–4. Later pl. B'way shows, moved to Calif., where he was active as a freelance and studio mus.; then to LV. CDs: w. A. Shaw (MM); Raeburn; D. Gillespie (Sav.); Kenton (Cap.).

KLUGH, EARL, gtr; b. Detroit, MI, 9/16/54. Stud. pno. then gtr. at 10. First prominent on Yusef Lateef's album, *Suite 16* 1970. Shortly thereafter he tour. and rec. w. George Benson. Joined Chick Corea's Return to Forever '74. Began rec. as a leader '76; also rec. "One on One" w. Bob James. From early '80s his work took on an increasingly pop-oriented style which had in its better moments traces of r&b. Infls: Chet Atkins, Lenny Breau, Laurindo Almeida. CDs: Manh.; BN; WB; w. Benson; B. James (Col.); Yusef Lateef (Rh.).

KNEPPER, JIMMY (JAMES MINTER), tbn, bs-tbn, v-tbn, bari horn, arr; b. Los Angeles, CA, 11/22/27; d. Triadelphia, WV, 6/14/03. Wife tptr. Maxine Fields. Began on bari. horn, then sw. to tbn. at age 9. Stud. w. Doc Edward Hiner, then at LA City and State Colls. Pl. w. Chuck Cascales '43–4; Tommy Reynolds, Kenny Baker, Red Dorris '45; Freddy Slack '48; Roy Porter '49; Joe Maini '49–51; Charlie Spivak, Charlie Parker '50; Charlie Barnet '51; Woody Herman '56; Claude Thornhill '56–7. Became widely known through his assoc. w. Charles Mingus '57–61. Pl. w. Stan Kenton '59; Gil Evans '60–77; Benny Goodman '62 (incl. USSR tour); Thad Jones–Mel Lewis Orch. '68–74; Joe Albany '70s. Pl. and arr. for Lee Konitz Nonet '75–81; Mingus Dynasty '79–89. Also pl. for B'way shows, incl. *Funny Girl* '64–6. He also worked w. Jimmy Zito; Johnny "Scat" Davis; Wingy Manone; Shorty Rogers; Jimmy McPartland; Buck Clayton; Clark Terry; Toshiko Akiyoshi; Pepper Adams; Gary Smulyan. In later yrs. he perf. and rec. w. several repertory ens., incl. AJO; Nat'l Jazz Ens.; Smithsonian Jazz Orch. Frank Van Dixhoorn wrote: "Every inflection in Jimmy Knepper's phrases, every move from third to fourth position is a split-second victory of form over vacuum. His wit, the veil over one measure and the razor-sharp intonation which reveals another, all these might be described. But they can't be predicted." Fav: Charlie Parker. Polls: *DB* New Star '58; *DB* '81–5. Fests: Eur., Japan, Africa since '60. CDs: Steep.; CC; SN; Beth.; tracks in *The Debut Story* (Deb.); w. Mingus (Atl.; Col.; RCA; Deb.: Imp.); G. Smulyan (CC); G. Gruntz (TCB); L. Konitz (Chiaro; SN; Steep.); Mingus Dynasty; Mingus BB; George Adams (SN); Clark Terry (Cand.); C. Bley (ECM); J. Breakstone (Cont.); K. Burrell (Verve); Dolphy (Cand.; Enja); Gil Evans (Imp.; Enja; Ant.); Goodman (MM); C. Hawkins (Imp); Joe Henderson (BN); Jones-Lewis (LRC).

KOFFMAN, MOE (MORRIS), fl, saxes, cl, comp, arr; b. Toronto, Ont., Canada, 12/28/28; d. Toronto, 3/28/01. Son Herb is tptr. Began on vln. at age 9, alto sax at age 13. Stud. at Toronto Cons. w. Herbert Pye, Samuel Dolin; later priv. w. Gordon Delamont. Pl. w. dance bands incl. Horace Lapp, Leo Romanelli, Benny Louis '40s. Koffman was among the first Canadian jazz mus. to adopt the bebop style. Made rec. debut w. US mus. in Buffalo, N.Y. '48. Moved to NYC '50. Pl. w. Sonny Dunham '50; Ralph Flanagan '50–1; Buddy Morrow '51; Jimmy Dorsey '51–2; Tex Beneke '52–3; Don Rodney '53–4; also freelanced w. Charlie Barnet, Art Mooney, Tito Rodriguez, Chico O'Farrill early '50s. Stud. in NYC w. Harold Bennett, Leon Russianoff. Ret. to Toronto '55. Worked as booking agent and pl. one night a week at George's Spaghetti House '56–90; also extens. studio work. Had hit single on fl. w. "Swingin' Shepherd Blues" '58. Rec. pop-jazz albums fr. '70s, incl. arrs. of comps. by Bach, Mozart, Vivaldi, etc. Pl. w. Boss Brass fr. '72. Led house band on TV show *Everything Goes* '74. App. as fl. soloist w. Toronto Symph. '75, also w. other Can. orchs. In '82 Koffman's qnt. began an assoc. w. Dizzy Gilles-pie, pl. several concerts in Can. each yr. Pl. w. Gilles-pie's United Nation bb at Du Maurier JF, Toronto '88. Koffman's qnt. perf. w. Peter Appleyard at fests fr. '91. Polls: CBC Jazz Unlimited '48; Toronto Arts Award '91. Fests: Austral. '80; So. Amer. '85; Germ. '90; many apps. in US. TV: Can. Timex jazz show '59; *Tonight Show* mid '60s. CDs: Soundwings; Duke Street; w. Boss Brass (Conc.; Imp.); Phil Nimmons (Sack.).

KOHLMAN, FREDDIE, dms, voc, lead; b. New Orleans, LA, 8/25/18; d. New Orleans, 9/29/90. Studied w. Louis Cottrell Sr., Manuel Manetta; pl. w. bands of A. J. Piron; Joe Robichaux; Papa Celestin; Sam Morgan. Moved to Chi. in mid 1930s, pl. in qt. w. Albert Ammons, Stuff Smith; also worked w. Earl Hines, Lee Collins. Ret. to NO '41, lead. own band fr. '44. Six mos. w. Louis Armstrong in mid '50s; then house dmr. at Jazz Ltd. in Chi. bef. ret. to NO in '60s. Pl. w. Louis Cottrell Jr., Dukes of Dixieland, and Onward Brass Band, the latter in '68. App. at NOJF '69. In '70s and '80s he app. at Eur. fests w. own gp.

and w. Milan-based Jambalaya Four. Rec. as lead. w. his Mardi Gras Loungers (MGM) '53; w. Chris Barber and Dr. John (BL) '80. CDs: w. Albert Nicholas–Art Hodes (Del.); Bob Wilber (Cir.); Excelsior Brass Band; Heritage Hall Jazz Band (GHB).

KOIVISTOINEN, EERO, tnr, sop saxes, comp; b. Helsinki, Finland, 1/13/46. Studied at Sibelius Acad. 1968–70. Led own gps. fr. '64; one of first Finnish mus. to pl. free jazz. Pl. w. rock gp. Blues Section '66–7. Led trio '67–9, qt. '69–71. Won int'l competition at Montreux JF '69 and was rewarded w. app. at the NJF. Stud. w. Herb Pomeroy, Joe Viola at Berklee Coll. of Mus. '71–3, then ret. to Sibelius Acad. '73–4. Co-led qt. w. Heikki Sarmanto '71–3; own gp. Music Society fr. '73. Tour. Eur. w. own gp. '70s. Pl. w. Helsinki New Music Orch. (UMO) fr. '75 to '88. He cond. it frequently thereafter and in May '96 was named artistic dir. for two yrs. Many apps. as cond. w. bbs in Germ., Nor., Den., incl. Hessicher Radio bb; Danish Radio Jazz Orch. Taught jazz in Faeroe Islands '79 and at Sibelius Acad. in Helsinki. Koivistoinen's ballet *Mother Earth* was perf. at the Helsinki City Theater '79. Won award for best arr. in Nordring radio competition for suite *Ultima Thule* '81; first prize in competition of Foundation for Promotion of Finnish Music for *Kukonpesa*. Established Pro rec. label '83. Chairman of Zone, a society of comp. '91; form. Trio X '95. His work as a comp. has been described as "cleverly exploiting different elements; national influences and hints of rock and ethno combine with jazz in an idiom rich in rhythmic variety." Fav: John Coltrane; comps: Duke Ellington, Gil Evans. Polls: Georgie Award as Best Finnish Jazz Mus. '67. CDs: Pro (some feat. such mus. as Jon Scofield; Tom Harrell; Jim McNeely; Randy Brecker; Jack DeJohnette); SN.

KOLLER, HANS, tnr, sop saxes, cl, comp; b. Vienna, Austria, 2/12/21; d. Vienna, 12/21/03. Studied cl. at Vienna Mus. Acad. '35–9. Made prof. debut on tnr. '38. In Germ. army '40–6; he was one of the few who pl. during the Nazi yrs. Led house band at Hot Club Vienna '47–50. Moved to Germ. '50; pl. w. Freddie Brocksieper, then led own qt. and New Jazz Stars w. Jutta Hipp, Albert Mangelsdorff. Pl. in Eur. w. Dizzy Gillespie '53; Lee Konitz–Lars Gullin '54; own qnt. w. Roland Kovac '54–6; Stan Kenton Orch. '55; Eddie Sauter's Baden-Baden radio bb '57–8; Benny Goodman '58. Led qt. w. Attila Zoller, Oscar Pettiford, Kenny Clarke or Jimmy Pratt late '50s. Dir. Norddeutscher Rundfunk jazz wkshps. '58–65; taught at Deutsches Schauspielhaus '68. Ret. to Vienna in '70; form. Free Sound w. Wolfgang Dauner, Adelhard Roidinger, Zbigniew Seifert. Led

Int'l Brass. Co. w. Kenny Wheeler, Mangelsdorff, Dauner '75–80. Pl. w. Fritz Pauer, Warne Marsh in '80s. Koller's extended comps. incl. the ballet *New York City* '68. He was also active as an abstract painter, exhibiting in Germ., Austr., France fr. '57. Polls: Austr. poll '72; *Podium* and *Jazz-Echo* polls many times. Fests: all major in Eur. Film: *Jazz Gestern und Heute.* TV: many apps. on Eur. TV. CDs: L&R; In + Out; w. Dauner; M. Solal (MPS); O. Pettiford (BL); Wolfgang Puschnig (Amadeo); Zoller (MPS; L&R).

KOMEDA, KRZYSZTOF (Krzystof Trzcinski), comp, pno; b. Poznan, Poland, 4/27/31; d. Warsaw, Poland, 4/23/69. Youngest student at Poznan Cons.; later took priv. pno. lessons and stud. mus. theory. Fr. 1950 closely assoc. w. jazz; co-creator of Polish jazz movement. Since government frowned on jazz, he began using the name Komeda to protect himself in his profession as doctor. Rose to local popularity w. perf. at Sopot JF '56. Led own free jazz qnt. at fests in Moscow; Kongsberg; Bled; clubs in Swed., Den. Active in jazz-poetry fusion. As songwriter won special award at National Song Fest, Opole '64. Comp. for ballet, mus. theater, and films incl. dirs. such as Jerzy Skolimowski, Henning Carlsen, and Roman Polanski. Those w. the latter incl. *Knife in the Water; The Vampire Killers; Cul-de-Sac; Rosemary's Baby.* Moved to Hollywood, Calif. in '67 to work w. Polanski. After being injured in an LA accident Jan. '69, he underwent brain surgery but never regained consciousness. Flown to Warsaw in April, he died a few days later. In '73 he was honored w. an entire concert of his mus. at the 15th Int'l Warsaw Jazz Jamboree. A four-volume LP set of his mus. was issued by the Polish label Muza. CDs: (w. more in production) on the Polonia label, entitled *The Complete Works of Krzysztof Komeda*; Power Bros.

KONITZ, LEE, alto sax, sop sax; b. Chicago, IL, 10/13/27. Began on cl. Stud. in Chi. w. Lou Honig, Santy Runyon, later w. Lennie Tristano. Pl. w. Gay Claridge, Jimmy Dale bb, Lennie Tristano in Chi. mid 1940s; Teddy Powell, Jerry Wald '45; Claude Thornhill '47–8; Miles Davis Nonet '48–50; recs. and occ. gigs w. Tristano late '40s. Tour. as single in Scand. '51. Pl. w. Gerry Mulligan '52; Stan Kenton Orch. '52–3; own gps. in US and Eur. fr. '53; Tristano '54–5, '59, '64. After app. on Miles Davis Nonet's "Birth of the Cool" sessions, Konitz became known as a chief exponent of the cool alto style, at a time when most altoists were under the overwhelming infl. of Charlie Parker. He taught and perf. infreq. in Calif. '62–4, then reemerged in the mid '60s. Tour. Eur. as single '65–6 and in '70s. In '75 he resumed his assoc. w. Warne Marsh, his former Tristano colleague, and

the duo released a series of albums. Konitz led a nonet, modeled after the Miles Davis Nonet, in the '70s. He has taught priv. since '52, and conducted lessons via tape with students all over the world. Author of an instruction book, *Jazz Lines* (William H. Bauer Publ.). In the '80s, made duo recs. w. Hal Galper, Martial Solal, Harold Danko, etc.; in '90s also led Brazilian qt. that incl. pnst. Peggy Stern. One of the true jazz improvisers. Awarded the Jazzpar Prize in Den. '92; Order of Arts and Letters fr. French government, NYC '98. Favs: C. Parker, Johnny Hodges, Ornette Coleman. Fests: all major fr. '50s; at Umbria Jazz '98, pl. w. Ornette Coleman and in a trio w. Paul Bley and Charlie Haden. Polls: *Met.* '54; *DB* Critics '57–8; TDWR '69. Video: *Lee Konitz: Portrait of an Artist* (Rhap.). CDs: Enja; Steep.; Atl.; Verve; Prest.; Mile.; Mos.; Phil.; BN; Vogue; BL; PJ; Owl; Sonet; Musidisc; LRC; BL; PJ; Owl; Sonet; SN; IAI; Label Bleu; M.A. Music; MM; Cand.; Evid.; Prog.; Story.; *Complete Tristano, Konitz & Marsh* (Mos.); w. Thornhill (Col.); M. Davis (Cap.; Prest.); Tristano (Cap.; Atl.); Marsh-Konitz (Mob. Fid.); Kenny Wheeler (ECM); Corea (Stretch); Lars Gullin (Drag.); Kenton (Cap.; Mos.); Mingus (Rh./Atl.; Deb.); Gil Evans (Verve; Prest.); Bill Evans (Fant.); G. Mulligan (PJ).

KOONSE, DAVE (DAVID L.), gtr; b. St. Joseph, MO, 8/26/37. Father a steel gtrst., taught him to pl. fr. age 4. Pl. and traveled w. Harry James band; George Shearing; Les Elgart; Chico Hamilton; Red Norvo. Son is gtrst. Larry Koonse. Recs. w. Charlie Barnet; James; Shearing; Gary Foster; Rod McCuen; et al. CDs: w. J. Rowles (JVC).

KOTICK, TEDDY (THEODORE), bs; Haverhill, MA, 6/4/28; d. Boston, MA, 4/17/86. Guitar at 6; bs. in hs. Gigged in New Engl.; to NYC 1948, pl. w. Johnny Bothwell; Buddy Rich; Tony Pastor. With Buddy DeFranco '49, '52; Artie Shaw '50; Stan Getz '51–3; Charlie Parker on and off '51–4; Bill Evans '56; George Wallington '56–7; Horace Silver '57–8; Al Cohn–Zoot Sims '59. Tour. w. Claude Thornhill early '60s; Martial Solal in US '63. Ret. to Mass. in early '70s, working locally and occ. rec. w. J. R. Monterose '79; Allen Eager '82. A reluctant soloist, he was a very strong accomp., referred to by Charlie Parker as "my heartbeat." Favs: Jimmy Blanton, Ray Brown, Tommy Potter. CDs: w. C. Parker (Verve; Jazz Classic; Rhino); S. Getz (Roul.; Roost; Mos.); B. Evans (Riv.; Mile.); G. Wallington; Jimmy Raney; Jon Eardley (Prest.); George Russell (BB); Teddy Charles (Atl.); Herbie Nichols; Horace Silver (BN); Phil Woods (Prest.; NJ); Rene Thomas (Jzld.); Al Haig (FS).

KRAL, IRENE, voc; b. Chicago, IL, 1/18/32; d. Encino, CA, 8/15/78. Sister of Roy Kral. Pl. pno., cl. in hs. Began singing at 16 w. Jay Burkhart Orch.; briefly w. Woody Herman, Chubby Jackson. Join. voc. gp. Tattle Tales, leaving in 1955 to work as a single. Worked w. Maynard Ferguson '57–8; Stan Kenton, Herb Pomeroy, Shelly Manne in early '60s. Moved to LA and freelanced there in '60s and '70s. Fav: Carmen McRae. Recs: own sess. for UA; DRG; Main.; Choice; Ava; w. Ferguson (Em); Pomeroy (UA); L. Almeida; S. Manne (Cap.). CDs: FS; Just Jazz.

KRAL, ROY JOSEPH, pno, voc, arr; b. Chicago, IL, 10/10/21; d. Montclair, NJ, 8/2/02. Sister, Irene Kral. Stud. classical pno. in Ill. 1927–35, inspired to pl. jazz after hearing Earl Hines on radio. Pl. w. own bb in Cicero, Ill. '39–40; Charlie Agnew '40–1; army bands in Mich. '42–6. Worked as staff arr. at Det. radio station '46–7. Made rec. debut w. Geo. Auld '47, then pl. w. Geo. Davis in Chi. '47. Kral met Jackie Cain when she joined Davis end of '47. Kral and Cain perf. together w. Dave Garroway in '48, then w. Charlie Ventura '48–9. They married in '49 and worked together as "Jackie and Roy," rec. over thirty albums. They had their own jingle prod. co. in the '60s and were active in the commercial field but later ret. to their jazz roots. Favs: Bill Evans, Tommy Flanagan, Jim McNeely. Polls: *DB, Met.* Fests: Eur., Asia, etc. since '49. TV: own progs. on PBS, CBC; also *Kraft Music Hall, Tonight Show*, Merv Griffin, Dinah Shore, Andy Williams, Smothers Bros. CDs: as Jackie & Roy, Col.; Koch; Red. Brn.; Sav.; Aud.; Disc.; DRG; BL; w. Ventura (Dec.; GNP Cres.).

KRALL, DIANA JEAN, voc, pno; b. Nanaimo, B.C., Canada, 11/16/64. Great-great-aunt, Jean, was in vaudeville in NYC. Both grandmoth. and moth. singers; fath. pl. pno. Began on pno. at age 4. Stud. harm. in jr. hs. Bryan Stovell, band dir. at Nanaimo District Senior Secondary Sch., taught her how to write charts for trio. Learned fr. her fath.'s and Stovell's rec. collections. Own trio in the summer after tenth grade. Att. Phil Nimmons Music Camp in Toronto, stud. w. Don Thompson. Pl. solo in restaurant, accomp. singer fr. age 15 to 17. Had duo at 15, trio at 16. Awarded scholarship to Berklee Coll. of Mus. fr. New Westminster JF 1982–3. Back to Nanaimo, summer '84; to Bud Shank's Jazz Wkshp., Port Townsend, Wash. Met Jeff Hamilton and, through him, Ray Brown '84, who encouraged her to come to LA. In fall '84 stud. there w. Alan Broadbent on Canada Arts Council Grant. Fr. '85 to '87, stud. w. Jimmy Rowles and cont. w. Brown. A job in Long Beach '86 required her to sing as well as play. Cont.

to pl. solo gigs into '87; ret. home again in second half of yr., remain. until spring '88. Then a scholarship enabled her to stud. w. Thompson in Toronto '88. Pl. solo pno. and sang in Toronto; pl., w. very little vocalizing, in Swed. and Switz. '89. Moved to NYC '90, worked there and w. her trio in Bost. Favs: Rowles, Jamal, Bill Evans, Peterson, Monty Alexander; vocs: grandmoth., Jean Krall, Bing Crosby, Maxine Sullivan, Ernestine Anderson. First rec. for Justin Time '93. After her dedication CD to Nat Cole, *All For You* (Imp.), she began tour. w. own trio w. Russell Malone, gtr., and Paul Keller, later Ben Wolfe, bs., app. at festivals worldwide and at Algonquin Hotel, NYC. Took part in tributes to Ella Fitzgerald, Carnegie Hall; and Benny Carter, Lincoln Center. Krall's accomplishment as a pianist certainly informs her convincing vocal delivery on rhythm numbers. Her hip, cool, yet intense ballad style sometimes makes her seem as if she stepped off the screen of a film noir. CDs: GRP; Imp.; JT; w. B. Carter (MM); Mark Whitfield (Verve).

KREITZER, SCOTT EDWARD, saxes, fl, cl; b. Brooklyn, NY, 11/2/64. Father pl. cl., tnr. sax; two sists. pl. gtr. and sang. Began on cl. at age 12. Stud. at U. of Miami 1982, William Paterson Coll. '84; later stud. w. Eddie Daniels. Pl. club dates while in hs in Miami. Pl. w. Ira Sullivan in Fla. '82–3; Blood, Sweat & Tears '85; Chuck Mangione. Pl. and rec. w. pop acts incl. Dionne Warwick; Julio Iglesias; David Lee Roth. Kreitzer was a winner in the Hennessy Jazz Search '88. He is active as a prod. and pop songwriter and leads his own qt. Favs: Rollins, Coltrane, Getz. Fests: Germ., Japan w. own qt. '90. CDs: Pony Canyon; Cexton; w. Spyro Gyra (GRP).

KRESS, CARL, gtr; b. Newark, NJ, 10/20/07; d. Reno, NV, 6/10/65. Began on bjo., then sw. to gtr. First prominent in Paul Whiteman Orch. dur. Bix-Trumbauer era, rec. w. the latter pair in 1927 on Chicago Loopers' date, and w. Red Nichols, Miff Mole; Dorsey Bros.; etc. '27–9. In the '30s he was a successful radio gtrst. and also a partner in the orig. Onyx Club on 52nd St. He rec. gtr. duets w. Eddie Lang '32, and Dick McDonough in '34. Cont. in commercial radio and TV work, incl. the Garry Moore show, for the most part, but pl. bjo. w. Clarence Hutchenrider trio '60. In the early '60s he and George Barnes recreated his Lang gtr. duets. He died of a heart attack while app. w. Barnes in a Nev. casino. One of the best and earliest rhythm gtrsts., Kress was the quintessential accompanist. CDs: ten tracks as leader on *Classic Capitol Jazz Sessions* (Mos.); w. Barnes (Jass); J. Teagarden (BB); (Dec.); Benny Goodman; B. Holiday (Dec.); Capitol

Jazzmen (Jazz Unlimited); E. Condon (Jazz.); Beiderbecke (Col.); Lang (Yazoo); Red Nichols (Tax); Edmond Hall (BN).

KRIVDA, ERNIE (ERNEST PAUL), tnr, alto, sop, saxes, cl; b. Cleveland, OH, 2/6/45. Father is prof. reed pl.; two uncles are amateur mus. Stud. cl. w. father fr. age of 7, then w. Dave O'Rourke at Phil Rizzo's Mod. Mus. Sch. Pl. w. Italian, Polish, and Hungarian bands fr. age 14; led own bb in hs. Stud. at Cleveland Institute of Mus., Baldwin-Wallace Cons. Pl. w. Jimmy Dorsey Orch. 1963; various show bands '64–7; Eddie Baccus, William "Weasel" Parker bb '65–7; Bill Dobbins '69; house band at Smiling Dog, Cleveland, Bill DeArango '70–4; Groove Holmes, Kenny Davis '74; Quincy Jones '75. Led own qt. in NYC '76–80, then ret. to Cleveland '80. Formed Cleveland Jazz All-Stars '82. Pl. w. Kenny Davis '82–4; Cadence Jazz All-Stars fr. '89. Krivda has led his own qt. in Cleveland fr. '80. He has taught jazz history and improv. at Lakeland Comm. Coll. fr. '89 and has been active as a clinician fr. '82. Favs: Getz, C. Hawkins, C. Adderley. Polls: all Cleveland magazine polls fr. '72. Fests: Japan w. Q. Jones '75; North Sea JF '81. TV: local PBS jazz specials. CDs: Cad.; Koch; CIMP; w. Cadence All-Stars (Timel.).

KRONOS QUARTET. String qt. formed in 1978 and based in SF: Donald Harrington, first vln. and mus. dir.; John Sherba, second vln.; Hank Dutt, vla.; Joan Jeanrenaud, cello. Noted for its interpretations of comp. such as Philip Glass, John Cage, and Terry Riley, Kronos rec. two albums on Landmark: *Monk Suite* '84, music by Thelonious Monk w. guests Ron Carter, Chuck Israels, and Eddie Marshall; and *Music of Bill Evans* '85 w. guests Jim Hall and Eddie Gomez. Arrs. and adaptations on both projects by Tom Darter. CD: 32.

KRUPA, GENE, dms, lead; b. Chicago, IL, 1/15/09; d. Yonkers, NY, 10/16/73. Played first gigs w. Frivolians in Chi. in 1921. Studied w. Edward B. Straight, Roy Knapp early '20s. Attended St. Joseph's Coll., Ind. '24–5. Made rec. debut 12/9/27 w. Red McKenzie–Eddie Condon Chicagoans. Pl. in Chi. w. Thelma Terry, Joe Kayser, Leo Shukin, Benson Orch. '27–8. Came to NYC w. McKenzie '29. Pl. w. Red Nichols at Hollywood Restaurant '29; Bix Beiderbecke, Adrian Rollini; also commercial bands incl. Irving Aaronson, Russ Columbo, Mal Hallett, Buddy Rogers early '30s. Join. Benny Goodman '34. Krupa was feat. on the hit "Sing Sing Sing" and became hugely popular while w. Goodman; leaving to form his own bb in '38–43. This band was especially popular in '42–3 when it featured Anita O'Day and Roy

Eldridge. Pl. w. Goodman '43; Tommy Dorsey '43–4; own bb '44–51 w. such sidemen as Charlie Kennedy, Buddy Wise, Don Fagerquist, Frank Rosolino, Red Rodney. JATP '51–3; own trio w. Charlie Ventura or Eddie Shu early '50s. Stud. tympani w. Saul Goodman (NY Philharm.) '51. Started own drum sch. w. Cozy Cole '54. Back w. JATP '59; own qt., often w. Ventura, fr. early '60s; occ. reunions w. Goodman, own bb in '60s. Made last publ. app. w. Goodman at NJF-NY '73. Krupa was the first musician to bring widespread public attention to the role of the drummer in jazz. He is widely regarded as one of the great technical masters and a lifelong student of the dms. Films: *Ball of Fire* '41; *Syncopation* '42; *Book Revue* (cartoon) '45; *Beat the Band* '47; (shorts) *Follow That Music* '46; *Drummer Man* '47; *Deep Purple* '49; w. Goodman, *Hollywood Hotel* '37; *Benny Goodman Story* '55. A fictionalized account of his life, *The Gene Krupa Story*, was released in '59. Favs: Cozy Cole, Buddy Rich, Dave Black. Polls: *Met.* '37–45; *DB* '36–9, '43, '52–3; *Esq.* Silver Award '46. TV: *Chicago and All That Jazz* '61; many apps. on *Tonight Show*, Merv Griffin, Mike Douglas, Sammy Davis Jr., etc. CDs: Col.; Verve; Jazz Unlimited; Hep; w. Goodman (BB; Col.; Dec.); Billie Holiday (Col.); Roy Eldridge (Col.; Verve); Hoagy Carmichael (BB); Condon (Jazz.); T. Dorsey (Hep; Jass); Red Nichols (Tax); O. Peterson (Pab); Teagarden; Waller (BB); T. Wilson (Hep); JATP (Verve; Pab.)

KRYSTALL, MARTY (MARTIN), tnr sax, bs cl, various reeds; b. Los Angeles, CA, 4/12/51. Studied classical cl. fr. age 11, later pl. in community orchs. At 15, heard Eric Dolphy's version of "Epistrophy," learn. tnr., later stud. fl. and oboe. Gigged w. Albert Collins 1970; closely assoc. w. Buell Neidlinger fr. '71; in El Monte Art Ensemble '71–77; Krystall Klear and the Buells '78–84; Buellgrass (later Stringjazz); Thelonious '86–90; and own qt. Also w. Peter Ivers Band '72–74; Jaco Pastorius's Word of Mouth Orch. '82; Charlie Haden's Liberation Orch. '86–8. Krystall combines the huge tone of a Ben Webster w. the interval jumps and adventurous spirit of an Eric Dolphy. CDs: Den.; M.A. WH; w. Neidlinger (SN; K2B2).

KÜHN, JOACHIM KURT, pno, comp; b. Leipzig, Germany, 3/15/44. Brother of Rolf Kühn. Classical career until 1961, when he became jazz artist w. S & H Qnt. in Prague, and for many yrs. off and on co-led qt. w. his bro. Dur. '70s he worked in NYC, also at NJF. Many other fests throughout Eur. Inspired by Franz Schubert, Miles Davis, John Coltrane. Won *Jazz Forum* poll for several yrs. fr. '70. Structurally and harmonically, Kuhn became known as an adventurous soloist and comp., occ. doubling on alto sax. Comps: *Paris/71/72 for Piano and Orchestra; Piano Solos 1–12*. CDs: CMP; co-lead. w. O. Coleman (Verve); Helen Merrill (Em.); L. Coryell (Act); D. Humair (Label Bleu; Blue Flame); Rolf Kühn (Blue Flame; L&R); M. Solal (Drey.).

KÜHN, ROLF, cl; b. Cologne, Germany, 9/29/29. Brother, pnst. Joachim Kühn. Stud. pno. for three yrs. Pl. cl. in Germ. bands and frequent radio apps. dur. 1940s and '50s. Fr. '56 to '61 he was based in NYC, where he subbed for Benny Goodman, pl. in Tommy Dorsey band led by Warren Covington. Rec. w. Dick Johnson, Toshiko Akiyoshi, et al. Back in Germ., he led various gps., worked w. Friedrich Gulda, toured and rec. w. his bro. Kühn was one of the few clsts. to work in a wide range of areas that incl. swing, bop, free jazz and jazz rock. CDs: Intuit; Blue Flame; Miramar.

KUHN, STEVE (STEPHEN L.), pno; b. Brooklyn, NY, 3/24/38. Studied w. Margaret Chaloff (Serge Chaloff's mother) fr. 1950, then at Harvard '55–9. Pl. solo and trio around Bost. fr. '51. Pl. w. Kenny Dorham '59–60; John Coltrane '60; Stan Getz '61–3; Charles Lloyd '64; Art Farmer '65–6; Art Blakey '66. Moved to Stockholm, Sweden '67, perf. and rec. in Eur. Ret. to US '71, led own gps., incl. a qt. w. Sheila Jordan, Bob Moses, Harvie Swartz in the late '70s. Kuhn pl. for jingles, TV, etc. in the early '80s but has since ret. to pl. jazz w. his own duo and trio. He has also been active as an educ., teaching at Harvard, Berklee, the New Sch., Eastman Sch. of Mus., New Engl. Cons. Frequently app. at Knickerbocker, NYC in '90s. Favs: Art Tatum, Bud Powell, Bill Evans. Fests: Eur. since '67. TV: many apps. on Eur. TV. CDs: ECM; Post.; Conc.; Owl; Evid.; Res.; w. Steve Swallow (ECM; XtraWatt); Dorham (Time); Getz (Verve); Joe Henderson (BN); Bob Moses (Gram.); O. Nelson (Imp.).

KYLE, BILLY (WILLIAM OSBORN), pno; b. Philadelphia, PA, 7/14/14; d. Youngstown, OH, 2/23/66. Studied org., pno.; pl. w. local bands fr. 1930; Tiny Bradshaw and Mills Blue Rhythm Band, under Lucky Millinder, bef. join. John Kirby '38–42. After army service '42–5, rejoin. Kirby briefly '46. then worked intermittently w. Sy Oliver '46–52; B'way pit bands, incl. two and a half yrs. w. *Guys and Dolls*. Fr. '53 until his death, brought on by an ulcer attack, he tour. worldwide w. Louis Armstrong's gp. Kyle was important in that he broke with the prevailing Teddy Wilson style of the early '30s. He was noted for his unique single-note style, infl., he claimed, by a saxophonist he had worked w. in '34. It was dynamically reminiscent of Earl Hines, but melodically quite original and often humorous in spirit. CDs: Class.; two tracks w. own gp. on *Giants of Small Band Swing, Vol. 1* (Riv.); w. Billie Holiday (Col.; Dec.); Anita O'Day (Sig.); Louis Armstrong (Col.; Dec.; Milan; Mos.; Verve; Pab.; BL; Story.); Buck Clayton (Mos.); Rex Stewart (Riv.); tracks w. J. Kirby and Leonard Feather All-Stars on *52nd Street Swing* (Dec.); Maxine Sullivan (Cir.); L. Hampton (BB); Benny Carter (B&B); Brubeck (Col.); Red Allen (Tax); Teddy Grace (Timel.).

KYNARD, CHARLES E., org, pno, tba, comp, arr; b. St. Louis, MO, 2/20/33. Mother pl. pno., fath. pl. alto sax. Stud. pno. in KC fr. 1942. Received B.A. in mus. ed. fr. U. of Kansas. Tour. world w. US Army show '56–7. Perf. w. KC Philharm. '61. Worked as studio mus. in LA '60s. Also pl. w. own gps. in clubs and taught mentally retarded children in LA public sch. Cross-country jazz and religious concert tour '67–8. Scored film, *Midtown Madness* '69. Supervised mus. and acted in film, *Love Sweet Love* '74. Favs: Jimmy Smith, Milt Buckner, Wild Bill Davis, Bill Doggett, Jack McDuff. LPs: PJ; Main,; Prest.; w. Sonny Stitt; Les McCann (PJ). CDs: BGP; one track in *Texas Tenors* (Prest.)

l

LA PORTA, JOHN D., cl., saxes, comp, arr; b. Philadelphia, PA, 4/1/20; d. Sarasota, FL, 5/12/04. Began on cl. at age 9. Stud. cl. w. Wm. Dietrich, Joseph Gigliotti, Leon Russianoff 1932–57. Pl. in Youth Symph. cond. by Leopold Stokowski '37–8. Stud. comp. w. Ernst Toch, Alexis Haieff '45–6; improv. w. Lennie Tristano '47–8; received B. Mus. '56, M. Mus. Ed. '57 fr. Manh. Sch. of Mus. Pl. w. Bob Chester, Richard Himber, Ray McKinley early '40s; Woody Herman '44–6; Tristano late '40s; Charles Mingus '50–67; Metronome All-Stars '51–2; own gps '51–62. Founding member and mus. dir. of Jazz Composers Wkshp. '52–4. App. w. Gunther Schuller at Brandeis Mus. Fest. '57; Leonard Bernstein and N.Y. Philharm. perf. Teo Macero's *Fusion* '58–9. Taught at Parkway Mus. Inst., Bklyn. '48–51. Reed coach for Marshall Brown's Newport Youth Band '53–8. Active as clinician '59–81. Taught at Manh. Sch. of Mus. '60–2; Berklee Sch. of Mus. fr. '62. Dir. Greater Bost. HS Stage Band '64–5. Pl. w. Bost. Sax Qt. w. Charlie Mariano '60s; Berklee Sax Qt. fr. '62; Herb Pomeroy Orch fr. '76; John La Porta–Bob Winter Duo fr. '81. La Porta was a founding member of the Nat'l Assoc. of Jazz Educs. and the author of eight instructional texts, incl. *Tonal Organization of Improv. Techniques* (Kendor); *Guide to Improv.* (Berklee); *Guide to Jazz Phrasing and Interpretation* (Berklee). His numerous arrs. for hs band are publ. by Berklee, Kendor, and Marshall Brown Music. La Porta taught and lectured at Berklee and in Fla. Polls: *Play.* '61; NAJE Award '86; Berklee Award '87. Fests: all major '50s–'60s. Film: *Trocadero* w. Bob Chester Orch. perf. La Porta comp. '42. CDs: w. C. Parker (Verve); T. Macero (Stash); C. Mingus (Deb; Sav.; Atl.); W. Herman (Col.); H. Mobley (Sav.); H. Merrill (Em.; Verve).

LaBARBERA, JOE (JOSEPH JAMES), dms; b. Dansville, NY, 2/22/48. Played in family band w. parents and bros., Pat and John. Father taught him dms., sax, and cl., which he pl. through hs. Stud. w. Alan Dawson at Berklee 1966. Prof. debut w. Sam Noto-Joe Romano qnt. in Buffalo, N.Y. '66. Pl. w. Chuck Israels trio '66; Frankie Randall '67. After army service '68–70, he worked w. Gap Mangione '70, '72–6; Gary Burton '77. Freelanced in NYC w. Phil Woods; Jim Hall; Art Farmer; Art Pepper; Zoot Sims; Bob Brookmeyer; John Scofield; et al. '77–8. Pl. w. Bill Evans '78–80; Tony Bennett fr. '80; occ. leads own small gps. in LA. Rec. debut w. Woody Herman on *The Raven Speaks* '71. Rec. *Land of Make Believe* w. Mangione (Merc.); *Paris Concerts* w. Evans (Elek. Mus.). CDs: Sack.; w. Lanny Morgan (Cont.); Harold Danko (Sunny.); J. Scofield (Enja); W. Herman (Fant.); Gary Foster; R. Clooney; Alan Broadbent (Conc.); Tad Weed (Nine Winds); Bill Evans (Drey.; WB; Timel.); Conte Candoli (FS).

LaBARBERA, JOHN P., comp, arr, pno, tpt; b. Warsaw, NY, 11/10/45. Raised in Mt. Morris, N.Y. Father pl. many instruments, had family band; moth. pl. bs.; bros. are Pat and Joe LaBarbera. Stud. w. fath., then at SUNY-Potsdam 1962–3; Berklee Coll. of Mus. '64–5; stud. comp. w. Rayburn Wright and Manny Albam at Eastman Arr. Wkshp. Pl. w. family band, r&b gps. early '60s. Recommended to Buddy Rich by bro. Pat. Pl. w. Rich '68; Glenn Miller Orch. w. Buddy DeFranco '69–71. LaBarbera has worked mainly as a comp./arr. fr. '71. He arr. for the Buddy

Rich band fr. '71 until the leader's death. Also wrote charts for Harry James; Woody Herman; Count Basie; Bill Watrous; Dizzy Gillespie; Mel Tormé; Doc Severinsen; Al Cohn; Phil Woods; and many commercial arrs. Helped form Diva '93, contributing strongly to the band's book. LaBarbera has taught at Alfred U. and Cornell and fr. '91 has been on the faculty at the U. of Louisville (Kentucky), where he teaches arr., ens., and computer mus. Favs: Kenny Dorham, Lee Morgan, Clifford Brown, Joe Gordon; arrs: Bill Holman, Gil Evans, Thad Jones. Fests: Eur., Japan, Korea w. DeFranco-led Miller band. TV: Johnny Carson, Mike Douglas, Merv Griffin, Dick Cavett w. Rich. CDs: w. Rich (RCA); Diva (Diva).

LaBARBERA, PAT (PASCEL), tnr sax; b. Warsaw, NY, 4/7/44. Played in family band. Stud. at Potsdam St. Teachers Coll. and Berklee Sch. 1964–7. Worked w. Buddy Rich '67–74. Moved to Toronto '74 for TV and studio work. Rec. and pl. w. Elvin Jones '75–8, then off and on '84–8. Infl: Coltrane. LPs: PM; JT. CDs: Sack.; w. Elvin Jones (Evid.); Buddy Rich (PJ; BB); Dave McMurdo (Sack.; JA); Sam Noto (Unisson).

LABORIEL, ABE (ABRAHAM), bs; b. Mexico City, Mexico, 7/17/47. Studied at Berklee Sch. of Mus.; rec. w. Gary Burton 1973. Worked extensively w. pop acts and briefly w. Count Basie in '70s. To LA '77; since then active in wide variety of commercial and jazz settings. Has often taken part in annual concert and seminars at U. of Pittsburgh w. Nathan Davis. Many albums w. Lee Ritenour; also rec. w. Joe Pass; Freddie Hubbard; Milt Jackson; and others. CDs: w. Burton (ECM); Joe Williams (Tel.); M. Davis; Al Jarreau (WB); B. Cobham (GRP); Tom Ranier (Cont.); Luis Bonilla (Cand.); Pass; E. Fitzgerald (Pab.); John Handy (Inak); S. Turrentine (BN); David Newman (Mile.); Grover Washington (Elek.).

LACY, KU-UMBA FRANK, tbn, flg, voc; b. Houston, TX, 1958. Father, Frank Sr., pl. gtr. locally w. Arnett Cobb, Russell Jacquet. Physics degree fr. Texas Southern U. Stud. at Berklee Coll. of Mus. (M.A.) and Rutgers U. Pl. w. bbs of Illinois Jacquet and Dizzy Gillespie; rec. w. Carla Bley; Henry Threadgill sxt.; Lester Bowie and Brass Fantasy. Acclaimed for his work as soloist and mus. dir. w. Art Blakey's Jazz Messengers fr. 1988 to '90. In the '90s worked w. Mingus bb and the bbs of Bobby Watson; McCoy Tyner; David Murray; Roy Hargrove; also Hargrove's Crisol; own gps. Album debut as leader, *Blue Fire* '91. Rec. *Journey to Iceland* (PS:Músík), in Reykjavík, Iceland, w. local musicians '91. A techni-

cally impressive trombonist with a shouting, often flamboyant style. Polls: *DB* TDWR five times. CDs: Tutu; Blakey (Timel.); w. Jay Collins (Res.); Roy Hargrove (Verve; Novus); H. Threadgill (Novus); McCoy Tyner (Verve); Illinois Jacquet (Atl.); Ralph Peterson (BN); Steve Turre (Ant.); Mingus bb (Drey.); Lester Bowie (ECM; DIW); David Murray (DIW); Bobby Watson (Col.); M. Formanek (Enja).

LACY, STEVE (Steven Lackritz), sop sax comp; b. NYC, 7/23/34; d. Boston, 6/4/04. Wife, cellist Irene Aebi. Stud. w. Cecil Scott; Harold Freeman; Joe Allard; Cecil Taylor in NYC; also at Schillinger Sch., Bost. 1953; Manh. Sch. of Mus. '54. Sat in w. C. Scott fr. '52. Pl. in gps. w. Max Kaminsky; Jimmy McPartland; Rex Stewart; Buck Clayton, Charlie Shavers, Zutty Singleton; Hot Lips Page early '50s. Stud. and pl. w. Cecil Taylor '55–7. Pl. w. Gil Evans Orch. off and on fr. '57; Jimmy Giuffre at Five Spot '59; Thelonious Monk '60, '63. Led own qt. w. Roswell Rudd and Dennis Charles, perf. Monk's mus. in NYC and Eur. early '60s. Pl. in Eur. w. Kenny Drew '63; free jazz w. Carla Bley '65; Don Cherry mid '60s. Tour. So. Amer. w. own gp. w. Enrico Rava, Johnny Dyani, Louis Moholo '65. In Rome '67–70 pl. w. Musica Elettronica Viva, other Italian musicians. Settled in Paris '70. Formed qnt. to perf. own comps. w. Aebi, Steven Potts, Kent Carter, Oliver Johnson early '70s. In '81 pnst. Bobby Few joined the gp. and Carter was repl. by Jean-Jacques Avenel. Lacy perf. extensively as an unaccomp. soloist, and, in the '80s, worked w. Japanese kabuki dancers and Indian classical musicians. Also led gps. w. Misha Mengelberg '80s. Billed as "The Bechet of Today" in the '50s, Lacy evolved through Lester Young to Cecil Taylor and Monk. He was comfortable in many genres but never lost this adventurous spirit, often informed by writers and painters as well as musicians. Favs: Rollins, Parker, Pee Wee Russell, Coltrane; comps: Ellington, Monk, Miles Davis. Polls: *Met.* New Star '57. Fests: all major fr. '60s. Films: short films in Rome; *Free Fall* (US); *Alfred R.* (Switz.). Rec. debut w. tptr. Dick Sutton '54. CDs: NJ; Prest.; hatArt; Novus; Evid.; Cand.; Red; SN; BS; Freelance; IAI; FMP; Silk.; w. C. Taylor (BN; Cand.); G. Evans (Prest.; Verve; Owl); T. Monk; M. Davis (Col.); Joe McPhee (Adda); H. Merrill (Owl; Em.); Gary Burton (BB); Globe Unity Orch. (FMP); Mengelberg; Rudd (SN); M. Waldron (Enja; SN; PW).

LADNIER, TOMMY (THOMAS), tpt; b. Florenceville, LA, 5/28/1900; d. NYC, 6/4/39. Studied w. Bunk Johnson. Moved to Chi. ca. 1917. Pl. on riverboats w. Charlie Creath '21. In Chi. w. Roy Palmer, Milton Vassar, Lovie Austin, Ollie Powers,

Fate Marable early '20s. Joined King Oliver '24; to Eur. w. Sam Wooding orch. for *Chocolate Kiddies* revue in Berlin, Germ. '25. Pl. w. Fletcher Henderson '26–7; rejoin. Wooding for Eur. tour '28–9. Pl. Eur. w. Benny Peyton, Herb Flemming, Louis Douglas, Noble Sissle, and own band '29–'31. During the Depression operated a Harlem tailor shop w. Sidney Bechet and also co-led NO Feetwarmers w. him '32–3. Rec. as leader (BB) '38; and in '20s-'30s w. O. Powers; Ma Rainey; Ida Cox; Lovie Austin; Bessie Smith; Henderson; Wooding; Mezz Mezzrow. Pl. Carnegie Hall *From Spirituals to Swing* concert w. Bechet '38. Some critics name Ladnier among the greatest trumpeters in the Armstrong-Oliver tradition. CDs: track in *The Jazz Trumpet Vol. 1* (Prest.); w. Sidney Bechet (BB); Bessie Smith; Henderson (Col.); Teddy Bunn; Jimmy O'Bryant (RST, Austral. label); Ida Cox (Black Swan).

LaFARO, (ROCCO) SCOTT, bs; b. Newark, NJ, 4/3/36; d. Geneva, NY, 7/6/61. Studied cl. and sax, took up bs. in 1953. Pl. w. Buddy Morrow '55; Chet Baker in Calif. '56; Ira Sullivan and Pat Moran in Chi '57. Back in So. Calif. '58 with Baker; B. Kessel; H. Rumsey, V. Feldman; S. Getz; and Cal Tjader. Closely assoc. w. Bill Evans fr. Dec. '59 until his death in a car crash. Won New Star Award in the *DB* Critics Poll '59. LaFaro's method of creating stimulating, rhythmically original, and often melodic counterlines was so infl. that even in the '90s many bssts. cont. to cite him as a major force in revolutionizing the use of the instrument. "He was one of the most talented youngsters to come up in years," said Ray Brown. "I was amazed by his facility, his intonation, and his ideas." Gary Peacock, Steve Swallow, Eddie Gomez, and Albert Stinson were clearly infl. by LaFaro. CDs: w. Bill Evans (Riv; *The Secret Sessions* boxed set, Mile.); Booker Little (Time); Ornette Coleman (Atl.); Tony Scott (Sunny.); Victor Feldman (Cont.).

LAFITTE, GUY, tnr sax; b. Saint Gaudens, France, 1/11/27; d. Gers, Simorre, France, 7/10/98. Self-taught, he pl. cl. w. gypsy bands bef. starting on tnr. sax; made prof. debut 1945; pl. w. vln. Michel Warlop '47; led Hot Club of Toulouse orch. until '48. Tour. w. Big Bill Broonzy '50; Mezz Mezzrow '51; Bill Coleman and Dicky Wells '52. Perf. w. Duke Ellington in film, *Paris Blues*. Led small gp. in Paris late '50s; won Grand Prix Django Reinhardt '54, Grand Prix du Disques '57. Tour. and rec. w. Lionel Hampton; Lucky Thompson; Emmett Berry in mid '50s. Rec. w. own trio on French Col. '56; Milt Buckner '77; Wallace Davenport '78; Bobby Durham, Arnett Cobb '80; Oliver Jackson and Jimmy Woode '81. Lived in

NYC briefly in early '80s. Was a vice president of the Marciac JF where w. his gp. he accomp. Getz; Benny Carter; Hampton; and Clark Terry. A warm-toned player whose strong ballad work was infl. by Coleman Hawkins. CDs: B&B; w. Bill Coleman (B&B); Hampton (EMI Jazztime).

LAGRENE, BIRELI, gtr, voc; b. Soufflenheim, France, 9/4/66. First gtr. lessons fr. fath. 1971. Rec. debut as leader, *Routes to Django* '80. App. on TV, at a Jazz fest. in Frankfurt, and on tour w. John McLaughlin, Al Di Meola, and Paco DeLucia in '80s. Rec. film soundtrack, *First Tango* '82. American debut at Kool JF "Tribute to Django" w. own gp. incl. gtr. Diz Disley '84. Lagrene's prodigious career, which incl. gigs w. Benny Carter; Benny Goodman; Stephane Grappelli; Jaco Pastorius; and Pat Metheny, found him eventually changing his style to pl. jazz rock, using gtr. synth. and various electronic accessories, but ret. to pl. acoustically w. Richard Galliano, etc. *Blue Eyes*, his tribute to Sinatra '98, revealed his talent as a voc. Fests: many in Eur. incl. Vienne, France, w. Galliano; Patrimonio, Corsica, w. Babik Reinhardt; etc. CDs: BN; Drey.; Ant.; Jazzpoint; w. *Tribute to Gil Evans* (SN).

LAHM, DAVID, pno, arr; b. NYC, 12/12/40. Son of lyricist Dorothy Fields; wife is cabaret singer Judy Kreston. Stud. pno. w. priv. teachers 1946–52. Lived in Indiana in '60s, encouraged by David Baker, Jamey Aebersold. Pl. w. D. Baker '64–5; J. Aebersold '65–6; Buddy Rich '68–70; Richie Cole, Ted Curson, Attila Zoller '71–5; own gp., Prism, w. Lyn Christie, Randy Brecker, A. Zoller, Dave Friedman; also gp. w. Janet Lawson '71–6; own gps. w. sidemen Joe LaBarbera, Cameron Brown, Jon Burr, Mike Formanek, Jane Ira Bloom, John Purcell, D. Friedman, etc. fr. '76. Has written lyrics to bebop tunes and solos. Worked mainly as accomp. and arr. for cabaret singers since '79; w. Kreston since '80. Through reharmonization and use of various time signatures Lahm brings freshness to his writing and playing without veering radically from the core of jazz. Fests: Engl. w. B. Rich '69; Germ. w. Zoller '71, '74. LPs: Palo Alto; Generation; Plug. CDs: Ark.; Generation.

LAINE, CLEO (Clementina Dinah Campbell), voc; b. Southall Middlesex, England, 10/28/27. Wife of John Dankworth; moth. of Alec Dankworth. Began singing at age 3. Worked w. J. Dankworth Seven and bb fr. 1951–7. Married Dankworth in '58 and pursued solo and stage career, making only guest apps. w. the band. Fr. the '70s, she has cont. to work w. her husband, app. worldwide w. his orch., incl. many TV specials. Awarded OBE '79; Hon. M.A., Open U.

'75; Hon. D. Mus. Berklee '82. Was named Personality of the Yr. by Variety Club '77; Singer of the Yr., *TV Times* '78; Grammy for Best Female Jazz Vocalist '86. With J. Dankworth, estab. Wavendon Sch. in Engl., where she teaches master classes for the All-Music Plan; master classes at Berklee Sch., Bost. App. in numerous prods fr. '70 to '90s, incl. *The Mystery of Edwin Drood* on B'way, for which she received *Theatre World* award and Tony nomination for Best Actress in a Musical '86. Rec. w. John Williams; James Galway; Ray Charles (RCA); Dudley Moore (CBS); and numerous others. "One of her most interesting features is her extraordinarily broad range," noted Don Heckman in the *LA Times*. "She swings with an easy groove, effortlessly popping out airy falsetto high notes that have become her trademark." CDs: RCA; w. Mel Tormé (Conc.).

LAINE, JULIAN, tbn; b. New Orleans, LA, ca. 1907; d. New Orleans, 9/10/57. Played in dance halls w. Louis Prima and Sharkey Bonano 1928; Johnny Bertucci '29; riverboats w. Tony Almerico early '30s. Pl. w. Bonano again '36. Worked w. various bands, incl. Prima, Almerico, and Joe Venuti in late '30s. Own band in '40. Army service '42-4. Worked w. Leon Prima, Almerico, and Bonano bands in late '40s; Muggsy Spanier in Chicago and SF; and Bonano in NO '50. Also pl. w. Johnny Wiggs in early '50s. Rec. w. George Hartman (Key.) '41.

LAINE, PAPA JACK (GEORGE VITAL), dms, alto horn; b. New Orleans; LA, 9/21/1873; d. New Orleans, 6/1/66. Formed first band in 1888; claimed to have been one of the first to perf. ragtime, imitating early black stomps and perf. Scott Joplin's "Shadow Rag" as a specialty number. Led the Reliance Brass Band, incl. Nick LaRocca, Sharkey Bonano, and the Brunies brothers, and said to be precursor of ODJB fr. 1890s into '30s. His gps. were so popular that Laine organized similar bands, booking up to five Reliance Bands simultaneously. Described as "the first white jazz musician" and "the father of white jazz," he was actually more an entrepreneur and booking agent.

LAKE, OLIVER EUGENE, alto, sop saxes, fl, comp; b. Marianna, AK, 9/14/42. Family moved to St. Louis, Mo., in 1943. Moth. sang in church choir. Son is dmr. Gene Lake. Started in drum and bugle corp. in St. Louis. Att. hs w. Lester Bowie; Philip Wilson; John Hicks; began pl. sax at age 18. Received B.A. in mus. ed. fr. Lincoln U., Jefferson City '68. Taught mus. in St. Louis publ. sch. '68-72. Founded Black Artists Gp. '68. Stud. comp. and arr. w. Oliver Nelson, Ron Carter '70. Lived in Paris, taught at Amer. Ctr. for Artists and Students '73.

Moved to NYC '74. Co-founded World Sax. Qt. w. Hamiet Bluiett, David Murray, Julius Hemphill '76; also led trio w. Michael Gregory Jackson, Pheeroan Ak Laff. Form. own jazz/funk/reggae gp., Jump Up '81; tour. Africa, spons. by USIA '82. Comp. two commissioned pcs. for Bklyn. Philharm. '83; many other commissions and grants fr. mid '80s. Founded Mus. of Bklyn. Initiative w. Lester Bowie, Cecil Taylor '85. Formed experimental qt., Blue Star '86. Participated in comps. exchange program in USSR '87. Perf. and rec. w. Max Roach; Donal Fox; Andrew Cyrille; Reggie Workman; Hannibal Peterson; James Newton; Abbey Lincoln; Michelle Rosewoman; and at numerous jazz fests. and concerts in the '80s and '90s, usually leading a qt., qnt., nonet, or bb. Favs: Ellington, Jackie McLean, Dolphy. Fests: Eur., Africa, Asia fr. late '70s. TV: *Night Music*. CDs: BS; Gram.; hatArt; M&A; w. World Sax Qt. (BS; JT; Elek. None.); Cyrille (DIW); Michael Gregory Jackson (IAI); Bennie Wallace (Den.); Reggie Workman (Leo).

LALAMA, DAVE (DAVID S.), pno, synth, arr; b. Aliquippa, PA, 4/23/54. Brother is Ralph Lalama. Fr. a mus. family; fath., Nofrey, a dmr., and moth., Jennie, a singer, gigged together in Pitts. area. Began on tpt. at age 9, sw. to pno. at 11. Stud. voice w. Rose Lasala 1970-2; pno. and comp. at Youngstown St. U. '72-6; comp. at NYU w. Paul Alan Levi '82-3, Tom Boras '90-2. Pl. in house trio at club in Warren, Ohio, w. R. Lalama '73-7; house rhythm section at Jazzmania, NYC, backing Claudio Roditi, Red Rodney, Pepper Adams, Sonny Fortune, and others '77-8. Pl. w. Eddie Jefferson-Richie Cole '77-8; then pl. and arr. for Woody Herman '78-80; Buddy Rich '81. Pnst. and arr. for singers, incl. Jimmy Witherspoon, Helen Forrest, Marion Cowings, Carol Fredette, Anita O'Day fr. '81. Subbed in Mel Lewis Orch.–Vanguard Orch. fr. '83. Pl. pno. and synth. w. Roland Vasquez '87-9; co-led Lalama Bros. Qt. w. R. Lalama, Dennis Irwin, Adam Nussbaum fr. '87. Lalama has been an assoc. prof. of mus. at Hofstra U. since '86. Received Ph.D. in comp. fr. NYU in '94. Favs: Hancock, Monk; arr: Thad Jones. Fests: Eur. w. W. Herman '78-9; UK w. B. Rich '81. TV: PBS and Eur. TV w. W. Herman '78-9. CDs: w. W. Herman (ITM; Conc.); Mike Carubia (KamaDisc); R. Vasquez (Soundwings); Perry Robinson (Jazzmania); M. Cowings (GoodGuise); Joe Ascione (Arb.).

LALAMA, RALPH NOFREY, tnr sax, cl, fl; b. Aliquippa, PA, 1/30/51. Grandfather pl. sax. and cl.; fath. pl. dms; moth. is singer; bro. Dave is pnst.-arr. Began on cl. at age 9, sax at 13. Pl. in local band at 14. Grad. fr. Youngstown St. U. 1975. Pl. w. Woody Herman '76–7; Buddy Rich '80–1; Mel Lewis Jazz Orch.–Vanguard Orch. fr. '83; Pete Malinverni fr. '87; Jack McDuff '88; Bopera House fr. '88; Rich Vitale fr. '90. Also freelanced w. Junior Cook; Sal Nistico, Joe Lovano; Kirk Lightsey; Harold Danko; Thad Jones–Mel Lewis Qnt. Teaches at William Paterson Coll. and NYU. Lead. Thurs. night jam sessions at Savoy Lounge '98. Favs: Rollins, Joe Henderson, Hank Mobley, Coltrane. Polls: *DB* TDWR '78. Fests: Eur., Jap. fr. '80. TV: Jerry Lewis Telethon; Italian TV. CDs: CC; w. W. Herman (Conc.); Mel Lewis Orch. (MM); Renée Manning (Ken); Joe Morello (DMP).

LAMARE, NAPPY (HILTON NAPOLEON), gtr, bjo, voc; b. New Orleans, LA, 6/14/10; d. Newhall, CA, 5/8/88. Brother, Jimmy, pl. saxes w. Charlie Barnet. In the teens, Nappy pl. bjo. w. local NO gps. that incl. Sharkey Bonano, Monk Hazel, and Johnny Bayersdorffer; gtr. and voc. w. Ben Pollack 1930–5; Bob Crosby '35–42; then freelanced in LA, often in reunions w. ex-Crosby colleagues; co-led combo with Ray Bauduc '55–68; w. Joe Darensbourg '69–83. Rec. w. own gps.; Nellie Lutcher; Julia Lee; Jessie Price; Eddie Miller. A capable rhythm guitarist rather than a soloist. CDs: as lead. and sideman in *Classic Capitol Jazz Sessions* (Mos.); w. Crosby (Dec.); R. Eldridge (Col.); B. Hackett (Dormouse Int'l); Judy Garland (Dec.); J. Teagarden (Mos.).

LAMB, JOHN, bs; b. Vero Beach, FL, 12/4/33. Played w. Red Garland and led own sxt. in Phila. 1950s. Mainly prominent w. Duke Ellington orch. '64–7, later rejoining the band fr. time to time. CDs: w. Ellington (Laser.; MM; BB; Fant.); J. Hodges (Suisa); Ella Fitzgerald (Verve).

LAMBERT, DAVE (DAVID ALDEN), voc, voc arr; b. Boston, MA, 6/19/17; d. Westport, CT, 10/3/66. No mus. educ. other than dms. at 10 for a yr. Spent three summers in late 1930s as dmr. w. Hugh McGuinness Trio in New Engl. Tree surgeon in Westchester bef. army service '40–3. Active duty as paratrooper, etc. bef. discharge in '43. After singing w. Johnny Long's band and Hi, Lo, Jack and the Dame, he teamed w. Buddy Stewart in Gene Krupa's band '44–5, rec. *What's This*, the first bop vocal record. Led voc. qt. in B'way show, *Are You With It* '46–7. Formed Dave Lambert Singers in early '50s, rec. background on Charlie Parker's *Old Folks* '53. Worked as contractor for voc. gps. and wrote background arrs. for Carmen McRae bef. teaming w. Jon Hendricks and Annie Ross in '57 to form Lambert, Hendricks and Ross, later Lambert, Hendricks and Bavan. Left gp. in Feb. '64. Own radio show on WBAI and freelance work in NYC until killed in highway accident. Film: jazz short, *Audition*. Recs. w. Red Rodney '46; own gp. (Cap) '49. LP: *Sing, Swing Along With Dave Lambert* (UA). CDs: w. L,H&R (Col.; Roul.; Imp.; Rh.); Lambert, Hendricks & Bavan (BB); Gene Krupa (Col.); Dave Lambert Singers w. C. Parker (Verve); King Pleasure (Prest.); w. Rodney in *Early Bebop* (Merc.).

LAMBERT, HENDRICKS & ROSS. Vocal. trio form. in late 1957 by Dave Lambert, Jon Hendricks, and Annie Ross to rec. *Sing Along with Basie*, but album—overdubbed voc. emulations of Basie band arrs.—was such a hit that L,H&R bec. a working gp. Established as definitive vocalese gp., L,H&R rec. several albums and toured, expanding repertoire w. clever lyrics—mainly by Jon Hendricks—based on established improv. solos and ens. In '62, when Ross left the gp. due to illness, it was renamed Lambert, Hendricks & Bavan (Yolande Bavan). L,H&B disbanded after Lambert left in '64. CDs: Imp.; Col.; Roul.; BB.

LAMOND, DON (DONALD DOUGLAS), dms; b. Oklahoma City, 8/18/21; d. Orlando, FL, 12/23/03. Raised in DC; stud. at Peabody Inst., Balt. Prof. debut w. Sonny Dunham 1943. With Boyd Raeburn '44; Woody Herman '45–9. In the '50s freelanced in NYC; pl. on many TV shows, incl. Steve Allen; Garry Moore; Ed Sullivan. Many dates and recs. w. Dick Hyman; Stan Getz; Bud Powell; Charlie Parker; Lester Young; Coleman Hawkins; Roy Eldridge; others. With George Wein's Newport Festival All-Stars in late '60s. In '70s he rec. w. Maxine Sullivan, Bucky Pizzarelli. Moved to Fla.; led his own bb late '70s and '80s. Also worked w. Harry Wuest's Top of the World Band at Disney World. Versatile and highly adaptable, he was perfect for Herman's "Four Brothers" orch. "After Don Lamond left," said Terry Gibbs, "we must have had six or seven of the greatest drummers, but they didn't fit. It was Don's band." Favs: Sid Catlett, Philly Joe Jones, Buddy Rich. CDs: RCA; w. Woody Herman (Col.; Cap.; BB; Evid.; Conc.); Serge Chaloff (Mos.); C. Parker (Verve; Stash); B. Holiday; A. O'Day (Verve); Lee Wiley (BB; Aud.); R. Braff; B. Freeman (BL); M. Ferguson (BB); S. Getz (Prest.; Roul.); B. Goodman (MM); Maxine Sullivan (Audio.); Z. Sims (Prest.).

LANCASTER, (WILLIAM) BYARD (aka THUNDERBIRD), saxes, fls, picc, cl, bs-cl; b. Philadelphia, PA, 8/6/42. Parents and grandfath. were amateur mus.; sist. is public sch. mus. teacher. Stud. in Phila. publ. sch. (Kenny Barron was a classmate), then at Shaw U. 1960–1; Berklee Coll. of Mus. '61–3; Bost. Cons. '62–3. Pl. w. J. R. Mitchell-

Jerome Hunter '56–9; Dave Burrell '61–4; Sunny Murray off and on fr. '65; Burton Greene, Bill Dixon '66; Sun Ra '69; McCoy Tyner '70; own gp. Sounds of Liberation '71–3; Walt Miller '74; Le Grand Prix w. Philly Joe Jones '75. Also pl. w. Ronald Shannon Jackson; Johnny Copeland; David Eyges; New African Griots; Jamaaladeen Tacuma. Co-mus. dir. of Miss Black Amer. pageant w. Philly Joe Jones '76. Comp. ballet-opera *Sweet Evil Miss* '70s. Lancaster has worked as a concert promoter and jazz educ. in Phila. fr. '70s. Received the Temple U. PASCEP Achievement Awd. in '92. Favs: Cecil Taylor, Sunny Murray, Barbara Walker. Polls: *Phila. Mag.* Best Street Mus. '90. Fests: Paris '69–79; Kingston, Jamaica, fr. '83; Belgium '87–90. TV: Miss Black Amer. '76. CDs: Gazell; Dogtown; w. J. Tacuma (Gram.); Khan Jamal (Story.; Stash); S. Murray (ESP Disk); Doug Hammond (DIW); Odean Pope (SN).

LAND, HAROLD DE VANCE, tnr sax; b. Houston, TX, 2/18/28; d. Los Angeles, 7/27/01. Raised in San Diego, Calif. Pl. w. Max Roach–Clifford Brown qnt. 1954–5; Curtis Counce '57–8; co-led qnt. w. Red Mitchell '61–2. Pl. many clubs in LA and SF w. Philly Joe Jones, Bobby Hutcherson; w. Gerald Wilson in '50s and '60s and intermittently into '90s. Fr. '68 to '71, he co-led gp. w. Hutcherson; also co-led qnt. w. Blue Mitchell '75–8. In '70s his gp. frequently incl. his son, Harold C. Land (b. 4/25/50), on pno. In '80s Land was part of the Timeless All-Stars Eur. trip; also freq. trav. as a single. In '92 he tour. Eur. w. Steve Grossman gp. Pl. w. Billy Higgins in Italy at Umbria Jazz '98. First taken with Coleman Hawkins, Land was then infl. by Lucky Thompson and Charlie Parker. The result was a mellow, swinging bop attack that occasionally sounded like Wardell Gray. After a period in which he was strongly swayed by John Coltrane, he went back toward his prior style with a Tranish residue. Film soundtracks: *The Young Savages* '61; *Seven Days in May* '64; *They Shoot Horses, Don't They?*, also on screen '69. CDs: Jzld.; Cont.; Mus.; Post.; w. C. Brown–M. Roach (Em.); Elmo Hope; B. Hutcherson (BN); Counce (Cont.); Bill Evans (Fant.); J. Faddis (Conc.); Red Garland; P. J. Jones (Gal.); F. Hubbard (Pab.); F. Rosolino (Spec.); Timeless All-Stars (Timel.); Dinah Washington (Em.); King Pleasure (HiFiJazz); Monk (Mile.).

LANG, EDDIE (Salvatore Massaro), gtr; b. Philadelphia, PA, 10/25/02; d. NYC, 3/36/33. Parents fr. Italy. Fath. was gtrst. and gtr./mandolin maker who taught his children music incl. Salvatore (his youngest), who adopted the name of his boyhood basketball hero. Stud. vln fr. age 7; then bjo. and gtr. Pl. in sch. band w. Joe Venuti; also pl. duets w. him.

Pl. at Shott's Cafe w. pnst. Chick Granese 1917; bjo. then gtr. w. Ch. Kerr '20; w. Venuti in Bert Eslow Qnt., Atlantic City '23; teamed w. Carl. Kress '23; pl. w. Dorsey Bros. in Scranton Sirens '24. Join. and visited Engl. w. Red McKenzie's Mound City Blue Blowers '25. Frequent associate of Joe Venuti fr. '26–33; their duo and qt. recs., such as *Stringing the Blues*, are classics of early jazz. As "Blind Willie Dunn" (to hide his racial identity) he rec. gtr. duets w. Lonnie Johnson, who said: "Lang could play guitar better than anyone I knew; the sides I made with him were my greatest experience." Pl. in bands of Don Voorhees; Roger Wolfe Kahn; Jean Goldkette, Paul Whiteman; app. w. Venuti in '30 Whiteman film, *King of Jazz*. Was Bing Crosby's accomp. '31–2; app. w. him in film, *The Big Broadcast* '32. Died following a tonsillectomy. Lang's many recs. established him as the first influential jazz gtrst.; his single string acoustic solos, incl. his own unaccompanied "Perfect," were prominent on countless sess. w. Red Nichols; Bix Beiderbecke; Frankie Trumbauer; King Oliver; Venuti–Lang All-Stars; and others. A week-long Eddie Lang JF in the towns of Oratino, Isernia, and Monteroduni, Italy, was held in Aug. '97. CDs: ASV; Yazoo; Timel.; Venuti-Lang (JSP); w. Beiderbecke; duets w. L. Johnson; Louis Armstrong (Col.); J. Venuti (BBC); B. Goodman (Dec.); Mound City Blue Blowers (Class.).

LANG, MIKE (MICHAEL ANTHONY), pno, kybd; b. Los Angeles, CA, 12/10/41. Studied at U. of Michigan (B.M.) 1963. Worked w. Paul Horn '64–5; Stan Kenton's Neophonic Orch. '66; Don Ellis '67; Tom Scott '68. Mainly active as studio mus. since late '60s; also comp. mus. for TV and films, occ. ret. to jazz. Comps. incl. "Karen's World" w. Paul Horn; "Rural Still Life" w. Tom Scott. CDs: Varese; w. Ellis (Col); Teresa Brewer (Col.); Dennis Rowland (Conc.).

LANG, RONNIE (Ronald Langinger), alto sax, fl, other reeds; b. Chicago, IL, 7/24/27. Started w. Hoagy Carmichael's Teenagers band. Worked w. Earle Spencer, Ike Carpenter, Skinnay Ennis 1947; Les Brown '49–50 and '53–6. Since then—although he has mainly been active outside of jazz, working on film, TV, and jingle sess.—he has perf. w. Stan Kenton; Pete Rugolo; Dave Pell; Earl Hines; and Frank Sinatra. Solos w. Les Brown incl. "Midnight Sun"; "Invitation"; "One O'Clock Jump"; "Happy Hooligan." LP: bari. sax w. Bobby Troup (Mode). CDs: w. Erroll Garner (Tel.).

LANGOSCH, PAUL RUSSELL, bs, comp; b. Dayton, OH, 11/4/57. Following a move to Wash., D.C., at age 11, he stud. bs. w. Albert Webster and Bill Vaughan of the Nat'l Symph. and w. Keter Betts. Prof. debut at age 15. Completed B.A. degree at Northwestern U. and M.M. at U. of Arizona. Taught at the Duke Ellington Sch. for the Arts 1977–78. Worked w. Herb Ellis; Barney Kessel; Phil Woods; Al Cohn; Tal Farlow; Tiny Grimes; Bud Shank; Johnny Hartman; Carol Sloane; Chris Connor; George Shearing; Mel Torme; others. With Tony Bennett fr. '85, incl. many TV apps. Favs: LaFaro, Ray Brown, Mingus. CDs: w. T. Bennett (Col.).

LANIGAN, JIM (JAMES WOOD), bs, tba; b. Chicago, IL, 1/30/02; d. Elburn, IL, 4/9/83. Member of Austin HS Gang. In 1920s he pl. w. Husk O'Hare; Bill Paley; Art Kassel; Johnny Maitland; Ted Fio Rito; then radio and theatre work. Pl. jazz occ. on gigs or recs. w. Jimmy McPartland; Danny Alvin; Bud Freeman; et al. Member of Chi. Symph. Orch. for many yrs. App. w. Austin High Gang at Playboy Fest. '59. Lanigan is best remembered as the bassist on the famous Dec. '27 McKenzie–Condon Chicagoans' rec. date that produced "Sugar"; "China Boy"; "Liza"; and "Nobody's Sweetheart." CDs: w. Condon (Class.).

LANPHERE, DON (DONALD GALE), saxes; b. Wenatchee, WA, 6/26/28; d. Redmond, WA, 10/9/03. Father, a former sax pl., owned a mus. store. Stud. priv. and in sch. through hs. Public debut on alto in 1941 w. father on bs. Fr. age 13 to 16 he pl. in local Elks Club under parental supervision; fr. 12 to 16 led hs sxt. for dances and programs around Wash. Stud. at Northwestern U. '45–7. Dur. summer of '46 he sat in w. Jimmie Lunceford band in Wenatchee. With Johnny Bothwell gp. in Chi. and to NYC '48. Rec. on tnr. sax for Dial w. Max Roach, Fats Navarro, Earl Coleman '48; w. own gp., feat. Fats Navarro, for Prest. '49. Worked w. Jerry Wald, Woody Herman, and Artie Shaw '49–50; was arrested on drug charges '51. Off the mus. scene '51–7, he worked in fath.'s mus. shop. Reappeared in the bands of Herb Pomeroy and W. Herman '59–61. Rearrested, Lanphere was mostly inactive until '82, when he made numerous rec. and received NEA grant for rec. project. Pl. the West End Cafe, NYC '83; KC '83; Eur. '85. In '90s, he taught mus. and cond. clinics for a sax manufacturer. Following an early chaotic career due to drug and alcohol problems, Lanphere, a born-again Christian, maintained a busy playing, teaching, and rec. schedule in the Wash. area. Primarily known as a tnr. player, his mature style was inspired by Lester Young, Charlie Parker, John Coltrane, Stan Getz, and Joe Henderson. CDs: Hep; Resource; DGL; Don Lanphere–Pete Christlieb (Origin); tracks as lead. in

Prestige First Sessions, Vol. 1 (Prest.); w. Jay Clayton (Hep); Herman (Mob. Fid.); New Stories (Origin).

LARKIN, MILT (MILTON aka TIPPY), tpt, v-tbn, voc; b. Houston, TX, 10/10/10. Inspired by Bunk Johnson in early 1930s; self-taught on tpt. Pl. w. Chester Boone '34–6. Organized own band in Chi. '36. Larkin's gp. was among top Midwestern territory bands of the late '30s and early '40s; sidemen incl. Eddie Vinson; Illinois Jacquet; Wild Bill Davis; Arnett Cobb. Began pl. tbn. while in army band '43–6. Reformed bb '46 but failed to recapture earlier success. Tour. w. own gps. until '56, when he settled in NYC. Led own spt. at Celebrity Club, NYC fr. '56. Retired to Houston mid '70s. CDs: w. Arnett Cobb (Del.).

LARKINS, ELLIS LANE, pno; b. Baltimore, MD, 5/15/23; d. Baltimore, 9/29/02. Studied at Peabody Cons.; Juilliard 1940. Made prof. debut '40 w. Billy Moore at Café Society Uptown, where he later led a trio. Worked off and on at Blue Angel, NYC '43–52; w. Edmond Hall Sxt. at Café Society '45–6. Accomp. Ella Fitzgerald, Helen Humes '50s-60s. Tour. w. hca. virtuoso Larry Adler '59. After several yrs. of relative obscurity, Larkins enjoyed renewed popularity in the late '60s and early '70s. Accomp. Joe Williams '68–9, '72. Extended engagements at NYC clubs and restaurants, incl. Gregory's, Michael's Pub, The Cookery, Tangerine, Carnegie Tavern '70s. Tour. So. Amer. w. Teddy Wilson, Marian McPartland, Earl Hines '74. Recital at Maybeck Hall '92. TV: Art Linkletter, Joe Franklin, Merv Griffin, Mike Douglas in '70s. CDs: Conc.; JA; B&B; Arb.; *Concert in Argentina* w. M. McPartland, Earl Hines, Teddy Wilson (JA); w. E. Fitzgerald (Dec.; Col.); Chris Connor (Beth.); R. Braff (Vang.; Arb.).

LaROCA, PETE. See **SIMS, PETE.**

LaROCCA, DOMINIC JAMES (NICK), crnt; b. New Orleans, LA, 4/11/1889; d. New Orleans, 2/22/61. Professional career began in 1905 w. Henry Young. Form. own band in '08. Pl. w. Brunies Bros.; Papa Laine; Johnny Stein; and others in NO. To Chi. w. Stein '16; formed Original Dixieland Jazz Band that yr. w. Alcide Nunez (later Larry Shields), Eddie Edwards, and Henry Ragas—dmr. Tony Spargo join. three wks. later. In early '17, while pl. successful engagement at Reisenweber's in NYC, the ODJB made history's first jazz rec. After pl. and rec. w. ODJB in London '19, LaRocca led the band in US until it broke up in '25. Moving back to NO, he operated construction business, ret. briefly to mus. for revival of ODJB '36–8. Ceased regular pl. ca. '40.

Although LaRocca's claims that the ODJB "invented jazz" were far over the top, those first recordings helped to popularize jazz, and LaRocca was an influence on Bix Beiderbecke's earliest efforts. Tulane U.'s archives contain LaRocca's originals and other ODJB scores. CDs: w. ODJB (BB).

LASHA, PRINCE (William B. Lawsha), saxes, fl, comp; b. Ft. Worth, TX, 9/10/29. During student yrs., he led a gp. w. Ornette Coleman. Lived in NYC in early 1950s, then to LA '54; worked intermittently w. Sonny Simmons, making joint rec. debut w. him on the '62 Cont. album *The Cry*. Rec. w. Elvin Jones '63. To Eur. '65; rec. again w. Simmons '67. In early '70s he worked w. Harold Land; Joe Henderson; vln. Michael White; rec. w. Herbie Hancock '80. To Eur. '84 and '87, when he pl. at the Magnetic Terrace in Paris. CDs: Cont.

LaSPINA, STEVE (STEVEN FRANK), bs, el-bs; b. Wichita Falls, TX, 3/24/54. Father pl. bs., grandfath. pl. tpt. in family club date band dur. 1930s. Stud. w. fath., then at U. of Illinois and w. Warren Benfield at DePaul. Introduced to prof. mus. by Rufus Reid in Chicago area. Pl. in Chi. w. Bunky Green, Larry Novak, Joe Daley '75–9, Chet Baker '78; Marian McPartland in Chi. and NYC '78–86. Moved to NYC '79; pl. w. Mel Lewis Orch. '78–82; Stan Getz '86–7; Jim Hall since '88; Andy LaVerne since '89; Benny Carter in mid '90s. Also pl. w. Toots Thielemans; Joe Williams; Dave Liebman; Richie Beirach; Bob Brookmeyer; Al Cohn; Zoot Sims; Pat Martino; Tommy Flanagan. LaSpina teaches bs. and improv. at NYU and at the Coll. of St. Rose in Albany, N.Y. Favs: LaFaro, Mingus, Chambers. Fests: Eur. since '75, Japan since '86. TV: *Today* w. M. McPartland '79; *Tonight Show* w. J. Hall '92. CDs: Steep.; w. J. Hall (Den.; Conc.; MM); Mary Osborne (Stash); Susannah McCorkle (Pausa; Conc.); M. McPartland (Conc.); Dick Katz (Res.); Vic Juris; Louis Smith; John Abercrombie (Steep.); Peggy Lee (Chesky); Benny Carter (MM); Fred Hersch (Red; Angel); LaVerne (Steep.; Tri.; Musidisc); Pat Martino; Mark Murphy (Muse).

LATEANO, VINCE (VINCENT JAMES JR.), dms; b. Sacramento, CA, 9/23/42. Played tpt. fr. fourth to ninth grade, then dms. w. priv. teacher. First road gig w. Carmen Cavallaro 1961–2; army band '63–5. Settling in SF in '66, he played locally w. Eddie Duran; Vince Guaraldi; Johnny Coppola; Al Plank; and many world-class visiting mus. Tour. w. Woody Herman for three mos. in '71; pl. and rec. w. Cal Tjader '78–82, incl. Grammy-winning album *La Onda Va Bien*. In early '90s he worked and rec. w.

Bruce Forman; w. Scott Hamilton '95. Rec. w. his wife, voc. Madeline Eastman. A discreet and dependable dmr., highly respected in the SF Bay area. Fests: 1995 Fujitsu-Concord JF. CDs: w. D. Gillespie (Mesa/Blue Moon); Tania Maria; C. Tjader (Conc.); M. Eastman (Mad Kat); Turtle Island String Qt. (WH); Smith Dobson–Dave Bendigkeit (Quartet).

LATEEF, YUSEF (William Emanuel Huddleston), tnr sax, fl, oboe, bassoon, comp, lead; b. Chattanooga, TN, 10/9/20. Started on alto, then tnr. sax while at Miller HS in Det. 1937; stud. tnr. w. Teddy Buckner. On recommendation of Lucky Thompson, got job w. Lucky Millinder in NYC '46. Pl. w. Hot Lips Page, Roy Eldridge, Herbie Fields '46–8. Tour. (as William Evans) w. Dizzy Gilles-pie '49–50. Ret. to Det. '50. Stud. fl., comp. at Wayne State U. Led own gps. w. Curtis Fuller, Wilbur Harden '55–9; also pl. w. Kenny Burrell. His gp. worked mainly in Det. but visited NYC several times '57–9. Began using unusual instr. incl. argol, rebob, earth-board late '50s. Moved to NYC and led own qt. there Jan. '60. Pl. w. Charles Mingus '60–1; Babatundi Olatunji '61–2; Cannonball Adderley '62–4; also Donald Byrd; Grant Green. Tour. US, Eur., Asia w. own gps. fr. '64. Pl. on Mal Waldron's soundtrack score for *The Cool World* '63 and Chas. Mills's *Tracks in the Sand* '60s. Stud. w. Dr. Allen Kimbler, a student of Karlheinz Stockhausen; also stud. fl. w. Howard Jones. Taught sax at Stan Kenton summer jazz clinics '63. Middle Eastern and Asian infls. bec. increasingly apparent in Lateef's work dur. the '60s. Added new instruments to his media of expression, incl. Taiwanese fl., shanai, and various bamboo fls. Active as abstract painter in '60s. Majored in fl. and received M.A. in Mus. Educ. at Manh. Sch. of Mus. Doctorate in Educ. fr. U. of Mass. '75. Assoc. profess. of music at Manh. Community Coll. in the late '70s; taught in Nigeria in the '80s. Ret. to US to teach at U. Mass. and Amherst. Grammy Award, Best New-Age Perf. '87. Most of his work in the '80s and '90s is outside of jazz although he did record, w. Ricky Ford, a tribute to various tnr. players on his own YAL label. Lateef's instructional books incl. two-vol. *Flute Book of the Blues* and many arrs. of his comps. A book of poetry, philosophical essays, and short stories, *Something Else*, is a collaborative effort w. Kenny Barron, Bob Cunningham, and Albert Heath. Comp: *Tahira*, rec. w. Hamburg Radio Orch.; *The African-American Suite* '93, rec. w. qnt. and WDR orch. CDs: Sav.; Prest.; NJ; Riv.; Imp.; Act; Rh./Atl; YAL; w. Gillespie (BB); C. Adderley (Riv.; Mile.; Land.; Cap.); Nat Adderley (Riv.); Donald Byrd (Del.); C. Fuller (Sav.); Grant Green (BN); Mingus (Rh.); C. Terry (Cand.).

LaVERE, CHARLIE (Charles Levere Johnson), pno, voc, comp; b. Salina, KS, 7/18/10; d. Aspen, CO, 4/28/83. Extensive classical ed. on pno.; self-taught on brass and reed instruments. Early assoc. of Charlie and Jack Teagarden; rec. debut w. the latter in 1933. Pl. w. Wingy Manone in Chi. '33. Rec. w. own band '35. Pl. w. Paul Whiteman in NYC '37-8. To Calif. in '38; pl. w. Frankie Trumbauer and did radio work w. Skinnay Ennis, John Scott Trotter, and Bing Crosby '47. Perf. voc. on Gordon Jenkins' "Maybe You'll Be There," which sold over a million copies. Rec. dates for the Jump label w. own gp., the Chicago Loopers, in '44, '50. Pl. w. Dale "Deacon" Jones '61; Bob Crosby '61-2. Was off-screen voc. on *Bell Telephone Hour* w. Gordon Jenkins. Worked for Lester Lanin, wrote arrs. for Jack Teagarden. Later worked as voc. coach and was first mus. dir. at Disneyland. Also in '60s w. Wingy Manone; Jackie Coon; Russ Morgan; Nappy Lamare. Semi-retired in early '70s. Best known comps: "Mis'ry and the Blues"; "The Blues Have Got Me"; "Cuban Boogie-Woogie." CDs: w. Billie Holiday; Judy Garland (Dec.); J. Teagarden (Conifer).

LaVERNE, ANDY, pno, kybds, comp; b. NYC, 12/4/47. Attended Ithaca Coll., then stud. briefly at Berklee Coll. of Mus. Stud. w. Bill Evans. Pl. w. pop bands in Boston dur. early 1970s. Tour. Eur. and rec. w. Woody Herman '73-5, then pl. w. Miroslav Vitous, Lee Konitz '76; Eddie Daniels '77. Formed duo w. Mike Richmond '77; also rec. w. own gps. fr. '77. Pl. w. Stan Getz '77-80; comp. close to sixty tunes while w. Getz, incl. extended work perf. by Getz and Buffalo Philharm. Pl. w. Brubeck-LaVerne Trio w. Chris and Dan Brubeck '80s and w. Carmen McRae; Thad Jones–Mel Lewis Orch.; and Dizzy Gillespie. Awarded four NEA Jazz Perf. grants. CDs: DMP; Conc.; Steep.; Musidisc; Tri.; Jazzline; D-T; w. Getz (Col.); Herman (Fant.); John Abercrombie (Steep.; Musidisc); J. Bergonzi (Red); Larry Schneider (Steep.).

LAWRENCE, ARNIE (Arnold Lawrence Finkelstein), alto, sop saxes; b. Brooklyn, NY, 7/10/38; d. Jerusalem, 4/22/05. Began on cl. then pl. tnr. sax fr. age 13. First prof. gigs at hotel in Catskill Mts., N.Y. 1951. Pl. w. Mat Mathews '55-6; Chico Hamilton off and on fr. early '60s; Rusty Dedrick '65; Urbie Green, Dick Hyman '65-8; Frank Foster mid '60s; Warren Chiasson-Jimmy Garrison '66; Doc Severinsen sxt. '65-7; Duke Pearson bb '67-8; NBC *Tonight Show* orch. w. Severinsen '67-72; Johnny Richards '68; Joe Newman '69-70; Les De Merle '69; Clark Terry fr. '70; Blood, Sweat & Tears '74; Rod Levitt '74-5; Chuck Israels' Nat'l Jazz Ens. '70s; Liza Min-

nelli '78; Louis Bellson bb '80; also extens. freelance w. Dizzy Gil-lespie; Elvin Jones; Jimmy Heath; Howard McGhee; others. Pl. w. own gps. Children of All Ages and Treasure Island fr. mid '60s. In the '80s he pl. a key role in developing the jazz BFA prog. at the New Sch., where he served as dir. of instruction into the late '90s. Moved to Israel '98 and opened his own jazz school. Perf. w. own gp. Blues Co-Elation '92. Lawrence prod. recs. w. John Coltrane; Kirk Nurock; and Tom Harrell. Fests: all major '73-82; Cork, Ireland '90. LPs: Adamo; Project 3; w. Severinsen (Command); C. Hamilton (BN). CDs: w. Frank Vignola (Conc.); Hamilton (Imp.).

LAWRENCE, DOUG (DOUGLAS MARSHAL), tnr, sop saxes, cl, fl; b. Lake Charles, LA, 10/11/56. Father and two bros. are prof. mus. Stud. cl. w. fath., then pl. w. fath.'s band in Albuquerque, N.M., fr. age 13. Worked w. show bands in Texas, New Mexico, and LV 1974-9; West Point Jazz Band '79-86, also freelanced w. show bands in the Catskills. Began coming into NYC '84, pl. w. Swing Street; Grover Mitchell bb; Loren Schoenberg bb; Buck Clayton; Benny Goodman; Mel Lewis; Jay McShann bb; Glen Zottola; Widespread Jazz Orch.; Teri Thornton. Moved to NYC in '86, pl. w. Mitchell, Schoenberg, Clayton, Geo. Benson, Lionel Hampton, Barry Harris, Urbie Green, Warren Vaché late '80s. Subbed for Kenny Hing w. Basie band. Favs: Lester Young, Wardell Gray, Paul Gonsalves, Hank Mobley. Fests: JVC JF since '88; Eur. '88, '91. TV: *Joe Temperley's Town*, Ch. 4, NYC. CDs: Fable; w. B. Clayton (Stash); G. Mitchell (Ken); L. Schoenberg (MM).

LAWRENCE, ELLIOT (Elliot Lawrence Broza), pno, arr, comp, cond; b. Philadelphia, PA, 2/14/25. Co-led *Horn & Hardart Children's Hour* band w. Buddy DeFranco on WCAU in Phila. 1937-41. Stud. at U. of Pa. Led own bb at WCAU '41-5 and in NYC '46-59. Sidemen incl. Gerry Mulligan; Red Rodney; Nick Travis; Johnny Mandel; Al Cohn; Tiny Kahn; Earl Swope; Al Porcino; Gene Quill; Hal McKusick; Eddie Bert. Led small gp. on Jack Sterling radio show '50s. Rec. w. Manny Albam, Woody Herman '57-8. Cond. in Moscow and Leningrad on St. Dept. tour '59. Mus. dir. and arr. for B'way shows, incl. *Bye Bye Birdie* '61; *How to Succeed in Business* '62; *Here's Love* '64; *Golden Boy* '65. Also arr. for films and TV, incl. Tony Awds. 25th Anniversary; *Irving Berlin 100th Anniversary Show*; Emmy Awards. Lawrence has been honored w. seven Emmy awds., a Tony, an Oscar, and the Hurley Cross Gold Medal and Alumni Prize of U. of Pa. Worked as a mus. consultant for N.W. Ayer Advertising fr. '78. Fav. arrs: Al Cohn, Gerry Mulligan, Johnny Mandel, Billy Byers. CDs:

Fant.; Col.; Mob. Fid.; w. Sims, Getz, etc., *Four Brothers Together Again* (RCA).

LAWS, HUBERT JR., fl, kybds, comp; b. Houston, TX, 11/10/39. Brother of Ronnie and voc. Eloise. Stud. at hs, Tex. So. U., LA State Coll., Juilliard. Prof. debut age 13 in Houston; later joined gp. variously known as Modern Jazz Sxt., Night Hawks, and (Jazz) Crusaders. After leaving Crusaders in 1960, he pl. at the Berkshire Fest. 1961; w. Mongo Santamaria '63–67; NY Metropolitan Opera Orch. '69–72. NY Philharm. '69–72. Freelanced and rec. w. Quincy Jones; Paul Simon; Paul McCartney; Natalie Cole; Aretha Franklin; Chick Corea; others. Prof. of fl. at Calif. Inst. of Arts. Winner of many *DB* polls, incl. Readers Poll annually fr. '71 and Critics Poll from '75. Favs: Julius Baker, fl.; Don Sebesky, arr. Laws, who teamed w. the classical flst. Jean-Pierre Rampal for several concerts dur. the '80s, is respected in both classical and jazz circles for his full sound and flawless intonation. CDs: CTI/Col., MM; Rh./Atl.; w. Chet Baker; Q. Jones (A&M); G. Benson; Weather Report (Col.); Ron Carter; F. Hubbard (CTI); S. Turrentine (MM); M. Tyner (Mile.); Corea (LRC); H. Mabern (Prest.); Gil Evans (Enja).

LAWS, RONNIE (RONALD), tnr sax; b. Houston, TX, 10/3/50. Brother of Hubert and Eloise Laws. Started on sax 1962; stud. fl. at Stephen F. Austin St. U; also attended Tex. So. U. Relocated to LA in '71; pl. w. Quincy Jones; Hugh Masekela; Kenny Burrell; rec. w. Walter Bishop Jr. '73. Fr. mid '70s, he was active in pop-oriented jazz; rec. w. bro. Hubert '74; Ramsey Lewis '77; pl. and rec. w. Earth, Wind and Fire; cont. to work in pop-jazz vein into early '90s. CDs: BN; w. Wayne Henderson (Whirl).

LAWSON, (RICHARD) HUGH (JEROME), pno, comp, arr; b. Detroit, MI, 3/12/35; d. White Plains, NY, 3/11/97. Attended Cass Tech. HS and Wayne St. U., where he stud. tnr. sax and pno. Pl. w. Yusef Lateef 1956–60. Came to NYC w. Lateef '60. Freelanced in '60s w. Sonny Rollins; Roy Eldridge; Sweets Edison; Roy Brooks; George Coleman; Charles McPherson; Grady Tate; Stanley Turrentine; Dinah Washington. In late '60s-early '70s, he pl. w. Lockjaw Davis; Joe Williams (w. S. Edison–Jimmy Forrest); Betty Carter; Joe Henderson; Kenny Burrell; Y. Lateef. Comp. and arr. for Piano Choir, which he helped found in '72. Led own trio fr. '75. Tour. Eur. w. C. Mingus '75; Eastern Eur. '77; Middle East '81–2. Rec. in late '70s-early '80s w. Charlie Rouse; Geo. Adams–Dannie Richmond; own gps. Taught at Henry Street Settlement, NYC in '70s. Pl. w. own trio and freelanced in NYC '80s-90s. App. w. Sweets Edi-

son at Tavern on the Green '94, '95. Favs: Bud Powell, Monk, E. Garner. CDs: SN; w. Lateef (Sav.; NJ; Prest.; Riv.; Rh.); G. Adams (BN; SN); Edison (Riv.; Cand.); J. Forrest (Prest.); J. Williams (Roul.); Mingus Dynasty (WW).

LAWSON, JANET, voc; b. Baltimore, MD, 11/13/40. Raised by a mus. family, Lawson sang on radio fr. age 3. Moved to NYC 1960. Stud. w. Hall Overton, Warne Marsh. Tour. extens. as nightclub singer; worked at Village Vanguard '65; and on TV w. Steve Allen '68–9. Perf. w. Duke Ellington '71. By '76 she had developed into an excellent jazz singer, an intelligent scatter with a four-octave range. Form. own qnt. that later rec. two albums; also rec. w. Eddie Jefferson; David Lahm. Feat. in *Five Ladies of Jazz* series at Metropolitan Museum of Art, NYC '83. Very active as an educator. Headed jazz voc. program at William Paterson Coll., Wayne, N.J. '81–8. Faculty member at Janice Borla Vocal Jazz Camp, Lisle, Ill. fr. '89. In '90s adjunct profess. at NYU; City Coll., NY; New School, where she developed a course '95, *Jazz Anatomy: Theory for Singers*, w. Sheila Jordan, Amy London. Has cond. clinics at Manh. Sch. of Mus.; Berklee Coll. of Mus.; U. of Indiana; U. of Calgary. Received grants fr. Rockefeller Foundation; NEA. Favs: Sarah Vaughan, Annie Ross, Sheila Jordan, Bobby McFerrin. Theater: soprano soloist w. Alvin Ailey in *Blood Memories* at City Center, NYC; comp. and created a musical, *Jass Is a Lady*, w. lyricist Diane Snow, prod. by Playwrights Horizons, NYC. Video: *Jazz Journey*, program for children, co-written w. Lenore Raphael. CDs: HokanZee; Cambria; w. Bob Dorough (Laissez-Faire).

LAWSON, YANK (JOHN RHEA), tpt; b. Trenton, MO, 5/3/11; d. Indianapolis, IN, 2/18/95. Mother pl. pno. Began on pno., sax, tpt. Stud. w. Carl Webb, Del Staigers at U. of Mo. Pl. w. Slaty Randall 1931; Ben Pollack '32–4. Founding member of Bob Crosby Orch. '35–8. Pl. w. Tommy Dorsey '38–40; Crosby '41–2; Benny Goodman '42. Pl. w. radio orchs. fr. '42 incl. *Kate Smith Show; Your Hit Parade*. Rec. w. Frank Sinatra '44. On staff at NBC '50–68; feat. w. Bobby Byrne on Steve Allen TV show '53–4; also Milton Berle; Perry Como, *Tonight Show*; etc. Led dixieland band w. Bob Haggart '50s. Played the King Oliver parts on Louis Armstrong's Decca album, *Satchmo: A Musical Autobiography* '57; pl. w. Armstrong at NJF '62. Pl. at Eddie Condon's in NYC '63–6. Tour. Asia w. Bob Crosby '64. Rec. w. Teresa Brewer; Judy Garland; Barbara Lea; Roy Eldridge. With help fr. Denver-based jazz patron Dick Gibson, Lawson and Haggart formed World's Greatest Jazz Band in '68; members incl. Billy Butterfield; Lou

McGarity; Carl Fontana; Bob Wilber; Bud Freeman; Ralph Sutton; Morey Feld. The WGJB enjoyed considerable success in the US and Eur. bef. disbanding in '78. Perf. in '80s w. own gps., reunions of WGJB, Crosby band. Favs: Armstrong, Butterfield, Warren Vaché. CDs: Sig.; Aud.; Jazz.; w. Armstrong (Dec.); WGJB (Atl.); T. Dorsey (BB); B. Crosby; R. Eldridge (Dec.); Swingville All-Stars (GTJ); Condon (Dec.).

LE SAGE, BILL (WILLIAM), vib, comp, arr, pno, acdn; b. London, England, 1/20/27. Father was semi-prof. dmr. in 1920s. Self-taught on pno. fr. '43. In army bands '45–8; made prof. debut in '48. Stud. w. Lennie Tristano in NYC '50. Orig. pnst. in Johnny Dankworth Seven '50–4. Began pl. vib. '53; member of Tony Kinsey Trio '54–61. *Lilywhite Boys*, a musical by Le Sage and Kinsey, opened in London in '60. Arr. for TV and films fr. '61. Co-led qt. w. Ronnie Ross '61–5. Formed 10-pc. gp., Directions In Jazz, incl. four cellos '63; the gp. perf. concerts in Engl. and at the Hamburg Jazz Wkshp. '64. Led Bebop Preservation Society '70–86. Pl. w. Barbara Thompson '71–8; J. Dankworth '79–83; Charlie Watts fr. '85. Favs: Lionel Hampton, Bud Powell. Polls: *MM* '56–61. Rec. w. Dankworth Seven for Esquire label; own LPs for Brit. Philips.; also w. Kinsey.

LEA, BARBARA (Leacock), voc; b. Detroit, MI, 4/10/29. Descendant of French comp. Alexander Chas. LeCoq. Stud. mus. theory at Wellesley Coll. 1951. Worked mainly as single fr. early '50s; w. Bob January bb '78–90; Loren Schoenberg bb fr. '81; Benny Goodman Orch. '86; Hi-Tones vocal qt. fr. '92. App. at the Oak Room of the Algonquin Hotel '98. Lea also worked as a musical and dramatic actress '63–80. She taught acting at Cal. State-Northridge '70, Hofstra U. '72; speech at Amer. Acad. of Dramatic Arts '72; also taught Actualism Lightwork meditation fr. '88. Mike Butcher called her "that rarity in this day and age, a singer whose voice is a musical instrument, whose reading of a lyric makes complete sense, who knows how to phrase and shade, has style, charm, and the ability to evoke the opulent glamour of a night on the town with caviar and champagne." Favs: Mildred Bailey, Billie Holiday, Lee Wiley. Polls: *DB* New Star '56. TV: *Tonight Show* w. Steve Allen. LPs: Jazz.; w. Yank Lawson–Bob Haggart; Mr. Tram Associates (Aud.). CDs: Aud.; Prest.; Chall.; w. Yank Lawson (Jazz.).

LEARY, FORD, tb, voc; b. Lockport, NY, 9/5/08; d. NYC, 6/4/49. Played in NYC w. Bunny Berigan 1936–7; Larry Clinton '38–40; Charlie Barnet '40–1; Mike Riley '41; Muggsy Spanier '42. Later worked as an actor. CDs: w. Barnet (BB).

LEARY, JAMES (JAMES HOUSTON III), bs; b. Little Rock, AR, 6/4/46. Studied at No. Tex. St., later U. of Arizona and Cal. State U.-SF. Voted best soloist at intercollegiate jf in St. Louis 1968. In '70s worked w. Bobby Hutcherson; Earl Hines; Dexter Gordon; Woody Shaw; also w. stage shows, incl. *Eubie* and *Ain't Misbehavin'*. In '80s he worked w. Count Basie; Dorothy Donegan; Ernie Andrews; toured w. Sammy Davis Jr. '84–9. Eur. tour w. Eddie Harris '90. Back w. Basie band late '90s. Rec. w. Hines, Hutcherson and own gps. CDs: w. C. Basie (Pab.; MAMA); Carmen Bradford (Evid.); Tito Puente (Trop.); Harold Land (Post.); John Handy (Inak); Gene Harris (Conc.); E. Hines (B&B); Eddie Marshall (Timel.).

LeDONNE, MIKE (MICHAEL ARTHUR), pno, org; b. Bridgeport, CT, 10/26/56. Father had mus. store, pl. gtr., and led own trio in Bridgeport. Pl. w. father's gp., then stud. at Manh. Sch. of Mus. and w. Jaki Byard at New Engl. Cons.; later stud. w. Nicholas Rodrigues and Jimmy Rowles in NYC. Pl. w. Widespread Jazz Orch. 1978; Panama Francis '81; house band at Jimmy Ryan's '81–2; Benny Goodman '82–3; also worked w. Scott Hamilton; Ruby Braff; Buddy Tate; Al Grey; Vic Dickenson; Doc Cheatham. Pl. w. Art Farmer–Clifford Jordan '88–9; Grady Tate '89; Milt Jackson since '89; also own gps. since '81. Pno. and org. w. Benny Waters '97. LeDonne, a versatile pianist, at home in several genres, is also effective on the Hammond B-3, as he demonstrates on Hamilton's *Organic Duke*. Favs: Hank Jones, Wynton Kelly, Cedar Walton, Tatum, Garner. Polls: *JJ* Rec. of Yr. Fests: Eur. since '81. CDs: CC; w. Chris Flory; Scott Hamilton (Conc.); Tad Shull (CC); Widespread Orch.; Mike Hashim (Stash); Milt Jackson; Joshua Redman (WB); Benny Golson (Mile.).

LEE, BILL (WILLIAM JAMES EDWARDS), bs, comp; b. Snow Hill, AL, 7/23/28. Mother, Alberta G. Lee, was a concert pnst.; fath., Arnold W. Lee, pl. tpt. and crnt.; son is filmmaker Spike Lee. Began pl. dms. in family band at age 8, then sw. to fl. at age 11. Stud. at Snow Hill Inst., then w. Kemper Harold, musicologist Willis James at Morehouse Coll. 1947. Began pl. bs. in '50. Moved to Chi. '52. Israel Crosby recommended him for a job w. Buster Bennett. Pl. w. Johnny Griffin; Billy Wallace; Clifford Jordan; Andrew Hill; Vernel Fournier; John Gilmore; Geo. Coleman; Frank Strozier; and others. Moved to NYC '59. Rec. in NYC w. Ray Bryant '60–1; Frank Strozier '60–2; John Handy '61. Worked in '60s w. Philly Joe Jones; Phineas Newborn; Harold Mabern; also folk and gospel gps., incl. Josh White; Odetta; Theodore Bikel; Judy Collins. Founder and leader of NY Bass Violin Choir '68; co-leader of Brass Company w. Bill Hardman, Billy Higgins '72–80s. Mus. dir. for Muriel Winston's *A Fresh Viewpoint*. Led a family band, Descendants of Mike and Phoebe, named for his ancestors fr. the 1800s—personnel incl. Consuela Lee Morehead, pno.; A. Grace Lee Mims, vocs.; and A. Cliffton Lee, tpt. Lee is the comp. of folk-jazz operas, incl. *The Depot; One Mile East; Baby Sweets; The Quarter*; and *Little Johnny*. Comp. mus. for the B'way prod. of *The Hand Is on the Gate*. Rec. in '70s w. Clifford Jordan, Stanley Cowell. Since '86, he has contributed mus. to his son's films, incl. *She's Gotta Have It* and *School Daze*. Fav: Jimmy Blanton. Fests: all major, also Newport Folk Fests. TV: *Today*; Harry Belafonte specials. CDs: w. Frank Strozier (VJ); *She's Gotta Have It* (Ant.).

LEE, GEORGE E(WING), voc, bari sax, lead; b. Booneville, MO, 4/28/1896; d. San Diego, CA, ca. 10/58. Brother of Julia Lee. Pl. w. army band 1917; sang w. vocal qt. Form. own gp. w. sister '20; perf. mainly at Lyric Hall, KC. Formed larger band '27. In '29 w. the intention of competing w. Bennie Moten, Lee signed up Jesse Stone, an arr. and manager, who hired modern mus., incl. Eddie Tompkins; Budd Johnson; Keg Johnson; Tommy Douglas; Herman Walder; Baby Lovett. Lee merged his gp. w. Moten's briefly '33–4; cont. to lead a bb into '35; then scaled it back to a small gp. Moved to Jackson, Miss. '40; relocated to Det. '42 to manage nightclub. Settled in San Diego after WWII. LP: Retrieval. CDs: tracks in *The Real Kansas City of the '20s, '30s and '40s* (Col.).

LEE, JEANNE, voc, comp; b. NYC, 1/29/39; d. Tijuana, Mexico, 10/25/00. Father was concert singer. Stud. modern dance, choreography, pno. Was feat. w. pnst. Ran Blake in concerts and recs., incl. 1962 MJF and Eur. tours. Later assoc. w. Gunther Hampel. Dur. late '60s and '70s rec. w. Sunny Murray; Archie Shepp; Anthony Braxton; Carla Bley; Andrew Cyrille. In '80s active as a comp., wrote oratorio, and form. a vocal summit w. Jay Clayton, Urszula Dudziak, and Lauren Newton. Lee was a singer of rare virtuosity whose work ranged fr. great complexity to basic simplicity; she has been called the most creative new vocal artist to emerge fr. the avant-garde of the '60s. CDs: Word of Mouth; Jeanne Lee–Ran Blake (BB); Owl); Jeanne Lee–Mal Waldron (Owl); Andrew Cyrille–Jeanne Lee–Jimmy Lyons (BS).

LEE, JOHN GREGORY, bs, el-bs, comp; b. Boston, MA, 6/28/52. Father pl in navy band dur. WWII. Stud. bs. and tbn. in hs, then bs. w. Dr. Edward Arian at Phila. Mus. Acad. Pl. w. local bands in Phila. fr. 1969; Carlos Garnett '71–2; then sub. for

Stanley Clarke w. Joe Henderson, Pharoah Sanders. Pl w. Max Roach '72; Chris Hinze in Eur. '72–4; Charlie Mariano, Joachim Kuhn, Norman Connors '74; Larry Coryell's Eleventh House '75–7; Alphonse Mouzon '77; own gp. w. dmr. Gerry Brown; also trio w. Brown, Philip Catherine '78–81; McCoy Tyner '82–4; various Dizzy Gillespie bands, incl. United Nation Orch. '84–92. Lee has also pl. w. Gary Bartz; Gil Evans; Walter Davis Jr.; Jimmy Heath; Lonnie Liston Smith; John Blake; Rodney Franklin; John Stubblefield; and worked as a rec. prod. More than eighty of his comps. have been rec. by other artists. He is involved w. many bands incl. the Fantasy Band w. Chuck Loeb, Marion Meadows, and Dave Samuels but most prominently the Dizzy Gillespie Alumni All-Stars; also dir. for *Dizzy: The Man and the Music*, the official concert and clinic program celebrating Gillespie's life and work. Favs: Jaco Pastorius, Marcus Miller, Ron Carter, Stanley Clarke. Polls: *Record World* '76. Fests: Eur., Asia, Africa, etc. since '72. Film: *A Night in Havana* w. Gillespie '87. TV: *Tonight Show*; Arsenio Hall w. Gillespie. CDs: John Lee–Gerry Brown, Mood–Hot Wire; Lime.; Japanese BN & Col.; w. Gillespie (Enja; Imp.; Projazz; Timel.); Gillespie Alumni All-Stars (Shan.); Mike Longo (CAP); Claudio Roditi (Res.); Fantasy Band (DMP; Shan.); T. Thielemans; C. Mariano; Jasper van't Hof (Lime.).

LEE, JULIA, voc, comp, pno; b. Booneville, MO, 10/31/02; d. Kansas City, MO, 12/8/58. Sang in children's band w. Walter Page; turned prof. as voc. w. Page's KC band in 1916. Worked as pnst. w. her bro. George E. Lee's band '20–33; as a single at Milton's Tap Room in KC '34–48. Her '44 recs. w. Jay McShann led to a Capitol contract and numerous sides until '52, often backed by top jazz mus., incl. Benny Carter; Vic Dickenson; Red Nichols; and Red Callender. Infl. by Jimmy Rushing and Joe Turner. CDs: Charly; Bear Family; tracks on *Reefer Songs* (Jass); *Christmas Kisses* (Cap.); *The 1940s Mercury Sessions* (Merc.); *The Real Kansas City of the '20s, '30s, and '40s* (Col.).

LEE, PEGGY (Norma Deloris Egstrom), voc, comp; b. Jamestown, ND, 5/26/20. Sang in local choir and on WDAY radio in Fargo, N. Dak.; worked w. Sven Olson and Will Osborne 1940–41. Discovered while working w. vocal gp. in Chi. '41; join. the Benny Goodman band. First hit record, "Why Don't You Do Right?" '42; married Goodman's gtrst., Dave Barbour, March '43 (div. '51). In the mid '40s, Ms. Lee began prolific rec. activity that yielded several major pop hits on Dec. and Cap., incl. "Golden Earrings" '47; "Manana" '48; "Lover" '52; "Fever" '58; "I'm a

Woman" '63; "Is That All There Is?" '69. App. in films, *Mr. Music* '50 *The Jazz Singer* '53; and *Pete Kelly's Blues* '55, the latter earning her an Academy Award nomination. Comp. music for films, incl. *Lady and the Tramp; Johnny Guitar; The Russians Are Coming; The Heart Is a Lonely Hunter;* and *About Mrs. Leslie.* Songwriting collaborators incl. Duke Ellington ("I'm Gonna Go Fishin'"); Quincy Jones ("New York City Blues"); Johnny Mandel ("The Shining Sea"); and Dave Grusin ("The Heart Is a Lonely Hunter"). First tour of Europe '61. A popular TV guest, she app. on *TV's Top Tunes* '51; *Songs for Sale* '51–2; *The Revlon Revue* '60; and shows hosted by Jack Paar; Frank Sinatra; Nat King Cole; Andy Williams; Dean Martin; Judy Garland; also her own "special." App. at Basin Street East and The Copacabana, NYC, and other major clubs and concert halls, sometimes w. Benny Carter, Quincy Jones, and Lou Levy as cond.-arrs. Won a Grammy for "Is That All There Is?" '69. Though sometimes sidelined by illness, Lee remained active as pop/jazz singer-songwriter throughout the '80s and into the '90s, app. in Engl. early in the decade. Some of her accomps. cont. to be jazz oriented, w. pnst. Mike Renzi as her mus. dir. App. at Peggy Lee Celebration Concert '94. Early infl: Billie Holiday. Films: *Pete Kelly's Blues*; others (see above). CDs: Cap.; Angel; MM; Dec.; w. B. Goodman (Col.); as voc. w. Capitol Jazzmen and dmr. w. Ten Cats and a Mouse in *Classic Capitol Jazz Sessions* (Mos.).

LEEMAN, CLIFF (CLIFFORD), dms; b. Portland, ME, 9/10/13; d. NYC, 4/26/86. Studied xyl. and perc.; pl. w. Portland Symph. 1927; w. Dan Murphy in Bost. '33; Hank Biagini '35; Artie Shaw '36–9; Tommy Dorsey '39; Charlie Barnet '40–3; Woody Herman '43; John Kirby and Raymond Scott '44; Jimmy Dorsey '45; Glen Gray '47. Dur. the '50s he worked mainly in NYC w. Bobby Hackett at Nick's and Eddie Condon at Condon's. Int'l tours w. many dixieland gps., incl. "Wild Bill" Davison. Worked w. Bob Crosby in LV '60; Dick Haymes '63, Dukes of Dixieland '63–4; Peanuts Hucko, NYC '64; toured Far East w. Condon '64 and '67. Many apps. at Colo. JP. "We don't seem to know what a drummer really is," said Buddy Rich. "He is not the showman—the guy who sits the highest or has his cymbals on backwards. He's the guy who makes the band sound good. That was Cliff Leeman." CDs: w. Charlie Barnet (BB; Dec.); J. Venuti (Sonet); Venuti–Z. Sims; Condon; Hackett (Chiaro.); Davison (Jazz.); T. Dorsey; Shaw (BB).

LEFEBVRE, GARY CHARLES, tnr, sop, alto saxes; cl, fl; b. Columbus, OH, 2/18/39. Family members all pl. various instr. Beginning in 1953 he stud.

priv. in San Diego w. Russ Cheevers, Dan Magnusson, others. In '57 he join. qnt. w. Mike Wofford, John Guerin, Don Sleet. Pl. w. Terry Gibbs '59; then Stan Kenton; Illinois Jacquet; Louie Bellson; Nelson Riddle. Worked in LV, LA, and San Diego '60s-90s. App. in Sweden w. Red Mitchell. Known mainly as superb section man. LPs: Disc.; w. Shorty Rogers-Jeri Southern (Studio West).

LEGGE, WADE, pno; b. Huntington, WV, 2/4/34; d. Buffalo, NY, 8/15/63. Parents both pnsts. Raised in Buffalo, where Milt Jackson heard him in 1952 and recommended him to Dizzy Gillespie, w. whom he pl. bs. for two weeks bef. sw. to pno. Left Gillespie '54; pl. w. Johnny Richards '55. Worked w. many other small gps., incl. those of Jimmy Knepper; Bill Hardman; Pepper Adams; Sonny Rollins; Charles Mingus. Later ret. to Buffalo and freelanced. Infl. by Bud Powell. CDs: w. Rollins; Jackie McLean (Prest.); Mingus (Rh./Atl.; Deb.); Gillespie (Verve; Vogue); M. Jackson (Sav.); Gigi Gryce (Riv.).

LEGGIO, CARMEN (CARMELO JOHN), tnr, alto sax, cl; b. Tarrytown, NY, 9/30/27. Father, Frank, pl. gtr. and mand.; bro. is a singer. Took cl. lessons in elem. sch., then self-taught. Pl. local dances fr. 1940. Pl. w. Terry Gibbs at Birdland '50–1. Freelanced in NYC w. Marty Napoleon mid '50s; Sol Yaged '56; Benny Goodman '57; Maynard Ferguson '58–9; own gp. fr. '60; Mel Lewis '61–78; Woody Herman, Gene Krupa mid '60s; Jake Hanna '70s. Also pl. w. Gene Krupa; Buddy Rich; Mel Tormé; Doc Severinsen; Al Cohn; Dinah Washington; Dizzy Gillespie; Nancy Wilson; Count Basie; Frank Sinatra Jr.; Bobby Darin; Paul Anka; etc. Leggio has taught at Trenton St. Coll., Glassboro St. Coll., and the US Air Force Band Sch. He owns a rec. label, Leggio Records. Favs: Artie Shaw, Coleman Hawkins, Charlie Parker. Fests: So. Amer. w. Krupa '65. Film: app. in *The Brotherhood* w. Kirk Douglas. TV: Mike Douglas, Johnny Carson, Dean Martin, Joe Franklin. CDs: Leggio; w. M. Ferguson (Roul.); Eddie Bert (FS); W. Herman (Jazz Hour).

LEGRAND, MICHEL, comp, arr, pno, cond; b. Paris, France, 2/24/32. Father, Raymond, was cond. and comp. in France. Stud. w. Nadia Boulanger at Paris Cons. 1943–52. First prof. gigs accomp. singers. Cond. and arr. for Maurice Chevalier, Edith Piaf. Arr. for Dizzy Gillespie w. Strings '52, then had hit w. own LP, *I Love Paris* '54. Legrand beg. comp. for films and TV in the late '50s. Although he is known mainly as a film comp., he has rec. w. many jazz artists, incl. Miles Davis; Bill Evans; Ben Webster; John Coltrane (all on the album *Legrand Jazz,*

Col. '58); Stan Getz '69; Sarah Vaughan '72; Phil Woods '73, '75; Bud Shank. Perf. in US and Eur. w. Woods '70s. Favs: Monk, Tatum, Peterson; bands: Ellington, Basie, Gillespie, Kenton. Legrand's film scores incl. *The Umbrellas of Cherbourg* '64; *The Thomas Crown Affair* (Best Song Oscar '68); *Summer of '42* (Oscar '71); *Lady Sings the Blues* '72; Orson Welles' *F for Fake* '75; *Yentl* (Oscar '83); *Dingo* (w. Miles Davis) '91. He won an Emmy for his score to the popular TV movie *Brian's Song* '70. Many of Legrand's songs have become standards, incl. "The Windmills of Your Mind"; "You Must Believe in Spring"; "Watch What Happens"; "What Are You Doing the Rest of Your Life?"; "The Summer Knows"; "Once Upon a Summertime"; "Pieces of Dreams." Among the artists who have rec. his comps. are Chet Baker; Bob Cooper; Art Farmer; Stanley Turrentine; Freddie Hubbard; Joe Pass; Oscar Peterson; Frank Sinatra; Susannah McCorkle; Lena Horne; Anita O'Day; Tony Bennett; Rosemary Clooney; and Cleo Laine. Dir., scored, and co-wrote the '89 film *Five Days in June*; dir. *Chase the Moon* w. Rudolf Nureyev for UK TV '89. Arr. four songs for Natalie Cole's hit CD *Unforgettable* '92. Legrand has won several Grammys as a comp. and arr., and was inducted into the Songwriters Hall of Fame '90. He has rec. extensively as a jazz pnst. and cont. to work all over the world as a freelance comp., arr., and orch. cond. TV: *Michel Legrand in Concert* UK '85; *Grand Piano,* w. Oscar Peterson, Claude Bolling CBC '84; Ann Margret, Dick Van Dyke specials; Danny Kaye; Maurice Chevalier. CDs: Col.; Verve; Gryphon; w. Vaughan (Main.); Natalie Cole (Elek.). Soundtracks: Philips; Bell; Motown.

LEIBROOK, MIN (WILFORD F.), bs sax, tba, bs; b. Hamilton, OH, 1903; d. Los Angeles, CA, 6/8/43. Played w. Wolverines; then to NYC to work w. Paul Whiteman 1927–31 (pl. bs.-sax solo on Whiteman rec. of "San"). Dur. this time he also rec. in small gp. w. Bix Beiderbecke. Worked w. Eddie Duchin '35 and Lennie Hayton orch. Last well-known jazz app. was a brief gig w. the Three T's (Jack and Charlie Teagarden and Frank Trumbauer) '36. Moved to Calif. w. Duchin, did studio and theatre work on bs. CDs: w. Beiderbecke (Mile.; Col.).

LEIGHTON, BERNIE (BERNARD SIDNEY), pno; b. West Haven, CT, 1/30/21; d. NYC 9/16/94. Began pl. pno. at age 6. Family moved to NYC in 1930. Pl. w. Bud Freeman at Kelly's Stables late '30s; Raymond Scott '40; Benny Goodman '40–1; Enric Madriguera '42; also studio work for CBS. In army '43–6, then stud. w. Bruce Simonds at Yale Sch. of Mus. '46–9. Perf. classical recital at Carnegie Hall

'49; worked mainly as studio mus. fr. mid '40s, rec. w. Dave Tough; Billie Holiday; Charlie Parker (w. strings); Benny Goodman; Artie Shaw; James Moody; Bob Wilber; and others. Also worked w. singers, incl. Frank Sinatra; Peggy Lee; Rosemary Clooney; Tony Bennett; Maxine Sullivan. Perf. on the soundtracks of several Woody Allen films. Favs: Tatum, T. Wilson, Lou Levy. Fests: Brussels w. Caterina Valente '63; UK w. Bennett '72–3. CDs: w. Parker (Verve); Joe Williams (BB); Roy Eldridge (Merc.); Oscar Brown Jr. (Col.); Goodman (MM); Holiday (Dec.); Mark Murphy (Riv.).

LEITCH, PETER JOHN, gtr, comp, arr; b. Ottawa, Ont., Canada, 8/19/44. Mostly self-taught but stud. classical gtr. in 1960s. Gigs in Montreal, Vermont, upstate NY in '60s and '70s. Moved to Toronto '78; pl. w. Peter Appleyard; Phil Nimmons; Rob McConnell; also w. own qt. and visiting soloists, incl. Milt Jackson; Red Norvo; Clark Terry; Kenny Wheeler; Al Grey–Jimmy Forrest; Judy Niemack; Bennie Wallace; Bobby Watson; John Hicks; James Williams. Moved to NYC '83. Leitch has worked extens. as an educ. and as a prod. for the Criss Cross label. Led his own gp. w. John Hicks, Ray Drummond, and Smitty Smith fr. '80s. In late '90s regular Sunday night gig at Walker's, NYC, w. various guests. Has annotated CDs for Res. Favs: Wes Montgomery, Kenny Burrell, Jim Hall, René Thomas. Fests: USSR '81 w. Fraser McPherson; Eur. since '86. CDs: Conc.; CC; Res.; w. Renee Rosnes; Jeri Brown (JT); Dominique Eade (RCA); J. Byard (SN); O. Peterson (Pab.); Woody Shaw (Muse).

LEITHAM, JENNIFER (né **JOHN DAVID**), bs; el-bs; b. Scott Air Force Base, IL, 8/10/53. Sang in hs chorus. A left-handed bs., he began stud. w. Al Stauffer in Phila. 1974. Tour. w. Woody Herman '81, incl. Playboy and Kool-NY fests. Moved to LA in '86; worked w. Jack Sheldon; Bob Cooper; Bill Watrous; Bud Shank; Bill Perkins; George Van Eps; Tommy Newsom; Joe Pass; Warne Marsh; Frank Sinatra Jr.; Bill Holman; Milcho Leviev; others. Leader of own gps. in LA fr. '87; pl. w. George Shearing and Mel Tormé. Pl. Otter Crest and Santa Fe Jazz Parties; Floating Jazz Fest. and Elkhart Jazz Fest. App. in film *Cool World*; TV incl. General Hospital, Night Court, Tonight Show w. E. Shaughnessy. Video: Impressions of Hollywood Boulevard w. Tommy Tedesco. Favs: Ray Brown, Pettiford, G. Mraz. CDs: USA; w. Tormé; G. Shearing–Tormé; Cleo Laine-John Dankworth (Conc.); E. Shaughnessy (Chase); Tedesco; Lorez Alexandria (Disc./Trend); Tom Talbert (SB); Dick Hafer (Prog.); Herb Geller (Hep; FS).

LEMON, BRIAN, pno; b. Nottingham, England, 11/2/37. Both parents semi-pro mus. Stud. at sch. Pl. w. Freddy Randall; Sandy Brown; Danny Moss; George Chisholm; Alex Welsh; Kenny Baker. Dur. 1970s–'80s he accomp. visiting Amers.: Milt Jackson; Ray Brown; Benny Goodman; Ben Webster; Harry Edison; Lockjaw Davis; Ruby Braff. Also was member of Lawson-Haggart band. In NYC '84 worked w. Bobby Rosengarden; tour. Switzerland, Japan, Brazil, US. Backed Warren Vaché, Scott Hamilton on their Brit. tours in '90s. Rec. w. Moss; Chisholm; S. Brown; Bud Freeman; Spike Robinson; et al. App. on radio w. Goodman; TV w. Ray Brown. Five-time winner, pro section, Brit. Jazz Awards '87–91. Strongly infl. by Tatum, Waller, Teddy Wilson. Solo pno. at Cork JF '94. CDs: w. Hamilton (Conc.); B. Kessel (BL); D. Moss; Vaché (N-H); Joe Temperley (Hep); Charlie Watts (Contin.); The Great British Jazz Band (Cand.).

LEONARD, HARLAN QUENTIN (aka MIKE), sax, lead; b. Kansas City, MO, 7/2/05; d. Los Angeles, CA, 1983. Early exp. w. George E. Lee, Bennie Moten 1923–31. Took over leadership of Moten's Kansas City Sky Rockets '34. In '38 he formed his own band in KC, the Rockets, which incl. such outstanding sidemen as Fred Beckett, tbn.; Henry Bridges, tnr. sax; Jesse Price, dms.; w. arrs. by Tadd Dameron. Charlie Parker was also in the band briefly. In '45 Leonard dissolved the band and went to work for the Internal Revenue Service in LA. LP: RCA. CDs: w. Bennie Moten (BB; Class.); tracks as lead. & sideman in *The Real Kansas City* (Col.).

LEONHARDT, DAVID EMIL, pno, bs, synth, comp; b. Louisville, KY, 9/2/56. Studied w. Jamey Aebersold in Louisville. Pl. in rock band as teenager, then w. J. Aebersold 1975–80. Pnst. and mus. dir. for Jon Hendricks '82–6; then co-led gp. w. Michelle Hendricks '86–90. Pl. w. David "Fathead" Newman fr. '86; Mickey Roker '91–2. Scored film *Ain't No King Comin'* '87. Mus. dir. for Manh. Tap dance co. '87–91; Maison de la Dance, Lyon, France '91. Led own gp. at fests in Atlanta; Winnipeg; and Shenzen, China '90–3. Taught at Jazz Ctr. of NY, Jazzmobile '89; New Sch. '89–90; Berkley Carrol Sch. '89–91. Lecturer and perf. for Young Audiences in NYC public sch. '89–91. Received comp. grants fr. Meet the Composer and the Nat'l Endowment for the Arts, and has been a columnist for *Keyboard Classics* mag. (formerly *Piano Stylist*) fr. '88. Favs: Hancock, Wynton Kelly, Bud Powell. Fests: Eur. fr. '82; So. Amer. '86; Japan '87, '89; China '89. TV: *Today*. CDs: Big Bang; w. M. Hendricks (Muse); H. Mann (Light.); David Newman (Koko.); String of Pearls (Alfa).

LEONHART, CAROLYN, voc; b. NYC, 7/10/71. Father, Jay Leonhart; bro., Michael Leonhart; moth., voc. Donna Leonhart. Stud. at HS of Mus. and Art, then at U. of Rochester and Eastman Sch. of Mus. fr. 1989. Sang on commercials and children's recs. as a child. Perf. w. Jay Leonhart '89–91; Eric Reed '90; Phil Woods '92. Favs: Holiday, Vaughan, Aretha Franklin. Polls: *DB* student voc. '92. Fests: Santa Fe '90. CDs: Toshiba-EMI; w. J. Leonhart (Sunny.).

LEONHART, JAY (JAMES CHANCELLOR), bs, el-bs, song writer, voc; b. Baltimore, MD, 12/6/40. Many mus. in family, incl. four sists., a bro., his wife, Donna, and two children, Michael and Carolyn. Began on pno., gtr., bjo. Stud. at Peabody Inst. 1946–8, '56–7; Berklee Coll. of Mus. '60–1; Oscar Peterson's Advanced Sch. of Contemp. Mus. '61–2; also stud. w. Wm. Curtis; Ray Brown; Orin O'Brien. Pl. in Balt. w. Divcus Chambers Orch. '49; bjo. duo w. bro. '51–5; Pier Five Jazz Band '55–9; Buddy Morrow '60–1; Mike Longo '62–3; Ethel Ennis '63–7. Also worked in insurance business and as a commercial pilot '63–7. Moved to NYC '68; pl. w. Urbie Green '68–70; Marian McPartland '70–3; Jim Hall '71–3; Tony Bennett '71–4; Thad Jones–Mel Lewis Orch. '74–5. Freelanced in '70s w. Zoot Sims; Lee Konitz; Buddy Rich; Gene Bertoncini; Tal Farlow; others. Pl. w. Mel Tormé '80–90; Louis Bellson fr. '85; also much commercial studio work fr. '70. Leonhart perf. at the Blue Note's weekend brunch in NYC fr. '86 into '90s. Writes personal songs about his life as a mus. and sings them acc. himself on bs, selling over 100,000 albums worldwide. Favs: Ray Brown, Pettiford, Blanton. Polls: NARAS Most Val. Player, five times. Fests: Eur., Japan fr. '75. TV: PBS tribute to Milt Hinton; *Today; Tonight Show*. CDs: DMP; Sunny.; Nesak Int'l; w. Dave Grusin (GRP); L. Bellson (MM); Gerry Mulligan (GRP; Conc.); John Bunch (LRC); G. Niewood (DMP); Tormé (DCC); Konitz (Sunny.).

LEONHART, MICHAEL J.C., tpt, pno, comp; b. NYC, 4/21/74. Father, Jay Leonhart; sist., Carolyn Leonhart; moth., voc. Donna Leonhart. Began on vln. Stud. classical tpt. w. Jim Hamlin 1985–92. Feat. soloist in all-city and tri-state jazz bands fr. age 13; also pl. w. father at NYC Blue Note and w. own gps. Leonhart's *Suite for Jazz Trumpet* was premiered w. Clark Terry, Bill Mays, and Gene Bertoncini in '91. In '92 he app. w. Wynton Marsalis, Jon Faddis, Harry Edison, Doc Cheatham, and others at JVC salute to Dizzy Gillespie and was named a Presidential Scholar in the Arts, perf. at the Kennedy Center in Wash., D.C. He has pl. w. Phil Woods; James Moody; Jon Faddis; Stanley Turrentine; Milt Hinton; and the

Mel Lewis Orch. and has been a member of the Philip Morris Superband. Favs: Miles Davis, Clifford Brown, Louis Armstrong. Polls: numerous student awards incl. *DB* comp. '90–2; arr. '91–2; soloist '90, '92; IAJE awards. Fests: Santa Fe '90; JVC '92. TV: ABC, CBS News; *Today*. CDs: Sunny.; w. Jay Leonhart (Sunny.).

LESBERG, JACK, bs; b. Boston, MA, 2/14/20; d. Englewood, NJ, 9/17/05. Brother Richard Burgin was prof. vln. and cond.; sist. also musical. Stud. vln. in Bost. 1930–7, and pl. it in local speakeasies dur. '30s, then sw. to bs. w. Muggsy Spanier '40. Worked w. Mickey Alpert at Boston's Cocoanut Grove, survived infamous fire that destroyed the club in '42. Moved to NYC '43; first gigs. w. James P. Johnson, Willie "The Lion" Smith. On staff at NBC fr. '44. Assoc. principal w. Leonard Bernstein–NY City Center Symph. '45–8; Eddie Condon '44–50. Stud. w. Fred Zimmerman '46–53. Freelanced w. Sarah Vaughan; Benny Goodman; Louis Armstrong; Jack Teagarden; Earl Hines; Wild Bill Davison; Coleman Hawkins; Peanuts Hucko; others fr. late '40s; Kai Winding; Jimmy McPartland; Max Kaminsky; Billy Butterfield; Billie Holiday; others '50s. Pl. w. Raymond Scott on *Lucky Strike Hit Parade* '50–7. Tour. Eur. w. Armstrong '56; w. Teagarden-Hines '57. Pl. and rec. w. Bobby Hackett; Ruby Braff; Joe Venuti; Georgie Auld; Doc Severinsen; Tony Bennett; others '60s. Lived in Austral. '71–4; pl. w. Sydney Symph. and led own qt. Studio mus. in LA '75–80; pl. on soundtracks to *Funny Girl, King Kong, Silent Movie*, etc. Tour. w. all-star bands, incl. Newport All-Stars; *Tribute to Louis Armstrong* w. Ruby Braff, Yank Lawson '80s. App. w. Braff in *A Night For Lady Day at Town Hall* '88. Org. jazz parties in Odessa and Midland, Tex., and Minneapolis '60s to '80s. Favs: Blanton, Ray Brown, Hinton, Duvivier. Fests: all major fr. '50s. TV: Milton Berle '48; *Bell Telephone Hour* '50; *Hit Parade* '50–7; *Texaco Swing into Spring* '59; *Tonight Show*. CDs: w. Howard Alden (Chiaro.); Braff (Conc.; BL); Dan Barrett; Flip Phillips; W. Vaché (Conc.); B. Hackett–Vic Dickenson (Chiar.); L. Armstrong; C. Hawkins (BB); J. Teagarden (BB; Mos.); Goodman (Col.); Condon (Dec.; Chiaro.; Mos.; Jazz.); Holiday (Dec.); P. Hucko (Timel.).

LETMAN, JOHNNY (JOHN BERNARD), tpt, voc; b. McCormick, SC, 9/6/17; d. NYC, 7/17/92. Studied tpt., mello. in Chi.; soloist w. Nat Cole's band 1933. Pl. w. Scatman Crothers in Columbus '35; tour. w. Jimmy Raschel '36. Ret. to Chi., working w. local bands and own qnt. '38–40; Horace Henderson '41; Red Saunders '42. Worked at a Det. aircraft factory and pl. w. Ted Buckner in '43. Moved to NYC '44,

working w. Lucky Millinder; Claude Hopkins; John Kirby; Phil Moore. Pl. w. Cab Calloway '47–9; C. Basie, Sammy Benskin '51; Wilbur De Paris at Jimmy Ryan's '56. Eur. tours: w. Tiny Grimes, Milt Buckner in '60s; Sammy Price '77; NO Blue Serenaders '85–6; Harlem Blues and Jazz Band '90; Lars Edegran orch. '89–92. Int'l tour w. show *One Mo' Time* in '80s. B'way credits incl. *Marathon '33: Never Live Over a Pretzel Factory* '64. Rec. Beth. LP, *The Many Angles of John Letman* '60; rec. w. Bernard Addison for British 77 label '61. CDs: w. Edegran (GHB); Lena Horne (BB); S. Price (B&B); Buck Clayton (Stash).

LEVALLET, DIDIER, bs, comp; b. Arcy-sur-Cure, France, 7/19/44. Studied at Lille Cons. To Paris 1969, working w. Ted Curson; Hank Mobley; Mal Waldron; Johnny Griffin; and in '70s w. free jazz gp., Perception. Pl. in US w. Byard Lancaster '74–6. Very active in '80s as comp. and perf. w. qnt., 12–pc. band, the Swing Strings System. In '90s he rec. w. Charles Tyler; Anthony Ortega; and own tentet. Taught jazz at Ecole National de Musique in Angouleme. A highly regarded, prolific, eclectic composer. CDs: w. Harry Beckett (Evid.); *The International Pescara Jam Sessions, 1970–75* (Phil.).

LEVEY, STAN, dms; b. Philadelphia, PA, 4/5/26; d. Van Nuys, CA, 4/19/05. Professional heavyweight boxer 1942–4. Rec. debut w. Barney Bigard '44. An early bebop dmr., he worked in the '40s w. Oscar Pettiford; Dizzy Gillespie–Charlie Parker; George Shearing; also w. bbs of Georgie Auld and Woody Herman. Join. Stan Kenton '52; later w. Howard Rumsey at Lighthouse. In '60s acc. Peggy Lee; Ella Fitzgerald; Pat Boone; comp. mus. for five Disney industrial films. Active as prof. photographer in mid '60s, retiring fr. mus. by end of decade to pursue photography full time. Made several LPs as leader for Beth.; rec. w. Gillespie; Parker; Ben Webster; Roy Eldridge; Gerry Mulligan; and others. CDs: V.S.O.P.; Aff.; w. Herb Ellis; Gillespie; Stitt; Webster; Fitzgerald; Mulligan (Verve); Getz (Prest.; Verve); Lee; Kenton (Cap.); Parker (Stash); Fats Navarro (Sav.); Chet Baker–Art Pepper (PJ); Konitz (RCA/Vogue); Lars Gullin (Drag.); V. Feldman; H. Rumsey (Cont.); C. Mariano (FS; Aff.); R. Kamuca (FS; HiFi); F. Rosolino (Sav.; Spec.); Bill Harris (Fant.).

LEVIEV, MILCHO, pno, kybds, comp; b. Plovdiv, Bulgaria, 12/19/37. Graduated fr. Bulgaria State Cons. in Sofia 1960. Leader, comp./arr. Bulgarian Radio-TV Big Band '62–6; w. A. Mangelsdorff '70–1. Emigrated to US '71 Pl. w. Don Ellis orch. '71–4; Willie Bobo gp. '73; Billy Cobham '74; also

Carmen McRae; John Klemmer; Airto; Lee Ritenour; and others. In late '70s he pl. w. Art Pepper; Bill Holman; Gerald Wilson; Lainie Kazan. Co-founder and leader of Free Flight '80–3. In '80s he worked w. Charlie Haden; Joe Farrell; Lingua Franca; w. Alexei Zoubov and Dusan Bodganovic '83–6; LA Jazz Choir fr. '85. Form. trio, Katoomi, w. Karen Briggs and Tootie Heath '89; duo dates w. Dave Holland fr. '87. Many foreign tours in '80s, incl. return trips to Bulgaria. Comps. incl.: *Sympho-Jazz Sketches* '82 and *Orpheus Rhapsody* '88, both commissioned by New Amer. Orch.; *The Green House*, a jazz cantata, commissioned by LA Jazz Choir '91. One of the most important or infl. player/comp. to emerge fr. Eastern Eur. in the '70s. CDs: Vart. Jazz; Disc.; M.A. Records; Alpha; TBCD; w. Art Pepper (Mole; Story.).

LEVINE, MARK JAY, pno, tbn, comp, arr; b. Concord, NH, 10/4/38. Studied at Bost. U. Active in NYC w. Houston Person and Mongo Santamaria in 1960s; in '70s pl. w. Joe Henderson, Gabor Szabo. Moved to SF; pl. w. Woody Shaw '75–6; Blue Mitchell–Harold Land '76–9. Has since worked w. Latin and jazz gps, many in the SF Bay area, incl. Stan Getz; Moacir Santos; Luis Gasca; and Cal Tjader. Also occ. led own qnt. in '80s. Received NEA grant for jazz comp. '77. Rec. w. own qnt. fr. '81. CDs: w. Cal Tjader (Conc.); Mark Lewis (Quartet); Joe Henderson; Afro Blue Band (Mile.); B. Shew (MAMA).

LEVINOVSKY, NICK (NIKOLAY), pno, comp, lead; b. Saratov, Russia, 12/14/44. Parents opera singers; bros. mus. and dir. Stud. at Saratov Mus. Coll. 1959–63, degree in pno.; L.B. Sobinov St. Cons. in Saratov '68–74, degrees in comp., theory, musicology. Pl. w. local bands and began to form own combos '60–3; pl. w. Soviet Army jazz orch. '64–7; began writing for bb. Led own qt., bb '68–9. Worked w. Eddie Rosner bb '70–1; Anatoly Kroll bb '71–2; Moscow Radio Orch. '73–5; Germann Lukianov gp. '75–6. Led Sympho-jazz orch., Azerb. '75–78; then form. Allegro, an oct. which he fronted until '89; tour. in Eur.; India; and Sri Lanka. Moved to US '90; app. at NY version of Moscow's Bluebird club at Irving Plaza w. own trio, spring '90. Gigged in NYC w. Victor Jones, Joe Locke, Igor Butman at Russian Samovar in mid '90s. Start. own bb '94, perf. w. it at Birdland '96. Favs: B. Evans, Hancock, Corea; arrs: O. Nelson, Thad Jones. Fests: Jazz Yatra, Bombay, New Delhi '84; w. reunion of Allegro at JVC-NY '95; Wade Barnes, JVC-NY '97. CDs: NLO; w. Barnes (360 Degrees).

LEVITT, AL (ALAN), dms; b. NYC, 11/11/32; d. Paris, France, 11/28/94. Wife, voc. Stella Levitt; son,

Sean, pl. gtr. Stud. pno. w. Moses Chusids in hs.; dms. w. Irv Kluger 1949–50. Pl. w. Barbara Carroll '50; Chuck Wayne '50–1; Charles Mingus '51; Lennie Tristano '52; Stan Getz '53; Paul Bley '54–5; Lee Konitz fr. '54. To Eur. in '56. Pl. in Netherlands w. Pia Beck '56; then moved to Paris, pl. w. Sidney Bechet; Rene Urtreger; Allen Eager; Martial Solal; Guy Lafitte; Stephane Grappelli; Barney Wilen. Ret. to US in '58. Pl. w. Toshiko Akiyoshi '58; Shirley Horn '59; Scott LaFaro Trio, accomp. Dick Haymes '59–60; Ronnie Ball Trio, accomp. Chris Connor '60–1; Candido Camero '62–3; Teddy Edwards '64; Stella Levitt fr. '64; Georgie Auld '65–6; Jackie Paris–Ann Marie Moss '67; Lionel Hampton's Inner Circle '67–8; C. Connor, David Allyn '70; Mingus '72. Rec. album for ESP w. wife and son '68. Moved to Las Palmas, Canary Islands, to work at Half Note club '73. Pl. in Spain w. Pedro Itturalde, own gp. '74. Moved to Paris in '75. Tour. Netherlands w. Peter Ind; pl. in Eur. w. M. Solal, G. Lafitte, R. Urtreger, Slide Hampton, Lee Konitz–Warne Marsh '76; Konitz–Jimmy Raney, Chet Baker '78; Alain Jean-Marie fr. '78; Kai Winding, Kenny Drew '79; Sonny Stitt, James Moody '81; Horace Parlan '84; Steve Grossman, Benny Carter '85; K. Drew, Teddy Edwards '86–7; H. Parlan, Great Guitars '87; Duke Jordan '90, '93. Co-led a gp. w. Belgian pnst. Nathalie Lorier. Levitt cond. clinics in France and Belgium. Favs: K. Clarke, Shadow Wilson, Roach, Philly Joe Jones, Rich. Fests: all major in Eur. Film: *Round Midnight* '86. TV: Eur. TV w. Lionel Hampton late '60s; *To Tell The Truth* '68; *Today* w. David Allyn '70. CDs: w. Lennie Tristano (Jazz Records); Getz; Grappelli (Verve); Marsh–Konitz (Mob. Fid.); Nathan Davis; Dusko Goykovich (DIW); Mingus (Deb.; Rh./Atl.).

LEVITT, ROD (RODNEY CHARLES), tbn, comp, arr; b. Portland, OR, 9/16/29. Parents pl. pno. Pl. w. Dizzy Gillespie bb 1956–7; Ernie Wilkins '57; Kai Winding '58; Gil Evans '59; Sy Oliver '59–60; Mundell Lowe '60; Quincy Jones '61; Oliver Nelson '62; Chuck Israels '70s; also arr. for Cedar Walton, Blue Mitchell. Led own oct '60s–70s. Levitt has taught arr. at City Coll. NY, Hofstra U., Hunter Coll., Fairleigh-Dickinson U. In recent yrs. he has worked as a commercial arr. Favs: Gil Evans, Duck Ellington. Own LPs on RCA and Riv. Fests: Middle East, Eur., S. Amer. CDs: BB; w. Gillespie (Verve; CAP).

LEVY, HANK (HENRY J.), comp, bari sax; b. Baltimore, MD, 9/27/27; d. Parkville, MD, 9/18/01. Studied at Balt. City Coll.; Navy Sch. of Mus.; Coll. of Wm. & Mary; Peabody Cons.; Catholic U.; Towson St. Coll. Pl. bari. w. Stan Kenton Orch. 1953. Arr.

for Sal Salvador Orch. '60–2; Don Ellis fr. '66; Kenton fr. '69. Taught at Towson St. Coll. fr. '68; his coll. band won many contests, incl. Notre Dame Coll. JF '70–2, and rec. an album every year fr. '76. Also taught at Kenton clinics. Premiered work *Opus for Overextended Jazz Ensemble* w. Balt. Symph. '71. Conducted own comps. at Manh. Sch. of Mus. concert of Kenton charts in '90s. Characterized by his use of unusual meters, Levy's comps. incl. "Chain Reaction"; "Whiplash"; "Passacaglia and Fugue"; "Indra"; "Ambivalence." Some of Levy's arrs. were publ. by Creative World in the '70s. His writing is represented on LPs by Kenton and Ellis and on CD w. Salvador (Stash).

LEVY, JED ALAN, tnr, sop saxes, fl; b. Bryn Mawr, PA, 8/12/58. Brother is classical clst. Stud. at New Engl. Cons. 1976–80. Pl. w. local r&b bands in N.J., then w. Frank Conroy '78; Jun Miyake '78–80; Jaki Byard since '79; Jack McDuff '83–4; Peter Leitch since '84; Kiyoto Furiwara '84–9; Don Patterson '86–7; Eliot Zigmund–Jack Walrath since '88; Bill Mays since '91; own gps. Freelanced w. Cedar Walton; Curtis Fuller; Miroslav Vitous; Tom Harrell; and others. Levy has taught at McGill U., William Paterson Coll., and Berklee Coll. of Mus. Favs: Rollins, Shorter, Joe Henderson, Lucky Thompson. Fests: Japan '90. CDs: Steep.; Res.; w. J. Byard (SN); P. Leitch (CC).

LEVY, JOHN O., bs; b. New Orleans, LA, 4/11/12. Raised in Chicago. Vln. at 8, pno. at 15; pl. w. Ray Nance in hs. Bs. at 17; worked w. Earl Hines; Tiny Parham; Red Saunders. Joined Stuff Smith trio (w. Jimmy Jones) in 1943, came to NYC w. him in '44. In NYC he pl. w. Ben Webster; Erroll Garner; Don Byas; Charlie Ventura; Phil Moore; rec. w. Lennie Tristano, Billy Taylor, Rex Stewart '47. Joined George Shearing '48 and toured w. his qnt. '49–51, after which he gave up perf. to become a personal mgr. for Shearing and, later, many other artists, incl. Joe Williams, Nancy Wilson. Honored with a concert at JVC-NY '98. CDs: w. Stuff Smith (Prog.); G. Shearing; Erroll Garner; Eddie Condon (Sav.); Billie Holiday (Dec.).

LEVY, LOU (LOUIS A.), pno; b. Chicago, 3/5/28; d. Dana Point, CA, 1/23/01. Studied at Roosevelt Coll. Worked w. Jay Burkhart, Jimmy Dale big bands. Georgie Auld combo in Chi. 1947. Accomp. Sarah Vaughan '47; tour. Scand. w. Chubby Jackson '47–8. Pl. w. Boyd Raeburn; then, most prominently w. Woody Herman '48–9. In early '50s pl. w. Charlie Shavers–Louis Bellson–Terry Gibbs sxt.; Tommy Dorsey; Auld; Flip Phillips. Retired to work in med-

ical publ. business in Minneapolis '51–4; in Nov. '54 he ret. to mus. as house pnst. at Chi.'s Blue Note. Starting in '56 he spent many yrs. accomp. Peggy Lee; tour. w. Ella Fitzgerald '58–61. In the late '60s accomp. Nancy Wilson and freelanced in LA. Fr. '73 he worked w. Supersax; pl. frequently w. Stan Getz fr. '50s. Well known as a vocal accomp., incl. Lena Horne '76–7; Tony Bennett '78–9; Frank Sinatra '86. Taught accomp. class at Dick Grove Sch. of Mus. Pl. often at Knickerbocker, NYC '80s-90s. Infl. by Bud Powell, he played with intensity and clarity at up tempo and harmonic intricacy on ballads, always remaining melodious. One of *Three Getz Pianos* at JVC-NY '96. CDs: Em.; Verve; Bud Shank Qnt.–Lou Levy Trio (Noct.); w. Virgil Gonsalves (Noct.); Fitzgerald; L. Hampton; G. Mulligan; A. O'Day (Verve); Stan Getz (Verve; Conc.); Chubby Jackson (EPM); Shorty Rogers (Mos.); Warne Marsh (CC); Art Farmer; Frank Morgan; Terry Gibbs (Cont.); Al Cohn (Conc.); Bob Cooper (Cont.; FS); Herb Geller (FS); Johnny Hodges; Bill Perkins (Story); Warne Marsh (CC); C. Hawkins (Pab.); Shorty Rogers (Mos.).

LEWIS, ED (BIG ED), tpt; b. Eagle City, OK, 6/22/09; d. Blooming Grove, NY, 9/18/85. Studied bari. horn w. fath.; prof. debut on tpt. with Jerry Westbrook in KC 1924. Pl. w. Benny Moten '26–31; Thamon Hayes '32–34; Harlan Leonard '34–6; Count Basie '37–47. Retired fr. mus. and worked as taxi driver, occ. pl. club dates; ret. in '80s, touring Eur. w. gp. known as the Countsmen. Best known comp., "It's Sand, Man," was rec. by Basie and later sung by L,H&R; highly regarded as lead tpt., he rarely pl. solos. CDs: w. Moten (BB); Basie (BB; Dec.; Col.).

LEWIS, GEORGE (George Joseph François Louis Zenon), cl; b. New Orleans, LA, 7/13/1900; d. New Orleans, 12/31/68. Started on pennywhistle, never learned to read mus.; sw. to cl. at 16. Pl. w. Black Eagle Band and Buddy Petit; then own band feat. Henry "Red" Allen 1923–4; Olympia Brass Band '28; also worked in Evan Thomas band w. Bunk Johnson ca. '32. Working by day as a stevedore, Lewis pl. odd jobs around NO and was largely unknown outside of the city until '42, when a small gp. of trad. jazz rec. collectors reunited him w. Bunk Johnson. By the mid '40s, Lewis had become a major figure in the NO jazz revival, visiting NYC w. Johnson in '45. The following yr., he went on his own, touring as far as Eur. and Japan in the late '50s and app. at the NJF in '57. In his book, *Shining Trumpets*, Rudi Blesh described Lewis as "Perhaps the finest jazz clarinetist since Johnny Dodds." CDs: BN; DCC Jazz; Story.; Mos.; Amer. Mus.; Biog.; George Lewis–Don Ewell (Del.) w. B. Johnson (GTJ; Amer. Mus.).

LEWIS, GEORGE E., tbn, comp; b. Chicago, IL, 7/14/52. Began on tbn. at age 9. Stud. w. Frank Tirro, Dean Hay at U. of Chi. Laboratory Sch. By age 12 he was transcribing Lester Young solos. Join. AACM 1971. Stud. theory w. Muhal Richard Abrams and perf. w. AACM members, incl. Abrams, Roscoe Mitchell, Douglas Ewart, Anthony Braxton '71–7. Stud. philosophy at Yale U. '72–4, B.A. '74; organized and led gps., Advent and Experimental Ens., while at Yale. Also stud. w. Anthony Davis, Fred Anderson. Pl. for two mos. w. Count Basie Orch. '76. Worked extensively w. Ewart, Braxton '76–80. Dir. of The Kitchen cultural ctr. in NYC '80–2. Became interested in computer mus. in the late '70s and perf. freq. as tbn. soloist accomp. by electronics and in a duo w. Richard Teitelbaum fr. '79. Rec. w. Gerry Hemingway '78; Leroy Jenkins, Karl Berger '79; Anthony Davis '79–81; David Murray '80; Gil Evans Orch. '81–2; Joachim Kühn '83; Steve Lacy fr. '84. Eur. tours w. Lacy, Misha Mengelberg perf. mus. of Thelonious Monk and Herbie Nichols '85; mus. of Cecil Taylor Orch. '87; John Zorn–Bill Frisell '89. Lewis has said that he does not consider himself a jazz musician and has called his instrument "a fifteenth-century anachronism that will probably not survive the next century in its present form." He taught computer mus. courses at the Royal Cons., the Hague '86; Simon Fraser U., Burnaby, B.C., Canada fr. '89; Banff Ctr. for the Arts, Banff, Alberta; U. Cal.-San Diego. Taught audiokinetic sculpture design and sonic art at the Art Inst. of Chi. '89–91. Major comps. incl. *Rainbow Family* '84; *The Empty Chair* '86; *Voyager* '87; *Changing with the Times* '91; *Nightmare at the Best Western* '92. Favs: Coltrane, Parker, Braxton, Mitchell, Ewart, Abrams, Zorn, Lacy. Polls: *DB* TDWR '77–8, '80. Fests: New Mus. fests in Eur., Asia. TV: French docu., *Rainbow Family* '84; British docu., *Improvisation* '91. CDs: BS; w. Zorn–Frisell; Braxton; Teitelbaum (hatArt); Lacy (hatArt; BS); James Newton (Audq.); Gil Evans (Evid.); Mengelberg (SN); Abrams; David Murray (BS); Mitchell (Chief); Vienna Art Orch. (Moers).

LEWIS, JIMMY (JAMES), bs, cello, uke, bjo, gtr, el-bs; b. Rutherford County, TN, 4/11/18. Mother pl. fife and dms.; grandmoth. pl. org.; aunt taught mus. at Fisk U.; Tenn. St. U. Began on uke., self-taught. Sang and pl. tnr. gtr. in Nashville 1939–44; owned tailor shop in Nashville '42–7. Pl. w. Tenn. St. U. band; Bill Readus, who sw. him to bs. '42–4; Leo Hines '45–7; Jimmy Hinsley '48–9; Count Basie '50–3; Cootie Williams '54–5; Duke Ellington '55–6; King Curtis '57–62; extensive freelancing. Pl. el-bs. for B'way musical *Hair* '65–71. Accomp. Alberta Hunter '77–82; own trio fr. '83. Favs: Blanton, Ray Brown,

Pettiford. Polls: *DB* TDWR '50–1. Fests: Eur. '58. TV: apps. on Germ. TV; PBS; NBC *Today*, w. Alberta Hunter; conversation video w. Basie. CDs: w. Basie (Col.); Lou Donaldson; Grant Green; Reuben Wilson (BN); King Curtis (R&T).

LEWIS, JOHN AARON, pno, comp, arr, lead; b. La Grange, IL, 5/3/20; d. NYC, 3/29/01. Raised in Albuquerque, N. Mex. Moth. stud. classical voice. Stud. pno. fr. 1927; anthropology and mus. at U. of New Mexico until '42. Met Kenny Clarke while in army '42–5. Joined Dizzy Gillespie bb in NYC '46; also stud. at Manh. Sch. of Mus. (M. Mus. '53). Premiered first major comp., *Toccata for Trumpet*, w. Gillespie at Carnegie Hall Sept. '47; other early arrs. for Gillespie incl. "Two Bass Hit"; "Emanon." Tour. Eur. w. Gillespie, then pl. for two mos. w. Tony Proteau in Paris '47. Ret. to US, pl. w. Illinois Jacquet '48–9; also freelanced w. Lester Young; Charlie Parker; Ella Fitzgerald. Pno. and arr. w. Miles Davis Nonet '49; arrs. incl. "Move"; "Budo"; "Rouge." Pl. w. Milt Jackson Qt. '51–2; by the end of '52, gp. had been renamed the Modern Jazz Qt. Lewis was mus. dir. of the MJQ fr. '52 until it disbanded temporarily in '74. His piece *Django* has been rec. by many musicians. Dur. his time w. the MJQ he also took jobs as a comp.-arr., incl. film scores for *Odds Against Tomorrow*; *No Sun in Venice*; *Storia Milanese*; *Kemek*. Head of faculty at Lenox Sch. of Jazz, Lenox, Mass. late '50s; mus. dir. of MJF '58–82. Tour. Eur. w. MJQ yearly fr. '60. Comp. ballet, *Original Sin*, premiered by SF Ballet '61. Org. and led Orch. USA, which perf. and rec. his comps. '62–5. Also arr. dates combining the MJQ w. string qt., large orch., etc. Appointed to bd. of trustees of Manh. Sch. of Mus. '66. Taught at Harvard '75; City Coll. NY '75–82; Appointed mus. dir. of AJO in late '80s; also served on NEA panel for Jazz, Folk & Ethnic Music. App. as solo pnst. at NJF-NY '75. Other comp. credits incl. scores for the TV series *Night Gallery* and for docu. films *Hope Through Water*; *Cities and People*; *Exposure*. When the MJQ re-formed in '82, resumed his role as mus. dir. until '95 when gp. again disbanded. Lewis was an elegant soloist with a great command of thematic invention, subtle sense of swing, and a deep feeling for the blues that, not being obvious, is sometimes overlooked. As a composer he was able to fuse classical devices with jazz in what has been called "Third Stream" and in shorter pieces use fugal material with élan, i.e., "Vendome" and "Concorde." He held honorary doctorates fr. U. of N. Mex., Berklee Coll. of Mus., Manh. Sch. of Mus., and New Engl. Cons. In '89 he was named an Officier Des Arts et Lettres by the French government. Favs: Tatum, Hank Jones, Ivan Pogorolich. Polls: *Met.* '60 as arr. Fests: all major w. MJQ. TV: many apps. w. MJQ. CDs: BN; Atl.; Em.; Red Brn.; DRG; w. MJQ (Prest.; Pab.; Atl.; LRC; BN); Douglas (Mob. Fid.); AJO (Atl., MM); Miles Davis (Cap.; Sav.; Prest.); C. Parker (Sav.; Verve); Gillespie (BB; Sav.; Verve; Vogue); Parker-Gillespie (Roost); Sonny Rollins; King Pleasure; Z. Sims; S. Stitt (Prest.); Illinois Jacquet (BB; Mos.); L. Young (Verve); M. Jackson; Cliff. Brown (BN); Mingus (Deb.); J. J. Johnson (Sav.; BN; Prest.); Helen Merrill (Verve); Fitzgerald (Dec.); Joe Newman (BL); G. Mulligan (GRP).

LEWIS, MARK, alto sax, comp; b. Tacoma, WA, 1/26/58. Blind fr. birth, he gained partial vision after a series of operations at age 2. First pl. alto sax at age 10, form. first gp. four yrs. later and pl. for local events. Moving to Seattle he became prominent on jazz scene but settled in Amsterdam, Netherlands, in 1978, making several ret. trips to US. Rec. debut as leader '87; also teamed w. pnst. Ted Gioia for duo album, *Tango Cool*. CDs: Quartet; w. Woody Herman (Conc.); Smith Dobson (Quartet).

LEWIS, MEADE LUX, pno, comp; b. Chicago, IL, 9/4/05; d. Minneapolis, MN, 6/7/64. Started on vln. Moved w. family to Chi. and sw. to pno., inspired by Jimmy Yancey. A master boogie-woogie pnst., Lewis rec. his own "Honky Tonk Train Blues" for Para. in 1927; released '29. In '35 Lewis was working as a cab driver and in a car wash while pl. gigs at night, when John Hammond, intrigued by "Honky Tonk Train," rec. a new version for the British Parlophone label. Another version was rec. for Vict. '37. Lewis was one of the key figures in the boogie-woogie craze of the late '30s-early '40s, along with Albert Ammons and Pete Johnson. The three started it all when they opened the historic '38 Carnegie Hall concert, *From Spirituals to Swing*, and cont. at Café Society '39, rec. for Col. as a three-piano team. Rec. for BN, initiating that label. Settled in LA in '41 but cont. tour., occ. doubling on celeste and harpsichord. He died in an automobile accident. "Honky Tonk Train Blues" and "Yancey Special" are considered classics of the boogie-woogie genre. CDs: Riv.; Verve; tracks in *Barrelhouse Boogie* (BB); w. Boogie-Woogie Trio (Story.); Edmond Hall (BN).

LEWIS, MEL (Melvin Sokoloff), dms, lead; b. Buffalo, NY, 5/10/29; d. NYC, 2/2/90. Father was a dmr. Worked w. Boyd Raeburn 1948; Alvino Rey '48–53; Ray Anthony '49–50, '53–4; Tex Beneke '50–3. Co-led a gp. with Bill Holman, and rec. '59–62 w. Terry Gibbs bb. Dates in LA w. Gerald Wilson; NYC w. Gerry Mulligan's Concert Jazz Band; Eur. w. Dizzy Gillespie '61; tour. USSR with Benny Goodman '62.

House dmr. MJF '59–62; Eur. concerts w. Friedrich Gulda fr. '64. Settled in NYC, form. Thad Jones–Mel Lewis Jazz Orch. '65. Band pl. regularly at the Village Vanguard and tour. US and overseas, incl. USSR. On Jones's departure in '79, Lewis became sole leader, w. Bob Brookmeyer principal arr. One of the most gifted bb dmrs. in a musical style often recalling the late Tiny Kahn. CDs: A&M; MM; Tel.; Red Brn.; w. Kenton (Cap.); Jimmy Rushing; Shorty Rogers; Joe Williams; Paul Desmond–Gerry Mulligan (BB); Mulligan (Verve; RTE); B. Goodman; Jay McShann (MM); E. Fitzgerald; Ben Webster; Jimmy Smith (Verve); AJO (Atl.; MM); Stephane Grappelli (BL); John Colianni; Howard Alden; Jon Faddis (Conc.); J. Lovano (SN); Warne Marsh; J. Knepper (CC); Art Pepper (PJ); Gillespie; Joe Henderson (BN); Gibbs; Bob Cooper (Cont.); Chet Baker (Gal.); Brookmeyer; Eddie Daniels (Prest.); Pepper Adams (Fant.).

LEWIS, RAMSEY EMMANUEL JR., pno; b. Chicago, IL, 5/27/35. Began pno. lessons at age 6. Stud. at Chi. Mus. Coll. 1947–54; U. of Ill. '53–4; and De Paul U. '54–5. Formed trio in 1956; has rec. profusely w. trio and orch. since '58, also w. Sonny Stitt; Clark Terry; Max Roach; others. In summer of '65 his trio scored a national hit with an album and hit single, "The 'In' Crowd," winning first of several Grammy awards. Rec. w. London Philharm. Orch. '88. Since '90 he has hosted *Sound and Style*, a weekly jazz TV show on BET cable network. Over the yrs., Lewis's mus. became increasingly commercial, but he maintained a limited jazz following. Fests: Randall's Island Jazz Fest., NYC '59; Saugatuck Jazz Fest., Mich. '60; NJF '61, '63. CDs: Col.; Chess; GRP; w. GRP All-Star Band (GRP); Bill Henderson (Vee-Jay).

LEWIS, ZABBY (WILLIAM SEBASTIAN), pno, lead, arr; b. Middleburg, NC, 11/1/14; d. Marston Mills, MA, or Boston, 7/9/94. Raised in Phila. Began pl. jazz after moving to Bost. 1932. Pl. w. Tasker Crosson's Ten Statesmen '34, then form. own 7–pc. band '36. Led bbs and small gps. mainly in Bost. but also in NYC '36–late '70s. Sidemen incl. Paul Gonsalves; Sonny Stitt; Cat Anderson; Alan Dawson; Roy Haynes; Al Morgan; Irving "Mouse" Randolph; Idrees Sulieman, and Freddie Webster.

LEWIS, TED (Theodore Leopold Friedman), lead, voc, cl, sax; b. Circleville, OH, 6/6/1892; d. NYC, 8/25/71. Active as bandleader, comedian, singer, and vaudevillian fr. 1910. Rec. frequently as leader in '20s and '30s, but despite such first-rate sidemen as Fats Waller; Benny Goodman; George Brunis;

Muggsy Spanier; Jimmy Dorsey; and Frank Teschemacher, Lewis's style was considered the epitome of "corn" by jazz musicians in many of his orchs. Best known for his early hits, "Me and My Shadow" and "When My Baby Smiles at Me." CDs: JSP.

LEWIS, VIC, lead, tbn, crnt, gtr; b. London, England, 7/29/19. Began on bjo., then sw. to gtr.; stud. w. grandfather fr. age 3. As a teenager, he led own gp. w. Carlo Krahmer, George Shearing; the gp. perf. on the BBC and Radio Luxembourg. Jammed in London clubs w. Django Reinhardt; Stephane Grappelli; Shearing; George Chisholm. Sat in w. Bobby Hackett; Tommy Dorsey, Jack Teagarden; and Louis Armstrong, and organized rec. sess. w. Hackett; Eddie Condon; Zutty Singleton while visiting NYC in 1938. While in Royal Air Force, pl. gtr. w. Buddy Featherstonhaugh '41–4. Worked w. Stephane Grappelli in London '44–5; Ted Heath '45. Led dixie. band w. Jack Parnell '44–6; band was freq. feat. on BBC. Form. own bb in '46; by '48 it was modeled after the Stan Kenton Orch. Sidemen incl. Ronnie Chamberlain; Bob Efford; Gordon Langhorn. Tour. US '56–7, '58–9. Led orch. backing Louis Armstrong and Johnny Ray in UK '50s. Sat in on tbn. w. Armstrong and Kenton on UK tours. Rec. bossa nova album w. Tubby Hayes, Ronnie Scott, and various Kenton alumni '63. Active as booking agent and mgr. fr. '59, booking tours for Count Basie; Carmen McRae; Nina Simone; Judy Garland; Dudley Moore; others. Also booked rock acts incl. The Beatles and Elton John. In the '80s formed a new bb for jazz dates and recs., some feat. visiting Amer. mus., incl. Shorty Rogers and Bud Shank. His autobiography, *Music and Maiden Overs: My Show Business Life*, was co-written w. Tony Barrow. CDs: Baldwin; Cand.

LEWIS, VICTOR VANN, dms, comp; b. Omaha, NE, 5/20/50. Parents, Richard and Camille, were classically trained mus. who pl. w. territory bands in 1940s. Father took him to hear Duke Ellington, Count Basie, Woody Herman. Began on cello at age 10, then sw. to dms. a yr. later; also stud. classical pno. Pl. prof. gigs fr. age 15, incl. jingles, circus, *Bob Hope Show*; also led own jazz gp. First important jazz gig accomp. Hank Crawford in Omaha. Stud. at U. of Neb. but left sch. to join a cabaret show in Minneapolis '73. Moved to NYC '74. Met Woody Shaw at first NYC gig w. Buster Williams' gp. Pl. w. Shaw mid '70s-80s; Dexter Gordon '77; Stan Getz '80–91. Freelanced w. Joe Farrell, Earl Klugh, Hubert Laws, David Sanborn '70s; Carla Bley, Art Farmer, J. J. Johnson, Mike Stern, John Stubblefield '80s. Perf. w. Bobby Hutcherson at Lincoln Ctr. Dexter Gordon

tribute '91; also tour. Russia w. Mingus Epitaph. Lewis pl. w. Kenny Barron Qnt.; co-led Horizon w. Bobby Watson; and leads own qnt. He conts. to be active as a freelancer, rec. in the '90s w. Gary Bartz; Eddie Henderson; Geoff Keezer; Janis Siegel; Larry Willis. Lewis's comps. have been rec. by Sanborn, Shaw, Watson, others. He teaches at the New Sch. Favs: Billy Hart, Eric Gravatt, Blakey. Polls: *DB*. Fests: all major fr. '70s. CDs: Enja; AudQ.; Red; w. K. Barron (Enja; Em.; Verve); Horizon (BN; Col.); W. Shaw (Col.; Mos.); D. Gordon (Col.); J. J. Johnson (Ant.); Willie Williams; Franco Ambrosetti; Stubblefield (Enja); Stephen Scott (Verve); G. Cables; Larry Willis (Steep.); Farmer (Cont.); Getz (Em.; Conc.; Sonet); J. Gourley (Up.); Benny Green (BN); John Hicks (DIW); Hutcherson (Land.) Mingus Dynasty (Col.); Watson (BN; Col.); G. Russell (SN); Brian Lynch (CC); L. Tabackin (Conc.).

LEWIS, WILLIE (WILLIAM T.), alto, bari saxes, cl; b. Cleburne, TX, 6/10/05; d. NYC, 1/13/71. Raised in Dallas; stud. at New Engl. Cons. Pl. briefly w. Will Marion Cook and The Musical Spillers bef. joining Sam Wooding orch. in NYC. To Berlin, Germ., in 1925 w. Wooding and *Chocolate Kiddies Revue*; toured int'l w. Sam Wooding until '31. Led own bands in Brussels and NYC '32–4. Fr. '34 to '39 he led one of the most popular bands in Eur., pl. Paris club engagements with such sidemen as Herman Chittison, Benny Carter, and Bill Coleman. In '40, when the Nazis invaded the Netherlands, Lewis and his band escaped to Switz., then pl. in Portugal before ret. to the US in '41. Settling in NYC, he worked mainly as waiter and bartender after the war, pl. only occ., incl. an app. in a '51 B'way show, *Angel in the Pawnshop*. LP: French Swing. CD: w. Bill Coleman (Topaz).

LIEBMAN, DAVE (DAVID), tnr and sop saxes; b. Brooklyn, NY, 9/4/46. Studied priv. w. Joe Allard; Ch. Lloyd; Lennie Tristano. Degree in Amer. History, NYU 1968; formed musicians' collective, Free Life Communication, w. Bob Moses in '69. Pl. w. Ten Wheel Drive '70; worked and rec. five albums w. Elvin Jones '71–3; rec. LP *My Goals Beyond* w. John McLaughlin. Pl. w. Miles Davis '73–4; while still w. Davis, rec. two albums w. Open Sky, a trio, and organized the gp. Lookout Farm. Tour. w. Chick Corea '77; fr. '78 to '80 he led his own qnt., feat. John Scofield. Since the mid-'70s has written numerous articles and rec. reviews for such publications as *DB*, *Coda*, and *Musician*; his books incl. *Lookout Farm: Improvisation for Small Jazz Groups* and *A Self Portrait of a Jazz Artist: Thoughts and Realities*, and he co-authored *Chromaticism in Jazz Improvisation*. In the '80s he was assoc. w. pnst. Richie Beirach, doing clinics and concerts; since '90 he has cont. to teach, perf., and rec. An eclectic offspring of John Coltrane and the avant-garde energies of the '60s, Liebman has widened his range considerably in the last decades, both as perf land educ. "Teaching," he says, "is like a pay-back for the privilege of living the life of an artist which, although a precarious one, has immense personal rewards." CDs: SN; CMP; Timel.; Story.; Red; Cand.; Heads Up; Evid., Owl; w. Miles Davis (Col.); Afro Blue Band (Mile.); Motohiko Hino (Gram.); Vince Mendoza (Act); Riccardo Del Fra (IDA); P. Fresu (Spl.); Lars Danielsson (Drag.; L+R); S. Swallow (ECM); Tom Harrell (Cont.); John McNeil; Niels Pedersen (Steep.); B. Moses (Gram; Open Minds); Pete "LaRoca" Sims (BN).

LIGHTHOUSE ALL-STARS. In 1990, a gp. billed as Shorty Rogers, Bud Shank, and the Lighthouse All-Stars began app. at US and Eur., feat. several of the mus. who had pl. at the Lighthouse in Hermosa Beach, Calif., dur. the '50s. CDs: Cand.; Cont. *See also* **RUMSEY, HOWARD.**

LIGHTSEY, KIRK (KIRKLAND), pno, fl, bassoon; b. Detroit, MI, 2/15/37. Studied pno. w. Johnson Flanagan, Tommy Flanagan's bro., fr. age 6; later stud. w. Gladys Wade Dillard. Introduced to jazz by Hugh Lawson, Paul Chambers at Cass Tech. HS.; pl. cl. in sch. orch. w. Ron Carter, Kiane Zawadi. Turned down cl. scholarship to Wayne St. U. to pl. w. Harold "Beans" Bowles 1954. In the mid '50s he tour. w. Arthur Bragg's Rhythm & Blues Show, w. Della Reese; T-Bone Walker; also pl. w. Yusef Lateef, Melba Liston; Ernestine Anderson. Pl. cl. and fl. in army band at Ft. Knox '60–2. Ret. to Det. after discharge, forming a duo w. Cecil McBee. Pl. for Motown rec. sess. and stud. w. Boris Maximovich early-mid '60s. Rec. w. Sonny Stitt '65; five albums w. Chet Baker '66. In the late '60s he worked w. Damita Jo and dir. theater gp., In Stage '65. Moved to Calif. '69; accomp. O.C. Smith '69–74; Lovelace Watkins '74–9, incl. int'l tours. Also pl. in Calif. w. Pharoah Sanders; Bobby Hutcherson; Esther Phillips; Harold Land. Came to prominence as sideman w. Dexter Gordon '79–83. Freelanced w. Jimmy Raney; Clifford Jordan; Don Cherry; Woody Shaw; Sonny Fortune; others '80s. Pl. w. Leaders, w. Lester Bowie, Arthur Blythe, Chico Freeman fr. late '80s; then led a qt. w. Santi Debriano, Eddie Gladden, Jerry Gonzales. He has taught at Howard U. and the New Sch. Living in Paris fr. the mid '90s. A world-class pianist who is often overlooked because he is not on the American scene but a musician of vast technique, repertoire, resourcefulness, and emotion. Favs: Art Tatum, Vladimir Horowitz, Thelonious Monk. Fests: all major fr. '70s incl. Cork '94; own trio, incl. Debriano, Ambassadeur Hotel, Juan-Le-Pins jf '94–7. Film: *Such Good Friends*, w. Abbey Lincoln. TV: Gene Kelly special w. Damita Jo. CDs: CC; Timel.; Sunny.; w. Leaders (BS); Clifford Jordan; Brian Lynch; J. Raney (CC); Peter Leitch (Res.); Satchmo Legacy Band (SN); Steve Nelson (Sunny.); James Moody (Novus); Chet Baker (Prest.; Timel.; Phil.); Woody Shaw (Muse); H. Land (Conc.).

LINCOLN, ABBEY (Anna Marie Woolridge aka Aminata Moseka), voc, songwriter, actress; b. Chicago, IL, 8/6/30. Raised in Calvin Ctr., Mich. Sang and acted while in hs., then tour. Mich. as dance band vocalist. Moved to Calif. 1951, working in local clubs. Sang under name Gaby Lee in Hawaii '52–3. Perf. in Hollywood clubs '54–6. Rec. debut album for Liberty label in '56, changing her name to Abbey Lincoln at the suggestion of promotion people; also rec. w. Benny Carter. App. in film *The Girl Can't Help it* '57, and tour. in leading role in road co. of stage show *Jamaica*. Rec. *We Insist! Freedom Now Suite* w. Max Roach, Oscar Brown Jr. '60. Married Roach, with whom she freq. collaborated '62–70. Lincoln began comp. her own songs in the late '50s. By the '60s, she was incorporating cultural and political themes into her lyrics, with an emphasis on themes of racial identity and equality. Starred in films *Nothing But a Man* '64; *For Love of Ivy* '68. Moved to LA after divorcing Roach '70. App. as actress on *Mission Impossible; Name of the Game; NBC Movie of the Week*, etc. '70s. Active in community affairs; taught drama at Cal. State U.-Northridge '74. In '75 she visited Africa, where the names Aminata and Moseka were conferred on her by leaders in Guinea and Zaire respectively. As Abbey Lincoln, she revived her career in the '90s w. a series of Verve CDs. CDs: Verve; Riv.; Enja; Liberty; w. Roach (Cand.; Imp.).

LINCOLN, ABE (ABRAHAM), tbn; b. Lancaster, PA, 3/29/07. Started on tbn. at age 5. Worked in NYC w. Adrian Rollini; replaced Tommy Dorsey in California Ramblers 1926; also pl. w. Roger Wolfe Kahn, Paul Whiteman, and Ozzie Nelson in '30s. Active in Hollywood studios, he participated in the Dixieland revival of the early '40s. Pl. w. Pete Fountain, Red Nichols, Matty Matlock, Wild Bill Davison, and the Village Stompers in '50s and '60s. App. at Sacramento Dixieland Jubilee '76. Inactive in mus. in recent yrs. CDs: w. Jack Teagarden (Mos.); California Ramblers (Biog.).

LINDSAY, JOHN, bs, tbn; b. Algiers, LA, 8/23/1894; d. Chicago, IL, 7/3/50. Doubled on tbn.

and bs., first with John Robichaux in early 1920s, then w. A. J. Piron until '24. Tour. w. King Oliver, then join. Dewey Jackson in late '25. To Chi. '25, where he began concentrating on bs. Rec. w. Jelly Roll Morton in '26; tour. w. Louis Armstrong '31–2. Worked w. Lil Armstrong; Jimmie Noone; Richard M. Jones; the Harlem Hamfats; and others in Chi. '30s. Rec. w. Johnny Dodds '40; Richard Miller '44. Worked w. own qt. in Chi in late '50s. A powerful bs. in the trad. style of Pops Foster. CDs: w. Morton; Bechet (BB); Armstrong (BB; Col.).

LINN, RAY (RAYMOND SAYRE), tpt; b. Chicago, IL, 10/20/20; d. Columbus, OH, 11/96. Father pl. tpt. Pl. w. local society band bef. join. Tommy Dorsey at 18. Pl. w. Woody Herman 1941–2; Artie Shaw '44; then ret. to Herman intermittently until late '50s. Also w. Boyd Raeburn '46. In '50s he pl. w. Bob Crosby; Shorty Rogers; Maynard Ferguson; Buddy DeFranco; and Les Brown. Form. own band, Chicago Stompers '74. Active w. studio work, rec. w. Frank Sinatra; Ella Fitzgerald; Sarah Vaughan. Comp. "The Way It Was in LA," rec. by Mark Murphy, and "Where's Prez," rec. by Les Brown. Received NEA award '81. Lived in Vienna, Va., in '80s. An early West Coast Gillespie disciple, he gravitated toward mainstream and dixie expressions later on. CDs: w. T. Dorsey; Shaw; Rogers (BB); J. Dorsey (Hep; Dec.); Herman (Dec.; Col.); Anita O'Day (Verve; Sig.); Raeburn (Sav.; Hep); Barney Kessel (Cont.).

LISTON, MELBA DORETTA, comp, tbn; b. Kansas City, MO, 1/13/26; d. Los Angeles, CA, 4/23/99. Raised in LA fr. 1937; stud. tbn. and pl. in pit band '42; worked w. Gerald Wilson fr. '43–7, dur. which time she began to arr. Pl. on small gp. rec. date w. Dexter Gordon '47; tour. w. Count Basie '48–9; Billie Holiday '49. After temporarily retiring fr. mus., she joined Dizzy Gillespie in '50. Occ. worked as film extra in mid '50s; rejoined Gillespie for several int'l tours, Middle East '56 and So. America '57. With Quincy Jones '59 as part of the musical show, *Free and Easy.* Dur. the '60s she worked freq. for Randy Weston as comp. and arr.; co-led a bb w. Clark Terry; wrote for Ellington; Tony Bennett; Eddie Fisher; the Buffalo Symph. Orch. In the '70s she divided her time between working. w. youth orchs. in Watts, Calif., and writing for Basie; Ellington; Abbey Lincoln; and, as a staff arr. at Motown, for Marvin Gaye; Diana Ross; and Billy Eckstine. Moving to Jamaica, she taught at the U. of the West Indies and worked as the dir. of Pop. Mus. Stud. at Jamaica Inst. of Mus. in Kingston. Ret. to NYC, she led an all-female gp. for a while but had difficulty maintaining it. In '85 a severe stroke left her paralyzed, ending her

playing career. In the '90s, living in LA, she was able to resume comp. on a limited basis w. the aid of a computer. Liston was an accomplished artist who, at a very difficult time, transcended the problems of being a woman comp.-mus. in a male-oriented jazz society. Early favs: T. Dorsey; Lawrence Brown. Fests: Women's JF, KC '79. Award: NEA Jazz Masters Fellowship '97. LP: *Melba Liston and Her Bones* (MGM) '58 and wrote for Johnny Griffin, Milt Jackson sessions. CDs: w. Dinah Washington (Em); Art Blakey (BB); J. Coltrane (Beth.); R. Weston (Verve; Ant.; Roul.); Betty Carter (Imp.; Verve); Dexter Gordon (Stash); D. Gillespie (Verve; CAP); Q. Jones (Merc.; Qwest; Imp.); C. Adderley; Sam Jones (Riv.); Lockjaw Davis; O. Nelson (Prest.).

LITTLE, BOOKER JR., tpt, comp; b. Memphis, TN, 4/2/38; d. NYC, 10/5/61. Raised in a musical family; sist. sang with London Opera Co.; fath. pl tbn., moth. a pnst. and singer. Jammed w. Phineas Newborn while still a teenager att. Manassas HS; later pl. w. Johnny Griffin and Walter Perkins' gp., MJT + 3, while a student at the Chi. Cons. Was introduced to Max Roach by Sonny Rollins; joined Roach's gp. June 1958, app. w. him at '58 NJF. Freelanced in NYC w. Mal Waldron '59; John Coltrane and Roach '60. Most important job was w. qnt. co-led w. Eric Dolphy at Five Spot, NYC in summer of '61, which also incl. Waldron, Richard Davis, and Ed Blackwell. By the time of his death, he had bec. one of the most promising tpt. innovators of the '60s. Recs. of the Five Spot dates suggest that his style was moving away fr. the infl. of Miles Davis and Clifford Brown into a more complex, dissonance-oriented style, somewhat related to the free jazz improv. of the early '60s. CDs: BN; Time; Cand.; Beth.; w. Dolphy (NJ; Prest.); Roach (Riv.; Imp.); Coltrane (Imp.).

LITTLE, (WESTON) WILBUR, bs; b. Parmele, NC, 3/5/28; d. Amsterdam, Netherlands, 5/4/87. Played pno w. air corps on Guam 1946, then sw. to bs. Worked w. local gps. in Wash., D.C. late '40s; tour. w. Griffin Bros. and Margie Day '49–51; led own trio, backing such visiting mus. as Miles Davis; Kenny Dorham; and John Coltrane. Intermittently worked day job for US Dept. of Interior while gigging w. Sir Charles Thompson, Leo Parker. Pl. w. J. J. Johnson '55–8. Freelanced w. Sonny Stitt; Shirley Horn; Nina Simone; Roland Kirk; off and on in NYC w. Elvin Jones '67–70. Moved to Amsterdam '77, tour. Eur. extensively w. Charles Tolliver; Archie Shepp; Barry Harris; et al. Inspired by Ray Brown, Little was a resourceful soloist and accomp. capable of pulling his weight in any setting. Infl: Ray Brown. CDs: w. Tommy Flanagan (DIW); Bobby Jaspar (Riv.); J. J.

Johnson (Col.); Elvin Jones (BN; Enja); Duke Jordan; Horace Parlan (Steep.); L. Konitz (Sonet); C. Terry (Vang.); A. Shepp (WW).

LIVINGSTON, FUD (JOSEPH ANTHONY), sax, cl, comp; b. Charleston, SC, 4/10/06; d. NYC, 3/25/57. Played acdn. and pno. bef. sw. to sax. Arr. and saxist w. Ben Pollack band and the California Ramblers in 1920s; also tour. w. Jean Goldkette; Nat Shilkret. In Engl. w. Fred Elizalde at Savoy Hotel '29. Many rec. dates w. Red Nichols; Miff Mole; Joe Venuti; Eddie Lang; et al. Briefly w. Paul Whiteman in '30, after which he concentrated on arr. for Pinky Tomlin, Bob Zurke, and others. Again active w. Jimmy Dorsey '35–7. Worked in Hollywood, Calif., dur. '40s, then to NYC, where he sometimes pl. pno. in bars until his death. Considered a star perf. in the white avant-garde movement of his day, w. a style similar to that of Pee Wee Russell. CDs: w. Louis Armstrong; J. Dorsey (Dec.); Bix Beiderbecke (Col.); Nichols in *The Jazz Age* (BB).

LIVINGSTON, ULYSSES, gtr; b. Bristol, TN, 1/29/12; d. Torrance, CA, 10/7/88. Worked in variety shows and carnivals. Pl. w. Lil Armstrong in Buffalo 1936; then in NYC w. Stuff Smith; Frankie Newton; and Sammy Price. Join. Benny Carter '38–9; Ella Fitzgerald '40–2. After army service, he lived in LA; launched the Four Blazers '46; rec. w. Spirits of Rhythm; JATP; Illinois Jacquet; Wilbert Baranco; and led own gp. To Hawaii w. Cee Pee Johnson '47. Sw. to el. bs. for studio work, then withdrew fr. mus. and bec. an electronic engineer, occasionally ret. for rec. sess. Rec. w. Jac McVea '62. CDs: w. Pete Johnson (Milan); Benny Carter (B&B); Billie Holiday (Col.); Newton (Aff.); Jacquet (Mos.); JATP (Verve).

LLOYD, CHARLES, tnr sax; b. Memphis, TN, 3/15/38. Studied w. Phineas Newborn; pl. locally w. Booker Little; Hank Crawford; B. B. King; Bobby Blue Bland. Moved to LA in the mid 1950s; while majoring in comp. at USC, he met and occas. jammed w. Harold Land; Eric Dolphy; Buddy Collette; and Ornette Coleman; pl. w. Gerald Wilson's bb. Pl. w. and was principal arr. for Chico Hamilton's gp. '61–4. Worked w. Cannonball Adderley '64; organized gp. w. Gabor Szabo, Herbie Hancock '65; Keith Jarrett and Cecil McBee '66–9; highly successful app. at MJF '66. First jazz mus. invited by Russian People's Gp. to tour Soviet Union '67; also app. at fests. in Poland and Czechoslovakia. First jazz mus. to pl. Fillmore West '67; tour. Far East for US St. Dept. '68. Pl. over 100 coll. concerts in early '70s; fr. '70 to '74 he did doctoral work at Cal Tech., where he was artist-in-residence '72–3. Poetry and mus. read-

ings in mid '70s w. Allen Ginsberg, Lawrence Ferlinghetti, et al. In '80s he pl. w. Michel Petrucciani in Calif. and tour. Eur. w. him; occ. app. at jazz fests. in late '80s and early '90s. Related stylistically to Coltrane, Lloyd was one of the few who successfully reshaped many elements of the avant-garde mus. of the '60s into a more commercially palatable form of creative expression. CDs: ECM; Atl.; BN; A&M; w. Cannonball Adderley (Cap.; Night); Chico Hamilton (Imp.); Joe Sample (WB).

LOCKE, EDDIE (EDWARD), dms; b. Detroit, MI, 8/2/30. Studied at Miller HS. First gigs w. local gps. at age 14. Pl., sang, and danced in duo Bop and Lock w. Oliver Jackson in Det. theaters early 1950s. Perf. at Apollo Thea., NYC '54, then remained in NYC. Pl. w. Red Allen; Dick Wellstood; Tony Parenti at Metropole Café fr. mid '50s; Tyree Glenn; Teddy Wilson; Willie "The Lion" Smith; Roy Eldridge '58–89; Coleman Hawkins '60–9. Freelance and rec. w. Ray Bryant, Duke Ellington, Kenny Burrell, Earl Hines '60s; Earle Warren, Lee Konitz, Tiny Grimes '70s. Led trio w. Roland Hanna mid '80s; own gps. since. Taught at the HS. of Perf. Arts and the Day Sch. in NYC. Favs: Jo Jones, Sid Catlett, Sonny Greer. Fests: app. often at JVC-NY '90s. TV: *Tonight Show* w. Hines; *Dial M for Music; Mike Douglas*. CDs: w. Hawkins (Verve; Imp.; JVC); Hines (Col.); Eldridge (Verve; Story.; Pab.); Konitz (LRC); Eddie Bert (FS); Irvin Stokes (Arb.)

LOCKE, JOE (JOSEPH P.), vib, pno, comp; b. Palo Alto, CA, 3/18/59. Began on dms. at age 8; stud. at Hochstein Sch. of Mus., Rochester, N.Y. 1968–71. Sw. to vib. at age 13; stud. w. John Beck, Gordon Stout, Bill Dobbins; Warren Benson at Eastman Sch. of Mus. '72–80. Taught at Hochstein Sch. '77. After grad. fr. hs., Locke tour. and rec. w. Spider Martin, then formed own qnt. which bec. popular in upstate N.Y. As a teenager, he jammed w. Dizzy Gillespie; Pepper Adams; Jimmy Owens; Billy Hart. Moved to NYC '81. Rec. orig. score for docu. film *El Salvador—Another Vietnam* '83. Pl. in duo w. Phil Markowitz '84–5. Tour. w. Mingus Epitaph Orch. '91. In addition to leading his own gp., pl. w. Mingus Dynasty; Mingus BB; Eddie Henderson; Ronnie Cuber; Ronnie Burrage; Alex Foster. Freelanced w. Kenny Barron; Victor Lewis; Michel Petrucciani; George Cables; Rufus Reid; Bob Mintzer; Gary Bartz; Kirk Lightsey; Jerry Gonzalez; Igor Butman. Lectured and cond. clinics at Eastman Sch. of Mus., LIU, Ithaca Coll., SUNY-Purchase, Crane Sch. of Mus. On the faculty of Manh. Sch. of Mus. and the Drummers Collective. Favs: Hutcherson, Milt Jackson, Dave Pike. Fests: Scotland w. own gp. fr. '87;

Eur. w. own gp.; Mingus Epitaph; Ronnie Burrage; Al Foster; Santi Debriano '90–2. CDs: Mile.; Steep.; Chief; Joe Locke–David Hazeltine (Sharp Nine); w. Eddie Henderson (Mile.; Cad.); Freddy Cole (Fant.); Peter Delano (Verve); Jay Collins (Res.); G. Cables (Steep.); R. Cuber (FS); Santi Debriano (Freelance); Butman (Russian Prestige).

LOEB, CHUCK (CHARLES SAMUEL), gtr, comp, arr; b. Suffern, NY, 12/7/55. Began on cello. Stud. w. Dennis Sandole; Jim Hall; Richie Hart; and at Berklee Coll. of Mus. 1974–6. Pl. w. local rock bands, then w. fusion gp. Exit '76; Chico Hamilton '77–8; Ray Barretto '78–9; Hubert Laws '79; Stan Getz '79–81; Steps Ahead '85–6; Michael Franks since '89. Accomp. comedian Robert Klein since '87; led own gps. since '85. Loeb has comp. for TV and prod. recs. for the DMP label. Favs: Wes Montgomery, Jim Hall, Jimi Hendrix, B. B. King; arrs: Thad Jones, Dave Grusin, Bob Mintzer, Don Sebesky. Fests: Eur. since '76; Asia since '79. TV: many apps. w. S. Getz. CDs: DMP; w. Getz (Em.); Kenia (Zebra); Nelson Rangell (GRP); Sergio Salvatore (N2K); Bob Mintzer (DMP); Donald Harrison (CTI); Danny Gottlieb (Atl.); Michel Camilo (Verve).

LOFTON, "TRICKY" (LAWRENCE ELLIS), tbn; b. Houston TX, 5/28/30. Began pl. in sch.; army band 1948–53. In '50s tour. w. Joe Liggins; T-Bone Walker; Lowell Fulson; Big Joe Turner; Bill Doggett; and others; in the '60s worked w. Richard Groove Holmes; in '70s w. J. McGriff; Ray Charles; Bill Berry Band; and Jon Hendricks' *Evolution of the Blues* '74–6. From late '70s w. local gps. in SF area. Favs: J. J. Johnson, J. Cleveland, J. C. Higginbotham, Tricky Sam Nanton, Jon Hendricks. LP: PJ. CDs: w. Holmes (PJ); Berry (Conc.).

LOKUMBE, HANNIBAL (Marvin Charles Peterson), tpt, comp, koto; b. Smithville, TX, 11/11/48. Mother is amateur jazz pianist. Began on dms., crnt. Led own gp., Soul Masters 1961. First instruction in harm. and theory fr. James Wilson '62–5. Pl. w. Chuck Jackson, T-Bone Walker '65–7. Stud. at No. Texas St. U. '67–9. Moved to NYC '70. Tour. Eastern US w. Rahsaan Roland Kirk '70. Pl. w. Gil Evans Orch. '71–80s. Also pl. in '70s w. Roy Haynes; Elvin Jones; Pharoah Sanders; Archie Shepp. Formed Sunrise Orch. w. cellist Diedre Murray '74. Also led free-jazz gp. in mid '70s w. Enrico Rava; Roswell Rudd; Ken McIntyre; Pat Patrick. Form. own Sunrise Orch. '74. Tour. in UK w. Don Weller–Bryan Spring qt. '84. During late '80s-early '90s in NYC pl. in churches, prisons, and schools more than in clubs. His *African Portraits* was premiered at Carnegie Hall '90. Moved back to Texas '93 but cont. to perform and teach worldwide. App. in *Portrait of the Artist as a Soul Man Dead* at Penumbra Theatre Company in St. Paul, Minn. '96. Comp. piece about Chief Crazy Horse for Kronos String Qt. '93. Favs: Coltrane, Ellington, Leos Janacek, B. B. King, Sun Ra, Cecil Taylor, Leadbelly. Fests: many incl. Berlin w. George Adams '76. TV: Eur. TV. CDs: Teldec/Atl.

LONGO, MIKE (MICHAEL JOSEPH), pno, comp, kybds; b. Cincinnati, OH, 3/19/39. Worked w. Cannonball Adderley while att. hs. in Ft. Lauderdale, Fla. Bach. degree in mus. fr. Western Kentucky U. 1959. Priv. lessons fr. Oscar Peterson 1961–62; and Hall Overton '70–72. Pl. w. Hal McIntyre orch. '57. House pnst. at Metropole Café, NYC '60–1. Form. own trio, worked as accomp. for vocs. in NYC, incl. Nancy Wilson; Joe Williams; Jimmy Rushing; Gloria Lynne. Trio also pl. regularly at Basin St. East, Embers, Hickory House. Pnst. and mus. dir. w. Dizzy Gillespie fr. '66 to '74, writing much of the gp.'s repertoire. Awarded NEA grant to write string qt. '72. Freelanced w. James Moody and Buddy Rich. Intermittently back w. Gillespie until '92. Wrote orch. work, *A World of Gillespie*, which was perf. by Gillespie and Det. Symph. '91. By the late '90s some seventy comps. by Longo had been rec. by himself on Main; Pablo; Groove Merchant; CAP, his own company; and by others. Re-formed trio '73, working many clubs around NYC, incl. Sweet Basil, Bradley's, Michael's Pub. Taught jazz course at Mozart Fest., Salzburg '82. Solo pnst. at Bemelmann's Bar at the Hotel Carlyle, NYC '81–92. Active as a teacher, his textbooks on harmony and pno. are used worldwide and sold on his web site. CDs: CAP; w. Gillespie (Imp.; GRP; MPS); Adam Rafferty; Nobby Totah (CAP); James Moody (Novus); Konitz (Den.).

LOPEMAN, MARK AARON, saxes, fl, cl, arr; b. Akron, OH, 12/2/57. Grandmother pl. stride pno. Member of Akron Jazz Wkshp., pl. w. local gps., club dates fr. 1971. Stud. at Eastman Sch. of Mus. '76–8; then in NYC w. Joe Allard '83; Billy Kerr '85; John Purcell '90. Pl. w. Glenn Miller Orch. '79; Tommy Dorsey Orch. '80–1; *Annie* touring co. '81–2; Woody Herman '83; Buddy Rich bb '83–4; Toshiko Akiyoshi–Lew Tabackin bb '84–6; Loren Schoenberg, Vince Giordano '85–90; Mel Lewis Orch. '87. Also pl. w. Buck Clayton bb; Grover Mitchell bb; Bill Kirchner; B'way shows. Arr. for Gil Evans Orch.; Helen Merrill; John Hendricks; John Lewis; Manh. Transfer; AJO; others. Favs: Getz, Parker, Adderley, Coltrane; arrs: Gil Evans, Bill Holman, Thad Jones. Fests: Japan '86 w. Akiyoshi; Eur. '87 w. M. Lewis.

CDs: w. H. Merrill–G. Evans (Em.); J. Hendricks (Den.); as arr: w. L. Schoenberg (MM).

LOUISS, EDDY (Edouard Louise), org, pno, tpt, voc; b. Paris, France, 5/2/41. Father, Pierre, who came from Martinique, pl. tpt. and led dance band in Paris. Took pno. lessons fr. moth.; pl. in father's band fr. 1954. Formed first gp. w. teenage friends. Stud. at Paris Cons. Pl. w. Double Six of Paris '61–3, incl. US-Can. tour. Awarded Prix Django Reinhardt fr. Academie du Jazz '64. Pl. pno. w. Johnny Griffin mid '60s; org. w. Art Taylor '66; Stan Getz, Jean-Luc Ponty late '60s-early '70s. Pl. in trio w. Kenny Clarke, Rene Thomas '68–70s. In the '80s Louiss led a bb, Multicolor Feeling. In '95 he join. forces w. Michel Petrucciani for a unique org.-pno duo, rec. *Conference de Presse* in concert and also app. at the Pescara JF. Polls: *DB* Critics TDWR '68, '71–4; *Jazz Forum* readers '71–2, '74. Fests: all major in Eur. TV: Eur. TV. CDs: Drey.; duo w. Petrucciani (Drey.); w. S. Getz (Verve; LRC); S. Grappelli (Musidisc; Accord); D. Humair (Drey.; Blue Flame); A. Mangelsdorff (Konnex); Rene Thomas (RTBF).

LOVANO, JOE (JOSEPH SALVATORE), tnr, alto, sop saxes, alto cl; b. Cleveland, OH, 12/29/52. Inspired by fath., Tony "Big T" Lovano, a well-regarded local Cleveland tnr. pl., he acquired an alto at age 5, sw. to tnr. 1964. Stud. at Berklee Coll. of Mus., grad. in '72. Tour. w. Tom Jones and Jack McDuff '73. To NYC '74, rec. w. Lonnie Liston Smith and George Benson. Feat. w. Woody Herman '74–6; joined Mel Lewis Jazz Orch. '80, remained through '80s. Also worked w. Paul Motian gp. and w. Motian in Charlie Haden's Liberation Music Orch. In '90 he joined John Scofield's gp. and also perf. as a lead. in many contexts: rec. w. pnsts. such as M. Petrucciani and Gonzalo Rubalcaba; Gunther Schuller's writing for the widely praised *Rush Hour*, in which Lovano incorporated the voice of his wife, Judi Silvano; and a trio w. Dave Holland and Elvin Jones. Regarded as a unique, mature voice among tnr. players of the '90s, Lovano had drawn on a wide variety of influences, from the classic saxophonists of the pre-bop period through to Coltrane and Coleman, to form his own expression. Awards: *DB* Readers, tnr. sax '95; *DB* Critics, Jazz Artist of the Year '95–6; Honorary doctorate fr. Berklee '98. CDs: BN; Evid.; Enja; w. M. Mainieri (NYC); B. DeArango (GM); Dave Brubeck (Tel.); Lee Konitz (Evid.); Branford Marsalis (Col.); P. Motian (ECM; SN; JMT); Charlie Haden; Yosuke Yamashita (Verve); Mel Lewis (MM); Lou Rawls (Manh.; BN); Jim Hall; Ray Brown (Tel.); John Scofield (BN); Tom Harrell (Cont.; Vict.); Peter Erskine (Novus; Den.);

Ray Drummond (Arab.); K. Werner (Sunny.); W. Herman (BB; WW).

LOVE, PRESTON, alto sax; b. Omaha, NE, 4/21. Brother, Tommy "Dude" Love, prof. saxist. Self-taught on sax but made prof. debut on dms. w. Warren Webb at age 15. Heard Earle Warren w. Count Basie and bec. serious about pl. alto sax. Pl. w. Lloyd Hunter 1941–2; Nat Towles '42; back w. Hunter briefly bef. gigging in Omaha. Took Warren's place as lead alto w. Basie for six weeks '43. Pl. intermittently w. Lucky Millinder '44–5 and w. Harlan Leonard. Rejoin. Basie '45–7; later formed r&b band, rec. for Federal in early '50s. Org. rec. co. w. Johnny Otis early '60s; tour. extens. w. own territory band in '50s-60s. Led West Coast Motown orch. late '60s-70s. Tour. in Eur. w. The Countsmen '83. Later living in Omaha, worked as teacher, dj, and writer. Perf. w. Otis at Monterey Pop Fest '70. Autobiography: *A Thousand Honey Creeks Later* (Wesleyan U. Press) '97. CDs: w. Basie (BB)

LOWE, CURTIS SYLVESTER, bari and tnr saxes; b. Chicago, IL, 11/15/19. Professional debut w. local gps. in 1940; mil. service '42–5; pl. in navy band w. Jerome Richardson, Buddy Collette, Marshal and Ernie Royal. Many stints w. L. Hampton, incl. '49–51, '52, '55–7; concerts w. Dave Brubeck Oct. '52. Rec. w. Johnny Otis in LA, '52; pl. w. Johnny Hodges spt. in clubs '53; rec. w. Earl Hines '58–9. Sec.-Treas. of Local 669 of the African-American mus. union in SF '58–60 and later worked w. the merged Local 6 until retirement in '84. LP: w. Hines (Felsted). CD: w. Hampton (Accord).

LOWE, FRANK (aka MEMPHIS FRANK), tnr sax; b. Memphis, TN, 6/24/43; d. NYC, 9/19/03. Studied alto w. Tuff Green at Melrose Jr. HS, then worked as salesman, songwriter for Stax label 1959. Stud. at U. of Kansas '61–3, then w. Pete Magadini at SF Cons. Ornette Coleman brought him to NYC in '66. Pl. w. Sun Ra '66–8; Alice Coltrane '70–3; Don Cherry, Sunny Murray, Carla Bley, Milford Graves, Rashied Ali, Butch Morris, Ed Blackwell fr. '70s. Collaborated w. Cherry on soundtrack to film *The Holy Mountain*; also prod. and arr. own film, *Street Music*, in '70s. In late '90s Lowe led a 7–pc. gp., Sax-Ensemble, perf. orig. comps. and mus. of Hank Crawford and Jackie McLean. Favs: Lester Young, Rollins, Getz, James Clay. Polls: *DB* TDWR '74. Fests: Eur. fr. '76. CDs: CIMP; BL; WW; w. Cherry (A&M); SaxEnsemble (Qwest).

LOWE, (JAMES) MUNDELL, gtr., comp, arr; b. Laurel, MS, 4/21/22. Studied w. fath.; moved to NO at 13, pl. first jobs there w. Abbie Brunies, Sid Devilla, and various Bourbon St. gps. In 1939 he pl. Nashville w. Pee Wee King on *Grand Ole Op'ry* radio show. Work briefly w. Jan Savitt; entered army in '43. Joined Ray McKinley's band in NYC '45–47. App. as actor and gtr. in off-B'way plays in '49. Led qt. w. Dick Hyman, George Duvivier, and Ed Shaughnessy on Dave Garroway's *Today*. Worked concurrently w. Sauter–Finegan orch., Billy Taylor, and own qt. at Embers, NYC. Left NBC in '58; comp./arr. for own LPs and docu. films. Moved to LA in '65, working as comp. for films, TV shows, incl. *I Dream of Jeannie; Wild, Wild West; Hawaii Five-O*. Co-produced *Jazz in the Round* for PBS network and cond. band; comp./cond. mus. for film *Billy Jack* '72. Extensive freelancing, '73–4; arr/prod. albums; pl. gigs and taught clinics in LA. Worked in Eur. w. wife, singer Betty Bennett '74–5. Pl. MJF many times and served as mus. dir. '81–6. Worked w. Peggy Lee; Carmen McRae; Sarah Vaughan; Bill Berry; Duke Ellington; Ben Webster; André Previn; Ray Brown; Mike Wofford; Holly Hofmann; Bob Magnusson; others. Moved to San Diego in '89. Pl. w. Great Guitars in mid '90s. CDs: Riv.; JA; Conc.; w. A. Previn; R. Brown (Tel.); Great Guitars; C. Tjader (Conc.); Sarah Vaughan (Col.; Roul.); Billie Holiday (Dec.); Carmen McRae (Dec.; Beth.); Charlie Parker (Rh.; Jazz Classics); Ruby Braff; Joe Williams (BB); Benny Carter (MM; Pab.); J. Hodges (Verve); Tete Montoliu (FS); Mel Powell (Vang.); Spike Robinson (Capri).

LOWTHER, (THOMAS) HENRY, tpt, crnt, flg, picc tpt, vln; b. Leicester, England, 7/11/41. Father pl. crnt. in Salvation Army; bros., brass mus. First stud. crnt., vln. w. fath., later at Royal Acad., London. Self-taught in jazz idiom. Start. prof. career w. Manfred Mann and John Mayall, then variously w. John Surman Brass Project 1982–92; Berlin Contemp. Jazz Orch. '90–2; London Jazz Comp. Orch. '88–92; pl. lead tpt. w. Gil Evans '83–4; George Russell's Living Time orch. '91. Worked w. Charlie Watts '86–7; J. Dankworth '66–90. Led own gp., Still Waters, fr. '87. Perfs. in India and most of Eur. Heard on numerous radio broadcasts; own qt. on *TV Jazz at the Gateway*. Taught at Trinity Coll., Royal Coll., Royal Acad. Won *MM* poll on tpt. and misc. instrument (vln.). CDs: Deram; w. Kenny Wheeler; John Surman (ECM).

LUBAMBO, ROMERO, gtr, cavaquinho; b. Rio de Janeiro, Brazil, 7/20/55. Mother and uncle are pnsts. in Brazil. Stud. at Villa Lobos Sch. of Mus. in Rio 1972–8. Pl. w. Leny Andrade; Cama de Gato; Mauro Senise in Brazil. Moved to NYC in '86; pl. w. Astrud Gilberto '86–90; Herbie Mann fr. '87 in Jasil Brazz;

Paquito D'Rivera fr. '88. Form. Trio Da Paz in '90s. An accomplished gtr. in several idioms. Favs: Wes Montgomery, Scott Henderson, Helio Delmiro. Fests: Japan fr. '87; Eur. in '90s. TV: Brazil. CDs: Koko.; co-lead. w. Gil Goldstein (Big World.); w. A. Gilberto (Verve); D'Rivera (Mess.); Kathleen Battle (Col.); D. Gillespie–P. Woods (CTI); Mann (Chesky); Ernie Watts (CTI); M. Petrucciani (BN); Ali Ryerson (Conc.).

LUCAS, AL (ALBERT B.), bs; b. Windsor, Ont., Canada, 11/16/16; d. NYC, 6/19/83. Father pl. bs; stud. pno. w. moth. at age 6; bs. and tba. at 12. To NYC 1933; briefly w. Kaiser Marshall; then tour. w. Sunset Royal Orch. '33–42; also w. Ace Harris '37. In early '40s he worked w. Coleman Hawkins; Hot Lips Page; Eddie Heywood; Duke Ellington July-Sept. '45; Mary Lou Williams '46 (feat. on her *Zodiac Suite* album); Illinois Jacquet '47–54; rejoined Heywood '54–6. After new stints. w. Hawkins and Williams, he did studio work in the '60s and '70s; to Japan w. Sam "the Man" Taylor '70. A swinging section member and soloist, Lucas also used a bow effectively. CDs: w. Jacquet (BB; Roul.; Mos.); R. Eldridge; Hawkins (Keynote/Merc.); Dexter Gordon (BN); Jay & Kai; J. J. Johnson; Seventh Ave. Stompers (Sav.); S. Stitt–P. Gonsalves (Imp.); M.L. Williams (Smith./Folk.).

LUCIE, LAWRENCE (LARRY), gtr, bjo, mand, cl; b. Emporia, VA, 12/18/14. Father pl. vln., bro. pl. sax in family square-dance band. Stud. bjo. in 1923 by correspondence course, later w. Luther Blake and at Bklyn. Cons. in NYC. First prof. gig w. June Clark '31. Subbed for a week w. Duke Ellington at Cotton Club, then pl. w. Benny Carter '32–4; Fletcher Henderson '34; Mills Blue Rhythm Band '34–6; Fletcher Henderson '36–9; Coleman Hawkins bb '40; Louis Armstrong '40–5. Freelance on recs. w. Spike Hughes; Teddy Wilson; Billie Holiday; Putney Dandridge; Joe Turner; Jelly Roll Morton; Red Allen '30s-early '40s. Led combo w. wife, singer Nora Lee (Susan) King fr. '46. Pl. w. Luis Russell, Cozy Cole '50s; tour. w. Louis Bellson bb '59. Active as freelance studio mus. '60s-70s. Pl. at Count Basie and Lucky Millinder tributes at Carnegie Hall '73; w. reconstituted Chick Webb band at NJF-NY; Armstrong tribute band '74. Charter member of NY Jazz Repertory Co. '75. Taught at Manh. Comm. Coll. '70s. Had own NYC cable (public access) show w. his wife into late '90s. Author of *Lucie's Special Guitar Lessons* (Playton Mus. Publ.). Film: *Jam Session* w. Armstrong. CDs: w. B. Carter (B&B); F. Henderson (Col.; Dec.); JR Morton; Bechet; Hawkins (BB); Louis Armstrong (Dec.); B. Holiday; E. Fitzgerald;

R. Eldridge (Col.). T. Wilson (Hep); Red Allen (Tax); Bobby Watson (NN).

LUNCEFORD, JIMMIE (JAMES MELVIN), lead, fl; b. Fulton, MO, 6/6/02; d. Seaside, OR, 7/13/47. Studied several instruments, incl. alto sax., fl., and other reeds, as a child in Denver, Colo. First serious mus. educ. was under Wilberforce J. Whiteman, father of Paul Whiteman; B.A. fr. Fisk U. and later study at CCNY. Played w. the bands of Elmer Snowden, Wilbur Sweatman, and others in middle 1920s. Taught at Manassas HS, Memphis, where he organized student band, the Chickasaw Syncopators '27; band rec. two sides for Col. and worked in Cleveland and Buffalo areas bef. moving to NYC '33. Rec. under Lunceford's name for Vict. and pl. at Harlem's Lafayette Theatre and Cotton Club '34. Two '34 recs.—"Jazznocracy" and "White Heat," arr. by Will Hudson—brought national attention to the band. Tour. Scand. '37. Dur. the next decade, the band enjoyed a unique reputation as a disciplined, showmanship-oriented orch. w. unique, two-beat swing, powerful section work, and crisp, rhythmic arrs., mostly written by tptr. Sy Oliver and pnst. Eddie Wilcox. Vocals by Oliver, saxophonist Willie Smith, and singer Dan Grissom added commercial appeal. Dur. the key yrs., '35–7, basic personnel incl. Eddie Tompkins; Eddie Durham; Earl Carruthers; Laforet Dent; Joe Thomas; Dan Grissom; and Jimmy Crawford. Trummy Young, tbn. and vocs., join. in Nov. '37; Gerald Wilson replaced Oliver as tpt. and arr. in Aug. '39; and Billy Moore Jr. wrote arrs. fr. '39. Lunceford cond. the band, rarely pl. an instrument. After '42 the personnel changed more frequently and the Lunceford vogue slowly faded. The band rec. for the Dec. Label '34–45 (also for Vocalion), then Majestic, but in its later yrs. it mainly revisited its earlier hits. Lunceford suffered a fatal heart attack while touring. The band cont. under the leadership of Wilcox and Thomas for two yrs., then solely Wilcox. By the end of the decade it had dissolved. The distinctive Lunceford style, typified by such recs. as "For Dancers Only" '37 and "Margie" '38, infl. many bandleaders and arrs. up to the '50s, incl. Sonny Dunham; Sonny Burke; Stan Kenton; and Tommy Dorsey (for whom Oliver worked for several yrs.). Among the important bbs of the '30s, the Lunceford band ranked w. Ellington, Basie, and Goodman. Film: *Blues in the Night* '41. CDs: Class.; Dec.

LUNDGREN, JAN, pno; b. Kristianstad, Sweden, 3/22/66. Younger sist. classical pno. teacher. Lived in Olofstrom for first five yrs., then moved to Ronneby. Pno. lessons fr. age 6. One of his teachers introduced him to jazz and he bought an Oscar Peterson rec. when he was 15. Att. Malmo Coll. of Mus., grad. in 1991. Then taught jazz as member of the faculty. As teenager worked w. local jazz gps.; later w. Arne Domnerus, Putte Wickman; eventually w. Benny Bailey; Herb Geller; Vincent Herring; Johnny Griffin. First infl. by Peterson; Bud Powell; Erroll Garner; Bill Evans; Jan Johansson; Bengt Hallberg. Rec. in Sweden w. American saxophonist Ed Epstein for Olufsen label '90. In '94 rec. first trio album in Copenhagen for Four Leaf Clover. Tour. in Swed. w. Geller '94 Rec. w. Bill Perkins in Hollywood '95. Pl. concert at Royal Swedish Acad. of Mus. w. Wickman, Domnerus Dec. '95. Lundgren's repertoire includes the well-known and the obscure of the great songwriters plus modern jazz originals fr. the '40s and '50s and beyond. Favs: Teddy Wilson, Armstrong, Parker, L. Young, Earl Hines, B. Powell, J. Lovano, Clifford Brown. Fest: Uppsala '98. Awards: Swed. Radio Musician of the Year '94; *Orkester Journalen* Golden Record '97. CDs: FS; Four Leaf Clover; Alfa; Sittel; w. Geller; Perkins; Conte Candoli (FS); Domnerus–Lars Erstrand (Proprius); Domnerus–Wickman (LadyBird).

LUNDY, CARMEN LATRETTA, voc, pno; b. Miami, FL, 11/1/54. Mother gospel singer; bro., Curtis Lundy, bs. Sang gospel as a child. Turned prof. in teens in duo Salt and Pepper. Degrees in studio mus. and jazz fr. U. of Miami. While in coll., worked at local clubs, then moved to NYC and remain. active in clubs, TV, and occ. acting jobs for next 13 yrs. Pl. a lead in *Sophisticated Ladies*; role of Billie Holiday off-off B'way in *They Were All Gardenias*. App. at Montreux JF '77; Munich '88; Eur. clubs and concerts '89–91. Moved to LA Oct. '91, working as singer and actress. A trained mus. who writes her own lyrics and mus. ("Time Is Love," written in 5/4, is a good example of her work.) Although a major critic saw Lundy as a potential major voc. of the '90s, the prediction was not fulfilled. CDs: JVC; Arab.; w. Ernie Watts (JVC); Curtis Lundy (Evid.); Fred Wesley (Ant.); Kip Hanrahan (Panagea); D. Betti van der Noot (Innowo).

LUTHER, FRANK DANNY, bs, pno; b. Chicago, IL, 2/23/44. Began on pno. at age 4; vln. at age 6; bs. at age 15. Stud. at Milwaukee Cons. 1967–8. Pl. in Chi. w. Tommy Ponce '60–4; Herbie Hancock '60; Al Cohn–Zoot Sims '65; in Milwaukee w. Manty Ellis '64–8; Buddy Montgomery '68; in Atlanta w. Duke Pearson '69; w. Roger Powell in Woodstock, N.Y. '70; then moved to NYC. Pl. w. Chet Baker, Jack Wilkins '73; Don Elliot '74–79; Gerry Mulligan '74–84; Jimmy Giuffre '75–80; Lee Konitz '76–77;

Don Friedman, Attila Zoller '76–8; Joe Puma '78–80; Phil Woods '80; Lionel Hampton '84; J. R. Monterose '85–7; Jimmy Cobb, '85–90; Warren Bernhardt '88–91. Luther comp. mus. and perf. solo bs. for modern dance concert at SUNY-New Paltz '91. Favs: Paul Chambers, Scott LaFaro, Ray Brown, Wilbur Ware. Fests: all major '74–85. Film: app. in *The Happy Hooker*. TV: Dick Cavett; PBS *Jazz in America* w. Mulligan. LPs: w. Mulligan (Embassy); D. Friedman (Prog.); A. Zoller (Enja).

LYNCH, BRIAN HOLLISTER, tpt, flg; b. Champaign, IL, 9/12/56. Father a psychologist and amateur tpt; moth. a teacher and voc. Pl. w. rock, r&b bands in hs and sat in w. Buddy Montgomery, Melvin Rhyne in Milwaukee. Stud. at Wisconsin Cons. 1975–80; stud. w. Doug Myers '72–3; Lonnie Hillyer '81–2; William Vacchiano '82. In San Diego, pl. w. Charles McPherson and Rob Schneiderman '81. Moved to NYC '81, where he was encouraged by Claudio Roditi, who got him several jobs. Worked w. Brazilian, Puerto Rican, and Cuban gps. Pl. w. Geo. Russell bb, Junior Cook '82; Horace Silver '82–5; Toshiko Akiyoshi '83–7; Jim Snidero '84; Jack McDuff '86–7; Eddie Palmieri '87–8. Gained nat'l prominence w. Art Blakey's Jazz Messengers Dec. '88 to Oct. '90. To Eur. w. Benny Golson and Art Farmer in '89. App. w. Jazz Messengers Alumni '90; Philip Morris Superband '91; Benny Golson '92. Joined Phil Woods Qnt. '92. Lynch combines the lyricism and brassy, hard-edged swing typical of the best of the Messenger tpt. tradition and has shown talent as a writer as well. Favs: Lee Morgan, Kenny Dorham, Freddie Hubbard, Woody Shaw. Fests: Japan fr. '83; Eur. fr. '88; Turkey, Austral. '91. CDs: Sharp Nine; CC; Ken; w. Blakey (Timel.; A&M); J. Snidero (CC); Eddie Palmieri (Elek.); P. Woods (Mos.; Evid.; TCB; Conc.); Ted Rosenthal (JA); Conrad Herwig (Ast. Pl.); Ralph Moore; Schneiderman (Res.); Akiyoshi (Ken).

LYON, JIMMY (JAMES FREDERICK), pno; b. Camden, NJ, 11/6/21; d. Paramus, NJ, 12/84. First pno. lessons at age 8 for a yr.; then self-taught, practicing six hrs. a day. At Collingswood (N.J.) HS he led 10-piece band. Prof. debut in local club at 17. Heard Art Tatum on the radio and drove to Phila. to buy every Tatum rec. he could find. In army 1942–6. Solo pnst. at Fred Waring's estate, Shawnee on the Delaware, '46–8. Moved fr. Phila. to NYC, pl. w. Tal Farlow, Buddy DeFranco '48. Pl. w. Gene Williams Orch. '49, then worked as June Christy's accomp. on the road '50–1; tour. w. Stan Kenton, freelanced w. Sam Donahue, Connie Haines, Bobby Byrne, Benny Goodman sxt. '51–2. Led trio, incl. Jimmy Raney, at

Blue Angel, NYC '53–62. Pl. solo pno. at many NYC venues incl. Waldorf-Astoria's reopened Peacock Alley, pl. Cole Porter's music on Porter's Steinway '78. Accomp. many singers, most importantly Mabel Mercer. Richard Sudhalter decribed Lyon's playing as "subtly swinging simplicity and elegance that constantly reveals fresh facets in tunes that would seem, by now, to have been completely explored." LPs: Finnadar; w. Mercer–Bobby Short (Atl.). CD: w. Mercer (Rh.).

LYONS, JIMMY (JAMES), alto sax; b. Jersey City, NJ, 12/1/32; d. NYC, 5/19/86. Raised mostly in NYC; in 1941 he moved in w. his grandfath. who owned the Woodside Hotel restaurant in Harlem, where Count Basie and many other jazzmen often made their headquarters. Buster Bailey gave him an alto sax when he was in his teens. Lyons also was friendly with Elmo Hope, Bud Powell, and Thelonious Monk. Studied briefly w. saxophonist Rudy Rutherford but was mainly self-taught. Three yrs. w. army in Korea, then ret. to NYC but made little musical progress until '60, when he began a long assoc. w. pnst. Cecil Taylor. Taught mus. at Narcotic Addiction Control drug treatment center in NYC '70–71; artist-in-residence, along w. Taylor and dmr. Andrew Cyrille, at Antioch Coll. '71–73, where he comp. *Aztec Nights* for a 25–piece ens.; dir. Black Mus. Ens. at Bennington Coll. '75. For the last decade of his life, he perf. and rec. as a lead. w. gps. that often incl. Joseph Jarman; Cyrille; Don Moye; bassoonist Karen Borca; and dmr. Paul Murphy. A Parker-inspired player, Lyons will probably be best remembered for his seamless, almost symbiotically connected improvisations w. Taylor. CDs: hatArt; BS; w. Taylor (BN; Konnex; NW; hatArt; SN), Gil Evans (Imp.); Cyrille (BS); Carla Bley (JCOA/ECM).

LYTELL, JIMMY (James Sarrapede), cl; b. NYC, 12/1/04; d. Kings Point, NY, 11/28/72. Picked his prof. name fr. movie actor Bert Lytell. Start. pl. prof. at 14 in his uncle's roadhouse. Replaced Larry Shields in the ODJB for two yrs. 1922–24; also tour. w. the Orig. Memphis Five '22–25. Cond. and pl. in many mus. comedies and radio shows throughout the '30s and '40s; mus. dir. for NBC in mid '40s. His own radio show, *The Chamber Music Society of Lower Basin Street*, was on the network in '40, '41, and '44. Played w. reorganized Orig. Memphis Five in '49 and mid '50s; cont. to freelance and rec. as leader and soloist until his death. His style was close to Larry Shields, Leon Roppolo, and Jimmie Noone. LPs: w. Annette Hanshaw; Jay C. Flippen; Ladd's Black Aces (Fountain). CDs: w. Orig. Memphis Five (Collector's Classics); Maxine Sullivan (Aff.).

LYTLE, JOHNNY (JOHN DILLARD), vib, comp, dms; b. Springfield, OH, 10/13/32; d. Springfield, 12/15/95. Father pl. tpt., led band; moth. pl. pno. Began on dms. Stud. w. Miriam Vantrest Pence and at Wittenberg U. Pl. dms. w. father's band fr. age 9; then bec. a successful amateur boxer. Pl. w. Ray Charles, Jimmy Witherspoon 1950; Gene Ammons '53. Sw. to vib. '53. Pl. w. Boots Johnson '55–7; own gps. w. sidemen incl. Johnny Griffin, Frank Wess, Joe Farrell, Ron Carter fr. '57. App. w. trio in concerts w. Wes Montgomery, Nancy Wilson, Miriam Makeba, Ray Charles '60s. Won numerous awds. for his community service throughout his career, incl. Indianapolis's Wes Montgomery Award and awards fr. the Urban League, the NAACP, and the cities of Newark, Buffalo, and Cleveland. He led the bb at Central State U. and dir. the Davey Moore Foundation and Culture and Art Center in Springfield. His best known comp. is "The Village Caller." In his autobiography, *Hamp*, Lionel Hampton recalls a 7-yr.-old Lytle introducing him to Hampton's long-lost father, who had been convalescing in a Dayton Veterans hosp. since the end of WWI. Favs: Hampton, M. Jackson, Cal Tjader. Fests: Engl. '88–9, '91; Netherlands '90. TV: *Bob Braun Show* CDs: Riv.: Muse; 32; w. Bobby Timmons (Prest.).

LYTTELTON, HUMPHREY, tpt, cl, tnr horn, comp, lead; b. Windsor, England, 5/23/21. First pl. jazz while in sch. at Eton; cont. to perf. while w. Grenadier Guards dur. WWII. First prof. gig w. Geo. Webb's Dixielanders 1947. In '48 he formed his own band, which rec. for Parlophone throughout the '50s, incl. w. Sidney Bechet '49. Orig. a staunch traditionalist, Lyttelton's band became a favorite dur. the '50s trad. revival, but he gradually adopted a more orchestrated, swing-era style approach, adding saxist Bruce Turner. Host of *BBC Jazz Club* prog. fr. '52; other BBC progs. incl. *Best of Jazz* fr. '64. Tour. US under auspices of NJF '59. Worked in Germ. and/or Switz. annually fr. '61. Tour. Engl. and Eur. w. Buck Clayton '63–6; Engl. w. Joe Turner '65. Lyttelton is also a cartoonist and author who wrote and illustrated the books *I Play as I Please* '54, *Second Chorus* '58 (both MacGibbon & Kee), and *Take It from the Top* (Robson), as well as an autobiog.; he contributed regularly to *Melody Maker* in the '50s. His sidemen have incl. Tony Coe; Johnny Parker; Wally Fawkes; Jimmy Skidmore; Joe Temperley; Tony Mann; Dave Green; Mick Pyne; John Surman. He founded the Calligraph rec. label in '83. TV: many apps. on BBC, incl. *In Concert* '75. CDs: Parlophone; Callig.; BL; Dormouse; Philips; Stomp Off.

m

MABERN, HAROLD JR., pno, comp; b. Memphis, TN, 3/20/36. Started on dms., pl. w. Frank Strozier while in hs. Pursued serious pno. study after hearing Phineas Newborn Jr. Moved to Chi. 1954; pl. w. Morris Ellis bb; Walter Perkins' MJT+3; Bob Cranshaw; Frank Strozier; Bobby Bryant; Willie Thomas. Moved to NYC '59; pl. w. Harry "Sweets" Edison '59; Lionel Hampton '60; Art Farmer–Benny Golson Jazztet '61–2; Roy Haynes, Irene Reid, Arthur Prysock '62; Miles Davis in Calif.; J. J. Johnson '63–5; Wes Montgomery '64; Joe Williams '66–7; Lee Morgan '67; Walter Bolden Trio '73–4. Member of Stanley Cowell's 7-pno. Piano Choir '70. Pl. and/or rec. in '70s w. George Coleman; Danny Moore; Billy Harper; Roy Haynes; Freddie Hubbard; R. R. Kirk; Hank Mobley; Clark Terry; Joe Newman; and many others. Regular member of G. Coleman's qt. since the '80s. Taught pno. and improv. at William Paterson Coll. since '71. In '90 and '91 Mabern toured Japan w. the 100 Gold Fingers of Jazz, a gp. comprising 10 top jazz pnsts. "Music is my love," says Mabern. "I never take it for granted." A strong bebop-based, blues-grounded player, he has been unjustly neglected through much of his career. Favs: Phineas Newborn Jr., Ahmad Jamal; arr: Thad Jones. Polls: BMI Jazz Pioneer. Fests: Eur., Jap. w. Coleman, J. Newman. TV: *Jazz Set* w. Bobbi Humphrey '71; *Soul* w. Lucky Thompson '70s. CDs: Col.; Sack.; Prest.; w. G. Coleman (Evid.); Betty Carter (Cap.); Lee Morgan; Mobley; Hubbard (BN); J. J. Johnson (Imp.); Contemp. Pno Ens. (Evid.; Col.); Cecil Payne; Jimmy Forrest; Eric Alexander (Del.); Kirk (Merc.); Strozier; Louis Smith (Steep.); J. Griffin (Gal.); G. Benson (CTI).

MACERO, TEO (ATTILIO JOSEPH), comp, saxes, prod; b. Glens Falls, NY, 10/30/25. In navy 1942–6 incl. att. Navy Sch. of Mus '43–4. Taught and freelanced in Glens Falls '46–7, then moved to NYC '48. Studied at Juilliard, B.S., M.S. '53, where he organized a dance band that perf. on WOR; also taught in Ridgewood, N.J. sch. Pl. club dates w. Larry Clinton early '50s. Founding member of Chas. Mingus's Jazz Wkshp. Pl. and rec. w. Mingus '53–5; own gps. fr. '55; Teddy Charles Tentette '56. Active as comp. of jazz-infl. atonal classical works '55–60; received Guggenheim grants '57–8. Macero's comp., *Fusion*, was perf. by NY Philharm. '58. On staff of Col. recs. '57–75, first as mus. editor, then as prod., mainly jazz but also B'way and pop sess., incl. *A Chorus Line* cast album and Simon and Garfunkel's *The Graduate*. Supervised Miles Davis's *Kind of Blue* sess. '59, *Bitches' Brew* '69; also signed Mingus to Col. and prod. sess. by Thelonious Monk; Dave Brubeck; Ramsey Lewis; and others. Left Col. to form Teo Prod. '75 but cont. to prod. for Miles Davis until '83. Has prod. twelve Gold rec. and written more than 1,000 comps., incl. ballet, *Everything Goes* '82; film, *Top Secret: The Teddy Kennedy Jr. Story* '86; *Special Friendships* '87; and TV scores. He resumed pl. sax in the '80s and prod. an album of his own comps. for bb in '83. CDs: Prest.; Stash; Vintage Jazz; w. C. Mingus (Col.; Deb.); Michel Legrand (Philips).

MACHITO (Frank Raul Grillo), perc, lead, voc; b. Tampa, FL, 2/16/12; d. London, England, 4/15/84. Raised in Cuba but made many trips to US bet. 1929 and '59. In '30s he pl. w. bands in Cuba, incl. El Sexteto Nacional at Havana's Montmartre Club; back in

US in '37, he pl. w. Xavier Cugat, Noro Morales, and others. Form. own band for which his bro.-in-law, Mario Bauza, hired arrs. to lend the gp. a jazz quality. Its Afro-Cuban sound was heard in concerts shared w. Stan Kenton's orch. and later on recs. feat. such guest stars as Charlie Parker; Dizzy Gillespie; Flip Phillips; Howard McGhee; Brew Moore; Armando Peraza all in '48–9. Pl. at Palladium Ballroom in NYC into '80s and was subject of docu. film, *Machito: A Latin Legacy*, Carlos Ortiz '87. Though not strictly in the jazz idiom, Machito's bands had a big jazz following and infl. the mus. thinking of Kenton, Gillespie, and others. After his death, his son, Mario Grillo, cont. the band. CDs: Trop.; Imp.; Verve; GNP Cres.; Tumbao; Timel.; Sky Ranch; w. Gillespie (Pab.); Parker (Verve); Kenton (Mos.).

MacKAY, DAVE (DAVID OWEN), pno; b. Syracuse, NY, 3/24/32. Studied at Trinity Coll. and Bost. U. 1950–9; also w. L. Tristano. In Bost. pl. w. Bobby Hackett; Sonny Stitt; Charlie Mariano; Bob Wilber; Serge Chaloff; later worked in NYC w. Jim Hall and own gps. Settled in LA in mid '60s; pl. w. Don Ellis; Emil Richards; and own gp., feat. his wife, the late singer Vicky Hamilton. Later form. gp. w. singer Bill Henderson and pnst./voc. Joyce Collins; cont. gigging locally and teaching into '90s. CDs: MAMA; Disc.; w. Chet Baker (Baker); Stephanie Haynes (Why Not).

MACKEL, BILLY (JOHN WILLIAM), gtr; b. Baltimore, MD, 12/28/12. Studied priv.; began on tnr. bjo. Pl. w. Percy Glascoe 1932–5; Buddy Johnson in Balt. '35–40; own combo '40–4. Join. Lionel Hampton '44 and remained—w. few interruptions—until mid '70s, longer than any other Hampton sideman. One return was to replace Wes Montgomery. Rec. w. Milt Buckner, Arnett Cobb, Herbie Fields, other Hampton sidemen mid '40s. Accomp. Billy Williams' voc. qt. '60s. CDs: w. Hampton (Verve; Dec.; Col.; Imp.).

MACKREL, DENNIS M. JR., dms, bs, arr; b. Omaha, NE, 4/3/62. Grandfather pl. tpt. Self-taught on dms., bs., and as arr. First prof. gig at 10. Pl. for LV show bands while att. U. of Nevada 1979–80. Moved to NYC '81, pl. for B'way shows. Pl. w. Count Basie Orch. '83–7. Freelanced w. Woody Herman, Buck Clayton, Grover Mitchell, Benny Carter, AJO, Smithsonian Jazz Orch., and others '89–91. Succeeded Mel Lewis in Mel Lewis Orch. '90. Mackrel has also perf. w. Mingus Epitaph; Hank Jones; Monty Alexander; Charles McPherson; Joe Williams; Marian McPartland; Diane Schuur; and worked again w. Basie Orch. in '98. Lead. of Manhattan Symphony Jazz Orch. '99. Favs: Art Blakey, Mel Lewis, Grady Tate; arrs: Thad Jones, Rob McConnell, Oliver Nelson. Fests: Japan fr. '83; Eur. fr. '85. TV: videos w. C. Basie Orch., Diane Schuur. CDs: w. C. Basie Orch. (Pablo; Den.); Joey DeFrancesco (Col.); G. Mitchell (Ken); Mel Lewis (MM); Hank Jones; Joe Williams (Verve); Grady Tate (Mile.); Howard Alden; Carol Sloane; Frank Wess (Conc.); Carla Bley (Watt); D. Schuur (GRP).

MacPHERSON, FRASER JOHN, tnr, alto saxes, fl, cl; b. Winnipeg, Man., Canada, 4/10/28; d. Vancouver, B.C., Canada, 9/28/93. Raised in Victoria, B.C. Began on cl., pl. NO jazz. Moved to Vancouver in 1948. In NYC '56–7, stud. w. Vincent James "Jimmy" Abato, Henry Zlotnick. Pl. in Vancouver w. Chuck Barber, Bob Reid, Lance Harrison '50–4; Chris Gage '61–3; own gp. '64–7; also worked as studio mus. Pl. sax w. Vancouver Symph. occ. fr. '58. From the '50s he freq. perf. on CBC radio and TV, incl. apps. w. Ray Norris ca. '51; as lead. of nonet late '50s; w. string orch. on own program '63–4. Form. trio w. Oliver Gannon, Wyatt Ruther '75. Tour. USSR '78, '81, '84, '86. Cont. to app. on CBC progs., incl. *Jazz Radio-Can.* and *Jazz Beat*. Taught at Douglas and Vancouver Commun. Colls. and was made a member of the Order of Can. in '87. Polls: Juno Awd. '83. Fests: apps. in US; Austr. '86; all major in Can. TV: many apps. on CBC. CDs: Conc.; Sack.; JT; w. Anita O'Day (Star Line).

MADISON, JIMMY (JAMES HENRY), dms; b. Cincinnati, OH, 2/17/47. Mother and fath. amateur mus.; bro. is prof. rock bsst. Pl. w. Marian McPartland 1969–71; James Brown '69–75; Bobby Hackett '71; Roland Kirk '72; Lee Konitz '73–8; Joe Farrell '74–5; Dave Matthews '74–82; Chet Baker '75–80; Geo. Benson off and on fr. '76; Nina Simone '78; Art Farmer late '70s-80. Co-led bb w. Angel Rangelov at Blue Note, NYC '81–5. Pl. w. Red Rodney fr. '90; Maceo Parker since '91. Freelanced w. Stanley Turrentine; Hank Jones; Al Cohn–Zoot Sims; Stan Getz; Ted Curson; Jack Walrath; and others. Madison has also worked w. such dancers as Shirley MacLaine; Maurice Hines; and the Joffrey Ballet. Owns and operates his own rec. studio in NYC. Favs: Elvin Jones, Joey Baron, Jack DeJohnette. Fests: Eur. since '70s. TV: *Tonight Show*, other network shows w. J. Brown, G. Benson. CDs: w. Stanley Turrentine (BN); Red Rodney (Contin.; Chesky); Maceo Parker (Verve); J. Walrath; Mark Murphy (Muse); Jim Hall (CTI); Kirk (Aff.); Ron McClure (Ken).

MADISON, KID SHOTS (LOUIS), crnt; b. New Orleans, LA, 2/19/1899; d. New Orleans, 9/48. Drummer in Waifs' Home Band w. Louis Armstrong

1915. Stud. crnt. w. Dave Jones, Louis Dumaine, and Joe Howard. Second crnt. w. Orig. Tuxedo Orch. '23 under Oscar "Papa" Celestin; later w. Frankie Dusen; Big Eye Louis Nelson; Alphonse Picou; worked with WPA brass band during Depression yrs.; w. Eureka Brass Band in '40s. In late '40s he held day job w. the NO Board of Health and cont. pl. until Jan. '48, when he suffered a stroke. CDs: w. George Lewis, *George Lewis With Kid Shots* (Amer. Mus.)

MAGADINI, PETE (PETER C.), dms, perc, educ; b. Great Barrington, MA, 1/25/42. Moved to Palm Springs, Calif., at age 6. Pl. first snare drm. in fifth grade. Moved to Phoenix, Ariz.; got drum set at 15, after his parents took him to hear Duke Ellington. Pl. rock & roll at hs dances; then country & western in clubs. Stud. w. Don Bothwell at SF Cons., B. Mus. 1965; on scholarship at Ali Akbar Khan Sch. of North Indian Mus., SF '66; w. Roy Burnes at U. of Toronto, Master of Mus. '73. While at sch. in SF, worked w. George Duke; Al Jarreau; John Heard; then tour. for yr. w. Diana Ross. Has pl. w. Don Menza; Mose Allison; Don Ellis; John Handy; as perc. w. Oakland Symph. '63–6; Berkshire Music Fest. Orch. '68; Toronto Symph. '71–7; as studio mus. in SF, LA, Toronto. Teaching priv. fr. '60; at SF Cons. '67–9; Lake Tahoe Summer Music Camp '76; Toronto Music Camp '80; Concordia U. fr. '83; McGill U. fr. '88; active as clinician. Favs: Elvin Jones, Roach, Manne. Fests: w. own qnt., Montreal; Ottawa '90. TV: special w. Stephane Grappelli, Yehudi Menuhin. Videos: *The Polyrhythm Video* '91; *The Learn to Play the Drumset Video* '92. Books: *Learn to Play the Drumset; Musicians' Guide to Polyrhythms; Poly-Cymbal Time; The Hal Leonard Percussion Book.* Rec. w. Buddy DeFranco (Choice); Buddy Tate (Sack). CDs: Timel.; Sack.; w. Menza (Sack.).

MAGNARELLI, JOE (JOSEPH ANTHONY), tpt, fl; b. Syracuse, NY, 1/19/60. Started work in Syracuse area w. local gps.; nat'l tours w. show bands for *Ain't Misbehavin'* and *A Chorus Line*. Worked w. Lionel Hampton 1987–9; Jack McDuff '89–94. Currently pl. w. Buddy Rich Orch.; Toshiko Akiyoshi; Vanguard Orch; Maria Schneider; NY Hardbop Qnt. Frequent tours w. Hampton and Akiyoshi to Eur. and Japan fr. '87; So. Amer. '92; China '95. Favs: Armstrong, Fats Navarro, Clifford Brown, Roy Eldridge, Tom Harrell. CDs: CC; Magnarelli–J. Swana (CC); w. NY Hardbop Qnt. (TCB); Hampton (Glad Hamp); Akiyoshi (Col.; RCA); McDuff (Conc.); Ben Wolfe (Mons); *Burnin' for Buddy* (Atl.).

MAGNUSSON, BOB (WILLIAM (ROBERT)), bs; b. NYC, 2/24/47. Father, Dan, was principal cl. for San Diego Symph. for 30 yrs; moth. taught and pl. pno. He stud. pno., French horn, gtr., and bs. for many yrs. bef. settling on acoustic bs. Worked in LA area since late 1960s; pl. w. Buddy Rich; Sarah Vaughan; Art Pepper; Joe Farrell; Mike Wofford; Benny Golson; Linda Ronstadt–Nelson Riddle; Natalie Cole. App. in Eur., So. Amer., Japan, and Austral. Versatile, he has also worked w. the San Diego Symph. and pl. in such films as *Dick Tracy* and *Sharkey's Machine*. TV: PBS *Club Date* series w. Joe Pass; Bud Shank; Laurindo Almeida; Hank Jones; Kenny Barron; Grammy show w. Pepper Adams. Teaches priv. and, fr. '77, at the Musicians Institute in LA. CDs: w. Bud Shank (Cand.); John Klemmer (BB); Mundell Lowe (JA); Pepper (Story.; Laser.); Bill Perkins (Story.); Mavis Rivers (Delos); Golson (Timel.); Corea (Stretch); Shorty Rogers (Conc.); Richie Cole (Muse); Holly Hofmann (Capri).

MAHOGANY, KEVIN BRYANT, voc, bari sax, cl, comp; b. Kansas City, MO, 7/30/58. Began on cl. in grade sch. Stud. sax in hs w. Ahmad Aladeen of Charlie Parker Foundation. Stud. voice at Baker U. (Kansas) w. William Gaeddert. First gigs on sax w. Eddie Baker's New Breed Orch. early 1970s. Formed jazz choir at Baker U. '81. Sang w. r&b gp., Robinson Pike '82; w. own r&b gp., Mahogany '84–7; w. r&b gp., The Apollos '87–90. Re-formed Mahogany as jazz/r&b gp. '90–2. Solo career as jazz vocalist fr. '93. Hosts annual fundraiser for KC Musicians' Emergency Fund. Has an expansive, powerful, deep voice. App. in Robert Altman film *Kansas City* and at Carnegie Hall concert *Eastwood After Hours* '96. A blues and ballad interpreter whose style lies somewhere between Joe Turner and Joe Williams, Mahogany also uses scat singing to advantage. Favs: Jon Hendricks, Al Jarreau, George Benson, Joe Williams. TV: In 1998 he was the subject of a *CBS Sunday Morning* segment. Polls: *DB* TDWR '94. Fests: Red Sea and Eur. fests as lead. fr. '93. CDs: Enja; WB; w. Elvin Jones (Enja); Marlena Shaw (Conc.); T. S. Monk (N2K); *Eastwood After Hours* (Malpaso).

MAHONES, GILDO, pno; b. NYC, 6/2/29. First important prof. gig w. Milt Jackson at Minton's; army 1951–3; then pl. w. Lester Young '53–6; Les Jazz Modes '57–8, Sonny Stitt, et al. Joined L,H&R '59, remained until '64. Dur. the '60s he backed other singers, incl. O. C. Smith '66; later was mus. dir. for Lou Rawls for three and a half yrs. Worked many LA clubs w. own trio and as sideman for Joe Williams; Jimmy Witherspoon; Esther Philips; King Pleasure; Leon Thomas; Sonny Stitt; Art Farmer; and others. Pl. w. Benny Carter in Japan '73 and occ. thereafter;

toured Middle East mid '70s. Cont. to pl. clubs and concerts in LA area into '90s. Mus. dir. for stage shows, *Don't Bother Me I Can't Cope* and *Charlatan*. CDs: w. L,H&R (BB); Charlie Rouse (Biog.); Joe Turner (Pab.); Booker Ervin; Ted Curson (Prest.); Lorez Alexandria (Muse); L. Young (Verve).

MAIDEN, WILLIE (WILLIAM RALPH), tnr, bari sax, cl, pno, comp, arr; b. Detroit, MI, 3/12/28; d. Los Angeles, CA, 5/29/76. Started pno. stud. at 5, saxes at 11. Worked w. local bands while in jr. hs; began pl. prof. in 1950 w. Will Osborne, then w. Johnny Pineapple and Perez Prado. Start. writing for Maynard Ferguson's band in '52; join. the band as its tnr. sax soloist in '56; cont. to write and/or pl. for Ferguson until '66; worked w. Charlie Barnet and pl. casual gigs in So. Calif. '66–9; also part-time teacher at Cerritos Jr. Coll. Arr. and bari. sax w. Stan Kenton orch. '69–73; assoc. profess. of contemp. comp. at U. of Maine at Augusta '73–4. A hard-swinging soloist w. strong connections to Stan Getz and the Four Brothers style of tnr. playing, his arrs. were bright and brassy, making full use of the aggressive power of the Ferguson and Kenton ensembles. LP: w. Kenton. CDs: w. Ferguson (BB; Roul.; Mos.).

MAINI, JOE (JOSEPH JR.), alto and tnr saxes, cl, fl; b. Providence, RI, 2/8/30; d. Los Angeles, CA, 5/8/64. Came from a musical family; fath. a gtrst, bro. pl. mand., specializing in Italian folk mus.; studied alto sax w. Joe Piacitelli. Tour. w. bands of Alvino Rey and Johnny Bothwell 1948; Claude Thornhill '51, dur. which time he was given a tnr. sax by Charlie Parker. Moved to Hollywood in early '50s; app. w. Dan Terry orch. in short film, *Birth of a Band* '55, and pl. on soundtrack of *I Want To Live*; gigged in late '50s and early '60s w. Jack Sheldon; Lorraine Geller; Terry Gibbs bb.; Shelly Manne; and Gerald Wilson bb. Powerfully infl. by Charlie Parker, Maini never quite had the chance to fulfill his potential bef. he shot himself to death in a game of Russian roulette. CDs: w. Clifford Brown (Em.); Manne; Gibbs (Cont.); Kenny Drew (BN); Jimmy Knepper in *The Complete Debut Recordings*; *The Debut Records Story* (Deb.).

MAINIERI, MIKE (MICHAEL T. JR.), vib, kybds, dms, arr; b. Bronx, NY, 7/4/38. Grandfather pl. Fr. horn w. Philharm.; fath. and uncle tap dancers; many other perfs. and mus. in family. Stud. priv. w. Phil Kraus and others. Pl. at nightly jam sess. at home fr. age 12 and w. own trio on Paul Whiteman radio show in Phila. 1952; then tour. w. Whiteman Orch. Briefly att. Juilliard, then pl. and arr. for Buddy Rich '56–62. Freelanced w. Billie Holiday, Benny Good-

man, Coleman Hawkins, Wes Montgomery late '50s-60s. Pl. w. Jeremy Steig in Jeremy & The Satyrs '62. Mainieri earned his rep. as a sess. mus., and in the late '60s form. White Elephant, a jazz-rock band made up of top studio mus., which stayed together until '72. In '79, he founded the acclaimed fusion gp. Steps Ahead, whose personnel has incl. Michael Brecker; Steve Gadd; Eddie Gomez; Don Grolnick; Peter Erskine; Chuck Loeb; Warren Bernhardt; Mike Stern; Eliane Elias. Mid-'90 gp. incl. Alex Foster, Rachel Z., Billy Kilson. In recent yrs. he has been active as a rec. prod. and comp. of TV and film mus. while serving as head of A&R for Centerfield Prods. Start. own NYC Recs. '92. Pl. synthivibe, which clarifies the sound of the vib. electronically. A true eclectic who doesn't forget his jazz roots. His *American Diary* (NYC), explores works by Barber, Bernstein, Copland, Ives, Sessions, Wm. Grant Still, Cage, and Zappa. Favs: Hampton, Norvo, Jackson. Polls: *DB* '61; ASCAP awd. '69. Fests: Eur., Japan, etc. w. Steps Ahead since '79. TV: w. Branford Marsalis on *Tonight Show*. CDs: w. Steps Ahead (NYC; Elek.); D. Sanborn (WB); P. Erskine (Cont.).

MAIZE, BOB (ROBERT), bs, b. San Diego, CA, 1/15/45. Made prof. debut in father's band 1958. To SF in '63; worked w. Sonny Stitt, Philly Joe Jones. Tour. w. Jon Hendricks '66. In the '70s he was mainly active in SF, pl. w. Mose Allison; Jerome Richardson, Herb Ellis; many recs. w. Cal Collins, Scott Hamilton, Dave McKenna, for Conc. In '80s he worked w. Horace Silver, Sarah Vaughan, Mel Tormé. Rec. w. Linda Hopkins, Tal Farlow. CDs: w. Conc. Jazz All-Stars; Emily Remler; Scott Hamilton; F. Capp; Tormé; R. Clooney; Al Cohn; Woody Herman (Conc.); H. Silver (Col.); Pepper Adams (Just Jazz); Boots Randolph (Laser.).

MAKOWICZ, ADAM (Matyszkowicz), pno; b. Gnojnik, Czechoslovakia, 8/18/40. Family moved back to Poland 1946. Stud. class. pno. priv. and at cons. fr. age 9. Heard jazz on Willis Conover VOA broadcasts and became enthralled by Art Tatum. Between ages 17–18 he began pl. jazz in student clubs. Moved to Warsaw 1965; led own trio and worked w. Michal Urbaniak and Zbigniew Namyslowski; began to use the name Makowicz in late '60s. Worked w. Urszula Dudziak early '70s and co-led gp., Unit. Made US debut in '77 at the Cookery in NYC and first US recs. for Col.; w. the help of Conover and John Hammond, he moved to NYC in '78 and became a US citizen in '86. Fr. late '70s he worked mostly as solo pnst. In '89 he gave his first concert in Poland in ten yrs. Cont. to tour US and int'l in the '90s, usually as soloist but also w. bs. Jay Leonhart and pnst. Dick Hyman. His work—characterized by great musicality and impressive technique—is steadily maturing as he moves away fr. a strong Tatum infl. In '92 Makowicz was awarded NEA grant to perf. three Art Tatum tribute concerts in NYC, Wash., D.C., and Tatum's hometown, Toledo. Pl. *Rhapsody in Blue* at Pescara JF '98. CDs: Conc., Atl., Chiaro.; VWC.

MALACH, BOB (ROBERT), tnr sax, fl; b. Philadelphia, PA, 8/23/54. Brothers Ray and Ron are prof. mus. Stud. w. Eddie Daniels; John Krell; Harold Bennett. Pl. w. Stanley Clarke 1976–8; Alphonse Mouzon, '76–9; Ben Sidran, Jasper Van't Hof fr. '77; Geo. Gruntz fr. '78; Aldo Romano '79; Didier Lockwood '79–80; Stevie Wonder '80–5; Bob Mintzer bb fr. '84; Horace Silver '86; Robben Ford fr. '87. Malach has taught in Germ. at the Reimscheid Sch. for the Arts '83 and Bremen U. '92; and in the Netherlands at the U. of Rotterdam and the Utrecht and Hilversum Cons. '90–2. Perf. w. Miles Davis and Quincy Jones at MJF '91; pl. on the soundtrack of the Cosby Show '86–92; and perf. on pop recs. by Madonna; Eddie Murphy; Jermaine Jackson; Steve Miller. Favs: Ben Webster, Coltrane, Sal Nistico. Fests: Eur. fr. '77; Jap. fr. '79; Asia w. Gruntz '88. CDs: GoJazz; w. Gruntz (Enja); Mintzer (DMP); Hank Jones (Stash); Dominique Eade (RCA); Mike Stern (Atl.); Sidran (GoJazz).

MALACHI, JOHN, pno, arr; b. Red Springs, NC, 9/6/19; d. Washington, DC, 2/11/87. Self-taught. First prof. work w. Trummy Young 1943; pl. and wrote arrs. for Billy Eckstine's bb '44–5; accomp. for Eckstine '47. Accomp. and rec. w. many singers, incl. Pearl Bailey '50; Dinah Washington '51; Sarah Vaughan '52–4; Al Hibbler '55–8; Dakota Staton; Gloria Lynne; Joe Williams. Pl. w. short-lived Louis Jordan bb '51. Later freelanced in Wash., rec. LP, *Classic Rags and Ragtime Songs* w. T. J. Anderson (Smith.). CDs: w. Eckstine (Sav.); Vaughan (Em., Verve).

MALESON, BOOTS (LEON SOLOMON), bs, el-bs, cello; b. Arlington, MA, 5/7/54. Brother is prof. tpt. in Bost.; fath. and grandfath. amateur violinists. Began on cello and pno. Stud. cello w. Ran Blake 1969; cello and bs. at New Engl. Cons. '71–3; Lehman Coll. '83–5. Pl. at Wally's in Bost. w. Ricky Ford, Dave Stewart, Bunny Smith fr. '73; freelanced in Bost. w. Elvin Jones, Milt Jackson, Archie Shepp, Ran Blake, Bob Mover, Pete Chavez, Claudio Roditi, James Williams, Bill Pierce; others '73–9. Moved to NYC '80, pl. w. Ron Carter fr. '80; Jack Wilson '82–7; South Shore Mus. Circus '76–87; freelanced

w. Richie Cole; Stanley Cowell; Kenny Barron; Roland Hanna; Jaki Byard; Mel Lewis Orch; others. Subbed in B'way pit bands fr. '89. Pl. w. Daryl Sherman '99. Maleson has taught at the Henry St. Settlement fr. '91. Favs: Pettiford, Ron Carter, Geo. Mraz. Fests: Eur., Japan w. Carter, Wilson. CDs: w. Carter (JVC; Mile.).

MALINVERNI, PETE (PETER GAETANO), pno; b. Niagara Falls, NY, 4/16/57. Studied w. Laura Copia in Niagara Falls fr. age 6. Pl. in cousin's jazz band while in hs, then att. Crane Sch. of Mus. 1975–9. Moved to NYC '82, stud. w. Elena Belli '82–5. Pl. in duos w. Ray Drummond, Michael Moore, Major Holley, David Williams, etc. since '84; trios, qts. w. Dennis Irwin since '85; also occ. gigs w. Mel Lewis Orch.; Joe Lovano; Sam Noto; Don Menza; Michelle Hendricks; Joe Romano,; Jimmy Dorsey Orch. w. Lee Castle. In '90s Malinverni had a trio with Michael Moore and Vernel Fournier. Received an NEA perf. grant for '92. Favs: Sonny Clark, Erroll Garner, Bill Evans, Ahmad Jamal. Polls: *Musica Jazz*. Fests: Eur. since '85; Japan since '89. TV: *Today*; also Germ. and Japanese TV. CDs: SB; Res.

MALNECK, MATTY, vln, comp; b. Newark, NJ, 12/9/03; d. Hollywood, CA, 2/25/81. Public schs. in Denver; stud. vln. w. priv. teacher. Pl. w. dance bands fr. 1921; pl. and rec. w. Paul Whiteman '26–37, feat. on "San." App. on numerous recs. in '20s and '30s, incl. Frank Signorelli '27; Jack Pettis '29; F. Trumbauer '31; Annette Hanshaw '32–3. Dir. sess. w. members of Ellington orch. on '28 rec. Accomp. Mildred Bailey '31–2. Led and rec. w. own orch. for Dec., Col., and Brunswick in late '30s but is best remembered as comp. of hit songs, incl. "I'm Through with Love"; "I'll Never Be the Same"; "Goody Goody"; and "Eeny, Meeny, Miney, Mo." Feat. in docu. film *Bix, Ain't None of Them Play Like Him Yet*, done shortly bef. his death. CDs: w. Hoagy Carmichael (BB); B. Goodman (Dec.).

MALONE, RUSSELL, gtr; b. Albany, GA, 11/8/63. Self-taught. At 19, went on the road w. org. gp., then settled in Atlanta, working there w. local bands of every kind, incl. country. Join. Jimmy Smith 1988 and tour. w. him for two yrs., then pl. w. Harry Connick Jr. bb '90–94. In late '92 he pl. w. Branford Marsalis, incl. guest shot on a CD and on *Tonight Show*. In mid '90s, he join. Diana Krall's trio. App. in Robert Altman film *Kansas City* '96, as well as on the CD and video. Malone, who also occasionally sings, has studied guitar history and is an adept player, well versed in a wide range of styles; does not use his considerable technique for its own sake; and communicates with direct warmth. Favs: Chet Atkins, Wes Montgomery, B. B. King. CDs: Imp.; Col.; w. D. Krall (Imp.); Benny Green (BN); B. Marsalis; Connick (Col.); Stephen Scott; Christian McBride; Roy Hargrove; *Kansas City* (Verve); NY Voices (RCA); Gary Barz (Atl.).

MALONE, TOM "BONES" (THOMAS HUGH), tbn, arr, bs-tbn, tba, tpt, euph, sax, fl; b. Honolulu, HI, 6/16/47. Began on vln. at age 5; sw. to tba. at age 11; took up tbn. at age 14; sax at 15; fl. at 18. Stud. tbn. w. Raymond G. Young at U. of So. Miss. 1964–6. First prof. gig as Boy Scout camp bugler '60. Pl. sax in Miss. r&b bands '62–6; tbn. and sax. in coll. band '65–7; tpt. w. Brenda Lee Jackson '66; tbn. w. Warren Covington's Tommy Dorsey Orch. '66; Lee Castle's Jimmy Dorsey Orch '67. Stud. at No. Tex. St. (B.S. psychology) '69. Freelance w. Les Elgart, Buddy Morrow, Jerry Grey, Tex Beneke, Bob Crosby, Supremes, Temptations, Marvin Gaye, and others '67–9. Pl. tbn. w. Woody Herman '69. Moved to NYC '70; worked as studio mus. and freelancer w. Vaughn Monroe; Larry Elgart; Warren Covington; B'way shows. Also stud. at New Sch. Pl. w. Waldorf-Astoria show band, Duke Pearson '70; Ten Wheel Drive '71; tbn. and tba. w. Doc Severinsen's New Generation Brass '72; tbn., tba., sax, tpt., picc. w. Frank Zappa '72; tpt. and arr. w. Blood, Sweat and Tears '73; tbn. and arr. w. Gil Evans Orch. '73–4, off and on '74–88; Billy Cobham–Alex Blake '75; Saturday Night Live band '75–85, incl. mus. dir. '81–5; The Band '76; Levon Helm's RCO All-Stars '78. Pl. and arr. horns for the Blues Brothers '78–80; also scored film. Tour. w. Blues Brothers Band '88; Gil Evans Orch. '91. App. w. Miles Davis–Quincy Jones at '91 Montreux JF. Pl. and rec. w. Howard Johnson's gp., Gravity '96. Malone has comp. and arr. extensively for TV and film. Has led a spt. w. Jon Faddis, Alex Foster, Bill Evans; remains busy as a studio mus. Author of an instruc. book, *Alternate Position System for Trombone* (Synthesis Publ.) '74. Favs: J. J. Johnson, Urbie Green, Frank Rosolino, Curtis Fuller, Bill Watrous; arrs: Gil Evans, Don Sebesky, Oliver Nelson. Fests: Eur., Asia, etc. w. Blues Bros. Band, Gil Evans Orch. Films: *The Blues Brothers; The Last Waltz* w. The Band; video w. Blues Bros. Band. TV: David Letterman; *Tonight Show*; Atlantic Recs. Special. CDs: w. Gravity (Verve); Gil Evans (BB; Evid.); Joe Jackson (Mob. Fid.).

MANCE, JUNIOR (JULIAN CLIFFORD JR.), pno; b. Chicago, IL, 10/10/28. Grew up in Evanston, Ill. Fath. was amateur pnst. Stud. priv., then at Roosevelt Coll., Chi. 1945–7. Pl. w. Jimmy Dale bb;

Gene Ammons, Lee Konitz, Gene Wright in Chi. '46–7; Ammons '47–9; Lester Young '49–50; Ammons '50–1. Drafted in '51, he pl. in the US army band at Fort Knox w. Cannonball and Nat Adderley and Curtis Fuller '51–3. Join. house band at Beehive Club in Chi.; pl. w. Coleman Hawkins, Charlie Parker, Sonny Stitt, Lockjaw Davis, Lester Young, others '53–4. Accomp. Dinah Washington '54–6. Pl. w. Cannonball Adderley '56–8; Dizzy Gillespie '58–61; own trio '61; Lockjaw Davis–Johnny Griffin '61. Accomp. Joe Williams '63–5. Worked mainly w. his own gps. since the '60s, app. freq. at NYC jazz clubs. He has taught pno. and a course on the blues at the New Sch. since '88. Favs: Tatum, Hank Jones, Hancock. Polls: *DB* New Star '61; T. Monk Memorial Awd. '82. Fests: Eur. since '58; Japan since '77. TV: app. w. Gillespie; Washington; Adderley; Joe Williams; own trio. CDs: Enja; Sack.; Chiaro.; w. Ammons; Stitt (Prest.); Joe Williams (BB); Howard McGhee (BL); D. Gillespie (Tel.; Steep.); Lester Young (Sav.); Al Grey (Tel.); Clifford Brown; D. Washington (Em.); C. Adderley (Em.; Merc.); Bernard Purdie (Act); Ben Webster (Enja); Dexter Gordon (Prest.); Alvin Queen (Divox); Wilbur Ware; Eddie Jefferson (Riv.).

MANDEL, JOHNNY (JOHN ALFRED), tbn, bs tpt, comp, arr, cond; b. NYC, 11/23/25. An important comp. and arr., he pl. w. Boyd Raeburn, Jimmy Dorsey, Buddy Rich, Georgie Auld, Woody Herman, and Alvino Rey in the 1940s. As an instrumentalist, he prefers bs. tpt., but he is best known for his writing. Wrote for Artie Shaw in '49 and for TV's *Your Show of Shows* in early '50s. Tour. intermittently as tbn. w. Count Basie in '53. Wrote score for *I Want to Live* '58, first film to have jazz integrated into score. Won Academy Award for "The Shadow of Your Smile" fr. the '66 film *The Sandpiper*. Other movie scores incl. *The Americanization of Emily* and *Harper*. Mandel's TV work incl. *M.A.S.H., Mr. Roberts,* and *Ben Casey,* and he has album/CD arr. credits for Frank Sinatra; Tony Bennett; Mel Tormé; Anita O'Day; Barbra Streisand; Nancy Wilson; and Clayton-Hamilton Jazz Orch. Received Best Arr. Grammy awards for Natalie Cole's *Unforgettable* '91; Shirley Horn's *Here's to Life* '92. Comps: "Not Really the Blues: El Cajon"; "A Time for Love"; "Emily." CDs: w. Manh. Transfer (Col.); Earl Klugh (WB).

MANGELSDORFF, ALBERT, tbn, comp; b. Frankfurt am Main, Germany, 9/5/28; d. Frankfurt am Main, 7/25/05. Brother Emil is alto saxist. Vln. fr. age 12, then gtr. Tbn. 1951 w. Joe Klimm, later w. Hans Koller, Jutta Hipp, and own gps. After pl. w.

Joki Freund qnt., led own gp. on Frankfurt radio; won Germ. *Jazz Echo* poll every yr. fr. '54. To US w. Newport Int'l Band '58; also independently '67, '69. Fr. '76 to '82, pl. w. Michel Portal; '86 toured Eur. w. John Surman; Elvin Jones; Dave Holland. Won TDWR in '65 *DB* Critics Poll. He was the first tbnst. to make prominent use of multiphonics, a technique in which simultaneous singing/playing prod. several notes at once. A prolific comp., he rec. extensively w. John Lewis; Lee Konitz; Alphonse Mouzon; Jaco Pastorius; Peter Brotzmann. CDs: Enja; Verve; Mood; MPS; Konnex; Mangelsdorff–J. Scofield (TuTu); w. Heiner Stadler (JA); NDR bb (Act); Wolfgang Dauner (Mood); Globe Unity Orch. (FMP).

MANGIONE, CHUCK (CHARLES FRANK), flg, kybd, comp, arr, tpt; b. Rochester, NY, 11/29/40. Brother is Gap Mangione. Began on pno. at age 8. Fath. was an avid jazz fan who introduced him to musicians, incl. Dizzy Gillespie; Horace Silver; Art Blakey; Kai Winding. Gillespie gave Mangione a tpt. in the early 1950s. Stud. at Eastman Sch. of Mus. (B. Mus.) '63. Led bop gp., Jazz Brothers, w. bro. Gap and Sal Nistico '58–61; first recs. on Riv. prod. by Cannonball Adderley. Taught mus. in Rochester parochial sch. '63–4. Moved to NYC '65; pl. w. Woody Herman; Kai Winding; Maynard Ferguson; then join. Art Blakey. Pl. w. Blakey '65–7, then ret. to Rochester. Formed qt. w. Gerry Niewood '68; taught at Eastman '68–72. On the strength of two concerts of original orchestral mus., which he presented at Eastman in '69–70, Mangione was asked to guest-conduct the Rochester Philharm. in '70. The perf. was broadcast on PBS, and the exposure resulted in Mangione's first major-label rec. contract w. Mercury Rec. and tour. w. own qt. '70–4. Founded Sagoma Records to rec. Gap Mangione, Esther Satterfield, Gerry Niewood '74. Pl. w. Gillespie at MJF '74. Mangione's career took a pop turn following the success of his soundtrack to Oscar Lewis's film *Children of Sanchez* and his single, "Feels So Good," which reached number two on the pop charts in '77. In the late '70s-early '80s, he won numerous awards and made many TV apps., pl. the National Anthem at ball games, etc. Reunion tour w. Jazz Brothers '86. Founded another rec. label, Feels So Good, '89. Mangione has tour. extens. w. his own gps. and comp. for TV fr. '74. His many awards incl. NY Regents Medal of Excellence '84; Honorary Doctorate fr. Eastman '85; Grammy for tune "Bellavia" '77. A one-time perennial Grammy nominee, Mangione's career has leveled in the '90s. Favs: Dizzy Gillespie, Miles Davis, Clifford Brown. Polls: *Rec. World* '75, '79; *Cashbox; Billboard; Rolling Stone; Performance; Bost. Globe; NY Daily News* '79; *Circus* '79–81; *Play*

'79–81, '84; *Atlantic City* Mag. '85. Fests: all major fr. '60. TV: own specials on PBS; Dick Clark specials; *Tonight Show*; Dinah Shore; *Solid Gold; Soul Train*; Grammy awards; many others. CDs: Riv.; Jzld.; Col.; A&M; Verve; Merc.; Feels So Good; w. Blakey (Limel.); Jazz Bros. (Riv.).

MANGIONE, GAP (GASPARE CHARLES), pno, kybds, arr; b. Rochester, NY, 7/31/38. Brother is Chuck Mangione. Self-taught until 1961, then stud. w. George Pappa-Stavrou at Syracuse U. (B.A. mus. and liberal arts) '65. Pl. w. Salt City Six '58–9; Jazz Bros. w. Chuck Mangione '58–61; house band at Syracuse jazz club '61–2; Jazz Bros. '63–5; own trio fr. '65. App. as guest soloist w. Chuck Mangione '70–84. Feat. w. Rochester Symph. '64, '79; Syracuse Symph. '64, '84. Pl. w. Jazz Bros. reunion tour '86; Boys from Rochester w. C. Mangione, Steve Gadd, Joe Romano '89; Dizzy Gillespie '91. Led own bb at NJF '91. His trio toured No. Amer. extens. '73–82 and has perf. in Rochester clubs and hotels fr. '65. Mangione served on the exec. board of the Rochester Mus. Assn. '70–4. Has taught jazz history at Syracuse U. fr. '85 and previously worked as a consultant to the jazz progs. at Syracuse '84–5 and the U. of Maine '85–6. Favs: Oscar Peterson, Wynton Kelly, Red Garland; arrs: Gil Evans, Frank Foster, Chuck Mangione. Fests: all major w. C. Mangione fr. '70. TV: PBS *Gap's Generation* '71–2, '85; CBS *Sunday Morning* '87; many apps. w. C. Mangione. CDs: Cafe; JMI; A&M; w. Boys fr. Rochester (Feels So Good); C. Mangione (A&M; Riv.; Merc.); Jazz Bros. (Riv.).

MANHATTAN TRANSFER. Vocal gp. organized in 1972. Late 1990s personnel comprises Tim Hauser (b. Troy, NY, 12/12/41); Alan Paul (b. Newark, NJ, 11/23/49); Janis Siegel (b. Brooklyn, NY, 7/23/52) and Cheryl Bentyne (b. Mt. Vernon, WA, 1/17/54). Bentyne replaced Laurel Masse, an orig. member, who left in 1979. All four members are comps. Their '75 self-titled album garnered acceptance in both pop and jazz circles. Mus. dir. is pnst. Yaron Gershovsky. Between '80 and '83, the gp. won Grammys for "Birdland" (arranged by Siegel); "Boy from New York City"; "Until I Met You"; "Route 66"; and "Why Not?" On the gp.'s most successful jazz-oriented album, *Vocalese* '85, Jon Hendricks was feat. prominently as lyricist and singer. Spinoff albums by members of the gp. incl. Bentyne's *Something Cool* (Col.) and Siegel's *Short Stories* (Atl.). The qt. won several *DB* awards as No. 1 voc. gp. Predicated on jazz vocalese, Manhattan Transfer encompasses bop, swing, fusion, and a little bit of everything and has a tendency toward slickness. CDs: Atl.; Col.

MANN, HERBIE (Herbert Jay Solomon), fl, tnr sax, cl, comp; b. Brooklyn, NY, 4/16/30. Began on cl. at age 9. Pl. in army band in Trieste 1950–3. Pl. w. Mat Mathews '53–4; Pete Rugolo '54. Comp. and dir. mus. for TV dramas; also tour. Eur. as single '56. Freelanced in Calif. '57. Formed Afro Jazz Sxt. in NYC '59; US St. Dept. tour of Africa '59–60. After touring Brazil in '61, Mann revamped his gp. and introduced elements of Brazilian mus. into his style. Had hit w. "Comin' Home Baby" on LP, *Herbie Mann at the Village Gate* '62. Tour. Brazil again '62–3; Japan '64. Formed new gp. w. two tbns. and flg.; scored another major commercial success w. live rec. fr. the '65 NJF. Throughout the late '60s, Mann cont. to experiment w. elements of Afro-Latin, Brazilian, and Middle Eastern mus., as well as w. r&b and rock styles. Rec. as lead. w. Memphis r&b sess. mus. '69; rock gtrst. Duane Allman '71. Prod. sessions w. Ron Carter, Miroslav Vitous, and Attila Zoller for own label Embryo, distrib. by Atl. '70. In '73 Mann's gp., Family of Mann, feat. Pat Rebillot, David Newman. Rec. in Eng. w. British rock mus. '74, then w. Jamaican saxist Tommy McCook. Had disco hit w. "Hi-Jack" '75. After twenty yrs. and fifty-two albums, Mann left the Atl. label in '79; started own label Herbie Mann Music '81. Perf. as unaccomp. soloist, also in duo w. Nana Vasconelos '80. Led qt. '80–2; Flute Summit w. David Newman, Dave Valentin '83–4; NY Samba Band '84; Jasil Brazz fr. '85. Mann moved to Santa Fe, New Mex., in '89. Form. another rec. label, Kokopelli '92 but later shifted several of the prods. to the Lightyear label. Favs: Frank Wess, William Kincaid, Harry Klee. Polls: *DB* '57–9, '66–70. Fests: all major. CDs: Light.; Koko.; Chesky; Gaia; Beth.; Atl.; Verve; Sav.; Prest.; NJ; Riv.; w. Sarah Vaughan (Merc.; Em.); Carmen McRae (Dec.; Beth.); Chet Baker; Billy Taylor; PJ Jones (Riv.); Clifford Brown (Em.); Art Blakey (BN); Q. Jones (Imp.); D. Valentin (GRP); Jackie and Roy (Koch); Hank Jones; O. Pettiford (Sav.).

MANNE, SHELLY (SHELDON), dms, comp; b. NYC, 6/11/20; d. Los Angeles, CA, 9/26/84. Although fath. and two uncles were percs., he started out on alto sax. Sw. to dms when stud. w. Billy Gladstone. Entered mus. business pl. on trans-Atlantic liners. First rec. w. the orch. of tbnst. Bobby Byrne 1939; then replaced Dave Tough w. Joe Marsala '40; worked w. Bob Astor '41; Raymond Scott '41–2; Will Bradley and Les Brown '42. In Coast Guard '42–5. Played on Coleman Hawkins' rec. of "The Man I Love" '43; "Blue 'N' Boogie" w. Gillespie '45. Active on and off w. Stan Kenton fr. '46–52; also rec. dur. that period w. Stan Getz '46; and worked w. Charlie Ventura '47; the Bill Harris–Shelly Manne

Sxt. '48; JATP '48–9; Woody Herman '49. Settled in Calif. in '52 and became a principal player in the West Coast jazz movement, as well as a first-call dmr. for rec, film, and TV studio work. Pl. w. Howard Rumsey at the Lighthouse '53 and Shorty Rogers '54. Perf. on a remarkably diverse range of recs. in the '50s, incl. Jimmy Giuffre's *Abstract No. 1* '54; André Previn's *My Fair Lady* '56; *The Poll Winners* w. Barney Kessel and Ray Brown '57; Sonny Rollins' *Way Out West* '57; and Ornette Coleman's *Tomorrow Is the Question* '59. From the mid '50s, he led variety of small gps. that incl. at various times Conte Candoli; Joe Gordon; Stu Williamson; Leroy Vinnegar; Frank Strozier; Bill Holman; Charlie Mariano; Richie Kamuca; Monty Budwig. App. in *The Man with the Golden Arm* and instructed Frank Sinatra for his drumming sequence; pl. the role of Dave Tough in *The Five Pennies* '58 and *The Gene Krupa Story* '59. Operated own jazz club, Shelly's Manne Hole, fr. '60 to '74; w. LA Four (Ray Brown, L. Almeida, and Bud Shank) '74–7; led qt. that incl. Lew Tabackin '77; toured Japan w. Gentlemen of Swing (Benny Carter, Harry Edison, Teddy Wilson, and Milt Hinton) '80. As comp., Manne wrote TV scores for the *Daktari* series and film scores for *Young Billy Young* and *Trial of the Catonsville Nine*. He probably made over a thousand jazz recs. and was the premiere sess. percst. in LA for several decades. Whether working w. a trio or a vast studio orch., he played with an intelligence and sensitivity that added fire, color, and impetus to everything he touched. Book: *Sounds of the Different Drummer*, Jack Brand and Bill Korst (Percussion Express) '97. CDs: Cont.; Sig.; Imp.; Disc.; w. Bill Evans (Verve); Clifford Brown (PJ); B. Raeburn; D. Gillespie; Fats Navarro (Sav.); C. Parker (Verve; Stash); B. Goodman (MM); Oliver Nelson (BB; Imp.); Chet Baker (PJ; Cont.); Benny Carter (Cap.; Cont.); Stan Kenton (Cap.; Jazz Unlimited; Mos.); L. Hampton; Getz; Tormé (Verve); Barney Kessel; O. Coleman; Rollins; Previn; H. Rumsey; L. Niehaus; A. Farmer; H. Hawes; H. Humes; H. McGhee (Cont.); Metronome All-Stars; Esq. All-Amer. Award Winners (BB); W. Herman (Cap.); Q. Jones (Imp.); E. Fitzgerald (Pab.); Rogers (Cap.; BB); A. Pepper (PJ; BN; Cont.); LA Four (Conc.); Sonny Criss (Prest.); Hank Jones (Gal.); John Lewis (DRG).

MANNING, RENÉE, voc; b. Brooklyn, NY, 2/8/55. Married to tbnst. Earl McIntyre. Sang and danced fr. age 3 at Fournier-Greco Sch. Stud. w. Elliot Ames; Joe Locass; Carmine Caruso. Grad. fr. HS of Mus. and Art. Worked w. Lloyd Price fr. '71; Nat Adderley '72–3; Smokers' Union (later Ear Candy) '74–83; Mel Lewis Orch. '84–9; Nat Adderley Jr.; Ronnie Mathews '86; own gp. since '87. Rec. opera, *Cos-*

mopolitan Greetings, w. George Gruntz, Germ. '92. Favs: Ella Fitzgerald, Johnny Hartman. Fests: Eur. since '84. TV: Eur. TV '88. CDs: Ken; w. Gruntz (MGB).

MANONE, WINGY (JOSEPH MATTHEWS), tpt, voc; b. New Orleans, LA 2/13/04; d. Las Vegas, NV, 7/9/82. Lost his right arm at age of 10 after it was crushed between two streetcars. Began pl. tpt. shortly thereafter and worked on Miss. riverboats when he was 17. Worked in NYC and Chi. bef. join. Crescent City Jazzers in Mobile, Ala. Later played in Tex., New Mex., and Calif.; led his own band in Biloxi, Miss. 1926; rec. in NO and NYC '27; and w. Benny Goodman '29. First known nationally as a jazz figure with the advent of swing era; rec. frequently w. own small gps. '34–7; first big hit was swing version of "The Isle of Capri" '35. In '40s he was based on West Coast, acting as sort of court jester to Bing Crosby and frequently making radio apps w. him. Several films, incl. *Sarge Goes to College* and, w. Crosby, *Rhythm on the River* '40. Co-authored biography, *Trumpet on the Wing*, publ. in '48. Settled in LV '54; pl. The Roundtable, NYC '60; NJF, NY World's Fair, casino dates in LV in '60s; gigs in Copenhagen mid '60s; Nice Festival '75; largely inactive for the last decade or so of his life. A comedy personality and entertainer, Manone was a good performer in an Armstrong-inspired style. His "Tar Paper Stomp," rec. for Champion in '29, was the first version of a riff that later became famous as "In the Mood." CDs: Collectors Classics; Class; w. Papa Bue's Viking Jazzband (Story.); own gps. in *Swing Is Here* (BB); Rex Stewart and Wingy Manone, *Trumpet Jive*; "Tar Paper Stomp" in *The Jazz Trumpet, Vol. 1* (Prest.).

MANTILLA, RAY (RAYMOND), cga, perc, lead; b. Bronx, NY, 6/22/34. Mainly self-taught; stud. w. priv. teachers incl. Lou Perez. Pl. w. Latin bands in 1950s, incl. La Playa Sxt.; Xavier Cugat; Lou Perez; René Touzet; Miguelito Valdez; Monguito Conjunto. Accomp. Eartha Kitt '55. Tour. w. Herbie Mann '60. Rec. w. Max Roach '60; Al Cohn '61. Pl. traps, led Latin band in Puerto Rico '63–9. Pl. w. Max Roach–M'Boom Re:Percussion fr. '70. Tour. Eur. and Japan w. Art Blakey early '70s; then rec. w. Gato Barbieri, Joe Farrell '74; Richie Cole, Don Pullen '76–7; Blakey, Charles Mingus '77–8; Walter Bishop, Morgana King '79; additional recs. w. Freddie Hubbard, Buddy Rich, Larry Coryell, and others fr. '60s. Tour. Cuba w. Dizzy Gillespie '77. Mantilla has led his own gp., Space Station, fr. '79. Pl. w. Muhal Richard Abrams fr. '80s; Kenny Burrell, Shirley Scott, Warren Chiasson '91; Dance Theater of Harlem '92. He app. w. Roach, Tito Puente, Mario Bauza, and Patato

Valdez at Lincoln Ctr.'s Ritual Drums concert '91. Favs: Chano Pozo, Candido. Fests: Eur. w. Space Station; M'Boom. TV: *You Bet Your Life* w. Bill Cosby, Shirley Scott '91. CDs: Red; Jazz Today; w. Roach (Enja; Cand.); M'Boom (SN); Blakey (Timel.); C. Mingus (Rh./Atl.); Lou Donaldson; Bobby Watson (Col.); Richie Cole (MM); Kenny Burrell (Cont.); Amina C. Myers (Novus); James Spaulding (Muse); Billy Taylor (GRP); Mann (Atl.); Barbieri (Imp.); M. R. Abrams (BS); D. Amram (FF).

MANUSARDI, GUIDO, pno; b. Chiavenna, Italy, 12/3/35. Father is amateur gtr.; daughter pl. pno. Stud. priv. for seven yrs. in Milan. Pl. w. Fest. Sanremo Trio w. Bjorn Alke, Bosse Skoglund 1966. Worked w. Romanian mus. in Bucharest '66–74. Tour. Eur. w. Joe Venuti '71; pl. w. Roy Eldridge and Bobby Hackett in tribute to Louis Armstrong at Sanremo Fest '71. House pnst. at Jazz Power club in Milan '70–2, where he accomp. Art Farmer; Don Byas; Dexter Gordon; Slide Hampton; Johnny Griffin; Art Taylor. Tour. Eur. w. Gordon-Hampton '74. Pl. w. Red Mitchell '74–92. Perf. at Eur. fests w. Niels H. Ø. Pedersen '74; own qt., Eur. All-Stars w. Franco Ambrosetti '77; Curtis Fuller–Kai Winding; Cecil Payne–Tony Scott '80; Kai Winding '81; Jimmy Owens '86. Fav: Bill Evans. Polls: Ital. Critics Poll '75–7; Silver Mask '78; RAI Award '85. Fests: all major in Eur. fr. '71. TV: Eur. TV. Rec. w. Gianni Basso. CDs: SN; Spl.; Penta.

MARABLE, FATE, pno, lead; b. Paducah, KY, 2/12/1880; d. St. Louis, MO, 1/16/47. Worked almost continuously on Miss. riverboats fr. 1907. Starting in 1917, he led own gp., the Kentucky Jazz Band, on Streckfus Line boats into early '30s. Cont. on riverboats—alternating w. Charlie Creath—until '40. Marable recruited fr. NO most of his remarkable list of musicians; so many became well-known in later yrs. that his gp. was often referred to as the "floating conservatoire." Among his distinguished alumni were Louis Armstrong (on and off '18–22); Red Allen; Zutty Singleton; Johnny and Baby Dodds; Pops Foster; Emmanuel Perez; Johnny St. Cyr; Mouse Randolph; Earl Bostic; Gene Cedric; Al Morgan; and Jimmy Blanton. Despite his reputation, Marable only rec. two titles w. his band: "Frankie and Johnny" and "Pianoflage" (OK) '24. He died of pneumonia.

MARABLE, LARANCE (LAWRENCE NORMAN), dms; b. Los Angeles, CA, 5/21/29. Self-taught; fath. a pnst. Prof. debut 1947; many gigs w. Charlie Parker; Stan Getz; Zoot Sims; Hampton Hawes; Dexter Gordon; Chet Baker; Wardell Gray. Briefly w. George Shearing's bb '59. Relatively inactive in '60s and early '70s, he perf. w. Supersax '76 and later w. Frank Rosolino; Joe Farrell; Victor Feldman. Extensive freelancing in LA in '80s and '90s, incl. Lighthouse All-Stars. One of the first modern dmrs. to establish himself on the West Coast in the bebop era, Marable, who became a member of Charlie Haden's Quartet West in '92, has kept pace with changing times. CDs: BN; w. Charlie Haden; Anita O'Day (Verve); Teddy Edwards; Frank Morgan (Cont.); Chet Baker; Groove Holmes (PJ); Walter Norris (Conc.); Shorty Rogers (Cand.); Hampton Hawes–Freddie Redd; Wardell Gray (Prest.).

MARANO, NANCY FAITH, voc, pno; b. Weehawken, NJ, 1/24/45. Father, prof. pnst.; moth., singer; sisr., opera coach. Stud. pno. w. father, later w. Juilliard teacher; pno. and voc. at Manh. Sch. of Mus. First gigs w. father's band as teenager. Sang w. bbs, incl. Cab Calloway 1980; Bob Rosengarden '84; Lew Anderson; Dick Johnson; Dick Cone; Sal Salvador. Sang in duo w. Eddie Monteiro fr. '83 to '95; Dave McKenna; also w. combos, incl. Charlie Byrd; Stephane Grappelli; Remo Palmieri; Artie Baker. Led own gps. w. Harold Danko; Don Friedman; Steve Kuhn; Derek Smith; Tom Harrell. Marano has taught at Mannes Coll. of Mus. '87–91; Manh. Sch. of Mus. fr. '88. Summer voc. clinics w. Manh. Sch. faculty, Italy in mid '90s. Favs: Sarah Vaughan, Ella Fitzgerald, Frank Sinatra. Polls: *Backstage* Mag. Bistro Award. Fests: Eur. fr. '90; w. Benny Carter at Charlie Parker Fest., NYC '97. CDs: Marano–Monteiro (Perfect Sound, Den); Marano–Manny Albam (TMD); w. Benny Carter (MM); Dick Hyman (Ref.).

MARCUS, STEVE (STEPHEN DAVID), tnr, sop saxes; b. NYC, 9/18/39; d. New Hope, PA, 9/25/05. Studied w. Bill Sheiner 1955–9; at Berklee Coll. of Mus. '59–61; rec. w. Gary Burton. Pl. w. Stan Kenton '62–3. Moved back to NYC '64; pl. w. Donald Byrd '65; rec. *Tennessee Firebird* w. Burton '66; pl. w. Woody Herman off and on fr. '67; Herbie Mann '67–70; Larry Coryell '70–3; own gp. Count's Rock Band '73–5; Buddy Rich fr. '75 as feat. soloist; also own gps. fr. '76. When Rich died in '87, assumed leadership of band while cont. to lead own gps. In '95 the Rich band rec. *Burnin' for Buddy* in 2 vols. w. many guest drmrs., incl. sess. organizer Neal Peart, Rich (via tape), Max Roach, Joe Morello, Steve Gadd, Ed Shaughnessy, and Dave Weckl. Marcus was a hot, hard-swinging player. Favs: Coltrane, Getz, Rollins. Fests: all major fr. '63. TV: Johnny Carson, Mike Douglas, Merv Griffin, etc. CDs: Red Brn.; *Burnin' for Buddy* (Atl.); w. Lionel Hampton (Tel.); *Lionel Hampton Presents Buddy Rich* (Kingdom GATE); Jazz Composers Orch. (JCOA).

MARDIGAN, ART (ARTHUR), dms; b. Detroit, MI, 2/12/23; d. Detroit, 6/6/77. Played w. Tommy Reynolds 1942; army service '43–4. Worked w. Georgie Auld '45. Dur. the next five yrs., he was very active on the NYC scene, pl. and/or rec. w. Charlie Parker; Allen Eager; Dexter Gordon; Kai Winding; Wardell Gray, and Fats Navarro. In early '50s he tour. w. Woody Herman, Pete Rugolo. Led sxt., incl. Al Cohn, for tracks in *The Jazz School* on Wing label '54; also pl. and rec. w. Stan Getz '54; then moved back to Det. Rec. w. Jack Brokensha '63; worked w. Getz again late '70s. Infl: Max Roach. CDs: w. Gordon; Navarro (Sav.); Gray; Jimmy Raney (Prest.); Getz; Herman (Verve); Chris Connor (Beth.).

MARES, PAUL JOSEPH, tpt, lead; b. New Orleans, LA, 6/15/1900; d. Chicago, IL, 8/18/49. Self-taught. Worked Miss. riverboat, SS *Capitol*, in his teens; moved to Chi. 1919 and worked at the Blatz and Camel beer gardens. Join. Friars Society Orch. (later renamed New Orleans Rhythm Kings) at Friars' Inn w. Leon Roppolo, Georg Brunis, Arnold Loyocano in early '20s. Band rec. as NORK for Gennett label in '22 and '23, incl. eight sides w. Jelly Roll Morton on pno. After NORK disbanded, Mares and Roppolo moved to NYC and pl. w. Al Siegal band in Greenwich Village. Ret. to NO and reorganized NORK '25. The new NORK rec. in NO in '25, but Mares soon left mus. to work in family fur bus. He ret. to Chi. in '34, opened a barbecue restaurant there, and rec. four sides under Friars Society name for Okeh in '35. Although he played occ. in Chi. fr. '45–8, Mares' short-lived career peaked with the NORK; the gp. is often associated with the ODJB, in part because of the parallel nature of their activities. Although some critics suggest that the NORK's performances lacked the fire and originality of the ODJB, most others point out the greater sophistication of the NORK, its superior soloists—especially Roppolo—and the infl. the band had on the Austin HS Gang. CDs: Mile.

MARGITZA, RICK (RICHARD DEAN), tnr sax, comp; b. Detroit, MI, 10/24/61. Grandfather, Bill Bandy, pl. bs. w. Glenn Miller and cello on Bird w. Strings sess.; fath. pl. vln. w. Det. Symph. late 1950s-90. Stud. vln. at age 4; then pno. and oboe. Sw. to sax in hs, inspired by recs. of Charlie Parker, John Coltrane, Michael Brecker. Stud. informally w. Sonny Stitt '78; Gerry Neiwood '79; Michael Brecker (whom he met while pl. MJF w. Wayne St. U. ensemble) '80. Stud. at Berklee Coll. of Mus. '81; U. of Miami '82–4; also lessons w. Dave Liebman dur. this period; then Loyola U. '86–7 while working w. Ellis Marsalis in NO. Tour. and rec. w. Maynard Ferguson '84; Flora Purim Airto '85. In '88 he moved to

NYC to join Miles Davis, doing summer tour. w. him in '89. Form. own gp. in '89 w. Robert Hurst, Jeff Watts, Jeff Calderazzo, then w. Steve Masakowski, Marc Johnson, Adam Nussbaum, Peter Erskine Airto. Pl. w. Maria Schneider bb '93. Tour. w. Eddie Gomez '94. Own gp., Second Line, w. NO mus. '95. Margitza often comps. in minor keys, reflecting his Romanian Gypsy roots. Has written two symphs. and a sax. concerto. Favs: Coltrane, Parker, Rollins, Shorter. CDs: BN; Steep.; Chall.; w. M. Davis (WB); Masakowski; J. Walrath; Bob Belden (BN); Andy Laverne; Dave Stryker; Stanley Cowell (Steep.); E. Gomez (Stretch); Niels Lan Doky (Mile.); Maynard Ferguson (JA); Maria Schneider (Enja); John Fedchock (Res.).

MARGOLIS, KITTY (KATHERINE), voc; b. San Mateo, CA, 11/7/55. Played gtr. in bands fr. ages 12 to 22 incl. Western swing band in Cambridge, Mass. 1973. After ret. to SF in '76, she join. 12-voice a cappella gp., Jazzmouth. Start. solo career in '78. Gp. w. Joyce Cooling '80–6, sidemen incl. Eddie Henderson, Pee Wee Ellis. Since '86 Margolis has led trios; tour. Holland, France, Germ. and Japan '91; and become fixture in SF Bay area. Her bop-oriented style mixes elements of Anita O'Day and Betty Carter w. her own infectious personality. Fests: Lionel Hampton JF at U. of Idaho often in '90s. Favs: Mark Murphy, Sarah Vaughan, L, H&R. CDs: Mad-Kat.

MARGOLIS, SAM (SAMUEL D.), tnr sax, cl; b. Dorchester, MA, 11/1/23; d. Deerfield Beach, FL, 3/20/96. Brother a classical critic and comp. Principally self-taught, first on cl. then tnr. Infl. by Louis Armstrong, Bud Freeman, Lester Young. Pl. w. combos around Bost., incl. Vic Dickenson; Shad Collins; Bobby Hackett; Rex Stewart; and Nat Pierce. Friend and roommate of Ruby Braff w. whom he rec. in Bost. 1954 and app. at the '57 NJF. In '58. after working w. Braff in NYC, he ret. to Bost., where he cont. to pl. into the mid '80s. Moved to Fla., worked locally. Favs: Freeman, Young, Babe Russin, Ben Webster. CDs: w. Braff (Jazz Connoisseur; BL; Aff.).

MARGULIS, CHARLIE (CHARLES A.), tpt; b. Minneapolis, MN, 6/24/03; d. Little Falls, MN, 4/24/67. First worked in local movie theatres; then to Det., pl. w. Jean Goldkette's Orch. led by Joe Venuti 1924. Tour. w. Paul Whiteman '27–30. After recovering fr. a serious illness, he worked in NYC studios w. Dorsey Bros. et al. Led own band briefly '37; join. Glenn Miller '38; also ran own chicken farm late '30s. Worked in Calif. '41; back in NYC '42 freelancing for the balance of his career. CDs: Artie Shaw (BB).

MARIANO, CHARLIE (CHARLES HUGO), alto sax, nagasuram; b. Boston, MA, 11/12/23. Studied at Schillinger House, Bost. for three yrs. in mid 1940s. Pl. w. Shorty Sherock '48; Larry Clinton and Nat Pierce '49–50; Chubby Jackson–Bill Harris '53; Stan Kenton Orch. '53–5; Shelly Manne in LA '56–8. Ret. to Bost. '58; pl. w. Herb Pomeroy. Pl. w. Kenton '58–9. Married to Toshiko Akiyoshi '59–late '60s. Led qt. w. Akiyoshi '60–7. Pl. and rec. w. Charles Mingus '62–3; CD reissue of Town Hall concert on Blue Note wrongly attributes Charles McPherson's solos on "My Search" and at the end of "Epitaph" (pt. 1, alternate take) to him. He lived in Japan '63–4. Taught at Berklee Sch. of Mus. '65–6. Lived in Malaysia, spons. by USIS, teaching mus. to members of state radio orch. '66–7. Perf. and rec. in Japan summer '67. Taught at Berklee '67–8. Formed jazz-rock gp. Osmosis '67. Moved to Belgium, formed gp., Ambush '71. Rec. in US for Atl. label late '71; then pl. for the play *Marat/Sade* for four mos. in Zurich '72. Stud. nagasuram (wooden fl. w. an oboe-like sound) for four mos. in India '73. Tour. Eur. w. Dutch pop gp., Supersister. Pl. and rec. in Finland, then join. Germ. pop gp., Embryo '73. Led Pork Pie w. Philip Catherine, Jasper van't Hof at Eur. fests '73–5. Lived in The Hague, Netherlands, for most of '75, then ret. to US to teach again at Berklee. Pl. w. Eberhard Weber '75–80; United Jazz and Rock Ens. '75–93. Since late '80s feat. w. singer/songwriter Konstantin Wecker. Cont. to lead own gps. An early disciple of Charlie Parker with his own identifying characteristics, Mariano's geographical odyssey has has taken him on a musically evolutionary one as well. He is still capable of harking back as he did w. Kenton reunion band in Engl. '87. Fest: w. Wolfgang Dauner at Red Sea JF, Israel '94. CDs: Prest.; FS; Lip.; ECM; VeraBra; BL; Intuit. Mus.; w. Kenton (Cap.); Akiyoshi (FS; Cand.); Manne (Cont.); Mingus (Col.; Imp.; BN); Elvin Jones (Imp.); Serge Chaloff (Mos.; BL); Vince Mendoza (Act); Jackie & Roy (Koch); Edward Vesala; Weber (ECM); Dauner (Mood); Catherine (CMP); Rabih Abu-Khalil (Enja); Mike Gibbs (Ah Um); Harvie Swartz (Gram.); Q. Jones (Imp.); MJQ (Atl.); United Jazz & Rock Ens. (VeraBra).

MARICLE, SHERRIE (SHARON L.), dms, perc, comp; b. Buffalo, NY, 9/2/63. Began on cl., cello. Received B.A. fr. SUNY-Binghamtom, M.A. fr. NYU. Priv. studies w. Mel Lewis; Adam Nussbaum; Jeff Hamilton; Bob Brookmeyer. First prof. gig on dms. at age 16. Pl. w. Slam Stewart 1984–7; Emery Davis Orch. '86–7; Bill Lombardo Orch. '87; Bucky Pizzarelli, Jazz By Six, Peter Appleyard bb '88; Sonny Costanzo Orch. '89; Jimmy Heath, Al Grey,

Clark Terry '90; Lionel Hampton bb, Oliver Jones '91. Also pl. w. symph. orchs., incl. Catskill Symph.; NY Pops; New Haven Symph; and B'way shows. Led a jam sess. at the Village Gate fr. '87. She taught at SUNY-Binghamton '83–7 and has been dir. of perc. studies at NYU fr. '90. Her comps. incl. bb, chamber, and symph. works. One of the founders of all-female bb, Diva '93. Favs: Mel Lewis, Adam Nussbaum, Jeff Hamilton, Buddy Rich. Polls: *DB* TDWR. Fests: Eur., Japan, Barbados, Portugal '92. Film: *Rap to Rock: The NY Music Scene*. TV: CBC *Expressions in Jazz* '91; Montreal JF '92 video. CDs: Stash; JA; LRC; w. Diva (Perfect Sound); S. Costanzo (Stash); John Mastroianni (JA).

MARIENTHAL, ERIC, alto, tnr, sop saxes, cl, fl, picc, oboe, comp; b. Sacramento, CA, 12/19/57. Early infls. Cannonball Adderley, John Coltrane, Charlie Parker. App. at MJF while in hs. Stud. at Berklee Sch. in late 1970s, majoring in perf.; pl. w. Herb Pomeroy's band. First road gig w. singer Maureen McGovern; then w. Al Hirt. Moved to LA area in '80s; heard by Chick Corea, who feat. him on his Elektric Band albums; began tour. w. Corea into the '90s. First solo albums late '80s, for GRP; also many sess. w. others, incl. Patti Austin; Lee Ritenour; David Benoit; Keiko Matsui; and Dave Grusin. Rec. *Walk Tall*, a tribute to Cannonball '98. CDs: i.e. music; GRP; w. Corea; David Benoit; Dave Grusin; GRP All-Star Band (GRP); Dennis Rowland (Conc.); Keiko Matsui (MCA).

MARKHAM, JOHN GORDON, dms; b. Oakland, CA, 11/1/26. Self-taught. With Charlie Barnet 1950–52; Billy May '53; KGO-TV staff orch. '56–9; also accomp. Ella Fitzgerald and Peggy Lee '58. Joined Red Norvo '59 for Austral. tour; then to Eur. w. Norvo and Benny Goodman gps. in Oct. '59. Many TV shows, incl. Dinah Shore; Ed Sullivan; Perry Como; Kate Smith. In '60s he worked in LA w. Dick Stabile, Frank Sinatra; also *Tennessee Ernie Ford Show*, Playboy Club. Mostly local SF area dates in '70s, '80s, and into the '90s. Rec. w. Eddie Duran; Brew Moore; Vince Guaraldi for Fant. CDs: w. Norvo (Ref.); Goodman (MM; Phon.); Cal Tjader (Fant.).

MARKOWITZ, MARKY (IRVING), tpt; b. Washington, DC, 12/11/23; d. NYC, 11/11/86. Started pl. at Police Boys' Club. Pl. w. Charlie Spivak 1942–3; Jimmy Dorsey '43–4; Boyd Raeburn '44–5; Woody Herman '46 and '48–9; Buddy Rich '46–7. Fr. late '40s he freelanced in Wash. and NYC. Rec. w. Dizzy Gillespie; Gene Krupa, Art Farmer in the '50s; George Russell, Herbie Mann, Al Cohn in the '60s; Maynard Ferguson, Gato Barbieri in the '70s. LPs:

sideman on *Jazz Mission to Moscow* (Colpix); w. Sonny Berman, *Beautiful Jewish Music* (Onyx). CDs: w. Carmen McRae (Dec.); Dardanelle–Slam Stewart; Bucky Pizzarelli–Slam Stewart (Stash); as section man w. Herman (Col.); Krupa; Rich; Jimmy Smith (Verve); Blue Mitchell (Main.).

MARKOWITZ, PHIL (PHILIP L.), pno, kybd; b. Brooklyn, NY, 9/6/52. Studied priv. fr. age 6, then at Eastman Sch. of Mus. While at Eastman he form. fusion gp., Petrus, which app. at 1973 NJF-NY. Pl. w. Petrus '71–5; Nick Brignola '74–5. Moved to NYC, pl. w. Joe Chambers '76; Jack Wilkins '78–80; Chet Baker '79–83; Miroslav Vitous '81; Toots Thielemans '81–3; Mel Lewis Orch. '83–5; Angela Bofill '84–5; own duo w. Joe Locke '84–5; Al Di Meola '85–6; Bob Mintzer '88–91; Mike Davis '89–91; Dave Liebman since '91. Markowitz pl. solo pno. on soundtrack for film *The Cotton Club* '84 and has led his own trio since '88. He is also an exp. educ. and clinician. Comp: "Sno' Peas," rec. by Bill Evans. Fests: Eur. since '79 w. C. Baker; M. Lewis; Al Di Meola; B. Mintzer. CDs: Passage; Ken; w. Baker (EMI); Brignola (Res.); Locke (Chief); Jerry Hahn (Enja); Vic Juris (Steep.); Dave Liebman (Owl); Marvin Stamm (MM); Wilkins (Chiaro.).

MARKS, DENNIS JOEL, bs, el-bs, pno, comp; b. Miami, FL, 8/1/67. Father, two uncles are prof. mus. Received B. Mus. fr. U. of Miami 1989, M. Mus. '92. Pl. club dates in Miami fr. age 18. Pl. w. Ira Sullivan, Spider Martin, Mike Gerber '86; Duffy Jackson '88; Dave Liebman '89; Bob Mintzer '90; Woody Herman Orch., Maynard Ferguson '92. Favs: Dave Holland, Ray Brown, Jaco Pastorius; arrs: Gil Evans, Bob Brookmeyer, Maria Schneider, Jim McNeely. Polls: DB best coll. ens. '87, '89. CDs: w. David Lahm (Hoedown); M. Ferguson (JA; Hot Shot); Michael Orta; Eric Allison; Billy Marcus (Cont.).

MARMAROSA, DODO (MICHAEL), pno; b. Pittsburgh, 12/12/25; d. Lincoln Lemington, PA, 9/17/02. Studied classical pno. Pl. in local bands, then w. Gene Krupa 1942–3; Tommy Dorsey '44; Artie Shaw '44–5. Moved to LA '46; house pnst. for Atomic Recs.; rec. classic Dial dates w. Charlie Parker '46; in late '40s worked w. Slim Gaillard, rec. w. Lester Young, gigged w. Boyd Raeburn, Lucky Thompson, and was on Thompson's Lucky Seven RCA session. Won *Esq.* New Star award '47. Rejoined Artie Shaw '49–50; rec. w. Stan Hasselgard, Wardell Gray and Int. All-Stars '50. Family problems, a traumatic 3-mos. army exp., and mental problems made him ret. to Pitts. in '54, all but disappearing fr. public view. Made slight comeback w. a '61 Argo album *Dodo's*

Back, and perf. briefly at Colony Restaurant, Pitts. in late '60s; never app. in public after '68. He was one of the most brilliant young pianists to emerge in the bebop era. CDs: Up.; Jz. Class.; w. G. Ammons (Prest.); Artie Shaw (BB); Lester Young (BN); C. Parker (Rh.; Sav.; Stash); C. Barnet (Dec.); Slim Gaillard (Verve); Esq. All-Americans (BB); Howard McGhee (Jz. Class.); Tom Talbert (SB).

MAROCCO, FRANK, acdn; b. Chicago, IL, 1/2/31. At 17, he won a contest pl. w. Chi. Pops Orch. Traveled with own qt. bef. settling in LA. Worked w. Les Brown and Bob Hope on TV, cruises, etc., but has mainly been a studio mus. on hundreds of TV and film soundtracks. Winner of NARAS Most Valuable Player award 1985 & '86. Rec. w. Stix Hooper; John Tirabasso; Les Brown. Favs: Joe Mooney, Leon Sash, Art Van Damme, Mat Mathews. CDs: Disc.

MARQUEZ, SAL (JOSE SALVADOR), tpt, flg, voc; b. El Paso, TX, 12/21/43. Father a singer, moth. pl. pno. Stud. at Tex. A&M and No. Tex. St. U. Join. Woody Herman 1968 (pl. on *Light My Fire* LP); Buddy Rich '69; Gerald Wilson '70; Louie Bellson '71; Thad Jones–Mel Lewis at MJF '71; Dee Barton '71; Beach Boys '71–2; Frank Zappa '72–3; Greg Allman '76–7; Crusaders '85–6, incl. Japan. tour '86. Fr. '88 he was mainly active perf. in concert, on recs., etc. w. Dave Grusin. In May '92 he join. the *Tonight Show* band. Favs: Miles Davis, Kenny Dorham, Louis Armstrong, Freddie Hubbard. Fav. own solo: "Jack's Theme" on soundtrack for film, *The Fabulous Baker Boys*, w. Grusin. Also pl. on soundtrack for *Havana* '90. On his first solo album, *One for Dewey*, Marquez revealed a strong affinity for the M. Davis style of the '60s. CDs: GRP; w. GRP All-Star Band (GRP); Dennis Rowland (Conc.).

MARRERO, LAWRENCE HENRY, bjo, gtr; b. New Orleans, LA, 10/24/1900; d. New Orleans, 6/5/59. Started out on bs., stud. w. his bros., John and Simon, and fath., Billy, a bs. who led the Superior Orch. Began prof. career w. Wooden Joe Nicholas 1919, then pl. bs.-dm. in Young Tuxedo Brass Band in early '20s. Worked into the '30s w. Chris Kelly; Peter Bocage; Lee Collins; Geo. Lewis; and John Robichaux. Rec. w. Bunk Johnson in '42 and frequently w. others until mid '50s. Marrero became popular among traditionalists dur. NO revival of '40s; tour. w. Geo. Lewis until '55, when failing health confined him to NO, where he form. his own band, occ. pl. el. gtr. CDs: w. Johnson (Mos.; GTJ; Amer. Mus.; Comm.); Lewis (Amer. Mus.; Story.; Riv.; GTJ); Alvin Alcorn (Story.); Ken Colyer (504); Wooden Joe Nicholas (Amer. Mus.).

MARSALA, JOE (JOSEPH FRANCIS), cl, saxes; b. Chicago, IL, 1/4/07; d. Santa Barbara, CA, 3/3/78. Father pl. v-tbn. Self-taught, later stud. w. symph. clst. Pl. in local bands w. bro. Marty on dms. Worked w. Art Hodes, Floyd O'Brien 1925–26; left Chi. '29 to join Wingy Manone in Akron, Ohio. Rejoin. Manone at Hickory House in NYC '35; form. own band there, summer '36, one of the first interracial combos on 52nd St., w. Red Allen, Eddie Condon, Joe Bushkin, Bobby Hackett, and harpist Adele Girard, whom he married in '37. Opened Eddie Condon's club '45. Perf. at Hickory House off and on with various gps. through '48; also led own bb briefly. Inactive in mus. '49–53, he became mus. publisher in NYC '54. As songwriter, Marsala had three big hits: "Little Sir Echo"; "Don't Cry Joe"; and "And So To Sleep Again." Began prod. recs. for a juke box co. in '62. Occ. returned to pl., incl. apps. on Tony Bennett rec. of "Sweet Lorraine" and at Donte's in North Hollywood in early '70s. As a jazzman, Marsala was an inspired, liquid-toned clst. and an excellent tnr. and alto man who never achieved the prominence he deserved. CDs: BB; Class. 1936–42; 1944–45, which incl. tracks w. Dizzy Gillespie, Chuck Wayne, Gene Di Novi as sidemen; w. Eddie Condon (Sav.; Jazz.); Sharkey Bonano (Timel.); Charlie Parker (Stash); Adrian Rollini (Aff.); also tracks w. L. Feather All-Stars in *52nd Street Swing* (Dec.).

MARSALA, MARTY (MARIO SALVATORE), tpt, dms; b. Chicago, IL, 4/2/09; d. Chicago, 4/27/75. Brother of clst. Joe Marsala. Started out as a dmr. in Chi. but sw. to tpt. in the late 1920s. Moved to NYC to join bro.'s band '36–41; briefly w. Will Hudson '37. Led his own band '41; w. Chico Marx's band '42–3; own qt. '43. Served in the army '44–5; pl. w. his bro., Miff Mole, and Tony Parenti '45–6. Led his own gps. fr. mid '40s to mid '50s. Moved to SF in '55, where he worked w. Earl Hines and rec. w. Kid Ory. Marsala's playing activity was minimized by illness for the last decade and a half of his life, but he briefly led gps. at the Club Hangover in SF and at Chi.'s Jazz Ltd. in '62. An excellent, often underrated mus., his Chi. style was infl. in equal parts by Louis Armstrong and Bix Beiderbecke. CDs: w. Joe Marsala (Class., 1936–42); Pee Wee Russell (Comm.); represented in *Great Swing Jam Sessions* (Jazz Unlimited).

MARSALIS, BRANFORD, tnr, sop saxes; b. Breaux Bridge, LA, 8/26/60. Father is pnst. Ellis Marsalis; bros., trumpeter Wynton, trombonist/prod. Delfeayo, and drummer Jason. Stud. w. father at NO Center for the Creative Arts; then at Southern U. w. cl. Alvin Batiste and at Berklee 1979–81; while there pl. bari. sax. w. Art Blakey bb on Eur. tour '80. Also, in Dec. '80, pl. tnr. sax w. Lionel Hampton Orch. In Jan. '81 left Berklee to pl. w. Clark Terry band, then w. bro. Wynton in Art Blakey's Jazz Messengers. From '81 to '84 pl. w. Wynton's qnt.; also rec. *Decoy* w. M. Davis; pl. w. Herbie Hancock on world-wide VSOP II tour, summer '83. Rec. as lead. '84, and w. Wynton. Joined Sting April '85, app. in film *Bring on the Night*; rec. his first classical LP, *Romance for Saxophone*, w. the English Chamber Orch. in Lond. Tour. w. Herbie Hancock '86; organized own gp. w. Kenny Kirkland late '86. Tour. Eur. and Japan w. his qnt., summer '87. In early '88 rejoin. Sting for US tour and rec. soundtrack for Spike Lee films, *Do the Right Thing* '88; *Mo' Better Blues* '90; in May '89 pl con-cert w. Sonny Rollins at Carnegie Hall; cond. clinics and master classes at several colls. and hs '89. Tour. Japan early '90; pl. National Anthem at NBA All-Star Game; hosted series of shows for NPR during Black History Month. Many app. and/or recs. w. Chick Corea; Take 6; Harry Connick Jr.; Sonny Rollins. In May '92 he became mus. dir. for the *Tonight Show* w. Jay Leno. Form. gp., Buckshot LeFonque, which blended rock, hip-hop, jazz, reggae, and African ele-ments and incl. a rapper and a DJ. Rec. an eponymous CD '94; began tour. w. gp. '95 and resigned his lead-ership of *Tonight Show* band. In '98 Marsalis became a producer for Col./Sony Recs. He has rec. w. a wide variety of artists, ranging fr. blues singer Joe Louis Walker and Dirty Dozen Jazz Band to the MJQ and David S. Ware. His eclectic career placed him in the forefront of the young NO musicians who came to prominence in the '80s. Marsalis's tnr. style has ele-ments of Ben Webster, Sonny Rollins, and John Coltrane; his sop. sax. style was impacted by Wayne Shorter's w. touches of avant-garde elements. Has had several straight acting roles in films, incl. *Throw Momma from the Train* and *School Daze*. He imbues both his acting and his playing w. a strong sense of humor. Has own radio series on NPR. CDs: Col.; w. Rollins (Mile.); Roy Hargrove (Novus; Verve); Art Blakey (BN; Conc.; Timel.); T. Blanchard; Connick; M. Davis; Marlon Jordan; W. Marsalis; E. Marsalis; H. Silver (Col.); D. Marsalis (Novus; Evid.); Steve Coleman (Panagea); Charlie Haden; Shirley Horn (Verve); Billy Hart (Gram.); Robin Eubanks (JMT); D. Gillespie; D. Ellington Orch. (GRP); Joanne Brac-keen (Conc.); MJQ (Atl.); Robert Hurst; David Mur-ray (DIW); GI Evans (Jazz Door); R. Rosnes (BN); Ed Thigpen (Timel.).

MARSALIS, DELFEAYO, prod, tbn, comp; b. New Orleans, LA, 7/28/65. Son of Ellis Marsalis, bro. of Branford, Wynton, and Jason. Began tbn. studies at age 12; also stud. prod. and engineering for six yrs. at Berklee Coll. of Mus. Began prod. demo tapes for his bros. at age 13; at 17 prod. his first album, *Syndrome*, for his father. Since 1985 has prod. numerous albums w. bros. Branford and Wynton; Marcus Roberts; his father; Courtney Pine; Harry Connick Jr.; Kenny Kirkland; Marlon Jordan; Terence Blanchard; Min-gus Dynasty; Adam Makowicz; and others. Also worked on soundtrack for the films *Throw Momma from the Train* '87; *Do the Right Thing* '88; *Mo' Bet-ter Blues* '89; and *Jungle Fever* '90. Along w. all these activities cont. to pl. tbn., tour. w. Ray Charles, 85; Art Blakey, Abdullah Ibrahim '88; Fats Domino, No Corporate Rubbish (a.k.a. the Berklee Jazz Ensemble) '89. His first CD as an instrumentalist, *Pontius Pilate's Decision* '92, feat. ten orig. comps., w. the title track introducing "burnout," an innovative approach to tbn. improv. The album also feat. his 14–yr.-old bro. Jason on dms. In mid to late '90s pl. w. Elvin Jones Jazz Machine. Favs: J. J. Johnson, Michel Becquet, Jack Teagarden, Lawrence Brown; fav. prod.: Teo Macero. CDs: Novus; Evid.; w. Elvin Jones (Enja); Kermit Ruffins (Just.).

MARSALIS, ELLIS, pno, educ, comp; b. New Orleans, LA, 11/13/34. B.A. at Dillard U. While sta-tioned in Santa Ana w. Marine Corps., he pl. occ. w. Ornette Coleman; Billy Higgins; Charles Lloyd; and Don Cherry. Briefly ran a night club in NO, then taught in Breaux Bridge, La.; later became house bandleader at the Playboy Club, NO; joined Al Hirt 1967–70. In early '70s he pl. w. James Black at Lu and Charlie's Club in NO; in '74 he was hired to head jazz studies program at NO Center for Creative Arts. With the rise to fame of such former students as Harry Connick Jr. and his sons Branford, Wynton, and Delfeayo, he gained a reputation as one of the foremost jazz educs. Rec. *Homecoming*, a collabora-tion w. Eddie Harris '85. In '89 he was awarded an honorary doctorate by Dillard U. Marsalis's comps. incl. *Ballad for Jazz Trio and Symphony Orch.* '82 and numerous short works. In '91 he became v.p. of the Int'l Assn of Jazz Educs. CDs: Col.; Evid.; Round.; AFO; BN; w. Nat Adderley (Jazzl.); Court-ney Pine (Ant.); W. Marsalis; B. Marsalis; Connick (Col.); D. Marsalis (Evid.); Dave Young (JT); Ameri-can Jazz Qnt. (BS); Heritage Hall Jazz Band (GHB); Kermit Ruffins (Just.); Fathead Newman (Meteor); Marcus Roberts (Novus).

MARSALIS, JASON, dms.; b. New Orleans, LA, 3/4/77. Son of Ellis; younger bro. of Branford, Wyn-ton, and Delfeayo. Co-lead. of Los Hombres Calientes. CDs: Basin Street; w. Marcus Roberts; E. Marsalis (Col.); Marcus Printup (BN); D. Marsalis (Novus).

MARSALIS, WYNTON, tpt, comp, arr, educ; b. New Orleans, LA, 10/18/61. Father is pnst. Ellis Marsalis; bros. are Branford, Delfeayo, and Jason. Studied jazz and classical tpt. fr. early age. Join. Danny Barker's Fairview Baptist Church Band at age 8; played at NO Jazz and Heritage Fest. Performed the Haydn *Trumpet Concerto* w. NO Philharm. at age 14. Also pl. w. community and youth orchs. and local r&b and top 40 bands. Studied at NO Center for Performing Arts; Berkshire Mus. Center at Tanglewood; then att. Juilliard Sch. of Mus. 1979–81. Played in NYC w. salsa bands; B'way show *Sweeney Todd*; Bklyn. Philharm. Pl. w. Art Blakey's Jazz Messengers '80–1. Toured w. Herbie Hancock's V.S.O.P. qt. w. Ron Carter, Tony Williams '81. Formed own qnt. w. Branford Marsalis, Kenny Kirkland, Charles Fambrough, Jeff "Tain" Watts; rec. first album as leader '81. Rejoin. Blakey for six months '82. Toured w. Hancock's V.S.O.P. II '83. Became first mus. to win Grammy in both jazz and classical categories '84. Broke up. qnt. after four albums '85. Co-founder of Jazz at Lincoln Center '87, Marsalis serves as the program's artistic director. The success of this program at home and int'l may be his greatest achievement. He recorded a three-volume set of standards, then a series of albums focusing on the blues: *The Majesty of the Blues* and the three-volume *Soul Gestures in Southern Blue*. Debuted new spt. w. Herlin Riley, Eric Reed, Reginald Veal, Wess Anderson, Todd Williams, Wycliffe Gordon '91. He also leads the LCJO. In the '90s, Marsalis turned to comp. extended works: *Blue Interlude* '91; *Citi Movement*, the score to Garth Fagan's ballet; *New York Griot* '91; three-section suite, *In This House, On This Morning*, premiered at Lincoln Center '93; *Blood on the Fields*, an oratorio on slavery, which won the '97 Pulitzer Prize for music, the first awarded to a jazz composer. Marsalis made a three-month int'l tour w. *Blood on the Fields* in early '97. He has written music for ballets by Peter Martins and Twyla Tharp and collaborated w. Judith Jamison of the Alvin Ailey American Dance Theatre. Keenly interested in jazz education, Marsalis has made *Jazz for Young People* series a regular Lincoln Center feature; he also teaches master classes at schools and won '96 Peabody Award for NPR series, *Making the Music*. A related PBS-TV series, *Marsalis on Music*, has been compared to Leonard Bernstein's highly successful *Young People's Concerts*. Int'l honors incl. Grand Prix du Disque, France; Edison Award, Netherlands; Honorary Membership in England's Royal Academy of Music. He has also received honorary doctorates from Rutgers U., Amherst Coll., Howard U., and LIU '97. Films: soundtrack for *Tune in Tomorrow* '89. Videos: incl. *Making the Music*, Sony Mus. Book:

Sweet Swing Blues on the Road, Marsalis & Frank Stewart (W. W. Norton) '94. CDs: Col., incl. LCJO; Art Blakey (BN; Conc.; Imp.; Evid.); D. Gillespie (Tel.); Michael White; Steve Turre (Ant.); MJQ (Atl.); Joe Henderson; Roy Hargrove; Shirley Horn (Verve); B. Marsalis; H. Hancock; Valerie Capers (Col.); D. Marsalis; Marcus Roberts (Novus); Chico Freeman (Cont.); Charles Fambrough (CTI).

MARSH, WARNE MARION, tnr sax; b. Los Angeles, CA, 10/26/27; d. North Hollywood, CA, 12/18/87. Son of a vlnst., Marsh studied acdn., bs. cl., alto and tnr. saxes with priv. teachers. First job w. Hollywood Canteen Kids 1944, followed by one and a half yrs. w. Hoagy Carmichael's Teenagers. Army '46–7; while stationed in N.J. he met Lennie Tristano. Freelanced in LA after discharge and spent four mos. on tour w. Buddy Rich. Moved to NYC in '48 and became one of Tristano's principal students and sidemen. Through much of the '50s, he worked unrelated day jobs to support his mus. activities. Rec. w. Metronome All-Stars '53. Worked briefly w. Lee Konitz '55; perf. intermittently as leader in Calif. '56–7; then to NYC. Reunion tours w. Tristano and Konitz '59, '64–5. Ret. to West Coast '66; began teaching full time '68; join. Supersax in its rehearsal days, cont. w. gp. '72–7. Tour. Eur. and rec. again w. Konitz '75–76. Also occ. led qt. in mid '70s w. Lou Levy, Jim Hughart, Frank Severino. Ret. to NYC in late '70s and cont. to teach. Tour. Eur. as soloist '82, '83. Marsh was an underrated improviser whose sonority and assoc. w. Tristano mistakenly identified him as a "cool" and "intellectual" player. In fact, his long, muscular lines were unfailingly energized—often with extremely complex rhythmic ideas. Never highly visible, he was nonetheless one of the most innovative tnr. saxophonists of his generation. He died on the bandstand dur. perf. at Donte's in No. Hollywood. CDs; CC; Hat Hut; Inter.; Zianna; Story.; *Complete Tristano, Konitz & Marsh* (Mos); w. Tristano (Cap.; Jazz Recs.); Giuffre-Konitz (Verve); Sal Mosca (Zianna); Konitz (Prest.; Story.; Phil.); Joe Albany (Riv.); Art Pepper (Cont.); Bill Evans (Fant.); Rich (Hep); Chet Baker; Pete Christlieb (CC); Hans Koller (In+Out).

MARSHALL, EDDIE (EDWIN HAROLD), dms; also rcdr, pno; b. Springfield, MA, 4/13/38. Both parents pl. pno., fath. as prof., moth. for choir. Stud. w. Joe Sefchik, Geo. Stone, Jim Chapin. At 14 pl. w. father's dance band in Springfield. In early 1960s he worked in NYC w. Sam Rivers and Stan Getz; pl. and rec. w. Charlie Mariano and Toshiko Akiyoshi '61. Settled in SF '67. Pl. w. Almanac '67 and Fourth Way '68–71. House dmr. at Keystone Korner '71–early

'80s, accomp. George Benson; Dexter Gordon; Mary Lou Williams; Eddie Jefferson. Rec. w. John Klemmer '72; Bobby Hutcherson '74–8; Kenny Burrell, Jon Hendricks '75; and w. his own gp. '77. Worked with Bebop and Beyond in SF Bay area mid '80s. In mid '90s he form. a qnt. feat. own comps. Pl. w. Bobby McFerrin fr. '94; also cont. w. Hutcherson qt. incl. Vail JP '95. Has taught at Antioch U., Stanford Jazz Wkshp., and Banff Centre Sch. of Fine Arts; served as artist-in-residence w. SF Symph. Favs: Jack DeJohnette, Tony Williams, Smitty Smith. CDs: Mon.; Timel.; w. Hutcherson (Land.); Bruce Forman (Conc.); T. Akiyoshi (Conc.; Cand.; FS); Art Pepper (Cont.); John Handy (Mile.; Quartet); Klemmer (Imp.); Bebop and Beyond (BM); Eddie Harris (Night); Larry Vuckovich (Conc.); Ed Kelly (Evid.); A. Shepp (SN).

MARSHALL, JOHN STANLEY, dms; b. Isleworth, England, 8/28/41. Began pl dms. at sch. but became more involved while stud. psychology at Reading U. Stud. briefly w. Allan Ganley, Philly Joe Jones. Pl. w. Alexis Korner's Blues Inc. 1964; Graham Collier '65–70; Ian Carr's Nucleus '69–71, again in '80s; Mike Gibbs '69–72; Jack Bruce '71–2; Soft Machine '72–81; Pork Pie w. Charlie Mariano, Jasper van't Hof '75; Eberhard Weber's Colours '77–81. Also app. in '70–80s w. Anthony Braxton; Gil Evans; John Surman; Sarah Vaughan; Ben Webster; Uli Beckerhoff qt. '90; w. Surman fr. '90, incl. Japanese tour '94. Has also perf. w. Hamburg Radio Orch. Fests: Montreux; NJF; Red Sea w. Nucleus. CDs: Hired Gun; w. Sarah Jane Morris (JH); Surman; Weber (ECM); Gibbs (Ah Um); Ian Carr (MMC/EMI); Barney Kessel (BL).

MARSHALL, JOHN THOMAS, tpt; b. Wantagh, NY, 5/22/52. Began on tpt. at age 10. Stud. w. Clem DeRosa in Cold Spring Harbor, N.Y. After hs, moved to NYC 1971. Pl. w. Latin and r&b bands; also free jazz w. Jazz Composers Orch.; Ornette Coleman. Stud. w. Lonnie Hillyer '75–7; Carmine Caruso, '79–81. Pl. w. Buddy Rich '76–8; Lionel Hampton '78–83; Mel Lewis '79–83. Freelanced w. Gerry Mulligan; Al Porcino; Toshiko Akiyoshi; Benny Goodman; Mario Bauza; Buck Clayton. Co-founded qnt., Metropolitan Bopera House, w. Danny D'Imperio '83. Revived gp. '87–91; fr. '89 the gp. was known as Bopera House. Toured US and Eur. w. Dizzy Gillespie bb '88. Marshall has lived in Cologne, Germ., and pl. w. the West Deutscher Rundfunk bb fr. '92. He is on the faculty of the Cons. Musikhochschule Cologne. Favs: Gillespie, Navarro, Dorham. Fests: Eur. w. Gillespie '88. CDs: John Marshall–Tardo Hammer Bopera House (VSOP); w.

WDR; Eddie Harris (ACT); Rich (Sequel); Hampton (Timel.); Lewis (Tel.).

MARSHALL, (JOSEPH) KAISER, dms; b. Savannah, GA, 6/11/1899; d. NYC, 1/3/48. Raised in Bost.; stud. w. George L. Stone and pl. w. Charlie Dixon bef. moving to NYC in early 1920s. Pl. w. vlnst. Ralph "Shrimp" Jones bef. join. Fletcher Henderson (and other Jones sidemen) in the house band of the Club Alabam; w. Henderson '22–29, dur. the band's formative yrs. In '30s and '40s he pl. w. Duke Ellington; Cab Calloway; Art Hodes; Wild Bill Davison; Sidney Bechet; Bunk Johnson; Mezz Mezzrow; and others. Marshall is generally considered to have been one of the great dmrs. of the early jazz yrs. CDs: w. Fletcher Henderson (Col.; BB); Mezzrow-Bechet (Story.); McKinney's Cotton Pickers; Lionel Hampton; Jack Teagarden (BB); Louis Armstrong (Col.); Benny Carter (B&B).

MARSHALL, WENDELL, bs; b. St. Louis, MO, 10/24/20. First cousin of Jimmy Blanton, who gave him his first lessons. Prof. debut was a brief stay w. Lionel Hampton 1942 bef. ret. to Lincoln U. in Jefferson City, Mo. In '47, following army service '43–6, he pl. a few mos. w. Stuff Smith, then form. own trio in St. Louis. To NYC, where he pl. w. Mercer Ellington for four mos.; join. Duke Ellington fr. Sept. '48 to Jan. '55. Was prominently feat. on "Duet" w. Jimmy Hamilton. Freelanced in NYC; rec. w. Art Blakey '57–8. Pl. on dozens of jazz rec. dates; formed The Trio w. Hank Jones and Kenny Clarke for many Savoy recs. He also worked in many B'way pit bands, incl. *Mr. Wonderful* '56–7; *Say Darling* '58–9; *Gypsy* '59. In the '60s he app. regularly on Prest. sessions, accomp. a wide spectrum of artists, ranging from Lonnie Johnson to Eric Dolphy. Also pl. in the pit for *A Funny Thing Happened on the Way to the Forum* and *Fiddler on the Roof* bef. retiring in '68. Marshall is remembered for his powerful technique and exceptional tone; some of his best work was done dur. the yrs. w. Ellington. Rec. as leader w. the Billy Byers orch. for RCA '55; and in the same yr. *A Keyboard History* as sideman w. Mary Lou Williams for Jazztone. CDs: w. Ellington (Cap.; Col.; Verve; Laser.; Mos.); Ellington-Strayhorn (Riv.); Blakey; Ike Quebec (BN); Louis Jordan (Merc.); J. Coltrane (Beth.); Roland Kirk (Em.); Carmen McRae (Dec.); Stan Getz (Bio.); Milt Jackson; H. Jones–K. Clarke; H. Jones–Bobby Jaspar; Phil Woods; Ernie Wilkins; Joe Wilder; Hank Mobley; Eddie Bert; Nat Adderley (Sav.); Gigi Gryce (Riv.); C. Hawkins (Prest.; Dec.); Red Garland; Art Taylor; Tiny Grimes; Johnny Hodges; Betty Roche; G. Ammons; Lockjaw Davis (Prest.); Lem Winchester (NJ).

MARTIN, ANDY, tbn; b. Provo, UT, 8/10/60. Raised in Hayward, Calif., until age 8; then moved to Long Beach. Pl. w. H. Silver; L. Bellson; Poncho Sanchez; and has had a longtime assoc. w. Dick Berk's gp., Adoption Agency. A fluid improviser whose warm, beguiling tone reflects some of his influences. Favs: Rosolino, Fontana, J. J. Johnson, Clifford Brown. CDs: w. Sanchez; Bellson; Frankie Capp (Conc.); Tom Talbert (SB); Berk (Res.; Nine Winds); Bill Holman (JVC); Bluezeum (Tel.); James Zollar (Naxos).

MARTIN, MEL (MELVYN KENNETH), saxes, fl, etc., comp; b. Sacramento, CA, 6/7/42. Professional debut at 16. Stud. at SF St. U. 1963–5. In '70s worked w. Boz Scaggs; Van Morrison; Santana; Cal Tjader; Azteca. Form. the gp. Bebop and Beyond '83, rec. for Concord. Also feat. soloist w. Benny Carter in US and Japan. Pl. w. Dizzy Gillespie bb; Mingus Epitaph; Keystone All-Stars in SF. CDs: w. Bebop and Beyond, incl. Gillespie (BM); *Plays Benny Carter* (Enja).

MARTIN, PETER H., pno; b. DeLand, FL, 8/17/70. Father pl. vln. w. St. Louis Symph.; moth. is Suzuki vln. teacher. Began on vln. and pno. Stud. at Juilliard Sch. of Mus. 1987–8; Fla. St. U. '89–90. Pl. w. Marlon Jordan '90; Betty Carter, Mark Whitfield '91; Wynton Marsalis '92, '94; Roy Hargrove '94–5; Joshua Redman fr. '95; Dianne Reeves '96; 4–Sight '98. Favs: Hancock, Tyner, Jarrett. Fests: Eur. fr. '91; Japan fr. '94; Israel '95; Philippines '96. TV: PBS *Live From Lincoln Center* '94. CDs: w. 4–Sight (N2K); Redman (WB); Johnny Griffin (Verve); Rodney Whitaker (DIW); J. Davenport (Tel.); The New Orleans Collective (Evid.).

MARTIN, SKIP (LLOYD), sax, arr; b. Robinson, IL, 5/14/16. Raised in Indianapolis, Ind. In late 1930s he pl. and/or arr. for Gus Arnheim; Charlie Barnet; Jan Savitt; Benny Goodman; Glenn Miller; others. Wrote several arrs. for Count Basie, incl. "Tuesday at Ten" and "Our Love Was Meant to Be." Settled in LA in '50s; moved out of jazz into pop field as cond. and arr. Also rec. three commercial jazz albums as leader. Best known for his arr. of "I've Got My Love To Keep Me Warm" for Les Brown. CDs: w. Barnet (BB); Goodman (Col.; Hep); Cootie Williams (Class.).

MARTIN, STU (STUART VICTOR), dms; b. Liberty, NY, 6/20/38; d. Paris, France, 6/11/80. Fr. 1953 to '57 pl. in and around NYC and resort hotels in Catskill Mts. Awarded Doris Duke Scholarship to Manh. Sch. of Mus. '56. In '58–9 he worked w. bands

of Les and Larry Elgart; Jimmy Dorsey; Elliott Lawrence; Boyd Raeburn; Dan Terry; Nat Pierce; Billy May; Buddy Morrow; Sam Donahue; Ray Eberle. Fr. '59 to '64 worked at Metropole Café w. Sol Yaged; Red Allen; Claude Hopkins; Zutty Singleton; Kai Winding; Hal Singer; pl. in NYC and/or tour. w. Maynard Ferguson; Slide Hampton Oct.; Duke Ellington; Count Basie; Quincy Jones, with whom he made his first Eur. trip '61; L,H&R; Donald Byrd; Herbie Hancock; Freddie Hubbard; Oliver Nelson; Curtis Fuller; Sonny Rollins. In Spain w. Byrd and Steve Marcus '65; Paris w. Jean-Luc Ponty; Berlin w. Albert Manglesdorff; Benny Bailey; Herb Geller; and SFB Radio Orch. Made Netherlands home base fr. '65–6. Pl. there and in Germ. w. Dexter Gordon; Ake Persson; Rita Reys; Pim Jacobs; D. Byas; Nathan Davis; L. Konitz; A. Farmer; S. Shihab; A. Zoller; G. Gruntz. Ret. to US Oct. '66. App. w. Chris Swansen bb at Town Hall, NYC, and on soundtrack for his film, *Tuesday Afternoon*. Member of orig. Gary Burton qt., tour. US through NJF '67. Tour. Germ. w. Zoller for four weeks. Formed trio w. Marcus and David Izenzon to tour. Engl. Feb. '68. Germ. tour. w. Konitz, Zoller Mar.-Apr. '68. Moved to Belgium May '68, tour. all over Eur. for fests., TV w. many of the mus. mentioned above and also Teddy Wilson; Phil Woods; Hank Mobley; Kenny Drew; Eje Thelin; Join. rock band of Jess and James for tour of Spain and Belgium Feb. '69. In Oct. form. trio w. John Surman, Barre Phillips and tour. Eur. Form. Ambush w. Phillips, Charlie Mariano, and Peter Warren '71–2, at which point he began working w. el. synths.; perf. solo concerts w. dms. and synths. through '73. Comp. and rec. el. tapes for Belgian, Polish Radio; soundtrack for *Description du Pain* by Brussels filmmaker Guy LeFevre. From Jan. '74 to Dec. '75 faculty member of Int'l U. of Communications, Wash., D.C., and Creative Mus. Foundation, Woodstock, N.Y.; also visiting clinician in Eur. for Paiste Cymbals. Ret. to Eur. full-time Jan. '76; working w. Surman, Phillips. Perf. w. Carolyn Carlson and the gp. De Recherche of the Paris Opera '76; also app. at Germ. and Swiss fests. w. Manglesdorff; Friedrich Gulda; Cecil Taylor. In '77 form. Mumps w. Manglesdorff, Surman, Phillips; tour. to Jan. '78 when he semi-retired from public perf. until Jan. '79. Pl. w. Zoller in NYC; Clifford Jordan in Guadeloupe; solo at Warsaw Fest 'Oct. '79. Form. new trio in Paris w. Gerard Marais, Claude Bartelemy and rec. for Marge label Nov. '79. Gp. tour. France Apr. '80. Although a volatile, explosive player with a strong personality, Martin never lost sight of his primary role as underscored in his words; "The drummer is the keeper of the time—now isn't that true?" and "The drummer should keep his ears open to what's happening around him because drums are an accompanying instrument in the first place." CDs: w. Q. Jones (Merc.; R&T); B. Eckstine (Em.); Konitz (Phil.); Barre Phillips (ECM); Rollins (BB); Valdo Williams (Sav.).

MARTINO, PAT (Azzara), gtr, comp; b. Philadelphia, PA, 8/25/44. Father was a singer. Stud. w. cousin, a gtrst., then w. Dennis Sandole. Tour. fr. age 15 w. Willis Jackson; Red Holloway; Sleepy Henderson; Sonny Stitt; Lloyd Price. Made rec. debut w. Jackson 1963. Pl. w. org. combos in '60s, incl. Jimmy Smith; Jack McDuff; Groove Holmes; Jimmy McGriff; Don Patterson; Trudy Pitts. Ret. to Phila. '66. Pl. w. John Handy '66, then led own gps. whose sidemen incl. Cedar Walton; Richard Davis; Billy Higgins. Infl. by Indian mus. in late '60s. In the '70s, Martino developed an interest in mus. of Karlheinz Stockhausen and Elliot Carter. He suffered a brain aneurysm in '80 and lost his memory. An operation saved his life but he did not resume playing until '84, listening to his old records to reclaim himself. His return to public playing came in '87. *All Sides Now* for Blue Note includes collaborations with guitarists from Les Paul and Kevin Eubanks to Mike Stern and Charlie Hunter. He has rec. on both 6– and 12–str. gtr. Favs: Dennis Sandole, Billy Bean, Johnny Smith, Charlie Christian, Wes Montgomery. Polls: *DB* Critics '69; *DB* TDWR '69, '72. Books: method book, *Linear Expressions* '83; transcribed solos, *Pat Martino: The Early Years* (CPP/Belwin). Video/Book/CD combination (REH/Manhattan Mus.) '93. CDs: BN; Evid.; Muse; 32; Prest.; w. W. Jackson (Prest.).

MASEKELA, HUGH RAMOPOLO, tpt, flg, vcl, comp; b. Witbank, South Africa, 4/4/39. First heard jazz via parents' extensive rec. collection; decided to become mus. after seeing film *Young Man with a Horn*. At 19 he pl. a mixture of jazz and African pop mus., mbaqanga, w. African Jazz Review. At 20 he was a member of Jazz Epistles (w. pnst. Dollar Brand), the first black jazz band to rec. an LP in So. Africa. Left Africa w. his then wife, singer Miriam Makeba; stud. at London's Guildhall Sch. of Mus. and NYC's Manh. Sch. of Music; tour. w. Harry Belafonte and released first solo album, *Trumpet Africaine*. In 1963 he formed his own rec. co., Chisa, for which he rec. eleven albums. Had major early '70s pop hit, "Grazing in the Grass"; toured Guinea and made series of recs. w. Ghanaian band, Hedzollah Zoundz '74. Joined the Kalahari Band in Botswana '82; in mid '80s he perf. w. Paul Simon's Graceland tour; co-wrote and comp. B'way musical *Sarafina!*; founded Botswana Int'l Sch. of Mus. In '91, after thirty-one yrs. of voluntary exile, he ret. to So. Africa w. *Sekunjalo*, a tour that feat. a fusion of musical

styles. Cont. working w. Kalahari Band into '90s. Initially infl. by Miles Davis, Masekela has also become a powerful singer whose comps. and perfs. in the '90s have reflected a rich fusing of African rhythms and Amer. jazz improv. CDs: Novus; Verve; w. 29th St. Sax. Qt. (Ant.); Dave Grusin (GRP).

MASON, HARVEY JR., dms, perc, comp; b. Atlantic City, NJ, 2/23/47. Studied at Berklee Coll. of Mus., New Engl. Cons. Tour. w. Erroll Garner 1969; George Shearing '70–1. Fr. '70s, he was in great demand as studio mus. in LA and as sideman for countless jazz and rock gps. Also w. symph. orchs. Pl. w. Duke Ellington; Quincy Jones; Red Norvo; Gerry Mulligan; Herbie Hancock; Grover Washington; Freddie Hubbard; Diane Schuur. Comps. incl. co-writer w. Hancock of "Chameleon." In recent yrs. he worked w. Dave Grusin; Lee Ritenour; George Benson; Frank Sinatra. Heard on film soundtracks: *The Fabulous Baker Boys* and *Havana*. In '91 he became a member of Fourplay w. Bob James. CDs: Atl.; w. M. Davis; Fourplay; G. Benson (WB); Herbie Hancock (Col.); Donald Byrd (BN); Joe Henderson; Ron Carter (Mile.); Joe Williams (Tel.); C. McRae (BN); Earl Klugh (BN; WB); C. Corea; Shirley Horn; Orquestra Was (Verve); Chet Baker (CTI); Joe Pass (Pab.); S. Turrentine (Fant.; BN); Washington (Elek.).

MASSEY, CAL ("FOLKS"), tpt, comp; b. Philadelphia, PA, 1/11/28; d. Brooklyn, NY, 10/25/72. Raised in Pitts.; cousin was Billy Massey, tpt. w. Gene Ammons; son, Zane Massey, tnr. sax. Tpt. at age 13, infl. by Freddie Webster. Tour. w. Jay McShann; Jimmy Heath; Billie Holiday; George Shearing. From mid 1950s he devoted most of his time to comp.; some of his works were rec. by McCoy Tyner; Jackie McLean; Freddie Hubbard; and others. Closely assoc. w. Archie Shepp fr. '69, tour. Eur. and No. Africa w. him. Comps: "Nakatini Suite," rec. by Lee Morgan; "Fiesta," rec. by C. Parker; and "Bakai," written for and rec. by J. Coltrane. Contributed songs and arrs. to *Lady Day: A Musical Tragedy*, a play about Billie Holiday which also feat. mus. by Shepp and Stanley Cowell. After att. a preview of the show, Massey died in his home, apparently of a heart attack. CDs: Cand.

MASSO, GEORGE PETER, tbn, pno, comp, arr; b. Cranston, RI, 11/17/26. Father pl. tpt., led prof. dance band in New Engl.; moth. was concert pnst. and org. Stud. at Bost. U., B. Mus. 1953, M. Mus. '59. Pl. w. Jimmie Palmer Orch. '44–5; army band in Germ. '45–6; Jimmy Dorsey Orch. '48; Latin Quarter Orch. '49–50. Taught mus. in Rhode Island public sch.

'55–66; U. of Conn. '66–74. Encouraged by close friend Bobby Hackett to resume pl. prof. Resigned teaching job in '74 to join Benny Goodman Sxt. '74–5; Hackett Qnt. '75; WGJB fr. '75; also freelanced w. Buck Clayton; Scott Hamilton–Warren Vaché; Charlie Ventura; Woody Herman; TV and film; etc. Masso's publ. arrs. incl. solo pcs. for tbn., tpt., tba., Fr. horn; brass trios and qnts.; stage band pcs. He pl. on the soundtrack of the films *The Gig* and *Crimes and Misdemeanors* and the NBC TV movie *Sunshine Is on the Way.* Fav: Lou McGarity. Fests: all major fr. '74. TV: hosted jazz history prog. in Rhode Island '70s. CDs: Arb.; Sack.; N-H; w. Arnie Krakowsky (Seaside); Shearing (Conc.); Peggy Lee (Angel); Barbara Lea (Aud.); Clayton (Chiaro.); Goodman (Lond.); Glenn Miller Orch. (GRP); Yank Lawson (Aud.; Jazz.); Spike Robinson (Hep).

MASTERS, MARK ALTON, tpt; b. Gary, IN, 11/13/57. Studied at Riverside City Coll. 1978–9; Cal. St. U. LA '80–83. Start. own band '82, while also working as clinician and judge at schs. Best known for app. at "Back To Balboa," a Stan Kenton reunion at which he revived the concert mus. of Bob Graettinger. Masters won critical acclaim for his ensemble's vigorous bb programs. Favs: Ellington, Gil Evans, Bill Russo. CD: Capri; SB; *Jimmy Knepper Songbook* (Focus); *Back to Balboa* (MAMA).

MASTREN, CARMEN NICHOLAS (Carmine Niccolo Mastandrea), gtr, b. Cohoes, NY, 10/6/13; d. Valley Stream, NY, 3/31/81. Played in family band w. his bros., one of whom, Al, went on to pl. tbn. w. Benny Goodman and Woody Herman. Took up vln., bjo. first; gtr. fr. 1931. Worked w. Wingy Manone in NYC '35; Tommy Dorsey '36–40; rec. w. Bechet-Spanier Big Four '40; Joe Marsala '40–1; then staff work at NBC. In army, pl. w. Glenn Miller AAF band in Eur. From early '46 active in studios; rejoined NBC staff '53, remaining until '70. At one time he was among the most popular jazz gtrsts., winning *DB* poll '37; *Met.* poll '39–40; pl. in the chordal style that preceded the electric solo style of Charlie Christian. In '70s he pl. w. NYJRC. CDs: w. Louis Armstrong (Dec.); Metronome All-Stars; T. Dorsey; Glenn Miller; Jack Teagarden (BB).

MASUO, YOSHIAKI, gtr, prod; b. Tokyo, Japan, 10/12/46. Father pl. pno. for silent movies in 1930s, then led jazz gp. at US mil. bases and later form. own bb. Began on pno., then sw. to gtr. at age 15. Self-taught. Join. jazz club at Waseda U., where he was discovered by Sadao Watanabe. Tour. Japan, Eur., US w. Watanabe '68–71. Won *SJ* poll for first time in '69. Moved to NYC '71. Rec. w. Elvin Jones '71; also pl.

w. Roy Haynes; Teruo Nakamura; Lenny White; Mike Brecker; Ashford & Simpson. Pl. w. Lee Konitz '72; Sonny Rollins '73–6. Tour. Eur. w. Jones '76. Led own gp. 78–81. Toured w. Jacksons '82, then rejoined Rollins '82–5. Formed own label, JazzCity, for distribution in Japan and Eur. '88, rec. Walter Davis; Steve Kuhn; Kenny Drew Jr.; Bill Stewart; Kevin Hays; etc. Some have been issued in US on Evidence in '98. Toured Japan after seven-yr. absence '90. Formed label, JazzCity Spirit '93. Fav: Wes Montgomery. Polls: *SJ* several times fr. '69. Fests: all major w. Rollins, Watanabe. CDs: JazzCity Spirit; JazzCity; Pony Canyon; Epic-Sony; w. S. Rollins (Mile.).

MATHEWS, MAT (Matthieu Schwartz), acdn; b. The Hague, Netherlands, 6/18/24. Took up mus. dur. Nazi occupation to avoid doing forced labor for Germans. Later sent to concentration camp but escaped back to Netherlands, where he hid for mos. in the attic of his mother's house. Inspired by a Joe Mooney broadcast, he took up acdn. after WWII. Within a yr. he was broadcasting w. qt. on Luxemburg radio and BBC. Worked w. Dutch gr., the Millers 1947–50. To NYC '52; developed contemp. jazz sound using button-key acdn. Started rec. '52, using such sidemen as Kenny Clarke; Percy Heath; Herbie Mann; Oscar Pettiford; and Art Farmer; also rec. w. Carmen McRae; Joe Puma; and Rita Reys. Mathews' albums failed to achieve much commercial success and he faded into relative obscurity, working locally in NYC before ret. to Netherlands '64. Arr. and prod. mus. for radio, TV, films. Pl. w. the Millers once more fr. '68 to '84. Fest.: Newport '57. CDs: FS; w. McRae (Dec.; Beth.); Pettiford (Sav.).

MATHEWS, RONNIE (RONALD ALBERT), pno; b. Brooklyn, NY, 12/2/35. Studied at Bklyn. Coll. and w. Hall Overton 1953–5; then at Manh. Sch. of Mus. '55–9. Pl. w. Gloria Lynne '58–60; Kenny Dorham '60–1; Max Roach '63–7; Roy Haynes '64–6; Freddie Hubbard '65–6; Woody Herman '68; Art Blakey '68–71; Louis Hayes fr. '72; Clark Terry fr. '74; Louis Hayes–Woody Shaw '76–7; Dexter Gordon '77; Johnny Griffin '78–82; Dizzy Gillespie '81, '88; since '80s w. Clifford Jordan and own gps. Pl. w. T. S. Monk gps. in late '90s. Mathews received a master's degree fr. Lehman Coll. in '87. B'way show *Black and Blue*; soundtrack of Spike Lee's film *Mo' Better Blues.* Teaches mus. theory at the New Sch. An underrated pianist, well schooled in Monk and Powell, who started out infl. by Horace Silver but developed his own voice, intelligently tempered by the post-bop waves made by Tyner and Hancock. A true master, as his recent work with T. S. Monk has demonstrated. Favs: Tatum, Bud Powell, Jamal, H. Silver. Fests: Eur., Japan, Austral. since '63. CDs: Red.; Timel.; Sack.; EastWind; DIW; w. F. Hubbard (BN); D. Gordon (Col.); Frank Morgan (Ant.); T. S. Monk (N2K); Clifford Jordan (Mile.); Renée Manning (Ken); L. Hayes (TCB); Roy Hargrove (Verve); Antoine Roney (Muse); Johnny Griffin (Gal.); Fiddler Williams (Arh.).

MATHEWSON, RON (ROGNVALD ANDREW), bs; b. Lerwick, Scotland, 2/19/44. From a musical family. Began on pno. at age 3; sw. to bs. at 16. Early exp. pl. reels and old-time dances in qt. w. vln., pno., acdn. Came to London w. Clyde Valley Stompers 1962. Ret. to Scotland, working for Herring Industry Board. Ret. to London to pl. w. Alex Welsh '64. Rec. w. Wild Bill Davison '65; Earl Hines, Rex Stewart, Bud Freeman '66. Pl. w. Tubby Hayes '66–73; Ronnie Scott fr. '68. Freelanced w. Philly Joe Jones, Kenny Clarke–Francy Boland bb late '60s, Ray Nance, Chas. Tolliver, Stan Getz, Brecker Bros., Roy Eldridge, Bill Evans, Joe Henderson, Oscar Peterson, Ben Webster, Phil Woods early '70s. Pl. w. British mus., incl. Gordon Beck, Stan Sulzmann, Charlie Watts, John Taylor, Kenny Wheeler '70s-80s. CDs: w. Tubby Hayes (Prog.; Mastermix; Harlequin); D. Humair (Blue Flame); P. J. Jones (BL); Arturo Sandoval; Ronnie Scott (JH); John Stevens (Konnex).

MATLOCK, MATTY (JULIAN CLIFTON), cl, arr; b. Paducah, KY, 4/27/09; d. Los Angeles, CA, 6/14/78. Studied cl. from age 12 in Nashville, then C-melody sax. With Blue Melody Boys, Tennessee Serenaders, then five years w. Beasley Smith Orch. Worked for eight months w. Jimmy Joy 1928–29; w. Tracy Brown in Pitts.; replaced Benny Goodman in Ben Pollack Orch. 1929. Stayed w. gp. when Pollack left in '34 and cont. as principal soloist when Bob Crosby took over leadership. From '38 to '42 Matlock concentrated on arr. for the orch., then moved to LA when it disbanded. Led his own gps., arr. for other bands and worked w., among others, Red Nichols; Pollack; and Rex Stewart. Led small gp. on radio and TV programs about the fictional Pete Kelly, as well as in film *Pete Kelly's Blues*. Many recs. w. various reformed Crosby bands '50–52, '56–57, '60, '66. In the '60s worked w. his own gps. in LA and LV; in Fla. w. Billy Maxted '65; w. Nichols '65; again with Crosby in NYC '66–67. Appeared on the Merv Griffin TV show '72; w. Ray McKinley at Disneyland '70; to Europe '72; many jazz parties, including Dick Gibson's Colo. JP; arr. and pl. on Disney film sound track featuring Phil Harris '74. An adroit cl. and an expert arr., he was a dependable exponent of the Chicago and dixieland styles. CDs: w. Pollack (Jazz.); Crosby

(Dec.; JA); Bobby Hackett (Dormouse Int'l); Jack Teagarden (ASV); Wingy Manone (Collector's Classics); Muggsy Spanier (Mob. Fid.).

MATTHEWS, DAVE (DAVID), alto, tnr saxes, arr; b. Chagrin Falls, OH, 6/6/11. Grew up in McAlester, Okla. Stud. at U. of Okla., Chicago Mus. Coll. to 1930. First known as alto saxophonist w. Ben Pollack '35–6; J. Dorsey '36–7; Benny Goodman '37–9; Harry James '39–40, writing arr. on "Two O'Clock Jump" '39. Briefly led own band early '40s bef. ret. to James as tnr. saxist in Hawkins-Webster style '41. Pl. w. Hal McIntyre '41–2; Woody Herman '42–3; Stan Kenton and Charlie Barnet '44. Settled first in NYC then in Calif. to work as arr. from late '40s to early '70s. Led own band in Lake Tahoe early '70s. Best known as an Ellington-infl. arr. ("Perdido" for Woody Herman '44) who often embodied actual passages from Ellington records in arrs. but was capable of excellent original work in the same style, such as "Portrait of Edward Kennedy Ellington" '49 for Barnet. CDs: w. Capitol Jazzmen; J. Teagarden in *Classic Capitol Jazz Sessions* (Mos.); L. Hampton (BB).

MATTHEWS, DAVID RICHARD, pno, comp; also Fr hrn, v-tbn, tpt; b. Sonora, KY, 3/4/42. Mother was pno. teacher and pl. organ in church. Matthews taught self to play by reading his mother's lesson books; pl. club dates while in hs. Stud. Fr. hrn., jazz, and comp. at Louisville Acad. of Mus. 1958–60. Stud. comp. w. Feliz Labunski at U. of Cincinnati '60–4 (B. Mus. '64). Led dance band on tour in Germany and Italy '66–8; pl. w. jazz gps. in Cincinnati '68–70. Arr. and band leader for James Brown '69–75. Stud. comp. w. Rayburn Wright, Manny Albam at Eastman Sch. of Mus. during summers '71, '73–5. Gigs at Bradley's, NYC, w. Sam Brown–Dave Matthews Trio '74–5. Led own bb at NYC clubs incl. Five Spot '74–83. Staff arr. for CTI label '75–8; arr. for Nina Simone; Hank Crawford; Art Farmer; Joe Farrell; Ron Carter; Idris Muhammad; Jim Hall; Geo. Benson. Arr. Simon and Garfunkel reunion concert in Central Park '80. Premiered comp. "La Zaragozana" on Metropole Dutch Radio '81. Form. Manhattan Jazz Qnt. w. Lew Soloff, Geo. Young, Charnett Moffett, Steve Gadd '84. Mus. dir. and arr. for Earl Klugh road show w. symph. orch. Cond. own comps. w. UMO Orch., Helsinki '90; Osaka Symph. Orch. '91. Mus. dir. and arr. for Manhattan Jazz Orch., an all-star orch. assembled by the Japanese Sweet Basil label, fr. '90. Has arr. for pop artists incl. Paul Simon; Billy Joel; Robert Plant; Julian Lennon; Paul McCartney; and has scored films incl. William Greaves's *The Fight* and Andrew Davis's *Stony Island*. Fav: Bill Evans; arr.: Gil Evans. Fests: Japan annually as guest artist, w. Manh. Jazz Qnt. or own trio fr. '83. Polls: *SJ* Rec. of Yr. '86, '88; *SJ* Combo '86, '88; *SJ* Arr-Comp. '89. CDs: PW; Sw. Bas.

MATTHEWS, ONZY DURRETT JR., pno, voc, arr; b. Ft. Worth, TX, 1/15/37; d. Dallas, TX, 11/15/97. Raised in LA fr. age 9. Stud. voice at Westlake Coll. of Mus. 1955–8. First job as arr. for Lionel Hampton '60; also arr. for singer Gene McDaniels. Form. own rehearsal bb in LA '61; sidemen incl. Dexter Gordon; Frank Morgan; Carmell Jones; Jack Sheldon; Bobby Bryant; Red Mitchell; Gabor Szabo; Frank Butler. Made rec. debut w. Lou Rawls '64. Also cond. own band on recs. w. Hampton; Ray Charles; Della Reese; Groove Holmes. Acted in play *The Last Mile*, Kraft Theater '65. Pl. and sang in hotels in Virgin Islands, Aruba, Curacao '69–72. Led 17–pc. band at NJF-NY '73. Collab. on arrs. w. Duke Ellington '73–4; subbed for Duke on tour w. Ellington orch. '74. Arr. for Earl Hines '73–4. Own bb in Paris '80–93. App. as an actor and/or musician in three films while living in Paris, incl. *Dingo*. Org. a bb in NYC in '93. Favs: Nat Cole, Ellington; arrs: Benny Carter, Ellington, Strayhorn. Fests: Eur., So. Amer. '79–91. CDs: w. Lou Rawls (Cap.).

MAUPIN, BENNY, saxes, bs cl, fl. etc.; b. Detroit, MI, 8/29/46. Extensive studies at school and w. priv. teachers 1954–62. Moved to NYC '63; freelanced w. rock and soul groups; also pl. w. Roy Haynes '66–8; H. Silver '68–70; and took part in M. Davis's *Bitches' Brew* recording '69. In '70s was chiefly heard w. Herbie Hancock; also rec. w. Woody Shaw. Settled in LA in early '70s. Rec. w. S. Rollins '75 and formed the sxt. Pulsation in the early '80s. Maupin's bass clarinet playing has been compared to that of Eric Dolphy; he also has frequently perf. on various unusual instruments incl. the saxello. CDs: w. M. Davis; Hancock (Col.); Rollins (Mile.); J. DeJohnette (Mile.; Prest.); C. Corea (LRC); W. Shaw (Cont.); Lee Morgan (BN); David Arnay (Band Together).

MAURO, TURK (Mauro Turso), tnr, bari saxes; b. NYC, 6/11/44. Father, Don, pl. tnr. sax; bro. Ron pl. dms. Began on cl. Stud. priv. fr. age 10, later w. Carmine Caruso. Began going to club dates w. father at age 11 to learn repertoire. Joined mus. union at age 15. First jazz gig w. Red Allen 1959. Grad. bs. '62, then tour. w. rock band Lou Dana and the Furys. Pl. w. Les Demerle, Leonard Gaskin, Bob Hammer at NYC World's Fair '64. Freelanced in NYC '65–75. Pl. w. own qt. in Catskills resorts '69–72. Led house band at Half Note club '73. Pl. w. Dizzy Gillespie bb '75; Buddy Rich bb '76–8; own gp. '78; Rich '79. Also pl. w. Blue Mitchell; Jon Faddis; Red Rodney;

Richie Cole; Roy Eldridge; Al Cohn. Artist-in-residence at Trenton St. Coll. '84. Drove limousine, did not play '86–7. Led a qt. and organ trio in Paris, where he lived fr. '87 before ret. to US and settling in Fla. June '94. Rec. tribute to Gene Ammons, *Hittin' the Jug* for Mile. A robust, hard-swinging player on both his horns. Fav. tnrs: Zoot Sims, Sonny Rollins; fav. bari: Gerry Mulligan, Pepper Adams. Fests: Eur. w. Rich '76; North Sea '81–2; France fr. '87. LP: *The Underdog* '77 w. Al Cohn as sideman (Story.). CDs: Mile.; Bloom.; w. Dave Frishberg (Bloom.).

MAXWELL, JIMMY (JAMES KENDRICK), tpt, bagpipes; b. Stockton, CA, 1/9/17; d. Great Neck, NY, 7/20/02. Grandfather crntst. in army band during Spanish-Amer. War, later pl. Fr. hrn. w. Walla Walla Symph.; fath. pl. cl.; moth., vln.; uncle, crnt. w. Paul Whiteman 1919. Self-taught fr. age 4; began stud. Louis Armstrong recs. '32. Stud. w. Benny Baker; Herbert Clarke; Lloyd Reese '39–49; learned harm. and theory by stud. recs. of Ellington; Stravinsky; Debussy; Ravel. Stud. Japanese at Columbia U. '40–5. Pl. w. Gil Evans '32–6; Jimmy Dorsey '36–7; Maxine Sullivan '37; Skinny Ennis '38–9; Benny Goodman '39–43; Raymond Scott '40; Paul Whiteman '43; CBS Staff orch. '43–5; Perry Como Show orch. '45–65; Whiteman '46; NBC Symph. '48–9; Great Neck (Long Island) Symph. '52–6; bbs incl. Quincy Jones, Oliver Nelson, Gerry Mulligan '58–66. Subbed for Cat Anderson w. Duke Ellington for 3 wks. '61. Tour. USSR w. B. Goodman '62. On staff at NBC '60–74, incl. *Tonight Show* orch. '65–73. Pl. w. Dave Berger Experimental Orch. '73–5; Ellington '74; NY Jazz Repertory Co. L. Armstrong Tribute band '75; Chuck Israels' Nat'l Jazz Ens. fr. '75. Lectured at the NY and Nat'l Brass Conferences. Pl. bagpipes in NYC St. Patrick's Day parade '58–64; also for *Shakespeare in the Park* '62; on rec. w. John Lennon. Solo tpt. on soundtrack to the film *The Godfather*. Favs: Armstrong, Eldridge, Berigan, Cootie Williams, Clifford Brown, Clark Terry. Films: *Powers Girl* w. Goodman; *Cabin in the Sky* w. Ethel Waters. CDs: w. Goodman (Col.; Cap.); Eldridge (Dec.); Cab Calloway (RCA); L. Hampton (Timel.); Q. Jones (Merc.); O. Nelson; C. Parker (Verve).

MAY, BILLY (WILLIAM E.), tpt, arr, comp; b. Pittsburgh, 11/10/16; d. San Juan Capistrano, CA, 1/26/04. Played and arr. for Charlie Barnet 1938–40; Glenn Miller '40–2. Pl. tbn w. NBC radio band; also worked w. Les Brown, Woody Herman while arr. for Alvino Rey. Settled in Hollywood '44; freq. pop record sessions. In '51 rec. own band for Capitol, feat. novel glissando sax section sound; its success led him to take a band on the road. In '54 Sam Donahue took over band; May resumed freelancing. Arr. for many singers, incl. Frank Sinatra, and was a major participant in Capitol's swing era revivals of the big bands. Best work as a jazz arr. incl. his charts for Barnet such as "In a Mizz"; "Lament For May"; "'Sposin'"; and the famous hit rec. "Cherokee." CDs: w. Barnet (RCA); J. Teagarden (Class.).

MAY, EARL, bs, el-bs; b. NYC, 9/17/27. Self-taught except for brief study w. Chas. Mingus 1952. Pl. w. Gene Ammons, Miles Davis, Sonny Stitt, Mercer Ellington '51; Billy Taylor Trio '51–9; Phineas Newborn briefly '59. Mus. dir. for Gloria Lynne '59–63. Freelanced w. singers incl. Carmen McRae, Sarah Vaughan mid '60s. Pl. w. Herbie Mann '65–7; Dizzy Gillespie '71–4; Joe Newman '72–3; Johnny Hartman '73; Frank Foster, Archie Shepp, Geo Benson late '70s. Pl. for Broadway shows incl. *Sophisticated Ladies* '81–5; *Big Deal* '86. Join. Doc Cheatham qt. '95. A busy freelancer w. a wide variety of gps. incl. Benny Waters at Birdland '97. Pl. left-handed but w. strings in normal tuning. Favs: Blanton, Pettiford, Ray Brown. CDs: w. J. Coltrane; B. Taylor; S. Stitt (Prest.); Irvin Stokes (Arb.); C. Rouse (Jzld.).

MAYERS, LLOYD G., pno, kybds, vln, arr; b. Brooklyn, NY, 11/11/29. Sister pl. pno. Began on vln., then stud. pno. at HS of Perf. Arts. Received B.A. fr. Manh. Sch. of Mus. Pl. w. Eddie Vinson 1949; Bennie Green '54; Dinah Washington '54–5; Josephine Baker '59–60; Nancy Wilson '62–3; Johnny Griffin–Eddie "Lockjaw" Davis '64; Joe Newman '65–6; Sammy Davis Jr. '67–72. Active as studio mus. fr. early '60s; also worked w. Etta Jones, Sam Taylor; as arr. for Redd Foxx's prod. co. '73; then join. Duke Ellington Orch. dir. by Mercer Ellington '74. Pl. for Broadway shows incl. *Bubbling Brown Sugar* '76; *Comin' Uptown*, '79; *Sophisticated Ladies*, '81. Pl. w. Anita Moore '83–4; then pl. w. revue, *Black and Blue*, in Paris '85–6. Worked w. Harold Ashby in mid '90s and pl. for the Ellington Society, NYC, w. own qt. '95. As an arr., wrote for Gloria Lynne; Lockjaw Davis; Ruth Brown; Charlie Rouse; and the Ellington Orch. Favs: Tatum, Bud Powell, Wynton Kelly, Hancock, Corea; arrs: Ellington, Oliver Nelson. TV: apps. w. S. Davis. CDs: w. Bennie Green (Prest.); Lockjaw Davis (Riv.); Irvin Stokes (Arb.).

MAYHEW, VIRGINIA, saxes, cl, fl; b. Palo Alto, CA, 5/14/59. Grandparents, parents are amateur mus. Start. on cl.; began pl. alto sax in hs jazz band. Moved to SF at age 20. Stud. priv. w. Johnny Coppola; Herbie Steward; Kirt Bradford and at various schls. Coppola gave her first prof. gigs. Pl. in SF w. Earl Hines;

Cab Calloway; Diahann Carroll; Frank Zappa; Johnny Coppola–Chuck Travis early-mid 1980s. Own gp. fr. '85. To NYC '87. Stud. at New Sch. where she received a Zoot Sims Scholarship. Pl. w. Norman Simmons; Sahib Shihab; Toshiko Akiyoshi; Slide Hampton; Rebecca Franks; and apps. w. the Jazz Nativity: *Bending Toward the Light* late '80s–'90s. Then w. Al Grey; Diva; cont. w. own gp. Wrote arrs. for Grey's Lincoln Center Battle Royale app. and his Telarc CD, *Centerpiece*. Mayhew is an assertive, melodic player on her main instrument, alto sax; she also exudes a tangible warmth on tenor. Favs: Charlie Parker, Ben Webster, John Coltrane. Fests: Italy '91. CDs: Chiaro.; w. Diva (Diva); R. Franks (Phil.); Al Grey (Capri); *Bending Toward the Light* (Milan).

MAYL, GENE, bs, tba, voc; b. Dayton, OH, 12/20/28. Started on bs. 1944. Pl. tba. in France '48–9, where he worked w. Claude Luter, Claude Bolling, and Don Byas. Best-known as founder of Dixieland Rhythm Kings, w. whom he tour. US and Can., app. freq. at trad. jazz fests in NO, etc. Also perf. w. Wild Bill Davison; Clancy Hayes; Georg Brunis; Muggsy Spanier; et al. Rec. w. Jimmy McPartland (Jazz.).

MAYS, BILL (WILLIAM ALLEN), pno, arr; b. Sacramento, CA, 2/5/44. Parents both musical. Started on pno. at age 5, then pl. tpt. and bari. horn fr. age 12. Pl. in navy band 1957–61; hotel and club date bands in Calif. '61–4. Pl. w. Bill Green bb in San Diego '65–9; then in LA w. Art Pepper; Howard Roberts; Bud Shank; Bobby Shew; Shelly Manne; Sonny Stitt; Red Holloway; Sarah Vaughan; Al Jarreau; Irene Kral; Peggy Lee; Anita O'Day; also own gps. Did much commercial studio work '74–84, then moved to NYC '84. Pl. in NYC w. Gerry Mulligan qt. and bb; Mel Lewis Orch.; Al Cohn–Clark Terry; Bob Brookmeyer; Teddy Edwards; Charles McPherson; Benny Golson; Bud Shank; own duos, trios, qts., qnts. Favs: Sonny Clark, Jimmy Rowles, Earl Hines. Polls: *DB* TDWR as arr. '82. Fests: Eur., Japan, Austral. since '67. TV: PBS w. Red Mitchell. CDs: Conc.; DMP; Trend; w. Freddie Hubbard (Elek.); B. Golson (Timel.); Mulligan (Tel.).

MAYS, LYLE DAVID, kybds, comp; b. Wisconsin, 1953. Attended No. Tex. St. U.; tour. US and Eur. w. Woody Herman 1975–6. Worked w. Pat Metheny on and off since '76; also pl. w. Eberhard Weber and Joni Mitchell. First album as leader '86, *Lyle Mays*; second '88, *Street Dreams*. Comp. music for film *The Falcon and the Snowman* '84; TV, *The Search For Solutions* PBS; and children's videos featuring Meryl

Streep, Max Von Sydow, et al. CDs: Geffen; w. Metheny (ECM; Geffen).

MAZUR, MARILYN, perc, b. NYC, 1/8/55. Danish and American parents. Lived in Denmark fr. 1961. Rec. and perf. as pnst. and dancer w. local gps. until early '70s; then sang and pl. dms. w. various bands incl. Feminist Improvising Gp. w. Irene Schweitzer, Lindsay Cooper in late '70s. Led own all-female music/theater gp., Primi Band '82-4; and worked w. Pierre Dorge and John Tchicai. Rec. *Aura* w. Miles Davis '85, and tour. w. him into '86. Worked w. Gil Evans '86; Wayne Shorter '87. Ret. to Denmark '89 to lead own gps., Future Song and Pulse Unit; also worked w. Mathias Ruegg; Charlie Mariano; and Jan Garbarek. CDs: Story.; w. Davis (Col.); Garbarek (ECM).

McBEE, CECIL, bs; b. Tulsa, OK, 5/19/35. Played cl. duets w. sist. Shirley in hs. Began pl. bs. at age 17. Stud. at Wilberforce U. Started prof. career w. Dinah Washington; then pl. cl. in army band at Ft. Knox, Kentucky 1959-61; also pl. bs. in trio w. Kirk Lightsey, Rudy Johnson. Moved to Det. '62; pl. w. Paul Winter '63-4; Grachan Moncur '64; Jackie McLean '64-5; Wayne Shorter '65-6; Freddie Hubbard, Miles Davis '66; Charles Lloyd '66-7; Yusef Lateef '67-9; Sam Rivers '67-73; Bobby Hutcherson '69; Pharoah Sanders, Alice Coltrane '69-73; Charles Tolliver '70; Lonnie Liston Smith '72-3; Sonny Rollins '73; Abdullah Ibrahim fr. '73; Chico Freeman fr. '76, tour. w. him '85-6; Leaders fr. '84. Also freelanced in late '70s-80s w. Art Pepper; McCoy Tyner; Mal Waldron; James Newton; Joanne Brackeen. Led his own gps. intermittently fr. '73. Taught at New Engl. Cons. and the New Sch. and has received two NEA comp. grants. Fests: all major fr. '60s. CDs: Palm.; Enja; Ind. Nav.; w. McLean; Shorter (BN); A. Coltrane; P. Sanders (Imp.); Dick Griffin (Konnex); C. Freeman (Ind. Nav.); John Hicks (Novus); G. Moncur; Hubbard–Woody Shaw; Geo. Adams (BN); Brackeen (Evid.); Steve Grossman (Drey.).

McBRIDE, CHRISTIAN LEE, bs; b. Philadelphia, PA, 5/31/72. Father, Lee Smith, is prof. el-bs.; greatuncle, Howard Cooper, is prof. bs. First prof. gig w. Lovett Hines at age 13. Stud. at HS for Perf. Arts, Phila., 1985-9; also w. Neil Courtney of Phila. Orch.; Juilliard Sch. of Mus. '89-90. Pl. intermittently w. Bobby Watson's Horizon fr. '89; Roy Hargrove '89-90; Freddie Hubbard, Benny Green fr. '90; Benny Golson fr. '91. Own gp. in late '90s. Member of Superbass w. Ray Brown, John Clayton. Howard Reich wrote in the *Chi. Tribune*: "He already sounds like no other bassist of his generation, his seemingly

nonchalant virtuosity counterbalanced by the deep maturity and self-assuredness of his playing." Favs: Brown, Pettiford, Paul Chambers. Fests: Eur. fr. '89; Japan fr. '91. Perf. his commissioned work, *Blues in Alphabet City*, w. LCJO. Comp. grants fr. Rockefeller Foundation and NEA '98. TV: CBS *Young Universe* '88; PBS *Edge* '92. CDs: Verve; McBride, Payton & Whitfield, *Fingerpainting* (Verve); w. F. Hubbard (MM); Joe Henderson (Verve); B. Green (BN); R. Hargrove (Novus); Wallace Roney (Muse); Ray Brown (Verve); Diana Krall (GRP).

McCALL, MARY ANN, voc; b. Philadelphia, PA, 5/4/19; d. Los Angeles, 12/14/94. Sang w. Buddy Morrow's house band at Phila, club; briefly w. Tommy Dorsey 1938. With Woody Herman '39-41 and '46-50; Charlie Barnet '41-3. Worked as a single in early '50s; briefly w. Charlie Ventura '54-5; then retired although occ. active. Rec. w. various accomps., incl. Ralph Burns '47; Phil Moore '48; Al Cohn '50; Ernie Wilkins '56. Won *DB* poll as best band vocalist '49. Infl: Mildred Bailey. Nat Hentoff called her "One of the few authentic jazz singers." Own rec. sess. for Col.; Roost. CDs: w. Barnet (BB); Ventura (Mos.); Herman (Cap.; Hep).

McCALL, STEVE, dms, perc; b. Chicago, IL, 9/30/33; d. Chicago, 5/24/89. Studied theory, Latin perc., classical perc. as teenager. Freelance work fr. 1957; to Montreal '59; pl. w. Bill Kersey. To NYC '60; worked w. Booker Ervin. Back to Chi. '61; worked w. Charles Stepney; Gene Shaw; Ramsey Lewis; and others. In '65 after pl. w. Muhal Richard Abrams' Experimental Band, he bec. a founding member of AACM. Freelanced in Chi. w. gps. ranging fr. bop to avantgarde. To Paris '67; rec. w. Marion Brown '68-9; Anthony Braxton '69-70. Ret. to Chi. '70; rec. w. Dexter Gordon; form. trio, Reflection, w. Fred Hopkins and Henry Threadgill. After spending a yr. in Eur., he ret. to NYC '75; re-form. the trio as Air; rec. and tour. widely bef. ret. to Chi. Other recs. w. Chico Freeman; Arthur Blythe; David Murray. In mid '80s he perf. w. Cecil Taylor's Unit and occ. as soloist, and w. the David Murray trio and oct. CDs: w. Chico Freeman (Ind. Nav.); Joseph Jarman (Del.).

McCANDLESS, PAUL, oboe, Eng hrn, bs cl, tnr sax, comp; b. Indiana, PA, 3/24/47. Oboe major at Duquesne U. and Manh. Sch. of Mus. Moved to NYC in 1967; pl. w. Paul Winter's Winter Consort '68-73. The gp. evolved into Oregon ca. '71; fr. '80 he also pl. in the gp. Gallery; and fr. late '80s also led own gps. McCandless had evolved into a more traditional-styled jazz tnr. sax soloist by the '90s. CDs: Access; WH; w. Oregon (ECM); Dean Peer (Fahrenheit).

McCANN, LES (LESLIE COLEMAN), pno, kybds, tpt, voc, comp, arr; b. Lexington, KY, 9/23/35. In 1956, after winning a navy talent contest as voc., app. on the *Ed Sullivan Show*. Moved to LA and form. a trio. Signed by the PJ label, he rec. numerous albums fr. '60 to '64, often feat. other artists, incl. Ben Webster; Stanley Turrentine; Joe Pass; Blue Mitchell; and the Gerald Wilson bb. Focusing on the then popular gospel-tinged "soul jazz" style, his lively pno. crossed idiomatic lines. Rec. for Limel. '65–7, then sw. to Atl. in '68. Hit recs. incl. "Compared to What," which was rec. w. Eddie Harris at '68 Montreux JF; it sold over a million copies, considerably enhancing McCann's standing in the pop field. Brought Roberta Flack to the attn. of Atl., launching her career. Worked w. Art Pepper, Stuff Smith, Coleman Hawkins, Klaus Doldinger, Stanley Turrentine, Leroy Vinnegar, Ron Jefferson, Johnny Griffin, Frank Zappa, Paul Chambers, Blue Mitchell, Zoot Sims '60s and '70s. In the '80s he emphasized vocs. and often pl. synths., diluting the jazz aspect of his perfs. A stroke suffered in mid '90s necessitated the hiring of a kybd. player, but McCann was well on his way to recovery by '97. TV commercials for US Sprint and the LA Lakers. TV: Bill Cosby Special; *Tonight Show*; Pat Sajak Show; *CBS Sunday Morning; Nightwatch; Jazz Counterpoint*; and acting role in *Police Woman*. Radio: Marian McPartland's *Piano Jazz*. Pl. every major US fest. except MJF; also app. and rec. at Montreux; and in Austral., Eur., Russia, Ghana, Israel, Tahiti, Japan, Mex., Can. As comp., collab. w. Morgan Ames; Johnny Mercer; Jon Hendricks; Gene McDaniels. Concerts incl. Carnegie Hall; MSG; Lincoln Center; Cincinnati Symph. Orch. McCann is a prolific, highly regarded watercolorist and photographer w. many exhibits in US. In '72 he became the first mus. to teach at Harvard's "Learning from Performers" program. Guest speaker at U. of Colorado Conference on World Affairs '89; twice a yr. since '89 at the Berkeley Unitarian Universalist Church—where he seeks ordination. Favs: Garner, Peterson, Wynton Kelly, Bill Evans. CDs: Night; MM; Rh./Atl.; w. Stanley Turrentine (BN); Marian McPartland (JA); Joe Pass (PJ); Richard "Groove" Holmes (PJ).

McCLURE RON (RONALD DIX), bs, el-bs, comp, arr, pno; b. New Haven, CT, 11/22/41. Began on acdn. at age 5. Received B. Mus. fr. Hartt Coll. of Mus. 1963. Stud. w. Hall Overton in NYC '65. Pl. w. Buddy Rich '63–5; Herbie Mann '64; Maynard Ferguson '64–5; Marian McPartland '65; Wes Montgomery, Wynton Kelly '65–6; Charles Lloyd '66–9; Miles Davis '68; Joe Henderson '70; Fourth Way Qt. '70–1; Freddie Hubbard, Pointer Sisters, Tony Ben-

nett, Thelonious Monk '72; Sarah Vaughan, Keith Jarrett '73; Blood, Sweat and Tears '74–6; Jack DeJohnette's Directions '76; Dave Liebman '80–90; Quest '83–91; Conrad Herwig fr. '85; Paul Bley '85–6; Michel Legrand '88; Richie Beirach fr. '89; Lee Konitz '90; Anders Bergcrantz '92. Also subbed in Mel Lewis and Gil Evans Orchs. in '80s. McClure taught at Berklee Coll. of Mus. '71–2 and at LIU '83–6. Worked extens. as a clinician and is currently on the jazz faculty at NYU. Favs: Geo. Mraz, Red Mitchell, Ron Carter; arrs: Gil Evans, Bill Holman. Fests: Eur., Jap., So. Amer., Austral. fr. '66. TV: NBC special on BS&T. CDs: Steep.; EPC, Ken; w. C. Herwig (Ken); D. Liebman (Timel.); BS&T (Col.).

McCONNELL, ROB (ROBERT MURRAY GORDON), v-tbn, comp, arr; b London, Ont., Canada, 2/14/35. Raised in Toronto; pl. slide tbn. in hs, later pl. w. dance bands. Worked three yrs. in Toronto brokerage house, ret. to mus. pl. v-tbn. Infl: Bob Brookmeyer. Stud. w. arr./comp. Gordon Delamont, then form. rehearsal band. Lived in NYC 1963–4; pl. in Maynard Ferguson band. Ret. to Toronto; became one of the top studio players, arr. and comp. for TV and recs. Pl. '65–9 in Phil Nimmons' gp., Nimmons 'N' Nine Plus Six. In '68 he form. first edition of the Boss Brass, a sixteen-pc. band without saxes, for transcriptions and commercial recs. Added saxes and expanded the Boss Brass to twenty-two later that yr. In '77 he rec. a two-disc direct-to-disc set, *Big Band Jazz*, that was widely acclaimed by musicians and critics. The Boss Brass—noted for its mixture of tight ensemble and such seasoned soloists as Guido Basso, Moe Koffman, Rick Wilkins, and Ed Bickert—established him as an important jazz comp. Moved to LA in '88 to teach at the Dick Grove Sch. and pl. locally. In '90 he reformed the Boss Brass in Toronto w. essentially the same personnel as in early '70s. Rec. w. the Singers Unlimited; Hi-Los; Phil Woods; Mel Tormé; and others but devotes most of his time to the Boss Brass. CDs: Imp.; SB; w. Dave Frishberg (Conc.).

McCORD, CAP (CASTOR), tnr sax, cl; b. Birmingham, AL, 5/17/07; d. NYC, 2/14/63. In 1924 he pl. in Edgar Hayes's Bluegrass Buddies w. his twin bro., saxophonist Ted McCord. After working w. Horace Henderson and Mills Blue Rhythm Band, he moved to France, pl. in Paris w. such visiting Amer. jazzmen as Louis Armstrong and Coleman Hawkins '34–8. Returning to US, he worked in NYC w. Leon Abbey and rec. w. Ethel Waters; Benny Carter; and, fr. '41–2, Claude Hopkins, after which he retired fr. mus. CDs: w. L. Armstrong (Col.); Benny Carter (Class.; BB); Mills Blue Rhythm Band (Hep).

McCORKLE, SUSANNAH, voc; b. Berkeley, CA, 1/1/49; d. NYC, 5/19/01. Self-taught. As a student in Eur. in the 1970s, she sang in Rome; then w. Bruce Turner; Wally Fawkes; other swing bands in London '72–7. Worked w. Keith Ingham late '70s-80s; own trio fr. '80s. Regular apps. at Oak Room, Algonquin Hotel, NYC, in late '90s. A published author of fiction and science fiction; articles on Bessie Smith and Ethel Waters app. in *American Heritage* '95, '97. McCorkle, said *Rolling Stone*, "utilize[d] the grammar of jazz with a sense of personal involvement that is often lacking in singers of American popular songs." Favs: Billie Holiday, Ella Logan, Ray Charles. Polls: *Stereo Review* Rec. of Yr.; *LA Times* '86. Fests: Eur. '73–4; London, Japan '91. TV: PBS *Susannah McCorkle and Friends* '88; *Nightline*; CBS *Sunday Morning*; Jap. TV. CDs: Conc.

McCRACKEN, ROBERT EDWARD (BOB), cl, tnr sax; b. Dallas, TX, 11/23/04; d. Los Angeles, CA, 7/4/72. Professional fr. the age of 17; stud. pno., dms., harm., cl. in Ft. Worth, Tex. Tour. w. Eddie Whitley band 1921; w. Jack Teagarden in Doc Ross band '24. Pl. w. Willard Robison in NYC '27–28; Hogan Hancock in Chi. '28. Worked in Tex. fr. '28–35. After pl. w. Frankie Trumbauer '35 and Joe Venuti '36, he moved to Chi. '39. Pl. w. Bud Freeman and Jimmy McPartland '39–40; Wingy Manone, Benny Goodman '41; Russ Morgan '42–4; Wayne King '45–6; and the house band at Chez Paree, Chi. '47–8. Toured Eur. and Africa w. Louis Armstrong '52. Moved to West Coast in early '50s and worked w. Kid Ory '53–4; Ben Pollack and J. Teagarden '54; tour. Eur. w. Ory '59; and worked w. Teagarden '62; Wild Bill Davison '67. TV: *The Untouchables* '63–4 CDs: w. Ory (GTJ).

McCURDY, ROY WALTER JR., dms; b. Rochester, NY, 11/28/36. Studied at Eastman Sch. of Mus. fr. age 10. After four yrs. in air force band, join. Chuck and Gap Mangione's Jazz Bros. 1960; then Art Farmer–Benny Golson Jazztet '61–2. Also pl. w. Mitchell-Ruff, Bobby Timmons, Betty Carter in early '60s; Sonny Rollins '63–4; and Cannonball Adderley Qnt. '65–75; traveling int'l w. Adderley, incl. successful tour of So. Amer '72. Worked as studio mus. for NBC *Movie of the Week* and did jingles w. Benny Golson. After death of Adderley in '75, McCurdy moved to LA and worked w. Kenny Rankin; Blood, Sweat & Tears; Nancy Wilson; Ella Fitzgerald. Toured US w. Freddie Hubbard; Stanley Turrentine; Jimmy Smith; Joe Williams; Billy Eckstine; Art Farmer; B. Golson; Sarah Vaughan; Ernestine Anderson. Teaches dms. priv. and at coll. clinics. Favs: Kenny Clarke, Max Roach, Philly Joe Jones, Elvin

Jones. CDs: w. Adderley (Cap.; Fant.; Night); N. Adderley (Atl.; Mile.); S. Rollins (BB); C. Basie (Pab.); Tom Talbert (SB); Betty Carter (Cap.); Scott Hamilton (Conc.); Joe Williams; Gene Ammons (Fant.); Clark Terry (Pab.); Sarah Vaughan (Pab.); Bobby Shew (MAMA); C. Candoli (BR).

McDONOUGH, DICK (RICHARD TOBIN), gtr, bjo; b. NYC, 7/30/04; d. NYC, 5/25/38. Mother pl. pno; start. on mand., then bjo. Made prof. debut on bjo. w. Ross Gorman 1925; sw. to gtr., backed singer Cliff Edwards ("Ukulele Ike"). Made hundreds of jazz rec. dates between '26 and mid '30s w. Red Nichols; Jack Teagarden; Jack Pettis; Miff Mole; Dorsey Bros.; Red Norvo; Benny Goodman; Adrian Rollini; Frank Trumbauer; Billie Holiday; Glenn Miller; et al. Frequently teamed up w. gtrst. Carl Kress dur. '30s. Led own band in NBC radio studios shortly bef. his death. An accomplished technician whose swinging gtr. sound was among the most highly regarded in the pre-electric era. CDs: w. Dorsey Bros.; B. Holiday (Col.); Fats Waller; Metronome All-Stars (BB); Goodman; Bud Freeman (Class.).

McDUFF, BROTHER JACK aka CAPTAIN JACK (Eugene McDuffy), org, comp, bs, pno; b. Champaign, IL, 9/17/26; d. Minneapolis, MN, 1/23/01. Self-taught, later stud, at NY Tech. in Cincinnati. Began as bs. pl. w. Denny Zeitlin and Joe Farrell. Led own gp. in Midwest early 1950s; then pl. w. Porter Kilbert, Eddie Chamblee in Chi. '57; Willis Jackson '57–8. Also pl. w. Johnny Griffin, Max Roach in Chi. '50s. A club owner suggested he sw. to organ. Own gp. fr. '59. Toured the US and Eur. and rec. w. such artists as Joe Henderson; Geo. Benson; Pat Martino. Made rec. debut as leader on Prest. '60; cont. on that label until '66, giving each sideman an opportunity to lead a rec. date (Geo. Benson's album debut as leader has him fronting McDuff's gp.). In the '80s McDuff sw. to synth. but w. little success. In '90s, back on B-3 organ, he signed w. Conc. label. App. in Japan, Bermuda. Fav. mus: Jimmy Smith; comps: Tadd Dameron, Horace Silver. Fests: all major fr. '60s; Vail Jazz Party '95. CDs: Prest.; BN; Conc.; w. Sonny Stitt; Gene Ammons; Roland Kirk (Prest.); Joey DeFrancesco (Col.; Conc.); Joshua Breakstone (Evid.); Joe Williams (Delos).

McEACHERN, MURRAY, tbn, alto sax; b. Toronto, Ont., Canada, 8/16/15; d. Los Angeles, CA, 4/22/82. Studied vln. for five yrs., winning medals and scholarships; fr. 1932 stud. w. Geo. Simms in Montreal, first cl., tnr. and alto sax, later tpt., tbn., tba., and bs. To Chi. '36, where he did a one-man-band novelty act. With Benny Goodman as tbnst. '36–7; pl. tbn. and alto w. Glen Gray's Casa Loma Orch. '37–41; asst. cond. w. Paul Whiteman's Orch. '41. Moved to Calif. to work as studio mus. Solo sound track work in films incl. *Glenn Miller Story, Benny Goodman Story*; TV series, *Pete Kelly's Blues* '59. In '60s and '70s he was one of LA's most active studio mus. Played briefly w. Duke Ellington, '73; led the Tommy Dorsey ghost band '74–6. Rec. w. Mary Ann McCall (Disc.); Willie Smith (Key.) CDs: w. B. Goodman (BB); Ernestine Anderson (Sav.); B. Holiday (BN); L. Armstrong (Class.)

McFARLAND, GARY, vib, comp/arr; b. Los Angeles, CA, 10/23/33; d. NYC, 11/3/71. A late starter, McFarland did not become serious about mus. until he took up vib. in the mid 1950s. Attended colls. in LA and San Jose bef. receiving scholarship to the Berklee Sch., where he spent a semester in '59. Also received scholarship to Lenox Sch. of Jazz in the summer of '60; then moved to NYC to work as comp. Wrote two arrs. for Gerry Mulligan Concert Jazz Band '61; album for Anita O'Day '61. Other significant early McFarland works incl. a strings and woodwinds album for Bill Evans; *Big Band Bossa Nova* for Stan Getz; *Point of Departure* for a sxt. '62–3. *Essence* for a John Lewis–led ensemble consisted of six McFarland origs. '64. A collab. w. choreographer Donald McKayle in '64 resulted in a two-act jazz ballet. McFarland's first commercial success was *Soft Samba*, a crossover effort that allowed him to take a qnt. on the road in '65; later that yr. he led the house orch. for the first *DB* Jazz Fest. in Chi. His suite, *America the Beautiful*, subtitled "A Jazz Lament for America," reached the top 200 LPs *Billboard* chart in '69. In the last yrs. of his life, McFarland increasingly turned to commercial projects. At his best, he was a comp./arr. w. a uniquely airy and open sound; unrestricted by any real technical educ., he frequently tried instrumental combinations which, though academically questionable, produced remarkably fresh-sounding music. Comps: "Chuggin'"; "Weep" for Mulligan; "Blue Hodge" for Johnny Hodges; also rec. by Al Cohn–Zoot Sims. CDs: Verve; DCC; w. Stan Getz; Anita O'Day; Bill Evans (Verve).

McFERRIN, BOBBY, voc, comp; b. NYC, 3/11/50. Parents are Robert and Sara McFerrin, both classical singers; father dubbed Sidney Poitier's singing voice in the film *Porgy and Bess*; moth. chairs voice dept. at Fullerton Coll.; and sist. Brenda is pop singer and voc. coach in LA. Stud. pno at Juilliard fr. age 6; family moved to LA in 1958; stud. mus. at Sacramento State U. and Cerritos Coll. Worked as journeyman pnst., pl. for *Ice Follies* and

w. lounge bands. In July '77, an inner voice told him he was a singer; worked as singer/pnst. at Salt Lake City pno. bar; moved to NO, then to SF, where he cont. to reside in the '90s. Until early '80s worked w. various musicians, incl. Wynton Marsalis and Wayne Shorter; released his first album, *Bobby McFerrin*, and tour. US w. all-star band, incl. Dizzy Gillespie and Herbie Hancock '82. In '83 remembering Keith Jarrett's solo pno. programs, he decided to try a similar approach w. solo voice. The reaction was overwhelmingly enthusiastic. McFerrin's ability to jigsaw together two and three seemingly simultaneously vocal lines, his astonishing range, and his superb harmonic sense resulted in unprecedented jazz solo perfs. His '89 rec., "Don't Worry, Be Happy," fr. the *Simple Pleasures* album, reached first place on the pop charts and won Grammy awards for Record and Song of the Year, bringing his Grammy count to nine. In '90 he tour. w. Voicestra, a 12–person a cappella voc. and theatre ens. In '91 he made a duet tour w. Chick Corea and added guest conducting to his activities, w. a two-mo. summer sched. of Bach, Tchaikovsky, etc. In '92 two duet albums were released: the '91 tour w. Corea and duet recs. w. classical cellist Yo-Yo Ma. A true Renaissance artist, McFerrin has successfully navigated virtually everything he's tried, fr. pop mus. to pure jazz improv., fr. the virtual creation of a new mus. form w. the Voicestra to well-received orchestral conducting. Despite the broad range of his activities, he cont., in '92, to justify his identification as perhaps the most gifted and certainly the most original jazz singer of his generation. Many TV apps., incl. subject of *60 Minutes* segment '97. CDs: Col.; BN; Sony; w. Gillespie (Tel.); Charles Lloyd (BN); MJQ (Atl.); Rob Wasserman (MCA).

McGARITY, LOU (ROBERT LOUIS), tbn, vln; b. Athens, GA, 7/22/17; d. Alexandria, VA, 8/28/71. Played vln. fr. age 7 and took up tbn. in hs. Worked w. Kirk Devore in Atlanta 1936; Nye Mayhew at Glen Island Casino '37; Ben Bernie '38–40. With Benny Goodman '40–2 and '46–7; Raymond Scott '42–3. Briefly in LA for studio work '47; then moved to NYC. Extensive radio, TV, and rec. activity for the next decade and a half, incl. Arthur Godfrey CBS radio show. Tour. Japan w. Bob Crosby '64 and became a charter member of WGJB '67. Despite ill health, he remained intermittently active until his death. McGarity is viewed by many as one of the best of the Jack Teagarden–infl. trombonists. CDs: w. B. Goodman (Col.; Cap.; MM); C. Parker (Verve); WGJB (Atl.); L. Armstrong (Dec.); Eddie Condon (Mos.; Dec.; Stash; Jazz.); World's Greatest Jazz Band (Atl.).

McGHEE, HOWARD B., tpt; b. Tulsa, OK, 3/6/18; d. NYC, 7/17/87. Raised in Det.; pl. cl. bef. sw. to tpt. Worked w. local bands. Join. Lionel Hampton Sept. 1941; Andy Kirk Nov. '41; rec. his own *McGhee Special* w. him '42. After a yr. w. Charlie Barnet '42–3, rejoin. Kirk until June '44. Pl. w. Georgie Auld for six mos. and briefly w. Count Basie. To Calif. w. Coleman Hawkins '44–5; stayed in LA, lead. own gp. '45–7. Rec. "Lover Man" and "Relaxin' at Camarillo" w. Charlie Parker '46–7; rec. and tour. w. JATP '45–8. Led own gp. at Paris JF '48; later led own band; pl. and rec. w. Machito; tour. Far East '51–2 w. Oscar Pettiford gp. In obscurity for most of the '50s due to drug problems, he ret. to prominence in '60s and was heard in concert gps. organized by George Wein; also pl. w. gp. feat. J. J. Johnson and Sonny Stitt which tour. Eur. and pl. at NJF. Pl. w. Duke Ellington orch. '61–2, '65 and '72. Led own bb at Harlem's Apollo Theatre '73; cont. to gig in N.Y. and N.J. through '70s, incl. perfs. at Rev. John Gensel's St. Peter's Lutheran Church. A heart ailment curtailed his pl. time and prowess, as evidenced by his app. on a Coleman Hawkins tribute at '84 Kool JF in NYC. McGhee forged a personal style out of a succession of infls., fr. Roy Eldridge to Dizzy Gillespie and Fats Navarro. He attributed his speed to early exp. pl. reeds. His early pl. feat. dazzling high-register flights; his post '60s was more middle range and introspective. CDs: BL; Cont.; Jz. Class.; w. Billie Holiday (Verve); C. Parker (Verve; Stash; Rh.); Lester Young (BN); Coleman Hawkins (Cap.); Johnny Hartman (Beth.); Fats Navarro (BN); Eddie Jefferson (Evid.); D. Ellington (Saja); Teddy Edwards (Cont.).

McGREGOR, CHRIS, pno; b. Umtata, South Africa, 12/24/36. Father a Scottish missionary. Stud. at Capetown Coll. of Mus. where he became infl. by the mus. of Webern, Schoenberg, and Bartok; pl. residency at Jazzhus Montmartre, Copenhagen in 1960s. Organized the Blue Notes '63; left So. Africa w. the gp. '64; pl. Antibes—Juan-les-Pins Jazz Fest bef. settling in London. The gp. became the genesis of a bb, the Brotherhood of Breath '70; rec. four albums in '80s. Also re-formed Blue Notes '75; led various small gps. in the '80s, and cont. app.; on and off w. new edition of Brotherhood of Breath, feat. singers and dancers. CDs: Vict.; Sonet.

McGRIFF, JIMMY (JAMES HARRELL), org, pno; b. Philadelphia, PA, 4/3/36. Parents both pnsts. Cousin of Benny Golson. Pl. sax, bs. in teens; bs. w. Big Maybelle. Stud. at Combs Sch. of Mus., Phila. and Juilliard. Worked as policeman, moonlighting as bs. His instrumental arr. of Ray Charles's "I've Got a Woman"

reached fifth position on *Billboard* r&b chart '55. Form. org. trio which rec. for Sue fr. 1962; Solid State '66–9; BN, Cap., and Groove Merchant in '70s; JAM, Mile. in '80s. Backed blues singer Junior Parker; teamed w. fellow organist Groove Holmes, whom he names as an infl. along w. Milt Buckner, Wild Bill Davis, Bill Doggett. Attributes much of his success to intermittent work w. Buddy Rich (on pno. and org.) fr. '69 to '74. Now pl. Hammond XB-3, which has an attachment that simulates the sound of other instruments. McGriff prefers not to be called a jazz artist: "Jimmy Smith is the jazz king on the organ, but when it comes to blues, I can do things where he can't touch me." CDs: Tel.; BN; Mile.; Headfirst; w. Harper Bros. (Verve); Hank Crawford (Tel.).

McINTOSH, TOM (THOMAS S.), comp, tbn; b. Baltimore, MD, 2/6/27. Studied voice at Peabody Cons. 1944; tbn. in US army band; grad. Juilliard '58. Active in NYC from '56; worked w. James Moody '59 and again '62; also w. Art Farmer–Benny Golson Jazztet '60. Wrote *Something Old, Something New* LP for D. Gillespie '63; writer and soloist fr. '64 w. N.Y. Jazz Sxt. which perf. his suite, *Whose Child Are You?*; also pl. w. Thad Jones–Mel Lewis fr. '69. After moving to LA '69, gave up pl. to comp. and arr. for TV and films, incl. *The Learning Tree; Soul Soldier; Shaft's Big Score; Slither; John Handy*. Comps: "The Cup Bearers"; "With Malice Toward None"; "Balanced Scales-Justice." CDs: w. Shirley Scott (Imp.); Freddy Cole (Fant.); Art Farmer–Benny Golson (Chess); Jimmy Heath (Riv.); Lee Morgan (BN); R. R. Kirk (Merc.).

McINTYRE, EARL PATRICK, tbn, bs-tbn, euph, tba, comp, arr; b. NYC, 11/21/53. Entire family are amateur brass players. Began on tpt. and vln., then sw. to tbn. and tba. Began pl. prof. while att. HS of Mus. and Art. Stud. at Mannes Coll. of Mus. and priv. w. Benny Powell; Alan Raph; Slide Hampton; Carmine Caruso. Pl. w. Taj Mahal 1970–1; Charles Mingus '72; Thad Jones–Mel Lewis Orch.–Vanguard Orch. since '73; Gil Evans '78; Carla Bley since '79; George Russell '80; Cecil Taylor '85–6; George Gruntz '91. Also pl. w. Billy Taylor; Howard Johnson; Clark Terry; James Spaulding; Paul Jeffrey; Sam Rivers. Comp. and arr. for Charlie Rouse; Lester Bowie's Brass Fantasy; Art Ens. of Chi.; Renée Manning; Mel Lewis. He is currently dir. of the Musicians of Brooklyn Initiatives bb and orch. Fav. tbn: Quentin Jackson; tba: Howard Johnson; arr: Thad Jones. Fests: Eur. and Japan w. Mel Lewis Orch.–Vanguard Orch. since '73. CDs: w. Jones-Lewis (A&M); Renée Manning (Ken); Gil Evans (Enja); George Russell (SN); Mingus bb (Drey.).

McINTYRE, HAL (HAROLD W.), alto sax, cl, lead; b. Cromwell, CT, 11/29/14; d. Los Angeles, CA, 5/5/59. Led his own band 1935–36 bef. joining Glenn Miller; was a key member of Miller's '37 gp., as well as the reorganized—and subsequently famous—Miller band of the following yr. Formed his own successful bb in '41 after leaving Miller; cont. as a leader until his death in a LA apartment fire. CDs: w. Glenn Miller (Col.; BB; Merc.).

McINTYRE, MAKANDA KEN (KENNETH ARTHUR), saxes, fl, oboe, Eng hrn, bsn, cl, pno, bs, dms, comp; b. Boston, MA, 9/7/31; d. NYC, 6/13/01. Father was mand. pl. Began on bugle at age 8; then pl. pno; heard Charlie Parker at age 16; took up sax at 19, fl. and cl. at 21. Pl. pno. while in army in Japan 1953. Stud. in Bost. w. Andy McGhee; Charlie Mariano; Gigi Gryce. B. Mus. in fl. and comp. fr. Bost. Cons. '58. M. Mus. in comp. '59. Rec. as lead. w. Eric Dolphy '60. Taught mus. in public sch. '61–7. Stud. oboe w. Harry Smyles in NYC '62. Pl. w. Jaki Byard, Bill Dixon, Jazz Comps. Orch. '62; Cecil Taylor '65–6. Received doctorate in educ. fr. U. of Mass. '75. Many recs. as lead. for Steep. in '70s. Pl. and rec. w. Nat Adderley '76; Beaver Harris '78–9; Craig Harris '80; Charlie Haden since '85. McIntyre held professorships at Central State U. '67–9; Wesleyan U. '69–71; Smith Coll. 70–80; SUNY-Old Westbury fr. '71 (founded Perf. Arts Dept.); Fordham U. 74–9; New School fr. '90. He cond. many jazz and African-Amer. mus. history wkshps. in the US, Eur., So. Amer., and Jamaica. Favs: Parker, Rollins, Coltrane. Fests: Eur., Japan, Africa, So. Amer., etc. TV: NYC and Bost. TV in '70s; *Night Music* '90. CDs: Steep.; BN; NJ; w. C. Haden (BN); E. Dolphy box (Prest.) includes the McIntyre–Dolphy NJ CD.

McKEE, ANDY (ANDREW G.), bs; b. Philadelphia, PA, 11/11/53. Grandfather was amateur vlnst. Began on alto sax at age 8, sw. to bs. in 8th grade. Stud. cello at Penn St. U. for two yrs. Later stud. w. Philly Joe Jones. Pl. w. Walt Dickerson 1977–9; Philly Joe Jones '79–80; Billy Harper '81. Freelanced in NYC w. Jaki Byard, Clifford Jordan, David Schnitter, Howard Johnson, Ted Curson, Sal Nistico, Charlie Rouse, Elvin Jones '80–4. Lived in Paris, freelanced w. Mal Waldron, Clark Terry, Chet Baker, Hank Jones, Joe Lee Wilson, Steve Lacy, Horace Parlan, Steve Grossman, Michel Portal, Daniel Humair, Martial Solal, Franco D'Andrea '84–5. Tour. w. Elvin Jones Jazz Machine '86–7, '90–2; Michael Petrucciani '87–91, '93; Von & Chico Freeman, Harry Sokal '92–3. Pl. in NYC w. Mingus bb fr. '92; also leads own gp. and teaches at New Sch. in NYC. Favs: Paul Chambers, Charlie Haden, Mingus. Fests: all

major fr. '77. TV: US, Eur., Jap. TV w. E. Jones; M. Petrucciani. CDs: w. Mingus (Drey.); Petrucciani (BN); Barry Altschul (SN); Dickerson; R. Cuber; Walt Dickerson (Steep.).

McKENNA, DAVE (DAVID), pno; b. Woonsocket, RI, 5/30/30. Mother pl. vln. and pno.; fath. pl. snare dm. in mil. band. Stud. w. Sandy Sandiford, A. Peloquin. Pl. w. own trio fr. mid 1940s; Boots Mussulli '47–8; Charlie Ventura '49; Woody Herman '50–1. Did not play while in army '51–3. Pl. w. Mussulli, Ventura '53; Gene Krupa, Stan Getz, Al Cohn–Zoot Sims, Buddy Morrow Orch. mid '50s; Dick Johnson '58–9; Bobby Hackett off and on fr. '58; Buddy Rich '59–60; Krupa '60. On staff at ABC early '60s. Pl. w. Peanuts Hucko, Buck Clayton, Yank Lawson, and others at Eddie Condon's '63–6. Moved to Cape Cod, Mass. '66 and since then has worked mainly as a solo pnst. in the Bost. area. He perf. w. Louis Armstrong at NJF '70 and has occ. pl. w. Scott Hamilton, Dick Johnson, Gray Sargent, Bob Wilber since '70s. Appeared often at Hanratty's, NYC in '80s; annual concerts for Heavenly Jazz concert series, NYC '90s. McKenna brings to the piano a prodigious left hand that is a rhythm section unto itself to go along with his dexterous right. Factor in the vast storehouse of songs at his fingertips and you have a most resourceful solo performer, celebrated for his theme medleys. He also is very effective in duo, trio, or any other combination. Fav: Louis Armstrong. Fests: Eur., Jap. TV: PBS w. Tony Bennett; Ed Sullivan; Steve Allen w. Ventura; W. Herman. CDs: Conc.; Chiaro.; w. Marian McPartland (JA); Al Cohn–Zoot Sims (BB); John Pizzarelli (Chesky); Ruby Braff (Conc.); Bobby Hackett (Chiaro.); G. Masso (Arb.).

McKENZIE, RED (WILLIAM), promoter, voc, comb; b. St. Louis, MO, 10/14/1899; d. NYC, 2/7/48. Started out as a jockey, but soon found a better outlet for his skills in the mus. business. From 1923 he pl. and rec. on comb with tissue paper (a kazoo effect) as leader of the Mound City Blue Blowers; also rec. w. Red Nichols '29–31; Adrian Rollini '33; and sang with Paul Whiteman '32–33. Ran a club on NYC's 52nd St., then retired fr. mus. '39–44. Ret. to NYC to sing with Eddie Condon at Town Hall; lead a band at Jimmy Ryan's; and rec. for National Recs. in '47. A prototype of the amateur musician, McKenzie was less important as a singer or perf. than as a promoter of jazz dur. the Depression yrs. As a talent scout, he was instrumental in obtaining rec. contracts for Bix Beiderbecke, the Chicago Rhythm Kings, the NORK, the Spirits of Rhythm, et al. CDs: Timel.; w. Jack Teagarden; C. Hawkins in *Three Great Swing Saxophones* (BB).

McKIBBON, AL (ALFRED BENJAMIN), bs; b. Chicago, IL, 1/1/19; d. Los Angeles, 8/29/05. Father pl tba., gtr. Stud. bs., pno. at Cass Tech HS in Det. Got into mus. through bro., a gtr. w. local bands of Kelly Martin, Ted Buckner. To NYC w. Lucky Millinder 1943. Pl. w. Tab Smith '45–6; Coleman Hawkins, J. C. Heard '46–7; Dizzy Gillespie '48–9, incl. Eur. tour. '48; Miles Davis '48. Count Basie '50; Thelonious Monk '51; Geo. Shearing '51–8, when he join. Cal Tjader until Aug. '59. In LA, freelanced, incl. work w. Calvin Jackson Duo. Staff mus. at NBC '65. In '71–2 tour. int'l w. Gillespie; Monk; and others in the gp. Giants of Jazz. Pl. w. Sammy Davis Jr. '75. Ret. to NYC ca. '90 to pl. in B'way show. McKibbon displayed exceptional style and technique in the Shearing gp., particularly in Latin works. Fest: NJF w. C. Hawkins '57. Recs. w. Neal Hefti; Ernie Freeman; Ray Charles. CDs: w. Gillespie (RCA); Monk (BN; BL); Davis (Cap.); Herbie Nichols (BN); Tjader (Fant.); B. Carter-D. Gillespie (Pab.).

McKINLEY, RAY (RAYMOND FREDERICK), dms, voc; b. Fort Worth, TX, 6/18/10; d. Largo, FL, 5/7/95. Began prof. career at age 9 w. bands in the Ft. Worth area. Left home at 15 and pl. w. territory bands such as Duncan Marion, Savage Cummings. In late 1920s he worked in NYC w. Milt Shaw Detroiters, which incl. tbn. Will Bradley. Pl. w. Smith-Ballew '32; Dorsey Bros. '34–5; J. Dorsey '35–9; then in mid '39 he became a founding partner of Bradley's newly formed band, which achieved popularity using a boogie-woogie beat and McKinley's vocals on such hits as "Beat Me Daddy Eight to the Bar" '40. Led own band briefly in '42; then pl. in Glenn Miller's AAF Band; while in Eur., he led Swing Shift, a contingent fr. the Miller band that incl. Mel Powell, Peanuts Hucko, Trigger Alpert. Following Miller's death in '44, he co-led the orch. w. Jerry Gray. After discharge, fr. '46 to '50, he led an adventurous, forward-looking band w. arrs. by Eddie Sauter and such soloists as Hucko; Vern Friley; Nick Travis; and Mundell Lowe. Fr. '50 to '56 he led own gps. and freelanced as TV singer in NYC. In May '56 he was commissioned by Miller's widow to organize a new Glenn Miller Orch., using the orig. library and style. He fronted the orch. until '66, incl. very successful tours of Iron Curtain countries '57 and Japan '64 and '65. Left Miller band in Jan. '66 and was replaced by Buddy DeFranco. Hosted US Treasury radio show *Bring Back the Bands* '67–8. Led own combo at Rainbow Grill '69; served as mus. consultant for Disney World '71; then in '73 he replaced Tex Beneke as leader of a Miller tribute band, heading it until '78. He cont. to freelance and, in '85, was on British TV w. Hucko and Zeke Zarchy. In the '90s he worked

mostly in Fla., where he resided. In Burt Korall's book, *Drummin' Men*, Lenny Hambro described McKinley's playing: "It's natural, often melodic, always pulsating, never fussy. He can play with anyone. Mac doesn't throw the kitchen sink in; he just makes everyone feel good. And his solos tell a story." Film: McKinley's '42 band in *Hit Parade of 1943*. TV: cond. orch. and co-hosted *Glenn Miller Time* CBS summer '61. Video: *Glenn Miller: America's Musical Hero*. CDs: Sav.; w. Dorsey Bros. (Cir.); J. Dorsey (Dec.); Glenn Miller (BB); Will Bradley (Col.).

McKINNEY, CARLOS, pno, comp; also dms, harp; b. Detroit, MI, 1/10/74. Belongs to prominent Det. jazz family. Nephew to pnst. Harold McKinney, bsst. Ray McKinney, tbnst. Kiane Zawadi (Bernard McKinney), dmrs. Earl McKinney and Walter Harris. Cousin to dmr. Ali Jackson and tptr. Khalil Jackson. Moth. Carolyn McKinney is voc., sist. Shani McKinney is pnst. Began stud. pno. at age 4 w. uncle Harold McKinney. First prof. gig at 12 w. r&b gp., Identity Band. Classical studies at Ctr. for Creative Studies 1983–91. While enrolled at Cass Tech HS, he also stud. w. Det. Symph. harpist Patricia Terry-Ross. Jazz stud. w. Ray McKinney, Harold McKinney, Marcus Belgrave '89–91. Pl. w. Legacy Qnt. '89–93. Moved to NYC '91; att. New Sch. (B.A. '95). Worked. w. Winard Harper '92–3; Antonio Hart '92–5; Buster Williams' Something More fr. '93; Wallace Roney '94–6; Sonny Rollins, Elvin Jones' Jazz Machine, Steve Turre fr. '96; Kenny Garrett–Charnett Moffett fr. '97. Asst. comp. to James Mtume for the hit TV show *New York Undercover*. Favs: Bud Powell, Hancock, H. McKinney. Fests: Eur. fr. '92; Senegal '94; Iceland '95; Turkey '97. CDs: Sirocco Jazz; w. Buster Williams; Bill Saxton (Jazzline); A. Hart (Novus); W. Roney (WB); Takashi Shimamoto (King).

McKINNEY'S COTTON PICKERS. Pioneer big band. An outgrowth of the Synco Jazz Band, formed in 1922 in Springfield, Ohio, by the dmr. William McKinney (b. Cynthiana, KY, 9/17/1895; d. Cynthiana, 10/14/69); in '23, McKinney turned the dms. over to Cuba Austin and became the band's non-perf. manager. The gp. became known as McKinney's Cotton Pickers in Det. '26. Early arrs. were by tptr. John Nesbitt. From early '27, w. Don Redman as mus. dir. and arr. and a series of superb recs. start. in '28, the band achieved a national reputation. On Redman's departure in '31, Benny Carter replaced him but remained for less than a yr. Members incl. Rex Stewart, Claude Jones, Dave Wilborn. Although the band survived until early '40s, its popularity had waned, and it had not rec. since '31. At its height, the band ranked artistically w. those of Ellington and Fletcher Henderson. CDs: (BB).

McKUSICK, HAL (HAROLD WILFRED), alto, tnr, sop saxes, cl, bs-cl, fl, picc, comp; b. Medford, MA, 6/1/24. Began on cl. but his main instrument bec. alto sax. Raised in Newton, where Ralph Burns was schoolmate. Pl. w. Don Bestor, Les Brown 1942; Dean Hudson, briefly w. Woody Herman '43; Boyd Raeburn '44–5. Moved to Calif. mid '50s. Pl. w. Johnny Otis, Alvino Rey, Al Donahue, Buddy Rich '48; Claude Thornhill '48–9; Terry Gibbs, '50–1; Elliot Lawrence, Don Elliot '51–6; Urbie Green, Geo. Williams '58. Between '55 and '58 made many recs., several reflecting his collab. w. George Russell. Form. own spt. w. four saxes '58–9; also much commercial work in late '50s. Staff mus. for CBS in NYC '58–72; freelanced extens. fr. late '50s. Began priv. tutoring in '52. Led gp. incl. Don Friedman or Hilton Ruiz on pno., Jeff Fuller or Harvey Swartz on bs., and Keith Copeland or Ray Mosca on dms. His comps. for Raeburn, Lawrence, and others were noted for their novel time signatures, modes, and counterpoint. Favs: Parker, Konitz, Davey Schildkraut, L. Young, Coltrane, Stitt, Rollins. CDs: Prest.; Dec.; BB; FS; w. Raeburn (Sav.); Geo. Russell (BB); Charlie Parker; J. Giuffre–L. Konitz (Verve); Gil Melle (Prest.).

McLAUGHLIN, JOHN, gtr, pno, synth, comp; b. Yorkshire, England, 1/4/42. Mother pl. vln. Pno. lessons fr. age 9. Self-taught on gtr.; orig. insp. by blues gtrs., later by jazz and flamenco players. First prof. gig w. Big Pete Deuchar's Professors of Ragtime late 1950s. Freelanced in London in early '60s w. Alexis Korner; Georgie Fame; Graham Bond; Herbie Goines; Brian Auger; also w. rock mus., incl. Jack Bruce; Mick Jagger; Eric Clapton. Pl. w. John Surman, Dave Holland mid '60s; also pl. in Germ. w. Gunter Hampel. Emigrated to US in '69. Pl. w. Tony Williams' Lifetime '69; Miles Davis '69–70, incl. landmark fusion albums *Bitches' Brew* and *In a Silent Way*. Became disciple of guru Sri Chinmoy '70. Led own gp., Mahavishnu Orch. '71–5; sidemen incl. Billy Cobham; Larry Young; Armando Peraza; Jean-Luc Ponty; John Surman; Tony Oxley. Form. gp. Shakti, w. Indian vlnst. L. Shankar, tabla player Zakir Hussain mid '70s; while with this gp., McLaughlin pl. an acoustic gtr. of his own design, based on the Indian vina. Moved to Paris late '70s. Briefly led own jazz-rock gp., One Truth, '78. Pl. acoustic gtr. in duos and trios w. flamenco gtr. Paco De Lucia, Al Di Meola, Larry Coryell, Christian Escoude early '80s. Re-form. Mahavishnu Orch. w. saxophonist Bill Evans '84. Rec. w. Miles Davis '84. Premiered gtr. concerto written for him by Mike Gibbs, w. LA Phil-

harm. '85. Pl. acoustic gtr. w. Trilok Gurtu '88–9. Premiered own *Mediterranean Concerto* w. Scottish National Orch. '90. Revived Shakti '99. McLaughlin is noted for his rock-infl. sound and rhythmic concept. In the '80s he began pl. the Synclavier gtr. synth. Fests: all major. CDs: CBS; Col.; JMT; Verve; w. Davis (Col.); Williams (Verve); Joe Farrell (CTI); Paco De Lucia (Philips); Luciano Pavarotti (Lond.).

McLEAN, JACKIE (JOHN LENWOOD), alto sax, fl, comp, dms, pno; b. NYC, 5/17/31; d. Hartford, CT, 3/31/06. Father, John, pl. gtr. w. Tiny Bradshaw. Began on sop. sax. Stud. in NYC w. Foots Thomas; Cecil Scott; Andy Brown; Joe Napoleon. Pl. w. Sonny Rollins 1948–9; Miles Davis '49–53; George Wallington '55–6; Art Blakey '56–7; Charles Mingus '57–8; Blakey '58; own qnt. fr. '58. Acted and pl. in off-B'way play *The Connection* '59–60; also starred in the film version '61. Tour. Japan w. all-star gp. '65. Began pl. fl. and working as bandmaster and counselor in N.Y. prisons '67. Co-founded Artists Collective in NYC early '70s. Taught at Hartt Coll. of Mus. fr. '68; it became part of the U. of Hartford '72, and he became head of the African-Amer. Mus. Dept.'s Jazz Degree Program. Perf. in a qnt. w. his son René fr. '75. In '90s he led a sxt. w. Raymond Williams, tpt.; Steve Davis, tbn.; Allan Palmer, pno.; qnt. w. Darren Barrett, tpt. While continuing to grow in all aspects of his music, McLean never lost the fire in his soul. In 1996 he said: "I'm looking to the future all the time and find what I can play that will be different and still keep the tradition of the music there." Comps: "Dig" (aka "Donna)"; "Dr. Jackyll"; "Little Melonae." Favs: L. Young, D. Gordon, Parker, Rollins, Coltrane; arrs: Ellington, Golson, Slide Hampton, Gil Evans. Polls: *DB* Critics TDWR '63; no. 1 alto '95. Fests: Eur. fr. '50s; Japan fr. '65. Films: *The Connection*; docu., *Jackie McLean on Mars* early '80s. TV: *Like It Is* w. Gil Noble, NYC; many apps. on Eur. TV. CDs: BN; Tri.; Prest.; Ant.; Verve; Mos.; w. M. Davis (Prest.; BN); Kenny Dorham; Lee Morgan; H. Mobley; D. Byrd; Walter Davis Jr. (BN); Blakey (Col.; BB; BN); D. Gordon (Steep.); Gillespie (Tel.); Abbey Lincoln (Verve).

McLEAN, RENÉ PROFIT, alto, tnr, sop saxes, cl, fl, bamboo fl, shakuhachi; b. NYC, 12/16/46. Father is Jackie McLean; moth., Dollie, is former actress and dancer. Began on gtr. Stud. sax w. father fr. age 9, then at Jazz Arts Society 1961–2; Haryou Act Cultural Prog. '63–6; N.Y. Coll. of Mus. '66–8; Clark Terry Youth Band Wkshp. '69–71. Also stud. priv. w. Joe Allard '69–70; Frank Foster '70–1; Jaki Byard '72; George Coleman '74–5; lessons w. Sonny Rollins, Kenny Dorham. First prof. gigs w. neighborhood bands. Pl. w. Monguito Santamaria '65–70; Jackie McLean fr. '70. Bandmaster at N.Y. State Narcotic Addiction Control Commission '70–3; also held other community service positions in downtown NYC at this time. Pl. w. Cesar Concepcion '71; Sam Rivers '71–2; Collective Black Artists bb '71–6; Doug and Jean Carn '72–3; Frank Foster's Loud Minority '72–5; Sivuca, Grachan Moncur III '73; Tito Puente '73–5; Arthur Prysock '74; Dizzy Gillespie bb, Horace Silver '75; Lionel Hampton Orch. '75–6; Woody Shaw–Louis Hayes '76–7. Feat. in NY Shakespeare fest.'s prod. of Aishah Rahman's *Unfinished Women in No Man's Land While a Bird Dies in a Gilded Cage* '77. Pl. w. S. Rivers bb, Hugh Masakela '77, '79–81; Lionel Hampton Orch. '77–8; Miriam Makeba '81. Led own gps. w. Harry Whitaker '77–9; Don De Palma '81–2. Guest soloist w. Joe Chambers, Bobby Sanabaria, Jaco Pastorius, Benny Powell, Abbey Lincoln, Tito Puente '85. McLean has co-led a gp. w. his father fr. '83. Awarded a Creative Arts Fellowship for perf. in Japan '85. Taught at the U. of Mass., the New Sch., and the U. of Hartford; also in So. Africa where he has lived since '85. Favs: Jackie McLean, Rollins, D. Gordon, Coltrane, Parker. Fests: all major w. J. McLean, W. Shaw, L. Hampton. Film: app. w. Cab Calloway in *The Cotton Club*. TV: many apps. on NYC local TV. CDs: Steep.; Tri.; w. J. McLean (Tri.); W. Shaw–Louis Hayes (TCB); Shaw (Col.; Mos.).

McMANUS, JILL, pno, comp; b. Englewood, NJ, 7/28/40. Studied classical pno. w. Heida Hermanns; jazz w. John Mehegan 1962–3; Roland Hanna '69–71; arr. at BMI Arr. Wkshp. '90–2. Led house trio at Concord Café NYC '72. Pl. w. Jazz Sisters w. Janice Robinson, Jean Davis, Willene Barton, Lynn Milano, Paula Hampton '74–7; own gps. w. Geo. Coleman, Jerry Dodgion, Bill Hardman, Tom Harrell, Rufus Reid, Sam Jones, Cameron Brown, Ben Riley, Billy Hart, Victor Jones, etc. fr. '76. Assembled and led all-star bb at KC Women's Jazz Fest '80. Pl. w. Pepper Adams '80–1; house band at Hanratty's '81; Frank Wess '87. Her '84 album, *Symbols of Hopi*, feat. adaptations of four Hopi songs pl. by jazz qnt. and two Native Amer. percs. Scored docu. film *In the Spirit of Haystack* '84. Taught at Third St. Settlement; Rutgers U., as sub. for Kenny Barron '78–80; Mannes Coll. of Mus. fr. '81. In addition to leading her duo and trio and occasional larger gps., McManus has worked as a stage manager for jazz concerts at Carnegie Hall. She is also a freelance writer, with articles publ. in *Ms.* mag., the *NY Post*, and the book *The Musical Woman* (Greenwood) '84. In '87 she prod. a video for Navajo teenagers on the subject of nutrition and diabetes prevention. Favs: Bill Evans,

Wynton Kelly, Kenny Barron, Tommy Flanagan. Fests: UK fr. '81; Switz. '89. LPs: Conc., Muse.

McNEELY, JIM (JAMES HARRY), pno, comp, arr; b. Chicago, IL, 5/18/49. Parents, grandfath. pl. pno.; bro. is prof. bs. in Chi. Stud. pno., sax, cl. w. Bruno Michelotti in Chi., then cont. pno. stud. w. John Garvey, Morgan Powell at U. of Ill. 1967–75. Moved to NYC '75; pl. w. Ted Curson '76–8; Chet Baker '78; Thad Jones–Mel Lewis Orch. '78–84; Stan Getz '81–8; Joe Henderson '84–9; Phil Woods '90–5; own trio since '83. Has also pl. w. Art Farmer, Bobby Watson. McNeely has taught at the Jamey Aebersold Summer Jazz Clinics since '79; NYU since '81; William Paterson Coll. (N.J.) since '85; BMI Comps. Wkshp. since '91. His writing for the CHJB and Vanguard Jazz Orch. incl. his own fresh, idiosyncratically modern originals and skewed versions of swing era warhorses. Favs: Monk, Tyner, Hancock. Fests: Eur. since '77; Austral. since '80; Japan '90. TV: *In Performance at the White House* w. Getz. CDs: Steep.; Conc., Lip.; w. Mel Lewis (Muse); Getz (Conc.; Drey.); Woods (Conc.; Mile.; Mos.; Evid.); John Handy (Quartet); Rufus Reid (Sunny.); Vanguard Jazz Orch. *Plays McNeely* (NW).

McNEIL, JOHN PATRICK, tpt, flg; b. Yreka, CA, 3/23/48. Heard Louis Armstrong on TV at age 8 and "fell in love with the idea of playing tpt." Self-taught. Pl. first prof. gig in hs; then pl. in Louisville, Ky. To NYC 1975. Encouraged by Clark Terry. Worked w. Horace Silver, Thad Jones–Mel Lewis orch. Tour. Denmark w. own gp. '79. Pl. in western Eur., Austral. in '70s, '80s. Taught priv. for many yrs.; in '90s at New. Engl. Cons., commuting fr. NYC to Bost. Gigs w. No Exit Sextet, NYC '95. Rec. debut NYC '78 for Steep. McNeil's style is well-grounded in the bop era and combined w. the modal to produce a personal expression. Fav: F. Hubbard. Comps: "The Glass Room"; "Faun"; "Sea Breeze"; "Greenwich"; "Out." CD: Steep.; John McNeil–Kenny Berger (Synergy).

McPARTLAND, DICK (RICHARD GEORGE), gtr, bjo, vln; b. Chicago, IL, 5/18/05; d. Elmhurst, IL, 11/30/57. Started on vln. at age 5, stud. w. his fath., a mus. teacher. Member of Chi.'s legendary Austin High Gang, along w. cornetist bro. Jimmy, Dave Tough, Bud Freeman, and others. Replaced Eddie Lang w. Mound City Blue Blowers in mid to late-1920s, then worked in Chi. w. local bands. When in his early thirties, suffered a heart attack, which forced his retirement from mus. Rec. w. Irving Mills and Jack Teagarden '28 and bro. Jimmy '39. Drove a cab in Elmhurst, a Chi. suburb, and made occ. playing apps., the last of which was in

1955 w. Baby Dodds, Jim Lanigan, and bro. Jimmy. CDs: w. Teagarden (Conifer).

McPARTLAND, JIMMY (JAMES DUGALD), crnt; b. Chicago, IL 3/15/07; d. Port Washington, NY, 3/13/91. Studied vln. at early age w. his fath., a music teacher, then sw. to crnt. at age 15. Started band in hs w. bro. Dick, Bud Freeman, and Frank Teschemacher, which became known as the Austin High Gang. Replaced Bix Beiderbecke in the Wolverines at age 17; worked w. Art Kassel 1926 and Ben Pollack '27–9. Rec. in '27 as McKenzie and Condon's Chicagoans w. members of the Austin High Gang, helping to define the Chi. jazz style. Worked in B'way pit bands '29–30; w. Russ Columbo '31–2; Horace Heidt, Smith Ballew, and Harry Reser '33–5. Led his own gp. '36–41, w. such sidemen as Rosy McHargue, cl.; Joe Harris, tbn.; Boyce Brown, alto sax; Geo. Wettling, dms. Toured w. Jack Teagarden's bb bef. entering army '42, where he served as combat soldier in Normandy invasion. While pl. w. USO unit in Belgium, he met pnst. Margaret Marian Turner (Marian McPartland), who became his wife in '45. Back in US in mid '40s, he led various gps., occ. w. his wife on pno. In the '60s and '70s he cont. to work around NYC and on int'l tours; w. Tony Parenti at Jimmy Ryan's '65–6; visited So. Africa '71–2; tour. w. Art Hodes '74; Nice Jazz Fest. '74; concerts and wkshps. in schs. '74–75; NJF '78. Tour. Engl. w. sxt. of Brit. mus. '85. App. w. M. McPartland on PBS special, *The McPartlands on New Year's Eve* '90; final concert perf. at U. of Chi. '90. Although the McPartlands were divorced in '70 (remarried two weeks before his death), they cont. to work together occ. McPartland, whose crnt. pl. was much admired by Beiderbecke (his musical role model), was, in his early years, one of the best players in the classic Bix style. Later on his approach, without abandoning its lyricism, became more personally rough and ready. Video: *Jazz at the Top: Remembering Bix Beiderbecke*. TV: *The Magic Horn* (Alcoa Presents '56); *The Sound of Jazz* (CBS '57); w. Bud Freeman, Joe Sullivan, Gene Krupa, et al., *Chicago and All That Jazz* (NBC '61). LP: *Shades of Bix*. CDs: Jazz.; w. M. McPartland (JA); J. Teagarden (BB); Beiderbecke (Mile.; Timel.); Condon; B. Goodman (Class.); Freeman (Jazz Classics in Digital Stereo); *Chicago Jazz Summit* (Atl.).

McPARTLAND, MARIAN (Margaret Marian Turner), pno, comp; b. Slough, England, 3/20/18. Great-uncle, Sir Frederick Dyson, mayor of Windsor, pl. cello. Moth. pl. classical pno. Stud. Guildhall Sch. of Mus., London 1937–8. Toured Engl. w. 4-pno. vaudeville act. While pl. for troops in Belgium dur. WWII as Marian Page, she met Jimmy McPartland; they married in '45 and moved to US in '46; pl. w. Jimmy's qnt. in Chi., then form. a trio to pl. at Embers in NYC '50. In '52 she opened at Hickory House and stayed there intermittently to '60. Pl. w. B. Goodman Sxt. '63. Own radio show on WBAI, NYC in mid '60s. Started own rec. comp., Halcyon '70. Active as teacher, indoctrinating young children and teenagers in understanding of jazz. Since '79 she has cond. *Marian McPartland's Piano Jazz*, an intimate radio series on the NPR network and its longest-running program, w. guest artists (mostly pnsts.); many of these broadcasts were issued on CD by JA. Numerous overseas tours, incl. So. Amer. w. Earl Hines, Teddy Wilson, Ellis Larkins '74; Japan '90; w. Benny Carter '91; fests. in Nice, Berlin, Copenhagen. Has perf. w. several symph. orchs. Celebrated her 80th birthday w. many guest stars, including her original Hickory House trio (Bill Crow, bs; Joe Morello, dms.), at a Town Hall concert, March '98. As her many recs. demonstrate, McPartland has over the years grown in harmonic sensitivity and subtlety of invention; she has been a consistently articulate spokesperson for jazz in the media and in her writings Awards: Deems Taylor; Peabody; *DB* Lifetime Achievement '97. Best known comp: "Ambiance"; Collab. w. Peggy Lee on "In the Days of Our Love"; w. Johnny Mercer on "Twilight World." Film: *Great Day in Harlem*. Video: *Jazz at the Top: Remembering Bix Beiderbecke*. TV: narrator for *Women in Jazz*, A&E. Book: *All in Good Time* (Oxford) '87. CDs: Conc.; JA; w. Ken Peplowski (Conc.); Helen Merrill (Merc.).

McPHEE, JOE, comp, poet, saxes, tpt, tbn; b. Miami, FL, 11/3/39. Began pl. tpt. in sch. band, then pl. w. army band in Germ. 1964–5. Made rec. debut on tpt. w. Clifford Thornton '67; pl. w. Matt Jordan Orch. late '60s. Self-taught on sax fr. '68. Rec. as unaccomp. soloist and lead. of free jazz ensembles fr. '69. Taught lecture course, The Revolution in Sound, at Vassar Coll. '69–71. Pl. in NYC w. Clifford Thornton, Don Cherry, Jazz Composers Orch. early '70s. Lived in Eur. '75–7; pl. w. Steve Lacy, others. In '81 the work of Dr. Edw. de Bono inspired him to adopt his "Lateral Thinking" approach, leading to what he terms "Po Music." Tour. Eur. w. trio and app. at Earshot Jazz Fest. in '95. Led gp. that incl. Joseph Jarman and Sunny Murray at Ayler Tribute in NYC '96. His work, *Unquenchable Fire*, was presented at Lincoln Ctr. in '97. Presented a series of concerts at Knitting Factory, NYC, Aug. '98; also concert at Merkin Hall. Rec. w. Jimmy Giuffre; Raymond Boni; Charles Moffett; André Jaume; Daunik Lazro; Evan Parker; Pauline Oliveros Deep Listening Band; and others. Despite his prolific rec. career, McPhee remains largely unknown in his homeland, but by '97 he was making more US apps. Received Earshot Golden Ear award for Best Concert '95 and '97. Fests: NJF '72; Willisau JF '76, '82; New Mus. Amer., SF '81; Cannes Film Fest. '87; and many others Eur. Fests. CDs: Hat Hut; hatArt; w. Jaume; Boni (Celp); Oliveros (Mode).

McPHERSON, CHARLES, alto, tnr saxes, pno, comp; b. Joplin, MO, 7/24/39. Moved to Det. at age 9; start. on alto at 13. Stud. w. Barry Harris at 18 and pl. first prof. gigs w. him at 19. To NYC 1959; on recommendation of Yusef Lateef join. Charles Mingus Jazz Wkshp. '60; pl. w. Mingus off and on until '74, incl. Eur. tour '72. Pl. and/or rec. w. Harris; Art Farmer; L. Hampton; D. Gillespie. Moved to San Diego '78; worked in the So. Calif. area in gps. that sometimes incl. his son, Chuck, on dms. Pl. on soundtrack of film, *Sweet Love Bitter* '66; and (in ens. only) *Bird*, '88; also worked w. gp., Uptown Express, incl. Tom Harrell. Taught at San Diego St. U. '83–5. A strong interpreter and extender of the Charlie Parker idiom w. a particularly singing tone. Several concert apps. for Jazz at Lincoln Center in late '90s. Favs: Parker, Hodges, Stitt. Poll: *DB* Critics TDWR '67. CDs: Arab.; Prest.; Main.; w. Mingus (Col., BN); Don Patterson; Eddie Jefferson (Prest.); Pepper Adams (FS); Dave Pike (Timel.); LCJO (Col.).

McPHERSON, ERIC CHRISTOPHER STE-PHENS, dms; b. NYC, 12/11/70. Studied w. Michael Carvin 1983–9, then at LaGuardia HS '86–9; cont. stud. w. Jackie McLean at Hartt Coll. of Mus. Pl. w. all-city hs band, McDonald's band '89; Jesse Davis, Collective Expression fr. '89; Roy Hargrove '90; Jackie McLean fr. '91. Favs: Blakey, Carvin, Elvin Jones. Polls: *DB* Best Student gp. and Soloist '89. Fests: Finland '90; Japan '90–1. CDs: w. J. Davis (Conc.); McLean (Ant.; BN).

McRAE, CARMEN, voc, pno; b. NYC, 4/8/20; d. Beverly Hills, CA, 11/10/94. Studied pno. priv. Discovered by Irene Wilson Kitchings (ex-wife of Teddy Wilson and comp. of "Some Other Spring"). Sang w. Benny Carter's band in 1944; later w. Count Basie; and in '46–7 w. Mercer Ellington, making her rec. debut w. him as Carmen Clarke (she was then married to dmr. Kenny Clarke); later married bsst. Ike Isaacs. Acquired a local following as intermission pnst. and singer at Minton's Playhouse, NYC; then sang often w. Mat Mathews Qnt. and rec. for small labels bef. signing w. Decca in '54. Winner of *DB* critics poll as New Star in '54, she moved gradually to the top echelons of jazz singers, achieving recognition through

tours of Eur. and Japan and, most notably, annual apps. at the MJF incl. in Dave Brubeck's *The Real Ambassadors* '62. Strongly infl. by Billie Holiday (her Col. album, *Lover Man*, was devoted to Holiday's repertoire) but never a sound-alike, McRae was a ballad singer of great subtlety and a jazz stylist whose bop infls. were noteworthy, particularly in her scat vocals. A capable pnst., she frequently accomp. herself. In May '91 after an appearance at the Blue Note in NYC, she had an attack of respiratory failure brought on by emphysema and was inactive at her home in Calif., except for some recording, during the next years. Comp: "Dream of Life." Ralph J. Gleason wrote of her: "She can make you believe any song she sings." Film: *Hotel*. TV: Numerous apps. in US and Eur.; seen in docus. *The Story of Jazz* and *Lady Day*: as actress in *Roots*. CDs: Qwest; Dec.; Novus; Den.; Atl.; Conc.; Dunhill; BN; Col.; Beth.; Verve; w. Betty Carter (Verve); Geo. Shearing (Conc.); Brubeck (Col.).

McRAE, TEDDY (THEODORE; "MR. BEAR"), tnr sax, comp, lead; b. Waycross, GA, 1/22/08; d. NYC, 3/4/99. Raised in Philadelphia. From mus. family. Stud. medicine first. Took mus. lessons fr. bro. and other priv. teachers. Pl. w. June Cole on and off fr. 1926. Organized band w. bros. around '28; then pl. w. other bands incl. Chick Webb, Charlie Johnson, Elmer Snowden '32; Stuff Smith '34; Lil Armstrong '35. Pl. w. Webb '36–9, also serving as arr., staying on when Ella Fitzgerald assumed leadership after Webb's death '39–41. Pl. w. Cab Calloway '41–2; J. Lunceford '42; L. Hampton '43. Staff arr. for Artie Shaw '43; mus. dir. of Louis Armstrong's bb '44–5; own band '45. Pl. in combos but was more occupied w. arr. and mus. publishing. Form. Enrica and Rae-Cox rec. labels w. Eddie Wilcox '59. Rec. in '30s w. Red Allen; Benny Morton; Putney Dandridge; Teddy Wilson; Chris Columbus. Comp. "Back Bay Shuffle," "Traffic Jam," both rec. by Shaw; "You Showed Me the Way." CDs: w. Webb; Fitzgerald (Dec.); Allen; Wilson; Dandridge; Louis Jordan (Class.).

McSHANN, JAY "HOOTIE" (JAMES C.), pno, voc; b. Muskogee, OK, 1/12/16 (he claimed that a 1909 birthdate, given elsewhere, is incorrect); d. Kansas City, MO, 12/7/06. Self-taught; stud. later at U. Missouri-KC 1952–3. Worked w. Al Denny in Tulsa '33; w. Ed Hill and His Bostonians in Albuquerque, New Mex. '35; w. Buster Smith, Dee Stewart and Elmer Hopkins Duo in KC '37. In '38 he form. a band that rec. a series of sess. for Dec. '41–2, incl. Charlie Parker's first recs. Drafted in late '43, he spent '44 in the army, then reorganized his band in

NYC. Moved to LA late '40s, rec. there w. small gps. for Aladdin and Merc. Fr. '50s he lived and worked mainly out of KC. In later yrs. he traveled extensively throughout France, Belgium, Engl., and Japan. Feat. in memorable jazz docu. film, *The Last of the Blue Devils* '79, also in video (Rhap.). Apps. in TV docus. *Celebrating Bird* '87 and *The Story of Jazz* '93. Awards incl. honorary doctorate from UM-KC and cert. of achievement from Rutgers U. Reg. participant in Colo. JPs. McShann developed a personal, percussive style, specializing in blues and boogie-woogie; sang w. a timbre almost exactly like that of his orig. band voc., Walter Brown. CDs: Mos.; B&B; Chiaro.; Dec.; Mile.; Stash; BL; MM; Sack.; McShann–John Hicks (Res); 24 tracks in *The 1940s Mercury Sessions* (Merc.); w. M. McPartland (JA); Ben Webster (Em.); Eddie Cleanhead Vinson (Del.).

McVEA, JACK (JOHN), tnr sax; b. Los Angeles, CA, 11/5/14; d. Los Angeles, 12/27/00. Father pl. bjo.; stud. alto sax w. a mus. in his father's band. Grad. Jefferson HS 1932; prof. debut w. Dootsie Williams' Harlem Dukes, Club Alabam; w. local bands through '30s. Joined orig. Lionel Hampton band on bari. sax '40; pl. w. Snub Mosley '43. Biggest hit was "Open the Door, Richard," which he introduced in '46 on recs. and in film *Sarge Goes to Washington.* Studio dates at MGM; pl. w. Dizzy Gillespie and Charlie Parker on Slim Gaillard's recs., *Slim's Jam,* etc. '45. Fr. '76 to '91, he worked at Disneyland. Retired in '91 for health reasons. CDs: w. T-Bone Walker (Mos.); L. Hampton (Dec.); JATP (Verve); C. Parker (Sav.); Duke Henderson in *West Coast Jive* (Del.).

MEADOR, DARMON AUGUST, voc, tnr and sop saxes, EWI; b. Waterville, ME, 8/26/61. Parents musical. Stud. at U. of Southern Mass. 1979–82; Ithaca Coll. '82–4. Moved to NYC '86; form. NY Voices '87 where he is mus. dir. and arr., as well as voc. and instrumentalist. Though sometimes compared to Manh. Transfer, the gp. developed a sound and style of its own. Meador is "especially interested in voc. improv., and bridging the gap between voc. and instrumental jazz." Fests: w. NY Voices, Berlin '89; Cascais '90; Bern '91. First rec. on GRP '89. CDs: GRP; Victor.

MEHEGAN, JOHN F., pno, educ; b. Hartford, CT, 6/6/20; d. New Canaan, CT, 4/3/84. Studied vln. but self-taught on pno. To NYC 1941; taught jazz priv. fr. '44; assist. Teddy Wilson at Metropolitan Mus. Sch. '45; head of jazz dept '46; taught jazz at Juilliard fr. '47; faculty, Columbia Teach. Coll '57–60; teacher at U. of Bridgeport '68; lectured at Yale '74–5. Pl. or rec. w. Lionel Hampton; Charles Mingus; Eddie

Costa. Pl. often w. own duo, trio at The Composer club, NYC '57. Two-month research and concert tour of So. Africa, summer '59; clinics in Scandinavia '74, '75. Fest: NJF as perf., panelist, critic '58. B'way: pl. in *Streetcar Named Desire.* TV: comp. and pl. soundtrack for Arthur Miller's *Story of Two Mondays* '73. Achieved prominence as pioneering pedagogue of jazz; author of *Jazz Improvisation,* first definitive text on jazz mechanics. Writer on jazz for *NY Herald Tribune, DB, Saturday Review,* etc. Rec. "Blowtop Blues" w. Hampton, Dec. '45. CDs: three tracks, backed by Mingus, K. Clarke, in *I Just Love Jazz Piano* (Sav.); w. Chuck Wayne (Sav.); Mingus box (Deb.).

MEHLDAU, BRAD, pno, comp; b. Jacksonville, FL, 8/23/70. Began experimenting with the pno. at age 4, took lessons fr. age 6. Lived in New York, New Hampshire, and Georgia. At age 10 his family moved to Connecticut. Att. Hall HS in Hartford. Pl. in sch.'s well-known jazz band and won Best All-Around Musician in Berklee Sch. of Mus. hs competition. Classically trained, he stud. jazz in the Jazz Program of the New Sch., NYC, w. Fred Hersch; Junior Mance; Kenny Werner; and Jimmy Cobb, who hired him for his gp., Cobb's Mob. Rec. w. Christopher Hollyday '91; Jesse Davis '93; own trio w. dmr. Jordi Rossy '94. In '94 Mehldau join. Joshua Redman's qt., tour. the Eur. festival circuit that summer and pl. w. Redman into '95. Form. trio w. Larry Grenadier and Rossy '95; rec. his first of three annual *Art of the Trio* albums and perf. internationally in trio and solo. Pl. in Lincoln Center's Piano Masters solo series, fall '98. Mehldau's body language at the keyboard and his introspective style have drawn comparisons with Bill Evans while some of his right-hand expositions bring Keith Jarrett to mind. These are two of the pnsts. that he cites as infls., along w. Peterson, Wynton Kelly, Tyner, Hancock, Miles Davis, and Coltrane; Schubert, Beethoven, and Schumann. It has been written that Mehldau "artfully combines the sophistication of classical training with a deep jazz sensibility." The classical influence turns up in the contrapuntal lines he weaves between his hands and the way he approaches his original comps., some of which, such as "Young Werther" and "Mignon's Song," reflect his abiding interest in German poetry and literature. He has also rec. the Beatles' "Blackbird" and "Exit Music (For a Film)" by Radiohead. Fests: Eur. w. Redman; Umbria Jazz '97–8; Umbria Winter Jazz. Polls: *DB* Critics TDWR '97; Best New Artist, *JT* Readers '97. Film: Soundtrack for *Eyes Wide Shut* '99. CDs: WB; FS; *Konitz, Mehldau, Haden* (BN); w. Jesse Davis (Conc.); C. Hollyday (Novus); J. Redman (WB).

MELDONIAN, DICK (RICHARD ANTHONY), cl, alto, tnr, sop saxes, fl, picc; b. Providence, RI, 1/27/30. Wife is singer-comp. Claire Zilles (aka Pinkie Corrigan). Stud. cl. and alto sax w. Joe Piacitelli 1938–46. Pl. w. local gps. and sat in w. Coleman Hawkins, Roy Eldridge, Ben Webster fr. '43. Led own qt. in Providence club '44. Family moved to LA '46. Pl. w. Freddie Slack '49. Pl. and rec. w. Charlie Barnet '50–1; Stan Kenton '52; Neal Hefti '53; Johnny Richards–Sarah Vaughan, Dick Collins, Noro Morales, Barnet '54; Kenton '55; Nat Pierce, Erroll Garner, Woody Herman '57; Tito Rodriguez, Tito Puente '58; Elliot Lawrence '58–64; Bill Russo, Marion Evans '59; Gerry Mulligan '60; Woody Herman, Gil Evans '61. Extensive freelance commercial and jazz studio work fr. '53. Regular sub in *Merv Griffin Show* band '68–73. Led own gps. fr. early '60s, incl. qt. at NJF '64; Jersey Swingers '78; orch. w. Sonny Igoe early '80s; duo and trio w. Marty Grosz fr. '80s. Meldonian has worked as a character model in TV and print ads fr. '70. Favs: Al Cohn, Zoot Sims, Phil Woods; arrs: Bill Holman, Gil Evans, Gene Roland. Films: app. w. Barnet '50, '67. TV: *Merv Griffin Show*; *Cavalcade of Bands* w. Barnet '50, w. Kenton '52, '55. CDs: Circle; w. S. Vaughan (Mer.); Kenton (Cap.); Mulligan (Verve); Garner (Col.).

MELILLO, MIKE (MICHAEL COSIMO), pno, comp; b. Newark, NJ, 6/9/39. Father was club date bsst.; uncle, club date pnst., and pres. of Newark mus. union. Stud. w. Achilles D'Amico and pl. tbn. in band at Arts HS, Newark; Woody Shaw, Larry Young, Andy Bey were classmates. Att. Rutgers U., where he form. a trio that became the house band at the Clifton Tap Room '62–4; accomp. Chet Baker; Phil Woods; Art Farmer; Clark Terry; Kenny Dorham; Coleman Hawkins; Ben Webster; Sonny Rollins; others. Pl. w. Rollins '65–6; then taught mus. in hs. Rejoin. Rollins '66–7; then form. gp., In Free Association, w. gtrst. Harry Leahey '67. Taught at NY Coll. of Mus. '67; N.J. St. Coll. '68–9; Tombrock Coll. '68–70. Moved to rural N.J. to concentrate on comp. Jammed w. neighbors Phil Woods, Bill Goodwin, Steve Gilmore fr. '73; form. the Phil Woods Qt. around '77. Pl. w. Woods until '81. In Italy '83–93, pl. w. trio and as solo pnst. Taught at Jazz U., Terni, Italy '86–93. Melillo ret. to live in the US in '93. Favs: Bud Powell, Monk. CDs: Phil.; SN; Red; w. Woods (Mos; Adelphi; SB; CleanCuts).

MELLE, GIL (GILBERT JOHN), bari, tnr saxes; comp; b. NYC, 12/31/31. Studied sax, oboe and cl. Self-taught. Occ. concert and club dates in 1950s; app. at NJF '54; rec. for BN and Prest. An early pro-ponent of el. mus.; comp. many film scores. From '60s mostly active in LA as comp. Wrote scores for more than 125 films. Built his own synths., drm. machine. Pl. Monterey JF '67, w. all-electronic jazz band, the Electronauts. Active fr. young age as painter and sculptor. Did covers for his own LPs as well as those by Monk; Miles Davis; Sonny Rollins. Worked on computer-based digital painting in mid '90s. Rec. electronic jazz album, *Tome VI* (Verve) '67. CDs: Prest.; BN.

MELROSE, FRANK (FRANKLYN TAFT), pno, comp; b. Sumner, IL 11/26/07; d. Hammond, IN, 1/9/41. Started on vln.; self-taught as pnst. Active in Chi. w. Wingy Manone, Bud Freeman 1928–9; sometimes rec. under the name of Kansas City Frank. Rec. w. Johnny and Baby Dodds in the Beale St. Washboard Band '29. Pl. w. Bud Jacobson at Chi. World's Fair '33; then inactive until '40, when he worked in Chi. clubs until his death. Last rec. w. Bud Jacobson's Jungle Kings in '41. Highly regarded in trad. jazz circles. CDs: w. Junie C. Cobb (Collector's Jazz).

MELVOIN, MIKE (MICHAEL), pno, kybds, comp; b. Oshkosh, WI, 5/10/37. Studied pno. fr. age 3 in Milwaukee; B.A. in English, grad. Dartmouth 1959. Moved to LA in '62; pl. w. Leroy Vinnegar; Frank Rosolino; Gerald Wilson bb; Paul Horn qnt.; Terry Gibbs. Accomp. and/or mus. dir. for many singers, incl. Joe Williams and Peggy Lee. Later became the first active mus. to serve as National Pres. of NARAS. Received three Most Valuable Player awards from NARAS, as well as the Emeritus Player award. Still active as jazz mus. in '90s. CDs: Voss; w. Manh. Transfer (Atl.).

MENGELBERG, MISHA, pno, comp; b. Kiev, USSR, 6/5/35. His fath., a Dutchman, led a studio orch. In late 1930s his family ret. to Netherlands, where he stud. pno. fr. age 5. Inspired by Ellington and Stravinsky, he cont. studies at a cons., won a prize at a jazz competition in '59; form. jazz gp. w. Han Bennink, which acc. Eric Dolphy shortly bef. his death; app. at '66 NJF. Many assoc. w. visiting US avant-gardists, incl., dur. the '80s, Steve Lacy; Roswell Rudd; George Lewis. An unorthodox and adventurous artist, he has been represented on many recs. w. Dolphy; Rudd; and others. CDs: SN; Avant; Hatology.

MENZA, DON (DONALD JOSEPH), saxes, fls, cls, comp, arr; b. Buffalo, NY, 4/22/36. Began cl. stud. at age 12; attended State U. of NY, Fredonia. Self-taught comp., arr. Join. 7th Army Jazz Orch., Stuttgart, Germ. 1956 w. Don Ellis; Cedar Walton;

Leo Wright; Lanny Morgan. Prof. rec. debut w. Al Belletto Sxt. '59. Pl. w. and arr. for bbs of Maynard Ferguson '60–62; Stan Kenton '62; led qt. w. Sam Noto '63. Worked in Munich '64–7 w. Max Greger TV Band; also co-leader of Bavarian Radio Jazz Ensemble, winning top award at first Montreux JF '67. Pl. w. Buddy Rich fr. '68. Settling in LA, he worked w. major film and rec. studios and TV networks; feat. soloist in several films, incl. *Havana* '89. With Louie Bellson Orch. and Qt. '70; Henry Mancini Orch. '70. Frequent sub in Woody Herman Band. Dur. '80s he went to Germ. w. Peter Herbolzheimer Orch. Back to LA w. bands of Bill Berry; Capp-Pierce; Benny Carter; and own orch. Pl. w. Bellson often in '90s. NEA grant to write three comps. for coll. wkshp. bands. Infl. by arrs. Bill Holman, Gil Evans, Oliver Nelson, Claus Ogerman. Fav. tnr. players: Ammons, Getz, Rollins. CDs: Voss; w. Bellson (MM); Ferguson (Roul.); Tito Puente (Conc.); Buddy Rich (PJ).

MERCER, JOHNNY (JOHN HERNDON), voc, comp; b. Savannah, GA, 11/18/09; d. Los Angeles, CA, 6/25/76. To NYC w. acting gp. 1927. By early '30s he had become well-known as outstanding lyricist and occ. singer on recs. w. Paul Whiteman; Dorsey Bros.; Benny Goodman; Bing Crosby; et al. In LA he co-founded Capitol Recs. label in '42, rec. own sess. and guest dates w. other artists. Among his best known songs were "If You Were Mine"; "Lazybones"; "Jeepers Creepers"; "Blues in the Night"; "One for My Baby"; "That Old Black Magic"; "Skylark"; "Come Rain or Come Shine"; and "Moon River." For a few songs, such as "Dream," he wrote music as well as lyrics. His last comp. was "I'm Shadowing You," w. mus. by Blossom Dearie. Although songwriting was his principal activity, Mercer had a distinctive, jazz-oriented voc. style and cont. to rec. through the yrs. Book: *Our Huckleberry Friend: The Life, Times and Lyrics of Johnny Mercer*, Robert Bach and Ginger Mercer, '82. CDs: Cap.; DRG; Conifer; Bobby Darin–Johnny Mercer (Atco); w. J. Teagarden (BB); Nat King Cole (Cap.).

MERRILL, HELEN (Helena Anna Milcetic), voc; b. NYC, 7/21/30. Mother and sis. were amateur singers; son is rock musician. Self-taught. Sang in amateur contests fr. 1944. Encouraged by Miles Davis; Stan Getz; Don Byas; Dizzy Gillespie; and others to pursue prof. career. Tour. w. Reggie Childs Orch '46–7. Married cl. Aaron Sachs '47 (divorced in mid '50s). Club dates w. Jerry Wald late '40s; then join. Earl Hines '52. Made rec. debut on Roost label in '53; signed w. Em. '54–8, where she was accomp. by Quincy Jones Orch. w. Clifford Brown; Gil Evans;

and others. Tour. Brazil in '57; lived and perf. in Eur. and Japan '59–63. Scarcity of work in NYC made her move to Tokyo in the mid '60s, where she perf. and occ. taught '67–72. Perf. in Japan w. Teddy Wilson, Gary Peacock. Lived in Hong Kong, '72; then moved to Chi. Pl. w. local mus., form. 10-pc. band w. Kenny Söderblom. Since ret. to NYC in the late '70s, has rec. w. Gil Evans; Gordon Beck; Stephane Grappelli; Roger Kellaway; Red Mitchell; Steve Lacy; Art Farmer; others. Tour. Japan w. Ron Carter '89. Rec. w. Wayne Shorter '92. Rec. of a commissioned work by comp. Jean-Yves Bosseur was selected to represent France in the Int'l Music Fest. Merrill is an intimate, moody singer with a quality that has often been described as "smoky" but which is also part velvet. Her care with a lyric, harmonic awareness, and warmth mark her as a subtle, superior stylist. Favs: Sarah Vaughan, Lucy Shelton. Polls: *SJ* '67–72. Fests: all major fr. '59. TV: Eur., Jap. TV. CDs: Merc.; Em.; Vict.; Ant.; PAR; Owl; Verve; w. Billy Eckstine (Merc.); Lee Konitz (Evid.).

MERRITT, JYMIE (JAMES), bs, el-bs, comp; b. Philadelphia, PA, 5/3/26. Mother was choral dir., pno. and voice teacher. Insp. by Ellington rec. feat. Jimmy Blanton. In mil. 1944–6; then stud. w. Carl Torello of Phila. Symph. and for three yrs. at Ornstein Mus. Sch. in Phila. First prof. gigs w. Tadd Dameron, Benny Golson, John Coltrane, Philly Joe Jones '49. Tour. w. Bull Moose Jackson '51–3; Chris Powell, B. B. King '55–7. Moved to NYC '57. Pl. w. Art Blakey '58–63; Chet Baker '64; Max Roach '65–8; Dizzy Gillespie '69; Lee Morgan '70–2. Formed own gp., the Forerunners, '62, which evolved into the cooperative unit, Forerunner, and cont. to be active in the Phila. area under Merritt's artistic guidance. Forerunner's repertoire incl. Merrit's extended comp., *The Spiritual Impulse*. Favs: Ray Brown, Mingus, Pettiford, Blanton. CDs: w. Blakey (BB; BN; Imp.; Select Jazz); Lee Morgan (BN).

METCALF, LOUIS, tpt; b. Webster Groves, MO, 2/28/05; d. NYC, 10/27/81. Started on dms., then crnt.; w. Charlie Creath in St. Louis off and on 1919–23. In NYC '23, pl. w. Jimmy Cooper's Black and White Review '23–4. Fr. '24 to '27 he pl. w. various gps., incl. Charlie Johnson; Willie "The Lion" Smith; Jelly Roll Morton; Sidney Bechet. Join. Duke Ellington '26–8; w. Luis Russell, King Oliver '29. In early '30s he briefly led own band; then to Montreal, Can., where he spent three years. working mostly in vaudeville as singer, dancer, and emcee. In late '30s pl. on riverboats out of St. Louis; moved to Can. '44–51, lead. his own int'l band in Montreal and on tour. From '51 he was mainly active as a freelancer in

NYC at Metropole Cafe, Embers, etc. One of the early practitioners of the muted, growl-style pl. assoc. w. Bubber Miley. Feat. on "West End Blues," "Call of the Freaks" w. Oliver; "Savoy Shout" w. Russell; "East St. Louis Toodle-oo," "Birmingham Breakdown" w. Ellington. Also rec. w. blues singers, incl. Bessie Smith and Rosa Henderson. CDs: w. D. Ellington (BB; Dec.); B. Smith (Col.).

METHENY, PAT (PATRICK BRUCE), gtr, comp; b. Lee's Summit, MO, 8/12/54. Younger bro. of tptr. Mike Metheny. Stud. tpt. fr. age 8, then, infl. by Wes Montgomery, sw. to gtr. in 1967. In '68 he perf. at a summer fest. w. Attila Zoller, who convinced him to go to NYC. Later was student and teacher at U. of Miami, Fla.; also stud. at Berklee Sch.; toured w. Gary Burton off and on '74-7. In '75 he worked w. kybdst. Lyle Mays, who became a frequent musical assoc. Rec. debut in '76 w. Jaco Pastorius and Bob Moses. Since then has led a gp. which has rec. profusely and made int'l tours. Among his sidemen have been Dewey Redman; Jack DeJohnette; Nana Vasconcelos; Mark Egan; Michael Brecker; Charlie Haden; and Billy Higgins. Pl. and/or rec. w. Julius Hemphill; Sonny Rollins; Abbey Lincoln; and others. As comp. Metheny has written TV and film scores, incl. *Amazing Stories* TV series and Schlesinger film, *The Falcon and the Snowman*. In recent yrs. he has pl. standard gtr., 12-string el., and gtr. synth. Especially popular in Can., where an entire Montreal fest. was dedicated to his mus. Always a highly proficient gtrst. w. a solid gift for melodic improv., he added a more unusual element to his style in the early '80s when he began to occ. incorporate Ornette Coleman–inspired free-jazz elements in his perf. Coleman recorded with him on *Song X* '85. Tour. and rec. w. Joshua Redman in '90s. Rec. collab. w. John Scofield; Derek Bailey. CDs: ECM; WB; Verve; Geffen; BN; KFW; w. Gary Burton (GRP); Mike Metheny; M. Brecker (Imp.); J. DeJohnette (MCA); Trilok Gurtu (CMP); Roy Haynes (Drey.); C. Haden; Abbey Lincoln (Verve); J. Redman; Kenny Garrett (WB); Tony Williams (Ark21).

METTOME, DOUG (DOUGLAS VOLL), tpt; b. Salt Lake City, UT, 3/19/25; d. Salt Lake City, 2/17/64. Inspired by Roy Eldridge; had own band in Salt Lake City. After three yrs. in army, worked w. Billy Eckstine 1946–7; Herbie Fields off and on '48–52. Was best known for his work w. Benny Goodman's '49 bebop bb and sxt., esp. on recs., "Bedlam"; "Blue Lou"; "Undercurrent Blues." Worked w. Woody Herman '51–2; Tommy Dorsey '53; Pete Rugolo '54; Johnny Richards; and the Dorsey Bros. Retired '58; then freelanced in NYC

early '60s, incl. own qt. at Roundtable, pl. in a style suggesting Roy Eldridge, his first infl., also elements of Bobby Hackett and Billy Butterfield. Greatly underrated soloist whose infls. incl. Fats Navarro and Red Rodney. CDs: w. Goodman (Mos.; Cap.; Hep); Herman (Disc.); Buddy Rich (Hep).

MEURKENS, (THOMAS) HENDRIK, hca, vib; b. Hamburg, Germany, 8/6/57. Began on vib. at age 16, hca. at 19. Mainly self-taught; stud. vib. w. Wolfgang Schluter. Pl. w. dixie. and swing bands in Germ. early to mid 1970s. Stud. theory, arr. at Berklee Coll. of Mus. '77–80, then ret. to Germ. Worked as studio mus. and comp. film scores '80–2. In Rio de Janiero '82–3. Led own qt. in Germ. '83. Tour. Eur. w. band pl. vib. '84–8; also pl. for Germ. TV series and w. Danish Radio bb. Rec. w. Sweets Edison mid '80s; David Friedman in Rio '89. Tour. Eur. pl. hca. w. Brazilian rhythm section '90. Rec. as lead. w. Paquito D'Rivera, Claudio Roditi '91. Moved to NYC '92. No one since Toots Thielemans has shown the saxophonic fluidity and invention on hca. like Meurkens. Favs: vib: Bobby Hutcherson, Milt Jackson, Victor Feldman; hca: Thielemans, Stevie Wonder. Polls: Germ. Phono Academy, '83. Fests: all major in Eur. CDs: Bella.; Conc.; w. Mary Stallings; Charlie Byrd; Manfredo Fest; Allen Farnham (Conc.).

MEZZROW, MEZZ (Milton Mesirow), cl, saxes; b. Chicago, IL, 11/9/1899; d. Paris, France, 8/5/72. Studied sax in Pontiac Reformatory 1917. Played around Chi. in '20s; rec. w. Jungle Kings and Chi. Rhythm Kings '27–8 and w. Eddie Condon '28; briefly worked in Paris '29. Dur. the '30s he was only occ. active in mus. Led bands for Brunswick and Victor-BB rec. dates '33–4, '38; briefly led an interracial band called The Disciples of Swing, NYC '37; but mainly made his living selling marijuana, for which he was jailed fr. '40 to '42. Rec. for his own King Jazz label w. Sidney Bechet, Hot Lips Page, Art Hodes, and others fr. '45 to '48. Played Nice JF '48; lived in France permanently fr. '51 until his death. Mezzrow was a highly controversial figure, often belittled as a mediocre mus.; Nat Hentoff dubbed him the "Baron Münchausen of jazz." A colorful autobiography, *Really the Blues*, written w. Bernard Wolfe '46, incl. his experience as an opium addict. The French critic Hugues Panassié, an ardent admirer, hailed Mezzrow as the greatest white clst. and perhaps the greatest white mus. Mezzrow, however, regarded himself as a "voluntary Negro." His best rec. perf. are found on his '34 Vict. sessions. CDs: Class.; Story.; BB; GHB; w. Benny Carter (BB; B&B); Armstrong; Bechet; Condon in *At the Jazz Band Ball* (BB).

MICHELOT, PIERRE, bs; b. St. Denis, France, 3/3/28; d. Paris, 7/3/05. Began on pno. at age 7, then sw. to bs. at age 16, stud. w. member of Paris Opera orch. Made prof. debut on USO tour. Pl. w. Rex Stewart 1948; Coleman Hawkins '49. Tour. France and Germ. w. Kenny Clarke '49–50. Worked at Club Saint-Germain w. Django Reinhardt '50; Stephane Grappelli '55. Generally recognized as the foremost French bsst., Michelot worked w. many Amer. mus., incl. Don Byas, John Lewis, and Thelonious Monk at the Ringside early '50s; Lester Young, Dexter Gordon, Stan Getz, Bud Powell at the Blue Note '56–60. Also rec. in France w. Zoot Sims '50; James Moody '50–1; Kenny Clarke '50–9; Dizzy Gillespie '52, '63; Martial Solal '53–68; Miles Davis '57; Bud Powell '60–1. Arr. for Chet Baker; K. Clarke; own bb. Member of Jacques Loussier's trio, Play Bach '59–74. Michelot received the Prix Django Reinhardt fr. the Academie du Jazz '63. He perf. w. Dexter Gordon in Bertrand Tavernier's '86 film *Round Midnight* and tour. the US w. Gordon the following yr. Fav: Pettiford. CDs: w. D. Gordon (BN); Miles Davis (Col.; Font.; Jazz Unlimited); Bud Powell (Drey.; BN; Col.); Don Byas (Col.); Lucky Thompson (FS); S. Grappelli; T. Thielemans (Verve); Clifford Brown (Vogue/RCA; Prest.).

MICKMAN, HERB, bs, pno; b. NYC, 3/1/40. Took up pno. in 1947, bs. in '55, el-bs. in '68. Toured as Sarah Vaughan's mus. dir. '65–8; then settled in LA. Has been active as a teacher and educ., making a lifetime study of jazz pno. styles. Formerly on faculty of LA Jazz Wkshp. and the Grove Sch. in Van Nuys, Calif., he was co-founder of the LA Bass Club. In '92 he taught jazz pno. classes at UCLA Extension. Feat. in bs. duets w. John Clayton in Clayton-Hamilton Orch '89–92. CDs: w. Clayton-Hamilton Orch. (Capri; Conc.).

MIDDLETON, VELMA, voc; b. St. Louis, MO, 9/1/17; d. Freetown, Sierra Leone, 2/10/61. Featured in night clubs as solo act fr. early 1930s. Joined Louis Armstrong's bb as voc. in '42 and remained w. him in various small gps. until her death. A fair jazz singer, her perfs., incl. duets w. Armstrong, were heavily interlaced w. comedy and dancing, which pleased audiences but was often frowned on by the jazz press. Rec. two albums under own name w. Earl Hines and Cozy Cole '48, '51. CDs: w. Armstrong (Dec.; Col.; Vict.; Story.).

MIGLIORI, JAY, tnr sax, cl, fl; b. Erie, PA, 11/14/30; d. Mission Viejo, CA, 9/21/01. Musical family: fath. pl. gtr. and mand., sists. pl. pno and vln. Stud. St. Louis Inst. of Mus. 1949–50; Berklee Sch.

of Mus. '53–5. Pl w. air force band in Tex. '51–2. In Bost. pl. w. house bands at Hi-Hat '53 and Storyville '54. With Woody Herman '56–9, incl. 4 mos. in So. Amer. Settled in LA '59. In '60s worked w. Charlie Barnet; Si Zentner; Gil Evans (at MJF); and the Terry Gibbs and Gerald Wilson bbs. Eur. tour w. Frank Zappa '71. Charter member of Supersax '72 to '90s. Also led his own small gps. CDs: Disc.; PBR; w. M. Davis; C. Parker (FS); Supersax (Cap.; Epic.).

MIKAMI, KUNI, pno; b. Tokyo, Japan, 12/19/54. Family incl. kabuki musicians. Stud. at Shobi Mus. Acad. in Tokyo 1960–72. First rec. w. singer Miyuki Kozaki '73. In NYC '74–80; stud. at Jazzmobile, Barry Harris Wkshp. Freelanced extensively; taught at Jimbo Mus. Sch, N.J.; wrote articles for Japanese community newspaper in NYC, *SJ, Jazz World*. Join. Lionel Hampton orch. April, '91 and toured int'l. CDs: Time USA.

MIKKELBORG, PALLE, tpt, comp; b. Copenhagen, Denmark, 3/6/41. Self-taught, but stud. cond. at Royal Mus. Cons. Began pl. at Vingaarden in Copenhagen 1961–4; w. Danish Radio Jazz Gp. '64–70, last four yrs. as leader; Danish Radio bb '65–70; Alex Riel–Mikkelborg qnt. '67–8; own qt. '65–7; oct. '67–91; Peter Herbolzheimer bb fr. '70; own spt. fr. '72. Has also worked w. George Russell; Dexter Gordon, Joachim Kuhn; Eje Thelin; Jan Garbarek; Dollar Brand; Johnny Dyani; Philip Catherine; Charlie Mariano; Maynard Ferguson; Ed Thigpen; Tootie Heath; Don Cherry; Bernt Rosengren; Ben Webster; Yusef Lateef; and, "for one unforgettable night," the Gil Evans orch. Infls: Albert Ayler, Gil Evans, Miles Davis, Clifford Brown, G. Russell, Bill Evans, Don Cherry, Charles Ives, Olivier Messiaen. TV: Has comp. mus. for several TV plays and films; TV prod. w. Bill Evans trio and symph. orch. '70; D. Gordon and strings '71; app. several times w. own gps. '67, '73–4; TV portrait of his mus. '75. Has perf. at most major Eur. fests., incl. Montreux where he won a first prize '68. Was voted Jazzman of the Yr. in Denmark '68; number one tpt. in *Jazz Forum* '69; received Cultural Government Scholarship '69. Mikkelborg, who states that he is strongly guided by Yoga philosophy, is highly regarded as one of Europe's most creative writer-players. Of his many extended instrumental works, the best known is *Aura*, a tribute to Miles Davis which he rec. in '84 w. Davis himself featured. CDs: w. Davis, *Aura* (Col); w. Ben Webster (Story.); Terje Rypdal (ECM); D. Gordon (Steep.).

MILES, BARRY (Barry Miles Silverlight), kybds, dms, comp, arr; b. Newark, NJ, 3/28/47. Two uncles were mus.; fath. owned rec. store. Stud. classical pno. w. Olga Von Till, Walter Klein; improv. w. John Mehegan; comp. w. Dika Newlin and at Princeton U. 1964–9; arr. w. Rayburn Wright; Manny Albam; Fred Karlin. First prof. gigs at age 5; joined mus. union at age 9. Pl. w. Woody Herman as child; own fusion gps. '63–80; Al Di Meola '91. Miles has been mus. dir. for Roberta Flack fr. '80. Favs: Tatum, Peterson, Glenn Gould. Fests: Eur., Japan. TV: PBS *Jazz Set* '71; *Fusion Suite* '73. CDs: T.C.; RCA; w. Di Meola (Col.); Nino Tempo (Atl.).

MILES, BUTCH (Charles J. Thornton Jr.), dms; b. Ironton, OH, 7/4/44. Started on snare dms. at age 9; stud. priv. in Charleston, West Va., then majored in mus. at West Va. St. Coll 1962–6. Worked w. local gps., then tour. w. Iris Bell's trio late '60s. Pl. w. Austin–Moro bb in Det. '70–1; Mel Tormé '71–4. Tour. w. Count Basie '75–9; app. in film *The Last of the Blue Devils* '79. After a few mos. w. Dave Brubeck '79, he tour. w. Tony Bennett '80–1. From '80s he pl. and/or rec. w. Peanuts Hucko; Al Cohn; Zoot Sims; Clark Terry; Woody Herman; Scott Hamilton; Warren Vaché; also wkshps. for drum companies and frequent apps. at Colo. and other jps. Miles's years with the Basie band yielded some of the ensemble's most dynamic recordings. Favs: Rich, Krupa, Jo Jones. Led series of LPs, incl. tributes to Chick Webb, Krupa, Basie for Famous Door. CDs: N-H; w. Basie (Pab.); Peter Appleyard; Flip Phillips (Conc.); T. Gibbs (Cont.); Amer. Comps. Orch.; D. Hyman (MM); N. Brignola; Phil Bodner (Stash); Ralph Sutton (Sack.); Danny Moss (N-H).

MILES, LIZZIE (Elizabeth Mary Landreaux), voc; b. New Orleans, LA, 3/31/1895; d. New Orleans, 3/17/63. Professional fr. 1909 w. King Oliver, A. J. Piron, et al.; to Chi. w. Manuel Manetta '18; later w. Oliver; Freddie Keppard; and Charlie Elgar; moved to NYC '21. Dur. '20s she rec. w. Oliver; Jelly Roll Morton; Clarence Williams; and others. Inactive in early '30s; w. Paul Barbarin at the Strollers Club, NYC '35; and Fats Waller '38. Out of mus. '42–50; then pl. clubs in SF and NO and rec. for Cap. CDs: w. Sharkey Bonano (Cap.; Story.); Geo. Lewis (Story.).

MILES, RON (RONALD GLEN), tpt; b. Indianapolis, IN, 5/9/63. B. Mus. fr. U. of Denver 1981–5; Manh. Sch. of Mus. '85–6. Master's fr. U. of Colo. '86–9. Based in Denver, he pl. w. Boulder Creative Mus. Ens. '84; Kim Stone '87–8. Best known for assoc. w. Duke Ellington Orch. under Mercer Ellington, tour. Italy w. *Sophisticated Ladies* revue May '92; Japan w. the Orch. Mar. '93. Pl. w. Bill Frisell fr. '94; also a member of John Gunther's Axis

Mundi. Asst. prof. at Metropolitan State Coll. of Denver fr. '91. Favs: Armstrong, Miles Davis, Lester Bowie. CDs: Gram.; Hess; Capri; w. Frisell (None.); Gunther (CIMP).

MILEY, BUBBER (JAMES), tpt; b. Aiken, SC, 1/19/03; d. NYC, 5/24/32. Studied tbn. bef. pl. crnt. Led own band and tour. w. Mamie Smith in early 1920s; join. Elmer Snowden's Washingtonians '23 just bef. the band came under Duke Ellington's leadership. Miley stayed w. Ellington until '29 and was replaced by Cootie Williams. With Noble Sissle '29; then Zutty Singleton and others. Led his own gp. in the show *Harlem Scandals* in Phila. dur. the last mos. of his life. In addition to his sides w. Ellington, Miley rec. in '30 w. King Oliver; Jelly Roll Morton; Hoagy Carmichael; and Leo Reisman, w. whom, because of segregation laws, he was required to perf. behind a stage curtain. Miley's "wa-wa" effects, which brought the sound of the tpt. close to that of the human voice, had great emotional value on the early Ellington recs. He was an expert in the use of the rubber plunger for special tonal variations. Collab. and co-wrote many of the early Ellington comps., incl. "East St. Louis Toodle-oo"; "Black and Tan Fantasy"; and "Creole Love Call." CDs: tracks on *New York Horns* (EPM); w. Ellington (Dec.; Col.; BB); Hoagy Carmichael (BB); Lee Wiley (JVC).

MILITELLO, BOB (ROBERT PHILIP), alto sax, cl, fl; b. Buffalo, NY, 3/25/50. Inspired by film, *The Benny Goodman Story*, he stud. cl., alto sax priv. 1965–8. Tour. w. Maynard Ferguson '75–9; pl. jazz clubs in Fla. '80. Living in Buffalo '81–4; pl. w. Buffalo Philharm.; off and on w. Dave Brubeck fr. '82. Moved to LA '84; fr. late '80s w. various bands, incl. Don Menza sxt.; Bill Holman and Bob Florence bbs; and own small gps. CDs: w. Ferguson (Col.); Holman (JVC); Brubeck (Tel.).

MILLER, BIG (CLARENCE HORATIO), voc, tbn, bs; b. Sioux City, IA, 12/18/22; d. Edmonton, Alb., Canada 6/9/92. Studied bs. and tbn. in sch. in Kansas. Pl. and sang in shows at Topeka Vocational Sch. Led own band 1947–9; then pl. bs. and sang w. Jay McShann '49–54. Sang w. Duke Ellington '55; then worked as a single. Scored a success at Great South Bay JF '57. App. w. Jon Hendricks' *Evolution of the Blues Song* revue at MJF '60. In Calif. in early '60s; then managed club in Honolulu, Hawaii '64–5. App. w. *Evolution of Blues Song* in Vancouver, Can. '66. After working around western Can., settled in Edmonton '70 and bec. a naturalized Can. citizen '73. Sang w. Tommy Banks bb at MJF '78; w. Jay McShann at reunion concerts in Edmonton '83, '89.

Also tour. w. Nimmons 'N Nine Plus Six and as single. Perf. w. Edmonton Symph '90. Taught at the Banff, Alberta, Jazz Wkshp. and at Grant MacEwan Coll., Edmonton. Favs: Walter Brown, Joe Turner. Polls: Juno Awd. '79. Fests: MJF '78; Edmonton Folk Fest '87–9; tours of Eur., Japan. Film: many apps. in Can. films incl. *Big Meat Eater* '82. TV: *Big and the Blues* '80. CDs: StonyPlain; South.

MILLER, DOUG (EDWARD DOUGLAS), tnr, sop saxes, cl, fl, comp, arr; b. No. Little Rock, AR, 6/10/52. Parents, two bros., sist. amateur mus. Stud. pno. fr. age 6, cl. fr. 10. Stud. sax w. Joe Allard; Andy McGhee; Joe Henderson; Pharoah Sanders. Had dance band w. bro. in Hays, Kansas 1967–70. Pl. w. Johnny Chambers in Kansas '72–5; 6th Army band '76–9; Ed Kelly in SF '79–80; Karlton Hester '79–80. Moved to NYC '82, pl. w. Geo. Russell, Machito '82; Lionel Hampton '82–8; mus. dir. '85–8; Art Blakey bb '83; McCoy Tyner bb; Jack McDuff '88; Larry Ridley '88–9; Count Basie Orch. fr. '89. Miller taught woodwinds and beginning pno. at Polomba Sch. of Mus., Bronx '88–9. Favs: Joe Henderson, Coltrane, Ben Webster; arrs: George Russell, Quincy Jones, Frank Foster, Bela Bartok. Fests: Eur. fr. '82; Japan '91. TV: PBS, NJF '88, '90; Arsenio Hall w. Basie Orch. '91. CDs: w. Basie Orch. (MAMA; BJ); Geo. Benson and Basie Orch (WB); Joe Williams and Basie Orch. (Tel.); L. Hampton (GladHamp); T. Puente (Trop.); Mark Murphy (Vict.).

MILLER, EDDIE (Edward Raymond Mueller), tnr sax, cl, voc; b. New Orleans, LA, 6/23/11; d. Los Angeles, CA, 4/1/91. Played in NO Owls and the Half Way House Orch. 1928. To NYC, where he pl. w. dance bands '29–30; then w. Ben Pollack '30–4; studio sess. w. Dorsey bros, Bunny Berigan. Join. Bob Crosby '36, staying until band broke up '42. After army service '43–4 settled in LA, leading own gp., movie studio jobs, and frequent Dixieland revival combo work, incl. Nappy Lamare '45–7; also many reunions w. Crosby off and on. Tour. Engl. w. Alex Welsh orch, '67; pl. w. Pete Fountain at his club in NO '67–76. Ret. to LA, freelancing in small gps.; tour. Eur. w. Yank Lawson and Bob Haggart '78, '84; pl. at LA Classic Jazz Society '87. Assoc. w. *Pete Kelly's Blues* on radio, TV, film. Comps. incl. "Lazy Moon" and "March of the Bobcats." Miller's style was often compared to that of Bud Freeman, but his personal version was smoother and, although it certainly swung, less pointedly rhythmic. CDs: Del.; w. Bob Crosby (Dec.); J. Teagarden (BB, Mos.); Muggsy Spanier (Mob. Fid.); Judy Garland (Dec.); Capitol Jazzmen (Jazz Unlimited).

MILLER, (ALTON) GLENN, lead, comp, tbn; b. Clarinda, IA, 3/1/04; d. ca. 12/16/44 en route from England to France in a small plane that was never seen again. Grew up in Fort Morgan, Colo. Studied briefly at U. of Colo. Experience w. territory bands bef. pl. w. Ben Pollack 1926–27; Paul Ash '28; Red Nichols '29–30. Freelanced in NYC as arr. and tbn. w. Nichols; Dorsey Bros.; Benny Goodman; and tour. w. Smith Ballew '32–34; form. Amer. orch. for British bandleader Ray Noble '35. While w. Noble, Miller began studies w. Joseph Schillinger and first discovered the clarinet-over-four saxes reed section voicing that later proved a key factor in the success of his own orch. After a short-lived attempt at leading a band in '37, Miller organized a second gp. in '38 w. Hal McIntyre, Tex Beneke, Al Klink, Chummy MacGregor, and vocs. Marion Hutton and Ray Eberle. Broadcasts fr. the Glen Island Casino, its summer location in '39, helped popularize the band and in that yr. and '40 its Bluebird recs. enjoyed a great reception fr. the public. Among the more successful numbers were "Moonlight Serenade," the band's theme song; "American Patrol"; "Little Brown Jug"; "Tuxedo Junction"; "String of Pearls"; "In the Mood." From that time until he disbanded to enter the service in '42, Glenn Miller had a following among young swing fans unmatched since the first Benny Goodman reign in '35. He later assembled a large orch. for the AAF which played in Engl. and broadcast to the armed forces '44. After his disappearance, the band carried on under Jerry Gray and Ray McKinley, pl. in Paris in '45. After WWII, a series of bands imitated the Miller style, incl. those of Tex Beneke; Ralph Flanagan; Jerry Gray; Ray Anthony. In the late '50s a band toured under his name, dir. by Ray McKinley and officially endorsed by the Miller estate. Several other leaders, incl. Buddy DeFranco, have since led a band under Miller's name. Films: *Sun Valley Serenade* '41; *Orchestra Wives* '42. *The Glenn Miller Story* '53 starred Jimmy Stewart as Miller. Book: *Glenn Miller and His Orchestra*, George T. Simon, '74. CDs: RCA; BB; Col.; Merc.

MILLER, MARCUS, el-bs, kybds, perc; b. NYC, 6/14/59. Began on el-bs. as teenager. Pl. first prof. gigs at age 15 w. r&b gp., Harlem River Drive. Pl. w. flst. Bobbi Humphrey 1977; then tour. w. Lenny White. Worked as studio mus. in NYC fr. late '70s; rec. w. Bob James; Grover Washington Jr.; Roberta Flack; Aretha Franklin. Pl. w. Miles Davis '80–2; David Sanborn early '80s. Co-prod. Sanborn's album *Backstreet* '82. Pl. several instr., comp., and arr. for Miles Davis' album *Tutu* '86; also credited as prod. on several tracks. Miller has led the gp. Jamaica Boys

w. L. White fr. early '80s. Pl. on soundtrack of film, *Love Jones* '97. Rec. w. Kazumi Watanabe '83–4; McCoy Tyner–Jackie McLean '85; Kevin Eubanks '86; also r&b acts, incl. Luther Vandross. App. w. own gp. at Juan-Les-Pins JF '97; w. The Legends, incl. Eric Clapton, David Sanborn, Steve Gadd, Joe Sample at Umbria JF '97. Film: comp. mus. for *Siesta* '87. CDs: Pra; w. M. Davis (Col.; WB); M. Tyner (Den.); J. McLean (BN); Victor Bailey; Kenny Garrett; Hannibal Peterson (Atl.); Kevin Eubanks; Jay Hoggard (GRP); Rodney Jones (Imp.); Cont. Pno. Ensemble (Col.); Wayne Shorter (Verve); Geo. Benson; Joe Sample (WB).

MILLER, MULGREW, pno, comp; b. Greenwood, MS, 8/13/55. Piano lessons at age 8. Early mus. experience in Baptist church and r&b gps. bef. entering jazz. Stud. at Memphis St. U. 1973–5, and w. Margaret Chaloff in Bost. '75. Tour. w. Mercer Ellington '77–9; worked w. Betty Carter '80; Woody Shaw '80–3; Art Blakey '83–6; Tony Williams '86–94. Rec. w. own trio '85. Led own gp., Wingspan, fr. '80s. Tour. w. Benny Golson '88. Rec. extensively w. various gps. in '80 and '90s. Miller, steeped in the blues and gospel of his youth, understands well the music of Bud Powell and such post-bop pnsts. as McCoy Tyner. He is at home in a trio but an asset to combos of any size. CDs: Land.; Novus; DIW; w. Blakey (Conc.; Timel.; PW; Evid.); Antonio Hart (Novus); Betty Carter (Verve); Eddie Daniels–Gary Burton (GRP); B. Marsalis (Col.); B. Hutcherson (Land.); T. Williams (BN); B. Golson (Den.); Steve Nelson; Steve Wilson (CC); Cassandra Wilson (JMT); D. Liebman (Red).

MILLER, PUNCH (Ernest Burden; aka **KID PUNCH**), tpt, voc; b. Raceland, LA, 6/10/1894; d. New Orleans, LA, 12/2/71. Cornetist w. local gps., then army bands in WWI; w. tbnst. Jack Carey in NO 1919; settled in Chi. '26; replaced Louis Armstrong in Kid Ory Band. Went to Dallas, Tex., w. Mack's Merrymakers; then to Chi., where he pl. and/or rec. w. Albert Wynn; Freddie Keppard; Chippie Hill; Tiny Parham; Omer Simeon; Jimmy Bertrand; Jelly Roll Morton; pl. w Erskine Tate; Frankie Franko's Louisianians. Worked mainly in Chi. until mid '40s; accomp. Big Bill Broonzy and Tampa Red on recs. A tour w. a carnival brought him briefly to NYC where took part in Rudi Blesh's Mutual Radio Network series *This Is Jazz* '47. Pl. w. rock 'n' roll revue in circus '54–6. Returned to NO '56, working as handy man and gigging occ. Toured Japan w. George Lewis '63; was subject of docu. film *'Til The Butcher Cuts Him Down* '71. Miller had speed and an affinity for the blues. Although he thought of himself as the equal

of Louis Armstrong, he had neither his authority nor creative powers. CDs: RST.

MILLINDER, LUCKY (LUCIUS VENABLE), lead; b. Anniston, AL, 8/8/1900; d. NYC, 9/28/66. Active as dance band lead. fr. the early 1930s. Tour. Eur. 1933; took over leadership of Mills' Blue Rhythm Band '34. In the earlier yrs., his sidemen incl. Red Allen; Charlie Shavers; Harry Edison; J. C. Higginbotham; Wilbur De Paris; Joe Garland; Tab Smith; Buster Bailey; Edgar Hayes; Billy Kyle; and John Kirby. In the '40s band members incl. Joe Guy; Freddy Webster; Dizzy Gillespie; Lucky Thompson; Eddie "Lockjaw" Davis; Bull Moose Jackson; Ellis Larkins; Bill Doggett; Clyde Hart; Sir Charles Thompson; Geo. Duvivier; and vocs. Sister Rosetta Tharpe; Trevor Bacon; and Wynonie Harris. In later yrs. he was active as disc jockey, mus. publisher, and liquor salesman. Though not a mus., Millinder was an animated and precise cond. whose bands were important breeding grounds for talent. Films: *Paradise in Harlem* '39; *Boarding House Blues* '48. CDs: Class.; tracks on *An Anthology of Big Band Swing, 1930–55* (Dec.); w. Mills Blue Rhythm Band (Class.).

MILLS BLUE RHYTHM BAND. Organized in late 1929 w. dmr. Willie Lynch as leader, the band followed Cab Calloway into the Cotton Club in early '30 and, under the management of Irving Mills, achieved some renown dur. the next few yrs., variously led by Baron Lee fr. '32 and Lucky Millinder fr. '34. Some of the best arrs. were contributed by the pnst. Edgar Hayes. Sidemen incl. Red Allen; Charlie Shavers; Sweets Edison; J. C. Higginbotham; Buster Bailey; Joe Garland. The band broke up in '38, but the name was later used for occ. recs. CDs: Class.; tracks on *Swingtime* (Col.); *An Anthology of Big Band Swing 1930–55* (Dec.).

MILLS BROTHERS, voc. gp; JOHN H. MILLS, b. Bellefonte, PA, 2/11/1882; d. Bellefontaine, OH, 12/8/67; and his sons, all born in Piqua, Ohio: HERBERT MILLS, b. 4/2/12; d. Las Vegas, NV, 4/12/89; HARRY MILLS, b. 8/19/13; d. Los Angeles, 6/28/82; DONALD F. MILLS, b. 4/29/15; d. Los Angeles, 11/13/99. When they started as youngsters, Herbert was an apprentice barber; Harry, a shoeshine boy; and Donald, a student. After singing in vaudeville shows in small Ohio theaters and on Cincinnati radio, they went to NYC and were famous by 1931. Made many recs. and app. in such films as *The Big Broadcast of 1932*. Early recs., labeled as "four boys and a guitar," feat. unique voc. emulations of instruments. Father, a barber, join. the act in January '36 to replace his eldest son, John C. Mills, b. 10/19/10, who died in

Bellefontaine, Ohio, 1/54/36. The Mills Bros. had more hits than any other voc. gp., about seventy between '31 and '68. In later yrs. the gp. rec. w. Duke Ellington; Bing Crosby; Louis Armstrong; Ella Fitzgerald; and Cab Calloway. Hits incl. "Paper Doll"; "Glow Worm"; "Lazy River"; "Opus One"; and "Sleepy Head." After John H. Mills's retirement in '56, the gp. app. as a trio, but by the '90s, it was reduced to one original member, Donald, and his son, John. Won *DB* Poll '51–2. CDs: Dec.

MILLS, JACKIE, dms; b. Brooklyn, NY, 3/1/22. Studied gtr. at Wurlitzer Music Co., NYC 1931; sw. to dms. '32. Gigged around NYC w. own band fr. age 13. In '40s pl. w. C. Barnet; Teddy Powell; D. Gillespie; Raymond Scott; Glen Gray; B. Raeburn; B. Goodman; also w. René Touzet '46; Gene Norman's Just Jazz concert '47. Fr. '49 to '62 pl. intermittently w. Harry James and worked as studio mus. From '60 to '65 served as a&r man for Ava Recs.; later in same capacity w. Mainstream. Favs: Jo Jones, Krupa. Rec. w. Red Norvo on Cap. CDs: w. Babs Gonzales (BN); L. Hampton (Dec.); Benny Carter (BB; Verve); Gerry Wiggins (Cont.); Dodo Marmarosa (Jz. Class.).

MINCE, JOHNNY (John Henry Muenzenberger), cl, saxes; b. Chicago Heights, IL, 7/8/12; d. Boca Raton, FL, 12/23/94. To Tulsa, OK, 1929 w. Joe Haymes band (later taken over by Buddy Rogers). Well known as jazzman w. Ray Noble's first US band '34–5 and T. Dorsey bb and Clambake Seven '36–41; also 2 mos. w. Bob Crosby '36. Tour. w. Irving Berlin's *This Is the Army* show; discharged fr. mil. '45. Fr. '46 to '66 feat. on radio and later TV w. Arthur Godfrey. Replaced Buster Bailey in L. Armstrong band '67. Active pl. club dates in NYC area and jazz parties such as Colo.; Odessa, Tex. Jazz fest. in Hanover, Germ. '74; tour. Engl. w. Kings of Jazz late '74. Pl. w. new Paul Whiteman Orch. '76; tour. w. Yank Lawson and Bob Haggart '82. Feat. in Keith Smith's *100 Years of American Dixieland* Engl. tour in '80s. His big, clear sound was powered by a formidable technique, placing him in the upper echelon of swing-era clarinetists. Favs: Goodman, Dodds, Fazola. Fests: Hanover, Germ. '74; Fest. of Traditional Jazz, Chi. '80; Nice JF '84. Rec. w. B. Hackett (Flying Dutchman; Col.); WGJB (Fly. Dutch.) G. Brunis (Comm.) Solos w. Dorsey: "Old Black Joe"; "Blue Danube"; "Panama": "Milenberg Joys." CDs: w. Dorsey (BB); Rick Fay (Arb.); Barbara Lea (Aud.).

MINE, KOSUKE, tnr, sop saxes; b. Tokyo, Japan, 2/6/44. Studied cl. at Toho Gokuen hs. First prof. gig on alto sax w. Kyuchin Kato's Blue Seven 1963–7. Switched to tnr. sax while w. Masabumi Kikuchi '69–73. In NYC '73–5. Ret. to Japan, pl. w. own gp. and Tsutomu Okada '76. Co-led fusion gp. Native Sun w. Takehiro Honda '78–85. The gp. tour. Africa, Brazil, USA '81. Led own straight-ahead jazz gp. fr. '85. Pl. w. Dizzy Gillespie in Osaka '87. Pl. w. all-star gp. Four Sounds, T. Honda, Masahiko Sato's Randooga, Masahiko Tagashi's J. J. Spirits fr. late '80s. Pl. 30th anniv. concert in Nagoya w. M. Kikuchi '92. Fav: Coltrane. Polls: *SJ* Readers sop. '73–83; *SJ* Readers tnr. '75–6, '91–3; *SJ* Critics tnr. '90–2. CDs: JVC; w. Native Sun (JVC); M. Tagashi (Verve); M. Sato (Epic-Sony; NipponCrown); T. Honda (Fun-House).

MINERVE, HAROLD "GEEZIL," alto sax, cl, fl, picc; b. Havana, Cuba, 1/3/22; d. New Rochelle, NY, 6/4/92. Raised in Orlando, Fla.; private lessons on cl. at age 12. Left home 1940 w. Ohio band led by dmr. Jeff Gibson; after hs grad., tour. w. back-up band for Ida Cox. Played in NO band formerly led by Joe Robichaux but fronted by Joan Lunceford (no relation to Jimmie Lunceford) of Mobile, Ala. Then pl. w. Clarence Love, Ernie Fields. Mil. service '43–6; back w. Fields until '50, when he join. Buddy Johnson. To NYC '57; pl. w. Mercer Ellingon '60; Ray Charles '62–4. Mus. dir. for Arthur Prysock; join. D. Ellington 9/7/71; after Duke's death, remain. off and on w. Mercer Ellington, also freelancing around NYC. CDs: w. D. Ellington (BN).

MINGER, PETE (GEORGE ALLEN), tpt, flg, pno; b. Orangeburg, SC, 1/22/43; d. Pompano Beach, FL, 4/14/00. Brother Jimmy is prof. jazz pnst.; moth. and grandmoth. pl. pno. in church. Began on sax. Mainly self-taught. Pl. in army band in Japan 1967–9. Att. Berklee Coll. of Mus. '69–70, then join. Count Basie Orch. '70. Pl. w. Basie '70–80; Al Grey '77; Curtis Fuller '77–8. Stud. at U. of Miami '81–5 (B.A. in mus. '85). Pl. w. Philip Morris Superband '89; Frank Wess bb '90; own gp. w. Curtis Peagler, Billy Mitchell fr. '80s. Taught in the Fla. publ. schs. fr. '85; Florida Int'l U. '87–9; Florida Memorial Christian Coll. fr. '89. Favs: Clifford Brown, F. Hubbard, Gillespie, C. Terry. Fests: all major w. Basie. TV: Timex jazz special '71. CDs: Conc.; JA; w. Basie (Pab.); Mel Tormé; Wess (Conc.); Hilton Ruiz (Dragon Rose); Melton Mustafa (Cont.); Turk Mauro (Mile.).

MINGUS, CHARLES JR., bs, pno, comp/arr, lead; b. Nogales, AZ, 4/22/22; d. Cuernavaca, Mexico, 1/4/79. Raised in the Watts section of LA; two sists. stud. pno. and vln. Mingus started on tbn., w. help from Britt Woodman, then sw. to cello; took up bs. at age 16, stud. w. Red Callender and former NY Philharm. bsst. Herman Rheinschagen; comp. study w. Lloyd Reese, which resulted in two early comps., "What Love" 1939 and "Half-Mast Inhibition" '40–41, both of which were rec. in the '60s. Got into the mus. business while in hs w. Buddy Collette. Pl. w. Lee Young '40; Louis Armstrong '41–3; Kid Ory, Alvino Rey, Lionel Hampton '46–8. Record debut w. Hampton '47 on own comp. "Mingus Fingers"; also rec. as accomp. for r&b singers and led various ensembles as "Baron Mingus." His first nat'l visibility was w. Red Norvo Trio '50–51. Left Norvo and settled in NYC and waited out his union card in '52; then worked w. Billy Taylor Trio '52–3, as well as Charlie Parker; Stan Getz; Duke Ellington; Bud Powell; and Art Tatum. He also spent some time working at the post office in a period when he became disenchanted w. the jazz scene. With his then wife Celia and Max Roach, he started Debut Records April '52, releasing early Mingus Jazz Workshop recs. and the famous Toronto concert, *Jazz at Massey Hall*, w. Charlie Parker, Dizzy Gillespie, Bud Powell, and Max Roach. The label lasted into the late '50s and eventually was sold to Fantasy Records. Various Jazz Workshop groups from late '50s incl. such musicians as John Handy; Booker Ervin; Eric Dolphy; Jimmy Knepper; Ted Curson; Clifford Jordan; Charles McPherson; Rahsaan Roland Kirk; Jackie McLean; Mal Waldron; Paul Bley; Jaki Byard; and long-time associate, dmr. Dannie Richmond, w. whom he developed a method of acceleration and deceleration they called "rotary motion." His mid '70s band included Jack Walrath, George Adams, Don Pullen, along w. Richmond. Late in '77 Mingus learned that he had amyotrophic lateral sclerosis (Lou Gehrig's disease) and by '78 he was confined to a wheelchair. Mingus led rebel festival w. Max Roach at Cliff Walk Manor in Newport '60 as an alternative to the NJF. Other fests incl. Antibes '60; MJF '64. Subject of docu. film, *Mingus*, Thomas Reichman '67. Video: *Triumph of the Underdog*, Dan McGlynn and Sue Mingus (Shan.) '98. His '71 autobiography, *Beneath the Underdog*, is a word improvisation that blends fact and fiction, while Brian Priestley's *Mingus:A Critical Biography* '82 is a well-researched work.

Mingus was a brilliant, volatile artist whose work, inspired by Ellington and Parker, married the past with the present into innovative, sometimes deliberately chaotic and provocative social commentary. His bass playing was as powerful as his personality, prodding and supportive, simultaneously, in ensemble, and hornlike in solo. As a composer he became increasingly important from the mid '50s. His work continues to inspire new generations of musicians due in no small part to his widow, Sue Mingus, who has continued his legacy through reissues; issuing

new material on the Revenge label to keep it from bootleggers with projects such as *Epitaph*, his extended, multi-segmented work reconstructed and conducted by Gunther Schuller for a double CD and concert tour; and Mingus Dynasty, a band founded after his death, consisting of alumni and others. In '88 it became the Mingus Big Band and from '91 has appeared every Thursday night at the Time Cafe, NYC. The player pool the band draws upon is so large that it has been able to maintain the Thursday night gig while touring the European summer festival circuit. Comps: "Goodbye Pork Pie Hat"; "Better Git It in Your Soul"; "Duke Ellington's Sound of Love"; "Fables of Faubus"; "Black Saint and the Sinner Lady." CDs: Deb.; *Charles Mingus: The Complete Debut Recordings*, 12–CD box (many of these sessions are also available as single CDs, incl. *Jazz at Massey Hall* which is listed under Parker as *The Quintet*); *The Debut Records Story*, 4–CD box; Rh./Atl. box; Cand.; Atl.; Col.; RCA; Sav.; Em.; Imp.; BB; Den.; Mos.; Beth.; BN; Roul.; Revenge; VDJ; w. C. Parker (Verve; Up.); Norvo (Sav.); Teddy Charles (Prest.; Atl.); Miles Davis; George Wallington (Prest.); Q. Jones (Imp.); L. Hampton (Dec.; Tel.); Bud Powell (Deb.); Ellington (BN); Joni Mitchell (Elek.). Mingus Dynasty: SN; Col.; Story; Mingus Big Band: Drey.; SN.

MINOR, DAN ("SLAMFOOT"), tbn; b. Dallas, TX, 8/10/09; d. NYC, 4/11/82. Played in local church band; then w. Blue Moon Chasers. First major prof. job w. Walter Page's Blue Devils 1927–9; Ben Smith '29–30; Earl Dykes '30; Alphonso Trent and others '31; w. Benny Moten '31–4. Pl. w. Count Basie briefly in Little Rock, Ark. '34, rejoin. him in KC '36 and remain. until July '41. During '40s worked briefly w. bands of Cab Calloway; Mercer Ellington; Buddy Johnson; Lucky Millinder; and, in '44, Willie Bryant. Then semi-inactive except for occ. gigs. Known mainly as a strong section player who generally did not take solos. CDs: w. Bennie Moten (BB); C. Basie (Dec.; Class.).

MINTZER, BOB (ROBERT), tnr, sop saxes, bs-cl, arr; b. New Rochelle, NY, 1/27/53. Studied at Hartt Coll. of Mus. 1970–2; Manh. Sch. of Mus. '72–4. Pl. w. Tito Puente early '70s; Eumir Deodato '74; Buddy Rich '75–7; Thad Jones–Mel Lewis Orch. '78; Sam Jones '79; Jaco Pastorius '81. Formed own bb in '84. Joined Yellowjackets '90. Mintzer has also worked w. Art Blakey; Hubert Laws; Mike Mainieri; Joe Chambers; Randy Brecker; Louie Bellson; Liza Minnelli; Steps Ahead; and maintains a busy schedule of commercial studio work. Form. qnt. for acoustic jazz CD on TVT '98. Teaches sax at Manh. Sch. of Mus. Favs:

Rollins, Lester Young, Coltrane, Geo. Coleman; arrs: Thad Jones, Gil Evans, Ellington. Polls: Best bb, *JT* and *Jazziz*. Fests: Eur., Asia. CDs: Novus; DMP; TVT; w. Steve Kuhn (Post.); Marvin Stamm (MM); Yellowjackets; GRP All-Star BB (GRP); Randy Brecker (Conc.); Peter Erskine (Den.); Bob Moses (Gram.).

MITCHELL, BILLY (WILLIE MELVIN), tnr, also alto, sop saxes, fl, cl; b. Kansas City, MO, 11/3/26; d. Rockville Centre, NY, 4/18/01. Family moved to Det. in 1929. Pno. lessons at age 6; stud. cl. in junior hs at 10; tnr. sax at Cass Tech. HS. After working w. Nat Towles he came to NYC w. Lucky Millinder '48; pl. briefly w. Jimmie Lunceford; Milt Buckner; and Gil Fuller. Replaced Gene Ammons in Woody Herman orch. '49. Rec. debut w. Kenny Clarke '49. Ret. to Det. and led own combo feat. Thad and Elvin Jones, Tommy Flanagan, and/or Terry Pollard. Tour. w. Dizzy Gillespie to Middle East spring '56, So. Amer. summer '56. Mus. dir. of band until he left to join Count Basie in late '57. Left Basie '61. Form. gp. w. Al Grey '62–4. Ret. to Basie mid '66 to mid '67. Mus. dir. for Stevie Wonder. In '70 tour. Eur. w. Clarke-Boland band of which he had been a founder-member in '63. Alto sax, mus. dir. for Gillespie orch. at Buddy's Place and Avery Fisher Hall '75. Fr. '70 very active as perf.-educ. w. Jazzmobile; Jazz Interactions; Henry St. Settlement Mus. Sch.; seminars at Hofstra U.; Yale '75 under the aegis of Billy Mitchell, Inc. which also prod. a film *The Marijuana Affair* w. a score by Melba Liston and soundtrack pl. by Mitchell. Rec. for Xan. at Montreux Fest. '78. Pl. many Eur. fests. in '80s incl. Italy; tour. Engl. '84; Mediterranean jazz cruises annually '88–90; Japan tour w. Frank Wess '89–90; Concord JF '91; Berlin and other Germ. venues in '90s. Wed. night gigs at Sonny's Place in Seaford, LI on and off from '63. LPs: Xan. CDs: own gp. in *Swing . . . Not Spring* (Sav); w. M. Jackson (Sav.); Basie (Roul.; Mos.); Gillespie (Verve; CAP); S. Vaughan (Verve); Lee Morgan–Wynton Kelly (Spec.); F. Wess; F. Vignola (Conc.); R. Charles-Milt Jackson (Atl.); L,H&R (Roul.).

MITCHELL, BLUE (RICHARD ALLEN); tpt; b. Miami, FL, 3/13/30; d. Los Angeles, CA, 5/21/79. Began pl. tpt. in hs. Worked w. Paul Williams 1951; freelanced in NYC '52; w. Earl Bostic until '55. Concert tour w. Red Prysock; Sarah Vaughan; Al Hibbler. Join. Horace Silver '58–64; own gp. w. Junior Cook, Chick Corea, Al Foster '69; tour. w. Ray Charles '69–71; John Mayall '71–3. Moved to LA in '74; freelanced w. Bill Berry; Bill Holman; Jack Sheldon; Richie Kamuca; and tour. w. Louis Bellson. LP: w.

Dexter Gordon (Xan.). CDs: Riv.; BN; w. Horace Silver; Jimmy Smith; Lou Donaldson; Stanley Turrentine (BN); Joe Turner (Pab.).

MITCHELL, GEORGE, crnt, tpt; b. Louisville, KY, 3/8/1899; d. Chicago, IL, 5/22/72. Studied tpt from age 12, join. Louisville Musical Club Brass Band 1916–7. Toured South w. minstrel show before settling in Chi., where he worked in early '20s w. Tony Jackson; Carroll Dickerson; Doc Cook; Jimmie Noone. Rec. w. NO Wanderers '26; Jelly Roll Morton '26–7; and own gp. '27. Pl. w. Lil Armstrong at Dreamland '25–6; Dave Peyton '27; Earl Hines at Grand Terrace '29–31. After leaving Hines, gave up mus. and worked as bank teller. Often regarded as having been in a class with Louis Armstrong and King Oliver among pioneers of the NO tpt. style. CDs: w. J. R. Morton (BB); Johnny Dodds (Dec.); Jimmie Noone (Collector's Classics).

MITCHELL, GROVER CURRY, tbn, arr; b. Whatley, AL, 3/17/30; d. NYC, 8/6/03. Moved to Pitts. 1938. Began pl. bugle, then tbn. in public sch. Pl. w. local bands in Pitts., then an Indiana territory band '47–8; Earl Hines in SF early '50s; Lionel Hampton late '50s; sub. in Duke Ellington Orch. '60–1. With Count Basie Orch. '62–70. After leaving Basie, worked as a studio mus. in LA, then rejoin. Basie '80; began lead. own bb full time after Basie's death in '84. Took Frank Foster's place as lead. of Basie band July '95. Held a B.A. in mus. fr. Empire State Coll. Favs: Urbie Green, J. J. Johnson, Bennie Green, Bill Harris; arrs: Ernie Wilkins, Ellington, Strayhorn, Thad Jones. CDs: Ken; Stash; as lead. of Basie band (MAMA; Act; Jazz); w. Basie (Verve).

MITCHELL, J. R. (JAMES R.), perc, educ, comp; b. Philadelphia, PA, 4/15/40. At 19 on road w. Red Prysock band. After that, B.A. in perc. at Combs Coll., master's degrees from Temple U. and the New Engl. Cons. Headed African-American mus. depts. at Ohio St. U. and Northeastern U. Play. and rec. w. Nina Simone; Betty Carter; Sonny Stitt; Dewey Redman. Formed own rec. label, Doria Recs. "J. R. Mitchell is one of the renaissance men of jazz," said Royal Stokes, *Washington Post*. Rec. w. Jaki Byard (Muse); Kalaparush Maurice McIntyre (Cad.). CD: w. Sonny Stitt (Prog.).

MITCHELL, LOUIS, dms, lead; b. Philadelphia, PA, 12/17/1885; d. Washington, DC, 9/12/57. Led one of first jazz bands in NYC. First black perf. to pl. a London West End Theatre 1914. Pl. with James Reese Europe; went to Paris in '16 and operated Grand Duc club there. Organized Mitchell's Jazz

Kings, which toured Eur. '18. Worked in Eur. after WWI and gave up mus. in the '30s.

MITCHELL, RED (KEITH MOORE), bs; pno; b. NYC 9/20/27; d. Salem, OR, 11/8/92. Played pno. and alto sax in army; later sw. to bs. Played bs w. Jackie Paris and Mundell Lowe; pno. w. Chubby Jackson's bb at Bop City '49. Then bs. w. Ch. Ventura and, later, Woody Herman '49–51. Worked w. Red Norvo '52–4, incl. Eur. tour; Gerry Mulligan '54; Hampton Hawes '55–6; rec. and pl. w. André Previn and Shelly Manne. Briefly w. D. Gillespie '68, before moving to Eur. Although he traveled extens. and occ. ret. to US, Mitchell was based in Stockholm, free-lancing all around the Continent for the next twenty-four years. In Mar. '92 settled in Salem. Gifted with a phenomenal technique, using double and triple stops, glissandos, etc., he established himself as a preeminent virtuoso of the acoustic bs. From '66 Mitchell explained he was "involved in the evolution of the bass, especially the survival of the string bass, by reverting to its original tuning (from top down, A, D, G) plus the addition of the 4th string, low C. Tuning the bass this way, in fifths, being the only way to play all the music written for the bass on one and the same instrument." Also occasionally pl. fluent pno. and sang his own songs. Wrote words and sang them to Tony Fruscella's solo on "I'll Be Seeing You." In '92, six mos. bef. suffering a fatal stroke, he rec. a duo album w. Roger Kellaway for Conc. CDs: Cont.: Capri; Mitchell–Harold Land (Atl.); Mitchell–Warne Marsh (Story.); w. B. Holiday (Verve); Benny Carter (BB); Stan Getz (Prest.; Mos.); Chet Baker (PJ); Helen Merrill (Ant.); Barney Kessel; Herb Ellis (Conc.); Hank Jones (Timel.); Mel Tormé (Stash); C. Terry (Enja); Kellaway (Conc.; Stash); Jimmy Raney (Vogue/RCA); Jimmy Rowles; Ellen Rucker (Capri).

MITCHELL, ROSCOE, alto sax, fl, comp; b. Chicago, IL, 8/3/40. Studied cl. and sax in hs. Early infls. incl. mus. fr. his uncle's store-front spiritualist church. Pl. in army band in Heidelberg, Germ., prior to beginning prof. career in hard bop gp. w. Henry Threadgill and Joseph Jarman 1961. In the same yr. he joined Muhal Richard Abrams' Experimental Band, a gp. that paved the way for the AACM; Mitchell served 10 yrs. as dean of educ. for the AACM Sch. of Mus. Founder and pres. of the Creative Arts Collective in East Lansing, Mich. '74–7. During '70s and '80s was active as educ. and artist in residence at various venues, incl. U. of Wisconsin and Banff Center in Alberta, Can. The Art Ensemble of Chi. evolved from Mitchell's sxt. and qt. Mitchell and the Art Ensemble of Chi. have won many honors, incl. Number One Combo awards from *DB* Critics

polls '71, '73, and '85. Also the *DB* Comp. of the Yr. award '80. In '82 Mitchell and the Art Ensemble received the NAACP Image Award. In '88 he was recognized for Outstanding Service to Jazz Educ. by the National Assoc. of Jazz Educs., and in '91 he received the Jazz Masters Award from Arts Midwest. Mitchell, who employs many handmade wind and perc. instruments and uses voc. sound effects, has been directly infl. by the free jazz idiom and the work of Eric Dolphy. Mitchell has rec. over fifty albums w. the Art Ensemble of Chi. since '68 and several dozen under his own name. CDs: Del.; BS; w. Art Ensemble of Chi. (Col.; Del.); Anthony Braxton (BB); Jodie Christian (Del.).

MITCHELL, (STEPHEN) TYLER, bs, el-bs; b. Chicago, IL, 10/7/58. Father is a muralist, friends w. many jazz mus. Stud. at So. Illinois U. 1976–8; Roosevelt U., Chi. '78–9; Howard U. '79–80. Pl. w. Von Freeman '82–4; Sun Ra '85–7; Chet Baker '86; Rashied Ali '86–7. Lived in Japan for six mos. in '88, then moved to NYC, pl. w. Jesse Davis '89–90; Art Taylor fr. '89; Jon Hendricks fr. '89. Also worked w. Al Grey; Dakota Staton; Walter Davis; Walter Bishop; Jackie McLean; Junior Cook; Annie Ross; Frank Morgan; Clifford Jordan; Freddie Redd; Barry Harris; Billy Bang; etc. Favs: Paul Chambers, Jimmy Garrison, Ron Carter. Fests: Eur. since '86; Japan since '88. CDs: w. Sun Ra (BS); J. Hendricks (Den.); J. Davis (Conc.); Steve Grossman (Drey.); A. Taylor (Enja; Verve).

MITCHELL, WHITEY (GORDON B.), bs; b. Hackensack, NJ, 2/22/32. Brother of Red Mitchell. Stud. cl., then tba. and bs. in hs. Worked w. Shep Fields 1952 before army service. Settled in NYC '54; gigged w. Tony Scott; Kai Winding–J. J. Johnson. Toured w. Pete Rugolo; Ch. Ventura; Gene Krupa; led own gps. late '50s; rec. w. Oscar Pettiford; Gene Quill; Betty Roche; Steve Lacy; Red Mitchell; Blue Mitchell; and André Previn. Tour. w. Benny Goodman '63–4; pl. w. Previn '64–5; then settled in LA, working as TV writer and producer. CDs: w. Pettiford (Imp.); Betty Roché; Herbie Mann (Beth.).

MIYAMA, TOSHIYUKI, lead; b. Chiba Pref., Japan, 10/31/21. In navy band 1939–45. After WWII, pl. reeds w. Lucky Puppy Orch. at US mil. camps '46–7. Organized 10-pc. band, Jive Aces; pl. at Johnson Air Base, Yokosuka '50. In '58 he expanded the band to 16 pcs. and renamed it the New Herd Orch. Expanded to 18 pcs. '60. The band became very popular in the '70s, largely on the strength of arrs. by Kozaburo Yamaki. The New Herd rec. w. Thelonious Monk '70; Chas. Mingus '71; also rec. w. M. Sato, M.

Tagashi as feat. soloists early '70s. Performed w. Dizzy Gillespie, John Faddis at MJF '74. The New Herd perf. at Carnival club in Shinjuku, Tokyo, and at colls. throughout Japan. Feat. at Nippon Express JF '93. Miyama received the Fumio Nanri awd. for contrib. to Japanese jazz '84. Polls: Jazz Disc '70–1; *SJ* Readers '71, '73–7. Fests: all major in Japan; MJF '74; NJF-NY '75; Jazz Yatra, India '82; Nice JF '84. CDs: Nippon-Col.; ThreeBlindMice; Teichiku-Union; w. Sadao Watanabe (Den.).

MIYANOUE, YOSHIAKI, gtr; b. Tokyo, Japan, 10/7/53. Self-taught from age 10. Int'l active since early 1970s, rec. regularly from '78 and feat. on Japanese TV & radio. Pl. in Australia '83; China '84; many visits to US incl. Int'l Jazz Parties in LA. An outstanding soloist clearly inspired by Wes Montgomery, to whom some of his albums on the Japanese King label are dedicated; also rec. w. Isao Suzuki; Toshihiko Kankawa; Shuji Atsuta.

MOBLEY, BILL (JOSEPH WILLIAM), tpt, flg, arr; b. Memphis, TN, 4/7/53. Mother pl. pno.; fath., who sings, pl. tpt., tbn., gave him a crnt. at age 5; join. sch. band at age 12. Mainly self-taught; did not take a priv. lesson until age 25. Pno. lessons in sch., grades 3–6. Stud. mus. educ. at No. Tex. St. U. '71–2. Pl. in Memphis w. Herman Green where a bandmate was pnst. James Williams '72–4. Pl. w. Williams fr. '74. Received B.S. fr. Rhodes Coll., Memphis '76. Pl. in Bost. w. Greg Hopkins–Wayne Naus bb '81–2; Bill Pierce '81–5. Taught ens., harm., arr., ear training at Berklee Coll. of Mus. '82–6. Tour. w. Artie Shaw Orch. '85–6. Pl. w. Donald Brown '85–8; Geoff Keezer '88–94; Marvin "Smitty" Smith '91–4; Clifford Jordan bb '92. Received master's in perf. fr. Manh. Sch. of Mus. '87. Taught tpt. at City Coll., NYC '90. Mobley's bb arr. of "Affaire D'Amour" by Donald Brown is publ. by Second Floor Music. Favs: Armstrong, Miles Davis, Woody Shaw. Fests: France w. D. Brown '89. CDs: w. J. Williams (Somethin' Else; DIW); D. Brown (Muse; Sunny.); Harold Mabern (Col.; DIW); Bill Easley (Mile.; Evid.); G. Keezer (DIW; Sunny.).

MOBLEY, HANK (HENRY), tnr sax; b. Eastman, GA, 7/7/30; d. Philadelphia, PA, 5/30/86. Raised in Newark, N.J.; stud. priv. for a yr. Worked w. Paul Gayten r&b band 1950–1; Max Roach on and off '51–3; Dizzy Gillespie '54; then join. co-op gp. w. Kenny Dorham, Art Blakey, Doug Watkins, and Horace Silver that became the Jazz Messengers '54–6. Pl. w. Horace Silver '56–7; Roach late '57–8; gigs w. Thelonious Monk '58. Back w. Blakey '59. App. at many Mon. night sessions at Birdland, NYC;

pl. w. Dizzy Reece '60; Miles Davis '61–2. Rec. an impressive series of LPs for Blue Note w. own gps. throughout the '60s. Lived in Eur. '68–70; back in US, co-led qnt. w. Cedar Walton. In late '70s, a lung problem rendered him all but inactive. A major instrumentalist in the hard bop style of the late '50s, Mobley's style was distinguished by a mellower tonal approach, which had many critics overlooking his prepossessing subtlety, harmonic sophistication, and considerable talent for structure, both as player and writer. CDs: Prest.; BN; w. Blakey (BN; Col.); M. Davis (Col.); Gillespie-Getz; Roach (Verve); Lee Morgan (Sav.); Dorham; D. Byrd; F. Hubbard (BN); *Tenor Conclave* w. Coltrane, Al Cohn, Zoot Sims (Prest.).

MODERN JAZZ QUARTET (aka MJQ). Group whose original members Milt Jackson, John Lewis, Ray Brown, and Kenny Clarke first perf. together as members of the Dizzy Gillespie Orch. in 1946. This lineup rec. as the Milt Jackson Qt. in '51–2. Percy Heath replaced Brown in late '52, and the gp. changed its name to the Modern Jazz Qt., perf. regularly in concert halls and clubs fr. '54. In '55 Clarke was replaced by Connie Kay. Beginning in the early '60s, the MJQ disbanded during the summer months in order to allow its members to work in other contexts. The gp. broke up in '74 but reunited in the early '80s and cont. to rec. and tour into the '90s. Mickey Roker filled in for Kay when the latter bec. ill. Kay returned but when he died in '94, Tootie Heath was his replacement. By the end of the year, however, due to Jackson's desire to be completely on his own, it appeared that the qt.'s existence had ended. While also noted for its recs. of "third stream" comps. by Lewis, Gunther Schuller, André Hodeir, and others, the MJQ is best known as a superior jazz ens. shaped by Lewis comps., Jackson's blues pieces, and a sophisticated style with heat at its core. CDs: Atl.; LRC; BN; Douglas Mus.; w. Paul Desmond (Red Brn.). *See also* **JACKSON, MILT and LEWIS, JOHN.**

MOER, PAUL (Paul E. Moerschbacher), pno, comp; b. Meadville, PA, 7/22/16. Studied theory and comp at U. of Miami, grad. 1951. In '50s pl. w. Benny Carter; Vido Musso; Zoot Sims; Stan Getz; Bill Holman; Shorty Rogers; etc. Rec. w. Bob Gordon; Jack Montrose; Bill Perkins. Performed regularly w. Paul Horn qt. '60–8; w. Les Brown fr. '65. Wrote arrs. for Jack Sheldon; Steve Allen; Bob Hope; Rosemary Clooney; et al.; mus. cond. for Clooney '65–80. CDs: w. Paul Horn (Hi Fi Jazz; Black Sun).

MOFFETT, CHARLES MACK, dms, tpt, orch bells, comp; b. Fort Worth, TX, 9/11/29; d. NYC,

2/14/97. Studied tpt. pno. priv. Pl. w. r&b combo at age 13; also w. Jimmy Witherspoon. Pl. tpt. in hs band. At 19 was welterweight boxing champ, Pacific Fleet, US Navy. Dms. in dance band at coll. in Austin; B.A. in mus. educ. Taught in Tex. hs for eight yrs., lead. sch. band to first place in state fests. Also app. w. Little Richard 1953. In NYC pl. w. boyhood friend Ornette Coleman '61; Sonny Rollins '63; own gp. w. Pharoah Sanders, Alan Shorter, Carla Bley '64. Mus. dir. of recreation center on Lower East Side. Instructor for Presbyterian Church Drum and Bugle Corps. Tour. Eur. w. Coleman '65–6, pl. concerts and fests in France Germ., Scand., Italy. Worked w. bs. Ron Brooks in NYC pl. dms. and tpt., sometimes simultaneously. Living in SF in mid '70s, app. w. the Charles Moffett Family incl. his sons (*see* **MOFFETT, CHARNETT**) at Keystone Korner, etc. Operated a mus. sch. and led a band, the Moffettes, made up of his students. Perf. w. Steve Turre; Keshavan Maslak; and Prince Lasha. Ret. to NYC in '80s; pl. w. Ahmed Abdullah's Solomonic Qt. Taught in sch. system for many yrs, incl. work w. mentally retarded children. His light, dancing way on the dms., particularly in his expressive cymbal work, was grounded in tradition but complemented avant styles, especially Coleman's. Film: *Who's Crazy* w. Coleman, Paris '66. Comps: "Yelvihs Overture"; "Adnerb"; "Last Night and Tomorrow." CDs: Sav.; w. Coleman (BN); Abdullah (Silk.); Frank Lowe (SN); Lasha (Cont.); Charles Tyler (ESP); Charnett Moffett (Manh.; BN); Archie Shepp (Imp.); General Music Project (Evid.).

MOFFETT, CHARNETT, bs, comp; b. NYC, 6/10/67. Father, dmr. Charles. Pl. half-sized bs. at age 7 in family band, which incl. bros. Codaryl, dms.; Charles Jr., alto, tnr. saxes; and Mondre, tpt.; with sist. Charisse, voc. Stud. at NYC's HS of Mus. and Art and the Juilliard Sch. Join. Wynton Marsalis at 16; later pl. w. Tony Williams; Slide Hampton; Mulgrew Miller; Monty Alexander; Sonny Sharrock; Stanley Jordan; and David Sanborn. Made rec. debut as leader in 1987. Doubles on acoustic and picc. bs. as well as five-string el-bs. in styles that range from jazz to funk and r&b. CDs: BN; Manh.; Evid.; w. Kenny Garrett (Atl.); Courtney Pine (Ant.); Sonny Sharrock (Axiom); Kevin Eubanks; Stanley Jordan (BN); Kenny Kirkland (GRP); Wallace Roney (Muse); James Williams (Em.); Ornette Coleman (Verve).

MOLE, MIFF (IRVING MILFRED), tbn; b. Roosevelt, LI, NY, 3/11/1898; d. NYC, 4/21/61. First gig Bklyn. 1914 for silent films. Form. Original Memphis Five w. Jimmy Lytell, Frank Signorelli, et al. Joined Sam Lanin, Roseland '19; rec. frequently w.

Memphis Five under various names (Cotton Pickers, Tennessee Tooters, Orig. Tampa Five, etc.), feat. Phil Napoleon; Frankie Trumbauer; Arthur Schutt; Red Nichols; Vic Berton; Rube Bloom; et al. Join. Red Nichols & His Five Pennies in mid '20s; rec. more than 100 sides under dozens of names incl. Miff Mole's Little Molers, Red & Miff's Stompers, Charleston Chasers. On staff WOR w. Don Voorhees; later 10 years w. NBC, pl. mostly classical mus. With Paul Whiteman '38; B. Goodman '42–3; four years at Nick's in NYC w. own Dixieland combo. Freelanced, then w. Muggsy Spanier in Chi., where he settled in '48; pl. w. small gps. at Blue Note, Jazz Ltd., and Bee Hive through '53. Mole became less active due to illness in the late '50s. When it was learned that he had become a street vendor in NYC, friends arr. a benefit, but the gesture came too late. Mole died shortly afterwards of a stroke. Tommy Dorsey called Mole the Babe Ruth of the trombone. His role in the history of jazz was particularly important for the attention he brought to the instrument's potential as a medium for melodic playing. He is at least as important as Jimmy Harrison, who was his contemporary, and such slightly later figures as Jack Teagarden, J. C. Higginbotham, and Dorsey. LPs: Frog; Jazz. CDs: track in *The Commodore Story* (Comm.); w. B. Beiderbecke (Col.; Mile.); Red Nichols (Biog.).

MONCUR, GRACHAN JR., bs; b. Miami, FL. 9/2/15. Father of Grachan Moncur III; half-bro. of Al Cooper. Began pl. bs., tba., tbn. ca. 1930. Worked in Miami w. Geo. Kelly early '30s. Moved to Newark, N.J. where John Hammond heard him pl. bs. on a local radio show. Rec. w. Bud Freeman, Putney Dandridge, Bunny Berigan, Mildred Bailey '35; Teddy Wilson '35–6. Founding member of Al Cooper's Savoy Sultans '37–45. Rec. w. Ike Quebec '45. Coled gps. w. Ace Harris '47; former Lunceford saxophonist Joe Thomas '48. Freelanced in Miami '50s-late 60s. CDs: w. I. Quebec in *The Blue Note Swingtets* (BN); B. Holiday (Col.).

MONCUR, GRACHAN III, tbn, comp; b. NYC, 6/3/37. Father is bs. Grachan Moncur Jr.; uncle Al Cooper pl. alto, arr., led Savoy Sultans. Began on pno. and cello, then tbn. at age 11. Stud. at Laurinburg Inst., Laurinburg, No. Caro. early 1950s; Manh. Sch. of Mus., Juilliard Sch. '56–9. Pl. w. Nat Phipps in Newark mid '50s; Ray Charles '58–60; Art Farmer–Benny Golson Jazztet '60–2. Mus. dir. for Ray Charles '62. Pl. w. Jackie McLean, Sonny Rollins, Archie Shepp, Joe Henderson '63–9. Also worked in '60s w. Herbie Hancock; Tony Williams; Bobby Hutcherson; Wayne Shorter; Marion Brown. Acted and pl. in James Baldwin's play *Blues for Mr.*

Charlie in London and NYC '64–5. Founded 360 Degree Music Experience w. Beaver Harris, Dave Burrell '68. Dir. of Creative Black Mus. Wkshp. in Newark, also co-led qt. w. John Patton early '70s. Perf. and rec. orig. comp. "Echoes of Prayer" w. 22-pc. orch. '74. Worked w. choreographer Keith Lee '78. Perf. w. Blue Ark, Amiri Baraka early '80s; Frank Lowe '84–5; Cassandra Wilson '85; Nathan Davis's Paris Reunion Band '86. Moncur was composer-in-residence at the Newark Community Sch. of the Arts '84–90. He has received comp. grants fr. NEA and N.J. Council for the Arts. Favs: J. J. Johnson, Sonny Rollins. Polls: *DB* TDWR '64. Fests: Eur., Japan, Africa '69–87. CDs: BN; Den.; BYG; w. McLean; Hancock (BN); Chris White (Muse); Golson (Prest.).

MONDRAGON, JOE (JOSEPH), bs; b. Antonito, CO, 2/2/20; d. Hilton Head, SC, 3/12/87. Self-taught; started career by chance when a band needed a bassist; worked w. many local bands around LA. First prominent in jazz w. Woody Herman 1946; rec. w. Alvino Rey, June Christy, Shelly Manne, Buddy Rich, Shorty Rogers, Buddy DeFranco late '40s–late '50s. Played on many film soundtracks, incl. *The Wild One* and *Pete Kelly's Blues*. Reg. apps. w. Ella Fitzgerald early '60s. Known for his strong tone and firm sense of swing, he was much in demand for West Coast jazz dates in '50s and early '60s. CDs: w. Fitzgerald; Billie Holiday (Verve); Gerry Mulligan; Chet Baker; Clifford Brown (PJ); Art Pepper (Sav.); Benny Carter; Shorty Rogers (BB).

MONK, T. S. (THELONIOUS SPHERE JR.), dms; b. NYC, 12/27/49. Grandfather Thelonious Monk pl. gtr. Fath. was the famous pnst. and comp. Initially pl. tpt. but sw. to dms. Stud. priv. w. Max Roach and Stanley Spector, also pno. lessons. After pl. dance mus. w. local top 40 gps. in NYC, joined father's band at age 20, toured w. him for two yrs. and again periodically fr. 1973–5. Also w. fusion band Natural Essence '73–5; Paul Jeffrey band and qt. '74–6. Led r&b gp., T. S. Monk '76–83. In '86 he established the Thelonious Monk Inst. of Jazz, sponsoring educ. programs and an annual instrumental competition w. major scholarship awards that launched the careers of Marcus Roberts, Joey DeFrancesco, and others. Served as consultant for Monk film *Straight, No Chaser* in '89. In '91 he organized a new jazz-oriented sxt., T. S. Monk, rec., tour., app. at Playboy JF in '92. Cont. to lead T. S. Monk and also Monk on Monk Tentet at major int'l fests. and clubs. Sidemen incl. Don Sickler, tpt., arr.; Bobby Porcelli, alto sax; Willie Williams, tnr. sax; Ronnie Mathews, pno. Favs: Roach, Blakey. CDs: BN; N2K; N-Coded Music.

MONK, THELONIOUS SPHERE, comp, pno; b. Rocky Mount, NC, 10/10/17; d. Weehawken, NJ, 2/17/82. Family moved to NYC ca. 1918. Began on pno. at age 6. Att. Stuyvesant HS. Tour. w. an evangelist in his mid teens. At Minton's Playhouse (where he was house pianist), Monroe's Uptown House, and other Harlem clubs Monk was one of a handful of innovators who, in the years before WWII, worked together informally on the harmonic and rhythmic innovations that evolved into a new jazz style: bebop. Dizzy Gillespie, Charlie Parker, Bud Powell, and Kenny Clarke were part of the same clique of visionary jazzmen. Monk pl. w. Lucky Millinder's orch. '42, then rec. w. Coleman Hawkins '44. Pl. briefly in mid '40s w. Dizzy Gillespie bb at Spotlite club on 52nd St., NYC. Other than these associations, he worked almost entirely as a leader of small combos. Rec. as lead. for BN label '47–52; w. Gillespie–Charlie Parker for Verve '50; Miles Davis, Sonny Rollins, and as lead. for Prest. '52–5. After many yrs. of neglect by critics, fans, and fellow musicians, Monk grad. began to acquire popularity ca. '55 when Prest. sold his contract to Riv., for whom he rec. '55–61. Quartet w. John Coltrane, Wilbur Ware, Shadow Wilson at Five Spot, NYC '57; led 10-pc. band w. arrs. of his comps. by Hall Overton at Town Hall concert Feb. '59; quartet w. Charlie Rouse '59–70. Signed w. Columbia Recs. '62. App. on cover of *Time* magazine '64. Tour. Eur., Mex., Japan late '60s. Pat Patrick, Paul Jeffrey replaced Rouse in qt. '71. Tour. w. Giants of Jazz w. Gillespie, Sonny Stitt, Kai Winding, Al McKibbon, Art Blakey '71–2. Rec. in solo and trio settings for Black Lion in London Nov. '71. Less active due to illness '72–3, then app. w. N.Y. Jazz Repertory Co. at Carnegie Hall April '74. Led qt. at NJF-NY w. son, Thelonious Monk Jr., on dms. '75. Monk spent his final yrs. in seclusion at the Weehawken, New Jersey, home of his lifelong friend and patron, the Baroness Pannonica de Koenigswarter. Monk's comps. that became jazz standards incl. "'Round Midnight"; "Well You Needn't"; "Straight No Chaser"; "Ruby My Dear"; "Off Minor"; "Epistrophy"; and "Blue Monk." Monk generally based his writing on conventional 12- and 32-bar structures; his comps. are distinguished by their melodic originality and the harmonic substructure. As a pianist, he employed a highly idiosyncratic style based on the Harlem stride tradition. In his solos he combined a highly original, often surprising sense of rhythm and melody, with a distinctive attack and timbre. Fav: Bud Powell. Film: app. in *Jazz on a Summer's Day*; docu. *Straight No Chaser*. TV: CBS *The Sound of Jazz* '57; all three available on video. CDs: BN; Prest.; Riv.; Col.; Mos.; Mob. Fid.; BL; Monk–Joe

Turner (Vogue/RCA); w. C. Parker–D. Gillespie (Verve); Davis; Rollins; Hawkins (Prest.); Hot Lips Page (High.); Blakey (Atl.).

MONTEIRO, EDDIE (EDWARD J.), acdn, el-acdn, synth, pno, voc.; b. Newark, NJ, 3/26/48. Studied acdn. w. Chas. Nunzio in Newark 1953–66; forced to take up pno. to study at NYU '66–7, where he received degree in theory as well. Pl. pno. on classical gigs, acdn. w. Latin band in N.J. late '60s. Began pl. acdn. on club dates while in coll., later w. Skitch Henderson; Ray Bloch; Peter Duchin. Pl. w. Bobby Rosengarden; Buddy Yannon. Duo w. Nancy Marano '83–92. Favs: Sivuca, Frank Marocco; arrs: Gene Puerling, Johnny Mandel, Robert Farnon, Pat Williams, Rob McConnell. Polls: *Backstage* mag. Bistro Awd. '89. Fests: Morocco '81–2; Canary Islands 83; Eur. fr. '90. Monteiro, expert in Brazilian mus., is an excellent scat singer in any idiom and particularly exciting when he plays and scats simultaneously. Film: app. in *Mortal Thoughts* w. Bruce Willis. TV: Jerry Lewis Telethon w. Rosengarden fr. '86. CDs: Marano–Monteiro, Den., w. guests Gerry Mulligan, Claudio Roditi, Roger Kellaway; Perfect Sound; w. Ronny White (Aud.).

MONTEROSE, J. R. (FRANK ANTHONY JR.), tnr sax; b. Detroit, MI, 1/19/27; d. Utica, NY, 9/16/93. Family moved to Utica 1928. Began on cl. at age 13, tnr. sax at 15. Pl. cl. w. Utica Jr. Symph. Worked w. territory bands '48–9; Henry Busse '50. Moved to NYC '51. Pl. w. Buddy Rich '52, then worked around Syracuse, NY '52–4. Ret. to NYC w. Claude Thornhill '54; pl. and rec. w. Teddy Charles, Jon Eardley, Ralph Sharon, Eddie Bert '55; Charles Mingus, Kenny Dorham's Jazz Prophets '56; also pl. w. Dan Terry, Terry Gibbs bbs. Rec. w. own gps. fr. '56; Geo. Wallington '57; René Thomas '60; Rein de Graaff '70. Pl. w. own gps. in upstate N.Y. fr. '80s. Monterose was reunited w. Eddie Bert for a rec. sess. at Birdland, NYC '91. A hard-bopping tenorman who took to doubling soprano late in his career. Favs: Parker, Rollins, Stitt, Coltrane. CDs: BN; FS; w. Teddy Charles (Atl.); E. Bert (FS); Kenny Dorham (BN); René Thomas (Jzld.).

MONTGOMERY, BUDDY (CHARLES F.), pno, vib, comp; b. Indianapolis, IN, 1/30/30. Brother of Monk and Wes. Self-taught; started w. local gp., the Hampton Bros., incl. Slide Hampton. Led qt. in army 1954; pl. w. Montgomery–Johnson qnt. '55–7. Switched from pno. to vib. '57, formed Mastersounds w. bro. Monk on el-bs. '57–60 and intermittently until '63; spent several mos. w. Miles Davis; then formed Montgomery Bros. Qt. in SF and pl. w.

George Shearing '62. After freelancing in NYC dur. '60s moved to Milwaukee in '69, teaching briefly at Wisconsin Coll. Cons. and working w. community orgs. Performed w. own gps. and solo fr. '68 in Milwaukee, then Oakland, Calif., and Bay Area fr. early '80s. In '86 he founded Oakland Jazz Alliance, which sponsors clinics and brings jazz to public schs.; organized first Oakland JF in '87. Tour. and rec. w. Marlena Shaw. In mid '90s was resident pnst. at Parker-Meridien Hotel, NYC. Favs: Tatum, Bud Powell, Garner. Polls: *DB* New Star vib. '58. Fests: Paris '92. TV: Johnny Carson, Arthur Godfrey. CDs: Conc.; Sharp Nine; Mile.; Land; w. Wes Montgomery (PJ; Mile.); Montgomery Bros. (Riv.); Marlena Shaw (Verve); Charlie Rouse (Land.); John Handy (Quartet); Frankie Lee (Blind Pig); Pete Escovedo (Conc.); Shearing (Jzld.).

MONTGOMERY, MARIAN (Maud Runnels), voc; b. Natchez, MS, 11/17/34. Professional debut on TV in Atlanta; pl. Chi. clubs under name of Pepi Runnels. Signed w. Cap. Recs. '63; perf. in clubs in NYC, LV, and LA bef. moving to London '65. Married pianist Laurie Holloway; often apps. w. him on British TV. Also collaborated w. pnst. Richard Rodney Bennett in clubs and on recs. Capable of singing with a distinctive jazz timbre, sensitive phrasing, and fine projection. CDs: JH; Browstone.

MONTGOMERY, MONK (WILLIAM HOWARD), bs, el-bs; b. Indianapolis, IN, 10/10/21; d. Las Vegas, NV, 5/20/82. Mainly self-taught; did not take up bs. until age of 30. Toured US and Eur. w. L. Hampton 1950–53; became known as the first major jazz musician to use the Fender el-bs.; later pl. w. Georgie Auld, Art Farmer. With his brother Buddy, vib.; Richie Crabtree, pno.; and Benny Barth, dms.; formed The Mastersounds '57–60; then form. combo w. his bros. Buddy and Wes. During early '60s doubled on acoustic bs.; pl. w. Cal Tjader '66; moved to LV '70; w. Red Norvo '70–72; also active with LV Jazz Soc. and as disc jockey. Leader of first black Amer. jazz gp. to tour S. Africa '74. CDs: w. Wes Montgomery (PJ; Riv.); L. Hampton (Vogue); Art Farmer (Prest.).

MONTGOMERY, WES (JOHN LESLIE), gtr, comp; b. Indianapolis, IN, 3/6/25; d. Indianapolis, 6/15/68. Self-taught. After working w. local bands, pl. w. L. Hampton 1948–50; ret. to Indianapolis and was barely known until he and bros. Buddy and Monk, who at that time were in a gp. called The Mastersounds, rec. together w. Wes as lead. for PJ in late '50s. Own trio '59; app. w. Coltrane Sxt. at MJF '60 Rec. for Riv. w. short-lived Montgomery Bros. band but mostly own gps. fr. '59 to '61. Tour. and rec. (incl.

Smokin at the Half Note) w. Wynton Kelly's trio '62–6. By then, Montgomery was already exerting enormous infl. on a new generation of guitarists, but in the mid 60's Verve prod. Creed Taylor steered him in a commercial dir. w. velvety, carefully charted accomps. that considerably increased Montgomery's income, but seriously diluted the jazz value of his recs. Among his major hits was "Goin' Out of My Head," which won a Grammy, followed by many *DB* and *Playboy* awards. Cont. rec. in the pop format w. Taylor at A&M. He was at the height of his commercial success when he succumbed to a heart attack. Montgomery, who did not read music and used his thumb instead of a plectrum, developed a much-imitated style based on parallel octaves played with an exceptionally strong sense of swing. He was considered by many to be the most influential guitarist since Charlie Christian. CDs: PJ; Riv.; Mile.; Verve; A&M; w. Harold Land (Jzld.); Wynton Kelly; Jimmy Smith (Verve); Nat Adderley; Milt Jackson (Riv.).

MONTOLIU, TETE (Vincente Montoliu Massana), pno; b. Barcelona, Spain, 3/28/33; d. Barcelona, 8/24/97. Father pl. oboe and English hrn. in Barcelona Symph. Blind from birth, he learned to read mus. in Braille at age 7. Became interested in jazz after hearing Duke Ellington recs. ca. 1940. Stud. informally and jammed w. Don Byas, who lived in the Montoliu home fr. '43. Stud. classical pno. at Barcelona Cons. fr. '46. Led Sun. morning jam sess. in Barcelona theater '50s; unknown for many yrs. due to lack of jazz activity in Spain. Rec. w. Lionel Hampton in Madrid '56; pl. at fest. in Cannes w. Doug Watkins, Art Taylor '58; Archie Shepp in Copenhagen '63–4; tour. Eur. w. Roland Kirk '64. Rec. in '60s and '70s w. Kirk; Kenny Dorham; Dexter Gordon; Ben Webster; Lucky Thompson; Anthony Braxton. Pl. solo pno. at Top of the Gate, NYC '67. Came to prominence in mid '70s as lead. of trios w. Niels-Henning Ørsted Pedersen–Albert Heath, and Geo. Mraz–Al Foster. Illness slowed him in the mid '90s. He was scheduled to duet w. Hank Jones at San Sebastian JF but was unable to fulfill the engagement and died shortly thereafter. CDs: Steep.; Enja; Timel.; SN; Conc.; FS; Montoliu-Mundell Lowe (FS); w. Braxton; Dorham; Gordon; C. Mariano; Shepp (Steep.); Geo. Coleman (Timel.); L. Hampton (BB); Kirk (Merc.).

MONTROSE, JACK, tnr sax, comp; b. Detroit, MI, 12/30/28; d. Las Vegas, 2/7/06. Played cl. alto sax in Chattanooga, Tenn., hs band. B.A. fr. Los Angeles St. Coll. '53. With Jerry Gray '53; Art Pepper Qnt. '54. Pl. on and provided arrs. for Clifford Brown rec. for Pacific Jazz '54; then pl. and rec. w. Bob Gordon;

Red Norvo; Shorty Rogers; et al. In '60s pl. LA clubs and worked as studio mus. Moved to Nevada '66; pl. at casinos in Reno, LV, and Lake Tahoe, only occ. ret. to jazz. Worked w. Frank Butler mid '70s; rec. w. Pete Jolly '86. His tenor was cool-toned but his delivery was rhythmically staccato. CDs: Holt; w. Chet Baker; Clifford Brown (PJ); Art Pepper (Sav.).

MOODY, JAMES, tnr, alto, sop saxes, fl, voc; b. Savannah, GA, 3/26/25. Raised in Reading, Pa., and Newark, N.J. Fath. pl. tpt. w. Tiny Bradshaw. First mus. training was in 1946 in the segregated Air Force Band. Credits Dizzy Gillespie and Tom McIntosh w. teaching him chord changes later on. Join. Gillespie's bb on tnr. sax in '46 on recommendation of singer Babs Gonzales and remain. into '48. To Paris in '48, remaining in Eur. for three yrs. Pl. the Paris JF w. Tadd Dameron–Miles Davis gp. '49. Rec. alto sax solo of "I'm in the Mood for Love" for Metronome Recs. in Sweden '49, which became famous in a later vocalese version by King Pleasure, "Moody's Mood for Love." During '50s and into '60s led own spt.; short-lived three-tnr. gp. w. Ammons, Stitt '62. From '63 to '71 pl. in Gillespie's qnt. where the two were musically en rapport and Moody's sense of humor and timing further dovetailed w. Dizzy's. In '75 moved to LV and worked in band at Hilton Hotel backing shows w. Bill Cosby; Tony Bennett; Lou Rawls; others. Moved to NYC in '79, led qt. that incl. Mike Longo's Trio. In '89 moved to San Diego. During a TV show celebrating his 70th birthday, Gillespie said, "Playing with James Moody is like playing with a continuation of myself." Has pl. w. D. Reinhardt; Benny Carter; O. Peterson; Barry Harris; Getz; Pettiford; Rich; Q. Jones; M. McPartland; E. Jefferson; T. Flanagan. Member of L. Hampton's Golden Men of Jazz gp. for a time in the '90s. Taught master classes and clinics and was an artist in residence at Florida U.; Berklee Coll.; U. of Alabama; U. of Oregon; Harvard; Cornell. Moody is an improviser of relentless energy, with masterful breath control and distinct flavors on his different horns but with certain consistencies: a vocalized tone, replete with cries; serpentine runs; and an outer-edge, harmonic sense. Favs: Coltrane, Gillespie; arrs: T. McIntosh, Slide Hampton, Al Cohn, Torrie Zito, Paul Hindemith. TV interviews in Africa, Japan, Israel, Eur., Asia, Australia, and Amer. Amer. TV apps. incl. '87 Wolftrap celebration of Gillespie's 70th birthday and Kennedy Center honoring of Gillespie; the *Tonight Show* and the *Ben Sidran Show* in NYC. Polls: *DB* Critics, TDWR, fl. '65; '67–74. CDs: Novus; BN; Tel.; Prest.; WB; w. Gillespie (Sav.; BB; Philips; Imp.; Verve; Vogue); L. Hampton (Tel.); Eddie Jefferson (Evid.); Tito Puente (Trop.); O. Peterson (Verve);

Jay McShann; Milt Jackson (MM); Gene Harris (Conc.); Q. Jones (Qwest); D. Brubeck (Tel.).

MOONEY, JOE, org, acdn, voc; b. Paterson, NJ, 3/14/11; d. Fort Lauderdale, FL, 5/12/75. Made debut in local radio act w. brother in late 1920s. Mooney—who was blind—took up acdn. '35; formed sxt., which was incorporated into Frank Dailey's band '37. Wrote arrs. for Dailey; Paul Whiteman; Larry Clinton. Later had qt. w. Russ Morgan. In '46 Mooney form. qt. w. Andy Fitzgerald, cl., feat. his own arrs. and intimate vocs. (i.e. "Tea for Two") which enjoyed a brief surge of popularity. After qt. disbanded Mooney took up Hammond org.; he app. as a singer with the Sauter–Finegan Orch. '52, remembered for his rendition of "Nina Never Knew." From '50s he worked mainly in Fla. but ret. occasionally to NYC for concerts and club dates. Won *DB* Critics poll on org. '54. CDs: Atl.; w. Sauter-Finegan (BB).

MOORE, "BIG CHIEF" RUSSELL, tbn; b. Komatke (on Native American reservation), AZ, 8/13/12; d. Nyack, NY, 12/15/83. A member of the Pima tribe. Stud. w. uncle at Blue Island, Ill.; pno., tpt., dms., euph. Worked on railroads before stud. at Sherman Inst. in Calif. Pl. bari. hrn. in National Guard band, Chi. 1928–9. Worked w. Tony Corral's band in Tucson, Ariz.; Lionel Hampton '35; Eddie Barefield '36. Freelanced and tour. until '39, when he began working in NO w. Papa Celestin, other local gps. Later pl. w. Harlan Leonard '41; Noble Sissle '42; L. Armstrong bb '43–5; app. in film *New Orleans* '46. Worked w. Sidney Bechet at Jimmy Ryan's, NYC '46–8. Went to Eur. '49 for Paris JF; tour. the Continent '53; rec. in Paris w. Buck Clayton; Mezz Mezzrow. Join. Jimmy McPartland '54. In late '50s worked w. Lester Lanin; pl. jazz concerts at the Metropole and Central Plaza, coll. dates. Two concert tours as lead. to So. Dakota, Arizona under the sponsorship of Nat'l Congress of American Indians to help build morale of Indian students and raise scholarship funds for them. During '60s pl. w. Armstrong's All-Stars until hospitalization forced temporary retirement '65. Tour. w. own gp. and rec. w. Cozy Cole '70s; tour. Engl. w. Keith Smith '81; in '83 tour. Engl. w. gp. of fellow Armstrong alumni. Moore had a strong, dramatic vibrato and pl. convincingly in the early NO contrapuntal style. CDs: w. Swingville All-Stars (GTJ); Armstrong (Class.; Verve); Charlie Parker (Phil.); Keith Smith (Lake).

MOORE, BILLY JR. (WILLIAM), comp, pno; b. Parkersburg, WV, 12/7/17; d. Copenhagen, Denmark, 2/28/89. Raised in NYC from 1932; worked five yrs. in a butcher shop bef. replacing Sy Oliver as arr. for Jimmie Lunceford '39–40. Moore's brittle, swinging scores, reflecting Oliver's infl., were heard in such first-class Lunceford perfs. as "Belgium Stomp"; "What's Your Story, Morning Glory"; "Chopin Prelude No. 7"; "Bugs' Parade"; "Monotony in Four Flats"; "Battle Axe." Fr. '40 to '44 arr. for Ch. Barnet ("Skyliner," etc.); Jan Savitt; then T. Dorsey. Was mus. publisher late '40s but became disillusioned w. mus. business in Amer. and moved to Eur. ca. '50. Wrote for French bands, tour. as mus. dir. for the Peters Sisters fr. '53; staff arr. for Berlin Radio, then tour. Eur. w. Delta Rhythm Boys. Eventually settled in Copenhagen. CDs: w. Lunceford; Barnet (Dec.).

MOORE, BREW (MILTON AUBREY JR.), tnr sax; b. Indianola, MS, 3/26/24; d. Copenhagen, Denmark, 8/19/73. Briefly pl. hca., tpt., and tbn. bef. taking up tnr. sax. Played in Fred Ford's band, NO 1942 and w. other gps. in Memphis and NO. To NYC briefly in '43; led qt.; ret. to NYC in '48, join. Claude Thornhill. Pl. w. Kai Winding; Machito '49; with Stan Getz, Zoot Sims, Al Cohn, and Allen Eager as part of a "Five Brothers" rec. gp. for Prest. '49; pl. w. Warne Marsh, Lennie Tristano '52–3; jammed w. Charlie Parker and others at the Open Door '53–4; then moved to SF, working w. tbnst. Bob Mielke; Cal Tjader; own gp. Was seriously ill in '59 but resumed pl. weekend jams at the Tropics and occ. Matson Line steamer trips to the Orient. After six mos. at Blue Note in Paris w. Kenny Clarke '61, moved to Copenhagen '65–7. From '67 to '70 pl. in NYC at Half Note and other Manh. club. After pl. in Canary Islands '70, he ret. to Denmark. He died after falling down a flight of stairs. Despite an erratic career marred by alcohol problems, Moore was among the most outstanding Lester Young–inspired tenor players. CDs: BL; Steep.; Fant.; four tracks w. own qt. in *In the Beginning . . . Bebop* (Sav.); w. C. Parker (Up.); Geo. Wallington; Chuck Wayne (Sav.); K. Winding in *Trombone By Three*; Getz (Prest.); Tjader (Fant.).

MOORE, DANNY (DANIEL WILLIAM), tpt, flg; b. Waycross, GA, 1/6/41; d. NYC, 2/16/05. After grad. fr. Center HS, att. Fla. A&M U. Tour. w. Paul Williams in US 1962. Pl. w. A. Blakey '64; five mos. w. C. Basie '66; also w. Ruth Brown, Q. Jones, Apollo Theater house band in '60s; Aretha Franklin in '70s. Reg. member of the Thad Jones–Mel Lewis orch. '69–72; flg. w. George Coleman Oct. fr. '72 off and on into '80s; D. Gillespie bb '75. Own gps. fr. '81. App. w. Max Roach and Abbey Lincoln at Lincoln Center in early '90s. Taught tpt., tbn., harm. at Henry Street Settlement House and Ethical Culture Sch., NYC '80s. Peter Watrous wrote of him in the *New York Times*: "His basic vocabulary comes from the mid-'50s trumpet lexicon, but the way he phrases, and all the embellishments he uses, made his improvisations swell with meaning." Favs: C. Brown, T. Jones, Gillespie. Fests: Montreux w. O. Nelson '73; also tour. in Japan in '70s; Eur. in '80s, '90s. Film: w. Paul Newman, *The Last Chance* '96. TV: app. in first jazz postage stamp commercial '95; *Good Day New York* '96. CDs: Top Talent; w. Freddy Cole (Fant.); G. Coleman (Charly); Jones-Lewis (Mos.; LRC); Pharoah Sanders (Evid.).

MOORE, DUDLEY (STUART JOHN), pno, actor; b. Dagenham, Essex, England, 4/19/35; d. Plainfield, NJ, 3/27/02. Studied at Guildhall Sch. of Mus.; B.A. fr. Oxford U. 1957; B. of Mus. degree '58. Made stage debut w. Oxford U. Drama Soc. '55. Pl. w. Vic Lewis '58–9; J. Dankworth '59–60; comp. incidental mus. for Royal Court Theatre '58–60. Teamed w. comedian Peter Cook in '60s. Led own trio intermittently fr. '61. Starred in *Beyond the Fringe* in London '61 and on B'way '62–4. Comp. background scores for films, plays, ballets, docus, and TV dramas. Tour. US w. trio '75, making numerous radio and TV apps. Long known as a brilliant comic actor, w. a string of successful films to his credit, Moore continued to appear and record as a pianist. Strongly influenced by Erroll Garner. CDs: w. Cleo Laine (RCA); Vic Lewis (Cand.).

MOORE, EDDIE, dms; b. San Francisco, CA, 9/14/40; d. Oakland, CA, 5/21/90. Worked w. cousin, orgst. Merl Saunders; the Mastersounds; and Dewey Redman, all in the 1960s. Tour. Vietnam w. singer Barbara Virgil '68; to Eur. late '60s to become house dmr. at Montmartre in Copenhagen; pl. w. Dexter Gordon. In '70s pl. and/or rec. w. Stanley Turrentine; Sonny Rollins; Redman; Woody Shaw; Bennie Wallace; tour. w. Rollins to India '78; and w. Redman '81; rec. w. Peter Sprague '83. Moore died in action, on the bandstand at Yoshi's. A memorial service in Aug. '90 grew into an annual fest. in SF. CDs: w. Mal Waldron–Steve Lacy (Evid.); Waldron (SN); Mark Lewis; Ted Gioia (Quartet); Rollins (Mile.); Pharoah Sanders; Barney Wilen (Timel.); Bennie Wallace (Enja).

MOORE, FREDDIE, dms, voc, wshbd; b. Washington, NC, 8/20/1900; d. Bronx, NY, 11/3/92. Learned dms. at age 12; ran away fr. home to pl. w. minstrel show; tour. extens. w. trav. shows in La., Fla., Cuba. Pl. w. Charlie Creath in St. Louis ca. 1927; own 7-piece band at the Savoy, Det., bef. join. Wilbur Sweatman in NYC '28–31. Tour. w. King Oliver '31–2; fr. '33 to '37 pl. w. own trio incl. Peter Brown, Don Frye. Worked regularly w. Art Hodes in mid '40s

and again in Chi. '50; w. S. Bechet '45, '47; Conrad Janis '51; Wilbur De Paris '52–4. Tour. Eur. w. M. Mezzrow '54–5; Sammy Price '55. Cont. to pl. in '60s; w. Tony Parenti '68–70; Roy Eldridge at Ryan's '71. During the '70s worked regularly w. Graham Stewart. From '76 pl. weekly w. Bob Cantwell's Saturday Night Stompers at the Red Blazer in NYC, sw. fr. dms. to wshbd. at age 87 due to failing health. He officially retired in Mar. '92 but sat in occasionally. As percussionist and vocalist, Moore was a personality as much as musician, using such props as oversized glasses and a fright wig. In his last yrs., he called himself "the world's oldest, continuous performing entertainer." Recs. w. Oliver '33; Bechet, Hodes '45; S. Price '55; Emmett Berry '56. CDs: w. K. Oliver (BB); Bechet (BN); Bunk Johnson (Amer. Mus.).

MOORE, GLEN R., bs; b. Portland, OR, 10/28/41. First prof. gig at age 14. Stud. in Copenhagen before moving to NYC; worked w. Jake Hanna; Zoot Sims; etc.; rec. w. Nick Brignola; pl. w. Paul Bley Synthesizer Show 1969–71. In '70, after pl. w. Paul Winter Consort, he organized the ensemble Oregon. Ret. to live in Oregon from '79; rec. first album as a lead. the same year; active as teacher. In early '90s worked and rec. a highly regarded duo album w. singer Nancy King. CDs: VeraBra; w. Oregon (ECM); Nancy King (Just.); Jerry Granelli (ITM Pacific); Ralph Towner (ECM).

MOORE, MARILYN, voc; b. Oklahoma City, OK, 6/16/31; d. Ft. Lauderdale, FL, 3/19/92. First perf. w. parents' vaudeville act at age 3; sang w. band in hs, then w. local bands in Okla. City and Chi. Briefly w. Woody Herman, Ch. Barnet 1952. Married Al Cohn '53; retired for several years; rec. debut, *Moody Marilyn Moore*, backed by Cohn, Beth. '57. Occ. active fr. 60s. A singer with a natural jazz timbre and sense of phrasing, her career was handicapped by critical resentment of her stylistic resemblance to Billie Holiday. Her son, Joe Cohn, is a talented gtrst.

MOORE, MICHAEL WATSON, bs, pno; b. Cincinnati, OH, 5/16/45. Father, Clarence, pl. jazz gtr. in Cincinnati on radio, TV; moth. grad. fr. Cincinnati Cons., taught voice and pno; maternal grandmoth. pl. pno. for silent movies in Ripley, Ohio. Pl. acdn. fr. age 7 to 9; tba. in hs. Stud. bs. w. Harold Roberts (Cincinnati Symph.) 1960; Frank Proto '66–8; Orin O'Brien in NYC '69–70. First gigs w. father while in hs. Pl. in Cincinnati w. David Matthews '63–5; Woody Evans at Playboy club '64–6. Tour. w. Woody Herman '67; then pl. w. Cal Collins at Cincinnati Playboy club '67–8. Moved to NYC '68. Pl. w. Marian McPartland '69–72; James Brown '71; Lee Konitz–Marshall Brown '72–3; Freddie Hubbard '73–4; Ruby Braff–Geo. Barnes '74–6; Benny Goodman '74–8; Bill Evans '77–8; also freelance w. Zoot Sims; Jimmy Rowles; Bob Brookmeyer; Hank Jones; Gerry Mulligan; Stan Getz; Teddy Wilson; Tommy Flanagan; Jack Wilkins; Jimmy Raney; Scott Hamilton; Warren Vaché; Chet Baker; Kenny Barron; Toshiko Akiyoshi; Herb Ellis; Tony Bennett; others late '70s-80s. Pl. in duo w. Gene Bertoncini fr. '71. Moved to Engl. '89; pl. w. Jim Mullen; Dave Cliff; Brian Spring; Brian Lemon; Spike Robinson; John Crichinson; Tony Lee; Jack Parnell. Ret. to US '92; pl. w. Howard Alden; Harry Allen; Ken Peplowski; Phil Woods. Moore taught at Eastman Sch. of Mus. summer prog. '76–88; U. of Bridgeport '81–2. Favs: Slam Stewart, Red Mitchell, Paul Chambers, Scott LaFaro. Fests: Africa w. W. Herman '66; Japan '71–80, '86; Germ. '75; Engl. '98–92. TV: *Tonight Show* w. Bertoncini '78; other TV w. Ed Sullivan; Dick Cavett; Merv Griffin. Profiled by Whitney Balliett in *The New Yorker* '80. CDs: Conc. (duo w. Bill Charlap); w. H. Alden; R. Braff; R. Clooney (Conc.); H. Allen (Mastermix); H. Danko (Sunny.); Gil Evans (BB); B. Goodman (Lond.); R. Kellaway (Chiaro.); M. McPartland (JA); J. Raney (Steep.).

MOORE, OSCAR FREDERIC, gtr; b. Austin, TX, 12/25/16; d. Las Vegas, NV, 10/8/81. Professional debut 1934 w. bro., gtrst. Johnny. Join. Nat King Cole '37, remain. w. him for exactly ten yrs., dur. which time he earned acclaim as the first of the modern combo gtrsts., pl. single-string amplified solos and chord work in a style that was a highly attractive element in Cole's recs. Settled in LA, worked mostly w. bro's. gp, the Three Blazers, rec. occasionally. By '60 had been virtually inactive in mus. and took work as a bricklayer but did ret. to playing. Tremendously popular in the heyday of the King Cole Trio, Moore won *DB* and *Metronome* polls as the country's No. 1 gtr. every yr. fr. '45–8; also won *Esq.* Silver Award '44–5, Gold Award '46–7. CDs: V.S.O.P.; w. Nat King Cole (Laser.; Cap.; Dec; M&A; Mos.); Joe Turner (Dec.); Capitol Jazzmen (Jazz Unlimited); Lester Young (Jass); L. Hampton; Art Tatum (Class.); I. Jacquet (Verve).

MOORE, PHIL, comp, voc coach, pno, voc; b. Portland, OR, 2/20/18; d. Los Angeles, CA, 5/13/87. Pioneered "block chord" pno. style 1939, later popularized by Milt Buckner, Geo. Shearing. Led own qt. at Café Society mid '40s. As one of the first blacks to break into the field, he was staff arr.-cond. for MGM in Hollywood for five years in late '40s. Accompanied Dorothy Dandridge, Lena Horne;

coached many singers, incl. Frank Sinatra; Marilyn Monroe; Ava Gardner. Best known pop song, "Shoo Shoo Baby." In later yrs. had own studio in Hollywood, coaching many singers. CDs: w. Lavern Baker; Bobby Short (Atl.); Ernestine Anderson (Sav.); Dizzy Gillespie (BN).

MOORE, RALPH ALGERNON, tnr, sop saxes; b. London, England, 12/24/56. Mother and uncle are tap dancers. Began on tpt. at age 13; tnr. sax at 14. Stud. at Berklee Coll. of Mus. 1975–8. Pl. w. local gps. in hs and coll., then w. Horace Silver '81–5; Roy Haynes '81–8; Mingus Dynasty '85; Freddie Hubbard '86–9; Dizzy Gillespie bb '87. Pl. w. J. J. Johnson fr. '88; also w. McCoy Tyner–Freddie Hubbard; Ray Brown; Gene Harris–Phillip Morris Superband; Cedar Walton's Eastern Rebellion; own qt. and qnt. Member of *Tonight Show* orch. fr. '95. Favs: Parker, Coltrane, Stitt. Fests: all major fr. '81. CDs: Land.; CC; Res.; Sav.; w. J. J. Johnson (Ant.); Ray Brown (Conc.); F. Hubbard (MM; BN); Eastern Rebellion (MM); Kenny Drew Jr.; Charlie Sepulveda (Ant.); Gene Harris–P. Morris Superband (Conc.); Don Sickler (Up.).

MOREHOUSE, CHAUNCEY, dms, perc; b. Niagara Falls, NY, 3/11/02; d. Philadelphia, PA, 11/3/80. First start. working for fath., a ragtime pnst. for silent films in Chambersburg, Pa. Stud. pno. w. Catholic nuns; later pl. w. Gettysburg Coll. dance band and w. the nucleus of Ted Weems band at Ocean City, N.J. After pl. w. Weems 1924 and Jean Goldkette '25–7, worked w. Don Voorhees orch. in the pit for B'way show, *Come Rain or Come Shine* '28. From '29 was in commercial radio, later TV, and also had own advertising agency, writing and making jingles. Developed a set of chromatically tuned dms. which he used for Afro-Cuban effects, etc. while leading his own band in '38. His importance to jazz lay in his participation in a number of classic recs. '26–30, with Bix Beiderbecke; Frank Trumbauer; Joe Venuti; Hoagy Carmichael; Red Nichols; Miff Mole; the Dorsey Bros.; et al. Considered one of the early pioneers of jazz drumming bef. he began to concentrate on studio work. CDs: w. B. Beiderbecke (Col.); Dorsey Bros. (Hep); The Georgians (Retrieval); Manone (Collector's classics); Mole (Frog); Adrian Rollini (Topaz).

MOREIRA, AIRTO GUIMORVA, perc, dms, voc; b. Itaiopolis, Brazil, 8/5/41. Studied acoustic gtr. and pno. 1948–50; perf. on radio at age 6; pl. in small bands at 12. Went to São Paulo and Rio at 16; pl. in many Brazilian cabarets. Own trio at 22, feat. Hermeto Pascoal, w. whom he later assembled the Quarteto Novo. To LA '68; stud. w. Moacir Santos '70. Rec. w. M. Davis '70; worked w. Lee Morgan and pl. on first Weather Report album '71. With wife, Flora Purim, worked in Chick Corea's Return to Forever gp. '73. Rec. and pl. w. dozens of mus., incl. Stan Getz; Cannonball Adderley; Gato Barbieri; etc.; moved to Berkeley, Calif. '73. For the past twenty-five yrs. while working mainly w. his wife in various gps., incl. Fourth World fr. '90, he has also freelanced extensively in perfs. and recs. w. H. Hancock; Q. Jones; Gil Evans; Hubert Laws; George Benson; George Duke; F. Hubbard; and scores of others. Moreira was among the first to play an important role as a supplementary percussionist in jazz rhythm sections; he helped introduce such instruments as the cuica and the berimbau to Amer. audiences. CDs: Ref.; Conc.; Epic; w. M. Davis (Col); G. Benson; Deodado; H. Laws (CTI); Wayne Shorter (Col.; Verve); F. Hubbard (Col.); Corea (Stretch); Donald Byrd; Duke Pearson (BN).

MORELL, JOHN E., gtr; b. Niagara Falls, NY, 6/2/46. Grandfather, fath., and bro. all pl. gtr. Self-taught. Pl. w. Les Brown 1967–70; Gil Evans–Miles Davis at Berkeley Fest. '68; Shelly Manne '70–4. Active in rec. and TV field w. Henry Mancini, et al; led own gps. fr. '75. In '92 led qt., pl. for Calif. Arts Council w. Joel Di Bartolo; Alan Estes; Tom Peterson; also pl. gigs w. Peter Erskine. LPs: w. Pete Chrislieb (Bosco); Shelly Manne (Main.). CD: w. Manne (Cont.).

MORELL, MARTY (MARTIN MATTHEW), dms, vib, perc; b. NYC, 2/15/44. Studied pno. and cl., then began pl. dms. at age 12. Stud. perc. at Manh. Sch. of Mus. '60. Pl. w. Al Cohn–Zoot Sims '66. Rec. w. Red Allen; Gary McFarland; Steve Kuhn '66; Gabor Szabo '67. Pl. w. Bill Evans trio '68–75. Moved to Toronto, Can. '74. Worked as studio mus. and pl. vib. in own Latin-jazz bands fr. mid-'70s. Pl. w. Rob McConnell's Boss Brass '78–81. CDs: w. B. Evans (Col.; Mile.; Verve); R. McConnell (Conc.).

MORELLO, JOE (JOSEPH A.), dms; b. Springfield, MA, 7/17/28. Began on vln; sw. to dms. in hs. Pl. in hs w. Phil Woods, Sal Salvador. Pl. w. Whitey Bernard, then join. Glen Gray 1950. Moved to NYC '52. Pl. w. Johnny Smith, Stan Kenton '52; Gil Melle '53; Marian McPartland '53–6; also freelance and rec. w. Woods, Salvador, Melle, Tal Farlow, Jimmy Raney, Jackie and Roy, etc. '54–6. Achieved wide recog. as a member of the Dave Brubeck Qt. '56–67. Worked mainly as teacher and clinician for Ludwig Drum Corp. fr. '67 when his eyesight began to fade. He became blind in '76. Occ. recs. and gigs

w. Brubeck; McPartland; Salvador. Led own gps. in NYC fr. '70s. Reunited w. McPartland and Bill Crow at McPartland's 80th birthday concert at Town Hall '98. His method books are publ. by Ludwig. Favs: Krupa, Dave Tough, Don Lamond, Rich, Bellson. Polls: *DB* '62–4. CDs: BB; DMP; w. D. Brubeck (Col.; LRC); *Burnin' For Buddy* (Atl.); Art Pepper (BN); *The Real Ambassadors* w. L. Armstrong (Col.); Tal Farlow (Verve); M. McPartland (Conc.; Sav.).

MORGAN, AL (ALBERT), bs; b. New Orleans, 8/10/08; d. Los Angeles, CA, 4/14/74. Brothers tptrs. Sam and Isaiah, reedman Andrew, all prof. mus. Played cl. and dms. at age 9, bs. at 10. Pl. w. bro. Isaiah's band; then w. Lee Collins 1923; tour. Fla. Pl. w. saxist David Jones in NO. Worked on riverboats w. Fate Marable '25–9. Rec. w. Jones-Collins Astoria Hot Eight, Vict. '29. Pl. w. Cab Calloway '32–6. Worked in Calif. w. Eddie Barefield '36–7; then freelanced bef. pl. w. Les Hite '42. Settled in Bost. w. Sabby Lewis band most of next decade; also w. Louis Jordan '45. Rec. w. Chu Berry; Eddie Condon; and others. Back in Calif. in '57, working w. Jack McVea and Nellie Lutcher; Joe Darensbourg; also duo with pnst. Buddy Banks. Morgan, who tied w. Milt Hinton for the *Esq.* Silver Award '44, was an exponent of the '30s quarter note bs. style. Films: w. Calloway, *The Big Broadcast* '32; *The Singing Kid* '36. CDs: w. Jack Teagarden (BB); T-Bone Walker (Mos.); Louis Jordan; Jay McShann (Stash); Red Allen (Collector's Classics).

MORGAN, FRANK, alto, sop saxes; b. Minneapolis, MN, 12/23/33. Studied gtr. w. fath., who pl. gtr. w. the Ink Spots. Later lived in Det., where, after hearing Charlie Parker w. Jay McShann Orch., he studied cl. Switched to alto sax in 1944. Made prof. debut in '48, while att. hs in LA. At 15, won a talent contest and rec. for RCA w. Freddie Martin. Rec. w. Wardell Gray on date prod. by Teddy Charles '53; Kenny Clarke '54; under own name '55. By then had become a heroin addict and was in and out of prison, incl. San Quentin, where he pl. w. Art Pepper and Dupree Bolton. Resumed app. in LA clubs in '70s and rec. a new album in '85. It was not until he played in NYC in late '86 that the East Coast critics, who had previously ignored him, hailed Morgan as a major alto virtuoso. Moved to NYC, later to Corrales, New Mex. First identified as a Charlie Parker stylist, Morgan later adapted a more personal and less rhythm-oriented approach, often graced w. tender lyricism. CDs: Cont.; GNP Cres.; Ant.; Tel.; Verve; Frank Morgan–Bud Shank (Cont.) w. L. Subramaniam–S. Grappelli (Mile.); Abbey Lincoln (Verve); Gray (Prest.)

MORGAN, LANNY (HAROLD LANSFORD), alto sax, fl, cl; b. Des Moines, IA, 3/30/34. Studied vln. from age 6. Fath. pl. alto sax w. own band and w. Ted Weems; family moved to LA '44. In '50s worked w. C. Barnet; Tommy Alexander; Si Zentner; Bob Florence; followed by mil. service. Based in NYC, he toured w. Maynard Ferguson '60–6. Later was active in studio work while freelancing in LA fr. '69 w. Bill Berry; Bill Holman; Terry Gibbs; and Florence; regular member of Supersax from early '70s. From '92 tour. w. Natalie Cole as a feat. soloist. Also active as teacher at Stanford U., etc. A fluent improviser in the Charlie Parker tradition. CDs: Cont.; V.S.O.P.; FS; w. Holman (JVC).

MORGAN, LEE, tpt; b. Philadelphia, PA, 7/10/38; d. NYC, 2/19/72. Studied tpt. priv. and at Mastbaum Tech.; pl. w. local gps. fr. 1953. Tour. w. Dizzy Gillespie '56–8; Art Blakey '58–61. With Jimmy Heath in Phila., then rejoined Blakey '64–5. In '65 rec. his hit comp., "The Sidewinder," for BN. Freelanced w. his own gps. During an app. at Slug's in the East Village, he was shot and killed by a woman friend while sitting at a table between sets. Strongly infl. by Clifford Brown, Morgan later developed an individual identity marked by a surging rhythmic attack that uses long, spinning phrases as well as choked notes; and a brassy, biting tone that is not without warmth, particularly on ballads. One of his earliest solos was "Night in Tunisia" w. Gillespie. Morgan was an activist and member of the Jazz and People's Movement which, in '70–71, protested media neglect of and indifference to jazz artists. Book: work in progress, *Pure Jazz Cooker* by Earle R. Gullins Jr. CDs: BN; Sav.; Roul.; Spec.; Jzld.; w. Blakey (BN; BB; Fontana; Imp.); Gillespie (Verve); Coltrane; Jimmy Smith; H. Mobley; Larry Young (BN); Curtis Fuller (Sav.).

MORGANELLI, MARK CHRISTOPHER, tpt, flg, pno, prod; b. Chincoteague, VA, 5/15/55. Own combo in hs. in Glen Head, N.Y., then stud. at Bucknell U., Pa. 1973–7. Pl. w. own qt. in Pa. and Fla. '77, then moved to NYC '78. Pl. w. Bob January, Don Redman '78; own rehearsal bb '78–9; also own gps. Pl. w. David Amram fr. '85; Tiny Grimes '89; Fathead Newman '90; Paquito D'Rivera '91. Prod. many recs. for the Candid label since '89. Owned Jazz Forum jazz club in NYC '79–83. He founded the Riverside Park Arts Festival in '85 and fr. '88 was the music coordinator for Birdland, when it was at 105th & B'way, NYC. In '90s functioning more as prod. for Jazz Forum Arts in Westchester. Favs: Miles Davis, F. Hubbard, Clifford Brown, Lee Morgan, C. Terry. Fests: MJF '76; Italy '89, '91; Club Med since '85.

TV: Joe Franklin. CDs: JazzForum; Cand.; w. P. D'Rivera (Cand.).

MORGERA, FABIO, tpt, flg, comp; b. Naples, Italy, 4/24/63. Studied at Scuola Di Fiesole 1980–4. Moved to USA '86. Stud. at Grove Sch. of Mus., LA '87; Berklee Coll. of Mus. '89–90. Pl. w. Eurojazz Orch. '82–5; Giorgio Gaslini '83–6. Led own bb and qt. '87. Pl. w. Quest–Toscana Jazz Pool '87; Igor Butman '88; Dave Holland–Toscana Jazz Pool; Eurojazz Orch. '89; own qnt. fr. '89. Taught at Umbria clinics in Italy '87–91. Member of Groove Collective in mid '90s. Favs: Lee Morgan, Miles Davis, Woody Shaw; comp: Wayne Shorter. Fests: many Eur. fr. '83; Mid. East '84; Russia '87. TV: Italian TV. CDs: Red; Ken; w. Groove Collective (Imp.).

MORONI, DADO (EDGARDO), pno, bs; b. Genoa, Italy, 10/20/62. Grandfather Enrico was opera singer; fath. sang w. dance bands 1940s-50s; moth. and sist. are amateur mus. Began on pno. at age 3; began pl. bs. at age 13. Mainly self-taught; stud. harmony w. Flavio Crivelli. First gig on radio show w. Franco Cerri at age 13. Pl. w. local gps. '76–80; Franco Ambrosetti '80–5; Gianni Basso '81–8. Pl. w. Jimmy Woode Trio '83–9; accomp. Amer. mus. incl. Johnny Griffin; Clark Terry; Bud Shank; James Moody; Freddie Hubbard; etc. Pl. w. Geo. Robert '85; Adrienne West '85–90; Mingus Dynasty '87; Two Bass Hit w. Ray Brown, Pierre Boussaguet fr. '89; Wolfgang Haffner fr. '89; Geo. Robert–Clark Terry on Swiss-spons. tour of Eur., Asia, Mid-East '91. In '87 Moroni was a judge for the Thelonious Monk Inst. Jazz Pno. Competition. He has led his own trio w. Rosario Bonaccorso, Gianni Cazzola fr. '91. Favs: Tatum, Wynton Kelly, Tyner; bs: Ray Brown, Paul Chambers, Ron Carter. Polls: many Eur. awds. Fests: US and Can. fr. '86; Africa '88; Asia, Mid-East '91. TV: Eur. TV fr. '76. CDs: Em.; w. G. Robert–C. Terry (TCB); w. Alain Guyonnet–Lee Konitz (TCB); Tom Harrell (Cont.); Jesse Davis; Hendrik Meurkens (Conc.); Ray Brown Tel.).

MORRIS, DINKY (JAMES EDWARD JR.), sop, alto, tnr, bari saxes; sop, alto, bs cls; fl; b. Chicago, IL, 7/9/36. Self-taught sax and cl. player. Played w. The Clefs 1951. This Chi. teenage gp., led by Wallace Burton, incl. Kirk Stuart, Ramsey Lewis, Eldee Young, and Red Holt. The Clefs were a dance hall house band that pl. w. and opposite such artists as Earl Hines; Art Blakey; Gene Ammons; Wardell Gray; James Moody; and Dinah Washington. After army stint '71, Morris pl. w. T-Bone Walker; Otis Rush; Von and George Freeman. Degree in sociology from Loyola U. '78. Acct. exec. at AT&T '71–89.

Joined Jeannie and Jimmy Cheatham's Band in Calif. '86. CDs: w. Cheathams (Conc.).

MORRIS, JOE (JOSEPH), tpt, bs; b. Montgomery, AL, 1922; d. Phoenix, AZ, 11/21/58. Studied w. bro., who pl. gtr. w. Erskine Hawkins. With L. Hampton 1942–6, rcc. his own comps. "Chop Chop"; "Punch & Judy"; "Tempo's Birthday." Backgrounds on Dinah Washington's "Evil Gal Blues." After working w. Buddy Rich '46, formed own band which incl. Johnny Griffin, Elmo Hope, Percy Heath, and Philly Joe Jones; rec. for Dec. and Atl.; later active pl. and singing w. r&b gps. CDs: w. L. Hampton (Dec.); Dinah Washington (Em.).

MORRIS, MARLOWE, pno, org; b. NYC, 5/16/15; d. NYC ca. '77. Nephew of cornetist Thomas Morris, w. whose gp. Fats Waller rec. in 1927. Stud. dms., hca., and uke. bef. taking up pno. Pl. w. June Clark '35–6; Spirits of Rhythm '39–40; Coleman Hawkins '40. After mil. service '41 pl. w. Scoville Brown; Al Sears; Sid Catlett; Eddie South; and Tiny Grimes; app. in classic jazz film short, *Jammin' the Blues* '40. Semi-retired fr. mus., working at post office until '49, after which he mainly pl. org. LP: *Play the Thing* (Col.) '62, which won the French Grand Prix du Disque; Ike Quebec box (Mos.). CDs: w. L. Hampton (BB); Jimmy Rushing (Vang.); w. Sid Catlett in *The Commodore Story* (Comm.); Tiny Grimes in *The Blue Note Swingtets* (BN).

MORRISON, JAMES, multi-instrumentalist; b. Boorowa, Australia, 11/11/62. Grandmother was still pl. pno. for a dance school into her late '80s; moth. teaches dance and pl. sax; bro. pl. dms.; sist. dancer and occ. mus. Began on crnt. at age 7 shortly after family moved to Sydney. Then, within a yr., took up tbn., tba., euph.; a few yrs. later alto sax. Form. own trad. gp. at 9; at 13 start pl. in night clubs. Entered New South Wales Cons. at 16, doubling at Paradise Jazz Cellar in Sydney. At 18 join. Don Burrows' qnt. Learned pl. and arr. and how to be a perf. fr. Burrows during his two yrs. w. him. After grad. fr. Cons., he became a teacher/lecturer in the Jazz Stud. Dept. First heard in the US at MJF 1979. Pl. w. Red Rodney for five mos. in '87. Pl. Colo. JP '87. Tour. US w. Australian Jazz Orch. '88. App. as soloist on Eur. jf circuit '88 where he was rec. by Nesuhi Ertegun for East-West (Atl.) label. World tour w. Philip Morris Superband '89. Rec. qt. tracks w. Ray Brown, Jeff Hamilton, Herb Ellis, and bb numbers for which he wrote the arrs. and overdubbed all horn parts—four tpts., four tbns., five saxes, and pno.—for Atl. CD, *Snappy Doo*. Rejoin. Superband for three mos., world tour '90. App. at Bern JF '90; w. Lalo Schifrin at

Juan-Les-Pins JF '94. Acknowledging Morrison's talent on tpt. and tbn., Larry Kart added: "And on baritone horn and euphonium—well, he appears to have virtually reinvented those marching-band stalwarts, bringing them fully to life in jazz terms." CDs: Atl.; w. Gene Harris & Phil. Morris Superband (Conc.).

MORRISON, PECK (JOHN A.), bs; b. Lancaster, PA, 9/11/19; d. NYC, 2/25/88. Studied tpt., dms., and bs.; army band in Italy 1946. Toured w. Lucky Thompson '50–3; in early '50s pl. and rec. w. Bill Graham; H. Silver; Gigi Gryce; Zoot Sims; pl. w. J. J. Johnson–Kai Winding Qnt. '54; Duke Ellington, Lou Donaldson, Gerry Mulligan '55; Johnny Smith '56. House bs. at Five Spot, NYC '57–9; tour. w. Carmen McRae '58. App. w. Newport Rebels JF '60; rec. w. Shirley Scott; Johnny Coles; Red Garland; D. Ellington; et al. Pl. el-bs. w. Sy Oliver '73 in Paris. In mid '80s freelanced in NYC and on the road w. various gps., incl. Harlem Blues and Jazz Band. CDs: w. Charlie Rouse (Epic); G. Mulligan (Verve; Em.); Betty Carter (Imp.); Randy Weston (Roul.).

MORRISSEY, DICK (RICHARD EDWIN), tnr, sop saxes, fl, cl; b. Horley, England, 5/9/40. Played cl. w. Gus Galbraith 1957; then sw. to tnr. sax. Pl. in India w. Harry South '60–1 bef. form. own gp. w. South, Phil Bates, Phil Seamen. Rec. as lead. fr. '61. Co-led jazz-rock gp. If ca. '70–4. Lived in Sweden '74–5. Pl. w. Herbie Mann, Average White Band mid '70s. Led funk-jazz gp., Morrissey–Mullen, w. Jim Mullen, mid '70s to '85. Morrissey ret. to leading a more mainstream jazz-oriented combo in the mid '80s. His pl. career was halted by ill health in the '90s. CDs: JH; Redial; Home.; Beggars Banquet; Coda; w. Mike Carr (Cargogold).

MORROW, BUDDY (Muni "Moe" Zudekoff), tbn, lead; b. New Haven, CT, 2/8/19. Played w. local bands, incl. Yale Collegians, as a teenager; moved to NYC 1934; stud. at Institute of Musical Art. In '30s pl. w. Paul Whiteman; orig. Artie Shaw band w. strings; T. Dorsey; B. Berigan; Eddie Duchin; Vincent Lopez. Naval service WWII. Pl. w. Bob Crosby '41; J. Dorsey '45; rec. w. Sharkey Bonano '36; Lee Wiley '43; Bob Crosby '42; Red McKenzie '44. Led own band '45–6, then did studio work in NYC. Reorganized band '51 and found success w. pop-style versions of r&b tunes for RCA. Ret. to studio work in '60s; led T. Dorsey ghost band in '70s and '80s. CDs: Aerospace.

MORROW, GEORGE WASHINGTON, bs; b. Pasadena, CA, 8/15/25; d. Orlando, FL, 5/26/92. First stud. vln.; then cello at age 13; and bs. in LA at Fine Arts Cons. Served in mil. 1943–6. Freelanced in LA w. Teddy Edwards; Charlie Parker; Sonny Criss. From '48 to '53, mainly in SF incl. Bop City, pl. w. Billie Holiday; Wardell Gray; Dexter Gordon; Sonny Clark. Best known as member of Clifford Brown–Max Roach gp. '54–6, and again when Roach re-organized '56–8. Later pl. w. Sonny Rollins; Anita O'Day; Chet Baker. App. at Nice JF '75. After settling in Fla. in '76 he worked in house band at Disney World, pl. w. many visiting soloists incl. Barney Kessel, Art Farmer. A strong-walking, supportive section player. Favs: Blanton, Pettiford, Ray Brown. CDs: w. Clifford Brown; Dinah Washington (Em.); M. Roach (Em.; Verve); Brown-Roach (Em.; GNP Cres.); Rollins (Prest.); Baker (Riv.); Anita O'Day (Evid.); Curtis Amy (PJ).

MORSE, ELLA MAE, voc; b. Mansfield, TX, 9/12/24; d. Bullhead City, AZ, 10/16/99. Sang w. father's jazz band; sist., Flora Ann, sang prof. as Flo Handy. Worked w. J. Dorsey 1939; first hit, "Cow Cow Boogie," rec. w. Freddie Slack orch. for Cap. '42. Other '40s hits incl. "Mr. Five by Five" and "House of Blue Lights." In '51 she rec. another hit, "Blacksmith Blues," w. Nelson Riddle orch. Thereafter worked primarily as a single until '57, when she retired again. An excellent swing era band vocalist, she came to be regarded more as a pop artist in the '50. CDs: Cap.; Pathé; box set (Bear Family Records).

MORTON, BENNY (HENRY STERLING), tbn; b. NYC, 1/31/07; d. NYC, 12/28/85. Played w. Billy Fowler 1923–6; Fletcher Henderson '26–8; Chick Webb '30–1; Don Redman '32–7; Count Basie '37–9, after which he worked w. various bands at NYC's Café Society, incl. Joe Sullivan, Teddy Wilson, and Edmond Hall; own band '46. From '46 he worked in B'way pit bands for such shows as *Memphis Bound; St. Louis Woman; Lend an Ear; Guys and Dolls; Silk Stockings*; and *Jamaica*. From '50s also active in jazz w. Bobby Hackett; Wild Bill Davison; Henry "Red" Allen. Toured w. WGJB '73–4. One of the most personal tbn. stylists with a vibrant, intense solo talent well represented on recs. w. Teddy Wilson; Benny Carter; et al. CDs: two tracks in *The Blue Note Swingtets* (BN); w. B. Holiday (Col.; Jazz Unlimited); Ruby Braff; Benny Carter (BB); Count Basie (Dec.; Class.); Eddie Condon (Stash); Roy Eldridge (NW); Wild Bill Davison (Sack.).

MORTON, JELLY ROLL (Ferdinand Joseph La Menthe), pno, comp, leader, voc; b. Gulfport, LA, 9/20/1885; d. Los Angeles, CA, 7/10/41. Started on gtr. 1892; pno '95. From '02 pl. pno in bordellos in NO's Storyville district. Spending only part of his time as a prof. mus., he was heard in Memphis, St. Louis, and KC. During this time, he was exposed to a wide range of mus., incl. ragtime, light classics, vocal and instrumental blues, and minstrel music, all of which impacted his own compositions. From '17 to '22, he spent much of his time in Calif., but his career as a recording artist began w. a series of solos made in Richmond, Indiana '23–4. The principal source of his fame was an impressive series of Victor sessions by Jelly Roll Morton's Red Hot Peppers made between Sept. '26 and Oct. '30, mostly in Chi. and NYC. The gp. incl. George Mitchell, Kid Ory, Omer Simeon, Johnny and Baby Dodds. During his successful years of the '20s, at the peak of his success, Morton—like many show business figures of the era—was an ostentatious presence, sporting a diamond-embedded tooth and elegant clothes. However, his star faded in the '30s with the emergence of the new swing styles advanced by Fletcher Henderson, Don Redman, Benny Carter, et al. By '37 Morton lived in relative obscurity, running a night club in Wash., D.C. Returning to NYC, he made a series of recordings in '39–40, spurred by a short-lived renewed interest in earlier jazz forms. He stayed in NYC until late '40, when—his health failing—he moved to Calif. where he died a few months later. Because of his boastful claims—notably that he had "invented jazz in 1902" and that many famous compositions were stolen from him—Morton became a controversial figure, but many of his claims were true. In the '50s, an era of "progressive" jazz, Dave Brubeck noted: "You can't really call today's jazz progressive, because Jelly Roll Morton was doing the same thing thirty years ago." *Jelly's Last Jam*, a Broadway musical of the early '90s starring Gregory Hines, did Morton an injustice by portraying him as a racist egotist while skirting his many accomplishments, but his melodies held up remarkably well. A more accurate picture of the man is painted by a spoken autobiography, recorded for the Library of Congress in '38 by Alan Lomax; it offers a fascinating insight to Morton, his music, and the early days of jazz. Book: *Mr. Jelly Roll*, Alan Lomax, '50 (Pantheon '93). His best known comps. incl. "King Porter Stomp"; "Milenberg Joys"; "Wolverine Blues"; "The Pearls"; "Wild Man Blues"; and "Kansas City Stomps." CDs: altered pno. rolls (None.); BB; Biog.; Retrieval; Rounder (Lib. of Cong. recs. without Morton's commentary); Comm.; GTJ; Mile.; Class.

MOSCA, JOHN, tbn; b. NYC, 6/22/50. Began on fl. Studied tbn. w. Dan Plumby; Jack Raines; "Charlie Small"; then w. Per Brevig at Juilliard. Pl. w. Larry Elgart 1968; rehearsal bands led by Jerry Kail, Al

Porcino, Gene Roland, Dave Berger, Dick Cone early '70s; Buddy Rich bb '70s; Thad Jones–Mel Lewis Orch. fr. '75 to '90, when it bec. the Vanguard Jazz Orch. w. Mosca as co-lead. He has taught at NYU; William Paterson Coll.; and Manh. Sch. of Mus. Favs: J. J. Johnson, Frank Rosolino, Bob Brookmeyer. An engaging, bop-oriented soloist. Fests: Japan '75; Eur. since '76 w. Mel Lewis Orch–Vanguard JO. CDs: w. Thad Jones–Mel Lewis (A&M; Atl.; MM); Christopher Holiday (Novus); Vanguard Jazz Orch. (NW); John McNeil–Kenny Berger (Synergy).

MOSCA, RAY (RAYMOND JR.), dms, timbales, tymp; b. NYC, 7/26/32. Played w. uncles (who pl. w. Paul Whiteman, Joe Venuti) fr. age 8, then at parties in Catskills fr. age 14. Stud. w. Jo Jones fr. age 16; also at Manh. Sch. of Mus. Pl. w. house band at Desert Inn, LV 1954; Alex Kallao '54–5; Cy Coleman, Oscar Pettiford '56; Mary Lou Williams '56–7; Lennie Tristano '56–8; Al Cohn–Zoot Sims '56–78; Geo. Wallington, Hampton Hawes '57; Geo. Shearing '58–60; Billy Taylor '60–2; Monty Alexander '61–78; Teddy Wilson '63–6; Benny Goodman '63; Dorothy Donegan fr. '63; Bobby Hackett '64–70. Rejoin. Goodman '68, then pl. w. Marty Napoleon '68–9; Oscar Peterson '69–70; Ray Nance '72–3; Earl Hines '72–5; Goodman again '75; Tyree Glenn '76–8; Phineas Newborn '80; Terry Gibbs–Buddy DeFranco '83–4. Has also done much commercial studio work. Favs: Krupa, Rich, Jo Jones. Fests: Eur. since '59 w. Shearing, Goodman, Donegan; Japan '75 w. Hines. Film: *Jazz on a Summer's Day* w. Shearing '58. TV: *Tonight Show*, Dean Martin, Arthur Godfrey, etc. CDs: w. Shearing (Cap.); B. Goodman (MM); Mike Longo (CAP); Dave McKenna; Dorothy Donegan (Chiaro.).

MOSCA, SAL (SALVATORE JOSEPH), pno; b. Mt. Vernon, NY, 4/27/27. Uncle pl. tpt. Stud. w. Wilbur Jessup in Mt. Vernon, then pl. w. army band 1945–7; Saxie Dowell '47. Stud. w. Lennie Tristano '47–55; then at NY Coll. of Mus. and NYU '48–51. Pl. and rec. w. Lee Konitz '49–65; Konitz–Warne Marsh in '70s; own gps. since late '70s. Mosca also has extensive teaching experience. Favs: Tatum, Bud Powell, Tristano. Fests: Eur. since '80. TV: Germ. '80. CDs: Jazz Records; Zianna; Disc.; Atl.; Mosca–Marsh (Zianna); w. Miles Davis (Prest.); Konitz (Prest.; Wave).

MOSES, BOB (ROBERT LAURENCE aka Rahboat Ntumba), dms, perc, comp; b. NYC, 1/28/48. Self-taught fr. age 10. Pl. vib. w. Latin bands in Bronx, then dms. w. early jazz-rock gp. Free Spirits

w. Larry Coryell 1966. Pl. w. Rahsaan Roland Kirk '67; Gary Burton '67–8. Freelanced in NYC w. Coryell; Steve Marcus; Free Life Communication w. Dave Liebman, Randy Brecker; Compost w. Jack DeJohnette '69–73. Formed gp. Open Sky w. Liebman late '60s. Tour. Engl. w. Mike Gibbs' bb '74. Pl. w. G. Burton '74–5; Pat Metheny mid '70s; Hal Galper, Gil Goldstein '78; Steve Swallow '79; Steve Kuhn–Sheila Jordan '79–82; Geo. Gruntz '83; Emily Remler '83–4; Mister Spats w. Steve Evans, June Bisantz early '80s. Comps. incl. "Our Life"; "Dancing Bears"; "Bittersweet in the Ozone"; "Arb Om Souple." Author of a drum method, *Drum Wisdom* (Clifton Publ.). Favs: Roach, Roy Haynes. Fests: all major w. Burton. CDs: Gram.; w. Burton (BB); Galper; Remler (Conc.); Michael Gibbs (Act).

MOSES, J. C. (JOHN CURTIS), dms; b. Pittsburgh, PA, 10/18/36; d. Pittsburgh, 1977, Played w. saxist Walt Harper 1958–60 and in NYC w. Clifford Jordan, Herbie Hancock, Kenny Dorham, Eric Dolphy '62–3. To Copenhagen as member of NY Contemp. Five w. Archie Shepp, John Tchicai, Don Cherry, and Don Moore. Later worked w. Roland Kirk; Sonny Stitt; Jackie McLean; Willie Bobo; cont. off and on w. Shepp. Returned to Den. '69; worked w. visiting Amers., incl. Coleman Hawkins; Dexter Gordon; Red Mitchell. Back in US, worked sporadically w. Eric Kloss, Nathan Davis in Pitts. until ca. '72, when illness forced him into semi-retirement. CDs: w. Kenny Dorham (BN).

MOSLEY, SNUB (Lawrence Leo Mosely), tbn, slide sax, voc, comp; b. Little Rock, AR, 12/29/05; d. NYC, 7/21/81. Studied at Cutaire Sch. of Music, Cincinnati, Ohio. Worked w. Alphonso Trent 1925–31; Claude Hopkins '34–6; L. Armstrong '36–7; Fats Waller '37. Form. own combo '38; because of the slide sax, which he designed, Mosley was dubbed "The Man with the Funny Horn" (rec. a tune "The Man with the Funny Little Horn" for Dec. '40). Led band in So. Pacific for first black USO troupe, which was headed by Alberta Hunter '45; other USO tours to Engl., France, and Germ. '52. From early '50s led own gps. in NYC; perf. in Engl. '78–81. Best known comp., "Pretty Eyed Baby," written w. Mary Lou Williams. Rec. LP, *Live at the Pizza Express*, for Pizza label, Lond. '78. CD: w. Armstrong (Class.).

MOSS, DANNY (DENNIS), tnr sax; b. Redhill, England, 8/16/27. Wife is vocalist Jeannie Lamb. Began pl. prof. at age 16. Rec. fr. late 1940s w. British bbs incl. Oscar Rabin, Vic Lewis, Ted Heath '53–5; John Dankworth '57–61; Humphrey Lyttelton '62.

Led own qt. fr. '62. Rec. w. Buck Clayton '63; Adelaide Hall ca. '69. Tour. w. Freddy Randall–Dave Shepherd '72–3. Freelanced fr. early '70s, rec. w. visiting Amer. singers incl. Tony Bennett; Bing Crosby; Ella Fitzgerald; Sarah Vaughan; Rosemary Clooney; also pl. w. symph. orchs. Founding member of educ. ens., Jazz College '79. Pl. w. Bobby Rosengarden, Pizza Express All-Stars '80; Jeannie Lamb fr. '80s. Moved to Australia '90. His pl. shows a liking for Hawkins and Webster. Moss received the M.B.E. medal from Queen Elizabeth in '90. CDs: Prog.; N-H; w. Randy Sandke (N-H); Susannah McCorkle (JA).

MOSSE, SANDY (SANFORD), tnr sax; b. Detroit, MI, 5/29/29; d. Amsterdam, The Netherlands, 7/1/83. Mother a singer. Start. on cl., 1939. Stud. in Chi. w. Buck Wells '43, later Chi. Mus. Coll. and arr. w. Bill Russo. Tnr. sax. '50; pl. w. Jimmy Dale, Jay Burkhart, et al. Moved to Eur., pl. w. Wallace Bishop, Henri Renaud, Django Reinhardt '51–3. Worked and rec. in Chi. w. Russo; Chubby Jackson; Cy Touff; tour. w. Woody Herman '53; M. Ferguson '56; B. Rich, '58; Ray Eberle '59. Worked in Chi. w. Dave Remington '68. Rec. two LPs as lead. for Argo '50s. CD: tracks in *A Night to Remember: Birmingham Jazz Festival* (CAP).

MOSSMAN, MICHAEL PHILIP, tpt, picc-tpt, flg, tbn, pno, dms; b. Philadelphia, PA, 10/12/59. Father pl. theramin. Self-taught, then stud. at Oberlin Coll., Rutgers U.; also stud. w. Vincent Cichowicz (Chi. Symph.); arr. w. Don Sebesky. Tour. Eur. w. Anthony Braxton 1978; Roscoe Mitchell–Leo Smith '79. Moved to Chi. '82; pl. w. Jazz Members bb '82–3; Chi. Chamber Orch. w. Bill Russo '83; R. Mitchell '83. Moved to NYC '83; pl. w. Machito, Lionel Hampton, Art Blakey '84; OTB '84–90; Michael Camilo fr. '85; Count Basie Orch., Mercer Ellington Orch. '85; Gerry Mulligan '85–6; Toshiko Akiyoshi bb on and off since '87; McCoy Tyner bb '87; Eddie Palmieri, Tito Puente, Mario Bauza, Daniel Ponce fr. '87; Dizzy Gillespie United Nation Orch. '88; Horace Silver fr. '89; Gene Harris Superband; Jack McDuff '89; Geo. Gruntz '89–91; Gil Evans Orch. '90; Slide Hampton's Jazz Masters, CHJB, Chico O'Farrill bb in '90s. Mossman is also an accomplished classical soloist, having app. w. the Naumburg Orch., Jupiter Symph., Garden St. Chamber Orch., and NJ Symph. Orch. Appointed head of Jazz Dept. at Queens Coll. Sept. '97. A powerhouse lead. tpt. w. great range and the same qualities, along w. agility in mind and fingers, as a soloist. Convincing on tbn. as well. Favs: F. Hubbard, Gillespie, Adolph Herseth. Polls: *SJ* Silver Disc '86. Fests: Eur., Asia, Africa, etc. since '78.

Film: soundtrack of *Me Amo Tu Cama Rica*, scored by Camilo. TV: Eur. CDs: Claves; Red; w. OTB (BN); Daniel Schnyder; Geo. Gruntz (Enja); R. Barretto (Owl); Benny Carter (MM); Kevin Mahogany (Enja); Chico O'Farrill (Mile.); Bob Mintzer (DMP).

MOST, ABE (ABRAHAM ELIJAH), cl, alto sax, fl; b. NYC, 2/27/20; d. Los Angeles, 10/10/02. Brother, Sam Most. Stud. priv. in Atlantic City, N.J. 1929–32. Prof. debut in Catskill Mts., N.Y., and at Kelly's Stables, NYC '39. Two yrs. w. Les Brown; army '42–5. After lead. own qt. and working w. Tommy Dorsey, he settled in LA as studio mus. From '50s was on staff at 20th Cent. Fox. In early '70s he reproduced the styles of many clarinetists in the Time-Life *Swing Era* series of re-recordings. Voted Most Valuable Player, Emeritus Award, by NARAS '86. In mid '90s tour. w. *A Tribute to Artie Shaw* package. CDs: Camard; w. Lyle Murphy (Cont.).

MOST, SAM (SAMUEL), fl, saxes, cl, voc; b. Atlantic City, NJ, 12/16/30. Brother of Abe Most. Stud. at Manh. Sch. of Mus. Worked in late 1940s w. Tommy Dorsey, Shep Fields. One of the first jazz flutists, he pl. w. his own qt. off and on from '53 and w. Mat Mathews '54. Tour. w. Teddy Wilson '57; Teddy Charles '58; Buddy Rich '59–61. Later w. Louis Bellson in LA and LV; led qt. at Shelly's Manne Hole in Hollywood. Worked w. Red Norvo '63–6, mostly pl. alto fl. In '70s and '80s cont. to freelance in LA, occ. w. his bro. Pl. Montreux JF '78 w. Xanadu All-Stars. Tour. Japan w. Tal Farlow '80 and w. Hank Jones–Ray Brown '85. Won *DB* Critics New Star fl. '54. LPs: Xan. CDs: Ray Brown–Monty Alexander–Sam Most (Conc.).

MOTEN, BENNIE (BENJAMIN), pno. comp, lead; b. Kansas City, MO, 11/13/1894; d. Kansas City, 4/2/35. Studied w. two pupils of Scott Joplin; led ragtime trio 1918–22, then led sxt. First rec. for Okeh, St. Louis '23; in the East w. bb fr. '26; rec. for Victor, Camden, N.J. '32, incl. such important sidemen as his bro., Buster Moten, acdn.; Count Basie, second pno.; singer Jimmy Rushing; and Hot Lips Page; Ed Lewis; Joe Keyes; Dan Minor; Eddie Durham; Harlan Leonard; Jack Washington; Eddie Barefield; Ben Webster; Buster Smith; and Walter Page. After his death (during a tonsillectomy), the band was briefly co-led by Basie and Buster Moten. Later, w. the help of Buster Smith, it became the nucleus of the Count Basie orch. CDs: BB; Class.

MOTEN, BENNY (CLARENCE LEMONT), bs; b. NYC, 11/30/16; d. New Orleans, LA, 3/27/77. Not related to Bennie Moten. Local bands in Tarrytown,

N.Y., then to NYC to pl. w. Hot Lips Page, Jerry Jerome 1941; Red Allen '42–9, '54–5, and '63–5; also w. Eddie South and Stuff Smith trios '49–51; Ivory Joe Hunter '52; Arnett Cobb '53–54; six mos. w. Ella Fitzgerald trio '56; tour. Africa w. Wilbur De Paris '57. In later yrs. he mainly freelanced in NYC. Fest: NJF w. Buck Clayton '56, rec. for Columbia. Rec. *Jazz at the Metropole* w. Red Allen & Charlie Shavers (Beth.) '55. CDs: w. Red Allen (Collectors Classics).

MOTIAN, PAUL (STEPHEN PAUL), dms, comp, lead; b. Philadelphia, PA, 3/25/31. Grew up in Providence, R.I. Began on gtr., then stud. dms. priv. 1943–6. In navy during Korean War, then stud. w. Billy Gladstone in NYC '53. Stud. at Manh. Sch. of Mus. '55–6. Pl. w. Geo. Wallington, Jerry Wald, Russell Jacquet '56; Tony Scott '56–8; Oscar Pettiford '57; Zoot Sims '58; Lennie Tristano '58–9; Al Cohn–Zoot Sims at Half Note '59. After freelancing w. Gil Evans; Geo. Russell; Stan Getz, Thelonious Monk; Coleman Hawkins; Roy Eldridge; Mose Allison; Art Farmer; etc., Motian came to prominence as a member of the Bill Evans Trio '59–64. Pl. w. Paul Bley '63–4. Active member of Jazz Composers' Guild fr. '64. Pl. w. Keith Jarrett off and on '66–9; folksinger Arlo Guthrie '69–71; Jarrett '71–6. Also worked w. Charles Lloyd, Karl Berger, Morgana King, Carla Bley, Charlie Haden, Roswell Rudd, Gato Barbieri, Don Cherry late '60s-early 70s. Comp. for films in '70s incl. *Punishment Park* and short films by Stan Vanderbeek. Pl. and rec. w. own gps.—incl. Electric Bebop Band—fr. '72. Led trio w. Chas. Brackeen, David Izenzon '76–80; qnt. w. Joe Lovano, Billy Drewes, Ed Schuller, Bill Frisell '80–5 (Jim Pepper repl. Drewes '83); trio w. Lovano, Frisell since '84, tour. Eur. '98. Motian also pl. w. Geri Allen and Charlie Haden and leads a trio w. Haden and Paul Bley. Autobiography, *We Couldn't Find Philadelphia* remains unpublished. Favs: Kenny Clarke, Blakey, Roach. Fests: all major fr. '50s. CDs: JMT; ECM; W&W; SN; w. Geri Allen–C. Haden (JMT; SN); K. Jarrett (ECM; Imp.; Atl.); B. Evans (Riv.; Verve); Frisell; P. Bley (ECM).

MOUND CITY BLUE BLOWERS. A traditional gp. using such devices as comb and tissue paper pl. by Red McKenzie, kazoo by Dick Slevin, and gtr. and bjo. by Jack Bland. The name was also used for gps. of varying personnel led by McKenzie 1924–36. The best known recs. under this name are two '29 sides, "One Hour" and "Hello, Lola," feat. McKenzie's hot comb w. Coleman Hawkins, Glenn Miller, Pee Wee Russell, Eddie Condon, Bland, Pops Foster, and Gene Krupa. CDs: tracks on *Three Great Swing Saxophones:* and *RCA Victor Jazz—The First Half Century* (BB).

MOUZON, ALPHONSE, dms, perc, pno, kybds, tpt; b. Charleston, SC, 11/21/48. Sister played cl. Stud. dms. at Bonds-Wilson HS. Prof. debut at 14 w. Claude Ray's org. trio. Early work w. Ross Carnegie society orch.; Shirley Scott–Stanley Turrentine; Horace Parlan (in B'way show *Promises, Promises*); Roy Ayers; McCoy Tyner; the Eleventh House w. Larry Coryell. Since 1975 led own band, also rec. w. Stanley Clarke; Herbie Hancock; Dave Grusin; Lee Ritenour; Chet Baker; Dizzy Gillespie; et al. Toured Eur. and Japan extens. as lead. and w. Weather Report; Tyner; Eleventh House. Mouzon has said, "Jazz rock drummers like myself, Billy Cobham and Lenny White bring jazz polyrhythms to a rock pulse." CDs: BN; Pausa; MPS; MPC; w. Passport (Atl.).

MOVER, BOB (ROBERT ALAN), alto, sop, tnr saxes, comp; b. Brookline, MA, 3/22/52. Father pl. tpt. w. Tommy Dorsey; Ina Ray Hutton; Charlie Spivak; Jerry Wald; later led band in Bost. in '50s, still active in Fla. Moth. sang w. Al Donahue band; cousin Jonathan Mover is prof. pop dmr. Began on pno. at age 5, then pl. tpt., gtr., dms. bef. sw. to sax at age 13. Stud. w. Ted Rosen, Joseph Brindisi '65; Phil Woods, Gordon Brisker '67; Richie Kamuca '68; Lee Konitz '69; Al Cohn, Danny Bank, Joe Allard, Jimmy Mosher '69–70. Stud. comp. w. Joe Maneri '71. Pl. w. Ira Sullivan in Miami '68; Chubby Jackson, Duffy Jackson, own trio w. Jaco Pastorius in NYC '69; Charles Mingus briefly '70; Jazz Wkshp, Bost. '71; Mingus '73; Chet Baker '73–4. Pl. in Brazil w. Lucio Alves, Johnny Alf '74; then rejoined Baker '75. Pl. w. Warren Chiasson; own qnt. w. Tom Harrell, Jimmy Garrison '75; Art Blakey Jr., Evelyn Blakey, Vinnie Burke, Albert Dailey '76. Co-led gp. w. Lee Konitz '77; led own gps. at Sweet Basil, NYC '77–80. Taught at Berklee Sch. of Mus. '80–1; pl. w. Art Mathews and led own gps. w. Joe Cohn; Mick Goodrick; Hal Crook; Bobby Ward. Pl. w. Chet Baker '81–2; own gps. fr. '82. Taught at Concordia U., Montreal '83–6. Returned to NYC, pl. w. Walter Davis Jr. '87–9. Perf. at Paris Alto Summit w. Phil Woods; Jackie McLean; C Sharpe; others '89. Perf. solo concert at Eddie Lang JF, Monterodoni, Italy '92. Pl. w. Toronto Jazz Qt. '95. Back in NYC in late '90s. Active as a clinician at universities in the US, Can., and Eur. Taking Charlie Parker, Lee Konitz, and Sonny Rollins as exemplars early on, Mover is the sum of his parts with a mind and a heart of his own. Other favs: Stitt, McLean, Woods, I. Sullivan, Frank Strozier, Charles McPherson. Fests: Brazil '74; Eur. fr. '75; Japan fr. '89. TV: Eur. TV w. C. Baker. CDs: JC; JT; DSM; w. W. Davis (JC).

MOYE, FAMOUDOU DON, dms, perc; b. Rochester, NY, 5/23/46. Raised in a family of musicians; stud. perc. at Wayne State U., Det. 1965–6. Took some lessons w. tptr. Charles Moore and pl. w. the gp. Detroit Free Jazz, tour. Eur. '68–9. Worked w. Steve Lacy in Rome and Paris. Also pl. there w. the Gospel Messenger Singers; Sonny Sharrock; Dave Burrell; Gato Barbieri; Pharoah Sanders; Alan Shorter. Join. the Art Ensemble of Chi. in Paris '70; also pl. and rec. w. the Black Artists Gp. in St. Louis. To Chi. '71. Artist-in-residence at Mich. St. U. '73. Pl. w. Randy Weston at Montreux JF '74; worked as a duo w. Steve McCall and pl. w. the bb of the AACM. Led a perc. ensemble, Malinke Rhythm Tribe; free-lanced w. a variety of other gps., pl. a wide range of styles. Recs. w. Joseph Jarman '78–81; Don Pullen '78–9; and in the late '70s w. Cecil McBee; Hamiet Bluiett; Julius Hemphill; Chico Freeman; et al. In mid '80s was a member of cooperative all-star gp., The Leaders, w. Don Cherry (later replaced by Lester Bowie), Arthur Blythe, Chico Freeman, Kirk Lightsey, and Cecil McBee. Fest: Umbria Jazz w. Lester Bowie's Brass Fantasy '96. CDs: AECO; Moye-Jarman (BS); w. Art Ens. of Chi. (Col.; Del.); Freeman; McBee (Ind. Nav.); Lightsey (Evid.); The Leaders (Sunny.).

MRAZ, GEORGE (JIRI O.), bs, comp; b. Pisek, Czechoslovakia, 9/9/44. Studied at Prague Cons. 1961–6. Rec. w. Karel Velebny '64–6. Moved to W. Germ. '66, pl. in Munich w. Pony Poindexter; Hampton Hawes; Benny Bailey. Moved to US '68. Stud. at Berklee Sch. of Mus.; pl. w. Dizzy Gillespie fr. late '60s; Oscar Peterson, Ella Fitzgerald '70–2; Thad Jones–Mel Lewis Orch. '72–6; Stan Getz '74–5; Walter Norris '75; Zoot Sims '75–83; Tommy Flanagan, NY Jazz Qt. fr. '77; John Abercrombie fr. '78; Pepper Adams, Roland Hanna '70s; Hank Jones fr. '80s. Mraz teaches bs. and ens. at the New Sch. Best known in recent years for a long association w. Tommy Flanagan, he is an exceptionally gifted bassist, using rapid single note runs and multi-stopped chordal passages to create solos on a par with players of any instrument. Favs: Ray Brown, Scott LaFaro, Ron Carter. Polls: *DB* TDWR '70s. Fests: all major fr. '70s. Pl. w. Joe Henderson at Texaco JF, NYC '98. Rec. three dates as lead. for Milestone '95–7. CDs: Mile.; w. Tommy Flanagan (Prog.; Enja; Timel.; Up.); Steve Kuhn (Post.); Carmen McRae (Novus); O. Peterson (MPS); C. Mingus (Atl.); T. Akiyoshi (Evid.); Gillespie (Tel.); Hank Jones (Verve); Art Pepper (Cont.); Bud Shank (Mile.).

MUHAMMAD, IDRIS (Leo Morris), dms; b. New Orleans, LA, 11/13/39. Father pl. bjo.; bros. all dmrs.

Began on dms. at age 8; first prof. gig at age 10. On grad. fr. hs he joined Larry Williams band. Pl. w. gtr. Joe Jones, Dee Clark late 1950s; Lloyd Price, Impressions early '60s. Mus. dir. for Sam Cooke, Jerry Butler '62–5, then pl. w. Lou Donaldson '65–7; B'way show *Hair* '69–73. House dmr. for Prest. label '70–2. Trav. to India '72. Tour. w. rock gp., Emerson, Lake & Palmer '72–3; Roberta Flack '73–7. Led own gp. '77–8; then pl. w. Johnny Griffin '78–9; Pharoah Sanders fr. '80. Pl. w. Larry Goldings trio on QE2 cruise, summer '96. A versatile dmr. who certainly carries the NO rhythmic essences within his style. CDs: Lip.; Mile.; Ther.; w. L. Donaldson (BN); Randy Weston (Verve); F. Hubbard (BN); Pharoah Sanders; John Hicks (Evid.); David Murray (DIW); Ahmad Jamal (Verve).

MUKAI, SHIGEHARU, tbn, lead; b. Nagoya, Japan, 1/21/49. Played w. Doshisha U. Mod. Jazz Gp. and Third Orch.; won Yamaha Light Mus. contest 1970. Moved to Tokyo '71; pl. w. Yoshio Otomo; Fumio Itabashi; Ryo Kawasaki; Terumasa Hino; Sadao Watanabe; Yosuke Yamashita; two-tbn. gp. w. Hiroshi Fukumura. Formed own gp. '72. Won first Shinjuku JF awd. as best new gp. '74. Disbanded gp., briefly lived in NYC '77–8. After ret. to Japan, led various gps. incl. Spik & Span; Morning Flight; Orissa; also pl. w. Kazumi Watanabe's KYLYN; Naoya Matsuoka's Wing; Akira Sakata; Yamashita; and visiting Amer. mus. incl. Elvin Jones, Billy Hart. Formed qt., Hot Session, w. Ryojiro Furusawa, Fumio Itabashi, Mitsuaki Furuno. Tour. Japan '91–2, celebrating twenty yrs. in mus. Considered best tbn. pl. in Japan; also noted for unique blending of Latin and other ethnic rhythms in his various gps. Favs: J. J. Johnson, Slide Hampton, Wayne Henderson, Coltrane. Polls: *SJ* Readers '75–93; *SJ* Critics '90–2. CDs: Nippon-Col.; Den.; Pro Arte; Teichiku-Union.

MULLIGAN, GERRY (GERALD JOSEPH aka JERU), bari, sop saxes, cl, pno, comp, arr, lead; b. NYC, 4/6/27; d. Darien, CT, 1/20/96. Parents pl. pno. Began on pno., ocarina. Family lived in Ohio, Mich. before settling in Phila. 1944. Stud. w. Sam Correnti in Reading, Pa. Self-taught as arr.; later stud. informally w. Johnny Warrington, Gil Evans. Pl. w. Harvey Marburger, Chuck Gordon '44–5; Alex Bartha, Geo. Paxton on tnr. sax '45. Arr. for Tommy Tucker, Elliot Lawrence, Warrington '45. Moved to NYC '46, arr. also pl. some tnr. sax for Gene Krupa '46–7, arrs. incl. "How High the Moon"; "Disc Jockey Jump." Pl. bari. sax w. Kai Winding, arr. for Claude Thornhill '47. Pl. and arr. w. Miles Davis "Birth of the Cool" Nonet '48–50; his arrs. incl. "Jeru"; "Boplicity"; "Rocker"; "Venus de Milo"; "Godchild." Pl. and arr.

w. Lawrence, Thornhill '50–1. Rec. own tentet for Prest. bef. moving to Calif. '51; arr. for Stan Kenton; pl. w. Howard Rumsey's Lighthouse All-Stars '51–2. In '52 Mulligan formed his first pianoless qt. w. Chet Baker, Bob Whitlock, Chico Hamilton. Over the next two yrs. Baker was repl. by Bob Brookmeyer and Jon Eardley, Whitlock by Red Mitchell, and Hamilton by Frank Isola. Mulligan began making frequent trips to Eur. in the early '50s and achieved int'l fame after a sensational app. at the Salle Pleyel, Paris '54. Led sxt., incl. Zoot Sims, in US and Eur. '55–8, then formed gp. w. Art Farmer '58. Originated 13-pc. Concert Jazz Band in NYC '60; led qnt. '66–8. Collab. w. Bill Holman on *Music for Baritone Saxophone and Orch.*, premiered w. LA Neophonic Orch. '66. Guest soloist w. Dave Brubeck Trio '68–72, then formed bb, The Age of Steam '72. Artist-in-residence at U. of Miami '74. Reunion concerts w. Chet Baker '74–5. Led sxt. w. Dave Samuels in NYC and Italy '74–7, also began pl. sop. sax. Re-formed Concert Jazz Band '78. Mulligan led a 20-pc. bb in the early '80s and experimented w. electronic mus '82–3. His qt. in the late '80s consisted of Dean Johnson, bs.; Richie DeRosa, Ron Vincent dms.; Bill Charlap, pno. From '92 Ted Rosenthal was the pnst. Rec. *Re-Birth of the Cool* w. Wallace Roney, Phil Woods, John Lewis, Bill Barber, etc., '92, and tour. w. it. Mulligan initially made his reputation as an arr. of exceptional subtlety. Then he established himself as the preeminent baritone saxophonist. As both writer and player he was a master of dynamics, able to swing at any decibel level, and a superb melodist. He was a fixture on the int'l scene fr. the mid 50's, app. w. all kinds of gps. incl. dixieland, in which he pl. cl. He received numerous awards, incl. a Grammy for his rec. "Walk on the Water"; Connecticut Arts Award '82; Viotti Prize '84; Yale U. Duke Ellington Fellowship '88; Phila. Mus. Assoc. Hall of Fame '90. A consistent winner on bari. sax in *DB, Met., Play.* polls, as well as in foreign magazines fr. '50s, as well as in foreign publications. Fests: all major fr. '54.; perf. "Prima Bara Dubla," duet w. Harry Carney and Ellington orch., NJF '58. Film: *Jazz on a Summer's Day* '58; *I Want To Live* '58; *The Subterraneans* w. Art Farmer '60; *The Rat Race; Bells Are Ringing; Hot Rocks* w. Quincy Jones; *La Memosa; Luv*; docu., *Listen: Gerry Mulligan*, Thor Raxlen '96. Video: *The Gerry Mulligan Workshop: A Master Class on Jazz and Its Legendary Players* (Hal Leonard) '95. TV: *The Sound of Jazz* CBS '57; CBS Timex Jazz w. Art Farmer '58; many other apps. Comps: "Line for Lyons"; "Walkin' Shoes"; "Song for Strayhorn." CDs: Prest.; PJ; Vogue; Verve; RTE; Col.; Chiaro.; A&M; GRP; Conc.; Tel.; Mulligan–Astor Piazzola (Accord); w. M. Davis (Cap.; BN); Thelonious Monk (Riv.); Stan

Getz; Ben Webster (Verve); Paul Desmond (RCA); Lee Konitz (Evid.); Dave Brubeck; L. Hampton (Tel.); Gerry Mulligan–Chubby Jackson (Prest.).

MULLINS, RILEY III, tpt, pno; b. Chicago, IL, 7/2/66. Studied at Carver HS 1981–5; Amer. Cons. '88–90; Berklee Coll. of Mus. '90–2; Rutgers U. fr. '92. Pl. w. Illinois Jacquet bb fr. '92; Mingus bb, Roy Hargrove bb, Louis Hayes Qnt. '95. Betty Carter *Jazz Ahead* program '95. Favs: Fats Navarro, Miles Davis, Clifford Brown; arr: Wayne Shorter. Fests: Brazil, Eur. w. Jacquet. TV: *Like It Is* w. Jacquet; PBS w. Betty Carter, CDs: w. L. Hayes (TCB; Sharp Nine); Duffy Jackson (Mile.).

MUNDY, JIMMY (JAMES), arr; b. Cincinnati, OH, 6/28/07; d. NYC, 4/24/83. Played vln. fr. age 6 to 21, working for a tour. evangelist. Stayed in Wash., D.C. after being fired for having an amorous relationship. By this time, he was pl. tnr. sax and doubling cl. and sop. sax. Join. White Bros. band on tnr. sax and remain. when dmr. Tommy Myles took it over. In late 1932 Earl Hines heard Mundy's comp. "Cavernism" at Crystal Caverns in Wash. and offered him a job. Mundy moved to Chi. w. Hines, join. the reed section but soon was concentrating solely on arr. Worked w. Hines at Grand Terrace in Chi. and on the road until '36, when he join. Benny Goodman as arr. for three yrs. Goodman rec. over 40 Mundy arrs., incl. "Sing, Sing, Sing"; "Swingtime in the Rockies"; and "Solo Flight" (feat. for Charlie Christian). After '39 briefly led own band and wrote arrs. for several bb, incl. Gene Krupa, Harry James, T. Dorsey; and, most prominently, Count Basie, who rec. "Super Chief"; "Louisiana"; "Queer Street"; "Feather Merchant." Mundy's "Fiesta in Blue" feat. Cootie Williams w. Goodman and Buck Clayton w. Basie, both recs. '41. In Calif. fr. '41 to '42, doing radio work w. Paul Whiteman for Gracie Allen and others (wrote "Travelin' Light," rec. by B. Holiday w. Whiteman). Served in army '43–5. To NYC in '48, where he freelanced as comp./arr., incl. film *The Man on the Eiffel Tower* and B'way show *The Vamp*, starring Carol Channing. Wrote for Gene Ammons, Sonny Stitt '50–5. To Paris '59, working as mus. dir. for Barclay Disques. From '60s was mainly active in studio and film mus. but contributed to Chet Baker Qnt. Prest. sessions '65. One of the busiest and best arrs. of the Swing Era, Mundy's charts have stood the test of time. Own LPs for Epic, long out of print. CDs: w. Earl Hines (BB).

MURANYI, JOE (JOSEPH P.), cl, sop, alto, tnr saxes, tarogato; b. Martins Ferry, OH, 1/14/28. Many mus. in family. Pl. in classical balalaika orch. as a youth. First prof. gig at age 16. Stud. w. Lennie Tristano while in army, then at Manh. Sch. of Mus., Columbia U. in early 1950s. Pl. w. Red Onion Orch. '52–4; Danny Barker '58; Bobby Hackett–Vic Dickenson, Marian and Jimmy McPartland, Wingy Manone '50s; also pl. at Stuyvesant Casino, NYC, w. Manone; Red Allen; Edmond Hall; etc., and at Eddie Condon's w. Condon; Geo. Wettling; Max Kaminsky; Geo. Brunis; etc. Pl. and tour. w. Village Stompers in mid '60s; Louis Armstrong All-Stars '67–71. Pl. at Jimmy Ryan's w. Roy Eldridge, Wild Bill Davison, Herman Autrey, Max Kaminsky, Zutty Singleton '70–83; also WGJB '70s. In recent yrs. has freelanced and rec. w. Classic Jazz Qt. w. Dick Sudhalter; Marty Grosz; Yank Lawson-Bob Haggart; Louisiana Repertory Jazz Ens. Muranyi is also an accomplished rec. prod. and has authored hundreds of liner notes. He is working on a book about Louis Armstrong. Favs: Omer Simeon, J. Dodds, Goodman, Shaw, K. Davern. Fests: Eur. since '68. TV: PBS, *GI Jive* w. Roy Eldridge; *American Masters: Louis Armstrong*; other apps. w. Armstrong. Many LP recs. w. Armstrong. CDs: Jazz.; w. Grosz (Stomp Off); Y. Lawson (Jazz.); Barbara Lea (Aud.); Louisiana Rep. Jazz Ens. (Nax.).

MURPHY, MARK, voc; b. Syracuse, NY, 3/14/32. Studied pno. at age 7. In 1950s sang in East Side NYC bars, accomp. himself on pno.; also worked as accomp. for Don Rickles. First recs. for Dec., Cap. '56; began extens. tour. and rec. in US late '50s. App. on TV shows *Jazz Scene USA, Tonight*, etc.; NJF '62. From '63 to '73 was based in London, frequently tour. Eur. In '70s and '80s in US, he was closely identified w. scat singing and vocalese, sometimes writing his own lyrics. Rec. *Bop for Kerouac* for Muse '81. App. and rec. w. George Gruntz orch. Added Brazilian mus. to his repertoire in early '80s. In '90s he cont. tour. while based in the SF area. Murphy has been accused of forcing hipness, but *Rolling Stone* observed that "when the glitter is stripped away, Mark Murphy is a singer of great power, depth and skill." App. w. Gruntz in "jazz opera," *Cosmopolitan Greetings* in Germ. '92. CDs: Vict.; Riv.; Mile.; Dec.; Muse; w. Madeline Eastman (Mad Kat); UFO (Verve); Gruntz (MGB).

MURPHY, SPUD (Miko Stephanovic), arr, comp, alto sax; b. Salt Lake City, 9/19/08; d. Hollywood, CA, 8/5/05. Played cl. fr. early childhood; stud. tpt. w. Red Nichols' father; pl. cl. in ship's band on US.–China run. First arr. for Tracy–Brown Orch. 1929–30; many arrs. for Benny Goodman and Glen Gray '35–7, incl. "Jingle Bells" and "Get Happy" for Goodman. Own band '38–41. Freelance arr. and

teaching in LA. In mid '50s developed own 12–tone system, which was stud. by Curtis Counce; Oscar Peterson; Gerald Wiggins; and others. CDs: Cont.; w. Charlie Barnet; Lena Horne (BB).

MURPHY, TURK (MELVIN EDWARD ALTON), tbn, lead; b. Palermo, CA, 12/16/15; d. San Francisco, CA, 5/30/87. Self-taught on crnt. and tbn. A force in the pre-war jazz revival movement, he helped organize Lu Watters Yerba Buena Jazz Band 1940, rec. w. them in '41. From '47 led his own band for recs. and night clubs; in '51 w. Marty Marsala; signed w. Col. Recs. '54 and acquired national reputation pl. in NYC, NO, and Newport; later toured Eur. and Australia. Had his own club, Easy Street, in SF, as well as a long-term booking at Earthquake McGoon's; opened a traditional jazz museum, In the Front Page. Murphy was an outspoken opponent of the conventional neo-Dixieland jazz of the Eddie Condon variety, preferring to use lesser-known material in place of the usual standard tunes. CDs: GTJ.

MURRAY, DAVID, tnr sax, comp, lead; b. Oakland, CA, 1/19/55. Started on pno., stud. w. his moth., a well-known gospel pnst.; alto sax at age 9, tnr. sax at 12. As teenager, co-led 15-pc. Notations of Soul band w. Rodney Franklin. Encouraged by Stanley Crouch and Bobby Bradford, moved to NYC 1975 and bec. involved in the Greenwich Village/Lower East Side–based loft jazz movement. First recs. w. Sunny Murray (no relation); work w. Lester Bowie, Fred Hopkins, and Steve McCall '75. From '75 to '80 took top honors as tnr. sax TDWR in *DB* polls. Co-founded World Saxophone Quartet w. Oliver Lake, Julius Hemphill, and Hamiet Bluiett '76; organized Clarinet Summit w. John Carter, Alvin Batiste, and Jimmy Hamilton '84. Since mid '80s perf. w. his own qts. Led own bb fr. '84 (w. "conduction" by Butch Morris), until '96, when Benny Russell became the lead. of the renamed Next Legacy Jazz Orch. He has also app. w. Jack DeJohnette's Special Edition; James "Blood" Ulmer; Ronald Shannon Jackson; McCoy Tyner; Randy Weston; et al. Received Guggenheim Fellowship '89; won Danish Jazzpar Award '91. Continues to tour and perf. at fests and major venues in US and overseas. Rec. w. African perfs. in Dakar '96. Originally identified w. Albert Ayler–Archie Shepp-style avant-garde playing, Murray's approach nevertheless incorporates huge-toned, romantic ballad playing in a Hawkins-Webster vein along with the inevitable rasping and upper-reaches screeching also employed at other tempos. Fav: Paul Gonsalves. CDs: DIW; Col.; Red Brn.; hatArt; Sound Hills; FS; Tutu; WW; Cecma; Stash; BS; Evid.; JT; w. World Saxophone Quartet (Elek. Mus.; None.; BS; Moers);

Clarinet Summit (Ind. Nav.); McCoy Tyner (Red Brn.); Steve Coleman (RCA); D. D. Jackson (JT); Barbara Dennerlein (Verve); DeJohnette; John Hicks (ECM); Dave Burrell (Gazell).

MURRAY, DON (DONALD LEROY), cl, sax; b. Joliet, IL, 6/7/04; d. Los Angeles, CA, 6/2/29. Father a minister. Pl. tnr. sax w. NORK 1923, then to Det., where he was feat. off and on w. Jean Goldkette through '27. Rec. w. Bix Beiderbecke '25 and '27; Frankie Trumbauer, Adrian Rollini '27; Joe Venuti '27–8. Pl. in B'way theater bands w. Don Voorhees and others '28. Was involved in a fatal alcohol-related accident while w. Ted Lewis band in Hollywood, filming *Is Everybody Happy*. His early death was commonly believed to have cut short what could have been an outstanding career as a jazz clarinetist. CDs: w. Bix Beiderbecke (Col.; Mile.).

MURRAY, SUNNY (JAMES MARCELLUS ARTHUR), dms, comp, arr; b. Idabel, OK, 9/21/37. Raised in Phila. Began stud. w. bro. at age 9. Moved to NYC 1956. Pl. w. Red Allen, Willie "The Lion" Smith, Jackie McLean, Ted Curson late '50s; Cecil Taylor fr. '59; Albert Ayler '65–7; also pl. in '60s w. Archie Shepp, Gil Evans. Made rec. debut as lead. '66. Active in France late '60s-early '70s. Co-led own gp., Untouchable Factor, w. Khan Jamal fr. '70s; own qnt. w. Grachan Moncur III, Steve Coleman, Curtis Clark, William Parker '80s; also led qnt. w. two saxes, two vlns. Rec. w. Cecil Taylor, David Eyges early '80s. Scored films incl. *In the Beginning* (Nigeria); *Walking Woman* (Canada); *The Party* (France); and several plays. Murray is a key figure in the development of a nonmetrical commentary style of freejazz drumming. Polls: *DB* Critics TDWR '66. Fests: Eur., Africa fr. late '60s. CDs: Enja; w. Gil Evans (Imp.); Cecil Taylor (Revenant).

MUSIKER, LEE ELLIOT, pno, kybds; b. Brooklyn, NY, 5/26/56. Father prof. cl., alto sax, fl.; moth. pl. and taught pno.; uncle, Sam Musiker, pl. cl. w. Gene Krupa. Early stud. w. father. Received B.A. in mus. theory, Manh. Sch. of Mus. 1978; M.A. jazz studies, Eastman Sch. of Mus. '81. Pl. club dates in NYC area, then w. Buddy Rich bb '82–3. Freelance w. Bob Mintzer; Jerry Dodgion; Lew Soloff; Jay Leonhart; Richie Cole; Grady Tate; Richard Davis. Also accomp. voc. incl. Chris Connor; Susannah McCorkle; Julie Wilson. Perf. w. classical and pops orchs. incl. Cincinnati Pops, Rochester Philharm., Little Rock Symph. Pl. for B'way shows *City of Angels* and *Starlight Express*, and perf. on the soundtrack of Woody Allen's *Crimes and Misdemeanors*. Taught at Eastman Sch. of Mus. '79–81; Jersey City

St. Coll. '90; Mannes Coll. of Mus. fr. '90. Favs: Bill Evans, Corea, Clare Fischer. Polls: *DB* Best College Gp. '81. Fests: Engl. '82–3; Dominican Rep. '82. TV: CBS *Nightwatch*; Phil Donahue. CDs: w. McCorkle (Conc.); NY Pops (Angel/EMI); Tyzik (Amherst).

MUSSO, VIDO WILLIAM, tnr sax, cl; b. Carrini, Sicily, 1/17/13; d. Rancho Mirage, CA, 1/9/82. Settled in Det. 1920, where he took up cl. Moved to LA '30, working there w. Everett Hoagland '33 and Gil Evans. Pl. w. Benny Goodman '36–8; Gene Krupa '38; Harry James '40–1; back w. Goodman '41; Woody Herman '42. While w. Stan Kenton '45–7, rec. "Come Back to Sorrento," which earned him popularity for his full-toned, Coleman Hawkins–inspired solo style. Also took part in Gene Norman's Just Jazz concert series '47. In later yrs. Musso led small gps. and freelanced, mainly in LV and LA. CDs: four tracks w. own gp. and four w. Eddie Safranski in *Loaded* (Sav.); w. Kenton (Cap.; Mos.); T. Dorsey; Goodman; L. Hampton (BB).

MUSSOLINI, ROMANO, pno; b. Carpena, Italy, 9/26/27; d. Rome, 2/3/06. Younger son of the dictator Benito Mussolini. His interest in jazz was due to recs. bought by his jazz-fan bro. After his father's death in 1945 he went into exile in Ischia w. his mother and sister. During an illness there, he took up pno. and acdn. as a hobby. For yrs. he had to work under a pseudonym, Romano Full, but he began app. under his own name at jazz fests. in the mid '50s. Rec. w. Nunzio Rotondo '54; pl. the first San Remo JF w. Rotondo and Gil Cuppini '55. From '56 to 62 led various small gps.; rec. w. Carlo Loffredo '57; pl. w. Lars Gullin on tour of Italy '59; also w. Chet Baker. Worked often w. Oscar Klein in Eur. Mussolini, who visited the US briefly a few times, was originally inspired by George Shearing and later by Oscar Peterson. Fest: duo w. Klein at L. Hampton JF, Idaho '95. CDs: w. Klein (N-H).

MUSSULLI, BOOTS (HENRY W.), alto, bari saxes; b. Milford, MA, 11/18/17; d. Norfolk, MA, 1967. Played alto sax and cl. from age 12. Worked w. local Bost. bands, incl. Mal Hallett; replaced Irving Fazola in Teddy Powell's orch. 1942. Pl. w. Stan Kenton '44–7; Vido Musso All-Stars '47; G. Krupa '48; Charlie Ventura '49; Kenton '52–4. In the late '50s Mussulli settled in Bost., teaching and pl. w. Toshiko Akiyoshi, Herb Pomeroy, and Serge Chaloff. Opened own club in Milford '59; led Milford Youth Band at NJF '67. A listing of his favs. indicates how his style was influenced with the advent of bop: Hodges, Carter, Parker, Konitz, C. Mariano, J. Dorsey. CDs: w. Chaloff (Mos.); Kenton (Cap.; Mos.); Ventura (Dec.); Musso in *Loaded* (Sav.).

MUSTAFA, MELTON SHAKIR, tpt, flg, comp/arr; b. Miami, FL, 11/23/47. Mother, Verrie Jones, pl. pno.; bro., Jesse Jones Jr., pl. cl., fl.; sist., Yvonne Peebles, is voc. Began pl. prof. while in hs. Mus. ed. major at Mississippi Valley St. U. 1965–7; stud. at Berklee Coll. of Mus. '66; B.S. in mus. ed. fr. Fla. A&M U. '67–69. Worked w. L. Hampton '80; Peter Graves Atlantean Driftwood Band '82; Jaco Pastorius gp., Word of Mouth '83; Bobby Watson qnt., Horizon '83–90; Jon Hendricks & Co. '84; Frank Foster Loud Minority, Duke Ellington Orch. '85; Count Basie '85–92; C. Mingus Epitaph Orch. w. G. Schuller '90, '93; led own orch. fr. '94 for such So. Fla. events as Birthday Celebration for Miami Beach; Summit of the Americas; National Women's Org.; Mayors' Convention; and the Hollywood JF w. Joe Williams. Head of mus. dept. of African Heritage Cultural Arts Center, Miami, fr. '93. Member of IAJE. Favs: Booker Little, F. Hubbard, Woody Shaw; arrs: Thad Jones, Frank Foster. Fests: *Play.*; No. Sea; Chi.; Montreal; Pori; Montreux: Lugano. TV: w. B. Watson; Bill Cosby Show w. Basie. Rec. debut w. Watson '83. CDs: Cont.; w. C. Basie Orch. (Den.; Tel.); Joe Williams (Tel.); Watson (BN; Col.; Evid.); Eric Allison (Cont.); Afro Blue Band (Mile.); Diane Schuur (GRP).

MYERS, AMINA CLAUDINE, pno, org, voc; b. Blackwell, AR, 3/21/42. Began mus. stud. at age 7. Dir. and perf. w. gospel gps. while in sch. Pl. in jazz and rock gps., then moved to Chi. mid 1960s. Joined AACM; also pl. w. Sonny Stitt, Gene Ammons. Worked w. other AACM artists incl. Kalaparush Maurice McIntyre; Muhal Richard Abrams; Henry Threadgill, Lester Bowie. Moved to NYC '76, cont. to work w. AACM artists. Rec. album of blues dedicated to Bessie Smith '80. Moved to Eur. ca. '81; rec. w. gospel singers Martha and Fontella Bass, David Peaston. Ret. to NYC, pl. w. Charlie Haden's Liberation Music Orch. fr. mid '80s. CDs: Novus; Leo; BS; Min. Mus.; w. M. McPartland (JA); Greg Osby (JMT); Charlie Haden (BN); Third Rail (Ant.).

MYERS, BUMPS (HUBERT MAXWELL), tnr sax; b. Clarksburg, WV, 8/22/12; d. Los Angeles, CA, 4/9/68. Moved to Calif. 1921. First prof. work w. Earl Whaley in Seattle '29. Freelanced in LA in early '30s, then to China in '34 w. Buck Clayton and Teddy Weatherford; remain. in Shanghai for 18 mos. From '36 back in LA w. Lionel Hampton; Les Hite; briefly in NYC w. Lee & Lester Young '42; then w. Jimmie Lunceford and Benny Carter. After brief stint in army, Myers rejoined Carter. Pl. w. Sid Catlett '45; Benny Goodman '47; Louis Bellson, Red Callender et al. '50s. After tour. w. Horace Henderson '62, Myers' failing health rendered him inactive. He had a vigorous, full-toned style in the Coleman Hawkins tradition. Fav: Don Byas. CDs: tracks w. Sid Catlett gp., Benny Carter bb in *Classic Capitol Jazz Sessions* (Mos.); w. T-Bone Walker (Mos.); Don and Dewey (Spec.).

MYERS, WILSON ERNEST "SERIOUS," bs, voc, arr; b. Germantown, PA, 10/7/06. Nickname came fr. his love of classical music. Debut at age 20, pl. dms. in a band accomp. Bessie Smith on tour. Took up bjo. and gtr. after tbn. and cl. Sw. to bs., pl. w. King Oliver 1931; New Orleans Feetwarmers of Sidney Bechet and Tommy Ladnier '32–3. Trav. to France w. Lucky Millinder '34; back in US work. w. the Spirits of Rhythm '34–7. From the spring of '37 worked in Paris w. Bill Coleman; pl. w. and wrote arrs. for Willie Lewis '37–8. Worked w. Oscar Aleman '39; led own band '38–9. Ret. to US '39, pl. w. Bechet, Spirits of Rhythm '40; Everett Barksdale '42; Mezz Mezzrow '43; DeParis bros. '44. Also led own combos and wrote arrs. for J. Dorsey band. Fr. '46 led own gp. in Phila. for many yrs. but eventually gave up music for mysticism. Rec. w. Ellington, Rex Stewart '46. CDs: w. Bechet (BB); Aleman (Acoustic Sound); Benny Carter (Class.); D. Reinhardt (Aff.); Rex Stewart in *The 1940s Mercury Sessions* (Merc.).

n

NAKASIAN, (PATRICIA) STEPHANIE, voc; b. Washington, DC, 8/29/54. Mother sang w. Meyer Davis for troops in WWII. Grew up in Bronxville, N.Y. Stud. classical pno., vln., sang in church choirs for 13 yrs. Stud. voice w. Joe Scott, NYC 1980–5. Degrees from Northwestern U. in economics; worked in banks in Chi. and NYC and as consultant at NY Stock Exchange. Met Hod O'Brien '80 and began working w. him. In '81 she quit finance job to become full-time jazz singer, working w. O'Brien (whom she married) into '90s.; also w. Andy LaVerne's Paradise, various bbs '81–2; Jon Hendricks voc. gp. '83–4. Annual trips to Eur.; tour. Den. w. Danish Radio Band '90. Has taught singers priv. and at clinics in US; in '90s at U. of Virginia; Va. Commonwealth U. Eur. Favs: E. Fitzgerald, B. Holiday, Chet Baker, Nat Cole, Irene Kral. Fests: many in Eur., US incl. North Sea; Kool; Delaware Water Gap; Columbia, So. Carolina. Rec. debut w. O'Brien on Criss Cross '85. CD: VSOP; w. O'Brien (CC).

NAMYSLOWSKI, ZBIGNIEW, alto sax; b. Warsaw, Poland, 9/9/39. Began pno. at age 4; cello at 12. Stud. theory at HS of Mus. in Warsaw. Pl. tbn. w. trad gp.; cello w. modern band. Took up alto sax 1960. Tour. US and Eur. w. Jazz Wreckers early '60s; form. own qt. '63; also pl. w. Krzystzof Komeda, Novi Singers, and rock singer Czeslaw Niemen. With George Arvanitas in Paris summer '70; fr. '71 led own qnt. His gps. incl. Adam Makowicz and other leading Polish mus. Namyslowski, who has written for radio, TV, and films, combines modern jazz and rock elements w. Polish folk mus. His alto pl. mixes bebop characteristics w. third stream, rock, and r&b. Favs: Parker, Coltrane, Rollins. Fests: many in Poland; NJF w. Wreckers '62; Cascais (Portugal) '74; first Jazz Yatra Bombay '78. CDs: Polskie Nagrania; Polonia; Koch Int'l.

NANCE, RAY (WILLIS), tpt, crnt, vln, voc; b. Chicago, IL, 12/10/13; d. NYC, 1/28/76. Studied pno. and vln. 1920; self-taught on tpt. Entertainer, lead. of own sxt. '32–7; pl. w. Earl Hines '37–8; Horace Henderson '39–40. Replaced Cootie Williams in Duke Ellington band '40–44. Because he pl., sang, danced, and mugged effervescently, Ellington dubbed him "Floorshow." Briefly led own trio '44. Rejoined Ellington '45, remaining intermittently until '63. Between '66 and '71 he worked mainly w. Sol Yaged at the Gaslight, NYC, but also in Switzerland w. pianist André Chaix; occ. rejoin. Ellington. With Brooks Kerr at Churchill's '73; tour. Eur. w. Chris Barber '74; freelanced NYC w. Kenny Burrell (Town Hall concert Dec. '75) et al. but was hampered by a kidney ailment. Nance, though popular as an entertainer, established himself during the Ellington years as a brilliant trumpeter and an exceptional vlnst. Although he inherited the Cootie Williams role in the Ellington orch. he was not best known for growl or wa-wa playing. His best known solo was on "Take the 'A' Train," where, after a tasty muted solo, he returns for some gorgeous open horn. It all became so much a part of the arrangement that when Williams came back into the band in the '60s he pl. Nance's solo verbatim. Nance's vln. can be heard to advantage on "Moon Mist"; "Bakiff"; and "Come Sunday." He won the *Esq.* New Star Awards on vln. '54. CDs: w. Ellington (Atl.; Saja; Laser.; Em.; Pab.; Red Brn.; MM; Roul.; Mos.; Beth.; Col.; RCA); Earl Hines (BB; Apollo); Jimmy Rushing (BB); Babs

490

Gonzales (BN); Johnny Hodges (Imp.); Shelly Manne (Sig.); Ella Fitzgerald (Verve); P. Gonsalves (BL); J. Bothwell (Hep); Chris Barber (Timel.); Doug Duke (Valley Vue).

NANTON, JOE "TRICKY SAM" (JOSEPH), tbn; b. NYC, 2/1/04; d. San Francisco, CA, 7/20/48. Started w. Cliff Jackson 1925; Frazier's Harmony Five '23–4; Elmer Snowden '25. Then w. Duke Ellington from '26 until his death. Nanton, who specialized in the use of the rubber plunger, set a style in his "wa-wa" solos that was comparable to Bubber Miley's tpt. effects, giving the instrument an almost human sound. Saxophonist Otto Hardwicke gave him the nickname. On some of Ellington's earlier recs., he pl. open solos with a full tone and forceful style. Notable rec. solos w. Ellington: "Black and Tan Fantasy"; "Echoes of the Jungle"; "Jack the Bear"; "Ko Ko"; "A Portrait of Bert Williams"; "Chloe"; and the "Work Song" (from *Black, Brown and Beige*). CDs: w. Ellington (BB).

NAPOLEON, MARTY (Matthew Napoli), pno; b. Brooklyn, NY, 6/2/21. Many mus. in family, incl. Phil, Teddy, Andy Napoleon. Began on vln., tpt., then, due to heart problems, sw. to pno. Pl. w. Bob Astor 1941; Chico Marx bb '42; Geo. Auld, Joe Venuti, Charlie Barnet, Teddy Powell, Lee Castle '40s; Gene Krupa '46; uncle Phil Napoleon's Memphis Five late '40s; Charlie Ventura bb '50; Big Four w. Ventura, Buddy Rich, Chubby Jackson '51; Louis Armstrong '52–4; two-pno. qt. w. bro. Teddy '55–6; own gp. and w. Red Allen at Metropole, NYC '56–8. Pl. w. Coleman Hawkins–Charlie Shavers gp. '58–9. Mostly led his own gps. in the early '60s but rejoin. Armstrong '66–71. Led own trio at NYC Playboy Club '71. Pl. w. Krupa, Pee Wee Erwin, Chris Griffin '71–2; Benny Goodman, WGJB, Peanuts Hucko '70s. In the mid '70s he wrote a series of pno. instruction books for Chas. Hansen Publ. Napoleon perf. in the '80s w. Lionel Hampton sxt. at White House and in a solo pno. concert at Carnegie Hall. A very accomplished pnst., comfortable in swing or bop, ensemble or solo. Favs: Erroll Garner, Dudley Moore; arrs: Neal Hefti, Johnny Mandel, Wes Hensel. Polls: *Play*. Fests: Eur., Asia, Africa since '52. Films: *Beat the Band* w. Krupa; *The Glenn Miller Story* w. Armstrong; *All That Jazz; Raging Bull; Tootsie*. TV: Dean Martin; Dick Cavett; Jackie Gleason; *Tonight Show*; etc., many apps. w. Armstrong. Fests: JVC-NY; North Sea; other Eur. and Can. JFs. Video: Armstrong '88. CDs: w. Krupa (Col.); Ventura (Mos.); Armstrong (Dec.; Mos.); Henry "Red" Allen (BB); Phil Bodner (Stash); w. Kai Winding, Allen Eager, etc. (originally Teddy Reig All-Stars) in *In the Beginning . . . Bebop* (Sav.).

NAPOLEON, PHIL (Filippo Napoli), tpt, lead; b. Boston, MA, 9/2/01; d. Miami, FL, 9/30/90. Nephews, Teddy and Marty Napoleon. Trained formally and pl. classical pieces as a teenager, he opted for jazz upon hearing the bands of the day while living in NYC. Form. the Original Memphis Five in 1921 w. Miff Mole, Frank Signorelli, Jimmy Lytell. Also rec. in '20s w. Charleston Chasers incl. the Dorsey Bros.; Benny Goodman; the Cotton Pickers; and Napoleon's Emperors. Entered studio work '28, and worked in radio and around NYC w. the orchs. of Sam Lanin; B. A. Rolfe; Leo Reisman. Own bb '38; pl. w. J. Dorsey '43. Re-form. Original Memphis Five '49, pl. for seven yrs. at Nick's in Greenwich Village. Then moved to Miami and opened own club, Napoleon's Retreat, where he led his own band. Pl. at NJF '59. CDs: Jazz.; w. J. Dorsey (Dec.); Mole (Frog); Original Memphis Five (Collectors Classics); Jack Pettis (Kings Cross); Boyd Senter (Timel.).

NAPOLEON, TEDDY (Edward George Napoli), pno; b. Brooklyn, NY, 1/23/14; d. Elmhurst, NY, 7/5/64. Nephew of Phil Napoleon; bro. of Marty Napoleon. A bandmate of Lee Castaldo (Castle) in Chinese restaurant 1933; tour. w. Tommy Tompkins for a few yrs; freelanced in NYC and environs late '30s. Pl. w. bbs of Johnny Messner, Bob Chester early '40s. Best known for a long, intermittent assoc. w. Gene Krupa bb and small gps. '44–58; also worked w. Eddie Shu and bro. Marty in NYC. Worked for a short time w. Tex Beneke; then moved to Fla. '59 where he led his own trio which, at times, backed soloists such as Flip Phillips and Bill Harris. A swinging exponent of the Earl Hines school, Napoleon named Oscar Peterson as his favorite pnst. CDs: w. Krupa (Hep); Krupa trio in *The 1940s—The Small Groups: New Directions* (Col.).

NARELL, ANDY, steel pans, pno, comp; b. NYC, 3/18/54. Introduced to steel pans at age 8 by his father; joined Musicians' Union at 10; played on TV and cruise ships as teenager. To Trinidad 1966, where he met great steel pan tuner, Ellie Mannett. Has made many trips to Trinidad since. Moved to Calif w. family '70; grad. U. Cal.-Berkeley '73; form. his own band late '70s; founded a rec. co., Hip Pocket '81. European and Asian tours '80s; recs. for Windham Hill; frequent tours of Caribbean. Pl. on film soundtracks for *Ghostbusters;Cocoon; Gorillas in the Mist*; etc.; album apps. w. Aretha Franklin; Pointer Sisters; Manh. Transfer; et al. Rec. producer for Windham Hill; prod. albums by Billy Childs; Ray Obiedo; and Kit Walker. Caribbean Jazz Project, form. by Dave Samuels '93, incl. Narell, Paquito D'Rivera; tour. Eur. jazzfest. circuit '95. Narell has single-handedly made the steel pan an accepted voice in the jazz pantheon of instruments. Because, as he explains, "There wasn't anyone doing jazz on this instrument when I started." Infls: Miles Davis, Coltrane, Bobby Hutcherson. CDs: WH; w. Carib. Jazz Project (Heads Up).

NASH, DICK (RICHARD TAYLOR), tbn; b. Somerville, MA, 1/26/28. Parents, siblings, wife, and son all musical. Started on tpt. 1938–40, bari. horn '40–2. Stud. in Bost. Prof. debut w. Sam Donahue '47; later w. Glen Gray, Tex Beneke, and army band in Korea. After working w. Billy May, freelanced in LA, then joined CBS staff '57. In early '70s Nash recreated solos by Tommy Dorsey and others for Time-Life Swing Era LP series. Active in '90s teaching and as freelance mus. Also gave priv. lessons. Recipient of many Most Valuable Player awards. His son, Ted Nash, is a talented NYC-based saxophonist. CDs: w. E. Fitzgerald (Verve); Erroll Garner (Tel.); Natalie Cole (Elek.); Sue Raney (Disc.).

NASH, LEWIS DOUGLAS, dms; b. Phoenix, AZ, 12/30/58. Studied at Arizona St. U., then in NYC w. Freddie Waits and Max Roach. First prof. gig. w. Jerry Byrd in Ariz. 1977; pl. w. visiting soloists in Phoenix incl. Sonny Stitt; Art Pepper; Red Garland; Lee Konitz. Moved to NYC '81. Pl. and tour. w. Betty Carter '81–4; Ron Carter '84–6; Branford Marsalis '86–8; J. J. Johnson '88; Don Pullen–Geo. Adams '88–9; Sonny Rollins '89; rec. w. own gp '89. A much-in-demand freelancer w. Jon Faddis; Stan Getz; Art Farmer; Clark Terry; Roland Hanna; Toots Thielemans; Steve Kuhn; Milt Jackson. Pl. w. Tommy Flanagan fr. '90. Member of CHJB. Own gp. at Vanguard, NYC fall '98. Perhaps the most talented dmr. of his generation, equally effective in small gp. or bb. Favs: Blakey, R. Haynes, P. J. Jones, Roach. Fests: Eur., So. Amer., Africa, Asia, Carib. since '81. CDs: Evid.; w. Betty Carter (Verve); B. Marsalis (Col.); Ron Carter (JVC); C. Terry (Delos; Chesky); Don Pullen; Jackie McLean; Don Pullen (BN); Antonio Hart (Novus); Justin Robinson (Verve); Flanagan (BN; Timel.).

NASH, TED (THEODORE MALCOLM), tnr sax; b. Somerville, MA, 10/31/22. Became known w. Les Brown 1944–6; Jerry Gray '47–52. Also many recs. w. Bob Crosby; Dave Barbour; Pete Rugolo; and Billy May. Later was staff member of Mort Lindsay band on Merv Griffin TV show and freelancer in LA. One of the first saxophonists to make expert, extensive use of the saxophone's high harmonics, effectively expanding the instrument's range by an extra octave. He published a primer on this aspect of the saxophone. CDs: four tracks w. own qt. in *The*

Keynote Coll. (Merc.); w. Les Brown (Col.); Joe Thomas in *Giants of Small Band Swing* (Riv.); Barney Kessel (Cont.); Ella Fitzgerald (Verve).

NASH, TED (THEODORE RUSSELL), alto, other saxes; b. Los Angeles, CA, 12/28/59. Father is tbnst. Dick Nash; uncle is Ted Nash. Stud. tbn. w. father 1965; reeds w. Ethmur Roten '71–3; improv. w. Charlie Shoemake '73; comp. w. Manny Albam, Bob Brookmeyer '89. Pl w. Quincy Jones, Lionel Hampton '75; Don Ellis '77–8; Toshiko Akiyoshi '77–90; Louis Bellson '77–91; Nat'l Jazz Ens. '79–81; Shelly Manne '80; Gerry Mulligan bb '80–7; Mel Lewis Orch. '81–92; Bob Brookmeyer '85; Benny Goodman '86; St. Luke's Ens. fr. '86; Bklyn. Philharm. fr. '88; AJO '89–91; Jay McShann, Ella Fitzgerald, Natalie Cole, Aretha Franklin, Jimmy Heath '91. Nash has led his own qt. fr. '89. Touring w. LCJO in late '90s. Teaches improv. at NYU. Active in Jazz Comp. Collective. Comp "5½ Weeks." Fests: Eur. fr. '77; Hong Kong '83; Japan '87, '89. CDs: Maple.; w. E. Fitzgerald (Verve); Louie Bellson (MM; Tel.); Mel Lewis Orch (MM); DMP Big Band (DMP); CHJB (BN); Marcus Roberts (Col.); John Pizzarelli (Novus); Ben Allison (Koch).

NASSER, JAMIL SULIEMAN (George Leon Joyner), bs; b. Memphis, TN, 6/21/32. First stud. w. moth., who was a church pnst. Golden Gloves bantamweight boxer at 15; got first bs. at age 16 and pl. first gig two wks. later. Led dance band at Arkansas St. U. 1949–52. Pl. tba. in army band '53–5; el-bs. w. B. B. King '55–6. To NYC w. Phineas Newborn '56. Stud. w. Michael Krasnapolsky; pl. w. Teddy Charles; Sonny Rollins; Sonny Stitt. Pl. and rec. w. Lester Young in Paris '59; Idrees Sulieman in No. Africa '59–60. Lived in Milan, Italy '61; comp. mus. for Tennessee Williams' *Blues at Teatro San Marco*. Ret. to US '62. Pl. w. own trio '62. Pl. w. own trio '62–4; Ahmad Jamal '64–72; Al Haig '75–8; Clifford Jordan, own gps., freelance fr. '80s; pl. w. Randy Weston; George Coleman; Idris Muhammad; Benny Green. Favs: Ray Brown, Mingus, Pettiford. Fests: all major fr. '60s. CDs: w. Jamal (Imp; Bird.); Lou Donaldson (BN); Red Garland; Coltrane (Prest.); G. Coleman (Evid.); Eric Dolphy (Enja); A. Haig (Prog.); Booker Little (BN); R. Weston (Verve).

NAVARRO, FATS (THEODORE), tpt; b. Key West, FL, 9/24/23; d. NYC, 7/7/50. Piano at age 6; tpt. at 13. Played tnr. sax briefly w. Walter Johnson's band in Miami 1939. After grad. hs '41, join. Sol Allbright in Orlando and trav. to Cincinnati w. him. Stud. w. another teacher there bef. going to Indianapolis, where he pl. tpt. w. Snookum Russell '41–2; w. Andy

Kirk '43–4. In Jan. '45 recommended by Dizzy Gillespie to join the Billy Eckstine band, where he remained for 18 mos. "A week or two after he'd joined us, you'd hardly know Diz had left the band." Eckstine recalled, "He played Dizzy's solos, not note-for-note, but his ideas and feeling were the same and there was just as much swing." With Illinois Jacquet '47–8, and briefly w. Tommy Reynolds; Lionel Hampton; and Coleman Hawkins. Played in Tadd Dameron's house band at Royal Roost, NYC '48–9. After that occ. gigs at Birdland, but Navarro was semi-inactive for over a yr. bef. his death from drug abuse and TB. Navarro was one of the bop era's most gifted and original stylists. His precise execution and pure tone were extraordinary, reaching their peak in the series of sides he rec. for Blue Note as leader or w. Tadd Dameron, Bud Powell, and others. Also notable was one unique side with a Benny Goodman sxt., "Stealin' Apples." Navarro's playing influenced many of the trumpeters who came on the scene in the '50s, particularly Clifford Brown and, through Brown, many of the next generation. CDs: BN; Sav.; Mile.; w. Coleman Hawkins (BB; Prest.); Metronome All-Stars; Gillespie (BB); Bud Powell (BN); B. Goodman (Cap.); Illinois Jacquet (Mos.); Eckstine (Sav.); w. Don Lanphere in *Prestige First Sessions, Vol. 1* (Prest.); Parker (French Col.).

NEIDLINGER, BUELL, bs, cello, educ; b. Westport, CT, 3/2/36. Studied at St. Thomas Choir Sch., NYC 1943; also at Mannes Sch. of Mus., pno., tpt., cello, then bs. Led own band while at Yale U.; worked as dj. From '55 freelanced in NYC w. Zoot Sims; Vic Dickenson; Tony Scott; C. Hawkins. Assoc. w. Cecil Taylor from '57 and dur. '60s pl. w. Jimmy Giuffre; Freddie Redd; Don Cherry; Alan Francis; and w. symph. orchs. in Houston and Bost. Rockefeller grant in '64 to study new music at SUNY-Buffalo. Perf. w. Budapest Qt. at Tanglewood '65. Solo bs. recitals in NYC. Taught at New Engl. Cons. of Mus., USC, Harvard-Radcliffe, Calif. Inst. of Arts, Rotterdam Cons. Feat. artist at US and Eur. jfs and soloist w. London Symph. Rec. w. Anthony Braxton; Steve Lacy; Frank Zappa; Jean-Luc Ponty; Elvis Costello; Bob Seger. Awards incl. NARAS Most Valuable Player '78. Music consultant to Francis Ford Coppola and CBS; creator of music specials for WGBH-TV; and numerous TV and film rec. sessions. Favs: Pettiford, Percy Heath, Walter Page. CDs: SN: K2B2; w. C. Taylor (BN; Cont.; Mos.); Ivo Perelman (K2B2); S. Lacy (NJ; Prest.); A. Braxton (BS); J. Ponty (BN).

NELOMS, BOB (ROBERT JAMES), pno, comp; b. Detroit, MI, 3/2/42. Studied pno. priv. fr. age 5. Inspired by such house guests as Art Tatum and Coleman Hawkins, but during early teens pl. in country & western bands in Eureka, Calif. At age 17, won *DB* scholarship to stud. at Berklee Coll. Original Motown Recs. staff pnst. 1961–3; helped create the "Motown Sound." Ret. to West Coast in mid '60s; formed jazz-rock fusion gp., The Flower, in SF and gigged w. Sly Stone, et al. Moved to Bost. late '60s; again stud. at Berklee. To NYC '73; pl. w. Pharoah Sanders; Roy Haynes; Pepper Adams; Clifford Jordan; et al.; from '76 to '78 worked w. Charles Mingus' last band; tour. more than thirty countries w. Mingus. Since early '80s cont. to refine his pno pl. working regularly in clubs; was artist-in-residence at SUNY-Binghamton; also perf. or rec. w. James Newton; Abbey Lincoln; Buddy Tate; Hamiet Bluiett. Jon Pareles of the *New York Times* describes Neloms as "a thoroughly up-to-date player whose strong sense of history is underlined by a solid left hand." CDs: w. Mingus (Atl.; Rh.); L. Hampton (Tel.).

NELSON, "BIG EYE" LOUIS (Louis Nelson DeLisle), cl; b. New Orleans, LA, 1/28/1880 or '85; d. New Orleans, 8/20/49. Studied w. Luis and Lorenzo Tio. May have pl. w. Buddy Bolden in early yrs. of century. Except for a period in Chi., 1916–8, Nelson spent much of his life in NO, working there w. King Oliver, Jelly Roll Morton, the Imperial Orch., the Golden Rule Orch., the Superior Orch., all before WWI. Largely inactive in mus. for twenty-five yrs., until the early '40s, when he pl. w. Kid Rena and led his own qt. In the mid '40s, Belgian critic Robert Goffin found him working as a doorman. Rec. two sess. '49 under the name of Louis Delisle. Nelson supposedly gave lessons to Sidney Bechet, and his style is alleged to have infl. Johnny Dodds and Jimmie Noone, although the paucity of rec. evidence makes it impossible to assess his work accurately. Rec. w. Kid Rena '40; Wooden Joe Nicholas '49. CDs: Amer. Mus.

NELSON, DAVE (DAVIDSON C.), tpt, pno, comp; b. Donaldsonville, LA, ca. 1905; d. NYC, 4/7/46. Played w. Ma Rainey; Jelly Roll Morton; Richard M. Jones. In 1927 join. Edgar Hayes, then led own band. After working w. Luis Russell '29, tour. w. King Oliver for four mos. '30; then again led his own gp. off and on, sometimes on pno. From '42 to '46 was staff arr. for a mus. publisher. Nelson, who was heard on some of King Oliver's later recs., had a style that clearly reflected Oliver's infl. CDs: w. King Oliver (BB; Class.).

NELSON, OLIVER EDWARD, comp, saxes, cl, fl; b. St. Louis, MO, 6/4/32; d. Los Angeles, CA, 10/28/75. Brother pl. alto w. Cootie Williams, 1940s;

sist. pnst. w. local bands. Studied pno. at age 6, sax at
11. First prof. job while in grade sch. Worked w.
Jeter-Pillars and George Hudson orchs. '47–48; Nat
Towles '40; Louis Jordan bb '50–1. In marines
'52–54; pl. in 3rd Division Band, also in officers'
clubs in Japan. Stud. comp. and theory at Washington
U., St. Louis '54–57, Lincoln U. '57–58. To NYC
where he rec. his first LP as a lead. on tnr. sax, New
Jazz '59; *Screamin' the Blues* on alto sax w. Eric Dolphy, NJ '60. Pl. w. Erskine Hawkins, Wild Bill Davis,
Louis Bellson '59, Eddie "Lockjaw" Davis '60;
briefly w. Duke Ellington '61. Settling in LA in '67,
Nelson became involved in writing for TV and films.
Except for a tour of Africa '69, he became semi-inac-
tive as a saxophonist; app. w. bb at Bottom Line,
NYC, June '75. The day after taping mus. for a *Six
Million Dollar Man* TV episode, Nelson suffered a
fatal heart attack. TV music: *Matt Lincoln; Six Mil-
lion Dollar Man; Ironside; It Takes a Thief; Name of
the Game; Mr. Broadway.* Film music: *Death of a
Gunfighter; Zig Zag; Skullduggery*; educ. film,
Encounter and Response. Comps: "Stolen
Moments"; *Afro-American Sketches* '61; *Jazzhattan
Suite* for BMI '67. Classical comps: woodwind qnt.
'60; song cycle for contralto and pno. '61; *Dirge for
Chamber Orchestra* '62; *Soundpiece for String Quar-
tet and Contralto* '63; *Soundpiece for Orchestra,*
which he pl. and cond. for Light Music Week,
Stuttgart, Germ. '64. Nelson's most acclaimed
albums—such as *Blues and the Abstract Truth*—have
been reissued on CD. CDs: BB; Prest.; NJ; Imp.;
Verve; w. J. J. Johnson (BB); Wes Montgomery;
Jimmy Smith (Verve); Sonny Rollins; Q. Jones
(Imp.); Thelonious Monk (Col.); Eric Dolphy
(Prest.); Nancy Wilson (Cap.).

NELSON, STEVE, vib; b. Pittsburgh, PA, 8/11/54.
Received B.F.A. in mus. fr. Rutgers U. 1983; M. Mus.
'89. Pl. w. David Newman; Kirk Lightsey; Geoff
Keezer; Kenny Barron; James Spaulding; Freddie
Waits; Mickey Bass; Curtis Fuller–Charli Persip;
Bob Cunningham; Mulgrew Miller; Lewis Nash. In
the '90s he has been part of Miller's Wingspan; Dave
Holland qt.; G. Shearing qnt; led own gp. Nash says
of him: "He swings hard like Milt Jackson and
stretches harmonically like Bobby Hutcherson."
Favs: Jackson; Hutcherson. Polls: *DB* Critics TDWR
'89, '91; *DB* Readers TDWR '91. Fests: Eur. fr. '90.
CDs: Sunny.; TCB; CC; Sack.; Red; w. Keezer
(Sunny.; BN); Johnny Griffin; Jackie McLean (Ant.);
David Newman (Atl.; Muse); Curtis Lundy (NN;
Evid.); M. Miller (Land.); D. Holland (ECM); Christ-
ian McBride (Verve); Donald Brown; Chris White
(Muse); Bobby Watson; Lewis Nash (Evid.); Kenny
Drew Jr. (TCB).

NEPUS, IRA, tbn; b. Los Angeles, CA, 9/5/45.
Father was one of the founders of the Hot Club of
France. Perf. in his first jazz concert at age 15. In
1960s worked w. Rex Stewart; Barney Bigard;
Johnny St. Cyr; Kid Ory; lead tbn. w. Woody Herman
'69–71. To Hawaii '72–82 to study at U. of Hawaii
and pl. w. Trummy Young. From '82 in LA, freelancing in studios for films, TV, and commercials. Lead
tbn. and soloist w. Clayton-Hamilton Orch. fr. '87. M.
Mus. degree from USC '89; on faculty of USC Jazz
Studies Dept. fr. '89. Tour. w. and served as asst. contractor for Benny Carter. CDs w. Clayton-Hamilton
(Capri); Gerald Wilson (MAMA); Michael Bloomfield (Takoma).

NERO, PAUL, vln, comp; b. Hamburg, Germany,
4/29/17; d. Los Angeles, CA, 3/21/58. Father taught
vln. NYC. Pl. with dance bands of Jan Savitt 1937;
Gene Krupa '45; w. symph. orchs. in Pitts., NYC, and
Phila. Commercial radio on West Coast from '48.
Best known comp. "The Hot Canary." Nero died after
several years of illness; his few recs for Cap. and
Sunset have not been issued in CD format.

NESTICO, SAMMY (Samuel Nistico), comp, arr; b.
Pittsburgh, PA, 2/6/24. Self-taught as tbn. Stud. at
Duquesne U. 1946–50. Staff arr. for USAF band '51.
Att. Catholic U., Wash., D.C. '51–52. After fifteen
years writing for the Air Force and the Marine bands,
he was recommended to Count Basie by his cousin,
Sal Nistico, and tbnst. Grover Mitchell; he began arr.
regularly for the Basie Orch. in '68. Four of his
albums of original music for Basie won Grammy
Awards. Also wrote music for TV and films; collaborated w. Steve Allen; Bobby Troup; and Johnny Mercer on songs; and orchestrated for most major movie
studios. Active in the field of jazz educ. w. many
works published for coll. and u. bands. Frank Capp's
Conc. CD, *Play It Again Sam*, is devoted entirely to
Nestico comps. CDs: w. Basie (Pab.); Capp (Conc.).

NEUMEISTER, ED (EDWARD P.), tbn, comp,
arr; b. Topeka, KS, 9/1/52. Father pl. tpt. Began on
tpt. at age 5, sw. to tbn. at 9. Pl. in amateur gp., Pieces
Of Eight, as teenager. Stud. w. Bob Szabo at San Jose
St. U. 1970–3; w. Mitchell Ross '75–8. Stud. comp.
w. Bob Brookmeyer, Manny Albam at BMI Comp.
Wkshp. '87–9. Pl. in SF w. Noel Jewkes, Bennett
Friedman, Mark Levine '75–80. Moved to NYC '80.
Pl. w. Lionel Hampton '80–1; Buddy Rich '81; Gerry
Mulligan '82; Mercer Ellington's Duke Ellington
Orch. '81–7; Mel Lewis Jazz Orch.–Vanguard Orch.
fr. '81. Led own qt. and qnt. fr. '78. Debuted own gp.,
New Hat, at Knitting Factory '91. Tour. Eur. as single
incl. perfs. w. UMO band in Helsinki; Hessischer

Rundfunk Jazz Ens. in Frankfurt '91–3. Pl. w. Phil Woods bb '98. Active as a clinician in the US and Eur. Received NEA grants in '90 and '91 and has arr. for the Mel Lewis Orch.–Vanguard Orch. and the Belgian Radio bb. An all-purpose tbnst. who is exceptionally adept at plunger pl. and whose writing can be quite experimental. Favs: J. J. Johnson, Frank Rosolino; arrs: Thad Jones, Brookmeyer, Ellington, Strayhorn, Gil Evans. Fests: all major fr. '80. CDs: w. Christopher Hollyday (Novus); Mel Lewis; M. Ellington (MM); Bill Mays (Conc.); Vanguard Jazz Orch. (NW).

NEVILLE, CHRIS, pno; b. Boston, MA, 10/15/55. Studied pno. and org. w. grandmother at age 4; at New Engl. Cons. Prep fr. 7 to 12; later at Berklee Coll. of Mus. and U. of Maine, where his teachers were extremely supportive and helped him get his prof. start. Perf. w. David Mallett, a country singer/songwriter 1983–91; led own gps.; worked w. many Bost. pls., incl. Herb Pomeroy, Alan Dawson. With Artie Shaw Orch. '92–95. Start. attracting attention through his work w. Benny Carter, whom he first pl. w. in '88; has rec. and pl. with Carter frequently from '89 to present, incl. perfs. at Lincoln Center and tours of US, Japan, Thailand, Germ. Perf. concerts w. Dizzy Gillespie; Claudio Roditi; Nick Brignola; Richie Cole. Also active as B'way mus. and accomp. prominent cabaret singers Mary Cleere Haran and Marlene Ver Planck. Favs: Jamal, Hancock, Vladimir Horowitz. TV: w. Benny Carter All-Stars, NHK-TV, Japan; Telfilm, Int., Thailand. CDs: w. Carter (MM); Greg Abate (Cand.).

NEW ORLEANS RHYTHM KINGS. Included Paul Mares, Georg Brunis, and Leon Roppolo, who grew up together in NO and pl. in local bands as teenagers. Featured from 1921–2 at Friar's Inn in Chi., afterward rec. as Friar's Society Orchestra. Other members incl. at various times Ben Pollack; Elmer Schoebel; Jack Pettis; et al. After a few more dates, incl. rec. sess. w. Jelly Roll Morton '23 (one of the first integrated jazz dates), ret. to NO and broke up in '25. In '34 another gp. using the same name rec. for Dec., feat. Wingy Manone and Brunis. Generally considered to be the first important white jazz band after the ODJB, whose ideas they blended with black influences from gps. like King Oliver's. CDs: Mile.

NEWBORN, (EDWIN) CALVIN, gtr; also pno, fl, picc; b. Memphis, TN, 4/27/33. Studied at Booker T. Washington HS; LeMoyne Coll. Pl. w. father's band and Roy Milton 1953; also in qt. w. pnst. bro. Phineas. With Earl Hines '59; Lionel Hampton '60–1; Bill Davis '62. Freelanced in Memphis in '60s

and '70s and in LA in '80s, rec. w. Linda Hopkins and others. A superior, swinging guitarist, Newborn never achieved the reputation he deserved. CDs: w. Booker Little (BN); Phineas Newborn (BB).

NEWBORN, PHINEAS JR., pno, comp; b. Whiteville, TN, 12/14/31; d. Memphis, TN, 5/26/89. Musical family. Stud. reed and brass instruments as well as pno. Played in r&b bands in Memphis w. his fath., a dmr., and others. With L. Hampton 1950 and '52; army band '53–5. Made his first major impact as a jazz artist at Basin St., NYC in '56. Duo w. Charles Mingus in '58; pl. w. Mingus on soundtrack of John Cassavetes' film *Shadows*. Tour Eur. '58 and '59. Highly praised by Nat Hentoff, Ralph Gleason, and other critics, he went into decline in the '60s as the result of emotional illness. Confined to Camarillo St. Hospital intermittently; when in better health, Newborn was frequently heard around LA. In early '75 he pl. briefly at World Jazz Association's first concert in LA. Virtuoso pnst. in the tradition of Art Tatum and such beboppers as Bud Powell. Remarkable left-hand player who dazzled with his flying parallel lines up and down the keyboard; also known for his locked-hands, block chord interludes. CDs: Steep.; BB; Cont.; Pab.; w. Booker Little (BN); Roy Haynes (NJ).

NEWMAN, DAVID (aka "FATHEAD"), tnr, alto saxes, fl; b. Dallas, TX, 2/24/33. As teenager pl. w. Buster Smith, later w. Ornette Coleman in band led by Red Connors. Pl. w. blues and r&b mus. incl. Lowell Fulson 1952–3; T-Bone Walker '54. Join. Ray Charles on bari. '54; later became feat. tnr. soloist. Pl. w. Charles '54–64. Began to acquire reputation in jazz circles and made first rec. as lead. w. Charles and Hank Crawford as sidemen '58. Freelanced in Dallas '64–6, then moved to NYC '66. Pl. and rec. w. own gps. fr. '66; w. King Curtis's Kingpins late '60s; Ray Charles '70–1; Red Garland, Herbie Mann's Family of Mann '72–4. Also worked as studio mus. w. pop and r&b acts. Ret. to Dallas '75. Rec. w. Junior Mance '83. App. in and pl. on soundtrack of Altman film, *Kansas City* '96. A descendant of the big-toned Texas Tenor legacy, Newman also blows blues-soaked alto and fl. His interpretations of Ellingtonia on his Kokopelli CD shows another side of him, Favs: Parker, Rollins, Stitt. Film: w. Charles '64. CDs: 32; Rh./Atl.; Mile; Muse; Koko.; Cand.; w. R. Charles (Atl., Pab.); Johnny Copeland (Verve); Roy Hargrove (Novus; Verve), James Clay (Ant); Blue-siana (WH); Hank Crawford (Mile); Lou Rawls (BN); Jimmy McGriff (Mile.); Roseanna Vitro (Tel.).

NEWMAN, JOE (JOSEPH DWIGHT), tpt, comp, b. New Orleans, LA, 9/7/22; d. NYC, 7/4/92. His fath., Dwight, a pnst., led band at Absinthe House, NO, and on radio. Stud. at Alabama St. Teacher's Coll., where Lionel Hampton heard and hired him 1941. Left Hampton '43 to join Count Basie for the first of several stints '43–6 and '52–61, also pl. w. J. C. Heard, Illinois Jacquet in '47. Mainly freelanced fr. '60; settling in NYC, he became a key figure (and, in '57, pres.) of Jazz Interactions, Inc.—an org. designed to promote jazz educ.—and in its orch., for which he wrote *Suite for Pops*, dedicated to L. Armstrong. To USSR w. Benny Goodman '62; and NY Jazz Repertory Co. '74. In '70s, he also pl. in B'way pit bands and was active cond. workshops and master classes; collab. w. Rev. John Gensel on two religious works. Cont. to work in B'way shows, TV, recs. until '91, when he suffered an incapacitating stroke. Newman, who conducted many university seminars, was one of the most consistent and spirited of the modern, transitional trumpeters, skillfully blending elements of swing and bop. He pl. quite often in Eur. and was a regular at the Colo. JP. Best known comp. "The Midgets," rec. by Basie. CDs: Prest.; Swing.; BL; Phon.; Newman–Joe Wilder (Conc.); w. I Jacquet (BB); Count Basie (Verve; Mos.); Billie Holiday; Wes Montgomery; Jimmy Smith (Verve); Milt Jackson (Atl.); Mel Tormé (Conc.); L. Hampton (Imp.; Dec.).

NEWSOM, TOMMY (THOMAS PENN), saxes, fl, cl, comp; b. Portsmouth, VA, 2/25/29. Studied at Peabody Cons. 1948–52. Tour. Eur., No. Africa, Saudi Arabia '55 w. USAF band; Latin America '61; and USSR '62 w. Benny Goodman. In Oct. '62 join. the NBC-TV staff, working on the *Tonight Show* w. Skitch Henderson, later w. Doc Severinsen. Switched from tnr. sax to alto in '68 and became asst. cond., contributing many of the band's most creative arrs. and some original comps., remaining in this capacity until the band left the show in spring of '92. Throughout this time Newsom made frequent local apps. in LA as leader or sideman w. small jazz gps. Won two Emmy awards for arranging and honorary doctorate from Old Dominion U. Favs: L. Young, Z. Sims, S. Getz, B. Webster. CDs: Laser.; w. J. J. Johnson (BB); Jack Lemmon; Boots Randolph (Laser.); Rosemary Clooney; Louie Bellson (Conc.); Jake Hanna (Arb.).

NEWSOME, SAM, tnr, sop saxes; b. Salisbury, MD, 4/28/65. Raised in Hampton, Va. A schoolmate of James Genus; att. Kecoughtan HS w. him and pl. in the same funk band. Began on alto sax at age 12, sw. to tnr. when he join. the sch.'s jazz ens. at 13. Alto sax Steve Wilson, also fr. Hampton, helped him w. his technique, harm. knowledge, and pl. recs. fr. his collection for him. While in sch. Newsome and Genus

would drive to Norfolk to play with and listen to dmr. Billy Drummond. Won Kool Jazz scholarship to Berklee, stud. comp. and arr. w. Bill Pierce, Andy McGhee; gigged in Bost. w. Donald Brown, Alan Dawson. With Brown did a Eur. tour w. Donald Byrd's qnt. In NYC he was heard by Terence Blanchard and began working w. his qnt. fr. 1989 to '94, tour. the US, Mex., Eur., Japan. Took up sop. sax as main horn '95, when rehearsing his band, Motivic Development, later renamed Global Unity. "The register of the soprano suited the way I wanted to play," says Newsome. "I felt I could be more melodic and free. I felt I could shed the past a bit, be more of an individual." Rec. first album as lead. Nov. '90 for Criss Cross. Favs: Rollins, Coltrane, Webster, L. Young, Parker, Shorter, O. Coleman. Film: soundtrack for *Malcolm X* w. Blanchard. CDs: CC; w. Blanchard; Monte Croft (Col.).

NEWTON, FRANKIE (WILLIAM FRANK), tpt; b. Emory, VA, 1/4/06; d. NYC, 3/11/54. Played w. Lloyd Scott 1927–29; first national exposure when he rec. w. Cecil Scott '29, pl. w. him into '30. In '30s worked w. Elmer Snowden; Charlie Johnson; Teddy Hill; orig. member John Kirby Sxt. '37. Own band at Café Society and Kelly's Stable, NYC '39–44. Often sidelined by illness, spent time painting and pl. only intermittently in later yrs. Noted for his use of mutes. Considered, with Roy Eldridge and Charlie Shavers, as one of the precursors of the modern tpt. style. CDs: Aff.; w. S. Bechet (BN); Bessie Smith (Col.); Billie Holiday (Comm.); Mezz Mezzrow (Class.); Teddy Wilson (Hep); Willie "The Lion" Smith (Timel.); Maxine Sullivan (Aff.); Mary Lou Williams (Suisa).

NEWTON, JAMES, fl, comp, educ; b. Los Angeles, CA, 5/1/53. Played el-bs. and saxes in hs; fl. fr. age 17; stud. w. Buddy Collette. B.A. from Cal. St., LA 1980. Perf. in LA w. Stanley Crouch's gp., along w. David Murray and Arthur Blythe. While in NYC '78, led a small gp. w. Anthony Davis. From '85 assoc. prof. of mus., teaching comp. and improv. at Cal Arts in Valencia, Calif. Visiting prof. of mus., Bennington Coll. '82; USC '88; U. of Calif., San Diego '91. NEA Fellow '80, '91; Guggenheim Fellow '92. Working exclusively as a flutist since late '70s, he has won several *DB* polls on that instrument. In '92, pl. concerts w. Kei Akagi. A highly unusual soloist who uses avant-garde wind techniques on his instrument, Newton is also an impressive mainstream improviser. His comps. range from jazz chamber ensembles to classical-style wind qnts. Comp: *Suite for Frida Kahlo* '91, rec. on Audq. CD. Other CDs: Audq.; ECM; Gram.; w. Chet Baker (Stash).

NICHOLAS, ALBERT, cl; b. New Orleans, LA, 5/27/1900; d. Basel, Switzerland, 9/3/73. Nephew of the clst. and crntst. "Wooden Joe" Nicholas. Stud. w. "Big Eye" Louis Nelson and Lorenzo Tio Sr. & Jr. Served in navy 1916–19; then in '20s and '30s worked w. Luis Russell, King Oliver, Chi.; Luis Russell, NYC '28–33; Sam Wooding; Chick Webb; Alex Hill; rejoin. Russell under L. Armstrong's dir. '35–9. Left mus. dur. early part of '40s; ret. to work w. Art Hodes; Bunk Johnson; Kid Ory in latter half of the decade. Lived mainly in Paris, Basel, etc. from '53 until his death. One of the best clarinetists in the NO Creole tradition, Nicholas rec. w. his own gps. and Red Allen; King Oliver; Luis Russell; Jelly Roll Morton; Rex Stewart; et al. CDs: w. Sidney Bechet (BB; Laser.); J. Teagarden; Jelly Roll Morton; Fats Waller (BB); Louis Armstrong (Dec.; Col.); King Oliver (Dec.).

NICHOLAS, "BIG NICK" (GEORGE WALKER), tnr sax, voc; b. Lansing, MI, 8/2/21. Began on pno., cl. Fath. pl. sax, got him start. w. local gps. 1939–40. Pl. w. Kelly Martin at Club Congo, Det. 1942; Earl Hines, Tiny Bradshaw '42–3. Moved to Bost. '44. Stud. theory, harm. at Bost. Cons. and pl. w. Sabby Lewis '44–6. Moved to NYC '46. Pl. w. Claude Hopkins, J. C. Heard, Lucky Millinder '46–7; Hot Lips Page off and on '47–54; Dizzy Gillespie Orch. '48; Cozy Cole, Timmie Rogers–Jonah Jones '53; Buck Clayton '55; Shorty Allen '57–9. Nicholas led a jam sess. at the Paradise Club in Harlem where he developed his stentorian style of scat singing '50–2. Led his own gps. in NYC fr. '53; in Virginia '77–9. Taught music in Va. publ. sch. '77–9 and made his rec. debut as lead. '83. John Coltrane's '62 comp. "Big Nick" was named for him. Favs: C. Hawkins, Coltrane; arrs: Strayhorn, Jimmy Jones. Fests: Eur. fr. '80; Hawkins Tribute at NJF-NY '83. Film: app. in Kiss of Death. Rec. "Open the Door, Richard" w. Dusty Fletcher (National); "La Danse" w. Hot Lips Page (Col.). Fav. solos: "Baby, Baby All the Time"; "Sposin'," w. Frankie Laine–Buck Clayton (Col.). CDs: Ind. Nav.; w. Gillespie (BB); Bennie Green in Prestige First Sessions, Vol. 3 (Prest.).

NICHOLAS, WOODEN JOE (JOSEPH), crnt, cl; b. New Orleans, LA, 9/23/1883; d. New Orleans, 11/17/57. Uncle of Albert Nicholas. Start. on cl.; learned crnt. under infl. of Buddy Bolden and Bunk Johnson. His reputation for power and stamina in street parades led to his own nickname. Played w. King Oliver 1915; led own gp., Camelia Band or Wooden Joe's Band, fr. '18. During Depression, he taught and played occasionally. Rec. as leader '45 and '49; and, under Raymond Burke, w. Johnny St.

Cyr '49. CDs: Amer. Mus.; w. Raymond Burke; Big Eye Louis Nelson; Baby Dodds (Amer. Mus.).

NICHOLS, HERBIE (HERBERT HORATIO), pno, comp; b. NYC, 1/3/19; d. NYC, 4/12/63. Early associate of Thelonious Monk, he also pl. frequently w. dixieland and swing bands in 1940s and '50s, incl. Snub Mosley; Rex Stewart; Milt Larkin; and with r&b bands. His harmonically venturesome style was first revealed in a '55 Blue Note album. Composer of "Lady Sings the Blues," which was rec. by Billie Holiday and was title of her autobiography; also wrote "The Bebop Waltz," a.k.a "Mary's Waltz," rec. by Mary Lou Williams. Other comps: "The Gig"; "Shuffle Montgomery." Nichols died after an erratic career, plagued by bad luck and obscure groups. Favs: John Lewis, Vladimir Horowitz; arr: Ellington. The Herbie Nichols Project, a concert of his music, was perf. by The Jazz Composer's Collective at Greenwich House, NYC, winter '94. CDs: BN; Mos.; Sav.

NICHOLS, RED (ERNEST LORING), crnt; b. Ogden, UT, 5/8/05; d. Las Vegas, NV, 6/28/65. Studied w. fath., a coll. mus. prof. In NYC 1925–32, worked off and on w. Sam Lanin, Paul Whiteman; led his own pit orch. for such shows as Strike Up the Band and Girl Crazy. Most active early white jazz band lead., his gp., Red Nichols and His Five Pennies, at various times incl. Joe Venuti; Eddie Lang; Jimmy Dorsey; Miff Mole; Benny Goodman; Pee Wee Russell; Jack Teagarden; Glenn Miller; Artie Shaw. A '59 Hollywood film, The Five Pennies, starred Danny Kaye as Nichols (who dubbed the crnt. tracks) and purported to be based on a part of his life, but it grossly sensationalized, sentimentalized, and fictionalized the truth. However, it was well received by the public. Nichols also app. in The Gene Krupa Story '60. Nichols' style, though often compared w. Bix Beiderbecke's, was neither as emotional nor as rhythmically complex. Whatever his value as a soloist, he made a unique contribution by assembling for recs. some of the best-remembered small gps. of the first so-called Golden Age of Jazz. CDs: Biog.; Cir.; Jazz.; also various collections (BB; Dec., Rhino).

NIEHAUS, LENNIE (LEONARD), alto sax, arr, comp; b. St. Louis, MO, 6/1/29. Studied at Cal. St. U. in LA 1946–51. Pl. in jam sess. w. Chet Baker; Hampton Hawes; Russ Freeman; Teddy Edwards. Join. the Stan Kenton Orch. '52; left for the army (where he met Clint Eastwood); rejoin. Kenton fr. '54 to '59. Concurrently had own qnt. w. Bill Perkins in LA. Since early '60s has been a prolific comp./clinician for university and concert bands, orchs., and small ens. From '84 has written scores for several of Eastwood's films, incl. *Unforgiven; Bird; Tight Rope; City Heat;* and *Pale Rider*. Wrote mus. for Billy Crystal's TV series, *Sessions* '91. Won *DB* New Star alto sax '55; British Academy Award nomination for Best Score for film *Bird* '88; Grammy award for *Follow That Bird* film soundtrack (Children's Album of the Year) '86; two BMI film awards for scores, *Pale Rider* and *Heartbreak Ridge*. CDs: Cont.; FS; w. Kenton (Cap.); Eastwood (WB).

NIEMACK, JUDY (JUDITH A.), voc; b. Pasadena, CA, 3/11/54. Many amateur singers in family. Stud. at Pasadena City Coll. 1972–4; New Engl. Cons. '74–5; Cleveland Inst. of Mus. '75; also stud. piano w. Lino Puccinelli '70–4; and improv. w. Warne Marsh '75–81. Perf. w. own qnt., Niemack's Pack '77–81; Warne Marsh '79–80; Pipe Dreams w. Janet Lawson, Perry Robinson, Scott Hardy '82–3; Riffs voc. qt. '83; Jazz Babies voc. trio '83–8; Larry Elgart Orch. '85–8; Cayenne Jazz Band '85–8; Swing Street '86–90; Peter Duchin Orch. '88–92; K.D.'s Pretty Big Basement Party since '91; own qt. since '78. Recs. as lead. w. Cedar Walton; Ray Drummond; Curtis Fuller; Joe Lovano; Kenny Barron. Niemack has taught voice and improv. at LIU, City Coll. of NY, William Paterson Coll., and the New School. In mid '90s she became profess. of jazz voice at the Hanns Eisler Hochschule in Berlin. She has written lyrics for the mus. of many contemp. jazz composers. incl. John Scofield; Don Grolnick; Mike Stern; and Steve Slagle. Favs: Betty Carter, Diane Reeves, Billie Holiday. Fests: Eur. since '82; Japan since '90. TV: Eur. and Jap. CDs: Stash; Freelance; co-lead. w. Konitz (Evid.); Cedar Walton (Freelance).

NIEWOOD, GERRY (Gerard J. Nevidosky), saxes, fl, picc, cl; b. Rochester, NY, 4/6/43. Studied at Hochstein Sch. of Mus. 1953–8; Eastman Sch. of Mus. '67–70. First prof. gigs in Rochester at age 11. Pl. w. Chuck Mangione '68–76; Thad Jones–Mel Lewis Orch.; Timepiece w. Ron Davis; Dave Samuels '76; Chuck Israels Nat'l Jazz Ens. '76–80; David Matthews '77–86; Gil Evans Orch. '78; Gerry Mulligan bb fr. '79; Teruo Nakamura '80–2; Joe Morello '80–3; Lynn Welshman fr. '80; Mel Lewis Orch. '82 Led own gps. and freelanced in '80s and '90s w. Astrud Gilberto; Butch Miles; Maureen McGovern; Jean-Luc Ponty; Jimmy McGriff; Nat Adderley; Grady Tate; Walt Levinsky; Frank Sinatra; etc. Niewood taught at Ramapo Coll. '80; Wm. Paterson Coll., U. of Bridgeport '91. Favs: C. Adderley, Rollins, Coltrane. Polls: *DB* TDWR sop. sax '74–5.

Fests: Eur., Japan, etc. fr. '70s. CDs: DMP; Perfect Sound; w. C. Mangione (Merc.; A&M; Verve); David Matthews–Jim Hall (Elec. Bird); Peggy Lee (Chesky); John Serry (Tel.).

NIMITZ, JACK (JEROME), bari sax, fl, cl; b. Washington, DC, 1/11/30. Mostly self-taught; first prof. gigs w. Bob Astor; Darryl Harpa. Pl. w. Joe Timer–Willis Conover's "The Orchestra" 1951–3; W. Herman '53–5; S. Kenton '55–6, '58–60. In '60s and '70s pl. w. Gerald Wilson; Oliver Nelson; Mike Barone; Bill Berry. Charter member of Supersax '73. Pl. w. Louie Bellson '73; Chuck Mangione '74. In '80s worked w. Don Menza bb; own qnt. w. Lanny Morgan, Benny Carter '81 and '83; MJF All-Stars '89. CDs: FS; w. H. Mann (Riv.); Terry Gibbs (Cont.); Q. Jones; O. Nelson (Imp.); Gerald Wilson (MAMA); Frank Capp (Conc.); Earl Klugh (BN).

NISTICO, SAL (SALVATORE), tnr sax; b. Syracuse, NY, 4/12/40; d. Berne, Switzerland, 3/3/91. Cousin, Sammy Nestico. Pl. w. r&b bands in upstate N.Y., then w. Mangione Bros. 1959–1. Feat. soloist w. Woody Herman '62–5 and again off and on into the '80s. Five mos. w. C. Basie '65; rejoin. '67; in LA w. Don Ellis '70. From '72 lived in NYC; freelanced w. Tito Puente; Chuck Israels' Nat'l Jazz Ensemble; tour. Eur. w. Slide Hampton; w. Buddy Rich combo at Rich's club, NYC '74. A hard-driving soloist in a style derived from Charlie Parker, Gene Ammons, and Sonny Rollins, Nistico was capable of negotiating the fastest tempos w. ease and great fire; he could also could impart a thoughtful lyricism to his ballad performance LPs: Jzld.; Bee Hive; CDs: Red; w. Mangione (Riv.); Herman (Chess); Mel Tormé (Stash); Buck Clayton (Chiaro.); Michael Bloomfield (Takoma).

NOBLE, RAY (RAYMOND STANLEY), lead, comp; b. Brighton, England, 12/17/03; d. London, England, 4/2/78. Led own band in Engl., fr. 1929 to 34, when he was mus. dir. for HMV. His New Mayfair Orch. was launching pad for singer Al Bowlly and trumpeter Nat Gonella. Moved to US and led all-star band at Rainbow Room in NYC '35–7 w. such sidemen as Glenn Miller; Claude Thornhill; Charlie Spivak; Will Bradley; et al. Later moved to Calif. where he was active leading bands on radio shows (i.e., Edgar Bergen) and accomp. such stars as Fred Astaire and Buddy Clark. Noble is best known in jazz as the comp. of such standards as "Cherokee"; "The Very Thought of You"; "I Hadn't Anyone Til You"; "The Touch of Your Lips"; and "Love Is the Sweetest Thing." CDs: EMI; RCA; also tracks on anthologies (Jass; Col.).

NOCK, MIKE (MICHAEL ANTHONY), pno, comp; b. Christchurch, New Zealand, 9/27/40. Moved to Australia 1958, remain. three yrs. and rec. two albums w. a trio. Stud. at Berklee in Bost.; while there, pl. w. Herb Pomeroy; Sam Rivers; Tony Williams. In mid '60s rec. w. Yusef Lateef, Art Blakey; joined John Handy in SF '67. Form. the fusion gp. Fourth Way, feat. at Montreux JF '70. Awarded NEA fellowships in comp. '72, '75, and '78. Assisted producer Teo Macero on LP and TV projects '76 to '85. After twenty-five years in the US he returned to Austral., pl. concert w. Australian Chamber Orch., hosting and co-producing own TV series. An innovative artist, he was much in demand dur. his yrs. in the US. Living in Sydney, active in a wide range of creative activities as pnst. and comp. CDs: Nax.; ECM; Timel.; Tom.; ABC/Polyg.; Ode; w. John Klemmer (Imp.).

NOONE, JIMMIE (JAMES), cl; b. Cut Off, LA, 4/23/1895, d. Los Angeles, CA, 4/19/44. Took up gtr. and cl. 1905; stud. briefly w. Lorenzo Tio Jr. and Sidney Bechet, replacing the latter in Freddie Keppard's band '13–14. He form. the Young Olympia Band w. Buddy Petit and played with Kid Ory and Papa Celestin bef. moving to Chi. in '17. Pl. w. Freddie Keppard in and around Chi. for several mos., ret. briefly to NO, then back to Chi. to work w. Bill Johnson's band (which also incl. King Oliver) at Royal Gardens. From '20s to 26 worked w. Doc Cook's Dreamland Orch. and, until '28, w. own small gp. at the Nest (later renamed the Apex Club), where dmr. Zutty Singleton recalled seeing, at different times, Benny Goodman; Artie Shaw; Carl Sandburg; and Maurice Ravel taking in Noone's cl. In and out of Chi. dur. '30s. In '35 pl. one month at Savoy Ballroom NYC; then back to Chi., which was his base as he tour. widely until '43 when he moved to LA. Pl. w. Kid Ory in LA and took part in Orson Welles' radio series until his death of a heart attack. Noone's recs. incl. his theme song, "Sweet Lorraine," which inspired Nat Cole; also "Apex Blues"; "I Know That You Know"; "Four or Five Times." A major infl. on early reed players, incl. Benny Goodman; Joe Marsala; Jimmy Dorsey; Buster Bailey; and Barney Bigard. Modern players like Eric Dolphy have also praised Noone's work. CDs: Dec.; Milan; Collector's Classics; w. Capitol Jazzmen in *Classic Capitol Jazz Sessions* (Cap.).

NOONE, JIMMIE JR. (JAMES FLEMING), cl, tnr sax, comp, arr; b. Chicago, IL, 4/21/38; d. San Diego, CA, 3/29/91. Son of Jimmie Noone, the famous NO clst. Family moved to LA in 1943. First cl. teacher was his father. Following fath.'s death, family moved to San Diego in the late '40's. He also stud. tnr., sop., alto sax, bjo., pno., and dms. In the '50s he pl. w. Teddy Picou and Daniel Jackson in San Diego. Pl. w. bands in the navy until he lost an eye while in Vietnam '58. Returning to San Diego from the war, he worked in the postal service fr. '60 and cont. pl. w. Cottonmouth D'Arcy's Jazz Vipers; also pl. and tour. Eur. w. Jeannie and Jimmy Cheatham's Sweet Baby Blues Band. In the '80s he led his own band, The New Orleans Good Time Society and Marching Band. He app. at many West Coast fests. and the NO Jazz Heritage Fest. w. the Cheathams. TV: *Club Date,* PBS w. Cheathams. CDs: w. Cheathams (Conc.).

NORRIS, AL (ALBERT), gtr; b. Kane, PA, 9/4/08; d. NYC, 12/26/74. Started on vln., bjo. w. gps. in Buffalo 1927–32. Join. Jimmie Lunceford, remain. throughout the band's existence w. time out for army service. Feat. on "Cheatin' on Me"; "Put on Your Old Grey Bonnet"; "Organ Grinder's Swing"; "Sweet Sue." After Lunceford's death cont. w. the band under Ed Wilcox; then retired, and in the '50s worked for post office in NYC. CDs: w. Lunceford (Dec.; Class.).

NORRIS, WALTER, pno, comp; b. Little Rock, AR, 12/27/31. Studied pno. fr. age 5; pl. w. Howard Williams' racially mixed orch. fr. age 10 until 1950; army service '51–2. Pl. w. Jimmy Ford in Houston '52–3; own trio in LV '53–4. Moved to LA '54; pl. w. own trio and F. Rosolino; J. Sheldon (w. whom he made his rec. debut '54); Zoot Sims; Teddy Edwards; Sonny Criss; tour. w. Stan Getz; Shorty Rogers–Bill Holman Qnt.; pl. on first Ornette Coleman album '58. Pl. in SF w. Getz '58; Johnny Griffin '59. To NYC '60; lead. and mus. dir. at Playboy Club '63–70; stud. at Manh. Sch. of Mus. '64–9; pl. w. Thad Jones–Mel Lewis Orch., tour. Eur. and Japan '74–6. Became an expatriate fr. '76, worked in a Berlin radio band from '77 and taught improv. at the Berlin Hochschule fr. '84. Norris's rhythmic mastery and harmonic imagination belatedly came to the attention of Amer. audiences in '90 when he began rec. a series of albums for Conc. Solo pno. at JVC-NY '92. Favs: Tatum; arr: Thad Jones. CDs: Conc.; Enja; w. O. Coleman (Cont.); Pepper Adams; C. Baker; H. Geller (Enja); Joe Pass; NDR Big Band (Act).

NORVO, RED (Kenneth Norville), vib, xyl; b. Beardstown, IL, 3/31/08; d. Santa Monica, CA, 4/6/99. Piano at age 8; after pl. xyl. while in high school, left for Chicago 1925; led a marimba septet, The Collegians. Worked w. Paul Ash, toured in vaudeville as solo act and tap dancer. Worked as staff musician at NBC, Chi., w. Victor Young, Ben Bernie, et al. Pl. NBC radio series w. Paul Whiteman; singer was Mildred Bailey, whom he married. Left White-man in NYC, leading pianoless octet, incl. Eddie Sauter on mellophone; Herbie Haymer, tnr. sax; and Dave Barbour, gtr., at Hickory House on 52nd St. From '36 led a 12-piece band, highly praised for its subtle brand of swing music, w. Sauter as arr. and, for the first few years, Bailey as vocalist. On 52nd St. Norvo and Bailey were billed as "Mr. & Mrs. Swing." In '43 Norvo led the first of a series of combos; that year he switched from xyl. to vib. Featured w. B. Goodman '45; in the same year, rec. a classic all-star session w. Dizzy Gillespie and Charlie Parker as side-men. With Woody Herman '46. Settled in Calif. '47. Continued to lead small groups, incl. one in NYC '49 that incl. Tony Scott, Mundell Lowe, and Dick Hyman. In '50s worked mostly w. trio, feat. Charles Mingus or Red Mitchell on bs. and Tal Farlow or Jimmy Raney on gtr. First overseas tour w. trio, Jan. '54. Rejoined Goodman several times, tour. Europe w. him '59. In '60s and '70s, despite hearing prob-lems, worked mainly in Las Vegas lounges. In '86 Norvo suffered a stroke that put an end to his playing, though he did perform briefly w. one hand during a cruise appearance w. Lionel Hampton, Terry Gibbs, and Gary Burton in late '90. Norvo was the first to introduce mallet instruments as valid vehicles for jazz. His early small group recordings from '33 became collectors' items: among his sidemen were Jack Jenney; Artie Shaw; Charlie Barnet; Teddy Wil-son; Bunny Berigan; Johnny Mince; Chu Berry; Gene Krupa. He won an *Esq.* Gold Award '44; tied w. Hampton '45-7. Films: *Screaming Mimi* '57; *Ocean's 11* '60. CDs: CBS/Portrait; MM; Stash; Sav.; Cont.; BB; Prest.; Fant.; Ref.; Hep; Merc.; four ses-sions as leader and one sess. as sideman w. Stan Has-selgard in *Classic Capitol Jazz Sessions* (Mos.); w. B. Goodman; W. Herman (Col.); Herman's Woodchop-per's in *The 1940s—The Small Combos: New Direc-tions* (Col.); F. Sinatra (BN).

NOTO, SAM, tpt, flg; b. Buffalo, NY, 4/17/30. Studied tpt. in grade sch.; went on road w. band at age 17. Join. Stan Kenton 1953, tour. Eur., US. Tour. w. Louie Bell-son–Pearl Bailey show '59; then pl. w. Count Basie '64-5, '67. Quintet w. Joe Romano in Buffalo '65; pl. for yr. at own coffee house, Renaissance. From '69 to '75 worked in show bands at Flamingo and other hotels in LV. Sectionmate Red Rodney recommended him to pro-ducer Don Schlitten who rec. the two tpts. for Muse '74 and, later, Noto for Xanadu '75, '77, '78. Moved to Toronto '75, working in the studios and w. Rob McConnell's Boss Brass. In '90s active freelance in Toronto. Known in his Kenton yrs. as a strong lead man and high note specialist, he emerged in the '70s as a vir-tuosic soloist inspired by Clifford Brown. Favs: Fats Navarro, Gillespie, Miles Davis, Brown. Fest: Montreux '78, rec. w. Xanadu All-Stars. LPs: Xan; w. Kenny Drew; Jimmy Rowles, etc. (Xan.). CDs: w. Kenton (Mos.; BN); McConnell (SB).

NOTTINGHAM, JIMMY (JAMES EDWARD), tpt, flg; b. Brooklyn, NY, 12/15/25, d. NYC, 11/16/78. With Willie Smith's navy band 1944–5; L. Hampton '45–7; Charlie Barnet, Lucky Millinder '47; Basie '48–50. After pl. w. Herbie Fields and several Latin bands, had gp. w. Budd Johnson '62. Join. CBS staff until '73 but cont. to play jazz w. Dizzy Gillespie; Quincy Jones; B. Goodman; Ray Charles; the Thad Jones–Mel Lewis Band, Clark Terry. Best known as exceptional lead trumpeter and adept w. a plunger mute. CDs: w. Shirley Scott (Imp.); Ruth Brown (Cap.); King Curtis; Chuck Willis (R&T); Joe Williams (BN); Coleman Hawkins (RCA).

NUNEZ, ALCIDE "YELLOW," cl; b. New Or-leans, LA, 3/17/1884; d. New Orleans, 9/2/34 Started on gtr.; cl. from 1902. Worked w. local bands, incl. Papa Jack Laine fr. '12 to '16. To Chi. '16 w. Johnny Stein's gp., which became nucleus of ODJB; left gp. in Oct. '16 bef. the first recs. were made. After lead. own band, tour. w. Bert Kelly; then joined Anton Lada's Louisiana Five, rec. w. them fr. '19 to '20 for Columbia, Emerson. Later led own qt. in Okla. and Tex., ret. to NO '27 and pl. w. the NO Police Band. Nunez is said to have a warm tone and a florid style; some observers criticized his use of novelty effects and animal sounds in his solos.

NUROCK, KIRK, comp, pno; b. Camden, NJ, 2/28/48. Father pl. pno. Pl. jazz and club dates in Phila. and Trenton, N.J. Stud. at Stan Kenton Clinics and w. Johnny Richards while in hs, then at Juilliard 1967–72 and Eastman Arr. Lab. Pl. w. Lee Konitz; Phil Woods; Dizzy Gillespie; Jane Ira Bloom; Arnie Lawrence; Tom Pierson; Sonny Stitt; Doc Severinsen; etc., but mainly worked as comp./arr. Founded Natural Sound Wkshp. '71 on the belief that natural sounds are inherently cre-ative. This philosophy is incorporated in many of Nurock's jazz-classical comps., incl. *Sonata for Piano and Dog* and *The Bronx Zoo Events*. Nurock has writ-ten comps. for Theo Bleckmann and Sheila Jordan, as well as numerous theater gps.; also commercial work for B'way, films, TV incl. Woody Allen's *Stardust Memories* and the *Tonight Show*. He is a charter mem-ber of the bd. of dirs. of "Meet the Composer," and teaches at the New Sch. A book of his comps., *The Music of Kirk Nurock, Vol. I,* was publ. in '91. Favs: Monk, Ellington, Tristano. Fests: Germ. '83, '91; France '78, '86. CDs: Wergo; Adamo.

NUSSBAUM, ADAM, dms; b. NYC, 11/29/55. Studied in Norwalk, Conn., then w. Joe Cusatis and Charli Persip in NYC. Pl. w. Monty Waters, Albert Dailey 1976; Dave Liebman '78–81; John Scofield '78–83; Bob Brookmeyer '82–3; Stan Getz '82–4; Jim McNeely since '84; Geo. Gruntz since '84; Randy Brecker–Eliane Elias '84–5; Gary Burton '85; Richie Beirach–Ron McClure since '85; Gil Evans Orch. '83–6; Mike Stern '85–8; Toots Thielemans since '86; Michael Brecker '87–90; Eliane Elias since '88; Doky Bros. since '89; own trio w. John Abercrombie, Dan Wall since '91; James Moody in '90s. Has done extens. freelance work and is an adjunct profess. at NYU, the New Sch., and LIU. Favs: Baby Dodds, Elvin Jones, Mel Lewis, Roy Haynes, Sid Catlett. Fests: Eur., Asia since '78. Videos w. S. Getz; M. Brecker; G. Burton; J. Scofield; Gil Evans; D. Liebman. CDs: w. M. Brecker (GRP); John Scofield (Enja; Novus); Joey Calderazzo; Rick Margitza (BN); Tom Harrell (Cont.); Gil Evans (Evid.); Lee Konitz (MM); George Gruntz (TCB).

a

OATTS, DICK (RICHARD DENNIS), alto, tnr saxes, cl, fl; b. Des Moines, IA, 4/2/53. Father, Jack, pioneered jazz educ. in Iowa; bro. Jim pl. w. Kenton, Thad Jones–Mel Lewis. Stud. w. fath., then for one yr. at Drake U. Pl. club dates fr. age 13. Freelanced in Minneapolis-St. Paul 1972–7 bef. moving to NYC. Pl. w. Thad Jones–Mel Lewis Orch. '77–9; Mel Lewis Orch. and Qnt. '79–90, then Vanguard Jazz Orch., Bob Brookmeyer '81–4; Ray Mantilla '82–6; Joe Haider '82–91; Red Rodney '86–90; Eddie Gomez '87–91; Dial and Oatts w. Garry Dial since '89; also pl. w. Tito Puente; Machito; Fred Hersch; Jack McDuff; Teo Macero; Joe Morello; Flora Purim. Taught at NYU '81–4; Manh. Sch. of Mus. fr. '91. Fav. arrs: Brookmeyer, Dial. Fests: Eur., Japan, So. Amer., etc. since '77. TV: David Letterman. CDs: Steep.; Dial and Oatts (DMP); w. Mel Lewis (Tel.; M M); R. Rodney (Steep.; Den.); T. Talbert (Chart.); H. Meurkens; A. Farnham (Conc.); Bill Mays; Ted Rosenthal (JA); Gary Smulyan (CC); Vic Juris (Steep.); A Donelian (Sunny.); Stockholm Jo (Drag.).

O'BRIEN, FLOYD, tbn; b. Chicago, IL, 5/7/04; d. Chicago, 11/26/68. Frequent pl. w. the Austin High Gang in Chi. To NYC 1933; rec. w. Eddie Condon; Benny Carter; Albert Nicholas; Mezz Mezzrow; Gene Krupa; Jack Teagarden. Tour. w. Phil Harris '35–9; G. Krupa '35–40; Bob Crosby '40–42. Settled in LA '43–48; pl. w. J. Teagarden; Wingy Manone; S. Sherock; Freddy Slack. From '48 in Chi. w. Bud Freeman; Art Hodes; et al. One of the first white trombonists to emulate the classic NO style; admired for the warmth of his solo work and the high quality of his perf. in improvised ensembles. CDs: w. Benny Carter (BB, Class.); Fats Waller (BB; BBC); Mezz Mezzrow (BB); Krupa; Condon; Bud Freeman (Class.); Bob Crosby (Swaggie); Jess Stacy (ASV).

O'BRIEN, HOD (WALTER HOWARD), pno; b. Chicago, IL, 1/19/36. Professional mus. in family on mother's side. Stud. priv., then at Oberlin Cons., Manh. Sch. of Mus. 1954–7. Made prof. debut in Conn. '50. Subbed for Randy Weston in Lenox, Mass. '55. Led own gp. at Avaloch in Lenox '56–7; then pl. w. Oscar Pettiford in NYC '57–8; J. R. Monterose–Elvin Jones in Albany '58–9; house band at club on Staten Island, backing Phil Woods, Freddie Hubbard, Charlie Rouse, Lee Konitz, etc. '60–3. Stud. math and psych. at Col. U. '64–9 (B.S. '69); then worked as computer programmer, research assistant at NYU '69–74; also stud. comp. w. Hall Overton, Chas. Wuorinen during this time. Owned jazz club, St. James Infirmary, in NYC '74–5; pl. in house rhythm section w. Beaver Harris, Cameron Brown backing Roswell Rudd; Sheila Jordan; Chet Baker; Zoot Sims; Al Cohn; Pepper Adams; Archie Shepp; etc. Pl. w. Marshall Brown '75; Russell Procope–Sonny Greer '77; trio w. Joe Puma at Gregory's, NYC '77–82. Tour. w. Stephanie Nakasian (later his wife) fr. '82. O'Brien taught at Turtle Bay Mus. Sch., NYC '72–5; in '90s at U. of Va. where he did two-pno. concert w. Barry Harris '95. Favs: Dave McKenna, Tommy Flanagan, Hank Jones. Fests: Eur. w. Nakasian fr. '84. CDs: CC; Res.; VSOP; w. Nakasian (VSOP); Chet Baker–Warne Marsh (CC); *Three Trumpets* w. Donald Byrd, A. Farmer, I. Sulieman (Prest.); Danny D'Imperio (Sack.).

O'BRYANT, JIMMY, cl, alto sax; b. Arkansas or Louisville, KY, ca. 1896–1900; d. Chicago, IL,

6/24/28. Best known for his recs. on cl. w. Lovie Austin's Blues Serenaders 1923–26. Also rec. w. Ida Cox, King Oliver '34; led his own Washboard Band '23–26. One of the most frequently rec. Chi. jazz clarinetists, his melodic style was often compared with that of Johnny Dodds. CDs: RST; w. Austin (Class.); Cox (Black Swan).

O'DAY, ANITA (Anita Belle Colton), voc; b. Chicago, IL, 10/18/19; d. W. Los Angeles, 11/23/06. Dance marathon contestant in the early 1930s; started singing prof. while still a teenager; worked w. Max Miller combo at Three Deuces in Chi. Join. Gene Krupa early '41, quickly establishing a reputation w. her husky sound and strong rhythmic phrasing. Biggest hits w. Krupa were "Let Me Off Uptown" (duet w. Roy Eldridge) and a wordless vocal on "That's What You Think." Sang w. Stan Kenton '44–5; rec. pop hit, "And Her Tears Flowed Like Wine." Rejoin. Krupa '45–6 bef. start. to work as a solo act. Rec. several important albums for Verve in mid '50s; had intermittent problems caused by heroin addiction. App. at NJF '58 in a perf. memorialized in the classic docu. film, *Jazz on a Summer's Day*; video (New Yorker). Tour. Japan '63 and '66. After nearly losing life to a drug overdose, finally broke a sixteen-year addiction in '68. Tour. Engl. '70; Eur. '71; perf. at Berlin JF, NJF, and MJF in early '70s; to Japan again in mid '70s. 50th year in jazz concert at Carnegie Hall '86. From late '80s cont. to tour, do club dates and jazz fests; app. at the Vine St. Bar & Grill, July '92. Describing her style, O'Day said, "I started out learning riffs, and I used to try to put a riff into everything I did until I got to where I could really do it. And then somebody said, 'Hey, we've got a jazz singer here.' So I guess that's what I am." In '89 John Wilson of the *New York Times* called her "funny, swinging and convincingly the best jazz singer performing today." Polls: *Esq.* Silver Award '45; *DB* '44–5; NEA Jazz Masters Award '97. Films: *The Gene Krupa Story; Zig Zag; The Outfit*. TV: *60 Minutes* '80. Book: autobiography, *High Times, Hard Times* w. George Eels (Putnam) '81. CDs: Sig.; Verve; DRG; Evid.; Pab.; w. Krupa (Col.); Kenton (Mos.; M&A); Nat King Cole (M&A).

O'FARRILL, ARTURO JR., pno, kybds, arr; b. Mexico City, Mexico, 6/22/60. Father, Chico O'Farrill. Stud. priv. fr. age 6, then at HS of Mus. and Art 1974–6; Manh. Sch. of Mus. '87–9; comp. w. David del Tredici at City Coll., NYC. First prof. exper. w. club date bands in hs. Pl. w. Artie Simmons' Jazz Samaritans '75; own sxt. The Untouchables '75–8; Manny Duran bb '76; own qt. Trachus '76–7. Guest soloist w. Machito '77. Pl. w. Carla Bley '79–82; Earl

McIntyre '80–91; Tony Dagradi '81; D. Sharpe, Band, Noel Pointer '81–2; Renée Manning '81–91; Gary Valente, Bobby Reveron's Jazz Criollo, own gp. '82. Mus. dir. for gospel gp., Liberate Wailing Wall '83–6. Had number one single in UK w. rap gp., J. Walter Negro and the Looze Jointz '84. Pl. w. Mobi Jazz Band '87–91; Dreamtime '88–90. Mus. dir. for Harry Belafonte '88–91. Pl. w. Lester Bowie '89; Latin Jazz USA bb; Howard Johnson's Gravity '90–1; Mobi Sxt. '91. Chico O'Farrill bb, pno. & mus. dir., fr. '91. Worked extensively as a commercial studio mus. fr. '77. Also dir. of the Center for Mus. Perf. at NYU. Favs: Monk, Herbie Nichols, Hancock. App. in solo pno. series at Kool JF, NYC. CDs: Mile.; w. C. O'Farrill (Mile.); Renée Manning (Ken); Carla Bley (Watt).

O'FARRILL, CHICO (ARTURO), comp, arr, cond; b. Havana, Cuba, 10/28/21; d. NYC, 6/27/01. Son, Arturo O'Farrill. Began pl. pno. at age 19; first stud. in comp. w. Felix Guerrero in Havana. Stud. law for a year. In US he took up tpt. while att. mil. sch. in Gainesville, Ga 1936–40. Pl. w. Armando Romeu at Tropicana, other Cuban bands until '48; worked as arr. fr. '46. Moved to NYC '48. Stud. w. Bernard Wagenaar; Stephan Wolpe; Hall Overton. Arr. for Benny Goodman ("Undercurrent Blues" '49), Machito, Miguelito Valdes, Stan Kenton, Dizzy Gillespie '50s. Wrote *Afro-Cuban Jazz Suite* '50; *Manteca Suite* '54. Tour. and pl. at Birdland w. own band '53–late '50s. Moved to Mexico late '50s. Presented jazz concerts in Mexico City '62–3; also feat. w. own orch. on TV series. Premiered Wind Qnt. '63. Ret. to US '65. Worked briefly in LV bef. ret. to NYC. Arr. and mus. dir. for CBS TV prog. *Festival of the Lively Arts* '65. Arr. for Count Basie Orch. fr. '65; Buddy DeFranco's Glenn Miller Orch., Cal Tjader '67; Clark Terry '70. Involved in commercial arr. for radio and TV spots fr. '71. First Symphony premiered in Mexico City '72. Comp. and arr. for Kenton, Candido '73; Frank Wess, Gato Barbieri '74. Cond. concerts by Machito, Dizzy Gillespie, others fr. mid '70s. Cond. concerts by Miami U. Jazz Band '88; UMO Orch. in Helsinki '89; Carnegie Hall Jazz Orch. '90; Mario Bauza '91–2. Own bb for Jazz at Lincoln Center, Nov. '95; weekly at Birdland, NYC fr. '98. Cond. his *Manteca Suite* and *Afro-Cuban Jazz Suite* at Lincoln Center '98. Comps. incl. *Tanga Suite in Five Movements* and *Carnegie 100*, commemorating the 100th anniv. of Carnegie Hall, both '91. Favs: Gil Evans, Sy Oliver. TV: Mex. TV late '50s-early '60s. Fest: Chicago JF '98. CDs: Verve; Mile.; w. M. Bauza (Mess.); Gillespie (Verve; Pab.); C. Parker (Verve); Basie (MPS); w. Goodman; Kenton (Cap.).

OGERMAN, CLAUS (Klaus Ogermann), comp, pno; b. Ratibor, Germany (since WWII, Raciborz, Poland), 4/29/30. Studied classical pno. in Nüremburg; pl. and rec. w. Kurt Edlehagen and Max Greger 1950s. Moved to US '59; had almost immediate success as arr. conducting orch. on countless albums by jazz, pop, and r&b artists. Arr. memorable albums for Antonio Carlos Jobim; Oscar Peterson; Bill Evans; Frank Sinatra; Wes Montgomery; Stan Getz; et al. Composed more jazz works in '70s, incl. *Some Times*, a jazz ballet '72; *Time Present and Time Past*. Rec. several albums feat. Michael Brecker in late '70s, early '80s, and early '90s. Despite his great variety of technical skills, Ogerman expresses a direct and simple explanation of his music: "I want it to sound good and hopefully it will mean something." CDs: GRP.

O'HARA, BETTY (IRENE), all brass instruments, voc, comp-arr; b. Morris, IL, 5/24/25; d. Sherman oaks, CA, 4/18/00. Mainly self-taught, first on tpt. Worked extensively around US and overseas w. Billy Vaughn in '70s. Active as studio tpt. player; also acquired a jazz reputation in such gps. as Dick Cary fr. '70; Maiden Voyage fr. '80; Jazz Birds Qnt; Dick Cathcart fr. '89. Rec. LP for Magnagraphic '85, overdubbing all the horns, arr., and singing. Mainly known as a valve trombonist, she made a feature of the double-bell euph., flg., etc., and was a singer of personal charm. CDs: Del.; w. Rick Fay (Arb.).

O'HIGGINS, DAVID, saxes, fl, EWI; b. Birmingham, England, 9/1/64. Studied mus, at City U., London 1983–5. First instrument, tpt., at age 7. Began prof. career at age 14, start. the Derbyshire Youth Jazz Orch. Moved to London '83; worked w. NYJO '83–6; Mezzoforte '85–9; Cleo Laine–J. Dankworth from '86; various others gps. incl. Jason Rebello '90–1; own gps. since '83. Tours throughout Eur.; Malta; Ireland; Iceland; Tunisia; Japan w. Salif Keita; app. at Montreux JF w. own gp., Roadside Picnic '89. Much TV work, incl. *Meeting the Queen* w. NYJO; *Wogan* w. Laine; numerous radio broadcasts w. own band and others. Received Cleo Laine Personal Awards to a Young All-Musician; has taught at Laine and Dankworth's Wavendon Sch., as well as Royal Acad. of Mus. and Guildhall Sch. of Mus. Also perf. w. Nancy Wilson; John Williams; Randy Crawford; Shorty Rogers; Jimmy Witherspoon; The Four Tops; and others; also as classical musician w. London Symph. Orch., Scottish Chamber Orch. Favs: C. Parker, S. Turrentine, B. Mintzer, M. Brecker. CDs: EFZ; BMG; Hep; w. Rebello (Novus); J. Dankworth (Sepia).

OHNO, SHUNZO (aka Shunzo Ono), tpt, flg; b. Gifu, Japan, 3/22/49. Cousin pl. vln. Pl. euph. in hs;

self-taught on tpt. Pl. in Tokyo w. Keiichiro Ebihara's Lobsters fr. 1968; Sound Limited, Soul Media late '60s–'70; Geo. Otsuka '70–3. Join. and tour. w. Art Blakey's Jazz Messengers '73, then moved to NYC. Pl. in NYC w. Blakey '74; Roy Haynes' Hip Ensemble '75; Norman Connors '75–7; Machito's Afro-Cuban Orch '81–3; Gil Evans '83–8. Tour. Japan w. Super Sounds w. Herbie Hancock, Wayne Shorter, Larry Coryell, Buster Williams '85–7. Pl. w. Williams fr. '91. Favs: Miles Davis, Lee Morgan; arr: Gil Evans. Fests: all major fr. '73. TV: *Music of the World* w. Blakey; MJF w. Gil Evans, Eur TV w. G. Evans, B. Williams, CDs: King; ProJazz; InnerCity; w. Gil Evans (Evid.); Buster Williams (Den.).

OKEGWO, UGONNA, bs, el bs; b. London, England, 3/15/62. Raised in Münster, Germ. Began on el. bs. Stud. in Berlin w. Walter Norris, Jay Oliver 1987. Pl. in Berlin w. Chas. Tolliver, Dizzy Reece July '88. Moved to NYC '90, stud. w. Cecil McBee. Pl. w. Jon Hendricks fr. '92; Jacky Terrasson fr. '93. Freelanced in NYC w. Jean Du Shon, Big Nick Nicholas '89; Carrie Smith, Joseph Jarman '91; Clifford Jordan bb, Monte Croft, Steve Davis, Tess Marsalis, Leon Parker, Geoff Keezer, Peter Leitch, Mingus Dynasty, Joshua Redman, Tolliver–Reece '92. Favs: Jimmy Garrison, Paul Chambers, Buddy Catlett. Fests: all major w. Hendricks. CDs: w. C. Tolliver (Strata East); Leon Parker (Col.); Hendricks (Tel.); Terrason (BN).

OKOSHI, TIGER (TORU), tpt, comp; b. Ashita, Japan, 3/21/50. Started pl. at age 11; pl. in local bands; stud. w. Sadao Watanabe. Came to US on his honeymoon in 1972; enrolled at Berklee Sch. and grad. '75. Pl. w. Buddy Rich; Gary Burton; Michael Franks; John Scofield; et al. Organized his own gp., Tiger's Baku; tour. US, Can., So. Amer., and Eur.; app. at Montreal JF and NJF. First album, *Tiger's Baku*, released '80; app. in his gps. have been Mike Stern; Vinnie Colaiuta; and Jeff Berlin. Fourth JVC album, *That Was Then, This Is Now*, rel. '91. Much infl. by Miles Davis's early jazz-rock-fusion bands, Okoshi's mus. mixes lyrical tpt. lines w. brisk synth. and perc. accents and funk-driven rhythms. Rec. w. Burton (ECM) '78. CDs: JVC; w. Mordy Ferber (Enja); D. Grusin (GRP); Cercie Miller (Stash); Jerry Bergonzi (Evid.); Bob Moses (Gram.); Lorraine Desmarais (Scherzo).

OLIVER, KING (JOE), crnt, lead; b. on plantation near Abend, LA, 5/11/1885; d. Savannah, GA, 4/8/38. Blinded in one eye by an early childhood accident; pl. tbn. briefly, then crnt. Pl. in the Melrose Brass Band 1907; the Olympia Band under A. J. Piron '12–14; own band w. Sidney Bechet '15; Eagle,

Onward, and Magnolia bands; Kid Ory's band '17, where he was first billed as "King" Oliver. Moved to Chi. in '19, pl. in Lawrence Duhé and Bill Johnson bands. Later took over Duhé's band, named it King Oliver's Creole Jazz Band, and pl. at Deluxe Café, Peking Cabaret, and Dreamland '20–1; took band to SF and Bay Area '21–2, then ret. to Chi. to pl. Lincoln Gardens. In '22 Oliver sent for Louis Armstrong to join band, which now became popular for its unique two-crnt. breaks. Band's April '23 Gennett sess. marked its (and Armstrong's) rec. debut. The Creole Jazz Band feat. Honore Dutrey, Johnny Dodds, Lil Hardin (later Lil Armstrong), Bill Johnson, and Baby Dodds; it remains one of the most celebrated of all jazz orchs. When band broke up, Oliver went to NYC alone '24, then ret. to Chi.; form. his Dixie Syncopators. Pl. Plantation Café, Chi. '24–7; then tour., incl. Savoy Ballroom, NYC '27. For next three yrs. Oliver was based in NYC, lead., tour., and rec. w. pickup bands. Moved to Nashville, Tenn., briefly, then cont. tour. w. ever-changing band until '37, by which time dental problems had him assigning tpt. solos to others. After several unsuccessful Southern tours, settled in Savannah, doing menial work in obscurity until his death. Throughout his life, Armstrong cited Oliver as his true idol and only real musical mentor. Comps. incl. "Canal Street Blues"; "Dippermouth Blues" (aka "Sugarfoot Stomp"); and "West End Blues"; and w. Richard M. Jones, "Riverside Blues" aka "Jazzin' Baby Blues," which evolved into "Dixieland Shuffle," rec. by Bob Crosby. Books: *King Joe Oliver*, Walter Allen & Brian Rust, 1955, rev. by L. Wright, etc., Engl., 1987; chapter in *Jazz Masters of New Orleans*, Martin Williams, Da Capo. CDs: BB; Dec.; *Louis Armstrong/King Oliver* (Mile.): w. Clarence Williams (Collector's Classics).

OLIVER, SY (MELVIN JAMES), comp/arr, tpt, voc, lead; b. Battle Creek, MI, 12/17/10; d. NYC, 5/28/88. Parents both mus. teachers; stud. tpt. w. fath. Pl. w. Zack Whyte band; freelanced in Columbus, Ohio. Join. Jimmie Lunceford 1933 and quickly rose to prominence as trpt., voc., and arr. of charts that gave the band its distinctive sound; his style was marked by simple swinging effects, staccato phrases w. a touch of humor, and a brilliant sense of continuity and climax. His most widely acclaimed arrs. incl. "Stomp It Off" and "Dream of You" '34; "Four or Five Times"; "Swanee River"; "My Blue Heaven"; "Organ Grinder's Swing"; "For Dancers Only"; "Raggin' the Scale"; "Posin'"; "Annie Laurie" '37; "Margie"; "Sweet Sue"; "By the River St. Marie" '38; " 'Tain't Whatcha Do"; "Cheatin' on Me"; "Le Jazz Hot"; "Ain't She Sweet" '39. In Oct. '39 Oliver left Lunceford to join Tommy Dorsey band as arr. and

occasional voc., contributing such originals as "Easy Does It"; "Opus 1"; "Well Git It"; and arrs. of such standards as "Sunny Side of the Street" and "Yes Indeed"—all definitive in establishing the more jazz-oriented style of the band. After lead. his own band in the army '43–45, cont. working for Dorsey, but also led his own bands from '46 on recs. and in person; mus. dir. for Dec. and other rec. labels from '47. Led band in Paris '68–69; lengthy engagements w. his band at the Rainbow Room, NYC in '70s and '80s. Led repertory bands in concerts of mus. by Lunceford, Dorsey, Ellington, and Henderson. In '95 his widow, singer Lillian Clark, donated his manuscript band arrs. to the N.Y. Public Library for the Perf. Arts. CDs: Mob. Fid.; w. Lunceford (Dec.; Class.); T. Dorsey; Metronome All-Stars (BB); Billie Holiday (Dec.); Chris Connor (Beth.).

O'NEAL, JOHNNY, pno; b. Detroit, MI, 10/10/56. Father, Johnny, was singer-pnst. Self-taught. Pl. gospel pno. fr. 1969; first jazz gig w. Kenny Gooch in St. Louis '76. Pl. in Det. w. Bennie Carew '77; tour. midwest w. Clifford Murphy '78. Discovered by Ray Brown in Chi. and rec. first album as lead. w. Brown for Conc. '78 (not released until '83). Pl. w. Milt Jackson '78–9; Lionel Hampton '80. Led own trio in Atlanta, backing Lockjaw Davis, Nat Adderley, Dexter Gordon, Clark Terry '81. Moved to NYC '82; hired by Clark Terry for gig at the Blue Note on first day in NYC. Pl. w. Art Blakey '82–4, inc. fests in Japan. Perf. solo pno. (at which he excels) concert at Carnegie Recital Hall '84. Led own trio w. Dave Young; Terry Clarke fr. '85. Pl. w. Clifford Murphy–Kermit Walker '89; Buddy DeFranco–Herb Ellis '90. CDs: JT; Parkwood; Sophia; w. Blakey (Timel.).

ONISHI, JUNKO, pno, comp; b. Kyoto, Japan, 4/16/67. Family moved to Tokyo, where she began taking pno. lessons 1971. Decided to pursue jazz after hearing a Thelonious Monk rec. while in hs. Stud. in US at Berklee Coll. of Mus. '86–9; jammed w. Delfeayo Marsalis; Roy Hargrove; Masahiko Osaka; Sam Newsome; Antonio Hart. Tour. Eur. w. Slide Hampton '88. Moved to NYC '89. Pl. w. Jesse Davis at Augie's and on tour of Japan '90. Also tour. Japan w. Gary Thomas '90; Kenny Garrett '91; and worked w. Greg Osby, Joe Henderson, Ralph Peterson, Mingus bb '90–2. Ret. to Japan '92. Formed trio w. Tomoyuki Shima, Dairiki Hara; pl. w. Shigeharu Mukai; Motohiko Hino. Favs: Monk, Tatum, Ellington, Mingus, O. Coleman. Fests: JVC-NY w. Osby '90; NJF-Saratoga w. J. Davis '90; Mt. Fuji JF w. Rodney Whitaker, Billy Higgins. CDs: BN; w. Jackie McLean (BN).

O'QUINN, KEITH OLAN, tbn; b. Lebanon, MO, 4/21/52. Began on pno. and vln. bef. sw. to tbn. at age 10. Stud. w. Phil Wilson at Berklee Coll. of Mus. 1970–3. Pl. w. Buddy Rich bb '73–4; Lin Biviano bb '74; Maynard Ferguson '75. Moved to NYC late '75; pl. w. Lionel Hampton '75–7; Chuck Mangione '77–82; Gerry Mulligan '78–81; Louie Bellson bb '88–91; Bob Mintzer bb '84–91; Dizzy Gillespie bb '88. O'Quinn has also worked extens. as a studio mus. Favs: J. J. Johnson, Jack Teagarden, Urbie Green. Fests: Eur. since '73. CDs: w. Charles Mingus (Atl.); L. Bellson (MM; Tel.); G. Mulligan (DRG); B. Mintzer (DMP); Maria Schneider (Enja); John Fedchock (Res.); DMP bb (DMP).

ORCHARD, FRANK (FRANCIS), v-tbn; b. Chicago, IL, 9/21/14; d. NYC, 12/27/83. Grandmother owned Orchard Sch. of Mus. Stud. vln. fr. age 6 to 12; bjo., tbn., and tba. in hs; Juilliard Sch. (Inst. of Mus. Art) 1932–3. Pl. w. Stanley Melba '33; then out of mus., working as a salesman late '30s. Joined J. McPartland '41; pl. w. Bobby Hackett, Bill Reinhardt, Max Kaminsky, Wingy Manone, Joe Marsala early- to mid-'40s. Freelanced w. various Dixieland gps. in NYC to mid '50s; moved to Dayton, Ohio, then St. Louis. Ret. to NYC in '60s; perf. w. Billy Butterfield '69; occasionally app. at Jimmy Ryan's, early '70s. CDs: w. E. Condon (Sav.); Manone in Rex Stewart–Wingy Manone, *Trumpet Jive* (Prest.); Marsala (Class.).

ORE, JOHN THOMAS, bs; b. Philadelphia, PA, 12/17/33. Father pl. cello; moth. pl. pno. Stud. cello at New Sch. of Mus., Phila. 1943–6; bs. at Juilliard '52. Pl. briefly w. Tiny Grimes '53; then w. Geo. Wallington, Lester Young '54; Ben Webster, Coleman Hawkins '55; Bud Powell '55, '57. Led own trio in Hempstead, LI '58. Freelanced in NYC '59–60. Pl. w. Thelonious Monk '60–3; Double Six '64; Teddy Wilson '64–5; Powell '65; Earl Hines '77. App. w. True Blue All-Stars at the Jazz Standard '99. Fests: Eur.; NJF w. Monk. TV: *Tonight Show* w. Teddy Wilson '65. CDs: w. T. Monk (Col.; Riv.; Story.; LRC); L. Young (Verve); Elmo Hope (Evid.; Prest.); Cecil Payne (Del.).

OREGON. Jazz chamber gp. formed in 1971 by members of the Paul Winter Consort: Paul McCandless, Glen Moore, Ralph Towner, and Collin Walcott. Walcott was replaced by the Indian dmr./perc. Trilok Gurtu '86. Began rec. for ECM '83. Employing techniques from jazz, classical, and folk mus. and combining them w. a wide range of acoustic instrumental colors, Oregon's non-el. fusion occupied a unique place in jazz, being the antithesis of the more electronic sounds of the '70s and '80s. CDs: ECM; Vang.

ORENDORFF, GEORGE, tpt; b. Atlanta, GA, 3/18/06; d. Los Angeles, CA, 4/13/84. Early experience in Chi.; to LA 1925. Pl. w. Paul Howard '25–30; Les Hite '30–9, incl. recs. when Armstrong was fronting the Hite band. Pl. w. Ceele Burke in early '40s. After army service in '43 was semi-inactive in mus., working for post office but still pl. occ. w. Maxwell Davis, Ben Pollack, and others. CDs: w. Armstrong (Col.); L. Hampton (Jazz Class. in Digital Stereo).

ORIGINAL DIXIELAND JAZZ BAND. Quintet of white musicians in New Orleans, organized 1916. Original personnel comprised Nick La Rocca, leader and crnt.; Alcide "Yellow" Nunez, cl. (replaced in Oct. '16 by Larry Shields); Eddie Edwards, tbn; Henry Ragas, pno. (replaced in '19 by J. Russel Robinson); and Johnny Stein, dms. (replaced in '16 by Tony Sbarbaro, aka Spargo). The band was a sensational success in Chi. '16, then moved to NYC. During a residency at Reisenweber's Restaurant, started in '17, the band rec. and became, in effect, the first jazz band to do so (James Reese Europe's orch. rec. a few borderline jazz perfs. '13–14). The ODJB enjoyed great favor in London, working and rec. there dur. '19–20. The gp. disbanded '24 but reorganized briefly in '36. Sbarbaro, the last surviving sideman, died in '69. Although they were musically limited, both as improvisers and as rhythmic players, and despite the inability of most of them to read mus., they helped to draw worldwide attention to jazz and steer young musicians in that direction. Other bands, both black and white, were active when the ODJB emerged, but only the ODJB had the promotional advantage of recs. Among the tunes popularized by the band are "Tiger Rag"; "Livery Stable Blues"; and "Sensation Rag." CDs: BB.

ORIGINAL MEMPHIS FIVE. Dixieland jazz gp. led by Phil Napoleon and feat. Frank Signorelli, Jimmy Lytell, Miff Mole, dmr. Jack Roth, and, at various times, many other players. Rec. frequently between 1921 and '31. The name was occasionally used again in the '40s and '50s by Napoleon and Signorelli. One of the first white bands to establish major jazz popularity after the ODJB, w. particularly impressive solos by Lytell. CDs: Collector's Classics.

O'ROURKE, DAVID FRANCIS, gtr; b. Dublin, Ireland, 2/7/60. Father and bro. pl. gtr. Some pno. lessons at age 9. Mostly self-taught on gtr. Form. own qnt., Giant Steps 1981. Pl. duet engagement w. Louis Stewart; also subbed as lead. of Stewart's trio at Peacock Theatre; won RTE "Young Musician of the Future" competition and pl. w. RTE Concert Orch.

'82. Visited NYC for first time '83, jamming w. Bucky Pizzarelli and taking "one, five-hour lesson w. Pat Martino that really turned me around." Pl. concert w. 5-gtr. gp. incl. Stewart '88. Moved to NYC '89. In '91 rec. w. Larry Willis, Bob Cranshaw, Al Harewood; arr. and orchestrated *Porgy and Bess* medley for Bklyn. Philharm. Orch. w. Willis as soloist. Pl. at Tramps w. Kirk Lightsey, Donald Harrison '92; form. org. trio w. Oliver Von Essen, Dave Gibson; tour w. org. Seleno Clarke's qnt. fr. '93. Has taught gtr. at New Sch. Jazz Program. Favs: L. Stewart, W. Montgomery, P. Martino, G. Benson, G. Green. Fests: Cork JF w. Ronnie Ross '85; Teddy Edwards, Turk Mauro '88; Charles McPherson '90; K. Lightsey '94; C. Walton '95; JVC-NY w. H. Ousley, V. Fournier '92. CDs: Nighttown.

ØRSTED PEDERSEN, NIELS-HENNING (HNØP), bs; b. Osted, Denmark, 5/27/46; d. Ishoj, Den., 4/19/06. Mother a church organist. Stud. pno. first; took up bs. ca. 1958; Oscar Pettiford dur. his yr. in Copenhagen. By '62 was pl. w. such visiting Americans as Bud Powell; later pl. w. Roland Kirk; Brew Moore; Bill Evans; John Lewis. House mus. w. Kenny Drew at Montmartre Cafe in Copenhagen; while still in teens turned down offer to join Basie. Worked frequently in '60s and '70s w. Dexter Gordon; in '70s and early '80s int'l w. Oscar Peterson. Duo w. Allan Botschinsky in '80s. Also rec. w. Basie; T. Montoliu; Don Byas; et al. An astonishing virtuoso with a flawless sense of time, capable of some of the most creative solos ever played on the instrument. CDs: Steep.; Pab.; Mile.; Enja; Verve; w. Botschinsky (M.A. Mus.); Peterson; Joe Pass (Pab.).

ORTEGA, ANTHONY ROBERT (aka BATMAN), alto sax, cl, fl; b. Los Angeles, CA, 6/7/28. First prof. gigs w. Earle Spencer, LA late 1940s. To Eur. w. Lionel Hampton '53, where he freelanced after tour. Balance of '50s and early '60s pl. w. Sonny Stitt; Q. Jones; Herbie Mann; Maynard Ferguson; Blue Mitchell. In '60s many app. w. Gerald Wilson and Groove Holmes. Moved to Encinitas, Calif. '75; improv. soundtrack for film, *An Unmarried Woman*; works frequently w. wife, Mona (pno., vib.). An adept bebop pl., Ortega began to incorporate avant-garde elements into his pl. in the late '60s. Favs. incl. Ch. Parker, Stan Getz, Dexter Gordon. CDs: Hat Hut; w. Ella Fitzgerald (Rep.); Billy Taylor (Imp.); Johnny Hartman (Beth.); Jackie and Roy (Koch).

ORY, KID (EDWARD), tbn, comp, lead; b. La Place, LA, 12/25/1886; d. Honolulu, HI, 1/23/73. Began pl. bjo. in string band; went to NO w. Lewis Mathews; took over leadership of the band 1917; sidemen incl.

Johnny Dodds; King Oliver; and (later) Louis Armstrong; Johnny Dodds; Sidney Bechet; Jimmie Noone; and George Lewis. Moved to Calif. '19; in '22 rec. "Ory's Creole Trombone" and "Society Blues" as Ory's Creole Jazz Band (aka Spike's Seven Pods of Pepper); these were the first jazz rec. by a black gp. and, to some, the first genuine jazz rec. ever made. To Chi. '24; pl. w. King Oliver '25-7; Dave Peyton, Clarence Black, the Chi. Vagabonds, Leon Rene '27-9. During '25 and '26, Ory rec. w. Armstrong's famous Hot Five gp., incl. his own comp. "Muskrat Ramble." Retired from music dur. '30s to run poultry farm w. his bro.; returned to mus. during early '40s NO jazz revival w. Barney Bigard band '42 and on Orson Welles '44 network radio series. App. w. Armstrong in the '46 film *New Orleans*. Back in prominence, tour. successfully w. own band. In '54 "Muskrat Ramble" received a new lease on life when it was fitted w. lyrics and rec. by many pop artists. Acting/playing role in *The Benny Goodman Story*, '56; NJF and other JFs in late '50s. Retirement in '60s, moving to Hawaii '66. The most famous of the original "tailgate" tbn. players, Ory used the instrument for rhythmic effects, fills, and glissandi, but also pl. solos in a rough and forceful style. He had a profound infl. on many musicians, both in his early yrs. and after the NO revival. Won the *Record Changer* All-Time, All-Star Poll '51. CDs: Story.; Verve; GTJ; w. L. Armstrong (Col.; RCA); Jelly Roll Morton (BB); King Oliver (Dec.); Albert Burbank (Story.).

OSAKA, MASAHIKO, dms; b. Akita Pref., Japan, 9/28/66. Father pl. gtr. Began on dms. at age 10. Stud. in US at Berklee Coll. of Mus. 1986-9. Dur. this time, he worked reg. with Delfeayo Marsalis and jammed w. Roy Hargrove; Antonio Hart; Wynton Marsalis; Branford Marsalis. Won first prize at Music Fest USA w. D. Marsalis '89. Moved to NYC, tour. France w. Bill Evans '89. Ret. to Japan '90, settled in Tokyo. Pl. w. Mikio Masuda; Issei Igarashi Twin Horn Band; Shigeo Murayama's Suikyoza Orch.; Yutaka Shiina; Yoshihiko Katori bb; Makoto Kuriya's X-Bar Trio; etc. Form. own qnt. w. Tomonao Hara. Polls: *SJ* Critics New Star '93. CDs: PW (co-lead. w. Hara); w. Now's the Time Wkshop. (FunHouse); M. Masuda (JVC); M. Sato (JVC); Jazz Networks w. R. Hargrove, A. Hart (Novus); M. Kuriya (PW).

OSBORNE, MARY, gtr; b. Minot, ND, 7/17/21; d. Bakersfield, CA, 3/4/92. Studied vln. at age 9. Heard guitarist Charlie Christian w. Alphonso Trent's orch. in Bismarck, No. Dakota, in late 1930s; soon after, she sw. to el. guitar. In NYC in the early '40s, she rec. w. Mary Lou Williams; C. Hawkins; Mercer Ellington. In '46 led her own trio at Kelly's Stable; fr. '52 to

'63 pl. daily on Jack Sterling radio show. Perf. on Art Ford TV show in '50s. Freelance gigs and teaching '64–70. In '68 moved w. her husband, trptr. Ralph Scaffidi, to Bakersfield, cont. to perform occ. there, in LA, and NYC into the '90s. CDs: Stash; w. Esq. All-Amer. Poll Winners (BB); Ethel Waters (Milan); C. Hawkins (RCA); track on *The Women* (BB).

OSBY, GREG, alto, sop saxes, comp, lead; b. St. Louis, MO, 8/3/60. Professional debut at age 15. In 1978, after working w. local pop, blues, and top-40 gps., won scholarship to Howard U., Wash., D.C. Stud. at Berklee Coll. of Mus., Bost. 1980–3, majoring in comp. and arr. To NYC '83 to join Job Faddis. Began developing his own style w. the help of fellow saxist Steve Coleman, w. whom he formed M-Base (Macro Basic Array of Structured Extemporization), a collective of Bklyn.-based musicians dedicated to developing a new vocabulary utilizing highly stylized compositional and improvisational methods. In '85 Osby join. and rec. w. Jack DeJohnette's Special Edition. Made his rec. debut as a leader on JMT '87. Tour. and rec. w. Andrew Hill '89. Osby describes himself as a left-of-center player who refuses to play "token phrases, funk clichés, simplistic blues scales—to me that's a cop-out." Names Andrew Hill, Muhal Richard Abrams, and Von Freeman as "*my* mentors." CDs: BN, JMT; w. Terri Lyne Carrington (Verve); S. Coleman (DIW; Panagaea); DeJohnette (BN; Imp.); Robin Eubanks; Cassandra Wilson (JMT); Lonnie Plaxico (Muse); Rodney Jones (MM); Jim Hall (Tel.).

OTIS, JOHNNY (John Veliotes), dms, vib, pno, comp, lead; b. Vallejo, CA, 12/28/21. Self-taught on dms. From a Greek immigrant family. Grew up in the black section of Berkeley, Calif. Pl. w. territory bands of George Morrison, Lloyd Hunter, and Harlan Leonard bef. lead. own bb at Club Alabam, LA 1945; tour. w. great success as r&b star, introducing such singers as Little Esther and Willie Mae Thornton. Occ. jazz gigs, incl. rec. date w. Lester Young. Radio dj and host of weekly live TV music show for several yrs. '50s. Has owned rec. labels and mus. publ. cos. over the yrs. but cont. to lead jazz and r&b bands around Calif. into '90s. *Listen to the Lambs*, an autobiog., was publ. in '66 by W. W. Norton. CDs: w. Lester Young (BN); Illinois Jacquet (Mos.).

OTIS, SHUGGIE (Johnny Alexander Veliotes), gtr; also bs, dms, pno; b. Los Angeles, CA, 11/30/53. Studied dms. w. fath. Johnny Otis, at age 4; took up gtr. at age 11; mainly self-taught. Stud. film scoring w. Albert Harris. Rec. debut at age 13 in father's album, *Cold Shot* on Kent. Toured int'l off and on w. Johnny Otis show 1965–89. Led own band; gigged

and/or rec. w. Gerald Wilson (his father-in-law); Red Holloway; Al Kooper; Don "Sugar Cane" Harris; Gene "Mighty Flea" Conners; Preston Love; Ginger Baker; Charlie Haden. Active in blues and rock in '70s and '80s, rec. own albums for Epic. Favs: Jimi Hendrix, B. B. King, T-Bone Walker. CDs: Epic; w. Gerald Wilson (Disc.).

OTTAVIANO, ROBERTO, sop, sopranino, alto, tnr saxes, cl, bs-cl, comp, arr; b. Bari, Italy, 12/21/57. Began on dms., then sw. to cl. and sax. Stud. at Bari U. Mus. Ctr. 1972–6; Cons. of Bari '77–80; also priv. w. Steve Lacy; Evan Parker; Federico Mondelci; Charlie Mariano. Pl. w. Andrea Centazzo '80–6; Enrico Rava fr. '80; studio orch. w. soloists Art Farmer; Ernie Wilkins; Dizzy Gillespie; Buck Clayton '82–5; Georg Grawe fr. '83; John Lindberg Revolving Ens. '85–6; Franz Koglmann, Franco D'Andrea fr. '85; Nexus '86–8; Maarten Altena '88; Giorgio Gaslini fr. '88; duos w. Ernst Reiseger, Keith Tippett, Franco D'Andrea, Francis Bebey, Pierre Favre, Barre Phillips fr. '90; Albert Mangelsdorff, Oliver Johnson, Mal Waldron, Ran Blake, Phil Minton, Steve Swallow, Sergei Kuryokhin, Tony Coe fr. '91; Tom Varner, Gerry Hemingway, Grand Orch. Nazionale, New Mus. Ens. fr. '92. Ottaviano has led his own trio '79–80; sxt. '83; qt. '84–5; Six Mobiles fr. '86; Network w. Ray Anderson, Henry Texier, Barry Altschul '91; Osservatori Silenziosi w. E. Rava, Stefano Battaglia, B. Phillips, P. Favre. He is the author of two instructional books, *Il Sax: Lo Strumento* (Padova Press), *La Itoria, Le Techniche*; and *Expanding the Horn*. Comp. film mus. for the French dir. Raimond Depardon. On the faculty of the Cons. of Bari fr. '89. Favs: Steve Lacy, Dave Liebman, Evan Parker. Polls: *Cadence* '89; *Musica Jazz* '87, '91. Fests: all major in Eur.; India '84; US '88; No. Africa '90. TV: *Agenda* w. Steve Lacy '81; *Jazz Yatra*, Bombay '84. CDs: Red; Spl.; w. Favre (ECM); F. Koglmann; G. Grawe (hatArt); G. Gaslini (SN).

OTTER, NED (NELSON), tnr sax; b. Huntington, NY, 5/29/59. Began on alto, inspired by older bro. Stud. at HS of Perf. Arts 1974–7; w. Geo. Coleman fr. '77. Pl. w. Red Rodney '79; Clark Terry bb '81; Geo. Coleman Octet fr. '87; Dizzy Gillespie bb '88. Otter, who worked as a pno. tuner fr. '81 to '88, works as a computer programmer. Did series of concerts at Stella Adler Theater in late '90s. Rec. as a sideman w. Shirley Scott for Muse '91. Favs: Geo. Coleman, Sonny Rollins, Hank Mobley. Fests: Eur. '81, '88. CDs: NO 1.

OUSLEY, HAROLD LOMAX, tnr, alto saxes, fl, digital horn; b. Chicago, IL, 1/23/29. Studied w. Walter Dyett at DuSable HS. Pl. w. circus bands 1949–55; King Kolax, Miles Davis early '50s; Billie Holiday, Joe Williams, Howard McGhee mid '50s; Dinah Washington '58. Pl. w. Clark Terry, Bud Powell in Paris '59. Returned to US '60, pl. w. Terry, McGhee, Machito, Joe Newman fr. early '60s; Jack McDuff fr. mid '60s; own gps. fr. '66; L. Hampton '70s; C. Basie mid '70s; also sub. for Paul Gonsalves w. Duke Ellington. Perf. w. many blues and r&b mus. incl. Ruth Brown; Percy Mayfield; Sunnyland Slim; Big Maybelle; Jimmy Witherspoon; Charles Brown. Pl. w. Bill Doggett '92. Ousley presents a variety of jazz and jazz hist. progs. in NYC schs. and is a staff member of the Groves Therapeutic Counseling Service, specializing in mus. therapy. Heads jam sessions at Jamaica Market, Queens, N.Y. Favs: Gene Ammons, Lester Young, Don Byas, Ben Webster, Charlie Parker. Polls: BMI Jazz Pioneer. Fests: Eur., Asia, So. Amer., Carib. fr. '60. Film: app. in *Cotton Comes to Harlem*. TV: own cable show in NYC, *Harold Ousley Presents* '92; Joe Franklin. CDs: J's Way; Beth.; Atl.; w. Geo. Benson (Col.); D. Washington (Em.).

OVERTON, HALL F., pno, comp, teacher; b. Bangor, MI, 2/23/20; d. NYC, 11/25/72. Studied at Juilliard 1947–51; priv. study w. Darius Milhaud and Wallingford Riegger. Army 1942–5; occ. jazz perfs. and recs. in late '40s and early '50s w. Teddy Charles; Jimmy Raney (two of many who also stud. w. him); Stan Getz; P. Woods; O. Pettiford; etc.; duo rec. w. Dave McKenna (Beth.). Primarily a classical comp.; pno. sonata and string qt. presented at Composer's Forum concert, NYC '54; *Symphony for Strings* perf. at Cooper Union '56. Best-known in jazz as a comp./teacher who understood the special demands of improv. and as arr. (incl. an orchestration of a Monk solo) for concert by Thelonious Monk Orch. at Town Hall '59. Favs: Bud Powell, Silver, Monk. Also contributed articles to *DB* and *Jazz Today*. CDs: w. Raney (Prest.); Monk (Riv.; Col.).

OWENS, CHARLES (Charles M. Brown), tnr sax, fl, woodwinds, comp; b. Phoenix, AZ, 5/4/39. Studied at San Diego St. Coll., in air force, and at Berklee Coll. in early 1960s. Pl. w. Buddy Rich '67–9; Mongo Santamaria '69–70. During '70s worked w. jazz gps., incl. Gerald Wilson; Bobby Bryant; Paul Humphrey; blues musicians—incl. John Mayall— and rock musicians, such as Frank Zappa, with whom he toured Eur. in '72. In '80s worked frequently on oboe, Eng. horn, and fl. w. James Newton and John Carter; also toured Eur. w. Horace Tapscott '87 and pl. bari. sax w. Mercer Ellington. A skillful soloist on a number of different instruments. CDs: w. Carmen

Bradford (Evid.); Jimmy and Jeannie Cheatham (Conc.); Buddy Rich (PJ); Jazz Underground (Imp.).

OWENS, JIMMY (JAMES ROBERT JR.), tpt, flg; b. NYC, 12/9/43 Studied w. Donald Byrd at HS of Mus. and Art 1958–61; w. Carmine Caruso, Henry Brant '61–2. Later stud. w. Roland Wiggins at U. of Mass. (M. Ed. '75). Jammed w. Miles Davis '58. Pl. w. Marshall Brown's Newport Youth Band '59–60; Slide Hampton '62–3; L. Hampton '63–4; M. Ferguson, Gerry Mulligan '64; Chas. Mingus, Hank Crawford '64–5; Herbie Mann '65–6; Max Roach mid '60s; Thad Jones–Mel Lewis Orch. '66; NY Jazz Sxt. '66–8; Clark Terry bb; Billy Taylor band on David Frost TV show late '60s. Perfs. and tours w. Duke Ellington Orch. '67–9; Dizzy Gillespie bb '68; Young Giants of Jazz '73; C. Basie Orch, Chuck Israels' Nat'l Jazz Ens. '70s. Also pl. w. Eur. radio orchs. Founding member of Collective Black Artists '69. Led own gps. fr. '69. Active in arts admin. in NYC, serving on the boards of NARAS '71–4; NEA jazz panel '72–6; NY Jazz Repertory Co. '74–5; NY State Council on Arts '75–81; Amer. Arts Alliance '77–83. Taught at Jazzmobile '75–84; dir. of wkshp. prog. '84–5. Tpt. chairman of Nat'l Assoc. of Jazz Educs. '82–4. His comp. credits incl. scoring off-Bway play, *Split Second*; PBS-TV film, *Conversations With Roy De Carava*, and ballets for the Rod Rodgers Dance Co. Leads two gps., Jimmy Owens Plus and Jazz in the Middle Ages. The latter feat. such middle-aged musicians as Billy Harper; Gary Bartz; Sonny Fortune; Kenny Barron; Buster Williams, who are frequently overlooked by the mainstream media. Vice-president of Jazz Foundation of America which administers the Jazz Musicians Emergency Fund. Owens cont. to be very active as a teacher and clinician on the subjects of jazz, jazz hist., and the business of mus. On faculty at SUNY-Old Westbury '81–6; Queensborough Comm. Coll. '84–5. Cond. wkshps. for high schools in Wash., D.C.; Va.; Miss. and Virgin Islands, late '90s. Polls: *DB* Critics TDWR '67; *Black Enterprise* mag. TV: David Frost w. Billy Taylor; *Black Journal*; Eur. TV w. Ellington. Under commission from Martin Luther King HS, NYC, wrote *Martin Luther King Suite* '98. CDs: w. Norman Simmons (Milljac); Jazzmobile All-Stars (Taylor-Made); Donald Byrd (BN); Mike Longo (CAP); Heiner Stadler (JA); Joe Henderson (Verve); Kenny Burrell (Conc.); Pete LaRoca Sims (BN); Booker Ervin (Prest.); Mingus Dynasty (Elek.).

OXLEY, TONY, dms, perc, comp; b. Sheffield, Yorkshire, England, 6/15/38. In Black Watch mil. band 1957–60. Led own qnt. in Sheffield '60–4, then pl. w. Derek Bailey '64–7. Moved to London

'67, where he bec. house dmr. at Ronnie Scott's, accomp. such visiting mus. as Sonny Rollins; Bill Evans; Stan Getz; Lee Konitz; and Charlie Mariano. Co-founded Incus rec. label w. D. Bailey and other mus., also founded Jazz Composer Orch. '71. Organized and taught jazz courses at Barry Summer Sch. '73. Formed own gps.: Angular Apron '74; SOH w. Alan Skidmore, Ali Haurand. Perf. and tour. Eur. w. Johnny Griffin; Art Farmer; Joe Henderson; Chas. Tolliver; John McLaughlin; Barry Guy; many others. Worked w. Geo. Gruntz on the mus. to the film *Steppenwolf*, prod. by Gruntz. Moved to Germ. in '79, where he conts. to lead his Celebration Orch. Favs: Blakey, Elvin Jones, Dolphy, Coltrane, Bill Evans. Polls: numerous awds. and commission from Arts Council of Gt. Britain. CDs: Incus; w. T. Stanko; John Surman; Paul Bley (ECM); J. McLaughlin (Polyd.; Marmalade); Cecil Taylor (FMP); E. Rava (SN); London Jazz Composers' Orch. (Intakt); Tony Coe; Anthony Braxton (hat Art); Derek Bailey (Ihens).

OZONE, MAKOTO, pno; b. Kobe, Japan, 3/25/61. Father, Minoru, a TV personality and club owner, pl. pno and org. Started on organ at age 10, pl. jazz in the style of Jimmy Smith; sw. to pno. two yrs. later after hearing Oscar Peterson perf. At 15 pl. w. Tadao Kitano and the Arrow Jazz Orch. Moved to US '80 to study at Berklee Sch.; pl. w. Gary Burton's band for six yrs. Debut album released on Col. '84; other albums incl. *After* and *Starlight* '90. Based in Japan fr. '89 to '92, he had a successful radio interview show. Returned to US '92, tour. w. Burton and Eddie Daniels in a show dedicated to Benny Goodman. A big hero in Japan, Ozone has become a major player in the int'l community, maintaining homes in Tokyo and Bost. "Makato," says Burton, "is the ideal combination of a talented musician and a talented performer, which is what makes him an instant success with audiences." Fest: Kool-NY JF '83. Won DB College Competition as Best Jazz Instrumentalist '82. CDs: Col.; Verve; JVC; GRP; w. Burton (ECM); Marc Johnson (Em.).

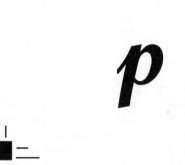

P

PAGE, HOT LIPS (ORAN THADDEUS), tpt, voc, lead; b. Dallas, TX 1/27/08; d. NYC, 11/5/54. Started pl. at age 12; was member of children's brass band w. Budd Johnson; pl. in band that accomp. Bessie Smith, Ma Rainey. With Walter Page's Blue Devils 1927–30; Bennie Moten, KC '31–5; briefly w. Basie '35–6; then led own bands in NYC. Rec. "Blues in the Night"; "Take Your Shoes Off, Baby"; "Motherless Child"; "St. James Infirmary" w. Artie Shaw in '41–2. Pl. the Paris JF '49. Page, who was infl. by Armstrong, both as singer and player (but certainly was his own man), perf. in a febrile style that was at its most impressive on his many successful blues records. Although no one truly posed a threat to Armstrong's throne, it has been said that Joe Glaser, Armstrong's mgr., signed Page in order to keep him out of his top client's way. CDs: High.; Story.; tracks on *52nd Street Swing* (Dec.); w. Billie Holiday (Col.; Story.); Bennie Moten; Artie Shaw (BB); Joe Turner (Dec.); Pete Johnson (Milan); Eddie Condon (Stash); M. Mezzrow (Story.); Ben Webster (Prog.); w. Basie in *Spirituals to Swing* (Vang.).

PAGE, WALTER SYLVESTER (aka BIG "UN"), bs; b. Gallatin, MO, 2/9/1900; d. NYC, 12/20/57. Not related to Hot Lips Page. Inspired by singing of folk songs and spirituals by his family. Pl. bs. drum w. neighborhood band, then horn in hs. Played bs. w. Bennie Moten off and on 1918–23; left to go w. roadshow band, which incl. Count Basie and Jimmy Rushing, and later stayed intact under his name as Walter Page's Blue Devils. Rejoin. Moten '31–4; briefly w. Jeter-Pillars Orch. in St. Louis. Join. Basie band '36, remaining until late '43 as integral part of legendary "All-American" rhythm section that was

one of the most important elements of Basie's success. App. w. Basie at *From Spirituals to Swing* Carnegie Hall concert '38. With Basie again '46–8; Hot Lips Page '49; Jimmy Rushing '51–2; Jimmy McPartland '52; then regularly in the band at Eddie Condon's club from November '52 until a few months before he died of pneumonia. Appeared on live CBS *Sound of Jazz* TV special '57, but was too ill to participate in the Col. rec. sess. that recreated the event. Page was considered the pioneer of walking bass. Fest: w. Ruby Braff, NJF '57. CDs: w. Basie (BB; Col.; Class.; Dec.); in *Spirituals to Swing*, Vang.); Billie Holiday (Col.); Moten; R. Braff (BB); Lester Young (Comm.); Buck Clayton; Eddie Condon (Mos.); Paul Quinichette (Prest.).

PAICH, MARTY (MARTIN LOUIS), pno, comp, arr; b. Oakland, CA, 1/23/25; d. Santa Ynez, CA, 8/12/95. First prof. job w. Gary Nottingham 1941–3 (other arr. was Pete Rugolo). Air Force band '43–6; after the war, stud. w. Mario Castelnuovo-Tedesco, earning B.A. and M.A. at LA Cons. In '50s worked freq. w. Jerry Gray; Shelly Manne; Peggy Lee; Shorty Rogers. Accomp. Dorothy Dandridge in London '56; pl. and arr. mus. for Disney film *Lady and the Tramp*. In '60s Paich became one of the most active comp./arrs. in Hollywood studios; staff arr. at NBC for the Dinah Shore and Andy Williams shows; comp./orchestrator of several works for the LA Neophonic Orch. '65–6; arr., cond., and rec. mus. for Ray Charles; Sammy Davis Jr.; Lena Horne; and Astrud Gilberto. In '89 he revived the Dek-tette, which acc. Mel Tormé on '50s recs., for a Japanese tour w. the singer. In '91 received the arr.'s award from the 6th annual Singers' Salute to the Songwriters. A dependable pnst., he was a prominent perf. on the Southern Calif. jazz scene of the '50s. CDs: VSOP; Disc.; Cand.; Conc.; w. H. Babasir–B. Enevoldsen (Noct.); Tormé (Conc.; Beth.; Stash); Ella Fitzgerald (Verve); Julio Iglesias (Col.).

PALMER, EARL C., dms, perc; b. New Orleans, LA, 10/25/24. Mother and aunt were a vaudeville team. Stud. pno., perc. at Grüenwald Cons. 1948–51. After tour. w. moth. and aunt as dancer, he settled in LA in '57 and soon earned a reputation as an all-round dmr., heard on countless pop, jazz, r&b recs. and TV shows. Pl. in films: *Hot Spot, Top Gun, Pretty Woman, The Fabulous Baker Boys, In Cold Blood.* Wide experience as teacher, giving clinics in US, Russia, Israel, many other countries. Executive on many committees; secretary-treasurer of Local 47 Mus.' Union '82–4; treasurer '90–2. Frequent jazz apps. w. Buddy Collette; Red Callender; Benny Carter; tour. Middle East w. Carter '75–6. CDs: w. Eddie Vinson (BB); D. Washington (Em.); Sam Cooke (Spec.); D. Gillespie (BN); Little Richard (Spec.).

PALMER, SINGLETON NATHANIEL, bs, tba; b. St. Louis, MO, 11/13/13. Studied pno. at age 12. Pl. bs. w. George Hudson in St. Louis and NYC fr. 1942–8. Rec. w. Clark Terry; join. C. Basie '48–50; left to form own gp., the Dixieland Six, pl. clubs in St. Louis. Fav: "The tuba player with Coon-Sanders." CDs: w. Basie (BB).

PALMIER, REMO PAUL (Palmieri), gtr; b. NYC, 3/29/23; d. NYC, 2/2/02. Planned to be an artist; pl. club dates to pay for art sch. Stud. harm., theory w. Tibor Serly. Made prof. debut w. Nat Jaffe 1942; then pl. w. Coleman Hawkins '43; Red Norvo; own gp. backing Billie Holiday on 52nd St. '44. Pl. on CBS radio series w. Mildred Bailey '44. With Phil Moore at Café Society '44–5. Rec. "All the Things You Are," "Groovin' High" w. Dizzy Gillespie '45; Teddy Wilson–Sarah Vaughan '46. Join. CBS staff '45; feat. on Arthur Godfrey show '45–72. Form. jazz qt. w. Hank Jones '72. Pl. night clubs w. Bobby Hackett early '70s; concerts w. Benny Goodman, Dick Hyman fr. '74. Perf. at Conc. JF "Guitar Explosion" w. Herb Ellis, Emily Remler, Howard Roberts, Tal Farlow, Barney Kessel '75. Concert in NYC w. Red Norvo, Louis Bellson, Teddy Wilson '85, issued on LP box *Swing Reunion* by Book-of-the-Month Club. Polls: *Esq.* New Star '45; Silver Awd. '46. CDs: Conc.; w. L. Bellson; Benny Carter–Amer. Jazz Orch. (MM); Gillespie (Sav.); Esq. All-Amer. Poll Winners; Lena Horne (BB); C. Parker (Rh.); L. Armstrong (RCA).

PAPA BUE (Arne Bue Jensen), tbn, lead; b. Copenhagen, Denmark, 5/8/30. Began as a merchant sea-man. Founding member of Royal Jazz Band 1953, which became Bohana Jazz Band, and, in '56, Papa Bue's Viking Jazz Band. Under his leadership, the band became an enormous success in Eur. jazz revival period. Pl. and rec. w. Chris Barber; Adrian Bentzon; Henrik Johansen; and many Amer. mus., incl. Geo. Lewis; Champion Jack Dupree; Art Hodes; Wild Bill Davison; Wingy Manone; and Edmond Hall. Papa Bue has cont. to lead this gp. into the '90s. Fest: NO '69. CDs: Timel.; Bell; Story.; as co-lead. w. Chris Barber (Story.).

PARENTI, TONY (ANTHONY), cl; b. New Orleans, LA, 8/6/1900; d. NYC 4/17/72. Played jazz on riverboats and in local clubs fr. 1914; led own band at Bienville Hotel '21. To NYC '27, subbed for B. Goodman in Ben Pollack band. After staff work at CBS, tour. w. Ted Lewis '36–42; led own band at Jimmy Ryan's. After two yrs. at Eddie Condon's club, worked in Miami Beach. Back in NYC '54, pl. in trio w. Zutty Singleton, Joe Sullivan. Pl. in house bands at Condon's and Ryan's in '60s, also TV w. Louis Armstrong, many studio dates, etc. One of the best all-around traditionalist musicians to emerge from the early NO jazz scene. He rec. LPs for Riv., Jazz., and other labels. CDs: Jazz.; Frog.; w. E. Condon (Dec.); Wild Bill Davison (Jazz.); Eddie Lang (Timel.); Jack Pettis (Kings Cross).

PARHAM, TINY (HARTZELL STRATHDENE), pno, org, comp; b. Kansas City, MO, 2/25/1900; d. Milwaukee, WI, 4/4/43. Led own gps. and app. as sideman in variety of Chi. clubs, incl. the Dreamland Café, during the 1920s. From the '30s worked as org. soloist in theaters and hotels until his death. Rec. w. own band for RCA Vict. '28–9. CDs: Class.; w. Junie C. Cobb (Collector's Classics); Johnny Dodds (Class.).

PARHAM, TRUCK (CHARLES VALDEZ), bs; b. Chicago, 1/25/13; d. Chicago, 6/5/02. Inspired by Walter Page. Pl. w. Zack White, doubling tba. and voc. 1932–4; Zutty Singleton '35; Roy Eldridge and/or Art Tatum '36–8 at Three Deuces in Chi. Came to prominence in the bands of Earl Hines '42 and J. Lunceford '42–7. Freelanced w. Muggsy Spanier '50–55; Louie Bellson, Herbie Fields '56–7; Art Hodes off and on fr. '57; and gigged w. Dorothy Donegan, Big Chief Russell Moore. Fest: JVC-NY JF '86. CDs: w. Earl Hines (BB); Little Bro. Montgomery (Earwig); Art Hodes; Edith Wilson (Del.); *Chicago Jazz Summit* (Atl.); Roy Eldridge (Topaz); M. Spanier (Story.).

PARIS, JACKIE, voc, gtr; b. Nutley, NJ, 9/20/27; d. NYC, 6/17/04. Uncle, Chick Paris, pl. gtr. w. Paul

Whiteman. Mainly self-taught. Won amateur contests as a child. Rec. for first job by Mills Bros. Pl. gtr. in trio w. Nick Jerret early '40s. In army '44–6, then stud. briefly at Scott Sch. of Mus. Rec. debut as leader on MGM '47 incl. "Skylark." Pl. and sang w. many 52nd St. combos, incl. Charlie Parker–Miles Davis '48. Made first vocal rec. of "'Round Midnight" w. Dick Hyman, Tommy Potter, Roy Haynes '49. Tour. w. Lionel Hampton as voc. '49–50. Worked as single in nightclubs fr. '50. Rec. w. Gigi Gryce–Donald Byrd '57. Began tap dancing late '50s. Perf. w. Lenny Bruce '59. Duo at Playboy clubs, resorts, etc., w. wife, Anne Marie Moss '60s. Rec. *Duke Ellington's Sound of Love* w. C. Mingus '74. Paris rec. as the leader of a qt. w. Jim McNeely and Adam Nussbaum '88. Taught at the New Sch. '89–91. His voice was a real jazz sound, whether on ballads or scatting. Favs: Anne Marie Moss, Ella Fitzgerald. Polls: *DB* New Star voc. '53; *Play.* '57–61. TV: Steve Allen '56; Music for Fun '59; Johnny Carson '60s; Mike Douglas '70s; Joe Franklin '70s-80s; CBC w. Rob McConnell. CDs: Em.; Aud.; Imp.; w. Mingus (Atl.); tracks in *The Complete Debut Recordings* (Deb.).

PARKER, CHARLIE (CHARLES CHRISTO-PHER JR.; "BIRD"; "YARDBIRD"), alto sax, tnr sax, comp, lead; b. Kansas City, KS, 8/29/20; d. NYC, 3/12/55. Moved to KC, Mo. in 1927. Pl. bari. horn in sch. band; moth. bought him an alto sax in '31. Left sch. at 15 to become full-time mus. Local musicians were critical of his work, but he matured dramatically after a summer resort job with George E. Lee's band. After that, intermittently w. Jay McShann, Lawrence Keyes, and Harlan Leonard '37–9. By the time he moved to NYC in '39, Parker's style already revealed aspects of the influential ideas associated with his mature yrs. Worked at Clark Monroe's Uptown House; made his first commercial recs. w. McShann '41; tour. w. McShann '40–42. Around this time met Dizzy Gillespie when he sat in w. McShann at the Savoy Ballroom. The styles of both players were uniquely individualistic and maturing rapidly along similar lines. They would become known in '45 as partners and virtual co-founders of the new jazz movement known as bebop. Regrettably, an Amer. Federation of Mus. strike, which started in Aug. '42, left a fascinating period in both Parker's and Gillespie's musical evolution undocumented for nearly two years. On leaving McShann, Parker ret. to NYC, where he often sat in at Minton's Play House and worked (cl. and alto sax) w. the bands of Noble Sissle '42 and (on tnr. sax) w. Earl Hines '43 (w. Gillespie in the tpt. section). Played briefly w. the Cootie Williams and Andy Kirk orchs., then went on

the road in '44 w. the orig. Billy Eckstine band, the first bb with a clear-cut policy of featuring the new bebop style in its solos and arrangements, but soon returned to New York and gigs on 52nd Street. First small group rec. w. Tiny Grimes for Sav. '44. Seven tunes for the Guild label w. Gillespie in Feb. and May '45 were considered the definitive sides that established the arrival of a new generation of jazz. Soon after the release of these recs., Parker and Gillespie became the twin focal points of interest in the then intensely active jazz world of 52nd St. Although respected by a growing number of young musicians, Parker—and Gillespie—had to deal with the antagonism of many mainstream jazz musicians and critics who actively opposed the new mus.

In late '45 (after having rec. his classics—"Now's the Time," "Billie's Bounce," and "Koko") Parker went to Hollywood to work w. Gillespie at Billy Berg's but found the local attitude hostile. Parker, who had been an active user of narcotics since his teens, broke down completely after a chaotic record session on the night of July 29, '46; he was arrested and committed to Camarillo State Hospital. After six mos. in the institution, he returned to LA, rec. two superb sessions for Dial (one featuring Erroll Garner) and then came back to NYC, opening at the Three Deuces with his own quintet. Worked in this format for the next few years, usually in NYC and Eastern cities. His sidemen during this time incl. Miles Davis, Red Rodney, and Kenny Dorham, tpt.; Duke Jordan and Al Haig, pno.; Tommy Potter, bs.; and Max Roach and Roy Haynes, dms. He also appeared intermittently with JATP from '46. The period from '47 to '51 was clearly Parker's most creatively productive. He was busy with concerts, night club gigs, radio apps., and recs.; his ensembles included his regular quintet; Machito's Afro-Cubans; and a string ensemble. After '51 he often worked as a traveling soloist with a variety of rhythm sections and back-up groups. His visits to Europe '49 and '50 (incl. the Paris JF and Scandinavia) were further documented by recordings. The last five years of Parker's life were beset by cycles of illness and cure, irregular and unpredictable performances, and difficulties with various authorities. In July '51, his NYC cabaret license was revoked—a common ploy by the Narcotics Squad to bring attention to the substance abuse problem. For Parker, the loss of the license meant that he could no longer work in NYC, forcing him to pick up work wherever he could until his reinstatement in '53. Plagued by uncertain employment, serious financial problems, and a complex of illnesses that included ulcers and cirrhosis of the liver, Parker suffered from a series of emotional and physical difficulties. In '54, after two suicide attempts, he voluntarily committed himself to Bellevue Hospital, NYC. Yet, remarkably, he appeared at a Town Hall, NYC, concert only a few months before his death, playing with a command as great as at any period in his career. On Mar. 4, '55, he made his final public app. at Birdland, the club that was named after him. He died a week later in the Stanhope Hotel apartment of his friend, the Baroness Pannonica de Koenigswarter.

Parker is the jazz world's Mozart, a musical genius who gathered together the traditional styles that had preceded him and transformed them into a brilliant new design. Like Mozart, his music was as fresh as it was whole; every note, every riff, every off-beat rhythm and extended harmony sounded precisely right. Even spontaneous improvisations sounded as well-planned and logical as carefully thought-out compositions. Despite little formal training, he was a man of remarkable technical skill, a fast reader, and a gifted composer/arranger. His best recordings were made with a small, informal combo, but he was proudest of his series of albums w. strings and woodwinds made fr. '50. His spontaneity was highlighted in recordings of unrehearsed appearances with the Woody Herman band in Kansas City and "The Orchestra" in Washington, D.C. In bringing the art of improvisation to a new peak of maturity, Parker had an inestimable influence on jazz musicians, regardless of their instrument. Since the mid 40's it has been almost impossible for new jazz players (and many pop and rock players) not to reflect, to some degree, a Parker influence. Acknowledging the world's debt to him, Lennie Tristano once observed: "If Charlie wanted to invoke plagiarism laws, he could sue almost everybody who's made a record in the last ten years." Parker comp. (usually for rec. dates) a series of instrumental numbers designed for unison interpretation by a quintet, but despite their casual genesis, these compositions display the same strikingly original melodic sense that was inherent in his improvised solos. His best known works are numerous, and incl. "Now's the Time" (later used as the basis for a r&b hit, "The Hucklebuck"; "Yardbird Suite"; "Confirmation"; and "Relaxin' at Camarillo." Video: *Bird*, Clint Eastwood (Warner) '88. Books: *Bird: The Legend of Charlie Parker*, Robert Reisner (Da Capo) '62; *Bird Lives*, Ross Russell (Quartet) '72; *Celebrating Bird*, Gary Giddins (Beechtree) '87. CDs: Sav.; Roost; Verve; BN; Rh.; Mos.; Stash; Up.; Jazz Classics; w. Jay McShann (Dec.); Metronome All-Stars (BB); Miles Davis (Sav.; Prest.); Gillespie (Verve; BB); Red Norvo (Jazz Classics).

PARKER, ERROL (Raphael Schecroun), dms, pno, comp, arr; b. Oran, Algeria, 10/30/25; d. NYC, 7/2/98. Mother was classical pnst., daughter, Elodie

Lauten, a comp. Began on African dms. at age 6, pno. at 14. As Ralph Schecroun, he pl. pno. w. Kenny Clarke–James Moody in Paris 1948–50; Django Reinhardt in Rome '50; Don Byas '50–9. Led own org. trio. Changed name to Errol Parker '60 in order to avoid litigation while simultaneously rec. as leader for two different labels. Led trio w. Geo. Lucas in Paris '60–4. Had a hit single w. "Lorre" in '64, then injured shoulder in car accident. By '67 Parker had changed his pno. style to accommodate his injury. Met Duke Ellington, who publ. two of his comps. through Tempo Mus. and encouraged him to come to the US in '67. Scored film *Des Garcons et Des Filles* by Etienne Perier '67. Moved to NYC '68. Founded own label, Sahara '71. Pl. pno. and dms. in the Errol Parker Experience w. Richard Davis, Bruce Johnson, Cornell Dupree, Monty Waters, Dewey Redman, Jimmy Owens, and others '72–81; dms. only in Errol Parker Tentet w. Wallace Roney, Philip Harper, Steve Coleman, Bill Saxton, Donald Harrison, Robin Eubanks, Patience Higgins, and others fr. '82. Parker occ. taught at the New Sch. Favs: Art Blakey; arr: Duke Ellington. Fests: Paris '83, '87; Antibes '64, '85; Netherlands '89. Book: *A Flat Tire on My Ass* (Cadence) '95; (Filipacchi) '96. LP: w. Kenny Clarke, *Paris Bebop Sessions* (Prest.). CDs: Sah.

PARKER, EVAN, tnr, sop saxes; b. Bristol, England, 4/5/44. Studied w. James Knott 1958–62. First gigs in Birmingham w. gp. inspired by John Coltrane Qt. early '60s. Moved to London '65. Pl. w. Spontaneous Music Ens. '66–8; Tony Oxley '69–72; Pierre Favre '69–71. Co-led Music Improv. Co. w. Derek Bailey '69–72. Pl. w. Peter Brotzmann, Chris McGregor '70; Globe Unity Orch., Alexander Von Schlippenbach fr. '70. Pl. in duo w. Paul Lytton '71–6; w. Brotherhood of Breath fr. '73; also perf. as unaccomp. soloist fr. '70s. Parker co-founded the Incus rec. label w. Bailey and Oxley '70. Author of *New/Rediscovered Musical Instruments* (Quartz/Mirliton). Favs: Coltrane, Dolphy, Bailey. Fests: all major in Eur. TV: Eur. TV. CDs: Incus; ECM; Leo; FMP; Ogun; Maya; Emanem; Chronoscope; Konnex; Ah Um; w. Music Improv. Co.; Derek Bailey (Incus).

PARKER, KIM, voc; b. NYC, 8/22/46. Won radio talent show as child. Mother, Chan, lived w. Charlie Parker 1950–4. Adopted Parker name and sang in musical theater while stud. jazz w. L,H&R. Moth. married Phil Woods '57. Traveled to Eur. w. Woods and Quincy Jones Orch. '59. Stud. drama at Hofstra U. '64; was named best vocalist at Villanova Intercollegiate JF. Did not perf. '67–79. Ret. to music w. perf. at Delaware Water Gap JF w. Al Cohn, Phil Woods '79. Worked as single at fests. and clubs in US and

Eur. fr. '79. Rec. w. pnsts. incl. Larry Gelb; Kenny Drew; Tommy Flanagan; Mal Waldron. Was the off-screen singing voice of Julie Christie in the French film *La Memoire Tatouee* '85. Fests: US and Eur. fr. '79. Films: *Nobody Knows Indio* '83; *Bizarre Rituals: Dances Sacred and Profane* '87. TV: Delaware Water Gap JF '83; Joe Franklin '83–5; *Jazz-In* in Swiss and Ger. TV '86. CDs: Musidisc; SN.

PARKER, KNOCKY (JOHN W.), pno; b. Palmer, TX, 8/18/18; d. Los Angeles, CA, 9/3/86. Played w. Tex. swing bands; rec. w. the Wanderers 1935; pl. w. Light Crust Doughboys while at Trinity U. in Waxahachie, Tex. '37–9. After army discharge, joined Zutty Singleton–Albert Nicholas trio in LA. Earned Ph.D. in Amer. studies, Kentucky Wesleyan Coll. and U. of South Fla. Gigged around NYC while teaching Eng. at Col. U; simultaneous careers as Eng. teacher and jazz concert lecturer at which he often demonstrated mus., ranging fr. Scott Joplin and James Scott to Dave Brubeck. Perf. and rec. w. Omer Simeon, Doc Evans, Tony Parenti, Carol Leigh '50s; also pl. w. Inez Cavanaugh at Chez Inez in Paris '52. Taught at Kent. Weslyn., Peabody Teachers Coll., U. of Kent. Rec. in '86 w. Joe Turner for Southland. Nominated for Grammy award. CDs: Jazz.

PARKER, LEO, bari sax; b. Washington, DC, 4/18/25; d. NYC, 2/11/62. Not related to Charlie Parker. First rec. on alto sax w. Coleman Hawkins 1944; bari. sax w. Billy Eckstine '44–46. Pl. w. Benny Carter; at Spotlite on 52nd Street w. Dizzy Gillespie gp. early '46. Earned some popularity as feat. soloist on Sir Charles Thompson's "Mad Lad." Rec. for Sav. Worked w. Illinois Jacquet gp. '47–50. During the '50s his career was hampered by problems w. drugs. He began a comeback in '61, rec. two albums for BN, but died of a heart attack early the following yr. A romping, deep-toned player infl. by the rhythmic side of Lester Young, and by Charlie Parker, he could also invest a ballad with tenderness. CDs: six tracks in *Prestige First Sessions. Vol. 1* (Prest.); w. Milt Jackson–Sonny Stitt (Gal.); Jacquet (BB; Mos.); Dexter Gordon (Sav.); Thompson (Del.).

PARKER, LEON EVANS JR., dms, perc; b. White Plains, NY, 8/21/65. Grandfather pl. dms.; moth. is semi-prof. jazz and r&b voc.; wife Lisa pl. fl. Primarily self-taught. Pl. w. Melvin Sparks, Carmen Leggio off and on 1984–6. House dmr. at El-C's in East Orange, N.J., also briefly w. Philip Harper at Blue Note club's after-hours jam '87. Pl. w. Jesse Davis, Peter Bernstein, Larry Goldings at Augie's '87–8; Kenny Barron at Fortune Garden '88; own gp. w. Lisa Parker in Eur. '89; own trio fr. '90; Sheila Jordan

in Japan '91; Joshua Redman fr. '92; Dewey Redman incl. three Eur. tours. Also worked w. Square Root; Danilo Perez; Geoff Keezer; Walter Bishop Jr.; Bill Mays; Gene Bertoncini; Arnie Lawrence; Jacky Terrasson. Parker's basic set up is a spare one: ride cymbal, snare dm., floor tom, and bs. dm.; but he also can perf. miracles w. only a ride a cymbal by using his sticks, mallets, and brushes to extract a variety of sounds and feelings that usually come from other parts of a regular drum kit. Also a very effective hand dmr. His rhythms creatively mix elements from Latin, funk, and world mus. with his solid grounding in jazz. Favs: Ray White, Ben Riley, Gene Jackson. Fests: Eur. fr. '89; Japan fr. '91. CDs: Col.; w. Terrasson (BN); Harvie Swartz (BM); Jesse Davis (Conc.); Dewey Redman; Bruce Barth (Enja); David Sanchez (Col.); V. Mayhew (Chiaro.).

PARKER, MACEO, alto, tnr saxes; b. Kingston, NC, 2/14/43. Inspired by uncle's band, "Bobby Butler and the Mighty Blue Notes." Maj. in music at No. Carolina A & T. Joined James Brown 1964 and remained off and on for 20 yrs. When Brown was jailed on a drug charge, Parker went out on his own, making his first album, *Roots Revisited*, which reached the #1 spot in *Billboard's* jazz charts. He went on to achieve consistent success in the r&b area, leading his own band. CDs: Verve; Novus; w. Fred Wesley (Ant.).

PARKER, WILLIAM, bs; b. Bronx, NY, 1/10/52. After learning cello, began pl. bs. in last yr. of hs. Stud. w. Milt Hinton; Richard Davis; Wilbur Ware; Jimmy Garrison. Pl. w. comedians, poets, folk bands. Became involved in New York "loft jazz" scene at the Firehouse; Studio Rivbea; Studio We 1971–5. Pl. w. Don Cherry at Five Spot. From late '70s part of collective gp., Other Dimensions Music. Pl. w. various Cecil Taylor gps. '80–91; then w. Charles Gayle; David S. Ware; Matthew Shipp. Own bands, fr. mid-'90s, incl. combo, In Order to Survive; and bb, Little Huey's Creative Music Orchestra. Favs: Jimmy Garrison, Wilbur Ware. CDs: BS; Zero In; Centering; Eremite; FMP; Silk.; Aum Fidelity; w. Taylor (Leo; FMP; hatArt; SN; Nica); D. S. Ware (Col.; DIW; Homestead; Silk.); Gayle (BS; Silk.; KFW); Shipp (Rise; Silk; Infinite Zero; hatArt); Roscoe Mitchell (BS); John Zorn–Derek Bailey (Avant).

PARLAN, HORACE LUMONT, pno; b. Pittsburgh, PA, 1/19/31. Private study from 1942. After a childhood attack of polio left his right hand partially paralyzed, Parlan developed a predominantly left-hand style. Pl. w. local gps. '52–7; worked in Wash., D.C. w. Sonny Stitt. Joined Ch. Mingus' Jazz Workshop '57–9; pl. w. Lou Donaldson '59–60; Booker Ervin '60–1; Eddie Lockjaw Davis–Johnny Griffin '61–2; Roland Kirk '63–6. Moved to Copenhagen '73. Tour w. Al Cohn–Zoot Sims '74; St. Dept. African tour w. Hal Singer; Japan w. J. Griffin '76. Fr. mid '70s extensive freelance work in Copenhagen; also tours from '80 w. Archie Shepp in US and Japan. Tour. Japan w. own trio, '86; Mt. Fuji JF w. Griffin; Joe Henderson; Jackie McLean '88; pl. Moscow w. Red Mitchell '91. CDs: Story.; Steep.; Enja; SN; BN; w. D. Gordon; Lou Donaldson (BN); Tubby Hayes–Clark Terry (Col.); C. Mingus (Rh.; Beth.); Harold Ashby (Timel.); Benny Bailey; Tony Coe (Hot House); Johnny Cole (CC); Booker Ervin (Cand.)

PARLATO, DAVE (DAVID CHARLES), bs; b. Los Angeles, CA, 10/31/45. Played and rec. w. Don Ellis 1966–8; Paul Horn '68–71; Gil Melle '69–74. Also worked w. Warne Marsh, Frank Strazzeri late '60s; and John Klemmer and Frank Zappa early '70s; w. Gabor Szabo '74–5. Cont. club dates and studio work in LA area into '90s. CDs: w. Ellis (Col.); Marsh (hatArt).

PARNELL, JACK, dms, comp, arr, lead; b. London, England, 8/6/23. Began on pno., then sw. to dms. at age 14. While in Royal Air Force, he pl. w. Buddy Featherstonhaugh's Radio Rhythm Club Sxt. 1943–4; then w. Vic Lewis '44–5; Kenny Baker '46–7. Came to prominence pl. and singing w. Ted Heath bb '44–51. Led own bb '51–5; sidemen incl. Jimmy Deuchar; Ronnie Scott; Phil Seamen; Hank Shaw; Joe Temperley. Stud. conducting '56, then was mus. dir. for Associated TV '57–late '70s. During the '60s he conducted the pit band for popular TV show *Sunday Night at the London Palladium*. Mus. dir. for many TV specials starring Lena Horne, Tony Bennett, Barbra Streisand, others '70s; *The Muppet Show* early '80s. Pl. w. gp., Best of British Jazz, fr. mid '70s; other members incl. Kenny Baker, Don Lusher, Betty Smith. Pl. at Pizza Express, London, w. Ruby Braff and others '80s. Dir. the BBC Big Band '94 CDs: w. Dick Sudhalter (Chall.); Joe Temperley (Hep).

PARRIS, REBECCA (Ruth Blair MacCloskey), voc; b. Needham, MA, 12/28/51. Parents both pnst. and org. Fath. introduced her to mus. theatre and summer stock at age 6. Stud. priv. w. uncle, David Blair McCloskey, who developed voc. technique utilized by many speakers, actors, stage perfs., and vocalists. Graduated Bost. Cons of Mus. Worked w. Top 40 bands through '70s; Freestyle (rock gp.) '80–1; Reminiscence (jazz voc. ensemble) '81–3; then as jazz soloist. Since then, she has been a priv.

voice coach, also teaching stage presence and technique; artist-in-residence and master classes at U. of New Hampshire, Howard U., and other schs. Made rec. debut w. Reminiscence '83, then LPs w. Phil Wilson and Eddie Higgins. Many fest. apps., incl. NJF at Saratoga, Int'l Floating JF. A full-toned, extrovert performer, Ms. Parris has long been popular in the Boston area. Joe Williams described her as having "a warm, vibrant sound." CDs: Weston-Blair; Entertainment Exclusives.

PARRISH, AVERY, pno; b. Birmingham, AL, 1/24/17; d. NYC, 12/10/59. Attended Alabama St. Coll.; pl. with coll. band, which later went out prof. under Erskine Hawkins' name. His blues solo rec., "After Hours" w. Hawkins, Jun. 1940, won vast popularity and was still being directly imitated in the '90s. Parrish was forced to retire from mus. after suffering near-fatal injuries in an accident '42. CDs: w. Hawkins (BB).

PARSON, DION G., dms, perc; b. St. Thomas, Virgin Islands, 6/11/67. As a child was exposed to a broad range of mus. styles. Started on tbn. w. considerable encouragement fr. his family and community. Changed to dms. at age 15, won a grant to attend Interlochen Mus. Acad., Mich.; after he ret. to St. Thomas, was selected the Virgin Islands' representative in McDonald's All-American HS Band. Received Bach. of Mus. from Rutgers U. 1990. Settled in NYC after grad. His first prof. job was w. Ray Anderson '90–1. Has perf. w. many prominent contemp. mus. incl. Donald Harrison '93–7; David Sanchez '95–6; Don Byron '95–7; and such veteran jazz stars as Lee Konitz; Milt Jackson; Monty Alexander. Tour. US, Eur., Japan, Can., West Indies. Worked w. Laurent de Wilde. Has taught at Rutgers U.; Arts HS, Newark; Cheney U., Westchester, Pa.; and master classes at So. Illinois U., Edwardsville. Also involved w. various mus. theater prod., incl. *Lulu Noir*, a jazz opera by Lee Breur w. mus. by Jon Faddis. Favs: Roy Haynes, Elvin Jones, Tony Williams, and "Michael Carvin, a master drummer" with whom he still studies and "who encourages me to take a worldly and spiritual approach to my instrument." CDs: Dion Parson–Ron Blake (Tahmun); w. Stephen Scott (Verve); Donald Harrison (Imp.); Justin Robinson (Arab.).

PASCOAL, HERMETO, pno, acdn, sax, fl, tpt, gtr, comp, arr, lead; b. Lagoa da Canoa, Brazil, 6/22/36. Family musical. Beg. by pl. in gps. w. fath., an acdnst. bro. Family moved to Recife '50. Pl. in Brazil w. various gps., incl. bro. on radio '58. Start. first gp., Som Quatro; then, w. Airto Moreira, form. Quarteto

Novo, achieving great popularity. Pl. in Rio, São Paulo. Visited France '68; to NYC '70, rec. w. Miles Davis and visiting Calif. briefly bef. going back to Brazil. Tour. in Mex. '72; US '74. Pl. often in Eur. incl. many times at Montreux, beginning in '79. Other Eur. fests. in '80s, '90s. His gp. does all manner of doubling, particularly in the perc. dept., and Hermeto creates a seemingly endless fountain of music, pl. anything that isn't nailed down, and a few instruments that are, possessed by the sheer joy of making music that combines multiple genres. CDs: Philips; w. Miles Davis (Col.); Donald Byrd (BN); Antonio Carlos Jobim (Sony/CTI); Sergio and Odair Assad (None.); Cal Tjader (Fant.); Flora Purim (Mile.).

PASS, JOE (Joseph Anthony Jacobi Passalaqua), gtr; b. New Brunswick, NJ, 1/13/29; d. Los Angeles, CA, 5/23/94. Studied w. Nick Gemus in Johnstown, Pa. 1939–40. Local gigs and tour w. Tony Pastor Orch. while still in sch. Pl. w. Charlie Barnet briefly '47. After navy service, his career was seriously held up by problems w. narcotics, which ended when he entered the Synanon Foundation in Santa Monica '61. His pl. on an album rec. at that institution, *Sounds of Synanon* (PJ) '61, brought him to the attention of the jazz public. He worked w. many West Coast gps. fr. '62, incl. Bud Shank; Gerald Wilson; Bobby Troup; Julie London; Clare Fischer; Bill Perkins; Earl Bostic; Les McCann; Groove Holmes; Page Cavanaugh. Won *DB* New Star award '63. Toured w. George Shearing '65–7. Frequent studio work in LA; jazz gigs at Donte's, incl. gtr. duets w. Herb Ellis '72–4. Sponsored by Norman Granz, he began rec. extens. for Granz's Pab. label, on his own, and w. Oscar Peterson; Ella Fitzgerald; Duke Ellington; Count Basie; Benny Carter; Roy Eldridge; Zoot Sims; Milt Jackson. He also rec. a series of solo albums entitled *Virtuoso*. Tour. Austral. w. B. Goodman '73; pl. Ronnie Scott's club in London '74. Seen w. increasing frequency overseas, he established a home in Hamburg, Germ. '89 but cont. to divide his time between the US and Eur. Pass is regarded by fellow jazzmen as an incomparable soloist, a virtuoso so totally in command of the instrument that he has sometimes been called the Art Tatum of the gtr. He was capable of swinging fiercely at fast tempos and of exceptional harmonic imagination on ballads. Many examples of his work have been published: *Joe Pass: Improvising Ideas*, co-written w. Jude Hibler; *Joe Pass Guitar Style; Chord Book; Jazz Guitar Solos*, etc. CDs: Pab. incl. 4–CD box; Laser.; Em.; Tel.; Ranwood; PJ; Act; w. Eddie Vinson and Otis Spann (BB); André Previn (Tel.); Peterson; Basie; Zoot Sims (Pab.); Richard "Groove" Holmes (PJ); NDR bb (Act).

PASTOR, TONY (Antonio Pestritto), tnr sax, voc, lead; b. Middletown, CT, 10/26/07; d. Old Lyme, CT, 10/31/69. Early assoc. of Artie Shaw and the bands of Irving Aaronson, Vincent Lopez, and Shaw's own bands from 1936–40. Form. own bb, which in late '40s feat. vocs. by Clooney sisters, Rosemary and Betty. From '59 formed a voc. act that incl. his sons, Tony Jr. and Guy. Retired in '68. Pastor was a capable tnr. sax. soloist and Armstrong-inspired singer. CDs: w. Artie Shaw (BB; Jazz Unlimited).

PASTORIUS, JACO (JOHN FRANCIS), el bs, comp; b. Norristown, PA, 12/1/51; d. Fort Lauderdale, FL, 9/21/87. Raised in Fort Lauderdale from age 7. Fath. pl. dms. and sang. Start. on dms., then pno., sax., gtr. After an interruption due to a broken arm, he resumed pl. in 1968, concentrating on el-bs. from '69. Taught at U. of Miami, pl. w. Ira Sullivan. Pl. and rec. w. Pat Metheny, Paul Bley. Discovered by Bobby Colomby of Blood, Sweat & Tears in '75, he rec. w. Colomby as prod.; H. Hancock; W. Shorter, et al. Pl. at Berlin Festival '76, shortly thereafter replacing Alphonso Johnson in Weather Report, and remaining w. the gp. until '82. During that time he also rec. w. his own gp., Word of Mouth, and app. w. Mike Stern; Bireli Lagrene; and Brian Melvin. Joe Zawinul, co-founder of Weather Report, called Pastorius "the greatest bass player of his time . . . a phenomenal musician, also a fine composer." Pastorius's career was hindered by serious drug problems and erratic behavior on stage, but many considered him to be the world's greatest el-bs. player. Beaten in a fight with a bouncer outside a Fort Lauderdale club, he died after nine days in a coma. CDs: DIW; Epic; Timel.; Sound Hills; Big World; Jazzpoint; WB; IAI; w. Weather Report; Hancock (Col.); Pat Metheny (ECM); Albert Mangelsdorff (MPS); B. Lagrene (Jazzpoint).

PATE, JOHNNY (JOHN WILLIAM), comp, arr, cond, pno, bs, tba; b. Chicago Heights, IL, 12/5/23. Son Don Pate is bsst.; Johnny Griffin is a cousin. Self-taught as bsst. and arr. while with 218th Army Band 1944–6. Pl. w. Coleridge Davis bb '46; Red Allen–J. C. Higginbotham '47–9; Stuff Smith '49–51. Stud. at Midwestern Cons., Chi. '50–3. Pl. w. Eddie South '51–3; Dorothy Donegan '53–4; Ahmad Jamal '56. Led own gp. '57–60; made rec. debut as lead. for Federal label '57. During '50s worked as house bs. at Blue Note, Chi., accomp. S. Vaughan; E. Fitzgerald; Ellington; et al. Arr. and bs. for *Last Train from Overbrook* w. James Moody '58. Rec. on bs. w. Ellington for Roulette '59. Arr. Wes Montgomery's *Movin' Wes* album for Verve '65. Arr. and prod. recs. for Shirley Horn '65; S. Getz, K. Burrell '68; P.

Woods, M. Alexander '69. In '70s comp., arr., and cond. for movies, TV incl. *Brother on the Run* '73; *Shaft in Africa* '75; *Bucktown USA; Shaft* TV series '76; *Dr. Black and Mr. Hyde* '77; *Satan's Triangle* '78; *Bustin' Loose* '80. Arrs. for Jimmy Smith rec. '92. Favs: John Clayton, bs., arr.; Johnny Mandel, arr.; O. Peterson, pno. LPs as lead. on Federal, King, Gig, Salem, MGM. CDs: as arr. w. J. Smith (Mile.); W. Montgomery (Verve).

PATITUCCI, JOHN, bs; b. Brooklyn, NY, 12/22/59. His bro. pl. gtr. so he tried one but didn't take to it. Started on el-bs. at age 10. Eventually pl. at rock 'n' roll parties. Heard Wes Montgomery who became a strong infl. Later, listening to Ron Carter inspired him to pick up acoustic bs. Family to Calif. 1978. Stud. at Cal. St.-SF and Cal. St.-Long Beach Moved to LA '82. Freelanced w. Freddie Hubbard; the Crusaders; Hubert Laws; Larry Carlton; Stan Getz. Pl. w. Chick Corea's Elektric Band '85–91; also w. Corea's Akoustic Band; led own gps. fr. '91; four albums under own name on GRP and numerous recs. w. Corea. One of the most highly regarded young bassists to emerge in the the '80s. CDs: GRP; Stretch; w. Corea (GRP); Bobby Shew (MAMA; Delos); Michel Camilo (Trop.).

PATRICK, PAT (LAURDINE KENNETH JR.), saxes; b. East Moline, IL, 11/23/29; d. Moline, 12/31/91. Studied tpt. at age 9 w. fath. and Clark Terry, both of whom pl. w. Speckled Red's Band. To Chi. at 12; sw. to sax; pl. in famous DuSable HS band w. Clifford Jordan, John Gilmore, John Jenkins, Julian Priester, Richard Davis, et al. Gigged around Chi. late 1940s and '50s w. local mus. as well as Muddy Waters; Gene Ammons; Dinah Washington; etc. With Sun Ra off and on for 35 yrs., tour. Eur. w. him in the '70s. Pl. tnr. sax w. Monk for short time '71. Through '80s tour. w. Illinois Jacquet; Mercer Ellington; L. Hampton; Lennie Drayton. Rec. w. James Moody; Clifford Jordan; John Coltrane; Sun Ra. Best known as bari. saxophonist. Prof. at SUNY in '70s. CDs: w. Coltrane (Imp.); Sun Ra (Del.; Evid.); Roland Kirk (Atl.); David Amram (Sav.); Blue Mitchell; Sam Jones; J. Heath (Riv.).

PATTERSON, DON, org; b. Columbus, OH, 7/22/36; d. Philadelphia, PA, 2/10/88. Pianist, originally infl. by Carmen Cavallaro, later by Erroll Garner. After hearing Jimmy Smith in 1956 took up org., making debut as orgst. in '59. Gigged and rec. w. Sonny Stitt; Gene Ammons; Eddie "Lockjaw" Davis; Kenny Burrell; Wes Montgomery; Eric Kloss; also often in duo w. dmr. Billy James. Mainly associated dur. the last decade of his life w. trombonist Al Grey.

Patterson said of his org. work, "I've tried to keep the piano sound—playing piano licks—and the organ helps my piano playing too." CDs: Prest.; Muse; w. S. Stitt (Del.; Prest.); G. Ammons; Lockjaw Davis (Prest.).

PATTON, BIG JOHN, org; b. Kansas City, MO, 7/12/35. Mother pl. pno. in church. Began pl. pno. at age 13. Toured w. Lloyd Price 1954–9. Took up Hammond org. ca. '61. Rec. in '60s w. Johnny Griffin; Harold Vick; Clifford Jordan; Grant Green; and w. Lou Donaldson '62–4. Led own trio '63–9; sidemen incl. Green; James "Blood" Ulmer; Clifford Jarvis. Living in East Orange, N.J. since the '70s. In '85 John Zorn used him on one track of his album *The Big Gundown*, rekindling interest in Patton's career. Tour. UK w. Jean Toussaint '89. Pl. w. Zorn at Knitting Factory, NYC '93. CDs: BN; DIW; Evid.; w. Zorn (Elek./None.); Donaldson (BN).

PAUER, FRITZ, comp, pno; b. Vienna, Austria, 10/14/43. From early 1960s worked w. Hans Koller and w. many visiting Americans in Berlin and Vienna. Rec. w. own gps. in '70; also w. Friedrich Gulda, Art Farmer. A talented comp. whose works incl. "Fairytale Countryside," which was rec. by Farmer and others. CDs: w. Farmer (SN; L+R); P. Herbolzheimer (Rare Bid); Koller (L+R).

PAUL, LES (Lester William Polfus), gtr; b. Waukesha, WI, 6/9/15. Began on hca. at age 8. Took up gtr. w. local pls. incl. Sunny Joe Wolverton, who dubbed him Rhubarb Red. Pl. w. Rube Tronson's Cowboys early 1930s; then left hs to join Wolverton's band on radio station KMOX, St. Louis. Pl. in duo w. Wolverton, Springfield, Mo. '32. In Chi. '34, was on radio as Rhubarb Red, pl. hillbilly mus. and, as Les Paul, reflecting the infl. of Django Reinhardt w. a jazz qt. He also interacted w. Louis Armstrong; Art Tatum; Roy Eldridge; Eddie South. Form. trio w. Jim Atkins (Chet's half-bro.) '36. He join. Fred Waring's Pennsylvanians, NYC '38, remain. into '41. After more radio work in Chi. '41–2, moved to Hollywood and form. new trio. In July '44 took part in first JATP concert: his duet w. Nat Cole on "Blues" a highlight. Feat. on Bing Crosby's radio show, he also rec. for Decca in a variety of genres, incl. backing singers such as Dick Haymes, the Andrews Sisters. An automobile accident in '48 halted his pl. career into mid '49. Meanwhile Paul, who had start. designing new el. gtrs. in the mid '30s, rec. himself, after much experimentation, as eight gtrs. in a souped-up version of "Lover." Released by Capitol Recs. '48, it set the stage for a collab. w. his soon-to-be-wife, voc.-gtr. Mary Ford (married 12/29/49) that resulted in multitracked hits of "How High the Moon" and "Tiger Rag." They were divorced '64. Paul retired fr. music '67. Ret. in '76, rec. w. Chet Atkins for RCA. Rec. on Al Di Meola album '80. In '84 began a regular Monday night series at Fat Tuesday's, NYC; similarly at Iridium fr. '96, where he jams w. jazz, country, and rock guitarists, an icon to the latter gp. who are familiar w. the Les Paul model gtrs. Polls: *DB* '51–3. CDs: Dec.; Laser.; Pair; w. JATP, *The First Concert* (Verve); Pat Martino (BN).

PAVAGEAU, "SLOW DRAG" (ALCIDE), bs; b. New Orleans, LA, 3/7/1888; d. New Orleans, 1/19/69. Wife, Annie, a singer, rec. w. Jim Robinson for Riv. '61. First known as gtrst. and celebrated dancer. Took up bs. in late 1920s; rec. on bs. w. Magee String Band '28. Worked w. Buddy Petit; Emile Barnes; and others. Play., rec., and tour. w. George Lewis '44–65. Also rec. and pl. w. Bunk Johnson '44–46, visiting NYC w. him '45. Became a major figure in the NO revival of mid '40s. Worked at Preservation Hall, NO, in the '60s. Tour. Eur. '57–9; Japan '64. "His amazing tone and forcefulness place him in the front rank of jazz bassists," wrote William Russell in '44. CDs: w. Jim Robinson (Riv.; Biog.); Lewis (Story.; BN; GTJ; *Hot Jazz* box [BN]).

PAYNE, BENNIE (BENJAMIN), pno. voc; b. Philadelphia, PA, 6/18/07; d. Los Angeles, CA, 9/2/86. Early friend and protegé of Fats Waller, w. whom he rec. a pno. duo of "St. Louis Blues." Visited Eur. w. *Blackbirds of 1929* revue. Rec. w. Duke Ellington; best known for long assoc. w. Cab Calloway band 1931–43 and again briefly after army service '46. Later accomp. Pearl Bailey and fr. '50 spent more than 20 years acc. Billy Daniels. CDs: w. Chu Berry (Class.; Topaz); Calloway (Class.).

PAYNE, CECIL McKENZIE, bari, alto saxes, fl, cl, bs-cl, comp; b. Brooklyn, NY, 12/14/22. Father pl. C-melody sax; sist. Cavril, is prof. voc.; many other mus. in family. Stud. gtr. at Christian Sch. of Mus., Bklyn. 1937, then alto sax w. Pete Brown '38–41. Pl. cl. in army band '43–6; then made rec. debut on alto w. J. J. Johnson and Bud Powell. Pl. bari. sax briefly w. Roy Eldridge bb '46; then join. Dizzy Gillespie bb, where he was feat. on "Ow!" and "Stay on It" '46–9. Freelanced in NYC w. James Moody, Tadd Dameron, Coleman Hawkins, etc. '49–52. Pl. w. Illinois Jacquet '52–4. Many recs. in '50s w. Kenny Dorham; Gigi Gryce; Jimmy Cleveland; Duke Jordan; Randy Weston; John Coltrane; and own gps. In '61 a band led by Payne and Kenny Drew repl. Freddie Redd–Jackie McLean gp. in the off-Bway play *The Connection*. Pl. w. Machito '63–4; Lionel Hampton

'64. Perf. and rec. in Engl. '66; then pl. w. Woody Herman '67; Slide Hampton '67–8; Dizzy Gilliespie '68–9; Count Basie Orch. '69–71; own gps. in '70s; NY Jazz Repertory Orch. '74; Benny Carter '77–9. With Dameronia fr. early '80s; own gps. in Phila. and NYC late '80s-90s. In his 70s, Payne's eyesight was failing but his songful baritone sax, with its nimble lines and warm, throaty tone, was still flying. Favs: Leo Parker, Harry Carney, Sonny Stitt. Polls: *DB* New Star '50; BMI Composer Award; Barry Harris "Barry" Award '90. Fests: Eur., Asia, Africa, etc. Films: apps. w. Illinois Jacquet, Benny Carter. TV: apps. w. Gillespie, Woody Herman, Randy Weston. CDs: Sav.; Strata-East; Stash; Del.; w. J. J. Johnson; Gryce (Sav.); Blakey; Gillespie (BB); Gillespie-Parker (Roost); Coltrane; B. Golson; Dameron (Prest.); Blakey–J. Moody; Dorham (BN); Weston (Biog.; Roul.); D. Washington (Em.); Eric Alexander (CC).

PAYNE, SONNY (PERCIVAL), dms; b. NYC, 5/4/26; d. Los Angeles, CA, 1/29/79. Son of veteran dmr. Chris Columbus. Stud. w. Vic Berton, 1944–45; pl. w. Baskin Bros, Hot Lips Page '44, Earl Bostic '45–7; Tiny Grimes '47–50; Lucille Dixon '48. After three yrs. w. Erskine Hawkins, led own band for two years. Join. Count Basie for the first of a series of stints '55–65, '73–74; also w. Frank Sinatra '65–7; Harry James '67–73 and again shortly bef. his death. Tour. Eur. w. Illinois Jacquet and Milt Buckner '76. A flashy and showmanly perf. in the spirit of Jo Jones and Gus Johnson, his contributions to the Basie band have been disputed, though many feel he was a first-rate bb dmr. CDs: w. Basie (Roul.; Verve; Mos.); E. Fitzgerald; S. Vaughan (Verve); M. Buckner (Prog.); Mel Tormé (Stash); L,H&R (Roul.); Getz; Paul Quinichette (Biog.).

PAYTON, NICHOLAS ANTHONY, tpt; b. New Orleans, LA, 9/26/73. Father a jazz and classical bsst.; moth. a former operatic singer and classical pnst. Fath. began teaching him tpt. at age 4. Stud. w. a variety of teachers incl. Ellis Marsalis at NOCCA. Also stud. at U. of NO w. Harold Battiste, Victor Goines. Encouraged early on by Wynton Marsalis, who taught him improv. Worked w. W. Marsalis; Clark Terry; E. Marsalis; Art Blakey; Marcus Roberts. Pl. w. Carl Allen fr. '91. Tour. w. Jazz Futures II in US and Eur. 1992; Elvin Jones, where he was mus. dir., '92–4. Regular at Lincoln Center concerts from '91; tour. w. LCJO '94. Has also app. w. CHJB; Newport JF All-Stars. Led. own qnt. at JVC-NY; Eur. fests '97. Capable of convincing solos of lyricism, power, range, and glowing sound in NO and bop idioms, reflecting his influences, but with a strong personal presence. Favs: Armstrong, M. Davis, Clifford Brown. Perf. in film *Kansas City* '96; at Grammy Awards TV show '98. CDs: Verve; Doc Cheatham–Nicholas Payton; Payton–Christian Mc-Bride; Payton–Mark Whitfield (Verve); w. Whitfield; Jimmy Smith; Joe Henderson (Verve); E. Jones (Enja); Jesse Davis (Conc.); M. Roberts (RCA); Teresa Brewer (Red Brn.); NO Collective (Evid.); Pete Yellin (Mons); Courtney Pine (Ant.).

PEACOCK, GARY, bs; b. Burley, ID, 5/12/35. Played pno. while in army in Germ., then sw. to bs. Remain. in Eur., pl. w. Albert Mangelsdorff; Attila Zoller; Tony Scott. Pl. w. Don Ellis, Barney Kessel, Shorty Rogers, Paul Horn in LA 1958–'60. Joined Bill Evans trio in NYC '62–3; tour. w. Miles Davis and pl. w. Paul Bley, J. Giuffre, Geo. Russell, Albert Ayler '64. Rec. w. Paul Bley '67 and '70. After stud. Eastern philosophies and medicine, he moved to Japan in '69. Stud. biology at U. of Wash. '72. Tour. Japan w. Bley and Barry Altschul '76. Worked in trio w. Keith Jarrett and Jack DeJohnette. In '80s taught at Cornish Inst. of Allied Arts in Seattle, Wash. An exceptional musician with a full sound that applies itself to many contexts, he uses double tones and harmonics w. remarkable celerity. CDs: ECM; Post.; JMT; w. B. Evans (Verve); D. Pullen (BN); K. Jarrett (ECM); L. Konitz (Evid.); Laurindo Almeida–Bud Shank (WP).

PEAGLER, CURTIS GREGORY, alto, tnr. saxes, pno; b. Cincinnati, OH, 9/17/30; d. Los Angeles, CA, 12/19/92. Studied at the Cosmopolitan Sch. of Mus. as a teenager, then at the Cincinnati Cons. of Mus. under Artie Matthews. Pl. w. r&b gps. in the 1950s and led his own, The Jazz Disciples, fr. late '50s to early '60s. With Ray Charles '64–9; Count Basie '70–7. Freelanced on West Coast as a single; pl. w. Jimmy Smith; Jimmy McGriff; Harry "Sweets" Edison; Jeannie and Jimmy Cheatham. App. in films *New York, New York; Roots; Brewster's Millions*; and *Bird*. Perf. at jfs. in Nice; North Sea; Chi.; NO; Conc.; Playboy; Colo. JP; Carnegie Hall. Infl: C. Parker, Eddie Vinson. LPs: Sea Pea; Pab. CDs: w. Cheathams; Frank Wess; Mel Tormé (Conc.); Freddie Redd (Mile.); C. Basie (Pab.); Teresa Brewer (Sig.; Dr. Jazz).

PEARSON, DUKE (COLUMBUS CALVIN JR.), pno, comp, lead, tpt; b. Atlanta, GA, 8/17/32; d. Atlanta, 8/4/80. Played tpt. in hs and coll. Army 1953–54; pl. Special Services show w. Wynton Kelly, Phineas Newborn, and George Joyner. Gigged on piano around Fla. and Ga. '54–59. Moved to NYC '59; during '60s worked frequently w. Donald Byrd

who rec. his comps., "Cristo Redentor"; "Chant"; "Noah"; and "March Children." Best-known comp., "Jeannine," has become a jazz standard. In '60s worked as prod. for BN label and led bb w. soloists overlapping personnel of Thad Jones–Mel Lewis Band. Accomp. Nancy Wilson, Dakota Staton, and other singers; tour. w. Carmen McRae and Joe Williams '73. His ability to pl. was impaired by multiple sclerosis. Pearson's bb albums for BN enjoyed wide critical acclaim, displaying his arrs., mixing swing and post-bop styles. Favs: Hank Jones, Wynton Kelly. CDs: BN; BL; w. Donald Byrd; Johnny Coles; S. Turrentine (BN).

PECORA, SANTO JOSEPH (Pecoraro), tbn; b. New Orleans, LA, 3/31/02; d. New Orleans, 5/29/84. Played Fr. hrn. first; then sw. to tbn. Best known for assoc. w. NORK 1924–5. After working in bbs led by Buddy Rogers, Ben Pollack, and others, he pl. tailgate tbn. in mid-to-late '30s w. Paul Mares; Sharkey Bonano; and Wingy Manone. Later worked in Hollywood studios; seen w. Manone in film *Rhythm on the River* '40; also in *Blues in the Night* '41. From late '40s was mainly in NO where he rejoin. Bonano and led own gps. His best known comps. were "I Never Knew What A Gal Could Do" and "She's Crying for Me" w. NORK. CDs: tracks w. his Tailgaters in *The Good Time Jazz Story* (GTJ); w. Geo. Girard (Story.).

PEER, BEVERLY A., bs; b. NYC, 10/7/12; d. NYC, 1/16/97. First prof. gigs as a pnst.; sw. to bs. 1928. Pl. w. Eddie Williams at Savoy Ballroom ca. '35. Chick Webb heard him and asked him to join his bb '36. Pl. w. Webb '36–9; when Webb died in '39, Peer stayed on under Ella Fitzgerald's leadership until '42. Stud. w. Max Zimmerman of N.Y. Philharm. '40. Pl. w. Taft Jordan '42; Sabby Lewis in NYC and Bost. '43–5. Att. Bost. Cons. '45, then ret. to NYC. Pl. w. Lucky Millinder '46–7; Mercer Ellington '47; Lucky Thompson '48; Ellis Larkins at Blue Angel '49–53. Worked w. Jimmy Lyon at Blue Angel in '50s; also accomp. singers incl. Pearl Bailey; Johnny Mathis; Barbra Streisand; Sarah Vaughan; etc. Peer met Bobby Short at the Blue Angel in the late '50s and worked w. him fr. that time, incl. several apps. at the White House. Peer perf. w. Short on the soundtrack to Woody Allen's *Hannah and Her Sisters* and also worked in pit bands at the Westbury Mus. Fair on Long Island, N.Y. Favs: Blanton, Ray Brown. Polls: *N.Y. Journal-American* All-American Swing Band '36. Fests: Eur. w. Short. CDs: w. Webb (Dec.); Fitzgerald (Dec.; Col.; Class.); Esq. All-Amer. Poll Winners (BB); Short (Rh.; Atl.; Tel.); Louis Jordan (JSP); Chris Connor (Charly).

PEIFFER, BERNARD, pno, synth, comp; b. Epinal, France, 10/22/22; d. Philadelphia, PA, 9/7/76. Family moved to Marseilles 1940. Stud. at Marseilles Cons. and Ecole Normale de Paris. Worked w. André Ekyan '43; Django Reinhardt, Hubert Rostaing '44. He accomp. Josephine Baker, dur. remainder of his mil. service. On his discharge, rejoin. Ekyan, backing Jean Sablon '46. He pl. on the Riviera and in Switz. and Tunisia '47. Tour. and rec. w. Rex Stewart '48; and many other visiting Americans incl. Bill Coleman; Don Byas; Bechet; James Moody. In '49 appeared in the film *Rendevous de Juillet*, which won Grand Prix du Disque. Pl. at Club St. Germain w. Reinhardt, Hubert Fol in early '50s. Moved to NYC '54, pl. the Embers; later Birdland. Though widely praised by critics, Peiffer's career suffered as the result of his desire to stay close to his home in Philadelphia. Compositions include "Blues for Django"; "Homage to J. S. Bach"; "Poem for a Lonely Child." Greatly underrated, he was described by John S. Wilson as "that rarity among jazz pianists—a legitimately schooled musician with brilliant technique who can transfer much of this brilliance to jazz performances without necessarily falling into the trap of believing that technique is all." Infls: Tatum, Waller, Garner; later, Tristano, Phineas Newborn, John Lewis. Fests: NJF '57-8; Montreal JF '64. Recs. for Dec.; Blue Star; Em.; Laurie. LP: w. Don Byas (Prest., out of print).

PELL, DAVE (DAVID), tnr, other saxes, cls; oboe, prod; b. Brooklyn, NY, 2/26/25. Clarinet at 13, then tnr. sax. Pl. w. Bob Astor, Tony Pastor. To LA 1945, pl. w. Bob Crosby, Les Brown. Led own oct. off and on fr. '53. During '60s and '70s mainly active as studio mus. but in '78 rec. w. Prez Conference, a sax gp. that pl. the solos of Lester Young and featured guests soloists Joe Williams and Sweets Edison. In later yrs. Pell was less active as a jazz soloist, frequently prod. albums for Liberty, Motown, and other labels, incl. his own co., Headfirst. He also prod. the Stan Kenton 50th Anniversary celebration, *Back to Balboa*, at Newport Beach, Calif. '91. CDs: Headfirst; GNP Cres.; FS; w. Chet Baker (FS); Benny Goodman (MM).

PEMBERTON, BILL (WILLIAM McLANE), bs; b. Brooklyn, NY, 3/5/18, d. NYC, 12/13/84. Studied vln. fr. 1926, then bs. at age 18. Club dates in NYC w. Frankie Newton '41-5; in late '40s and '50s pl. w. Herman Chittison; Mercer Ellington; Eddie Barefield; Billy Kyle; Barbara Carroll; et al. Rec. and perf. w. A. Tatum '56; mostly studio work in NYC '60-6; pl. w. Earl Hines qt. '66-9. Form. and pl. in JPJ Qt. w. Budd Johnson, Oliver Jackson, and Dill Jones

'69-75. Also worked w. Ruby Braff, Max Kaminsky, and Vic Dickenson early '70s. In late '70s and early '80s rec. and pl. w. Panama Francis and the Savoy Sultans; rec. w. Doc Cheatham '84. CDs: w. Panama Francis (Stash; B&B); Ivory Joe Hunter (R&T); JPJ Qt.; Dickenson (Story.); Cheatham (Park.); Hines (B&B; NW).

PEÑA, RALPH RAYMOND, bs, comp; b. Jarbridge, NV, 2/24/27; d. Mexico City, Mexico, 5/20/69. Studied gtr., bari. horn, and tba. Prof. debut at age 15 w. Jerry Austin. Played w. Nick Esposito 1949; Art Pepper; Cal Tjader; Stan Getz '50-52; Billy May '53; Barney Kessel '53-5; Charlie Barnet '54; Jimmy Giuffre trio '56-7. Rec. w. Shorty Rogers '55-8; short stints w. B. DeFranco '56-9; led band at Sherry's Hollywood, incl, Hamp Hawes, Carl Perkins '57; worked in duo w. Pete Jolly '58-62. Dur. the '60s pl. w. Ben Webster; world tour w. Frank Sinatra; and in Eur. w. Shearing '62. Led own 9-pc. band around LA '63. Peña was noted for a rich, full sound, particularly in arco passages. He was in Mexico to score a film when he was hit by a car; he died in a local hospital two wks. later. Favs: Blanton, Red Mitchell. CDs: w. J. Giuffre (Atl.; FS); Chico Hamilton (FS); Shelly Manne (Cont.); Shorty Rogers (RCA).

PENLAND, RALPH MORRIS, dms; b. Cincinnati, OH, 2/15/53. Studied and taught at New Engl. Cons.; in 1970 pl. w. Webster Lewis; Freddie Hubbard; Charles Lloyd. Own gp., Penland Polygon, debuted in '75 and cont. active, w. various personnel, into mid '90s. One of LA's most active and dependable rhythm section players, a first call for musicians of every style. CDs: w. Chet Baker (Novus); C. Rouse (Land.); Eddie Daniels (GRP); F. Hubbard (Evid.); Joe Sample (WB); Carmen Bradford (Evid.); Janis Siegel-Fred Hersch (Col.); Bunky Green (Delos).

PENN, CLARENCE LACQUESE, dms, mrba, tympani; b. Detroit, MI, 3/2/68. Played tpt. briefly, then sw. to dms. Stud. at Northwestern HS 1982-5; Interlochen Arts Acad. '86; U. of Miami '86-7; Virginia Commonwealth U. '87-91. Pl. w. Ellis Marsalis '87-90; Joe Kennedy '88-91; Betty Carter fr. '91. Favs: Philly Joe Jones, Jo Jones, Frankie Dunlop. Polls: *DB* Outstanding Student Soloist '86. Fests: all major w. Carter '91-2. TV: *Entertainment Tonight* w. Ellis Marsalis-Dizzy Gillespie; Montreux and Det. JFs w. Carter '92. CDs: w. Carter (Verve); Joshua Redman (WB); Cyrus Chestnut (Atl.).

PENSYL, KIM (KIMOTHY C.), pno, kybds, tpt, flg; b. Columbus, OH, 7/20/57. Studied at Ohio St. U.,

Eastman, Cal. St.-Northridge. First prof. gig w. Guy Lombardo as lead and solo tpt; also pl. w. Don Ellis; Hubert Laws; Gerald Wilson; and Louie Bellson. Rec. debut 1988 w. first of *Pensyl Sketches* series on Optimism label. Signed w. GRP Recs. '91. "The classic jazz forms that I have learned, studied, practiced and performed," says Pensyl, "have not been so much abandoned in my current work as they have been incorporated in a new manner." CDs: Optimism; GRP.

PEPLOWSKI, KEN (KENNETH JOSEPH), cl, tnr, alto saxes; b. Garfield Heights, OH, 5/23/59. As pre-teenager, gigged w. brother in Polish polka band late 1960s. Worked w. T. Dorsey band '78–80; then mostly w. own gps. through '80's; w. B. Goodman '85; Leon Redbone '84–91; also Loren Schoenberg bb, off and on '82–91; dates w. Rosemary Clooney; Eddie Condon house band; as well as Dixieland gigs w. Jimmy McPartland. Though an excellent tnr. sax pl. inspired by Sonny Stitt and others, Peplowski is most outstanding as one of the few major clarinetists to come to prominence in the late '80s. Fav. cl: Goodman, Jimmie Noone, Jimmy Hamilton; fav. sax: Stitt, Parker, B. Webster, Getz, C. Hawkins. CDs: Conc.; w. Charlie Byrd; Howard Alden; Hank Jones; Susannah McCorkle; M. Tormé; R. Braff (Conc.).

PEPPER, ART (ARTHUR EDWARD), alto, tnr saxes, cl; b. Gardena, CA, 9/1/25; d. Panorama City, CA, 6/15/82. Played w. Benny Carter at age 18; gigged around LA w. Gus Arnheim, Lee Young. Join. Stan Kenton Nov. '43 for three mos. Two yrs. in the army, then freelanced in LA from May '46 to Sept. '47; w. Kenton again on and off until early '52. Inactive for next few yrs. while serving jail terms for drug abuse. Rec. for Cont. fr. '56; worked in LV and LA '57–60, pl. w. Latin bands as well as jazz gps. Took up tnr. sax briefly '64; lead alto w. Buddy Rich '68–9; then entered Synanon rehab. center for three yrs. With Don Ellis '75; fr. '77 frequently tour. US and Japan w. qt. feat. George Cables; rec. *The Trip* and *No Limit* (Cont.); also cond. clinics at schs. and colls. Took part in film, *Art Pepper: Notes from a Jazz Survivor* '82. Pepper, who felt his infl. came from Lester Young and Lee Konitz rather than Charlie Parker, left a series of exceptional albums that demonstrated his warm, melodically oriented style that shifted to a Coltrane infl. Despite his chaotic career, he was established as one of the most important alto players of his day; occasionally very effective on tnr. and cl. Film: soundtrack solos for *Heart Beat* '79. Book: autobiography, *Straight Life*, w. Laurie Pepper (Da Capo) '79. CDs: *The Complete Art Pepper Galaxy Recordings*, 16–CD boxed set (Gal.); others: Gal.; PJ; Cont.; Tampa; Story.; Laser.; Drey.; Sav.; VSOP;

Time Is; Art Pepper–Zoot Sims (Pab.) w. Babs Gonzales (BN); Chet Baker; Rich (PJ); Elvin Jones (Evid.); Joe Farrell (Drive Archive); S. Kenton (Cap.; Mos.); Tom Talbert (SB); Shorty Rogers (RCA); Shelly Manne (Sav.); Helen Humes; Art Farmer; Barney Kessel (Cont.); Elvin Jones (Konnex).

PEPPER, JIM, tnr, sop saxes, comp; b. Portland, OR, 6/17/41; d. Portland, 2/10/92. Grew up in Okla. Fath. pl. sax. Tap-danced as a youth. Self-taught on tnr. sax and cl. Moved to NYC in mid 1960s. Pl. in gp. Free Spirits w. Larry Coryell. Worked w. Don Cherry, Dewey Redman. Rec. "The Ballad of the Fallen" w. Charlie Haden's Liberation Music Orch. '82. Pl. w. Paul Motian; collab. w. Mal Waldron; led own gps. His best-known comp. "Witchi-Tai-To," based on a peyote chant, reflected his Native American heritage. Video: *Pepper's Pow Wow*. CDs: Enja; Pepper–Claudine François (Pan Music); w. Haden (ECM); Bob Moses (Gram.); Motian (SN); Waldron (Tutu), and in *The Art of the Duo* (Enja).

PERAZA, ARMANDO, perc; b. Havana, Cuba, 5/30/24. Self-taught on bongos, congas. Pl. in various Cuban bands 1943–49, replacing Mongo Santamaria in two gps., Los Dandys and Chano Pozo's band. After six mos. in Mexico City, moved to NYC '49; two days later rec w. Machito's band feat. Charlie Parker. Tour. and rec. w. Slim Gaillard '50–51; pl. and instructed baseball and boxing in Tijuana, Mex. '51–53; then moved to SF, rec. w. Cal Tjader; tour. and rec. w. George Shearing '55–64. Returning to SF rejoin. Tjader '66–72. Then tour. the world for eighteen yrs. w. Carlos Santana, rec. 20 albums w. him. Best recs. incl. Tjader's first album, *Ritmos Calientes*; also *Mood Latino; Latin Lace; Velvet Carpet* w. Shearing. Other sessions w. Perez Prado; Buddy Collette; Rene Touzet. CDs: w. John McLaughlin (Col.); Tjader (Fant.; Verve).

PERCIFUL, JACK T., pno, org; b. Moscow, ID, 11/26/25. Began pno. at age 7. Stud. classical pno. and received degree in mus. educ. from U. of Idaho. Began career pl. in coll. dance bands. From 1945 to '46 pl. in army service band in Japan. Moved to LA where he worked in films and TV and app. in the Dicky Wells Qt. w. Ernie Andrews '53–4; Jerry Fuller Qt. '54–5; Milt Herth Trio '55; Charlie Barnet '58. For more than twenty yrs., fr. '56, he was assoc. w. the Harry James Orch., tour. w. him in Mex. and So. Amer. in '61 and Japan in '64. Pl. w. the Buddy Catlett Trio '89–91. Apps. at Red Kelly's, Tacoma in '90s. Fests: w. James, MJF; and NJF '74. Favs: Jimmy Rowles, Nat Cole, Teddy Wilson, Tatum. CDs: w. Harry James (Verve).

PEREZ, DANILO (Danilo Enrico Perez Samudio), pno, comp; b. Monte Oscuro, Panama, 12/29/66. Father sings; uncle and cousin are mus. Stud. at Nat'l Cons., Panama 1978–82; w. Donald Brown at Berklee Coll. of Mus. '85–7. Pl. w. Edgardo Quintero '78–82; Victor Mendoza '85–6; Jon Hendricks '87–9; Paquito D'Rivera fr. '88; Terence Blanchard '89; Dizzy Gillespie United Nation Orch. fr. '89; Mauricio Smith '90; Tom Harrell since '90; Claudio Roditi, Steve Turre '91; also own trio. As educ. Perez, who teaches improv. and jazz stud. at New Engl. Cons., was artist-in-residence at the Irving Gilmore Int'l Kybd. Fest., Kalamazoo, Mich. '98. Perez, who mixes Latin and jazz with elan and imagination followed his first Impulse album, the acclaimed *Pana-Monk*, with *Central Avenue*. At the time he said: "So far in Latin jazz we have been mixing our rhythms with the melodic elements of bebop. Here I'm trying to do something different: I'm trying to find a common denominator, I'm trying to include our own blues from Latin America." Favs: Tatum, Hancock, Jarrett. Fests: Japan fr. '88; Eur. fr. '91. Film: heard on soundtrack and contributed orig. mus. to *Winter in Lisbon*, starring Gillespie '90. TV: *Latin Jazz* w. own trio. CDs: Imp.; Novus; w. P. D'Rivera (Town Crier; Chesky); C. Roditi (Chesky; Cand.); T. Harrell (Cont.); Gillespie (Tel.; Milan); D. Sanchez (Col.); Jeanie Bryson (Tel.); T. S. Monk (N2K).

PEREZ, MANUEL (EMANUEL aka EMILE), crnt, lead; b. New Orleans, LA, 12/28/1871; d. New Orleans, 1946. Like many NO musicians of the period he made a primary income at a trade, in his case cigar maker. He bec. a member of the Onward Brass Band in 1900, lead. it fr. '03 until its end in '30. Also pl. w. the Imperial Orch. w. George Baquet and George Filhe. Went to Chi. '15, pl. in a gp. w. Louis Cottrell, Lorenzo Tio, and Eddie Atkins. Ret. to NO he worked on the SS *Capitol* '18; at the Oasis and Pelican Ballroom '21–2. Cont. to pl. in parades w. the Onward Brass Band and the Maple Leaf Orch. Ret. to Chi. '27–30, pl. Charlie Elgar; then back to NO, pl. w. the Onad and John Robichaux. In '31 retired fr. music to concentrate once more on making cigars. Noted for his precise attack and pure tone.

PERKINS, BILL (WILLIAM REESE), saxes, cl, bs cl, fl, comp; b. San Francisco, CA, 7/22/24; d. Sherman Oaks, CA, 8/9/03. Raised in Chuquicamata, Chile, and Santa Barbara, Calif. Held degrees in electrical engineering fr. Cal. Tech. and mus. fr. U. Cal.-Santa Barbara. Army 1943–5; then stud. mus. under GI Bill at Westlake Coll. of Mus. Began his prof. mus. career full time '50. Pl. w. Jerry Wald '50–1. Shorty Rogers recommended him to Woody Herman,

whose band Perkins pl. w. '51–3. Pl. w. Stan Kenton '53–4. Tour. Eur. w. Herman spring '54; back w. Kenton '55–9; fr. Jan. '59 gigged w. Terry Gibbs, Allyn Ferguson; stud. engineering, worked for World Pacific as engineer, mixer, tape editor. Fr. '63 to '69; engineer at United-Western Recording. Pl. w. Marty Paich; Rogers; New Amer. Orch.; Doc Severinsen's *Tonight Show* band; Lennie Niehaus; Johnny Mandel; John Williams; Dave Grusin; Billy Byers; Billy May. With Akiyoshi-Tabackin bb '74–7, most often on bari. sax. With the rejuvenated Lighthouse All-Stars on tnr. and bari. fr. '89 w. Bud Shank and Shorty Rogers as co-leaders; also worked w. Shank sxt. in '90s and rec. on his own. Inventor of Saxophone-Synthesizer-Interface and co-inventor of Trumpet-to-Synthesizer-Interface. Favs: Lester Young, Coltrane, Rollins, Joe Henderson. Won *DB* Critics Poll as New Star tnr. sax '55. CDs: FS; Riv.; Cand.; Inter.; Story.; Perkins–Richie Kamuca (PJ); w. Terry Gibbs (Cont.); John Lewis (BN); Oliver Nelson (Imp.); Annie Ross; Chet Baker (PJ); Herman (Conc.); Kenton (Cap.); Rogers (Time Is); Lighthouse All-Stars w. Rogers & Shank (Cand.); Bill Holman (JVC).

PERKINS, CARL, pno; b. Indianapolis, IN, 8/16/28; d. Los Angeles, CA, 3/17/58. Not related to singer of same name. Bro. Ed Perkins is bs. Self-taught. Worked w. Tiny Bradshaw and Big Jay McNeely 1948–9; then settled in Calif. Dec. '49. Worked mostly as single, pl. dates w. Miles Davis '50. Army '51 and '52. With Oscar Moore off and on '53–5; later w. Harold Land and Chet Baker; rec. w. Max Roach–Clifford Brown '54. Also worked w. Art Pepper; Curtis Counce; Dexter Gordon; Buddy DeFranco. Unorthodox technique in which his left hand, which had been impaired by polio in childhood, paralleled the keyboard. He played bass notes with his elbow. Comp: "Grooveyard." Favs: Tatum, Hamp Hawes, Bud Powell, Peterson, Garner. CDs: FS; w. Roach-Brown (GNP Cres.); Harold Land; Leroy Vinnegar; Counce (Cont.); Pepper (BN); Baker (PJ).

PERKINS, WALTER, dms; b. Chicago, IL, 2/10/32. Studied at DuSable HS. Att. Wilson Jr. Coll. on basketball scholarship, then drafted into mil. After discharge, stud. at Cosmopolitan Sch. of Mus. Pl. in Chi. w. Ahmad Jamal 1956–7; Coleman Hawkins '59; freelanced. Formed own gp. MJT+3 (trio w. Harold Mabern, Bob Cranshaw plus Frank Strozier and tpt. Willie Thomas) and moved to NYC '60. Pl. w. MJT+3 '60–2; Carmen McRae '61–3; Sonny Rollins '62; Art Farmer '63; Teddy Wilson '64; Billy Taylor '65; Charles Mingus on and off fr. '67. Also pl. and rec. in '60s-70s w. J. J. Johnson; Geo. Shearing; Gene Ammons; Billy Taylor; Booker Ervin; Clark Terry;

Jaki Byard; Lucky Thompson; Pat Martino; Mabern; Sonny Stitt; Roland Kirk; Lightnin' Hopkins. Pl. w. Erroll Garner early '70s; Illinois Jacquet '80. Gigging on Long Island in '90s. Taught in the NYC publ. schs. and at York Coll. Perf. and taught w. Mus. for Young Audiences fr. '85. Fav: Sid Catlett. Fests: Eur. fr. '65; Mexico '69; Japan '87; Antigua '79–83. CDs: w. Booker Ervin (Prest.); C. McRae (Col.); Mingus (Imp.); R. Kirk (Limel.); Johnny Coles (BN).

PERKO, JUKKA, alto, sop saxes; b Huittinen, Finland, 2/18/68. Began pl. sax 1982. Nicknamed Little Bird after making debut at Pori JF '85. Pl. w. Dizzy Gillespie bb '87–8. Stud. at Sibelius Acad. fr. '88. Pl. w. Helsinki New Mus. Orch. (UMO) fr. '89. Led own qt. fr. '90. Pl. w. Horace Tapscott at Ultra Mus. Meeting Workshop, Pori '90. In '93 form. gp. w. vibist Severi Pyysalo. CDs: Andania; Perko-Pyysalo (Ondine Octopus).

PERRY, P. J. (PAUL JOHN), alto, other saxes, fl; b. Calgary, Alb., Canada, 12/2/41 Father, Paul, pl. tnr. sax, led well-known Can. dance band. Began on pno., cl. Join. father's band on bari. sax 1955. Pl. at Vancouver clubs, Sylvan Lake resorts '55–9. Moved to Toronto '59, pl. alto w. Ron Collier; Sonny Greenwich; others. Pl. w. Maury Kaye in Montreal '62. In Eur. worked w. Annie Ross, Brian Auger '63–6, then ret. to Vancouver. Pl. w. Pacific Salt '72–5, then moved to Edmonton. Pl. w. Tommy Banks, own gps. '75–9; also pl. sax w. Edmonton Symph. In Toronto '81–4, perf. in clubs w. Boss Brass; Dizzy Gillespie; Slide Hampton; Woody Shaw; Herbie Spanier; others. Ret. to Edmonton '85; pl. w. Tommy Banks bb; Edmonton Symph.; also duos w. pnsts. incl. Banks, Bill Emes. Tour. western Can. w. own qt. '90. CDs: JA; IGMOD.

PERRY, RAY, alto sax, el vln; b. Boston, MA, 2/25/15; d. NYC, 10/50. Brother of saxophonist Joe Perry and dmr. Bay Perry. As vlnst., sang and pl. in unison in a style later popularized by Slam Stewart. Pl. w. Blanche Calloway 1940; Lionel Hampton '40–3; J. C. Heard Sxt. '46; rec. w. Ethel Waters '46. In '46–50 worked off and on w. Illinois Jacquet; Sabby Lewis; and own bands. Perry was a capable mainstream saxophonist and an underrated vln. soloist, perhaps the first vlnst to play in the bebop style. CDs: w. Jacquet (BB; Mos.); Hampton (Class.; Dec.); Ethel Waters (Milan).

PERRY, RICH (RICHARD), tnr, sop saxes, fl; b. Cleveland, OH, 7/22/55. Began on alto sax. Stud. at Bowling Green St. U. 1973–5. Pl. w. Glenn Miller Orch. '75–6; Thad Jones–Mel Lewis Orch. '77–8;

Mel Lewis Orch. '78–81 and fr. '87; John Fedchock–Maria Schneider bb fr. '89; Fred Hersch fr. '90. Perry app. as a soloist w. UMO in Helsinki '90. Leads a gp. w. Harold Danko. Favs: Wayne Shorter, Joe Henderson, Coltrane. Fests: Eur. '77–8, '80, '88 w. Jones-Lewis-Mel Lewis Orch. CDs: Steep.; w. Hersch (Chesky); Stefan Karlsson (Just.); Nora York (Polystar); Bill Warfield (Inter.); Fedchock (Res.).

PERSIANY, ANDRÉ PAUL STEPHANE (Persiani), pno, comp; b. Paris, France, 11/19/27. Musical family. Pl. at US Army bases in Germ. 1945. Rec. debut in France '46. In '47 worked w. Hubert Fol and Be Bop Minstrels, rec. w. Kenny Clarke, Dick Collins. After army service, tour. and rec. w. Buck Clayton; Big Bill Broonzy; Mezz Mezzrow; later w. Lionel Hampton; Sidney Bechet. Visited US in '56, app. at Metropole Café w. Charlie Shavers; Roy Eldridge; and others. In NYC again in '61 worked w. Bud Freeman, Jonah Jones, remaining until '69. In Paris in '70s worked w. Carrie Smith, Jonah Jones. A swinging pnst. infl. by the block chord style of Milt Buckner, he also earned recognition as arr. Infl. by Benny Carter, Gil Evans. CDs: w. Cat Anderson; Buckner; Arnett Cobb (B&B); B. Clayton (Vogue).

PERSIP, CHARLI (CHARLES LAWRENCE), dms, perc, lead; b. Morristown, NJ, 7/26/29. Two uncles were mus. Stud. in Newark, N.J., then at Juilliard for two yrs. in late 1940s. Pl. w. Joe Holiday and local bands in Newark. Pl. w. Tadd Dameron '53; Dizzy Gillespie '53–8, incl. St. Dept. tours of Middle East, So. America '56; Johnny Richards Orch. '58–9; Harry James Orch. '59; also pl. and rec. in '50s w. Lee Morgan; Dinah Washington; Kenny Dorham; Zoot Sims. Formed own gp., the Jazz Statesmen, w. Freddie Hubbard and Ron Carter '60. Pl. w. Gil Evans Orch. '60–1; house band at Apollo Theatre '62–6; Billy Eckstine '66–73; Archie Shepp '76–80; Frank Foster '77–8. Taught dms. and theory at Jazzmobile since '74 and is the author of a book entitled *How Not to Play Drums*. Pl. w. own bb, the Superband, since '81; own qnt., Persipitation, since '92. Favs: Elvin Jones, Roach. Fests: Eur., Africa, Asia since '56; NJF w. Gillespie '57. TV: Dizzy Gillespie 70th Birthday at Wolftrap. CDs: SN; w. Gillespie (Verve; CAP); Q. Jones (Imp.); Roland Kirk (Merc.); Kenny Burrell (Verve).

PERSON, HOUSTON STAFFORD JR., tnr sax; b. Newberry, SC, 11/10/34. Father sang in church choir; moth. pl. pno. Stud. w. Aaron Harvey at So. Carolina St. Coll. 1952–5. In army 1955–8; pl. w. Eddie Harris; Lanny Morgan; Don Menza; Don Ellis; Leo Wright; Cedar Walton; Lex Humphries while stationed in Germ. Stud. at Hartt Coll. of Mus. '58–61. Pl. w. Johnny Hammond Smith '61–3; own gp. fr. '63; also pl. w. Groove Holmes; Charles Earland; Ran Blake. Has teamed w. Etta Jones since '68 and prod. recs. for Bill Hardman; Charles Earland; Charles Brown; Johnny Lytle; Dakota Staton; Jimmy Ponder; etc. Pl. on many jazz cruises. A blues-oriented player with a large, warm sound. Favs: Jacquet, Getz, Ammons, Stitt. Received the Eubie Blake Jazz Awd. in '85. Fests: Eur., Japan. CDs: Prest.; 32; Muse; Savant; SN; High.; Person–Buddy Tate–N. Simpkins (Muse) w. Ron Carter; Etta Jones; Joey De Francesco (Muse).

PERSSON, ÅKE, tbn; b. Hassleholm, Sweden, 2/25/32; d. Stockholm, Sweden, 2/5/75. Hailed as Swedish counterpart to J. J. Johnson, he pl. w. many bands incl. Simon Brehm; Arne Domnerus; Harry Arnold; Lars Gullin. After tour. w. Quincy Jones 1959–60, he settled in Berlin '61, working w. radio house band until '75. Also pl. w. Clarke-Boland bb; C. Basie; D. Ellington; D. Gillespie. Rec. w. Stan Getz; Herbie Mann; Geo. Wallington; Roy Haynes. Died after reportedly deliberately driving his car off a bridge in Stockholm. CDs: w. Basie (Roul.; Mos.); Clarke-Boland (MPS); Clifford Brown (Prest.); Q. Jones (Merc.; Qwest); Getz (Drag.).

PETERSON, HANNIBAL. *See* **LOKUMBE, HANNIBAL.**

PETERSON, OSCAR EMMANUEL, pno, comp, educ, lead; b. Montreal, Que., Canada, 8/15/25. Father an amateur mus. who trained his five children on piano and brass instruments. Oscar's second instructor was sist. Daisy, later a prominent piano teacher. Both she and Oscar studied with Paul de Marky, a Hungarian concert pianist trained by a student of Liszt and later a teacher at McGill U. Peterson's classical training was extensive. He attended Montreal HS with Maynard Ferguson and played in a band led by Ferguson's brother Percy. Peterson won a Canadian Broadcasting Corp. amateur contest and was given his own regular 15–minute program 1939. The broadcasts revealed a strong Teddy Wilson influence. In 1944 he began to play with Johnny Holmes's dance band. Signed to a contract by Canadian RCA Victor, he made recordings 1945–9, most exploiting his prowess at boogie-woogie but not representative of his playing at the time. Leading a trio at the Alberta Lounge he was heard by many American musicians visiting Montreal, including Ray Brown and Coleman Hawkins. He was offered a job by Jimmie Lunceford and urged to move to the US by Count Basie and others.

Norman Granz, at first unimpressed by the boogie-woogie recordings, heard a broadcast from the Alberta in '49 and went to the club. He booked Peterson for a surprise appearance, backed by Ray Brown and Buddy Rich, with JATP at Carnegie Hall that September. In '50 Peterson became a regular with JATP and also toured in a duo with Brown, then added Irving Ashby on guitar. Barney Kessel replaced Ashby and, a year later, Herb Ellis took Kessel's place to form one of the most celebrated trios in jazz history. Ellis left in '58, drummer Edmund Thigpen joined the group to form another illustrious trio until '65 when Thigpen left and Brown dropped out to settle in California. Various rhythm teams included bassists Sam Jones '66–70, and George Mraz '70; and drummers Louis Hayes '65–6; Bobby Durham '67–70. In '72, when Granz formed the Pablo label, Peterson was often allied with Niels Pedersen and Joe Pass. He recorded a series of duets with trumpeters Dizzy Gillespie; Roy Eldridge; Sweets Edison; Clark Terry; and Jon Faddis; collaborations with Count Basie; and all-star jam groups as in the series of albums done at the Montreux JF '75, '77. Granz also recorded him with big bands and strings. Martin Drew became his regular drummer in '80. In the late '80s and early '90s there were reunion tours and recordings with Brown, Ellis, and Durham. In May '93 while appearing at the Blue Note, NYC, Peterson suffered a stroke which cost him the use of his left hand. After two years of therapy he returned to active playing. His guitarists, whether Lorne Lofsky, Ellis, or Ulf Wakenius, became important in a new way, having to compensate for Peterson's disability. The pianist's right hand, however, is as dazzling as ever in its single line and is now also used for strong chordal contributions. From '95 he has appeared at international festivals and played club and concert engagements.

Most of Peterson's voluminous discography is under Granz's aegis, but for five years, beginning in the late '60s, he made private recordings (including several solo sessions) for Hans-Georg Brunner-Schwer, who later released them on his MPS label. From '90 he has been affiliated with the Telarc label. The number of awards he has received are legion. He won the *DB* Readers poll in '50 and on into the '60s incl. '63, '65–7; *Playboy* Musicians' Musician ten times; at least ten honorary doctorates; Medal of Service of the Order of Canada '73; and invested as a Companion of the Order of Canada '83. Always interested in education, he founded, in company with Brown and Thigpen, a jazz school which became known as the Advanced School of Contemporary Music '60. Before it closed it turned out such students as Mike Longo and Jay Leonhart.

Peterson's playing is a compendium of the history of jazz piano. In its clarity and brilliance it is reminiscent of Liszt, but the knowledge of Bach, Chopin, and Debussy is also evident. The jazz influences include Nat Cole (an obvious influence on his vocals as well), Teddy Wilson, and Art Tatum, but he is capable of Basie-like simplicity and able to utilize the powerful stride style. After the innovations of Bill Evans, some of that pianist's approach to tone and voicing appeared in his work. His playing from the earliest days embraced both the swing era and bebop. His noted compositions include the *Canadiana Suite* '64 and *Hymn to Freedom*, which became one of the crusade hymns during the civil rights movement in the US. His earlier collaboration with animator Norman McLaren, *Begone Dull Care*, won awards worldwide. Other works include "Fields of Endless Day"; his score for Les Ballets Jazz du Canada contains a special waltz for the city of Toronto called "City Lights." TV: CBC documentary produced by his niece, Sylvia Sweeney. Biography: *Oscar Peterson: The Will to Swing*, Gene Lees '88. CDs: Verve; Pab.; MPS; Tel.; w. Lester Young; Getz (Verve); Count Basie; Benny Carter; Lockjaw Davis; Edison; Eldridge; Gillespie; Terry, etc. (Pab.).

PETERSON, RALPH, dms; b. Pleasantville, NJ, 5/20/62. Family of dmrs; start. pl. at age 3. Stud. at Rutgers U.'s Livingston Coll., maj. in tpt. before sw. to dms. While in coll. pl. w. Sonny Stitt; Curtis Fuller; Nat Adderley; Joanne Brackeen; and Jimmy Heath. Later w. Walter Davis; Art Blakey; Jon Faddis; David Murray; et al.; also pl. w. OTB on three albums. Since 1987 led his own gps. feat. many of his own comps. Also rec. w. Charles Lloyd and Michelle Rosewoman. Peterson is an adventurous dmr.-comp. who has dealt w. unusual meters, such as 17/8, and made use of unusual instrumentations involving cl., bs. cl., and vib. CDs: BN; Cap.; Evid.; Somethin' Else; w. R. Hargrove (Novus); OTB (BN); Lloyd Charles (ECM); J. Spaulding (Muse).

PETIT, BUDDY (JOSEPH CRAWFORD), b. White Castle, LA, ca. 1897; d. New Orleans, LA, 7/4/31. Played w. Jimmie Noone and Honore Dutrey band 1916; briefly w. Jelly Roll Morton in LA '17; led bands, Young Olympians and Black and Tan Orch., in NO and Tex.; pl. on SS *Madison* riverboat excursions. Petit never rec. but was described by other NO trumpeters as an important infl. in the early yrs. of the century.

PETRUCCIANI, MICHEL, pno, comp; b. Orange, France, 12/28/62; d. NYC, 1/6/99. Of Italian descent, the son of jazz gtrst. Antoine "Tony" Petrucciani.

Born with a rare growth-stunting bone disease, his career was interrupted as the result of broken bones. Pl. dms. in family band w. brothers; stud. classical pno. for several yrs.; first prof. concert at 13. By 17, he had moved to Paris and rec. his first album. Arriving in US in '81, he introduced himself to saxophonist Charles Lloyd and they went on tour together. App. at Kool JF in NYC '84 with own band; in '85 he pl. w. duo/trio at the Montreux JF. First BN album in '86; in '89 he briefly explored a synth. and el-bs. sound, but his '91 album, *Playground*, marked a ret. to more basic values, w. French, Italian, Brazilian, and Jamaican references. Won the French Prix Django Reinhardt and Grand Prix Du Disque–Prix Boris Vian (equiv. to the Amer. Grammy Award) and the Italian Government Cultural Office award for Best Eur. Jazz Musician. Standing three feet high and weighing 65 pounds, Petrucciani overcame his physical disability to enjoy int'l success, perf. w. such mus. as Freddie Hubbard; Joe Henderson; Charlie Haden; Jack DeJohnette; Jim Hall; Buster Williams; John Abercrombie; Roy Haynes; and Gary Peacock. In the '90s he rec. as a team w. orgst. Eddy Louiss and app. w. him at Pescara JF. Petrucciani pl. two concerts at Umbria JF '96, one solo, the other a duet w. Tony Petrucciani. His remarkable technique and powerful rhythmic pl. were countered with a lyrical, almost Impressionistic character uniquely his own. CDs: BN; Owl; EPM; Drey.; Petrucciani–Eddy Louiss (Drey.); w. J. Lovano (BN).

PETTIFORD, OSCAR, bs, cello, comp, lead; b. Okmulgee, OK, on Indian reservation, 9/30/22; d. Copenhagen, Denmark, 9/8/60. Father, Doc Pettiford, orig. a veterinarian, formed family band w. his wife, a mus. teacher, and eleven children, incl. Oscar. Raised mainly in Minneapolis; tour. w. family band until 1941. Toured in Charlie Barnet band as half of two-bs. team w. Chubby Jackson '43. With Roy Eldridge at the Onyx Club; co-leader w. Dizzy Gillespie (at the same club) of first bebop gp. to pl. 52nd St. late '43–4; made his rec. debut w. Esq. All-Stars Dec. '43. With Coleman Hawkins; Boyd Raeburn in LA '45; Duke Ellington Nov. '45 to Mar. '48 and subsequently rejoin. him many times. With Woody Herman '49. After breaking an arm pl. softball while w. Herman, began experimenting w. jazz cello '50; rec. on the instrument for Mercer Recs. '50. Freelanced in early '50s w. Louis Bellson–Charlie Shavers and his own gps.; occasionally led a 13–pc. band. Left for Eur. '58 and lived in Copenhagen until his death from a "polio-like virus," working w. Stan Getz; Bud Powell; and other expatriates. He was a direct infl. on Niels-Henning Ørsted Pedersen. Pettiford was the most melodically inventive and technically agile bassist in jazz after Jimmy Blanton. He showed unusual skill in adapting his style to the cello, where his pizzicato sounded like Charlie Christian's gtr. lines. A talented writer, his comps incl.: "Blues in the Closet"; "Tricrotism"; "Swingin' Till the Girls Come Home"; "Bohemia After Dark." Won *Esq.* Gold Award '44–5; *Metronome* poll '45; *DB* Critics poll '53, '55–7. CDs: Imp.; Topaz; Sav.; BL; w. Ellington (RCA; Prest.); R. Charles–Milt Jackson (Atl.); Wynton Kelly (BN); J. Coltrane (Beth.); Coleman Hawkins (Cap.; Story.; Riv.; Del.); C. Parker (Stash); Miles Davis (Prest.; BN); Thelonious Monk (Riv.); B. Holiday (Story.); S. Chaloff (Mos.); Lucky Thompson (Imp.); R. Rodney (Sav.); Earl Hines (Del.).

PETTIS, JACK, tnr sax, lead; b. Danville, IL, 1902. Started on C-Melody sax, age 16. Moved to Chi. and pl. w. Elmer Schoebel bef. joining NORK. To NYC as accomp. to vaudeville singer; stayed, sw. to tnr. sax, and join. Ben Bernie 1929–30; then led own band (for Bernie) on board SS *Leviathan*. Made several recs. for Vict., Okeh with personnel incl. Adrian Rollini; Joe Venuti; Eddie Lang; Tommy Dorsey; Jack Teagarden; Benny Goodman. Own bands at New Yorker Hotel '32 and in LA '37, then retired from mus. LP: Retrieval. CDs: Kings Cross; w. NORK (Mile.; Village); Red Nichols (Jazz Oracle).

PHILLIPS, BARRE, bs, comp; b. San Francisco, CA, 10/27/34. Took up bs. at age 13, classical stud. w. Fred Zimmerman in NYC. Pl. w. Don Heckman, Don Ellis 1962; Eric Dolphy, Gunther Schuller '63–4; J. Giuffre trio '63–5; tour. Eur. w. George Russell '64. Rec. w. Bob James; pl. w. Archie Shepp at NJF. From '67 he divided his time among London, Paris, and the US, working in France w. Marion Brown; Germ. w. Gunter Hampel; and in a gp. known as Music By '79–80. In '80s mus.-in-residence at Mus. Gallery, Toronto. Later in the decade feat. w. Derek Bailey and British bs. Barry John Guy. Many recs. w. John Surman; Dave Holland; the classical · ensemble Accroche Note. Phillips has been called a major link between the Eur. and Amer. free jazz scenes. CDs: ECM; w. Heiner Stadler (JA); Archie Shepp (Imp.).

PHILLIPS, FLIP (Joseph Edward Filipelli), tnr sax, bs cl; b. Brooklyn, NY, 3/26/15; d. Fort Lauderdale, FL, 8/17/01. Took up cl. in 1927. Stud. cl., theory w. cousin Frank Reda who also gave his prof. start through club dates. Worked as cl. in Bklyn. restaurant '34–9; then w. Frankie Newton at Kelly's Stable '40–1. Sw. to tnr. sax w. Larry Bennett at Hickory House '42–3. Came to prominence w. Woody Herman '44–6; then joined JATP as a regular through

'57, his frenetic solo on "Perdido" winning public acclaim. Starting in the spring of '52, he visited Eur. annually w. JATP for several yrs.; also w. Gene Krupa Trio in summer of '52. Tour. Eur. w. Benny Goodman '59. Settled in Pompano Beach, Fla., in '60s, working w. own qt. and managing a condominium. In '70 he pl. at the Colo. JP, the first of many apps. there; also pl. Pasadena JF. In '72 took part in Woody Herman alumni reunion at NJF-NY. Returned to full-time pl. '75, app. w. Teddy Wilson at Michael's Pub, NYC; W. Herman 40th anniversary Carnegie Hall concert '76. Tour. Eur. '82 and cont. to pl. in concert, fests. and jazz cruises aboard the SS *Norway* and *Song of America*. Celebrated his 80th birthday w. party/fest. in Fla. His warm-toned tnr. sax effectively caressed a ballad and swung with vibrant authority on medium and up tempos, reflecting Webster, Hawkins, and, occasionally, Young. Fav: Frankie Trumbauer. Polls: *Esq.* New Star '45; *Metronome* '48; *DB* '48–9. Films: w. Herman, *Sensations of 1945; Earl Carroll's Vanities* '45; *Hit Parade of 1947; New Orleans* '47. TV: JATP on Nat Cole Show. Some of his fav. solos are incl. in Fred Astaire's recs. for Norman Granz. CDs: Verve; Conc.; Chiaro.; w. Herman (Col.; BB; Conc.); Red Norvo (Stash); B. Goodman (MM); Charlie Parker (Verve); JATP (Verve; Pab.); B. Holiday; F. Astaire (Verve); *Town Hall Concert* (Comm.); Metronome All-Star Band (BB); Nat Cole (Cap.); S. Kenton (Mos.).

PHILLIPS, SONNY (ROOSEVELT; aka Jalal Sabir Rushdan), org, pno; b. Birmingham, AL, 12/7/36. Studied priv. w. Ahmad Jamal 1955; prof. start through tnr. sax players Nicky Hill, Paul Bascomb, and Eddie Harris. In '60s worked w. Eddie Harris; Gene Ammons; Jimmy Witherspoon; Arthur Prysock; and Rusty Bryant. From '70s mostly pl. and rec. w. Houston Person and Etta Jones. Began teaching regularly '77 in Bklyn. and later in Pasadena, Calif. After a serious struggle w. cancer '80–1, he moved to Altadena, Calif. '82 and resumed teaching. CDs: w. Houston Person–Etta Jones (Muse).

PHYFE, EDDIE (EDWIN LLOYD), dms; b. LaCrosse, WI, 8/24/29; d. Bethesda, MD, 7/29/92. Raised in Westchester County, N.Y. Stud. w. Fred Albright; pl. w. Dick Wellstood; Dick Hyman; Bob Wilber; et al.; first recs. at age 16 w. Wilber's Wildcats. As teenager worked w. Pee Wee Russell; Mezz Mezzrow; Red McKenzie; Eddie Condon; Wild Bill Davison; at Jimmy Ryan's, Nick's, Stuyvesant Casino, etc. In early 1950s worked w. Wilber; Marian McPartland; Bobby Hackett; rec. w. Mel Powell; tour. w. and co-led The Six '54–5. Moved to Wash., D.C. '56. Led house band at Patio Lounge. Pl. w.

Charlie Byrd gp. '57–8; own trio at Charlie's Cafe '58–60; freelanced w. Lester Young; Billie Holiday; Sonny Stitt; Billy Butterfield mid to late '50s. From '60s worked primarily in film, theatre, and TV recs.; occasionally as writer, actor, dir., and prod. incl. film *Dead to the World* '59. Recs. w. Byrd; Joe Bushkin; Sidney Bechet; Hot Lips Page; Billie Holiday; et al. CDs: w. all-star gps. incl. Bechet, Hot Lips Page in *World's Greatest Jazz Concert #1, #2* (Jazz.).

PICHON, FATS (WALTER), pno; b. New Orleans, LA, 1906; d. Chicago, IL, 2/26/67. Studied pno. fr. age 8 to 16; also stud. at New Engl. Cons. Worked in NO in 1920s w. the Tulane Orch.; led own band at Pelican Café; worked w. Sidney Desvigne on the SS *Island Queen*. Also tour. Mex. and Tex., and pl. in NYC w. Luis Russell; Elmer Snowden; Fess Williams, and Lucky Millinder. Rec. as leader of trio w. Henry "Red" Allen and Teddy Bunn. Ret. to NO '31; again worked w. Desvigne and led band on SS *Capitol*; hosted TV show from the Absinthe House late '50s; cont. to work as soloist into '60s. CDs: w. Russell; Red Allen (Collectors Classics).

PICKENS, WILLIE L., pno, arr; b. Milwaukee, WI, 4/18/31. Mother was amateur pnst.; stepfath. was prof. alto sax. Pl. in hs band w. Bunky Green, Frank Morgan. Stud. at Wisc. Cons. 1947–54 (Teacher's Certificate '54); U. of Wisc.-Milwaukee '54–8 (B.S. in mus. educ. '58). App. at '61 NJF w. Eddie Harris. Worked as mus. teacher in Chi. schs. '66–90. Chairman of mus. dept. at Wendell Phillips HS '76–90. Freelanced, mainly in Chi. and Midwest, w. Arturo Sandoval; Jackie McLean; Jon Faddis; James Moody; Nancy Wilson; Joe Williams; Art Farmer; Stanley Turrentine; Ray Brown; Charles McPherson; Tom Harrell; Steve Grossman; Nat Adderley; et al. Worked w. Wynton Marsalis–Elvin Jones at Bottom Line, NYC '90. Member of Elvin Jones Jazz Machine fr. '91. Led qt. w. Joe Henderson, Buster Williams, Billy Higgins in concert at Webster U., St. Louis '93. Concerts, jazz cruises w. Clark Terry, Louie Bellson fr. '94. Pickens' trio perf. w. the Chi. Children's Choir at the Chi. JF '95; he wrote voc. arrs. for concert. Taught jazz pno. at Northern Ill. U. '95. Since '94, he has participated in the Chi. Public Schs.' Jazz Mentors program. Favs: Tatum, B. Powell, Kenny Kirkland, Monk; arrs: Tadd Dameron, Klaus Ogerman, Gil Evans. Fests: Red Sea JF w. Chi. Jazz All-Stars '90; Eur., Japan w. Jones fr. '91; Bern JF w. C. Terry '95. CDs: Southport; w. E. Harris (VJ); E. Jones (Enja); L. Bellson; Clark Terry (Chiaro.); S. Grossman (Drey.).

PICOU, ALPHONSE FLORISTAN, cl; b. New Orleans, LA, 10/19/1878; d. New Orleans, 2/4/61.

Started on gtr. at age 14; cl. at 15. Pl. in Accordiana band 1894; his own Independence band 1897; Oscar Duconge 1899; Excelsior Band 1900; Keppard's Olympia Band 1901. Later w. Bunk Johnson; Emanuel Perez; Dave Peyton; Wooden Joe Nicholas. Active w. many bands, symph. orchs., etc. in NO in '20s; w. Crescent City Orch. '32; then in retirement until '40. Rec. w. Kid Rena '40 and Papa Celestin '47; both times repeated the famous "High Society" solo (supposedly originated by George Baquet) with which he was most closely associated. In '60 he was the owner of a bar and occ. still active w. the Eureka Band. CDs: w. Papa Celestin, *The 1950s Radio Broadcasts* (Arh.).

PIERANUNZI, ENRICO, pno; b. Rome, Italy, 12/5/49. Father, a gtrst., introduced him to jazz recs. at age 6. Stud. classical pno. w. Dante Ullu 1957–71. First prof. gig w. Marcello Rosa '68. Pl. in Italy w. visiting mus. incl. Kenny Clarke; Sal Nistico; Johnny Griffin; Art Taylor; Kai Winding; Chet Baker; Art Farmer; Sonny Stitt; Lee Konitz; Jim Hall '73–early '80s. Led own gps. and perf. as solo pno. fr. '75. Pl. w. Dino Piana–Oscar Valdambrini Sxt. '76–82; trio w. Marc Johnson, Joey Baron '84–6; duo w. Johnson '90; duo w. Paul Motian '92. Perf. at Angry Squire, NYC w. Michael Moore, Joey Baron; also at Condon's w. Lew Soloff and in Bost '85; w. Johnson, Peter Erskine at Blue Ridge Mus. Fest in Lynchburg, Va. '90. Leads a trio w. Enzo Pietropaoli, Fabrizio Sferra. He has perf. on numerous film soundtracks for composers Armando Trovaioli and Ennio Morricone, incl. *Nuovo Cinema Paradiso*. Taught seminars fr. '75; at Siena dur. summers '80–5. Teaches at the Siena winter sess. and at Frosinone Cons., where he is a full professor. "Behind his improvisations, behind his brilliant compositional talent one recognizes an authentic musical culture, although Enrico never shows it off, never underlines it. This is his great quality, and a rare one as well." —Pino Candini. Favs: Bill Evans, Chick Corea, Keith Jarrett. Polls: Ital. Critics Poll '82; *Musica* Jazz '82, '88–9. Fests: all major in Eur.; USA '82, '85, '90. CDs: Timel.; SN; IDA; yvp; w. C. Baker; L. Konitz (Phil.).

PIERCE, BILL aka BILLY (WILLIAM WATSON III), tnr, sop saxes, comp; b. Hampton, VA, 9/25/48. At age 13 began pl. tnr. sax; also alto sax, cl., bs. cl. in sch. band. Stud. in Tenn., then at Berklee Coll. of Mus. in Boston (B.A. 1973). Pl. w. James Williams in duo, bbs and Alan Dawson's qt. Worked w. Marvin Gaye; Stevie Wonder; D. Gillespie; Art Farmer; Sam Jones. Pl. w. Williams '79–80 and again in '84–5. By this time he had achieved prominence w. Art Blakey's Messengers '80–2, where he also served as mus. dir.

Tour. w. Tony Williams qnt. '86–94. Professor at Berklee. A solid, modern mainstream player called by Branford Marsalis, "my first major influence." CDs: Sunny.; PW; w. Blakey (Conc.; Timel.); A. Hart (Novus); G. Keezer (Sunny.); J. Swana (CC); J. Williams (Sunny.; DIW); T. Williams (BN).

PIERCE, BILLIE (Wilhelmina Goodson), pno, voc; b. Marianna, FL, 6/8/07; d. New Orleans, LA, 9/29/74. At age 15, played for Bessie Smith for a week in Pensacola, Fla. To NO 1929 to temporarily replace her sist., Sadie, in Buddy Petit's band on the SS *Madison*. Returned to NO in '30, working at the Blue Jay, where she met cornetist DeDe Pierce, whom she married. Well known in NO for thirty yrs., the Pierces gained int'l recognition through two '60 Riv. albums. Soon also rec. for Atl. and various smaller labels. Throughout '60s, she frequently perf. at Preservation Hall in NO as well as on many coll. campuses and jazz fests. CDs: Riv.

PIERCE, DEDE (Joseph De Lacrois), tpt, crnt, voc; b. New Orleans, LA 2/18/04; d. New Orleans, 11/23/73. First pl. w. Arnold Dupas' Olympia Band 1924. He and his wife, Billie, were regulars at Luthjens fr. '35 to mid '50s, when illness hospitalized them both and blinded DeDe. Recovered, they rec. for Riv. '60 and rekindled their careers which, for the most part, ran parallel. DeDe accomp. Ida Cox on her last Southern tour. Originally infl. by Chris Kelly and Kid Rena, his style in later yrs. also had distinct traces of Louis Armstrong. Pl. for dances and parades. CDs: Riv.

PIERCE, NAT (NATHANIEL), pno, comp; b. Somerville, MA, 7/16/25; d. Los Angeles, CA, 6/10/92. Studied at New Engl. Cons. Mainly active in 1943–51 w. small gps. in Bost., incl. Nick Jerret, Shorty Sherock. Tour. w. Larry Clinton '48; then ret. to Bost. to form own bb, which rec. for Motif label and lasted until early '50. In '51 he began a long assoc. w. Woody Herman as pnst. and arr., remaining until '55 and writing for him off and on for many yrs. Pierce rec. an album for RCA Vict. in Feb. '57 at Harlem's Savoy Ballroom; his was the last bb to pl. there bef. it was demolished. From '61 he doubled as Herman's arr. and road mgr., pl. a major role in the orch.'s resurgence. From '66 he was mainly active in LA, writing for Carmen McRae; Louie Bellson; Anita O'Day. Wrote orchestrations for Erroll Garner's *Other Voices* and was his road manager for tour of Japan, Austral., and New Zeal. Jun. '72; also subbed for eight wks. in Stan Kenton band '72 and for several mos. w. Basie band in '76, dur. those leaders' illnesses. With Frankie Capp form. Capp-Pierce Orch.

(later billed as Capp-Pierce Juggernaut) '75, enjoying local success in LA; also rec. frequently w. Scott Hamilton; Warren Vaché; Rosemary Clooney. Pierce took part in many hs and coll. clinics and was seen in almost all major US and Eur. fests., often w. Herman. He was an exceptional rhythm pnst. in the style of Count Basie. As arr., he contributed many works to the Herman book, among them his own "Poor House Blues"; "Kissin' Cousins"; and arrs. of such standards as "Days of Wine and Roses"; "Body and Soul"; "Jazz Me Blues"; "Blue Monk." After Pierce's death, Capp cont. to perf. w. the band, retaining the Capp–Pierce billing for a time. Fests: Eur. fests. w. One O'Clock Jumpers '89. TV: wrote the arrs. for *The Sound of Jazz* '57. CDs: w. Capp–Pierce Juggernaut (Conc.); Freddie Green–Al Cohn (BB); L,H&R (Imp.); R. Eldridge (NW); S. Getz (Biograph); S. Chaloff (Up); W. Herman (RCA).

PIETROPAOLI, ENZO, bs, el-bs; b. Genoa, Italy, 9/29/55. Studied briefly w. Massimo Giorgi 1974; John Neves '75; mainly self-taught. Pl. w. Enrico Pieranunzi fr. '82; Rita Marcotulli–Pietro Tonolo '83–88; Lingomania '86–9; Lanfranco Malaguti fr. '87; Roberto Gatto fr. '89; Enrico Rava fr. '91. Also freelanced in Eur. w. Chet Baker; Woody Shaw; Lester Bowie; Kenny Wheeler; Toots Thielemans; Bob Berg; Johnny Griffin; Lee Konitz; Archie Shepp; Phil Woods; Curtis Fuller; Jimmy Knepper; Albert Mangelsdorff; Ray Bryant; Ben Sidran; Cedar Walton; Joe Pass; Kenny Clarke; others. Pietropaoli taught at Jazz U., Terni '85–9. Favs: Milt Hinton, Paul Chambers, Charlie Haden. Polls: *Musica Jazz* '87–9. Fests: all major in Eur.; US '87. CDs: Gala; w. Malaguti (Nueva); Baker; Konitz (Phil.); C. Fuller (Timel.).

PIKE, DAVE (DAVID SAMUEL), vib, comp; b. Detroit, MI, 3/23/38. Studied dms. fr. 1946. To LA '54, concentrating on vib. and mrba. and working w. Elmo Hope; Harold Land; Carl Perkins; and Dexter Gordon bef. moving to NYC in '60. Tour. w. Herbie Mann '61–4; then settled in Eur., pl. at fests., writing for TV, and rec. w. Clark-Boland band. Back in US '73, freelanced w. Buddy DeFranco; Nelson Riddle; Ray Anthony. Ret. to NYC '80. A broken arm, suffered in a fall fr. a loft bed, set him back about three yrs. A gig at the Bonaventure Hotel in downtown LA helped him to rehabilitate and he moved to Ghent, Belgium, two and a half yrs. later. Ran own jazz club and rec. for Criss Cross '86; Timeless '88. Ret. to US '90s, working first in Fla., then Wilmington, No. Carolina, bef. settling once more in LA. A superior, self-taught vibraphonist. Favs: Lionel Hampton, Milt Jackson. Infls: Parker, Rollins, Bud Powell. CDs:

MPS; CC; Muse; Timel.; CBS Portrait; w. Bill Evans (Col.); H. Mann (Atl.).

PINE, COURTNEY, tnr, sop saxes, bs cl, fl; b. London, England, 3/18/64. Of Jamaican origin; start on cl., then tnr. sax, in reggae and funk gps. Sw. to jazz from early 1980s in various wkshp. groups such as Spontaneous Music Ensemble and the Freebop Band. In mid '80s founded the Abibi Jazz Arts, an association dedicated to the advancement of jazz among black British musicians. Worked with all-black big band, The Jazz Warriors, and small gps., among them, The World's First Saxophone Posse. Worked w. Geo. Russell; Art Blakey; Elvin Jones; and a bb led by Rolling Stones drummer Charlie Watts. From mid '80s led own qt. or qnt.; tour. US '90. Strongly infl. by John Coltrane, Pine has also incorporated reggae and free jazz elements in his music. Visited Egypt and So. Africa in the mid '90s. His '97 release, *Underground*, done w. Nicholas Payton, Mark Whitfield, and DJ Pogo, reflected some of his experiences in those countries. Pine has become one of the most acclaimed British jazz players of recent years. CDs: Ant.; Island; w. Bheki Mseleku (World Circuit).

PINKETT, WARD (WILLIAM), tpt; b. Newport News, VA., 4/29/06; d. NYC, 3/15/37. Trumpet at age 10; stud. in Meridian, Miss. Joined White Bros. Orch. in Wash., D.C.; pl. w. Charlie Johnson at Small's Paradise, NYC. With Jelly Roll Morton 1928 and '30; feat. on "Shoe Shiner's Drag"; also rec. w. King Oliver, Bubber Miley, Clarence Williams, James P. Johnson. '29–31. From '33 pl. w. Rex Stewart; Teddy Hill; and in qt. led by Albert Nicholas at Adrian Rollini's Tap Room '35. CDs: w. Morton (BB); Chick Webb (Dec.); Clarence Williams; King Oliver (Class.).

PIRON, A. J. (ARMAND JOHN), vln, comp, lead.; b. New Orleans, LA, 8/16/1888; d. New Orleans, 2/17/43. Musical training from his fath., an orch. lead.; first prof. gig 1904. Led own band '08; pl. w. Peerless Orch. ca. '12; front man for Olympia Orch. fr. '12. Established publishing co. w. Clarence Williams '15; publ. his own works, incl. "I Wish I Could Shimmy Like My Sister Kate." Pl. w. Papa Celestin '16; occasionally app. w. W. C. Handy's Orch. '17. From '18 to '28 led the Piron Orch., perf. mostly in NO; pl. at the Cotton Club and the Roseland Ballroom, NYC early '20s. Led various small gps. on riverboats in '30s and early '40s. Other best-known comp. is "The Purple Rose of Cairo," written w. pnst. Steve Lewis. Piron died in a NO charity hospital. CDs: Azure.

PISANO, JOHN, gtr, comp; b. Staten Island, NY, 2/6/31. Began stud. pno. at age 10. Sw. to gtr. at 13. Stud. w. Chuck Wayne. Pl. in air force band from 1951–6. Paul Horn recommended him to Chico Hamilton, w. whom he pl. until '58. Worked as Peggy Lee's mus. dir. and w. Herb Alpert and the Tijuana Brass; Benny Goodman; Joe Pass. Much studio work in LA fr. '60. First rec. w. Chico Hamilton '57 on PJ. Own LP: *Velas* (Voss). CDs: Pab.; w. Pass (Pab.; PJ); Bill Perkins (Riv.); Hamilton (SN); F. Capp (Conc.).

PIZZARELLI, BUCKY (JOHN PAUL), gtr; b. Paterson, NJ, 1/9/26. Sons are gtrst./voc. John; bsst. Martin; daughter Mary is also gtrst.; uncle, Bobby Domenick, pl. gtr. w. name bands. Educ. at Central HS, Paterson. Self-taught while sitting in w. Joe Mooney. Tour. w. Vaughn Monroe 1943. Army service in Eur. and Philippines '44–6. With Monroe '46–52. On staff at NBC in NYC '52–66 w. time out to tour. w. Three Suns trio '56–7. On staff at ABC, pl. w. Bobby Rosengarden on Dick Cavett Show late '60s. Tour. Eur. w. Benny Goodman '70, '72–4. Pl. in duos w. Geo. Barnes; Zoot Sims; Bud Freeman; Stephane Grappelli; Joe Venuti '70s. Duo w. son John fr. '81. Tour. Canada w. Peter Appleyard '85–8; Japan w. Benny Carter '87; Switz. w. Yank Lawson, US w. Charlie Byrd, Barney Kessel '89; and w. S. Grappelli '90. Pl. at JVC fest. w. Bobby Short '90. Guest of honor at Eddie Lang gtr. fest. in Monterodoni, Italy '90. Perf. at Grappelli's 85th birthday concert, Carnegie Hall '93. Pizzarelli, who is a veritable storehouse of songs, plays a 7-string electric guitar. The extra string, tuned to A, lets him play a bass line to his own solos and makes this guitar a great overall accompanying instrument. He is also an accomplished classical guitarist. Taught at William Paterson Coll. '71–88 and is the author of the gtr. book *Touch of Class* (Keith Perkins Publ.). Fav: George Van Eps. Fests: Eur., Japan; US jazz parties. CDs: Stash; Story.; Scott Hamilton–Bucky Pizzarelli (Conc.); w. John Pizzarelli (Stash; Chesky; Novus); Johnny Frigo (Chesky); B. Wilber–K. Davern; Flip Phillips (Chiaro.); S. McCorkle (Conc.); Miles Davis (Col.); Hank Jones (Stash); L. Hampton (Tel.); Grappelli (Angel; Omega; Tel.); Lee Wiley (Aud.); K. Davern (Arb.).

PIZZARELLI, JOHN (JOHN PAUL JR.), gtr, voc; b. Paterson, NJ, 4/6/60. Father is Bucky Pizzarelli. Stud. bjo. w. uncles, then pl. tpt. fr. age 9. Mostly self-taught on gtr. w. help from father. Pl. and sang in a duo w. father fr. age 17. Sat in w. Bucky and Zoot Sims at a Highlights in Jazz concert, NYC '80. Perf. and rec. w. own gps. since early 1980s. His '90s trio includes pno.

Ray Kennedy and bs., bro. Martin Pizzarelli. He has developed into a gtrst. adept at blazing tempos or on romantic ballads. As a vocalist he exudes a boyish charm, vulnerable on ballads and hiply rhythmic on the swinging numbers. Pizzarelli was voted the best male jazz vocalist in '88 and '89 by the Manh. Assoc. of Cabarets. The trio has app. several times at the Algonquin Hotel, NYC. Favs: Oscar Moore, Freddie Green, George Barnes, Bucky Pizzarelli. Polls: Garden State Mus. Awds. '90. Fests: Eur., Asia since '86. Video: *Jazz Guitar Virtuoso* (Mel Bay) '98. TV: apps. on ABC soaps *All My Children* and *Ryan's Hope*; NBC's *Today*; also Eur. TV. B'way: *Dream* '97. CDs: Novus; Chesky; Stash; w. Bucky Pizzarelli (Stash); Grappelli (Tel.); K. Lockhardt-Bost. Pops Orch. (RCA).

PIZZI, RAY (RAYMOND MICHAEL), saxes, fl, bsn; b. Everett, MA, 1/19/43. Studied at Bost. Cons. and Berklee Sch. 1960–64. Tour. w. Woody Herman '66; to LA '69, freelancing w. Dizzy Gillespie; Louie Bellson; Willie Bobo; Milcho Leviev. Rec. as lead. and sideman in a wide variety of settings, he became one of the few jazzmen to improvise on the bsn., though best known as a saxophonist. CDs: w. J. Chiodini (MCA); Joe Henderson (Mile.).

PLANK, JIM (JAMES M.), dms, perc, comp; b. San Diego, CA, 2/4/43. Musician-parents encouraged his interest in mus. John Guerin and Shelly Manne were key infl.; Mike Wofford and Don Sleet were musical role models who helped him get started professionally. A gifted dmr./percst., he pl. in diverse settings: jazz, symphonic (SD Symph. fr. 1961), and opera (SD Opera fr. '75). Pl. in band w. Bill Mays, Bob Magnusson, Peter Sprague '79–82. Pl. w. A. Farmer; B. Golson; K. Burrell; Wofford; H. Jones; L. Almeida; J. Pass; J. Moody; M. Lowe; J. Henderson; B. Kessel; D. Schuur. Fests: Playboy: Telluride; Tour Japan w. Schuur '91. TV: Many PBS *Club Date* series w. artists listed above. CDs: w. Almeida (Conc.); Wofford; Magnusson (Disc); Checkfield (Amer. Gramophone).

PLATER, BOBBY (ROBERT), alto sax, cl, fl, arr/comp; b. Newark, NJ, 5/13/14; d. Lake Tahoe, NV, 11/20/82. Father pl. dms. Worked w. Savoy Dictators 1937–9; Tiny Bradshaw '40–42. While w. Bradshaw comp. and arr. "Jersey Bounce." After leading own band in army, spent most of the rest of his career primarily with two leaders: eighteen years each w. Lionel Hampton and Count Basie, later becoming the latter's mus. dir. Mainly known as an excellent section man. CDs: w. Basie (Pab.); Teresa Brewer (Dr. Jazz); Hampton (BB).

PLAXICO, LONNIE LUVELL, bs, el-bs, pno; b. Chicago, IL, 9/4/60. Older bro. is dmr; moth. pl. pno. Began on el-bs. at age 12; learned to play by watching bro.'s band. Pl. w. local bands fr. 1973, incl. one gig backing Sonny Stitt '76. Pl. acoustic bs. fr. '76. Pl. w. Von Freeman '79–80; Oscar Lindsay '80–1; Wynton Marsalis '82. Freelanced w. Chet Baker, Hank Jones, Sonny Fortune, Harold Vick, Slide Hampton, Woody Shaw, etc. '83; Dexter Gordon, David Murray, Art Blakey '84. Pl. and rec. w. Dizzy Gillespie '85–6. Extens. freelance w. Dakota Staton, Jack DeJohnette, Kenny Burrell, Stanley Turrentine, Abbey Lincoln, Ronnie Mathews, Don Pullen, Clifford Jordan, Steve Coleman, Greg Osby, etc. fr. '86. Plaxico teaches at the New Sch. Favs: Ray Brown, Ron Carter, Paul Chambers. Fests: all major fr. '83. TV: Joan Rivers; *Today*. CDs: Muse; w. Terence Blanchard; W. Marsalis (Col.); Blakey (Conc.; Evid.); Steve Coleman (Pangaea); DeJohnette (Imp.; BN; Manh.); R. Eubanks; Cassandra Wilson (JMT); Osby (JMT; BN); B. Dennerlein (Verve).

PLEASURE, KING (Clarence Beeks), voc, lyricist; b. Oakdale, TN, 3/24/22; d. Los Angeles, CA, 3/21/81. Raised in Cincinnati. Won amateur night contest at Harlem's Apollo Theater, NYC 1951, singing his words to James Moody's solo on "I'm in the Mood for Love" (some credit the lyrics to Eddie Jefferson). He rec. this and several other vocalese numbers for which he wrote the words for Prest., incl. "Parker's Mood" and "Jumpin' with Symphony Sid." Moved to West Coast '56 and was based in SF. His later yrs. were spent living in relative obscurity, but he has been acknowledged as a founder of the vocalese movement that Lambert, Hendricks & Ross popularized in the '60s. CDs: Prest.; BN; HiFi Jazz.

POINDEXTER, "PONY" (NORWOOD), alto, and sop sax, voc; b. New Orleans, LA, 2/8/26; d. Oakland, CA, 4/14/88. Studied cl. in elementary sch.; attended Candell Cons. of Mus. in Oakland. Prof. debut in NO at Cave Club w. Sidney Desvigne 1940. Tour. w. Billy Eckstine '47–8.; pl. w. Vernon Alley, '50; Lionel Hampton '51–2; then own gp. at Bop City, SF. Tour. in small gps. on West Coast to March '59 when he took own gp. into Jazz Cellar, SF, remain. into '60. In '61 join. accomp. gp. for L,H&R. To Eur., Aug. '64; lived there for fifteen yrs. In '79 when illness curtailed his pl. career, he turned to singing. When Neal Hefti heard Poindexter pl. a Charlie Parker–style phrase in a solo, he wrote a piece based on it and called it "Little Pony," rec. by Count Basie '51; lyrics were added by Jon Hendricks '58. Autobiography: *The Pony Express*, Frankfurt,

Germ. '85. CDs: w. L,H&R (Col.); L,H&Bavan (BB); Wes Montgomery (PJ).

POLCER, ED (EDWARD JOSEPH), crnt; b. Paterson, NJ, 2/10/37. Father and uncle were prominent horn players in N.J. Began on xyl. at age 6. Stud. tpt. w. Prof. James V. Dittamo 1944–50; pl. solo crnt. in Paterson Civic Orch. at age 13. Pl. w. Knights of Dixieland at Hawthorne, N.J., HS '50–4. With Stan Rubin's Tigertown Five while stud. engineering at Princeton U. '54–8, incl. Eur. tours, Carnegie Hall, Grace Kelly's wedding, etc. Freelance in NYC fr. '58, frequently subbing for Max Kaminsky at Jimmy Ryan's. In air force early '60s. Pl. w. Red Balaban and Cats off and on '69–85; Benny Goodman '73; Bob Greene '75. Dir. of touring prog. at NY Jazz Museum '75. Manager and co-owner of Eddie Condon's '75–85. Led own gp. Midtown North at Condon's '83–5. Pres. of jazz educ. organization Int'l Art of Jazz '82–9. Tour. w. Condon's All-Stars fr. '90. Polcer cont. to be active on the fest. and jazz party scene. He perf. w. Jane Jarvis at Zinno in NYC early '93. Favs: R. Braff, Armstrong, B. Hackett, M. Spanier. Film: app. in *The Bell Jar*. TV: apps. on ABC soap opera *Ryan's Hope*. CDs: Jazz.; N-H.

POLLACK, BEN, lead, dms; b. Chicago, IL, 6/22/03; d. Palm Springs, CA, 6/7/71. First prominent as dmr. w. Friars Society Orch. (NORK); rec. for Gennett 1922–3. Form. his own band in Calif. '25; dur. next decade, band members incl. Glenn Miller; Benny Goodman; Jack Teagarden; Jimmy McPartland; Charlie Spivak; Matty Matlock; Yank Lawson; Harry James; Freddie Slack; Muggsy Spanier; Ray Bauduc; Dave Matthews; Irving Fazola. After breakup of band '34, many of the members reassembled under the leadership of Bob Crosby. Later Pollack form. other bands incl. one fronted by comedian Chico Marx '41; ran his own rec. co., Jewel, in mid '40s. Owned restaurants, pl. at them occasionally. Settled in Palm Springs, where he committed suicide. Although not an important mus. himself, Pollack consistently led the best white jazz orchs. of his era. CDs: Jazz.; w. NORK (Mile.).

POLLARD, TERRY JEAN, pno, vib; b. Detroit, MI, 8/15/31. Self-taught. Pl. "Star Dust" at age three and a half. Pl. w. Johnny Hill 1948–9; Emmit Slay Trio '50, '52; Billy Mitchell '52–3. Best remembered as pnst. and co-vib. in Terry Gibbs Qt. '53–7. App. w. him on Steve Allen TV show and tour. w. Birdland All-Stars. Leaving Gibbs, she settled in Det., working locally w. Yusef Lateef. She opted to remain in Det. in order to raise a family but cont. for many yrs. to lead a trio. A sparkling modern soloist showing Bud Pow-

ell and Gibbs influences, she was incapacitated after suffering a major stroke ca. '80. LPs: w. Gibbs (Merc.); Dorothy Ashby (Jzld.).

POLO, DANNY, cl; b. Toluca, IL, 12/22/01; d. Chicago, IL, 7/11/49. Grew up in Clinton, Ill.; first prof. jobs w. Elmer Schoebel in Chi. 1923. Played w. Ben Bernie '24–6; Joe Venuti; Jean Goldkette. Moved to France '28; mainly in Engl. in '30s as jazz soloist w. Ambrose Orch. Rec. w. all-star jazz ensembles for Dec. Back in US '39; rec. w. Coleman Hawkins; pl. w. Joe Sullivan at Café Society '39–40; app. w. Jack Teagarden in film, *Birth of the Blues*; pl. w. Claude Thornhill fr. '42 until his death. Also tour. briefly w. Dave Barbour '48. CDs: w. George Chisholm (Timel. Historical); Coleman Hawkins; two tracks in *The Women* (BB).

POMEROY, HERB (IRVING HERBERT III), tpt, comp, arr, lead, educ; b. Gloucester, MA, 4/15/30. Studied dentistry at Harvard; theory, comp., pno., tpt. at Schillinger House (later Berklee Coll. of Mus.) in Bost. Worked w. Charlie Parker, Charlie Mariano in Bost. 1953; then tour. w. Lionel Hampton '53–4. Led own bb in Bost. briefly bef. joining Stan Kenton Sept. '54. On faculty of Berklee Coll. of Mus. fr. '55. Led bb at The Stables, Bost. w. sidemen incl. Joe Gordon; Jaki Byard (on tnr. sax); Boots Mussulli; Charlie Mariano; Bill Berry. Taught at Lenox Sch. of Jazz '59–60. Led bb w. sidemen incl. Dusko Goykovich; Michael Gibbs; Sam Rivers; Hal Galper; Alan Dawson. Working for the Cultural Exchange Prog. of the US St. Dept., Pomeroy dir. the Radio Malaya Orch. in Malaysia '62. Pl. w. John Lewis's Orch. USA '62–3. Dir. Mass. Inst. of Tech. Concert Jazz Band fr. '63. Also taught at summer jazz clinics mid '60s. Hosted jazz TV show in Bost. '65–6. Comp. ballet scores *The Road of the Phoebe Snow; Wilderness of Mirrors* for Bost. dance co. early '70s. Extended work *Jolly Chocolate* commissioned by Nat'l Jazz Ens. and prem. at Lincoln Ctr. '74. Formed bb '75 incl. students, former sidemen, other Bost. mus. incl. John La Porta, Phil Wilson. Other Pomeroy sidemen have incl. Alan Broadbent; Lin Biviano; Joe and Pat LaBarbera; Harvey Mason; Miroslav Vitous; Ernie Watts; Mike Mantler; Gene Perla. Favs: Dizzy Gillespie, Miles Davis, Kenny Dorham. CDs: Daring; w. Mariano (Prest.; FS); Serge Chaloff (Mos.; BL); Charlie Parker (Stash); John Lewis (Atl.); Donna Byrne (Stash).

PONOMAREV, VALERY, tpt; b. Moscow, Russia, 1/20/43. Mother pl. pno. Began on dms., sw. to tpt. at age 16. Became interested in jazz after hearing Clifford Brown on shortwave radio; stud. bebop fr. recs.

he bought on the black market. Perf. at youth club in Moscow 1965–9; rec. on Melodiya label w. Vadim Sakun. Defected to Italy '71; pl. in Rome w. Romano Mussolini. Came to NYC '73; pl. club dates and worked as dept. store clerk; then sat in w. Art Blakey, who later sent for him to join the Jazz Messengers. Pl. w. Blakey '77–81. Ponomarev has led his own band, Universal Language, fr. '80; sidemen have incl. Ralph Moore; Larry Willis; Hideki Takao; Dennis Irwin; Kenny Washington; Victor Jones. He perf. w. Max Roach; Harold Land; Sam Dockery; Geo. Morrow in Clifford Brown memorial concert in Wilmington, Del. '91. Perf. at first Moscow Int'l Jazz Fest. '92. Favs: Clifford Brown, Freddie Hubbard, Fats Navarro, Lee Morgan, Blue Mitchell, Nat Adderley. Fests: all major w. Blakey. Film: *Frozen in Amber*, docu. about Russian expatriates in the arts. TV: many apps. w. Blakey. CDs: Res.; Vart.; w. Blakey (Timel.); Junior Cook (Steep.).

PONTY, JEAN-LUC, vln, kybds, comp; b. Avranches, Normandy, France, 9/29/42. Father taught vln. and moth. taught pno. Ponty stud. both from age 5. In 1955 he quit sch. to practice as concert vlnst., winning a prize at the Cons. in '60. First pl. jazz on sax; by '64 had become a jazz vlnst., pl. w. small gps. in clubs around France. Visited US in '67 when John Lewis invited him to take part in a vln. workshop at MJF. To LA '69, pl. and rec. w. Frank Zappa; settled permanently in US in '73, tour. w. Zappa. After pl. w. the Mahavishnu Orch., he form. his own jazz-rock gp. and soon found a wide audience for his original comps. pl. on el. vln. Throughout the '70s and '80s he produced and perf. on numerous albums, using synths. and, fr. '77, a 5-string el. instrument, known as the violectra. He teamed w. violinists Svend Asmussen, Stuff Smith, and Stephane Grappelli for an album, *Violin Summit* '66 and again w. Grappelli in a '73 album. Heard as guest soloist w. several symph. orchs., Ponty enjoyed success as a vlnst. who pioneered jazz, rock, bop, and modal jazz crossovers. CDs: Atl.; Epic; BN; PJ; Drey.; Verve; MPS; Ponty-Grappelli (MPS); w. Elton John (MCA); Mothers of Invention (Discreet); Mahavishnu Orch. (Col.); C. Corea (Polyd.); George Duke (Elek.).

POPE, ODEAN, tnr sax, oboe, fl, cl, pno; b. Ninety Six, SC, 10/24/39. Family moved to Phila. in early 1940s. Moth. pl. pno. and org. in church; fath. pl. tbn. and dms. Stud. fr. age 14 at Midway Mus. Sch. and Granoff Sch. of Mus., Phila. Pl. in Phila. w. Lee Morgan '55–6; Jimmy Smith '56–7; Chet Baker '64. In pit band at Uptown Theatre '65–71, backing Gladys Knight; Stevie Wonder; Temptations; etc. Pl. w. Max Roach '67–8; Billy Paul '69–71; fusion gp., Catalyst

'71–4; Geo. Taylor '78; Max Roach fr. '79; Philly Joe Jones, Archie Shepp '80; Magnificent Seven '81–3. Led the Odean Pope Saxophone Choir fr. '77. Taught at the Model Cities Cultural Arts Assoc. '71–5; Settlement Mus. Sch. Summer Mus. Camp '77–9; John Bartram HS. '79. Artist-in-res. at Amherst Coll. fr. '79; Community Coll. of Phila. and Cleveland's Cuyahoga Comm. Coll. '85; Phila. Perf. Arts HS '87. Favs: Hassan Ibn Ali, Charlie Parker. Polls: *DB; Musician; Billboard.* Fests: Eur.; Turkey w. Roach '91. CDs: Enja; SN; Moers; w. Roach (SN; BM).

PORCELLI, BOBBY (ROBERT A.), alto sax, fl; b. NYC, 12/16/37. Father was prof. saxophonist, moth. taught pno. Pl. w. Tito Rodriguez early 1960s; Duke Pearson, Joe Henderson–Kenny Dorham bb mid '60s; Machito '65–6; Tito Puente fr. '66; Mongo Santamaria '67, '88–91; Chuck Israels mid '70s. Since the early '80s, Porcelli has also perf. as a single in Eur. An original member of T. S. Monk's sxt.; also w. Monk on Monk Tentet. An exciting, Parker-based soloist. Favs: Parker, Stitt, Adderley, Kenny Garrett, Dick Oatts. Polls: *Latin NY* mag. '77. Fests: Eur. since early '80s. Film: *Radio Days* w. Tito Puente. CDs: Spl.; w. T. S. Monk (BN; N2K); M. Santamaria (Conc.); T. Puente (Conc.; Trop.); The Bronx Horns (Top Ten); Don Sickler (Up.).

PORCINO, AL, tpt, lead; b. NYC, 5/14/25. After hs stud. w. Charles Colin. Join. Louis Prima April 1943. Pl. w. Tommy Dorsey '44; Georgie Auld '45; Gene Krupa, Woody Herman '46; Stan Kenton '47–8; Chubby Jackson '49; and again w. Herman '49–50. During '50s he rejoined Herman and Kenton, also pl. w. Pete Rugolo, Charlie Barnet, Count Basie '51; Elliot Lawrence '52. Moved to LA '57; organized band w. Med Flory; solidified reputation as powerful lead tpt. w. Terry Gibbs orch. '59–62. Tour. w. singers incl. Sinatra, Judy Garland, Peggy Lee in '60s. Pl. w. Buddy Rich '68; Thad Jones–Mel Lewis '69–70, '75–6 incl. Eur., Japan tours in latter yrs. Concerts w. Chuck Mangione and Rochester Philharm. '70, '71. Led own bb intermittently in '70s, rec. w. Mel Tormé at the St. Regis Hotel, NYC '74. Moved to Munich '77, working w. SDR, SFB radio bands and own bb. Tour. US universities as a clinician for band wkshps. '83. Many concerts for Munich radio. William Whitworth wrote of him: "I think Al has been more successful than any other jazz lead player in combining bigness with brilliance." Favs: Gillespie, Conte Candoli; arrs: B. Holman, A. Cohn, Brookmeyer. Fests: MJF '59–62; own band w. Al Cohn, Burghausen JF '87. TV: w. Judy Garland for six mos. '63. Film: pl. on soundtracks for *I Want to Live* '58; *The Cincinnati Kid* '65. Rec. debut w. Auld '45. Solo on "Lover" w.

Charlie Parker '51, but own fav. solo w. Krupa on "Valse Triste" '46. CDs: Jazz Mark feat. Al Cohn; Cohn w. Porcino bb (Red Brn.; Raz-M-Taz); w. Parker; Gillespie; E. Fitzgerald (Verve); Shorty Rogers (BB); Terry Gibbs (Cont.); Oliver Nelson (Imp.); Kenton (Mos.); Buddy Rich (PJ); Herman (Cap.).

PORTER, ROY LEE, dms, comp; b. Walsenburg, CO, 7/30/23; d. Los Angeles, 1/25/95. Self-taught. First prof. job tour. w. Milt Larkin. Small gp. gigs in 1940s w. Teddy Bunn; Howard McGhee; Benny Carter; Dexter Gordon; own bb in LA '48–50. Pl. on Charlie Parker's first Dial rec. date '46; rec. w. Teddy Edwards, D. Gordon. In '50s pl. w. Earl Bostic; Louis Jordan; Perez Prado. Inactive in '60s but led another gp. in '70. Retired from drumming in '78. Autobiography, *There and Back: The Roy Porter Story* (LSU Press) '91. CDs: w. Parker (Stash; Rh.; Mos.); Gordon (Stash); McGhee (Jazz Class.).

PORTER, YANK (ALLEN), dms; b. Norfolk, VA, 1895; d. NYC, 3/22/44. Active in NYC from 1926 w. Cliff Jackson and in '30s w. Louis Armstrong; James P. Johnson; Fats Waller. In '40 pl. w. Joe Sullivan and Teddy Wilson bands at Café Society. Also rec. w. Benny Carter and Art Tatum. CDs: L. Armstrong (BB; Col.); B. Holiday; Joe Turner (Dec.).

POTTER, CHRIS (JOSEPH CHRISTOPHER), tnr, alto, sop saxes, cl, fl, pno; b. Chicago, IL, 1/1/71. Studied w. Bryson Borgstedt, John Emche in Columbia, So. Carolina 1981–5. Began pl. prof. gigs while in hs. A Presidential Scholar in the Arts in '89, he moved to NYC at 18 to stud. at the New School (one of his professors was Kenny Werner w. whom he later rec. a duo CD for Conc.) and the Manh. Sch. of Mus. Join. Red Rodney '89. Has pl. w. Paul Motian; Renee Rosnes; Jon Scofield; Mingus bb; Mike Mainieri; Dave Douglas; Dave Holland. Favs: Sonny Rollins, John Coltrane, Charlie Parker. Polls: *DB* Best HS Instrumentalist '89. Award: third place in Thelonious Monk Competition '91. Fests: Eur. since '90. TV: PBS w. R. Rodney. CDs: Conc.; w. Red Rodney (Elek.; Contin.); S. McCorkle; John Patitucci; John Hart; M. McPartland (Conc.); Urbie Green (Chiaro.); P. Motian (JMT); Mingus bb (Drey.); J. Moody (Tel.).

POTTER, TOMMY (CHARLES THOMAS), bs; b. Philadelphia, PA, 9/21/18; d. Philadelphia, 3/3/88. Raised in Cape May, N.J. Stud. pno. and gtr. in Jersey City; took up bs. 1940. Worked w. John Malachi in Wash., D.C.; Trummy Young in Chi. and NYC; Billy Eckstine bb '44–5; John Hardee, Max Roach, etc. in NYC '46–7. Best known as sideman w. Charlie

Parker from '47–9, also tour. w. JATP. Six mos. w. Stan Getz, a few weeks w. Basie '50; concert tours w. Eckstine. Worked w. Earl Hines '52–3; Artie Shaw, Sept. '53–July '54; Eddie Heywood trio '55; Bud Powell trio '56. Tour. Sweden's folk parks w. Rolf Ericson summer '56; own trio at Lamplighter Club, Valley Stream, Long Island, N.Y. '57. Pl. w. Tyree Glenn '58–60; Sweets Edison '60–1; Buck Clayton '63. Tour. Eur. w. NJF gp. '65. Pl. w. Al Cohn–Zoot Sims '65. Later freelanced w. J. McPartland, Buddy Tate. Semi-inactive in '70s, working as civil service employee in Bklyn. Hospital recreation dept. Own gp. for club dates '75. While not renowned as a soloist Potter was an excellent rhythm section pl. whose work w. Parker established him as one of the leading bassists of the early bebop era. Favs: Pettiford, Ray Brown, Mingus. Fest: Charlie Parker tribute at NJF-NY '80. TV: *Like It Is*, ABC '75. CDs: w. Parker (Sav.; Stash; Verve; Rh.); B. Powell (BN); M. Davis; Jimmy Forrest; Wardell Gray (Prest.); Getz (Prest.; Roul.; Biog.; Roost); E. Condon (Sav.); Artie Shaw (MM).

POTTS, BILL (WILLIAM ORIE), pno, arr, comp; b. Arlington, VA, 4/3/28; d. Plantation, FL, 2/16/05. During jr. hs in Wash., D.C. 1941–3, pl. gtr., acdn.; pno. in hs '44–6. Att. Catholic U. briefly late '46–early '47 but mostly self-educated. Got into jazz by listening to Count Basie; Lester Young; Nat Cole. Took up comp., arr. Own gp. under stage name, Bill Parks, tour. in Fla. and Mass. '47. Changed name back to Potts. Tour. south w. bands of Marvin Scott, Bob Astor '48. In Wash. w. army band '49–56, tour. numerous times in Canada and Iceland. Dur. these yrs. was chief arr. for "The Orchestra," led by dmr. Joe Timer and presented by Willis Conover. Also arr. "Jersey Bounce" for Tony Pastor, first rec. arr. '55. After service, worked in local clubs w. own combo. Backed Lester Young at Patio Lounge '56. Pl. w. Norman Williams New Jazz Qnt. incl. Earl Swope, tbn. Pl. w. Woody Herman '57–8. Tour. w. Ralph Marterie, Bobby Vinton as pnst., cond., and arr. '60s; in same capacity w. Paul Anka in US, Eur. '63–7. In '70, living in NYC, pl. w. Clark Terry; S. Getz; Phil Woods; Al Cohn; Zoot Sims; Charlie Byrd; Jeri Southern; Eddie Fisher; Ella Fitzgerald. Fr. '80 to '87 app. twice a year w. his bb at Blues Alley, Wash., D.C. Fr. '74 to '90 at Montgomery Coll., Rockville, MD, taught arr., theory; rehearsed and cond. stage band; and was audio engineer. In Aug. '95 moved fr. Maryland to Fla. Wrote comps., arrs. for rec. dates by The Six; Al Cohn; Phil Woods–Gene Quill; Al Cohn–Zoot Sims; Bob Brookmeyer; Quincy Jones '50s; Buddy Rich '60s; Charlie Byrd '80s. Favs: Dave McKenna, Nat Cole, Tommy Flanagan; arrs: Bill Holman, Al Cohn, Don Menza. As engineer rec. *One*

Night in Washington, Charlie Parker w. The Orchestra '53; *One Night in Washington*, Dizzy Gillespie w. The Orchestra '55, both on Elektra Musician. LP: four comps. for *Willis Conover's House of Sounds* (Bruns. '53); pl. pno. and wrote 10 comps. for *Jazz Under the Dome*, Freddie Merkle (Vik '58); own LPs for Dec.; Colpix; Jazz Mark. Most acclaimed work was *The Jazz Soul of Porgy and Bess* w. bb feat. Sims, Cohn, Brookmeyer, Art Farmer, Sweet Edison, etc. for United Artists '59. CDs. *Jazz Soul of Porgy and Bess* (BN); w. Lester Young (Pab.).

POWELL, BENNY (BENJAMIN G.), tbn, bs-tbn; b. New Orleans, LA 3/1/30. Mother pl. pno., sist. also musical. Began on dms. Stud. tbn. w. Eddie Pearson in NO. Made prof. debut w. USO band 1/1/1944, then stud. at Alabama St. Teachers Coll. where he pl. with the Collegians. Pl. w. Dooky Chase '45; King Kolax '46–7; Ernie Fields '47; L. Hampton '48–51; C. Basie '51–63; Thad Jones–Mel Lewis Orch. '65–9; Duke Pearson '65–72; Merv Griffin Show band '70–78; Bill Berry '75–80; Terry Gibbs '76–7; B. Goodman '78; Bill Holman '78–80; Basie alumni bands '80–5; Slide Hampton's World of Trombones '81–2; John Carter '83–6; Randy Weston fr. '83; Amer. Jazz Orch. fr. '85; Benny Carter '92; Joe Williams at Rainbow and Stars mid '90s. Powell has taught at LIU and the Jazzmobile Wkshp. Organized and participated in jazz concert-lecture programs in NYC and LA public schs. Favs: J. J. Johnson, Frank Rosolino, Steve Turre; arrs: Thad Jones, Duke Pearson, Frank Foster, Frank Wess. Polls: *DB* '56. Fests: all major fr. '50s. Films: app. w. Sammy Davis in *A Man Called Adam*; Mel Brooks's *Blazing Saddles* w. Basie. TV: Merv Griffin '78–88. CDs: w. Basie (Mos.; Verve; Roul.); Conc. JF; K. Burrell; Bill Berry (Conc.); F. Wess (Sav.; Conc.); Benny Carter (MM); John Carter (Gram.); Frank Foster (Sav.); Dameronia (SN); L. Hampton (BB; Timel.); Abdullah Ibrahim (Enja); Talib Kibwe (Evid.); Joe Newman (FS); D. Ellington (Pab.).

POWELL, BUD (EARL RUDOLPH), pno, comp; b. NYC, 9/27/24, d. NYC, 8/1/66. Father, Wm. Powell, and grandfath. were mus., bro. Richie a pnst. Leaving sch. at 15, he gigged around Coney Island, pl. at Canada Lee's Chicken Coop and w. Valaida Snow's Sunset Royals. A frequent visitor to Minton's, mentored by T. Monk, he revealed an incipient bop style on first recs. w. Cootie Williams 1943–4. Leaving Williams, he was in and out of the 52nd St. scene but suffered a nervous breakdown in '45 and for the rest of his life was intermittently in mental hospitals, often depending on alcohol and narcotics. He worked w. John Kirby; D. Gillespie; Allen Eager; Sid Catlett;

Don Byas in '40s. Own trio at Birdland '50s. In '59 his health improved, he lived in Paris, pl. at the Chat Qui Peche and working in trio w. Kenny Clarke and Pierre Michelot. In the early '60s he was diagnosed w. TB and hospitalized until Francis Paudras opened his home to him and helped to restore his health. Although he now was faring much better, Powell longed for home and ret. to NYC in '64, and pl. once again at Birdland. He found himself surrounded by aggravating reminders of his chaotic past. Then, except for an app. at Carnegie Hall in '65, he was largely inactive until his death. Powell's status as the first and foremost bop pianist is beyond dispute. Charged with a fantastic dynamic energy and a fast flow of original ideas, he produced solo albums that made him the idol of young pnsts. in the '40s and '50s. Technically, he showed a mastery of the keyboard and a tonal individuality in his attack that no other pianist quite duplicated. Among Powell's countless admirers were Ellington, Tatum, and Basie. His best known comps. incl. "Glass Enclosure"; "Parisian Thoroughfare"; "Tempus Fugue-It"; "Dance of the Infidels"; "Bouncing with Bud"; "Celia"; "Un Poco Loco"; "I'll Keep Loving You"; and "Hallucinations" (also known as "Budo"). In the '86 film *Round Midnight*, Dexter Gordon portrayed a character based in great part on Powell. Books: *La Danse des Infidèles*, Francis Paudres '86; *Dance of the Infidels* (DaCapo) '98; *Wail: The Bud Powell Story*, Peter Pullman (Farrar, Straus Giroux). CDs: Col.; Verve; Deb.; Roul.; BN; BB; Del.; Drey; MS; Steep; Story.; Mythic Sound; w. C. Parker (Sav.; Stash; Deb.); J. J. Johnson; Fats Navarro (Sav.); D. Gillespie (Verve; Philips); D. Gordon (Sav.; BN); C. Mingus (Atl.); J. Griffin (BL); Cootie Williams (Class.); S. Stitt (Prest.).

POWELL, JESSE, tnr sax; b. Fort Worth, TX, 2/27/24; d. NYC, 10/19/82. Studied mus. at Hampton U. 1939–42. Tour. w. Hot Lips Page 42–3; Louis Armstrong '43–4; Luis Russell '44–5. Relocated to Calif. w. C. Basie when he replaced Illinois Jacquet Sept. '46. Led own band; then feat. w. Howard McGhee sxt. at Paris JF '48. Pl. w. D. Gillespie bb, '49–50. From '50 freelanced in NYC, often pl. r&b. Rec. w. McGhee; Gillespie. CD: track in *Texas Tenors* (Prest.).

POWELL, MEL (Melvin Epstein), pno, comp; b. NYC 2/12/23; d. Sherman Oaks, CA, 4/24/98. After working w. Bobby Hackett; George Brunis; Muggsy Spanier 1939–40 and Wingy Manone '41, he joined Benny Goodman at age 18, and dur. two yrs. w. the band, comp. and was featured on "The Earl"; "Mission to Moscow"; "Clarinade." After a stint w. Raymond Scott on CBS, he toured w. Glenn Miller's Army Air Force Band, rec. in Paris w. Django Reinhardt in '45. Rejoined Goodman '45. To LA; worked in studios but ret. East, stud. comp. w. Paul Hindemith at Yale. Except for occasional reunions w. Goodman, he remained inactive in jazz for many yrs., stud. and lecturing under a Guggenheim Fellowship. Joined Cal Arts in Valencia, Calif., as founding dean of the mus. sch. until '76 when his status changed to that of member of the faculty w. a chair in comp. In '82, impressed by the all-female jazz orch. Maiden Voyage, he wrote a suite for the gp., *Setting for Jazz Band*, which was perf. at Cal Arts Fest. In '86 perf. jazz in public for first time in many yrs., he pl. w. various gps. on the SS *Norway* Jazz Cruise, app. there again in '87 and '88; subsequently a muscular illness curtailed his playing career. He cont. to teach at Cal Arts, and in '90 his comp., *Duplicates*, a concerto for two pnos., earned him a Pulitzer Prize. Despite his long absences, Powell remained an adroit and inspired jazz soloist in a personal style that incl. elements of Earl Hines and Teddy Wilson. CDs: Chiaro.; 12 tracks in *Classic Capitol Jazz Sessions* (Mos.); w. B. Goodman (Col.; Cap.; MM); Glenn Miller (BB; Vict.); C. Parker (Verve).

POWELL, RICHIE (RICHARD), pno; b. NYC, 9/5/31; d. Pennsylvania Turnpike, near Bedford, PA, 6/26/56. Father and bro. Bud pnsts. Stud. City Coll. of NY 1950–1; priv. w. W. F. Rawlins. Pl. at Baby Grand Café, NYC w. Jimmie Carl Brown '49–50. Worked around Phila. '50–1; w. Paul Williams r&b band '51–2; Johnny Hodges orch. '52–4. Joined Max Roach–Clifford Brown qnt. '54; did most of writing and arranging for the gp. Killed in car crash w. Clifford Brown. CDs: w. C. Brown–M. Roach (Em.); S. Rollins (Prest.); D. Washington (Em.).

POWELL, RUDY (EVERARD STEPHEN aka Musheed Karweem), cl, saxes; b. NYC, 10/28/07; d. NYC, 10/30/76. Studied pno., vln., sax. In late 1920s pl. w. June Clark; Gene Rodgers; Cliff Jackson at Lenox Club '28–31; Fats Waller off and on fr. '34; Eur. w. Edgar Hayes '37; then w. Claude Hopkins, Teddy Wilson big band '38–40; Andy Kirk '40; Fletcher Henderson '41–2; Don Redman '43; Claude Hopkins, Cab Calloway '45–8; Lucky Millinder '48–51; briefly w. Ch. Ventura, then w. Jimmy Rushing band '51–2; Buddy Tate '53. Also heard w. Arnett Cobb; Erskine Hawkins; and in '60s w. Ray Charles; Buddy Johnson; Joe Marshall. Tour. extensively w. the Saints and Sinners '65–9. In ill health but occ. active in '70s. Well known for his caustically colorful growl cl., he was also a fine, melodic alto soloist. Favs: Benny Carter, Goodman, Bigard. CDs: w. Fats Waller (BB); Ellington (Red Brn.); Ray Charles (Pab.); Red Allen; Edgar Hayes; T. Wilson; Rex Stewart (Class.); A. Kirk (B&B); B. Holiday; J. Rushing; Ellington, small gps. (Col.).

POWELL, SELDON, tnr sax, other saxes, cl, fl, picc; b. Lawrenceville, VA, 11/15/28; d. Hempstead, NY, 1/25/97. Studied at Brooklyn and NY Cons. 1947–49; grad. Juilliard '57. First job w. Betty Mays' Swingtet '49. Pl. w. Tab Smith at Savoy Ballroom '49; Lucky Millinder, Dec. '49–Jan. '51; army '51–2, pl. w. service bands in Germ. and France. To NYC on return, pl. dates and recs. w. Sy Oliver, Erskine Hawkins, Neal Hefti, Louie Bellson, Don Redman '52–5; rec. w. Eddie Jefferson for Prest. '53. App. w. Friedrich Gulda sxt. at Birdland '56; worked w. Johnny Richards on and off fr. '57; Billy VerPlanck '57–8; Brussels World's Fair and Eur. tour w. B. Goodman '58; W. Herman, briefly, '59; concerts w. Jimmy Cleveland. Staff work at ABC-TV '60; pl. w. B. Rich qnt. '60; Bellson '62, '64; Clark Terry '63; Ahmed Abdul-Malik '64. In pit band of B'way show *Fade In–Fade Out* w. Carol Burnett '64. Staff mus. at Westbury Music Fair; many recs. w. studio bbs backing Groove Holmes; Gato Barbieri; Anthony Braxton; Dizzy Gillespie. Orig. inspired by Lester Young, he pl w. a light but firm sound and buoyant sense of rhythm. Favs: Young, Stitt. Fests: NJF w. Gulda '56; Don Butterfield '58; JVC-NY w. G. Mulligan '87. Film: *A Man Called Adam* w. Sammy Davis '66. TV: *Schaeffer Circle Theatre; Merv Griffin Show;* w. Billy Taylor Orch. on *David Frost Show;* led band for Leon Bibb's *Someone New*. Rec. LPs as a lead. for Roost, Epic. CDs: w. Teresa Brewer (Sig.); Joe Williams (BB); King Pleasure (BN); Gato Barbieri (Imp.); Ray Bryant–Betty Carter (Col.); Charlie Byrd; B. Taylor (Riv.); Clark Terry (Cand.); Seventh Ave. Stompers; Marlene VerPlanck (Sav.); Goodman (Limel.; MM); MJQ (Atl.).

POWELL, SPECS (GORDON), dms; b. NYC, 6/5/22. Played w. Edgar Hayes 1939, Eddie South '39–40, John Kirby '41, Benny Carter '41–2, Benny Goodman '44, Red Norvo '44–5. From '43 was staff mus. at CBS in NYC under Raymond Scott, Raymond Page, Leopold Stokowski. In '45, Powell took part in a celebrated Red Norvo swing-cum-bop session that featured Dizzy Gillespie, Charlie Parker, Flip Phillips, Teddy Wilson, and Slam Stewart. Won *Esquire* New Star Award '45. In later yrs., retired fr. mus. to work as a real estate dealer in So. Calif. CDs: w. Norvo (Stash); B. Holiday (Dec.); C. Hawkins (Del.); Mildred Bailey; Charlie Ventura (Sav.); Erroll Garner (Col.); Jerry Jerome (Arb.); L. Feather; Earl Hines; John Kirby; Eddie South; Jess Stacy; Mary Lou Williams; T. Wilson (Class.).

POZO, CHANO (Luciano Pozo y Gonzales), perc, dancer, voc; b. Havana, Cuba, 1/7/15; d. NYC, 12/2/48. Fascinated w. West African rhythms fr. his boyhood; fr. the late 1930s belonged to a Nigerian cult, the Abakwa, that provided much of the rhythmic excitement at the local Mardi Gras celebrations. Soon won high acclaim in Cuba as a dmr., dancer, and comp. On 9/29/47 he and bongo player Chiquitico perf. at Carnegie Hall w. Dizzy Gillespie's bb in the first serious attempt to combine jazz and Afro-Cuban music; their recs. of *Cubana Be–Cubana Bop*, and "Manteca" (co-written w. Gillespie as was "Tin Tin Deo") launched the concept of "Afro-Cuban Jazz." Tour. Eur. and US w. Gillespie '48, who told Ira Gitler: "Chano personally was a roughneck." Indeed, his life came to a violent end—after only a yr. in US, he was fatally shot in a Harlem bar, the Rio Café. In one yr., the man Marshall Stearns called "the greatest of all Cuban drummers" had made a lasting impression and added a new chapter to jazz history. Comps: "El Pin Pin"; "Vogue." CDs: tracks in *Legendary Sessions: 1947–53* (Tumbao); w. Gillespie (RCA; Vogue; GNP (Res.); Roost); James Moody (BN); C. Parker; I. Jacquet; C. O'Farrill (Verve); Milt Jackson (Gal.).

POZO, CHINO (FRANCISCO), bgo, cga dms, tmbls; b. Havana, Cuba, 10/4/15; d. NYC, 4/28/80. Cousin of Chano Pozo. (Some people claimed not.) Self-taught on pno., bs. To US 1937; pl. w. Machito '41–3; Jack Cole Dancers '43–9. Active in many jazz and Latin gps. fr. late '40s, incl. Jose Curbelo; Noro Morales; Tito Puente; Tito Rodriguez; Enric Madriguera; Perez Prado; Josephine Premice; Tadd Dameron; Charlie Parker; and Dizzy Gillespie. Tour. w. Peggy Lee '54–5; pl. w. Stan Kenton '55; Herbie Mann '56; Xavier Cugat, Rene Touzet '59. Rec. w. Illinois Jacquet, Phineas Newborn in '50s; Gabor Szabo '65; later w. singer Paul Anka. Favs: Chano Pozo, Candido. CDs: w. Fats Navarro (BN); Billy Taylor (Riv.); Peggy Lee (Cap.); Harry Betts (Mob. Fid.); Louis Jordan (Merc.).

PRATT, BOBBY, tbn, pno; b. South Glen Falls, NY, 5/23/26; d. NYC, 1/7/94. Studied tbn. w. bro. Norman. First gigs in burlesque clubs in Schenectady, N.Y., at age 15. Moved to NYC 1942. Pl. w. Charlie Barnet '43–4; Tommy Reynolds, Johnny Richards, Geo. Auld '44; Stan Kenton '45; Raymond Scott '45–6; Lennie Lewis '47; Sam Donahue '48–9; Johnny Bothwell '49–50. While dental work was being completed in '50, he taught himself pno. Jammed w. Charlie Parker, Ben Webster, Coleman Hawkins, Big Sid Catlett, Trummy Young, Max Roach, Lester Young, Slam Stewart, etc. '40s-50s.

Subbed for Vic Dickenson in Eddie Heywood sxt. Pl. w. Ruby Braff, Billy May, Jimmy McPartland '60s. Pno. at Jimmy Ryan's '67–70; tbn. fr. '70. Worked at Ryan's w. Tony Parenti; Max Kaminsky; Zutty Singleton; Marshall Brown; Roy Eldridge; Jimmy McPartland; Herman Autrey. Perf. on soundtrack to film *Book of Numbers* early '70s. Fr. '79 to '90 pno. and/or tbn. w. Ernie Lumer at the Cajun. Solo pno. weekdays at the Park Ave. Plaza fr. '89. Pno. in duo w. Pete Compo fr. '86; Steve Berger at Arturo's fr. '90. A musicians' musician. Fav. tbn: Vic Dickenson, Trummy Young; fav. pno: Billy Kyle, Count Basie. TV: NJF-NY w. Eldridge on PBS '73; special w. Bobby Hackett, Nicol Williamson. LP: w. Eldridge (Pab.). CDs: Take 12.

PRESENCER, GERARD, tpt, flg; b. London, England, 9/12/72. Father was opera singer, owned jazz club in London. Began on pno. First experience sitting in at father's club. Pl. w. Nat'l Youth Jazz Orch., then pl. and rec. w. Charlie Watts Qnt. fr. 1987. Also freelanced w. Conte Candoli; Bill Watrous; Shorty Rogers; Bill Holman; Stan Tracey; Teddy Edwards; Harold Land; Niels H. Ø. Pederson; Herb Geller; Kenny Drew; Roy Hargrove; Ronnie Scott; John Dankworth; Peter King; Nigel Hitchcock; Louis Bellson. Leads a qt. One of the brightest talents to emerge in the UK in the '90s. Favs: Miles Davis, Kenny Wheeler, Freddie Hubbard. Polls: British Jazz Rising Star '92. Fests: US, Eur., Japan, So. Amer.; Appleby JF, Engl. '98. Film: *Blue Ice* w. Michael Caine. CDs: BN; w. C. Watts (UFO; Contin.).

PRESERVATION HALL JAZZ BAND. A varied gp. of NO musicians organized in the 1950s by art dealer Larry Borenstein to pl. in his gallery. From 1961, perfs. took place in a nearby building, renamed Preservation Hall (opened by tba. pl. Allan Jaffe, who died in '87), which soon became a popular tourist attraction. In '63 the band, led by George Lewis and Kid Thomas, toured the US; later that year and in '64–5, Lewis led Punch Miller, Louis Nelson, et al. on tours of Japan. A Eur. tour in '67 featured DeDe Pierce, Willie Humphrey, Nelson, et al. Apps. at the Stanford Summer Fest, Calif., and NYC's Lincoln Center Fest '67–8 brought the gp. national attention. In '68 the band represented the US at the "cultural Olympics" during the Mexico City games. Kid Thomas led the band on a tour of the Far East, Can., and Eur. in '71; fr. mid '70s Percy Humphrey took over leadership of the principal touring band. Other gps. occasionally toured with alternate personnel. In the early '90s the best version of the band incl. Wendell Brunious, tpt.; Michael Whire, cl.; Narvin Kimball, bs.; Frank Demond, tbn.; James Prevost, bs.; John Royen, pno.; and Joseph

Lastie Jr., dms. As it entered its third decade the aura of history that had always surrounded the band was gone forever. CDs: Col.

PRESTON, DON (DONALD W.), pno, synth, bs; b. Flint, MI, 9/21/32. Father Donn Preston, a tptr. and comp. whose works were perf. by Det. Philharm. Stud. and pl. in army w. Herbie Mann; att. U. of Miami; pl. in Det. w. Elvin Jones and Yusef Lateef; in LA w. Carla Bley and Charlie Haden late '50s. Joined Frank Zappa and the Mothers of Invention fr. 1967 to '74 off and on. During that time, he also pl. w. Gil Evans and Buell Neidlinger's gp., Thelonious. Eur. and overseas tours w. Michael Mantler; Michael Hoenig; Gil Evans. Active in LA studios from '70s as synth. player and kybdist. Taught at Wind Coll., LA Recording Wkshp., etc. Many sound designs for films and stage plays. CDs: w. Michael Mantler (ECM; WATT); John Carter (Gram.); *Escalator Over the Hill* w. Carla Bley (Watt); Bobby Bradford–John Carter Qnt. (hat Hut); Peter Erskine (Den.); Ivo Perelman (K2B2).

PREVIN, ANDRÉ GEORGE (Andreas Ludwig Priwin), pno, comp; b. Berlin, Germany, 4/6/29. Studied at Berlin Royal Cons. and Paris Cons. To US 1939; stud. pno. w. fath., a mus. teacher. Rec. debut '45 for Sunset. After hs, hired as arr. at MGM Studios '48 but rec. jazz for RCA w. own gps. '49–55. From '56 to '60 took leaves of absence from studio to pl. jazz w. trio in clubs and on recs. His '57 album of *My Fair Lady* w. Shelly Manne became best-seller that started trend of show-score jazz albums. Previn went to Paris in '57 to score film *Gigi*, for which he won the Oscar. Other film scores: *Porgy and Bess, The Subterraneans* (also on screen); *Bells Are Ringing*. In early '60s he rec. jazz for Col., but by mid '60s had moved entirely into classical area, conducting Houston and London Symphs. and major orchs. in US and Eur., and tour. worldwide. Returned occasionally to jazz; album w. Ella Fitzgerald in early '80s, own trio albums into the '90s. Rec. at the Musikverein in Vienna w. Ray Brown, Mundell Lowe (Verve '97). Though no longer mainly identified w. jazz, Previn in his earlier yrs. proved to be an astonishing soloist, heard in collaborations w. Shorty Rogers; Benny Carter; Benny Goodman; Pete Rugolo; Barney Kessel. He was clearly infl. by Art Tatum, Oscar Peterson, Bud, Powell, and Horace Silver. In the '50s he was married to singer Betty Bennett, for whom he wrote and conducted; later married to singer/songwriter Dory Langdon and actress Mia Farrow. His '61 album *Previn Plays Harold Arlen* won a Grammy. CDs: Tel.; Col.; Verve; Cont.; Deutsche Grammophon; w. Benny Carter; Lyle Murphy (Cont.).

PREVITE, BOBBY (ROBERT), dms, comp; b. Niagara Falls, NY, 7/16/51. Studied at U. of Buffalo 1969–73. Pl. w. local gp. in Buffalo in '60s using homemade dms. Led own gps. in NYC fr. mid '70s; also pl. w. Wayne Horvitz; Robin Holcomb; Butch Morris; John Zorn; John Clark; etc. Favs: Tony Williams, Ginger Baker. Polls: *DB* TDWR comp. '91; *Rolling Stone* '91. Fests: Eur., Japan, etc. fr. '80. TV: *Sat. Night Live*, Eur. TV. CDs: Gram.; Enja; w. Jane Ira Bloom (Arab.); w. Zorn, *Voodoo: The Music of Sonny Clark* (BS).

PRICE, JESSE, dms, voc; b. Memphis, TN, 5/1/09; d. Los Angeles, CA, 4/19/74. Played in pit band in Memphis; tour. w. blues singers. Moved to KC 1934–6; pl. w. C Basie '36; own band late '30s; Harlan Leonard '39–41; Louis Armstrong '43; Stan Kenton '44; Benny Carter '48. Sidelined by illness in later yrs. CDs: w. Jay McShann in *The 1940s Mercury Sessions* (Merc.); Kenton; Red Norvo in *Classic Capitol Jazz Sessions* (Mos.); Dexter Gordon (BN); Pete Johnson (Del.).

PRICE, MIKE (MICHAEL BURR), tpt, flg; b. Chicago, IL, 1/26/41. Cornet at age 12; majored in mus. at Northwestern U. Prof. debut at 17. Stud. comp. for three yrs. at Berklee. Local bands in Chi.; pl. w. Ralph Marterie; Les Elgart; Tex Beneke. First tpt. w. Stan Kenton 1967–8; Buddy Rich '69–70. Member of Akiyoshi-Tabackin band in Calif. '73–83; Gerald Wilson Orch. '83–9. Also led own jazz-rock gp., Blue Guitar '76–83 and own spt. in LA '85–8. Moved to Tokyo '89, pl. jazz solo chair w. Nobuo Hara and Sharps & Flats Orch., also own sxt. and qt. A superior all-around leader and solo perf., Price has given tpt. and band clinics throughout the US and Japan. Favs: Gillespie, C. Brown, Lee Morgan. CDs: w. Akiyoshi (RCA).

PRICE, RUTH, voc; b. Phoenixville, PA, 4/27/30. Originally stud. ballet 1952; self-taught as singer. Inspired by Charlie Parker, she sang w. Charlie Ventura '54, then freelanced in Phila. clubs. Spent several mos. at Village Vanguard in NYC and cont. to work occasionally as a dancer. Moved to Hollywood '57; sang at Jazz City; danced in stage show, *Vintage '60*; sang and rec. at Shelly's Manne Hole; worked w. Harry James band '64–5. Semi-retired fr. mus. dur. marriage to Dave Grusin but fr. mid '80s coordinated talent at several LA clubs, incl. Central Park West and the Jazz Bakery. Noted for her natural phrasing, individual sound, and sure sense of intonation. CDs: Cont.; w. Herb Geller (Hep).

PRICE, SAMMY (SAMUEL BLYTHE), pno, voc, comp; b. Honey Grove, TX, 10/6/08; d. NYC,

4/14/92. Studied w. Booker T. Washington's daughter. Prof. debut 1923 in Dallas, Tex.; tour. as dancer w. Alphonso Trent band. Worked w. Lee Collins '25; toured TOBA circuit '27–30. During '30s rec. in Dallas, pl. in Chi. and Det. Settled NYC '38 and was virtual house mus. at Dec. for many years, pl. r&b and pop sess. w. Sister Rosetta Tharpe, Trixie Smith, etc. Led series of small band dates w. his own gp., Texas Blusicians, early '40s; one date incl. Lester Young. Rec. and worked w. Mezz Mezzrow, visiting Nice JF '48. After three yrs. back in Tex., he ret. to NYC, working w. Red Allen, Tony Parenti. Frequent Eur. tours thereafter, incl. fests in Antibes and Lugano. Cont. to perf. in NYC, solo and w. Doc Cheatam and others until his death. Excellent early-style blues and boogie-woogie pianist. CDs: Story.; Sack. (co-lead w. D. Cheatham); two tracks w. Texas Blusicians in *52nd Street Swing* (Dec.); w. Ida Cox (Riv.); Joe Turner (Dec.); Mezzrow-Bechet (Story.).

PRIESTER, JULIAN ANTHONY, tbn, b. Chicago, IL, 6/29/35. Studied pno. bari. horn bef. taking up tbn. at DuSable HS. Pl. w. Sun Ra 1953–4; Lionel Hampton '56; Dinah Washington '57–8. To NYC June '58; worked w. Max Roach '59 in gp. incl. Booker Little, Eric Dolphy, and Clifford Jordan; w. Slide Hampton '59. Freelanced in NYC '60s; six mos. w. D. Ellington late '60s; pl. w. Herbie Hancock sxt. '70–3. Took Swahili name Pepo Mtoto while w. Hancock. In SF area from mid '70s, working w. Stanley Cowell and Red Garland; rec. w. Dave Holland, George Gruntz early '80s. Active in Seattle area from late '80s. CDs: Riv.; w. T. Monk and M. Roach (LRC); Sun Ra (Del.); Jane Ira Bloom (Arab.); Sam Rivers; Reggie Workman; Ralph Simon (Post.).

PRIMA, LOUIS, tpt, voc; b. New Orleans, LA, 12/7/11, d. New Orleans, 8/24/78. Brother Leon pl. tpt. Stud. vln. for seven yrs., then tpt.; in 1930 made prof. debut in NO theater. Worked w. Red Nichols in Cleveland '31–2; rose to national popularity in '34–5 when he led small bands in 52nd St. clubs, notably the Famous Door, and rec. a series of sess. w. all-star gps. that incl. Eddie Miller; George Brunis; Nappy Lamare. Became a star of the swing era, leading a bb in the '40s; in '50s he often app. in LV w. his wife, singer Keely Smith, to whom he was married from '53 to '61, and tnr. sax Sam Butera. His guttural singing and Armstrong-inspired tpt. style became highly commercialized, making his later perfs. of little jazz interest. Best known comp.: "Sing, Sing, Sing." Film: *The Benny Goodman Story* '55. CDs: Sav.; Viper's Nest; w. Joe Venuti (IAJRC).

PRINTUP, MARCUS, tpt; b. Conyers, GA, 1/24/67. Raised in the Baptist church by parents who are "both good singers and into gospel music." Earliest jazz infl. was his older sister, who pl. tnr. sax in a hs band. Began tpt. in fifth grade but was 21 bef. he "developed a taste for jazz history." While in hs, he listened to Earth, Wind & Fire and Kool and the Gang. Played in a tentet, Soul Reason for the Blues, while at U. of No. Fla., where pnst. Marcus Roberts heard him in 1991. Began tour. w. Roberts in '92, also app. w. the LCJO and at Betty Carter's Jazz Ahead concert. Bill Kohlhaase, in the *LA Times*, called him "A musician of uncommon communication and emotion, confident without being brash, technically accomplished without being cold." Favs: Booker Little, Freddie Hubbard, Fats Navarro. Film: *Dancing About Architecture* '98. Rec. *Hubsongs*, a tribute to Hubbard for BN w. labelmate, tprt. Tim Hagans. CDs: BN; w. W. Marsalis (Col.); M. Peyroux (Atl.).

PRIVIN, BERNIE (BERNARD), tpt, flg; b. Brooklyn, NY, 2/12/19; d. White Plains, NY, 10/8/99. Sister sang on club dates w. Meyer Davis Orch. Learned mello. in orphanage 1926–30; sw. to tpt. after hearing Louis Armstrong at age 13. Earning a living on club dates at age 15. Pl. w. Harry Reser 1937; Bunny Berigan, Tommy Dorsey '38; Artie Shaw '39–40. Also worked w. Buddy Rich at Picadilly Hotel late '30s. Pl. w. B'way show *Kiss Me Kate* '40; then freelanced w. Perry Como; Jan Savitt. Pl. w. Charlie Barnet '40–1; Mal Hallett '41; Benny Goodman '41–2; Barnet, Jerry Wald '43. In army '43–6, soloist w. Glenn Miller's Army Air Force band. Pl. w. Goodman '46–8; then on staff at CBS '50–73. Rec. w. Sy Oliver '49–51; Goodman off and on '51–61. Visited Sweden as a single '69, rec. live for the Bernie Privin Admiration Society. Tour. Eur. w. Pee Wee Erwin; Warren Covington's Tommy Dorsey Orch. '74; Russia w. NY Jazz Repertory Co. '75; and Eur. as soloist '70s. Favs: Armstrong, Bobby Hackett, Roy Eldridge, Zoot Sims. Fests: Eur. fr. '70s. Film: *Dancing Co-Ed* w. Artie Shaw, Lana Turner; also app. in film w. Charlie Barnet. LPs: Regent; HMT (Swed.). CDs: w. Goodman (Cap.); A. Shaw (BB; Jazz Unlimited); Glenn Miller; Lena Horne; C. Barnet (BB); Charlie Parker (Verve); Al Caiola (Sav.).

PROCOPE, RUSSELL, alto sax, cl; b. NYC, 8/11/08; d. NYC, 1/21/81. Studied vln. for eight yrs. bef. taking up sax and cl. Pl. and rec. w. Jelly Roll Morton 1928; later alto sax and cl. w. Benny Carter '29; Chick Webb '29–3; Fletcher Henderson '31–4. Toured Engl. and France w. Teddy Hill '37. Came to prominence dur. his yrs. w. the John Kirby Sxt. '38–43. Join. Duke Ellington '46. Left immediately after Ellington's death '74; pl. w. Brooks Kerr and in B'way musical *Ain't Misbehavin'*. Won *DB* Critics Poll on cl. '70–73. His principal solo reputation derives from his alto work with Kirby and his cl. work off and on with Ellington. Also considered a superb section man. CDs: w. Ellington (BB; BN; Atl.; Col.); Jelly Roll Morton; Kirby; Buster Bailey; Billy Kyle (Class.).

PROFIT, CLARENCE, pno, comp; b. NYC, 6/26/12; d. NYC, 10/22/44. Child prodigy, pl. fr. age 3, broadcasting as teenager w. schoolmate Edgar Sampson. Led own ten-piece band in Harlem; w. Teddy Bunn's Washboard Serenaders 1930–1; then spent six yrs. in the West Indies. Back in US in '37, he led a trio in various NYC and Bost. clubs until his death. Profit was first known as a stride pianist, but his few recordings display a later harmonically rich style that was years ahead of its time. Co-comp. of "Lullaby in Rhythm" w. Sampson. Rec. w. Washboard Serenaders (Vict. '30); Teddy Bunn (Vict. '30); own trio (Bruns. '39); Dec. '40; solos, Col. '40. CD: Memoir.

PRYSOCK, ARTHUR W. JR., voc; b. Spartanburg, SC 1/2/24; d. Hamilton, Bermuda, 6/17/00. Brother Red pl. tnr. sax. Self-taught, sang in church. Moved to Hartford, 1940; worked as cook, sang w. local bb. To NYC '44; sang w. Buddy Johnson Orch. '44–52, prod. 15 hit recs.; worked as single fr. '51. Very popular '64–65, when he app. several times on *Tonight Show*. Rec. w. Count Basie Orch. '65. In the '80s was a guest lecturer for 3 yrs. at Five Towns Coll. of Mus., LI. Favs: Basie, L. Hampton; arrs: Mort Garson, Quincy Jones. Fests: Eur., etc. fr. '50s. TV: own special *This Is My Beloved*; Mike Douglas, etc. CDs: Old Town; Verve; Mile.; w. Basie (Verve).

PRYSOCK, RED (WILBERT), tnr sax; b. Greensboro, NC, 2/2/26; d. Chicago, IL, 7/18/93. Studied pno., then sax. Join. Tiny Grimes after mil. service 1947. Left Grimes '49 but ret. occ. for rec. dates w. him on Atl., Gotham, United. With Roy Milton '50; Tiny Bradshaw '51–3, feat. on "Soft" for King label; Cootie Williams '53. Often assoc. w. Alan Freed in rock 'n' roll shows '54–6. Own band from '54, rec. for Merc. '54–61. Led organ trios in '60s but more often led band for bro. Arthur Prysock. CDs: w. A. Prysock (Mile.).

PUENTE, TITO (ERNESTO ANTONIO JR.), vib, tmbls, perc, lead; b. NYC, 4/20/25. Became prof. at early age, pl. w. Noro Morales; Pupi Campo; and other Latin bands early 1940s; stud. at Juilliard Sch. of Mus., mid '40s. Since then has led his own gps.;

often collaborated w. such jazz artists as Cal Tjader; Woody Herman; and Doc Severinsen. App. reg. all over Eur. and at NJF, Montreux JF, and MJF; app. TV: Bill Cosby show. Released well over 100 albums; has received five Grammy awards. A pioneer in the mixing of jazz and Latin rhythms. Helps to drive his band from in front with a variety of timbales. A participant as one of the "three kings" in the *Jazz Nativity*. CDs: Conc.; Trop.; w. Sheila E. (Verve); Daniel Ponce (Ant.); Poncho Sanchez (Conc.); Hilton Ruiz (Trop.; Tel.); Ray Barretto (Col.); TropiJazz All-Stars (Trop.); B. Golson (Mile.).

PUGH, JIM (JAMES EDWARD), tbn, comp, arr; b. Butler, PA, 11/12/50. Began on pno. at age 5; then sw. to tbn. at 10. Stud. in Atlanta 1960–3 and Pitts. '63–8, then att. Eastman Sch. of Mus. '68–72. Pl. w. Chuck Mangione '71–2; principal tbn. w. Rochester Philharm. summer '72; pl. w. Woody Herman '72–6; Chick Corea '76–8; Gerry Mulligan '79; Jay Leonhart since '88; also w. Joe Roccisano orch. Pugh has worked extens. as a studio mus.; pl. on numerous film and TV soundtracks; and has comp. jingles and film mus., as well as jazz and classical pieces. His comp. *Lunch with Schroedinger's Cat* was premiered at Lincoln Center in '91 by Concordia Chamber Orch. In '92 the Williamsport Symph. premiered his *Concerto for Trombone and Orchestra*. Teaches at NYU; lecturer/perf. at Eastman; North Tex. St.; etc. Favs: Urbie Green, C. Fontana, F. Rosolino, B. Brookmeyer. Polls: NARAS Most. Val. Player, five times. Fests: Eur. since '72. CDs: DMP; Pewter; w. Herman (Fan.; BB); B. Mintzer (DMP); John Scofield (BN); J. Pizzarelli (Novus); A. Di Pippo (Stash); The Gospel Hummingbirds (Blind Pig).

PUKWANA, DUDU (MTUTUZEL), saxes, pno; b. Port Elizabeth, South Africa, 7/18/38; d. London, Engl., 6/30/90. Moved to London w. Chris McGregor's Blue Notes when the apartheid regime banned mixed gps. 1965. Made 2 recs. w. the gp. Spear '73–4; also pl. and comp. for bb, the Brotherhood of Breath; in late '70s, tours w. band Zila. Recs. w. H. Masekela and Johnny Dyani. He pl. w. an unusual mixture of infls., ranging from So. African township mus. to the mainstream of Coleman Hawkins and the free form of Ornette Coleman CDs: Ah Um; w. Blue Notes; Brotherhood of Breath (Ogun); Dyani (Steep.).

PULLEN, DON (GABRIEL), pno, org, comp; b. Roanoke, VA, 12/25/44; d. NYC, 4/22/95. Musical family; fath. a dancer, gtrst, singer; uncle a singer; cousin, Clyde "Fats" Wright, pnst. Stud. at J. C. Smith U. in No. Caro. Moved to NYC early 1960s, pl.

org. w. r&b gps. bef. joining avant-garde jazz scene; pl. w. Milford Graves; Albert Ayler; Giuseppi Logan; Sonny Murray; et al. Worked w. Nina Simone '70–1; Art Blakey '74; Ch. Mingus '72–5. From mid '70s to mid '80s pl. w. Don Pullen–George Adams Qt. (w. Dannie Richmond and Cameron Brown), rec. ten albums w. the gp. From mid '80s worked as a soloist. An extremely versatile pnst., capable of pl. "outside" or in straight-ahead mainstream style, Pullen in the last ten yrs of his life proved to be one of the most original players on the scene. His '92 album *Kele Mou Bana* revealed an emerging interest in the spirit and rhythms of Brazil and So. Africa, and he was experimenting w. Native American mus. at the time of his death. "I finally feel more free . . . to play what I feel like playing," he said in early '92. CDs: BS; BN; w. Adams (Timel.; SN); David Murray (DIWA); Maceo Parker (Verve); Ivo Perelman; Roy Brooks (Enja); Jane Bunnett (Evid.); C. McBee (Ind. Nav.); Conjure (Roundup); Mingus (Rh./Atl.)

PUMA, JOE (JOSEPH J.), gtr; b. Bronx, NY, 8/13/27; d. Bronx, NY, 5/31/00. Father built gtrs. and mands.; bros. and sists. pl. pno., uke., gtr. Self-taught, orig. inspired by Django Reinhardt. Worked as army aircraft mechanic in Rome, NY 1944; heard Charlie Parker while working as draftsman in NYC '45–7. Joined mus. union '48. Pl. w. Cy Coleman '50; Frank Damone '51; Sammy Kaye, Louie Bellson, Don Elliot '52; Sal George, Joe Roland, Bobby Corwin '53; Artie Shaw's Gramercy Five, Les Elgart, Graham Forbes '54; Peggy Lee '54–5. Led own trio w. Bill Evans, Pete Compo at Left Bank, NYC '57. Pl. w. Lee Konitz, Dick Hyman, Herbie Mann–Sam Most '58; Dick Katz at Sch. of Jazz in Lenox, Mass. '59; Jimmy Lyon at Blue Angel '59–63. Rec. album of songs based on bird calls, *Like Tweet* '61; title song was later used in film *Good Morning Vietnam*. Tour. w. both Morgana King, Fran Jeffries as accomp. and conductor late '60s. Duo w. Chuck Wayne '72–4; various gps. w. Al Cohn; Jimmy Raney; Jim Hall; Warren Vaché; Chuck Wayne; Cecil Payne; Carmen Leggio at Strykers '75–8; trio w. Hod O'Brien, Frank Luther at Gregory's '78–82. Moved to Fla. '85, pl. w. Joe Roland '85–7. Ret. to NYC '88. Led duo at restaurant in Bklyn., also rec. w. Morgana King; Helen Merrill; Carol Sloane. Pl. w. Warren Vaché fr. '92. Puma taught briefly at Housatonic Coll. in Bridgeport, Conn. '70s Favs: Reinhardt, Christian, Geo. Van Eps; arrs: Gordon Jenkins, Billy May, Bill Finegan, Puccini. Polls: *Met.* '57. Fests: Eur. '85–6. TV: Mike Douglas w. Morgana King; NBC *Sunday* w. C. Wayne. CDs: Res.; Muse; w. A. Shaw (Verve; MM); Carmen McRae (Col.).

PURDIE, BERNARD LEE (aka PRETTY), dms, perc, bells, tymp; b. Elkton, MD, 6/11/41. Began on tpt, fl.; dms. at age 6. Stud. at Geo. Washington Carver Sch. and w. Clyde Bessicks, Leonard Hayward 1948–57; later at Morgan St. Coll. in Balt. Pl. w. Bessicks' bb '50–6; Jackie Lee and the Angels '53; carnival and circus bands '53–4. Perfs. and session work w. r&b acts incl. Ray Charles '57–61; Lloyd Price '57–75; James Brown '57–68; Les Cooper '60–2; Lonnie Youngblood '60–4; Otis Redding '61–3; Aretha Franklin fr. '66, incl. mus. dir. '70–5; B. B. King fr. '68; also w. rock acts incl. Rolling Stones '62–5; Beatles fr. '62; Animals '63–4; Monkees '65–8; Steely Dan '70–5; Jeff Beck '75–8. Pl. w. King Curtis '65–72; Groove Holmes '65–75; Geo. Benson '65–79; Jack McDuff '65–85; Grover Washington '67–75; Johnny Hammond Smith '69–75; Gato Barbieri '69–87; Count Basie '70–1; Jimmy McGriff '70–91; Louis Armstrong '71–2; Hank Crawford fr. '71; Duke Ellington '72; Humming Bird '76–9; Dizzy Gillespie '82–5. House dmr. for CTI label '68–74. Among the busiest sess. dmrs. in pop and jazz for more than three decades, Purdie is generally credited as an innovator of the funk drumming style. He has taught priv. fr. '62; at New Sch. fr. '87; at Five Towns Coll. fr. '88. Favs: Bellson, Billy Cobham, Jo Jones. Fests: Eur. fr. '64; Africa '64–85; So. Amer. '67–79; Australia '68; Japan w. Gillespie '82. CDs: Act; w. Gillespie (Pab.); Eddie Harris (Act); Leon Thomas (Portrait); Bennie Wallace; Randy Brecker (BN); Hank Crawford; Lou Donaldson (Mile.); Jimmy Smith (Verve); Houston Person (Prest.; Savant); James Brown (Atl.).

PURIM, FLORA, voc; b. Rio de Janeiro, Brazil, 3/6/42. Worked in Brazil in Quarteto Novo w. Airto Moreira (whom she later married) and Hermeto Pascoal. Moved to US 1967; toured Eur. w. Stan Getz '68; rec. w. Duke Pearson '69–70; worked w. Gil Evans, then tour. w. Chick Corea and Moreira in Return to Forever '72–3. After incarceration on drug charges in San Pedro, Calif., she resumed working with Moreira in Jan. '76 and cont. into '90s, occ. leading and rec. w. her own gps. In '74 she won *DB* Readers Poll and the Critics TDWR. CDs: Conc.; Sound Wave; w. Elements (Novus); Ivo Perelman (K2B2; Enja); Corea (Stretch); Pearson (BN); Joe Henderson (Mile.).

PURNELL, ALTON, pno, voc; b. New Orleans, LA, 4/16/11; d. Inglewood, CA, 1/14/87. Performed as voc. until late 1920s, when he focused on pno. Worked w. various bands in NO until mid '40s, incl. Alphonse Picou; "Big Eye" Louis Nelson; and Sidney Desvigne. His stint w. Bunk Johnson, incl. perf.

in NYC '45, brought Purnell wider renown. He remain. w. Johnson band after George Lewis became leader. From '57 lived in LA, pl. w. Teddy Buckner; the Young Men of New Orleans; and Kid Ory. Tour. Eur. extens. in '70s w. Legends of Jazz. Rec. own album in Japan '76. CDs: GHB; w. Geo. Lewis (Story.; Mos.); *Legends of Jazz & Barney Bigard* (GHB); Keith Smith (Lake).

PURNELL, KEG (WILLIAM), dms; b. Charleston, WV, 1/7/15; d. NYC, 6/25/65. Studied at Sch. of Amer. Mus., NYC. Pl. w. Chappie Willett at W.Va. St. Coll.; King Oliver 1934–5; own trio in NYC '38–9; Benny Carter bb '39–41; Claude Hopkins '41–2; Eddie Heywood '42–8 and '51–2. Rec. w. Rex Stewart; Teddy Wilson; Willie "The Lion" Smith; et al. Worked w. Heywood again '51–2, and freelanced in NYC area into the '60s, often w. Snub Mosley. CDs: w. Carter (BB; Class.) ; Rex Stewart (Class.)

PURRONE, TONY (ANTHONY MICHAEL), gtr, el-bs; b. Bridgeport, CT, 10/18/54. Brother is classical pnst. Began pl. prof. at age 14. Stud. at U. of Bridgeport and NYU, then w. Sal Salvador, Barry Galbraith. Pl. w. Heath Bros. 1978–82; Jimmy Heath since '78; Ed Thigpen since late '80s. Pl. w. own gps. since '78 and w. Gerry Mulligan; Lee Konitz; Billy Eckstine; Lew Soloff; Freddie Hubbard; Dave Liebman; Frank Foster; Dizzy Gillespie; Lionel Hampton; Al Cohn; Pepper Adams; Milt Jackson; Joe Pass; Geo. Benson; etc. Pl. and rec. w. Heath Bros. '98. Favs: Johnny Smith, Tal Farlow, Wes Montgomery Fests: Eur., So. Amer., Japan since '81. TV: *Big Band Bash* '78; *Bill Cosby Live* '80; 1980 Winter Olympics. CDs: w. Heath Bros. (Conc.); J. Heath (Land.; Steeple.; Verve); w. Thigpen (JT; Reckless).

PURTILL, MOE (MAURICE), dms; b. Huntington, LI, NY, 5/4/16; d. Fairlawn, NJ, 3/9/94. First prominent on recs. w. Red Norvo, Mildred Bailey 1936–7,

he was also briefly w. Glenn Miller in late '37. Pl. w. T. Dorsey '38–9; then rejoin. Miller and became well known during Miller's three yrs. of major successes until the band broke up in '42. After navy service '44–6, worked briefly w. Tex Beneke and the Miller Memorial Orch.; later w. Richard Himber and Billy Maxted, but mainly known thereafter as a NYC studio mus. CDs: w. Miller (BB); Bobby Hackett (Jazz.).; T. Dorsey (BB; Jass); M. Bailey (Topaz); Bunny Berigan (Class.); R. Norvo (Hep).

PURVIANCE, DOUG, bs-tbn; b. Baltimore, MD, 7/18/52. B.S. in mus. perf. fr. Towson St. U. 1975; M. Mus. fr. Manh. Sch. of Mus. '92. Pl. w. local soul and jazz bands in Balt., then w. Stan Kenton '75–6. Moved to NYC '77, pl. w. Slide Hampton's World of Tbns. fr. '77; Thad Jones–Mel Lewis Orch. fr. '78, incl. Vanguard Jazz Orch. Also pl. w. Frank Wess Orch., Bill Kirchner Nonet. Purviance has his own prod. co., which oversaw the rec. of Dizzy Gillespie's score for the '92 film *Winter in Lisbon*. Favs: J. J. Johnson, Slide Hampton, Tony Studd. Fests: Eur., Asia, etc. since '80. Film: app. in Spike Lee's *Malcolm X*. CDs: w. Kenton (CW); Mel Lewis Orch (MM); Vanguard JO (NW); Frank Wess; Mel Tormé (Conc.); Bill Warfield (Inter.).

PURVIS, JACK, tpt, tbn; b. Kokomo, IN, 12/11/06; d. San Francisco, CA, 3/30/62. First prominent w. the Original Kentucky Night Hawks. Freelanced in late 1920s as tptr, and arr.; briefly w. Hal Kemp; also made rec. w. his own all-star gps., Okeh '29–30; best known side was "Copyin' Louis." Later worked off and on w. the Dorsey Bros.; Charlie Barnet; Joe Haymes. Between '37 and '47 served prison term for armed robbery. A wildly eccentric character, Purvis in his day was one of the few white mus. to be closely assoc. w. black artists and styles. Infl. Armstrong. CDs: one track in *The 1930s—The Small Combos* (Col.); w. Coleman Hawkins (Class.).

QUEALEY, CHELSEA, tpt; b. Hartford, CT, 1905; d. Las Vegas NV, 5/6/50. First prominent dur. visit to Engl., where he rec. for Parlophone w. Fred Elizalde 1927. Back in US, worked w. California Ramblers; Paul Whiteman; to Calif. w. Ben Pollack. Rec. w. Mezz Mezzrow in NYC (Vict.) '34 ("Apologies," etc.); pl. w. Isham Jones '35–6; Joe Marsala '36; F. Trumbauer briefly '37; Bob Zurke '39–40. After freelancing w. small gps. at Nick's in NYC, returned to Calif. '46 working there and in LV. Rec. w. Goofus Five (Okeh) '25, '27; Isham Jones Juniors (Dec.) '36. CDs: w. Mezzrow (Class.); The Little Ramblers (Timel.); Adrian Rollini (Topaz); Benny Carter (BB).

QUEBEC, IKE ABRAMS, tnr sax; b. Newark, NJ, 8/17/18; d. NYC, 1/16/63. Started as dancer and pnst. First gig on tnr. sax w. Barons of Rhythm 1940; later worked w. Frankie Newton; Hot Lips Page; Roy Eldridge; Trummy Young; Sunset Royals; Ella Fitzgerald; Benny Carter; Coleman Hawkins. Intermittently w. Cab Calloway '44–51. From '44 to '46 he rec. for BN, incl. one of the label's early hits, "Blue Harlem." In '50s his pl. career slowed considerably. Worked as a&r assistant and talent scout for BN recs. and then, in '59, rec. some 45s for the label. In the '60s, a series of fine LPs on BN heralded a strong comeback, but it was halted by lung cancer. Quebec was a superior tnr. man of the Hawkins sch. w. a big tone and firm, vigorous style, notably in the blues idiom. CDs: BN; eight tracks in *The Blue Note Swingtets* (BN); w. Grant Green–Sonny Clark (Mos.); Jimmy Smith; Dodo Greene; Grant Green; Sonny Clark (BN); Roy Eldridge (Dec.); Hot Lips Page (Class.); Oscar Pettiford (Topaz).

QUEEN, ALVIN, dms; b. Bronx, NY, 8/16/50. Played for Ruth Brown at the age of 16. In 1970 join. Horace Silver for two yrs.; then George Benson for a yr.; pl. w. Charles Tolliver for eight yrs. (incl. Eur. tour). Later lived in Montreal, working w. Sadik Hakim. Moved to Switz. in '79 and founded Nilva Recs. in Geneva. Took part in many sess. as sideman or producer; rec. w. John Collins; Junior Mance; et al. Accomp. Sweets Edison, Lockjaw Davis. Tour. France w. Plas Johnson and Edison '82. Worked in Zurich w. Wild Bill Davis '83. His adaptability enabled him to pl. with a variety of gps. at the Nice JF '85. Traveled between US and Eur. more often in mid '90s, app. w. Edison at Tavern on the Green, NYC '95. Fest: Vitoria (Spain) w. David Sanchez–Danilo Perez '94. CDs: Nilva; Divox; w. G. Coleman; John Hicks; Pharoah Sanders (Evid.); Niels Lan Doky (Story.); Kenny Drew (Timel.); Lou Levy (Verve); H. Parlan (Enja); Bennie Wallace (Audq.).

QUICKSELL, HOWDY (HOWARD), bjo, gtr; b. Fort Wayne, IN, 1901; d. Pontiac, MI, 10/30/53. Best known for associations w. Bix Beiderbecke, first as a member of Jean Goldkette Orch. 1922–7, then on recs. w. Bix and F. Trumbauer. When Goldkette broke up, Quicksell went w. other bands (although he remained on Goldkette's personal staff until '32), pl. w. orch. of Frank Jones (bro. of Isham Jones) in Saginaw, Mich. '28. In the '30s, he did movie studio work in Hollywood but ret. to Saginaw '35, reduced his mus. activities and held a variety of jobs such as General Motors inspector, insurance salesman, and representative for a Mich. distillery. At one point he moved to Des Moines, Iowa. Quicksell, who once roomed w. Beiderbecke, is mentioned extensively in the book

Bix: Man and Legend by Richard Sudhalter and Philip Evans. Recs. w. Goldkette; Red Nichols '26. CDs: w. Beiderbecke (Mile.; Col.; Timel.).

QUILL, GENE (DANIEL EUGENE), alto sax, cl; b. Atlantic City, NJ, 12/15/27; d. Atlantic City, 12/8/88. Father, Daniel Leroy Quill, pl. vln. and had own band in Delaware dur. 1920s; nephew Gary Quill Jr. pl. sax, gtr. Took up alto sax in pre-teen yrs. Won "Stars in the Making" contest which made him eligible for app. w. J. Dorsey orch. at Steel Pier at age 11. Join. AFM Local 661 at age 15. Had own band while in hs, pl. army bases and USO dances. At 16 pl. in Alex Bartha's pit band at Steel Pier; at 18 joined Jerry Wald orch., then pl. w. Art Mooney, B. De Franco, C. Thornhill, G. Krupa, Dan Terry in '50s. Co-led combo, Phil and Quill, w. Phil Woods '57–8; worked w. Johnny Richards and Nat Pierce bands in same period. Pl. w. Gerry Mulligan Concert Jazz Band in early '60s, then freelanced in NYC. Lead alto w. Buddy Rich '66–7; in late '60s and early '70s worked w. a variety of local bands at clubs in Atl. City; also pl. in LV w. Dan Terry, Ray Anthony, Billy Daniels '73. Fr. '74 to '77 pl. lead alto in Steel Pier show band; also did jazz concerts w. John Andrews band at Stockton St. Coll., N.J. '74, '76. In what was believed to be a robbery, he was mugged on Memorial Day weekend '77, leaving him paralyzed on his right side and blinded in one eye. At a '79 benefit for Quill, Phil Woods pl. and presented him w. a new alto. Quill, having revised his fingering to compensate for his lame right hand, pl. at the benefit. In the '80s he pl. w. his church orch.; in '82 w. Mike Reed trio. A fiery player w. a cutting edge sound in a style

inspired by Charlie Parker, he was also an excellent jazz clst. as illustrated by his solos in the album *Gerry Mulligan* '63. Favs: Parker, Woods, C. Mariano, H. Geller. Rec. LP, *Wide Range*, w. J. Richards incl. what he considered his best solo on "Ballad of Tappan Zee." CDs: w. Woods (Prest.); Gil Evans; Q. Jones (Imp.); Mulligan (Verve; RTE); B. Potts (BN); Billie Holiday (Verve); Joe Newman (BL); Rich (PJ).

QUINICHETTE, PAUL, tnr sax; b. Denver, CO, 5/17/16, d. NYC, 5/25/83. Studied at Denver U.; majored in mus. at Tenn. St. Coll. Pl. w. local bands in Omaha, Neb., and, in late 1930s, w. Shorty Sherock in Chi. With Jay McShann '42–4; Johnny Otis '45–7; Benny Carter and Sid Catlett in Calif. Went to NYC w. Louis Jordan. With Lucky Millinder '48–9; Red Allen, Hot Lips Page '51. Tour. w. Count Basie '51–3, where he earned the nickname "Vice Pres" because of his tonal and stylistic similarities to Lester Young. Later worked w. Benny Goodman and Nat Pierce '55. Inactive in mus. for many yrs. but pl. w. Brooks Kerr; Sammy Price; Buddy Tate in mid '70s. CDs: Prest.; Biog.; w. John Coltrane; Gene Ammons; Webster Young (Prest.); Billie Holiday (Verve); S. Vaughan (Verve; Merc.); McShann (Dec.); Goodman (MM); Clifford Brown; Dinah Washington (Em.); Eddie Vinson (Beth.); Woody Herman (Evid.); Oscar Pettiford (Sav.); Nat Pierce (Hep); Buddy Tate (NW).

QUINTET OF THE HOT CLUB OF FRANCE. Organized in Paris in 1934 by an association of jazz enthusiasts. *See also* REINHARDT, DJANGO, and GRAPPELLI, STEPHANE.

RABINOWITZ, MICHAEL HARRIS, bsn, pno, bs-cl; b. New Haven, CT, 11/27/55. Mother pl. vln. Started on pno., cl. Stud. in New Haven at Neighborhood Mus. Sch., Educ. Ctr. for the Arts. Pl. w. Eddie Buster Trio, then w. jazz sxt. at SUNY-Purchase 1974–8 (B.F.A. in music '78). Pl. w. Blow Band on streets of Amsterdam; Paris; Scotland '80–2. While in Eur. perf. w. Ed Thigpen; Horace Parlan; Kenny Drew. Led own duo, trio, qt. in NYC fr. '83. Worked w. Mosaic Sextet w. Dave Douglas, Mark Feldman '86–9; Bill Kirchner Nonet '89–93; Mingus Epitaph Band '89–91; Gunther Schuller's New England Ragtime Orch. '91–6; Rush Hour Orch. w. Schuller, Joe Lovano '94–6. Has taught privately for last ten years. Formed gp. Bassoon In The Wild w. bassoonist Paul Hanson '96. A fiery, articulate pl. of whom Jamey Aebersold wrote: "Finally! The bassoon enters the world of jazz . . . for real." Favs: Hanson, Coltrane, M. Davis, Rollins. Fests: Eur. '90; Russia '91; Finland '95. TV: Bravo; BBC w. Mingus Epitaph. CDs: JF; Cats Paw; w. Mingus Epitaph (Col.); Ira Sullivan (Muse).

RACHEL Z (Rachel C. Nicolazzo), pno, synth, voc, cl, oboe, fl; b. NYC, 12/28/62. Mother is opera singer, fath. an artist who pl. pno. Voice lessons fr. age 2; piano lessons fr. 7. Stud. pre-college at Manh. Sch. of Mus.; Berklee. Wanted to become jazz mus. after hearing *Miles Smiles* while at Berklee summer session. Pl. in NYC w. Nardis Qnt. 1979; Oracle '80. Ret. to Boston to attend New Engl. Cons. '82. Pl. w. Bob Moses '83, then led own trio '84–6; combo feat. Geo. Garzone '84–8. Worked in Boston w. Dave Hann '84–6; Bill Banfield, Thania Sanchez, El Eco '86; Bruce Arnold '87. Ret. to NYC '88. Pl. w. Najee

for three mos. '88–9; Jimi Tunnell '88–91; Will Downing, Nicki Richards '89; Angela Bofill, Geo. Howard '90; Steve Smith's Vital Information '91; Bobby Watson '93; Special EFX, Larry Coryell '94; Sophie B. Hawkins '95. With Mike Mainieri's Steps Ahead '89–95; Wayne Shorter '93–6. Pl. w. Charnett Moffett, Susan Weinhardt, Gino Vanelli, Cindy Blackman '96. Led own trio and qt. fr. '90. Favs: Hancock, Corea, Jarrett. Fests: all major. TV: *Tonight Show* '94. CDs: NYC; Col.; w. Shorter (Verve); Steps Ahead (NYC); Bobby Waltson (Koko.).

RADER, DON (DONALD ARTHUR), tpt, flg, comp; b. Rochester, PA, 10/21/35. Father pl. tbn in dance bands. Stud. w. his fath. and at US Naval Sch. of Mus. 1954–5. Worked primarily w. bbs, incl. Woody Herman, Maynard Ferguson, Count Basie, Terry Gibbs, and Louis Bellson in the '60s; three world tours w. Les Brown, starting in '67; w. Stan Kenton, Toshiko Akiyoshi '70s; on radio staff at SDR in Stuttgart '82; three tours of Japan w. Benny Carter in late '80s. As educ. ran clinics all over the world. Favs: Freddie Hubbard, Chet Baker, Oscar Brashear. Comp: "Greasy Sack Blues" for Woody Herman. CDs: L&R; w. C. Basie–E. Fitzgerald (Verve); Herman (Fant.); Bill Holman (JVC); Ferguson (Roul.); Bob Curnow (MAMA).

RAE, JOHNNY (John Anthony Pompeo), vib, perc, dms; b. Boston, MA, 8/11/34. Studied at New Engl. Cons. and Berklee Sch. Worked w. Herb Pomeroy 1953–4; pl. vib. w. George Shearing '55–6. Later w. small gps. led by Johnny Smith, Ralph Sharon, Cozy Cole '57–8; Herbie Mann '59–60. Pl. dms. w. Cal Tjader '61–6; also rec. w. Stan Getz '62; pl. dms. and vib. w. Gabor Szabo. Rejoin. Tjader '68–70; in mid '70s pl. w. Charlie Byrd and Great Guitars. From late '70s freelanced in show bands and pl. Latin jazz; also took part in drm. clinics at hs and colls. and repaired dms. at Drumland, SF. Author of instruction books for dms. and mallet instruments. CDs: w. Getz; Tjader (Verve).

RAEBURN, BOYD (Boyde Albert Raden), lead, saxes; b. Faith, SD, 10/27/13; d. Lafayette, LA, 8/2/66. Led various commercial bands bef. building new jazz-oriented unit 1944. One of the two main bb gathering places for young talent in mid '40s. Sidemen incl. Dizzy Gillespie; Sonny Berman; Benny Harris; Trummy Young; Tommy Pedersen; Earl Swope; Don Lamond; Johnny Bothwell; Al Cohn; Ed Finckel; Oscar Pettiford; arrs. George Handy, Ed Finckel. Raeburn played saxes (principally bs. sax) but was not a soloist. In '45 reorganized in Calif. w. Johnny Mandel, Dodo Marmarosa, David Allyn and others. Orch. was quite avant-garde even for these years of changing styles. Later in NYC w. a band that incl. Buddy DeFranco w. arrs. by Johnny Richards. Having failed to gain commercial success by '52, he left mus. and went into the tropical furniture business. Later moved to Nassau, the Bahamas. Raeburn was married in '46 to Ginnie Powell, his voc., who died in Nassau '59. Despite the enthusiastic support of Duke Ellington and other admirers and a brief series of recs., Raeburn's adventurous ensembles never achieved the success they deserved. Recs. for Guild; Jewel. CDs: Sav.; Hep; Cir.

RAGAS, HENRY, pno; b. New Orleans, LA, 1891; d. NYC, 2/18/19. To Chi. w. Johnny Stein band 1916; soon after, became a part of ODJB, perf. on its history-making recs. in '17 and again in '18. Comp. "Bluin' the Blues." His career was cut short by the widespread influenza epidemic of 1918. CDs: w. ODJB (BB).

RAGLIN, JUNIOR (ALVIN REDRICK), bs; b. Omaha, NE, 3/16/17; d. Boston, MA, 11/10/55. Best known as bs. w. Ellington orch. replacing Jimmy Blanton in 1941 and remaining until '45. Also worked w. Ellington alumni Rex Stewart, Ray Nance, and Al Hibbler. Rejoin. Ellington briefly '46–7 but was sidelined by illness. CDs: w. Ellington (Vict.; Prest; Col.; Class.); Ella Fitzgerald (Dec.); Rex Stewart in *Trumpet Jive* (Prest.); Edmond Hall (BN).

RAINEY, CHUCK (CHARLES W. III), bs, el-bs; b. Cleveland, OH, 6/17/40. Studied at Lane U., Jackson, Tenn. Tour. w. Big Jay McNeely 1960–1; Sil Austin '61–2; Sam Cook '63; Jackie Wilson '64. Pl.

w. King Curtis in NYC from '64; became extremely active in rec. studios late '60s, early '70s, pl. and/or rec. w. Jerome Richardson; Grady Tate; Al Kooper; H. Belafonte; Mose Allison; Hamp Hawes; and dozens of others. Perf. w. Eddie "Cleanhead" Vinson at Montreux JF '71; tour. and rec. w. Aretha Franklin '71–5. Moved to LA and pl. w. the Crusaders '72–3 and Hampton Hawes '74–5; rec. in mid '70s w. Donald Byrd; Sonny Rollins; John Handy; et al. An extremely versatile mus. much praised for his ability to adapt to a wide variety of mus. styles. CDs: w. Geo. Benson (Verve); Byrd; R. Brecker (BN).

RAINEY, MA (Gertrude Malissa Nix Pridgett), voc; b. Columbus, GA, 4/26/1886; d. Rome, GA, 12/22/39. Made debut 1898, singing and dancing in show, *A Bunch of Blackberries*; then married Will "Pa" Rainey in '04 and tour. w. him in the Rabbitfoot Minstrels. In '12 she tour. w. the Moses Stokes Co., which picked up a young Bessie Smith in Chattanooga, Tenn. It was Smith's first prof. gig, and Rainey became a mentor of sorts. Rec. nearly one hundred sides for Paramount '23–8, accomp. first by Lovie Austin's Blues Serenaders, then her own band. Accomps. incl. Tommy Ladnier; Joe Smith; Fletcher Henderson; Louis Armstrong; Tampa Red; and Thomas A. Dorsey, who became her mus. dir. Less active in the '30s, she retired to Georgia in '35. Known as the "mother of the blues," Ma Rainey was hailed by connoisseurs as one of the idiom's greatest female exponents, second only to Bessie Smith. She was the earliest known link between the male country blues artists who roamed the streets and back roads of the South and their female counterparts, the so-called classic blues singers. Often accomp. by jug and washboard bands, she had a rough-edged, compelling voice. CDs: Mile.

RAMEY, GENE (EUGENE GLASCO), bs; b. Austin, TX, 4/4/13; d. Austin, 12/8/84. First pl. tpt. then sousaphone. To KC 1932; learned to pl. bs. fr. Walter Page. Pl. w. Countess Johnson '36; Jay McShann '38–44; Luis Russell '44–5. Worked on 52nd St. w. Hot Lips Page; Charlie Parker; Coleman Hawkins; Ben Webster. Three mos. w. C. Basie '52–3; tour. w. Dorothy Donegan, Art Blakey '54. Extensive freelancing from mid '50s, incl. Eur. tours w. Buck Clayton; McShann; also pl. w. Muggsy Spanier; Eddie Vinson; Teddy Wilson. Lived in Tex. fr. '76, working locally into '80s. In his most active yrs. dur. the '50s was one of the most sought-after bassists. CDs: w. Parker; McShann (Stash); Monk (BN); Fats Navarro; J. J. Johnson; D. Gordon (Sav.); Getz (Prest.); Clayton (Story.); Jimmy Forrest (Del.).

RAMIREZ, RAM (Roger Ameres), pno, org, comp; b. San Juan, PR, 9/15/13; d. Forest Hills, NY, 1/11/94. Grew up in NYC. A pno. prodigy at age 8, he was prof. at 13. In the early 1930s pl. w. Louisiana Stompers. Pl. w. Rex Stewart '32–4; accomp. Monette Moore '33. Join. Spirits of Rhythm '34; Willie Bryant '35. Trav. to Eur. w. tptr. Bobby Martin '37. In '39 back in NYC, working w. Ella Fitzgerald; then w. Charlie Barnet '42; Frankie Newton '43; John Kirby, Hot Lips Page '44; Sid Catlett '45; then worked as solo pno. and in trios. In '53 took up Hammond org. after hearing Wild Bill Davis. Pl. extens. in NYC. Tour. Eur. w. T-Bone Walker '68. Pl. w. Harlem Blues and Jazz Band '79–80, incl. Dixieland Fest., Dresden, Germ; also tour. w. HB&JB for Caribbean cruise '87. Died of kidney failure. Renowned for his song "Lover Man," he comp. many other originals, notably "Mad About You," rec. for BN w. Ike Quebec '44. LPs: RCA; Master Jazz. CDs: w. Fitzgerald (Dec.); Ellington (Col.); Rex Stewart (Aff.); King Pleasure–Annie Ross (Prest.); Quebec in *The Blue Note Swingtets* (BN).

RAMSAY, BILL (WILLIAM G.), bari sax, other saxes, cl, fl; b. Centralia, WA, 1/12/29. Army service 1948–52. In '60s and '70s worked w. Buddy Morrow; M. Ferguson; Montgomery Bros.; et al.; pl. tnr. sax w. B. Goodman '79–82; bari. sax w. C. Basie 3/84–3/85. Off and on since '88 w. Grover Mitchell; fr. '89 w. Frank Wess–Harry Edison Orch. In April of '92 pl. at the Blue Note, NYC, w. Joe Williams and Frank Wess Orch. Clinician w. Bud Shank Jazz Wkshp. annually in Port Townsend, Wash. CDs: w. Wess-Edison; Wess (Conc.); G. Mitchell (Ken).

RANDALL, FREDDY (FREDERICK JAMES), tpt, crnt; b. London, England, 5/6/21. Began pl. tpt. at age 16; self-taught. Form. St. Louis Four 1939. In army '40–2. Led own dixieland band '43, then pl. w. Freddy Mirfield and his Garbage Men '44 (J. Dankworth was also in the band). Formed own gp. '45; toured Eur. and pl. on BBC Jazz Club radio series. Perf. as guest soloist w. British mus. incl. Ted Heath; Henry Hall; Harry Parry, Bert Ambrose; also w. visiting US mus. incl. Pee Wee Russell; Wild Bill Davison; Bud Freeman; Teddy Wilson; Sidney Bechet; Bill Coleman; Jimmy and Marian McPartland. Tour. southern US w. own spt. '56. Retired fr. mus. due to lung ailment '58. Returned to pl. part-time '63. Pl. w. Dave Shepherd '71; Britain's Greatest Jazz Band, later known as the Randall-Shepherd All-Stars, fr. '72. In virtual retirement since. Moved fr. East London to Devon '93. Favs: Armstrong, Bobby Hackett, Billy Butterfield, Charlie Teagarden. Fests: Montreux JF w. Randall-Shepherd All-Stars '73. LPs: Dormouse; BL. CD: Jazz.

RANDOLPH, IRVING "MOUSE," tpt; b. St. Louis, MO, 6/22/09; d. NYC, 12/10/97. Pl. w. Walt Farrington 1923–4; Willie Austin '25–6; Art Sims–Norman Mason '26; Fate Marable '27; Floyd Campbell '27–8; Alphonso Trent '28; J. Frank Terry '29–30. Moved to KC, pl. w. Andy Kirk '31–4. Came to NYC w. Fletcher Henderson '34. Pl. w. Benny Carter '34; Luis Russell '34–5; Cab Calloway '35–9. Also rec. in '30s w. Teddy Wilson, Lionel Hampton. Pl. w. Ella Fitzgerald band (formerly Chick Webb Orch.) '39–42; Don Redman at Zanzibar '43; Edmond Hall at Café Society, both Uptown and Downtown, '44–7; Eddie Barefield '50. Tour. US and Latin Amer. w. Marcelino Guerra early '50s. Rec. in '50s w. Pearl Bailey, also various r&b acts. Worked w. Bobby Medera at Savoy Ballroom '55; Chick Morrison '58–70s. CDs: w. Hampton (BB); Fitzgerald; Henderson (Dec.); Carter; Chu Berry; Edmond Hall (Class.); Calloway; T. Wilson; Billie Holiday (Col.); Mildred Bailey (Sav.).

RANDOLPH, ZILNER T(RENTON), tpt, comp; b. Dermott, AR, 1/28/1899; d. Chicago, IL, 2/2/94. Studied pno., tpt., harm., theory, etc., until 1926. Pl. w. Bernie Young in Milwaukee '27–31. Best known as arr. and tptr. '31–5 w. L. Armstrong, for whom he comp. "Ol' Man Mose." In Chi. he arr. for many bands, incl. Earl Hines; D. Ellington; Fletcher Henderson, Woody Herman. In late '40s built a musical act w. his son and two daughters; in '70s was working as teacher. CDs: w. L. Armstrong (BB; Vict.; BBC; Col.).

RANEY, DOUG, gtr; b. NYC, 8/29/56. Son of Jimmy Raney; bro. Jon a pnst. At age 13 stud. dms. but soon sw. to gtr. and began listening to B. B. King, Muddy Waters. He then heard jazz through his father's rec. collection and changed his style. Stud. w. Barry Galbraith; then w. J. Raney in 1972 when the latter ret. fr. Louisville. Prof. debut w. Al Haig at Gregory's; rec. debut in duet track w. father for Choice '75. In '77 pl. in duo w. him at Bradley's and on Eur. tour. Settled in Copenhagen and rec. as a lead. fr. '77–85 (co-lead. w. J. Raney '79) for Steep.; also as sideman for the label. Tour. in France and Italy w. Chet Baker '79. Fr. '90 pl. w. tnr. sax Thomas Franck; also co-led gp. w. Bernt Rosengren. Fr. '93 member of Eur. Gtr. Jazz Orch., dir. by Louis Stewart. CDs: Steep; w. Haig-Raney (Choice); Jesper Thilo (Story.); Chet Baker (Steep.); Eur. Gtr. Jazz Orch. (Jardis); Joe Cohn (D-T).

RANEY, JIMMY (JAMES ELBERT), gtr, comp; b. Louisville, KY, 8/20/27; d. Louisville, 5/10/95. Father a prominent newspaperman. Moth. pl. gtr.

Stud. w. A. J. Giancoll and Hayden Causey; the latter recommended Raney to replace him in Jerry Wald band, NYC 1944. After two mos. w. Wald he went to Chi. '45, working there w. Max Miller; Lou Levy; Lee Konitz; and many local combos. Tour. w. Woody Herman Jan.-Sept. '48. Worked in trio w. Al Haig, then Buddy DeFranco sxt. and intermittently w. Artie Shaw '49–50. Pl. briefly w. Terry Gibbs bef. becoming part of the Stan Getz qnt. where he was responsible w. Getz for the unique sound achieved by the gp. '51–2. Pl. w. Teddy Charles; then fr. Mar. '53 he spent a yr. w. the Red Norvo trio, tour. Eur. w. him in early '54. After three mos. w. Les Elgart he join. the Jimmy Lyon trio at the Blue Angel, remaining there until he pl. w. Don Elliot qt. in the B'way show *A Thurber Carnival* '60. Rejoin. Getz '62–3. Then did TV jingles, recs., priv. teach., and pl. for singers and for B'way shows. Ret. to Louisville in late '60s, teach., working in non-music jobs, and doing some pl. In the summer of '72 he visited NYC, pl. at The Guitar; Gulliver's (N.J.); and Bradley's. App. in concert w. Haig at Carnegie Recital Hall Nov. '74. Fr. the mid '70s began tour. in Japan, Holland, France, Switz., Engl., Den., Belgium; collab. w. son Doug; and w. Attila Zoller in Germ. In the early '90s his career was slowed by Meniere's Disease and his perfs. became sporadic. A pure-toned player, amplifier down, Raney was appraised by Teddy Charles as "one of the first to grasp the Charlie Parker lyricism into long, flowing lines of his own. He went through the chord changes melodically, not just running them. . . . He foreshadowed things that Coltrane, Miles and Gil Evans did later. I don't think he influenced them, but the abstract harmonies and the use of the upper functions of the chords are things that Coltrane later reintroduced." Favs: Christian, Farlow. Comps: "Signal"; "Parker 51"; "Motion"; "Momentum"; "We'll Be Together"; *Suite for Guitar Quintet;* "Double Image." CDs: Prest.; CC; Steep.; B&B; *Two Jims and Zoot* (Main); w. Haig (Choice); Norvo (Fant.); B. Brookmeyer (Prest.); Getz (Prest.; BN; Verve; Mos.); B. Holiday (BN); T. Charles (Prest.; Atl.).

RANEY, SUE (Charlene Claire Clausen), voc; b. McPherson, KS, 6/18/36. Raised in Albuquerque, NM; child prodigy, had own TV show at age 14; rec. first album w. Nelson Riddle arrs. at 17 in LA. Ret. briefly at 24 after car accident, then became intensely active rec. commercial jingles in Hollywood studios. Returned to in-person apps. at jazz clubs mid '70s. Worked w. Supersax and Voices gp.; rec. w. Michel Legrand, Henry Mancini. Admired by many of her peers, she is a compelling and consistently underrated jazz singer. CDs: Disc.; w. Vic Lewis (Cand.).

RANGELOV, ANGEL G., comp, arr, tbn, pno, gtr; b. Rousse, Bulgaria, 5/10/53. Began on acdn. at age 5; gtr. at age 10. Stud. at Rousse Mus. Sch. 1965–70; classical comp. and tbn. at Cons. of Sofia, Bulgaria '74–7; jazz comp. and perf. w. Dieter Glawishnig at Graz and Vienna Cons., Austria '77–80. Cond. orig. mus. w. Rousse Jazz Orch., Bulgarian Radio and TV bb; pl. w. Peter Herbolzhimer bb, own sxt. in Austria '76–9. Immigrated to US '80. Stud. w. Phil Wilson, Herb Pomeroy, Mike Gibbs, Greg Hopkins at Berklee Coll. of Mus. '80–2. Led own bb and pl. w. Slide Hampton's tbn. choir while at Berklee. Moved to NYC '81. Stud. arr. priv. w. Gil Evans, Thad Jones '81–6. Orig. comp. "Eclipse" premiered by Gil Evans Orch. '84. Arr. for Thad Jones's Count Basie Orch. early '80s; Skitch Henderson–NY Pops Orch. '85. Form. management co., Jazz For Cats, only to represent artist Tony Munzlinger '86; organized art exhibitions at Eur. JFs '87–8. Join. Dizzy Gillespie All-Star bb '87. Conducted all-star bb at Pori JF '88; London Symph. Orch. for Geo. Benson, rec. '88; UMO Orch. in Finland '89. Rangelov has taught priv. fr. '81 and has produced recs. for Kenny Werner and Geo. Benson. He has co-led a bb w. Jimmy Madison fr. '82. Comps. incl. "Samba Dei-der," written for McCoy Tyner bb. Exhibited his paintings of jazz musicians at Sweet Basil, NYC '96. Favs: Thad Jones, Gil Evans, Robert Farnon. Polls: Austrian Int'l Jazz Seminar prize. TV: Joe Franklin. CDs: as arr. w. Tyner (Verve).

RANGER, CLAUDE, dms, comp, arr; b. Montreal, Que., Canada, 2/3/41. Mainly self-taught; stud. arr. w. Frank Mella. Pl. w. showbands in Montreal early 1960s; Pierre Leduc, Ron Proby fr. mid '60s; Lee Gagnon '67–9; Aquarius Rising w. Brian Barley, Michel Donato '69–71; also led gps. on CBC prog. *Jazz En Liberté.* Moved to Toronto '72. Pl. w. Moe Koffman '78–80; freelanced w. Lenny Breau; Geo. Coleman; Larry Coryell; Sonny Greenwich; James Moody; Doug Riley; Don Thompson; Phil Woods. Led own gps. fr. '82. Ranger moved to Vancouver, Can., in '87 and has been a mainstay of the Du Maurier JF there. He has led a bb, the Jade Orch. fr. '90. Favs: Roach, Tony Williams, Elvin Jones. TV: many apps. on CBC. LP w. Breau (Adelphi). CDs: w. Jane Bunnett (Dark Light).

RANIER, TOM (THOMAS JOHN RAINIERI), pno, cl, saxes, fl, synths; b. Chicago, IL, 7/13/49. Father pl. cl. and saxes; moth. was a singer. Bach. degree in comp. from Cal. St.-Fullerton; classical pno. study at USC and CalArts. Pl. w. Dave Pike 1974; Don Ellis, Carmen McRae, Dexter Gordon '75; Joe Farrell '76; Harold Land '77. Also pl. w. Milt Jackson '80–2; trio w. John Heard and Sherman Ferguson off and on

'80–3. During balance of '80s occasionally w. Terry Gibbs; Supersax; w. James Moody '89; Lee Konitz '91; Lanny Morgan and Med Flory '91–2. Most often heard on pno., Ranier also doubled on saxes and cl. in many dates. An accomplished classical cl., he has perf. the Mozart *Clarinet Concerto*, the Artie Shaw *Concerto for Clarinet*, and other classical works w. several LA symph. ens. Favs: Peterson, Corea, Bill Evans; arrs: M. Legrand, Nelson Riddle, Eddie Sauter. CDs: Cont.; *Heard, Ranier and Ferguson* (ITI); w. Joe Pass (Tel.); Lanny Morgan (Cont.); Frank Capp; Capp–R. Woodard (Conc.); Herb Geller (Hep; FS; VSOP); *Jackson, Johnson, Brown and Co.* (Pab.).

RANK, BILL (WILLIAM C.), tbn; b. Lafayette, IN, 6/8/04; d. Cincinnati, OH, 5/20/79. Professional debut in Fla. w. Collins Jazz Band 1921; pl. w. Jean Goldkette '23–7. Many small gp. rec. dates w. Bix Beiderbecke; Adrian Rollini; et al.; worked w. Paul Whiteman orch. '27–38. Studio work in LA late '30s, then led own band in Cincinnati in '40s. Cont. part time in mus. while working as insurance agent; active on recs. and at fests. until shortly before his death. CDs: w. Beiderbecke (BB; Col.).

RASKIN, MILT (MILTON WILLIAM), pno, comp; b. Boston, MA, 1/27/16; d. Los Angeles, CA, 10/16/77. Studied at New Engl. Cons. Pl. w. Gene Krupa 1938; Tommy Dorsey '42; studio mus. in LA from '44. Cond. and arr. for Nancy Wilson, George Shearing in '60s. Wrote lyrics for *Naked City* theme, "Somewhere in the Night," and for instrumentals assoc. w. Stan Kenton, who rec. them as *Artistry in Voices and Brass*. Active as mus. dir. and cond.; also a gifted painter w. several showings in So. Calif. CDs: w. Krupa (Class.); Dorsey (BB; Jass); Billie Holiday (Verve).

RATAJCZAK, DAVE (DAVID C.), dms, perc; b. Buffalo, NY, 12/24/57. Grandfather pl. vln w. Paul Whiteman; bro. is freelance pnst. in Houston, Tex. Began on pno. Stud. w. John Rowland (Rochester Philharm.) 1968–75; at Eastman Sch. of Mus. '76–80 (B. Mus.) '80 Pl. w. Woody Herman '80–2; Glenn Miller band '82; Bob Mintzer '84; Chris Connor '85–9; Jackie and Roy '86–8; Susannah McCorkle '86–9; Bob Wilber Orch. '87–90; B'way show *City of Angels* '89–92; Walt Levinsky bb fr. '89; Eddie Daniels '90; Gerry Mulligan Qt. fr. '90. Ratajczak taught at U. of Conn. '86–9 and Hofstra U. He pl. on the soundtrack to the films *Brighton Beach Memoirs* and *Biloxi Blues*. Favs: Philly Joe Jones, Jack DeJohnette, Sid Catlett. Fests: Eur. fr. '80s. CDs: w. Milt Hinton (Col.); John Fedchock (Res.); Kenny Rankin (Chesky); Mark Vinci (Flat Cat).

RAVA, ENRICO, tpt, flg, comp, lead; b. Trieste, Italy, 8/20/39. Mother was amateur classical pnst., grad. fr. Cons. di Torino. Began on tbn. at age 16 then sw. to tpt. after seeing Miles Davis perf. Self-taught, later stud. w. Carmine Caruso in NYC. Pl. w. Gato Barbieri in Rome 1964; Steve Lacy in Eur., So. Amer., US '65–9; also freelanced in mid '60s w. Mal Waldron, Lee Konitz. Moved to NYC, pl. w. Roswell Rudd '69–76; Jazz Composers Orch., Globe Unity Orch. '70s. Tour. Eur., So. Amer. w. own qt. '73–84; sidemen incl. John Abercrombie; Rudd; Aldo Romano; F. Di Castri; Bruce Ditmas. Also led trio w. Philip Catherine and Miroslav Vitous or Niels H.Ø. Pederson. Ret. to Italy '85; led own qt. of Ital. mus. fr. '85. Rec. w. Tony Oxley, berimbau player Nana Vasconcelos as Rava String Band '84. Pl. w. Archie Shepp, Cecil Taylor '85; Joe Henderson–Paul Motian '87; C. Taylor '88; Quatre w. M. Vitous, Daniel Humair, F. D'Andrea fr. '88. Rec. album of Ital. opera themes w. gp. Ravalopera, comprising Rava's reg. qt. feat. French accordionist Richard Galliano plus string qt. '92. Rec. album of orig. songs in the French and Ital. tradition w. Galliano, pnst. Rita Marcotulli, bassist Enzo Pietropaoli '93. No matter the setting, Rava has an exciting edge to his playing, whether cooking straight-ahead or pushing the envelope in other, varied directions. He perf., rec., and cond. a 13–piece ens. in a unique version of the music fr. *Carmen* w. arrs. by Bruno Tommaso at Umbria Jazz '96, Montreal JF '97; rec. it for Label Bleu '95. Another brilliant project is his interpretation of the music of Nino Rota fr. the Fellini films. Rava has scored many Ital. films incl. *Oggetti Smarriti* by Giuseppe Bertolucci. He has taught at the Siena jazz wkshp. fr. '81. Favs: Miles Davis, Chet Baker. Polls: Ital. critics '82, '88. Fests: all major. Film: app. in Ital. films *O.R.G.* '70s. TV: Eur., So. Amer. TV. CDs: MM; SN; *Rava Carmen; Rava "Noir"* (Label Bleu); w. Quatre (Gala); Rava-D'Andrea; Konitz-Rava (Phil.); Abdullah Ibrahim (Enja); S. Lacy (ESP).

RAZAF, ANDY (Andreamenentania Paul Razafinkeriefo), songwriter; b. Washington, DC, 12/16/1895; d. Hollywood, CA, 2/3/73. Occasionally rec. as a singer but not primarily known as a mus. or a perf. Important in jazz as lyricist for many songs that became jazz standards and as close friend and songwriting partner of Fats Waller. Wrote mus. for revues, *Connie's Hot Chocolates of 1928* and *Lew Leslie's Blackbirds of 1930*; lyrics for "Honeysuckle Rose"; "Ain't Misbehavin'"; "Keepin' Out of Mischief Now"; "Black and Blue"; "S'posin'"; "Massachusetts"; "Memories of You"; "Stompin' at the Savoy"; "In the Mood"; "Christopher Columbus"; and hundreds of others. Book: *Black and Blue: The Life and*

Lyrics of Andy Razaf, Barry Singer (Macmillan) '92. CDs: as voc. w. Waller (BB); F. Henderson (Class.); Maxine Sullivan, *Tribute to Andy Razaf* (DCC).

REA, DANILO, pno, comp; b. Vicenza, Italy, 8/9/57. Received diploma fr. Santa Cecilia Cons., Rome 1980. Member of Roma Jazz Trio '75–85 incl. perfs. w. Lee Konitz, Steve Grossman '76; Albert Mangelsdorff '77; Art Farmer '78; Chet Baker '80; Bob Berg '82; Curtis Fuller '83. Led own trio fr. '83. Pl. w. Giovanni Tommaso fr. '83; Jimmy Knepper '85; Lingomania '85–8; Big Bang bb feat. Phil Woods '87; Umbria Jazz All-Stars '86–7; Dave Liebman '88; duo w. R. Gatto '89. Rea led a qnt. w. Tony Oxley, Paolo Fresu '91. Perfs. as a solo pnst. and leads a duo and trio w. Aldo Romano. Has also perf. on film and TV soundtracks and as a classical soloist w. orch. He has taught at clinics in Italy fr. '86. Favs: Bill Evans, Bud Powell, Paul Bley. TV: Italy. CDs: Gala; w. C. Fuller–Roma Trio (Timel.); Lingomania (Gala); Big Bang (Phil.).

REARDON, CASPER, harp; b. Little Falls, NY, 4/15/07; d. NYC, 3/9/41. Played mainly w. symph. orchs. in Phila. and Cincinnati. On radio he used the stage name Arpeggio Glissandi. Became first to pl. jazz on harp, rec. w. Jack Teagarden and Paul Whiteman. Occ. led his own small gps. in NYC and Chi. CDs: w. Teagarden (Conifer).

REBELLO, JASON MATTHEW, pno, kybds, comp; b. Carshalton, England, 3/29/67. Cousin, Simone Rebello, is percst. Stud. at Guildhall Sch. of Mus., London, 1987–90. Formed first gp. at age 15 w. sch. friends. At 18 made rec. debut in Netherlands w. Jean Toussaint, *Impressions of Coltrane*. Since '88 has perf. at jfs in Engl., Eur., and Japan w. own gp. and Tommy Smith; Toussaint; Wayne Shorter; James Moody; Cleveland Watkiss; Bud Shank; et al. Taught jazz courses at the Royal Acad., London; teaches priv. Two-time winner of *Wire* Award; Brit. Jazz Awards "Best Newcomer" '91. Rebello combines a sense of respect for the early masters w. a keen ear for the most contemporary concepts. CDs: Novus; w. Tony Rémy (GRP); Julian Joseph (East West); Alan Skidmore (Miles Music); Jean Toussaint (World Circuit; NN).

REBILLOT, PAT (PATRICK EARL), pno, org, harpsichord, kybds, comp, arr; b. Louisville, OH, 4/21/35. Father amateur singer; moth. amateur pnst. Principal church orgst. in Louisville 1947–52. Stud. at Mt. Union Coll. '49–53; w. Jeno Takacs at Cincinnati Cons. '53–7 (B.S., mus. ed. '57). In army, arr. and tour. w. army entertainers '58–60. Moved to NYC after discharge, working w. Benny Powell,

Chris Connor, Jeremy Steig, Benny Goodman, Paul Winter, Sarah Vaughan '60s. Pl. at Half Note w. Zoot Sims; Roy Eldridge; James Moody; Jimmy Rushing; Sonny Rollins; also w. own gps. at Greenwich Vill. clubs. Conductor for show *Jacques Brel Is Alive and Well*. Pl. w. Gary Burton '71–2; kybds. and mus. dir. w. Herbie Mann '72–7. Pl. w. Thad Jones–Mel Lewis late '70s. Rebillot has worked mainly as a studio mus. fr. '79. Worked w. Mann intermittently in the '80s. Favs: Monk, Ellington. Polls: NARAS M.V.P. Awds. on kybd. '79–81, '86; on pno. '82; NARAS Virtuoso Awd. '87. Fests: Brazil w. P. Winter '65; Japan, Austral., Eur. w. Mann '72–7; MJF w. Airto & Flora Purim '74. LP: Atl. CDs: w. Frank Foster (Prest.); Mark Murphy (Muse); Chuck Loeb (JC); Nnenna Freelon (Col.); Patti Austin (Epic); B. Belden (BN); Gloria Lynne (Muse); David Newman (Mile.).

RED, SONNY (Sylvester Kyner), alto sax; b. Detroit, MI, 12/17/32; d. Detroit, 3/20/81. First prof. gig w. Barry Harris 1949. Pl. tnr. sax w. Frank Rosolino '54; back to alto sax w. Art Blakey late '54. To NYC '57 w. Curtis Fuller; ret. to Det. Aug. '58. Tour. in Seattle, Wash., Vancouver and Edmonton, Can., in first half of '59 before ret. to NYC in June. Rec. several albums as leader '58–62 for BN, Jzld. In '60s and '70s pl. and/or rec. w. Donald Byrd; Kenny Dorham; Pony Poindexter; Yusef Lateef; Clifford Jordan; Howard McGhee; et al. A soulful pl. w. a penchant for blues-based pieces. Early infl: Sonny Stitt. CDs: BN; w. P. Quinichette (Prest.); Curtis Fuller; Tommy Flanagan (Sav.); D. Byrd (BN); Lateef (Atl.)

REDD, CHUCK (CHARLES RANDOLPH), dms, vib; b. Takoma Park, MD, 9/10/58. Younger bro. Robert is jazz pnst. in Wash., D.C. Began on pno. at age 7. Stud. dms. w. John Richardson fr. age 10; then for two yrs. at Montgomery Coll., Rockville, Maryland, at age 16. Pl. dms. w. Bill Potts bb, Mike Crotty bb '77–9; Charlie Byrd Trio fr. '80; Tal Farlow, Emily Remler, Red Norvo, Laurindo Almeida '80–8; Great Gtrs. w. Byrd, Barney Kessel, Herb Ellis '80–9; Monty Alexander '87–8; Tommy Flanagan '89; Dizzy Gillespie Qnt. in Africa '90. Pl. vib. w. Mel Tormé '91. Also freelance w. Scott Hamilton; Ken Peplowski; Howard Alden; Widespread Jazz Orch.; Bud Shank; etc. Redd pl. vib. in his own qt. Fav. dmrs: Shelly Manne, Philly Joe Jones, Buddy Rich; vib: Milt Jackson. Fests: Austral., Eur. fr. '80; Asia fr. '86; Africa '90. TV: *Tonight Show* '83. CDs: Exclusive Arts; w. Byrd; S. McCorkle; K. Peplowski (Conc.).

REDD, FREDDIE, pno, comp; b. NYC, 5/29/28. Fath. was pno. teacher but Redd resisted lessons.

First became interested in jazz while in the army in Korea when a friend pl. a Gillespie-Parker rec. Self-taught, also stud. at Greenwich House, NYC. First job w. Jo Jones in early 1949. Worked w. dmr. Johnny Mills in Syracuse, N.Y., then pl. in NYC w. Oscar Pettiford '49; Cootie Williams, Jive Bombers '53; Joe Roland, Art Blakey '54. Rec. w. Art Farmer–Gigi Gryce, May '55; Gene Ammons June '55. Tour. Sweden in '56 w. Rolf Ericson and Ernestine Anderson; rec. w. Ericson and own trio album. Pl. w. Charles Mingus in SF '56, remaining there to become house pnst. at Jimbo's Bop City for six mos. Ret. to NYC in summer '57 and rec. his *San Francisco Suite* for Riv. in Oct. Own trio '57–8. He led a qt., wrote the score, and perf. as an actor in the seventeen-month run of the Off-B'way play *The Connection*, '59–60; also rec. mus. fr. the play on Blue Note w. Jackie McLean. Tour. w. *The Connection* in London and Paris '61. Remained in Europe, pl. in France, Den., and the Netherlands. Back to SF '63; then to Guadalajara, Mex., for a yr. The peripatetic Redd then went back to NYC '66, on to London, rec. on organ w. James Taylor and Paul McCartney, bef. winding up in Berlin at end of '69 for three mos. After a couple of yrs. in Paris, spent a yr. in Amsterdam. Ret. to US '74, settling in LA in the '70s and '80s. Represented Mississippi Art Council at NO World's Fair '84. In '88 began a yr.'s gig at Studio Grill in Hollywood. Moved to Pacific, Calif., near SF, in '90. His playing merges blues and bop elements into a robust, two-handed style; as a comp. has created memorable, long-lined melodies incl. "Time to Smile"; "Thespian"; "So Samba"; and "After the Show." Favs: Bud Powell, C. Parker, Monk. Film: *The Connection*, dir. by Shirley Clarke '61. TV: *Jazz a la Noche*, Guadalajara mid '60s; own gp. w. Slide Hampton, Barcelona, early '70s. LPs: Inter.; Futura. CDs: Mos.; Up.; BN; Tri.; Riv.; Mile.; Hampton Hawes–Freddie Redd, *Piano: East/West*; w. Gene Ammons; Art Farmer (Prest); Rolf Ericson (Drag.).

REDD, VI (ELVIRA), alto, sop saxes, voc; b. Los Angeles, CA, 9/20/28. Father, Alton, a NO dmr., pl. w. Les Hite and Kid Ory. Stud. w. great-aunt, Alma Hightower, who also taught Melba Liston. Local dance dates while in sch. Briefly retired from mus. 1957–60. In early '60s pl. LA clubs; rec. two albums; pl. w. Earl Hines '64. Led qt. in SF w. her then husband, dmr. Richie Goldberg. Briefly w. D. Gillespie and C. Basie '68. From early '70s was school teacher in LA, pl. occasional gigs. Strongly infl. by Charlie Parker, she is also an exceptional singer w. a warm and personal timbre. LPs: UA; Atl.; w. Marian McPartland (Halcyon). CDs: w. Gene Ammons (Prest.).

REDMAN, (WALTER) DEWEY, tnr, alto saxes, cl, musette, comp; b. Ft. Worth, TX, 5/17/31; d. Brooklyn, NY, 9/2/06. Son, Joshua Redman. Began on cl. at age 13; mainly self-taught. Pl. in church and marching bands. Att. Tuskeegee Inst. briefly to study el. engineering; then transferred to Prairie View A&M in Tex. (B.S., 1953). Received Master's in educ. fr. No. Texas St. '59. Taught and dir. bands in Tex. public schs. '57–9, then moved to LA '59. In SF '59–67, pl. w. Pharoah Sanders; Don Garrett; Smiley Winters; Wes Montgomery. Also co-led bb w. Monty Waters; led after-hrs. sess. at Soulville. Moved to NYC '67. Pl. w. Sunny Murray, then joined Ornette Coleman. Pl. w. Coleman '67–74; Charlie Haden Liberation Mus. Orch. '69; Keith Jarrett '71–6; Jazz Comp. Orch., Alice Coltrane, own gps. '70s. Feat. w. N.Y. Jazz Repertory Co. in concert of Coltrane's mus. '74. Co-led gp. Old and New Dreams w. Don Cherry, C. Haden, Ed Blackwell, '76–80s. Pl. w. Pat Metheny, '80–1; Henri Texier. He cont. to lead his own small gps. Acknowledged as a leading "free" player, he was capable of convincing solos in a Lester Young style. Fests: Eur., incl. Umbria Jazz '95; Japan, Australia. TV: Eur. and Austral. TV. CDs: Mons; Evid.; ECM; w. O. Coleman (BN); C. Haden (BN; ECM); Randy Weston (Ant.); P. Motian (JMT); K. Jarrett (Imp.); R. Kendrick; P. Delano (Verve).

REDMAN, DON (DONALD MATTHEW), comp/arr, lead, saxes, voc; b. Piedmont, WV, 7/29/1900; d. NYC, 11/30/64. Father pl. in brass band; moth. sang contralto. Child prodigy who learned to pl. most orch. instruments. Graduated from Storer Coll., West Va., w. a mus. degree 1920; further studies at Bost. and Det. cons. Worked in NYC w. saxophonist Billy Paige '23; rec. w. Fletcher Henderson '23 and joined the Henderson band soon after at the Club Alabam. During next three yrs. he wrote most of the band's arrs. and rec. accomps. for Bessie Smith; Ma Rainey; and Ethel Waters. Rec. w. Duke Ellington '26; Louis Armstrong and Savoy Ballroom Five '28. After leaving Henderson, he became mus. dir. of McKinney's Cotton Pickers—also pl. and sang w. the band, helping to establish it as one of the most important bbs of the day. During this time he rec. two of his best-known comps, "Cherry" and "Gee, Ain't I Good to You?" In '28 rec. two sessions under the name *Chocolate Dandies*. Redman led his own big band from Oct. '31 to Jan. '40, featuring such players as Horace Henderson; Henry "Red" Allen; Benny Morton; and Harlan Lattimore. During this time Redman also wrote arrs. for Paul Whiteman; Ben Pollack; Isham Jones; et al. His harmonically advanced comp., "Chant of the Weed," was the band's radio theme on remote broadcasts in the '30s. Through much of the

'40s he freelanced as comp./arr. for numerous radio shows and Cab Calloway; Jimmy Dorsey; Count Basie; et al. In '46 he organized the first Amer. jazz orch. to tour Eur. after World War II. Sidemen incl. Don Byas, Billy Taylor. From '51 until his death, he was mus. dir. for Pearl Bailey and pl. a small acting role in her musical, *House of Flowers* '54–5. Redman was one of the first significant comp./arrs. in jazz history. Many of the devices he employed became basics in the jazz arranging style book. When Louis Armstrong joined Henderson, Redman seized the opportunity to transform the Armstrong improvisational style into a new kind of swinging bb style as exemplified by "Sugarfoot Stomp" and "The Stampede." He was a fine soloist, especially on alto and soprano saxes, and a delightful vocalist with an engaging, informal, semi-conversational style. CDs: Class.; Hep; Steep.; w. Henderson (Col.); McKinney's Cotton Pickers (BB); Louis Armstrong (Col.; BBC); Babs Gonzales (BN); Fats Waller (BBC); B. Holiday (Jazz Unlimited).

REDMAN, JOSHUA, tnr, sop, alto saxes; b. Berkeley, CA, 2/1/69. Father, Dewey Redman; moth. a dancer. Graduated fr. Harvard. Gave up law studies when he won Thelonious Monk competition 1991 and was signed by Warner Bros. Rec. and tour. w. Chick Corea sxt. in "Tribute to Bud Powell" '96 but mostly leads own gp. Sidemen have incl. Brad Mehldau; Christian McBride; Larry Grenadier; Brian Blade. Redman has been among the most successful of his generation because he has brought together his influences and reflected them through his intelligence and persona. Favs: Rollins, Dexter Gordon, Coltrane, S. Turrentine, Jacquet. Fests: all the int'l fests. TV: Profiled on CBS *Sunday Morning* '97. Film: Perf. in Altman film, *Kansas City* '96. CDs: WB; w. Corea (Stretch); Kenny Drew Jr. (Ant.); P. Motian (JMT); Dewey Redman (Evid.); Dave Brubeck; Ray Brown (Tel.); McCoy Tyner (Mile.); Delfeayo Marsalis; John Hicks (Novus).

REECE, DIZZY (ALPHONSO SON), tpt; b. Kingston, Jamaica, 1/5/31. Father pnst. for silent films. Stud. bari. horn at age 11; sw. to tpt. at 14. Schoolmates were Joe Harriott, Bogey Gaynair. Went to Eur. 1948; pl. w. Don Bya, Jay Cameron in Paris '49–50. Later worked in Germ. and the Netherlands w. dmr. Wallace Bishop, Sandy Mosse, and Byas. To London '54, working in clubs and w. Tony Crombie's band. Spent '56–7 in Paris, Portugal, and London; in '58 worked in France w. Jacques Helian's bb. Then gigged in London clubs w. Victor Feldman; Tubby Hayes; Ronnie Scott; Jimmy Deuchar w. occ. vists to France bef. migrating to US Oct. '59. Rec. deb. on

Tempo 10–inch LP, London, May '55. Introduced to NYC by Blue Note, which had released his first LP in the US (rec. in Paris), *Blues in Trinity* via gig at Wells'. Led own gp. at Village Vanguard May '60. Freelanced as sideman and led own gp. for experimental films at Bridge Theater '66. Traveled to Eur. w. D. Gillespie Reunion BB '68; Paris Reunion Band '85. In the early '90s was a member of Clifford Jordan's weekly bb at Condon's, NYC. Pl. w. own gp. at Lenox Lounge in Harlem '98. Reece plays in an energetic, personal bop style that owes more to the modern trumpet lineage than to other individuals. He picked up the nickname Dizzy as a young prankster in Jamaica before he ever heard Gillespie, whom he named as a favorite on his arrival in New York. Film: score and soundtrack for *Nowhere to Go*, UK '58. Comp: "Con Man," rec. by Tommy Flanagan. LPs: BN; Bee Hive; w. Paris Reunion Band (Sonet). CDs: NJ; w. V. Feldman (Cont.); C. Jordan (Mile.).

REED, ERIC SCOTT, pno; b. Philadelphia, PA, 6/21/70. Father, David, a former gospel singer, taught him basic harmony. Grew up pl. org., pno., and dms. in church. Stud. at Settlement Mus. Sch. 1977–81 and R. D. Colburn Sch. of Arts '82–88. Met jazzmen through Harold Battiste; worked w. Teddy Edwards, Clora Bryant at age 16. While in coll. at Cal. St.-Northridge pl. w. John Clayton, Gerald Wilson and learned the inner workings of a bb. Many overseas tours from '89. Pl. w. Wynton Marsalis spt. '90–1 and again in '92; also w. F. Hubbard, Joe Henderson '91–2. Own trio fr. '93. Reed is fluent in modern styles and is able to bring his gospel feeling into them with conviction and flair. Favs: M. Tyner, A. Jamal, W. Kelly. Fest: Juan Les Pins '95–6. CDs: Imp.; MoJazz; Cand.; w. Wynton Marsalis; Marlon Jordan (Col.); West Coast Jazz Summit (Mons).

REED, WAYMON, tpt; b. Fayetteville, NC, 1/10/40; d. Nashville, TN, 11/25/82. Studied at Eastman Sch. of Mus. Pl. w. Ira Sullivan and Pee Wee Ellis in Miami, Fla.; tour. w. James Brown 1965–9; Count Basie '69–73 and '77–8; also in '75 w. Frank Foster and Thad Jones–Mel Lewis. In '78 left Basie to tour as cond. and soloist w. Sarah Vaughan, to whom he was then married. CDs: w. C. Basie; Joe Turner (Pab.); T. Brewer (Sig.; Dr. Jazz).

REEDUS, TONY (ANTHONY), dms, comp; b. Memphis, TN, 9/22/59. Took up dms. at age 14. As a sideman worked w. Milt Jackson; Billy Taylor; Jackie McLean; Bobby Hutcherson; Benny Golson; Mercer Ellington. Rec. w. Woody Shaw '81; Phineas Newborn Jr. 1987; later rec. w. Kenny Garrett; Geoff Keezer; Benny Green; Steve Nelson. First album as leader, *Incognito*, on Enja '91. In '90s tour. w. Freddie Hubbard; Mulgrew Miller; also feat. w. Smithsonian Jazz Orchestra. CDs: Enja; w. K. Garrett (Atl.); Mulgrew Miller (Novus; Land.); Contemporary Pno. Ens. (Col.); F. Hubbard (MM); B. Golson (Drey.; Evid.); James Williams (Evid.); B. Easley (Sunny.).

REEVES, DIANNE, voc, comp; b. Detroit, MI, 10/23/56. Raised in Denver, Colo., fr. age 2. Discovered at 16 by Clark Terry; worked w. him at jazz fests. Moved to LA; began stud. w. Phil Moore 1980; worked w. Billy Childs' Night Flight '79–81; tour. w. Sergio Mendes '81. Introduced to rhythms of West Africa and West Indies while working w. Harry Belafonte '83–6. From late '80s worked as single, specializing in pop, Brazilian, and scat singing. First solo album for Blue Note '87. After several yrs. of straddling pop/jazz fence, she started focusing on the latter in mid '90s. App. w. Benny Carter at Lincoln Center '96. CDs: BN, incl. reissue of recs. done for Palo Alto '81–5; w. McCoy Tyner; Terri Lyne Carrington (Verve); Geo. Duke; Joe Sample (WB); Lou Rawls (BN); T. S. Monk (N2K); Benny Carter (MM).

REEVES, NAT (NATHANIEL GARFIELD), bs.; b. Lynchburg, VA, 5/27/55. Grandfather pl. blues gtr., bjo., hca. Self-taught. El. bs. at age 16 for six yrs. Form. a Top 40 band. Acoustic bs. at 22, perf. in Richmond, Va., w. Russell Wilson. To NYC 1979, pl. w. Kenny Garrett; Mulgrew Miller; Jo Jones Jr.; jamming at Jazz Forum '79–81. Infl. by Sam Jones. Worked two weeks w. Sonny Stitt '82. Met Jackie McLean in Hartford, Conn., and moved there to become part of his gp. and to teach at the U. of Hartford and Artists Collective. Toured w. McLean in Eur., So. Africa '93; SS *Song of America* cruise w. McLean '94. So. Africa w. T. S. Monk '95. Join. K. Garrett '95. Favs: Blanton, Paul Chambers, Slam Stewart, Ray Brown, Ron Carter. TV: WBET *Jazz Central* w. Garrett June '95. CDs: w. McLean (Ant.; Verve; Tri.; Bird.; BN); Garrett (CC; WB); Randy Johnson (Muse); M. Musillami (Stash).

REHAK, FRANK JAMES, tbn; b. NYC, 7/7/26; d. Badger, CA, 6/26/87. Took up tbn. while serving in navy dur. WWII. Pl. in many bands, incl. Gene Krupa; Jimmy Dorsey; Claude Thornhill; Sauter-Finnegan; Benny Goodman. Tour. Middle East and Latin Amer. w. Dizzy Gillespie 1957. Play. on large ensemble recs. w. Miles Davis–Gil Evans '57–62. Left Woody Herman in '69 to enter Synanon drug rehabilitation center, eventually becoming dir. of one of its branches. During the '50s Rehak was one of the outstanding bop trombonists infl. by J. J. Johnson, Earl Swope. CDs: w. Gillespie (Verve; CAP); Rollins

(Verve); Geo. Russell (Imp.); Johnny Hartman; Coltrane (Beth.); M. Davis–G. Evans (Col.); T. Macero (Stash); Ivory Joe Hunter (R&T); *Roots* w. Prestige All-Stars (Prest.).

REICHENBACH, BILL (WILLIAM FRANK), tbn, tba, euph; b. Takoma Park, MD, 11/30/49. Father (also Bill Reichenbach, b. Wash., DC, 12/18/23) pl. dms. w. T. Dorsey and was a member of C. Byrd trio 1962–73. Stud. tbn., arr. at Eastman Sch. Pl. w. Chuck Mangione '69–71; bs. tbn. w. Buddy Rich '72; tbn. w. Akiyoshi-Tabackin bb '75–8; Don Menza Sxt. and bb '76–'84. Tba. w. Steve Huffstetter Band '85. Own qt. off and on from '88. From '75 when he moved to LA, his career was devoted mainly to recs., TV, and film gigs; also gave jazz clinics at universities. Tour. Japan w. Akiyoshi; Austral. and N. Zealand w. Bobby Shew; Switz. and the Netherlands w. Paulinho da Costa. First album as leader for Silver Seven Recs. Favs: J. J. Johnson, Frank Rosolino. CDs: w. Akiyoshi-Tabackin (RCA); Booker T. Jones (MCA); Spyro Gyra; Patti Austin (GRP); Joe Sample (MCA); Boney James (WB); D. Marsalis (Evid.).

REID, RUFUS L., bs; b. Atlanta, GA, 2/10/44. Started on tpt. In 1961 joined USAF band and learned to pl. bs. using method developed by Bob Haggart. Pl. w. Buddy Montgomery '66; to Chi. '69, working w. Curtis Fuller; Dizzy Gillespie; Lee Konitz; James Moody; Gene Ammons; et al. Toured w. Bobby Hutcherson–Harold Land qnt. '71; Freddie Hubbard and Nancy Wilson '71; Eddie Harris '71–4. Moved to NYC '76; worked w. Thad Jones–Mel Lewis '76–7; D. Gordon '77–8; taught at Wm. Paterson Coll., N.J. '79–80. First album as lead., *Perpetual Stroll*, w. Kirk Lightsey '80. Also rec. in '80s w. Ricky Ford; Jack DeJohnette's Special Edition; Art Farmer; Kenny Burrell; Jimmy Heath; et al. Co-led TanaReid qnt. w. dmr. Akira Tana from '90, rec. for Conc. Perf. on soundtrack of Spike Lee's *School Daze* and *Do the Right Thing*. A schooled and adaptable musician, Reid has written two bass instruction books, *The Evolving Bassist* and *Evolving Upward*. CDs: Sunny.; w. TanaReid (Evid; Conc.); duo w. Harold Danko (Sunny.); Kenny Barron (Up.); D. Gordon (Col.); A. Farmer (Cont.).

REINHARDT, DJANGO (JEAN-BAPTISTE), gtr; comp; b. Liverchies, Belgium, 1/23/10; d. Fontainebleau, France, 5/16/53. Raised in a Gypsy encampment, Reinhardt roamed through Belgium and France; picked up vln., bjo., and gtr. Seriously burned in a caravan fire 11/1928, he lost the use of two fingers of his left hand and spent a year recovering from injuries. He quickly developed new technique to overcome the handicap and, after hearing jazz, began fusing it with an engaging Gypsy flavor. His unique style was first heard in such bands as Andre Ekyan's fr. '31. A chance encounter w. vlnst. Stephane Grappelli in '34 led to the creation of the Quintet of the Hot Club of France; the other three members were his bro., Joseph Reinhardt (b. Paris, 3/1/12; d. Paris, 2/82), and Roger Chaput on gtrs. and Louis Vola on bs. The qnt. worked together on and off until '39, rec. w. such visiting Amers. as Coleman Hawkins; Benny Carter; Rex Stewart; Dicky Wells; Eddie South; et al. In London at the outbreak of WWII, Grappelli decided to stay while Reinhardt ret. to France and replaced him with clarinetist Hubert Rostaing. Visiting the US in '46, Reinhardt toured w. Ellington and pl. at Café Society Uptown. The reception was disappointing, perhaps because Reinhardt pl. el. gtr. This was his only visit to the US; he cont. to rec. and tour in France until shortly bef. his death. Reinhardt was the first Eur. jazz perf. to infl. Amer. musicians, many of whom acknowledged their debt to him. His most effective perfs. were done w. the QHCF, which made over two hundred recs. His rhapsodic brand of melodic improvisation is especially effective on slower tempo numbers, but he had the capacity to swing at any tempo. His best known comp. is "Nuages"; others are "Djangology"; "Swing Guitars"; "Minor Swing"; "Daphne"; and "Manoir de Mes Reves (Django's Castle)." Film: documentary, *Django Reinhardt*, dir. by Paul Paviot '58. Book: *Django Reinhardt*, Charles Delaunay (DaCapo) '61. CDs: BB; BN; Stash; Verve; Ark.; Prest.

REMLER, EMILY, gtr, comp; b. NYC, 9/18/57; d. Sydney, Australia, 5/7/90. First attracted to folk and rock mus., she turned to jazz while stud. at Berklee Coll. and listening to Wes Montgomery, Charlie Christian, and others. Prof. debut in NO, where she accomp. singers. Discovered by Herb Ellis, she pl. at the Conc. JF. 1978; tour. for three yrs. w. Astrud Gilberto; fr. '81 rec. regularly for Conc. Played in pit band for *Sophisticated Ladies*. Worked primarily as tour. soloist in the last yrs. of her life. Married for three yrs. to pnst. Monty Alexander. Equally adept at mainstream and jazz fusion, Remler was becoming one of the most respected young guitarists at the time of her allegedly drug-related death. CDs: Conc.; Just.; w. R. Clooney; S. McCorkle (Conc.); D. Benoit (GRP); R. Cole–H. Crawford (Mile.).

RENA, KID (Henry René), tpt; b. New Orleans, LA, 8/30/1898; d. New Orleans, 4/25/49. Older bro., Joseph, pl. dms w. him. Was a student, along w. L. Armstrong, at Joseph Jones's Colored Waifs' Home.

Replaced Armstrong in Kid Ory's band 1919. After Ory left for Calif., start. his own gp., Dixieland Jazz Band, w. George Lewis on cl. For several yrs. thereafter led the Tuxedo Brass Band and the Pacific Brass Band. Rec. only once, in '40, w. Louis Nelson, Alphonse Picou, and Jim Robinson. In later yrs. Rena was inactive due to ill health. Rec. for Delta, NO, '40. CD: *Prelude to the Revival, Vol. 2* (Amer. Mus.).

RENAUD, HENRI, pno, comp; b. Villedieu, Indre, France, 4/20/25; d. Paris, 10/17/02. Studied vln. and pno. To Paris 1946, gigging there w. Don Byas; Buck Clayton; James Moody; Roy Eldridge; formed own trio at Tabou; accomp. Sarah Vaughan; Lester Young; Clifford Brown. In '54 rec. series of sessions in NYC w. M. Jackson; Al Cohn; J. J. Johnson; Oscar Pettiford; Max Roach; et al. In France formed qt. w. Jay Cameron; they backed June Richmond '57. Pl. at Birdland w. Philly Joe Jones '59; then in Paris w. Kenny Clarke and Buck Clayton. Deejay on Radio Monte Carlo '62. In '64 gave up full-time pl. to become head of jazz production for CBS France where he was responsible for many important projects, particularly reissues. Contributed articles to *Jazz Hot, Jazz Magazine*. Also prod. shows for TV and radio fr. '70s. Film: comp. part of soundtrack for *Murmur of the Heart* '70; served as advisor for *Round Midnight* '86. Jimmy Rowles and Michael Moore rec. an album of Renaud's comps. for French Col. Combo won *Jazz Hot* poll '53. Fest: own qnt., Antibes '68. A cool, understated player whose single-note lines showed the infl. of his favs: G. Wallington, Al Haig, Thelonious Monk. CDs: w. Pettiford; Konitz-Brookmeyer; James Moody–Frank Foster; Zoot Sims (Vogue); Clifford Brown (Vogue; Prest.); J. J. Johnson–Al Cohn (FS).

RENDELL, DON (DONALD PERCY), tnr, sop, alto saxes; fl, cl; b. Plymouth, England, 3/4/26. Father pnst., orgst., mus. dir.; moth. voc. in mus. shows. Self-taught, took up alto sax at 15. Began prof. career in show band 1943. Pl. w. US mus. in band backing USO perfs. '44. Worked w. Oscar Rabin '50–3. Pl. w. J. Dankworth Seven of which he was a founding member. With Tony Crombie '55; T. Heath '55–6; Eur. w. S. Kenton '56; Woody Herman Anglo-American Herd '56, '59. Led own gp. fr. '53 to '55, then fr. '60 incl. qt. co-led w. Ian Carr '63–9. Taught at various jazz summer schs.; at Royal Acad. of Mus. '74–7 and Guildhall Sch. of Mus. fr. '84. Has also taught Bible studies. Comps: "Antibes"; "Jubal"; "Trane Ride." Orig. infl. Lester Young, later John Coltrane. One of the respected veterans of Brit. jazz. Publs: *A Saxophone Selection* (Guildhall School); *Introduction to the Flute: Advanced Flute Method*

(EMI Music Co.). Recs. for Jazzland; Decca; EMI; Col.; live recs. w. Kenton and Herman. CDs: Spot.; w. Dankworth (Hallmark); Michael Garrick (Jaza 3).

RETURN TO FOREVER. Jazz fusion gp. active in '70s. CDs: Col.; Polyd. *See* **COREA, CHICK.**

REUSS, ALLAN, gtr; b. NYC, 6/15/15. Studied w. George Van Eps, who recommended that he replace him in B. Goodman orch. 1934–8; pl. w. Paul White-man '38; Jack Teagarden '39–40; Ted Weems '40–1; J. Dorsey '41–2. Rejoin. Goodman '43; Harry James '43–4; then freelanced in Hollywood. Best remem-bered for recs. w. Teddy Wilson, Billie Holiday, and L. Hampton late '30s; feat. in solos w. Teagarden and Corky Corcoran. A superior rhythm guitarist and occasional soloist. Won *DB* poll for best guitarist '44. CDs: Goodman (BB); C. Hawkins (Cap.); Armstrong (Vict.); Benny Carter in Key. Coll. (Merc.).

REYS, RITA (MARIA EVERDINA), voc; b. Rot-terdam, Netherlands, 12/21/24. Father was mus.; moth. was dancer; bro. pl. alto sax. Sang w. Hawaiian band 1940; theater band led by her father '42; Lex Van Spall '42–4; Ted Powder '45; Piet Van Dijk '47–50, incl. tour of No. Africa '49. Married Wes Ilcken '45; she sang w. Ilcken's gp. until his death '57. On tours of US, she sang w. Mat Mathews, Art Blakey '56; Chico Hamilton, Jimmy Smith '57. Worked w. Kurt Edelhagen, Bengt Hallberg in Germ. and Sweden '58. Married Pim Jacobs '60. Rec. and perf. as soloist fr. '60. Received Edison awd. fr. Dutch Rec. Industries '61. Favs: Billie Holiday, Car-men McRae, Ella Fitzgerald. LP: Epic, backed by the Jazz Messengers '56. CD: w. Lars Gullin (Drag.).

RHODES, TODD WASHINGTON, pno, arr; b. Hopkinsville, KY, 8/31/1900; d. Flint, MI, 2/16/63. Best known as a member of McKinney's Synco Jazz Band 1922, which evolved into McKinney's Cotton Pickers '22–34. To Det., where he was active w. r&b and pop mus. into '50s. Discovered LaVern Baker, who sang w. his band in '52; also gave Johnnie Ray his start. CDs: w. McKinney's Cotton Pickers (BB).

RICH, BUDDY (BERNARD), dms, voc, lead; b. Brooklyn, NY, 9/30/17; d. Los Angeles, CA, 4/2/87. A child prodigy, he worked w. his parents' vaudeville act fr. the age of 18 mos., dancing and singing. Led his own stage band fr. age 11 for a yr. and a half. His jazz career began when he joined Joe Marsala 1938; then pl. briefly w. Bunny Berigan, Artie Shaw '39; Tommy Dorsey '39–42; and Benny Carter '42. After serving in marines '42–4, he rejoined Dorsey for two more yrs., guesting on *Rattle and Roll* w. Benny

Goodman and *Your Father's Moustache* w. Woody Herman '45. With the help of Frank Sinatra formed his own bop-oriented band, incl. Red Rodney, Earl Swope '46, the first of several bbs. In this period he also showed his skills as a tap dancer in his band's stage shows. Starting in '47 toured several times as a single w. JATP. Pl. short stint w. Les Brown; formed Big Four w. Charlie Ventura, Chubby Jackson, Marty Napoleon '51. Pl. w. Harry James '53–6. A heart attack incapacitated him winter '59–60, but he returned to playing and singing later in '60. Rejoin. James '61; left to form his own band '66–74. Led small band, singing and pl. at his own club, Buddy's Place, in '74. Alternated small gps. and bbs until the early '80s, when he organized a series of bbs feat. a new generation of young players. Rich's acid wit was often in evidence on the bandstand; he frequently dis-played his quick way with a put-down in his many apps. on late-night TV talk shows, esp. w. Johnny Carson, where he also sat in w. Doc Severinsen's orch. Rich was one of the greatest natural technicians on his instrument. Though unable to read mus., he was capable of following the most intricate arrs. after hearing them once. His fluency with regular eighth-note patterns made it possible for him to bridge the gap between jazz phrasing and contemporary rock music. Fests: many int'l apps. w. bb; also drum battle w. Blakey, Roach, Elvin Jones at Radio City jam ses-sion, NJF-NY '74. Fav: Jo Jones. Polls: won *DB* Readers '67, '70–2; Hall of Fame, Reader's Poll '74; band won *DB* Critics TDWR '68. Films: apps. w. Shaw; Dorsey. Video: DCI. Books: *Super Drummer: A Profile of Buddy Rich*, Whitney Balliett (Bobbs-Merrill) '68; *Traps, the Drum Wonder*, Mel Tormé (Oxford) '91. CDs: PJ; Hep; RCA; BGO; 12 tracks w. '46 bb in *The 1940s Mercury Sessions* (Merc.); co-lead w. G. Krupa (Verve); M. Roach (Merc.); w. T. Dorsey; Metronome All-Stars; Artie Shaw (BB); C. Parker (Verve; Rh.); B. Powell; Armstrong; L. Young; JATP (Verve); Nat Cole (Cap.); A. Tatum (Pab.); L. Hampton (Tel.).

RICH, FREDDY, pno, lead; b. Warsaw, Poland, 1/3/1918; d. California, 9/8/56. Best known as leader of popular band, some of whose recs. incl. Bunny Berigan; Benny Goodman; Dorsey Bros.; and, later, Benny Carter and Roy Eldridge.

RICHARDS, ANN (Margaret Ann Borden Kenton), voc; b. San Diego, CA, 10/1/35; d. Hollywood Hills, CA, 4/3/82. Sang w. local gps. in Oakland and SF; four mos. w. Charlie Barnet combo; six mos. w. George Redman in Hollywood. Join. Stan Kenton band 1955; married Kenton in Oct. of that yr. A few mos. later, shortly bef. winning the *DB* poll as no. 1

band singer, she gave up her career except for a few rec. sess. both w. and without Kenton. Divorced from Kenton in '61; club dates in LA throughout '60s. CDs: w. Kenton (Mos.).

RICHARDS, EMIL (Emilio Joseph Radocchia), vib, perc; b. Hartford, CT, 9/2/32. Xylophone at age 6; att. Hartford Sch. of Mus. 1949–52; pl. w. several symph. orchs. '50–54; army band '54–5. Tour. w. Geo. Shearing '56–9. Settled in LA; pl. mrba. in own qnt; w. Paul Horn '59–62; Shorty Rogers '63–5; Don Ellis '64–9; own Microtonal Blues Band '69. In the same yr. he went to India, stud. meditation and Indian mus.; pl. w. Roger Kellaway Cello Qt. '70–4. Tour. w. Ravi Shankar; Tom Scott; George Harrison '74; w. Frank Zappa Electric Symph. '75–7. Concerts w. Stan Kenton Neophonic in late '60s and w. New Amer. Orch. '77–88. Own qt. fr. '89. A gifted mus. whose style reflects both swing and bebop elements, Richards also experimented w. unusual perc. instruments. Movie soundtrack work incl. ethnic perc. sounds for *Prince of Tides; Hook; Dying Young; Robin Hood;* and *Star Trek VI.* Taught extensively at Grove Sch. and as clinician for instrument manufacturers. CDs: w. Paul Horn (Black Sun); Louie Bellson (Pab.; Conc.).

RICHARDS, JOHNNY (John Cascales), comp/arr, lead; b. Queretaro State, Mexico, 11/2/11; d. NYC, 10/7/68. Raised in Schenectady, N.Y. Moth. was prof. pnst. who stud. w. Paderewski. Richards learned bjo., pno., vln., and tpt. as child; in a vaudeville act, "The Seven Wonders of the World," ages 10–12; saxophonist and house orchestrator at Phila.'s Mastbaum Theatre at age 17. Attended Syracuse U., then to London to comp. film scores for Gaumont 1932–3; to Hollywood as Victor Young's assistant at Paramount '33–40. While in LA, stud. w. Arnold Schoenberg and received master's degree from UCLA. Led own band '40–5, playing tnr. sax, cl., tpt.; early sidemen incl. Paul Smith, later Pete Rugolo, on pno.; singer Andy Russell on dms.; Bob Graettinger, bari. sax and arr. Freelance arrs. for Boyd Raeburn '46–7; Charlie Barnet; Stan Kenton. Cond./arr. for Dizzy Gillespie date w. strings, woodwinds Oct. '50; film scores in Mexico '48 and '50. To NYC in early '50s; arrs. for rec. dates by Sarah Vaughan; Sonny Stitt; Helen Merrill; Gillespie; et al. Occasionally led own bb in NYC '56–60, '64–5. Despite his reputation as an uncompromising mus. iconoclast, Richards' best-known comp. is probably "Young at Heart," a pop hit for Frank Sinatra in '54. His most widely heard orchestral works are "Soliloquy"; "Prologue"; "Bags and Baggage," written for and rec. by the Kenton band. Richards wrote in a heavy-textured, skillfully orches-

trated style that was sometimes painfully top-heavy, but which often resulted in remarkably colorful timbres. LPs: CW; Beth. CDs: w. S. Kenton (Cap.); Helen Merrill (Em.).

RICHARDS, RED (CHARLES COLERIDGE), pno; b. Brooklyn, NY, 10/19/12; d. Scarsdale, NY, 3/12/98. Studied classical pno. for six yrs. w. Profess. Weeks in Harlem. Began pl. jazz after hearing Fats Waller; Willie "The Lion" Smith; James P. Johnson at parties. First gig w. own sxt. at Wonder Bar in Fallsburg, N.Y. summer 1937. Pl. w. Horse Collar Williams–Kermit Scott at Monroe's Uptown House fall '37; Skeets Tolbert '38–41. Made rec. debut w. Tolbert '38. In army '42–4, then pl. w. Tab Smith at Savoy Ballroom '45–9; Sidney Bechet '51; Bob Wilber–DeParis Bros.–Sid Catlett at Storyville, Bost. '51. Also freelance w. Roy Eldridge; Bobby Hackett; Jimmy McPartland; Rex Stewart; Buster Bailey. Pl. w. Buck Clayton, Mezz Mezzrow in Eur.; also tour. w. Frank Sinatra '53. Tour. w. Muggsy Spanier '53–7, then worked as single in Columbus, Ohio '57–8. Freelanced w. Fletcher Henderson Alumni '58; Wild Bill Davison '58–9. Formed Saints & Sinners w. Vic Dickenson '60; the group received much critical acclaim until it disbanded in '70. Pl. w. own qt. w. Herb Hall in Syracuse, N.Y. '72–4; solo pno. at Eddie Condon's '75–7, trio '77–8. Worked mainly as solo pnst. fr. '79; also pl. w. Panama Francis's Savoy Sultans. Favs: Tatum, Teddy Wilson, Waller. Fests: Eur. and Tokyo as soloist '80–90. CDs: Sack.; w. Rex Stewart–Fletcher Henderson Orch. (FS); Savoy Sultans (Stash); Milt Hinton (Chiaro.); Seventh Ave. Stompers (Sav.); M. McPartland (JA); Swingville All-Stars (GTJ).

RICHARDS, TIM, pno, comp; b. London, England, 6/23/52. Studied classical pno. first; then jazz w. Hal Galper et al.; mostly self-taught. First band, Spirit Level, fr. 1979; trio '88, tour. Eur. w. both. Also tour. Eur. w. trumpeter Jack Walrath '87. Formed London Blues Band '93. Teacher of blues pno., U. of London; Westminster Adult Educ. Inst. CDs: Spot.; Future Music; 33.

RICHARDSON, JEROME C., tnr, alto, sop, bari saxes, fl, woodwinds, voc; b. Sealy, TX, 11/15/20; d. Englewood, NJ, 6/23/00. Began on alto sax at age 8; stud. at SF State Coll. Local mus. Ben Watkins and Wilbert Baranco helped him get first prof. gig at age 14. Pl. w. local bands 1934–41, then briefly as Willie Smith's replacement w. Jimmie Lunceford. In navy '42–5, pl. w. dance band under Marshal Royal. Tour. w. Lionel Hampton '49–51, first flute solo on "Kingfish." Pl. w. Earl Hines '52–3. Moved to NYC '53;

freelanced w. Lucky Millinder, Cootie Williams. Subbed w. Chico Hamilton Qnt. and pl. in pit band at the Roxy '54–6. Led own qt. at Minton's Play House, NYC '55–60s. As studio mus., app. on *Your Hit Parade* and other commercial NYC broadcasts fr. '56. Pl. w. Oscar Pettiford '56–7; Quincy Jones Orch. fr. '59, incl. Eur. tour '60. Also freelanced in '50s w. Lucky Millinder; Cootie Williams; Johnny Richards; Gerry Mulligan; Gerald Wilson. Led own gp. at Jazz Gallery in '60s and freelanced w. Kenny Burrell; Peggy Lee; Billy Eckstine; Brook Benton; Julie London; Oliver Nelson. Own band at Basin Street East '64. Lead alto w. Thad Jones–Mel Lewis Orch. '65–70; pl. w. Bobby Rosengarden band on Dick Cavett TV show '70–1. Studio mus. in LA '71. Tour. Japan w. Q. Jones '72–3; Percy Faith '74. Worked in LA w. own gps., Louis Bellson, Dave Grusin '70s. Tour. Eur. w. Nat Adderley '80. Ret. to NYC '89. Pl. w. Clifford Jordan bb in early '90s; Art Farmer qnt., sxt. fr. mid '90s. B'way: pl. for *Ain't Misbehavin';* *Black and Blue; Dream Girls; The Tap Dance Kid.* Although primarily known as a versatile and dependable sess. mus., Richardson was also an excellent jazz soloist and a capable ballad singer. Favs: Parker, Stitt, Getz, F. Wess (fl.). Fests: NJF; MJF; Northsea; San Remo. TV: apps. w. Sammy Davis Jr. '60; pl. for Bing Crosby Special; *Baryshnikov On Broadway*; major award shows.; Dick Cavett '70–1. CDs: NJ; TCB; w. C. Jordan bb (Mile.); Gillespie; Milt Jackson (Pab.); Mingus Dynasty (Col.); J. J. Johnson; Oliver Nelson; Joe Williams (BB); K. Burrell (Prest.; Fant.); W. Montgomery; Jimmy Smith (Verve); Q. Jones: (Merc.; Imp.).

RICHMAN, BOOMIE (ABRAHAM SAMUEL), tnr sax; b. Brockton, MA, 4/2/21. Club dates in Bost.; to NYC 1942; pl. w. Muggsy Spanier; Jerry Wald; w. T. Dorsey '46–52; B. Goodman '53–4. In '50s freelanced in NYC studios; rec. w. Sauter-Finegan; Neal Hefti; Peanuts Hucko; Al Cohn; Ruby Braff; Urbie Green; and Red Allen. Cont. studio work from '60s. CDs: w. Dorsey (BB); Goodman (Cap.); Pee Wee Russell (Comm.).

RICHMOND, DANNIE (CHARLES D.), dms, tnr sax; b. NYC, 12/15/35; d. NYC, 3/16/88. A tnr. saxophonist into his early 20s, self-taught on dms. w. help from Charles Mingus. Was Mingus's regular dmr. on and off fr. 1956–70. Jazz-rock w. the Mark-Almond Band; accomp. Joe Cocker and Elton John. Briefly w. Chet Baker bef. rejoining Mingus '74. After Mingus's death in '79, pl. w. Mingus Dynasty and co-led a qt. w. George Adams and Don Pullen. Richmond pl. w. the melodic abandon of a horn player. Although his time was excellent, he often pl.

in swirls of rhythmic energy that seemed to supersede the timekeeping function. Mingus felt, rightly, that Richmond was the perfect dmr. for his music and developed with him a technique that used acceleration and deceleration which Mingus called "rotary motion." CDs: Red; Timel.; SN; w. Mingus (BB; Beth.; Col.; Mos.; Atl.; Rh.); L. Hampton (Tel.); John Jenkins (BN).

RICHMOND, JUNE, voc; b. Chicago, IL, 7/9/15; d. Gothenburg, Sweden, 8/14/62. Sang w. Les Hite; J. Dorsey; Cab Calloway; and, fr. 1939–42, Andy Kirk. To Eur. '48, where she became enormously popular as a solo act, though mostly in the pop field. Rec. under her own name in Stockholm '51; w. Q. Jones, '57. Along w. Billie Holiday, Richmond was among the first African-American singers to be feat. w. a white band (during her stint w. Dorsey). CDs: w. Calloway (Class.); in *The Legendary Big Band Singers*; J. Dorsey (Dec.); Andy Kirk (B&B).

RICHMOND, MIKE (MICHAEL), bs, el-bs; b. Philadelphia, PA, 2/26/48. Studied at Temple U. 1965–70, then w. Jimmy Garrison '70–2. Pl. first prof. gig at age 14. Pl. w. Chico Hamilton '72–4; Billy Eckstine '73–6; Jeremy Steig '73–81; Joe Farrell '74–8; Gil Evans '74–9; Dannie Richmond '74–89; Hubert Laws, Jack DeJohnette, Mose Allison '75–8; Stan Getz; Pat Metheny '76–9; Chet Baker '77–81; Art Farmer '78–81; John Handy '80–3. Also pl. in '70s w. Ray Nance; Paul Gonsalves; Bobby Timmons; Buddy DeFranco; Thad Jones–Mel Lewis; Roland Kirk; Cedar Walton; Clifford Jordan; etc. Perf. in Bombay w. Ravi Shankar '80. Pl. w. Arnie Lawrence since '73; Geo. Gruntz since '78; Lee Konitz since '82; Paul Motian since '88. Taught at CUNY since '78 and at NYU and the New Sch. since '88. Favs: Red Mitchell, Eddie Gomez, Ludwig Streicher. Fests: Eur., Africa, Asia since '73. Film: app. in *Dirty Mouth* w. Lenny Bruce. TV: docus. of Miles Davis, Stan Getz; Dick Cavett; *Tonight Show.* CDs: Steep., Polyg., Nomad; w. Getz (Col.); Konitz (MM); Jackie Paris (Aud.); Bill Warfield (Inter.; SB); John Clark (Post.); Gruntz (TCB; Enja; A. LaVerne (Steep.).

RIDDLE, NELSON, comp, arr; b. Oradell, NJ, 6/1/21; d. Los Angeles, CA, 10/6/85. Trombonist and arr. for T. Dorsey; B. Crosby; Charlie Spivak. Extremely active rec. and TV comp. arr. whose assoc. w. jazz traces to his arrs. for Peggy Lee; Nat "King" Cole; Ella Fitzgerald; and, most notably, Frank Sinatra, who credited much of his success to Riddle's charts. In early 1980s he arr. and cond. a series of highly successful albums of standards for pop singer

Linda Ronstadt. CDs: w. T. Dorsey (BB); E. Fitzgerald (Verve); F. Sinatra (Rep.); Antonio Carlos Jobim (WB).

RIDLEY, LARRY (LAURENCE HOWARD JR.), bs; b. Indianapolis, IN, 9/3/37. Brother pl. tpt. Began on vln., then sw. to bs. after hearing Ray Brown. Early experience w. Freddie Hubbard, James Spaulding. First prof. gig w. Wes Montgomery 1953. Stud. at Indiana U. '55–9; w. Percy Heath at Lenox Sch. of Jazz '59. Later received B.S. in mus. educ. fr. NYU '71; M.A. cultural policy studies, SUNY-Empire State Coll. '92. After coll., pl. in NYC w. Hubbard '59; tour. w. Slide Hampton '60. Fr. '60 to '65, freelanced w. Philly Joe Jones; Lou Donaldson; Randy Weston; Dinah Washington; Carmen McRae; Red Garland; Barry Harris; Coleman Hawkins; Jackie McLean; Horace Silver; Sonny Rollins; Max Roach; Roy Haynes; etc. W. Dizzy Gillespie, Thelonious Monk, McCoy Tyner, Jazz Comps. Orch. late '60s; Newport All-Stars fr. '68. Orig. member of NY Bass Violin Choir; NY Jazz Repertory Co. Tour. Eur. w. Young Giants of Jazz '73. Beginning w. his appointment to the faculty of Rutgers U. in '71, Ridley has been very active in educ. Dir. of jazz prog., chairman of mus. dept. at Rutgers fr. '72. Guest lecturer on jazz and black cultural issues at hs and colls. fr. '70s. Artist-in-res. at several universities, incl. Utah, Creighton, Southern, Grambling Coll., Colorado Coll., Montana fr. '70s. Bass chairman of Nat'l Assoc. of Jazz Educs. '82–4, '90–2. Designed jazz educ. courses for M. L. King HS, NYC '83–4. Consultant to NJ Dept. of Higher Educ. '89. Cont. to teach at Rutgers; New School. Published interview w. Milt Hinton in IAJE Journal '91. Led own jazz repertory gp. Jazz Legacy Ens. fr. '80s; sideman incl. Virgil Jones; David "Fathead" Newman; Ronnie Mathews, Larry McClellan; Brian Kirk; Bud Revels, Kenny Washington, others. Pl. w. Dameronia fr. '81; David Baker–L. Ridley–Joe Kennedy string qnt. fr. mid '80s. Also freelanced extensively w. Lionel Hampton; Kenny Burrell; Geo. Benson; Harold Ashby; Norman Simmons: Muhal Richard Abrams; D. Gillespie; Curtis Fuller; Joe Newman; Kenny Barron; Hank Jones; Dakota Staton, etc. Pl. w. Smithsonian Jazz Orch. fr. '92. Served as a panelist or consultant w. the Rutgers Paul Robeson Cultural Ctr.; NY State Council on the Arts; Nat'l Jazz Service Org.; Penn. Arts Council; Wisconsin Arts Council; Harlem Chamber of Commerce; Charlotte Afro-Amer. Cultural Ctr. Founder and pres. of a production co., Jazz Legacy, Inc. Favs: Ray Brown, Percy Heath, Pettiford, Paul Chambers, Wilbur Ware. Fests: all major. Won Mid-Atlantic Arts Foundation Living Legacy Jazz Award '97. TV: NJ public TV; video

interview w. Doc Cheatham, *Jazz Legacy.* CDs: Jazz Legacy; Strata East; w. Dameronia (SN); Dexter Gordon (Prest.); J. McLean; H. Silver; Lee Morgan; F. Hubbard (BN); Bill Barron–Booker Ervin (Sav.).

RIEDEL, GEORG, bs, comp; b. Karlsbad, Czechoslovakia, 1/8/34. Classically trained. Worked w. Lars Gullin 1953–4; Arne Domnerus off and on for many yrs. fr. '55. Composed "Dizzy" for Gillespie and bb; "Kind of Requiem" for Ellington; won Prix Italia for his TV ballet, *Riedaiglia;* music for many films; also awards for children's mus. CDs: w. Arne Domnerus (Phon.); *Jazz at the Pawnshop, Vol. 3* (Proprius).

RIEL, ALEX POUL, dms; b. Copenhagen, Denmark, 9/13/40. Studied in Copenhagen 1955; one term at Berklee Sch. 1966, where he stud. w. Alan Dawson; pl. in Bost. w. Roland Kirk; Toshiko Akiyoshi, Herb Pomeroy. Made rec. debut w. Stuff Smith '56; worked w. various trad. gps. to '60s. Pl. and rec. w. Brew Moore–Don Byas qt. '59–61. House dmr. at Montmartre, Copenhagen backing many American mus. '63–5; also worked w. Erk Moseholm trio '64–7; Danish Radiojazzgruppen '65–8. Form. qnt. w. Palle Mikkelborg '66 and oct. V8 '70–5. Pl. in rock gp., Savage Rose '68–72. Worked w. Six Winds. Has rec. extensively w. Ben Webster; Dexter Gordon; Sahib Shihab; Jackie McLean; Archie Shepp; Peter Herbolzheimer; Wild Bill Davison; Champion Jack Dupree; Clara Ward; Niels Lan Doky; Karin Krog; et al. He pl. an unaccompanied solo, "In a Way," on his own trio rec. for the Fona label '63; his '97 rec. for Stunt, *Unriel,* incl. sidemen Jerry Bergonzi; Michael Brecker; Mike Stern; Eddie Gomez; N. Lan Doky. Fests: qnt. w. Mikkelborg won first prize at Montreux '68; then pl. at NJF. Award: Danish jazz mus. of the yr. '65. CDs: Red; Stunt; w. Webster (BL; Steep.); Gordon; McLean; Eddie Davis; Ken McIntyre; K. Dorham (Steep.); N. Lan Doky (Mile.).

RIGGS, CHUCK (CHARLES), dms; b. Westerly, RI, 8/5/51. Mainly self-taught. Stud. one yr. at Rhode Island Sch. of Mus. Encouraged to come to NYC by Roy Eldridge 1976. Pl. w. Hamilton-Bates Blue Flames '72–6; Bob Wilber '78; Smithsonian Jazz Ens., Benny Goodman Sxt. '78–80; Kenny Davern–Dick Wellstood '83–5; Wilber '84; Flip Phillips '85–6; Ruby Braff '85–7; Jay McShann '88–9. Riggs has been a member of the Scott Hamilton Qt. fr. '76. Favs: Jo Jones, Sid Catlett, Jake Hanna, Philly Joe Jones, Jimmy Cobb. Fests: all major w. Hamilton, Braff, McShann. Film: pl. on soundtrack of *The Cotton Club.* CDs: w. Hamilton (Conc.; Chiaro.; King); F. Phillips (Chiar.; Conc.); Chris Flory; Maxine Sullivan; Conc. All.-Stars (Conc.).

RILEY, BEN (BENJAMIN ALEXANDER JR.), dms; b. Savannah, GA, 7/17/33. Family moved to NYC when he was 4. Stud. w. Cecil Scott while in jr. hs. Pl. in hs band; then, while in service, 187th Airborne band 1951–2. First prof. job. w. Bobby Brown '56. Bet. '56–65 gigged w. Gene Rodgers; R. Weston; N. Simmons; K. Burrell; E. Davis–J. Griffin '60–2; then freelanced w. J. Mance; Stitt; Getz; Woody Herman; Paul Winter; A. Jamal; Ray Bryant; Rollins; Dick Katz; R. Hanna; Walter Bishop Jr.; Billy Taylor; Mary Lou Williams; K. Winding. Join. Thelonious Monk '64–7. Taught in Wyandanch, LI, elementary sch. system, jr. coll.; USDAN summer camp '68–70. Pl. w. NY Jazz Qt. fr. '71, incl. Japanese tour '74. Alice Coltrane on and off '68–75; Ron Carter qt. '75–7; Jim Hall '81; Abdullah Ibrahim fr. '83–4. With Charlie Rouse, Kenny Barron, and Buster Williams founded Sphere in '82 and tour. w. it through '86. Pl. w. Chet Baker, Getz late '80s; Barron trio late '80s-90s. Own qt. w. Ted Dunbar, Steve Nelson '95–6. Sphere revived w. Gary Bartz '98. Favs: Clarke, Roach, Blakey, P. J. Jones, R. Haynes, Jo Jones. Fests: NJF '59; w. Monk '64–5; w. NYJQ, NJF-NY '74; Umbria Jazz '86 w. Sphere; '88 w. Getz. Film: *Straight No Chaser* w. Monk, also in video. TV: *Positively Black* w. Carter; apps. w. Nina Simone; Rollins; Monk; Paul Winter. CDs: Joken; w. Monk (Col.); Sphere (Verve); Rollins (RCA); Davis-Griffin (Prest.; Jzld.); Alice Coltrane (Imp.); Phil Woods–Griffin (BN); Sam Jones (Riv.); K. Barron (CC); C. Roditi; Larry Gales (Cand.).

RILEY, HERLIN, dms; b. New Orleans, LA, 2/15/57. From a mus. family. Began pl. dms. at age 3. Stud. tpt. through hs and two yrs. of coll. Perf. briefly as a tpt. but stayed w. the dms. Worked w. Ahmad Jamal 1984–87. Join. Wynton Marsalis spt. '88 and has tour. w. him since, incl. LCJO from '92. Pl. for theatre productions, incl. *One Mo' Time; Satchmo: America's Musical Legend.* CDs: w. W. Marsalis; B. Marsalis; E. Marsalis; H. Connick (Col.); Marcus Roberts (Novus); Monty Alexander (Chesky); Michael White (Ant.); Wycliffe Gordon; Jamal (Atl.); Clayton Bros. (WB).

RILEY, HERMAN, tnr sax, woodwinds; b. New Orleans, LA, 8/31/33. High school band, then army and study at Southern U. To San Diego 1957–63 to attend City Coll. Moved to LA '63, where he pl. frequently w. Bobby Bryant and app. w. him at MJF '69. Also in '60s, worked w. Shelly Manne; Q. Jones; Benny Carter; Donald Byrd; Joe Williams; Count Basie. In '70s rec. w. Gene Ammons, Blue Mitchell; toured So. Africa w. Monk Montgomery '74. Rec. w. Capp-Pierce Juggernaut '78; L. Hampton '80–1.

Tour. int'l w. Mercer Ellington in late '80s and w. orgst. Jimmy Smith '90; also to Japan w. B. Carter '90. CDs: w. Jeannie and Jimmy Cheatham (Conc.); Jimmy Smith (Mile.).

RILEY, (JOHN) HOWARD, pno, comp; b. Huddersfield, Yorkshire, England, 2/16/43. Father a semi-prof. dance band pnst. Began pno. at age 6, earned B.A. 1964; M.A. '66, U. of Wales; M. Mus., Indiana U. '67; M. Phil., York U. '67. After living in US ret. to Eng. '67, began prof. jazz career. Besides own jazz trios has worked w. John McLaughlin '68; Barbara Thompson qnt. '69–70; Jazz Comps. Orch. fr. '70; Tony Oxley Qnt./Sxt. fr. '72; Keith Tippett fr. '81; in duo w. Jaki Byard fr. '82; Evan Parker Qt. fr. '83. Has tour. in UK, Eur, Can., and US. Many radio broadcasts. Awarded UK/USA Bicentennial Fellowship in the Arts '67. Has taught jazz pno. classes at London's Guildhall Sch. of Mus. fr. '69; Goldsmith's Coll. fr. '75; many jazz wkshps., summer schs. Creative Assoc. at Center of Creative and Perf. Arts, Buffalo, N.Y. '76–7. Favs: Bill Evans, Monk, Tatum, Dick Twardzik. His LPs incl. *The Toronto Concert* (Spot.); *Live at Royal Festival Hall* w. Byard (Leo). CDs: w. Elton Dean (Slam; VP); Barry Guy (Intakt).

RILEY, JOHN BERNARD, dms; b. Aberdeen, MD, 6/11/54. Mother is amateur pnst. Pl. w. rock bands in Maryland, then stud. at No. Texas St. U. and Manh. Sch. of Mus. Pl. w. Larry Elgart bb, Milt Jackson '76–7; Woody Herman '78; Rich Boukas '79–82; Kenny Werner fr. '79; Joe Lovano fr. '84; Bob Mintzer fr. '86; Red Rodney fr. '87; John Scofield fr. '89. Also extensive freelancing in '80s w. Dave Liebman; Stan Getz, Dizzy Gillespie; Jimmy Heath; Randy Brecker; Phil Woods; Mel Lewis Orch; Vanguard Jazz Orch. App. w. Miles Davis and Quincy Jones at Montreux JF '91. Pl. w. Clayton bros. in '90s. Riley taught at No. Texas St. fr. '75–6; U. of Bridgeport '79–81; Manh. Sch. of Mus. '90s. Favs: Philly Joe Jones, Tony Williams, DeJohnette. Fests: Eur. since '78, Japan since '89. TV: Eur. and Jap. TV. CDs: w. Werner (Sunny.); Mintzer (DMP); John Hart (BN); Mike Metheny (Imp.); John Serry (Tel.); DMP bb (DMP); Vanguard Jazz Orch. (NW).

RILEY, MIKE, tbn; b. Fall River, MA, 1/5/04; d. Redondo Beach, CA, 12/87. Well known briefly as co-leader w. Ed Farley as popularizer of "The Music Goes Round and Round." Later led own gps. incl. some jazz soloists. In 1951 he led a trio w. John Benson Brooks on pno. and Bill Crow (best known as a bassist) on dms.

RIMINGTON, SAMMY, cl, alto sax; b. London, England 4/29/42. Professional debut w. Barry Martyn 1959. Established himself w. Ken Colyer '60–5. Worked in US in '65, pl. w. such veterans as Red Allen, Zutty Singleton. In NO pl. w. Hall bros.; rec. w. Kid Thomas; pl. w. Don Ewell, Max Morath. Back in Eur., worked w. Martyn again '69; led own band; and experimented w. jazz-rock in his gp. Armada '71. Pl. w. George Webb '73; Martyn '74; Duke Burrell '74–5; Chris Barber '77–9. Rimington is widely admired as a clst. in the early tradition but has extended his style when pl. alto. CDs: GHB; w. Jim Robinson (Biog.); Colyer (Lake); Ginger Pig New Orleans Band (GHB).

RINGWALD, BOB (ROBERT SCOTT), pno, bjo, bs, voc; b. Roseville, CA, 11/26/40. Father of actress Molly Ringwald, who sang with his band for several yrs. Best known as leader of Great Pacific Jazz Band from 1979. Heard at Sacramento Jazz Jubilee and other traditionalist venues. Playing the mus. of Louis Armstrong and others, the band was popular in the LA area.

RITENOUR, LEE (MACK), gtr; b. Los Angeles, CA, 1/11/52. Studied priv. w. Duke Miller; Joe Pass; Howard Roberts; Christopher Parkening; then at USC Sch. of Mus. under Jack Marshall. Prof. debut at age 12 w. The Esquires (19-pc. orch.); w. Afro Blues Qnt., Craig Hundley Trio 1969. Traveled w. Sergio Mendes, later freelancing extensively in LA studios. Formed first gp. '73 w. John Pisano, second gp. w. D. Grusin '74, for local dates. Began teaching classical gtr. at USC in same yr. and in '75 coordinated new studio gtr. program. Form. gp. Friendship w. Ernie Watts, Abe Laboriel, etc., beginning late '70s. Many recs. fr. '76 usually blending r&b, pop, and jazz. Tours of Brazil in late '80s added So. Amer. elements to his pl. of the period. A prodigious and versatile perf. who pl. acoustic and el. gtrs., bjo., mand., and el-bs., Ritenour by '92 had numerous best-selling albums. Favs: Wes Montgomery, K. Burrell, Gabor Szabo. Despite early infl. fr. Montgomery, Ritenour's style and phrasing more strongly reflected the work of such blues and rock players as B. B. King and Eric Clapton. CDs: GRP; w. Oliver Nelson (BB); LA Workshop (Den.); S. Turrentine (Fant.); David "Fathead" Newman (Mile.); Dave Grusin (GRP; N2K); Stanley Clarke (Epic); Joe Henderson (Mile.); Harvey Mason (Atl.); Fourplay (WB); John Pisano (Pab.).

RITZ, LYLE (JOSEPH,) bs, vln, uke; b. Cleveland, OH, 1/10/30. While in army, introduced to jazz through Lennie Niehaus 1954. In LA, rec. two LPs on uke. '57–8. Pl. w. Paul Horn '58–9; Les Brown '59; Bob Florence Combo and Band '61–77; Barney Kessel Trio '65. Mainly commercial jobs in '70s and '80s. Moved to Hawaii '89 where he taught and pl. bs. and uke., working w. Gabe Baltazar; Del Courtney; and other local gps.

RITZ, THE. Vocal gp. form. in Bost. 1982; dedicated to extending jazz voc. tradition of L,H&R. Varying personnel; in '91 incl. Daryl Bosteels, Melissa Hamilton, Val Hawk, and Chris Humphrey. Numerous world tours on fest. and club circuit; seven albums on Pausa and Denon labels. The gp.'s expressed aim is to "embody the timeless excitement and warmth of the jazz vocal genre." CDs: Den.

RIVERA, MARIO, tnr, alto, sop, bari saxes, fl, tpt, tambora; b. Santo Domingo, Dominican Republic, 7/22/39. Son, Phoenix, pl. pno., dms. Stud. w. Tavito Vasquez. Pl. w. top merengue bands in his homeland before coming to NYC at age 21. Tour. w. Tito Rodriguez 1963–5. Pl. w. Machito, Tito Puente; later w. S. Stitt, Roy Haynes; in '70s Eddie and Charlie Palmieri, Tipica 73; own gp., the Salsa Refugees; bari. sax w. George Coleman's Oct. A member of D. Gillespie's United Nation orch. fr. '88; also w. Slide Hampton's Jazz Masters. In '90s cont. to work w. Puente's Latin Jazz Ensemble and Golden Men of Latin Jazz; Chico O'Farrill Orch. App. in concert, "The Latin Tinge," at Lincoln Center '95. Adept in both Latin and jazz music, he is a volatile, Coltrane-inspired tenor saxophone soloist and an equally commanding, fiery presence on flute. Favs: Coltrane, C. Parker, Dexter Gordon, C. Adderley. Fests: worldwide w. Puente; United Nation orch.; Jazz Masters. CDs: GH; w. Puente (Conc.; Trop.); O'Farrill (Mile.); G. Coleman (Charly); Gillespie (Enja).

RIVERS, SAM (SAMUEL CARTHORNE), tnr sax, comp; also sop sax, pno, bs-cl, fl, viola; b. Reno, OK, 9/25/23. Mother a pnst., fath. a member of Fisk Jubilee Singers and Silvertone Qt. Raised in Little Rock, Ark., and Chi., pl. in sch. and local bands. Stud. at Bost. Cons. 1947–52; later att. Bost. U. Pl. in Bost. w. Jaki Byard; Joe Gordon; Herb Pomeroy; Gigi Gryce. Pl. two mos. w. Miles Davis '64, incl. tour of Japan. First rec. w. own gp. '65. Moved to NYC, began teaching at own studio in Harlem '67. Pl. w. Cecil Taylor '67–71; six mos. w. McCoy Tyner '71. Comp.-in-res. w. Harlem Opera Society '68–70s. Opened perf. space, Studio Rivbea, w. wife Bea in lower Manh. '71; perf. w. own gp.; Dewey Redman; Frank Lowe; Chas. Tyler; Clifford Jordan; Sonny Fortune. Artist-in-res. at Wesleyan U. '70–3; lecturer on Afro-Amer. mus. history at Conn. Coll. '72. App.

as guest soloist w. SF Symph. '75. Pl. w. Dave Holland fr. early '70s; D. Gillespie in late '80s, incl. Eur. Fests. Rivers has cont. to tour and rec. w. his own gps. He has pl. pno. more freq. since the late '70s. Living in Orlando, Fla, in '90s. Polls: *DB* Critics TDWR fl. '75. Fests: all major fr. '70s. CDs: Vict.; BN; Mos.; Post.; Timel.; BS; w. Dave Holland (ECM; IAI); R. Workman (Post.); H. Ruiz (Novus); B. Ditmas (Post.); Dick Griffin (Konnex); James Blood Ulmer (Col.).

RIZZI, TONY (TREFONI), gtr; b. Los Angeles, CA, 4/16/23. Studied vln., then tpt. bef. taking up gtr. After army service in WWII, pl. w. Boyd Raeburn; Milton Delugg; Alvy West; Les Brown. Staff mus. at NBC for many yrs.; active studio mus.; pl. a wide variety of stringed insts. In 1973 organized a 5-gtr. gp. that interpreted harmonized versions of of the comps. and improvised solos of Charlie Christian; rec. on LP for the Milagro label. CD: w. Paul Smith (Tampa).

ROACH, MAX (MAXWELL), dms, comp; b. New Land, NC, 1/10/24. Family moved to Brooklyn when he was 4. Moth. was gospel singer. Pl. dms. in gospel band fr. age 10. Stud. at Manh. Sch. of Mus. House dmr. at Monroe's Uptown House, pl. w. Charlie Parker; Dizzy Gillespie; Thelonious Monk; Bud Powell; et al. fr. 1942. Also pl. in early bop jam sess. at Minton's and other clubs. Made rec. debut w. Coleman Hawkins '43. Pl. w. Gillespie, briefly w. Ellington '44; Benny Carter '44–5; C. Parker '45; Stan Getz, Allen Eager, Hawkins '46; Parker '47–9; Miles Davis '48–50; C. Parker intermittently '51–3; JATP '52; Harold Rumsey at the Lighthouse, Calif. '54; also freelanced w. Louis Jordan, Red Allen. Roach led an infl. hard bop qnt. that feat. Clifford Brown '54–6; other sidemen fr. '50s to '60s incl. Harold Land; Sonny Rollins; Richie Powell; George Morrow; Kenny Dorham; Booker Little; George Coleman; Tommy Turrentine; Stanley Turrentine. Co-founded Debut Recs. w. Charles Mingus '52; took part in the famed Massey Hall concert w. Parker; Gillespie, Bud Powell, Mingus, Toronto '53. In the late '50s Roach began incorporating free jazz elements into his mus. From the '60s and '70s his mus. incl. references to the struggle for racial equality, e.g. *We Insist! Freedom Now Suite* '60. Married to Abbey Lincoln '62–70; many comps. fr. this period use solo voice or chorus. Comp. for B'way shows, films, TV, also extended orch. works fr. '60s. Led M'Boom Re: Percussion, a perc. ens., fr. '70; sidemen incl. Roy Brooks; Joe Chambers; Freddie Waits. Led combos w. Cecil Bridgewater, Odean Pope, Billy Harper, Reggie Workman '70s. Perf. w. J. C. White Singers

gospel chorus at fests. '72–75; took part in drum concert w. Art Blakey, Buddy Rich, Elvin Jones at Radio City for NJF-NY '74. Rec. w. Abdullah Ibrahim; Anthony Braxton; Archie Shepp; Cecil Taylor late '70s. In addition to M'Boom, Roach has led the Double Qt., which combines his combo w. the Uptown String Qt., led by his violist daughter Maxine. Pl. w. his So What Brass Qnt. at Blue Note Club, NYC Nov. '98. Roach has been active as a lecturer on jazz fr. the late '60s and has been a profess. at the U. of Mass.-Amherst fr. '72. He holds numerous honorary degrees and was awarded a MacArthur Fellowship in '88. The following yr. he was named Commander of the Order of Art and Letters in France. In '92 he collab. w. librettist Amiri Baraka on an opera, *The Life and Life of Bumpy Johnson,* premiered by the San Diego Repertory Theater. Presented a series of concerts at the 92nd St. Y., NYC late '90s. An architect of modern jazz drumming, he built on the innovations of Kenny Clarke, elaborating the style, bringing more complex cross-rhythms into play, and employing greater textural variety. Roach was elected to the Amer. Acad. and Inst. of Arts and Letters '92. Polls: *Met.* '51, '54; *DB* '55; *DB* Critics '57–9. Fests: all major. Film: *Freedom Now* (Ital. short film) '66. CDs: BN; Col.; Cand.; Imp.; Mesa–Blue Moon; Em.; SN; LRC; Merc.; Deb.; Riv.; Fant.; as co-leader w. Clifford Brown (Em.); w. Carter (Class.); Parker (Verve; Sav.; Stash); J. J. Johnson (Sav.; Col.); S. Rollins (Riv.; Prest.); S. Getz (Verve); Thelonious Monk; Clifford Brown; S. Stitt (Prest.); M. Davis (Cap.; Prest.); Bud Powell (BN; Verve); Hawkins (Del.; Prest.); duets w. Gillespie (A&M); Braxton (BS); C. Taylor (SN).

ROBERT, GEORGE PAUL, alto sax, cl; b. Geneva, Switzerland, 9/15/60. Started on pno. at age 9; then cl., stud. at Cons. de Musique fr. ages 10–19. Took up sax at 18. Formed a jazz gp. w. his five brothers, which was coached by such visiting mus. as Sam Woodyard and Jimmy Woode. B. Mus., Magna Cum Laude, fr. Berklee Coll. of Mus. 1984; M. Mus. from Manh. Sch. of Mus. '87. From '80s pl. w. Toshiko Akiyoshi; L. Hampton; Ray Drummond; Billy Hart; Billy Higgins; and Buster Williams. Own qt. fr. '84; fr. '87 co-leader of The George Robert–Tom Harrell Qnt.; fr. '91 new qt. w. Dado Moroni, Isla Eckinger, Peter Schmidlin. Clark Terry tour. w. them in his 70th birthday yr. in Switzerland, Germ.; again in '91 (US) and '93. Robert, whose main infl. is Phil Woods, tour. w. Woods's bb on Eur. fest. circuit '98. Fests: Montreux; Lugano; Geneva; Vienne; Spokane; L. Hampton Idaho; all Canadian fests '94. Taught master classes at U. of Calgary; U. of Brit. Columbia; Swiss Jazz Sch.; hs in Switz., Can.; also on faculty of

Courtenay Summer Jazz Workshop., Can. fr. '92. CDs: Mons; Cont.; TCB; w. Harrell (Cont.).

ROBERTS, HOWARD MANCEL, gtr; b. Phoenix, AZ, 10/2/29; d. Seattle, WA, 6/28/92. Mostly self-taught on gtr. except for lessons w. a former bomber pilot at the end of WWII; stud. Schillinger system, orchestration and comp. in LA, 1950s. First prof. gig at age 11 in Phoenix. Moved to LA '50 and was continuously active in studios for TV, movies, and rec. work for the next three decades. App. as sideman on recs. w. Shorty Rogers; Lennie Niehaus; Buddy Collette; Paul Horn; Bud Shank; Buddy De Franco; et al. Co-founder of Gtr. Institute of Technology (Musicians Institute) '77. CDs: w. Shorty Rogers (BB); Diane Schuur (GRP); Buddy Collette (Cont.); Hank Jones; Art Pepper (Gal.); Wardell Gray; Frank Morgan (FS); Pete Jolly; Jack Sheldon (VSOP); G. Mulligan (A&M).

ROBERTS, LUCKEY (CHARLES LUCK-EYETH), pno, comp; b. Philadelphia, 8/7/1887; d. NYC, 2/5/68. Child actor and acrobat bef. taking up pno. A versatile ragtime perf., he published several orig. pno. rags 1913–23. Composed mus. for fourteen comedies, prod. bef. and after WWI, incl. his first, *My People* '11. During the '20s he was a favorite bandleader in high society, w. orchs. in N.Y., Newport, Palm Beach, etc., and a great favorite of the Duke of Windsor (then the Prince of Wales). In later yrs. the owner of the Rendezvous, a bar on St. Nicholas Ave. in Harlem, but cont. active in mus. App. at Carnegie Hall '39; Town Hall '41. Best known comps. incl. "Moonlight Cocktail" '41 and "Massachusetts" '42. Suffered a stroke in the late '50s and went into almost total retirement. A powerful ragtime pl., he was an important early infl. on Duke Ellington, James P. Johnson, and many other Harlem pnsts. of the early '20s. CD: Solo Art; Luckey Roberts–Willie "The Lion" Smith (GTJ).

ROBERTS, MARCUS (MARTHANIEL), pno, comp; b. Jacksonville, FL, 8/7/63. Blind from the age of 4. His moth., a gospel singer, inspired him in the church; when he was 12 his parents bought him a pno. and he began formal training. His nine yrs. of classical studies incl. four yrs. as a mus. major with Leonidus Lipovetsky at Fla. St. U., Tallahassee. After meeting Wynton Marsalis, he was invited to replace Kenny Kirkland in the trumpeter's gp. in 1985. From '85 to '91 he pl. and rec. nine albums w. Marsalis, then form. his own gp., having meanwhile begun a solo career. Won first prize at first T. Monk Int'l Jazz Competition. Began rec. under own name '89. His comp. "Romance, Swing and the Blues" was com-

missioned and premiered by Jazz at Lincoln Center '93. In early '94 he served as mus. dir. of LCJO for a US tour. His late '90s trio incl. Roland Guerin, bs; and Jason Marsalis, dms. Won Helen Keller Achievement Award '98. A mus. of eclectic taste, Roberts has devoted much of his time to rediscovering the mus. of such predecessors as D. Ellington, T. Monk, and Jelly Roll Morton, with a clear affinity for stride pno. Also active cond. seminars and clinics. Some of his rec. work indicated a desire to recall the entire history of jazz pno., possibly at the expense of the development of a personal style. Nevertheless, his work was widely praised and some of his comps. are graceful and sensitive, often with a well-developed feeling for the blues. His recs. of *Rhapsody in Blue,* James P. Johnson's *Yamekraw,* and *The Joy of Joplin* are on Sony Classical. CDs: Novus; Col.; Sony Classical; w. W. Marsalis (Col.); D. Marsalis (Novus); Tough Young Tenors (Ant.); Wycliffe Gordon–Ron Westray (Atl.); M. Printup (BN).

ROBERTSON, ZUE (C. ALVIN), tbn; b. New Orleans, LA, 3/7/1891; d. Watts, CA, 1943. Studied pno. first but took up tbn. at 13. Pl. extensively in circus and show bands incl. Kit Carson's Wild West Show 1910. With Olympia Band ca. '14; then Manuel Perez; Richard M. Jones. John Robichaux. Moved to Chi. '17 to work at De Luxe Café. Pl. in Chi. w. Jelly Roll Morton '23; King Oliver '24. Tour. w. W. C. Handy; then ret. to Chi to pl. w. Dave Peyton's theater orch. In '29 he moved to NYC where he pl. pno. and org. at the Lincoln and Lafayette Theaters fr. '30. Moved to Calif '32, pl. pno. and bs. there for the rest of the decade. Many credited him with setting what came to typify the New Orleans tbn. style of the '20s. Rec. w. Morton for OKeh '23. CD: w. Morton (Class.).

ROBICHAUX, JOE (JOSEPH), pno; b. New Orleans, LA, 3/8/1900; d. New Orleans, 1/17/65. Nephew of John Robichaux. Stud. w. Steve Lewis before moving to Chi. 1918 w. tptr. Tig Chambers. Ret. to NO to work w. Papa Celestin; Lee Collins; and the Black Eagle Band. Pl. and rec. w. the Jones-Collins Astoria Hot Eight. In '30s worked w. Kid Rena and Willie O'Connell, form. his own band, the New Orleans Rhythm Boys, '33–9. Perf. as soloist in NO in '40s; accomp. Lizzie Miles in Calif. in '50s; join. George Lewis's band, replacing Alton Purnell, '57–64. Rec. as leader, Voc. '33; w. Jones-Collins (Vict.) '28. CD: w. G. Lewis (Milneburg; Drag.; GHB).

ROBICHAUX, JOHN, vln, bs, dms, acdn, leader; b. Thibodaux, LA, 1/16/1886; d. New Orleans, LA,

1939. Pl. bs. dm. w. Excelsior Brass Band 1892–03. Organized his own band 1893, perf. as a vlnst; maintained a variety of bands, incl. a 36–piece ens. in '13, until his death. Described by the "NO Family Album" as "the most continuously active dance-band leader in NO history." Among the mus. who work. for him were Lorenzo Tio and Manuel Perez. He was a proficient arr. and comp. of more than 350 songs. Many of his arrs. are in the Tulane U. jazz archive. His nephew, John Robichaux (b. NO, ca. 1915), also a dmr., pl. w. the NO Ragtime Orch. '71 and tour. w. the musical show, *One Mo' Time*.

ROBINSON, ELI, tbn; b. Greenville, GA, 6/23/11; d. NYC, 12/24/72. Studied tbn. in hs in Charleston, West Va. Moved to Det. after graduation in 1928. Club dates w. various bands, incl. Alex Jackson; Speed Webb; Zack White; McKinney's Cotton Pickers. First recs. w. Blanche Calloway '35. To NYC in '36, work w. Teddy Hill; Willie Bryant. Briefly w. Roy Eldridge in Chi. '39. Pl. w. Count Basie fr. '41 to '47, then w. Lucky Millinder, and Buddy Tate's band '50s and '60s. Lung surgery in '69 curtailed his pl. career. CDs: w. Basie (BB; Hep; Class.); Lester Young (Sav.).

ROBINSON, FRED (FREDERICK L.), tbn; b. Memphis, TN, 2/20/01; d. NYC, 4/11/84. To Chi. 1927; pl. w. Carroll Dickerson alongside L. Armstrong; pl. on "West End Blues" and other well-known Armstrong Hot Five recs. '28. To NYC '29; in '30s pl. w. Edgar Hayes; Don Redman; Benny Carter; Andy Kirk; F. Henderson; feat. on a '39 Jelly Roll Morton sess. for BB. In '40s pl. w. Cab Calloway; Sy Oliver; w. Noble Sissle '50–1. Gave up full-time mus. '54 but cont. to pl. occasionally into '60s. CDs: w. L. Armstrong (Col.; BBC); J. R. Morton (BB); F. Henderson (Jazz Unlimited); Benny Carter (Class.).

ROBINSON, J(OSEPH) RUSSEL, pno, comp; b. Indianapolis, IN, 7/8/1892; d. Palmdale, CA, 9/30/63. Mainly self-taught. While in teens, pl. for silent movies. Rec. many pno. rolls 1918–26. Accomp. Lizzie Miles and other blues singers in '20s but is most noted for replacing Henry Ragas in ODJB '19–21. Tour. Eng. w. ODJB '19. His best-known songs range fr. "That Eccentric Rag" '12 to "Margie"; "Singin' the Blues"; "Beale Street Mama"; and the '48 Nat Cole hit, "A Portrait of Jenny." Highly respected by black musicians of the era for his ability to play and compose in the Afro-American idiom. CDs: w. ODJB (BB).

ROBINSON, JIM (JAMES), tbn; b. Deer Range, LA, 12/25/1892; d. New Orleans, LA, 5/4/76. Started

out on gtr.; took up tbn. dur. army service in France 1917. First prof. work w. Kid Rena in NO '17; then w. Lee Collins in the Golden Leaf Band. In '23 joined the Morgan Band, rec. w. it in '27 and perf. in Chi. '29. Worked mostly as longshoreman during '30s except for gigs w. Capt. John Handy and Kid Howard. Rec. w. Kid Rena '40; Bunk Johnson and George Lewis '42–46. Toured Eur. and US w. Lewis in '50s; rec. as lead. for Riv. in '60. App. regularly at Preservation Hall '61–75. A strongly individualistic player who managed to maintain the traditional tailgate role of the tbn. in the NO style while still retaining a powerful melodic presence. CDs: GHB; Riv.; Biog.; w. Bunk Johnson (Story.); Geo. Lewis (Mos.; Story.; Biog.; Del.).

ROBINSON, JUSTIN JAY, alto, sop saxes; b. NYC, 8/14/68. Mother pl. cl., fath. pl. alto and tnr. saxes. Stud. at Sch. of Perf. Arts NYC, then at LIU. Made perf. debut in First Generations of Jazz show at Village Gate. Pl. w. McDonald's HS Jazz Band 1984–6; Harper Bros. '86; Betty Carter '88. Freelance around NYC since '87. Robinson hosted the nightly jam sess. at the Blue Note, NYC fr. '87–9. Rec. for Arabesque in late '90s. "And no matter how far Robinson stretches form, the language of Charlie Parker is firmly imprinted on his inner spirit."—Ted Panken, WKCR-FM. Favs: Parker, Adderley, Stitt. Fests: Eur. and Japan since '88. TV: *Tonight Show*. CDs: Arab.; Verve; w. R. Kendrick; Harper Bros.; Stephen Scott; Abbey Lincoln (Verve); C. Brooks III (Muse).

ROBINSON, ORPHY EVERTON, vib, mrba, perc, sax; b. London, England, 10/13/60. Mostly self-taught, but pl. w. Hackney and Islington Youth Band 1973–77, start. on tpt., dms. First prof. band, Savannah '78–81; Jazz Warriors '86–92; feat. soloist w. Courtney Pine '86–8; Andy Sheppard '87–91; Mica Paris '89; co-led Annavas Project w. kybd. player Joe Bashorun '90; mrba. w. Shiva Nova. Named "Most Promising Newcomer" '89 by *Wire* magazine. Since '86 many tours to Eur., Japan, Austral., Poland. Prod., wrote, arr. mus. for soundtrack to BBC TV series *Blood Rights*. Early infl: Roy Ayers. Concurrent w. mus. career works as stand-in/double in films. CDs: BN; w. Jazz Warriors (Island); A. Sheppard; C. Pine (Ant.).

ROBINSON, PERRY MORRIS, cl; b. NYC, 8/17/38. Father is comp. Earl Robinson. Began on pno., then sw. to cl. at age 9. Att. HS of Mus. and Art, NYC 1952–6; Manh. Sch. of Mus. '58. Bec. interested in free jazz after meeting Ornette Coleman at Lenox Sch. of Jazz '59. Further studies w. Eric Simon at Mannes Coll. of Mus.; Kalman Black of LA Symph. Tour. Spain, Portugal '59–60; pl. w. Tete Montoliu in Spain '60. Pl. w. Sunny Murray, Paul Bley in NYC '62; Don Friedman, Archie Shepp, Bill Dixon in Eur. '60s. Form. gp. w. Bill Folwell, Tom Price while pl. in US navy band. Pl. w. Roswell Rudd's Primordial Qnt. '68. Co-led trio w. David Izenzon, Randy Kaye late '60s. Pl. w. Carla Bley's Jazz Comps. Orch. late '60s–'70s; Two Generations of Brubeck '73–5; Gunter Hampel's Galaxie Dream Band late '70s–'80s. In the '80s Robinson led several gps. incl. Pipe Dreams, a qt. w. two singers and a gtr. He is also a prof. magician. Favs: Sonny Rollins, Pee Wee Russell, Charlie Parker, Tony Scott. Polls: *DB* Critics TDWR '67; *Jazz and Pop* '69; *Jazzwerld*, The Netherlands '70. Fests: Eur. '70s. CDs: w. Carla Bley (JCOA); Ray Anderson (Enja); Dave Brubeck (Col.); Henry Grimes (ESP); Archie Shepp; Charlie Haden (Imp.); Gunther Hampel (Birth).

ROBINSON, PRINCE, cl, tnr sax; b. Portsmouth, VA, 6/7/02; d. NYC, 7/23/60. Self-taught on cl; pl. w. Lilian Jones orch. locally 1919–21; Quentin Redd in Atlantic City '22, before moving to NYC. Pl. w. Lionel Howard '23; Elmer Snowden; June Clark. With Ellington '25–6; Billy Fowler. To So. Amer. w. Leon Abbey '27. A mainstay of McKinney's Cotton Pickers '28–35; Blanche Calloway '35–6; Willie Bryant '37–8; Roy Eldridge '38–9; Armstrong '40–2; L. Millinder '42–4, incl. app. at Café Society. From '45 to '52 mainly w. Claude Hopkins; Red Allen '54; led own gp. on Long Island, N.Y. until '59. Though respected as a clst., Robinson was at one time also considered to be a potential rival to Coleman Hawkins on tnr. sax. He felt his best solos were "Crying and Sighing" and "Rainbow 'Round My Shoulder" w. McKinney. CDs: W. McKinney (BB); D. Ellington (Dec.); Clarence Williams (Collector's Classics).

ROBINSON, SCOTT, all saxes incl. contrabs, bs, cl, fl, tpt, euph, v-tbn, theremin, comp; b. Pompton Plains, NJ, 4/27/59. Grew up in Va. fr. age 5. Moth. was pno. teacher; grandfath. pl. alto sax; bro. David is trad. jazz crntst. in Wash., D.C., area. Grandfath. gave him an alto sax at age 10. Fluent on all woodwinds and valve brass. Led own gps. fr. hs. Stud. at Berklee Coll. of Mus. 1977–81. Pl. w. Phil Wilson bb '80; Klaus Suonsaari off and on fr. '80; Tom Pierson Orch. '85–91; Illinois Jacquet bb '87; Toshiko Akiyoshi Orch., Louie Bellson bb fr. '87; Lionel Hampton '88–9; John Fedchock–Maria Schneider bb, Vince Giordano's Nighthawks fr. '89; Mel Lewis Orch. as sub. fr. '89; Mario Bauza '89–91; Buck Clayton bb '90–2; Joe Roccisano bb fr. '90; Pheeroan Aklaff

'91–2; Frank Wess bb, Grover Mitchell Orch. fr. '91. Pl. tpt. w. T. Akiyoshi Qnt. '92. Also misc. gigs w. Bob Mintzer bb; Peter Erskine; Doc Severinsen; Chico O'Farrill Orch.; Mingus bb. Robinson has led a qt. w. Horace Parlan, a trio w. P. Aklaff and Jules Thayer, and also rec. w. A. Braxton. His comps. incl. *Point, Line and Plane*, an extended work insp. by the paintings of Kandinsky; he has also worked w. the Penn. Dance Theater and sculptor Rob Fischer. Taught instrument repair and jazz courses at Berklee '82–4; Kistner Jazz Camps, Canada '82–9; Turtle Bay Mus. Sch., NYC fr. '87. Worked as an instrument repairman in Bost. and NYC '80–7. As versatile w. styles as he is w. instruments. Favs: Ben Webster, Louis Armstrong, John Coltrane. Fests: Eur. fr. '84; Japan fr. '91. TV: Eur. TV. CDs: Arb.; Bliss; Ken; w. B. Mintzer (DMP); T. Akiyoshi (Col.); Gary Smulyan (CC); Christopher Hollyday; John Pizzarelli (Novus); Suonsaari (SN); Randy Sandke (Conc.; N-H); Ruby Braff; Bob Wilber; Bobby Gordon; Daryl Sherman (Arb.); Caecilie Norby (BN); Maria Schneider (Enja); F. Wess; Carol Sloane (Conc.); Marty Grosz (Jazz.; N-H); John Fedchock (Res.).

ROBINSON, SPIKE (HENRY BERTHOLF), tnr sax; b. Kenosha, WI, 1/16/30; d. Writtle, Engl., 10/28/01. Studied cl. 1938–49; in '48 attended Navy Sch. of Mus. and in '49 became the only American member of the London Jazz Club 11. Rec. for English Esquire '51, pl. alto sax w. Victor Feldman. Back in US '52, he sw. to tnr. sax; earned engineering degree at U. of Colo. In Boulder, Colo., he became a full-time production and engineering manager by day, pl. w. David and Don Grusin, Johnny Smith, Gus Johnson, and others '56–85. Took up mus. full time in '85, pl. jazz parties and fests., working w. such perfs. as Peter Appleyard and Bob Brookmeyer, and earning renewed popularity in Engl. Feat. on many radio and TV programs in US, the UK, and Eur. By '90 he was living mainly in Engl. but ret. occasionally to the US to pl., usually in Colo. A cool-toned player with a Getzian bent. CDs: Disc.; Capri; Hep; OMD; Cargo; w. Scott Hamilton (Conc.).

ROCCISANO, JOE (JOSEPH LUCIAN), alto sax, woodwinds, comp, lead; b. Springfield, MA, 10/15/39; d. NYC, 11/9/97. Studied priv. w. Harry Huffnagle 1956; Ascher Slotnick '57; Albert Harris, '74; Potsdam St. U. (B.S. in mus. ed. '63. Prof. debut w. Warren Covington '57–9; tour. w. T. Dorsey band led by Sam Donahue '64; then settled in LA, working w. Don Ellis '66–8; Ray Charles '67–8; freelanced w. L. Bellson; T. Gibbs; Don Menza; B. Holman; and led own 12-piece band. From '76 occasionally led own 15-piece band, Rocbop; in '80s rec. w. Capp-

Pierce Juggernaut and gigged with many bands in the LA area. Wrote arrs. for Bellson; Ellis; Doc Severinsen; Woody Herman, "Green Earrings" '78; Pete Christlieb–Warne Marsh, "Tenors of the Time" '78. Moved to NYC '85 and led bb at Fat Tuesdays, etc; nonet at Blue Note for Sunday brunches fr. '96. On his way to that gig he died of a heart attack. Infls: P. Woods, Parker, Coltrane, Rollins. Fests: MJF, NJF w. Ellis; also Japan '64. Publ: *Stage Band Arr. & Comp.* (Life Line Music Press, Agoura, Calif.). CDs: Land.; w. L. Bellson (MM; Tel.); Capp-Pierce (Conc.); Ellis (Col.; GNP Cres.).

ROCCO, MAURICE JOHN, pno, voc; b. Oxford, OH, 6/26/15; d. Bangkok, Thailand, 3/24/76. Mother was mus. teacher. A prodigy and prof. pnst. fr. childhood, he popularized the practice of pl. pno. while standing and was more of an entertainer than a jazz mus., despite the intensity of his fast boogie-woogie perfs. Popular attraction in US clubs and Hollywood musicals during the '40s. He lived in Paris and Hong Kong bef. moving to Bangkok in the early '60s and was a fixture at the Bamboo Bar of the Oriental Hotel until he was knifed to death in his apartment. Films: *Vogues of 1938; 52nd Street; Incendiary Blonde*; and several shorts. Recs: Dec.; Vict., etc.

ROCHÉ, BETTY (MARY ELIZABETH), voc; b. Wilmington, DE, 1/9/18; d. Pleasantville, NJ, 2/16/99. Raised in Atlantic City; to NYC 1939; won amateur contest at Apollo Theatre; worked w. Savoy Sultans '41–2. After joining D. Ellington, she became the first singer to perf. the blues sequence in "Black, Brown and Beige" at the band's Carnegie Hall concert Jan. '43. She impressed many listeners as the best female voc. ever heard w. Ellington. Sang and rec. w. Earl Hines '44; rejoin. Ellington '52–3, earning popularity w. her humorous, bop-inspired version of "Take the 'A' Train." Though she rec. occasionally in '50s and early '60s, she was relatively obscure; illness prevented her from working for many yrs. CDs: Beth.; Prest.; w. Ellington (Prest; Col.); Earl Hines (Del.).

RODGERS, GENE (EUGENE R. JR.), pno, comp; b. NYC, 3/5/10; d. NYC, 10/23/87. Father taught at Bost. Cons. Led The Revellers 1928; pl. w. bands of Billy Fowler; Chick Webb; and Bingie Madison. Formed vaudeville act w. another pianist, Fred Radcliffe, which app. in London '36; also rec. there w. Benny Carter. Arr. and pl. w. Coleman Hawkins, taking part in his celebrated '39 "Body and Soul" sess. From '40s was heard in Calif., and seen in several films; from '50s worked mainly as soloist or w. trio. In last yrs., toured Eur. and Japan w. the

Harlem Blues and Jazz Band. CDs: w. C. Hawkins (BB); B. Carter; King Oliver; Clarence Williams (Class.); Slam Stewart (B&B).

RODIN, GIL (GILBERT A.), prod, sax, comp; b. Russia, 12/09/06; d. Palm Springs, CA, 6/17/74. Studied reeds, fl., tpt. while att. sch. in Chi. First prominent with Ben Pollack band 1927–35, then became charter member of Bob Crosby Orch. on alto sax (no solos) and as mus. dir. Later led mil. band w. Ray Bauduc '44–5, rejoin. Crosby; but fr. the '50s was active as TV producer, mainly at MCA Universal. Comp. "Boogie-Woogie Maxixe." CDs: w. J. Teagarden (BB); Crosby; Judy Garland (Dec.).

RODITI, CLAUDIO, tpt, flg, perc, pno; b. Rio de Janeiro, Brazil, 5/28/46. Father pl. gtr. and vln. Stud. in Brazil and Austria, later at Berklee Coll. of Mus. Worked as studio mus. in Brazil, then moved to Bost., pl. w. Alan Dawson–Tony Teixeira, also own bb w. Mark Harvey. Moved to NYC in early 1980s, pl. w. Bob Mover; Charlie Rouse; Mike Morgenstern; Thiago de Mello; Herbie Mann; Paquito D'Rivera; Dizzy Gillespie United Nation orch. fr. '88; Slide Hampton Jazzmasters fr. '93; own gps. in '90s. App. w. Gillespie Alumni All-Stars at Blue Note, NYC '98. A fine brassman in the tradition of his favored players who, within his own groups, is able to combine Brazilian mus. and jazz in a most energetic and felicitous manner. Favs: Gillespie, Lee Morgan, F. Hubbard, Booker Little. Fests: Eur., Asia, So. Amer., etc. TV: Gillespie at Royal Fest. Hall. CDs: Mile.; Mons; Cand.; Res.; Summit; w. D'Rivera (Town Crier; Mess.); Rouse (Up.); Gillespie; Slide Hampton (Tel.); H. Meurkens (Conc.); Dave Valentin (Trop.); J. Heath (Verve); H. Silver (Imp.); Chip White; Jorge Sylvester (Post.)

RODNEY, RED (Robert Rodney Chudnick), tpt, fl; b. Philadelphia, PA, 9/27/27; d. Boynton Beach, FL, 5/27/94. Began on tpt. at age 13. Stud. at Mastbaum Vocational HS. On road at age 15, pl. w. Jerry Wald, Jimmy Dorsey 1944; Elliot Lawrence '45; Gene Krupa, Buddy Rich '46; Claude Thornhill '47; Oscar Pettiford at the Roost '48; Woody Herman '48–9; also worked w. Tony Pastor, Les Brown, Georgie Auld '40s. Pl. w. Charlie Parker '49–52; Charlie Ventura '52. Pl. w. local bands and worked as club date booking agent in Phila. '52–7; w. Ira Sullivan at Bee Hive Club, Chi. '56; Sammy Davis Jr., O. Pettiford '57. Inactive in jazz '57–72, pl. in Las Vegas show bands in late '60s-early '70s. Began pl. jazz again ca. '72; tour. Eur. w. *Musical Life of Charlie Parker* '74. Lived in Denmark, pl. in Eur. '74–8. Ret. to NYC '79. Co-led qnt. w. Ira Sullivan '80–5; own qnt. fr. '85, incl. Garry Dial; Dick Oatts; Chris Potter. App. as soloist in Jazz at Lincoln Center concert w. W. Marsalis, R. Hargrove et al. '93. Rodney held an honorary doctorate fr. Harvard U. A volume of solo transcriptions was publ. in '83. One of Gillespie's earliest disciples, Rodney always brought fire and lyricism to his improvisations. Favs: Fats Navarro, Clifford Brown, Miles Davis, Dizzy Gillespie. Polls: *DB* Hall of Fame. Films: shorts w. Krupa '46; *Beat the Band* w. Krupa '47. Consultant for and character in *Bird* '88. CDs: Sav.; Den.; Contin.; Chesky; Muse; tracks in *Early Bebop* (Merc.); tracks in *Prestige First Sessions, Vol. 3* (Prest.); w. C. Parker (Verve; Stash); W. Herman (Cap.); D. Gillespie (Tel.); C. Thornhill (Col.); Serge Chaloff (Mos.); T. Brewer (Red Brn.); w. B. Rich in *The 1940s Mercury Sessions* (Merc.).

RODRIGUEZ, JAY (Hernan Ramiro Rodriguez Sierra), tnr, alto, bari saxes, fl, bs cl, comp/arr; b. Baranquilla, Colombia, 9/17/67. Family moved to NYC 1971. At age 8 stud. cl. in grade sch. Fr. ages 10–15 stud. in N.J. w. Tito D'Rivera, Paquito's father; also w. Mark Friedman. Stud. harm., theory at HS of Perf. Art. Schoolmates were Bill Charlap; Justin Robinson; Stephen Scott. Then further reed stud. '82–4 w. Phil Woods; summer classes w. Joe Allard at Manh. Sch. of Mus. '84. Stud. pno. w. Michael Wolff; fl. w. Julius Baker '84. Semester at Manh. Sch. '85. Att. New Sch.'s Jazz Program '86–9, incl. lessons fr. Jimmy Heath; George Coleman; Joe Lovano. First job was a rumba in Weehawken, N.J. w. voc. Narcisso Valdes '81. Worked w. Vincente Pacheco, Tito Puente '81; Butch Johnson, Marco Rizo '82. Jammed in Harlem w. Victor Venegas, Bross Townsend, Herman Foster '83. Fr. '86 pl. w. funk ens., did studio work on jingles. Pl. w. Charlie Sepulveda; Eddie Palmieri; in LV w. Natalie Cole '86. Worked w. Bill Ware '88; Bobby Sanabria '90; Dizzy Gillespie's United Nation Orch. '91; Rashied Ali fr. '91; Ray Barretto '91–2; Gil Evans Orch. '92–4; Groove Collective fr. '93; Medeski, Martin & Wood fr. '94; subbing in Mingus bb fr. '94. Pl. w. Roy Hargrove bb, Chucho Valdes '98. Early infls. incl. Charlie Parker, John Coltrane, Stanley Turrentine, Michael Brecker, P. D'Rivera, Rahsaan Roland Kirk. Favs: Joe Henderson, Illinois Jacquet, Lester Young. Fests: Montreux w. Barretto '91; Groove Collective '94; Madarao w. Gr. Collect., CHBB '94; Montreal w. Steps Ahead '95; Nice w. Barretto, Gr. Collect., own trio '97; Umbria, Baranquilla, Havana '98. Video: w. Gr. Collect. CDs: Funk the Planet; w. Groove Collective (Shan.; WB; Imp.); Barretto (Conc.); Sanabria (FF); Ware (KFW); Medeski, Martin & Wood (Gram.); Victor Jones (New Frontier); Josh Roseman (BN).

ROGERS, REUBEN RENWICK, bs, el-bs; b. Brooklyn, NY, 11/15/74. Raised in St. Thomas, V.I., fr. age 2. Moth. pl. church org. Began on cl., then pno., sax, dms., gtr., before settling on bs. at 14. Gigged in hs w. St. Thomas jazz musicians incl. Louis Taylor; Eddie Russell; Ron Blake. Received scholarships fr. St. Thomas Arts Council to att. Interlochen Arts Camp and Berklee Coll. of Mus. 1991–2. Received B. Mus. fr. Berklee '97. Worked w. Betty Carter, Marlon Jordan '93; Marcus Roberts '93–5; Teodross Avery '93–7; Carl Allen, Marcus Printup '94–6; own trio, qt. '94–7; Roy Hargrove qnt., bb '95; Nicholas Payton qnt. fr. '95; Eric Reed '95–6; W. Marsalis '95–7; Terrell Stafford, Jesse Davis, Mulgrew Miller '96; Donald Harrison '96–7. Freelance work w. Billy Pierce; Johnny Griffin; Doc Cheatham; Phil Woods; Clark Terry. Favs: Ron Carter, Paul Chambers, Ray Brown. Fests: worldwide w. Payton, Avery, Marsalis, Roberts, Hargrove. CDs: w. Avery; Harrison (Imp.); Printup (BN); Payton (Verve); Allen (Atl.); Anthony Wonsey (Alfa); *Alto Summit* (Mile.).

ROGERS, SHORTY (Milton Michael Rajonsky), tpt, flg, comp/arr, lead; b. Great Barrington, MA, 4/14/24; d. Van Nuys, CA, 11/7/94. Studied at HS of Mus. & Art, NYC, where he grew up; later at LA Cons. In 1940s pl. w. bbs of Will Bradley; Red Norvo; Woody Herman. Settled in Calif. '46; pl. w. C. Barnet; Butch Stone (w. S. Getz, Herbie Steward); w. Herman again as tpt. and arr. '47–9; same capacities w. Stan Kenton '50–1. Pl. w. Howard Rumsey at Lighthouse '51–3; form. Shorty Rogers and the Giants '53. His stud. w. Dr. Wesley LaViolette was reflected in experimental works in the '50s w. Teddy Charles and others using modes, bi-tonalities, and other unusual techniques. Thereafter for many yrs. mostly worked in studios, often providing backgrounds for pop singers. During '80s gradually ret. to active perf.; many int'l tours fr. '82. In '89 he and Bud Shank reorganized the Lighthouse All-Stars for recs. and concert tours. Inspired by Miles Davis as a soloist, Rogers was far more original as a comp./arr. He had a profound impact on the West Coast jazz scene from the early '50s. In '50 named Al Cohn and Neal Hefti as fav. arrs. Comp. and/or arr. "Keen and Peachy"; "Keeper of the Flame"; "That's Right"; "More Moon"; and "Lemon Drop" for Herman; "Jolly Rogers"; "Round Robin"; "Viva Prado"; "Maynard Ferguson"; "Art Pepper"; and "Coop's Solo" for Kenton. Film: Pl. and had acting role in *Man with the Golden Arm*; soundtracks for *The Wild One; Private Hell 36.* CDs: Mos.; BB; Cand.; Conc.; Time Is; w. S. Getz; Teddy Charles (Prest.); C. Parker (Stash); Herman (Col.; Cap.); Kenton (Cap.); S. Manne; H. Rumsey (Cont.); Red

Norvo (BB); Shank (Noct.); four tracks w. K. Winding, Getz in *Loaded* (Sav.).

ROKER, MICKEY (GRANVILLE WILLIAM), dms; b. Miami, FL, 9/3/32. Began pl. dms. in drm. and bugle corps while in army 1953–5. Stud. briefly at Music City, Phila. '56. Pl. in Phila. w. Jimmy Divine, King James, Sam Reed, Jimmy Oliver, Jimmy Heath '56–9; also jammed w. Lee Morgan; Reggie Workman; Kenny Barron; McCoy Tyner. Moved to NYC '59. Pl. w. Gigi Gryce '59–61; Ray Bryant '61–3; Joe Williams–Junior Mance '63–5; Nancy Wilson '65–7; Duke Pearson big band '67–9. Also freelanced in '60s w. Mary Lou Williams; Milt Jackson; Clifford Jordan; Sonny Rollins; Art Farmer; Stanley Turrentine; et al. Pl. w. Lee Morgan '69–71; Dizzy Gillespie '71–9; Ella Fitzgerald '80. Freelanced extens. fr. '80s w. Oscar Peterson; Zoot Sims; Milt Jackson; Ray Brown. Replaced Connie Kay in MJQ '92 and early '93. In mid '90s house dmrs. at Ortlieb's in Phila. Gillespie said of him: "Once he sets a groove, whatever it is, you can go to Paris and come back and it's right there. You never have to worry about it." Favs: Blakey, P. J. Jones, Tony Williams, Elvin Jones. Fests: all major incl. Phila. Mellon JF which honored him. CDs: w. Gillespie; M. Jackson (Pab.); Herbie Hancock; D. Pearson (BN); S. Rollins (Imp.); R. Bryant (Col.); NY Hardbop Qnt., *Rokermotion* (TCB).

ROLAND, GENE, tpt, tbn, mello, saxes, comp/arr; b. Dallas, TX, 9/15/21; d. NYC, 8/11/82. Studied at No. Texas St. 1940–2; classmates were Herb Ellis, Jimmy Giuffre; form. air force band w. Giuffre. Pl. and arr. for Stan Kenton '44; briefly w. L. Hampton and Lucky Millinder and again w. Kenton mid '40s. In NYC wrote arrs. for 4-tnr. sax ensembles '46, and brought them to some Calif. ens. which eventually led to Woody Herman's Four Brothers sound. Pl. tbn. w. C. Basie; Millinder; C. Barnet; arr. for A. Shaw and Claude Thornhill late '40s. Led 26-piece band that incl. D. Gillespie, M. Davis, C. Parker, Zoot Sims, G. Mulligan, et al. '50. Arr. for Woody Herman and Kenton in '50s, introducing a new sound—four mellophoniums—to Kenton's band, captured on LP, *Adventures in Blues* '61, where Roland solos on both mello. and sop. sax. Led his own large group in NYC early '60s. Comp. for and cond. Radiohus Orch., Copenhagen '67. Tour. w. Kenton '73; work in NYC, occ. w. own bands, occ. heard as a singer late '70s. A musician/composer of rare versatility who has rarely been properly credited for the significant effect his arranging had on the post-WWII big band sound. LPs: *Swingin' Friends*, own oct. w. Al Cohn, Zoot Sims, Clark Terry, et al. (Brunswick); *The Band That*

Never Was (Spot.); w. J. Knepper (Beth.) '57. CDs: w. P. Quinichette (Biog.); Kenton (Class.; Cap.; Status); Oscar Pettiford (Sav.).

ROLLINI, ADRIAN, bs sax, vib, xyl, dms, comp; b. NYC, 6/28/04; d. Homestead, FL, 5/15/56. Played w. California Ramblers, first on xyl., then bs. sax, of which he became the only prominent soloist in late 1920s and early '30s. Pl. in London w. Fred Elizalde '27–8. In NYC rec. many sessions w. Red Nichols; F. Trumbauer; Joe Venuti; Bix Beiderbecke; occasionally playing novelty instruments, "hot fountain pen" and "goofus." Phased out sax to concentrate on vib., rec. as lead. Operated Adrian's Tap Room at President Hotel, NYC '34–6. To Fla. in early '50s as proprietor of hotel. Rollini earned a unique place in jazz history through his inventive work on bass sax both as soloist and in rhythmic bass function. CDs: Topaz; Aff.; w. Beiderbecke (Col.); Bud Freeman; C. Hawkins (Class.); The Little Ramblers (Timel.); Joe Venuti; Eddie Lang (Jazz Classics in Digital Stereo); California Ramblers (Biog.)

ROLLINI, ARTHUR FRANCIS, tnr sax; b. NYC, 2/13/12; d. Florida, 12/30/93. Brother of Adrian Rollini. In Engl. w. Fred Elizalde 1929. In early '30s pl. w. California Ramblers, Paul Whiteman; w. B. Goodman '34–9 (solos on recs. "Bugle Call Rag"; "Sent for You Yesterday"). Worked w. Richard Himber '40–1; Will Bradley '41–2. Staff mus. at ABC, NYC '43–58; out of mus. fr. '59 except for occasional club dates. Autobiography: *Thirty Years with the Big Bands* '87. CDs: w. Goodman (BB; Col.); Adrian Rollini (Aff.; Topaz).

ROLLINS, SONNY (THEODORE WALTER), tnr sax; b. NYC, 9/7/30. An older bro. pl. vln. Sonny took pno. lessons briefly at age 9; stud. alto sax fr. 1944, sw. to tnr. sax in '46. Pl. w. neighborhood gp. incl. Jackie McLean, Kenny Drew, Art Taylor for dances, cocktail "sips." Through tptr. Lowell Lewis rehearsed w. Thelonious Monk in '48. Made his rec. debut w. Babs Gonzales on Cap. '49. The same yr. he rec. as a sideman on two occasions w. J. J. Johnson, who rec. several Rollins comps. incl. "Audubon," and Bud Powell. Pl. w. Art Blakey '49; Tadd Dameron, Powell '50. Pl. in Chi. w. dmr. Ike Day '50; six mos. w. Miles Davis '51. Despite problems with heroin he rec. extensively as a leader and sideman w. Davis, Monk, Art Farmer; MJQ for Prest. fr. '51 to '54. In '55 he voluntarily spent four and a half mos. in the federal narcotics hospital in Lexington, Kentucky, before settling at a YMCA in Chi. He worked as a janitor and truck loader and practiced assiduously, sometimes joined by tptr. Booker Little. Late in the yr. he pl. w.

the Clifford Brown–Max Roach qnt. at the Bee Hive, subbing for Harold Land. He became regular in the qnt., remaining a yr. after Brown's death in June '56. During this period he again rec. prolifically w. Roach, Davis, and as a leader, establishing himself as the tenor sax force in jazz. Albums such as *Saxophone Colossus* garnered praise from both the critical fraternity and the listening public. His jazz calypso, "St. Thomas," echoed his roots (both parents emigrated from the Virgin Islands) and began a long line of calypso-based originals, i.e., "Don't Stop the Carnival" and "Duke of Iron." His recording of "Way Out West" further demonstrated his ability to creatively use songs that would not ordinarily seem likely vehicles for valid jazz interpretation and also put him in a trio context with bass and drums (Ray Brown and Shelly Manne) that he would employ often in the late '50s.

In '59, dissatisfied with the nightclub scene and his own playing in the light of all the accolades being heaped upon him, Rollins took a sabbatical which became a well-publicized part of his legend when he was discovered practicing in the upper reaches of the Williamsburg Bridge. He returned to public playing with a quartet featuring Jim Hall at the Jazz Gallery, NYC '61 and rec. *The Bridge* for RCA '62. In July of that year he made an excursion into "free jazz," recording *Our Man in Jazz* at the Village Gate with Don Cherry and Billy Higgins. In '66 he began using a piano in his gps. again. While pl. at Ronnie Scott's in London '65, he comp., arr., and rec. the soundtrack for the film *Alfie* '66. From '68 to '71 Rollins took another leave of absence from the commercial jazz world. In '59–61 he had investigated Rosicrucianism; here he visited Japan and India, studying zen, yoga, and the theories of Ghita. He ended his retreat in June '71 and by '72 was tour. again in Eur., playing festivals and, in the US, college concerts. Tour. Far East from '73. Generally he has eschewed clubs for the most part, certainly anything over two nights. In the '80s he did a series of concerts in NYC featuring various young musicians individually, such as Branford Marsalis; Terence Blanchard; and Roy Hargrove. At one of these presentations, in April '83 with Wynton Marsalis at Town Hall, he collapsed from exhaustion during the second number but was back playing in a June concert at the Beacon Theater. In '85 he played a rare solo concert at the Museum of Modern Art.

From the '70s his recordings have reflected the influence of pop, rock, and r&b. He occasionally pl. sop. sax. Some feel that to really experience Rollins one must hear him in person where he remains the only improviser able to effectively sustain inventiveness in extended solos. In recent years his front line collaborator has been tbnst. Clifton Anderson;

pianists have incl. Mark Soskin, Stephen Scott, Kevin Hays; longtime stalwart Bob Cranshaw, el. bass; and a gaggle of drummers, the best of whom was Al Foster. Polls: countless wins in *DB* Readers and Critics polls, Hall of Fame '73. Awards: Guggenheim Fellowship '72; Doctor of Arts fr. Bard Coll. '92; Lifetime Achievement Award fr. Tufts U. '96. TV: BBC Special, filmed at Ronnie Scott's and in various London locations '74. Videos: *Live at Laren,* '73; *Saxophone Colossus* '86 (Rhap.). Comps: "Oleo"; "Airegin"; "Doxy"; "Alfie's Theme"; "Silver City." CDs: boxed sets: Prest.; RCA; Mile.; also BB; Verve; Imp.; BN; Riv.; w. M. Davis (Prest.); S. Stitt; Gillespie (Verve); Babs Gonzales (BN); M. Roach (Em.; Merc.); F. Navarro–T. Dameron; B. Powell (BN); J. J. Johnson (Prest.; Sav.); Monk (Prest.; Riv.).

ROMANIS, GEORGE ZACHERY (Roumanis), bs, comp; b. Trenton, NJ, 2/11/29. Played and arr. for Charlie Spivak 1949; Ralph Flanagan '50. Air Force '50–5; pl. and arr. for air force dance band and symph.; after discharge fr. service, worked w. B. Goodman; Johnny Smith; Claude Thornhill, etc. From '60s active w. commercials and studio work. Film scores incl. *Of Mice and Men.* In early '90s he was completing work on *Phaedra,* an opera in three acts, for Opera San Jose. Favs: Gerry Mulligan, Sy Oliver, Count Basie. LPs: *Modern Sketches in Jazz* (Coral); w. Sal Salvador as pl. and arr., *Colors in Sound* (Dec.); Johnny Smith (Roost). CDs: w. Bud Shank as comp./arr. (Capri).

ROMANO, ALDO, dms; b. Belluno, Italy, 1/16/41. Raised in France. Began on gtr., then sw. to dms. at age 20. Self-taught. Pl. in Paris w. Barney Wilen; Michel Portal; Jean-Luc Ponty; and Amer. mus. incl. Jackie McLean; Bud Powell; Stan Getz; Don Cherry. Known mainly as a free-jazz dmr. fr. 1965. Rec. w. D. Cherry '65; Steve Lacy '65–6; Giorgio Gaslini, Jazz Realities w. S. Lacy; Carla Bley '66; Gato Barbieri, Rolf Kuhn '67; Joachim Kuhn '69; Karin Krog '70; Robin Kenyatta '72. Led own rock gp. '71–3, then pl. w. Philip Catherine, Charlie Mariano, Jasper van't Hof in band Pork Pie '73–5; François Jeanneau '76–7; Enrico Rava fr. '78. Rec. as lead. fr. '78. Pl. w. Michel Petrucciani '80s. CDs: MLP; Verve; Owl; Enja; w. Petrucciani (EPM); Joe Albany (FS); P. Catherine (Inak); European Music Orch. (SN); E. Rava (ECM); Henri Texier (L. Bleu); Pietro Tonolo (Spl.).

ROMANO, JOE (JOSEPH), tnr sax, alto sax; also cl, fl; b. Rochester, NY, 4/17/32. Studied alto fr. age 8; cl. at Eastman Sch. of Mus. ages 10–12; tnr. for one yr. First prof. gigs w. local bands at age 14. Pl. w. air force bands in Alaska, Texas, New York 1949–early '50s. Joined Woody Herman Orch. in Calif. '56; pl. w. Herman off and on until '66. Worked in Las Vegas '60–1; also two yrs. w. Chuck Mangione in Rochester '60s. Pl. w. Sam Noto in Bufffalo '66–7. Living in Calif., worked w. Buddy Rich off and on '68–70. Pl. briefly w. Stan Kenton '70; then pl. w. L. Bellson, Les Brown '70–2; B. Rich '72–4. Freelanced in Roch. '74–5. Moved to NYC '75. Pl. w. Chuck Israels' Nat'l Jazz Ens.; subbed in Thad Jones–Mel Lewis Orch. mid to late '70s. Also freelanced w. W. Herman; Bellson; Bill Watrous fr. late '70s. In mid '80s pl. w. Don Menza, Bill Berry in Calif. A fluid, swinging player on alto and tnr. Favs: Parker, Rollins, Bud Powell, Coltrane, Hawkins, Young. Fests: MJF w. W. Herman '60s; also NJF, KCJF. MJF w. L Bellson '71; fest. apps. w. Rich. TV: Pearl Bailey, Bob Hope shows w. L. Brown '70–2. LPs: w. Noto (Xan.); Herman (Philips). CDs: w. Mangione (Jzld.); Bellson (DRG); Rich (PJ); Capp-Pierce (Conc.).

RONEY, ANTOINE, tnr, sop saxes; b. Philadelphia, PA, 4/1/63. Grandmother and aunt pl. pno. and sang in church choir; aunt also pno. teacher. Grandfath., Roosevelt Sherman, pl. gtr., tba., tpt. and worked in Frankie Fairfax band. Older bro. Wallace start. him in music: "Harmony, rhythm. Everything he would learn in lessons or his discoveries he would show me." Began on cl., then alto sax and tnr. sax. Stud. w. Jackie McLean at Hartt Sch. of Mus. at U. of Hartford. Worked w. Donald Byrd 1983; McLean '84; Clifford Jordan, Ted Curson, John Patton '86; Rashied Ali '87–8; Arthur Taylor '89; Jesse Davis '89–90, making rec. debut on Davis's *Horn of Passion*; Jacky Terrasson '91–2; w. Ravi Coltrane in gp. Grand Central '92–3; Michael Carvin '95–6; fr. '97 in qnt. w. Wallace Roney. Has taught saxophone and jazz ensemble at McLean's Artists Collective in Hartford, Conn. Roney says: "I had a chance to see groups like the Giants of Jazz with Monk, Art Blakey, Sonny Stitt, Dizzy Gillespie. All these people played like there was no tomorrow *every time* they played their instruments." Roney, a powerful and passionate player, follows this example. He comes to post-Coltranism from his own oblique angle with deep spiritualism. Favs: Coltrane, Shorter, Rollins. Tour. in all major Eur. countries, Israel, Malta, Japan. CDs: w. W. Roney (WB; Muse); J. Davis (Conc.); Carvin (Muse); *Endless Miles* (N2K).

RONEY, WALLACE, tpt, flg; b. Philadelphia, PA, 5/25/60. Brother Antoine Roney. Theory and pno. lessons at 5; stud. at Settlement Mus. Sch.; in 1969 advanced tpt. stud. w. symph. mus. Moved to Wash., D.C. First prof. band at 13 while cont. stud. at Duke

Ellington Sch. for the Arts. After further stud. at Howard U. and Berklee Coll., join. Art Blakey briefly in '82. Rejoin. him in '87 also serving as mus. dir. For the next two yrs. doubled bet. the gps. of Blakey and Tony Williams. In July '91 Miles Davis invited Roney to pl. w. him at the Montreux JF in Switz. The perf., comprising Gil Evans' arrs., was highly acclaimed and released on CD and in video (both WB) '93. He has often been compared to Davis and has tour. w. a Davis tribute band of Wayne Shorter, Herbie Hancock, Ron Carter, and Tony Williams and participated in Gerry Mulligan's *Rebirth of the Cool.* Tour. w. Chick Corea's "Tribute to Bud Powell" '96. Married pnst. Geri Allen with whom he collab. in qt., incl. Antoine Roney, fr. '97. CDs: WB; Muse; w. G. Mulligan (GRP); *Tribute to Miles* (Qwest); Tony Williams; Geri Allen (BN); Corea (Stretch); *Warner Jam, Vol. 1* (WB); Blakey (Delos); *Endless Miles* (N2K); Marvin Smith (Conc.); Kenny Barron (Enja).

ROPPOLO, (JOSEPH) LEON, cl; b. Lutcher, LA, 3/16/02; d. New Orleans, LA, 10/5/43. Studied vln., cl., and gtr. Worked w. Georg Brunis and Paul Mares 1916; Eddie Shields and Santo Pecora '17. Pl. on riverboats. Went to Chi. w. Brunis and Mares, join. Mares' Friars Society Orch. '21, which became the New Orleans Rhythm Kings, in which he established his reputation. Traveled to NYC w. Mares '23. Worked in Texas w. Peck Kelley '24 bef. ret. to NO. Pl. w. Abbie Brunies' Halfway House Orch. and the reorganized NORK '25; soon after suffered a mental breakdown and was institutionalized for the rest of his life. Form. a band in sanitorium, pl. tnr. sax. One of the most gifted musicians in jazz at a stage when many of its participants were self-taught and technically limited. Roppolo brought to his performances a soaring, spirited style that gave him legendary stature. He was comp. or co-comp. of "Farewell Blues"; "Milenberg Joys"; "Sugar Babe"; and "Tin Roof Blues." CD: w. NORK (Mile.).

ROSENBERG, ROGER MARK, bari, sop saxes, bs-cl, cl, fl, tnr, alto saxes; b. NYC, 5/26/51. Studied w. Phil Woods at Ramblerny jazz camp, New Hope, Pa. 1965–7; Indiana U. '69–70; New Engl. Cons. '71–3; then w. Vic Morosco, Danny Bank, Keith Underwood in NYC. Stud. classical comp. w. Harold Seletsky '71–81. Pl. w. Tito Puente '74; Buddy Rich '75; Mongo Santamaria '75–7; Chet Baker '77–9. Founded Latin jazz gp. Jasmine in late '70s. Pl. fr. late '70s w. Lee Konitz; Walter Bishop Jr.; Eddie Palmieri; Ray Barretto; Janet Lawson; David Lahm; David Matthews; Don Sebesky; Bob Mintzer; Geo. Russell; Dr. John; Mel Lewis Orch.; Tom Harrell; etc. Pl. in '90s w. Mingus Orch.; Gil Evans Orch. w.

Miles Davis at Montreux JF '91. Rosenberg has also worked extens. as a Broadway and studio mus. Favs: bari: Ronnie Cuber, Pepper Adams, Harry Carney; sop: Coltrane. Polls: NARAS Most Val. Player on bari. sax '86; San Souterio Int'l Poll '84. Fests: Eur. since '79. Video: Miles Davis–Montreux (WB). Recs. w. J. Lawson; D. Lahm. CDs: w. B. Mintzer (DMP); Mingus Epitaph; David Sanchez (Col.); Mingus BB (Drey.); Monk on Monk (N2K); George Russell (SN); John Scofield (Verve).

ROSENGARDEN, BOBBY (ROBERT M.), dms, perc; b. Elgin, IL, 4/23/24. Mother pl. pno. for silent movies. Sons Mark and Neal are musicians. Stud. w. Oliver Coleman in Chi. 1935–6; w. Roy Knapp while in hs. Music scholarship to U. of Michigan, where he stud. w. Dr. Wm. D. Revelli '42–3. Pl. w. army band in Missouri '43; air force band in Mississippi '44–5; Teddy Phillips '45; Henry Busse '45–6. Moved to NYC '46, pl. w. Charlie Spivak; Raymond Scott; Alvy West's Little Band; also house bands at the Copacabana; Bill Miller's Riviera '46–8; Skitch Henderson '48. On staff at NBC, incl. NBC Symphony '49–68. Busy as studio mus. fr. '50s, rec. w. Duke Ellington; Lena Horne; Billie Holiday; J. J. Johnson–Kai Winding; Joe Williams; Doc Severinsen; Frank Sinatra; Ella Fitzgerald; Tito Puente; Dick Hyman; N.Y. Philharm. concerts w. Miles Davis–Gil Evans, '50s. Pl. w. Benny Goodman off and on '65–86. Led band for Dick Cavett TV show on ABC '69–74. Mus. dir. at Waldorf-Astoria's Empire Room '73. Pl. w. World's Greatest Jazz Band '74–8; N.Y. Jazz Repertory Co. fr. '74, incl. Russian tour '75; Soprano Summit '75–8; Gerry Mulligan fr. '76; Blue Three w. Kenny Davern, Dick Wellstood '81–3. Led his own bb at the Rainbow Room in NYC. Living in Fla., cont. to freelance in '90s. A swinging dmr. who says he picked up his infectious "near shuffle" beat fr. Jimmy Crawford, Rosengarden is also expert w. various So. American and Caribbean rhythms. Favs: Chick Webb, O'Neil Spencer, Gene Krupa, Buddy Rich, Jo Jones. Film: *C-Man* w. Conrad Nagel; many soundtracks. Fests: all major w. various bands; own gp. at Cork JF '94. CDs: w. Goodman; Brubeck (Col.); Jimmy Smith (Verve) ; Joe Venuti–Zoot Sims; Mulligan; K. Davern; Soprano Summit (Chiaro.).

ROSENGREN, BERNT AAKE, tnr sax, fl, comp; b. Stockholm, Sweden, 12/24/37. Accordion at age 10; tnr. sax at 15. Tour. and rec. w. Jazz Club '57 combo. Heard in Newport w. Int'l Youth Band 1958; perf. as soloist on soundtrack of Roman Polanski's film, *Knife in the Water*, '62. In '60s and '70s pl. w. George Russell; Don Cherry; Lars Gullin; also led own bands. CDs: Steep.; EMI (Swed.); Drag.;

Liphone; w. Rolf Ericson (Amigo); Doug Raney (Steep.); Russell (SN); Don Cherry (Verve); Lars Gullin (Drag.); Monica Zetterlund (RCA).

ROSENTHAL, TED (THEODORE MARCUS), pno, comp, arr; b. Great Neck, NY, 11/15/59. Began on gtr. and tpt. Stud. at Manh. Sch. of Mus., then stud. arr. w. Manny Albam; Bob Brookmeyer; Meyer Kupferman. Pl. w. Jay Leonhart since 1988; Joe Roccisano bb '91; Jon Faddis '92; Gerry Mulligan fr. '92; also own trio and qnt. Rosenthal won first prize in the 1988 Thelonious Monk Int'l Jazz Piano Competition. He currently teaches piano and theory at Mannes Coll. of Mus. Favs: Tatum, Bud Powell, Hancock. Fests: Eur. w. Mulligan '92. TV: Night Music w. David Sanborn, Jean-Luc Ponty '89. CDs: Conc.; Ken; CTI; Rosenthal–Bill Charlap, *The Gerry Mulligan Songbook* (Chiaro.); w. Mulligan (Tel.); Randy Sandke (Conc.).

ROSNES, RENÉE (IRENE LOUISE), pno, comp; b. Regina, Sask., Canada, 3/24/62. Sisters pl. vln. and cello. Husband is dmr. Billy Drummond. Stud. vln. at Royal Cons. of Mus. in Vancouver, then introd. to jazz by hs mus. teacher. Stud. classical pno. at U. of Toronto for two yrs., then ret. to Vancouver and pl. w. visiting soloists incl. Dave Liebman, Joe Farrell. Moved to NYC 1986, pl. w. Out of the Blue '87–9; Joe Henderson '87; Wayne Shorter, J. J. Johnson '88; Jon Faddis '88–91; James Moody, Frank Morgan, Robin Eubanks–Steve Turre '90; Buster Williams since '90; David "Fathead" Newman '91; Ralph Moore since '91; also own trio. Favs: Cedar Walton, Hancock, Monk, Tyner. Polls: *DB* TDWR '88–90; *Radio & Records* '90. Fests: Eur. since '87; Jap. since '89; New Zealand '90. TV: Chicago JF video w. Ralph Moore '91. CDs: BN; w. B. Drummond (CC); OTB (BN); H. Alden (Conc.); Ray Drummond (Arab.); Joe Henderson (BN); V. Herring (MM); J. J. Johnson (EM.; Verve); NH Ø Pederson (Mile.); Greg Osby (JMT).

ROSOLINO, FRANK, tbn, comp, voc; b. Detroit, MI, 8/20/26; d. Los Angeles, CA, 11/26/78. All-musical family. Gtr. at 10; tbn. in hs. Army band at age 18 for two yrs. Pl. w. Bob Chester 1946–7; Glen Gray '47; Gene Krupa '48–9; earning recognition there as a tbnst. and scat/comedy singer; later w. Tony Pastor end of '49; Herbie Fields '50; Geo. Auld '51; own gp. in Detroit in early '50s; Stan Kenton '52–4. Settled in Calif., working at Lighthouse in late '50s. Countless sound track and rec. dates w. Quincy Jones, Elmer Bernstein, et al; Eur. visits w. Conte Candoli; tour. US w. Benny Carter; pl. w. Supersax in '70s. Rosolino's expressive style, individual sound, and humorous touches, both in his playing and singing, established him as an outstanding performer on the LA scene. He died tragically, a suicide, killing one small son and wounding another. Fests: MJF; Concord; Charlie Parker Memorial, KC, w. Supersax; Dick Gibson Colo. JPs. Poll: tied for first, *DB* Critics New Star '53. Film: short, *Deep Purple* w. Krupa, in which he sings "Lemon Drop," '49; on screen and soundtrack, *I Want to Live* '58; soundtracks: *Hotel* '67; *The Hot Rock* '71. TV: w. Steve Allen '62–4; *M Squad*; Merv Griffin Show. Comp: "Blue Daniel." CDs: D-T; VSOP; Spec.; own qt. in *Swing . . . Not Spring* (Sav.); w. Kenton (Cap.); B. Collette; Bob Cooper; T. Gibbs; H. Humes; B. Carter; Howard Rumsey (Cont.); Z. Sims (Vogue; Pab.); Chet Baker (PJ); C. Candoli; Dexter Gordon; Richie Kamuca (FS); Jack Sheldon (VSOP); S. Stitt (Verve).

ROSS, ANNIE (Annabelle McCauley Allan Short), voc, songwriter; b. Mitcham, England, 7/26/30. To US 1933 w. her aunt, singer and actress Ella Logan; raised in Los Angeles. App. in *Our Gang* comedies and pl. Judy Garland's sister in *Presenting Lily Mars* '42. Stud. acting NYC. Ret. to Engl. '47, pl. lead in *Burlesque*; teamed w. songwriter Hugh Martin in night club act. Worked in France w. bands of Bernard Hilda; Emil Stern; Jack Dieval. Ret. to US '50 and created a sensation with her vocalese lyrics to Wardell Gray's "Twisted" and Art Farmer's "Farmer's Market." Tour. for two wks. w. L. Hampton's orch. in Eur. summer '53; then, after ret. to the Paris night club circuit, sang in Engl. w. bands of Jack Parnell and Tony Crombie. Scored a hit in London revue, *Cranks*, and later, after pl. in it on Broadway, remain. in the US. While working w. a vocal gp. on the Patrice Munsel TV series '57–8, she teamed with Dave Lambert and Jon Hendricks to record a multi-taped LP titled *Sing a Song of Basie* using vocalese techniques. The success of the album led to the formation of Lambert, Hendricks & Ross on a permanent basis in Sept. '58. Rec. for Columbia, they soared to national popularity. In '62 Ross left the group to pursue solo interests as an actress and singer, freelancing in Engl. Partner in club, Annie's Room '65–6; also app. at Ronnie Scott's and Eur. fests. incl. Warsaw, Bologna '65; Frankfurt '66. From '70s starred w. Vanessa Redgrave in *The Threepenny Opera*; app. in Kurt Weill program w. André Previn at Royal Fest. Hall; *Seven Deadly Sins* w. Royal Ballet; and *Tonight We Improvise*. Ret. to US '85, she acted in many films and has cont. to perform as a vocalist on both sides of the Atlantic, fr. the Algonquin, NYC, to Pizza on the Park, London, mostly as a single but incl. a brief reunion w. Hendricks at the Blue Note in mid '90s. In '98 she and Hendricks began perf. together again. She remains a definitive exponent of pure, jazz-inspired singing. Favs: David Allyn, Ernestine Anderson, Gladys Knight, Gail Wynters. Other lyrics: "Jackie"; "Music Is Forever." Films: *Throw Mama from the Train: Superman; Pump Up the Volume; The Player; Short Cuts*. English TV series: *Send in the Girls*. CDs: PJ; DRG; *King Pleasure Sings/Annie Ross Sings; The Bebop Singers* (Prest.); w. L,H&R (Col.; Rh.; Imp.); soundtrack fr. *Short Cuts* (Imago).

ROSS, ARNOLD (Rosenberg), pno; b. Boston, 1/29/21; d. Venice, CA, 6/5/00. Studied cl., sax, vln., pno. Tour. So. America, West Indies in ships' orchs. 1937–8; pl. Hammond organ w. Frank Dailey '38–9; pno. w. Jack Jenney '39; Vaughn Monroe '40–2; Glenn Miller's army band '43–4; Harry James '44–7. Pl. w. JATP '46; Charlie Parker '47. In late '40s, early '50s freelanced in California; toured Europe w. Lena Horne '52. Pianist, arr., and cond. for Bob Crosby TV show '54–6; Spike Jones TV series '57–8. Led various gps. of his own late '50s; accomp. Billy Eckstine; rec. w. Dave Pell; Barney Kessel; Nelson Riddle; et al. Narcotics addiction caught up with him in the late '50s. Entered the Synanon Foundation in Santa Monica, Calif., July '60. Cured, he became active in the organization of Synanon. Took part in LP, *Sounds of Synanon*, w. Joe Pass and others for Pacific Jazz. From mid '60s to mid '70s worked w. Riddle; other studio work w. Paul Weston, Johnny Mann; accomp. for Edie Adams; Jane Russell; Frances Wayne. Rec. w. own trio for Nocturne '73. Cont. perf. into '90s. Film: *Synanon* '64. CDs: w. JATP (Verve); D. Gillespie (Vogue); tracks in *Sunset Swing* (BL); Willie Smith w. Harry James (Col.).

ROSS, RONNIE (ALBERT RONALD), bari sax; b. Calcutta, India, 10/2/33; d. London, England, 12/12/91. Started on tnr. sax. Went to Engl. 1946. In mid '50s pl. w. Tony Kinsey; Ted Heath; Don Rendell, where he sw. to bari. sax. App. w. Marshall Brown's Int'l Youth Band at NJF '58. Form. Jazz Makers w. Alan Ganley '58; tour. US '59. Tour. Eur. w. MJQ '59. Later pl. in Engl. w. Anglo-American band led by Woody Herman. Led qnt. w. Bill Le Sage '61–5. Led own qt. '86. Generally acknowledged to be one of England's outstanding bari. sax soloists. Dur. '60s rec. w. John Dankworth; Clark-Boland; Friedrich Gulda; and in '70s w. Clark Terry. LP: *European Windows* w. John Lewis (RCA) '58. Solo on singer Lou Reed's *Walk on the Wild Side* '72. CDs: w. Reed (RCA); Clark Terry (MPS).

ROSSY, JORDI (JORGE), dms, tpt, pno; b. Barcelona, Spain, 8/21/64. Father pl. acdn., gtr. Bro. Mario is prof. bassist; late sist. Mercedes pl. pno. and comp. Stud. classical perc. in Barcelona 1976–81; tpt. major at Berklee Coll. '89–90. Worked w. many bands in Spain, pl. dms. and tpt., rec. ten LP. Occ. pl. for rec., TV, and fests. w. Woody Shaw; Jack Walrath; Dave Schnitter; Kenny Wheeler '85–9. In Boston '89–90, pl. w. Bill Pierce; Danilo Perez; Joshua Redman; Paquito D'Rivera. Tour. Eur., US, Japan w. D'Rivera; gigs in NYC and Spain w. Brad Mehldau '91–2; Mehldau, Mark Turner qt., Perico Sambeat, Kurt Rosenwinkel, Chris Cheek, Seamus Blake, and Int'l Hashua Orch. '93–5. Worked primarily w. Mehldau but also w. the Bloom Daddies (Blake and Cheek, etc.) and occ. the Int'l Hashua Orch. '97–8. Taught dms., tpt., combo (improv.), Barcelona '85–9. Favs: Ed Blackwell, Elvin Jones, Al Foster. Won several awards in Spain: classical perc. '82; comp. '86; w. bands of which he was a member, Spanish TV '85–9. Awarded second prize in Thelonious Monk Drum Competition '92. CDs: Mehldau-Rossy Trio (FS); w. Mehldau (WB); Sambeat; Cheek; Mercedes Rossy Memorial Concert; Rosenwinkel (FS); Avishai Cohen (Stretch); Mark Turner; The Bloom Daddies (CC).

ROSTAING, HUBERT, tnr sax, cl; b. Lyons, France, 9/17/18. Studied at cons. in Algiers, where he pl. w. the Red Hotters. Moved to Paris 1939; pl. sax and bandoneon at Mimi Pinson's Club. Replaced Stephane Grappelli in Quintet of Hot Club of France, mainly pl. cl. '40–8; also rec. w. Aime Barelli during same period. From '60s was mainly involved in writing music for films. CDs: w. Reinhardt (EMI; DRG; Verve; GNP Cres.).

ROTONDI, JIM (JAMES ROBERT), tpt, pno; b. Butte, MT, 8/28/62. Mother, Ruth, is pno. teacher. Took up pno. at 8; parents required all five children to do so fr. that age. Stud. tpt. fr. 12 in Butte public sch. system. Grad. fr. No. Tex. St. U., B. Mus., 1985. Worked for six mos. on Premier Cruise Lines, Cape Canaveral, Fla. '86; tour. US w. Off-B'way revue *Beehive* for two mos. '87; tour. in US, Eur., Japan and rec. w. Ray Charles Orch. '91–2. Pl. w. Junior Cook and Cecil Payne '91–5; w. Lionel Hampton Orch. fr. '95. Pl. w. George Coleman Oct., NYC '95; Michael Weiss Sxt. '95–7; Lou Donaldson Qt., Qnt. '96–7. Co-founded gp. One For All w. Eric Alexander, Steve Davis, Dave Hazeltine, Peter Washington, Joe Farnsworth '96. Pl. w. Curtis Fuller Sxt. fr. '97. Teaches priv. Favs: Cliff. Brown, F. Hubbard, Miles Davis. Fest: Nice w. Hampton '97. Co-winner, Int'l Trumpet Guild Jazz Tpt. Competition '84. TV: w. Ray Charles, *50 Years in Show Business*, Fox. Rec. debut w. E. Alexander '92. CDs: CC; w. One For All (Sharp Nine); Alexander (Del.; Alfa); Steve Davis

(CC); Hazeltine; Ray Appleton (Sharp Nine); Charles Earland (High.); John Pizzarelli (RCA).

ROUSE, CHARLIE (CHARLES), tnr sax; b. Washington, DC, 4/6/24; d. Seattle, WA, 11/30/88. Studied cl. at Howard U., pl. tnr. sax w. B. Eckstine Orch. 1944; D. Gillespie bb '45; recs. w. Tadd Dameron, Fats Navarro '47; R&B dates in Washington, NYC; D. Ellington May '49–Mar. '50. Briefly w. Basie small group '50. Rec. w. Clifford Brown '53, pl., w. tbnst. Bennie Green's qnt., O. Pettiford Sxt. Co-leader w. Julius Watkins of Jazz Modes '56–8; w. Buddy Rich '59. Main association w. T. Monk Quartet 1959–70; also freelanced extensively. Inactive in music for a while, then w. cellist Calo Scott bef. join. the cooperative group Sphere '82. Though his long tenure w. Monk led to his being called a virtual extension of the pianist, Rouse was a strong, bop-rooted individualist whose mastery was well displayed in his work w. Sphere. Video: *Straight No Chaser* w. Monk. CDs: 32; Col.-Epic; Jzld.; Land.; Up.; Enja; W. Les Jazz Modes (Biog.); Monk (Riv.; Col.); *Fats Navarro and Tadd Dameron*; Clifford Brown (BN); Sphere (Verve; Red); G. Mulligan (Col.).

ROVERE, BIBI (GILBERT), bs; b. Toulon, France, 8/29/39. Studied Nice Cons. 1954. After working w. Barney Wilen '57–9, was heard in '60s at Blue Note in Paris w. Bud Powell; Kenny Drew; Johnny Griffin; Dexter Gordon; Kenny Clarke; briefly w. D. Ellington '64. Pl. w. pnst. Art Simmons at Living Room in Paris '64–5; member of Martial Solal Trio '62–74. Also worked w. Clark Terry; Sonny Stitt; Stephane Grappelli; et al. Retired in '78 but ret. to active pl. in '86, app. w. Steve Grossman; Bud Shank; Jackie McLean. Highly regarded by both French and American jazz men as a strong section and solo bassist. Fests: many in France; Pescara w. Tom Kirkpatrick '98. Won Prix Django Reinhardt fr. French Jazz Academy '67. CDs: w. S. Grossman (Timel.); B. Powell (MS).

ROWLES, JIMMY (James Polk Hunter), pno, comp, voc; b. Spokane, WA, 8/19/18; d. Burbank, CA, 5/28/96. Began pl. in freshman yr. at Gonzaga U. Self-taught. Pl. in local bands. Moved to LA 1940, pl. first w. the dance bands of Garwood Van and Muzzy Marcellino. Ben Webster helped him get start. in jazz w. Slim Gaillard '41; join. Lester and Lee Young's gp. '41–2; also worked w. Billie Holiday. Five mos. w. Benny Goodman '42; Woody Herman '42–3. While in service pl. w. Skinnay Ennis's army band. Rejoin. Herman '46. Worked w. Les Brown, T. Dorsey, Goodman, Butch Stone '47; Bob Crosby '47–51. Freelanced extensively in LA w. Peggy Lee;

Betty Hutton; Josephine Premice; Billie Holiday; Stan Getz; Chet Baker; Charlie Parker; Benny Carter; Zoot Sims. Very active movie studio and TV work '40s-60s, incl. ongoing collab. w. Henry Mancini. In '73 took part in tribute to Art Tatum at NJF-NY. After living in NYC off and on for five years, pl. at The Cookery, Bradley's, etc., tour. w. Ella Fitzgerald for three years, then ret. to Calif. Semi-inactive from late '80s due to ill health but appeared often w. his daughter, tptr. Stacy Rowles. In later yrs. he became well known as a composer: his "Ballad of Thelonious Monk" was rec. by Carmen McRae; "The Peacocks" was feat. in the film *Round Midnight*, and rec. by Stan Getz, Marian McPartland, Branford Marsalis, Gary Foster, and Rowles himself. In '86 he was the honoree of the LA Jazz Society. Frequently cited as the favorite accompanist of many singers, Rowles was an artist of consummate harmonic imagination. For many years he specialized in building a repertoire of Ellington and Strayhorn compositions. Fav: Tatum. LPs: as lead. and sideman *America the Beautiful* w. Al Cohn, French Col.; Xan. CDs: Capri; Delos; JVC; Koko.; w. Ray Brown (Conc.); S. Getz (Col.); Herbie Harper; H. Babasin; B. Shank (Noct.); Zoot Sims (Pab.); Dexter Gordon (Stash).

ROWLES, STACY, tpt, flg, voc; b. Los Angeles, LA, 9/11/55. Father, pnst. Jimmy Rowles, showed her the scales on his old army trumpet; stud. priv.; voted "best soloist" on flg. in contest at Orange Coast Coll. Pl. in. all-female band led by Clark Terry 1975; start. in '79, was founding member of Maiden Voyage bb; also pl. w. Jazz Birds, an off-shoot of the band; app. at. Women's Jazz Festival, KC '80; toured w. female gp., sxt., Alive! '80s. Made rec. debut '84 on Concord. Pl. w. guitarist Nels Cline '87; app. frequently with her fath. in nightclubs and on records. A respected and creative artist, Rowles plays w. the kind of warmth and precision long associated w. her fath, music. CDs: w. Jimmy Rowles (Delos); Nels Cline (Enja).

ROWSER, JIMMY (JAMES EDWARD), bs; b. Philadelphia, PA, 4/18/26. Studied w. Anthony Quintelli in Phila. Pl. w. house band at Blue Note, Phila. '54–6; Dinah Washington '56–7; Maynard Ferguson '57–9; Red Garland, Lee Morgan '59; Dinah Washington '59–60; Junior Mance '61; Herb Ellis, Illinois Jacquet '62; Benny Goodman '63; Frederich Gulda '64; also freelanced w. Ray Bryant, Al Cohn–Zoot Sims. Pl. w. Les McCann fr. '69; Ray Bryant '80s-90s; duo w. Hilton Ruiz since '84. Rowser received a B.S. and M.A. from the City Univ. of NY in '88 and teaches beginning strings in the South Orange-Maplewood, N.J. school system. Fests: Eur., Asia,

Africa, So. Amer., etc., since late '50s. Film: *Soul to Soul* w. Les McCann '71. CDs: w. D. Washington (Em.); R. Bryant (Pab.); Red Garland (Prest.).

ROY, TEDDY (THEODORE GERALD), pno; b. Duquoin, IL, 4/9/05; d. NYC, 8/31/66. Cornet for seven years, then pno.; in Chi. w. Coon-Sanders Orch.; Bost. w. Pee Wee Russell, Bobby Hackett 1933; own band in Mass., w. Max Kaminsky 45–6; pl. w. revived Original Dixieland Jazz Band '46, but many jobs outside music in early '40s; army '43–5. Freelanced in NYC w. Miff Mole; Wingy Manone; at Condon's Club. CDs: w. Eddie Edwards and ODJB in *The Commodore Story* (Story.).

ROYAL, ERNIE (ERNEST ANDREW), tpt.; b. Los Angeles, CA, 6/2/21; d. NYC, 3/16/83. Brother of Marshal Royal. Att. LA Jr. Coll. Worked w. Les Hite 1937–8; Cee Pee Johnson '39; Lionel Hampton '40–2; navy band '42–5. With Vernon Alley in SF; in Hollywood w. The Phil Moore Four, Count Basie '46. Join. Woody Herman's Second Herd '47–9. Then Ch. Barnet, D. Ellington summer '50. Two years in Paris with Jacques Helian; tour. Europe and No. Africa. Combo w. Wardell Gray '52; Stan Kenton Jan.-Aug. '53 and again '55. Staff musician ABC in NYC '57–72; also countless dates w. Q. Jones; O. Nelson; G. Evans; also Broadway shows, etc. Europe w. Friedrich Gulda, later with NYJRC. Although renowned for his lead playing and high note finales, Royal was also a talented soloist coming out of a swing-era background but not untouched by Gillespie and Navarro. CDs: Herman (Col.; Cap.); C. Hawkins (Drive Archive); Billy Taylor (Imp.).

ROYAL, GREGORY CHARLES, tbn; b. Greensboro, NC, 10/10/61. Studied from 4th grade in Washington, D.C., Youth Orch. prog. until 1978. Toured w. Art Blakey '79–80; Slide Hampton's World of Trombones '83–84. Stud., later taught music theory at D. Ellington Sch. of Arts '85; instructor and band member at Clark Terry Jazz Camp '85. Tour. Africa w. Howard U. Sxt. '87. Pl. in show *Ain't Misbehavin'* at Nat'l Theater '88. Joined Ellington Orch. '88, tour. extensively in Eur., Japan, and US under Mercer Ellington's leadership. Favs: Curtis Fuller, Slide Hampton, Buster Cooper. CD: Mercer Ellington (MM).

ROYAL, MARSHAL WALTON, alto sax, cl; b. Sapulpa, OK, 12/5/12; d. Inglewood, CA, 5/8/95. Studied vln., gtr., reeds; prof. debut at age 13. Worked w. local bands and Curtis Mosby 1929; w. Les Hite '31–9. Pl. w. Cee Pee Johnson '40; L. Hampton '40–2. Navy service '42–6. Pl. in NYC w. Eddie Heywood '46; then moved to West Coast and studio work '46. After pl. w. C. Basie Octet '50, helped him to organize new band '51, remaining until '70. Free-lanced in LA w. various big bands, incl. Bill Berry and Capp-Pierce Juggernaut. In '89 was lead alto sax w. F. Wess bb. A fine lead alto player and an effective soloist in many styles of jazz and pop music, he has often been compared to Benny Carter. Film: w. Ellington, *Belle of the Nineties* '34. Stage: nine months pl. for LA prod. of *Sophisticated Ladies*. Book: *Marshal Royal, Jazz Survivor* w. Claire Gordon (Cassell). Rec. w. Art Tatum Swingsters (Decca) '37. CDs: Conc.; Royal–Snooky Young (Conc.); w. Tatum (Dec.); Basie (Verve; Roul.; Mos.); L. Hampton (BB; Class.); Capp-Pierce; Berry (Conc.).

RUBALCABA, GONZALO, pno, comp; b. Havana, Cuba, 5/27/63. Offspring of a long line of musicians; studied at Havana Cons. Began rec. while still a teenager, prod. nearly an album a yr., incl. one w. Dizzy Gillespie, rec. live in Havana. Since 1980 frequently worked outside Cuba; tour. France and Africa w. Orquesta Aragon; also pl. Germ. and Engl. w. his own fusion gp., Projecto. Until '92 political differences between Cuba and the US made it impossible for Rubalcaba to receive a visa to visit the US. He has been best known via recs. made in Can. and Eur. and released in the US on the Rounder and Blue Note labels. A powerful pnst. with a strong, articulate touch. Some felt Rubalcaba's rec. work brings a startling new perspective to such familiar works as Thelonious Monk's "Well You Needn't" while others put it in the category of grandstanding. CDs: BN; Mess.; w. J. Bunnett (Den.).

RUBIN, VANESSA KAY, voc, fl, pno; b. Cleveland, OH, 3/14/57. Brother Michael is percst.; bro. Quentin is gtrst. Stud. classical voice and led r&b vocal trio in hs; later stud. w. Newman Copeland; John Motley; Barry Harris in NYC. Received B.A. in journalism fr. Ohio St. U. 1978; taught English in Cleve. publ. schools '79–82. Sang in Cleve. w. Blackshaw Bros.; Dewey Jeffries; Willie Smith's Little Big Band. Jazz All-Stars '80–2. Moved to NYC '82. First NYC gig w. Pharaoh Sanders at Vanguard '82. Sang w. Mercer Ellington '83; Frank Foster's Loud Minority '85; Lionel Hampton Orch. '87; also w. Kenny Barron; John Hicks; Kirk Lightsey; T. Blanchard. Led a sxt. w. Aaron Graves, Tarik Shaw, Aaron Walker, Eddie Allen, Roger Byam. She was dean of students at Prospect Hts. HS in Bklyn. '84–91. Favs: Vaughan, McRae, Nancy Wilson, Fitzgerald. Fests: Eur. fr. '87; Asia fr. '88. TV: Jap. TV '90; *Tonight Show* '92. CDs: Novus; w. Cecil Bridgewater (BM).

RUCKER, ELLYN KAY, kybds, voc; b. Des Moines, IA, 8/29/37. Musical family; stud. pno from age 8. Worked in local clubs through 1960s and '70s, occ. accomp. such perf. as Kenny Burrell; James Moody; Roy Eldridge; etc. Began to tour int'l in mid '80s, sometimes w. Spike Robinson qt., sometimes w. own gps. or as soloist. Many apps. at North Sea JF, Cork JF, as well as France, Germ., Holland, Switz., etc., '85–91. CDs: Capri.

RUDD, ROSWELL HOPKINS JR., tbn, comp; also Fr horn, pno, perc; b. Sharon, CT, 11/17/35. Parents both amateur musicians. Studied Fr. horn fr. age 11; self-taught on tbn. Stud. at Yale U. 1954–8. Pl. in NYC w. Eli's Chosen Six '54–9; Herbie Nichols '60–3; also freelanced w. Wild Bill Davison; Bud Freeman; Ed Hall; Eddie Condon early to mid-'60s. Pl. w. Steve Lacy–Dennis Charles '61–3; Bill Dixon '62; NY Art Qt. w. John Tchicai, Milford Graves '64–5. Worked as staff musicologist for folklorist-ethnomusicologist Alan Lomax fr. '64. Tour. Denmark, Netherlands '65. Pl. w. Archie Shepp '65–7; then led own gp., Primordial Qt., w. Robin Kenyatta, Karl Berger, Lee Konitz '68–70. Also pl. w. Charlie Haden's Liberation Music Orch. '69; Gato Barbieri '69–70. Freelanced w. Chas. Davis; Perry Robinson; Albert Ayler; Cecil Taylor; Enrico Rava; others late '60s-70s. Led own gp. Roswell Rudd and Friends w. Sheila Jordan, Beaver Harris, early '70s. Pl. w. Jazz Composers Orch. '70–80s. Taught world music and jazz improv. at Bard Coll. '73–5. Led own combo at St. James Infirmary, NYC '74–5. Pl. w. Monk Project w. S. Lacy, Misha Mengelberg '82. Rudd was professor of music ethnology at the U. of Maine in '80s. Many of his comps. attempt to illustrate the connections bet. jazz, European classical music, and various world musics. Pl. trad. jazz w. local bands in upstate NY early '90s. Reunited w. NY Art Qt. at Bell Atlantic JF, NYC '99. Fav. comps: Ellington, Monk. Polls: *DB* New Star '63. Film: app. as dixie. mus. in *The Hustler*. CDs: *The Unheard Herbie Nichols* (CIMP), w. Archie Shepp (Imp.); Cecil Taylor (Cand.; Mos.); Lacy (BS).

RUEGG, MATHIAS, comp/arr, cond, pno; b. Zurich, Switzerland, 12/8/52. Studied comp. and arr. in Graz and Vienna while working as a pnst. during the 1970s. He moved fr. Switz. to Austria in '76 and the following yr. founded the Vienna Art Orch., a scaled-down big band incl. tba.; and vocalese fr. Lauren Newton. The orch. pl. the Berlin JF '81; Jazz Yatra, Bombay; US; Can. '84; toured extensively in Eur. '85. Key sidemen incl. Herbert Joos, Karl "Bumi" Fian, tpt.; Roman Schwaller, Wolfgang Puschnig, saxes; Woody Schabata, vibes; Uli Scherer, pno. Guest artists have incl. Art Farmer; John Surman; Karin Krog; and tbnst. George Lewis. Ruegg's eclecticism is displayed in his repertory, which encompasses Scott Joplin; Jelly Roll Morton; Mingus; Hans Koller; Ornette Coleman; Anthony Braxton; Lennie Tristano; and Erik Satie. He devoted an entire album to interpreting Satie's themes: *The Minimalism of Erik Satie*. In '83 he form. the Vienna Art Choir, which consists of ten to twelve singers and has been accomp. by members of the VAO. Polls: *DB* Critics best bb '84–5; best arr. '81–6. CDs: hatArt; Moers; Amadeo.

RUFF, WILLIE HENRY JR., bs, Fr horn; b. Sheffield, AL, 9/1/31. Learned Fr. horn while in army; met Dwike Mitchell while pl. in band at Lockbourne, Ohio, army base. Stud. w. Paul Hindemith at Yale U. (B. Mus, 1953, M. Mus. '54). While at Yale, gigged w. Benny Goodman. Pl. w. Lionel Hampton '55, then formed duo w. Mitchell. In '59, while on tour w. the Yale Russian Chorus, the Mitchell-Ruff duo became the first modern jazz gp. to perf. in Moscow at an impromptu concert at the Tchaikovsky Cons. In the early '60s the gp. added drummer Charlie Smith (later repl. by Helcio Milito). Pl. at Hickory House, NYC '66. Mitchell and Ruff traveled w. Pres. Johnson on goodwill diplomatic mission to Mexico '66. Made film in Brazil, tracing African roots of Brazilian music '67. As a professor of music at Yale, Ruff founded the Duke Ellington Fellowship Prog. '72. Rec. w. Mitchell and Dizzy Gillespie '70–1. Rec. version of *Harmonices Mundi*, a treatise by the German mathematician and music theorist Johannes Kepler, w. help of scientist John Rodgers '81. Perf. w. Mitchell in China '79; rec. as unaccomp. soloist in St. Mark's Basilica, Venice '83. Favs: Ray Brown, Pettiford. Book: *Willie and Dwike: an American Profile*, William Zinsser, '84. LP: w. Dizzy Gillespie & Mitchell-Ruff (Main.). CD: Mitchell-Ruff in *Atlantic Jazz Keyboards* (Rh.); w. Gil Evans (Prest.).

RUGOLO, PETE, arr; comp; b. San Piero, Sicily, 12/25/15. Came to the US at age 5. Raised in Santa Rosa, Calif. Stud. at Mills College in Oakland w. Darius Milhaud. Best known as chief arr. for Stan Kenton 1945–9 and as rec. producer for Cap. (responsible for the famous Miles Davis "Birth of the Cool" sess. '49–50). Led bb in '54, rec. for Col. With Mercury Recs. as rec. dir. '57; rec. w. his own band in late '50s, mainly active outside jazz, writing for movies and TV. Among the jazz-related perfs. he has arr. and cond. for are Nat "King" Cole; Billy Eckstine; Dinah Washington; Peggy Lee; Woody Herman; Mel Tormé. He won the *DB* poll as Best Arr. '47, '49–51, '54; also received several Emmy awards and nomina-

tions. CDs: w. Ernestine Anderson (Merc.); B. Eckstine (Em.); Nat Cole; Stan Kenton (Cap.).

RUIZ, HILTON, pno, kybd; b. NYC, 5/29/52; d. New Orleans, 6/6/06. Studied w. Santiago Messorana 1957–9; classical w. Geo. Armstrong fr. '59; Mary Lou Williams '71; Cedar Walton '72; Harold Mabern '72–3; Chris Anderson '75. Perf. at Carnegie Recital Hall at age 8. Pl. w. Joe Newman '70–92; Geo. Coleman, Clark Terry fr. '70; Cal Massey bb '71–2; Frank Foster '71–4; Major Holley '71–90; Freddie Hubbard, Joe Henderson '72; Jackie McLean, Charles Mingus '73; Rahsaan Roland Kirk fr. '73; Betty Carter '74; Rashied Ali '74–5; Pharaoh Sanders '79–80; F. Hubbard, Paquito D'Rivera '82–3; Abbey Lincoln '84–5; duo w. Jimmy Rowser fr. '84; also perf. on soundtrack to Woody Allen's *Crimes and Misdemeanors* '91. Co-author of a pno. method, *Jazz and How to Play It*. Guest of honor at the Heineken JF in San Juan, PR '89. A fiery player, adept in Latin, jazz, and any combination of the two. Infls: Tyner, Monk, Waller, Tatum, Hancock. Fests: Japan w. P. D'Rivera, F. Hubbard '83. CDs: Novus; Stash; Trop.; Dragon Rose; Tel.; w. R. R. Kirk (Atl.; Night); David "Fathead" Newman (Mile.); T. Puente (Trop.; Conc.); Afro Blue Band (Mile.); M. Santamaria (Mile.); Mario Rivera (GH).

RUMSEY, HOWARD EUGENE, bs; b. Brawley, CA, 11/7/17. Studied bs. in Chi. and LA. Pl. w. Vido Musso 1938; Johnny "Scat" Davis '39–40; Stan Kenton '41–42; Freddie Slack '44; Charlie Barnet '45. Organized Lighthouse All-Stars '50–60, incl. Bob Cooper; Shorty Rogers; Bud Shank; Max Roach; Stan Levey; et al. Rumsey operated the Lighthouse in Hermosa Beach fr. '61–71 (he gave up pl. bs. around '68), and fr. '72 to '85 had his own club, Concerts by the Sea, in Redondo Beach. In '85 he retired to Hemet, Calif. CDs: Lighthouse All-Stars (Cont.); w. C. Barnet (Dec.); S. Kenton (M&A).

RUSHEN, PATRICE LOUISE, pno, synths, comp; b. Los Angeles, CA, 9/30/54. Studied at USC; pno. w. Earl Hultberg 1960–3; Dorothy Bishop '63–72. Won awards w. Locke HS band in LA. In teens, tour. w. Leslie Drayton; Melba Liston; Abbey Lincoln; Gerald Wilson Orch. Pl. w. The Meeting '80–93; Santana-Shorter Project '88; Prince '90; TV/film comp. for *Women of Brewster Place; Hollywood Shuffle*. Mus. dir. for many shows incl. *Robert Townsend Comedy Hour* '89; *NAACP Image Awards* annually from '89; *Emmy Awards* '91, '92; *Sandra Bernhard After Dark* '92; *Comic Relief V* '92. Rushen, who names Herbie Hancock, McCoy Tyner, Keith Jarrett, Thad Jones, Gil Evans, Joe Henderson, and Oscar

Peterson as infl., is an artist of great talent who has shown increasing maturity as comp., cond., and pnst. CDs: Prest.; w. J. McLaughlin; Wayne Shorter (Col.); S. Rollins (Mile.); Terri Lyne Carrington (Verve); Jean-Luc Ponty (Atl.; WB); Paul Jackson Jr. (Atl.); S. Turrentine (Fant.); Joe Williams (Tel.); Gene Dunlap (Avenue Jazz).

RUSHING, JIMMY (JAMES ANDREW; aka MR. FIVE-BY-FIVE), voc; b. Oklahoma City, OK, 8/26/03; d. NYC, 6/8/72. Musical family; pl. vln., pno. by ear. Early gigs in So. Calif. w. Jelly Roll Morton; Harvey Brooks; Paul Howard 1920s. Member of Walter Page Blue Devils '27–9; Bennie Moten orch. '29–35; Count Basie '35–50. Toured w. own spt. for two yrs., then as single from June '52. Eur. w. Humphrey Lyttelton, Buck Clayton, B. Goodman '61; Japan w. E. Condon '64. Acting role in film, *The Learning Tree*. His last album, *The You and Me That Used To Be*, was voted Record of the Year in the '72 *DB* Critics Poll; also voted Best Male Singer in the same poll. In last yrs, often seen at the Half Note in NYC w. Al Cohn, Zoot Sims. Rushing's distinctive timbre, ebullient delivery, and rhythmic drive established him as an outstanding blues shouter, although he himself considered the blues tag to be too restricting. Indeed, he was a warm, personal interpreter of non-blues material. CDs: Col.; BB; w. Basie (Dec.; Col.; Verve); Moten (BB); Goodman (MM); Brubeck (Col.).

RUSHTON, JOE (JOSEPH AUGUSTINE JR.), bs sax, cl; b. Evanston, IL, 4/19/07; d. San Francisco, CA, 3/2/64. Played all other saxes bef. concentrating on bs. sax in 1928. Played in Chi. w. his own band '28–32; w. Ted Weems '34; Jimmy McPartland, Bud Freeman, et al. NYC w. B. Goodman '42–3; soundtrack of film, *The Gang's All Here* '43. Settled in Calif. '43; w. Horace Heidt '43–5; Red Nichols '47–63. Film, *The Five Pennies* '58. Various nonmusical jobs in aircraft industry in '40s. Only mus. after Adrian Rollini to make effective use of the bs. sax as a solo vehicle until Scott Robinson. CD: w. Nichols (Jazz.).

RUSSELL, CURLY (DILLON), bs; b. NYC, 3/19/20; d. NYC, 7/3/86. Played tbn. and bs. in YMCA Symph. Worked w. Don Redman 1941; Benny Carter '43. In NYC from '44; pl. on first Dizzy Gillespie combo dates and was best-known and possibly most-rec. bebop bassist. Worked w. Art Blakey, Stan Getz, Coleman Hawkins, Charlie Parker, M. Davis, B. Powell to mid 50s. Tour. w. Buddy DeFranco '52; from late '50s w. local r&b gps. CDs: w. Parker (Sav.; Verve; Rh.); Gillespie (Verve);

Blakey (BN); Bud Powell (Roul.; Verve); Clifford Jordan; F. Navarro–T. Dameron (BN); Clifford Brown (PJ); S. Stitt (Prest.).

RUSSELL, GENE (WILLIAM EUGENE), pno, comp; b. Los Angeles, CA, 12/2/32; d. Los Angeles, 5/3/81. Cousin of Charlie Christian. Stud. w. Hampton Hawes, et al. Active in LA in 1960s writing mus. for films and TV. Also app. as actor and founded Black Jazz Recs in '70s. Pl. in gps. led by Rahsaan Roland Kirk; Zoot Sims; Leroy Vinnegar; Dexter Gordon; Wardell Gray; Miles Davis. Black Jazz rec. Harold Vick, Walter Bishop Jr., and Doug and Jean Carn.

RUSSELL, GEORGE ALLAN, comp, pno; b. Cincinnati, OH, 6/23/23. Father was mus. profess. at Oberlin Coll. As a child, pl. dms. in drum and bugle corps, then w. local bands in hs. Stud. at Wilberforce U. and pl. w. Collegians, who also incl. Ernie Wilkins. Contracted TB at age 19, stud. arr. w. another patient while recovering. Wrote first arrs. for A. B. Townsend Orch. at Cotton Club, Cincinnati. Arr. and pl. dms. for Benny Carter mid 1940s, then arr. show mus. for clubs in Chi.; also arr. for Earl Hines. In the late '40s moved to NYC where he met Charlie Parker; a health relapse prevented him fr. joining Parker's gp. Wrote historic Afro-Cuban arr. *Cubano Be–Cubano Bop* for Dizzy Gillespie Orch. '47; also comp. and arr. for Charlie Ventura; Claude Thornhill; Artie Shaw; Buddy DeFranco. Comp. and arr. for Lee Konitz, incl. "Ezz-thetic," "Odjenar." Completed thesis on compositional theory, *The Lydian Chromatic Concept of Tonal Organization* '53. Rec. w. own gps. fr. '56. Taught at Lenox Sch. of Jazz '58–9. Tour. w. own sxt. '60–4. Moved to Scand. to teach, study, and exper. w. el. sound, mid '60s. Ret. to US '69. Has taught at New Engl. Cons. fr. '69. Comp. *Listen to the Silence* ("a mass for our times") '71. Worked on second volume of *Lydian Chromatic Concept*, did not compose '72–9. Formed NY bb '78. Formed Living Time Orch. '83. Russell has received numerous fellowships incl. MacArthur Found., Guggenheim (twice), NEA Jazz Master, six other NEA grants. He has taught and lectured at numerous Amer. and Eur. univs. Polls: British Jazz Awd., Oscar du Disque du Jazz, many other awds. Fests: all major fr. '60. His *New York, N.Y.* reissued on Impulse CD '98. CDs: BB; Imp.; Dec.; Stash; SN; BN; Riv.; Elec. Bird; w. H. Merrill (Merc.).

RUSSELL, LUIS CARL, lead, comp, pno; b. Careening Cay, a small island near Bocas Del Toro, Panama, 8/6/02; d. NYC, 12/11/63. Studied gtr., vln., and pno. At 17 won $3,000 in lottery and brought mother and sister to US. Pl. w. Albert Nicholas, B. Bigard, P. Barbarin, NO 1920; w. Ch. Cook, Freddie Keppard, and Jimmie Noone, Chi. '25; joined King Oliver at Plantation Club, Chi. '25; then to St. Louis and the Savoy Ballroom in NYC '27. Led own band fr. '27; rec. w. Louis Armstrong '29; Armstrong fronted Russell's band '35–43; back lead. own band '43–8; then quit mus. business to run candy and gift shops, and teach pno. and org. Russell led one of the outstanding bands of the late '20s w. such sidemen as Henry "Red" Allen; J. C. Higginbotham; Albert Nicholas; Charlie Holmes; and Teddy Hill. CDs: Collector's Classics; w. L. Armstrong (Dec., Col.); King Oliver (Dec.).

RUSSELL, PEE WEE (CHARLES ELLS-WORTH), cl; b. St. Louis, MO, 3/27/06; d. Alexandria, VA, 2/15/69. Studied priv. and att. Western Mil. Acad. and U. of Missouri. Prof. debut on the riverboats in St. Louis 1920; then to Mexico and the West Coast w. Herbert Berger. Worked w. Peck Kelley, Leon Roppolo. To Chi. in mid-20s to work w. Bix Beiderbecke, Frankie Trumbauer. Rec. "Feelin' No Pain" w. Red Nichols '27; thereafter, scores of small rec. gps. Moved to NYC '27; w. Louis Prima '35–7; often w. Eddie Condon, Red McKenzie, et al. Rare bb app. in '38 w. Bobby Hackett on cl. and (reluctantly) alto sax. Frequently at Nick's in Greenwich Village and Eddie Condon's in the '40s. Near fatal illness in SF 1951–3 brought national attention. Toured Eur. w. Geo. Wein '61; Japan, etc., w. E. Condon '64. Apps. at Newport and other jfs; rec. for Col. and perf. w. Thelonious Monk at NJF '63. One of the most distinctive musicians of Prohibition era, Russell had a plaintive tone and style, using so-called "dirty" tone and growl effects. In his later yrs. he worked seamlessly w. mus. of various styles and eras; also became an accomplished abstract painter. TV: *The Sound of Jazz*, CBS '57. CDs: Comm.; Prest.; w. Beiderbecke; R. Braff (BB); Fats Waller (BBC); E. Condon (Dec.; Mos.; Stash); Wild Bill Davison (Comm.); M. Kaminsky (Jazz.).

RUSSIN, BABE (IRVING), tnr sax; b. Pittsburgh, PA, 6/8/11; d. Los Angeles, CA, 8/4/84. Brother Jack a pnst. who pl. w. Red Nichols. Self-taught; pl. w. California Ramblers 1926; Smith Ballew Orch. '26–7; rec. and pl. off and on w. Red Nichols '27–32. B. Goodman orch.; Ben Pollack; and studio work; T. Dorsey '42–3. Rejoin. Goodman several times; seen in films *The Benny Goodman Story* and *The Glenn Miller Story*. In '70s tour. w. nostalgia bb shows; took part in Time-Life "Swing Era" re-creations on LP led by Glen Gray and Billy May. A strong exponent of the Coleman Hawkins sch. CDs: B. Holiday (Col.); T.

Dorsey (BB); B. Goodman (BB; Dec.); L. Armstrong (Vict.; Mos.); Raymond Scott (Stash); E. Fitzgerald (Verve); Tom Talbert (SB).

RUSSO, ANDY (ANTHONY C.), tbn; b. Brooklyn, NY, 7/8/03; d. Brooklyn, 9/16/58. Own NO jazz band in early 1920s. Radio staff work '30s; Jimmy Dorsey '42–5. From '49 until his death worked under various leaders in small gps., mostly at Nick's in Greenwich Village, NYC. Rec. w. Phil Napoleon for Jazzology. CDs: w. B. Berigan (Hep); J. Dorsey (Dec.).

RUSSO, BILL (WILLIAM JOSEPH), tbn, comp, lead; b. Chicago, IL, 6/25/28; d. Chicago, 1/11/03. Studied w. Lennie Tristano 1943–6 while pl. w. local bands. Led Experiment in Jazz orch. '48–9. Pl. w. and wrote for Stan Kenton '50–4; led own qnt. in Eur. '55; dur. late '50s moved to NYC and taught at Sch. of Jazz in Lenox, Mass. In Rome and London '61–5; worked for the BBC and Brit. jazz orch. Returned to Chi. '65 as dir. of Center for New Mus. at Columbia Coll. Wrote for Kenton Neophonic '66. Form. Chi. Jazz Ensemble. In '70s spent a yr. as comp. in SF; then back to Chi. Led Kenton alumni gp. at reunion in Newport Beach, Calif. '91. Re-org. Chi. Jazz Ens. in '90s. Russo's work, often characterized as Third Stream, incl. some of the most adventurous and experimental writing ever perf. by Kenton. CDs: Chicago Jazz Ensemble (CMG); w. Kenton (Cap.; Mos.); L. Konitz–J. Giuffre (Verve).

RUSSO, SONNY (SANTO J.), tbn; b. Brooklyn, NY, 3/20/29. Father was prof. tptr., vlnst., alto sax pl; grandfath. prof. tbnst.; moth. pl. pno. Began on pno., vln. Stud. w. fath. and grandfath. Sat in w. fath. fr. age 15. Pl. w. Buddy Morrow 1947; Lee Castle '48; Sam Donahue '49; Artie Shaw '49–50; Art Mooney '50; Tito Puente early '50s; Jerry Wald, Tommy Tucker, Buddy Rich, Ralph Flanagan '51–2; Sauter-Finegan Orch. '53–5; Neal Hefti '54–5; Dorsey Bros. '55–6; Maynard Ferguson Birdland Band '56. Pl. w. B'way show bands fr. mid 50s. Pl. w. Sauter-Finegan '56–61; Louis Bellson '57; Machito, Bobby Hackett, Benny Goodman early '60s; Doc Severinsen '67; *Tonight Show* orch. in NYC '67–73; Frank Sinatra off and on '67–88; Urbie Green and 21 Tbns. '68; WGJB '70s. Also many recs. w. singers incl. Jimmy Rushing; Tony Bennett; Lena Horne; Perry Como; Dinah Washington; etc. Favs: Teagarden, Vic Dickenson, Urbie Green, Carl Fontana. Polls: *DB* New Star. Fests: So. Amer. w. Goodman '61; Eur. w. WGJB '75; So. Amer. w. Sinatra '80–1. TV: *Tonight Show* w. Louis Armstrong '71; Concert for the Americas w. Sinatra, Buddy Rich. CDs: w. M. Ferguson; Sauter-Finegan (BB).

RUTHERFORD, RUDY (ELMAN), cl, alto & bari sax; b. Arizona, 6/18/24; d. NYC, 3/31/95. Clarinet, bari. sax w. L. Hampton 1943–4; C. Basie '44–7. Join. Ted Buckner in Det. '47. Work. w. Basie again '51. App. w. Chuck Berry at NJF in film *Jazz on a Summer's Day* '58. Perf. and rec. w. Wilbur De Paris; worked w. Ram Ramirez Trio '59; Buddy Tate '60, '64; Earl Hines in mid-70s; I. Jacquet Orch. in '80s-90s. Led own combos at Count Basie's; other NYC area clubs; Ramapo Country Club '50s and '60s. Also served as mus. dir. for singer Marion Williams. Cl. solo with Basie on "High Tide" '45. Recs. w. De Paris, Hines. CDs: C. Basie (BB); I. Jacquet (Atl.); Lester Young (Sav.).

RYERSON, ALI, fl; b. NYC, 10/21/52. Father, Art, well known jazz gtrst. in bbs and NYC studios; bros. organized jazz-rock gp. in which she did first prof. pl. 1968. Began on fl. at age 8. Stud. classical; jazz. Applied Mus. major, Western Conn. St. U.; priv. stud. w. Harold Bennett '70–3. Tour. w. pop gps, incl. Sandler and Young, in clubs, concert halls, and LV main rooms '73–7. Grad. cum laude fr. Hartt Sch. of Mus., U. of Hartford (B. Mus. 1979). Won Hartt Concerto Competition '78–9; Applied Mus. Award '79. Principal fl. w. Hartt Orch. '77–9. Priv. instruction w. John Wion; master classes w. Julius Baker. Form. the Ryerson Baroque Trio '79. Freelanced w. Conn. Opera Co.; Hartford Symph.; Chamber Orch. of Hartford. Form. own jazz qnt. '80. In Montreal as freelance '81–2, incl. long duo job at Hotel Meridien. Fr. '82–7 lived in NYC, working as commercial studio mus. and freelance in jazz, classical fields. Perf. w. Lou Donaldson, Chico Hamilton, Grady Tate, Frank Foster, Frank Wess, Maxine Sullivan, Clark Terry, Chuck Wayne '85.

Tour. in Eur. as jazz soloist and guest artist w. Stephane Grappelli; Oliver Jackson; rec. first solo album in London for Baron label. App. at major fests., home and abroad, incl. several perfs. w. mentor, Julius Baker. In '88 relocated to Brussels, rec. three albums w. Belgian pnst./comp. Charles Loos for EMD, Igloo, B Sharp labels. Also did radio, TV projects in Engl., Spain, Belgium '88–90. Signed by Red Baron label after her perf. w. Grappelli at Carnegie Hall. Rec. two CDs using guests such as Kenny Barron; Roy Haynes; Red Rodney; Cecil McBee. Engaged as principal fl. of Monterey Bay (Calif.) Symph. '91–2. Freelanced in Calif. w. Pavarotti; Laurindo Almeida; Bill Watrous; Art Farmer. In '93–6 rec. three CDs for Concord incl. Brazilian album w. Joe Beck. Ret. to NYC area and cont. tour. int'l. Fr. '96 duo w. Beck, alto fl. and alto gtr. (invented by Beck), rec. *Alto* for DMP. Versatile virtuoso performer. Favs: Julius Baker; Bill Evans. Fest: w. Big Apple All-Stars at Cork JF, Ireland '94. CDs: Conc.; Red Brn.; DMP.

RYPDAL, TERJE, gtr, fl, saxes, comp; b. Oslo, Norway, 8/23/47. Studied pno. fr. age 5, gtr. at 13. In late 1960s, pl. w. Jan Garbarek gp., also w. Geo Russell, w. whom he stud. Lydian Concept. First prominent as soloist in free-jazz fest, Baden-Baden '69. Own trio at Berlin JF '72. Started new gp, Rypdal Odyssey, which in late '75 pl. its first concert in Engl. Led trio incl. Palle Mikkelborg, tour. Continent '80. Award fr. Norwegian Jazz Federation '85. Regarded as one of Eur.'s outstanding comps.; has written extended works for symph and theatre. Pl. at Umbria JF '96. CDs: ECM; w. Ketil Bjørnstad (ECM); Tomasz Stanko (BMG).

SAARSALU, LEMBIT, tnr sax; b. Roosna-alliku, Estonia, 7/8/48. Played acdn., cl. Led own qt. 1978–81. Stud. cl. at Tallinn Music Sch., grad. 1975. Has pl. in Africa, Cuba, the Near East and all over Eur. Pl. and rec. in duo w. pnst. Leonid Vintskevich, rec. for Melodiya and app. w. Vintskevich in Moscow, Idaho, '89, 90, and '92 at Lionel Hampton JF. An adventurous and unconventional soloist. Favs: S. Getz, J. Coltrane, S. Rollins. TV: film, *Old Melody* '81.

SACHS, AARON, cl, tnr sax; b. NYC, 7/4/23. Early experience w. the bands of Babe Russin 1941; Van Alexander '42–3; Red Norvo on and off '41–5; Benny Goodman '45. In '52–3 he and his then wife, singer Helen Merrill, tour. w. Earl Hines. Later freelanced in NYC w. Latin and jazz gps., incl. Tito Rodriguez; tour. w. Louie Bellson '59. Freelancing and teaching but no longer prominent on the jazz scene, Sachs is a talented clst. and one of the first to translate the bop style to that instrument in the '40s. Won *Esq.* New Star '45. Rec. w. Eddie Heywood, Sarah Vaughan '44; own gp. incl. Terry Gibbs for Manor '47. Own LP for Rama. CDs: w. Norvo (Comm.); Tom Talbert (SB; Chartmaker; Modern Concepts); S. Manne (Cont.).

SADI, FATS (Sadi Lallemand), vib; b. Andenne, Belgium, 10/23/26. Started on xyl., pl. in circus ca. 1937. Led own gp., Sadi's Hot Five '45; pl. w. Bobby Jaspar in Bob Shots '46; Don Byas '47. In Paris '50–61; pl. and made movie short w. Django Reinhardt, Aime Barelli '53; Martial Solal '55; own band '55; André Hodeir's Jazz Groupe de Paris; Don Byas; Michel Legrand; et al. Many recs. in '50s, incl. vocs.

w. Blossom Dearie's Blue Stars voc. gp. Settled in Brussels in early '60s; worked occ. w. Clarke-Boland bb. From '72 he had his own TV show; also pl. bongos, sang, and acted. Rec. w. Byas in mid '50s. CD: w. Klaus Doldinger (ACT).

SAFRANSKI, EDDIE (EDWARD), bs; b. Pittsburgh, PA, 12/25/18; d. Los Angeles, CA, 1/10/79. Violin at 8, then cello and bs. Played w. Hal McIntyre Orch. 1941–5; Stan Kenton '45–8; Charlie Barnet '48–9. Mainly studio work in '50s, incl. educ. TV series *The Subject Was Jazz* '58. Freelance pl. and teaching in LA fr. '60s. Won *DB* polls '46–52; *Met.* poll '47–54; *Esq.* Silver Award '47. Safranski was a superior rhythm and solo bassist who, alongside Shelly Manne, made invaluable contributions to the Kenton rhythm section. CDs: w. Kenton (Mos.; Hep; Class.); Nat Cole (Cap.); Johnny Smith (Roul.); Vido Musso in *Loaded*; Kai Winding in *In the Beginning ... Bebop*; Marian McPartland; Jay and Kai (Sav.); S. Getz (Roost); D. Gillespie; Metronome All-Stars (BB); Hot Lips Page (Story.); André Previn (BL).

ST. CYR, JOHNNY (JOHN ALEXANDER), bjo, gtr; b. New Orleans, LA, 4/17/1890; d. Los Angeles, CA, 6/17/66. Studied w. his fath., who pl. fl. and gtr. Long association w. Armand Piron, then two yrs. w. Martin Gabriel 1913–14; Kid Ory '14–16; pl. on riverboats w. Fate Marable '17–19. To Chi. '23; pl. w. King Oliver; Jimmy Noone; and, fr. '25 to '29, w. Doc Cook. Best known for his participation in the Louis Armstrong Hot Five and Hot Seven sess. '25–7 and on Jelly Roll Morton dates '26. Retired to NO '30, working mainly as a plasterer, but pl. w. local gps., incl. Paul Barbarin, Alphonse Picou. Led own band in LA fr. '55 and pl. on riverboat at Disneyland, leading the Young Men From NO '61–6. CDs: w. L. Armstrong (Col.; BBC); J. R. Morton (BB); Jimmie Noone (Milan); Percy Humphrey–P. Barbarin (Story.).

SALVADOR, SAL (Silvio Smiragha), gtr; b. Monson, MA, 12/21/25d. Stamford, CT, 9/22/99. Mainly self-taught. Gigs in Springfield, MA, w. Phil Woods and Joe Morello, then moved to NYC 1949; roomed w. Tal Farlow, Jimmy Raney, Johnny Smith. Pl. w. Mundell Lowe '49; Terry Gibbs '50. Staff mus. for Col. Recs. '50–1. Pl. w. Stan Kenton Orch. '52–3; own qt. '54–60; also extensive freelancing. Led own bb, Colors in Sound '60–5; then worked accomp. singers, incl. Tony Bennett; Paul Anka, Eydie Gormé; Johnny Mathis '65–70. Formed gtr. duo w. Alan Hanlon '71–3; taught and lectured in '70s. Pl. in '80s w. own qt., qnt., bb; also in gps. w. Dave Weckl, Joe Morello. Pl. w. qnt., Crystal Image, fr. '89. Owned a rec. label, Danbar; authored ten guitar methods, incl. the popular *Single String Studies* and *Complete Chord Book* (Mel Bay). Favs: Tal Farlow, Johnny Smith, Tony Purrone, John Collins, Emily Remler. Polls: *Play.; DB*; many ASCAP awds. Fests: all major. Films: *Jazz on a Summer's Day* '58. TV: *Music '55* w. Kenton; Merv Griffin; Joe Franklin. CDs: BN; Stash; w. S. Kenton (Cap.); N. Brignola (Stash).

SAMPLE, JOE (JOSEPH LESLIE), pno, comp; b. Houston, TX, 2/1/39. Founding member of a gp. known as The Swingsters, The Nighthawks, and fr. 1961 The Jazz Crusaders. In '72 the gp. was shortened to The Crusaders; by this time, Sample was involved heavily w. people in the pop field, incl. Diana Ross; Joni Mitchell; Ray Charles; tour. w. Tom Scott's LA Express in '73 and w. the Rolling Stones. His activities in later yrs. were of less interest to jazz purists, though he continued to comp. and perf. in many jazz-related fields. CDs: MCA; WB; w. Jazz Crusaders (PJ, GRP); D. Byrd (BN); E. Fitzgerald (Rep.); S. Turrentine (Fant.); Miles Davis (WB); Les McCann (Night); Dennis Rowland (Conc.); Ramsey Lewis (GRP); Randy Crawford (WB).

SAMPSON, EDGAR (MELVIN), comp, saxes, vln; b. NYC, 8/31/07; d. Englewood, NJ, 1/16/73. Studied vln. as a child, sax in hs. First job in vln.-pno. duo w. Joe Coleman 1924; w. Duke Ellington summer '27. Worked w. orchs of Arthur Gibbs at Savoy, Charlie Johnson '28–30. Alto and vln. w. Fletcher Henderson '31–3; Chick Webb '33–7. While w. Webb, he wrote a series of instrumentals that were among the biggest hits of the swing era: "Stompin' at the Savoy"; "Blue Lou"; "Don't Be That Way"; "If Dreams Come

True"; "Lullaby in Rhythm"—all rec. by Benny Goodman, mostly in Sampson's own arrs. After leaving Webb, he stopped pl.; arr. for Red Norvo; B. Goodman; C. Webb; A. Shaw; T. Wilson; et al. Resumed pl. in '40s w. Al Sears and own band; in late '40s and early '50s he worked and rec. w. Latin bands, incl. Marcelino Guerra; Tito Puente; Tito Rodriguez. Only occ. heard as soloist (vln. on "House of David Blues" w. Henderson; bari. sax on Lionel Hampton's "Ring Dem Bells"). Sampson's melodic, swinging scores were outstanding examples of bb writing, which made him a central figure in the late '30s. CDs: w. B. Holiday (Col.); L. Armstrong; L. Hampton (BB); Chick Webb (Dec.); F. Henderson (Sav.); Charlie Johnson (Hot 'N Sweet).

SAMUELS, DAVE (DAVID ALAN), vib, mrba; b. Waukegan, IL, 10/9/48. Studied dms. and perc. w. Jake Jerger in Ill. 1954–66; self-taught on vib. and mrba. Received B.A. in psychology fr. Bost. U. '71. Moved to NYC '74; pl. w. Gerry Mulligan '74–7; Carla Bley '75; Gerry Niewood '77; Paul McCandless '79; Gallery fr. '80; Art Lande '81; Anthony Davis '83; Spyro Gyra fr. '83; Bobby McFerrin '84. Own duo, Double Image, w. Dave Friedman fr. '75. Samuels taught vib. at Berklee Coll. of Mus. '72–4 and jazz studies at William Paterson Coll. '79–89. He is on the board of dirs. of the Percussive Arts Society. Favs: Red Norvo, Milt Jackson. Polls: *Mod. Drummer* '87, '89; *Jazziz* '87, '89. Fests: Eur. since '75. TV: *Masters of Percussion* on PBS. CDs: ECM; MCA; GRP; w. G. Mulligan–C. Baker (Col./CTI); G. Mulligan (Tel.; LRC); J. Beck (DMP); P. D'Rivera (Mess.); O. Peterson (Tel.).

SANABRIA, BOBBY (ROBERT D.), dms, vib, perc, comp-arr; b. Bronx, NY, 6/2/57. First pl. on car bumpers, then conga dms. Inspired by father's recs. of Machito; Tito Puente; Tito Rodriguez; Brazilian mus.; r&b; and folkloric mus. of PR. B. Mus. fr. Berklee Coll. 1975–9. Pl. w. Marco Rizo fr. '80; T. Puente bb on and off fr. '81; Mongo Santamaria '82–4; Perico Ortiz '86–7; Mario Bauza '87–93; Paquito D'Rivera '86, '93; H. Threadgill '88–9; Xavier Cugat '89–91. Fr. '80 Sanabria has also led his own band, Ascension. Since '90, he has taught dms. and perc. at Mannes Coll. of Mus.; faculty member of Drummers' Collective, NYC; worked nationally and int'l as clinician. Rec. debut w. Santamaria on Roul. '82. Favs: Buddy Rich, T. Puente, Art Blakey, Shelly Manne, Willie Bobo; arrs: Rene Hernandez, Puente, Ray Santos, Don Ellis. Fests: many major fests. int'l fr. '82. Awards: NEA '83. TV: film, *Rivkin the Bounty Hunter* '84; PBS docu. on Mongo Santamaria '84; M. Bauza '90; Bill Cosby show '92;

own apps. on WGBH, Bost. '85–6; *Visiones*, WNBC '94. Pubs: contributor to *Modern Drummer; NY Latino*; and newsletters: *Descarga; Highlights in Percussion*. CDs: FF; w. Bauza; P. D'Rivera (Mess.); Norman Simmons (Milijac); Scott Robinson (Ken); Jorge Sylvester (Post.); Michael Mossman (Claves); *Mambo Kings* sound track (Elek.).

SANBORN, DAVID (WILLIAM), alto sax; b. Tampa, FL, 7/30/45. Raised in St. Louis. Started on alto sax at age 8; later advised to play it as physical therapy dur. recovery fr. polio. Played prof. in St. Louis fr. age 14, backing Albert King, Little Milton. Stud. music at Northwestern U. 1963–4 while active on Chi. blues scene; also stud. at U. of Iowa '65–7. Moved to SF; pl. and rec. w. Paul Butterfield Blues Band '67–71. Lived in Woodstock, NY, for a yr. and resumed w. Butterfield '72. Pl. w. Stevie Wonder '72–73, tour. w. Rolling Stones US tour '72. Many rec. and solos w. pop acts, incl. David Bowie; James Brown; the Eagles; Bruce Springsteen. Pl. w. Gil Evans '74 to mid '80s and Brecker Bros '75. From mid '70s, he toured w. own bands and made his debut album as leader, *Taking Off*. By '91 Sanborn had rec. nine albums, five of which won Grammy Awards. Also app. regularly as a guest soloist on the David Letterman TV show, hosted his own NBC TV show, *Night Music*, and cond. a widely syndicated radio program, *The David Sanborn Show*. Strongly infl. by Hank Crawford, Sanborn's approach is passionate and intense and more blues than jazz-oriented, but his improvisations often don't seem fully developed. CDs: WB; w. Esther Phillips (CTI); Brecker Bros. (Novus); Gil Evans (BB); R. Cuber (ProJazz); A. Jarreau (WB); Tim Berne (JMT).

SANCHEZ, DAVID, tnr sax, sop sax; b. Hato Rey, PR, 9/3/68. Originally wanted to pl. tpt., but took up conga dms. at 8; three yrs. later, a sch. band dir. started him on sax. Classical studies at Free Sch. of Mus. fr. age 12. First infl. by Afro-Cuban danza and other trad. Latin mus., he turned to jazz after hearing Miles Davis, John Coltrane, and Billie Holiday recs. Pl. w. local bands while in hs, then moved to NYC in late 1980s. Att. Rutgers U. and stud. priv. w. Ted Dunbar, John Purcell, Kenny Barron '86–88. Gigs w. Eddie Palmieri, Hilton Ruiz, Daniel Ponce, Paquito D'Rivera, Larry Ridley '89–90. Tour. Eur. and US w. Dizzy Gillespie's United Nation Orch. '91. Sanchez also perf. in combos w. Gillespie and participated in his month-long Diamond Jubilee celebration at NYC's Blue Note in January '92. Tour. w. Philip Morris Superband '92. Pl. w. Slide Hampton's Jazz Masters fr. '92. Guest soloist w. Kenny Barron trio at Village Vanguard, April '93. Worked w. Danilo Perez

'93. Own gp. fr. '94. Favs: Sonny Rollins, John Coltrane, Don Byas, Dexter Gordon. Fests: all major w. Gillespie '91. CDs: Col.; w. Gillespie (Telarc); H. Ruiz (Tel.); Kenny Drew Jr. (Ant.); Slide Hampton (Tel.); Roy Hargrove (Verve); Mingus Big Band (Drey.); Ryan Kisor (Col.); Santi Debriano (Evid.); Danilo Perez (Novus).

SANDERS, PHAROAH (Farrell Saunders), tnr sax; b. Little Rock, AR, 10/13/40. Worked in r&r in SF Bay Area bef. settling in NYC in 1962, working there w. Don Cherry; Albert Ayler; Sun Ra; and, fr. '65, John Coltrane's final gp. After Coltrane's death he remained w. the unit under Alice Coltrane. Led his own combo w. singer Leon Thomas '69–70; also w. Mike Mantler and Carla Bley in Jazz Composers Orch. '68. In the '70s and '80s, his playing offered a diverse blend of jazz, fusion, modal mus., bop, and other elements. In '82 he led a qt. w. John Hicks, Walter Booker, and Idris Muhammad. Altered his outer-edge stance in the '90s to a degree. CDs: Evid.; Imp.; Axiom; Verve; ESP; Timel.; w. Sonny Sharrock (Axiom); Randy Weston (Ant.); J. Coltrane; A. Coltrane (Imp.); Bheki Mseleku; Terry Callier (Verve); Don Cherry (BN); Wallace Roney (WB); Steve Turre (Ant.); Benny Golson (Timel.); Art Davis (SN); Elvin Jones (Konnex); Jazz Composers Orch. (JCOA).

SANDKE, JORDAN LEWIS, tpt, flg, crnt; b. Chicago, IL, 2/20/46. Mother pl. pno. as hobby; bro. is tptr. Randy Sandke. Took up dms. at age 11, then tpt. at 13. Stud. tpt. in Chi. w. Ronald Schilke; later w. Charles Lewis at New Engl. Cons. (B. Mus. 1977); then w. Bob McCoy, NYC. After pl. "for kicks" through academic yrs. (B.A. in ancient hist., Chi. U.), he began working w. local blues bands, incl. Mighty Joe Young '67–9; Junior Parker '70–1; then soul and top-40 gps. First rec. w. Johnny Ross & the Soul Explosion '68. Worked w. local bop qnt. and Latin bands in Bost. '77–8. Moved to NYC '78. Formed ongoing assoc. w. Widespread Depression Orch., Vince Giordano's Nighthawks, both in '79; and also frequented Jimmy Ryan's, listening to Roy Eldridge. Other assoc. incl. Jaki Byard's Apollo Stompers '79–87; Buck Clayton Swing Band '88–91; Panama Francis '83; Walt Levinsky's Great Amer. Swing Band '87–89. Since '84 he has worked w. "almost every band" at Roseland, incl. his own '91–2. App. w. Allen Toussaint, Off-B'way, in *Staggerlee* '87. Received NEA Grant in '90 to perf. the music of Coleman Hawkins and Roy Eldridge w. a qnt. at Saratoga JF '91; Ottawa JF '92; NY Brass Conf. '94. A versatile tptr. Favs: Eldridge, Clifford Brown, Beiderbecke. Rec. w. Mighty Joe Young (Del.); Howlin'

Wolf (Chess). CDs: Stash; w. Widespread Depression (Stash).

SANDKE, RANDY (RANDALL), tpt, comp, arr, gtr; b. Chicago, IL, 5/23/49. Brother is tptr. Jordan Sandke. Stud. at Indiana U. 1966–9, later w. Vince Penzerella. First gigs while in hs. Stud. gtr. and pno. while recovering fr. throat injury '70–80. Pl. w. Bob Wilber '83–5; Benny Goodman '85–6; Newport All-Stars fr. '85; Buck Clayton '86–91; own qt. fr. '88; R. Sandke's Metatonal Band fr. '91. Also concerts and fests. w. Flip Phillips; Ralph Sutton; Ken Peplowski; Milt Hinton; others. Although Sandke is best known as a mainstream trumpeter, his comps. employ an orig. harmonic approach which he calls "metatonal." He premiered *The Mystic Trumpeter*, an extended work for qnt. based on the Whitman poem, at Greenwich House and the Knitting Factory '92. Favs: Beiderbecke, Armstrong. Fests: Eur. fr. '83; India '84; Japan fr. '88; JVC-NY '98–9. Film: *The Cotton Club*. TV: PBS Benny Goodman special. CDs: Conc.; N-H; Jazz.; Stash; w. J. Pizzarelli (Novus); Mel Tormé; S. McCorkle (Conc.); Barbara Carroll (DRG); Buck Clayton Swing Band; Buck Clayton Legacy; NY All-Stars (N-H); B. Goodman (MM).

SANDOVAL, ARTURO, tpt, pno, perc, voc; b. Artemisa, Havana, Cuba, 11/6/49. Studied at National School of Arts. Co-founded the gp. Irakere, which Dizzy Gillespie heard on a visit to Havana in 1977. In '89 he and Gillespie perf. in the Can. premiere of *A Night in Havana*. Gillespie became his mentor and hired him for his United Nation Band; while on tour with it in Italy in '90, Sandoval defected to US and settled in Fla. He has perf. as soloist w. the National Symph. Orch., the Leningrad Symph. and at jfs around the world; rec. in Finland w. Gillespie and in Venezuela, Mexico, Germ., Engl., and France. A trumpeter of extraordinary technical ability; his high notes have pl. a large role in establishing his fame, but he is capable of lyrical improv. as well. He is also an exceptional pnst. and a scat singer with a unique and humorous style. Favs: Gillespie, Clifford Brown, Woody Shaw. TV: '96 Grammy awards. CDs: Mess.; JH; GRP; w. Irakere (Col.); J. Moody (Tel.); D. Gillespie (Pab.); GRP All-Star bb (GRP); T. S. Monk (N2K); D. Grusin (N2K; GRP).

SANTAMARIA, MONGO (RAMON), congas, perc, comp; b. Havana, Cuba, 4/7/22; d. Miami, FL, 2/1/03. Studied vln. but sw. to dms., inspired by Chano Pozo. Pl. in leading Cuban clubs until 1948, when he left for Mexico and the US w. his cousin, Armando Peraza. Worked w. Gilberto Valdez, Perez Prado, Geo. Shearing '53; and Tito Puente. Best

known for his collab. w. Cal. Tjader '57–61, dur. which time he rec. as leader for Riv. and Col.—later Atl. and Vaya—scoring a major hit w. his version of Herbie Hancock's "Watermelon Man." Santamaria cont. to tour and rec., straddling the pop-jazz fence as he pl. Latin, soul-jazz with salsa roots, occ. collaborating w. jazz mus. such as Dizzy Gillespie and Jack McDuff. Fests: Montreux JF '71 and w. Gillespie '81. CDs: Conc.; Aud.; Mile.; w. D. Gillespie (Pab.); M. Ruiz (Novus); Tito Puente (Trop.); Valerie Capers (Col.); Poncho Sanchez (Conc.); Steve Turre (Verve).

SANTISI, RAY (RAYMOND), pno, comp, arr; b. Boston, MA, 2/1/33. Mother was opera fan; sists. were amateur singers. Classical pno. lessons fr. early age, then stud. at Schillinger House, precursor of Berklee Coll. of Mus. '51. Made rec. debut w. Boots Mussulli 1954. Stud. theory and comp. w. Dr. Richard Bobitt '54; comp. at Boston Cons. '55; piano w. Margaret Chaloff '60. Co-managed club, The Stable, late '50s-mid '60s. When the club changed its name to the Jazz Workshop, Santisi gave up his managerial status and joined the house rhythm section, backing Getz; Hawkins; Golson; H. Edison; B. Clayton; C. Baker; D. Gordon; Z. Sims; Stitt; et al. Taught summers at Stan Kenton jazz clinics '60–72; also was on-call jazz pianist w. Boston Pops. Tour. in late '60s, early '70s w. Buddy Rich, Gabor Szabo. Recipient of NEA grants for comp. and perf. mid '70s. Santisi has been a faculty member at Berklee fr. '57 and has been part of Berklee at Umbria Jazz dur. summers. Favs: T. Flanagan, B. Evans, B. Powell; arrs: Ellington, Johnny Richards, G. Russell. Fests: Scand. w. Buddy DeFranco early '70s; Japan w. own trio mid '80s. TV: WGBH-Boston. LPs: w. Donald Byrd (Transition); B. DeFranco (Sonet). CDs: w. Serge Chaloff (Mos.); Herb Pomeroy (FS).

SARGENT, GRAY, gtr; b. Attleboro, MA, 6/10/53. Mother and bro. were amateur mus. but no longer play. Took pno. lessons fr. age 7–9; began on gtr. at age 11. Mainly self-taught. First prof. gigs at age 12; began working full-time after grad. fr. hs. Pl. w. Illinois Jacquet (small gps. on and off 1977–85, bb '90). Freelanced extensively in Bost. and NYC w. Benny Carter; Phil Woods; Marshall Royal; Bob Wilber; Kenny Davern; Arnett Cobb; Buddy Tate; Peanuts Hucko; Frank Wess; Scott Hamilton; Vic Dickenson; Dicky Wells; Al Grey; Slide Hampton; Dizzy Gillespie; Roy Eldridge; Joe Newman; Clark Terry; Chet Baker; Barry Harris; Duke Jordan; Dick Katz; Dave McKenna; Ruby Braff; Milt Hinton; Jo Jones; Sam Woodyard; Maxine Sullivan; Sheila Jordan; others. Taught at Jamey Aebersold Jazz Camp, Nova Scotia '82; Harvard U. '88–9 as artist-in-residence. Fests: Eur. w. Jacquet '80–90; w. McKenna '89–91. TV: PBS *Big Band Ballroom Bash* w. Dick Johnson's Artie Shaw Orch. CDs: Conc.; w. D. McKenna; Lou Columbo; Scott Hamilton; NJF All-Stars; Conc. All. Stars (Conc.); Donna Byrne (Stash).

SARMANTO, HEIKKI, pno, comp; b. Helsinki, Finland, 6/22/39. Brother is Pekka Sarmanto. Stud. priv. fr. age 13. Stud. at Helsinki U., Sibelius Acad, 1962–4; Berklee Coll. of Mus. '68–71; also stud. priv. w. Margaret Chaloff while in Bost. Pl. w. Esa Pethman, Christian Schwindt, own gps. fr. '62. Tour. Eur. w. own gps. fr. early '70s; made regular visits to NYC and Bost. Worked or sat in w. Sonny Rollins, Art Farmer, Clark Terry, Joe Henderson, Geo. Russell, Charlie Mariano, '60s–70s. In the '70s, Sarmanto's extended comps. incl. the *New Hope Jazz Mass*, which premiered at St. Peter's Church in NYC '78, and a jazz opera. The jazz mass was later perf. at NJF '79. Comps. in '80s incl. three large suites, incl. a suite for jazz ens. and strings, and a ballet suite. Other comps. incl. songs w. lyrics by Finnish poets and mus. for TV and radio plays. Became assoc. w. Opera Ebony in NYC '93, which has presented his oratorio, *Perfect Harmony*, and other works. In Sept. '98 he was appointed Artistic Director of the UMO Jazz Orch. Video: *Saxophone Colossus* (Sony) '87, by Robert Mugge, in which Sonny Rollins plays Sarmanto's orchestrations of Rollins' themes; *Concerto For Tenor Saxophone and Orchestra*, cond. by Sarmanto in Tokyo, '86. Favs: Tatum, Bud Powell. Polls: Best Finnish Jazz Mus. '70; Best Pnst., Montreux JF '71. CDs: Finlandia.

SARMANTO, PEKKA, bs; b. Helsinki, Finland, 2/15/45. Brother is Heikki Sarmanto. Stud. vln. and bs. at Sibelius Acad., then joined bro.'s band in 1965. Played and rec. w. Eero Koivistoinen fr. '65. Rec. w. Edward Vesala '69; Ted Curson '70; Charlie Mariano, Juhani Aaltonen '74. As house bs. at Groovy Club in late '70s he backed such visiting mus. as Benny Carter; Toots Thielemans; Clifford Jordan; Joe Newman; Bob Berg; Tom Harrell. Feat. in H. Sarmanto's suite *Song for My Brother* '82. Rec. w. D. Gillespie–A. Sandoval '82; E. Vesala '83. Pl. in duo w. Juhani Aaltonen '80s. Sarmanto is the most rec. Finnish jazz artist. CDs: w. Edward Vesala (ECM); Gillespie-Sandoval (Pab.).

SARPILA, ANTTI, cl, saxes; b. Finland, 6/11/64. Father a reed pl., encouraged him to travel to the US for study. Befriended by Bob Wilber at Pori JF '80. Pl. w. Zoot Sims, Frank Wess, Marshal Royal, Buddy Tate at Colo. JP '82. Played in '88 Benny Goodman tribute at Carnegie Hall; Royal Ellington Concert at

Royal Festival Hall '89. In late '90s he lead a swing bb in Finland. CDs: own label, Antti Sarpila; w. Buck Clayton Legacy; Ralph Sutton (N-H); Swedish Swing Society (Sittel); Ulf Johansson (Phon.); Bob Wilber (N-H; Phon.).

SASAJIMA, AKIO, gtr; b. Hakodate, Japan, 3/14/52. Self-taught on gtr; listened to Amer. movie soundtracks and pop gps., then fell under infl. of Baden Powell and Wes Montgomery. Played semi-prof. in Sapporo, sometimes w. Sadao Watanabe. Moved to Tokyo, translated a number of the Berklee Coll. of Mus. textbooks, thereby absorbing their contents. To Chi. in 1977; pl. Chi. JF '79, rec. w. Brazilian gp. Som Brasil; Judy Roberts; Victor Lewis; Harvie Swartz; Joe Henderson; Ron Carter. In '91 tour. Japan. w. Randy Brecker; Don Friedman; Jimmy Cobb; Harvie Swartz. Based in Chi. and SF. CDs: Muse.

SATO, MASAHIKO, pno, keyb, comp, arr; b. Tokyo, Japan, 10/6/41. Started pno. lessons at age 5. Stud. w. Fusako Uenuma 1947–51; Hiroshi Ito '51–6. Also stud. vln. w. Hiroshi Hatoyama '47–50. First prof. gig w. Geo. Kawaguchi's Big Four + 1 while still at Keio U. HS '58. Stud. at Keio U. Sch. of Economics '60–4; pl. w. Jiro Inagaki; Kenzo Takami's Midnight Suns; and led own trio concurrently. Won *DB* scholarship '66; stud. comp. and arr. at Berklee Coll. of Mus. '66–8. Pl. in Bost. w. Clark Terry; Charlie Mariano; others. Ret. to Japan, pl. concert w. 18-pc. orch. in Tokyo '68. Formed trio w. Yasuo Arakawa, Masahiko Togashi '69. Active fr. '70s w. own gps. incl. Garando '71–4; CPU Qt. w. M. Togashi '74–6; MSB (Medical Sugar Bank) qnt. '79–80; SAIFA Oct. '86. Rec. in Tokyo w. Chas. Mingus, Helen Merrill '71; in Germ. w. Attila Zoller, Karl Berger '71. Won Japan Arts Fest. Award '70, '72; Fumio Nanri award for contribution to Japanese jazz '83. Rec. w. Art Farmer and strings '83. Premiered new int'l gp., Randooga, at Select Live Under the Sky concert in Tokyo '90; sidemen incl. Wayne Shorter; Ray Anderson; Nana Vasconcelos. Won *SJ* poll in three categories '91. Pl. monthly concerts w. Randooga at Pit Inn, Tokyo, feat. Kosuke Mine, Kazutoki Umezu, Hedefumi Toki, others '91. Pl. concert w. 1,000 chanting Buddhist priests at Budokan '93. Sato has comp. numerous film and TV scores and has arr. for singers incl. Kimiko Ito, Nancy Wilson. Japan's best and most-in-demand comp.-arr. Best-known comps. incl. "Tenbinza No Uta," "Yamataifu," both rec. by T. Miyama's New Herd orch.; "Escape Velocity," rec. w. Eddie Gomez, Steve Gadd '86. Favs: Yuji Takahashi, Olivier Messiaen, Akira Miyazawa. Polls: Jazz Disc '90; *SJ* Readers pno. '70–1; *SJ* Readers kybd. '85–93; *SJ* Readers comp./arr. '71–3, '84–93; *SJ* Critics kybd., comp./arr. '90–2. Fests: Berliner Jazztage '71; Montreux JF '72; Donaueschinger Musiktage '80; Moers Int'l New JF '82, '91; Kool JF-NY '83; JVC JF-NY '87; Paris JF '91. CDs: Enja; Teichiku-Union; Sony; NEC-Avenue; Epic-Sony; w. C. Mingus (Den.); Masami Nakagawa (JVC); Randooga (Epic; Nippon Crown).

SAUNDERS, CARL, tpt, flg, comp, arr; b. Indianapolis, IN, 8/2/42. Mother Gail was first voc. w. Stan Kenton at Rendezvous Ballroom, Balboa, Calif.; her bro. was band lead. Bobby Sherwood. Self-taught; first prof. gig w. Kenton 1961–2. Pl. w. Si Zentner, Prez Prado '62; Harry James '66. Also worked occ. as pnst. and dmr. '60s. Lead tpt. w. M. Ferguson, C. Barnet, B. Goodman '67; E. Fitzgerald '68. Soloist w. B. Rich '67–8. Tour. w. Robert Goulet '69–70; Paul Anka '70–1. Lived in LV, working in show bands '72–84. Freelanced in LA fr. 84; soloist w. Supersax; Dave Pell Octet; Bob Florence Limited Edition bb. First tpt. w. Bill Holman bb fr. '84. In '96 a book of Saunders' tunes, entitled *The Cookbook*, was published by SNL. Favs: K. Dorham, Don Fagerquist, F. Hubbard; arrs: Holman, Brookmeyer, Thad Jones. CDs: SNL; w. Holman (JVC); Kenton (Cap.); H. Silver (Silveto); Anthony Wilson; Gerald Wilson (MAMA).

SAUNDERS, KEITH LEO, pno, comp/arr; b. Wilkes-Barre, PA, 8/25/60. Family moved to Van Nuys, Calif. 1964. Stud. classical pno. ages 8–15. Jazz stud. w. Charlie Shoemake '75–8; Horace Silver '82. Pl. in LA w. Roy McCurdy, Bill Watrous '80–2; Dick Berk's Adoption Agency, for which he was mus. dir. '80–3. Rec. w. Berk for Disc. Gig w. Tom Harrell '83. Moved to NYC '84. Worked w. Richie Cole '83–9; gigs w. Harrell '85; Lionel Hampton '88. In '90 became lead. of NY Hardbop Qnt. which began as a cooperative. Fr. '96 Bim Strasberg has been co-lead. Saunders is also pno./mus. dir. for tap dance company, Manhattan Tap, fr. '92. Has taught priv. fr. '94. Favs: Bud Powell, Silver, Tyner, Wynton Kelly. Pl. a month in Nagoya, Japan '90 w. Hardbop Qnt.; Engl. w. Manhattan Tap '95. CDs: w. Hardbop (TCB).

SAUNDERS, RED (THEODORE), dms, tymp, vib, leader; b. Memphis, TN, 3/2/12; d. Chicago, IL, 3/5/81. Studied dms. at St. Benedict the Moor Sch. in Milwaukee, Wisc., where he was raised. Moved to Chi. and worked w. pnst. Stomp King in clubs, early 1930s, and w. Tiny Parham at Savoy Ballroom '34, bef. join. the house band at Club DeLisa, which he led fr. '37 to late '50s, when club closed. In the course

of his career, he worked w. Louis and Lil Armstrong, Duke Ellington, Woody Herman. Feat. soloist w. Louis Bellson–Pearl Bailey show at Chéz Parée '59; led house band at Regal Theater '60–7. Rec. w. sxt., '45–6, and bb, '49–54; *Mistreatin' Woman Blues* for Okeh '51, feat. singer Joe Williams. Perf. w. Art Hodes '68; Little Bro. Montgomery '69. Led own band '70; also active as booking agent. LP: w. L. Bro. Montgomery (Earwig); Edith Wilson (Del.); Guy Warren (Dec.). CDs: w. Junie C. Cobb (Riv.); Joe Williams (Sav.).

SAUTER, EDDIE (EDWARD ERNEST), comp; b. NYC, 12/2/14; d. Nyack, NY, 4/21/81. First prominent playing mellophone and arr. for Red Norvo's small combo at NYC's Hickory House 1935; later arr. for Norvo's larger ens. '36–8. From '39 he enjoyed great success writing charts for Benny Goodman (incl. his comps. "Benny Rides Again" and "Clarinet à La King"), Artie Shaw, and others. Co-led bb w. arr. Bill Finegan '52–7. Though its instrumentation was unorthodox and it was not a jazz band per se, the Sauter-Finegan Orch. reflected the Swing background of its co-leaders and often featured jazz soloists. Sauter arr. for radio house band in Baden Baden '57–60. Several admirable works for Stan Getz, incl. Getz's album *Focus* in '61 and the soundtrack collab. w. Getz for film *Mickey One* '65. Sauter's best works place him among the compositional giants of the swing era. CDs: Sauter-Finegan Orch. (BB); w. R. Eldridge; Red Norvo (Col.).

SAVAGE, RON (RONALD; "DOC"), dms; b. New Brunswick, NJ, 8/8/62. Studied at Berklee Coll. 1986–9 and priv. w. Alan Dawson. In late '80s and early '90s he pl. w. Cecila Smith's gp. (w. Mulgrew Miller, et al.); Ricky Ford; Julius Hemphill bb; James Williams; and Mark Whitfield. With Christopher Hollyday fr. '89, incl. perf. at Montreux, Berlin, Nice, Northsea, Stuttgart JFs. On faculty at Berklee Coll. of Mus. CDs: w. C. Hollyday (Novus); Darrell Katz (Cad.).

SAVOY SULTANS. A 9-piece band dir. by Al Cooper. The resident alternate gp. at Harlem's Savoy Ballroom fr. 1937 to '46, it swung infectiously in the "jump" style of its day and feat. such outstanding soloists as Rudy Williams, alto sax, and Sam Massenberg, tpt. A gp. w. the same name and similar instrumentation was organized in '74 by dmr. Panama Francis—it worked regularly fr. '79 through the early '90s, occ. reviving the repertoire of the earlier band and incl. tnr. sax-arr. George Kelly, who was a member of the original Sultans. CDs: Al Cooper (Class.); Panama Francis (Stash).

SAXTON, BILL (WILLIAM EDWARD), saxes, cl, fl; b. NYC, 6/28/46. Studied sax at New Engl. Cons. Frank Foster, Clark Terry, Sonny Stitt helped to start his prof. career. Worked w. Mongo Santamaria, Roy Haynes Hip Ensemble, Tito Puente, Machito in 1970s; C. Terry bb, Mercer Ellington, Frank Foster, Charli Persip Superband, Freddie Hubbard qnt., Count Basie, Mingus Dynasty, Roy Ayers in '80s; Errol Parker fr. '80s; Louis Hayes qt., Randy Weston African Rhythms, own qt. in '90s. Has pl. in Eur., mainly Germ., w. qt. twice a yr. Associate instruct. LIU; adjunct faculty at The New Sch.; priv. instruct. Henry St. Settlement; also teaches theory, woodwinds at Elma Lewis Sch. of Fine Arts., Bost.; jazz and improv. at New Engl. Cons. Cond. master classes, lectures, and clinics at Del. St.; U. of Mass.; York Coll. Consultant for Perf. Arts Prog., N.Y. Housing Authority. Comp: more than thirty, incl. "One for Booker"; "Priorities"; "Beneath the Surface." Arrs. for Alvin Queen; Hilton Ruiz; Young Mus. of NYC bb; LIU Jazz Ens.; York U. jazz wkshp. Favs: C. Parker, S. Rollins; arrs: Thad Jones, F. Foster. Film: Cotton Club. TV: Reading Rainbow. Rec. debut w. Billy Gault (Steep.) '72. Rec. w. M. Santamaria (Atl.) '73. CDs: Nilva; Divox; Trion; Jazzline; w. B. Watson (Col.); Dick Griffin (Konnex); Errol Parker (Sah.); John Patton (Evid.; PW).

SAYLES, EMANUEL RENÉ (aka MANNY), bjo, gtr; b. Donaldsonville, LA, 1/31/07; d. New Orleans, LA, 10/5/86. Son of NO gtrst. George Sayles. Self-taught, he moved to NO, worked w. Fate Marable on riverboat SS Capitol 1928. Rec. w. Jones and Collins Astoria Hot Eight '29. Worked as lead. and sideman in Chi. '39–49; in NO fr. '49. Rec. w. Peter Bocage, Louis Cottrell, and Percy Humphrey in '61 and as lead. '61–3. Toured Japan w. Geo. Lewis '63–4; Sweet Emma Barrett '64. Freelanced in Chi. '65–8; then perf. at Preservation Hall, NO '68. Toured UK as soloist '69. Pl. in NO '70s-80s; also toured w. Pres. Hall Jazz Band '70s. Rec. in '70s w. Kid Thomas, Earl Hines. CDs: w. Peter Bocage; Percy Humphrey; Louis Cottrell (Riv.).

SCHAEFER, HAL (HAROLD HERMAN), pno, comp; b. NYC, 7/22/25. Wife is lyricist Brenda Schaefer. Stud. pno. at HS of Mus. and Art, then w. Laura Dubman. Stud. comp. w. Mario Castelnuovo-Tedesco, Henry Brandt. Played w. bbs in Catskills fr. age 13; w. Lee Castle 1940; Ina Ray Hutton '41; Benny Carter '42; Harry James, Boyd Raeburn '43; Billy Eckstine '44; Peggy Lee–Dave Barbour '45–7. Worked w. own gps. and arr. for recs. and films fr. '47. Schaefer comp. scores for the films The Money Trap '62 and The Amsterdam Kill '77; arr. for shows, incl. Foxy and A Funny Thing Happened on the Way to the Forum. Worked as a vocal coach in NYC fr. '50s and perf. reg. in NYC clubs. Favs: Art Tatum, Roland Hanna. Polls: DB New Star '45. Fests: Cuba '59; Eur. '60; So. Amer '61; Kool and JVC fests. in '80s. Films: With a Song in My Heart; I'll Get By. CDs: Disc.; w. B. Raeburn (Sav.).

SCHEPS, ROB (ROBERT ALLEN), tnr, sop, fl, bari, alto, picc; b. Eugene, OR, 12/30/65. Uncle, Eric Goldberg, is comp. Began on recorder at age 7; pl. tnr. fr. age 9, fl. fr. age 13. Played w. local bands, own gps. fr. '77. Stud. at Eastman summer prog. '81; New Engl. Cons., '82–6 (B. Mus. '86); also at Banff Center for the Arts '84–5, '87. Perf. at NEC and Banff w. Dave Liebaman; Dave Holland; John Abercrombie; Cecil Taylor; Steve Coleman; Gil Evans; Jaki Byard; Anthony Braxton; others. Pl. w. Geo. Russell, Bob Moses fr. '87; Terumasa Hino '89; Al Grey fr. '91. Also freelanced in Bost. w. Mick Goodrick; John Lockwood; Tim Hagans; Gary Valente; in NYC w. Jack McDuff; Larry Moses; Harvie Swartz; Greg Bandy; Greg Kogan; Clark Terry. Scheps has taught at Mannes Coll. of Mus. fr. '90. Leads own gps., the Core-Tet and Bartokking Heads. Pl. w. Roswell Rudd in co-led qt., SF '99. Favs: John Coltrane, Sonny Rollins, Joe Henderson, John Gilmore, Billy Harper. Polls: DB Student Awds. '84–5, '87. Fests: Japan w. Hino '90; Eur. fr. '84. TV: Merv Griffin Show w. Buddy Rich '82; NYC Live at 5. CDs: w. Terumasa Hino (BN); Darrell Katz (Cad.); Jazz Comp. Alliance (Northeastern); Duffy Jackson (Mile.).

SCHIAFFINI, GIANCARLO, tbn, tba, comp, arr; b. Rome, Italy, 10/23/42. Played tpt. for two yrs. then sw. to tbn. Self-taught fr. age 15. Pl. w. Gruppo Romano Free Jazz 1965–70; duo w. Andrea Centazzo; own trio '77–80; Giorgio Gaslini '78; own tentet '80–1; duo w. Tiziana Ghiglioni '84–9; Dino Betti Van Der Noot bb '87–9; Ital. Instabile Orch. fr. '90; own nonet fr. '92. Schiaffini has taught tbn. and tpt. at the Pesaro and Liaquila Cons. fr. '75 and at the Siena jazz clinic every summer fr. '83. He is active in mus. theater as both a comp. and an actor. He is also involved in el. mus. and contemporary classical mus., and has collab. w. such composers as Giacinto Scelsi and Luigi Nono. Holds a doctorate in physics fr. Rome U. and worked as a physicist at a nuclear research center in Rome '67–75. Favs: Tricky Sam Nanton, J. J. Johnson; arr. Gil Evans. Fests: all major in Eur.; also U.S., Japan, India, Austral., Mex. TV: Eur. TV. CDs: Cramps; Spl.; BMG-Ariola; Leo; Pentaflowers; w. T. Ghiglioni (Spl.); L. Nono (Ed.RZ; Ricordi).

SCHIFRIN, LALO (BORIS), comp, pno; b. Buenos Aires, Argentina, 6/21/32. Father was cond. of Buenos Aires Philharm. Extensive pno. stud., incl. scholarship at Paris Cons. Pl. at jf while in Paris. In Argentina, form. a bb that was heard by Dizzy Gillespie 1956. After '58 moved to NYC where he worked w. jazz trio and arr. for Xavier Cugat; he gave his *Gillespiana Suite* to Gillespie, who hired him for his qnt. After tour. w. Gillespie for three yrs. he worked for Quincy Jones, then concentrated entirely on comp. Scored dozens of films and TV series, w. occ. jazz interludes such as his *Jazz Suite on the Mass Text,* for Paul Horn; *Reflections* for Stan Getz; *The Cat* for Jimmy Smith; and *Dialogues for Jazz Quintet and Orchestra* for Cannonball Adderley. In '67 he comp. the Grammy-winning theme for *Mission Impossible,* a long-running TV series that later became a film. His jazz score for the film *El Jefe* won Argentinian Academy Award; other film scores incl. *Dirty Harry* '71; *Magnum Force* '73; *The Eagle Has Landed* '77; *Voyage of the Damned* '76; *The Sting II* '85. Reunited intermittently w. Gillespie, but in recent yrs. has been active mainly as cond. of the Glendale Symph. Tour. Eur. fests. at head of all-star horns, incl. Phil Woods, James Morrison, Jon Faddis '94. Commissioned by Bix Beiderbecke Society in '95 to write *A Rhapsody for Bix.* CDs: Aleph (own co.); Atl.; w. D. Gillespie (Philips; Verve); Jimmy Smith; Cal Tjader (Verve); Eric Dolphy (Enja); Coleman Hawkins (Pab.); Q. Jones (Merc.).

SCHILDKRAUT, DAVEY (DAVID), alto sax; b. NYC, 1/7/25; d. NYC, 1/1/98. Professional debut w. Louis Prima 1941; later w. Buddy Rich, Anita O'Day '47; Stan Kenton '53–4; Pete Rugolo '54. Rec. w. Oscar Pettiford '54; Miles Davis (incl. *Solar*) '54. Also worked w. George Handy '55; rejoined Kenton '59; freelanced fr. '60s, incl. gig w. Eddie Bert at West End Café, NYC. Strongly infl. by Charlie Parker. Drifted away from jazz scene in later yrs. Rec. w. Bert; Handy. CDs: w. Miles Davis (Prest.); S. Kenton (Natasha; Astral Jazz).

SCHLIPPENBACH, ALEX (ALEXANDER VON), pno, comp; b. Berlin, Germany, 4/7/38. Classical studies fr. age 8. Pl. w. Gunter Hampel 1963–5; also w. Manfred Schoof '64–7. Earned wide praise for his comp. *Globe Unity,* perf. at '66 Berlin fest. by Globe Unity Orch. From '67 he led various small gps. and occ. perf. and rec. as soloist. Cont. off and on w. Globe Unity Orch. which at times incl. Kenny Wheeler; George Lewis; Evan Parker; and Steve Lacy. A key figure in the interrelationship of improv. and comp. employing avant-garde classical and free jazz elements. CDs: FMP; w. Berlin Contemporary Jazz Orch. (ECM; DIW); Globe Unity (FMP); Evan Parker (Leo); Aki Takase (FMP).

SCHMIDLIN, PETER, dms; b. Basel, Switzerland, 12/28/47. Self-taught; made prof. debut in Switz. 1965. From '70 he worked w. many touring US mus., incl. Johnny Griffin; Dexter Gordon; Slide Hampton; Lee Konitz; Dizzy Reece. Member of Jazz Live Trio of Radio Zurich '70–83; Swiss sxt., Magog '72–7; Dusko Goykovich Qnt. '78–9; Horace Parlan Trio '80–4; Benny Bailey Qnt. '86–91; George Robert Qt. (gp. has also incl. Clark Terry) since '89, incl. US club apps. in '91. Won first prize as best dmr. at Int'l JF Zurich '62. President and executive producer of TCB label. CDs: w. G. Robert; B. Bailey; Alice Day and CoJazz Plus (TCB); C. Terry–G. Robert (Mons).

SCHNEIDER, MARIA LYNN, comp, arr, pno; b. Windom, MN, 11/27/60. Studied pno., theory w. Evelyn Butler in Windom 1965–78; at U. of Minn. '79–83 (B. Mus. '83); U. of Miami '84; w. Rayburn Wright at Eastman Sch. of Mus. '84–5 (M. Mus. '85). Moved to NYC '85; stud. priv. w. Bob Brookmeyer '86–7. Arr. for Woody Herman Orch., Mel Lewis Orch. Assist. arr. to Gil Evans on film *The Color of Money;* also on Sting's Eur. tour w. Gil Evans Orch. '87. Co-led John Fedchock–Maria Schneider bb '88–91. Received Gil Evans Fellowship Awd. fr. Int'l Assoc. of Jazz Educs. '91. Cond. own mus. w. Stockholm Jazz Orch.; Danish Radio Orch.; Cologne Radio Orch.; Norrbottens bb (Lulea, Sweden) '93. Cond. Gil Evans' mus. at Spoleto Fest. '93. Has led her own jazz orch. on Mon. nights at Visiones in NYC fr. '93. Taught harmony and arr. at New Sch. '93–4; arr. at Manh. Sch. of Mus. '94. Favs: Bob Brookmeyer, Gil Evans, Duke Ellington. Comp: three-part *Scenes From Childhood.* CDs: Enja; w. Kevin Mahogany (Enja).

SCHNEIDERMAN, ROB (ROBERT ROLAND), pno; b. Boston, MA, 6/21/57. Grew up in Palo Alto, Calif., fr. age 5. Moth., classical pnst. and teacher, gave him lessons at age 8. Moved to San Diego at age 12. At 16 he form. a band in hs w. Peter Sprague. Stud. informally w. pnst. Butch Lacy. Played in San Diego w. Charles McPherson, Eddie Harris late 1970s-82. Moved to NYC '82. Pl. w. Chet Baker; Art Farmer; Clifford Jordan; James Moody; Zoot Sims; Slide Hampton; Jimmy Heath; Junior Cook; Harold Land; J. J. Johnson; TanaReid. Schneiderman taught jazz courses at Queens Coll. and William Paterson Coll. '85–92. Awarded NEA Jazz Fellowship '87. From '88 to '94 he attended City Coll., where he earned a B.A. in math. and pl. four yrs. of varsity soccer. Moved to Berkeley, Calif., in Aug. '94. Received

Doctorate in math. fr. U. of Calif., '95. Active as math. profess. while working w. own trio on weekends in SF. Comps. incl. "New Outlook"; "Radio Waves;" "Dark Blue"; all title tracks from his Res. recs. Favs: Bud Powell, Erroll Garner, Sonny Clark. Fests: Eur. w. C. Baker '85; E. Harris '90; Japan w. J. J. Johnson '91. CDs: Res.; w. J. J. Johnson; TanaReid; Rufus Reid (Conc.); Fred Hersch (Classical Action).

SCHNITTER, DAVE (DAVID BERTRAM), tnr sax, sop sax, cl, fl; b. Newark, NJ, 3/19/48. Began on cl. at age 9, then sw. to sax at age 15. Received B.A. fr. N.J. St. Coll. Pl. w. r&b, Latin, and club date bands in hs and coll. Began visiting NYC for jam sess., rehearsals, Latin gigs 1972. Sat in w. Joe Newman; Frank Foster; Howard McGhee; then began working w. Ted Dunbar, Wilbur Little '73. Led own gp. at Boomer's three nights a week '73–4. Join. Art Blakey Nov. '74. Pl. w. Blakey '74–80; Walter Bishop Jr. Sxt. '79–80; Freddie Hubbard '80–2; Vibration Society (Rahsaan Roland Kirk tribute band) '83–4. Also pl. in early '80s w. Frank Foster; Charles Earland; Groove Holmes; Johnny Lytle. Lived in Valencia, Spain '83–90, working w. Tete Montoliu; Daniel Humair; Mal Waldron; Sal Nistico; Marion Brown; Barney Kessel. Also freelanced throughout Eur. Toured Spain w. Slide Hampton's Echoes of Bebop bb '86. Tour. Spain w. Blakey; Jackie McLean; Benny Golson; Curtis Fuller; and then Jazz Messengers; Javon Jackson; Brian Lynch; Geoff Keezer; Essiet Essiet '90. Moved to NYC in '90. Worked w. Mickey Bass '95. Favs: John Coltrane, Joe Henderson, Dexter Gordon. Fests: all major w. Blakey, Hubbard. TV: Eur., Jap., Brazilian TV w. Blakey. LPs: Muse. CDs: w. A. Blakey (Conc.; Timel.); F. Hubbard (Pab.); S. Stitt (Muse).

SCHOEBEL, ELMER, pno, comp; b. East St. Louis, IL, 9/8/1896; d. St. Petersburg, FL, 12/14/70. Played pno. in silent films and vaudeville shows fr. age 14. To Chi. after WWI; pl. and wrote for Friar's Society Orch. (aka NORK) 1922–3. For many yrs. he worked as staff arr. for Warner Bros. in NYC. Resumed pl. pno. in 40s; joined Conrad Janis '50–53. Settled in Calif. in late '60s. Schoebel was one of the first important comp.-arrs. in jazz. In the early '20s, he prepared many King Oliver, Louis Armstrong and Jelly Roll Morton works for publication. As a songwriter, his many hits incl. "Farewell Blues"; "Bugle Call Rag"; "Nobody's Sweetheart"; "Prince of Wails"; "Spanish Shawl"; "House of David Blues"; CDs: w. New Orleans Rhythm Kings (Mile.).

SCHOENBERG, LOREN, lead, tnr sax, pno; b. Fairlawn, NJ, 7/23/58. Began on tpt. and cl. in jr. hs. Stud. pno. w. Sanford Gold, Hank Jones 1973–6; sax w. Joe Allard '78–80; Lee Konitz '76; John Purcell '86. Pl. w. Eddie Durham '76–80; Harold Ashby '78–81 (pno.); Harlem Blues and Jazz Band '78–9; Sammy Price '79; Joe Albany '79–80; Jo Jones '80; Jabbo Smith '80–4; Panama Francis's Savoy Sultans '83. Also worked as Benny Goodman's personal manager '80–5. Led own bb since '80; in '85 entire band was hired by Goodman. Pl. w. Buck Clayton '85–7; AJO fr. '86; Benny Carter fr. '88; Harold Nicholas '89; Peanuts Hucko, Sylvia Syms '90; Smithsonian Jazz Orch. '91. Radio host on NYC jazz stations fr. '82. Gave lecture at Int'l Ellington Conf. in Manchester, Engl. '88. Schoenberg cond. the Germ. Radio Orch. of Cologne '88–9 and cond. the AJO '91–2; Smithsonian Jazz Orch, fr. '91. Mus. dir. and tnr. sax for Bobby Short small band; guest soloist w. LCJO, late '90s. Fav. tnrs: Lester Young, Coleman Hawkins, Sonny Rollins, Bud Freeman; fav. pnos: Art Tatum, Fred Hersch, Kenny Werner. Polls: *DB* TDWR '89. Fests: Eur., Austral., Asia since '81. TV: *Let's Dance* w. B. Goodman on PBS; *Today*. CDs: TCB; MM; w. AJO (EW); B. Goodman; Benny Carter (MM); David Murray (Stash); T. Talbert (Chartmaker); K. Peplowski (Conc.); B. Short (Tel.)

SCHOOF, MANFRED, tpt, flg, pno, perc, comp; b. Magdeburg, Germany, 4/6/36. Studied at Mus. Akademie, Kassel 1955–8, later in Cologne. Pl. w. Gunter Hampel '63–5; led own gp. fr. '65. Worked occ. w. A. Mangelsdorf; w. Geo. Russell '69 and '71. Comp. concerto for tpt. perf. by Berlin Phil. '69. Pl. w. Clarke-Boland orch. '69–71; toured Asia w. own sxt. '75; comp. *Ode* for Globe Unity Orch. Worked w. Mal Waldron '74–80; formed own bb '80. CDs: Wergo; w. Heiner Stadler (JA); European Jazz Ens. (Ear-Rational; M.A. Music); Globe Unity Orch. (FMP); Gunther Hampel (Birth): George Russell (SN).

SCHROEDER, GENE (EUGENE CHARLES), pno; b. Madison, WI, 2/5/15; d. Madison, 2/16/75. Musical family; stud. pno. and cl. in Wisc. To NYC 1939; pl. w. Joe and Marty Marsala; also Wild Bill Davison in Chi. and NYC. In '43 he began a long assoc. w. Eddie Condon at his club, on a TV series, and on tour. In '60s w. Dukes of Dixieland and Tony Parenti. CDs: w. Eddie Condon (Col.; Sav.; Mos.; Stash); Esq. All-Amer. Poll Winners (BB); S. Bechet (Laser.); J. Teagarden (BB;Mos.); Bud Freeman (RCA); Bobby Hackett (Dormouse)

SCHULLER, ED (EDWIN G.), bs, comp; b. NYC, 1/11/55. Father is Gunther Schuller. Began on gtr., cl. Began pl. bs. at age 15; pl. first prof. gig w. Ricky Ford the same year. Stud. at New Engl. Cons. Pl. w.

Lee Konitz; Joe Lovano; Ted Curson; Dave Liebman; Jimmy Knepper; Clark Terry; Ran Blake; Paul McCandless; Billy Hart; Marty Ehrlich; Roland Hanna. Tour. w. Lovano; Paul Motian; Tim Berne; Jim Pepper; Pat Martino; Mal Waldron; Gerry Hemingway; Mingus Epitaph Orch.; Jaki Byard. Taught at Newark Acad., Berklee Coll. of Mus. Headed the jazz dept. at the Schweitzer Inst. of Mus. in Sandpoint, Idaho, fr. 1988. Favs: Pettiford, Mingus, Dave Holland. Fests: Eur., Australia, Venezuela fr. '80. CDs: Tutu; GM; Timescraper; w. Mingus Epitaph (Col.); Lovano (BN); Motian (ECM; SN); Tom Varner; Tim Berne (SN); Franco Ambrosetti (Enja); George Schuller; Bill De Arango (GM); Perry Robinson (WW); Waldron; J. Pepper (Tutu).

SCHULLER, GEORGE A., dms, perc; b. NYC, 12/29/58. Grandfather Arthur Schuller, vln., NY Philharm. 1924–65; fath., Gunther Schuller; moth., Marjorie Schuller, concert pno. and voc. in early '40s; bro., bsst. Ed Schuller. Moved to Boston '67. Stud. cl. ages 11–13; dms. fr. 11. Bachelor's degree in jazz perf. fr. New Engl. Cons. '82; then worked on Bost. scene for twelve yrs. w. Herb Pomeroy; J. Byard; J. Bergonzi; G. Garzone; Mick Goodrick; Ran Blake; Bill Pierce; Bruce Gertz; John LaPorta; Hal Crook. Co-founded 12-pc. ens. Orange Then Blue '84 and has tour. with it since in US, Can., Middle East, Eur. Moved to Bklyn. '94. Pl. and/or rec. w. Joe Wilder; Britt Woodman; Mose Allison; L. Konitz; Danilo Perez; T. Harrell; George Adams; Attila Zoller and the Smithsonian Jazz Masterworks Orch. Current bands incl. Lisa Thorson fr. '87; Tom Beckham fr. '96; Tom Varner Trio; Jim Pepper Remembrance Band fr. '97. Asst. rec. engineer, Tanglewood (Mass.) '75–82; Jazz dir., deejay, WMBR, Cambridge, Mass. '76–84. Comps. and arrs. have been rec. by Mike Metheny; Orange Then Blue; Ed Schuller; LaPorta-Wilder-Woodman Sxt. Favs: Elvin Jones, Tony Williams, DeJohnette. Fests: Berlin JF w. Orange Then Blue '95; Nijmegen (Netherlands) '95; Montreux-Detroit JF '96; Linz (Austria) w. Gunther Schuller dur. weeklong fest. of Gunther's compositional works; Jazz But, Munich, w. Pepper Remembrance Band '97; many Can. fests. Awards: NEA Rec. Grant '88; Comp. Grant '95. TV: soundtrack to *Face Down* w. Joe Lovano, mus. by Gunther Schuller, Showtime Prod. '96. CDs: GM; w. Orange Then Blue (GM); Lovano (BN); Gunther Schuller; Eugene Maslov; LaPorta-Wilder-Woodman; Bill De Arango (GM); Miles Donahue (Timel.); Thorson; Rob Levit (Brown.); Mili Bermejo (Xenophile).

SCHULLER, GUNTHER ALEXANDER, comp, cond, Fr hrn; b. Jackson Heights, NY, 11/11/25.

Father was violinist in N.Y. Philharm. Stud. w. principal horn of Met. Opera and w. Robert Schulze; also stud. fl. Pl. w. Amer. Ballet Theatre 1943; Cincinnati Symph. '43–5; Met. Opera '45–59. Pl. and rec. w. Miles Davis nonet '49–50. Coined term "third stream" to describe synthesis of jazz and classical forms '57; Schuller was the first classical mus. to be prominently identified w. this movement. Early third stream comps. incl. "Transformation" '57; *Concertino for Jazz Qt. and Orch.* '59; *Abstraction* '59; and *Variants on a Theme of Thelonious Monk* '60. Schuller collab. freq. w. John Lewis fr. the late '50s, and many of his comps. were rec. by the Modern Jazz Qt. Wrote articles of criticism and analysis for *Jazz Review* '58–60. Taught jazz styles and comp. at Lenox Sch. of Jazz, which he co-founded w. Lewis and others late '50s. Perf. at MJF '59. Premiered comp. *Conversation* w. MJQ and Beaux Arts String Qt. at Town Hall, Sept. '59. Premiered jazz ballet *Variants*, choreographed by Geo. Balanchine '61. Acting mus. dir. at MJF '61; mus. dir. at Int'l JF, Wash., D.C. '62. Cond. of John Lewis Orch. USA '62–5. Produced first jazz concert at Tanglewood, Mass. '63. Lectured on jazz in Poland, Yugoslavia, Germ., spons. by US St. Dept. '63. President of New Engl. Cons. '67–77. While in this position, he formed the New Engl. Cons. Ragtime Ens., which pl. reworked arrs. of Scott Joplin rags fr. the original Red Back Book; these arrs. were used on the soundtrack for film *The Sting* '74. Also formed New Engl. Cons. Jazz Repertory Orch., which perf. the arrs. of Duke Ellington; Fletcher Henderson; Don Redman; others. Publ. *Early Jazz: Its Roots and Musical Development* (Oxford), a book of jazz history and analysis '68. Produced monumental weekly radio series, *Music in Evolution*, for WBAI, NYC early '60s. Premiered comps. *Triplum 2* w. Balt. Symph., *Four Sound Scopes* w. Hudson Valley Philharm. '75. Formed mus. publ. cos. Margun Music '75, Gunmar Music '79. These firms publ. jazz and third stream works by Charles Mingus; George Russell; Johnny Carisi; Ran Blake; Jimmy Giuffre; as well as editions of mus. by Joplin; Joseph Lamb; Eubie Blake. Establ. GM Recs. label '80. In '89, he received Col. U.'s William Schuman award and publ. *The Swing Era: The Development of Jazz, 1930–1945* (Oxford), the second volume in a planned trilogy of which *Early Jazz* was the first. CDs: w. M. Davis (BN; Cap.); John Lewis (Atl.); Chas. Mingus (Rh.); Gigi Gryce (Sav.); M. Davis–Gil Evans (Col.); D. Gillespie (Verve); as comp. w. MJQ (Atl.).

SCHULMAN, IRA, fl, saxes, reeds; b. Newark, NJ, 1/12/26. Played in Chi. bands in 1950s. Moved to Calif. '59, working there w. Onzy Mathews; Don

Ellis (four yrs.); Dave Mackay–Vicky Hamilton (two yrs.). Fr. '70 he gave many clinics in LA schs., offering a varied program of Bach; Mozart; Debussy; Ellington; Parker; Monk; Clifford Brown. In early '80s he form. a sax/woodwind qt., The Four Winds, which perf. jazz and classical works in LA area. Jazz and poetry apps. w. Frankie Nemko; LP on Trend. CDs: w. Ellis (Col.).

SCHUMACHER, DAVE (DAVID MICHAEL), bari sax, saxes, fl, bs cl; b. Chicago, IL, 3/24/60. Studied, start. w. alto sax, at Rutgers U. w. Paul Jeffrey, Kenny Barron 1979–82. Pl. w. Bill De Arango, Cleve. '78; Tommy Ponce, Carl Leukaufe, Lin Halliday, Chi. '79; Eddie Gladden Sxt., Newark '80; Lionel Hampton bb '83–9, incl. extensive world touring; Art Blakey bb, Japan '87; Mel Tormé '93; Harry Connick Jr. fr. '90, incl. Eur., Japan; Jason Lindner bb fr. '96; Monk on Monk Tentet fr. '97, incl. Eur. fest. circuit. A robust, hard swinger who favors the baritone's lower register, reflecting some of his infls. Favs: Pepper Adams, Cecil Payne, Leo Parker, Carney. Awards: NEA Perf. Grants '91, '95. TV & Radio: w. Hampton; Connick. Co-founder of Amosaya Recs. CDs: Amo.; w. Hampton (Atl.; Glad Hamp); Tormé (Tel.); Connick (Col.).

SCHUTT, ARTHUR, pno; b. Reading, PA, 11/21/02; d. San Francisco, CA, 1/28/65. Professional debut pl. for silent movies 1916. Pno. and arr. w. Paul Specht '18. In NYC w. with Roger Wolfe Kahn orch., playing second pno. to Vincent Lopez. Best known through many famous jazz rec. dates w. Frankie Trumbauer, Bix Beiderbecke '27; Red Nichols '26–8 and '31; Joe Venuti '27–9; Miff Mole '27–9; Dorsey Bros. '28–9; Eddie Lang '29; Cotton Pickers '29; Charleston Chasers '29–30; Benny Goodman '31, '34; Adrian Rollini '33. From late '30s he was in Calif. as studio staff mus. and freelancer. Schutt—who in '22 pl. what was considered a precedent-setting ad lib solo chorus on Paul Specht's "All Muddled Up"—was, according to John Hammond, "the first jazz pianist with a big technique ever to become prominent on records." CDs: w. L. Armstrong; B. Beiderbecke; Emmett Miller (Col.); Judy Garland; B. Goodman (Dec.); E. Lang (ASV; Yazoo); Red Nichols (Village; ASV; Tax); King Oliver (CDS); J. Teagarden (BB; ASV); J. Venuti (JSP).

SCHUUR, DIANE JOAN, voc, pno; b. Tacoma, WA, 12/10/53. Blinded in a hospital accident at birth. Studied mus. at Wash. Sch. for the Blind; stud. jazz voc. and pno. improv. while in her twenties. Discovered by Ed Shaughnessy, who feat. her w. bb, Energy Force, at MJF '75. Rec. career began on GRP w. *Dee-*

dles '84. Won Grammys for *Timeless* '86, and *Diane Schuur with the Count Basie Orchestra* '87. App. w. Stan Getz at White House '82, and on Carnegie Hall TV Special '87. Rec. duets. w. B. B. King in '94. Although gifted with a fine voice, an excellent ear for harmony, and solid jazz rhythms, Schuur sometimes fails to exercise restraint and oversteps the bounds of good taste. She has occasionally been misdirected toward superficial pop recs. CDs: GRP; Atl.

SCOBEY, BOB (ROBERT ALEXANDER JR.), tpt; b. Tucumcari, NM, 12/9/16; d. Montreal, Que., Canada, 6/12/63. Raised in Stockton, Calif.; army band 1942–6. Prominent w. Lu Watters Yerba Buena Band throughout '40s, playing second crnt./tpt. in Oliver-Armstrong style. Led own band in Oakland, Calif., in '50s; moved to Chi. in early '60s. Key figure in West Coast revival of traditional jazz, in which ensembles took precedence over solos. His sidemen on recs. incl. Matty Matlock; Ralph Sutton; Art Hodes. Rec. as a sideman w. Sidney Bechet '53 and Bing Crosby '57. CDs: w. Clancy Hayes; Lu Watters (GTJ).

SCOFIELD, JOHN, gtr, comp; b. Dayton, OH, 12/26/51. Raised in Wilton, Conn. Took up gtr. at age 11. Played in rock and r&b gps. as a teenager but studied jazz fr. 1966. Pl. bs briefly prior to entering Berklee Coll., where he studied w. Mick Goodrick and Gary Burton '70–3. Carnegie Hall concert w. Gerry Mulligan–Chet Baker '74; then joined Billy Cobham–George Duke jazz/rock gp. Rec. w. Charles Mingus; rejoined G. Burton; tour. Japan w. Terumasa Hino; in '77 he led a band tour. Eur. In '79 he led trio w. Steve Swallow and Adam Nussbaum; in late '82 he join. Miles Davis, whose gp. also incl. gtrst. Mike Stern. After leaving Davis in '85, he again led and rec. w. his own gps. Perf. at tribute concert for Tal Farlow w. John Abercrombie and Larry Coryell. Joined Marc Johnson's Bass Desires gp; rec. w. Jay McShann; toured Eur. w. Mike Gibbs bb '91. From early '90s, his regular gp. incl. Joe Lovano, Dennis Irwin, and Bill Stewart. In '91 the *DB* poll named him the number one guitarist and positioned his band, Electric Jazz, equally. A strongly linear player, Scofield mixes feedback and avant-garde electronic effects w. a strong melodic flow. CDs: BN; Novus; Gram.; Verve; Enja; w. G. Mulligan–C. Baker (CTI); Tal Farlow (Verve); L. Coryell (Novus); C. Baker (CTI; A&M); M. Davis (Col.); C. Mingus (Atl.); McCoy Tyner (BN); Gary Burton (Conc.; GRP); H. Hancock; Joe Henderson (Verve); George Adams (Timel.); Franco Ambrosetti; Ray Anderson (Enja); Jim Hall (MM); Paul Bley (SN); Marc Johnson (ECM).

SCOTT, BOBBY, pno, comp, vocals; b. Bronx, NY, 1/24/37; d. NYC, 11/5/90. Studied at La Follette Sch. of Mus. in NYC 1945; w. Edvard Moritz, a former pupil of Debussy, '49. During his teens, he pl w. Louis Prima, Tony Scott (no relation); w. Gene Krupa 1955. Pl. w. Lester Young. As a singer, he had a '56 hit w. an ABC single, "Chain Gang." Played club dates and taught theory in the late '50s; worked w. Quincy Jones at Mercury Recs. as pnst, arr., and a&r man in the '60s, often not, he claimed, getting proper credit for his work. The title song of his score for the film *A Taste of Honey* was a major pop hit, as was his tune "He Ain't Heavy, He's My Brother," rec. by Neil Diamond in '70. A versatile artist whose comps. went beyond jazz and pop to embrace concert mus. in a wide variety of areas. Was writing autobiography at time of death (unpubl.); comp. "Solitude Book" for guitarist Carlos Barbosa-Lima, arr. for Lou Rawls, rec. w. L. Hampton. Favs: Bill Evans, Dave McKenna; comp: Bela Bartok, Roy Harris. LPs: Beth.; ABC-Par.; Verve. CDs: MM; w. L. Hampton (MM); Wes Montgomery (Verve); Lou Rawls (BN); Q. Jones (Merc.; Imp.); Shirley Horn; R. R. Kirk (Merc.).

SCOTT, BUD ARTHUR, gtr, bjo, voc; b. New Orleans, LA, 1/11/1890; d. Los Angeles, CA, 7/2/49. In the teens, he pl. w. Buddy Bolden; John Robichaux; Freddie Keppard; sang, pl. in vaudeville tours fr. 1913. To NYC '15; pl. in pit bands. To Chi. in '23 where he pl. and rec. on bjo. w. King Oliver, originating the traditional "Oh, play that thing!" shout on "Dippermouth Blues." Back and forth between LA and Chi., working w. Kid Ory (LA), Oliver again (Chi.). With Erskine Tate in Chi. '26, then Dave Peyton. Also worked w. Jimmie Noone at Apex Club, Chi. '28; then settled in LA, working w. Mutt Carey in '30s, leading own gp. late '30s. Back w. Kid Ory '44–8. App. w. L. Armstrong in film *New Orleans* '47. CDs: w. L. Armstrong (Col.; Vict.; Dec.); King Oliver (Dec.); J. R. Morton (BB); Johnny Dodds (Dec.); J. Noone (Milan; Collectors' Classics).

SCOTT, CECIL XAVIER, saxes, cl; b. Springfield, OH, 11/22/05; d. NYC, 1/5/64. Played w. his bro., Lloyd (b. 1902), in Scott's Symphonic Syncopators; cont. to work together under Cecil's or Lloyd's name through 1920s. Cecil later worked w. various Clarence Williams units, the Missourians, and Fletcher Henderson. Pl. w. Teddy Hill '36–7; Alberto Socarras '37–42. In '40s led own bb, then small gps. w. Hot Lips Page; Art Hodes; and, in '50s, Jimmy McPartland; Willie "The Lion" Smith; and others. A versatile mus./showman, Scott sometimes pl. three clarinets simultaneously. CDs: w. Billie Holiday (Col.); Alberta Hunter; Rex Stewart (Prest.); Henry Red Allen (Tax; Collector's Classics); Teddy Wilson (Hep); Willie "The Lion" Smith (Timel.); Clarence Williams (CDS).

SCOTT, HAZEL DOROTHY, pno, voc; b. Port of Spain, Trinidad, 11/11/20; d. NYC, 10/2/81. To US in 1924 w. moth., who led an all-female band. A child prodigy; stud. at Juilliard from age 8; own radio series '36; sang in B'way show, *Sing Out the News* '38; earned big following at Café Society '39–45. Married Rev. Adam Clayton Powell '45; app. w. Billie Holiday for FDR at White House dur. WWII; worked in movies, concerts, and clubs to '57; lived in France for two yrs. Best rec., *Relaxed Piano Moods* '55, for C. Mingus's Debut Records, w. Mingus and Max Roach. Known for jazz interpretations of classical pieces. Infl. by Tatum, Hines, Teddy Wilson, and, later, Bud Powell. Films: *I Dood It*: *Rhapsody in Blue*. TV: Own show. CDs: Debut; two tracks on *The Women* (BB).

SCOTT, LITTLE JIMMY (JAMES VICTOR), voc; b. Cleveland, OH, 7/17/25. Mother, a church pnst., was killed in auto accident when Scott was 13; he was raised in a foster home. First prof. gigs touring Midwest and South w. Estelle "Caledonia" Young mid '40s. Scott's diminutive stature and baby face led listeners to assume he was a child, thus the nickname. Joined Lionel Hampton 1948; rec. his first hit record, "Everybody's Somebody's Fool," w. Hampton '50. Solo career in early '50s; rec. for Roost, incl. "The Masquerade Is Over." From the '50s Scott's career was a roller coaster of occ. rec. deals and long absences fr. the mus. business. Ray Charles, a long-time admirer, rec. him for his Tangerine label, but the record was withdrawn for contractual reasons and Scott lapsed into a twenty-yr. oblivion. Resumed perf. in mid '80s, helped by such admirers as Ruth Brown and songwriter Doc Pomus. He ret. to recs. and club apps. in '92. CDs: Spec.; WB; w. David Sanborn (Elek.); Hampton (Dec.).

SCOTT, RAYMOND (Harry Warnow), comp; b. 9/10/08; d. North Hills, CA, 2/8/94. Worked w. bro. Mark Warnow's orch. 1932–4. Best known as leader of a qnt. that in '30s rec. a series of novelty tunes, such as "Huckleberry Duck"; "Dinner Music for a Pack of Hungry Cannibals"; "Confusion Among a Fleet of Taxicabs Upon Meeting with a Fare"; "Twilight in Turkey." Led bb '39–41; then at CBS '42, cond. the first interracial orch. to work as a house band; members incl. Charlie Shavers; Ben Webster; Cliff Leeman; Johnny Guarnieri. Later pioneered development of el. mus. devices. Inactive due to illness from '80s. Married to voc. Dorothy Collins of '50s *Hit Parade* TV show. CDs: Col.; Stash.

SCOTT, RONNIE, tnr sax, lead; b. London, England, 1/28/27; d. London, 12/23/96. Began on sop. and sw. to tnr. at age 15. Pl. w. Johnny Claes 1944–5; Ted Heath '46; Cab Kaye. Pl. on the *Queen Mary* '46–8; heard Dizzy Gillespie; Charlie Parker; Bud Powell when ship docked in NYC. Co-founded Club Eleven '48. Pl. w. Tito Burns, Jack Parnell '52; then formed own 9-pc. band w. Jimmy Deuchar, Derek Humble, Victor Feldman, Phil Seaman '53. Toured US in '55. Formed Jazz Couriers w. Tubby Hayes '56; pl. in Eur. '57–9. Operated own club, Ronnie Scott's, in London '59–67, pl. there w. own gp. w. Stan Tracey. Pl. w. Kenny Clarke–Francy Boland bb '62–73. Led own gp. w. Deuchar, Ronnie Ross at Half Note, NYC '63. Led oct. w. Kenny Wheeler '68–9; trio w. Mike Carr '71–5. Perf. at Carnegie Hall, NYC '74. Led qt. and qnt. w. Dick Pearce fr. '75. Ronnie Scott's moved to a larger location in Frith St. in '67; it remains the main venue for visiting Amer. mus. Club has own Jazz House label. Scott was awarded the OBE in '81. Fests: all major in Eur.; Jazz Yatra, Bombay '84. TV: Eur. TV; concert on ABC '74. CDs: JH; w. Clarke-Boland (MPS); Victor Feldman (Cont.).

SCOTT, SHIRLEY, org, pno, comp; b. Philadelphia, PA, 3/14/34; d. Philadelphia, 3/10/02. From musical family. Stud. pno. at Ornstein Sch. of Mus., Phila. Took up tpt. in hs and won scholarship. Pl. pno. w. bro.'s band in father's priv. club. Began playing org. at Phila. club in 1955; worked w. Eddie "Lockjaw" Davis '56–60. Led own trio briefly, then worked w. Stanley Turrentine '60–71. Scott and Turrentine were married in '61 and divorced in '71. Toured w. own gp. and rec. for Chess label '71–4. Formed bop trio w. Harold Vick '74. Rec. w. Jimmy Forrest '78; Dexter Gordon '82. In the '90s, Scott ret. to pl. pno. and org. She led the house band on Bill Cosby's *You Bet Your Life* TV show '92. Hospitalized after severe side effects fr. diet pills '97–8. Favs: Milt Buckner, Jackie Davis, Jimmy Smith. TV: many apps. on NYC and Phila. TV in '60s-70s. CDs: Imp.; Muse; Cand.; w. E. Davis (Prest.); S. Turrentine (BN; Imp.); Antonio Hart (Imp.).

SCOTT, TOM (THOMAS WRIGHT), tnr sax, comp; b. Los Angeles, CA, 5/19/48. Father is Nathan Scott, a film and TV comp. (*Dragnet, My Three Sons*); moth. a pnst. Started on cl.; self-taught as comp.-arr.; his Neoteric Trio won combo division of Teenage Battle of the Bands at Hollywood Bowl 1965. Pl. w. Don Ellis; Oliver Nelson; Roger Kell-

away; and Howard Roberts while still a teenager; at 19 made first rec., *Honeysuckle Breeze*, which incl. one of his best-known comp., "Blues for Hari." In late '60s and early '70s, he worked as a studio mus. and comp. of TV scores for such series as *Streets of San Francisco; Cannon; Baretta*; etc., and film scores for *Conquest of the Planet of Apes* and *Uptown Saturday Night*. As a player he was closely associated w. Kellaway; John Guerin; Max Bennett; and others. Formed jazz-fusion gp. L.A. Express '73; rec. and toured w. Joni Mitchell. Toured w. Ravi Shankar and George Harrison '75; cont. studio work into '80s and '90s; mus. dir. for *The Pat Sajak Show* fr. '87; rec. w. Gerry Mulligan; George Benson; Tony Williams; and Woody Herman; and under own name for GRP. After many jazz-fusion and jazz-rock hybrid recs., he ret. to mainstream jazz in '92 w. rec. *Born Again*. CDs: GRP; Epic; w. LA Workshop (Den.); De Novo (Interface); Manh. Transfer (Atl.); GRP All-Star bb (GRP); Jonathan Butler (N2K); Earl Klugh (BN).

SCOTT, TONY (Anthony J. Sciacca), cl, saxes, comp, pno, voc; b. Morristown, NJ, 6/17/21. From a family of musicians; stud. at Juilliard 1940–2; led own band in army '42–5. Made transition fr. Benny Goodman to Charlie Parker. Pl. w. Buddy Rich, Ben Webster, Trummy Young, Charlie Ventura, Sid Catlett late '40s; also occ. worked as pnst. for singers. Worked w. Claude Thornhill band '49; wrote arr. for Billie Holiday, Sarah Vaughan; pl. w. Duke Ellington for a mo. '53. For balance of '50s, he wrote charts and pl. cl., pno., and saxes. Worked at Minton's, NYC; as mus. dir. for Harry Belafonte; and led his gp. on tours and at fests. Spent first half of '60s traveling in Far East, playing mus. drawn fr. Indian and Asian sources. In '64 he rec. *Music for Zen Meditation*, one of the first New Age recs. Worked w. own gps. in late '60s, incl. a concert of Indian music w. Collin Walcott '67. Based mainly in Italy since '70 he cont. to travel internationally, often perf. w. Romano Mussolini qt. and own gps. CDs: Verve; Sunny; Phil.; 32; Core; FS; RCA; Verve; SN; w. Benny Carter; Sarah Vaughan; D. Gillespie (Class.); Coleman Hawkins (Dec.); B. Holiday (Verve); C. McRae (Beth.); Max Roach (SN).

SEALES, MARC ANTHONY, pno, synth; b. Tacoma, WA, 7/23/54. From a musical family. Began taking pno. lessons while in hs. Stud. at Western Wash. U. and w. Jerome Graj in Seattle. First prof. job pl. in bro.'s rock band. Led own gp. in Seattle 1982–8. Pl. w. Ernestine Anderson '82–3. Gigs w. Joe Henderson '82–5; Kenny G '83; Slide Hampton, Bobby Hutcherson '84; James Newton '85. Pl. w. Mark Murphy off and on fr. '82; Don Lanphere fr.

'85. Freelanced w. Clark Terry, Art Farmer, Eddie Vinson '87; Julian Priester, Frank Morgan '88; Red Holloway '89. Led own trio fr. '90; own gp., New Stories fr. '92. Freelanced w. Larry Coryell '90; Benny Golson–Slide Hampton '92; Jon Faddis '93; Pete Christlieb, Teddy Edwards, Eddie Daniels '94. On faculty of the U. of Wash. Favs: Herbie Hancock, Wynton Kelly, Bill Evans. Fests: North Sea '85 and DuMaurier-Vancouver '91, both w. Lanphere; JVC-Russia w. New Stories '93. CDs: w. New Stories (Origin); Mark Murphy (Vict.); Lanphere (Hep).

SEAMEN, PHIL (PHILIP WILLIAM), dms; b. Burton-on-Trent, England, 8/28/26; d. Lambeth, England, 10/13/72. Played w. Nat Gonella, Ken Turner in 1940s; w. Jack Parnell, Ronnie Scott, Kenny Baker in '50s; also w. Tubby Hayes; Joe Harriot, and, in '60s, w. Georgie Fame. House dmr. at Ronnie Scott club '64–8. In the '60s, he was rated most inventive and versatile dmr. in Engl. CDs: w. D. Morrissey (Home.); Tony Coe (Hep); Victor Feldman (Cont.); Tubby Hayes (JH); Bruce Turner (Lake).

SEARS, AL (ALBERT OMEGA), tnr sax; b. Macomb, IL, 2/21/10. Played w. Paul Craig in Buffalo, NY, 1927; Chick Webb at Savoy Ballroom, NYC late '28. Toured w. *Keep Shufflin'* revue; pl. w. Zack Whyte '29; Elmer Snowder '31–2. Led own gps. in '30s, first in Buffalo, later in Newport, Ky. (incl. singer Helen Humes), and at the Renaissance Ballroom, NYC. In early '40s, he worked w. Andy Kirk, Lionel Hampton; took own band (w. Lester Young) on USO tour. Feat. w. D. Ellington '43–9 and on and off until '51, as prominent soloist. Mus. dir. of Johnny Hodges band '51; scored first big hit as comp. of "Castle Rock." Quit Hodges '52 to settle in NYC and concentrate on mus. publishing, espec. in area of r&b. Sears's best solos w. Ellington were characterized by unusually brisk, choppy phrasing, a staccato articulation, and a vociferous emotionalism. CDs: Prest.; w. D. Ellington (Vict.; Col.; Prest.); Hodges (Prest.; Verve); L. Hampton; Rex Stewart; H. James (Class.); C. Hawkins (Prest.); Buddy Rich (Hep);

SEATON, LYNN EARL, bs; b. Tulsa, OK, 7/18/57. Sister pl. fl. Began on gtr., then sw. to bs. at age 9. Stud. at U. of Okla.; received NEA grant in 1980 to stud. w. Rufus Reid. Pl. w. rock, blues, and jazz gps. in Okla., then moved to Cincinnati, Ohio '80, where he pl. w. Blue Wisp bb; Steve Schmidt Trio w. visiting soloists, incl. Herb Ellis; Scott Hamilton; Warren Vaché; Al Cohn; Nick Brignola; Maxine Sullivan; Carol Sloane; also occ. w. Cincinnati Pops Orch. Adjunct prof. of mus. at U. of Cincinnati '82–4. Join. Woody Herman '84. Pl. w. Count Basie Orch. '85–7;

Tony Bennett '87. Moved to NYC '87, pl. w. George Shearing '87–8. Freelanced since '88 w. Mel Lewis; Toshiko Akiyoshi–Lew Tabackin; Howard Alden; Ernestine Anderson; Joe Williams; Buck Clayton bb; others. Pl. w. Monty Alexander since '89; also own trio. Stud. w. François Rabbath in Paris '91. Favs: Slam Stewart, Major Holley, Rufus Reid, Ray Brown. Fests: Eur., Japan, Carib., etc., since '84. TV: Cosby Show w. C. Basie Orch. CDs: w. H. Alden (Conc.); C. Basie Orch. (Den.; Philips); Frank Wess; John Colianni; Ernestine Anderson (Conc.); Milt Hinton (Col.); DMP bb (DMP); John Fedchock (Res.); Kenny Drew Jr. (Mile.).

SEBASTIAN, RICKY (JAMES), dms, perc, pno; b. Opelousas, LA, 12/5/56. Studied at U. of SW La., then at Berklee Coll. of Mus. First prof. gig w. Emmet Kelly Circus at age 16. Pl. w. Ellis Marsalis; Harry Connick Jr.; Dr. John; and others in NO bef. moving to NYC '83. Pl. w. Mike Stern; Sam Rivers; Jaco Pastorius; Bobby McFerrin; John Scofield; Dave Valentin; Claudio Roditi; Herbie Mann; Gil Evans. Sebastian has been on teaching staff at Dmrs.' Collective since '85. He app. w. Gil Evans on the soundtrack of the film *The Color of Money*. Favs: Tony Williams, Elvin Jones, Steve Gadd. Fests: Eur., Asia, Austral. CDs: w. Herbie Mann (Chesky); Tania Maria (Conc.); C. Fambrough (Evid.).

SEBESKY, DON (DONALD J.), comp, arr, pno, tbn; b. Perth Amboy, NJ, 12/10/37. Brother Jerry pl. pno., tbn. Began on acdn. Stud. tbn. w. Warren Covington at Manh. Sch. of Mus. 1953–7; stud. comp. '55–9. Pl. w. Covington '55–6; Kai Winding '56–7; Claude Thornhill '57; Maynard Ferguson '57–8; Stan Kenton '58–9; Gerry Mulligan '60. Since '60s worked mainly as arr., incl. many charts for A&M and CTI label artists. Arr. for own bb; Wes Montgomery '65–8; Buddy Rich '68–9; Paul Desmond '69; Freddie Hubbard '71, '74; Sonny Stitt '73; also Carmen McRae; Astrud Gilberto; Charlie Mariano. He has also done extens. comp. for film and TV and is the author of *The Contemporary Arranger* '75. He has taught priv. seminars on arr. since '76. Favs: Bill Holman, Marty Paich, Gerry Mulligan. CDs: CTI; Angel-EMI; w. F. Hubbard; Geo. Benson; Larry Coryell (CTI); Wes Montgomery (Verve); Erroll Garner (Tel.); Astrud Gilberto (Verve).

SEDRIC, GENE (EUGENE, aka HONEY BEAR), cl, tnr sax; b. St. Louis, MO, 6/17/07; d. NYC, 4/3/63. Father was a ragtime pnst. Early jobs on riverboats w. Charlie Creath, Fate Marable. Joined Sam Wooding 1923, tour. Eur. and So. Amer. w. him for much of next decade; also briefly w. Fletcher

Henderson. Best known for long assoc. w. Fats Waller '32–42, app. on most of his recs. Later w. Jimmy McPartland, Bobby Hackett; to France w. Mezz Mezzrow '53. Joined Conrad Janis '53. Rec. for Prest. w. band of Waller alumni (led by Dick Wellstood) '61; retired soon thereafter due to illness. Superior cl. soloist and Coleman Hawkins–inspired tenor. CDs: w. Waller; Lena Horne (BB); Wellstood (Prest.); Bobby Hackett (Story.); T. Wilson; Don Byas; Putney Dandridge; James P. Johnson (Class.); Pee Wee Russell; Don Redman (Topaz).

SEGURE, ROGER, arr; b. NYC 5/22/05. Self-taught until 1945, when he stud. Schillinger system. Started out as accomp. for singers; toured US and Asia w. Midge Williams 1930s. Starting in '38 he wrote arr. for Louis Armstrong; Andy Kirk; Alvino Rey; others. Best known for numerous Jimmie Lunceford charts, incl. "What'cha Know Joe" and "Blue Afterglow." Scored mus. for *Blues in the Night*, a film feat. Lunceford band. Mus. dir. for Ralph Edwards TV show '51; taught at Westlake Coll of Mus. in LA fr. '50s; later in LA hs. CDs: w. Lunceford (Class.).

SEIFERT, ZBIGNIEW, vln, alto sax, comp; b. Cracow, Poland, 6/6/46; d. Munich, Germany, 2/15/79. Won awards in Poland and Hungary as best Coltrane-oriented saxophonist. Took up vln. while w. Tomasz Stanko gp. Many recs. and fests. throughout Eur.; MJF w. John Lewis 1976; comp. concerto for vln, orch., and jazz gp. for Radio Hamburg. His final sess. was rec. in US w. John Scofield; Jack DeJohnette; and others. Greatly respected as modern violinist using modal concepts. CDs: w. Stanko (Power Bros.); Wolfgang Dauner (MPS); Oregon (Vang.).

SELF, JIM, tba, bs; b. Franklin, PA, 8/20/43. B.S. Indiana, U. of Pa 1961; M. Mus., Catholic U '67; Dr. of Mus. Arts, USC '76; stud. w. Harvey Phillips; Charlie Shoemake; et al. Tba. and bs. w. army band, Wash., D.C. '65–7. Active as teacher '69–74, U. of Tenn. To LA '74, freelancing in studios, incl. mus. for over 400 films, incl. the "Voice of the Mother Ship"; tba. solo for *Close Encounters of the Third Kind*. Toured Eur. and rec. w. Don Ellis '77; pl. w. Jon Hendricks in *Evolution of the Blues* '78–9; toured Japan four times, once w. Mel Tormé and Marty Paich Dektette. Received NARAS Most Valuable Player Award three times; named Emeritus VP '87. Ambition is to "expand the tuba as a jazz solo instrument—without compromise and with no excuses for its size or difficulty." CDs: Conc.; d'Note; Trend; w. Gary Foster; Mel Tormé–M. Paich (Conc.).

SENATORE, PAT; bs; b. Newark, NJ, 8/19/35. Studied at Juilliard 1958–60. To LA '60; pl. w. Stan Kenton; Dick Stabile; Les Brown. With Herb Alpert Tijuana Brass '65–70; tour. w. various small gps. '70–77. From '78 to '83 he operated Pasquale's, a popular jazz club at Malibu, Calif.; fr. '84 prod. sess. and rec. w. Cedar Walton and Billy Higgins; also prod. albums for Cand.; tour. w. Peggy Lee. CDs: w. VIP Trio (Hi-Brite).

SENENSKY, BERNIE (BERNARD MELVIN), pno, kybd, comp; b. Winnipeg, Man., Canada, 12/31/44. Studied pno. w. Clara Perlman fr. age 9 to 16, then w. jazz pnst. Bob Erlendson. Pl. in Winnipeg and Edmonton clubs 1962–6; hotel engagements across Can. '66–8. Moved to Toronto '68. Accomp. visiting mus., incl. Joe Williams, Art Farmer, Red Rodney, Zoot Sims, Phil Woods, Buddy DeFranco, Frank Morgan, Art Pepper, and Sonny Stitt at Bourbon Street and the Colonial in Toronto mid '70s. Pl. w. Moe Koffman fr. '79; Peter Appleyard fr. '80s; Terry Gibbs, Buddy DeFranco, Herbie Mann in Eur. '89. Senensky's own gps., ranging fr. trio to spt., have app. at clubs and fests across Can. His comps. have been rec. by DeFranco; Rodney; Koffman; and Don Thompson. Favs: Keith Jarrett, McCoy Tyner, Bill Evans, Chick Corea. TV: *Oscar Peterson Presents*, CTV '74. CD: Unity.

SEPULVEDA, CHARLIE (Charles Sepulveda Rivera), tpt, flg; b. Bronx, NY, 7/15/62. Family moved to Puerto Rico 1970, where he stud. w. Juan Pacheco at Escuela Libre de Mus. '74–9; Cons. de Musica de PR '79–81; CUNY '85–8. Pl. w. Willie Rosario, Ralphy Levit '78; Julio Castro '78–9; various salsa gps. '79; Bobby Valentin '80–3; El Cano Estramera '83–4; Eddie Palmieri since '84; Ray Barretto '85–6; Hector La Voe '85–7. Freelance w. Tito Puente, Celia Cruze, Johnny Pacheco, Dr. John, David Byrne, Fania All-Stars '90–1. Lead tpt. w. Dizzy Gillespie since '91. Pl. w. own gps. since '89. Favs: Lee Morgan, Freddie Hubbard, Clifford Brown, Miles Davis, Gillespie. Fests: US, Eur., Jap., So. Amer., Africa, etc. TV: *Night Music* w. Eddie Palmieri '88; *Kojak* '90. CDs: Ant.; Trop.; w. Palmieri (Fania); Tito Puente (Conc.; Tropi.); H. Ruiz; Gillespie (Tel.); Dave Valentin (GRP); Trop. Jazz All-Stars (Trop.); Manny Oquendo (Mile.).

SETE, BOLA (Djalma de Andrade), gtr, comp; b. Rio de Janeiro, Brazil, 7/16/28; d. Greenbrae, CA, 2/14/87. Studied at Nat'l Sch. of Mus. in Rio; staff mus. for Braz. radio, then to US 1960. Discovered by Dizzy Gillespie; pl. w. him at MJF '62; rec. for Fant., soloist w. V. Guaraldi; formed own gp. '66. Inspired by Andres Segovia and in jazz by George Van Eps; Barney Kessel; Tal Farlow; he achieved a rhythmic sensitivity equal or superior to that of any other Brazilian guitarist who became involved in jazz. In addition to gtr., he played lutar, a lute-shaped instrument of his own design. CDs: w. Vince Guaraldi (Fant.).

SEVERINSEN, DOC (CARL HILDING), tpt, bandleader; b. Arlington, OR, 7/7/27. Studied w. fath.; won many state and national contests as cornetist. Worked w. Ted FioRito 1945; Charlie Barnet '47–9; Sam Donahue '48; Tommy Dorsey '49. Joined NBC staff '49; feat. on Steve Allen Show '54–5; member of Billy Taylor's house band for NBC-TV series, *The Subject Is Jazz.* In Oct. '62 he became asst. cond. of Skitch Henderson's band on the *Tonight Show* and in '67 its leader. In '72, he moved with the show to Burbank, Calif., and remained until May '92, after which he occ. reunited the band for tours but was mainly active cond. symph. orchs. Also worked often as brass clinician and has led jazz gp., Xebron. A versatile trumpeter who initially showed a bebop infl., Severinsen later pl. in a more mainstream style. CDs: Passport; w. Lena Horne; Joe Morello; Sauter-Finegan Orch. (BB); G. Mulligan; S. Getz; Jimmy Smith (Verve); Gil Evans (Imp.); Sunset Mus. Band (SSR).

SHAFRANOV, VLADIMIR, pno; b. Leningrad, Soviet Union, 12/31/48. Father pl. tpt. in army band, pno. at home; moth. sang; cousin Boris is prof. jazz pnst. and arr. Began on vln. at age 4; pno. at age 5. Stud. at Children's Mus. Sch. 1952, then at Rimsky-Korsakov Cons. Heard jazz on Voice of Amer.; also met and jammed w. Duke Ellington, Thad Jones–Mel Lewis when they came to the USSR. Made rec. debut w. Dobry Molodsy Band on Melodia label '71; rec. sold seven million copies. Lived in Finland '74–83; pl. w. visiting mus., incl. Joe Newman; Clifford Jordan; Al Grey; Zoot Sims; Bob Berg. Pl. w. Dexter Gordon in Stockholm '75. Moved to NYC '83; freelance w. Dizzy Gillespie; Johnny Griffin; Benny Golson; Jon Faddis; Woody Shaw; Freddie Hubbard; Sonny Fortune; Bobby Hutcherson; Pepper Adams, Ron Carter; Geo Mraz; Al Foster; Roy Haynes; Lewis Nash; Victor Lewis fr. '84. Pl. in duos in NYC clubs w. Red Mitchell; Ron Carter; George Mraz; Rufus Reid; Buster Williams; Bob Cranshaw '84–6. Also accomp. singers, incl. Ernestine Anderson; Diane Schuur; Bobby McFerrin. Shafranov taught at Sibelius Academy, Helsinki '74–6; Pori Cons. '79–80; Ovlunkyla Pop & Jazz Cons., Helsinki '80–3. Favs: Bill Evans, Tommy Flanagan, Cedar Walton, Sviatoslav Richter. Polls: *Rytmi* mag.

(Finnish) '92; numerous awds. fr. Finnish gvt. Fests: Pori JF fr. '74; rest of Eur. fr. '84. Film: Japanese prod. of *Breakfast at Tiffany's* '91. TV: Finnish TV; Hungarian TV '89. CDs: JA.

SHANE, MARK A., pno; b. Perth Amboy, NJ, 4/14/46. Studied priv. 1953–63. Pl. in '70s and '80s w. Benny Goodman; Buck Clayton, Ruby Braff; Wild Bill Davison; Doc Cheatham; Vic Dickenson; Scott Hamilton; Peanuts Hucko; Bob Wilber; Flip Phillips; Bobby Rosengarden; Buddy Tate; Ken Peplowski; Earle Warren; Kenny Davern; Milt Hinton; Warren Vaché Jr.; also solo gigs. Shane apps. on the film soundtracks of *The Cotton Club; Brighton Beach Memories; Biloxi Blues*; and *Working Girl.* Favs: Teddy Wilson, Art Tatum, Fats Waller. Fests: Eur., Japan since '80s. TV: BBC w. B. Wilber '89. CDs: Kamadisc; w. Sam Pilafian; Empire Brass (Tel.); B. Wilber (Jazz.; N-H); Back Bay Stompers (Sound Off); Joe Ascione (N-H); Scott Robinson (Arb.); R. Sandke (Jazz.); M. Grosz (J&M).

SHANK, BUD (CLIFFORD EVERETT JR.), alto sax; b. Dayton, OH; 5/27/26. Extensive studies in Dayton; Durham, NC; NYC, and LA. Cl. at age 10, alto sax at 12. After pl. w. coll. band 1943–46, moved to LA and join. Charlie Barnet '46–'48; Alvino Rey '49; Stan Kenton '50–'52; George Redman '53; Lighthouse All-Stars '53–'55; own qt. '56–63. Freelance work in TV and film studios, LA jazz clubs '63–'75. Pl. many coll. concerts and cond. clinics throughout US. In '75 he, Shelly Manne, Ray Brown, and Laurindo Almeida formed the L.A. Four, which rec. and worked intermittently until '83. Later worked mainly w. own qt., moving to Port Townsend, Wash. where he cond. jazz workshops. Returned to LA in '89 for reunion of Lighthouse All-Stars which also tour. int'l. Winner of *DB* awards on alto sax and fl. and named Most Valuable Player by NARAS. Shank was best known in '60s as a superior jazz soloist and all-around studio mus. He later gave up other instruments to concentrate on alto. His style by now displayed considerable diversity, extending beyond its bop-inspired beginnings. Has also been active as a comp. of jingles and TV spots. Perf. in Eur. almost annually since '80. CDs: Cont.; WP; Mile.; Cand.; Capri; Conc.; FS; WW w. Roumanis String Qt. (Capri); Lighthouse All-Stars (Cont.; Cand.); Shorty Rogers (Cand.; Conc.; BB); Lorez Alexandria (Imp.); C. Baker (PJ; Cont.; FS); M. Tormé (Stash); E. Fitzgerald (Verve); Billy Eckstine (Em.); Miles Davis; B. Kessel; Frank Morgan (Cont.); G. Mulligan (Cap.; A&M); Art Pepper (PJ); Charlie Byrd; L.A. Four (Conc.); Jiggs Whigham (Capri); Kenton (Cap.).

SHAPIRO, ARTIE (ARTHUR), bs, el-bs; b. Denver, CO, 1/15/16; d. Las Vegas, 3/24/03. Sister a concert pnst. Pl. tpt fr. age 13, sw. to bs. at 18. Pro. career began in 1934, when Wingy Manone brought him to the Mus. Union. In the '30s he pl. and/or rec. w. Frank Froeba; Sharkey Bonano; Red McKenzie; the reborn ODJB; Bud Freeman; Chu Berry; Eddie Condon; Paul Whiteman; and Bobby Hackett. In '40 he worked w. Joe Marsala; then moved to Hollywood '41; freelanced w. J. Teagarden; Joe Sullivan; Eddie Miller. Army service, then w. Charlie Ventura; Artie Shaw; Benny Goodman. Active as MGM studio mus. and on recs. w. Bing Crosby and Frank Sinatra, late '40s–'50s. He was an early adherent of what he describes as "freedom of movement" in bs. playing. CDs: w. Billie Holiday (Verve); Cap. Jazzmen (Jazz Unlimited); Teagarden; Marsala; Manone; C. Hawkins; Freeman; L. Feather; B. Berigan; Condon; Goodman; Chu Berry (Class.); Bonano (Timel.); Nat Cole (Cap.); Shaw (MM); Jess Stacy (ASY); R. Eldridge; Pee Wee Russell (Topaz).

SHARON, RALPH, pno, arr; b. London, England, 9/17/23. Studied pno w. moth., an Amer. pnst. Prof. debut w. Ted Heath 1946; later w. Frank Weir's Orch. Formed own sxt. incl. Victor Feldman, at London's Stork Club; won *MM* poll for four yrs. To NYC '53; made Amer. debut at Embers. Rec. w. Teddy Charles, Charles Mingus, Kenny Clarke, Lucky Thompson, and Chris Connor '55–9; Johnny Hartman and Mel Tormé '56. Best known as mus. dir. for Tony Bennett '56–68 and fr. '80. Between stints w. Bennett he was mus. dir. for Peggy Lee; Robert Goulet; and Rosemary Clooney. Made a series of pno. trio recs. for release in Engl. CDs: DRG; w. C. Basie–T. Bennett (Roul.); T. Bennett (Col.); Chris Connor (Beth.).

SHARPE, AVERY GEORGE, bs, el-bs, comp; b. Valdosta, GA, 8/23/54. Mother pl. pno. and dir. gospel choirs. Began on pno. and acdn. At U. of Mass. he stud. economics 1972–6 and mus. w. Archie Shepp '78–80. Worked as insurance adjustor, '76–9, then pl. w. Shepp '79–80; Art Blakey '80; Young Lions, Cab Calloway, Fred Hopkins–Daniel Ponce '82; McCoy Tyner Trio fr. '84; Freddie Hubbard '86; Geo. Benson '89; own gp. fr. '90. Sharpe has taught in wkshps. and clinics at many US universities. He comp. scores to the films *An Unremarkable Life* and *Lydia*, and produced a 6–hr. jazz and blues prog. for Mass. cable TV that feat. Phil Woods, Taj Mahal, others. He has received several NEA comp. and perf. grants. Favs: Milt Hinton, Charles Mingus, James Jamerson. Fests: Eur. w. Hubbard, Tyner. TV: Mass. cable. CDs: Sunny.; JKNM; w. McCoy Tyner (PW;

Fant.; Den.; Enja; Timel.; Mile.; Bird.); Frank Morgan (Cont.); John Blake (Gram.); Marc Puricelli (MM); Jeri Brown (JT); S. Grossman (Drey.); A. Shepp–Yusef Lateef (YAL).

SHARROCK, SONNY (WARREN HARDING), gtr, comp; b. Ossining, NY, 8/27/40; d. Ossining, 5/25/94. Sang in rock gp. 1954–9; self-taught on gtr. fr. age 19; one semester at Berklee Sch. of Mus. To NYC '65. Pl. w. Olatunji '65; Byard Lancaster '66–7; Pharoah Sanders '66–7; Sunny Murray '67; Herbie Mann '67–73. Pl. w. Don Cherry in Berlin '68; Miles Davis summer of '69; Cannonball Adderley '70. In early '70s he and voc. wife Linda toured w. their own gp.; fairly inactive in late '70s and early '80s; pl. and rec. w. art rock gp., Material, alongside George Lewis, Henry Threadgill, Billy Bang. In late '80s he worked w. Last Exit, which incl. Ronald Shannon Jackson and Bill Laswell; tour. w. his own small gps. early '90s. He died just as his career was showing new promise. Joachim Berendt called Sharrock "the free jazz guitarist *par excellence*," who "plays clusters, sounding all the notes imaginable simultaneously . . . with the ecstatic vitality of harmonically unchained free jazz." CDs: Enemy; Axiom; CMP; w. P. Sanders (Imp.); B. Cosby (Verve); Last Exit (Enemy); H. Mann (Atl.); W. Shorter (BN).

SHAUGHNESSY, ED (EDWIN T.), dms, perc; b. Jersey City, NJ, 1/29/29. Mostly self-taught on dms. but later stud. tympani, vib., and tablas (w. Allah Rakha). In late 1940s he pl. w. George Shearing; Jack Teagarden; Georgie Auld; first prominent w. Charlie Ventura '48–9. Toured Eur. w. Benny Goodman '50; pl. w. Tommy Dorsey, Eddie Lawrence, Jerry Wald, Johnny Richards '51–2. Subbed w. Duke Ellington orch. '52. Freelanced '50s w. Charles Mingus; Mundell Lowe; Teddy Charles; Horace Silver; pl. in house rhythm section at Birdland and Downbeat clubs; toured w. Lucky Millinder band. In '60s he made five albums w. Count Basie's orch. Joined *Tonight Show* band, moving to LA w. the show in '72. Discovered Diane Schuur and presented her at MJF '76. Pl. w. own qnt. at fests and coll. gigs fr. '86. Well-schooled in all phases of percussion, he was inspired by Big Sid Catlett, Dave Tough, and Jo Jones; Shaughnessy is among the first jazz dmrs. to employ two bass dms. CDs: Chase; w. Teddy Charles; Chris Connor (Atl.); C. Ventura (Dec.); Tommy Newsom; Jack Lemmon (Laser.); R. Eldridge (Vogue); Shirley Scott (Imp.); Can. Brass (Vict.); Doc Severinsen (Amherst); J. Hodges; B. Holiday (Verve); C. Terry (Cand.); Q. Jones; R. R. Kirk (Merc.); Gene Ammons; B. Brookmeyer; Etta Jones; O. Nelson (Prest.); Mundell Lowe (Riv.).

SHAVERS, CHARLIE (CHARLES JAMES), tpt, comp; b. NYC, 8/3/17; d. NYC, 7/8/71. Father pl. tpt. Shavers started on pno., then bjo. bef. sw. to tpt. Played in NYC w. Willie Gant; in Phila. w. Frankie Fairfax 1935. With Tiny Bradshaw, Lucky Millinder in NYC '37. Rose to prominence w. John Kirby Sxt., which he joined in '37; comps. incl. "Undecided." Briefly w. Raymond Scott; then Tommy Dorsey '45–9, rejoined him several times. Co-led gp. w. Louis Bellson, Terry Gibbs '50; tour. Japan w. Tommy Dorsey ghost band led by Sam Donahue '64; many other tours in '50s and '60s w. Benny Goodman; Frank Sinatra; et al. A true virtuoso, Shavers was a leading infl. on trumpeters in the '40s, bringing great range and technique to his work in an original and immediately identifiable style and timbre. As arr. he molded the personality of the Kirby gp. w. his deft blending of tpt., cl., and alto sax. Won *Esq.* Silver Award '46; *DB* poll '48. CDs: B&B; w. Billie Holiday (Col.; Verve); T. Dorsey (BB; Hep); Esq. All-Amer. Poll Winners (BB); Coleman Hawkins (BB; Apollo; Prest.; Key. Coll.); C. Parker; Fred Astaire (Verve); B. Goodman (Cap.); L. Hampton (Dec.); Alberta Hunter (Stash); D. Byas (Sav.); Hal Singer (Prest.); Bechet (BB; JSP); T. Dameron (Riv.); J. Dodds (B&B); C. Barnet (Evid.); Nat Cole (BL); Teddy Grace (Timel.); O. Peterson (Pab.).; B. Rich (Hep); Kirby (Class.).

SHAW, ARTIE (Arthur Jacob Arshawsky), cl, comp; b. NYC, 5/23/10; d. Thousand Oaks, CA, 12/30/04. Took up sax in hs; prof. debut on sax and later cl. w. Johnny Cavallaro. Pl. w. Austin Wylie in Cleveland, Ohio 1927–9; Irving Aaronson '29–31. After freelancing in NYC w. Red Nichols, Vincent Lopez, et al. he retired fr. mus. '34–5, reappearing w. a string qt. at NYC's Imperial Theatre summer '35. The sensation caused by this unusual use of strings in a swing context led to his first bb, feat. brass, strings, rhythm, and saxophonist Tony Pastor. The venture was short-lived; in early '37 Shaw formed a new band w. four saxes, five brass, and four rhythm. His first big hit w. the band, "Begin the Beguine," rec. July '38, made him a national figure. His band at one time incl. Buddy Rich, Georgie Auld, Helen Forrest, and Billie Holiday. After retiring to Mexico for a few mos. in Dec. '39, Shaw ret. to rec. w. a larger ensemble, incl. a full string section, and a hit w. "Frenesi." His Gramercy Five combos featured at one time or another Billy Butterfield, Johnny Guarneri, and Roy Eldridge. His bb feat. Hot Lips Page, who sang and pl. on "Blues in the Night." Many arrs. for Shaw's bands were written by Jerry Gray; William Grant Still; Lennie Hayton; and Shaw himself. After leading a final bb in '50 and a '54 Gramercy Five gp. w.

Tal Farlow, Hank Jones, et al., he retired permanently from perf. and never pl. again. In '83 he organized a new band, but the leader and feat. clst. was Dick Johnson, and Shaw rarely app. w. the gp. Living in Newbury Park, CA, he was writing fiction in the '90s. Shaw's virtuosity was impressive and demonstrated to good advantage on such recs. as *Concerto for Clarinet, Blues,* and the Gramercy Five releases. His imaginative efforts to bring new ideas into jazz and swing were sometimes overshadowed by his highly publicized marriages to Lana Turner, Ava Gardner, Evelyn Keyes, and five others, as well as by his outspoken opinions. Films: *Dancing Co-ed* '39; *Second Chorus* '40. Books: autobiography, *The Trouble with Cinderella* '52; fiction, *I Love You, I Hate You, Drop Dead* '65. CDs: BB; Col.; MM; Jazz Unlimited; Class.; Musi.; Hep; Tax; w. Lena Horne; Benny Carter (BB); Raymond Scott (Stash);' B. Berigan (Jass); B. Holiday (Col.); Red Norvo (Hep); Fats Waller (ASV).

SHAW, ARVELL JAMES, bs; b. St. Louis, MO, 9/15/23; d. Roosevelt, NY, 12/5/02. Played w. Fate Marable on riverboat 1942; navy band '42–5; Louis Armstrong bb '45–7. Pl. w. Louis Armstrong All Stars '47–50, then stud. harmony in Geneva '51. Pl. w. Armstrong on and off until '60, also w. Teddy Wilson; Coleman Hawkins; Lionel Hampton; Charlie Shavers; Red Allen; Rex Stewart; Cozy Cole; Vic Dickenson; Roy Eldridge; Benny Goodman. Rejoin. All Stars '60–5; tour. Eastern Eur. w. Armstrong '66, then pl. w. him intermittently until '71. Pl. w. own trio fr. '70; Dorothy Donegan, Teddy Wilson '72–4; Barney Bigard, Earl Hines in France '74. Presented jazz programs w. own sxt., Jazz Giants of the Golden Age, in public sch. dur. '70s. Pl. in B'way pit bands for *Bubblin' Brown Sugar* and *Ain't Misbehavin'* in '80s. Pl. in '90s w. Lionel Hampton's Golden Men of Jazz; own gp., Louis Armstrong Legacy All-Stars. Fests: US, Eur., Asia, Africa w. Armstrong. Films: *New Orleans* w. Armstrong, Billie Holiday '47; *The Strip* w. Armstrong All Stars '51; *Glenn Miller Story; High Society; Saga of Satchmo.* TV: many apps. w. Armstrong. CDs: w. Armstrong (Dec.; Col.; Story.; Mos.); Herb Hall (Sack.); L. Hampton (Tel.); Sammy Price (Story.); Keith Smith (Lake); Doc Cheatham (Jazz.); B. Goodman (MM); Coleman Hawkins (Dec.).

SHAW, CHARLES ("BOBO"; WESLEY JR.), dms; b. Pope, MS, 9/15/47. Studied tbn., bs., perc., theory, and comp. w. Hamiet Bluiett; dms. w. Ben Thigpen. A key figure in creation of Black Artists Gp. in St. Louis. Also worked w. Julius Hemphill; Ike and Tina Turner; Roland Hanna; Reggie Workman. To Paris for a yr. in early 1970s working w. Anthony

Braxton; Steve Lacy; Alan Silva; et al. Also led Human Arts Ensemble in US and Eur. dur. '70s; rec. w. Joseph and Lester Bowie; Oliver Lake; Frank Lowe; Hemphill. Rec. w. Billy Bang '84; inactive in late '80s. His use of polyrhythms has been compared to that of Elvin Jones. CDs: w. Billy Bang (SN); O. Lake (BL); Frank Lowe (BS).

SHAW, MARLENA, voc; b. New Rochelle, NY, 9/22/44. First prof. job. w. Howard McGhee 1964. Concerts in Catskill Mts., also w. Marian McPartland. Began rec. for Cadet '66. After singing at Playboy clubs, tour. w. Basie band off and on '68–70. From early '70s living in LV, she diversified her repertoire to aim at the pop and r&b market but since late '80s has taken part in several jazz cruises and app. at jazz clubs, displaying the characteristics of a well-qualified jazz singer. CDs: Verve; BN; Conc.; w. Joe Williams (Verve; Tel.); Jimmy Smith (Mile.); *Benny Carter Songbook* (MM).

SHAW, WOODY (HERMAN II), tpt, comp; b. Laurinburg, NC, 12/24/44; d. NYC, 5/10/89. Father was member of gospel gp. in Newark, N.J. Started on tpt in 1955; gigs w. Larry Young, Tyrone Washington; w. Eric Dolphy in early '60s. In Paris w. Kenny Clarke; Bud Powell; Johnny Griffin; rec. in Germ. w. Nathan Davis. Back in US he joined Horace Silver '65–6; w. Chick Corea '66; Jackie McLean '67; McCoy Tyner off and on '68–early '70s. Also worked w. Max Roach; in pit band for B'way shows; qnt. w. Joe Henderson '70; w. Gil Evans, Art Blakey '71–3; led combo in SF w. Bobby Hutcherson; back to NYC '76 w. Junior Cook–Louis Hayes Qnt. Thereafter mainly led his own small gps. Originally compared to Freddie Hubbard, Shaw was an accomplished soloist who, dur. the '70s, moved away from strictly chordal work into a controlled freedom. In the mid '80s rec. an exciting two-CD set w. Hubbard for BN. His last yrs. were tragic: he was plagued by failing eyesight and a drug problem, and he lost an arm in a subway accident. He had the potential for becoming the most infl. trumpeter of the '90s. CDs: Mos.; Enja; Timel.; Red; 32; Cont.; BN; TCB; w. Blakey (BN; Prest.); D. Gordon (Col.); W. Herman (Conc.); L. Hampton (Tel.); Larry Young; H. Silver; Bobby Hutcherson; H. Mobley; Joe Henderson; J. McLean (BN); Roy Brooks (Enja); Nathan Davis (MPS); Dolphy (Charly); Kenny Garrett (CC); B. Golson (Timel.); Mal Waldron (SN).

SHEARING, GEORGE ALBERT, pno, comp; b. London, England 8/13/19. Blind from birth; stud. at Linden Lodge Sch. for Blind. Pl. jazz in clubs after hearing Fats Waller and Teddy Wilson recs. After hearing him at a Rhythm Club jam sess., L. Feather set up his first rec. date, 1937 (later arr. for his immigration to US). After pl. in 17-pc. blind band led by Claude Bampton, he worked as a single bef. join. Ambrose and His Orch. for two yrs. Won *MM* poll as top Brit. pnst, for seven yrs. Pl. acdn. in Frank Weir orch '47. In Dec. '46, he made a three-mos. visit to US, which incl one Sav. rec. date; ret. to US, Dec '47, spent much of '48 at Three Deuce on 52nd St., first as soloist, then w. gps. In Jan. '49, while leading a qt. that incl. Buddy DeFranco at Clique Club, he rec. for the Disc. label w. a qnt. that became his reg. gp. for club apps. Orig. members were Margie Hyams, vib.; Chuck Wayne, gtr; Denzil Best, dms.; John Levy, bs. First big hit was MGM rec. of "September in the Rain," on which Shearing's locked-hands style blended w. gtr. and vib. to give the gp. a distinct sound and enormous commercial appeal worldwide. Later members of the gp., which he maintained for almost thirty yrs. (w. brief hiatus in '64), incl. Cal Tjader, Toots Thielemans, Gary Burton, Joe Pass, Andy Simpkins, and Israel Crosby. From the mid '70s he worked mainly in duo format w. bs. but also pl. classical concerts w. many symph. orchs. Among his numerous albums are an LP w. Peggy Lee and award-winning CDs w. Mel Tormé. His best-known comp is "Lullaby of Birdland," comp. in '52 as a theme song for the legendary NYC jazz club. Shearing was the first British mus. to exert a major infl. on jazz; his qnt. style of the '50s was widely imitated. Revived qnt. format for rec. and tour. in '90s for a brief time. CDs: Tel.; Cap.; MPS; Sav.; Conc.; Mos.; Jzld.; Verve; w. M. Tormé; Ernestine Anderson; Hank Jones; Carmen McRae (Conc.); S. Grappelli; B. Eckstine (Verve); Joe Williams (Tel.). Cleo Laine (Vict.); D. Brubeck (Tel.).

SHELDON, JACK, tpt; voc; b. Jacksonville, FL, 11/30/31. Professional debut in Det. at 13; to LA at 17; att. LA City Coll. Air force bands to 1952. Pl. several mos. at Lighthouse, then w. Jack Montrose; Art Pepper; Wardell Gray; Dexter Gordon; Jimmy Giuffre; Herb Geller. Pl. w. Curtis Counce '56; Dave Pell, Stan Kenton '58; Benny Goodman '59. In the '60s he rec. a standup comedy album for Cap. and was seen on TV as actor and comedian; reg. on Merv Griffin Show; in '70s and '80s worked w. Bill Berry; Goodman; Woody Herman; and various small gps. Led own bb in LA in early '92. Along with an extroverted comedic style and personality, Sheldon remains a fluent and compelling jazz improviser. CDs: BN; Conc.; Up.; w. Harry Betts (Mob. Fid.); K. Drew (BN); S. Kenton (Cap.); M. Tormé; Rosemary Clooney; Bill Berry; Victor Feldman (Conc.); B. Goodman (MM); Curtis Counce (Cont.); A. Pepper (Cont.; BN).

SHEPARD, ERNIE (ERNEST JR.), bs; b. Beaumont, TX, 7/19/16; d. Hamburg, Germany, 11/23/65. Early work in Texas, then to Calif. to pl. w. Gerald Wilson and Phil Moore, Perf. w. Dizzy Gillespie–Charlie Parker qnt.; rec. on bs. and as voc. w. Slim Gaillard 1951; also rec. w. Sonny Stitt; Gene Ammons; and Johnny Hodges. Toured Eur. w. Duke Ellington '62; rec. on bs. and as voc. w. Paul Gonsalves '63. Settled in Germ. '64 to do sess., studio, and TV work. CDs: w. D. Ellington (Atl.; Pab.; MM); J. Hodges (Imp.); Ammons; Stitt (Prest.); Stayhorn (Red Brn.).

SHEPHERD, SHEP (BERISFORD), dms; b. Honduras, 1/19/17. Raised in Phila.; worked w. Jimmy Gorham in 1930s. Pl. w. Benny Carter '41–2; rec. w. Artie Shaw '41. In late '40s worked as arr.; tour. w. Cab Calloway, Earl Bostic; pl. w. Bill Doggett '52–9. His comp., "Honky Tonk," was a big hit for Doggett. Pl. for B'way shows bef. moving to SF Bay area in '60s, where he was still freelancing in '90s; also worked as cabinet maker. CDs: w. Benny Carter (BB).

SHEPP, ARCHIE, tnr, sop saxes, comp; b. Ft. Lauderdale, FL, 5/24/37. Father pl., bjo., gtr., mand., semiprof. Grew up in Phila.; stud. tnr. w. Tony Mitchell. Pl. cl. in hs band, which also incl. Reggie Workman, and sax in r&b band w. Lee Morgan 1953. Stud. dramatic lit. at Goddard Coll. (B.A. '59), also stud. pno. w. Margaret Coleman. Moved to NYC '59. Pl. w. Cecil Taylor '60–1, and app. w. Taylor in off-B'way play, *The Connection*. Co-led gp. w. Bill Dixon '62–3; NY Contemp. Five w. Don Cherry, John Tchicai '63–4. Led own gps. w. Bobby Hutcherson, Roswell Rudd, Beaver Harris, Grachan Moncur III, and others fr. '64; pl. w. John Coltrane off and on fr. '65. Beginning in the '60s Shepp began to incorporate original poems into his perfs.; his use of mus. to convey specific political messages made him a controversial figure. Original play, *The Communist*, produced in NYC '65. Worked w. Cal Massey fr. '69; co-wrote mus. theater piece *Lady Day: A Musical Tragedy* w. Massey '72. Shepp has taught at SUNY-Buffalo '69–74 and at U. of Mass.-Amherst fr. '70. He has toured and rec. mainly in Eur. fr. '70s and cont. to be active in theater. In later yrs. he retrenched fr. earlier free jazz style to incorporate mainstream elements into his playing. Cont. to tour int'l and rec. into mid '90s. Award fr. New Engl. Foundation for the Arts '95. Outspoken on social issues, Shepp has incorporated his views in such poems and comps. as "Malcolm, Malcolm, Semper Malcolm" and "Attica Blues." Favs: John Coltrane, Sonny Rollins, "the entire tradition." Polls: *DB* New Star. Fests: Eur. fr.

'61. Film: various short films. TV: PBS, Eur. TV. CDs: Enja; Imp.; Steep.; hat Art; Sack.; SN; Timel.; w. Coltrane; Gil Evans; Chico Hamilton (Imp.); Charlie Haden (A&M); Yusef Lateef (YAL); Cecil Taylor (Cand.).

SHEPPARD, ANDY, tnr, sop saxes; b. Warminster, England, 1/20/57. Grandparents were musical. Self-taught, first on gtr. and fl. In early 1980s he was part of Sphere (no connection w. American gp. of same name); worked w. Laurent Cugny bb w. Gil Evans '87. Since the mid '80s has app. w. Urban Sax; George Russell Living Time Orch.; Carla Bley bb; Carla Bley–Steve Swallow Trio; Nana Vasconcelos; Keith Tippett; Michael Mantler. Various gps. of his own since '88, incl. the Balanescu String Qt.; In Co-Motion; Big Co-Motion. Rec. w. Bley; Russell; Evans; Tippett. Wrote music for *Natural World* TV docus., plus other TV and radio apps. Was named Best Newcomer in '88 by the British *Wire*; also Best Album, Best Instrumentalist '89; Best Album '90. Sheppard's varied career has taken him to such far-flung places as Mongolia, Nigeria, Israel, as well as most of Eur. and the U.S. CDs: Ant.; WATT; BN; L. Bleu; Verve; w. C. Bley (WATT; ECM); B. Dennelein (Enja); George Russell (Stash).

SHEPPARD, BOB (ROBERT), tnr, sop saxes; b. Trenton, NJ, 5/4/52. Raised in Levittown, Pa.; grad. Bucks County Comm. Coll. 1973 and Eastman Sch. of Mus. Taught at Loyola U., NO fr. 76. Moved to Calif. in early '80s; cont. to teach regularly. Worked regularly in TV talk show bands and in TV and film studios; back-up for Madonna; Brandon Fields; Michael Franks; Scott Henderson; Rickie Lee Jones; et al. Also pl. w. Freddie Hubbard; T. Akiyoshi–L. Tabackin bb; Billy Childs; etc. First solo album, *Tell Tale Signs*, on WH released in '91. Favs: J. Coltrane, C. Adderley, J. Henderson. Josef Woodard wrote in *DB* that Sheppard's playing "sits comfortably between the poles of 'fusion' accessibility and the bedrock of traditional jazz values." CDs: WH; w. Akiyoshi–Tabackin (RCA); Billy Childs (Stretch; WH); Bob Curnow (Mama); Bill Cunliffe (Disc.); John Beasley (WH).

SHEPPARD, HARRY, vib, dms; b. Worcester, MA, 4/1/28. Professional debut at 15 on dms.; stud. vib. at Berklee 1948. Pl. w. Cozy Cole–Sol Yaged Band '56; in '60s rec. or tour. w. Georgie Auld, Doc Severinsen, and Benny Goodman. From '70s local engagements, mainly in Houston, Texas. CDs: Justice.

SHERMAN, DARYL, pno, voc; b. Woonsocket, RI, 6/14/49. Father, Sam Sherman, pl. tbn. w. Buddy

Morrow, Sonny Dunham. Began on pno. at age 7. Attended U. of RI, then stud. voice beginning in 1970s. Joined mus. union at age 16, pl. w. father's qt. Taught mus. in Rhode Island sch. system '71–3. Worked w. own duo, trio since '77; own qt. w. Dick Sudhalter '82–3. Sang w. new Artie Shaw band '83 Pl. w. Paul Whiteman Orch. retrospective '85–6; duo w. Dave McKenna '85–90; John Goldsby '91; Gray Sargent '90–2. Collaborators have incl. Jay Leonhart; Harvie Swartz; Eddie Barefield; Howard Alden; Gene Bertoncini; Mel Lewis. Worked in Cologne, Germ. '90. Duo w. bs. Boots Maleson at Firebird Cafe, NYC '99. A hip singer with a wide range of material. Favs: Dave McKenna, Bill Evans, Tommy Flanagan, Mildred Bailey, L. Armstrong, Sylvia Syms. CDs: Arb.; Audio.

SHERMAN, RAY, pno; b. Chicago, IL, 4/15/23. To LA w. family 1939. Played and/or arr. w various bands, incl. Gus Arnheim and Jan Savitt. Army '43–6; w. Ray Bauduc gp. '46. Mainly worked as studio mus., incl. film *Pete Kelly's Blues,* '54; in '55 began long assoc. w. Bob Crosby, incl. TV series. Comp. *Theme, Variations and Fugue,* perf. in '68 by LA Neophonic Orch. under Stan Kenton. Renewed activity in jazz in '80s w. Crosby; Jack Sheldon; Abe Most; Dick Cathcart; Henry Cuesta; Pete Fountain. Fests at the Hague, Nice, etc. Popular pnst. in traditional circles. CDs Arb.; w. J. Teagarden (Mos.); Jack Sheldon (Conc.); Dan Barrett; Bobby Gordon (Arb.); Nick Fatool (Jazz).

SHEROCK, SHORTY (Clarence Francis Cherock), tpt; b. Minneapolis, MN, 11/17/15; d. Northridge, CA, 1/26/80. Played w. Ben Pollack 1936; Jimmy Dorsey '37–8; Bob Crosby '39; Gene Krupa '40–1; Tommy Dorsey '41; Horace Heidt '41–5. Also app. w. JATP '44. Led own band '45–8; later mainly studio work in LA; many rec. w. Frank Sinatra. A superior swing tptr. infl. by Roy Eldridge, Sherock was under-represented on recs. CDs: w. Muggsy Spanier (Mob. Fid.); E. Fitzgerald; JATP (Verve); Cap. Jazzmen (Jazz Unlimited); Benny Carter (Cap.; Prest.).

SHERTZER, HYMIE (Herman Schertzer), alto sax; b. NYC, 4/2/09; d. NYC, 3/22/77. Played vln. at 9, sax at 16. Auditioned for Benny Goodman 1934; had to double on vln. for a job w. Billy Rose at Music Hall. In late '30s he rec. w. Bunny Berigan; Lionel Hampton; Teddy Wilson–Billie Holiday. Stayed w. Goodman as lead alto until '38; spent a yr. w. Tommy Dorsey; rejoined Goodman until '40; then spent another yr. w. T. Dorsey; final bb work in '42, again w. Goodman. Settled in NYC, became NBC staff

mus. mid '40s. Rec. in studio gps. led by Ella Fitzgerald; Sarah Vaughan; Sy Oliver; Louis Armstrong; Artie Shaw; and Goodman. Primarily a section man and an excellent lead alto, he pl. an important role in such celebrated Goodman perfs. as "Sing, Sing, Sing," and "Stompin' at the Savoy". CDs: w. L. Hampton (BB); B. Holiday (Col.).; Goodman (BB; Col.).

SHEW, BOBBY (Robert Joratz), tpt, flg, Shewhorn, comp, b. Albuquerque, NM, 3/4/41. Most valuable training came from pl. for dances while in early teens. Started on gtr. at age 8; sw. to tpt. same yr. Pl. w. Tommy Dorsey orch. fr. 1964–65. Since '66 pl. w. Woody Herman; Buddy Rich; Benny Goodman; Terry Gibbs; Maynard Ferguson; Louis Bellson; Toshiko Akiyoshi–Lew Tabackin; Nat Pierce–Frank Capp Juggernaut; Neal Hefti; Peter Herbolzheimer (Germ.); Frank Strazzeri; Art Pepper; Bud Shank; Horace Silver; Chuck Flores; Pepper Adams–B. Shew; Teddy Edwards; and has led own gps. Hosted TV series *Just Jazz* in New Zealand '80–81. Grammy nomination in '80 for *Outstanding in His Field.* An active clinician–jazz educ.–perf. all over the world. Acted as Nat'l Tpt. Chairman for the IAJE fr. '75; served on the board of dir. of the Int'l Tpt. Guild. Authored numerous articles of educ. interest in trade magazines. Favs: Blue Mitchell, Chet Baker, Art Farmer, Clifford Brown, Conte Candoli. TV/Video: *Club Date* as special guest w. Holly Hofmann Qt. CDS: MAMA; D-T; Delos; w. W. Herman (Col.); B. Rich (Sequel; BGO); Akiyoshi-Tabackin (RCA); Louie Bellson (Pab.; Conc.); Bud Shank; F. Capp (Conc.).

SHIELDS, LARRY (LAWRENCE), cl, comp; b. New Orleans, LA 9/13/1893; d. Los Angeles, CA, 11/21/53. Best-known member of a mus. family; bros. were Pat (gtr.), 1891–d.?; Eddie (pno), 1896–1936; Harry (bari. sax), 1899–1971. Joined Nick La Rocca at 15; w. Bert Kelly in Chi. '15; replaced Alcide Nunez in ODJB Oct. '16–21, performing on its historic '17 session which marked the debut of jazz on recs. Played w. Paul Whiteman, then moved to Calif. until late '20s. To Chi. and NO in '30s; w. revived ODJB '36–8; then semi-inactive in Calif. Was considered by some to be the most capable member of the ODJB. CDs: w. ODJB (BB).

SHIHAB, SAHIB (Edmund Gregory), bari, alto saxes, fl; b. Savannah, GA, 6/23/25; d. Tennessee, 10/24/89. Studied w. Elmer Snowden in Phila., then at Bost. Cons. 1941–2. Lead alto w. Fletcher Henderson '44–5; then w. Roy Eldridge, Ray Perry to '47; and in NYC w. Art Blakey; Thelonious Monk; Dizzy

Gillespie; Buddy Johnson; Illinois Jacquet. To Eur. w. Quincy Jones '59–60; remained in Eur., settling in Den.; pl. w. Clarke-Boland Band, Ernie Wilkins. Returned to US '73, living first in LA, then in the '80s in NYC. Comp. score for ballet based on *The Red Shoes*. Though fluent on all saxes and fl., Shihab was best known as a bari. soloist with a deep, cutting sound and a creative style. Scored and perf. soundtrack to Danish film *Sextet* '64. *Conversations*, a 23–minute suite, is the title number of his Black Lion CD '63. CDs: BL; Sav.; w. Monk (BN); Art Blakey (BB; BN); LaVern Baker; Milt Jackson (Atl.); R. Eldridge (Dec.); Jay McShann (MM); Ben Webster (Story.); Betty Carter (Imp.); Clarke-Boland (MPS); Eddie Jefferson (Evid.); Randy Weston (Roul.); M. Waldron; T. Dameron; Phil Woods; J. Coltrane (Prest.); Oscar Pettiford (Imp.); Charlie Rouse (Up.); Brew Moore (BL); Benny Golson (Cont.).

SHIM, MARK, tnr sax; b. Kingston, Jamaica, 11/11/73. Family migrated to Can. when he was 8 mos. old. After five yrs. moved to Richmond, Va. Began pl. alto sax in seventh grade and by the time he reached tenth grade was pl. concert and regional band, pl. classical repertoire. At this time he heard Charlie Parker recs., sw. to tnr. sax in the advanced jazz band and began stud. Parker's transcribed solos. Grad. fr. hs in 1991 and stud. at Virginia Commonwealth U. Transferred to Wm. Paterson Coll. in N.J. '93 but in '94 moved to Bklyn. and start. pl. at jam sessions, etc. Met Hamiet Bluiett at a Harlem session and rec. w. him. Through Bluiett join. David Murray bb. Mentored by Betty Carter in Jazz Ahead program and feat. w. her trio. Fr. '97 pl. and rec. w. Mingus bb. Uses computer for comp.; favors odd-measured pieces. Favs: Rollins, "Lockjaw" Davis, Joe Henderson, Gene Ammons. CDs: BN; w. Mingus bb (Drey.); Mose Allison (BN).

SHIRLEY, DON (DONALD), pno, org, comp; b. Kingston, Jamaica, 1/29/27. First studies w. moth. Was invited to stud. w. Mittolovski at Leningrad Cons. at age 9. Holds a B.A., M.A., and Ph.D. in psychology fr. Harvard and a Ph.D. in liturgical art fr. Catholic U. Already known as a classical concert pnst. when he began pl. jazz at the urging of George Shearing, Duke Ellington, and Nat Cole. Began rec. in '54, accomp. by bsst. Richard Davis; numerous LPs for Audio Fidelity, Col., Cadence, and Atl. '54–74.

SHIRLEY, JIMMY (JAMES ARTHUR), gtr, el-bs; b. Union, SC, 5/31/13; d. NYC, 12/3/89. Raised in Cleveland, Ohio; stud. w. fath., a prof. mus. Pl. in Cincinnati w. Frank Terry 1934; own qt. w. three gtrs.

and bs. '35–6. With Clarence Profit in NYC '37–41; then led own trio in Phila. '41–2. Toured w. Ella Fitzgerald and The Four Keys '42–3. Rejoined Profit briefly bef. his death '43; then pl. w. Herman "Ivory" Chittison off and on '43–54. Dur. this time he also led a trio and freelanced in NYC w. Phil Moore, Toy Wilson, Bill Williams '50; Vin Strong '53. In the '40s he was known for his use of the "vibrola" or tremolo bar. Pl. el-bs. w. George James, Buddy Tate '60s. In the '70s he rec. in Paris w. Johnny Guarnieri and Stephane Grappelli and as a leader. CDs: w. Benny Carter; Lena Horne (BB); B. Holiday; E. Fitzgerald (Dec.); Earl Bostic (King); Sid Catlett; C. Hawkins (Class.); S. Grappelli; Slam Stewart (B&B); Pete Johnson (Sav.); tracks w. Edmond Hall and Art Hodes in *Hot Jazzbox* (BN).

SHOEMAKE, CHARLIE (CHARLES EDWARD), vib, pno; b. Houston, TX, 7/27/37. Studied pno. as a child, then at So. Methodist U. 1955–6; later informally w. Jimmy Rowles. Self-taught on vib.; moved to LA in '56, pl. w. Charles Lloyd; Art Pepper; Lighthouse All-Stars; then studio and club work late '50s-early '60s. Pl. w. G. Shearing Jan. '67 through '73; formed qnt. w. Pete Christlieb, pl. LA clubs '75–7. Has led own small bands since '81. Fr. '73 to '90 he operated an in-home improv. studio in Sherman Oaks, Calif. Using no vibrato motor, Shoemake plays in a distinctive, clean style that is rooted in bebop. Favs: C. Parker, F. Navarro, B. Powell. CDs: Chase; Disc.; Bruce Eskoritz (Koch).

SHOEMAKE, SANDI (SANDRA MARIE), voc; b. Rochester, MN, 10/9/38. Father a dixieland dmr./voc. Stud. pno. as child, voice lessons at 17; attended LA City Coll., perf. in bands led by Bob MacDonald; w. Si Zentner 1958–60; studio work in '60s; staff NBC-TV voc. on shows starring Andy Williams; Dean Martin; Red Skelton; Jerry Lewis '65–70; w. Nelson Riddle orch. '64–70; rec. and perf. w. husband, Charlie Shoemake, fr. '60s. Fav: Dick Haymes, B. Eckstine. Her approach favors purity of sound and lacks dramatics, though she can still be emotional. CDs: w. C. Shoemake (Disc.).

SHORT, BOBBY (ROBERT WALTRIP), pno, voc; b. Danville, IL, 9/15/24; d. NYC, 3/21/05. Child prodigy; app. in vaudeville fr. age 10. Feat. at Blue Angel, NYC; the Haig in LA; and the Gala in Hollywood. Worked at clubs in Paris 1950s and '60s. In residence off and on at the Café Carlyle, NYC fr. '68. In late '90s accomp. by ens. w. horns. Spent summers in south of France; occ. concert tours. Acquired an int'l reputation for his interpretation of sophisticated lyrics. Fav. pnst., Dick Hyman. Whitney Balliett called Short "one of the last examples (and indubitably the best) of the café singer or the supper club singer or 'troubador'." CDs: Atl.; Tel.; w. M. McPartland (JA); *Benny Carter Songbook* (MM).

SHORTER, WAYNE, tnr, sop saxes, comp; b. Newark, NJ, 8/25/33. Majored in fine arts in hs and has cont. to paint. Cl. at 16, then tnr.; mus. ed. at NYU 1956–8; briefly w. Horace Silver '56. After army service he pl. w. Maynard Ferguson, Jul.-Aug. '59, then joined Art Blakey as mus. dir. and sideman until early '64. Soon after leaving Blakey, he joined Miles Davis, Sep. '64 to spring of '70. Took up sop. sax. in '68. While with Davis he earned a reputation as comp. of such tunes as "E.S.P."; "Prince of Darkness"; "Nefertiti"; "Fall"; "Paraphernalia"; "Sanctuary"—important contemp. works that updated the Davis gp.'s repertoire. In late '70s Shorter and fellow Ferguson and Davis alumnus Joe Zawinul formed Weather Report, which stayed together fifteen yrs. and perf. such Shorter comps. as "Mysterious Traveler"; "Tears"; "Eurydice"; "The Moors"; "Manolete." Shorter began rec. as a leader in '59, and he cont. to do so while w. Davis and Weather Report, often rec. his own comps. His own albums, which sometimes reflect a Latin Amer. infl., are generally less abstract than his work w. Weather Report. For his '75 album, *Native Dancer*, he feat. Milton Nascimento as comp. and perf. After Weather Report disbanded, Shorter toured extensively as a solo artist and led various small gps. Appeared in the film *Round Midnight* '86. Toured with Carlos Santana and a Latin jazz-rock gp. '88. Although Shorter found the sop. sax more compatible to his style than the tnr., he cont. to use both instruments. Won the *DB* award on sop. for thirteen yrs. straight, starting in '69. Favs: Charlie Parker, John Coltrane, Lester Young; comps. incl.: Gil Evans, Gil Fuller, Stravinsky, Ravel. CDs: Vee-Jay; BN; Verve; Col. w. Weather Report; Miles Davis (Col.); Gil Evans (Verve); Art Blakey (BN; Imp.; DIW; FS; Riv.); H. Merrill (Ant.); Lee Morgan–Thad Jones (Roul.); McCoy Tyner; R. Rosnes; Lee Morgan; T. Williams; Donald Byrd; M. Petrucciani (BN); T. S. Monk (N2K); Buster Williams (In & Out); Marcus Miller (Drey.); J. Pastorius (Sound Hills); H. Hancock (Col.; Qwest).

SHU, EDDIE (Edward Shulman), multi-instrumentalist; b. NYC, 8/18/18; d. St. Petersburg, FL, 7/4/86. Started on vln., gtr., and hca.; at 17, he tour. w. hca. band, then worked as ventriloquist and hca. soloist w. Major Bowes. Studied all reed and brass instruments but most often heard on tnr. sax. After army service he played w. Tadd Dameron 1947; George Shearing '48; Buddy Rich, Lionel Hampton '49–50; Charlie

Barnet '50–1; Chubby Jackson '52. Mainly known in '50s as member of Gene Krupa Trio '54–8. Worked in Cuba and Miami; rejoined Krupa several times '58–59. Pl. cl. on tour w. L. Armstrong '64–5. In later yrs. pl. and taught in St. Croix, the Virgin Islands, then settled in Fla. A capable trumpeter, Shu's versatility allowed him to easily shift fr. modern tnr. sax w. Krupa to traditional cl. w. Armstrong. CDs: w. Joe Bonner (Evid.); Armstrong (EPM); R. Eldridge; Anita O'Day (Verve)

SHULL, TAD (THOMAS BARCLAY JR.), tnr sax, cl; b. Norwalk, CT, 10/15/55. Uncle was prof. dmr. in Atlanta. Began on alto. Stud. w. John Mehegan, Dave Liebman and pl. w. youth swing band in Westport, Conn. 1967–70. Att. New Engl. Cons. '74–6. Pl. w. own gps. fr. '76; Bob Wilber, Smithsonian Jazz Orch. '81; Widespread Jazz Orch. fr. '81. Shull received a B.A. and M.A. in political science fr. Columbia U. '89. Favs: Don Byas, Coleman Hawkins, Ben Webster. Fests: Eur. '83–5. CDs: CC; w. Jordan Sandke in *The Sandke Brothers* (Stash).

SHULMAN, JOE (JOSEPH), bs; b. NYC, 9/12/23; d. NYC, 8/2/57. First prof. gig w. Scat Davis 1940; Les Brown '42. In army '43. Rec. w. Django Reinhardt while in Eur. w. Glenn Miller's Army Air Force Band. Back in US he pl. w. Buddy Rich; Claude Thornhill; and Miles Davis (on the "Birth of the Cool" sess.). Worked w. Peggy Lee '48–50; Lester Young '50. Rec. trio date w. Billy Strayhorn and Duke Ellington, '50. Married pnst. Barbara Carroll '54, and tour. w. her until his death. CDs: w. G. Miller (BB); M. Davis (Cap.); Lester Young (Verve); Claude Thornhill (Hep); Ellington-Strayhorn (Riv.).

SICKLER, DON, tpt, arr; b. Spokane, WA, 1/6/44. Mother taught pno., org., acdn., and pl. org. for silent movies. Stud. pno. w. moth. fr. age 4. Began pl. tpt. at age 10. Started dixieland band at age 12; within a yr. the band had expanded and was pl. hs and coll. dances. Stud. tpt. w. Donald Byrd; arr. w. Russ Garcia, Johnny Richards at Stan Kenton Mus. Camp late '50s-early '60s. Received B.A. in mus. fr. Gonzaga U., Spokane, Wash. '67. Moved to NYC '67. Studied at Manh. Sch. of Mus., freelanced in B'way show bands late '60s. Worked mainly in mus. publ. in '70s, incl. managing editor, E.B. Marks Mus. Corp. '71–3; freelance mus. editing and prod. '73–4; prod. manager, Big 3 Mus. Corp. '75–9. Pl. w. Philly Joe Jones late '70s. Founded two full-service jazz publ. companies, Second Floor Mus. and Twenty-Eighth Street Mus. in '80. Mus. dir. and member of Dameronia fr. '82; Thelonious Monk Reunion Orch. '86–7. Pl. and arr. w. Art Blakey bb in Japan '87–9; own qt. in Paris '87; Superblue fr. '88;

Birdology w. Jackie McLean, Johnny Griffin '89; BN
bb in Japan '90; Clifford Jordan bb fr. '90; T. S. Monk
band fr. '91. Also pl. w. Candido; Charli Persip; James
Williams; Jaki Byard; Panama Francis. Cond. Gil
Evans Retrospective at Lincoln Ctr. '83; Howard
McGhee Tribute at New Sch. '87; Mus. of Jackie
McLean at Lincoln Ctr. '90; Jack Walrath w. Strings
'90; Joe Henderson–Freddie Hubbard bb '92. In '90
produced an all-star concert at Carnegie Recital Hall
dedicated to the mus. of Hank Mobley. Sickler's arrs.
have been rec. by Art Blakey; Freddie Hubbard;
Woody Shaw; Joe Henderson; others. Prod. recs. for
Hubbard; Shaw; Henderson; Larry Coryell; Donald
Brown; Wallace Roney; Renee Rosnes; etc. Taught at
Bklyn. Mus. Sch. '68–72; Hunter Coll. '84–5, '88;
Hartt Sch. of Mus. (master classes) fr. '86. Dir. bb at
Col. U. fr. '86. Favs: Dizzy Gillespie, Clifford Brown,
Freddie Hubbard. Polls: *DB* TDWR arr. '90. Fests:
Eur., Japan fr. '87. CDs: Res.; Up.; w. Superblue (BN);
T. S. Monk (BN; N2K); Cedar Walton (Delos); Birdol-
ogy (Verve); C. Jordan bb (Mile.); Jack Sheldon; Fred-
die Redd; Jimmy Gourley (Up.).

SIDES, DOUG (DOUGLAS JOSEPH), dms, perc,
comp; b. Los Angeles, CA, 10/10/42. Began on pno.
Stud. at U. of So. Calif.; w. Alan Dawson at Berklee
Coll. of Mus.; NYU. Pl. in Bost. w. Illinois Jacquet
1961; then in LA w. Teddy Edwards, Lionel Hampton
'62; Howard Rumsey '62–3; Johnny Griffin, Curtis
Amy–Dupree Bolton, Harold Land '63; Charles
Kynard '64. In mil. '64–6. Worked in SF w. Tommy
Butler '66; Merle Saunders '67; John Handy '67–8.
In LA w. Harold Land–Bobby Hutcherson '69–70;
Phineas Newborn Jr. '70; O. C. Smith '70–2; Blue
Mitchell–Jimmy Forrest, Harold Land '72. Pl. w. Joe
Henderson; Joe Sample; Buddy Collette; Jack Wilson
early '70s; Rudolph Johnson; H. Land; Sammy Davis
Jr.; Harry "Sweets" Edison; Eddie "Lockjaw" Davis
late '70s. Toured Eur. w. Abbey Lincoln '80; US,
Can. w. Jon Hendricks '82–3. Led own gp. at Yale
Club, NYC '87. Toured Eur. w. show *Sophisticated
Ladies* '88. Moved to Amsterdam '89. Since '91
Sides has worked locally w. Benny Bailey and tour.
w. J. Griffin; Tete Montoliu; Steve Grossman; Tom
Harrell; Walter Bishop Jr.; Ralph Sutton; Ranee Lee;
Hank Jones; Oliver Jones. Favs: Frank Butler, Elvin
Jones, Philly Joe Jones, Alan Dawson. Fests: Eur. fr.
'80. TV: *Jazz Scene USA* w. Teddy Edwards; March
of Dimes telethon w. Lionel Hampton; Dutch TV w.
Oliver Jones. Rec. w. John Handy (Col.); Blue
Mitchell (Main.). CDs: w. Walter Bishop Jr. (Red);
Joe Van Enkhuizen (Timel.); Don Bennett (Cand.).

SIDRAN, BEN, pno, comp, author; b. Chicago, IL,
8/14/43. Raised in Racine, Wisc.; stud. pno fr. age 5;

met Steve Miller and Boz Scaggs in coll.; rec. w.
Miller Band 1969. Occ. pl. w. Eric Clapton; Peter
Frampton; et al. while stud. at U. of Sussex, Engl.
First album of his own, *Feel Your Groove* '71; his
book of jazz essays, *Black Talk* '71, was ill-
researched. In the '70s worked w. Woody Shaw; Blue
Mitchell; and Tony Williams; rec. w. Lee Ritenour,
Joe Henderson, and Steve Gadd '79. In the '80s prod.
jazz video discs feat. Phil Woods; Richard Davis; et
al. and hosted a jazz radio show on NPR '81–3; perf.
as soloist at Paris fest. '86; toured Eur. with a gp. '88.
In '92 began running his own co., Go Jazz. CDs:
A&M; Arista; Ant.; WH; BB; BM; w. Van Morrison
(Verve); Richie Cole (Mile.).

SIGNORELLI, FRANK, pno, comp; b. NYC
5/24/01; d. NYC, 12/9/75. Early reputation w. Original Memphis Five 1917 and '26–31; also ODJB '21.
In the next few yrs. he was part of a pioneering circle
of white jazz mus., incl. Bix Beiderbecke; Frank
Trumbauer; Joe Venuti; Eddie Lang; and Adrian
Rollini, who rec. frequently. Rejoined ODJB '36–8;
w. Paul Whiteman '38. Dur. '40s he pl. at Nick's and
other NYC clubs w. Phil Napoleon, Bobby Hackett;
in '50s he re-formed Original Memphis Five for radio
and TV. Well-known as comp. of "I'll Never Be the
Same"; "Stairway to the Stars"; "A Blues Serenade."
His pno. comps. incl. "Park Avenue Fantasy"; "Midnight Reflections." Signorelli was an important jazz
figure in the '20s and early '30s. CDs: w. ODJB
(BB); Bix Beiderbecke (Col.); J. Teagarden; B.
Goodman (Dec.); Original Memphis Five (Village);
Joe Venuti; (JSP); Eddie Lang (ASV; Yazoo).

SILVA, ALAN TREADWELL, bs; b. Bermuda,
1/22/39. Raised in Bklyn., stud. tpt. w. Donald Byrd.
Attended N.Y. Coll. of Mus.; took up bs. 1962. Pl. in
free gps., incl. Cecil Taylor '65–9; Sun Ra '65–70;
Albert Ayler '66–70; Sunny Murray and Archie
Shepp '69. Moved to France '70; formed Celestrial
Communication Orch. but also worked in smaller
gps. w. Frank Wright; Bobby Few; and Muhammad
Ali. From mid '70s lived and taught in NYC and
Paris; rec. w. C. Taylor, Bill Dixon, Andrew Hill in
'80; Globe Unity Orch. '82. He then became semi-
inactive for several yrs. but ret. to play pno. w. British
percst. Roger Turner and tnr. saxophonist Gary Dodd
'90–1. CDs: ESP; w. Albert Ayler (Imp.); B. Dixon
(SN); Jazz Composers Orch. (JCOA); Sunny Murray
(ESP); A. Shepp (Aff.); C. Taylor (BN; hatArt
Charly).

SILVER, HORACE WARD MARTIN TAVARES,
(Silva), pno, comp; Norwalk, CT, 9/2/28. Father, of
Portuguese descent, pl. folk mus. fr. Cape Verdean

Islands; uncle pl. tbn. in pit bands for silent movies. Stud. sax in hs, pno priv. w. a church organist. Pl. local gigs on tnr. sax and pno. Discovered by Stan Getz while pl. a gig w. local Hartford band led by Harold Holdt. Toured w. Getz 1950–1. Moved to NYC; worked frequently w. Art Blakey '51–2; Terry Gibbs, Coleman Hawkins '52. After rec. w. Lou Donaldson for Blue Note in '52, the label signed him and rec. him regularly for almost thirty yrs. Worked w. Oscar Pettiford, Bill Harris, Lester Young '53. In '56, after co-leading Jazz Messengers w. Art Blakey for two yrs., he formed a qnt. Like Blakey, Silver helped pioneer the development of hard bop and nurtured sidemen who became leaders of similar ens., incl. Donald Byrd; Blue Mitchell; Junior Cook, Art Farmer, Joe Henderson; and, later, Tom Harrell; Randy and Michael Brecker. After leaving BN in the early '80s, he formed Silveto Records and spent much of his time managing his rec. and publ. businesses, occ. reorganizing a tour gp. Dur. this time he also became a prolific, if simplistic, lyricist and comp. of large-scale voc. works, many of them dedicated to his philosophy of self-help via holistic and metaphysical means. Among his most famous comps. are "The Preacher"; "Señor Blues"; "Doodlin'"; "Opus De Funk"; "Nica's Dream"; "Song for My Father"; "Sister Sadie"; "Blowin' the Blues Away"; "Filthy McNasty"; "Peace." Silver lectured at El Camino Coll. in Torrance, Calif., on "The Art of Small Combo Jazz Playing." Won *DB* Critics Poll '54, New Star pno. Originally inspired by Bud Powell, Silver, who features a percussive, hard-driving attack, himself became the source of much inspiration and imitation. His early yrs. as a saxophonist may have infl. the strongly melodic character of his music. CDs: BN; Col.; Imp.; Verve; w. A. Blakey (Col.; BN); S. Getz (Mos.; Roost; Roul.); Milt Jackson (Atl.; Prest.); M. Davis (Prest.; BN); Sonny Rollins; Kenny Dorham; J. J. Johnson; Clifford Brown (BN); K. Clarke; Al Cohn; Hank Mobley (Sav.); Art Farmer (Prest.); Lester Young (Story.).

SIMEON, OMER VICTOR, cl, saxes; b. New Orleans, LA, 7/21/02; d. NYC, 9/17/59. Studied w. Lorenzo Tio Jr. Pro. debut w. his bro., violinist Al Simeon, 1920. In Chi. dur. '20s he pl. w. Charlie Elgar; Luis Russell; Erskine Tate; and rec. w. Jelly Roll Morton; King Oliver; and others. With Earl Hines '31–7; Horace Henderson '37–8; Walter Fuller '39–40; Coleman Hawkins '40. With Jimmie Lunceford '42, remaining w. the band under Eddie Wilcox's leadership until '50. Then freelanced w. Bud Freeman; Bobby Hackett; mainly w. Wilbur DeParis from '51–59, incl. African tour '57. CDs: w. K. Oliver (Dec.); L. Hampton; J. R. Morton; E. Hines (BB);

Kid Ory (GTJ); Bunk Johnson (Amer. Mus.); F. Henderson (ASV); Lunceford (Class.); Sidney DeParis in *Hot Jazz* (BN); Art Hodes (Dormouse).

SIMMONS, JOHN JACOB, bs; b. Haskell, OK, 6/14/18; d. Los Angeles, CA, 9/19/79. Daughter, Sue, is NBC-TV anchorwoman. Attended sch. in Okla. and Calif., where he pl. in San Diego and LA night clubs w. Nat King Cole and others, and rec. w. Teddy Wilson 1937. Moved to Chi. and worked w. Johnny Letman, Roy Eldridge '40. With Benny Goodman in NYC '41; Cootie Williams and Louis Armstrong '42. Pl. w. CBS radio orchestras and app. in film, *Jammin' the Blues* '44; also w. Louis Armstrong's bb, Eddie Heywood, Illinois Jacquet in mid '40s. In the same period he rec. w. James P. Johnson; Hot Lips Page; Sid Catlett; Ben Webster; Billie Holiday; Erroll Garner; Coleman Hawkins; Benny Carter; and Don Byas; later rec. w. Ella Fitzgerald; Thelonious Monk; and Sir Charles Thompson. Pl. w. Erroll Garner trio, NYC '49–52; in Scand. w. Rolf Ericson and Duke Jordan '55. Rec. w. Harry Edison '58; pl. w. Phineas Newborn '59–60. Largely inactive thereafter due to illness. CDs: w. Erroll Garner (Col.; Sav.; Verve); B. Holiday (Dec.; Comm.; Verve); Lena Horne (BB); Sir Charles Thompson (Apollo); C. Hawkins (Cap.); Art Tatum (Pab.); Tadd Dameron; Dameron-Coltrane (Prest.); Lester Young; Hot Lips Page (Comm.); I. Jacquet (Mos.); Nat Cole; André Previn (BL); Teddy Wilson (Hep); Buddy Rich (Sequel); Monk; Milt Jackson (BN).

SIMMONS, (SARNEY) NORMAN, pno, comp; b. Chicago, IL, 10/6/29. Studied at Chi. Sch. of Mus. 1945–9. Began pl. prof. w. Clifford Jordan '46. Own trio fr. '49. Pl. w. Claude McLin qt. '50; Gus Chapell qnt, Paul Bascomb qnt. '51. Also worked gigs in Chi. w. Flip Phillips–Bill Harris; Coleman Hawkins–Roy Eldridge '51. Dur. long engagement as house pnst. at Bee-Hive in Chi. '53, he pl. for Ch. Parker; Dexter Gordon; and others. Freelanced w. trio and led C&C Orch. w. sidemen such as Gene Ammons, Frank Strozier, Booker Little '56–7. Noted as an outstanding accomp. to singers, he moved to NYC and worked w. Dakota Staton '58; Ernestine Anderson '59; Carmen McRae '61; Betty Carter '73, and others. Also worked w. Lockjaw Davis–Johnny Griffin qnt. '59–60; Eldridge '70–1; Tyree Glenn '71; J. McPartland '75; Anita O'Day '75–81; Scott Hamilton '77. House pno. at Lulu's, Bost. '78; Hopper's, NYC '79. Recs. as pnst./arr./cond. w. Staton; Helen Humes; Teri Thornton, Johnny Griffin; Mongo Santamaria. Throughout most of the '80s and '90s he toured w. Joe Williams. Taught for Jazzmobile fr. '73; at William Paterson Coll. fr. '82; New Sch. in '90s.

NEA Grant for comp. '74. Formed Milljac Rec. and Publ. Co. Favs: Hank Jones, Oscar Peterson, Ellington. Fests: Austral., Engl., Japan. CDs: Milljac; w. Joe Williams (Delos; Verve); Scott Hamilton (Conc.); Al Grey; Frank Wess; Harold Ashby (Gem.); Carmen McRae (Col.); J. Griffin (Riv.); Milt Hinton (Chiaro.); Betty Carter (Roul.; Verve); Les McCann (Night); Roy Eldridge (Pab.).

SIMMONS, SONNY (HUEY), alto, tnr saxes, English horn, comp; b. Sicily Island, LA, 8/4/33. Raised in Oakland, Calif., fr. age 8. Bought sax at 17; met and worked w. Prince Lasha for a decade, forming several gps. From mid 1960s he worked clubs in NYC and Calif. Rec. debut in '62 w. Lasha. Concerts and clubs w. gp. feat. his wife, trumpeter Barbara Donald. Together they started the Woodstock fest. '69. Pl. at Nairobi Fest. '71 w. Bobby Hutcherson and Lasha. Comps incl. "City of David"; "Dolphy's Days"; "Coltrane in Paradise"; "Seven Dances of Salome." First inspired by Charlie Parker, Simmons was later infl. by Ornette Coleman. Dur. the '80s he devoted much time to studying, writing, and teaching. CDs: ESP; Qwest; CIMP; w. Lasha (Cont.); E. Dolphy (Charly); Elvin Jones (Imp.).

SIMON, ED (Edward Simon Morillo), pno; b. Cardon, Falcon, Venezuela, 7/27/69. Father is amateur gtrst.; bros. Marlon and Michael pl. dms. and tpt., respectively. Began on el-org., then pno. Pl. tbn. in middle sch. band. Stud. at Perf. Arts HS, Phila. 1984–6; U. of the Arts, Phila. '86–9; Manh. Sch. of Mus. '89. Pl. in family band fr. age 10. Worked w. Greg Osby '89; Kevin Eubanks '89–93; Bobby Watson and Horizon '89–94; Paquito D'Rivera Havana–NY Ens. off and on '90–4; Herbie Mann '90–4; Victor Lewis '92–3; United Nation Orch. fr. '93; Terence Blanchard fr. '94. Simon placed third in the Thelonious Monk pno. competition in '93 and currently teaches the Latin-jazz ensemble at the U. of the Arts in Phila. Favs: Keith Jarrett, Herbie Hancock, Chick Corea. Fests: Eur., So. Amer., Central Amer., Caribbean, Japan, Australia. CDs: Audioq.; w. Blanchard (Col.); Watson (BN; Col.); Eubanks (GRP); Osby (GRP; JMT; BN); Mann (Chesky); Lewis (Audioq.; Red); Claudio Roditi (Cand.).

SIMON, JOHN DAVID, tnr, sop saxes, fl; b. Philadelphia, PA, 5/2/59. Grandmother pl. pno.; uncle pl. hca. Began on pno. at age 4. Stud. pno. priv. 1969–75; then sax w. Joe Fortunato '75–7 and at Phila. Coll. of Perf. Arts '77–81 (B. Mus. '81); Manh. Sch. of Mus. '95–7 (M. Mus. '97). First experience while in hs, sitting in w. Joe Fortunato Trio w. John DeFrancesco. Pl. w. org. trios in Phila., incl. Herb Nix

at Gert's Lounge '82–6; Don Patterson '82–8; own trio at Jewel's '87–7. Pl. w. Odean Pope sax choir fr. '86. Moved to NYC '87; pl. w. Charles Earland '87–8; Illinois Jacquet bb '88–95; Panama Francis's Savoy Sultans '89–93. Received NEA grant to study w. Joe Henderson '88; also stud. w. Frank Wess, Vince Trombetta. Occ. gigs w. Shirley Scott '88–91; Mickey Roker fr. '91. Pl. w. Ella Fitzgerald and Clark Terry bb at Radio City, also subbed in T. S. Monk band '92. Simon has led a qnt. w. John Swana, John DiMartino, Matthew Parrish, Mark Johnson fr. 91. Guest w. Mickey Roker qt., Phila. in late '90s. On the faculty of the Settlement Mus. Sch. in Phila. fr. '82; Jazz Combo Instructor, Manh. Sch. of Mus. '95–7; Ridgewood Cons. faculty fr. '98. Favs: Sonny Stitt, Stan Getz, Sonny Rollins. Fests: Eur., Japan, Carib. w. Jacquet, Francis. Film: *Texas Tenor* w. Jacquet. CDs: Muse; w. O. Pope (SN); Joe Sudler–Clark Terry (TJA); Manh. School of Mus. Jazz Orch. at Montreux (SB).

SIMON, MAURICE JAMES, tnr, bari saxes; b. Houston, TX, 3/26/29. Played w. Russell Jacquet band in Texas 1943–4; moved to LA, where he worked w. Gerald Wilson; toured w. Illinois Jacquet. Led gp. w. bro. Freddie late '40s-53; in '50s worked w. Count Basie, Cootie Williams; backed Billy Williams and Cab Calloway. In '60s he backed singers in LV and LA; pl. bari. sax w. Ray Charles '67. Off and on w. Mercer Ellington fr. '74 through '80s. In his early yrs. Simon was known for his rousing Illinois Jacquet–inspired style. CDs: w. I. Jacquet (BB; Mos.).

SIMONE, NINA (Eunice Waymon), voc, pno; b. Tryon, NC, 2/21/33; d. Carry-le-Rouet, France, 4/21/03. One of 8 children, all of whom sang or pl. an instr. Self-taught on pno. fr. age 6, org. fr. age 9. Moved to Phila. '50; stud. at Curtis Inst. of Mus. and taught pno.; later stud. at Juilliard. Worked as accomp. to singers '50–4, then began to sing herself. First gig as singer/pnst. at Atlantic City gay bar '54. "I Love You Porgy," fr. her deb. Bethlehem album, was a huge hit in '59. Tour. w. own gp. fr. '60, w. a repertoire that incl. such songs of social protest as "Mississippi Goddam"; "Why? (the King of Love is Dead)." She was an engaging pianist w. a distinct vocal style who effectively lent that style to a wide variety of material. In the '60s her political stance brought her a near-cult following, but bizarre personal behavior and lateness for bookings eventually dimmed her spotlight. Continued rec. into the late '90s but not w. the impact of old. CDs: Beth.; Roul.; Philips; Col.; Verve.

SIMPKINS, ANDY (ANDREW H.), bs; b. Richmond, IN, 4/29/32; d. Culver City, CA, 6/2/99.

Started on cl. at 10, pno at 14, and bs while in army 1953. Joined Gene Harris and Bill Dowdy to form the Three Sounds, a popular gp. that rec. numerous BN albums fr. '57. After moving to LA '66, he freelanced, then tour. w. George Shearing '68–76. Worked w. Sarah Vaughan '79–89; to Japan w. Lorez Alexandria '91. Dur. the '70s and '80s he pl. and rec. w. Monty Alexander; Kenny Burrell; Freddie Hubbard; Chick Corea; Oscar Peterson; Carmen McRae; and his own qnt. A dependable bassist known for his buoyant swing and commanding sound. CDs: Disc; MAMA; w. Three Sounds; S. Turrentine (BN); S. Vaughan (Pab.; Col.; J. Pass; Benny Carter; Sweets Edison (Pab.); G. Wiggins; M. Stallings; Scott Hamilton (Conc.); Teddy Edwards; Anita O'Day (Verve); Terry Gibbs (Cont.); V. Feldman (Riv.).

SIMS, PETE "LaROCA" (PETER), dms, comp; b. NYC, 4/7/38. Father pl. tpt., moth. pno. Stud. perc. in NYC public sch. system; then at HS of Mus. and Art; CCNY; Manh. Sch. of Mus. Max Roach heard him at a Jazz Unlimited session at Birdland and recommended him to Sonny Rollins. As Pete LaRoca, he pl. w. Rollins 1957–9; Tony Scott '59; Slide Hampton; Jackie McLean late '50s; John Coltrane '60; own gp. intermittently '61–2; Marian McPartland '62. House dmr. at Jazz Wkshp., Bost. '63–4; then pl. w. Art Farmer '64–5; Chas. Lloyd '66; Paul Bley, Steve Kuhn late '60s. Discouraged by the dominance of rock and jazz-rock, LaRoca abandoned his mus. career in '68 to bec. a lawyer, using his birth name, Peter Sims. He resumed perf. occ. in '79 and returned full-time in the '90s—as Pete "LaRoca" Sims—lead. a sxt. called Swingtime. Favs: Philly Joe Jones, Elvin Jones. CDs: BN; 32; w. S. Rollins; McLean; Johnny Coles; Joe Henderson (BN); P. Bley (Sav.); J. Byard (NJ); George Russell; Don Friedman (Riv.); J. R. Monterose (FS); K. Dorham (BL).

SIMS, RAY C., tbn, voc; b. Wichita, KS, 1/18/21; d. Cedar City, UT, 3/14/00. Brother of Zoot Sims. Pl. w. Jerry Wald, Bobby Sherwood; rec. w. Anita O'Day 1947; pl. and rec. w. Benny Goodman. Pl. and sang ballads w. Les Brown '47–57; also worked w. Dave Pell Oct. '53–7. Pl. w. Harry James '57–69; rec. w. Bill Holman, Red Norvo, Charlie Barnet late '50s. Rec. w. James '73; as voc. w. Corky Corcoran '73; also rec. w. bro.'s qnt. as tbnst. and voc. '79–80. Active in studios from '80s. CDs: w. Z. Sims (Pab.); A. O'Day (Sig.); Jackie and Roy (Koch); Harry James (Verve); Red Norvo (RCA);

SIMS, ZOOT (JOHN HALEY), tnr, alto, sop saxes, cl.; b. Inglewood, CA, 10/29/25; d. NYC, 3/23/85. Raised in a family of vaudeville artists, he started on

dms. and cl., then tnr. sax at 13. Prof. mus. fr. age 15. Pl. w. Ken Baker 1941; Bobby Sherwood '42–3; Sonny Dunham, Bob Astor '43; Benny Goodman, Sid Catlett '44. Army '44–46; then pl. and rec. w. Bill Harris and Joe Bushkin '46; and back again w. Goodman. Also w. Gene Roland '47; and Woody Herman's bb '47–49, where he gained fame as a member of the famous tenor-led saxophone section known as the Four Brothers. Settled in NYC, working w. Buddy Rich '49; Artie Shaw '49–50; Goodman's gp. '50, incl. Eur. tour. Then w. Roy Eldridge in Paris and Birdland, NYC '50; Chubby Jackson '50; and Elliot Lawrence '51. With Stan Kenton '53. Ret. to Calif., where he freelanced bef. ret. east as a member of Gerry Mulligan's sxt. '55–6. From '57 he worked regularly in gps. co-led w. Al Cohn. Tour. w. Mulligan bb '60. Rejoined W. Herman for a concert in early '70s; then w. Goodman for tours of Eur., Austral., and US. Tour. int'l w. JATP '67, '75. His later yrs. were marked by fine collaborations w. Jimmy Rowles. One of a generation of young post-WWII tnr. players who integrated some of Charlie Parker's spirit into a Lester Young–derived style to find a voice of their own. In his later yrs., Sims reincorporated some of his early Ben Webster infl. Always a natural swinger, he brought a shimmering, mellow warmth to his ballad performances. Film: w. Don Albert, *Beale Street Mama* '46. Video: Rhap. CDs: 32; BN; Mob. Fid.; FS; Prest.; Riv.; Story.; Pab.; Biog.; RCA/Vogue; co-lead w. Al Cohn (BB; Dec.; BN; Evid.); co-lead w. Art Pepper (Pab.); co-lead w. Bucky Pizzarelli (Story.); w. C. Baker; C. Mingus (Col.); G. Mulligan (Verve; PJ); Eldridge (Vogue); Booker Ervin (Aff.); Herman (Col.; Cap.; BB; Conc.); Goodman (MM); S. Getz; Miles Davis; John Coltrane (Prest.); Carmen McRae (Novus; Decca); Joe Venuti (Chiaro.); Jimmy Rushing; Joe Williams (BB); Basie (Pab.); Kenton (Cap.; Mos.).

SINATRA, FRANK (FRANCIS ALBERT), voc; b. Hoboken, NJ, 12/12/15; d. Los Angeles, CA, 5/14/98. As a teenager he sang locally, sometimes w. the Hoboken Four, a gp. w. which he won *Major Bowes Amateur Hour* radio show talent contest in Sept. 1935; tour. w. Bowes show for three mos., sometimes broadcasting. From '37 to '39 worked as singer-waiter at Rustic Cabin roadhouse, Englewood, N.J., incl. radio remotes carried by WNEW. Toured and rec. w. Harry James fr. summer of '39–40. Joined Tommy Dorsey Orch. and rose to enormous popularity by '43, when Col. reissued his '39 rec. w. James of "All or Nothing At All." It became a hit in '43, by which time his popularity—through recs., radio exposure, and live apps.—was such that he left Dorsey to pursue a solo career. Over the next few yrs., Sinatra attained world-wide fame, app. in a dozen major movies and rec. profusely. Through '49 he was with Col., where his assoc. w. comp.-arr. Axel Stordahl set the standard for modern ballad style. Rec. "Sweet Lorraine" w. Metronome All-Stars '46. In the late '40s, when Col. steered him toward novelty material, sales sagged, press relations deteriorated, and his career went into decline, albeit a short-lived one. He made a stunning comeback as a dramatic actor in the '53 film *From Here to Eternity*, which won him an Oscar. On his new label, Capitol, charts by such arrs. as Nelson Riddle, Billy May, and Gordon Jenkins combined with his classy demeanor and hip delivery to make him the personification of "cool." Harry "Sweets" Edison was a frequent accompanist. Forming his own rec. label, Reprise, in the '60s, Sinatra rec. w. Count Basie; Duke Ellington; and Antonio Carlos Jobim. He retired in '71 but began a gradual return to do concerts in '73. Continued to tour into mid '90s, when illness curtailed his perf. activity. Over the yrs., Sinatra won countless awards fr. *DB, Met., Playboy*, etc. and, in '85, was given the Presidential Medal of Freedom. Although not generally viewed as a jazz singer, he has cited Louis Armstrong and Billie Holiday as infl. and is admired by jazz musicians and fans for his phrasing, which he attributed in large measure to Mabel Mercer. Books: *Sinatra*, by Arnold Shaw (Holt, Rinehart and Winston); *His Way*, by Kitty Kelley (Bantam); *The Revised Compleat Sinatra*, Albert Lonstein and Vita Marino (Cameron Publication); *The Frank Sinatra Reader*, Steven Petkov and Leonard Mustazza (Oxford) '95; *Sinatra! The Song Is You*, Will Friedwald (DaCapo) '97. CDs: Col.; Cap.; Rep.; BN; WB; w. T. Dorsey (Vict.; Buddha).

SINGER, HAL (HAROLD JOSEPH; CORNBREAD), tnr sax; b. Tulsa, OK, 10/08/19. Started on vln. at age 8; sax and cl. in hs; alto sax at Hampton U. where he grad. w. a degree in agriculture. Later stud. w. Eddie Barefield in NYC and at Juilliard. Worked as prof. mus. dur. summer vacations fr. coll. First name job w. T. Holder 1938. Pl. w. Geechie Smith '39; Ernie Fields '39–40; Lloyd Hunter '41; Nat Towles '41–2; Tommy Douglas in KC '42; Jay McShann '43; Willie "The Lion" Smith, NYC '43–4; Chris Columbus, Earl Bostic, Roy Eldridge (incl. rec. debut on *Fish Market*), Sid Catlett '44; Don Byas, Trummy Young '45; Red Allen '46; Hot Lips Page '47; Lucky Millinder, Bull Moose Jackson '48; Duke Ellington '48. Singer also had own gps. fr. '45. In '48 his r&b hit, "Cornbread," gave him a nickname and sufficient recognition to take own gp. on the road. Tour. US to '58, incl. as leader of a bb for heavyweight champ Joe Louis's revue '53; became a regu-

lar at the Metropole Café in NYC, where he teamed w. Charlie Shavers '58–61. Moved to Paris '65. Tour. w. own gp. in Eur., Turkey, Africa. Taught at clinics in France, Belg. fr. '72. Fests: many in Eur., Coleman Hawkins Tribute at NJF-NY '83. Awarded Chevalier of Arts and Letters by French Cultural Ministry '90. Films: w. Kenny Clarke in *The Only Game in Town*; w. tnr. saxist V. Chekasin in *Taxi Blues* '89. Favs: Hawkins, Young, Rollins, Coltrane. Book: autobiography, *Jazz Roads* '90. CDs: FNAC; Prest.; Sav.; w. Lonnie Johnson (Prest.); T-Bone Walker (Del.); R. Eldridge (Dec.); J. McShann (MM); Eddie "Cleanhead" Vinson (Del.).

SINGLETON, ZUTTY, dms; b. Bunkie, LA, 5/14/1898; d. NYC, 7/14/75. Mainly self-taught, he was directed toward a mus. career by an uncle, Willie Bontin Bontemps, who pl. bs. and gtr. First pro jobs at the Rosebud Theatre w. Steve Lewis 1915. Then w. Big Eye Louis Nelson; the Tuxedo Band; John Robichaux; and the Maple Leaf Band. Pl. w. Fate Marable's riverboat gps. '21–23; first recs. w. Marable '24. In Chi. fr. mid '20s he pl. w. Doc Cook; Dave Peyton; Jimmie Noone. Became known to wider jazz audience via recs. w. Louis Armstrong '28; and Jelly Roll Morton and Barney Bigard '29. Active in the '30s w. Roy Eldridge; Bobby Hackett; Sidney Bechet; and others, often at Nick's in NYC. Moved to Calif. in early '40s; app. in films, *Stormy Weather* '43 and *New Orleans* '47. Rec. w. Dizzy Gillespie and Charlie Parker under Slim Gaillard's leadership '45. In Eur. w. Mezz Mezzrow in early '50s. Back in NYC in mid '50s he pl. dixieland sess. at Metropole Café and Jimmy Ryan's in early '60s. Freelanced until '69, when a stroke forced his retirement. With Baby Dodds, Singleton was a pioneer NO-style dmr., but he moved away fr. the style's limitations by assimilating Chi. style technique (incl. the use of sock cymbals and brushes). Known for his imaginative use of cymbals, rim shots, etc. in his breaks and fills, Singleton was a superb accomp. who could pl. effectively in a variety of styles. LP: Fat Cat's Jazz. CDs: w. S. Bechet; L. Hampton (BB); J. R. Morton (BB; Comm.); Fats Waller (BB; CDS); L. Armstrong (Col.; BB); Victoria Spivey–Lucille Hegamin (Prest.); S. Gaillard, C. Parker (Sav.); Henry Red Allen (Hep; Tax); NJ. Teagarden–Pee Wee Russell (Riv.); Eldridge (Col.); tracks as lead. of spt. and trio in *Classic Capitol Jazz Sessions* (Mos.); also w. Capitol Jazzmen in same boxed set.

SIPIAGIN, ALEX (ALEXANDER), tpt, flg; b. Yaroslavl, Russia, 6/11/67. Great-granduncle, Leonid Sobinov, famous operatic baritone. Began mus. ed. at age 12 in Children's Brass Orch. Accepted as tpt.

major under Mikhail Tsomaev at Sobinov Mus. Coll., Yaroslavl 1982. Transferred to Gnesin Mus. Inst., Moscow '83. Did not grad. until '90 due to military service. Dur. this time became involved w. jazz. Began pl. prof. while a student. Worked w. Melodiya Rec. Co. Won first prize in first All-Russia Competition for Young Performers of Jazz Music, Rostov-on-Don '89. Gained fourth place in Int'l Thelonious Monk Competition, Wash., D.C., and was presented a Bach tpt. by Clark Terry '90. At the end of that yr. relocated in US. Has been a member of Gil Evans Orch. fr. '91; Gil Goldstein's Zebra Coast Orch. fr. '92; Bob Moses Mozamba '93–4; George Gruntz Concert Jazz Band fr. '93; Mingus bb fr. '95; Charlie Haden Liberation Orch., July '97. Also pl. w. Eric Clapton–Dr. John band; St. Luke's Symph. Orch.; David Binney gp.; Bob Brookmeyer–Lee Konitz; Teo Macero. Tours in Eur., Russia, Egypt w. Gruntz '94–8; Mingus, Eur., Brazil, US '96; own band in Texas '91–4; also tour. w. Christoff Schweitzer, Eur.; Alex Foster, Japan. Has perf. w. Randy Brecker; James Moody; Tom Harrell; Slide Hampton; Lew Soloff; Frank Wess; Craig Handy; Gary Bartz; Igor Butman. Has taught priv. in NYC fr. '91. Favs: Miles Davis, Kenny Wheeler; arr: Gil Goldstein. CDs: TCB; w. Mingus (Drey.); Macero (Col.); Larry Coryell (Shan.); Binney (Audq.); Moody (WB); Conrad Herwig (Conc.); Gruntz (TCB).

SISSLE, NOBLE LEE, voc, vln; b. Indianapolis, IN, 7/10/1889; d. Tampa, FL, 12/17/75. Served as dm. major in Jim Europe's 369th Div. Band dur. WWI and until 1919. Formed long-time partnership w. Eubie Blake, producing and comp. such shows as *Shuffle Along* '21, *Chocolate Dandies* '24. Worked in Engl. as voc. w. local gps. '28. Back in US he led bands in the '30s w. Sidney Bechet; Tommy Ladnier; Buster Bailey; Bill Coleman; and in '35, Lena Horne, who also cond. the band for awhile. Led band at Diamond Horseshoe in NYC '38–50; later active mainly as publisher and occ. leader. CDs: tracks on collections (Dec.; Col.; Jass); w. Bechet (Class.).

SIX, JACK, bs, tpt, comp; b. Danville, IL, 7/26/30. Studied tpt. in Chi., comp. at Juilliard, 1955–6. Worked w. Claude Thornhill '58; Woody Herman '59–60; Herbie Mann '59–64; Don Elliott '60–64; Jimmy Raney '61; Dukes of Dixieland '64. Became int'l known as bassist on tours w. Dave Brubeck '68–74. Pl. w. Jim Hall '76–8. Pl. in house band on Merv Griffin TV show, backing Benny Goodman, Buddy Rich, etc. '78–9. Mus. dir. for Claridge Hotel, Atlantic City '81–5. Back w. Brubeck '89–98. Rec. w. Tal Farlow, Illinois Jacquet, Jay McShann. Favs: Percy Heath, Ray Brown, Scott LaFaro, Eddie

Gomez. Fests: many int'l w. Brubeck; Nice JF w. Hank Jones, Roy Haynes as house rhythm section '80. CDs: w. Brubeck (Col.; Atl.; MM; Tel.); Brubeck–G. Mulligan (Col.); Farlow (Prest.); S. McCorkle (JA).

SKIDMORE, ALAN RICHARD JAMES, tnr, sop saxes, fl, alto fl; b. London, England, 4/21/42. Father, Jimmy, pl. tnr. sax w. George Shearing, Jack Parnell, Vic Lewis, Humphrey Lyttelton in 1950s. Aided by fath., but mainly self-taught. Since late '60s he has perf. and rec. w. John Mayall; Georgie Fame; John Surman; Clark Terry; Britt Woodman; Stan Tracey; Van Morrison; Mose Allison; Charlie Watts; and others. Joined Alexis Korner's Blues Inc. '64; pl. w. Ronnie Scott's qnt. '65. Formed own qnt. '69. Featured soloist w. West and North Germ. Radio Orchs. in '70s and '80s. From '76–82 he tour. and rec. w. George Gruntz Concert Jazz Band. Own gp. SOH w. Tony Oxley, Ali Haurand fr. '78. Pl. at Ronnie Scott w. Elvin Jones '86. Perf. Duke Ellington's Sacred Mus. in Durham Cathedral '90. Taught summer sch. in Bavaria. Has pl. in India, S.E. Asia, Hong Kong, Manila, Singapore, Eur., and US. Fests. w. Tracey, Fame, et al. Won many *MM* polls fr. '71. TV: concert, *Tribute to John Coltrane*, Dublin '86. Favs: Coltrane, Rollins, Dexter Gordon, Michael Brecker, Gerd Dudek, Ronnie Scott. Recs. w. Mayall; Korner; Surman; Michael Gibbs; Rolf Kuhn; Weather Report + 3. CDs: Miles Music; w. V. Morrison–G. Fame (Verve); Danny Thompson (Ant.).

SLACK, FREDDIE (FREDERICK CHARLES), pno, comp, lead; b. La Crosse, WI, 8/7/10; d. Los Angeles, CA, 8/10/65. Recorded and tour w. Ben Pollack's band 1934–36; then w. Jimmy Dorsey '36–9; Will Bradley–Ray McKinley band '39–41. Best known for such boogie-woogie recs. as "Beat Me Daddy Eight to the Bar" '40 but also was a convincing blues pl. as he demonstrated on a '41 Joe Turner Dec. sess. Led own band '42 and had a hit rec., "Cow Cow Boogie." Led various bands and gps. in Calif. in '40s and '50s. CDs: w. Bradley-McKinley (Col.); T-Bone Walker (Mos.); Jimmy Dorsey; Joe Turner (Dec.).

SLAGLE, STEVE (STEVEN), alto sax, sop sax, fl, alto-cl, comp; b. Los Angeles, CA, 9/18/51. Grandfather was swing dmr. in St. Louis, Mo. Fath. was first teacher. Pl. in local dance bands fr. age 16. Received *DB* grant to study at Berklee Coll. of Mus. 1970. Tour. w. Stevie Wonder and pl. in qt. w. John Scofield '72. Freelanced in Bost., then moved to NYC '76. Received M. Mus. fr. Manh. Sch. of Mus. Lead alto w. Machito's Afro-Cubans '76–7; Steve Kuhn–Harvie Swartz '78–9. Pl. tnr. briefly w. Woody

Herman Orch. '80; lead alto w. Lionel Hampton Orch. '80–2; Bro. Jack McDuff '82; Carla Bley '82–5; Charlie Haden Liberation Mus. Orch. '83; in Brazil w. Milton Nascimento '86. Tour. w. own qt. w. Mike Stern, Jaco Pastorius, Adam Nussbaum '86. Mus. dir. for Ray Barretto's Latin Jazz Band '88–91. In the early '90s Slagle has cont. to freelance and lead his own gps. In Nov. '93 he debuted a 10-pc. band at Greenwich House, NYC. His comps. have been perf. by the Mingus bb, in which he pl. a prominent part on alto. He leads a sax qt. at the Manh. Sch. of Mus and has been the recipient of three NEA comp. and perf. grants. Favs: Art Pepper, Charlie Parker. Fests: Eur., Japan, So. Amer. fr. '77. TV: Japanese TV w. C. Bley. CDs: Steep.; Panorama; Polyd.; w. S. Kuhn (ECM); C. Bley (Watt); R. Barretto (Conc.); C. Haden (ECM); Mingus bb (Drey.); D. Stryker (Steep.).

SLOANE, CAROL SPURR, voc; b. Providence, RI, 3/5/37. Uncle pl. pno. and sax in Ed Drew's Orch. and arranged to secure her first gig at age 14. Perf. w. Ed Drew 1952–4; mus. theater '55–7; Larry Elgart '58–60. Moved to NYC '60. Subbed for Annie Ross in L,H&R, then perf. at '61 NJF. Rec. w. Tommy Flanagan; Frank Wess; etc., since '60s. Sloane fulfills all the requisites to be called a true jazz singer. Favs: Carmen McRae, Shirley Horn. Fests: Japan since '77. TV: many apps. on *Tonight Show*. CDs: CBS; Cont.; Conc.; Koch Jz.; Century; co-lead w. Clark Terry; w. Conc. All-Stars; Phil Woods (Conc.).

SLON, CLAUDIO, perc; b. Brazil, 11/12/43. Studied fr. age 14; won New Star award in Brazilian jazz critics' poll at age 16. Principal percst. w. São Paulo Philharm. for two yrs. Drummer w. Sergio Mendes 1970–76, tour. the world and rec. 15 albums. Worked in NYC; then moved to LA, rec. w. Willie Bobo; Bola Sete; Dave and Don Grusin; John Pisano; Joe Pass; Stan Getz; Laurindo Almeida; and many others. CDs: w. J. Pisano; Joe Pass (Pab.).

SMALLS, CLIFF (CLIFTON ARNOLD), pno, arr, tbn; b. Charleston, SC, 3/3/18. Studied w. fath. While w. Carolina Cottonpickers, he att. KC Cons. From 1942 to '46 w. Earl Hines as tbn., second pno., and arr. From late '40s to '60s he cond. and arr. for Billy Eckstine; Clyde McPhatter; Brook Benton; et al.; also accomp. Ella Fitzgerald; Roy Hamilton; Smokey Robinson. In '70s pl. w. Sy Oliver; rec. w. Eddie Barefield; Buddy Tate; Oliver Jackson; et al. Infl. by Art Tatum and Earl Hines. CDs: tracks in *Master Jazz Piano* (Mos.); w. E. Fitzgerald (Col.); B. Tate (NW); Bennie Green (Prest.); Paul Gonsalves–Roy Eldridge (Fant.).

SMIETANA, JAROSLAW, gtr, comp; b. Krakow, Poland, 3/29/51. Studied at Katowice Acad. of Mus.; prof. debut 1972. Led band, Extra Ball '74–84, winning awards at the Jazz on the Odra competition '75. Band pl. important role in Polish jazz, app. at North Sea and other fest; Polish jazz mus. Vladislaw Sendecki, Andrzej Olejniczak, et al. made debuts w. band. From '86–91 he led qt., Sounds, and pl. w. visiting artists, incl. Freddie Hubbard; Manfred Schoof; Alex Riel; Milan Svoboda. Winner of several *Jazz Forum* polls as gtr. CDs for Muza and other Polish labels.

SMITH, BESSIE, voc; b. Chattanooga, TN, 4/15/1894; d. Clarksdale, MS, 9/26/37. Born and raised in poverty, Smith was still in her teens when her bro. Clarence, a comedian, ret. to Chattanooga w. the Moses Stokes Co., a small troupe that incl. Ma Rainey. She worked w. Moses Stokes Co. in honky tonks, carnivals, and traveling tent shows for the next few yrs., but left to go on her own, using 81 Theatre, Atlanta, Ga., as her base. By early 1920s she had established a reputation in Northeast and settled in Phila. Signed w. Col. in '23, scoring a hit w. first release, "Downhearted Blues." Quickly became reigning queen of female blues singers, top act on TOBA (Theatre Owners Booking Association) circuit, and the highest-paid black entertainer of her day, earning as much as $2,000 per week. At the height of her popularity, she spent winter mos. tour. TOBA theatres w. her own often elaborate shows and took her tent show through the South each summer, using her own custom-built railroad car. Regular rec. sess. in NYC '23–31 yielded over 156 sides for Col. w. accomp. incl. Louis Armstrong; Joe Smith; Tommy Ladnier; James P. Johnson; Fletcher Henderson; Charlie Green; and Clarence Williams. Rapidly changing taste, the advent of talking pictures, and, eventually, the Depression were factors contributing to the decline of her career in the late '20s. In '29 she starred in a seventeen-minute film short, *St. Louis Blues*, and app. in a major B'way flop, *Pansy*, but she never stopped singing. Soon after Col. dropped her in '31, she began working in small Phila. clubs, and tour. on a shoestring budget. A stormy marriage to Jack Gee was over and she was now living w. Lionel Hampton's uncle, Richard Morgan. In '33 she again rec., making four sides for Okeh w. a band that incl. Frankie Newton, Jack Teagarden, Chu Berry, and—on one selection—Benny Goodman. It was Bessie's most modern accomp. to date, and she was now making herself over to better suit the oncoming Swing Era. With swept-back hair, elegant satin gowns, and a repertoire that incl. popular ballads, she app. at the Apollo Theatre and subbed for Billie Holiday at Connie's Inn on Times Square. She seemed to be on the verge of making a comeback in late '37 when her car was involved in a fatal accident on a Mississippi road. For decades it was believed that Bessie Smith bled to death after being refused admission to a white hospital, but that story turned out to be apocryphal. There were many so-called classic blues singers, but none approached the magnetism of "The Empress of the Blues." Frank Schiffman, at whose Lafayette and Apollo theatres Bessie often app., observed: "Whatever pathos there is in the world, whatever sadness she had, was brought out in her singing—and the audience knew it and responded to it." Book: *Bessie*, Chris Albertson '71. CDs: Col.; BBC.

SMITH, BILL (WILLIAM OVERTON), cl, comp; b. Sacramento, CA, 9/22/26. Took up cl. at 10. To NYC to stud. at Juilliard, then w. Darius Milhaud at Mills Coll. in Oakland, Calif., where he met Dave Brubeck and formed an oct. w. him. M.A. in mus. 1952. Taught at USC and rec. in LA w. Shelly Manne, Red Norvo '57. Won Prix de Rome and a Guggenheim Fellowship; settled in Rome '60–6. Formed Amer. Jazz Ens. w. Bill Eaton, touring US and Eur.; dir. Contemp. Mus. Gp. at U. of Wash., Seattle fr. '66. Frequently reunited w. Brubeck fr. '81, often using el. effects in his cl. solos. Smith is a man of prodigous talent, both as a comp. and cl. Early works incl. *Concerto for Clarinet and Combo*, rec. w. Manne, and *Divertimento*, w. Norvo. CDs: w. Brubeck (MM; Tel.; Col.; Fant.; Conc.).

SMITH, BOBBY (ROBERT), alto sax, arr; b. Providence, RI, 1/3/07; d. Los Angeles, CA, 6/6/95. Mother pl. pno. Took up pno., then dms. bef. stud. w. Hilton Jefferson's teacher. First job w. Banjo Burney's band. Worked w. the Sunset Royals in the 1930s. Join. Erskine Hawkins in early '40s as lead alto and arr. Wrote and was feat. on the hit "Tippin' In," which became the band's theme. Rec. thirty-four titles w. small gps. for the Apollo, Ruby, and Honey labels fr. '49–51. Lived in LA dur. latter part of his career. CDs: Del.; w. E. Hawkins (BB).

SMITH, BUSTER (HENRY), alto sax, cl, comp; b. Ellis County, TX, 8/26/04; d. Dallas, TX, 8/10/91. Self-taught; worked on cl. w. local gps. in Dallas 1923; alto w. Walter Page Blue Devils '25. Jimmy Rushing, Hot Lips Page, Count Basie, and Eddie Durham worked w. Page in the Blue Devils. From '31 Smith led the band, which by then incl. Lester Young. From '33 to '35 he was in KC w. Bennie Moten, upon whose death he became part of a small Basie gp. at the Reno Club '36. He contributed a large portion of the book, incl. parts of the orig. "One O'Clock

Jump." When Basie went North, Smith, who had no faith in the enterprise, remained in KC, pl. w. Claude Hopkins and Andy Kirk. In '37 he formed his own gp., which briefly incl. the 17–year-old Charlie Parker. Later moved to NYC as arr. for Basie, Benny Carter; et al. Returned to Dallas in '42, where he cont. to lead small gps. Rec. an r&b-oriented album as leader for Atl. in '59 and gave up sax the same yr.; played pno., gtr., and bs. App. in the film *The Last of the Blue Devils* '74. Retired in late '80s. Smith's place in jazz history is largely due to his reputation as Charlie Parker's mentor. Parker once said, "Buster was the guy I really dug." His few recs. reveal a stylistic resemblance to Parker in terms of linearity and phrasing. CDs: w. Hot Lips Page in *52nd Street Swing* (Dec.); Pete Johnson; Page (Class.).

SMITH, CARL (TATTI), tpt; b. Marshall, TX, 1908. Toured w. Midwest road shows; then w. Terence Holder's band in KC 1931; to West Coast in early '30s w. Gene Coy. Joined Count Basie at Reno Club in KC '36 and made first Basie rec. date under the name Jones-Smith, Inc., a sxt. that incl. Lester Young and Jimmy Rushing. Left Basie early '37; played w. Skeets Tolbert's Gentlemen of Swing '38–40. In '40s he worked briefly w. Leon Abbey; Benny Carter; and Chris Columbus. Moved to So. Amer., pl. in Argentina and Brazil in late '40s and '50s. CDs: w. C. Basie (Col.).

SMITH, CARRIE LOUISE, voc, pno; b. Ft. Gaines, GA, 8/25/41. Sang in church choir in Newark, N.J.: choir app. at NJF 1957. Perf. w. Big Tiny Little '70–2; Tyree Glenn '73; NY Jazz Repertory Co. fr. '75, incl. USSR tour; Cab Calloway '77. Many recs. as lead w. Buddy Tate; Budd Johnson; Art Farmer; Doc Cheatham; Vic Dickenson; Art Hodes; Hank Jones; Marty Napoleon; Richard Wyands; George Duvivier; Major Holley; etc., fr. '76. Perf. freq. at Rainbow Room in NYC fr. '70s. Perf. w. WGJB '87; in Paris show, *Black and Blue*, which moved to B'way '89–91; Wynton Marsalis at NJF '91. Smith sang for Pres. Carter at the White House in '80. She received an Achievement Awd. from the Nat'l Urban League in '91. Although she sings in the tradition of Bessie Smith—to whom she has been likened—the resemblance is closest in the gowns and feathers. Fav. arr: Budd Johnson; pno: Bross Townsend. Fests: Eur. since '77. TV: PBS, *Today* w. Bobby Short '81; Benny Goodman special CDs: Evid.

SMITH, CARSON RAYMOND, bs; b. San Francisco, CA, 1/9/31; d. Las Vegas, NV, 11/2/97. Brother is Putter Smith. At age 5 studied pno. for a yr. Took up bs. at Bell HS 1944. Stud. w. H. Rheinschagen in

LA '49–50. First came to prominence in LA w. Gerry Mulligan's pianoless qt. '52–3; briefly tour. w. Charlie Parker, Chet Baker '53. Orig. member of Baker Qt., pl. first NJF '54. Pl. w. Russ Freeman '55; Chico Hamilton '56–7. Freelanced in LA, incl. a rec. date w. Stan Kenton '59; also worked w. Charlie Barnet '58, '59, '60; Vido Musso '59–60; Carl Fontana '60; three yrs. at Silver Slipper in LV w. Charlie Teagarden '60–62. Pl. in LV show bands '63–75; also w. Buddy Rich '68; Fontana '76; P. Hucko Qnt. '77, '85; Hucko All-Stars, Tokyo '91. Tour. Japan w. Georgie Auld Oct. '64, '67, '68. Pl. w. C. Hamilton Reunion in Calif., Eur. '89; a regular at Colo. JP in '80s, '90s. Comp: "Carson City Stage." Favs: Niels H. Ø Pedersen, George Mraz, Red Mitchell. Film: *Sweet Smell of Success* w. Hamilton '57. TV: Steve Allen show w. Baker '54; S. Kenton special w. Dick Clark '59. CDs: w. B. Holiday (Verve); G. Mulligan (Fant; PJ); C. Baker (PJ; Up.); C. Parker (Stash); B. Rich (Sequel); C. Baker–S. Getz; Clifford Brown; Lee Konitz (PJ); Hamilton (SN); Kenton (Status).

SMITH, CHARLIE (CHARLES), dms; b. NYC, 4/15/27; d. New Haven, CT, 1/15/66. Raised on Long Island, N.Y., gigged around N.Y.C. until he joined trio accomp. Ella Fitzgerald (w. Hank Jones, Ray Brown) 1948. Later worked w. the Erroll Garner Trio; George Shearing; Slam Stewart; Benny Goodman; Oscar Peterson; Artie Shaw; Joe Bushkin; Slim Gaillard; also briefly w. Duke Ellington. Pl. w. Billy Taylor trio '52–4; Aaron Bell trio '54–6; Wild Bill Davison '59; moved to New Haven to pl. w. Dwike Mitchell and Willie Ruff; worked as comp. and teacher in last yrs. of his life. TV: Earl Wilson show w. Dizzy Gillespie and Charlie Parker '52. LP: own trio on Dawn. CDs: w. E. Garner (Sav.; Verve); S. Gaillard (Verve); Taylor (Prest.); O. Pettiford (Sav.); J. J. Johnson (FS); Mitchell-Ruff (32); Herbie Mann (Riv.).

SMITH, CLARA, voc; b. Spartanburg, SC, 1894; d. Detroit, MI, 2/3/35. In vaudeville fr. 1910; tour. fr. '18, incl. TOBA circuit. Settled NYC '23; owned and operated Clara Smith Theatrical Club fr. '24. Rec. regularly for Col. '23–32 w. accomps. incl. Louis Armstrong; Fletcher Henderson; and Lonnie Johnson. Recs. incl. four duets w. Bessie Smith (no relation); fr. mid 20s to mid 30s she app. in numerous revues and theatrical musicals, sometimes billed as "The World's Champion Moaner." Although her voice did not have the power of Bessie Smith's, Clara ranked among the best of the so-called classic blues singers. Carl Van Vechten, a true connoisseur of the classic blues genre, described her as having "a voice that is powerful or melancholy by turn." CDs: Col.; VJM; duets w. B. Smith (Col.).

SMITH, DEREK GEOFFREY, pno; b. London, England, 8/17/31. Became full-time mus. at age 23, pl. w. the Johnny Dankworth band. Then worked w. small gp. bef. immigrating to US 1957. Led trio w. Percy Heath and Connie Kay; frequently pl w. Benny Goodman in the '70s and '80s. Worked w. Marlena Shaw; Bill Watrous; Buddy DeFranco; Sal Salvador; Arnett Cobb; others in '70s. Toured Japan '83 w. Benny Carter. App. often at Colo. JP in late '80s. Trio w. Milt Hinton, Bobby Rosengarden fr. early '80s. Cork JF w. Rosengarden '94. Busy freelancer at jazz parties, etc. Duo w. Dick Hyman; many apps. as solo pnst. in '90s. Perf. on Woody Allen soundtracks: *Hannah and Her Sisters; Radio Days; Crimes and Misdemeanors.* Fav: Oscar Peterson. An incisive, confident stylist in a variety of settings. CDs: Chiaro.; Prog.; Dick Hyman–Derek Smith (Arb.); w. M. Hinton (Col.; Chiaro.); L. Bellson (MM; Tel.); S. Asmussen (Sig.); Flip Phillips (Chiaro.); T. Brewer (Sig.); D. Hyman (MM).

SMITH, FLOYD ("WONDERFUL"), gtr; b. St. Louis, MO, 1/25/17; d. Indianapolis, IN, 3/29/82. A pioneer of the el-gtr., which he first used on a rec. w. the Jeter-Pillars Orch 1937–8 and most notably on "Floyd's Guitar Blues" w. Andy Kirk's band '39; remained w. Kirk off and on until '46. Led own trio in Chi. and worked w. Wild Bill Davis and Chris Columbus '54–7; toured w. Bill Doggett in US and Eur. '59–64. In early '70s he ret. to Eur. and was feat. on recs. w. Al Grey; Buddy Tate; and Davis. CDs: w A. Kirk (Class.).

SMITH, HOWARD HAROLD, pno; b. Ardmore, OK, 10/19/10. Briefly w. Benny Goodman 1934; Ray Noble '35; Isham Jones '35–6; Glenn Miller '37. Well-known for his pno. solo on "Boogie-Woogie" w. Tommy Dorsey, in whose band he pl. fr. '37 to '40. CDs: w. T. Dorsey (BB).

SMITH, JABBO (CLADYS), tpt, v-tbn, voc; b. Pembroke, GA, 12/24/08; d. NYC, 1/16/91. Played w. Jenkins' Orphanage Band, Charleston, So. Caro. Prof. mus. at 16; pl. w. Cecil Scott, Charlie Johnson, and Erskine Tate early 1920s. Rec. "Black and Tan Fantasy" w. Duke Ellington '27. Pl. w. Fats Waller '28; later w. Earl Hines and own bands in Chi. and Milwaukee; Claude Hopkins '36–8; led own gp. in Newark, N.J. early '40s, then ret. to Claude Hopkins '44. Retired to Milwaukee for many yrs. but cont. to pl. periodically. App. at NJF '75. In '78 he perf. w. the show *One Mo' Time* at Village Gate, NYC, and tour. w. it. Sang at Berlin JF '86 w. Don Cherry, also app. w. him at Village Vanguard. A powerful trumpeter whose energy and improvisational skill invited comparison with Armstrong in the '20s. CDs: Biog.; Class.; Topaz; w. Ellington (Dec.); Willie "The Lion" Smith; Clarence Williams; Hopkins (Class.); Charlie Johnson (Hot 'N Sweet); Thomas Morris (Frog); Fats Waller, one track in *Great Trumpets* (BB).

SMITH, JIMMIE (JAMES HOWARD), dms; b. Newark, NJ, 1/27/38. Studied at Juilliard Sch. 1959–60. First prominent w. L,H&R '62–3; Erroll Garner '67–74; then freelanced in LA area w. Benny Carter, Harry "Sweets" Edison. In '80s he worked w. Barney Kessel; Herb Ellis; and Terry Gibbs–Buddy DeFranco qnt. A dependable, swinging mus., Smith has been in frequent demand in Southern Calif. CDs: w. L,H&B (BB); Benny Carter; D. McKenna; Ray Brown; Ernestine Anderson; Al Cohn (Conc.); E. Garner (Tel.); C. Basie; P. Newborn; Sweets Edison (Pab.); T. Gibbs (Cont.); K. Burrell (Fant.).

SMITH, JIMMY (JAMES OSCAR), org; b. Norristown, PA, 12/8/25; d. Scottsdale, AZ, 2/8/05. At age 6 teamed w. fath. in song-and-dance routine at local clubs. After navy service stud. bs. at Hamilton Sch. of Mus. and pno. at Ornstein Sch. of Mus. 1948–50. Played pno., then org. w. Don Gardner's Sonotones '51–4. Began rec. for BN w. own org. trio Sept. '55, rising quickly to int'l. prominence as revolutionary new stylist on el-org. Rec. for Verve in '60s, sometimes w. bb, occ. also singing. In LA for several yrs. dur. '70s, operating his own supper club. Frequent apps. at fests world-wide. In '87 he pl. a brief solo on Michael Jackson's album, *Bad*; in '92 pl. small gp. dates in Japan, Eur., Mexico, and US, usually w. Herman Riley; also occ. duet dates and recs. w. Jimmy McGriff. Used a great variety of org. stops and had a unique gift for astonishing improvs. at fast tempi, producing unique tone colors and showing phenomenal technique w. hands and feet. Although Larry Young, others exerted infl. in later yrs., Smith cont. into the '90s to win polls and be the primary infl. on jazz org. CDs: Verve; Mile.; BN; w. Wes Montgomery (Verve); B. Gonzales (BN); S. Criss (Muse); S. Turrentine (BN).

SMITH, JOE (JOSEPH), tpt; b. Ripley, OH, 6/28/02; d. NYC, 12/2/37. Brother of tptr. Russell Smith. Small gps. in St. Louis, Mo., then to NYC 1920. Joined Kaiser Marshall band; accomp. Ethel Waters; Bessie Smith (whose favorite tpt. he was); and Mamie Smith '22–3. Led a gp. backing Noble Sissle and Eubie Blake '24; off and on w. Fletcher Henderson '25–8; w. Bennie Moten briefly, then McKinney's Cotton Pickers intermittently '29–34. In the early '30s his health broke down and he worked

infrequently. He spent the last four yrs. of his life in a Long Island, N.Y., hospital. A spirited, sensitive artist whose tone and warmth of style were frequently compared to Bix Beiderbecke's, he ranked w. Tommy Ladnier among the most underrated tpt. players of the '20s. CDs: w. Bessie Smith; F. Henderson (Col.); McKinney's Cotton Pickers (BB); Ethel Waters (Milan).

SMITH, JOHNNY (JOHN HENRY JR.), gtr; b. Birmingham, AL, 6/25/22. Father pl. bjo. Self-taught, pl. tpt., vla., and vln. bef. gtr. Moved to Portland, Maine, at age 13. Debut pl. hillbilly mus. w. Fenton Bros. band 1939; trio in Bost. '40–41; army '42–46; pl. tpt. in air force band; vln. and vla. in concert gp.; gtr. w. Eugene Ormandy and Phila. Orch. NBC staff in NYC '47–53; pl. gtr., tpt. w. pop and symph. orchs. While at NBC, he start. qnt. and rec. "Moonlight in Vermont," feat. Stan Getz, voted one of two top jazz recs. of '52 in *DB* poll. Own gps. at Birdland '53–60. Moved to Colorado Springs in '64 where he owned and operated a mus. store until '91. Tour. Engl. w. Bing Crosby in '70s. Won *DB* Critics poll as new star '53; *DB* poll '54; *Met.* poll '54–5. Received honorary doctorate fr. U. of Colo. Book: *The Complete Johnny Smith Approach to Guitar* (Mel Bay) '80, unique in notating mus. in actual pitch. Favs: Django Reinhardt, Andres Segovia. CDs: Roul.; Conc.; w. S. Getz (Roost).

SMITH, JOHNNY "HAMMOND" (JOHN ROBERT), org, pno; b. Louisville, KY, 12/16/33; d. Victorville, CA, 6/4/97. Studied pno. w. private teacher at age 13. St. pl. prof. at 15 w. Kenny Hale. Later w. Paul Williams; Chris Columbus. Inspired by Wild Bill Davis, took up org. and form. own combo in Cleveland 1957. Worked w. Nancy Wilson '58; and as a sideman w. Columbus before lead. own gp. at Harlem spots such as Count Basie's, Minton's, Shalimar-By-Randolph, etc. Rec. for Prest. fr. '59 to '70 and was one of the popularizers of jazz org. in the wake of Jimmy Smith. In the '70s, rec. for Kudu, experimented w. other el. kybds. and synths. but thereafter perf. mainly w. his org. gp. Favs: Wild Bill Davis, Tatum. CDs: Prest.; Mile.; w. G. Ammons (Prest.); O. Nelson; L. Winchester (NJ).

SMITH, KEITH ("MR. HEFTY JAZZ"), tpt, voc; b. London, England, 3/19/40. Studied w. Profess. Philip Parker, Henry "Red" Allen in US. In 1964 he tour. US as "exchange band" for Wild Bill Davison. Pl. NO w. George Lewis; Calif. w. Johnny St. Cyr; Barney Bigard; Alton Redd; Chi. w. Lil Hardin Armstrong; Muddy Waters; Otis Spann; Paul Butterfield; NYC w. Eddie Condon; Tony Parenti; Zutty Singleton; Kenny Davern; Dick Wellstood. In '72 he joined Papa Bue's Viking Jazz Band, touring Eur. and Far East. In '81 he fronted Louis Armstrong All Stars in a tribute to Satchmo for a total of 100 concerts. Prod. and perf. in "100 Years of Dixieland Jazz," feat. George Chisholm. In '84 he prod. *Stardust Road*, the mus. of Hoagy Carmichael, starring Georgie Fame. He has app. regularly w. own band in US. Tour. w. Armstrong tribute in UK w. guest clst. Joe Muranyi. TV: *The Wonderful World of Louis Armstrong*. CDs: Let's Do It; GHB; Lake.

SMITH, DR. LONNIE, org, pno, kybds; b. Buffalo, NY, 7/3/42. From mus. family; grandmoth., moth., and aunt had gospel qt. Self-taught. Began on tpt. and tba. in sch. but did not read mus. First prof. gigs as doo-wop voc. w. Teen Kings 1950s; later led voc. gp. the Supremes (pre-Motown); Smith Bros. early '60s. Received first Hammond B-3 as gift from mus. store owner; later rented it to Jack McDuff, which led to acquaintance w. Lou Donaldson. Tour. w. Sammy Bryant, also backed Motown artists in Buffalo '63–4. Met Geo. Benson while sitting in w. McDuff in Buffalo mid '60s. Later joined Benson's gp. in Pitts., then came w. him to NYC late '60s. Smith has more than thirty albums under his own name, w. sidemen incl. Lee Morgan; David Newman; King Curtis; Blue Mitchell; Joe Lovano. Tour. w. Dizzy Gillespie; Grover Washington Jr.; Ron Carter; Jimmy McGriff; Frank Foster; Leon Thomas; Willis Jackson. Also worked w. r&b artists incl. Gladys Knight; Dionne Warwick; Etta James; Esther Phillips; Impressions; Coasters. Pl. w. Lou Donaldson in '90s. With right-hand flights and chordal warmth he is able to build waves of mesmerizing excitement, even when playing "air" keyboard. Favs: Jimmy Smith, Larry Young, Don Patterson; arrs: Oliver Nelson, Gil Evans. Polls: *DB* '69. CDs: BN; LRC; Venus; *Jazz Funk Masters* (P-Vine); w. Benson (Col.); Donaldson (Mile.; Col.); Ron Holloway; Turk Mauro; J. McGriff (Mile.); R. Cuber (Pro Jazz); J. Ponder (Muse); Essence All-Stars (Hip Bop); Chartbusters (NYC; Prest.).

SMITH, LONNIE LISTON, pno, kybd; b. Richmond, VA, 12/28/40. Father sang w. gospel gp., the Harmonizing Four; two bros. are prof. mus. Stud. tpt. at Armstrong HS in Richmond, then received B.S. in mus. ed. fr. Morgan State U. 1961. Moved to NYC '62, pl. w. Betty Carter '62–3; Max Roach '64–5; Art Blakey '65–6; Roland Kirk '66–7; Joe Williams '67–8; Pharoah Sanders–Leon Thomas '68–71; Gato Barbieri '71–3; Miles Davis '73–4. Formed crossover gp., Cosmic Echoes, w. bro. Donald Smith '74; pl. w. Cosmic Echoes since '74. Smith has app. as a lecturer

and clinician at many Amer. and Eur. universities. Favs: Art Tatum, Fats Waller, Oscar Peterson. Polls: *Billboard*; also Eur. and Jap. awards. Fests: Eur. and Jap. since '70. TV: many apps., incl. *Jazz Set* '71; *In Concert* w. M. Davis '73. CDs: BB; Startrak; w. Oliver Nelson (BB); Pharoah Sanders (Imp.); M. Davis (Col.); Stanley Turrentine (CTI).

SMITH, MAMIE (née Robinson), voc; b. Cincinnati, OH, 5/26/1883; d. NYC, 10/30/46. Having built a reputation as a vaudeville act in the teens, she was starring in *Maid of Harlem* at the Lincoln Theatre, NYC, in 1920, when she turned one of the show's songs into the world's first voc. blues recording. "Crazy Blues," originally named "Harlem Blues," started the trend that saw rec. labels scrambling to sign up blues women. In the early '20s she tour. and rec. w. own band, Mamie Smith's Jazz Hounds, which incl. Coleman Hawkins, Bubber Miley, Elmer Snowden, and Perry Bradford. App. in film short *Jailhouse Blues* '29 and a series of features aimed at black audiences: *Othello in Harlem* '39; *Mystery in Swing* '40; *Sunday Sinners*, and *Murder on Lenox Avenue* '41; on *Because I Love You*, a '43 soundie, she was backed by Lucky Millinder's orch. CDs: tracks on various Col. collections.

SMITH, MARVIN "SMITTY" (O. II), dms, perc; b. Waukegan, IL, 6/24/61. Father, Marvin, is a dmr. Stud. w. fath. for two yrs. Att. Berklee Coll. of Mus., then pl. w. Jon Hendricks 1980–2; Frank Foster–Frank Wess '83–4; Hamiet Bluiett, Kevin Eubanks, David Murray '84. Freelanced in early-mid '80s w. John Hicks; Bobby Watson; Slide Hampton; Ray Brown; Ron Carter; Dave Holland; Hank Jones; Art Farmer–Benny Golson. Pl. w. Steve Coleman in early '90s; made rec. debut as lead. '87; also rec. w. Sonny Rollins; Donald Byrd. Tour. w. Sting '87. Since the mid '90s, he pl. w. Kevin Eubanks in *Tonight Show* band, also doing comedy skits in the show. CDs: Conc.; w. S. Coleman (JMT; Novus); D. Holland (ECM); Gil Evans (BB; Evid.); Benny Golson (Den.); Kevin Eubanks (GRP; BN); George Shearing (Conc.); S. Rollins (Mile.); Peter Leitch (Res.; CC; Conc.); Ray Drummond (Arab.; CC); B. Marsalis (Col.); Art Farmer (Cont.); Monty Alexander; Frank Foster (Conc.).

SMITH, MIKE (MICHAEL ALAN), alto, sop saxes, fl; b. Chicago, IL, 3/3/57. Studied at No. Tex. St. U. 1975–80. Pl. bari. w. Maynard Ferguson '80–1; alto w. Buddy Rich '81–2; Clark Terry, Frank Sinatra '85; Art Farmer '86; Nat Adderley off and on fr. '87; Ira Sullivan off and on fr. '89. Smith worked full-time for Frank Sinatra fr. '87. Favs: Cannonball Adderley,

Charlie Parker, Benny Carter. Fests: world tours w. Sinatra fr. '87. TV: apps. w. Sinatra. CDs: Del.; w. Buddy Childers (Trend); Bobby Lyle (Atl.); Les McCann (Night).

SMITH, PAUL THATCHER, pno; b. San Diego, CA, 4/17/22. Parents were entertainers. In 1940s pl. w. Johnny Richards (whose ward he was); Ozzie Nelson; Ziggy Elman (in army band); Les Paul '46–7; Tommy Dorsey '47–9. Settled in LA '49; freelanced in LA area, rec. w. Dizzy Gillespie; Ray Anthony; Buddy Rich; Buddy De Franco. Frequently accomp. Ella Fitzgerald in person and on recs. fr. '56 into '90s Smith is a highly accomplished pnst., but excessive displays of technical prowess detract from his performances. CDs: Tampa; w. E. Fitzgerald; Anita O'Day (Verve); Karrin Allyson (Conc.); Gary Sivils (Altenburgh); T. Dorsey (Hep); JATP (Pab.).

SMITH, PINE TOP (CLARENCE), pno, voc, comp; b. Troy, AL, 6/11/04; d. Chicago IL, 3/15/29. Raised in Birmingham, Ala. Pianist, dancer, and comedian on TOBA theatre circuit, accomp. Butterbeans and Susie and other popular acts; also accomp. Ma Rainey. Discovered by "Cow Cow" Davenport. Only rec. twice: first in Dec. 1928 for Brunswick in Chi., second shortly bef. he was killed by a stray bullet. Six yrs. after his death, his orig. pno. solo w. monologue, "Pinetop's Boogie-Woogie," officially named the genre. It was rec. by many artists in the '30s, most notably in Dean Kincaide's '38 arr. for the Tommy Dorsey orch. Possibly infl. by Jimmy Yancey, he was among the first to play boogie-woogie. CDs: *The Boogie-Woogie Masters* (Charly).

SMITH, PUTTER (PATRICK VERNE), bs; b. Bell, CA, 1/19/41. Brother of bs. Carson Smith; stud. w. him and Bob Enevoldsen. Pl. w. Alan Broadbent; Thelonious Monk; George Foster; Warne Marsh; Akiyoshi-Tabackin bb; et al. In 1971 while working w. Monk at Shelly's Manne Hole, he was cast as a killer in the film *Diamonds Are Forever.* Teacher of rhythm section techniques at Pasadena City Coll. and mus. reading at the Mus. Institute. CDs: w. Walter Norris; Karrin Allyson (Conc.); Broadbent (Conc.; Disc.); Mose Allison (Elek.); Bill Perkins (Inter.); Dick Sudhalter (Aud.).

SMITH, RUSSELL T., tpt; b. Ripley, OH, 1890; d. Los Angeles, CA, 3/27/66. Brother of Joe Smith. Moved to NYC 1910; worked w. army bands and revues. From '25 to '41 he was lead tpt. for Fletcher Henderson orch.; also perf. dur. this period w. Horace Henderson '33; Claude Hopkins '35–6; and Benny Carter '34 and '39–40. Later worked w. Cab Cal-

loway '41–6 and Noble Sissle. Settled in Calif. in '50s, teaching and occ. perf. An impeccable technician and excellent sight reader, Smith was greatly admired by other trumpeters. CDs: w. Benny Carter (BB); F. Henderson (Col.); Red Allen–Coleman Hawkins (Hep); Chu Berry (Topaz); C. Hawkins (Class.)

SMITH, SEAN CHRISTOPHER, bs; b. Norwalk, CT, 11/11/65. Grandmother pl. pno. and wrote songs. Began on alto sax, then pl. el-bs. Stud. at U. of Bridgeport 1983–5; Manh. Sch. of Mus. '87–90 (B. Mus. '90). Pl. w. Bill Charlap fr. '87; Gerry Mulligan '88; Bill Mays fr. '89; Tom Harrell '90; Gene Bertoncini, Hugh Lawson, Allen Mezquida fr. '90; Lee Konitz '92; Don Friedman fr. '92; Jon Gordon fr. '93. Smith has also worked w. singers incl. Peggy Lee, Mark Murphy '90; Diane Schuur '91; Rosemary Clooney '94. He has led his own duo and trio fr. '94. Favs: Red Mitchell, Scott LaFaro, Michael Moore, Paul Chambers, Geo. Mraz. CDs: w. Bill Charlap (Prog.; Chiaro.); A. Mezquida (TDJ); Carol Sloane; Bill Mays (Conc.); Bob Kindred (Conawago); J. Gordon (Chiaro.); Peter Leitch (Res.).

SMITH, STUFF (HEZEKIAH LEROY GORDON), vln, voc, comp; b. Portsmouth, OH, 8/14/09; d. Munich, Germany, 9/25/67. Studied w. his fath., a mus. and amateur boxer, in Cleveland, Ohio. Began his career as a dancer and violinist w. the Aunt Jemima Revue 1924. Worked w. Alphonso Trent in Dallas, Tex. '26–9, then w. Jelly Roll Morton. Formed his own band, mostly around Buffalo, N.Y. fr. '30. Took a sxt. that incl. Cozy Cole and Jonah Jones into the Onyx Club, NYC in late '35, drawing crowds w. a novelty song, "I'se a Muggin'," with which he made his rec. debut '36. More recs. by Stuff Smith and His Onyx Club Boys followed, some of the best w. Jonah Jones on tpt. Smith, who pioneered the use of the amplified vln., led Fats Waller's band after the pianist's death in '43. After keeping a relatively low profile in the late '40s and early '50s, he ret. to prominence in '57 w. a series of recs. for Norman Granz and tour. extensively in the '60s, settling in Copenhagen in '65. Although his popularity in Eur. remained high, Smith became ill and perf. only rarely in the last yr. of his life. In his amplified solos, he broke all the traditional violin rules, giving the rhythmic beat precedence over academic accuracy. His unique style was imitated by virtually all jazz violinists who followed him. His comps. incl. "Time and Again" (rec. by Sarah Vaughan); "Desert Sands"; "Skip It"; and "Midway." Won the *Esq.* Silver Award '46. CDs: Verve; Story.; Prog.; Class.; w. Nat Cole (Cap.); Sun Ra

(Evid.); D. Gillespie (Verve; Sav.); E. Fitzgerald (Verve); S. Grappelli–Stuff Smith (Pab.)

SMITH, TAB (TALMADGE), alto, tnr saxes; b. Kingston, NC, 1/11/09; d. St. Louis, MO, 8/17/71. Started on C-melody sax at 13. First prof. job w. Carolina Stompers 1929; then w. Fate Marable; Dewey Jackson; Eddie Johnson. First prominence as jazz man w. Lucky Millinder '35–9. Played w. Count Basie '40–2; Millinder again '42–3. Formed own combo from late '40s as r&b attraction. Popular at Savoy ballroom in '40s and '50s. Later became a real estate agent in St. Louis, occ. playing locally. CDs: Del.; w. B. Holiday (Col.; Comm.); R. Eldridge; C. Hawkins (Key. Coll.); D. Washington (Merc.); Henry "Red" Allen (Collector's Classics); Basie; Mills Blue Rhythm Band; L. Millinder (Class.).

SMITH, TOMMY, tnr sax; b. Edinburgh, Scotland, 4/27/67. Father exposed him to jazz via concerts and recs. Inspired by Coleman Hawkins at age 12. Won several first prizes at Edinburgh JF and a Berklee Coll. scholarship 1984–6. After Eur. tour, he perf. briefly w. Chick Corea, then became regular member of Gary Burton band '86–8. Played w. Niels Lan Doky '90–1; Daniel Humair '92. Debut album w. John Scofield, Jack DeJohnette, Eddie Gomez, et al. Radio work incl. *Take the Jazz Train* '83–5 and *National Big Band Competition* '87; hosted *Tommy Smith Jazz Types,* a six-part BBC-TV series w. Burton, Corea, Bobby Watson, BBC Symph. Orch. '89. His work in the '80s was strongly infl. by Coltrane but became more personalized in '90s. He has said of his orig. infl., Coleman Hawkins, "[He] made the hairs stand up on the back of my neck. From that day on, my romance was with jazz." Comp. *Saxophone Concerto* for the Scottish Ensemble, premiered in '90; second concerto, based on Scott's *The Lay of the Last Minstrel* '91. CDs: Linn; BN; w. N. L. Doky (BN); G. Burton (ECM).

SMITH, TRIXIE, voc; b. Atlanta, GA, 1895; d. NYC, 9/21/43. Moved to NYC after attending Selma U. 1915. Toured as feat. singer on TOBA circuit fr. '18 into early '20s; rec. for Black Swan label, accomp. by James P. Johnson '21; and Fletcher Henderson '22–3; then on Para. w. Henderson; Louis Armstrong; Buster Bailey; et al. In late '30s rec. for Dec. w. Charlie Shavers; Sidney Bechet; Teddy Bunn; and others. From mid 20s to mid 30s she perf. in many musical shows and revues. Small acting roles in films dur. early '30s, incl. *The Constant Sinner* w. Mae West '31. Rec. for Dec. '38–9, then largely inactive except for a few charity appearances. CDs: w. Sidney Bechet; Johnny Dodds (Class.).

SMITH, WADADA LEO, tpt, flgl, fl, etc.; b. Leland, MS, 12/18/41. In 1967 after early work in blues and r&b bands, and mil. service, he became a member of AACM, working w. Roscoe Mitchell; Anthony Braxton; Leroy Jenkins; and, in '70, in the Creative Construction Co. w. Steve McCall, Richard Davis, and Muhal Richard Abrams. In '70 he also made docu. film, *See the Music,* w. Marion Brown and tour. Eur. w. Henry Threadgill; began rec. for own label, Cabell in '71. Formed New Dalta Ahkri for series of concerts and recs. w. Anthony Davis; Oliver Lake; et al. Dur. the '70s Smith's tpt. was compared favorably to Miles Davis and Booker Little by some critics. He stud. ethnomusicology at Wesleyan U. '74–5. Active as writer on mus. topics, he made several trips to Eur. in late '70s, rec. w. Derek Bailey and in '79 w. Peter Kowald and Gunter Sommer. In '83 he rec. *Procession of the Great Ancestry,* then visited Can., where he rec. *Rastafari* w. Bill Smith trio. Active as a teacher fr. mid '80s. His lyricism has set him apart from many other figures in free jazz. CDs: Tzadik; ECM; w. A. Braxton (BB; Del.).

SMITH, WARREN, perc, dms, vib, tymp, comp; b. Chicago, IL, 5/14/34. Father, Warren, pl. reeds w. Noble Sissle and Jimmy Noone and taught in Chi.; moth. was prof. harpist and pnst.; many other mus. in family. Stud. cl. w. fath. 1937–40; first gigs as dmr. w. fath. and uncles. Received B.S. in mus. ed. fr. U. of Ill. '57; M. Mus., perc., Manh. Sch. of Mus. '58. Pl. in B'way pit bands and w. Gil Evans '58. Formed Composers' Wkshp. Ens. '61. Pl. w. Aretha Franklin, Nina Simone, Lloyd Price '60s; Nat King Cole '64; Sam Rivers '64–76; NY Jazz Repertory Co., Gil Evans Orch. '68–76. Mus. dir. for Lloyd Price's Turntable Club '68. Pl. w. Janis Joplin '69; Tony Williams Lifetime '71. Founding member of M'Boom collective perc. ens. '70. Pl. w. M'Boom fr. '70; also pl. w. Andrew White; Julius Hemphill; Muhal Richard Abrams; Nancy Wilson; Quincy Jones; Count Basie; Carmen McRae. Smith has worked extensively in the rock and pop field and on B'way, incl. *Jelly's Last Jam* '92. He has perf. w. the Bklyn. Philharm.; Amer. Symph. Orch.; Vermont State Symph.; Chi. Civic Orch.; w. the NYC Ballet; Dance Theatre of Harlem; Merce Cunningham; Alvin Ailey. He has taught in NYC publ. schs. '58–68; at Third St. Settlement '60–7; Adelphi U. (chair of African-Amer. Studies) '70–1; SUNY-Old Westbury fr. '71; also numerous lectures and clinics. In '91 Smith was an exchange professor at Kangnung Nat'l U. in Kangnung, Korea. Favs: Tony Williams, Elvin Jones, Max Roach, Art Blakey; comp/arr: Duke Ellington, Chas. Mingus, Thelonious Monk, Gil Evans, Horace Silver. Fests: Eur. fr. '60s. Film: app.

w. Cab Calloway in *The Cotton Club*. CDs: w. Hannibal Peterson (Atl.); Kenny Barron (Muse); Dick Griffin (Konnex); Ken McIntyre (BN); M'Boom (SN; Col.); M. R. Abrams (BS); Gil Evans (BB); T. Williams Lifetime (Verve; Polyd.).

SMITH, WILLIE (WILLIAM McLEISH), alto sax, cl, voc; b. Charleston, SC, 11/25/10; d. Los Angeles, CA, 3/7/67. Studied at Fisk U. in Nashville, Tenn., where he met Jimmie Lunceford, whose band he joined fr. 1929 to '42. After a yr. w. Charlie Spivak, joined the navy, leading an all-star gp. at Great Lakes Naval Training Station in Chi. Feat. w. Harry James '44–51 and '54–64. Replaced Johnny Hodges in the Duke Ellington band '51; left in late '52, joined Billy May; tour. w. JATP. Along with Johnny Hodges and Benny Carter, Smith was one of the first great bb alto players. His buoyant, happy tone and rhythmic style, employing fewer glissandi than Hodges, was one of the most distinctive characteristics of the Lunceford band. He also has shown talent as a cl. (notably on Lunceford's "Sophisticated Lady"; "Rose Room"; and "What's Your Story, Morning Glory") and as a voc. ("Wham"; "Put It Away"; "Rhythm Is Our Business"). CDs: w. H. James (Cap.; Col.); Nat King Cole (Cap.); B. Holiday; *The Jazz Scene*; C. Parker; JATP (Verve); L. Hampton (Dec.); J. Lunceford (Dec.; Class.); Lester Young (BN); R. Eldridge (Key. Coll.); Ellington (Col.); O. Peterson (Pab.); André Previn (BL); J. Hodges (Prest.)

SMITH, WILLIE "THE LION" (William Henry Joseph Bonaparte Bertholoff), pno, comp; b. Goshen, NY, 11/25/1887; d. NYC, 4/18/73. Claims mixed parentage: Mohawk Indian, French, Spanish, and Negro on his moth.'s side; part Jewish on his fath.'s side. Raised in Newark, N.J., where he made his prof. debut 1914. Into army '17, served in Eur. where, according to his story, he earned his nickname as the result of bravery w. an artillery unit at the front. Led own band at Leroy's in Harlem '20. Toured Canada and US mainly as a single in the '20s; worked at Onyx Club on 52nd St. in late Prohibition days, as well as Pod's and Jerry's in Harlem. Largely unknown to the public until '35 when he began rec. regularly for Dec. w. a series of small gps. Recs. feat. many of his own comps., some of them lacy, charming melodies that contrasted with stride passages of great intensity. Freelanced in NYC clubs in '40s; toured Eur. and So. Africa '49–50; and worked frequently at the Central Plaza, NYC. Appeared in film, *Jazz Dance* '54; on TV in Dupont Show of the Month *Chicago and All That Jazz* '61. Cont. to perf. at fests. and tour. Eur. '65, '66. His best-known comp. was "Echoes of Spring"; others were "Passionette"; "Rip-

pling Waters"; "Concentrating"; "Contrary Motion"; "Zig Zag"; also "Portrait of the Duke." The last was a reciprocal salute to Duke Ellington, who considered Smith his one major mentor and influence and who in '39 comp. and rec. "Portrait of the Lion." Book: *Music on My Mind*, autobiography w. George Hoefer. CDs: Timel.; Vogue; BL; Class.; Milan; w. Alberta Hunter (Prest.); S. Bechet; Benny Carter (BB); E. Condon (Jazz.)

SMULYAN, GARY, bari sax; b. Bethpage, NY, 4/4/56. Began on alto sax. Encouraged by Joe Dixon while in hs; sat in w. Chet Baker; Lee Konitz; Jimmy Knepper; Ray Nance. Studied at SUNY-Potsdam 1974–5; Hofstra U. '76–8. Pl. w. Woody Herman '78–80; Mel Lewis Orch. since '80; Mingus Epitaph '89; Philip Morris Superband '89–91; Smithsonian Jazz Masterworks Orch. since '91. Also freelanced since '80 w. Konitz; George Coleman; Red Rodney; Lionel Hampton; Toshiko Akiyoshi–Lew Tabackin; Machito; Tito Puente; Clark Terry; Louis Bellson; etc. With Three Baritones band in late '90s. Favs: Pepper Adams, Harry Carney. Polls: *JT* TDWR '90. Fests: Eur.; Asia, etc., since '78. TV: Mingus *Epitaph*. CDs: CC; w. M. Lewis; F. Hubbard (MM); Gene Harris; Woody Herman (Conc.); K. Mahogany (Enja); M. Camilo (Col.); Mingus bb; Three Baritones (Drey.); DMP bb (DMP); Don Sickler (Up.); T. Harrell (Vict.); Vanguard Jazz Orch. (NW); Benny Green (BN); Joe Henderson (Verve); Mike Le Donne (CC); Rob Schneiderman (Res.)

SNIDERO, JIM (JAMES J.), alto, sop saxes; b. Redwood City, CA, 5/29/58. Studied at No. Tex. State U. 1977–81. Pl. w. Jack McDuff '81–3; Frank Wess '83; Toshiko Akiyoshi since '83; own qt. since '85; own qnt. w. Tom Harrell since '90; Frank Sinatra '91–2. Snidero has taught at various universities in the US and Eur., and at the Jamey Aebersold Wkshp. Favs: Charlie Parker, Cannonball Adderley, Sonny Stitt. Fests: Japan since '84; Eur. since '86. TV: CBS *Sunday Morning* w. Akiyoshi; also w. Akiyoshi on Laserdisc and Germ. TV. CDs: Ken; Red; CC; D-T; Toshiba; w. Akiyoshi (Col.; Ascent); Brian Lynch (Ken; CC); C. Herwig (Ken); Greg Hatza (Palm.); Walt Weiskopf (CC).

SNOW, VALAIDA, tpt, voc; b. Chattanooga, TN, 6/2/1900; d. NYC, 5/30/56. In mid 1920s she and her sister Lavaida worked w. Jack Carter's band in Shanghai; pl. w. Earl Hines in Chi. '29. Rec. w. Washboard Rhythm Kings '32. To Engl. w. *Blackbirds of 1934*, then worked in Calif., incl. apps. in two films, *Irresistible You* and *Take It From Me*. Rec. w. Noble Sissle '35, and under her own name '36. From '36 to

'40 she was active in Engl. and on the Continent, where she pl. w. Django Reinhardt. Arrested by local police while tour. Sweden in '41, she was deported. Stories of her spending the next two yrs. in a Nazi concentration camp in Denmark have never been confirmed, but she ret. to US in '43 and cont. to work until her death. Though she was a talented trumpeter/singer, Valaida Snow's handful of recordings are hard to find LP: Rosetta; Swing. CD: w. Washboard Rhythm Kings (Collectors Classics)

SNOWDEN, ELMER CHESTER (POPS), bjo, gtr, saxes; b. Baltimore, MD, 10/9/1900; d. Philadelphia, PA, 5/14/73. Played in Balt. w. Eubie Blake 1915. Had own combo in Wash., D.C. 1921. Took band to NYC in '23. Told that the band—now The Washingtonians—must have a pnst., Snowden sent for Duke Ellington, who eventually took over as leader (so said Snowden; others have recalled the events differently). In late '20s and early '30s he led bands w. such sidemen as Count Basie; Claude Hopkins; Jimmie Lunceford; Bubber Miley; Frankie Newton; "Tricky Sam" Nanton; Chick Webb; and Benny Carter. At the Hot Feet Club in Greenwich Village (1928–9) he had Waller; Garvin Bushell, Otto Hardwicke; Webb; and others. In '30 his band at The Nest in NYC feat. Rex Stewart, Jimmy Harrison, Prince Robinson, Joe Garland, Freddy Johnson. In '32 his Smalls Paradise orch. (R. Eldridge, Dicky Wells, Al Sears, and Sid Catlett) were feat. in a short film, *Smash Your Baggage.* Had five bands working simultaneously under his name (one led by Cliff Jackson) in NYC. Taught mus. in Phila late '30s; led various gps. there and in NYC throughout the '40s. Worked as a Phila. parking lot attendant in '50s but ret. to mus. in '59. Rec. for Prest., Riv., and other labels '60–61. Later spent three yrs. teaching at Berkeley Sch. of Mus. in Calif.; played MJF '63; toured Eur. w. the Newport Guitar Workshop '67. Many traditional jazz enthusiasts regard Snowden as one of the foremost exponents of jazz bjo. Was planning to open a gtr. sch. at the time of his death. CDs: Riv.; Prest.; Fontana; duo w. Lonnie Johnson (Prest.).

SOCARRAS, ALBERTO, fl, saxes, cl; b. Manzanillo, Cuba, 9/19/08. Local orchs. in Cuba bef. moving to US late 1920s; rec. w. Clarence Williams; pl. w. *Blackbirds* shows '28–33, incl. tour of Eur. Played fl. on Lizzie Miles's "You're Such a Cruel Papa to Me" '28; rec. on cl. and alto w. Bennett's Swamplanders '30. Pl. w. Benny Carter '33; briefly formed own band; toured Eur. as leader of all-female band '34. Pl. w. Sam Wooding '35; Erskine Hawkins for Cotton Club Parade '37. Led own bands at Harlem Uproar House; Glen Island Casino; Ren-

dezvous Inn; etc; sidemen incl. Edgar Sampson; Cab Calloway; Mongo Santamaria; etc. Later specialized in classical fl.; solo recital at Carnegie Hall '45; taught fl. into '70s. Rec. w. Babs Gonzales '49. CDs: w. Babs Gonzales (BN); Clarence Williams (Class.)

SOCOLOW, FRANK, tnr and alto saxes, cl; b. Brooklyn, NY, 9/18/23; d. NYC, 4/29/81. Studied w. Leon Russianoff at 13. Sideman in the '40s w. Boyd Raeburn; Buddy Rich; Chubby Jackson; Georgie Auld; tour. Scand. w. Jackson 1947–8; later w. Artie Shaw '49–50; then freelanced in NYC, mainly w. Johnny Richards orch. Rec. w. gps. led by Edmond Hall and Sid Catlett '44; as lead. w. Freddie Webster, Bud Powell '45. Active w. many bop stars dur. '50s, incl. Charlie Parker; Buddy DeFranco; Charlie Ventura; Terry Gibbs; Gene Krupa. LPs: several apps. in *Bebop Revisited* series on Xanadu. CDs: w. M. Ferguson; Joe Morello (BB); Sid Catlett (Class.); Hal McKusick (Dec.); Raeburn; Phil Woods (Sav.); Shaw (FS); w. Chubby Jackson in *The Jazz Arranger, Vol. 2* (Col.).

SOLAL, MARTIAL, pno, comp; b. Algiers, Algeria, 8/23/27. Studied pno at age 6 w. his moth., an opera singer. Dur. mil. service in late 1940s, he pl. on radio in Algeria and Morocco. To Paris '50; pl. and rec. w. Django Reinhardt; Don Byas; Lucky Thompson; Kenny Clarke; and Sidney Bechet. In late '50s he formed a qt. and began comp. mus. for films; led trio w. Guy Pedersen and Daniel Humair in '60s. In early '60s he made first of annual apps. in US; rec. an album w. Lee Konitz '68 and later app. w. him as a duo and in small gps. off and on '74–82. From the early '80s he occ. led a bb or trio and participated in concerts of contemporary classical mus. A superb pnst. in a wide variety of styles, Solal has perhaps been too chameleonic a player to have made a large impact on US jazz audiences, but his originality and ability to swing are beyond question. CDs: Vogue; MPS; Drey.; SN; JMS; w. S. Getz (LRC); S. Grappelli (Owl; Atl.); D. Humair (Blue Flame; L. Bleu); Konitz (Steep.); Reinhardt (Musidisc); Lucky Thompson (Vogue); Attila Zoller (MPS)

SOLOFF, LEW (LEWIS MICHAEL), tpt, flg, picctpt; b. NYC, 2/20/44. Father, Buddy Soloff, was a vaudeville soft shoe dancer; moth. a vaudeville violinist. Stud. uke. w. fath. at age 5; pno. fr. age 5 to 13; began pl. tpt. in fifth grade in Lakewood, N.J. Stud. at Juilliard Prep. Dept. 1955–61; w. Edward Treutel at Eastman Sch. of Mus. '61–5 (B. Mus. '65). Also stud. w. Carmine Caruso and members of Rochester, Phila., and Chi. symphs. First prof. experience w. show bands in Catskills '58–65. Freelanced w.

Machito; Tito Puente; Vincent Lopez; Maynard Ferguson; Joe Henderson; Kenny Dorham; Clark Terry; Barry Miles; Gil Evans; Chuck Jackson; Chuck Mangione; Urbie Green; Slide Hampton; Radio City orch. '65–8. Feat. w. Blood, Sweat & Tears '68–73. Pl. w. Thad Jones–Mel Lewis Orch. off and on '68–76. Feat. soloist w. Rochester, Utica, and NO symphs. '73. Pl. w. Gil Evans Orch. '73–83; also app. w. Chuck Mangione as feat. soloist '70s. Co-led qnt. w. Jon Faddis '75. Rec. w. Sonny Stitt '76; Stanley Turrentine '76–7; Geo. Russell '78, '80. Lead tpt. w. Frank Sinatra in Atlantic City '80s; also worked w. rock acts, incl. Sting, Mick Jagger. Soloff pl. w. the Manh. Jazz Qnt., the Lincoln Ctr. Jazz Orch., and leads two bands, one el. and one acoustic. Cont. to be in high demand as a studio player, rec. in the '90s w. Dr. John and Marianne Faithful. He is active as a clinician and is on the faculties of Manh. Sch. of Mus., the New Sch., and NYU. A subtle and idiosyncratic improviser. Favs: Louis Armstrong, Miles Davis, Dizzy Gillespie. Polls: *SJ*. Fests: all major. CDs: Mile.; Evid.; Sw. Bas.; PW; w. H. Ruiz (Novus); C. Bley (WATT); F. Hubbard (DRG); Helen Merrill; Jimmy Heath; Joe Henderson (Verve); M. Gibbs (Act); Manh. Jazz Qnt. (ProJazz; King; Bellaphon); Gil Evans (BB; Evid.; ProJazz); D. Ponce (Ant.); C. Earland (Muse); F. Ambrosetti; Daniel Schnyder (Enja); Jim Hall; Ted Rosenthal (CTI); D. Gillespie (Tel.); George Russell (SN); LCJO (Col.).

SOPH, ED (EDWARD B.), dms; b. Coronado, CA, 3/21/45. Studied w. Elder Mori, Houston, Tex. 1960–3; att. No. Tex. State U. '63–8, pl. w. Lab band. Worked locally w. Arnett Cobb; Jimmy Ford; Don Wilkerson; pl. w. Stan Kenton and Ray McKinley dur. summers '65–6; tour. and rec. w. Woody Herman '68, '70, '71. Moved to NYC '71; dur. '70s he pl and rec w. Herman; Bill Watrous; Clark Terry; Joe Henderson; and Dave Liebman. Has taught priv. and at workshops and colls. since late '70s, ret. to teach at No. Tex. St. U. in mid '80s. Often identified as a power player via his work w. Herman, Kenton, et al., Soph says, "I would like to rid myself of the stigma of being a big band drummer. I prefer small groups, with two exceptions: Woody and those bands at North Texas." CDs: w. W. Herman (Conc.; Fant.); M. Bloomfield (Takoma); Joe Henderson (Enja); John McNeil (Steep.); Clark Terry (Vang.).

SOSKIN, MARK SAMUEL, pno, synth, comp, arr; b. Brooklyn, NY, 7/12/53. Studied at Colo. State U. 1972–3; Berklee Coll. of Mus. '73–4. Pl. w. local bands in Bost. and SF, then w. Pete and Sheila Escovedo '74; Mel Martin '75; Eddie Henderson '76; Joe Henderson '77; Bill Cobham '77–8; Sonny

Rollins '78–93; Astrud Gilberto '81–2; Geo. Russell, Jon Lucien '83; Stanley Turrentine '88–91; Herbie Mann '88–91; Ronnie Cuber, Steve Slagle, Roland Vasquez '91; own trio and w. Claudio Roditi '93. Very involved w. Brazilian music. Soskin comp. and pl. for TV series *The Equalizer*. Favs: Stanley Cowell, Egberto Gismonti. Fests: Eur., Japan, etc., since '77. LP: Prest. CDs: King; Vartan Jazz; TCB; Jazz City; w. S. Rollins (Mile.); Geo. Russell (SN); H. Mann (Chesky); Roland Vazquez (RVCD); H. Meurkens (Conc.); Kenia (Zebra); Steve Slagle (Panorama); C. Roditi (Res.); Joe Locke (Steep.); Bobby Watson (Koko.).

SOUCHON, EDMOND II, M.D. (DOC), archivist, gtr, bjo, voc; b. New Orleans, LA, 10/25/1897; d. New Orleans, 8/24/68. While studying medicine, he developed an intense interest in NO jazz, which he cont. to pursue after gaining prominence as a surgeon. A member of the Sixth and Seven Eighths String Band dur. and after WWI, he also pl. w. many local mus., incl. Johnny Wiggs, Papa Jack Laine, and Paul Barbarin. Rec. w. own gps. in 1950s. As a jazz archivist, Souchon had a weekly local radio show, edited *Second Line*, the journal of the NO Jazz Club, and wrote *New Orleans Jazz. A Family Album* w. Al Rose. Helped establish the National Jazz Foundation in the '40s and the NO Jazz Museum in the '50s. His archives were left to Tulane U., which houses the museum. CDs: w. Johnny Wiggs (Story.).

SOUTH, EDDIE (EDWARD OTHA), vln; b. Louisiana, MO, 11/27/04; d. Chicago, IL, 4/25/62. Extensive classical studies in Chi., Paris, and Budapest but racial barriers made him turn to jazz. Played w. Jimmy Wade, Charlie Elgar, and Erskine Tate orchs. in early 1920s. In '31 he organized his own gp. w. Everett Barksdale and Milt Hinton. Returned to Paris '37 and took part in classic series of recs. w. Django Reinhardt, Stephane Grappelly, and Michel Warlop. In '45–6 pl. daily w. studio band at WMGM, NYC; in '50s he occ. app. on TV w. Dave Garroway; Fran Allison; Herb Lyons; and on WGN, Chi. Because the jazz vln. was considered an anomaly in his early yrs., South's work went largely unappreciated, but keen ears were aware of his uniquely rhapsodic style at slow tempos and his powerful swing in rhythm tunes. CDs: Class.; w. Reinhardt (Swing).

SOUTHERN, JERI (Genevieve Hering), voc, pno, comp; b. Royal, NE, 8/5/26; d. Los Angeles, 8/4/91. Fifteen yrs. of classical pno. study fr. age 5. Graduated fr. Notre Dame Academy in Omaha, Neb., where she made her prof. debut in 1944. Worked as intermission pnst. and accomp. (for Anita O'Day and others) at several Chi. night clubs incl. the Hi Note bef. beginning to attract attention as a singer. Active on radio and TV, she signed w. Dec. in '50s. and scored first rec. hit w. "You'd Better Go Now." Moving to Calif., she worked at local clubs but became tired of personal apps. From early '60s she devoted herself to teaching voice, pno., and comp. Greatly admired by singers and pnsts. of her day, incl. Frank Sinatra. She was planning to resume her career on recs. at the time of her death. CDs: Dec.; w. Shorty Rogers (Studio West). Southern is sampled in Charlie Haden's *Haunted Heart* (Verve).

SPANIER, HERBIE (HERBERT ANTHONY CHARLES), tpt, flg, pno, comp; b. Cupar, Sask. Canada, 12/25/28; d. Toronto, 12/13/01. Father and two uncles pl. instr. Began on gtr., hca. at age 5, then pl. bugle in cadet band in Regina. Stud. tpt. briefly in hs; mainly self-taught. One of Can.'s first beboppers, he pl. in Regina w. Paul Perry and led his own gp., the Boptet, ca. 1948. In Chi. '49–50; Toronto '50–4. Moved to NYC '54; pl. w. Paul Bley '54–5; Claude Thornhill, Hal McIntyre '55. In Montreal '56–8. Pl. w. Bley in LA '58–9; McIntyre in Reno, Nev. '59. Ret. to Montreal '60. Pl. in dance and hotel bands, CBC orchs., and w. own gps. on CBC and in clubs, incl. Tete De L'Art; Black Bottom; Jazz Workshop '60–71. Also taught briefly at Sir Geo. Williams U. Moved to Toronto '71. Feat. soloist w. Nimmons 'N Nine Plus Six '71–80. Led own gps. fr. '70s, often at George's Spaghetti House. Spanier comp. mus. for the film *Via Montreal* '75. Favs: Roy Eldridge, Dizzy Gillespie, Miles Davis. TV: many apps. on CBC; Timex jazz prog. '59. CDs: w. Phil Nimmons (Sack.); Paul Bley (JT).

SPANIER, MUGGSY (FRANCIS JOSEPH), crnt; b. Chicago, IL, 11/9/06; d. Sausalito, CA, 2/12/67. Played dms., crnt. in sch. band fr. age 13. Early jobs w. Sig Mayer; Elmer Schoebel; Charlie Pierce; Charlie Straight. First rec. at age 18 w. Bucktown Five. Prominent w. Ted Lewis 1929–36 and Ben Pollack '36–8. In '39 formed his Ragtime Band, an 8-pc. gp. that rec. sixteen highly praised sides for RCA. Rejoined Ted Lewis briefly, then w. Bob Crosby '41; led own bb thereafter but in later yrs. led small combos or worked w. Earl Hines in SF. Sometimes compared to King Oliver, Spanier's distinctive style was characterized by his effective use of mutes. CDs: BB; Mob. Fid.; ASV; w. Eddie Condon (Class.; Stash; Jazz.); Ted Lewis (JSP); Fats Waller (CDs); six tracks w. The Bucktown Five in *Bix Beiderbecke and the Chicago Cornets* (Mile.); *World's Greatest Jazz Concert #1, #2* (Jazz.).

SPANN, LES (LESLIE L. JR), gtr, fl; b. Pine Bluff, AR, 5/23/32. Studied at Tenn. State U. 1950–7; pl. and rec. w. Phineas Newborn '57; Dizzy Gillespie '58–9; to Eur. w. Quincy Jones in the show *Free and Easy* '59–60. Many rec. sess. w. Duke Ellington; Ben Webster; Curtis Fuller; Charles Mingus; and own qnt. in which he pl. fl. In '60s he rec. or pl. w. Jerome Richardson; Nat Adderley; Ella Fitzgerald; Duke Pearson; Sonny Stitt; among others. CDs: w. Bill Coleman (Polyd.); D. Gillespie; D. Ellington (Verve); Q. Jones (Merc.; Qwest); Randy Weston (Roul.); Abbey Lincoln; Nat Adderley; Sam Jones (Riv.); Red Garland (Jzld.); Benny Goodman (MM); Benny Bailey (Cand.); J. Hodges (Verve; BB).

SPARGO, TONY (Antonio Sbarbaro), dms; b. New Orleans, LA, 6/27/1897; d. NYC, 10/30/69. Early gigs w. Papa Jack Laine and Merrit Brunies; to Chi. in 1916, replaced Johnny Stein in ODJB. App. on the band's pioneering Vict. recs. and remained until it disbanded, then rejoined when it was revived '36–9. In NYC he worked w. Phil Napoleon; Eddie Condon; Miff Mole; Tony Parenti. His flamboyant style represented the earliest ragtime-based form of jazz drumming. He was the last surviving member of the ODJB. CDs: w. ODJB (BB); E. Condon (Class.); Phil Napoleon (Jazz.).

SPAULDING, JAMES RALPH JR., alto sax, fl; b. Indianapolis, IN, 7/30/37. Father pl. gtr. prof. in Ind. and Midwest early 1920s; grandfath. pl. bjo. Began on bugle, tpt., cl. Mainly self-taught. Formed own gp., the Monarch Combo, while in hs. In army bands '54–7. First prof. gig w. Jazz Contemporaries in Indianapolis '56. Moved to Chi. '57; stud. briefly at Cosmopolitan Sch. of Mus. Pl. w. Sun Ra '57–8; Sonny Thompson '58–9; own qt. '60–3. Moved to NYC '63. Pl. w. Freddie Hubbard '63–6; Max Roach, Randy Weston '65; Wayne Shorter '65–6; Bobby Hutcherson, Roy Haynes '66; Roach '67; Leon Thomas, Hutcherson '70; Weston, Art Blakey, Horace Silver, Pharoah Sanders, George Wein's Newport All-Stars early '70s; Mercer Ellington's Duke Ellington Orch '74–5. Led own gps. in NYC and at colls., incl. NYU, Cornell, Vassar, Utica Coll., Manh. Coll. '68–early '70s. Received B.A. fr. Livingston Coll., Rutgers U. '75. Spaulding was an adjunct profess. at Rutgers '72–5; also participated in wkshps. at Rutgers w. Budd Johnson; Clark Terry; Sonny Rollins; Jo Jones; Milt Hinton; Milt Jackson; Randy Weston; and others. Spaulding cont. to lead his own gps. in the late '70s and early '80s but rarely rec. w. them. Rec. w. Ricky Ford '84–7. Began rec. regularly as a leader for Muse Recs. in '88; also teaching priv. Pl. w. Billy Higgins and True Blue All-Stars '99. Favs: Charlie

Parker, John Coltrane. Polls: *Cadence* '88; *Billboard* '90. Fests: Eur. w. Roach, Weston; Japan w. BN all-star tour '87. TV: *Dial M for Music* w. Hubbard; *Positively Black* w. L. Thomas. CDs: Muse; w. David Murray bb (DIW); F. Hubbard; S. Turrentine; Larry Young; B. Hutcherson; W. Shorter; H. Silver; Duke Pearson; H. Mobley (BN); Sun Ra (Evid.); Bheki Mseleku (Verve); Woody Shaw (Mos.); Max Roach (Atl.); World Saxophone Qt. (BB).

SPEIGHT, ANDREW, saxes; b. Sydney, Australia, 3/23/65. Parents both involved w. jazz; fath. dir. several mus. fests. in Austral. Pl. w. Northside Big Band; James Morrison qnt.; Sydney Cons. combos; and own hard bop qnt., Now's the Time. Finalist in 1991 Thelonious Monk sax competition. Active as teacher in Austral. fr. '85 and at Mich. State U. fr. '91. Also working locally w. trumpeter Louis Smith in Lansing, Mich.

SPENCER, (WILLIAM) O'NEIL, dms, voc; b. Cedarville, OH, 11/25/09; d. NYC, 7/24/44. School in Springfield, Ohio. Joined Al Sears in Buffalo, N.Y. 1930. Renowned for his brush work, he was well known for long stint w. Mills Blue Rhythm Band, later known as the Lucky Millinder Orch. '31–6. From '37 to '41 he was a regular member of the John Kirby Sxt., a delicate chamber ens. that comprised Charlie Shavers, Buster Bailey, Russell Procope, and Billy Kyle, w. vocs. by Maxine Sullivan. In '41 when TB rendered him inactive, he was replaced by Specs Powell, but he ret. to Kirby briefly in '42. CDs: w. Henry "Red" Allen (Collector's Classics); J. Kirby (Class.; Col.); J. Dodds (Class.; B&B); Mildred Bailey (Dec.); Lil Hardin Armstrong; Sidney Bechet; Buster Bailey; Andy Kirk; Billy Kyle; Mills Blue Rhythm Band; F. Newton; Willie "The Lion" Smith; Maxine Sullivan (Class.).

SPERLING, JACK, dms; b. Trenton, NJ, 8/17/22. Worked w. Bunny Berigan and Tex Beneke 1940s; Les Brown, Bob Crosby, and Dave Pell's oct. '50s. Rec. w. Pell; Eddie Miller; Benny Goodman; Charlie Barnet; Bob Florence; and others. App. w. Brown '83 at Aurex JF, Tokyo. CDs: w. Les Brown (Fant.); B. Berigan (Class.); Tom Talbert (Modern Concepts); P. Fountain (Dec.); Abe Most (Camard).

SPIRITS OF RHYTHM. Instrumental gp. Variously known in earlier yrs. as Ben Bernie's Nephews or the Five Cousins, the gp. was principally popular for the vocs. of Leo Watson and the gtr. work of Teddy Bunn, who joined in 1932. Orig. the bros. Wilbur and Doug Daniels were feat., singing and pl. tiples (small gtrs.). The band occ. assembled to work in Hollywood,

Calif., and on 52nd St. in NYC. It broke up in the early '40s; Bunn and Watson were reunited by Black and White Recs. for a '45 sess. The gp.'s strong points were its humor-tinged informality and Watson's manic comedy vocals. CDs: JSP.

SPIVAK, CHARLIE (CHARLES), tpt; b. Kiev, Ukraine, 2/17/07; d. Greenville, SC, 3/1/82. To US in infancy, raised in New Haven, Conn. Took up tpt. in 1917. Played w. Paul Specht in '20s; Ben Pollack, Dorsey Bros. in early '30s; Ray Noble '35; Bob Crosby '37–8; Tommy Dorsey '38–9. In '40s he led his own band, backed by Glenn Miller. Though not a jazz soloist, he was a highly proficient studio mus. w. a sweet style; his sidemen incl. Dave Tough and Willie Smith. He cont. to lead bands in '50s and '70s. CDs: Cir.; w. Glenn Miller (Col.); Met. All-Stars (BB); J. Teagarden (ASV; Class.).

SPIVEY, VICTORIA REGINA, voc, pno; b. Houston, TX, 10/15/06; d. NYC, 10/3/76. Professional from age 12 in Dallas, Tex.; rec. for Okeh in St. Louis, Mo. 1926–9, accomp. by gps. incl. King Oliver; Louis Armstrong; Clarence Williams; and Lonnie Johnson, w. whom she rec. several double-entendre voc. duets. First rec., "Black Snake Blues," became a hit. Switched to Vict. '29–30; Vocalion '31 and '36–7. Feat. in King Vidor's *Hallelujah*, the first all-black musical film '29. In the early '40s she tour. w. Olsen and Johnson's *Hellzapoppin'* show but had withdrawn fr. mus. by '50s. Was reunited w. L. Johnson for Prest. recs. in '61; app. in Engl. in early '60s; the folk-blues renaissance was on and Spivey once again attracted attention. One admirer was Bob Dylan, who heard her perf. at Gerdes Folk City in Greenwich Village and made a guest app. on her own Spivey label. Spivey's prestige rose considerably in '70 when Dylan had her photo placed on the back of his *New Morning* album. CDs: Prest.; BB; w. L. Johnson (Col.; Prest.); Red Allen (Class.).

SPRAGUE, PETER TRIPP, gtr, comp; b. Cleveland, OH, 10/11/55. Raised in Colo. until 1963, when family moved to Del Mar, Calif. Infl. by his dmr. fath., Hall. Bro. Tripp, prof. tnr. saxist and flst. Took up gtr. at age 12. Stud. w. Bill Coleman in San Diego. Pl. in hs stage band; form. first gp., Minor Jazz Qnt. Att. Interlochen Arts Academy, Mich. Moved to Bost. '76; stud. w. Pat Metheny at Berklee; Margaret Chaloff and Albin Czak, New Engl. Cons. Back in SD began gigging through efforts of Bob Magnusson and Charles McPherson. Pl. w. Road Work Ahead w. Bill Mays, Magnusson, and Jim Plank in late '70s. Has worked w. McPherson; Chick Corea; Hubert Laws. Fr. '88 has taught at the Musicians Institute in

LA; worked in Spain, Netherlands, Argentina. Favs: P. Metheny, J. Pass; infls: Rollins, Corea; Bach. LPs: Xan.; w. McPherson (Xan.). CDs: Conc.; w. Billy Childs (Conc.); Bill Mays (JA).

SPROLES, VICTOR, bs; b. Chicago, IL, 11/18/27. Studied under Walter Dyett at DuSable HS 1942–6, then pl. in army band. Gigged w. Coleman Hawkins in Milwaukee, Wisc. '52. In Chi. pl. w. Ira Sullivan in house bands at the French Poodle '52–3; Bee Hive w. Norman Simmons, Vernel Fournier '54–7. While at the Bee Hive, Sproles backed Lester Young; Sonny Stitt; Charlie Parker; Wardell Gray; Dexter Gordon. Rec. w. Stan Getz '58. Pl. w. Johnny Griffin–Lockjaw Davis '58–60; N. Simmons '60–2; Carmen McRae '62–4; Art Blakey off and on '64–8. Rec. w. Lee Morgan, Andrew Hill late '60s. House bs. at Half Note, NYC '69–72; pl. w. Al Cohn–Zoot Sims; Anita O'Day; Jimmy Rushing; James Moody; w. Clark Terry '69–70s; Hazel Scott '70; N. Simmons fr. early '80s. Favs: Junior Raglin, Slam Stewart, Wilbur Ware, Paul Chambers, Ray Brown. Fests: all major w. McRae, Blakey. TV: apps. w. McRae, Blakey, H. Scott, Johnny Hartman. CDs: w. Lee Morgan (BN); Sun Ra (Evid.); John Young (Del.); S. Getz–C. Baker (Verve); B. DeFranco (Cand.); Johnny Griffin (Riv.).

STABULAS, NICK (NICHOLAS), dms; b. NYC, 12/18/29; d. Great Neck, NY, 2/6/73. Studied w. Henry Adler 1945–8. Did commercial work bef. pl. and rec. w. Phil Woods '54–7. Also pl. and/or rec. in late '50s and early '60s w. Jon Eardley; Jimmy Raney; Eddie Costa; George Wallington; Al Cohn; Zoot Sims; Gil Evans; Mose Allison; Carmen McRae; et al. In '60s worked w. Chet Baker; Kenny Drew; Bill Evans; in '64 pl. w. Lennie Tristano at Half Note in concert that was initially broadcast and later released on rec. Stabulas died in an auto accident. A strong, swinging style made him a favorite of many N.Y. musicians in the '50s and '60s. CDs: w. A. Cohn–Z. Sims (Dec.); J. Derise (Beth.); G. Wallington (NJ; Sav.); Mose Allison; Jon Eardley; Gil Evans; Jimmy Raney; Phil Woods–Gene Quill (Prest.); P. Woods (NJ); Konitz (Verve); Tristano (Jazz).

STACY, JESS ALEXANDRIA, pno; b. Bird's Point, MO, 8/11/04; d. Los Angeles, CA., 1/5/94. Played on riverboats w. Tony Catalano, et al. 1920–2. In Chi., he freelanced w. Muggsy Spanier; Frank Teschemacher; and many other local bands, until July '35, when he joined Benny Goodman in NYC. Dur. four yrs. w. Goodman his immortality as an artist was assured by a memorable, impromptu solo on "Sing, Sing, Sing" at the historic '38 Carnegie Hall concert. Also made first rec. version of Bix Beiderbecke's

piano comps. "Flashes" and "In the Dark." Worked w. Bob Crosby, '39–42; rejoined Goodman '42–4; w. Tommy Dorsey '42–5; own band in '45. Married to singer Lee Wiley '43–6. In the '40s he rec. w. Gene Krupa; Harry James; Lionel Hampton; Eddie Condon; Ziggy Elman; Metronome All-Stars; etc. In later yrs. worked in local bars in LA, then became disillusioned and more or less retired fr. mus., but appeared at '74 NJF. Rec. for Chiaro. '74 and '77. Inspired by Earl Hines and Bix Beiderbecke, Stacy pl. w. dynamic articulation, strong harmonic conception, and a powerful capacity to swing. CDs: Class.; ASV; four tracks in *Classic Capitol Jazz Sessions* (Mos.); Chiaro.; w. B. Goodman (Col.; BB); L. Hampton (BB); M. McPartland (JA); Spanier; Cootie Williams; Bud Freeman; Harry James (Class.); Bob Crosby (Dec.); E. Condon (Stash; Jazz.); Count Basie (Hep); T. Dorsey (Jass).

STAFFORD, TERELL LAMARK, tpt, flg; b. Miami, FL, 11/25/66. Mother pl. tpt.; fath. dms. Wife is voc. Melissa Walker. Began stud. at age 13 in Elk Grove Village, Ill.; first vla., then gtr., finally tpt. Met Bobby Watson at jam sess. in Wash., D.C., in 1991 and join. his gp., Horizon, into '95. Also worked w. Justin Robinson '91; Victor Lewis '91, '95; Kenny Barron '92; Shirley Scott '93; Lafayette Harris '94; Stephen Scott, Herbie Mann, Cornell Dupree, Don Braden '95. Co-led qnt. w. Tim Warfield '94–5; own qnt. '95. Euro. tours and fests. w. Watson. TV: Bill Cosby w. Shirley Scott '92; *Tonight Show* w. Watson '93. Rec. debut on Watson's *Present Tense* (Col); also rec. sound track for film *A Bronx Tale* w. Watson. Band dir. and tpt. instr. at Cheyney U. fr. '93. Favs: C. Brown, F. Hubbard. A hard-driving soloist w. elements fr. swing tptrs. added to his basically power bop style. CDs: Cand.; w. B. Watson (Col.); Stephen Scott (Verve); C. Dupree (Koko.); T. Warfield (CC); Craig Bailey (Cand.); Cecil Brooks; L. Harris (Muse).

STAMM, MARVIN, tpt, flg; b. Memphis, TN, 5/23/39. Studied tpt. fr. age 12; grad. No. Tex. State U. 1961. Worked through coll. w. Tex. mus. James Clay; Leroy Cooper; et al. Worked w. Stan Kenton '61–2; Woody Herman '65–6; Thad Jones–Mel Lewis '66–72; Duke Pearson '68–72; Bob Mintzer '84; AJO '86; George Gruntz Concert Jazz Band fr. '87 Led his own gps. intermittently fr. '70s; one of most active NYC studio mus. throughout '70s and '80s; ret. to full-time jazz pl. '90s. Recs. w. Kenton; Oliver Nelson; Pearson; Jones-Lewis; Patrick Williams; Chuck Mangione; Bill Evans; feat. solos on Paul McCartney's "Uncle Albert" and "Admiral Halsey" and Carly Simon's "Wee Small Hours."

Favs: Clifford Brown, Kenny Wheeler, Dizzy Gillespie, Miles Davis. CDs: MM; w. Deodado (CTI); L. Bellson (MM); Oliver Nelson (BB); AJO (Atl.); Bob Mintzer (DMP); Bill Mays (Conc.); M. Tormé (Stash); G. Miller Orch (GRP); E. Garner (Tel.); S. Kenton (Cap.); G. Gruntz (TCB).

STANKO, TOMASZ, tpt; b. Rzeszow, Poland, 7/11/42. Took up tpt. at age 16. Formed qt., Jazz Darings, w. Adam Makowicz, which was one of first Eur. gps. infl. by Ornette Coleman 1962. Pl. w. Krzysztof Komeda '63–7; Andrzej Trzaskowski mid '60s; later led own qnt., incl. Zbigniew Seifert, Janusz Muniak '68–73. In '70s he pl. w. Global Unity Orch. and Michal Urbaniak; fr. '74 to '78 and into '80s co-led qt. w. Edward Vesala. Rec. unaccomp. solos at Taj Mahal '80. From early '80s he worked w. many US mus., incl. Chico Freeman; Jack DeJohnette; Rufus Reid; Lester Bowie; David Murray; and, in '84, Cecil Taylor's bb. Greatly respected in Eur. for his free form jazz work. First infl. by Chet Baker, he then listened to Miles Davis; Clifford Brown; and Don Cherry. Describing his improv. melodies, Polish critic Kazimierz Czyz wrote, "Lyricism and sharp expression here are not a contradiction but a symbiosis." CDs: GOWI; Polonia; Konnex; Jam; Power Bros.; Polskie Nagrania; Muza; ECM; as co-lead w. Matka Joanna (ECM); w. C. Taylor (SN; FMP); Gary Peacock (ECM); Christian Muthspiel (Amadeo); A. Trzaskowski (Polskie Nagrania; Muza).

STARK, BOBBY (ROBERT VICTOR), tpt; b. NYC, 1/6/06; d. NYC 12/29/45. Studied w. Eugene Mikell Sr. Extensive freelance work in NYC w. Leon Abbey, Billy Butler. Briefly w. McKinney's Cotton Pickers; Chick Webb 1926–7; Fletcher Henderson '28–33; then rejoined Webb '34–9, staying on w. the band under Ella Fitzgerald's dir. after Webb's death. After army service pl. w. Garvin Bushell '43; Benny Morton '44. Stark's work w. Fletcher Henderson and rec. gps., such as the Chocolate Dandies, variously recalled the styles of Joe Smith and Bill Coleman. He was said to have been an infl. on Roy Eldridge. CDs: w. E. Fitzgerald (Dec.; Class.); C. Webb (Hep.; Dec.); F. Henderson (Col.); Red Allen (Hep); Benny Carter (Charly; B&B); Louis Jordan (JSP).

STARR, KAY (Kathryn La Verne Starks), voc; b. Dougherty, OK, 7/21/22. Joined Joe Venuti at age 13, remaining for four yrs.; also worked briefly w. Glenn Miller and Bob Crosby 1939. Best known for her recs. w. Charlie Barnet '43 and Cap. Jazzmen, an all-star gp. that incl. Nat Cole, Coleman Hawkins, Max Roach. Achieved wide popularity from late '40s w. purely commercial pop hits like "Wheel of Fortune"

and "Side by Side" but retained some of her jazz qualities. Often used such jazz mus. as Venuti, Ben Wester, Red Norvo, and Red Nichols on her recs. Still active in '90s. CDs: eight tracks in *Classic Capitol Jazz Sessions* (Mos.); w. Cap. Jazzmen (Jazz Unlimited); Nat Cole (Cap.).

STATON, DAKOTA (Aliya Rabia), voc; b. Pittsburgh, PA, 6/3/32. Sang w. bro.'s orch. locally, then club dates in US and Can. The success of her Cap. album, *The Late, Late Show*, brought her national attention in 1957. Rec. w. George Shearing, tour. w. Benny Goodman. In mid '60s she lived and worked in Engl. and Germ. Returned to US in '70s and has since been active as a blues and jazz perf. In late '90s did a series of gigs at Danny's Skylight Room. CDs: Muse.

STEGMEYER, BILL (WILLIAM JOHN), cl, arr; b. Detroit, MI, 10/18/16; d. Long Island, NY, 8/19/68. Early experience w. Austin Wylie; Glenn Miller; and Bob Crosby. From '40s he arr. and pl. w. Billy Butterfield; Yank Lawson; and Bobby Hackett in NYC; also accomp. Billie Holiday and Pearl Bailey. Arr. music for TV show, *Hit Parade,* in '50s; also pl. in Lawson-Haggart band off and on fr. '51; in '60s was staff cond. at CBS. CDs: w. L. Amstrong (Class.); Bob Crosby (Halcyon); B. Holiday (Dec.); Jerry Jerome (Arb.); G. Wein (Vict.); tracks w. Frankie Trumbauer in *Classic Capitol Jazz Sessions* (Mos.).

STEIG, JEREMY, fl; b. NYC, 9/23/42. From an artistic family; fath. is illustrator William Steig, moth. and sist. also artists. Jeremy painted the cover for his Columbia LP 1963. Started on recorder; took up fl. at age 11, stud. w. Paige Brook of N.Y. Phil. Orch. Attended HS of Mus. & Art. First club date was w. Jim Hall and Paul Bley; pl. w. Bley and Gary Peacock '61. Motorcycle accident in '62 paralyzed right side of his face and left him deaf in one ear for six mos.; had to use prosthetic device for a yr. to enable him to pl. fl. Debut solo album, *Flute Fever* '63; worked w. jazz gp. backing Tim Hardin '66–7. Formed Jeremy and the Satyrs '67, and has led own gps. ever since; in late '60s and '70s rec. w. Bill Evans; Jan Hammer; and Eddie Gomez; perf. w. Jimi Hendrix and Art Blakey; began to utilize el. devices w. his fl. in early '70s. In the '80s mostly active doing soundtrack work for animated cartoons. Returned to rec. in '92 w. release of *Jigsaw.* An inventive improviser, he has pioneered in the aural expansion of the fl.'s capabilities w. a variety of techniques ranging from electronics to flutter tonguing, humming, and singing. TV: *The Jazz Set* (PBS) '71. LP: *Flute Fever* (Col.). CDs: Tri.; w. Bill Evans (Verve); Joe Henderson (Mile.); Eddie Gomez (Stretch).

STEIN, ANDY (ANDREW ERNEST), vln, saxes, comp, arr; b. NYC, 8/31/48. Father is pnst. and comp.; aunt, cousins pl. strings. Stud. vln. w. Charles Avsharian; Hamao Fujiwara; Joseph Fuchs; Burton Kaplan. Pl. sax w. rock gp. Commander Cody and his Lost Planet Airmen '69–76; also Vince Giordano; Swing Fever bb; Victor Lombardo bb. Pl. vln. w. Giordano '80–7; Maurice Peress Orch.; Paquito D'Rivera; Dick Hyman; John Hendricks; Eddie Daniels; Ken Peplowski; etc.; also many special concerts, incl. tribute to Joe Venuti at Michael's Pub '85; Lincoln Center Classical Jazz '88, '91. Arr. for Giordano; Bobby Short; Manh. Rhythm Kings. Stein, an accomplished classical violinist, has perf. and rec. w. Itzhak Perlman; Placido Domingo; Marilyn Horne. He has also pl. country fiddle w. Willie Nelson; Merle Haggard; and regularly on Garrison Keillor's radio progs. since '89. He app. on the soundtracks to the films *The Cotton Club* and *Bix: Interpretation of a Legend* and scored the Oscar-winning short film *Sundae in New York* '84. Favs: Eddie South, Fritz Kreisler, Joseph Szigetti, Joe Venuti. Fests: Eur., Asia. CDs: w. J. Hendricks (Den.); LCJO (Col.); Bay Bay Ramblers; Keith Ingham (Stomp Off).

STEIN, LOU (LOUIS), pno; b. Philadelphia, PA, 4/22/22; d. Litchfield, CT, 12/10/02. Began on alto sax; pl. first prof. gig on pno. at 14. Participated in jam sess. at Billy Kretchmer's w. Buddy DeFranco; Charlie Ventura; Bill Harris late 1930s. Pl. w. Ray McKinley '42; Glenn Miller's Army Air Force band in New Haven, Conn. After discharge he rejoined McKinley '46–7; then pl. w. Charlie Ventura, who rec. his comp. "East of Suez" '47. Freelanced in '50s w. Yank Lawson–Bob Haggart; Billy Butterfield; Kai Winding; Benny Goodman; Sarah Vaughan; Sauter-Finegan Orch.; Neal Hefti; Joe Newman; Louis Bellson; Edgar Sampson; Peanuts Hucko; Red Allen; Coleman Hawkins; Lester Young; also commercial work. Active as jingle writer and commercial studio mus. fr. '58. Rec. and tour. w. Joe Venuti '69, '71–2. Rec. as lead. and unaccomp. soloist fr. '70s. Rec. in '80s w. R. McKinley; Flip Phillips; Nick Fatool; Lawson-Haggart. CDs: Pullen Music; w. Glenn Miller (BB); L. Konitz–J. Giuffre (Verve); J. J. Johnson–Kai Winding (Sav.); Nick Fatool (Jazz.); C. Hawkins (Jass.); Yank Lawson (Aud.)

STERN, MIKE (MICHAEL PHILIPS), gtr; b. Boston, MA, 1/10/53. Mother was amateur pnst. Began on pno., then sw. to gtr. at age 12. Stud. w. Pat Metheny, Mick Goodrick at Berklee Coll. of Mus. 1971–4; then stud. w. Charlie Banacos. Recommended by Metheny to Blood Sweat & Tears '74. Pl. w. BS&T '74–6; Jerry Bergonzi, Tiger Okoshi '76–8;

Billy Cobham '78–9; Miles Davis '80–3; Jaco Pastorius '83–4; David Sanborn '85; Steps Ahead '86; Miles Davis '86–7; Michael Brecker '87–90; Mike Stern–Bob Berg Band fr. '89; Brecker Bros. fr. '92. Pl. w. Joe Henderson at Blue Note, NYC Feb. '93. Stern curr. leads a trio w. Lincoln Goines and Ben Perowsky. Favs: Jim Hall, Jimi Hendrix, Wes Montgomery. Fests: all major fr. '70s. TV: *Tonight Show* w. Branford Marsalis; *Saturday Night Live* w. M. Davis; Mike Douglas, Dinah Shore w. BS&T. CDs: Atl.; w. M. Davis (Col.); M. Brecker (Imp.); Harvie Swartz (BM); Arturo Sandoval (GRP); Pat Martino (BN); Tom Harrell (Vict.); Jim Hall (Tel.); Bob Berg (Den.); Michael Brecker (Imp.).

STEVENSON, GEORGE EDWARD, tbn; b. Baltimore, MD, 6/20/06; d. NYC, 9/21/90. Studied tbn. and sax w. Albert Jack Thomas, in whose city concert band he made prof. debut. Formed Balt. Melody Boys 1925. Relocated to NYC, pl. w. Irwin Hughes at the Arcadia Ballroom '30; w. Charlie Johnson at Small's '32; Fletcher Henderson at Roseland '35; Claude Hopkins at the Cotton Club '36; Ovie Alston at Ubangi Club '37. Also pl. w. Hot Lips Page, Jack Carter '38; Lucky Millinder '39–43; Cootie Williams '44; Roy Eldridge '44–6; and Cat Anderson '47. Later toured Eur. w. Sammy Price; in NYC w. Don Redman; Rex Stewart; and many others; led own band in Wantaugh, N.Y. '59. In '60s worked w. Joe Thomas; Lem Johnson; and Max Kaminsky. Pl. sax occasionally, but mainly known as tbnst. in the Tricky Sam Nanton tradition. CDs: w. Earl Hines (Del.); Ellington small gps. (Col.); Hot Lips Page; Rex Stewart; Cootie Williams (Class.); B. Holiday (Dec.).

STEWARD, HERBIE (HERBERT), tnr sax, alto sax, cl; b. Los Angeles, CA, 5/7/26. Quit sch. at 16 to join Bob Chester; later freelanced around LA w. Barney Bigard, Freddy Slack. Pl. w. Artie Shaw 1944–6; later w. Alvino Rey, solo on "Cement Mixer." In late '47 dur. three mos. w. Woody Herman Band, he was one of the feat. soloists on the orig. version of "Four Brothers." Later worked w. Red Norvo; Tommy Dorsey; Harry James; but lapsed into obscurity as casino and studio mus. in LV and the SF Bay area, often doubling on alto and fl. Strongly infl. by Lester Young, he was greatly admired by Stan Getz and others as one of the pioneer cool tnr. saxists. Own sessions for Roost '50, '51. CDs: Mob. Fid.; w. Herman (Col.); Harry Betts (Mob. Fid.); Benny Goodman; Artie Shaw (MM); B. Holiday (Story.); Barney Kessel (Conc.); George Handy in *The Jazz Scene* (Verve).

STEWART, BILL (WILLIAM HARRIS), dms; b. Des Moines, IA, 10/18/66. Father pl. jazz tbn.; moth.

is choral dir. Named after tbnst. Bill Harris. Stud. at Wm. Paterson Coll., Wayne, N.J. 1984–8. Pl. w. Larry Goldings Trio fr. '89; Lee Konitz Qt. '90; Maceo Parker '90–1; John Scofield Qt. fr. '90. Also freelanced in NYC w. Scott Kreitzer; Armen Donelian; Bryan Lynch–Jim Snidero '87–8; James Moody; Joe Lovano; Richie Beirach; Marc Copland; Lew Tabackin; Dieter Ilg '88–90. Favs: Roy Haynes, Elvin Jones, Philly Joe Jones. Fests: all major fr. '89. TV: HBO special w. James Brown–Maceo Parker '91. CDs: BN; Evid.; w. J. Lovano (BN); L. Konitz (SN); A. Donelian (Sunny.); J. Scofield (BN; Verve); L. Goldings (Verve; Novus); André Jaume (Celp); Maceo Parker (Verve; Novus); Fred Wesley (Ant.); M. Copland (Evid.); Seamus Blake; Bill Charlap (CC); Jon Gordon (Chiaro).

STEWART, BOB, tba; b. Sioux Falls, SD, 2/3/45. Wife is folk-jazz vlnst. Elektra Kurtis. Stud. tpt. at age 10; then tba. at Phila. Coll. of the Perf. Arts 1962–6. To NYC '68; joined Howard Johnson's tba. ensemble, Substructure (later renamed Gravity) '68. Worked w. Carla Bley; Frank Foster's Loud Minority; Gil Evans; and Sam Rivers late '60s. In '71 joined Collective Black Artists Ens.; also w. Arthur Blythe; Charles Mingus; McCoy Tyner; Globe Unity Orch. in '70s. Co-led gp. w. French hornist John Clark. In '80s began assocs. w. David Murray's bb; Lester Bowie's Brass Fantasy; and Henry Threadgill Orch. Pl. w. Christof Lauer's qt. in '90s. Rec. as leader, *First Line*, in '87. Exhibits rare speed and subtlety in his command of this demanding instrument. CDs: Post.; w. Bley (WATT); H. Johnson Gravity (Verve); A. Blythe (Ind. Nav.); L. Bowie (In + Out); Lauer (CMP).

STEWART, BUDDY, voc; b. Derry, NH, 9/22/22; d. New Mexico, 2/1/50. Toured in vaudeville as 8-yr.-old child prodigy; formed vocal trio 1937. In NYC '40, worked w. and married singer Martha Wayne (later known as Martha Stewart, film actress). Both sang w. voc. gps. in Glenn Miller and Claude Thornhill bands. After army service '42–4, he teamed w. Dave Lambert in Gene Krupa orch.; they sang together on the band's rec. of "What's This," the first bebop vocal rec. Later worked w. Red Rodney, Charlie Ventura '46–7; Kai Winding '48; Charlie Barnet '49. Ironically, like Lambert, he died in an auto accident. Excellent ballad singer and pioneer vocal bebopper. CDs: w. Krupa (Hep); Charlie Parker; George Wallington (Sav.); Red Rodney in *Early Bebop* (Merc.).

STEWART, JIMMY (JAMES OTTO), gtr; b. San Francisco, CA, 9/8/37. Piano at age 4, gtr. the following yr., mand. and bjo. at 9. Stud. at Coll. of San Mateo; Chi. Sch. of Mus.; Berklee. Prof. debut w. Earl Hines at 15. Pl. w. Gabor Szabo 1967–73; Gary McFarland '69; Vince Guaraldi '69–70; Louis Bellson '71; Mercer Ellington '81; own gps. Arr. and cond. for many pop singers, extensive studio work, app. on over 1200 recs., also feat. soloist w. SF Symph. Orch. and Civic Light Opera. Prolific author/educ. incl. *Wes Montgomery Jazz Guitar Method* among twenty-two books. Elected to Alabama Jazz Hall of Fame '91; winner of numerous *Guitar Player* magazine polls. A brilliant guitarist, Stewart's own solo career in jazz is often overshadowed by his remarkable eclecticism. Rec. w. Szabo for Skye label. Favs: Wes Montgomery, Charlie Christian, Segovia. CDs: Blackhawk; w. Gabor Szabo (Imp.).

STEWART, LOUIS, gtr; b. Waterford, Ireland, 1/5/44. Became int. in jazz after traveling to NYC w. showband led by cl. Jim Doherty 1961. Studied in Ireland, then pl. w. Noel Kelehan. Won awd. for outstanding Eur. soloist at Montreux JF '68. Pl. w. Tubby Hayes '68; Benny Goodman '69–71; Ronnie Scott '75–9; Geo. Shearing '77–80. Freelanced in UK and abroad fr. early '80s. Founded Eur. Gtr. Jazz Orch., a 5-gtr. gp. that pl. bb charts. Rec. in '80s w. Martin Taylor; Brian Dunning; Spike Robinson. Fests: app. often at Cork JF incl. w. Bobby Rosengarden '94. CDs: Hep; Eur. Gtr. Jazz Orch.; solo; duet w. Martin Taylor (Jardis); w. Shearing (Tel.; MPS); J. J. Johnson (Verve); Spike Robinson (Hep).

STEWART, REX WILLIAM JR., crnt; b. Philadelphia, PA, 2/22/07; d. Los Angeles, CA, 9/7/67. Musical family. Grew up Washington, D.C., where he first met Duke Ellington. Quit hs to gig w. Ollie Blackwell's Ragtime Clowns. Toured w. Danny Doy's Melody Mixers. To NYC late 1921, playing tnr. sax w. Willie Lewis's Musical Spillers; several other jobs, mainly on crnt., in Harlem cabarets; w. Elmer Snowden at Small's Paradise '24–5. Pl. w. Fletcher Henderson for a few mos. in '26; then two yrs. w. Horace Henderson; and back again w. Fletcher off and on '28–33. Also pl. w. McKinney's Cotton Pickers and Fess Williams. Led own bb at Empire Ballroom, NYC '33–4. Joined Luis Russell band briefly, then to Duke Ellington in late '34, remaining (w. occ. leaves of absence) until '45. Dur. that period he evolved the squeezed-tone, half-valve effect that became famous via an Ellington rec., "Boy Meets Horn." He was featured in small gp. sess., usually w. other Ellington sidemen, incl. a '39 Paris qt. date w. Barney Bigard and Django Reinhardt. Later toured Eur. as freelance and with JATP. Studied cooking at Paris's Cordon

Bleu and became a much-admired amateur chef; also lectured on jazz at the Paris Cons. In later yrs. living in LA, he was semi-active but began a new career as a writer of books (*Jazz Masters of the Thirties*), magazine and newspaper articles for the *Los Angeles Times, DB*, etc. He died suddenly after a brain hemorrhage. Stewart's work during the Ellington yrs. was as distinctive and valuable as that of Cootie Williams and Ray Nance, though he never quite achieved their level of recognition. His autobiography, *Boy Meets Horn*, was written w. Claire P. Gordon and published (by U. of Mich. Press) in '91 but takes his story only to '48. TV & video: *The Sound of Jazz* (Vintage Jazz Class.). CDs: Aff.; B&B; Prest.; *Key. Coll.* (Merc.); w. S. Bechet; L. Hampton; McKinney's Cotton Pickers (BB); F. Henderson (Col.; BB; Sav.); D. Ellington (Col.; BB; Prest.; Vict.); C. Hawkins (Dec.); Earl Hines (Del.); J. Hodges (Suisa); D. Reinhardt (Aff.; Verve); Cootie Williams (FS); Benny Carter (Charly).

STEWART, SLAM (LEROY), bs; b. Englewood, NJ, 9/21/14; d. Binghamton, NY, 12/10/87. Studied at Bost. Cons. Pl. w. Peanuts Holland in Buffalo, N.Y. 1936. Formed team w. Slim Gaillard '38 and scored hit w. their rec. of novelty song, "Flat Foot Floogee." Team broke up in '42; Stewart appeared in film *Stormy Weather* '43. Toured, rec. w. Art Tatum Trio '43–4 and again in '46–50. Many apps. w. Benny Goodman, starting in '44. Own trio w. Billy Taylor (later Beryl Booker) on pno., John Collins on gtr. Stewart gained fame through his use of bowing the bs. and simultaneously humming his solos an octave higher. After working w. pnst. Rose Murphy, he settled in Binghamton, N.Y., and taught there at the State U. in the '70s. Rejoined Goodman and teamed up w. Bucky Pizzarelli in '78. Heard on many recs. w. Gaillard; Lester Young; D. Gillespie; Don Byas; Erroll Garner; Tatum; R. Murphy; Johnny Guarnieri; Goodman; Lionel Hampton. Won *Esquire* Silver Award '45–6. CDs: Delos; B&B; co-lead w. Gaillard, Slim & Slam (Col.); w. Pizzarelli; Dardanelle (Stash); B. Goodman (Col.); F. Waller (BB); A. Tatum (Cap.); D. Gillespie; E. Garner (Sav.); L. Hampton (Dec.); Lester Young; C. Hawkins (Merc.); Red Norvo (Rh.; Stash); S. Grappelli (B&B); A. Tatum (Dec.; Cap.; BL).

STINSON, AL (ALBERT FORREST JR.), bs; b. Cleveland, OH, 8/2/44; d. Boston, MA, 6/2/69. Played w. Terry Gibbs 1961; Chico Hamilton '62–5; Charles Lloyd '65–6; John Handy '67; Larry Coryell 69. Freelanced in LA from mid '60s. Considered an exceptional bassist with a brilliant technique and adventurous ideas. CDs: w. Bobby Hutcherson (BN); C. Hamilton (Studio West; Imp.).

STITT, SONNY (Edward Boatner), alto, tnr, bari saxes; b. Boston, MA, 2/2/24; d. Washington, DC, 7/22/82. Father a mus. teacher, bro. a concert pnst.; sist. a singer. Stud. pno. at age 7, then cl. and alto sax. Lived for a while in Saginaw, Mich., where he worked w. Thad Jones, then in Det. and Newark, N.J. Stitt claimed he had his style bef. he heard early recs. of Jay McShann feat. Charlie Parker. When he and Parker met in 1943, each was surprised to find that the other had developed a virtually identical style. After tour. w. Tiny Bradshaw in '43, Stitt joined the Billy Eckstine band for eight mos., then became a key figure in the NYC bebop movement; rec. on alto w. Dizzy Gillespie '46 and led his own first sess. in Aug. '46. He later pl. tnr. and occ. bari. but was equally fluent on all saxes. Often engaged in tenor "battles" w. Gene Ammons, w. whom he co-led a gp. '50–2; Eddie "Lockjaw" Davis; and others; tour. w. JATP fr. '56; trio w. org. Don Patterson '61. To Japan in sxt. w. Clark Terry, J. J. Johnson '64; pl. in Giants of Jazz '71–2 w. Gillespie, Thelonious Monk, Kai Winding. Stitt won *Esq.* New Star Award on alto '47. He and Parker were mutual admirers. Stitt had a wealth of ideas that were often similar to Parker's but with a distinctive rhythmic thrust. Film & video; *Jazz on a Summer's Day* '58. CDs: Verve; Atl.; Muse; Roul.; Imp.; Del.; Prest.; 32; as co-lead. w. P. Gonsalves (Imp.); Lockjaw Davis (Roul); G. Ammons (Verve; Prest.); D. Gillespie (Verve; Sav.); Art Blakey (Imp.); S. Getz; O. Peterson; R. Eldridge; E. Fitzgerald (Verve); D. Gordon (BN); Milt Jackson–Sonny Stitt (Gal.); Miles Davis (Drag.); Fats Navarro (Sav.); Ronnie Scott (JH).

STITZEL, MEL (MELVILLE J.), pno, comp; b. Germany, 1/9/02; d. Chicago, IL, 12/31/52. Raised in Chi. Best known for recs. w. NORK 1923; comp. "Tin Roof Blues." Arr. for Chi. bands incl. Louis Panico. Benson Orch. fr. '25. Led own band in '40s and pl. w. Danny Alvin in early '50s until shortly bef. his death. Rec. w. Muggsy Spanier in Bucktown Five '24; Stomp Six '25; and trio sess. w. Benny Goodman '28. Both Jelly Roll Morton and Fletcher Henderson rec. his comp., "The Chant." CDs: w. New Orleans Rhythm Kings; Bucktown Five in *Bix and the Chicago Cornets* (Mile.); B. Goodman (Class.); Muggsy Spanier (Verve).

STOBART, KATHY (FLORENCE KATHLEEN), tnr sax; also alto, sop, bari saxes; b. South Shields, England, 4/1/25. From mus. family. Began on pno., then sw. to sax. Joined local band in Newcastle at age 14. Moved to London in 1942, pl. w. local gps. In the mid '40s she pl. w. Art Pepper, then a serviceman stationed in London. Worked w. Canadian pnst. Art

Thompson, to whom she was married late '40s. Toured w. Vic Lewis '49; then led own gp. '50–1. Married trumpeter Bert Courtney early '50s. Pl. in '50s w. V. Lewis, Humphrey Lyttelton. Pl. w. Lyttelton '69–77. Led own gps. fr. mid '70s; sidemen have incl. Harry Beckett; John Burch; Lennie Best. Stobart has also freelanced w. Johnny Griffin; Al Haig; Earl Hines; Buddy Tate; Zoot Sims; Dick Hyman. Headlined at first British Women's JF '82. Pl. w. all-female bb, Gail Force 17, mid '80s. Toured w. H. Lyttelton '92. CDs: Parlophone; w. Lyttelton (BL; Callig.); Buddy Tate (BL).

STOCKHAM, JEFF (JEFFREY RALPH), Fr hrn, tpt, flg, v-tbn; b. Rochester, NY, 11/12/58. Studied pno. 1965–74. Fr. hrn. fr. '67; tpt. fr. '77. B. Mus., Syracuse U. '80; M. Mus., Eastman Sch. '82. Joined funk band Airport in Syracuse '79. In Rochester w. Nirvana jazz qt. '80; Eastman Jazz Ens., Well-Tempered Brass Qnt. '80–2; Nate Rawls bb '80–4. On faculty of SUNY-Geneseo '81–3. Pl. w. Geneseo Chamber Symph. and Woodwind Qt. '81–3; fusion band Jacknife '82–4; Veralyn & Eloquence '83–6; Stan Colella Orch. '86–94; Full Swing '94; Danny D'Imperio's Boilermakers, Little Georgie's Shufflin' Hungarians fr. '94; Bearcat Jass Band fr. '95; Central N.Y. Jazz Orch.; Salt City Jazz Collective fr. '96. Tour. Eur. w. bluesman Jimmy Johnson '96–7. Pl. w. T. S. Monk fr. '97. Worked as graphic artist fr. '86. Favs: Fr. hrn: John Clark, Julius Watkins; tpt: Clifford Brown, Miles Davis, Chet Baker. Fests: Eur. and Africa w. Jimmy Johnson '96; Eur. w. T. S. Monk '97. CD: T. S. Monk (N2K).

STOKES, IRVIN SONNY, tpt, flg; b. Greensboro, NC, 11/11/26. Mother pl. pno. Began on tpt. at age 12. Stud. w. Isaac Johnson at James P. Dudley HS, then w. B. L. Mason at A&T Coll. 1943–7. Pl. w. Lou Donaldson in local bands, incl. Billy Toles, Max Westerbrand. Moved to NYC '47. Jammed w. Ernie Henry; Cecil Payne; Randy Weston; Duke Jordan; Leonard Gaskin; Max Roach; etc., at Putnam Central Club, Bklyn., then join. Mercer Ellington Orch. '48, remain. into '49; sub. for Shorty Baker w. Duke Ellington '49–50. Pl. w. Erskine Hawkins, Eddie Wilcox's Jimmie Lunceford Orch. early '50s; Buddy Johnson Orch. '56–8; Andy Kirk Orch., Tiny Bradshaw '50s; house band at Apollo Theater, NYC '59–60; Austin Powell at Bklyn. supper club '60. Pl. club dates and freelanced '60–70; B'way shows incl. *Hair, The Wiz* fr. '71. Pl. w. Thad Jones–Mel Lewis Orch. '78–9; Panama Francis's Savoy Sultans fr. '79; Illinois Jacquet–Arnett Cobb '82; Oliver Jackson '82–9; I. Jacquet bb '88–9. Pl. w. Frank Foster's Count Basie Orch. '90. Subbed for Doc Cheatham at

Sweet Basil fr. '80s and became regular w. Chuck Folds there '97. Works often in Paris w. George Arvanitis, Danny Doriz, etc. Stokes is a member of the Screen Actors Guild and has app. in films and commercials. He taught jazz improv. at Queens Coll. '78. Polls: Hot Club de France Awd. '85. Fests: Eur. fr. '78; Japan fr. '88. Film: app. in *Angel Heart; Jersey Girls; Malcolm X.* TV: commercials in NYC and Eur. CDs: Arb., w. P. Francis (B&B; Stash); I. Jacquet (Atl.); O. Jackson (Muse); Bobby Watson (Evid.); Tad Shull (CC).

STOLLER, ALVIN, dms; b. NYC, 10/7/25; d. Los Angeles, CA, 10/19/92. Played w. many name bands fr. 1941, incl. Vaughn Monroe; Benny Goodman; Tommy Dorsey; Charlie Spivak; Harry James; Sy Oliver; Bob Crosby; Billy May. Also many rec. dates w. JATP; Charlie Shavers; Ben Webster; Flip Phillips; and others. From the '50s he was mainly involved in commercial work. Rec. w. Art Tatum–Roy Eldridge; Fred Astaire; Oscar Peterson; Hawkins-Webster; Paul Smith; Frank Sinatra. A first-rate swinging dmr., better known for his many yrs. of studio work. CDs: w. Billie Holiday (Verve); Benny Carter (BB; Verve); Phineas Newborn (BB); B. Holiday; JATP; F. Astaire; E. Fitzgerald (Verve); A. Tatum (Pab.); E. Garner (Sav.; Tel.).

STONE, DAVE (DAVID), bs; b. Glendale, CA, 7/14/55. Father and uncle pl. bs., the latter w. LA Philharm. Pl. w. Ray Anthony 1974; Woody Herman, Stan Kenton '75; Harry James '76; Nancy Wilson '77; then extensive freelance work in LA area, incl. Louie Bellson band off and on fr. '84; Jack Sheldon; Les Hooper. CDs: w. Bellson; Sheldon; H. Alden–G. Van Eps; Scott Hamilton (Conc.); Bill Perkins (Jazz Mark); T. Newsom; Jack Lemmon (Laser.).

STONE, FRED, flg, tpt, comp; b. Toronto, Ont., Canada, 9/9/35; d. Toronto, 12/10/86. Made prof. debut at 16 w. father's orch. Lead tpt. in CBC Symph. Orch late 1950s, early '60s; pl w. Ron Carter and Phil Nimmons '60s; Rob McConnell '68–70; toured w. Duke Ellington '70–1. Led own bands in Toronto; also many TV app. as soloist and cond. Best known for work on Ellington's *New Orleans Suite* album. CDs: w. Ellington (Atl.; Pab.).

STONE, JESSE, pno, arr; b. Atchison, KS, 11/16/01; d. Altamonte Springs, FL, 4/1/99. Raised in Mo. Toured w. his family's minstrel show fr. age 5. In 1920s, led the Blues Serenaders; later was mus. dir. for George E. Lee and Terrence Holder. Led KC Rockets w. Thamon Hayes '32–4; fr. '35, led the Cyclones, feat. Jabbo Smith and Budd Johnson, in

Chi. Cont. to lead bands through '40s and was mus. dir. for the Int'l Sweethearts of Rhythm. Retired from pl. to work as a&r for rec. companies, most notably as songwriter, prod., and arr. for the Atlantic label, collab. w. Ray Charles, Ruth Brown, Big Joe Turner, the Clovers, and the Drifters. In the '40s his "Idaho" was a bb hit and became a jazz standard. His r&b hits incl. "Shake, Rattle and Roll" and "Money Honey." CDs: track w. Blues Serenaders in *The Real Kansas City* (Col.); w. E. McGee Stone (Atl.).

STONE, RICK (RICHARD JOHN), gtr, bs, pno; b. Fairview Park, OH, 8/13/55. Grandmother pl. pno. for silent movies; younger bro., Bill, pl. gtr. Stud. at Heights Acad. of Mus. fr. 1964. Developed interest in jazz w. help of cartoonist-jazz critic Harvey Pekar. Stud. classical gtr., harm. at Cuyahoga Comm. Coll. '75–7 (A.A. '77); pl. in Cleveland w. Tom Moore. Stud. at Berklee Coll. of Mus. '78–80 (B. Mus. '80); pl. in Bost. w. Frank Sikora. Ret. to Cleveland '80; pl. w. him '82; wedding bands '83; Marc Bernstein, Preston Trombly, C. Sharpe '84–5, '87; own qt. and qnt. '85–6; Jimmy Robinson at U. of the Streets '86–8; own gps. fr. '88. Pl. bs. w. Evelyn Blakey '91. Pl. in duo w. Victor Gaskin or Yosuke Inoue '92. Studied w. Hal Galper '92. Stone's NYC gps. have incl. Junior Cook, Richard Wyands, Kenny Barron, Ralph Lalama, Dennis Irwin, Vernel Fournier. Taught at Parma, Ohio, Comm. Arts Prog. '76–7; Amer. Inst. of Gtr. '83–4; Pace U. '84–90; Jazzmobile Workshop fr. '91. He has worked part-time as a computer systems analyst fr. '86. Favs: Wes Montgomery, Pat Martino, Jimmy Raney. TV: *A.M. Cleveland* '85. CDs: Jazzland.

STOVALL, DON (DONALD), alto sax; b. St. Louis, MO, 12/12/13; d. NYC, 11/20/70. Studied vln., then took up sax and worked w. Dewey Jackson 1930–1; Fate Marable '32–3; Lil Armstrong in Buffalo '36. In '36–8 pl., w. Peanuts Holland; also led own band in Buffalo '37–8. Moved to NYC '39, rec. w. Lil Armstrong; Pete Johnson; Sammy Price; Snub Mosley; worked w. Price, Eddie Durham '40; Cootie Williams orch. '41. Best known for his hot, jumping style w. Red Allen sxt. '42–50. Retired fr. mus. and took a job w. the telephone co. '51. Favs: J. Hodges, Tab Smith. CDs: w. Pete Johnson (Sav.; Class.; Milan); Red Allen; Lil Hardin Armstrong; Hot Lips Page; Sammy Price (Class.).

STOWELL, JOHN, gtr; b. NYC 7/30/50. Studied priv. Best known for work w. bassist David Friesen 1976–83, w. whom he rec. several albums for Inner City; and with flst. Paul Horn fr. '83, incl. a visit to Russia in '83. Other jobs w. Milt Jackson '77; Pete

Christlieb, Bill Watrous, Conte Candoli '80; Art Farmer '85. Extensive teaching experience at dozens of coll. clinics in US and Can. Favs: Jim Hall, Wes Montgomery, Ed Bickert. CDs: GSPJAZ.

STRASBERG, BIM ERIK, bs; b. La Jolla, CA, 1/21/60. Started on gtr. age 4, switched to bs. at 15. Grew up near other young mus.: Peter Sprague, gtr.; Rob Schneiderman, pno.; John Leftwich, bs., who introduced him to jazz and eventually hired him for gigs. Stud. w. Bertram Turetsky. Pl. w. Peter Sprague and in San Diego area w. Charles McPherson, whom he still considers a mentor, 1982–5. Settled in NYC '85; pl. w. Valery Ponomorev '89. Currently works w. several gps., incl. N.Y. Hardbop Qnt. since '90, acting as co-lead. fr. 96; Mickey Roker Qt. fr. '94; Fukushi Tainaka fr. '96. Tour. Japan fall '90 w. what bec. Hardbop Qnt.; Engl., Oct. '95 w. Hardbop Trio backing Manhattan Tap, a troupe it accomp. '92–6; and perf. w. other tap legends incl. Buster Brown; Chuck Green; and Gregory Hines. Radio: Live on WBGO w. N.Y. Hardbop Qnt.; WNYC, *Around New York* '93. TV: *The Naked Gershwin* w. Cecil Lytle, pno., PBS. Favs: Doug Watkins, Paul Chambers, Sam Jones. CDs: w. Hardbop Qnt. (TCB; Amo.); Manhattan Jazz Orch. (Blue Lion).

STRAYHORN, BILLY (WILLIAM; "SWEE'-PEA"), comp, pno, lyricist; b. Dayton, OH, 11/29/15; d. NYC, 5/31/67. Raised in Hillsboro, N.C., then in Pitts., where he had extensive mus. training and developed an interest in all the arts, along with an ability to write both lyrics and mus. Mainly interested in classical mus., he played Grieg's *Piano Concerto in A Minor* at his hs graduation; he was almost 20 before jazz began to interest him, mainly through the recs. of Duke Ellington. He arr. to meet Ellington backstage when the band visited Pitts. and demonstrated several of his songs, incl. "Lush Life," a song of rare sophistication written when he was a 16-yr.-old drugstore soda jerk. Impressed, Ellington offered to take the songs, and thus began a long and fruitful relationship. A comp. and arr. as well as lyricist, Strayhorn wrote several charts for small Ellington units led by Barney Bigard and Johnny Hodges, and wrote or co-wrote hundreds of works for the orch., incl. "Take the 'A' Train"; "Satin Doll"; *The Perfume Suite*; *Such Sweet Thunder*; *A Drum Is a Woman*; and *The Far East Suite*. He won the *Esq.* Silver Award as arr. in '45 and '46. Except for a Eur. tour by the band in '50, he rarely app. in public with Ellington. So similar was their creative thinking that the band's members often could not tell where one man's contribution ended and the other's began. Strayhorn's origs. incl. the Ravel-tinged "Chelsea

Bridge"; "Day Dream"; "After All"; "Raincheck"; "Johnny Come Lately"; "Passion Flower"; "A Flower Is a Lovesome Thing"; "Midriff"; "Smada"; "Boodah"; "The Intimacy of the Blues"; and "Isfahan." His last work, "Blood Count," was comp. in the hospital where he died after a ten-year battle w. cancer. Strayhorn occ. pl. pno. duets w. Ellington, mainly at private parties, but their orig. pno duet piece, "Tonk," was rec. twice: first at an Esq. All-Stars sess. for RCA, later as part of a two-pno. sess. for Mercer Recs. He rarely rec. as a gp. leader; one sess., *The Peaceful Side,* was rec. in Paris for United Artists; there were dates w. gps. called the Coronets, the Ellingtonians, etc., but most went out of print dur. the '70s and '80s. Dur. the '80s, Strayhorn's work became so popular that such artists as Art Farmer, Marian McPartland, and Toshiko Akiyoshi devoted albums to his comps. But most memorable is Ellington's earlier tribute, *And His Mother Called Him Bill,* taped three mos. after Strayhorn's death. Despite his considerable talent and the exposure given his work through Ellington, Strayhorn preferred to stay in Ellington's shadow—thus, he may well be the most underrated major comp. in the history of jazz. As Mercer Ellington observed, "Strayhorn was a tremendous help. Pop was really stimulated by his presence. It worked both ways—Billy was inspired to show what he could contribute, while Pop, who wanted Billy to hear what he could do, started writing more himself." Book: *Lush Life: A Biography of Billy Strayhorn,* David Hajdu '96. CDs: Red Brn.; BN; w. Ellington, pno. duets (Riv.); J. Hodges (B&B; Prest.); Cootie Williams (B&B); Clark Terry (Riv.); L. Armstrong (Class.; Vict.); Carmen McRae (Dec.); Sathima Bea Benamin (Enja); *Billy Strayhorn Songbook* (Verve); *Portrait of a Silk Thread,* by Dutch Jazz Orch. (Koko.).

STRAZZERI, FRANK JOHN, pno; b. Rochester, NY, 4/24/30. Studied at Eastman Sch. of Mus., starting out on sax and cl. In 1952 he was house pnst. at a Rochester club, acc. such perf. as Roy Eldridge; J. J. Johnson; and Billie Holiday. Moved to NO in '54 to play w. Sharkey Bonano Dixieland Band. Pl. w. Charlie Ventura '57–8; Woody Herman '59. Moved to LA '60; rec. for Atl.; Verve; and PJ w. Terry Gibbs; Carmell Jones; Herb Ellis; et al. Toured w. Maynard Ferguson; Cal Tjader; Howard Rumsey; Les Brown in '60s and '70s. From mid 70s he worked w. various gps. Many LPs w. Louie Bellson; Bob Summers; Sonny Stitt; Don Menza; Bill Perkins; Cal Tjader. CDs: FS; Jazz Mark; Disc.; w. Chet Baker (Novus); L. Bellson (Pab.; Conc.); Curtis Amy; Lennie Niehaus; Art Pepper (FS); Conte Candoli (Best Recordings); Bill Perkins (Jazz Mark; Inter.).

STRIPLING, (LLOYD), BYRON, tpt; b. Atlanta, GA, 8/20/61. Studied at Interlochen Arts Acad., then Eastman Sch. of Mus. Pl. w. Clark Terry bb 1981; Lionel Hampton bb '84; Woody Herman bb '85; Count Basie Orch. '85–9; also Buck Clayton bb; Dukes of Dixieland; Lester Bowie; Jazz Arts Gp.; Arvell Shaw. Stripling is an accomplished classical soloist, having perf. w. the Baton Rouge, Virginia, and Midland Symphs. He has done extensive studio work and pl. lead tpt. w. the B'way shows *City of Angels* and *Jelly's Last Jam.* In '87 he pl. and portrayed Louis Armstrong in *Satchmo: America's Musical Legend.* Tour. Eur. fests. w. D. Gillespie bb '88. Favs: Maurice André, Roy Eldridge, Clark Terry, Cootie Williams, Kenny Dorham. Fests: Eur., Japan since '84. TV: PBS w. Boston Pops '88. CDs: w. C. Basie Orch. (Den.); Grover Mitchell (Ken); Pam Tate (Left Field); Freddy Cole (Fant.); G. Mulligan (Tel.); S. Rollins (Mile.); Carmen Bradford (Evid.); Diane Schuur (GRP); Paquito D'Rivera (Mess.).

STRONG, JIMMY, cl, tnr sax; b. 8/29/06; d. 1940s. Played w. Lottie E. Hightower's Nighthawks in Chi., early 1920s. Toured w. show '25, then pl. w. various bands in Calif. Ret. to Chi.; worked w. Carroll Dickerson '27–9; Clifford King bb '28. Best known for his participation on classic Louis Armstrong Hot Five and Savoy Ballroom Five recs. '28–9. Led own gp. fr. '30s; also pl. w. Zinky Cohn '37; Jimmie Noone bb '39. Strong moved to Jersey City, N.J., and worked there w. local bands until his death. CDs: w. L. Armstrong (Col.; BBC).

STROZIER, FRANK R., alto sax, fl, cl, comp; b. Memphis, TN, 6/13/37. Early associate of Harold Mabern; George Coleman; Hank Crawford; Phineas and Calvin Newborn; and Booker Little. To Chi. in 1954; pl. w. Walter Perkins' gp., MJT+3; also w. Roy Haynes '61 and briefly w. Miles Davis '63. Moved to LA, where he worked w. Shelly Manne '65–7 and Don Ellis '68. Back to NYC '71; joined Jazz Contemporaries and the NYJRC; also pl. w. George Coleman Oct. First rec. as leader '76–7; pl. w. Horace Parlan '77. To Eur. '78; Town Hall concert '80; has since freelanced as player and teacher. A powerful perf. in a style rich with blues and bebop elements. TV: *The Jazz Set* (PBS) '71. CDs: Steep.; w. Booker Little (BN); McCoy Tyner (Imp.); Chet Baker (Verve); Booker Ervin (Prest.); Johnny Griffin; Sam Jones (Riv.); Horace Parlan (Steep.).

STRYKER, DAVE (DAVID MICHAEL), gtr; b. Omaha, NE, 3/30/57. Primarily self-taught; stud. in LA w. Billy Rogers 1979–81. Pl. w. rock bands fr. age 12, then w. Jack McDuff '84–5; Stanley Turrentine fr.

'86; Steve Slagle fr. '87; own gps. fr. '81. Also extensive freelance w. Jimmy Smith; Lonnie Smith; Freddie Hubbard; Dizzy Gillespie; and others. Stryker received NEA perf. grants in '88 and '90. Comps: "Swamp Dog"; "Nomand"; "Lonnie." Favs: Wes Montgomery, Grant Green, Geo. Benson, Pat Martino. Fests: Japan '89. TV: w. Turrentine, *Say Brother*, WGBH, Bost. '89. CDs: Ken; Steep.; w. Turrentine (Blues Alley); Slagle (Panorama); Bill Warfield (SB); K. Mahogany (WB); Billy Rogers (Stash); Mike Freeman (Best Rec.).

STUART, KIRK (Charles Kincheloe), pno; b. Charleston, WV, 4/13/34; d. 12/17/82. Conservatory training. Accomp. Billie Holiday 1956; arr./cond./pno. for Della Reese '57–9; Sarah Vaughan '61–3. In mid '60s he led own gp. in LA; rec. w. Al Grey and Reese. Then taught at Howard U., occ. leading own gps. in LV and accomp. Joe Williams in NYC and LA. CDs: w. Vaughan (Merc.); Basie and Vaughan (Roul.).

STUBBLEFIELD, JOHN (JOHNNY IV), tnr, sop saxes, fl, cl, arr; b. Little Rock, AR, 2/4/45; d. Bronx, NY, 7/4/04. Studied at Horace Mann HS 1960–3; U. of Ark. at Pine Bluff '63–7; Vandercook Coll. of Mus. '67–70; U. of Ind. '67. Pl. in Ark. w. Eddie Fischer Band '59; York Wilburn '60–3; Art Porter, Jackie Wilson, Solomon Burke '64; O. V. Wright '65; Drifters '66; own qnt. '67. Moved to Chi. '67, pl. w. AACM '67–70; Joseph Jarman, Little Jr. Parker '68; Art Ens. of Chi. '69. Moved to NYC '71, pl. w. Collective Black Artists' bb, Mary Lou Williams, Stanley Cowell '71; Charles Mingus '72–3; Roy Brooks '73–4; Gil Evans Orch. '74; Frank Foster, Tito Puente '72–4; Dollar Brand, Marvin Gaye '73; Cecil McBee, Roy Haynes '74–5; Billy Taylor, Thad Jones–Mel Lewis Orch. '75; Nat Adderley '76–7; Mayuto, Benny Powell '78; Manh. Blaze '79; Reggie Workman '79–83; McCoy Tyner bb since '84; Freddie Hubbard, Randy Weston, George Russell '85; World Sax. Qt. '86–8; Kenny Barron since '86; Teruo Nakamura '86–91; Jerry Gonzalez '87–8; Louis Hayes '89–90; Billy Hart gp., Mingus bb in '90s. Own qt. since '80. Stubblefield worked extensively as an educ., teaching at Chi. public sch. '67–70; Jazzmobile fr. '74; Rutgers U. '83–4; Wesleyan U. '90s. Favs: Coleman Hawkins, Don Byas, Lester Young, Charlie Parker, John Coltrane; arrs: Don Redman, Benny Carter, Budd Johnson. Polls: *DB* '73, '76–7. Fests: Eur., Asia since '69. TV: apps. in US and Eur. CDs: Enja; SN; w. Miles Davis (Col.); McCoy Tyner (Bird.; Mile.); K. Barron (Verve; Enja); A. Ibrahim; Jerry Gonzalez (Enja); Victor Lewis (Audioq.); Mingus bb (Drey.); Harvie Swartz (Gram.); N. Adderley

(Steep.); A. Braxton (hatArt); Louis Hayes (Steep; Cand.); Miles Davis (Col.).

SUDHALTER, DICK (RICHARD MERRILL), tpt, crnt, flg; b. Boston, MA, 12/28/38. Father, Al, was altoist in 1920s-30s; sist. and bro. pl. sax. Began on pno., then inspired by Bix Beiderbecke to pl. crnt. Stud. w. Armando Ghitalla (Bost. Symph.), then at Oberlin Coll. Later stud. in NYC w. Jim Maxwell, Carmine Caruso. Pl. w. classmates Steve Kuhn, Roger Kellaway in Mass., then sat in w. Pee Wee Russell; Bud Freeman; Jimmy McPartland. Pl. w. Riverboat Seven in Germ. '60–6; then moved to Engl., pl. w. Anglo-Amer. Alliance '66–8; Sandy Brown '72–4. Formed New Paul Whiteman Orch. '74; Commodore Spt. '74. Ret. to US '75, pl. w. NYJRC '75–8; New Calif. Ramblers '76–8; Loren Schoenberg orch. fr. '81; Classic Jazz Qt. w. Marty Grosz, Joe Muryani '85–7; Mister Tram Associates '87–8; Vineyard Jazz Ens. w. Schoenberg, Muryani since '89. Also pl. on soundtracks of several Woody Allen films. Sudhalter has taught at Brown U. and Oberlin Coll. He is also a journalist, having worked as Eur. corresp. and bureau chief for UPI '64–72; jazz reviewer for *N.Y. Post* '78–84; also much freelance activity. He received a Grammy for his liner notes to Time-Life's Bunny Berigan collection. Books: *Bix: Man and Legend* (Schirmer) '74 (nominated for the Nat'l Book Awd. in '74); *Lost Chords* (Oxford) '99. Favs: Beiderbecke, Berigan, Bobby Hackett, Johnny Windhurst. Fests: Eur. since '60. TV: hosted *In the Key of Jazz* on WNYC '80–1. CDs: Aud.; Chall.; Stomp Off; w. Mister Tram (Aud.); Classic Jazz Quartet (Jazz.); Tom Saunders (N-H).

SUDLER, MONNETTE LEIGH, gtr, dms, voc, comp, pno; b. Ridley Park, PA, 6/5/52. Mother sings, pl. pno.; great-uncle pl. pno., org. Began on pno. Stud. comp./arr. at Combs Coll. of Mus. 1970–1; gtr. at Berklee Coll. of Mus. '71–2; also stud. priv. w. Bob Zatzman; Harold Golden; Joe Sgro. Pl. w. Sounds of Liberation w. Khan Jamal '70–2; Change of the Century Orch. '75; Sam Rivers bb '77; C.O.C. Orch. '80; Dameronia '83; Hugh Masekela '85; Grover Washington Jr. '86–7; Sunny Murray's Untouchable Factor, C.O.C. Orch. '87; own gps. fr. '70s. Stud. at Esther Boyer Coll. of Mus.–Temple U. '87–8. Comp. the score to the film *Dumped On* for ABC-TV. Fr. '77 to '92 Sudler was married to saxophonist Kenzel Honesty. Favs: Wes Montgomery, Bola Sete, Jimi Hendrix; arrs: Charles Mingus, Oliver Nelson, Randy Weston. Fests: Germ. '73; Eur. '78. CDs: Steep.

SULIEMAN, IDREES DAWUD (Leonard Graham), tpt, alto sax; b. St. Petersburg, FL, 8/27/23; d. St.

Petersburg, 7/26/02. Studied at Bost. Cons. Dur. 1940s he pl. w. Sid Catlett; Cab Calloway; Mercer Ellington; Illinois Jacquet; Earl Hines; Count Basie; Lionel Hampton; Erskine Hawkins; Dizzy Gillespie; Gerry Mulligan. With Friedrich Gulda at Birdland and NJF '56; Randy Weston '58–9. Settled in Stockholm, '61, took up alto sax. Moved to Copenhagen, '64. Member of Clarke-Boland bb fr. mid '60s. Worked in radio bb fr. early '70s. One of the first trumpeters after Gillespie to be identified w. bebop, but because of his extended time overseas, his impact has been less than notable. In the '90s he occ. visited US; pl. concert at Mannes Sch. of Mus., NYC early '90. He rec. w. Mal Waldron; Horace Parlan; Thelonious Monk; Coleman Hawkins; Teddy Charles. Favs: Rafael Mendez, Clifford Brown; Dizzy Gillespie. CDs: Steep.; Clarke-Boland (MPS); Ella Fitzgerald (Dec.); B. Powell–D. Byas (Col.); T. Monk (BN); C. Hawkins (Prest.; Riv.); R. Weston (Ant.); C. Brown; G. Ammons (Prest.); J. Coltrane (Prest.; Beth.); J. Henderson (Verve); D. Gordon; Red Mitchell; H. Parlan (Steep.); Thad Jones; Lester Young (Story.); *The Cats* w. K. Burrell, T. Flanagan; *Coolin'* w. Teddy Charles (NJ); Bobby Jaspar (Riv.); Donald Byrd; Mae Waldron (Prest.); Max Roach (Deb.); Eric Dolphy (Enja).

SULLIVAN, CHARLES. *See* **ADILIFU, KAMAU.**

SULLIVAN, IRA BREVARD JR., tpt, flg, saxes, fl, comp; b. Washington, DC, 5/1/31. Father, moth., fourteen siblings all mus.; many other mus. in family. Stud. tpt. w. fath., sax w. moth. Pl. first gig at age 7; was an important part of the mod. scene in Chi. fr. 1949. As a member of the house band at the Bee Hive club in Chi. '52–5, Sullivan pl. w. Charlie Parker; Lester Young; Wardell Gray; Roy Eldridge; Sonny Stitt; Howard McGhee; Bennie Green; etc. Pl. w. Bill Russo mid '50s; Art Blakey in NYC '56. Ret. to Chi. '57. Moved to Miami area in early '60s, pl. w. own gps., local bbs. Contractor-percussionist for Miami prod. of *Hair* '71. Sullivan has perf. in Fla. schools fr. '60s and has taught at the U. of Miami fr. '70s. He was rarely heard outside of Fla. until '80, when he formed a qnt. w. Red Rodney to perf. orig. comps. A high-level player on all his instruments. Fav: Gerald Schwarz. Polls: *DB* TDWR. Fests: Colombia '68; Eur. '70s-80s; JVC-NY '99. CDs: Chess; Del.; w. A. Blakey (Col.); R. Rodney (32; Sav.); Hank Jones (Stash); J. R. Monterose (BN); Melton Mustafa (Cont.); Jim Cooper; Lin Halliday (Del.); R. R. Kirk (Chess); Red Garland (Gal.); Joe Diorio (Ram).

SULLIVAN, JOE (Dennis Patrick Terence Joseph O'Sullivan), pno, comp; b. Chicago, IL, 11/5/06; d. San Francisco, CA, 10/13/71. Studied at Chi. Cons.;

own qt. 1923; rec. debut w. McKenzie & Condon's Chicagoans '27. Worked in many pop bands; also in NYC w. Red Nichols; accomp. Bing Crosby in Calif.; w. Bob Crosby band '36–7; then sidelined by illness until '39, when he rejoined Crosby briefly; then formed own interracial sxt. for Café Society. His many rec. sessions incl. "Knockin' a Jug" w. Louis Armstrong '29; his own comp. "Gin Mill Blues" '33; others w. Lionel Hampton, Sidney Bechet. Pl. at Condon's club in NYC '46–7; mainly in SF Bay area in '50s; at Hangover Club in SF; MJF '63; NJF '64; comp. and pl. in docu. film, *Who's Enchanted?* '63. Ill and infrequently active in later yrs. Sullivan was a sensitive and inventive soloist whose infls. were Earl Hines and Fats Waller. Comp: "Little Rock Getaway." CDs: Class.; w. Louis Armstrong; B. Holiday (Col.); M. Spanier; C. Hawkins; Lionel Hampton; Jack Teagarden (BB); B. Goodman; Condon; Bing Crosby (Dec.); S. Bechet (Laser.); Henry "Red" Allen (Hep; Collector's Classics); Capital Jazzmen (Jazz Unlimited); nine trio tracks, also tracks w. Capitol Jazzmen; Jack Teagarden in *Classic Capitol Jazz Sessions* (Mos.).

SULLIVAN, MAXINE (MARIETTA WILLIAMS), voc; b. Homestead, PA, 5/13/11; d. NYC, 4/7/87. Discovered by pnst. Gladys Mosier while singing in a Pitts. club. Mosier introduced her to Claude Thornhill, who arranged her rec. debut and briefly acted as her mus. dir. Sang at Onyx Club on NYC's 52nd St., where she began a partnership w. John Kirby, whom she married, 1937–41. Her hit rec. of "Loch Lomond" and his popularity enabled them to launch their own radio series. Dur. their marriage, she app. in the films *St. Louis Blues* and *Goin' Places*; also seen as Titania in '39 stage production, *Swingin' the Dream.* Though long identified with jazz versions of folk songs, Sullivan's gentle, melodic sound and style displayed a rare, cool subtlety. Dur. a long solo career (interrupted by a few yrs.' retirement in the '50s) she studied and pl. valve tbn. and flg. Ret. to recs. on Period label '56–7; worked as nurse; active in community affairs in Bronx; founded House That Jazz Built, a nonprofit recreation center, while married to stride pnst. Cliff Jackson. Toured int'l w. WGJB fr. '69 through '70s; many new albums in later yrs.; also jazz cruises on SS *Norway*, recs. w. Bob Wilber, Dick Hyman. In her 70s she effectively combined a smoother, more mature voice w. the graceful characteristics that endeared her to swing-era audiences. CDs: Conc.; Class.; DCC; Cir.; Aud.; Kenneth; Mob. Fid.; w. Benny Carter (BB); Kirby (Col.); Teddy Wilson (Class.).

SUMMERLIN, ED (EDGAR E.), tnr sax, comp; b. Marianna, FL, 9/1/28; d. Rhinebeck, NY, 10/10/06.

B. Mus. degree, Central Mo. State U. 1951; master's degree, Eastman Sch. of Mus. '52; comp. study w. Samuel Adler, Gunther Schuller; Hall Overton. Taught jazz comp., theory, and sax at No. Tex. State late '50s and at Sch. of Jazz '60. In '60s he freelanced w. bands of Sonny Dunham; Ted Weems; Tony Pastor; and Don Ellis; comp. for films and TV; mus. consultant to Playwrights' Unit of Actors Studio; arr./comp. for Freddie Hubbard; Sheila Jordan; Steve Kuhn; Toshiko Akiyoshi; Ron Carter; and Lee Konitz. Co-led experimental mus. gp. w. Don Heckman that incl. Steve Swallow, Ed Shaughnessy, Ron Carter, Charli Persip, et al. Dir. of the Jazz Program at City Coll. of N.Y. '71–89. Arr. for numerous RCA and Caedmon recs. Perf. his work, "Musings," for saxophone and strings in Urbino, Cattolica, and Rimini, Italy '90; formed string and jazz rhythm section ens. '90, w. guest soloists Ron Carter and Lee Konitz; perf. at Black Hills Jazz Fest. '92. LPs: Jax or Bett. Jazz Workshop (Engl.); *Ring Out* Joy (Avant-Garde); *Liturgical Jazz* (Ecclesia Recs). Named BMI Jazz Pioneer '84; received Distinguished Alumni Award from Missouri State U. An extremely versatile player/comp. whose work ranged freely from mainstream to avant-garde jazz. CDs: Ictus.

SUN RA (Herman "Sonny" Blount or Lee; aka Sonny Bourke; Le Sony'r Ra), pno, kybd, comp, arr, lead; b. Birmingham, AL, 5/22/14; d. Philadelphia, PA, 5/30/93. Studied w. Lula Randolph in Wash., D.C. Pl. pno. w. Fletcher Henderson Orch. at the Club DeLisa in Chi. 1946–7; first attracted attention as an arr. Led own gp.—known as the Myth-Science or Solar Arkestra—fr. the mid '50s in Chi., where it became significant in the avant-garde movement. Moved to NYC '60. Associated w. Jazz Composers Guild '64–6. In the '70s Sun Ra and the Arkestra settled in Phila., gaining a large following through freq. tours of Eur. and US colleges; concerts were visual as well as musical events, with costumes, dancers, and, occ., films and circus-type performers. Many of Sun Ra's sidemen showed an intense loyalty; John Gilmore, Marshall Allen, and Pat Patrick joined him in '56; other members incl. Ronnie Boykins, Craig Harris, Lex Humphries, Clifford Jarvis, Julian Priester, Tommy Turrentine. Sun Ra claimed to have come to Earth as a goodwill messenger from outer space, and much of his music invoked the outer-space theme. In later yrs., the Arkestra was known as the Intergalactic Arkestra. Building on the modest mainstream success of '90 CD, *Blue Delight*, the Arkestra presented a series of concerts feat. mus. from Walt Disney films at NYC's Bottom Line club '91. Sun Ra was one of the first jazz musicians to use el. instruments; he pl. the el-pno. fr. '56, clavioline fr. '63, and

Moog synth. fr. '69. After his death, the Arkestra cont. to perf. under the direction of either John Gilmore or Marshall Allen. Polls: Arkestra won *DB* Critics TDWR '71–2; *DB* TDWR org. '75; *DB* synth. '75. Fests: Eur. fr. '70s; Mexico '74. TV: *Saturday Night Live* '76. Films: *The Cry of Jazz* '59; *Sun Ra: A Joyful Noise* '80. Book: *Space Is the Place*, John Szwed (Pantheon) '97. CDs: Del.; Sav.; Evid.; IAI; ESP; BL; Imp.; Leo; DIW; hatArt; BS; A&M; Enja; w. Billy Bang (SN); Walt Dickerson (Steep.).

SUONSAARI, KLAUS HENRIKKI, dms, comp, arr, pno; b. Iitti, Finland, 11/7/59. Mother and sist. pl. pno.; great-uncle, Harry Bergström, is well-known Finnish film comp. Began on pno. at age 6, sw. to dms. at 14. Stud. at Oulunkyla Pop/Jazz Cons., Lahti Cons. 1973–9; Eastman Sch. of Mus. '76–7. Moved to US '79, stud. at Berklee Coll. of Mus. '79–84. Pl. w. Heinola bb, Blue Train '74–9; Scott Robinson, Niels Lan Doky fr. '80; Herb Pomero–Berklee bb '81–4; Angel Rangelov bb '83; LaVerne Butler fr. '85; Muhal Richard Abrams–UMO '88; Diana Krall; Bobby Short fr. '89; Vanguard Jazz Orch. '91. Pl. and rec. w. own gps. fr. '84. Arr. for Empire Brass Qnt., Bobby Short. Pl. w. Short fr. '97. Suonsaari taught at Oulunkyla Cons. '79, '89. His qnt., Blue Train, was voted the number one jazz gp. in Finland in '78. Favs: Philly Joe Jones, Elvin Jones, Billy Higgins. Fests: Eur. fr. '74. TV: CBS: *Music and Things*; Finnish TV. CDs: Story.; JA; L+R; SN; w. M. R. Abrams (UMO); N. Lan Doky (BN); Scott Robinson (Arb.); Short (Tel.)

SUPERSAX. A nonet feat. five saxophones, tpt. and rhythm section pl. a repertoire based mainly on the solos of Charlie Parker. Formed by Med Flory and Buddy Clark in Los Angeles 1972. Although Clark left in '75, the personnel has remained relatively stable. In early '92 it consisted of Flory and Lanny Morgan, Jay Migliori, Ray Reed, and Jack Nimitz on saxes; Conte Candoli, tpt.; and a rhythm section comprising Lou Levy, Dave Carpenter, and Frankie Capp. At time the brass spot was filled by tbnsts. Frank Rosolino or Carl Fontana. For some apps. and recs., four vocalists were added and billing changed to Supersax and Voices. Numerous tours of Japan and Eur. Supersax won a Grammy award as Best Jazz Instrumental gp. '73. Though sometimes dismissed as a gimmick, the harmonization of Parker's work (now mostly by Flory) is ingenious and effective. CDs: Col.; Cap.

SURMAN, JOHN, bari, sop saxes, bs-cl, synth, comp, arr; b. Tavistock, England, 8/30/44. First experience pl. in wkshps. organized by Mike Westbrook

1958–62. Stud. at London Coll. of Mus. '62–5; London U. Institute of Educ. '65–6. Pl. w. Westbrook until '68, incl. Montreux JF '68. Pl. w. Mike Gibbs, Graham Collier, Chris McGregor, Dave Holland, John McLaughlin '64–8. Pl. in The Trio w. Stu Martin, Barre Phillips in Eur. '69–72; SOS sax trio w. Alan Skidmore, Mike Osborne '73–5. Worked w. Carolyn Carlson Dance Co. at Paris Opera '74–9. Formed Mumps w. S. Martin, B. Phillips, Albert Mangelsdorff '77. Rec. in duo w. Karin Krog '77; Stan Tracey '78. Pl. w. Miroslav Vitous, Azimuth '79–82; own 11-pc. gp. Brass Project fr. '81; Graham Collier's Hoarded Dreams, Gil Evans' British band '83. Tour. w. Gil Evans '86–7. Favs: Johnny Dodds, Harry Carney, Duke Ellington, Charlie Parker, John Coltrane, Sonny Rollins. Polls: *MM* '68–74; *DB* TDWR '69; Best Soloist at MJF '68. Fests: all major in Eur. CDs: ECM; w. John Abercrombie; Paul Bley; Mick Goodrick; B. Phillips; M. Vitous (ECM); Gil Evans (Jazz Door); A. Mangelsdorff (Konnex); Stan Tracey (BN); John McLaughlin (Polyd.); Mike Westbrook (Novus); Tim Brady (JJ).

SUTTON, RALPH EARL, pno; b. Hamburg, MO, 11/4/22; d. Denver, CO, 12/30/01. Played w. his father's band around St. Louis, fr. 1936. Toured w. Jack Teagarden bef. army service. After discharge '45, worked locally in St. Louis. To NYC '47 to rejoin Teagarden; pl. at Eddie Condon's as intermission pnst. '48–56. Moved to SF, pl. at clubs in Bay Area, MJF '61. Moved to Aspen, Colo. '64 and worked in his wife's supper club, Sunnie's Rendezvous. Worked w. Bob Crosby in NYC '66. Played in Denver w. the Ten Greats of Jazz, which evolved into the WGJB. Tour. through '74, when he settled in Pine, Colo. Made series of duo recs. in early '80s; app. at Kool JF, NYC '83; JVC-NY '98. Regular participant at Colo. JPs (and other similar jazz parties) for many yrs. Orig. inspired by Fats Waller and James P. Johnson, Sutton matured into an artist with a powerful left hand and an excellent rhythmic and harmonic sense, capable of pl. in a broad range of styles. Biography: *Piano Man*, James D. Shacter (Jaynar Press) '75. CDs: Chiaro.; Story.; Mile.; Conc.; Sack.; Solo Art; N-H; Flyright; w. WGJB (Atl.); E. Condon (Story.; Mos.); Barbara Sutton Curtis (Sack.); Dick Hyman (Mile.; Conc.); Wild Bill Davison (Jazz.; Story.); Bunk Johnson (Amer. Mus.); Bob Wilber (Arb.).

SUZUKI, CHIN (YOSHIO), bs, el-bs, pno, comp; b. Nagano, Japan, 3/21/46. From mus. family. Stud. pno. and vln. as child; began pl. gtr. in hs. Pl. pno. in coll. band at Waseda U., Tokyo. Stud. w. Sadao Watanabe; took up bs. at his suggestion, then pl. w. him 1969–71; Masabumi Kikuchi '71–3. Moved to

NYC Oct. '73. Pl. w. Stan Getz '74; Art Blakey's Jazz Messengers '75–6; Bill Hardman–Junior Cook '76–80; own gp. w. Dave Liebman '70s. Stud. comp. at Juilliard Sch. of Mus. Ret. to Tokyo '84. Formed gp. Matsuri '85; perf. concert at Sogetsu Kaikan, Tokyo '86. Built rec. studio in Tokyo, late '80s. Reunited w. S. Watanabe at Yoshiaki Masuo's homecoming concert '93. Polls: *SJ* Readers '72–4, '89, '93; *SJ* Critics '90–2. CDs: King; JVC; Video Arts; Nippon Crown; GRP.

SWAINSON, NEIL (JAMES SINCLAIR), bs, comp; b. Victoria, B.C., Canada, 11/15/55. Studied briefly w. Robert Meyer in Victoria; mainly self-taught. Pl. w. Paul Horn 1975–7, then moved to Toronto. Pl. w. Moe Koffman '78–82. Worked w. dmr. Jerry Fuller in Toronto clubs accomp. US mus., incl. Joanne Brackeen; Doc Cheatham; George Coleman; Al Cohn; Johnny Griffin; Jay McShann; Bob Mover; Red Rodney. Pl. w. Woody Shaw intermittently '83–7. Began subbing for Don Thompson w. George Shearing '85 and replaced him full-time '88. Fests: all major w. Shearing; Eur. w. W. Shaw. CDs: Conc.; Sack.; w. Shearing (Conc.; Tel.); Mel Tormé; Ed Bickert; Peter Leitch; Rob McConnell; Walter Norris (Conc.); Pat LaBarbera; Jay McShann; Doc Cheatham (Sack.); Renée Rosnes; Jon Ballantyne (JT); Sam Noto (Unisson); Woody Shaw (In + Out; Muse).

SWALLOW, STEVE (STEPHEN WALCOTT), bs, el-bs, comp; b. NYC, 10/4/40. Began on pno., tpt., sw. to bs. at 18. While stud. at Yale, he began pl. prof. w. visiting jazz mus., incl. Pee Wee Russell; Buck Clayton; and Vic Dickenson. Moved to NYC in 1960 and pl. w. Paul Bley; the Jimmy Giuffre Trio; George Russell; and others. Pl. w. Art Farmer Qt. and began writing mus. Tour. w. Stan Getz '65–7; joined Gary Burton Qt. '68, remaining for twenty yrs. w. occ. interruptions. Sw. to el-bs. in '70 and was instrumental in developing a jazz vocabulary for that instrument. Moved to Bolinas, Calif. '70; worked in SF w. Art Lande, Mike Nock '70–3. Taught for two yrs. at Berklee Coll. of Mus. fr. '74. Tour. w. Burton, Carla Bley, John Scofield '80–4. Also active as rec. producer for such artists as Scofield; Bley; Lew Soloff; and Niels-Henning Ørsted Pedersen. In '94 he tour. Japan w. Steve Kuhn and Eur. w. Carla Bley bb; Andy Sheppard; Jimmy Giuffre; and Paul Motian Electric BeBop Band. Cont. to tour and rec. through '90s. Comps. incl. "Domino Biscuit"; "Arise, Her Eyes"; "Eiderdown"; "General Mojo's Well Laid Plan"; "Home," a setting of poems by Robert Creeley. Favs: Charles Mingus, Charlie Haden, Wilbur Ware, Red Mitchell. Polls: *DB* critics New Star '64. CDs: ECM;

WATT; XtraWATT; w. Gary Burton (BB; ECM); P. Motian (JMT); Joe Henderson; Joe Lovano (BN); J. Scofield (Novus; BN; Enja;Verve); S. Getz (BB; Col.); J. Giuffre (Owl; hatArt; ECM); P. Bley (Sav. ; SN; ESP); G. Russell (Riv.); Carla Bley (WATT); Don Ellis (Cand.); Art Farmer (Atl.); B. Goodman (MM); Jazz Composers Orch. (JCOA); Roger Kellaway (FS).

SWANA, JOHN, tpt, flg, EVI (el valve instr); b. Norristown, PA, 4/26/62. Took up tpt. at age 11. Became interested in jazz after hearing a Dizzy Gillespie rec. at 17. Stud. tpt. at Temple U. in Phila. w. Mike Natale; B. Mus. 1987. Transcribed solos by Freddie Hubbard; Clifford Brown; Miles Davis; Tom Harrell. From mid '80s perf. in Phila. w. Don Patterson; Shirley Scott; Mickey Roker; and Cecil Payne. Also worked w. Joe Sudler Swing Machine, backing guests Frank Foster; Eddie "Lockjaw" Davis; Phil Woods; et al. Freelance in '90s w. Bootsie Barnes; Charles Fambrough. Gigs in Phila., incl. gp. co-led w. Johnny Coles '96–7. Pl w. Gerry Gibbs in NYC, LA, Paris '96–8. Favs: Hubbard, Miles Davis, Dorham, Harrell. Fest: Molde w. Eric Alexander '96. CDs: CC; w. Alexander; Chris Potter (CC); B. Golson (Ark.); Fambrough (Evid.; Audq.; CTI); P. Leitch (Conc.).

SWARTZ, HARVIE (HARVIE S), bs, pno, comp; b. Chelsea, MA, 12/6/48. Studied pno. and comp. at Berklee Coll. of Mus., then bs. w. Orrin O'Brien (N.Y. Philharm.). Pl. in Eur. w. Dexter Gordon; Kenny Drew; Art Taylor; Brew Moore; Jimmy Heath; Johnny Griffin 1970; and in Bost. w. Fred Taylor; Chris Connor; Mose Allison; Jaki Byard; Charlie Shavers. Came to NYC w. Mike Abene '73. Pl. in early '70s w. Thad Jones–Mel Lewis Orch.; Gil Evans; Lee Konitz; Chet Baker; Jackie Paris; Sheila Jordan since '73; Barry Miles '74–6; David Friedman '75–81. Co-led Double Image w. Dave Samuels '77. Pl. w. Steve Kuhn '77–81; Stan Getz late '70s. Own gps. since '80, incl. Harvie Swartz String Ens. '82–3; Double Bass w. Jeff Andrews since '91. Swartz has taught at Manh. Sch. of Mus. since '84; a clinician at Eastman Sch. of Mus. since '89. Fests: Eur. since '70. TV: PBS *Women in Jazz* w. S. Jordan. CDs: Gram.; as co-lead w. S. Jordan, M. A.; Randy Klein (Jazzheads); w. S. Jordan (Muse); Mick Goodrick (CMP); Bill Mays (JA); S. Kuhn (NW); A. Farmer–L. Konitz (Stash); L. Bellson (Tel.); L. Konitz (SN; Evid.); V. Mayhew (Chiaro.); P. D'Rivera (Cand.); Mike Stern (Atl.); T. Thielemans (Conc.); Daniel Humair (Owl).

SWEATMAN, WILBUR C., comp, cond, cl; b. Brunswick, MO, 2/7/1882; d. Washington, DC, 3/9/61. Traveled w. circus band; pl. w. Mahara's Minstrels; organized all-black orch. in Minneapolis, Minn. 1902. A cylinder of "Maple Leaf Rag," purportedly rec. by him in '04, has never been found. Became well-known in Chi. '10; wrote such comps. as "Old Folks Rag"; "Boogie Ray"; "Down Home Rag." Moved to NYC '13; led Sweatman's Original Jazz Band '18–21. Rec. for various labels incl. Col. '16–35 but jazz value is, in the main, minimal. In '23 he was a player in the scenario that brought Duke Ellington; Elmer Snowden; Sonny Greer; and Toby Hardwicke to NYC (Ellington apps. on Sweatman's '24 rec. "Battleship Kate"). He later stopped perf. and became a booking agent, publicist, and mus. publisher. Primarily a novelty artist known for his ability to play three clarinets simultaneously, Sweatman nonetheless had a significant impact on jazz via his rag tunes, his early jazz-styled recs., and his involvement in Ellington's early career.

SWINGLE SINGERS. Formed in 1962 by the Amer. saxophonist Ward Swingle (b. Mobile, AL, 9/21/27) and Christiane Legrand (b. Aix-le-Bain, France, 8/21/30). The octet developed a unique style, singing Bach and other Baroque works with jazz inflections. Made Eur. and US tours and several recs. bef. disbanding '73. Swingle formed another voc. gp. in Engl., Swingle II, which specialized in scat singing, early jazz, pop tunes, and contemp. classical mus. CDs: w. MJQ (Atl.).

SWOPE, EARL BOWMAN, tbn; b. Hagerstown, MD, 8/4/22; d. Washington, DC, 1/3/68. Family all musicians. Pl. w. Sonny Dunham 1942; Boyd Raeburn '43–4; Georgie Auld, Don Lamond '45; Buddy Rich '46–7; Woody Herman '47–9; Elliot Lawrence '50–1. Worked in Wash., D.C., w. The Orchestra under Joe Timer: joined Jimmy Dorsey '57, remaining w. band under Lee Castle after Dorsey's death. Worked w. Louie Bellson '59; and was freelancing in Wash. w. Bob Cross when he died. One of the first bebop-influenced trombonists who did not follow directly in the musical footsteps of J. J. Johnson. CDs: w. Serge Chaloff (Mos.); Woody Herman (Cap.; Story.); S. Getz (Prest.); B. Raeburn (Cir.); Buddy Rich (Hep; *The 1940s Mercury Sessions*, Merc.); L. Bellson (Jazz Hour).

SWOPE, ROB (GEORGE ROBERT), b. Washington, DC, 12/2/26; d. Washington, 1/9/67. Brother of Earl Swope, whom he replaced in Buddy Rich band 1947. Also pl. w. Chubby Jackson; Gene Krupa; Elliot Lawrence; Boyd Raeburn; Claude Thornhill; Jimmy Dorsey; Louie Bellson. Led a trio in Wash., D.C., in '50s and played in Joe Timer's Orch. CDs: w. Buddy Rich (Hep).

SYRACUSE, RICH, bs, el-bs; b. Connecticut, 4/19/61. Played first gigs while in jr. hs. Stud. at Manh. Sch. of Mus. 1979–83. Pl. w. Joey Calderazzo Trio '84–8 accomp. Mike Brecker; Dave Liebman; Benny Powell; Bucky Pizzarrelli; and others. Pl. fr. late '80s w. Eddie Henderson; Peter Yellin; Nick Brignola; Danny Brubeck; Jerry Bergonzi; Lew Soloff; Dick Berk; Mike Holober; etc. Syracuse has also perf. w. New Jersey Lyric Opera; Hartford Ballet; Gp. for Contemp. Mus. He has worked as a counselor for troubled adolescents fr. '90. Favs: Jimmy Garrison, Ron Carter, Dave Holland. Fests: Scan. '83. CDs: w. Nick Brignola (Res.); David Torn (WH); Bob Smith (DMP).

SZABO, GABOR, gtr; b. Budapest, Hungary, 3/8/36; d. Budapest, 2/26/82. Father gave him gtr. for his 14th birthday; self-taught, he listened to jazz on Voice of America; acc. singers and wrote for films and radio 1954–6; then left after the revolution and stud. at Berklee '57–9; also w. Newport International Band '58. Pl. w. Chicago Hamilton '61–4; Charles Lloyd '65; Gary McFarland '65; own gp. '66–8. Toured and rec. w. Lena Horne. Scored Chico Hamilton's music for Roman Polanski film *Repulsion*. After a period showing strong bop infl., became involved with jazz-rock, Indian mus., and el. distortions. Seriously ill, he returned to Budapest and was hospitalized there in Dec. '81. Won *DB* New Star award 1964. CDs: Imp.; w. P. Desmond (CTI); Chico Hamilton (Imp.); Lena Horne (DCC).

t

TABACKIN, LEW (LEWIS BARRY), tnr sax, fl; b. Philadelphia, PA, 3/26/40. Began pl. in hs 1955. Flute major at Phila. Cons. '58–62 (B. Mus. '62). In army '62–5, pl. in N.J. w. Tal Farlow, Don Friedman. Moved to NYC '65; freelanced w. Maynard Ferguson; Cab Calloway; Urbie Green; Bobby Rosengarden; Buddy Morrow; Clark Terry; Duke Pearson; Thad Jones–Mel Lewis; Joe Henderson; Chuck Israels; Doc Severinsen; also small gp. gigs w. Donald Byrd; Elvin Jones; Attila Zoller; D. Friedman; Roland Hanna; Toshiko Akiyoshi. Led trio at La Boheme in '68–9. Pl. w. Dick Cavett show band '69; also in Eur. w. Israels' Int'l Jazz Qt., Danish Radio Orch '69. Married Toshiko Akiyoshi, co-led qt. w. her fr. '70. Moved to LA '72, pl. w. *Tonight Show* band '72–83. Since '73 feat. soloist w. Akiyoshi-Tabackin bb; concert apps., tours of Japan, and a series of LPs on RCA. The orch. rose rapidly in popularity and earned many awards for Akiyoshi as arr. and comp. It was voted the Best Band in the *DB* poll annually fr. '80 to '84; Grammy nominations for Best Big Band Performance annually fr. '76 to '81 and several times subsequently. The band also won several awards fr. *SJ* in Japan and other publications. Moved back to NYC '83. In recent yrs. Tabackin has focused on small gp. projects. Pl. in duo w. Dave Holland '89; qt. w. Randy Brecker, Peter Washington, Lewis Nash '91; all-star gp. NY Jazz Giants '92. Own trio fr. mid '90s. He has perf. and rec. annually w. the Metropole Orch. in the Netherlands fr. '80s; tour. G. Wein's Newport All-Stars fr. late '80s. Tabackin is an exceptional tnr. saxophonist, inspired by Sonny Rollins and other early giants. However, as he puts it, "Instead of emulating, copying their notes, I try to absorb certain abstract qualities—an aura or essence that I hear, which to me is the spirit of the music, and it becomes part of my musical expression." In contrast to his forceful tnr. pl., Tabackin tends more to be a gentle classicist on fl.; as A. James Liska wrote in the *LA Daily News*, "He established standards of the jazz flute for future generations of players." Favs: Coleman Hawkins, Sonny Rollins, Don Byas, Zoot Sims. Polls: *DB* Critics flute '80–1, '83; *DB* Readers flute '81–2. Fests: all major. CDs: Conc.; Vartan Jazz; w. Akiyoshi-Tabackin bb (Col.); Donald Byrd (BN); AJO-Benny Carter (MM); Duke Pearson (BN); Carla White (Evid.); J. Colianni; Bill Berry; NY Jazz Giants; H. Alden (Conc.); Jazz Composers Orch. (JCOA); G. Gruntz (MPS).

TAKAS, BILL (WILLIAM J.), bs, el-bs, comp, arr; b. Toledo, OH, 3/5/32; d. NYC, 11/8/98. Played w. Zoot Sims, Tal Farlow, Marian McPartland, Pee Wee Russell late 1950s; Gerry Mulligan Concert Jazz Band '60; Paul Anka, Gene Krupa '61–2; Vic Damone '63–4; Judy Collins, Theodore Bikel, Anka '65; Doc Severinsen '66; Benny Goodman '67; Ten Wheel Drive '68–9. Pl. w. house band at Half Note NYC, backing Al Cohn–Zoot Sims, Kai Winding, Bob Brookmeyer, Jimmy Rushing, Anita O'Day, and others '68–9. On NBC staff w. Severinsen, early '70s. Led bands for theater prod. *Elephant Steps* '70; *Dr. Selavey's Magic Theatre* '72–3. Pl. el-bs. w. house band at Bradley's, backing Al Haig, Jimmy Rowles, Jimmy Raney, Mike Longo, Barry Harris, Bob Dorough '74–5. Pl. in Calif. w. B. Dorough, Manh. Transfer '75. Cont. to perf. w. Dorough into '90s. Scored NBC special *Earth Year One* '71. Fests: NJF-NY w. Mulligan '60. CDs: w. Mulligan (Verve); Dorough (Beth.; Laissez-Faire).

TALBERT, TOM (THOMAS), comp, arr, pno; b. Minneapolis, MN, 8/4/24; d. Los Angeles, 7/2/05. Self-taught. Led own band in LA 1946–9. Arr. for Boyd Raeburn; Stan Kenton; Claude Thornhill; Buddy Rich; et al. Moved to NYC '50, arr. for Oscar Pettiford; Kai Winding; Sammy Davis Jr., Charlie Ventura. Ret. to LA '75; scored many TV dramatic shows; led own gps. New bb recs. in '90s. Headed his own foundation, which awarded grants to students and working mus. In '96 recipients in the latter category were comps. Maria Schneider of NYC and Kim Portnoy of St. Louis. Rec. LP, *Bix, Fats, Duke*, Atl. '56, reissued on Modern Concepts. Favs: Ellington, Billy Moore Jr., Eddie Durham. CDs: SB; ChartMaker, Modern Concepts; w. Patty McGovern (Inter.).

TANA, AKIRA, dms, perc, kybd; b. San José, CA, 3/14/52. Mother pl. koto; cousin pl. baroque org. Raised in Palo Alto, Calif. Att. Harvard 1970–4. Stud. w. Alan Dawson '73; later w. Vic Firth, Fred Buda at New Engl. Cons. Pl. w. Geo. Russell, Paul Winter '77; Helen Humes '77–8; Jaki Byard, Sonny Stitt, Hubert Laws, Sonny Rollins '78; Art Farmer '78–86; Johnny Hartman, Milt Jackson '79; Jimmy and Percy Heath '79–82; Stanley Cowell '80; Sylvia Syms '80–4; Zoot Sims '80–5; Al Cohn '82–5; Jimmy Rowles, Slide Hampton '83; Cedar Walton, Van Dyke Parks '84; Charles Aznavour '84–5; Jim Hall '85–6; Art Farmer–Benny Golson Jazztet '85–7; Maurice Hines, Lena Horne '86; Geo. Coleman '86–7; V. D. Parks '87–91; Paquito D'Rivera '88–9; James Moody fr. '89; Chita Rivera, Frank Wess '90; Ray Bryant, J. J. Johnson, Manhattan Tap '91. Tana has co-led TanaReid w. Rufus Reid fr. '91. He has taught at Queens and Wm. Paterson Colls. Moved to Belmont, Calif. '99. Favs: K. Clarke, Blakey, P.J. Jones, Elvin Jones, Tony Williams. Fests: all major fr. late '70s in Eur., Japan. Film: acted in *Collision Course* w. Jay Leno. CDs: PW; w. TanaReid (Evid.; Conc.); A. Farmer (Conc.; SN); J. Moody (Novus); Jim Hall; J. J. Johnson; Tete Montoliu (Conc.); Carl Fontana (Up.); Giacomo Gates (DMP); Rob Schneiderman (Res.); Warne Marsh (Inter.); C. Roditi (Mile.; Cand.); Zoot Sims (Pab.); Asian American Trio (PW).

TANIA MARIA (Tania Marie Reis Leite), pno, voc, comp; b. São Luis, Brazil, 5/9/48. Father was guitarist and singer. Stud. classical pno. ages 7–13. From age 13, led gp. organized by fath. Rec. five albums while still in her teens; moved to Paris in 1974, perf. in clubs and tour. extensively; rec. for Eur. labels '74–81. Perf. at NJF '75. Charlie Byrd heard her at an Austral. JF and recommended her to Carl Jefferson of Conc. Records. Moved to NYC, made first rec. for

Concord '81. She had great commercial success w. rec. *Come with Me* '83. Rec. for Manh., Cap., and BN in '80s, then ret. to Conc. '93. Fav. pno: Oscar Peterson, Bill Evans, Luiz Eca; voc: Sarah Vaughan, Ella Fitzgerald, Dinah Washington, Nat King Cole. Fests: all major fr. '74. CDs: Conc.; BN; Cap.; Manh.; w. M. Petrucciani (BN).

TAPSCOTT, HORACE, pno, comp; b. Houston, TX, 4/6/34; d. Los Angeles, CA, 2/27/99. Studied pno. w. moth. at age 6, also learned tbn. Moved to LA in 1945. Stud. w. Gerald Wilson (tbn.); Lloyd Reese. Pl. in hs band; Gerald Wilson orch. start. in '51; AAF band '53–7. Tour. w. Lionel Hampton, pl. tbn. and pno. '58–9; resettled in LA. Led Pan-Afrikan People's Arkestra '59–82 and many small gps.; pl. the Vanguard in NYC in the '90s. A remarkably original pnst. comp., straddling the line between advanced bop and free jazz while retaining his own mus. personality. His gps. incl. Arthur Blythe, Azar Lawrence, Roberto Miranda, Michael Session, and Thurman Green. His comps. are the focus of Sonny Criss's *Sonny's Dream*. Favs: Randy Weston, Andrew Hill, Mal Waldron. Rec. solo pno. dates for Nimbus label in '80s. CDs: Arab.; hatArt; w. Criss (Prest.); Blythe (Novus).

TARDY, GREG (GREGORY JOHN), tnr sax, B-flat sop cl, fl; b. New Orleans, LA, 2/3/66. Father an opera singer in NO; moth. an opera singer turned jazz singer who perf. regularly in Milwaukee and St. Louis. Rec. two CDS. Sist. classical fl.; bro., tpt., began jazz before Greg but, like their father, gave up musical career to help support family. In last two yrs. of hs, Greg stud. cl. priv. w. Carol Tilbury. Stud. classical cl. perf. at Carroll Coll., Waukesha, Wisc. 1984–86 and at U. of Wisc.-Milwaukee '86–88; jazz harm. at Wisc. Cons. of Mus. '88; U. of New Orleans '91; but "learned more from experience than at any of these schools." Switched to tnr. sax at age 21. Start. pl. in funk/fusion bands in Milwaukee to raise money to finish classical cl. course. "Discovered jazz and eventually took it seriously." Worked w. pop bands fr. rock, rap, and reggae to blues, country, Latin, and gospel in Milwaukee, St. Louis, NO '85–91. NO bands incl. Neville Bros, Allan Toussaint. Pl. w. Nichols Payton Qnt; also occ. gigs w. Ellis Marsalis, Olympia Brass Band '92–3; Elvin Jones Jazz Machine '93–5. Freelanced w. John Hicks, Jay McShann, TanaReid, Roy Hargrove, Rashied Ali, Brian Lynch, Steve Coleman, Russell Gunn, Dave Schumacher '95–6. Pl. w. Jason Lindner bb, Omer Avital Sxt. '96–8; own qnt., Tom Harrell gp. fr. '97. Bet. '84 and '90 worked in a steel foundry, fireplace company, food service jobs, selling shoes at Kmart, gardening, on a strawberry farm, et al. Counselor at Maine Jazz Camp, summers '96–7; also taught cl., sax, priv. Favs: Shorter, Hawkins, Coltrane; comp: Harrell, Shorter, Donald Brown. Awards: while in hs, All-State Orch. feat cl. soloist; also All-State Band; offered full-tuition scholarship to U. of Wisc.-Madison. Fr. '91 has pl. in Eur., Japan, Brazil. Fest: Bell Atlantic w. Dave Douglas '99. Rec. debut was a gospel session in Milwaukee. First rec. as a lead. for Du Bat label '92. CDs: Imp.; Du Bat; w. Steve Coleman; Harrell (RCA); Gunn (Muse; High.); Andy LaVerne (Steep.).

TATE, BUDDY (GEORGE HOLMES), saxes, cl, fl; b. Sherman, TX, 2/22/15; d. Chandler, AZ, 2/11/01. First prof. gig 1927. Made rec. debut w. Troy Floyd in San Antonio, Tex. '31. Worked w. Terrence Holder '30–3; Count Basie '34; Andy Kirk '34–5; Nat Towles '35–9. Replaced Herschel Evans in Count Basie band '39. Pl. w. Basie '39–49; briefly w. Lucky Millinder, Hot Lips Page, Jimmy Rushing '50–2. Formed own band '53; in res. at Celebrity Club '53–mid '70s. Gigs at Savoy Ballroom, Biltmore, and Waldorf-Astoria hotels. Led qt. and spt. fr. early '70s; many tours of Eur. and Japan. Also tour. Eur. w. Saints and Sinners, and pl. occ. w. Basie. Made docu. film w. Roger Vadim in Paris '74. Co-led gp. Two Tenor Boogie w. Paul Quinichette at West End, NYC '75. Pl. w. Jay McShann, Jim Galloway in Canada late '70s. Toured w. Texas Tenors w. Illinois Jacquet '80s. Also perf. w. Countsmen in NYC. Pl. w. Lionel Hampton's Golden Men of Jazz at Blue Note, NYC '91. Despite his ill health in the early '90s, Tate made a rare app. in '93 at the Long Island JF, but was unable to play in the late '90s. Favs: Arnett Cobb, Illinois Jacquet, Stan Getz, Lester Young. Polls: rec. of yr., Academie du Disque Français '68. Fests: all major. CDs: Muse; Story.; Chiaro; BL; B&B; NW; Sack.; Res.; Prest.; w. C. Basie (BB; Hep; Col.); L. Hampton (Dec.; Tel.); I. Jacquet (BN); Joe Turner (Evid.); Buck Clayton (Prest.; Col.; Mos.); Milt Buckner (B&B; Prog.); Ruby Braff (BL); Al Cohn; Concord All-Stars (Conc.); Sweets Edison; Nancy Harrow (Cand.); Slim Gaillard (Verve; Hep); B. Goodman (Lond.; MM); Milt Hinton; Flip Phillips (Chiaro.); Helen Humes (Muse); J. Rushing (Vang.); Coleman Hawkins (Prest.).

TATE, ERSKINE, vln, leader; b. Memphis, TN, 12/19/1895; d. Chicago, IL, 12/17/78. Moved to Chi. while in his teens. Stud. at Amer. Cons. of Mus.; debut on vln. 1912. Led orch. at Vendome Theater '19–28, later at various theater and ballrooms. His sidemen incl. Louis Armstrong (who was asked to sw. fr. cnt. to tpt. in the band for appearance's sake); Earl Hines; Punch Miller; Freddie Keppard; Buster Bai-

ley; Milt Hinton; Jimmy Bertrand. A skilled teacher on various instruments, Tate ceased perf. in the mid '40s to concentrate on tutoring. His orch. rec. for Okeh and Vocalion in the '20s. CDs: w. L. Armstrong (Col.).

TATE, FRANK EASTMAN, bs; b. Washington, DC, 7/18/43. Att. Greensboro Coll. (B.A. bus. admin. 1965). Pl. tpt. w. Burt Massengale Orch. '64–7; Massengale sw. him to bs. Freelanced in Wash., D.C. '68–72; then led house band at Blues Alley '72–4, accomp. Wild Bill Davison; Zoot Sims–Al Cohn; Hank Jones; Teddy Wilson; Eddie Daniels; Bobby Hackett; Urbie Green; etc. Pl. w. Hackett '74. Moved to NYC '75; pl. w. Marian McPartland and freelanced w. Milt Jackson; Joe Venuti; Zoot Sims; Ray Bryant; Jimmy Rowles; John Bunch; Benny Goodman; Red Norvo; etc. Worked w. Ronny Whyte since '77; Pearl Bailey–Louis Bellson '85–90; Ruby Braff, Howard Alden–Dan Barrett since late '80s; Bobby Short in '90s. Favs: Ray Brown, Milt Hinton, Scott LaFaro. Fests: Eur. since '81. TV: apps. w. P. Bailey, Dave McKenna, Teddy Wilson, Alden-Barrett. CDs: w. Bobby Short (Tel.); H. Alden; Ruby Braff (Conc.); Zoot Sims (Pab.); Dardanelle–S. Stewart (Stash).

TATE, GRADY, dms, voc; b. Durham, NC, 1/14/32. Self-taught fr. age 5. Stud. jazz drumming while in air force 1951–5. After discharge ret. to Durham to att. N. Caro. Coll. Moved to Wash., D.C. '59 and pl. there w. Wild Bill Davis late '59–62; then moved to NYC. Pl. w. Jerome Richardson, Quincy Jones Orch. '62–3. Worked extensively as studio mus. fr. early '60s. Pl. w. Cy Coleman on Les Crane TV show for three mos. '65; Billy Taylor Trio '66. Also freelanced in '60s w. Duke Ellington; Count Basie; Oliver Nelson; Bill Evans; Jimmy Smith; Wes Montgomery; Stanley Turrentine; Stan Getz; Roland Kirk; Donald Byrd; Kenny Burrell; J. J. Johnson; Oscar Peterson; Lalo Schifrin; Kai Winding; Zoot Sims; others. Toured w. Peggy Lee '67, then pl. w. NBC *Tonight Show* Orch. '68–74. Other singers Tate has accomp. incl. Sarah Vaughan; Ella Fitzgerald; Astrud Gilberto; Chris Connor; Ray Charles; Blossom Dearie; Lena Horne. Active as voc. fr. '72. An extremely versatile dmr., Tate cont. to freelance extensively. Fests: all major fr. '63. TV: Les Crane '65; *Tonight Show* '68–74; Joey Bishop, Merv Griffin, Joe Franklin, *Black Journal* '70s. CDs: Mile.; w. John Hicks (Novus); J. Smith (Verve; BN; Mile.); Stan Getz (Verve; Col.); J. J Johnson (BB); J. Hodges (Verve; Imp.); G. Mulligan; Ray Brown (Conc.); B. Evans; K. Burrell (Verve); O. Nelson (BB; Imp.); L. Hampton (MM; Tel.); Geo. Shearing (Tel.); Zoot Sims; S. Vaughan; Benny Carter (Pab.).

TATUM, ART (ARTHUR JR.), pno; b. Toledo, OH, 10/13/09; d. Los Angeles, CA, 11/5/56. Born into a musical family, he stud. vln. and gtr. bef. concentrating on pno. at mus. institutes in Columbus and Toledo. Blind in one eye and w. very limited vision in the other, he was largely self-taught, using Braille, listening to radio and recs. and local musicians; his primary jazz infl. was Fats Waller, his main pop source Lee Sims. Made prof. debut in 1926; hired by Speed Webb '28; had his own radio series '29–30. In '32 he went to NYC as accomp. for Adelaide Hall, and while there rec. his first solo sess. in March '33, pl. four tunes that revealed a creative and technical mastery already far beyond that of any of his contemporaries. Fr. '34 to '41 he rec. several sess. for Dec., mostly solos but also a small swing band date '37; two memorable sess. w. blues singer Joe Turner '41. An early perf. on NYC's 52nd St. in the '30s, he was internationally known by '38 when he app. at Ciro's Club in London. He was praised by many classical pnsts. (He and Horowitz were mutual admirers who attended each other's concerts.) Earned the lifelong respect of fellow musicians; won the *Esq.* Gold Award '44 (ironically, never a *DB* Readers poll); perf. at first jazz concert ever given at the Metropolitan Opera House Jan. '44 and a Commodore rec. sess. w. Esq. All-Stars, released shortly afterward. To many, Tatum's most memorable period began when he pl. 52nd St. clubs accomp. by Tiny Grimes, gtr., and Slam Stewart, bs. The interaction among these three was masterful. Later Tatum worked on his own but reorganized w. Everett Barksdale replacing Grimes. Despite the acclaim and respect he enjoyed, Tatum's jobs were largely confined to clubs; he pl. relatively few concerts, and when he did play a concert tour in the US, it was not on his own but as part of a package with Stan Kenton's Orch., Shorty Rogers' gp., and others. Tatum's film apps. were brief: a 13–sec. solo in a jam session scene in *The Fabulous Dorseys* '47 and a fleeting app. in a '44 *March of Time* segment. He rec. only intermittently bef. '54, when Norman Granz produced a long series of solo and gp. sessions, the latter incl. Louie Bellson; Benny Carter; Red Callender; Buddy DeFranco; Sweets Edison; Roy Eldridge; Lionel Hampton; Jo Jones; Barney Kessel; Buddy Rich; and Ben Webster. Pianists of every school fr. swing to the avant-garde continue to be inspired by Tatum. Book: *Art Tatum: A Guide to His Recorded Music,* a discography by Arnold Laubach and Ray Spencer '82. CDs: Pab.; Verve; Dec.; Cap.; Story.; M&A; BB; Col.; JVC; BL; High.; w. Esq. All-Amer. Poll Winners (BB); B. Holiday (Story.); L. Armstrong (Class.); w. Coleman Hawkins in *The Commodore Story* (Comm.).

TAYLOR, ARTHUR S. JR. (aka A. T.), dms, comp, lead; b. NYC, 4/6/29; d. NYC, 2/6/95. Studied w. Chick Morrison. Pl. w. teenage band in Harlem's Sugar Hill neighborhood w. Sonny Rollins, Jackie McLean, Kenny Drew. First prof. job w. Howard McGhee in 1948; then worked w. Coleman Hawkins '50–1; Buddy DeFranco '52; Bud Powell '53; Geo. Wallington, Art Farmer '54; Powell and Wallington trios again '55–6; Gigi Gryce–Donald Byrd Jazz Lab gp.; also led own Taylor's Wailers at The Pad in Greenwich Village '56. Pl. w. Miles Davis on and off '55–7. During this period he also worked and rec. often w. Red Garland's trio and qnt. Tour. France, Belg. w. Byrd, Bobby Jaspar, July-Dec. '58. In '59 he rec. w. J. Coltrane and Thelonious Monk. Moved to Paris '63 where he stud. w. Kenny Clarke for four yrs. Worked w. Don Byas; Ben Webster; Dexter Gordon; Kenny Drew; but most often w. Johnny Griffin in Eur.; and made periodic visits to the US. Based in Belgium fr. '70, he ret. to the US in '84. Led gp. in Bud Powell tribute for UN Jazz Society '84, which was incorporated as part of a Powell tribute at NJF-NY '85. In '91 he revived Taylor's Wailers w. such sidemen as Abraham Burton, alto sax; Willie Williams, tnr.; Marc Cary, Jacky Terrasson, pno.; Tyler Mitchell, bs. From a crisply swinging, archetypical bebop dmr., reflecting a personal blend of Clarke, Roach, and Blakey, Taylor grew in his role as a leader in the '90s to shape and inspire his young soloists with fiery, sophisticated patterns. Favs: J. C. Heard, Philly Joe Jones. Fests: numerous major fests. incl. NJF-NY '92. Films: w. Monk, *Liaisons Dangereuses* '59; w. Mal Waldron, D. Gillespie, *The Cool World* '63. Radio: own interview show on WKCR, NYC '84. Book: *Notes and Tones* '77, rev. ed., Da Capo '92. Rec. debut w. O. Pettiford for Mercer '51. CDs: Verve; Enja; Prest.; NJ; w. B. Powell (BN; Verve); C. Parker (Verve); Coltrane (Prest.; Atl.); T. Monk (Riv.); M. Davis (Prest.; Col.); D. Gordon (BN); Gene Ammons; Red Garland; J. McLean; S. Rollins; Mal Waldron; G. Wallington (Prest.); J. Griffin (Timel.); Tristano (Atl.).

TAYLOR, BILLY (WILLIAM SR.), bs, tba; b. Washington, DC, 4/3/06; d. Fairfax, VA, 9/2/86. Son, Billy Jr., was also a bassist. Start. on tba.; moved to NYC 1924, pl. w. Elmer Snowden '25; Charlie Johnson '27–9; Duke Ellington '28. Tour. w. McKinney's Cotton Pickers '29–31; worked again w. Johnson '32–3; Fats Waller '34; also briefly w. Fletcher Henderson. Best known for his subsequent stay w. Ellington '35–40, incl. the band's dual bs. period, when he pl. alongside Hayes Alvis and/or Jimmy Blanton. Worked w. Coleman Hawkins '40; Red Allen '40–1; Joe Sullivan '42; Cootie Williams '44; Barney Bigard

'44–5; Benny Morton '45; freelanced in NYC w. Cozy Cole '45, '49 bef. ret. to Wash., D.C. Taylor was greatly admired as a bassist in the fluent tradition of Blanton. Rec. his own "Taylor Made" w. Bennie Morton '34. Rec. for Col. w. Bigard, Cootie Williams, and Johnny Hodges gps. '36–9. Own gp., Big Eight, for Keynote '44. CDs: w. Ellington (Col.; BB); Bessie Smith (Col.); Lester Young (Sav.); R. Eldridge; Joe Turner (Dec.); Benny Carter; L. Hampton; McKinney's Cotton Pickers; J. R. Morton (BB); Charlie Johnson (Hot 'N Sweet); Buck Clayton (Riv.).

TAYLOR, BILLY (WILLIAM EDWARD JR.), pno, comp, arr; b. Greenville, NC, 7/24/21. Father sang, pl. pno. and brass instruments, and dir. choir. Began on dms., gtr., sax. Stud classical pno. in Wash., D.C. w. Elmira Streets, Henry Grant; w. Undine Moore at Virginia St. Coll. 1938–42 (B. Mus. '42). Later stud. w. Richard McClanahan in NYC; earned Ph.D. fr. U. of Mass. '75. First gig w. Ben Webster at Three Deuces '44. Pl. w. Billie Holiday, Stuff Smith, Eddie South, Dizzy Gillespie, Foots Thomas '44–5; Cozy Cole in *Seven Lively Arts* at Billy Rose Theater '45; Machito briefly '46; Slam Stewart at Three Deuces '46. Tour. Eur. w. Don Redman '46, then freelanced in Paris '46–7. Pl. in duo w. organist Bob Wyatt '48, then led own qt. '49–50. In '50 Artie Shaw fronted Taylor's gp., calling it the Gramercy 5. House pnst. at Birdland '51. Led own trio fr. '52, beginning w. Earl May, bs., and Charlie Smith, dms.; over the yrs. sidemen have incl. some of the top bassists and drummers. Wrote several instructional books, also articles for *DB, Sat. Review, Esq.*, and other publ. in '50s. Jazz dj on WLIB, WNEW in NYC '59–66; prog. dir. for WLIB '66–9. Perf. concerts and lectured in schs. fr. '62. Organized wkshp. series w. Geo. Wein at NJF and Hunter Coll. '64. Founder, president of Jazzmobile fr. '65. Hosted jazz TV show in NYC '66. Mus. dir. for David Frost TV show '69–72; general manager at WLIB briefly in early '70s, then founded Billy Taylor Productions, a publishing and advertising production co., '73. While cont. to lead his trio, he hosted numerous jazz radio and TV progs. in the '70s and '80s, incl. several progs. on the PBS and BRAVO networks and a 13–segment radio show *Taylor Made Piano*. Arts correspondent for CBS *Sunday Morning* since '81. Portrayed Jelly Roll Morton in the CBS prog. *You Are There*, and app. in TV commercials, incl. McDonald's, Pepsi Cola, Budweiser. Own concert series at Metropolitan Museum of Art, NYC; programs at Kennedy Center, Wash., DC, Founded own rec. labels BETCO '87, Taylor-Made '88. Recipient of an Emmy and numerous other awards and honorary degrees. Comp. credits incl.

Peaceful Warrior, in honor of M. L. King; *Make A Joyful Noise*, a suite commissioned by Tufts U.; *Suite for Jazz and Orch.*; and more than 300 songs, incl. "I Wish I Knew How It Would Feel To Be Free." Also comp. ballet mus. for B'way show *Your Arms Too Short To Box with God* '76; music for TV incl. *Sesame Street*. Has taught at Yale U., Manh. Sch. of Mus., C. W. Post Coll., Howard U., U. of Calif., U. of Mass., Fredonia St. U., and numerous clinics in the US and abroad. Books: *Jazz Piano: A Jazz History* (Wm. C. Brown Co.); instructional books incl. *Sketches for Jazz Trio, Ragtime Pno. Solos, Mambo Pno. Solos, Billy Taylor's Bebop, Combo Arranging* (all Hansen Publ.). Favs: Art Tatum; arrs: Duke Ellington, Billy Strayhorn. Polls: *DB* New Star '53; Lifetime Achievement '84. TV: CBS *Sunday Morning*; David Frost; *That Was the Week That Was*; PBS incl. *Memories of Eubie, Swingin' the Blues, Salute to Duke, Jazz at Spoleto*; also *Today, Tonight Show*, etc. CDs: Ark.; Taylor-Made; Conc.; Prest.; Riv.; Sav.; FS; GRP; w. Turtle Island String Qt. (WH); Q. Jones (Imp.); O. Pettiford (Sav.); Coleman Hawkins (FS; Story.); Lucky Thompson (FS).

TAYLOR, CECIL PERCIVAL, pno, comp; b. NYC, 3/15/29. Mother pl. pno. Began on pno. at age 5. Stud. at N.Y. Coll. of Mus., then at New Engl. Cons. 1952–6. Gigs w. Hot Lips Page; Lawrence Brown, Johnny Hodges; then pl. and rec. w. qt., incl. Steve Lacy, Buell Neidlinger, Dennis Charles '56–7. This gp. held an extended engagement at the Five Spot and app. at NJF '57. Led qt. w. Archie Shepp, Neidlinger, Charles at Five Spot and in Jack Gelber's play *The Connection* '61. In the '60s Taylor's sidemen incl. Shepp; Albert Ayler; Jimmy Lyons; Sunny Murray; Roswell Rudd; Andrew Cyrille. Tour. Eur. w. Lyons, Murray '62. Co-founded Jazz Comp. Guild '64–5. Although he received much critical acclaim for his impressive technique and orig. ideas, Taylor was freq. unemployed and rec. little in the late '60s and '70s. Tour. Eur. w. Lyons, Cyrille, Sam Rivers '69. Taught courses in Black Mus. at U. of Wisc. '70–1 but resigned after failing two-thirds of his students for lack of seriousness; taught at Antioch Coll., Ohio '72–3; Glassboro St. Coll., N.J. '73. Tour. as solo pnst. and leader fr. '73. Worked w. Friedrich Gulda '76. Carnegie Hall concert w. Mary Lou Williams '77; assoc. w. dancer Dianne McIntyre '77, '79; comp. ballet mus. for Baryshnikov '79. Pl. duet concerts w. Max Roach at Columbia U. '79. Pl. w. int'l all-star gp. incl. Enrico Rava; Tomasz Stanko; John Tchicai '84; Art Ens. of Chi. '85; Berlin JF w. many different gps. fr. bb to individual dmrs., incl. Tony Oxley; Louis Moholo; Han Bennink '88; a recent combo, the Feel Trio, incl. Oxley and bs.

William Parker. Awarded a Guggenheim fellowship in '73. Favs: Thelonious Monk, Duke Ellington, Horace Silver. Polls: *DB* Rec. of Year, Hall of Fame '75. Fests: Eur. fr. '62 Film: French docu. '66. CDs: BN; Cont.; Sound Hills; FMP; Leo; SN; Revenant; Konnex; NW; hatArt; Cand.; BL; w. Art Ensemble of Chi. (Col.); J. Coltrane (BN); G. Evans (Imp.); Tony Williams (Col.); Mary Lou Williams (Pab.)

TAYLOR, GENE (CALVIN EUGENE), bs; b. Toledo, OH, 3/19/29; d. Sarasota, FL, 12/22/01. Moved to Det. in 1936. Pl. sousaphone and pno. bef. sw. to bs. Moved to NYC '58; pl. w. Horace Silver '58–64; Blue Mitchell '64–6; Nina Simone, who rec. his song, "Why (The King of Love is Dead)" '66–8. Pl. and sang w. folksinger Judy Collins '68–76. Worked in '70s w. Duke Jordan; Junior Mance; Billy Taylor; Lou Donaldson; Stanley Turrentine; Buddy Rich–Louis Bellson; etc. Taught mus. in NYC publ. schs. '85–8. Pl. w. Barry Harris fr. '70s. Favs: Ray Brown, Percy Heath. Fests: Eur., Japan, etc. TV: Mike Douglas, Dick Cavett, *Tonight Show* w. Collins, Simone. CDs: w. H. Silver; Duke Pearson; Blue Mitchell; S. Turrentine (BN); N. Simone (RCA); Miles Davis (Phon.); Coleman Hawkins (Enja).

TAYLOR, MARK ANTHONY, dms; b. London, England, 11/7/62. Self-taught at age 5; began sitting in w. local bands at 9. Turned prof. at 16; worked w. Ronnie Scott qnt., Stan Tracey qt. and bb, backing up visiting mus., incl. Kenny Barron; George Coleman; Monty Alexander; George Cables; Teddy Edwards; James Moody; Eddie Davis; Pharoah Sanders; Kenny Drew; Philip Catherine–N-H. Ø. Pedersen; Ray Brown; Lew Tabackin. Tour. Eur. extensively since 1985. Moved to NYC in mid '90s. An extremely hard-swinging dmr. Favs: P. J. Jones, Elvin Jones, Art Blakey, Max Roach, Roy Haynes, Billy Higgins. Fest: Cork JF, Ireland, w. Franco Ambrosetti–George Gruntz qnt. '94. Film: *Stormy Monday* w. Sting. CDs: w. L. Tabackin (Conc.); Spike Robinson–Louis Stewart (Hep.); Herb Geller (FS).

TAYLOR, MARTIN, gtr; b. Harlow, Essex, England 10/20/56. Father, Buck Taylor, prof. bs. pl. Self-taught fr. age 4; pl. in father's band at 13; first prof. job at 16 on cruise ship betw. Engl. and US. Worked w. Stephane Grappelli fr. 1979 to '90, rec. and tour. the world, incl. an app. on the *Tonight Show* and a Royal Command Perf. in London. Dur. same period tour. w. Buddy DeFranco, making two albums. In '89 he joined The Great Guitars w. Barney Kessel, Charlie Byrd; also worked in Austral. w. Joe Pass. Of his twelve albums w. Grappelli, three feat. Yehudi Menuhin. Films incl. Louis Malle's *Milou en Mai*;

comp. music for BBC docu. *Where Eagles Fly*; many TV commercials; plus numerous TV apps. w. Grappelli. Pl. NJF-NY w. Grappelli '84. Voted top gtrst. in British Jazz Awards '87–91; *DB* TDWR '83. Has given seminars and master classes in US and Eur., also at U. of Ghana and Cons. of Mus., Western Austral. Tour. exclusively as soloist in '90s. Video: *Martin Taylor, Jazz Guitarist* (Warner Chappell). CDs: Linn; w. Grappelli (Linn); DeFranco (Hep; ProJazz).

TCHICAI, JOHN MARTIN, tnr, sop, alto sax, bs-cl; b. Copenhagen, Denmark, 4/28/36. Father a Congolese diplomat, moth. Danish. Raised in Aarhus, Den. Began on vln. at age 10, then sw. to alto and cl. at 16. Stud. alto for three yrs. at Royal Cons., Copenhagen. Pl. at fests in Helsinki and Warsaw, where he met Archie Shepp and Bill Dixon, who encouraged him to come to US. In NYC worked as restaurant chef and formed N.Y. Contemporary Five w. Shepp, Don Cherry 1963; other sidemen incl. bs. Ronnie Boykins or Don Moore, dmrs. Sunny Murray or J. C. Moses. In '63 the gp. tour. Sweden, where it rec. mus. for the film *Future One*. Co-led N.Y. Art Qt. w. Rowell Rudd, Lewis Worrell, Milford Graves '64–5. Member of Jazz Composers Guild '60s. Rec. *Ascension* w. John Coltrane '65; also rec. w. Shepp, Albert Ayler. Ret. to Den. '66. Pl. in Eur. w. Don Cherry, Gunter Hampel; led wkshp. ens. Cadentia Nova Danica '67–71. Cut down on perf. in order to focus on teaching '72–7. Dur. this time Tchicai pl. w. Johnny Dyani; Instant Composers Pool; Geo. Gruntz; Irene Schweitzer. Pl. w. Strange Bros. '76–81. Ret. to pl. full-time '77. Pl. w. Pierre Dorge's New Jungle Orch. fr. '77. Heard mainly on tnr. and sop. saxes fr. '83. Also pl. in '80s w. Chris McGregor's Brotherhood of Breath; all-sax gp. De Zes Winden; J. Dyani. Reunited w. N.Y. Art Qt. at Bell Atlantic JF, NYC '99. CDs: Steep; Freedom; BS; Enja; w. J. Coltrane; A. Shepp (Imp.); J. Dyani; P. Dorge (Steep.); Albert Ayler; N.Y. Art Qt. (ESP); Charles Gayle (Silk.); Cecil Taylor (SN).

TEAGARDEN, CHARLIE (CHARLES), tpt; b. Vernon, TX, 7/9/13; d. Las Vegas, NV, 12/10/84. Brother of Jack ("Big T"), he was sometimes known as "Little T." Prof. debut w. Herb Brooks' Oklahoma Joy Boys; tour. w. Frank Williams' Oklahomans. To NYC, where he joined Ben Pollack 1929–30; Red Nichols '30–31; Roger Wolfe Kahn '32; w. Paul Whiteman fr. '33 to '40, taking leave of absence in '36 to pl. w. his bro. and Frank Trumbauer in "Three T's" gp. at Hickory House and other NYC clubs. Occ. pl. in Jack's bb dur. '40s. After army service, join. Harry James '46 and Jimmy Dorsey '48–51; then rejoin. Jack Teagarden; studio band led by Jerry Gray in late '51; also rejoin. Ben Pollack briefly. Own trio w. Ray Bauduc, Jess Stacy '51–2. Many dates w. Bob Crosby's Bob Cats '54–8; then settled in LV, freelancing extensively but gradually withdrawing fr. pl., taking an executive job with the local Mus. Union. His clear tone and style suggested a Bix Beiderbecke infl. CDs: w. J. Teagarden (BB; Dec.; Mos.); B. Goodman (Dec.); B. Holiday (Col.); Fats Waller; Red Nichols (ASV); Joe Venuti (Yazoo).

TEAGARDEN, JACK (WELDON JOHN), tbn, voc, lead; b. Vernon, TX, 8/29/05; d. New Orleans, LA 1/15/64. Musical family; fath. pl. tpt., moth. pno.; his sist. Norma and younger bros., Charles and Cub, pl. in his band at various times. Studied pno. at 5; took up tbn. 1915. Infl. by blues and spirituals and by Peck Kelley, a pnst. in whose band he pl. '21–2. Led own band in KC, worked w. Doc Ross, Willard Robison. Moved to NYC in '27; made rec. debut w. Eddie Condon '28. Pl. w. Ben Pollack band fr. June '28 to May '33, also freelanced on many rec. dates w. Red Nichols; Louis Armstrong; Eddie Condon. Gained prominence while w. Paul Whiteman band fr. Dec. '33 to Dec. '38. Dur. this time he also pl. w. "The Three Ts," a contingent fr. the band w. Charlie Teagarden and Frank Trumbauer. From Jan. '39 until late '46 Teagarden led a bb and gp, and won the *Esq.* Gold Award, app. w. an all-star band in an *Esq.* concert at the Metropolitan Opera House, NYC. From '47 to 51, he tour. w. Louis Armstrong and extensively w. his own traditional band. Reunited w. his bro. Charlie, sister Norma, and mother at the '63 MJF. Soon thereafter his health declined and he died of bronchial pneumonia. Teagarden's importance as a tbnst. and singer kept him in the forefront almost from the time of his arrival in NYC. He associated w. black musicians more closely than most of his white contemporaries. He used various mutes, and occ. pl. with the bell of the tbn. removed. His control of the upper register was exceptional, his use of trills remarkable, and his melodic sense impeccable. Teagarden was featured in such films as *Me and the Boys* '29; *Thanks a Million* '35; *Birth of the Blues* '41; *The Strip* '51; *Glory Alley* '52; and *Jazz on a Summer's Day* '58. CDs: Arb.; BB; Dec.; Mos.; Laser.; Jazz.; w. Louis Armstrong (BB; Col.; Dec.; Mos.); B. Holiday (Col.; Story.); Bessie Smith (Col.); Esq. All-Amer. Poll Winners; Metronome All-Stars (BB); E. Condon (Dec.); Cap. Jazzmen (Jazz Unlimited); Pee Wee Russell (Comm.); B. Goodman (Dec.; BB); Muggsy Spanier; Fats Waller (BB); Rex Stewart; Adrian Rollini (Aff.); J. Venuti (Yazoo); Red Nichols (Tax).

TEAGARDEN, NORMA (Norma Teagarden Friedlander), pno.; b. Vernon, TX, 4/28/11. Sister of Jack and Charlie Teagarden. Began stud. vln. but soon sw. to pno. Pl. w. territory bands in New Mex. Made rec. debut in NYC w. bro. Jack for Decca in 1944. Perf. in gps. w. Matty Matlock; Muggsy Spanier; Wild Bill Davison; and Turk Murphy. Tour. Netherlands '77; Engl. '86; app. on NPR radio w. Marian McPartland; received many awards incl. Certificate of Honor fr. Int'l Inst. for Study of Women in Jazz. Guest of honor at Dixieland fests throughout US. Perf. and rec. at MJF. Favs: Dick Hyman, Paul Smith, Dave McKenna. CDs: w. Jack Teagarden (Arb.; Dec.); E. Condon (Jazz.).

TEDESCO, THOMAS, gtr, educ; b. Los Angeles, CA, 2/2/43. Studied liberal arts at U. of Nebraska 1964; formal mus. studies fr. '68. By '73 he was teaching gtr., bs., theory, and comp. classes in LA. Perf. w. Bobby Bradford; Ray Draper; John Carter; and others; received a degree fr. Santa Monica Coll. and a B.A. in mus. comp. fr. Cal State Dominguez Hills. In a review of his '83 Nimbus album, *Tommy Tedesco and Ocean, DB* called him "a flawless technician who tends toward intricate, yet never routinely virtuosic, single-note lines."

TEDESCO, TOMMY (THOMAS J.), gtr; b. Niagara Falls, NY, 7/3/30; d. Northridge, CA, 11/10/97. Began pl. gtr. at age 11. While at Niagara U. at age 22 auditioned for Ralph Marterie and went on road w. his bb through Oct. 1953. Moved to LA in '50s. Led own trio at the Lighthouse; pl. w. Joe Burton trio; worked w. Dave Pell; Chico Hamilton; Bill Holman; Mel Lewis; Buddy Collette; in '60s w. Benny Goodman; Shelly Manne; Red Callender; Oliver Nelson; in '70s w. John Lewis; Ray Brown; Herbie Hancock; Harvey Mason; Dave Grusin; Tom Scott. In '80s, primarily w. his own gp. on recs. and in live apps. Favs: Kessel, Howard Roberts, J. Raney, Farlow. Called the Most Recorded Guitarist in the history of the music business, he began working in the studios in the '50s. Pl. on the soundtracks of *The Deer Hunter; The Godfather; Field of Dreams.* TV: as a regular on *Fernwood Tonight.* As educ., in charge of studio gtr. studies at Mus. Institute of Technology. Cond. clinics for Fender, Gibson, and Yamaha. Wrote many gtr. books incl. autobiography, *Confessions for a Guitar Player*; articles for *Guitar Player* magazine. Elected to *Guitar Player* magazine Hall of Fame '74. Received NARAS Award '78, for the Mus. Business of Rec. Rec. w. Sinatra, Ella Fitzgerald, Elvis Presley, Barbra Streisand. LP: *Hot Coles* w. Manne (Flying Dutchman). CDs: Disc.; w. Fitzgerald (Pab.).

TEELE, PHIL (PHILIP ALLEN), bs, tbn, contrabass tbn, euph, ophicleide, comp; b. Ottumwa, IA,

6/6/42. Began wind studies in LA schs. at age 13. Between 1958 and '64, he stud. bs-tbn. w. Ernie Smith, George Roberts, and Dick Nash. Perf. in late '50s with Onzy Matthews; George Andrews; Gerald Wilson. After pl. w. the Army Norad Band '61–63, ret. to LA and perf. w. Tex Beneke, Bob Knight. Between '73 and 89 tour. in Japan, Eur. w. Akiyoshi-Tabackin bb. Dur. '80s and '90s worked w. bands of Bill Watrous; Shorty Rogers; Gordon Brisker; Vinny Golia; Jack Elliot; smaller ensembles w. Steve Huffsteter, Bruce Fowler. Co-founder w. B. Fowler of gp., Enormous Bones. Taught master classes at USC, Cal State-Northridge; clinics and seminars in Japan. Favs: George Roberts, Kenny Shroyer, Bill Reichenbach. LPs: *Synthetic Division* (Fossil Records) and w. Akiyoshi-Tabackin Orch. (RCA; Conc.). CDs: w. Vinny Golia (Nine Winds); Rosemary Clooney (Conc.).

TEMPERLEY, JOE (JOSEPH), bari, sop sax, bs-cl; b. Cowdenbeath, Scotland, 9/20/29. Self-taught. Rec. on tnr. sax w. Harry Parry; Jack Parnell; Tony Crombie; then pl. bari. w. Tommy Whittle 1955–6; Humphrey Lyttleton '58–65. Moved to NYC '65, pl. w. Woody Herman '66–7; Thad Jones–Mel Lewis Orch. '68–70; Clark Terry '68–73; Duke Ellington Orch '74; Duke Pearson; Charles Mingus. Pl. w. Buck Clayton bb '85–91; Lincoln Ctr. Jazz Orch. fr. '87; Wynton Marsalis, Benny Carter '90. Also pl. in '80s-90s w. Mingus Epitaph; Geo. Wein All-Stars; Arvell Shaw; Doc Cheatham; Dave McKenna. Temperley pl. on the soundtracks of *The Cotton Club; Biloxi Blues*; and *When Harry Met Sally*. Favs: Harry Carney, Cecil Payne. Fests: Eur., Asia, Africa, So. Amer. TV: apps. w. Ellington, Lincoln Ctr. Orch. CDs: Hep; Naxos; w. Benny Carter (MM); W. Marsalis; LCJO (Col.); Deodado (CTI); Floating JF Trio (Chiaro.); Clark Terry; Ellington Orch. (MM); Buck Clayton (Chiaro.; N-H); Joe Henderson bb (Verve); Benny Waters; Jimmy Knepper (Hep); H. Lyttleton (Callig.); Dave McKenna (Conc.).

TEMPO, NINO, tnr sax; b. Niagara Falls, NY, 1/6/35. Started on cl., then tnr. sax in hs dance bands; moved to Calif. as a teenager, became child actor in movies. In the mid 1960s he shared a series of pop hits w. his sister, April Stevens, for Atl. label, most notably "Sweet and Lovely"; "Paradise"; and "Deep Purple." After pl. solos on various albums w. Frank Sinatra, Eydie Gormé, and Steve Lawrence, he left music until late '80s. At a memorial service for Atl. co-founder Nesuhi Ertegun, he pl. a tnr. sax solo and was subsequently rec. by Ahmet Ertegun in his first album as an instrumentalist. His tone has been compared to that of Stan Getz. CDs: Atl.; w. MJQ; Diane Schuur (Atl.).

TERRASSON, JACKY (JACQUES-LAURENT), pno; b. Berlin, Germany, 11/27/65. Father is French, moth. is African-Amer. Raised in Paris fr. age 2; began classical stud. on pno. at 5. Studied w. Amer. expatriate Jeff Gardener at 13; then att. Lycée Lamartine, a hs for perf. arts, where he stud. theory, ear training, classical mus. history. Fellow student was Stephane Paudras, son of Francis Paudras. Terrasson was able to access Paudras's extensive collection of jazz recs. and films. Moved to Bost. in '85, where he spent two semesters at the Berklee Coll. of Mus.; then led trio at Blondies in Chi. '86. Ret. to Paris '87 to fulfill mil. obligation. Pl. in Eur. w. Barney Wilen, Dee Dee Bridgewater '88; Guy Lafitte '88–9; Ray Brown's Two Bass Hit '89–91. Moved to NYC '90. Pl. w. Jesse Davis '91; Wallace Roney '91–2; Arthur Taylor's Wailers '91–2; Steve Grossman '93; Betty Carter for eight mos. '93. Own trio fr. '94. Favs: Bud Powell, Thelonious Monk, Herbie Hancock. Fests: all major in Eur. fr. '86; Japan '90. Won Thelonious Monk Competition '93. CDs: BN; JAR; Venus; w. A. Taylor (Verve); W. Roney (Muse); R. Brown (GML); Javon Jackson (BN); Jesse Davis (Conc.); Grand Central (Evid.); Sebastian Whittaker (Justice); Eddie Harris (MM); Jimmy Scott (WB).

TERRY, CLARK (aka CEE TEE), tpt, flg, voc; b. St. Louis, MO, 12/14/20. Brothers Charles and Virgil were amateur mus. who pl. dms., and tba. and uke., respectively. Cousins Lesa Terry vlnst. w. Uptown String Qt.; Zela Terry cellist w. Nice Symph. Pl. "G" bugle in Tom Powell Drum and Bugle Corps 1935; then stud. v-tbn. in hs. Pl. on riverboats in St. Louis, then w. navy band at Great Lakes Naval Station '42–5. After discharge pl. briefly w. Lionel Hampton '45; Geo. Hudson in St. Louis '45–6; Charlie Barnet in Calif. '46; Eddie Vinson, Charlie Ventura, G. Hudson '47; Count Basie Orch. '48–9; Basie small gp. '50–1. Came to prominence w. Duke Ellington '51–9. Pl. w. Quincy Jones '59; on staff at NBC in NYC '60–72, also much freelance studio work. As a popular member of the *Tonight Show* orch., Terry became known for his mumbling style of scat singing. After tour. Japan w. J. J. Johnson '64, he had a hit rec. "Mumbles," rec. w. the Oscar Peterson Trio. Tour. Eur. w. Peterson and Ella Fitzgerald '65. Co-led qnt. w. Bob Brookmeyer '60s, then led own combo and Big Bad Band in clubs, concerts, fests fr. '72; also app. as soloist for George Wein, Norman Granz at fests. Pl. mainly flg. fr. early '70s. Very active as clinician and teacher fr. '70s. In the '80s Terry cont. to work as a studio mus. and tour. w. own gp. and Oscar Peterson's. In the '90s led own gps., incl. The Spacemen, and was feat. w. Lionel Hampton's Golden Men of Jazz. In '95 his dir. of annual summer bb camps in

Iowa and Okla. evolved into his own mus. sch. at Teikyo Westmar U. in Le Mars, Iowa. Coming out of Roy Eldridge and Charlie Shavers, he picked up on the innovations of Dizzy Gillespie and incorporated them into his style, which also sometimes echoes the choked notes of Rex Stewart. Favs: Duke Ellington, Louis Armstrong, Oscar Peterson, Count Basie. Polls: *DB* TDWR bb '75. Fests: all major. TV: *Tonight Show*, many other apps. Books: *Let's Talk Trumpet*, Vols. 1–3; w. Phil Rizzo, *Interpretation of the Jazz Language* (C.J.C. Publ.). CDs: Mons; Riv.; Cand.; Pab.; Vang.; Chiaro.; Chesky; Delos; w. C. Barnet (Evid.); Ellington (BB; Saja/Atl.; Col.); C. Basie (BB; Pab.; Col.); Red Mitchell (Enja); O. Peterson (Verve; Em.; Pab.).; Wardell Gray; Lockjaw Davis (Prest.); C. Adderley; T. Dameron; J. Heath; J. Griffin; M. Jackson; Budd Johnson; Sam Jones (Riv.); L. Hampton (Tel.); J. McShann; Flip Phillips (Chiaro.); Cecil Taylor (Cand.); Dinah Washington (Em.); Gillespie (Pab.).

TESCHEMACHER, FRANK, cl, saxes; b. Kansas City, MO, 3/14/06; d. Chicago, IL, 2/29/32. Attended Austin HS in Chi. w. Jimmy McPartland; Bud Freeman; and others of the legendary "Austin High Gang" who pl. gigs together in 1924–5. The gp. expanded to become Husk O'Hare's Wolverines in Des Moines, Iowa; later a similar unit w. Teschemacher and Muggsy Spanier pl. at the Midway Gardens in Chi. "Tesch" worked w. Sig Meyers, Art Kassel, Floyd Towne in Chi. and w. Red Nichols and others in NYC. He met his death in an auto accident while driving to a rehearsal w. Wild Bill Davison. Infl. by Johnny Dodds and Jimmy Noone, he was a trailblazer in white Chi.-style jazz. CDs: W. E. Condon; B. Freeman; M. Mezzrow (Class.); Wingy Manone (Collectors Class.); M. Mole (Frog); M. Spanier (Verve).

THARPE, SISTER ROSETTA (Rosetta Nubin), voc, gtr; b. Cotton Plant, AR, 3/20/21; d. Philadelphia, PA, 10/9/73. Grew up in Chi. where her mother, Katie Nubin Bell, sang in church choir and taught her mus. Joined Cab Calloway revue '38; Lucky Millinder Orch. '41–3. She mainly sang gospel songs, but her powerful, highly rhythmic gtr. style had the sound of rock to come, and when she combined it w. her rich melodic voice, idiomatic barriers vanished. Signed w. Dec. '38–56; rec. numerous sides as solo '38–69; duets w. her mother '49; w. Millinder '41–3 (incl. three Soundie films). Her '51 marriage to Russell Morrison attracted 25,000 paying guests and was rec. by Dec. In the '40s she also rec. superb voc. duets w. Marie Knight, most notably "Didn't It Rain" and "Up Above My Head, I Hear Music in the Air." Rec. for Merc., MGM, and Verve

fr. '56 to '69. Dur. her secular period also worked at Café Society, NYC. App. in London and Paris in late '50s w. M. Knight and Chris Barber. CDs: Milan; w. L. Millinder (Dec.); D. Gillespie (Verve).

THIELEMANS, TOOTS (JEAN), hca, gtr, whistler, comp; b. Brussels, Belgium, 4/29/22. Played acdn. fr. age 3; began pl. chromatic hca. at age 17. Self-taught. Family fled to France dur. WWII; ret. to Belg. 1941. Bought gtr. after hearing Django Reinhardt; pl. in American G.I. clubs fr. '44. Visited US '47. Discovered by Benny Goodman at Paris JF '49. Tour. Eur. w. Goodman Sxt. '50. Immigrated to US '51. Pl. w. Geo. Shearing Qnt. '53–9. Led own gps. in US and Scand. '59–63. Best known comp., "Bluesette," rec in Stockholm '61, feat. him whistling in unison w. his gtr. On staff at ABC in NYC '63–mid '60s; many studio dates as instrumentalist and whistler. Feat. w. Quincy Jones Orch. on recs. and soundtracks '69–70s. Led own bop gps. in US and Eur. fr. early '70s. Tour. USSR w. own qt. '72. Thielemans perf. on the soundtrack to films *Midnight Cowboy; Getaway; Cinderella Liberty; Sugarland Express* '70s; also perf. theme music to PBS prog. *Sesame Street*. App. at Montreux JF in '70s-80s w. Oscar Peterson; Dizzy Gillespie; Paquito D'Rivera. Thielemans was the first mus. to pl. bebop on the hca. and remains the most prominent jazz hca. player. In addition to perf. w. his gp. in the US, he pl. in a duo w. Martial Solal in France. He rec. as lead. w. Shirley Horn '93. Favs: Miles Davis, John Coltrane, Bill Evans. Fests: all major. CDs: Riv.; Pab.; Verve; Em.; Stash; Milan; Den.; w. David Grisman (Zebra); Marc Johnson (Em.); Jim Hall (MM); Shirley Horn (Verve); J. J. Johnson (Imp.); M. Legrand; L. Konitz (Evid.); Richard Galliano (Drey.); Q. Jones (Merc.; A&M); Eliane Elias (Den.); O. Peterson; Ella Fitzgerald (Fab.).

THIGPEN, BEN (BENJAMIN F.), dms, voc; b. Laurel, MS, 11/16/08; d. St. Louis, MO, 10/5/71. Father of Ed Thigpen. Toured Midwest w. Doc Cheatham and others; best known for his long tenure with Andy Kirk 1930–47. Later moved to St. Louis and worked w. local gps. CDs: w. A. Kirk (Dec.); Mary Lou Williams (Class.).

THIGPEN, ED (EDMUND LEONARD), dms, comp; b. Chicago, IL. 12/28/30. Son of Ben Thigpen. Pl. w. Cootie Williams, Johnny Hodges, Lennie Tristano, Bud Powell in 1950s; Billy Taylor '56–9; Oscar Peterson Trio '59–65; Ella Fitzgerald '66–7 and again '68–72. Moved to Copenhagen, Den., in '72, earning worldwide recognition as a percst., lecturer, and freelance touring musician. Frequently ret. to US, incl. annual visits to Colo. JP. Has written instruction books such as *Talking Drums*, publ. in Toronto, Can. in '65; also *The Sound of Brushes* Copenhagen '81. CDs: Timel.; JT; Reckless; w. O. Peterson (MPS; Verve); E. Fitzgerald; Ben Webster; S. Stitt; Blossom Dearie (Verve); Z. Sims; Teddy Wilson; Benny Carter (Story.); Jutta Hipp (BN); Eddie Vinson; Teddy Charles (Beth.); Monty Alexander (Conc.); J. Coltrane–P. Quinichette; Mal Waldron (Prest.).

THOMAS, BOBBY (ROBERT CHARLES), dms; b. Newark, NJ, 11/14/32. Played in army bands, then stud. at Juilliard Sch. of Mus. Pl. in Newark w. Nat Phipps early 1950s; army bands mid '50s; Sir Roland Hanna, Illinois Jacquet late '50s. Pl. in '60s-70s w. Wes Montgomery; Gigi Gryce; Junior Mance; Hubert Laws; Don Ellis; Herbie Mann; Cy Coleman; Gerry Mulligan; Quincy Jones; Ray Charles. Pl. w. Billy Taylor since '60s. Thomas has worked extensively on B'way and was mus. coord. for *A Chorus Line*. His comps. have been rec. by Wayne Shorter; Hubert Laws; Junior Mance; Dave Pike. Not to be confused w. percst. Bobby Thomas. Favs: Max Roach, Elvin Jones, Jack DeJohnette; arrs: J. J. Johnson, Manny Albam. Fests: Eur., Japan, So. Amer. in '60s. CDs: w. W. Montgomery (Riv.); Hubert Laws (Atl.); Billy Taylor (Taylor-Made; GRP); as part of Taylor trio w. Turtle Island String Qt. (WH).

THOMAS, FOOTS (WALTER PURL), tnr sax, fl; b. Muskogee, OK, 2/10/07; d. Englewood, NJ, 8/26/81. Brother of Joe Thomas. Raised in Topeka, Kansas; began to work as mus. while attending Kansas Vocational Coll. To NYC 1927; pl. w. Jelly Roll Morton '27–9; Joe Steel '29; The Missourians '29, remaining w. band when it was taken over by Cab Calloway. Arr. "Minnie the Moocher" for Calloway, rec. in '31. Left Calloway '43; pl. w. Don Redman at the Zanzibar, NYC; briefly led own band '44. Quit pl. and was active as manager, agent, and mus. publ. fr. '48; clients incl. Dizzy Gillespie; Bill Doggett; Bill Davis; et al. CDs: w. J. R. Morton (BB); Coleman Hawkins; Calloway (Class.); O. Pettiford (Topaz).

THOMAS, JAY, tpt, flg, saxes, fl; b. Seattle, WA, 10/27/49. While in hs received scholarship to Berklee in Bost. Moved to NYC; stud. tpt. w. Carmine Caruso; pl. w. Machito; rec. w. James Moody. Back in Seattle, took up fl. and tnr. Tour. UK w. Slim Gaillard in early 1980s. Visited Japan, representing Seattle in jazz exchange. Tour. clubs and clinics w. David Friesen. Can. gigs w. John Stowell. Was a frequent member of house band at Parnell's jazz club dur. '80s, working w. visiting jazz artists incl. George

Cables; Bill Mays; Harold Land. A personable and versatile multi-instrumentalist, Thomas is comfortable in a variety of jazz environments. CDs: Disc.; w. Herb Ellis (Justice); Jessica Williams (JF); Slim Gaillard; Jay Clayton (Hep); Jim Knapp (SB).

THOMAS, JOE (JOSEPH JR), comp, tnr sax; b. Muskogee, OK, 12/23/08. Brother of Walter "Foots" Thomas. To NYC w. Jelly Roll Morton 1929. Worked w. Blanche Calloway and other bands dur. '30s; w. Dave Martin early '40s; then gave up pl. to become voc. coach. Later was a&r executive for Dec. '49–50; Victor '51–2. Dir. and wrote innumerable r&b rec. dates from late '40s. CDs: w. J. R. Morton (BB).

THOMAS, JOE (JOSEPH VANKERT), tnr sax; b. Uniontown, PA, 6/19/09; d. Kansas City, KS, 8/3/86. Played alto sax w. Horace Henderson 1929–30; to tnr. w. Stuff Smith in Buffalo '30–1. Tnr., cl., and voc. w. Jimmie Lunceford fr. '32 until Lunceford's death '47. Took over the band jointly w. Ed Wilcox; later led own small gp. In business as undertaker fr. early '50s but cont. to pl. occ.; app. at '70 NJF; rec. for Uptown w. Jimmy Rowles '79 and Jay McShann '82, as sidemen. A big-toned, melodious, and inspired soloist, he was one of the Lunceford band's great personalities in the halcyon days. Memorable perfs. incl. "Baby Won't You Please Come Home"; "Wham"; "Bugs Parade"; "Posin"; and "What's Your Story, Morning Glory?" CDs: w. J. Lunceford (Dec.); Billie Holiday (Col.; Dec.).

THOMAS, JOE (JOSEPH LEWIS), tpt; b. Webster Groves, MO, 7/24/09; d. NYC, 8/6/84. Played w. local Midwest bands into early 1930s. To NYC, worked w. Fletcher Henderson '34, '36–7; Benny Carter '39–4. Briefly led own band, then pl. w. James P. Johnson, Joe Sullivan '40–1; Teddy Wilson '42–3; Barney Bigard '44–5. From late '40s worked mostly in NYC, sometimes w. own gps., occ. w. wife, voc. Babe Mathews. Relatively inactive fr. '70s due to ill health. One of the most underrated trumpeters of the Swing Era, his fine tone and relaxed style can be heard on many recs. w. Lil Armstrong; Barney Bigard; Pete Brown; Don Byas; Harry Carney; Cozy Cole; Red Norvo; Art Tatum; Fats Waller; George Wettling; and his own gps. CDs: tracks as leader in Key. Coll.; as sideman in Key. Coll. w. Cozy Cole; Red Norvo (Merc.); Lil Hardin Armstrong; Don Byas (Class.); Benny Carter (B&B); Art Tatum (Dec.); Fats Waller (BB).

THOMAS, KID (Thomas Valentine), tpt; b. Reserve, LA, 2/3/1896; d. New Orleans, LA, 6/16/87. Joined Pickwick Brass Band 1910; formed band w. Edmond

Hall and other members of Hall family '14. To NO in '22; led own bands fr. early '30s; worked regularly at Moulin Rouge in '40s and '50s. Made first recs. in '51; leader on two albums in Riverside "New Orleans: The Living Legends" series, rec. '60–1. Began working at Preservation Hall when it opened '61; cont. into mid '80s, occ. leading own gp., Algiers Stompers. CDs: Riv.; Amer. Mus.; 504; GHB. w. Jim Robinson (Biog.); Capt. John Handy (GHB); De De Pierce (504).

THOMAS, (AMOS) LEON (JR. aka LEONE), voc; b. East St. Louis, IL, 10/4/37; d. NYC, 5/8/99. Studied mus. at Lincoln HS; Tenn. St. U.; sang w. Ben Thigpen; tour. theaters w. Art Blakey and others; rec. w. Mary Lou Williams *Live at Town Hall*; replaced Joe Williams in Count Basie orch. 1961. Sang w. Basie at inaugural balls of Presidents Kennedy and Johnson. Worked w. Pharoah Sanders '69–72; joined Santana '73; then worked mainly on his own, receiving recognition as a lyricist and scat singer, and for his unusual voc. style, which incorporated a form of yodelling patterned after the mus. of Central African pygmy tribes. In late '90s app. at Lenox Lounge, NYC. CDs: Soul Brothers; Portrait-CBS; w. Oliver Nelson (BB); Malachi Thompson (Del.); P. Sanders (Imp.; Evid.); Basie (Rep.).

THOMAS, RENÉ, gtr, comp; b. Liege, Belgium, 2/25/27; d. Santander, Spain, 1/3/75. Guitar at 8; Django Reinhardt was role model. After working locally w. Bobby Jaspar and others, moved to Paris in 1953, rec. there in '54. Moved to Can. '56. Dur. five yrs. in Can. he worked w. Al Haig; Miles Davis; Jackie McLean. Also took part in Sonny Rollins rec. date in NYC. Back in Eur., formed qnt. w. Jaspar. After Jaspar's death, led own gp. accomp. Stan Getz and rec. extensively. In later yrs. Thomas was infl. by Jimmy Raney. He died suddenly of a heart attack. CDs: Jzld.; RTBF w. S. Rollins (Verve); Chet Baker (WW; BB); Getz (Verve; LRC); D. Humair (Blue Flame); Jaspar (FS); L. Konitz (Phil.).

THOMPSON, BARBARA GRACEY (Hiseman), sop, alto, tnr saxes, cl, fl, alto fl, picc, rcdr; b. Oxford, England, 7/27/44. Married to Jon Hiseman; they have owned rec. studio fr. 1982. Two grandparents musical. Stud. at Royal Coll. of Mus. '64–7. Began pl. in many student bands; helped and encouraged by Don Rendell; Art Themen; Bill Le Sage; Mike Gibbs; et al. In stage band for London prod. of *Cabaret* '67–8. Since '64 she has worked w. New Jazz Orch.; Gibbs; Le Sage; Rendell; Johnny Dankworth; The United Jazz & Rock Ens. w. W. Dauner, Kenny Wheeler, Albert Manglesdorff, Charlie Mariano, et al.; own

gps., Jubiaba and Paraphernalia, and Moving Parts, a 19–pc. jazz band. TV: wrote mus. for and/or app. in BBC TV and radio shows, incl. two-hr. BBC film, *Sweet Nothing*. Conducted improv. and contemp. mus. wkshps. in Austr., Switz., Germ., and UK. Regards herself as "more a composer than a player . . . my influences range from Duke Ellington and Gil Evans to Stravinsky and Messaien." Rec. w. Andrew Lloyd Webber and pl. for his stage and TV projects. CDs: Black Sun; VeraBra.

THOMPSON, DON (DONALD WINSTON), bs, pno, vib, dms; b. Powell River, B.C., Canada, 1/18/40. Worked in Vancouver w. Dave Robbins; Chris Gage; Conte Candoli; Barney Kessel. First US job on pno., then bs., w. John Handy in mid 1960s. Worked in Vancouver and Toronto studios. Played bs. w. Paul Desmond '75–6; bs. and pno. w. Jim Hall to '82; then bs. (occ. doubling as second pnst.) w. George Shearing '82–7. Though best known as a bs. player, Thompson is an artist of unusual versatility, an admirable soloist on vib. and pno., a capable dmr. and comp. For some yrs. he has been a teacher at the Banff Center in Alberta. Rec. an album of his own comps. w. Kenny Wheeler in '90, pl. pno. w. Dave Holland on bs. CDs: JA; Conc.; w. R. McConnell (SB; Conc.); Jim Hall (Conc.; MM); P. Desmond (Tel.); E. Remler (Conc.); Brass Connection (JA); G. Shearing–M. Tormé (Conc.); D. McMurdo (Sack.; JA); Pat LaBarbera; Jay McShann; Buddy Tate (Sack.).

THOMPSON, LUCKY (ELI), tnr, sop sax; b. Columbia, SC, 6/16/24; d. Seattle, WA, 7/30/05. Raised in Detroit. Acquired first sax at 15. Pl. in local gps. w. Hank Jones, Sonny Stitt, et al. Four mos. w. Lionel Hampton band 1943. In '44 he pl. w. Sid Catlett; Hot Lips Page; Billy Eckstine band; in late '44 he joined Count Basie for a yr. Living in Calif. '46–7, he rec. extensively w. Boyd Raeburn, Dizzy Gillespie; joined Louis Armstrong band briefly; won *Esq.* New Star award on tnr '47. In April '47, led own all-star gp. for RCA sess. that yielded one of his most moving ballad solos, "Just One More Chance." Back in NYC in '48, he worked w. Oscar Pettiford at Clique Club, freelanced, led own band off and on for two yrs. at Savoy Ballroom, but was relatively inactive until his role in the '54 Miles Davis *Walkin'* sess. brought him back to prominence. In Feb. '56 he joined Stan Kenton's band in Paris, pl. bari. sax; later pl. tnr. on Kenton's *Cuban Fire* LP. By this time he had also taken up sop. sax. Thompson lived in Eur. '57–63. Back in US he rec. several albums for Prest., some feat. his distinctive work on sop. sax, and kept a relatively low public profile as a single parent raising two sons. Ret. to Eur. for three yrs. in '68. His last known recs. were made in NYC '72-3. In '73-4 he taught at Dartmouth and Yale, then withdrew fr. the public arena, reportedly embittered and disillusioned with the jazz scene. As one of the great tnr. stars in the Coleman Hawkins–Ben Webster tradition, he was a superb artist whose retirement was greatly regretted. CDs: Prest.; Imp.; Vogue; IAJRC; LRE; Ensayo; Cand.; w. Benny Carter (BB); Milt Jackson (Sav.); O. Pettiford (Imp.); Esq. All-Amer. Poll Winners (BB); Miles Davis; King Pleasure (Prest.); C. Parker (Sav.; Rh.; Stash); L. Armstrong (Mos); J. Hartman (Beth.); L. Hampton (Tel.); Q. Jones (Imp.); Duke Henderson (Del.); D. Washington (Del.; Em.); Hot Lips Page.; Basie (Class.); Thelonious Monk (BN); Dodo Marmarosa (FS); Kenton (Cap.); Martial Solal (Vogue).

THOMPSON, MALACHI RICHARD, tpt, comp; b. Princeton, KY, 8/21/49; d. Chicago, 7/16/06. Cousin, James Spinks, is actor/singer/comedian. Grew up in Chi. Began on pno. at age 5. Received A.A. fr. Malcolm X Coll. 1972; B.A. fr. Governor's St. U. '74; later stud. tpt. w. Freddie Hubbard; Woody Shaw; Joe Summerhill. Pl. w. Troy Robinson's Jazz Wkshp. Ens. '66. Joined AACM '67; pl. w. Muhal Richard Abrams; Henry Threadgill; Leroy Jenkins; John Stubblefield; Kalaparusha Maurice McIntyre. Also began long assoc. w. Lester Bowie around this time. Pl. w. Gallery Ens. w. Joe Williams, Calvin Jones, Bobby Miller; at jam sess. w. Von Freeman, John Young, Lefty Bates. Pl. in Operation Breadbasket Orch. w. King Kolax, Murray Watson, Raymond Orr '68-72. Led own gps. in Chi. fr. '70 w. Ari Brown; Sonny Seals; Ron Muldrow; Kirk Brown; Buddy Butler; others. Received NEA comp. grant '72. Moved to NYC '74. Pl. w. Collective Black Artists Orch., Sam Rivers bb, Joe Henderson, Jackie McLean '74; also led qnt. w. Carter Jefferson, Victor Lewis '74. Pl. w. Roland Alexander '75-9; K. M. McIntyre fr. '75. Co-led Brass Proud w. Norman Spiller '75-80. Pl. w. Sam Wooding fr. '76. Mus. dir. for Inner Space–Outer Space multimedia project '78. Pl. w. Jazzmobile-CETA bb fr. '78; Archie Shepp off and on '79-88; Lester Bowie's Sho'Nuff Orch. '79; own gps. w. James Spaulding, Oliver Lake, Joe Ford, Gary Bartz, David Murray, Geo. Adams, Billy Harper, Paul Quinichette fr. '80; Lester Bowie's NY Hot Trumpet Repertory Co. '82-4 and his Brass Fantasy '84-8. Thompson was diagnosed w. cancer in '89. While undergoing treatment and unable to perf., he wrote a mus. play, *The Jazz Life*, which premiered in '90. Began perf. and rec. w. his own gp. again '90; feat. soloist in revival of Duke Ellington musical *Jump for Joy* '91. Formed 10-pc. gp., Africa Brass

'91. Thompson taught in the Chi. public schs. '73-4; New Muse Children's Museum, Bklyn. '78-81; Virginia Commonwealth U. '85-6. He lectured extens. on jazz history fr. '78; syndicated column "State of the Art," '90s. Favs: Clifford Brown, Freddie Hubbard; arr: Thad Jones. Fests: Eur. fr. '78. TV: *The Federal Artist* (docu.). CDs: Del.; w. L. Bowie's Brass Fantasy (Virgin; ECM); Willie Kent (Del.).

THOMPSON, SIR CHARLES PHILLIP, pno, comp, org; b. Springfield, OH, 3/21/18. Father was Methodist minister. Began on vln., then sw. to pno. ca. 1930. Left home at 15 to join Lloyd Hunter Orch. in Omaha, Neb. Pl. w. midwestern territory bands, incl. Nat Towles '37-9; Floyd Ray. Pl. w. Lionel Hampton '40; then w. Lester and Lee Young at Café Society '41. Pl. in 52nd St. clubs w. Roy Eldridge, Don Byas, Hot Lips Page, et al. mid '40s. To Calif. w. Coleman Hawkins–Howard McGhee '44-5. Ret. to NYC, rec. as leader w. Charlie Parker '45. While w. Illinois Jacquet '47-8, he comp. "Robbin's Nest," which became Jacquet's biggest hit rec. Lived in Cleveland '48-9, then freelanced w. Charlie Barnet and others. Rejoined Jacquet briefly in '52. Worked mainly as orgst. in '50s, leading combos in Harlem bars. Made Eur. tour as pnst. '59. Pl. w. Coleman Hawkins at Berlin JF '64. Sporadically active '64-74, then underwent major surgery '74. Made comeback concert June '75 at Pilgrimage Theatre. Married a Japanese woman in NYC, summer of '90, moving to Matsudo near Tokyo, in Feb. '92. Occ. works in small clubs in Japan. Rec. for Japanese label, Paddle Wheel '93. CDs: B&B; Del.; tracks in *Master Jazz Piano* (Mos.); w. Buck Clayton (Col.; Prest.; Story.; Mos.); I. Jacquet (BB; Col.; Verve; Mos.); C. Hawkins (Cap.); J. Rushing (Col.); Ike Quebec; Dodo Greene; Charlie Parker (BN); Milt Jackson (Gal.); L. Hampton (BB); Vic Dickenson (Vang.); Joe Newman (FS).

THORNHILL, CLAUDE, comp, pno, leader; b. Terre Haute, IN, 8/10/09; d. NYC, 7/1/65. Studied at Cincinnati Cons. and Curtis Inst. First job w. Austin Wiley through band member Artie Shaw, who became a close friend. Arr. for Hal Kemp; Bing Crosby; Benny Goodman. Pnst. and arr. for Ray Noble 1935-6. He pl. in various small gps. in late '30s w. Billie Holiday; Louis Prima; Benny Goodman; Bud Freeman; Glenn Miller. Sponsored Maxine Sullivan's NYC debut and cond. her rec. of "Loch Lomond." Own band '40-2. Pl. w. Artie Shaw and his own service band in the navy, '42-5. Formed new band in '46, impressing audiences w. a rich range of sounds and blend of classical, pop, and jazz material. He was the first to give prominence to the arrs. of Gil

Evans and to make use of French horns in a modern dance band. Some of his sidemen—incl. Lee Konitz, Bill Barber, Joe Shulman, and arr. Evans—formed the nucleus of Miles Davis's Birth of the Cool band on Cap. Thornhill cont. to lead a band periodically, using his own arrs. as well as those of Gerry Mulligan and Ralph Aldridge. The tonal texture of his original band, notably the manner in which he used French horns, earned him great prestige among musicians. Dur. the '50s he led small gps., occ. assembled a bb, and worked for Tony Bennett bef. going into semi-retirement in NYC. CDs: Col.; Hep; w. B. Holiday (Col.); Bunny Berigan (Topaz); Bud Freeman; Benny Goodman; Maxine Sullivan (Class.); Wingy Mahone (Collectors Classics).

THORNTON, TERI, voc, pno, songwriter; b. Detroit, MI, 9/1/34; d. Englewood, NJ, 5/2/00. Raised in mus. environment and mainly self-taught. Sang in gospel gp. w. moth. and grandmoth. Made prof. debut in 1956 at the Ebony Club in Cleveland. Worked in and around Chi. and the Midwest for four yrs. Johnny Griffin brought her to Riverside, where she rec. in '60–1. In '63 had a hit for the Dauntless label w. "Somewhere in the Night," theme song of the TV series *Naked City*. Pl. clubs and tour. Eur., Austral., Japan early '60s. After rec. for Columbia in mid '60s, retired to raise a family. During the next twenty yrs., living in Calif., Det., NYC, Wash., D.C., Calif. again, then NYC in mid '80s, her only mus. activity was local gigs and songwriting. Perf. at Berlin JF '95. Sang at Arthur's in Greenwich Village '96–7, accomp. herself at the pno., as she has throughout the yrs. Felled by cancer in Oct. '97, she recovered sufficiently to sing w. Diva at the Bern JF, Switz., April '98. Hospitalized for exhaustion, she learned in June '98 that her cancer had disappeared. In Sept., in a dramatic perf., she won first prize in the Thelonious Monk Jazz Competition, Wash., D.C. Favs: Nat Cole, Carmen McRae, Sarah Vaughan, Ella Fitzgerald, Lena Horne, Judy Garland. LPs: Riv. CDs: Riv.; Verve.

THREADGILL, HENRY LUTHER, alto sax, comp; b. Chicago, IL, 2/15/44. Played perc. in marching bands as a child; pl. bari. sax and cl. in hs. Pl. w. Joseph Jarman, Roscoe Mitchell, and Muhal Richard Abrams' Experimental Band (the precursor of the AACM) early '60s; tour. w. gospel gp. '65–7. Dur. army service pl. pop, jazz, and rock in service gps.; ret. to Chi. '69, worked with AACM, pl. in house band at a blues club and rec. w. Abrams. Earned B. Mus. fr. Amer. Cons. of Mus. early '70s and pl. w. Amina Claudine Myers. Organized co-op trio, Reflection, w. Steve McCall and Fred Hopkins '71; reassembled in '75 as Air, it rec. ten albums in

the next decade. Name changed to New Air fr. '82 to '86, the yr. of its disbandment. Moved to NYC in mid '70s, working and rec. w. R. Mitchell; David Murray; et al. In late '70s organized and rec. w. the X-75 gp., incl. four strings, four winds, and voice; the ens. evolved into Sextett (which actually has seven members: Threadgill counts the two percs. as one) and, in the '90s to Very Very Circus. Awards incl. Best Comp. in *DB*'s '88 and '89 Readers Poll and '90 Critics Poll. More than 150 of his comps. have been rec.; others incl. *First and Second Quintets for String Quintet*, premiered at Carnegie Recital Hall '84–5, and *Hymn to Wright Reverend* for fl. qt. '90. A complex comp. and improv., Threadgill rigorously mixes planned and spontaneous elements in his works. Peter Watrous of the *NY Times* has called him "perhaps the most important jazz composer of his generation." CDs: Novus; TMR; Axiom; BS; Col.; w. Bahia Black (Axiom); M. R. Abrams (Del.; BS); Air; D. Murray (BS); R. Mitchell (Chief).

TIBERI, FRANK, saxes, fl, bsn; b. Camden, NJ, 12/4/28. Played in clubs fr. age 13, then w. Bob Chester 1948. Freelanced in '50s; pl. w. Benny Goodman, Urbie Green. Joined Woody Herman '69 as lead tnr; also pl. bsn. Cont. w. Herman, taking over as the band's dir. on his death in '87. Cond. coll. mus. seminars at most leading jfs in US and Eur. A major voice on tnr. w. the Herman band, he is also a proficient leader and one of the few effective jazz bassoon soloists. CDs: w. W. Herman (Fant.; Story.; Conc.); Rosemary Clooney w. Herman (Conc.); Billy Ross (Cont.).

TIMER, JOE (Joseph Michael Theimer), dms, comp; b. Alexandria, VA, 3/21/23; d. Washington, DC, 5/15/55. Studied at Navy Sch. of Mus. 1943, Catholic U. '47–8. Pl. w. Johnny Scat Davis '47; Lennie Tristano '49; Elliot Lawrence '51. Rec. own LP, *House of Sounds*, Brunswick. TV shows and concerts w. Willis Conover–produced programs by *The Orchestra* fr. '51. Chief arr. was Bill Potts. CDs: *One Night in Washington*, Charlie Parker w. The Orchestra (BN).

TIMMONS, BOBBY (ROBERT HENRY), pno; b. Philadelphia, PA, 12/19/35; d. NYC, 3/1/74. Studied w. uncle at 6; attended Phil. mus. acad. for a yr. Local dates bef. joining Kenny Dorham's Jazz Prophets Feb. 1956. Later w. Chet Baker '56–7; Sonny Stitt '57; Maynard Ferguson '57–8; Art Blakey '58–9; Cannonball Adderley '59–60; then briefly back w. Blakey. Best-known comps., "Moanin'," "Dis Here," and "Dat Dere," helped generate the gospel-tinged "soul jazz" style of late '50s and early '60s. In the

'6os he worked mainly in NYC bars and restaurants w. his own trio, and occ. pl. vib. Died of cirrhosis of the liver. A talented pnst. and imaginative comp., Timmons occ. revealed a broader—if never fully realized—range of creative potential but never quite managed to move beyond the approach that brought him popularity. CDs: Riv.; Prest.; w. A. Blakey (BB; Fontana; BN; Imp.; Select Jazz); K. Burrell; K. Dorham; Lawrence Marable (BN); Lee Morgan (Roul.; BN); S. Stitt (Verve); Chet Baker (PJ); Pepper Adams; Cannonball Adderley; Nat Adderley; Sam Jones; Johnny Griffin (Riv.).

TIO, LORENZO JR., cl; b. New Orleans, LA, 4/18/1893, d. NYC, 12/24/33. Father, Lorenzo Sr. (1866–1920), and uncle, Papa (Luis) Tio (1863–1927), also well-known NO clarinetists. Pl. in parade bands fr. age 9; in 1897 he pl. w. Lyre Club Symph. Orch.; fr. '10 he pl. w. the Onward and Excelsior brass bands. His cl. students incl. Barney Bigard; Albert Burbank; Johnny Dodds; Albert Nicholas; and Jimmie Noone. Pl. w. Papa Celestin fr. '13, then to Chi. to work w. Manuel Perez, Charlie Elgar '16–17. Ret. to NO, rejoined Papa Celestin; pl. off and on w. Armand Piron, incl. periods in NYC '18–28. Briefly ret. to NO, pl. w. Tuxedo Brass band; then back to NYC to freelance; pl. on NYC-Albany steamboats. Residency at Nest Club in Harlem until his death. CDs: w. Armand Piron (Azure); Clarence Williams (Hot 'N Sweet).

TIZOL, JUAN, valve tbn, comp; b. San Juan, PR, 1/22/1900; d. Inglewood, CA, 4/23/84. Played in San Juan bef. moving to US in 1920. While at Howard Theater in Wash., D.C., he met Duke Ellington whom he joined in '29. Dur. the next fifteen yrs. he contributed many comps. to the band's repertoire, incl. "Moonlight Fiesta"; "Pyramid"; "Caravan"; and his widely-played "Perdido." After seven yrs. w. Harry James, he rejoined Ellington '51–3; then back w. James '53–60. Final stint w. Ellington '60–1, after which he was in virtually total retirement except for an office job in the local Musicians Union. CDs: Key. Coll. (Merc.); w. D. Ellington (BB; Dec.; Mos.; RCA; Col.; Prest.; Laser.); Nat King Cole (Cap.); E. Fitzgerald (Verve); J. Hodges (Prest.); Harry James (FS; Col.).

TJADER, CAL (CALLEN RADCLIFFE JR.), vib, dms, perc; b. St. Louis, MO, 7/16/25; d. Manila, Philippines, 5/5/82. Mother pl. pno; fath. was in vaudeville. Grad. SF State w. mus. ed. degree. Pl. w. Dave Brubeck trio and oct. 1949–51; George Shearing Qnt. Jan. '53–Apr. '54; then led own gp. in SF, specializing in Latin Amer. jazz. Signed w. Fant. in early '50s but sw. to Verve in '60s, by which time he had gained int'l popularity and become a regular on campus dates. Such Verve albums as *Several Shades of Jade* '63 and *Soul Sauce* '65 generated huge rec. sales. Cont. to tour and rec. for the Conc. Picante label in '70s. Died of heart attack while touring, Tjader achieved an effective synthesis of Latin and Afro-Cuban elements along with traces of *salsa*. His sidemen, at various times, incl. Willie Bobo; Mongo Santamaria; and Clare Fischer. CDs: Fant.; Prest; Conc.; Verve; PJ; w. Brubeck; Charlie Byrd; Stan Getz (Fant.); Anita O'Day; Shearing (Verve); Woody Herman; Rosemary Clooney; Carmen McRae (Conc.).

TOGASHI, MASAHIKO, dms, perc, comp, lead; b. Tokyo, Japan, 3/22/40. Father pl. vln. and cello. Stud. vln. as child; began pl. dms. while in jr. hs. Made prof. debut w. Naoya Matsuoka Trio at age 14, then pl. w. Sadao Watanabe 1956. Organized Jazz Academy w. other young mus., incl. Masayuki Takayanagi, Hideto Kanai, Masabumi Kikuchi '61. Formed own gp. w. Yosuke Yamashita, Kuniro Takimoto, Kazumori Takeda '65; although short-lived, this gp. is considered to be the first Japanese free jazz gp. Pl. w. S. Watanabe '66–8; then formed trio w. Masahiko Sato, Yasuo Arakawa. An accident in '69 left him unable to pl. dms. for a yr. Despite being confined to a wheelchair, he was able to ret. to pl. using a specially designed drum kit. Comp. suite *Ohitsuziza No Uta* for T. Miyama's New Herd Orch. '71. Pl. w. M. Sato '70s-80s; Richie Beirach '78; Steve Lacy, Kent Carter '81; Leo Smith '82. Received Fumio Nanri awd. for contrib. to Japanese jazz '79; also tour. Eur. w. Steve Lacy; Don Cherry; Charlie Haden. Tour. Japan in duo w. S. Lacy '83; qt. w. Lacy, D. Cherry, Dave Holland '86; trio w. Gary Peacock, M. Sato '87; trio w. tbn. Geo. Lewis '89; duo w. Yosuke Yamashita '90. Formed J. J. (Japan Jazz) Spirits w. Kosuke Mine, Nobuyoshi Ino '91; won *SJ* poll in three categories '92. Polls: Jazz Disc '69, '74–6, '79–80, '82, '91; *SJ* Readers dms. '70; *SJ* Readers perc. '82–4, '93; *SJ* Readers Jazzman of Yr. '92–3; *SJ* Critics perc., best combo, Jazzman of Yr. '92. Fests: all major in Japan; Paris JF w. Lacy '91. CDs: Japan-Victor; East Wind; Cornelius; Paddle Wheel; Japan-Verve; Nippon Crown; w. S. Lacy (NEC-Avenue).

TOLLIVER, CHARLES, tpt, comp, arr; b. Jacksonville, FL, 3/6/42. Self-taught. Grew up in NYC. Att. Howard U. for three yrs. Pl. w. Jackie McLean, Joe Henderson, Edgar Bateman 1963–5; Art Blakey '65. Moved to LA, '66; pl. w. Willie Bobo, Gerald Wilson bb '66. Ret. to NYC '67; pl. w. Max Roach '67–9; own gp. Music, Inc. fr. '69. Co-founded Strata-East Records w. Stanley Cowell '71. Pl. and rec. w. McCoy Tyner; Horace Silver; Booker Ervin; Andrew Hill; Gary Bartz; Roy Ayers; Oliver Nelson. Tour Eur. w. own qt., also arr. for Eur. radio bb '80s-90s. Tolliver is on the faculty of the New Sch. Polls: *DB* TDWR '68. Fests: Eur. fr. '70s. CDs: BL; Strata-East; w. J. McLean; H. Silver (BN); Louis Hayes (Steep.); McCoy Tyner (Mile.).

TOMMASO, GIOVANNI, bs, comp, arr; b. Lucca, Italy, 1/20/41. Brother Vito is pnst.; cousin Bruno is bassist. Began on pno. at age 12; bs. at age 16. Self-taught. Pl. w. bro. Vito's gp. Quintetto di Lucca 1957–62, incl. US tour '59–60. Moved to Rome '67. Worked as studio mus., comp. mus. for films and TV, incl. scores for silent films by Chaplin, Keaton, Lloyd, John Ford. Led fusion gp. Perigeo '72–7; own qnt. fr. '77; own trio w. Franco D'Andrea, Roberto Gatto fr. '84; Ital. TV bb '80s. Pl. w. his qnt. at Blue Note, NYC, '86. Worked w. singers incl. Mina; Lucio Dalla; Riccardo Cocciante; Anna Oxa; choreographers incl. Kelly Armah; Roberta Garrison; Patrizia Cerroni. Tommaso has been dir. of the Umbria Jazz Clinics in conjunction w. Berklee Coll. of Mus. since '86. Favs: Slam Stewart, Paul Chambers, Scott LaFaro, Henry Grimes, Ray Brown, Dave Holland. Fests: many major fr. '72. TV: Eur. TV. CDs: Red; w. Perigeo (RCA); Massimo Urbani; D'Andrea (Red); Enrico Rava (SN).

TOMPKINS, ROSS, pno, comp, kybd, synth; b. Detroit, MI, 5/13/38; d. St. Augustine, FL, 6/29/06. Studied priv. and at New Engl. Cons. Active in NYC in '60s, he pl. w. Kai Winding '60; Eric Dolphy '64; J. J. Johnson. Pl. also w. many gps. at Half Note, NYC, incl. Wes Montgomery '66; Bobby Brookmeyer–Clark Terry, Joe Newman, Illinois Jacquet '67. Joined NBC staff orch., pl. *Tonight Show* '67; Roy Eldridge, Al Cohn–Zoot Sims '68–72; Bobby Hackett '65–70; Benny Goodman '68; James Moody, NYC and Calif. In '72 he moved to CA w. *Tonight Show* band, remaining w. it until May '92; then freelanced in LA. Frequent local apps. w. jazz combos and bands, incl. Louie Bellson orch.; also occ. led small gps. at Donte's and elsewhere. Many apps. at Colo. JP. Tompkins, who named Ellington, Armstrong, Earl Hines, and Fats Waller as sources of inspiration, was an eclectic, technically outstanding mainstream-modern soloist. CDs: Prog.; w. T. Newsom; Jack Lemmon (Laser.); Herb Ellis; Jack Sheldon (Conc.); Bellson (Pab.; Conc.); Bob Cooper–Conte Candoli (VSOP); Dick Hafer (Prog.); Spike Robinson (Capri); Zoot Sims (Pab.); Doc Severinsen (Amherst).

TONOLO, PIETRO, tnr, sop saxes, fl; b. Mirano, Italy, 5/30/59. Brother Marcello is jazz pnst. Began on pno. at age 6, then pl. vln. fr. age 9–17; pl. sax fr. age 15. Introduced to jazz by bro. ca. 1974. Pl. in Jazz Studio gp. w. bro. '76–9; Gianni Cazzola '79–81. Moved to Milan '80. Pl. off and on in Eur. w. Enrico Rava '81–6; Gil Evans Orch., Kenny Clarke '82; Sal Nistico, Chet Baker, Lee Konitz, John Surman, Aldo Romano, Kenny Wheeler, Dave Holland '80s. Led own trio and qt. fr. '82; duo w. Rita Marcotulli fr. '86. Pl. w. Gil Evans Orch., C. Baker in NYC '85; Gil Evans at Umbria JF '87. Pl. in Eur. w. Henri Texier fr. '88; Joe Chambers '89–91; also w. Enrico Pieranunzi, Giovanni Tommaso. Tonolo leads a qt. w. Roberto Rossi, Piero Leveratto, Alfred Kramer, and pl. and arr. w. Keptorchestra bb. He teaches sax, arr., and ensemble in Venice and Florence. Favs: Ben Webster, Lester Young, Sonny Rollins, Sal Nistico, Dewey Redman. Fests: all major in Eur.; US '85, '87. CDs: Spl.; w. J. Chambers (Penta.); Augusto Mancinelli; Giuseppe Emmanuele; Paolo Carrus (Spl.).

TORFF, BRIAN QUADE, bs, el-bs; b. Chicago, IL, 3/16/54. Father was amateur singer. Began on pno. Stud. at Berklee Coll. of Mus. 1973; Manh. Sch. of Mus. '74. First gig w. Cleo Laine–John Dankworth at Carnegie Hall '74. Pl. w. Laine '74–6; Erroll Garner, Mary Lou Williams '75; Oliver Nelson, Sonny Stitt '76; Stephane Grappelli fr. '76; Marian McPartland '77–8; Thad Jones–Mel Lewis Orch., Hank Jones '78; Geo. Shearing '79–82, incl. perf. at White House '82; own trio fr. '83. Formed fusion gp. Etosha '86. Pl. w. Clark Terry, James Moody, Jimmy Cobb '89–91; Red Rodney '91. Torff has been dir. of jazz studies at U. of Bridgeport since '89. Favs: Paul Chambers, George Mraz. Fests: Eur., Asia, etc. '77–82. TV: PBS, etc., w. Shearing. CDs: Aud.; w. Shearing; Tormé; M. McPartland (Conc.); Mary Lou Williams (Chiaro.); M. Hinton (Col.).

TORMÉ, MEL (MELVIN HOWARD), voc, comp, dms, pno; b. Chicago, IL, 9/13/25; d. Los Angeles, CA, 6/5/99. Six mos. singing w. Coon-Sanders Orch. at Blackhawk 1929, cont. to sing dur. hs yrs. w. Buddy Rogers and other name bands. Stud. dms. at age 7; acted in radio soap operas '34–40. First song, "Lament to Love," rec. by Harry James '41. Tour. w. Chico Marx band '42–3; movie debut in *Higher and Higher* '43; led vocal gp., the Mel-Tones, in Calif.; army '45–6. From '47 was a major attraction as a single; also known for comps. incl. "Stranger in Town"; "County Fair"; "Born to Be Blue"; and the perennial favorite, "The Christmas Song." Among literally hundreds of recs., his most unusual was undoubtedly a Bethlehem set on which he played Porgy to Frances Fay's Bess. It was a radio DJ who dubbed him "The Velvet Fog," a tag he came to dislike. Indeed, his sound was much fuller and richer than the nickname implied. A uniquely sophisticated and versatile artist who often wrote his own arrs. Tormé is greatly admired by his peers. In the '80s he frequently app. as himself on the TV series *Night Court* and began rec. for the Concord label, often w. George Shearing, but also w. Cleo Laine, Marty Paich, and Rob Mc-Connell. In Aug. '96 he suffered a stroke that incapacitated him for the rest of his life. Tormé was also a gifted writer whose books incl. *The Other Side of Midnight*, tracing his experience dur. a TV series w. Judy Garland; and *Traps, the Drum Wonder*, a sensitively written biography of his long-time friend Buddy Rich. CDs: Dec.; Conc.; Stash; Tel.; Cap.; Beth.; Col.; Verve; Atl.; FS; Rh.; w. Peggy Lee (Cap.); Chico Marx (Laser.); G. Mulligan (GRP); Artie Shaw (MM).

TORRES, NESTOR, fl; b. Mayaguez, PR, 4/21/57. Started on dms, then sw. to fl. at age 12. Infl. by Tito Puente; moved to NYC after hs graduation; then commuted to Bost. to study at Berklee Coll. and New Engl. Cons. From 1977 to '81 he gigged in NYC w. Puente; Eddie Palmieri; and local charanga bands. Moved to Miami '81; pl. So. Fla. club and coll. circuit; signed multi-album contract w. Polygram '89 and released first album, *Morning Ride* '90. In May '90 Torres was seriously injured in a celebrity powerboat race accident that crushed his upper body and damaged his lungs. Began his comeback in Aug. '91 with the release of *Dance of the Phoenix*. *Jazziz* described Torres' first album as "an exotic music travelogue through American, Colombian, Brazilian and Afro-Cuban stylings piloted by Torres' forceful, often fiery flute solos." CDs: Verve; Polyg.; Sony Int'l; Shan; w. Billy Ross (Cont.).

TOTAH, NOBBY (NABIL MARSHALL), bs; b. Ramallah, Palestine (after WWII, Jordan), 4/5/30. Father was headmaster of sch. in Ramallah, Jordan. Moth., a drama teacher, started him on pno. Later sw. to vln. Moved to US 1944, attending Moses Brown sch. in Providence, R.I.; graduated w. degree in political science from Haverford Coll., where he also began to pl. bs. '53; army service '53-4; pl. w. Toshiko Akiyoshi and Hampton Hawes while in Japan. After discharge worked w. Charlie Parker '54. The following yr. he began the first of numerous sporadic gigs w. Gene Krupa and Johnny Smith. In late '50s he worked w. Les Elgart; Cy Coleman; Zoot Sims; Eddie Costa; Herbie Mann; in '60s pl. w. Bobby Hackett; Teddy Wilson; Sol Yaged; et al.; in '70s w. Benny Goodman; Max Kaminsky; Hazel Scott. Rec. w. Lee Konitz '77. Has led various small gps. with such sidemen as Attila Zoller; Pepper

Adams; Horace Parlan; and Mike Longo. CDs: CAP; w. Tal Farlow (Verve); H. Mann (Atl.); Z. Sims (Chess); George Wallington (Sav.).

TOUFF, CY (CYRIL JAMES), bs-tpt; b. Chicago, IL, 3/4/27; d. Evanston, IL, 1/24/03. Began on pno. at age 6; later pl. C-melody sax, tpt., xyl. Pl. tbn. in army band w. Conte Candoli, Red Mitchell 1944-6. After discharge stud. w. Lennie Tristano. Pl. w. Jimmy Dale; Jay Burkhart; Bill Russo; Charlie Ventura; Shorty Sherock; Ray McKinley; Boyd Raeburn; also NYC Opera Co. late '40s. Sw. to bs.-tpt. after hearing Johnny Mandel pl. one in late '40s. Tour. w. Woody Herman Orch. '53-6. Rec. w. Nat Pierce '54; as lead. in Calif. '55. Freelanced in Chi. w. Chubby Jackson fr. '56. Also rec. as lead. of dixieland and hard bop gps. mid '50s. Rec. w. Clifford Jordan, Von Freeman for Bee Hive label '81. Freelanced as a studio mus. and w. local gps. LPs: w. Herman (Cap.). CDs: PJ.

TOUGH, DAVE (DAVID JARVIS), dms; b. Oak Park, IL, 4/26/08; d. Newark, NJ, 12/6/48. Son of Scottish immigrants. After att. Oak Park HS he studied for three yrs. at Lewis Institute in Chi., simultaneously becoming one of the legendary Austin HS Gang, a gp. that incl. Bud Freeman, Frank Teschemacher, Eddie Condon 1925-7. Worked w. various Chi. bands, incl. Husk O'Hare's Wolverines, bef. going to Eur. w. Danny Polo in mid '27. Pl. in France, Belgium, and Germ., where he also rec. Around '29 he played his way back to US aboard the liner *Ile de France*; freelanced briefly in NYC; then ret. to France, working w. Mezz Mezzrow and George Carhart in Paris. Back in US he went on the road w. Red Nichols late '29. In '32 illness all but rendered him inactive for three yrs.; he ret. in '35 to work w. Ray Noble, then Tommy Dorsey '36-8; Red Norvo; Bunny Berigan; Benny Goodman (replacing Gene Krupa) '38; briefly rejoined T. Dorsey; then Jimmy Dorsey; Jack Teagarden; and Bud Freeman's Summa Cum Laude Orch. until poor health struck him again. The '40s cont. the pattern of work, interrupted by periodic bouts w. alcoholism. After working w. Artie Shaw and Charlie Spivak '41-2, he toured the South Pacific w. Shaw's navy band. Back in NYC he sparked the Woody Herman band '44-5. His last yrs. were also marked by indecision as to whether he should stay w. traditional or modern jazz, since he was highly accomplished in both areas. He pl. w. Joe Marsala at the Hickory House in '45, the Charlie Ventura–Bill Harris gp. in '47, and periodically w. Eddie Condon. While on leave from a N.J. veteran's hospital he fell on a Newark street and suffered a fractured skull. Originally inspired by Baby Dodds and other NO pioneers, Tough evolved with the music, later idolizing Max Roach. His playing was marked by elegance, finesse, and an unerring sense of swing. Frustrated by a desire to become a writer, he contributed a valuable series of articles to *Metronome*. He won the *Esq.* Armed Forces Award in '44; Silver Award '45 & '47; Gold Award '46. Also *DB* poll '45, '46. CDs: w. B. Goodman (Col.; BB); T. Dorsey; Teagarden; Artie Shaw (BB); W. Herman (Col.); Esq. All-Amer. Poll Winners (BB); Flip Phillips (Sig.); Wild Bill Davison (Comm.); Condon (Dec.); Freeman (CDS); Nichols (Tax); Rex Stewart (Prest.); B. Berigan (Class.).

TOUSSAINT, JEAN, tnr, sop saxes; b. Aruba, Netherlands Antilles, 7/27/60. Father and uncle both mus. Raised on St. Thomas, where he stud. pno., fl., and sax in sch. Pl. first w. calypso band in St. Thomas. Stud. at Berklee Coll. 1977–80; while there pl. w. r&b band '79; then had own qt. w. Wallace Roney in Bost. Recommended as replacement in Art Blakey's Jazz Messengers in '82, he remained with the gp. into '86, also lead. late-hour jam sessions at the Blue Note, NYC, dur. this period. Pl. w. Jerry Gonzalez '85–6. Moved to Engl. to teach at the Guildhall Sch. of Mus. '86 and has made his home in London since. Form. own gp., which incl. Jason Rebello and Alec Dankworth, and el. band. Pl. w. Cedar Walton '89; tour. Spain and Mid. East w. Max Roach '91; Julian Joseph qt. fr. '90. Won *DB* TDWR '84. TV: *Sesame Street* w. W. Marsalis '85; *Father Time* w. Blakey. CDs: JH; WC; w. Blakey (Conc.; Evid.; PW; Timel.; Delos); J. Joseph (Atl.); Conjure (Pangaea); Nathan Davis (DIW); Andy Hamilton; Bheki Mseleku (WC).

TOWNER, RALPH, gtr, pno; b. Chehalis, WA, 3/1/40. Parents both musical. Improv. at pno. fr. age 3; pl. tpt. at 5, and in dance band at 13. Stud. theory and comp. at U. of Oregon 1958–63; grad. work '64–6. Classical gtr. study w. Karl Scheit at Vienna Acad. of Mus. '63–4, '67–8. To NYC '69, working w. various gps., often on pno.; pl. w. Jimmy Garrison '69–70; Jeremy Steig '69–71; Paul Winter '70–1; Weather Report '71, pl. 12-string gtr. on *I Sing the Body Electric*; off and on w. Gary Burton '74–5. His original plan to pl. jazz on pno. and classical mus. on gtr. was sidetracked by exposure to Brazilian mus. In '71 he was co-founder of the gp. Oregon—w. Collin Walcott, Glen Moore, and Paul McCandless—an ens. that pl. a significant role in the advancement of a form of chamber jazz that incorporates folk, classical, and world mus. elements. Also led a gp. called Solstice in mid '70s. In '85, a yr. after Walcott died in an auto accident, Oregon resurfaced w. Indian drummer Trilok Gurtu. Since then Towner, McCandless, and

Moore have also worked as a trio. Tour. and rec. w. John Abercrombie '70 and '80s; frequent concerts and recs. w. such perfs. as Egberto Gismonti; Gary Burton; Jan Garbarek; Kenny Wheeler. Cont. to explore chamber jazz into '90s, often via recs. on ECM, his home base label for twenty-five yrs. Despite a lack of widespread recognition, Towner is one of the true orig. voices on contemp. jazz gtr. w. a style based not on a gtr. model but on technical and emotional inspiration fr. the pno. of Bill Evans. Other favs: Scott LaFaro, Paul Bley, Keith Jarrett, Julian Bream. Fests: Woodstock w. Tim Hardin; NJF-NY, solo '73, w. Oregon '74–5; Pori, Bergamo, Molde, Berlin, Istanbul '95. Poll: *DB* Critics TDWR '74. CDs: ECM; w. Oregon (ECM; Vang.; VeraBra); Weather Report (Col.); T. Gurtu (CMP); Duke Pearson (BN); Vince Mendoza (Manh.); G. Burton (ECM; GRP); Arild Andersen (ECM); J. Abercrombie; Gary Peacock; Jan Garbarek; K. Jarrett (ECM).

TOWNSEND, BROSS E., pno; b. Princeton, KY, 10/18/33. Grandmother was mus. teacher; fath. pl. pno. in family movie theater. Pl. for church fr. age 11. Pl. w. Woody Herman; Erskine Hawkins; Gene Ammons; Milt Jackson; John Coltrane; Dicky Wells; Rex Stewart; Sonny Stitt; Philly Joe Jones; Clark Terry–Bob Cunningham; Frank Wess; Frank Foster; Earle Warren's Countsmen; Geo. Kelly's Savoy Sultans; Russell Procope; etc. Accomp. many singers incl. Dinah Washington; Little Jimmy Scott; Carrie Smith; Jimmy Reed. In '90s working w. Dakota Staton and teach. at Jazzmobile and the New Sch. He has lectured at many Amer. colls. and pl. for the B'way musicals *Dinah* and *Black and Blue*. Favs: Art Tatum, Phineas Newborn, Duke Ellington. Fests: Eur. w. Staton, Buddy Tate, etc. Films: *Sweet Sweetback's Baadasssss Song* '71. TV: Docu., *Women in Jazz*. CDs: Claves; w. D. Staton (Muse); Greg Bobulinski (Cat's Paw).

TRACEY, CLARK, dms; b. London, England, 2/5/61. Father is pnst. Stan Tracey; wife is voc. Tina May. Stud. mus. at summer schs., initially on pno. Stud. dms w. Brian Spring. Began pl. w. father in 1978; w. Tommy Smith; Don Weller; Dee Dee Bridgewater in show *Lady Day*; Buddy DeFranco; tribute to Art Blakey '91. Dates w. Pharoah Sanders; Johnny Griffin; Charlie Rouse; John Hicks trio; George Cables; Bud Shank. Led own qnt. fr. '84; sxt. fr. '92. Tours of S. Amer., Mid. East, India, Far East, East and West Eur.; Chi. JF '89. Many apps. on BBC Radio's *Sounds of Jazz*. TV: *Father & Son*. Soundtrack to film *Stormy Weather*. Recs. w. DeFranco, Stan Tracey (sm. gps. and orch.), own qnt. on Steam Records. CDs: 33 Jazz; w. Tina May; Mike Hashim

(33 Jazz); Guy Barker (Spot.); Alan Barnes; Warren Vaché (Zephyr); NDR bb (ACT); Alan Skidmore (Miles Mus.); Stan Tracey (BN; Steam; Cadillac); Bobby Wellins (Jazzizit); Bob Wilber (Arb.).

TRACEY, STAN (STANLEY WILLIAM), pno, comp, arr; b. London, England, 12/30/26. Started on acdn. Self-taught on pno.; pl. w. Jack Parnell; Ted Heath; Ronnie Scott. House pnst. at Scott's club fr. its opening in 1960 to '68, pl. there and on TV w. Scott; Zoot Sims–Al Cohn; Sonny Rollins; Dexter Gordon; R. R. Kirk; Ben Webster; Stan Getz; Freddie Hubbard; J. J. Johnson; et al. Local and continental gigs w. qt. and bb '69–71. Form. duo w. Mike Osborne '72. Concerts in Engl. w. 10-pc band, qt., trio, duo, solo '73. Led oct. '76–85; qt. fr. '78; sxt., Hexad, fr. '79. Has tour. worldwide. Worked w. Tony Coe; Alan Skidmore; Keith Tippett; John Surman. Taught at City Literary Inst.; Goldsmiths' Coll.; Guildhall Sch. of Mus. Comps: "Under Milkwood" '65; "Alice in Jazzland" '66; "Baby Blue," rec. by Harry Carney, Paul Gonsalves. Comp. and perf. for Southwark Cathedral Shakespeare birthday concert. Infls: Ellington, Monk. Received OBE '86; awards fr. *Wire/Guardian* for pno., comp., best album. Honored w. commemorative concert '93. Film: w. S. Rollins on soundtrack of *Alfie* '66. CDs: BN; Steam; w. NDR Big Band (ACT); Guy Barker (Spot.); Benny Golsori; Don Byas; R. R. Kirk; Wes Montgomery; Ronnie Scott (JH); Alan Skidmore (Miles Mus.); Keith Tippett (Ogun).

TRAVIS, NICK (Nicholas Anthony Travascio), tpt; b. Philadelphia, PA, 11/16/25; d. NYC, 10/7/64. Studied at Mastbaum Sch. of Mus. Pl. w. Johnny McGee, Mitchell Ayres, Vido Musso 1942; Woody Herman Dec. '42 until drafted '44. Pl. jazz concerts in Paris while in service; off and on '46–9 w. Ray McKinley, where his feature was "I Cover the Waterfront"; later six mos. w. Benny Goodman '48–9; Jerry Wald, Gene Krupa, Ina Ray Hutton in late '40s; Tommy Dorsey, Tex Beneke '50; Herman '50–1; Jerry Gray, Bob Chester. Pl. w. pit band for *Top Banana* on B'way; Elliot Lawrence '51; Jimmy Dorsey '52–3. Prominent w. Sauter-Finegan Orch. 53–6; then worked at NBC fr. '57 and was active in the studios into the '60s. Pl. w. Gerry Mulligan Concert Jazz Band '60–2. Pl. Lincoln Center concert w. Thelonious Monk '63. Hospitalized w. ulcers shortly before his death. Favs: Clifford Brown, Miles Davis, Harry Glantz. An eclectic soloist who combined swing and bop, he was heard to advantage in small gps. led by Al Cohn and others. Rec. own LP for Vict. '54, and others w. Cohn; Billy Byers (Vict.); T. Aless (Roost); M. Albam (Vict.; Coral); B. Holman (Cap.).

CDs: w. C. Hawkins; Maynard Ferguson; Joe Morello (BB); T. Talbert (SB); S. Getz (Verve); E. Lawrence (Fant.); G. Shearing; A. Cohn; E. Condon (Sav.); G. Mulligan (Verve; RTE); Sauter-Finegan; Lee Wiley (BB); Z. Sims (Riv.); E. Lawrence (Fant.).

TREADWELL, GEORGE McKINLEY, tpt; b. New Rochelle, NY, 12/21/19; d. NYC, 5/14/67. Worked in house band at Monroe's Uptown House 1941–2. Pl. w. Benny Carter '42–3; Sunset Royals '43; Cootie Williams '43–6. While w. J. C. Heard at Café Society he met Sarah Vaughan, who headlined there. They were married in '47. After acting as her mus. dir. and helping to develop her public image, he quit pl. but cont. to work as her manager even after their divorce. In the '50s he also represented the Drifters and Ruth Brown; worked as an a&r man and, fr. '59, as a songwriter. Rec. in the mid '40s w. Heard; Ethel Waters; Dicky Wells; S. Vaughan. CDs: w. E. Waters (Milan); Vaughan; C. Williams (Class.).

TRENT, ALPHONSO (ALPHONSE), pno; bandleader; b. Fort Smith, AR, 8/24/05; d. Fort Smith, 10/14/59. Began mus. in hs; stud. at Shorter Coll., Little Rock, Ark.; organized first band 1923, gaining wide territorial fame with long-run gig as first African-Amer. band to be booked at the Adolphus Hotel, Dallas, Tex. '25–6. One of the most successful bands to emerge fr. the Southwest, the gp. toured nationally w. dates at Savoy Ballroom, NYC, and on Strekfus Great Lakes steamers; but Trent's refusal to play a regular schedule on the East Coast lowered the band's visibility and probably diminished its potential for commercial success, despite the quality of its mus. Collectively, sidemen incl. Peanuts Holland; Mouse Randolph; Snub Mosley; Stuff Smith; Sy Oliver; and Harry Edison. In an amazing stroke of bad timing, Trent gave up the band in '34, just bef. the dawn of the bb Swing Era. Ret. to mus. in mid '30s w. a sxt. which, at one time in '38, incl. Charlie Christian. In the '40s and '50s Trent concentrated on territory work, then ret. to Fort Smith, where he occ. pl. at a local restaurant. Rec. for Gennett '28, '30; Champion '33.

TRISTANO, LENNIE (LEONARD JOSEPH), pno, comp, educ; b. Chicago, IL, 3/19/19, d. NYC, 11/18/78. Vision-impaired fr. birth by influenza, he was totally blind by the age of 9. Extensive studies, incl. the Amer. Cons. of Mus. Pl. locally fr. 1931, leading his own Dixieland band on cl. Encouraged by Chubby Jackson, he came to NYC in '46. Dur. next five yrs. while pl. intermittently w. his own combos, he worked successfully to expand the harmonic horizons of jazz improv. By the late '40s he was the leader of an informal cult, a sch. of progressive ideas in which his principal disciples were Lee Konitz, Warne Marsh, Billy Bauer—key participants in a remarkable '49 series of Cap. recs. that realized some of Tristano's harmonic and rhythmic theories. After '51 when he opened his own studio, Tristano rarely appeared in public, focusing on his work as a teacher. His students incl. such exponents of early jazz as Bud Freeman and Bob Wilber. Toured Eur. '65; reunited w. Konitz and Marsh at Half Note '66; last app. in public '68. French TV docu. on his life and mus. '73. One of the least visible but most infl. jazz voices, Tristano was the first perf. to attempt free improv. in a jazz context ("Intuition" and "Digression") in '49, ten yrs. bef. the app. of Ornette Coleman. Tristano's playing style—built upon long, unrelentingly propulsive eighth-note phrases and harmonically dense block chording—impacted not only the players assoc. w. his "school" but also such artists as Bill Evans and Clare Fischer. CDs: Cap.; *Key. Coll.* (Merc.); Jazz Records; Rh./Atl.; w. Metronome All-Stars; D. Gillespie (BB); L. Konitz (Prest.); Charlie Parker (Phil.)

TROTMAN, LLOYD NELSON, bs, comp; b. Boston, MA, 5/25/23. Studied at New Engl. Cons. Pl. w. Joe Nevils' Alabama Aces on tour w. Blanche Calloway 1941. Moved to NYC '45. Pl. w. Eddie Heywood, Hazel Scott, then joined Duke Ellington for two mos. '45. Freelanced w. Pete Brown, Geo. James, Edmond Hall, Wilbur DeParis mid '40s. Pl. w. Boyd Raeburn '48–9; Johnny Hodges '51–2; also pl. w. Sonny Dunham, Jerry Wald. Worked as studio mus., mainly in r&b field, fr. late '40s. Rec. w. Lucky Millinder '52; Ray Charles '53; Bud Powell '55; Joe Turner '56–8; Red Allen '57. Pl. w. Red Allen at NJF '59. Favs: Jimmy Blanton, Oscar Pettiford, Slam Stewart, Richard Davis. CDs: w. J. Hodges; Bud Powell (Verve); Henry Red Allen (BB); Chuck Willis; Ivory Joe Hunter (R&T); Ellington-Strayhorn (Riv.).

TROTTER, TERRY WILLIAM, pno; b. Los Angeles, CA, 10/5/40. Mother is an amateur pnst., sist., Linda Trotter, an opera singer. Stud. fr. age 5 w. priv. teachers incl. Marjorie Duncan Baker; Earl Voorhies; Pete De Santis; Victor Aller; Leonid Hambro. First prof. gigs w. Chas. Lloyd–Don Cherry 1955. Pl. w. Bobby Hutcherson, Herbie Lewis, Walter Benton '55; Lenny McBrowne, Teddy Edwards '56–7; Les Brown '58; Lighthouse All-Stars w. Art Pepper, Conte Candoli '59–60; Lena Horne '61–2; Joe Pass, Chet Baker off and on '68–73; Charlie Shoemake late '60s-80s. Trotter has been a member of Larry Carlton's gp. fr. '84. Favs: Glenn Gould, Bud Powell, Bill Evans. Fests: Eur. '80s-90s. LPs: w. L. Carlton (MCA); L.

McBrowne (WP; Riv.). CDs: MAMA; w. Jim Self (d'Note); Jeanie Bryson (Tel.); Ella Fitzgerald (Pab.).

TROUP, BOBBY (ROBERT WILLIAM), voc, pno, comp; b. Harrisburg, PA, 10/18/18; d. Sherman Oaks, CA, 2/7/99. Self-taught pnst. Early mus. experience working in family mus. stores. Wrote first hit song, "Daddy," while dancing in Mask & Wig show at U. of Pa.'s Wharton Sch. of Business 1941. With Tommy Dorsey as staff songwriter 41; US Marine capt. '42–6. After WWII moved to LA, where he wrote next hit, "Route 66." Rec. his song "Brand New Dolly" w. Count Basie Band '48. Worked in bars w. trios late '40s and early '50s. Rec. debut as leader on Cap. '52. Moderated TV series, *Stars of Jazz* '56–8. Produced many LPs feat. his wife, singer Julie London '60s. Portrayed pnst. Arthur Schutt in film *The Five Pennies* '59 and Tommy Dorsey in *The Gene Krupa Story* '60. Portrayed Dr. Joe Early on NBC-TV show *Emergency*. Best known songs incl. "Girl Talk"; Meaning of the Blues"; "Baby, Baby All the Time"; "Snooty Little Cutie"; and "You're Looking at Me." LP: VSOP. CD: Star Line

TROVESI, GIANLUIGI (GIOVANNI LUIGI), sop, alto saxes, cl, picc-cl, alto-cl, bs-cl; b. Nembro (Bergamo), Italy, 1/10/44. Father is amateur dmr.; daughter is vlnst. Began on dms., then sw. to cl. Stud. cl., comp. at Instituto Musicale G. Donizetti, Bergamo 1960–72. Pl. w. Cichellero bb w. Dusko Goykovich '72–4; Franco Cerri '74–7; Giorgio Gaslini '77–82; own trio fr. '77; Misha Mengelberg ICP Orch. '79; Trovesi-Conrad Bauer duo '79–80; Italian Radio and TV bb fr. '79; int'l qt. w. Barre Phillips, Gunter Sommer, Manfred Schoof '81; Trovesi-Centazzo duo '83–4; Trovesi-Damiani Qnt. '84–5; Paolo Fresu fr. '90; Ital. Instabile Orch., own oct. fr. '91; Grand Orch. Nazionale '92. Also freelanced and rec. w. Anthony Braxton; Evan Parker; Kenny Wheeler; Tony Oxley; Albert Mangelsdorff, Steve Lacy; Horace Tapscott; others. Trovesi taught in Ital. secondary schs. '67–78; hs in Stockholm '79; Brescia Conservatorio '83–5. He has been on the faculty of the Siena Seminari Estivi fr. '80. Favs: Charlie Parker, Eric Dolphy, Ornette Coleman. Polls: Ital. Critics prize '78; Rai Radiounojazz '83; *Musica Jazz* '88, '92. Fests: US '80–1; India '82; Austral. '91. TV: Eur. TV. CDs: Spl.; SN; Red; w. P. Fresu; Pietro Tonolo; Paolo Damiani (Spl.); G. Gaslini (SN; DDQ); Tiziana Ghiglioni (yvp); Ital. Instabile Orch. (Leo); Guido Manusardi (SN); Enrico Rava (L. Bleu).

TROWERS, ROBERT, tbn; b. Brooklyn, NY, 3/3/57. Father pl. gtr., hca; moth. pl. pno.; many other mus. in family. Began on pno., then pl. viola for one yr. Pl. tbn. fr. age 15. Stud. at CCNY 1975–80. Pl. w. various rehearsal bands, then w. Ray Draper bb '78; Jaki Byard's Apollo Stompers '78–9; Abdullah Ibrahim '79; Cecil Payne '80; Ibrahim '81; Lionel Hampton Orch. '82–5; Sam Wooding bb '84; Illinois Jacquet bb '86–7; Count Basie Orch. fr. '87. Trowers taught science in Bklyn. public schs. '84–7. He is on the faculty of the Bklyn. Cons. Favs: Jimmy Cleveland, J. J. Johnson, Tyree Glenn. Fests: all major w. Hampton, Jacquet, Basie Orch. CDs: Conc.; w. Susannah McCorkle; Jesse Davis (Conc.); C. Basie Orch. (Telarc; Den.).

TRUJILLO, BILL (WILLIAM L.), saxes and other woodwinds; b. Los Angeles, CA, 7/7/30. Played w. dance bands while still in hs. With Alvino Rey 1950; Woody Herman '53–4; Charlie Barnet '57; Stan Kenton '58–9. From '60 he worked in LV, backing such singers as Ella Fitzgerald; Sarah Vaughan; and Peggy Lee; in late '80s tour. w. Frank Sinatra. CDs: w. S. Kenton (Cap.; CW).

TRUMBAUER, FRANKIE ("TRAM"), saxes; b. Carbondale, IL, 5/30/01; d. Kansas City, MO, 6/11/56. Mother a concert pnst. Formed first gp. at age 17. Served in navy dur. WWI. In 1921 he pl. w. local band of pnst. Gene Rodemich. In Chi. fr. '22; pl. in Benson orch. '22–3; Ray Miller '23–4. In '25 he became mus. dir. for Jean Goldkette at Arcadia Ballroom in St. Louis, Mo., where he began an assoc. w. Bix Beiderbecke that cont. in the Paul Whiteman orch. and out of which came Trumbauer's most important contribution to jazz, a series of small gp. sess. feat. Beiderbecke. Trumbauer also led rec. bands fr. '29 to '36, using sidemen from Whiteman's band. After almost a decade w. Whiteman, he led his own band fr. '37 to '39, but in March '39 gave up mus. to join Civil Aeronautics Authority. Dur. WWII he also worked as test pilot. He ret. to NYC in '45 to do studio work w. Raymond Paige but was largely inactive in mus. for the rest of his life. Trumbauer perf. on the C-melody sax, a rare instrument pitched between alto and tnr. His tone was exceptionally clear and his ideas were melodically and harmonically influential. Musicians who have cited him as an inspiration incl. Lester Young and Benny Carter. As the catalyst of some of the most notable recorded jazz of the late '20s, Trumbauer is an important link in jazz history. CDs: own sessions in *Classic Capitol Jazz Sessions* (Mos.); w. Beiderbecke (Col.; BB); J. Teagarden (BB); Eddie Lang (Timel.); J. Venuti (Jazz Classics in Digital Stereo).

TRUNK, PETER, bs, tpt, cello; b. Frankfurt am Main, Germany, 7/17/36; d. NYC, 12/31/73. Broadcasts and concerts w. Kenny Clarke, Zoot Sims 1957; member of Albert Mangelsdorff spt. '58–9. Recs. w. Hans Koller; Sims; Mangelsdorff. In '60s he pl. w. Klaus Doldinger, Dusko Goykovich; rec. w. Tete Montoliu; Benny Bailey; Don Byas; Ben Webster; et al. Worked w. Manfred Schoof in New Jazz Trio, Kurt Edelhagen '72. Died in an auto accident. CDs: w. K. Doldinger (ACT); D. Goykovich (Enja); Lucky Thompson (Cand.).

TRZASKOWSKI, ANDRZEJ, pno, comp; b. Cracow, Poland, 3/23/33; d. Warsaw, Poland, 9/16/98. Studied pno., comp., musicology, etc. fr. 1950s to '74. Formed Melomani '51; worked w. Jazz Believers '59; formed the Wreckers '59; perf. in Wash., D.C., and NJF '62. His gps. in the '60s incl. M. Urbaniak; Z. Namyslowski; and Ted Curson. From '60 pl. and rec. w. Stan Getz; Art Farmer; Phil Woods; Lucky Thompson; Idrees Sulieman; et al. From '65 to '70 he worked regularly in NDR Radio's *Jazz Workshops* series in Hamburg, Germ. Worked as dir. of Polish Radio and TV Orch. in Warsaw fr. early '70s, cont. to comp., cond., and write jazz criticism. In late '80s won several prizes for his comp. from Polish Composers' Union. His comps. incl. "Nihil, Novi," written in '62 for Don Ellis and the Polish Nat'l Philharm. Orch.; other comps. incl. "Synopsis"; "Bluebeard"; "The Quibble"; scores for about thirty films. CDs: Muza; Pol. Col.; Sonoton; w. *Stan Getz in Warsaw* (Muza).

TSILIS, GUST WILLIAM, dms, vib, mrba, pno; b. Chicago, IL, 4/14/56. Began on dms., then pno. Pl. w. own gps. fr. 1986; Herb Robertson in Eur. '87; Wilber Morris in Phila. '88; Arthur Blythe '90–1. Tsilis's sidemen have incl. Blythe; Joe Lovano; John Abercrombie; and Billy Hart. Did production and promotional work for the Enja and Ken Music labels Managed Visiones jazz club in NYC. Favs: Milt Jackson, Vladimir Ashkenazy, Kenny Barron. Fests: Eur. '87; Jap. w. own gp. '91. CDs: Ken; w. The Enja Band; Blythe; Ron Getz (Enja); Karl Denson (Minor Mus.).

TSUKAHARA, KOTARO, pno; b. Tokyo, Japan, 8/19/52. Piano at 3, later vln., vla., tpt., tbn., bn. Frequent apps. in Japan, Austral., US w. Buddy DeFranco; also in Japan w. Jimmy Smith, Milt Jackson, and in US w. Scott Hamilton, Red Holloway. Perf. at the Int'l Jazz Party in LA in 1993, he made a strong impression w. his powerful neo-bop style. Favs: Bud Powell, Hank Jones, Phineas Newborn. Feat. at MJF '89, '91, '92. His CDs, mostly available only in Japan, have incl. sess. w. Milt Jackson; Jimmy Smith; and Eiji Kitamura.

TUCKER, BEN (BENJAMIN MAYER), bs; b. Nashville, TN, 12/13/30. Studied tba. in hs 1948–49; maj. in mus. at Tenn. St. U. and start. on bs. there. Pl. in Nashville clubs for two yrs., then mil. service for four. After discharge in '50s he join. Warne Marsh in LA; worked w. Art Pepper briefly, then Carl Perkins at Tiffany Club. To NYC '59, gigging w. various gps. bef. join. Roland Hanna. Tour. w. Chris Connor fall '59. Pl. w. Herbie Mann, Billy Taylor in '60s. To Rio de Janeiro w. Kenny Dorham, Zoot Sims, Curtis Fuller, and others '61. Rec. w. own qnt. for Ava '63. Active in '60s and '70s w. Yusef Lateef; Marian McPartland; Illinois Jacquet; Mose Allison; Pat Martino; Harold Vick. Bought and operated radio station WSOK, Savannah, Ga., fr. '72. Pl. at JVC-NY; and w. Mann at Blue Note '95. Favs: Ray Brown, Oscar Pettiford. Early recs. w. Freddie Gambrell; Dempsey Wright; W. Marsh; K. Burrell; R. Hanna; in '60s w. G. Mulligan, Grant Green. Comp: "Comin' Home Baby," rec. w. H. Mann. CDs: w. Bob Dorough (Evid.); Lou Donaldson; Grant Green (BN); Ray Crawford (Cand.); K. Dorham (BL); Gil Evans; Jimmy Smith (Verve); P. Martino; I. Jacquet (Prest.); H. Mann (Atl.); A. Pepper (BN; Tampa-OJC); Tristano-Marsh (Cap.).

TUCKER, BOBBY (ROBERT NATHANIEL JR.), pno; b. Morristown, NJ, 1/8/23. Began gigging at age 14. Stud. under Cecily Knechtel at Juilliard; later stud. at N.Y. Inst. of Mus. Art. Pl. w. Barons of Rhythm 1932. Entered service in '43 for three yrs. and pl. tbn. in mil. band; pnst.-arr.-leader for post dance band. Best known as accomp. for Mildred Bailey briefly in '46 and Billie Holiday '46–9, incl. rec. dates until '55. He also pl. in clubs on 52nd St. w. gps. led by Lucky Thompson; Stuff Smith; and Babs Gonzales. Became Billy Eckstine's mus. dir. in '49, writing arrs. and tour. int'l w. him until his final dates in '92. Tour. w. Tony Bennett in mid '90s. Because of his subsidiary role as an accomp., Tucker—whose approach ranged from sensitive and lyrical on ballads to a swinging bopper at faster tempos—never achieved the recognition he deserved as a soloist. CDs: w. B. Holiday (Dec.; Verve; BN); B. Eckstine (Roul.; Verve; Merc.); Eckstine-C. Basie (Roul.); Joe Wilder (Eve. Star); B. Gonzales in *East Coast Jive* (Del.).

TUCKER, GEORGE ANDREW, bs; b. Palatka, FL, 12/10/27; d. NYC, 10/10/65. While in army he became interested in mus. through Ellington rec. w. Oscar Pettiford. Moved to NYC 1948. Stud. at NY Cons. of Modern Mus. and later w. Fred Zimmerman at Juilliard '57–8. Early experience w. Earl Bostic; Sonny Stitt; John Coltrane. Became house bs. at Continental Lounge in Bklyn. In '58–9 became house bs.

at Minton's Playhouse, working as leader and sideman w. Jerome Richardson and, in early '60s, w. Horace Parlan and Booker Ervin. Rec. w. Howard McGhee '61. Pl. w. Junior Mance. Tour. w. Lambert, Hendricks & Bavan '62–3; also app. w. Jaki Byard; Kenny Burrell; Earl Hines. Died of cerebral hemorrhage. A powerful and positive force in any gp. to which he lent his presence. Favs: Miles Davis, Charlie Parker, Pettiford. CDs: w. Lucky Thompson; Charles McPherson; J. Byard (Prest.); H. McGhee (BL); L,H&B (BB); Freddie Redd (Riv.); Walt Dickerson; Oliver Nelson; Eric Dolphy (NJ); Curtis Fuller (Sav.); Cliff Jordan; D. Gordon; K. Burrell; S. Turrentine (BN); E. Hines (Merc.; Verve); Z. Sims (Beth.); Jackie McLean; Joe Zawinul (FS); Booker Ervin (Cand.; Sav.).

TUCKER, MICKEY (MICHAEL B.), pno, kybd, comp, oboe, Engl. horn; b. Durham, NC, 4/28/41. Lived in Pitts. until 1954, then ret. to Durham. Piano lessons fr. age 6. Att. Morehouse Coll. Taught at Roosevelt HS, Lake Wales, Fla.; Mississippi Valley St. Coll. Worked w. Damita Jo '65; Timmie Rogers '66–7; Little Anthony and the Imperials '67–8; James Moody '69–71; org. w. Roland Kirk '71; three mos. w. Thad Jones–Mel Lewis late '73; Eddie Jefferson, Eric Kloss, Frank Foster, Sonny Red, Willis Jackson, Cecil Payne, Roy Brooks '73–5; Final Edition '75. Tour. Eur., No. Africa w. Art Blakey '76. Rec. in NYC w. Philly Joe Jones, Billy Harper, Junior Cook '77. Tour. and rec. w. F. Foster '77–9; Art Farmer–Benny Golson Jazztet early '80s. Favs: Fats Waller, Art Tatum, Hampton Hawes, Phineas Newborn, Oscar Peterson, Herbie Hancock. TV: Mike Douglas, Ed Sullivan '60s-70s. CDs: Steep; w. Eddie Jefferson (Muse); Junior Cook; Ted Dunbar; Bill Hardman (Steep.); Art Farmer–The Jazztet (SN); R. R. Kirk (Rh./Atl.); Louis Hayes (Cand.).

TURNER, JOE (JOSEPH H.), pno; b. Baltimore, MD, 11/4/07; d. Montreuil, France, 7/21/90. Not related to blues singer of same name. Early experience in Harlem bands w. Jimmy Harrison, June Clark; also w. Louis Armstrong in 1930s; accomp. Adelaide Hall on Eur. tour. Pl. in Sy Oliver's army orch. '44–5; Rex Stewart '46. Ret. to Eur. after WWII; took up residence in Hungary and Switzerland '49–62, then settled in Paris where he became a fixture at La Calvados. Pl. long engagement at The Cookery, NYC '76, then ret. to Paris. Infl. by James P. Johnson and Fats Waller, Turner was a powerful stride pnst., possibly the last of the idiom's original exponents. LP: Pab. CDs: Solo Art; B&B; w. L. Armstrong (Col.); Django Reinhardt (Class.); Adrian Rollini (Topaz).

TURNER, JOE (JOSEPH VERNON; "BIG JOE"), voc; b. Kansas City, MO, 5/18/11; d. Los Angeles, CA, 11/24/85. Worked fr. teens in KC as singing bartender, often in partnership w. Pete Johnson, who came w. him to NYC for historic 1938 *From Spirituals to Swing* concert. Accomp. by Johnson at concert and subsequent Vocalion rec. date. From '40–9 he made numerous recs. w. Johnson and gps., incl. pnsts. Joe Sullivan; Art Tatum; Willie "The Lion" Smith; Sammy Price; Freddie Slack; and Albert Ammons. Won *Esq.* Silver Award '45. After rec. for several small labels, he signed w. Atl. '51–9; his mus. became more r&b-oriented, hitting the charts w. such hits as "Chains of Love" and "Shake, Rattle and Roll," which some regard as seeds of r&r. Living in LA fr. '60s, Turner worked w. Johnny Otis Show, often perf. at the MJF. In '74 he app. in the docu. film *Last of the Blue Devils*. More noted for the power and intensity of his style than for the clarity of his readings of lyrics, Turner brought a unique personal warmth to the blues at every tempo. Comps: "Cherry Red"; "Wee Baby Blues"; "Roll 'em Pete"; "Piney Brown Blues." CDs: BB; Dec.; Pab.; Evid.; Rh.; w. C. Basie; *Joe Turner Meets the Trumpet Kings* (Pab.); Tatum (Dec.); Joe Sullivan; Willie "The Lion" Smith (Class.)

TURNER, MARK, tnr sax; b. Wright Patterson Air Force Base, Fairborn, OH, 11/10/65. Raised in southern Calif. fr. age 4. Stud. alto sax in hs but intended to be an illustrator when he att. Long Beach Coll. In 1987, now pl. tnr. sax, he enrolled at Berklee Coll. in Boston, where he stud. w. Billy Pierce; Joe Viola; George Garzone; jammed w. Joshua Redman; Seamus Blake; Antonio Hart; Geoff Keezer; Dwayne Burno. He names Hal Crook's book, *How to Improvise,* as "invaluable." Grad. w. B. Mus. in performance '90, and moved to NYC. Jammed at Smalls, other small lower Manhattan bars. Pl. w. TanaReid; leads own qt. Also perf. w. Charlie Haden; Slide Hampton; Lionel Hampton; Tom Harrell; and Brad Mehldau. Mehldau wrote of Turner: "Mark's output involves very little affectation. He doesn't court the theatrics often associated with his instrument . . . [playing] with a candor usually reserved for older players." Favs: Coltrane, Warne Marsh, Joe Henderson. In addition, he acknowledges Lennie Tristano, Keith Jarrett, and Steve Coleman as infls., as well as Bartok, Schoenberg, Webern, and Messiaen. Also enjoys Bach and Monteverdi. CDs: CC; WB; *Jazz Christmas Party: Warner Jams Vol. 2: The Two Tenors* (WB); Tad Shull–Mark Turner, *Ballads* (CC); w. Jimmy Smith (Verve); Leon Parker; Ryan Kisor (Col.); Delfeayo Marsalis (Novus); Ed Simon (Koko.); Russell Gunn (High.); TanaReid (Evid.);

Seamus Blake; Jon Gordon; Jonny King (CC); George Colligan (Steep.).

TURNEY, NORRIS WILLIAM, alto, tnr, sop, saxes, cl, fl; b. Wilmington, OH, 9/8/21; d. Kettering, OH, 1/17/01. Brother pl. dms., sist. pl. pno. Stud. pno., C-melody sax, alto, and cl. w. Inez Jones in Wilmington. Cont. stud. w. Geo. Carr, Artie Matthews in Cincinnati, Ohio, where he pl w. Virgil Tucker, Little Jimmy Washington in 1930s; A. B. Townsend Band at Cincinnati Cotton Club '41–3. To St. Louis '44; pl. briefly w. Fate Marable, then w. Jeter-Pillars Orch. Tour. w. Tiny Bradshaw '45; moved to NYC. Pl. w. Billy Eckstine Orch '46–7, then ret. to Ohio. Taught and pl. w. own gps. in Ohio, Ind., Ky. in early to mid '50s, except for '51 in NYC. Pl. w. Elmer Snowden in Phila. and Johnny Lynch in Atl. City late '50s, then ret. to NYC '60. Pl. w. orchs. of Clark Terry; Erskine Hawkins; Frank Foster; Duke Pearson; Howard McGhee; co-led rehearsal band w. Danny Small. Pl. w. Ray Charles '67; Duke Ellington '69–73; B'way pit bands '75–85; Geo. Wein, Panama Francis, AJO in '80s. Back to Ohio '89. Favs: Willie Smith, Benny Carter, Johnny Hodges. Comp: "The Checkered Hat," dedicated to Hodges. Polls: *DB* TDWR on fl. '70–1. Fests: Eur., Asia, Austral., etc., w. Ellington. TV: apps. w. R. Charles, Ellington. CDs: Maple.; w. Ellington (BN; Atl.); R. Eldridge (Pab.); AJO (Atl.); NJF All-Stars (Conc.); Randy Weston (Verve); Jodie Christian (Del.); Cat Anderson; Panama Francis (B&B); Paul Gonsalves (BL); LCJO (Col.).

TURRE, STEVE, tbn, conch shells, comp, arr; b. Omaha, NE, 12/8/49. Wife is cellist Akua Dixon. Stud. at U. of Mass.-Amherst (B.A.); No. Tex. St. U. 1968–9; in SF w. Norman Williams '70; Manh. Sch. of Mus. '86. First prof. gig at age 13. Pl. w. Rahsaan Roland Kirk in SF '70; Van Morrison '71; bs-tbn. w. Ray Charles '72; Charles Moffett, Art Blakey '73; Thad Jones–Mel Lewis '73; Woody Shaw '74–5. Pl. tbn. and el-bass w. Chico Hamilton '74–6. Pl. w. R. R. Kirk '76–7; Woody Shaw Concert Ens., Slide Hampton and Collective Black Artists '77–8; Elvin Jones Jazz Machine, Cedar Walton '79; Jon Faddis, Archie Shepp bb, Reggie Workman, Lester Bowie's Sho 'Nuff Orch. '80; Pharoah Sanders, Slide Hampton's World of Tbns., Hugh Masekela '81; Woody Shaw '82–7. Guest soloist at Salsa Meets Jazz concerts at Village Gate w. Tito Puente, Johnny Ventura, Ruben Blades '83. Pl. w. Lester Bowie's Brass Fantasy fr. '83; Jay McShann; Benny Powell; Celia Cruz; Lou Rawls; Oscar DeLeon; Patti LaBelle; Gladys Knight; also B'way shows and opera, *X,* w. Springfield Symph. '85; Cedar Walton fr. '85. Led own qt., qnt., and shell choir fr. '86. Pl. w. James Newton;

Jack Walrath; Jerry Gonzalez' Fort Apache Band; Jose Alberto; Libre; Vibration Society '86; Art Farmer-Benny Golson Jazztet; McCoy Tyner bb; Dave Valentine; Daniel Ponce; Hilton Ruiz; Freddie Hubbard; Buddy DeFranco; Dizzy Gillespie bb, Bill Lee Orch.; Mercer Ellington; Celia Cruz; Conjunto Libre '87. Turre has arr. for Ray Charles; Max Roach; Woody Shaw; Dexter Gordon; Slide Hampton. He has taught at U. of Hartford; Berklee Sch. of Mus.; U. of Mass.; LIU; William Paterson Coll.; Manh. Sch. of Mus. *Sanctified Shells*, an album which focuses on Turre's conch shell pl., was released on Ant. in '93. Fests: all major fr. '73. Polls: *DB* TDWR, *JT, Jazziz* '87; Outstanding Mus. Jazz Yatra JF, Bombay '84. TV: *Sat. Night Live* band fr. '86. CDs: Ant.; Verve; Stash; w. Robin Eubanks (JMT); Fred Wesley (Minor Mus.); M. Tyner (Mile.; Bird.); D. Gillespie; J. Gonzalez (Enja); Antonio Hart (Novus); Frank Wess (Conc.); W. Shaw (Col.; Muse; Elek.; Mos.); H. Ruiz (Novus; Stash); P. Sanders (Evid.); L. Bowie (ECM; DIW); Mingus bb (Drey.); S. Hampton (BL); Cedar Walton (Delos); Don Braden; Ralph Moore (CC); Johnny Griffin (Ant.); Bobby Watson (Col.).

TURRENTINE, STANLEY WILLIAM, tnr sax, comp; b. Pittsburgh, PA, 4/5/34; d. NYC, 9/12/00. Father, Thomas, was amateur saxophonist, pl. w. Pitts. Savoy Sultans. Bros. are Tommy and dmr. Marvin Turrentine. Stud. tnr. w. fath. fr. 1947. Pl. w. Ray Charles '52; Earl Bostic '53; Max Roach '59–60. Formed own gp. ca. '60, rec. for BN. In '61 he married orgst. Shirley Scott, a member of his gp. (divorced '71). Led own gp., also rec. w. larger ens. for CTI label, which brought him to a wider pop audience early '70s. From '75 he cont. to rec. as a leader in a pop-soul vein for Fant. and Col. In the early '90s he signed w. MM and ret. to pl. and rec. mainstream acoustic jazz. His most famous comp. is "Sugar." Favs: Don Byas, Coleman Hawkins, Sonny Rollins. CDs: Imp.; Fant.; MM; BN; CTI; Time; w. Max Roach (Enja); K. Burrell; I. Quebec; Benny Green; D. Byrd (BN); T. Monk–M. Roach (LRC); David Newman (Atl.); Jimmy Smith (BN; Mile.); Abbey Lincoln (Riv.; Verve); Diana Krall (GRP); Shirley Scott (Imp.; Prest.); Roy Hargrove (Verve); F. Hubbard (CTI); Gene Harris (Conc.).

TURRENTINE, TOMMY (THOMAS WALTER JR.), tpt, comp; b. Pittsburgh, PA, 4/22/28; d. NYC, 5/13/97. Father was amateur saxophonist, pl. w. Pitts. Savoy Sultans; moth. pl. pno., aunt pl. tpt. Bros. are Stanley Turrentine and dmr. Marvin Turrentine. Began on vln., then sw. to tpt. at age 11. First studies w. aunt and cousin Horace Turner. Pl. w. Snookum Russell 1945–6; Benny Carter in Calif. '46. Stud. w.

Ronald Lavalle in Pitts. '46–7, then join. Geo. Hudson '47. Pl. w. Hudson '47–9; Dizzy Gillespie bb for one week '49. In army '50, then w. Count Basie orch. '51–2; Gay Crosse in Cleveland, Ohio '52; Earl Bostic '52–3; local bands in Pitts. '53. Led rehearsal band w. bro. Stanley in Pitts. '53–4. Ret. to NYC '55. Pl. w. Chas. Mingus, Lloyd Price '56. Worked briefly w. r&b mus. Chuck Edwards in Pitts., then join. Max Roach w. bro. Stanley '59. Pl. w. Roach '59–60, then freelanced in early '60s w. Paul Chambers; Booker Ervin; Stanley Turrentine; Ahmed Abdul-Malik; Jackie McLean; Sonny Clark; Dexter Gordon; Lou Donaldson; Rufus Jones; John Patton. Sporadically active fr. mid '60s. In the '70s and '80s Turrentine was assoc. w. the U. of the Streets on NYC's Lower East Side, freq. perf. there w. saxophonist Clarence "C" Sharpe. App. w. Barry Harris at Symph. Space, NYC '80s. Pl. and rec. w. Sun Ra '88. Although ill health forced Turrentine to stop pl. in '88, he cont. to write and contribute comps. to recs. by his bro. Stanley and others. Favs: Miles Davis, Ray Nance, Thad Jones, Clifford Brown, Fats Navarro, Dizzy Gillespie. CDs: Time; w. S. Turrentine; Sonny Clark (BN); M. Roach (Enja; Time); Sun Ra (A&M); B. Rich (Verve); Abbey Lincoln (Riv.); P. J. Jones (Sonet); Booker Ervin (Aff.).

TURSO, RON (RONALD DOMINICK), dms; b. NYC, 7/29/48. Father, Duke, and bro., Turk Mauro, pl. sax and sing; moth. is amateur pnst. Stud. at Newtown HS, then w. Nick Stabulas, Charlie Perry. First gigs w. father, then freelance in NYC 1966–7. In army '68–70. Pl. w. Turk Mauro '70–3; Vinnie Burke '74. House dmr. at Sonny's Place, Long Island, N.Y. '75; pl. in LI sch. w. Billy Mitchell; Mauro; Hugh Lawson; also Club Med w. Joe Newman '75–6. Pl. w. Dakota Staton '77–8; Eddie Jefferson '79. Subbed for Eddie Locke w. Roy Eldridge '79–80. Pl. w. Zoot Sims '81–5; B. Mitchell–T. Mauro '85; Joe Newman '86–9; T. Mauro fr. '87; Sol Yaged '92. Favs: Buddy Rich, Max Roach, Tony Williams. Fests: Scand. w. D. Staton '77; Paris '87–91, Belgium '88 w. Mauro. TV: Swedish TV w. Staton '77. CDs: w. T. Mauro (Bloom.).

TURTLE ISLAND STRING QUARTET. Members incl. vln. Darol Anger; vln. David Balakrishnan; vla. Katrina Wreede; and cello Mark Summer. Self-described as specialists in "American vernacular music," the qt.'s first album, *The Turtle Island String Quartet* (WH), revealed an ens. whose members were surprisingly competent improv. Balakrishnan, who writes many of the group's arrs., performs with a firm command of jazz rhythms. Anger, a folk-oriented perf. bef. he joined the gp., brings a loose, country feeling to his solos. Summer and Wreede tend to pl. supporting roles, although Wreede is an effective improv. on vla. and Summer's crisp accents give the gp. its solid, rhythmic foundation. In '92 Wreede was replaced by Tanya Kalmanovitch. CDs: WH; *On the Town* feat. the Billy Taylor Trio.

TWARDZIK, DICK (RICHARD), pno; b. Danvers, MA, 4/30/31; d. Paris, France, 10/21/55. Studied classical pno. w. Margaret Chaloff, att. Longy Sch. of Music, Cambridge, Mass., and New Engl. Cons. Prof. debut w. Serge Chaloff in Bost. 1951. Later pl. w. Charlie Parker; Charlie Mariano; and Herb Pomeroy; tour. w. Lionel Hampton. Rec. w. Chaloff, Mariano, and as a leader bef. joining Chet Baker for Eur. tour '55; while on tour died of a drug overdose, robbing jazz of an outstandingly individual stylist. His best work is contained in half a Pacific Jazz LP shared with Russ Freeman and includes his provocative comps: "A Crutch For the Crab"; "Albuquerque Social Swim"; and "Yellow Tango." Favs: Bud Powell, Art Tatum. CDs: New Artists; w. C. Parker (Up.); C. Baker (Em.; Verve); S. Chaloff (Mos.); C. Mariano (Prest.).

29th STREET SAXOPHONE QUARTET. A vital, cohesive, and lucid gp. w. Bobby Watson, Ed Jackson, altos; Rich Rothenberg, tnr.; and Jim Hartog, bari.; all four saxophonists doubling as comps. CDs: Ant.; Red. *See also* **WATSON, BOBBY.**

TYLER, CHARLES LACY, alto, sop, bari saxes, cl; b. Cadiz, KY, 7/20/41; d. Toulon, France, 6/28/92. Studied alto sax and cl. Pl. bari. sax in an army band. Pl. w. Albert Ayler 1965; rec. first album as a leader w. Henry Grimes, Charles Moffet, others '66. Formed the New Mus. Orch. w. Arthur Blythe, Oliver Lake, Julius Hemphill, and others. Rec. w. Billy Bang '81–3. Toured Eur. w. Sun Ra and settled in Den. '84; moved to France '85. Rec. w. Steve Lacy '86; from late '80s worked w. Alan Silva; Bobby Few; Chris Henderson; et al. CDs: Silk.; ESP; w. Ayler (ESP); Hal Russell (Chief); Steve Lacy (Silk.); Khan Jamal (Steep.); Billy Bang (SN).

TYNER, (ALFRED) McCOY (aka Sulaimon Saud), pno; b. Philadelphia, PA, 12/13/38. Piano studies fr. age 13 at Granoff Sch. of Mus. First important prof. gig w. Benny Golson–Art Farmer Jazztet 1959; but major recognition came when he pl. w. John Coltrane Qt. '60–5. In the '60s he also rec. under his own name for Imp. and BN w. Ron Carter; Lee Morgan; Joe Henderson; and others. In '71 he signed w. Mile.; toured and rec. w. Milestone Jazzstars (Ron Carter, Sonny Rollins, and Al Foster) '78; led qnt. w. Gary Bartz and vlnst. John Blake mid '80s. In '87 toured int'l w. Avery Sharpe and Louis Hayes in a tribute to Coltrane. In the '90s his trio has incl. bs. Sharpe and Aaron Scott—who became his regular dmr. He also formed a bb, pl. in clubs and on int'l tours. Tyner has been infl. in the use of rich-textured harmonies as rhythmic devices, sometimes based on fourths and fifths, often with extensive use of modes. His pl. also has been greatly infl. by African and Asian elements. CDs: Imp.; Mile.; Den.; BN; Bird.; Verve; Evid.; Chesky; Enja; Red Brn.; Timel.; w. J. Coltrane (Atl.; Imp.; Roul.; Rh.); A. Sharpe (Sunny.); Hank Mobley; Joe Henderson; Grant Green; Lee Morgan; Wayne Shorter (BN); The Jazztet (Chess); J. J. Johnson; A. Blakey (Imp.); Curtis Fuller (Sav.); Steve Grossman (Drey.); Rollins; Grappelli (Mile.); David Murray (DIW); Frank Morgan (Cont.).

u

ULANO, SAM (SOLOMON PAUL), dms; b. NYC, 8/12/20. Brother Ben pl. acdn.; a niece, Ellen Payne, is prof. concert vlnst. Stud. dms. and tympani at Harlem Sch. of Mus. 1935. Pl. w. army band in Hawaii and Japan '42–6. Owned drm. shop in NYC '46–70. Taught at NY Coll. of Mus. '52–62. Wrote articles for *Int'l Musician* mag early '50s and later for *Big Bands* mag. Pl. w. Bill Snyder '56–60; Tony Parenti–Dick Wellstood at Metropole Café, NYC '60–4; Sol Yaged '64–75; own gp. at Gaslight club '75–80; Max Kaminsky at Eddie Condon's late '70s; own qt. at Red Blazer '87–92; Bob Cantwell's NY Stompers fr. '89. Ulano led a 9–pc. band, Sammy's Double-Dixie Band, at the Red Blazer fr. '92. Ulano is the subject of a biographical docu. film, *Mr. Rhythm* '93. He has produced instructional material for dmrs., incl. books and videos, and publ. a magazine, *Drum Files Revisited.* Favs: Buddy Rich, Gene Krupa, Max Roach, Louis Bellson, Philly Joe Jones, Sid Catlett, Tony Briglia. Film: *Mr. Rhythm.* TV: Garry Moore, Ernie Kovacs, Steve Allen, Shari Lewis '50s–'60s; Cerebral Palsy telethons w. Yaged '67–70; Joe Franklin '80s; David Letterman '92. LPs: Lane; w. S. Yaged (Lane).

ULMER, JAMES BLOOD (Damu Mustafa Abdul Musawwir), gtr, comp, arr, fl; b. St. Matthews, SC, 2/2/42. Self-taught fr. age 4; stud. w. fath., James David Ulmer, fr. age 14. Pl. w. father's gp. 1951–5; pl. and sang w. gospel gp. Southern Sons. Moved to Pitts. '59, pl. w. r&b gps. Savoys, Del Vikings, Jewel Brenner's Swing Kings '59–64. Moved to Columbus, Ohio '64, stud. jazz and pl. w. Hank Marr '64–7. Moved to Det. '67, pl. w. Big John Patton and local gps. '67–71. Moved to NYC '71. Pl. nine mos. at Minton's Playhouse, then w. Art Blakey; Rashied Ali, Larry Young; Joe Henderson; Paul Bley; Arthur Blythe. Stud. and perf. w. Ornette Coleman '73–8; pl. w. own gps. fr. '78. Fr. the late '80s Ulmer has led several gps., each one dedicated to a particular mus. style., incl. The J. B. Ulmer Blues Experience; the Music Revelation Ens., a "pure" jazz gp.; The Odyssey Band, devoted to Ornette Coleman's "harmolodic concept"; and the Intercity String Qt. w. J. B. Ulmer, for which he is comp. and arr. Polls: Individual Jazz Award '79; Jazz Broke Out Award '82. Fests: Eur., Japan fr. '70s. CDs: Phalanx; Col.; DIW; In + Out; w. Sola (Axiom); Joe Henderson (Mile.); Third Rail (Ant.); John Patton (BN); Karl Berger (In + Out); David Murray (BS); Music Revelation Ens. (Moers; DIW).

UMEZU, KAZUTOKI, alto sax, cl, bs-cl; b. Sendai, Japan, 10/17/49. Began on cl. at age 13. Stud. at Kunitachi U. of Mus., where he formed duo w. pnst. Yoriyuki Harada. After graduating, moved to NYC '74. Formed gp. Seikatsu Kojo Iinkai w. Harada. Also pl. w. Lester Bowie, Ted Daniel, Arthur Blythe, Oliver Lake, others '74–7. Ret. to Japan '77; reformed Seikatsu Kojo Iinkai w. Harada, also gp. Shudan Sokai (Mass Evacuation). In '80s formed free-jazz gps. D-U-B (Doctor Umezu Band) and DIVA, and tour. Eur. Also pl. w. Yosuke Yamashita; Masahiko Togashi; rock gp. R. C. Succession. Tour. Austral. w. Fumio Itabashi, Nobuyoshi Ino '90. Pl. w. Masahiko Sato's Randooga fr. '90; Kazumi Watanabe's Asian Fantasy '91. Pl. w. Tom Cara at Knitting Factory in NYC '93. Mal Waldron rec. w. him on Teichiku-Union. Polls: *SJ* Critics misc. instr. '91; *SJ* Critics New Star cl. '91–2. CDs:

Teichiku-Union; w. D-U-B (Omagatoki); Tom Cara (Umiushi); DIVA (NEC-Avenue).

UMO JAZZ ORCHESTRA. Internationally known orch. from Helsinki, Finland, established in 1975 w. Esko Linnavalli as conductor, and supported by the Finnish Ministry of Educ.; Finnish Broadcasting Co. (YLE); and the city of Helsinki. It became full-time orch. in '84. "The very highest praise for UMO. What other band could do "African Game," "All About Rosie" and "Ezz-thetic" in three rehearsals!?" — George Russell. CDs: *UMO Plays the Music of Muhal Richard Abrams* (UMO); UMO Jazz Orch. (Naxos).

UPCHURCH, PHIL, gtr, bs, dms, synth, comp; b. Chicago, IL, 7/19/41. Father a pno. pl., introduced him to uke. 1952. Self-taught. Began rec. career at age 17 w. gps. of Curtis Mayfield; Otis Rush; Jimmy Reed. After tour. w. r&b gps. ret. to Chi., pl. and rec. w. Woody Herman; Stan Getz; Groove Holmes; B. B. King; Dizzy Gillespie. Drafted into mil. in '65, he pl. jazz clubs in Germ. w. Special Services. Ret. in '67 to rec. w. Richard Evans; Grover Washington; Cannonball Adderley. Joined Ramsey Lewis '70. To LA '71 for film work. Tour. Japan w. Quincy Jones '72. Led qnt. w. Tennyson Stephens; album w. CTI '75. Perf. w. George Benson '75–81; Mose Allison '82; Gary Burton; Joe Williams; Natalie Cole; Carmen McRae; Michael Jackson. Taught seminars at Duquesne U. and in Japan. In LA fr. '77. Tours w. Julio Iglesias '84; Jimmy Smith '90; and in Eur. w. Jack McDuff '91. Pl. own custom-made gtr. Infls: Kenny Burrell, Albert King, B. B. King, Muddy Waters. Book: subject of *What It's Like to Be a Musician* by Arthur Shay (Reilly & Lee, Chi.). CDs: King; Jam; Pro Jazz; w. Joe Williams (Tel.; Delos); Red Holloway–C. Terry; J. McDuff (Conc.); Gtr. Wkshp. (JVC); Booker T. Jones (MCA); Dennis Rowland (Conc.); J. Pisano (Pab.); Geo. Benson (WB).

URBANI, MASSIMO, alto sax; b. Rome, Italy, 5/8/57; d. Rome, 6/24/93. Brother, Maurizio, pl. tnr. Began on cl. Stud. at Cons. di S. Cecilia 1971. Pl. w. Giorgio Gaslini '71–3; jazz rock gp. Area '73; Enrico Rava '74–7; Lester Bowie '77–8; Eur. Jazz Orch., Kenny Clarke '78; Enrico Pierannunzi '79–84; Five for Jazz '83–4; Giovanni Tommaso '85–7; Eur. All-Stars '89. Urbani taught clinics in the US at Duke U. and Berklee Coll. of Mus. Favs: Charlie Parker, Sonny Stitt. Polls: Ital. Critics Poll '80; Top Jazz Awd. '82; Charlie Parker Awd. '85. Fests: All major in Eur.; US '75, '85–6; Austral. '75. Films: *Sconcerto Rock* w. Gianna Nannini, Bernardo Bertolucci. TV: Ital. TV. CDs: BMG-Ariola; Red; Spl.; w. G. Tommaso (Red); Mario Schiano (Spl).

URBANIAK, MICHAL, vln, tnr, sop saxes; b. Warsaw, Poland, 1/22/43. Studied at Warsaw Acad. of Mus. Became interested in jazz after hearing Willis Conover show on Voice of Amer. Pl. tnr. w. Zbigniew Namyslowski 1961; Andrzej Trzaskowski '62–4; Krzysztof Komeda '62–5; also worked as classical vlnst. dur. this time. Led own gp. w. Urszula Dudziak in Scand. '65–9; Constellation in Poland '65–early '70s. Moved to NYC in early '70s. Pl. w. own gp., Fusion '74–7; Larry Coryell '80s; also pl. w. Archie Shepp; Bill Cobham; Oliver Nelson; Miles Davis. Urbaniak comp. the score to film *On the Road*. He was given the Grand Prix for Best Soloist at the Montreux JF '71. Favs: Stuff Smith; comps: Miles Davis, Stevie Wonder, Duke Ellington, Wayne Shorter. Polls: *DB; Jazz Forum* '72–3. TV: Eur. TV. CDs: Steep.; L+R; Polskie Nagramia; Story.; Milan; w. Miles Davis (WB); Paul Bley; Larry Coryell (Steep.); K. Komeda (Polonia).

URSO, PHIL, tnr sax; b. Jersey City, NJ, 10/2/25. Raised in Denver, Colo.; self-taught, first on cl, then tnr. sax; US Navy. To NYC 1947. Pl. w. Elliot Lawrence '48–50; Woody Herman '50–51; Terry Gibbs, Miles Davis '52; Oscar Pettiford '53. Many gigs at Birdland w. bop gps., where he met Chet Baker. Starting '55, they worked together intermittently until '72. With Claude Thornhill late '50s. Between jobs, he frequently ret. to Denver and was still living and working there in the mid '90s. Infl. by Zoot Sims and Sonny Rollins. "Perhaps not an innovator," *Jazz Journal* noted, "but a very polished and stylish tenor saxophonist." CDs: Sav.; w. Chet Baker (PJ; FS; Verve); Art Pepper (Mos.); w. Pettiford in Mingus: *The Complete Debut Recordings* and *The Debut Records Story* (Deb.).

URTREGER, RENÉ, pno; b. Paris, France, 7/16/34. Lived in Southern France and No. Africa 1939–45. After yrs. of classical training took up jazz in '51. First prof. gig w. Pierre Michelot '53; worked w. Don Byas and Buck Clayton; rec. w. Chet Baker '55. Toured the Continent w. Birdland show, backing Miles Davis, Lester Young, John Lewis, et al. '56; reg. accomp. at Paris' Club Saint-Germain for many visiting Amer. soloists, incl. Davis, Young, Lionel Hampton, Stan Getz late '50s. Awarded Prix Django Reinhardt '61; rec. w. Stephane Grappelli and Stuff Smith '65; also worked on mus. for films and TV and accomp. the Double Six of Paris. Except for a period in '64 when he tour. w. a pop singer, Urtreger remained active in jazz. In '80s he worked regularly at The Montana Club in Paris and appeared regularly in concerts and jazz fests. One of France's outstanding pnsts. in the Bud Powell tradition. CDs: w. S.

Getz (LRC); L. Young (Verve); Chet Baker (Em.; Verve); M. Davis (Fontana); Kenny Clarke (Philips).

UTESOV (or UTYOSOV), LEONID OSIPO-VICH, voc, vln; b. Odessa, Ukraine, Russia, 3/21/1895; d. Moscow, USSR, 3/10/82. Involved in the theater fr. his early yrs., he established his Theatrical Jazz Ens. in 1921, adapting Russian folk songs. Inspired by Sam Wooding's Chocolate Kiddies band, which visited the USSR in the '20s, and by Ted Lewis, Utesov app. in concerts and on recs. and became the most popular entertainer in Stalin's Russia. His film, *The Happy Guys*, was a great success at the '35 Venice Film Festival and supposedly earned him Stalin's approval. Although he placed a heavy accent on comedy and entertainment, the band usually incl. a number of jazz-oriented sidemen and arrs. of works by Duke Ellington, Frankie Trumbauer, and others. In '65 Utesov was named a People's Artist of the USSR. He cont. to lead a band until '75. Recs. on Melodiya label.

VACHÉ, WARREN WEBSTER JR., crnt, tpt, flg, pno; b. Rahway, NJ, 2/21/51. Father, Warren, is bs. and jazz writer; bro. Allan pl. cl., sax w. Jim Cullum band in Tex. Began on pno., then sw. to brass instr. in elem. sch. Stud. w. Jim Fitzpatrick, then at Montclair St. Coll.; w. Pee Wee Erwin 1970–80. First gigs in N.J. w. father. Pl. w. NYJRC at Carnegie Hall, recreating solos of Bix Beiderbecke '75; Benny Goodman off and on '75–85; house band at Eddie Condon's '76–9; Scott Hamilton fr. '76; Concord Super Band '79–82; Concord All-Stars fr. '79; Geo. Wein's Festival All-Stars fr. '84. Played, led orch. for, and co-produced w. Ira Gitler Swing: 40 and Over for JVC-NY '91. Vaché acted and pl. in the '85 film The Gig. He coached actor Richard Gere for his role as a tpt. player in the film The Cotton Club and was mus. dir. for the stage revival of Private Lives starring Richard Burton and Elizabeth Taylor. Fests: all major fr. '75. TV: Today. CDs: Conc.; N-H; Zephyr; Aud.; w. H. Alden; Dan Barrett; R. Clooney; Conc. All-Stars; S. Hamilton; W. Herman; NJF All-Stars; Geo. Shearing (Conc.); B. Goodman (Lond.); Bobby Short; G. Mulligan (Tel.); D. Hyman (MM); Judy Carmichael (Jazz.); G. Wein (Col.); B. Goodman (Verve; Lond.).

VALDAMBRINI, OSCAR, tpt, flg; b. Turin, Italy, 5/11/24; d. Rome, Italy, 12/26/97. Father, Agostino, was vlnst. Stud. vln. at Turin Cons., later stud. tpt. priv. Pl. in Switzerland mid 1940s, then in Turin bef. settling in Milan in early '50s. Jammed w. Rex Stewart '48. Led qnt. w. Gianni Basso '52; Sestetto Italiano '55–7. Formed new qnt. w. Basso '55 which became best-known modern jazz gp. in Italy. Basso-Valdambrini Qnt. was house band at Taverna Mexico, Milan, backing Gerry Mulligan, Chet Baker, Lars Gullin, Stan Getz, Miles Davis, Conte Candoli '55–60. Pl. w. Armando Trovajoli bb '57–8. Added tbn. Dino Piana to Basso gp., visited NYC '62. Pl. in Eur. w. bbs of Gil Cuppini '64–71; Giorgio Gaslini '68–9; Duke Ellington '68–9; Maynard Ferguson '70–1; Lionel Hampton. Re-formed Basso-Valdambrini Sxt. '72; cont. to lead gp. after Basso left '74. Pl. w. TV Orch. of Rome fr. '72, incl. concerts w. Frank Rosolino; Freddie Hubbard; Ernie Wilkins; Mel Lewis. Pl. w. Dusko Goykovich, Kai Winding '80s. Concerts in NYC '93. Led a sxt. w. Dino Piana. Favs: Armstrong, Roy Eldridge, Chet Baker, Miles Davis, Tom Harrell. Polls: Ital. Critics '74. Fests: all major in Eur. CDs: w. Piana-Valdambrini Sxt. (Penta.); Basso-Valdambrini Sxt. (Fonit Cetra).

VALDES, CHUCHO (JESUS), kybds, comp; b. Quivican, Cuba, 10/9/41. Father, Bebo, an important Cuban lead.; dur. 1950s Chucho cond. the band. Studied w. Zenaida Romeu; Rosario Franco. Worked w. Ernesto Lecuona; Benny More. Led first trio at age 16. Pl. w. Elio Reve Orch. '65–7. Formed the Orquesta Cubana de Musica Moderna in '67. This evolved into the gp. known as Irakere, formed in '73 w. Valdes as leader, Arturo Sandoval and Paquito D'Rivera as sidemen. He continues to lead this band in the '90s, w. new personnel, combining Afro-Cuban, jazz, and classical infls. Also leads own qt. and perf. as solo pnst. In '80 founded Havana Int'l JF, which has grown in stature through '98. Guests over the yrs. have included Tania Maria, Ronnie Scott, Dizzy Gillespie, Carmen McRae, and Roy Hargrove. At the '96 fest. Hargrove put together the gp. Crisol with American and Cuban mus., incl. Valdes. It tour. int'l and rec. for Verve. As a soloist and lead. Valdes app. several times at Lincoln Center; w. qt. at the Village Vanguard plus sist., voc. Mayra Valdes. A highly skilled composer/arranger, he employs his formidable keyboard technique to bring forth, in the words of writer Raquel Vallejo, "double-handed arpeggios, Afro-Cuban passages, stunning chords and blazing rhapsodies." Comps: "Missa Negra"; "Tierra En Trance"; "Cantata a Babalu"; "Yemaya"; "La Explosion." Favs: Kenny Barron, McCoy Tyner, Bill Evans, Tommy Flanagan, Brad Mehdau. Fests: NJF-NY '78; Montreal '93; Umbria '98; w. Crisol, JVC-NY '97. CDs: BN; VV; Bembe; Import; Int'l Mus.; Mess.; RMM; JH; w. Irakere (Col.; BN; Mess.); Hargrove (Verve); Sandoval (JH).

VALDES, PATATO (Carlos M. Valdes-Galan), cga, perc; b. Havana, Cuba, 11/4/26. Father pl. el tres (Cuban gtr.). Began on el tres at age 12, then pl. bs. bef. sw. to cga. Pl. in Cuba w. La Sonora Mantancera fr. 1944; also w. Conjunto Casino; Conjunto Kubavana; Conjunto Azul; Chano Pozo. Moved to US '53. Pl. w. Machito '53–7; Tito Puente '57–9; Herbie Mann '59–72. Also freelanced and rec. w. Kenny Dorham; Art Blakey; Billy Taylor; Grant Green; Max Roach; Mike Longo; Willie Bobo; Cal Tjader; Quincy Jones; Alfredo Rodriguez; Elvin Jones; Dizzy Gillespie; Jorge Dalto. Tour. Eur. w. Mario Bauza '91. Valdes made several recs. demonstrating Latin perc. techniques '74–80 and is the designer of Latin Perc. Inc.'s Patato model cga. Favs: Armando Peraza, Francisco Aquavella, Giovanni Hildalgo. Fests: Eur., Africa w. Mann. Film: *And God Created Woman* w. Brigitte Bardot. TV: Jerry Lewis telethon; *Bill Cosby Show; You Bet Your Life* w. Cosby. CDs: w. Grant Green; A. Blakey; K. Dorham (BN); M. Longo (CAP); Roy Hargrove; Cal Tjader (Verve); Q. Jones (Merc.); H. Mann (Atl.); Hilton Ruiz (Tel.); Benny Golson (Mile.); Ronnie Cuber (FS).

VALENTIN, DAVE (DAVID), fl; b. Bronx, NY, 4/29/52. Started on cgas. and bongos at age 7; joined a local gp. at 13 as a timbales pl.; att. HS of Mus. and Art; stud. perc. and fl. Rec. debut w. Ricardo Marrero's gp. 1977; also rec. w. vlnst. Noel Pointer that yr. Signed w. newly formed GRP label and went on to rec. fourteen albums. Named best fl. in *Jazziz* Readers Poll '89, '90, '91. A firm believer in the world-related aspects of his instrument, he usually tours w. fifteen fl. of various sizes and materials. "What I want to do," says Valentin, "is portray a whole tapestry of sound and bring a full interpretation of what the flute is all about." CDs: GRP; Trop.; w. S. Turre (Ant.); GRP All-Star bb; Jay Hoggard (GRP); T. Puente (Trop.); C. Fambrough (Evid.); Memo Acevedo (JA); Adela Dalto (Mile.); D. Grolnick (WB); D. Grusin (N2K).

VALENTINE, JERRY (GERALD), arr, tbn; b. Chicago, IL, 9/14/14. Studied comp.; self-taught on tbn. Joined Earl Hines on tbn. 1940; many arr. for Hines, incl. "Second Balcony Jump." Worked in Chi. w. Dallas Bartley; King Kolax; arr. for shows at club DeLisa '43. Best known as arr. and pl. w. Billy Eckstine orch. '44–7; among his charts was Sarah Vaughan's only rec. w. the band, "I'll Wait and Pray," and the instrumental, "Blowing the Blues Away." A&R adviser for National Recs. in early '50s. He later wrote arrs. for Art Farmer; Coleman Hawkins; and Pepper Adams. CDs: w. C. Hawkins (Prest.); Hines (Class.); Eckstine (Sav.); arrs. & cond. for Prestige Blues-Swingers, *Outskirts of Town* (Prest.).

VAN EPS, GEORGE ABEL, gtr; b. Plainfield, NJ, 8/7/13; d. Newport Beach, CA, 11/29/98. Noted mus. family incl. fath., ragtime bjo. pl. and arr. Fred Van Eps; bros. Bobby, pno. and arr.; John, saxes. Self-taught on bjo. 1924; pl. w. Smith Ballew '29–31; Freddy Martin '31–3; Benny Goodman '34–5; Ray Noble '35–6 and '39–41; freelance radio and recs. in Hollywood '36–9 and '45–55, incl. house band work w. Paul Weston since '45. Worked for father in sound rec. research lab., Plainfield '42–4. Freelanced in Calif., incl. studio work; feat. w. Dick Cathcart band in film and TV series, *Pete Kelly's Blues* '55. App. at Colo. JPs in '60s. Inactive after suffering heart attack but pl. occ. at Donte's in Hollywood. Tour. UK in '86. A pioneer expert in chord-style acoustic gtr., Van Eps designed a unique 7-string gtr. w. additional bs. string, allowing him to accomp. himself. In the '90s he formed a partnership w. Howard Alden, making occ. apps. and recs. CDs: Conc.; w. B. Goodman (BB; Dec.); H. Alden; Johnny Smith (Conc.); Judy Garland (Dec.); Red Norvo (Hep).

VAN MANEN, WILLEM, tbn, comp; b. Amsterdam, Netherlands, 9/3/40. Studied sociology; became prof. mus. at age 27. In 1970s and '80s pl. w. Günter Hampel and Willem Breuker Kollektief. Founded his own gp., the ContraBand, '85, active throughout Eur. More than 100 jazz comps. Professor of tbn. at Sweelinck Cons., Amsterdam. CDs: w. Breuker (Entr'acte); ContraBand (Bvhaast; VPRO); Leo Cuypers (Bvhaast.).

VAN ROOYEN, ACK, tpt, flg, arr; b. The Hague, Netherlands, 1/1/30. Studied at Royal Cons., The Hague 1947–50. Pl. w. Ernst van't Hoff '51; his bro. Gerry Van Rooyen '54; the Ramblers '55–7. Worked in France w. Aime Barelli '57–60; Kenny Clarke. Pl. in Germ. w. Sender Freies Berlin '60–7; Erwin Lehn '67. Freelanced in Germ. and the Netherlands w. Peter Herbolzheimer bb fr. '70; Charlie Antolini bb

'72–80; United Jazz and Rock Ens. '75; Gustav Brom bb '76; Hans Koller bb '77; Stephan Dietz '78; H. Koller bb '80. Toured w. Clark Terry, Gil Evans '79. Also arr. for radio orchs. '70s. Freelanced in Netherlands, also taught in cons '80s. CDs: w. Miles Davis (WB); Paul Heller (Mons); Mark Murphy (September); Eberhard Weber (ECM).

VANCE, DICK (RICHARD THOMAS), comp, arr, tpt; b. Mayfield, KY, 11/28/15; d. NYC, 7/31/85. Grew up in Cleveland, Ohio. Began on vln., then sw. to tpt. Tour. w. Frank Terry 1932–4, then worked w. Lil Armstrong in Buffalo '35. Moved to NYC '36. Pl. w. Kaiser Marshall, Willie Bryant '36; Fletcher Henderson '36–8. Pl. and arr. for Chick Webb–Ella Fitzgerald '38–41. Staff arr. for Cab Calloway, Don Redman, Glen Gray '39–41; also arr. for Sarah Vaughan–Earl Hines; Billy Eckstine bb; Lena Horne; Harry James Orch. Pl. w. Eddie Heywood '44–5; Charlie Barnet, Don Redman '40s; extens. work in B'way pit bands '40s. Stud. comp. and tpt. at Juilliard '44–7. Pl. w. Duke Ellington Orch. '51–2 and arr. several selections on Ellington '55 LP. Freelanced and pl. in Radio City orch. '60s. Pl. for B'way shows incl. *Hallelujah Baby* '67; *No, No, Nanette* '71–2; *Seesaw* '73. Toured Africa as cond. w. Jazz Dance Theater '69. Freelanced and pl. w. Eddie Barefield's Bearcats '70s; also some arr. for Duke Ellington, Mercer Ellington. Vance taught musicology and jazz perf. at Manh. Community Coll. fr. '70. CDs: w. F. Henderson (Col.); E. Fitzgerald (Dec.; Col.); C. Webb (Dec.); Chu Berry; Vic Dickenson (Topaz); C. Hawkins; Billy Kyle; Mary Lou Williams (Class.); Billie Holiday (Dec.)

VAN'T HOF, JASPER, kybds, pno; b. Enschede, Netherlands, 6/30/47. Both parents were musicians. Took six yrs. of classical pno. lessons. Led qt. w. gtrst. Toto Blanke 1970, then pl. w. Pierre Courbois' Association PC '70–2; Chris Hinze '73–4; Pno. Conclave, Archie Shepp '74; Zbigniew Seifert mid '70s. Rec. as lead. fr. '73. Co-led gp. Pork Pie w. Charlie Mariano, Philip Catherine mid '70s. Van't Hof cont. to pl. w. former Pork Pie sidemen, incl. Mariano, Jean-Luc Ponty, Alphonze Mouzon, into the '80s. Rec. w. Total Music trio w. C. Hinze, Sigi Schwab '82. Led own gps. in '80s incl. Eyeball w. Didier Lockwood; Pili Pili, which incorporated African perc. and computer mus. Rec. in '80s w. A. Shepp. CDs: w. Philip Catherine (CMP); Lol Coxhill (See For Miles); George Gruntz; Wolfgang Dauner (MPS); C. Mariano (Lipstick); A. Shepp (Steep.).

VARNER, TOM (THOMAS L.), Fr horn, comp; b. Morristown, NJ, 6/17/57. Raised in Millburn, N.J.

Pno. at 9; Fr. horn at 10. Stud. in public sch. and at New Engl. Cons., where his instructors incl. Peter Gordon; Jaki Byard; George Russell. Grad. in 1979 w. B. Mus. Stud. priv. w. Julius Watkins, Dave Liebman under NEA Grant '81. Began pl. prof. in Bost. in late '70s. Moved to NYC '79; was helped by John Clark. Did early work in Eur. as leader and w. George Gruntz orch. Pl. w. Dave Liebman sxt. '82; Gruntz '83–91; Bobby Previte '83–90; John Zorn '84–90; Urs Blochlinger Ens. '85–9; N.Y. Composers Orch. fr. '87; La Monte Young bb '90; Ton Art '90–4; fr. '90 w. Peter Scharli sxt.; fr. '91 w. Neil Kirkwood Oct.; fr. '92 w. George Schuller's Orange Then Blue; Franz Koglmann's Pipetet, Bobby Watson bb '93; Steve Lacy Oct. '93–5; fr. 94 w. Ed Jackson Oct.; East Down Spt.; fr. '95 w. Hans Kennel's Habarigani Brass. Also pl. w. Thomas Chapin; Mel Lewis orch.; Jane Ira Bloom. As a leader has app. at Knitting Factory, incl. such sidemen as L. Konitz, Previte, Mark Feldman; The Kitchen; Roulette; Greenwich House; various NYC churches. Has tour. in So. Amer. '84; Far East '87; Eur. fr. '82. Has given lectures/wkshps. for Int'l Horn Society. Favs: J. Watkins; comp. Henry Threadgill, Dave Douglas. Polls: *DB* '83; *JT* '90, '93. Video: *Miles and Quincy at Montreux*; wrote and perf. score *Saints and Sinners*. Rec. debut w. own qt. for SN, NYC '80. Fav. own solo: "How Does Power Work" on album *The Mystery of Compassion*. CDs: SN; NN; NW; w. Previte (Gram.); Gruntz (ECM; Enja; Hat Hut); Zorn (None.); Watson (Col.); Lacy (SN); Allan Harris; Chris Kase (Mons); Roberto Ottariano (Spl.).

VARRO, JOHNNY (JOHN ROBERT), pno; b. Brooklyn, NY, 1/11/30. Studied priv. Played at Central Plaza, NYC fr. 1946; after army service, tour. w. Bobby Hackett '53. In '50s often app. at Nick's and Eddie Condon's in NYC. To Fla. '65. Tour. Far East w. Dukes of Dixieland; then settled in Miami, where he led his own trio for almost ten yrs. Based in LA fr. '79; pl. at local clubs. Toured Eur. several times w. Wild Bill Davison and Peanuts Hucko; many jazz parties in US and Can. CDs: Arb.; w. Eddie Miller; Chuck Hedges (Del.); Davison (Timel.); R. Braff; Rick Fay; Tom Saunders (Arb.); Danny Moss; Bill Allred; Allan Vaché (N-H); Dick Hafer (Prog.).

VASCONCELOS, NANA (JUVENAL DE HOLLANDA), perc; b. Recife, Brazil, 8/2/44. Debut w. fath.'s gp. at age 12; later pl. dms. in bossa nova band. Moved to Rio to join Milton Nascimento in mid 1960s, stud. berimbau. Toured Argentina, US, and Eur. w. Gato Barbieri; then stayed in Eur. for two yrs., rec., pl., and working with handicapped children. Toured w. Egberto Gismonti '77. In '78 founded the trio Codona w. Don Cherry and Collin Walcott. After Walcott's death in '84, he worked in a gp. w. Cherry. Led his own unit, Bush Dance. Worked w. Jan Garbarek gp. in late '80s. Vasconcelos has contributed a broad variety of tonal effects through the use of the cuica and many other perc. instruments. CDs: Ant.; w. Jim Pepper (Ryko; Island); J. DeJohnette (Imp.); Eliane Elias (BN); Trilok Gurtu (CMP); J. Garbarek (ECM); J. Hoggard (GRP); P. Metheny (ECM); Ivo Perelman (GM).

VAUGHAN, SARAH LOIS ("SASSY"), voc; b. Newark, NJ, 3/27/24; d. Los Angeles, CA, 4/3/90. Sang at the Mt. Zion Baptist Church, Newark, N.J., as a child; pno lessons 1931–9; also pl. org. Won amateur contest at Apollo Theatre, NYC; was recommended to Earl Hines by Billy Eckstine. Made debut as voc. and second pnst. w. Hines orch. at the Apollo, Apr. '43. Joined Eckstine's new band '44–5; first solo rec. Dec. '44. Sang briefly w. John Kirby combo '45–6, otherwise worked mainly as a solo act after leaving Eckstine. Rec. for Musi. '46. Aided by the praise and enthusiasm of such mus. as Dizzy Gillespie and Charlie Parker, she slowly gained wider public acceptance under the guidance of her first husband, George Treadwell. Starting in '49 she rec. for Col. and moved into the upper echelons of show business via TV, recs., concerts, and int'l tours. In '54 she made a classic sess. w. Clifford Brown for the Em. label and later a bb sess. led by Ernie Wilkins. In '60s rec. w. bands led by Count Basie; Benny Carter; Frank Foster; Quincy Jones; and others on Merc. and Roul. From the '60s she visited over sixty countries, app. in a variety of environments w. accomps. ranging fr. trio to symph. orch. In US she sang w. the Boston Pops; LA Philharm.; the Cleveland and SF Symphs.; and numerous others. In '72 she rec. an LP for the Main. label w. Michel Legrand as comp., arr., and cond. From '78–80 she was backed by her then-husband, tptr. Waymon Reed's qt. In '80s she enjoyed great public success. Although she was never a best-selling rec. artist—in the pop music sense—she had one hit, "Broken-hearted Melody" '58, and her albums are perennial catalog items. Sarah Vaughan's voice, completely different from those of Billie Holiday, Ella Fitzgerald, or any of the great jazz stylists before her, brought to jazz an unprecedented combination of attractive characteristics: a rich, beautifully controlled tone and vibrato; an ear for a song's chord structure that enabled her to change or inflect the melody as an instrumentalist might; a coy, sometimes archly naïve quality alternating w. a great sense of sophistication. Her numerous awards incl. the *Esq.* New Star Award '47; *DB* polls '47–52.

CDs: Col.; Verve; Em.; Mob. Fid.; Main.; Merc.; Roul.; Laser.; Pab.; BN; w. C. Basie (Pab.; Mos.); B. Eckstine (Class.; Verve); D. Gillespie; John Kirby (Class.).

VEAL, REGINALD, bs; b. Chicago, IL, 11/5/63. Grew up in NO. Pl. pno. at 8; then started pl. el-bs. w. father's gospel gp. After hs graduation, he was encouraged by Wynton and Branford Marsalis to take up acoustic bs. Attended Southern U. in Baton Rouge, La., stud. bs. tbn. w. Alvin Batiste and pl. tbn. in marching band. As bassist worked w. Ellis Marsalis, incl. tour of southeast Asia. Joined Terence Blanchard–Donald Harrison gp. in July 1986. Member of Wynton Marsalis band fr. Dec. '87 to Dec. '93, dur. which time he also tour. w. the LCJO. With Eric Reed Trio '98. CDs: w. B. Marsalis; E. Marsalis; W. Marsalis; Elvin Jones; Leroy Jones; LCJO (Col.); Nicholas Payton (Verve); Michael White; Courtney Pine (Ant.); D. Marsalis (Novus); M. Roberts (Novus; Col.); Eric Reed; Greg Tardy (Imp.); Tough Young Tenors (Ant.); Junko Onishi (BN).

VENTURA, CHARLIE (Charles Venturo), tnr sax; also bari, bs saxes; b. Philadelphia, PA, 12/2/16; d. Pleasantville, NJ, 1/17/92. Pl. w. local bands in 1930s; then feat. w. Gene Krupa's bb and particularly within Krupa's trio '42–6, except for a stint w. Teddy Powell '43–4. After leading a short-lived bb that rec. for National, he formed his "Bop for the People" gp., which enjoyed great popularity, due in large measure to his Chu Berry–Ben Webster-infl. tnr. and the vocal duo of Jackie Cain and Roy Kral. The horns were Bennie Green, tbn.; Conte Candoli, tpt.; and Boots Mussilli, alto sax. In '51 he was part of the Big Four w. Marty Napoleon, Buddy Rich, and Chubby Jackson. Rejoined Krupa many times in '50s and '60s. Lived in LV '58–61; then to Denver, working there w. gtrst. Johnny Smith bef. moving to Minneapolis. Following a long bout w. a stomach ailment, ret. to LV '70–2, working on radio as a dj. Fr. '72 to '75 lived in Windsor, Conn., and led house band at Sheraton Tobacco Valley Inn w. guest stars Bobby Hackett, Dave McKenna, et al. Heard to advantage w. Teddy Wilson at Michael's Pub, NYC '74 and freelanced into the '80s. A driving soloist who—particularly in the earlier yrs., when he tour. w. JATP—played tastefully for a couple of choruses but then would take to grandstanding. Won *Esq.* New Star Award '46; *DB* Poll for tnr. sax '45; *DB* Poll for Small Combo '48; *Met.* Poll for Small Combo and tnr. sax, '49. Solos w. Krupa: "Leave Us Leap"; "Dark Eyes." CDs: Dec.; GNP Cres.; *The Complete Charlie Ventura and Flip Phillips on Clef and Norgran* (Mos.); w. Chu Berry (Class.); Krupa (Hep); Krupa Trio in *1940s,*

The Small Groups: New Directions (Col.); Dizzy Gillespie (BB); Jackie & Roy; Charlie Parker (Sav.); JATP (Verve); Neal Hefti in *Early Bebop* (Merc.).

VENUTI, JOE (GIUSEPPE), vln; b. Lecco, Italy, 9/16/1894, or Philadelphia, PA, 9/16/03; d. Seattle, WA, 8/14/78. From age 7, he grew up in Phila., where he met Eddie Lang. Worked in Atlantic City w. a gp. feat. Lang 1919; later that yr. he went to NYC w. Lang to work w. Red Nichols. Pl. w. Bert Eslow's qt. in Atlantic City '21; he and Lang joined Jean Gold-kette orch. in Det. '24 and made their rec. debut w. him. Moved to NYC '25; numerous recs. w. Lang, incl. the celebrated "Stringin' the Blues" '26. Other dates w. Frank Trumbauer; Paul Whiteman; the Dorsey Bros.; Hoagy Carmichael; Adrian Rollini; and Red McKenzie. In Sept. '26 he began a series of recs. w. Joe Venuti's Blue Four, whose members incl. Lang and occ. Rollini, Trumbauer, Lennie Hayton, Jimmy Dorsey. They developed a unique style, a tonal finesse and chamber mus. quality hitherto unknown in jazz. Putting his classical training to unprecedented use, he became the first well-known jazz vlnst. One of his innovations was to tie the bow around the instrument and pl. all four strings simulta-neously for chordal passages. World-renowned by the early '30s, Venuti pl. in Engl. in '34 and for the next two decades tour. w. his own gps., incl. a bb '35–43. Pl. lounges in LA, LV, and Seattle (his home base) in the '60s. In '67, after a period of relative obscurity, he began perf. regularly at Colo. JPs. Also app. at the '68 NJF; London Jazz Expo '69. Began rec. w. Marian McPartland; Zoot Sims; Earl Hines; and others. In '75 Venuti pl. an important role in a NJF-NY tribute to Bix Beiderbecke. He maintained his musicianship and ardor into his last years. CDs: Chiaro.; JSP; Topaz; w. B. Beiderbecke (Col.; BB); J. Teagarden (Dec.); L. Armstrong (Col.); *Violin Jazz* (Yazoo); Dorsey Bros. (Hep).

VERPLANCK, BILLY (JOHN FENNO); comp, arr, tbn; b. Norwalk, CT, 4/30/30. Played first prof. job w. Jess Stacy at age 15. Arr. for many popular bbs in 1950s; also pl. w. Claude Thornhill '52; Dorsey Bros. '56. Married Marlene when both were w. Tommy Dorsey's band late '50s. Worked mainly as commercial studio arr. and mus. fr. '60s. Favs: Tommy Dorsey, Bill Harris; arrs: Marion Evans, Neal Hefti, Billy Strayhorn, Hall Overton, Count Basie, Duke Ellington. CDs: Sav.; w. C. Hawkins (Sav.).

VERPLANCK, MARLENE (Pampinella), voc; b. Newark, NJ, 11/11/33. Began singing at age 19. Sang w. bbs of Tex Beneke; Charlie Spivak; Tommy Dorsey. Married trombonist-arr. Billy VerPlanck

when both were with Dorsey. Worked as commercial studio mus. w. husband fr. 1960s; sang on hundreds of jingles. Began working in jazz clubs in '70s, then sang at Carnegie Hall and Kool JF. Began touring internationally early '90s. App. at Ronnie Scott's, Birmingham, Engl. '95. Rec. w. Saxomania, all-French reed section led by Claude Tissendier. CDs: Aud.; Sav.

VICK, HAROLD EDWARD, tnr, sop saxes; b. Rocky Mount, NC, 4/3/36; d. NYC, 11/13/87. Uncle was reedman Prince Robinson. Grad. fr. Howard U; tour. w. r&b bands bef. settling into small gp. work in NYC early 1960s. Pl. for Jean Erdman Dance Co. '66–7; w. Walter Bishop, Grant Green '67; own qnt. '67–8; Negro Ensemble Co., incl. Eur. tour '69; D. Gillespie bb; King Curtis '69–70. Gave lectures and demonstrations w. Benny Powell for Jazz Interactions '70; w. Aretha Franklin '70–4; Shirley Scott '74; rec. w. Jimmy McGriff '80–1. App. w. Slim Gaillard at Village West, NYC '83. Mainly identified w. soul jazz gps., Vick was a potent blues pl. Awarded NEA comp. grant '73. CDs: BN; w. Abbey Lincoln (Enja); Grant Green; B. Cosby (Verve); Groove Holmes; Jack McDuff (Prest.); Milt Jackson (Pab.); Big John Patton (BN).

VIENNA ART ORCHESTRA. *See* **RUEGG, MATHIAS.**

VIG, TOMMY, vib, dms, comp; b. Budapest, Hun-gary, 7/14/38. Toured Eur. as drumming prodigy at age 7. Grad. Bartok Cons.; left Hungary dur. 1956 revolt; stud. at Juilliard. Lived in LV bef. moving to LA. Guest soloist w. LA Neophonic, gave own con-certs, scored several films, and concentrated mainly on studio work. Won *DB* Critics Poll on vib. TDWR '67. Still freelancing in LA area in '90s, w. occ. gigs in jazz clubs. CD: Disc.

VIGNOLA, FRANK J., gtr, bjo, mand, uke; b. West Islip, NY, 12/30/65. Father pl. acdn.; bro. Michael pl. tpt. Stud. w. Jimmy George fr. age 5. Pl. w. own gp., Silver Lake, at church functions late 1970s; Jim Plosha '82–6; Ken Peplowski '86–8. Formed Hot Club Quintette '88, tour. and perf. at Michael's Pub in NYC '88–90. Freelanced '90–1. Formed Travelin' Light w. tba. Sam Pilafian '91. Favs: Joe Pass, Wes Montgomery, Django Reinhardt. Fests: Eur. w. Peplowski '91–2. Film: app. w. Vince Giordano in *Bloodhounds on Broadway*. CDs: Tel.; Conc.; w. Travelin' Light; Empire Brass: S. Pilafian (Tel.); S. McCorkle; K. Peplowski; C. Byrd; *Concord Jazz Collective* w. Howard Alden, Jimmy Bruno (Conc.); Roy Gerson (JA).

VINCENT, RON (RONALD DAVID), dms; b. Warwick, RI, 10/18/51. Began on pno., then pl. tba. in hs. Gigs at local Elks Club fr. 1967. Received B.A. in mus. ed. fr. Berklee Coll. of Mus. '73. Pl. w. Carmell Jones in KC '79–82; Diane Reeves '80; John McNeil '83–8; Bill Kirchner Nonet '87–91; Nancy Kennedy '89; Helen Merrill '90–1; Gerry Mulligan '90–2; Marion Cowings–Kim Kalesti '91. Pl. w. own qt. since '90. Vincent teaches at the Jamey Aebersold Jazz Camp and has lectured at many universities. Favs: Elvin Jones, Jack DeJohnette, Roy Haynes. Fests: Eur., Japan, Brazil since '89. TV: Gerry Mulligan at North Sea JF '91. CDs: w. B. Charlap (Chiaro.); Eden Atwood (Conc.); G. Mulligan (Tel.; GRP); C. Sloane; Phil Woods (Conc.).

VINCI, MARK ALBERT, alto sax, fl; also tnr, sop saxes, cl, picc; b. Xenia, OH, 1/26/60. Father is musicologist, moth. is church orgst. and pnst. Began on pno. and tpt., then stud. sax w. father fr. age 7. Pl. w. local gps. in Canton area fr. 1971. Pl. w. Marian McPartland at Carlyle Hotel '77; Glenn Miller Orch. '79–81; Woody Herman '81–2; Gerry Mulligan '85, '88; own qnt. w. Jerry Dodgion '86; duo w. Milt Hinton '90; own qnt. fr. '92. Vinci has taught at Skidmore Coll. fr. '89. Favs: Cannonball Adderley, Johnny Hodges. Fests: Eur. w. Herman, Mulligan. TV: apps. w. Mulligan; Miller Orch. CDs: Flat Cat; w. W. Herman (Conc.); J. Fedchock (Res.); M. Schneider (Enja).

VINDING, MADS, bs, el-bs; b. Copenhagen, Denmark, 12/7/48. Started pl. bs. at age 11, became prof. at 16. Worked and rec. w. Danish gp., Burnin' Red Ivanhoe, 1969; in the '70s he worked and rec. w. numerous Scand. gps. and individuals, incl. Svend Asmussen; Kjell Øhman; Rune Gustavsson; Sylvia Vrethammar; Christian Sievert; and Bengt-Arne Wallin; also w. Ed Thigpen; Duke Jordan; and Johnny Griffin, w. whom he tour. Japan '76. His reputation solidly established, Vinding was greatly in demand dur. the '80s and '90s, working and/or rec. w. Ernie Wilkins; Herbie Hancock; Kenny Drew; Hank Jones; Gary Burton; Ben Webster; Sonny Stitt; Al Foster; Stan Getz; Dizzy Gillespie; Joanne Brackeen; Quincy Jones; Bob Brookmeyer; Wayne Shorter; and the Danish Radio BB. He has participated on over 500 recs. and toured throughout Eur. and in the US, Brazil, and Japan. Also produced recs. and written film scores. Awards incl. Best Soloist, Nordring, '70; Ben Webster Prize, '82; Palœ Jazz Prize '97. "What makes Mads Vinding an outstanding artist and a sought-after soloist is his unique musical command and his great maturity," said Danish Radio commentator Peter H. Larsen. Favs: All creative people. CDs:

duo w. Bob Brookmeyer, Chall.; w. K. Drew; Art Farmer; Kim Parker (SN); J. Griffin; Howard McGhee; D. Jordan; D. Raney (Steep.); R. Hanna; Hank Jones; Thomas Clausen (Story.).

VINNEGAR, LEROY, bs, comp; b. Indianapolis, IN, 7/13/28; d. Portland, OR, 8/2/99. In LA fr. 1954, played w. Shelly Manne '55–56; app. on best-selling *My Fair Lady* LP w. Manne, André Previn. Won the *DB* New Star Award '57. Won reputation as "walking bass" stylist; was dubbed "The Mighty Walker." Freelanced in Hollywood dur. '70s and pl. in movies, TV, and radio. Pl. w. Art Tatum; Stan Getz; Teddy Edwards; Les McCann; Gerald Wilson; Barney Kessel; Bobby Troup; Julie London; Red Garland; Miles Davis; Carmen McRae; Sonny Criss; Earl Hines; Harold Land; Art Blakey; Lionel Hampton; Lou Rawls; Pearl Bailey; Helen Humes; Ben Webster; Kenny Clarke; Max Roach; many others. First rec. w. Frank Morgan on Gene Norman Presents. Favs: Percy Heath, Ray Brown. CDs: Cont.; w. B. Collette; Benny Carter; S. Manne; Helen Humes; H. Land; H. McGhee; Phineas Newborn; S. Rollins (Cont.); F. Rosolino (Spec.); C. Walton (Prest.); L. Hampton–S. Getz; G. Mulligan; Jimmy Smith (Verve); Elmo Hope; Kenny Dorham; Kenny Drew (BN); Joe Pass; Jazz Crusaders; Chet Baker; A. Pepper–C. Baker (PJ); Teddy Edwards (Ant.; Cont.); Dexter Gordon (Beth.); Q. Jones (Imp.); L. McCann–Eddie Harris (Atl.); S. Chaloff (Mos.)

VINSON, EDDIE (CLEANHEAD); alto sax, voc; b. Houston, TX, 12/18/17; d. Los Angeles, CA, 7/2/88. Professional debut w. Milton Larkins 1936–40; worked w. Floyd Ray orch '40–1, then joined Cootie Williams bb '42. Quickly established himself as a powerful blues singer w. a personal, broken-toned style. Big hits w. Williams were "Cherry Red" and "Somebody's Got To Go." Formed own gp. '45; had big hit w. "Kidney Stew Blues"; worked at the Zanzibar on B'way w. 16–pc orch. '47; tour. US '48–9. After his popularity waned, he worked w. small gps. and as a single, then rejoined Williams briefly '54. Worked mainly as a single for the balance of his career, living in LA in later yrs., but working many int'l jfs. Vinson pl. alto in a coarse-toned, ruggedly swinging blues vein enriched w. bop inflections. He is acknowledged by many mus. as being the actual writer of "Tune Up" and "Four," which are normally assoc. w. Miles Davis. CDs: BB; Del.; Beth.; Merc.; Pab.; B&B; BL; w. Joe Williams (Delos); C. Basie Sarah Vaughan; Joe Turner (Pab.); Cootie Williams (Class.; tracks in *Classic Capitol Jazz Sessions*, Mos.); Roomful of Blues (32).

VINTSKEVICH, LEONID, pno, comp; b. Kursk, Russia, 4/1/49. All-musical family. Stud. at Kazan Cons. 1967–72. Pl. solo classical mus. to '77; jazz w. own trio '78–81. Best known as partner of Lembit Saarsalu, w. whom he app. '89–90, '92 at Lionel Hampton JF in Moscow, Idaho. Favs: Garner, Peterson. Number one pno. in Soviet jazz critics' poll '89. Rec. for Russian Melodiya label.

VIOLA, AL (ALFRED), gtr; b. Brooklyn, NY, 6/16/19. Self-taught. Toured w. Page Cavanaugh Trio 1947–9 and into '90s; Bobby Troup '50–4; Ray Anthony '55–6; Harry James '57. Buddy Collette Qnt. fr. '57 off and on into '90s. Many TV apps. on *Stars of Jazz*, Andy Williams, Jonathan Winters, et al. App. in movies, *Romance on the High Seas* and *A Song Is Born.* Perf. background mus. for many other films. LPs w. Julie London; Bobby Troup; June Christy; Helen Humes; Mavis Rivers; Kay Starr; Linda Ronstadt; Hadda Brooks; The Four Freshmen; also instrumental LPs w. Shelly Manne; Laurindo Almeida; Pete Rugolo; Buddy Collette; Terry Gibbs; and others. CDs: w. F. Sinatra (Cap.; Rep.); H. Brooks (Pointblank); Buddy Collette (Studio West); Page Cavanaugh (Starline); Natalie Cole (Elek.).

VITOUS, MIROSLAV LADISLAV, bs, gtr, comp; b. Prague, Czechoslovakia, 12/6/47. Father pl. sax. Began on vln. at age 6, pno. at 9, then sw. to bs. at 14. While stud. at Prague Cons., pl. w. Junior Trio feat. Jan Hammer and bro. Alan Vitous; also worked w. dixieland gp. A Vienna contest spons. by Friedrich Gulda won him a scholarship to Berklee Coll. of Mus. Arrived in US Aug. 1966. Offered job w. Cannonball Adderley but declined and att. Berklee for eight mos. Moved to NYC summer '67; worked w. Art Farmer; Freddie Hubbard; Bobby Brookmeyer–Clark Terry. Pl. briefly w. Miles Davis, then join. Herbie Mann '68–70. Rec. w. Donald Byrd '67; Chick Corea, Jack DeJohnette '68; Wayne Shorter '69; Larry Coryell '70. Pl. w. Stan Getz '70; H. Mann '71; Miles Davis briefly '71; Weather Report '71–3. In '74–5 Vitous lived in LA while practicing a new instrument, a double-necked gtr. and bs., made especially for him. Dur. this period he made only one public perf., w. Airto. Rec. w. all-star gp. feat. Herbie Hancock, Airto, Jack DeJohnette '75. Led own gp. fr. '76. Joined faculty of New Engl. Cons. '79; head of jazz dept. fr. '83. Led qt. w. John Surman, Kenny Kirkland or John Taylor, Jon Christensen '79–82. Pl. in Trio Music w. Chick Corea, Roy Haynes fr. '81. CDs: Evid.; ECM; w. Weather Report (Col.); Terje Rypdal; Jan Garbarek (ECM); Franco Ambrosetti (Enja); Trio Music (ECM); Corea (BN; ECM); Franco D'Andrea; D. Humair; (L. Bleu); J. DeJohnette (Mile.); H. Mann; Joe Zawinul (Atl.); W. Shorter (BN)

VITRO, ROSEANNA (Wickliffe), voc, pno; b. Hot Springs, AR, 2/28/51. Began career in Houston, Tex., in mid 1970s. Stud. w. voc. Ray Sullenger and Arnett Cobb. Two yrs. at Green Room while hosting weekly radio broadcast. Oscar Peterson and Tommy Flanagan encouraged her to move to NYC, where she sang and tour. w. Lionel Hampton's band '81. App. in major NYC clubs. Cont. classical voice training at Manh. Sch. of Mus., jazz improv., and—to enhance Brazilian style—Portuguese at New Sch. Sang at jazz fests. in Hollywood, Calif., Clearwater, Fla., and Houston. Perf. w. Buddy Rich; Kenny Barron; Buster Williams; Hank Jones; Junior Mance; Mel Lewis; TV w. Steve Allen; Keter Betts; Ramsey Lewis; and Steve Kuhn. Described by *LA Times* as "a first rate improviser determined to use her voice with the same musical breadth and density with which instrumentalists use their horns." Favs: Ella Fitzgerald, Sarah Vaughan, Nancy Wilson. CDs: Conc.; Tel., Chase Music.

VLATKOVICH, MICHAEL PIERRE, tbn, comp; b. St. Louis, MO, 5/4/51. Studied at St. Louis Inst. of Mus. Has worked mainly with his own gps. but also w. Vinny Golia. Started own label, Thankyou Records, to make self-produced album in 1981. Co-leader of Transvalue w. poet Charles Britt. Accomp. Peggy Lee, Toni Basil, and pl. on soundtracks for many TV and film projects. Vlatkovich is an emotionally charged perf. capable of adapting to many mus. environments. CDs: w. Transvalue; Vinny Golia (Nine Winds).

VOGEL, VIC (VICTOR STEFAN), comp, arr, tbn, tba, vib; b. Montreal, Que., Canada, 8/3/35. Studied pno. as a child; pno., theory, analysis w. Michel Hirvy 1954–5. Mainly self-taught. Pl. w. dance bands of Hugh Sealey, Geo. Sealey, Boogie Gaudet, Steve Garrick late '50s. Led own gp. at Chez Paree ca. '60. Pl. pno. w. Double Six of Paris in Quebec '61. Pl. pno., tbn., tba w. Lee Gagnon Tentet early '60s. Vogel has worked as comp., mus. dir., or accomp. for many CBC radio and TV progs. He has led his own bb which has perf. at Canadian fests w. guest soloists incl. Zoot Sims; Phil Woods; Mel Tormé; Dizzy Gillespie. He has comp., arr., and conducted for events, incl. Montreal Olympics '76; Canada Games '85. In '78 he arr. a concert for Woody Shaw w. the Quebec Symph. Fests: all major in Canada. TV: CBC progs. incl. *Music Hall, Les Couche-tard, Vedettes En Direct.* Has own record label, VV. CDs: Audiogram; Grudge.

VON OHLEN, JOHN ("BARON"), dms; b. Indianapolis, IN, 5/13/41. Played w. Billy Maxted Manh. Jazz Band 1967–8; Woody Herman '68–9; Stan Kenton '70–2; then settled in Cincinnati, where his bb pl. at the Blue Wisp club and he established a reputation through recs. Comps: "A Walk Through Bombay"; "Red Man." CDs: Blue Wisp BB (Sea Breeze); w. Kenton (CW); Mel Tormé (Conc.).

VON SCHLIPPENBACH, ALEX (ALEXANDER), pno, comp; b. Berlin, Germany, 4/7/38. Studied comp., pno. in Cologne. Joined Günter Hampel qnt. in Paris 1963; tour. w. Manfred Schoof '64–7. From '66 he enjoyed great success w. his Globe Unity Orch. which over the yrs. incl. such sidemen as Kenny Wheeler; Schoof; Enrico Rava; Albert Mangelsdorff; George Lewis; Evan Parker; Steve Lacy; and Alan Silva. Pl. a major role in the Eur. evolution of the free jazz movement; comfortable in bb and small gp. settings, his pl. incl. many elements of Eur. classical avant-garde mus., stride, and bop. CDs: Globe Unity Orch. (FMP).

VOYNOW, DICK (RICHARD F.), pno; b. 1900; d. Los Angeles, CA, 9/15/44. Replaced Dud Mecum in The Wolverines' first booking at the Stockton Club in Hamilton, Ohio. Became the band's business manager and functional leader, cont. in those roles after the orig. members had departed. Toured frequently until 1926; irregularly after that. From late '20s, he was rec. manager for Brunswick-Decca and other labels; worked as rec. exec. on West Coast in early '40s. CDs: w. Beiderbecke (Mile.; Timel.).

V.S.O.P. Initially the title of a Herbie Hancock album chronicling a 1976 concert of his mus. at the NY-NJF. The letters refer to a "Very Special One-time-only Performance." A qnt. from the concert—Hancock, Ron Carter, Wayne Shorter, Tony Williams, and Freddie Hubbard (all but Hubbard had pl. w. Miles Davis's mid '60s qnt.)—made several highly praised tours as V.S.O.P. in the late '70s and w. Wynton and Branford Marsalis in place of Hubbard, and also called The Quintet, '83. CD: Col.

W

WADENIUS, GEORG, gtr, bs; b. Stockholm, Sweden, 5/4/45. Professional debut in Sweden 1968. Came to US to join Blood Sweat & Tears '72 and tour. w. the gp. internationally. CDs: w. Blood, Sweat & Tears (Col.); Ronnie Cuber (Steep.; ProJazz; Mile.); Howard Johnson (Verve); Dexter Gordon (Steep.); Joe Henderson (Mile.).

WADSWORTH, DEREK, tbn, arr, comp; b. Bradford, England, 2/5/39. From 1950 he studied w. brass bands, initially on crnt. Self-motivated, he worked w. dance bands until joining Georgie Fame's band in '63. Since heard w. Humphrey Lyttelton '68–75; Graham Collier '70–8; Maynard Ferguson '72–4; Diana Ross Orch '75; Johnny Dankworth '68–75. In US w. Ferguson '72; several visits to Eur. w. Fame. Founder/lecturer Musicians Union Rock Wkshp. series '76–81; comp. and pl. on 24-part TV series, *Space 1999*. Recs. incl. Dick Tracy, feat. his orch. w. Al Jarreau (WB); w. Fame; Collier; Mike Westbrook; and Ferguson.

WAITS, FREDDIE (FREDERICK DOUGLAS), dms, perc, fl, comp; b. Jackson, MS, 4/27/43; d. NYC, 11/18/89. Son is dmr. Nasheet Waits. Pl. w. such bluesmen as John Lee Hooker and Memphis Slim; then w. Motown artists bef. moving to NYC. In 1960s he worked w. Sonny Rollins; Cedar Walton; Wild Bill Davis; w. McCoy Tyner '67–70; M'Boom fr. '71. Accomp. Ella Fitzgerald, Lena Horne, Carmen McRae '71–3. With Billy Taylor trio '71–2, '75. Pl. w. NYJRC '74–5; Mercer Ellington, incl. tours of Africa, Eur. '75; Teddy Edwards '76; Curtis Fuller '78. Also pl. in Colloquium III with Horacee Arnold and Billy Hart. Pl. and/or rec. w. Abbey Lincoln, Archie Shepp,

Marion Brown '80. In '80s tour. France and rec. w. M'Boom; also gave many perfs. in schs. and joined the faculty of Rutgers U. Pl. w. Cecil Taylor qnt. '87. CDs: w. Ray Bryant (Em.); Kenny Barron (Muse; Up.); Dick Griffin (Konnex); D. Byrd (BN); Buck Hill; J. Hoggard (Muse); Stanley Cowell; R. Hanna (DIW); Richard Davis (DIW; Hep); R. "Groove" Holmes (Prest.); Abbey Lincoln (ITM); Sam Noto (Xan.); J. DeJohnette (Land.); Lee Morgan (FS).

WAKENIUS, ULF KARL ERIK, gtr; b. Halmstad, Sweden, 4/16/58. Mother pl. Swed. folk songs on acoustic gtr. Mostly self-taught, stud. pno. first, then gtr. at Gothenburg Cons. Began pl. prof. in 1979. Pl. w. Guitars Unlimited '80; Airto Moreira–Flora Purim, Larry Coryell '83; Sivuca '84–7. Own gp. feat. Bob Berg '87–9. Pl. w. Niels Pedersen fr. '88; Doky bros. '88–94; Jack DeJohnette, Bill Evans, Randy Brecker, Dave Liebman, Berg, Herbie Hancock '92; Graffiti feat. Dennis Chambers '92–4; Jim Hall, Joe Henderson, Peter Erskine, Albert Mangelsdorff '94; Ray Brown fr. '94; Johnny Griffin '96; Milt Jackson, Art Farmer, Max Roach, Phil Woods, Benny Golson, Toots Thielemans '97; Oscar Peterson fr. '97. Has taught at clinics worldwide. A mobile single-stringer with the ability to keep up with Peterson, Wakenius shows in his own recordings a penchant for tender ballads. Favs: Wes Montgomery, Jim Hall, Joe Pass. TV: w. Peterson, US, Germ.; also w. Henderson, Farmer, Jackson, Thielemans, Griffin, Golson. Rec. debut a solo LP (Drag) '83. CDs: Drag.; Sittel; w. Peterson; Brown (Tel.); Pedersen (Verve); Doky bros. (BN).

WALCOTT, COLLIN, sitar, tabla, perc; b. NYC, 4/24/45; d. Magdeburg, Germany, 11/8/84. Studied vln., perc., majored in perc. at Indiana U; stud. sitar w. Ravi Shankar and tabla w. Alla Rakha in LA. Moved to NYC; perf. and rec. w. Tony Scott 1967–9; rec. on sitar w. Miles Davis '72. Pl. w. Paul Winter Consort '70–1; Oregon '70–84; Codona, w. Dan Cherry and Nana Vasconcelos, '78–84. Died in automobile accident while tour. w. Oregon. CDs: w. Oregon (ECM); Jim Pepper (Ryko; Isl.).

WALD, JERRY, cl, leader; b. Newark, NJ, 1/15/19; d. Las Vegas, NV, 9/73. Studied sop. sax, alto sax, and cl. at early age w. private teachers. Led band at Childs' Spanish Gardens, NYC, 1941 (incl. Billy Bauer); at Lincoln Hotel '42. Led swing-style band, pl. in Artie Shaw style, throughout '40s. Sidemen over the yrs. incl. Al Cohn (also as arr.), Lee Konitz. Led gp. and managed Studio Club in Hollywood, Calif. '49–51. Sidemen incl. Bill Perkins. Led gps. in NYC on and off fr. '52. Not related to motion picture producer of same name. Recs. for Decca, Col., MGM, Merc. LP: Kapp.

WALDO, TERRY (RALPH EMERSON III), pno, comp, arr; b. Ironton, OH, 1/26/44. Mother pl. pno. Stud. priv. in Columbus, Ohio 1953–67. Also pl. tpt., tba., bs., org., tympani, cello in hs. App. on Ted Mack's Amateur Hour w. own gp., Fungus 5 ("Our Music Grows on You"). Pl. in NO w. Red Garter and Preservation Hall bands '67; in SF w. Red Garter, Ted Shaeffer, Turk Murphy '68–9. While stud. communications at Ohio St. U. (M.A. '70), he pl. w. Gene Mayl's Dixie. Rhythm Kings. Waldo met Eubie Blake in '71 and became his student, protegé, and sometime collaborator. Led own gps., Waldo's Gutbucket Syncopators '69–83; Waldo's Ragtime Orch. fr. '78; Waldo's Gotham City Band fr. '84. Also freelanced extensively w. Black Eagle Jazz Band; Ernie Carson; Vince Giordano; Harlem Blues Band; Louisiana Repertory Jazz Ens.; Woody Allen; Leon Redbone; others. Feat. soloist w. Columbus, Sacramento, and San Antonio Symphs. '70s. Prod. NPR series *This Is Ragtime* '73. Waldo scored the off-B'way musical *Capitol Cakewalk* '91; other comp. credits incl. musical *Warren G.* '76; PBS educ. prog. '86; much commercial work. Worked as mus. dir. for several productions of *One Mo' Time* fr. '84; also *Mr. Jelly Lord, Hoagy Carmichael Review* '84; *The Odetta Show* '84–5; *No Maps on My Taps*, Waldo's Ragtime Orch. vaudeville show '86. He is the arr. of a folio of rags by Eubie Blake (Marks Music '75), and the author of articles and a historical book, *This Is Ragtime* (Hawthorne '76). Other projects incl. scoring a BBC special on the history of movies '92; scoring silent films for American Movie Classics cable channel '93. Favs: Bob Wright, Eubie Blake, Paul

Lingle, Don Ewell. Fests: Germ. '75; Nice JF '78; JVC Fests in NYC. TV: Hosted TV specials in Columbus '74–9; consultant to Eubie Blake special on PBS '83. LP: w. Blake. CDs: Stomp Off; Musical Heritage Society; w. Louisiana Repertory Jazz Ens. (Naxos).

WALDRON, MAL (MALCOLM EARL), pno, comp; b. NYC, 8/16/26; d. Brussels, Belgium, 2/2/02. Originally wanted to be a classical pnst. Began pl. alto sax, then sw. to pno. in coll. Received B.A. in comp. fr. Queens Coll., where he stud. w. Karol Rathaus. Worked in NYC w. Big Nick Nicholas, Ike Quebec 1949–53; made rec. debut w. Quebec '50. Pl. briefly in rock 'n' roll bands, then w. Chas. Mingus '54–7; Lucky Thompson, Lucky Millinder '55. Formed own qnt. w. Idrees Sulieman, Gigi Gryce '56. Rec. extens. as lead. and sideman for Prest. label '56–8. Accomp. Billie Holiday fr. '57 until her death in '59; worked w. Abbey Lincoln fr. '59. Led own combo at Five Spot, NYC fr. late '50s. Also wrote modern ballet scores for Henry Street dance gp. '50s. In '61–2 app. at the Five Spot w. a qnt. led by Eric Dolphy and Booker Little. Scored films: *The Cool World* '63; *Three Bedrooms In Manhattan, Sweet Love Bitter* '65. Also comp. mus. for LeRoi Jones's plays *The Slave* and *The Dutchman*. Tour. Eur. '65; then settled in Italy '66. Pl. first free-jazz concert in Italy opposite Gato Barbieri '66. Moved to Munich '67; also tour. Poland, Switz., Germ., Italy. Active in Eur. as comp. for recs., TV, films fr. late '60s. Perf. w. other expatriate mus. incl. Archie Shepp, Steve Lacy. Tour. Japan fr. '70. Rec. in Japan w. singer Kimiko Kasai '71. Began making return visits to the US in '75. His comps. incl. the jazz standard "Soul Eyes." Favs: Bud Powell, Thelonious Monk, Herbie Nichols; arrs: John Lewis, Duke Ellington. Polls: *SJ* Silver Disc '69; Album of Yr. '71. Fests: NJF w. Mingus '55–6; all major in Eur. fr. '65; Japan fr. '70. TV: featured on TV classic *The Sound of Jazz* '57. CDs: Novus; Evid.; ProJazz; Beth.; SN; NJ; ECM; BL; Prest.; Freelance; PW; Timel.; w. C. Mingus (Rh./Atl.; Sav.; Debut); John Coltrane; K. Burrell; Thad Jones; J. McLean; P. Woods; T. Macero (Prest:); Ron Carter (NJ); E. Dolphy (Cand.; NJ; Prest.); Max Roach (Fant.; Imp.); S. Lacy (SN; Novus; NJ; Slam); A. Braxton; Chico Freeman; K. Parker (SN); Teddy Charles (Atl.); Jeanne Lee (Owl).

WALKER, JIM (JAMES), fl, picc; b. Muncie, IN, 3/10/44. Pno. and fl. lessons fr. age 6. Played club dates w. fath., cl. and public sch. band dir., but first half of career was involved primarily in classical mus. as assoc. principal fl. w. Pitts. Symph. 1969–77 and LA Phil. '77–85. Formed Free Flight, a qt. feat. a mixture of classical, bop, and fusion '80. Since '84 he has also pl. many duet concerts w. the gp.'s kybd. pl. Mike Garson, often employing stunning rapid unison lines; rec. "Sierra" w. Miles Davis; "Atlantis" w. W. Shorter; cond. master classes in fl. and tour. Can., So. Amer. '82; Eur. '83; and Russia '89. One of the very few classical virtuosos to make a successful transition to jazz. Favs: Hubert Laws, James Moody, James Galway. CDs: Tall Tree; w. Free Flight (CBS); Pat Coil (Sheffield Labs).

WALKER, MELISSA, voc; b. Edmonton, Alb., Canada, 7/3/64. Sister pl. fl. and pno. but not prof. Married to tptr. Terell Stafford. Pl. bsn. in jr. hs and hs. Began priv. voice lessons while in hs and sang at grad. Att. Brown U. and enrolled in voc. program as an elective for two yrs., also stud. priv. Had been interested in Billie Holiday while in hs; Sarah Vaughan and Dinah Washington while at coll.; but considered music a hobby and was pursuing a law degree. Moved to Va. in late 1980s after grad. and took part in jazz wkshps. under Ronnie Wells, Wash., D.C., which pointed her toward a singing career. Further stud. w. Ron Ellison also in Wash. Has cont. coaching on informal basis w. Norman Simmons, voice stud. w. Yvonne Hachet, both in NYC. First gig in Wash. '90. Sang at jazz fests. in Chile, Alberta, Hungary '93. Rec. debut on CD she released independently. Has never worked w. any band but her own except for jam sessions. Has worked in retail management '86–7; law firm paralegal '87–91; substitute teacher of English, music '92–3; senior legal analyst, Prudential Ins. Co., Newark, N.J. fr. '93. App. at The Jazz Standard, NYC early '98. Walker has a flexible, rangy, expressive voice. Whether treating lyrics intelligently or scatting she shows a fine sense of rhythm and emanates a jazz feeling without strain. Favs: McRae, Vaughan, Holiday, Nina Simone. CD: Enja.

WALKER, T-BONE (AARON THIBEAUX), voc, gtr; b. Linden, TX, 5/28/10; d. Los Angeles, CA, 3/16/75. Mother pl. gtr., fath. pl. bs. Grew up around church mus. and blues. As a boy, he led Blind Lemon Jefferson around; pl. bjo. in medicine shows 1924. Studied gtr. w. Chuck Richardson, who also taught his childhood friend Charlie Christian. Briefly w. Ida Cox show—where he danced and pl. bjo.—and three days w. Ma Rainey show in Houston, Tex. '26. Made rec. debut in Tex. '29 as "Oak Cliff T-Bone." Worked w. Milton Larkin; accomp. Ma Rainey '33. Moved to Calif. '34; gained popularity w. Les Hite Band—w. whom he rec. "T-Bone Blues" twice—in Calif. and NYC '39–40. Rec. w. Freddie Slack '42. Throughout the '40s and '50s he worked as a single, pl. amplified gtr., and laid a foundation for the rock and roll el-gtr.

dominance to come. Tour. Eur. '62, '68. Walker's most popular comp. is "They Call It Stormy Monday," which has been widely rec. by him and others since '47. "Nobody has contributed as much, as long or as variously to the blues," observed critic Pete Welding. Book: *Stormy Monday: The T-Bone Walker Story*, by Helen Oakley Dance (foreword by B. B. King) '87. CDs: BB; Del.; Mos.; w. Eddie Vinson (Del.).; *JATP in London 1969* (Pab.); Jay McShann (B&B).

WALL, MURRAY JAMES, bs; b. Melbourne, Australia, 9/28/45. Older bro. pl. dixieland cl. and sax. Began on tpt. Taught self to play bs. by listening to Oscar Pettiford recs. Pl. in Melbourne w. visiting soloists, incl. Clark Terry, Mel Tormé, Billy Eckstine 1962–79. Moved to NYC '79; pl. w. Jon Hendricks '81–5; Benny Goodman '85–6. Pl. fr. late '80s w. Warren Vaché; Buck Clayton bb; Scott Hamilton; Anita O'Day; Jimmy Ryan's All-Stars; Grover Mitchell Orch.; Annie Ross; Richard Wyands. Favs: Oscar Pettiford, Wilbur Ware, Percy Heath. Fests: Eur. and Israel w. Hendricks; Japan '88–9. TV: PBS T. Monk tribute w. Hendricks. CDs: w. Benny Goodman (MM); K. Peplowski; Sweets Edison (Conc.); Joel Helleny (Arb.); Keith Ingham (Jump; Sack.); Marty Grosz (Jazz.; J&M; N-H); W. Vaché (N-H).

WALLACE, BENNIE LEE JR., tnr sax, cl; b. Chattanooga, TN, 11/18/46. Began on cl. at age 12. Stud. at U. of Tenn. (B.A. 1968), then pl. w. local gps. While working in Denver, Colo., he met Gary Burton, who encouraged him to move to NYC. Pl. w. Monty Alexander '71, then active on NYC loft scene. Pl. w. Sheila Jordan '76; Ray Anderson off and on fr. '76. Led own trio fr. '77 w. sidemen incl. Eddie Gomez; Eddie Moore; Dannie Richmond; Alvin Queen. Tour. US, Eur., Japan w. qt. in '80s. Pl. w. Anthony Wilson at Izzy Bar, NYC '97. Films: mus. dir. for *Blaze; White Men Can't Jump*; animated short *Redux Riding Hood;* comp. *Little Surprise* for Jeff Goldblum–dir. short. CDs: BN; Audq.; Enja; Den.; w. Mose Allison (BN); George Gruntz (MPS); Anthony Wilson (MAMA).

WALLACE, CEDRIC, bs; b. Miami, FL, 8/3/09; d. NYC, 8/19/85. Professional debut w. Honey Boys Orch. in Fla. In NYC pl. w. Reggie Johnson at Saratoga Club, then w. Jimmie Lunceford. Best remembered for his tenure w. Fats Waller 1938–42; later worked w. Gene Cedric and Garland Wilson, then led own gp. in NYC clubs. CDs: w. F. Waller (BB; Buddha).

WALLACE, SIPPIE (Beulah Thomas), voc, kybds; b. Houston, TX, 1/11/1898; d. Detroit, MI, 1/11/86.

Musical family, her bro. was pnst. Hersal Thomas, niece was blues singer Hociel Thomas; first sang and pl. org. in local Baptist church where fath. was a deacon. Moved to Chi. and made rec. debut for Okeh in 1923, accomp. by Eddie Heywood; later rec. accomps. incl. King Oliver; Louis Armstrong; Sidney Bechet; Natty Dominique; and Johnny Dodds. Regular theatre tours on T.O.B.A. circuit in '20s; retired fr. mus. in '30s, moving to Det. Revived career in '45, rec. Merc. sess. w. Albert Ammons Rhythm Kings. Rec. again in '59 and '62. In mid '60s the blues/folk revival gave her career a boost, incl. tours throughout US and Eur. and recs. In '83 her album, *Sippie*, received a Grammy nomination. CDs: Story.; Allig.; w. L. Armstrong (Aff.); Clarence Williams (EPM/Hot 'n Sweet); Axel Zwingenberger (Vagabond); two tracks w. A. Ammons in *The 1940s Mercury Sessions* (Merc.).

WALLACE, STEVE (STEVEN SCOTT), bs; b. Toronto, Ont., Canada, 8/16/56. Studied gtr. w. Gary Benson; bs. w. Lenny Boyd at Humber Coll. 1975–6. Pl. in Toronto jazz clubs backing mus. incl. Pepper Adams; Ed Bickert; Geo. Coleman; Lockjaw Davis; Sweets Edison; Scott Hamilton; Warren Vaché; Pat LaBarbera; Rob McConnell; Sam Noto; Zoot Sims '79–84. Pl. w. Fraser MacPherson off and on '81–6; Boss Brass fr. '83; Woody Herman All-Stars '85; Concord All-Stars '87; Moe Koffman briefly '88; Oscar Peterson '88–9; Olive Jones fr. '89. Fests: Eur., Japan w. W. Herman and Conc. All-Stars; all major w. Peterson. CDs: w. Boss Brass; Conc. All-Stars; Rosemary Clooney; Ed Bickert; Mel Tormé; Ernestine Anderson (Conc.); Fraser McPherson (Conc.; JT; CBC); Oliver Jones (JT); S. Noto (Unisson).

WALLER, FATS (THOMAS), pno, org, voc, comp; b. NYC, 5/21/04; d. Kansas City, MO, 12/14/43. At age 5, he learned to pl. harmonium but soon spent more time at a neighbor's pno. Played vln. and pno. in Public Sch. 89 orch. dir. by Edgar Sampson. His father, a church deacon, recognized Waller's talent and tried to dir. it toward classical mus., but the Lincoln Theatre's pipe org. was a bigger lure. In 1919 he was hired as the Lincoln's house orgst. Stud. priv. w. James P. Johnson and George Gershwin's bro.-in-law, Leopold Godowsky. Made numerous pno. rolls and solo recs. fr. '22; also voc. accomps. and sess. w. Fletcher Henderson; McKinney's Cotton Pickers; Ted Lewis; and Jack Teagarden. A prolific comp., he teamed up w. lyricist Andy Razaf for some of the era's most enduring songs, incl. "Ain't Misbehavin'" and "Honeysuckle Rose." Between '23 and '27 he rec. some 20 tunes on pno. rolls, incl. his first comp., "Squeeze Me." Worked in many nightclubs and the-

atres dur. '20s, pl. org. and pno. (he was the first successful jazz orgst.), and accomp. Sara Martin; Bessie Smith; Alberta Hunter; et al. In Chi. he worked w. Erskine Tate '27. Collaborated w. lyricist Andy Razaf on a series of highly successful songs for such shows as *Keep Shufflin'* '28, and *Hot Chocolates* '29. In '28, Waller made his first Carnegie Hall app. in James P. Johnson's *Yamekraw*. From '26 he made a series of solo recs. for Vict., pl. own comps., incl. "Handful of Keys"; "Valentine Stomp"; "Smashing Thirds"; and "My Fate Is in Your Hands." He made a brief trip to France and Engl. in '32; then began a successful series of radio broadcasts, *Fats Waller's Rhythm Club*, over WLW in Cincinnati, Ohio '33–4. In May '34 he initiated a series of Vict. sess. w. own gps., Fats Waller and His Rhythm, pl. a mixture of orig. songs and current pop tunes. In '38 he ret. to London, where he led an Engl. gp. on recs. While in Engl. he also comp. and rec. *London Suite*. This work was also on the program of his '42 Carnegie Hall concert, but the evening was ill-produced and critics found the proceedings laborious. They received more favorably his mus. for the '43 B'way mus. *Early to Bed*. Returning to NYC from a Calif. engagement, Waller died aboard the train of influenzal bronchial pneumonia. After his death, many pnsts.—notably Count Basie, Johnny Guarnieri, Ralph Sutton, Joe Sullivan, and Dick Hyman—kept the Waller tradition alive. Waller added to the James P. Johnson style a symmetry and delicacy without precedent in jazz. At times light and airy but occasionally forceful with a mighty "stride" left hand, he could turn the tritest pop song into a gem. He app. in several films, incl. *King of Burlesque* and *Hooray For Love* '35; *Stormy Weather* '43; and several shorts. Among his comps., which numbered in the hundreds, were "Blue Turning Gray Over You"; "Keepin' Out of Mischief Now"; "How Can You Face Me"; "Black and Blue"; "The Joint Is Jumpin'"; "Zonky"; "Viper's Drag"; and "Willow Tree." Theater: musical revue, *Ain't Misbehavin'* '78. Books: *Fats Waller*, Maurice Waller and Anthony Calabrese '79; *Fats Waller: His Life and Times*, Joel Vance '77; *Ain't Misbehavin'*, Ed Kirkeby '66. CDs: BB; BBC; Buddha; w. McKinney's Cotton Pickers; Met. All-Stars; J. Teagarden (BB); Alberta Hunter (Stash); F. Henderson (Col.); Red Allen (Collector's Classics); Pee Wee Russell (Comm.).

WALLINGTON, GEORGE (Giacinto Figlia), pno, comp; b. Palermo, Sicily, Italy, 10/27/24; d. NYC, 2/15/93. Family emigrated to NYC one yr. after his birth. Stud. pno. w. his fath., an opera singer, fr. age 9. Dur. teens he began pl. at clubs in Bklyn. and Greenwich Village; met Clarence Profit, a major infl. Played in first bop gp. on 52nd St. w. Dizzy Gillespie,

Don Byas, Max Roach, and Oscar Pettiford 1943–4. Dur. next few yrs. he was intensely active on bop scene w. gps. led by Charlie Parker; Terry Gibbs; Allen Eager; Serge Chaloff. In early '50s he pl. w. Red Rodney; Al Cohn; Zoot Sims; tour. briefly w. L. Hampton band in mid '53. Led qnt. w. Donald Byrd and Phil Woods at Café Bohemia. Left mus. in late '50s to work in his father's air-conditioning business, occ. reemerging for apps. and recs. Moved to Fla. Made a comeback in the '80s; tour. and rec. in Japan; pl. in Italy. App. at '85 JVC-NY. His best-known comps. are "Godchild," rec. by Chubby Jackson, Miles Davis; and "Lemon Drop," rec. by Woody Herman, Gene Krupa, Phil Woods, and Jackson. A contributor to the bop movement, Wallington was among the few white mus. to play a significant role in the evolution of the idiom. Though he was often compared to Bud Powell, his style was formed bef. he heard Powell, and—typical of bop pnsts.—dominated by fluent single-note right hand lines with occ. rhythmic left-hand punctuations. CDs: Den.; Interface; Sav.; Prest.; NJ; Vogue; VSOP; w. S. Chaloff (Mos.; Cool + Blue); Al Cohn (Sav.); Bobby Jaspar (Riv.); G. Mulligan; S. Getz (Prest.); Tom Talbert (Modern Concepts); L. Hampton (Natasha); w. Annie Ross in *The Bebop Singers* (Prest.).

WALRATH, JACK ARTHUR JR., tpt, flg, comp, lead; b. Stuart, FL, 5/5/46. Began on tpt. at age 9. Won contests throughout sch. in Montana. Stud. at Arranger's Stage Band Camp, Calif. 1963–4; Berklee Coll. of Mus. '64–8 (B. Mus. '68). Led own gps. in Bost. w. Miroslav Vitous, Pat and Joe LaBarbera. Moved to LA '68, pl. w. r&b gps., incl. Drifters; Platters; Jackie Wilson. Co-led avant-r&b band, Change, w. Billy Elgart, Gary Peacock; jazz gp. Revival w. Glenn Ferris '69–71. Tour. w. Ray Charles '72. Pl. and comp. for Chris Poehler band in SF. Moved to NYC '73. Pl. w. Paul Jeffrey Oct., latin bands, then joined Charles Mingus '74. Pl. w. Mingus '74–8; Charli Persip Superband '78–90; Dannie Richmond '79–81; Sam Rivers '79–84; Carlos Ward '87; Muhal Richard Abrams '88–91; Mingus Epitaph '89–91; Geo. Gruntz '91; Jazz Tribe w. Walter Bishop, Bobby Watson. Walrath was lead. and mus. dir. of Mingus Dynasty '89–early '90s. He has led his own gps. fr '80; Jack Walrath and Masters of Suspense fr. '86. Many comps., incl. "Revenge of the Fat People"; "Killer Bunnies"; "Village of the Darned." His '88 rec. w. country singer Willie Nelson, "I'm So Lonesome I Could Cry," received a Grammy nomination. Has been an outspoken opponent of the neoclassical movement in jazz, arguing that innovation not emulation is the core of the jazz tradition. Favs: Louis Armstrong, Nat Adderley, Dizzy Gillespie, Sonny Rollins,

Eric Dolphy; comps: Duke Ellington, Ornette Coleman, Charles Mingus, Joe Henderson, Polls: *DB* TDWR. Fests: Eur., Asia, So. Amer. fr. '74. TV: Eur., MJF '77 w. Mingus; Mingus Epitaph video. CDs: Muse; BN; Evid.; JA; Steep.; TCB; ACT; w. Mingus Dynasty (Col.); Mingus (Atl.; Rh.; Jazz Door; Jazz Classics); Miles Davis (WB); M. R. Abrams (BS); Ricky Ford (Muse); Lou Rawls (BN); B. Purdie (ACT); Mike Clark (Stash); L. Hampton (Tel.); Hamiet Bluiett (Mapleshade); Bob Nel; NY Comp. Orch. (NW); Charli Persip (SN); Dannie Richmond (Timel.; Tutu).

WALTON, CEDAR ANTHONY JR, pno, comp; b. Dallas, TX, 1/17/34. Studied w. moth. and at U. of Denver, Colo. To NYC 1955; army service '56–8. Joined J. J. Johnson qt. '58–60; Jazztet '60–1; Art Blakey '61–4. Dur. '60s he was a member of BN label's virtual house rhythm section, rec. w. Blue Mitchell; Lee Morgan; Kenny Dorham; Freddie Hubbard; Donald Byrd; Milt Jackson; and others. Accomp. Abbey Lincoln '65–7. Freq. in Eur. fr. '70s. From time to time led a gp., Eastern Rebellion, w. Clifford Jordan; Sam Jones; Billy Higgins, et al; in mid 70s led Soundscapes, a jazz-funk band. Through '80s pl. w. Timeless All-Stars and led his own trios or qts., often w. Jordan. Best-known comps incl. "Bolivia"; "Ugetsu"; "Ojos de Rojo"; "Cedar's Blues"; "Mode for Joe"; "Twilight Waltz"; and "Midnight Waltz." Although Walton frequently plays the bop repertoire, he is a lyrical, idiomatically versatile perf. who also embraces elements of blues and modality. CDs: Ast. Pl.; Delos; Steep.; Timel.; Red; CC; Evid.; Conc.; Mon.; Ther.; Prest.; Imp.; Disc.; Early Bird; w. J. Coltrane (Atl.); C. Hollyday (Novus); Benny Carter (MM); Timel. All-Stars (Delos); Milt Jackson (EW; MM; Limel.; Pab.; Qwest; Rep.); Eastern Rebellion (Imp.; MM); F. Hubbard (BN; MM); Lee Morgan; J. Henderson (BN); Clifford Jordan; Blue Mitchell; J. Heath; K. Dorham (Riv.); Sam Jones (Xan.); Steve Turre (Stash); James Clay (Ant.); Wayne Shorter (Aff.); A. Blakey (BN; Imp.; MCA; Riv.); K. Burrell (Cont.); J. J. Johnson (Col.); Pat Martino (Prest.); Lucky Thompson (LRC); Steve Grossman (Drey.; Red).

WANZO, MEL, tbn; b. Cleveland, OH, 11/22/30. Studied at Youngstown U. 1948–52; pl. w. army band led by Cannonball Adderley '52–4; further studies at Cleveland Inst. of Mus. '58–61. ABC-TV staff mus. in Cleveland '61–3; Glenn Miller Orch. led by Ray McKinley '63–7. After US and Eur. tour w. Woody Herman '67–8, he joined Count Basie as lead tbn. '69–80. Rejoined the Basie band in '84 after four yrs. of freelancing, mainly in LA. Not primarily a soloist, he is a valuable lead tbn. CDs: w. C. Basie (Tel.; Pab.); Frank Capp (Conc.); Milt Jackson w. Basie (Pab.).

WARD, CARLOS NATHANIEL, alto, tnr saxes, fl; b. Ancon, Panama, 5/1/40. Family moved to Seattle, Wash. 1953; started on cl. at 13. Studied at Navy Sch. of Mus. while in mil. Stationed in Germ., he pl. w. Albert Mangelsdorff and was infl. by Eric Dolphy. Back in Seattle he pl. w. John Coltrane '65 and cont. after moving to NYC. Freelanced in NYC dur. loft scene of the '60s, pl. w. Don Cherry; Sam Rivers; Sunny Murray; Rashied Ali; Karl Berger; Paul Motian; and David Izenzon. As a member of Jazz Comp. Orch. and the pop gp. BT Express, Ward showed his versatility. Settled in SF '67; ret. to NYC 69; longtime assoc. w. Abdullah Ibrahim since '73, later assoc. w. pnst. Don Pullen into the '90s. Dur. '80s he pl. w. Don Cherry and briefly '86 w. Cecil Taylor Unit. TV: *The Jazz Set* '71. CDs: Leo; w. Don Pullen (BN); Bob Stewart (Post.).

WARD, HELEN, voc; b. NYC, 9/19/16; d. Arlington, VA, 4/21/98. Studied pno. in childhood. Sang fr. her teen yrs. Heard on WOR radio. First prominent tour. w. Benny Goodman 1934–6; also rec. w. Gene Krupa, Teddy Wilson, Bob Crosby late '30s. Toured w. Hal McIntyre '42–3; joined Harry James '44; prod. and dir. mus. shows at radio station WMGM '46–7. Remained semi-retired but in '50s worked w. Peanuts Hucko and occ. rejoined Goodman. Rec. album, *The Helen Ward Song Book* '81. Superior jazz-inflected bb singer. CDs: w. B. Goodman (BB); Red Norvo (MM); one track w. Krupa in *The Women* (BB).

WARE, DAVID S., tnr sax; b. Plainfield, NJ, 11/7/49. Played bari. sax, alto sax, and, finally, tnr. sax as a teenager. Att. Berklee Coll. 1967–9. Form. gp., Apogee, in Bost. '70, perf. there until moving to NYC '73. Pl. in Cecil Taylor's orch., Carnegie Hall '74; pl. and rec. w. Andre Cyrille '74–6; pl. in trio w. tptr. Raphe Malik mid '70s; tour. Eur. w. Taylor '76–7. Pl. in duo w. Barry Harris '77. Assoc. w. Cyrille again '78, '80. Own qt. fr. late '80s. Rec. for Silkheart label in late '80s-early '90s, then for Homestead, DIW. Signed by Branford Marsalis for Columbia '98. Ware features a grinding, raspy modality, delivered in a wide-toned style replete with honks, squeals, and rapid, repetitious runs generic to the avant-garde saxes of the '60s. On a standard such as "Autumn Leaves" he hews close to the melody with virtually no improvisation but imbues it with a passion akin to Albert Ayler's. Most proponents emphasize his great energy. CDs: Col.; DIW; Silk.; w. Cyrille (BS; DIW); Taylor (Enja).

WARE, LEONARD, gtr, comp; b. Richmond, VA, 12/28/09. Started on oboe at Tuskeegee Inst.; sw. to gtr. early 1930s. Best known for the rec. of his comp. "Hold Tight" w. Sidney Bechet '38. In '40s rec. w. Joe Turner; Buddy Johnson; Albinia Jones. Inactive since late '40s. CDs: w. Joe Turner (Dec.); Bechet; Don Byas (Class.).

WARE, WILBUR (BERNARD), bs; b. Chicago, IL, 9/8/32; d. Philadelphia, PA, 9/9/79. Studied bjo., bs.; prof. debut w. Stuff Smith; rec. w. Sun Ra early 1950s. Rec. w. Johnny Griffin; pl w. T. Monk mid '50s. Settled in NYC, worked w. Art Blakey '56; also w. Buddy DeFranco; rejoined Monk '57–8. As staff bs. for Riv. label, he rec. w. a variety of mus. and his own gp. late '50s, early '60s. To Chi '63; semi-inactive for several yrs., working sporadically w. A. Shepp and Sun Ra into '70s. Viewed by some observers as a linking pl. between the bop of Paul Chambers and the contemp. work of Charlie Haden, et al. CDs: Riv.; w. Blakey (Col.); K. Dorham; K. Drew; J. Griffin; E. Henry; B. Mitchell; Monk; G. Mulligan; Z. Sims; T. Thielemans (Riv.); S. Rollins (BN).

WARFIELD, BILL (WILLIAM LEONARD JR.), tpt, cnt, flg, fl, pno, arr; b. Baltimore, MD, 3/2/52. Studied at Peabody Cons. 1966–70; Towson State U. '70–4; U. of Md., Balt. '78–80; Manh. Sch. of Mus. '91–3. Played w. local top-40 and show bands '67–77, then w. fusion bands Mystical Bone '74–5, Both Worlds '77–8. Dir. Port City Jazz Ens., also gigs in Balt. and Wash., D.C., w. Sonny Stitt, Lee, Konitz, Charles Covington '78–80. Perf. commissioned work w. Balt. Symphony '79. Moved to NYC '80, pl. w. Mel Lewis Jazz Orch. '80–1; Bill Kirchner Nonet fr. '80. Tour. w. Paul Anka '81–2. Joined Mus. of Bklyn. Initiative '82. Pl. w. Sheila Jordan '87; Amer. Jazz Orch. '88; Lester Bowie, Oliver Lake at Town Hall '90; Roland Vasquez '92. Warfield has led his own bb in NYC clubs since '88. He has taught at the Dalton Sch. since '89; Bklyn. Coll. since '90, and Towson State U. since '92. He has received comp.'s grants fr. Mus. of Bklyn. Initiative, the Bklyn. Dance Consortium, and Meet the Composer. Favs: Freddie Hubbard, Lee Morgan, Miles Davis; arrs: Charles Mingus, Thad Jones, Bob Brookmeyer. CDs: Interplay; SB; w. B. Kirchner (SB); Dave Stryker (Steep.).

WARLOP, MICHEL, vln; b. Douai, France, 1/23/11; d. Bagneres-de-Luchon, France, 3/6/47. A child prodigy, he met Stephane Grappelli while pl. w. Gregor and his Gregorians. Accomp. Maurice Chevalier and other singers; rec. w. Grappelli and Django

Reinhardt mid '30s; in vln. trio w. Grappelli and Eddie South 1937. In '40s pl. w. Raymond LeGrand and led own string spt. An exceptional technician who was considered Grappelli's peer. CDs: w. Reinhardt; South (Class.).

WARREN, BUTCH (EDWARD RANDOLPH), bs; b. Washington, DC, 9/8/39. Played in band led by his father in 1953, then worked in Wash., D.C., w. Gene Ammons, Stuff Smith ca. '56–7. Moved to NYC, worked w. Kenny Dorham '58–60. House bs. at BN Recs. '61–3; rec. w. Jackie McLean; Donald Byrd; Herbie Hancock; Stanley Turrentine; Joe Henderson; Sonny Clark; Dexter Gordon. Pl. w. Thelonious Monk '63–4, incl. Eur. and Japan tours. Ret. to Wash., D.C., and pl. on local TV show '65– 6, then tour. w. r&b gps., incl. The Platters '66. Did not perf. due to illness late '60s-early '70. Ret. to mus. parttime in mid '70s; pl. w. Howard McGhee, Richie Cole '75. Fests: Eur., Japan w. Monk. CDs: w. Monk (Col.); D. Byrd; Dexter Gordon; I. Quebec; H. Hancock; J. Henderson; Grant Green (BN); McCoy Tyner (Imp.); Elmo Hope; W. Bishop Jr. (FS); K. Dorham (FS; Time).

WARREN, EARLE RONALD (Earl), alto sax, voc, comp; b. Springfield, OH, 7/1/14; d. Springfield, 6/4/94. Father pl. mand.; twin bro., Robert, pl. dms. Played pno., bjo., uke. in family band bef. taking up C-melody sax. Added "e" to name ca. 1930 to distinguish himself from Earl Hines and other jazz mus. named Earl. Led own gp. in Springfield, then pl. w. Marion Sears in Cleveland '33–5 and again in '36. Led own bb in Cincinnati, where Count Basie heard him. Joined Basie April '37, splitting lead alto and bari. sax duties w. Jack Washington. By '38 he had establ. himself as lead alto and ballad voc. With Basie, Warren was noted as an excellent section leader, and for his solos on such recs. as "Out the Window"; "Sent for You Yesterday"; "Pound Cake." His comps. incl. "Tom Thumb"; "Circus in Rhythm"; "Rockin' the Blues"; and, w. Buster Harding, "9:20 Special." Pl. w. Basie until '45, then led own gp. in Cincinnati and NYC. Rejoined Basie briefly '48, '49–50. Managed Johnny Otis early '50s, then worked in NYC and Wash., D.C., theaters as freelance mus. dir. Alto sax, manager, mus. dir. w. Eddie Heywood '54–5. Tour. and rec. w. Buck Clayton '57–62. Dir. shows at Apollo Theater in NYC and theaters in Wash., D.C., Balt., Chi. Also emcee and dir. for Alan Freed stage shows in NYC '50s-60s. Tour. Eur. w. Lena Horne '61. Pl. in nightclubs w. Emmett Berry mid '60s; also owned furniture store dur. this time. Reunion w. Basie and Eur. tour. w. revue *Jazz From a Swinging Era* '67. Mus. dir. for Platters '69; Drifters '70. Led own band at the

Lorelei, NYC '71–2, and the Countsmen, a Basie alumni band, off and on '72–91. Orig. Countsmen incl. Buddy Tate, Doc Cheatham, Dill Jones, Benny Morton, or Vic Dickenson. Cond. NY Jazz Repertory Orch. in Basie tribute '75. Led own gps. w. Dicky Wells; Joe Newman; Taft Jordan; Paul Quinichette; Jimmy Lewis; Dill Jones at West End Café '75–early '80s. In the early '80s Warren lived and perf. in Geneva, Switzerland. Tour. Eur. w. Buck Clayton's Basie Alumni band '83. Pl. in NYC at Sweet Basil's '80s. Ret. to Springfield and lived w. sister Nancy Mitchell '87. Pl. w. Johnny Lydell, own gp. in Indiana late '80s. Fests: Eur. w. Clayton; Benny Carter; own gps. Film: *Born to Swing* '72. CDs: w. Basie (Col.; Dec.; BB; Class.); Lester Young (Sav.); B. Clayton (Steep.; Chiaro.; Story.); Milt Jackson–Ray Brown (Verve); Arnett Cobb; L. Hampton (Timel.); B. Holiday (Col.); I. Jacquet (Verve).

WARREN, PETER, bs, cello, comp; b. Hempstead, NY, 11/21/35. Father pl. bs,; family incl. many other string players. Stud. cello at Juilliard w. Josef Emonts, principal w. N.Y. Philharm.; also studied at Adelphi Coll. Self-taught on bs. Played solo cello concert at Carnegie Hall 1962; cello w. NYC Ballet, Atlanta Symph. '63–5. Began pl. bs. in LV show bands '66. Tour. w. Tommy Dorsey Orch. '66; Dionne Warwick '66–9. In NYC '69–72, formed 10-bs. gp., NY Bass Revolution, and el-mus. gp., Interchange. Also stud. w. Chuck Israels and pl. w. Chick Corea; Larry Coryell; Herbie Mann; Barry Altschul; Bob Moses; el-bs. w. Danny Kalb's Blues Project. In Eur. '72–8, pl. w. Jean-Luc Ponty; Phil Woods; Daniel Humair; Michel Portal; Joachim Kuhn; Stu Martin; John Surman; Anthony Braxton; pl. cello w. Ambush w. Martin; Charlie Mariano; Barre Phillips. Received NEA grant to comp. for cello '76. Ret. to US, pl. w. Jack DeJohnette's Directions and Special Edition '78–83. Cond. wkshps. at Creative Music Foundation '70s. Led own gp. w. John Scofield, Mike Stern, Steve Slagle, Victor Lewis fr. '83. Warren became active as a clinician and has contrib. articles to *Bass Player* mag. Favs: Gary Peacock, Paul Chambers, Eddie Gomez. Polls: *DB* Rec. of Yr. '80; Prix Du Disc '88 (both w. Special Edition). TV: Eur. TV. CDs: w. J. DeJohnette (ECM); A. Mangelsdorff (Enja).

WASHINGTON, BUCK (FORD LEE), pno, voc, dancer; b. Louisville, KY, 10/16/03; d. NYC, 1/31/55. Spent virtually his entire career in partnership w. John Sublett ("Bubbles"). The "Buck & Bubbles" team began in 1912; then both came to NYC as teenagers '19. Washington achieved a secondary reputation as a competent, Hines-inspired pnst. In '30 he rec. w.

Louis Armstrong, incl. "Dear Old Southland" and "My Sweet." Led the accomp. band on Bessie Smith's final session '33 and rec. w. Coleman Hawkins '34. Buck & Bubbles app. together in *Porgy and Bess* and in the films *Cabin in the Sky* and *A Song Is Born*. The team broke up in '53; the following yr. Washington tour. w. comedian Timmie Rogers' combo. CDs: w. B. Smith: L. Armstrong (Col.); Coleman Hawkins (Class.).

WASHINGTON, DINAH (Ruth Jones), voc; b. Tuscaloosa, AL, 8/29/24; d. Detroit, MI, 12/14/63. Raised in Chi.; played pno. and dir. church choir. From age 15 she perf. in nightclubs and in Sallie Martin's Gospel Choir. Played pno. at Three Deuces; sang at Garrick Stage Lounge where she was heard by Louis Armstrong's manager, Joe Glaser, who brought Lionel Hampton in to hear her. She joined the Hampton band in 1943 and made her rec. debut the same yr., accomp. by a Hampton contingent. "Evil Gal Blues," fr. the sess., became a hit and eventually led to her working as a single fr. '46. Over the yrs. Washington added r&b and pop songs to her repertoire, incl. "What a Difference a Day Made" and "This Bitter Earth." Dur. her prolific rec. career, Washington reached a broad audience w. material ranging fr. the forthright blues style of a Bessie Smith tribute to a jam sess. w. Clifford Brown and Max Roach, and middle-of-the-road ballads. Her distinct, gospel-bred delivery was perfectly suited for a growing urbanized rhythm & blues audience. Part of her perf. at '57 NJF is seen in film, *Jazz on a Summer's Day*. CDs: Merc.; Em.; Verve; Del.; Roul.; w. L. Hampton (Dec.); C. Brown–M. Roach (Em.); first recs. in *Keynote Collection* (Merc.).

WASHINGTON, GEORGE, tbn, arr; b. Brunswick, GA, 10/18/07. Raised in Jacksonville, Fla., he stud. at Edward Waters Coll. 1922. Moved to Phila. in '25; then to NYC, where he stud. w. Walter Damrosch at the NY Cons. In '20s he pl. w. Luckey Roberts; Charlie Johnson; Vernon Andrade; in '30s w. Don Redman; Benny Carter; pl. and arr. for Mills Blue Rhythm Band '32–6. Also w. Fletcher Henderson '37; L. Armstrong '37–43. To Calif. w. Horace Henderson '45; led own bands in LA and LV fr. '50s; also pl. w. Johnny Otis and rec. w. Bill Darensbourg. Later freelanced as tbnst. and arr. CDs: w. Benny Carter (Class.); Ben Webster (Em.); Henry Red Allen (Collector's Classics).

WASHINGTON, GROVER JR., tnr, alto, sop, bari saxes, fl, cl, el-bs, pno; b. Buffalo, NY, 12/12/43; d. NYC, 12/1/99. Father pl. tnr. sax; moth. sang in choir; bro., Darryl, pl. dms. w. Groove Holmes. Father

bought him a sax at age 10; lessons at Wurlitzer Sch. of Mus. Pl. in hs band, also all-city hs band. Stud. chord progressions w. Elvin Shepherd. Left Buffalo at age 16 w. Columbus, Ohio-based gp., the Four Clefs. After its breakup in '63, he pl. w. orgst. Keith McAllister for two yrs. In army 1965–7; while stationed at Ft. Dix, N.J., he pl. in Phila. w. org. trios and rock gps. Also worked in NYC w. Billy Cobham for Jazz Interactions dur. this time. Pl. in Phila. w. Don Gardner's Sonotones '67–8. Worked for local rec. distributor '69–70, then ret. to full-time pl. w. Chas. Earland late '70. Rec. as sideman on soul-jazz dates for Prest. label '70–1. Rec. w. gtrst. Joe Jones, Leon Spencer, Johnny Hammond Smith early '70s. Rec. first album as lead., *Inner City Blues*, for Kudu label '71. The rec. was a hit, and Washington formed a tour. band shortly thereafter. His '75 album, *Mister Magic*, was the first of his many gold and platinum recs. Began rec. on fl. late '70s. Washington's style, a combination of jazz and gentle r&b, played a role in shaping the so-called "smooth jazz" of the '90s. He was, however, also capable of playing more substantive jazz. Favs: John Coltrane, Joe Henderson, Oliver Nelson. Fests: all major fr. '71. TV: numerous apps. on US, Eur., Jap. TV. CDs: Col.; BN; GRP; w. John Blake (Sunny.); Vanessa Rubin (Novus); Freddy Cole (Fant.); James Moody (Tel.); Eddie Henderson (Mile.); Mal Waldron (Evid.); Kathleen Battle (Col.); G. Mulligan (Tel.); T. S. Monk (N2K).

WASHINGTON, JACK (RONALD), bari and alto sax; b. Kansas City, KS, 7/17/10; d. Oklahoma City, OK, 11/28/64. Professional debut in 1926 w. Paul Banks. Worked w. Bennie Moten '27–35; Bus Moten '35; Leslie Sheffield '35–6; Count Basie '36–43. Army service '43–6; then w. Basie again '46–50. Moved to Oklahoma City where he worked at the airport but also pl. w. Bobby Knott's orch. dur. '50s. Seldom featured as soloist w. Basie, he was highly regarded by his colleagues. His fluid, personal style can be heard on such early recs. as "Doggin' Around"; "Topsy"; "Jive at Five"; "Somebody Stole My Gal"; and on "Lopin" w. the post-war band. In '58 he drove to NYC for the Paul Quinichette Prest. session, *Basie Reunion*. CDs: w. Basie (Dec.; BB; Class.); Quinichette (Prest.); B. Holiday (Col.); B. Moten (BB).

WASHINGTON, KENNY, dms; b. Brooklyn, NY, 5/29/58. Raised on Staten Island. Pl. dms. at age 7. Stud. at Music & Art HS, NYC, w. Justin DiCioccio. Pl. w. Lee Konitz 1977–8; Betty Carter '78–9; Johnny Griffin fr. '80. Fr. '89 into early '90s w. Tommy Flanagan trio; also w. trios of George Cables, Larry Willis. Pl. and/or rec. w. Kenny Burrell; Ron

Carter; Frank Wess; Milt Jackson; George Coleman; Walter Davis; Walter Bishop; Cedar Walton; Benny Carter; Clark Terry; Dizzy Gillespie; Dameronia; subbed in Mingus Dynasty. A keen student of jazz history w. a vast album collection. Does weekly deejay show on WBGO-FM, Newark, N.J. Favs: P. J. Jones, Jo Jones, Shadow Wilson. CDs: w. Konitz (Chiaro.; Evid.); Griffin (Gal.; Ant.); Tommy Flanagan (Timel.); M. Jackson (MM); Arturo Sandoval (GRP); Joshua Breakstone (Cont.); Burrell; Bobby Watson (BN); Dameronia (SN); Teddy Edwards (Muse); Jim McNeely (Steep.); Mingus Dynasty (Story.); Terry; Phil Woods (Chesky); G. Wein's Newport All-Stars (Col.); John Swana (CC).

WASHINGTON, PETER MARK, bs, gtr; b. Los Angeles, CA, 8/28/64. Self-taught. Stud. Engl. lit. at U.C.-Berkeley 1982–6; a few lessons w. Herbie Lewis. First gig in uncle's church at age 15. Freelanced in SF Bay Area w. John Handy; Bobby Hutcherson; Lorez Alexandria; Johnny Coles; Harold Land; Frank Morgan; Ernestine Anderson; Ernie Andrews; Chris Connor; others. Moved to NYC '86 at invitation of Art Blakey. Pl. w. Blakey '86–8. Freelanced in NYC fr. '88 w. Benny Golson; Milt Jackson; Mingus Dynasty; Bobby Hutcherson; Dizzy Gillespie; Johnny Griffin; Teddy Edwards; Tommy Flanagan; Hank Jones; Ralph Moore; Lew Tabackin–Toshiko Akiyoshi; Randy Brecker; Fathead Newman; Charles McPherson; Geoff Keezer; Mulgrew Miller; Tom Harrell; others. Favs: Doug Watkins, Paul Chambers, Albert Stinson, Ron Carter. Fests: Eur., Japan, So. Amer. fr. '86. CDs: w. Blakey (Delos; Evid.; BS; Arco); Gillespie (Tel.); R. Moore; M. Miller (Land.); T. Akiyoshi (Col.); Justin Robinson; Stephen Scott (Verve); T. Harrell (Chesky); Jim Snidero (CC; Red); J. Griffin (Ant.); L. Tabackin (Conc.); D. Hazeltine (Sharp Nine); Geoff Keezer; T. Flanagan (BN); Eric Alexander; Michael Weiss; Benny Green; Brian Lynch (CC).

WASHINGTONIANS, THE. See **SNOWDEN, ELMER,** and **ELLINGTON, DUKE.**

WATANABE, KAZUMI, gtr, comp, lead; b. Tokyo, Japan, 10/14/53. Began on gtr. at age 14. Pl. first prof. gigs while in mid-teens. Stud. jazz gtr. w. Sadanori Nakamura at Yamaha Mus. Sch., Tokyo 1969–70; jazz theory w. Makoto Uchibori '70–1; Sadao Watanabe (not related) '71–2. Further gtr. study w. Masayuki Takayanagi '72–4; classical gtr. w. Tamaki Shimizu '70–1. Pl. w. Sadanori Nakamura; Masaru Imada; Isao Suzuki; Shigeharu Mukai; Sadao Watanabe; Takehiro Honda; own gps '70s. Formed gp. KYLYN w. Ryuichi Sakamoto '79. Made world tour

w. YMO fall '79. Rec. album *To Chi Ka* (Nippon-Col.), prod. by Mike Mainieri '80; also tour. Japan w. Marcus Miller, Omar Hakim, M. Mainieri '80. Freelanced w. visiting US gps. incl. Steps Ahead '80, '82; Brecker Bros. '82; Jaco Pastorius '82. Formed own fusion gp. Mobo '83. Tour. US w. Mobo III Band '85; rec. album *Spice of Life* in London w. Bill Bruford '86. Pl. concert in Tokyo dedicated to Django Reinhardt '89; at Montreux JF '89. Received Fumio Nanri awd. for contrib. to Japanese jazz '90. Active w. Asian trad. mus. gps. early '90s; formed gp. Asian Mobo '90. Organized mus. event Asian Fantasy w. Yosuke Yamashita, Akira Sakata, Kazutoki Umezu '91. Formed gp. Resonance Vox, which often feat. guest soloists incl. Kosuke Mine, Asuka Kaneko, Yasuhiro Kobayashi '92. Most of Watanabe's albums have been released in the US on the Denon and Rhino labels. Favs: Jim Hall, Wes Montgomery, S. Nakamure, Takayanagi, John Coltrane, Larry Coryell, Julian Bream. Polls: *Jazz Disc* '84; *SJ* Readers '76–93; *SJ* Readers Rec. of Yr. '84; *SJ* Critics '90–2. CDs: Den.; Rh.; Polyd.-Domo; Nippon-Col.

WATANABE, SADAO, alto, sop saxes, fl, comp, lead; b. Utsunomiya, Japan, 2/1/33. Father pl. and taught biwa, a Japanese lute. Began pl. cl. in jr. hs. Moved to Tokyo in 1951 and pl. in dance bands at US mil. bases. Studied fl. w. Ririko Hayashi of Tokyo Philharm. '53. Joined Toshiko Akiyoshi Qt. '53, then led gp. after she left to study in US '56–8. Won first of many *SJ* polls '59. In US stud. at Berklee Coll. of Mus. '62–5. Pl. w. Gary McFarland, Chico Hamilton '65, then ret. to Japan. Appointed dir. of Yamaha Inst. of Pop. Mus., formed qt. w. M. Kikuchi, M. Togashi '66. Won *SJ* award for best album for rec. w. Charlie Mariano '67. Visited Brazil, rec. w. Brazilian mus.; also made first app. at NJF '68, Montreux and NJF '70. Rec. w. Charlie Mariano '68; Chick Corea, Miroslav Vitous, Jack DeJohnette in NYC '70. Visited Africa '74. Rec. w. Hank Jones, Ron Carter, Tony Williams '76. Became first jazz mus. to receive Grand Prix Awd. fr. Japanese govt. '76; also won Fumio Nanri awd. for contribution to Japanese jazz. Rec. in LA w. Dave Grusin, Lee Ritenour '78. Pl. landmark concert at Budokan w. Tokyo Philharm. cond. by Dave Grusin '80. Tour. US annually fr. '80 into early '90s; prod. annual concert series in Tokyo fr. '85. Tour. Japan w. Sonny Rollins '90. Led own gp. at Ronnie Scott's, London '91; So. African tour '92. Watanabe publ. a book of color photos, *La Fiesta: Mille Miglia* (Fujitelevision Publ. Inc.) '92. He was a feat. guest soloist at Yoshiaki Masuo's homecoming concert in Tokyo '93. His autobiography is entitled *Jazz for Myself* (Arachi Publ.). Polls: *SJ* alto '59–93; *SJ* Jazzman of Year '68–9, '74,

'76–81, '84–9; *SJ* Rec. of Year '80–1, '85–6, '88; *Jazz Disc* '67, '72. Fests: all major fr. '68. CDs: King; Vict.; Den.; Vang.; Elek.; Sony; Verve.

WATANABE, TAKESHI, dms; b. Tokyo, Japan, 6/7/52. Studied w. Motohiko Hino, later w. Billy Hart; Jimmie Smith; Alan Dawson; et al. Joined bs. Yoshio Ikeda's band in 1973, remaining until '79. From then until '81 w. Isao Suzuki's gp.; from '81 w. Eiji Kitamura. Heard at several JFs incl. MJF '89, Mt. Hood '91, LA Jazz Party '92, '93. Favs: Elvin Jones, Buddy Rich, Billy Higgins.

WATERS, BENNY (BENJAMIN), alto, tnr saxes, cl, voc; b. Brighton, MD, 1/23/02; d. Columbia, MD, 8/11/98. Self-taught on org. fr. age 3, then pno. Began perf. at 7 after older bro. gave him a sax. At 18 stud. at New Engl. Cons.; later taught mus. One of his students was Harry Carney. Pl. and wrote arrs. for Charlie Johnson 1926–31; in the same period rec. w. King Oliver and Clarence Williams. In '30s and '40s he worked w. Fletcher Henderson; Hot Lips Page; Claude Hopkins; Jimmie Lunceford. In the '40s he led his own band for four yrs.; to Eur. w. Jimmy Archey's NO jazz gp. '52; settled in Eur. at that time. Pl. in Paris at the club La Cigale for fifteen yrs. w. Jacques Butler; took over leadership of the band in '67. Played many fests and rec. in Eur. dur. '70s and '80s; worked in NYC briefly in '80s but moved back permanently in '92. Although he turned blind after '87 he maintained a busy schedule. Celebrated his 95th birthday w. a perf. at Birdland, NYC, and remained active until his death. Has been compared to Coleman Hawkins and Sidney Bechet. On alto he sometimes sounded like a cross between Benny Carter and Earl Bostic. CDs: Story.; Hep; JP; Enja; Jazz.; w. Clarence Williams (Collector's Classics); Archey (Story.); King Oliver (Jazz Class. in Digital Stereo); Charlie Johnson (Hot 'N Sweet); Lunceford; Hot Lips Page; Claude Hopkins (Class.); Keith Smith (Lake).

WATERS, ETHEL, voc, actress; b. Chester, PA, 10/31/1896; d. Los Angeles, CA, 9/1/77. Made debut singing in church choir at 5. After winning talent contest, began app. in Phila. and Balt. theatres, eventually billed as "Sweet Mama Stringbean." Worked w. partner Ethel Williams as "The Two Ethels" bef. moving to NYC in 1917. Began rec. for Black Swan label in '21; also tour. and rec. w. Fletcher Henderson's Black Swan Troubadours '22. By mid '20s, she was rec. w. great success for Col. and app. in such shows as *Blackbirds* and the *Black Bottom Revue*; throughout '30s she cont. to perf. in hit shows, incl. *As Thousands Cheer* and *Heat Wave*, and rec. w. such

accomps. as Duke Ellington '32; Benny Goodman '33; and Victor Young '34. By the early '40s she had gained nationwide acceptance as a stage star w. many acting roles, incl. the highly successful *Mamba's Daughters* '39. Highlights of her film career were *Cabin in the Sky; Tales of Manhattan; Pinky; The Sound and the Fury*; and *Member of the Wedding* '53, in which she reprised her stage role. A superb singer, Ethel Waters' vocal range was wide and her phrasing strongly jazz-tinged. She moved effortlessly among slightly raunchy material, such as "Do What You Did Last Night" and "My Handy Man," sweet love songs like "Memories of You" and "Am I Blue?," and—in later yrs.—religious songs such as "His Eye Is on the Sparrow." Lee Wiley, Connee Boswell, Mildred Bailey, and Lena Horne were among contemporary singers whom she infl. In later years, she abandoned popular mus. and turned to religion, sometimes touring w. evangelist Billy Graham. Her autobiography, *His Eye Is on the Sparrow*, was published in '51. CDs: Col.; w. Benny Carter (BB); Dorsey Bros. (Hep); Duke Ellington (Class.).

WATKINS, DOUG (DOUGLAS), bs, cello; b. Detroit, MI, 3/2/34; d. Holbrook, AZ, 2/5/62. Schoolmates at Cass Tech HS incl. Paul Chambers (who was his cousin by marriage) and Donald Byrd. Left Det. w. James Moody in summer of 1953 and ret. the next yr. to work w. Barry Harris trio, backing such visiting stars as Stan Getz; Charlie Parker; Coleman Hawkins. Relocated to NYC Aug. '54, working at Minton's and w. Kenny Dorham and Hank Mobley; then joined Art Blakey's Jazz Messengers. Pl. w. Horace Silver '56 and Charles Mingus Jazz Workshop (when Mingus pl. pno.) '60–61; recs. w. Silver; Byrd; Art Blakey; Art Farmer; Gene Ammons; Sonny Rollins; Jackie McLean; Pepper Adams; Phil Woods; et al. Pl. cello on own New Jazz album, *Soulnik*. One of the brightest talents among the wave of mus. who came to NYC from Det. in the mid '50s. Killed in an auto accident near Holbrook. CDs: w. A. Blakey (Col.; BN); D. Byrd (Polyd.; BN); J. McLean (Prest.; BN); S. Rollins (Prest.; BN); Lee Morgan (Sav.; BN); H. Mobley; Y. Lateef (Sav.); Mingus (Rh./Atl.); K. Burrell; Coltrane; Art Farmer; G. Ammons; C. Fuller; C. Hawkins; Phil Woods (Prest.); H. Silver (BN); Pepper Adams (Riv.)

WATKINS, JULIUS, Fr horn; b. Detroit, MI, 10/10/21; d. Short Hills, NJ, 4/4/77. Took up French horn in grammar sch. at age 9, but also pl. tpt. w. Ernie Fields 1943–6, Milt Buckner '49–50. Stud. at Manh. Sch. of Mus. Rec. w. Kenny Clarke, Babs Gonzales '49; Thelonious Monk and Sonny Rollins '53. Tour. w. Pete Rugolo Orch. '54. In '56, he and

Charlie Rouse formed the gp. Les Jazz Modes, intermittently rec. and tour. w. it for the next three yrs. App. w. Oscar Pettiford bb '56–8, where he was feat. w. David Amram on "Two French Fries." With George Shearing bb '59. From early '60s he was mainly active in studios and B'way shows; also pl. w. Charles Mingus brass ens. '65; rec. w. John Coltrane; Tadd Dameron; Freddie Hubbard; Gil Evans; Curtis Fuller; et al. Watkins was the first French hornist to play in the bop style and bring a personal quality to his improvs. Due to the limited demand for his instrument in jazz, he never achieved recognition commensurate w. his talent. An annual Julius Watkins Jazz French Horn Festival was inaugurated in NYC '94. CDs: Biograph (w. Les Jazz Modes); w. Kenny Clarke (Sav.); M. Davis–G. Evans (Col.); D. Gillespie; K. Burrell (Verve); Randy Weston (Roul.); J. Heath (Riv.); T. Monk (Prest.); O. Pettiford (Imp.); D. Amram; Gigi Gryce (Sav.); B. Gonzales (BN); Q. Jones (Merc.; R&T; Qwest); Benny Bailey; Cal Massey; Phil Woods (Cand.); G. Evans (Verve; Enja); Milt Jackson (Sav.; Riv.); McCoy Tyner (Mile.); B. Golson (Cont.); tracks w. Pettiford in *Charles Mingus: The Complete Debut Recordings*; and *The Debut Records Story* (Deb.).

WATKISS, CLEVELAND, voc, pno; b. London, England, 10/21/59. Studied priv. at Guildhall Sch. of Mus. 1987–8. Worked w. Jazz Warriors; Art Blakey; Kenny Wheeler; Courtney Pine; Stevie Wonder; et al. In US, he pl. w. Cassandra Wilson, Branford Marsalis. Many radio and TV apps., incl. *Club Mix* w. Blakey, jingles, mus. videos. App. at Guitar Legends Fest., Seville, Spain '91. *Wire* award, "Best Vocalist" '87–9. Rec. w. James Taylor. CDs: w. Jazz Warriors (Ant.); C. Pine (Island).

WATROUS, BILL (WILLIAM RUSSELL II), tbn, comp; b. Middletown, CT, 6/8/39. Father pl. tbn. w. swing bands. Stud. harmony at New London HS, then spent four yrs. in navy. Settled in NYC, pl. w. Kai Winding; Roy Eldridge; Quincy Jones; Woody Herman; Johnny Richards; Count Basie. Staff orch. for Merv Griffin Show 1964–7; staff mus. at CBS '67–9; *Dick Cavett Show*, NBC '68–70. After pl. w. Ten Wheel Drive in '71, he formed his own bb, Manhattan Wildlife Refuge, which rec. two LPs for Col. Relocated to LA in late 70s, cont. freelance work and occ. led bb. Pl. w. Trombone Summit (Winding and Albert Mangelsdorff) in Germ. '80. Annual apps. at Colo. JPs. One of the most versatile, all-around artists on his instrument, he was for some time a first call studio player in LA. Favs: Clifford Brown, Charlie Parker, Carl Fontana, Vic Dickenson, Johannes Brahms, Dizzy Gillespie. CDs: D-T; GNP Cres.;

Soundwings; w. Deodado (CTI); W. Montgomery; Chick Corea (Verve); Brass Connection (JA); A. Sandoval (GRP); Gene Harris; Bill Berry (Conc.); E. Fitzgerald (Pab.); John Leitham (USA).

WATSON, BOBBY (ROBERT MICHAEL JR.), alto sax; b. Lawrence, KS, 8/23/53. Father pl. tnr. sax. Started on pno., then cl. Played in church. Grad. KC Junior Coll. 1973; rec. B.A. in mus. theory fr. U. of Miami '75. Moved to NYC, where he joined Art Blakey's Jazz Messengers '71; became mus. dir. eight mos. later and app. on a dozen recs. w. the gp. '77–81. Worked and rec. on and off w. his own gp., Horizon, fr. '80; also pl. w. George Coleman '81; Louis Hayes '82; rec. w. Ricky Ford and Sam Rivers '82; Charli Persip '84; John Hicks; Lou Rawls; and Teramasu Hino. From '82 worked w. cooperative gp., the 29th St. Saxophone Qt.; in summer of '89 he participated in all-star version of Jazz Messengers at Mt. Fuji Fest., Japan; later that yr. led his "High Court of Swing" at Rotterdam's Heineken Fest. Co-leader w. Victor Lewis of gp. Horizon. Own bb fr. '92. Pl. lead alto on soundtrack of Spike Lee film, *School Daze*. Comps. incl. "Ms. B.C."; "Love Remains." Polls: *DB* Alto Sax TDWR. CDs: Col.; BN; Evid.; Red; w. 29th Street Saxophone Quartet (Red; Ant.); Blakey (Red; BN; Col.; Timel.); Louis Hayes (Steep.); Bob Belden (BN); Sam Rivers (BS); John Hicks (DIW); Peter Leitch (CC); Victor Lewis (Audq.); Ray Mantilla; Steve Nelson (Red); Charli Persip (SN)

WATSON, LEO, voc; b. Kansas City, MO, 2/27/1898; d. Los Angeles, CA, 5/2/50. Came to prominence singing and pl. tiple (a small uke-like instrument) w. a qnt. originally known as Ben Bernie's Nephews but later better-known as the Spirits of Rhythm (w. gtrst. Teddy Bunn as his main partner). The gp. made a few recs. and app. at the Onyx Club on 52nd St., NYC, w. Watson occ. doubling on tbn. or dms. He is mainly known for his highly individual style of "scat" singing, which combined unpredictable rhythmic gyrations w. a manic stream-of-consciousness sense of humor. He tour. for eight mos. w. Gene Krupa's band 1938 and is heard briefly on three Artie Shaw recs. Made one sess. under his own name for Dec. Moved to Calif. '40, where he was reunited a few times w. Bunn. App. in films, incl. *Panama Hattie* '42. Some of his best work was heard on a sess. backed by the Vic Dickenson qnt.—"Jingle Bells," "Sonny Boy"—and a final rec. w. the Spirits of Rhythm, "Scattin' The Blues," "Coquette." CDs: w. Spirits of Rhythm (JSP); Washboard Rhythm Kings (Collectors Class.); L. Feather; Slim Gaillard; Krupa; Shaw (Class.); B. Goodman (Phon.); Billie Holiday (Col.).

WATTERS, LU (LUCIOUS), tpt, comp; b. Santa Cruz, CA, 12/19/11; d. Santa Rosa, CA, 11/5/89. Led swing and dance bands until late 1930s, when the NO style inspired him to form the SF Bay Area–based Yerba Buena Jazz Band, whose members incl. Turk Murphy, Clancy Hayes, and Bob Scobey. The gp. enjoyed great success in an era that saw renewed interest in NO-style jazz. Watters gave up band while serving in navy dur. WWII but reassembled it after the war until '50. In early '50s he left mus. to study geology, returning briefly until final retirement in '57. His band pl. a major part in stimulating the int'l post-war revival of traditional jazz. CDs: GTJ.

WATTS, ERNIE (ERNEST JAMES), saxes, fl, etc.; b. Norfolk, VA, 10/23/45. Family lived in Det. 1948–57, then in Wilmington, Del. Started on bari. sax. in jr. hs; classical training. Won *DB* scholarship to Berklee Coll.; dur. his second yr. there, left to join Buddy Rich, touring w. him '66–8. Settling in LA, he pl. w. Gerald Wilson; Toshiko Akiyoshi; Wayne Henderson; tour. Africa w. Oliver Nelson. Joined NBC staff '72 w. *Tonight Show* band; freelanced extensively w. Lee Ritenour's gp., Friendship, dur. the next decade. Toured w. Rolling Stones '81. From late '80s Watts had overlapping jobs w. the Patrice Rushen-Ndugu Chancler gp., The Meeting; Charlie Haden's Qt. West; and his own gp.; also cond. hs and coll. clinics. He became a key figure in music educ. and was frequently voted Most Valuable Player by the LA chapter of NARAS. His stylistic adaptability enabled him to fit into a broad variety of settings, pl. everything from straight-ahead jazz to fusion. He has been heard in many film & TV scores incl. *The Fabulous Baker Boys; Midnight in the Garden of Good and Evil; The Color Purple; Fame; Night Court; Dynasty.* CDs: CTI; JVC; w. Charlie Haden–Qt. West (Verve); E. Fitzgerald (Rep.); Joe Henderson (Mile.); B. Rich (PJ); L. McCann (MM); Lee Ritenour (JVC; GRP); A. Sandoval; GRP All-Star bb (GRP); H. Hancock; Monk (Col.); Geo. Cables (Cont.); J. J. Johnson (Pab.); Carmen McRae; Jean-Luc Ponty (BN); G. Mulligan (A&M); A. O'Day (GNP Cres.).

WATTS, JEFF "TAIN," dms, comp; b. Pittsburgh, PA, 1/20/60. Began stud. at age 10; acquired own drm. set at 15 and was inspired by Charlie Parker and John Coltrane to explore jazz history. After hs he enrolled in cons. program at Duquesne U., transferring two yrs. later to Berklee Coll. in Bost., where he met Branford Marsalis. Later became member of Wynton Marsalis's first qnt. for four yrs. After tour. w. George Benson and McCoy Tyner for the next yr., he joined Branford Marsalis's Qnt. Played on soundtrack of Spike Lee's *Do the Right Thing* and por-

trayed a dmr. in his *Mo' Better Blues.* In May 1992, Watts moved to Calif. w. B. Marsalis's *Tonight Show* band, but left after Marsalis resigned in mid '90s. One of the most versatile dmrs. on the contemporary scene, he is in frequent demand for rec. sess. CDs: Sunny.; w. S. Rollins (Mile.); S. Fortune (BN); T. Blanchard; W. Marsalis; B. Marsalis (Col.); Victor Bailey (Atl.); E. Marsalis (Col.; BN); James Williams (Em.); Courtney Pine (Ant.); Geri Allen; Stanley Jordan (BN); D. Marsalis (Novus); Betty Carter; Stephen Scott (Verve); McCoy Tyner (Den.); Larry Willis (Steep.).

WAYNE, CHUCK (Charles Jagelka), gtr, comp, arr; b. NYC, 2/27/23; d. Jackson, NJ, 7/29/97. Many amateur mus. in family. Self-taught, began on mandolin. Pl. w. a Russian balalaika band. Led own trio in hs, then pl. w. Bklyn. band that incl. Al Cohn. Pl. w. Clarence Profit in Greenwich Village; 52nd St.; w. Nat Jaffe at Kelly's Stables 1941. In army '42–4. Pl. w. Benny Harris, Barney Bigard '44; Joe Marsala '44–6; Dizzy Gillespie, Red Norvo–Slam Stewart '45; Woody Herman, Ralph Burns '46; Jack Teagarden, Coleman Hawkins, Phil Moore '47; Bud Powell, Lester Young, Barbara Carroll, Alvy West '48; Geo. Shearing '49–52; own gps. fr. '52; Geo. Wallington '53; Brew Moore; Zoot Sims '53–4; Tony Bennett '54–7. Comp. score for Broadway prod. of *Orpheus Descending* '57, then pl. w. Gil Evans Orch. '58–9. On staff at NBC '59; CBS '60–70. Pl. in duo w. Joe Puma '72–6. Freelance in '70s-80s w. Duke Jordan, Frank Wess. App. regularly at Gregory's fr. '74 until it closed, '79. Also B'dway shows, jingles, and accomp. vocalists incl. Frank Sinatra, Dick Haymes, Morgana King, Billy Eckstine, Sarah Vaughan, Steve Lawrence and Eydie Gorme, etc. Wayne taught at New Engl. Cons., Westchester Cons., Mannes Coll. of Mus., and Coll. of Staten Island. One of the first gtrsts. to take part in the bebop movement, rec. w. Gillespie in '45. Favs: Charlie Christian, Julian Bream; arrs: Johnny Mandel, Gil Evans. Polls: *DB, Play.* Fests: UK, '85; Argentina '86; Italy '88. Films: app. in *Miss New Orleans*; shorts w. Geo. Shearing. TV: Garry Moore, Carol Burnett, Ed Sullivan, Merv Griffin, also PBS. Publ: three books: *Scales; Chords; Arpeggios* under the general title *The School of Chuck Wayne* (Second Floor Music). Comps: "Zero Hour"; "Slightly Dizzy"; "Sonny," written for Sonny Berman but appropriated by Miles Davis as "Solar." LPs: Vik; Focus; Prog.; Wayne-Puma (Choice). CDs: Sav.; w. Marsala (Class.); D. Gillespie (Sav.); G. Shearing (Sav.; Verve); W. Herman (Col.); C. Hawkins (RCA); Duke Jordan (Steep.); G. Wallington; Wingy Manone in *Trumpet Jive* (Prest.); S. Chaloff (Mos.); B. Goodman (MM).

WAYNE, FRANCES (Chiarina Francesca Bertocci), voc; b. Boston, MA, 8/26/19; d. Boston, 2/6/78. Started w. bro. Nick Jerret's gp. in 1942. Worked w. Charlie Barnet '42, but enjoyed bigger popularity while w. Woody Herman '43–6, mainly through her rec. of "Happiness Is a Thing Called Joe." Married tptr.-arr. Neal Hefti '45; moved to Calif. '46 where she worked briefly as a single bef. going into semi-retirement. In '50s through '70s, she occ. rec. and gigged w. Hefti. Last apps. at Donte's in North Hollywood. Won *Esq.* New Star Award '46. Rec. for Atl. '57. CDs: w. C. Barnet (Dec.); W. Herman (Col.; RST; Hep.).

WEATHER REPORT. Jazz fusion gp. formed Dec. 1970; orig. members were Joe Zawinul, kybd.; Wayne Shorter, saxes; Miroslav Vitous, bs.; Alphonse Mouzon, dms.; Airto Moriera, perc. Until mid 80s Zawinul and Shorter were the only continuous members, w. other personnel changing frequently, incl., at various times, Peter Erskine; Jaco Pastorius, Omar Hakim, Alex Acuna. In '85 Shorter was replaced by Steve Khan and the name changed to Weather Update. From '88 the gp., under Zawinul, was known as the Zawinul Syndicate. Some of its best-known albums are *Weather Report* '71; *I Sing the Body Electric* '72; *Sweetnighter* '73; *Mysterious Traveler* 74; *Tale Spinnin'* '75; *Black Market* '76; and *Heavy Weather* '76 (which incl. Zawinul's hit, "Birdland"); *Mr. Gone* '78; *Night Passage* '80; *Domino Theory* '83; and *Sportin' Life* '85. Despite the prominence of its leaders and soloists, Weather Report's success depended primarily on its use of ensemble colors and textures, collective improvisation, and a rhythmic foundation that contemporary audiences found accessible. Over the yrs., Zawinul became increasingly dominant and Shorter's role diminished. CDs: see above, all on Columbia.

WEATHERFORD, TEDDY, pno; b. Bluefield, WV, 10/11/03; d. Calcutta, India, 4/25/45. Was raised in NO fr. age 12; began pno at 14. To Chi. in early 1920s; pl. at the Moulin Rouge w. Jimmy Wade and the Vendome Theatre w. Erskine Tate. Considered one of the most advanced pnsts. of the '20s, he was sometimes compared favorably w. Earl Hines. In '26 he went to Calif. and subsequently to China w. Jack Carter's band (which incl. Albert Nicholas). Remaining in the Far East, he led own band in Singapore, Manila, Shanghai, etc. Returned to US briefly in '34; recruited Buck Clayton's bb for gig at Canidrome Ballroom, Shanghai. Pl. at Taj Mahal Hotel in Bombay '36–40; rec. in Paris, and pl. in Ceylon; long residency pl. at Grand Hotel in Calcutta. Died prematurely of cholera. LP: tracks in *Piano & Swing*

(Pathé). CDs: w. L. Armstrong (Col.); Eddie South (Class.).

WEBB, CHICK (WILLIAM), dms, leader; b. Baltimore, MD, 2/10/02; d. Baltimore, 6/16/39. Born w. a physical deformity described as TB of the spine, Webb sold newspapers to purchase first set of dms. Worked w. gtrst. John Trueheart in Jazzola Orch. To NYC ca. 1924, briefly w. Edward Dowell; led qnt. at Black Bottom Club, oct. at Paddock Club, then formed Harlem Stompers for Savoy Ballroom, Jan. '27. A yr. later he added three mus. to pl. at Rose Danceland. After several other NYC residencies, he began long regular stints at Savoy Ballroom; sidemen incl. Johnny Hodges; Bobby Stark; Jimmy Harrison; Benny Carter. By '34, when band began rec. regularly, Edgar Sampson was a key figure as alto saxist and arr., and Ella Fitzgerald was the main voc. Helped by frequent broadcasts fr. the Savoy, tours, and many recs., the band reached the peak of success in the mid '30s. By '38 Webb's health began to fail, and when he died, the band cont. for several yrs. under the mus. leadership of Teddy McRae and Eddie Barefield but fronted by Fitzgerald. Webb was a powerful, pulsating dmr. whose magnificent control of bs. drm. and cymbals lent the band much of its personality in ensemble work and in his occ. solos. He was, according to critic Barry Ulanov, "perhaps the greatest of jazz drummers, a gallant little man who made his contribution to jazz within an extraordinary framework of pain and suffering." CDs: Dec.; Hep; Tax; w. L. Armstrong; Benny Carter (BB); Ellington (Col.).

WEBB, LAWRENCE ARTHUR ("SPEED"), voc, dms; b. Peru, IN, 7/18/06. Played in local gps. bef. forming a co-op gp., the Hoosier Melody Lads, in 1925. While in Calif., the band app. in silent films, incl. *Riley the Cop, Sins of the Father* '28, and a '29 Ethel Waters short. Until '38, Webb led such bands as The Hollywood Blue Devils, The Dixie Rhythm Kings, Jack Jackson's Pullman Porters, and the Brown Buddies, w. sidemen incl. Roy Eldridge, Teddy Buckner, Vic Dickenson, Henderson Chambers, Teddy Wilson, and Art Tatum. Left mus. in '38 to pursue a degree in embalming, a skill he had originally studied at U. of Illinois in the '20s; settled in South Bend, Ind., running own mortuary and writing for the *Indiana Herald*; also became politically active.

WEBBER, JOHN ROBERT, bs; b. St. Louis, MO, 8/5/65. Mother pl. pno. Began on el-bs. at age 11; sw. to double bs. at 15. Pl. first prof. gigs while in hs. Stud. at Northern Ill. U. 1983–4; Roosevelt U. '84–5.

Pl. in Chi. w. Von Freeman '85–6; then moved to NYC '87. Pl. w. Bill Hardman, Junior Cook '87–8; Metropolitan Bopera House, Lou Donaldson '88; Christopher Hollyday '90; Jimmy Cobb '91. Favs: Oscar Pettiford, Paul Chambers, Sam Jones. Fests: Eur. w. Donaldson '88; Eur., So. Amer. w. Hollyday '90. TV: Scottish, Yugoslavian TV. CDs: w. J. Cook (Steep); C. Hollyday (Novus); Peter Bernstein (CC); Eric Alexander (Del.); Chris Flory (Conc.); Boptism (Boptism).

WEBER, EBERHARD, bs, comp; b. Stuttgart, Germany, 1/22/40. Father began teaching him cello in 1946; took up bs. in '56, but did not make prof. debut until '72. Worked w. Wolfgang Dauner in '60s. In '72, after developing 5–string bs., he rec. *The Colours of Chloe,* which won him int'l acclaim. In mid '70s he worked w. Ralph Towner and Gary Burton and led the gp. Spectrum w. Volker Kriegel. Formed band, Colours, tour. US w. it in '76, '78–9. In '80s he frequently worked as a member of Jan Garbarek band, gave solo bs. concerts, and wrote film mus. Weber's compositional concepts owe more to the comp. Steve Reich than to African-Amer. sources. Over the yrs., he has been active as a film & TV dir. CDs: ECM; w. Jan Garbarek; G. Burton; P. Metheny; R. Towner (ECM); Benny Bailey (Enja); S. Grappelli (Verve).

WEBSTER, BEN (BENJAMIN FRANCIS), tnr sax; b. Kansas City, MO, 2/27/09; d. Amsterdam, Netherlands, 9/20/73. Studied vln. and pno., pl. the latter in silent movie houses and in several Oklahoma territory bands; stud. sax w. Budd Johnson but mainly self-taught. First prof. job on sax was a three-mo. stint w. family orch. led by Lester Young's father 1930. Worked w. a succession of bands in the early '30s, incl. Jap Allen '30; Blanche Calloway '31; Bennie Moten '31–2; Andy Kirk '33. To NYC in '34, where he joined Fletcher Henderson, Benny Carter, Willie Bryant '33–4; briefly w. Duke Ellington '35; Cab Calloway '36–7; Stuff Smith, Roy Eldridge '38. With Teddy Wilson's bb '39–40, then back w. Ellington '40–3. Also pl. w. Raymond Scott; John Kirby; and Sid Catlett. In NYC and Chi. clubs w. own gp. fr. '44. Rejoined Ellington for ten mos '48–9; then briefly w. Jay McShann in KC and tour w. JATP. From early '50s he led own gps. Worked in NYC and Calif. '63, then moved to Eur. '64, settling first in Amsterdam; then Copenhagen. Webster was one of the warmest perfs. in the Coleman Hawkins tradition and among the first to bring the tnr. sax to full maturity as a jazz instrument. His unique vibrato sometimes ended w. more breath than tone but his work has been respected and eulogized by critics, fans, and

musicians of every era. He is best remembered for recs. made w. the Ellington band of '40–2, inc. "Cotton Tail"; "Chelsea Bridge"; "All Too Soon"; "Conga Brava"; "C Jam Blues"; "Just A-Settin' And A-Rockin." TV: Appeared on *Sound of Jazz,* CBS-TV '57. Film: *Big Ben,* Netherlands '67; also app. in the film *Quiet Days in Clichy.* CDs: Vict.; Riv.; Cont.; JH; BL; Verve; Em.; Story.; Imp.; Sack.; w. B. Holiday (Col.; Verve); Bennie Moten (BB); Benny Carter (BB; Cont.; Class.); Art Tatum (Pab.); L. Hampton; R. Norvo; Joe Williams (BB); Charlie Parker; I. Jacquet; G. Mulligan; C Hawkins; Slim Gaillard (Verve); D. Washington (Merc.); Oliver Nelson (Imp.); Bill Harris (Fant.).

WEBSTER, FREDDIE, tpt, b. Cleveland, OH, 1917; d. Chicago, IL, 4/1/47. At 16 he formed a band in Cleveland w. Tadd Dameron. Then w. Marion Sears, Erskine Tate, and Earl Hines 1938; w. Benny Carter off and on '39–43; Lucky Millinder '41–2; Jimmie Lunceford '42–3; Sabby Lewis '44; Cab Calloway '45; John Kirby '45–6. In '45 he also pl. w. Dizzy Gillespie's bb and rec. w. Georgie Auld. Webster was greatly admired by Miles Davis, whom he infl. (e.g., solos on "Now's the Time" and "Billie's Bounce"), and Dizzy Gillespie, who said he had "the most beautiful sound I've ever heard on the trumpet." He is best known for his brief apps. on Sarah Vaughan's "You're Not the Kind" and "If You Could See Me Now." Rec. "The Man I Love," "Reverse the Charges" w. F. Socolow (Duke) '45, reissued on Xan. LP *Bebop Revisited, Vol. 6.* CDs : w. S. Vaughan (Class.).

WEBSTER, PAUL FRANCIS, tpt; b. Kansas City, MO, 8/24/09; d. NYC, 5/6/66. Studied at Fisk U. Prof. debut w. George E. Lee 1927; also pl. w. Bennie Moten; Tommy Douglas; Eli Rice. Jimmie Lunceford, for whom he had worked briefly in '31, hired him again in '35. He remained for seven yrs. and became closely identified w. the horn's upper register via such solos as on "For Dancers Only." After leaving Lunceford, he pl. w. Cab Calloway off and on '44–52; Charlie Barnet '46–7 and '52–3; Sy Oliver '47; Ed Wilcox '48–9; Count Basie '50. Semi-inactive from mid '50s but cont. to make occ. apps. w. Oliver and others. CDs: w. B. Moten (BB); J. Lunceford (Dec.; Class.).

WEED, TAD, pno, comp, arr; b. Detroit, MI, 5/5/57. Moved to LA 1978. Toured int'l w. Carmen McRae; Anita O'Day; Paul Anka; Jack Jones. Pl. w. Charles Lloyd; Nick Brignola; Chaka Khan; Al Cohn; Woody Herman; Vinny Golia; Kenny Burrell; Richie Cole; Teddy Edwards. In '90s pnst. and mus. dir. for Dick

Berk's Jazz Adoption Agency. CDs: Nine Winds; w. Berk (Res.; Nine Winds); Vinny Golia; Rob Blakeslee (Nine Winds); Kim Richmond (USA).

WEIN, GEORGE THEODORE, pno, lead, producer; b. Boston, MA, 10/3/25. Studied w. Margaret Chaloff, Sam Sax 1933–43; Teddy Wilson at Juilliard, summer '48. Formed 13-pc. band late '30s. In army stationed in Eur '44–6. Pl. in local clubs while att. Bost. U. '46–50. Pl. w. Max Kaminsky '46; Edmond Hall '47; Wild Bill Davison '49. Opened Storyville jazz club in Bost. '50. Pl. at Storyville w. Bobby Hackett, Pee Wee Russell, Jo Jones, Vic Dickenson, Jimmy McPartland, others '50–4. Founded Storyville rec. label (not to be confused w. Danish Storyville Rec.), opened Mahogany Hall dixieland club '52. Rec. w. Mahogany All-Stars w. Dickenson, Doc Cheatham '53. Wein is best known for establishing the NJF in '54. Rec. w. Ruby Braff '54–69. Taught Jazz History at Bost. U. mid '50s. Prod. jazz week at Amer. Pavilion at Brussels World's Fair '58. Tour. Eur. w. Newport All-Stars fr. '59. Formed Festival Productions Inc. '60. Founded Newport Folk Fest; Ohio Valley JF; Bost. Globe JF '62; Newport Opera Fest. '66; Hampton JF '68; NO Jazz and Heritage Fest. '70; NJF-NY '72. Established NYJRC '73. Founded La Grande Parade du Jazz, Nice '74; NJF-Saratoga '78; Playboy JF, LA '79; Jazz at the Bowl w. LA Philharm '80; Budweiser-NJF, Madarao, Japan '81. Tour. w. Newport All-Stars w. Scott Hamilton, Oliver Jackson, Harold Ashby, Slam Stewart, Norris Turney, Warren Vaché '82. Prod. Geo. Wein Collection for Conc. rec. label '83. Visiting artist at Harvard U. '83–4. Wein began working w. JVC in '84 to prod. four major int'l fests in Eur. and Newport, R.I. Founded Mellon JF, Phila. '86. As president of Festival Productions Inc., Wein curr. prods. over twenty-five major fests in the US, Eur., and Japan, and organizes Eur. tours for more than 200 Amer. musicians. In '78 Pres. Carter honored Wein at the White House on the 25th anniversary of the NJF. In '91 France named Wein Chevalier de la Legion d'Honneur and Commandeur de l'Ordre des Arts et des Lettres. Other awards incl. R.I. Hall of Fame '90; Louisiana Governor's Award '89; BMI, Nat'l Music Council Awards '85; Conn. Arts Awd. '82; Honorary Degree, Berklee Coll. of Mus. '76; US Dept. of St. Tribute of Appreciation '71; Hampton Inst. Centennial Medallion '68. Polls: *DB* Lifetime Achievement '82; *Billboard* Trendsetter Awd. '73. CDs: Col.; w. Lee Wiley (Aud.); Newport Fest. All-Stars (Conc.).

WEISKOPF, WALT (WALTER DAVID), tnr sax; b. Augusta, GA, 7/30/59. Father pl. pno., classical and show tunes. Bro. Joel, pno. At age 16 his first jazz

teacher in Syracuse, N.Y., recommended him for prof. work. Stud. cl. first, then sax. B. Mus., Eastman Sch. of Mus., Rochester, N.Y. 1980; M.A., Queens Coll., NYC '88. Pl. w. Buddy Rich '81–2, incl. *Concert for the Americas* w. Sinatra; Toshiko Akiyoshi Orch. and small gp. '83–96, tour. in Eur., Japan.; own qt. w. Joel Weiskopf, Jay Anderson, Jeff Hirshfield '85; Roland Vasquez Oct. and Qt. '87–97. Also has pl. w. Renee Rosnes; Eliot Zigmund; Carnegie Hall Jazz Band; and Pete "LaRoca" Sims. Cl. teacher was Leon Russianoff '88–9. As clst. app. w. American Ballet Theatre Orch; American Comp. Orch.; and Concordia Chamber Orch. Perf. Aaron Copland *Concerto for Clarinet* as guest soloist w. Gotham Chamber Orch., NYC '94. Taught at Jersey City St. Coll.; teaches improv. and jazz sax as faculty member at Princeton U. Saxophonist Mel Martin wrote: "Walt Weiskopf's main influence seems to be John Coltrane but he is no slavish imitator." Favs: Coltrane, Dewey Redman, Joe Henderson, Getz. Awards: Perf. Grants fr. NEA '89, '91, '94. Publs: *Coltrane: A Player's Guide to Understanding His Harmony* '91 and *The Augmented Scale* (Jamey Aebersold) '93, both w. his former sax teacher fr. Eastman, Ramon Ricker; *Intervallic Improvisation* (Aebersold) '95. CDs: CC; Iris; D-T; w. Akiyoshi (Col.); Vasquez (RVCD); Billy Drummond; Jim Snidero (CC); Mark Soskin (TCB); Rich bb (Atl.).

WEISS, MICHAEL DAVID, pno, comp; b. Dallas, TX, 2/10/58. Studied priv. 1964–76; at Interlochen Camp '73; Berklee Coll. of Mus. '74; Indiana U. '76–81. Organized and led own gps. in hs and coll. Pl. w. Jon Hendricks and Co. '82; Bill Hardman–Junior Cook '83–7; Lou Donaldson '84–8; Slide Hampton's World of Tbns. '87; Johnny Griffin fr. '87; Art Farmer–Clifford Jordan '88–9; Ralph Moore '89; Idrees Sulieman, Frank Wess, Geo. Coleman, Fathead Newman, Gary Bartz '90; Mingus Epitaph Orch., Chas. McPherson '91; Smithsonian Jazz Orch., Vanguard Jazz Orch. fr. '91. Weiss has led his own trio, qt., and qnt. fr. '85 w. sidemen incl. Junior Cook; Larry Gales; Al Harewood; Lew Tabackin; Lewis Nash; Dennis Irwin; Peter Washington; Ben Riley; Slide Hampton; Chas. McPherson; Tom Harrell. He taught at Ind. U. '81 and has cond. clinics at univs. in the US and Eur. Favs: Barry Harris, Buddy Montgomery, Cedar Walton. Fests: Eur. fr. '82. TV: app. w. trio on CBS *Nightwatch* '89. CDs: Steep.; DIW; CC; w. J. Griffin (Verve; Ant.); C. McPherson (Arab.).

WEISS, SID, bs; b. Schenectady, NY, 4/30/14. First prof. gigs in mid 1930s w. Louis Prima; Wingy Manone; Charlie Barnet; Artie Shaw; Joe Marsala;

Tommy Dorsey. Rec. w. Benny Goodman '41–5; tour. Eur. w. Hal McIntyre '45. Mainly studio work to '54, when he moved to LA and retired fr. full-time playing. Elected officer of Musicians Union '70–1; Calif. Deputy Labor Commissioner '74–9. CDs: w. B. Goodman (Col.); T. Dorsey; Ellington; A. Shaw (BB; Phon.); Buck Clayton (Riv.); Eddie Condon (Dec.; Jazz.); Jerry Jerome (Arb.); Mound City Blue Blowers (Timel.); Rex Stewart; Joe Marsala (Class.)

WELDON, JERRY (GERARD JOSEPH), tnr sax; b. NYC, 9/27/57. Studied w. Paul Jeffrey in NYC and at Rutgers U. 1978–81. Pl. w. Paul Jeffrey bb 1978–81; Bobby Forrester fr. '81; Lionel Hampton '82–8; Machito '83–4; Jack McDuff '88–90; Harry Connick Jr. fr. '90; the NY Hard Bop Qnt. fr. '91. A thoughtful soloist whose subtle swing has plenty of fiber. Favs: Sonny Rollins, Dexter Gordon, Paul Gonsalves, Lester Young. Fests: Eur., So. Amer., Japan w. Hampton; Connick. TV: *Tonight Show* '90; Arsenio Hall '90–1. Video: w. Connick, *Swing Out w. Harry.* CDs: Cat's Paw; w. NY Hard Bop Qnt. (TCB); Jack McDuff (Conc.); Al Grey (Pullen); H. Connick (Col.).

WELLINS, BOBBY (ROBERT COULL), tnr, sop saxes, comp; b. Glasgow, Scotland, 1/24/36. Studied alto sax, harmony w. fath.; later kybd. harmony. Moved to London in mid 1950s. Pl. w. Buddy Featherstonehaugh; Tony Crombie; Vic Lewis. Premiered extended comp., *The Battle of Culloden Moor,* in London '61. Pl. w. New Departures jazz and jazz poetry gps. fr. '61, incl. Stan Tracey Qt. mid '60s. Feat. w. Tracey in *Under Milk Wood* suite '65–6. Inactive for several yrs., then resumed perf. in '77 as co-leader w. Don Weller of hard-bop combos. Active as an educ. in UK fr. late '70s. Rec. *Birds of Brazil,* aka *Endangered Species* suite '89. CDs: Hep; Hot House; Cadillac; Jazzizit; w. Jimmy Knepper (Hep); Spike Robinson (Essential Jazz).

WELLS, DICKY (WILLIAM), tbn; b. Centerville, TN, 6/10/09; d. NYC, 11/12/85. Raised in Louisville, Ky.; studied mus. fr. 1919, pl. bari. horn in community center band. Tbn. at age 16. To NYC in '26 w. Lloyd Scott band, later led by Lloyd's bro. Cecil. With Elmer Snowden '30–31, app. w. his band in film *Smash Your Baggage.* Pl. w. many bbs in NYC, incl. Chick Webb; Benny Carter; Teddy Hill (Eur. tour '37); but best known for long stay w. Count Basie, July '38–Dec. '45 and again '47–50. Between the two stints, he worked w. J. C. Heard; Willie Bryant; Sy Oliver. Dur. '50s he worked w. Jimmy Rushing; Earl Hines; Buck Clayton; in the '60s w. Ray Charles; B. B. King; Buddy Tate; also Eur. tours. Took day job ca.

1970 but cont. to gig occasionally, mostly w. Earle Warren. In an essay, *The Romantic Imagination of Dickie Wells,* André Hodeir analyzed the symmetry and contrasts of Wells's work, his ability to use subtle inflections and vibratos to optimum effect, and the skillful technique employed on his early recordings. Book: *The Night People, Reminiscences of a Jazzman,* with Stanley Dance (Smithsonian) '71. CDs: w. C. Basie (Dec.; BB; Hep; Col.; Class.); Benny Carter (BB; Class.); Henry Red Allen (Tax; Collector's Classics); Lester Young (Merc.; Comm.); Buck Clayton (Steep.; Riv.; Story.); J. Rushing; R. Eldridge (Col.); B. Holiday (Col.; Dec.); D. Reinhardt (ASV); Jack Teagarden–Pee Wee Russell (Prest.); Teddy Hill (Hep; Class.).

WELLSTOOD, DICK (RICHARD MacQUEEN), pno; b. Greenwich, CT, 11/25/27; d. Palo Alto, CA, 7/24/87. Studied in Bost. and NYC until 1946. Pl. swing, stride, and boogie-woogie w. Bob Wilber '46–50; pl. and rec. w. Sidney Bechet in '47 and '49. Joined Jimmy Archey '50, touring Eur. w. him in '52. With Roy Eldridge '53; mainly w. Conrad Janis through '60. Many gigs w. traditional gps. at Eddie Condon's, etc., fr. '60s. Tour. So. Amer. w. Gene Krupa '65. In '70s he frequently worked in N.J. and N.Y. clubs, and at jazz parties. Tour. Eur. w. WGJB. In the '80s he briefly practiced law; also pl. frequently w. Kenny Davern. An uncommonly versatile pnst. whose scope incl. all traditional forms but whose harmonic ideas were advanced, enabling him to work in almost any setting. Favs: Wynton Kelly, T. Monk, James P. Johnson, Ray Charles. CDs: Chazz Jazz; Solo Art; Arb.; Chiaro; w. M. McPartland (JA); Davern; Classic Jazz Qt. Wild Bill Davison (Jazz.); Bunk Johnson (Amer. Mus.); Dan Barrett (Conc.); J. Archey (Story.); Doc Cheatham (Park.); Roy Eldridge (Verve); Vince Giordano (Cir.); Bob Wilber (Prog.).

WELSH, ALEX, crnt, voc, lead; b. Edinburgh, Scotland, 7/9/29; d. London, England, 6/25/82. Moved to London in 1954. Led own band at British concerts, fests., and clubs fr. '55. From '63 the band tour. Engl. accomp. such visiting mus. as Bud Freeman; Red Allen; Pee Wee Russell; Earl Hines; Ruby Braff; Dicky Wells; Rex Stewart; Ben Webster; and Lockjaw Davis. In the '70s he cont. to tour. Engl. and Eur. w. an eclectic program of dixieland and mainstream jazz. After many personnel changes, Welsh stuck to dixieland for the last four yrs. of his life. He died after a long illness. Fests: Barcelona '66; Antibes '67; NJF '68; Jazz Expo, London '67–70; Leipzig '73; Edinburgh '74; Breda '75. Pl. Louis Armstrong Memorial Concert at Royal Fest.

Hall, London '75. Won *MM* poll as best small band '70. CDs: BL; Lake; w. Braff (BL).

WENDHOLT, SCOTT, tpt; b. Patuxant River, MD, 7/21/65. Raised in Denver, Colo.; parents very musical. Attended Indiana U. 1983–7, where he received a B. Mus. in jazz perf.; started pl. locally there and in Cincinnati. Since moving to NYC in '90, has worked w. several prominent big bands, incl. CHJB, Vanguard Jazz Orch., Mingus bb, and the orchs of Maria Schneider, Toshiko Akiyoshi, Louis Bellson, Bob Mintzer, Woody Herman, and Joe Roccisano. Also perf. w. his own gps. and has worked w. Fred Hersch, Vincent Herring, and Don Braden. Has tour. in Eur., Scand., Japan, and So. America. Teaches at jazz clinics. Favs: Miles Davis, Woody Shaw, Freddie Hubbard. Radio: w. CHJB, NPR broadcasts. CDs: CC; D-T; w. Bruce Barth (Enja); Kevin Hays (Steep.); Herring (MM); Braden; Darryl Grant; Roberta Piket (CC); K. Suonsaari (SN); Tim Ries (Moo; CC); B. McFerrin (BN); Akiyoshi; Junko Sumi (Nippon Crown); Manhattan Jazz Orch.; Manhattan Super Spt. (SB); J. Fedchock (Res.); Vanguard Jazz Orch. (NW); Mintzer bb (DMP); Buddy Rich bb (Atl.).

WERNER, KENNY (KENNETH), pno; b. Brooklyn, NY, 11/19/51. Played stride pno. on TV at age 11. Studied classical pno. at Manh. Sch. of Mus. 1969–70; jazz at Berklee Coll. of Mus. '71–3. Rec. own LP in '77; then pl. w. Charles Mingus, Archie Shepp '80–4; Mel Lewis Orch. fr. '84; Joe Lovano fr. '80s; much freelance work w. Bob Brookmeyer; Ron Carter; Dizzy Gillespie; Chico Freeman; and others. Many apps. pl. solo and duo w. Rufus Reid; Ray Drummond; Jaki Byard. Own trio w. Ratzo Harris, Tom Rainey since '80s. Werner has taught at the New Sch., NYC, since '87 and is a frequent lecturer and clinician. Favs: Bill Evans, Keith Jarrett, Fats Waller, Jaki Byard. Fests: tour w. own gps. since late '80s. CDs: Conc.; Sunny.; Steep.; w. C. Mingus (Atl.); M. Lewis Orch. (MM); J. Lovano (BN); L. Konitz (SN; Evid.); Peter Erskine (Novus; Den.); Maria Schneider (Enja); Jim Pepper (Ryko; Island); R. Eubanks (JMT); Chris Potter (Conc.); T. Harrell (Vict.); Joe Locke (Steep.); Jane Ira Bloom (Arab.); Santi Debriano (Freelance).

WERTICO, PAUL DAVID, dms, perc; b. Chicago, IL, 1/5/53. Primarily self-taught; studied briefly at Western Ill. U. 1971. Pl. w. Pat Metheny fr. '83; Ken Nordine; Earwax Control in Chi. fr. late '80s; Paul Winter '90; own gps. Trio New, Strapagander, Quintet Thing. Freelance w. Jerry Goodman; Dave Liebman; Larry Coryell, Eddie Harris; Ben Sidran; Lee Konitz; Bob Mintzer; Herbie Mann; Lew Tabackin;

Chico Freeman; Terry Gibbs; Buddy DeFranco; Sam Rivers; etc. in Chi. fr. '76. Wertico is on the bd. of governors of the Chi. chapter of NARAS, is a reg. contributor to drum magazines, and has taught at Northwestern U. fr. '91. Favs: Roy Haynes, Elvin Jones, Art Blakey. Polls: NARAS Outrageous Rec. Awd. '90. Fests: all major w. Metheny fr. '83. Film: app. in *The Babe.* TV: *Tonight Show, Today,* etc., w. Metheny. CDs: Pony Canyon; w. Metheny (WB; ECM; EMI; Geffen); Rich Corpolongo (Del.); Earwax Control (Depot).

WESS, FRANK WELLINGTON, tnr, alto saxes, fl; b. Kansas City, MO, 1/4/22. Family moved to Sapulpa, Okla. ca. 1930, then to Wash., D.C. '35. Stud. at Dunbar HS, then at Howard U. '37–8. Pl. w. local dance and show bands '37–41. Assistant bandleader and solo cl. in army band in No. Africa '41–5; also led swing band that accomp. Josephine Baker in concerts for Allied troops. Ret. to US '45, pl. w. Billy Eckstine Orch '46–7; Eddie Heywood '47; Lucky Millinder Orch. '48; Bullmoose Jackson '48–9. Ret. to Wash., D.C., stud. fl. at Modern Sch. of Mus. '49–53. Pl. w. Count Basie Orch. '53–64. Freelanced in NYC fr. '64, incl. B'way shows, jingles, TV, films, etc. Member of New York Jazz Qt. w. Roland Hanna, Ron Carter, and Ben Riley fr. '75. Also pl. w. Two Franks w. Frank Foster; NY Jazz Qt. w. Hanna, Geo. Mraz, Smitty Smith; Dameronia '81–5; Two at the Top w. Johnny Coles; Benny Goodman; Slam Stewart; Billy Taylor; Toshiko Akiyoshi bb; Walt Levinsky bb; Elliot Lawrence bb; Bobby Rosengarden bb; NY Repertory Orch.; Tony Cabot bb; Benny Carter bb; Dizzy Gillespie Dream Band; Philip Morris Superband. Accomp. vocs. incl. Nat Cole; Ella Fitzgerald; Sarah Vaughan; Frank Sinatra; Tony Bennett; Joe Williams; Dinah Washington; Harry Connick Jr.; others. Wess has worked extensively as a clinician at Miami U., No. Tex. St. U., U. of N.H., Cornell U., Oberlin Cons., etc. Robust tnr. pl. and excellent lead and solo alto saxist, Wess is considered to be the first of the modern jazz flsts. Has led a bb fr. '89. Favs: Young, Webster, J. Griffin, H. Mobley. Polls: *DB* '54–62; *MM* '57. Fests: all major fr. '53. Film: *Rhythm in a Riff* w. B. Eckstine. TV: Dick Cavett, David Frost, *Night of a Hundred Stars,* PBS special w. Helen Forrest, *Saturday Night Live,* Jerry Lewis Telethon, etc. CDs: Conc.; Sav.; Ref.; Gem.; w. Basie (Verve; Roul.; Mos.); J. Coltrane; Gene Ammons; Thad Jones (Prest.); J. J. Johnson; O. Nelson (BB); The Ritz (Den); Norman Simmons (Milljac); Gene Harris; Susanah McCorkle (Conc.); Benny Carter (MM); Frank Foster (Sav.; Conc.); Toshiko Akiyoshi; Dexter Gordon; LCJO (Col.); New York Jazz Qt. (Enja); Joe Newman (Prest.; BL; FS; Sav.);

Kenny Clarke; Milt Jackson (Sav.); B. Goodman (Lond.); B. Taylor (Riv.; Taylor-Made).

WEST, DOC (HAROLD), dms; b. Wolford, ND, 8/12/15; d. Cleveland, OH, 5/4/51. Studied pno., cello, dms. Worked w. Tiny Parham 1932; later Erskine Tate, Roy Eldridge. Subbed for Chick Webb in Webb's band '38; also for Jo Jones in Basie band in early '40s. Pl. w. Hot Lips Page '39–41 and frequented the legendary dawn-of-bop sessions at Minton's. Made the transition fr. swing to bop and was much in demand on 52nd St. Pl. w. Tiny Grimes '44; Slam Stewart trio '45–6; Erroll Garner trio '47. Rec. for Sav. w. Grimes–Charlie Parker '44; also dates w. Stewart; Garner; Don Byas; Leo Watson–Vic Dickenson. Rejoined Roy Eldridge and died while on the road w. him. CDs: w. Parker (Sav.; Stash); E. Garner (Sav.); Wardell Gray (BL); Don Byas; Slam Stewart; Sammy Price (Class.); Eldridge (Dec.; Col.; Class.); B. Holiday (Col.); J. McShann (Dec.); O. Pettiford (Topaz).

WEST, PAUL E., bs, vln, vla, comp, arr; b. NYC, 1/28/34. Mother. was pno. teacher. Stud. vln. w. Albert Polnarioff 1940–58; began pl. bs. in '53. Att. HS of Mus. and Art; Wagner Coll. (B.A. mus. ed.). Won classical vln. competition and cond. sch. orch. while in hs. Organized and led 50–member orch. and chorus '50–3. Pl. bs. w. Ray Charles '55; Dizzy Gillespie '56–8; Dinah Washington '58–9; house band at Concord Hotel '59–63; Johnny Mathis '60; house band at Playboy club '63–6; Petula Clark '66; Charles Aznavour '66–7; Monty Alexander '67–8; D. Gillespie '68–9. Worked on East Coast w. vocalists, incl. Carmen McRae '69–83; Billy Eckstine fr. '70; Joe Williams fr. '73; Peggy Lee '80–90. Pl. fr. '80s w. Milt Jackson; Cedar Walton; Kenny Barron; w. Roland Hanna in '90s. Exec. dir. of Jazzmobile Inc. '69–73; helped found Jazzmobile Wkshp. '69. West has been dir. of the Henry St. Settlement Mus. Sch. in NYC fr. '73. Favs: Jimmy Blanton, Oscar Pettiford, Ray Brown. Film: *Dream Lover* w. Kristy McNichol '84. TV: David Frost; *Soul; Positively Black.* CDs: w. Mike Longo (CAP); Les Jazz Modes (Biog.); E. Fitzgerald; Gillespie (Verve); Harold Ashby; Al Grey (Gem.); D. Washington (Em.); Lee Morgan (Spec.).

WESTBROOK, MIKE (MICHAEL JOHN DAVID), pno, comp, arr; b. High Wycombe, England, 3/21/36. Mother, pno. teacher; wife, Kate Barnard Westbrook, voc., tnr. horn, picc. Mostly self-taught. Stud. painting, but became interested in jazz through recs. Ran jazz wkshp. at Plymouth Art Center w. 8–pc. band that incl. John Surman. Moved to London in 1962. Form. sxt., again w. Surman; own Con-

cert Jazz Band '67. Fr. '70 to '72 he co-led, w. John Fox, the multimedia Cosmic Circus; rock-oriented gp., Solid Gold Cadillac '71–4. Own brass band '73; orch. 74; trio. w. wife '82; cont. w. orch. to present. Has tour. Eur. regularly since '70s; NYC '73; Can. '79; Austral. '84. Comp. for Arts Council film, *Music in Progress* '78. BBC-TV apps. incl. *The Cortege* '82; *Mama Chicago* '80 for BBC2. Many concert films in Eur., often w. wife. Fest: Montreux JF '68. Awarded OBE '88. An eclectic who draws on poetry, theater, and a wide variety of musics in his writing. Favs: Ellington, Monk, Jimmy Yancey; comps: Ellington, Monk, Mingus, Morton, Stravinsky, Brecht-Weill. CDs: Tip Toe; hatArt; Enja ; Novus; Venture; ASC.

WESTON, RANDY (RANDOLPH E.), pno, comp; b. Brooklyn, NY, 4/6/26. Son Azzedin Niles Weston, perc. Studied w. private teacher. Teenage musical colleagues were Cecil Payne, Ray Copeland. Served overseas in army 1945. Owned restaurant '47–9. Began in music prof. w. George Hall, Art Blakey '49; then w. Frank "Floorshow" Culley '50; Bull Moose Jackson '51; Eddie Vinson, Kenny Dorham '53; Payne '54. Worked at Riverside Recs. '54–5; also at Music Inn, Lenox, Mass., as second cook in summer; pl. pno there at night. Bill Grauer of Riverside heard him and Weston rec. a Cole Porter LP for the label '54. Pl. many summers in Mass.'s Berkshire Mts. at Music Inn and Avaloch w. own trio, qt. Worked at NYC clubs such as Café Bohemia, Vanguard, Five Spot, Composer. Tour. colleges w. qt. and jazz dancers annually fr. '59 to '64. Did history of jazz lecture-concerts at NYC hs and libraries. Together w. Rev. John Gensel presented jazz services in various churches '63–6. His gp. began the jazz policy at the Half Note, 57. Pl. concerts for the United Nations Jazz Society. Weston's interest in Africa, sparked in childhood by his father, was actualized in '61 when he pl. at Performing Arts Fest. in Nigeria. Visited Nigeria again '63. Calif. coll. lecture-concert tour fall '66. St. Dept. tour of West Africa, Jan. '67. Visited Morocco, Tunisia, Aug.-Sept., remaining in Morocco where he pl. in major cities. Lived in Rabat '67–8; moved to Tangier where he opened his African Rhythms Club '69 and became involved w. the Gnawan and Berber musicians, later reflected in his albums *Blue Moses, Tanjah,* and *The Splendid Master Musicians of Morocco.* Ret. to US '72. Lived for a time in Annecy, France, but basically has a residence in Brooklyn and travels in the US, Europe, and Africa. His gp., which in the '60s had Booker Ervin and Ray Copeland in the front line, has Talib Kibwe and Benny Powell in the '90s. Weston, whose vibrant, expressive comps. incl. "Hi-Fly", "Little

Niles"; Berkshire Blues"; "African Cookbook"; "Ganouah"; and suite *Uhuru Africa*, is a rhythmically powerful, two-handed pnst. of deep feeling whether pl. solo, in trio, or gp. Favs: Tatum, Bud Powell, Monk. Early infls. also incl. Basie, Nat Cole, Ellington. Fests: NJF '58, '73; MJF '66; org. and pl. at Fest. of American, African & Moorish Mus., Tangier '72; Montreux '74; many others in Eur., Afr. Poll: *DB* Critics, TDWR '72. CDs: Riv.; Biog.; Enja; Verve; Free.; BN; w. David Murray (BS); Kibwe (Evid.); Roy Brooks (Enja).

WESTRAY, RONALD, tbn; b. Columbia, SC, 6/13/70. Began pl. at age 10. B.A. fr. So. Carolina St. U. 1991. Feat. on Marcus Roberts' rec. *As Serenity Approaches* '91. Later tour. w. Roberts' spt. in US; in Eur. w. Jazz Futures II '92. Perf. w. Wynton Marsalis and NYC Ballet '93; w. LCJO. Favs: J. J. Johnson, Trummy Young, Lawrence Brown. CDs: co-lead. w. Wycliffe Gordon (Atl.); w. Roberts (RCA); LCJO (Col.).

WETTLING, GEORGE GODFREY, dms; b. Topeka, KS, 11/28/07; d. NYC, 6/6/68. Raised in Chi., where he stud. w. Roy Knapp and was infl. by Baby Dodds. Prof. jobs in 1920s and early '30s w. Floyd Towne; Seattle Harmony Kings; Paul Mares. From '35 to '36 he pl. and tour. w. Jack Hylton's Amer. band. With Wingy Manone in Pitts. '36; then w. Artie Shaw bb in NYC; Bunny Berigan '37; Red Norvo '37-8; Paul Whiteman '38-41; in the next two yrs. he also worked w. Muggsy Spanier; Bobby Hackett; and the Chico Marx band. From '43 to '52, while he was a staff mus. at ABC in NYC, Wettling freelanced at rec. sessions and w. various gps., often at Eddie Condon's club. In the '50s he pl. w. Jimmy McPartland; Muggsy Spanier; and, in '57, tour. Engl. w. Condon. In '60s he tour. w. Bud Freeman, worked w. Dukes of Dixieland, and led own trio in NYC. As a writer he contributed to *DB* and other publications; also spent last twenty-five yrs. of his life creating Stuart Davis–infl. paintings that graced several album covers and were exhibited in NYC. CDs: w. L. Armstrong; A. Shaw; Metronome All-Stars; B. Berigan; J. Teagarden; F. Waller (BB); B. Holiday (Dec.); Coleman Hawkins (Merc.); E. Fitzgerald (Dec.); E. Condon (Dec.; Col.; Mos.; Jazz.); Wild Bill Davison (Jazz.); C. Parker (Stash).

WETZEL, BONNIE (née Jean Addleman), bs; b. Vancouver, WA, 5/15/26; d. Vancouver, B.C., Canada, 2/12/65. Extensive studies on vln. but self-taught on bs. Join. Ada Leonard all-female band in 1945; gtr. w. Marion Gange's trio '47-8. Married trumpeter Ray Wetzel '49, pl. w. him in Tommy Dorsey band '51. Gigged w. Charlie Shavers and Roy Eldridge in NYC. Worked w. Herb Ellis, Lou Carter in Soft Winds trio and w. Beryl Booker trio (w. Elaine Leighton, dms.) in mid '50s. Tour. Eur. w. Booker in *Jazz USA* show (incl. Billie Holiday, Buddy DeFranco, Red Norvo) Jan.-Feb. '54 Recs. w. Booker for Gotham '47; w. D. Byas for Vogue '54.

WETZEL, RAY, tpt; b. Parkersburg, WV, 1924; d. Sedgwick, CO, 8/17/51. Wife was bassist Bonnie Wetzel. First prominent as section member of Woody Herman band in 1943-5 on such recs. as "Apple Honey"; "Caldonia"; "Northwest Passage." Heard w. Stan Kenton in lead and solo roles '45-8, incl. "Intermission Riff"; "Dynaflow." Feat. on "Over the Rainbow" while w. Ch. Barnet '49. Sang and pl. w. Henry Jerome '50; rejoined Kenton '51; Tommy Dorsey '51; died in auto accident while on the road w. Dorsey. Rec. w. Vido Musso for Trilon; Eddie Safranski for Atl. '47. CDs: w. W. Herman (Col.); S. Kenton (Cap.; Mos.); C. Parker (Verve); T. Dorsey (BB).

WHEELER, KENNY (KENNETH VINCENT JOHN), tpt, flg, arr, comp; b. Toronto, Ont., Canada, 1/14/30. Introduced to tpt. by fath., a part-time tbnst. in St. Catherines, Ont., where Kenny pl. in local bands. Stud. tpt. w. Ross McClanathan; harmony at Toronto Cons. in early 1950s w. John Weinzweig, first Can. comp. to practice serial technique. In Montreal '52 and unable to get visa to US, he moved to Engl. Stud. comp. w. Richard Rodney Bennett in early '60s; counterpoint w. William Russo '63-4. Fr. '59 to '65 pl. w. Johnny Dankworth Orch. for which he wrote *Windmill Tilter*. Pl. w. Mike Gibbs fr. '69; Globe Unity Orch. fr. '72; assoc. w. Anthony Braxton fr. '72; Azimuth fr. 76; Bill Bruford '77; Spontaneous Mus. Ens. '66-70; Tony Oxley '69-72; United Jazz and Rock Ens. fr. '78; Dave Holland qnt. '83-7. Noted for the broad range of his work, he has also pl. w. Ronnie Scott; Tubby Hayes; Friedrich Gulda; Clarke-Boland bb; George Lewis; Stan Getz; Keith Jarrett; Jack DeJohnette; and own gps. in concerts and recs. Considered a superb tpt. and flg. soloist, he is also a highly individual comp. whose work in recent yrs. has had a widening infl. Perf. w. radio orchs. in Rome, Helsinki, Stockholm. Taught at Banff Sch. of Fine Arts in Alberta, Can. '90s. Infls: Booker Little, A. Farmer, B. Bailey, M. Davis, F. Hubbard, Buck Clayton.; other infls: Gil Evans, Bill Evans, Ellington. Fests: NJF w. Dankworth '59; Berlin Anti-Fest. w. Globe Unity '74; Berlin w. M. Gibbs '75; Antibes, Montreux w. Braxton '75. Tied w. Woody Shaw for TDWR in *DB* Critics Poll '70. CDs: ECM; Ah Um, SN; Musi.; w. A. Braxton (hatArt); S. Coleman; Mike Westbrook (Novus); Jane Ira Bloom

(Arab.); Azimuth; D. Holland; Bill Frisell; Berlin Contemporary Jazz. Orch.; Ralph Towner (ECM); Pepper Adams (Res.); Philly Joe Jones (BL); Globe Unity Orch. (FMP); Michael Gibbs (Ah Um).

WHETSOL, ARTHUR (Arthur Parker Schiefe), tpt; b. Punta Gorda, FL, 1905; d., NYC 5/1/40. Raised in Wash., D.C., where Duke Ellington was a childhood friend. Worked w. Ellington under his and Elmer Snowden's dir.; also worked in Wash., D.C., w. Claude Hopkins; the White Bros.; and other local gps. Worked briefly w. Ellington in NYC 1923, then ret. to Wash. to study medicine at Howard U. Rejoined Ellington in '28 and stayed through Oct. '36, when illness forced him to retire, though he made brief efforts to rejoin. Primarily known for his section work, but he was heard prominently on such '20s Ellington recs. as "Dicty Glide"; "Stevedore Stomp"; "Black Beauty"; "Jungle Jamboree"; "Rocky Mountain Blues"; "Misty Morning." CDs: w. D. Ellington (BB).

WHIGHAM, JIGGS (OLIVER HAYDN III), tbn, comp, arr; b. Cleveland, OH, 8/20/43. Studied pno at age 7 at Cleveland Institute of Mus.; a self-taught tbnst., he made his rec. debut at 17 w. Glenn Miller Orch., dir. by Ray McKinley. Living and working in Germ. since 1964, he received a full professorship at the Musikhochschule Köln (Cologne) in '79. He has taught and pl. throughout the world and done considerable radio, TV, and film work. Pl. w. Stan Kenton; George Gruntz; Gerry Mulligan; Stan Getz; Peter Herbolzheimer; Bud Shank; Bill Holman; Carl Fontana. Won first prize at the Int'l Competition for Modern Jazz in Vienna '66. Favs: Michael Bequet, Jimmy Knepper, Jack Teagarden, J. J. Johnson. CDs: Capri; Mons; w. The Brass Connection (JA); Allen Farnham (Conc.); Joe Pass (ACT); Gruntz (MPS); German Jazz Orch. (Mons); Carl Fontana (TNC-Jazz).

WHITAKER, RODNEY, bs, comp, arr; b. Detroit, MI, 2/22/68. Studied vln. at age 8; sw. to bs. at 13. Became interested in jazz after hearing Paul Chambers on Coltrane's LP *Soultrane*. Stud. w. Ed Quick, Jerome Stasson in Det. sch. system; priv. w. members of Det. Symph. Participated in Marcus Belgrave's Jazz Wkshps.; perf. classical mus. w. Det. civic orch.; pl. w. Donald Washington's Bird/Trane/Sco/Wow! in 1980s. At age 15, he was hired by dmr. Leonard King for Strata Nova; pl. w. other local gps., incl. Kenny Cox, Donald Walden. In '88 he moved to NYC to join Terence Blanchard and Donald Harrison. Worked w. Blanchard's new gp. '91–3, then joined Roy Hargrove for three and a half yrs. Later ret. to the Det.

area to pl. and teach at Mich. St. U. With LCJO fr. '96. Favs: Chambers, Ray Brown. CDs: Koch Jz.; w. T. Blanchard (Col.); Antonio Hart (Novus); R. Hargrove (Novus; Verve); Johnny Griffin (Verve); Kevin Mahogany; Kenny Garrett (WB); Eric Reed (MoJazz); Teodross Avery (Imp.); Junko Onishi (BN).

WHITE, ANDREW (NATHANIEL III), woodwind; also pno, bs, comp; b. Washington, DC, 9/6/42. Uncle, Addison White, is a multi-instrumentalist. Att. Howard U. 1960–4; extensive classical studies '64–8. Organized JFK Qnt. early '60s. Pl. oboe w. Amer. Ballet Theatre Orch '68–70, dur. which time he also pl. bs. w. Stevie Wonder. Pl. Engl. horn and bs. w. Weather Report on *I Sing the Body Electric* and *Sweetnighter*. Dur. '70s he started his own rec. co., Andrew's Music, releasing recs. and transcriptions of John Coltrane; Eric Dolphy; Charlie Parker; et al. Worked w. Mal Waldron; Elvin Jones; and Beaver Harris in '80s. Rec. on oboe w. McCoy Tyner for BN LP *Cosmos*. A versatile comp.-perf. who, despite his many activities, remains relatively obscure. Books: *Hey Kid! Do You Wanna Buy A Record?*, Washington; *Andrew's X-Rated Band Stories*, Washington. CDs: w. Weather Report (Col.); Julius Hemphill (BS).

WHITE, CARLA RUTH, voc; b. Oakland, CA, 9/15/51. Father pl. tpt. and recorder. Began as an actress, then stud. w. Lennie Tristano 1971–5; Warne Marsh '78–81; Jill McManus '82–3; Colin Romoff '85–7; Don Sebesky '87; Erik Thorendahl '87–91. Perf. w. own qnt. w. Manny Duran '80–5; own trios since '85. Favs: Mark Murphy, Sarah Vaughan, Shirley Horn. Fests: Trinidad w. W. Marsh '83; Mexico '89; Jap. '90–1. TV: Mex. and Jap. TV. CDs: Evid.; Mile.; w. Patricia Barber (Ant.).

WHITE, CHRIS (CHRISTOPHER WESTLEY), bs, comp; b. NYC, 7/6/36. Studied pno. priv. in Bklyn. Pl. w. Cecil Taylor off and on fr. 1955 to '59; Bernard Pfeiffer '60; Nina Simone '60–1; Dizzy Gillespie Qt. '62–6; Billy Taylor Trio '66–70s. Stud. at Manh. Sch. of Mus. late '60s. Also freelanced w. James Moody; Teddy Wilson; Willie "The Lion" Smith; Eubie Blake; Earl Hines; Thad Jones–Mel Lewis Orch. Rec. w. Jimmy Owens–Kenny Barron '67; Mary Lou Williams '69. Active as educ. and administrator fr. late '60s. Founded Rhythm Associates jazz sch. '66. Jazzmobile Community Liaison '67; exec. dir. '68. Member of NYC Mayor's Urban Action Task Force '68; special assist. in community relations to N.Y. governor '68–9. Exec. prod. of Black Expo at N.Y. City Center '69. Artistic dir., *Black on Black* series at Carnegie Recital Hall '72.

Consultant to MUSE jazz wkshp. early '70s. Dir. of Rutgers Inst. of Jazz Studies '70s. Rec. w. Andrew Hill '74–5; K. Barron '75; Kalaparusha Maurice McIntyre '76. Scored West Indian film *Aggro Sieze-man* '75. White has lectured on jazz at univs. in the US and abroad. He is the author of numerous articles on jazz publ. in *Amer. Mus.*, Grove *Dictionary of Music and Musicians*, etc. Jazz editor for *The Black Perspective in Music* '70s. Taught at Newark Community Sch. of Arts '80s. White's comps. incl. the suites *Dana's Basement* and *Fantasy*. Fests: all major w. Gillespie. CDs: Muse; w. D. Gillespie (Philips; Verve); Nina Simone (Roul.); A. Hill (Steep.); Q. Jones; R. R. Kirk (Merc.).

WHITE, DR. MICHAEL, cl.; b. New Orleans, LA, 11/29/54. Relatives incl. such early NO players as bs. "Papa John" Joseph, cl. Willie "Kaiser" Joseph, and saxophonist Earl Fouché. Pl. cl. fr. age 13; was member of St. Augustine HS band. Earned doctorate in foreign languages and teaches Spanish and African-Amer. mus. at Xavier U. Pl. w. Doc Paulin marching jazz band for, three and a half yrs. fr. 1975; regular member of Young Tuxedo City Jazz Band, the Royal Brass Band, and the Orig. Crescent City Jazz Band. App. w. the show *One Mo' Time* '80s; began pl. at Preservation Hall '81; many int'l and US tours, incl. two trips to Japan. Rec. w. Wynton Marsalis on *The Majesty of the Blues*, as well as on the soundtrack for feat. film, *Tune in Tomorrow*. App. on Lincoln Center's Classical Jazz Series w. own band '89 and '90. Regular New Yr.'s apps. at Village Vanguard in '90s. Favs: Johnny Dodds, Sidney Bechet, Omer Simeon, George Lewis, Willie Humphrey. CDs: Ant.; w. W. Marsalis (Col.).

WHITE, HARRY ALEXANDER (FATHER), comp, arr, tbn; b. Bethlehem, PA, 6/1/1898; d. NYC, 8/14/62. Worked off and on w. Elmer Snowden and Duke Ellington in Wash., D.C., and NYC 1923–9, incl. several mos. w. Ellington at Cotton Club. Also w. Luis Russell '27–8. Joined Cab Calloway '30; led Mills Blue Rhythm Band jointly w. Edgar Hayes '31–2; back w. Calloway '32–5. Comp. and arr. "Evenin'" for Calloway—it was later made famous by Jimmy Rushing w. Count Basie. Back w. Russell (then directing Louis Armstrong band) '35–6, but illness forced him to retire, and—except for a recovery in '47—he was only occ. active in mus. while mainly working in a NYC bank. White pl. and arr. for Manzie Johnson, Hot Lips Page, and Bud Freeman; he doubled on alto sax for some later jobs. While with Calloway, he coined the term "jitterbug." CDs: w. L. Armstrong; Calloway; Hot Lips Page (Class.); Mills Blue Rhythm Band (Hep).

WHITE, LENNY (LEONARD III), dms, comp; b. Jamaica, NY, 12/19/49. Self-taught on dms. fr. age 14. Attended N.Y. Institute of Technology. Pl. w. Jazz Samaritans '67; Jackie McLean '68. Rec. w. Miles Davis '69 (incl. *Bitches' Brew*), then pl. w. Joe Henderson '70–1; Gil Evans '71; Freddie Hubbard, Stan Getz, Luis Gasca '72; Azteca '73. Also rec. w. Gato Barbieri, Stanley Clarke early '70s. Pl. w. Wallace Roney gp. in late '90s. Orig. member of Chick Corea's Return to Forever '73–6. Rec. w. Chaka Khan, Nancy Wilson '81–2. White is also an accomplished photographer and painter. Favs: Philly Joe Jones, Tony Williams, Elvin Jones. Fests: all major '70s. TV: Eur. TV w. Corea; Don Kirshner Rock Concert. CDs: Atl.; w. F. Hubbard (CTI); Return to Forever (Polyd.; Col.); Al Di Meola; Miles Davis (Col.); M. Urbaniak (EW; Milan); C. Corea; Eddie Gomez (Stretch); Joe Henderson (Mile.); Wallace Roney (WB); Jaco Pastorius (Epic); Charles Fambrough (Audq.); Gato Barbieri; Gil Evans (A&M); Geri Allen (Story.).

WHITE, MICHAEL WALTER, vln; b. Houston, TX, 5/24/33. Raised in Oakland, Calif.; stud. vln. fr. age 9. Came to public attention w. John Handy qnt. at MJF 1965. Later worked w. jazz-rock gp., the Fourth Way; rec. w. Pharoah Sanders, McCoy Tyner, and Joe Henderson early '70s. Also pl. w. Prince Lasha; Sun Ra; Coltrane; Dolphy; Wes Montgomery; Kenny Dorham; Richard Davis. Made series of albums for Impulse, one of which introduced his suite, *The Land of Spirit and Light*. Though much of his mus. communicates an intense energy, White can also convey a sense of peace, tranquillity, and spirituality that is clearly a part of his nature. Infl. by Coltrane, Dolphy. CDs: w. Tyner (Mile.); Teddy Edwards (Verve); Lonely Universe (CMP); Pharoah Sanders (Imp.; Verve); Joe Henderson (Mile.); George Duke (WB).

WHITE, ROCKY (QUINTEN), dms; b. San Marcos, TX, 11/3/52. Studied at Tex. Southern U. 1971–3. Joined the Duke Ellington Orch. a yr. bef. Duke's death and cont. playing w. the band off and on through the '90s, under Mercer Ellington's leadership. CDs: w. Mercer Ellington (GRP; MM).

WHITE, SONNY (ELLERTON OSWALD), pno; b. Panama City, Canal Zone, 11/11/17; d. NYC 4/28/71. A cousin of Kenny Clarke, he began pno. study at 8. Debut with Jesse Stone at 19. Worked w. Willie Bryant 1937; Teddy Hill '38. In '40 he accomp. Billie Holiday and pl. w. Frankie Newton; off and on w. Benny Carter for several yrs. After army service, pl. w. Hot Lips Page '44–5; Harvey Davis Band at the Cinderella Club '47–54. Several yrs. w.

Wilbur De Paris, incl. gigs at Jimmy Ryans on 52nd St. and African tour '57. After three yrs. w. Louis Metcalf, he joined Jonah Jones in '69 and remained w. him for the next two yrs. Infl. by Teddy Wilson. CDs: w. S. Bechet; Lena Horne (BB); R. Eldridge (Col.); Benny Carter (BB; Merc.); Vic Dickenson (Topaz); B. Holiday (Col.; Comm.).

WHITEMAN, PAUL, leader; b. Denver, CO, 3/28/1890; d. Doylestown, PA, 12/29/67. Father, Wilberforce J. Whiteman, was a Denver hs mus. teacher whose students incl. Jimmie Lunceford. Orig. pl vla., first in the Denver Symph. Orch fr. 1907, then in the SF Symph. Orch '14. Led a 40–pc. navy band dur. WWI. Organized dance band on West Coast '18; worked in Atlantic City '19, NYC '20. Began rec. '20; his recs. of "Whispering" and "Japanese Sandman" were multi-million sellers; by the early '20s he was the world's biggest pop band-leader. In Feb. '24, he premiered George Gershwin's *Rhapsody in Blue* at Aeolian Hall, NYC; later, he introduced Gershwin's *Concerto in F,* Ferde Grofé's *Grand Canyon Suite,* and commissioned works fr. Duke Ellington, William Grant Still, et al. In the '20s and '30s his sidemen and vocs. incl. Bix Bei-derbecke; Frank Trumbauer; Jack and Charlie Tea-garden; Miff Mole; Joe Venuti; Bunny Berigan; Eddie Lang; Tommy and Jimmy Dorsey; Matty Mal-neck; Hoagy Carmichael; Bing Crosby; Mildred Bailey. Johnny Mercer; Don Redman; Bill Challis; and Tom Satterfield were among the arrs. Whiteman was feat. in many films, incl. *King of Jazz* '30; *Thanks a Million* '35; *Strike Up the Band* '40; *The March of Time* '43 and '48; *Atlantic City* '44; *Rhap-sody in Blue* '45; *The Fabulous Dorseys* '47. His orch. also provided the mus. for six B'way shows, incl. *Scandals of '22; Lucky* '27; and *Jumbo* '35. Although he was dubbed the "King of Jazz" by his promoters, the title did not fit his music. "Whiteman drew very little from the jazz language except some of its simpler rhythmic patterns," wrote Wilder Hob-son. "There was little more than a trace of the per-sonal expression, improvisation, counterpoint, or rhythmic subtlety of natural jazz." Nevertheless, such recs. as "San"; "Sugar"; "Wang Wang Blues"; "Washboard Blues" and later items feat. Trumbauer, J. Teagarden, et al. had fairly strong jazz content. He also was a mus. dir. at ABC in NYC in the late '50s. In '56 Whiteman rec. a 50th anniversary album feat. several of his alumni. The last decade of his life was spent in virtual retirement, running a farm in N.J. Books: *Pops: Paul Whiteman, King of Jazz,* by Thomas DeLong (New Century) '83. CDs: ASV; Cap; Vict.; Pro Arte; seven tracks in *Classic Capitol Jazz Sessions* (Mos.).

WHITFIELD, MARK ADRIAN, gtr; b. Linden-hurst, NJ, 10/6/66. Raised in Syosset, Long Island, N.Y. Began on acoustic bs. at age 7, later sw. to alto sax, and took up gtr. around 1980 after family moved to Seattle. Pl. club dates while in hs '82. Stud. at Berklee Coll. of Mus. '83–7. Moved to NYC '87. Pl. w. Donald Harrison, Jack McDuff '88–90. Made rec. debut w. Donald Harrison–Terence Blanchard '89. Pl. w. Roy Hargrove '90; Jazz Futures '91. Whitfield has led his own gp. since '90. App. in Robert Altman film, *Kansas City* '96. A fluent soloist whose single-string and chordal style has prepossesing intensity, he is a fine ballad interpreter, steeped in the blues. Favs: Charlie Christian, Wes Montgomery, George Benson. Polls: *Jazziz* New Artist of Yr '90. Fests: Eur., Japan, So. Amer. fr. '89. TV: *Nightline, Tonight Show, Today.* CDs: WB; Verve; w. Nicholas Payton; Jimmy Smith (Verve); Jazz Futures; Cleo Laine (Novus); Courtney Pine (Ant.); Ernie Watts (JVC); D. Harrison (Sw. Bas.) Allan Harris (Mons).

WHITFIELD, SCOTT JAMES, tbn, comp, arr, voc; b. West Islip, NY, 3/10/63. Began on tbn. at age 9. Became int. in comp. at 14, just prior to form. first band in Inverness, Fla., 1977. Pl. w. Scott Whitfield's Cheshire Cats '77–82; Sugarfoot Stompers '82–3; own gp. Jazz Express '83–4; Pete Peterson Orch. '85–7. B. Mus, Fla. St. U. '84; M. Mus., No. Texas St. U. '87. Director of Five O'Clock lab band at No. Tex. '86–7, also taught jazz history. Led own qt. and bb, also pl. and arr. for various combos and show bands at Walt Disney World '87–93. Pl. w. Bill Allred Classic Jazz Band fr. '92; Sam Rivers bb '93; Nat Adderley '93–4; Lew Anderson bb; Walt Levinsky Swing Band fr. '93; Vince Giordano's Nighthawks '93–6; DMP bb; Dean Pratt bb; Tom Talbert Orch. fr. '96. Adjunct Profess. of tbn., U. of No. Fla., Jacksonville '93. Fr. '94 Whitfield has been lead and solo tbn. w. the Toshiko Akiyoshi Orch. and has led his own gp., the Manhattan Vocal Project. He is considered one of the most highly skilled trombonists active on the New York scene. Favs: Fontana, Rosolino, J. J. Johnson; arrs: Thad Jones, Sammy Nestico, Gil Evans, Akiyoshi; vocs: Jack Jones, Joe Williams, Tormé. Fests: Japan '94–6; Eur. '95–6; China '95. CDs: Amo.; w. Cedar Walton (Ast. Pl.); Akiyoshi (RCA; Col.; Nippon Crown); N. Freelon (Col.); Talbert (Chart.); DMP Big Band (DMP); as arr. w. Allred (Sunjazz); Diva (Diva).

WHITTLE, TOMMY (THOMAS), tnr sax, wood-winds; b. Grangemouth, Scotland, 10/13/26. Wife is voc. Barbara Jay. Self-taught. Pl. w. many Engl. gps., incl. Ted Heath, Lew Stone, Jack Parnell, Robert Farnon, Pizza Express All-Stars. Rec. w. Benny

Goodman; tour. US 1956–57; led own band early '60s; many fests in '80s, incl. Nice, North Sea, Edinburgh. Won *Jazz Rag* British Jazz Award for tnr. sax '91; pl. w. Ted Heath revival band led by Don Lusher early '90s. CDs: Teejay; w. G. Shearing (Tel.); Bob Wilber (Arb.); J. J. Johnson (Verve).

WICKMAN, PUTTE (HANS-OLOF), cl; b. Falun, Sweden, 9/10/24; d. Falun, 2/14/06. Began his prof. career in a swing style 1945 but the post-war influx of bebop led him to add some modern elements. Pl. w. Simon Brehm, Charlie Norman, he led his own gp. fashioned instrumentally after the Goodman sxt. and feat. pnst. Reinhold Svensson at Nalen in Stockholm '48. In May '49 app. at Paris JF. Rec. in '50s w. Jimmy Raney; Lars Gullin; and Svend Asmussen. From late '50s led a bb for dancing at Grand Hotel, Stockholm, in addition to tour. w. jazz sxt. In spring '59 gigged in NYC, incl. Sidney Bechet Memorial concert at Carnegie Hall. From mid 70s, he made int'l tours, usually as solo act. Tour. U.S. and Can. w. qt. '91. Was considered by many to be Sweden's foremost clst. Roger Kellaway and Red Mitchell were among his rec. sidemen for Dragon in late '80s. CDs: Phon.; Drag.; Bluebell; four tracks in *North American Tour 1991*, Caprice; w. Benny Carter; Alice Babs; Georg Riedel; Roy Williams (Phon.); Arne Domnerus (Phon.; Ladybird).

WIGGINS, GERALD FOSTER, pno, org; b. NYC, 5/12/22. Father of J. J. Wiggins. Worked briefly w. Stepin Fetchit and Joe Carroll, then tour. w. Les Hite 1940; Louis Armstrong '40–41; pl. w. Benny Carter on and off '42–92. Toured US and Eur. w. Lena Horne '50–2; accomp. Kay Starr '53–63; rehearsal pnst. for Marilyn Monroe; many tours w. Helen Humes '74–81. Based in LA, he pl. at many of the leading jazz fests and parties in '70s and '80s; app. often w. Scott Hamilton '89–91. His many app. in movies and TV shows established Wiggins as one of the most accomplished all-around pnsts. Video: *Tomorrow* w. Quincy Jones. CDs: Conc.; B&B; Cont.; w. Red Holloway–Clark Terry; F. Capp; S. Hamilton; F. Wess (Conc.); B. Webster (Em.); Z. Sims; R. Eldridge (Vogue); L. Armstrong (Vict.; BB); Joe Pass (Pab.); Benny Carter (Cap.; Verve); Kenny Clarke; Milt Jackson (Sav.); Sweets Edison; Major Holley (B&B); I. Jacquet (Verve); Art Pepper (BN); Buddy Collette (Cont.); Helen Humes (Muse; B&B); Mercer Ellington (GRP); King Pleasure (Hi Fi Jazz).

WIGGINS, J. J. (GERALD FOSTER JR.), bs; b. Los Angeles, CA, 4/15/56. Son of pnst. Gerald Wiggins. Stud. at Henry Grant Studio. Made many concert and TV apps. w. Craig Hundley trio 1968; won trophy as outstanding instrumentalist in Hollywood

Bowl Teenage Battle of the Bands even though he was not yet a teenager. Pl. w. own trio; also worked w. his father. Pl. w. Duke Ellington Orch. under Mercer Ellington's leadership fr. '74. CDs: w. Bill Easley (Mil.); Mercer Ellington (GRP; MM); Al Grey (Chiaro.; Capri; Arb.).

WILBER, BOB (ROBERT SAGE), cl, sop, alto, and tnr saxes; b. NYC, 3/15/28. Wife is voc. Joanne "Pug" Horton. Studied under Willard Briggs at Scarsdale HS 1941–3; then w. Paul Dahm (cl. in Goldman Band) '43–5; Eastman Sch. '45–6; and priv. w. Sidney Bechet '47–9; Lennie Tristano and Lee Konitz '50–1; Leon Russianoff and Joe Guidice (sax) '52–7; Manhattan Sch. of Mus. '54–5; Sanford Gold (pno.) '65–6. B.A. fr. SUNY '83. In '47 w. Bechet's help, he organized The Wildcats, a band that helped to spark the post-WW II traditional jazz revival on East Coast; made rec. debut on Comm. the same yr. Led band at the Savoy, Bost. '47–9. Pl. w. Mezz Mezzrow at Nice JF '48. Opened Storyville Club, Bost. '51 w. band feat. Sid Catlett and DeParis bros. Army service '52–4. Member of co-op gp., The Six '54–6; in late '50s he pl. w. Bobby Hackett, Max Kaminsky, Benny Goodman, and Eddie Condon, incl. tour of Engl. An orig. member of WGJB '68, he left it in '73; co-led Soprano Summit w. Kenny Davern '74–9. In late '70s he began transcribing classic perfs. for his Jazz Repertory Orch. and other gps., incl. the mus. of Jelly Roll Morton; King Oliver; and early Duke Ellington. Dir. concerts at Nice JF '78–9. Tour. w. NYJRC Armstrong repertory program in Russia '75; also Soprano Summit tour in South Africa '75. Dir. of Smithsonian Jazz Repertory Ens. '81–4, incl. national tours; re-created B. Goodman's '38 Carnegie Hall concert '88 and tour. US and UK w. bb Goodman tributes. Presented world premiere of Ellington's *The Queen's Suite*, London '89 w. attendant TV show and video cassette. In '92 he brought Artie Shaw to London to cond. perfs. of Mozart's *Clarinet Concerto* and Shaw's *Concerto for Clarinet*, w. himself as soloist. Formed a record company, Bodeswell, in '79. Led the Bechet Legacy fr. '80–3. Reunions w. Davern at Colo. JPs, SS *Norway* cruises and recs. in '80s, '90s. Artist-in-residence at Oberlin '81; Rutgers '83; dir. of Jazz Studies at Wilkes Coll., Pa. '83. Wilber is a fluid clst. whose devotion to Sidney Bechet has not prevented him from developing a strongly original sop. sax sound and individual style. Moved to Engl. in late '80s. Favs: Goodman, Bechet, Hodges, C. Hawkins. Films: Mus. dir for *Cotton Club* '84; also for *Brighton Beach Memoirs; The Untouchables; Tucker* '85–90. Mus. dir. for *Bix* '90. TV: mus. dir. and emcee for *Young Jazz Musician of the Year*, BBC '91–2. Autobiography: *Music Was Not Enough*

(Oxford) '88. CDs: Conc.; Story.; Chiaro.; Cir.; Jazz.; Phon.; Arb.; N-H; w. S. Bechet (Laser.); WGJB (Atl.); Condon (Col.; Mos.); Soprano Summit; Teddy Wilson; Summit Reunion (Chiaro.).

WILCOX, EDDIE (EDWIN FELIX), pno, arr; b. Method, NC, 12/27/07; d. NYC, 9/29/68. Studied at Fisk U., where he pl. in band led by Jimmie Lunceford. Rejoined Lunceford in 1929 and contributed some of the bands most successful arrs., incl. "Flaming Reeds and Screaming Brass"; "Miss Otis Regrets"; "Rhythm Is Our Business"; "Impromptu"; "Like a Ship at Sea"; "Knock Me a Kiss"; "Easy Street." After Lunceford's death in '47, Wilcox led the band w. tnr. sax Joe Thomas for two yrs. Became sole leader, then, after band broke up, led own gps in NYC until early '50s. Subsequently worked as arr. and a&r man, writing for many pop hit recs. CDs: w. Lunceford (Dec.; Sav.; Class.; Cir.).

WILCOX, SPIEGLE (NEWELL), tbn; b. Cortland, NY, 5/2/03; d. Cortland, 8/25/99. Began on valve tbn. but sw. to slide while stud. at Manlius Mil. Sch. near Syracuse, N.Y., in 1918. Pl. in Paul Whiteman's Collegians '24; then w. Calif. Ramblers bef. joining Jean Goldkette band in Det. '25, sharing the bandstand w. Bix Beiderbecke and Frank Trumbauer. In '27 he ret. to Cortland; entered the family coal business, playing only for weekend dances. Joe Venuti brought him back to mus. w. a Carnegie Hall reconstruction of the Goldkette band w. Venuti for Chiaro. '75. In early '99 Wilcox, who had pl. all over the US and Eur. w. Warren Vaché, Romano Mussolini, and Can.'s Climax Jazz Band, could claim to be one of the two or three oldest jazz musicians still active. CDs: Timel.; w. Bill Challis (Cir.); w. California Ramblers in *New York Jazz in the Roaring Twenties*, Vol. 2 (Biog.).

WILDER, JOE (JOSEPH BENJAMIN), tpt, flg; b. Colwyn, PA, 2/22/22. Raised in Phila., where his fath. led a band. Made debut as child on radio talent show. Stud. at Mastbaum Sch. of Mus.; classmates incl. Red Rodney, Buddy DeFranco. Pl. w. Les Hite 1941–2; Lionel Hampton '42–3. Asst. bandmaster in marines '43–5, then rejoined Hampton '45–6. Pl. w. Jimmie Lunceford '46–7, then w. Lucky Millinder; Sam Donahue; Herbie Fields; Noble Sissle. Pl. in B'way pit bands, incl. *Guys And Dolls* '51–4; Count Basie Orch. incl. Eur. tour '54; pit bands '54–7. On staff at ABC '57–73. Pl. in band for Dick Cavett, Jack Paar TV shows. Toured Soviet Union w. Benny Goodman '62. First tpt. w. Symph. of the New World '65–71. Worked w. Tony Bennett–Lena Horne; Michel Legrand '74; Steve Allen–Terry Gibbs '75. Four concerts as member of NY Philharm. '75. Many

freelance studio dates in '70s, incl. r&b, jingles. Supplied tpt. solos for soundtrack of film *The Wild Party*, w. James Coco, Raquel Welch. Rec. w. Benny Carter '85. Wilder cont. to be active in B'way pit bands and as a freelance studio mus. in NYC. An all-purpose player but particularly a golden-toned balladeer. Saluted at a concert in which he played, JVC-NY '98. TV: Bill Cosby, Sammy Davis, Howard Cosell '70s. CDs: Eve. Star; Sav.; w. C. Basie; Joe Williams; Jimmy Smith; B. Holiday; D. Gillespie (Verve); Hank Jones (Sav.); Lena Horne; J. J. Johnson (BB); Benny Carter (Conc.); G. Evans; Q. Jones (Imp.); Carmen McRae (Dec.); O. Brown Jr.; C. Mingus; Terence Blanchard (Col.); Tom Talbert (Modern Concepts); L. Bellson; B. Goodman (MM); L. Hampton; C. Hawkins (Dec.); T. Dameron (Riv.).

WILEN, BARNEY (BERNARD JEAN), tnr, sop saxes, comp; b. Nice, France, 3/4/37; d. Paris, France, 5/25/96. Raised in US age 3 to 9. Pl. in family band in Nice; won prize for best "cool" gp., Paris, 1953. First prominent w. Henri Renaud; rec. w. Roy Haynes and Jay Cameron. Worked in Club St. Germain, Paris, w. Kenny Clarke, Bud Powell, et al. '55. Won French Jazz Academy's Django Reinhardt prize '57. Rec. w. Miles Davis on soundtrack of *Ascenseur Pour L'Echafaud* '57; tour. Eur. w. Davis '57–8; pl. NJF '59. Rec. w. Milt Jackson '58; Kenny Dorham '59. Rec. Thelonious Monk's mus. for *Les Liaisons Dangereuses*; comp. sound tracks for two other films, *Les Femmes Disparaissents* and *Un Temoin dans un Ville* '58–9. Experimented w. Indian mus. and free jazz-rock in '60s, rec. an album, *Dear Professor Leary* '68. App. at Berlin JF '67. To Africa in '69, where he engineered Archie Shepp's set at Algiers Fest.; stud. indigenous mus., using it in an album, *Moshi* '72. After a period of relative obscurity, he ret. to visibility at the Paris Fest '87. In his early yrs., Wilen was considered to be one of the most authentic disciples of Lester Young. A later infl. was Sonny Rollins. Favs: Parker, Stitt, Rollins, Coltrane. His experimentations of the '60s and '70s were abandoned in the '80s when he returned to his original bop style. CDs: Timel.; Deux; IDA; Fontana; Sunny.; w. M. Davis; A. Blakey (Fontana); Bud Powell (Mythic Sound).

WILEY, LEE, voc, songwriter; b. Fort Gibson, OK, 10/9/08; d. NYC, 12/11/75. Partially of Native Amer. heritage; studied briefly in Tulsa, Okla. To NYC 1930; joined Leo Reisman '31–3; swiftly earned popularity via rec. and broadcasts w. Reisman; Paul Whiteman; and Willard Robison. Dur. the '30s she was closely assoc. w. Victor Young, w. whom she comp. "Got the South in My Soul"; "Eerie Moan"; and her best known song, "Anytime, Anyday, Anywhere." From '39 she was closely assoc. w. Eddie Condon, rec. several albums of show tunes w. such mus. as Max Kaminsky; Joe Bushkin; and Fats Waller. Married to Jess Stacy for five yrs. fr. '43, she toured briefly w. his short-lived bb. In the late '40s she worked as a night club single but was in virtual retirement in the '60s and '70s. Her final app. was w. Condon at the '72 NJF-NY. In '63 a romanticized TV biography of her life starred Piper Laurie. Wiley's was one of the few completely distinctive voices in jazz. Her husky, erotic warmth and wide vibrato gave her a distinctive sound. Her knack for selecting superior tunes, combined w. her sensitive interpretations of them, produced many memorable recs. CDs: Aud.; Col.; BB; Up.; BL; w. Bing Crosby; Eddie Condon (Dec.).

WILKERSON, DON, tnr sax, comp; b. Moreauville, LA, 7/32; d. Houston, TX, 7/18/86. After informal mus. educ. at home, he began pl. alto sax while in hs in Houston. Made prof. debut in Dayton, Texas. Joined Amos Milburn 1948; also worked in LA w. Chas. Brown '48–9. In Houston '50–4, then joined Ray Charles. Featured on such early Charles recs. as "Come Back Baby"; "I Got a Woman"; and "This Little Girl of Mine." Rec. debut as leader on Riv. album, *Texas Twister*, prod. by Cannonball Adderley '60. Rec. three albums for BN, prod. by Ike Quebec '62–3. CDs: track in *Texas Tenors* (Prest.); w. Ray Charles (Rh./Atl.).

WILKINS, ERNIE (ERNEST BROOKS), comp, saxes; b. St. Louis, MO, 7/20/19; d. Copenhagen, Denmark, 6/5/99. Studied at Wilberforce U.; dur. three yrs. in navy, he pl. at Great Lakes w. Clark Terry; Willie Smith; Gerald Wilson. Pl. w. Earl Hines's last bb 1948. Pl. alto and tnr. saxes w. Count Basie '51 but soon gave up playing to focus on comps. and arrs. Wrote for Tommy Dorsey; Basie; Harry James; pl. sax. again w. Dizzy Gillespie dur. overseas tours. In '60s he divided his time between NYC and Det., where he wrote for his bro. Jimmy's bb. Joined Clark Terry as mus. dir. and comp. '68, then led own band at Montreux JF. In early '70s he became an a&r exec. for Mainstream Recs. Choral suite, *Four Black Immortals*, perf. at Town Hall and Avery Fisher Hall '75. In '79 after tour. w. Terry again, he took up residence in Copenhagen, where he led his own gp., The Almost Big Band. Inactive in '90s after suffering a paralyzing stroke '91. Wilkins' arrangements were a vital factor in the success of the Basie and James bands. CDs: Steep; Kenny Clarke–Ernie Wilkins (Sav.); w. M. Ferguson (Verve; BB); S. Rollins; Gillespie (Verve); Clifford Brown (Em.); LaVern Baker (Atl.); S. Vaughan (Em.; Merc.; Verve); Basie (Tax); Danish Radio BB (Hep).

WILKINS, JACK, gtr; b. Brooklyn, NY, 6/3/44. Began pl. gtr. at age 14, then studied w. John Mehegan, Rodrigo Riera. Pl. w. Chuck Wayne in all-gtr. gp. 1964, then w. Earl Hines; Buddy Rich; Stan Getz; Dizzy Gillespie; Pearl Bailey; Sarah Vaughan; Mel Tormé; Ray Charles; Bill Evans; Phil Woods; Chet Baker; own trio. Teaches at Manh. Sch. of Mus. and leads a qt., Alien Army. Favs: Tal Farlow, Barney Kessel, Django Reinhardt, Johnny Smith, Wes Montgomery. Fests: Eur., Asia, etc. TV: *The Guitar Show*. CDs: MM; Chiaro.; Claves; String Jazz; Arab.; w. Mike Clark (Stash); Nora York (Evid.); Earl Hines (BL).

WILKINS, RICK, comp, arr, tnr sax; b. Hamilton, Ont., Canada, 2/1/37. Began writing for dance bands in Hamilton. Moved to Toronto in 1957; stud. arr. w. Phil Nimmons at the Advanced Sch. of Contemp. Mus. headed by Oscar Peterson. Wrote extensively for TV in Toronto and LA. Gene Lees has praised "his big, strong, extroverted tenor sound, one of the important voices of Rob McConnell's Boss Brass for which he writes as well as plays." CDs: w. McConnell (Conc.); McConnell–Phil Woods (Imp.); Frank Wess; Peter Appleyard (Conc.).

WILLIAMS, AL (ALFRED G. JR.), dms; b. Pasadena, CA, 1/8/43. Started on cl. Stud. at Compton Coll. and Billy Moore Sch. of Drumming. While in coll., he formed The Modern Jazz Majors; perf. at the Lighthouse. Rec. debut w. Leroy Vinnegar 1974; also tour. and/or rec. w. Hampton Hawes; Teddy Edwards; Kenny Burrell; Roy Ayers; Eddie Harris; others. Opened Jazz Safari, the first jazz club in Long Beach, Calif. '78. In '86 the club—renamed Birdland West—expanded and moved to downtown Long Beach. Promoter of annual Long Beach JF; awarded Black Business Prof. Association Genesis Award '89. From late '80s he has made local club and jf apps. w. own gp., The Al Williams Jazz Society. CDs: w. Gerald Albright (Atl.); H. Hawes (Cont.).

WILLIAMS, BUSTER (CHARLES ANTHONY JR.), bs, el-bs, comp; b. Camden, NJ, 4/17/42. Father, Chas. Williams, taught him to pl. bs. and dms. Williams decided to focus on bs. after hearing an Oscar Pettiford rec. Att. Combs Coll. of Mus. 1960–1. Pl. w. Gene Ammons–Sonny Stitt '60–1; Dakota Staton, Betty Carter, Lee Morgan '61–2; Jimmy Heath, Benny Golson '62–3; Sarah Vaughan '63–4; Nancy Wilson, Jazz Crusaders, Donald Byrd, Miles Davis '64–8; Bobby Hutcherson–Harold Land '67–8; Herbie Hancock, Herbie Mann, Art Blakey '69–72; Dexter Gordon, Billy Taylor, Wynton Kelly, Illinois Jacquet, McCoy Tyner, Mary Lou Williams

'73–5; Jimmy Rowles, Ron Carter, Art Farmer, Kenny Burrell, Woody Shaw, Slide Hampton '75–9. Won Grammy in '79 for rec. w. Great Jazz Trio (w. Hank Jones, Tony Williams). Feat. soloist w. London Symph. on Phillipe Sarde's soundtrack for film *Les Choix Des Armes* '81. Pl. w. Sphere '82–5; Timeless All-Stars fr. '85. Freelanced in US, Eur., Japan w. H. Hancock, Branford Marsalis, Larry Coryell, Wayne Shorter fr. '86. Led own qnt. w. Ralph Moore, Shunzo Ono, Benny Green, Billy Drummond fr. '90. Pl. w. Sphere fr. '98. Taught at the Jazzmobile Wkshp. '73–5. Williams has app. on more than 400 recs. Favs: Oscar Pettiford, Paul Chambers, Ray Brown, Ron Carter. Fests: all major fr. '63. TV: *Sesame Street, Today*, Grammy Awds., Mike Douglas. Comps: "Tokudo"; "Christina"; "Deceptakon." CDs: Muse; In&Out: Den.; TCB; w. S. Vaughan (Merc.); N. Wilson (Cap.); D. Gordon (Prest.); H. Hancock (BN); Sphere (Elek.; Verve; Red); Nnenna Freelon (Col.); G. Ammons–S. Stitt; Shirley Horn (Steep.; Verve); Timeless All-Stars (Timel.); S. Turre (Ant.; Stash); Frank Morgan (Cont.; Ant.); C. Walton; K. Drew Jr. (Evid.); S. Getz–J. Rowles; M. Davis (Col.); K. Barron; Benny Green; Ralph Moore (CC); Franco Ambrosetti; E. Hubbard; Chet Baker (Enja); L. Konitz; Buck Hill; Hilton Ruiz; Mary Lou Williams (Steep.)

WILLIAMS, CLARENCE, pno, comp, publ; b. Plaquemine, LA, 10/8/1893; d. NYC, 11/6/65. Father was a mus.; family moved to NO in 1906. From '10 Williams took part in minstrel shows as voc. and m.c., later as pnst. and comp. Worked w. Bunk Johnson, Sidney Bechet, et al. Active as a song publ. and writer fr. '13; early hits incl. "Royal Garden Blues" (co-authored w. Spencer Williams—no relation); "Sugar Blues"; "Baby Won't You Please Come Home"; "Gulf Coast Blues"; and "I Ain't Gonna Give Nobody None of My Jelly Roll." A pedestrian pnst., Williams is mainly remembered as publisher of works by Spencer Williams; Willie "The Lion" Smith; James P. Johnson; and others, and for organizing rec. dates by his own Blue Five and such blues singers as Bessie Smith; Eva Taylor (his wife fr. '21); Sara Martin; and Sippie Wallace. His daughter Irene (b. '31) sang w. the Herman Chittison trio in the '50s. The Clarence Williams Blue Five recs. helped bring attention to Louis Armstrong and Sidney Bechet, among others. Dur. the '30s Williams also rec. w. washboard bands. CDs: Collector's Classics; w. B. Smith (Col.; BBC); King Oliver (Dec.); Lonnie Johnson; L. Armstrong; Josh White (Col.); Ethel Waters (Milan).

WILLIAMS, CLAUDE "FIDDLER," vln, gtr, bs; b. Muskogee, OK, 2/22/08; d. Kansas City, MO,

4/25/04. Worked in Okla. w. Pettiford family band 1927. Joined T. Holder '28, remaining when Andy Kirk took over the band. After working in Chi. w. Eddie and Nat Cole, he pl. gtr. and occ. vln. w. Count Basie fr. late '36. Rec. w. Basie in Jan. '37; replaced by Freddie Green 2 mos. later. After yrs. of obscurity, he ret. to mus. activity as vlnst. and gtrst., mainly tour. w. Jay McShann in the '70s and '80s and app. at many jfs. Still active in '90s, he app. w. Jay McShann at '96 Carnegie Hall concert tribute to Clint Eastwood. Dan Morgenstern described him as "a swing fiddler in the Stuff Smith tradition." He has also been compared to Joe Venuti. CDs: Steep.; Arh.; Prog.; w. C. Basie (Dec.); J. McShann (Sack.; B&B); Karrin Allyson (Conc.); Clint Eastwood (WB); A. Kirk (Class.).

WILLIAMS, COOTIE (CHARLES MELVIN), tpt, comp; b. Mobile, AL, 7/24/10; d. NYC, 9/14/85. Started on bsn., tba., and dms.; self-taught on tpt. Tour. w. the Young Family Band (w. Lester Young on tnr. sax) at 17. Worked w. Eagle Eye Shields' band in Fla. 1925–6; to NYC w. Alonzo Ross '28. After working briefly w. Chick Webb and a few mos. w. Fletcher Henderson, he replaced Bubber Miley w. the Duke Ellington band in Feb. '29. His open and plunger solos were among the Ellington band's most distinctive sounds through '40. Best known for "Echoes of Harlem" '36 and "Concerto for Cootie" (which became "Do Nothing 'Til You Hear From Me") '40. In late '30s he made numerous rec. dates his own gps.; Teddy Wilson; Lionel Hampton; and Ellington contingents led by Barney Bigard and Johnny Hodges. In Nov. '40 his move fr. Ellington to Benny Goodman inspired Raymond Scott's "When Cootie Left the Duke." Williams contributed to such memorable Goodman sxt. sides as "Wholly Cats" and "Royal Garden Blues," and the full band's "Superman." Left Goodman after a yr., forming his own bb until late '40s; later reduced it to gp. size. In the early '50s he sometimes obscured his jazz talent in r&b bands that featured exhibitionistic tnr. saxes. Pl. Savoy ballroom until it closed; toured Eur. for several weeks and pl. Embers and other clubs '59. From '62 to the late '70s he pl. mostly w. the Ellington orch. Among his later work w. Ellington were "New Concerto for Cootie"; "The Shepherd" '68; "Portrait of Louis Armstrong" '70. Won the *Esq.* Gold Award '45–6; Silver Award '44. In his heyday Williams combined the best of Bubber Miley and Louis Armstrong and may have been the best all-around tpt. player in jazz. CDs: Class.; tracks w. bb in *Classic Capitol Jazz Sessions* (Mos.); FS; w. B. Goodman (Col.; Jazz Unlimited); D. Ellington (BB; Col.; Prest.; Pab.; MM; Atl.; Dec.; BN; Verve; Saja); J. Hodges (B&B); L. Hampton; Met. All-Stars (BB); E.

Fitzgerald–D. Ellington (Verve); Gabrielle Goodman (JMT); T. Wilson (Hep); B. Strayhorn (Red Brn.); Bud Powell (Mythic Sound); B. Holiday (Col.).

WILLIAMS, DAVID (aka "HAPPY"), bs; b. Trinidad, West Indies, 9/17/46. Father is bsst. in West Indies; bro. Ira "Buddy" Williams is dmr., sist. is concert pnst. Moved to London, then to NYC 1969. Worked w. Beaver Harris '69 and stud. w. Ron Carter. Pl. w. Chuck Mangione '69–70; Roberta Flack '70–2; then w. Ornette Coleman, Donald Byrd, Charles McPherson, Billy Taylor, Donny Hathaway, Duke Jordan '73; Charles Davis, Kenny Barron '74; Elvin Jones '75–6, incl. Eur. and S. Amer. tours. With Art Pepper '76, '81; Slide Hampton '85; rec. and tour. w. Cedar Walton mid '80s into '90s. Joined Woody Shaw '86; Stan Getz '88; Kenny Barron, Frank Morgan '90–1; Freddie Hubbard, Clifford Jordan bb '91. Fav: Ron Carter. CDs: Timel.; w. C. Hollyday (Novus); James Clay; F. Morgan (Ant.); Eastern Rebellion; F. Hubbard (MM); Clifford Jordan (Mile.); Art Pepper (Gal.); Billy Higgins; C. Walton (Evid.; CC; Timel.; Red); K. Barron (CC; Enja; Verve); Larry Willis (Steep.); Slide Hampton; Warne Marsh; Dave Pike (CC); Steve Grossman (Drey.; Red.); Ronnie Mathews (DIW)

WILLIAMS, EARL CONROY, dms; b. Detroit, MI, 10/8/38. Father Paul "Hucklebuck" Williams, pl. bari. and alto, had hit single in 1948. Began on pno. Stud. at Det. Cons. '47–9; Det. Inst. of Mus. Arts '49–51. Pl. gigs in Det. w. Lester Young '54; Barry Harris; Della Reese; Yusef Lateef; then tour. w. father. Pl. w. Eddie Heywood '59–63; Cootie Williams '60s; Major Holley–Tommy Flanagan '61; Dwike Mitchell–Willie Ruff '62; Big Nick Nicholas, Mary Lou Williams '64; Sam "The Man" Taylor '64–5; Diahann Carroll, Jaki Byard '65–6; Billy Mitchell '67–77; Swingle Singers '68; Seldon Powell '69–72; Sam Taylor '72; Charlie Green, Tyree Glenn, Lena Horne '73; Grant Green '74; Teddy Wilson; Sy Oliver '74–5; Hal McKusick '75–6; Ed. Heywood '75–88; Earle Warren '79; Patti Bown '79–80; Warne Marsh, Sonny Stitt, Jean-Pierre Rampal '80; Ron Carter '80–1; Claude Bolling–J. Rampal '81; Melba Liston '82; Valerie Capers since '86; Shirley Vincent '88. Favs: Chick Webb, Max Roach, Elvin Jones. Fests: Japan fr. '64–5, '72; So. Amer. '81; France '89. TV: Jack Paar w. C. Green '73; PBS *Gala of Stars* w. Bolling-Rampal '81. CDs: w. Romi Akiyama (Elec. Bird); Randy Weston (Verve); Hal Singer (FNAC).

WILLIAMS, ELMER A., tnr sax, cl; b. Red Bank, NJ, 1905; d. Red Bank, 6/62. Played w. Claude Hopkins 1936–7; Chick Webb '27–34; also briefly w. McKinney's Cotton Pickers '31; Fletcher Henderson '36–9; Horace Henderson '39; Ella Fitzgerald '41. Worked w. Lucky Millinder '44–5; rejoined Hopkins '46; also rejoined F. Henderson '50. In late '50s worked in Milan until disability from diabetes limited his activities. CDs: w. L. Armstrong (BB); Chick Webb (Dec.); F. Henderson; Horace Henderson (Class); Ivory Joe Hunter (R&T); Chu Berry; Roy Eldridge (Topaz).

WILLIAMS, FESS (STANLEY R.), sax, cl, leader; b. Danville, KY, 4/10/1894; d. NYC, 12/17/75. Musical family; Charles Mingus was his nephew. Studied vln., cl. fr. 15; own band in Cincinnati at 20; renamed as Royal Flush Orch. after he moved to NYC in 1925, pl. at Savoy Ballroom '26–8. Was dir. of Dave Peyton band in Chi. late '28. Back in NYC, led own band in '30s w. such sidemen as Rex Stewart; Albert Nicholas; and Garvin Bushell. Semi-retired in '60. CDs: w. Sammy Price (Class.); Reuben Reeves (Timel.).

WILLIAMS, FRANC (FRANCIS), tpt; b. McConnell's Mills, PA, 10/20/10; d. Houston, PA, 10/2/83. Son was Greg Morris of *Mission Impossible* TV series. Pl. w. many bbs, incl. Claude Hopkins; Edgar Hayes; Ella Fitzgerald; Sabby Lewis; and Machito in 1940s. Best known for work w. Duke Ellington Orch. '45–9, playing on "Three Cent Stomp" and "Trumpet No End." Chiefly w. Latin bands in '50s and '60s; briefly back w. Ellington '51, then w. Clyde Bernhardt; toured Eur. Charter member of NYJRC '74, pl. on Eur. tour of Charlie Parker tribute; Bix Beiderbecke tribute at NJF-NY '75. Own qt., Swing Four w. Eddie Durham, twice weekly at West End Café '75–6. Featured w. Harlem Blues and Jazz Band and from late '70s w. Panama Francis's Savoy Sultans. CDs: w. D. Ellington (Vict.; Prest.; MM; Col.); Panama Francis; I. Jacquet (B&B); J. Hodges (Suisa).

WILLIAMS, JACKIE (ARTHUR), dms; b. NYC, 1/2/33. Began on pno., then studied dms. w. Aubry Brooks 1949–51. Freelanced in NYC in mid '50s. Pl. w. Buck Clayton fr. late '50s; Edmond Hall '62; Red Richards '64–5; Earl Hines '67–8; Teddy Wilson fr. '69; also pl. in '60s w. Roy Eldridge; Eddie Condon; Illinois Jacquet; Clark Terry; Odetta; own trio. Pl. w. Bobby Hackett, Buddy Tate fr. early '70s; Slam Stewart–Johnny Guarnieri '75; Jay McShann '80; Doc Cheatham fr. early '80s; Ralph Sutton, Harold Ashby, Billy Mitchell, Howard Alden–Dan Barrett '89. Favs: Jo Jones, Roy Haynes, Jimmy Cobb, Rich, Roach, Blakey. Fests: Eur. since '60s; JVC–NY in '90s. TV: apps. w. Earl Hines, Doc Cheatham. CDs:

w. Alden-Barrett (Conc.); Milt Hinton; Junior Mance (Chiaro.); Zoot Sims (Pab.); E. Garner; Bobby Short (Tel.); Doc Cheatham (Park.; Col.); Stephane Grappelli; Slam Stewart (B&B); Benny Waters (JP); Buddy Tate (NW).

WILLIAMS, JAMES, pno, org, comp; b. Memphis, TN, 3/8/51; d. NYC, 7/20/04. Tony Reedus is nephew. Began on pno. at age 13, then stud. w. Russell Wilson, Daniel Fletcher at Memphis State U. Pl. in Memphis w. Herman Green; Sylvester Semple; Bill Mobley; Bill Easley; and as church org. Moved to Bost. 1974; taught at Berklee Sch. of Mus. '74–7; and worked w. Alan Dawson; Joe Henderson; Woody Shaw; Milt Jackson; Clark Terry. Pl. w. Art Blakey '77–81; then freelanced w. Sonny Stitt; Louis Hayes; Slide Hampton; and others. Led own gps. in NYC fr. late '70s. Williams also taught at the U. of Hartford and perf. on the soundtrack to Spike Lee's film *Do the Right Thing*. Williams' Finas Prods. has presented a series of concerts at Merkin Hall which honor various jazzmen and perpetuate Phineas Newborn's name. From '93 member of Contemporary Piano Ensemble w. Mulgrew Miller, Harold Mabern, Geoff Keezer, Donald Brown. Favs: Herbie Hancock, Phineas Newborn Jr., Wynton Kelly, Hank Jones, Mulgrew Miller. Polls: *DB* TDWR '88. Fests: Eur., Japan, Carib. since '77. CDs: Em.; Col.; Conc.; Evid.; Sunny.; BN; w. A. Blakey (Conc.; BN; Imp.; Evid.; Timel.); Emily Remler; M. "Smitty" Smith (Conc.); Art Farmer; Tom Harrell (Cont.); B. Easley (Mile.); E. Gomez (Stretch); Howard Johnson (Verve); Contemporary Piano Ens. (Evid.; Col.); K. Burrell (Evid.); Curtis Fuller (Timel.); Joe Wilder (Eve. Star); Bobby Watson (Col.); Billy Pierce (Sunny.).

WILLIAMS, JESSICA, pno, comp; b. Baltimore, MD, 3/17/48. Began pno. lessons at age 4. Classical stud. at Peabody Cons. Pl. w. Buck Hill in local club at 16. Moved to Phila. 1968. Pl. in qnt. w. Philly Joe Jones and Tyree Glenn in early '70s; also w. Joe Morello and in local rock gps., sometimes on org. Led own pno. trio fr. same period. Moved to SF '77, becoming house pnst. at Keystone Korner. Pl. w. featured guests, incl. Stan Getz; Bobby Hutcherson; Charlie Haden; Tony Williams; Eddie Harris; Eddie Henderson. Worked mainly in SF Bay Area, but also in Portland, Oregon, and Seattle w. Red Mitchell; Leroy Vinnegar; David Friesen. In '80s she pl. synthesizer, overdubbing on bs. and dms. for recs. on her own Quanta and EarArt labels. Beginning w. Northsea JF '91, she has made frequent trips to Eur. for concerts, fests. Though her style and touch have been compared to those of Bill Evans, her improvs. also show a Monk infl. w. a touch of whimsy. Received

NEA grant to prod. and perf. her comp. "Tutu's Dream," dedicated to Archbishop Desmond Tutu, '88; for comp. and arr. a Thelonious Monk tribute for bb and string ens. '89; Guggenheim Fellowship '94. CDs: Timel.; Conc.; Hep; JF; Cand.; w. C. Rouse (Land.).

WILLIAMS, JOE (Joseph Goreed), voc; b. Cordele, GA, 12/12/18; d. Las Vegas, NV, 3/29/99. Lived in Chi. fr. age 3. Prof. debut w. Jimmie Noone in 1937. Dur. '40s he sang w. local gps., also Coleman Hawkins bb '41; Lionel Hampton '43; Andy Kirk '46. After teaming w. boogie-woogie pnsts. Albert Ammons and Pete Johnson, he worked mainly w. Red Saunders '50–53; also briefly w. Count Basie spt. at Brass Rail. His reunion w. Basie late '54–60 yielded his first rec hits, incl. "Every Day"; "Alright, Okay, You Win"; and "The Comeback." His phenomenal success w. Basie helped fill a gap left by the departure of Jimmy Rushing. In '60s he toured w. various accomps., incl. Sweets Edison Qnt. and the Junior Mance and Norman Simmons trios. Dur. this period Williams remained a convincing urban blues perf., but he also expanded his scope and with his rich, warm baritone developed into a superior balladeer and all-purpose singer. Dur. the '70s and '80s he lived in LV but seldom worked there, concentrating instead on int'l concert tours, jazz cruises, and golf tournaments. He received NARAS's Governor's Award in '83 and a Grammy for the album *I Just Want To Sing* in '85. Voted Best Jazz Singer many times by *DB*. Had acting roles in the film *The Moonshine War* and on TV's *The Bill Cosby Show*. Also numerous apps. on the *Tonight Show*. Honored by the Society of Singers at an all-star concert in LV '91. Received the American Jazz Masters Award fr. NEA '93. CDs: Delos; BN; Roul.; Tel.; Fant.; Sav.; RCA; Verve; w. C. Basie (Verve; Phon.); Count Basie Orch. (Tel.); M. McPartland (JA); Frank Capp (Conc.); Milt Jackson (Qwest); Arturo Sandoval (GRP).

WILLIAMS, JOHN B. JR., bs; b. NYC, 2/27/41. Started on dms.; self-taught on bs. dur. marine corps service, later stud. for two yrs. w. Ron Carter. With Horace Silver 1967–9; Kenny Burrell, Leon Thomas, Kai Winding '69; Dizzy Gillespie, Hugh Masekela '70. Rec. w. Mose Allison, Count Basie, Roy Ayers, Bobby Hutcherson–Harold Land qnt., et al. Joined *Tonight Show* orch. '72. Worked w. Billy Cobham, Benny Carter early '70s; rec. w. Louis Bellson late '70s; Jon Hendricks '82: Gerald Wilson, Art Farmer–Benny Golson Jazztet '82. Was a member of Arsenio Hall TV show band, early '90s LPs: w. Silver; Cobham. CDs: w. L. Bellson (Conc.); Hutcherson-Land (BN); Gerald Wilson (Disc.).

WILLIAMS, JOHN C. JR., bari sax, bs cl; b. Orangeburg, SC, 10/31/36. Father pl. vln., moth., pl. pno. Guitarist John Collins was his uncle and mentor. Prof. debut w. local LA bands 1961; army '62–5; toured w. Ike and Tina Turner '66; Ray Charles '68. With Count Basie '70–5, and again '80; after Basie's death, he cont. w. orch. into '90s. Between the two stints, he worked in LA w. Capp-Pierce Juggernaut; Louis Bellson; Gerald Wilson; and Stevie Wonder. Favs: Harry Carney, Pepper Adams. CDs: w. C. Basie (Den.; Tel.; Pab.).

WILLIAMS, JOHN OVERTON, alto, bari saxes, cl; b. Memphis, TN, 4/13/05; d. Columbus, OH, 11/24/96. Attended hs in KC; mostly self-taught, he launched his prof. career w. Paul Banks 1922. Had own band '24–8; his pnst., Mary Lou Scruggs, later became his wife. Joined Terrence Holder in Oklahoma City '28, remaining when Andy Kirk became the leader '29. Left Kirk in '39 and retired from mus. until '42 when he joined Cootie Williams. Pl. bari. sax on Kirk's "Blue Clarinet Stomp" '29. Co-wrote "Froggy Bottom" for Kirk w. Mary Lou Williams '36. It was revived in the film *Kansas City* '96. Rec. w. Cecil Scott for Vict. CDs: w. Kirk (Dec.).

WILLIAMS, JOHNNY (JOHN JR.), bs; b. Memphis, TN, 3/13/08; d. NYC, 10/23/98. Studied vln., tba. Went to Atlanta to attend coll. but joined Graham Jackson orch. on tba. Sw. to bs. after stud. w. William Graham. Pl. in southern territory bands dur. 1930s. Moved to NYC early '36, pl. w. Mills Blue Rhythm Band '37–8, then for a short time w. Benny Carter. Pl. w. Frankie Newton '39; Coleman Hawkins '39–40; Louis Armstrong to '42; Teddy Wilson '42–4; Edmond Hall '44–7; Tab Smith '48–52; Johnny Hodges '54–5. Active sporadically until tour. in France w. Buddy Tate '68. Assoc. often w. Red Richards in '70s; tour. w. Bob Greene's World of Jelly Roll Morton '78–82. Worked w. Harlem Blues and Jazz Band fr. '78. CDs: w. Billie Holiday (Comm.); Edmond Hall (BN); Hodges (Verve); Mills Blue Rhythm Band; L. Armstrong (Class.).

WILLIAMS, JOHNNY (JOHN THOMAS), pno; b. Windsor, VT, 1/28/29. Played church org. in Windsor. At 16 he joined Mal Hallett in Bost.; at 19 pl. w. Johnny Bothwell. Moved to NYC 1949; mil. service to '53. Worked briefly w. Charlie Barnet Feb. '53; then six mos. w. Stan Getz; Don Elliot; and others, bef. rejoin. Getz for eight mos. in Oct. '54; later w. Bob Brookmeyer. Rec. w. Med Flory, Bill De Arango, Paul Quinichette, Art Mardigan '54; own trio for Em. '54–5 (re-issued on double LP); Cannonball Adderley, Phil Woods '55; Al Cohn, Zoot Sims '56; in

Calif. w. Buddy Collette '59; Pete Rugolo Orch. '60. Not related to film comp./cond. John Towner Williams. Worked as a city manager in Fla. in '90s. Infl. by Bud Powell, but his percussive comping and rhythmic style also reflected Horace Silver. CDs: w. Woods (Prest.); Getz (Verve); Sims (Biog.; Chess).

WILLIAMS, LEROY, dms; b. Chicago, IL, 2/3/37. Mother and sist. pl. pno. Self-taught fr. age 15. Pl. in Chi. w. Wilbur Ware, Scotty Holt, John Gilmore, Gene Ammons, Sonny Stitt, Bennie Green, Judy Roberts '59–64. Moved to NYC '67, pl. w. Booker Ervin '67; Sonny Rollins, John Patton '68; Clifford Jordan '68–9; Barry Harris since '69; Charles McPherson, W. Ware '69; Hank Mobley '70; Yusef Lateef, Thelonious Monk, Ray Bryant, Dizzy Gillespie '72; Andrew Hill, James Moody, Stan Getz, Geo. Coleman '73; Junior Cook–Bill Hardman '76; Slide Hampton, Sonny Stitt '79; Johnny Griffin '80; Pepper Adams, Jimmy Slyde '81; Dewey Redman '87. Favs: Philly Joe Jones, Art Blakey, Sid Catlett, Max Roach, Roy Haynes. Fests: Eur., Japan. Many sess. for Xan. w. Jimmy Raney; Al Cohn; Barry Harris et al. CDs: w. H. Mobley (BN); B. Harris (Tel.); J. Cook (Steep.; Muse); F. Morgan (Tel.); J. Helleny (Arb.); C. McPherson (Xan.); J. Patton (BN); Pete Malinverni (Res.); Slide Hampton (BL); Richard Wyands (DIW); Jaco Pastorius (Sound Hills); Bertha Hope; Bill Hardman; Louis Smith (Steep.).

WILLIAMS, MARY LOU (Mary Elfrieda Scruggs), pno, arr; b. Atlanta, GA, 5/8/10; d. Durham, NC, 5/28/81. Inspired to comp. by Lovie Austin. To Pitts. w. moth. at 4; stud. pno. Appeared publicly w. vaudeville act, Seymour & Jeanette 1925. Joined band led by John Overton Williams, who became her first husband, '25. Sub-pnst. and arr. in Terrence Holder's band (which was later taken over by Andy Kirk) '29; became full-time member '30 and remained until '42. Williams' first arr. for Kirk was "Mess-a-Stomp" '29. Dur. her yrs. w. Kirk, she became known for the bb arrs. She wrote for Benny Goodman; Tommy Dorsey; Earl Hines; Louis Armstrong; Jimmy Lunceford; et al. In '42 she led a small gp. w. her second husband, Harold "Shorty" Baker, on tpt. She also wrote for Duke Ellington "Trumpet No End" '46; and Dizzy Gillespie "In the Land of Oobladee" '49. Part of her original *Zodiac Suite* was performed by the N.Y. Philharm. at Carnegie Hall in '46. A close assoc. of the bebop movement, she befriended Gillespie; Bud Powell; Thelonious Monk; and Tadd Dameron. Dur. two yrs. spent in Eur., she pursued religious interests, later writing such spiritual works as *Black Christ of the Andes* and *Mary Lou's Mass* (commissioned by the Vatican '69). During the '60s she cont. to work in clubs, write sacred works, and teach. In '77 she rec. a controversial pno. duo album w. Cecil Taylor, received honorary doctorates fr. several universities, and joined the faculty of Duke U. in No. Caro. A superlative stride and swing pnst. and expert boogie-woogie player, Williams was practically the only significant female jazz instrumentalist/comp. of the '30s. Always alert to changing developments in jazz, she worked w. such emerging talent as Herbie Nicholas; Hilton Ruiz; and Horace Parlan. Using bop and avant-garde techniques, her style cont. to evolve in later yrs. but she is best remembered for her contributions to the Andy Kirk band of the '30s—incl. "Froggy Bottom"; "Walkin' and Swingin'" (from which came Monk's "Rhythm-a-ning"); and "Little Joe from Chicago." The hit "Black Coffee" is obviously borrowed from Williams' "What's Your Story, Morning Glory." Fests: NJF '57 w. Gillespie; MJF '65; Montreux JF '68. CDs: Pab.; Chiaro.; Smith.; Vogue; Steep.; w. A. Kirk (Dec.); C. Taylor (Pab.); B. Goodman (Hep; Lond.; Cap.); M. McPartland (JA); D. Gillespie (Verve).

WILLIAMS, MIDGE, voc; b. California ca. 1908; d. 1940s. Started singing w. family qt., turning prof. in 1927. Made several tours to the Far East in the early '30s, perf. in Shanghai and Tokyo. Ret. to US '34; cond. own radio series in LA '34–6. Rec. in NYC w. Teddy Wilson '36; also several sess. for Variety and Vocalion as Midge Williams and Her Jazz Jesters, w. changing personnel that incl. Charlie Shavers, Edmond Hall, Buster Bailey, Pete Brown, Frankie Newton, and the John Kirby gp. '37–8. Rec. two sides in Tokyo, singing in Japanese. Toured w. Louis Armstrong's bb '38–41; then perf. as a single. CDs: w. Lil Hardin Armstrong; Bunny Berigan; Teddy Wilson (Class.).

WILLIAMS, NELSON "CADILLAC," tpt; b. Birmingham, AL, 9/26/17; d. Voorburg, Netherlands, 11/15/73. In the 1930s he toured briefly w. boogie-woogie pnst. Cow Cow Davenport; played w. Trianon Crackerjacks and Brown Skin Models '36; then became mus. dir. for Dixie Rhythm Girls in Birmingham, Ala. Joined Tiny Bradshaw in Phila. '39; after three yrs. in an army band he worked w. Billy Eckstine bb, then w. John Kirby and Billy Kyle Qt. '48. Best known for his work w. Duke Ellington '45–51. Leaving Ellington, he settled in Paris, pl. at the Trois Mailletz and other clubs around Eur. Rec. w. Dutch Swing Coll. Band in '56. Rejoined Ellington several times between '56 and '70. An expert employer of the wah-wah mute, Williams modeled himself after Roy Eldridge and Dizzy Gillespie but also sang in the style of Louis Armstrong. CDs: w. Ellington (Col.); Dutch Swing Coll. (Philips).

WILLIAMS, RICHARD GENE (aka NOTES), tpt; b. Galveston, TX, 5/4/31; d. NYC, 11/5/85. Started on tnr. sax, took up tpt. in his teens. Pl. w. local bands in Tex.; received mus. degree from Wiley Coll.; served four yrs. in air force. Joined Lionel Hampton for Eur. tour 1956; earned master's degree fr. Manh. Sch. of Mus. Between '59 and '64 he worked w. Charles Mingus; Gigi Gryce; Oliver Nelson; Yusef Lateef; Quincy Jones; Lou Donaldson; Slide Hampton; and Orch. USA. Rec. w. D. Ellington '65 and '71; toured w. Thad Jones–Mel Lewis '66–70; pl. w. Gil Evans '72–3; Clark Terry '73; rejoined Hampton '75. Later worked in pit bands for B'way musicals and in early '80s was member of Mingus Dynasty. CDs: Cand; w. D. Ellington (Saja); R. R. Kirk (Merc.); C. Mingus (Col.; BN); Mingus Dynasty (SN); C. McRae (Dec.); Randy Weston (Roul.); Y. Lateef (Riv.; Imp.); Jones-Lewis (LRC); Booker Ervin (Sav.; BN); E. Dolphy; Lockjaw Davis (Prest.); Oliver Nelson; Gigi Gryce (NJ); Red Garland (OJC); Clark Terry (Vang.).

WILLIAMS, ROY, tbn; b. Bolton, Lancashire, England, 3/7/37. First experience in Manchester-based trad. jazz band. In 1960 after mil. service, he pl. in London w. tptr. Mike Peters; then Terry Lightfoot '61 and Monty Sunshine. Came to prominence w. Alex Welsh band '65–78. Pl. w. Humphrey Lyttelton '78–82. Freelanced fr. '83 w. Pizza Express All-Stars; Five-A-Slide; Spike Robinson; others. Perf. at Colo. JP and in NYC '80s. CDs: BL; Hep; Phon.; Sine; N-H; w. Peter Meyer; Tom Saunders; Bill Allred (N-H); Ruby Braff (BL; Arb); Five-A-Slide; H. Lyttelton; Sammy Price; Alex Welsh (BL); Brian Lemon; George Masso (Zephyr); Doc Cheatham (Sack.); Dick Sudhalter (Chall.); Benny Waters (Hep).

WILLIAMS, RUBBERLEGS (Henry Williamson), voc, dancer; b. Atlanta, GA, 7/14/07; d. NYC 10/17/62. Known mainly as dancer in vaudeville and tent shows of the 1920s and '30s. Featured w. Elmer Snowden in the film short, *Smash Your Baggage* '33. Sang "My Buddy" at Bessie Smith's funeral '37. Also app. in shows at the Apollo, NYC, and other theatres singing and dancing to bb accomps. by Fletcher Henderson; Chick Webb; Dicky Wells; and Count Basie, who wrote "Miss Thing" for him. Although his career flourished in an earlier era, Williams perf. and rec. w. some of the biggest names in bop dur. the mid '40s., incl. Dizzy Gillespie; Charlie Parker; and Miles Davis, who made his rec. debut backing Rubberlegs on a '45 Sav. rec., "That's the Stuff You Gotta Watch." CDs: w. M. Davis (Sav.); Gillespie (Class.); Parker (Phil.).

WILLIAMS, RUDY, alto, tnr, bari saxes, cl; b. Newark, NJ, 1919; d. Cape Cod, MA, 9/54. Played sax fr. age 12. Feat. on alto w. Al Cooper's Savoy Sultans 1937–43; w. Hot Lips Page and Chris Columbus '43. Led own band Feb. '44; then briefly w. Henry Jerome; Dud Bascomb; and John Kirby Sxt.; led own band again at Minton's, NYC '45. In late '40s toured Far East w. USO show; pl. w. Jazz-in-Bebop Orch; led own bands in Bost. and NYC. To Calif. in early '50s; pl. w. Illinois Jacquet and Gene Ammons; toured mil. bases in Far East w. Oscar Pettiford's gp. '51–2. Recs. w. Don Byas; Babs Gonzales; Tadd Dameron; Eddie "Lockjaw" Davis; Gene Ammons; Johnny Hodges; and others. Led own bands fr. '52 bef. he was drowned in a fishing boat accident. His solos on "Looney" and "Little Sally Water" w. Al Cooper were played in a rubbery Willie Smith–derived but highly personal style that, in some ways, prefigured Ornette Coleman. In the mid '40s he showed a Charlie Parker infl. CDs: w. Gonzales (BN); Bennie Green (Prest.); D. Byas (Sav.); T. Dameron; Fats Navarro (Mile.); Charlie Christian (Jazz Anthology); Al Cooper (Class.).

WILLIAMS, SANDY (ALEXANDER BALOS), tbn; b. Somerville, SC, 10/24/06; d. NYC, 3/25/91. Father was a minister. Stud. tba. bef. sw. to tbn. Launched career w. Miller Bros. in Wash., D.C., then worked w. Claude Hopkins 1927–9; Horace Henderson '29; Fletcher Henderson '32–3. Join. Chick Webb '33 and after his death remained w. band under Ella Fitzgerald's leadership until '40. Worked w. Benny Carter '40; Coleman Hawkins '42–3; D. Ellington '43; F. Henderson again '41–2. While w. Henderson he also pl. w. Lucky Millinder; Cootie Williams; and Sidney Bechet. Worked w. Art Hodes '47; tour. Eur. w. Rex Stewart '47–8. In '55 he was hospitalized for six mos. and lost his teeth, but fr. late '57—in a determined effort to make a successful comeback—he gigged intermittently, pl. dixieland dates at Central Plaza and Local 802–sponsored concerts in NYC parks. Williams, who made his rec. debut w. Jelly Roll Morton '30, was one of the best tbnsts. of that decade, pl. in a style reminiscent of his first idol, Jimmy Harrison. CDs: own Big Eight in *Giants of Small Band Swing*, vols. 1&2 (Riv.); w. Webb (Hep; Dec.); Bechet (BB; BN); Jelly Roll Morton (BB).

WILLIAMS, SPENCER, comp, pno; b. New Orleans, LA, 10/14/1889; d. Flushing NY, 7/14/65. Studied at St. Charles U. in NO. Worked as pnst. and voc. in Chi. fr. 1907 bef. moving to NYC '16. Early assoc. of Clarence Williams (no relation). Began active songwriting w. Fats Waller (with whom "Squeeze Me" was an early collaboration '18). To

Paris '25; wrote for Josephine Baker in *La Revue Negre*; back to US '28. Became famous via such songs as "I Ain't Got No body"; "Basin Street Blues"; "Mahogany Hall Stomp"; "Royal Garden Blues"; "I Found a New Baby"; "Everybody Loves My Baby"; "Shim-me-sha-wobble"; "I Ain't Gonna Give Nobody None of My Jelly Roll"; and "Tishomingo Blues." In '30 he sang and pl. on recs. w. Lonnie Johnson and Teddy Bunn. After vacationing w. Fats Waller in France '32, he moved to Engl. where in '36, he wrote the lyrics for Benny Carter's "When Lights Are Low." Moved to Sweden '51 and lived there until '57 when ret. to NYC. CDs: w. Arthur Briggs (Jazz Archives); Teddy Bunn (RST).

WILLIAMS, TODD MAXWELL, tnr sax, cl, fl; b. St. Louis, MO, 7/16/67. Influenced by older bro., who started mus. instruction at a very young age. Todd started on alto sax in fifth grade; picked up tnr. as a teenager, also learned doubling instr. Start. pl. prof. w. local gps. around St. Louis as teenager. Attended Eastman Sch. of Mus. 1986–7; grad. w. honors fr. Manh. Sch. of Music '97. Became prominent through working w. Wynton Marsalis '87–93, incl. recs., concerts, and extensive int'l tours. Active in LCJO '89–92; Jazz at Lincoln Center Children's Concerts. Teaches priv. and is active clinician. Very active as staff writer/band dir. and teacher w. Times Square Church Mus. Ministry, NYC. ASCAP "Special Awards" '95, '96. Fav: J. S. Bach. TV: *Tonight Show*; *Shannon's Deal*; Arsenio Hall; music for Charlie Brown Special; *Sesame Street*. CDs: w. W. Marsalis; LCJO (Col.); Marcus Roberts (Novus); Tough Young Tenors (Ant.); Manhattan Sch. of Mus. Orch. at Montreux (SB).

WILLIAMS, TONY (ANTHONY), dms; b. Chicago, IL, 12/12/45; d. Daly City, CA, 2/23/97. Grew up in Bost.; began pl. dms. at the age of 8. First mentor was his fath., Tillmon, a saxophonist. Studied w. Alan Dawson 1955. Later stud. in harmony and comp. w. teachers fr. Juilliard and U. of Calif., Berkeley. Gained early advice and guidance fr. Sam Rivers w. whom he collaborated on a series of experimental concerts with the Bost. Improv. Ens. Moved to NYC in Dec. 1962, pl. w. Jackie McLean's gp. Miles Davis heard him and hired him for his qnt. '63. Along w. Herbie Hancock and Ron Carter in Davis's rhythm section, he helped give jazz a new texture, expanding—w. his personal sense of freedom and dynamics—Elvin Jones's concept of stating the beat all over the drum set. While with Davis he also led BN rec. dates that utilized his comps. and illustrated his avant-garde inclination. In the late '60s when his attention was drawn to the prevailing rock beat, he left Davis to form one of the first fusion gps., Life-time, w. John McLaughlin, Jack Bruce, and Larry Young. It was a high-decibel mixture of jazz and rock, chordal and free form approaches. Although it set the pace for an era of jazz-rock fusion, Lifetime—whose personnel changed often—never achieved the commercial recognition some thought it deserved. In the mid '70s Williams rec. his comp. "There Comes a Time" w. Gil Evans. In '76 he joined Hank Jones and Ron Carter to form The Great Jazz Trio; the following yr. he began tour. and rec. w. V.S.O.P., a gp. that mir-rored the '60s Miles Davis qnt. and feat. Herbie Han-cock, Carter, Wayne Shorter, and Freddie Hubbard. This gp. resurfaced periodically in the '80s and in the '90s w. Wallace Roney replacing Hubbard. Williams also tour. the US, Eur., and Japan w. Hancock, Carter, and Wynton Marsalis '82. Fr. the mid '80s he led his own gps. w. Roney; Donald Harrison; Mulgrew Miller; Bobby Hutcherson; Carter; Billy Pierce; et al. Williams mixed his jazz w. rock, funk, and, as in *Wilderness*, classical music. Two days after undergo-ing a gall bladder operation, he suffered a fatal heart attack in the hospital. Polls: *DB* Critics as New Star '64. CDs: BN; Col.; Verve; Ark21; Polyd.; w. Davis; J. McLaughlin; W. Marsalis; Weather Report; S. Getz (Col.); Chet Baker (A&M); D. Pullen; Wayne Shorter (BN); S. Rollins; Ron Carter; McCoy Tyner (Mile.); E. Dolphy; Andrew Hill; Grachan Moncur III (BN); Michel Petrucciani; Marcus Miller (Drey.); Hancock (BN; Col.; Qwest); Joe Henderson (BN; Cont.); Hal Galper (Enja); Mulgrew; Miller (Land.).

WILLIAMS, WILLIE, tnr, sop saxes, cl, fl; b. Wilm-ington, NC, 11/1/58. Family moved to Phila. when he was an infant. Started pl. cl. at 6. Pl. w. r&b gps., Crosstown Traffic fr. age 13. Studied in public sch. 1967–76; Better Break Mus. Camp '73–6; Settlement Mus. Sch. '74–6. Pl. w. Sumi Tonooka '75. After hs graduation he att. Phila. Coll. of the Perf. Arts '76–80, pl. w. local org. trios and in studio for Phila. International Recs. at night. When Bobby Watson heard him play, he encouraged him to come to NYC, where he worked w. Odean Pope sax choir '78–82; Don Patterson, Herb Nix, Johnny Williams '80–1; Art Blakey, Woody Shaw, Ronnie Mathews, Curtis Lundy, Rashied Ali, Zahir Batin '82; Charles Fam-brough since '82; Jimmy Madison–Angel Rangelov bb at Blue Note '82–3; Arthur Taylor fr. '88; Sonny Fortune '89; Abdullah Ibrahim '89–90; Ray Mantilla '89–91; Butch Morris '90; Clifford Jordan bb fr. '91; T. S. Monk fr. '91; own qnt. fr. '87. Also many pop and r&b gigs w. the Spinners; Temptations; Four Tops; Diana Ross; Johnny Mathis; Lou Rawls; Frank Sinatra; etc. Pl. for B'way shows incl. *Ain't Misbe-havin'; A Chorus Line; 42nd St.; Sophisticated*

Ladies; The Wiz; Uptown It's Hot. Williams has taught at CCNY since '90. Favs: John Coltrane, Lucky Thompson, Sonny Rollins. Polls: Phila. Mus. Society '89. Fests: Eur., Asia since '82. CDs: NN; w. Bobby Watson (BN); C. Jordan bb (Mile.); T. S. Monk (BN; N2K); K. Mahogany (Enja); A. Taylor (Enja; Verve).

WILLIAMSON, CLAUDE BERKELEY, pno; b. Brattleboro, VT, 11/18/26. Brother of Stu Wil-liamson. Stud. classical mus. fr. age 7, later at New Engl. Cons. Pl. in father's orch. To LA 1947. Pl. w. Charlie Barnet '47–9 (feat. on *Claude Reigns*); June Christy '50–1; Lighthouse All-Stars (replaced Russ Freeman) '53–6; co-led qt. w. Bud Shank '56–8; Red Norvo Qnt. '59–60. Mil. service '52–3. Also worked w. Barney Kessel; Art Pepper; and Frank Rosolino. After some yrs. away from jazz, he taught at U. of Mass. '76; toured Japan '77; taught at Orange Coast Coll. '89. Williamson's playing strongly reflects the infl. of Bud Powell, who is a favorite, along w. Wyn-ton Kelly. CDs: V.S.O.P.; Interplay; w. Lighthouse All-Stars; Chet Baker; Barney Kessel (Cont.); Char-lie Mariano (Aff.; FS); Art Pepper (Sav.); Bud Shank (WW); G. Mulligan (LRC; Verve).

WILLIAMSON, STU (STUART LEE), tpt, valve tbn; b. Brattleboro, VT, 5/14/33; d. Studio City, CA, 10/1/91. Brother of pnst. Claude Williamson. To Calif. in 1948. Toured w. Stan Kenton '51; Woody Herman '52–3. Took up valve tbn. '54; pl. regularly w. Lighthouse All-Stars '54–5; off and on w. Shelly Manne '55–8; pl. MJF '58. Rec. w. Howard Lucraft; Shelly Manne; Marty Paich; Stan Kenton; Light-house All-Stars; etc. In the '50s Williamson was one of the West Coast's most fluent and articulate tptrs. Inactive fr. '68, he spent his last years fighting a drug habit. CDs: w. Zoot Sims (Prest.); Elmo Hope (BN); W. Herman (Disc.); Clifford Brown; Art Pepper (PJ); Benny Carter; Stan Kenton (Cap.); Jackie and Roy (Koch Jz.) Anita O'Day; Mel Tormé (Verve); Terry Gibbs; Lighthouse All-Stars; Helen Humes; Lennie Niehaus (Cont.).

WILLIS, LARRY (LAWRENCE ELLIOT), pno; b. NYC, 12/20/42. Voice major at HS of Mus. and Art; grad. Manh. Sch. Music; stud. priv. w. John Mehegan. Pl. w. Jackie McLean 1962; H. Masekela '64; Kai Winding '65–7; Stan Getz '69; Cannonball Adderley '71; Earl May '71–2; Blood, Sweat & Tears, '72. Freelanced fr. '75 in NYC; rec. fr. late '70s w. Ryo Kawasaki, Sonny Fortune; in 80s w. David "Fathead" Newman, Nat Adderley; also own trio fr. '80s. Pl. w. Branford Marsalis, Woody Shaw '86; Carla Bley–Steve Swallow '86–7; Ft. Apache Band fr. '88;

Roy Hargrove fr. '97. Comps: "To Wisdom the Prize"; "Isabelle the Liberator." Favs: Hancock, Wynton Kelly, Bill Evans. CDs: Audioq., Steep.; Maple.; Sound Hills; w. B. Marsalis (Col.); Carmen McRae (Novus); F. Hubbard (BN); Carla Bley (WATT); J. McLean (BN); N. Adderley (Evid.); Jerry Gonzalez–Ft. Apache (Sunny.; Mile.); R. Hargrove (Verve); Hamiet Bluiett (Maple.); Freddy Cole (Fant.); H. Masekela (Verve); Geo. Mraz (Mile.); Chip Jackson (JazzKey).

WILSON, ANTHONY JAY, gtr, comp, arr; b. Los Angeles, CA, 5/9/68. Father is comp./arr. and bb lead. Gerald Wilson. Began gtr. lessons at age 7; self-taught fr. age 12. Stud. at Tanglewood Music Ctr.; B.A. in comp. fr. Bennington Coll. Pl. w. Gerald Wilson Orch. fr. 1984; Harold Land late '80s; Ed Schuller '90–2; pop singer Vanessa Paradis in Eur. '93–4; Al McKibbon '95. In late '90s working w. own qt. and nonet; Bennie Wallace; Dave Pike. Pl. Izzy Bar w. NYC version of nonet, incl. Wallace, '97. Won an award from the Thelonious Monk Inst. in '95 for his composition "Karaoke"; first CD, *Anthony Wilson,* won IAJE Gil Evans Fellowship Award '97. Gunther Schuller wrote: "Solid, intelligent, mainstream ensemble jazz, that looks both back to the heyday of the 1950s and forward to a spikier future." Favs: Wes Montgomery, Johnny Smith; arrs: Ellington, Gil Evans. Fests: Monterey '85–7; '90–7; Verona '86; North Sea '90. CDs: MAMA; w. G. Wilson (Disc.; MAMA).

WILSON, CASSANDRA, voc, gtr, lyricist, comp; b. Jackson, MS, 12/4/55. Father, Herman Fowlkes, was gtrst., bsst. Performed fr. the time she sang at her bro.'s kindergarten grad. when she was 5. Pno. lessons for seven yrs. fr. age 9. Pl. in hs marching band and had own gp. w. two gtrsts. Early infls. were Robert Johnson, Joni Mitchell. Perf. folks songs in coffeehouses in Miss. and Ark., accomp. herself on gtr. Stud. jazz w. Alvin Fielder and sang w. Black Arts Music Society in Jackson. Degree in mass communications fr. Jackson St. U. '81; worked in public affairs at TV station in NO. Sang w. alto saxist Earl Turbinton and became more interested in Ella Fitzgerald, Sarah Vaughan, and Betty Carter. Moved to NYC in early '80s, working w. Steve Coleman, the M-Base Collective, Henry Threadgill's New Air, and Bob Belden's Rhythm Club. Began rec. for the JMT label '85. Signed w. Blue Note '93 and, keeping her eclecticism intact, returned to her basic blues roots. Major role in Wynton Marsalis's *Blood on the Fields* '97. Wrote lyrics for her Miles Davis tribute *Traveling Miles* '99. David Browne described her as "treating pop songs without snobbery, unafraid to muddy the

perceptions of what a jazz singer should and shouldn't do." Other critics felt that a true jazz singer shouldn't, but Mike Joyce wrote of her ability "to get to the soul of a song that make comparisons moot." CDs: BN; JMT; w. Air (BS); Bob Belden; Javon Jackson (BN); Steve Coleman (Novus); Robin Eubanks (JMT).

WILSON, DENNIS EDWARD, tbn, comp; b. Greensboro, NC, 7/22/52. B. Mus. fr. Berklee Coll. 1974. Pl. w. Lionel Hampton '74–5. Lead tbn. w. Tommy Dorsey Orch '75. Toured w. Count Basie Orch. '77–87, after which he took on a new assignment as education projects dir. for Count Basie Enterprises. Lead tbn., actor, and arr. w. the mus. show *Satchmo* '87; lead tbn. w. Dizzy Gillespie '88; Frank Wess Orch. '90. Fav. own recs. w. Wess. Many clinics at universities and hs throughout US '86–92. Fest. duet w. Robert Trowers on Rev. Gensel tribute at JVC-NY '95. CDs: w. Basie; Ella Fitzgerald–Basie; Milt Jackson–Basie (Pab.); Benny Carter (MM); Wess (Conc.).

WILSON, DICK, tnr sax; b. Mt. Vernon, IL, 11/11/11; d. NYC, 11/24/41. Raised in Seattle; stud. alto sax w. Joe Darensbourg; sw. to tnr., pl. w. Don Anderson in Portland, Ore. 1929; later w. Darensbourg, Gene Coy '33–4; Zack Whyte '34–5; and Andy Kirk fr. '35 until his death. An individual tnr. stylist recalling Herschel Evans and Chu Berry, he was described by Mary Lou Williams as "very advanced." Feat. w. Kirk on "Bearcat Shuffle"; "Steppin' Pretty"; "Christopher Columbus"; "Lotta Sax Appeal"; "A Mellow Bit of Rhythm"; "Wednesday Night Hop"; "Froggy Bottom"; "Little Miss"; "Walkin' and Swingin." CDs: w. Kirk (Dec.; Class.); Mary Lou Williams (Class.).

WILSON, GARLAND LORENZO, pno; b. Martinsburg, WV, 6/13/09; d. Paris, France, 5/31/54. In 1932, after pl. for two yrs. in NYC clubs and rec. for Col. in 1931, he went to Eur. as accomp. for singer Nina Mae McKinney. Remaining on the Continent, he pl. at clubs in Paris, mainly at Boeuf sur le Toit; tour. Engl. w. Jack Payne's band '35–6; rec. in Paris as soloist and w. Jean Sablon, Danny Polo '39. Back in US '39–40, he rec. w. Cedric Wallace and accomp. Thelma Carpenter. Back to Eur., where he worked mainly in Paris and London from 1951 until his death. A powerful pianist infl. by Earl Hines. CDs: Class.

WILSON, GERALD STANLEY, comp, tpt, lead; b. Shelby, MS, 9/4/18. Studied pno. w. moth., later at hs in Memphis 1932–3. Moved to Det. '34, stud. at Cass

HS. Worked w. Plantation Club Orch., then tour. w. Chic Carter. Replaced Sy Oliver in Jimmie Lunceford band fr. late '39 to April '42. Settled in LA '42; pl. w. Les Hite; Benny Carter; Phil Moore; then in Willie Smith's band at Great Lakes Naval Training Station in Chi. Formed own band Dec. '44; pl. and arr. for Count Basie off and on '47–8; Dizzy Gillespie '48. After a brief period of mus. inactivity, he ret. to full-scale activity in LA and SF in late '50s. Organized a rehearsal band '57; app. w. band at The Flamingo in LV '61; LA clubs and MJF '63. From early '60s he intermittently led his own bbs, rec. for PJ w. such sidemen as Harold Land, Joe Pass, Oscar Brashear, Teddy Edwards, Carmell Jones, Ernie Watts, Snooky Young, and Bobby Bryant. He scored scenes for such films as *Where the Boys Are* '60; *Love Has Many Faces* '64. Won *DB* Critics Poll in bb category '63 and in comp. category '64. In '65 led bb for Al Hirt at Carnegie Hall. Arr. and comp. for Stan Kenton's Neo-phonic Orch.; E. Fitzgerald; D. Ellington; and the LA Philharm. Orch. under Zubin Mehta. Hosted daily radio show on KBCA (now KKGO), LA '68–73. Faculty member at Cal. State U. Northridge '70–83 and at Cal State, LA '80. In '88 he celebrated his 70th birthday by cond. the AJO in a NYC concert of his works. His best-known comp, "Viva Tirado," was rec. by El Chicano; Percy Faith; the Fifth Dimension; and others. Other comps, many infl. by Mexican themes, incl. "Josefina"; "Moment of Truth"; "Carlos"; "The Golden Sword"; and "Feelin' Kinda Blue." CDs: PJ; Disc.; Trend; MAMA; w. Ben Webster (Em.); Ernestine Anderson (Sav.); S. Vaughan (Roul.); Joe Pass (PJ); Basie (BB); Benny Carter; Sid Catlett (Class.); Buddy Collette; Curtis Counce (Cont.); D. Ellington (Col.).

WILSON, JACK JR., pno, comp; b. Chicago, IL, 8/3/36. Studied in Ft. Wayne, Ind.; first prof. gigs 1950. Pl. w. James Moody '53; then went to Indiana U '53–5; moved to Columbus, Ohio; had own gp.; also pl. w. Roland Kirk. With Dinah Washington '56–7; freelanced in Chi.; after mil. service, he ret. to gig w. Washington '61. Extensive freelance work in LA throughout the '60s. Pl. and/or rec. w., among others, Roy Ayers; Gerald Wilson; Harold Land; Shelly Manne; Jimmy Witherspoon; Clark Terry–Bob Brookmeyer qnt.; rec. w. Terry '80. Prod. mus. scores for such TV shows as *Peyton Place, Bob Hope Presents*, and *Repertoire Workshop*. Cont. to be active as pnst., mus. dir., and arr./comp. CDs: BN; w. Eddie Harris (Night); G. Wilson (PJ); D. Washington (Em.); C. Terry (Pab.).

WILSON, JOE LEE (JOSEPH), voc; b. Bristow, OK, 12/22/35. Sang in church as child; stud. jazz at

LA City Coll. Prof. debut 1958; moved to NYC '62. Worked w. Sonny Rollins; Freddie Hubbard; Lee Morgan; Miles Davis; Roy Haynes; Jackie McLean; Frank Foster; and Pharoah Sanders. Feat. on Archie Shepp album *Attica Blues* in early '70s; also rec. as leader. State Dept. tour w. own gp., Joy of Jazz; app. at NJF-NY and Live Loft Fests mid '70s. Settled in Engl. late '70s; toured Eur. and UK. Living in France since '80s. A strongly individual stylist w. elements of gospel and blues in his often arhythmic perfs. Rec. w. Charles Earland for Prest. '72. CDs: Drey.; Oblivion; w. Archie Shepp (Imp.); Billy Gault (Steep.).

WILSON, MATT (MATTHEW E.), dms; b. Knoxville, IL, 9/27/64. Jazz Studies Grant fr. NEA to study w. Ed Soph in Conn. 1984; B. Mus. fr. Wichita St. U., Kansas, '86. In Wichita pl. w. Steve Story band; Jerry Hahn '82–7; in Boston w. Either/Orchestra; Charlie Kolhase; Dominique Eade; Bevan Manson Trio; John Medeski; Mandala Oct. '87–92. Moved to NYC '92. Pl. w. Dewey Redman Qt., Cecil McBee band, Lee Konitz '94. Own qt. fr. '96; has also worked w. Fred Hersch; Dave Liebman; Thomas Chapin; Joanne Brackeen; Ted Rosenthal; Mario Pavone; Marty Ehrlich; Sam Newsome; Bill Mays; Sheila Jordan. Favs: Ed Blackwell, Billy Higgins, Shelly Manne, Elvin Jones, Roy Haynes. Fests: Umbria; JVC-Paris w. Redman '95; Colombia w. Jordan '98; Bell Atlantic w. qt. '99. Poll: Best New Artist, N.Y. Jazz Critics Circle '97. CDs: Palm.; w. Konitz; Vic Juris (Steep.); Redman; McBee; Joel Frahm (Palm.); Eade (Vict.); Alan Chase; Either/Orchestra; Kolhase (Acc.).

WILSON, NANCY SUE, voc; b. Chillicothe, OH, 2/20/37. Performed in club and on TV in Columbus, Ohio; tour. w. Rusty Bryant band 1956–8. Discovered in Columbus by Cannonball Adderley, who advised her to go to NYC. She made a succession of popular recs. for Cap. in the '60s, incl. sessions w. the Adderley and Geo. Shearing gps. Praised in her early yrs. for a timbre similar to that of Dinah Washington, she has occ. worked in jazz settings, incl. w. Hank Jones Trio in Japan; Oliver Nelson; Gerald Wilson; Jimmy Jones and the revived Jazztet '82. Occasional acting roles on TV; hosted her own Emmy-winning show on KNBC '74. Cont. to tour w. great commercial success into the '90s. CDs: Den.; Cap.; Col.; BN.

WILSON, PHIL (PHILLIPS ELDER JR.), tbn, educ, comp; b. Belmont, MA, 1/19/37. Studied at New Engl. Cons. and Navy Mus. Sch. In late 1950s pl. w. Herb Pomeroy and Jimmy Dorsey; fr. '60 to '62 pl. in North Amer. Air Defense Command Band. After three yrs. w. Woody Herman, he was appointed to Berklee Sch. as head of tbn. dept., also teaching theory and comp. Cont. to arr. for Buddy Rich, incl. "Mercy, Mercy, Mercy," and others. Numerous other activities as educ. and cond., incl. heading jazz division of Afro-Amer. Dept. of New Engl. Cons. Cond. Bost. Symph in his own work, *The Earth's Children*. Wilson was one of the first tbnsts. to make effective use of multi-phonics. CDs: Cat's Paw; w. Joe Pass (ACT); w. Herman (Jazz Hour; BB; Verve).

WILSON, SHADOW (ROSSIERE), dms; b. Yonkers, NY, 9/25/19; d. NYC, 7/11/59. Professional debut in 1938 w. Frankie Fairfax; soon after joined Lucky Millinder '39; Jimmy Mundy bb, Benny Carter '39–40; Tiny Bradshaw '40; Lionel Hampton '40–41; Earl Hines '41–3; Georgie Auld, Louis Jordan '44; Count Basie '44–6 and '48; Illinois Jacquet '46–7, '50, '53–4; Woody Herman '49; Erroll Garner Trio '51–2; Ella Fitzgerald '54–5; Thelonious Monk at Five Spot '57–8; then freelanced in NYC w. Lee Konitz; Joe Newman; Sonny Stitt; et al. Won New Star award from *Esq.* in '47 and was considered an expert both for bb and small gp. work. CDs: w. Erroll Garner (Col.); Esq. All-Amer. Poll Winners (BB); Illinois Jacquet (BB; Mos.); Louis Jordan (Dec.); Sir Charles Thompson (Del.); J. Coltrane (Rhino); Sonny Stitt; Stan Getz; Gil Melle; Tadd Dameron (Prest.); Lester Young (Sav.); Milt Jackson; J. J. Johnson; Fats Navarro (BN); G. Mulligan (Riv.); Monk (BN; Jzld.); Basie (Cir.).

WILSON, STEVE (STEVEN), alto, sop saxes, fl, cl; b. Hampton, VA, 2/9/61. Father sang in spiritual choir. Began on alto sax in jr. hs, later pl. oboe and fl. Became interested in jazz dur. last yrs. in hs, pursuing it further at Va. Commonwealth U., Richmond 1980–1, '82–5. Pl. w. local r&b and funk bands '73–9; Stephanie Mills '81–2. Worked as studio mus. and pl. w. fusion gp., Secrets, in Richmond '85; also occ. gigs w. Ellis Marsalis. Joined Out of the Blue (OTB) '86, then moved to NYC '87. Pl. w. OTB '86–9; tour. US and Eur. for a yr. w. Lionel Hampton '89–90; Ralph Peterson Jr., Michelle Rosewoman fr. '88; AJO '90–2; Buster Williams Qnt. '89; Renee Rosnes fr. '90; Smithsonian Jazz Orch. fr. '91; Jimmy Heath bb '95. Since '91 he has been an adjunct faculty member of William Paterson Coll. jazz program, N.J., and cont. to occ. lead a qnt. In the late '90s he worked w. Chick Corea's gp., Origin; Dave Holland Qnt.; Bruce Barth Qt.; his own gp.; and others. Favs: Wayne Shorter, Joe Henderson, Johnny Hodges. Polls: *DB* student award '83; *DB* TDWR '97. Fests: Eur., Asia fr. '86. TV: Japan. CDs: Stretch; CC; w. OTB (BN); R. Peterson (BN; Evid.); R. Rosnes; Bill Stewart (BN); Kevin Hays (Evid.); L. Bellson (Tel.);

K. Mahogany; Bruce Barth (Enja); James Williams (Evid.); DMP bb (DMP); Scott Wendholt; Don Braden; Billy Drummond; Dave Hazeltine (CC); Terell Stafford (Cand.).

WILSON, TEDDY (THEODORE SHAW), pno, comp; b. Austin, TX, 11/24/12; d. New Britain, CT, 7/31/86. Piano and four years of vln. study at Tuskegee U., Ala.; mus. theory major at Talladega Coll. First prof. dates in Det. 1929, incl. Speed Webb band; in '31 repl. Art Tatum in Milton Senior band in Toledo, Ohio. Went to Chi. w. Senior, working briefly w. Erskine Tate; Clarence Moore; Eddie Mallory. In early '33 he worked for two mos. w. Louis Armstrong's bb, then w. Jimmie Noone bef. joining Benny Carter in NYC. Gained int'l recognition after rec. w. Carter's Chocolate Dandies for Eur. market ("Once Upon a Time"; "Blue Interlude"; etc). Played and rec. w. Willie Bryant's band 1934–5. In July of '35 he rec. and subsequently tour. w. Benny Goodman, forming, w. Gene Krupa, the Goodman Trio and—when joined by Lionel Hampton—Quartet. Its integrated personnel was considered daring. Fr. '35 he made numerous recs. w. own star-studded gps., incl. voc. accomps. for Lena Horne; Ella Fitzgerald; Thelma Carpenter; and, most notably, Billie Holiday. On leaving Goodman in '39, Wilson led a bb for a yr., then a sxt. '40–4, often at both Café Society Downtown and Uptown, NYC. His ret. to Goodman in '44 was the first of many reunions, incl. '62 tour of USSR. He worked for CBS radio in '46 and for a while ran his own mus. sch. Staff mus. at WNEW Radio, NYC '49–52. Rec. a series of trio dates for Norman Granz '52–8, and app. as himself in *The Benny Goodman Story* '55. Wilson's distinct, elegant style evolved fr. a synthesis of Hines, Tatum, and Waller w. a neat, often understated symmetry in single-note lines and effective use of 10ths in the left hand. He was the most infl. young pnst. of the late '30s and early '40s, but his considerable talent as arr. was largely overlooked. Won the *Esq.* Gold Award '45 and '47; Silver Award '46; *DB* poll '36–8. CDs: Story.; Hep; BL; Timel.; B&B; Mos., Chiaro.; JA; w. B. Goodman (Col.; BB; MM); B. Holiday (Col.; Story.); L. Armstrong (BB; Col.); Benny Carter; T. Dorsey; Esq. All-Amer. Poll Winners; Met. All-Stars (BB); C. Hawkins (Merc.); L. Hampton (Tel.); Ben Webster (Verve; Story.); R. Norvo (Stash); L. Wiley (Aud.); Lester Young (Verve); Zoot Sims (LRC); Roy Eldridge (Col.).

WINCHESTER, LEM (LEMUEL DAVIS), vib; b. Philadelphia, PA, 3/19/28; d. Indianapolis, IN, 1/13/61. Studied saxes; took up vib. 1947. In the '50s he was member of Wilmington, Del., police force, pl.

local jobs as sideman. Featured at NJF '58, he subsequently made rec. debut on MGM, his gp. sharing LP *New Faces at Newport* w. Randy Weston's gp. Quit police force in '60 to devote full time to mus. Rec. w. Oliver Nelson; Johnny Hammond Smith; and under own name. Killed himself pl. Russian roulette while on tour. Keenly interested in jazz history, Winchester was considered one of the most promising young vib. artists of the Milt Jackson school. CDs: NJ; Prest.; w. Etta Jones; Jack McDuff; Johnny "Hammond" Smith (Prest.); Oliver Nelson (NJ).

WINDHURST, JOHNNY (JOHN HENRY), tpt; b. Bronx, NY, 11/5/26; d. Poughkeepsie, NY, 10/2/81. Self-taught. Sat in at Nick's in Greenwich Village at age 15. Prof. debut in 1944. Pl. w. Sidney Bechet at Savoy Café, Bost. '45. Worked in Bost., often at Storyville, w. own qt. and w. Ruby Braff. Pl. Town Hall concert w. Art Hodes, James P. Johnson, NYC '46. To LA where he pl. Gene Norman's Dixieland Jubilee w. Louis Armstrong; dates w. Nappy Lamare '47–8. Led own Riverboat Five in Columbus, Ohio, and Bost. In '52–3 he worked at Eddie Condon's for fourteen mos., then six mos. w. George Wettling '53; pl. w. J. Teagarden '54. Pl. for Huntington Hartford's prod. *Joyride*, Hollywood and Chi. '56. Own gps. in Columbus and Dayton, Ohio; concert tours on eastern coll. circuit; gigs in Fla. '57–9. Fr. Oct. '59 into early '60s pl. at Condon's again. In late '60s he moved to his mother's house in Poughkeepsie and fr. '70s worked at local club. He was supposed to app. at the Manassas JF in '81 but died of a heart attack bef. he could leave for Va. A superior swing-styled artist with a distinctively beautiful tone. Favs: Armstrong, Hackett, Gillespie. Rec. w. Teagarden for Decca. CDs: w. Condon (Story.); Barbara Lea (Prest.); Lee Wiley (Aud.).

WINDING, KAI CHRESTEN, tbn; b. Aarhus, Denmark, 5/18/22; d. Yonkers, NY, 5/7/83. With family to US in 1934; pl. acdn., then tbn. w. Shorty Allen, Sonny Dunham, Alvino Rey '40–1. After service in coast guard, joined Benny Goodman for three mos., then tour. w. Stan Kenton Feb. '46–Apr.'47. His sound became the model for Kenton's tbn. section. In '48 he worked w. Charlie Ventura's gp. and teamed w. singer Buddy Stewart in a small unit. Until '54 he doubled between jazz combos at Royal Roost, Bop City, etc., and radio and TV studio work, then united w. tbnst. J. J. Johnson for a highly successful qnt., Jay and Kai, whose considerable popularity in the mid '60s brought the relatively neglected instrument to the forefront of modern jazz. In the '60s he led a 4–tbn. sxt. '56–61; then his own spt. w. four tbns. Winding was reunited briefly w. Johnson in '58 for a

Eur. tour. From '62 he was mus. dir. of Playboy club in NYC. Wrote jingles and scores for industrial films. Briefly co-led all-star band w. Eddie Condon at Roosevelt Grill, NYC '69. To West Coast w. *Merv Griffin Show* studio band. Tour. Eur. and US w. Giants of Jazz (incl. Gillespie and Monk) '71–2. In 1977 he gave up studio work, moved to Spain, and concentrated on writing, also pl. at many Eur. fests. Formed new tbn. duo w. Curtis Fuller '79. In '82 he toured Japan w. J. J. Johnson. CDs: Jay and Kai, Imp.; Sav.; Beth.; Col.; Status; own gp. in *Trombone By Three* (Prest.); *Four Trombones*, Winding, Johnson, Bennie Green; Willie Dennis (Deb.); T. Dameron (FS); F. Navarro (Mile.); Miles Davis (Cap.); Getz (Prest.); W. Herman (Disc.); G. Wallington (Sav.).

WINESTONE, BENNY (BENJAMIN), tnr sax, cl, fl; b. Glasgow, Scotland, 12/20/06; d. Toronto, Ont., Canada, 6/10/74. In 1930 he worked in London w. Ted Heath, Sid Lipton. In Toronto w. Frank Bogart '41–2; briefly w. Jess Stacy band in US '45; Maynard Ferguson in Montreal, Can. '47–8. Own gp. w. Herbie Spanier in Toronto '51, various other jobs in Can. Film: *A Yank at Oxford* '38. Best known through his early recs. in Engl. w. Geo. Chisholm.

WINTERS, TINY, bs; b. London, England, 1/24/09. Prominent in 1930s w. bands of Roy Fox; Bert Ambrose; Lew Stone; Ray Noble; and on recs. w. Coleman Hawkins. Resident mus. at Hatchett's club in London 1948–55. In '60s he spent three yrs. w. George Chisholm's band. After brief retirement in '70s he ret. to work w. Digby Fairweather but retired again in the '90s. Active on radio and as annotator for disc notes. Winters was one of Britain's most important jazz bassists. CDs: w. Coleman Hawkins (ASV); Benny Waters (Jazz.).

WISE, BUDDY (ROBERT RAYMOND), tnr sax; b. Topeka, KS, 2/20/28; d. Las Vegas, NV, 7/15/55. Professional debut 1943. Pl w. Hal Wasson, Mal Hallett to '45, then five yrs. w. Gene Krupa; nine mos. w. Woody Herman; eighteen mos. w. Ray Anthony. Recs. w. Krupa, incl. "Lemon Drop"; "These Foolish Things"; "Disc Jockey Jump." Fav. own solos on Fats Waller tunes rec. by Krupa for Vict. Although he named Al Cohn and Zoot Sims as favs., he was also infl. by Wardell Gray. CDs: w. Virgil Gonsalves (Noct.); Krupa (Hep).

WISE, FRITZ LARON, dms, perc; b. Houston, TX, 8/18/54. Grandfather, from La., played delta blues gtr. and pno. Stud. in LA; in 1973, shortly after graduation, he joined Gerald Wilson Orch. and for five yrs. doubled between Wilson and the Harold Land–Blue

Mitchell Qnt. In the '70s he also pl. w. Kenny Burrell; Ernie Andrews; Bobby Bryant; Johnny "Hammond" Smith; Hampton Hawes; and singer Leon Thomas. Worked w. Horace Tapscott gps. off and on fr. '87; Buell Neidlinger's gp., Thelonious; Ernestine Anderson '89; Larry Gales Qt. '90–92. Favs.: Elvin Jones, Freddie Waits, Philly Jo Jones.

WITHERSPOON, JIMMY (JAMES), voc; b. Gurdon, AR, 8/8/23; d. Los Angeles, 9/18/97. No musical training but sang in Baptist church choir at 7. While w. merchant marine in the Pacific 1941–3, he sang blues in Calcutta w. Teddy Weatherford band. Replaced Walter Brown w. Jay McShann Orch. in Vallejo, Calif., touring w. McShann '44–8. As solo artist, he had big hit w. "'Tain't Nobody's Business" on Supreme Records in '47; other hits followed, incl. "Big Fine Girl" and "No Rollin' Blues." Worked sporadically dur. '50s; made a strong comeback at MJF in Oct. '59. From then on he made numerous albums and firmly established himself as an artist in the tradition of Big Joe Turner and Jimmy Rushing. Eur. tour '61; own radio series '72. TV: *Midnight Special* '74; film: *Black Godfather* '75. Overcoming serious health problems in the '70s, he cont. into the '90s to make int'l tours fr. his base in LA. CDs: Spec.; Prest.; BL; Chess; Fant.; w. Buddy Tate; Jay McShann (Class.).

WOFFORD, MIKE (MICHAEL RILEY), pno, comp; b. San Antonio, TX, 2/25/38. Mother a singer in So. Calif. Stud. pno., tbn. at age 7; priv. pno lessons in San Diego, Calif. At age 18 won competition for young comp.; cond. San Diego Symph. feat. his own songs. Active fr. late 1950s in LA area, w. Shorty Rogers All-Stars at Lighthouse in Hermosa Beach; Shelly Manne off and on fr. '66–78; accomp. Sarah Vaughan; June Christy; Ruth Price. Gigs in LA or San Diego w. Kenny Burrell; Benny Carter; Stan Getz; Zoot Sims; Holly Hofmann; Joe Pass; accomp. Ella Fitzgerald fr. '89. Many jazz fests fr. early '70s at MJF; Carnegie Hall; Berlin; Otter Crest; etc. A diverse and imaginative perf. TV: PBS *Club Dates* w. Art Farmer, Harry Edison. CDs: Disc.; Conc.; w. Bud Shank (Conc.); Mundell Lowe (JA); J. Pass (PJ); Madeline Eastman (Mad-Kat); P. Christlieb (Capri); E. Fitzgerald; S. Vaughan (Pab.); Shelly Manne (Cont.).

WOLFE, BEN (BENJAMIN JONAH), bs, comp; b. Baltimore, MD, 8/3/62. Father pl. vln. w. San Antonio Symph. 1965–6. Grew up in Portland, Ore., where he began to pl. mus., first on tba., bs-tbn. Studied bs. fr. age 20 w. Larry Zgone; Ray Brown; Homer Mensch; Orin O'Brien. Freelanced in Portland area w. Bud Shank, Bobby Shew, Woody Shaw

'84; moved to NYC and gigged w. Junior Cook; Duke Jordan; Ted Curson; Charles Davis; Eddie Henderson; Benny Powell. Worked w. Woody Herman '86; Dakota Staton, Jimmy Scott '87; Mel Lewis orch. '88; Harry Connick '88–93; also led own trio at Village Gate fr. '89; at Smalls in mid '90s. In Jan. '94 he join. Wynton Marsalis; pl. w. LCJO '95; Eric Reed trio '96. Favs: P. Chambers, Oscar Pettiford, Ray Brown, J. Blanton; com.: Strayhorn, Mingus. Fests: int'l w. Connick; Marsalis; Reed. Film soundtracks w. Connick. Rec. debut on Danish label w. Lars Møller, feat. Jimmy Cobb '88. CDs: Mons; w. Connick; B. Marsalis (Col.); Carl Allen; Wess Anderson (Atl.); Manh. Projects (Evid.); Mary Stallings (Conc.); James Moody; Kevin Mahogany (WB).

WOLFF, MICHAEL BLIEDEN, pno, kybds; b. Victorville, CA, 7/31/52. Father, a doctor, pl. as amateur w. Brew Moore. Stud. UCLA, UC-Berkeley, and Manh. Sch. of Mus. in 1970s. Pl. w. Cal Tjader '72–4; Airto Moreira and Flora Purim '74–5; Cannonball Adderley '75; Jean-Luc Ponty '76, Thad Jones–Mel Lewis '76; Sonny Rollins '76–78; Ray Barretto and Joe Farrell '77. In '89 he formed The Posse, which in '90 became the house band on the Arsenio Hall TV show. Taught music priv. in NYC for ten yrs. LP w. C. Adderley (Fant.). CDs: Col.; w. Dave Samuels (Verve).

WOOD, BOOTY (MITCHELL JR.), tbn; b. Weedowee, AL, 12/27/19; d. Dayton, OH, 6/10/87. Attended public schls. in Dayton, stud. w. Clarence François at Dunbar High. Entered music prof. through Snooky Young, first locally, then in Chick Carter's Dixie Rhythm Boys 1938–9. Pl. w. Jimmy Raschel '40–1; Tiny Bradshaw 42–3; Lionel Hampton between '43–7, excepting navy band under Willie Smith at Great Lakes Naval Training Station '44–5; Arnett Cobb '47–8; Erskine Hawkins '48–9. After a yr. back w. Cobb, Hawkins again to early '51, and six mos. w. Count Basie, he ret. to Dayton and worked as a postman '51–9; also led his own local gp. fr. '54. Joined Duke Ellington Sept. '59, pl. w. him to '60 and, again, in '63 and the early '70s. Tour. w. Earl Hines '68; pl. w. Mercer Ellington '70s; Basie '79–mid '80s. In the mid and late '60s he att. Central St. U. and taught jazz studies at Dunbar HS. Ret. to Dayton after retiring fr. the bbs in Jan. '84. At the time of his death teaching jazz studies at Central St. and making preparations to perf. at the Edinburgh JF in Scotland. While w. Ellington, Wood proved quite adept in the role of plunger specialist. Favs: Fred Beckett, Trummy Young. Own LP for Engl. Col. '60. CDs: w. Ellington (Col.; Pab.; Fant.; Saja); Basie

(Pab.); Cat Anderson (B&B); L. Hampton (Dec.); Willis Jackson (Del.).

WOOD, ELISE APRIL, fl, alto-fl, picc; b. Philadelphia, PA, 7/6/52. Mother is pnst. Began on pno. and gtr. Grad. fr. U. of Mass. Studied w. Charles Majeed Greenlee; Frank Wess; Barry Harris; arr. w. Frank Foster; Don Sebesky. First prof. gigs w. dance cos., incl. Rod Rodgers; Morse Donaldson; Negro Ens. Co. Co-led gp. Safari East w. Vishnu Wood 1971–90. Pl. w. Archie Shepp '73; Clifford Jordan '80; Roland Hanna '87–9. Worked mainly w. John Hicks in a variety of settings fr. '82. Wood taught at Hampshire Coll. '75–7. She received an NEA study grant '80, perf. grant '84. Favs: James Moody, Frank Wess, Yusef Lateef, Eric Dolphy, Miles Davis. Fests: Guadaloupe '78, '80, '82; Brazil '84; Japan '85, '90–2; Canada '89–91; Eur. '91. TV: Brazil, Eur. TV. CDs: w. J. Hicks (Evid.).

WOOD, VISHNU (WILLIAM CLIFFORD), bs, oud; b. North Wilkesboro, NC, 11/7/37. Father pl. reeds; bro. Max pl. bs. Family moved to Det. in late '40s. Pl. tpt. and perc. in hs, then sw. to bs. Studied w. members of Det. Symph., then at Det. Inst. of Musical Arts-U. of Det. '59–61. Later studied at U. of Mass. '76–8. Pl. w. harpist Dorothy Ashby on and off '57–61; Yusef Lateef, Joe Henderson late '58–61. Moved to NYC '61. Pl. w. Kenny Dorham at Jazz Gallery '61; Randy Weston fr. '62; Decomier Singers mid '60s; Horacee Arnold–Sam Rivers in NYC publ. schs. '65. Toured Africa w. Weston '66–7. Moved to Rabat, Morocco, at invitation of Moroccan govt. '68. Perf. w. Weston, Ed Blackwell in Africa '68–9. Ret. to NYC '70. Pl. bs. and oud w. Here and Now Co., Pharoah Sanders–Leon Thomas, Alice Coltrane '70. Tour. Japan w. Drum Wkshp. late '70. Pl. bs. and oud w. dance-mus. gp., Impulses, in NYC '71. Artist-in-residence at Lafayette Theater, Harlem '71. Freelanced w. Thelonious Monk; Dizzy Gillespie; Max Roach; Elvin Jones; Roy Haynes; Jack DeJohnette; Archie Shepp; Barry Harris; Slide Hampton; Art Farmer; Clifford Jordan; etc. Wood has extensive experience in the educ. field. He was dir. of mus., Stockbridge Sch., Stockbridge, Mass. '73–5; artist-in-res., U. of Mass. '75–7, '81–4; profess. of mus., Hampshire Coll. '76–80; lecturer, Rutgers U. '80–1; lecturer, Vassar Coll. '84. Wood's own educ. org., Safari East Cultural Presentations, Inc., has presented progs. of mus. in NYC, Chi., and London publ. schs. since '84. Favs: Paul Chambers, Charles Mingus. Fests: Africa, Asia, Carib., etc. fr. mid '60s. CDs: w. A. Coltrane (Imp.); R. Weston (Verve; BL).

WOODARD, RICKEY, saxes, fl, cl; b. Nashville, TN, 8/5/50. Started briefly on cl., then pl. sax in fam-ily band w. sister, two bros., concentrating mainly on r&b until Gene Ammons inspired him to concentrate on jazz. Majored in mus. at Tenn. State U. Stud. sax in LA w. Bill Green; joined Ray Charles; then freelanced extensively in LA area w. Clayton-Hamilton band; Capp-Pierce Juggernaut; Jimmy and Jeannie Cheatham; also worked w. Jimmy Smith; Ernestine Anderson; and led own qt. Many jazz parties and fests., incl. Concord; MJF; North Sea; and all leading clubs in LA area. Favs incl. Coleman Hawkins, Ben Webster, Hank Mobley. An inspired, charging soloist, he favors tnr. but doubles on alto. CDs: Cand.; FS; Conc.; w. Clayton-Hamilton (Capri); J. and J. Cheatham; F. Capp; Nnenna Freelon; Mary Stallings (Conc.); John Leitham (USA); Horace Silver (Col.); Jimmy Smith (Mile.).

WOODE, JIMMY (JAMES BRYANT), bs, comp, pno; b. Philadelphia, PA, 9/23/28; d. Lindenwold, NJ, 4/23/05. Father, a mus. teacher, pl. bari. horn w. dixieland bands. Studied pno. at Phila. Acad. of Mus. Stud. w. Clarence Cox; later at Bost. U., Bost. Cons., and under bs. Paul Gregory in Calif. Sang w. navy band 1945. Pl. pno. and sang w. voc. gp., the Velvetaires; formed own trio '46. Toured w. Flip Phillips '49; Sarah Vaughan, Ella Fitzgerald '50. Pl. w. Nat Pierce off and on '51–2. House bs. at Storyville, Bost. '53–5; then pl. w. Duke Ellington '55–9. Also rec. as lead. '57; w. Johnny Hodges '55–8; w. Clark Terry '56–9. Moved to Stockholm, '60. Pl. w. radio and TV bands and club dates w. top Swedish jazz mus. Became well known as TV vocalist and sideman on Swedish recs. Rec. w. Eric Dolphy '61. Moved to Cologne, Germ. '64 to manage own publishing co. Pl. w. Cologne-based Kenny Clarke–Francy Boland band '64–73. Rec. w. Don Byas; Albert Nicholas '63; Johnny Griffin '64–8; Sahib Shihab '64–8; Ted Curson–Booker Ervin '66; Milt Buckner '66–9; Benny Bailey '68; Mal Waldron '68–77; Helen Humes '74. Lived in Netherlands mid '60s, then moved to Munich early '70s. Moved to Vienna early '80s; Switzerland in '90s. Pl. occasionally w. Nathan Davis's Paris Reunion Band. Favs: Jimmy Blanton, Oscar Pettiford, Ray Brown, George Duvivier, Paul Chambers, Richard Davis. Fests: all major in Eur. TV: many Eur. apps. CDs: w. D. Ellington (Pab.; Col.; Roul.; Beth.; Saja; Em.); C. Hawkins (Stash); J. McShann (MM); C. Parker (BN; Up.); S. Chaloff (BL; Mos.); Clarke-Boland (MPS); Bechet (BL; Laser.); Tony Coe (Hot.); Dusko Goykovich; Nathan Davis (DIW); Dolphy (Enja); Hampton Hawes; B. Holiday (BL); Ernie Wilkins (Bird.); Doc Cheatham; Sweets Edison (Orange Blue); Clark Terry (Riv.).

WOODING, SAM (SAMUEL DAVID), pno, comp; b. Philadelphia, PA, 6/17/1895; d. NYC,

8/1/85. Made prof. debut in NYC clubs in 1912; after army service in WWI, he worked as a pnst. in Atlantic City, N.J. Moved to NYC and formed band that pl. at Smalls Paradise where it was heard by a Russian impresario, Leonidoff, who hired it for a hastily assembled, all-black revue, *Chocolate Kiddies*, which opened in Berlin, Germ. 1925. Wooding's arrs.—which incorporated what he called "symphonic syntheses" of Eur. classical mus.—were a great success, leading to further engagements in Russia and So. Amer. Pl. and rec. in Barcelona, Spain '29; Copenhagen in early '30s; then disbanded, but organized another gp. in NYC area '35. By that time many bbs had come to prominence, so Wooding—who had been on the cutting edge ten yrs. earlier—never regained his popularity. From '37 to '41 he led the Southland Spiritual Choir. In the '50s he taught mus. in Wilmington, Del., where students incl. Clifford Brown, and later teamed up w. voc. Rae Harrison for apps. in Iceland and Eur. (they were married in the '80s). In the '70s Wooding formed a new bb with which he rec. an album and pl. a concert in Switzerland. Though he remained relatively unknown at home, Wooding was a key figure in spreading the popularity of jazz in Eur. dur. the period between world wars. Rec. "Shanghai Shuffle" (for which he wrote the arr.) Vox '25; other recs. for Parlophone; Pathé '29.

WOODMAN, BRITT BINGHAM, tbn; b. Los Angeles, CA, 6/4/20; d. Hawthorne, CA, 10/13/00. Musical family. Pl. pno., tbn., tnr. sax, and cl. w. his bros. in a family band 1937–9. Worked w. Phil Moore '38; Les Hite '39–42. Army service '42–6; w. Boyd Raeburn '46; then w. Eddie Heywood and Lionel Hampton '46–7. Stud. at Westlake Coll. in LA '48–50. Replaced Lawrence Brown in Duke Ellington orch. '51, remaining until '60; w. Charles Mingus '61, '66; Quincy Jones, Johnny Richards, and Chico Hamilton '63; Benny Goodman sxt. '67. Also pl. for several B'way shows in '60s and worked occ. w. Oliver Nelson; Ernie Wilkins; and Lionel Hampton. Ret. to Calif. '70; pl. w. Bill Berry; Akiyoshi-Tabackin; Capp-Pierce; Nelson Riddle; tour. Japan w. Benny Carter '77–8. Back to NYC in '80s; pl w. NYJRC and did studio work. Feat. w. Ellington on "Theme for Trambean"; "Sonnet to Hank V"; "Red Garter." A highly inventive mus., comfortable in a variety of musical styles. CDs: w. C. Mingus (Col.; Deb.; Cand.; Imp.; Rh.; BN); D. Ellington (Em.; Roul.; Beth.; Saja; Laser.; Mos.; Red Brn.); T-Bone Walker (Mos.); D. Gillespie (Verve); E. Fitzgerald (Rep.); J. Coltrane (Imp.); Mingus bb (Drey.); J. Hodges (Imp.); AJO–Benny Carter (Pab.; MM); S. Turre (Ant.); DMP bb (DMP); T. Akiyoshi

(Novus); Bill Berry; Frank Capp (Conc.); Miles Davis (Deb.); C. Terry (Chiaro.); B. Raeburn (Sav.).

WOODS, CHRIS (CHRISTOPHER COLUMBUS), alto sax, woodwinds, comp; b. Memphis, TN, 12/25/25; d. Brooklyn, NY, 7/4/85. Early idol was cousin Bob Mabane, who pl. tnr. sax w. J. McShann in swing era. Studied. alto and cl. priv. in St. Louis dur. 1930s and '40s; theory and harmony at Mus. and Arts U. '48–51. Played w. Tommy Dean, Jeter-Pillars, and George Hudson in St. Louis '48–51; Ernie Fields '51; own gp. '52–62. Moved to NYC, worked w. Dizzy Gillespie; Clark Terry; Howard McGhee; Sy Oliver; Buddy Rich; et al. Eur. tours as sideman and soloist '73–4. Jazz fest app. at NJF; Pori; Nancy; San Sebastian. Authorship of "Blues Walk" (aka "Loose Walk") was claimed by Woods who rec. it as "Somebody Done Stole My Blues" on a Del. LP of the same title. LPs w. C. Basie; Clark Terry; D. Gillespie; Ernie Wilkins; Sy Oliver; and others. CDs: Del.; w. Carla Bley (ECM).

WOODS, PHIL (PHILIP WELLS), alto sax, cl, comp; b. Springfield, MA, 11/2/31. Inherited alto sax fr. uncle; began pl. at age 12. Stud. w. Harvey LaRose in Springfield, then moved to NYC 1948. Studied w. Lennie Tristano, also one semester at Manh. Sch. of Mus. '48; studied cl. w. Jimmy Abate at Juilliard Sch. of Mus. '48–52 (B. Mus. '52). First prof. job w. Westover Air Force Band. Pl. w. Richard Hayman, Charlie Barnet '52; Jimmy Raney '55; Geo. Wallington, Friedrich Gulda, Dizzy Gillespie, Kenny Dorham '56; co-led Phil & Quill w. Gene Quill '57; Buddy Rich '58–9; Quincy Jones '59–61, incl. many trips to Eur. Freelanced in '50s-60s w. Geo. Russell; Neal Hefti; Jackie Cain–Roy Kral; Joe Newman; Manny Albam; Al Cohn–Zoot Sims; Oliver Nelson; Thelonious Monk; many others; also worked extens. as studio mus. Rec. extended comp. *Rights of Swing*, premiered comps. for sax qt. at Town Hall '60. Toured Russia w. Benny Goodman Orch. '62. Headed jazz dept. of Ramblerny arts camp '66–7. In Paris led gp. Eur. Rhythm Machine w. Geo. Gruntz, Henri Texier, Daniel Humair '68–73. In LA for ten mos. '73, pl. in electronic qt. w. Pete Robinson. Moved to Pa. '74. Founding member of Clark Terry bb, pl. concerts w. Michel Legrand '70s; also on film soundtracks of *The Hustler, Blow-Up*. Led own qt. '74–83, when it was expanded to qnt.; also a larger ens., the Little Big Band; all have incl. Steve Gilmore, bs.; Bill Goodwin, dms. Tour. w. own bb '99. Woods is devoted to playing acoustically and exhibits a corresponding fidelity to the music, burning with a passion that has always been a hallmark of his style. His gps. won Grammys in '77, '82–3. In '89 he was named Officer of the Order of Arts and Letters by the French govt. He serves on the boards of the Del. Water Gap Celebration of the Arts and the Al Cohn Memorial Jazz Collection at East Stroudsburg U. Author of a saxophone method (Creative Jazz Composers Publ.); CD-Rom: *Jazz Tutor* (Master-Class Prods); and continues to teach priv. and cond. master classes. Favs: Charlie Parker, Johnny Hodges, Benny Carter. Fests: all major and numerous jazz cruises. Polls: *DB* New Star '56; TDWR cl. '62; Critics alto '75–90; Critics gp. '88–91; Readers alto '75–91; Readers gp. '85, '88–9, '91; *Play.* '72; NAJE poll '87; *JT* Critics, Readers '90–1. CDs: Den.; BN; Imp.; Muse; MM; Evid.; Mos.; TCB; Conc.; Chesky; Prest.; Mile.; FS; Phil.; w. Benny Carter (Conc.; Imp.; MM); D. Gillespie (CAP; Verve); Q. Jones (Merc.; Qwest); T. Monk (Riv.); O. Nelson (Imp.); S. Turrentine; Lee Morgan (BN); S. Rollins (Imp.); Gil Evans; Jimmy Smith (Verve); Richie Cole (32); Benny Bailey (Cand.); B. Goodman (MM); G. Mulligan (GRP); C. Terry; Jon Gordon (Chiaro.); G. Wallington (Sav.; Prest.); Joe Williams (BB); Al Cohn–Zoot Sims (BN); Carol Sloane (Conc.).

WOODYARD, SAM (SAMUEL), dms; b. Elizabeth, NJ, 1/7/25; d. Paris, France, 9/20/88. Self-taught; sat in w. local gps in and around Newark, N.J. Joined Paul Gayten r&b band 1950–1; Joe Holiday '51; Roy Eldridge '52; Milt Buckner '53–5. Joined Duke Ellington in July '55 and remained, w. periodic absences, through Nov. '66; also w. Mercer Ellington Orch. at Birdland while Duke was in Eur. summer of '59. Accomp. Ella Fitzgerald; moved to LA and was only periodically active due to ill health, sometimes pl. dms. or congas w. Bill Berry; D. Ellington; Buddy Rich. Tour. Eur. fr. late '70s, often w. Claude Bolling. Though Duke Ellington praised him highly, opinions varied; Whitney Balliett wrote that he "handles every number as if he were breaking rocks." He spent his last yrs. freelancing in Eur. CDs: w. D. Ellington (BB; Saja; Atl.; Em.; Pab.; MM; Roul.; Beth.; Vict.; Red Brn.); J. Coltrane; J. Coltrane–D. Ellington (Imp.); E. Fitzgerald–D. Ellington (Verve); Cat Anderson–Sir Charles Thompson; (B&B); J. Hodges (Story.; Pab.); Steve Lacy (Novus); B. Strayhorn (Red Brn.); C. Terry (Riv.); B. Rich (LRC).

WOOTTEN, RED (LAWRENCE B.), bs, gtr; b. Social Circle, GA, 11/05/21. Parents both musical; grandfath. a choir dir. Prof. debut w. Gene Austin 1940. In '40s pl. bs. w. Jan Savitt; Randy Brooks; Tony Pastor; Tommy Dorsey; in '50s w. Woody Herman; Charlie Barnet; Red Norvo. Toured Eur. w. Benny Goodman dectet '59. Studio work in '60s and '70s; many c&w recs.; rec. w. Anita O'Day mid '70s.

Won three West Coast awards from Academy of Country Mus. '67, '68, 82. Films: w. Norvo, *Screaming Mimi; Kings Go Forth*. Favs: Jimmy Blanton, Bob Haggart, Eddie Safranski, Don Costa, and Nelson Riddle. CDs: w. Goodman (MM); Norvo (Ref.; RCA).

WORKMAN, REGGIE (REGINALD DAVID), bs, perc; b. Philadelphia, PA, 6/26/37. Began on pno., then sw. to bs., euph., and tba. in hs. Pl. w. local r&b bands fr. 1955. First jazz gig w. Gigi Gryce '58. Pl. w. Freddy Cole '58; Red Garland '59; Roy Haynes '59; John Coltrane '60; James Moody '62; Art Blakey '63–4, incl. Eur., Japan tours; Albert Heath '64; Yusef Lateef '65; Herbie Mann '66; Thelonious Monk '67; Alice Coltrane late '60s. Also worked in '60s w. Freddie Hubbard; Archie Shepp; Lee Morgan; Cedar Walton; Jackie McLean; Gary Bartz; Wayne Shorter; and others. State Dept. tour to Brazil w. Music Inc. '72. Pl. in Italy w. Max Roach '73–4; Charles Tolliver, Billy Harper, Shepp, Art Farmer, others '70s; David Murray, Mal Waldron, Elvin Jones, others '80s; Marilyn Crispell fr. '88; Oliver Lake fr. '91. Workman has been heavily involved in jazz educ. since the late '60s: Perf. and lectured for Young Audiences, Inc., and coordinated mus. prog. at Samuel Tilden Commun. Ctr. '67–70; created mus. prog. at Central Bklyn. Summer and Winter Acad. '70; artist-in-res. at Wilmington Sch. of Mus. '71–2; dir. mus. curriculum for N.J. Bd. of Educ. '72; assoc. prof. at U. of Mass.-Amherst '73–4; dir. of mus. dept. at New Muse Community Museum '75–81; assoc. prof. at LIU, Bklyn. '85–8. Served as Dir. of Artist Relations for Nippon Col. '77–81. Taught at the New Sch., NYC fr. '87 and has been prog. dir. for the jazz dept. fr. '89. Received numerous honors, incl. El Hajj Malik Shabazz Award '75; Eubie Blake Award '78; IAJE Award '91. Co-prod. tributes to Coltrane and Charlie Parker at Bklyn. Acad. of Mus., '90–1. Active as lecturer, clinician, and consultant. Leads the Reggie Workman Ens. w. Marilyn Crispell, Don Byron, Gerry Hemingway, Jeanne Lee, Oliver Lake, Andrew Cyrille, Michele Navazio. Favs: Oscar Pettiford, Ray Brown, Paul Chambers, Jymie Merritt, Eddie Gomez, Cecil McBee. Fests: all major fr. '60. TV: many apps. as panelist and perf. CDs: Post.; M&A; Leo; w. A. Cyrille (DIW); C. Rouse (Col.); M. Crispell (M&A; Leo); O. Lake (Gram.); Coltrane (Atl.; Imp.); M. Waldron–S. Lacy (Evid.); Freddie Hubbard; Lee Morgan; Wayne Shorter (BN); A. Blakey (BN; Riv.); Shepp (Den.); D. Byron (None.); B. Ervin (Prest.); D. Murray (BS).

WORLD SAXOPHONE QUARTET. Founded in 1976, its orig. members were David Murray, tnr. sax.;

Oliver Lake and Julius Hemphill, altos; and Hamiet Bluiett, bari., doubling on other saxes and fl. Gp. has toured regularly in Eur. since '78, drawing on the avant-garde as well as more traditional sources to build a unique and challenging repertoire. Albums incl. *WSO Plays Duke Ellington* '86; *Rhythm and Blues* '89; *Metamorphosis* '91. In '91 Hemphill was replaced by Arthur Blythe, who later was succeeded by John Purcell. CDs: JT; BS; None.

WORLD'S GREATEST JAZZ BAND. An outgrowth of a band formed in the late 1960s by Colo.-based impresario Dick Gibson, this gp. was co-led by tptr. Yank Lawson and bs./arr. Bob Haggart. Members incl. Billy Butterfield, tpt.; Bob Wilber, Bud Freeman, saxes; Lou McGarity, Carl Fontana, Benny Morton, Vic Dickenson, tbn.; Morey Feld, Gus Johnson, dms. WGJB built an interesting repertoire comprising standards and jazz arrs. of current pop songs. Guests app. w. the band incl. Bobby Hackett, Eddie Miller, and singer Maxine Sullivan. As demand for the band waned, its size diminished, and the original ens. was virtually defunct by '78. CDs: Atl.

WRIGHT, GENE (EUGENE JOSEPH; "SENATOR"), bs.; b. Chicago, IL, 5/29/23. Mainly self-taught until 1952 when he stud. w. priv. teachers. Led Dukes of Swing in Chi. 1943–6; pl. w. Gene Ammons '46–8; Count Basie '48–9; Ammons '49–51; Arnett Cobb '51–2; Buddy De Franco '52–5, incl. Eur. tour. Best known for int'l tours w. Dave Brubeck Qt. '58–68. Own gp. in concerts at black colls. '69–70; w. Monty Alexander Trio '70–4; then moved to Calif., where he freelanced extensively w. Karen Hernandez; Gene Harris; Jack Sheldon; Erroll Garner. Occasional reunions w. Brubeck incl. State dinner for Ronald Reagan and M. Gorbachev in Moscow '88. Tour. w. Herbie Mann in Eur. '90. Infl. by Walter Page. Named an honorary senator by the US State Dept. in '58. Fests: many w. Brubeck, incl. NJF-NY '85. CDs: w. D. Brubeck (Col.; LRC); Paul Desmond (BB); Hadda Brooks (Pointblank); L. Armstrong (Col.); Dorothy Ashby; Sonny Stitt (Prest.); Buddy Collette (Cont.); Cal Tjader (Fant.).

WRIGHT, HERMAN AUSTIN, bs; b. Detroit, MI, 6/20/32; d. NYC, 6/25/97. Started on dms. at Greusel Intermediate Sch.; bs. at Cass Tech HS. Pl. in Det. w. Yusef Lateef, Terry Pollard. To NYC '60, pl. w. Terry Gibbs; Lateef; Rollins; Basie; Shearing; and Archie Shepp. Failing health stopped him fr. trav. but in '92 he became a regular at the Monday night jam session held by the Jazz Foundation of America at Local 802's Club Room. CDs: w. Lateef (Riv.; NJ); Shepp (Timel.).

WRIGHT, LAMMAR SR., tpt; b. Texarkana, TX, 6/20/07; d. NYC, 4/13/73. Studied in KC; w. Bennie Moten 1923–8; Missourians (later led by Cab Calloway) '27–42. Ret. to him occ., but also pl. w. Don Redman '43; Claude Hopkins '44–6; Cootie Williams '44; Lucky Millinder off and on '46–52; Sy Oliver; Louis Armstrong; and own band. In 1950s he was active as teacher and studio mus., also rec. w. Arnett Cobb; C. Basie, Sauter-Finegan; Geo. Shearing's bb in '59. Father of Lammar Jr. and Elmon, both trumpeters who played with Dizzy Gillespie's big bands. CDs: w. B. Moten (BB); L. Hampton (Dec.); D. Gillespie (Vict.).

WRIGHT, LEO NASH, alto sax, fl, cl; b. Wichita Falls, TX, 12/14/33; d. Vienna, Austria, 1/4/91. Father pl. alto sax w. Boots and His Buddies. Stud. w. father in Calif. dur. WWII. Ret. to Tex. to complete hs and study w. John Hardee. Att. Huston-Tillitson Coll. and SF St.; then pl. w. Saunders King in SF. To NYC, where he pl. w. Charles Mingus; joined Dizzy Gillespie Aug. 1959 and pl. w. him through '62; then w. Kenny Burrell; Gloria Coleman; and briefly w. own qnt. In '62–3 he rec. w. Lalo Schifrin; Jack McDuff; Jimmy Witherspoon; Johnny Coles; Antonio Carlos Jobim; Bob Brookmeyer. To Eur. in late '63, freelancing mainly in Scand. '63–4; then pl. at the Blue Note in Berlin, Germ., and settled there. Became member of the house band at Dug's and Radio Free Berlin Studio Band for over a decade. Rec. w. Geo. Gruntz '65; Lee Konitz '68. Moved to Austr. Pl. and rec. w. Red Garland at Keystone Korner, SF '78. App. in Paris Reunion Band '86. Early favs: Hodges, Carter, Willie Smith, Jimmy Dorsey; then Charlie Parker. He combined the Hodges tonality and the Parker lines w. an inherent blues feeling. Fests: MJF; NJF; Antibes w. Gillespie; also Germ.; Switzerland; Finland. CDs: w. Richard Williams (Cand.); D. Gillespie (Philips; Steep.; Omega; Verve); Tadd Dameron (Riv.); Johnny Coles (BN); J. McDuff (Prest.); Red Garland (32).

WRIGHT, SPECS (CHARLES), dms; b. Philadelphia, PA, 9/8/27; d. Philadelphia, 2/6/63. Army band 1946–7; six mos. w. Howard McGhee, incl. '48 trip to France. Dizzy Gillespie band and combo '49–51; Earl Bostic '52–3; Kenny Drew '53; freelanced in Phila., tour. w. Cannonball Adderley '55–6. Accomp. Carmen McRae '57–8; Sonny Rollins '58; various bebop gps. at Birdland, NYC; pl. and rec. w. Red Garland '59; then traveled w. L,H&R '60–61. CDs: w. A. Blakey (BN); J. Coltrane (Rh.); Betty Carter (Imp.); C. Adderley (Verve); Ray Bryant; Red Garland (Prest.).

WRIGHTSMAN, STAN, pno; b. Gotebo, OK, 6/15/10; d. Palm Springs, CA, 12/17/75. Joined father's band in 1924 in Springfield, Mo.; later in hotel band in Gulfport, Miss. From 1930 w. Ray Miller in NO; w. other bands in Tex., La., and Okla. Joined Ben Pollack '35 for a yr.; moved to LA '37 and app. on many Dixieland sess. w. Santo Pecora, Joe Yukl, Wingy Manone, Eddie Miller; also rec. w. Artie Shaw; Nappy Lamare; and Bob Crosby. In '50s he rec. w. Rampart Street Paraders; Matty Matlock; Pete Fountain; in '58 w. Bob Scobey; Ray Bauduc; and Wild Bill Davison. Played on soundtrack of film, *The Five Pennies.* On TV, *M Squad, Bourbon St. Beat,* and others LPs: w. Pete Fountain. CDs: w. Sharkey Bonano (Timel.); Artie Shaw (BB).

WYANDS, RICHARD FRANCIS, pno; b. Oakland, CA, 7/2/28. Mother pl. pno. and sang in church; cousin pl. dms. Joined mus. union at age 16. Stud. at SF St. Coll. 1945–50. Pl. w. SF club house band in early '50s, backing visiting soloists. Accomp. Ella Fitzgerald '56; Carmen McRae '57. Moved to NYC '58; pl. w. Roy Haynes; Charles Mingus; Kenny Burrell; Jerome Richardson '59; Gigi Gryce; Oliver Nelson; Etta Jones; Lockjaw Davis; Gene Ammons '60–1. Tour. w. Kenny Burrell '65–74 and freelanced extensively in NYC. Pl. w. Budd Johnson '74; Benny Bailey '78; Illinois Jacquet '79–90; Zoot Sims '81–2; Geo. Kelly '81–5; Frank Wess. Also pl. in '70s and '80s w. Major Holley; Slam Stewart; Al Cohn; Benny Carter; The Duke's Men. Perf. on the film soundtrack *Moscow on the Hudson.* Favs: Hampton Hawes, Tommy Flanagan, Herbie Hancock, Erroll Garner, Phineas Newborn. Fests: Japan w. Burrell '72; Eur. fr. '84. CDs: Steep.; DIW; CC; Jazzcraft; w. Benny Carter (MM); C. Mingus (BN); M. Hinton (Col.); I. Jacquet (Atl.); Carl Fontana (Up.); C. Payne: Harold Ashby (Stash); Roland Kirk (Merc.); E. Dolphy; G. Ammons; Lockjaw Davis; Etta Jones (Prest.); F. Hubbard (CTI); E. Andrews (Muse); J. Helleny (Arb.); Eric Alexander (CC); Gigi Gryce; O. Nelson (NJ); Buddy Tate (Res.); Cal Tjader (Fant.); Richard Williams (Cand.); Hal Singer (FNAC).

WYBLE, JIMMY, gtr; b. Port Arthur, TX, 1/25/22. Studied priv. 1935. Pl. in Houston, Tex., w. Peck Kelley, et al. On staff at Houston Radio '41–2; army '42–6. Studio work in LA; tour. w. Red Norvo '59–60; Benny Goodman in '60, '63; Frank Sinatra. Cont. studio work in LA; also pl. at Donte's w. Tony Rizzi's 5-gtr. gp. He has written instruction books and tutored. Wyble, who stud. classical gtr. w. Laurindo Almeida, has long been noted for his eclecticism. Favs: C. Christian, T. Farlow, J. Raney. Films: *Kings Go Forth, Screaming Mimi* w. Norvo. CDs: w. B. Goodman (Phon.; TCB; MM); Norvo (RCA; Ref.).

WYNN, ALBERT, tbn; b. New Orleans, LA, 7/29/07; d. Chicago, IL, 5/73. Prominent in Chi. in 1920s w. Earl Hines; led own band '26–8; toured Eur. w. Sam Wooding '28. During '30s he was active in Chi. w. Carroll Dickerson and at Apex Club w. Jimmie Noone. After working w. Fletcher Henderson '37–9, he rejoined Noone; also pl. w. Baby Dodds, Lil Armstrong, Little Brother Montgomery, and Franz Jackson '56–60. After leading own gp. for Riv. Rec.'s Living Legends series '61, he worked w. Little Brother Montgomery '64, but spent last yrs. inactive due to failing health. Wynn was infl. more by Jimmy Harrison and Jack Teagarden than by the early tailgate style. CDs: Riv.; w. Lil Hardin Armstrong (Riv.); Richard M. Jones; F. Henderson (Class.).

WYNTERS, GAIL (Nancy Gail Shivel), voc; b. Ashland, KY, 2/17/42. Family had gospel gps. Shivel Singers, Shivel Sisters fr. 1930s; sons are prof. mus. in Ky. Self-taught. Sang w. family gp. at song fests, revivals, etc., and w. local gps. in Lexington, Ky., while in coll., then signed by Cap. in Nashville. Wynters works mainly as a single and has perf. and rec. w. Roger Kellaway; Jay Leonhart; Arnie Lawrence; Dr. John; Rufus Reid; James Moody; Dick Katz; etc. She taught at the New Sch., NYC '88–9. Favs: Sarah Vaughan, Louis Armstrong, Billie Holiday, Marvin Gaye. Fests: Chile, Cuba. TV: PBS w. Dick Katz; ABC News—*Guns in America.* CDs: VWC.

x, y

XIQUES, EDWARD F. JR., bari, other saxes, fl, cl; b. Staten Island, NY, 10/9/39. Began on sop. sax. Pl. w. Jaki Byard, Herb Pomeroy while at Bost. U. 1957–62. Moved to NYC, taught mus. in N.Y. and N.J. schs. '62–8. Pl. w. Buddy Morrow, Les and Larry Elgart, Tex Beneke, Duke Pearson, Herbie Mann, Donald Byrd, Chris Swansen '60s; Woody Herman '70; Thad Jones–Mel Lewis Orch. '72–9; Bill Watrous '74–5; Frank Foster '77; B'way show *Best Little Whorehouse in Texas* '78–82; Toshiko Akiyoshi–Lew Tabackin bb '84–5; Liza Minnelli fr. '87. Xiques has also taught at City Coll.; U.. of Bridgeport; Western Conn. State Coll. Favs: Charlie Parker, Johnny Hodges, Ornette Coleman, Joe Henderson. Fests: Eur., Asia w. W. Herman, Jones-Lewis. Film: *A Tuesday Afternoon* w. Swansen. CDs: Edex; w. Jones-Lewis (A&M).

YAGED, SOL (SOLOMON), cl; b. Brooklyn, NY, 12/8/22. Inspired by Benny Goodman radio broadcasts. Stud. w. Simeon Bellison of NY Philharm. 1935–45. Pl. w. Bklyn. Doctor's Orch.; Gotham Symph.; offered job w. Buffalo Symph. Led trio w. Hank Duncan, Danny Alvin at Jimmy Ryan's '41. Led own gps. at NYC clubs, incl. Swing Club; Nick's; Onyx; Three Deuces; Village Vanguard; Eddie Condon's; Birdland fr. '42. Pl. w. Phil Napoleon's Memphis Five '45; Red Allen, Dizzy Gillespie, Woody Herman, Roy Eldridge, et al. at Metropole '54–62. As technical advisor to film *Benny Goodman Story,* he taught Steve Allen to pl. cl. '55. Led own combo at NYC World's Fair '63–4; in residence at Gaslight Club '66–76, Red Blazer Too fr. '66. Yaged was feat. in a concert at Carnegie Hall w. Eddie Barefield, Bucky Pizzarelli, Spanky Davis '79. He was a feat. perf. in the Highlights in Jazz concert series in NYC in '89 and '92. Fav: Benny Goodman. Film: app. in *Carnegie Hall* '47. TV: *Tonight Show* w. Steve Allen; Jerry Lewis telethon; Joe Franklin. LPs: as lead (Herald; Lane); w. Jack Teagarden (Urania); Chubby Jackson (Everest). CD: w. Coleman Hawkins (Jass).

YAMASHITA, YOSUKE, pno, comp, lead; b. Tokyo, Japan, 2/26/42. First prof. gig at age 17. Stud. at Kunitachi Coll. of Mus., Tokyo 1962–7. Pl. in '60s w. Masahiko Togashi; Sadao Watanabe; Terumasa Hino; et al. Led own trio '69–83; pl. free jazz feat. such saxophonists as Kazunori Takeda; Seiichi Nakamura; Akira Sakata. Very popular in '70s; pl. in Germ. '74; at Montreux JF '76; at NJF-NY '79. Primarily active as solo pnst. '84–8. Pl. w. trad. Japanese drum ens., Kodo '85. Tour. US '85; perf. *Rhapsody in Blue* w. Osaka Philharm. '86. Pl. annually at Sweet Basil, NYC, in trio w. Cecil McBee, Pheeroan Aklaff fr. '88. Received Fumio Nanri award for contrib. to Japanese jazz '89. Tour. US, Can., Japan '92. Led New Trio w. Yasushi Komatsu, Akira Horikoshi fr. '90; tour. Eur. '91–2. Made unprecedented 88–city tour of Japan '93. Yamashita is the author of more than ten books about his life in jazz. Fests: all major in Japan, Eur. Polls: *SJ* Readers '80–93; *SJ* Readers Jazzman of Year '82; *SJ* Readers Rec. of Year '82, '91; *SJ* Critics '90–2. CDs: Ant.; Verve; DIW; Victor; King; Enja; Frasco; Kitty; one track in *Jazz Masters: Verve at 50* (Verve).

YANCEY, JIMMY (JAMES EDWARD), pno; b. Chicago, IL, 2/20/1898; d. Chicago, 9/17/51. Father a gtrst. and singer. Toured US and Eur., tap-dancing and singing in vaudeville shows from 1900 until '15, incl.

Buckingham Palace for royal family '13. Settled in Chi. '15; made his living mainly as groundskeeper for the Chi. White Sox at Comiskey Park, also playing blues pno. at clubs and rent parties. In '19 he married singer Estella Harris (better known as Mama Yancey, a name under which she rec. for Riv. '61), whom he often accomp. Began rec. after his name became well-known via recs. of "Yancey Special" by Meade Lux Lewis and Bob Crosby '39–40. Said to have infl. Lewis, Albert Ammons, Pete Johnson, Pine Top Smith, and others, Yancey pl. occ. at Bee Hive club in Chi.; also in '48 w. his wife at Carnegie Hall. One of the most original of the boogie-woogie pnsts., his bs. lines were highly unconventional. CDs: Document; *Chicago Piano, Vol. 1* (Atl.); tracks on *Barrelhouse Boogie* (BB); *Atlantic Blues: Piano* (Atl.); *Juke Joint Jump: A Boogie-Woogie Celebration* (Col.).

YELLIN, PETE (PETER), alto, sop saxes, fl, cl; b. NYC, 7/18/42. Mother was concert vlnst., fath. was NBC staff pnst. and arr. Stud. w. Joe Allard, Harold Bennett at Juilliard 1963–7. Pl. w. Lionel Hampton '63–5, then off and on '66–77; Buddy Rich '67; Tito Puente since '69; Joe Henderson '70–6; Charles Earland '73; Charles Mingus '74; Jaki Byard, Sam Jones '75; B. Rich '75–7; Maynard Ferguson '78; Bob Mintzer since '83. Also Mel Lewis, Eddie Palmieri, own gps. Yellin has been dir. of the jazz prog. at LIU-Bklyn. fr. '81. Favs: Charlie Parker, Sonny Stitt, Eric Dolphy, Cannonball Adderley. Polls: *Play.* and *DB* TDWR '73–4. Fests: Asia w. Hampton '71–3; So. Amer. '75; Eur. fr. '88. CDs: Metro.; Mons.; w. B. Mintzer (DMP); J. Henderson (Verve; Mile.); Buddy Rich (PJ).

YOUNG, DAVE (DAVID ANTHONY), bs, comp; b. Winnipeg, Man., Canada, 1/29/40. Sister, Sydney Young McInnis, classical pnst. Stud. at Berklee Coll. of Mus. w. William Curtis 1962 and w. Thomas Monohan at RCMT '67–9. Active in both jazz and classical mus. Worked w. both Moe Koffman and Hagood Hardy's Montage in Toronto late '60s. With Edmonton Symph. '70–2; Hamilton Philharm. '72–4; Winnipeg Symph. '74. Tour. w. Oscar Peterson '75 but ret. to Hamilton orch. later in the yr., remain. w. it on and off into early '80s and through the '80s w. COC orch. In the late '70s was part of the Carol Britto and Bernie Senensky trios at Bourbon Street backing visiting US mus. Pl. w. Wray Downes fr. '76; also w. Joe Sealy, Johnny O'Neal. Pl. w. Britto '82; Lenny Breau '83. Tour. w. own bands '83–7. Worked again w. Peterson '86–8, '89–90. Tour. w. Oliver Jones '88–9. Int'l tours w. Peterson; P. Appleyard; Africa w. O. Jones; '91 in Japan w. Barney Kessel. Excellent arco soloist. CDs: JT; w. Peterson; Benny Carter (Pab.); Breau (Guitarachives); Oliver Jones (JT); Don Menza (Sack.); Kenny Wheeler (Just A Memory).

YOUNG, ELDEE, bs, el-bs, cello; b. Chicago, IL, 1/7/36. Father pl. mand. Stud. gtr. w. bro., then bs. in hs and at Amer. Cons. of Mus., Chi. Pl. w. King Kolax 1951; Chuck Willis '54; other blues and r&b singers, incl. Joe Turner, T-Bone Walker, Joe Williams mid '50s. Pl. bs. and cello w. Ramsey Lewis Trio '56–66; also rec. w. Lorez Alexandria '57; James Moody '59; as lead. '61. In '66 Young and dmr. Red Holt left Lewis to form Young-Holt Unlimited. Young pl. bs. and el-bs. in this gp. Fav: Ray Brown. CDs: Argo; w. R. Lewis (Argo; Cadet; Chess); John Young (Del.); Eden Atwood (Conc.)

YOUNG, GEORGE ERNEST (Opalisky Jr.), saxes, cl, fl; b. Philadelphia, PA, 10/7/37. Raised in Germantown, Pa. Fath., a steelworker and coal miner, pl. sax; cousin Louis Opalesky is classical tptr. Studied in Phila. w. Paul Ferra; Leroy Hitchner; Carl Waxman; later in NYC w. Harold Bennett. Pl. in Phila. Orch. while in hs. Tour. w. own gp. George Young Revue late 1950s, incl. extended engagements in LV and Wildwood, N.J. Worked as studio mus. in NYC fr. early '60s. Pl. in '60s in Phila. w. Phila. Orch.; Mike Douglas; Gerry Blauit. Pl. in NYC w. Gene Roland bb; Al Porcino's Band of the Century mid '60s; Mike Mainieri–White Elephant late '60s; Ten Wheel Drive '60s; Joel Kaye–Johnny Richards bb '65–73; *Purlie Victorious* theater band late '60s-early '70s. Orig. member of Chuck Mangione Qt. '68–76. Tour. w. Liza Minnelli, Benny Goodman mid '70s; also w. Paul Simon mid '70s–'80. Pl. w. Teo Macero's All-Stars, Mel Tormé; Michel Legrand mid '70s; Louis Bellson fr. mid '70s; Chuck Israels' Nat'l Jazz Ens. '76–80; Timepiece w. Ron Davis, Dave Samuels '76–83; Dave Matthews '77–86; Gerry Mulligan bb off and on fr. '79; Mulligan-Tormé at Carnegie Hall '80–1; Teruo Nakamura '80–2; Joe Morello '80–3; Lynn Welshman fr. '80; Astrud Gilberto '81; own qt. w. Harold Danko, Rick Laird, Butch Miles '81–2; Mel Lewis Orch., David Grusin '82; Frank Sinatra early '80s; Manh. Jazz Qnt. w. Lew Soloff fr. early '80s; *Saturday Night Live* band fr. '88; Phi Woods bb in late '90s. Led a qt. w. Warren Bernhardt, Tony Marino, Tom Whaley fr. '92. He has pl. on numerous, movie soundtracks, incl. *All That Jazz: Star 80; Silent Movie; New York, New York; Another You.* Favs: Charlie Parker, Lester Young, John Coltrane; arrs: Bob Brookmeyer, Billy Byers, Ralph Burns, Dave Matthews, Frank Foster, Mike Abene. Polls: NARAS Most Val. Player five consec. times; NARAS Virtuoso Awd. Fests: Portugal '65; Eur. '75, '80; Japan fr. '82. TV: Ed Sullivan '61; *Sat. Night Live* fr. '88. CDs: Chiaro.; PW; w. Manh.

Jazz Qnt. (PW; SB); Randy Weston (Roul.); Louie Bellson (MM; Chiaro.); Jim Pugh; Joe Beck; John Tropea (DMP); Jay Leonhart (Sunny.); D. Grusin (GRP); B. Goodman (Verve; Lond.); David Sanchez (Col.); Phil Woods (Conc.).

YOUNG, KAREN ELIZABETH, voc, gtr, perc; b. Montreal, Que., Canada, 6/19/51. Raised in Hudson, Que. Began on gtr. at age 14; had minor folk hit "Garden of Ursh" at age 19. Stud. voice w. Jane Ellison. Founding member of Bug Alley Band 1975–9, sang under name Karen Egan. Led own gps. fr. '81 incl. All Smiles; Young Latins; Unclassified w. Helmut Lipsky. Came to prominence in duo w. Michel Donato '83–90. Young's repertoire incl. jazz, pop, and light classical material. In the '80s she perf. in church choirs, classical and new music ensembles, and musical theater. She has taught at the U. of Montreal fr. '88 and has led a trio w. Norman Lachapelle and Francine Martel fr. '91. Polls: Felix Awd. '88. Fests: all major in Can.; France; UK; USA w. Donato. CDs: as co-lead. w. Donato (JTR).

YOUNG, LARRY (Khalid Yasin Abdul Aziz), org; b. Newark, NJ, 10/7/40; d. NYC, 3/30/78. Father an orgst.; stud. classical pno. Prof. debut c. 1957 w. Lou Donaldson; Kenny Dorham; Hank Mobley; Tommy Turrentine; Grant Green; as well as r&b gps. in N.J. Formed own gp. w. gtr. and dms; first album, *Groove Street*, rec. '60. In Paris '64 w. Donald Byrd and Nathan Davis at Chat Que Peche. Dur. late 60s and early 70s his pl. moved into new areas, showing influences from Jimi Hendrix and John Coltrane, using modality and free jazz techniques. Pl. w. Miles Davis '69; John McLaughlin '70; and Tony Williams Lifetime '69–71. Because of his advanced ideas, Young has been named as an important influence by younger organists such as Barbara Dennerlein. CDs: BN; w. Grant Green and Donald Byrd (Verve); G. Green; Joe Henderson (BN); Tony Williams (Verve); Woody Shaw (Muse); Miles Davis (Col.); Jimmy Forrest (NJ).

YOUNG, LEE (LEONIDAS RAYMOND), dms; b. New Orleans, LA, 3/7/17. Started in Minneapolis, pl. saxes and tbn. in family band w. bro. Lester, sist. Irma, and father/leader pnst. Willis Handy Young. In LA fr. 1934; worked w. Mutt Carey '34–5; Buck Clayton '36; Eddie Barefield '36–7; pl and rec. w. Fats Waller '37. After working briefly as voc. and dmr. w. Lionel Hampton '40–1, he formed a sxt. w. Lester Young fr. early '41, pl. in LA and at Café Society in NYC. In mid '40s rec. w. Dinah Washington; Ivie Anderson; and Mel Powell; pl. w. JATP '44–6; again w. Hampton '47; Benny Goodman '47–8. An

occ. early assoc. of Nat King Cole, Young joined Cole's trio as a regular member fr. '53 to '62. From the mid '60s stopped pl. and became rec. exec. w. VeeJay and, later, Motown Recs. CDs: w. C. Parker (Verve); L. Hampton (Dec.); Nat Cole (Cap.); Ernestine Anderson (Sav.); JATP (Verve); Duke Henderson (Del.); Judy Garland (Dec.); Capitol Jazzmen (Jazz Unlimited).

YOUNG, LESTER WILLIS ("PREZ", "PRES"), tnr sax, cl, comp; b. Woodville, MS, 8/27/09; d. NYC 3/15/59. Raised in NO and, fr. age 11, in Minneapolis. In 1919 pl. dms. in family band led by his fath., Willis Handy Young, w. bro. Lee and sist. Irma. Also stud. tpt. and vln but sw. to alto sax at 13. Traveled w. family band, tour. the Dakotas, Kans., and Neb. dur. carnival season. After leaving family band in '27, he took up bari., then tnr. sax while w. Art Bronson's Bostonians. During the next five yrs. he was in and out of many bands, incl. Frank Hines; Eugene Schuck; Walter Page's Blue Devils; Eddie Barefield; and Boyd Atkins. Settled in KC after leaving Blue Devils '33; pl. w. Clarence Love and King Oliver. Was hired briefly by Fletcher Henderson, who was dissatisfied w. Young's frostier-than-Hawkins tone. After six mos. w. Andy Kirk he joined Count Basie, w. whom he had worked previously. Played at the Reno Club in KC in the summer of '36, then went to Chi., where he made rec. debut w. a qnt., Jones-Smith Inc., from Basie's band. With Basie to NYC, where his laid-back phrasing and light, cool tone set him apart fr. other tnr. players and brought him attention. He always cited Frankie Trumbauer as his original idol but also admired Jimmy Dorsey. Rec. w. Basie, staying w. him until Dec. '40. Dur. the Basie yrs. he made numerous recs. w. Billie Holiday; Teddy Wilson; and others. When he named Holiday "Lady Day," she gave him his nickname, "Prez." In early '41 Young opened w. his own small gp. at Kelly's Stable in NYC, then co-led a band in Calif. and NYC w. his bro. Lee. After tour. w. Al Sears' USO Camp Shows band, he rejoined Basie, Dec. '43. Drafted into the army '44, Young spent fifteen mos. in the service, suffering traumatic experiences w. racism and ending up in detention barracks bef. his release in Dec. '45. It has been said that the army experience had a devastating effect on his life and prof. career.

Back in civilian life he began tour. and rec. w. Norman Granz's JATP and was a key player in the classic Gjon Mili–Granz film, *Jammin' the Blues*. He feat. at Birdland, NYC when it opened Dec. '49. Cont. to tour int'l through the '50s, but heavy drinking increasingly impaired his health and affected his playing. The last three yrs. of his life were marked by a series of catastrophes, incl. a nervous breakdown and hospitalization for malnutrition and alcoholism. In '57 he app. w. Basie at the NJF and on the celebrated CBS TV show, *The Sound of Jazz.* Young visited Paris in Jan. '59, made his final rec. date there, and died the day after his ret. to the US. His rise to the forefront of the jazz scene in the '40s launched a new sch. of airy-toned, melodically-oriented tnr. pl. that seemed the antithesis of Coleman Hawkins's full sound and harmonic complexities. He could also take one note and generate tremendous swing. Young's tone and style had a powerful impact upon the post-war generation of tnr. saxophonists, incl. Stan Getz; Al Cohn; Zoot Sims; Paul Quinichette; Wardell Gray; and Gene Ammons. He also significantly infl. the stylistic development of Dexter Gordon and, through him, Sonny Rollins and John Coltrane. Although he also was an engaging clarinetist, "Blue and Sentimental" (w. the Basie Band) and "I Want a Little Girl" (w. the KC Six) are rare instances of his rec. on that instrument. Video: *Lester Young—Song of the Spirit,* Bruce Fredericks '88. Books: *Lester Young Reader,* Lewis Porter (Smithsonian) '85; *You Just Fight For Your Life,* Frank Buchmann-Moller (Greenwood Press) '90. CDs: Verve; Sav.; BN; Story.; Comm.; Pab.; w. Billie Holiday (Col.; Dec., Verve); Charlie Parker (Verve); Count Basie (Col.; Verve; Dec.; Class.); JATP (Pab.; Verve); Benny Goodman (BB); E. Fitzgerald; Hawkins and Eldridge (Verve); Miles Davis (Jazz Unlimited); *Story of Jazz* (Col.).

YOUNG, SNOOKY (EUGENE EDWARD), tpt; b. Dayton, OH, 2/3/19. Brother was trumpeter Granville "Catfish" Young. Pl. in family band; later in Atlanta w. Eddie Heywood Sr. and Graham Jackson. While still in teens pl. w. Wilberforce Collegians and Clarence "Chic" Carter 1937–9. First prominent as lead and solo tpt. w. Jimmie Lunceford '39–42; pl. on soundtrack of film, *Blues in the Night* '41. Worked briefly w. Count Basie, then in Calif. w. Lionel Hampton; Les Hite; Benny Carter; and Gerald Wilson. Rejoined Basie on several occ., the last time being Oct. '57 to June '62. Then joined NBC as staff mus.; also worked w. Benny Goodman; Thad Jones–Mel Lewis; Charlie Barnet; and Kenny Clarke–Francy Boland in '60s. Moved to LA '72 as member of Doc Severinsen's *Tonight Show* band, staying until '92 when Severinsen left the show; also freelanced locally w. Bob Cooper; Marshal Royal; rec. for Conc.; Capp-Pierce; et al. For over fifty yrs. Young remained a consummate lead and solo player, greatly in demand at rec. sess. CDs: w. Basie (BB; Verve; Mos., Roul.; Pab.); Donald Byrd (BN); C. Hawkins (Imp.); Geo. Benson (Verve); C. Mingus (Col.); Frank Wess; Dave Frishberg; Mel Tormé (Conc.); Jack Lemmon (Laser.); Oliver Nelson (BB);

L,H&R (Roul.); L. Hampton (Dec.); Lunceford (Class.); and many others.

YOUNG, TRUMMY (JAMES OSBORNE), tbn, voc; b. Savannah, GA, 1/12/12; d. San Jose, CA, 9/10/84. Raised in Wash., D.C.; prof. debut 1928 in Booker Coleman's Hot Chocolates. Later worked w. Hardy Bros. and Tommy Miles. Rose to prominence dur. engagements w. Earl Hines '34–7 and Jimmie Lunceford '37–43. Also briefly w. Charlie Barnet, own band on 52nd St. and in Chi. '43–4. Rec. w. Charlie Parker, Dizzy Gillespie '45. After pl. w. Boyd Raeburn and app. w. JATP and in other gps., moved to Hawaii where he lived '47–52. From summer '52 to Jan. '64, tour. the world w. Louis Armstrong, then ret. to Hawaii. From mid '60s worked mainly as a single, pl. Nice JF, Colo. JPs, etc.; worked w. Chris Barber in Eur. Young's extroverted, technically brilliant tbn. solos, and his intimate breathless vocal style with its humorous touches were outstanding features of the Armstrong gps. and the Lunceford band (incl. his biggest hit, "Margie," which he rec. in '38). Won *Esq.* New Star award '47. CDs: w. L. Armstrong (Dec.; Col.; Milan); Billie Holiday (Col.; Verve); J. Lunceford (Dec.; Class.); Coleman Hawkins (Merc.); Illinois Jacquet (Mos.); Buck Clayton (Class.; Riv.); Gillespie; E. Hines (Class.); Dexter Gordon; B. Raeburn (Sav.); Peanuts Hucko (Timel.); C. Parker (Phil.).

YSAGUIRRE, BOB (ROBERT), bs, tba; b. Belize, British Honduras, 2/22/1897; d. NYC, 3/27/82. Started on tba. at age 18. Pl. in mil. band 1917–19. Lived in NO '20. Pl. w. Amos White '22. To NYC w. Armand J. Piron in '22, pl. and rec. w. Piron '23–5; joined Elmer Snowden band '25–6; Alex Jackson's Plantation Orch. '26–9. Also short stints w. Fletcher and Horace Henderson bef. beginning long assoc. w. Don Redman's band '31–40. Remained active in NYC into the late '60s, though mostly as painter. CDs: w. F. Henderson (Col.).

YUKL, JOE (JOSEPH), tbn; b. NYC, 3/5/09; d. Los Angeles, CA, 3/15/81. Started on vln. but sw. to tbn. while at U. of Maryland in mid 1920s. Worked in NYC w. Red Nichols; Dorsey Bros.; Joe Haymes; and CBS Orch. late '20s and early '30s. Freelanced in Balt., '31–3. Joined Dorsey Bros. Orch., then w. Jimmy Dorsey until '37. Worked in Calif. w. Ray McKinley; Ben Pollack; Frank Trumbauer; Ted Fio Rito. Studio work in Hollywood fr. '40s; also rec. dates w. Wingy Manone, Charlie Lavere. Played bit part and perf. in film *Rhythm Inn* '51; coached and tracked solo for James Stewart's jam sess. scene in *The Glenn Miller Story* '54. CDs: w. Louis Armstrong (Mos.); J. Dorsey (Dec.); Dorsey Bros. Orch. (Cir.).

ZARCHY, ZEKE (RUBIN), tpt; b. NYC, 6/12/15. Musical family. Pl. w. Joe Haymes 1935; Benny Goodman '36; Artie Shaw '36; Bob Crosby '37. Joined Red Norvo in NYC, then back w. B. Crosby '38. With Tommy Dorsey '39; Glenn Miller '40; NBC staff, NYC '40–2. Mil. service '42–5; overseas w. Glenn Miller AAF Band '44–5. Freelance work in LA after WWII and w. Frank Sinatra; lead tpt. w. Paul Weston for over twenty yrs. Many foreign tours, incl. eighteen trips to Japan since '73 w. Billy Vaughn Orch. Also tour. w. Benny Goodman Tribute Band; w. Ray Conniff to Brazil several times fr. '83; three Glenn Miller Reunion tours '85–91. Zarchy cont. to pl. lead and solo tpt. into his late seventies. CDs: w. Glenn Miller (BB; Vict.); Goodman (BB); T. Dorsey (Tax); Artie Shaw (Class.); Bob Crosby (Dec.).

ZARDIS, CHESTER, bs; b. New Orleans, LA, 5/27/1900; d. New Orleans, 8/14/90. Worked w. Kid Rena, Chris Kelly, and A. J. Piron in NO dur. 1920s. Pl. tba. and bs. w. Sidney Desvigne and Fats Pichon on riverboats in '30s (also pl. w. Pichon in '39). Pl. briefly w. Count Basie at Apollo Theatre, NYC while w. Duke Dejan's Dixie Rhythm Band '36–7. Rec. w. Bunk Johnson '42; George Lewis '43. Pl. at Preservation Hall and toured US and Eur. w. its resident band '66–7. Led own Legends of Jazz band in early '80s. CDs: w. Geo. Lewis (Mos.); Bunk Johnson (Story.).

ZAWADI, KIANE (Bernard McKinney), tbn, euph; b. Detroit, MI, 11/26/32. Mother, four bros., two sists. mus.; many other mus. in family. Stud. at Cass Tech. HS, Wayne St. U.; later stud. w. Britt Wood-

man. First prof. gig w. Barry Harris–Sonny Stitt at Madison Ballroom 1951. Pl. w. Art Blakey in Phila. '54; Donald Byrd '55; Alvin Jackson '55–6; Yusef Lateef, Pepper Adams '58. Moved to NYC '59; pl. w. Illinois Jacquet '59; Slide Hampton '60; Sun Ra, Freddie Hubbard '60s; Archie Shepp, McCoy Tyner, Dollar Brand, Charles Tolliver, Harold Vick early '70s; Frank Foster late '70s. Also pl. w. Philly Joe Jones; Randy Weston; Ahmad Jamal; Jimmy Owens; Babs Gonzales; Les McCann; James Moody; Howard McGhee; Lionel Hampton; Roland Alexander; Joe Henderson; Clark Terry bb; Brass Co.; etc. Pl. w. Illinois Jacquet bb '90; Clifford Jordan bb fr. '90. Zawadi has worked extens. on B'way and w. r&b acts, incl. Aretha Franklin; Jackson Five; Four Tops; Supremes; Kool and the Gang; etc. He has taught in Bklyn. pub. sch. '67–8; at New Muse Community Museum, Bklyn. '69–82; Jazzmobile Wkshp. fr. '72. Favs: J. J. Johnson, Slide Hampton, Britt Woodman, Lawrence Brown. Polls: *DB* TDWR. Fests: Eur. w. Jacquet, D. Brand, C. Jordan; Africa w. Tolliver. Film: app. in *Seven Deadly Sins*. CDs: w. Clifford Jordan bb (Mile.); Donald Byrd (Del.); Sun Ra (Sav.); Illinois Jacquet (Atl.); Hank Mobley; F. Hubbard (BN); R. Kendrick (Verve).

ZAWINUL, JOE (JOSEF ERICH), kybds, comp; b. Vienna, Austria, 7/7/32. Played acdn. as a child; stud. at Vienna Cons. Pl. w. Austr. radio and dance bands; pl. and comp. for Friedrich Gulda. Immigrated to US on Berklee scholarship in 1959. After working briefly w. Maynard Ferguson's band he accomp. Dinah Washington '59–61, then joined Cannonball Adderley and remained w. him as pnst. and principal comp. until '70. While w. Adderley he

715

wrote such hits as "Mercy, Mercy, Mercy" and "Walk Tall." His comp. "In a Silent Way" became the title tune of a classic Miles Davis album on which he pl. kybds.; he also app. on Davis's pace-setting *Bitches' Brew.* In Dec. '70 Zawinul and Wayne Shorter founded Weather Report, a gp. that stayed together with occ. personnel changes until '85 and bec. the most influential fusion gp. of its day. A decidedly electronic olio of jazz and rock, the gp. had Zawinul playing synths. After the breakup of Weather Report, Zawinul founded his own gp., The Zawinul Syndicate, and began using the korg-pepe, an instrument he designed with a bassoon-like mouthpiece and acdn.-type buttons. He also briefly ret. to playing acdn. for the first time in many yrs. Some of the works perf. by this gp. incl. lyrics or narrations. A '91 album produced by Zawinul for West Afr. singer Salif Keita was well received. He ret. to Berklee to receive an honorary Doctor of Mus. degree at the '91 convocation. Although he has called The Syndicate the best band he's ever had, Weather Report is probably the gp. for which he will best be remembered. CDs: Col.; Philips; w. Weather Report; The Zawinul Syndicate (Col.); Cannonball Adderley (Riv.; Cap.; Night); Miles Davis (Col.); Gerald Veasley (Heads Up); Trilok Gurtu (CMP); Joe Henderson (Mile.); Katia Labeque (Drey.); Y. Lateef (Riv.; Rh./Atl.); Ben Webster; Eddie Jefferson; Sam Jones (Riv.).

ZEITLIN, DENNY (DENNIS JAY), pno, synth, comp; b. Chicago, IL, 4/10/38. Parents both pl. pno; stud. priv. 1944–52; stud. comp. w. George Russell. Gigged w. various local gps. around Champaign, Ill., Chi., and Balt., where he became resident at Johns Hopkins, studying medicine. Toured Eur. summer of '60, pl. w. gps. in Paris, incl. Oscar Pettiford's. Rec. several albums for Col. and app. at Newport and Monterey JFs mid '60s. Dual career in psychiatry and mus. since mid '60s. Withdrew fr. active jazz scene late '60s to concentrate on study of el. instruments. Worked mainly in SF area until mid '70s, when he once again increased his concert schedule. Wrote film score for *Invasion of the Body Snatchers* '78. Continued with career as psychiatrist, occ. tour. w. trios and, in late '80s, rec. for WH. Originally infl. by Lennie Tristano, Bill Evans (who rec. his comp. "Quiet Now"), and George Russell, his playing in the late '80s and early '90s added more conventional mainstream elements. CDs: WH; Conc.; ECM.

ZENTNER, SI (SIMON H.), tbn, bandleader; b. NYC, 6/13/17; d. Las Vegas, 1/31/00. Played w. Les Brown, Harry James, Jimmy Dorsey early '40s; w. various bands and studio gps. in Hollywood '44–57

until he started his own dance band. In '60 he had a popular hit, "Lazy River," arr. by Bob Florence. Continued to tour w. bands, pl. in LV, backing such singers as Johnny Mathis and Nancy Wilson. CDs: w. J. Teagarden (Mos.); L. Armstrong (Vict.).

ZETTERLUND, MONICA, voc; b. Hagfors, Sweden, 9/20/37; d. Stockholm, 5/12/05. First prominent w. Arne Domnerus's band in Stockholm 1958–9. Toured UK and US '59–60. Rec. w. Bill Evans Trio '64 and w. a band led by Thad Jones. Admired early on for her jazz sensitivity, she eventually became better known as a film and stage actress. CDs: Swed. EMI; Phon.; w. B. Evans; N. H. Ø. Pedersen (Verve).

ZITO, RONNIE (RONALD), dms; b. Utica, NY, 2/17/39. Father, three bros. all musicians. Began pl. w. family. Pl. w. J. R. Monterose in Utica 1958; Bobby Darin '58–61; Frank Rosolino in LA '61; Peggy Lee '62; Woody Herman '65–6. A popular sess. player, Zito perf. on numerous pop and jazz dates, incl. Bobby Scott; Helen Merrill; Astrud Gilberto; Barry Manilow; and Bob Stewart. Film: soundtrack of *A League of Their Own* '92. B'way: *Chicago,* late '90s. Rec. w. Freddy Cole '95. Favs: Elvin Jones, Philly Joe Jones, Buddy Rich, Max Roach, Art Blakey. CDs: w. W. Herman (Col.); Jay Leonhart (Nes); F. Cole (After 9).

ZITO, TORRIE, comp/arr, pno; b. Utica, NY, 10/22/33. Father pl. bs.; pno. for silent films at movie house in Utica. Bro. Freddie pl tbn. w. C. Barnet, Kenton, A. Shaw, L. Millinder; bro. Ronnie, dmr. Early interest in pno.; some tutelage fr. fath. Took up tpt., fl. in hs but cont. as self-taught pnst. w. gigs after grad. Stud. pno. formally for yr. To NYC, stud. comp. w. Vittorio Giannini at Manh. Sch. of Mus. 1956–7. After tour. w. singer Jerry Vale '58–9, ret. to NYC, working in jingle studio and freelancing. Wrote albums for James Moody, Argo '61; Herbie Mann, Atl.; on staff for Quincy Jones at Merc., albums w. Harry Lookofsky and Double Six of Paris; B. Eckstine; S. Vaughan; also for Bobby Darin; Barbra Streisand. Mus. dir. for Tony Bennett '73–9; Helen Merrill fr. '79. Writing for Marvin Hamlisch concerts w. Pitts., Balt. Symphs. Comps: "Lisa" (for Cannonball Adderley); "Somerset"; "A Summer Thing" (for Zoot Sims); *Concert Waltz for Harp & String Qt.; Divertimento for Clarinet & Strings.* Favs: Bill Holman, Horace Silver, Robert Farnon; pno: Bill Evans, Red Garland, Silver. TV: writing for *Miss Universe; Tony Awards; Kennedy Center Honors.* Awards: Emmys for *Tony Awards; Night of 100 Stars.* CDs: w. Merrill (Verve; JVC; Par); Sabine Meyer–Eddie Daniels (EMI).

ZOLLAR, JAMES DELANO, tpt, pno; b. Kansas City, MO, 7/24/59. Mother was cabaret singer; bro. Tony is songwriter; sist. Jawole Willa Jo Zollar leads dance troupe, Urban Bush Women. Began on bugle at age 9; tpt. at age 12. Family moved to SF 1971; stud. w. Woody Shaw; Norman Bishop Williams. Moved to San Diego, Calif. '74. Stud. at Mission Bay HS; San Diego City Coll.; U. of Cal.-San Diego w. Jimmy Cheatham '82-4. First prof. gig w. Mercer Ellington's Duke Ellington Orch. '83. Pl. in San Diego w. Jay McShann; Eddie Vinson; Jeannie and Jimmy Cheatham; in LA w. Leslie Drayton; Big Joe Turner; Roger Newman's Rather Large Band. Moved to NYC to rejoin Ellington band '85. Rec. debut w. Claude Williamson on Bopland label '85. Also worked w. Panama Francis; Lester Bowie; Sunny Murray; Craig Harris; Charli Persip; Cab Calloway. Toured Eur. w. Bob Stewart First Line Band '87, '91; Japan w. Steve Coleman and Five Elements '88; Japan w. Ellington '89; Engl. w. Ellington '92. Lived in Geneva, Switz. '92-4; taught at jazz sch. in Bern, where he rec. his own sess. and w. Joe Heider bb. Pl. w. Mongo Santamaria at Heineken JF, PR '93. Toured Eur. w. David Murray bb '93. Ret. to NYC '94; worked w. Mongo Santamaria; David Murray; Don Byron; Henry Threadgill. Toured Eur. w. Murray, Byron '95. Worked w. Frankie Ruiz fr. '95; Hilton Ruiz fr. '96. Fav: as tpt. and arr., Thad Jones. Film: *Kansas City*. TV: as pianist in Madonna's music video *Secret*. CDs: Naxos; w. D. Murray (DIW; Astor Place); B. Stewart (JMT; Post.); Nancie Banks Orch. (CAP); Kansas City Band (Verve); Ed Jackson (NW).

ZOLLER, ATTILA CORNELIUS, gtr, comp; b. Visegrad, Hungary, 6/13/27; d. Newdale, VT, 1/25/98. Started on vln at age 4; pl. tpt. in hs symph. orch. After WWII, pl gtr. in Budapest clubs; in Vienna 1948 formed gp. w. vibist Vera Auer. To Germ. '53, pl. w. Jutta Hipp '54-5; w. Hans Koller '56-9. Moved to US '59, stud. at Sch. of Jazz in Lenox, Mass. Briefly w. Chico Hamilton, then w. Herbie Mann '62-5. Own qt. w. Don Friedman mid '60s; also w. Klaus Doldinger, Red Norvo, and Benny Goodman late '60s. Toured Japan w. Astrud Gilberto '70 and as part of Guitar Festival w. Jim Hall, Kenny Burrell '71. In '71 he was granted patent for electronic pick-up device for gtr. and elec. bs. App. at Berlin Jazztage '73; worked weekly concerts and clinics in Vermont '75. Worked and rec. w. Jimmy Raney in duo '79-80. Reunited w. Koller in NYC '79; rec. w. Daniel Humair, Kirk Lightsey, etc. '86. Active as teacher primarily at his Vermont Jazz Center. Yearly tours of Germ., Austr., Switz., Hungary, etc. Died after long bout w. colon cancer in

Vermont, where he had lived for twenty-five yrs. Award fr. New Engl. Foundation for the Arts '95. CDs: Enja; MPS; ACT; L + R; Bhakti; w. B. Goodman (MM); Lee Konitz (Phil.); O. Pettiford (BL); Martial Solal (MPS); Klaus Doldinger (ACT).

ZOTTOLA, GLENN PAUL, tpt, flg, alto sax; b. Port Chester, NY, 4/28/47. From mus. family; fath. was arr. and tpt. player for Claude Thornhill; bro., Bob, a tptr. pl. w. Slide Hampton. Stud. w. father, first perf. at age 13 in family's jazz club, Something Else, in N.Y. w. such players as Tommy Flanagan; Booker Ervin; and Ray Bryant. In 1960s pl. w. Bobby Hackett; Lionel Hampton; various clubs; B'way shows '66-77; B. Goodman '77-9. In '80s w. Bob Wilber; Butch Miles; Maxine Sullivan; Peggy Lee; et al. and in '90s w. John Clayton and Peanuts Hucko. Though known primarily as a trumpeter, Zottola is also a competent alto player. Favs: Louis Armstrong, Charlie Parker, and Clifford Brown. CDs: w. Maxine Sullivan (Mob. Fid.); Peggy Lee (Angel); Steve Allen (Conc.); Bob Wilber (Jazz.); Doc Cheatham (Natasha).

ZURKE, BOB (ROBERT ALLEN; Boguslaw Albert Zukowski), pno, comp; b. Detroit, MI, 1/17/12; d. Los Angeles, CA, 2/16/44. Child prodigy. Pl. and rec. fr. mid 1920s to mid '30s w. various local gps. around Phila. Came to prominence in late '36, replacing Joe Sullivan w. Bob Crosby band. During the boogie-woogie craze of the late '30s and early '40s he was considered a leading exponent. Won '39 *DB* poll as Best Pianist. Left Crosby in mid '39; led own short-lived bb; then pl. solo in various Chi., Det., and LA clubs until his death. CDs: w. J. Teagarden (BB); Bob Crosby; Judy Garland (Dec.).

ZWEIG, BARRY KENNETH, gtr; b. Detroit, MI, 2/7/42. Studied vln. and theory at No. Hollywood HS. Began gtr. at age 15. Rec. debut at age 18 w. Bill Baldwin. First major jazz gig w. Eddie Miller, Nappy Lamare, Charlie Lodice 1962. Drafted into army '64, he pl. in World Band w. Bobby Shew and others. After army, he tour. for eight mos. w. Buddy Rich Band. Freelanced in LA fr. '66 to '70, incl. tours w. Andy Williams; Henry Mancini; Sammy Davis Jr. With Willie Bobo '70. TV and film work w. Dinah Shore; Don Ellis Orch. Taught gtr., incl. seminar w. Shelly Manne, and at Grove Sch. of Mus. Own trio w. Paul Gormley, Gene Estes. Also pl. w. Gene Estes Qt. Favs: Wes Montgomery, Joe Pass, John Pisano. CDs: w. Buddy Rich (PJ); Dave Pell (JVC; Headfirst); Frank Capp (Conc.); Bill Holman (JVC); John Leitham (USA).

ZWERIN, MIKE (MICHAEL), tbn, comp, writer; b. NYC, 5/18/30. Studied vln; att. HS of Mus. and Art. While at sch. pl. tbn. briefly w. Miles Davis "Birth of the Cool" band. After living in Paris for several yrs., he worked in NYC w. Billy May; Sonny Dunham; toured w. Claude Thornhill 1958–9; Maynard Ferguson '59–60; Bill Russo '60. Though still active in jazz, Zwerin was president of Capitol Steel Corp. fr. '60. Member of Orch. USA w. Gunther Schuller and John Lewis '62–5; toured USSR w. Earl Hines '66. In Eur. fr. '69; pl. w. George Gruntz's Concert Jazz Band. Living in Paris since late '60s, he is best-known as jazz columnist for the Int'l *Herald Tribune*. Authored several books, incl. *Close Enough for Jazz* '84; *Tristesse de St. Louis* (about jazz under Nazi regime) '87; has also written numerous witty, incisive columns for the *Village Voice* and *DB* and continues to play occ. CDs: w. Sxt. of Orch. U.S.A. (BB); Miles Davis (Cap.); Gruntz (MPS); Big Band Charlie Mingus (SN).; Zip (Verve/Gitanes Jazz).